THE NEW GROVE
DICTIONARY OF MUSIC AND MUSICIANS®

Volume Fifteen

The New
GROVE
Dictionary
of Music and
Musicians®

EDITED BY

Stanley Sadie

15

Playford–Riedt

GROVE

MACMILLAN PUBLISHERS LIMITED, LONDON
GROVE'S DICTIONARIES OF MUSIC INC., NEW YORK, NY
MACMILLAN PUBLISHERS (CHINA) LIMITED, HONG KONG

© Macmillan Publishers Limited 1980

First Edition of *A Dictionary of Music and Musicians*, planned and edited by SIR GEORGE GROVE, DCL, in
four volumes, with an Appendix edited by J. A. Fuller Maitland, and an Index by Mrs Edmond
Wodehouse, 1878, 1880, 1883, 1890.
Reprinted 1890, 1900

Second Edition, edited by J. A. FULLER MAITLAND, in five volumes, 1904–10

Third Edition, edited by H. C. COLLES, in five volumes, 1927

Fourth Edition, edited by H. C. COLLES, in five volumes, with Supplementary Volume, 1940

Fifth Edition, edited by ERIC BLOM, in nine volumes, 1954; with Supplementary Volume, 1961
Reprinted 1961, 1973, 1975

American Supplement, edited by WALDO SELDEN PRATT, in one volume, 1920
Reprinted with new material, 1928; many later reprints

The New Grove Dictionary of Music and Musicians,®
edited by STANLEY SADIE, in twenty volumes, 1980

The New Grove and *The New Grove Dictionary of Music and Musicians* are registered trademarks
in the United States of Macmillan Publishers Limited, London.

Macmillan Publishers Limited, London and its associated companies are the proprietors of the trademarks
Grove's, The New Grove, and *The New Grove Dictionary of Music and Musicians* throughout the world.

First published 1980 in hardback edition.
Reprinted with minor corrections, 1981, 1984, 1985, 1986, 1987, 1988, 1989, 1990, 1991, 1992, 1993, 1994, 1995.
Reprinted 1995 in paperback edition.
Published by Macmillan Publishers Limited, London. Both editions are distributed outside the United
Kingdom and Europe by Macmillan Publishers (China) Limited, Hong Kong, a member of the Macmillan
Publishers Group, and by its appointed agents. In the United States of America and Canada, Macmillan
Publishers (China) Limited, Hong Kong have appointed Grove's Dictionaries of Music Inc., New York,
NY, as sole distributor.

Text keyboarded, corrected, page-made-up and filmset by
Richard Clay (The Chaucer Press) Ltd, Bungay, Suffolk, England

Illustrations originated by Fletcher & Son Ltd, Norwich, England

Music examples processed by Halstan & Co.Ltd, Amersham, England

Printed and bound in the United States of America by R. R. Donnelley & Co., Crawfordsville, Indiana

British Library Cataloguing in Publication Data

The New Grove dictionary of music and
musicians.®

A catalogue record for this book is available
from the British Library.

ISBN 0–333–23111–2 (hardback)
ISBN 1–56159–174–2 (paperback)

Library of Congress Cataloging in Publication Data

Main entry under title:

The New Grove dictionary of music and musicians.®
Includes bibliographies.
1. Music-Dictionaries.
2. Music-Bio-bibliography.
I. Grove, George, Sir, 1820–1900.
II. Sadie, Stanley.
ML100.N48 780'.3   79-26207

ISBN 0–333–23111–2 (hardback)
ISBN 1–56159–174–2 (paperback)

Contents

General Abbreviations

A	alto, contralto [voice]		Bte	Benedicite
a	alto [instrument]		Bucks.	Buckinghamshire (GB)
AB	see BA		Bulg.	Bulgarian
ABC	American Broadcasting Company; Australian Broadcasting Commission		BVM	Blessed Virgin Mary
			BWV	Bach-Werke-Verzeichnis [Schmieder, catalogue of J. S. Bach's works]
Abt.	Abteilung [section]			
acc.	accompaniment, accompanied by			
AD	anno Domini			
add, addl	additional			
add, addn	addition		c	circa [about]
ad lib	ad libitum		Calif.	California (USA)
Ag	Agnus Dei		CanD	Cantate Domino
all	alleluia		carn.	Carnival
AM	see MA		CBC	Canadian Broadcasting Corporation
a.m.	ante meridiem [before noon]		CBE	Commander of the Order of the British Empire
amp	amplified			
AMS	American Musicological Society		CBS	Columbia Broadcasting System (USA)
Anh.	Anhang [appendix]		CBSO	City of Birmingham Symphony Orchestra
anon.	anonymous(ly)		CeBeDeM	Centre Belge de Documentation Musicale
ant	antiphon		cel	celesta
appx	appendix		CEMA	Council for the Encouragement of Music and the Arts [now the Arts Council of Great Britain]
arr.	arrangement, arranged by/for			
ASCAP	American Society of Composers, Authors and Publishers			
			cf	confer [compare]
attrib.	attribution, attributed to		c.f.	cantus firmus
Aug	August		CH	Companion of Honour
aut.	autumn		chap.	chapter
			Chin.	Chinese
			chit	chitarrone
			Cie	Compagnie
B	bass [voice]		cimb	cimbalom
B	Brainard catalogue [Tartini]		cl	clarinet
b	bass [instrument]		clvd	clavichord
b	born		cm	centimetre(s)
BA	Bachelor of Arts		CNRS	Centre National de la Recherche Scientifique (F)
Bar	baritone [voice]			
bar	baritone [instrument]		Co.	Company; County
BBC	British Broadcasting Corporation		Cod.	Codex
BC	British Columbia (Canada)		col.	column
BC	before Christ		coll.	collected by
bc	basso continuo		collab.	in collaboration with
Bd.	Band [volume]		comm	communion
Berks.	Berkshire (GB)		conc.	concerto
Berwicks.	Berwickshire (GB)		cond.	conductor, conducted by
bk	book		Conn.	Connecticut (USA)
BLitt	Bachelor of Letters/Literature		cont	continuo
BM	British Museum		Corp.	Corporation
BMI	Broadcast Music Inc. (USA)		c.p.s.	cycles per second
BMus	Bachelor of Music		Cr	Credo, Creed
bn	bassoon		CSc	Candidate of Historical Sciences
Bros.	Brothers		Ct	countertenor
Bs	Benedictus		Cz.	Czech

D	Deutsch catalogue [Schubert]; Dounias catalogue [Tartini]	GmbH	Gesellschaft mit beschränkter Haftung [limited-liability company]
d.	denarius, denarii [penny, pence]	govt.	government [district in USSR]
d	died	grad	gradual
Dan.	Danish	GSM	Guildhall School of Music and Drama, London
db	double bass		
DBE	Dame Commander of the Order of the British Empire	gui	guitar
dbn	double bassoon		
DC	District of Columbia (USA)	H	Hoboken catalogue [Haydn]; Helm catalogue [C. P. E. Bach]
Dec	December		
ded.	dedication, dedicated to	Hants.	Hampshire (GB)
DeM	Deus misereatur	Heb.	Hebrew
Dept	Department	Herts.	Hertfordshire (GB)
Derbys.	Derbyshire (GB)	HMS	His/Her Majesty's Ship
dir.	director, directed by	HMV	His Master's Voice
diss.	dissertation	hn	horn
DLitt	Doctor of Letters/Literature	Hon.	Honorary; Honourable
DMus	Doctor of Music	hpd	harpsichord
DPhil	Doctor of Philosophy	HRH	His/Her Royal Highness
DSc	Doctor of Science/Historical Sciences	Hung.	Hungarian
		Hunts.	Huntingdonshire (GB)
		Hz	Hertz [c.p.s.]
ed.	editor, edited (by)		
edn.	edition		
e.g.	exempli gratia [for example]	IAML	International Association of Music Libraries
elec	electric, electronic		
EMI	Electrical and Musical Industries	ibid	ibidem [in the same place]
Eng.	English	i.e.	id est [that is]
eng hn	english horn	IFMC	International Folk Music Council
ens	ensemble	Ill.	Illinois (USA)
esp.	especially	IMS	International Musicological Society
etc	et cetera [and so on]	Inc.	Incorporated
ex., exx.	example, examples	inc.	incomplete
		incl.	includes, including
		Ind.	Indiana (USA)
f, ff	following page, following pages	inst	instrument, instrumental
f., ff.	folio, folios	int	introit
f	forte	IPEM	Institute for Psycho-acoustics and Electronic Music, Brussels
facs.	facsimile		
fasc.	fascicle	ISCM	International Society for Contemporary Music
Feb	February		
ff	fortissimo	ISM	Incorporated Society of Musicians (GB)
fff	fortississimo	ISME	International Society of Music Educators
fig.	figure [illustration]	It.	Italian
fl	flute		
fl	floruit [he/she flourished]		
fp	fortepiano	Jan	January
Fr.	French	Jap.	Japanese
frag.	fragment	*Jb*	Jahrbuch [yearbook]
FRAM	Fellow of the Royal Academy of Music, London	Jg.	Jahrgang [year of publication/volume]
		jr	junior
FRCM	Fellow of the Royal College of Music, London	Jub	Jubilate
FRCO	Fellow of the Royal College of Organists, London	K	Kirkpatrick catalogue [D. Scarlatti]; Köchel catalogue [Mozart; no. after / is from 6th edn.]
FRS	Fellow of the Royal Society, London		
		kbd	keyboard
		KBE	Knight Commander of the Order of the British Empire
Gael.	Gaelic		
Ger.	German	KCVO	Knight Commander of the Royal Victorian Order
Gk.	Greek		
Gl	Gloria	kHz	kilohertz
Glam.	Glamorgan (GB)	km	kilometre(s)
glock	glockenspiel	Ky	Kyrie
Glos., Gloucs.	Gloucestershire (GB)	Ky.	Kentucky (USA)

£	libra, librae [pound, pounds sterling]
L	Longo catalogue [D. Scarlatti]
Lancs.	Lancashire (GB)
Lat.	Latin
Leics.	Leicestershire (GB)
lib	libretto
Lincs.	Lincolnshire (GB)
lit	litany
LittD	Doctor of Letters/Literature
LlB	Bachelor of Laws
LlD	Doctor of Laws
LP	long-playing record
LPO	London Philharmonic Orchestra
LSO	London Symphony Orchestra
Ltd	Limited
M.	Monsieur
MA	Master of Arts
Mag	Magnificat
mand	mandolin
mar	marimba
Mass.	Massachusetts (USA)
MBE	Member of the Order of the British Empire
Mez	mezzo-soprano
mf	mezzo-forte
mic	microphone
Mich.	Michigan (USA)
Minn.	Minnesota (USA)
Mlle	Mademoiselle
mm	millimetre(s)
Mme	Madame
MMus	Master of Music
mod	modulator
Mon.	Monmouthshire (GB)
movt	movement
MP	Member of Parliament (GB)
mp	mezzo-piano
MS	manuscript
MSc	Master of Science(s)
Mt	Mount
MusB, MusBac	Bachelor of Music
MusD, MusDoc	Doctor of Music
MusM	Master of Music
NBC	National Broadcasting Company (USA)
n.d.	no date of publication
NJ	New Jersey (USA)
no.	number
Nor.	Norwegian
Northants.	Northamptonshire (GB)
Notts.	Nottinghamshire (GB)
Nov	November
n.p.	no place of publication
nr.	near
NSW	New South Wales (Australia)
Nunc	Nunc dimittis
NY	New York State (USA)
ob	oboe
obbl	obbligato
OBE	Officer of the Order of the British Empire

Oct	October
off	offertory
OM	Order of Merit
Ont.	Ontario (Canada)
op., opp.	opus, opera
op cit	opere citato [in the work cited]
opt.	optional
orch	orchestra, orchestral
orchd	orchestrated (by)
org	organ
orig.	original(ly)
ORTF	Office de Radiodiffusion-Télévision Française
OUP	Oxford University Press
ov.	overture
P	Pincherle catalogue [Vivaldi]
p.	pars (1p. = *prima pars*, etc)
p., pp.	page, pages
p	piano
p.a.	per annum
PC	number of chanson in A. Pillet and H. Carstens: *Bibliographie der Troubadours* (Halle, 1933)
Penn.	Pennsylvania (USA)
perc	percussion
perf.	performance, performed (by)
pf	piano
PhD	Doctor of Philosophy
pic	piccolo
pl.	plate; plural
p.m.	post meridiem [after noon]
PO	Philharmonic Orchestra
Pol.	Polish
Port.	Portuguese
posth.	posthumous(ly)
POW	prisoner of war
pp	pianissimo
ppp	pianississimo
pr.	printed
PRO	Public Record Office, London
prol	prologue
PRS	Performing Right Society (GB)
Ps	Psalm
ps	psalm
pseud.	pseudonym
pt.	part
ptbk	partbook
pubd	published
pubn	publication
qnt	quintet
qt	quartet
R	[in signature] editorial revision
R.	number of chanson in G. Raynaud: *Bibliographie des chansonniers français des XIIIe et XIVe siècles* (Paris, 1884) and H. Spanke: *G. Raynauds Bibliographie des altfranzösischen Liedes* (Leiden, 1955)
R	response
R	Ryom catalogue [Vivaldi]
R	photographic reprint
r	recto

RAF	Royal Air Force
RAI	Radio Audizioni Italiane
RAM	Royal Academy of Music, London
RCA	Radio Corporation of America
RCM	Royal College of Music, London
re	response
rec	recorder
recit	recitative
red.	reduction, reduced for
repr.	reprinted
Rev.	Reverend
rev.	revision, revised (by/for)
RIdIM	Répertoire International d'Iconographie Musicale
RILM	Répertoire International de Littérature Musicale
RISM	Répertoire International des Sources Musicales
RMCM	Royal Manchester College of Music
RNCM	Royal Northern College of Music, Manchester
RO	Radio Orchestra
Rom.	Romanian
RPO	Royal Philharmonic Orchestra (GB)
RSFSR	Russian Soviet Federated Socialist Republic
RSO	Radio Symphony Orchestra
Rt Hon.	Right Honourable
RTE	Radio Telefís Eireann (Ireland)
Russ.	Russian
RV	Ryom catalogue [Vivaldi]
S	San, Santa, Santo, São [Saint]; soprano [voice]
S.	south, southern
$	dollars
s	soprano [instrument]
s.	solidus, solidi [shilling, shillings]
SACEM	Société d'Auteurs, Compositeurs et Editeurs de Musique (F)
San	Sanctus
Sask.	Saskatchewan (Canada)
sax	saxophone
Sept	September
seq	sequence
ser.	series
sf, *sfz*	sforzando, sforzato
sing.	singular
SJ	Societas Jesu (Society of Jesus)
SO	Symphony Orchestra
SPNM	Society for the Promotion of New Music (GB)
spr.	spring
SS	Saints
Ss	Santissima, Santissimo
SSR	Soviet Socialist Republic
St	Saint, Sint, Szent
Staffs.	Staffordshire (GB)
Ste	Sainte
str	string(s)
sum.	summer
Sup	superius
suppl.	supplement, supplementary
Swed.	Swedish
sym.	symphony, symphonic
synth	synthesizer

T	tenor [voice]
t	tenor [instrument]
TeD	Te Deum
Tenn.	Tennessee (USA)
timp	timpani
tpt	trumpet
Tr	treble [voice]
tr	tract; treble [instrument]
trans.	translation, translated by
transcr.	transcription, transcribed by/for
trbn	trombone
U.	University
UHF	ultra-high frequency
UK	United Kingdom of Great Britain and Northern Ireland
unacc.	unaccompanied
unattrib.	unattributed
UNESCO	United Nations Educational, Scientific and Cultural Organization
unperf.	unperformed
unpubd	unpublished
US	United States [adjective]
USA	United States of America
USSR	Union of Soviet Socialist Republics
V	versicle
v, vv	voice, voices
v., vv.	verse, verses
v	verso
va	viola
vc	cello
vcle	versicle
VEB	Volkseigener Betrieb [people's own industry]
Ven	Venite
VHF	very high frequency
vib	vibraphone
viz	videlicet [namely]
vle	violone
vn	violin
vol.	volume
W.	west, western
Warwicks.	Warwickshire (GB)
Wilts.	Wiltshire (GB)
wint.	winter
Wisc.	Wisconsin (USA)
WoO, woo	Werke ohne Opuszahl [works without opus number]
Worcs.	Worcestershire (GB)
WQ	Wotquenne catalogue [C. P. E. Bach]
ww	woodwind
xyl	xylophone
Yorks.	Yorkshire (GB)
z	Zimmerman catalogue [Purcell]

Bibliographical Abbreviations

All bibliographical abbreviations used in this dictionary are listed below, following the typography used in the text of the dictionary. Broadly, *italic* type is used for periodicals and for reference works; roman type is used for anthologies, series etc (titles of individual volumes are italicized).

Full bibliographical information is not normally supplied in the list below if it is available elsewhere in the dictionary. Its availability is indicated as follows: D – in the article 'Dictionaries and encyclopedias of music'; E – in the article 'Editions, historical'; and P – in the list forming §III of the article 'Periodicals' (in this case the number in that list of the periodical concerned is added, in brackets). For other items, in particular national (non-musical) biographical dictionaries, basic bibliographical information is given here; and in some cases extra information is supplied to clarify the abbreviation used.

Festschriften and congress reports are not, in general, covered in this list. Although Festschrift titles are usually shortened in the dictionary, sufficient information is always given for unambiguous identification (dedicatee; occasion, if the same person is dedicatee of more than one Festschrift; place and date of publication; and where the dedicatee has an entry the editor's name may be found); for fuller information on musical Festschriften up to 1967 see W. Gerboth: *An Index to Musical Festschriften and Similar Publications* (New York, 1969). The only congress report series listed below are those of the international and the German musicological associations; for others cited in the dictionary, sufficient information is always given for identification (society or topic; place; date of occurrence); full information may be found in J. Tyrrell and R. Wise: *A Guide to International Congress Reports in Music, 1900–1975* (London, 1979).

AcM	*Acta musicologica* P [Intl 5]
ADB	*Allgemeine deutsche Biographie* (Leipzig, 1875–1912)
AM	*Antiphonale monasticum pro diurnis horis* (Paris, Tournai and Rome, 1934)
AMe (AMeS)	*Algemene muziekencyclopedie* (and suppl.) D
AMf	*Archiv für Musikforschung* P [D776]
AMI	L'arte musicale in Italia E
AMP	Antiquitates musicae in Polonia E
AMw	*Archiv für Musikwissenschaft* P [D552]
AMZ	*Allgemeine musikalische Zeitung* P [D32, 154, 170]
AMz	*Allgemeine Musik-Zeitung* P [D203]
AnM	*Anuario musical* P [E91]
AnMc	*Analecta musicologica* (some vols. in series Studien zur italienisch-deutschen Musikgeschichte), Veröffentlichung des Musikabteilung des Deutschen historischen Instituts in Rom (Cologne, 1963–)
AnnM	*Annales musicologiques* P [F638]
AntMI	Antiquae musicae italicae E
AR	*Antiphonale sacrosanctae romanae ecclesiae pro diurnis horis* (Paris, Tournai and Rome, 1949)
AS	*Antiphonale sarisburiense*, ed. W. H. Frere (London, 1901–25/R1967)
Baker 5, 6	*Baker's Biographical Dictionary of Musicians* (5/1958 and 1971 suppl., 6/1978) D
BAMS	*Bulletin of the American Musicological Society* P [US540]
BeJb	*Beethoven-Jahrbuch* [1953–] P [D925]
BJb	*Bach-Jahrbuch* P [D434]
BMB	Biblioteca musica bononiensis E
BMw	*Beiträge zur Musikwissenschaft* P [D1013]
BNB	*Biographie nationale [belge]* (Brussels, 1866–)
BordasD	*Dictionnaire de la musique* (Paris: Bordas, 1970–76) D
Bouwsteenen: JVNM	*Bouwsteenen: jaarboek der Vereeniging voor Nederlandsche muziekgeschiedenis* P [NL20]
BrownI	H. M. Brown: *Instrumental Music Printed before 1600: a Bibliography* (Cambridge, Mass.; 2/1967)
BSIM	*Bulletin français de la S[ociété] I[nternationale de] M[usique]* [previously *Le Mercure musical*; also other titles] P [F364]

BUCEM	*British Union-catalogue of Early Music*, ed. E. Schnapper (London, 1957)
BurneyH	C. Burney: *A General History of Music from the Earliest Ages to the Present* (London, 1776–89) [p. nos. refer to edn. of 1935/R1957]
BWQ	*Brass and Woodwind Quarterly* P [US756]
CaM	Catalogus musicus E
CEKM	Corpus of Early Keyboard Music E
CEMF	Corpus of Early Music in Facsimile E
CHM	*Collectanea historiae musicae* (in series Biblioteca historiae musicae cultores) (Florence, 1953–)
CM	Le choeur des muses E
CMc	*Current Musicology* P [US747]
CMI	I classici musicali italiani E
CMM	Corpus mensurabilis musicae E
CMz	*Cercetări de muzicologie* P [R29]
CS	E. de Coussemaker: *Scriptorum de musica medii aevi nova series* (Paris, 1864–76/R1963)
ČSHS	*Československý hudební slovník* D
CSM	Corpus scriptorum de musica E
CSPD	*Calendar of State Papers (Domestic)* (London, 1856–1972)
Cw	Das Chorwerk E
DAB	*Dictionary of American Biography* (New York, 1928–)
DAM	*Dansk aarbog for musikforskning* P [DK88]
DBF	*Dictionnaire de biographie française* (Paris, 1933–)
DBI	*Dizionario biografico degli italiani* (Rome, 1960–)
DBL	*Dansk biografisk leksikon* (Copenhagen, 1887–1905, 2/1933–)
DBP	*Dicionário biográfico de musicos portuguezes* D
DČHP	*Dějiny české hudby v příkladech* E
DDT	Denkmäler deutscher Tonkunst E
DHM	Documenta historicae musicae E
DJbM	*Deutsches Jahrbuch der Musikwissenschaft* P [D980]
DM	Documenta musicologica E
DNB	*Dictionary of National Biography* (London, 1885–1901, suppls.)
DTB	Denkmäler der Tonkunst in Bayern E
DTÖ	Denkmäler der Tonkunst in Österreich E

EDM	Das Erbe deutscher Musik E	JbMP	Jahrbuch der Musikbibliothek Peters P [D336]
EECM	Early English Church Music E	JEFDSS	The Journal of the English Folk Dance and Song Society P [GB341]
EIT	Ezhegodnik imperatorskikh teatrov P [USSR17]		
EitnerQ	R. Eitner: Biographisch-bibliographisches Quellen-Lexikon D	JFSS	Journal of the Folk-song Society P [GB183]
		JIFMC	Journal of the International Folk Music Council P [Intl 10]
EitnerS	R. Eitner: Bibliographie der Musik-Sammelwerke des XVI. und XVII. Jahrhunderts (Berlin, 1877)	JMT	Journal of Music Theory P [US683]
EKM	English (later Early) Keyboard Music E	JRBM	Journal of Renaissance and Baroque Music P [US590]
EL	The English Lute-songs		
EM	The English Madrigalists E	JRME	Journal of Research in Music Education P [US665]
EM	Ethnomusicology P [US664]	JVNM	see Bouwsteenen: JVNM P [NL20]
EMDC	Encyclopédie de la musique et dictionnaire du Conservatoire D		
EMN	Exempla musica neerlandica E		
EMS	The English Madrigal School E	KJb	Kirchenmusikalisches Jahrbuch P [D284]
ES	Enciclopedia dello spettacolo D	KM	Kwartalnik muzyczny P [PL35, 64]
ESLS	The English School of Lutenist-songwriters E		
		LaborD	Diccionario de la música Labor D
FAM	Fontes artis musicae P [Intl 16]	LaMusicaD	La musica: dizionario D
FasquelleE	Encyclopédie de la musique (Paris: Fasquelle, 1958–61) D	LaMusicaE	La musica: enciclopedia storica D
		LM	Lucrări de muzicologie P [R27]
FCVR	Florilège du concert vocal de la renaissance E	LSJ	The Lute Society Journal P [GB487]
FétisB (FétisBS)	F.-J. Fétis: Biographie universelle des musiciens (2/1860–65) (and suppl.) D	LU	Liber usualis missae et officii pro dominicis et festis duplicibus cum cantu gregoriano (Solesmes, 1896; many later edns., incl. Tournai, 1963)
GerberL	R. Gerber: Historisch-biographisches Lexikon der Tonkünstler D		
GerberNL	R. Gerber: Neues historisch-biographisches Lexikon der Tonkünstler D	MA	The Musical Antiquary P [GB240]
		MAB	Musica antiqua bohemica E
GfMKB	Gesellschaft für Musikforschung Kongressbericht [1950–]	MAM	Musik alter Meister E
		MAP	Musica antiqua polonica E
GMB	Geschichte der Musik in Beispielen, ed. A. Schering (Leipzig, 1931) E	MAS	[publications of the British] Musical Antiquarian Society E
GR	Graduale sacrosanctae romanae ecclesiae (Tournai, 1938)	MB	Musica britannica E
		MC	Musica da camera E
Grove 1(–5)	G. Grove, ed.: A Dictionary of Music and Musicians, 2nd–5th edns. as Grove's Dictionary of Music and Musicians D	MD	Musica disciplina P [US590]
		ME	Muzïkal'naya entsiklopediya D
		MEM	Mestres de l'escolania de Montserrat E
Grove 6	The New Grove Dictionary of Music and Musicians D	Mf	Die Musikforschung P [D839]
		MGG	Die Musik in Geschichte und Gegenwart D
GS	Graduale sarisburiense, ed. W. H. Frere (London, 1894/R1967)	MH	Musica hispana E
		MJb	Mozart-Jahrbuch des Zentralinstituts für Mozartforschung [1950–] P [A254]
GS	M. Gerbert: Scriptores ecclesiastici de musica sacra (St Blasien, 1784/R1963)	ML	Music and Letters P [GB280]
		MLMI	Monumenta lyrica medii aevi italica E
GSJ	The Galpin Society Journal P [GB415]	MM	Modern Music P [US488]
		MMA	Miscellanea musicologica [Australia] P [AUS19]
HAM	Historical Anthology of Music, ed. A. T. Davison and W. Apel, i (Cambridge, Mass., 1946, rev. 2/1949); ii (Cambridge, Mass., 1950) E	MMB	Monumenta musicae byzantinae E
		MMBel	Monumenta musicae belgicae E
		MMC	Miscellanea musicologica [Czechoslovakia] P [CS191]
HawkinsH	J. Hawkins: A General History of the Science and Practice of Music (London, 1776) [p. nos. refer to edn. of 1853/R1963]	MME	Monumentos de la música española E
		MMFTR	Monuments de la musique française au temps de la renaissance E
HJb	Händel-Jahrbuch P [D712, 968]	MMg	Monatshefte für Musikgeschichte P [D188]
HM	Hortus musicus E	MMI	Monumenti di musica italiana E
HMT	Handwörterbuch der musikalischen Terminologie D	MMN	Monumenta musicae neerlandicae E
HMw	Handbuch der Musikwissenschaft, ed. E. Bücken (Potsdam, 1927–) [monograph series]	MMP	Monumenta musicae in Polonia E
		MMR	The Monthly Musical Record P [GB75]
HMYB	Hinrichsen's Musical Year Book P [GB381]	MMRF	Les maîtres musiciens de la renaissance française E
HPM	Harvard Publications in Music E		
HR	Hudebni revue P [CS80]	MMS	Monumenta musicae svecicae E
HRo	Hudebni rozhledy P [CS176]	MO	Musical Opinion P [GB90]
HV	Hudebni věda P [CS204]	MQ	The Musical Quarterly P [US447]
		MR	The Music Review P [GB376]
		MRM	Monuments of Renaissance Music E
IIM	Izvestiya na Instituta za muzïka P [BG14]	MRS	Musiche rinascimentali siciliane E
IMa	Instituta et monumenta	MS	Muzïkal'nïy sovremennik P [USSR37]
IMi	Istituzioni e monumenti dell'arte musicale italiana E	MSD	Musicological Studies and Documents, ed. A. Carapetyan (Rome, 1951–)
IMSCR	International Musicological Society Congress Report [1930–]	MT	The Musical Times P [GB33]
		MVH	Musica viva historica E
IMusSCR	International Musical Society Congress Report [1906–11]	MVSSP	Musiche vocali strumentali sacre e profane E
IRASM	International Review of the Aesthetics and Sociology of Music P [Intl 32]	Mw	Das Musikwerk E
		MZ	Muzikološki zbornik P [YU37]
IRMO	S. L. Ginzburg: Istoriya russkoy muzïki v notnïkh obraztsakh D		
IRMAS	The International Review of Music Aesthetics and Sociology P [Intl 32]	NA	Note d'archivio per la storia musicale P [I186]
		NBJb	Neues Beethoven-Jahrbuch P [D636]
IZ	Instrumentenbau-Zeitschrift P [D806]	NBL	Norsk biografisk leksikon (Oslo, 1921–)
		NDB	Neue deutsche Biographie (Berlin, 1953–)
		NM	Nagels Musikarchiv E
		NNBW	Nieuw Nederlandsch biografisch woordenboek (Leiden, 1911–37)
JAMS	Journal of the American Musicological Society P [US613]	NÖB	Neue österreichische Biographie (Vienna, 1923)

NOHM	*The New Oxford History of Music*, ed. E. Wellesz, J. A. Westrup and G. Abraham (London, 1954–)	*SartoriB*	C. Sartori: *Bibliografia della musica strumentale italiana stampata in Italia fino al 1700* (Florence, 1952–68)
NRMI	*Nuova rivista musicale italiana* P [I 282]	*SBL*	*Svenska biografiskt leksikon* (Stockholm, 1918–)
NZM	*Neue Zeitschrift für Musik* P [D75, 1088]	*SchmidlD (SchmidlDS)*	C. Schmidl: *Dizionario dei musicisti* (and suppl.) D
OHM	*The Oxford History of Music*, ed. W. H. Hadow (Oxford, 1901–5, enlarged 2/1929–38)	SCMA	Smith College Music Archives E
OM	*Opus musicum* P [CS222]	*SeegerL*	H. Seeger: *Musiklexikon* D
ÖMz	*ÖsterreichischeMusikzeitschrift* P [A233]	SEM	[University of California] Series of Early Music E
		SH	*Slovenská hudba* P [CS192]
		SIMG	*Sammelbände der Internationalen Musik-Gesellschaft* P [Intl 2]
PalMus	Paléographie musicale (Solesmes, 1889–) [see entry SOLESMES]	*SM*	*Studia musicologica Academiae scientiarum hungaricae* P [H49]
PAMS	*Papers of the American Musicological Society* P [US543]	*SMA*	*Studies in Music* [Australia] P [AUS20]
PÄMw	Publikationen älterer praktischer und theoretischer Musikwerke E	SMd	Schweizerische Musikdenkmäler E
PBC	Publicaciones del departamento de música de la Biblioteca de Catalunya E	*SML*	*Schweizer Musiker Lexikon* D
		SMM	Summa musicae medii aevi E
PG	*Patrologiae cursus completus*, ii: *Series graeca*, ed. J.-P. Migne (Paris, 1857–1912)	*SMN*	*Studia musicologica norvegica* P [N45]
PGfM	Publikationen der Gesellschaft für Musikforschung E	*SMP*	*Słownik muzyków polskich* D
		SMw	*Studien zur Musikwissenschaft* P [D536]
PIISM	Pubblicazioni dell'Istituto italiano per la storia della musica E	*SMz*	*Schweizerische Musikzeitung/Revue musicale suisse* P [CH4]
PL	*Patrologiae cursus completus*, i: *Series latina*, ed. J.-P. Migne (Paris, 1844–64)	SOB	Süddeutsche Orgelmeister des Barock E
PM	Portugaliae musica E	*SovM*	*Sovetskaya muzïka* P [USSR66]
PMA	*Proceedings of the Musical Association* P [GB80]	*STMf*	*Svensk tidskrift för musikforskning* P [S46]
PMFC	Polyphonic Music of the Fourteenth Century E		
PNM	*Perspectives of New Music* P [US724]	TCM	Tudor Church Music E
PRM	*Polski rocznik muzykologiczny* P [PL85]	TM	Thesauri musici E
PRMA	*Proceedings of the Royal Musical Association* P [GB80]	*TVNM*	*Tijdschrift van de Vereniging voor Nederlandse muziekgeschiedenis* P [NL26]
PSB	*Polskich słownik biograficzny* (Kraków, 1935)		
PSFM	Publications de la Société française de musicologie E	UVNM	Uitgaven der Vereniging voor Nederlandse muziekgeschiedenis E
Quaderni della RaM	*Quaderni della Rassegna musicale* P [I 272]	VMPH	Veröffentlichungen der Musik-Bibliothek Paul Hirsch E
		VMw	*Vierteljahrsschrift für Musikwissenschaft* P [D282]
Rad JAZU	*Rad Jugoslavenske akademije znanosti i umjetnosti* (Zagreb, 1867–)	*VogelB*	E. Vogel: *Bibliothek der gedruckten weltlichen Vocalmusik Italiens, aus den Jahren 1500 bis 1700* (Berlin, 1892); rev., enlarged, by A. Einstein (Hildesheim, 1962); further addns in *AnMc*, nos.4, 5, 9 and 12; further rev. by F. Lesure and C. Sartori as *Bibliografia della musica italiana vocale profana pubblicata dal 1500 al 1700* (?Geneva, 1978)
RaM	*La rassegna musicale* P [I 197]		
RBM	*Revue belge de musicologie* P [B126]		
RdM	*Revue de musicologie* P [F462]		
ReM	*La revue musicale* [1920–] P [F475]		
RHCM	*Revue d'histoire et de critique musicales* [1901]; *La revue musicale* [1902–10] P [F320]		
RicordiE	*Enciclopedia della musica* (Milan: Ricordi, 1963–4) D	*WaltherML*	J. G. Walther: *Musicalisches Lexicon oder Musicalische Bibliothec* D
RiemannL 12	*Riemann Musik Lexikon* (12/1959–75) D	WDMP	Wydawnictwo dawnej muzyki polskiej E
RIM	*Rivista italiana di musicologia* P [I 280]	WE	Wellesley Edition E
RISM	*Répertoire international des sources musicales* [see entry under this title]	WECIS	Wellesley Edition Cantata Index Series E
RMARC	*R[oyal] M[usical] A[ssociation] Research Chronicle* P [GB496]	*YIFMC*	*Yearbook of the International Folk Music Council* P [Intl 31]
RMFC	*Recherches sur la musique française classique* P [F677]		
RMG	*Russkaya muzïkal'naya gazeta* P [USSR19]	*ZfM*	*Zeitschrift für Musik* P [D75]
RMI	*Rivista musicale italiana* P [I 84]	ZHMP	Zrodła do historii muzyki polskiej E
RMS	Renaissance Manuscript Studies E	*ZI*	*Zeitschrift für Instrumentenbau* P [D249]
RN	*Renaissance News* P [see US590]	*ZIMG*	*Zeitschrift der Internationalen Musik-Gesellschaft* P [Intl3]
RRMBE	Recent Researches in the Music of the Baroque Era E	*ZL*	*Zenei lexikon* D
RRMR	Recent Researches in the Music of the Renaissance E	*ZMw*	*Zeitschrift für Musikwissenschaft* P [D556]

Library Sigla

The system of library sigla in this dictionary follows that used in its publications (Series A) by Répertoire International des Sources Musicales, Kassel, by permission. Below are listed the sigla to be found; a few of them are additional to those in the published RISM lists, but have been established in consultation with the RISM organization. Some original RISM sigla that have now been changed are retained here.

In the dictionary, sigla are always printed in *italic*. In any listing of sources a national sigillum applies without repetition until it is contradicted. For German sigla, the intermediate *brd* and *ddr* are excluded; the list below shows in which part of Germany or Berlin each library is located.

Within each national list, entries are alphabetized by sigillum, first by capital letters (showing the city or town) and then by lower-case ones (showing the institution or collection).

A: AUSTRIA

Ee	Eisenstadt, Esterházy-Archiv
Eh	——, Haydn Museum
Ek	——, Stadtpfarrkirche
F	Fiecht, Benediktinerordensstift St Georgenberg
Gd	Graz, Diözesan Archiv
Gk	——, Hochschule für Musik und Darstellende Kunst
Gl	——, Steiermärkische Landesbibliothek am Joanneum
Gmi	——, Musikwissenschaftliches Institut der Universität
Gu	——, Universitätsbibliothek
GÖ	Furth bei Göttweig, Benediktinerstift
GÜ	Güssing, Franziskaner Kloster
H	Herzogenburg, Chorherrenstift
HE	Heiligenkreuz, Zisterzienserstift
Ik	Innsbruck, Konservatorium
Imf	——, Museum Ferdinandeum
Imi	——, Musikwissenschaftliches Institut der Universität
Iu	——, Universitätsbibliothek
Iw	——, Prämonstratenserordensstift Wilten
KN	Klosterneuburg, Augustiner-Chorherrenstift
KR	Kremsmünster, Benediktinerstift
L	Lilienfeld, Zisterzienser-Stift
LA	Lambach, Benediktinerstift
LEx	Leoben, Pfarrbibliothek St Xaver
LIm	Linz, Oberösterreichisches Landesarchiv
LIs	——, Bundesstaatliche Studienbibliothek
M	Melk an der Donau, Benediktinerstift
MB	Michaelbeuern, Benediktinerabtei
MÖ	Mödling, Pfarrkirche St Othmar
MZ	Mariazell, Benediktiner-Priorat
N	Neuburg, Pfarrarchiv
NS	Neustift, Pfarrarchiv
R	Rein, Zisterzienserstift
Sca	Salzburg, Museum Carolino Augusteum
Sd	——, Dom-Musikarchiv
Sk	——, Kapitelbibliothek
Sm	——, Internationale Stiftung Mozarteum
Smi	——, Musikwissenschaftliches Institut der Universität
Sn	——, Nonnberg, Benediktiner-Frauenstift
Ssp	——, St Peter Benediktiner-Erzabtei
SB	Schlierbach, Stift
SCH	Schlägl, Prämonstratenser-Stift
SE	Seckau, Benediktinerabtei
SEI	Seitenstetten, Benediktinerstift
SF	St Florian, Augustiner-Chorherrenstift
SH	Solbad Hall, Franziskaner-Kloster
SL	St Lambrecht, Benediktiner-Abtei
SP	St Pölten, Diözesanarchiv
SPL	St Paul, Stift
ST	Stams, Zisterzienserstift
STE	Steyr, Stadtpfarrarchiv
TU	Tulln, Pfarrkirche St Stephan
Wd	Vienna, Stephansdom
Wdo	——, Zentralarchiv des Deutschen Ordens
Wdtö	——, Gesellschaft zur Herausgabe von Denkmälern der Tonkunst in Österreich
Wgm	——, Gesellschaft der Musikfreunde
Wh	——, Pfarrarchiv Hernals
Whb	——, Hauptverband des Österreichischen Buchhandels
Wk	——, Pfarrkirche St Karl Borromäus
Wkann	——, Hans Kann, private collection
Wkh	——, Kirche am Hof
Wkm	——, Kunsthistorisches Museum
Wl	——, Archiv für Niederösterreich (Landesarchiv)
Wm	——, Minoritenkonvent
Wmg	——, Pfarre, Maria am Gestade
Wmi	——, Musikwissenschaftliches Institut der Universität
Wmk	——, Akademie für Musik und Darstellende Kunst
Wn	——, Österreichische Nationalbibliothek, Musiksammlung
Wögm	——, Österreichische Gesellschaft für Musik
Wp	——, Musikarchiv, Piaristenkirche Maria Treu
Wph	——, Wiener Philharmoniker, Archiv und Bibliothek
Wps	——, Priesterseminar
Ws	——, Schottenstift
Wsa	——, Stadtarchiv
Wsp	——, St Peter, Musikarchiv
Wst	——, Stadtbibliothek, Musiksammlung
Wu	——, Universitätsbibliothek
Ww	——, Pfarrarchiv Währing
Wweinmann	——, Alexander Weinmann, private collection
Wwessely	——, Othmar Wessely, private collection
WAY	Waydhofen an der Ybbs, Pfarre
WE	Wels, Stift
WIL	Wilhering, Zisterzienserstift
Z	Zwettl, Zisterzienserstift

B: BELGIUM

Aa	Antwerp, Stadsarchief
Aac	——, Archief en Museum voor het Vlaamse Culturleven
Ac	——, Koninklijk Vlaams Muziekconservatorium
Ak	——, Onze-Lieve-Vrouwkathedraal
Amp	——, Museum Plantijn–Moretus
Apersoons	——, Guido Persoons, private collection
As	——, Stadsbibliotheek
Asa	——, Kerkebestuur St-Andries
Asj	——, Collegiale en Parochiale Kerk St-Jacob
Averwilt	——, F. Verwilt, private collection
AN	——, Anderlecht, St-Guiden Kerk
Ba	Brussels, Archives de la Ville
Bc	——, Conservatoire Royal de Musique
Bcdm	——, Centre Belge de Documentation Musicale [CeBeDeM]
Bg	——, Eglise de Ste Gudule
Bi	——, Institut de Psycho-acoustique et de Musique Electronique

Br	——, Bibliothèque Royale Albert 1er/Koninklijke Bibliotheek Albert I
Brtb	——, Radiodiffusion-Télévision Belge
Bsp	——, Société Philharmonique
BRc	Bruges, Stedelijk Muziekconservatorium
D	Diest, St Sulpitiuskerk
Gar	Ghent [Gent, Gand], Stadsarchief
Gc	——, Koninklijk Muziekconservatorium
Gcd	——, Culturele Dienst Province Ost Vlaanderen
Geb	——, St Baafsarchief med Bibliotheek Van Damme
Gu	——, Rijksuniversiteit, Centrale Bibliotheek
K	Kortrijk, St Martinskerk
Lc	Liège, Conservatoire Royal de Musique
Lu	——, Université de Liège
LIc	Lier, Conservatoire
LIg	——, St Gummaruskerk
LV	Louvain, Dominikanenklooster
LVu	——, Université de Louvain
M	Mons, Conservatoire Royal de Musique
MA	Morlanwelz-Mariemont, Musée de Mariemont
MEa	Mechelen, Archief en Stadsbibliotheek
MEs	——, Stedelijke Openbare Bibliotheek
OU	Oudenaarde, Parochiale Kerk
Tc	Tournai, Chapitre de la Cathédrale
Tv	——, Bibliothèque de la Ville
TI	Tienen, St Germanuskerk
Z	Zoutleeuw, St Leonarduskerk

BR: BRAZIL

Rem	Rio de Janeiro, Escola de Música, Universidade Federal do Rio de Janeiro
Rn	——, Biblioteca Nacional

C: CANADA

E	Edmonton, University of Alberta
Fc	Fredericton, Christ Church Cathedral
Ku	Kingston, Queens University, Douglas Library
Lu	London, University of Western Ontario, Lawson Memorial Library
Mc	Montreal, Conservatoire de Musique et d'Art Dramatique
Mfisher	——, Sidney T. Fisher, private collection [in *Tu*]
Mm	——, McGill University, Faculty and Conservatorium of Music and Redpath Libraries
On	Ottawa, National Library of Canada
Qc	Quebec, Cathédrale de la Sainte-Trinité
Qul	——, Université Laval
SAu	Sackville, Mt Allison University
SJm	St John, New Brunswick Museum
Tb	Toronto, Canadian Broadcasting Corporation
Tm	——, Royal Ontario Museum
Tolnick	——, Harvey J. Olnick, private collection
Tp	——, Toronto Public Library, Music Branch
Tu	——, University of Toronto, Faculty of Music
Vu	Vancouver, University of British Columbia Library, Fine Arts Division
W	Winnipeg, University of Manitoba

CH: SWITZERLAND

A	Aarau, Aargauische Kantonsbibliothek
AShoboken	Ascona, Anthony van Hoboken, private collection
Bchristen	Basle, Werner Christen, private collection
Bm	——, Musikakademie der Stadt
Bmi	——, Musikwissenschaftliches Institut der Universität
Bu	——, Öffentliche Bibliothek der Universität, Musiksammlung
BA	Baden, Historisches Museum (Landvogtei-Schloss)
BEk	Berne, Konservatorium
BEl	——, Schweizerische Landesbibliothek
BEms	——, Musikwissenschaftliches Seminar der Universität
BEsu	——, Stadt- und Universitätsbibliothek; Bürgerbibliothek
BI	Biel, Stadtbibliothek
C	Chur, Kantonsbibliothek Graubünden
D	Disentis, Stift
E	Einsiedeln, Benediktinerkloster
EN	Engelberg, Stift
Fcu	Fribourg, Bibliothèque Cantonale et Universitaire
Ff	——, Franziskaner-Kloster
Fk	——, Kapuziner-Kloster
Fsn	——, Kapitel St Nikolaus
FF	Frauenfeld, Thurgauische Kantonsbibliothek
Gamoudruz	Geneva, Emile Amoudruz, private collection
Gc	——, Conservatoire de Musique
Gpu	——, Bibliothèque Publique et Universitaire

GLtschudi	Glarus, A. Tschudi, private collection
Lmg	Lucerne, Allgemeine Musikalische Gesellschaft
Ls	——, Stiftsarchiv St Leodegar
Lz	——, Zentralbibliothek
LAc	Lausanne, Conservatoire de Musique
LAcu	——, Bibliothèque Cantonale et Universitaire
LU	Lugano, Biblioteca Cantonale
Mbernegg	Maienfeld, Sprecher von Bernegg, private collection
MO	Morges, Bibliothèque de la Ville
MÜ	Müstair, Frauenkloster
N	Neuchâtel, Bibliothèque Publique
R	Rheinfelden, Christkatholisches Pfarramt
S	Sion, Bibliothèque Cantonale du Valais
Sa	——, Staatsarchiv
Sk	——, Kathedrale
SA	Sarnen, Bibliothek des Kollegiums
SAf	——, Frauenkloster
SCH	Schwyz, Kantonsbibliothek
SGs	St Gall, Stiftsbibliothek
SGv	——, Stadtbibliothek
SH	Schaffhausen, Stadtbibliothek
SM	St Maurice, Bibliothèque de l'Abbaye
SO	Solothurn, Zentralbibliothek, Musiksammlung
TH	Thun, Stadtbibliothek
W	Winterthur, Stadtbibliothek
Wpeer	——, Peer private collection
Zi	Zurich, Israelitische Kulturgemeinde
Zjacobi	——, Erwin R. Jacobi, private collection
Zk	——, Konservatorium und Musikhochschule
Zma	——, Schweizerisches Musik-Archiv
Zms	——. Musikwissenschaftliches Seminar der Universität
Zp	——, Pestalozzianum
Zz	——, Zentralbibliothek
ZG	Zug, Stadtbibliothek
ZO	Zofingen, Stadtbibliothek
ZU	Zuoz, Gemeindearchiv

CO: COLOMBIA

B	Bogotá, Catedral

CS: CZECHOSLOVAKIA

Bb	Brno, Klášter Milosrdných Bratří [in *Bm*]
Bm	——, Ústav Dějin Hudby Moravského Musea, Hudebněhistorické Oddělení
Bu	——, Státní Vědecká Knihovna, Universitní Knihovna
BA	Bakov nad Jizerou, pobočka Státní Archívu v Mladé Boleslavi
BEL	Bělá pod Bezdězem, Městské Muzeum
BER	Beroun, Okresní Archív
BRa	Bratislava, Okresní Archív
BRe	——, Evanjelícka a. v. Cirkevná Knižnica
BRhs	——, Knižnica Hudobného Seminara Filosofickej Fakulty University Komenského
BRnm	——, Slovenské Národné Muzeum, Hudobné Oddělenie
BRsa	——, Štátny Ústredný Archív Slovenskej Socialistickej Republiky
BRsav	——, Slovenská Akadémia Vied
BRu	——, Univerzitná Knižnica
BREsi	Březnice, Děkanský Kostel Sv Ignáce
BSk	Banská Štiavnica, Farský Rímsko-Katolický Kostol, Archív Chóru
CH	Cheb, Okresní Archív
CHOd	Choceň, Děkanský Úřad
CHOm	——, Městské Muzeum
H	Hronov, Muzeum Aloise Jiráska
HK	Hradec Králové, Muzeum
HOm	Hořice, Vlastivědné Muzeum
J	Jur pri Bratislave, Okresní Archív, Bratislava-Vidick
JIa	Jindřichův Hradec, Státní Archív
JIm	——, Vlastivědné Muzeum
K	Český Krumlov, Pracoviště Státního Archívu Třeboň, Hudební Sbírka
KL	Klatovy, Okresní Archív
KO	Košice, Městsky Archív
KOL	Kolín, Děkanský Chrám
KRa	Kroměříž, Státní Zámek a Zahrady, Historicko-Umělecké Fondy, Hudební Archív
KRA	Králíky, Děkanský Úřad
KRE	Kremnica, Městsky Archív
KU	Kutná Hora, Oblastní Muzeum
KVd	Karlovy Vary, Děkanský Úřad
KVso	——, Karlovarský Symfonický Orchestr
L	Levoča, Rímsko-Katolický Farský Kostol
LIa	Česká Lípa, Okresní Archív

LIT	Litoměřice, Státní Archív
LO	Loukov, Farní Úřad
Mms	Martin, Matica Slovenská, Oddělenie Hudobných Pamiatok
Mnm	——, Slovenské Národné Muzeum, Archív
MB	Mladá Boleslav, Okresní Archív
ME	Mělník, Okresní Archív
MH	Mnichovo Hradiště, Vlastivědné Muzeum
N	Nítra, Státní Archív
ND	Nové Dvory, Farní Úřad
NM	Nové Mesto nad Váhom, Rímsko-Katolický Farský Kostol
OLa	Olomouc, Státní Oblastní Archív v Opava
OLu	——, Státní Vědecká Knihovna, Universitní Knihovna
OP	Opava, Slezské Muzeum
OS	Ostrava, Československý Rozhlas, Hudební Archív
OSE	Osek, Klášter
Pa	Prague, Státní Ústřední Archív
Pak	——, Archív Metropolitní Kapituly
Pdobrovského	——, Knihovna Josefa Dobrovského
Ph	——, Československá Cirkev Holešovice
Pis	——, Československo Hudební Informační Středisko
Pk	——, Archív Státní Konservatoře v Praze
Pnm	——, Národní Muzeum, Hudební Oddělení
Pp	——, Archív Pražského Hradu
Ppp	——, Památník Národního Písemnictví na Strahově
Pr	——, Československý Rozhlas, Hudební Archív Různá Provenience
Pra	——, Rodinní Archív Karla Kovařovice
Ps	——, Strahovská Knihovna [in *Ppp*]
Psf	——, Kostel Sv Franciscus
Psj	——, Kostel Sv Jakuba
Pu	——, Státní Knihovna ČSSR, Universitní Knihovna
PLa	Plzeň, Městsky Archív
PLm	——, Západočeské Muzeum
PLA	Plasy, Okresní Archív
POa	Poděbrady, pobočka Státní Archívu Nymburk
POm	——, Helichovo Muzeum
PR	Příbram, Okresný Muzeum
PRE	Prešov, Rímsko-Katolický Farský Kostol
RA	Rakovník, Státní Archív
RAJ	Rajhrad, Klášter [in *Bm*]
RO	Rokycany, Okresný Muzeum
ROZ	Rožnava, Biskupský Archív
RY	Rychnov, Muzeum Orlicka
Sk	Spišská Kapitula, Katedrálny Rímsko-Katolický Kostol, Knižnica Spišskej Kapituly
SNV	Spišská Nová Ves, Rímsko-Katolický Farský Kostol
SO	Sokolov, Státní Archív
TC	Třebíč, Městsky Archív
TN	Trenčín, Okresní Archív
TR	Trnava, Dóm Sv Mikuláša
TRB	Třebenice, Klášter
TRE	Třebón, Státní Archív
TU	Turnov, Okresný Muzeum
VE	Velenice, Farní Úřad
VM	Vysoké Mýto, Okresný Muzeum
ZA	Zámrsk, Státní Archív

CU: CUBA

Hn	Havana, Biblioteca Nacional
Hse	——, Biblioteca de la Sociedad Económica de Amigos del País

D: GERMANY

Aa	Augsburg, BRD, Kantoreiarchiv St Annen
Af	——, Bibliothek der Fuggerschen Domänenkanzlei
Ahk	——, Dominikanerkloster Heilig-Kreuz
As	——, Staats- und Stadtbibliothek
Asa	——, Stadtarchiv
AAd	Aachen, BRD, Bischöfliche Diözesanbibliothek
AAg	——, Kaiser Karl-Gymnasium, Lehrerbibliothek
AAm	——, Domarchiv
AAst	——, Stadtbibliothek
AB	Amorbach, BRD, Fürstlich Leiningische Bibliothek, private collection
ABG	Annaberg-Buchholz, DDR, Pfarramt, Kirchenbibliothek
ABGa	——, Kantoreiarchiv St Annen
AD	Adolfseck bei Fulda, BRD, Schloss Fasanerie, Bibliothek der Kurhessischen Hausstiftung
ALa	Altenburg, DDR, Landesarchiv (Historisches Staatsarchiv)
ALs	——, Stadtarchiv
ALt	——, Bibliothek des Landestheaters
AM	Amberg, BRD, Staatliche Provinzialbibliothek
AN	Ansbach, BRD, Regierungsbibliothek
AÖ	Altötting, BRD, Kapuziner-Kloster St Konrad
ARk	Arnstadt, DDR, Kirchenbibliothek
ARsk	——, Stadt- und Kreisbibliothek
ARsm	——, Schlossmuseum
ASh	Aschaffenburg, BRD, Hofbibliothek
ASm	——, Stadtbücherei
ASsb	——, Stiftsbibliothek
B	Berlin, Staatsbibliothek Preussischer Kulturbesitz [W]
Ba	——, Amerika-Gedenkbibliothek (Berliner Zentralbibliothek) [W]; Deutsche Akademie der Künste [E]
Bch	——, Musikbücherei Charlottenburg [W]
Bdhm	——, Deutsche Hochschule für Musik Hanns Eisler [E]
Bds	——, Deutsche Staatsbibliothek (formerly Königliche Bibliothek; Preussische Staatsbibliothek; Öffentliche Wissenschaftliche Bibliothek), Musikabteilung [E]
Bdso	——, Deutsche Staatsoper [E]
Be	——, Institut für Musikerziehung der Humboldt-Universität [E]
Bgk	——, Streit'sche Stiftung [in *Bs*] [E]
Bhbk	——, Staatliche Hochschule für Bildende Kunst [W]
Bhesse	——, A. Hesse, private collection [E]
Bhm	——, Staatliche Hochschule für Musik und Darstellende Kunst [W]
Bim	——, Staatliches Institut für Musikforschung Preussischer Kulturbesitz [W]
Bk	——, Staatliche Museen Preussischer Kulturbesitz [W]
Bko	——, Komische Oper [E]
Blk	——, Bezirks-Lehrerbibliothek Kreuzberg [W]
Bm	——, Marienkirche [E]
Bmb	——, Internationale Musikbibliothek, Verband Deutscher Komponisten und Musikwissenschaftler [E]
Bmi	——, Musikwissenschaftliches Institut der Freien Universität [W]; Musikwissenschaftliches Institut der Humboldt-Universität [E]
Bmm	——, Märkisches Museum [E]
Bn	——, Nikolaikirche [E]
Bp	——, Pädagogisches Zentrum [W]
Br	——, Deutscher Demokratischer Rundfunk, Notenarchiv [E]
Bs	——, Berliner Stadtbibliothek [E]
Bst	——, Stadtbücherei, Hauptstelle Berlin-Wilmersdorf [W]
Btu	——, Universitätsbibliothek der Technischen Universität [W]
Btum	——, Lehrstuhl für Musikgeschichte der Technischen Universität [W]
Bu	——, Universitätsbibliothek der Freien Universität [W]
Buh	——, Universitätsbibliothek der Humboldt-Universität [E]
BAa	Bamberg, BRD, Staatsarchiv
BAf	——, Franziskaner-Kloster
BAs	——, Staatsbibliothek
BAL	Ballenstedt, DDR, Stadtbibliothek
BAR	Bartenstein, BRD, Fürst zu Hohenlohe-Bartensteinsches Archiv, private collection
BAUd	Bautzen, DDR, Domstift und Bischöfliches Ordinariat
BAUk	——, Stadt- und Kreisbibliothek
BB	Benediktbeuren, BRD, Pfarrkirche
BD	Brandenburg an der Havel, DDR, Domstift
BDH	Bad Homburg von der Höhe, BRD, Stadtbibliothek
BE	Berleburg, BRD, Fürstlich Sayn-Wittgenstein-Berleburgsche Bibliothek, private collection
BEU	Beuron, BRD, Benediktiner-Erzabtei
BEV	Bevensen, BRD, Superintendantur, Ephoratsbibliothek und Bibliothek Sursen
BFa	Burgsteinfurt, BRD, Gymnasium Arnoldinum
BFb	——, Fürstlich Bentheimsche Bibliothek [in *MÜu*]
BG	Beuerberg über Wolfratshausen, BRD, Pfarramt, Stiftskirche
BGD	Berchtesgaden, BRD, Katholisches Pfarramt
BH	Bayreuth, BRD, Stadtbücherei
BI	Bielefeld, BRD, Städtisches Ratsgymnasium
BIB	Bibra, DDR, Pfarrarchiv
BIR	Birstein über Wächtersbach, BRD, Fürst von Ysenburgisches Archiv und Schlossbibliothek, private collection

BIT	Bitterfeld, DDR, Kreismuseum
BK	Bernkastel-Kues, BRD, Cusanusstift
BKÖ	Bad Köstritz, DDR, Pfarrarchiv
BMek	Bremen, BRD, Bücherei der Bremer Evangelischen Kirche
BMs	——, Staats- und Universitätsbibliothek
BNba	Bonn, BRD, Beethoven-Haus und Beethoven-Archiv
BNek	——, Gemeindeverband der Evangelischen Kirche
BNms	——, Musikwissenschaftliches Seminar der Universität
BNu	——, Universitätsbibliothek
BO	——, Bollstedt, Pfarramt
BOCHb	Bochum, BRD, Bergbaumuseum
BOCHmi	——, Musikwissenschaftliches Institut der Ruhr-Universität
BOCHs	——, Stadtbibliothek, Musikbücherei
BORp	Borna, DDR, Pfarrkirche
BS	Brunswick, BRD, Stadtarchiv und Stadtbibliothek
BTH	Barth, DDR, Kirchenbibliothek
BÜ	Büdingen, BRD, Fürstlich Ysenburg- und Büdingisches Archiv und Schlossbibliothek
BW	Burgwindheim über Bamberg, BRD, Katholisches Pfarramt
Cl	Coburg, BRD, Landesbibliothek
Cm	——, Moritzkirche
Cv	——, Kunstsammlung der Veste Coburg
CA	Castell, BRD, Fürstlich Castell'sche Bibliothek
CD	Crottendorf, DDR, Kantoreiarchiv
CR	Crimmitschau, DDR, Stadtkirche St Laurentius
CZ	Clausthal-Zellerfeld, BRD, Kirchenbibliothek
CZu	——, Universitätsbibliothek
Dhm	Dresden, DDR, Hochschule für Musik Carl Maria von Weber
Dkh	——, Katholische Hofkirche
Dl	——, Bibliothek und Museum Löbau [in *Dlb*]
Dla	——, Staatsarchiv
Dlb	——, Sächsische Landesbibliothek
Dmb	——, Musikbibliothek
Ds	——, Staatstheater
DB	Dettelbach über Kitzingen, BRD, Franziskanerkloster
DEl	Dessau, DDR, Universitäts- und Landesbibliothek
DEs	——, Stadtarchiv, Rathaus
DI	Dillingen an der Donau, BRD, Kreis- und Studienbibliothek
DIp	——, Bischöfliches Priesterseminar
DIN	Dinkelsbühl, BRD, Katholisches Pfarramt St Georg
DIP	Dippoldiswalde, DDR, Evangelisch-Lutherisches Pfarramt
DL	Delitzsch, DDR, Museum und Bibliothek
DM	Dortmund, BRD, Stadt- und Landesbibliothek
DO	Donaueschingen, BRD, Fürstlich Fürstenbergische Hofbibliothek, private collection
DÖ	Döbeln, DDR, Pfarrbibliothek St Nikolai
DÖF	Döffingen über Bölingen, BRD, Pfarrbibliothek
DS	Darmstadt, BRD, Hessische Landes- und Hochschulbibliothek
DSim	——, Internationales Musikinstitut
DSk	——, Kirchenleitung der Evangelischen Kirche in Hessen und Nassau
DT	Detmold, BRD, Lippische Landesbibliothek
DÜgg	Düsseldorf, BRD, Staatliches Görres-Gymnasium
DÜha	——, Hauptstaatsarchiv
DÜk	——, Goethe-Museum
DÜl	——, Landes- und Stadtbibliothek
DÜmb	——, Stadtbüchereien, Musikbücherei
DÜR	Düren, BRD, Stadtbücherei, Leopold-Hoesch-Museum
Ek	Eichstätt, BRD, Kapuzinerkloster
Es	——, Staats- und Seminarbibliothek
Ew	——, Benediktinerinnen-Abtei St Walburg
EB	Ebrach, BRD, Katholisches Pfarramt
EBS	Ebstorf, BRD, Kloster
EF	Erfurt, DDR, Wissenschaftliche Bibliothek der Stadt
EFd	——, Dombibliothek
EFs	——, Stadt- und Bezirksbibliothek
EIa	Eisenach, DDR, Stadtarchiv
EIb	——, Bachhaus und Bachmuseum
EIl	——, Landeskirchenrat
EIHp	Eichtersheim, BRD, Pfarrbibliothek
EL	Eisleben, DDR, Andreas-Bibliothek
EM	Emden, BRD, Grosse Kirche
EMM	Emmerich, BRD, Staatliches Gymnasium
EN	Engelberg, BRD, Franziskanerkloster
ERms	Erlangen, BRD, Musikwissenschaftliches Seminar der Universität

ERu	——, Universitätsbibliothek
ES	Essen, BRD, Musikbücherei der Stadtbücherei
EU	Eutin, BRD, Kreisbibliothek
F	Frankfurt am Main, BRD, Stadt- und Universitätsbibliothek
Fkm	——, Museum für Kunsthandwerk
Fmi	——, Musikwissenschaftliches Institut der Johann Wolfgang von Goethe-Universität
Fsg	——, Philosophisch-Theologische Hochschule St Georgen
Fsm	——, Bibliothek für Neuere Sprachen und Musik
FBa	Freiberg, DDR, Stadtarchiv
FBb	——, Bergakademie, Bücherei
FBo	——, Geschwister-Scholl-Oberschule, Historische Bibliothek
FBsk	——, Stadt- und Kreisbibliothek
FF	Frankfurt an der Oder, DDR, Stadt- und Bezirksbibliothek
FG	Freyburg, DDR, Pfarrarchiv
FLa	Flensburg, BRD, Stadtarchiv
FLs	——, Staatliches Gymnasium
FRcb	Freiburg im Breisgau, BRD, Collegium Borromaeum
FRms	——, Musikwissenschaftliches Seminar der Universität
FRu	——, Universitätsbibliothek
FRIs	Friedberg, BRD, Stadtbibliothek
FRIts	——, Theologisches Seminar der Evangelischen Kirche in Hessen und Nassau
FS	Freising, BRD, Dombibliothek
FUf	Fulda, BRD, Kloster Frauenberg
FUl	——, Hessische Landesbibliothek
FUp	——, Bischöfliches Priesterseminar, Bibliothek der Philosophisch-Theologischen Hochschule
Ga	Göttingen, BRD, Staatliches Archivlager
Gb	——, Johann Sebastian Bach-Institut
Gms	——, Musikwissenschaftliches Seminar der Universität
Gs	——, Niedersächsische Staats- und Universitätsbibliothek
GA	Gaussig bei Bautzen, DDR, Schlossbibliothek
GAH	Gandersheim, BRD, Stiftsbibliothek
GAM	Gau-Algesheim, BRD, Stadtarchiv
GAR	Gars am Inn, BRD, Philosophisch-Theologische Ordenhochschule der Redemptoristen
GBB	Grossbrembach, DDR, Pfarrarchiv
GBR	Grossbreitenbach bei Arnstadt, DDR, Pfarrbibliothek
GD	Gaesdonck über Goch, BRD, Collegium Augustinianum
GE	Gelenau, DDR, Pfarrarchiv
GERk	Gera, DDR, Kirchenarchiv
GERs	——, Stadtmuseum
GERsb	——, Stadt- und Bezirksbibliothek
GEY	Geyer, DDR, Kirchenbibliothek
GF	Grossfahrer, DDR, Pfarrarchiv Starcklof-Eschenberger
GHk	Geithain, DDR, Evangelisch-Lutherisches Pfarramt
GHNa	Grossenhain, DDR, Archiv
GHNk	——, Kirche
GI	Giessen, BRD, Justus Liebig-Universität
GL	Goslar, BRD, Marktkirchenbibliothek
GLA	Glashütte, DDR, Pfarrarchiv
GM	Grimma, DDR, Göschenhaus, Johannes Sturm, private collection
GMl	——, Landesschule
GO	Gotha, DDR, Evangelisch-Lutherische Stadtkirchengemeinde
GOa	——, Augustinerkirche
GOg	——, Gymnasium
GOl	——, Forschungsbibliothek [former Landesbibliothek]
GOs	——, Stadtarchiv
GOsk	——, Stadt- und Kreisbibliothek
GÖp	Görlitz, DDR, Evangelischer Parochialverband
GÖs	——, Stadtbibliothek
GÖsp	——, Pfarramt St Peter
GOL	Goldbach bei Gotha, DDR, Pfarrarchiv
GRim	Greifswald, DDR, Institut für Musikwissenschaft
GRk	——, Konsistorialbibliothek
GRu	——, Ernst-Moritz-Arndt-Universität
GRÜ	Grünhain, DDR, Pfarramt
GÜ	Güstrow, DDR, Heimatmuseum
GZ	Greiz, DDR, Stadt- und Kreisbibliothek
GZbk	——, Staatliche Bücher- und Kupferstichsammlung

GZmb ——, Städtische Musikbibliothek
GZsa ——, Historisches Staatsarchiv
Ha Hamburg, BRD, Staatsarchiv
Hch ——, Gymnasium Christianeum
Hhm ——, Harburg, Helmsmuseum
Hj ——, Gelehrtenschule des Johanneum
Hkm ——, Kunstgewerbemuseum
Hmb ——, Musikbücherei der Hamburger Öffentlichen Bücherhallen
Hmg ——, Museum für Hamburgische Geschichte
Hmi ——, Musikwissenschaftliches Institut der Universität
Hs ——, Staats- und Universitätsbibliothek
Hsa ——, Senatsarchiv
Hth ——, Universität, Theatersammlung
HAf Halle an der Saale, DDR, Hauptbibliothek und Archiv der Franckeschen Stiftungen [in *HAu*]
HAh ——, Händel-Haus
HAmi ——, Institut für Musikwissenschaft der Martin-Luther-Universität
HAmk ——, Marienbibliothek
HAs ——, Stadt- und Bezirksbibliothek
HAu ——, Universitäts- und Landesbibliothek Sachsen-Anhalt
HAI Hainichen, DDR, Heimatmuseum
HB Heilbronn, BRD, Stadtarchiv
HCHs Hechingen, BRD, Stiftskirche
HD Hermsdorf, DDR, Pfarrarchiv
HEk Heidelberg, BRD, Evangelisches Kirchenmusikalisches Institut
HEms ——, Musikwissenschaftliches Seminar der Universität
HEu ——, Universitätsbibliothek
HER Herrnhut, DDR, Archiv der Brüder-Unität
HEY Heynitz, DDR, Pfarrbibliothek
HG Havelberg, DDR, Museum
HHa Hildburghausen, DDR, Stadtarchiv
HIb Hildesheim, BRD, Beverin'sche Bibliothek
HIm ——, St Michaelskirche
HIp ——, Bischöfliches Priesterseminar
HL Haltenbergstetten, BRD, Schloss über Niederstetten, Fürst zu Hohenlohe-Jagstberg'sche Bibliothek, private collection
HLN Hameln, BRD, Stadtbücherei des Schiller-Gymnasiums
HN Herborn, BRD, Evangelisches Theologisches Seminar
HO Hof an der Saale, BRD, Jean Paul-Gymnasium
HOr ——, Stadtarchiv, Ratsbibliothek
HOE Hohenstein-Ernstthal, DDR, Kantoreiarchiv der Christophorikirche
HOG Hofgeismar, BRD, Predigerseminar
HOR Horst, BRD, Evangelisch-Lutherisches Pfarramt
HR Harburg über Donauwörth, BRD, Fürstlich Oettingen-Wallerstein'sche Bibliothek, private collection
HSj Helmstedt, BRD, Juleum
HSk ——, Kantorat zu St Stephani [in *W*]
HSm ——, Kloster Marienberg
HSwandersleb ——, Bibliothek Pastor Wandersleb
HTa Halberstadt, DDR, Stadtarchiv
HTd ——, Dombibliothek
HTg ——, Gleimhaus
HVh Hanover, BRD, Staatliche Hochschule für Musik und Theater
HVk ——, Arbeitsstelle für Gottesdienst und Kirchenmusik der Evangelisch-Lutherischen Landeskirche
HVl ——, Niedersächsische Landesbibliothek
HVs ——, Stadtbibliothek
HVsa ——, Staatsarchiv
HVth ——, Technische Hochschule
HX Höxter, BRD, Kirchenbibliothek St Nikolaus
Iek Isny, BRD, Evangelische Kirche St Nikolai
Iq ——, Fürstlich Quadt'sche Bibliothek, private collection
ILk Ilmenau, DDR, Kirchenbibliothek
ILs ——, Stadtarchiv
IN Indersdorf über Dachau, BRD, Katholisches Pfarramt
Jmb Jena, DDR, Ernst Abbe-Bücherei, Musikbücherei
Jmi ——, Musikwissenschaftliches Institut der Friedrich-Schiller-Universität
Ju ——, Universitätsbibliothek der Friedrich-Schiller-Universität
JA Jahnsdorf bei Stollberg, DDR, Pfarrarchiv
JE Jever, BRD, Marien-Gymnasium
Kdma Kassel, BRD, Deutsches Musikgeschichtliches Archiv

Kl ——, Murhardsche Bibliothek der Stadt und Landesbibliothek
Km ——, Musikakademie
Ksp ——, Louis-Spohr-Gedenk- und Forschungsstätte
KA Karlsruhe, BRD, Badische Landesbibliothek
KAsp ——, Pfarramt St Peter
KAu ——, Universitätsbibliothek
KAL Kaldenkirchen, BRD, Pfarrbibliothek
KARj Karl-Marx-Stadt, DDR, Jacobi-Kirche
KARr ——, Ratsarchiv
KARs ——, Stadt- und Bezirksbibliothek
KBs Koblenz, BRD, Stadtbibliothek
KBEk Koblenz-Ehrenbreitstein, BRD, Provinzialat der Kapuziner
KFm Kaufbeuren, BRD, Stadtpfarrkirche St Martin
KFs ——, Stadtbücherei
KIl Kiel, BRD, Schleswig-Holsteinische Landesbibliothek
KImi ——, Musikwissenschaftliches Institut der Christian-Albrecht Universität
KIu ——, Universitätsbibliothek
KIN Kindelbrück, DDR, Pfarrarchiv, Evangelisches Pfarramt
KMk Kamenz, DDR, Evangelisch-Lutherische Hauptkirche
KMl ——, Lessingmuseum
KMs ——, Stadtarchiv
KNd Cologne, BRD, Erzbischöfliche Diözesan- und Dombibliothek
KNh ——, Staatliche Hochschule für Musik
KNhi ——, Joseph Haydn-Institut
KNmi ——, Musikwissenschaftliches Institut der Universität
KNu ——, Universitäts- und Stadtbibliothek
KÖ Köthen, DDR, Heimatmuseum
KPk Kempten, BRD, Kirchenbibliothek, Evangelisch-Lutherisches Pfarramt St Mang
KPs ——, Stadtbücherei
KPsl ——, Stadtpfarrkirche St Lorenz
KR Kleinröhrsdorf über Bischofswerda, DDR, Pfarrkirchenbibliothek
KT Klingenthal, DDR, Kirchenbibliothek
KU Kulmbach, BRD, Stadtarchiv
KZa Konstanz, BRD, Stadtarchiv
KZr ——, Rosgarten-Museum
KZs ——, Städtische Wessenberg-Bibliothek
Lm Lüneburg, BRD, Michaelisschule
Lr ——, Ratsbücherei
LA Landshut, BRD, Historischer Verein für Niederbayern
LAU Laubach, BRD, Gräflich Solms-Laubach'sche Bibliothek
LB Langenburg, BRD, Fürstlich Hohenlohe-Langenburg'sche Schlossbibliothek, private collection
LCH Lich, BRD, Fürstlich Solms-Lich'sche Bibliothek, private collection
LEb Leipzig, DDR, Bach-Archiv
LEbh ——, Breitkopf & Härtel, Verlagsarchiv
LEdb ——, Deutsche Bücherei, Musikaliensammlung
LEm ——, Musikbibliothek der Stadt
LEmh ——, Hochschule für Musik
LEmi ——, Musikwissenschaftliches Institut der Karl-Marx-Universität
LEsm ——, Museum für Geschichte der Stadt
LEt ——, Thomasschule
LEu ——, Universitätsbibliothek der Karl-Marx-Universität
LFN Laufen an der Salzach, BRD, Stiftsarchiv
LHD Langhennersdorf über Freiberg, DDR, Pfarramt
LI Lindau, BRD, Stadtbibliothek
LIM Limbach am Main, BRD, Pfarramt
LL Langula über Mühlhausen, DDR, Pfarramt
LM Leitheim über Donauwörth, BRD, Schlossbibliothek Freiherr von Tucher
LO Loccum über Wunstorf, BRD, Klosterbibliothek
LÖ Lössnitz, DDR, Pfarrarchiv
LR Lahr, BRD, Lehrerbibliothek des Scheffel-Gymnasiums
LST Lichtenstein, DDR, Kantoreiarchiv von St Laurentius
LÜd Lübeck, BRD, Distler Archiv
LÜh ——, Bibliothek der Hansestadt
LUC Luckau, DDR, Nikolaikirche
Ma Munich, BRD, Franziskanerkloster St Anna
Mb ——, Benediktinerabtei St Bonifaz
Mbm ——, Metropolitankapitel
Mbn ——, Bayerisches Nationalmuseum
Mbs ——, Bayerische Staatsbibliothek

Mcg	——, Georgianum, Herzogliches Priesterseminar	*NBss*	——, Studienseminar
Mdm	——, Deutsches Museum	*NEhz*	Neuenstein, BRD, Hohenlohe-Zentral-Archiv
Mh	——, Staatliche Hochschule für Musik	*NEschumm*	——, Karl Schumm, private collection
Ml	——, Evangelisch-Lutherisches Landeskirchenamt	*NERk*	Neuenrade, BRD, Kirchenbibliothek
Mmb	——, Städtische Musikbibliothek	*NEZp*	Neckarelz, BRD, Pfarrbibliothek
Mms	——, Musikwissenschaftliches Seminar der Universität	*NGp*	Neckargemünd, BRD, Pfarrarchiv
Msl	——, Süddeutsche Lehrerbücherei	*NIw*	Nieheim über Bad Driburg, BRD, Weberhaus
Mth	——, Theatermuseum der Clara-Ziegler-Stiftung	*NL*	Nördlingen, BRD, Stadtarchiv, Stadtbibliothek und Volksbücherei
Mu	——, Universitätsbibliothek		
Mwg	——, Wilhelms-Gymnasium, Lehrerbibliothek	*NLk*	——, Kirchenbibliothek St Georg
MAk	Magdeburg, DDR, Kulturhistorisches Museum, Klosterbibliothek	*NM*	Neumünster, BRD, Schleswig-Holsteinische Musiksammlung der Stadt [in *Kll*]
MAkon	——, Konsistorialbibliothek	*NO*	Nordhausen, DDR, Humboldt-Oberschule
MAl	——, Landeshauptarchiv	*NS*	Neustadt an der Aisch, BRD, Evangelische Kirchenbibliothek
MAs	——, Stadt- und Bezirksbibliothek		
MB	Marbach an der Neckar, BRD, Schiller-Nationalmuseum	*NSg*	——, Gymnasialbibliothek
		NT	Neumarkt-St Veit, BRD, Pfarrkirche
MBG	Miltenberg am Main, BRD, Franziskanerkloster	*NW*	Neustadt an der Weinstrasse, BRD, Heimatmuseum
MCH	Maria Laach über Andernach, BRD, Benediktinerabtei	*OB*	Ottobeuren, BRD, Benediktiner-Abtei
		OF	Offenbach am Main, BRD, Verlagsarchiv André
ME	Meissen, DDR, Stadt- und Kreisbibliothek	*OH*	Oberfrankenhain, DDR, Pfarrarchiv
MEIk	Meiningen, DDR, Evangelisch-Lutherische Kirchengemeinde	*OLl*	Oldenburg, BRD, Landesbibliothek
		OLns	——, Niedersächsisches Staatsarchiv
MEll	——, Staatsarchiv	*OLH*	Olbernhau, DDR, Pfarrarchiv
MEIo	——, Opernarchiv	*ORB*	Oranienbaum, DDR, Landesarchiv–Historisches Staatsarchiv
MEIr	——, Staatliche Museen mit Reger-Archiv		
MEL	Meldorf, BRD, Joachimsche Bibliothek, Dithmarsches Landesmuseum	*OS*	Oschatz, DDR, Ephoralbibliothek
		OSa	Osnabrück, BRD, Niedersächsisches Staatsarchiv
MERa	Merseburg, DDR, Domstift	*OSm*	——, Städtisches Museum
MERr	——, Regierungsbibliothek	*Pg*	Passau, BRD, Gymnasialbibliothek
MERs	——, Stadt- und Kreisbibliothek	*Pk*	——, Bischöfliches Klerikalseminar
MERz	——, Deutsches Zentral-Archiv, Historische Abteilung	*Po*	——, Bischöfliches Ordinariat
		Ps	——, Staatliche Bibliothek
MFL	Münstereifel, BRD, St Michael-Gymnasium	*PA*	Paderborn, BRD, Erzbischöfliche Akademische Bibliothek
MGmi	Marburg an der Lahn, BRD, Musikwissenschaftliches Institut der Philipps-Universität		
		PI	Pirna, DDR, Stadtarchiv
MGs	——, Staatsarchiv und Archivschule	*POh*	Potsdam, DDR, Pädagogische Hochschule
MGu	——, Universitätsbibliothek der Philipps-Universität	*PR*	Pretzschendorf über Dippoldiswalde, DDR, Pfarrarchiv
MH	Mannheim, BRD, Wissenschaftliche Stadtbibliothek und Universitätsbibliothek		
		PU	Pulsnitz, DDR, Nikolaikirche
MHrm	——, Reiss-Museum	*PW*	Pesterwitz bei Dresden, DDR, Pfarrarchiv
MHR	Mülheim, BRD, Stadtbibliothek	*Q*	Quedlinburg, DDR, Stadt- und Kreisbibliothek
MI	Michelstadt, BRD, Evangelisches Pfarramt West	*QUh*	Querfurt, DDR, Heimatmuseum
MK	Markneukirchen, DDR, Gewerbemuseum	*QUk*	——, Stadtkirche
MLHb	Mühlhausen, DDR, Blasiuskirche	*Rim*	Regensburg, BRD, Institut für Musikforschung [in *Ru*]
MLHr	——, Ratsarchiv im Stadtarchiv		
MMm	Memmingen, BRD, Evangelisch-Lutherisches Pfarramt St Martin	*Rp*	——, Bischöfliche Zentralbibliothek
		Rs	——, Staatliche Bibliothek
MMs	——, Stadtbibliothek	*Rtt*	——, Fürstlich Thurn und Taxis'sche Hofbibliothek, private collection
MÖ	Mölln, BRD, Evangelisch-Lutherische Kirchengemeinde St Nikolai		
		Ru	——, Universitätsbibliothek
MOSp	Mosbach, BRD, Pfarrbibliothek	*RAd*	Ratzeburg, BRD, Domarchiv
MR	Marienberg, DDR, Kirchenbibliothek	*RB*	Rothenburg ob der Tauber, BRD, Stadtarchiv und Rats- und Konsistorialbibliothek
MS	Münsterschwarzach über Kitzingen am Main, BRD, Abtei		
		RE	Reutberg bei Schaftlach, BRD, Franziskanerinnen-Kloster
MT	Metten über Deggendorf, BRD, Abtei		
MÜd	Münster, BRD, Bischöfliches Diözesanarchiv	*REU*	Reuden, DDR, Pfarrarchiv
MÜms	——, Musikwissenschaftliches Seminar der Universität	*RH*	Rheda, BRD, Fürst zu Bentheim-Tecklenburgische Bibliothek [in *MH* and *MÜu*]
MÜp	——, Bischöfliches Priesterseminar und Santini-Sammlung	*RIE*	Riesa, DDR, Heimatmuseum
		RL	Reutlingen, BRD, Stadtbücherei
MÜrt	——, Seminar für Reformierte Theologie	*RMmarr*	Ramesloh über Winsen, BRD, G. Marr, private collection
MÜs	——, Santini-Bibliothek [in *MÜp*]		
MÜsa	——, Staatsarchiv	*ROmi*	Rostock, DDR, Institut für Musikwissenschaft der Universität
MÜu	——, Universitätsbibliothek		
MÜG	Mügeln, DDR, Pfarrarchiv	*ROs*	——, Stadt- und Bezirksbibliothek
MWR	Marienweiher über Kulmbach, BRD, Franziskanerkloster	*ROu*	——, Universitätsbibliothek
		RÖ	Röhrsdorf über Meissen, DDR, Pfarrbibliothek
MZfederhofer	Mainz, BRD, Hellmut Federhofer, private collection	*RÖM*	Römhild, DDR, Pfarrarchiv
MZgm	——, Gutenberg-Museum	*ROT*	Rotenburg, BRD, Predigerseminar
MZgottron	——, Adam Gottron, private collection	*ROTTd*	Rottenburg an der Neckar, BRD, Diözesanbibliothek
MZmi	——, Musikwissenschaftliches Institut der Universität		
		ROTTp	——, Bischöfliches Priesterseminar
MZp	——, Bischöfliches Priesterseminar	*RT*	Rastatt, BRD, Friedrich-Wilhelm-Gymnasium
MZs	——, Stadtbibliothek und Stadtarchiv	*RUh*	Rudolstadt, DDR, Hofkapellarchiv
MZsch	——, Musikverlag B. Schotts Söhne	*RUl*	——, Staatsarchiv
MZu	——, Universitätsbibliothek der Johannes-Gutenberg-Universität	*RÜ*	Rüdenhausen über Kitzingen, BRD, Fürst Castell-Rüdenhausen Bibliothek
Ngm	Nuremberg, BRD, Germanisches National-Museum	*Seo*	Stuttgart, BRD, Bibliothek und Archiv des Evangelischen Oberkirchenrats
Nla	——, Landeskirchliches Archiv		
Nst	——, Stadtbibliothek	*Sh*	——, Staatliche Hochschule für Musik und Darstellende Kunst
NA	Neustadt an der Orla, DDR, Pfarrarchiv		
NAUs	Naumburg, DDR, Stadtarchiv	*Sl*	——, Württembergische Landesbibliothek
NAUw	——, Wenzelskirche	*SAh*	Saalfeld, DDR, Heimatmuseum
NBsb	Neuburg an der Donau, BRD, Staatliche Bibliothek	*SAAmi*	Saarbrücken, BRD, Musikwissenschaftliches Institut der Universität

SAAu	——, Universitätsbibliothek
SBg	Straubing, BRD, Johannes Turmair-Gymnasium
SBj	——, Kirchenbibliothek St Jakob
SBk	——, Karmeliter-Kloster
SCHhv	Schwäbisch Hall, BRD, Historischer Verein für Württembergisch-Franken
SCHm	——, Archiv der St Michaelskirche
SCHr	——, Ratsbibliothek im Stadtarchiv
SCHEY	Scheyern über Pfaffenhofen, BRD, Benediktiner-abtei
SCHM	Schmölln, DDR, Archiv der Stadtkirche
SCHMI	Schmiedeberg bei Dresden, DDR, Pfarramt
SCHWherold	Schwabach, BRD, Herold collection
SCHWk	——, Kirchenbibliothek
SDF	Schlehdorf, BRD, Katholische Pfarrkirche
SF	Schweinfurt-Oberndorf, BRD, Kirchen- und Pfarr-bibliothek des Evangelisch-Lutherischen Pfarramts
SFsj	——, Pfarramt St Johannis, Sakristei-Bibliothek
SGh	Schleusingen, DDR, Heimatmuseum
SHk	Sondershausen, DDR, Stadtkirche
SHs	——, Stadt- und Kreisbibliothek
SHsk	——, Schlosskirche
SI	Sigmaringen, BRD, Fürstlich Hohenzollernsche Hofbibliothek, private collection
SLk	Salzwedel, DDR, Katharinenkirche
SLm	——, J. F. Danneil-Museum
SLmk	——, Marienkirche
SNed	Schmalkalden, DDR, Evangelisches Dekanat
SNh	——, Heimatmuseum Schloss Wilhelmsburg
SO	Soest, BRD, Stadtbibliothek im Stadtarchiv
SÖNp	Schönau bei Heidelberg, BRD, Pfarrbibliothek
SPlb	Speyer, BRD, Pfälzische Landesbibliothek, Musik-abteilung
SPlk	——, Bibliothek des Protestantischen Landes-kirchenrats der Pfalz
SPF	Schulpforta, DDR, Heimoberschule
SSa	Stralsund, DDR, Bibliothek des Stadtarchivs
ST	Stade, BRD, Predigerbibliothek [in *ROT*]
STO	Stolberg, DDR, Bibliothek
SUa	Sulzenbrücken, DDR, Pfarrarchiv
SUH	Suhl, DDR, Stadt- und Bezirksbibliothek Martin Andersen Nexö
SWl	Schwerin, DDR, Wissenschaftliche Allgemein-bibliothek [former Mecklenburgische Landes-bibliothek]
SWs	——, Stadt- und Bezirksbibliothek, Musikabteilung
SWsk	——, Schlosskirchenchor
SWth	——, Mecklenburgisches Staatstheater
SZ	Schleiz, DDR, Stadtkirche
Tes	Tübingen, BRD, Evangelisches Stift
Tl	——, Schwäbisches Landesmusikarchiv [in *Tmi*]
Tmi	——, Musikwissenschaftliches Institut der Eberhard-Karls-Universität
Tu	——, Universitätsbibliothek
Tw	——, Bibliothek des Wilhelmstiftes
TAB	Tabarz, DDR, Pfarrarchiv, Evangelisch-Lutheri-sches Pfarramt
TEG	Tegernsee, BRD, Pfarrkirche, Katholisches Pfarr-amt
TEI	Teisendorf, BRD, Katholisches Pfarramt
TH	Themar, DDR, Pfarramt
TIT	Tittmoning, BRD, Kollegiatstift
TO	Torgau, DDR, Johann-Walter-Kantorei
TOek	——, Evangelische Kirchengemeinde
TOs	——, Stadtarchiv
TRb	Trier, BRD, Bistumarchiv und Dombibliothek
TRp	——, Priesterseminar
TRs	——, Stadtbibliothek
Us	Ulm, BRD, Stadtbibliothek
Usch	——, Von Schermar'sche Familienstiftung
UDa	Udestedt über Erfurt, DDR, Pfarrarchiv, Evangelisch-Lutherisches Pfarramt
V	Villingen, BRD, Städtische Sammlung
VI	Viernau, DDR, Pfarramt
W	Wolfenbüttel, BRD, Herzog August Bibliothek
Wa	——, Niedersächsisches Staatsarchiv
WA	Waldheim, DDR, Stadtkirche St Nikolai
WAB	Waldenburg, DDR, Kirchenmusikalische Bibliothek von St Bartholomäus
WB	Weissenburg, BRD, Stadtbibliothek
WBB	Walberg, BRD, Albertus-Magnus-Akademie, Biblio-thek St Albert
WD	Wiesentheid, BRD, Musiksammlung des Grafen von Schönborn-Wiesentheid, private collection
WE	Weiden, BRD, Pfannenstiel'sche Bibliothek, Evan-gelisch-Lutherisches Pfarramt
WEH	Weierhof, BRD, Mennonitische Forschungsstelle
WEL	Weltenburg, BRD, Benediktinerkloster
WER	Wernigerode, DDR, Heimatmuseum, Harzbücherei
WERk	Wertheim am Main, BRD, Evangelisches Pfarramt
WERl	——, Fürstlich Löwenstein'sche Bibliothek, private collection
WEY	Weyarn, BRD, Pfarrkirche [in *FS*]
WF	Weissenfels, DDR, Heimatmuseum
WFg	——, Heinrich-Schütz-Gedenkstätte
WGk	Wittenberg, DDR, Stadtkirche
WGl	——, Reformationsgeschichtliches Museum, Luther-halle
WGp	——, Evangelisches Predigerseminar
WH	Windsheim, BRD, Stadtbibliothek
WIl	Wiesbaden, BRD, Hessische Landesbibliothek
WILd	Wilster, BRD, Stadtarchiv (Doos'sche Bibliothek)
WL	Wuppertal, BRD, Wissenschaftliche Stadtbibliothek
WM	Wismar, DDR, Stadtarchiv
WO	Worms, BRD, Stadtbibliothek
WRdn	Weimar, DDR, Deutsches Nationaltheater
WRgm	——, Goethe-National-Museum
WRgs	——, Goethe–Schiller-Archiv und Franz-Liszt-Museum
WRh	——, Franz-Liszt-Hochschule
WRhk	——, Herderkirche
WRiv	——, Institut für Volksmusikforschung
WRl	——, Landeshauptarchiv
WRs	——, Stadtbücherei, Musikbücherei
WRtl	——, Thüringische Landesbibliothek, Musiksamm-lung
WRz	——, Zentralbibliothek der Deutschen Klassik
WS	Wasserburg am Inn, BRD, Chorarchiv St Jakob, Pfarramt
WÜms	Würzburg, BRD, Musikwissenschaftliches Seminar der Universität
WÜsa	——, Stadtarchiv
WÜu	——, Universitätsbibliothek
X	Xanten, BRD, Stifts- und Pfarrbibliothek
Z	Zwickau, DDR, Ratsschulbibliothek
Zmk	——, Domkantorei der Marienkirche
Zsch	——, Robert-Schumann-Haus
ZE	Zerbst, DDR, Stadtarchiv
ZEo	——, Bücherei der Erweiterten Oberschule
ZGh	Zörbig, DDR, Heimatmuseum
ZGsj	——, Pfarramt St Jacobi
ZI	Zittau, DDR, Stadt- und Kreisbibliothek
ZIa	——, Stadtarchiv
ZL	Zeil, BRD, Fürstlich Waldburg-Zeil'sches Archiv, private collection
ZW	Zweibrücken, BRD, Bibliotheca Bipontina, Wissen-schaftliche Bibliothek am Herzog-Wolfgang-Gymnasium
ZZ	Zeitz, DDR, Heimatmuseum
ZZs	——, Stiftsbibliothek

DK: DENMARK

A	Århus, Statsbiblioteket
Dschoenbaum	Dragør, Camillo Schoenbaum, private collection
Hfog	Hellerup, Dan Fog, private collection
Kc	Copenhagen, Carl Claudius Musikhistoriske Sam-ling
Kh	——, Københavns Kommunes Hovedbibliotheket
Kk	——, Det Kongelige Bibliotek
Kmk	——, Det Kongelige Danske Musikkonservatorium
Km(m)	——, Musikhistorisk Museum
Ks	——, Samfundet til Udgivelse af Dansk Musik
Kt	——, Teaterhistorisk Museum
Ku	——, Universitetsbiblioteket 1. Afdeling
Kv	——, Københavns Universitet, Musikvidenskabeligt Institut
Ol	Odense, Landsarkivet for Fyen, Karen Brahes Bib-liotek
Ou	——, Universitetsbibliotek
Rk	Ribe, Stifts- og Katedralskoles Bibliotek
Sa	Sorø, Sorø Akademis Bibliotek

E: SPAIN

Ac	Ávila, Catedral
Asa	——, Monasterio de S Ana (Real Monasterio de Encarnación)
Ast	——, Monasterio del S Tomás, Archivo de la Iglesia
AL	Alquezar, Colegiata
ALB	Albarracín, Colegiata
AS	Astorga, Catedral
Ba	Barcelona, Real Academia de Ciencias y Artes
Bac	——, Corona de Aragón

Bc	——, Biblioteca de Cataluña
Bca	——, Catedral
Bcapdevila	——, Felipe Capdevila Rovira, private collection
Bcm	——, Conservatorio Superior Municipal de Música
Bih	——, Instituto Municipal de Historia (formerly Archivo Histórico de la Ciudad)
Bim	——, Instituto Español de Musicología
Bit	——, Instituto del Teatro (formerly Museo del Arte Escénico)
Boc	——, Biblioteca Orfeó Catalá
Bsm	——, S María del Mar
Bu	——, Biblioteca del Universidad
BA	Badajoz, Catedral
BUa	Burgos, Catedral
BUlh	——, Monasterio de Las Huelgas
BUm	——, Museo Arqueológico
BUp	——, Biblioteca Provincial
BUse	——, Parroquia de S Esteban
C	Córdoba, Catedral
CA	Calahorra, Catedral
CAL	Calatayud, Colegiata de S María
CAR	Cardona, Archivo Comunal
CU	Cuenca, Catedral
CUi	——, Instituto de Música Religiosa
CZ	Cádiz, Archivo Capitular
E	El Escorial, Real Monasterio de S Lorenzo
G	Gerona, Biblioteca Catedralicia
Gm	——, Museo Diocesano
Gp	——, Biblioteca Pública
Gs	——, Seminario Gerundense
GRc	Granada, Catedral
GRcr	——, Capilla Real
GU	Guadalupe, Real Monasterio de S María
H	Huesca, Catedral
J	Jaca, Catedral
JA	Jaén, Catedral
LPA	Las Palmas, Catedral de Canarias
La	León, Catedral
Lc	——, Colegiata de S Isidoro
Lp	——, Biblioteca Pública Provincial
LEc	Lérida, Catedral
LEm	——, Museo Diocesano
Ma	Madrid, Real Academia de Bellas Artes de S Fernando
Mah	——, Archivo Histórico Nacional (Real Academia de la Historia)
Mam	——, Biblioteca Musical Circulante
Mat	——, Museo-Archivo Teatral
Mc	——, Conservatorio Superior de Música
Mca	——, Casa de Alba, private collection
Mcns	——, Congregación de Nuestra Señora
Mic	——, Instituto de Cultura Hispánica, Sección de Música
Mit	——, Ministerio de Información y Turismo
Mlg	——, Fundación Lazaro Galdiano
Mm	——, Biblioteca Municipal
Mmc	——, Casa Ducal de Medinaceli, Bartolomé March Servera, private collection
Mn	——, Biblioteca Nacional
Mp	——, Palacio Real
Mpm	——, Patronato Marcelino Menéndez y Pelayo del Consejo Superior de Investigaciones Científicas
Mrt	——, Radio Nacional de España-Televisión
Msa	——, Sociedad General de Autores de España
Msi	——, Ciudad Universitaria, Facultad de Filosofía y Letras, Biblioteca de S Isidoro
MA	Málaga, Catedral
MO	Montserrat, Monasterio de S María
MON	Mondoñedo, Catedral
OL	Olot, Biblioteca Popular
OR	Orense, Catedral
ORI	Orihuela, Catedral
OS	Osma, Catedral
OV	Oviedo, Catedral Metropolitana
P	Plasencia, Catedral
PAc	Palma de Mallorca, Catedral
PAp	——, Biblioteca Provincial
PAMc	Pamplona, Catedral
PAMm	——, Museo Sarasate
PAS	Pastrana, Iglesia Parroquial
RO	Roncesvalles, Monasterio de S María
Sc	Seville, Catedral
Sco	——, Biblioteca Capitular Colombina [in *Sc*]
SA	Salamanca, Catedral
SAcalo	——, José López-Calo, private collection
SAu	——, Universidad Pontificia, Biblioteca Universitaria

SAuf	——, Universidad Pontificia, Facultad de Filosofía y Letras
SAN	Santander, Biblioteca de Menéndez y Pelayo
SC	Santiago de Compostela, Catedral
SCu	——, Biblioteca Universitaria
SD	Santo Domingo de la Calzada, Archivo
SE	Segovia, Catedral
SEG	Segorbe, Catedral
SI	Silos, Monasterio Benedictino (Abadía) de S Domingo
SIG	Sigüenza, Catedral
SIM	Simancas, Archivo General
SO	Soria, Biblioteca Pública
Tc	Toledo, Archivo Capitular
Tp	——, Biblioteca Pública Provincial y Museo de la Santa Cruz
TAc	Tarragona, Catedral
TAp	——, Biblioteca Pública
TO	Tortosa, Catedral
TU	Tudela, Colegiata (formerly Catedral) de S María
TZ	Tarazona, Catedral
U (also *SU*)	Seo de Urgel, Catedral
V	Valladolid, Catedral
Vp	——, Parroquia de Santiago
VAa	Valencia, Archivo, Biblioteca y Museos Municipales
VAc	——, Catedral
VAcm	——, Conservatorio Superior de Música
VAcp	——, Colegio y Seminario del Corpus Christi del Patriarca
VAim	——, Instituto Valenciano de Musicología
VAu	——, Biblioteca Universitaria
VI	Vich, Museo Episcopal
VIT	Vitoria, Catedral
Zac	Saragossa, Archivo de Música del Cabildo
Zcc	——, Colegio Calasanci
Zfm	——, Facultad de Medicina
Zp	——, Biblioteca Pública
Zs	——, Biblioteca Capitular de la Seo
Zsc	——, Seminario de S Carlos
Zu	——, Biblioteca Universitaria
Zvp	——, Iglesia Metropolitana [in *Zac*]
ZA	Zamora, Catedral

EIRE: IRELAND

C	Cork, University College
Da	Dublin, Royal Irish Academy
Dam	——, Royal Irish Academy of Music
Dcb	——, Chester Beatty Library
Dcc	——, Christ Church Cathedral
Dm	——, Marsh's Library
Dmh	——, Mercer's Hospital
Dn	——, National Library and Museum of Ireland
Dpc	——, St Patrick's Cathedral
Dtc	——, Trinity College
Duc	——, University College

ET: EGYPT

S	Mt Sinai

F: FRANCE

A	Avignon, Bibliothèque Municipale, Musée Calvet
Aa	——, Archives Départementales de Vaucluse
AB	Abbeville, Bibliothèque Municipale
AG	Agen, Archives Départementales de Lot-et-Garonne
AI	Albi, Bibliothèque Municipale
AIXc	Aix-en-Provence, Conservatoire
AIXm	——, Bibliothèque Municipale, Bibliothèque Méjanes
AIXmc	——, Maîtrise de la Cathédrale
AL	Alençon, Bibliothèque Municipale
AM	Amiens, Bibliothèque Municipale
AN	Angers, Bibliothèque Municipale
ANG	Angoulême, Bibliothèque Municipale
ANN	Annecy, Bibliothèque Municipale
APT	Apt, Cathédrale Ste Anne
AR	Arles, Bibliothèque Municipale
AS	Arras, Bibliothèque Municipale
ASO	Asnières-sur-Oise, François Lang, private collection
AU	Auxerre, Bibliothèque Municipale
AUT	Autun, Bibliothèque Municipale
AV	Avallon, Société d'Etudes d'Avallon
AVR	Avranches, Bibliothèque Municipale
B	Besançon, Bibliothèque Municipale
Ba	——, Bibliothèque de l'Archevêché
Be	——, Ecole Nationale de Musique
BD	Bar-le-Duc, Bibliothèque Municipale
BE	Beauvais, Bibliothèque Municipale
BER	Bernay, Bibliothèque Municipale

BG	Bourg-en-Bresse, Bibliothèque Municipale et Musée de l'Ain	*NO*	Noyon, Bibliothèque Municipale
		NS	Nîmes, Bibliothèque Municipale
BL	Blois, Bibliothèque Municipale	*NT*	Niort, Bibliothèque Municipale
BO	Bordeaux, Bibliothèque Municipale	*O*	Orleans, Bibliothèque Municipale
BOI	Boisguillaume, Musée Boieldieu	*Pa*	Paris, Bibliothèque de l'Arsenal
BOU	Bourbourg, Bibliothèque Municipale	*Pal*	——, American Library in Paris
BR	Brest, Bibliothèque Municipale	*Pbf*	——, Centre de Documentation Benjamin Franklin
BS	Bourges, Bibliothèque Municipale	*Pc*	——, Conservatoire National de Musique [in *Pn*]
BSM	Boulogne-sur-Mer, Bibliothèque Municipale	*Pcf*	——, Comédie-Française, Bibliothèque
C	Carpentras, Bibliothèque Inguimbertine et Musée de Carpentras	*Pcrs*	——, Centre National de la Recherche Scientifique
		Pe	——, Schola Cantorum (Ecole Supérieure de Musique, Danse et Art Dramatique)
CA	Cambrai, Bibliothèque Municipale		
CAc	——, Cathédrale	*Pgérard*	——, Yves Gérard, private collection
CAD	Cadouin, Bibliothèque de l'Abbaye	*Pi*	——, Bibliothèque de l'Institut
CAH	Cahors, Bibliothèque Municipale	*Pim*	——, Institut de Musicologie de l'Université, Bibliothèque Pierre Aubry
CAL	Calais, Bibliothèque Municipale		
CC	Carcassonne, Bibliothèque Municipale	*Pis*	——, Institut Supérieur de Musique Liturgique
CF	Clermont-Ferrand, Bibliothèque Municipale et Universitaire, Section Centrale et Section Lettres	*Pm*	——, Bibliothèque Mazarine
		Pma	——, Musée National des Arts et Traditions Populaires
CH	Chantilly, Musée Condé	*Pmeyer*	——, André Meyer, private collection
CHA	Châteauroux, Bibliothèque Municipale	*Pmg*	——, Musée Guimet
CHE	Cherbourg, Bibliothèque et Archives Municipales	*Pmh*	——, Musée de l'Homme
CHM	Chambéry, Bibliothèque Municipale	*Pn*	——, Bibliothèque Nationale
CHR	Chartres, Bibliothèque Municipale	*Po*	——, Bibliothèque–Musée de l'Opéra
CN	Caen, Bibliothèque Municipale	*Pphon*	——, Phonothèque Nationale, Bibliothèque et Musée
CNc	——, Conservatoire National de Musique	*Ppincherle*	——, Marc Pincherle, private collection [dispersed 1975]
CO	Colmar, Bibliothèque Municipale		
COs	——, Consistoire de l'Eglise de la Confession d'Augsbourg à Colmar	*Ppo*	——, Bibliothèque Polonaise de Paris
		Prothschild	——, Germaine, Baronne Edouard de Rothschild, private collection
COUm	Coutances, Bibliothèque Municipale		
COUs	——, Grand Séminaire	*Prt*	——, Office de Radiodiffusion-Télévision Française
CSM	Châlons-sur-Marne, Bibliothèque Municipale	*Psc*	——, Société des Auteurs et Compositeurs Dramatiques
CV	Charleville, Bibliothèque Municipale		
Dc	Dijon, Bibliothèque du Conservatoire	*Pse*	——, Société des Auteurs, Compositeurs et Editeurs de Musique
Dm	——, Bibliothèque Municipale (Bibliothèque Publique)		
		Psg	——, Bibliothèque Ste Geneviève
DI	Dieppe, Bibliothèque Municipale	*Pshp*	——, Bibliothèque de la Société d'Histoire du Protestantisme
DO	Dôle, Bibliothèque Municipale		
DOU	Douai, Bibliothèque Municipale	*Psi*	——, Séminaire Israélite de France
E	Epinal, Bibliothèque Municipale	*Pthibault*	——, Geneviève Thibault, private collection
EP	Epernay, Bibliothèque Municipale	*PAU*	Pau, Bibliothèque Municipale
EV	Evreux, Bibliothèque Municipale	*PE*	Périgueux, Bibliothèque Municipale
F	Foix, Bibliothèque Municipale	*PO*	Poitiers, Bibliothèque Municipale
G	Grenoble, Bibliothèque Municipale	*POu*	——, Faculté des Lettres de l'Université de Poitiers, Section de Musicologie
Ge	——, Ecole Régionale de Musique, de Danse et d'Art Dramatique		
		Rc	Rouen, Conservatoire
GAP	Gap, Archives Départementales des Hautes-Alpes	*R(m)*	——, Bibliothèque Municipale
H	Hyères, Bibliothèque Municipale	*RE*	Rennes, Bibliothèque Municipale
Lc	Lille, Conservatoire	*RO*	Roanne, Bibliothèque Municipale
Lfc	——, Facultés Catholiques	*RSc*	Rheims, Bibliothèque de la Cathédrale
Lm	——, Bibliothèque Municipale	*Sc*	Strasbourg, Conservatoire
LA	Laon, Bibliothèque Municipale	*Sg(sc)*	——, Grand Séminaire (Séminaire Catholique)
LB	Libourne, Bibliothèque Municipale	*Sim*	——, Institut de Musicologie de l'Université
LG	Limoges, Bibliothèque Municipale	*Sm*	——, Archives et Bibliothèque Municipale
LH	Le Havre, Bibliothèque Municipale	*Sn*	——, Bibliothèque Nationale et Universitaire
LM	Le Mans, Bibliothèque Municipale	*Ssa*	——, Société des Amis des Arts de Strasbourg
LO	Louviers, Bibliothèque Municipale	*Ssp*	——, Séminaire Protestant
LP	Le Puy-en-Velay, Bibliothèque Municipale	*SA*	Salins, Bibliothèque Municipale
LR	La Rochelle, Bibliothèque Municipale	*SAU*	Saumur, Bibliothèque Municipale
LV	Laval, Bibliothèque Municipale	*SCL*	St-Claude, Bibliothèque Municipale
LYc	Lyons, Conservatoire National de Musique	*SDE*	St-Denis, Bibliothèque Municipale
LYm	——, Bibliothèque Municipale	*SDI*	St-Dié, Bibliothèque Municipale
Mc	Marseilles, Conservatoire de Musique et de Déclamation	*SE*	Sens, Bibliothèque Municipale
		SEL	Sélestat, Bibliothèque Municipale
Mm	——, Bibliothèque Municipale	*SERRANT*	Serrant, Château
MAC	Mâcon, Bibliothèque Municipale	*SO*	Solesmes, Abbaye St-Pierre
MD	Montbéliard, Bibliothèque Municipale	*SOI*	Soissons, Bibliothèque Municipale
MEL	Melun, Bibliothèque Municipale	*SQ*	St-Quentin, Bibliothèque Municipale
MH	Mulhouse, Bibliothèque Municipale	*T*	Troyes, Bibliothèque Municipale
MIL	Millau, Bibliothèque Municipale	*TH*	Thiers, Bibliothèque Municipale
MIR	Mirecourt, Bibliothèque Municipale	*TLc*	Toulouse, Conservatoire
ML	Moulins, Bibliothèque Municipale	*TLd*	——, Musée Dupuy
MLN	Montluçon, Bibliothèque Municipale	*TLm*	——, Bibliothèque Municipale
MO	Montpellier, Faculté de Médecine de l'Université	*TO*	Tours, Bibliothèque Municipale
MOv	——, Bibliothèque de la Ville et du Musée Fabre	*TOgs*	——, Grand Séminaire
MON	Montauban, Bibliothèque Municipale	*TOul*	——, Bibliothèque Universitaire, Section Lettres
MZ	Metz, Bibliothèque Municipale	*TOur*	——, Centre d'Etudes Supérieures de la Renaissance
Nd	Nantes, Bibliothèque du Musée Dobrée	*TOU*	Toulon, Ecole Nationale de Musique
Ne	——, Ecole Nationale de Musique, d'Art Dramatique et de Danse	*TOUm*	——, Bibliothèque Municipale
		TOUs	——, Société des Amis du Vieux Toulon
Nm	——, Bibliothèque Municipale	*TU*	Tulle, Bibliothèque Municipale
NAc	Nancy, Conservatoire	*V*	Versailles, Bibliothèque Municipale
NAm	——, Bibliothèque Municipale	*VA*	Vannes, Bibliothèque Municipale
NAR	Narbonne, Bibliothèque Municipale	*VAL*	Valenciennes, Bibliothèque Municipale
NI	Nice, Bibliothèque Municipale	*VE*	Vesoul, Bibliothèque Municipale
NIc	——, Conservatoire de Musique	*VN*	Verdun, Bibliothèque Municipale

GB: GREAT BRITAIN

A	Aberdeen, University Library, King's College
AB	Aberystwyth, National Library of Wales
AM	Ampleforth, Abbey and College Library, St Lawrence Abbey
Bp	Birmingham, Public Libraries
Bu	——, University of Birmingham, Barber Institute of Fine Arts
BA	Bath, Municipal Library
BEas	Bedford, Bedfordshire Archaeological Society
BEcr	——, Bedfordshire County Record Office
BEp	——, Public Library Music Department
BENcoke	Bentley (Hants.), Gerald Coke, private collection
BEV	Beverley, East Yorkshire County Record Office
BO	Bournemouth, Central Library
BRb	Bristol, Baptist College Library
BRp	——, Public Libraries, Central Library
BRu	——, University of Bristol Library
Ccc	Cambridge, Corpus Christi College
Cchc	——, Christ's College
Cclc	——, Clare College
Cfm	——, Fitzwilliam Museum
Cgc	——, Gonville and Caius College
Cjc	——, St John's College
Cjec	——, Jesus College
Ckc	——, Rowe Music Library, King's College
Cmc	——, Magdalene College
Cp	——, Peterhouse
Cpc	——, Pembroke College
Cpl	——, Pendlebury Library of Music
Ctc	——, Trinity College
Cu	——, University Library
Cumc	——, University Music Club
Cus	——, Cambridge Union Society
CA	Canterbury, Cathedral
CAR	Carlisle, Cathedral
CDp	Cardiff, Public Libraries, Central Library
CDu	——, University College of South Wales and Monmouthshire
CF	Chelmsford, Essex County Record Office
CH	Chichester, Diocesan Record Office
CHc	——, Cathedral
DRc	Durham, Cathedral
DRu	——, University Library
DU	Dundee, Public Libraries
En	Edinburgh, National Library of Scotland
Enc	——, New College Library
Ep	——, Public Library, Central Public Library
Er	——, Reid Music Library of the University of Edinburgh
Es	——, Signet Library
Eu	——, University Library
EL	Ely, Cathedral
EXc	Exeter, Cathedral
EXcl	——, Central Library
EXed	——, East Devon Area Record Office
EXu	——, University Library
Ge	Glasgow, Euing Music Library
Gm	——, Mitchell Library
Gsma	——, Scottish Music Archive
Gtc	——, Trinity College
Gu	——, University Library
GL	Gloucester, Cathedral
H	Hereford, Cathedral
HAdolmetsch	Haslemere, Carl Dolmetsch, private collection
Lam	London, Royal Academy of Music
Lbbc	——, British Broadcasting Corporation
Lbc	——, British Council
Lbm	——, British Library, Reference Division (formerly British Museum) (= *Lbl*)
Lcm	——, Royal College of Music
Lco	——, Royal College of Organists
Lcs	——, Vaughan Williams Memorial Library (Cecil Sharp Library)
Ldc	——, Dulwich College
Lgc	——, Gresham College (Guildhall Library)
Lkc	——, University of London, King's College
Llp	——, Lambeth Palace
Lmic	——, British Music Information Centre
Lmp	——, Marylebone Public Library
Lpro	——, Public Record Office
Lsc	——, Sion College
Lsm	——, Royal Society of Musicians of Great Britain
Lsp	——, St Paul's Cathedral
Ltc	——, Trinity College of Music
Lu	——, University of London, Music Library
Lva	——, Victoria and Albert Museum
Lwa	——, Westminster Abbey
Lwcm	——, Westminster Central Music Library
LA	Lancaster, District Central Library
LAu	——, University Library
LEbc	Leeds, University of Leeds, Brotherton Collection
LEc	——, Leeds Public Libraries, Music Department, Central Library
LF	Lichfield, Cathedral
LI	Lincoln, Cathedral
LVp	Liverpool, Public Libraries, Central Library
LVu	——, University Music Department
Mch	Manchester, Chetham's Library
Mcm	——, Royal Northern College of Music
Mp	——, Central Public Library, Henry Watson Music Library
Mr	——, John Rylands University Library, Deansgate Branch
Mrothwell	——, Evelyn Rothwell, private collection
Mu	——, John Rylands University Library
NO	Nottingham, University Library
NW	Norwich, Central Library
NWr	——, Norfolk and Norwich Record Office
Ob	Oxford, Bodleian Library
Obc	——, Brasenose College
Och	——, Christ Church
Ojc	——, St John's College
Olc	——, Lincoln College
Omc	——, Magdalen College
Onc	——, New College
Ooc	——, Oriel College
Oqc	——, Queen's College
Ouf	——, University, Faculty of Music
Oumc	——, University Music Club and Union
P	Perth, Sandeman Music Library
R	Reading, University, Music Library
RI	Ripon, Cathedral
RO	Rochester, Cathedral
SA	St Andrews, University Library
SB	Salisbury, Cathedral
SH	Sherborne, Sherborne School Library
SHR	Shrewsbury, Shropshire County Record Office
SOp	Southampton, Public Library
SR	Studley Royal, Fountains Abbey MS 23 [in *LEc*]
STb	Stratford-on-Avon, Shakespeare's Birthplace Trust
STm	——, Shakespeare Memorial Library
T	Tenbury, St Michael's College [Toulouse–Philidor collection now largely in *F-Pn*, *V*]
W	Wells, Cathedral
WB	Wimborne, Minster
WC	Winchester, Chapter Library
WCc	——, Winchester College
WI	Wigan, Public Library
WO	Worcester, Cathedral
WRch	Windsor, St George's Chapter Library
WRec	——, Eton College
Y	York, Minster
Yi	——, Borthwick Institute of Historical Research

GR: GREECE

Ae	Athens, Ethnike Biblioteke tes Hellados
AT	Mt Athos, Koutloumousi Monastery
ATSch	——, Chilandari Monastery
ATSdionision	——, Dionision Monastery
ATSgreat lavra	——, Monastery of the Great Lavra
ATSiviron	——, Iviron Monastery
ATSserbian	——, Serbian Monastery
ATSvatopedi	——, Vatopedi Monastery
LA	Lavra
P	Patmos

H: HUNGARY

Ba	Budapest, Magyar Tudományos Akadémia Régi Könyvek Tára és Kézirattár
Ba(mi)	——, Magyar Tudományos Akadémia Zenetudományi Intézet Könyvtára
Bb	——, Bartók Béla Zeneművészeti Szakközépiskola Könyvtára
Bev	——, Evangélikus Országos Könyvtár
Bf	——, Belvárosi Föplébániatemplom Kottatára
Bj	——, Józsefvárosi Evangélikus Egyházközség Kottatára
Bl	——, Liszt Ferenc Zeneművészeti Főiskola Könyvtára
Bm	——, Budavári Nagyboldogasszony Templom Kottatára

Bn	——, Országos Széchényi Könyvtára
Bo	——, Állami Operaház
Bp	——, Piarista Gimnázium Könyvtára
Br	——, Ráday Gyűjtemény, Könyvtár és Levéltár
Bs	——, Központi Szemináriumi Könyvtár
Bst	——, Szent István Bazilika Kottatára
Bu	——, Egyetemi Könyvtár
BA	Bártfa, church of St Aegidius [in *Bn*]
CSg	Csurgó, Csokonai Vitéz Mihály Gimnázium Könyvtára
DR	Debrecen, Tiszántúli Református Egyházkerület Nagykönyvtára
DRm	——, Déri Múzeum
DRu	——, Kossuth Lajos Tudományegyetem Könyvtára
Ea	Esztergom, Komárom Megyei Levéltár
Efko	——, Főszékesegyházi Kottatár
Efkö	——, Főszékesegyházi Könyvtár
Em	——, Keresztény Múzeum Könyvtára
EG	Eger, Főegyházmegyei Könyvtár
EGb	——, Bazilika Kottatára
Gc	Győr, Püspöki Papnevelő Intézet Könyvtára
Gk	——, Székesegyházi Kottatár
Gm	——, Xántus János Múzeum
Gz	——, Zeneművészeti Szakközépiskola Könyvtára
GGn	Gyöngyös, Országos Széchényi Könyvtár, Bajza József Müemlékkönyvtár
GYm	Gyula, Múzeum
KE	Keszthely, Országos Széchényi Könyvtár Helikon Könyvtára
KI	Kiskunhalas, Református Egyházközség Könyvtára
KŐ	Kőszeg, Plébániatemplom Kottatára
KŐm	——, Jurisich Múzeum
MOp	Mosonmagyaróvár, 1. sz Plébániatemplom Kottatára
NY	Nyiregyháza, Református Városi Egyházközség Könyvtára
P	Pécs, Székesegyházi Kottatár
PA	Pápa, Dunántuli Református Egyházkerület Könyvtára
PH	Pannonhalma, Szent Benedekrend Központi Főkönyvtára
Se	Sopron, Evangélikus Egyházközség Könyvtára
Sg	——, Berzsenyi Dániel Gimnázium Könyvtára
Sl	——, Liszt Ferenc Múzeum
Sp	——, Szentlélekröl és Szent Mihályról Nevezett Városplébánia Kottatára
Sst	——, Storno Gyűjtemény
SA	Sárospatak, Tiszáninneni Református Egyházkerület Nagykönyvtára
SD	Szekszárd, Balogh Ádám Megyei Múzeum
SFk	Székesfehérvár, Püspöki Könyvtár
SFm	——, István Király Múzeum
SFs	——, Székesegyházi Kottatár
SG	Szeged, Somogyi Könyvtár
SGm	——, Móra Ferenc Múzeum
SGu	——, Szegedi Orvostudományi Egyetem Könyvtára
SY	Szombathely, Püspöki Könyvtár
SYb	——, Berzsenyi Dániel Megyei Könyvtár
SYm	——, Smidt Múzeum
T	Tata, Plébániatemplom Kottatára
V	Vác, Székesegyházi Kottatár
VE	Veszprém, Püspöki Könyvtár
VEs	——, Székesegyházi Kottatár

I: ITALY

Ac	Assisi, Biblioteca Comunale
Ad	——, Cattedrale S Rufino
Af	——, S Francesco
AC	Acicatena, Biblioteca Comunale
AG	Agrigento, Biblioteca Lucchesiana
AGI	Agira, Biblioteca Comunale
AGN	Agnone, Biblioteca Emidiana
AL	Albenga, Cattedrale
ALEa	Alessandria, Archivio di Stato
ALEi	——, Istituto Musicale Antonio Vivaldi
AN	Ancona, Biblioteca Comunale
ANcap	——, Biblioteca Capitolare
ANd	——, Archivio della Cappella del Duomo
AO	Aosta, Seminario Maggiore
AP	Ascoli Picena, Biblioteca Comunale
AQ	Aquileia, Archivio della Basilica
ARc	Arezzo, Biblioteca Consorziale
ARd	——, Duomo
ASc(d)	Asti, Archivio Capitolare (Duomo)
ASi	——, Istituto Musicale Giuseppe Verdi
ASs	——, Seminario Vescovile

AT	Atri, Museo della Basilica Cattedrale, Biblioteca Capitolare
Baf	Bologna, Accademia Filarmonica
Bam	——, Biblioteca della Casa di Risparmio (Biblioteca Ambrosini)
Bas	——, Archivio di Stato
Bc	——, Civico Museo Bibliografico Musicale
Bca	——, Biblioteca Comunale dell'Arciginnasio
Bl	——, Conservatorio di Musica G. B. Martini
Bof	——, Oratorio dei Filippini
Bpm	——, Facoltà di Magistero dell'Università degli Studi, Scuola di Perfezionamento in Musicologia
Bsd	——, Convento di S Domenico
Bsf	——, Convento di S Francesco
Bsm	——, Biblioteca Conventuale S Maria dei Servi
Bsp	——, Basilica di S Petronio
Bu	——, Biblioteca Universitaria
BAca	Bari, Biblioteca Capitolare
BAcp	——, Conservatorio di Musica Nicola Piccinni
BAgiovine	——, Alfredo Giovine, private collection
BAn	——, Biblioteca Nazionale Sagarriga Visconti-Volpi
BAR	Barletta, Biblioteca Comunale Sabino Loffredo
BDG	Bassano del Grappa, Biblioteca Civica
BE	Belluno, Biblioteca del Seminario
BEc	——, Biblioteca Civica
BGc	Bergamo, Biblioteca Civica Angelo Mai
BGi	——, Civico Istituto Musicale Gaetano Donizetti
BI	Bitonto, Biblioteca Comunale Vitale Giordano
BRa	Brescia, Ateneo di Scienze, Lettere ed Arti
BRd	——, Duomo
BRi	——, Istituto Musicale A. Venturi
BRp	——, Archivio di S Maria della Pace
BRq	——, Biblioteca Civica Queriniana
BRs	——, Seminario Vescovile
BRsg	——, S Giovanni Evangelista (Cappella del Ss Sacramento)
BRsmg	——, Madonna delle Grazie
BRss	——, S Salvatore
BRE	Bressanone, Seminario Vescovile Vicentinum
BRI	Brindisi, Biblioteca Pubblica Arcivescovile Annibale de Leo
BV	Benevento, Archivio Capitolare
BVa	——, Archivio di Stato
BVam	——, Biblioteca e Archivio Storico Provinciale Antonio Mellusi
BVT	Borgo Val di Toro, Biblioteca Comunale Manara
BZa	Bolzano, Archivio di Stato
BZc	——, Conservatorio di Musica Claudio Monteverdi
BZd	——, Duomo
BZf	——, Biblioteca dei Minori Francescani
BZtoggenburg	——, Count Toggenburg, private collection
CAc	Cagliari, Biblioteca Comunale
CAcon	——, Conservatorio di Musica Giovanni Pierluigi da Palestrina
CAsm	——, Cattedrale S Maria
CAu	——, Biblioteca Universitaria
CAP	Capua, Museo Provinciale Campano
CARcc	Castell'Arquato, Chiesa Collegiata
CARc(p)	——, Archivio Capitolare (Archivio Parrochiale)
CATa	Catania, Archivio di Stato
CATc	——, Biblioteche Riunite Civica e Antonio Ursino Recupero
CATm	——, Museo Belliniano
CATss	——, Società di Storia Patria per la Sicilia Orientale
CC	Città di Castello, Duomo
CCc	——, Biblioteca Comunale
CDA	Codogna, Biblioteca Civica Popolare L. Ricca
CEb(sm)	Cesena, Badia S Maria del Monte
CEc	——, Biblioteca Comunale Malatestiana
CEN	Cento, S Biagio
CF	Cividale del Friuli, Archivio Capitolare
CFm	——, Museo Archeologico Nazionale
CHR	Chieri, Facoltà Teologica dei Gesuiti
CHT	Chieta, Biblioteca Provinciale Angelo Camillo de Meis
CHV	Chiavenna, Biblioteca Capitolare Laurenziana
CLE	Corleone, Biblioteca Comunale Francesco Bentivegna
CLO	Corlono, Chiesa della Reggia Ducale
CMac	Casale Monferrato, Archivio Capitolare
CMbc	——, Biblioteca Civica
CMs	——, Seminario Vescovile
CMI	Camogli, Biblioteca Comunale Nicolo Cueno
CMO	Camerino, Biblioteca Valentiniana e Comunale
COc	Como, Biblioteca Comunale
COd	——, Duomo

CORc	Correggio, Biblioteca Comunale
COS	Cosenza, Biblioteca Civica
CPa	Carpi, Archivio Paolo Guaitoli della Commissione di Storia Patria de Carpi
CPc	——, Biblioteca Comunale
CR	Cremona, Biblioteca Statale
CRd	——, Duomo
CRE	Crema, Biblioteca Comunale
CREi	——, Istituto Musicale L. Folcioni
CT	Cortona, Biblioteca Comunale e dell'Accademia Etrusca
CZorizio	Cazzago S Martino, Orizio private collection
DO	Domodossola, Biblioteca e Archivio dei Rosminiani di Monte Calvaro
E	Enna, Biblioteca Comunale
Fa	Florence, Ss Annunziata
Faq	——, Pius XII Institute, Graduate School of Fine Arts, Aquinas Library
Fas	——, Archivio di Stato
Fc	——, Conservatorio di Musica Luigi Cherubini
Fd	——, Duomo
Ffabbri	——, M. Fabbri, private collection
Fl	——, Biblioteca Medicea-Laurenziana
Fm	——, Biblioteca Marucelliana
Fn	——, Biblioteca Nazionale Centrale
Folschki	——, Olschki private collection
Fr	——, Biblioteca Riccardiana e Moreniana
Fs	——, Seminario Arcivescovile Maggiore
Fsa	——, Biblioteca Domenicana, Chiesa S Maria Novella
Fsm	——, Convento S Marco
Fu	——, Università degli Studi, Facoltà di Lettere e Filosofia
FA	Fabriano, Biblioteca Comunale
FAd	——, Duomo
FAN	Fano, Biblioteca Comunale Federiciana
FBR	Fossombrone, Biblioteca Civica Passionei
FEbonfigliuoli	Ferrara, Bonfigliuoli private collection
FEc	——, Biblioteca Comunale Ariostea
FEd	——, Duomo
FEmichelini	——, Bruto Michelini, private collection
FELc	Feltre, Biblioteca Comunale
FELd	——, Duomo
FELm	——, Museo Civico
FEM	Finale Emilia, Biblioteca Comunale
FERc	Fermo, Biblioteca Comunale
FERd	——, Duomo
FERl	——, Liceo Musicale Girolamo Frescobaldi
FERmichelini	——, Bruno Michelini, private collection
FOc	Forlì, Biblioteca Comunale Aurelio Saffi
FOd	——, Duomo
FOG	Foggia, Biblioteca Provinciale
FOLc	Foligno, Biblioteca Comunale
FOLd	——, Duomo
FOSc	Fossano, Biblioteca Civica
FZac(d)	Faenza, Archivio Capitolare (Duomo)
FZc	——, Biblioteca Comunale
FZsavini	——, Ino Savini, private collection
Gc	Genoa, Biblioteca Civica Berio
Gf	——, Biblioteca Franzoniana
Ggrasso	——, Lorenzina Grasso, private collection
Gi(l)	——, Conservatorio di Musica Nicolò Paganini
Gim	——, Istituto Mazziniano
Gsc	——, S Caterina
Gsmb	——, S Maria della Castagna
Gsmd	——, S Maria di Castello, Biblioteca dei Domenicani
Gu	——, Biblioteca Universitaria
GA	Ganna, Badia Benedittina
GE	Gemona, Duomo
GN	Giulianova, Biblioteca Comunale Vincenzo Bindi
GO	Gorizia, Seminario Teologico Centrale
GR	Grottaferrata, Badia Greca
GUA	Guastalla, Biblioteca Municipale Maldotti
GUBsp	Gubbio, Biblioteca Comunale Sperelliana
I	Imola, Biblioteca Comunale
IE	Iesi, Archivio Comunale
IV	Ivrea, Biblioteca Capitolare
La	Lucca, Archivio di Stato
Lc	——, Biblioteca Capitolare Feliniana
Lg	——, Biblioteca Statale
Li	——, Istituto Musicale Luigi Boccherini
Ls	——, Seminario Vescovile
LA	L'Aquila, Biblioteca Provinciale Salvatore Tommasi
LE	Lecce, Biblioteca Provinciale Nicola Bernardini
LI	Livorno, Biblioteca Comunale Labronica Francesco Domenico Guerrazzi
LOc	Lodi, Biblioteca Capitolare
LOcl	——, Biblioteca Comunale Laudense
LT	Loreto, Archivio Storico della Cappella Lauretana
LU	Lugo, Biblioteca Comunale Fabrizio Trisi
Ma	Milan, Biblioteca Ambrosiana
Malfieri	——, Trecani degli Alfieri, private collection
Mb	——, Biblioteca Nazionale Braidense
Mc	——, Conservatorio di Musica Giuseppe Verdi
Mca	——, Archivio della Curia Arcivescovile
Mcap(d)	——, Cappella Musicale del Duomo
Mcom	——, Biblioteca Comunale
Md	——, Archivio della Cappella Musicale del Duomo
Mdonà	——, Mariangelo Donà, private collection
Mr	——, Archivio Storico Ricordi (Casa Editrice)
Ms	——, Biblioteca Teatrale Livia Simoni
Msartori	——, Claudio Sartori, private collection
Mt	——, Biblioteca Trivulziana
Mvidusso	——, Carlo Vidusso, private collection
MAa	Mantua, Archivio di Stato
MAad	——, Archivio Storico Diocesano
MAav	——, Accademia Virgiliana di Scienze, Lettere ed Arti
MAc	——, Biblioteca Comunale
MAi	——, Istituto Musicale Lucio Campiani
MAp	——, Duomo S Pietro
MAs	——, Seminario Vescovile
MAC	Macerata, Biblioteca Comunale Mozzi-Borgetti
MACa	——, Archivio di Stato
MC	Monte Cassino, Biblioteca dell'Abbazia
ME	Messina, Biblioteca Universitaria
MEmeli	——, Alfonso Meli, private collection
MEnicotra	——, Arturo Nicotra, private collection
MEs	——, Biblioteca Painiana del Seminario Arcivescovile
MFc	Molfetta, Biblioteca Comunale Giovanni Panunzio
MFsr	——, Pontificio Seminario Regionale Pio XI
MFsv	——, Seminario Vescovile
MOa	Modena, Accademia Nazionale di Scienze, Lettere ed Arti
MOd	——, Duomo
MOdep	——, Deputazione di Storia Patria per le Antiche Province Modenesi
MOe	——, Biblioteca Estense
MOf	——, Archivio Ferni
MOl	——, Liceo Musicale Orazio Vecchi
MOs	——, Archivio di Stato
MTventuri	Montecatini-Terme, Antonio Venturi, private collection
MV	Montevergine, Biblioteca del Santuario
MZ	Monza, Insigne Basilica di S Giovanni Battista
MZc	——, Biblioteca Civica
Na	Naples, Archivio di Stato
Nc	——, Conservatorio di Musica S Pietro a Majella
Nf	——, Biblioteca Oratoriana dei Filippini
Nlp	——, Biblioteca Lucchesi-Palli [in *Nn*]
Nn	——, Biblioteca Nazionale Vittorio Emanuele III
Ns	——, Seminario Arcivescovile
Nsn	——, Società Napoletana di Storia Patria
Nu	——, Biblioteca Universitaria
NO	Novacello, Biblioteca dell'Abbazia
NON	Nonantola, Seminario Abbaziale
NOVc	Novara, Biblioteca Civica
NOVd	——, Archivio Musicale Classico del Duomo
NOVg	——, Archivio e Biblioteca di S Gaudenzio
NOVi	——, Civico Istituto Musicale Brera
NOVsg	——, Archivio Musicale di S Gaudenzio
NT	Noto, Biblioteca Comunale
Oc	Orvieto, Biblioteca Comunale Luigi Fumi
Od	——, Biblioteca dell'Opera del Duomo
OR	Oristano, Seminario Arcivescovile
ORT	Ortona, Biblioteca Comunale
OS	Ostiglia, Biblioteca Musicale Greggiati
OSI	Osimo, Biblioteca Comunale
Pbonelli	Padua, E. Bonelli, private collection
Pc	——, Biblioteca Capitolare
Pca	——, Biblioteca Antoniana, Basilica del Santo
Pci	——, Museo Civico, Biblioteca Civica e Archivio Comunale
Pi(l)	——, Istituto Musicale Cesare Pollini
Ppapafava	——, Novello Papafava dei Carreresi, private collection
Ps	——, Seminario Vescovile
Pu	——, Biblioteca Universitaria
PAac	Parma, Archivio Capitolare
PAas	——, Archivio di Stato
PAc	——, Conservatorio di Musica Arrigo Boito
PAi	——, Istituto di Studi Verdiani
PAsg	——, S Giovanni Evangelista
PAst	——, Madonna della Steccata

PAt	——, Teatro Regio
PAL	Palestrina, Biblioteca Comunale Fantoniana
PAVc	Pavia, S Maria del Carmine
PAVi	——, Civico Istituto Musicale Franco Vittadini
PAVs	——, Seminario Vescovile
PAVsm	——, S Michele
PAVsp	——, S Pietro in Ciel d'Oro
PAVu	——, Biblioteca Universitaria
PCa	Piacenza, Collegio Alberoni
PCc	——, Biblioteca Comunale Passerini Landi
PCcon	——, Conservatorio di Musica G. Nicolini
PCd	——, Duomo
PCsa	——, Biblioteca e Archivio Capitolare di S Antonino
PCsm	——, S Maria di Campagna
PEc	Perugia, Biblioteca Comunale Augusta
PEd	——, Cattedrale
PEl	——, Conservatorio di Musica Francesco Morlacchi
PEsp	——, S Pietro
PEA	Pescia, Biblioteca Comunale Carlo Magnani
PESc	Pesaro, Conservatorio di Musica Gioacchino Rossini
PEScerasa	——, Amadeo Cerasa, private collection [now *VTcerasa*]
PESd	——, Duomo
PESo	——, Biblioteca Oliveriana
PIa	Pisa, Archivio di Stato
PIarc	——, Biblioteca Arcivescovile Cardinale Pietro Maffi
PIc	——, Museo Nazionale di S Matteo
PIca	——, Biblioteca Cateriniana
PIcc	——, Archivio e Biblioteca Certosa di Calci
PIp	——, Archivio Musicale dell'Opera della Primaziale
PIr	——, Biblioteca Raffaelli
PIraffaelli	——, Raffaelli private collection
PIs	——, Fondo Simoneschi
PIst	——, Chiesa dei Cavalieri di S Stefano
PIN	Pinerolo, Biblioteca Comunale Camillo Allinudi
PLa	Palermo, Archivio di Stato
PLcom	——, Biblioteca Comunale
PLcon	——, Conservatorio Vincenzo Bellini
PLd	——, Duomo
PLi	——, Istituto di Storia della Musica, Facoltà di Lettere, Università degli Studi
PLm	——, Teatro Massimo
PLn	——, Biblioteca Nazionale
PLpagano	——, Roberto Pagano, private collection
PLs	——, Baron Pietro Emanuele Sgadari di Lo Monaco, private collection [in Casa di Lavoro e Preghiera Padre Massini]
PLsd	——, Archivio Storico Diocesano
PO	Potenza, Biblioteca Provinciale
POa	——, Archivio di Stato
POd	——, Duomo
PR	Prato, Duomo
PS	Pistoia, Cattedrale
PSc	——, Biblioteca Comunale Forteguerriana
Ra	Rome, Biblioteca Angelica
Rac	——, Accademia di Francia
Raf	——, Accademia Filarmonica Romana
Ras	——, Archivio di Stato
Rc	——, Biblioteca Casanatense
Rcg	——, Curia Generalizia dei Padri Gesuiti; Pontificio Collegio Germano-Ungarico
Rchristoff	——, Boris Christoff, private collection
Rcns	——, Archivio della Chiesa Nazionale Spagnuola
Rco	——, Congregazione dell'Oratorio
Rcsg	——, Oratorio di S Girolamo della Cantà
Rdi	——, Discoteca di Stato
Rdp	——, Archivio Doria-Pamphili, private collection
Rf	——, Archivio dei Filippini
Rgiazotto	——, Remo Giazotto, private collection
Ria	——, Istituto Nazionale di Archeologia e Storia dell'Arte
Rif	——, Istituto di Fisiologia dell'Università
Rig	——, Istituto Storico Germanico
Rims	——, Pontificio Istituto di Musica Sacra
Rla	——, Biblioteca Lancisiana
Rli	——, Accademia Nazionale dei Lincei e Corsiniana
Rlib	——, Basilica Liberiana
Rn	——, Biblioteca Nazionale Centrale Vittorio Emanuele III
Rp	——, Biblioteca Pasqualini [in *Rsc*]
Rps	——, Pio Sodalizio de Piceni
Rsc	——, Conservatorio di Musica S Cecilia
Rsg	——, S Giovanni in Laterano
Rsgf	——, Arciconfraternità di S Giovanni dei Fiorentini
Rslf	——, S Luigi de' Francesi
Rsm	——, Archivio Capitolare di S Maria Maggiore [in *Rvat*]
Rsmm	——, S Maria di Monserrato
Rsmt	——, S Maria in Trastevere
Rsp	——, Santo Spirito in Sassia
Rss	——, S Sabina (Venerabile Convento)
Rv	——, Biblioteca Vallicelliana
Rvat	——, Biblioteca Apostolica Vaticana
RA	Ravenna, Duomo
RAc	——, Biblioteca Comunale Classense
RAs	——, Seminario Arcivescovile dei Ss Angeli Custodi
REas	Reggio Emilia, Archivio di Stato
REc	——, Archivio e Biblioteca Capitolare del Duomo
REd	——, Archivio Capitolare del Duomo
REm	——, Biblioteca Municipale
REsp	——, Archivio Capitolare di S Prospero
RIM	Rimini, Biblioteca Civica Gambalunga
RO	Rosate, S Stefano
RVE	Rovereto, Biblioteca Civica Girolamo Tartarotti
RVI	Rovigo, Accademia dei Concordi
Sac	Siena, Accademia Musicale Chigiana
Sas	——, Archivio di Stato
Sc	——, Biblioteca Comunale degli Intronati
Sd	——, Archivio Musicale dell'Opera del Duomo
Smo	——, Biblioteca annessa al Monumento Nazionale di Monte Oliveti Maggiore
SA	Savona, Biblioteca Civica Anton Giulio Barrili
SAL	Saluzzo, Archivio del Duomo
SAS	Sassari, Biblioteca Universitaria
SDF	San Daniele del Friuli, Biblioteca Civica Guarneriana
SE	Senigallia, Biblioteca Comunale Antonelliana
SI	Siracusa, Biblioteca Comunale
SML	Santa Margherita Ligure, Biblioteca Comunale Francesco Domenico Costa
SO	Sant'Oreste, Collegiata di S Lorenzo
SON	Sondrio, Biblioteca Civica Pio Rajna
SPc	Spoleto, Biblioteca Comunale
SPd	——, Duomo
SPE	Spello, Collegiata S Maria Maggiore
ST	Stresa, Biblioteca Rosminiana
SUsb	Subiaco, Biblioteca S Benedetto
SUss	——, Monumenta Nazionale dell'Abbazia di S Scolastica
Ta	Turin, Archivio di Stato
Tb	——, Convento di Benevagienna
Tci	——, Biblioteca Civica Musicale Andrea della Corte
Tco	——, Conservatorio Statale di Musica Giuseppe Verdi
Td	——, Duomo
Tf	——, Accademia Filarmonica
Ti	——, Istituto Salesiano Valsalice
Tmc	——, Museo Civico
Tn	——, Biblioteca Nazionale Universitaria
Tr	——, Biblioteca Reale
Trt	——, Archivio Musicale Radiotelevisione Italiana
TE	Terni, Istituto Musicale G. Briccialdi
TEc	——, Biblioteca Comunale
TI	Termini-Imerese, Biblioteca Liciniana
TLP	Torre del Lago Puccini, Museo di Casa Puccini
TOD	Todi, Biblioteca Comunale Lorenzo Feoni
TOL	Tolentino, Biblioteca Comunale Filelfica
TRa	Trent, Archivio di Stato
TRc	——, Biblioteca Comunale
TRmd	——, Museo Diocesano
TRmn	——, Museo Nazionale
TRmr	——, Museo del Risorgimento
TRE	Tremezzo, Count Gian Ludovico Sola-Cabiati, private collection
TRN	Trani, Biblioteca Comunale G. Bovio
TRP	Trapani, Biblioteca Fardelliana
TSci(com)	Trieste, Biblioteca Civica
TScm	——, Civici Musei di Storia ed Arte
TScon	——, Conservatorio di Musica G. Tartini
TSmt	——, Civico Museo Teatrale di Fondazione Carlo Schmidl
TSsc	——, Fondazione Giovanni Scaramangà de Altomonte
TSsg	——, Archivio della Cappella della Cattedrale S Giusto
TVca(d)	Treviso, Biblioteca Capitolare (Duomo)
TVco	——, Biblioteca Comunale
Us	Urbino, Cappella del Sacramento (Duomo)
Usf	——, S Francesco [in *Uu*]
Uu	——, Biblioteca Universitaria
UD	Udine, Duomo
UDa	——, Archivio di Stato

UDc	——, Biblioteca Comunale Vincenzo Joppi
UDi	——, Istituto Musicale Jacopo Tomadini
URBc	Urbania, Biblioteca Comunale
URBcap	——, Biblioteca Capitolare (Duomo)
Vas	Venice, Archivio di Stato
Vc	——, Conservatorio di Musica Benedetto Marcello
Vcg	——, Biblioteca Casa di Goldoni
Vgc	——, Biblioteca e Istituto della Fondazione Giorgio Cini
Vlevi	——, Fondazione Ugo Levi
Vmarcello	——, Andrighetti Marcello, private collection
Vmc	——, Museo Civico Correr
Vnm	——, Biblioteca Nazionale Marciana
Vqs	——, Accademia Querini-Stampalia
Vs	——, Seminario Patriarcale
Vsf	——, Conventuale di S Francesco
Vsm	——, Procuratoria di S Marco
Vsmc	——, S Maria della Consolazione detta Della Fava
Vt	——, Teatro la Fenice
VAa	Varese, Archivio Prepositurale di S Vittore
VAc	——, Biblioteca Civica
VCc	Vercelli, Biblioteca Civica
VCd	——, Duomo (Biblioteca Capitolare)
VCs	——, Seminario Vescovile
VD	Viadana, Biblioteca Civica
VEaf	Verona, Società Accademia Filarmonica
VEas	——, Archivio di Stato
VEc	——, Biblioteca Civica
VEcap	——, Biblioteca Capitolare (Cattedrale)
VEs	——, Seminario Vescovile
VEsg	——, S Giorgio in Braida
VG	Voghera, Collegiata di S Lorenzo
VIb	Vicenza, Biblioteca Civica Bertoliana
VId	——, Duomo
VImc	——, Museo Civico
VImr	——, Museo del Risorgimento
VIs	——, Seminario Vescovile
VIGsa	Vigévano, Duomo S Ambrogio
VIGsi	——, S Ignazio
VIM	Vimercate, S Stefano
VO	Volterra, Biblioteca Guarnacci
VTc	Viterbo, Biblioteca Comunale degli Ardenti
VTcarosi	——, Attilio Carosi, private collection
VTcerasa	——, Amadeo Cerasa, private collection
VTp	——, Biblioteca Pio XII, Pontificio Seminario Regionale
VTs	——, Seminario Diocesano
VTM	Ventimiglia, Civica Biblioteca Aprosiana

IL: ISRAEL

J	Jerusalem, Jewish National and University Library
Jp	——, Patriarchal Library
S	Mt Sinai
SS	St Sabas, Monastery

IS: ICELAND

Rn	Reykjavik, National Library

J: JAPAN

Tm	Tokyo, Musashino Ongaku Daigaku
Tma(Tmc)	——, Bibliotheca Musashino Academia Musicae
Tn	——, Nanki Music Library, Ohki private collection

N: NORWAY

Bo	Bergen, Offentlige Bibliotek
Bu	——, Universitetsbiblioteket
Oic	Oslo, Norwegian Music Information Centre
Oim	——, Institutt for Musikkvitenskap, Universitet
Ok	——, Musik-Konservatoriet
Onk	——, Norsk Komponistforening
Or	——, Norsk Rikskringkastings
Ou	——, Universitetsbiblioteket
Oum	——, Universitetsbiblioteket, Norsk Musikksamling
T	Trondheim, Kongelige Norske Videnskabers Selskab
Tmi	——, Musikkvitenskapelig Institutt

NL: THE NETHERLANDS

Ad	Amsterdam, Stichting Donemus
At	——, Toonkunst-Bibliotheek
Au	——, Universiteitsbibliotheek
Avnm	——, Bibliotheek der Vereniging voor Nederlandse Muziekgeschiedenis [in *At*]
AN	Amerongen, Archief van het Kasteel der Graven Bentinck, private collection

BI	Bilthoven, Stichting Gaudeamus
D	Deventer, Stads- of Athenaeumbibliotheek
DHa	The Hague, Koninklijk Huisarchief
DHgm	——, Gemeentemuseum
DHk	——, Koninklijke Bibliotheek
DHmw	——, Rijksmuseum
G	Groningen, Universiteitsbibliotheek
Hs	Haarlem, Stadsbibliotheek
HIr	Hilversum, Radio Nederland
L	Leiden, Gemeentearchief
Lml	——, Museum Lakenhal
Lt	——, Bibliotheca Thysiana [in *Lu*]
Lu	——, Bibliotheek der Rijksuniversiteit
Lw	——, Bibliothèque Wallonne
LE	Leeuwarden, Provinciale Bibliotheek van Friesland
R	Rotterdam, Gemeentebibliotheek
'sH	's-Hertogenbosch, Archief van de Illustre Lieve Vrouwe Broederschap
Uim	Utrecht, Instituut voor Muziekwetenschap der Rijksuniversiteit
Usg	——, St Gregorius Vereniging, Bibliotheek [in *Uim*]
Uu	——, Bibliotheek der Rijksuniversiteit

NZ: NEW ZEALAND

Ap	Auckland, Public Library
Au	——, University Library
Dp	Dunedin, Public Library
Wt	Wellington, Alexander Turnbull Library

P: PORTUGAL

AN	Angra do Heroismo, Biblioteca Pública e Arquivo Distrital
AR	Arouca, Museu Regional de Arte Sacra do Mosteiro de Arouca
AV	Aveiro, Museu de Aveiro, Mosteiro de Jesus
BA	Barreiro, Biblioteca Municipal
BRp	Braga, Biblioteca Pública e Arquivo Distrital
BRs	——, Sé de Braga
C	Coimbra, Biblioteca Geral da Universidade
Cm	——, Biblioteca Municipal
Cmn	——, Museu Nacional de Machado de Castro
Cs	——, Sé Nova
Cug	——, Biblioteca Geral da Universidade
Cul	——, Faculdade de Letras da Universidade
CA	Cascais, Museu-Biblioteca Condes de Castro Guimarães
Em	Elvas, Biblioteca Públia Hortênsia
EVc	Évora, Arquivo da Sé
EVp	——, Biblioteca Pública e Arquivo Distrital
F	Figueira da Foz, Biblioteca Pública Municipal Pedro Fernandes Tomás
G	Guimarães, Arquivo Municipal Alfredo Pimenta
La	Lisbon, Palácio Nacional da Ajuda
Laa	——, Academia de Amadores de Musica (Conservatorio Municipal)
Lac	——, Academia das Ciencias
Lan	——, Arquivo Nacional de Torre do Tombo
Lc	——, Conservatorio Nacional
Lcg	——, Fundação Calouste Gulbenkian
Lf	——, Fábrica da Sé Patriarcal
Lif	——, Instituto de Franca
Ln	——, Biblioteca Nacional
Lr	——, Emissora Nacional de Radiodifusão
Ls	——, Sociedade de Escritores e Compositores Portugueses
Lt	——, Teatro Nacional de S Carlos
LA	Lamego, Biblioteca da Sé
LE	Leiria, Biblioteca Erudita e Arquivo Distrital (Biblioteca Pública)
Mp	Mafra, Palácio Nacional
Pa	Oporto, Ateneu Comercial
Pc	——, Conservatorio de Musica
Pcom	——, Biblioteca Comunale
Peh	——, Museu de Etnografia e Historia
Pf	——, Clube Fenianos Portuenses
Pm	——, Biblioteca Pública Municipal
PD	Ponta Delgada, Biblioteca Pública e Arquivo Distrital
PL	Ponte de Lima, Arquivo da Misericórdia
PO	Portalegre, Arquivo da Sé
Va	Viseu, Arquivo Distrital
Vm	——, Museu Grão Vasco
Vs	——, Arquivo da Sé
VV	Vila Viçosa, Casa da Bragança, Museu-Biblioteca

PL: POLAND

B	Bydgoszcz, Biblioteka Miejska
BA	Barczew, Archiwum Kościoła Parafialnego
Cb	Cieszyn, Biblioteka Śląska, Oddział Cieszyn
Cp	——, Biblioteka Tschammera w Kościele Ewangelickim
CZp	Częstochowa, Klasztor OO. Paulinów na Jasnej Górze
GD	Gdańsk, Biblioteka Polskiej Akademii Nauk
GNd	Gniezno, Archiwum Archidiecezjalne
GR	Grodzisk, Klasztor OO. Cystersów
Kc	Kraków, Biblioteka Czartoryskich
Kcz	——, Biblioteka Czapskich
Kd	——, Klasztor OO. Dominikanów
Kj	——, Biblioteka Jagiellońska
Kk	——, Kapituła Metropolitalna
Kp	——, Biblioteka Polskiej Akademii Nauk
Kpa	——, Archiwum Państwowe
Kz	——, Biblioteka Czartoryskich
KA	Katowice, Biblioteka Śląska
KO	Kórnik, Polska Akademia Nauk, Biblioteka Kórnicka
Lk	Lublin, Biblioteka Katolickiego Uniwersytetu
Lw	——, Biblioteka Wojewódzka i Miejska im. H. Łopacińskiego
ŁA	Łańcut, Muzeum
ŁO	Łowicz, Biblioteka Seminarium
MO	Mogiła, Klasztor OO. Cystersów
OB	Obra, Klasztor OO. Cystersów
Pa	Poznań, Biblioteka Archidiecezjalna
Pr	——, Miejska Biblioteka Publiczna im. Edwarda Raczyńskiego
Pu	——, Biblioteka Uniwersytecka
PE	Pelplin, Biblioteka Seminarium Duchownego
PŁp	Płock, Biblioteka Towarzystwa Naukowego
R	Raków, Archiwum Kościelne
SA	Sandomierz, Seminarium Duchownego
SZ	Szalowa, Archiwum Parafialne
Tu	Toruń, Biblioteka Uniwersytecka
TA	Tarnów, Archiwum Archidiecezjalne
Wm	Warszawa, Biblioteka Muzeum Narodowego
Wn	——, Biblioteka Narodowa
Wp	——, Biblioteka Publiczna
Ws	——, Biblioteka Synodalna Ewangelicka
Wtm	——, Biblioteka Warszawskiego Towarzystwa Muzycznego
Wu	——, Biblioteka Uniwersytecka
WL	Wilanów, Biblioteka, Oddział Muzeum Narodowego Warszawy
WRol	Wrocław, Biblioteka Ossolineum Leopoldiensis
WRu	——, Biblioteka Uniwersytecka

R: ROMANIA

Ab	Aiud, Biblioteca Documentară Bethlen
Ba	Bucharest, Biblioteca Academiei Republicii Socialiste România
Bc	——, Biblioteca Centrală de Stat
BRm	Brașov, Biblioteca Municipală
Sb	Sibiu, Muzeul Brukenthal
TMt	Tîrgu Mureș, Biblioteca Documentară Teleki

S: SWEDEN

A	Arvika, Folkliga Musikskolan
E	Enköping, Samrealskolans Arkiv
ES	Eskilstuna, Stadsbiblioteket
Gem	Göteborg, Etnografiska Museet
Ghl	——, Hvitfeldtska Högre Allmänna Läroverket
Gu	——, Universitetsbiblioteket (formerly Stadsbiblioteket)
GÄ	Gävle, Vasaskolans Bibliotek
Hfryklund	Hälsingborg, D. Daniel Fryklund, private collection [in *Skma*]
Hs	——, Stadsbiblioteket
J	Jönköping, Per Brahegymnasiet
K	Kalmar, Stifts- och Gymnasiebiblioteket
KA	Karlstad, Stadsbiblioteket
KAT	Katrineholm, Stadsbiblioteket
KH	Karlshamn, Museums Biblioteket
L	Lund, Universitetsbiblioteket
Lbarnekow	——, Barnekow private collection
LB	Leufsta Bruk, De Geer private collection
LI	Linköping, Stifts- och Landsbiblioteket
M	Malmö, Stadsbiblioteket
N	Norrköping, Stadsbiblioteket
Ö	Örebro, Karolinska Skolans Bibliotek
ÖS	Östersund, Jämtlands Läns Bibliotek
Sdt	Stockholm, Drottningholms Teatermuseum
Sic	——, Stims Informationscentral för Svensk Musik
Sk	——, Kungliga Biblioteket
Skma	——, Kungliga Musikaliska Akademiens Bibliotek
Sm	——, Musikmuseet
Smf	——, Stiftelsen Musikkulturens Främjande
Sn	——, Nordiska Museet
Ssr	——, Sveriges Radio
St	——, Kungliga Teaterns Bibliotek
SK	Skara, Stifts- och Landsbiblioteket
STd	Strängnäs, Domkyrkobiblioteket
STr	——, Roggebiblioteket
Uifm	Uppsala, Institutionen för Musikforskning vid Uppsala Universitetet
Uu	——, Universitetsbiblioteket
V	Västerås, Stadsbiblioteket
Vll	Visby, Landsarkivet
VIs	——, Stadsbiblioteket
VX	Växjö, Landsbiblioteket

SF: FINLAND

A	Turku [Åbo], Sibelius Museum Musikvetenskapliga Institutionen vid Åbo Akademi, Bibliotek & Arkiv
Aa	——, Åbo Akademis, Bibliotek
Hko	Helsinki, Helsingin Kaupunginorkester
Hmt	——, Musiikin Tiedotuskeskus
Hr	——, Oy Yleisradio AB, Nuotisto
Hs	——, Sibelius-Akatemian Kirjasto
Hy	——, Helsingin Yliopiston Kirjasto
Hyf	——, Helsingin Yliopiston Kirjasto, Department of Finnish Music
TA	Tampere, Tampereen Yliopiston Kansanperinteen Laitos

US: UNITED STATES OF AMERICA

AA	Ann Arbor, University of Michigan Music Library
AB	Albany, New York State Library
AL	Allentown (Penn.), Muhlenberg College, John A. W. Haas Library
AM	Amherst (Mass.), Amherst College, Robert Frost Building
ATu	Atlanta (Georgia), Emory University Library
AU	Aurora (NY), Wells College Library
AUS	Austin, University of Texas
Ba	Boston, Athenaeum Library
Bhs	——, Bostonian Society
Bc	——, New England Conservatory of Music
Bco	——, American Congregational Society, Congregational Library
Bfa	——, Fine Arts Museum
Bge	——, School of Fine Arts, General Education Library
Bh	——, Harvard Musical Association
Bhh	——, Handel and Haydn Society
Bhs	——, Massachusetts Historical Society
Bl	——, Grand Lodge of Masons in Massachusetts, A. F. and A. M. Library
Bm	——, University, Mugar Memorial Library
Bp	——, Public Library, Music Department
Bth	——, University, School of Theology
BAep	Baltimore, Enoch Pratt Free Library, Fine Arts and Music Department
BAhs	——, Maryland Historical Society
BApi	——, City Library, Peabody Institute
BAu	——, Johns Hopkins University Libraries
BAw	——, Walters Art Gallery
BAT	Baton Rouge, Louisiana State University Library
BE	Berkeley, University of California, Music Library
BER	Berea (Ohio), Baldwin-Wallace College, Ritter Library of the Conservatory
BETm	Bethlehem (Penn.), Archives of the Moravian Church in Bethlehem
BETu	——, Lehigh University, Lucy Packer Lindeman Memorial Library
BG	Bangor (Maine), Public Library
BK	Brunswick (Maine), Bowdoin College, Department of Music
BLl	Bloomington, Indiana University, Lilly Library
BLu	——, Indiana University, School of Music Library
BO	Boulder, University of Colorado Music Library
BRc	Brooklyn, Brooklyn College Music Library
BRp	——, Public Library
BU	Buffalo, Buffalo and Erie County Public Library
Charding	Chicago, W. N. H. Harding, private collection [in *GB-Ob*]
Chs	——, Chicago Historical Society Library
Cn	——, Newberry Library

Cu	——, University Music Library
CA	Cambridge, Harvard University Music Libraries
CAR	Carlisle (Penn.), Dickinson College
CDhs	Concord, New Hampshire Historical Society
CDs	——, New Hampshire State Library
CG	Coral Gables (Florida), University of Miami Music Library
CHua	Charlottesville, University of Virginia, Alderman Library
CHum	——, University of Virginia Music Library
CHH	Chapel Hill, University of North Carolina Music Library
CIhc	Cincinnati, Hebrew Union College
CIu	——, University of Cincinnati College-Conservatory of Music
CLm	Cleveland, Museum of Art, Cantatorium
CLp	——, Public Library, Fine Arts Department
CLwr	——, Western Reserve University, Freiberger Library and Music House Library
COu	Columbus, Ohio State University Music Library
CR	Cedar Rapids, Iowa Masonic Library
Dp	Detroit, Public Library, Music and Performing Arts Department
DB	Dearborn (Mich.), Henry Ford Museum and Greenfield Village
DE	Denver (Colorado), Public Library, Art and Music Division
DM	Durham (North Carolina), Duke University Libraries
DN	Denton, North Texas State University Music Library
DO	Dover (New Hampshire), Public Library
Eg	Evanston (Ill.), Garrett Theological Seminary
Eu	——, Northwestern University, Music Library
ECstarr	Eastchester (NY), Saul Starr, private collection
EXd	Exeter (New Hampshire), Phillips Exeter Academy, Davis Library
EXp	——, Public Library
FW	Fort Worth, Southwest Baptist Theological Seminary
G	Gainesville, University of Florida Library, Rare Book Collection
GA	Gambier (Ohio), Kenyon College Divinity School, Colburn Library
GB	Gettysburg, Lutheran Theological Seminary
GR	Granville (Ohio), Denison University Library
GRE	Greenville (Delaware), Eleutherian Mills Historical Library
Hhs	Hartford, Connecticut Historical Society Library
Hm	——, Case Memorial Library, Hartford Seminary Foundation
Hp	——, Public Library, Art and Music Department
Hs	——, Connecticut State Library
Hw	——, Trinity College, Watkinson Library
HA	Hanover (New Hampshire), Dartmouth College, Baker Library
HB	Harrisonburg (Virginia), Eastern Mennonite College, Menno Simons Historical Library and Archives
HG	Harrisburg, Pennsylvania State Library
HO	Hopkinton, New Hampshire Antiquarian Society
HU	Huntingdon (Penn.), Juniata College, L. A. Beechly Library
I	Ithaca (NY), Cornell University Music Library
IO	Iowa, University of Iowa Music Library
K	Kent (Ohio), Kent State University Library
Lu	Lawrence, University of Kansas Libraries
LAu	Los Angeles, University of California, Walter H. Rubsamen Music Library
LAuc	——, University of California, William Andrews Clark Memorial Library
LAusc	——, University of Southern California School of Music
LB	Lewisburg (Penn.), Bucknell University, Ellen Clark Bertrand Library
LChs	Lancaster (Penn.), Lancaster County Historical Society
LCm	——, Lancaster Mennonite Historical Library and Archives
LCts	——, Theological Seminary of the United Church of Christ
LEX	Lexington, University of Kentucky, Margaret I. King Library
LOs	Louisville (Ky.), Southern Baptist Theological Seminary, James P. Boyce Centennial Library
LOu	——, University, School of Music Library

LU	Lincoln University (Penn.), Vail Memorial Library
M	Milwaukee, Public Library, Art and Music Department
MI	Middletown (Conn.), Wesleyan University, Olin Memorial Library
MORduncan	Morgantown, Richard E. Duncan, private collection
MSp	Minneapolis, Public Library
MSu	——, University of Minnesota Music Library
MV	Mt Vernon (Virginia), Mt Vernon Ladies Association of the Union Collection
Nf	Northampton (Mass.), Forbes Library
Nsc	——, Smith College, Werner Josten Music Library
NAZ	Nazareth (Penn.), Moravian Historical Society
NBs	New Brunswick, Theological Seminary, Gardner A. Sage Library
NBu	——, Rutgers University Library
NEm	Newark (NJ), Newark Museum
NEp	——, Public Library
NH	New Haven, Yale University, School of Music Library
NORts	New Orleans, Theological Seminary
NORtu	——, Tulane University, Howard Tilton Memorial Library
NP	Newburyport (Mass.), Public Library
NYcc	New York, City College Library, Music Library
NYcu	——, Columbia University Music Library
NYfo	——, Fordham University Library
NYfuld	——, James J. Fuld, private collection
NYgo	——, University, Gould Memorial Library
NYgr	——, Grolier Club
NYhc	——, Hunter College Library
NYhs	——, New York Historical Society
NYhsa	——, Hispanic Society of America
NYj	——, Juilliard School of Music
NYlateiner	——, Jacob Lateiner, private collection
NYma	——, Mannes College of Music, Clara Damrosch Mannes Memorial Library
NYmc	——, City Museum, Theatre and Music Department
NYmm	——, Metropolitan Museum of Art, Thomas J. Watson Library
NYp	——, Public Library at Lincoln Center, Library and Museum of the Performing Arts
NYpm	——, Pierpont Morgan Library
NYq	——, Queens College of the City University, Paul Klapper Library, Music Library
NYts	——, Union Theological Seminary
OA	Oakland (Calif.), Public Library
OAm	——, Mills College, Margaret Prall Music Library
OB	Oberlin, Oberlin College Conservatory of Music
Pc	Pittsburgh, Carnegie Library
Pfinney	——, Theodore M. Finney, private collection [in *Pu*]
Ps	——, Theological Seminary, Clifford E. Barbour Library
Pu	——, University of Pittsburgh, Theodore Finney Music Library
PD	Portland, Maine Historical Society
PER	Perryville (Missouri), St Mary's Seminary
PHbo	Philadelphia, St Charles Borromeo Theological Seminary
PHbs	——, William Bacon Stevens Library
PHchs	——, American Catholic Historical Society of Philadelphia
PHci	——, Curtis Institute of Music
PHem	——, Eric Mandell Collection of Jewish Music
PHf	——, Free Library of Philadelphia
PHhs	——, Historical Society of Pennsylvania
PHkm	——, Lutheran Theological Seminary
PHlc	——, Library Company of Philadelphia
PHma	——, Musical Academy
PHphs	——, Presbyterian Historical Society
PHps	——, American Philosophical Society
PHr	——, Philip H. and A. S. W. Rosenbach Foundation
PHtr	——, Trinity Lutheran Church of Germantown
PHts	——, Westminster Theological Seminary
PHu	——, University of Pennsylvania, Otto E. Albrecht Music Library
PIlevy	——, Pikesville (Maryland), Lester S. Levy, private collection
PL	Portland (Oregon), Library Association of Portland, Music Department
PO	Poughkeepsie, Vassar College, George Sherman Dickinson Music Library
PRs	Princeton, Theological Seminary
PRu	——, University, Harvey S. Firestone Memorial Library

PROhs	Providence, Rhode Island Historical Society
PROu	——, Brown University Libraries
R	——, Rochester, University, Eastman School of Music, Sibley Music Library
RI	Richmond, Virginia State Library
Sp	Seattle, Public Library
Su	——, University of Washington Music Library
SA	Salem (Mass.), Essex Institute, James Duncan Phillips Library
SB	Santa Barbara, University of California, Library
SFp	San Francisco, Public Library, Fine Arts Department, Music Division
SFs	——, Sutro Library
SFsc	——, San Francisco State College Library, Frank V. de Bellis Collection
SHE	Sherman (Texas), Austin College, Arthur Hopkins Library
SLc	St Louis, Concordia Seminary
SLf	——, Fontbonne College
SLkrohn	——, Ernst C. Krohn, private collection
SLug	——, Washington University, Gaylord Music Library
SLC	Salt Lake City, University of Utah Library
SM	San Marino (Calif.), Henry E. Huntington Library and Art Gallery
SPmoldenhauer	Spokane (Washington), Hans Moldenhauer, private collection
STu	Stanford, University, Division of Humanities and Social Sciences, Music Library
SW	Swarthmore (Penn.), Swarthmore College Library
SY	Syracuse, University Music Library and George Arents Research Library
Tm	Toledo, Toledo Museum of Art
TA	Tallahassee, Florida State University, Robert Manning Strozier Library
U	Urbana, University of Illinois Music Library
Ufraenkel	——, Fraenkel collection
UP	University Park, Pennsylvania State University Library
Wc	Washington, DC, Library of Congress, Music Division
Wca	——, Cathedral
Wcu	——, Catholic University of America Music Library
Wgu	——, Georgetown University Libraries
Ws	——, Folger Shakespeare Libraries
Wsc	——, Scottish Rite Masons, Supreme Council
Wsi	——, Smithsonian Institution, Music Library
WA	Watertown (Mass.), Perkins School for the Blind
WC	Waco (Texas), Baylor University Music Library
WE	Wellesley (Mass.), Wellesley College Library
WELhartzler	Wellman (Iowa), J. D. Hartzler, private collection
WGc	Williamsburg (Virginia), College of William and Mary
WGw	——, Colonial Williamsburg Research Department, historical collection
WI	Williamstown (Mass.), Williams College, Chapin Library
WM	Waltham (Mass.), Brandeis University Library, Music Library, Goldfarb Library
WOa	Worcester (Mass.), American Antiquarian Society
WS	Winston-Salem (North Carolina), Moravian Music Foundation

USSR: UNION OF SOVIET SOCIALIST REPUBLICS

J	Jelgava, Muzei
Kan	Kiev, Tsentral'naya Naukova Biblioteka, Akademiya Nauk URSR
Kk	——, Biblioteka Gosudarstvennoy Konservatoriy imeni P. I. Chaykovskovo
KA	Kaliningrad, Oblastnaya Biblioteka
KAg	——, Gosudarstvennaya Biblioteka
KAu	——, Universitetskaya Biblioteka
KI	Kishinev, Biblioteka Gosudarstvennoy Konservatoriy imeni G. Muzichesku
Lan	Leningrad, Biblioteka Akademii Nauk SSSR
Lia	——, Gosudarstvennïy Tsentral'nïy Istoricheskïy Arkhiv
Lil	——, Institut Russkoy Literaturï
Lit	——, Leningradsky Gosudarstvennïy Institut Teatra, Muzïki i Kinematografii
Lk	——, Biblioteka Leningradskoy Gosudarstvennoy Konservatoriy imeni N. A. Rimskovo-Korsakova
Lph	——, Muzïkal'naya Biblioteka Leningradskoy Gosudarstvennoy Filarmonii
Lsc	——, Gosudarstvennaya Ordena Trudovovo Krasnovo Znameni Publichnaya Biblioteka imeni M. E. Saltïkova-Shchedrina
Lt	——, Leningradskiy Gosudarstvennïy Teatral'nïy Muzey
Ltob	——, Tsentral'naya Muzïkal'naya Biblioteka Gosudarstvennovo Akademicheskovo Teatra Operï i Baleta imeni S. M. Kirova
LV	L'vov, Biblioteka Gosudarstvennoy Konservatoriy imeni N. V. Lysenko
Mcl	Moscow, Gosudarstvennïy Tsentral'nïy Literaturnïy Arkhiv
Mcm	——, Gosudarstvennïy Tsentral'nïy Muzey Muzïkal'noy Kul'turï imeni M. I. Glinki
Mk	——, Gosudarstvennaya Konservatoriya imeni P. I. Chaykovskovo, Nauchnaya Muzïkal'naya Biblioteka imeni S. I. Taneyeva
Ml	——, Gosudarstvennaya Ordena Lenina Biblioteka SSSR imeni V. I. Lenina
Mm	——, Gosudarstvennïyi Istoricheskïyi Muzei
Mt	——, Gosudarstvennïyi Teatral'nïyi Muzei imeni A. Bakhrushina
MI	Minsk, Biblioteka Belorusskoy Gosudarstvennoy Konservatoriy
O	Odessa, Biblioteka Gosudarstvennoy Konservatoriy imeni A. V. Nezhdanovoy
R	Riga, Biblioteka Gosudarstvennoy Konservatoriy Latviyskoy imeni J. Vitola
TAu	Tartu, Universitetskaya Biblioteka
TAL	Tallinn, Biblioteka Gosudarstvennoy Konservatoriy
TB	Tbilisi, Biblioteka Gosudarstvennoy Konservatoriy imeni V. Saradzhisvili
V	Vilnius, Biblioteka Gosudarstvennoy Konservatoriy Litovskoy SSR

YU: YUGOSLAVIA

Bn	Belgrade, Narodna Biblioteka N. R. Srbije
Dsd	Dubrovnik, Knjižnica Samostana Dominikanaca
Dsmb	——, Franjevački Samostan Mala Braća
La	Ljubljana, Knjižnica Akademije za Glasbo
Lf	——, Knjižnica Franćiskanškega Samostana
Ls	——, Škofijski Arhiv in Biblioteka
Lsa	——, Slovenska Akademija Znanosti in Umjetnosti
Lsk	——, Arhiv Stolnega Kora
Lu	——, Narodna in Univerzitetna Knjižnica
MAk	Maribor, Glazbeni Arhiv Katedrale
MAs	——, Knjižnica Škofijskega Arhiv
NM	Novo Mesto, Knjižnica Frančiskanškega Samostana
NMc	——, Glazbeni Arhiv Katedrale
O	Ohrid, Narodno Museum
Sk	Split, Glazbeni Arhiv Katedrale
Ssf	——, Knjižnica Samostana Sv Frane
Za	Zagreb, Jugoslavenska Akademija Znanosti i Umjetnosti
Zda	——, Državni Arhiv
Zha	——, Hrvatski Glazbeni Zavod
Zk	——, Glazbeni Arhiv Katedrale
Zs	——, Glazbeni Arhiv Bogoslovnog Sjemeništa
Zu	——, Nacionalna i Sveučilišna Biblioteka

Volume Fifteen

Playford – Riedt

A Note on the Use of the Dictionary

This note is intended as a short guide to the basic procedures and organization of the dictionary. A fuller account will be found in the Introduction, vol.1, pp.xi–xx.

Abbreviations in general use in the dictionary are listed on pp.vii–x; bibliographical ones (periodicals, reference works, editions etc) are listed on pp.xi–xiii.

Alphabetization of headings is based on the principle that words are read continuously, ignoring spaces, hyphens, accents, bracketed matter etc, up to the first comma; the same principle applies thereafter. 'Mc' and 'M'' are listed as 'Mac', 'St' as 'Saint'.

Bibliographies are arranged chronologically (within section, where divided), in order of year of first publication, and alphabetically by author within years.

Cross-references are shown in small capitals, with a large capital at the beginning of the first word of the entry referred to. Thus 'The instrument is related to the BASS TUBA' would mean that the entry referred to is not '**Bass tuba**' but '**Tuba, bass**'.

Work-lists are normally arranged chronologically (within section, where divided). Italic symbols used in them (like *D-Dlb* or *GB-Lbm*) refer to the libraries holding sources, and are explained on pp. xiv–xxx; each national sigillum stands until contradicted.

P

CONTINUED

Playford. English family of music publishers and booksellers.

(1) John Playford (i) (*b* Norwich, 1623; *d* London, ?Dec 1686). Music publisher and bookseller, clerk to the Temple Church and vicar-choral of St Paul's Cathedral. During the period 1651–84 he dominated the music publishing trade (then virtually confined to London) in a business to which his son (2) Henry Playford succeeded. For the printing of his books he engaged the services of THOMAS HARPER (successor to THOMAS EAST), WILLIAM GODBID (successor to Harper) and his own nephew (3) John Playford the younger, who, apprenticed to Godbid, entered business in 1679 with the latter's widow Anne. The format, style and printing of Playford's books, together with evidence from the stationers' registers, suggest with some certainty that they were printed with East's types, although for title-pages, other than those engraved, a less florid style than the earlier borders was preferred. In many instances Playford adopted East's device and its surrounding motto, 'Laetificat cor musica' (see fig.1).

1. LIFE. A monument at St Michael-at-Plea, Norwich, to his father, John, a mercer, and local records show that he was one of a large family many of whom were scriveners or stationers. Since there is no record of his entry at the grammar school his brother Matthew attended, he was probably educated at the almonry or choir school attached to the cathedral, where he acquired a knowledge of music and the 'love of Divine Service' to which he later referred. Shortly after the death of his father (22 March 1639) he was apprenticed to John Benson, a London publisher of St Dunstan's

1. Device adopted by Playford's printer, Thomas Harper, from Thomas East

Churchyard, Fleet Street (23 March 1639/40), for seven years, achieving his freedom on 5 April 1647, when he became a member of the Yeomanry of the Stationers' Company. This entitled him to trade as a publisher.

He lost no time in securing the tenancy of the shop in the porch of the Temple Church from which all his publications were issued until his retirement. It was one of the addresses of (2) Henry Playford until 1690, when the stock was auctioned. Royalist by family and by personal inclination, Playford began publishing political tracts culminating in *The Perfect Narrative of the Tryal of the King* and others relating to the executions of royalist nobility (reprinted in 1660 as *England's Black Tribunal*). In November 1649 a warrant was issued for the arrest of Playford and his associates. Nothing more is known of him until a year later, when on 7 November 1650 he entered in the stationers' registers 'A booke entituled The English Dancing Master'. Although registration before publishing was theoretically obligatory he entered so few of his music books that it is impossible to tell if this, subsequently published in 1651, was his first.

In 1653 he was admitted clerk to the Temple Church, an office he held with some distinction to the end of his life, devoting himself to the repair and maintenance of the building and to promoting the seemly ordering of the services both there and, through his publications, elsewhere. At about this time he married. When his wife Hannah inherited from her father, Benjamin Allen, publisher of Cornhill, the Playfords moved (1655) from the neighbourhood of the Temple to Islington, where she established a boarding-school for girls, which she maintained until her death in 1679. Playford then moved back to London, taking a house in Arundel Street, Strand, which later passed to his son.

Temperley's examination of the court books of the Stationers' Company shows that Playford was called to the livery in 1661. In 1681 a letter from the king to the master and wardens required that he and others named be admitted to the court of assistants. He attended most of its meetings until 1684 when he declared his retirement from business in favour of his son (2) Henry Playford and another young man, Richard Carr. A number of books, however, retained his imprint until 1686. In his will of that year he desired to be buried in the Temple Church, or in St Faith's, the stationers' chapel in the undercroft of St Paul's, but no record of the burial is known in either place. On his death Purcell wrote the *Elegy on my friend, Mr John Playford*.

1

2. John Playford in 1663 (the two musical phrases indicate his membership of the Catch Club): engraving by Richard Gaywood

reflects a new fashion for this 'brisk and airy' instrument that lasted for the next 30 years, but the lessons for the cittern and the virginals, which did not last much beyond the mid-17th century, are evidence of declining sympathy with Playford's nostalgia for these instruments.

The same is true of the hymns and psalm paraphrases (as distinct from the psalter), which were an ordained part of Anglican worship, and of the songs and instrumental pieces addressed to the proficient performer. As examples of the creative genius of Henry Purcell, Matthew Locke, William and Henry Lawes, Christopher Simpson and Richard Dering, they afford interest to the scholar, but are without those qualities which enabled the vocal music of the Tudor period eventually to outlast them. These had been the copyright of Thomas East, and his rivals failed to find a transferee after the death of William Stansby, who had acquired them in 1625. It is possible, even probable, that they were part of the stock of East's printing house in Little Britain bought by Thomas Harper in 1634, later the workshop of (3) John Playford. In 1653 (1) John Playford offered them as part of his bookseller's stock in his *Catalogue of All the Musick Bookes printed in England*; they reappeared in the advertisements appended to many of his books. In 1690 when the stock of his shop by the Temple Church was to be sold by auction, they were again catalogued for the benefit of 'those remote from London' and offered to buyers for a few pence. The dedications and prefaces to these and his other publications reflect Playford's commercial acumen, his xenophobia, and his devotion to the restoration of the monarchy and to the divine service decently ordered.

2. PUBLICATIONS.

Playford's publications, apart from the political tracts and miscellaneous non-musical works, fall into three categories: theory of music and lesson books for various instruments, which usually contain brief instructions followed by 'lessons' or short pieces derived from popular airs; collections of songs and instrumental pieces; and psalms, psalm paraphrases and hymns, including *The Whole Book of Psalmes* for the Stationers' Company. He began to publish music in 1651; the list shows how rapidly new books succeeded one another in the early years, becoming more sparse later. Examination of the contents, however, shows that often a 'new edition' differs little from its predecessor although new 'lessons' may have been added and some others subtracted, and the later songbooks may be selections or rearrangements of earlier titles under new names. It is generally assumed that *The English Dancing Master or Plaine and easie Rules for the Dancing of Country Dances with the Tune to each Dance* addressed to the 'Gentlemen of the Innes of Court' came first, but *A Musicall Banquet* bears, as well as Playford's imprint, that of John Benson, his former master. *The English Dancing Master*, with many enlarged editions until 1728, is probably Playford's best-known work, because of the modern revival of the country dance and as the largest single source of ballad airs. *A Musicall Banquet* contains the genesis of later books: *Musick's Recreation* (1652), *Catch that Catch Can* (1652; for illustration *see* CATCH), *Court Ayres* (1655) and *A Breefe Introduction to the Skill of Musick* (1654). All but the first continued in new and enlarged editions. *Apollo's Banquet for the Treble Violin* (1669)

PUBLICATIONS
(selective list)

(all published in London; Playford's printers and partners not cited)
A Musicall Banquet in 3 Choice Varieties: The First . . . New Lessons for the Lira Viol: the Second, Musica Harmonia, New Allmans . . . for Tr and B Viol, by W. Lawes and other Authors: the Third . . . New Catches and Rounds: to which is added Rules . . . for such as learne to Sing or to Play on the Viol (1651⁶) [each part was later expanded into a book]; The (English) Dancing Master (1651/*R*1957; numerous rev. edns. to 1728); A Booke of New Lessons for Cithern and Gittern (?2/1652; enlarged 3/1666); Musick's Recreation on the Lyra Viol (1652⁷, 4/1682⁹); Select (Musicall) Ayres and Dialogues (1652⁸; enlarged 2/1653⁷; selections 3/1659⁵); J. Hilton, ed.: Catch that Catch Can (1652¹⁰; enlarged 7/1686⁴; other edns. to *c*1720) [entitled The (Pleasant) Musical Companion in some later edns.]
A Catalogue of All the Musick Bookes . . . Printed in England (1653); H. Lawes: Ayres and Dialogues . . . the First Booke (1653); J. Playford: A (Breefe) Introduction to the Skill of Musick (1654; other edns. to 1730 incl. to 1680 [having as pt ii T. Campion's Art of Composing with adds C. Simpson]; 1657 [omitting Campion, but incl. Directions for Playing the Viol de Gambo and Tr Vn]; 1660 [having as bk 3 Campion's Art of Descant with adds C. Simpson]; 1674 [incl. Order for Performing Divine Service in Cathedrals]); H. Lawes: The Second Book of Ayres and Dialogues (1655); Court Ayres . . . of 2 Parts, Tr, B, for viols/vns (1655⁵; rev. 2/1662⁸ as Courtly Masquing Ayres) [enlarged from Musica Harmonia in A Musicall Banquet]
W. Child: Choise Musick to the Psalmes of David (1656) [variant repr. of First Set of Psalms, 1639, advertised in A Musicall Banquet, but no earlier exemplar known]; M. Locke: His Little Consort (1656); H. Lawes: Ayres and Dialogues . . . the Third Book (1658); M. Locke and C. Gibbons: Cupid and Death . . . reprinted with Scenes and Music (1659) [originally pubd without music, 1653]; J. Playford, ed.: The Whole Book of Psalmes collected into English Meeter (1661) [for the many later edns. see Temperley (1972)]; R. Dering: Cantica sacra, 2, 3vv, bc (org) (1662) [ded. by Playford to Queen Henrietta Maria]; Musick's Hand-maide presenting New and Pleasant Lessons for Virginals or Harpsycon (1663⁷)
Musick's Delight on the Cithren, Restored and Refined (1666⁴); The Treasury of Musick (1669⁵) [incl. the 1659 selection of Ayres and Dialogues, bks 2, 1655, and 3, 1658, of Lawes's Ayres and

Dialogues]; Apollo's Banquet for the Tr Vn (1669; other edns. to 1701); J. Playford: Psalms and Hymns in Solemn Music, 4vv, on the Common Tunes . . .; also 6 Hymns, 1v, org (1671) [ded. to the Dean of St Paul's]; T. Greeting: The Pleasant Companion . . . for the Flageolet (1672, 4/1682); London Triumphant (1672) [Lord Mayor's Show]; Choice Songs and Ayres, 1v, theorbo/b viol: being Most of the Newest Songs sung at Court and at the Publick Theatres (1673³; enlarged 3/1676); M. Locke: The Present Practice of Musick Defended and Vindicated against the Exceptions . . . lately published by Thomas Salmon . . . together with a Letter from John Playford (1673)

T. Jordon: The Goldsmith's Jubilee or London's Triumphs (1674) [Lord Mayor's Show]; Cantica Sacra containing Hymns and Anthems, 2vv, org, both Latine and English . . . the Second Sett (1674²) [ded. to the king]; The Triumphs of London (1675) [Lord Mayor's Show]; G. Sandys and H. Lawes, rev. J. Playford: A Paraphrase upon the Psalms (1676) [originally pubd in 1638]; The Whole Book of Psalmes (1677; 20 edns. to 1757) [not identical with the 1661 publication]; Musick's Hand-Maid: New Lessons and Instructions for the Virginals (1678⁶); Short Rules and Directions for the Tr Vn (1679) [lost]; Choice Ayres and Songs . . . the Second [–Fifth] Book (1679⁷, 1681⁴, 1683⁵, 1684³); T. Jordon: London's Glory (1680) [Lord Mayor's Show]; H. Purcell: Sonnata's of III Parts (1681); G. Dieseneer: Instrumental Ayres in 3 and 4 Parts . . . in 3 Books (1682); The Triumphs of London (1683) [Lord Mayor's Show]

(2) Henry Playford (*b* ?Islington, *c*1657; *d c*1707). Music publisher. He was the younger son and only known survivor of the several children of (1) John Playford (i) and godson of Henry Lawes. He was called to the livery of the Stationers' Company in February 1680/81 and in 1684 attended the court of assistants representing his father with whom he was in business. For a short time he joined with Richard Carr 'near Middle Temple Gate', then continued independently in Fleet Street, in Arundel Street where his father had lived and at the old shop by the Temple Church. He may have

retired or died in 1707 when his publications were taken over by JOHN CULLEN of The Buck, Fleet Street, and John Young of St Paul's Churchyard.

Henry Playford did not do so much as his father to revive the practice of music in church and home, nor did he express himself, his ideals and ambitions, as his father had done in dedications and introductions. Much of what he published was ephemeral and much continued what his father had begun, updated and amended to meet changing and more informed taste. He supported the introduction to music printing of the 'new tied-note or London character' (see *Twelve Songs by John Blow and Others*, 1699, and later publications), and thoroughly revised *The Dancing Master* to provide the 'longways' type of country dance more suited to the assembly room than the figure-dances of earlier editions. In all he showed a lively perception of the requirements of public entertainments and the pleasure garden concerts which created a market for 'favourite songs' and instrumental pieces. But where his father had dominated the field of music publishing, he faced strong competition in a developing trade that was breaking away from the book publishing trade of which it had formerly been a part. His most memorable and lasting publications are probably Tom D'Urfey's songs to popular tunes in *Wit and Mirth* and Henry Purcell's *Orpheus Britannicus*.

PUBLICATIONS
(selective list)
(all published in London; Playford's printers and partners not cited)
Works first pubd by (1) John Playford (i): The Dancing Master (8/1690, 12/1703; other edns. to 1728); The Second Book of the

The English Dancing Mafter :

O R,

Plaine and eafie Rules for the Dancing of Country Dances, with the Tune to each Dance.

LONDON,

Printed by *Thomas Harper*, and are to be fold by *John Playford*, at his Shop in the Inner Temple neere the Church doore. 1651.

3. Title-page of 'The English Dancing Master', printed by Thomas Harper and published by John Playford in 1651

Pleasant Musical Companion (2/1694, 5/1707/*R*1709); An Introduction to the Skill of Musick (11/1687; 15/1703; other edns. to 1730); Apollo's Banquet (5/1687[5], 6/1690[4]; bk 2, 1691[5]; other edns. to 1701); The Second Part of Musick's Hand-maid (1689[7]); T. Greeting: The Pleasant Companion . . . for the Flageolet (5/1683); The Whole Book of Psalms (numerous edns. to 1757)

Works pubd by Henry Playford: The Theater of Music (1685[5], 1685[6], 1686[3], 1687[5]); Harmonia Sacra or Divine Hymns and Dialogues (1688[1], 1693[1]); The Banquet of Music (1688[6], 1688[7], 1689[5], 1690[5], 1691[6], 1692[8]); Thesaurus musicus . . . the Second Book (1694[7]) [the 1st pubd 1693 by J. Hudgebut]; Deliciae musicae (1695[7], 1695[8], 1696[5], 1696[6], 1696[7]); The A'Lamode Musician . . . ingraved from the Originalls (1698[2]) [the 'Originalls' were pbd separately, early examples of sheet music]; Wit and Mirth (1699[6], 1700[4]); Mercurius musicus (1699[4]–1702); Tunes to the Psalms (1700); The Divine Companion (1701); H. Purcell: Orpheus Britannicus . . . the Second Book (1702); The Diverting Post (1706) [house journal]

(3) John Playford (ii) (*b* Stanmore Magna, *c*1655; *d* ?20 April 1685). Music printer. He has been confused with other members of the family also named John, and with one, believed to be a bookseller, who spelt his name Playfere, but there is now no doubt that he was the son of the Rev. Matthew Playford (brother or half-brother of (1) John Playford (i)), vicar of Stanmore Magna, who forfeited both livelihood and property because of his royalist sympathies.

At some time, probably in the 1670s, WILLIAM GODBID, a printer of scientific books and music, took young John Playford as apprentice; at Godbid's death in 1679, his widow, Anne, took John into the partnership and advertised in *The Art of Descant* (refashioned from Campion's *Art of Composing* published by 'Snodham alias Este') that 'the only Printing-house in England for Variety of Musick and Workmen that understand it, is still kept in Little Britain by A. Godbid and J. Playford Junior'. An examination of the publications suggests that much of the type and many of the ornaments and other features, including the device 'Laetificat cor musica', originally belonged to THOMAS EAST and was used successively by Harper and Godbid.

In 1682 Playford seems to have acquired the ownership of the business and in the same year his name appears in the livery list of the Stationers' Company; in 1683 he attended the company's court of assistants. He died between 20 April 1685, when he signed his will, and 29 April when the will was proved, bequeathing the business to his sister Eleanor.

A year later the *London Gazette* of 3–6 May 1686 advertised 'An Ancient Printing-house in Little Britain, late in possession of Mr John Playford deceased, well-known and ready fitted . . . with good Presses and all manner of Letter for . . . Musick, Mathematicks, Navigation and all Greek and Latin Books . . . to be Sold . . . or Lett by Lease'. From subsequent events it seems that the royal printers bought some of the material; but early in 1687 Eleanor requested permission from the king to continue to print music, 'having nothing else to subsist by, yo'r Petitioner prayes that she may continue her Printing-house . . . and may have the honour to be your Majesty's servant for printing the said Musick [and] Mathematick . . . there being no other . . . that can doe the same'. She sought to further her case by referring to her father Matthew Playford, who 'suffered sequestration and was ruined', and to the continuous business carried on 'above forty years' in the same place; but James II, unlike Charles, was not well disposed to the Playford family. The royal printers were happy to assert that there were 'more Master-printers set up than there is work to be had', and to emphasize their own willingness to serve His Majesty 'in all mat-

ters of musick etc'. The petition was dismissed; the royal printers, who had 'already bought much of the Petitioner's materials', were ready to buy the rest and with that the continuity of an established business ended.

BIBLIOGRAPHY

E. Arber and G. E. B. Eyre: *Archives of the Worshipful Company of Stationers . . . Transcript of the Registers 1554–1708* (London, 1875–1914)

F. A. Inderwick: *Calendar of the Inner Temple 1505–1714* (London, 1895)

? F. Kidson: 'The Petition of Mrs Eleanor Playford', *The Library*, 3rd ser., vii (1916), 346

F. Kidson: 'John Playford and 17th Century Music Publishing', *MQ*, iv (1918), 516

C. L. Day and E. B. Murrie: 'English Song-books and their Publishers 1651–1702', *The Library*, 4th ser., xvi (1936), 355

W. C. Smith: 'Some Hitherto Un-noticed Catalogues of Early Music', *MT*, lxxvii (1936), 636, 701

C. L. Day and E. B. Murrie: *English Song-books 1651–1702* (London, 1940)

M. J. Dean-Smith: *Playford's English Dancing Master 1651* (London, 1957) [annotated facs. edn.]

M. Tilmouth: 'Some Early London Concerts and Music Clubs 1670–1720', *PRMA*, lxxxiv (1957–8), 13

C. Blagden: 'The Stationers' Company in the Civil War Period', *The Library*, 5th ser., xiv (1959), 1

——: *The Stationers' Company* (London, 1960)

M. Tilmouth: 'A Calendar of References to Music in Newspapers . . . 1660–1719', *RMARC*, i (1961), 1–107

L. Coral: 'A John Playford Advertisement', *RMARC*, v (1965), 1

N. Temperley: 'John Playford and the Metrical Psalms', *JAMS*, xxv (1972), 331–78

——: 'John Playford and the Stationers' Company', *ML*, liv (1973), 203

MARGARET DEAN-SMITH

Plaza(-Alfonzo), Juan Bautista (*b* Caracas, 19 July 1898; *d* Caracas, 1 Jan 1965). Venezuelan composer and musicologist. He began music studies at the age of 15 with Jesús María Suárez; within a year he was asked to lead the choir and to teach music to his fellow pupils in the Caracas French School. Thereafter he studied law and medicine at the university while continuing to act as choirmaster at the French School, where he produced his first large work, the zarzuela *Zapatero a tus zapatos*. In 1920 a scholarship took him to the Scuola Superiore di Musica Sacra in Rome; there he was taught by Casimiri, Manari, Ferretti and Dagnino, taking the degree of Master of Sacred Composition (1923). Returning to Caracas in that year, he was appointed choirmaster of the cathedral (1923–47) and professor of harmony at the Escuela Nacional de Música (1924–8), where he later instituted and taught courses in music history (1931–62) and aesthetics (1948–62). From 1936 to 1944 he undertook the study and cataloguing of a large quantity of colonial music that had been discovered in 1935; this work led to the publication of the 12-volume collection *Archivo de Música Colonial Venezolana* (Montevideo, 1943). While serving as director of culture in the Ministry of Education (1944–6) he established the Escuela Preparatoria de Música, which, under his direction (1948–62), became one of the most vital music schools in the country. Throughout these years he also appeared as an organist and as conductor of the Venezuela SO. After retiring in 1962 he gave his attention to further researches in the colonial music archive and to the cataloguing of his own work.

The most productive period of Plaza's life coincided with his tenure as cathedral choirmaster. After 1947 he wrote less, and the later works show an increasing abandonment of traditional tonality and a tendency towards introspection. Most of his compositions are vocal pieces, written for the church or for the choruses at the schools in which he taught; notable within this group are the Requiem (1933) and *Las horas* (1930). The principal influences on his early music were those of Puccini and Perosi; later pieces show his interests in impressionism and in Stravinsky's music. But his music was always individual and deeply rooted in the romantic Venezuelan folksong tradition.

WORKS
(selective list; most unpublished)

CHORAL

Masses: Misa breve, e, TB, orch, org, 1924; Misa en honor de S Inés, unison vv, org, 1925; Requiem, unison vv, org, 1926; Misa en honor de Santiago Apóstol, STB, orch, 1926, arr. TTB, org, 1944; Requiem, TTBB, orch, 1933; Mass, TTB, 1936; Misa 'Popule meus', TTB, orch, 1937; Misa en honor de S Juan de la Cruz, 2vv, org, 1947; Misa litúrgica de la esperanza, TB, org, 1962

Other sacred: many motets, psalms, offertories, etc

Secular: Las horas (F. Paz Castillo), SATB, orch, 1930; many unacc. pieces

OTHER WORKS

Orch: Elegía, eng hn, str, 1923; El picacho abrupto, sym. poem, 1926; Vigilia, sym. poem, 1928; Campanas de pascua, sym. poem, 1930; Fuga criolla, str, 1931; Fuga romántica venezolana, str, 1950; Elegía, str, timp, 1953; Marcha nupcial, 1959

Songs for 1v, pf: 7 canciones venezolanas (L. Barrios Cruz), S, pf, 1932; many others

Chamber pieces, many pf compositions, works for org and gui, educational music, arrs. of Venezuelan national anthem

Principal publishers: Associated, Institución José Angel Lamas

WRITINGS

'Music in Caracas during the Colonial Period (1770–1811)', *MQ*, xxix (1943), 198

'Música colonial venezolana', *Letras venezolanas* (Caracas, 1958), no.11

Other essays in *Revista nacional de cultura*

BIBLIOGRAPHY

Compositores de Américas/Composers of the Americas, ed. Pan American Union, ix (Washington, DC, 1963), 105

E. Plaza-Alfonzo: 'Apuntes sobre la persona, la vida y la obra de Juan Bautista Plaza', *Cultura universitaria*, lxxxix (1965), Oct–Dec, 46

ALEJANDRO ENRIQUE PLANCHART

Plaza (y Manrique), Ramón de la (*b* Caracas, *c*1835; *d* Caracas, 15 Dec 1886). Venezuelan music historian. After his marriage to the wealthy Mercedes Ponce Valdés he became a deputy to the Venezuelan Congress in 1870. In recognition of his services as head of a legislative commission concerned with religious matters he was made a general. By presidential decree he became first director of the newly created Instituto Nacional de Bellas Artes on 3 April 1877. He was an amateur cellist and composer whose sensitivity, practical musicianship, wide reading, extensive European travels and informed patriotism made him the ideal interpreter of his nation's artistic past. His luxuriously printed *Ensayos sobre el arte en Venezuela* (Caracas, 1883/*R*1977), published to commemorate Bolívar's birth, was the first Latin American music history and is still one of the best; it has been drawn upon extensively in later writings on the subject, particularly those of L. Cortijo Alahija. It combines extensive analysis of aboriginal music with a precise and extremely valuable history of European music in Venezuela from the founding of Caracas to Plaza's time; it includes a 56-page musical appendix. He also published *El drama lírico y la lengua castellana como elemento musical* (Caracas, 1884), a study of Spanish as a vehicle for opera.

BIBLIOGRAPHY

M. L. Sánchez: *La enseñanza musical en Caracas* (Caracas, 1949), 34

A. R. Villasana: *Ensayo de un repertorio bibliográfico venezolano (años 1808–1950)* (Caracas, 1976), v, 583f

J. A. Calcaño: 'Nuestro primer libro sobre arte', introduction to facs. of *Ensayos sobre el arte en Venezuela* (Caracas, 1977), p.xiiiff

ROBERT STEVENSON

Pleasants, Henry (*b* Wayne, Penn., 12 May 1910). American author and critic. He trained as a singer and pianist at the Philadelphia Musical Academy and Curtis Institute of Music, with subsequent private studies in singing, piano and composition. In 1930 he became music critic for the *Philadelphia Evening Bulletin*, and music editor from 1934. After army service (1942–50), mostly in North Africa and Europe, he joined the US Foreign Service and was based successively in Munich, Berne and Bonn. During this time (1945–55) he was also central European music correspondent for the *New York Times*. Since 1967, when he settled in London, he has been London music critic for the *International Herald-Tribune* and London music editor of *Stereo Review*, as well as a frequent contributor to the musical press in Britain and the USA. He is married to the harpsichordist Virginia Pleasants.

His writings extend and elaborate a critical principle which accords serious attention to the popular musical vernacular of the 20th century (jazz, theatre music, rock and pop), in the belief that these styles have gained a dominant position in world music not only as commercial entertainment, but also as art. His study of great singers is related to this in suggesting that the art of singing reached its zenith in the Baroque period; since then it has been in conflict with the demands of emotional expression and compositional techniques and cannot survive if lyrical grace is not the chief element of its style.

WRITINGS

ed. and trans.: *E. Hanslick: Vienna's Golden Years of Music, 1850–1900* (New York, 1950)

The Agony of Modern Music (London, 1955)

Death of a Music?: the Decline of the European Tradition and the Rise of Jazz (London, 1961)

ed. and trans.: *The Musical Journeys of Louis Spohr* (New York, 1961)

ed. and trans.: *The Musical World of Robert Schumann* (New York, 1965)

The Great Singers (New York, 1966)

'Great Popular Singers', *Music and Musicians*, xvii/4 (1968), 40

Serious Music – and all that Jazz! (London, 1969)

ed. and trans.: *The Music Criticism of Hugo Wolf* (New York, 1978)

NOËL GOODWIN

Plectrum (Fr. *médiator*, *plectre*; Ger. *Dorn*, *Kiel*, *Plektrum*, *Schlagfeder*; It. *plettro*). A general term for a piece of material with which the strings of an instrument are plucked. Tinctoris called the plectrum of antiquity 'pecten' and that of the Middle Ages 'penna' (quill). Ancient Greek sources used the terms 'plectron' and 'pecten'. Lute-type instruments – such as the guitar, the *biwa* of Japan, or the Western lute itself before about 1450 – have often been played with a plectrum, in some instances a rather large one (*see* JAPAN, fig.17), in others a more delicate type (*see* LUTE, fig.7).

Medieval Arabic writings describe plectra made from eagles' talons as well as ones of wood, ivory, bone, tortoise-shell and quill. The initial sound of a string set into vibration by a plectrum is naturally more akin to that of a string plucked by a fingernail than by the flesh of the finger. A plectrum facilitates tremolando effects (as on the mandolin) and vigorous strumming, but does not favour the kind of polyphonic texture that was cultivated on the high-Renaissance lute and vihuela. Psaltery-type instruments, such as the zither and the Middle Eastern *qānūn*, are likely to be played with a plectrum (*see* QĀNŪN, fig.1), but harps virtually never are, as the player often has a relatively unclear view of the strings and so tends to rely on the sense of touch to help distinguish them. The term also refers to the small tongue which plucks the string of a harpsichord (it may be of leather or plastic instead of quill).

BIBLIOGRAPHY
J. Tinctoris: *De inventione et usu musicae* (Naples, c1487)
W. Bachmann: *Die Anfänge des Streichinstrumentenspiels* (Leipzig, 1964, 2/1966; Eng. trans., 1969)

Pleeth, William (*b* London, 12 Jan 1916). English cellist. He studied with Julius Klengel at the Leipzig Conservatory, making his début in Leipzig in 1932 and at the Grotrian Hall, London, in 1933. As a soloist (several composers have dedicated works to him), as a sonata player with his wife, Margaret Good, and as a chamber music player (Blech Quartet, 1936–41, and Allegri Quartet, 1952–67), he is distinguished by an exuberant, extrovert style, combined with a passionate conviction which is embodied in the full and colourful tone he produces from his 1732 Stradivari. He became professor of cello and chamber music at the Guildhall School of Music in 1948. Among his pupils were his son Anthony (*b* London, 11 May 1948), a leading Baroque cellist, and Jacqueline Du Pré.

WATSON FORBES

Plein jeu (Fr.: 'full registration'). Possibly a corruption of *plain jeu*, 'integrated registration'. While modern composers often use the phrase loosely to denote 'full organ' at the player's discretion, *plein jeu* has two particular meanings in the history of the organ. The phrase itself seems to have arisen some time in the 16th century to describe the combination of stops that gave the same Principal chorus as the old undivided, stop-less BLOCKWERK, i.e. Principals 16', 8', 4' (etc), Fourniture and Cymbale, perhaps with Bourdons. At Notre Dame, Alençon (1537–40), the term *principal du corps* is still used, corresponding to the Dutch, German and probably English term 'principal', i.e. not a single rank but the Diapason chorus as a whole. At Chartres in 1542, the contract refers to the *plain jeu* as an even bigger Diapason chorus, complete with the eight 32' pedal pipes and the doubled and tripled ranks at 8' and 4' pitch. For Mersenne (1636), *plain jeu* included a Tierce but not the highest Cymbale mixture. The second purpose of the term was to denote one of two distinct choruses in the great corpus of Classical French organ music from 1670 to 1770, namely the Diapason chorus or *plein jeu* as distinct from the Flute, Cornet, mutation and reed combination of *grand jeu*. Like the other regular and systematic registrations of the Classical French organ, the *plein jeu* became associated with (a) particular interludes in the Mass (*plein jeu* for the opening Kyrie, *grand jeu* for the closing, etc), and (b) a particular musical style, usually sustained, with constant and slowly resolving suspensions, in four or five parts, massive in texture rather than strictly contrapuntal.

PETER WILLIAMS

Plena. A song genre of Puerto Rico, believed to have originated in the early 20th century, with a binary form consisting of solo or duet melodies followed by choral refrains. Narrative texts, often humorous and picaresque, are sung in the high and strident nasal singing style typical of Puerto Rico, frequently in parallel 3rds. The *plena* is characterized by extensive syncopation,

1. Ignace Joseph Pleyel: stipple engraving (1793) by W. Nutter after T. Hardy

and the use of triplet figures in vocal lines creates rhythmic contrast with the duple metre accompaniment of guitars, *panderetas* (tambourines) and *congo* drums.

WILLIAM GRADANTE

Plenary mass. A unified musical setting of both the Ordinary and the Proper of the Roman Catholic Mass. Examples are rare, except as settings of the REQUIEM MASS.

Plessis. *See* DUPLESSIS family.

Plessis, Hubert du. *See* DU PLESSIS, HUBERT.

Pleyel (i). Austro-French family of composers, musicians, publishers and piano makers, active in France. (For the firm of piano makers, *see* PLEYEL (ii).)

(1) Ignace Joseph [Ignaz Josef] **Pleyel** (*b* Ruppersthal, Austria, 18 June 1757; *d* Paris, 14 Nov 1831). Austrian composer, music publisher and piano maker, active in France. He founded a major publishing house and a piano factory and his compositions achieved widespread popularity in Europe and North America.

1. LIFE. Pleyel's baptismal certificate in the parish office names his father Martin, a schoolteacher, and his mother Anna Theresia (Maria Christina Theresa in *MGG*). He is said to have studied with Vanhal while very young, and in about 1772 he became Haydn's pupil and lodger in Eisenstadt, his annual pension being paid by Count Ladislaus Erdődy, whose family at Pressburg was related to Haydn's patrons, the Esterházys. The count showed his pleasure at the progress of his protégé by offering Haydn a carriage and two horses, for which Prince Esterházy agreed to provide a coachman and fodder.

Little is known of the daily activities of Haydn's

several pupils. A few incidents concerning Pleyel's apprenticeship are recounted in Framery's *Notice sur Joseph Haydn*, in which the author claimed that 'these various anecdotes were furnished me by a person who spent his entire youth with him and who guarantees their authenticity'. That person is generally identified as Pleyel, living in Paris when the *Notice* appeared there in 1810. The assumption is strengthened by the manner in which the narrative favours Pleyel, always emphasizing the closeness of his relationship with Haydn and the master's affection and esteem for him.

During this period Pleyel's puppet opera *Die Fee Urgele* was first performed at Eszterháza (November 1776), and at the Vienna Nationaltheater. Haydn's puppet opera *Das abgebrannte Haus*, or *Die Feuersbrunst*, was also first performed in 1776 or 1777, with an overture (or at least its first two movements) now generally accepted as being by Pleyel.

Pleyel's first position seems to have been as Kapellmeister to Count Erdődy, but again that period of his career is undocumented. He and the count were members of the masonic Lodge 'Zum goldenen Hirschen', founded by the count's brother Ludwig, and located from 1778 in the town of Fidisch, near Eberau in Burgenland. The musical importance of the count's chapel is affirmed in the notice published after his death on 13 July 1786: a variety of instruments as well as several hundred symphonies, concertos, quintets, operas, masses and other works were to be sold two years later in Vienna for the benefit of the poor (*Wiener Zeitung*, 9 Aug 1788). Pleyel's String Quartets op.1 (1782–3, Ben 301–6) are dedicated to Count Erdődy for his 'generosity, paternal solicitude and encouragement'.

During the early 1780s Pleyel travelled in Italy. Through Norbert Hadrava, an ardent music lover and part-time composer attached to the Austrian embassy in Naples, Pleyel was asked to compose lyra (hurdy-gurdy) pieces for performance by Ferdinand IV, the 'Lazzarone' King of Naples; Hadrava had instructed the king in an elaborate version of the instrument, and also procured commissions for Haydn and Sterkel. Two of Pleyel's works for the hurdy-gurdy survive in autographs (Ben 202 and 202.5). In 1784 Hadrava engineered the commissioning of an opera: Pleyel's *Ifigenia in Aulide* had its première at the S Carlo theatre on the king's name day, 30 May 1785, and there were 18 further performances that summer.

Meanwhile (probably in 1784) Pleyel had become assistant to F. X. Richter, Kapellmeister of Strasbourg Cathedral, and he succeeded to the post when Richter died in 1789. From 1786 he also conducted and organized a series of public concerts in collaboration with J. P. Schönfeld, Kapellmeister of the Strasbourg Temple Neuf. On 22 January 1788 he married (Franziska) Gabrielle (Ignatia) Lefebvre, daughter of the *tapissier* Stephen Laurence Lefebvre, with whom Pleyel was later involved in a variety of business investments. Four children survived the union, the eldest of whom was (2) Camille Pleyel. The Strasbourg period was Pleyel's most productive musically; most of his compositions date from the years 1787–95. His pupils of that time included Ferdinand Fränzl, who dedicated his op.1 to Pleyel, and P.-J. Pfeffinger.

The Revolution having abolished the cathedral's religious functions and the city's secular concerts, Pleyel accepted an invitation to conduct the

Professional Concerts in London, and stayed there from December 1791 until May 1792 (thus, contrary to some sources, he cannot have composed the *Marseillaise*, which had been written in Strasbourg by Rouget de Lisle in April). There is no evidence for the assertion that Pleyel let himself be used by the entrepreneur Wilhelm Cramer of the Professional Concerts to draw listeners away from Haydn's concurrent series with the impresario Salomon, nor even that he was aware of Haydn's plans when he accepted the invitation. The composers remained unaffected by the rival publicity, expressing mutual affection, dining together, performing each other's music and attending each other's concerts. Haydn generally received more critical and popular acclaim, but Pleyel's concerts were also well attended; and his compositions, especially the *symphonies concertantes* and quartets, were highly praised in the press.

During Pleyel's London stay, George Thomson of Edinburgh asked him to compose the introduction and accompaniments for a series of Scottish airs and to write a set of piano trios. Thomson's remarks in a letter to Kozeluch about having been 'juggled, disappointed and grossly deceived by an eminent musical composer with whom I entered into an agreement some years ago' and his decision to use Kozeluch's settings for the second volume of Scottish songs have been construed to mean that Pleyel had in some way behaved dishonourably. But Thomson evidently retained no animosity, for during a trip to Paris in 1819 he paid a friendly visit to Pleyel's shop and in a letter home praised his publications extravagantly.

2. *Title-page, engraved by Aubert, of Pleyel's 'Collection complette des quatuors d'Haydn, dédiée au Premier Consul Bonaparte' (1801)*

After returning to the Continent, Pleyel bought the large Château d'Itenwiller at St Pierre, near Strasbourg, probably with the considerable earnings of his London concerts (the last, on May 14, had been the usual 'benefit'). According to a dramatic story (which remains undocumented despite searches in Strasbourg archives, and varies in each telling) Pleyel was repeatedly arrested during 1793 by Revolutionary authorities who suspected him of pro-Austrian or aristocratic sympathies; he was released only after writing (while under guard) the rather banal patriotic hymn *La révolution du 10 août 1792, ou Le tocsin allégorique* (Ben 706). This includes references to the popular *Ça ira* and to several works by Grétry, and requires a large ensemble of voices and instruments, including church bells and cannons. The première in Strasbourg Cathedral (on 10 August 1793) used bells chosen by Pleyel from those requisitioned from churches of the region no longer holding services. The last of subsequent performances occurred in 1799 at the inauguration of the concert hall of the city's Réunion des Arts.

Early in 1795 Pleyel settled in Paris, opened a music shop and founded a publishing house, which issued some 4000 works during the 39 years it existed, including many by Boccherini, Beethoven, Clementi, Cramer, J. L. Dussek, Haydn and other friends of Pleyel and his son. Some of them (e.g. Dizi, Kalkbrenner, Méhul, Rossini) were involved in the firm by financial investment. Pleyel established agents for the sale of his publications all over France, and maintained an active exchange of letters and music with some of the foremost European music publishers (e.g. Artaria of Vienna, Böhme of Hamburg, Breitkopf of Leipzig, Hoffmeister of Vienna, Hummel of Amsterdam and Simrock of Bonn), sometimes arranging for reciprocal engraving of their issues.

The most important achievement of the Maison Pleyel was probably its issue of the first miniature scores, a series entitled Bibliothèque Musicale. It began in 1802 with four of Haydn's symphonies, and continued with ten volumes of his string quartets, followed by chamber works by Beethoven, Hummel and Onslow (the last in 1830). In 1801 Pleyel also issued a *Collection complette des quatuors d'Haydn, dédiée au Premier Consul Bonaparte*, the title-page beautifully engraved by Aubert (see fig.2), the separate parts engraved by Richomme and probably edited by the violinist Baillot. The prefatory material includes a handsome portrait of Haydn by J. Guérin and a thematic catalogue 'of all Haydn's quartets, sanctioned by the author and arranged in the order in which they appeared'. This statement and Haydn's earlier relationship with Pleyel have involved the edition in the debate concerning the authenticity and order of certain quartets generally attributed to Haydn. The edition also includes two pages of subscribers' names, many of them notable musicians (e.g. Cherubini, Dussek, Grétry, Kreutzer, Méhul, Salomon, Viotti) or aristocracy centred on Vienna (e.g. Erdődy, Esterházy, Golitsïn, Harrach, Lobkowitz, Razumovsky, Swieten, and Thurn and Taxis). The first edition contained 80 quartets, subsequent editions adding two, then one, as Haydn composed them.

In 1805 Pleyel travelled with his son (2) Camille to Vienna, where his string quartets were warmly received. They also paid several visits to the aging Haydn; they heard Beethoven play the piano and were greatly impressed by his brilliant improvisational technique. But one of the primary reasons for the visit, the establishment of a branch publishing office, failed despite the support of local friends. The firm had been plagued since its inception by a series of legal contests that were not exceptional but sapped Pleyel's energy and financial resources. In 1813 he made a determined effort to sell the publishing enterprise, describing his stock in a letter to a prospective buyer as 48,000 plates of pewter (*fin étain*) or copper, printed music he had published or for which he was agent, instruments (violins, violas, double basses, trumpets, trombones, bows, strings etc), manuscripts not yet engraved and unused paper. 'In the last two years I have published more than 200 new works, of which 29% to 30% have not yet been put on sale . . . Most of my editions have been engraved by Richault, Lobry, Petit and Marquerie, the best engravers in Paris.'

During the 1820s Ignace Pleyel indulged his love of rural life by spending increasing amounts of time on a large farm about 50 km from Paris. During the same period the firm's output became more predominantly popular, as symphonies, sonatas and quartets were replaced by *romances*, *chansonnettes* and similar genres by Bayle, Bizot, Georgeon, Panseron and (especially) Pauline Duchambge, whose songs were always issued with alternative piano and guitar accompaniments. The firm also issued many fantasias, variations, rondos and potpourris of operatic *airs* by Adolphe Adam, Carulli, Duvernoy, Mayseder, Pixis and others. In 1834 the Maison Pleyel ceased its publishing activities entirely, selling its stock of plates and printed works to various Paris publishers including Lemoine, Prilipp, Delloy, Richault and Schlesinger.

2. WORKS. The enormous popularity of Pleyel's music during his lifetime is reflected in the testimony of contemporary journals and of early writers like Gerber and Fétis. The small town of Nantucket (Mass.), then still a whaling port, formed a Pleyel Society in 1822 'to chasten the taste of auditors', according to a newspaper announcement. The most telling evidence of the appeal of his music lies in the thousands of manuscript copies that filled the shelves of archives, libraries, churches, castles and private homes and in the thousands of editions produced in Europe and North America. In quality the works vary greatly, although most show considerable facility and a thorough technical grounding. The earlier works in particular display thematic originality and ingenious developments that make them fresh and attractive. After about 1792 his talent seems to have diminished; his inventiveness waned and he occasionally succumbed to routine procedures.

An insufficiently recognized aspect of Pleyel's production is the extent to which whole works, movements or parts of movements were re-used. Some of the borrowing was obviously by the composer, but much was perpetrated by publishers, probably without his knowledge or consent. Most of the songs with keyboard accompaniment, for example, which were highly popular around the turn of the 19th century especially in English-speaking countries, are settings of movements from symphonies or quartets (e.g. *Henry's Cottage Maid*, from Ben 137; *Time a Favorite Sonnet*, from Ben 327A; *Fanny's Worth*, from Ben 350; and the ubiquitous *German Hymn*, from Ben 349). Never-

3. Title-page of Pleyel's 'Six Grand Lessons for the Harpsichord or Piano-forte' (London: Preston, between 1787 and 1810)

theless many of the songs have considerable charm. Certain categories of the instrumental works consist entirely of arrangements: the quartets for keyboard and strings, the four-hand keyboard works and all ensembles that include guitar or harp. Working in an age when music was considered a commodity to be put to the widest possible use, Pleyel did not hesitate to issue a concerto with alternative solo parts for flute, clarinet or cello (Ben 106), or to transform a set of piano trios (Ben 465–70) into flute quartets (Ben 387–92) or string trios (Ben 410–15) by 'scrambling' the original 18 movements into an almost entirely new juxtaposition of movements in transposed keys. Such procedures reflect Pleyel's total acceptance of the tastes and values of contemporary music lovers, which may explain his widespread popularity. The duets for violins, flutes or other combinations have never lost their appeal as teaching pieces. Many works of other genres merit resuscitation for study and performance.

WORKS

Most printed works appeared in multiple editions and in arrangements for various combinations of instruments. Dates in parentheses indicate the earliest editions. Letters appended to Ben numbers indicate works in which some movements are different from those in the preceding work. For a complete concordance of prints and thematic catalogue, see R. Benton: *Ignace Pleyel: a Thematic Catalogue of his Compositions* (New York, 1977) [Ben]

* – autograph

SYMPHONIES
(*nos. refer to Benton, 1977*)

121, c, 1778, *F-Pn (inc.) (1787), ed. A. Carse (London, 1949); 122, A, 1778, *A-Wgm (inc.) (1786); 123, F, 1782–4 (1788); 124, D, 1782–4 (1790); 125, B♭, 1782–4 (1787); 126, D (1785), ed. in Smith (1968); 127, B♭ (1785–6); 128, C (1786); 129, C (1786); 130, G (1786); 131, C (1786); 131A, C, ?1786–93, *A-R, ST, CS-OP, D-HR, Mbs, Rtt, TEG, I-CR, Mc, MOe, US-Wc*; 131B, C, 1786 or after, *A-ST, D-HR, Mbs, I-Mc, MOe*; 132, B♭ (1786), ed. in Smith (1968); 132A, B♭, ?1786–90, *CH-Zz, D-DO, HR, Rtt, I-MOe, Vnm*; 133, D,

1786 (1787); 134, E♭, 1786 (1787), ed. J. L. Petit (Paris, 1973); 135, B♭, 1786 (1787); 136, F, 1786 (1787), ed. in Smith (1968); 136A, F, *US-Wc*; 137, A, 1786 (1787); 138, f, 1786 (1787); 139, E♭ (1789); 140, F (1789), ed. F. Oubradous (Paris, 1957); 140A, F (1791–2); 141, G (1789); 142, c (1790); 143, C (1790), ed. in Smith (1968); 144, E♭ (1790); 145, D (1790); 146, G (1790); 147, d (1791), ed. in Smith (1968); 147A, D, 1791 or after, *F-Pn (inc.); 148, E♭ (1793); 149, B♭ (1794); 150, B♭ (1799); 150A, B♭, 1799–1800, *Pn, *GB-Lbm; 151, C, by 1800, *Lbm; 152, E♭, ?1801, *F-Pn, *GB-Lbm; 153, f, ?1801, *F-Pn (inc.); 154, C, *Pn (inc.) (1803); 155, a, ?1803, *Pn, *GB-Lbm; 156, G (1804); 157, C (?1804–5); 158, C, *A-Wn, D-AB, HR, GB-Lbm, I-Fc*; 159, F, *D-Rtt*; 160, d, *I-MOe*; 161, D, *D-DO, I-MOe*

CONCERTOS, SYMPHONIES CONCERTANTES

Ben	
101	Vc conc., C, *F-Pn*, 1782–4
102	Vc conc., D, 1782–4, lost
111	Symphonie concertante, E♭, solo vn, va, vc, ob, perf. 1786
103	Vn conc., D, 1785–7 (1788)
103A	Vn conc., D (1788)
104	Vc conc., C (1788)
105	Va/Vc conc., D (1790); ed. C. Hermann (Frankfurt am Main, 1951)
112	Symphonie concertante, B♭, solo vn, va (1791)
113	Symphonie concertante, F, 2 solo vn, va, vc, fl, ob, bn, perf. 1792
106	Cl/Fl/Vc conc., C (1797)
114	Symphonie concertante, A, 2 solo vn/solo pf, vn, perf. 1792
115	Symphonie concertante, F, solo (fl, ob, bn, hn)/(pf, vn) (1802 or 1805); ed. F. Oubradous (Paris, 1959)
107	Bn conc., B♭, *CS-Pnm*
108	Vc conc., C, *A-Wgm
116	Symphonie concertante, F, solo pf, vn, *I-Gi(l)*

MISCELLANEOUS ORCHESTRAL AND CHAMBER

201	Nocturne, D, ob, 2 hn, vn, va, vc, vle, 1780, *F-Pn
201A	Nocturne [Serenade], D, solo vn, solo vc, 2 hn, vn, va, b, 1780–90 (1790)
202	[Untitled work], C, 2 hn, 2 vn, va, b, 2 hurdy-gurdies, c1785, *Pn (inc.)
202.5	Nocturne, 2 cl, 2 hn, 2 va, b, 2 hurdy-gurdies, 1785, *D-Bds
203–14	Twelve Minuets (6 with trios), 2 ob, 2 hn, 2 vn, b, 1785–7 (1787)
215	Nocturne [Serenade], C, ob, 2 hn, 2 va, vc, b (1787)
216	Serenade, F, ob, 2 hn, 2 vn, va, b (1790)
217	Nocturne, B♭, ob, 2 hn, 2 va, b, *A-Wgm*
218	Adagio, a, solo vn, 2 ob, 2 bn, hn, 2 vn, va, b, *F-Pn
219	Serenade [Parthia], 2 cl, 2 bn, 2 hn [transcr. from recording, source unknown]
220	Divertimento, G, 2 hn, 2 vn, va, vc, *A-Wgm*, *F-Pn (inc.)

QUINTETS, SEXTETS, SEPTETS

271–2	Str Qnts, E♭, g, 2 vn, 2 va, vc (1785)
273	Str Qnt, C, 2 vn, 2 va, vc (1786)
276	Str Qnt, a, 2 vn, 2 va, vc (1786)
277	Str Qnt, f, 2 vn, 2 va, vc, perf. 1786
251	Septet, E♭, 2 vn, va, vc, db, 2 hn (1787)
274–5	Str Qnts, D, B♭, 2 vn, 2 va, vc (1787)
280–82	Qnts, G, C, E♭, fl, ob, vn, va, vc (1788); no.282 ed. H. Steinbeck (Vienna, 1968)
283–4	Str Qnts, F, D, 2 vn, 2 va, vc (1788)
278–9	Str Qnts, B♭, G, 2 vn, 2 va, vc (1789)
285	Str Qnt, F, 2 vn, 2 va, vc (1789)
261	Sextet, F, 2 vn, 2 va, vc, b (1791)
286	Qnt, g, hpd, fl, vn, va, b, *A-Wgm
287	Str Qnt, g, 2 vn, 2 va, vc, *F-Pn

QUARTETS

301–6	Str Qts, C, E♭, A, B♭, G, D, op.1, *USSR-Lsc (1782–3, nos.303–4, inc.)
307–12	Str Qts, A, C, g, E♭, B♭, D (1784)
313–18	Str Qts, B♭, A, e, C, E♭, D, 1785 (1786)
319–24	Str Qts, C, G, F, A, B♭, D, 1786 (1786)
325–30	Str Qts, E♭, B♭, A, C, G, F, 1786 (1787); 326A, 327A, 329A (1787); 325A, 328A, 330A (1788)
331–3	Str Qts, B♭, G, d, 1786 (1787), ded. King of Prussia
334–6	Str Qts, C, A, E♭, 1786 (1787), ded. King of Prussia
337–9	Str Qts, D, F, g, 1786 (1787), ded. King of Prussia
340–42	Str Qts, G, c, D, 1786 (1787), ded. King of Prussia
343–5	Str Qts, F, A, F (1788)
346–51	Str Qts, C, F, E♭, G, B♭, A (1788), ded. Prince of Wales; 348A, 350A (1788)
352	Qt, F, vn, 2 va, vc (1788); ed. U. Drüner (Zurich, 1976)
381–6	Str Qts, D, F, A, G, B♭, C, fl/vn, va, vc (1789)
353–8	Str Qts, C, B♭, e, G, A, f (1791), ded. King of Naples
359–64	Str Qts, F, B♭, D, E♭, G, E (1792)

387–92 Qts, D, F, A, C, G, A, fl, vn, va, vc (1797); nos.387–9 ed. J.-P. Rampal (New York, 1977)
393–4 Qts, D, G, fl, vn, va, vc (1799)
365–7 Str Qts, C, Bb, f (1803), ded. Boccherini
367A Str Qt, f, *F-Pn
367B Str Qt, f, Pn
368–9 Str Qts, Eb, D (?1810), ded. Viotti, *Pn (no.368, inc.)
369A Str Qt, D, *Pn
369B Str Qt, D, *Pn
370 Str Qt, g, *Pn
395 Qt, Eb, fl, 2 cl, bn, D-ASh; ed. G. Meerwein (London, 1970)

TRIOS
(Kbd Trio = Trio [Sonata] for kbd, fl/vn, vc)
428–30 Kbd Trios, C, F, G, 1783–4 (1785); nos.428–9 ed. W. Stockmeier (Munich, 1976); Ben 430 is by Haydn: H XV:5
401–3 Str Trios, Eb, D, F, vn, va, vc (1787); ed. B. Päuler (Zurich, 1971)
404–9 Str Trios, C, Eb, D, e, Bb, G, 2 vn, vc (1788 or 1789)
431–6 Kbd Trios, C, G, Bb, A, e, D (1788), ded. Queen of Great Britain
437–9 Kbd Trio, F, G, Eb (1790), ded. Elizabeth Wynne
440–42 Kbd Trio, Bb, C, f (1791), ded. Mme de Marclésy
443–5 Kbd Trios, C, F, D (1793) (Scottish Airs, bk 1)
446–8 Kbd Trios, G, Bb, A (1794) (Scottish Airs, bk 2)
449–51 Kbd Trios, C, G, Bb (1794) (Scottish Airs, bk 1)
452–4 Kbd Trios, D, Bb, A (1794–5) (Scottish Airs, bk 2)
455–7 Kbd Trios, C, G, Bb (1795–6) (Scottish Airs, bk 3)
461 Kbd Trio, D (1795–6)
458–60 Kbd Trios, G, D, C (1796–8) (Scottish Airs, bk 4)
462–4 Kbd Trios, F, D, Bb (1796) (with favourite airs)
465–7 Kbd Trios, F, C, Eb (1796), ded. Eugénie Beaumarchais
468–70 Kbd Trios, Bb, A, C (1796–7), ded. Mme de Gramont
410–15 Str Trios, D, F, G, Bb, G, A, 2 vn, vc (1797); nos.410–12 ed. B. Päuler (Zurich, 1974)
471–3 Kbd Trios, Bb, D, Eb (1798), ded. Mme Martilière
474–6 Kbd Trios, F, Bb, Eb (1803), ded. Empress of Russia
416 Str Trio, Bb, 2 vn, va, *F-Pn

DUOS
571–2 Duos, Bb, G, kbd, vn (1787)
573 Duo, Bb, kbd, vn (1788)
501–6 Duos, C, D, F, G, A, Bb, vn, vc (1788)
507–12 Duos, Bb, F, C, G, D, A, 2 vn/fl, or fl, vn (1788)
513–18 Duos, Bb, D, A, F, C, e, 2 vn (1789)
519–24 Duos, C, g, A, Bb, G, d, 2 vn (1789)
525 Duo, C, va, vc (1792)
526–8 Duos, C, F, Eb, vn, va (1795)
529–31 Duos, G, Bb, c, vn, va, or 2 vn (1796)
531A Duo, d, 2 fl (1796)
574–9 Duos, C, F, G, Bb, D, Eb, kbd, fl/vn (1796)
575A Duo, F, 2 vn (1796–7)
580–85 Duos, F, D, Bb, e, C, A, kbd, fl/vn (1798)
532–4 Duos, C, g, D, 2 vc (1799/R1970)
532–7 Duos, C, g, Eb, G, Bb, D, 2 vn, *F-Ppincherle (no.536) (1799)
538–43 Duos, C, G, a, F, D, e, 2 vn (1806); ed. G. Maglioni (Milan, 1954)
544–9 Duos, D, Eb, C, Bb, f, G, vn, va (1808–12)

KEYBOARD, HARP SOLOS
601–12 12 German dances, kbd (1792)
613 Rondo, Eb, harp/kbd (1796)
614 Swiss Air with Variations, Bb, kbd/harp (1796)
615 Air with Variations, Bb, pf (1798)
616–17 Pieces, c, Bb, harp/hpd (1798)
618–24 7 Pieces, pf (?1799)
625–7 Sonatas, a, F, G, kbd (1800)
628–63 36 Ecossaises, pf (1803)
664–9 6 Ecossaises, pf (?c1810)
670 Sonata, Bb, kbd, A-Wn, B-Bc, D-WRl, I-OS
801–27 27 instructional exercises pubd in a pf method (1796), incl. 3 for pf 4 hands; also attrib. Dussek

STAGE, VOCAL
701 Die Fee Urgele (marionette opera, 4, von Pauersbach, after C. S. Favart), Eszterháza, Nov 1776, *A-Wn
702 Overture to J. Haydn: Die Feuersbrunst, H XXIXb:A, 1776 or 1777, US-NH
703 Ifigenia in Aulide (opera, 3, ? A. Zeno), Naples, S Carlo, 30 May 1785, I-Nc
704 Deutsche Aria, Eb, v, pf (1790)
705 Hymne à la liberté (Rouget de Lisle), Revolutionary song, v, pf (1791)
706 La révolution du 10 août 1792, ou Le tocsin allégorique, Revolutionary hymn, vv, orch, 1793, F-Pn
707–38 32 Scottish songs, arr. 1–2vv, pf, vc, 1792–3, *Pn, *GB-Lbm (1793–9)
739 Hymne du temple de la raison, v, pf, ?1792–4
740 Hymne à la nuit (Viscount de Parny), v, pf (1795)
741 Mass, G, 1796–7, CS-Pnm, D-BAR, I-Fc
742–53 Winter-Unterhaltung (12 songs), v, pf (c1798)
754 Requiem, Eb, *F-Pn
755 Cum Sancto Spiritu, fugue, D, chorus, orch, *A-Wgm
756 Mass, D, *Wn, I-Fc

(2) (Joseph Stephen) Camille Pleyel (*b* Strasbourg, 18 Dec 1788; *d* Paris, 4 May 1855). Composer, pianist and business associate of his father (1) Ignace Pleyel. He studied with his parents and with Desormery (probably Jean-Baptiste, the son), Dussek and Steibelt. In 1813–14 he toured southern France, giving piano recitals and arranging for the sale of music and pianos, sometimes in exchange for wood, wine or other materials, in Montpellier, Bordeaux and Toulouse. On 1 January 1815 he became a legal partner of the firm, after which it used the trade name 'Ignace Pleyel et fils aîné'. Nevertheless he spent the period from 16 March to 21 July of that year in London, perhaps to avoid the danger of conscription created by Napoleon's return to power for 100 days (the period corresponded almost exactly with his stay abroad).

In London Pleyel was introduced by the elderly Salomon to the prince regent, and on the queen's 71st birthday, 19 May, he performed for a company that included the prince, Queen Charlotte and Princess Charlotte. He also gave several public performances, including one at the Philharmonic Society on 1 May and a two-piano recital with Kalkbrenner. In addition he gave piano lessons, examined pianos and reported to his father on their construction, arranged for the purchase and delivery of mahogany, looked without success for an able piano builder to work for the firm and tried to collect various debts due to the firm. His frequent companions were the pianists Cramer, Kalkbrenner and Ries and the piano makers Broadwood and Tomkison.

After his return to Paris Pleyel gradually assumed more responsibility for the running of the firm, especially the piano-building side of its activities. On 5 April 1831 he married the pianist Marie Moke (see (3) below); they separated after four years.

Pleyel was a close friend of Chopin, who made his Paris début on 26 February 1832 (and gave his final Paris concert on 16 February 1848) in the Salle Pleyel, opened by the firm in 1830. After Camille's death the firm was taken over by Auguste Wolff. (For its later history *see* PLEYEL (ii)) In the summer of 1837 Pleyel accompanied Chopin to London in an unsuccessful effort to cheer the pianist, who was suffering from his unrequited love for Marie Wodzińska. According to Legouvé, who admired Pleyel for his generous nature as well as his exceptional capacity for administration, Chopin was often heard to say 'There is only one man left today who knows how to play Mozart; it is Pleyel, and when he is willing to play a four-hand sonata with me, I take a lesson'.

Before devoting himself entirely to commercial activities, Pleyel wrote a number of compositions for the piano (the last being op.51). They were issued by the Pleyel firm and in London; apart from a few sonatas and trios they are chiefly fantasias, potpourris of opera airs, rondos, nocturnes, airs, caprices and *mélanges*.

(3) (Camille) Marie (Denise) Moke Pleyel (*b* Paris, 4 Sept 1811; *d* St Josse-ten-Noode, nr. Brussels, 30 March 1875). French pianist, teacher and composer, wife of (2) Camille Pleyel. At an early age she displayed talent for the piano. She studied successively with Jacques Herz, Ignaz Moscheles and Frédéric Kalkbrenner and at the age of 14 performed Kalkbrenner's first concerto at the Brussels Théâtre Royal. By 1830 she was teaching the piano at a girls' school (the Institut Orthopédique in the Marais section of Paris), where her colleagues and admirers included Ferdinand Hiller and Berlioz (who taught the piano and the guitar respectively). She became engaged to Berlioz after her mother's objections to him were weakened by his having finally won the Prix de Rome. Three months after his departure for Rome in December 1830, however, she married (2) Camille Pleyel. She continued her piano teaching, writing to a friend in July of her fond husband, who 'has willingly consented to my continuing to give lessons; you know that I am very attached to my independence'. Chopin dedicated to her his three Nocturnes op.9 in 1833, the same year that Kalkbrenner did the same with his *Fantaisie et variations sur une mazourka de Chopin* op.120.

After legal separation from her husband (1835) Mme Pleyel resumed her performing career, reaping enormous successes in Bonn, Dresden, Leipzig, Vienna, St Petersburg, Paris and London; one of her English performances prompted De Quincey to write of her as 'the celestial pianofortist'. Heaven nor earth has yet heard her equal'. In 1842 she requested and received permission to establish her domicile in Belgium. From 1848 until 1872 she was a piano teacher at the Brussels Conservatory, of which the director was F.-J. Fétis. Fétis wrote that she was responsible for the establishment of a true school of piano playing in Belgium; that her playing was notable for astonishing technical facility, but also for strength, tonal modifications, charm and poetry; and that among the many famous pianists heard by him, no other gave the feeling of perfection that her playing created. She was also appreciated by Mendelssohn and Liszt and the latter, a personal friend with whom she performed four-hand works, dedicated to her his *Réminiscences de Norma* (1841) and the *Tarantelle di bravura d'après la Tarantelle de 'La muette de Portici' d'Auber* (1846). Pleyel composed several works for the piano, including a *Rondo parisien pour piano* op.1, a Fantasia on motifs from Weber's *Preciosa* and an Andante.

BIBLIOGRAPHY

N. E. Framery: *Notice sur Joseph Haydn* (Paris, 1810)
J. F. Lobstein: *Beiträge zur Geschichte der Musik im Elsass und besonders in Strassburg* (Strasbourg, 1840), 33ff
J.-B. Weckerlin: *Musiciana* (Paris, 1877) [incl. several letters to Pleyel]
O. Comettant: *Un nid d'autographes* (Paris, 1885, 2/1886) [incl. letters to Pleyel]
C. Pierre: *Les hymnes et chansons de la Révolution* (Paris, 1904)
M. Vogeleis: *Quellen und Bausteine zu einer Geschichte der Musik und des Theaters in Elsass* (Strasbourg, 1911/R1978)
M. Pincherle: 'L'édition musicale au dix-huitième siècle', *Musique*, i (1928), 493 [incl. letter from George Thomson to Pleyel]
A. Hedley: *Chopin* (London, 1947, rev. 2/1974 by M. J. E. Brown)
A. Carse: 'A Symphony by Pleyel', *MMR*, lxxix (1949), 231
H. C. R. Landon: *The Collected Correspondence and London Notebooks of Joseph Haydn* (London, 1959)
J. Klingenbeck: 'Ignaz Pleyel und die Marseillaise', *SMw*, xxiv (1960), 106
A. Tyson: 'Haydn and Two Stolen Trios', *MR*, xxii (1961), 21
B. S. Brook: *La symphonie française dans la seconde moitié du XVIIIe siècle* (Paris, 1962)
J. Klingenbeck: 'Ignaz Pleyel: sein Streichquartett im Rahmen der Wiener Klassik', *SMw*, xxv (1962), 276
——: 'Pleyel, Ignaz Joseph', *MGG*
G. de Rothschild: *Luigi Boccherini: sa vie, son oeuvre* (Paris, 1962; Eng. trans., 1965)
R. Benton: 'Ignace Pleyel, Disputant', *FAM*, xiii (1966), 21
——: 'London Music in 1815, as seen by Camille Pleyel', *ML*, xlvii (1966), 34
R. B. Smith: *The Periodical Symphonies of Ignaz Pleyel* (diss., U. of Rochester, NY, 1968) [incl. scores of syms. Ben 126, 132, 136, 143, 147]
R. Benton: 'A la recherche de Pleyel perdu, or Perils, Problems and Procedures of Pleyel Research', *FAM*, xvii (1970), 9
J. Zsako: 'Bibliographical Sandtraps: the Klavierschule, Pleyel or Dussek?', *CMc* (1971), no.12, p.75
R. Benton: 'Pleyel's *Bibliothèque musicale*', *MR*, xxxvi (1975), 1
——: 'Bemerkungen zu einem Pleyel-Werkverzeichnis', *Mf*, xxviii (1976), 280
——: *Ignace Pleyel: a Thematic Catalogue of his Compositions* (New York, 1977)
——: 'A Résumé of the Haydn–Pleyel Trio Controversy, with some Added Contributions', *Haydn-Studien*, iv (1978)
——: 'Pleyel as Music Publisher', *JAMS*, xxxii (1979), 125

RITA BENTON

Pleyel (ii). French firm of piano makers. It was founded in 1807 at Paris by the composer Ignace Pleyel (*see* PLEYEL (i)). The firm quickly adopted and improved the best features of English piano making; JEAN HENRI PAPE helped Pleyel from 1811 to 1815 with the building of cottage pianos or 'pianinos', small vertically strung uprights invented by the English maker Robert Wornum (ii) which were new to France. In 1815 Ignace's son Camille Pleyel joined the firm; 14 years later the pianist Frédéric Kalkbrenner joined too, and did much to publicize Pleyel pianos. Chopin became closely associated with the firm; he made his début in Paris at the Salle Pleyel, and later owned a Pleyel grand of 1839. Cramer, Moscheles and Steibelt were also friends of the firm. Business increased so much that the firm claimed 250 employees and, probably with exaggeration, an annual production of 1000 pianos in 1834. By the 1870s the annual output had increased to 2500, a level which was maintained for the rest of the century.

In 1855 Camille died and was succeeded by his son-in-law, Auguste Wolff (*b* Paris, 3 May 1821; *d* Paris, 9 Feb 1887), the firm becoming Pleyel, Wolff & Cie. After Wolff's death his son-in-law Gustave Lyon (*b* Paris, 19 Nov 1857; *d* Paris, 12 Jan 1936) assumed control of 'Pleyel, Lyon et Cie'. Lyon developed a *harpe éolienne* (*see* AEOLIAN HARP), but is more famous for his development of the chromatic harp at the end of the 19th century. It dispensed with pedals, substituting a string for each semitone of the octave. Debussy wrote for it, but it has never achieved the popularity of the double-action harp, as the number of strings is nearly double and it requires a totally different finger technique. Under Lyon the firm also made chromatic timpani, chimes, practice keyboards and two-manual pianos.

At the turn of the century Pleyel began making two-manual harpsichords, with $2 \times 8'$ and $1 \times 4'$, six pedals and classical casework (*see* HARPSICHORD, §5 (i)). Wanda Landowska suggested a new design in 1912, a modern departure having little in common with the classical instrument, with a heavy case including a cast-iron frame, and a 16' register. About two such instruments were made annually. It was this instrument that Landowska played throughout her career. In 1961 the firm was merged with Gaveau-Erard, but it continued to make pianos under the name of Pleyel. In 1976 the merged firm was bought out by Schimmel of Brunswick.

BIBLIOGRAPHY

J. Turgan: *Les grandes usines de France: la manufacture de pianos de MM. Pleyel, Wolf* [sic] *et Cie* (Paris, 1862)
O. Comettant: *Histoire de cent mille pianos* (Paris, 1890)

T. de Fourcaud: *La Salle Pleyel* (Paris, 1893)

A. Dolge: *Pianos and their Makers* (Covina, Calif., 1911/*R*1972)

R. E. M. Harding: *The Piano-forte: its History Traced to the Great Exhibition of 1851* (Cambridge, 1933, rev. 2/1978)

A. Loesser: *Men, Women and Pianos: a Social History* (New York, 1954)

C. Ehrlich: *The Piano: a History* (London, 1976)

MARGARET CRANMER

Plica (Lat.: 'fold'). The name used in the 13th and 14th centuries for liquescent neumes. It describes their usual shape: a single stroke doubling back on itself to make a 'U' or inverted 'U', thicker at the curve. The plica was not a single note but a two-note neume, containing the pitch where the plica was placed on the staff plus a higher ('U' shape) or lower (inverted 'U') note. The second note was semi-vocalized to provide a passing note or anticipatory note before the next note. The semi-vocalization was most commonly practised on the consonants 'l', 'm', 'n', 'r', before another consonant (2452 out of 3500 cases in the study in PalMus, ii, 1891), sometimes when they were the only consonant between vowels; on the second vowel of diphthongs; the consonant pair 'gn'; sometimes 'd' and 't' at the ends of words (particularly *et, sed, ut*); sometimes soft 'c' and soft 'g' (before 'e' and 'i'); sometimes also 'd', 's', 't', 'x', before other consonants; and 'i' or 'j' when used as a consonant.

While early writers on neume shapes and names (see Huglo) called the ascending form *epiphonus* and the descending form *cephalicus*, 13th-century theorists used the term 'plica'. Thus Jehan des Murs (*GS*, iii, 202):

Clives, plicae, virga, quilismata, puncta, podati,
Nomina sunt harum; sint pressi consociati.

The plica retained its basic function of indicating liquescence in all plainchant manuscripts, in most manuscripts containing non-mensural secular monophony and in most manuscripts containing polyphony until the 14th century. The situations where Mocquereau found liquescent neumes used in 10th–11th-century manuscripts (see PalMus, ii, 1891) are distinguished in the same way in later sources (with minor differences due to different pronunciation practice, to which, in fact, liquescent neumes are a guide). Of later theorists only Lambertus (Pseudo-Aristotle) attempted a description of the method of voice production involved (*CS*, i, 273): 'The plica is sung by narrowing or closing the epiglottis while subtly including a vibration of the throat'; this seems to be a picturesque way of saying that the forethroat is formed as for consonants while the vocal chords are still vibrating.

In Parisian repertories of polyphony of the early 13th century, however, the plica was also used in melismatic music, without liquescent function. Five of the rhythmic modes, which were the basis of the method of indicating rhythm in this music, did not provide for a note on at least one beat of a ternary measure (i.e. one quaver out of every three in 3/8 transcription; or two out of six in 6/8 transcription). Ex.1 shows how plica strokes added to patterns of 1st- and 2nd-mode ligatures provide these notes (see Apel, pp.228f, for more complex examples). The plica most often implies an added note at the interval of a 2nd. Definite instances of larger intervals are rare, one such being found in the conductus *Deduc Syon uberrimas*: in *E-Mn* 20486 on the syllable '-tas' of 'gravitas' there is a two-note descending ligature *d–G* (f.84r, staff 4); in *D-W* 677 there is a plica on *d* with a slight thickening at the end of the stroke on *G* (f.160r [151r], staff 10); while *I-Fl* 29.1 and *D-W* 1206 have a plica with stylized square note head and a long descending tail to the right (f.336v, staff 4, f.94r, staff 6, respectively).

In the second half of the 13th century discrete note shapes were evolved for plica longa and plica brevis, to complement the standard long and breve shapes; Table 1 gives the commonest forms. The Parisian repertories of the second half of the 13th century are however largely of syllabic music (i.e. motets), and the plica retained its basic function of denoting liquescence. Walter Odington, who called it 'semitonus et semivocalis' (*CS*, i, 236), preferred to use the longer method of writing 6th-mode passages (continuous breves): 'certior est et acceptior' (*CS*, i, 245), presumably to avoid confusion between the two functions.

TABLE 1

	long		or		plica longa ascendens
					plica longa descendens
	breve				plica brevis ascendens
					plica brevis descendens

The plica was frequently preceded by another note of the same pitch; the reason for this is not always clear. The group can usually be confidently transcribed as equivalent to a long (crotchet or dotted crotchet) rather than a breve (quaver), but this is by no means a universal rule (see Tischler). It was to some extent interchangeable with the simple plica, with a two-note ligature or with a three-note group of which the first two notes were of the same pitch. A comparison of the notation of *D-W* 677, 1028, *E-Mn* 20486 and *I-Fl* 29.1 for the tenor parts of the 17 polyphonic conductus they have in common shows 50 or so simple plicas found alone above a single syllable, 100 or so 'compound' plicas, and 170 or so binaria or single note + binaria, in any one manuscript: 12–15% are found in an alternative form in one or more of the other three manuscripts. *E-Mn* 20486 shows a preference for simple plicas, *D-W* 1028 for binaria or single note + binaria; sometimes *D-W* 677 and *E-Mn* 20486 use a binaria with elongated first element where the other manuscripts have a compound plica or single note + binaria. More detailed statistics both depend on and help investigation of the layering of the repertory as a whole.

Ex.1

1st-mode ligature pattern

1st-mode with plicas

2nd-mode ligature pattern

2nd-mode with plicas

The single note + binaria is the usual form in square staff notation of the *pressus* (descending) and *pes quassus* (ascending) compound neumes. Although these neumes originally entailed a special manner of performance (Jehan des Murs said the *pressus* should be performed evenly and swiftly; *GS*, iii, 202), they have no special shape in, for instance, Parisian 13th-century chant manuscripts, to draw attention to this characteristic. Kuhlmann (p.111) suggested that in Parisian polyphony the note-group denoted a vibrato, being what Jerome of Moravia called *flores* (*CS*, i, 91–2). At any rate the compound plica was usually used in situations where liquescence was appropriate.

TABLE 2

I – Fl 29.1	∩	⁊∩	▪	⁊▪	Total
total number of occurrences on liquescent consonant	165 *38.6%*	164 *38.4%*	85 *19.9%*	13 *3%*	427
in conductus, also found in other sources	143 *41.7%*	138 *40.2%*	53 *15.5%*	9 *2.6%*	343
in unica	22 *26.2%*	26 *31%*	32 *38.1%*	4 *4.8%*	84

The Fathers of Solesmes (PalMus, ii, 1891) said that not every such situation was matched by a liquescent neume, but did not give figures to show how often. Table 2 gives statistics for the tenor parts of the three- and two-part conductus in *I-Fl* 29.1; it shows the number of times a syllable ending 'l', 'm', 'n', or 'r' and followed by another consonant (words such as *salve*, *omnes*, *cantat*, *virgo*) is matched by a simple plica, a compound plica, a binaria or a single note + binaria (ascending or descending forms). The use of binaria may possibly be a tendency in later pieces or in those that are more certainly Parisian; separate figures are therefore given for pieces which are also found in other sources and for unica, to show approximately how the repertory of the manuscript is divided.

The polyphonic pieces of the Roman de Fauvel (*F-Pn* fr.146), the last source in mensural music to use plicas to any great extent, still used the plica for liquescence. Counting the same situations where 'l', 'm', 'n' and 'r' occur as in Table 2, there are 51 instances of a plica in the polyphonic pieces and 27 of a binaria. If the pieces using 3 or fewer semibreves to the breve are counted separately from those using 4 or more, the figures are as follows: in polyphonic pieces using 3 or fewer semibreves to the breve, 29 plicas and 9 binaria; in those using 4 or more semibreves, 22 plicas and 18 binaria.

BIBLIOGRAPHY
A. Mocquereau: 'Neumes-accents liquescents ou semi-vocaux', *Le répons-graduel Justus et palma*, PalMus, ii (1891), 37–86
J. Pothier: 'De la plique dans le plain-chant', *Revue du chant grégorien*, iii (1895), 55 [summarized by P. Bohn, *MMg*, xxvii, 1895, p.47]
G. M. Suñol: *Introducció a la paleografia musical gregoriana* (Montserrat, 1925; Fr. trans., rev. and enlarged 2/1935)
H. Freistedt: *Die liqueszierenden Noten des gregorianischen Chorals* (Fribourg, 1929)
G. Kuhlmann: *Die zweistimmigen französischen Motetten des Kodex Montpellier, Faculté de médecine H 196* (Würzburg, 1938)
W. Apel: *The Notation of Polyphonic Music 900–1600* (Cambridge, Mass., 1942, rev. 5/1961)
M. Huglo: 'Les noms des neumes et leur origine', *Etudes grégoriennes*, i (1954), 53
H. Tischler: 'Ligatures, Plicae and Vertical Bars in Premensural Notation', *RBM*, xi (1957), 83
H. Anglès: 'Die Bedeutung der Plika in der mittelalterlichen Musik', *Festschrift Karl Gustav Fellerer* (Regensburg, 1962), 28

DAVID HILEY

Plicka, Karel (*b* Vienna, 14 Oct 1894). Czech ethnomusicologist, artist and photographer. Plicka attended a teachers' institute in Hradec Králové (1909–13) and, after playing in a chamber ensemble in Sweden and studying violin in Berlin, he began teaching in the east Bohemian town of Úpice. He left to study art in Vienna (1916–18) and then music in Prague from 1919, where he became choirmaster of the Philharmonic chorus (1922–4). He had collected folksongs as a boy and after he joined the Matica Slovenská (Slovak Foundation) in the town of Turčiansky Svätý Martin in 1924 he spent 15 years collecting and classifying over 40,000 folksongs, many of them from remote areas. In 1929 he brought a group of folk musicians from 50 Slovak villages to Prague, where valuable documentary recordings were made. The results of his work he publicized with a lecture tour of America (1935–6), through his folk music editions, both scholarly and popular, and with his films and photographs of folk life and costumes.

WRITINGS
'Sbieranie ľudových piesní' [Collecting folksongs], *Slovenské pohľady*, xl (1924), 239
'Slovenské uspaványky' [Slovak lullabies], *Slovenské pohľady*, xliii (1927), 460
'Svetová vojna v ľudových piesňach slovenských' [The world war in Slovak folksongs], *Slovenské pohľady*, xlv (1929), 445
'Lyrické piesne zbojnícke' [Lyrical brigand songs], *Slovenské pohľady*, l (1934), 290

FOLKSONG EDITIONS
Eva Studeničová spieva [Eva Studeničová sings] (Turčiansky Svätý Martin, 1928)
Tance z Piešťan [Dances from Piešťany] (České Budějovice, 1928)
Slovenské pesničky [Slovak songs] (Turčiansky Svätý Martin, 1937)
Český zpěvník [A Czech songbook] (Prague, 1940, 3/1957)
Slovenský spevník [A Slovak songbook] (Bratislava, 1961)
with J. Horák: *Zbojnícke piesne slovenského ludu* [Brigand songs of the Slovak people] (Bratislava, 1965)

BIBLIOGRAPHY
J. Horák: 'Karel Plicka', *HRo*, vii (1954), 683
J. Potúček: *Súpis slovenských hudobnoteoretických prác* (Bratislava, 1955), 336 [bibliography and list of writings]
V. Šolín: 'Na besede u Karly Plicky' [Plicka in conversation], *HRo*, xxii (1969), 673

JOHN TYRRELL

Plinthamer, Adolf. See BLINDHAMER, ADOLF.

Plishka, Paul (*b* Old Forge, Penn., 28 Aug 1941). American bass. He began singing lessons at the age of 18 at Montclair State College, and two years later became a pupil of Armen Boyajian, director of the Paterson Lyric Opera, New Jersey, receiving his initial stage experience with this company. In 1965 he joined the Metropolitan Opera National Company, singing Mozart's Bartolo and Puccini's Colline. When the touring company was disbanded, he was invited to join the Metropolitan Opera at Lincoln Center, where he made his début as the Monk in *La Gioconda* in September 1967. Gradually he took on leading roles in both the serious and *buffo* repertories, among them Leporello, Oroveso (*Norma*), King Marke, Procida (*Les vêpres siciliennes*), and both Varlaam and Pimen in *Boris Godunov*. He has appeared with numerous orchestras in the USA. He sang in Verdi's Requiem at the Las Palmas Festival in the Canary Islands, took the title role in

Verdi's *Oberto* in Bologna, and appeared as Gounod's Mephistopheles in Bari. In 1975 he sang Marcel in a rare revival of *Les Huguenots* in New Orleans. He made his La Scala début in *La damnation de Faust* in 1974, and in 1975 sang Philip II at Strasbourg. His mellow, voluminous bass can be heard in recordings of *Anna Bolena*, *I puritani* and *Norma*.

MARTIN BERNHEIMER

Plocek, Alexandr (*b* Prague, 26 Feb 1914). Czech violinist. He studied the violin under A. Svoboda in Plzeň, then with Otakar Ševčík in Písek (1927–33) and Jaroslav Kocian at the Masters School of the Prague Conservatory (1931–4), at the same time reading law at Prague University. In 1935 he was co-founder of the Czech Trio. He spent 1936 and 1937 at the Ecole Normale de Musique in Paris in the chamber class of Alexanian and Thibaud, making his British début with a tour in 1937. He led the Czech PO from 1937 to 1942, but concentrated more on chamber playing with the Czech Trio and the Prague Quartet (1941–6), and gave frequent concerts with Páleníček. Appointed a soloist of the Czech Philharmonic in 1949, he toured widely in Europe, and with the Czech Trio in India and Japan in 1960. The intellectual discipline of his playing controls a balanced, refined tone and sense of style in a wide repertory of standard and contemporary works. In 1946 he was appointed to teach at the Prague Academy of Music, and he worked at the Janáček Academy in Brno from 1948 to 1952.

BIBLIOGRAPHY

ČSHS

V. Pospíšil: 'Alexandr Plocek', *HRo*, vi (1953), 161

K. P. Sádlo: 'Bilance k padesátinám' [Balance sheet at 50], *HRo*, xvii (1964), 111

J. Kozák: *Českoslovenští koncertní umělci a komorní soubory* [Czechoslovak concert artists and chamber ensembles] (Prague, 1964), 138f

R. Budiš: *Slavní čeští houslisté* [Famous Czech violinists] (Prague, 1966), 170f

J. Creighton: *Discopaedia of the Violin 1889–1971* (Toronto, 1974)

ALENA NĚMCOVÁ

Plocek, Václav (*b* Prague, 28 Aug 1923). Czech musicologist. He studied composition with Šín and Krejčí at the Prague Conservatory (1942–7), the piano with Jan Heřman (1942–5) and musicology and aesthetics at Prague University (1945–8), where he took the doctorate under Hutter in 1948 with a dissertation containing an analysis of the St Vít troper of 1235. Subsequently he joined the music section of the Prague University library, where he took a diploma in librarianship (1950). In 1964 he moved to the Musicology Institute of the Czechoslovak Academy of Sciences, where he devoted himself to the systematic study of Czech medieval music, analysing and editing sources, and Czech musical palaeography. In 1967 he obtained the CSc with a catalogue of music manuscripts in Prague University library.

WRITINGS

Původ svatováclavského responsoria 'Laudemus Dominum' [The origin of the St Vit responsory *Laudemus Dominum*] (diss., U. of Prague, 1948; extracts in *Ročenka Universitní knihovny v Praze 1957*, 130 [with Eng., Ger., Russ. summaries]

'Nově nalezená sekvence o svaté Dorotě a její poměr k Jenštejnově "Decet huius" ' [A newly discovered sequence on St Dorothy and its relation to Jenštejn's *Decet huius*], *Ročenka Universitní knihovny v Praze 1956*, 69; Ger. trans. in *De musica disputationes Pragenses*, i (1972), 120

'Nejstarší dvojhlasy v rukopisech Universitní knihovny' [The oldest two-part song manuscripts in Prague University library], *Ročenka Universitní knihovny v Praze 1960–1961*, 129; Ger. trans in

J. Fukač, V. Plocek and M. K. Černý: *Bydgoszcz 1966: Beiträge zur Geschichte der tschechischen Musik* (Prague, 1966), 65–109

'Die Katalogisterung der lateinischen Handschriften in der Staatsbibliothek der Tschechoslowakischen sozialistischen Republik in Prag', in J. Fukač, V. Plocek and M. K. Černý: *Bydgoszcz 1966: Beiträge zur Geschichte der tschechischen Musik* (Prague, 1966), 1

Catalogus codicum notis musicis instructorum, qui in Bibliotheca publica rei publicae Bohemicae socialisticae – in Bibliotheca universitatis Pragensis servantur (diss., Czechoslovak Academy of Sciences, 1967; Prague, 1973)

'Zásady popisu rukopisů psaných ve starých notačnich systémech' [Principles in the description of manuscripts written in early systems of notation], *HV*, v (1968), 230–63 [with Eng., Ger., Russ. summaries]

'K problematice našich nejstarších tanečních skladeb' [Some questions concerning the oldest Czech dance compositions], *HV*, vi (1969), 3 [with Eng., Ger., Russ. summaries]

'Ještě k problematice Czaldy waldy' [More about the Czaldy waldy], *HV*, vii (1970), 46 [with Eng., Ger., Russ. summaries]

'Zur Problematik der ältesten tschechischen Tanzkompositionen', *SM*, xiii (1971), 241

K počátkům středověkého dramatu v Čechách: transkripce a analýza neumatického zápisu z rukopisu XIV D 12 Národního muzea v Praze [The beginnings of medieval drama in Bohemia: transcription and analysis of the neumatic notation of *CS-Pnm* XIV D 12] (in preparation)

JOSEF BEK

Plocka, Marek z. *See* MAREK Z PŁOCKA.

Plomer [Plourmel], John. *See* PLUMMER, JOHN.

Plousiadēnos [Plousiadenus], Joannēs. Byzantine 15th-century composer and theorist; *see* BYZANTINE RITE, MUSIC OF THE, §17.

Plüddemann, Martin (*b* Kolberg, Pomerania [now Kołobrzeg, Poland], 29 Sept 1854; *d* Berlin, 8 Oct 1897). German composer and singer. As a child, Plüddemann heard chamber and operatic music in his home, which stimulated an early love of music. He studied at the Leipzig Conservatory (1871–6) under E. F. Richter. After a brief service as Kapellmeister in St Gall (1878), Plüddemann left for Munich to study singing with Julius Hey and Friedrich Schmitt. There he also began a writing career with the publication of several polemical articles on music. The loss of his voice in 1880 forced him to give up singing. At first he turned to music criticism in Munich. After years of travel, including a stay in Berlin, he conducted the Singakademie in Ratibor (1887), taught singing at the Steiermärkische Musikschule in Graz, and on his return (1894) to Berlin, where he remained until his death, he wrote music criticism for the *Deutsche Zeitung*.

Plüddemann's lifelong ambition was to rekindle interest in a neglected area of German song: the ballad. He established 'ballad schools', first in Berlin (1886) and later in Graz (1890), where he strove to realize his ideal in collaboration with young singers and composers. Although his efforts prompted numerous ballad-evenings, he laboured on behalf of the declining genre without accomplishing any lasting success.

He held that most composers, notably excepting Loewe, conceived the ballad incorrectly in terms of the lied's pervasive lyricism and evocation of a single mood. Plüddemann, however, recognized the ballad's distinctive characteristics, its emphasis on epic and narrative elements, its structural correspondences of one musical section for each dramatic situation in the narrative, and its graphic delineation of characters in dialogue. Taking his revered Loewe as a model, Plüddemann developed a vocal style suitable for narration, which he termed his 'parlando-ballad style'. His ballads achieve unity through the modified recurrence of musical sections and with leitmotifs. Their declamation is lively and faithful to the verses, and the dramatic characterization (influenced by Wagner) is, at its best, vividly etched and gripping. The piano parts are symphonically complex and rich in imagery – some look like piano reductions of orchestral scores. Plüddemann explored the early German Romantic poetry based on sagas, fairy tales and medieval historical subjects to find ballad texts. Outstanding examples of his settings include *Siegfrieds Schwert* (Uhland), *Der alte Barbarossa* (Rückert) and *Der Taucher* (Schiller), all in volume i of his *Balladen und Gesänge*. He also wrote lieder and arranged folksongs for chorus.

WORKS
(published in Nuremberg unless otherwise stated)

[48] Balladen und Gesänge, 8 vols. (1891–9); [8] Lieder und Gesänge (1893)
Works for chorus incl. [8] Altdeutsche Liebeslieder, 4 male vv (Berlin, 1879); 6 Lieder (Eichendorff), 4 male vv (1901)

WRITINGS

Die Bühnenfestspiele in Bayreuth (Leipzig, 1876)
Aus der Zeit, für die Zeit (Leipzig, 1880)
'Karl Loewe', *Bayreuther Blätter*, xv (1892), 318
Introduction to *Balladen und Gesänge* (Nuremberg, 1891–9)

BIBLIOGRAPHY

R. Batka: *Martin Plüddemann und seine Balladen* (Prague, 1896)
L. Schemann: 'Uber die Bedeutung der Ballade für unsere Zeit und unsere Zukunft: ein Brief an Martin Plüddemann', *Bayreuther Blätter*, xx (1897), 34
R. Bilke: 'Martin Plüddemann', *Die Musik*, vii (1907–8), 89
L. Schemann: *Martin Plüddemann und die deutsche Ballade* (Regensburg, 1930) [with portrait, selected writings and letters]
H. Engel: 'Martin Plüddemann', *Pommersche Lebensbilder*, i (1934), 395
W. Suppan: 'Martin Plüddemann und seine Grazer Balladenschule', *Südost-Tagespost* (1960), suppl.59

EDWARD F. KRAVITT

Pludermacher, Georges (*b* Guéret, Creuse, 26 July 1944). French pianist. He started piano lessons at the age of four and at 11 entered the Paris Conservatoire where he studied with Lucette Descaves and Jacques Février and was awarded many honours. He continued his studies with Géza Anda in Lucerne in 1963–4, and won prizes in international competitions. Pludermacher has toured widely in France and throughout Europe, both as soloist and in chamber music, becoming particularly well known as an interpreter of contemporary music: he gave the first performance of Boucourechliev's *Archipel 1* at Royan in 1967 and has appeared frequently with the Domaine Musical and with Musique Vivante, directed by Diego Masson. He has also given many concerts of music for two pianos with Yvonne Loriod. Besides contemporary works his repertory includes most of the Classical and Romantic concertos.

RONALD KINLOCH ANDERSON

Plummer [Plomer, Plourmel, Plumere, Polmier, Polumier], **John** (*b* ?c1410; *d* c1484). English composer. By 1441 he was a member of Henry VI's Chapel Royal; from 1444 to 1455 he was the first to hold the title (though not to perform the duties) of Warden or Master of the Chapel Children. By 1449 he had joined the London Gild of Parish Clerks. As late as 1467 he was still nominally a Gentleman of the Chapel Royal under Edward IV; but he settled in Windsor c1458 and by 1460 had beome verger of the Royal Free Chapel of St George in Windsor Castle, remaining in that position until 1483–4. Until 1967 only four works by Plummer were known, three votive antiphons and a motet. These

showed him as a suave but progressively minded composer who experimented with invertible counterpoint and imitation: *Anna mater*, for three tenors and an optional triplex, is particularly remarkable in the latter respect. The recent discovery of a Kyrie and Gloria demonstrates that he also wrote large-scale isomelic masses; this in turn suggests that the anonymous mass on ff.107*v*–16 of *I-TRmn* 89, which resembles *Anna mater* both in its general style and in its very unusual disposition for three equal tenors, may also be by Plummer.

More recently, Staehelin has pointed out that the Mass 'Omnipotens Pater' in the opening 'English fascicle' of *B-Br* 5557 had an ascription 'Plourmel' until the mid-19th century. This ascription is now replaced by an unacceptable one to 'G. Binchois' in what is clearly a 19th-century hand; and Curtis has shown that the cycle is stylistically compatible with the more securely ascribed works of Plummer.

WORKS

Edition: *Four Motets by John Plummer*, ed. B. Trowell (Banbury, 1968) [T]

Mass with Kyrie trope 'Omnipotens Pater', 3vv, *B-Br* 5557 (ed. in Curtis)
Kyrie 'Nesciens mater', Gloria 'Nesciens mater', 4vv, *GB-Lbm* Add.54324 (fragmentary, chant in iv; Ky with trope 'Deus creator omnium'; Gl anon., but paired with Ky)
Anna mater matris Christi, 4vv; T 24, ed. in EECM, viii (1968), 34 (text from responds, rhymed office of St Anne)
Descendi in hortum meum, 3vv; T 13 (fragmentary kbd arr. in Buxheim Organbook, ed. in EDM, xxxviii, 1958, p.216)
Tota pulcra es, 3vv; T 16
Tota pulcra es, 3vv; T 20, ed. in EECM, viii (1968), 28

DOUBTFUL WORKS

Kyrie 'Deus creator omnium', Gl, Cr, San, Ag, 3vv, *I-TRmn* 89 (anon. but scoring and style suggest Plummer's authorship)
Ibo michi ad montem mirre, 3vv, *TRmn* 90 (anon., attrib. Plummer by Scott on stylistic grounds; for edn. see Scott)
Qualis est dilectus tuus, 3vv; ed. in CMM, xlvi/2 (1969), 74 (also attrib. Forest; probably by Forest)

BIBLIOGRAPHY

C. Johnson: 'John Plummer, Master of the Children', *Antiquaries Journal*, i (1921), 52, 94
W. H. Grattan Flood: 'The Beginnings of the Chapel Royal', *ML*, v (1924), 85
J. Harvey: *Gothic England* (London, 2/1948), 87, 115, 141
A. Seay: 'The Dialogus Johannis Ottobi in arte musica', *JAMS*, viii (1955), 93 [Hothby's praise of 'Plumere']
H. Baillie: 'A London Gild of Musicians, 1460–1530', *PRMA*, lxxxiii 1956–7), 15
J. N. Dalton, ed.: *The Manuscripts of St. George's Chapel, Windsor Castle* (Windsor, 1957)
B. L. Trowell: *Music under the Later Plantagenets* (diss., U. of Cambridge, 1960), i, 62, 68; ii, 185, 289
M. and I. Bent: 'Dufay, Dunstable, Plummer – a New Source', *JAMS*, xxii (1969), 394–424
A. B. Scott: 'Ibo michi ad montem mirre: a New Motet by Plummer', *MQ*, lviii (1972), 543
M. Staehelin: 'Möglichkeiten und praktische Anwendung der Verfasserbestimmung in anonym überlieferten Kompositionen der Josquin-Zeit', *TVNM*, xxiii/1 (1973), 79
G. R. K. Curtis: *The English Masses of Brussels, Bibliothèque Royale, MS. 5557* (diss., U. of Manchester, 1979)

BRIAN TROWELL

Pluriarc [bow lute]. A multiple-necked lute of the Congo basin, made by fitting a number of musical bows together into a single resonator so that each string has its own string-bearer. For illustration *see* GABON, fig.5. *See also* entry 'Pluriarc' in Appendix A.

Plutarch (*b* before AD 50; *d* after AD 120). Greek philosopher and biographer. References to music in his philosophical works are fairly frequent and provide good evidence for the musical information and vocabulary current among educated persons of the period. The treatise *Peri mousikēs* ('On music') is of doubtful authenticity and is generally cited as Pseudo-Plutarch, although some regard it as an early genuine work. It contains miscellaneous information, especially about the history of Greek music, and often depends upon good authorities, e.g. lost works of Aristoxenus. The edition by Weil and Reinach has a useful but incomplete review of passages of Plutarch which deal with music.

EDITIONS
Plutarque: De la musique, ed. and Fr. trans. H. Weil and T. Reinach (Paris, 1900)
Plutarque: De la musique, ed. and Fr. trans. F. Lasserre (Olten and Lausanne, 1954)
De musica, ed. K. Ziegler, Plutarchi moralia, vi/3 (Leipzig, 2/1959)
Plutarch's Moralia, xiv, ed. and trans. B. Einarson and P. H. De Lacy (London and Cambridge, Mass., 1967)

BIBLIOGRAPHY
R. P. Winnington-Ingram: 'The Spondeion Scale', *Classical Quarterly*, xxii (1928), 81
K. Ziegler: 'Plutarchea, I: zu *De musica*', *Studi in onore di L. Castiglioni*, ii (Florence, 1960), 1107
——: *Plutarco*, Biblioteca di studi classici, iv (Brescia, 1965)
E. K. Borthwick: 'Notes on the Plutarch De Musica and the Cheiron of Pherecrates', *Hermes*, xcvi (1968), 60

For further bibliography see GREECE, §I.

R. P. WINNINGTON-INGRAM

Pneuma. A category of neume in Byzantine chant; *see* NEUMATIC NOTATIONS. *See also* NEUMA.

Pocci, Franz Graf von (*b* Munich, 7 March 1807; *d* Munich, 7 May 1876). German composer and writer on music. In childhood he showed talent for drawing, painting and music, and although he studied law at the universities of Landshut and Munich, he continued his artistic activities, composed and performed at the piano. From 1847 to 1863 he was a musician at the Bavarian court. As a composer, Pocci excelled at writing miniatures, and was at his most characteristic in children's songs, for which he showed a special gift. His plays with musical settings for the Munich Marionette Theatre added new vitality to puppet opera; he also designed the scenery for these productions. He was less successful in composing in larger forms. Pocci was extremely versatile not only as a musician but also as a writer; he wrote independent literary works and song texts, in addition to writing on music.

WORKS
(*most MSS in Pocci family archives, Ammerland am Starnbergersee*)

STAGE
Der Alchymist (Singspiel, 2, L. Koch), Munich, 1840
Der Ronga (incidental music, F. von Kobell), Munich, 1847
Puppet operas, for the Munich Marionette Theatre

OTHER WORKS
Vocal: 22 choruses, 3 qts, 3 trios, 9 duets, 20 solo songs, 95 children's songs
Inst: Zum Zeitvertreib, 6 ländler, 2 zithers; 2 pf sonatas; 12 other pf pieces; Soldatenmarsch, 2 fl, ?pf; Morgenlied, hn, ?pf

WRITINGS
'Über die Romantik der modernen Musik', *Deutsche Blätter für Literatur und Leben*, ed. F. von Elsholtz, A. von Maltitz and F. A. von Zu-Rhein (Munich, 1840), 93
'Über Ouverturen', ibid, 158
'Musikalischer Sonnenaufgang', ibid, 205
Many articles in the *Münchner allgemeine Zeitung*, 1839–53

BIBLIOGRAPHY
H. Holland: *Zur Erinnerung an F. Pocci* (Munich, 1877)
——: 'Pocci', *ADB*
L. Hirschberg: 'Franz Pocci der Musiker', *ZMw*, i (1918–19), 40–70 [with complete list of works]
F. Pocci: *Franz Poccis lustiges Komödienbüchlein* (Munich, 1921)
——: *Das Werk des Künstlers Franz Pocci* (Munich, 1926)
K. Pastor: *Franz Pocci als Musiker* (diss., U. of Munich, 1932)
H. R. Purschke: 'Pocci', *ES*

GAYNOR G. JONES

Poche [pochette]. *See* KIT.

Pochettino. *See* POCO.

Pochetto. *See* KIT.

Pochissimo. *See* POCO.

Pociej, Bohdan (*b* Warsaw, 17 Jan 1933). Polish music critic. He studied musicology under Zofia Lissa, Chomiński and Feicht at Warsaw University (1953–9). Since 1959 he has been a member of the editorial board of the bi-weekly *Ruch muzyczny*. He also writes for *Tygodnik powszechny*, *Polska* and *Polnische Perspektive*. Possessing one of the keenest minds in contemporary Polish music criticism, Pociej combines in his analyses both a technical and an aesthetic approach. His writings have been strongly influenced by the philosopher Roman Ingarden.

WRITINGS
'O twórczości Bogusława Schäffera' [The works of Bogusław Schäffer], *Muzyka*, ix/3–4 (1964), 44
Klawesyniści francuscy [French harpsichord composers] (Kraków, 1969)
'Opis – analiza – interpretacja' [Description – analysis – interpretation], *Res facta*, iv (1970), 151
Bach: muzyka i wielkość [Bach: music and greatness] (Kraków, 1972)
Idea – dźwięk – forma [Idea, sound, form] (Kraków, 1972)
'Uwagi o wartościach w muzyce' [Considerations on values in music] *Res facta*, vi (1972), 140

ZYGMUNT M. SZWEYKOWSKI

Pockorny, Franz Xaver. *See* POKORNY, FRANZ XAVER.

Poco (It.: 'little', 'somewhat'). A direction that modifies many tempo, expression and dynamic marks in music. In strict Italian, *poco forte* and *poco allegro* would mean the opposite of *forte* and *allegro*; and Grove 5 drew attention to the slovenliness of that usage, pointing out that *un poco forte* and *un poco allegro* were correct. But *poco allegro* is current, for better or worse, and must be considered part of 'musicians' Italian' (*see* TEMPO AND EXPRESSION MARKS, §3). *Pochettino*, the diminutive, and *pochissimo*, the superlative, are also current in musical scores.

Podatus (from Gk. *pous, podos*: 'foot'). *See* PES (ii).

Poděšt, Ludvík (*b* Dubňany u Hodonína, 19 Dec 1921; *d* Prague, 27 Feb 1968). Czech composer and administrator. In 1941 he changed from language studies in Brno to enter the conservatory of that city, but his musical education was interrupted by World War II. He returned to study composition under Kvapil at the Brno Conservatory (1945–8) and musicology under J. Racek and B. Štědroň at Brno University (1945–9), receiving a doctorate for his thesis on socialist realist music, *Hudba v pojetí socialistického realismu*. Poděšt worked for Czech radio (1947–51), was artistic director of the V. Nejedlý Army Arts Ensemble in Prague (1953–6) and then directed music for Czech television from 1958. His administrative activities also involved him in the Union of Czechoslovak Composers and other artists' organizations. Towards the end of his life he spent much of his time in Casablanca and concerned himself intensively with theory.

The source of his music's spontaneity may be found in the folk music of Moravian Slovakia, his native region. In his music of the 1940s (piano pieces, chamber music, songs on contemporary Czech poetry and a symphony of 1947–8) he followed the post-Janáček tradition. In about 1950 he began to respond to the new policy of socialist realism, writing orchestral works (such as the symphonic poem *Raymonde Dien* of 1950–51) that were melodically conventional and readily comprehensible in general; during this period he was closely associated with youth and army ensembles. His suites and dances for orchestra drew on Czech and Moravian folk music, and he also produced around 300 mass songs, a fifth of which were recorded on disc. Similar characteristics are displayed in his early operettas (both for radio and for the stage), incidental music and film scores; these prepared the way for a series of operas, including *Hrátky s čertem* ('Gossip with the Devil', after Drda, 1957–60) and *Tři apokryfy* ('Three apocryphas', after Čapek, 1959), which are singularly successful treatments of popular conversational comedies.

JIŘÍ FUKAČ

Podešva, Jaromír (*b* Brno, 8 March 1927). Czech composer. He was born into an artistically talented family; his father, a leading Brno violin maker, took charge of his early musical studies. He studied composition under Kvapil, from 1946 at the Brno Conservatory and then at the Janáček Academy of Music in Brno (1947–51), where he continued as a postgraduate assistant. He served as secretary of the Union of Czechoslovak Composers in Prague (1956–9) and later as chairman of the Brno branch for some years. A UNESCO scholarship took him on an eight months' trip to France, the USA and England (1960–61) to study with Dutilleux and Copland. In 1969 he was appointed to teach composition at the Ostrava Conservatory, although he retained contacts with Brno. His early music was greatly influenced by that of Novák and Janáček. In the 1950s he was involved with the popular music and mass political songs that were being developed, but his concert music was becoming more subjective, more concerned with a personal response to poetry. For example, his Third Symphony (1966) was based on the verse of M. Kundera and B. Hrabal. His music has changed from a free tonality to a simultaneous use of tonality and dodecaphony; the procedures are discussed in his treatise (1973). Podešva has also produced some popular educational works.

WORKS
(selective list)

Stage: Opustíš-li mne [If you leave me] (opera, Podešva, after Z. Pluhař), 1962–3, rev. 1965–6; Bambini di Praga (ballet-opera buffa, after B. Hrabal), 1968
Orch: 6 syms., 1951–73; Conc., pf trio, orch, 1956–7; Sinfonietta, str, 1959; 4 sym. poems
Inst: 5 str qts, 1948, 1950, 1951, 1955, 1965; many duos with pf, other chamber music, pf pieces
Vocal: 17 cycles of popular songs, 4 other song cycles, 2 cantatas, 27 choral pieces and cycles

Principal publishers: Český Hudební Fond, Panton, Supraphon, Ústřední Dům Lidové Umělecké Tvořivosti

WRITINGS
Současná hudba na západě [Contemporary music in the west] (Prague, 1963)
Možnost kadence v dvanáctitónovém poli [The possibility of cadence in the dodecaphonic field] (Prague, 1973)

BIBLIOGRAPHY
J. Trojan: 'Tvůrčí profil J. Podešvy' *HRo*, xviii (1965), 936
——: 'Symfonické paralely J. Podešvy', *HRo*, xxi (1968), 149

JIŘÍ FUKAČ

Podio, Francesco. *See* DEL POMO, FRANCESCO.

Podio [Puig], Guillermo de [Despuig, Guillermo] (*fl* 2nd half of the 15th century). Spanish priest and music theorist. Born possibly in Valencia or Tortosa, he is usually identified with the Guillermo de Puig who was curate of S Catalina de Alcira, Valencia, from 1479 to 1488. A Guillermo Molins de Podio held a benefice at Barcelona Cathedral, and was a chaplain to John II of Aragon in 1474. The relationship between these two clergymen has not been established. The theorist wrote *Ars musicorum* (Valencia, 1495; ed. A. Seay, Colorado Springs, 1978) and *In enchiridion de principiis musicae* (MS, *I-Bc*). The latter, apparently intended for Spanish students at Bologna, may be evidence that Podio visited that city. The first treatise comprises eight books and sets out to be exhaustive; an expanded treatment of part of it appears anonymously in *In enchiridion*. Podio's musical aesthetic was based on the ideas expounded by Boethius; thus, he regarded music as a mathematical and physical science, integrated into the Quadrivium according to the Pythagorean system. He classified musicians as theoretical or practising exponents, the former, as was customary, being regarded as superior. On several important points he opposed Ramos's innovations, particularly in his discussion of the sizes of intervals, where he adhered to Pythagorean arithmetic. In the same way, he retained and discussed the use of Guidonian solmization, rather than adopt Ramos's syllabic notation. Podio attributed the growth of Roman chant, and its relationship to polyphony, to Pope Vitalian. *Ars musicorum*, with its traditional bias, is an important source of information on the mensural notation of the 15th century. In it Podio drew attention to certain 'errors' in Gaffurius, thereby highlighting the differences between contemporary Italian and Spanish notational practice. In many ways Podio was the most influential Spanish theorist of his time. Ramos was barely known or mentioned by Iberian writers, whereas Podio was regularly cited and commended even in the 18th century. In particular, he influenced Bizcargui, the other leading theorist in Spain active in that period.

BIBLIOGRAPHY
J. Ruiz de Lihory, Barón de Alcahalí: *La música in Valencia* (Valencia, 1903), 378
H. Anglès: 'La notación musical española de la segunda mitad del siglo XV: un tratado desconocido de Guillermo de Podio', *AnM*, ii (1947), 151 [incl. text of *In enchiridion*]
R. Stevenson: *Spanish Music in the Age of Columbus* (The Hague, 1960)
F. J. León Tello: *Estudios de historia de la teoria musical* (Madrid, 1962)

F. J. LEÓN TELLO

Podius, Francesco. *See* DEL POMO, FRANCESCO.

Poe, Edgar Allan (*b* Boston, Mass., 19 Jan 1809; *d* Baltimore, 7 Oct 1849). American writer. Beyond its bizarre and macabre surface, his work consistently reveals a concern with neurotic states, with frequent hints of interpretation in Freudian terms. This, and his technique of symbol and suggestion, recommended his writings to many composers at the turn of the century. Debussy, who was fascinated by the tales in Baudelaire's translation, planned a work based on *The Fall of the House of Usher* at least as early as 1890; 18 years later he was projecting a double bill of Poe operas for the New York Metropolitan. Poe's view of music as 'suggestive and indefinite' – 'sensations which bewilder while they enthral' – bears comparison with that of the symbolists. The sympathy he found between musical sounds and mental states, most fully expounded in *The Bells*, is also seen in the linking of the sensitive and troubled Roderick Usher with the vibrating strings of a guitar.

WORKS SET TO MUSIC
(publication dates follow titles)

TALES

Ligeia (1838): used as subject of Cl Qnt no.2, op.27/2, by Holbrooke, 1910; inserted poem (trans. Bal'mont) set by Gnesin as The Conqueror Worm, op.12, 1v, orch, 1913
The Devil in the Belfry (1839): scenario and sketches for opera by Debussy, 1902–12; ballet by Inghelbrecht, 1921; opera by Lualdi, 1919–23; orch work by Vallerand, c1923
The Fall of the House of Usher (1839): inserted poem (trans. Mallarmé) used as subject of sym. study Le palais hanté op.49 by Schmitt, 1900–04; lib and sketches for opera by Debussy, 1908–17; sym. poem by E. B. Hill, op.27, 1919–20; opera by Sitsky, 1965
The Island of the Fay (1841): work for pf/orch by H. F. B. Gilbert
Eleonora (1842): work for small orch by Baudrier, 1938
The Masque of the Red Death (1842): lib by Schreker, 1911; ballet by C. Scott, 1932; ballet by N. N. Tcherepnin; ballet by Holbrooke
The Pit and the Pendulum (1843): work for orch by E. S. Kelley, 1930; opera by B. Bettinelli, perf. 1967

POEMS

Al Aaraaf (1829): work for str sextet by Holbrooke, op.43, 1902
Israfel (1831): used as subject of Sextet op.33a for pf and wind by Holbrooke, 1906
The Raven (1845): sym. poem by Holbrooke, op.25, 1900; sym. poem Nevermore, op.9 by Myaskovsky, 1909; work for reciter and pf by S. Hawley; sym. poem Nevermore by Morawski; work for chorus and orch by B. Shapleigh, op.50; work for Bar and orch by E.-W. Sternberg
Ulalume (1847): sym. poem by Holbrooke, op.35, 1901–3; sym. poem by Morawski
Annabel Lee (1849): work for reciter and pf by Ireland, c1910
The Bells (1849): poem for chorus and orch by Holbrooke, op.50, 1903; poem (trans. Bal'mont) for solo vv, chorus and orch by Rakhmaninov, op.35, 1913; work for chorus and pf by E. L. Diemer; work for reciter and pf by S. Hawley

MISCELLANEOUS

Homage to E. A. Poe: dramatic choral sym. by Holbrooke, op.48, 1908
Edgar Poe: sym. impression by Zanella, 1923

BIBLIOGRAPHY

M. G. Evans: *Music and Edgar Allan Poe* (Baltimore and Oxford, 1939/*R*1968)
E. Lockspeiser: *Debussy et Edgar Poe* (Monaco, 1961) [incl. lib, scenario and sketches by Debussy for Poe operas]

PAUL GRIFFITHS

Poelchau, Georg Johann Daniel (*b* Kremon, nr. Riga, 23 June 1773; *d* Berlin, 12 Aug 1836). German music collector and singer. He became a student at the University of Jena in 1792, and later lived in Hamburg, where he made several appearances as a solo tenor and probably started his music collection. In 1813 he moved to Berlin and in the following year joined the Singakademie. For the rest of his life he was chiefly concerned with augmenting his rich collection of music manuscripts and editions; this involved extensive travel and frequent correspondence, particularly with the Viennese collector Aloys Fuchs. He became director of the library of the Singakademie on C. F. Zelter's death in 1832.

Poelchau possessed valuable printed books from the 16th and 17th centuries and original manuscripts of the works of Haydn, Mozart and Beethoven. But the greatest value of his collection lay in the many priceless Bach autographs and manuscript copies that he owned at a time when the Bach renaissance was still in its early stages. When he died, his son Hermann took charge of the collection until it was purchased by the Königliche Bibliothek, Berlin, in 1841 (it is now in *D-Bds*).

BIBLIOGRAPHY

G. Schünemann: *Die Singakademie zu Berlin, 1791–1941* (Regensburg, 1941)
G. von Dadelsen: *Bemerkungen zur Handschrift Johann Sebastian Bachs, seiner Familie und seines Kreises* (Trossingen, 1957)
P. Kast: *Die Bach-Handschriften der Berliner Staatsbibliothek* (Trossingen, 1958)
F. W. Riedel: 'A. Fuchs als Sammler Bachscher Werke', *BJb*, xlvii (1960), 83
W. Virneisel: 'Poelchau, Georg Johann Daniel', *MGG*
K. Engler: *Georg Poelchau und seine Musikaliensammlung: ein Beitrag zur Überlieferung Bachscher Musik in der ersten Hälfte des 19. Jahrhunderts* (Göppingen, 1974)

RICHARD JONES

Poenicke, Johann Peter. *See* PENIGK, JOHANN PETER.

Poggioli, Antonio (*b* Samarugio, Rome, c1580; *d* Rome, 10 March 1673). Italian music publisher and dealer. He published most types of instrumental and sacred and secular vocal music, including reprints of Arcadelt, Lupacchino and Tasso, a complete edition of Cifra's motets (1638) and an important anthology, *Scelta di motetti* (1643). His publications date from 1620 to 1668 and he drew on seven Roman printers including Robletti, Masotti, Grignani and Mascardi. Poggioli built up his publishing concern from a book-dealer's business that he had probably founded himself. It was in central Rome (Parione), and his sign, which appeared in his publications, was a hammer. He married in 1607 and had at least four children of whom one, Giovanni Poggioli (*b* Rome, 17 July 1612; *d* Rome, 30 Sept 1675), followed his father's occupation. Giovanni is known only as the editor of the later of the two, slightly different, editions of the *Scelta* that appear to have been published within two days of each other in July 1647. This representative anthology of the Roman motet in the mid-17th century was also issued, with further slight changes, by Phalèse in 1652 as *Delectus sacrarum cantionum* (in *GB-Och*; not in *RISM*).

BIBLIOGRAPHY

H. Leichtentritt: *Geschichte der Motette* (Leipzig, 1908)
C. Sartori: *Dizionario degli editori musicali italiani (tipografi, incisori, librai-editori)* (Florence, 1958)
P. Kast: 'Biographische Notizen zu Römischen Musikern des 17. Jahrhunderts', *AnMc*, no.1 (1964), 58

COLIN TIMMS

Pögl, Peregrinus (*b* Sandau, nr. Magdeburg, 1 March 1711; *d* Neustadt am Main, 15 Nov 1788). German composer. He entered the Benedictine monastery at Neustadt am Main in 1735. He was a prolific composer of church music, but only two of his many publications appear to have survived. He was regarded by his contemporaries as a leading church composer, but his surviving publications suggest that this reputation was exaggerated. In his *Antiphonale marianum* (1763) the vocal solos are heavily decorated in an instrumental rather than a vocal idiom, and the quality of musical invention is not commensurate with their technical difficulty. The choral writing in this volume is repetitive and dull in texture. In general, Pögl's music lacks rhythmic life and his attempts to use chromatic harmony are unsuccessful.

WORKS

Obiectum pinnarum tactilium, op.1 (Neustadt am Main, 1746), 6 trio sonatas
Sacrificium Deo vespertinum, 4vv, 2 vn, org, op.3 (Bamberg, 1747), 4 vespers
Incensum dignum in odorum, 4vv, 2 vn, org, op.5 (Neustadt, 1754), 19 offertories
Antiphonale marianum, 4vv, 2 vn, 2 clarinos, org, vc, op.7 (Neustadt, 1763), 32 antiphons
6 masses: the title-page of the only extant volume in *D-Mbs* is missing; perhaps these form op.2, 4 or 6

ELIZABETH ROCHE

Poglietti, Alessandro [Boglietti, Alexander de] (*b* ?Tuscany, 1st half of the 17th century; *d* Vienna, July 1683). Austrian composer, organist and teacher of Italian birth. He may have received his musical training in either Rome or Bologna. He later settled in Vienna. At the beginning of 1661 he is known to have been organist and Kapellmeister to the Jesuits at the Kirche zu den neun Chören der Engel. On 1 July of the same year he was appointed court and chamber organist in the Kapelle of the Emperor Leopold I. He was very highly regarded as a teacher of keyboard playing and composition, and monks came from all over Austria to be taught by him. He formed particularly close ties with the Benedictine foundation of Göttweig, Lower Austria, where he occasionally stayed as a guest, and it was there in 1677 that his only known opera, *Endimione festeggiante*, was performed, on the occasion of a visit by the emperor. He also enjoyed the friendship of Count Anton Franz von Collalto and the Prince-bishop of Olomouc; in 1672 he inherited large estates near their residences at Brtnice and Kroměříž. He was held in such esteem that the emperor raised him to the ranks of the aristocracy, and the pope created him a Knight of the Golden Spur. He lost his life during the siege of Vienna by the Turks.

Poglietti is primarily important for his keyboard music. After Froberger and together with Kerll he represents one of the most vital links between Frescobaldi and composers of the late Baroque era such as Bach, Handel, Fux and Gottlieb Muffat. His sketchbook, discovered a few years ago (see Riedel, 1968), and his *Compendium oder kurtzer Begriff, und Einführung zur Musica* of 1676 offer guidance to students of 17th-century keyboard playing and an introduction to the art of composition. The 12 ricercares, many copies of which have survived, belong to the series of significant contrapuntal compositions that started with Frescobaldi's *Fiori musicali* (1635) and ended with Bach's *Die Kunst der Fuge* and were regarded as models of the strict style. Poglietti was particularly interested in musical imitations. In his *Compendium* he noted down many themes for 'all manner of capriccios, variously imitating on an instrument the songs of birds and other sounds'. They occur in the section in which he is concerned with the imitation of natural sounds (e.g. nightingale, canary, cuckoo, cock and hen) and of the sounds of bells, work and war. Many pieces by him on such themes have survived, for example *Über das Henner- und Hannergeschrei, Teutsch Trommel und Franzoik Trommel* and battle music such as the *Toccatina sopra la ribellione di Ungheria* (1671) and the *Toccata fatta sopra l'assedio di Filippsburgo* (1676). *Rossignolo*, a cycle dedicated to the Emperor Leopold I in 1677 on the occasion of his marriage to his third wife, is specially rich in programmatic movements. It is mainly musical instruments that Poglietti imitated here, though he also used elements from the folk music of particular countries and regions, as in *Böhmisch Dudlsack, Hollandisch Flagolett, Franzosische Baiselements, Pollnischer Sablschertz, Soldaten Schwebelpfeif, Ungarische Geigen* and *Steyermarckker Horn*. The keyboard writing in these pieces is unusually full and brilliant. By virtue of its overall structure, symbolic content and skilful handling of form and variation technique, *Rossignolo* must rank as one of the most important cycles in the literature of keyboard music.

WORKS

VOCAL

(*in the castle archive, Kroměříž, unless otherwise stated*)

Endimione festeggiante (opera, J. Dizent), Göttweig, 12 Jan 1677
Missa, 4vv; Missa, 5vv, insts; Missa, 3vv, vn, bc, 1680
Requiem aeternam
Magnificat, 3vv, vn, org
Litaniae Lauretanae, 8vv, insts
Ave regina coelorum, 5vv
2 motets, 5, 8vv, insts

INSTRUMENTAL

Toccatina sopra la ribellione di Ungheria, kbd, 1671 [with dance movts]; ed. in DTÖ, xxvii, Jg.xiii/2 (1906/*R*)
Toccata fatta sopra l'assedio di Filippsburgo, kbd, 1676
Rossignolo, kbd, 1677; ed. in DTÖ, xxvii, Jg.xiii/2 (1906/*R*)
Toccata del 7. tono, kbd [with canzon and dance movts]
12 ricercares, kbd; ed. in Die Orgel, ii/5–6 (Lippstadt, 1957)
Many suites, canzonas, capriccios, short preludes and fugues, kbd
8 sonatas, many balletti, str insts
For sources see Riedel, 1960

WRITINGS

(*only those on music*)

Compendium oder kurtzer Begriff, und Einführung zur Musica, 1676, A-KR
Regulae compositionis (for sources see Federhofer)

BIBLIOGRAPHY

A. Koczirz: 'Zur Lebensgeschichte A. de Pogliettis', *SMw*, iv (1916), 116
P. Nettl: 'Der Wiener Tanzkomposition in der 2. Hälfte des 17. Jahrhunderts', *SMw*, viii (1921), 45–175
G. Frotscher: *Geschichte des Orgel-Spiels und der Orgel-Komposition*, i (Berlin, 1935, enlarged 3/1966), 479ff
A. Kellner: *Musikgeschichte des Stiftes Kremsmünster* (Kassel, 1956), 245
H. Federhofer: 'Zur handschriftlichen Überlieferung der Musiktheorie in Österreich in der 2. Hälfte des 17. Jahrhunderts', *Mf*, xi (1958), 264
R. Pečman: 'Lidové taneční motivy v Pogliettiho suitě *Rossignolo*', *Sborník prací filosofické fakulty brněnské university*, F9 (1960), 47
F. W. Riedel: *Quellenkundliche Beiträge zur Geschichte der Musik für Tasteninstrumente in der 2. Hälfte des 17. Jahrhunderts* (Kassel, 1960), 80ff, 142ff
——: 'Neue Mitteilungen zur Lebensgeschichte von Alessandro Poglietti und Johann Kaspar Kerll', *AMw*, xix–xx (1962–3), 124
——: 'Alessandro Pogliettis Oper *Endimione*', *Festschrift Hans Engel* (Kassel, 1964), 298
W. Apel: *Geschichte der Orgel- und Klaviermusik bis 1700* (Kassel, 1967), 551ff; (Eng. trans., rev., 1972), 566ff
J. Sehnal: 'Die Musikkapelle des Olmützer Bischofs Karl Liechtenstein-Castelcorn in Kremsier', *KJb*, li (1967), 79–123
H. Knaus: *Die Musiker im Archivbestand des kaiserlichen Obersthofmeisteramtes (1637–1705)*, ii (Vienna, 1968), 20f, 23, 57f, 110, 116f, 133
F. W. Riedel: 'Ein Skizzenbuch von Alessandro Poglietti', *Essays in Musicology: a Birthday Offering for Willi Apel* (Bloomington, Ind., 1968), 145
S. Wollenberg: *Viennese Keyboard Music in the Reign of Karl VI* (diss., U. of Oxford, 1975)

FRIEDRICH W. RIEDEL

Pohanka, Jaroslav (*b* Olešnice, Moravia, 29 June 1924; *d* Brno, 28 April 1964). Czech music historian. He studied composition, flute and piano at Brno Conservatory (1940–43, 1946–7) and after teaching music at a gymnasium in Brno (1948–50), he became director of a music school in Šlapanice, near Brno (1951–60), and then a research assistant in the music history department of the Moravian Museum (1960–64). He was able to put to use his interest in early Czech music and his extensive knowledge of its sources both in his transcriptions for the ensemble Collegium Musicum Brunense, of which he was co-founder and artistic director, and in his *Dějiny české hudby v příkladech* ('The history of Czech music in examples', 1958). This major Czech compilation is a critical edition of basic Czech sources from the earliest times to the first half of the 19th century. In it, just as in the 13 volumes of Musica Antiqua Bohemica which he prepared for publication, Pohanka was responsible for revealing many new sources and bringing to notice a number of neglected composers of worth, such as J. A. Losy, J. K. Tolar and P. J. Vejvanovský. Pohanka's edition of Vejvanovský was intended to supplement a projected monograph on this composer. In his last years his energy was concentrated principally on amassing and working on material for a book on Czech lute music which he left incomplete at his death.

WRITINGS

'Loutnové tabulatury z rajhradského klástera' [Lute tablatures from the Rajhrad monastery], *Časopis moravského musea*, xl (1955), 193 [incl. Fr. résumé]
'O nejstarších českých skladbách pro loutnu' [The oldest Czech works for lute], *HRo*, viii (1955), 245
'Satirický popěvek z 15. století' [A satirical song from the 15th century], *HRo*, x (1957), 172
'Výkonní hudebníci v Brně: příspěvek k sociálnímu postavení hudebníků ve 14. století' [Performing artists in Brno; a note on the social status of musicians in the 14th century], *HRo*, xi (1958), 387
'Lidové tance z pozůstalosti Kristiána Hirschmentzla' [Folkdances from the estate of Kristián Hirschmentzl], *Radostná země*, x (1960), 105 [incl. Ger. résumé]
'Neznámá kantáta L. van Beethoven?' [An unknown cantata by Beethoven?], *Časopis moravského musea*, xlvi (1961), 137 [also in Ger.]
'Historické kořeny české kramářské písně' [The historical roots of Czech fairground songs], *Sborník Václovkova Olomouc 1961* (Prague, 1963), 89
'Bohemika v zámecké hudební sbírce z Náměšt' n. Osl.' [Bohemica in the music collection of the castle of Náměšt' nad Oslavou], *Časopis Moravského musea*, xlviii (1963), 235 [incl. Ger. résumé]
Loutna a její podíl na vývoji instrumentální hudby v Čechách [The lute and its part in the development of instrumental music in Bohemia] (MS, owned by Heda Pohanková Brno) [incl. transcrs. of lute tablatures]

EDITIONS

V. J. Tomášek: Tre ditirambi op.65, MAB, xxix (1956)
Dějiny české hudby v příkladech [The history of Czech music in examples] (Prague, 1958)
J. A. Losy: Pieces de guitarre, MAB, xxxviii (1958)
P. J. Vejvanovský: Serenata e sonate per orchestra, MAB, xxxvi (1958); *Composizioni per orchestra*, MAB, xlvii–xlix (1960–61)
J. K. Tolar: Balletti e sonate, MAB, xl (1959)
F. Krommer: II. Quartetti per oboe, MAB, xlii (1959)
J. Zach: Cinque sinfonie d'archi, MAB, xliii (1960)
A. Filtz: Sei sinfonie per orchestra op.2, MAB, xliv (1960)
G. Benda: Sinfonie, MAB, lviii; lxii; lxvi (1962–5)
W. A. Mozart: Quartette mit einem Blasinstrument, Neue Mozart-Ausgabe, viii/20/2 (Kassel, 1962) [к285, 285a, 285b, 298, 370/368b]

BIBLIOGRAPHY

'In memoriam Jaroslava Pohanky', *Časopis Moravského musea*, xlix (1964), 285
R[udolf] P[ečman]: 'In memoriam Jaroslava Pohanky', *HRo*, xvii (1964), 468
ALENA NĚMCOVÁ

Pohl, Carl Ferdinand (*b* Darmstadt, 6 Sept 1819; *d* Vienna, 28 April 1887). German music historian, organist and composer. He came of a musical family, his grandfather having been a maker of glass harmonicas, his father (*d* 1869) chamber musician to the Duke of Hessen-Darmstadt, and his mother a daughter of the composer Bečvařovsky. He was trained as an engraver, but in 1841 he settled in Vienna and after studying under Sechter became in 1849 organist of the new Protestant church in the Gumpendorf suburb. His compositions, of which at least 14 collections of songs and keyboard pieces were printed, date mostly from these years. In 1855 he resigned his post for reasons of health and devoted himself thereafter to teaching and writing.

In 1862 he published a pamphlet on the history of the glass harmonica. From 1863 to 1866 he lived in London, occupied in research at the British Museum on Haydn and Mozart; the result was *Mozart und Haydn in London*, a work whose accurate detail makes it still very useful. In 1866, through the influence of Jahn, Köchel

and others, Pohl was appointed archivist and librarian to the Gesellschaft der Musikfreunde in Vienna. As custodian of the society's large collections he produced monographs describing their history and extent, and collaborated with Haberl and Lagerberg in Eitner's *Bibliographie der Musik-Sammelwerke* (1877). By far his most important work was the biography of Haydn, which he undertook at the instigation of Jahn, and whose final volume was completed after his death. Although it contains errors and omissions, Pohl's work has nevertheless remained the basis for all serious Haydn biographies since its publication.

WRITINGS

Zur Geschichte der Glas-Harmonica (Vienna, 1862; Eng. trans., 1862)
Mozart und Haydn in London (Vienna, 1867)
Die Gesellschaft der Musikfreunde . . . und ihr Conservatorium (Vienna, 1871)
Denkschrift aus Anlass des hundertjährigen Bestehens der Tonkünstler-Societät . . . in Wien (Vienna, 1871)
Gebäude und Kunstsammlungen der Gesellschaft der Musikfreunde (Vienna, 1872)
Joseph Haydn (Leipzig, 1875–82; final vol., ed. H. Botstiber, Leipzig, 1927)
Denkschrift . . . des Singverein der Gesellschaft der Musikfreunde (Vienna, 1883)
Festschrift . . . der . . . Philharmonischen Concerte in Wien (Vienna, 1885)
Articles and reviews in *AMZ*, *MMR*, *Jb des Conservatorium der Gesellschaft der Musikfreunde*, *ADB*, *Grove 1* and many others

BIBLIOGRAPHY

E. Mandyczewski: 'Pohl, Karl Ferdinand', *ADB*
K. Geiringer: 'Der Brahms-Freund C. F. Pohl: unbekannte Briefe . . . an Johannes Brahms', *ZfM*, Jg.102 (1935), 397
FRANZ GEHRING/BRUCE CARR

Pohl, David. *See* POHLE, DAVID.

Pohl, Richard (*b* Leipzig, 12 Sept 1826; *d* Baden-Baden, 17 Dec 1896). German critic. After studying philosophy, chemistry and physics in Karlsruhe and Göttingen, he was given basic musical training by E. Wenzel in Leipzig. There he made friends with Schumann; he later planned an oratorio on Luther with Schumann, wrote for him the linking text for the concert version of *Manfred* and helped him with other texts. After a brief period as professor at the Johanneum in Graz, he moved to Dresden where he worked with K. F. Brendel on the *Neue Musikzeitung* (1852–4). Already a committed Wagnerian, he became the declared voice of Wagner, Liszt, Berlioz and other progressive musicians in opposition to Hanslick; all three composers were his close friends, especially during his years in Weimar (1854–64). He was an editor of the *Neue Zeitschrift für Musik*, writing under the pseudonym 'Hoplit' (doubtless a reference to the heavily-armed infantry of ancient Greece). Berlioz sought him out on a visit and arranged for him to play the cymbals in a performance of *Harold en Italie*, in which the harp was played by Pohl's first wife, the virtuoso Johanna Eyth (*b* Karlsruhe, 19 March 1824; *d* Baden-Baden, 25 Nov 1870). Liszt later expressed his gratitude for Pohl's 'faithful and noble devotion which you always showed to the Weimar Progressive Period in the years 1849–58' (letter of 12 September 1884). Wagner was appreciative of Pohl's championship; later, however, coolness arose over Pohl's published view (not denied in private) that Wagner had derived his chromatic harmony in *Tristan* from Liszt. Though not a major critic, Pohl was scrupulous and well informed and did much to arouse interest in his chosen composers. He also wrote some poetry, a novel (*Richard Wiegand*) based on Wagner, a

number of songs and instrumental pieces. In 1864 he
retired to Baden-Baden.

WRITINGS

Akustische Briefe (Leipzig, 1853)
Bayreuther Erinnerungen (Leipzig, 1877)
'Erinnerungen an Robert Schumann', *Deutsche Revue*, ii (1878), 169
Richard Wagner (Leipzig, 1883)
Gesammelte Schriften über Musik und Musiker (Leipzig, 1883–4/*R*) [3
  vols.: Wagner, Liszt, Berlioz]
Die Höhenzüge der musikalischen Entwickelung (Leipzig, 1888)
'Bülows Briefe', *Neue deutsche Rundschau*, v (1894), 446, 783
ed. L. Pohl: *Hector Berlioz's Leben und Werke* (Leipzig, 1900)
Texts for Schumann (*Manfred*) and Liszt (*Prometheus*); Ger. trans. of
  Berlioz's collected writings (Leipzig, 1864) and Saint-Saëns (*Samson
  et Dalila*)

BIBLIOGRAPHY

R. Pohl: 'Autobiographisches', *Musikalisches Wochenblatt*, xii (1881),
  3
H. R. Schäfer: *Neue Musikzeitung*, xiv (1893), 211
A. Seidl: 'Richard Pohl', *Bayreuther Blätter*, xx (1897), 116
O. Kitzler: *Musikalische Erinnerungen mit Briefen von Wagner,
  Brahms, Bruckner und Pohl* (Brno, 1904)
H. Schorn: 'Richard Pohl', *NZM*, Jg.83 (1916), 393

JOHN WARRACK

Pohle [Pohl, Pohlen, Pole, Pol, Bohle], **David** (*b*
Marienberg, nr. Chemnitz [now Karl-Marx-Stadt],
1624; *d* Merseburg, 20 Dec 1695). German composer
and instrumentalist. He received his musical training
from Schütz at Dresden. He worked for short periods at
the courts at Dresden, Merseburg (as an instrumentalist
in 1648–9), Kassel (about 1650), Weissenfels, Zeitz and
Merseburg again (all during the 1650s) before settling at
Halle, were he is listed as Konzertmeister in 1660 and
as Kapellmeister in 1661. At Halle he composed and
directed many large masses and sacred concertos at the
cathedral and wrote at least six Singspiels, most of them
to texts by the court secretary, David Elias Heidenreich.
Between 1674 and 1677 he also worked at the related
courts at Weissenfels and Zeitz. He was Kapellmeister
at Zeitz from 1678, and when the Halle court was
transferred to Weissenfels in 1680 he was replaced as its
Kapellmeister by J. P. Krieger, who in 1678 had been
appointed his assistant. He remained at Zeitz until
1682, when he moved to a similar position at
Merseburg; he remained there until his death. He published none of his music, and much of it is lost. The
earliest surviving pieces are the arias to strophic poems
by Paul Fleming composed at Kassel in 1650. All of his
other extant vocal music is sacred; it shows his strong
preference for Latin texts, both biblical and non-biblical,
which he set as concertos for few voices. In 1663–4 he
composed cantatas for the entire church year, each
consisting of a concerto based on a biblical verse combined with an aria to a strophic ode by Heidenreich. The
one extant work from this cycle, *Siehe, es hat
überwunden der Löwe*, appears to be the earliest surviving concerto-aria cantata. Pohle's sonatas are distinguished by cantabile melody, rich harmony and a dark
sound resulting from scoring that favours the middle
and lower instruments.

WORKS

SACRED LATIN VOCAL

Amo te Deus, 3vv, 3 insts, bc, *D-GMl*, *S-Uu*
Benedicam Dominum (2 versions), 2vv, 3 insts, bc, *Uu* (tablature)
Bonum est, 3vv, bc, *Uu*
Diligam te Domine, 1v, 2 insts, bc, *D-Kl*
Domine ostende, 5vv, 5 insts, bc, *S-Uu*; ed. B. Grusnick (Stuttgart,
  1975)
Domine quis, 4vv, 5 insts, bc, *Uu*
In te Domine speravi, 3vv, 3 insts, bc, *Uu*
Jesus auctor, 3vv, 2 insts, bc, *Uu*
Jesu care, 1v, 2 insts, bc, *Uu*

Miserere mei Deus, 5vv, 5 insts, bc, *D-Kl*
Nascitur Immanuel, 5vv, 5 insts, bc, *GMl*
Oculi mei, 3vv, 2 insts, bc, *S-Uu*
Paratum cor, 1v, 2 insts, bc, *Uu*
Te sanctum, 5vv, 7 insts, bc, *Uu*
Tulerunt Dominum, dialogue, 6vv, 6 insts, bc, *Uu*
Verbum caro factum est, 3vv, 2 insts, bc, *Uu*
Vox Domini, 1v, 2 insts, bc, *Uu*

SACRED GERMAN VOCAL

Der Engel des Herrn, 4vv, 4 insts, bc, *Uu* (tablature)
Es wird ein Stern aus Jacob aufgehen, 4vv, 3 insts, bc, *D-B*
Herr, wenn ich nur dich habe, 1v, 5 insts, bc, *B*
Herr, wenn ich nur dich habe, 3vv, 3 insts, bc, *S-Uu*; ed. H. J. Moser
  (Stuttgart, 1964)
Ihr Völker bringet her, 3vv, 3 insts, bc, *D-B*
Jesu, meine Freude, 4vv, 3 insts, bc, *B*
Nur in meines Jesu Wunden, 6vv, 6 insts, bc, *S-Uu*
Siehe, es hat überwunden der Löwe, 5vv, 7 insts, bc, *D-B*
Wie der Hirsch schreiet, 1v, 3 insts, bc, *S-Uu*; ed H. Winter (Hamburg,
  1965)

For lost works see Serauky

SECULAR VOCAL

13 arias (P. Fleming), 2vv, 2 vn, bc, 1650, *D-Kl*; 12 ed. W. Gurlitt,
  David Pohle: Zwölf Liebesgesänge nach Paul Flemming (Kassel,
  1938)
Kein Augenblick vergeht, madrigal, 3vv, bc, *S-Uu*
Marindchen, du siehst hold und schöne, aria, 2vv, 5 insts, bc, *Uu*
Weiss und Schwarz, 2vv, 2 insts, bc, *Uu*

SINGSPIELS

(all lost; librettos mostly by D. E. Heidenreich)
Liebe krönt Eintracht, 1669; Der singende Hof-Mann Daniel, 1671;
  Aspasia, 1672; Der glückselige Liebes-Fehl Prinz Walrams aus
  Sachsen, 1673; Der verliebte Mörder Herodes, 1673; Das ungereimte
  Paar Venus und Vulcanus, 1679

INSTRUMENTAL

25 sonatas, a 4–8, bc, *D-Kl*, *S-Uu*; Sonata a 8, C, ed. H. Winter
  (Hamburg, 1965), Sonata a 6, F, ed. H. Winter (Hamburg, 1968)
2 suites, a 4, *D-Kl*; 1 ed. J. Ecorcheville, *Vingt suites d'orchestre du
  dix-septième siècle français* (Paris and Berlin, 1906/*R*1970)
Ballet, *PL-GD* (lute tablature)

BIBLIOGRAPHY

E. H. Meyer: *Die mehrstimmige Spielmusik des 17. Jahrhunderts in
  Nord- und Mitteleuropa* (Kassel, 1934)
W. Serauky: *Musikgeschichte der Stadt Halle*, ii/1 (Halle and Berlin,
  1939/*R*1970)
C. Engelbrecht: *Die Kasseler Hofkapelle im 17. Jahrhundert* (Kassel,
  1958)
F. Krummacher: *Die Überlieferung der Choralbearbeitungen in der
  frühen evangelischen Kantate* (Berlin, 1965)
G. Gille: *Der Schützschüler David Pohle (1624–1695): seine
  Bedeutung für die deutsche Musikgeschichte des 17. Jahrhunderts*
  (diss., U. of Halle, 1973)
——: 'Die geistliche Vokalmusik David Pohles (1624–1695)', *Musik
  und Kirche*, xlv (1975), 64

KERALA JOHNSON SNYDER

Pohlmann, Johannes (*fl* 1767–93). English harpsichord
and piano maker, of German origin. He worked in
London, first in Compton Street, Soho, and later at 113
Great Russell Street, Bloomsbury. He was one of the
instrument makers known as the '12 Apostles' who
emigrated from Germany after the Seven Years War.
Pohlmann was probably the second piano maker in
London after JOHANNES ZUMPE, building similar
instruments to Zumpe's and filling the orders Zumpe
could not handle. No harpsichords by him survive, and
his earliest known piano is a square one dated 1767. His
pianos usually have a range of five octaves, *F'–f'''* (some
missing *G♯'*); early instruments by him with the shorter
compass *G'–f'''* are also known (Brussels Conservatoire
collection). His pianos include two hand stops to raise
the dampers in the treble and the bass; occasionally
there is a third, to operate the 'lute'. A half-blow
mechanism, where the hammer's resting-point is raised
nearer to the strings, is found in some of his pianos; the
sound it produces is disappointing and it was never
generally adopted. Pohlmann appears to have made only

square pianos in which the English single action with overdampers was used.

BIBLIOGRAPHY

E. F. Rimbault: *The Pianoforte: its Origins, Progress and Construction* (London, 1860)

R. E. M. Harding: *The Piano-forte: its History Traced to the Great Exhibition of 1851* (London, 1933, rev. 2/1978)

A. Loesser: *Men, Women and Pianos: a Social History* (New York, 1954)

MARGARET CRANMER

Poikilorgue. A free-reed instrument built by Cavaillé-Coll in 1834; *see* HARMONIUM.

Point [pointe, poynte, poyncte]. An English term in use from the 16th century to the beginning of the 18th signifying a motif, or more generally a theme, suitable for treatment in an imitative style, and by extension a piece or passage in such a style. Butler (*Principles of Musik*, 1636) defined the point as 'a certain number and order of observable Notes in any one Part, iterated in the same or in divers Parts: within the time commonly of two Sem[i]briefs in quick Sonnets, and of four or five in graver Musik'. The word was apparently derived from the Italian *punto*, which was used in the same sense by Nicola Vicentino in his *L'antica musica ridotta alla moderna prattica* (1555), and perhaps ultimately from the Latin PUNCTUM, used by some medieval theorists (Anonymous IV, Johannes de Grocheo) to designate individual phrases or sections of a piece.

In discussing 'fuga' (i.e. imitation) Morley (1597) observed that the 'way of two or three several points going together is the most artificial kind of composing which hath been invented either for Motets or Madrigals'; the maintenance of a point in imitative writing could justify certain technical irregularities, but it was 'better to leave the point and follow none at all than for the point's sake . . . make . . . hard unpleasant music, for music was devised to content and not offend the ear'. Writers such as John Coprario (*Rules how to Compose*, c1610), Christopher Simpson (*A Compendium of Practical Music*, 1667), and Roger North (early 18th century) used the term in a similar way when discussing imitation, but in his *Division Viol* (1659) Simpson also stressed the importance of sometimes developing a point in making divisions on a bass: here he was clearly thinking of a point as a motif rather than as a theme for imitative treatment.

The Mulliner Book (MB, i) contains six pieces with the title 'Point', one each by Sheppard and Tallis and four anonymous pieces perhaps by Mulliner himself though sometimes attributed to Redford. With the exception of Tallis's piece, which is somewhat more extended, they are simply extremely short fugues with one entry in each part. It was rare at this period in instrumental music for a single theme to dominate an extended imitative piece, and even in the next century a piece 45 bars long by Tomkins bears the title 'A substantial verse maintaining the point' (MB, v, no.31). One lyra viol tablature (*GB-Mp*) contains an anonymous 'point or prelud[ium] to be playde before the Lancashire pipes'. This is not an imitative piece but merely develops the motif stated at the outset.

The term 'point' (and its German equivalent *Punkt*) is still used with reference to 16th-century music. A section of music generated by the imitative treatment of a motif is commonly called a 'point of imitation', and the

motets of Gombert, Crecquillon and their contemporaries are said to be made up of several such 'points', usually eliding one with the next (see HAM, no.114).

BIBLIOGRAPHY

C. van den Borren: *Les origines de la musique de clavier en Angleterre* (Brussels, 1912; Eng. trans., 1913), 11

J. Caldwell: *English Keyboard Music Before the Nineteenth Century* (Oxford, 1973), 57

MICHAEL TILMOUTH

Point d'orgue (Fr.). (1) A harmonic pedal or PEDAL POINT or ORGAN POINT.

(2) A pause or FERMATA.

(3) A cadenza such as is commonly implied by a fermata in appropriate situations, for example in concertos.

Pointer (Fr.). In French music of the 17th and 18th centuries, *pointer* requires that notes (especially quavers) written as equal be played 'dotted', so that the first of the series is lengthened, the second decreased by as much (e.g. a dotted quaver followed by a semiquaver). As late as 1768 Rousseau gave substantially this definition (*Dictionnaire*, article 'Pointer'). However, he distinguished between French and Italian usage: while (he wrote) the French 'point', as a matter of course, those notes written as equal, the Italians play the notes as written (i.e. as equal) unless the specific term *pointé* is given in the music. In this sense *pointer* is a species of *notes inégales*. For another meaning of *pointer* ('separated'), *see* PIQUER.

DAVID D. BOYDEN

Poise, (Jean Alexandre) Ferdinand (*b* Nîmes, 3 June 1828; *d* Paris, 13 May 1892). French composer. He studied under Adam at the Paris Conservatoire and gained second place in the Prix de Rome of 1852. He devoted himself immediately to *opéra comique*, and found popularity for his works by exploiting a gift for unpretentious melody. His *La surprise de l'amour* was specially admired and successful. In 1867 he arranged and reorchestrated Philidor's *Le sorcier* for a Parisian revival.

WORKS

Unless otherwise stated, all *opéras comiques*, first performed in Paris and published (vocal score) in same year.

BP – *Bouffes-Parisiens*; OC – *Opéra-Comique*; TL – *Théâtre-Lyrique*

Bonsoir, voisin (1, Brunswick, A. de Beauplan), TL, 18 Sept 1853 (1854)

Les charmeurs (1, M. de Leuven), TL, 17 March 1855

Thé de Polichinelle (1, E. Plouvier), BP, 4 March 1856, not pubd

Le roi Don Pèdre (2, Cormon, E. Grangé), OC, 30 Sept 1857

Le jardinier galant (2, de Leuven, Siraudin), OC, 4 March 1861

1 piece for La poularde de Caux, Palais-Royal, 17 May 1861; collab. Bazille, Clapisson, Gautier, Gevaert, Mangeant

Les absents (1, A. Daudet), OC, 26 Oct 1864

Jean Noël (1, E. Dubreuil), 1865, not perf., pubd (vocal score) in *Le magasin des demoiselles*

Les moissonneurs (cantata), OC, 15 Aug 1866, not pubd

Le corricolo (3, Labiche, Delacour), OC, 28 Nov 1868, not pubd

Les deux billets (1, J. P. de Florian), Athénée, 19 Feb 1870

Les trois souhaits (1, J. Adenis), OC, 29 Oct 1873

La surprise de l'amour (2, C. Monselet, after Marivaux), OC, 31 Oct 1877

La cigale et la fourmi (1, A. Beaumont, after Lafontaine), 1877, not perf., pubd (vocal score) in *Le magasin des demoiselles*

La dame de compagnie (1, Beaumont), 1877, not perf., pubd (vocal score) in *Le magasin des demoiselles*

L'amour médecin (3, Monselet, after Molière), OC, 20 Dec 1880

La reine d'une heure (1, Beaumont), not perf., pubd (vocal score) in *Le magasin des demoiselles*

Le médecin malgré lui (after Molière), 1887, not pubd

Carmosine, Monte Carlo, 1928

Cécile, oratorio, Dijon, 1888
Several choruses, 4 male vv, cited in *FétisB*; songs

DAVID CHARLTON

Poissl, Johann Nepomuk, Freiherr von (*b* Haukenzell, Lower Bavaria, 15 Feb 1783; *d* Munich, 17 Aug 1865). German composer. He came from an aristocratic family of Lower Bavaria and the Upper Palatinate and was the son of an electoral chamberlain. After attending school in Straubing and Munich, he went to the University of Landshut in 1800; he devoted himself entirely to musical studies. In 1805 he took up permanent residence in Munich, where he met Danzi (then still assistant Kapellmeister at the Munich Court Opera) and the Abbé Vogler, both of whom taught him composition and gave him decisive encouragement. As early as 1806 he came before the public with a comic opera, *Die Opernprobe*, although he had considerably more success with the serious opera *Antigonus* two years later and with the *dramma eroico Ottaviano in Sicilia* in 1812. His meeting with Weber (1811) was as important for his artistic development as was his contact with Danzi; from the intellectual rapport between the three artists there rapidly grew a genuine and mutually beneficial friendship. Later, as an opera conductor in Prague and Dresden, Weber continued to champion Poissl's works.

Despite increasing success, which reached a peak with the grand operas *Athalia* (1814) and *Der Wettkampf zu Olympia* (1815), both acclaimed in Munich and other German towns, Poissl found himself for many years in impoverished circumstances as an independent composer with a large family to support; in order to hold his own, he was repeatedly compelled to rely on gratuities and the support of the King of Bavaria. But his hopes for a position at the Darmstadt theatre, for which he had composed the successful *Nittetis* (1817) and also *Issipile* (not performed), were not fulfilled; and he had to wait until he was 40 for an appointment at the Munich Opera, for which he had long hoped. Finally in 1823 he was made assistant superintendent of court music, and two years later was also entrusted with the court theatre directorship, a post which brought him 4500 florins annually. Yet only eight years later he was forced to yield to a successor, Theodor von Küstner; although his superiors were perfectly satisfied with the artistic qualities and intentions of his planning of the repertory, they were by no means happy about the theatre's dwindling receipts and mounting debts under his management. He was left with directing only court music until 1847, when he was named first chamberlain and dismissed. During his tenure at the court theatre he seldom had his own operas performed. His still popular magical opera *Die Prinzessin von Provence* (with whose première the Nationaltheater, rebuilt after the great fire of 1823, reopened in 1825) and the two Romantic operas *Der Untersberg* (1829) and *Zaide* (1843) constitute the last examples of his work for the stage. He spent the last years of his life again in poverty, oppressed by illness and family worries. When he died, his life's work as a musical dramatist had long been forgotten.

Poissl's works, though constructed with assured skill and in many details valuable, interesting and prophetic, nevertheless lack originality. However, seen in the context of the history of opera, he was a significant figure in the evolutionary phase between Mozart and Weber and a noteworthy representative of that transitional period which was marked in Germany by the efforts of various composers to overcome all reliance on Italian and French models and to strive towards an independent German through-composed grand opera. Alongside such powerful works as Weber's *Der Freischütz* and *Euryanthe*, Poissl too made notable contributions; the high esteem in which his operas were held during the years of his best work is evidenced by the widespread performances of many of his stage works and by many admiring contemporary judgments, above all Weber's description of Poissl's musical language in the introduction he wrote for the Dresden performance of *Der Wettkampf zu Olympia* (1820): 'Especially characteristic of Baron Poissl – besides the great attention he gives to declamation, his rich harmonic sequences and his apt and varied scoring – is his flowing, clearly constructed melodic style which is not only delicate but has the added virtue of being extremely singable.' Earlier (1814), Weber had recommended *Athalia* to the Prague public in similar terms; at the time, the work was extolled by the newspapers as 'German grand opera' and, indeed, a 'national achievement'.

Poissl also wrote incidental music for the stage and insertions to operas by other composers; he composed various sacred musical works (including three masses), cantatas, oratorios, a series of concertante instrumental compositions, and songs, duets and canzonets with piano accompaniment. He was a gifted author, and was in advance of his time in that most of his opera librettos were his own work, many of them adaptations of Metastasio. He produced metrical translations of plays, including a German adaptation of Racine's *Andromaque* which was performed in Stuttgart in 1815. In 1820 he took over the position of Munich correspondent for the Viennese *Allgemeine musikalische Zeitung*. His essays include ideas on the direction of the German court theatre and recommendations for the foundation of a society for the benefit of theatre poets and composers.

WORKS

MSS in *D-Mbs*; except where otherwise indicated, operas and incidental music first performed at Court Opera, Munich.

OPERAS

Die Opernprobe (comic opera, 2, Poissl, after It. lib), 23 Feb 1806

Antigonus (3, Poissl, after Metastasio), 12 Feb 1808

Ottaviano in Sicilia (dramma eroico, 3, Poissl, after Metastasio), 30 June 1812, ov. pubd

Aucassin und Nicolette (Singspiel, 3, F. K. Hiemer, after Sedaine), 28 March 1813

Athalia (grand opera, 3, G. Wohlbrück, after Racine), 3 June 1814, ov. pubd

Der Wettkampf zu Olympia oder Die Freunde (grand opera, 3, Poissl, after Metastasio), 21 April 1815, ov. pubd

Dir wie mir oder Alle betrügen (comic opera, 2, von Zahlhans), 1816, unperf.

Nittetis (grand opera, 3, Poissl, after Metastasio), Darmstadt, 29 June 1817

Issipile (grand opera, Poissl, after Metastasio), 1818, unperf.

La rappresaglia (opera semiseria, 2, Poissl, after F. Romani), 7 April 1820

Die Prinzessin von Provence (magical opera, 3, Poissl, after Romani), 23 Jan 1825

Der Untersberg (romantic opera, 3, E. von Schenk), 30 Oct 1829

Zaide (romantic-tragic opera, 4, Poissl), 9 Nov 1843

Additions to operas by Dittersdorf, Nasolini, Pilotti, Rossini

INCIDENTAL MUSIC

Renata (F. Heyden), 12 Oct 1823

Belisar (von Schenk), 23 Feb 1826

Kaiser Ludwigs Traum (Festspiel, von Schenk), 27 March 1826

Hermannschlacht (Kleist), 1 double chorus, 1826, ?unperf.

ORATORIOS AND SACRED CHORAL

Méhuls Gedächtnisfeyer (J. Sendtner), Munich, 22 Dec 1817

Judith (oratorio), excerpts perf. Munich, 11 April 1824

Der Erntetag (oratorio, Poissl), Munich, 4 April 1835

3 masses: C, 1812, A♭, c1816, E♭, 1817; Stabat mater, 8vv (Munich, 1821); Miserere, 8vv, 1824, arr. 6vv, 1833; Ps xcv, solo vv, chorus, orch; Omnes gentes, off, S, chorus, orch; Salve regina, 8vv

OTHER VOCAL

Der Sommertag (pastoral cantata, ?Poissl), Munich, March 1814
Die Macht des Herrn (cantata, F. Bruckbräu), Munich, 21 April 1826
Vergangenheit und Zukunft (dramatic poem, Poissl), Munich, 30 Nov 1832
Ein baierisches Volkslied (Sendtner), chorus, 1824; arias and duets, 1–2vv, orch; 10 canzonettas, 1–3vv, pf, 4 pubd (Munich, n.d.); songs, 1–2vv, pf

INSTRUMENTAL

Concs., incl. Cl Conc., 1812; Vc Conc., 1817 (Leipzig, 1818)
Harmoniemusik für die königliche Tafelmusik, c1845 [after Donizetti, Auber and I. Lachner]
6 variations, vn, bn, hpd

BIBLIOGRAPHY

M. M. von Weber: *Carl Maria von Weber* (Leipzig, 1864–6)
C. M. von Weber: *Sämtliche Schriften* (Leipzig, 1908)
E. Reipschläger: *Schubaur, Danzi und Poissl als Opernkomponisten* (diss., U. of Rostock, 1911; Berlin, 1911)
M. Zenger: *Geschichte der Münchener Oper* (Munich, 1923)
E. Bücken: *Der heroische Stil in der Oper* (Leipzig, 1924)
L. Schrott: 'Aus dem Ringen um die deutsche Oper', *Die Musik*, xxxii (1939–40), 299

ANTON WÜRZ

Poisson, Jakub Jan. See RYBA, JAKUB JAN.

Poitevin, Guillaume (*b* Boulbon, nr. Arles, 2 Oct 1646; *d* Aix-en-Provence, 26 Jan 1706). French composer. He was trained as a choirboy at St Trophime, Arles. On 17 November 1663 he was engaged to serve the Cathedral of St Sauveur, Aix-en-Provence, on the strength of his serpent playing. He received the tonsure on 8 March 1665 and on 23 April 1667 was named *maître de musique* of the cathedral. He was ordained on 2 April 1672 and became a prebendary of St Sauveur on 14 May 1677. At his request he retired from his post on 4 May 1693 and was succeeded by his pupil Jean Gilles, who was in turn followed by Jacques Cabassol. On 5 May 1698 at the chapter's request he returned to his post and held it until his death. The successes of his students indicate that he must have been an able teacher. Two of his pupils, Campra and Blanchard, served in the royal chapel, and two others, Gilles and Belissen, had distinguished careers in the cities of Toulouse and Marseilles respectively.

Poitevin's few extant works reveal a mastery of harmony and counterpoint. The requiem attributed to him is rich in prepared dissonances and chromatic movement, more so than the mass fragments. His word-setting is generally syllabic, with occasional melismas on appropriate words such as 'laudamus', 'gloria' and 'ascendit'. Though none of the extant works requires instruments beyond the basso continuo, a list at Arles mentions a lost *Dixit en symphonie*, evidence that he, like his students, composed works with orchestra.

WORKS

Fragments of four masses, 4vv, *F-AIXmc*: Messe 'Ave Maria'; Messe 'Speciosa facta es'; Messe 'Benedicta tu'; Messe 'Dominus tecum'
Messe des morts, 4vv, bc; edn. (Paris, 1962)
De profundis and Libera me, both 4vv, bc, *AIXmc*
3 Dixit en symphonie, lost

BIBLIOGRAPHY

J. Bougerel: *Mémoires pour servir à l'histoire de plusieurs hommes illustres de Provence* (Paris, 1752)
C. F. Achard: *Dictionnaire de la Provence et du Comté-venaissin*, iv (Marseilles, 1787), 98
E. Marbot: *Gal et Guillaume Poitevin* (Aix-en-Provence, 1887)
S. d'Arve: *Miettes de l'histoire de Provence* (Marseilles, 1902)
L. de La Laurencie: 'Notes sur la jeunesse d'André Campra', *SIMG*, x (1908–9), 159
F. Raugel: 'La maîtrise de la cathédrale d'Aix-en-Provence', *Bulletin de la Société d'étude du XVIIe siècle*, xxi–xxii (1954), 422

——: 'La maîtrise et les orgues de la primatiale St. Trophime d'Arles', *RMFC*, ii (1961–2), 105, 115
M. Frémiot: 'L'école provençale', *Encyclopédie des musiques sacrées*, ed. J. Porte, ii (Paris, 1969), 544

JOHN H. HAJDU

Poitiers. French university city, capital of Poitou. Poitiers is richly endowed with sacred buildings whose organs are well equipped to meet the varied requirements of all organ music, with the possible exception of the early Baroque period. The well-known cathedral organ, built by François-Henri Clicquot (author of the treatise *Théorie pratique de la facture de l'orgue*, 1789), is in a perfect state of preservation and specially suited to the performance of French Classical organ music.

Although the existence of numerous church organs has prompted frequent concerts of sacred music, the main musical life of Poitiers is concentrated in the Théâtre Municipal (which has 900 seats) and in two halls (with 650 and 450 seats respectively), which are suitable for recitals and chamber music. The Orchestre de Chambre de Poitiers, consisting of 15 string players, is the only professional instrumental ensemble in the city and has toured in France and abroad. There is also an amateur string ensemble (the Orchestre J. S. Bach) and a municipal wind band.

Choral singing is cultivated by numerous amateur choirs. The most noteworthy are the Rencontres Musicales de Poitiers, the Jeunesses Musicales de France, the Amis de l'Orgue and the Collegium Musicae Antiquae. This last body, an ensemble which uses old instruments, is attached to the university and directed by Antoine Geoffroy-Dechaume.

The chief concern of the Conservatoire de Musique et de Danse (1100 students in the early 1970s) is the education of those who intend to go on to the Paris Conservatoire; there are, however, other pupils in its 'amateur' section. The Institut de Musicologie at the university specializes in the study of medieval music.

As a regional capital Poitiers is the centre of musical education and concert promotion for the four départements that make up the region. It is also the home of the celebrated organ builder Jean Boisseau, and at least four well-known composers were born or have lived there: Hilaire Penet (*fl* early 16th century), Michel Lambert (1610–96), Louis Vierne (1870–1937) and Pierre Petit (*b* 1932).

BIBLIOGRAPHY

R. Favreau: 'Orgues et psallettes à Poitiers à la fin du Moyen Age', *Bulletin de la Société des antiquaires de l'Ouest et des musées de Poitiers*, xii (1973), 47

LUCIEN JEAN-BAPTISTE

Pokorny [Pokorný]. The name of a large number of Bohemian musicians and composers of the 18th and 19th centuries; Dlabač mentioned 12 of them. Because the name (meaning 'humble') is so common, it is impossible to establish whether all the musicians who bore it were related. The most important of them, Franz Xaver (Thomas) Pokorny (1729–94), is considered separately below (with his sons Bonifaz, 1757–89, and Joseph Franz, *b* c1760).

Jan Pokorny (*b* Milevsko, 16 May 1689; *d* Bechyně, 27 Dec 1783) was a singer at the Premonstratensian church of St Benedict at Prague from 1697 to 1700, and then choral director and organist at Bechyně for 40 years; he may have been a composer. Václav Pichl was one of his pupils. In about 1789 his son Josef was organist and director of music at Pont-à-Mousson, near

Metz in France. František Pokorny (*b* ?Vlasim; *d* Ronov, 13 Aug 1797) studied at Prague in about 1750 and later took a post as organist at Ronov where he was also active as a teacher. He composed a number of sacred works. Gotthard Pokorny (*b* Český Brod, 16 Nov 1733; *d* Brno, 4 Aug 1802) was first employed as a school assistant in his home town; from 1760 he was conductor at the cathedral of St Peter at Brno. He composed church music, violin concertos and other works.

Stephan Johann Pokorny (*b* Chrudim, *c*1740; *d* Vienna, 1792) studied at Německý Brod from 1755 to 1760; he then entered the Augustinian order at Prague and became a pupil of Kajetan Mara. From 1780 he was organist of an Augustinian monastery in Vienna. Johann Ferdinand Pokorny (*b* Koloveč u Domažlic, 1797; *d* Jihlava, 3 March 1870) was the son of a teacher and studied at Prague; he later became a singer at the Premonstratensian monastery at Strahov near Prague. In 1819 he became director of a new music society in Jihlava where, for more than 20 years, he conducted the theatre orchestra in performances of operas by Mozart, Weber and others; from 1836 he was also director of the choir. His manuscript *Geschichtliche Skizze des Musikvereins in der k.k. Stadt Iglau* (in the collection of the Männergesangverein, Jihlava) contains the programmes of all his concerts.

Franz [František Xaver Jan] Pokorny (*b* Lstiboř [now Ctiboř, Benešov district], 22 Dec 1797; *d* Meidling, nr. Vienna, 7 Aug 1850) was the son of a teacher. In 1819 he joined the orchestra of the Josefstadt Theater in Vienna as a clarinettist and from 1822 he played in theatre orchestras in Pressburg (now Bratislava) and Baden. In 1827 he became conductor of the theatre orchestra in Pressburg and in 1835 director of the theatre. In 1836 he also took over direction of the theatre in Baden, and in 1837 that of the Josefstadt Theater. His opera company performed at Pressburg during the winter, at Vienna in the spring and at Baden in the summer. In 1845 he acquired the Theater an der Wien and he soon resigned all his directing posts except those in Vienna. His main interest was the narrative Singspiel, the most successful of which, performed under his direction, was *Der Zauberschleier* (1842) by his conductor A. E. Titl. Other conductors engaged by Pokorny included Suppé and Lortzing. Johann Baptist Pokorny (*d* Munich, after 1840) was a pupil of Fracassini, and entered the service of the Bamberg court some time before 1796. In that year he became a court musician, in 1800 was appointed assistant director of music, and in 1802 director of music at the court. After the dissolution of the Kapelle he became conductor of the music society.

A number of masses, litanies, Rorate, *Te Deum* and *Regina coeli* settings, offertories and Czech pastorellas (in *CS-Pnm* and many church libraries) are attributed simply to Pokorny.

BIBLIOGRAPHY
ČSHS; *EitnerQ*; *GerberNL*

G. J. Dlabacž: *Allgemeines historisches Künstler-Lexikon* (Prague, 1815/*R*1973)

C. von Wurzbach: *Biographisches Lexikon des Kaiserthums Oesterreich* (Vienna, 1856–91)

Z. Nejedlý: *Bedřich Smetana*, ii (Prague, 1925, rev., enlarged 2/1951 [as vol.iii])

K. Benyovsky: *Das alte Theater* (Bratislava, 1926)

O. Rommel: *Die Alt-Wiener Volkskomedie* (Vienna, 1952)

B. R. Schimscha: *Das Josefstädtertheater als Operbühne* (diss., U. of Vienna, 1965)

TOMISLAV VOLEK

Pokorny [Pokorný, Pockorny], **Franz** [František] **Xaver** **(Thomas)** (*b* Mies [now Stříbro, Czechoslovakia], 20 Dec 1729; *d* Regensburg, 2 July 1794). Bohemian composer. He may have been related to other Bohemian musicians named Pokorny. In the early 1750s, after studying at Regensburg with Riepel, he was sent by Count Philipp Karl of Oettingen-Wallerstein for further study with Johann Stamitz, Richter and Holzbauer at Mannheim. In March 1754 Pokorny had to return to Wallerstein where his services were required in the Kapelle. In November 1754 he was promised the position of choral director but this failed to materialize, despite a petition of 12 May 1766. On 13 July 1766 he submitted a symphony to the court of Thurn and Taxis at Regensburg with an application for admission to the royal Kapelle. His inclusion in a salary list of the Kapelle for the same year shows that his application was successful. His gravestone describes him as a musician of the royal chamber.

Of the considerable number of works attributed to Pokorny, many can be identified as the work of other composers. Conflicting attributions exist for 57 symphonies (see LaRue) and only a few works can be authenticated by details of place and date. Pokorny's symphonies are mostly in four movements and are usually scored for strings, two flutes and two horns (oboes, trumpets, timpani and clarinets are used only occasionally). His music contains a strong element of popular melody, which is expanded by sequential methods rather than by true thematic development.

Pokorny's son Bonifaz (Franz Xaver Karl) (*b* Wallerstein, 24 Jan 1757; *d* Scheyern Abbey, 5 Aug 1789) took vows at Scheyern Abbey in 1780 and was ordained a priest in 1783. As *regens chori*, organist and teacher he became one of the abbey's leading musicians. None of his compositions has survived. Another son, Joseph Franz (*b* Regensburg, *c*1760), is mentioned in Eitner and Mettenleiter as a musician employed at the court of Thurn and Taxis at Regensburg, though his name does not appear in the court records. The horn virtuoso Beate Pokorny, who achieved great success at the Concert Spirituel in Paris in 1780, was not the daughter of Franz Xaver Pokorny, as is sometimes stated, but she may have been his sister.

WORKS
(attribution often uncertain)

Orch: *c*100 syms., *D-DO*, *HR*, *Rtt*, *SI*, 1 ed. in DTÖ, xxxi, Jg.xv/2 (1908/*R*) attrib. G. M. Monn; *c*50 hpd concs., *Rtt*; fl conc., ed. in NM, clxxii (1954) attrib. Boccherini; 2 cl concs., *Rtt*, ed. in EDM, 1st ser., xli (1957); 2 ob concs., hn conc., 3 concs. for 2 hn, *Rtt*; Concerto da camera a 6, E♭, *Rtt*; serenades, marches, dances, *Rtt*

Chamber: str qt, *SI*; trio, 2 vn, b, *SI*; sonata, hpd, str, *Rtt*

BIBLIOGRAPHY
EitnerQ

D. Mettenleiter: *Musikgeschichte der Stadt Regensburg* (Regensburg, 1866)

L. Schiedermair: 'Die Blütezeit der Oettingen-Wallerstein'schen Hofkapelle', *SIMG*, ix (1907–8), 83–130

H. Becker: 'Zur Geschichte der Klarinette im 18. Jahrhundert', *Mf*, viii (1955), 271

R. Quoika: *Musik und Musikpflege in der Benediktinerabtei Scheyern* (Munich, 1958) [refers to Bonifaz Pokorny]

J. LaRue: 'Major and Minor Mysteries of Identification in the 18th-century Symphony', *JAMS*, xiii (1960), 181

J. M. Barbour: 'Pokorny Vindicated', *MQ*, xlix (1963), 38

based on *MGG* (x, 1380–82) by permission of Bärenreiter

AUGUST SCHARNAGL

Pol. *See* POLICKI.

Pol, David. *See* POHLE, DAVID.

Polacca (It.: 'Polish'). A term applied to compositions in a Polish style ('alla polacca'); it is usually taken as the Italian equivalent of POLONAISE. The term was used by Bach (Brandenburg Concerto no.1, finale) and Telemann (Concerto in F, DDT, xxix–xxx); in the 19th century it came to be applied to instrumental or vocal pieces related tenuously or not at all to the polonaise, for example Schubert's setting of Scott's 'Lay of the Imprisoned Huntsman' from *The Lady of the Lake* (D843). Instrumental polaccas are often showy and ornate, gaining in brilliance what they lose in national character. Thus Chopin in a letter to Tytus Woyciechowski (14 November 1829) wrote of his 'alla polacca' with cello accompaniment op.3 as 'nothing more than a brilliant drawing-room piece – suitable for the ladies'; evidently he did not put it in the same class as his polonaises, even of that early period.

Polaccas frequently appeared in 19th-century operas, usually as vocal bravura pieces, or as cheerful concerted numbers, for example those in Bellini's *I puritani* and Rossini's *Il barbiere di Siviglia* (the finale). Instrumental movements with the designation 'alla polacca' also occur, like the finale of Sibelius's Violin Concerto.

WILLIAM BARCLAY SQUIRE/MAURICE J. E. BROWN

Polacchina, La. *See* COSTANTINI, LIVIA.

Polacco, Giorgio (*b* Venice, 12 April 1875; *d* New York, 30 April 1960). Italian conductor. After studies in Venice, at the Milan Conservatory, and in St Petersburg, he was engaged as an assistant at Covent Garden in 1890 and made his début the next year at the Shaftesbury Theatre, conducting Gluck's *Orfeo ed Euridice*. He quickly became a successful opera conductor in many European cities, in Russia and in South America (including four seasons in Buenos Aires and seven in Rio de Janeiro), and conducted for Tetrazzini's American début in 1905 in Mexico and San Francisco. In 1911 he directed the first English production in the USA of Puccini's *La fanciulla del West* by the Savage company and took the production on tour in the USA; he made his Metropolitan début the next year. There he remained, succeeding Toscanini in charge of the Italian repertory, until 1917. He conducted in Chicago (1918–19) and returned there in 1921 from Europe at the invitation of Mary Garden; the Chicago Civic Opera was formed in 1922, and Polacco was principal conductor until ill-health forced him to retire in 1930. His performances were noted for precision and vigour and, in addition to Wagner and Italian operas, he became a leading conductor of French opera under Garden's influence at Chicago. He appeared at Covent Garden in 1912–13, and made his last appearances there, in 1930, conducting *Pelléas et Mélisande* with Maggie Teyte, who, in her autobiography (1958), described him as that opera's 'ideal interpreter'.

RICHARD D. FLETCHER

Polaczek, Dietmar (*b* Bendsburg [now Będzin, Poland], 26 Oct 1942). German music critic and composer. He began studying architecture (1961–5) and then changed to musicology with Wessely and art history with Franz at Graz University (1965–71) while also studying the violin, viola, organ and composition. He won the first prize for composition in 1964 at the International Youth Music Festival, Innsbruck, and in 1969 and 1970 took part in the Darmstadt summer courses for new music. Polaczek was arts editor of the *Neue Zeit* (Graz) in 1967–8; in 1971 he began working as a freelance composer and journalist in Munich, writing reviews and theoretical essays on contemporary music for the *Süddeutsche Zeitung, Melos, Musica* and other German, Austrian and Swiss newspapers, and in 1976 he was appointed music critic of the *Frankfurter Allgemeine Zeitung*. He is also known as a broadcaster.

WORKS
(selective list)

5 analoge Sonatinen, vn, pf, 1963; Variazioni della moderna, pf, 1963; Duellett, vn, pf, 1964; Laternengesänge, 1v, pf, 1964; Vernissage septenaire, orch, 1964; Concertino, str, 1964–5; Partita 'Christ ist erstanden', org, 1963–5; Metamorfosen und Fuge, gui, 1965; Lesabéndio, wind qnt, 1966; Lobgesang (Brecht), chorus, 9 insts, 1966; Pf Conc., pf, 6 sax, 6 trbn, 4 timp, str, 1967–8; Die Reihenreihe, fl, 1968; Applaus I–II, conductor, speaker, chorus, 2 perc, public, 1969–70; Kleine Gebläsemusik, S, T, B, harmonium, positive org, 6 wind, 1968–73

Principal publisher: Modern Edition (Munich), Universal (Vienna)

ALFRED GRANT GOODMAN

Polak, Jakub. *See* REYS, JAKUB.

Polak, Jan. *See* POLONUS, JOHANNES.

Poland (Pol. Polska). Republic in eastern Europe. Christianity was introduced in the late 10th century, and in 1025 Bolesław I became the country's first king. With the death of Bolesław III (1138) the kingdom was divided into principalities and was threatened by outside powers, but it was reunited in the 14th century by Wladisław I and his son Kasimir the Great. By the Union of Lublin (1569) Poland absorbed Lithuania, thus reaching its maximum extent, and subsequently prospered both economically and culturally. In the 18th century the country was attacked by both Sweden and Russia, losing considerable territory; by the First Partition of Poland (1772) much of the country became West Prussia, while Lithuania was lost to Russia and Galicia to Austria. By the Second Partition (1793) further territory was lost and the country was reduced to a third of its former size; with the Third Partition (1795) the remaining territory was divided between Russia, Prussia and Austria. A result of the constant interchanges of domination of parts of present-day Poland, notably Silesia, Pomerania and West Prussia, is that at times they have partaken of German cultural traditions, especially such cities as Wrocław (Breslau), Gdańsk (Danzig), Szczecin (Stettin) and Legnica (Liegnitz); while L'vov (Pol. Lwów; Ger. Lemberg), now in the Ukrainian SSR, has partly Polish traditions.

There were suppressed insurrections and changes of territory during the 19th century, but it was not until 1918 that Poland achieved independence. By that time more than a third of the population consisted of minorities, Germans, Ukrainians, Belorussians, Lithuanians and Jews, all of whom influenced musical life. The German invasion of Poland precipitated World War II, after which the country became a socialist state.

I. Art music. II. Folk music.

I. Art music

1. To 1600. 2. 1600–1850. 3. Since 1850.

1. TO 1600. The introduction of Christianity at the end of the 10th century led to the development of choral singing. The earliest sources of church music in notation were found in Płock, and date from about 1130; an antiphon in honour of St Wojciech, *Magna laus voce sonora*, dates from the period 1090–1127. The

Dominican Wincenty z Kielc, the earliest known Polish composer, wrote an Office in honour of St Stanisław, *Dies adest celebris* (1255). The oldest surviving song in Polish is *Bogurodzica*. Although the first known written version dates from 1407 (*PL-Kj* 1619), the song itself is much earlier, with a 12th-century melody; according to Jan Długosz, *Bogurodzica* was a national song sung by Polish knights on the battlefields (for example in 1410 and 1431). From the beginning of the 15th century carols (*kolędy; see* KOLĘDA) and Marian songs, sometimes of Latin origin, appear. Some songs have a dance-like character, such as *Pieśń o Bożym umęczeniu* ('Song of God's martyrdom') by Ładysław z Gielniowa (1488). Secular songs were recorded considerably later; not until the 15th century do surviving manuscripts indicate their existence. However, music did flourish relatively early among the middle classes, and musicians enlivening festivities appear as early as the first half of the 14th century. Troubadours were active in the 11th century; most songs of chivalry originated in the time of the reign of Bolesław Krzywousty ('the wry-mouthed'), though no knights' songs survive. Court music did not appear in Poland until the end of the 14th century.

The earliest sources of Polish polyphony date from the 14th century: *Surrexit Christus hodie* in two- and three-part organum, the two-part *Benedicamus Domino* and two Latin motets. Wincenty z Kielc wrote polyphonic religious songs which show folk influence. From its origins Polish music was partly dependent for its development on Western music, and around 1427 Nicolaus de Radom composed a series of works in the Burgundian style, including a fine *Magnificat* setting. In the 15th century there were music lectures at the University of Kraków, and during that period instrumental music developed at the court of the Polish king. Works by other Polish composers which merit attention are *Cracovia civitas* with one vocal and two instrumental parts by Stanisław Ciołek, and a march by Kraków students, *Breve regnum erigitur*. The activity of Kraków University, the fact that the works of the Burgundian and Netherlands schools were well known in Poland, and the close contact of foreign musicians with Poland (Heinrich Finck studied in Kraków around 1450), all indicate that there was a high level of musical creativity in Poland.

The Polish Renaissance proper was manifested in music in the 16th century, when Kraków became the main centre of musical life, particularly through the royal chapel, in which Polish, Italian, Netherlands and Hungarian musicians performed. In 1540 King Sigismund I founded the Capella Rorantistarum, an unaccompanied male-voice ensemble, at the cathedral. Other ensembles were also active in Kraków, such as groups of dignitaries and monastic ensembles. The nonconformist movement publicized music and founded a printing house, making the music of the period more widely available. In the 16th century and at the beginning of the 17th century Marenzio, Pacelli, Wincenty Lilius, Annibale Stabile and Merula were among the foreign composers active in Poland, and had a great influence on the development of Polish music. The native composers Sebastian z Felsztyna, Mikołaj z Krakowa, Mikołaj z Chrzanowa, Marcin Leopolita, Krzysztof Borek, Tomasz Szadek and Wacław z Szamotuł wrote all forms of church music, including masses, motets and Lamentations. Many Polish works from this period survive, most notable of which are the organ tablatures

(such as those of Mikołaj z Krakowa, which include transcriptions of secular songs). The Reformation brought both monophonic and polyphonic chorales to Poland; some were elaborately conceived, and some had associations with folklore (like the song for the marriage of Jan Kostka ze Stymbarku, 1554). Krzysztof Klabon cultivated the epic song, and other outstanding composers of Polish songs at that period were Wacław z Szamotuł and Cyprian Bazylik. In 1580 the richest source of Polish Renaissance song appeared in print, the *Melodie na Psałterz Polski* ('Melodies for the Polish Psalter') of Mikołaj Gomółka, a singer and instrumentalist in Kraków; the collection contains 150 psalm settings on Polish texts by Jan Kochanowski, and is characterized by highly developed harmony.

Predominant among the instrumental music of the period was lute music; the Hungarian Bálint Bakfark and the Italian Diomedes Cato were active in Poland. The appearance of dance music was linked with the development of instrumental music, both for dancing and in stylized form: court dances, dances of the nobility and of the bourgeoisie, and regional dances. Their abundance and richness led them to survive for many years, and they were not ousted by Italian and French dances as happened elsewhere. Polish dances possessed no less fascination for foreign composers than did foreign ones for Polish composers, and there are 41 collections from Germany, Switzerland, Hungary, Czechoslovakia, England and the Netherlands, containing over 300 dances with titles indicating Polish origin.

2. 1600–1850. In the 17th century Polish music became less dependent on foreign music, and the period is now regarded as the golden age of Polish music. Mikołaj Zieleński, the foremost Polish composer of the early Baroque, who used antiphony in his offertoriums, had his works published in Venice in 1611. In the three fantasias for cornett, bassoon, strings and organ in the collection *Communiones totius anni* Zieleński adhered to the Venetian style, with ricercare form and echo effects. The period saw the flourishing of Polish music theory, particularly in Kraków (Sebastian z Felsztyna, Jan z Legnicy, Marcin Kromer, Stefan Monetarius and others). Instrument making also developed, and new chapels appeared, maintained not only by the ruling class but also by the monasteries, particularly those of the Jesuits. Italian opera was performed at court as early as 1633; the first opera by a Polish composer, *La fama reale* by Piotr Elert, has not survived. By 1646 11 operas, often staged with ballet, had been presented at the king's castle. During the period of the Swedish invasion of Poland the activities of the court opera came to an end, and the devastations of World War II make access to the musical sources of this period difficult. Besides Zieleński, Marcin Mielczewski, who composed the first Polish concertato works and religious music, was active in the 17th century. Church music of various kinds flourished in the work of Bartłomiej Pękiel, who wrote the first Polish oratorio, *Audite mortales*, and the monumental *Missa 'La Lombardesca'* for voices and instruments. Damian Stachowicz, who worked in Łowicz, wrote a fine work in concertato style, *Veni consolator* for soprano, trumpet and continuo. The most representative composer of instrumental music was Adam Jarzębski, a violinist and architect, and composer of 27 *Canzoni e concerti*. The outstanding composers at the turn of the 17th century were S. S. Szarzyński, G.

G. Gorczycki (director of the cathedral chapel in Kraków and author of about 12 concertato compositions and a cycle of psalm settings, *Completorium*), Jacek Różycki, Jan Podbielski and Andrzej Niżankowski (a pupil of Frescobaldi and composer of organ music).

During the Enlightenment, in Poland as elsewhere, musical culture became a middle-class pursuit. In 1724 the first public opera house was founded, although the first public opera performance in Polish did not occur until 1778 (Maciej Kamieński's *Nędza uszczęśliwiona*, 'Misery made happy'). J. D. Holland and Jan Stefani composed operas, based, like the work of Kamieński, on Polish folklore. Around 1740 Jacek Szczurowski wrote the first Polish symphony. The work of Antoni Milwid (symphonies in pre-Classical style) was also important for the development of the symphony in Poland. Many symphonies by contemporary Polish composers were discovered much later, greatly altering the picture of the development of Polish music.

In the late 18th century partitions of Poland and uprisings played a part in the development of the patriotic song. Polish folklore played an important role, particularly in stylized dances such as the mazurka, krakowiak and polonaise; this is typified by the development of the polonaise for piano (M. K. Ogiński, Jozef Kozłowski, Józef Deszczyński and Joachim Kaczkowski). Jan Kleczyński was one of the first representatives of Classicism, and was influenced by Haydn, whose music was well known in Poland. A combination of Classical and Romantic elements is seen in the works of Franciszek Lessel, composer of numerous instrumental works, Franciszek Mirecki (piano concertos and opera), and also in the works of the violinist Karol Lipiński. M. A. Szymanowska wrote miniatures for the piano. The works of the greatest significance for Polish music at that time were those of J. A. F. Elsner (operas and church music) and K. K. Kurpiński (operas on Polish themes).

With Chopin, Polish music became internationally influential; although confined almost without exception to the piano, his works evolved a highly individual style through their original harmony and their transformation of folk music elements. In Poland the opera composer Stanisław Moniuszko was no less important than Chopin; his outstanding work is *Halka* (1847, his first important opera), to a libretto by Wolski. He also wrote cantatas and religious works. Other composers of the period include Józef Nowakowski, Józef Deszczyński, T. N. Nidecki, Antoni Orłowski and Julian Fontana. The outstanding performer of the time was the virtuoso violinist Henryk Wieniawski, who wrote two violin concertos and numerous solo works; his brother Józef was an organizer of Warsaw's musical life. The Warsaw Institute of Music (later the conservatory) was founded by the violinist Apolinary Kątski. Other noteworthy performers were I. M. Komorowski, Stanisław Duniecki, Ignacy Krzyżanowski, Emanuel Kania and Nikodem Biernacki.

3. SINCE 1850. The main representatives of late 19th-century Polish music were Władysław Żeleński (1837–1921), composer of Romantic operas and programmatic overtures, and Zygmunt Noskowski, a natural symphonist and outstanding teacher, whose finest works are the Overture *Morskie Oko*, the symphonic poem *Step*, and his symphonic variations. Other prominent composers were Aleksander Zarzycki, Adam Münchheimer (1831–1904), Gustaw Roguski (1839–1921), Antoni Stolpe, Henryk Jarecki, the songwriters J. K. Gall and Stanisław Niewiadomski, Eugeniusz Pankiewicz, Antoni Rutkowski and Juliusz Zarębski.

At the end of the 19th century Polish musical life had a firm basis, through the activities of the conservatories, music societies and the development of choirs and musical literacy, and there were a number of composers of considerable ability. Six composers won well-deserved reputations: the pianist Ignacy Paderewski, a virtuoso of genius and composer of the opera *Manru* and a symphony among other works, the well-known teacher Roman Statkowski, Henryk Melcer-Szczawiński, Zygmunt Stojowski (who worked in the USA), the musicologist and composer Henryk Opieński, and the conductor and composer Emil Młynarski. They represented a conservative tendency, while the composers of the emergent generation, the 'Young Poland' group, were following new directions. Among the latter were Mieczysław Karłowicz, composer of six symphonic poems and a violin concerto; Grzegorz Fitelberg, famous as a conductor; Ludomir Różycki, who composed symphonic poems and operas; and above all Karol Szymanowski, whose outstanding works include operas, four symphonies, two violin concertos and a *Stabat mater*. In his later works – e.g. in the ballet *Harnasie* and *Pieśni kurpiowskie* – Szymanowski drew on Polish folk music. Of the composers working outside the 'Young Poland' group the most noteworthy are Eugeniusz Morawski-Dąbrowa, L. M. Rogowski, Juliusz Wertheim and Feliks Nowowiejski.

Between the wars Polish music developed in two directions. The first was characterized by the influences of German and Russian music, the second (rather later) by the influence of French music, particularly neo-classicism. Many leading Polish composers studied in Paris, mostly with Nadia Boulanger. To the first trend belonged composers who developed from the Romantic tradition: Piotr Rytel, Witold Friemann and Witold Maliszewski. Józef Koffler was the only Polish composer of 12-note music. The neo-classical trend reached its peak after World War II (Grażyna Bacewicz and Michał Spisak). The foremost Polish composers of the 1970s besides Lutosławski and Penderecki, who have international reputations, were Stanisław Wiechowicz, Kazimierz Sikorski, Bolesław Szabelski, Tadeusz Szeligowski, Alexandre Tansman, Bolesław Woytowicz, J. A. Maklakiewicz, Piotr Perkowski, Michał Kondracki, Jerzy Fitelberg, T. Z. Kassern, Artur Malawski, Roman Palester, Antoni Szałowski, Grażyna Bacewicz, Andrzej Panufnik, Michał Spisak, Kazimierz Serocki, Włodzimierz Kotoński, Tadeusz Baird, Bogusław Schäffer, Wojciech Kilar and H. M. Górecki.

Avant-garde music has flourished in postwar Poland to a higher degree than in any other European socialist state, and some of its composers have achieved international fame. The country's active musical life results partly from the relative autonomy enjoyed by the government, and thus by its artistic institutions; it is also supported by many fine performers (worthy successors to Wieniawski and Paderewski), music education, festivals (notably the 'Warsaw Autumn', from 1956), folk music research (some 70,000 folktunes have been collected since 1945) and musicology, as shown by the collections Antiquitates Musicae in Polonia and Monumenta Musicae in Polonia.

See also GDAŃSK, KRAKÓW, L'VOV (i), POZNAŃ, SZCZECIN, WARSAW, WROCLAW.

BIBLIOGRAPHY

A. Sowiński: *Les musiciens polonais et slaves* (Paris, 1857; Pol. trans., Paris, 1874)

A. Poliński: *Dzieje muzyki polskiej w zarysie* [A history of Polish music in outline] (Lwów, 1907)

H. Opieński: *La musique polonaise* (Paris, 1918, 2/1929)

L. Bernacki: *Teatr, dramat i muzyka za Stanisława Augusta* (Lwów, 1925)

Z. Jachimecki: 'Muzyka polska' [Polish music], *Polska, jej dzieje i kultura* (Warsaw, 1929–31)

J. W. Reiss: *Polskie skrzypce i polscy skrzypkowie* [Polish violins and violinists] (Warsaw, 1946)

Z. Jachimecki: *Muzyka polska w rozwoju historycznym od czasów najdawniejszych do doby obecnej* [Polish music in historical development from the earliest times to the present day] (Kraków, 1948–51)

A. Chybiński: *Słownik muzyków dawnej Polski do roku 1800* [Dictionary of early Polish musicians to 1800] (Kraków, 1949)

K. Michałowski: *Opery polskie* [Polish operas] (Kraków, 1954)

T. Strumiłło: *Szkice z polskiego życia muzycznego XIX w.* [Sketches of Polish musical life in the 19th century] (Kraków, 1954)

K. Michałowski: *Bibliografia polskiego piśmiennictwa muzycznego* [A bibliography of Polish music literature] (Kraków, 1955)

T. Strumiłło: *Źródła i początki romantyzmu w muzyce polskiej* [The sources and origins of Romanticism in Polish music] (Kraków, 1956)

J. M. Chomiński and Z. Lissa, eds.: *Kultura muzyczna Polski Ludowej 1944–1955* [The musical culture of People's Poland, 1944–55] (Kraków, 1957)

J. Reiss: *Najpiękniejsza ze wszystkich jest muzyka polska* [The finest of all is Polish music] (Kraków, 1958)

Z. M. Szweykowski, ed.: *Z dziejów polskiej kultury muzycznej* [From the history of Polish musical culture], i (Kraków, 1958)

H. Feicht and Z. Lissa: 'Polen', *MGG*

L. T. Błaszczyk: *Dyrygenci polscy i obcy w Polsce działający w XIX i XX wieku* [Polish and foreign conductors working in Poland in the 19th and 20th centuries] (Kraków, 1964)

J. M. Chomiński, ed.: *Słownik muzyków polskich* [Dictionary of Polish musicians] (Kraków, 1964–7)

S. Jarociński, ed.: *Polish Music* (Warsaw, 1965)

H. Feicht: *Muzyka staropolska* [Music of old Poland] (Kraków, 1966)

M. Hanuszewska and B. Schäffer: *Almanach polskich kompozytorów współczesnych* [Almanac of contemporary Polish composers] (Kraków, 1966)

P. Podejko: *Nieznani muzycy polscy ... 1585–1820* [Unknown Polish musicians, 1585–1820] (Bydgoszcz, 1966)

Z. Lissa, ed.: *Polsko-rosyjskie miscellanea muzyczne* [Polish–Russian musical miscellany] (Kraków, 1967)

J. Chomiński: *Muzyka Polski Ludowej* [Music of People's Poland] (Warsaw, 1968)

E. Dziębowska, ed.: *Polska współczesna kultura muzyczna 1944–1964* [Musical life in modern Poland, 1944–64] (Kraków, 1968)

H. Feicht: 'Polska pieśń średniowieczna' [Polish medieval song], *Musica medii aevi*, ii (1968), 52

J. G. Görlich: 'Deutsch-polnische Beziehungen in der Musik', *Musik des Ostens*, v (1969), 49

M. Przywecka-Samecka: *Drukarstwo muzyczne w Polsce do końca XVIII wieku* [Music printing in Poland up to the end of the 18th century] (Kraków, 1969)

Z. M. Szweykowski: 'Styl koncertujący w polskiej muzyce wokalno-instrumentalnej' [Concertato style in Polish vocal–instrumental music], *Muzyka*, xv/1 (1970), 3

Z. Chechlińska, ed.: *Szkice o kulturze muzycznej XIX w.* [Outlines of musical culture in the 19th century] (Warsaw, 1971)

J. Kłobukowska: 'Muzyka francuskiego renesansu w Polsce' [French Renaissance music in Poland], *Muzyka*, xvii/2 (1972), 29

A. and E. Mrygoń: *Bibliografia polskiego piśmiennictwa muzykologicznego* [A bibliography of Polish musicological literature] (Warsaw, 1972)

Z. Chechlińska and J. Stęszewski, eds.: *Polish Musicological Studies*, i (Kraków, 1977) [incl. list of Pol. dissertations 1947–74]

T. Ochlewskiego, ed.: *Dzieje muzyki polskiej w zarysie* [A history of Polish music in outline] (Warsaw, 1977)

R. Jasinski: *Na przełomie epok: muzyka w Warszawie, 1910–1927* [At the turning point of the age: music in Warsaw, 1910–27] (Warsaw, 1979)

II. Folk music

1. Introduction. 2. Sources and research. 3. Function and context. 4. General characteristics. 5. Instruments. 6. Music regions.

1. INTRODUCTION. The 'Polishness' of Polish folk music does not reside in its stylistic uniformity, but in its use of the Polish language, one of the western family of Slavonic languages. The concept of 'folk' usually denotes a local collection of integrated, rural communities with a traditional culture but in the 20th century research has been broadened to include the working urban environment and the oral tradition of religious songs. Poland has a population of about 35 million, half of which is urban and approximately 1·5% of which represents national minorities (Lithuanians, Belorussians, Ukrainians, Ruthenians, Slovaks and Czechs). Polish has a number of dialects which differ in varying degrees from the literary language and there are numerous cultural regions (see fig.1). Since 1945 the west of the country has been the scene of intensive resettlement, which precludes discussion of the characteristic features of this culture in terms of geographical categories.

2. SOURCES AND RESEARCH. There are a number of important sources for the pre-folkloristic period (before the 18th century). Excavations from the Palaeolithic era to the Middle Ages have revealed ceramic rattles (including zoomorphic and ornithomorphic types), ceramic hourglass drums, bone and clay whistles, panpipes (from the 8th century to the 6th century BC, in Małopolska) made from nine bone pipes and probably constructed in an anhemitonic pentatonic scale, pipes and chordophones, including five-string zithers of the KANTELE type (fig.2). Written sources include the reports of travellers and merchants (e.g. the Arab geographer Ibn Rustah, *fl* 903), of writers (e.g. Theophylactus Simokatta, 7th century) and of foreign and Polish chroniclers (e.g. Wincenty Kadłubek), sermons, statutes and synodal resolutions, economic accounts and tax registers dealing with such varied items as Slavonic chordophones, Polish trumpets, pipes and the distribution of pipers, superstitions and songs (e.g. historical songs, midsummer night customs and the songs that were sung at them). In literature there are references to customs and songs (e.g. by Jan Kochanowski) and instruments (e.g. by Kasper Miaskowski). Musical sources yield quotations of melodies and metrorhythmic features in compositions from the Renaissance onwards, including contrafacta and dances. Further information comes from iconography, especially wall-paintings (e.g. the earliest Polish representation of bagpipes, in the church at Mieronice, early 14th century) and woodcuts in printed works (fig.3); and from organological literature (e.g. Agricola, *Musica instrumentalis deudsch*, Wittenberg, 1529, on Polish violins).

In the 19th century the first attempts were made to note down folk music, inspired partly by the ideas of Romanticism (the search for 'Slavonic antiquities'), and later by 'positivism' (a desire for scientific documentation). Folk art was also looked to for confirmation of the national identity by a nation deprived of its existence as an independent political unit. The year 1802, when Hugo Kołłataj first formulated the needs of Polish historiography, is regarded as the date when the study of Polish folklore began. The first collections of songs, most often without melodies, were made by Joachim Lelewel, Adam Czarnocki (under the pseudonym Zorian Dołęga-Chodakowski), Kazimierz Wójcicki, Wacław Zalewski (pseudonym Wacław z Oleska), Karol Lipiński, Żegota Pauli, Józef Konopka, Ludwik Zejszner and Jan J. Lipiński. The first articles on folklore were written by Paweł Woronicz on folksong and Karol Kurpiński on folk music (1820).

An important change of direction was effected by the work of Oskar Kolberg (1814–90), who collected and published ethnographic collections, including some on folklore, arranged in volumes according to region and

1. Map of Poland showing the major cultural regions

encompassing Polish, Lithuanian, Belorussian and Ukrainian ethnic areas. 33 volumes were published during his lifetime. The reprinting of these, and publication of the unpublished manuscripts (begun in 1961), will amount to about 80 volumes, containing about 25,000 songs and dances and about 15,000 melodies. Other important collectors of Kolberg's period and later were Gustaw Gizewiusz, Florian Cenowa, Józef Lompa, Andrzej Cinciała, Jan Kleczyński and Zygmunt Gloger.

From about 1904 folk music began to be recorded on the gramophone: musicologists engaged in this work included Adolf Chybiński, Helena Windakiewicz, Łucian Kamieński, Marian Sobieski and his wife Jadwiga, and the ethnographer Kazimierz Moszyński. Between 1930 and 1939 archives of recordings were built up in Poznań (under Kamieński) and Warsaw (director Julian Pulikowski), containing a total of 25,000 recordings. Individual collectors of folk music included Marian Stoiński, Władysław Skierkowski and Stanisław Mierczyński.

During World War II these collections of recordings were completely destroyed. Since 1945, under the direction of the Sobieskis, an important new collection has been built up totalling about 75,000 recordings and housed in the Institute of Fine Arts, Warsaw. Research

was begun in 1970 at the Catholic University of Lublin on the oral tradition of religious songs. Research in general is being carried out by Ludwik Bielawski, Anna Czekanowska, Adolf Dygacz and Jan Stęszewski.

3. FUNCTION AND CONTEXT. Folklore survives to varying degrees in different villages and regions. Until the mid-20th century everyone in the villages sang, and professional musicians, untrained in the Western sense, played for dances. The repertory of songs is divided in the communities into that of children and adults. The adults sing either in groups, as in some ritual songs, or solo, as in women's lullabies and men's and women's *przyśpiewki* (the *przyśpiewka* is associated with rituals or with the dance and consists of a short 'pre-dance' stanza sung by a dancer as a musical cue to the instrumentalists, followed by the playing of this melody for the dance by the ensemble). Some songs are led by individuals, such as the *czepiarka*, the woman who puts the married woman's headdress on the bride at the wedding. The musicians play local *przyśpiewki* for the dance, a small number of dances being purely instrumental, and a few melodies for ceremonial occasions. The relationship between the singers and players in performance of dance music is usually one of

two types: singing is followed by dancing with the instrumental group, followed by singing again; or, singing with the instrumental group is followed by dancing with the instrumental group, followed by singing with the instrumental group again. The first type of relationship is encountered in Wielkopolska and the Kielce and Lublin regions, and the second type in Podhale, Beskid Śląski, the Kraków area and Kielce region. A similar relationship between instrumental group and singers is found in ritual group songs (e.g. of weddings), although there are occasions when the ritual songs are sung by a group without instrumental accompaniment.

The most important ritual is the wedding, with a rich repertory of melodies. Some wedding songs have a wide

Ex.1 *Chmiel*, wedding song, Lublin region (Kolberg, 1883)

distribution (e.g. the *chmiel*), others are more local. The most important annual ceremonies are those clustered around Christmas, such as the singing of carols (*kolędowanie*) and processions with masked figures; spring customs of driving away winter and welcoming spring (*gaik, topienie marzanny, dyngus*) and *sobótki* (customs for midsummer night), traditions known to have existed from the Middle Ages; and ceremonies for summer, the harvest and the end of the harvest.

A considerable number of the melodies are for dances, and many others possess dance characteristics – the connection with the dance leaves its mark on the music. Dances are usually accompanied by instruments, but a few dances are accompanied by songs only: these are children's dances and a traditional women's dance at weddings in the Kurpie region, called *przytrampywanie*. Dances can be divided into group dances and couple-dances. Among those for groups are dances based on a circle (e.g. the *zbójnicki*, a men's dance, and the *przy-trampywanie*) and figure-dances (e.g. *szewc, miotlarz, kadryl*). Most common are round-dances for many couples, for instance the *kujawiak, oberek, okrągly, światówka, powolniak* and polka.

Song texts may be loosely associated with particular melodies, in which case they form a repertory primarily of single stanzas which are joined into cycles as needed, as in certain situations at a dance, for example. A closer link between melody and text is apparent in ritual and multi-stanza songs, such as ballads. Jan Bystroń distinguished three basic groups of songs: songs related to rituals; general songs, which can be sung at any time, anywhere, by anyone, and include ballads, comic songs and *przyśpiewki*; and occupational songs. The most

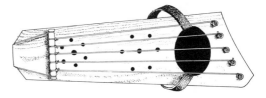

2. *Drawing of a 12th–13th-century gęśle (five-string zither) from Gdańsk*

numerous are the ritual and general songs, the most vital are the sub-group of *przyśpiewki*. The epic is not a characteristic genre.

Participants in a local musical culture have a system of concepts which class songs according to their ritual function, their place of performance and their dance type; these correspond to fairly distinct musical groups. In the terminology of Sandomierz (Table 1) *polne* ('field') songs are those sung in the open air; *światowe* ('worldly' songs) are *przyśpiewki* melodies and are sung to texts with varying content. In Podhale (Table 2) the word 'nuta' means melody; *wierchowe* ('peak' songs) are those versions of dance-tunes, called *ozwodne*, which are not danced to, and are sung as general songs in the open air. The people do not consider children's songs, funeral laments, shepherds' calls, etc, as music.

4. GENERAL CHARACTERISTICS. Vocal and instrumental music is based on a more or less equal-tempered tonal system. Two groups of forms, one recited rhythmically (children's play songs), the other without a fixed rhythm (laments), display the merest traces of melodic organization. In some types of scale (e.g. narrow-range or pentatonic) the 7th and the 3rd occur with a neutral pitch or are unstable (ex.1). Particular scales or types of scale predominate in the songs of a specific region, or are connected with certain genres. The melodic range of

3. *Entertainment in a hostelry with serby (fiddle), dudy (bagpipe), flute and bębenek (drum): woodcut from J. Haur's 'Skład albo skarbiec znakomitych sekretów ekonomii ziemiańskiej' (1693)*

TABLE 1

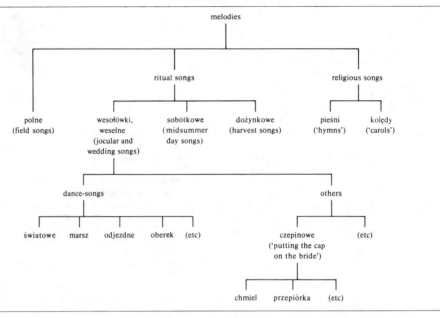

the songs varies from one region to another. Melodies with a range of a 3rd or a 4th are considered survivals and are found in wedding songs and annual rituals (ex.2). Many street vendors' calls are based on two pitches a 3rd apart, or three notes ranging over a 4th. The pentatonic scale is found in conservative regions (e.g. Kurpie region), but it is unknown in the Carpathian area (Orawa, Podhale, Pieniny). Major and minor modes are known all over Poland.

Most frequently, a single note is sung to each syllable of a text (syllabic song). A certain amount of melisma, generally of two notes (as in grace-, passing- and changing notes), occurs in about 10–20% of songs in the south and about 60–70% in the central regions, although these usually occur as isolated instances. More melismas are found in slower and ceremonial songs, fewer in the lively ones and in dance-songs. Glissando is frequent. Monophony predominates; the earlier polyphony is characteristic of the Carpathian area. Harmonic songs (i.e. in harmony of the Western type) in folk usage date from the 19th and 20th centuries and are rarely found. Folksong melodies usually move in 2nds and 3rds; larger intervals may occur at the beginning of a phrase, in *przyśpiewki*, and in songs from the western and north-western regions. The general melodic contour is undulating. The melody is divided into sections coinciding with the divisions of the text lines and limits of the beat. Melodic motifs, except in archaic ceremonial melodies, are sharply outlined and distinct.

In old songs syllabic verse forms predominate. Devia-

TABLE 2

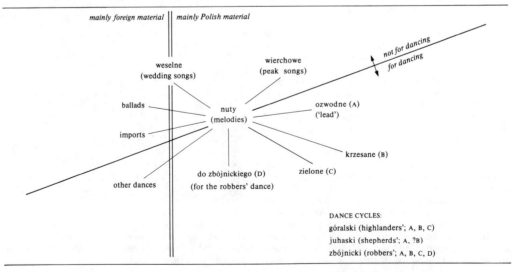

tion from the strict syllabic system does occur; there is, for instance, an asyllabic system, in which the number of syllables and accents in a line is variable, and a tonic system (e.g. in children's songs and those of annual rituals), in which there is a set number of accents in a line, but the number of syllables varies. In the syllabic system the most common divisions of syllables within the line are: 12 (6 + 6) and 6, 8 (4 + 4), 14 (4 + 4 + 6) as in ex.10, 10 (5 + 5) as in ex.1, 7 (4 + 3), 13 (4 + 4 + 5), 11 (4 + 4 + 3) and 10 (4 + 6). The frequency of their occurrence varies in different areas. Syllabic songs are generally composed of two- or four-line rhymed isorhythmic stanzas. Heterosyllabic stanzas are found, for instance *aaba* (where the third line is of a different length), *aabba*[1] (the fifth line being a section of the first) and *aabb*. 12- and 8-syllable lines are generally connected with *przyśpiewki*; the 10 (5 + 5)-syllable line is a verse-form used in northern Poland for *przyśpiewki*, or for wedding or harvest songs; 11-syllable lines are connected with pastoral and wedding songs. The basic words of the text are expanded with interjections (*oj, ej, dana*), a nonsense refrain or a meaningful one, and repetitions of the text (as in ex.2). Interjections are characteristic of dance-songs (ex.3), while a meaningful refrain is found in wedding songs, among others (e.g. ex.1, second part).

Ex.2 Midsummer Day song, Lublin region (Czekanowska, 1961)

There is a close correlation between syllabic versification and the repetitive and generative qualities of the rhythmic patterns. Some rhythms are particularly frequent, as are those of the mazurka, krakowiak and polonaise, which were the first 'national dances'. At the beginning of the 17th century 'Polish dances' based on the rhythm of the mazurka were fashionable outside Poland (but despite its reputation the rhythm noted in Jan z Lublina's tablature of *Wesel się polska korona* ('Rejoice, O Polish nation') from about 1540 is not a Polish mazurka rhythm). The mazurka rhythm is associated mainly with 8-, 14-, 12- (ex.3) and 13-syllable lines; it is in triple metre, often in fast time, the bar having a maximum of four syllables, condensed in the first part of the bar (ex.4a). The phrases vary in rhythm, depending on the proportions of the line (ex.4b). These rhythms are found in non-dance-songs all over Poland and in *przyśpiewki* in the central region. The dances with mazurka rhythms have various names, tempos and characteristics: *kujawiak* (ex.8), *obertas*, *powiślak*, *światówka* (ex.3), *mazur* and others.

12-syllable lines are the basis for a group of fast, duple-metre krakowiak dances, which are found mainly in Małopolska. Locally they assume various names (*szopieniak, mijany, suwany* and others). Most frequent are two forms of syncopated krakowiak rhythms (ex.5). The rhythmic formula of the *polonez* ('polonaise') is associated with some dance-songs, also with general ones and a few wedding songs. It is characterized by triple time with a fairly slow tempo; a maximum of six syllables to a bar; like the mazurka, a rhythm of four

Ex.3 *Światówka*, dance-song, rationalized rhythmic pattern, Sandomierz region (Stęszewski, 1974)

syllables; and special cadential turns and dotted rhythms (ex.6). The polonaise rhythm uses the rarer lines of 10 (4 + 6), 17 (4 + 6 + 4 + 3) and 19 (6 + 6 + 4 + 3) syllables, and polonaise dances have a number of names: *polski, chodzony, pieszy, wolny, wielki* and others.

Features common to the whole of Poland are absence of anacrusis and a preponderance of 'descendental' rhythm (i.e. progressively decreasing rhythmic density within each bar or phrase) and dotted descendental rhythm. Singing is in a natural chest voice, of medium intensity. Wedding songs are sung lower, dance-songs higher. Ritual songs and those sung out of doors have the slowest tempos.

The stanzaic form predominates in Polish folksongs. Those without stanzas are street vendors' and shepherds' calls (*wyskanie* in Podhale), children's play songs, songs for annual ceremonies and some *wierchowe* melodies from Podhale. The most frequent forms of musical stanza (where *R* is the refrain) are: AA', AA'A' (ex.10), AAR (ex.1), AA'RA', AB (ex.7), AA'B (ex.2), ABB' (ex.3), AAAA', AABA, ABAB', ABCA etc. Songs with a bar structure usually have 8 or 16 bars, but are

Ex.4 Common mazurka rhythms

(a)

(b)

Ex.5 The most common krakowiak rhythms

Ex.6 Common rhythmic patterns in the polonaise

4. *Trombita (long wooden trumpet), Beskid Śląski region*

expanded by repetitions and refrains. The arrangement of phrases is usually symmetrical, although other structures occur (ex.7). The most stable elements of the songs are form, versification and rhythm, and to a lesser degree, scale and, least of all, melody. The variability of the melody is, however, subject to certain limitations (ex.1 shows the variation in one bar of the melody).

5. INSTRUMENTS. Some instruments are used exclusively by children, and these are mostly toys producing one or a few notes, or percussion instruments. They include wooden *fujarki* (pipes) with six to eight or fewer finger-holes; *fujarki z kory*, pipes made from willow bark; *piszczałki* (reedpipes) made from the stems of plants, with single or double reeds; ivy leaves and pieces of birch bark; *gwizdki* (whistles) made from various materials; *klekotki* (rattles) or *kołatki* (clappers), and the *terkotki* (rattles) used on Good Friday; *grzechotki* (rattles); and the *diabełek* ('little devil'), which is a small friction drum. Larger and stronger friction drums known as *burczybas* or *huk* are used by adults in the Pomorze and Warmia regions as ritual instruments.

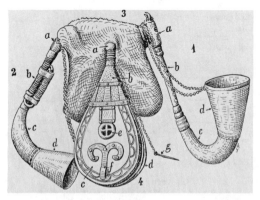

5. *Dudy (bagpipe) from Wielkopolska; (1) chanter: (a) wind cap, (b) chanter, (c) wooden horn, (d) metal bell; (2) drone: (a) wind cap, (b) drone-pipe, (c) horn, (d) metal bell; (3) bag; (4) bellows: (a) 'knee', (b) neck, (c) upper board, (d) leather casing, (e) vent with valve inside, (f) hook, (g) cleaning rod for removing excess wax from finger-holes*

Adults use many instruments, some of which are confined to particular regions. They can be divided according to usage into those for accompanying dances, and those which are used in other circumstances. Thus the violin and bagpipes are used to accompany dances, while the violin and various kinds of wooden flutes are also used to play solo music – *granie do słuchu* ('for listening') – in some areas.

Ex.7 Wedding song, Kurpie region (S. Jarociński, ed.: *Polish Music*, Warsaw, 1965)

"Oj, zza sto-la, pa-ni mło-da, zza sto-la, a po-dzię-kuj swam ce-piar-kóm we-so-ło.

There are three types of wooden trumpet, used by shepherds: the *bazuna* in Pomorze is about 2 metres long (it is also played by fishermen); the *ligawka* or *ligawa* from Mazowsze, about 1·5 metres long, can be straight or slightly curved, and is also played in the evenings during Advent; and the *trombita* (*trąbita, trębita*; fig.4) from Beskid Śląski, up to 5 metres long. The *bazuna* and *ligawka* are slightly conical; the *trombita* is cylindrical. The *trombita* is used for playing slow melodies but the *bazuna* and *ligawka* produce only four to eight harmonics. The *fujarki* (fipple flutes) are also shepherds' instruments and are of two types: the first has six to eight finger-holes; the second has no finger-holes, but by overblowing, and either opening or closing the distal end, two series of harmonics are produced, which are the basis of rich melismatic playing. In Mazowsze such pipes are made of willow bark, while in Beskid Żywiecki they are made from a hollowed-out branch about 60 cm long; they are usually played while herding a flock, or during Lent; hence the name *postna* ('Lenten') *fulyrka*.

There are five basic types of bagpipe in Poland, all with single reeds. The *kozioł* of western Wielkopolska has the deepest tone and the widest range: $b\flat-c'-d'-e\flat'-f'-g'-a\flat'-b\flat'-c''-d'-e\flat''$ (drone $E\flat$), the two highest notes being produced by overblowing. The hairy side of the skin is on the outside of the bag. The *dudy* (figs. 5 and 6), common in other parts of Wielkopolska, has a slightly smaller range and a higher pitch: $f'-a'-bb'-c''-d''-eb''-f''-g''$ (drone Bb), although it can be tuned higher or lower. In the Beskid Śląski region *gajdy* are used, tuned to $bb-eb'-f'-g'-ab'-bb'-c''$ (drone Eb), while in the Beskid Żywiecki there are *dudy*, similar to the *gajdy*, tuned to $c'-eb'-f'-g'-a'-b'-c''-d''$ (drone F). The *koza* of Podhale, with no bell, differs considerably from the other types in that it has three drones: one in the separate drone-pipe, and two in the chanter, which has three channels. Its scale is: $bb'-c''-d''-eb''-f''-g''$ (drones Bb, f' and bb'). All the bagpipes except those in Beskid Żywiecki and Podhale have bellows for filling the bag with air. Most types have a straight drone-pipe, while that in the *kozioł* and the *dudy* from Wielkopolska is bent twice, at an angle of 180° (see fig.5), and has a bell. Historical sources show clearly that the distribution of bagpipes in Poland was once much greater than it is now. Young people learning to play the *dudy* in Wielkopolska use a bladder pipe known as *siesieńki* or *pęcherzyna* (fig.7) with a scale similar to that of the *dudy*. The *siesieńki* has no drone or bellows, and the leather bag is replaced by one or two bladders.

Of the string instruments, the violin predominates throughout Poland. Common characteristics of violin playing are a general adherence to the 1st position; frequent use of the E and A strings for playing the melody and the occasional use of the D and G strings for drone accompaniment; arco playing, in a non-legato style apart from ornamentation; and 'playing for listening'.

Until the early 20th century, smaller string instruments of the kit type were played in Wielkopolska and Podhale: the *mazanki* (tuned $a'-e''-b''$) and *złóbcoki* or *gęśliki* (with three to four strings tuned like the violin) respectively (figs.8a and b). They were carved out of one piece of wood, except for the soundboard. In the 19th century there existed in the Lublin area a string instrument called the *suka*, similar in shape to the violin but with a shorter neck and three strings: the strings were stopped with the fingernails, and it was held like the viola da gamba (cf fig.3). Both the *suka* and *mazanki* had bridges constructed so that one foot rested on the soundboard and the other, longer, foot extended through the opening to rest against the back of the instrument: the *basy* in the Kalisz area had a similar bridge. *Mazanki* began to be replaced at the turn of the 20th

century by a violin with an artificial fret, designed to facilitate playing in the 1st position but in a higher register, required for playing with the *dudy*.

Various bass string instruments with two to four strings and of different shapes are used in Poland, including the *basetla* or *basy*, a type of local cello or double bass. Many are carved out of one piece of wood, apart from the soundboard, and are played as drone instruments with unstopped strings (e.g. in the Kielce and Kalisz areas) or with stopped strings in the Podhale and Rzeszów areas, although this is a newer practice. A popular instrument in the Rzeszów area is the locally made *cymbały* (dulcimer).

Of percussion instruments, the tambourine, usually with jingles around the rim, is known generally, as is a medium-sized double-headed drum, which has been supplemented since the 1940s and 1950s by the triangle or cymbals. The tambourine is struck either with a stick or with the hand, while the double-headed drums are struck only with sticks.

Wind instruments in folk ensembles are a relatively new addition and include clarinets (chiefly in C and E♭), cornets and trumpets. From the end of the 19th century concertinas and accordions began to appear in folk bands.

The most common type of folk band in the 19th century contained a melody instrument (e.g. the violin) and a rhythmic one (e.g. drum or *basy*), and such an ensemble survives in some regions such as Biłgoraj, Lublin, Sandomierz, Kielce and Mazowsze. In bagpipe-playing areas, an ensemble can be composed of bagpipes and a string instrument – *mazanki*, violin or violin with artificial fret. At the turn of the 20th century, a second violin, adding a chordal accompaniment, joined the violin and drum or violin and bass in Podhale, Rzeszów and other regions. Gradually, more instruments have been added to the basic ensemble, so that a band may now consist of, for instance, first violin, clarinet, trumpet, second violin and double bass (e.g. in the Kraków region).

In instrumental playing there are particular phrases which begin and end the melody, and also appear between stanzas (ex.8). An instrumental performance is based on frequent repetitions of the same melody, embellished each time with new ornaments, variants, rhythmic changes and transpositions. The basic repertory of a

6. *Dudy* (*bagpipe*), *Beskid Żywiecki region*

7. *Siesieńki jednopęcherzowe* (*single bladder pipe*)

folk band consists of *przyśpiewki*, dance-tunes, wedding tunes and marches.

6. MUSIC REGIONS. It is possible to distinguish five large music regions: central, north-western, north-eastern, eastern and southern Poland.

The whole of central Poland is marked by the predominance of mazurka triple time in the dance, associated with a fairly quick tempo and tempo rubato (ex.3 shows in brackets the basic, rationalized rhythmic pattern). The melodies are usually lively and often have a range of an octave or a 9th and a scale that cadences on

the lowest note and has its axis of melodic movement on the fourth degree from the lowest (cf the scales of various types of bagpipe): $d'-[e']-f\sharp'-g'-a'-b\flat'/b'-c''-d''-[e'']$. This type of scale is also found in other regions.

The sub-region of Wielkopolska is distinguished by a larger number of songs with different rhythms, polonaises and waltzes (*okrągłe*, *do koła* and others), duple time and figure-dances; a tendency for numerous repetitions of text and melody (as in Kujawy); and the instruments *mazanki*, *siesieńki*, *dudy*, *kozioł*, and the Kalisz two-string *basy*. West Wielkopolska possesses vocal melodies with the widest average range in Poland, which can be explained by the influence of the *kozioł* scale on singing. Characteristic of the Kujawy subregion are: *kujawiaki*, which are dances somewhat slower than those in, for example, Mazowsze and the Kielce region; dance cycles of various tempos; and a rich technique of violin playing (ex.8). Śląsk has many dances of the polonaise and figure type, and dance-games; ensembles with a relatively large number of wind instruments; and more homophonic songs than other regions. Many survivals of calendar ritual and wedding music are found in the Opole area of Śląsk. In Mazowsze, Kielce and Sandomierz mazurka rhythms are characteristic; the tradition of violin playing is extremely rich in Sandomierz and Kielce. Some characteristics of central Poland are common to the neighbouring regions.

The north-western region has lost its individuality: duple and triple metres are now equally common; the tempo is leisurely and the vocal register fairly low. There is wide use of major and minor scales, and in the Kaszuby region relatively wide melodic intervals are found.

Besides frequent duple and triple metres the north-

Ex.8 The *kujawiak* dance, Kujawy region, played on the violin by Władysław Kwiatkowski (*b* 1903) (Bielawski ed., 1973)

eastern region is characterized by five- and eight-beat bars, and apocope. *Przyśpiewki* in triple time usually contain three syllables to a bar. In five-beat metre a four-syllable group (ex.9a) plays a basic role, and can be seen in verse lines with eight, 11 (ex.7) and 13 syllables. Five-beat bars are mostly associated with wedding songs, fairly slow and not accompanied by dancing: they are found in Kurpie, Mazury and northern Podlasie. In the same area it is possible to find eight-beat bars associated with archaic scales of medium range (e.g. a pentachord, also the pentatonic), with 12-syllable lines, wedding texts and fairly slow tempo. There are

Ex.9 Typical rhythmic formulae in five- and eight-beat bars

two forms of eight-beat bars (exx.9b and c), which are reminiscent of the krakowiak, but are certainly earlier. The archaic manner of articulation of the apocope rests on the absence, or more rarely, the strong diminuendo of the final syllable of the stanza's text (ex.10). The distribution of apocope is similar to that of the five- and eight-beat bars. The songs from this region have

Ex.10 *Leśna* (outdoor) song, Kurpie region (Stęszewski, 1974)

relatively slow medium tempos; its open-air songs (*leśne*) are rich in melisma.

The eastern region is distinguished by its greater number of archaic, slow ritual songs (wedding, harvest and midsummer eve) without metre, which use narrow diatonic (e.g. tetrachordal) scales. In these melodies the highest ratio of melisma has been recorded, with the frequent appearance of somewhat syllabic and non-syllabic verse forms, texts in stichic form and non-stanzaic musical structure. Wedding songs make use of dance melodies to a lesser extent. The dance repertory is largely in triple time (e.g. the *oberek*), and shows a strong influence from central Poland.

The southern region is characterized by a marked preponderance of duple-metre melodies, which also

(a)   *(b)*

8. *Small string instruments of the kit type: (a) złóbcoki played by Adam Kuchta, Bukowina Tatrzańska, Nowy Sacz province, (b) mazanki from Grodzisk Wielkopolski, Poznań province (Państwowe Muzeum Etnograficzne, Warsaw)*

serve as dance *przyśpiewki*. In the lowland parts of the territory krakowiak rhythms are strongly represented, and have spread from there to the highland regions. Parts of the Carpathian district (e.g. Beskid Żywiecki, Podhale and Pieniny) possess their own repertory of dance melodies and dotted rhythms *alla zoppa*. In the Beskid Śląski region chromaticism plays a considerable part; Podhale, Orawa and Pieniny have produced a style of polyphonic singing that owes nothing to Western harmony. Podhale is distinguished by a descending melodic outline; the dance cycles *góralski* (for a pair of soloists) and *zbójnicki* (men's dances); the predominant range of a 6th (in about 30% of the repertory); the frequent occurrence of the F mode; a high vocal register and great tension of the voice in men's singing, and low women's voices; the *koza* and *złóbcoki* (see §5); a decided preponderance of 12-syllable lines; and the dance *ozwodny* with a five-bar phrase (ex.11), which occurs in dance cycles. The music of the mountainous regions is characterized by the narrowest average melodic range; dance- and wedding-songs are performed in tempo giusto, contrasting with the rigours of the slow metrical *wierchowe* and *wałęsane* melodies, sung in the open air.

Ex.11 *Ozwodny* dance, Podhale, two violins and bass (Mierczyński, 1930)

The geo-ethnic situation of Poland is reflected in the character of its folk music. This is connected with western Europe in the decided predominance of strophic song forms and in some of its song subjects (e.g. in the ballad). Polish folk music has the syllabic system of versification common to other western Slavs (except for the Czechs); with the Lusatians it shares the types of instrument which appear in Wielkopolska. With the Finns, Lapps, Estonians and Latvians, Polish folk music shares the five-beat bar structure; with them and with the eastern and southern Slavs, the apocope. The link with the eastern Slavs is also seen in the traces of non-syllabic versification, some common melodic motifs and narrow-range types of scale. With the Slovaks, Hutsuls (from the east Carpathians), Hungarians and Balkan peoples, southern Poles share many instruments, *alla zoppa* rhythms, polyphonic forms and some dances; these phenomena may be traces of the migrations of the Vlachs (Wallachians) who brought their pastoral culture from the south.

There is much to indicate that the boundaries of the Polish language are not barriers to musical phenomena. Polish folk music had a strong influence outside Poland, particularly with its mazurka rhythms, which spread as far as Scandinavia, where they appear in the *polska* dance.

BIBLIOGRAPHY

COLLECTIONS

Ł. Gołębiowski: *Lud polski, jego zwyczaje, zabobony* [The Polish people, their customs and beliefs] (Warsaw, 1830)

W. z Oleska [W. M. Zaleski]: *Pieśni polskie i ruskie ludu galicyjskiego* [Polish and Russian songs of the Galician people] (Lwów, 1833)

K. W. Wójcicki: *Pieśni ludu Białochrobatów, Mazurów i Rusi znad Bugu* [Songs of the people of Białochrobatie, Mazury and the Russians from across the Bug] (Warsaw, 1836/R1976)

J. Konopka: *Pieśni ludu krakowskiego* [Songs of the Kraków people] (Kraków, 1840/R1974)

O. Kolberg: *Pieśni ludu polskiego* [Songs of the Polish people] (Warsaw, 1857)

——: *Lud, jego . . . pieśni, muzyka i tańce* [The people, its . . . songs, music, dances] (Warsaw and Kraków, 1861–90/R1962–8)

——: *Pokucie: obraz etnograficzny* [Ethnographic sketch of Pokucie] (Kraków, 1882–9)

——: *Lubelskie: obraz etnograficzny* (Kraków, 1883)

——: *Mazowsze: obraz etnograficzny* (Kraków, 1885–90)

——: *Chełmskie: obraz etnograficzny* (Kraków, 1890–91)

Z. Gloger and Z. Noskowski: *Pieśni ludu* [Folksongs] (Kraków, 1892)

J. S. Bystroń: *Polska pieśń ludowa: wybór* [Polish folksong: a selection] (Kraków, 1920, 3/1945)

J. S. Bystroń, J. Ligęza, S. M. Stoiński and F. R. Ryling: *Pieśni ludowe z polskiego Śląska* [Folksongs from Polish Silesia] (Kraków, 1927–39, Katowice, 1961)

W. Skierkowski: *Puszcza kurpiowska w pieśni* [Kurpie green forest in song] (Płock, 1928–34)

S. Mierczyński: *Muzyka Podhala/La musique du Podhale* (Lwów and Warsaw, 1930, 3/1973)

E. Mika: *Pieśni orawskie* (Kraków, 1934, 2/1957)

Ł. Kamieński: *Pieśni ludu pomorskiego* [Folksongs from Pomorze] (Toruń, 1936)

J. Chorosiński: *Melodie taneczne Powiśla* [Dance melodies from the banks of the Vistula] (Kraków, 1949, 2/1953)

A. Dygacz and J. Ligęza: *Pieśni ludowe Śląska Opolskiego* [Folksongs from Opole Silesia] (Kraków, 1954)

S. Wallis: *Pieśni górnicze Górnego Śląska* [Mining-songs from Upper Silesia] (Kraków, 1954)

J. Sobieska and M. Sobieski: *Szlakiem kozła lubuskiego* [On the trail of the Lubus kozioł] (Kraków, 1954)

M. Sobieski: *Wybór polskich pieśni ludowych* [Selection of Polish folksongs] (Kraków, 1955)

M. Sobieski and M. Sobolewska: *Pieśni ludowe Warmii i Mazur* [Folksongs from Warmia and Mazury] (Kraków, 1955)

W. Poźniak: *Pieśni ludu krakowskiego* [Songs of the Kraków people] (Kraków, 1956)

E. Mika and A. Chybiński: *Pieśni ludu polskiego na Orawie* [Songs of the Polish people of Orawa] (Kraków, 1957)

J. Sadownik, ed.: *Pieśni Podhala: antologia* [Songs from Podhale: an anthology] (Kraków, 1957, 2/1971)

J. Sobieska: *Wielkopolskie śpiewki ludowe* [Folksongs from Wielkopolska] (Kraków, 1957)

A. Szurmiak-Bogucka: *Górole, górole, góralska muzyka: śpiewki Podhala* [Mountain music: songs from Podhale] (Kraków, 1959)

J. Tacina: *Gronie, nasze gronie* [Our mountain ridges] (Katowice, 1959)

A. Dygacz: *Pieśni górnicze* [Mining-songs] (Katowice, 1960)

J. Burszta, ed.: *O. Kolberg: Dzieła wszystkie* [Collected works] (Kraków, Wrocław and Poznań, 1961–)

A. Glapa and A. Kowalski: *Tańce i zabawy wielkopolskie* [Dances and games from Wielkopolska] (Wrocław, 1961)

J. Tacina: *Pieśni ludowe Śląska Opolskiego* [Folksongs from Opole Silesia] (Katowice, 1963)

S. M. Stoiński: *Pieśni żywieckie* [Songs from Żywiec] (Kraków, 1964) [with appx, *Dudy żywieckie* [Bagpipes from Żywiec]]

A. Oleszczuk: *Pieśni ludowe z Podlasia* [Folksongs from Podlasie] (Wrocław, 1965)

G. Dąbrowska: *Tańce Kurpiów z Puszczy Zielonej* [Kurpie dances from the green forest] (Warsaw, 1967)

J. Mikś: *Pieśni ludowe ziemi Żywieckiej* [Folksongs from Żywiec] (Żywiec, 1968)

W. Kirstein: *Pieśni z Kociewia* [Songs from the Kociewie region] (Gdańsk, 1970)

J. Lisakowski: *Pieśni kaliskie* [Songs from Kalisz] (Kraków, 1971)

B. Krzyżaniak, A. Pawlak and J. Lisakowski: *Polska pieśń i muzyka ludowa, i: Kujawy* [Polish folksong and music, i: Kujawy region] (Kraków, 1974–5)

BOOKS AND ARTICLES

K. Kurpiński: 'O pieśniach w ogólności' [On songs in general],

Tygodnik muzyczny (1820), no.8, p.29; no.9, p.33
H. Windakiewiczowa: 'Rytmika polskiej pieśni ludowej' [The rhythm of Polish folksongs], *Wisła*, ii (1879), 716
——: *Studia nad wierszem i zwrotką poezji polskiej ludowej* [Studies on the verse and stanza of Polish folk poetry] (Kraków, 1913)
B. Wójcik-Keuprulian: 'Polska muzyka ludowa' [Polish folk music], *Lud słowiański*, iii/B (1932), 3–33
K. Moszyński: 'Kultura ludowa słowian' [The culture of the Slav people], *Kultura duchowa*, ii/2 (Kraków, 1939, 2/1967), 1103–1347
S. Benet: *Song, Dance and Customs of Peasant Poland* (London, 1951)
W. Kotoński: 'Uwagi o muzyce ludowej Podhala' [Notes on the folk music of Podhale], *Muzyka*, iv (1953), nos.5–6, p.3; nos.7–8, p.43; nos.11–12, p.26; v/1–2 (1954), 14
C. R. Halski: 'Folk Music: Polish', *Grove 5*
A. Czekanowska: 'Pieśń ludowa Opoczyńskiego na tle problematyki etnograficznej' [Opoczno folksong against the background of ethnographic problems], *Studia muzykologiczne*, v (1956), 444–533
W. Kotoński: *Góralski i zbójnicki: tańce górali podhalańskich* [*Góralski* and *zbójnicki*: dances of Podhale mountaineers] (Kraków, 1956)
A. Wozaczyńska: *Pieśni kurpiowskie: ich struktura i charakterystyka w świetle zbiorów W. Skierkowskiego* [Kurpie songs, their structure and characteristics in the light of W. Skierkowski's collections] (Wrocław, 1956)
L. Bielawski, ed.: *A. Chybiński: O polskiej muzyce ludowej: wybór prac etnograficznych* [On Polish folk music: a selection of his ethnographical works] (Kraków and Warsaw, 1961)
A. Czekanowska: *Pieśni biłgorajskie* [Songs of Biłgoraj] (Wrocław, 1961)
O. Żeromska: *Tańce polskie narodowe i regionalne* [Polish national and regional dances] (London, 1963)
A. Czekanowska: 'The Diatonic Melodies of the Narrow Range in Slavic Countries', *Lud*, l (1964–5), 392
L. Bielawski: 'Muzyka ludowa polska' [Polish folk music], *Słownik folkloru polskiego*, ed. J. Krzyżanowski (Warsaw, 1965), 240
J. Stęszewski: '"Chmiel": szkic problematyki etnomuzycznej wątku' [*Chmiel*: a sketch of the ethnomusicological problems of the type], *Muzyka*, x/1 (1965), 3
R. Lange: 'Historia badań nad tańcem ludowym w Polsce' [A history of research on folkdances in Poland], *Lud*, li (1967), 415–49
J. Stęszewski: 'Die Apokope, eine Eigentümlichkeit im Volksliedervortrag', *Festschrift für Walter Wiora* (Kassel, 1967), 641
W. Kamiński: 'Instrumentarium muzyczne w Polsce średniowiecznej' [An inventory of musical instruments in medieval Poland], *Musica medii aevi*, iii (1968), 7
L. Bielawski: *Rytmika polskich pieśni ludowych* [The rhythm of Polish folksongs] (Kraków, 1970)
A. Czekanowska: *Ludowe melodie wąskiego zakresu w krajach słowiańskich* [Folk melodies of the narrow range in Slavonic countries] (Kraków, 1972)
J. Sobieska: *Ze studiów nad folklorem muzycznym Wielkopolski* [From studies on the folk music of Wielkopolska] (Kraków, 1972)
J. Stęszewski: 'Sachen, Bewusstsein und Benennungen in ethnomusikologischen Untersuchungen', *Jb für Volksliedforschung*, xvii (1972), 131–70
L. Bielawski: 'Polnische Volksgesänge ohne Strophenbau und primitive Strophenformen', *Analyse und Klassifikation von Volksmelodien* (Kraków, 1973), 53
J. Sobieska and M. Sobieski: *Polska muzyka ludowa i jej problemy: wybor prac* [Polish folk music and its problems: a selection of works], ed. L. Bielawski (Kraków, 1973)
J. Stęszewski: 'Polish Research on Musical Folklore after 1945', *9th International Congress of Anthropological and Ethnological Sciences: Chicago 1973*, 109
——: 'Uwagi o badaniu żywej tradycji polskich śpiewów religijnych' [Notes on the research of the living tradition of Polish religious songs], *Stan badań nad muzyką religijną w kulturze polskiej* (Warsaw, 1973), 110
——: 'Uwagi o etnomuzycznej regionalizacji Polski' [Notes on the ethnomusicological regionalization of Poland], *Dyskurs o tradycji* (Wrocław, 1974), 323
——: 'Geige und Geigenspiel in der polnischen Volksüberlieferung', *Die Geige in der europäischen Volksmusik*, ed. W. Deutsch (Vienna, 1975), 16

BOGUSŁAW SCHÄFFER (I), JAN STĘSZEWSKI (II)

Polani, Girolamo (*fl* Venice, 1704–17). Italian singer and composer. He sang as a soprano in the 36-member vocal establishment at St Mark's in Venice. The accounts record that in 1708 he was at the bottom of the pay scale, receiving 25 ducats (other sopranos there were paid as much as 100), as did a tenor on the same roster, Francesco Polani. To supplement this meagre

income he composed a number of operas and appears to have reached the peak of his career in 1709, when two of his works were performed at the Teatro di S Angelo; otherwise most of his operas were for the Teatro di S Fantino, a small, short-lived house specializing in low-budget productions. In 1717 the theatre introduced Venice's first season of comic opera, including Polani's *Chi la fà, l'aspetta*. This work, whose music is lost, is of interest as an early regional development in the genre. It is an urban domestic comedy with skilfully controlled and rapidly moving action, and its characters include a gondolier who speaks in Venetian dialect. Although exactly contemporary with similar developments in Neapolitan *opera buffa*, *Chi la fà* seems to be independent of southern models; rather its dramaturgy derives from the pastoral opera, having only five characters, relatively brief duration (only 25 musical numbers), and a short third act. Nearly all the numbers are da capo exit arias, and the only ensemble is the third act's brief, conventional *coro finale*. The S Fantino's venture into a new genre cannot have had more than moderate success, for it was not imitated by the city's other opera houses, and the theatre closed in 1719.

WORKS

(*opere serie, performed in Venice, unless otherwise stated*)
La costanza nell'honore (F. Passarini), Rovigo, ?Manfredini, 1703; as La vendetta disarmata dall'amore, S Fantino, 1704
Creso tolto a le fiamme (A. Aureli), S Angelo, 1705
Vindice la pazzia della vendetta (B. Pedoni), S Fantino, 1707
La Rosilda (Pedoni), S Fantino, 1707
Prassitele in Gnido (Aureli), SS Apostoli, 1707
Il cieco geloso (Aureli), S Fantino, 1708
La virtù trionfante d'amore vendicativo (Pedoni), S Fantino, 1708
Berengario rè d'Italia (M. Noris), S Angelo, carn. 1709
Il tradimento premiato (G. P. Candi), S Angelo, aut. 1709
Chi la fà, l'aspetta (comic opera, Passarini), S Fantino, carn. 1717

[6] Cantate da camera a voce sola, *GB-Lkc*

BIBLIOGRAPHY

F. Caffi: *Storia della musica sacra nella già cappella ducale di San Marco in Venezia dal 1318 al 1797*, ii (Venice, 1855/R1972), 30f, 45
T. Wiel: *I teatri musicali veneziani nel settecento* (Venice, 1897/R1975 and 1979), esp. pp.xliii f

JAMES L. JACKMAN

Polbero. *See* POWER, LEONEL.

Poldini, Ede (*b* Budapest, 13 June 1869; *d* Corseaux, Vaud, 28 June 1957). Hungarian composer and pianist. He studied with Stephan Tomka at the National Conservatory in Budapest and with Mandyczewski (theory) and Epstein (piano) in Vienna. His studies there were followed by a year in Geneva; then, in 1908, he settled permanently in Bergeroc, Vevey. He received the Hungarian Cross of Merit, second class (1935), and the Hungarian Medal for Artists (1948).

In Hungary Poldini was renowned chiefly for his stage works, but his success was not limited to his native country. *Vagabund und Prinzessin* and *Hochzeit im Fasching*, his two best operas, were both produced in London, the former at Covent Garden in 1906 and the latter, as *Love Adrift*, at the Gaiety Theatre in 1926; *Vagabund* was also seen in around 20 other European cities. His many piano compositions, too, achieved widespread popularity. Poldini's compositional style differs from most of his compatriots at the time in that his links were rather with contemporary French and German music, the Hungarian element serving merely as decoration.

WORKS
(selective list)

Stage: Cartouche (comic opera, 1), 1884, unpubd; Nordlicht (ballet, 1, V. Léon), Budapest, 1894; Dornröschen, Aschenbrödel, Die Knusperhexe (3 children's operas), 1899, Budapest, 1927, orchd T. Polgár; Vagabund und Prinzessin (opera, 1, A. F. Seligmann, after Andersen), Budapest, 1903; Hochzeit im Fasching (opera, 3, B. Diósy), Budapest, 1924; Die gute alte Zeit (operetta), Budapest, 1926; Das Seidennetz (comic opera), Budapest, 1927; Himfy (opera, P. Bodrogh), 1934, Budapest, 1938

Pf: Divertissements; Blumen, op.38, after Rückert; Dekameron, op.39; Walzerbuch, op.42; Masken, op.44; 3 études, op.45; Rosen, op.56, 5 waltzes; Walzerfrühling, op.59; Lustgärten, op.63; Poésies lyriques, op.68; Vortragsstudien, op.70

Other works: orch pieces, incl. arrs. of pf works; choral music, songs

Principal publishers: Bosworth, Challier, Hainauer, Méry, Schott, Simrock, Universal

MELINDA BERLÁSZ KÁROLYI

Pole, David. *See* POHLE, DAVID.

Pole, Hans. *See* POLONUS, JOHANNES.

Pole, William (*b* Birmingham, 22 April 1814; *d* London, 30 Dec 1900). English civil engineer and music scholar. He attained the highest distinction in both science and music. He was professor of civil engineering at University College, London, from 1859 to 1876. A keen student of music from his early years, he graduated at Oxford as BMus in 1860 (at the age of 46) and as DMus in 1867. His interest in music was not solely academic; he was organist in London at St Mark's, North Audley Street, from 1836 to 1866. For his scientific work he was elected a Fellow of the Royal Society of London in 1861 and of the Royal Society of Edinburgh in 1877. From 1878 to 1890 he was one of the examiners for music degrees in the University of London.

Pole is remembered today for his treatise *The Philosophy of Music*. This was not a work on aesthetics, but a reproduction of a series of lectures he had been invited to give in 1877 at the Royal Institution of Great Britain 'on the Theory of Music, as illustrated by the late researches of Helmholtz', i.e. on acoustics as a physiological basis for music theory. The book is still valuable to music students as an introduction to Helmholtz's *Lehre von den Tonempfindungen*.

Pole was active with A. F. Ellis and A. J. Hipkins in the movement that eventually succeeded in lowering the high 19th-century English concert pitch by some two-thirds of a tempered semitone. He contributed several articles to the *Musical Times* and to the first edition of Grove's *Dictionary*, including 'Pitch'. He edited *Three Songs* (London, 1872), providing them with four-hand piano accompaniment, and composed a *Psalm c* performed at Tenbury in 1861, from which he arranged an eight-voice motet (London, 1879) performed at the Chester Festival of 1882.

WRITINGS
Musical Instruments in the Great Industrial Exhibition of 1851 (London, 1851)
'Diagrams and Tables to Illustrate the Nature and Construction of the Musical Scale and the Various Musical Intervals', in F. A. G. Ouseley: *A Treatise on Harmony* (London, 1868)
The Story of Mozart's Requiem (London, 1879) [first printed in *MT*, xiv (1869–71)]
The Philosophy of Music (London, 1879, 6/1924 ed. H. Hartridge)
Notes from my Life and Work (London, 1898) [incl. list of writings]

BIBLIOGRAPHY
F. G. Edwards: Obituary, *MT*, xlii (1901), 103
E. J. Dent: Introduction to W. Pole: *The Philosophy of Music* (London, 6/1924)

GEORGE GROVE/LL. S. LLOYD

Poledňák, Ivan (*b* Velké Meziříčí, 31 Dec 1931). Czech musicologist. He studied musicology and aesthetics at Brno University (1951–6) under Jan Racek, Bohumír Štědroň and the aesthetician Oleg Sus, taking a diploma with a dissertation on Helfert's aesthetics which was accepted for his doctorate in Prague University in 1967. He took the CSc degree in 1969 at Prague with a work on jazz. After completing his studies he worked at the Institute of Educational Research, Prague (1959–68), and wrote a series of methodological papers, textbooks and other material for music education at state schools; at the same time he was vice-president of the Czech Society for Music Education (1969–71). He played an important part in Czechoslovak research into jazz and dance music, a field which had long suffered from dilettantism. As an expert on jazz he was appointed artistic director of the Reduta Intimate Theatre in Prague (1963–72), a small-scale stage specializing in musicals and some experimental work. In 1968 he became a member of the musicology institute at the Czech Academy of Sciences, where he has concentrated on the psychology of music. He is a part-time lecturer in musicology at Prague University.

WRITINGS
'Soupis prací Vladimíra Helferta' [A list of Helfert's works], *Musikologie*, v (1958), 253–313
Kapitolky o jazzu [Chapters on jazz] (Prague, 1961, 2/1964; Slovak trans., 1964)
'Některé problémy rozvoje hudební představivosti' [The development of musical imagination], *HV*, i (1964), 541; ii (1965), 3
with J. Budík: *Výchova hudbou* [Education through music] (Prague, 1964, 2/1972)
——: *Hudba – škola – zítřek* [Music – school – future] (Prague, 1965)
with L. Dorůžka: *Československý jazz: minulost a přítomnost* [Czechoslovak jazz: past history and present] (Prague, 1967)
K estetickým názorům Vladimíra Helferta [Helfert's aesthetics] (diss., U. of Prague, 1967; extracts in *HRo*, x, 1957, 500)
'K otázce specifičnosti jazzu' [What makes jazz specific], *HV*, vi (1969), 419
K problematice jazzové hudby [Questions of jazz music] (CSc diss., U. of Prague, 1969)
'Další poznámky k integraci hudby jazzové oblasti do základní hudební výchovy' [Further remarks on the integration of music from the sphere of jazz into basic music education], *Akcent*, i/2 (1970), 31
'K problému hudebního vkusu' [The problem of musical taste], *HV*, ix (1972), 99
'K metodologickým otázkám psychologie hudby' [Methodological questions of the psychology of music], *HV*, x (1973), 275; xi (1974), 3
with A. Matzner, I. Wasserberger and others: *Československá jazz & pop encyklopedie* (Prague, in preparation)

JOSEF BEK

Polewheel [?Wheeler, Paul] (*fl* 1650–60). English musician and composer. He achieved fame as a violinist during the Commonwealth, but no details of his life are known. His name appears as Paul Wheeler in Evelyn's Diary for 4 March 1656 and a further reference is in John Batchiler's *The Virgin's Pattern* (London, 1661). Two of his pieces for bass viol are in *US-NYp* Drexel 3551 and what appear to be three more are in *GB-Ob* Mus.Sch.C.39. The name 'Paulwheel' is attached to two pieces in Playford's *The Division Violin* (London, 1685) and 'Powlwheel' is also represented in the 1695 edition. *GB-Och* 1183 contains a bass instrumental part by him.

ANDREW ASHBEE

Policci, Giovanni Battista (*fl* 1665–84). Italian composer and organist. He competed unsuccessfully for the post of *vicemaestro di cappella* of St Maria della Steccata, Parma, in 1665 but obtained it on 22 July 1667 on the death of Francesco Manelli. On 23 May 1670 he was named organist of the same church, and on 3 October 1681 *maestro di cappella*. From 23

Scptcmbcr of that year to August 1684 he also served as *vicemaestro* of the Parma court, for which in 1681 he composed *Amore riconciliato con Venere*, an introduction to a ballet, and the opera *Amalasunta in Italia*, performed in the theatre of the Collegio dei Nobili, both to texts by Alessandro Guidi. None of his music is known to survive.

BIBLIOGRAPHY
EitnerQ; RicordiE
L. Balestrieri: *Feste e spettacoli alla corte dei Farnesi* (Parma, 1909)
N. Pelicelli: 'Musicisti in Parma nei secoli xv–xvi', *NA*, ix (1932), 217

Policki [Pol; first name unknown] (*fl c*1750). Polish composer. As many of his works are in the Cistercian monastery libraries at Mogiła and Obra, it is probable that he belonged to a Cistercian order, further implied by the monogram RP (? Reverendus Pater) which precedes his name in surviving manuscripts. Three masses with instruments and a shortened Vespers cycle, also with instruments (all *PL-MO*), provide interesting examples of the development of the Classical style in Poland, and also illustrate the infiltration of the polonaise into contemporary sacred music. These works adhere to the early *galant* style – though retaining the da capo form and two- to three-part vocal texture of the Italian Baroque tradition – and are distinguished by interesting melodic invention. A Benedictus is edited in Florilegium Musicae Antiquae, xxiii (1967), and in Musica Antiqua Polonica, Baroque (1969). Two further masses (formerly in *PL-OB*) were lost in World War II.

BIBLIOGRAPHY
A. Chybiński: 'Przyczyny do historii krakowskiej kultury muzycznej XVII i XVIII wieku' [Contribution towards the history of Kraków musical culture in the 17th and 18th centuries], *Wiadomości muzyczne* (1925), nos.5–6
——: *Słownik muzyków dawnej Polski* [Dictionary of early Polish musicians] (Kraków, 1949)
T. Strumiłło: *Źródła i początki romantyzmu w muzyce polskiej* [The sources of romanticism in Polish music] (Kraków, 1956), 72
Z. M. Szweykowski: 'Z zagadnień melodyki w polskiej muzyce wokalno-instrumentalnej późnego baroku' [The question of melody in Polish vocal-instrumental music of the late Baroque], *Muzyka*, vi/2 (1961), 53
K. Mrowiec: *Pasje wielogłosowe w muzyce polskiej XVIII wieku* [Polyphonic Passions in Polish music of the 18th century] (Kraków, 1972), 120, 172, 181
MIROSŁAW PERZ

Policreto [Policreti, Policretto], **Giuseppe** [Giosef] (*b* Treviso; *fl* 1571–80). Italian composer, writer and poet. He was a monk in the order of the Servi di Maria and appears not to have held any professional musical post. In the dedication of his *Il primo libro delle napolitane* (Venice, 1571⁹), for three voices, he referred to the contents as being his first works. He was probably active in Padua about 1580, for he signed the dedication of his *Boscareccie: terzo libro delle canzoni* (Venice, 1580) for three and six voices from there. His other known works are *Il secondo libro delle giustiniane* (Venice, 1575¹⁴), for three voices, and a five-voice madrigal in *Delli pietosi affetti* (Venice, 1598⁶).

BIBLIOGRAPHY
G. Alberti: *Selva letteraria d'uomini illustri per dottrina dei Servi di Maria* (MS, *I-Fn* Conv.sopp.1257, A.6), 86
G. Gaspari: *Catalogo della biblioteca del Liceo musicale di Bologna*, iii (Bologna, 1893/R1961), 250
A. M. Vicentini: 'Memorie di musicisti dell'ordine dei Servi di Maria', *NA*, viii (1931), 43
N. Bridgman: 'Musique profane italienne des 16e et 17e siècles dans les bibliothèques françaises', *FAM*, ii (1955), 52
PIER PAOLO SCATTOLIN

Polidori, Ortensio (*b* Camerino; *fl* 1621–54). Italian composer. He was *maestro di cappella* of Fermo Cathedral from 1621 to 1630, at Pesaro Cathedral in 1634 and at Chieti from 1639 to 1646. According to Schmidl he afterwards held a similar post at Palermo. Eight collections by him published before 1621 are lost. His surviving output consists entirely of sacred music, including a large proportion of mass and psalm settings. A number of these are for large forces – either the conventional double choir of opp.10 and 16 or more modern mixed concertato ensembles including violins and (in op.14) trombones or viols. His motet collections are for smaller combinations; op.13 includes competent solo motets with declamatory lines to which ornamental semiquaver runs are added sparingly for expressive effect. The time signature 6/4 is found in a duet in this volume – an early instance of its use in church music.

WORKS
(published in Venice unless otherwise stated)

Motecta, 2–4vv, liber I, op.2 (1612), lost
Il quinto libro de motetti, 2–5vv, bc (org), op.9 (1621)
[3] Messe a 2 chori, bc, libro I, op.10 (1622)
Messe, 5, 8vv, con ripieni e 2 vn, bc (1631)
Salmi, 5vv, bc, op.12 (1634)
Motetti, 1, 2vv, bc, op.13 (1637)
[2] Messe, 5, 8vv, bc, 2 vn ad lib, ed anche con ripieni, trbns/viols/other insts, op.14 (1639)
Salmi, 3, 5vv, bc, 2 vn ad lib ed anche con ripieni di trbns/viols/other insts . . . libro II, op.15 (1641)
Salmi a 2 chori, libro II, op.16 (1646)
Salmi a 2 chori, parte concertati e parte pieni, 8vv, bc, op.17 (Rome, 1654)

BIBLIOGRAPHY
SchmidlD
L. Virgili: 'La cappella musicale della chiesa metropolitana di Fermo', *NA*, vii (1930), 1–86
JEROME ROCHE

Poliński, Aleksander (*b* Włostów, 4 June 1845; *d* Warsaw, 13 Aug 1916). Polish writer on music, critic and journalist. He studied medicine and sang in the choir of an Augustine church in Warsaw. Cutting short his medical studies, he began a course at the Warsaw Conservatory with Żeleński, Noskowski and Minchejmer. From about 1880 until his death he was a music critic and journalist for the Warsaw newspapers and magazines *Kurier warszawski* (permanent reviewer from 1889 to 1914), *Tygodnik ilustrowany*, *Kłosy*, *Echo muzyczne, teatralne i artystyczne*, *Scena i sztuka* and many others. From 1903 to 1916 he taught at the Warsaw Conservatory, lecturing in Polish music history. He also composed (two masses and a number of religious songs), and edited a number of early works for performance and publication.

Poliński's main interest was the history of Polish music: he collected a large number of sources and materials (his rich collection, kept in the royal palace in Warsaw, was lost during World War II), published treatises, books and articles and organized concerts of early works. He was the author of the first broad history of Polish music (1907); in it he used source materials to outline the development of culture and musical life in Poland in a historical and social context. He also tried to bring about an appreciation of Polish music of specific periods; his writings include a monograph on the medieval religious song *Bogurodzica* (1903).

WRITINGS
'Mikołaj Gomółka i jego psalmy' [Gomółka and his psalms], *Echo muzyczne*, iv (1880)
'Wacław z Szamotuł Szamotulski, sławny muzyk z XVI wieku' [Szamotuł, a famous musician of the 16th century], *Echo muzyczne*, v (1881)

'Znakomitsi muzycy cudzoziemscy w Polsce' [Distinguished foreign musicians in Poland], *Echo muzyczne*, vi (1882)

'Notatki z bibliografii muzycznej' [Notes from musical biography], *Echo muzyczne i teatralne*, i (1884)

'Monumenta musices sacrae in Polonia', *Echo muzyczne, teatralne i artystyczne*, iii (1886)

'Walenty Greff Bakfark, nadworny lutnista Zygmunta Augusta' [Bakfark, court lutenist to Sigismund Augustus], *Echo muzyczne, teatralne i artystyczne*, iv (1887)

Katalog rozumowany pierwszej polskiej wystawy muzycznej [Catalogue raisonné of the first Polish music exhibitions] (Warsaw, 1888)

'O muzyce kościelnej i jej reformie' [On church music and its reform], *Echo muzyczne, teatralne i artystyczne*, vi (1889); also pubd separately (Warsaw, 1888)

Pieśń Bogurodzica pod względem muzycznym [Musical view of Bogurodzica] (Warsaw, 1903)

Dzieje muzyki polskiej w zarysie [History of Polish music in outline] (Lwów, 1907)

Chopin (Kiev, 1914)

Moniuszko (Kiev, 1914)

'Nieznany skarb muzyczny' [An unknown musical treasure], *Kwartalnik muzyczny*, i/3 (1912)

EDITIONS

Mikołaj Gomółka: 10 psalms, *Jana Kochanowskiego: dzieła wszystkie* [Complete works of Kochanowski], i (Warsaw, 1884), 253ff

Śpiewy chóralne kościoła rzymsko-katolickiego zebrane z zabytków muzyki religijnej polskiej z XVI i XVII wieku [Choral songs of the Roman Catholic Church collected from monuments of Polish religious music of the 16th and 17th centuries] (Warsaw, 1890)

BIBLIOGRAPHY

SMP

A. Chybiński: 'Poliński Aleksander: Dzieje muzyki polskiej w zarysie' [Poliński: *History of Polish music in outline*], *Przegląd powszechny*, xcviii (1908), 119; also in *Sfinks*, ii/4 (1908), 147

Z. Jachimecki: 'Najnowsze prace z dziedziny historii muzyki polskiej' [The newest work on the heritage of Polish music history], *Ateneum polskie*, i (1908), 407; also in *Przegląd polski*, clxvii/3 (1908), 150

M. Synoradzki: 'Z Warszawy' [From Warsaw], *Biesiada literacka*, lxxxii (1916), no.35, p.130

K. Morawska: 'Badania nad muzyką dawną w Polsce w XIX wieku' [Research on early music in Poland in the 19th century], *Szkice o kulturze muzycznej XIX w.: studia i materiały*, iii, ed. Z. Chechlińska (Warsaw, 1976), 69, 83, 123

KATARZYNA MORAWSKA

Poliphant [polyphon(e)]. An English plucked instrument of the early 17th century. John Playford attributed its invention to Daniel Farrant and described it as 'An Excellent Instrument . . . not much unlike a lute, but strung with wire'. Talbot mentioned its wire strings and scalloped shape. It seems to have been an attempt at a diatonically tuned hybrid of all the wire-strung instruments (including the harp), with short treble strings played open across a lute-shaped body, fingered strings over a fingerboard, and long bass diapasons like those of a theorbo. A 17th-century drawing by Randle Holme (*Academy of Armory*, GB-*Lbm* Harl.2034; see illustration) shows 41 strings, but Talbot mentioned only 37. John Evelyn's description of the poliphant in his diary for 14 August 1661 shows that by then it was

Drawing of an instrument described as a poliphant from Randle Holme's 'Academy of Armory', 17th century (GB-Lbm Harl.2034, f.207v)

considered very rare: 'the Polyphone, an instrument having something of the Harp, lute, Theorb &c: it was a sweete Instrument, by none known in England, or described by any Author'.

BIBLIOGRAPHY

M. Tilmouth: 'Some Improvements in Music Noted by William Turner in 1697', *GSJ*, x (1957), 57

D. Gill: 'The Orpharion and Bandora', *GSJ*, xiii (1960), 14

——: 'James Talbot's Manuscript: the Wire-strung Fretted Instruments and the Guitar', *GSJ*, xv (1962), 60

IAN HARWOOD

Polish Music Publications. *See* POLSKIE WYDAWNICTWO MUZYCZNE.

Poliziano [Ambrogini Poliziano], **Angelo** (*b* Montepulciano, Tuscany, 1454; *d* Florence, 1494). Italian humanist and poet. He spent most of his life in the service of the Medici family. He was close to Lorenzo de' Medici, whose children he taught, and on his death wrote a lament, *Quis dabit capiti meo aquam*, which Isaac set to music. Poliziano was equally at home in Latin or Tuscan verse. His poetry was set by contemporary Florentine composers such as Isaac, Bartolomeo degli Organi and Pintelli as well as by a younger generation, including Bernardo Pisano. Tromboncino, Cara and other frottolists also set occasional verse by him. Poliziano's celebrated *Fabula di Orfeo*, an entertainment written in various verse forms for a half-spoken, half-sung performance, was probably written for the Carnival season in Mantua in 1480 during one of his short periods away from Florence. No music has survived (an ascription of the music to 'Germi' is a misreading in Carducci's edition); the style was probably similar to that of an anonymous setting of Poliziano's *Canzone di maggio* in Razzi's *Libro primo delle laude spirituali* (*RISM* 1563⁶). *Orfeo*, long described as an epoch-making secularization of religious drama, is probably better considered as looking forward to the rise of both the *intermedio* and dramatic performances. The poem was twice recast as a drama.

BIBLIOGRAPHY

G. Carducci, ed.: *Le Stanze, L'Orfeo e le Rime de Messer Angelo Poliziano* (Florence, 1863)

I. Del Lungo, ed.: *Prose volgari inedite e poesie latini e greche . . . di Angelo Ambrogini Poliziano* (Florence, 1867)

N. Sapegno: *Commento alle rime del Poliziano* (Rome, 1949, 2/1955)

Il Poliziano e il suo tempo: IV convegno internazionale di studi sul Rinascimento: Firenze 1954

J. J. Gallucci: *Festival Music in Florence, ca. 1480–ca. 1520* (diss., Harvard U., 1966)

I. Maïer: *Ange Politien: la formation d'un poète humaniste, 1469–1480* (Geneva, 1966)

W. Osthoff: *Theatergesang und darstellende Musik in der italienischen Renaissance* (Tutzing, 1969)

N. Pirrotta and E. Povoledo: *Li due Orfei: da Poliziano a Monteverdi* (Turin, 1969, rev. 2/1975)

F. W. Sternfeld: 'The Birth of Opera: Ovid, Poliziano, and the *lieto fine*', *AnMc*, no.19 (1979), 30

JAMES HAAR

Polka. A lively couple-dance in 2/4 time. It originated in Bohemia as a round-dance, and became one of the most popular ballroom dances of the 19th century. Its origins are somewhat obscure; music with the polka's characteristics is in various collections written about 1800 for practical use by village musicians. It has been suggested that the name is derived either from the Czech *půlka* ('half'), the characteristic feature of the dance being its short heel-and-toe half-steps, or from *pole* ('field'); more probably it comes from the Czech term for a Polish girl, *polska*, either as the title of a vocal

Eight varieties of the polka: cover of 'Original Polka Quadrilles' (c1845) published by Louis Jullien

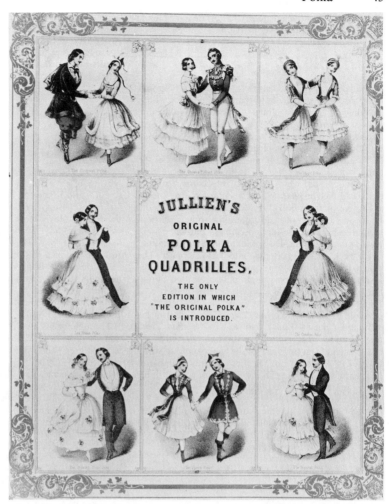

accompaniment to the dance or in reference to the krakowiak dance-songs which the Bohemians adapted for their polkas.

The polka was introduced to Prague in 1837 and appeared in print the same year in Berra's collection *Prager Lieblings-Galoppen für Pianoforte*. In the following years innumerable polkas were written by such composers as Hilmar, Joseph Labitzky and Josef Neruda, and were published in collections of dances or in special series with picturesque or topical titles. In 1839 the band of a Bohemian regiment took the polka to Vienna, and that year it also reached St Petersburg. The Prague dancing-master Johann Raab introduced it to Paris in 1840, though it was not until 1843–4 that it became the favourite dance of Parisian society. On 11 April 1844 the dance was first performed in London by Carlotta Grisi and Jules Perrot on the stage of Her Majesty's Theatre. The next month it appeared in the USA, where it gave rise to numerous jokes about the presidential candidate J. K. Polk. In 1845 the polka was danced at Calcutta at a ball given by the governor-general in honour of Queen Victoria. It attained extraordinary popularity, and clothes, hats, streets and even puddings were named after it. Magazines and newspapers of the time were full of news items, descriptions, illustrations and advertisements referring to the dance.

From Paris the correspondent of *The Times* reported that 'politics is for the moment suspended in public regard by the new and all-absorbing pursuit, the Polka'. *Punch*, in the year of the polka's arrival in London, despaired of the constant allusions to the dance heard in society: 'Can you dance the Polka? Do you like the Polka? Polka – Polka – Polka – Polka – it is enough to drive me mad'. In the early days of its triumphant round-the-world tour the polka was accompanied by related Bohemian dances, such as the *třasák* which became known in German-speaking countries as the *Polka tremblante*, the *skočná* which became known in Vienna as the *Zäpperlpolka*, and the 3/4 time *rejdovák* which became known in France and the USA as the *redowa*. However, local dancing-masters introduced their own variants; during the 1840s the polka-mazurka was popular, combining polka steps with the 3/4 time of the mazurka; in Germany the *Kreuzpolka* was the most popular form, and in Viennese ballrooms during the 1850s two distinct forms evolved, the graceful *Polka française* and the livelier *Schnell-Polka* which was similar to the galop.

According to Cellarius's *La danse des salons* (Paris, 1847) the tempo of the polka was that of a military march played rather slowly, at 52 bars (104 crotchets) per minute. The music was usually in ternary form with eight-bar sections, sometimes with a brief introduction and coda. The characteristic rhythm of the dance (ex.1) emphasizes the third quaver of the bar.

Ex.1

The polka was cultivated by all the leading ballroom dance composers of the latter part of the 19th century, including the Strausses, Gungl, Lumbye and Waldteufel. It even affected popular song, as attested by George Grossmith's *See me dance the polka* (1886). Along with the waltz it was a staple of military bands and mid-19th-century popular sheet music. But by the end of the century it was reverting to its position as a Czech national dance, of which the best 20th-century example is Jaromír Vejvoda's (*b* 1902) *Škoda lásky*, also known as the 'Rosamunde Polka' or 'Beer-barrel Polka'. In the USA polkas are still performed by some ballroom orchestras and accordion ensembles, particularly in areas with a large mid-European immigrant population.

The polka was also adopted into 'serious' music. The phases of this process are seen in Smetana's music: his piano pieces range from simple polkas, written during the 1840s, to refined and expressive pieces in the *Czech Dances* (1877–8); he used the polka in his operas *The Bartered Bride*, *The Kiss* and *Two Widows*, and in his symphonic poems *Vltava* and *From Bohemian Fields and Groves*. The polka was introduced into the cyclic sonata form by Fibich in the Scherzo of his String Quartet in A (1874), but the most famous example in this genre is by Smetana, in the second movement of his string quartet *From my Life* (1876). A noted 20th-century example is in Weinberger's opera *Shvanda the Bagpiper* (1927), and others are in Walton's *Façade* (1922), Shostakovich's ballet *The Golden Age* (1930) and Stravinsky's *Circus Polka* (1942).

BIBLIOGRAPHY

A. Waldau: *Böhmische Nationaltänze* (Prague, 1859–60)
Č. Zíbrt: *Jak se kdy v Čechách tancovalo* [How they used to dance in Bohemia] (Prague, 1895)
Z. Nejedlý: *Bedřich Smetana*, ii (Prague, 1925) [with list of early polkas]

For further bibliography *see* DANCE.

GRACIAN ČERNUŠÁK/ANDREW LAMB

Pollak, Anna (*b* Manchester, 1 May 1912). English mezzo-soprano. Born of Austrian parents, she spent much of her childhood in the Netherlands, returning to England to complete her education. She joined Henry Baynton's Shakespeare Company, playing juvenile roles; after a period in repertory, musical comedy, operetta and with the Entertainments National Services Association during the war, she began to study singing with Joan Cross. She made her début in Sadler's Wells Opera's first postwar season, as Dorabella in June 1945, and remained with the company until 1961, creating Lady Nelson (Berkeley's *Nelson*) and Mrs Strickland (Gardner's *The Moon and Sixpence*), and singing several travesty roles, including Cherubino, Siebel, Hänsel, Orlofsky and Lehl (*The Snow Maiden*); she also scored a great success as Carmen in Dennis Arundell's 1949 production. With the English Opera Group she created Bianca in *The Rape of Lucretia* (1946), the title role in Berkeley's *Ruth* (1956) and several parts in Williamson's *English Eccentrics* (1964). She sang Fatima in a rare revival of Weber's *Oberon*, at the 1950 Holland Festival, Cherubino at Covent Garden (1952) and Dorabella at Glyndebourne (1952–3). Her last public appearances

were as Public Opinion in Offenbach's *Orphée aux enfers* at the Coliseum in autumn 1968. Despite her virtual lack of formal musical or vocal training, Pollak was one of the most musical, versatile and satisfying singers in English opera of the postwar period and an actress of great accomplishment and style.

HAROLD ROSENTHAL

Pollak, Frank. *See* PELLEG, FRANK.

Pollak, Rose. *See* PAULY, ROSE.

Pollarolo, (Giovanni) Antonio (*b* Brescia, baptized 12 Nov 1676; *d* Venice, 30 May 1746). Italian composer, son of Carlo Francesco Pollarolo. He was a pupil of his father and perhaps of Lotti. When he was 13 years old the family moved from Brescia to Venice. His first employment at St Mark's began in 1702 as substitute for his father, who was *vicemaestro di cappella*. In 1723 Antonio assumed this office in his own right. When the *primo maestro*, Biffi, died in 1733, Pollarolo participated in an inconclusive competition for the vacated position. He served as acting *maestro* for three years until a second competition was won by Lotti, and in 1740 succeeded Lotti as *primo maestro*.

Throughout his life Pollarolo lived in the parish of S Simone Grande in Venice. His first wife died in 1709, leaving three young children; his second wife, whom he married in 1712, bore him four more children.

His first opera was *L'Aristeo*, performed at Venice in 1700, followed by *Griselda* (1701) and *Demetrio e Tolomeo* (1702). He began composing operas and oratorios again in 1714, starting with *Recognitio fratrum*, an oratorio written for the Ospedale degl'Incurabili, where his father was *maestro*. In 1716 Antonio was himself elected *maestro di coro* at one of the Venetian conservatories, the so-called Ospedaletto, for which he wrote the Latin oratorios *Sacrum amoris* (1716) and *Sterilis fecunda* (1717). In 1718 he composed the *Oratorio per il Ss Natale* for Rome. He contributed music to the opera *Nerone fatto Cesare* (Venice, 1715) and probably for a setting of *Venceslao* (1721). For a decade his operas were produced at Venetian theatres. *Cosröe* was performed in Rome in 1723 and the serenata *I tre voti* in Vienna in 1724.

In the early librettos Antonio Pollarolo is called the 'emulator' of his celebrated father, Carlo Francesco. That he was no longer so described in his second main series of operas, beginning in 1719, possibly signifies that he was then recognized as a composer in his own right. His operatic style can be only partly judged because his datable extant music comes from so short a period (1721–4) and consists chiefly of arias; only *I tre voti* survives complete. A eulogy of the Empress Elizabeth, the text offered little opportunity for dramatic development, but the music is rich in style, from the festive five-part sinfonia to the terzettos (marked 'coro') and the accompanied and ensemble recitatives. But the most worthwhile music is in the extended da capo arias, which exceed his father's in scope and virtuosity. The *A* section is tripartite, with an orchestral introduction. The return of *A* is often abbreviated, even to the point of recapitulating only the introduction. Basso continuo arias have almost entirely given way to orchestrally accompanied ones. The vocal themes are more interesting than his father's because of their lively, syncopatcd rhythms, and thcir widc-ranging coloratura is a true vehicle for the virtuoso singers of the period.

WORKS

Plautilla (opera, V. Cassiani), Venice, 1721, arias in *D-Mbs* 1117 and 1139

Cosröe (opera, A. Zeno), Rome, 1723, 13 arias in *F-Pc* D12707

I tre voti (serenata, Cassiani), Vienna, 1724, score *A-Wn* 17732

Cantatas: Dopo lungo, A, bc, *D-Mbs* 67/347; Stanco ormai di cercar, S, bc, *I-Nc* 22.2.16

Motets: Alleluia cigni canori, A, vn, va, bc; Quid quaeritis in terra, A, 3 insts; Silete gentes silete, A, bc; *D-B* 30260

Arias in *GB-Cfm* 45, *Lbm* Add.14215, *Lcm* 1741, *I-Mc* Arch.Mus.Noseda 0, 31–15, 31–16

Lost works include the operas: L'Aristeo (G. C. Corradi), Venice, 1700; Griselda (Zeno), Venice, 1701; Demetrio e Tolomeo (A. Marchi), Venice, 1702; Nerone fatto Cesare (M. Noris), Venice, 1715; Leucippo e Teonoe (P. M. Suarez), Venice, 1719; La figlia che canta (F. Passarini), Venice, 1719 (possibly by Pollarolo or 'diversi'); Lucio Papirio dittatore (Zeno), Venice, 1721; Venceslao (Zeno), Venice, 1721 (only Acts 2 and 3 by Pollarolo); Turia Lucrezia (D. Lalli), Venice, 1728; L'abbandono di Arminda (G. Boldini), Venice, 1729; Sulpizia fedele (Lalli, Boldini), Venice, 1729; and the oratorios: Recognitio fratrum, Venice, 1714; Sacrum amoris novendiale in Dei pariture virginis gloriam (G. Cassetti), Venice, 1716; Sterilis fecunda (Cassetti), Venice, 1717; Oratorio per il Ss Natale, Rome, 1718

OLGA TERMINI

Pollarolo, Carlo Francesco (*b* c1653; *d* Venice, 7 Feb 1723). Italian composer and organist. His works, especially the operas, illustrate the stylistic transition from the late Venetian to the Neapolitan school of opera composers.

1. LIFE. He was probably a pupil of his father, Orazio Pollarolo, organist in Brescia at the parish church of SS Nazaro e Celso (c1665–1669) and at the cathedral (1669–c1675). Before 1676, in which year his son Antonio Pollarolo was born, Carlo Francesco was organist at the Congregazione dei Padri della Pace, and he substituted for his father at the cathedral for more than a year before being named his successor on 18 December 1676 (it is not known when Orazio had left the city or where he went). On becoming organist at the cathedral Carlo Francesco relinquished his other post. The records of the parish church of SS Nazaro e Celso establish his marriage in 1674 and the baptisms of his first two children. The family moved at least twice to different parishes of the city, for the baptisms of the next two children, in 1678 and 1679, are recorded at the church of S Afra, whereas those of four more children between 1682 and 1689 are recorded at S Zeno.

During these years Pollarolo advanced rapidly in his profession. On 12 February 1680 the *maestro di cappella*, Pietro Pelli, resigned his position at Brescia Cathedral, and Pollarolo was elected *capo musico* in his place. On 7 June 1681 he assumed a comparable position in the Accademia degli Erranti, a society devoted to 'letters, arms, and music'; he probably continued in this capacity until 1689. A libretto records the performance in 1680 of his earliest oratorio, *La fenice*, whose music is lost. From 1685 on his activity as opera and oratorio composer intensified: *I delirii per amore* was given at Brescia, *La Rosinda* in Vienna (both in 1685), *Il demone amante, overo Giugurta* opened the 1686 season in Venice, followed the same year by *Il Licurgo, overo Il cieco d'acuta vista*. His *Rodrigo* (1687), *La costanza gelosa negl'amori di Cefalo e Procri* (1688) and *Alarico re de Gotti* (1689) were given at Verona, and a version of *Antonino e Pompeiano* with most of the music by Pollarolo at the Teatro Grande in Brescia in 1689. Thus he was an established composer before his arrival in Venice. He and his family must

have lcft Brcscia by thc cnd of 1689, when a new organist (Giovanni Battista Quaglia) was elected at the cathedral, but his younger brother Paolo (*b* 1672) and the latter's son Orazio (*d* 1765), who composed a few operas, pursued musical careers in Brescia. His daughter Giulia married the organ builder Giacinto Pescetti, a fellow Brescian, in 1697 and the opera composer GIOVANNI BATTISTA PESCETTI was their son.

On 13 August 1690 Carlo Francesco was elected second organist at St Mark's, Venice. Two years later he attained the position of *vicemaestro di cappella*, an unusually quick advancement. From 1691 his operas were performed in the Venetian theatres at the rate of one or more each year. He dominated the most reputable opera house in the city, S Giovanni Grisostomo, from about 1691 to about 1707 and also had works staged at S Angelo, S Cassiano, S Fantino and other theatres in and outside Venice.

The Pollarolo family settled in the parish of S Simone Grande in Venice, where a further son was born in 1692. Ten years later Carlo Francesco competed for the position of *primo maestro* at the cathedral but lost the election by one vote to Antonio Biffi. Three months later Pollarolo was 'giubilato', i.e. relieved of his regular duties without loss of status, and his son Antonio took over his duties as *vicemaestro*. But Pollarolo's activity as an opera composer had reached a peak and continued strongly until about 1720. His best works date from the period from 1690 to 1705. His tenure as musical director of the Ospedale degl'Incurabili, one of the four famous Venetian conservatories, can be ascertained from librettos and from Coronelli's *Guida de' forestieri*: it dated at least from 1696 to 1718, perhaps even to 1722. The librettos of the Latin oratorios *Tertius crucis triumphus* (1703), *Samson vindicatus* (1706), *Joseph in Aegypto* (1707), *Rex regum* (1716) and *Davidis de Goliath triumphus* (1718) establish his authorship of the music as well as his position at the Incurabili. He wrote music for other institutions and occasions too: in 1697 an oratorio, *Il combattimento degli angioli*, for the Oratorio of S Maria della Consolazione (La Fava), in 1699 an intermezzo, *Il giudizio di Paride*, for the Accademia degli Animosi, whose guiding spirit was Apostolo Zeno. Then in 1716 Pollarolo composed a cantata, *Fede, Valore, Gloria e Fama* (in which Faustina Bordoni sang the part of Faith), for the Austrian ambassador to Venice, and the wedding of the ambassador's son in 1721 was celebrated with Pollarolo's music to *Il pescator disingannato*. His last stage work was the opera *L'Arminio*, produced in November 1722, when he was already suffering from his final illness, which lasted six months. He was buried in S Maria di Nazaret, known as the Chiesa degli Scalzi, located on the bank of the Grand Canal in Venice.

2. WORKS. Pollarolo wrote some 85 operas and 13 oratorios over a period of 42 years (1680–1722). He belongs to the generation of Marc'Antonio Ziani and Perti. His operas were performed throughout Italy and in Vienna, Brunswick and Ansbach, but his popularity did not outlive him. His chief librettists were Corradi, Frigimelica Roberti, Noris, Silvani and Zeno. Of these Noris is known for his deference to the taste of the Venetian public, whereas Frigimelica Roberti and Zeno worked towards the reform of librettos.

Pollarolo's early operatic style, derived from Legrenzi and Pallavicino, reflects his attention to dramatic and textual expression. The recitatives range from an epic style with longer note values to a quasi-secco style with many repeated notes. A more florid melodic line often appears in cadences just before an aria. Even fully-fledged coloratura passages, whether intended as word-painting or not, occur in the recitatives. Pollarolo frequently alternated recitatives with ariosos of varying metre (4/4, 3/4, 3/2). These features contribute to the refreshing flexibility in compositional technique which is in strong contrast to the stereotyped scene structure of the later works of Pollarolo and his contemporaries. The melodic style had not yet congealed into formulae for questions, exclamations or cadences. Short exclamations by a group of people may be set as recitatives. Sometimes a repeated phrase, in recitative or arioso, functions as a refrain either to unify the section or to define a persistent mood; the result is a kind of miniature rondo form.

By *Il Faramondo* in 1699 ariosos had disappeared from Pollarolo's operas. Recitatives are more in the secco style; expression is now concentrated in harmonic shifts, modulations, affective intervals, chromatic bass lines and dissonances between vocal and bass lines. Accompanied recitatives become focal points of expression; the earliest example occurs in *La Rosinda* (1685). The early arias are brief, but already in *ABA* form with variations such as an abbreviated or an expanded reprise. Arias accompanied only by the basso continuo outnumber those with orchestra. The bass may simply give harmonic support or move in patterns totally independent of the vocal theme (e.g. 'Non lagrimate, no' from *Il Roderico*, 1686, Act 1 scene xiii).

The expansion and orchestral elaboration of the accompanied aria is one of Pollarolo's chief contributions to Venetian opera. Thematically the arias of the middle period are undistinguished, but formally they expand to da capo arias with a bipartite *A* section. The basic principle of da capo form is constantly varied by some unusual melodic, harmonic or formal trait. In the last works Pollarolo even approaches a tripartite *A* section (e.g. 'O sommo Apollo' from *Astinome*, 1719). Recitative interrupting an aria forms an effective dramatic device (e.g. 'Ha soave e dolce vita' from the undatable oratorio *Isabelle*). In the 1690s the orchestral arias began to increase in number; in *Ariodante* (1716) they outnumber continuo arias by a ratio of four to one. In his early works the accompaniments usually consist of three-part strings (unmarked in the scores) in which the two treble parts tend to be widely separated from the bass. During the 1690s a wide variety of instrumental combinations appears, ranging from one to eight parts but most often five. Interesting examples include a solo violin in duet with the voice without bass in 'Usignuoli che cantate' from *Onorio in Roma* (1692), Act 3 scene vi; three-part strings without bass in 'Il viver mio si chiude' from *La forza della virtù* (1693), Act 3 scene ii; cornett and bass in 'Aure vaghe' from *Ottone* (1694), Act 2 scene i; oboe and bass in 'Fede e onor' from *Le pazzie degli amanti* (1701), Act 2 scene iv; two tenor violas, violone and theorbo in 'In quel piè legato' from *Onorio in Roma*, Act 2 scene iv; five-part strings plus two oboes in 'O non ti rivedrò' from *Ottone*, Act 3 scene ix; and the same with timpani in 'All'armi' in *La forza della virtù*, Act 3 scene viii. Pollarolo was one of the first Venetian composers to introduce the oboe into the opera orchestra. In *Onorio in Roma* (Act 3 scene ii) he transfers the concerto grosso principle to the operatic

stage: the five-part orchestra on stage alternates with the three-part concertino off-stage. Elsewhere the alternation between tutti and concertino serves to reduce the accompanying sound during the singer's phrases. Devices such as offstage singing, offstage obbligatos, and echo effects are frequent in the oratorios as well as in the operas. In Pollarolo's late operas the variety of instrumental combinations and effects gives way to a basic four-part texture; and his instrumental style develops from simple chordal writing to idiomatic string writing of some virtuosity. The sinfonia of *Onorio in Roma* features five idiomatic string parts in addition to the simpler figured bass part. Others are scored for four-part strings and winds (oboes, trumpets or trombones), as in *La forza della virtù* and *Ariodante*. The form of the sinfonia loosely resembles the Scarlattian type, varied by elements from the French overture.

Ensemble singing is limited to relatively short duets; only in the finales do we find brief vocal trios, quartets or quintets. Choruses appear only in the oratorios *Jesabelle* and *Jefte* (1702); those in the latter score are exceptional in being written in a quasi-polyphonic style over a figured bass.

It is the increasing standardization in Pollarolo's later operas (scenes divided into long passages of secco recitative followed by large-scale da capo arias) coupled with a virtuoso vocal style that links him with the so-called Neapolitan school of opera.

WORKS

OPERAS

(sources in score unless otherwise stated)

Il Roderico [Rodrigo] (G. B. Bottalino), Mantua and Livorno, 1686, *I-MOe* Mus.F.954

Onorio in Roma (G. M. Giannini), Venice, 1692, *D-AN* VIg 39

La forza della virtù (D. David), Venice, 1693, *B-Br* 2529, *CS-K*

Alfonso primo (M. Noris), Venice, 1694, *US-SFsc*

Ottone (G. Frigimelica Roberti), Venice, 1694, *SFsc*, *CS-K*

La Santa Genuinda, Rome, Palazzo Doria Pamphili, 1694, *D-Mbs* 2985, *F-Pn*, *GB-Lbm* Add.16123–5 (Act 1 by G. L. Lulier, Act 2 by A. Scarlatti, Act 3 by Pollarolo or C. F. Cesarini)

Irene (Frigimelica Roberti), Venice, 1695, *CS-K*, Naples, 1704 (with additional arias by A. Scarlatti), 23 arias, 1 duet, *I-Nc* A512

Il pastore di Anfriso (Frigimelica Roberti), Venice 1695, nearly complete, *CS-K*

Gl'inganni felici (A. Zeno), Venice, 1696, *Gb-Lbm* Add.16209, arias, *I-Rvat* Barb.lat.4134 and 4143; facs. edn. (New York, 1977)

Almansore in Alimena (Giannini), Reggio Emilia, 1696, 6 arias, *I-Bc* V127

Tito Manlio (Noris), Florence, 1696, 58 arias, *Nc* 33.6.28

La Rosimonda (Frigimelica Roberti), Venice, 1696, *CS-K*

La clemenza d'Augusto (C. S. Capeci), Rome, Feb 1697, *E-Mn*, *GB-Lbm* (1 aria) (Act 1 by S. de Lucca, Act 2 by Pollarolo, Act 3 by G. Bononcini)

Il Faramondo (Zeno), Venice, 1699, *A-Wn* 17258

Il repudio d'Ottavia (Noris), Venice, 1699, 10 arias, *I-Bsp* Lib.P.63

Il colore fa' la regina (Noris), Venice, 1700, *CS-K*

Le pazzie degli amanti (F. Passarini), Vienna, 1701, *A-Wn* 17571

Semiramide (F. Silvani), Venice, 1713, 9 arias, *D-Dlb* B38P

Marsia deluso (A. Piovene), Venice, 1714, 5 arias, *Dlb* 1/F/30

Ariodante (A. Salvi), Venice, 1716, *US-Wc* M1500.P74A6 (20th-century copy of lost *D-Dlb* score), 22 arias, *I-Vc*

Astinome (? G. Lerner), Rome, 1719, 10 arias, *F-Pn* D12706

Giulio Cesare nell'Egitto, Acts 1 and 3, *US-Wc* M1500.P74G4, Act 2, *GB-BENcoke*

Pastorale à tre voci, *Mp* 580 Ps41

Lost operas include:

I delirii per amore (F. Miliati), Brescia, 1685; Il Licurgo, overo Il cieco d'acuta vista (Noris), Venice, 1686; Il demone amante, overo Giugurta (Noris), Venice, 1686; Enea in Italia (F. Bussani), Milan, 1686; La costanza gelosa negl'amori di Cefalo e Procri, Verona, 1688; Alarico re de Gotti, Verona, 1689; Antonino e Pompeiano (Bussani), Brescia, 1689

Alboino in Italia (G. C. Corradi), Venice, 1691, ? with G. F. Tosi; Il moto de le stelle osservato da Cupido (serenata), Padua, 1691; La pace fra Tolomeo e Seleuco (A. Morselli), Venice, 1691, revived as Il Seleuco, Rome, 1693; Venere travestita (A. Scappi), Rovigo, 1691; L'Ibraim Sultano (Morselli), Venice, 1692; Iole regina di Napoli

(Corradi), Venice, 1692; Marc'Antonio (Noris), Genoa, 1692

Gli avvenimenti di Erminda e di Clorinda sopra il Tasso (Corradi), Venice, 1693; Amage regina de' Sarmati (Corradi), Venice, 1694; La schiavitù fortunata (F. M. Gualazzi), Venice, 1694; Falsirena (R. Cialli), Ferrara, 1695; Ercole in cielo (Frigimelica Roberti), Venice, 1696; Amor e dovere (D. David), Venice, 1697; Circe abbandonata da Ulisse (A. Aureli), Venice, 1697

La forza d'amore (L. Burlini), Venice, 1697; Marzio Coriolano (Noris), Venice, 1697; L'Oreste in Sparta (P. Luchesi), Reggio Emilia, 1697; I reggi equivoci (Noris), Venice, 1697; L'enigma disciolto (G. B. Neri), Reggio Emilia, 1698, under the title Gli amici rivali, Venice, 1714; L'Ulisse sconosciuto in Itaca, Reggio Emilia, 1698; Il giudizio di Paride (intermezzo), Venice, 1699; L'oracolo in sogno (Silvani), Mantua, 1699 (Act 1 by Caldara, Act 2 by Quintavalle, Act 3 by Pollarolo)

Il delirio comune per l'incostanza dei genii (Noris), Venice, 1701; L'inganno di Chirone (D. P. d'Averara), Milan, 1700; Lucio Vero (Zeno), Venice, 1700; Ascanio (d'Averara), Milan, 1702; L'odio e l'amore (Noris), Venice, 1703; Venceslao (Zeno), Venice, 1703; L'eroico amore (M. A. Gasparini), Bergamo, 1704, under the title L'Alcibiade ovvero La violenza d'amore, Milan, 1709, under the title L'amante impazzito, Venice, 1714 (Act 2 by Pollarolo)

La fortuna per dote (Frigimelica Roberti), Venice, 1704; Il giorno di notte (Noris), Venice, 1704; Il Dafni (Frigimelica Roberti), Venice, 1705; La fede ne' tradimenti (G. Gigli, variants by G. Berretta), Venice, 1705; Filippo re della Grecia (P. G. Barziza), Venice, 1706; Flavio Bertarido re dei Langobardi (S. Ghisi), Venice, 1706; La vendetta d'amore, Rovigo, 1707; L'Ergisto (F. Passerino), Rovigo, 1708; Ginevra principessa di Scozia (Salvi), Brescia, 1708, under the title Ariodante, Venice, 1716 (see extant operas); Il falso tiberino (Zeno), Venice, 1708; L'Alcibiade ovvero La violenza d'amore, Milan, 1709 (see L'eroico amore, 1704)

La ninfa riconosciuta (Silvani), Vicenza, 1709; Amor per gelosia, Rome, 1710; Il Costantino Pio (P. Ottoboni), Rome, 1710; Engelberta o La forza dell'innocenza, Brescia, 1711; Eraclio (P. A. Bernardoni), Rome, 1712 (Act 3 by Pollarolo); L'infedeltà punita (Silvani), Venice, 1712; Peribea in Salamina, Padua and Vicenza, 1712; Publio Cornelio Scipione (A. Piovene), Venice, 1712; Spurio postumio (Piovene), Venice, 1712; L'amante impazzito, Venice, 1714 (see L'eroico amore, 1704); Gli amici rivali, Venice, 1714 (see L'enigma disciolto, 1698)

Il trionfo della constanza, Vicenza, 1714; Tetide in Sciro (C. S. Capece), Vicenza, 1715; Il germanico (Barziza), Venice, 1716; L'innocenza riconosciuta (T. Malipiero), Venice, 1717; L'amore in gara col fasto (F. Silvani), Rovigo, 1718; Farnace (Lalli), Venice, 1718; Il pescatore disingannato ('epitalamio musicale'), Venice, 1721; L'Arminio (Salvi), Venice, 1722

ORATORIOS

La Rosinda, Vienna, 1685, A-Wn Cod.18103

Jefte (Frigimelica Roberti), Venice, 1702, Wn Cod.16581

Jesabelle, B-Bc 1096

Sansone, GB-Mp F530 Ps41

Saule indemoniato, Mp F530 Ps44

Lost oratorios include:

La fenice, Brescia, 1680; Il combattimento degli angioli (Frigimelica Roberti), Venice, 1697; La clemenza di Salomone (Frigimelica Roberti), Venice, 1702; Le gare dell'India e di Roma, Brescia, 1703; Tertius crucis triumphus, Venice, 1703; Samson vindicatus, Venice, 1706; Joseph in Aegypto, Venice, 1707; Il convito di Baldassar (P. A. Ginori), Rome, 1708; Rex regum in veneti regia a regibus adoratus (G. Cassetti), Venice, 1716; Davidis de Goliath triumphus, Venice, 1718

OTHER WORKS

19 solo cantatas with bc or orch acc., D-B 30260 and 30136, CH-Zz, F-Pn D.14440, GB-Lbm Add.31518, Add.34057, I-REm 31, Pca D.5, Recueil de motets choisis de différents auteurs (Paris, 1712)

67 arias and 5 duets with bc or orch acc., D-B 30260 and 30136, Kl 4.Mus.14, XII, MÜs Sant HS174, SHsk, CH-Zz, F-Pn Rés.1800, GB-Lbm Eg.2961, I-Pca D.7, Rvat Barb.lat.4134 and 4143, Chigiani Q.20 and Q VIII 206, Vgc

Fugue in d, org, US-SFsc, I-Vnm; ed. AMI, iii (1897/R)

7 motets or sacred cantatas, D-B 17593, Dlb A285, F-Pn L.15302, I-Ac 303/3–5

Kyrie and Gloria, 6vv, orch, D-B 17740

Magnificat, 8vv, orch, B 17741

Mass, 5vv, I-Vnm Cl.Iv-1507 (11469), a recent copy marked 'Provenienza: Acquista Canal, 1928', authorship doubtful

Arias, Venetian songs, motets, capriccio and fugue, D-Dlb, destroyed during World War II

DOUBTFUL WORKS

(music lost unless otherwise stated)

Amage regina de' Sarnati, ?1693, ?Pollarolo, Act 2, P-La V-59

Alfonso il sesto re di Castiglia, Naples, 1694; composer uncertain but cast same as that of Alfonso primo, 1694 (see extant operas)

Il re infante (Noris), Bologna, 1694; music possibly by Pollarolo with additions by Perti

Gl'amori di Paride ed Ennone in Ida, ?1697; composer uncertain

Gl'amori tra gli odii o sia il Ramino in Norvegia (M. A. Remena), Venice, 1699; music by M. A. Ziani, not Pollarolo as is suggested elsewhere

Catone Uticenze (Noris), Venice, 1701; possibly by Pollarolo

De la virtude ha la bellezza onore (? P. Pariati), Venice, 1704; possibly by Pollarolo

Statira (Zeno, Pariati), Venice, 1705; music by F. Gasparini, not Pollarolo as is suggested elsewhere

La pace fra Pompeiano e Cesarini (A. Aureli), Venice, 1708; composer uncertain

Triumphus fidei, Venice, 1712; composer ? A. Lotti or Pollarolo

Il pescatore fortunato principe d'Ischia; lib and music by A. Novi

Berenice e Lucilla o L'amar per virtù, D-W Cod.Guelf.204; music by ? Pollarolo or Freschi; but cast listed is the same as that of Pollarolo's Lucio Vero of 1700; recits in German

La Proserpina, GB-Lbm Add.16110, attrib. to Pollarolo based on a pencil note on f.136

Il miracolo di Sant'Antonio di Padua, oratorio, I-MOe F.1546, attrib. 'Sig.Pol.'

BIBLIOGRAPHY

F. Caffi: Storia della musica sacra nella già cappella ducale di San Marco in Venezia dal 1318 al 1797 (Venice, 1854–5/R1972)

H. Kretzschmar: Geschichte der Oper (Leipzig, 1919)

H. C. Wolff: Die venezianische Oper in der zweiten Hälfte des 17. Jahrhunderts (Berlin, 1937)

O. Termini: Carlo Francesco Pollarolo: his Life, Time, and Music with Emphasis on the Operas (diss., U. of Southern California, 1970)

——: 'Carlo Francesco Pollarolo: Follower or Leader in Venetian Opera?', Studi musicali, viii (1979), 223–72

OLGA TERMINI

Polledro, Giovanni Battista (b Piovà, Casale Monferrato, nr. Turin, 10 June 1781; d Piovà, 15 Aug 1853). Italian violinist and composer. He studied in Asti, then, about 1796, was heard in Turin by Pugnani, who became his teacher for six months. This led to his appointment as a violinist of the royal orchestra at Turin, of which Pugnani was the leader. When the orchestra was dissolved, soon after the French forced the king to abdicate in 1798, Polledro gave concerts in northern Italy and in 1804 became leader of the theatre orchestra and a church musician in Bergamo. Soon after, he went to Moscow and spent about five years in the employ of Prince Tatishchev, who maintained his own serf orchestra. In 1811 he resumed his travels and was acclaimed in Germany as the best violinist since Viotti. In 1812 he performed with Beethoven in Karlsbad. In 1814 he became leader of the Dresden court orchestra, with a salary equal to that of Weber, the conductor. From 1824 to 1844 he was active in Turin as court maestro di cappella.

Polledro's playing was praised for its technical facility, especially in double stops and jumps across the fingerboard. His compositions were considered of only moderate interest even by his contemporaries; but they are elegant and exemplify the technical advances leading from Pugnani to Paganini. He wrote mainly for the violin, and also some church music, both vocal and instrumental. His six études have been reissued in a modern edition.

WORKS

Printed works published in Leipzig before 1812 unless otherwise stated

Vn concs.: G, op.6, autograph GB-Lbm; e, op.7, autograph Lbm; d, op.10

Variations, vn, orch: 'Nel cor più non mi sento' [Paisiello], op.3; C, op.5; d, op.8

Chamber: 3 trios, 2 vn, vc: G, op.2; d, op.4; A, op.9; Duets, 2 vn, op.11 (Vienna, n.d.)

Orch: Sinfonia pastorale (Milan, n.d.)

Sacred: Mass, vv, orch/org (Milan, n.d.); Miserere, 4vv, orch/org (Milan, n.d.)

Studies: Exercices amusants (Esercizi piacevoli), vn (after 1814); 6 études, vn (n.d.)

3 sinfonie ecclesiastiche; Bn Conc.; 5 vn concs.; 3 duos, 2 vn; all mentioned by Fétis

BIBLIOGRAPHY

FétisB

AMZ, xiv (1812), 280, 721; xv (1813), 499

G. Roberti: *La cappella regia di Torino 1515–1870* (Turin, 1880)

E. Anderson, ed.: *The Letters of Beethoven*, i (London, 1961), 384ff

BORIS SCHWARZ

Pollet. French family of musicians and at least one music publisher, active in the 18th and 19th centuries.

(1) Charles-François-Alexandre Pollet [*l'aîné*] (*b* Béthune, 1748; *d* Evreux, 1815). Cittern player, guitarist and composer. By 1771 he had settled in Paris where his performances on the cittern (English guitar) brought the instrument to considerable popularity. He is best known for his cittern method (op.5, 1775), and also published pieces and arrangements for the cittern, including the *Journal d'airs pour le cistre* (1778).

(2) (Jean-Joseph-)Benoît Pollet [*le jeune*] (*b* Béthune, 1753; *d* Paris, 16 April 1823). Harpist, composer and music publisher, perhaps also cittern player, brother of (1) Charles-François-Alexandre Pollet. He was a pupil of the harpist Jean-Baptiste Krumpholtz, and contributed to the development of performing harp harmonics. He established a music shop in Paris in 1791, and by 1802 was issuing his own publications. He published many of his own works for harp, including a method, a concerto, duos, sonatas and arrangements and variations on popular airs, in addition to many of his own romances. At his death the publishing firm was apparently discontinued, though it may have been carried on for a few years by his wife, the harpist Marie-Nicole (née Simonin, 1787–1864) and son L. M. Pollet (*c*1783–*c*1830), a guitarist; it then may have passed to the firm of Hanry or of Frère in about 1825.

(3) Joseph Pollet (*b* Paris, 30 April 1803; *d* Paris, 1883). Organist and choirmaster, son of (2) Benoît Pollet. He served as organist and choirmaster at Notre-Dame de Paris from 1831 to 1871; he was the father of the organist and composer Charles Pollet, who left some organ and vocal music and many didactic and characteristic pieces for piano.

A cittern player N. Pollet was a member of the Parisian Masonic lodge 'St Alphonse des Amis Parfaits de la Vertu'. His relationship to the family is not known, and he may have been the same person as (1) Charles-François-Alexandre Pollet.

BIBLIOGRAPHY

FétisB; *GerberNL*

A. Choron and F. Fayolle: *Dictionnaire historique des musiciens* (Paris, 1810–11)

C. Hopkinson: *A Dictionary of Parisian Music Publishers 1700–1950* (London, 1954)

R. Cotte: *Musiciens franc-maçons à la cour de Versailles* (in preparation)

ROGER COTTE

Pollier, Mathias. *See* POTTIER, MATHIAS.

Pollini, Francesco [Franz] **(Giuseppe)** (*b* Ljubljana, 25 March 1762; *d* Milan, 17 Sept 1846). Italian pianist, singer and composer of Slovene birth. He was a pupil of Mozart in Vienna. After 1786 he appeared as a pianist and violinist in various Italian cities, while in Verona, Bologna, Milan, Rome, Turin and Naples he became famous as an opera singer. In 1790, after moving to Milan, he studied composition under N. A. Zingarelli. He became a piano teacher at the new Milan Conservatory in 1809 and in that capacity is remembered as the first person after Rameau and J. S. Bach to encourage the technique of interlocking hand positions. In his *Trentadue esercizi* (1820) he used three staves, to encourage the performer to sustain a melody in the middle of the keyboard while playing more elaborate passages above and beneath it, thus producing with two hands almost the effect of four. In his preface he explained this technique:

I propose to offer a simple melody more or less plain, and of varied character, combined with accompaniments of different rhythms, from which it can be clearly distinguished by a particular expression and touch in the cantilena in contrast to the accompaniment.

His textbook, *Metodo per clavicembalo* (Milan, 1811), was long a standard work for conservatories. As a composer Pollini belonged to the early Classical school. His works were published by several European publishing houses, particularly Ricordi. In recognition of his renown, Bellini dedicated *La sonnambula* to him.

WORKS

(selective list; unless otherwise stated, all published Milan, n.d.)

VOCAL

Dramatic: L'orfanella svizzera (melodrama, 2), MS; Il genio insubre (opera, 2), MS; La casetta nei boschi (opera, 3), Milan, Cannobiana, 25 Feb 1798, MS

Songs, 1v, pf/hpd: 3 canzonette (Zurich, n.d.); Sai qual'è, romanza; Un'arietta e 3 canzonette; Vile un pensier, sonetto; Canto di Selma d'Ossian; Ah non trovo in seno il core, MS; L'Ave Maria – Preghiera, MS; Deh Vergin rimira, aria, MS

Other: Il trionfo della pace (cantata, A. Fugazza), Milan, La Scala, 30 April 1801, ?pubd; Stabat mater, S, A, 2 va, 2 vc, org (?1830); Kyrie, ?*D-Bds*

INSTRUMENTAL

Pf: Variazioni, op.10; Variations sur un air d'un ballet avec un rondeau, op.13 (Vienna, n.d.); 32 esercizi in forma di toccata (1820); Toccata, op.31 (?1810); Fantaisie sur 'Quel sepolcro che racchiude', op.32 (Paris, n.d.); Divertimento pastorale, op.34; Scherzo di fantasia, op.37; Fantasia sopra differenti motivi nell'opera 'La gazza ladra' di Rossini, op.40; Introduzione con variazioni sopra un tema originale, op.41; Introduzione e rondo, d, op.43, ed. in *L'arte antica e moderna*, vi (Milan, 1875); Preludio cantabile e rondo, op.44 (Vienna, n.d.); Introduction et Toccata, op.50 (Leipzig, n.d.); Variazioni e Toccata, op.53; Scherzo, op.56 (Leipzig, n.d.)

Hpd: 3 suonate, op.26 (*c*1810); Capriccio, op.28; 1 de' 32 esercizi in forma di toccata, E♭, op.42 (1820); Introduzione ed allegro pastorale, 4 hands, op.49; Estro armonico, op.57; Fantasia, op.58; Variazioni sopra la prima contradanza del ballo 'Il noce di Benevento'

Chamber: Sonata facile, hpd/harp, vn obbl, op.33, no.1; Ode Ill di Anacreonte, 2 vn, va, db, op.39; Sonata, C, hpd, vn obbl; Grande sonate-caprice et var., harp, pf (Vienna, n.d.)

BIBLIOGRAPHY

EitnerQ; *RiemannL 11*

H. Costa: 'Ein Porträten-Album aus dem vorigen Jahrhundert', *Mitteilungen des Historischen Vereines für Krain*, xviii (1863), 52

P. von Radics: *Frau Musica in Krain* (Ljubljana, 1877)

F. K. Lukman: 'Rod Pollinijev in ljubljanski zdravnik dr. Janez Krizostom Pollini' [The Pollini family and the physician Dr Janez Krizostom Pollini of Ljubljana], *Kronika*, vii (1940), 32

W. Georgii: *Klavier-Musik* (Zurich and Freiburg, 1950), 460

D. Cvetko: *Histoire de la musique slovène* (Maribor, 1967)

DRAGOTIN CVETKO

Pollini, Maurizio (*b* Milan, 5 Jan 1942). Italian pianist. He studied first with Carlo Lonati, and made his début at the age of nine. He then studied with Carlo Vidusso while continuing to perform, and in 1959 he graduated from the Milan Conservatory. He had already caught the attention of the Italian press in 1957 when he performed Chopin's studies in Milan; in 1959 he won the Ettore Pozzoli Competition in Seregno, and in 1960 the Warsaw Chopin competition. Since 1960 he has played regularly throughout Europe and in America, distinguishing himself as one of the most talented and profound performers of his generation. He has played with many leading conductors, notably with Claudio Abbado, with whom he is considered to have a special rapport owing to the analytical strictness of his interpretations. His repertory extends from Bach to contemporary music. In 1974, the Schoenberg centenary year, he gave the complete solo piano music in several capital cities, winning the highest praise for his clarity of exposition allied to the same refinement and freshness that he brings to Schubert and Schumann. In Bartók and Prokofiev he excels in masterful concentration. He also shows a keen interest in the most difficult 20th-century music; he has often performed Boulez's Second Sonata and he took part in the first performance of Nono's *Como una ola de fuerza y luz* (Milan, 1972). Among his recordings, Chopin's preludes, Stravinsky's Three Movements from *Petrushka* and Schoenberg's pieces are outstanding. In 1972 he gave an advanced course at the Accademia Chigiana in Siena.

PIERO RATTALINO

Pollitzer, Adolf [Adolphe] (*b* Budapest, 23 July 1832; *d* London, 14 Nov 1900). Hungarian violinist and teacher. The youngest of a family of 19, Pollitzer studied the violin under Böhm and composition under Preyer in Vienna, and later the violin under Alard in Paris. He played before the emperor as a child and at 13 won the friendship of Mendelssohn, in whose presence he played the E minor Violin Concerto. Settled in London by 1851, Pollitzer led at the Opera under Costa for many years, and also led the New Philharmonic and Royal Choral societies. In 1861 he was appointed professor of violin at the London Academy of Music, of which he became principal in 1890. His numerous pupils included Elgar, whose talent as 'a most earnest musician' he recognized and to whom he gave much encouragement. He produced Ten Violin Caprices and many editions of violin works by Alard, De Bériot, Vieuxtemps etc.

BIBLIOGRAPHY
Obituary, *Illustrated London News* (8 Dec 1900)
F. Boase: *Modern English Biography*, vi (London, 1921/*R*1965)
KEITH HORNER

Pollius, Daniel. *See* BOLLIUS, DANIEL.

Polmier, John. *See* PLUMMER, JOHN.

Pololáník, Zdeněk (*b* Brno, 25 Oct 1935). Czech composer. He studied the organ with Josef Černocký at the Brno Conservatory (1952–7) and composition with Petrželka and Schaefer at the Brno Academy of Music (1957–61). From 1963 he was a member of Tvůrčí Skupina A ('Creative Group A'). He associated himself with avant-garde ideas in the 1950s and 1960s, though his spontaneous inventiveness has not been subordinated to any particular new technique. Even his 12-note serial compositions, those from the Second Symphony (1962) to the ballet *Mechanismus* (1964), are by no means strict. Indeed, he inclines towards modality of the type which lies behind Moravian folksong. His music also shows an expressive feeling for rhythm and tone-colour, the latter being particularly evident in his collage and electronic pieces. Nor has he eschewed elements of pop music, which appear in the *Rytmická mše* ('Rhythmic mass') and the musical *Mladá garda* ('The young guard'), for the principle of combination is the decisive factor in his work.

WORKS
(*selective list*)

Stage: Mechanismus (ballet, R. Adler), 1964, Liberec, 1965; Popelka (marionette ballet), 1966; Mladá garda [The young guard] (musical), 1974; Pierot (ballet, 3), 1975, Olomouc, 6 April 1976; Silák Hungerfield [Hungerfield the strong man] (opera, Z. Kaloč, after R. Jeffers), 1975

Orch: Sinfonietta, 1958; Toccata, db, chamber orch, 1959; Divertimento, 4 hn, str, 1960; Sym. no.1, 1961; Sym. no.2, 11 wind, 1962; Sym. no.3, org, perc, orch, 1962; Concentus resonabilis, 19 insts, tape, 1963; Sym. no.4, 1963; Conc. grosso, gui, fl, hpd, str, 1966; Pf Conc., 1966; Sym. no.5, 1969; Suite, after Song of Songs, 1975

Vocal: Nabuchodonosor, chorus, 3 tpt, timp, 1960; Zpěv mrtvých dětí [Song of dead children] (J. Wenig, J. Šprincl), 15vv, 3 tpt, 2 perc, 1963; Vávra, children's vv, pf, 1964; Cantus psalmorum, B-Bar, harp, org, perc, 1966; Rumor letalis, chorus, 1966; Sheer hushsheereem [Song of Songs], oratorio, S, T, 2 Bar, B, vv, orch, 1970; Missa brevis, children's vv, org, 1970; Rytmická mše [Rhythmic mass], 1973

Chamber and inst: Variations, org, pf, 1956; Sonata bravura, org, 1959; Scherzo contrario, xyl/gui, b cl/cl, vn, 1961; Musica spingenta I, db, wind qnt, 1961; Musica spingenta II, str qt, hpd, 1962; Musica spingenta III, b cl, perc, 1962; Sonata laetitiae, org, 1962; 3 scherzi, wind qnt, 1963; 12 preludii, 2 pf, org, 1963; Musica concisa, fl, b cl, pf, hpd, perc, 1963; Allegro affanato, org, 1963; Oratio, 9 insts, 1968

Tape: 4 zvukové konverzace a finale [4 sound conversations and finale], 1965

Principal publishers: DILIA, General Music, Panton, Státní Hudební Vydavatelství, Zanibon

BIBLIOGRAPHY
J. Bártová: 'Tri mladí z Brna' [Three young men from Brno], *HRo*, xix (1966), 134
J. Smolka: 'Zdeněk Pololáník: Musica spingenta III', *HRo*, xix (1966), 54
F. Hrabal: 'Šír haš šírím' [Song of Songs], *HRo*, xxii (1970), 391
OLDŘICH PUKL

Polonaise (Fr.). A stately Polish processional dance or an instrumental piece; the latter developed largely outside Poland and is characterized by the rhythm shown in ex.1. The dance, which took on its French name in the

Ex.1

17th century, had vocal prototypes in old Polish folkdances, such as the *chodzony* (walking), the *wolny* and *powolny* (slow), the *wielki* (great), the *obracany* (turning), *okrągły* (round) and others. Sung as well as danced, they were, and still are, used during public ceremonies and festivities, particularly weddings. The melodies for the dances, many of which are found in Kolberg's collections, are in triple metre, consist of short phrases, usually without upbeat, and are simple in structure, often with a two-bar repeated section in the middle. One of the oldest of these folk polonaises is the *chmiel* (hops) or *chmielowy* (hops dance), which was danced and sung during the 'capping of the bride'. This pentatonic melody (ex.2) belonged to the Wielkopolska district,

Ex.2

Oj, chmie-lu,   chmie-lu,   ty buj-ne zie - le
Nie bę-dzie, bez cie   ża-dne we - se - le.

Oj, chmie-lu   oj nie-bo-że,   chmie-lu nie-bo-że
To na dól, to na gó-rze.

especially Kujawy, in the western regions of Poland, but in time developed variations each particular to its own region. In Mazowsze, the central territory of the Vistula, it took on the nature of a lively mazurka in a major key (ex.3). The rest of the melody is identical with the second

Ex.3

four bars of the original in ex.2 (this second version was used by Chopin during his celebrated improvisation in Vienna on 30 August 1829 and is echoed in his Nocturne op.9 no.1 written at the same time; ex.4).

From the western regions of Poland the dance found its way to the neighbouring countries of Moravia and

Ex.4

Hanaki, where it became popular as a maypole dance in a somewhat livelier tempo. It became the chief national dance of the Lusatian Wends, and was especially popular in Germany and Scandinavia (see POLSKA). Not until the 18th century did the dance actually bear the title 'polonaise' in Polish sources; a manuscript collection of 1772 made by Joseph Sychra contains 62 polonaises, and one dating from 1800 (*D-Bds* 38048) has 23. Besides the triple time and phrases without upbeat these pieces show the characteristic closing rhythm of the classic polonaise (ex.5), but many retain the struc-

Ex.5

ture of the two-bar repeated middle section similar to the older 'polonez'. These collections also contain polonaises in minor keys, called 'galantino', 'galanterie polone' or 'lente', which are in contrast to the briskly played polonaises in major keys. Many also have a contrasting trio section, a characteristic of the contemporary art polonaise.

In spite of its intrinsic charm the folk polonaise would never have become popular internationally had it not been taken up by the nobility. In the first phase of its development it appeared as a dance cultivated by the gentry and lesser aristocracy; this intermediate polonaise type still shows a close relationship with that of the common people and was still sung. The texts became more sophisticated and the rhythm began to approximate to that of the courtly polonaise, but it does not show the characteristic closing figure shown in ex.5. The court polonaise became an instrumental rather than a vocally accompanied dance and was played by musicians in the galleries of the great reception halls while the assembly, dressed in great splendour, danced it below in processional figures whose character suggested the name 'martial dance'. As a court dance it was transformed into the most highbred expression of the Polish national spirit and became in the process the most representative of Polish dances throughout Europe.

The terms 'polnischer Tanz', 'chorea polonica', 'polacca' etc appear in the Loeffelholtz manuscript (1585) and Nörmiger's *Tabulaturbuch* (1598), but the oldest source of a piece called a Polish dance is in Ammerbach's organ tablature book (1583); the piece is in 4/4 metre and is followed by a triple-time 'Proportz'. It is not certain whether these pieces and others found in late 16th-century sources were related to the elaborate processionals of the time, such as that performed by the nobility at the accession of Henry of Anjou in Kraków

in 1574. In any case, none of the 16th-century 'Polish dances' resembles the later polonaise. The polonaise is not mentioned in contemporary dance literature, such as Arbeau's *Orchésographie* (1588); according to Lindgren, the earliest account of a processional dance referred to specifically as Polish was made in 1733, in a description of a ball held at the court of Frederick the Great in 1709.

The origins of the stylized instrumental polonaise certainly go back to the 17th century and are intertwined with the instrumental accompaniments to the courtly polonaise. Important 17th-century collections that include polonaises are the lutebook of Virginia Renata of Gehemans (1640; *D-Bds* 20052) and Georg Neumark's *Poetisch- und musikalisches Lustwäldchen* (Hamburg, 1652[6]). A 17th-century dissertation (Wallerius-Retzelius: *De tactu musico*, Uppsala, 1698) discusses two types of polonaise, a 'proportio peritiorum' for the gentry and a 'proportio plebejorum' for the lower classes.

The 18th century brought about the stylization of the form. Among the first examples to have all the characteristics of the classic polonaise – triple metre, phrases without upbeat, a repeated rhythmic figure and the closing rhythm shown in ex.5 – are those of J. S. Bach (French Suite no.6; Orchestral Suite no.2). The Germans, for whom the polonaise represented 'Polish taste and Polish style', were enthusiastic propagators of the dance as a musical form. Mattheson (*Der vollkommene Capellmeister*, 1739) spoke highly of the melody, character and passion of the polonaises of his day, and Telemann, who visited Poland in 1704–7, praised the dance in a letter to Mattheson (*Grundlage einer Ehrenpforte*, 1740, p.175) and composed many examples himself. Sperontes included vocal polonaises in his *Singende Muse an der Pleisse* (1736–45), and J. G. Goldberg, for whom Bach wrote the Goldberg Variations, composed 24 polonaises in Rococo style. In the second half of the century W. F. Bach, Kirnberger and Schobert contributed to the genre, as did Mozart and Beethoven.

The change from a vocal to an instrumental form brought with it certain modifications, particularly in melodic style. The instruments were capable of wider range and greater mobility than the voices, which resulted in bolder sweeps and an elaborate figuration, 'breaking, like a gigantic reptile, into thousands of coils', as Adam Mickiewicz described it (*Pan Tadeusz*, pt.xii). This can be seen in an orchestral polonaise of 1782 by Grabowiecki (ex.6) and is even more marked in a work of W. F. Bach (ex.7). The characteristic cadence can be noted in ex.6 as well as in W. F. Bach's Polonaise in C minor (c1765; ex.8). Towards the end of the 18th century the repetition of the melody in the dominant was gradually replaced by a contrasting melody and later by

Ex.6

Ex.7 Adagio

Ex.8 Andante

a two-section trio. Rondo form was also used, as in Mozart's 'Polonaise en rondeau' (Piano Sonata in D K284/205*b*), which may have been inspired by Schobert's polonaises, and Beethoven's 'Rondo alla polacca' in the triple concerto for piano, violin and cello op.56.

Outside Germany, Handel, Couperin and Gabriel Guillemain contributed to the genre, and from about 1800 art polonaises began to be written in Poland. The 20 polonaises by Prince Ogiński (1765–1833), written for piano (some for four hands), were of the melancholy 'galantino' type and had programmatic titles (*Les adieux, Toten-Polonaise* etc); they became famous all over Europe and contributed to the spread of the polonaise across the Continent as a salon piece, vocal opera insert and occasional piece. The polonaise for piano was further developed by two of Chopin's teachers, Wojciech Zywny and Józef Elsner, 'the father of Polish music'. Józef Kozłowski wrote polonaises for piano, nearly 70 for orchestra and others for chorus and orchestra, including *Grom pobiedy rozdawajsia*, which up to 1833 was the Russian national hymn. Another of Kozłowski's polonaises, written in honour of Catherine II, was introduced by Tchaikovsky into his opera *The Queen of Spades* at the moment when the Tsaritsa appears.

Karol Kurpiński observed in 1820 that with the loss of Poland's independence the polonaise lost its noble character, and he sought to revive its vanished splendour with his 'Coronation' Polonaise for chorus and orchestra (1826). If Elsner's words of 1811 to Breitkopf & Härtel – 'everything that is pleasing nowadays may be converted into a polonaise' – need verification, it can be found in Kurpiński's work: in 1819, for instance, he dedicated a polonaise to the Duke of Cumberland, into which he introduced *Rule, Britannia* and *God Save the King*. Even Chopin was not immune to this tendency, for he introduced an air from Rossini's *La gazza ladra* into his Polonaise in Bb minor, and the finale of his variations on Mozart's 'Là ci darem', op.2, presents the theme in polonaise rhythms.

Beethoven's sole example for the piano, the Polonaise in C major op.89, was dedicated to the Empress of Russia, and Weber composed a *Grande polonaise* (op.21, 1808) and a *Polacca brillante* (op.72, 1819), later arranged by Liszt for piano and orchestra. Schubert's ten polonaises, all for four hands (four in op.75, 1818; six in op.61, 1826) are by far the finest examples of the dance between W. F. Bach and the mature Chopin. They are remarkable not only for the harmonic and rhythmic variety of the dances themselves, but for the lyrical beauty of the hitherto perfunctory trio sec-

tions.

But these, and those that came later, are overshadowed by the polonaises of Chopin, whose name is today inseparably associated with the form. As with many of the other small forms that he used, he brought it to its height of development as a piano piece, making it a musical symbol of Polish nationalism. The success of his polonaises was due in part to the enthusiasm for things Polish in western Europe around 1830, which contributed to the popularity of polonaises for salon and concert use. The figure from the end cadence (ex.9) appears in the polonaises, and is especially noticeable in the Polonaise in A op.40 no.1, whose second theme is possibly one of the best-known examples of the typical polonaise martial rhythm shown in ex.1. The great Polonaise in Ab op.53 exploits all the dramatic possibilities inherent in the polonaise, and is probably the finest example of the form in all music.

Ex.9

Polonaises for piano were also written by Schumann (eight for four hands, 1828; *Papillons* op.2 no.11), Liszt (1851; *Fest-Polonaise*, 1876) and Wagner (op.2). The polonaise also appeared in chamber music, concertos and opera, often with the title POLACCA; Weber included one, 'Kommt ein schlanker Bursch', in *Der Freischütz*. The Russian composers were attracted to the form as an evocative and symbolic adornment of their dramatic work: Musorgsky used the polonaise rhythm to good effect in the prologue to *Boris Godunov*, and Tchaikovsky wrote an original polonaise for *Sleeping Beauty* as well as *Eugene Onegin*, the latter arranged by Liszt for piano solo. As a neighbour of Poland, Russia quickly adopted the polonaise and it became popular as a dance for the peasantry as well as an art form. Glinka elevated the form to magnificent proportions and at the same time recalled earlier practices by composing one for chorus and orchestra which set the words 'Great is our God' (1837); he also composed a Polonaise in E for orchestra (1839).

BIBLIOGRAPHY

J. F. Reichardt: 'Der hanakische Tanz', *Musikalisches Kunst-Magazin*, i (1782), 157

O. Kolberg: *Lud, jego . . . pieśni, muzyka i tańce* [The people, its . . . songs, music, dances] (Warsaw and Kraków, 1861–90/*R*1962–8)

W. Gostomski: *Polonez i menuet* (Warsaw, 1891)

A. Lindgren: 'Die ältesten Polonaisen', *AMz*, xix (1894)

F. Starczewski: 'Contribution à l'histoire de la polonaise', *Congrès international d'histoire de la musique: Paris 1900*, 215

——: 'Die polnischen Tänze', *SIMG*, ii (1900–01), 673–718

T. Norlind: 'Zur Geschichte der polnischen Tänze', *SIMG*, xii (1910–11), 501

A. Chybiński: 'Die deutschen Musiktheoretiker im 16.–18. Jahrhunderts und die polnische Musik', *ZIMG*, xiii (1911–12), 56

A. Simon: *Polnische Elemente in der deutschen Musik* (Zurich, 1916)

L. Kamiński: 'Neue Beiträge zur Entwicklung der Polonaise bis Beethoven', *Beethoven-Zentenarfeier: Wien 1927*, 66

——: 'O polonezie staropolskim' [On old Polish polonaises], *Muzyka współczesna*, v/3 (1928), 99

H. Opieński: 'Przyczynek do dziejów poloneza w Polcew 18 wieku' [Study of the history of the polonaise in Poland in the 18th century], *KM*, vi/17–18 (1933), 36

C. Sachs: *Eine Weltgeschichte des Tanzes* (Berlin, 1933; Eng. trans., 1937/*R*1963)

H. Dorabialska: *Polonez przed Chopinem* [The polonaise before Chopin] (Warsaw, 1938)

J. Kurczewski: *Polonez w polskiej muzyce ludowej* [The polonaise in Polish folk music] (Poznań, 1950)

J. W. Reiss: 'Polonez, jego pochodzenie i rozwój' [The polonaise: its origin and development], *Poradnik muzyczny*, xl (1950); xli (1951)

A. Harasowski: *The Golden Book of Polish Song* (London, 1953)
C. de Nys: 'Note sur les polonaises de Wilhelm Friedmann Bach', *Chopin Congress: Warszawa 1960*, 578
A. Sławiński: 'Rytm a harmonia w polonezach Chopina' [Rhythm and harmony in the polonaises of Chopin], *Chopin Congress: Warszawa, 1960*, 241
Z. Stęszewska: 'Z zagadnień historii poloneza' [Problems of the history of the Polonaise], *Muzyka*, new ser., v/2 (1960), 77
F. Hoerburger and M. Sobieski: 'Polonaise', *MGG*

JÓZEF W. REISS/MAURICE J. E. BROWN

Polonus, Johannes [Polak, Jan; Pole, Hans] (*b* Breslau; *fl* 1590–1616). German composer and instrumentalist. He was appointed a court musician at Wolfsburg in 1590. In 1603 (according to *EitnerQ*) he was a violinist in the Berlin court orchestra, with a salary of 112 thalers and free board, which was raised to 144 thalers in 1612. The title-page of his *Canticum Sanctorum Ambrosii et Augustini* (Magdeburg, 1606), for five voices, names him as a musician of the Elector of Brandenburg, and in 1616 he became the elector's Kapellmeister. 13 of his motets, for four to six voices, appeared in the collection *Cantiones aliquot piae* (Helmstedt, 1590), and a manuscript wedding song, *Selig ist der gepreiset*, written for the Duke of Saxony in 1607 and signed 'Johannes Polonus Marchiacus' is extant (in *D-Dlb*).

RICHARD MARLOW

Polovinkin, Leonid Alexeyevich (*b* Kurgan, 13 Aug 1894; *d* Moscow, 8 Feb 1949). Russian composer and teacher. He entered the Moscow Conservatory in 1914 to study the piano with Konyus and Kipp and also the violin. In 1918 he enrolled in the composition classes of Myaskovsky and Vasilenko, and at the same time he studied harmony with Zolotaryov, counterpoint with Il'yinsky, fugue with Glier, form with Catoire and orchestration with Vasilenko. After graduating in 1924 he moved to Leningrad, and there he took part in the establishment of the studio of the Monumental'nïy Teatr Operï i Baleta, known as the Mamont (Mammoth). He was also music director at the Alexandrinsky Theatre, but soon returned to Moscow for postgraduate composition study at the conservatory (1925–6). There he did work on formal analysis and taught orchestration (1926–32). In 1927–8 he began a long career as music director of the Moscow Central Children's Theatre, and he organized and conducted the children's symphony orchestra. In his music he had to overcome a dependence on Skryabin before seeking a new language in connection with the Assotsiatsiya Sovremennoy Muzïki (Association for Contemporary Music). This development was influenced by Les Six, by Schoenberg and by an attraction towards urban life. A second phase in Polovinkin's work began with his appointment to the children's theatre, and was also spurred by the sharply negative press reaction to his music. In this later period he turned to a simpler, folksong-like style.

WORKS
(selective list)

STAGE

Operas: Zerkalo [The mirror] (after Synge: The Hero), 1924, unpubd; Skazka o rïbake i rïbke [The tale of the fisherman and the fish] (after Pushkin), perf. 1935, unpubd; Churila Plenkovich, n.d., unpubd
Musical comedies: Sirokko, op.32, perf. 1928; Dazhe v trikotazhe [Even in knitting], perf. 1931, unpubd
Children's ballets: Nagua (Negrityonok i obez'yana [The little negro boy and the monkey]), perf. 1927; Ya – malo, mï – sila [I am little, we are strong], perf. 1931
Incidental music

ORCHESTRAL

7 syms.: op.35, 1929, unpubd; n.d., unpubd; 'Romanticheskaya', 1932; 'Krasnoarmeyskaya' [Red army], 1933, unpubd; n.d., unpubd; n.d., unpubd; 1942
Prolog, op.17, 1924–5; Teleskop I, 1926; Teleskop II, 1928; Simfonicheskiy etyud, 1928, unpubd; Tantsï zagadok [Dances of mysteries] (1930); Mïs [Cape], dance suite, 1931, unpubd; Pervomayskaya [First of May], ov., 1931; Pf Conc., 1933; Pogranichniki [The border guards] (children's sym. ballad, A. Barto), S, Bar, orch (1937)

OTHER WORKS

Chamber: Na rassvete [At dawn], 1v, fl, cl, pf qt, perf. 1925–6; 2 str qts (1946), (1948); Pf Trio, n.d., unpubd
Pf: Sonata no.1, F, op.1, 1924; Proisshestviya (Evénements), opp.5, 10, 12, 20, 1922–9; 3 Pieces, op.9 (1925); Sonata no.2, E♭, op.13, 1925, unpubd; Sonata no.3, C, op.15 (1926); Sonata no.4, F, op.18 (1927); Prervannaya serenada [Interrupted serenade], op.20/1 (1926); Ironicheskaya novella (1926); Sonata no.5, A (1929); 2 Nocturnes (1933); Variations, a (1934); Dzyuba, suite (1936); Elegiya i fugirovannoye allegro, 1938; Toccata, f♯ (1939); 24 Postludes (1941); 2 divertissements (1946), (1947)
Songs: 5 Romances, op.14 (M. Tsvetayeva, Blok, T. Shchepkina-Kupernik, A. Tolstoy, Lermontov) (1926); 3 Romances, op.16 (P. Oreshin, B. Zubakin), n.d.; 7 Romances, op.23 (A. Golenishchev-Kutuzov, Bal'mont, A. Globa, S. Esenin) (1927); Myortvïy chas [Dead hour] (Barto) (1934); Kon' [Horse] (Pushkin) (1937); V 20-m godu [In '20] (V. I. Lebedev-Kumach) (1938); Vesenyaya pesnya [Spring song] (A. Zharov) (1940); Krasnoarmeytsu [For the Red Army man] (I. Utkin) (1942); Galya i Sharafat (E. Tarakhovskaya) (1943)
Children's songs and choruses, mass songs, film scores

Principal publishers: Muzsektor, Universal

BIBLIOGRAPHY
L. Polovinkin: 'K moyemu avtorskomu kontsertu', *Sovremennaya muzïka* (1928), no.30, p.140
G. Polyanovsky: 'O tvorchestve L. A. Polovinkina' [On Polovinkin's work], *SovM* (1934), no.5, p.13
M. Levashov: 'L. A. Polovinkin', *SovM* (1949), no.3, p.72
N. Sats: *Deti prikhodyat v teatr* [Children are coming to the theatre] (Moscow, 1961), 222ff
———: *Vsegda s toboy* [Always with you] (Moscow, 1965)
L. Rimsky: 'Materialï k biografii L. A. Polovinkina' [Materials towards a biography of Polovinkin]; 'Perepiska L. A. Polovinkina' [Polovinkin's correspondence], *Iz proshlovo sovetskoy muzïkal'noy kul'turï*, ed. T. Livanova (Moscow, 1975), 142–210

INNA BARSOVA

Polska. A collective name for a central and north European dance of the processional and rotating type ('ballatio'). It dates from the Renaissance and now exists under various regional names. Versions of it are found at all levels of society and fall into two groups – those in the polska's modern metre (C, ₵, 2/4) and those in its archaic metre (3/4, 3/8). Some archaic polskas are of particular interest as prototypes of the POLONAISE.

The polska entered the stream of European dance history in the first half of the 16th century, and its roots may be found in Polish folk choruses and dance pairs. Under the influence of a similar dance, the allemande, it developed into both duple- and triple-time versions, which then each had separate historical developments. Their chief features (particularly those of the triple-time version) became the basis of whole groups of folk-dances, such as the mazurka, *kujawiak* and *oberek*, as well as providing a pattern for new dance variations that adopted the folk characteristics of specific countries.

The Swedish polska has a rhythm similar to that of the mazurka (ex.1). It seems to have been danced mostly by peasants from the 16th century until the early 18th; during the reign of Charles XII, when Sweden and Poland were closely allied, it became popular with the upper classes for a time. Despite its foreign origins, it

Ex.1 'Näckans polska'

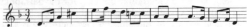

came to be considered one of the most characteristically national folkdances of Sweden, appearing in such important folk collections as Nils Andersson's *Svenska låtar* (Stockholm, 1922–40) (*see* SWEDEN, §II).

The dance was popular in all the Scandinavian countries. It retained the name 'polska' in Finland (ex.2) but was called simply 'Pols' in Norway or 'Polsk dans' in Denmark. In Poland the 'polski' (ex.3) was a richly developed dance stemming from the triple-time polska, and also became known by various other names, such as *chodzony*, *do przodka*, *pieszy*, *obchodny*, *wielki*, *powolny* and *obracany*; it is from this group that the polonaise evolved. In Lusatian Serbia the dance was called *serbski*, *stara serbska reja* ('old Serbian round'), *kwasna reja* or *nejwěććinska reja*. In Czechoslovakia the *starodávný*, *taněc*, *vałaský* (ex.4), *chodzony*, *hladky taněc* ('sweet dance') and *zatáčaný* were all dances of the polska type.

Ex.2

Ex.3

Mazur

Ex.4

Co su to za ti - ně, co su to za

ti - ně, v tej foj-to - ve du - bi - ně?

Pa-su se tam ko - ně, di dě-ve-čko pro né,

sy - ne-ček jich ši - ru - je.

The music for the dance did not become a part of the Renaissance and Baroque suites but remained in the vanguard of creative dance composition in Poland, Hungary and Germany, as seen in the work of Mikołaj z Krakowa and Wojciech Długoraj, the lute intabulations of Matthäus Waissel and the organ intabulations of Jan z Lublina, August Nörmiger and Christoph Loeffelholtz. Polskas for dancing are also found in the works of Hans Neusidler and Philipp Hainhofer, in manuscript collections. Stylized polskas are found in the work of 19th- and 20th-century European composers such as Dvořák (*Slavonic Dances* op.46 nos.4 and 6, op.72 nos.10, 12 and 14) and Grieg (*25 norske folkeviser og dandse* op.17 nos.1, 3, 5, 8 and 19). Janáček included two *starodávný* in his Wallachian Dances, and Tauno Marttinen a wedding-dance polska in *Legenda* op.83.

BIBLIOGRAPHY

Č. Zibrt: *Jak se kdy v Čechách tancovalo* [What used to be danced in Bohemia] (Prague, 1895, 2/1960)

T. Norlind: 'Zur Geschichte der polnischen Tänze', *SIMG*, xii (1910–11), 501

H. G. Nielssen: *Vore aeldste folkedanse* (Copenhagen, 1917)

——: *Folkelig vals* (Copenhagen, 1920)

T. Norlind: 'Svensk folkmusik och folkdans', *Natur och kultur*, xcvi (1930); pubd separately (Stockholm, 1930)

K. Semb: *Norske folkedansar* (Oslo, 1946–61)

J. M. Chomiński and Z. Lissa, eds.: *Muzyka polskiego odrodzenia* [Music of the Polish Renaissance] (Warsaw, 1953)

L. Burlas, J. Fišer and A. Hořejší: *Hudba na Slovensku v XVIII storoči* [Music in Slovakia in the 18th century] (Bratislava, 1954)

L. Janáček, ed.: *O lidové písni a lidové hudbě* [On folksong and folk music] (Prague, 1955)

E. Ala-Könni: *Die Polska-Tänze in Finnland* (Helsinki, 1956)

Lětopis Instituta za serbski ludospyt [Annual of the Institute for Serbian Folklore], ser.C (1959–60), no.4

Z. Stęszewska: *Tańce polskie z tabulatur lutniowych* [Polish dances from lute tablatures] (Warsaw, 1962)

M. Drabecka: *Polskie tańce ludowe w dziełach O. Kolberga* [Polish folkdances in the works of O. Kolberg] (Warsaw, 1963)

J. Raupp: *Serbische Volksmusikanten und Musikinstrumente* (Budyšin, 1963)

J. Kresánek, ed.: *Fontes musicae in Slovacia: melodiarum annae Szirmay-Keczer* (Bratislava, 1967)

J. Krogsaeter: *Folk Dancing in Norway* (Oslo, 1968)

J. Sobieska and M. Sobieski: *Polska muzyka ludowa i jej problemy* [Polish folk music and its problems], ed. L. Bielawski (Kraków, 1973)

FRANTIŠEK BONUŠ

Polskie Wydawnictwo Muzyczne [PWM; Polish Music Publications]. In 1928 a group of Polish musicologists and musicians led by Adolf Chybiński, Teodor Zalewski, Tadeusz Ochlewski and Kazimierz Sikorski organized the Towarzystwo Wydawnicze Muzyki Polskiej (TWMP; Polish Music Publishing Society), Warsaw, to publish authentic editions of Polish music. The catalogue includes music in all genres from the 15th century to the 20th. In 1934 TWMP began publishing the periodical *Muzyka polska*; the principal scholarly series is Wydawnictwo Dawnej Muzyki Polskiej, which includes early music by Szarzyński, Mielczewski, Pękiel, Gorczycki and Żeleński as well as 19th- and 20th-century music up to World War II. In April 1945 TWMP transferred its assets to PWM, organized by Tadeusz Ochlewski; Mieczysław Tomaszewski succeeded Ochlewski on the latter's retirement in 1965. The PWM-Edition is the only music publishing house in Poland and produces a wide range of music and music literature. It is particularly important for its publications of early and avant-garde Polish music and critical editions of Chopin, Moniuszko, Wieniawski and Szymanowski.

TERESA CHYLIŃSKA

Polumier, John. *See* PLUMMER, JOHN.

Polyakin, Miron Borislovich (*b* Cherkassï, 12 Feb 1895; *d* Moscow, 21 May 1941). Ukrainian violinist and teacher. He was taught the violin as a child by his father, a violinist and conductor. He studied with Efrem Bonsovsky at the Lysenko Music School in Kiev (1904–8), then entered Leopold Auer's class at the St Petersburg Conservatory and continued studying with him until 1917. He made his début in St Petersburg in 1909, and started giving frequent concerts in 1914, gaining international fame through tours in western Europe and the USA (1918–26); in 1926 he returned to live in the USSR. He became a professor at the Leningrad Conservatory in 1928 and at Moscow in 1936. Together with Heifetz, Elman and Zimbalist, Polyakin confirmed the world-wide importance and influence of Auer's 'St Petersburg school' of violin playing. He combined romantic expressiveness, warmth and deep humanity with refined elegance and virtuoso brilliance, in a repertory that ranged from the major works of Bach, Beethoven, Brahms and others to the showpieces of virtuoso technique. He exerted an important influence on the formation of a Soviet school of violin playing, and was made Honoured Art Worker of the RSFSR in 1940.

BIBLIOGRAPHY
I. Yampol'sky: 'Miron Polyakin: k 5-letiyu so dnya smerti' [On the 5th anniversary of his death], *SovM* (1946), no.7
L. Raaben: *Miron Polyakin* (Moscow, 1963)
J. Creighton: *Discopaedia of the Violin, 1889–1971* (Toronto, 1974), 592f
I. M. YAMPOL'SKY

Polyakova, Lyudmila Viktorovna (*b* Rostov-na-Donu, 4 Nov 1921). Soviet musicologist. She studied at the Gnesin Music School (1938–41) and in the department of theory and composition of the Moscow Conservatory (1943–8), where her teachers included R. I. Gruber. After her graduation in 1948 she carried on postgraduate studies in composition until 1952. She took the *kandidat* degree in 1955 with a dissertation on two Soviet operas set in World War II. She is a music critic, and from 1953 to 1960 was head of the music drama section in the editorial office of *Sovetskaya muzïka*, to which she has contributed many articles. Since 1961, when she became a senior research fellow at the Institute for the History of the Arts in Moscow, she has devoted much time to research into the history of Czechoslovak music, and also general aspects of 20th-century foreign music. She is principally concerned with problems of opera.

WRITINGS

Kartinki s vïstavki Musorgskovo [Musorgsky's *Pictures at an Exhibition*] (Moscow, 1951, 2/1960)
Vremena goda Chaykovskovo [Tchaikovsky's *The Seasons*] (Moscow, 1951, 2/1960)
Sem'ya Tarasa D. B. Kabalevskovo [Kabalevsky's *The Family of Taras*] (Moscow, 1953)
Vokal'nïy tsikl D. D. Shostakovicha Iz evreyskoy narodnoy poezii [Shostakovich's song cycle *From Hebrew Folk Poetry*] (Moscow, 1957)
'Nekotorïye voprosï dramaturgii sovetskoy operï' [Some questions of dramatic presentation in Soviet opera], *Voprosï muzïkoznaniya*, iii, ed. V. S. Vinogradov and others (Moscow, 1960), 86–123
Voyna i mir S. S. Prokof'yeva [Prokofiev's *War and Peace*] (Moscow, 1960, 2/1971)
La musique soviétique (Moscow, 1961; Eng. trans., 1961)
Vokal'nïye tsiklï G. V. Sviridova [Sviridov's song cycles] (Moscow, 1961, 2/1972)
'Voprosï tvorcheskovo stilya G. V. Sviridova' [Aspects of Sviridov's compositional style], *Muzïka i sovremennost'*, i (Moscow, 1962), 183–242

Opernoye tvorchestvo Leosha Yanacheka [Janáček's operatic works] (Moscow, 1968)
'Cheshskaya revolyutsionnaya muzïka mezhvoyennovo dvadsatiletiya' [Czech revolutionary music during the 20 years between the wars], *Iskusstvo revolyutsiyey prizvannoye*, i, ed. Institut istorii iskusstv (Moscow, 1969), 185–220
'Russkiye operï Yanacheka' [Janáček's Russian operas], *Puti razvitiya i vzaimosvyazi russkovo i chekhoslovatskovo iskusstva*, ed. Institut istorii iskusstv (Moscow, 1970), 190
'Pesni rumïnskovo revolyutsionnovo podpol'ya' [Songs of the Romanian revolutionary underground movement], *Iskusstvo revolyutsiyey prizvannoye*, ii, ed. B. I. Rostotskiy (Moscow, 1972), 179
'Bol'shoy teatr SSSR', *Muzïkal'noy entsiklopediya*, ed. Yu. Kel'dïsh, i (Moscow, 1973), 523
ed.: *Iz istorii muzïki sotsialisticheskikh stran Evropï* [From the history of music in European socialist countries] (Moscow, 1975) [incl. 'Obrazï russkoy literaturnoy klassiki v cheshskoy opere', 112–68]
Cheshskaya i slovatskaya opera XX veka [Czech and Slovak opera of the 20th century] (in preparation)
Georgy Sviridov (in preparation)
Otar Taktakishvili (in preparation)

BIBLIOGRAPHY
G. B. Bernandt and I. M. Yampol'sky: *Kto pisal o muzïke* [Writers on music], ii (Moscow, 1974) [incl. list of writings]
YURY KELDÏSH

Polychronion. A set of acclamations to the Byzantine Emperor and his family which were sung on ceremonial occasions in Constantinople. The singers addressed the person they greeted with wishes for many years. Nowadays polychronia are sung during the liturgy whenever a bishop is present.

Polyeleos. A chant in the Byzantine ORTHROS which is made up of verses from Psalms cxxxiv and cxxxv. Its name is derived from the repetition of the word 'eleos' ('mercy') in the refrain of Psalm cxxxv.

Polyhymnia [Polymnia]. The Muse of hymns, dance and mime, represented with the barbiton; *see* MUSES.

Polymnestus of Colophon (*fl* 7th century BC). Greek composer. He wrote nomes sung to the aulos and epic and elegiac poetry, but nothing of his work has survived. From Asia Minor he went to Sparta, where with Thaletas, Sacadas and others he brought about a revival of poetry and especially of music: so much, but probably no more, merits belief in the testimony of the Pseudo-Plutarchian *De musica* concerning him (chaps.3–12, §§1132*c*–1135*c* passim; chap.29, §1141*b*). Pindar (frag.178, ed. Bowra) spoke of him as a famous poet, and the comic dramatist Cratinus, Pindar's contemporary, mentioned his compositions (frag.305, ed. Kock). Later, however, Aristophanes (*Knights*, l.1287) associated them with sexual depravity. This divergence from the remainder of the tradition is puzzling, since the works of a poet-composer prominent in 7th-century Sparta are not likely to have been licentious.

BIBLIOGRAPHY
J. M. Edmonds, ed. and trans.: *Lyra graeca* (London and Cambridge, Mass., 1922–7, 2/1928–40), i, 38ff
B. Einarson and P. H. De Lacy, ed. and trans.: *Plutarch's Moralia*, xiv (London and Cambridge, Mass., 1967)
U. Knoche: 'Polymnestos', *Der kleine Pauly*, iv (Stuttgart, 1972), 1007
WARREN ANDERSON

Polynesia. One of the three groups of the PACIFIC ISLANDS. (For map *see* PACIFIC ISLANDS, fig.1.)

1. Introduction. 2. Cook Islands: (i) Vocal music (ii) Instruments. 3. Easter Island. 4. French Polynesia: (i) General (ii) Austral Islands (iii) Mangaréva (Gambier Islands) (iv) Marquesas Islands (v) Tahiti (Society Islands) (vi) Tuamotu Islands. 5. Hawaii: (i) Vocal music (ii) Instruments (iii) Modern Hawaiian music. 6. Samoa: (i) Vocal music (ii)

Instruments (iii) Stylistic characteristics (iv) Music in society. 7. Tonga. 8. Tuvalu (Ellice Islands).

1. INTRODUCTION. Polynesia (Gk. *poly*: 'many', *nēsos*: 'island') comprises 18 island groups lying in a rough triangle, with New Zealand at the southern point, Hawaii in the north and Easter Island in the east. Excluding New Zealand's substantial land area of about 260,000 sq km, the total land area is less than 25,000 sq km, of which about 15,000 sq km lie at the northern apex of the triangle, in the Hawaiian Islands. The remaining groups, comprising hundreds of islands, have a total land area of less than 9000 sq km dispersed in approximately 30,000,000 sq km of ocean: one and a third times the size of the North American continent. The chief island groups in western Polynesia are Samoa (divided politically into Western Samoa and American Samoa) and Tonga, both lying close to Fiji, which is usually classified with Melanesia, but is closely related in many aspects of culture, including music and dance, to Polynesia. Together with Tuvalu (until 1975 the Ellice Islands), Tokelau, Niue, Wallis and Futuna Islands they make up western Polynesia (a common and useful division though without official status). Eastern Polynesia comprises the Society, Tuamotu, Mangaréva (Gambier), Austral, Rapa and Marquesas Islands (now all part of French Polynesia, see §4), together with the Cook Islands, Pitcairn Island, Easter Island, New Zealand and some small islands between the central eastern islands and Hawaii. There are also several Polynesian outliers in Melanesia (e.g. Ontong Java in the Solomon Islands) and in Micronesia.

There are important differences between New Zealand, the volcanic islands, and the coral atolls in the resources available for cultural use. The people speak related Polynesian languages, and in most archipelagoes English or French as well (on Easter Island, Spanish). Polynesian people, in spite of their physical distance from one another, have a strong sense of kinship with each other. Migrations and intermarriage have contributed to this sense of kinship. The migrations, not only in the prehistoric past but also since Western powers have been active in the Pacific, have been to smaller, uninhabited islands as well as to larger islands, when commerce could support the development of urban centres (e.g. the migrations from the Tuamotus, Marquesas and other islands of French Polynesia to Papeete, Tahiti; and from Samoa to Hawaii). Since the 1960s the great increase in the number of non-Maori Polynesians in Auckland, especially Polynesians from the Cook, West Samoan and Tokelau islands, has given that city the largest concentration of Polynesians in the world.

The original settlement of Polynesia has been a subject of great interest and not a little controversy. The generally accepted theory is that peoples moved through Melanesia and perhaps through Micronesia, and that a settlement on Fiji was the base from which Polynesian culture, as a distinctive configuration of patterns, was derived, and from which settlement of Tonga and Samoa then took place. (A South American origin of Polynesians has also been proposed.) From Samoa, peoples are believed to have migrated into central eastern Polynesia and from there to Hawaii, New Zealand and Easter Island.

Traditional social organization in western Polynesia focussed on the lineage organization; in central eastern Polynesia (and Hawaii) it focussed on religious practices

centred on the *marae* ('temple'). Religious music is not known to have been associated with western Polynesian cultures before European contact, but it was an intrinsic part of the culture of eastern Polynesia, where the concepts of *mana* ('spiritual power' or 'cosmic energy') and *tabu* ('restriction') governed the life of the people, and temple ceremonies were believed to be essential. Temple priests were specialists, and chanters received long and arduous training not only in memorizing long texts (e.g. genealogical chants) on which the continuity of *mana* from one chief to the next depended, but also in mastering the extraordinary types of vocal production needed for performing the ceremonial music. Each song type had a prescribed organization of specified components, and extensive training and rehearsal were necessary to ensure that nothing would fail in the performance. Throughout central eastern Polynesia there was a fairly unified tradition – more elaborately performed in the high islands that could support more complex cultures, particularly Tahiti and the Marquesas.

Polynesians have always had a reputation for being extremely musical. Reports from early Western explorers and others in the Pacific noted the frequency and enjoyment of performance among Polynesians; missionaries found that singing was the most effective route to conversion; and the tourist industry now promotes an image of handsome, uninhibited people on a palm-lined beach, singing and dancing. This reputation for musicality seems to have arisen largely from the quality of their choral singing, in which large groups with clear voices achieve a fine tonal blend and precision in enunciation and ensemble; from their ability to join a group in informal, unrehearsed singing and find some melodic outline (not necessarily one of any written four-part setting – often more than four parts are sounding) which either enhances the balance of tones in simple harmonies or provides an obbligato that is interesting yet unobtrusive; from their ability to perform in large groups with no conductor (although now there often is one); and from the fact that it is virtually impossible to find a Polynesian who says he 'can't sing'. Polynesians on the whole unquestionably do enjoy making music together, finding social solidarity in group performance and aesthetic pleasure in a full, rich sound, rhythmically projected.

Polynesian music is essentially vocal music, although there are some traditional instruments, as well as some styles of guitar playing and of singing with guitar accompaniment readily identified by foreigners as Polynesian. Throughout Polynesia hymn singing is an activity much enjoyed – in many islands an activity not limited to church services. PAN-PACIFIC POP, which is an extension of pan-Polynesian pop, is an important source of social entertainment as well as of economic gain in commercial contexts.

See also PACIFIC ISLANDS and NEW ZEALAND.

2. COOK ISLANDS. The Cook Islands comprise 15 widely scattered islands lying between 8° and 23° S and 156° and 167° W, with a total land area of 241 sq km and a total population of 20,000; the islands fall naturally into two groups, the northern and the southern. They are a self-governing protectorate of New Zealand and the people speak both Cook Islands Maori and English. The music of the northern Cook atolls has just begun to be studied in depth; brief accounts of their music can be found in works by P. H. Buck (T. R.

Hiroa, 1932) and by E. and P. Beaglehole. This discussion is concerned primarily with styles in the southern Cook group, particularly those of Aitutaki and Mangaia where McLean conducted fieldwork in 1967. Much work remains to be done on this music, however, and the information given should accordingly be regarded as tentative and subject to review.

(*i*) *Vocal music.* There are at least 40 named song types in the southern Cook Islands. Some are purely vocal, others accompany dance; some are probably Tahitian importations, others are clearly indigenous; some are peculiar to particular islands and others are more widespread. Only the more common song types are discussed here.

Introduced song types include the *imene* and the *ute*. The term 'imene' is a transliteration of the English word 'hymn'. However, as a verb the word can mean simply 'to sing' and hence there are both sacred and secular *imene*. Those of the secular variety include *imene akaevaeva* ('laments') and *imene tārekareka* ('songs for pleasure'). By far the most common, however, are church hymns, sung in parts. These are known collectively as *imene tapu* ('sacred hymns'). On the island of Aitutaki there are two styles of polyphonic *imene tapu*: those whose texts are in the hymnbook of the local Cook Islands Christian church, and those which are settings of biblical texts. The latter, which are distinguished by rhythmic grunting in unison from the men, are called *imene tuki*. The grunting (*tuki*) is performed as an integral part of the composition, 'to decorate the hymn'. *Imene* singing was almost certainly introduced into Aitutaki in 1820, by two Tahitian pastors who were taken to the island by the missionary John Williams and left there to introduce Christianity. The style has developed continuously and new *imene* are constantly being composed. On Aitutaki, composers from each of the seven main villages are required to compose two new *imene* – one *imene tuki* and one with a hymnbook text – twice a year, for Christmas and for the New Year. These new hymns are first performed at combined services in the church at Arutanga. The best-liked of the *imene tuki* may remain in the repertory for 30 years or more, though this is exceptional: more usually, only the latest ones are still sung because the leading women for the earlier ones have died. There are six, or sometimes seven, named parts in *imene tuki*. Two are main parts, sung by groups of women and men respectively. Superimposed upon the main women's part are two upper solo women's parts, and one or two upper solo men's parts are added to the main men's part and the bass grunting (*tuki*). Typically the women sing at the top of their range, as loudly as possible.

Similar styles of hymn singing occur on the other islands of the Cook group with different names, and the names for the voice-parts also differ from island to island. On Mangaia, the men's grunting is called *engu*; the *imene tuki* song type is thus called *imene engu*. The hymnbook hymns on Mangaia are called *imene Āreti*, after a missionary named Harris (Āreti) who is credited with introducing the style.

The *ute* style was introduced to the Cook Islands from Tahiti. In the 1820s Ellis complained of Tahitian *ute* that 'they were, with few exceptions, either idolatrous or impure, and were consequently abandoned when the people renounced their pagan worship'. Unknown to Ellis, however, the *ute*, far from being aban-

doned, had merely been driven underground. The style subsequently spread not only to the Cook Islands, but also throughout French Polynesia. Many *ute* still contain Tahitian words. Although Ellis described them as 'historical ballads', they are now mostly love songs and topical songs. They are sung in parts like the *imene*, though in a different style. Unlike *imene*, *ute* are sometimes accompanied by guitars, ukeleles, mouth organs or accordions.

Indigenous song types include the *pe'e*, *amu* and *karakia*. *Pe'e* songs are found on all the islands of the southern Cooks as well as on Penrhyn, where they are called *pese*. The latter cognate form of the word also occurs in Samoa where it means simply 'song', as seems to have been the case in Tahiti, where the term was *pehe*. In Mangaia, similarly, the word seems to be a generic term for song, since love songs, welcome songs and hauling songs are all called *pe'e*. More usually, however, *pe'e* are historical songs commemorating particular events or the brave deeds of an ancestor; they were formerly used in oratory to demonstrate the knowledge and ability of the orator. They are now almost invariably associated with legends or other oral traditions, and are performed as an integral part of story-telling. Although *pe'e* can be sung, most, particularly in Aitutaki, are recited in 'speech-song' style.

In Rarotonga *amu* are praise songs which tell the life story or deeds of celebrated chiefs or warriors. On Atiu, they likewise describe 'brave deeds' or 'a love of affection', or alternatively may be songs of 'a joyous nature, as in canoe hauling'. On Aitutaki, as in Atiu, there are two varieties of *amu*, both of which are said to be sung in unison (although the few recorded by the writer were in parts). The first are songs of praise or farewell for the dead, intended for performance in the presence of the dead body. They are accompanied by wailing, and are sung not at the funeral service but immediately after death by women mourners and relatives of the deceased, gathered round the body. All songs of this type are said to have been composed by women, and they are sung mostly by women although sometimes old men will join in. The other kind of *amu* was sung while hauling logs or pulling up boats, to encourage the men. In Mangaia, the term *amu* does not appear to be used, but songs for lifting heavy loads – the equivalent of the second variety of *amu* in Atiu and Aitutaki – are called *tauamu*.

Karakia are incantations or invocations. They are found throughout the southern Cook group. According to Buck, the Mangaian variety formed part of the stock-in-trade of priests, and the set words were valuable intangible property. They are performed solo, by men, in recited style.

There are some song types specific to Mangaia: these are of particular interest because of changes which have taken place in them since missionary activity began. The missionary William Gill wrote at length in 1875 of ceremonies called *tara kakai* ('death talks'). These took place at night in large, specially constructed houses lit with candlenut torches. Each male relative of the deceased had to lead a unison unaccompanied *tangi* ('crying song'); these songs alternated with *tiau*, songs accompanied by the *ka'ara* (slit-drum). Besides the 'death talks', funeral games called *eva* ('dirge proper') were performed. Unlike the 'death talks', these took place by day. Four varieties were listed by Gill: *eva tapara* ('funeral dirge'), *eva puruki* ('war dirge'), *eva toki* ('axe dirge'), and *eva ta* ('crashing dirge'). All except the first were performed with weapons, presumably by men. In 1967 – less than 100 years later – no-one could be found on Mangaia who had ever heard of a *tara kakai*, *tangi*, or Gill's four varieties of 'dirge proper'. The term *eva*, however, is still extant as a type of song performed exclusively by men, concerned with such topics as battles or the honouring of a warrior.

Complementary to the *eva* is another song type, not mentioned by Gill at all, called *mire*, which was formerly sung only by women. Women still lead the song, but men may now take part. According to some informants, *eva* and *mire* are sung on special occasions to entertain important people visiting the island, unlike *pe'e*, which can be performed at any time. Both *eva* and *mire* are recited song types performed in unison by groups of singers; they may be accompanied by actions; many of the *mire* recorded by the writer were accompanied by vigorous hand-clapping.

(*ii*) *Instruments*. The only instruments still important are the percussion instruments used in ensemble to accompany dancing. They include slit-drums (*pātē* on Rarotonga; *tokere* (fig.1) on Aitutaki; *ove* on Mangaia), which are also used singly for signalling; *pa'u* (large and small drums with shark- or goatskin heads); and the *tini* (paraffin tin). Larger slit-drums, called *ka'ara*, played with two sticks instead of one to produce four notes instead of the two of the *tokere*, were typical of Mangaia, but had become obsolete as a traditional instrument by the late 1960s, surviving only as *tupāpaku* ('ghost voices') of the olden days which are said to be heard in the bush when a chief of the island is going to die. However, the *ka'ara* has now been revived by the Cook Islands National Theatre dance company. Bamboo flutes, apparently mouth-blown, were used as toys by children in the early 20th century, as were coconut-leaf whistles, palm-leaf trumpets and bamboo

jew's harps. According to Buck, another toy used was the bullroarer. The *pu* (shell trumpet), usually end-blown though sometimes side-blown, was formerly used as a signal to assemble the people or as a warning for warriors to mobilize. On Mangaia, the sound of the *pu* was the voice of the god Rongo, calling the people to rituals associated with his service. It is now more prosaically used by the baker, to signal when bread is ready.

3. EASTER ISLAND. Easter Island (Rapanui), lying 27° 10′ S and 109° 30′ W with a population of about 1500, is the furthest east of the Polynesian islands. According to a tradition still celebrated in song the ancestral settlers arrived from the west in two canoes. An impressive Polynesian culture flourished before the arrival of the first Europeans on Easter Sunday, 1722. Ceremonial dances performed at the *ahu* (sacred places at the site of the famous huge stone images) were a form of worship. Ancient stories, incised in post-European times in script or glyphs on *kohau rongo-rongo* (wooden tablets), were chanted by traditional specialists at the rites of the bird-man cult and other ceremonies, and are still chanted by some elderly people. Some examples still known include the creation myth, stories about ancestors, the bird and yam legend, laments and work chants. Catholic missionaries from Tahiti arrived in 1864 bringing a style of chant that was adopted by the islanders. But the death of the traditional priests and most of the population through a smallpox epidemic and 'blackbirding' (the forced recruitment of Polynesians for labour) resulted in the loss of much pre-contact culture by the 1870s. Secular Polynesian genres (mostly Tahitian) were absorbed from 1914 onwards, and Latin American and international popular styles from 1954 (e.g. the Mexican *corrido*, the Argentine tango, the waltz, foxtrot, etc). In

1. Dancers accompanied by tokere (slit-drums), Aitutaki, Cook Islands, 1967

that year a regular ship service was established with Chile, which had annexed the island in 1888. Since the opening of an airport in 1966, the demands of tourism have strongly influenced musical activity.

Both traditional and modern music are predominantly vocal. To the pre-missionary period, Campbell ascribed *aku-aku* (chants devoted to spirits), *riu* (laments recounting past events) and *riu-tangi* (funeral chants), *ate* (praise chants addressed to humans and things, with musical patterns similar to those of *riu*), *uté* (short songs with fixed forms), *kai-kai* (recitations for string games, some being *patautau* recitations (see below) of texts from the *rongo-rongo* tablets), and *ei* (provocative or insulting songs, consisting of improvised satirical couplets, which could lead to fights or even tribal war if the satirized person took offence). To the period from 1864 to 1914 he ascribed evolved types of *riu*, *kai-kai* and *ei* in addition to *hakakio* (chants expressing gratitude at feasts), *ha-ipo-ipo* (wedding chants of Tahitian origin), and *hīmene* (hymns). *Riu*, the broadest category, embraces some types (e.g. surfing chants) which have been classified separately by other authors. Early *riu* were historical accounts of local kings or wars, remembrance of ancestors, or expressions of mythical beliefs about *tangata manu* ('bird men'). Evolved *riu* concern more recent historical events.

Extant *ate*, considered by Campbell to be at least 200 years old, are rhythmically free and have wide ranges of pitch. *Patautau* are free rhythmic recitations without precise pitch. Musical styles within *riu* and other traditional song types vary because in many instances the music now sung is more recent in origin than the text. Tahitian *hīmene* style (see §4(v)) and other two- and three-part singing styles are found (in bourdon, organum, free counterpoint and homophonic harmony).

Dancing or body movements, such as the gentle swaying of torso and arms in *hīmene*, accompanies most singing. Clapping, striking hands on the ground and non-musical vocal sounds are common types of accompaniment. The instrumental inventory is small. The *keho* (a stone plate over a gourd resonator in a pit in the ground) was stamped rhythmically to accompany singing and dancing. A shell (trumpet) was listed by one early writer. The *kauaha* from South America (a rattle made from the jawbone of a horse) and guitars and drums said to have come from Tahiti are now considered traditional accompaniment to light songs and dances.

4. FRENCH POLYNESIA.

(i) General. The area of eastern Polynesia now known as French Polynesia includes Tahiti and the other Society Islands, as well as the archipelagoes east of Tahiti: the Tuamotus (76 coral atolls); the Marquesas (12 islands); the Australs (five islands); and the Mangaréva (Gambier) Islands.

The sequence of Polynesian settlement of eastern Polynesia is fairly well established. It is known that Polynesians from western Polynesia (probably Samoa) settled the central part of eastern Polynesia (i.e. the Marquesas and the Societies) about the 1st century AD. Migrations to other eastern Polynesian island groups followed. Voyages among island groups are known to have continued to take place after settlements had been established. By the time of European exploration in the Pacific, beginning in the 16th century, distinctive sociocultural patterns had evolved in all the archipelagoes,

although these were remarkably homogeneous considering the tremendous ocean distances involved. The islands with the most elaborate cultures were the high islands (the Marquesas and the Australs); the low coral atolls of the Tuamotus and others were less developed. Particularly on the high islands, chant (or song) and dance played an important part in religious and other ceremonial activities.

European discovery of the eastern Polynesian islands extended over two centuries. One Spanish navigator, Mendaña, is credited with the discovery of some of the Marquesas Islands in 1595, and another, Quiros, with the discovery of some of the Tuamotus in 1606. But it was not until 1767 that the English navigator, Samuel Wallis, landed on Tahiti, which thereafter became a favourite port of call for European ships in the central Pacific, and the centre from which European culture was introduced to Polynesia, and Polynesian culture to Europe (see §(v) below).

The music of eastern Polynesia was essentially vocal, in spite of the impressive drums played at the *marae* (temple) and their importance to society. Musical characteristics described in studies of the 1930s and 1940s reveal that there were two basic styles of chanting (or singing). One was a rhythmic recitation with fast tempo and indefinite pitch. The other was of more definite pitch with a small number of notes in a small range. The inventories of successive (i.e. melodic) and simultaneous (i.e. harmonic) intervals were noted as being the same, and consisted of major 2nd, minor 2nd and minor 3rd, although these must be considered only approximations. The sound recordings from these studies corroborate the description written by Forster in 1773 (*see* PACIFIC ISLANDS, §3). Two- and three-part textures predominated in the multi-part music recorded, but the vocabulary of the Marquesas clearly indicates three basic and three additional registers for women as well as additional parts for men. The most widespread form had a three-part organization consisting of a solo 'question', a solo 'answer' and a group refrain, this unit being repeated as many times as necessary to accommodate the long texts of traditional historical narrative songs; however, other types of form (e.g. *AB*, *ABA* and *ABCD*) were also noted. Performance required extraordinary types of vocal production and there were certain prescribed ways to end phrases, including terminal glides (a downward glissando to an indefinite pitch), trills and sustained tone.

Among the most widespread instruments in eastern Polynesia was the conch-shell trumpet, associated with ceremonies and used as a signalling device on canoe voyages. At the time of the first contact with Europeans, especially in the high-island cultures, large standing single-headed drums with sharkskin membranes and (in some cases) elaborately carved frames were integrally associated with ceremonies. Small drums and other percussion instruments were used for dance accompaniment. Bamboo nose flutes were widely distributed where bamboo was available.

Throughout French Polynesia, missionaries sought to substitute church music for the old traditional music; by the mid-20th century hymn singing was the predominant type of music among the older generation, while their children have become strongly attracted to Tahitian popular songs accompanied by guitar and *tini* (tin can drum) and play the ukelele and ad hoc instruments.

(ii) Austral Islands. The five islands of the Austral group lie south of Tahiti. Of these, Raivavae ('High Island') and Tubuai were the source of some of the handsomely carved eastern Polynesian tall drums now in European museums, which were collected before missionary influence had suppressed their use and construction. The shell trumpet was widespread. Surviving traditional folk tales and a recurrent motif in the artefacts consisting of a row of stylized dancers attest the interest in dance (and presumably in its associated music) in pre-missionary Raivavae.

Throughout the Austral Islands, the chief musical activity of adults is now hymn singing in Tahitian *hīmene* style (see §4(v) below). *Hīmene* singing is the outstanding feature of the New Year festival, one of the two great celebrations of the year. In Rapa, there is a friendly competition between communities in the singing of newly composed *hīmene*. In contrast, where church control does not forbid the modern equivalent of the traditional eastern Polynesian *taure'are'a* ('adolescent') life style, young people enjoy secular song and dance forms introduced from Tahiti by personal contact or through the radio. The 14 July festival is the yearly climax of young people's musical activities. Several types of instrument have been reported from the Australs but none appears to have been in use for very long.

(iii) Mangaréva (Gambier Islands). The Mangaréva islands lie east of the Tuamotus on the Tropic of Capricorn at 135° W. The most extensive study of traditional Mangarévan culture, carried out by a Bishop Museum expedition in 1934, found that music was essential to many rituals connected with food, religion, life-cycle events, etc. Singing, mostly accompanied by body movements or dance, was both solo and choral; group singing included two- and three-part textures. Some song types were accompanied by instruments, especially by the drum in important ceremonies. Songs were usually classified by subject matter and helped to perpetuate traditional knowledge. A particular example was the *kapa*, based on incidents in the *atoga*, an oral tradition shared with other Polynesian cultures and including folk tales of local origin. The importance of the role of the *pou-kapa* ('song leader') was widely recognized. The *kapa* consisted of successive verses in question and answer form, each verse followed by a refrain. The seven other song types noted in the 1934 study included laments, praise songs and love songs.

The principal instruments were the *pa'u* (drum), *puko'e* (nose flute) and *pu* (shell trumpet). One of the playing techniques for the *pu* was unusual for Polynesia: it was held under the arm and notes of low, medium and high pitch (each with special verbal designation) were played; a high shrill tone was produced by inhaling. The 1934 study also recorded Mangarévan names for a slit-drum, a stone which was beaten, several other inadequately described idiophones, an end-blown mouth flute, a rolled leaf (called a trumpet but possibly a double-reed whistle like the Hawaiian *pū lā'ī*) and a drum with a mat cover instead of the usual stretched sharkskin.

(iv) Marquesas Islands. Although the Marquesas were the eastern Polynesian islands first discovered by Europeans, Marquesans were notable among Polynesians for their resistance to much imported Western culture, including music. Therefore, recordings by a Bishop Museum expedition in 1920–21 may provide the most reliable indication of a style that, with regional variants, was widespread in eastern Polynesia at the time of the first European contact. According to Handy, no Polynesian people employed music more continually, for music was not only central to rites and festivities but also accompanied almost every kind of activity. The Marquesan language had an extensive vocabulary pertaining to music. There were many named kinds of chant (over 50 in one dictionary). There were terms for three basic 'voices' (i.e. registers) and three additional related voices for women, and the same for men. Three modes of clapping (each producing a different sound) and other types of body percussion were designated, and there were names for 16 kinds of drum.

Each song type had a prescribed organization of specified components, indicating a systematized performing practice in both sound and function. Marquesans classified song or chant as either *tapu* ('restricted', 'sacred') or non-*tapu*, but a *tapu* song could become non-*tapu* after its original purpose had been fulfilled. Handy's study presents the song types as recreational, eulogistic and religious. Marquesans believed that it was only through effective chanting or singing that a desired goal (spiritual, procreative, social, etc) could be achieved, and therefore great emphasis was placed on selecting not merely the right chant or song, but the right mode of performance. The *pu'e*, for example, a religious chant, was more a magic spell than a devotional chorus. It could be chanted only by old men, and contained non-lexical syllables believed to have magic power; it was slow, and was accompanied by large and small drums and clapping. There were both solo and choral songs and chants, but according to Handy, it was choral performance that was particularly cultivated in Marquesan music. All group performances were carefully and thoroughly rehearsed.

There is considerable variety among the ten recordings (each of a different song type) analysed by Winne. However, some generalizations can be made. Chants accompanied by powerful rhythmic effects (e.g. men's grunting – see §(v) below) tended to be simple melodically. Extraordinary types of vocal production were important. Melodic movement emphasized the repetition of certain intervals, both simultaneous and successive, mainly minor 3rds and major and minor 2nds, and some microtones. Tempo was predominantly fast, with contrasts between sections. Musical forms included the alternation of two phrase contours, *ABA* and *ABCD*, and characteristically included a refrain (see also §4(i) above).

The inventory of traditional musical instruments of the Marquesas was large for Polynesia. There were percussion sticks and a xylophone, jew's harp, a large variety of drums, a musical bow, both nose and mouth flutes, a single-reed aerophone, and both shell and wood trumpets.

(v) Tahiti (Society Islands). (a) Background. The island of Tahiti is so well known that the culture of the nine Society Islands (lying between 15° 48' and 17° 53' S and 148° 05' and 154° 43' W with a total of 1536 sq km of land) is usually called 'Tahitian'. Tahiti was the first of the Pacific Islands to attract widespread interest in Europe. In 1768, the French navigator, Bougainville, thinking he was the first European to discover Tahiti (although the English navigator Samuel Wallis had

2. *Tall drums played at a marae sacrificial ceremony on Tahiti: engraving from the atlas of Captain Cook's 'Voyage to the Pacific Ocean' (1784)*

3. *Tō'ere (slit-drum), Tahiti*

landed there in 1767), named it 'New Cythera' and took Aoutouru (Auturu), a native who exemplified the 'noble savage' from an island paradise, to France, where he was presented to the king and fascinated Madame de Pompadour and many leaders of the Romantic movement. In 1774, on Captain Cook's second voyage, Omai was taken from a neighbouring island, Huahine, to England, where he became the darling of English society and was the subject of O'Keefe's elaborate and popular musical of 1785, *Omai: or a Trip Round the World*, with music by William Shield.

Tahiti was also a centre for the introduction of European culture to much of Polynesia. Shanties sung by English sailors of the *Bounty* and other ships, and hymns taught by Protestant missionaries (from 1797), were adopted and adapted. Tahiti became a centre for missionary activity (first Protestant, then Catholic and, later, Mormon), from which Polynesian converts trained as missionaries carried not only their religious beliefs and the associated church music, but also, in many cases, some of their secular music, to widely scattered parts of the Pacific.

Papeete, Tahiti's largest town and principal communications centre, is now the administrative and commercial capital of French Polynesia. Its population includes people from throughout the Societies and from other French Polynesian islands, 'demis' (of mixed descent), Chinese, French and others. Some of these live in enclaves maintaining elements of their own ways of life and enjoying their own music. As elsewhere in the Society Islands, hymn singing is an important church activity, but European concert music is not widely known.

The predominant music of Papeete is Tahitian PAN-PACIFIC POP, which absorbs elements from international popular music introduced by radio, gramophone, cinema and television. Also prominent are slit-drum ensembles that accompany Tahitian dance. Both are enjoyed by Tahitians informally and as commercial entertainment at waterfront bars and luxurious tourist hotels, and both have been recorded. Tahitian popular music is disseminated from Papeete to all of French Polynesia via travel and radio, and throughout the world by recordings and an occasional touring dance troupe.

(*b*) *Early reports of Tahitian music.* Tahitians were very fond of music and dance, perpetuating their legends and traditions through stylized recitation and the singing of prayers, genealogies, laments, salutes, harangues and love lyrics at festive and religious ceremonies. Early accounts mention a little solo singing and chanting, but more group performances, including chorus, instruments and dance. Especially noted were the performances by groups of young men of the Arioi society (a cult of theatrics devoted to the god 'Oro) who travelled to villages throughout the islands. Because their dance was considered obscene, the Arioi were anathema to the Christian missionaries.

Only a few types of instrument are noted in early writings. The most elaborate and varied type was the *pahu*, a vertical cylindrical drum with a sharkskin membrane laced to the base (which in some *pahu* were elaborately carved). Tall *pahu* of both large and small diameter were highly valued properties of the *marae* ('temple') and the *ari'i* ('chief'). The drum names suggest their function in society, e.g. *pahu rutu mā'a na te 'ōpū-*

nui ('drum to beat for food for august stomachs'). In *marae* ceremonies a single drum was played for some functions, two or three in ensemble for others (fig.2). Only the largest were beaten with sticks; others were hand-beaten. A tall drum of small diameter and high pitch used in ritual human sacrifice was called *tō'ere*, a name now applied to the wooden slit-drum introduced from Rarotonga (in the Cook Islands) in the early 1800s and used for secular dance (fig.3). Conch-shell trumpets (*pū*) were also used in *marae* ceremonies and on voyages (fig.4). Some of them had long bamboo mouthpieces. Smaller drums, *pahu 'upa'upa*, were used for dance accompaniment in ensemble with the *'ihara* (an extinct idiophone) and the *vivo* (transverse nose flute). The *vivo* was also played solo and in duet. For a duet, if two *vivo* did not match in pitch, a leaf was wrapped around the end of the shorter one to lower its pitch.

(*c*) Traditional music in the mid-20th century. No thorough field study has yet been made of Tahitian music. However, a general description can be given of the traditional types of music and dance performed in the competitions of the annual July Fête, a celebration centring on Bastille Day which provides an approved outlet for the exuberance and display which had been highly valued in ancient *heiva* ('amusement dance') before their suppression by missionaries. These are: *hīmene tārava*, *'ōte'a*, *pā'ō'ā*, *hivinau*, *'utē* and *'aparima*.

The word *hīmene* (derived from 'hymn') is generally applied to the styles of both the Protestant hymn tune and the pre-existing multi-part (i.e. polyphonic) choral singing of traditional Polynesian texts, including the archaic *paripari fenua* about legendary heroes and chiefs. *Hīmene tārava* designates the traditional musical style (whether with Christian or traditional Polynesian text) in which women take the lead, some singing short repeated melodic patterns of small compass, others a steady, smooth drone. Men's voices enter later with an initial melodic contour that leads to vigorous pulsations on drone pitches with a strongly aspirated vocable (somewhat like 'hi' or 'hu' or blowing into a bottle, and variously described as ejaculations, grunts, etc). One person sings without text, soaring high over the other parts primarily on pitches that reinforce the acoustic overtones of the intense choral sound. At phrase endings, all voices merge into a long-sustained tonic during which the next phrase is begun by the women. Phrases of similar texture follow, with as many restatements as are needed for the text. Breath-taking is staggered to permit a continuous tone from the beginning to the end of the entire song, which may last 15 minutes or more.

The *'ōte'a* is a group dance with rapid hip movements for women and vigorous knee movements for men. The rhythmic counterpart for this is played by an ensemble of three to ten or more *tō'ere* (slit-drums) of contrasting size and pitch, one or more *tariparau* (double-headed barrel drum now often European in design), and in most performances (although excluded from some Fête competitions) a *tini* (five-gallon paraffin can). A performance typically begins with a series of shouts each answered by a short drum response that leads into the first statement of the short, fast, rhythmic motif in duple metre. Knowledgeable eastern Polynesians can identify the specific village or island source of many motifs. The first statement of the motif is played on a single *tō'ere*, and is followed by statements on the others at their

entrances. It is played on one or more *tō'ere* throughout the section until the cadential formula. After the first statement of the motif, complementary rhythmic patterns are played, increasing the complexity of the texture. Subsequent sections are based on different motifs and characteristically all instruments enter simultaneously. The climax may be frenetic; the ending is always abrupt. Great vigour and precision are required in the virtuoso drumming.

The satirical subject matter of the *pā'ō'ā* is performed by a male solo chanter-dancer accompanied by a seated male chorus who sing, produce extra-musical vocal sounds and strike their hands on the ground. The music for the circular dance, *hivinau* (perhaps from 'heave now'), is a solo–response song inspired by European sailors' shanties. *'Utē* are songs with optional

4. Conch-shell trumpet, Tahiti

accompaniment by instruments (guitar, harmonica and, formerly, accordion) or voices, or both. Music for the *'aparima* (a standing or sitting gesture dance) is another song type with optional instrumental accompaniment.

(*vi*) *Tuamotu Islands*. The Tuamotu archipelago of low coral islands lies between the Society and Marquesas Islands. Interaction with Tahiti and other islands began in prehistoric times and continues through government administration and the migration of young Tuamotuans to Papeete, seeking a way of life more exciting than that of their own islands. The Tuamotus, with limited natural resources and waters dangerous for navigation, have had fewer contacts with Europeans than Tahiti.

Although most socio-cultural patterns had been transformed by 1930, some of the Tuamotuan music recorded by a Bishop Museum expedition and analysed by Burrows is considered indigenous. It is simpler and probably more archaic than any extant in the Society Islands. Informal song festivals of *fakataratara* ('eulogy of lands') and *fakateniteni* ('eulogy of heroes'), some performed in old chant style and some in *hīmene* style (see §4(v) above), were held when people gathered for the pearl-diving season. Such eulogies, together with genealogical recitation and war, ceremonial and recreational dancing, were among the *vanaga* ('esoteric lore') traditionally taught to descendants of rulers.

A complete native classification of song types is not known, but Burrows's study presents: solemn chants, laments, incantation and prayers, dance music (ten kinds, including games played while chanting), love songs (three kinds), enumeration songs, work songs, chants of glory, enlivening chants, and the announcement of a turtle catch (the turtle was a highly esteemed food and was specially significant in Tuamotuan religious practice). The singing of Christian and secular songs is now an important social activity.

The Tuamotuan language has terms not only for chant and song categories (e.g. *fagu*: solemn, sacred chant handed down from ancestors without intended change) and dance types but also for qualities of vocalization (e.g. *tarava*: a steady tone; *fakatukutuku*: a special kind of quavering tone).

In 1930 no singing style was exclusively associated with a specific song type. Burrows did describe some general features characteristic of indigenous Tuamotuan music, however: special vocalization; simple non-metric rhythm; steady tempo; the use of indeterminate pitch in fast rhythmic recitation, and of definite pitches (two to six notes) in narrow compass in other song types; and two-part singing with preference for intervals of 3rds and 2nds. The predominant form is a short solo by one voice, a solo response by another voice, followed by the chorus; this tripartite design is repeated as many times as required by the text. Introduced music includes a three-part Tahitian *hīmene* style (see §4(v) above) (with a larger pitch range than the older Tuamotuan two-part singing) in which new songs are composed for some important occasions. A more recent introduction is PAN-PACIFIC POP.

Early instruments included a drum and conch trumpet characteristic of eastern Polynesia, and a bamboo nose flute which may have been imported from Tahiti. In the 1930s harmonica, guitar and a bottle blown across the top accompanied dancing on one island, and in 1952, on a different island, galvanized pots and a wooden slit-drum. Rhythmic stamping and other body percussion continue to be important.

In Papeete on Tahiti (and to a lesser extent elsewhere) there is modern music identified as Tuamotuan that includes not only specific songs, but also *tairi paumotu*, a style of percussive stroking of guitar and ukelele in very fast rhythmic patterns, which developed sometime between 1929 and 1934, a native adaptation of the guitar playing of Kenneth Emory, a Bishop Museum anthropologist engaged in field work in the Tuamotus.

5. HAWAII. Although the name actually refers only to the principal island of the Hawaiian Islands archipelago, it is now commonly used to designate all the islands of that group. Lying in the North Pacific about 3070 km south-west of San Francisco, Hawaii was the northernmost archipelago settled by Polynesians and had a flourishing Polynesian culture when discovered by Captain Cook in 1778. Since 1959 Hawaii has been a state of the USA, and its population of about 800,000 is known for its cultural pluralism; in addition to descendants of early Hawaiian Polynesians there are also Polynesians from other island groups (e.g. Samoa), as well as Asians (Chinese, Japanese, Korean, Filipino and Vietnamese) and Caucasians (European and American). Certain genres of the musical heritage of all these peoples are perpetuated, some primarily by the peoples themselves, others by all the inhabitants jointly, providing an annual calendar of many colourful festivals. The discussion here centres on music identified as Hawaiian, particularly traditional styles which existed before

European contact. Western art music is discussed separately; *see* HAWAII.

(i) *Vocal music.* In traditional Hawaiian culture before contact with Europeans, music was predominantly vocal in concept and form. The Hawaiians believed that all life contained *mana* (cosmic energy) and that this inspired musical creativity of a high degree. Surviving traditions reveal that Hawaiians attained some of the highest points in the Polynesian development of *mele* (chants), hula (dances which interpret texts) and musical instruments, mostly those played to accompany *mele hula* (dance-chants).

Some styles of chant are not intended for dancing, for example the *oli* and *kepakepa*. *Oli* is a term covering three sub-styles: *oli*, a chant with prolonged phrases sung in one continuous breath, *ho'āeāe* characterized by prolonged vowels, and *ho'ouwēuwē* which imitates wailing. The *kepakepa* style is a rapid and rhythmic recitation. Both *oli* and *kepakepa* are performed by trained, unaccompanied solo chanters. Two of the basic requisites for excellence in chanting are prolonged vowel fluctuation, and the admired technique of *'i'i* (rapid chest-tone tremor). Vowel fluctuation usually occurs at the initial syllable of the *mele*, and at the beginnings and particularly the endings of subsequent phrases. (Hawaiian syllables are characterized by a final vowel and an absence of consonant clusters.) *'I'i* usually occurs on back vowels and a strongly aspirated 'h'. It permeates the tone production in chanting, but is most frequently used at phrase endings.

In *oli* style (ex.1) it is considered desirable to chant long continuous phrases in a free flowing rhythm. There is no repetition of text lines. The chanter intones on what is spoken of as a single pitch, controlled by sustained breathing. However, although a text line (i.e. musical phrase) may begin directly on the predominant pitch it may also begin with an upward slur from about a minor 3rd below this pitch (ex.1a), and phrase endings are characterized by a terminal glide (ex.1b), followed by a quick intake of breath. The predominant pitch is determined by the chanter's experience and by what is the most comfortable level for projecting chest tones. Occasionally an individual prefers to raise the pitch between the phrases of a text or between texts in sequence.

The emotion of love, as in a lullaby or love poem, is conveyed through the prolonged use of *'i'i* on selected vowels in *ho'āeāe* style, in which case there are fewer words to a musical phrase. In *ho'ouwēuwē* style, the grief-laden emotional character of a dirge or lament is punctuated with outbursts of wailing. Sometimes,

Ex.1 *Oli* techniques; transcr. Z. Cambra

(a) Phrase beginning, showing upward slur and prolonged vowel fluctuation on initial syllable

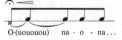

O-(uououou)   na - o - na...

(b) Phrase ending, showing prolonged vowel fluctuation and terminal glide

no- (uououououou) e,

because emotions of love and sorrow overlap and complement each other, *ho'āeāe* and *ho'ouwēuwē* blend. In *kepakepa*, the rapid rhythmic style of recitation requires that a chanter have thorough knowledge and unfailing recall of a genealogy, or skill at improvising a topical chant. Enunciation in this style is clear and precise, musical phrases are shorter than in *oli*, and there are no prolonged vowels.

Mele are chanted poems which document and comment on religious, psychological, historical and social aspects of the culture, and which also prescribe the specific musical style – whether *oli* or *mele hula* – through which they are to be projected. The interpretation and presentation of a *mele* is subject to the chanter's conceptualization of the composer-poet's (*haku mele*) meaning. Some *mele* have two meanings: the literal, and the 'hidden' (*kaona*). In religious *oli*, names of specific deities are sometimes disguised with vowel sounds to preserve the sacred *mana*. A *mele* would be presented as a personal gift to a designated individual who would then become the acknowledged and remembered 'owner' of the composition. The first performance of that *mele* would establish the recipient-owner's unwritten 'copyright'. Chanters exercise individual freedom in the intuitive development of certain aspects of performing style, but generally agree that one goal is to produce a pleasing and continuous sound throughout the chanting.

Mele hula (ex.2), which unlike *oli* accompanies dance, shares certain characteristics with *oli* style such as sustained breathing, chest-tone projection, control of vowel fluctuation and *'i'i*, and beginning a phrase either directly on the principal pitch or with an upward slur. But unlike *oli*, most *mele-hula* texts are in couplets and are usually repeated. The *mele-hula* style differs, too, in having simple regular duple or quadruple rhythmic organization, with a tonal content ranging from two or three notes in very old chants to five or six notes in compositions of the mid-19th century. (19th century transcriptions of *mele-hula* melodies show the minor 3rd occurring more frequently than other intervals, though this interval size must be considered an approximation only.) Other features of *mele-hula* style include ornamental slurs to and from upper and lower neighbouring notes; an undulating melodic contour; the consistent use of two short melodic phrases, with only slight melodic and rhythmic variations to accommodate the text of each verse; and instrumental and body-percussion accompaniment. There are prescribed rhythmic patterns for the accompaniment of all *mele hula*. Contrasting formulae are assigned to the introduction, each stanza, the interludes between stanzas, and the cadence. *Mele hula* are classed as *hula noho i lalo* ('sitting dance') and *hula ku i luna* ('standing dance'). Gestures illustrate or interpret key words of the text. In sitting dances the dancers usually accompany themselves with body percussion or instruments. Most standing dances are accompanied by one or more *ho'opa'a* (a seated chanter-drummer), but in one style of standing dance, the dancers accompany themselves with body percussion. Dances which depict the sounds and movements of animals (e.g. dog, plover, shark, turtle, spider and pig) are now seldom seen.

(*ii*) *Instruments*. Of the 18 traditional categories of instrument, 10 are primarily or exclusively associated with *mele hula*. Materials for making instruments were

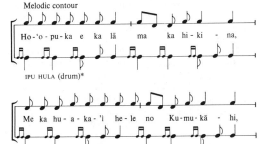

Ex.2 *Mele hula*, transcr. Z. Cambra

Melodic contour

Ho-'o-pu-ka e ka lā   ma   ka hi-ki - na,

IPU HULA (drum)*

Me ka hu-a-ka-'ī he-le no   Ku-mu-kā - hi,

*Upward stems indicate finger slaps
Downward stems indicate heavy beats

selected for their quality of sound.

The *pahu hula* ('dance drum'), a wooden hula drum (fig.5), is played by the *ho'opa'a* to accompany the *'ōlapa* ('dancer') in the *hula pahu* ('drum dance'). It is made from a log (either coconut or breadfruit) with one large upper and one smaller lower cavity carved out on each side of a thick partition. A sharkskin (now more often a calf or other type of skin) is stretched over the rim of the large cavity, and is secured in place with cord lashings drawn taut through the carved openwork patterns of the smaller cavity. The drummer strikes the membrane with one or both hands. According to Hawaiian tradition, the *pahu* was introduced about six centuries ago by the distinguished visitor, La'a-mai-Kahiki ('La'a-from-Tahiti'). Temple priests, impressed with the instrument, adopted it for religious ceremonies and called it *pahu heiau* ('temple drum'). Hula masters adapted it for sacred honorific temple dances.

The *pūniu* (coconut-shell knee drum) is made from a coconut shell covered with skin (traditionally that of a *kala*, or surgeon-fish; other types of skin are now used as well), which is firmly lashed to a ring under the shell. Cords are braided at the ring lashings to tie the *pūniu* to the player's thigh. The drum is struck with a braided thong of leaf or fibre. It is sometimes played in conjunction with the *pahu hula*, and at other times as self-accompaniment. When it is used together with the *pahu hula*, both drums are played by the same musician, who uses one hand for each as in fig.5*b*.

The *ipu hula* ('dance gourd'), now usually called gourd drum, is played by the *ho'opa'a* to accompany the *'ōlapa* in the *hula 'āla'apapa* ('formal dance'), and also in self-accompaniment in the *hula kuolo* ('kneeling dance'). It is made from two gourds (*Lagenaria siceraria*), the lower being large, long and globular and the upper short and squat (see fig.5*a*). Both are selected for the quality of sound produced by striking the dried, hard rind. The stem ends are cut off, inner seeds removed, and the two gourds are joined, forming a neck. A hole is centred above the resonance chamber. The player secures the instrument in one hand through a wrist loop, raises it, thumps it down on a mat, raises it again and gives it quick flexible slaps with the fingers of the other hand.

Kāla'au ('strike wood') are sticks played by the *'ōlapa* in self-accompaniment. They are made from two rods of hard, resonant wood; although traditionally *kauila* (*Alphitonia ponderosa*) was used, now rosewood and coffee (introduced by the Europeans) are also used. The older form of the instrument requires one rod about a metre long, and another about a third as long, both slightly thicker in the middle and tapered at each end. Using the left-hand fingers, the player holds the long rod loosely at the centre, balancing it over the left forearm, and beats a simple rhythm on the rod's extended portion with the short rod held in the right hand. A newer form dating from the 1870s is a matched pair of rods the size and shape of the smaller of the older rods. The *papa hehi* ('treadle footboard') is played by the *'ōlapa* in some *hula kāla'au* ('stick dances'; see fig.6).

The *'ulī'ulī* (gourd rattle) is played by the *'ōlapa* in self-accompaniment, in either sitting or standing dances. It is made from a single small gourd receptacle containing seeds, fitted with a fibre handle surmounted by an artistically designed flat circular disc fringed with feathers. In 1779, Captain James Cook and his men witnessed the *hula 'ulī'ulī* (gourd-rattle dance) at Kealakekua, Hawaii (see fig.7). The male *'ōlapa* wore *kūpe'e niho 'īlio* ('dog-teeth anklets') made from multiple rows of canine teeth strung on a net backing. Dancers now use two *'ulī'ulī*, the gourd having been replaced by the calabash (introduced from tropical America) or a hard coconut shell; the disc is now of dyed feathers, and occasionally ceramic facsimiles of the anklets are worn by male dancers.

The *pū'ili* (bamboo rattle) is played in self-accompaniment. It is made from a section of native Hawaiian bamboo (*Bambusa vulgaris*), about 50 mm or longer. One end with a node serves as a handle. Some narrow longitudinal slits, evenly spaced, are inserted in the remainder of the tube. The *'ōlapa* taps the *pū'ili* gently against the palm of the hand, the shoulders, or the ground. *Pū'ili* are now sometimes used in pairs and are struck together.

'Ili'ili ('pebbles'), sometimes referred to as stone castanets, are used as clappers in self-accompaniment. Two matched pairs of water-worn, dense (usually basaltic lava), flat, round or oval pebbles are selected both for quality of sound (lava from recent flows gives a preferred brighter sound) and for comfortable fit in the seated dancer's hands.

Kā'eke'eke (stamping pipes) are made of hard, thin-walled native Hawaiian bamboo (*Schizo-stachyum*) open at the top and with closed node end near the bottom. They are stamped vertically on a hard surface, and are played in pairs, each pair having two pipes of unequal length.

The *'ūlili* is a spinning rattle, played in self-accompaniment. It consists of three gourds, two of which spin when a cord wound around a stick is manipulated through a hole in the middle gourd (see fig.8).

Instruments for serenading include the *'ohe hano ihu* ('bamboo nose flute'; fig.9) which consists of a length of native Hawaiian bamboo with a nose hole cut at an angle above the closed node end and two or three finger-holes along the tube towards the open end; the *ipu hōkiokio* ('gourd whistle'), a globular flute; and *'ūkēkē*, a mouth bow with two or three fibre strings.

Sound-making devices include the *pū lā'ī* ('ti leaf trumpet') made of a rolled leaf; the *oeoe* (bullroarer); and the *nī'au kani* ('sounding coconut midrib'), a jew's harp. The *pū kani* ('sounding horn'), a shell trumpet used for blowing signals, is usually made from either the

(a)

(b)

5. *Ho'opa'a (chanter-drummer) playing: (a) ipu hula (gourd drum); (b) pahu hula (wooden hula drum) with left hand, and pūniu (coconut-shell knee drum) with right hand*

triton (*Charonia tritonis*) or the helmet shell (*Cassis cornuta*). It is similar to shell trumpets found elsewhere in Polynesia.

(*iii*) *Modern Hawaiian music*. Since 1820, when the first American Protestant missionaries arrived, traditional music in Hawaii has remained predominantly vocal as it was before; songs are still transmitted orally, use *kaona*, are phrased and slurred according to text, are learned by listening to and imitating experienced performers, are presented as gifts, are closely associated with hula, and are performed according to individual stylistic preferences. Melodic phrases are characteristically repeated, the melodies having undulating contours and enlarged pitch ranges except when they are simulating traditional chant. Rhythms are usually simple patterns derived from hula drum beats applied to strumming techniques on 'ukulele and guitar, and also used in symphonic arrangements.

Among the types of contemporary Hawaiian music derived from European contacts are HĪMENI (tunes derived from or composed in the style of hymns), anthems, marching songs, sea shanties, waltzes and old popular songs. Adopted stylistic characteristics include simple chordal harmonies, modulation, and, since the 1960s, close parallel and dissonant harmonies of college vocal trios and quartets. Introduced instruments include the 'ukulele (*see* UKELELE); the 'Hawaiian' guitar, the latter having been developed in several special forms (slack-key, steel and electric; *see* ELECTRIC GUITAR); European symphonic instruments (sometimes played in ensemble with traditional Hawaiian percussion); and, since the 1960s, electronic synthesizers and sophisticated recording apparatus. The development from the mid-20th century of publishing and recording industries is providing new impetus for the output of professional musicians.

In the 1970s there was a renaissance of interest in Hawaiian music, both of styles dating from before contact with Europeans and of later styles also identified as Hawaiian. Institutions involved in fostering this interest include the Bernice P. Bishop Museum (for collecting manuscripts and instruments); the Kamehameha Schools, the University of Hawaii, the State Council on Hawaiian Heritage and the Hawaiian Music Foundation (for perpetuating Hawaiian music as a performing art); and the Polynesian Culture Center (for tourist exhibitions). Hula continues to be prominent as entertainment but more frequently serves a commercial purpose rather than its traditional cultural role. Dance tempos are faster, medleys are appearing, and different types of traditional instruments are now used in alternate stanzas within one *mele hula*. Vocal soloists are reviving interest in *leo ki'eki'e*, a traditional falsetto singing style. Hawaiians view this commitment to Hawaiian music as being in harmony with traditional practices of perpetuating the *mana* of their lifestyle.

6. SAMOA. The Samoan Islands are in central Polynesia (14° S, 170–72° W). Their music, long the object of travellers' admiration and occasionally featured in a brief study, has only just begun to have extended and detailed investigation. The nine inhabited islands of the Samoan archipelago (the independent nation of Western Samoa, four islands; and the territory of American Samoa, five islands) form a homogeneous musical area whose style, on the evidence available, appears to be distinct from those of neighbouring island groups (although some of these, Tonga in particular, adopted Samoan songs and dances up to the 20th century).

(*i*) *Vocal music*. Samoan music is primarily vocal and is performed on a wide variety of public and private occasions; the songs themselves do not have titles, but are identified according to their use. In a few cases (e.g. dancing and paddling) virtually any composition will suffice as an accompaniment to the actions; but in general, textual content restricts the occasions on which a song is performed. Samoan speech distinguishes formal and colloquial systems of pronunciation; in song, however, only the formal type is used. The texts themselves usually have rhyming lines occupying an equal number of bars; non-rhyming lines or lines of unequal length tend to be followed by a refrain. Nonsense syllables are virtually unknown. Older songs often refer to practices now obsolete, such as traditional marriage ceremonies, food homages and some games. Words of unknown meaning are also occasionally found.

Ex.3 *Tagi*, rec. and transcr. R. Moyle

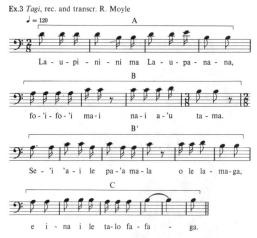

The most common song type is the *tagi* which is the sung section of a type of legend called a *fagono*; several hundred *fagono* are extant, and narrating them is a popular form of night-time entertainment. A large number of *tagi* use one or more of three stereotyped melodic phrases; the form of these tends to be *ABC*, with *B* always and *C* occasionally in series (see ex.3). Occasionally the *B* type of phrase occupies the entire *tagi* melody. *Fagono* may last from five minutes to more than an hour, and may contain from one to 16 *tagi*.

There are a few medicinal incantations performed by only one or two people in a village; nonetheless they are widely trusted to cure headache, choking on a fishbone, hiccoughs, skin blemishes and carbuncles. An incantation either addresses the malign spirit thought to be possessing the patient and threatens it with destruction, or else invokes the native doctor's family spirit to effect a cure. Samoan children have numerous group games incorporating songs, which are usually short and are performed in time to actions described in the texts. Many of the melodies centre on two notes a perfect 4th apart (see ex.4). Children also sing when gathering shellfish, massaging adults, teasing a cat, losing a tooth, etc. Chief among songs no longer performed in their original contexts are those of war and

Ex.4 Children's song, rec. and transcr. R. Moyle

'I - su - mu o le   va - i, so - a - 'a - i, so - a - 'a - i

paddling. Both types tend to be short, with alternation
between leader and unison chorus, and are capable of
indefinite repetition (see ex.5). Where they are still sung,
they often serve as dance-songs, two or more strung
together forming a longer composite whole. Despite this
change in purpose they continue to be identified
according to their former contexts. About the beginning
of the 20th century Samoan dance styles changed: the
large groups of singing performers carrying out
movements in unison were replaced by non-singing
dancers who performed independently. Very few songs
are composed specifically for dance accompaniment;
there are, however, a small number of mostly humorous
texts used exclusively for dances that imitate animal and
human behaviour. Modern group songs in traditional
style are composed for specific village occasions (e.g.

6. 'Ōlapa (dancer) playing kāla'au ('strike wood') and
papa hehi ('treadle footboard'), Hawaii

welcome, farewell, praise, sorrow), and are often freely
performed thereafter at festive gatherings. Other song
types performed less frequently include obscene, funeral
and marriage songs, lullabies and intoned historical
texts. There is no written record of music associated
with pre-Christian religion.

(ii) *Instruments.* Idiophones, membranophones and aerophones are found in Samoa, although aerophones are
now rare; there is no evidence of chordophones. The
three principal wooden slit-drums, the *pātē*, *lali* and
logo, serve to signal church events. The smallest, the
pātē, was brought from Tahiti by English missionaries;
the larger *lali* had its origin in Fiji, probably coming to
Samoa as part of the normal equipment of the large
Fijian double canoe. The largest of all, the *logo* (fig.
10b), appears to have been created by missionaries in
the 19th century for use as a church 'bell'; in design, it is
modelled on the Samoan *lali*. No particular rhythmic
patterns are evident for any instrument. The *pātē* and
logo are struck with single beaters, but *lali* are played
with two drumsticks, and they are always beaten in pairs
(fig.10a), one man to each instrument. Beating a rolled
floor mat is a common form of rhythmic
accompaniment to group singing; mat-flicking and
hand-clapping are also features of dance-songs. A jew's
harp, fashioned from two pieces of coconut leaf, is used
as a children's toy. Early writings indicate the former
presence of stamping tubes, sounding boards, half
coconut shells and at least one other type of slit-drum;
but these instruments are no longer seen.

Ex.5 Paddling song, rec. and transcr. R. Moyle

E   pe - i le po - po   e, e   pe - i 'o   le o -
- 'o   e Ta - u - ti - li i ga - ga - 'e, ___   Ga -
- lu - e fa - 'a- Ni - u - ē,   a - uē   fe - fē.

Flutes were once common, and included end-blown
and side-blown types, the syrinx and the nose flute. For
reasons not yet clear none of these types is still used,
although they are well remembered by older Samoans.
Finger-holes varied in number from two to eight, but
little is known of the scale patterns used. The conch-
shell trumpet is commonly employed as a signalling
device on both land and sea. Children sometimes make
toy whistles and squeakers out of grass. Drums with
single or double skin-heads are used principally as
signals for applause at cricket matches; these types of
drum may originally have been introduced from the
Marquesas Islands, although modern examples tend to
be European in design.

(iii) *Stylistic characteristics.* There are four sub-styles of
Samoan song, each distinguished on the basis of musical
texture – solo, unison, responsorial and part-singing.
Solo songs are characterized by a predominance of
stepwise movement, intervals smaller than a 4th, usually
rising, and descending intervals larger than a 4th at

7

9

8

7. *'Ōlapa (dancers) performing hula 'ulī'ulī (gourd rattle dance) with kūpe'e niho 'īlio (dog-teeth anklets): drawing (c1778) by John Webber, Captain Cook's artist, in the Bernice P. Bishop Museum, Honolulu*

8. *'Ūlili (spinning rattle), Hawaii*

9. *'Ohe hano ihu (bamboo nose flute), Hawaii*

10. *Slit-drums of Upolu, Samoa: (a) a pair of lali; (b) logo, struck with a single beater*

10a

10b

phrase endings. Unison songs contain a considerable amount of melodic repetition, especially at the opening of a song, and their melodies centre on two notes a perfect 4th apart, with cadences often rising a 4th before falling approximately one octave in a terminal glissando. Responsorial songs also concentrate on notes a perfect 4th apart. There are similarities too between the level opening of the unison song and the melodic repetition of the leader's line in the responsorial song. The cadential outline of the chorus line in the responsorial song also resembles that of the unison song. Overlap between leader and chorus is rare. Relatively few non-acculturated homophonic or polyphonic songs have been recorded: these songs appear to be characterized by movement in parallel 4ths and 5ths and a cadence formula in which the highest voice remains level above

two falling parts. Stylistic features common to Samoan music as a whole include a wide range of tempos, the frequent use of simple duple metre and a dactylic rhythmic figure, and the constant appearance of the perfect 4th, not only as a harmonic and melodic interval, but also as the total melodic range, and as an integral part of several cadence formulae.

(*iv*) *Music in society.* Larger villages have a resident composer, always a male, who provides songs for specific occasions: arrivals or departures, deaths, political and social achievements. The more renowned among them are often engaged by villages other than their own. The composer also teaches his songs to the village choir, and may even act as song leader for a first public performance. In return he is paid in fine mats, bark cloth and cash. In partsongs the lowest voice (*malū*) is taught first, a whole strophe at a time, before the upper parts (*usu* and *ato*) are added. Missionary influence, apart from introducing new melodic outlines and stereotyped harmonic progressions, has been responsible for two developments: four-part harmony (earlier songs were in two or three parts), and mixed choirs (earlier group songs appear to have been exclusively male).

There is no organized system of song ownership, but local pride discourages widespread use of a song that has specific references to a particular village, and because most group songs are composed for particular occasions, textual content tends to determine the appropriateness of further performances. Particular funeral and marriage songs may be performed only by certain villages or districts on pain of public shame or even physical violence, and medicinal incantations are sung only by the native doctor, whose supernatural power is essential to the cure. Where a song is known and sung over a wide geographical area and where its origin is not known, it is usually referred to simply as a 'Samoan song' and is the common property of the whole country; several paddling, war and game songs are of this type.

The attributes of a good singer include the ability to maintain a given pitch and tempo, to memorize a voice part and song text, and a strong, clear voice. A song leader is also expected to know all the voice parts and be prepared to correct any uncertainties in melody or text, to choose a comfortable pitch and tempo, and to introduce and regulate the hand-clapping which accompanies dance-songs. Most group songs are performed seated, sometimes with the leader standing in the middle of the group. In the older, standing, group dances, the dancers themselves sang, but for the newer, individualistic performances, a seated choir accompanies the dancers. Most funeral, food-homage and marriage songs are performed while walking or carrying out prescribed body movements. Lullabies, however, are always sung seated, while cradling the infant in the lap. Medicinal incantations are delivered from a variety of postures, as are children's game songs.

Samoan concepts of music have song as their focal point; all musical performances by voices or instruments are called 'songs' provided they have a melody; instruments producing unpitched rhythm, on the other hand, are said to be 'struck'. Samoans believe that all children are born with equal musical talent and seem to have no notion of the inheritance of such skills, although they appear to consider that musical ability is but one manifestation of a generally superior intelligence. The value of song is seen as twofold: it heightens emotions, especially humour and sorrow, through the compression and balance of contrasting ideas and rhyming lines; and, particularly in the form of group songs, it adds dignity and formal significance to any ceremonial occasion. For group songs there is no recognized optimal choir size: 'the more, the better' is generally the opinion. However, *kava* calls (the shouted parts of the *kava*-drinking ritual), intoned poetry, and incantations may not be performed by more than one person. Voice grouping in single-sex partsongs strongly favours the bass, which may have two or even three times the number of tenors; even the largest choirs, though, have but one leader, who sings the highest vocal line. Mixed choirs tend to have equal numbers in all parts.

7. TONGA. The kingdom of Tonga is an archipelago of 150 islands (population *c*80,000) lying south-west of Samoa between 18° and 23° S and between 173° and 176° W.

Its music has been known to the Western world since 1773 when, during the second voyage of Captain Cook, Forster described it as displaying 'inventive genius and elegant taste'. Elements of pre-European music still survive; but the indigenous music has become almost inextricably interwoven with music introduced from other Polynesian islands and with Western music, especially in its use of intervals and harmony characteristic of Protestant hymn tunes.

Tongan music is essentially poetry rendered melodically, sometimes accompanied by percussion instruments and body movement. Musical performances are predominantly group activities with a secular rather than a religious function. A large piece is usually composed for a specific occasion to honour an individual, social group, village or event. These pieces might be described as speeches which reflect and validate the stratified social system. Melodic range is narrow, often within a 5th, except for descending slides at ends of sections, and the pulse is usually organized in four or eight. The music usually begins slowly and accelerates, rhythm is often accentuated by drums or hand-clapping. According to 18th-century accounts, polyphony was indigenous and the six-part harmony now used appears to have evolved from a pre-European form with four men's parts and two women's parts. The two most important parts were *fasi* ('melody') and *laulalo* ('drone'), both sung by men. The other four were 'decoration' of the *fasi*, and were largely improvised.

Two melodic instruments were the *mimiha* (panpipes) with three main pitches and several secondary pitches, and the *fangufangu* (nose flute; for illustration, *see* FLUTE, fig.2*h*) with four pitches. *Mimiha* were played for amusement, while the *fangufangu* was used to awaken chiefs, substituting for the human voice when the latter was *tabu* ('forbidden'). Other indigenous instruments were percussive and used mainly to accompany sung dance-poetry. Bamboo stamping tubes, from 91 cm to 1·8 metres long, and sounding boards of hardwood or bamboo beaten with sticks, were played in ensembles. These two instruments, as well as the dance they accompanied (*me'elaufola*), are obsolete. The *nafa* (slit-drum), nearly circular in cross-section, is hollowed out to various thicknesses so that different notes may be obtained when it is struck with two wooden beaters; it is used to accompany the *me'etu'upaki* dance. In addition, a drum with a skin head and metal body is now called *nafa* and accompanies the *ma'ulu'ulu*, an acculturated sitting dance which evolved from the earlier sitting dance *'otu haka*. The latter was traditionally accompanied by a *tafua* (bamboos wrapped in a mat and struck with wooden beaters). The *lali*, a slit-drum of a different form, is used for signalling and was reputedly imported from Fiji. Today 'string bands' of ukelele, guitar and one-string bass are frequently heard accompanying the popular *hiva kakala* ('sweet songs').

The main genres of Tongan music are: *tau'a'alo* (work songs), sung for cooperative work such as dragging a boat to shore; game songs, sung by children to accompany juggling or exercises; *tengihea* (mourning songs) of two types, spontaneous wailing intoned at a funeral, and poetry sung in praise of the deceased; *fakaniua* (narrative songs) on historical and mythological subjects; *faiva* (dance-songs), songs invariably accompanied by dance; and *hiva kakala* ('sweet songs'), which are sometimes accompanied by the *tau'olunga* dance.

See also PACIFIC ISLANDS, §2.

8. TUVALU (ELLICE ISLANDS). Tuvalu (formerly the Ellice Islands) is an archipelago of nine low coraline islands, lying between 5° and 11° S and 176° and 180° E, some 1200 km north-west of Samoa. The inhabitants (*c*6000) speak a Polynesian language, except those of the island Nui, which was conquered by Gilbertese from Micronesia. The archipelago was first populated by Polynesians in the 16th century by migration from the west. Sporadic contacts with European sailors in the early 19th century and, after 1861, systematic Christianization, primarily through Samoan missionaries of the London Missionary Society, led to drastic changes in the religion, social organization and, consequently, music and dance of Tuvalu. The establishment of church choirs, mission and government schools, migratory work and the introduction of radios have contributed to an intensive process of cultural change. In the 1960s, music and dance in Tuvalu were dominated by European-American traits.

Before the arrival of missionaries, indigenous music and dance were closely connected with religious ceremonies and social organization. The only instruments were the *pu* (shell trumpet), used exclusively for signalling, and the *pātē* and *nafa* (slit-drums), which were used for signalling but also served to accompany dances (fig.11). Categories of song included *taanga* (genealogical songs), *onga* and *fakanau* (dance-songs), play songs, etc. These songs were typically in one of three styles: a kind of 'speech-song' (strophic, strictly metrical recitation without definite pitches); 'level recitative' (strophic, metrical recitation on two or more tonal levels simultaneously); and 'triadic melody' (strophic songs emphasizing the 3rd and the 5th, with a second line in parallel movement or as a bourdon). Both speech-song and level recitative are common phenomena throughout Polynesia; there are specific

11. Singing, hand-clapping and a small slit-drum accompany the onga dance, Niutao, Tuvalu, 1963

similarities between Tuvalu songs and those of the Tuamotu Islands. The 'triadic melodies' may represent influences from eastern Melanesia.

Another type of song structure, the 'pentatonic responsorial', which prevails in dance-songs of the categories *mako fakaseasea*, *mako fakatangitangi* and *fatele*, was introduced after the arrival of Samoan missionaries and flourished between 1890 and 1915. It is characterized by a melismatic, pentatonic solo line answered by an overlapping, syllabic chorus line a 5th to an octave lower. Outside Tuvalu, similar songs have been found only in Samoa; historical data make a Samoan derivation probable.

Since 1915, adaptations of tunes from Christian hymn books (e.g. those of Sankey) and functional-harmonic polyphony have gained prominence, shaping also the style of secular songs. In the 1950s, local composers began to create multi-part church and secular songs which combine local elements with those of Samoan and European derivation. For almost all dances rhythmic accompaniment is now provided by men sitting round a wooden crate and beating it with their hands.

BIBLIOGRAPHY

COOK ISLANDS

W. Ellis: *Polynesian Researches* (New York, 1829, enlarged 2/1832–4/*R*1969)
W. W. Gill: *Myths and Songs from the South Pacific* (London, 1876) [song texts in Polynesian and English]
T. R. Hiroa [P. H. Buck]: *The Material Culture of the Cook Islands, Aitutaki* (New Plymouth, 1927)
——: *Ethnology of Manihiki and Rakahanga* (Honolulu, 1932)
——: *Ethnology of Tongareva* (Honolulu, 1932)
E. and P. Beaglehole: *Ethnology of Pukapuka* (Honolulu, 1938/*R*1971)
T. R. Hiroa [P. H. Buck]: *Arts and Crafts of the Cook Islands* (Honolulu, 1944)
M. McLean: *Field Notes on the Music of Aitutaki and Mangaia* (MS, U. of Auckland, Archive of Maori and Pacific Music)

EASTER ISLAND

A. Métraux: *Ethnology of Easter Island* (Honolulu, 1940/*R*1971)
E. Pereira Salas: *La música de la Isla de Pascua* (Santiago, 1947)
R. Campbell: *La herencia musical de Rapanui: etnomusicologia de la Isla de Pascua* (Santiago, 1971)

FRENCH POLYNESIA

E. S. C. Handy and J. L. Winne: *Music in the Marquesas Islands* (Honolulu, 1925/*R*1971)
T. Henry: *Ancient Tahiti* (Honolulu, 1928/*R*1971)
E. G. Burrows: *Native Music of the Tuamotus* (Honolulu, 1933/*R*1971)
T. R. Hiroa [P. H. Buck]: *Ethnology of Mangareva* (Honolulu, 1938/*R*1971)
R. I. Levi: *Tahitians* (New York and Chicago, 1973)
D. Oliver: *Ancient Tahitian Society* (Honolulu, 1974)
K. Emory: 'Tuamotuan Chants and Songs from Napuka', *Directions in Pacific Traditional Literature* (Honolulu, 1976)

HAWAII

N. Emerson: *Unwritten Literature of Hawaii* (Washington, DC, 1909/*R*1965)
H. Roberts: *Ancient Hawaiian Music* (Honolulu, 1926/*R*1971)
T. R. Hiroa [P. H. Buck]: *Arts and Crafts of Hawaii* (Honolulu, 1957)
D. Kahananui: *Music of Ancient Hawaii* (Honolulu, 1962)
K. Wong: 'Ancient Hawaiian Music', *Aspects of Hawaiian Life and Environment* (Honolulu, 1965), 9ff
M. K. Pukui and S. H. Elbert, eds.: *Hawaiian Dictionary* (Honolulu, 1971)

SAMOA

J. Williams: *Journal of a Voyage to the Navigators . . . in the Olive Branch* (MS, 1832–3)
J. B. Stair: *Old Samoa; or, Flotsam and Jetsam from the Pacific Ocean* (London, 1897), 134f
T. R. Hiroa [P. H. Buck]: 'The Wooden Gongs', *Samoan Material Culture* (Honolulu, 1930/*R*1971), 575
R. M. Moyle: *Samoan Traditional Music* (diss., U. of Auckland, 1971)
——: 'Samoan Song Types', *SMA*, vi (1972), 55
——: 'Samoan Medicinal Incantations', *Journal of the Polynesian Society*, lxxxiii (1974), 155
——: 'Samoan Musical Instruments', *EM*, xviii (1974), 57

TONGA

E. W. Gifford: *Tongan Myths and Tales* (Honolulu, 1924/*R*1971)
E. E. V. Collocott: *Tales and Poems of Tonga* (Honolulu, 1928/*R*1971)
R. M. Moyle: 'Traditional Music of Tonga', Hibiscus HLS-65 [disc notes]
A. L. Kaeppler: *Tongan Musical Genres in Ethnoscientific and Ethnohistoric Perspective* (in preparation)

TUVALU (ELLICE ISLANDS)

D. Christensen: 'Old Musical Styles in the Ellice Islands, Western Polynesia', *EM*, xviii (1964), 34
D. Christensen and G. Koch: *Die Musik der Ellice-Inseln* (Berlin, 1964)
BARBARA B. SMITH (1, 3, 4), MERVYN McLEAN (2),
ZANETA HO'OŪLU CAMBRA (5), RICHARD M. MOYLE (6),
ADRIENNE L. KAEPPLER (7), DIETER CHRISTENSEN (8)

Polyphon. (1) A MUSICAL BOX invented in the 1880s with interchangeable metal discs in place of cylinders to pluck the teeth of a metal comb (or to activate a star wheel which plucked) and thus produce musical sounds. 'Polyphon' was originally a trade name, like Regina and Symphonion, but came to mean any instrument of this type. *See also* MECHANICAL INSTRUMENT.

(2) Another name for the POLIPHANT. The polyphon or polyphone is discussed by M. Tilmouth: 'Some Improvements in Music noted by William Turner in 1697', *GSJ*, x (1957), p.57 and by D. Gill: 'James Talbot's Manuscript: V. Plucked Strings – the Wire-strung Fretted Instruments and the Guitar', *GSJ*, xv (1962), p.60.

Polyphone. *See* POLIPHANT.

Polyphonia Orchestra. London orchestra founded in 1962; *see* LONDON, §VI, 2(ii).

Polyphony (Ger. *Mehrstimmigkeit, Vielstimmigkeit*). A term used in connection with the technique of composition to designate various important categories in European music: music in more than one part, music in many parts, and the style in which all or several of the musical parts move to some extent independently.

1. The term. 2. Multiplicity of parts. 3. Independence of parts. 4. 20th-century views.

1. THE TERM. The word and its adjectival form were already common in classical Greek (*polyphonia*: 'that which has many sounds, many voices'; *polyphōnos*: 'of many sounds', 'of many voices', 'loquacious', 'abundant in linguistic expression'). This does not, however, seem to be the usage underlying the musical term: it first appears as a parallel term to *diaphonia* (*see* DISCANT, §I, 1) in its technical sense and also as a neologism. In post-Hellenic times, while the noun was apparently used almost exclusively as a musical term, the adjective and its derivatives had other meanings too, including the classical ones. Thus in English 'polyphonist' refers to 'one who produces a variety of vocal sounds, a ventriloquist' (*Oxford English Dictionary*; see also 'Polyphonical', 'Polyphonous'). Since 1851 the English term 'polyphone' has been used in Assyriology to denote a written sign for different vocal sounds. 'Polyphone' is also the name of a lute-like instrument of the Elizabethan age 'of so different a stringing and tuning that it is impossible to play what is sett to it on any other hand instrument' (1655, cited in *OED*). The Italian *polifono* was the name given to an 'instrument invented in 1833, whose tone has the characteristics of the clarinet and the bassoon and can go from one to the other' (Mendel and Reissmann, *Musikalisches Conversations-Lexikon*, 1877). In 1890 an organ capable of imitating practically every orchestral instrument (notably strings and woodwind) was described as a 'polyphonic organ' (*OED*, 'Polyphonic'). The German POLYPHON is the name of an apparatus invented in the last quarter of the 19th century, initially called *Symphonion*, which was 'driven by clockwork or by hand, and capable of playing any tune when the corresponding perforated disc is inserted' (*OED*, 'Polyphone'). Since 1620 (G. Blancano: *Sphaera mundi seu cosmographia*, pp.436, 439), multiple echoes have been described as polyphonic (Schaeffner, 1966). Kircher (*Musurgia universalis*, 1650, ii, 256; *Phonurgia nova*, 1673) spoke of *polyphonismus* where a sound is reinforced by multiple echo; and 'polyphone' or 'polyacoustic' is the name given to a physical area through which 'one sound may be heard as many' (*OED*). In all of these cases the stem 'polyphon-' is selected with reference to the variety or multiplicity of notes, sounds or melodies; and the same applies to the word as a technical term in music.

2. MULTIPLICITY OF PARTS. In relation to the technique of composition the term was first used to mean 'music having many voices', its antithesis being 'monophony' or 'monody'. It is still current in this sense. The two earliest known examples of its use, in which it appears as a generic term for the concepts of *diaphonia*, *triphonia* and *tetraphonia basilica* (sustained-note organal writing) or *organica* (discant writing) (*Summa musice*, c1300, wrongly attributed to Jehan des Murs, *GS*, iii, 239ff), and as a description of discant writing (anon. 15th-century treatise in *B-Br* 10162–6), appear to be isolated cases. But from the time of Luscinius's *Musurgia seu praxis musicae* (1536), in which instruction in the notation and composition of music for several voices is given under the heading 'De concentus polyphoni ratione', there has been a continuous tradition for the concept, extending through Kircher and the musical historians of the later 18th century up to the 20th. Kircher (1650, i, 215, 539, 543), who used *polyphonia* alongside *polyodia* in the sense of 'music in more than one part' (though not only in this sense), distinguished between a *polyodia naturalis* (a rudimentary polyphony which the term may have denoted even in classical antiquity) and a *polyodia artificialis* (artistically composed polyphony whose origins lay with Guido). In historical writing of the late 18th century (Gerbert, *De cantu et musica sacra*, 1774 and *GS*, 1784; *HawkinsH*, 1776; *BurneyH*, 1782) the term, which after Kircher's time had also been used with other meanings, came to be used generally for music in more than one part. But this usage was less common than another tradition which became prevalent during the later 18th century and which is discussed below (see §3). It was used in this sense by Wagner in *Oper und Drama* (1851). Ever since non-European music has come within the scope of musicology, a number of writers have made a distinction between: (1) 'polyphony' or 'music in more than one part' as a case in which there is conscious structuring of the sound (Marius Schneider, *Geschichte der Mehrstimmigkeit*, i, 1934, p.30) or as a procedure in which one part is 'answerable to' the others (Boulez, 'Contrepoint', *FasquelleE*); and (2) phenomena involving simultaneous sounds in which this is not the case (e.g. heterophony), and which are not founded on the 'conception of a simultaneity of a number of parts' (Eggebrecht, 'Polyphonie', *RiemannL 12*).

Kircher (1650, e.g. vol.i, 322) also used *polyphonia* in

the sense of 'music in many parts', meaning compositions for more than four voices; and as well as implying writing for more than one voice, *polyphonium* could also specifically refer to writing for many independent voices (e.g. vol.ii, 159ff). J. G. Walther (*WaltherML*) seems to have had this narrower meaning in mind when he declared: 'Polyphonium ... [is] a composition in many parts' (cf J. H. Zedler, *Universal-Lexicon*, 1741; J. E. Häuser, *Musikalisches Lexikon*, 1828, 2/1833; Mendel and Reissmann, *Musikalisches Conversations-Lexikon*, 1877). At all events, Häuser stated expressly: ' "In many parts" [*vielstimmig*] or "polyphonic" are the terms used to describe writing which consists of more than four parts'. The Stössel brothers too (*Kurtzgefasstes musicalisches Lexicon*, 1737, 2/1749) probably had this meaning in mind when they rewrote Walther's definition as follows: 'Polyphonia, in music, are things for full chorus'. However, these interpretations are not absolutely clear; for both *vielstimmig* ('in many parts') and *vollstimmig* ('for full chorus') are also used in the sense of *mehrstimmig* ('in more than one part'), the latter term having become prevalent only in the course of the 19th century.

3. INDEPENDENCE OF PARTS. From the time of Koch's *Versuch einer Anleitung zur Composition* (1782–93) the term 'polyphony' has been used to describe a way of writing that is distinct from monody (though Koch referred to this contrasting way of writing as 'homophony'). Kircher had discussed 'voces ... *homophōnos*, sive aequali processu ... progredientes' in which 'semibrevium syncopae' and 'fugae' are avoided (1650, i, 314). Koch defined the two concepts in his *Musikalisches Lexikon* (1802) as follows:

Polyphonic writing: this is understood as referring to a piece of music in which a number of voices affirm the character of a principal part, and in which the feelings of several persons are expressed.

Homophonic writing: this is understood as referring to a sort of writing in which only one voice affirms the character of a principal part, and where the remaining voices present serve merely as an accompaniment.

In the *Versuch*, however, he spoke of three 'processes' of composition (p.82): one in which the expressive content of a piece is focussed on the main voice without expressive melodic projection in the accompanying voices; a second in which the main part is constructed with regard to subsidiary parts which can enhance the expression; and a third in which the expressive content is embodied in an indivisible combination of voices. The second of these processes doubtless still counts as 'homophonic writing' since a distinction is made between the principal and subsidiary voices; and only the third process should be referred to as 'polyphonic writing'. Similarly, Ambros (*Geschichte der Musik*, iii, 1868) still spoke of homophony even where there was a considerable degree of independence in the subsidiary parts (pp.121f): 'Even the richest, orchestrated etc. accompaniment will remain incomplete and unsatisfying without the principal part. In polyphony, on the other hand, every single part is equally important, each is quite self-dependent and yet again each is referred to the others: they all stand for one, and one for all'. By contrast, in Mendel and Reissmann (1877), where 'homophony' is already understood in a special sense as 'the chordal writing of parts by means of which they are to a certain extent unified as a single part', 'polyphony' is spoken of not only when 'the harmony is autonomously produced from parts written in a completely independent melodic manner', but also where harmonic writing breaks down 'into independent parts'. This classification

of types of writing (also found in A. B. Marx) has not, however, become established. It is now usual to define 'polyphony' as a kind of writing in which 'each part makes a claim to more or less independent writing (counterpoint in which all parts are essential)', and 'monody' as the 'predominance of a melody with various types of accompaniment which may be relatively free in movement or else may be kept in a strict contrapuntal relationship to the melody. Here use is also made of a style halfway between homophony and polyphony: pseudopolyphonic part-writing which is sometimes genuinely contrapuntal and sometimes more homophonic (in 3rds and 6ths)' (Adler, *Handbuch der Musikgeschichte*, i, 1924, 2/1930).

In the *Versuch* Koch illustrated the 'polyphonic process' with a concertante vocal duet in which the voices imitate each other, whereas in his *Lexicon* definition he appears to have had in mind a dramatic composition – possibly a Mozartian operatic ensemble. Gathy (*Musikalisches Conversationslexikon*, 1835) also took his example from opera, illustrating polyphony by the end of the first act of Spontini's *Olimpie*; moreover, the finale in grand opera is described as *polyphonium*. Authors after that time ceased to think specifically of a dramatically applied polyphony; Koch's definition was significantly weakened by the words 'as it were' in Schilling (*Encyclopädie der gesammten musikalischen Wissenschaften*, v, 1837): he described polyphony as the type of writing 'in which ... as it were, the feelings of several persons are expressed simultaneously'.

Since the middle of the 19th century it has also been recognized that the multiple-part music of the Middle Ages and the Renaissance is polyphonic; its harmony arises only as a secondary phenomenon (Helmholtz, *Die Lehre von den Tonempfindungen*, 1863; Ambros, 1868). Helmholtz regarded the early period precisely as the period of polyphony: he described the principal epochs of music as (p. 390):

(1) the homophonic (one-part) music of antiquity, with which is linked the music now being produced by the peoples of Oriental and Asiatic lands; (2) the polyphonic music of the Middle Ages – in many parts, but still without reference to the independent musical significance of the simultaneous sounds – extending from the 10th to the 17th century when it passes over into (3) harmonic or modern music, characterized by the independent significance accorded to harmony as such. Its origins lie in the 16th century.

In English usage 'polyphony' tends to be used 'for early music', while 'for later periods (16th to 18th century)' the term 'counterpoint' is preferred ('Counterpoint', *Harvard Dictionary of Music*, 2/1969). In the view of Stumpf (*Die Anfänge der Musik*, 1911), 'polyphony', as a genre distinct from 'harmonic music', has its place in a system of 'genres of music-making ranging from monophony to music in several parts', foreshadowed in non-European music, exemplified in 'the early years of our own epoch', and then gradually giving way to preoccupation with simultaneities – 'harmonic music'.

With the changes in handling of the word came differences also in the concept of polyphony. Most common is the concept of contrapuntal writing according to strict laws. It was with this in mind, for example, that after hearing Richard Strauss's Symphony in F minor in 1885 Brahms declared: 'One may weave together several triadic themes but that is still not polyphony' (quoted in 'Polyphonie', H. J. Moser, *Musik-Lexikon*, 1963 edn.). Mahler, on the other hand, described such things as the random sounds of a forest festival – noises from swings and roundabouts, shooting-galleries and puppet theatres, a military band and a male-voice choir, heard when he and a friend were out walking in the woods – as the archetype of his polyphony (N. Bauer-Lechner, *Erinnerungen an Gustav Mahler*, 1923, p.147):

Do you hear that? That is polyphony and that is where I have got it from. . . . Exactly like that, coming from quite different sides, this is how the themes must come, and they must be completely distinct in their rhythmic and melodic character (anything else is merely something written in many parts, disguised homophony): it only requires that the artist should organize it and unify it into a congruous and harmonious whole.

4. 20TH-CENTURY VIEWS. For Webern (*Der Weg zur neuen Musik*), polyphony embodied a musical coherence based on melodic relationships between the parts (p.56): 'We see an absolute movement away from homophonic music back to polyphonic music, a striving to make musical coherence deeper and clearer'; he developed this statement (p.28):

and now we see this process, this remarkable reaction: what we have observed in polyphony – as extensive a coherence as possible – and thus, what has been identified as the artistry of the Netherlands composers – this striving is gradually once more seizing possession of these things and a new polyphony is evolving.

Recent musical history in general (as also follows from the sentences quoted above) is conceived as a turning away from homophony and a renewed turning towards polyphony. H. Jalowetz and Adorno also affirmed a decline in homophony, but among the remaining possibilities they endeavoured to make a distinction between polyphony and a way of working 'which adds to one or more principal parts one or more equally independent parts which will remain relatively secondary, and will be graduated according to rank' – a way of working that they termed 'counterpoint'. According to Adorno, this second type is more essential to present-day practice because it preserves within itself monody as it has been dominant for about 400 years. The contrapuntal process generally 'maintains the idea of a songlike melody and hence of an autonomous subject in the midst of genuinely composed multiple part-writing so long as it does not impose upon it an ideal of pre-bourgeois collectivity' (1957).

Such processes tend still to be referred to indiscriminately as 'polyphony'. The extent to which one can speak of 'polyphony' is itself in doubt. Eggebrecht ('Polyphonie', *RiemannL 12*) doubts the equation of polyphony with counterpoint in 20th-century music because 'while in counterpoint a series of independent parts arises from conditions of simultaneous sound', in modern music the 'independence of the parts primarily serves the formation [justification] of new sounds'. In his view serial polyphony goes beyond the writing of true 'voices' and therefore beyond polyphony. According to Boulez (*Penser la musique aujourd'hui*, 1963, p.153), on the other hand, the compositional parts are not done away with, but are freshly defined, as:

constellations of events obeying a certain number of common criteria; distributions of families of evolving structures in a mobile and discontinuous time dimension, with variable density and using non-homogeneous timbre; these constellations are mutually dependent in a very special way as far as pitches and durations are concerned.

Correspondingly, when referring to his own technique of composition, Boulez also spoke of a polyphony in addition to monody (music in one part), homophony ('density-transformation of monody': 'the structure unfolds its objects horizontally, the vertical density of the object being variable', p.135) and heterophony ('the superposition upon a primary structure of a modified aspect of the same structure'). He defined polyphony as a combination of structures of which one is answerable to the other. The 'forms of syntactical organization' that he mentioned may also be combined to make a 'polyphony of polyphonies', a 'heterophony of heterophonies', a 'heterophony of polyphonies' and so on (p.133). Likewise, transitions may be effected between them; in other words, 'a monody may in fact represent a "reduced" polyphony, just as a polyphony will in actual fact be the distribution or "dispersion" of a monody' (pp.138f).

Zimmermann (1971) has proposed a distinction between 'homogeneous', 'heterogeneous' and 'polystylistic' polyphony. Polyphony is 'homogeneous' when there is an imitative relationship between the parts. If there is no imitation, or if (for instance, with a cantus firmus, or the bass line of a Baroque trio sonata) one of the parts is not involved in the imitation, there then arises 'heterogeneous' polyphony. In 'polystylistic' polyphony (which according to Zimmermann corresponds to a modern kind of musical awareness, and to which the future belongs) the composition is put together 'no longer from individual parts or distinguishable groups of parts, but from different pieces of music, from quite different manners of composition'.

See also COUNTERPOINT; DIAPHONIA; HETEROPHONY; ORGANUM.

BIBLIOGRAPHY
T. W. Adorno: 'Die Funktion des Kontrapunkts in der neuen Musik', *Klangfiguren: musikalische Schriften I* (Berlin, 1959)
B. Nettl: 'Notes on the Concept and Classification of Polyphony', *Festschrift Friedrich Blume* (Kassel, 1963), 247
A. Schaeffner: 'Variations sur deux mots: polyphonie, hétérophonie', *RBM*, xx (1966), 43
H. H. Eggebrecht: 'Polyphonie', *RiemannL 12*
H. W. Zimmermann: 'Über homogene, heterogene und polystilistische Polyphonie', *Musik und Kirche*, xli (1971), 218
WOLF FROBENIUS

Polyrhythm. The superposition of different rhythms or metres. It is an important characteristic of some medieval polyphony (particularly late 14th-century French secular song), and also a common technique of 20th-century composition (used successfully by such composers as Stravinsky, Bartók and Hindemith, as well as in modern jazz). The term is closely related to (and sometimes used synonymously with) CROSS-RHYTHM, though the latter is properly restricted to rhythm that contradicts a given metric pulse or beat.
See also RHYTHM.

Polytonality. The simultaneous presentation of more than two tonalities in a polyphonic texture, hence an extension of BITONALITY.

Polzelli [Polcelli, née Moreschi], **Luigia** (*b* Naples, *c*1760 [?1750]; *d* Kaschau [now Košice], 1832). Italian mezzo-soprano. In March 1779 she and her husband, the violinist Antonio Polzelli (*b* Rome; *d* Vienna, 1791), went to Eszterháza on a modest two-year contract, after having apparently lived in Bologna. Before their contract expired Prince Nikolaus commanded its termination, though the dismissal was later reversed. Despite their indifferent talents they remained in service until the dissolution of the Kapelle (1790) – probably through the intercession of Haydn, who, faced with an unhappy marriage, had taken on Luigia as a mistress. (According to Pohl, she was then 19, though her death date, also supplied by Pohl with the added comment 'in her 82nd year of life', seems to advance this by ten years.) In spite of Haydn's private instruction she was never assigned a leading role at Eszterháza, and her restricted range and musicality made it necessary for him to rewrite even secondary parts for her. She appeared only twice in Haydn's operas (as Silvia in *L'isola disabitata* and Lisetta in *La vera costanza*), though he composed most of his insertion arias specially for her. After the dissolution of the Kapelle and the death of her husband she appeared in lesser Italian theatres (Bologna, Piacenza). Haydn's letters from London still speak of his hope of marrying her. He willingly granted her continual requests for money, and oversaw the education of her sons Pietro and Antonio (who was rumoured without proof to be by Haydn). In 1800 he promised to marry no other, and assured her a lifelong pension (which he reduced by half in his final will). Polzelli, however, before Haydn's death, married the singer Luigi Franchi. They remained until 1815 in Bologna, and set out in 1820 from Cremona to Hungary, where she died impoverished.

BIBLIOGRAPHY

C. F. Pohl: *Joseph Haydn*, ii (Leipzig, 1882/*R*), 89ff
H. Botstiber: 'Haydn and Luigia Polzelli', *MQ*, xviii (1932), 208
R. Tenschert: *Frauen um Haydn* (Vienna, 1947)
H. C. R. Landon: *The Collected Correspondence and London Notebooks of Joseph Haydn* (London, 1959)
D. Bartha and L. Somfai: *Haydn als Opernkapellmeister: die Haydn-Dokumente der Esterházy-Opernsammlung* (Budapest, 1960), 50ff
D. Bartha: *Joseph Haydn: gesammelte Briefe und Aufzeichnungen* (Kassel, 1965)
J. Harich: 'Das Opernensemble zu Eszterháza im Jahr 1780', *Haydn Yearbook*, vii (1970), 12
——: 'Haydn Documenta IV', *Haydn Yearbook*, vii (1970), 103, 131
HORST WALTER

Pomius, Francesco. See DEL POMO, FRANCESCO.

Pommer. The German name for the alto, tenor and bass SHAWM (the treble being known as the *Schalmey*). The term is an alteration of *Bombarde* (the general 15th-century name for the alto shawm), through *Bomhart*, *Pumhart*, and *Pommert*, all of which are found in 16th-century German writings. The form *Pommer* occurs in Praetorius's *Syntagma musicum* (1618) and is much used by modern German writers and museum curators.

See also BASSOON, §3, and ORGAN STOP (*Bombardon*).
ANTHONY C. BAINES/R

Pommer, Josef (*b* Mürzzuschlag, Styria, 7 Feb 1845; *d* Gröbming, Styria, 25 Nov 1918). Austrian folk music collector. After studying at the University of Vienna (1864–70), where he took a doctorate in philosophy, he taught at Vienna Gymnasien (1874–1912). He was interested in folksongs as a schoolboy, and studied music so that he could transcribe those he heard. In 1885 he became director of the choir of the Verein der Deutschen Steirer in Vienna and in 1889 founded the Deutscher Volksgesang Verein to foster authentic folksong. In 1892 he founded the *Flugschriften zur Kenntnis und Pflege des deutschen Volksliedes* and in 1899 he launched the monthly journal *Das deutsche Volkslied*, which remained until 1949 the leading German-language publication in its field. He also took a major part in planning the state-sponsored project *Das Volkslied in Österreich*, which was prevented from publication because of World War I. Pommer's unshakable enthusiasm and thorough work made an inestimable and still influential contribution to folksong performance and research. He was the most important Austrian folksong collector, authority and pioneer; his collections of yodel songs are particularly valuable, for it was through them that this song form first became known to the musical world.

WRITINGS

Wegweiser durch die Literatur des deutschen Volkslieds (Vienna, 1896)
Über das älperische Volkslied und wie man es findet (Vienna, 1907)
Die Wahrheit in Sachen des österreichischen Volksliedunternehmens (Vienna, 1912)

FOLKSONG EDITIONS

Liederbuch für die Deutschen in Österreich (Vienna, 1884, 5/1905)
Jodler und Juchezer (Vienna, 1889)
252 Jodler und Juchezer, new ser. (Vienna, 1893)
444 Jodler und Juchezer aus Steiermark und dem steirisch-österreichischen Grenzgebiet (Vienna, 1902)
Blattl-Lieder (Vienna, 1910)

BIBLIOGRAPHY

K. Kronfuss: 'Josef Pommer: sein Leben und Wirken', *Das deutsche Volkslied*, xxi (1919)
M. Pommer: *Dr. Josef Pommer und das deutsche Volkslied* (diss., German U. of Prague, 1941)
WALTER DEUTSCH

Pommier, Jean-Bernard (*b* Béziers, 17 Aug 1944). French pianist. He started to play the piano at an early age, and studied with Yves Nat, Eugene Istomin and others. He went to the Paris Conservatoire in 1958, leaving in 1961 with a *premier prix*; he also studied conducting under Eugène Bigot. In 1962 he received a First Diploma of Honour in the Tchaikovsky Competition in Moscow. Since that date he has performed widely, in Europe, the USA and Japan, and has returned to the USSR several times. In 1971 he appeared at Salzburg under Karajan, and the next year he made his début under the same conductor with the Berlin PO. He appeared with the New York PO and the Chicago SO in the 1973–4 season. He has given several performances, particularly in England, with the Northern Sinfonia, as conductor–soloist, and is also actively engaged in chamber music.

Pomo, Francesco del. See DEL POMO, FRANCESCO.

Pompeati, Signora. See CORNELYS, THERESA.

Pomposo (It.: 'pompous', 'ceremonious'). A tempo (and mood) designation, but more often a qualification for such designations. Handel used it in the overture to *Samson*. Koch (1802) indicated that, like *grave*, *pomposo* implied the use of over-dotting; but his word is hardly authoritative and should not be taken as universally applicable. See also VIOLA POMPOSA.

For bibliography *see* TEMPO AND EXPRESSION MARKS.
DAVID FALLOWS

Ponape. See MICRONESIA, §2(iii).

Ponc, Miroslav (*b* Vysoké Mýto, 2 Dec 1902; *d* Prague, 1 April 1976). Czech composer and conductor. He graduated from Suk's master class at the Prague Conservatory in 1930 and from Hába's department of quarter-tone music in 1935 with his Suite for quarter-tone piano. Ponc also studied composition with Hába (1922–3, 1925–7) and took private lessons with Schoenberg, first probably in 1927 and then in 1932. He attended lectures on acoustics and on ethnomusicology at Berlin University; in Berlin he completed his piano studies with Breithaupt and his conducting studies with Scherchen. Apart from Hába, the most powerful influence on Ponc's career came from the Berlin avant-garde group Der Sturm, of which he became a member after the exhibition of his stage designs in 1927. He settled in Prague in 1932, by which time he had already produced a number of pieces following the principles of his teacher. On 11 May 1935 the Prague National Theatre produced his full-length ballet *Osudy* ('The Fates'), a work of little merit although it initiated a long period of work for the stage. In 1945 he established a permanent orchestra at the Stavoské (later Tyl) Theatre and joined the staff of the National Theatre; he worked as a conductor and composed more than 100 sets of incidental music. Ponc also wrote music for radio (in excess of 300 scores) and films.

WORKS
(selective list)

Dramatic: Svatebčané na Eiffelce [The wedding couple of the Eiffel Tower] (incidental music, Cocteau), orch, 1923; Předehra ka staro-řecké tragédii [Ov. to the ancient Greek tragedy] (Arnošt Dvořák: Oresteia), orch ¼-tone, 1929; Osudy [The Fates], ballet, 3 scenes, A, speaker, orch, 1934
Orch: Preludium, 1929; Concertino, pf, orch, 1930
Inst: 5 polydynamických skladeb [5 polydynamic compositions], cl, xyl, str qt, 1923; Study, 2 vc, ¼-tone, 1924; Little Passacaglia, va, vc, db, ¼-tone, 1924; 3 études, ¼-tone pf, 1927; Nonet, 1932; Str Trio, 1937; Malá suita [Little suite], pf (1954)
Vocal: Uličnické popěvky [Street urchins' songs], song cycle, 1923

Principal publisher: Nakladatelství krásné literatury, hudby a umění

BIBLIOGRAPHY
'O hudbě v činohře, hudební moderně a avantgardě s jubilantem Miroslavem Poncem' [On music in the theatre, modern music and the avant garde: an interview with Ponc], *HRo*, xv (1962), 894

JIŘÍ VYSLOUŽIL

Ponce, Juan (*b* *c*1480; *d* ?after 1521). Spanish composer. He may have been of the Andalusian noble family Ponce de León. He studied with Lucio Marineo, the Sicilian humanist who from 1484 to 1496 occupied a chair at Salamanca University; while there he composed a four-voice version of the student drinking-song, *Ave color vini clari*. A published exchange of Latin letters between Marineo and his pupil (Valladolid, 1514) identifies Ponce as a *cantor regius* ('royal singer'). On the death of Ferdinand in 1516 Ponce may have joined the household of Charles V. A version of his patriotic villancico *Françia, cuenta tu ganançia* refers to events of 1521.

Ponce's 12 partsongs (seven for four voices, four for three and one for two) in the *Cancionero musical de palacio* (MME, v and x) include a solmization villancico *La mi sola, Laureola* and a mirror canon *Para verme con ventura* which reveal him as one of the most polished and ingenious composers of his generation. His one surviving sacred work is a three-voice *Salve regina* (*E-Sco* 5–5–20) with alternating sections in plainsong and treble-dominated polyphony.

BIBLIOGRAPHY
R. Stevenson: *Spanish Music in the Age of Columbus* (The Hague, 1960), 184–9, 284f [incl. transcr. of *Salve regina*]

ROBERT STEVENSON

Ponce, Manuel (María) (*b* Fresnillo, Zacatecas, 8 Dec 1882; *d* Mexico City, 24 April 1948). Mexican composer and pianist. When two months old, he was taken to Aguascalientes, which he always regarded as his home. He took piano lessons with his sister Josefina from the age of six, and with Cipriano Ávila from the age of ten. In 1891 he composed *La marcha del sarampión*, in 1895 he was made assistant organist of S Diego, Aguascalientes, and in 1897 he became chief organist. Financial aid from his brother Antonio enabled him to study the piano in Mexico City with Vicente Mañas (1900–01). After a period of teaching in Aguascalientes, writing criticism for *El observador*, giving concerts and composing piano bagatelles, he left for Europe in 1904,

giving his first recitals in the USA (in St Louis) on the way. Antonio again supported his studies in Bologna with Torchi and at the Stern Conservatory, Berlin, where he gave a recital at the Beethovensaal on 18 June 1906. In 1909 he succeeded Castro as piano teacher at the Mexico City Conservatory, and from May 1915 to June 1917 (except for a trip to New York for an Aeolian Hall recital devoted to his work on 27 March 1916) he lived in Havana as music critic of *El heraldo de Cuba* and *La reforma social*.

Back in Mexico he married the singer Clema Maurel, taught again at the conservatory and at his own Beethoven Academy, conducted the National SO (1917–19), and, with Rubén M. Campos, edited the *Revista musical de México* (1919–20). He then moved to Paris (1925–33), where he edited the *Gaceta musical* (1928–9) and renewed his style after consultations with Dukas. Returning to Mexico City in 1933, he resumed piano teaching at the conservatory, which he directed in 1934–5, edited the conservatory's monthly *Cultura musical* (1936–7) and taught folklore in the newly established music faculty of the university (1933–8). He was the first Mexican composer honoured with an official invitation to tour South America (September–December 1942). Segovia, promoter of the invitation from Uruguay, gave the first performance of the *Concierto del sur* in Montevideo during the tour (4 October). The middle movement of his last major work, the Violin Concerto, includes strains from *Estrellita*, a song by him published in 1914 that had become the most widely sung art song in Latin America. At his death from uremic poisoning he was recognized as the one Mexican composer whose music appealed to all levels of society.

Not only his sentimental songs but also the early piano pieces in the brilliant salon style of Moszkowski and Chaminade then regnant were profusely published by the five leading houses of Mexico City. In later life he absorbed French impressionist methods and neo-classical counterpoint into a guitar literature that Segovia and his followers quickly established as part of the standard repertory.

WORKS
(selective list)

Orch: Pf Conc., 1912; Balada mexicana, pf, orch, 1914; Estampas nocturnas, 1923; Chapultepec, 3 bocetos sinfónicos, 1929, rev. 1934; Canto y danza de los antiguos mexicanos, 1933; 3 cantos de Tagore, 1v, orch, 1933; Poema elegíaco, chamber orch, 1935; Suite en estilo antiguo, 1935; Instantáneas mexicanas, 1938; Ferial, divertimiento sinfónico, 1940; Concierto del sur, gui, orch, 1941; Vn Conc., 1943; Suite sinfónica [after I. Albéniz: Merlin]
Chamber: Trio romántico, pf trio, 1911; Sonata, vc, pf; Cuarteto miniatura, str, 1929; Sonata, vn, pf, 1933; Str Trio, 1933; Sonata, vn, va, 1935
Gui: Sonata no.1 'Mexicana' (1967); 4 canciones mexicanas; Etude, d; Folias de España, 20 variations and fugue; 4 piezas; 5 preludios; 6 other sonatas; Thème varié et finale
Pf: 2 sonatas, 1913, 1968; 2 danzas, 2 études, Gavota, Gavotte et musette, Guateque, Horas angustas, Intermezzo, Juventud, Mazurkas nos.1, 2, 8, 10, 23, 27, Preludio cubano, Preludio galante, Preludio y fuga sobre un tema de Haendel, 3 preludios, Primer amor, 2 rapsodias mexicanas, Scherzino mexicano, Valse galante
Songs: A la orilla de un palmar, Acuérdate de mí, Adiós mi bien, Aleluya, La barca del marino, Cerca de mí, Cielito lindo, Cuiden su vida, La despedida, El desterrado, Dolores hay, Estrellita, Granada, Isaura de mi amor, Lejos de tí, Las mañanitas, Ofrenda, El olvido, Oye la voz, La pajarera, Para amar sin consuelo, Perdí un amor, 6 poemas arcáicos, 3 poemas de González Martínez, 3 poemas de Mariano Brull, 3 poemas de R. Tagore, Por tí mi corazón, Por tí mujer, Qué lejos ando, Serenata mexicana, Si algún ser, Si alguna vez, Soy paloma errante, Sperando sognando, Todo pasó, Toi, Trigueña hermosa, Valentina, Ven oh luna, Voy a partir, Ya sin tu amor, Yo mismo no comprendo, Yo te quiero

Principal publishers: Peer, Schott [guitar works]
MSS in *US-NYp*

BIBLIOGRAPHY
J. C. Romero: 'Efemérides de Manuel M(aría) Ponce', *Nuestra musica*,
v/2 (1950), 164–202 [incl. work-list]
Compositores de América/Composers of the Americas, ed. Pan
American Union, i (Washington, DC, 1954), 51ff
Dictionary Catalog of the Music Collection, xxiv (Boston, 1964), 545ff
[*NYp* publication]
ROBERT STEVENSON

Ponce de León, José María. Colombian composer; *see*
COLOMBIA, §I, 2.

Ponchielli, Amilcare (*b* Paderno Fasolaro [now Paderno
Ponchielli], nr. Cremona, 31 Aug 1834; *d* Milan, 17
Jan 1886). Italian composer. He was the most important
opera composer (Verdi apart) between the mid-19th century and the advent of the so-called 'Giovane Scuola'.

1. LIFE. The son of a shopkeeper who was organist in
the village church, he studied music first with his father
and then with the organist of a neighbouring village. He
was soon admitted without payment to the Milan
Conservatory, where he remained from 1843 to 1845, a
pupil of Pietro Ray (theory), Arturo Angeleri (piano),
Felice Frasi (composition to 1851) and Alberto
Mazzucato (music history and aesthetics, and composition from 1851). By the age of ten he had already
composed a symphony without orchestrating it; other
works followed, among them two pieces for the operetta
Il sindaco babbeo, composed in collaboration with three
fellow pupils in 1851, and the remarkable *Scena campestre* (1852).

Having taken his diploma on 4 September 1854,
Ponchielli settled in Cremona as a church organist with
the small annual stipend of 1000 lire, but as a protégé of
Ruggero Manna, who was in charge of the local Teatro
Concordia and *maestro di cappella* at the cathedral, he
was appointed by him his deputy at the theatre in 1855.
In 1860 he conducted several operas at the Teatro
Carcano in Milan and in Alessandria. He had made his
début as an opera composer in 1856 at the Teatro
Concordia with *I promessi sposi*, but its success (15
performances) was confined to that theatre; the impresarios of La Scala who went to hear it judged the
libretto (which Ponchielli himself, with a few friends,
had taken from Manzoni's novel) to fall below their
lowest standards.

A second opera, *Bertrando dal Bormio*, was put into
rehearsal at the Teatro Carignano in Turin in 1858, but
for unknown reasons it was not performed. *La
savoiarda* followed at Cremona in 1861 with results
upon which the sources are contradictory. On 6 May
1861 Ponchielli was appointed, after a competition,
conductor of the civic band of Piacenza for three years.
On 26 December 1863 he gave his opera *Roderico re
dei goti* at the local Teatro Comunale, but it had only
one performance. In 1864 he returned to Cremona as
conductor of the municipal band. There, in 1865, he
also conducted operas and gave one of his ballets, but
his aspirations as an opera composer long remained
disappointed (in 1867 Piave agreed to write him a
libretto, but then fell ill). His wish to leave the provinces
was likewise foiled; he won the competition for the chair
of counterpoint and fugue at the Milan Conservatory in
1870, but intrigues led to the appointment of Franco
Faccio. The quest ended only with the triumph in
December 1872 at the Teatro Dal Verme, Milan, of a
much-revised version of *I promessi sposi*. Two months

Amilcare Ponchielli

later, La Scala gave his ballet *Le due gemelle* with great
success (it may have already been performed elsewhere),
and the firm of Ricordi began to publish his music and
have it performed. Further, they commissioned a new
opera for La Scala, *I lituani* (6 March 1874). This was
successful, and meanwhile *I promessi sposi* had been
taken up by many Italian theatres. Ponchielli's greatest
triumph came in 1876 with *La Gioconda*, on a text
drawn by Boito from Hugo's *Angelo, tyran de Padoue*.

The operas that followed, although well received by
the critics and the public, did not enjoy wide circulation;
but Ponchielli's fame was now established, and he
received countless invitations and commissions during
the last nine years of his life. He held the chair of
composition at the Milan Conservatory from May 1880
(he resigned in September but returned at the beginning
of 1881). His pupils there included Puccini, whom he
persuaded to compose his first opera, and, for a short
time, Mascagni. In addition, he was *maestro di cappella*
at S Maria Maggiore in Bergamo, for which he composed much sacred music. In 1884 he was in St
Petersburg, where *La Gioconda* was given at the
Mariinsky Theatre, and also *I lituani* under the title of
Aldona. In 1874 he had married the soprano Teresina
Brambilla, who had starred in the 1872 *Promessi sposi*;
by her he had two sons and a daughter. His premature
death was mourned nationally.

2. WORKS. Of Ponchielli's numerous compositions, *La
Gioconda* is the only work that has survived in the modern
repertory, and that only to a limited extent. Even in their
day the others had little circulation (except *I promessi
sposi*, which, however, appeared only in less important
theatres) and later the wave of *verismo* opera easily
swept them away; but there are pages in them which are
not inferior. Their inconsistency is to be explained by

the inconsistency within Ponchielli: on the one hand, he had a strong musical talent, an imagination equal to the most varied situations and reinforced by solid and absolutely up-to-date workmanship; on the other, his character was not only meek (his kindliness was unlimited and the humour that seasoned it entirely without malice), but passive, and unsuited to exercising any kind of authority or self-defence. This explains the paradox of a man who, although he had been highly appreciated at the Milan Conservatory, waited 18 years in the neighbouring provinces before finding his way into the Milan theatres, where so many less important composers were admitted. It also explains why seizing on the *en plein* in an opera was a fortuitous event for him. He had a genuine dramatic instinct, which could move in any direction, but not the cultural or spiritual power necessary to direct it. From his letters (quoted copiously by De Napoli and Cesari), these limitations stand out clearly; the observations he made to his librettists were always acute, but they consisted mostly of objections, hesitations, entreaties and statement of impossibility. In contrast to Verdi, Ponchielli was not in charge of his librettist, but subject to him.

The singularity of *Gioconda* is rooted in the special character of its libretto, in which Boito (not without accepting modifications proposed by Ponchielli himself after the performance in Milan in 1876) returned to grand opera in the style of Scribe, but not in literal fashion. The result is a stylization; from the sensationalist technique of grand opera, Boito extracted a kind of Platonic ideal of Italo-French Romantic opera by means of a collection of conventional situations fittingly arranged and focussed. The libretto itself is artistically counterfeit. Boito even falsified Hugo's play by eliminating its raison d'être, the polemic against the devastation produced by the 'tyrant', since Boito's Alvise Badoero, Hugo's Angelo, is only a deceived husband and later a secondary character. But the opportunity for a composer like Ponchielli was inestimable. From it he derived the greatest stimulus to his inventiveness, creating music which is alive, varied and sensitive. In spite of public acclaim, 20th-century critical opinion (with rare exceptions, like Mila and Lanza Tomasi) and, indeed, the non-Italian criticism of the past century too, rejects this view with disgust (Hanslick) or vehemence (Shaw, Hugo Wolf), failing to understand that the libretto's grimness for the sake of effect is only a springboard.

Lying between Wagnerian music drama and late Verdi, and *verismo* opera and 'modern music', *La Gioconda* can moreover easily seem to lie out of its true period. But in fact it not only performed ideally the task – at the correct historical moment – of bringing a genre to a conclusion and of celebrating it while doing so, but it contains intensely inspired pages, for example, the highly original tenor *romanza* 'Cielo e mar', and that of La Cieca and the famous 'Suicidio'. It also contains anticipations of the future. Verdi's Iago is the outcome, even musically, of Barnaba in *Gioconda*; likewise, Puccini's 'Sì, pazzo son' (*Manon Lescaut*, end of Act 3) comes straight from the accented triplets of 'Suicidio'. Moreover, the vocal style of *Gioconda* foreshadows the temptations to which *verismo* opera would soon yield, and in the melodious flourishes of the woman who on the threshold of death feigns happiness before the villain Barnaba, it achieves with striking effect that *art nouveau* manner which Boito as composer had tried for, and only clumsily achieved, in *Mefistofele*.

Of Ponchielli's other operas, none possesses an equally effective dramaturgy, but many suggest a definite atmosphere, and it was from this that he gained his inspiration. Perhaps the most vivid example is in *I lituani*, where he created an imaginary Slav colouring which is often expressive and not without curious analogies to the contemporary and then unknown *Boris Godunov*. Another instance occurs in the biblical *Il figliuol prodigo*, where an equally imaginary oriental colouring often appears and where, moreover, a piece of rarefied symphonic writing of memorable quality emerges in the intermezzo preceding Act 4. Conversely, *Marion Delorme* is inspired by the style of *opéra comique*, not avoiding recollections of *La traviata*, while *Lina* (a reworking of *La savoiarda*) turns back to *opera semiseria* in the style of Donizetti. The most heterogeneous opera is *I promessi sposi*, in which, apart from isolated scenes, only the last tableau (the final expiation at the fever hospital, added in the second version) succeeds in being completely convincing in tones of a mellowed Verdianism. Ponchielli himself realized that the conventional verses of its clumsy libretto destroyed the effects of the realistic prose that made Manzoni's novel so revolutionary in Italian literature.

Ponchielli lacked a striking personality. His originality manifested itself more easily in certain details, but it also existed on a larger scale. The trite remark that makes him out to be a crude and trivial composer, a 'bandmaster', is, however, entirely unfounded. On the contrary, as Tebaldini observed, 'he did not bring the band into the orchestra, but rather, the orchestra into the band'. Indeed, his compositions for band are conceived in a truly symphonic spirit with complete formal freedom and sometimes with almost impressionistic touches, as with the hardly perceptible quotations from the popular *Inno di Garibaldi* (with the same lightness and restraint, themes by Donizetti are evoked in the highly attractive cantata *Omaggio a Donizetti*). Formal freedom and variety are to be found even in his operas, from *I lituani* onwards, fostered by the symphonic treatment and sometimes by themes which recur, either exactly or in subtle and meaningful variants. In grafting, to varying degrees, influences from Mendelssohn, early Wagner and contemporary French composers on to a musical language formed in the school of Meyerbeer and middle-period Verdi, Ponchielli proved himself the very antithesis of an uncultivated artist. He was also the antithesis of a pedant. His youthful compositions already proclaim this; in the Quartet for wind instruments and orchestra (1857) the form is capricious and is entirely in terms of a parodistic play of timbres (dominated by the strident colour of the piccolo clarinet) which even foreshadows Stravinsky. Remarkable, too, is the fact that many of his vocal chamber *romanze* are really operatic arias of wide-ranging span.

WORKS

OPERAS

Introduzione, 1 aria in Il sindaco babbeo (farsa, G. Giacchetti), Milan, Conservatory, March 1851, collab. C. Marcòra, D. Cagnoni, A. Cunio

I promessi sposi (melodramma, 4 pts., after Manzoni), Cremona, Concordia, 30 Aug 1856, excerpts, pf acc. (Milan, n.d.); rev. (E. Praga), Milan, Dal Verme, 4 Dec 1872; autograph *I-Mr*, vocal score (Milan, 1872 [defective], 1873)

Bertrando dal Bormio, 1858, not perf.; autograph *Mr*

La savoiarda (dramma lirico, 3, F. Guidi), Cremona, Concordia, 19 Jan 1861; rev. 1870, autograph *US-CA*; rev. as Lina (C. D'Ormeville), Milan, Dal Verme, 17 Nov 1877, vocal score (Milan, n.d.)

Roderico re dei goti (3, Guidi, after R. Southey: Roderick), Piacenza,

Municipale, 26 Dec 1863
Introduzione, 1 duet in La vergine di Kermo (Guidi), composed 1860, perf. Cremona, Concordia, 22 Feb 1870, collab. with 10 others; score *I-CR*
Il parlatore eterno (scherzo comico, 1, A. Ghislanzoni), Lecco, Sociale, 18 Oct 1873; vocal score (Milan, n.d.)
I lituani (dramma lirico, prol, 3, Ghislanzoni, after Mickiewicz: Konrad Wallenrod), Milan, La Scala, 6 March 1874; rev. La Scala 6 March 1875, autographs *US-NYpm* [rough draft], *NYpm*, *I-Mr*, vocal score (Milan, n.d.)
I Mori di Valenza (dramma lirico, 4, Ghislanzoni, after Scribe: Piquillo Alliaga, begun 1874, Act 4 completed by Annibale Ponchielli and A. Cadore, Monte Carlo, Opéra, 17 March 1914; vocal score (Turin, 1914)
La Gioconda (dramma lirico, 4, Tobia Gorrio [Boito], after Hugo: Angelo, tyran de Padoue), Milan, La Scala, 8 April 1876; rev. Venice, Rossini, 18 Oct 1876, autographs *US-NYpm* [rough draft], *I-Mr*, score (Milan and New York, n.d.)
Il figliuol prodigo (melodramma, 4, A. Zanardini), Milan, La Scala, 26 Dec 1880; autograph *Mr*, vocal score (Milan, n.d.)
Marion Delorme (melodramma, 4, E. Golisciani, after Hugo: Marion de Lorme), Milan, La Scala, 17 March 1885; autograph *Mr*, vocal score (Milan, n.d.)

BALLETS

Grisetta (azione mimica), Cremona, Concordia, carn. 1864–5; polka, arr. pf, pubd as Un bacio di più (Milan, n.d.)
Le due gemelle (azione coreografica, prol, 6, A. Pallerini), 1st known perf., Milan, La Scala, 4 Feb 1873; autographs *Mr*, *US-STu*, arr. pf (Milan, n.d.)
Il genio della montagna (Barracani), early work, perf. Milan, Canobbiana, Feb 1874; excerpts, arr. pf (Milan, n.d.)
Many others, lost

CANTATAS

Dante, solo vv, vv, orch, 1865
Omaggio a Donizetti (Ghislanzoni), solo vv, vv, orch, Bergamo, Riccardi, 13 Sept 1875; autograph *I-Mr*, vocal score (Milan, n.d.)
Cantata (Ghislanzoni), vv, orch, Milan, La Scala, for the monument to Manzoni, 22 May 1883
Cantata per [Papa] Gregorio [VII], T, B, vv, orch, Bergamo, Dec 1885; autograph *BGi*

SACRED

For solo vv, vv, orch, perf. Bergamo, S Maria Maggiore, autographs *BGi*: Mass, Qui tollis, Magnificat, all perf. Dec 1882; Miserere, Holy Week 1883; Lamentations nos.1–6, Holy Week 1886, sketches for later nos.
Others: Gloria, v, acc., autograph private library Treccani degli Alfieri, Milan; Solemn Mass, 3 male vv, org/pf (Milan, n.d.)

VOCAL CHAMBER
(for 1v, pf unless otherwise stated)

Accorse al tempio, scena, aria, 2 solo vv, pf, perf. 1854, autograph *US-STu*; Tanto gentile e tanto onesta pare (Dante), 1865; Il marinaio della Terribile, ballata, Bar; Piangea (M. M. Marcello), in *Palestra musicale*, ii (1867); Romanza, for his wife on wedding day (Milan, n.d.); Eternamente! (Marcello), romanza, S, vc obbl (Milan, 1874); Povera madre!, scena drammatica (Milan, 1883); Mattinata (E. Praga), autograph in facs. in *Auxilium*, only issue (Milan, 1884); Oh da qual mano gelida, romanza, Bar (Milan, n.d.); Dimenticar, ben mio (after Heine), romanza (Milan, n.d.); Preghiera (from S. Pellico: Ester d'Engaddi), 4 solo vv (Milan, n.d.); Un sogno (C. Monteggia) (Milan, n.d.)
Composizioni inedite (Turin, 1889): Noi leggevamo insieme (Ghislanzoni), romanza; Una notte al camposanto (Ghislanzoni), elegia; L'anello, il rosario, la ciarpa (Marcello), romanza; Voga sull'onda placida, piccola barcarola; Il povero Pieruccio, ballata; Il risorgimento (Leopardi), duettino; Vago augelletto (Petrarca), notturno, 4 solo vv; Il trovatore, aria, S; Dolor di denti (Ghislanzoni), aria buffa, B; L'accattone (Marcello), romanza, Bar; Luce! (F. Fontana), meditazione, S, T; Il pellegrino, il trovatore e il cavaliere, notturnino, 3 male vv; Vezzosa pescatrice, quartetto, S, A, T, B
Felice!, in *Natura ed arte*, xiii (1903–4); Storiella, A, in *Varietas*, i (1904); Povero fiorellino! (L. Stecchetti), in *Natura ed arte*, xvi (1906); Invocazione, in *Natura ed arte*; Perché?, in *Natura ed arte*; Eterna memoria, Il giuro, L'orfana, Pace ed oblio!, La povera, Barcarola, L'abbandono, L'eco (Aarau, 1906)

INSTRUMENTAL

Orch: Scena campestre, sym., perf. 1852, arr. pf 4 hands (Milan and Bologna, n.d.); Qt, fl, ob, pic cl, cl, orch, perf. 1857, score *I-Ria*, with pf acc. (Milan, n.d.)
Band: Fantasia militare, perf. 1863, rev. 1873 (Milan, 1874); Principe Umberto, march, perf. 1866, autograph *CR*; Il convegno, divertimento, 2 cl, band, perf. 1868, score *Ria*, arr. 2 cl (Milan, n.d.); Marcia funebre, 1869; Marcia funebre, for funeral of F. Lucca, 1872, score *CR*, arr. pf 4 hands, in *Fiori e foglie* (Milan, 1874); 29 Maggio 1873: Funerali di Alessandro Manzoni, funeral march (Milan, 1874);

Elegia funebre, for Manzoni, 1873, arr. pf (Milan, n.d.); Marcia funebre (Milan, 1874); Elegia funebre, perf. 1881, score *CR*, arr. pf 2/4 hands (Milan, 1882); Il Gottardo, triumphal hymn, orch, band, perf. 1882, score *CR*, arr. pf 2/4 hands (Milan, 1883); Sulla tomba di Garibaldi, elegia (Milan, 1882); Elegia funebre, for Ponchielli, perf. 1886
Undated: Viva il re, march, *Tr*; Carmelita, mazurka, *CR*; Carnevale di Venezia, variations, *CR*; Flugelhorn Conc., autograph Museo Civico, Cremona; Polka fortuna, autograph *CR*; Marcia funebre, orchd by B. Coppola, 1890, *CR*
Chamber: Capriccio, ob, pf, autograph *Mr* (Milan, n.d.); Elegia, vn, pf (Aarau, 1906)
Pf: Sinfonia, 4 hands, autograph *Mr* (Milan, n.d.), perf. Milan Conservatory, 1844, as orchd by P. Arrieta; Rimembranze dell'opera Il reggente di Mercadante, divertimento, 4 hands, 1858, autograph *Ms*; L'innamorata, mazurka, in *Palestra musicale*, i (1866); Amicizia, mazurka, in *Lo Strauss italiano* (Milan, 1873); La staffetta di Gambolò, polka impossibile, 1881 (Milan, n.d.); Tutti ebbri!, galop sfrenato, perf. 1882 (Milan, n.d.); Gavotte poudrée (Milan, 1884); Ricordanze dell'opera La traviata, 4 hands (Milan, 1886); T'amerò sempre, melodia, in *Album cosmopolite pour piano*, vi (1899); Fantasia sull'opera La favorita di Donizzetti [sic], 4 hands (Milan, n.d.); Saltarella, polka (Milan, n.d.); Il primo affetto, Notturno, Romanza (Aarau, 1906)

BIBLIOGRAPHY

E. Hanslick: 'Gioconda', *Die moderne Oper*, iv: *Musikalisches Skizzenbuch* (Berlin, 1888/*R*1971, 3/1911)
A. Mandelli: *Le distrazioni di A. Ponchielli* (Cremona, 1897)
S. Farina: 'Amilcare Ponchielli', *Gazzetta musicale di Milano*, lv (1900), 523, 535, 547
H. Wolf: 'Gioconda', *Musikalische Kritiken* (Leipzig, 1911), 54 [4 May 1884]; 152 [22 Feb 1885]
G. B. Shaw: *Music in London 1890–94*, i (London, 1932), 64ff [5 Nov 1890]
G. Adami: *Giulio Ricordi e i suoi musicisti* (Milan, 1933)
G. Cesari: *Amilcare Ponchielli nell'arte del suo tempo: ricordi e carteggi* (Cremona, 1934)
Cremona (1934), July [special issue]
M. Mila: 'Caratteri della musica di Ponchielli', *Pan*, ii/2 (1934), 481
G. Tebaldini: 'Amilcare Ponchielli', *Musica d'oggi*, xvi (1934), 239
A. Damerini: 'Una lettera inedita di A. Ponchielli', *Musica d'oggi*, xvii (1935), 141
U. Rolandi: *Nel centenario ponchielliano: Amilcare Ponchielli librettista* (Como, 1935)
G. De Napoli: *Amilcare Ponchielli (1834–1886); la vita, le opere, l'epistolario, le onoranze* (Cremona, 1936)
C. Sartori: 'Il primo rimaneggiamento dei *Promessi sposi*', *Rassegna dorica* (20 May 1938)
A. Damerini: *A. Ponchielli* (Turin, 1940)
N. Jacob and J. C. Robertson: *Opera in Italy* (London, 1948)
G. Tebaldini: 'Il mio maestro', *La Scala* (1952), March
M. Morini: 'Destino postumo dei *Mori di Valenza*', *La Scala* (1957), March
G. Gavazzeni: 'Considerazioni su di un centenario: A. Ponchielli', *Trent'anni di musica* (Milan, 1958), 57
J. W. Klein: 'Ponchielli: a Forlorn Figure', *The Chesterian*, xxxiv (1959–60), 116
G. Lanza Tomasi: *Guida all'opera* (Milan, 1971)

FEDELE D'AMICO

Pondelli, Jo. *See* RONDELLI, JO.

Pongrácz, Zoltán (*b* Diószeg, 5 Feb 1912). Hungarian composer. He studied composition with Kodály at the Budapest Academy of Music (1930–35), and then took lessons in conducting with Nilius in Vienna (1935–8) and with Krauss in Salzburg (1941). Pongrácz won the Ferenc József Prize in 1939 and worked on non-European music at Berlin University (1940–41) before becoming répétiteur at the Budapest Opera. He then worked for Hungarian radio as a music adviser, producer and choral conductor, and he was professor of composition at the Debrecen Conservatory from 1947 to 1958, a period when he was also active in the Hungarian Musicians' Union. An interest in exotic traditions influenced his early creative work. Later he turned in the direction of Schoenberg and Berg and, after a period of silence, began to work with tape, this latter development being stimulated by the Darmstadt summer courses which he attended in 1964, 1965 and

1972, and by his participation in Koenig's courses at Utrecht University (1965–6). In 1975 he was appointed professor of electronic composition at the Budapest Academy of Music.

WORKS
(selective list)

Stage: Az ördög ajándéka [The devil's present], ballet, 1936; Odysseus és Nausikaa, opera, 1949–50

Vocal: István, oratorio, 1938; Apollo musagètes, female chorus, cl, pf, perc, 1958; Negritude, chorus, perc, 1962; Ispirazioni, chorus, orch, tape, 1965; Rapszódia, vv, gypsy band, 1976

Inst: Pastorale, wind, pf, org, timp, 1941; Gamelan Music, 9 insts, 1942; Sym., 1946; Wind Qnt, 1956; 3 Etudes, orch, tape, 1963; Hangok és zörejek [Tones and noises], orch, 1966; 3 Improvisations, pf, 5–7 perc, 3 tapes, 1969–71; 3 Bagatelles, 4 perc, tape, 1972; Toccata, pf, 1977

Tape: Phonotese, 1965–6; Luna IX, 1966–7; Halmazok és párok [Piles and pairs], 1968; Mariphonia, 1971–2; Zoophonia, 1973; Rotációk [Rotations], 1975; Közeledni és távolodne [Approaching and moving off] (G. Rühm), 1975; Les parfumes, multi-media, 1976; 144 hang [144 sounds], 1977

Principal publishers: Editio Musica, Schott

WRITINGS

Népzenészek könyve [About gypsy music] (Budapest, 1965)
Mai zene – mai hangjegyírás [Contemporary music – contemporary notation] (Budapest, 1971)

F. ANDRÁS WILHEIM

Poniatowski, Józef Michał Ksawery Franciszek Jan (*b* Rome, 20 Feb 1816; *d* Chislehurst, 3 July 1873). Polish composer and tenor. He was related to the Polish king, Stanisław August Poniatowski, and to Prince Józef Poniatowski, a marshal of France who died at the battle of Leipzig (19 October 1813). He studied in Rome, then in Florence under C. Zanetti and F. Ceccherini. At the age of 17 he won a prize in mathematics, but devoted himself to music, first appearing as a singer in the theatres of Florence and Lucca. As a composer he is known for opera. His first, *Giovanni da Procida* (1838), was staged in Florence with Poniatowski singing the tenor part; it was well received, and was repeated in Lucca. His next opera, *Don Desiderio*, was performed in Pisa (1840) then, with great success, at Venice, Milan, Livorno, Bologna, Rome and Naples; in 1858 it was given at the Théâtre Italien in Paris. Of his other operas, two were particularly popular: *Bonifazio de' Geremei* (1843) and *Malek Adel* (1846), an *opera seria*.

Poniatowski was created Prince of Monte Rotondo in 1848, and, after the political upheavals of the same year, the Grand Duke of Tuscany appointed him ambassador, first in Brussels (1849), then in London (1850–53) and finally in Paris, where Napoleon III made him a senator of the French Empire. Poniatowski staged his four-act *Pierre de Médicis* at the Opéra, and his one-act *Au travers du mur* at the Opéra-Comique. He accompanied Napoleon into exile in England; his *Gelmina*, written for Adelina Patti, was performed in London, as were excerpts from his Mass in F. His operas are marked by melodic inventiveness, and his ballad *The Yeoman's Wedding Song* remained popular in England for a long time. He wrote a booklet, *Le progrès de la musique dramatique* (Paris, 1859).

WORKS
OPERAS
(MSS lost unless otherwise stated)

Giovanni da Procida (Poniatowski, after G. N. Niccolini), Florence, 25 Nov 1838
Don Desiderio, ossia Il disperato per eccesso di buon cuore (C. Zaccagnini, after G. Giraud), Pisa, 26 Dec 1840, F-Pn, excerpts arr. pf (Milan, c1841), lib in Pol. (Lwów, 1870)
Ruy Blas (after Hugo), Lucca, 2 Sept 1843
Bonifazio de' Geremei (Poniatowski), Rome, 28 Nov 1843, Po, excerpts (Milan, c1845); rev. as I Lambertazzi, Florence, 1845
La sposa d'Abido (G. Peruzzini, after Byron), Venice, Feb 1845, lib (Venice, 1845)

Malek Adel (after S. Cottins: Mathilde), Genoa, 20 June 1846
Esmeralda (F. Guidi, Poniatowski, after Hugo), Florence, 26 June 1847
Pierre de Médicis (J.-H. Vernoy de Saint-Georges, E. Pacini), Paris, 9 March 1860, vocal score (Paris, 1860–61), lib (Paris, 1860)
Au travers du mur (Vernoy de Saint-Georges), Paris, 9 May 1861, vocal score (Paris, 1861), lib (Paris, 1862)
L'aventurier (Vernoy de Saint-Georges), Paris, 26 Jan 1865, vocal score (Paris, 1870–72)
La contessina (A. de Lauzières, after Vernoy de Saint-Georges, J. Adenis), Paris, 28 April 1868, Pn, vocal score (Paris, n.d.), lib (Paris, 1868)
Gelmina (F. Rizzelli), London, 4 June 1872, lib (London, 1872)

OTHER WORKS

Messe solennelle, 4vv, vocal score (Paris, 1867); Mass, F, London, 27 June 1873, vocal score (London, n.d.); The Yeoman's Wedding Song, ballad (London, n.d.); Circé, scène dramatique (Paris, n.d.); Femme du contrabandier, scène (Paris, n.d.); Hochzeitsmorgen: Kling, Klang, wie schön der Sang (Leipzig, n.d.); Love's Oracle (London, n.d.); Ma cinquantaine (Paris, n.d.); Il était là, mélodie (Paris, 1863); 8 mélodie, 1v, pf (Paris, 1858); Stabat mater, frag., Pn; Boléro, pf (Paris, 1863)

BIBLIOGRAPHY

SMP
H. Mendel and A. Reissmann: Musikalisches Conversations-Lexikon, i–xii (Berlin, 1870–79, 3/1890–91/R1969)

IRENA PONIATOWSKA

Pönick, Johann Peter. See PENIGK, JOHANN PETER.

Pons, José (*b* Gerona, *c*1768; *d* Valencia, 2 Aug 1818). Spanish composer. He was a choirboy at Gerona Cathedral, where he studied with Jaime Balius and probably with Manuel Gonima. In 1789 he is mentioned as 'a musician of Madrid'. In 1791 he was made choirmaster at Gerona Cathedral, and subsequently was appointed vice-choirmaster at Córdoba Cathedral. In 1793 he was named choirmaster of Valencia Cathedral, where he remained until his death. All his known works are religious, apart from a few overtures and symphonies, which were, however, composed for the religious concerts that took place in some cathedrals at the more important feasts. He wrote masses, psalms, Lamentations for Holy Week, motets and villancicos. Particularly noteworthy are his responsories for Christmas. His work survives in several Spanish archives (E-VAc, G, C, SC, Bc). He was a gifted composer and a solid technician whose individuality emerges more vividly in large-scale works than in small. Pons enjoyed a considerable reputation in his lifetime.

BIBLIOGRAPHY

V. Ripollés: El villancico i la cantata del segle XVIII a València (Barcelona, 1935)
F. Civil Castellví: 'La capilla de música de la catedral de Gerona (siglo XVIII)', Anales del Instituto de estudios Gerundeses, xix (1968–9), 131–88
J. López-Calo: Catálogo musical del archivo de la Santa Iglesia Catedral de Santiago (Cuenca, 1972), 290ff [with additional bibliography]

JOSÉ LÓPEZ-CALO

Pons, Lily (Alice Joséphine) (*b* Draguignan, nr. Cannes, 16 April 1898; *d* Dallas, 13 Jan 1976). American soprano of French birth. A piano student at the Paris Conservatoire, she received her first vocal instruction from Alberti de Gorostiaga. She made her opera début in 1928 at Mulhouse, as Lakmé; Reynaldo Hahn conducted. She then sang in provincial houses (Cannes and Deauville). On the recommendation of Zenatello, she went to the Metropolitan Opera, making her début on 3 January 1931 as Lucia. She caused a sensation and remained at that house to celebrate her 25th anniversary. She had success as Gilda, Amina, Marie (*La fille du régiment*), Philine (*Mignon*), Olympia and, above all, Lakmé. Her name became a household word. She sang in South America, London (Covent Garden, 1935, Rosina) and made some films. In 1938 she married André Kostelanetz. A singer of international standing, Pons possessed an agile, fragile and extremely high coloratura voice; it suited her to sing the Mad Scene from *Lucia* a whole tone higher than written. Her intonation was not always accurate, but her technique was otherwise exceptionally secure.

BIBLIOGRAPHY
B. Park: 'Lily Pons', *Record Collector*, xiii (1961), 245 [with discography]

MAX DE SCHAUENSEE

Pons [Ponsetç, Ponset, Ponsett] **de Capdoil** [Cabdueill, Capdoilh, Capduoill, Capduch, Capduelh, Capdueil, Capduill, Chapdoill, Chapteuil] (*b* c1165; *d* c1215). French troubadour. Son of the lord of St Julien Capdoil, in Puy-Ste Marie-en-Velay (Haute-Loire), Pons de Capdoil was considered by his contemporaries to be the very epitome of the troubadour courtly knight: valiant in war, a master in the arts of music, poetry and love, highly polished and gracious in manners and speech, and of a genial and happy disposition. The many contemporary descriptions and references, including those in his own works, yield few precise dates, but it seems likely that he was born between 1160 and 1170. The last contemporary mention of him is in a document of the years 1218–20 where the context suggests he had already died. He was praised by other poets (for example Bertran de Born, Elias de Barjol and Folquet de Marseille) in works which date from as early as 1190 to as late as 1213, years which probably span the time of his greatest productivity and influence. His active life was spent mostly at Marseilles, where he was closely associated with the Count of Auvergne, whose wife, the beautiful Azalaïs de Mercoeur, was the inspiration for some of his finest love poetry, including a moving *planh* on her death. It is probable that, along with the Count of Auvergne, he accompanied Philippe Auguste and Richard I on the third crusade, and his crusading songs come from about that time.

In his poetry, Pons was less rich in imagery than Bernart de Ventadorn and less facile in the manipulation of words than Arnaut Daniel, though near in both respects. The rhythm of his poetry, however, is seldom surpassed for its adroit balance between regularity of metric flow and subtle deviation from it. In all, his poems are among the best representatives of troubadour art at the height of its excellence. Of his 27 known poems, four survive with music. His melodies deserve especial comment, for they are among the finest in the repertory. They show consummate skill in formal design, in graceful expressiveness and in the melodic variety within their limited resources. Other composers recognized their virtues, for his melodies were used as contrafacta in 12 compositions.

WORKS
Edition: *Der musikalische Nachlass der Troubadours*, ed. F. Gennrich, SMM, iii, iv, xv (1958–65) [G]

Lejals amics cui Amors te jojos, PC 375.14 [contrafacta: Pujol, 'Cel qi salvet Daniel dels leos', PC 386.1a; Anon., 'No·m platz rics hom, si non es amoros', PC 461.176; Uc de Saint Circ, 'Mesier Albric, so·m prega Ardisos', PC 457.20a]; G 77

Meills qu'om no pot dir ni pensar, PC 375.16 [contrafacta: Daude de Carlus, 'En re no me semblatz joglar', PC 123.1; Gui de Glotos, 'Diode, be sai mercandejar', PC 193.1; Guiraut Riquier, 'Guillem de Mur, que cuja far', PC 248.37; Sordel, 'Mant hom·m fan meravilhar', PC 437.20a; Uc de Saint Circ, 'Seign'en coms, no·us cal esmajar', PC 457.33]; G 78, ed. U. Sesini, *Le melodie trobadoriche della bibl. Ambrosiana* (Turin, 1942), 266

S'eu fis ni dis nuilla sazo, PC 375.19 [contrafacta: Bertran Carbonel (de Marseilla), 'Cor, digatz me per qual razo', PC 82.9; 'Un sirventes de vil razo', PC 82.18; 'Anc de joc no vi far son pro', PC 82.22; Peire d'Alvernhe, 'Lo seigner que formet lo tro', PC 323.22]; G 78, ed. U. Sesini, *Le melodie trobadoriche della bibl. Ambrosiana* (Turin, 1942), 266

Us gais conortz me fai gajamen far, PC 375.27; G 79

BIBLIOGRAPHY
F.-J. Fétis: *Histoire générale de la musique* (Paris, 1869–76/*R*)
M. von Napolski: *Leben und Werke des Trobadors Pons de Capdoil* (Halle, 1879) [incl. edn. of texts]
A. Thomas: 'L'identité du troubadour Pons de Chapteuil', *Annales du Midi*, v (1893), 374
R. Lavaud: 'Pons de Capdeuil', *Mémoires de la Société d'agricole et scientifique de la Haute-Loire*, xiii (1904), 292
H. Riemann: *Handbuch der Musikgeschichte*, i/2 (Leipzig, 1904–5), 251f
C. Fabre: 'Le troubadour Pons de Chapteuil: quelques remarques sur sa vie et sur l'esprit de ses poèmes', *Mémoires de la Société d'agricole et scientifique de la Haute-Loire*, xiv (1905), 25; see also review by S. Stronski, *Annales du Midi*, xix (1907), 547
S. Stronski: 'En Pons de Capdeulh', *Annales du Midi*, xviii (1906), 483
C. Fabre: 'Un poème inédit de Peire Cardinal: Cardinal et Pons de Chapteuil', *Archivum romanicum*, iii (1919), 37

For further bibliography *see* TROUBADOURS, TROUVÈRES.

GWYNN S. McPEEK

Pons d'Ortafas (*fl* 1200–40). Provençal troubadour. Two works are ascribed to this poet, probably identifiable with Pons I d'Ortaffa (in the vicinity of Perpignan), who appears in documents of 1214 and 1240. *Si ay perdut mon saber* (of contested authorship) survives with music. In bar form, the melody is interesting for the manner in which it develops in the cauda the opening motif of the second phrase.

See also TROUBADOURS, TROUVÈRES.

BIBLIOGRAPHY
H. Anglès: *La música a Catalunya fins al segle XIII* (Barcelona, 1935)
F. Gennrich, ed.: *Der musikalische Nachlass der Troubadours*, SMM, iii, iv, xv (Darmstadt, 1958–65), no.241

THEODORE KARP

Ponse, Luctor (*b* Geneva, 11 Oct 1914). Dutch pianist and composer of Swiss origin. He received *prix d'excellence* in theory and solfège (1930) and piano (1932) at the Valenciennes Conservatory, and continued his piano studies with Aubert at the Geneva Conservatory, receiving a *prix de virtuosité*. At the same time he was studying composition with Barblan, Lamy and Badings. In 1936 he settled in the Netherlands, where he established a reputation as an interpreter of new music, particularly that of Bartók. Since 1940 he has used a dodecaphonic style of composition. In 1964 he began work at the Instituut voor Sonologie, Utrecht, where he joined the teaching staff. His works received prizes in the Leboeuf Competition (Brussels, 1936), the Luxembourg International Competition (1952) and the Queen Elisabeth Competition (1953 and 1965).

WORKS
(*selective list*)

Orch: Divertissement, 1946; Pf Conc., 1951–5; 2 syms., 1953, 1957; Sinfonietta no.2, 1959; Conc. da camera, bn, orch, 1962; 2-pf Conc., 1962; Vn Conc. no.2, 1965

Inst: Str Qt no.2, 1946; Vn Sonata, 1948; Vc Sonata no.2, 1950; Variations, fl, hpd, 1962; Euterpe, 11 insts, 1964; Pf Suite, 1964; Studies, pf, 1974

Tape: Enchantement, 1962; Etude I, 1965; Nacht, 1966; Conc. I, pf, tape, 1967; Facettes tournantes, 1968; Radiophonie Ia, 1968, Ib, 1968, II, 1969, III, 1969

Principal publisher: Donemus

BIBLIOGRAPHY
J. Wouters: 'Dutch Music and the Queen Elisabeth Contest', *Sonorum speculum* (1962), no.10, p.17
——: 'Luctor Ponse: Concerto da camera', *Sonorum speculum* (1964), no.19, p.32

ROGIER STARREVELD

Ponselle [Ponzillo], **Rosa** (*b* Meriden, Conn., 22 Jan 1897). American soprano. After some experience in church singing, she began to appear in film theatres and vaudeville, often in duet with her elder sister Carmela (a mezzo-soprano who was to sing at the Metropolitan Opera from 1925 to 1935). In 1918 her coach William Thorner brought her to the attention of Caruso and Gatti-Casazza. In the first Metropolitan production of *La forza del destino*, she made an unprecedented début – the first operatic performance of her life – as Leonora (15 November 1918), opposite Caruso and De Luca. She had prepared the role with Romano Romani, who remained her principal operatic and vocal tutor throughout her career. She sang at the Metropolitan for 19 seasons, undertaking 22 roles in the dramatic and dramatic-coloratura repertories. Perhaps most celebrated as Norma, she also enjoyed extraordinary successes in *Oberon, Ernani, Don Carlos, La Gioconda, Andrea Chenier, Guillaume Tell, L'amore dei tre re, Don Giovanni* (Donna Anna), *Cavalleria rusticana, La traviata, La vestale* and *L'africaine*. She also participated in such little-known operas as Breil's *The Legend*, Montemezzi's *La notte di Zoraïma* and Romani's *Fedra*. In 1935 she attempted Carmen, perhaps unwisely, and experienced her only notable failure. Two years later she retired from opera, reportedly after her request for a revival of *Adriana Lecouvreur* was rejected, and vowed never again to set foot in the Metropolitan after her final performance (as Carmen, 15 February 1937). She made her Covent Garden début as Norma on 28 May 1929, returning as Violetta, Leonora (*La forza del destino*) and the heroine of Romani's *Fedra*; at the Florence Maggio Musicale in 1933 she sang Julia (*La vestale*). Although her repertory was broad, she never sang

Puccini or Wagner, about which she confessed regret in later years.

Ponselle's voice is generally regarded as one of the most beautiful of the century. She was universally lauded for opulence of tone, evenness of scale, breadth of range, perfection of technique and communicative warmth. Many of these attributes are convincingly documented on recordings. She sang briefly in concerts and at public ceremonials after her premature operatic retirement, then moved to Baltimore, where she concentrated on teaching. In 1954 she made a few private song recordings, later released commercially, revealing a still opulent voice of darkened timbre and more limited range. She has served as artistic director of the Baltimore Civic Opera, which commemorated her 70th birthday with a new production of *La forza del destino* on 10 March 1969.

BIBLIOGRAPHY

O. Thompson: *The American Singer* (New York, 1937), 335ff
I. Cook: 'Rosa Ponselle', *Opera*, iii (1952), 75
L. Riemens and R. Celletti: 'Ponselle, Rosa', *Le grandi voci* (Rome, 1964) [with opera discography by S. Smolian and R. Vegeto]
T. Villella and B. Park: 'Rosa Ponselle Discography', *Grand baton*, viii/1–2 (1970), 5
J. B. Steane: *The Grand Tradition* (London, 1974), 289ff
J. Ardoin: 'A Footnote to Ponselle's Norma', *Opera*, xxvii (1976), 225

MARTIN BERNHEIMER

Ponset [Ponsetç, Ponsett] **de Capdoil** [Cabdueill, Capduch, Chapdoill etc]. *See* PONS DE CAPDOIL.

Ponsonby, Charles Garrett. *See* DROGHEDA, 11th Earl of.

Pont [Ponte], **Jacques du** [Dupont, Jacques; Ponte, Giaches de; Pont, Jacobus de] (*b c*1500; *d* probably after 1564). French composer active in Italy. He was a priest. He was *maestro di cappella* at S Luigi dei Francesi, Rome, on 14 October 1536 and remained there until 31 January 1538. Frey suggested that he might have entered Pietro Bembo's service, for he set the whole of Bembo's *Cinquanta stanze* in 1545. The large number of collections that include works by Pont indicates his popularity. The madrigal *Con lei foss'io* appeared in 21 printed collections with an Italian text and in two collections with a French text. The humorous *Canzon di cald'arost* (in *RISM* 1549[31]), whose text deals with meat-selling, uses the dialect of the Marche. Cametti considered it likely that the melodic lines contained street cries. According to Einstein, Pont belonged to the circle of minor Venetian composers whose activity had ceased by the mid-16th century. However, many of Pont's works, particularly the motets, derive from the northern polyphonic tradition and do not contain elements of the polychoral style or the chromaticism typical of Rore and Willaert.

WORKS

Cinquanta stanze del Bembo, 4vv (Venice, 1545)
3 madrigals: 1543[18], ed. in Cametti; 1546[15]; 1549[31]
2 chansons, 1536[5], 1548[5] (1 contrafactum of madrigal)
3 motets, 1539[7], 1539[13], 1564[1]
For instrumental transcriptions see *BrownI*

BIBLIOGRAPHY

G. O. Pitoni: *Notitia de contrapuntisti e de compositori di musica* (MS, *I-Rvat* C.G.I/1–2, *c*1725)
A. Cametti: 'Jacques Du Pont e la sua "Canzon di cald'arost" (1549)', *RMI*, xxiii (1916), 273
A. Einstein: *The Italian Madrigal* (Princeton, 1949/*R*1971)
H.-W. Frey: 'Die Kapellmeister an der französischen Nationalkirche San Luigi dei Francesci in Rom im 16. Jahrhundert, 1514–1577', *AMw*, xxii (1965), 276
J. Haar: 'A Gift of Madrigals to Cosimo I: the Ms. Florence, Bibl. Naz. Centrale, Magl. XIX, 130', *RIM*, i (1966), 170

Rosa Ponselle in the title role of Ponchielli's 'La Gioconda'

P. A. Myers: *An Analytical Study of the Italian Cyclic Madrigals published by Composers Working in Rome ca.1540–1614* (diss., U. of Illinois, 1971), 4, 39, 47f, 84

PATRICIA ANN MYERS

Ponta [Ponte], Adamus de [Pontanus, Adamus] (*fl* 1563–85). South Netherlands composer. He may be identifiable with Adamus Scrinifici, *duodenus* from 1531 to 1538 and precentor from 1540 to at least 1548 at St Martin, Liège, with one of the two Adam Laurii, or with Adam Rickelt senior or junior, precentors and succentors at the same church between about 1531 and 1561. De Ponta was a singer at the *Hofkapelle* in Vienna from 1 January 1563 until 31 August 1564. On the death of the Emperor Ferdinand I both he and Castileti, the Kapellmeister, were pensioned off. From 1567 to 1569 he was succentor at St Jean l'Evangéliste, Liège, and rector of the altar of St Ambroise. He was succeeded in 1570 by J. Rolandi d'Oreye, and from that year his name appears in the payrolls of St Lambert Cathedral, Liège, as succentor and as beneficiary of the altar of St Denis, one of the 12 altars of the cathedral designated for musicians. On 3 October 1573 Castileti mentioned 'Adamus de Ponte' to the chapter of St Jean, Liège, in connection with the return of some priestly ornaments. On 15 September 1576, he was elected canon of St Materne in the cathedral. The appointment resulted in tensions between de Ponta and the cathedral chapter, and it was probably on this account that he was replaced as succentor on 26 October 1577 by Henri Sartoris and as canon by J. Rolandi in December. He may have returned directly to St Jean, but if so he can at best have been only second succentor, as the chapter had appointed T. Halloy as *maître de chant* on 18 May 1577 in succession to J. Rolandi. De Ponta and Fabri, who is described as an organist, are quoted as being witnesses at the appointment of a choirboy at St Jean on 10 February 1581; this may indicate that de Ponta was in charge of the instruction of the *duodeni*. On 1 March 1582 the chapter of St Jean named 'M. Adamus de Ponte' succentor. On 10 June 1585 'M. Adam sanckmeister zu S Johann zu Lüttich und seine zwey Jungen were among the 15 worthy musicians assembled by M. Peudargent to celebrate the marriage of William, Duke of Jülich-Clève, to the Countess Jacobea de Bade in Düsseldorf. This is the last known reference to de Ponta.

His style is predominantly imitative, characteristic of south Netherlands composers, showing considerable expertise and invention. The beginning of the motet *Apparuit* well illustrates his technique: the six voices are divided into two groups of three which repeat the same entry; two of the three sing a descending motif in canon at the octave, while the third takes up the same motif in inversion. Similarly, in the two parts of the motet *Tu es pastor* (*secunda pars: Quodcunque ligaveris*), four of the five voices sing a motif in canon and then they sing a number of imitative motifs, against which the fifth voice repeatedly states the first six notes of the plainsong *Tu es Petrus* in semibreves, spread out at intervals of eight breves. These highly organized works display an impressive technical facility. Four of de Ponta's motets, for four to five voices, are in *RISM* 1568³; another, *Apparuit caro suo Joanni*, for six voices, is in the second Aachen choirbook (in *D-AAm*).

BIBLIOGRAPHY

A. Smijers: *Die kaiserliche Hofmusik-Kapelle von 1543–1619*, (Vienna, 1922)

J. Quitin: 'Les maîtres de chant de la cathédrale Saint-Lambert à Liège', *RBM*, vii (1954), 1

G. Pietzsch: 'Die Jülich'sche Hochzeit, 1585', *Studien zur Musikgeschichte des Rheinlandes*, lii (Cologne, 1962)

JOSÉ QUITIN

Pontac, Diego de (*b* probably Saragossa, 1603; *d* Madrid, buried 1 Oct 1654). Spanish composer. For details of his early years we are indebted to his brief autobiography, *Discurso … remitido al racionero Manuel Correa*, which is dated 22 June 1633. He began studying music at the age of nine at Saragossa. By the age of 16 he was studying singing and 'a little counterpoint' there under Juan Pujol and Francisco Berge; he later studied counterpoint with Pedro Rimonte. In 1620 he won a competition and became *maestro de capilla* at the Hospital Real at Saragossa and later was sent to Madrid to study composition under Nicolás Dupont. After failing to obtain an appointment at Plasencia, Pontac received a prebend as *maestro de capilla* at Salamanca; he soon became examiner in singing at the university there. He was preferred to many other competitors for a chaplaincy at Madrid and later became *maestro de capilla* at the Iglesia Mayor at Granada. In each position he took pride in having many students. In 1644 he became *maestro de capilla* at Santiago de Compostela, and from 7 September 1649 to 8 July 1650 he held a similar position at the Cathedral of La Seo, Saragossa. He was at Valencia Cathedral from 1650 to 1653. Finally he moved to Madrid, where on 22 March 1654 he became deputy *maestro de capilla* of the royal chapel.

In 1631 Pontac prepared two large MSS of his works for publication, one of which, lacking about 20 leaves at the end, still exists and is owned by José Subirá. It was submitted to the critical scrutiny of numerous prominent musicians, who spoke highly of its contents, and Pontac wrote his autobiography to support publication. However, none of his music was ever printed. There are 20 works in the MS: six four-part masses, one for six voices and two four-part mass antiphons; four four-part and two five-part motets; three six-part responsories and two four-part settings of *Salve regina*. 16 other works, two of them secular, survive in other MS sources (at *E-E, MO, VAc* and *Zvp*); some (at *E* in particular) include works for up to 12 voices, with continuo.

BIBLIOGRAPHY

J. Ruiz de Lihori: *La música en Valencia: diccionario biográfico* (Valencia, 1903)

J. Subirá: 'Músicos espanyols del segle XVII: Diego de Pontac', *Revista musical catalana*, xxxi (1934), 417

BARTON HUDSON

Pontar [pontare] (It.). *See* PUNTATO.

Ponte, Jacques du [Giaches del]. *See* PONT, JACQUES DU.

Ponte, Lorenzo da. *See* DA PONTE, LORENZO.

Pontelibero, Ferdinando ['Ajutantini'] (*b* Como, 1770; *d* Milan, 1835). Italian violinist and composer. After working as an orchestral violinist in Como, he became a member of the La Scala orchestra at the end of the century. According to Rovani's historical novel *Cento anni* (1857), he composed the controversial republican ballet *Il Generale Colla in Roma* (1797). His nickname 'little adjutant' possibly derives from his part in this pro-Napoleonic work. He provided scores for at least ten more ballets between 1799 and 1812. A trip to Paris in 1806, mentioned by Fétis but otherwise unverified, may account for the publication there of his opp.3 and 4.

In 1814 Pontelibero became first violin for the ballet

at La Scala, a promotion criticized by the *Allgemeine musikalische Zeitung*: 'How they chose a Mr Pontelibero ... even the orchestra cannot comprehend'. During the tenure (1812–21) of Salvatore Viganò as principal choreographer of La Scala, he is known to have contributed to only a few ballets, since Viganò generally ignored local composers. Only one of these works, *Numa Pompilio* (1815), was choreographed by Viganò, whom the *Allgemeine musikalische Zeitung* reported to have 'done no one a favour' by choosing Pontelibero. During Pontelibero's last years at La Scala (1819–33), he appears to have composed only chamber music. The *Allgemeine musikalische Zeitung* also reported several unsigned collaborations in the 1820s with the Milanese amateur composer Count Cesare Castelbarco, in which Castelbarco provided 'the principal [first violin] part along with the obbligato portions of the others', and Pontelibero 'the accompaniment, which consists chiefly in *Brillen* [Alberti bass figures]'. In spite of his German critics, Pontelibero was admired by the Milanese, for whom his masterful string writing and brilliant, if less than profound, style had an immediate appeal. Two comedies by a Ferdinando Pontelibero, perhaps this one, were performed in Milan and published there in 1832.

WORKS

BALLETS

(performed at La Scala, Milan, unless otherwise stated)

Il Generale Colla in Roma (Il ballo del Papa), 25 Feb 1797; Gonzalvo in America, Jan 1799; I francesi in Egitto (Buonaparte in Egitto), 11 Feb 1799; Zulima, Jan 1800; Sadak e Kalasrad, Jan 1801; Il sagrifizio di Curzio, 26 Dec 1804; Alcina e Ruggiero, aut. 1805; Magri e grassi, 16 June 1806; Cambise in Egitto, 30 Sept 1807; La morte di Whaytsong, ultimo imperatore della dinastia chinese, 24 Jan 1809, Acts 2–5 by G. Ferliga

Dances in Azione da eseguirsi nella festa del Senato Consulente per la Pace di Vienna e pel ritorno dalla guerra di S.A.I. il Principe Vicere, 1810; Manco-Capac, Milan, Canobbiana, sum. 1812; Ov. to La noce di Benevento, 25 April 1812, *I-Mc*, ballet composed by F. Süssmayr; Numa Pompilio, 25 Feb 1815, 2 excerpts, arr. hpd (Milan, n.d.), with some music by others; dances in Il mistico omaggio (cantata), 15 March 1815

Dances in La mania del ballo, 9 Aug 1815, 2 excerpts, arr. pf (Milan, n.d.); 1 dance in Tamerlano, 29 May 1816 (Milan, n.d.); dances in Ramesse, o sia Gli arabi in Egitto, 5 June 1819; dances in Elena e Gerardo, Venice, La Fenice, carn. 1820

OTHER WORKS

Inst: 3 sinfonias, c, B♭, E♭, *Mc*; 3 duos, 2 vn (Milan, n.d.); 3 trii, vn, va, vc, op.3 (Paris, n.d.); 6 str qts: 3, op.4 (Paris, n.d.), 3, op.5 (Milan, n.d.); Solo per ballo, C, arr. org, *OS*

Vocal: Ottave di Torquato Tasso, S, hpd, op.6 (Milan, n.d.) [66 ottave from *Gerusalemme liberata*]

BIBLIOGRAPHY

FétisB

'Nachrichten', *AMZ*, xvi (1814), col.255; xvii (1815), col.290; xxix (1827), cols.635, 884

G. Rovani: *Cento anni* (Milan, 1857, 2/1934)

M. Chiesa: 'Pontelibero, Ferdinando', *MGG*

KATHLEEN KUZMICK HANSELL, GILDA GRIGOLATO

Ponticello (It.). (1) BRIDGE.

(2) *See* SUL PONTICELLO.

Pontifical (from Lat. *liber pontificalis ordinis*: 'book of pontifical ritual'). A collection of liturgical formularies for episcopal functions of the Western Christian church. Early medieval books containing such formularies do not follow a standard pattern but usually include material for such occasional services as the dedication of a church, confirmation, expulsion of penitents on Ash Wednesday, reconciliation of penitents on Maundy Thursday, ordination, consecration or benediction of people and objects, anointing of monarchs and for-

mularies on the occasion of a synod. Many early books contain a year's cycle of episcopal benedictions for Mass, but these are more often found in the BENEDICTIONAL.

In the mid-11th century, a type of pontifical originating at St Alban, Mainz (*c*960), became standard at Rome; it was revised by Innocent III (1198–1216). Guillaume Durand, Bishop of Mende (1285–96) and active at the papal court, made another revision incorporating material from French dioceses and reordering and excluding many non-essential rituals. It was adopted by Clement V (*d* 1314). There have been other revisions, most notably that of Agostino Patrizi de Piccolomini and Johannes Burckard (1497) and the *Pontificale romanum* of 1595. The edition of 1941 bears the names of Benedict XIV and Leo XIII on its title-page.

Prepared for princes of the church, pontificals were often splendidly decorated, which has ensured that many have survived. Most contain some simple notated chants and provide important information on the style of notation used in many medieval scriptoria. Leroquais described 250 pontificals in French libraries, Frere cited 39 English ones, and Andrieu listed and grouped sources of those favoured at Rome in the Middle Ages (the earliest is edited in Vogel and Elze).

See also LITURGY AND LITURGICAL BOOKS.

BIBLIOGRAPHY

W. H. Frere: *Pontifical Services*, Alcuin Club Collections, iii–iv (London, 1901)

V. Baudot: 'Bénédictions épiscopales', 'Bénédictionnaire', *Dictionnaire d'archéologie chrétienne et de liturgie*, ii/1 (1910)

——: *Le pontifical* (Paris, 1910)

P. de Puniet: *Le pontifical romain: histoire et commentaire* (Paris, 1930; Eng. trans., 1932)

V. Leroquais: *Les pontificaux manuscrits des bibliothèques publiques de France* (Paris, 1937)

M. Andrieu: *Le pontifical romain au moyen-âge*, Studi e testi, lxxxvi–lxxxviii, xcix (Vatican City, 1938–41)

H. Leclercq: 'Pontifical', *Dictionnaire d'archéologie chrétienne et de liturgie*, xiv (1939)

C. A. Bouman: *Sacring and Crowning* (Groningen, 1957)

C. Vogel and R. Elze: *Le pontifical romano-germanique du dixième siècle*, Studi e testi, ccxxvi–ccxxvii (Vatican City, 1963)

Pontio [Ponzio], **Pietro** (*b* Parma, 25 March 1532; *d* Parma, 27 Dec 1595). Italian theorist and composer. He was ordained and was appointed *maestro di cappella* of S Maria Maggiore, Bergamo, on 17 January 1565, a position for which Cipriano de Rore, who may have been his teacher, strongly recommended him. He was soon dismissed, however, as the result of a suit brought before the Council of the Misericordia on 3 January 1567. On 17 January he assumed the position of *maestro di cappella* at the Madonna della Steccata, Parma, where he remained until May 1569. He spent some time in the company of Girolamo Cornazzano, a cavalier to the Polish king. From 1577 to 26 November 1582 he held the post of *maestro di cappella* at Milan Cathedral, after which he returned to the Steccata in Parma. He was recommended by Cardinal Farnese to receive a prebend at Parma Cathedral on 22 May 1592. He was buried in the cathedral.

His extant music is mainly sacred and comprises several volumes published in Venice between 1580 and 1595. Some examples of his composition in his treatise, the *Ragionamento* (1588), show a greater proximity to the style of Gombert than to that of Palestrina. The melodies move conjunctly within a narrow range, points of imitation are often limited to four or five notes and repeated themes sometimes show subtle alterations of rhythm that disguise their identity. His principal fame, however, rests on his theories, as presented in two published treatises: the *Ragionamento* consists of four conversations that took place on consecutive days at the home of Count Mario Bevilacqua of Verona, to whom the volume is dedicated; the *Dialogo* (1595) is, as the title indicates, also laid out in the form of a discussion. The treatises display many similarities in their content, and prove Pontio to be a theorist who formulated the rules of good counterpoint and showed concern for the clear presentation of the text. He displayed a considerable knowledge of 16th-century music, holding as models in particular Josquin, Willaert, Gombert and Morales. Like earlier theorists he acknowledged his indebtedness to Gaffurius, Aaron and Zarlino: his discussion of melodic lines and proper melodic intervals, consonances, dissonances and of harmonic vocabulary in general owes much to Zarlino.

In the *Dialogo*, part of the discussion centres on achieving musical variety, through use of new subjects or of cadences outside the mode of a piece. A principal concern, however, is the appropriate setting of a text. Pontio maintained that texts of the lessons of Holy Week, the Passions and the *Miserere* should in particular be clearly understood, and passages such as 'Et incarnatus est' and 'Jesu Christe' in the Mass should be set in note-against-note style so that clarity of the text would heighten the spirit of devotion. The 2nd, 4th and 6th modes were, by virtue of their more sombre nature, considered suitable for the lessons. Pontio, like Zarlino, asserted that moods of sadness call for the minor 3rd and that the major 10th should be reserved for a lighter kind of music.

The *Ragionamento* is notable for its comments on individual musical forms. The polyphonic mass should be constructed on similar themes in each of its movements, although contrasting sections should be based on different material, with, for example, the Christe differing from the Kyrie. Motets should be based on appropriately serious themes, and should not contain sudden changes to rapid movement, a feature more suited to canzonas or madrigals. The themes of madrigals, however, should be abbreviated, and sections introduced in which the voices move in note-against-note style, using minims or semiminims. Concerning instrumental forms, he stated that a ricercare should be based on a lengthy subject which is often used in its entirety. A *versetto* should be shorter, and have no more than a semibreve or breve between the entries of the parts. In his writings Pontio drew a contrast of particular interest between an improvising performer, or 'contrapuntalist', whose abilities extend no further than adding a new part to a given melody, and a 'true musician', capable of combining a number of different melodies to form an entire composition.

WORKS
(all published in Venice)

Missarum, liber primus, 5vv (1580), lost
Missarum, liber secundus, 5vv (1581)
Motettorum, liber primus, 5vv (1582), lost
Modulationum, liber primus, 5vv, 1582[3]
Missarum, liber primus, 4vv (1584)
Magnificat, liber primus, 4vv (1584), lost
Missarum, liber tertius, 5vv (1585)
Modulationum, liber secundus, 5vv, 1588[10]
Psalmum vesperarum, liber secundus, 4vv (1589), lost
Missarum, liber tertius, 4vv (1592)
Hymni solemniores, 4vv (1595)
Sacred works, 1592[3], 1619[3]; 1 madrigal, 1596[11]

THEORETICAL WORKS
Ragionamento di musica . . . ove si tratta de'passaggi . . . et del modo di far motetti, messe, salmi et altre compositioni (Parma, 1588); facs. edn., DM, xvi (1958)
Dialogo . . . ove si tratta della theorica et prattica di musica (Parma, 1595)

BIBLIOGRAPHY
N. Pelicelli: 'Musicisti in Parma nei secoli XV–XVI', *NA*, viii (1931), 208
J. Armstrong: 'How to Compose a Psalm: Ponzio and Cerone Compared', *Studi musicali*, vii (1978), 103–39

ROLAND JACKSON

Ponty, Jean-Luc (*b* Arranches, 29 Sept 1942). French jazz violinist. His parents were both music teachers, and gave him instruction on the violin and piano from the age of five. In 1959 he entered the Paris Conservatoire, where he won a *premier prix* for violin after one year. He then played in the Concerts Lamoureux for two years, but in 1964, after a highly successful appearance at the Antibes Jazz Festival, he decided to become a full-time jazz musician. Since then Ponty has been considered the most important new violinist in jazz, with a style especially influenced by American avant-garde saxophonists of the 1960s. He has also taken part in progressive popular music, performing with such groups as Frank Zappa's Mothers of Invention and with the Mahavishnu Orchestra.

LAURENT GODDET

Ponzillo, Rosa. *See* PONSELLE, ROSA.

Ponzio, Giuseppe. *See* PONZO, GIUSEPPE.

Ponzio, Pietro. *See* PONTIO, PIETRO.

Ponzo [Ponzio], Giuseppe (*fl* 1759–91). Italian composer. He may have been born in Naples, and Milan's *Indice de' spettacoli teatrali* of 1791 listed him as 'still living'. The list of his operatic productions gives some indication of his travels. He also wrote instrumental music, dedicating a set of trio sonatas to the Princess Adelaide.

WORKS
OPERAS
Demetrio (opera seria, Metastasio), Genoa, carn. 1759; score, *P-La*
Arianna e Teseo (opera seria, Pariati), Milan, Ducale, Jan 1762; score, *La*, *I-Gi(l)*
Artaserse (opera seria, Metastasio), Venice, S Benedetto, Jan 1766; score, *P-La*
Il rè alla caccia (comic opera, Goldoni), ?Malta, Reale, ?1775; Vienna, 1777; score, *I-Gi(l)*, *Nc*
Doubtful: Alceste, Reggio Emilia, 1760, score in *P-La*; L'uomo femmina, Madrid, 1771, ?by Antonio Ponza

OTHER WORKS
6 trio o sian Sonate, 2 vn, vc (Paris, c1760)
6 sinfonie; sonata, fl, vn, b: *D-W*, *I-Gi(l)*, *Mc*
Credo, 4vv, insts, *I-Nc*
Ouverture, 1762, *Mc*
Arias, duets etc, *D-Dl*, *I-Gi(l)*, *Nc*

BIBLIOGRAPHY
FétisBS; Gerber L; GerberNL; SchmidlDS

JAMES L. JACKMAN

Poole [Poul], Anthony (*fl* c1670). English composer. The sources for his music date from about the 1670s. 15 solos for bass viol by him are in *GB-Ob* Mus.Sch.C.71; the authorship of one of these is uncertain. Two sets of elaborate 'divisions' for two bass viols and continuo are in *GB-DRc* D.4, where a third such work is probably wrongly attributed to him. Playford's *The Division Violin* (1695) includes two of his violin solos.

ANDREW ASHBEE

Poot, Marcel (*b* Vilvoorde, nr. Brussels, 7 May 1901). Belgian composer and teacher. A son of Jan Poot, director of the Royal Flemish Theatre, Brussels, he first took music lessons with the organist Gérard Nauwelaerts. At the Brussels Conservatory he studied harmony and the piano with Sevenants, Lunssens and de Greef; he was then a pupil of Mortelmans in counterpoint and fugue at the Royal Flemish Conservatory, Antwerp. In 1916 he went to Gilson for lessons in composition and orchestration. At this time Poot was greatly interested in the cinema: his three symphonic sketches *Charlot* (1926) were suggested by Chaplin's films. Later he composed numerous scores for silent films, particularly for documentaries on aspects of Belgian life. Also he discovered the possibilities of jazz, using them in *Jazz Music* and in his first ballet, *Paris in verlegenheid*, staged at the Royal Flemish Opera, Antwerp, in 1935. At the same time he composed music for several radio plays.

In 1925 Poot – together with Bernier, de Bourguignon, Brenta, de Joncker, Otlet, Schoemaker and Strens – formed the Synthétistes, an association of pupils of Gilson founded on his 60th birthday. They had no common aesthetic, but each sought the strength of the group in establishing his own style. This collaboration lasted for five years, assisted by performances given by the conductor Prévost and the pianist Scharrès. Poot won the Rubens Prize in 1930, and this enabled him to move to Paris, where he worked under Dukas at the Ecole Normale de Musique. On his return to Brussels he began a career as a teacher, at first in secondary schools, later at the Vilvoorde Music Academy and finally at the Brussels Conservatory, where he taught practical harmony and then counterpoint. He was also for a time reader at the Institut Supérieur des Arts Décoratifs, Brussels. With Gilson he founded the *Revue musicale belge*, and he wrote for many Belgian and foreign periodicals: for 15 years he was music critic of the Brussels newspaper *Le peuple* and from 1944 to 1949 that of *La nation belge*. In 1943 he was appointed inspector of Belgian music schools, but during the German occupation he was prevented from carrying out his duties. He directed the Brussels Conservatory from 1949 until his retirement in 1966. Poot is a member of the Royal Flemish Academy, chairman of the Queen Elisabeth competition and president of the SABAM; he has served on many national and international music committees.

A comparatively early work, the *Vrolijke ouverture* (1935), has many of the qualities that have remained characteristic of Poot's music. It is a short, gay piece, strongly rhythmic and essentially tonal; after Franck's works it is probably the most frequently played orchestral piece by a Belgian composer. Poot's brilliant and vigorous style – close to middle-period Stravinsky, or more particularly to Prokofiev – is often used to ironic or humorous effect, and has shown itself better suited to orchestral than to vocal music.

WORKS
(selective list)

STAGE AND VOCAL

Het ingebeeld eiland [The fancy isle], opera, 1925; Paris in verlegenheid, ballet, 1925; Het vrouwtje van Stavoren [The little woman of Stavoren], operetta, 1928; Moretus, chamber opera, 1944; Pygmalion, ballet, 1951

3 Negro Songs (trans. R. Herreman), 1v, pf, 1938; Le dit du routier, oratorio, 1943; Icare, oratorio, 1947; Chanson bachique, reciter, speaking vv, male chorus, n.d.

ORCHESTRAL

Variations in the Forms of Dances, 1921; Charlot, 1926; 5 syms., 1929, 1938, 1952, 1972, 1974; Fugato, 1932; Jazz Music, 1933; Rondo, pf, orch, 1935; Vrolijke ouverture, 1935; Symphonisch allegro, 1937; Epic Legend, pf, orch, 1938; Symphonisch triptiek, 1938; Ballad, str qt, orch, 1939; Concertstück, vc, orch, 1942; Fantasia, 1944

Rapsodie, 1948; Divertimento, 1952; Perpetuum mobile, 1953; Tarantella, 1953; Devils Rondo, 1958; Pf Conc., 1959; 2 Sym. Movts, 1961; Suite in the Form of Variations, 1963; English Suite, 1964; Conc. grosso, pf qt, orch, 1964; Tpt Conc., 1973; Concertante beweging, wind, 1975; Pf Conc. no.2, 1975; Symfonische ballade, 1976; Cl Conc., 1977

CHAMBER AND INSTRUMENTAL

Pf Qt, 1932; 3 Pieces in Trio, pf trio, 1935; 5 Bagatelles, str qt, 1939; Pf Suite, 1942; Pf Sonatine, 1945; Ballad, vc, pf, 1948; Ballad, sax, pf, 1948; Habanera, vn, 1949; Pf Etude, 1951; Ballad, vn, pf, 1952; Pf Variations, 1952; Pf Ballad, 1957; Wind Qnt, 1959; Concertino, 4 sax, 1962; Hn Qt, 1965; Légende, 4 cl, 1967; Musique de chambre, pf trio, 1972; Ob Concertino, ob, pf, 1972; Pf Sonatina no.2, 1975; Impromptu, brass qt, 1975; Alla marcia et barcarolle, pf, 1976

Principal publishers: CeBeDeM, Eschig, Universal

BIBLIOGRAPHY

F. de Wever: *Paul Gilson et les Synthétistes* (Brussels, 1949), 46ff
C. van den Borren: Introduction to *Catalogus van het werk van Marcel Poot* (Brussels, 1953)
Music in Belgium (Brussels, 1964) [CeBeDeM publication]
H. Heughebaert: 'Ontmoetinger met Vlaamse Komponisten: Marcel Poot', *Vlaams musiektijdschrift*, xxii/1 (1970), 3 [with list of works and discography]

CORNEEL MERTENS

Pope, Alexander (*b* London, 22 May 1688; *d* Twickenham, 30 May 1744). English critic, poet, satirist and wit. He was the son of a wealthy Catholic linen draper. The publication of *An Essay on Criticism* (1711) marked the beginning of his fame. He was acquainted with the leading political and artistic figures of his day including Lord Burlington, Lord Bolingbroke, the Earl of Oxford, Congreve, Addison, Steele, Aaron Hill, Swift, Gay, Arbuthnot, Greene and Handel. Pope's skill with the 'heroic couplet', his grammatical precision and his rhetoric supplemented his talent for irony, invective and satire.

Since theories of harmony were so much a part of the contemporary canon of taste, it was inevitable that Pope should explore musical terminology and theory. He was known as the 'little nightingale' for his sweet voice as a child, but his interest in music was not as profound as that of Dryden or Congreve. His comments on Bononcini, for example, in a letter to the Duchess of Buckingham (27 January 1722) declare approval for the man's 'great Fame' and a 'Personal Knowledge of his Character', but omit discussion of his music. About this time Pope was involved with the Burlington circle, and helped Handel in the preparation of *Haman and Mordecai*, a masque libretto based on the *Esther* of Racine and Brerton. Arbuthnot and Gay probably did most of the work on the libretto, which suffers from static episodes and a lack of sustained dramatic pace. Several Handel works incorporate lines from Pope: lines from the pastorals are inserted in *Acis and Galatea* and *Semele*, and Handel himself added the famous 'Whatever is, is right' (from the *Essay on Man*) to the final Act 2 chorus of *Jephtha*.

Pope supplied choruses, set to music by Bononcini in 1723, for the Duke of Buckingham's *Brutus*. He was also involved with operatic projects by Gay, including *Achilles* (for which he contributed the prologue) and *The Beggar's Opera*. He altered his own *Ode to St Cecilia* when Greene set it in 1730 and may have prepared the text of a cantata for Durastanti in 1724 on the insistence of Peterborough. Mainwaring claimed that Pope declared himself to be unmusical, but if so he certainly took his friend Arbuthnot's recommendations to heart since his defence of Handel in the 1742 *Dunciad* (iv, 45–70) is spirited. Of his own poems, the most frequently set to music was *The Dying Christian to his Soul*, particularly popular in a version of 1795 by a Methodist, E. Harwood. Parry, Schubert and Havergal Brian set texts derived from Pope.

BIBLIOGRAPHY
J. Mainwaring: *Memoirs of the Life of the late G. F. Handel* (London, 1760)
L. Stephen: 'Pope, Alexander', *DNB*
J. Butt, ed.: *The Poems of Alexander Pope* (London and New Haven, 1953–7)
O. E. Deutsch: *Handel: a Documentary Biography* (London, 1955/ R1974)
M. Goldstein: *Pope and the Augustan Stage* (Stanford and London, 1958)
D. Siegmund-Schultze: 'Alexander Pope und Händel', *HJb*, iv (1958), 81
W. Dean: *Handel's Dramatic Oratorios and Masques* (London, 1959)
E. R. Wasserman: 'Pope's *Ode for Musick*', *Essential Articles for the Study of Alexander Pope*, ed. M. Mack (London, 1968), 159
                                                    DUNCAN CHISHOLM

Pope [Conant], **Isabel** (*b* Evanston, Ill., 19 Oct 1901). American musicologist and philologist. She attended Radcliffe College, taking an AB in 1923, an MA in 1925 and a PhD in Romance philology in 1930. In 1935 she was appointed a tutor in French and Spanish literature at Radcliffe; from then until 1936 she studied musicology at Harvard with Hugo Leichtentritt. She remained at Radcliffe until 1940, then from 1941 to 1944 she worked in Mexico with Adolfo Salazar, whose *La música moderna* she translated for the Norton series. She was again at Radcliffe as tutor from 1945 to 1949. In 1950 she received a joint fellowship of the Mexican government and the Rockefeller Foundation which enabled her to travel to Spain to study Spanish musical influences in colonial Mexico. In 1951 she studied Spanish musical sources in Spain, Italy and France as a Guggenheim Fellow; she continued research in those countries from 1959 to 1960.

Pope is particularly interested in the relationship between music and poetry in Spanish vocal music of the Middle Ages and Renaissance. Her background in Romance philology enabled her to edit the literary texts in both Helen Hewitt's edition of the *Odhecaton* and Hans Tischler's edition of 13th-century French motets. She has studied the musical and literary aspects of the villancico, concluding that the 15th-century villancico still bore traits of the lyric type of 13th-century oral tradition. She has published studies of the manuscript *I-MC* 871, an important source of late 15th-century music from the Aragonese court of Naples.

WRITINGS
Musical and Metrical Forms of the Mediaeval Lyric in the Hispanic Peninsula (diss., Radcliffe College, 1930)
'Mediaeval Latin Background of the Thirteenth-century Galician Lyric', *Speculum*, ix (1934), 3
Review of H. Anglès: *La música a Catalunya fins al segle XIII* (Barcelona, 1935), *Speculum*, xii (1937), 404
'El villancico polifónico', *Cancionero de Upsala*, ed. R. Mitjana y Gordón and J. Bal y Gay (Mexico City, 1944)
Music in Our Time (New York, 1946) [trans. of A. Salazar: *La música moderna*, Buenos Aires, 1944]
'Documentos relacionados con la historia de la música en Mexico', *Nuestra musica*, vi (1951), 5, 245
'The "Spanish Chapel" of Philip II', *Renaissance News*, v (1952), 1, 34
'Notas sobre la melodía del *Conde claros*', *Nueva revista de filología hispánica*, vii (1953), 395
'La musique espagnole à la cour de Naples dans la seconde moitié du XVᵉ siècle', *Musique et poésie au XVIᵉ siècle: CNRS Paris 1953*, 35

'Musical and Metrical Form of the Villancico', *AnnM*, ii (1954), 189
'Vicente Espinel as a Musician', *Studies in the Renaissance*, v (1958), 133
'The Secular Compositions of Johannes Cornago, Part I', *Miscelánea en homenaje a Monseñor Higinio Anglés* (Barcelona, 1958–61), 689
'La vihuela y su música en el ambiente humanístico', *Nueva revista de filología hispánica*, xv (1961), 364
Review of M. Picker, ed.: *The Chanson Albums of Marguerite of Austria* (Berkeley, 1965), *Speculum*, xliii (1968), 373
'King David and his Musicians in Spanish Romanesque Sculpture', *Aspects of Mediaeval and Renaissance Music: a Birthday Offering to Gustave Reese* (New York, 1966), 693
with M. Kanazawa: 'The Musical Manuscript Montecassino N879' [*recte* 871], *AnM*, xix (1966), 123–53
'Villancico', *MGG*

EDITIONS
with H. Hewitt: *Harmonice musices odhecaton A* (Cambridge, Mass., 1942)
with M. Kanazawa: *The Musical Manuscript Montecassino 871* (Oxford, 1978)
with H. Tischler: *Thirteenth Century French Motets* (in preparation)
                                                    PAULA MORGAN

Popma van Oevering, Rynoldus [Reinolt] (*b* Warga, baptized 6 Jan 1692; *d* Leeuwarden, buried 6 April 1782). Netherlands organist and composer. He presumably studied music with his father Georgius (Jurjes) Oevering, schoolmaster and organist at Warga until 1707. He became organist of the Galileeërkerk in Leeuwarden on 16 September 1712, and of the Grote (Jacobijner) Kerk there on 26 February 1713. On 17 March 1727 van Oevering participated in the dedication of the new organ by Christiaan Müller at St Bavo in Haarlem. He remained organist at Leeuwarden until 1741, and was concurrently carilloneur until 1757. Later he was churchwarden of Warga, although he continued to live in Leeuwarden.

Oevering's works include a psalmbook (in *B-Bc*) and a collection of six keyboard suites op.1 (ed. H. Brandts Buys, Amsterdam, 1955). As Prince Johan Willem Frise, who died in 1711, is mentioned in the dedication it would seem that the work was published in about 1710, when van Oevering was only 18 years old. Each suite consists of an overture followed by several dances, in which a preponderance of triple rhythms betrays French influence, especially that of Couperin. The melodic invention is not profound, but the general style is fluent and attractive.

Pop music. A term that from the late 1950s has been applied to the central and most widely circulated kinds of popular music (analogously with 'pop art'), in particular rock and roll, reggae etc; *see* POPULAR MUSIC, §III.

Popov, Gavriil Nikolayevich (*b* Novocherkassk, 12 Sept 1904; *d* Repino, 17 Feb 1972). Russian composer and pianist. He studied at the Leningrad Conservatory with Shcherbachov for composition and Nikolayev for the piano. His symphonies, which follow the epic tradition of Borodin and Glazunov, occupy a central place in his output; the Second and Fourth are particularly characteristic. A monumental dramatic quality distinguishes his numerous choral compositions. There are interesting and varied links in his work with folklore: Russian in the first instance, though the Symphony no.3 draws on Spanish folk music.

WORKS
(selective list)
Orch: 5 syms., incl. no.2 'Rodina' [The homeland], no.4 'Slava otchizne' [Glory to the fatherland]; sym. suites
Chamber: Sextet, 1927; Str Qt, 1951; other pieces

Other works: cantatas, choral pieces, pf music, stage works, over 30 film scores, music for the radio

Principal publishers: Muzgiz, Sovetskiy Kompozitor

BIBLIOGRAPHY
A. Ogolevets: '2 simfoniya G. Popova', SovM (1946), no.5, p.84
D. Kabalevsky: 'O masterstve' [On mastery], SovM (1952), no.3, p.22 [on the Str Qt]
A. Medvedev: 'Master khorovo pis'ma' [A master of choral writing], SovM (1961), no.11, p.27
V. Bogdanov-Berezovsky: 'Bogatstvo tvorcheskoy naturï' [Richness of creative nature], SovM (1964), no.9, p.32
Obituary, Sovetskaya kul'tura (1972), no.4

GALINA GRIGOR'YEVA

Popov, Todor (*b* Drjanovo, 21 Jan 1921). Bulgarian composer. He graduated from the Sofia Music Gymnasium in 1942 and from the Sofia State Academy of Music in 1949. From 1946 to 1949 he was composer to the folksong and dance ensemble of the Ministry of the Interior, and for a short time he was musical director for Sofia Radio's children's broadcasting. Then after a period of five years as music editor for a youth publication, he continued his studies at the Moscow Conservatory (1952–7) under Sposobin, Skryabkov and Rakov. Popov was secretary (1962–5) and general secretary (1965–9) of the Bulgarian Composers' Union and in 1968 he began work as a composer to the army. Although he has written chamber music and some orchestral pieces, Popov has achieved popularity as a song composer. Primarily a melodist, he writes uncomplicated music bearing the stamp of national colour, derived mainly from folk music. His songs are easily understood yet markedly individual.

WORKS
(*selective list*)

Inst: Rojen, orch, 1954; 2 str qts (1956) (1965); Daletshno detstwo [Distant childhood], orch, 1957; Elegie, vc/db, str orch, 1965
Choral: Swetal prasnik [Bright festival], solo vv, chorus, orch, 1959; Pesen sa golemija den [Song for the great day], B, children's chorus, chorus, orch, 1968; 200 songs, folksong arrs., etc
Film scores, c20 solo songs

Principal publishers: Muzgiz, Nauka i Izkustvo (Sofia)

LADA BRASHOVANOVA

Popov, Valery (Sergeyevich) (*b* Moscow, 9 Sept 1937). Soviet bassoonist. After studies at the Moscow Conservatory he joined the USSR State SO in 1962. He won the all-Russian competition in 1963 and the Budapest competition two years later. In 1971 he was appointed to teach at the Moscow Conservatory. The outstanding Russian bassoonist of his generation, his playing is warm and virile. He has become well known in Russia through a number of recordings. He has given the premières of solo works by Alexeyev, Yury Levitin and Korndorf, and Lev Knipper and Sofya Gubaydulina have written concertos for him.

WILLIAM WATERHOUSE

Popovici, Timotei (*b* Tincova, nr. Lugoj, 1 Sept 1870; *d* Lugoj, 11 July 1950). Romanian choirmaster, composer and teacher. He studied in Caransebeş with Antoniu Sequens and Victor Nejedly, and in Iaşi with Gavriil Musicescu. As choirmaster of the music societies of Caransebeş, Braşov and Sibiu, as a prominent teacher in these cities, and as conductor of the Metropolitan Choir of Sibiu, Popovici was one of the leading artists in Transylvania at the beginning of the 20th century. His compositions, suited to the capacities of schoolchildren and amateurs, were designed to be both educational and patriotic. He wrote what was the first music dictionary in Romanian (1905), after the lexicon of Titus Cerne (1889).

WORKS
(*all published in Sibiu unless otherwise indicated*)

SACRED CHORAL
Irmosul Paştilor [Eastern hymn], 3 equal vv, 1896 (Leipzig, 1896); Troparele chemării Duhului Sfînt [Invocations to the Holy Ghost], mixed chorus (1901); Cuvine-se cu adevărat (Byzantine hymn), male vv (1902); Cîntări liturgice: liturghia Sf. Ioan Chrisostom [Songs on the liturgy of St John Chrysostom], children's chorus (1902); Liturghia pentru cor de bărbaţi: imn la centenarul I as Seminarului Andreian [Hymn for the centenary of St Andrew's Seminary] (I. Teculescu), male vv, 1912 (1912); Repertor coral, male vv (1914); Cîntările liturghiei [Liturgical songs], 2–3 equal vv, 1942 (1942); Cîntările liturghiei, mixed chorus, 1943 (1943)

SECULAR CHORAL
(*on popular texts unless otherwise indicated*)
Regele munţilor [The mountain king], S, T, chorus, 1924 (1924); La oglindă [The mirror] (G. Coşbuc), S, chorus, pf; Florile dalbe [White flowers], mixed and male choruses: i (Craiova, 1928), ii (Sibiu, 1945)
Male vv: M-aş mărita [I shall marry], 1895 (Leipzig, 1896 [for mixed chorus]); Foaie verde de trifoi [The green cloverleaf], op.5, 1898 (Brasov, 1898); Ştii, mîndro, cînd ne iubeam [You remember, dear, when we were in love], op.11, 1901 (1902); Cîntece naţionale [National songs] (Sibiu, 1919); Hora lui Iancu [Iancu's dance] (I. Soricu), 1940 (1940)
Equal vv: Fetele casni [The domestic girls] (N. Rădulescu-Niger), in România musicală, suppl. (1899); Cîntece naţionale (1919)

ORCHESTRAL
Potpuriu de cîntece populare; Poem despre Avram Iancu [Poem in honour of Iancu]; marches for military band

WRITINGS
Dicţionar de muzica (Sibiu, 1905)
Cum se face învăţămîntul cîntării în şcoalele primare [Teaching singing in the primary schools] (Sibiu, 1930)

BIBLIOGRAPHY
G. Şoima: Părintele Timotei Popovici la 75 ani [The priest Popovici at the age of 75] (Sibiu, 1945)
Z. Vancea: Creaţia muzicală românească, sec. XIX–XX, i (Bucharest, 1968)
V. Cosma: 'Popovici, Timotei', Muzicieni români: lexicon (Bucharest, 1970) [with complete list of works]

ROMEO GHIRCOIAŞIU

Popp, Lucia (*b* Bratislava, 12 Nov 1939). Austrian soprano of Czechoslovak birth. She studied at the Bratislava Academy of Music and privately. After her début there as the Queen of Night, she made her first appearance at the Vienna Staatsoper in 1963, in the same role. That year she played one of the Three Boys (*Die Zauberflöte*) at the Salzburg Festival. Since her 1966 début at Covent Garden as Oscar, her London roles have included Despina, Sophie, Aennchen and Gilda; in 1967 she was the Queen of Night at the Metropolitan Opera, in 1976 Sophie at the Paris Opéra. Other roles, sung throughout Europe, include Zerlina, both Blonde and Constanze, Marzelline (which she sang under Bernstein in the bicentenary production of *Fidelio* at the Theater an der Wien in 1970), Rosina and Zerbinetta. In lieder recitals she is accompanied by her husband, the conductor György Fischer. Her bright, soaring, highly individual timbre, charming personality and engaging presence are suited equally to the soubrette repertory and to the more intense emotions of roles such as Ilia, Susanna and, on record, Anita in Massenet's *La navarraise*. Other recordings include the Queen of Night and Despina under Klemperer, Blonde under Krips, Elisa in *Il rè pastore* and Sophie under Bernstein, and *Carmina burana* under Frühbeck de Burgos.

ALAN BLYTH

Popper, David (*b* Prague, 16 June 1843; *d* Baden, Vienna, 7 Aug 1913). Austrian cellist and composer.

Son of Anselmus Popper, Kantor of Prague, he studied the cello with Julius Goltermann at the conservatory and developed a remarkable talent. During his first tour in 1863 he met Bülow in Germany; impressed by Popper's virtuosity, Bülow accompanied him in concerts and arranged his appointment as Kammervirtuos to Prince Hohenzollern at the Löwenberg court chapel. In 1868, after many successful European tours, he was appointed principal cellist of the Vienna Hofoper; later he joined the Hellmesberger Quartet. He resigned in 1873 in order to continue touring, accompanied by Liszt's pupil Sophie Menter (daughter of the cellist Joseph Menter) whom he had married the previous year; the marriage was dissolved in 1886.

Popper settled in Budapest in 1896, becoming a professor at the Royal Conservatory (an appointment he held for the rest of his life); for a time he was a member of the Hubay Quartet. In London in 1891 he gave the first performance (with Howell and Delsart) of the *Requiem* op.66, for three cellos and orchestra; it remains one of his best-known compositions. He published over 75 works, the majority for his own instrument; although not profound, they are melodious and idiomatic. He had a polished technique, a full, warm tone and a classical style, and was acknowledged as one of the great virtuosos and teachers of his day; among his pupils were Jäger, Sulzer, Földesy and Lebell.

His brother Wilhelm (1846–1905) was a less remarkable performer but made a career as a distinguished orchestral player in London and New York, and in the Vienna PO (1880–1905). He wrote works for cello which were considered by his contemporaries to have merit.

WORKS

4 concs., vc, orch: d, op.8 (Offenbach, 1871); e, op.24 (Leipzig, 1880); G, op.59 (Hamburg, 1880); b, op.72 (Leipzig, 1900)
Requiem, 3 vc, orch, op.66 (Hamburg, 1892)
Str Qt, c, op.74, ed. B. Schmidt (Leipzig, 1905)
Suite, 2 vc, op.16 (Leipzig, 1876); Andante serioso, vc, op.27 (Leipzig, 1880)
Cadenzas for vc concs.: Haydn, D; Saint-Saëns, op.35; Volkmann, op.33; Schumann, op.129; Molique, op.45: ed. G. von Vikar (Vienna, 1924)
68 character- and salon pieces, mostly vc, pf, incl.: 6 Characterstücke, op.3 (Leipzig, 1880); 3 Stücke, op.11 (Leipzig, 1874); Im Walde, suite, op.50 (Hamburg, 1882); 3 Stücke, op.64 (Hamburg, 1892); Ungarischer Rhapsodie, op.68 (Leipzig, 1894)
Pf pieces, songs, transcriptions

TUTORS

Hohe Schule des Violoncello-Spiels, op.73 (Leipzig, 1901–5)
10 mittelschwere grosse Etüden, op.76 (Leipzig, c1905)

BIBLIOGRAPHY

J. W. von Wasielewski: *Das Violoncell und seine Geschichte* (Leipzig, 1889, 3/1925/R1970; Eng. trans., 1894/R1968), 150
B. Weigl: *Handbuch der Violoncell-Literatur* (Vienna, 1911, 3/1929)
                                          LYNDA LLOYD REES

Popular Concerts. London concert series established in 1858; *see* LONDON, §VI, 4(ii).

Popular music. The term 'popular music' has most commonly been applied to music of, and since, the 'Tin Pan Alley' era, i.e. the 1880s onwards in the USA and the early years of the 20th century in Europe. The social background in which that particular form of music-making flourished had however been developing for many decades previously. In this article the term is used in a somewhat wider sense to embrace the music that, with the growth of industrialization in the 19th century, began to develop distinctive characteristics in line with the tastes and interests of the expanding urban middle

classes. The repertories covered thus embrace certain types of comic opera and dance music as well as music covered by less specific terms such as 'light music' and the equivalent German *Unterhaltungsmusik*. Particularly during the 19th century the repertories covered overlap substantially with the main body of concert, theatre and domestic music. Nor can they always be sharply differentiated from music brought to urban areas from oral folk-music traditions.

The essence of popular music is that it should be readily comprehensible to (and perhaps also performable by) a large proportion of the populace, and that its appreciation presupposes little or no knowledge of musical theory or techniques. The music so defined thus comprises pieces of modest length with a prominent melodic line (often vocal) and a simple and restricted harmonic accompaniment. Pieces are often originally planned for performance in a theatrical or other public context and in consequence of their appeal come to be enjoyed domestically either in practical performance or in recorded reproduction. During the 19th and early 20th centuries the principal form of dissemination was sheet music, but after the advent of mechanical reproduction it gradually came to be the gramophone record or tape. Throughout the period an industry of publishers and composers has increasingly exploited the idioms of popular music for commercial gain, sometimes aiming at particular ethnic, social or age groups.

During the 20th century, in particular, the subject of popular music has become vast and diffuse, and its documentation at a serious level is poor. The general trend has been for traditional European forms to be overtaken by styles and techniques developed in North America, at least until the end of the 1960s; the resulting mixture has reached all parts of the world, being adopted with little change in countries with strong Western orientations (e.g. Australia and Japan) and affecting traditional idioms in India (particularly in film music), Africa (*see* HIGHLIFE; CONGOLESE MUSIC; KWELA) and most other countries with urban communities.

In this article, Europe and North America are considered separately for the period up to World War II and together thereafter, since developments in American popular music had by then come to dominate international trends. In the European section it is impracticable to treat the music and developments of each different country and language in detail; developments in Britain are therefore frequently given detailed consideration in §I as being broadly indicative of trends elsewhere in Europe. Certain local aspects of popular music in individual European countries, as well as the local popular traditions of countries outside Europe and North America, are discussed in the articles on those countries; for Central and South American traditions *see* LATIN AMERICA, §IV.

I. Europe to World War II. II. North America to 1940. III. Since 1940.

I. Europe to World War II

1. The Industrial Revolution. 2. 19th-century dance hall and pleasure garden. 3. 19th-century operetta and music hall. 4. Popular music versus serious. 5. American influences. 6. Between the world wars. 7. 20th-century popular song.

1. THE INDUSTRIAL REVOLUTION. The basic elements of popular music have existed for centuries. On the one hand, for example, there were the tunes played by itiner-

1. Home music-making (c1830): engraving by J. Bernstrom after A. B. Frost

ant musicians accompanying dancing on village greens or communal singing in village inns. On the other, there were songs that were composed for stage or concert performances and gained sufficient popularity to be passed from one person to another or published in printed form. But the market for printed music was severely limited, and social class barriers as well as the inadequacies of communications restricted the extent of international and even national currency of a piece of music. It was with the increasing industrialization of the 19th century and the reduction of the gap between social classes that this situation changed drastically. Improvements in transport by road, rail and sea opened up communications; there were advances in instrument design and printing; and education became available to an ever greater proportion of civilized populations.

In the expanding urban areas the public increasingly sought out musical entertainment in parks, pleasure gardens and music halls, and the latest popular tunes would be ground out in the streets on hurdy-gurdies and barrel organs. Music became a common link and a support of morale for a culturally limited industrial population. Concerts and theatres flourished; instrumental virtuosos, singers and composers were able to enlarge their sphere of activity, and some became popular idols. Conservatories of music were set up, and methods of learning were developed for the working classes, such as the Tonic Sol-fa system invented by John Hullah in England in 1840. Women's guilds and men's clubs practised community singing, and mills and factories formed brass bands for their employees.

Choral music and especially oratorios – encouraged for their moral value – flourished. Popular oratorios such as Handel's *Messiah* and Mendelssohn's *Elijah* (1846) were much performed and attended by large audiences. Amateur choral societies abounded. Particularly during the third quarter of the century many new hymn tunes and hymnals appeared, among them some still in use, such as *Hymns Ancient and Modern* (1861). Quite apart from their use in churches, such hymnals were present in homes for family singing around the piano or harmonium. The introduction of the upright piano around 1830 provided a particular stimulus for home music-making. In days when the mechanical reproduction of music in the home was virtually limited to the severely restricted cylinder music box, evenings spent around the piano singing hymns and ballads and playing on various instruments were a standard part of middle-class family life. The ability to sing and to play the piano or some other instrument was an important social attribute in Victorian Britain.

All of this helped create an active music-publishing industry; before the invention of player pianos, gramophone records and tapes, the printed page was the only means of making compositions available to the general public. Editions of Beethoven's piano sonatas, Chopin's waltzes and Mendelssohn's Songs without Words formed the basis of many home music collections: from about 1830 J. A. Novello in London was one of the first to realize the possibilities of cheap editions of the popular classics, and throughout the 19th century such editions were to be found in most publishers' catalogues. Publishers attracted regular buyers with series of standard format editions, for example Boosey's Royal Edition (of popular operas) or Novello's Original Octavo Edition of Operas and Oratorios. They also issued compendium albums of instrumental pieces and songs, specifically for domestic consumption, and there were further publications issued at regular intervals, such as Boosey's *Musical Cabinet* (1861–81) and Chappell's *Musical*

Magazine (founded 1861), which rang the changes between 'Nine Pianoforte Pieces by Brinley Richards', 'Twelve Songs by Bishop and Balfe', piano reductions of popular operas, etc. In addition popular musical journals such as *Pitman's Musical Monthly* (1883–93) and the *Strand Musical Magazine* (1895–9) mixed news and illustrated features on performers and composers with supplements of simple music for the home.

More general magazines also often had musical supplements; it was for the monthly issues of one such that Tchaikovsky composed his suite *The Seasons* (1875–6). This, and pieces such as Rubinstein's Melody in F (1853), typify the piano music played in the home. Besides the incidental output of composers of more lasting renown, there were also the salon pieces of such as Gustav Lange (1830–69) or the piano fantasias of Sydney Smith (1839–89), both of whom gained a certain vogue in their day as specialists in catering for the demand for music in the home. Alongside the purely instrumental pieces were the lieder of Adolf Jensen and French *mélodies* such as Massenet's *Ouvre tes yeux bleus* and Hahn's *Si mes vers avaient des ailes*. Above all, Italy produced such composers as Ciro Pinsuti, Luigi Denza and F. Paolo Tosti, whose works seldom rose above the level of the drawing-room ballad but who, in songs such as Tosti's *Non m'ama più*, *Vorrei morire*, *Goodbye* and *La serenata*, demonstrated a lightness of touch and a flow of warm, Italian melody that gave them great international currency.

The fact that Pinsuti, Denza and Tosti each at various times settled in England is perhaps an indication of the extent to which the sentimental ballad was prized above all in Victorian Britain (*see* BALLAD, §7). From 1867 Boosey & Co., followed by other London publishers, sponsored regular ballad concerts at which their latest products were introduced to the public by leading singers. This was the age of the royalty ballad, the royalty going not to the composer (who merely received a flat payment) but to the singer who launched the song. The texts were sentimental verses about love, gardens and birds, the music simple strophic settings marked by easy melody, stereotyped accompaniments and maudlin harmonic progressions. The genre was typified by Balfe's *Come into the garden, Maud* (1858), Sullivan's *The Lost Chord* (1877) and *Love's Old Sweet Song* (1882) by J. L. Molloy (1837–1909). Publishers required that such songs should contain no musical flights beyond the powers of the purchasing amateurs at whom they were aimed, and able composers such as Sullivan readily acknowledged them as mere potboilers which helped composers to earn a living.

Besides piano pieces and songs, there was a steady output of partsongs and pieces for the various instrumental combinations that were found in the home. Furthermore, the pieces specifically intended for the home were only a small part of the music that actually found its way there; most came from theatre, café or pleasure garden, to be turned into all manner of arrangements for domestic use. Czibulka's *Liebestraum nach dem Balle* (1889) was not unusual in being published in arrangements for some 30 different combinations, among them piano solo (standard and simplified), piano duet, violin and piano, flute and piano, cornet solo, string quartet, two mandolins with mandola and guitar, zither, and military band. With richly illustrated title-pages, publishers sought to attract popular fancy for their latest song or dance publications much as record companies now do with pictorial covers. Topicality of title or evidence of royal patronage was important in guiding popular taste. Such pieces were often of little intrinsic merit; but it was among the music that started life in the dance hall, music hall, pleasure garden or theatre that the most vital part of the popular music of the 19th century was to be found.

2. 19TH-CENTURY DANCE HALL AND PLEASURE GARDEN. Before the 19th century dancing had been clearly divided up between social classes: on the one hand there was country dancing or dancing at inns, with local musicians providing a simple accompaniment; on the other, there was dancing at court and in the homes of the aristocracy, with music provided by resident orchestras (*see* DANCE, §V, 2). During the early years of the 19th century large dance halls such as the Sperl (1807) and the Apollo (1808) opened in Vienna. There the public was able to enjoy dancing combined with drinking as an evening's entertainment. The dances of the time included the galop and the contredanse (later the 'quadrille de contredanses' or quadrille), but the mainstay soon came to be the waltz. Gradually developing into a more refined form, it became known throughout Europe. In the wake of the international interest in dancing that it encouraged, other dances enjoyed periods of fashion and popularity. Around 1840, for example, the polka spread across Europe, was danced in every ballroom, and gave its name to everything from clothes and hats to streets and inns.

The music for the fashionable Viennese balls of the 18th century had often been provided by composers of the stature of Haydn, Mozart and Beethoven. But as the growth of public dancing increased, a need arose for specialist musicians, and the music provided for dancing proved so popular that it came to be performed not only for its functional purpose but also as concert music. From the mid-1820s men such as Joseph Lanner and the elder Johann Strauss found themselves in great demand, playing at balls during Carnival, at cafés and inns, and during the summer at popular outdoor concerts. Much the same was happening elsewhere. In Paris, Philippe Musard began his series of promenade concerts in the rue St Honoré in 1833; Louis Jullien, after starting indoor concerts of dance music in the Jardin Turc, went to London and promoted a series of promenade concerts at Covent Garden Theatre from 1840. Such concerts of popular music, built around the dances of the time, were part of the attraction of the pleasure gardens that opened towards the mid-19th century, for example the Vauxhall at Pavlovsk near St Petersburg in 1838 and the Tivoli in Copenhagen in 1843, which took their names from existing pleasure gardens in London and Rome respectively.

Jullien's programmes give an idea of the music played at these promenade concerts. A popular overture by Rossini or Weber would be followed by the latest waltzes or quadrilles, vocal and instrumental solos, perhaps a movement from a symphony, and finally a potpourri of classical and popular themes decked out with fantastic effects. Jullien's descriptive piece *The Destruction of Pompeii*, for example, ended with 'explosion of the crater, falling temples and total destruction of the city'. Personal magnetism, which Jullien had to an exceptional degree, was important to the success of all the popular conductor–composers. For most of the 19th century these performers prospered in capital cities and spas, their dance compositions enjoying a double life in dance halls and pleasure-garden concerts before finding their way into the home as printed editions. Among the most successful were the Strausses in Vienna, Labitzky in Carlsbad, Gungl in Berlin and Waldteufel in Paris. Gungl's *Amoretten-Tänze* (1860), the younger Johann Strauss's *An der schönen blauen Donau* (1867) and Waldteufel's *Les patineurs* (1883) enjoyed particular acclaim and enabled their composers to travel widely conducting concerts of their music. Gungl was the first of them to visit the USA (1849), followed by Jullien (1853), the younger Johann Strauss (1872) and others.

Many of these musicians also had experience as military bandmasters; the 19th century was a period in which military bands particularly prospered. Advances

2. Programme for one of Jullien's concerts at the Theatre Royal, Covent Garden (31 January 1846), including pieces by Jullien

in instrument design greatly widened the scope for wind ensembles, and military training academies were set up on the model of the Royal Military School of Music at Kneller Hall, near London (1857). Military bands not only maintained the morale of regiments but also entertained the general public, often playing in the intervals of concerts given by spa orchestras or playing along with them to give extra weight to pieces such as Jullien's *British Army Quadrilles* (1846). In addition, military bands were to be found playing from bandstands in large parks or on piers at the increasingly popular seaside resorts. Their programmes were similar to those of the spa string orchestras, but with greater emphasis on more ebullient pieces such as overtures and marches.

Similar music was heard at the circus and the fairground. After the introduction of steam power in the 1860s, the design of fairground organs was perfected around 1870 by such manufacturers as the Italian Gavioli (working in Paris). The fairground organ sought to reproduce the sound of a full band, so that the more boisterous items were equally the basis of its repertory. Above all the military band, the circus band and the fairground organ needed a supply of stirring marches. The last two decades of the 19th century in particular produced many marches that have remained popular, among them Louis Ganne's *Marche lorraine*, J. F. Wagner's *Unter dem Doppeladler*, Carl Teike's *Alte Kameraden* and Julius Fučík's *Einzug der Gladiatoren* (this last especially popular with circus bands).

3. 19TH-CENTURY OPERETTA AND MUSIC HALL. Operatic music, although not strictly 'popular' as the term is here defined, often became widely popular during the 19th century. Singers such as Jenny Lind and Adelina Patti were popular figures, fêted wherever they appeared and with their portraits on the title-pages of sheet music editions. Even those who never visited an opera house might well have been familiar with the tunes of operas such as *Il barbiere di Siviglia* (1816), *Der Freischütz* (1821), *La sonnambula* (1831) or *The Bohemian Girl* (1843). The most celebrated operatic arias were sung at popular concerts; selections of the main numbers were churned out by barrel organs and published for all manner of combinations of instruments; and the main tunes were also arranged as waltzes and quadrilles for dancing. Many opera overtures went into the repertory of every spa orchestra or military band, as was notably the case with French operas such as Auber's *Masaniello* (1828), Hérold's *Zampa* (1831), Adam's *Si j'étais roi* (1852) and Thomas' *Mignon* (1866). Furthermore, English opera in particular produced ballad-like songs designed to be popular in the drawing-room: 'Home, sweet home' from Bishop's *Clari, the Maid of Milan* (1823), 'When other lips' and 'I dreamt that I dwelt in marble halls' from *The Bohemian Girl* have had a lengthy existence quite separate from the operas that served to launch them.

In due course, as Wagner and Verdi developed a more integrated and more intellectually demanding form, operatic music began to lose this accessibility to the general public. By then, however, OPERETTA had developed as an essentially popular form of theatrical entertainment and fulfilled much the same functions for the general public as opera had previously managed to do. Beginning with the one-act sketches which Offenbach produced in Paris during the 1850s, operetta

3. Scene at the Krollgarten, Berlin: engraving from the Leipzig 'Illustrirte Zeitung' (1875)

soon grew to encompass full-length works of international renown such as Offenbach's *La belle Hélène* (1864), Lecocq's *La fille de Madame Angot* (1872), the younger Johann Strauss's *Die Fledermaus* (1874) and Sullivan's *The Mikado* (1885). Operetta overtures such as Suppé's to *Leichte Kavallerie* (1866) and *Die schöne Galathé* (1865) took their place in the standard orchestral and band repertory, and operetta scores proved the perfect source of material for the dance floor. The younger Johann Strauss's *Rosen aus dem Süden* on themes from *Das Spitzentuch der Königin* (1880) is perhaps the best-known waltz arranged on themes from an operetta.

Further down the social scale came the songs sung in music halls. As urban populations expanded in the major cities of Europe, the demand increased for places of undemanding communal entertainment, mixing drinking with singing. By the 1840s London was acquiring its first recognizable music halls, large rooms set aside by publicans for their clientèle to drink at tables while entertainers performed on a platform (*see* MUSIC HALL). In Paris much the same was happening as *cafés chantants* came into vogue. The success of these places caused their proprietors to expand the entertainment provided, with perhaps a small orchestra rather than a piano and with a wider range of performers. The entertainment even came to embrace ballet and opera; music from Gounod's *Faust* was first heard in London in selections sung at the Canterbury Music Hall. But the songs of a comic, topical and often suggestive nature became the most important part of the entertainment. They had no serious musical aspirations, and relied for their success on the crude appeal of their topics and their simple, vulgar musical phrases which could readily be picked up and sung by the audience.

The success of individual songs depended a great deal on the personality and projection of the performers, who were able to build up personal reputations and widen their sphere of activity. Furthermore, it was to the performer rather than to the composer, author or publisher that a song essentially belonged. As with royalty ballads, the performer bought a song from a composer; but whereas the name of a composer of a royalty ballad at least was shown prominently on the sheet music or concert programme, it was the portrait of the performer that took precedence on the title-page of a music-hall song. Thus the name of George Leybourne has remained celebrated in the annals of music hall along with songs that he made famous, such as *Champagne Charlie* (1866) and *The Flying Trapeze* (1867), while that of Alfred Lee, who composed these and other successful songs of the time, has been forgotten. It was above all these features of music-hall song – the basic simplicity of the material, the immediacy of impact and the importance of performer rather than composer – that were to become increasingly typical of popular music as the social class to which they appealed gained status.

4. POPULAR MUSIC VERSUS SERIOUS. Developments during the 19th century increasingly took serious music out of the reach of the general public. Whereas a movement from a Beethoven symphony might have been included in a popular orchestral concert programme, the same was unlikely with a Bruckner movement; and whereas arias or orchestral selections from Rossini's operas became widely familiar, dance bands were unlikely to

4. Sheet-music cover of 'Champagne Charlie', first published in 1867

have played quadrilles on themes from the operas of Wagner. In any case, by then a plethora of music was being produced that was expressly tailored to meet the requirements of a wide public. The huge demand brought forward people of modest musical accomplishment who considered themselves equal to the requirements of producing a waltz or ballad, and if their technical ability was limited there were professional musicians willing to attend to such aspects as harmonizing, orchestrating and editing a piece for publication.

Thus there was a growing dichotomy between serious music and popular; and inevitably the greater rewards that might attend relatively less effort in the popular field caused bitterness and scorn among musicians who set their sights beyond current popular taste. Furthermore this dichotomy was accentuated by the development of musical criticism. Serious critics could for the most part ignore the apparently ephemeral music produced for the general public. But the appearance of musical dictionaries, in particular, made some semblance of critical comment necessary. Factors such as the disposition, training and social standing of commentators made them out of sympathy with popular styles of music, and where sheer bulk of output made assessment of quality difficult, the result was generally an ill-disguised scorn for the methods of popular music. The article on Offenbach in *Grove 1* (1878–89) demonstrates the open contempt for a composer who sought to give the public what they wanted. The tendency of intellectual musicians to condemn all that was readily approachable inevitably increased the gulf between

popular music and serious.

It was particularly towards the turn of the century that popular music showed signs of the greater commercialization that was to dominate it in the 20th century. There was, for example, a tendency to spin out melodies and make greater use of a limited amount of material: the classic 19th-century Viennese waltzes usually had five waltz sections, each containing two contrasted melodies, the whole preceded by an elaborate introduction and concluded by a coda; by the 1890s, however, the melodies had become broader, the waltz sections correspondingly of greater length and their number reduced to three. From Paris around the turn of the century came the 'valse lente', exemplified by Alfred Margis' *Valse bleue* (1900) and F. D. Marchetti's 'valse tzigane', *Fascination* (1904), slow waltzes in which the main theme is given greater prominence and the amount of original material correspondingly reduced.

Another important development was the expansion of music hall during the last decade of the 19th century. In Paris the Moulin Rouge (1889), Casino de Paris (1891) and other large music halls were opened. In Britain the banning of drink from the body of the hall led to the conversion of music hall into variety, and chains of variety theatres (e.g. the Hippodrome, Empire and Palace theatres) were established, with music-hall stars providing what increasingly became family entertainment. Music hall was moving nearer to the theatre, and operetta was increasingly acquiring some of the characteristics of music-hall entertainment. In Paris the stars of the *café-concert* were found in the new 'vaudeville operettas', while in London the comic operas of Gilbert and Sullivan were losing popularity in favour of the 'musical play' and MUSICAL COMEDY.

In the musical comedies of the Gaiety Theatre in London, such as *The Shop Girl* (1894) and *The Circus Girl* (1896), a credible story and real singing ability mattered less than a parade of attractive girls in fashionable dress and a quota of familiar comic characters. 'Hit' numbers were provided to meet the requirements of performers and for the immediate gratification of the public rather than as an integral part of a balanced and well-developed score. Indeed the music was generally the work of two men – one responsible for the technically more ambitious ensembles, the other for the leading performers' hit numbers; and interpolations of other songs were freely allowed. Even the dramatically and musically more integrated musical plays of Daly's Theatre, exemplified by Sidney Jones's *The Geisha* (1896), had insert numbers. The trend was also discernible in Berlin, where Paul Lincke, fresh from his experience in Berlin variety theatres and at the Folies-Bergère in Paris, launched the spectacular Berlin revue-operetta with *Frau Luna* (1899). Meanwhile the tendency for music hall to move to more pretentious surroundings had encouraged the development of a more intimate form of night-time entertainment. In Paris during the 1890s the bohemian population gathered at Montmartre cabarets to enjoy the satirical entertainments featuring the *diseuse* Yvette Guilbert, while in Berlin around 1900 Schoenberg and Oscar Straus were composing songs for the newly opened Überbrettl (*see* CABARET).

These were potentially great years for music publishers, who had a ready market for published editions of the currently popular songs. Many enjoyed particular prosperity, for example Francis, Day & Hunter (established 1877) in London, while others, such as Salabert in Paris (1898) and Apollo in Berlin (c1899), were newly set up and soon became prominent in popular music publishing. However, in Britain in 1900 the attractions of music publishing prompted pirate operators to exploit the lax British copyright laws by pirating editions of currently successful numbers. Sheet music of only two or three pages could readily be photographed and lithograph copies cheaply and quickly run off for sale at prices undercutting that of the copyright edition. Publishers trimmed their profit margins to the minimum with the introduction of the 'sixpenny edition', but without recourse to legal redress they were largely powerless against the pirate operators. The Musical Copyright Association, formed to fight the pirates, was reduced to raiding the stalls of pirate operators, seizing their copies and seeking out their printing presses. This at least aroused publicity for the cause of composers and publishers, leading to the eventual outlawing of the pirates through the copyright laws of 1906 and 1911. At around the same time efforts were being made to obtain fees not only for the sale of printed copies but also for the performance of a piece of music. Britain was again behind some continental countries; since 1880 a licence had been required for the performance of French compositions in Britain while British compositions could be performed freely without fee (for details see COPYRIGHT COLLECTING SOCIETIES). By the setting up of the Performing Right Society in 1914 this situation, too, was remedied.

A performing right was made even more relevant by the spread of recording, which had a profound effect on the development of popular music. In the first place, the medium disseminated and perpetuated individual interpretations of artists in the numbers associated with them. Music-hall performers such as Marie Lloyd and Eugene Stratton, and the songs they sang, thus achieved a place in popular awareness that had never been achieved by artists of an earlier generation. Furthermore the limitations of early gramophone records put a premium on short, two- or three-minute pieces that made an immediate impact on the listener. Not only music-hall artists but also singers of greater pretensions turned to the lighter repertory for material to record. Italian singers turned to the Neapolitan popular song, Viennese to the 'Heurige' song. It is no coincidence that songs from the early years of the century have remained in popular awareness as earlier ones generally have not, for example *Torna a Surriento* (1902) by the brothers Ernesto and G. B. De Curtis, or *Wien, du Stadt meiner Träume* (1913) by Rudolf Sieczynski (1879–1952). Such songs have remained inseparably linked with the gramophone through successive generations of singers. Much the same was achieved in Britain with Edwardian ballads such as *Because* (1902) by Guy d'Hardelot or *Somewhere a voice is calling* (1911) by Arthur F. Tate (1880–1950). These last two also demonstrate a feature of 20th-century popular music that was to become ever more important as American commercial methods were followed, namely the increasing popular awareness of a song which linked an easily memorable musical phrase to a key verbal one.

5. AMERICAN INFLUENCES. During the 19th century many European popular musicians had visited the USA as an extension of their international travels. The traffic was by no means one way; in 1878, for instance, Patrick

Gilmore took the band of the 22nd Regiment of New York to Europe and attracted high praise for his performances. However, this was still essentially a European style of music-making. Of more significance for the development of popular music in Europe were the essentially American forms of entertainment that became popular there. In 1843 Dan Emmett's Virginia Minstrels visited Britain, and the minstrel show was to remain for several decades a standard part of British popular music (see MINSTRELSY, AMERICAN). During the 1880s the barn dance arrived in Britain from America, and in the 1890s the whole of Europe succumbed to the strains of Henry J. Sayers's *Ta-ra-ra-boom-der-é* (1891) and Charles K. Harris's *After the Ball* (1892), which thus heralded the arrival of American popular song.

During the 1890s, too, the marches of Sousa became known in Europe, and the visit of his band to the Paris Exposition of 1900 and to Britain in 1901 increased public receptiveness to the lively rhythms of the cakewalk and the two-step march. These had already appeared in Europe through such pieces as Sousa's *Washington Post* (1889) and Kerry Mills's *At a Georgia Camp Meeting* (1897) and *Whistling Rufus* (1899). European composers were not slow to imitate the styles. A cakewalk dance by Leslie Stuart was published in London in 1897, and the lilting rhythms of Stuart's 'coon' songs such as *Little Dolly Daydream* (1897) and *Lily of Laguna* (1898) not only achieved great popularity on both sides of the Atlantic but helped pave the way for the syncopated rhythms that were soon to arrive from America in considerable force. In the early years of the century the American negro musical comedy *In Dahomey*, with music by Will Marion Cook (1869–

5. *Sheet-music cover of 'Little Dolly Daydream', first published in 1897 by Francis, Day & Hunter (London) and T. B. Harms (New York)*

1944), was produced in London (1903), and the cake-walk became a standard feature of both British musical comedy and European operettas, such as Lehár's *Die lustige Witwe* (1905).

The success of this and other operettas of the Viennese 'silver age', such as Leo Fall's *Die Dollarprinzessin* (1907) and Oscar Straus's *Ein Walzertraum* (1907), helped, along with British musical comedies, to retain for a time the dominance of European-style stage works even in the American theatre. But in Britain, American songs were becoming ever more popular, many of them introduced into musical comedies, as were Jean Schwartz's *Bedelia* (1903) in *The Orchid* and John H. Flynn's *Yip-i-addy-i-ay* (1908) in *Our Miss Gibbs* (both with scores largely by Caryll and Monckton). Most, however, made their appearance in Britain through the variety theatres, often adapted for British consumption. Thus Harry Von Tilzer's *Down where the Wurzburger flows* (1902) became *Riding on top of the car*, a tribute to the British tramcar, while his *Under the Anheuser Bush* (1903) became virtually the signature tune of British music hall as *Down at the old Bull and Bush*.

Dance styles were also beginning to show American influence. During the 1870s the 'boston', a variant of the waltz, had reached Europe from North America without making any great impact at the time (*see* BOSTON (ii)). However, the success of the slower form of waltz, the 'valse lente', led to a succession of pieces in similar style to which was danced the 'valse boston'. To the accompaniment of British compositions such as Archibald Joyce's *Dreaming* (1911) and Sydney Baynes's *Destiny* (1912), the 'valse boston' conquered Europe in the years immediately before World War I and established the slower waltz tempo that still prevails. At about the same time the tango, having reached Paris from South America, was beginning to spread through Europe. The publication of A. G. Villoldo's *El Choclo* (Paris, 1911) heralded the arrival of the genuine Argentine tango, and by 1912 'tango teas' – afternoon tea gatherings at which the dance was featured – were becoming fashionable in London. The dance was featured not only on the dance floor, but also in many stage shows such as the London revue *Hullo Tango* (1913).

In the marketing of popular music, too, American influences were making their mark. During the 19th century a British music-hall song had been the property of the performer rather than the composer or publisher, and it had been the performer who dictated when a piece should be published and who received a royalty on copies sold. Now British publishers switched to the American system of 'free' songs – 'free' in the sense that they could be sung by anyone. They thus had to follow Tin Pan Alley in setting up publicity departments with a staff of 'song-pluggers' whose job it was to press a song on performers and producers. By ensuring that a song was accepted for a London revue or musical comedy, for the provincial pantomimes or for seaside concert parties, the song-plugger could launch it on the road to popularity.

The real breakthrough for American popular music in Europe came with ragtime. The classical kind, as exemplified by the compositions of Scott Joplin, was not to make its greatest impact until some 70 years after it was written; but in the years immediately preceding World War I the commercial variety immediately made itself felt in such songs as Irving Berlin's *Alexander's Ragtime Band* (1911) and Lewis F. Muir's *Waiting for the Robert E. Lee* (1912). The latter was introduced to Britain by the American Ragtime Octette (curiously enough on the same bill as the première of Leoncavallo's *I zingari*), and they were followed by a succession of ragtime artists in revues and variety shows. This time no concession to British taste was needed, and the conquest of European popular music by American may be dated from these years. With the advent of ragtime revues such as *Hullo, Rag-time!* (1912), traditional musical comedy and music hall both began to lose favour, while ragtime dances such as the 'bunny hug', 'turkey trot' and 'grizzly bear' paved the way for the foxtrot, which took its place around Europe alongside the 'valse boston', the tango and the remnants of 19th-century forms as the foundation of a new era in social dance (*see* DANCE, §VII, 3).

6. BETWEEN THE WORLD WARS. World War I demonstrated wartime's traditional power to inspire successful pieces of popular music, but this time the European strains of Ivor Novello's *Keep the home fires burning* (1914) were joined by the American exuberance of George M. Cohan's *Over There!* (1917). Popular music was much affected by the changes brought about by the war, in particular the disappearance of the Austro-Hungarian Empire, and with it the society that had nurtured the Viennese waltz, the basis of much 19th-century popular music. America, by contrast, had emerged largely unaffected, and the hold that ragtime and the foxtrot had established on popular musical styles was consolidated. From now on, all major innovations in popular music were to come from America.

In the later stages of the war, American military bands had been amazing the allied troops with displays of jazz, and in 1918 the band of James Reese Europe had performed in Paris with what was, outside America, a revolutionary combination of instruments: cornet, trombone, clarinet, two violins, banjos, piano and percussion. In 1919 the Original Dixieland Jazz Band created a similar sensation in Britain with its revolutionary sounds and instrumental combinations. Pure jazz could never become an essentially popular form in the sense of being aimed at the masses; but Paul Whiteman was able to achieve the popular description of 'king of jazz'. In 1923 his band toured Europe, and the dance-band sound that made use of syncopated rhythms and jazz instrumentation flourished between the wars and provided a popular image of jazz. In 19th-century Britain dancing had not spread through society to the extent that it had in central Europe, but after World War I every major town in Britain acquired its 'palais de danse', where the public could enjoy the foxtrot and waltz as well as later fashions such as the charleston, 'black bottom' and quickstep. Hotels, too, sponsored regular dances and acquired resident bands with the popular new instrumental combinations, including saxophones, trombone, banjo and piano. Outstanding among them were those of London's Savoy Hotel during the 1920s (the Savoy Havana Band and the Savoy Orpheans).

In the theatre, too, American works became increasingly popular, whether in the older operetta style of Romberg and Friml or the newer American song-and-dance musical comedy style. The production of Jerome Kern's *Oh Boy!* in London in 1919 was followed by a steady flow of works by Kern, Gershwin, Rodgers and others. The major American musical comedies were seen in London shortly after New York, and indeed London was at times even more receptive than New York. Youmans's *No, No, Nanette!* was actually seen in London before New York, and Kern, Gershwin, Rodgers and Cole Porter all wrote scores specially for London. Later the London productions of many American shows were recorded while the Depression was preventing recordings in America.

Whereas in the 19th century popular music styles had tended to move westwards, during the 20th the direction was reversed. The crossing of the Atlantic was easily accomplished, but the language barrier made the further crossing to the Continent more difficult. Traditional forms showed greater resilience, and perhaps no American musical comedy other than *No, No, Nanette!* made a really big impact on the Continent until after World War II. The new dance styles and 'jazz' instrumentation, however, were readily accepted. Not only were American artists such as Whiteman welcomed, but so were British bands such as those of Jack Hylton and Ray Noble. Similar dance bands sprang up all over the Continent under band-leaders such as Ray Ventura in France and Dájos Béla in Berlin, though the rhythmic flexibility of American bands was not so readily acquired. The appeal of the new dance styles on the Continent is apparent in European popular song between the wars, while operetta scores such as Paul Abraham's *Viktoria und ihr Husar* (1930) and Henri Christiné's *Dédé* (1931) were largely a succession of pieces in the dance rhythms and instrumentation of the time. Above all, Weill's *Die Dreigroschenoper* (1929), designed to exploit popular music to political and satirical effect, survives as a remarkable fusion of contemporary styles such as the blues ('Moritat'), foxtrot ('Kanonen-Song'), boston ('Liebeslied'), tango ('Zuhälter-Ballade'), shimmy ('Ballade vom angenehmen Leben') and cabaret song ('Barbara-Song').

However, the real impact between the wars was made by the development of mechanical forms. Home entertainment no longer meant evenings around the piano. At the turn of a switch the sound of the popular dance bands could be enjoyed either on radio or on the gramophone. By 1926 electrical recording had brought greater fidelity into gramophone reproduction, and the use of the microphone resulted in new singing styles such as crooning and close harmony. The gramophone record was increasingly replacing printed sheet music as the means by which popular music was disseminated. From 1929 there was also the new medium of the talking picture, providing a form of entertainment that successfully competed with the live theatre for the attention of public, performers and composers alike. The silent cinema had given employment to musicians who provided piano or orchestral accompaniments to films, and had created a great demand for descriptive pieces such as Ketèlbey's *In a Monastery Garden* (1915). But the advent of the talking picture provided much greater challenges. Classically trained musicians such as Erich Wolfgang Korngold, expelled from their homeland by the rise of Hitler, were able to find employment in Hollywood providing background scores for dramatic films. In Europe, as in America, popular variety performers such as Maurice Chevalier, Marlene Dietrich and Gracie Fields found a new medium in the film musical, which thus provided yet

6. 'No, No, Nanette!' (first produced in London in 1925): with Jimmy (Joseph Coyne) and Billy (George Grossmith) singing 'I want to be happy'

another field for the purveyors of popular song.

7. 20TH-CENTURY POPULAR SONG. The 19th-century popular musical success had often been a purely instrumental composition – a waltz, march or overture for instance. Although the 20th century also produced successful instrumental pieces – notably syncopated piano novelty pieces such as Billy Mayerl's *Marigold* (1927) – the main 20th-century successes were vocal. In turning Chopin's *Fantaisie-impromptu* into *I'm always chasing rainbows* (1918) Tin Pan Alley had shown the commercial value of adding a verbal phrase to a musical one; in turning an Andantino in Db (1892) by Edwin H. Lemare (1865–1934) into *Moonlight and Roses* (1925) it had shown how the process could give a tune an instant recognizability that would otherwise be completely lacking. For commercial success a lyric thus became essential. Even the dance-band numbers were vocal pieces, so that all bands had a vocalist to sing a verse and a chorus or two of a number the band was playing.

European publishers learnt their techniques from America, and in 1925 the British publisher Lawrence Wright (established 1911) followed the American example and refurbished Beethoven's Minuet in G as *Mignonette*. Wright was the most progressive British publisher of the 1920s, and around his premises in Denmark Street there grew up London's equivalent of New York's Tin Pan Alley. In 1926 he founded the magazine *Melody Maker*, in which current popular music topics could be aired, and a regular 'hit parade' of best-selling numbers could be published. Under the name of Horatio Nicholls, Wright was himself the most

successful British popular song composer of the 1920s, and his foxtrot ballad *Shepherd of the Hills* (1927) typifies the light lyrical songs that British songwriters produced during the decade. The song was marketed as 'the 3000 miles a second New York–London hit', since Wright had composed it on board the *Majestic* and transmitted it from New York by telephone for performance the same night by Jack Hylton's orchestra. On another occasion, to publicize the song-foxtrot *Me and Jane in a Plane* (1927, music by 'Jos. Geo. Gilbert'), Wright hired an aeroplane to carry Hylton and his orchestra low over Blackpool playing the piece and dropping printed copies on to the beach. In the years immediately after World War I the success of a popular song depended a good deal on its reception by holiday-makers, who customarily took home from the seaside a copy of the latest hit. At the chief resorts rival publishers set up chains of demonstration stores along the sea front, where holiday-makers could join in the choruses of the latest releases, reading the words from large songsheets let down in front of them.

British composers never achieved the rhythmic freedom of their American counterparts, and their greatest successes were often with songs that met the continuing need for more traditional styles. Two big international successes of the 1930s were *Lady of Spain* (1931) and the old-time comedy chorus *Let's all sing like the birdies sing* (1932), both by Tolchard Evans (1901–78). Achieving worldwide success for their European warmth of melody were the tango and foxtrot ballads of the Austrian refugee Will Grosz (alias Hugh Williams), notably *Isle of Capri* (1934), *Red Sails in the Sunset* (1935) and *Harbour Lights* (1937). In another category were the slow, romantic ballads of Ray Noble, whose *Goodnight, Sweetheart* (1931), *Love is the sweetest thing* (1933) and *The very thought of you* (1934) captured some of the subtlety of American songwriting; being also a band-leader and arranger, Noble was able to settle successfully in the USA. Among theatre songs that managed to rank with the American output were *Limehouse Blues* (1922, lyrics by Douglas Wilmer) by Philip Braham (1881–1934) and *These Foolish Things* (1935, lyrics by Eric Maschwitz) by Jack Strachey (1894–1972). But only in Noël Coward did Britain have a composer–lyricist consistently able to match the sophistication of leading American songs in such numbers as *Parisian Pierrot* (1923) and *A Room with a View* (1928).

Continental songs that achieved the widest international success were often overtly European numbers that continued to provide relief from American styles. Often they were in traditional dance rhythms, such as the *paso doble* of José Padilla's *Valencia* (1925), the tango *Jalousie* (1926) by Jacob Gade or the Viennese waltz *Zwei Herzen im Dreivierteltakt* (1930) by Robert Stolz. Generally, however, the elements that went to make up a successful song – the linking of musical and verbal phrase, the vocal projection of a particular singer, the arrangement of a particular band, the promotion received, or even the mood of a country – were such that a 20th-century song rarely achieved a truly universal currency. Occasionally a song found an ideal interpreter in different countries, as did Maurice Yvain's *Mon homme* (1920) with Mistinguett in France and Fanny Brice in the USA; but more often the basic material was thoroughly overhauled for different countries. Thus when Whiteman took up the Austrian success

7. *Advertisement for the Edison home phonograph from the 'Illustrated London News' (3 February 1900)*

8. 'Parisian Pierrot' from the revue 'London Calling' by Noël Coward (first produced in London in 1923): with Gertrude Lawrence (left)

Madonna, du bist schöner als der Sonnenschein (1924) by Robert Katscher (1894–1942), he had it refurbished for his own orchestra with a new text as *When Day is Done* (1926). Similarly, the Italian song *Parla mi d'amore, Mariù* (1932) by C. A. Bixio (*b* 1896) might be readily recognizable in America as *Tell me that you love me*; but in Britain it became known as *Love's last word is spoken* and in France, where it was an immensely successful popular chanson, as *Le chaland qui passe*. In its transformation into the *Beer Barrel Polka* ('Roll out the barrel', 1939) Vejvoda's song *Škoda lásky* ('The harm of love', 1934), which also became a success in Germany as the *Rosamunde Polka*, underwent not only a change of words but also a change from minor to major key for its chorus.

Like so many successful songs of the 1930s, some of those mentioned were composed for films. Although the basic commodity was little changed in style, the methods of dissemination were changing yet again. With the advent of electrical recording in the mid-1920s new companies had sprung up with rival versions of current dance-band successes. Broadcasting had also increased the accessibility of musical entertainment to the general public, and dance bands were among the highlights of an evening's listening, bringing new songs to a vast audience. The seaside demonstration stores were thus no longer so important, and bribery of broadcasting bandleaders by song-pluggers ('plug money') was a more likely route to commercial success. Although a really successful British song could still sell a million sheet-music copies, the record sales would be more like three million, and the days of the music sheet as the prime means of disseminating popular music were over.

A simple piece of inspiration could thus reach many millions of people in little time and sometimes earn large sums of money for publisher, composer, lyricist and performer – though for every big hit there would be many more big flops. From different standpoints, two men closely involved with popular music between the wars summed up the situation: 'Strange how potent cheap music is', said a character in Noël Coward's play *Private Lives*, while in his book *Music Ho!* (1934) Constant Lambert reflected on 'the appalling popularity of music'.

BIBLIOGRAPHY

J. Abbott: *The Story of Francis, Day and Hunter* (London, 1952)

R. Nettel: *Seven Centuries of Popular Song* (London, 1956)

E. Rogers and M. Hennessey: *Tin Pan Alley* (London, 1964)

H. P. Hofmann and P. Czerny: *Der Schlager: ein Panorama der leichten Musik*, i (Berlin, 1968)

K. Young: *Music's Great Days in the Spas and Watering Places* (London, 1968)

E. Lee: *Music of the People: a Study of Popular Music in Great Britain* (London, 1970)

A. McCarthy: *The Dance Band Era* (London, 1971)

R. Pearsall: *Victorian Sheet Music Covers* (Newton Abbot, 1972)

M. R. Turner: *The Parlour Song Book* (London, 1972)

I. Whitcomb: *After the Ball* (London, 1972)

R. Pearsall: *Victorian Popular Music* (Newton Abbot, 1973)

——: *Edwardian Popular Music* (Newton Abbot, 1975)

——: *Popular Music of the Twenties* (Newton Abbot, 1976)

II. North America to 1940

1. English traditions. 2. Irish melodies. 3. Bel canto. 4. The expanding market. 5. Minstrel songs. 6. The first Americans: Stephen Foster. 7. Singing families: the Hutchinsons. 8. Piano music. 9. The Civil War. 10. Postwar years. 11. Tin Pan Alley. 12. Between the wars.

1. ENGLISH TRADITIONS. The tradition of broadside balladry (*see* BALLAD, §8) was transported to North America, and resulted in the first printed sheet music there. Broadsides printed in England have been retrieved in America; ballads were printed and sold in the American colonies in the 17th and 18th centuries, principally in such cities as Boston, Philadelphia and New York. These were commercial ballads, usually consisting of only a printed text, to be sung to a tune already familiar to the purchaser through oral tradition. Even when a melody was printed, it served only to jog the memory; it was never a newly written tune. Many of these tunes have survived in oral tradition, in notated instrumental music as airs for variation, or in tutors and such contemporary sources as Playford's *The English Dancing Master* (1650, many later editions) and *A Choice Collection of 180 Loyal Songs* (1685); *Wit and Mirth: or Pills to Purge Melancholy* (1699), an anthology in several volumes, contains the words and music to almost 1000 songs, some by known composers of the 16th to 18th centuries, some by unknown and probably earlier composers. The creation of new, narrative, usually topical texts to be fitted to already familiar tunes has continued (e.g. the songs of Woody Guthrie). Since the late 18th century such ballads have been a single and often unrecognized element in American popular music.

The printing of individual items of music began in

North America only after the Revolution. A few pieces were issued in the late 1770s and the 1780s, but it was not until the last decade of the century that they appeared in any great number. Early printers and publishers included Benjamin Carr (Philadelphia and New York), Joseph Carr (Baltimore), James Hewitt (New York), P. A. von Hagen (Boston) and George Willig (Philadelphia).

Musical life in the new nation was still closely linked with that of England. Nearly all professional musicians had been born and/or trained in London, and most of the music performed was that played there. English ballad operas were performed in North America as early as 1735, when *Flora: or, Hob in the Well* was given in Charleston, South Carolina. *The Beggar's Opera* had been staged in New York by 1750, and in 1752 an English company calling itself the Old America Company landed at Yorktown, Virginia, and gave its first performances at Williamsburg. The company remained in existence for almost 50 years, travelling throughout the American colonies and continuing to perform after the Revolution. Other local and visiting companies helped to popularize ballad opera. The works most often performed were *Love in a Camp*, *Rosina* and *The Poor Soldier* by William Shield, *The Children in the Wood* and *Zorinski* by Samuel Arnold, Charles Dibdin's *The Deserter*, Stephen Storace's *No Song, No Supper* and Thomas Arne's *Love in a Village*. There were repeated performances of these works in the late 18th century and the early 19th, and when American music publishers began bringing out single pieces of sheet music for performance in the home, songs from these operas made up a substantial part of the repertory.

The programmes of benefit and subscription concerts in various American cities similarly included those pieces most often performed in contemporary English concerts. Musical societies were formed in Charleston, New York, Boston and Philadelphia, and outdoor entertainments at such places as Nibblo's Garden in New York were patterned on London's pleasure gardens. All these concerts offered mixed programmes of instrumental and vocal music; a fixed and popular part of them was solo songs, the singer being accompanied by a keyboard instrument or instrumental ensemble.

All this music is in what might be called the 'London' style of the day, combining elements of English airs with those of works by such fashionable foreign composers as Handel and J. C. Bach. The songs are strophic; their melodies are mostly diatonic, built largely of scale passages and skips outlining basic triads, and the accompaniments are almost completely diatonic triads in simple figurations. Many songs have a pseudo-folk style; such 'Scottish' songs as James Hook's *Within a Mile of Edinboro Town* enjoyed wide popularity. Texts were mostly pastoral, comic or moralizing. Many of James Hook's songs, written for Vauxhall Gardens (1774–c1820), were published in annual collections, some of which were reprinted and sold in the USA, as were at least 200 other songs of his. Music of this sort continued to be printed and sung in the USA into the first decades of the 19th century. In addition, songs by the somewhat younger singer and composer John Braham, such as 'All's Well' (from *The English Fleet in 1342*), 'The Beautiful Maid' and 'Fair Ellen' (from *The Cabinet*), 'The Death of Nelson' (from *The Americans*), and the ballads *Is there a heart that never lov'd* and *The Willow*, were among the most popular pieces in the USA between 1800 and 1820. When Braham toured there with his son Charles in 1840–42 he was warmly received, largely because of his great fame as a songwriter.

Many versatile musicians who had been active in London went to the USA at this time and helped shape musical life in the new country through their playing, conducting and organization of musical events. Most of them composed, though none had outstanding talent, and some of their pieces were songs in the same style as the music just discussed. Benjamin Carr, who had been connected with the London Ancient Concerts, went to New York in 1793 and was active there and in Philadelphia as a pianist, singer, composer and music publisher; among the more successful of his several dozen published songs were Four Ballads (1794) to texts from Shakespeare. Alexander Reinagle arrived in 1786 and worked as a conductor, performer and manager in several cities; most of his published songs (about 50) were arrangements of pieces by Arnold, Kelly, Dibdin and Shield. James Hewitt went to the USA in 1792, and was active for many years as a conductor and composer, especially for ballad opera productions. Other song composers from England were George K. Jackson, whose popular Dirge for General Washington was written in 1800, and Raynor Taylor. These men lacked a distinctive style of composition but their songs enjoyed moderate success and were part of the first body of popular music printed in America.

2. IRISH MELODIES. Hook and his contemporaries sometimes wrote songs based on or derived from Scottish and Irish tunes. Interest in Irish song increased in England and America with the publication by Edward Bunting of several collections of traditional Irish melodies (1796–1840), and by 1800 such songs as *Drink to me only* and *The Blue Bells of Scotland* were widely printed and sung. By far the most influential collection of Irish songs was the ten-volume *A Selection of Irish Melodies*, with texts written by Thomas Moore and tunes harmonized by John Stevenson (i–vii, 1807–18) and Henry Bishop (viii–x, 1821–34). The tunes, originally in oral tradition, were polished and arranged for one to four voices with keyboard accompaniment. Their success in the USA was immediate and great. The first volume was reprinted by G. E. Blake in Philadelphia as early as 1808–9 and the publication of succeeding volumes followed as quickly on their first appearance in England and Ireland. Many of the songs (e.g. *Believe me if all those endearing young charms*, *The harp that once thro Tara's halls*, *The Last Rose of Summer* and *The Minstrel Boy*) were printed separately and repeatedly. They were sold first as printed sheet music, and eventually became an enduring part of the American musical heritage, some even entering oral tradition. The simplicity and directness of their melodies, and perhaps even more their direct expression of universal human sentiments through both words and music, reached more people than had previously responded to songs printed as sheet music.

3. BEL CANTO. The music of early 19th-century Italian opera had as profound an effect on popular song in the USA as Irish melodies. G. E. Blake published an aria from Rossini's *Tancredi* in sheet-music form in 1818 (the first music by this composer to be printed in the country) and, soon after, productions of Italian opera in

English became popular at the Park Theatre in New York and elsewhere. Rossini's *Il barbiere di Siviglia*, in an English version by Henry Bishop, was first staged at the Park in 1819 and was repeated many times in the next years, and similar reworkings of Italian operas for the English stage by Bishop and Rophino Lacey followed. Lacey's *Cinderella: or, The Fairy-queen and the Glass Slipper*, based largely on Rossini's *La Cenerentola*, was first performed at the Park in 1831 and repeated some 50 times in the first season alone. Bellini's *La sonnambula* was first performed in the USA in an English version in 1835, and *Norma* in 1841.

Professional European companies were concurrently performing Italian opera. Manuel Garcia brought an opera troupe to New York in 1825; they gave over 70 performances of nine Italian operas before moving on to other American cities with the same repertory. The Montresor Company, brought to the USA through the efforts of Lorenzo da Ponte (then a professor of Italian literature at Columbia College), gave about 30 performances of Italian operas in New York in autumn 1832. New Yorkers subsequently raised $150,000 for the construction of an Italian Opera House, and a company of professional European singers was assembled; the grand opening took place on 18 November 1833 with a performance of Rossini's *La gazza ladra*, and 80 performances of various operas were given in the first season.

In the decades after 1820 arias, ensembles and even choruses from the operas of Rossini, Bellini, Donizetti and their contemporaries, first presented on the stage, were arranged as simple strophic songs for one voice with keyboard accompaniment, fitted with English texts, and published as pieces of sheet music, many of which enjoyed excellent sales. Italian operatic music also reached America indirectly through the songs of several English composers so influenced by it that their music transmitted its most important stylistic features. The sheet-music songs of Henry Bishop, who was much concerned with (and influenced by) Italian opera in London, were the most widely sold in the USA in the first quarter of the 19th century. Some were airs from his stage works, some were his arrangements printed in the last volumes of Thomas Moore's *Irish Melodies* and in Moore's *National Airs* (1818–28), and some were airs and ballads written for Vauxhall Gardens. *Home, Sweet Home* is his most durable song; others popular at the time included *Tho 'tis all but a dream*, *Peace be around thee* and *Oft in the stilly night* (from Moore's *National Airs*), 'Love has Eyes' (from the comic opera *The Farmer's Wife*), the ballad *Sweet Maid* and many others no longer remembered. They all have an easy melodic charm, direct emotional expression and simple accompaniments that do not distract attention from the singer and the text.

Even more important in the history of American popular music was the Englishman Henry Russell. In about 1835 he arrived in the USA and embarked on a country-wide concert tour before returning to England in 1841. Once he had established his reputation, Russell performed only his own songs. Each dealt with some situation that his audiences could understand and respond to in a deeply and directly emotional way: many are nostalgic, speaking of lost youth, and friends and family who are gone; others deal with social (and other) injustices. The treatment of these subjects may now seem melodramatic, and Russell was quite aware that their effect on his audiences was to his financial advantage. Nevertheless, a concern for social issues was new to American popular music. Most of Russell's songs are simple strophic ballads, their melodies, harmonies and accompaniments obviously derived from Italian opera; some are more extended pieces not unlike a scena in contemporary Italian opera. Russell's voice, delivery and intensity of expression made him by far the most popular singer in the USA; his sheet music to be performed in the home was equally popular. His most successful songs were reprinted for many decades after he left the country, and many were sung throughout the 19th century.

4. THE EXPANDING MARKET. Sheet music is sold mostly to people with some degree of musical literacy. There were few such people in the decades immediately following the Revolution; music publishing was a small industry, mostly confined to the larger cities. People who could read music were usually those with a good general education; many of them had enough musical training to be responsive to art music. Stylistic differences between classical music and sheet music for home use were not great. But events in American music education led inevitably to a sharper distinction between art and popular music, and to a dramatic increase in the potential audience for the latter.

In New England the first singing schools, taught by William Billings and his contemporaries, trained great numbers of people who had had no opportunity for instruction in the basic skills of reading and singing music, and they continued to do so when the singing schools spread to the south and west in the early 19th century. Instruction in music became more common in private schools, particularly those for women, in the 19th century. Music became a desirable social skill for women and a symbol of culture and refinement. Innumerable academies and 'female seminaries' helped women 'to attain a moderate execution of music, with correct time and pure taste, so as to please others and amuse herself', as it was put in an anonymous essay entitled *Thoughts on Domestic Education* (1829).

A second group of New Englanders, including Thomas Hastings and Lowell Mason, began in the second and third decades of the century to develop methods of more 'scientific' instruction in music and of 'elevating the taste' of Americans. The Boston Academy of Music (established 1832) was dedicated to instructing as many people as possible and was a model for schools in other cities. In 1837 the Boston School Committee authorized music instruction in the public-school syllabus; Mason, working through his Academy of Music, directed the course and it became a model for countless others during the 19th century (*see* EDUCATION IN MUSIC, §VIA, 2).

As a result of these developments thousands and then millions of Americans became musically literate. Although their first instruction was in sacred and social ensemble music, they were able to apply their new skills to playing and singing popular sheet music in the home. By the 1830s and 1840s, when popular music began moving in directions that were to make it more appealing to vastly larger numbers of people, the potential market for such music had expanded enormously through the increasing numbers of Americans who had the basic musical skills to consume it.

5. MINSTREL SONGS. Songs of the late 18th or early 19th century occasionally used the negro slave as sub-

ject matter, and black characters were sometimes introduced into ballad operas. *I sold a guiltless negro boy* by a Mr Moulds (1796), Benjamin Carr's *A Negro Song* (1801) and the anonymous *Banjo Song* (1818) appeared as sheet music. Such pieces represented a minor current, however, and their music was in no way remarkable or different from other music of the time.

Charles Mathews, a British comedian who went to the USA in 1822, was fascinated by the speech of American negroes. After listening to and transcribing their characteristic pronunciations, rhythms and inflections he began introducing skits and mock-lectures in negro dialect into his stage acts; their success was partly responsible for a fashion in stage impersonations of negroes (*see* MINSTRELSY, AMERICAN). By the late 1820s several American entertainers, performing with blackened faces, were singing comic 'negro' songs as part of their acts. The most popular included George Nichols, Bob Farrell and George Washington Dixon, who was singing in 'blackface' in Albany by 1827. The music they sang was a shared body of material of uncertain origin, some of which was published as sheet music almost immediately. *The Coal Black Rose* (1830–31), one of Dixon's most popular songs, was followed by *De Boatman's Dance*, *Clare de Kitchen*, *Lucy Neal* and others. *Zip Coon* (c1834), the most enduring of these early minstrel songs, is known now as *Turkey in the Straw*.

In Louisville, Kentucky, in 1828 Thomas Dartmouth ('Daddy') Rice introduced the song *Jim Crow* between

9. Sheet-music cover of 'Jim Crow' (c1829) showing 'Daddy Rice'

acts of a local play, *The Rifle*, as part of an impersonation of an old negro doing a comic, shuffling dance; it had tremendous success both on stage and as sheet music (1829). Rice's performance was received with great enjoyment and acclaim in Cincinnati, Pittsburgh, Baltimore, Washington, New York and eventually London. Within a decade negro impersonations on stage were so popular that entire companies were formed to do dances, songs, jokes and skits. The Kentucky Minstrels, the Ethiopian Serenaders, the Sable Harmonists, the troupe assembled by E. P. Christy and particularly the Virginia Minstrels of Dan Emmett were all successful with shows of comic skits and dialogues interspersed with dances and songs. Minstrel shows continued to be the most popular form of stage entertainment in the USA until well after the Civil War and they persisted in amateur productions well into the 20th century.

Europeans regarded minstrel shows as a native American form of musical theatre unlike anything they had experienced before. Thomas Rice (1836) and the Virginia Minstrels (1843) performed with great success in England; minstrel songs were the first characteristically American music to be successful in Europe. Despite this, and despite the fact that the songs were sung in negro dialect by performers in blackface, the music of the songs was usually directly derived from European models. *Jim Crow* for example, which Gilbert Chase has called 'the first great international song hit of American music', does not differ in melody or harmony from European music. Musically, most minstrel songs are clearly in the current tradition of English–American popular music, indebted to European art music, Irish ballads and the melodies of Italian opera. A few, however, are different. A characteristic syncopated rhythmic pattern, probably derived from instrumental music played by American negroes, appears in many minstrel dances, banjo tunes and some songs. A handful of minstrel tunes (e.g. *Old Dan Tucker* and *De Boatman's Dance*) are based on pentatonic scales and repetitive melodic patterns, and are possibly derived from slave songs of African origin.

6. THE FIRST AMERICANS: STEPHEN FOSTER. Although nearly all the sheet music published in the USA before the 1820s was composed by Europeans, there were a few songs by native Americans. The earliest was Francis Hopkinson, who wrote songs as early as 1759, and his *Seven Songs for the Harpsichord* (1788; for voice and keyboard, despite the title, and dedicated to George Washington) was one of the first secular music publications in the country. Oliver Shaw published a number of songs in the early 19th century, but like Hopkinson's they had no distinctive style and no impact on the musical life of the country. There was no development of solo secular music at this time corresponding to the successful and distinctive part-music of William Billings and other New Englanders. John Hill Hewitt, son of James Hewitt, has often been named the first successful native American composer of songs. Certainly *The Minstrel's Return'd from the War* (1827) was widely performed and sold. But his most popular songs were written much later, many of them during the Civil War, by which time Stephen Foster had written his most popular songs and his impact on American music had already been felt.

Foster composed some 200 songs, beginning with

Open thy lattice, love (1844) and continuing to the month of his death 20 years later. Many were written for minstrel shows, and even more were ballads for home performance. The facts of his brief life afford few clues either to the phenomenal and lasting popularity of his songs or to the much debated topic of their 'American' nature. Much has been made of the 'folk nature' of these songs and of the fact that many have passed into oral tradition. But they were all newly composed, and there is no evidence that Foster had any direct or prolonged contact with any body of folk music, or that he would have been interested in such music. He did, however, have a broad and deep acquaintance with the various current types of popular music. He had an intimate knowledge of minstrel music; his own first minstrel songs, written in 1847 and 1848 (e.g. *Lou'siana Belle*, *Away Down South*, *Uncle Ned* and *Oh Susanna*), were solidly in the style of the day, and some have melodic similarities to the most popular songs of this kind. He knew the songs of Henry Russell, whom he heard in Pittsburgh, and the melodic style of Italian opera. *Foster's Social Orchestra*, a set of instrumental solo, duet, trio and quartet arrangements, contains many pieces by Donizetti, and others by Bellini, Mozart, Balfe and Wallace; his duet *Wilt thou be gone, love?*, with a text adapted from Shakespeare's *Romeo and Juliet*, could easily pass as part of an opera by Donizetti; to an attentive ear, many of the simpler songs have traces of the melodic style of Bellini and his contemporaries, and reminiscences of Irish airs run through many of his songs.

Foster was probably not familiar with music in the oral traditions of American negroes, the poor or rural Scottish–Irish or any other ethnic groups. But he did know the popular music that had become important in American culture. His melodies, drawing on and combining various threads of it, made his songs readily familiar to millions of Americans. His music is American in that it combines elements of English stage and concert music, Irish melodies, Italian opera and minstrel music (with its occasional references to the African heritage of American blacks) – bodies of music that came into contact with one another only in the USA. Foster's texts are rarely topical but deal with intensely nostalgic emotions, such as longing for the past or dreams of lost love. On one level they mirror events of his own unhappy life, on another they reflect a predominant mood in the USA during the decades before the Civil War, and that may account for their great popularity. The nation was suffering a crisis of conscience and identity; many Americans wished that matters could be simple and unspoilt as they had been, or were thought to have been, before the turmoils of the 1840s and 1850s.

The music of Foster's songs is astonishingly simple. The melodies are completely diatonic, built on conjunct movement with simple leaps, and their phrases and larger structures are symmetrical. They are always in major keys. Harmonies are diatonic, with only an occasional chromatically altered chord, usually a secondary dominant. Many of his songs, including some of the best known such as *Old Folks at Home* and *Oh Susanna*, use only the tonic, dominant and subdominant. This simplicity does not result from ignorance or poverty of invention; certain of his songs show that he was adept at using more varied harmonies and complex formal structures. He understood, as did no composer

10. *Sheet-music cover of an English edition of Stephen Foster's 'My Old Kentucky Home, Goodnight!', first published in America in 1853*

before him, that truly popular music must be grasped at first or second hearing, remembered with some accuracy after only a few more, and must be easily performable at home by those with rudimentary skills. Musicological methods, however, cannot adequately explain how he was able to write *Jeanie with the light brown hair*, *Camptown Races*, *Massa's in de cold ground* and the many other songs that have been popular for over a century. The means are so simple as to suggest that almost anyone could write such songs; yet no-one but Foster did.

7. SINGING FAMILIES: THE HUTCHINSONS. In 1839–43 an Austrian singing family, the Rainers, performed with great success in the USA; they wore Tyrolean costumes, yodelled, and popularized *Silent Night* and several other songs. Their greatest impact was indirect: their success gave great encouragement to an American singing family, the Hutchinsons, and helped prepare audiences for them.

There were 13 Hutchinson children, most of whom sang occasionally for church or social gatherings in their home town, Milford, New Hampshire. After the success of the Rainers, four of the most talented and ambitious formed a group which began performing in small towns in New Hampshire and Vermont, then moved on to such larger communities as Saratoga Springs and Albany. In September 1842 they sang for the first time in Boston, following this with concerts in Philadelphia, Baltimore and Washington (where they appeared before President Tyler in 1844). In 1845 they

11. Sheet-music cover of a collection of songs by the Hutchinson Family, with a copy of the famous lithograph (1843) by Endicott

went to England. For several decades they were a central force in American popular music, through their public appearances and the successful sales of their songs, published mainly by the Boston firm of Oliver Ditson.

The Hutchinsons sang the sentimental and melodramatic ballads popular at the time. Their first success was *The Snow Storm*, about a young couple freezing to death in a blizzard, and they often sang Henry Russell's *The Old Sexton*, *My Mother's Bible* and *The Child's First Lament* (about a child whose brother has died). But they were also strongly concerned with current social and political problems. All were teetotallers and included in even their earliest programmes the temperance songs *King Alcohol* and *Cold Water*. They allied themselves with the abolition movement in 1842 and insisted on including *The Bereaved Slave Mother*, *Slave's Appeal* and *Gone, Sold and Gone* in their concerts, even when faced with hostile audiences in Baltimore, Washington and St Louis. Their *Get off the Track* was felt to be such an inflammatory combination of an aggressively anti-slavery text with a rousing tune that no major publisher would bring it out. They took the ex-slave Frederick Douglass on their tour of England, to arouse abolitionist sentiments in that country; shunning London, they sang only in small towns for working-class audiences. By this time they thought of themselves as social reformers rather than entertainers. They sang for the first Women's Rights Convention (Akron, Ohio, 1851); *The Song of the Shirt* is an early popular song concerned with inequality in the treatment of women. They went to Kansas in 1855 during the violent controversy concerning the state's admission to the Union, and later they were among the popularizers of *John Brown's Body*, which contributed

to anti-slavery sentiment in the north. *The Indian's Lament* denounces the persecution of Red Indians, some of whom the Hutchinsons had met on a trip to Minnesota (1857). They campaigned for Abraham Lincoln, published political songs supporting him, and continued to work for temperance and universal suffrage after the war. A trip to the south after the war brought them into contact with ex-slaves, whose music they found so exciting that they later sang such spirituals as *My Jesus says there's room enough*.

The Hutchinsons sang music by many composers in their own arrangements for vocal quartet. Some songs were their own and some were their arrangements of such familiar tunes as *Old Dan Tucker* set to new words. Their music was distinctive only as a synthesis of many types of music currently popular; this synthesis was uniquely American. John Hutchinson wrote that 'not only during our foreign tour were we recognized as "American singers", but during our long career we were never anything else'. Their music was also American in its involvement with contemporary critical issues. The Hutchinsons demonstrated that popular song could be a potent force in arousing general sentiment on controversial matters, more potent perhaps than political oratory or crusading journalism.

8. PIANO MUSIC. A certain amount of the sheet music published consisted of pieces for the piano or other keyboard instruments. The publication of marches and waltzes, begun in the late 18th century, increased in the first quarter of the 19th. Few marches were composed for the piano; those that appeared in sheet-music form were either keyboard reductions of band music or arrangements of marches from operas and other 'classical' works. The former are particularly valuable because very little band music of the time is extant in its original instrumentation and its history can be reconstructed only from these keyboard versions.

Some of the waltzes published in America in the early 19th century are anonymous, identified usually by nationality; 'German Waltz' and 'Hungarian Waltz' are common labels. Some are simplified arrangements of pieces (not always waltzes) by European composers (Mozart, Clementi, Hummel, Beethoven etc). Others are original works written in America by such men as Charles Gilfert, active in Charleston and New York after his arrival from Prague; Peter K. Moran (d 1831), who came to New York from Dublin in 1813; and Peter Weldon (dates unknown), the most prolific composer of waltzes in the country before 1825. Whatever their origin, in their sheet-music form these waltzes all resemble one another: they were written or arranged as simple sectionalized pieces, and could be played by the amateur musician of modest technique who accompanied popular songs.

Polkas appeared in large numbers after their introduction to the USA in the early 1840s; quadrilles, mazurkas, polonaises, schottisches and other national dances were also published, and the keyboard repertory included programme music and sets of variations. There is not always a clear distinction between this music and concert pieces written by more accomplished pianists. Some more serious music was played in American parlours in the 19th century, just as some singers of popular songs had sufficient technique and taste to sing opera arias and art songs as well as songs by Henry Russell and Stephen Foster; but there was a clearly defined market throughout the 19th century for short piano works requiring modest technique and little musical sophistication, and these pieces were played by and for the same people who performed and listened to the popular songs.

9. THE CIVIL WAR. The drama, tension and excitement of the events leading to the secession of the several southern states from the Union and the horror and heroism of the war itself – all of a degree unprecedented in the country's history – came when popular music was reaching an unprecedented number of Americans and was beginning to deal directly with issues of the day. The result was that popular music just before and during the war not only concerned itself with political, military, social and personal events, but was absorbed into the events themselves. Songs of the Civil War cover the entire range of its events: there were patriotic rallying songs (*Battle Hymn of the Republic, Dixie, The Battle Cry of Freedom, The Bonnie Blue Flag*), songs dealing with individual heroes and military events (*The Drummer Boy of Shiloh, Stonewall's Requiem, Marching through Georgia*), songs about serious and humorous aspects of life in the army (*Goober Peas, Tenting on the Old Camp Ground, Grafted into the Army*) and countless others. Many of the best were expressions of the loneliness, fear and sadness of the soldiers and their families and friends (*When this cruel war is over, The Vacant Chair, When Johnny comes marching home*); these touched so directly on experience that they became part of the war and were remembered long after.

It was an American war, and its songs were all written or arranged by Americans. The most successful was

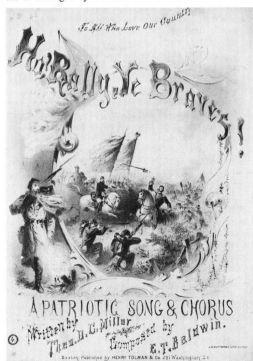

12. *Sheet-music cover of 'Ho! Rally, Ye Braves!', published in Boston in 1863 during the Civil War*

George F. Root from Massachusetts, who went to Chicago just before the war and had a long association there with the important publishing firm of Root & Cady. In addition to his immensely popular wartime songs (including *Battle Cry of Freedom* and *Just before the Battle, Mother*), he composed other successful ballads (*The Hazel Dell, Rosalie, the Prairie Flower*) and a vast amount of religious and instructional music. Henry Clay Work wrote as many 'hit' songs during the war as Root and was equally successful afterwards with such songs as *Come Home, Father* and *Grandfather's Clock*. John Hill Hewitt was the leading southern songwriter; his *All Quiet along the Potomac* is one of the most poignant of all anti-war songs, and like so many of the time was equally popular in the south and the north. Stephen Foster's numerous war songs are not among his best.

Musically, these war songs represented no new trends. Many of them, including *Dixie* and *Wait for the Wagon*, had originated in minstrel shows. Traditional and newly composed Irish tunes abounded. Southern troops marched to *The Bonnie Blue Flag*, based on the traditional *Irish Jaunting Car*, while northern bands played *We are coming, Father Abra'am*, which was *The Wearing of the Green* fitted with new words. Septimus Winner converted an 'old Irish song' into *Johnny is gone for a soldier*, and Patrick Gilmore, the Irish-born bandmaster of the Union army, was responsible for *When Johnny comes marching home*. The best of the ballads represent a fusion of the various types of music that had taken root in the country, a fusion that by the mid-century had led to a distinctly American style of song.

10. POSTWAR YEARS. During the decades before and after the Civil War many emigrated to the USA, particularly from the Germanic and Scandinavian countries. Many were professional musicians, some of whom merely visited, but a large number stayed, and the music they brought with them profoundly affected the development of American music.

The German pianist Leopold de Meyer toured the USA in 1845–7. P. T. Barnum brought the famous singer Jenny Lind over in 1850, launching her tour with the most imaginative and outlandish publicity campaign the ·country had ever seen. Though she was there for only two seasons of concerts, her effect on the musical consciousness of the country was incalculable. The Norwegian violinist Ole Bull played in the USA for the first time in 1843 and remained there for most of his life, playing in all parts of the country and composing pieces entitled *The Niagara, Solitude of the Prairie* and *To the Memory of Washington*. Henry Vieuxtemps performed there, as did many other violinists and pianists less well remembered. The Germania Musical Society, 25 instrumentalists from Berlin, gave orchestral concerts in 1848–54 and, when the orchestra dissolved, the members (all now American citizens) found positions as teachers, conductors and professors in various parts of the country.

There was a flow in the other direction as well. William Mason, probably the most talented American pianist to that date (excepting Gottschalk), studied in Germany (1849–54), where his teachers included Liszt. William B. Bradbury, a prolific composer of songs and other music for schools and the church, went to study in Leipzig in 1847; *The Jubilee*, his collection of music for schools and recreational music groups, sold over

250,000 copies, and it is estimated that more than two million of his music books were sold during his lifetime. H. C. Work, the composer of Civil War songs, also studied for several years in Europe.

The inevitable result of this movement of musicians to and from the USA and north-central Europe was that Germanic music became increasingly important in American musical life from the mid-19th century. This was reflected in popular music by the increasing number of German pieces published, and by the slow but unmistakable stylistic change in the songs of American composers. The anonymous *Ach wie ist's möglich*, translated as 'How can I love thee' and published in sheet-music form by F. D. Benteen (Baltimore, 1855), became one of the most widely bought songs of the decade. Alexander Reichardt's *Du bist mir nah und doch so fern* was brought out as 'Thou art so near and yet so far' (Cleveland, 1861). Anton Rubinstein's Melody in F became a staple item for parlour pianists, Schubert's songs began to be published, and several of the most memorable songs from Wagner's *Tannhäuser* and *Lohengrin*, simplified, trimmed to appropriate dimensions and fitted with English words, became widely sung and loved. Johann Strauss's *Blue Danube* waltz was first printed in the USA in 1867, Brahms's *Wiegenlied* in 1868.

The decades after the Civil War were not important ones for American popular music. There were no significant developments other than the gradual assimilation of German elements into the American mixture, and no new composers with the talent of a Stephen Foster or even a George Root. The fervour of the war years faded and again most songs were concerned with personal rather than public matters. Excellent individual songs of the period include Henry Tucker's *Sweet Genevieve* (1869), Hart Pease Danks's *Silver Threads among the Gold* (1873; it sold more than two million copies), H. C. Work's *Grandfather's Clock* (1876), *Carry me back to Old Virginny* (1878) by the negro composer James Bland and the tremendously successful *White Wings* (1884) by Banks Winter. Many of the most popular songs were imported from England or Ireland, for instance *In the Gloaming* (1877) by Annie F. Harrison, Sullivan's *The Lost Chord*, and *Love's Old Sweet Song* (1884) by James Molloy (1837–1909).

From the early 1870s the comedy team of Ned Harrigan (1845–1911) and Tony Hart (1855–91) with the London-born songwriter Dave Braham dominated the New York stage with shows made up of a succession of comic skits, dances, songs, jokes, impersonations and character sketches. Their first great success, *The Mulligan Guard* (1873), included a title song by Braham which, like many later numbers (until the partnership split up in 1885), was popular as sheet music. Braham's native musical language was that of the British music hall, but his style assimilated other elements as he became more familiar with musical life in the USA. The most important factor in the Harrigan–Braham song style, which dominated American popular music for several decades, is that the songs were written for stage productions whose intent was to entertain. Almost all were humorous or amusing, even when they dealt with politics, poverty or slavery, and did not attempt to educate or provoke an audience on any issue.

11. TIN PAN ALLEY. Until the last decades of the 19th century the important publishers of popular music had been scattered over much of the country. Some, such as Firth, Pond & Co. (Foster's chief publisher), had been in New York, but Root & Cady (Chicago), Oliver Ditson (Boston), G. E. Blake (Philadelphia), John Church jr (Cincinnati), J. L. Peters & Co. (St Louis), G. Willig jr (Baltimore), Joseph E. Winner (Philadelphia) and many others played important roles in the printing and dissemination of sheet music, and none had any monopoly of successful songs. Most of them also published other types of music: church music, vocal collections for schools and academies, instrumental instruction books, keyboard music and even some classical items.

In the last 15 years of the century New York became the focal point of the popular music industry. This was because of the growing importance of the city in musical and theatrical life generally; the continuing influence on popular music of the New York group Harrigan, Hart and Braham; and most of all the ambition, energy and foresight of a new generation of New York music publishers in the 1880s and 1890s. Of these the most successful were Thomas B. Harms (Harms Inc. began publishing in 1881), Willis Woodward (from 1883) and Isidore Witmark (M. Witmark & Sons first brought out music in 1885). These men concentrated on popular music, and the key to their success – in terms that were to be used in the next century – was their use of market research to select material and of marketing procedures to sell it. Song composers were employed under contract, the market was surveyed to see what types of song were selling best, and composers were expected to write in these styles; their songs were tested on potential performers and listeners to select those suitable for publication. 'Song-pluggers' were employed to do this, and performers were persuaded to include new songs in their acts to bring them to the attention of potential buyers of sheet music. By the end of the 19th century several of the most important publishers had offices in 28th Street between 5th Avenue and Broadway, near Union Square. This street became known as Tin Pan Alley, a name eventually used to refer to this entire period of American popular music.

During these years vaudeville replaced the minstrel show as the most popular form of stage entertainment. There were many similarities between the two, and each consisted of sequences of comic skits, songs, dances, larger production numbers and other acts. Tony Pastor's Music Hall became the first centre of American vaudeville soon after Lillian Russell's début there in 1881. A circuit of vaudeville theatres developed across the country, and more opened in New York, including Oscar Hammerstein's Victoria Theater (1904) and the Palace Theater (1913). An enormous quantity of music was needed for their entertainments; great amounts of money were to be made from the sale of songs popularized in vaudeville; and ties between this music and the most powerful New York publishers became increasingly close.

The first great songwriter of this era was Paul Dresser. His music, however, is closer to the best sentimental ballads of the previous decades than to the style that came to be identified with Tin Pan Alley. His songs (e.g. *The pardon that came too late*, 1891; *Just tell them that you saw me*, 1895; *On the banks of the Wabash*, 1899; and *My Gal Sal*, 1905) have the melodic simplicity, nostalgic texts and naive, direct appeal of Stephen Foster's. Their harmonic language is slightly more complex, particularly in the characteristic passages of 'barber-shop harmony' (chromatic passages at the ends of phrases).

In its first decades Tin Pan Alley produced a succession of songs, remarkable equally for their commercial success and for their permanence in American culture. The market potential was demonstrated early, when over five million copies were sold of Charles K. Harris's *After the Ball* (1892). Large numbers of songs from around the turn of the century became widely known and many entered oral tradition: *Daisy Bell* (Harry Dacre, 1892), *The band played on* (Charles B. Ward, 1895), *Sweet Rosie O'Grady* (Maud Nugent, 1896), *In the good old summertime* (George Evans, 1902), *Sweet Adeline* (Harry Armstrong, 1903), *Give my regards to Broadway* (George M. Cohan, 1904), *In the shade of the old apple tree* (Egbert Van Alstyne, 1905), *Shine on, harvest moon* (Nora Bayes and Jack Norworth, 1908), *By the light of the silvery moon* (Gus Edwards, 1909), *Put on your old gray bonnet* (Percy Wenrich, 1909), *Down by the old millstream* (Tell Taylor, 1910), *Let me call you sweetheart* (Beth Slater Whitson and Leo Friedman, 1910) and *When Irish eyes are smiling* (Ernest R. Ball, 1912). The texts of these songs suggest that the USA was a peaceful, happy, prosperous country during these decades, making an easy transition from rural to urban life. The many songs about the past describe warm memories of a happy and innocent childhood, usually in a rural or small-town setting. Songs about the present are nearly always set in the city, pictured as a gay, lively place. The persistent image of the 'Gay Nineties' as one of the happiest and least troubled times in American history has been derived largely from these songs. But Tin Pan Alley was interested in selling songs, not solving social problems; and the chosen method was to entertain people by giving them music divorced from the unpleasant or difficult realities of the time or of their own lives.

Stylistically this body of music is remarkably homogeneous. Melodies are symmetrical and diatonic. The composers made pervasive use of the sequence, one of the most effective devices for making a melody quickly memorable. The songs are strophic, with a verse followed by a chorus usually of 16 or 32 bars. Before the advent of Tin Pan Alley strophic forms had been the norm; whether texts were narrative or contemplative, popular songs had been written, performed and printed with several verses to the same music. Some had a short refrain or chorus (often for four voices) at the end of the verse; the music for this was often a repetition or extension of the music for the verse and could be omitted without serious damage to the song. It was for the music of the verse that the song was known and remembered. But in the late 19th century and the early 20th the chief melodic material began to be put in the chorus, and the verse took on the nature of preliminary or introductory music; these songs came to be known by their choruses and it is by their choruses that they are remembered.

As in Europe, by the turn of the century the musical vocabulary of popular music had become distinct from that of other types of music. Earlier, Hook, Shield and John Braham had written melodies and chords in the same general style as art music of their time, though much simpler; Bishop and Russell had used melodies, chords and accompaniment patterns similar to those in the music of Rossini, Bellini and Mendelssohn. But by the mid-19th century the situation was different: the songs of Foster and Root do not have the harmonic richness and variety or the melodic complexity of music by Verdi, Chopin or Wagner. The musical language of the Harrigan–Braham songs is still further removed from that of contemporary serious music. By the early 20th century the contrast was even more extreme; the songs discussed in this section have no affinity with, for instance, the music of Debussy, the early works of Stravinsky and Schoenberg, or the *Concord Sonata* and Second String Quartet of Ives.

The musical style of popular songs became relatively static in the mid-19th century. Art music continued to change and develop, becoming increasingly complex in harmony, melody, form and instrumentation; popular music continued to depend on simple, symmetrical, diatonic melodies supported by triads built mostly on the fundamental degrees of the major scale, cast in simple sectional forms. It was not uncommon for arrangements of serious works to become popular songs in the early decades of the 19th century, up to and including several early works by Wagner and Verdi, but the stylistic differences were later too great to be bridged, and there was no exchange between popular and serious music for almost 100 years. It was probably the extreme simplicity of this music that made it extraordinarily popular and accessible. It is not based on tradition – except the tradition of popular music – but rather created its own traditions. For example, there was no music indigenous to the favourite American sport of baseball, but *Take me out to the ball game* (written by Albert Von Tilzer, who had no knowledge of the sport and little interest in it) was so widely played during baseball games that it has become inextricably linked with the game in the minds of most Americans.

Several diverse currents in popular music at this time should be mentioned, not only because they produced some successful songs but also because of their impact on the following period. The early 20th century was the great era of RAGTIME, which gained currency at the end of the 19th century after the publication of piano rags (e.g. by Thomas M. Turpin and Scott Joplin) and became fashionable throughout the USA, remaining so until World War I. It was rooted in minstrel music and various aspects of black culture, but was not extemporized, and was written primarily for the piano. There has been a growing tendency to regard it as an art music form. Its performance required a considerable degree of skill and its chief form of dissemination was the piano roll rather than printed music. A number of songs of the period make such pervasive use of ragtime rhythmic patterns that they have a character somewhat different from that of other popular songs; one of the first was Ben R. Harney's *You've been a good old wagon but you've done broke down* (1895) and probably the most popular was Joe Howard's *Hello, ma baby* (1899). The historic significance of ragtime however lay not in the success of individual songs but in the way that some of its rhythmic patterns permeated the style of many composers of the next generation.

Other songs with more sophisticated musical content than those of Tin Pan Alley are typified in the work of Victor Herbert. He composed much art music and was most successful with operettas and musical comedies. Although he had no connection with the popular music industry, songs from his stage works (like 'Ah! Sweet mystery of life') sold as well in sheet-music form as the products of Tin Pan Alley. In harmonic vocabulary and melodic style his songs are much closer to European art music than are those of the contemporary professional songwriters. Reginald De Koven's songs which sold well commercially, such as 'Oh, promise me' from the opera *Robin Hood* (1890), are similarly related to European musical theatre, as are the songs of Ethelbert Nevin (*The Rosary*, 1898), Carrie Jacobs Bond (*I love you truly*, 1901) and Ernest R. Ball (*Love me and the world is mine*, 1906). None of these composers worked in Tin Pan Alley. Their songs have chromatic harmonies indebted to European art music of the second half of the 19th century; formally they are longer and more complex than those of Tin Pan Alley, their accompaniments are richer and more elaborate and sometimes as important as the vocal lines (which often rise to a climax on a high note just before the end and require a trained singer's skill in performance). They nevertheless enjoyed commercial success, and their musical style anticipated that of the next decades.

12. BETWEEN THE WARS. Changes in methods of dissemination and their effect on the place of music in American culture were the most important developments in popular music in the first half of the 20th century, indeed more important than changes in the music itself. At the end of World War I vaudeville, revue, operetta and musical comedy were still the principal vehicles for the introduction and popularization of songs, and money was made chiefly from the sales of sheet music for domestic performance. More than 100 American companies made pianos; almost every American family of some degree of education had a piano, and the introduction of mechanical pianos and devices attached to standard pianos for the playing of piano rolls enabled many people with little or no musical training to enjoy music in their homes.

Thomas A. Edison began experimenting with sound recording in 1877; by 1888 the 'talking machine' was sophisticated enough for a recording of classical music to be made; commercial gramophones and records were manufactured the following year in Germany; and in the 1890s the new invention became a commercial success in the form of 'nickel-in-the-slot' machines (later called juke-boxes) in public places. Spring-driven record-playing machines were first manufactured for home use in the last years of the century, and within a few years the Victor Talking Machine Company, Edison and Columbia were recording and marketing hundreds of cylinders and discs of various types of music, mostly for the home market. By the 1920s about 100 million records were being pressed each year. Popular music was a central part of this repertory almost from the beginning, and the new medium made it more readily available to a much larger audience.

The experiments by Frank Conrad of the Westinghouse Electric Company with radio transmission of records (begun in Pittsburgh in 1920) led to the establishment of KDKA, the first commercial radio station. Within a decade more than 600 commercial stations were operating in the USA; the number of radio sets in homes soared into the millions, and patterns of home life were changed as a result. From the start popular music was a staple of radio broadcasting. Many performers whose reputations had been made on the stage moved to the new medium, through which hundreds of new singers, including Rudy Vallee, Whispering Jack Smith, Kate Smith and Frank Parker,

became famous; by the 1930s the 'Lucky Strike Hit Parade', in which the most popular songs of the week were heard, had become a leading radio show and a potent force in the popular music industry.

The first film with continuous sound was *The Jazz Singer* (1927), with Al Jolson; thereafter popular music was irrevocably linked with the film industry. *Broadway Melody* (1929) was the first successful film musical; early examples of this genre were little more than filmed versions of Broadway revues, but with three great successes in 1933 (*Footlight Parade, Forty-second Street* and *Gold Diggers of 1933*) it took on new dimensions and a more distinct idiom through the direction and staging of extravagant production numbers by Busby Berkeley. Songs were also interpolated into most other types of film. By the mid-1930s films had become the chief form of American entertainment; about 60 million cinema tickets were sold each week and the demand for new songs was enormous. Film companies engaged hundreds of songwriters, including some whose reputations had already been established on Broadway and Tin Pan Alley.

When popular music had been disseminated only in the form of sheet music, it was intended chiefly for the home, for people who had enough skill in music to be able to play an instrument or at least sing with some accuracy. Songs were often introduced on the stage, but after that they were actively enjoyed by people who played and sang them. The sale of sheet music continued to be an important part of the popular music business in the 20th century, but records, radio and films brought popular songs to many millions of Americans who could not read music. The change was profound. Enjoyment of music, domestic as well as public, became increasingly passive, taking the form of listening rather than performing. A new type of consumer of popular music emerged in the 1920s and 1930s: he had no training in music but was nevertheless able to enjoy music through the convenient means of recordings, the radio and films.

The American Society of Composers, Authors and Publishers (ASCAP) was organized in February 1914 to protect performing rights, an issue which became much more acute with the increasing importance of new methods of dissemination. Victor Herbert sued Shanley's Restaurant for performing his music without permission, and the US Supreme Court ruled in 1917 that public performance for profit could not be given without the permission of the composer or his agent, on whatever terms might be agreed. ASCAP was then able to license and collect fees from thousands of restaurants, theatres and other establishments offering music for commercial purposes, and became a wealthy organization with great influence in the entertainment world.

In the early days of Tin Pan Alley the general style of songwriting was more important than the style of individual composers. A few, for example Harry Von Tilzer, enjoyed long careers and wrote large numbers of successful songs over several decades, but generally the most popular songs of the period had far more fame than their composers. This situation began to change around 1910, and between the wars a small number of extremely talented and successful songwriters dominated popular music with long successions of songs in their individual styles; they were well known as personalities, and people associated them with their songs.

From 1907 to the 1950s Irving Berlin wrote a series

13. Sheet-music cover of Irving Berlin's 'Alexander's Ragtime Band', first published in 1911

of songs that represent the core of the popular repertory of the period. Among his most famous individual songs, many of them written for insertion in stage revues and films, are *Alexander's Ragtime Band* (1911), *God Bless America* (1918) and *Always* (1925); his musicals, which include the *Ziegfeld Follies* (of 1919, 1920 and 1927) and *Annie, get your Gun* (1946), contain many more, among them 'Easter Parade', 'Oh, how I hate to get up in the morning' and one of the most successful of all American popular songs, 'White Christmas'. Berlin's position in American popular music was central for almost 50 years. His songs were performed on the stage, radio and in films by the best entertainers of several generations: Irene and Vernon Castle, Eddie Cantor, Fanny Brice, W. C. Fields, Grace Moore, the Marx Brothers, Ethel Waters, Ethel Merman, Al Jolson, Ginger Rogers and Fred Astaire, Rudy Vallée, Bing Crosby, Bob Hope and Judy Garland. His songs' lasting popularity is symptomatic of the long period of stylistic homogeneity in American popular music.

Others were scarcely less popular or influential. Jerome Kern produced a series of musicals and films with songs that were commercially successful, received critical acclaim, and have retained a place in American culture. They include 'Look for the silver lining' (from *Sally*, 1920), 'Ol' Man River' (*Show Boat*, 1927), 'Smoke gets in your eyes' (*Roberta*, 1933) and *The last time I saw Paris* (1940). George Gershwin was one of the most talented and skilful popular composers of the entire era; most of his songs were composed for revues, musicals or films such as *Lady be Good* (1924) and *Funny Face* (1927) and include 'Somebody loves me', 'Oh, lady be good' and 'Embraceable you'. Cole Porter's principal successes came in his stage musicals and film scores from the late 1920s onwards and include such songs as 'What is this thing called love?' (*Wake up and*

Dream, 1929), 'Night and Day' (*The Gay Divorcee*, 1932), 'Begin the Beguine' (*Jubilee*, 1933), 'In the still of the night' (film *Rosalie*, 1937) and 'So in love am I' (*Kiss me Kate*, 1948). Richard Rodgers collaborated with the lyricist Larry Hart on 21 musical comedies which included many popular songs, but it was after Hart's death that he wrote three sensationally popular musicals, *Oklahoma* (1943), *Carousel* (1945) and *South Pacific* (1949), with Oscar Hammerstein II; each had a number of songs that rapidly became classics of American popular music. He also wrote songs for films.

These men dominated the era, wrote the largest number of successful songs and set the style for others. There were also successful individual songs by many other talented but less prolific writers, including Joe Burke, Sammy Fain, Isham Jones, Jimmy McHugh, Harry Warren, Vincent Youmans, Harold Arlen, Hoagy Carmichael, Duke Ellington, Jimmy Van Heusen and Frank Loesser.

America's brief involvement in World War I had produced a few war songs, mostly patriotic (George M. Cohan's *Over there!*, 1917) or sentimental (Richard A. Whiting's *Till we meet again*, 1918). But the events of the postwar years – the Depression, the rise in Europe of totalitarian governments and the resulting flow of refugees to the USA from eastern and central Europe, and the outbreak of World War II – were almost completely disregarded in popular songs. The industry clung to the position, defined during the early days of Tin Pan Alley, that popular music was for entertainment only and that anything difficult, troublesome or controversial was to be avoided; the role of a song was to help the listener forget the real world and its problems. Love – romantic, sentimental love as defined by the mores of white, middle-class Americans – was the predominant subject matter. Even the country's active participation in World War II brought no more than a flurry of superficially cheerful patriotic songs and a few others childishly ridiculing the enemy.

ASCAP itself, organized to protect composers, lyricists and music publishers, became a powerful force for stability and orthodoxy. A very large amount of money was at stake: $80,000 accrued from fees for performing rights in 1921; by 1967 the amount had grown to $59 million. ASCAP was tightly restricted: no more than 1000 composers and lyricists and fewer than 150 music publishers held membership by the early 1940s. The organization's desire to perpetuate itself, coupled with the industry's aim of appealing to the largest possible audience, resulted in a period of popular song remote from most of the realities of American life.

In style, the popular songs written between the wars represent a continuation of the musical means of the songs from the first decades of Tin Pan Alley. Nearly all consist of a verse (usually omitted in all but stage performances) and a 32-bar chorus, most often in the form *AABA*. The principal composers were either born in Europe, or trained there, or had a good acquaintanceship with European music; in details of harmonic and melodic style their songs draw on an international style more than those of their predecessors at the turn of the century had done. Harmonies remain basically triadic, diatonic and tonal, but individual chords are more varied and complex, including 7th and 9th chords, chords with added 6ths and 2nds, and a wide variety of chromatically altered chords (including augmented and diminished ones). Modulations to remote keys occur between sections or even within a phrase. In general, the harmonic language of Kern, Gershwin and Porter borrows elements from such early 20th-century composers as Debussy, Grieg, Fauré, Puccini and Rakhmaninov. Melodies have more sense of direction and climax, in this respect resembling melodic lines in opera and art song.

For the first time in almost a century many stylistic details of American popular music were akin to those of serious music – but the serious music of several decades earlier, not that of such important contemporary composers as Stravinsky, Schoenberg, Bartók, Webern, Hindemith or Copland. Melodies from the classical repertory, adapted to the appropriate length, shape and words, were made into successful popular songs, as in the early 19th century. *Our Love* (1939) was taken from Tchaikovsky's *Romeo and Juliet*, *Moon Love* (1939) from his Fifth Symphony, *The Story of a Starry Night* from his Sixth Symphony and *Tonight we Love* from his First Piano Concerto, *The Lamp is Low* from Ravel's *Pavane pour une infante défunte*, and *Till the End of Time* from a Chopin polonaise.

The products and philosophy of Tin Pan Alley dominated American popular music during the first half of the 20th century. But despite the superficial continuity and consensus that appeared to persist after World War II, other types of music were attracting large and growing audiences through their freshness, vitality and direct appeal to huge numbers of Americans outside the orbit of Tin Pan Alley songs. This new type of popular music, which predominated after 1955, differed radically in musical style and content from what had preceded it.

BIBLIOGRAPHY

W. Chappell: *Popular Music of the Olden Time* (London, 1859, rev. 2/1965)
J. H. Hewitt: *Shadows on the Wall* (Baltimore, 1877)
Anon.: *Minstrel Songs: Old and New* (Boston, 1882)
G. F. Root: *The Story of a Musical Life* (Cincinnati, 1891)
H. Russell: *Cheer Boys, Cheer!: Memories of Men and Music* (London, 1895)
J. W. Hutchinson: *Story of the Hutchinsons* (*Tribe of Jesse*) (Boston, 1896)
O. G. T. Sonneck: *A Bibliography of Early Secular American Music* (Washington, DC, 1905, rev. 2/1945)
J. M. Chupple, ed.: *Heart Songs* (Boston, 1909)
H. E. Rollins: 'The Black-letter Broadside Ballad', *Proceedings of the Modern Language Association of America*, xxxiv (1919), 258–339
G. M. Cohan: *Twenty Years on Broadway* (New York and London, 1924)
C. K. Harris: *After the Ball: Forty Years of Melody* (New York, 1926)
P. Dresser: *The Songs of Paul Dresser: with an Introduction by his Brother Theodore Dreiser* (New York, 1927)
C. G. D. Odell: *Annals of the New York Stage* (New York, 1927–49, 2/1970)
C. Wittke: *Tambo and Bones: a History of the American Minstrel Stage* (Durham, North Carolina, 1930)
E. B. Marks: *They All Sang: from Tony Pastor to Rudy Vallée* (New York, 1934)
S. F. Damon: *Series of Old American Songs, Reproduced in Facsimile* (Providence, Rhode Island, 1936)
I. Witmark: *The Story of the House of Witmark: from Ragtime to Swingtime* (New York, 1939/R1976)
H. Dichter and E. Shapiro: *Early American Sheet Music: its Lure and its Lore, 1768–1889* (New York, 1941)
P. D. Jordan and L. Kessler: *Songs of Yesterday* (New York, 1941)
E. B. Marks: *They All Had Glamour: from the Swedish Nightingale to the Naked Lady* (New York, 1944)
S. Spaeth: *A History of Popular Music in America* (New York, 1948/R1962)
A. Shaw: *Lingo of Tin Pan Alley* (New York, 1950)
J. Burton: *The Blue Book of Tin Pan Alley* (Watkins Glen, NY, 1951, enlarged 2/1965)
J. Mattfeld: *Variety Music Cavalcade: a Chronology of Vocal and Instrumental Music Popular in the United States* (New York, 1952)
R. Gelatt: *The Fabulous Phonograph: from Edison to Stereo*

(Philadelphia, 1954, rev. 2/1965)
G. Chase: *America's Music: from the Pilgrims to the Present* (New York, 1955, rev. 3/1977)
E. J. Kahn, jr.: *The Merry Partners: the Age and Stage of Harrigan and Hart* (New York, 1955)
H. Meyer: *The Gold in Tin Pan Alley* (Philadelphia and New York, 1958)
P. Gammond: *Dictionary of Popular Music* (New York, 1961)
D. Ewen: *Popular American Composers, from Revolutionary Times to the Present* (New York, 1962; suppl. 1972)
H. Nathan: *Dan Emmett and the Rise of Early Negro Minstrelsy* (Norman, 1962)
D. Ewen: *The Life and Death of Tin Pan Alley* (New York, 1964)
P. Glass and L. C. Singer: *Singing Soldiers: a History of the Civil War in Song* (New York, 1964)
N. Shapiro: *Popular Music: an Annotated Index of American Popular Songs* (New York, 1964–)
R. J. Wolfe: *Secular Music in America, 1801–1825: a Bibliography* (New York, 1964)
I. Stambler: *Encyclopedia of Popular Music* (New York, 1965)
D. Ewen: *American Popular Songs from the Revolutionary War to the Present* (New York, 1966)
L. S. Levy: *Grace Notes in American History: Popular Sheet Music from 1820 to 1900* (Norman, 1967)
H. F. Mooney: 'Popular Music since the 1920s: the Significance of Shifting Taste', *American Quarterly*, xx (1968), 67
H. W. Hitchcock: *Music in the United States: a Historical Introduction* (Englewood Cliffs, NJ, 1969, rev. 2/1974)
L. S. Levy: *Flashes of Merriment: a Century of Humorous Songs in America, 1805–1905* (Norman, 1971)
I. Whitcomb: *After the Ball* (London, 1972)
A. Wilder: *American Popular Song: the Great Innovators, 1900–1950* (New York, 1972)
S. Applebaum, ed.: *Show Songs from 'The Black Crook' to 'The Red Mill': Original Sheet Music for 60 Songs from 50 Shows, 1866–1906* (New York, 1974)
R. D. Kinkle and N. McCaffrey: *The Complete Encyclopedia of Popular Music and Jazz, 1900–1950* (New Rochelle, NY, 1974)
R. C. Toll: *Blacking Up: the Minstrel Show in Nineteenth-century America* (New York, 1974)
W. W. Austin: *Susanna, Jeanie, and The Old Folks at Home: the Songs of Stephen C. Foster from his Time to Ours* (New York, 1975)
L. Engel: *Their Words are Music: the Great Theatre Lyricists and their Lyrics* (New York, 1975)
J. A. Stephens: *Henry Russell in America: Chutzpah and Huzzah* (diss., U. of Illinois, 1975)
I. Whitcomb: *Tin Pan Alley: a Pictorial History (1919–1939)* (New York, 1975)
R. Jackson: *Popular Songs of Nineteenth-century America* (New York, 1976)
L. S. Levy: *Picture the Song: Lithographs from the Sheet Music of Nineteenth-century America* (Baltimore and London, 1976)
R. Crawford, ed.: *The Civil War Songbook: Complete Original Sheet Music for 37 Songs* (New York, 1977)
D. L. Root: *American Popular Stage Music, 1860–80* (diss., U. of Illinois, 1977)
D. Ewen: *All the Years of American Popular Music: a Comprehensive History* (Englewood Cliffs, NJ, 1978)
C. Hamm: *Popular Song in America* (New York, 1979)

III. Since 1940. So far this article has discussed separately the distinct, though often closely related, traditions of popular music: those of Europe and of North America. From 1940 onwards, any such separation would be increasingly arbitrary. It is not simply that the situation was altered by the freer spreading of people across the world (and in particular the dissemination of American popular music through American servicemen in and after World War II), but that the internationalization of the commercial world, and in particular the record and music-publishing industries, tended to break down such national barriers as existed. The instantaneous and repetitive communications system through radio, television and records, so fundamental a part of 20th-century life, made it possible for music to be transported rapidly to any part of the world, and to be heard as endlessly as any individual might desire. It may be argued that such repetition has caused stylistic cycles in popular music to run their course more quickly than in the past: thus none of the important movements in popular music since the 1930s has lasted for more than six or eight years. These have been swing, with its new instrumentation, vibrant sound and powerful rhythmic drive; then rock and roll, in the mid-1950s, with a basic difference in sound, singing style, instrumentation and expressive intent (again with a fundamental driving rhythmic pulse); and, in the 1960s and 1970s, rock, with its variety and freedom of sound and form, and its strong links with political and social radicalism.

The discussion that follows takes account of certain trends of the 1920s and 1930s not dealt with in §I or §II as not strictly germane to popular music at that period.

1. Country music. 2. The influence of race records and jazz: big bands. 3. American domination. 4. Rock and roll. 5. The folk-music revival. 6. The rock movement. 7. The 1970s.

1. COUNTRY MUSIC. Wide areas of the rural south and west of the USA, particularly hilly and mountainous regions, were populated mostly by descendants of English and Scottish immigrants who remained largely isolated from urban America until well into the 20th century and maintained family, social and religious traditions brought across the Atlantic. Their chief types of music were of four kinds, two secular and two religious. One was the narrative ballad, about historical or mythical characters; such pieces were often variants of Child ballads, strophic unaccompanied songs with modal or pentatonic tunes. In the early 20th century they were often accompanied by the guitar, violin or banjo. A second secular type was the instrumental dance, such as the hornpipe or jig. These were originally played on the fiddle and later also on the guitar and banjo, in an ornamental, virtuoso style, with performers creating their own variations on tunes already known to their listeners; many tunes have been traced back to 16th- or 17th-century England. Of the religious types, one embraced the hymn, psalm and spiritual song; these were disseminated in shape-note collections, with melodies usually derived from or similar to the narrative ballads and instrumental dances, but with three- or four-part harmony, reflecting the modal or pentatonic nature of the tunes with frequent use of 4ths, 5ths and 7ths in vertical sonorities. Last there was gospel or revival hymnody, a type of religious music from the late 19th century which had many elements in common with mainstream American sacred music, including diatonic and tonal melodies, harmonized triadically and functionally, usually ending with refrains characterized by repeated words or phrases. The texts treated personal salvation in a highly emotional way, and were sung with great vigour. The vocal style in these types of music was nasal, harsh and often highly ornamented, continuing an ancient vocal tradition having little or no contact with western European art music. To urban Americans it seemed a crude, harsh, uncultivated sound.

The dissemination of this music by radio and record companies began in the south in the early 1920s (*see* COUNTRY MUSIC). Powerful stations in Atlanta, Fort Worth, Nashville and Chicago drew most of their audience from rural areas; country music was ignored or ridiculed by urban Americans even in the south and midwest. The music offered by these stations combined elements of the four types of rural Anglo-American music mentioned above. Much of it was vocal, often drawing on traditional ballad melodies, sung by one voice or by a small ensemble of singers using a harmonic style with roots in shape-note music; the accom-

14. *The Carter Family: Maybelle (guitar), Alvin Pleasant (standing) and Sara (autoharp)*

panying group consisted of a small number of guitars, banjos and sometimes other string instruments such as the fiddle and the mandolin. Some of the music was instrumental, played by small string bands of guitars, fiddles and banjos.

The most successful early performers of hillbilly music, as it was first called, were the Carter Family of Virginia. As the commercial potential began to be recognized and tapped, the nature of the music changed. Jimmie Rodgers, the first renowned figure of country music, had an authentic country background but early in his career was singing newly composed songs that shared elements of style with both traditional Anglo-American music and urban popular music. Later musicians (e.g. Gene Autry, Roy Acuff and Hank Williams) still had roots in the country tradition, and their audiences remained mostly rural, but their voices were less harsh, their accompaniments slicker and based more on the common harmonic practice of popular music, and their material all newly composed. Country music of the 1930s and 1940s was still unacceptable to urban audiences, but the differences between this music and urban popular music in America were not as great as they had been a generation earlier.

2. THE INFLUENCE OF RACE RECORDS AND JAZZ: BIG BANDS. At the time that traditional Anglo-American music was first commercialized as hillbilly music, another large and rich body of music was discovered by radio and the record industry: the music of black Americans. This was also regional and ethnic music, existing only in oral tradition. A historic disc by the blues singer Mamie Smith of *That thing called love* and *You can't keep a good man down* (1920) was followed by a flood of recordings of blues, jazz and black gospel music by both small and large record companies. The audience for 'race records' (as they were soon called), numbering millions, was altogether different from the one that consumed white urban popular music; yet at one point a certain development in jazz had a great stylistic influence on white popular music.

By the early 1930s many arrangers of big-band jazz were well-trained musicians with a knowledge of serious music and white commercial music; theirs was a hybrid style, in harmony and melody quite close to Tin Pan Alley and with instrumentation and rhythm derived

15. The Casa Loma Orchestra, 1930

from earlier jazz. It worked perfectly well for a black band to play an arrangement of a Gershwin song, for example, partly because Gershwin (and others) had already adapted jazz harmonies and rhythms to Tin Pan Alley. This music did not go unnoticed by white musicians. The first successful white big band was the Casa Loma Orchestra of Detroit, in great demand among college audiences as early as 1931. Playing arrangements by Gene Gifford, who had learnt his art largely from listening to black big bands, they alternated between slow numbers for dancing and faster 'swinging' arrangements. Their recordings, including *Black Jazz* (1932), *Smoke Rings* (1933) and *White Jazz* (1933), introduced the sound of big-band jazz to many whites who had never heard a black band.

Similar white bands played in clubs and at dances in the early 1930s. In 1934 Benny Goodman's orchestra and two other bands playing in different styles were engaged regularly for three-hour radio broadcasts. The Goodman band, with five brass, four saxophones and four rhythm men playing arrangements by Fletcher Henderson, including some that had been played by black bands for several years, quickly built a large, enthusiastic following, and made such best-selling records as *Blue Skies*, *King Porter Stomp* and *Goody-goody* (1936). The term 'swing' was coined for this music, probably by a BBC announcer in the early 1930s. The bands of Jimmy and Tommy Dorsey, Artie Shaw, Woody Herman, Harry James, Glenn Miller and other whites took big-band music to success. Many bands played both this 'sweet' style and the more black-derived variety of jazz, and their sudden fame brought some recognition and popularity to the black bands of Henderson, Duke Ellington and others on whom they had based their music.

Although Tin Pan Alley reached a peak in the early 1940s, the most popular recordings were swing numbers such as Goodman's *One o'clock Jump*, Shaw's *Begin the Beguine*, and Miller's *In the Mood* and *A String of Pearls*, and the bands playing this music were in the greatest demand.

Stylistically, 'sweet' swing stood somewhere between Tin Pan Alley and jazz. Most bands had one or more singers who sang ballads squarely in Tin Pan Alley style in their form, harmony and content, differing only in being accompanied by a band of brass, reed and rhythm instruments rather than a string-dominated studio orchestra. The most notable singers were Frank Sinatra, Jo Stafford, Doris Day, Perry Como, Dick Haymes and (after the war) June Christy, all known best for their ballad-style singing. Instrumental pieces were usually fast, with the rhythm section maintaining an absolutely steady beat, the brass and saxophones playing the syncopated patterns of arranged jazz, and the soloists taking improvised choruses, half-choruses and eight-bar strains – the same type of music played by the black bands of Duke Ellington, Count Basie, Jimmie Lunceford and Benny Carter.

3. AMERICAN DOMINATION. The musical style of American popular music of the first half of the 20th century was an international one. Some Tin Pan Alley composers had been born abroad, many others were first-generation Americans, and some spent a great deal of time abroad. Most worked in New York, the most international city in the USA. There was nothing provincial about the environment in which this music was composed and performed.

Not surprisingly, European songs easily became popular in the USA and vice versa. The songs of Gershwin and Porter were widely known in France and England, while *These Foolish Things* (1935), for example, written in England by Jack Strachey and Harry Link, became a favourite in America in the early 1940s; other popular songs were *Szomoru Vasárnap* ('Gloomy Sunday', 1936) by the Hungarian Rezső Seress, Hugh Williams's *Harbour Lights* and the Cuban song *Aquellos ojos verdes* ('Green eyes', 1931) by Nilo Menendez. While most songs popular in America were written by natives this reflected no stylistic difference between American songs and those of other countries with urban popular-music traditions.

The USA was in a strong position at the end of World War II. It had been unified by the wartime mobilization of its armed forces and industry. Its forces were stationed in many parts of the world, occupying defeated countries and maintaining bases in allied and neutral ones. It had escaped the physical devastation suffered by much of Europe, its casualties had been comparatively light, and it was industrially and economically healthy. American ideas, attitudes and culture were thus important in shaping the postwar world. The American troops stationed abroad were supplied with entertainment: American films, live entertainers, record shops, special radio broadcasts and soon the Armed Forces Network, which broadcast mostly American popular music. This entertainment inevitably reached the European friends and brides of American servicemen and the many more Europeans who heard American radio programmes.

The record and film industries of most European countries had been shattered, or had had their activities diverted, by the war. America's were intact, and in the years after the war Europe imported unprecedented numbers of American films and records, partly because they were available, partly because the demand for American products was growing. Although the decade after the war was not, artistically, a peak period for American popular music, its increasing domination of the world market was the most important development in international popular music. American popular styles even had an impact in Africa, particularly in the development of the pan-African style known as CON-GOLESE MUSIC. There was, however, some feeling in Europe that the situation was harmful and unfair to European musicians, and that Europe should resist being engulfed by low-level American culture.

With the recovery of the European record industry by the early 1950s, there was even more reason to resist American music. In some countries there was direct government support of native popular music. An annual festival of popular music begun in San Remo, Italy (1951), was supported largely by the national radio network, RAI, and broadcast in its entirety; it included a competition for Italian songwriters, judged by popular vote. From the mid-1950s similar festivals were held elsewhere in western Europe as well as such eastern European cities as Opole, Poland. The first Eurovision Song Contest, an annual event that is broadcast and televised, was in 1956. Each participating country (of which there were 18 in 1976) is represented by one song, often in English or French, and national juries cast votes. Most of the songs, particularly those which win the most votes, are ballads or lively catchy pop tunes with little national character, much in the style of Tin Pan Alley and film songs of the early 1950s.

4. ROCK AND ROLL.

(i) *The foundations.* Profound changes had taken place within America during and just after World War II. Millions of people from rural areas, particularly the south, flocked to the cities in search of jobs and a better way of life. Many large cities suddenly had greatly increased populations of rural whites and southern blacks, who brought their own cultures, creating a large urban audience for country and black music. At first there was little contact between these types of music and the popular music of white urban Americans. Most city radio stations continued to play Tin Pan Alley music, black musicians played in bars and dance halls where whites never went, poor whites recently from rural areas continued listening to the music they had always liked, and small record shops sold black and country records. Many young whites found interest and excitement in music other than that they were expected to enjoy.

White urban popular music continued to depend predominantly on ballad-type songs in the Tin Pan Alley tradition, with an occasional faster, novelty song (e.g. *The Thing*, by Phil Harris, 1950; *Doggie in the Window*, sung by Patti Page, 1953). But there were

hints of new directions. Frankie Laine, a white singer, had learnt much of his vocal style from blacks, and his rough, harsh, highly emotional, rhythmically flexible singing style (heard in *Mule Train*, 1949) represented a sharp break from the controlled, smooth, European style that dominated popular music and was represented at the time by Tony Bennett, Dinah Shore, Frank Sinatra, Eddie Fisher, Perry Como and Nat King Cole.

Other forms of novelty are represented by *Goodnight, Irene*, written by the black singer Huddie Ledbetter ('Leadbelly') in 1936, sung on a record of 1950 by the Weavers (see §5 below); by *Tennessee Waltz*, written in 1947 by Redd Stewart and Pee Wee King, first played on a country-music station in Louisville, Kentucky, and sung by Patti Page on a popular record of 1950; by *Cold, Cold Heart*, written by the country musician Hank Williams and recorded by Tony Bennett, 1951; and by *Cry*, sung on a 1951–2 recording by Johnny Ray, a white singer whose style, with sobs, gasps, vocal breaks, an unusually high range and unrestrained emotionalism, had much more in common with certain black singers. These songs still had string-dominated orchestras, conventional forms and the 19th-century-derived harmonizations of Tin Pan Alley. But their success indicated the existence of an audience for popular music that departed in some way from traditional Tin Pan Alley patterns.

(ii) *Early rock and roll.* 'Popular music' had been a term referring both to the body of music most widely played on radio, juke-boxes and recordings and to the style of this music. But in 1955 rock and roll, a type of music significantly different in style from what popular music had been, suddenly began to attract widespread enthusiasm. Its advent marked one of the most dramatic turning-points in the history of popular music.

Rock and roll is often reckoned to have begun in the second half of 1955 when *Rock around the Clock*, a recording by Bill Haley and the Comets heard in the film *Blackboard Jungle*, became popular first in America and soon afterwards in Europe. It was not, however, stylistically innovatory; *Crazy, Man, Crazy* (1953) and *Dim, Dim the Lights* by Bill Haley and his group, *Gee* by the Crows, *Work with me Annie* by the Midnighters, *Shake, Rattle and Roll* by Joe Turner and *Sh-boom* by the Chords (all 1954) were in the same general style, which had been developing for some years, mostly among blacks in the south and in northern urban areas populated by transplanted southern blacks. What was new in 1955 was the discovery by major record companies of this music's commercial potential in the white mass market of America and Europe. This had been anticipated; for years, college students in the south, along the Atlantic seaboard and in some large northern cities had been listening to black music on the radio and on records. Alan Freed (1922–65), a disc jockey, had coined the term 'rock and roll' in 1951. The music industry had been slow to recognize that, since the end of World War II, there was a new generation of potential consumers of recorded music with different tastes, attitudes and needs from those of their parents' generation.

The type of black music that developed into rock and roll is accurately described by the term RHYTHM AND BLUES. It used the traditional formal pattern of blues, each verse having three four-bar phrases with the harmonic scheme I–I, IV–I, V–(IV)–I. Most verses were

16. *Bill Haley and the Comets, c1955*

performed by a solo singer accompanied by piano and sometimes guitar, double bass, drums or other instruments used in jazz (e.g. saxophone or trumpet); usually one or more interior verses were played by one of the instruments (usually a saxophone) improvising over the same 12-bar pattern. The singing style was that of blues and authentic jazz: a harsh, hoarse, throaty vocal production, much vocal ornamentation, and a rhythmic style involving much singing slightly ahead of or behind the beat while the rhythm section maintained a steady pulse. Traditional blues had often been sung to a slow tempo, but this new hybrid form borrowed the rhythmic propulsion of jazz, usually proceeding in a moderately fast 4/4 metre with a heavy downbeat and strong rhythmic impulses on the upbeats. Lyrics were often sexually suggestive; the term 'rock and roll' itself had sexual innuendos to blacks. Nonsense syllables were often interpolated by the solo singer, frequently echoed by a small vocal group.

Bill Haley was white and had been a country musician with a group called the Saddlemen. His early rock and roll pieces such as *Rock around the Clock* were stylistically similar to the hybrid rhythm and blues with a few modifications: his instrumentation was that of country music rather than jazz or blues, with several guitars (one of them amplified), double bass and drums; his singing style was hoarse and declamatory but much more on the beat than that of many black singers; and the sexual implications of the music were played down.

Black musicians had sometimes been successful in the world of white urban popular music before 1955, but such people as Lena Horne, the Ink Spots and Nat King Cole had succeeded largely by performing Tin Pan Alley music in a style close to that of white performers. Less than a year after a mass response to rock and roll had been triggered by Haley's group, it was possible for large numbers of black performers playing and singing in their own style to succeed in the white commercial world. Successful recordings by blacks included *Maybellene* by Chuck Berry, *Tutti Frutti* by Little Richard (Penniman), *Bo Diddley* by Bo Diddley (Ellis McDaniel), *Earth Angels* by the Penguins and *The Great Pretender* by the Platters.

The most prominent rock and roll performer was Elvis Presley. He made his first recording in Memphis in 1954 as a country-music singer. The RCA Victor record company engaged him in 1955; early in 1956 his *Heartbreak Hotel* had great success, even among country-music and black audiences, and he had a series of further successes (among them *Hound Dog* and *Love me Tender*, 1956; *Jailhouse Rock*, 1957; *Don't*, 1958; *It's now or never*, 1960). His early hits were mostly in a fast, driving rock and roll style, many in 12-bar blues form, accompanied by his own guitar: basically the same elements from black rhythm and blues and white country music that Haley had used. But Presley was a much better musician and a more dynamic personality, and in his singing style, gestures and stage deportment he often emphasized the sexual implications of rock and roll more than other white musicians had dared. He became the biggest commercial success in the brief history of rock and roll, a film star, a personality idolized by millions of young people. His words and actions were unceasingly reported by the press; he was the symbol of a new era in popular music.

In the decade after 1955 rock and roll encompassed a number of related but distinct musical styles. The best black singers (Little Richard, Diddley, Berry, Fats Domino) continued to perform in the style of black rhythm and blues. The early white rock and roll stars (Presley, Jerry Lee Lewis, Buddy Holly, the Everly Brothers, Haley, the Big Bopper) all had southern country-music backgrounds, and their music synthesized rhythm and blues with white country music. Some black groups (e.g. the Drifters, the Penguins, the Coasters, the Spaniels and the Clovers) sang in a slower, less rhythmically driving tempo, with a smoother vocal sound to their three- and four-part harmonizations; texts were usually sentimental rather than sexual, and the forms were usually those of Tin Pan Alley (*AABA*, *ABAB*) rather than 12-bar blues. By 1957 another style of rock and roll had appeared: music by non-southern whites (e.g. Bobby Darin, Pat Boone, Dion, Paul Anka, Ricky Nelson) whose musical backgrounds were white urban music, not the antecedents of rock and roll. They sang softer, less driving, gentler versions of established rock and roll songs, and new songs with some of the external trappings of rock and roll but rooted in Tin Pan Alley. Their style omitted the raucous, earthy, harsh quality of rock and roll, and had white pre-rock and roll vocal styles, often a string-dominated studio orchestra accompaniment and sentimental or cute texts. With this music Tin Pan Alley was fighting the momentum of rock and roll by incorporating some of its elements and repertory, but creating a style that had almost none of the qualities that had made rock and roll so different from popular music.

(*iii*) *World reaction.* With rock and roll, the music industry had finally recognized that the number of adolescents and college students was so great that music geared to their taste could be financially profitable, even though their parents disliked and even feared it. The older generation found rock and roll loud, harsh, unpleasant, often unintelligible; its sexual innuendos were plain, and for most older people in America and Europe in the mid-1950s sex was not a proper subject for music of a blatant and coarse character. Further, it was clearly a part of such feared trends as racial mixing and the growing antagonism of younger people towards their parents. At first parents attempted to prevent their children from listening to it, radio stations were brought under pressure not to play it, ordinances were proposed to ban live performances, and ministers delivered sermons against it. Yet rock and roll spread rapidly, in both Europe and America.

Rock and roll had quickly reached Europe. By early 1956, the Armed Forces Network, Radio Luxembourg and the BBC were broadcasting many hours of Haley, Presley, Berry and the like. Young people in Germany, Britain, Scandinavia, Switzerland and even countries such as France that had resisted postwar American pop music responded to 'big beat' music (as it was often called) with the same enthusiasm and fanaticism as their

American counterparts. Rock and roll became an international musical language among a certain age group. The film *Rock around the Clock* with Haley and Freed was enormously successful in Europe, particularly in Britain and Germany; and the idiom was aggressively encouraged by American record companies. By early 1957, *Rock around the Clock* had become the first record to sell a million copies in Britain. It was reckoned that at least 75% of the records sold in western Europe at the peak of the rock and roll invasion were American. Eastern European youth was no less enthusiastic, though its access to the music was more difficult: it was officially condemned and records were not on open sale. But the music was widely heard in eastern Europe on the Armed Forces Network and Radio Luxembourg, from tapes and from pirated records.

Rock and roll was resisted in Europe for the same reasons as in America, for its blatant sexuality and its appeal to an age group not well understood and beginning to be feared by its elders. In Britain 'teddy boys' were among the first and most enthusiastic fans of rock and roll. Riots followed showings of the film *Rock around the Clock* in British cinemas, in Milan in 1957 (when rock and roll made a belated entrance into Italy) and in Germany, particularly Berlin, during a tour by Haley in 1958. A legal ban was discussed in France. But by the early 1960s rock and roll seemed to be dying of its own accord.

(*iv*) *British rock and roll: the Beatles.* The first wave of

17. Elvis Presley, 1956

rock and roll had been so strong and so completely American that European performers and writers had been submerged for some years. But by 1960 there were new European pop performers, such as the Italian Modugno, and that year British pop music too gained ground. In Britain in the mid-1950s skiffle bands playing music derived from the pre-rock and roll style of such black Americans as Big Bill Broonzy, Muddy Waters and Leadbelly had found modest and friendly support in coffee houses and had occasionally been recorded (e.g. Lonnie Donegan's *Rock Island Line*, 1956). Tommy Steele became the first successful British rock and roll singer, early in 1956, followed by Cliff Richard in 1958; their style was almost completely derived from that of Americans. Not until 1962–4 were there enough talented, original young British musicians to do more than copy American styles. Many groups (e.g. the Rolling Stones, Herman and the Hermits, the Dave Clark Five, Gerry and the Pacemakers) were successful at this time; the Beatles were the first to make an impact outside the country, alerting the world to the fact that British rock and roll had matured enough to rival American music.

The Beatles' first record, *Love me do* (1962), quickly became popular in Britain. Their climb in popularity and their domination of international popular music was unprecedented. Their first LP record, *Please please me* (1963), was the best seller in Britain for six months in 1963; the song *I want to hold your hand* was the best seller in America only two weeks after its release in early 1964. Their records accounted for an estimated 60% of the total record sales in the USA in the first quarter of 1964, and their first American tour, in February 1964, was one of the most publicized events of the decade. Their success in the USA, easy to document because statistics of record sales and playings were kept with considerable accuracy, was duplicated in every other country with a distribution network.

The Beatles' fantastic success is not easy to explain in terms of their musical style. At least at the beginning it was not distinct from that of many other groups, and was admittedly modelled on Berry, Buddy Holly and the Crickets, the Miracles and the Beach Boys, a Californian group that had also made its first recording in the early 1960s (emphasizing in its songs the freedom of fresh air, surf and sunshine). The Beatles used mostly moderately fast 4/4 tempos; the characteristic rock and roll emphasis on the second and fourth beats; the rock and roll ensemble of solo guitar, rhythm guitar, bass guitar and drums, occasionally piano or electric organ; moderate amplification; songs in *AABA* or *ABAB* forms rather than the 12-bar blues form; texts mostly about love, nice and sweet and rarely suggestive; frequent vocal solos, but, more importantly, ensemble singing with a smooth blend of all four voices in unison or harmony, frequently with very high or even falsetto singing; and harmonies neither as simple as the endlessly repeated I–IV–V chords of blues-based rock and roll nor as sophisticated as those of Tin Pan Alley, but characteristically the use of simple chords in unexpected sequences. The general tone and rhythmic character of their music had strong associations with their Liverpool origins.

Part of the Beatles' appeal lay in their charm, their

18. *The Beatles: (left to right) Paul McCartney, John Lennon, Ringo Starr and George Harrison*

apparent innocence and their direct and happy texts. They were a rock and roll group that even parents could enjoy. They were successful because they were enormously talented in using familiar musical elements to create songs of such apparent simplicity that one wonders why other musicians could not or did not do just what they were doing. John Lennon, George Harrison and Paul McCartney were able to produce lyrics and tunes that resembled those of other writers but were significantly better.

5. THE FOLK-MUSIC REVIVAL. In the 1930s and 1940s a handful of musicians made careers of singing their own arrangements of Anglo-American folksongs (e.g. Burl Ives and John Jacob Niles) to small but loyal audiences in college communities and in liberal circles in the eastern USA, and brought out records that were sometimes moderately popular. At the same time a politically orientated movement led by such musicians as Woody Guthrie, Leadbelly and Pete Seeger used the same body of music to publicize the deprived conditions in which many Americans lived and to rally support to radical political activity that promised to attack these problems. Seeger and Guthrie were members of the Almanac Singers, five or more musicians who performed for liberal and college audiences. Their music was based on traditional tunes, performed in a vocal style retaining much of the harsh, nasal character of country and mountain singing, and accompanied by guitars, banjos and harmonicas. Most of their songs dealt with harsh conditions of life for the poor and repressed in America; sometimes they were old tunes with new, topical texts. This group became the Weavers, who enjoyed commercial success with recordings of such songs as *Goodnight, Irene*, where they compromised their original style to attain popularity: although their most popular records had lush orchestral arrangements and included humorous or sentimental rather than protest songs, they met conservative opposition and were harassed and prevented from bringing out new records or appearing on commercial programmes.

The arrival in New York of Bob Dylan, a young singer from Minnesota, breathed new life into the folk revival. Dylan had gone east to seek out Guthrie, and he stayed to listen to other singers, try out his songs and write new ones. After a few appearances at folk-music clubs he signed a recording contract. He made an LP record, *Bob Dylan* (1961), sang at Carnegie Hall (1961), quickly wrote new songs (notably *Blowin' in the Wind*) and made new recordings; by 1963 he was the central figure in the newly vitalized field of popular folk music. Many of his early songs were based on traditional melodies, but soon he began writing his own words and music. He sang to his own guitar and harmonica accompaniment in a rasping, declamatory voice that combined elements of country music, black and rock and roll styles. His song texts were biting, bitter, satirical and intensely personal commentaries on his own life and the world around him; the language was often obscure, but filled with such vivid words and images that he was taken seriously as a poet. Although older folk musicians felt he was not an authentic member of their movement, Dylan accomplished what they had not: he introduced to millions of listeners a song style derived from traditional Anglo-American music, with texts of apparent protest against American society.

19. Bob Dylan

He claimed to be apolitical, but his songs were adopted by the generation of young political activists who greatly influenced American life in the 1960s. Dylan's success made it easier for other folk-orientated performers (e.g. Joan Baez, Phil Ochs, Tom Paxton, Gordon Lightfoot, Judy Collins) to reach larger audiences.

Another type of 'folk' music was enjoying success at the time. The Kingston Trio, three well-groomed young men, recorded the folksong *Tom Dooley* (1958) which sold in large numbers; a similar group, Peter, Paul and Mary, had a first big success with *Puff, the Magic Dragon* (1963). The music of these groups and many others that imitated them were much more in the tradition of urban popular music than Dylan: their singing style was smooth; their harmonizations were slick and professional; they accompanied themselves with gentle, strummed acoustic guitars; their music soothed while Dylan's assaulted; even though they called their music 'folk', they only occasionally used melodies from authentic traditional music. But with the recording of Dylan's *Blowin' in the Wind* (1963) by Peter, Paul and Mary, two strains of the folk revival came together, and for the rest of the 1960s some form of folk-based music was dominant in the complex web of popular music styles.

6. THE ROCK MOVEMENT.
(*i*) *The background*. Rock (as opposed to rock and roll), which dominated popular music over most of the world for almost a decade from the early 1960s, cannot be defined in terms of a single musical style. It was rather a conglomeration of styles unified by a common spirit, a common environment and a common objective. Clearly it is impossible to define in purely musical terms a style

encompassing, for example, the Rolling Stones, Country Joe and the Fish, Joni Mitchell, Sly and the Family Stone, Jefferson Airplane, Deep Purple, Led Zeppelin, Donovan, the Who, Jimi Hendrix, Paul Simon and Cream. The music of these and of many others, however, came to be understood by its listeners as a single body.

The rise of rock in the 1960s cannot be seen apart from socio-political events of the time. This was the period when many small countries were trying to gain freedom from domination by larger and stronger nations; when various racial and ethnic groups were fighting to overcome historical patterns of repression and persecution; and when individuals in many parts of the world began seeing the possibility of attaining personal liberation from social, cultural, political and sexual patterns that inhibited their free development.

With communications worldwide and instantaneous, there was a great deal of identification among these three kinds of struggle, and the student movement was concerned with them all. Student demonstrations in Paris, Warsaw, New York and Berkeley were part of the same pattern. A loosely organized, worldwide community of minority ethnic groups, politically repressed minorities, entire small countries and individuals set out in the 1960s to do what they could, by any means, to change patterns at all levels that they viewed as repressive and restrictive. Almost without exception, rock musicians belonged, in convictions and action, to this strange coalition. Their music became an inseparable part of many of the public and private acts of defiance and rebellion that characterized the era.

(ii) *The music: to 1970.* Rock differed from rock and roll in some obvious ways. It was electric, heavily dependent on amplification and electronic distortion, eventually even electronic generation, of sound. Forms became freer and more elastic, ranging from brief, traditional, sectional song forms to extended improvisations that often appear to be form-free. Texts sometimes dealt with social and political issues, sometimes with intensely personal experiences presented in introverted and often obscure language. Audiences continued to be predominantly young, but many older people, particularly those with liberal or radical political outlooks, began listening to rock. There was even the beginning of serious critical writing about this music, and the subject became one for study in universities.

There was no clear point of demarcation between, on the one hand, rock and roll and, on the other, rock, in the early 1960s. Some musicians, like the Beatles, went through a gradual change in style, retaining much of the musical language that had brought them popularity while gradually absorbing new elements. In *The House of the Rising Sun* (1965) an English group, the Animals, used a mixture of blues-derived sounds and forms, vigorous driving rhythms and imaginative amplification in sharp contrast to the scrubbed-up, commercial, international rock and roll style of the early 1960s. The Rolling Stones, from 1964, featured a more earthy sound, lyrics that often bordered on the scandalous, and personal appearance and stage deportment that were deliberately provocative. Bob Dylan, whose first use of amplification (Newport Festival, 1965) alienated many people, was in the vanguard of the rock style with the increasing harshness and bitterness of his lyrics and timbres.

In the mid-1960s San Francisco became a centre for the development of rock in the USA. This was attributable partly to the presence nearby of a strongly dissident student community at the University of California at Berkeley, which promoted the Free Speech Movement and the first serious protests against the war in Vietnam, and partly to the city's traditional tolerance, which led to its Haight-Ashbury district's becoming a centre for new types of urban commune in which drugs were freely used and many of the traditional modes of American life were increasingly abandoned. New forms of rock flourished in such a context. In October 1965 a community rock concert and dance at Longshoreman's Hall attracted the Charlatans, five musicians from Virginia City, Nevada, playing music based on country blues; the Great Society, with the singer Grace Slick; and Jefferson Airplane. Other dance concerts followed, and two 'rock palaces' were established to provide nightly music and dancing: the Avalon, founded by Chet Helms, with the band Big Brother and the Holding Company and the singer Janis Joplin; and Fillmore Auditorium, managed by Bill Graham. Within a year there were more than 1000 rock bands in the area, notably the Grateful Dead, Quicksilver Messenger Service, and Country Joe and the Fish.

The music of these pioneer San Francisco rock palaces was based on country and blues, with all instruments heavily amplified and often distorted. The lead guitar played a fluid, wailing, expressive line that owed much to blues singing techniques yet often sounded remarkably like a jazz saxophone. The rhythm and bass guitars often functioned as percussion, but also played solos and at other times took part in a dense, rich contrapuntal texture. The rhythm section – drums and sometimes piano – emphasized the heavy downbeats that characterized this music; they too had solos. One or more of the players also sang, with vocal techniques necessarily based on the use of the microphone. Lyrics were political, obscure, openly sexual and sometimes mystical. 'Light shows', projected on screens above and behind the musicians, used slides, moving film, strobe lights and the projection of oils swirling in water; the lights sometimes pulsed to the beat of the music, sometimes bathed the performers and audience in colour. Most of the audience danced, singly, improvising movements and motions suggested by the music, the lights, or the drugs that most of them took (usually LSD, giving the name 'acid rock' to the music).

The Byrds were the first west-coast group to bring this music to the east coast of the USA. Their recording of Bob Dylan's *Mr Tambourine Man* (1965), with amplified acoustic guitars, other folk instruments, and a singing style modelled on country and southern revival-hymn music, became particularly popular, and their performance in New York in early 1966 was the first elaborate light show to be given there; the nature of the audience helped give the movement respectability in intellectual circles. In early 1967 Jefferson Airplane, now with Grace Slick, went to New York. Later that year the east coast's first rock palaces opened in New York – Bill Graham's Fillmore East and the Electric Circus. In California, rock performers including Janis Joplin, Jimi Hendrix and the Grateful Dead performed in the Monterey Pop Festival for the first time in 1967, and a commercial film of the festival introduced the music to a national audience.

For a brief period, rock had little effect on popular

music. The most popular songs of 1965, including *Downtown* sung by Petula Clark, *This Diamond Ring* by Gary Lewis and the Playboys and *Mr Lonely* by Bobby Vinton, were indebted to commercialized rock and roll and to late Tin Pan Alley style, and in 1966 *Strangers in the Night*, sung by Frank Sinatra and solidly in the Kern and Berlin tradition, reached the top of the music industry's sales lists. The various forms of rock, however, soon became popular as the success of various recordings demonstrates, including *Mr Tambourine Man* and *Turn, Turn, Turn* (sung by the Byrds, 1965), and the Rolling Stones' erotic song *Satisfaction*. In late 1965 and 1966 the Beatles began using more obscure texts, with thinly veiled references to drugs, new instrumental sounds and more complex harmonies and rhythms (e.g. in *Norwegian Wood*, *Eleanor Rigby* and *Yellow Submarine*). In 1966 Paul Simon and Art Garfunkel, who had begun as folk-revival entertainers, unveiled their own style of rock in *Sounds of Silence*.

From the mid-1960s numerous black performers captured a large part of the pop market with styles derived from blues, rhythm and blues, gospel music and other forms, which collectively became known as SOUL MUSIC. An international adjunct to these styles was REGGAE, which originated in Jamaica.

In 1967 the Beatles' record *Sergeant Pepper's Lonely Hearts Club Band* appeared, containing songs covering an unprecedentedly wide stylistic and expressive range, and ending with a reprise of the first song, with the haunting, mysterious *A Day in the Life* as a sort of coda. The moods range from the rollicking good nature of the title song, through the amusing music-hall text and style of *When I'm Sixty-four*, the melodramatic *She's Leaving Home* and the obscure, surrealistic *Lucy in the Sky with Diamonds*; accompaniments include the traditional rock ensemble of two guitars, bass and drums, such instruments as the sitar, with natural sounds (e.g. cheering crowds, animal noises) and an instrumental ensemble approaching the sound of a symphony orchestra. These various elements are overlaid, mixed and superimposed on multiple taped tracks, creating sounds of great subtlety and complexity. This is a studio recording; its musical effects would be unobtainable in live performance.

1967 was also the year that Jim Morrison and the Doors, a group from California that had been popular underground, with an insolent, obscurely poetic, openly erotic style, achieved prominence: their first record (1967) begins with the ferocious *Break on through* and ends with *The End*, an 11½-minute piece in which Morrison, singing as if in a trance, works up to insane shrieks as the lyrics have him kill an imaginary father. The group reached national popularity in 1967 with *Light my Fire*, probably one of the most erotic songs then to have been commercially recorded. Jimi Hendrix, who also appeared in 1967, was a black, left-handed guitar player, using the most explosive, ear-splitting amplification yet heard, creating a volume and complexity of sound that almost literally deafened his audiences, while engaging in outrageous stage deportment that included simulated sexual acts with his guitar and concluded with a frenzied scene in which he doused the guitar with lighter fluid and burnt it, with amplification turned increasingly higher.

The Who, an English group consisting of Pete Townshend (guitar), John Entwistle (bass guitar), Keith Moon (drums; replaced, after his death in 1978, by Kenny Jones) and Roger Daltrey (voice), also exploited ear-splitting amplification, electronic feedback and a gymnastic stage act; the interpretative movement varied from song to song, but usually ended with Townshend smashing his guitar and tossing it to an audience almost wild with excitement. Janis Joplin, an energetic white blues singer, had a vocal technique ranging from almost inaudible whispers through straight blues singing to hoarse bellows, and was accompanied by the highly amplified Big Brother and the Holding Company. The Velvet Underground, working with Andy Warhol's 'total environment' show, *The Exploding Plastic Inevitable*, performed songs about sex, drugs, murder, sado-masochism and the like in a show integrating films, music, dancers, slides and the audience, who were part of the show. In another vein, the Moody Blues made the recording *Days of Future Passed* with the London Festival Orchestra, the first attempt to synthesize rock and classical music. *Nights in White Satin* from this record became popular in Britain and the USA. Cream, formed with extensive advance publicity as rock's first 'super-group', included Ginger Baker (percussion), Eric Clapton (guitar) and Jack Bruce (bass guitar), who had already achieved fame as virtuosos, particularly from their extended solo improvisations. They set new standards of ensemble playing and had a significant influence on other rock groups before disbanding in 1968.

One side of Simon and Garfunkel's record *Bookends* (1968) is a cycle of six songs about the various stages of life from youth to old age. The Beatles' *Abbey Road* (1969) also has an entire side devoted to a tightly unified piece. The Iron Butterfly's *In-a-gadda-da-vida* (1969) has one side of uninterrupted improvisation. The Yardbirds often played a 'rave-up', an improvised instrumental piece lasting as long as half an hour, with the guitar playing of Eric Clapton. The Who created *Tommy*, widely called the first 'rock opera', a long series of songs and instrumental pieces held together by a thread of a plot and recurring musical material; in 1971 they performed *Tommy* at the Metropolitan Opera House in New York before a socially mixed audience.

Donovan (Donovan Phillips Leitch), from Scotland, sang quiet songs that seemed to owe something to Dylan and something to the West Indies but were unmistakably his own (e.g. *Catch the Wind*, *Mellow Yellow* and *Jennifer Juniper*), accompanied by his guitar. The Incredible String Band consisted of a duo playing several instruments, including the guitar, sitar, dulcimer, electric organ, mandolin, panpipes, *gmbri* (a Berber lute), *shahnāī* (an Indian oboe) and harpsichord, creating a strange, mystical, ethereal mood. The sitarist Ravi Shankar was enthusiastically accepted by rock audiences. The American organist Virgil Fox played Bach on the electric organ, with a light show, at such places as Fillmore East, and this too was accepted as part of rock. The most significant single event of the period was the outdoor festival in Woodstock, New York, in August 1969, attended by at least half a million people in several days of rock, drugs, war protests and fellowship, with many well-known rock artists: it received considerable attention and was seriously discussed as representing an alternative world of peace, music and drugs.

(*iii*) *Later rock*. Later rock festivals were less pleasant than Woodstock, and at some there was violence and death. Rock became associated with less acceptable

20. *Free pop concert in Hyde Park, London, on 31 August 1974, with (from left to right) John Paul Jones (bass guitar), Steve Broughton (drums) and Roy Harper (lead guitar)*

forms of political radicalism and damaging excesses, an association reinforced by the deaths, many from drug-related causes, of rock performers such as Janis Joplin, Jimi Hendrix, Jim Morrison and Brian Jones of the Rolling Stones. Many of the best rock groups of the 1960s, however, continued into the 1970s, some (e.g. the Rolling Stones) with equal success. New and successful groups in the early 1970s included Jethro Tull, an English group featuring some of the most virtuoso playing ever heard in rock; America, building on the tradition of country rock; and Alice Cooper, featuring perhaps the most outlandish stage deportment ever, such as female dress and simulated murder scenes. Other groups, notably the Beatles, disbanded.

The most successful new performers were singers. James Taylor, who recorded *Sweet Baby James* (1970), had a style based on country music, nasal but clear and sweet, with a small ensemble of acoustic instruments. Carole King had been a successful songwriter for some years, and became prominent as a performer on the recordings *Tapestry* (1971) and *Music* (1972); her songs were simple, usually strophic, introspective and gentle, accompanied by a piano, one or two guitars and a bass guitar. Almost all rock performers had been male, but in the 1970s audiences were more receptive to women; veterans (some with folk affiliations) such as Judy Collins and Joni Mitchell were more successful.

A typical rock artist of the 1970s was Elton John, trained as a pianist for five years at the Royal Academy of Music, London, before playing in a series of rock and blues bands; with the lyricist Bernie Taupin he began writing songs in the late 1960s. His first record, *Elton John* (1970), was widely successful in Britain and America and was followed by *Tumbleweed Connection* (1971) and *Madman across the Water* (1972). His songs show a wide expressive and technical range, from tender and nostalgic to raucous and humorous, with a

recognizable musical style combining elements of rock and roll, country music, serious music and English music hall. Whether accompanied by a small group or a studio orchestra with strings, his virtuoso piano playing and his individual presence are always evident.

In rock music of the 1970s, political and sociological involvement had given way to personalization and introspection, and groups had given way to individual performers (just as the mass protests and demonstrations had largely disappeared). The popular music of the 1970s was quieter and simpler, using traditional song forms, simpler textures and chords, as opposed to improvisation, free forms and electronic distortion. Many stylistic elements of rock of the 1960s developed because the music was largely instrumental, but in the 1970s the music returned much more to the voice and to the text.

As with rock and roll a decade before, rock reached Europe through broadcasts, recordings and through tours by English and American groups. Rock palaces were established in such cities as Amsterdam, where tolerance of drugs enabled the San Francisco mixture of rock and drugs to be emulated. Rock groups were established in various European countries; their music was clearly derived from American and British rock. Outdoor rock concerts were held in various cities in western Europe and even in Budapest; outdoor festivals lasting several days and bringing together many groups also spread. Despite severe political disturbances at festivals in France during 1968, there were numerous peaceful festivals throughout the country in the early 1970s. Rock and pop festivals proliferated in Britain, the largest being the three-day Isle of Wight Festival in August 1970 which drew 200,000 people.

7. THE 1970S. There was no significant break during the 1970s in the Anglo-American domination of world popular music. There was, to be sure, a large and grow-

ing amount of indigenous popular music and rock in various countries around the globe: Japan had numerous rock bands; several Spanish-speaking countries in both Europe and the New World continued their lively tradition of vernacular song flavoured with local musical dialects; the African continent was teeming with 'highlife' and other regional types of popular music combining native languages and musical traditions with Western instruments, harmonies and song forms; even the USSR had popular groups mixing the musical idioms and instruments of various parts of the country with the rhythmic drive and stylistic clichés of 'soft rock'. None of this reached the world market in sufficient quantity to make an impact. Musically and economically, the hegemony of the USA and Britain continued, and in those countries most of the songs popular at any time were national products, with a smaller number imported from the other country. Elsewhere the pattern was of a fluctuating mixture of local repertory with British and American items; it continued to be unusual for a record from a country other than Britain or the USA to gain currency in a third country. The path to wider distribution for outsiders was that followed by the Australian singer Olivia Newton-John and the German group Tangerine Dream: performances and record distribution within one of the two dominant countries. Local dialects of the world popular music language are thus not central to the development of the genre.

In Britain and the USA, the main tendencies were eclecticism, consolidation and fusion. There were no new musical currents as powerful as the birth of rock and roll in the early 1950s or the emergence of rock in the 1960s. On popular radio, conservative rock and pop styles prevailed, and in some instances there was even a return to aspects of pre-rock Tin Pan Alley style. Several songwriters of the 1960s continued to be productive. Some of Paul Simon's songs were of a quality equalling or even surpassing his early ones; and Rod Stewart had a success in 1971 (*Maggie May*) after years as a journeyman singer for various British rock groups. Stevie Wonder began moving in more individual directions in the 1970s, making use of overdubbing techniques to play most of the instruments himself, and moving away from the MOTOWN sound of his early years to a distinctive mixture of soul, pop, gospel music and earlier Tin Pan Alley styles. Linda Ronstadt, the most successful female singer of the second half of the decade, was exceptional in that she did not write her own songs but depended on composers and arrangers to supply her with diverse material, drawing on rock and roll, folk rock, new pop songs, rearrangements of country-rock favourites and traditional Anglo-American ballads.

Established rock groups continued to be productive, and the most successful new ones worked within the now traditional rock styles. Among them were the California-based Eagles, Fleetwood Mac (an older group that succeeded only after many personnel and style changes) and the Bay City Rollers (who settled down to turning out pleasantly bouncy songs in their own version of the mainstream pop-rock style). In the USA the most significant change was geographical, as such southern groups as the Allman Brothers and the Marshall Tucker Band brought the centre of rock back to the region where its stylistic roots lie.

Stylistic mixtures of black and white music are common in Anglo-American music. Soul music was at first dominated by the Motown sound of Detroit, but the situation became more complex when Kenny Gamble and Leon Huff, in Philadelphia, joined the singer Jerry Butler to create a somewhat different sound, light and shimmering, with such instruments as the vibraphone and marimba combining with guitars, crisp drumming and falsetto singing to give a distinctive sensual effect; they later polished and refined this texture further. Others enjoyed similar success with the same sort of 'pop soul', a term correctly implying roots in both black and white music. Discotheques had flourished at various times in the 1960s and early 1970s; their peak popularity began in 1974, partly because of the practice of emphasizing the type of 'pop soul' music just mentioned. The new 'Philadelphia sound' – light, rhythmic, sensual and bouncy – suited the new style of dancing, and discotheque patrons danced to music of increasingly varied origin: records produced by small studios (such as TK in Florida), older soul records, music by white southern bands (for example the popular *Get down tonight* by KC and the Sunshine Band), novelties (such as *Disco Duck* by Ricky Dee's Cast of Idiots) and 'disco' versions of classical music (*A Fifth of Beethoven* by Walter Murphy). This was the most purely instrumental, dance-orientated popular music for two decades, and it quickly swept Britain, the USA and then the rest of the world. There was a similar cross-over between rock and country music, typified by the popularity in both contexts of many songs by Linda Ronstadt and Olivia Newton-John, as well as ones by Johnny Cash, Dolly Parton and Crystal Gayle.

The only significant international success of other than Anglo-American popular music came from Jamaica. Jamaican 'soul rock' came particularly to be known in 1973 with the film *The Harder they Come*, about the world of reggae. The most successful reggae group was Bob Marley and the Wailers, formed in 1964 but widely successful only in the mid-1970s. Featuring a hard, sparse, driving rock texture of amplified guitars and bass, hard and brittle drumming, combined with insistent Afro-Latin rhythms and call-and-response singing that often resembled African vocal production and techniques, their songs deal with the social and economic injustices of their country. Such protest music was strangely out of place in the 1970s, when audiences tended to listen to sounds rather than messages, and their biting lyrics rallied no other oppressed groups.

Within Anglo-American rock, the middle and late 1970s saw a return to the large groups and heavily amplified sounds of the previous decade. Elton John provides an instructive example. His early success had been as a writer of imaginative and often delicate songs; by 1975 he used a large supporting cast of instrumentalists and singers, with amplifiers, filling the largest available halls with very loud sound, and affecting outlandish costumes and stage deportment. During the 1970s the amplification of voices and instruments became routine in live performance. The traditional rock band of guitars, electric bass, keyboard and drums came regularly to be augmented by woodwind, brass and even strings. Such an orchestra became almost standard in all kinds of music – rock, pop, soul and country. The piano and electric organ were augmented, and often replaced, by synthesizers, which brought to the ensemble an increasingly wide range of colour and amplitude of sound.

Emerson, Lake and Palmer, a popular British group

of the 1970s, was typical of those dependent on electricity. Composed of only three musicians, it made use of sophisticated amplification and sound distortion, together with electrically produced sound, on a variety of instruments played with immense virtuosity to create a wide sonic spectrum ranging from occasional simple amplification of guitar, drums, bass and voice to enormous packages rivalling the symphony orchestra in richness, volume and complexity. The group played music of great stylistic diversity, from English folksongs to arrangements of hymns, fusions of jazz and rock, and versions of such works as Musorgsky's *Pictures at an Exhibition*, fugues and toccatas by J. S. Bach and Aaron Copland's *Rodeo*. Members of several other groups making important use of electricity were trained or had an interest in classical music, and their pieces often reflect the harmonies and sonorities of late 19th-century art music, notably that of Liszt and Debussy. The Moody Blues pioneered the synthesis of classical music and rock in the late 1960s, and Pink Floyd was probably the first group to depend on electronic technology to imitate orchestral sounds. King Crimson and Tangerine Dream were later practitioners of what has been called 'art rock'. Brian Eno, once connected with the avant garde in London and somewhat influenced by John Cage and La Monte Young, worked in the electronic medium (*Discreet Music*, 1975) and subsequently worked with Robert Fripp, once of King Crimson. The recording of Mike Oldfield's *Tubular Bells* (1973) is a spectacular demonstration of what can be done by one man in an electronic studio.

The growing use of electronics for live performance coincided with the use of increasingly complex and sophisticated lighting and other visual effects as part of a rock stage act. The groups Yes and Genesis, for example, combined their electric sound with spectacular light shows (recalling those of the California groups of the mid-1960s), incorporating such new technology as laser beams. The soul-rock Earth, Wind and Fire used holograms in their visual show. Other groups have made use of pervasive amplification and sound generation with music that in propulsion, rhythm and gesture continues the rock tradition of the 1960s. This trend extends from such 'heavy metal' groups as Led Zeppelin and Iron Butterfly to countless newer British and American bands, among them Deep Purple, Grand Funk Railroad, Black Sabbath and Queen.

The last two groups occasion mention of yet another important link between practices of the 1970s and the early tradition of rock. Provocative and outlandish stage attire and behaviour have been an important resource since the birth of rock and roll. The two decades following Presley witnessed a steady, ever changing parade of hair styles, costumes, gestures and props; as the level of tolerance and acceptance rose, rock stars adopted more bizarre and shocking images. The line extends from Presley through Little Richard, Jerry Lee Lewis, Jimi Hendrix, the Rolling Stones, Jim Morrison, the Who and Alice Cooper to Queen. It is in this context that 'punk' rock (and the related 'New Wave', seen by some as a startling new direction in the late 1970s, must be considered. Such groups as the Sex Pistols, with their loud and often extremely simple hard-rock sound, their stage conduct (vomiting, spitting, fighting and disrobing on stage), their texts with a range from obscene and blasphemous to inaudible, their peculiar attire and their anarchistic pose, were in many ways among the more traditional of the new rock groups, simply modernizing many important aspects of the rock scene. What was new about punk rock, however, was its inclusion of the rock 'establishment' among such traditional targets for scorn as governmental, religious, political and educational establishments and the police.

At the same time, however, rock achieved a new respectability and power. The journal *Rolling Stone*, a symbol of the dissident late 1960s, was a decade later filled with news of increasingly prosperous rock producers, backers and performers, and has a wider circulation of higher social standing. Serious newspapers in most Western countries began to carry regular reviews of rock and pop concerts and recordings as well as articles on rock music and musicians. Lectures and courses on rock have become commonplace in colleges and universities; papers dealing with this music and its sociological and cultural significance are read at meetings of learned societies; and dissertations have been written on the Beatles and their contemporaries. What started as a rebellious sub-culture has been embraced by large and important elements of mainstream culture in America and Europe.

BIBLIOGRAPHY

J. S. Patterson: *The Folksong Revival and some Sources of the Popular Image of the Folksinger: 1920–1963* (diss., Indiana U., 1963)
C. Belz: *The Story of Rock* (New York, 1969, 2/1972)
D. D. Braun: *Toward a Theory of Popular Culture: the Sociology and History of American Music and Dance, 1920–1968* (Ann Arbor, Mich., 1969)
N. Cohn: *Rock from the Beginning* (New York, 1969)
J. Eisen, ed.: *The Age of Rock* (New York, 1969–70)
D. Laing: *The Sound of our Time* (London and Sydney, 1969)
L. Roxon: *Lillian Roxon's Rock Encyclopedia* (New York, 1969, 2/1971)
A. Shaw: *The Rock Revolution* (London and New York, 1969)
L. Brown and G. Friedrich: *Encyclopedia of Rock & Roll* (New York, 1970)
T. Cash, ed.: *Anatomy of Pop* (London, 1970)
C. Gillett: *The Sound of the City: the Rise of Rock and Roll* (New York, 1970, 2/1972)
B. Larson: *Rock and Roll, the Devil's Diversion* (McCook, Nebraska, 1970)
R. Leydi: *Dizionario della musica popolare europea* (Milan, 1970)
R. Meltzer: *The Aesthetics of Rock* (New York, 1970)
L. Stanley: *Folk Rock: a Bibliography on Music of the Sixties* (San José, Calif., 1970)
R. S. Denisoff: *Great Day Coming: Folk Music and the American Left* (Urbana, Ill., 1971)
A. H. Goldman: *Freakshow: the Rocksoulbluesjazzsickjewblackhumorsexpoppsych Gig and Other Scenes from the Counter-culture* (New York, 1971)
L. Roxon: *Rock Encyclopedia* (New York, 1971)
G. Wood: *An A–Z of Rock and Roll* (London, 1971)
The Age of Paranoia: How the Sixties Ended (New York, 1972)
R. Hoffman: *Zwischen Galaxis und Underground: die neue Popmusik* (Munich, 1972)
T. Jasper: *Understanding Pop* (London, 1972)
J. Landau: *It's Too Late to Stop Now: a Rock and Roll Journal* (San Francisco, 1972)
I. Whitcomb: *After the Ball* (London, 1972)
P. Flattery: *The Illustrated History of Pop* (London, 1973; New York, 1975, as *The Illustrated History of British Pop*)
M. Friedman: *Buried Alive: the Biography of Janis Joplin* (New York, 1973)
P. Hesbacher: 'Contemporary Popular Music: Suggested Directions for Further Research', *Popular Music and Society*, ii (1973), 297
M. Jahn: *Rock: from Elvis Presley to the Rolling Stones* (New York, 1973)
A. Leibovitz, ed.: *Shooting Stars: the Rolling Stone Book of Portraits* (San Francisco, 1973)
G. Peellaert: *Rock Dreams: 20 Jahre Popmusik von A bis Z* (Munich, 1973)
E. Sanders: *Trips: Rock Life in the Sixties* (New York, 1973)
I. Stambler: *Encyclopedia of Popular Music and Rock* (New York, 1973)
J. C. Whitburn: *Top Pop Records 1955–1972* (Menomonee Falls, Wisc., 1973)

B. W. Anderson: *Popular American Music: Changes in the Consumption of Sound Recordings, 1940–1955* (diss., U. of Pennsylvania, 1974)

N. N. Nite: *Rock On: the Illustrated Encyclopedia of Rock 'n Roll* (New York, 1974)

L. N. Redd: *Rock is Rhythm and Blues: the Impact of the Mass Media* (East Lansing, Mich., 1974)

A. Shaw: *The Rockin' 50s: the Decade that Transformed the Pop Music Scene* (New York, 1974)

C. Hamm, B. Nettl and R. Byrnside: *Contemporary Music and Music Cultures* (Englewood Cliffs, NJ, 1975)

M. Nyman: 'Experimental Music and the American Vernacular Tradition', *1st American Music Conference: Keele 1975*, 142

S. Schmidt-Joos: *Rock-Lexikon* (Reinbek, 1975)

T. Souster: 'The Rock Influence', *1st American Music Conference: Keele 1975*, 134

I. Stambler: *Encyclopedia of Pop, Rock and Soul* (New York, 1975)

E. Stoelting: *Deutsche Schlager und englische Popmusik in Deutschland: ideologiekritische Untersuchung zur Textstile waehrend der Jahre 1960–1970* (Bonn, 1975)

L. Grossman: *A Social History of Rock Music* (New York, 1976)

D. Laing and P. Hardy, eds.: *The Encyclopedia of Rock* (St Albans, 1976–)

J. Miller, ed.: *The Rolling Stone Illustrated History of Rock & Roll* (New York, 1976)

T. Kneif: 'Rockmusik und Bildungsmusik', *IRASM*, viii (1977), 237

S. Borris: *Popmusik: Kunst aus Provokation* (Wiesbaden, 1978)

T. Kneif: *Sachlexikon Rockmusik* (Reinbek, 1978)

S. Nugent and C. Gillett: *Rock Almanac: Top Twenty American and British Singles and Albums of the '50s, '60s, and '70s* (Garden City, 1978)

C. Hamm: *Popular Song in America* (New York, 1979)

ANDREW LAMB (I), CHARLES HAMM (II–III)

Poquelin, Jean-Baptiste. *See* MOLIÈRE.

Poradowski, Stefan Bolesław (*b* Włocławek, 16 Aug 1902; *d* Poznań, 9 July 1967). Polish composer and teacher. He graduated in 1926 from the Poznań Conservatory, where he had studied composition and theory with Opieński, and at the same time he graduated in law from Poznań University. His music studies were continued with von Reznicek in Berlin (1929). From 1930 until the outbreak of World War II, and again from 1945, he was a professor of composition and theory at the Poznań Conservatory. He also taught at the Wrocław Conservatory from 1956, his pupils there including Koszewski and Natanson. Among the awards he received were two Warsaw Competition prizes (1935 for the Trio no.3, 1946 for the Sinfonietta) and the City of Poznań Prize (1960).

Poradowski's early works are in a Germanic late-Romantic style. He then attempted to develop a more individual style, drawing on impressionist features. During his subsequent career his style changed to some extent, but his basic approach remained the same: he ignored the newest techniques and wrote in a straightforward manner, mostly contrapuntal, melodically well-shaped, sometimes with rich harmonies, and formally classical. In later years he lacked consistency and self-criticism.

WORKS
(selective list)

ORCHESTRAL

Syms.: no.1, 1928; no.2, 1930; no.3, 1932; no.4, 1934; no.5, 1937–8; no.6 (Symfonia jubileuszowa), 1951–2; Sym. no.7, 1961; Sym. no.8, 1967

Other works: Classical Conc., va d'amore, str, 1925; Sinfonietta, small orch, 1925; Tryptyk, str; Db Conc., 1929; Classical Serenade, str, 1940; Polish Rhapsody, vn, orch, 1944–5; Concert Ov., 1947; Ratusz poznański [Poznań Town Hall], sym. poem, 1950; Conc., fl, harp, str, 1954; Nocturne, fl, harp, str, 1961; Vn Conc., 1965

VOCAL

Opera: Płomienie [Flames] (3, J. Cygańska), 1961–6; orch suite, 1963

Choral: Pieśń wiosenna [Spring song] (E. Zegadłowicz), S, chorus, orch, 1926; Koń Światowida [The horse of Światowid] (Zegadłowicz), T, Bar, chorus, orch, 1931; Odkupienie [Redemption]

(K. Trzywdar-Rakowski), Mez, chorus, orch, 1939–41; Rapsod poznański, cantata, 1950; Laur wawrzynowy (Poradowski), cantata, 1954; Pieśń o Wiśle, cantata, 1954; 3 masses, 4 hymns, many other pieces

Songs (Staff, Słoński, Zbierzchowski, etc); folksong arrs.

CHAMBER AND INSTRUMENTAL

Chamber: Str Qt no.1 'Metamorfozy', 1923; Str Qt no.2, 1923; Sonata, vn, pf, 1925; Trio no.1, vn, va, db, 1929; Trio no.2, vn, va, db, 1930; Trio no.3, vn, va, db, 1935; Str Qt no.3, 1936; Str Qt no.4, 1947; Trio no.4, 3 db, 1952; Trio no.5, vn, va, vc, 1955; Preludium i toccata, vn, pf, 1961; Capriccia, db, 1963

Pf: Preludium i fuga, 1925; Tryptyk, 1939–44; Preludium i fuga, 1956

Org: Tryptyk, 1926; Preludium i fuga [on themes from W. Gieburowski: Magnificat], 1946

Principal publisher: Polskie Wydawnictwo Muzyczne

WRITINGS

Nauka harmonii [Harmony treatise] (Poznań, 1931, rev. 5/1964)

Ogólne wiadomości z akustyki [General knowledge on acoustics] (Poznań, 1947)

BIBLIOGRAPHY
F. Dąbrowski: 'Stefan Bolesław Poradowski', *Ruch muzyczny* (1967), no.16, p.9

E. Drozdowski: 'Stefan Bolesław Poradowski', *Ruch muzyczny* (1968), no.19, p.18

BOGUSŁAW SCHÄFFER

Porcelijn, David (*b* Achtkarspelen, Friesland, 7 Jan 1947). Dutch composer and conductor. At the conservatory in The Hague he studied the flute with Vester (1964–8) and composition with Van Baaren and Van Vlijmen (1966–70), winning the composition prize in 1970. He then studied conducting with Stotijn, and composition and conducting with Tabachnik in Geneva, where he remained as Tabachnik's assistant.

WORKS
(selective list)

Continuations, 11 wind, 1968; Requiem, perc ens, 1970; Cybernetisch objekt, orch, 1971; 10-5-6-5(a), wind qnt, 2 vib, 2 str qt, 1972; Pulverizations, wind qnt, 1972; Pole II, b cl, 1973; Into the Earth, 14 brass, 2 perc, 1976; 12 November 1819, wind qnt, 1976

Principal publisher: Donemus

WRITINGS

Communications for (Easy) Flute and Modern Flutist (The Hague, 1971)

Method for the Flute (Wormerveer, 1971)

BIBLIOGRAPHY
E. Vermeulen: 'David Porcelijn: Cybernetica for Orchestra', *Sonorum speculum* (1971–2), no.49, p.13

ROGIER STARREVELD

Porcile, Giuseppe. *See* PORSILE, GIUSEPPE.

Pordenon, Marc'Antonio da (*b* Padua, 1535; *d* ?c1580–90). Italian composer, nephew of G. A. Licino detto il Pordenone. In 1571 he was *maestro di cappella* in the service of 'Ill.mo & Rever.mo Strozzi'. In 1578, as can be seen from his fifth book of five-part madrigals, he was *maestro di cappella* of S Marco at Pordenone, the town from which his family took its name. In November 1580 he applied for the position of *maestro di cappella* at Padua Cathedral, but received only two votes out of 23 and Giovanni Battista Mosto was the successful applicant. Pordenon's *Primo libro de madrigali à 4*, published in the same year, indicates that he was connected with the Accademici Olimpici of Vicenza.

WORKS
(all except anthologies published in Venice)

Il primo libro de madrigali, 5vv (1564)

Il secondo libro de madrigali, 5vv (1567)

Il terzo libro de madrigali, 5vv (1571)

Il quarto libro de madrigali, 5vv (1573)

Il quinto libro de madrigali, 5vv (1578)

Il primo libro de madrigali, 4vv (1580[11])

Messe, cited in 1628 inventory of Scuola degli Accoliti and Verona Cathedral, *I-VEcap*

Works in 1563[13], 1577[7], 1583[11], 1583[14], 1584[15], 1587[7], 1588[29], 1589[10], 1593[4]

BIBLIOGRAPHY

R. Casimiri: 'Musica e musicisti nella cattedrale di Padova', *NA*, xviii (1941), 112; xix (1942), 70

K. BOSI MONTEATH

Porena, Boris (*b* Rome, 27 Sept 1927). Italian composer. He studied in Rome under Petrassi and others, receiving diplomas in the piano (1948) and composition (1953) at the conservatory and graduating in literature at the university (1957). In 1957–60 he attended the Darmstadt summer courses and in 1965 he won the Città di Milano award with *Über aller dieser deiner Trauer*. He has contributed to RAI and specialist publications (e.g. the *Enciclopedia dello spettacolo*), and in 1972 he was appointed to hold an experimental course in composition at the Rome Conservatory, increasingly turning towards musical-pedagogic experiments. In 1974 he succeeded Petrassi as president of the Sindacato Musicisti Italiani.

Unlike those other Italian composers of his generation who are generally termed 'independents', Porena's independence has been constantly conditioned by the newest developments in music. He began to break out of the backwater of his early works (the Concerto with trombone obbligato still clumsily derives from pre-war Italian neo-classicism) in *Der Gott und die Bajadere*, a cantata setting Goethe's verse in the original and stylistically referring to middle-period Stravinsky. Immediately thereafter his attendances at Darmstadt, together with Nono's example, promoted the cautious serial apprenticeship shown in *Vor einer Kerze*, thus enabling Porena to achieve, in the succeeding *Vier Lieder aus dem Barock*, an outstanding concision. Already hostile to the 'rationalistic frenzy' he saw in post-Webernism, he subsequently developed a humanistic opposition to the capsizal of serialism into irrationality, proceeding – between the Gryphius Cantata (1959–61) and the *Musica per quartetto* (1967) – to the elaboration of a technique assuming a prototype of tonality. Not that this solitary effort prevents references to both the main compositional tendencies of the period: formal indeterminacy and social commitment. Quite consistently, however, the model of the rhythmically aleatory writing adopted in *Neumi* (a work involving perhaps Porena's most adventurous use of sound) goes back to plainsong, and the texts concerning the Nazi persecution of Jews, which he set in the Nelly Sachs Cantata and *Über aller dieser deiner Trauer*, focus on the archetypal features of such a historical tragedy.

In 1968 Porena ended his neo-tonal experiments with *La mort de Pierrot*, a 'melodrama' whose unpretentious Italian text strikingly contrasts with the German high literature employed in his preceding vocal works, and significantly supports a stylistic regression to pre-war modernism. This highlights that turning from his creative if polemic participation in the problems of contemporary music which eventually led to the recovery of a pure pleasure of music-making balanced by stoical surrender to the present. Hence his use – in the context of private or collective recreation – of radical techniques previously rejected, which the *Inquisizioni musicali* even introduce into a thought-provoking exhumation of Schubertian style, and which the educational collection *Kinder-Musik* fully exploits according to its cheerful 'musikantisch' purpose, recalling the youthful *Blockflöten-Album*.

WORKS
(selective list)

Orch: Conc. no.1, chamber orch, pf obbl, 1952; Conc. no.2, chamber orch, trbn obbl, 1956; Musica per archi no.1, 1960, no.2, 1967; Musica per orch no.1, 1963, no.2, 1966
Choral: 3 pezzi sacri, S, chorus, brass, 1953; 6 responsori per la settimana santa, 1955–6; Der Gott und die Bajadere (Goethe), S, Bar, chorus, orch, 1957; Todesfuge, 4vv, str qt, 1957; Cantata (Gryphius), 3 solo female vv, chorus, orch, 1959–61; Cantata da camera (N. Sachs), S, female vv, 8 insts, 1964; Cantata da camera (Trakl), B, male vv, 10 insts, 1959–64; Über aller dieser deiner Trauer (Celan, N. Sachs), S, B, chorus, orch, 1965
Solo vocal: 4 klassische Lieder (Goethe), S, pf, 1956; 4 kanonische Lieder (Celan), S, cl, 1958; Vor einer Kerze (Celan), Mez, insts, 1958; 4 Lieder aus dem Barock, S, hn, pf, 1959; 3 Trakl-Lieder, Bar, 3 trbn, 1960; La mort de Pierrot (I. Porena), Mez, 3 hn, 3 va, 1968
Inst: Blockflöten-Album, rec, 1955; 3 pezzi concertanti, 2 pf, brass, str, 1955; Neumi, fl, mar, vib, 1963; Cadenze, fl/vn, 12 insts, 1965; Musica per quartetto d'archi, 1967; D'après, fl, 1968; Inquisizioni musicali, 1971: 6 Laendler, pf, 5 bagatelle, pf, 30 canoni per Aldo Clementi, pf/insts, Per una schubertiade, pf, vc, 2 fughette e una fuga, pf, 15 finzioni, vc; early chamber works
Educational: Kinder-Musik, 1972

Principal publisher: Suvini Zerboni
For fuller list see 'Voci aggiunte' (1961)

WRITINGS

'L'avanguardia musicale di Darmstadt', *RaM*, xxviii (1958), 208
'Thomas Mann e la musica contemporanea', *Musica d'oggi*, new ser., i (Milan, 1958), 91
'Caso e necessità', *RaM*, xxxi (1961), 425
'Note sul più recente Petrassi', *Biennale di Venezia*, xiii/49 (1963), 38
with G. Baggiani: 'Ricorsi medioevalistici del novecento', *Terzo programma* (Rome, 1964), no.2, p.227
'Musica e avanguardia', *Discoteca*, vi/53–vii/58 (Milan, 1965–6)
'I concerti di Petrassi e la crisi della musica come linguaggio', *NRMI*, i (1967), 101
'Petrassi e la crisi della musica come linguaggio', *Biennale di Venezia*, xvii/61 (1967), 32
'Seguitando a parlare', *Spettatore musicale*, ii/6 (Bologna, 1967), 20
'Per un nuovo balletto di R. Vlad', *Chigiana*, xxv (1968), 295
'Questa è una finzione', *Spettatore musicale*, v (1970) July–Sept, 12
'Una nota su Strawinsky', *Studi musicali*, i/1 (1972), 187
Musica/società: inquisizioni musicali II (Turin, 1975)
'Per una normalizzazione sociale della musica', *NRMI*, x (1976), 442

BIBLIOGRAPHY

R. Boccia: 'Alcuni compositori romani del dopoguerra', *RaM*, xxviii (1958), 122
'Voci aggiunte e rivedute per un dizionario di compositori viventi', *RaM*, xxxi (1961), 45
A. Gentilucci: *Guida all'ascolto della musica contemporanea* (Milan, 1969), 319f
G. Zaccaro: 'Le pagine della musica nuova: criticismo e umanesimo di Boris Porena', *Discoteca*, x/88 (1969), 36
R. Zanetti: 'Gli indipendenti: Togni, Castiglioni, Porena', *Musica moderna*, iii/108 (Milan, 1969), 177

CLAUDIO ANNIBALDI

Porfirii [**Porfiri**], **Pietro** (*fl* 1687–1709). Italian composer. He was a member of the clergy and in 1692 was *maestro di cappella* of the collegiate church of S Nicolò at Fabriano. According to Radiciotti (1893) he lived for many years in the vicinity of Senigallia and was *maestro di cappella* at Ostra, Iesi, Arcevia and Pesaro. It is unclear whether he was born in that region or at Venice, as asserted by the revisers of Allacci. He was a canon at Urbino in 1709 (according to *RicordiE*); this information probably derives from the libretto to *La Leucippe*.

WORKS
OPERAS
(all lost)

Zenocrate ambasciatore a' Macedoni (M. A. Gasparini), Venice, Teatro S Moisè, 1687, attrib. by Ivanovich
Lo schiavo fortunato in Algeri (M. A. Gasparini), Treviso, Teatro di S Margarita, 1688 and perhaps earlier (pubd lib *I-Bc*); also perf. Pesaro, 1699, according to Radiciotti
Il Vespasiano (G. C. Corradi), Fabriano, 1 June 1692 (pubd lib *Vgc*), originally by C. Pallavicino, Porfirii composed only the changes
La forza del sangue, o vero Gl'equivoci gelosi (G. A. Lorenzani), Mondolfo, nr. Senigallia, 1696 (pubd lib *Vgc*), originally by F. Lanciani, Porfirii composed only the changes

L'Isifile amazzone di Lenno (A. Aureli), Pesaro, Teatro del Sole, 1697 (pubd lib *Rn*)

La Leucippe, Senigallia, 20 June 1709 [lib pubd at Urbino]

OTHER WORKS

Cantate da camera a voce sola . . . op.1 (Bologna, 1692)

BIBLIOGRAPHY

EitnerQ; RicordiE

G. Ivanovich: *Minerva al tavolino* (Venice, rev. 2/1688)

L. Allacci: *Drammaturgia* (Venice, enlarged 2/1755/*R*1961)

G. Radiciotti: *Teatro, musica e musicisti in Sinigaglia: notizie e documenti* (Tivoli, 1893), 43

——'La cappella musicale del duomo di Pesaro', *Santa Cecilia* (Turin, 1914)

Porphyry

Porphyry [Porphyrios, Porphyrius] (*b* Tyre or Bashan [Batanea], *c*234; *d* Rome, *c*301). Greco-Syrian neo-Platonic philosopher and scholar. His original name was Malchos ('king'). He was a pupil of Longinus at Athens, and of Plotinus at Rome, and spent much time in Sicily. Eunapius, in his *Lives of the Sophists* (late 4th century), praised Porphyry for having presented the doctrines of Plotinus in a clearly comprehensible manner. Plotinus denied the Aristotelian categories, however, whereas Porphyry wrote a commentary on them and added an introduction, which strongly influenced medieval logic through Boethius and others; Porphyry's central doctrine was the idea of submerging the soul in the Deity through an ecstasy which can be induced through magic (*theourgia*) and asceticism.

Porphyry's treatise *Against the Christians*, in 15 books (*Kata Christianōn*), was destroyed under Theodosius II in 448. Fragments of it quoted by the Church Fathers show, however, points of agreement with Christianity, especially concerning music. Porphyry may have been the first author to attack secular music for its sensual attraction; his treatise *De abstinentia* contains a polemic against dancing and the drama, and the music associated with them, for they deflect man from his true goal. Even though inferior deities (good and evil demons) could be influenced by orgiastic music, the highest deity should be approached only 'with pure silence and pure thoughts' (*De abstinentia*, ii, 34).

In his commentary on Ptolemy's *Harmonics* (*Eis ta Harmonika Ptolemaiou hypomnēma*), Porphyry showed a greater technical knowledge of music (*see* PTOLEMY, CLAUDIUS); it survives in 70 manuscripts and is quoted in numerous Byzantine scholia in manuscripts of Ptolemy's treatise. (Pappus is no longer considered to be the author of part of this commentary.) It extends only as far as the seventh chapter of the second book of Ptolemy, and is uneven in content: there is little on Ptolemy's doctrines of intervals, genera and modes (i, chap.4–15; ii, 1–7) but much on the introductory chapters setting out the structure of the work. Porphyry discussed in detail basic principles of harmonic theory (i, 1–2), and, above all, acoustics (i, 3); he compared sense perception and reason, the criteria by which former theorists had judged consonance. Porphyry assigned Ptolemy to an intermediate position between the Pythagorean and Aristoxenian schools of music theory, since Ptolemy had conceived of reason according to the former and sense perception according to the latter.

According to his Pythagorean point of view, Porphyry adopted the same numerical proportions as the foundation of both rhythm and melody (i.e. successions of pitches). Quantitative differences in the speed of vibrations determine whether a note is high or low; but Porphyry, unlike Ptolemy, went on to claim that

these differences of pitch are qualitative (especially p.58, ed. Düring, 1932).

One of the most valuable aspects of Porphyry's commentary results from his extensive use of earlier specialist treatises on music, some otherwise unknown. He quoted from the *Pythagorean Primer of Music* of Ptolemaïs of Cyrene, *Concerning the Difference between the Pythagorean and Aristoxenian Theories of Music* of Didymus, the *Compendium of Music* of Heraclides, an *Interpretation of the Timaeus* by Aelian, the *Likenesses* of Dionysius 'ho mousikos', the *Mathematics* of Archytas, the *Music* of Theophrastus and a *Sounds* (*Peri akoustōn*) of the school of Aristotle.

BIBLIOGRAPHY

EDITIONS

I. Düring, ed.: *Porphyrios Kommentar zur Harmonielehre des Ptolemaios*, Göteborgs högskolas årsskrift, xxxviii/2 (Göteborg, 1932)

I. Düring, ed. and trans.: *Ptolemaios und Porphyrios über die Musik*, Göteborgs högskolas årsskrift, xl/1 (Göteborg, 1934)

CRITICAL STUDIES

F. Boll: *Studien über Claudius Ptolemäus: ein Beitrag zur Geschichte der griechischen Philosophie und Astrologie* (Leipzig, 1894) [also pubd in *Jb für classische Philologie*, suppl.xxi (1894), 66–254]

C. Stumpf: *Geschichte des Konsonanzbegriffes*, i: *Die Definition der Konsonanz im Altertum*, Abhandlungen der philosophisch-philologischen Classe der Königlichen Bayerischen Akademie der Wissenschaften, xxi/1 (Munich, 1897)

H. Abert: *Die Musikanschauung des Mittelalters und ihre Grundlagen* (Halle, 1905)

J. Bidez: *Vie de Porphyre, le philosophe néo-platonicien* (Ghent and Leipzig, 1913)

L. Schönberger: *Studien zum 1. Buch der Harmonik des Claudius Ptolemäus: Beilage zum Jahresbericht des Humanistischen Gymnasiums Metten* (Augsburg, 1914)

O. J. Gombosi: *Die Tonarten und Stimmungen der antiken Musik* (Copenhagen, 1939)

J. Handschin: *Der Toncharakter* (Zurich, 1948)

R. Beutler: 'Porphyrios', *Paulys Real-Encyclopädie der classischen Altertumswissenschaft*, xliii (Stuttgart, 1953), 273–313

L. Richter: *Zur Wissenschaftslehre von der Musik bei Platon und Aristoteles*, Deutsche Akademie der Wissenschaften zu Berlin, Schriften der Sektion für Altertumswissenschaft, xxiii (Berlin, 1961)

B. Alexanderson: *Textual Remarks on Ptolemy's Harmonica and Porphyry's Commentary*, Studia graeca et latina Gothoburgensia, xxvii (Göteborg, 1969)

LUKAS RICHTER

Porpora, Nicola

Porpora, Nicola (Antonio) (*b* Naples, 17 Aug 1686; *d* Naples, 3 March 1768). Italian musician. He was internationally famous during his lifetime both as a composer (particularly of vocal music and opera) and as a singing teacher.

1. LIFE. Nicola Porpora was the third son of Carlo Porpora, a Neapolitan bookseller, who placed him in the Conservatorio dei Poveri di Gesù Cristo on 29 September 1696. The boy stayed there about ten years. For the first three he paid for his education and upkeep but thereafter was maintained free of charge (the conservatory gave free places to its best music students and by 1699 probably considered him among them). His first important commission after leaving the Gesù Cristo was for an opera, *Agrippina*, performed in the Neapolitan Royal Palace on 4 November 1708. Commissions for further major works came to him slowly at first. *Flavio Anicio Olibrio*, his second opera, was performed in Naples in 1711, and *Basilio re d'oriente*, his third, in 1713. The librettos of these two operas state the names of the patrons Porpora was then serving. That of *Flavio* calls him *maestro di cappella* to the Prince of Hessen-Darmstadt; that of *Basilio* names him *maestro di cappella* to the Portuguese ambassador. Of these, the Prince of Hessen-Darmstadt played the more important role in

Porpora's career. He went to Naples in the wake of the Austrian invasion and occupation of the city in 1707; between 1709 and 1713 he was general of the Austrian army there, and afterwards was governor of Mantua. In librettos of several of Porpora's works between 1711 and 1725 the composer is called either *maestro* or *virtuoso* of the prince, though he can hardly have served him directly after the prince's departure from Naples in 1713. Walker has suggested that the prince may have been responsible for securing the operatic commission Porpora received from the Viennese court in 1714: the work concerned was *Arianna e Teseo*, performed in Vienna on 1 October (the emperor's birthday). For a while Porpora enjoyed considerable favour both at the imperial court in Vienna and at the viceregal court in Naples. His opera *Temistocle* was presented in Vienna on 1 October 1718, his opera *Faramondo* in Naples on 19 November 1719 (the empress's name day), his serenata *Angelica* in Naples on the emperor's birthday, 1720 (repeated in Vienna the same year on the empress's name day and in Naples again on 28 August 1722, the empress's birthday), and his serenata *Gli orti esperidi* was given in Naples on the empress's birthday in 1721. The texts of both serenatas were by a young poet who was to become the greatest librettist of the century, Pietro Metastasio; *Angelica* was his first important poem intended for musical setting. One of Porpora's singing pupils, the later much-famed castrato Farinelli, made his début in this same work. By this time Porpora was beginning to make his mark as a teacher. Between April 1715 and the end of December 1721 he served as *maestro di cappella* (i.e. chief teacher of singing and composition) at the Neapolitan Conservatorio di S Onofrio. From his private singing classes there emerged around this period both Farinelli and the equally renowned castrato Caffarelli (who made his début in 1726). Another student with whom Porpora came into contact was the future composer Johann Adolf Hasse. When Hasse reached Naples from Germany in 1722, he took a few lessons from Porpora before deciding to study under Alessandro Scarlatti.

Porpora had to wait until the 1720s before acquiring popularity as a composer in Rome and northern Italy. The first Roman opera with which he was associated was in fact a joint venture, *Berenice regina d'Egitto*, produced at the Capranica theatre, Rome, in 1718 with music by Porpora and by Domenico Scarlatti. *Eumene*, his first complete opera for a Roman audience, was performed at the Alibert theatre in 1721, and must have been a success for he was invited to produce further operas for the theatre in 1722 and 1723. In 1725 he was for the first time active in northern Italy, providing an opera and an oratorio for Milan and an opera for Reggio Emilia. Fétis claimed to have seen an autograph letter proving that he was also in Vienna that year. In 1726 he settled in Venice, where he was appointed *maestro* to the girl students of the Ospedale degli Incurabili, where he stayed until 1733. In March that year he made an unsuccessful attempt to gain the post of *maestro di cappella* at St Mark's in Venice. Some time during the summer or early autumn he resigned from the Incurabili and travelled to London.

Porpora's invitation to London came from a group of English noblemen who were setting up an opera company, known as the Opera of the Nobility, in competition with the existing Italian opera company in England under Handel. The Opera of the Nobility opened its first season on 29 December 1733 with the première of a new opera by Porpora, *Arianna in Nasso*. Over the next two and a half years he composed four more operas, an oratorio, a serenata and items for three pasticcios, all for this company. In spite of the fact that he had with him one of the finest teams of Italian singers then assembled (it included the castrato Senesino, the soprano Cuzzoni, and from October 1734 Farinelli as well), Porpora and the Opera of the Nobility did not establish a clear superiority over Handel's rival concern. His last work written in London was the serenata *La festa d'Imeneo*, given four times between 4 May and 15 May 1736 in honour of the marriage of the Prince of Wales. Later that summer he left England: perhaps he already foresaw that the two rival companies could not be supported indefinitely by the London public (and in fact both closed for lack of money the following year). Porpora meanwhile returned to Venice where, about February or March of 1737, he took up his old post of *maestro* of the Incurabili on a temporary basis. The permanent holder of the post by this time was Hasse, who was away from Venice for most of 1737 and 1738 (he was Kapellmeister to the Saxon court at Dresden and had duties there). It seems that Porpora stayed at the Incurabili until about September 1738 when Hasse returned to Venice.

Porpora next moved to Naples, where he arrived on 11 October. On 1 July 1739 he was appointed *maestro di cappella* at the Neapolitan Conservatorio di S Maria di Loreto. His opportunities to teach and compose in Naples were many, but he had been there barely three years when he was seized once more with a desire to travel and change jobs. On 6 October 1741 the Loreto governors gave him leave to go to Venice to fulfil an operatic commission. Once in Venice however he ignored his obligations to the Neapolitans and on 26 January 1742 accepted the post of *maestro di coro* at the Venetian Ospedale della Pietà for the particularly handsome annual salary of 500 ducats. For some unknown reason he asked leave to resign from the Pietà on 15 February 1743, and thereafter gave his services to another of the Venetian musical establishments for young ladies, the Ospedaletto. It was while he was working at the Ospedaletto that he heard, in November 1744, of the death of Leonardo Leo, *maestro di cappella* at the Neapolitan court, and applied to Naples for the vacancy. The court for its part decided that the post was to be filled by competitive examination held in Naples in April 1745. Because Porpora was unable to go, he begged unsuccessfully for his case to be considered *in absentia*. He was still working at the Ospedaletto in June 1746 – a manuscript of his *Laudate pueri* (*GB-Lbm*) written for the girls there is so dated. But in 1747 he was on the move again, this time to Dresden.

From 1747 to 1751 Porpora was in Dresden as singing teacher to the Electoral Princess Maria Antonia. For her 23rd birthday (18 July 1747) he composed the opera *Filandro*, produced in the electoral theatre under Hasse's direction. It was the only opera he composed during his stay in Saxony. His time there is said to have been soured by an unfortunate rivalry that developed between his soprano pupil, Regina Mingotti, and the famous though by this time aging soprano Faustina Bordoni, Hasse's wife. Both singers were in the cast of *Filandro*. Porpora was made court Kapellmeister on 13 April 1748 with an annual salary of 1200 thalers. The appointment was 'until further notice', and may temporarily have seemed to undermine Hasse's position as chief musician at court. On 7 January 1749, however, Hasse was created Ober-Kapellmeister and so maintained his superior position. At the end of 1751 Porpora's salary ceased and in its place, from 1 January 1752, he was awarded a state pension of 400 thalers a year. Some time during 1752 or at the beginning of 1753 he moved to Vienna: this is clear from two letters of Metastasio, who had been Viennese court poet since

Nicola Antonio Porpora: engraving (1825) by Hasler

1730, to Farinelli (15 February and 17 March 1753), which show that, on Farinelli's suggestion, Metastasio had considered handing Porpora his new libretto *L'isola disabitata* to set, but had then, in March, changed his mind when Porpora became ill. Porpora afterwards gave singing lessons in Vienna to Wilhelmine, mistress of Pietro Correr, the Venetian ambassador, and also to Marianna Martinez, Metastasio's protégée. Metastasio was probably responsible, directly or indirectly, for the first meeting between Porpora and the young Joseph Haydn. In the mid-1750s Haydn lived in an attic of the Michaelerhaus in Vienna where Metastasio also lived. He became Porpora's valet, pupil and keyboard accompanist during his master's singing lessons. All that is known about the relationship between them comes from Haydn's autobiographical sketch. In it he made clear what he owed to Porpora: 'I wrote fluently, but not wholly correctly, until I had the good fortune to learn the true foundations of composition from the celebrated Porpora who was in Vienna at that time'.

Porpora's financial position in Vienna, which was never very sound, became precarious after the start of the Seven Years War in 1756 and the invasion of Saxony by Prussia. According to Walker he was still

drawing his Saxon pension in 1757, but it is unlikely that he was doing so by 5 March 1759 when Metastasio wrote Farinelli a letter describing Porpora's desperate financial situation 'after the noted misfortunes of Saxony'. By this time Porpora must already have made some intimation to his acquaintances in Naples that he wanted to return there. The governors of the Conservatorio di S Maria di Loreto, where he had served from 1739 to 1741, elected him 'another *maestro di cappella*' to join the two *maestri* already serving, at a meeting held, according to the minutes, on 25 January 1758. However, since these minutes are recorded between minutes of other governors' meetings on 4 January and 30 April 1759, it seems that the true date of his election was a year later. Porpora did not reach Naples until early in April 1760. He took up his responsibilities at the Loreto on 10 April and shortly after was invited to compose an opera to open at the S Carlo theatre on 30 May. This, his last opera, *Il trionfo di Camilla*, was a revision of an earlier opera of his heard at the same theatre in 1740, and was not a success. When the death of Abos in September 1760 created a vacancy for *maestro* at the Conservatorio di S Onofrio, the post was given to Porpora. The next year, however, he resigned from both his teaching appointments, leaving the Loreto on 30 April and the S Onofrio in September. His final years of retirement were spent in considerable poverty.

2. WORKS. Though Porpora wrote several instrumental works, his output in this field was small by comparison with that of his vocal works. These can be classified under the headings of secular operas, sacred operas and oratorios, secular serenatas and cantatas, other sacred compositions, solfège and other didactic pieces. In any assessment of the composer the secular operas have to be stressed as they comprise the largest and most important category. Though he wrote his first opera as early as 1708, he only gradually acquired sufficient fame to be constantly in demand as an opera composer. His great period of operatic composition occurred between 1718 and 1742, after which his popularity among theatre audiences declined.

Musical taste in Italy changed considerably during the first years that he was active as a composer. Styles emphasizing melody with a simple homophonic accompaniment (usually for full strings and continuo) came into fashion, and vocal melody acquired both more lyrical, lilting qualities and, at times, more decorative ornament. The development of Porpora's own style ran parallel with this general trend, and it may be argued that he was one of the composers chiefly responsible for the trend towards more embellishment in vocal melody. Being a great singing teacher, he understood as well as anyone the capabilities of the voice, and he exploited its range and flexibility in passages that were unusually florid and sustained. This deep understanding of the art of singing had its drawbacks, for there are signs in his operas of the 1720s and early 1730s that he came to rely too heavily on the ability of singers to sustain the musical interest through virtuoso display. He made little attempt at this stage of his career to strive for variety in his arias (the da capo structure was the norm), and he rarely applied unusual procedures for the sake of dramatic impact. To some extent this attitude changed when he arrived in London in 1733. Faced with competition from Handel, who had an uncommon flair for making opera theatrically effective, Porpora sharpened his powers of characterization: he aimed for more attractive melody, became more willing to vary the da capo formula of the arias, and made much more extensive use of accompanied recitative than hitherto. This stimulant to his ingenuity was no longer present, however, once he returned to Italy in 1736, and his last operas show a slow decline in his compositional powers and a return to conventionality.

Intricate embellished vocal writing was a characteristic of many of his sacred compositions too. In addition to his few sacred operas and oratorios, Porpora wrote several masses, two *Te Deum* settings, a large number of psalm settings, motets and canticles. Most of his surviving religious music represents his contribution to the concerts and other musical functions of the three Venetian hospitals which he served. The vocal parts in his music for the Incurabili and Ospedaletto are for sopranos and contraltos only, but his works for the Pietà (1742) contain chorus parts for basses and sometimes also for tenors, showing that the hospital assembled mixed choirs for its festivals. All these Venetian compositions are accompanied by strings and continuo. The pieces concerned vary from the very simple *In exitu Israel* of February 1744 with homophonic, antiphonal writing for two SAA choirs in one tempo to the very elaborate *Magnificat* in G minor of 1742 for SSATB and SSAB choirs (with additional solo parts for soprano and contralto) in nine movements, some for the choruses, some for soloists, and some for a mixture of both, written in a variety of homophonic and contrapuntal idioms. In addition to his other pieces Porpora wrote over 30 solo Latin motets for favourite female pupils at the Incurabili and Ospedaletto. Few of these survive, though many of their texts are extant. Four (in the British Museum) have solo parts as virtuoso as any the composer wrote for leading stars on the operatic stage. The admiration for the musical performances of the hospitals so often expressed by visitors to Venice in the mid-18th century is perfectly understandable on the evidence of these pieces.

WORKS

(music lost unless otherwise stated)

DRAMATIC

(heroic operas unless otherwise indicated)

Agrippina (N. Giuvo), Naples, Palazzo Reale, 4 Nov 1708, arias *I-Mc*, *Nc*
Flavio Anicio Olibrio (Zeno and P. Pariati), Naples, S Bartolomeo, carn. 1711, Acts 1–2 autograph *GB-Lbm*; rev. Rome, Alibert, carn. 1722, 10 arias *B-Bc*
Basilio re d'oriente (?G. B. Neri), Naples, Fiorentini, 24 June 1713
Arianna e Teseo (Pariati), Vienna, Hoftheater, 1 Oct 1714; rev. version, 30 arias, duet *GB-Cfm*, Act 2 autograph *Lbm*, Act 2 modern copy *US-Wc*
Berenice regina d'Egitto (A. Salvi), Rome, Capranica, carn. 1718, collab. D. Scarlatti
Temistocle (Zeno), Vienna, Hoftheater, 1 Oct 1718
Faramondo, Naples, S Bartolomeo, 19 Nov 1719
Eumene (Zeno), Rome, Alibert, carn. 1721
Adelaide (Salvi), Rome, Alibert, carn. 1723, *D-SWl*
Amare per regnare (?F. Silvani), Naples, S Bartolomeo, 12 Dec 1723
Damiro e Pitia (D. Lalli), Munich, 1724
Semiramide regina dell'Assiria (?Silvani), Naples, S Bartolomeo, spr 1724; 2 acts *I-MC*
Griselda (?Zeno), ?1724, *D-LEm*
Didone abbandonata (Metastasio), Reggio Emilia, Pubblico, Ascension 1725, Acts 2–3 autograph *GB-Lbm*
Siface (Metastasio), Milan, Ducale, 26 Dec 1725, *B-Bc*, *Br*, *GB-CDp*, Acts 1, 3 autograph *Lbm*; rev. version *B-Bc*
La verità nell'inganno (?Silvani), Milan, Ducale, carn. 1726
Meride e Selinunte (Zeno), Venice, S Giovanni Grisostomo, carn. 1726, *B-Bc*, *Br*, *Lbm*, *Lcm*; *I-Ac*, *Bc*, *Bsp*, *Fc*, *Gl*, *Mc*, modern copy *US-Wc*
Imeneo in Atene (S. Stampiglia), Venice, S Samuele, 1726, *D-Dlb*, *F-Pn*
Siroe re di Persia (Metastasio), Rome, Delle Dame, carn. 1727, arias *GB-Lcm*

Ezio (Metastasio), Venice, S Giovanni Grisostomo, aut. 1728, *B-Bc*, *GB-Lam*
Ermenegildo, Naples, 1729, according to Mondolfi
Semiramide riconosciuta (Metastasio), Venice, S Giovanni Grisostomo, carn. 1729, *GB-Lam*; rev. Naples, S Carlo, 20 Jan 1739, *D-Dlb*, *I-Nc*, modern copy *US-Wc*; facs. edn. (New York, 1977)
Mitridate (F. Vanstryp), Rome, Capranica, carn. 1730, *B-Bc*, *Br*, modern copy *US-Wc*
Tamerlano (A. Piovene), Turin, Regio, carn. 1730
Poro (after Metastasio: Alessandro nell'Indie), Turin, Regio, carn. 1731
Annibale (Vanstryp), Venice, S Angelo, aut. 1731, *B-Bc*, modern copy *US-Wc*
Germanico in Germania (N. Coluzzi), Rome, Capranica, carn. 1732
Issipile (Metastasio), Rome, Rucellai, carn. 1733, Act 1 *I-MC*, 4 arias *GB-Lcm*
Arianna in Nasso (P. Rolli), London, Lincoln's Inn Fields, 29 Dec 1733, *A-Wn*, *GB-Lbm*, modern copy *US-Wc*; Favourite Songs (London, 1734)
Enea nel Lazio (Rolli), London, Lincoln's Inn Fields, 11 May 1734, *GB-Lbm*
Polifemo (Rolli), London, King's, 1 Feb 1735, *GB-Lbm*, Act 3 autograph *Lbm*; Favourite Songs (London, 1735)
Ifigenia in Aulide (Rolli), London, King's, 3 May 1735, *Lbm*, Act 2 autograph *Lbm*
Mitridate (Gavardo da Gavardo [C. Cibber]), London, King's, 24 Jan 1736, *B-Bc*, Acts 2–3 autograph *GB-Lbm*
Lucio Papirio (Salvi, rev. G. Boldoni), Venice, S Cassiano, carn. 1737, 21 arias *A-Wn*
Rosbale (after C. N. Stampa: Eumene), Venice, S Giovanni Grisostomo, aut. 1737, Act 3 autograph *GB-Lbm*
Carlo il calvo, Rome, Delle Dame, spr. 1738, *I-Nc*, sinfonia, 14 arias, 1 duet *GB-Lcm*
Il barone di Zampano (comic opera, P. Trinchera), Naples, Nuovo, spr. 1739
L'amico fedele (comic opera, G. di Pietro), Naples, Fiorentini, aut. 1739
Intermezzo for the marriage of the Infante D. Filippo, Madrid, 1739
Il trionfo di Camilla (Stampiglia), Naples, S Carlo, 20 Jan 1740, ?*D-Dlb*
Tiridate (Metastasio: Zenobia), Naples, S Carlo, 19 Dec 1740
Partenope, Naples, 1742, according to Mondolfi
La Rosmene, Vienna, 1742, *GB-Lbm*
Statira (Silvani), Venice, S Giovanni Grisostomo, carn. 1742, *D-B*, *Dlb*
Temistocle (Metastasio), London, Haymarket, 22 Feb 1743, *A-Wn*; Favourite Songs (London, 1743)
Filandro (V. Cassani: L'incostanza schernita), Dresden, Hoftheater, 18 July 1747, *D-B*, *Dlb*
Il trionfo di Camilla (Stampiglia, rev. G. Lorenzi), Naples, S Carlo, 30 May 1760, Acts 1, 3 autograph *GB-Lbm*
Giasone, according to Walker a serenata, Naples, 1742, *I-MC*
Tolomeo re d'Egitto, *I-Nc*
Il trionfo di Camilla, ?third version, *US-Wc*

SECULAR CANTATAS, SERENATAS

Composizione drammatica [title unknown], Naples, palace of the Prince of Hessen-Darmstadt, Nov 1711
Cantata in honour of Charles VI, Rome, Nov 1712, pt.2 autograph *GB-Lbm*
Angelica (Metastasio), Naples, 1 Oct 1720, *A-Wn*, autograph *GB-Lbm*
Gli orti esperidi (Metastasio), Naples, Palazzo Reale, 28 Aug 1721, autograph *GB-Lbm*
Imeneo, cantata for the wedding of the Prince of Montemilletto (S. Stampiglia), Naples, 1723
Componimento per musica (G. L., 'Pastor Arcade'), Rome, 19 Nov 1732
Twelve solo cantatas dedicated to the Prince of Wales (Metastasio) (London, 1735)
La festa d'Imeneo (P. Rolli), London, King's, 4 May 1736, 2 copies, 1 autograph *GB-Lbm*
Le nozze d'Ercole e d'Ebe, Venice, S Giovanni Grisostomo, last evening of carn. 1744
Numerous other secular cantatas, incl. Odimi Alcide, part autograph *GB-Lbm*; Calcante ed Achille; and Non fuggir empia fortuna
132 solo cantatas in *A-Wgm*, *Wn*; *B-Bc*; *D-B*, *Dlb*, *LEm*, *Mbs*, *MÜs*; *GB-Cfm*, *Lbm*, *Lcm*; *I-Ac*, *Bc*, *Bsp*, *Fc*, *Gl*, *Mc*, *MTventuri*, *Nc*, *PAc*, *Rsc*, *Vc*, *Vlevi*, *Vnm*; *US-Wc*; thematic index in Sutton

ORATORIOS, SACRED OPERAS

Il martirio di S Giovanni Nepomuceno (Marchese d'Este Cristina), Naples, S Luigi dei Padri Minimi, 1 June 1711, *A-Wn*, *D-B*
Il trionfo della divina giustizia ne' tormenti e morte di Gesù Cristo, Naples, S Luigi di Palazzo, Saturday before Easter 1716, pt.1 *D-Ha*, pt.2 *F-Pn*
Il martirio di S Eugenia, Naples, Conservatory S Onofrio, 1721/2, autograph Acts 1, 3, *GB-Lbm*
Cantata per la notte di Natale, Rome, Palazzo Apostolico, 24/5 Dec 1732, pt.1 *I-Rc*
Sanctus Petrus Urseolus, Venice, Incurabili, 1733, lib *I-Vnm*
Davide e Bersabea (Rolli), London, Lincoln's Inn Fields, 12 March

1734, *A-Wn*, fragments *GB-Cfm*
Il Gedeone (A. Perrucci), Vienna, Hofkapelle, 28 March 1737, *A-Wn*, pt.2 *I-Nc*
Il verbo in carne, oratorio per la natività di Gesù Cristo, Dresden, 1748, *D-MÜs*, autograph *GB-Lbm*, *Lcm*
Israel ad Aegyptiis liberatus, Venice, Incurabili, 1759, 2 arias *GB-Lbm*; lib *I-Rsc*
Ripieno di una cantata in lode di S Gennaro (A. Gennaro, Duca de Belforte), Naples, Sedile di Portanova, 4 May 1765, *GB-Lbm*
Introduzione ad Psalmum Miserere ['Genas lacrymis rigate'], lib *I-Vmc*
Introduzione ad Psalmum Miserere ['Nos qui salvasti'], *I-Nc*
Introduzione ad Salmo Miserere ['Sacrum sumente Lyram'], *GB-Lbm*
Oratorio, 5vv ['Legan l'alme in dolci nodi'], *D-B*, doubtful authenticity

OTHER SACRED WORKS

Principal sources: *A-Wgm*, *Wm*, *Wn*; *D-B*, *Bds*, *Dlb*, *MÜs*; *GB-Lbm*, *Lcm*; *F-Pn*; *I-Ac*, *Baf*, *Bc*, *Fc*, *Mc*, *Nc*, *Nf*, *Vmc*; *US-MSu*, *Npl*, *Wc*
3 masses; 8 Kyrie–Gloria, 2 of doubtful authenticity; Kyrie; Gloria
57 choral motets and psalm settings, 5 inc.; 53 solo motets, 44 text only, 2 Te Deum, 1756, 1757; 14 solo antiphons, 1 fragmentary
3 Notturni de defonti; 13 solo Lessons for Holy Week, 1 inc.; 6 Latin duets for the Passion of Jesus Christ; 3 a cappella motets

INSTRUMENTAL

(thematic indexes in Mayeda and Degrada)
[6] Sinfonie da camera, 2 vn, bc, op.2 (London, 1736); as 6 concerti, *GB-Lbm*
6 Sonatas, 2 vn, vc, bc [vc, hpd] (London, 1745), collab. G. B. Costanza
12 sonate, vn, bc (Vienna, 1754)
Concerto, vc, str, bc, *Lbm*; concerto, fl, str, bc, *D-KA*; Ouverture roiale, insts, 1763, *I-Nc*; sonata, F, vc, bc, *GB-Lbm*; fugue, G, hpd, *I-Nc*
Several pieces attrib. Porpora in 18th- and 19th-century anthologies

BIBLIOGRAPHY

BurneyH; *FétisB*
G. Carpani: *Le Haydine, ossia lettere sulla vita e sulle opere di G. Haydn* (Milan, 1812)
M. Fürstenau: *Zur Geschichte der Musik und des Theaters am Hofe zu Dresden* (Dresden, 1861–2/*R*1971)
S. Fassini: *Il melodramma italiano a Londra nella prima metà del settecento* (Turin, 1914)
F. Walker: 'A Chronology of the Life and Works of Nicola Porpora', *Italian Studies*, vi (1951), 29
——: 'Porpora, Nicola', *Grove 5*
U. Prota-Giurleo: 'Per una esatta biografia di Nicolò Porpora', *La Scala* (1957), Jan, 21
A. Mondolfi: 'Porpora, Nicola', *MGG*
A. Mayeda: *Nicola Antonio Porpora als Instrumentalkomponist* (diss., U. of Vienna, 1967) [incl. thematic catalogue]
F. Degrada: 'Le musiche strumentali di Nicolò Porpora', *Chigiana*, xxv (1968), 99
S. H. Hansell: 'Sacred Music at the *Incurabili* in Venice at the Time of J. A. Hasse', *JAMS*, xxiii (1970), 282, 505
M. F. Robinson: 'Porpora's Operas for London, 1733–1736', *Soundings*, ii (1971–2), 57
——: 'The Governors' Minutes of the Conservatory S Maria di Loreto, Naples', *RMARC*, x (1972), 39, 43–5, 47, 94
E. L. Sutton: *The Solo Vocal Works of Nicola Porpora: an Annotated Thematic Index* (diss., U. of Minnesota, 1974)
C. Vitali: 'Un concerto per violoncello attribuito a Porpora', *Studi musicali*, viii (1979), 291

MICHAEL F. ROBINSON

Porrectus [flexa resupina] (Lat.: 'stretched out'). A neume signifying three notes, the second lower than the others. It is sometimes called *flexa resupina* because it is a *flexa* (two notes in descending order) which turns upwards again (is made *resupina*; see RESUPINUS; for illustration *see* NEUMATIC NOTATIONS, Table 1; Table 2 shows the *porrectus* in notations of different regions).

BIBLIOGRAPHY

M. Huglo: 'Les noms des neumes et leur origine', *Etudes grégoriennes*, i (1954), 53

Porrino, Ennio (*b* Cagliari, 20 Jan 1910; *d* Rome, 25 Sept 1959). Italian composer. He studied composition with Dobici and Mulè, took a diploma at the Rome Conservatory in 1932, and then attended a course under Respighi. After teaching at the conservatories of Rome, Venice and Naples, he was appointed director of the Cagliari Conservatory in 1956. The character of his music is Respighian: there is an indulgent use of illu-

strative colour and a nationalist rhetoric. A supporter of Salò's Fascist republic, he wrote for it the *Inno dei legionari*, performed in Venice in 1945.

WORKS
(selective list)

Operas: Gli Orazi (C. Guastalla), Milan, 1941; L'organo di bambù (G. Artieri), Venice, 1955; I Shardana (Porrino), Naples, 1959
Orch: Tartarin de Tarascon, 1932; Sardegna, 1933; 3 canzoni italiane, 1937; Sonata drammatica, 1947; Nuraghi, 1952; Conc. dell'Argentarola, gui, orch, 1953; Sonar per musici, 1959
Other works: Altair, ballet, Naples, 1942; Mondo tondo, ballet, Rome, 1949; Il processo di Cristo, oratorio, 1949

ALBERTO PIRONTI

Porro, Giovanni [Gian] **Giacomo** [Borro, Johann Jacob] (*b* Lugano [then in Italy], *c*1590; *d* Munich, Sept 1656). Italian composer and organist, later resident in Germany. He was appointed organist to the Duke of Savoy at the court in Turin on 10 June 1618. In autumn 1623 he moved to Rome, where he soon became *maestro di cappella* of S Lorenzo in Damaso. From 1626 he deputized as organist at St Peter's and after the death of Giacomo Guidi became Frescobaldi's substitute there from 26 August 1630. Although Frescobaldi did not return from Florence until 1 May 1634 Porro seems to have left St Peter's at the end of November 1633 and later left Rome. He was in Vienna when in September 1635 he was appointed, retrospectively from 15 August, vice-Kapellmeister of the court of the Elector Maximilian I of Bavaria in Munich, and he soon became Kapellmeister. During Maximilian's rule the music of the court centred on the chapel. This is reflected in Porro's output for Munich – now lost – as listed by Sandberger. It comprised 32 masses, 60 propers, a requiem, 64 settings of the *Magnificat*, two of the Te Deum and seven of the *Stabat mater*, 60 'cantiones', 187 psalms, 208 antiphons, 20 litanies and 274 other motets; he is also said to have written 200 madrigals and ten ballettos. When the Elector Ferdinand Maria succeeded in 1651, there was a new interest in secular art, and Porro was involved in the introduction of opera to Munich (G. B. Maccioni's *L'arpa festante*, 1653); he may have composed *La ninfa ritrosa* (given on 2 February 1654). He was well looked after at Munich, enjoying frequent increases in salary as well as gifts in cash and kind. In summer 1636 and in 1653 he was able to visit Italy to recruit musicians. He appears to have been an outstanding and meticulous administrator. In spite of illnesses after 1650, he opposed the appointment of an assistant until J. K. Kerll, his eventual successor, took the post in spring 1656. Only four pieces by Porro survive: a secular solo song in *RISM* 1622[2], two small-scale sacred pieces in 1628[5] and a vesper psalm in 1663[2].

BIBLIOGRAPHY

F. X. Haberl: 'J. J. Porro', *KJb*, xvi (1891), 70
A. Sandberger: preface to *J. K. Kerll: Ausgewählte Werke*, i, DTB, iii, Jg.ii/2 (1901)
A. Cametti: 'Girolamo Frescobaldi in Roma', *RMI*, xv (1908), 745
S. Cordero di Pamparato: 'I musici alla corte di Carlo Emmanuele I di Savoia', *Biblioteca della Società storica subalpina*, cxxi (1930), 101

JOHN HARPER

Porro [Porrot], **Pierre Jean** (*b* Béziers, *c*1759; *d* Montmorency, 31 May 1831). French guitarist, composer and music publisher. He began his musical studies in Béziers, then moved to Paris as a guitar teacher in 1783. He soon began publishing periodical guitar collections, and in 1786 he founded his own publishing house. By 1788 he had begun the successful *Journal de* *guitare*, a periodical collection of *airs* and guitar pieces which flourished into the 19th century. His connection with the Concert Spirituel (as an associate of Henri Joseph Rigel) may have led to his publishing the influential series *Collection de musique sacrée*, which included works by Jommelli, Pergolesi, Leo, Mozart and Haydn, in addition to some of his own pieces. Active during the transition from the five-course Baroque guitar to its Classical counterpart with six strings, Porro composed for both these instruments and for the lyre-guitar, which was popular in France around 1800.

WORKS
(all published in Paris)

Hymne à la liberté, 3vv (1794); Hymne religieux et patriotique, 3vv (1794); Panis angelicus, 4vv, org; Hymne à Ste Cécile, collab. Riegel; other vocal works

2 concertos, gui, orch; duos, 2 gui (opp.18, 28, 32); duos, gui, kbd (opp.33, 35); numerous pieces for gui, vn/fl (incl. opp.11, 17, 19, 20, 30, 36); trios, gui, vn, va (opp.26, 38); numerous pieces and arrs. for solo gui; other inst music

Numerous airs and romances, 1–2vv, gui/lyra-gui/harp/kbd, pubd singly and in collections, esp. Cent mélodies anciennes et modernes (c1810)

Methods for gui (incl. op.31), lyre-gui, flageolet

BIBLIOGRAPHY

FétisB; LaMusicaD

F. Donnadieu: 'Musiciens et compositeurs biterrois: Porro', *Bulletin de la Société archéologique, scientifique et littéraire de Béziers*, xxv–xxvi (1897)
C. Hopkinson: *A Dictionary of Parisian Music Publishers, 1750–1950* (London, 1954)
B. Bardet: 'Porro, Pierre-Jean', *MGG*

THOMAS F. HECK

Porsile [Persile, Porcile, Porsille], **Giuseppe** (*b* Naples, 5 May 1680; *d* Vienna, 29 May 1750). Italian composer and singing-master. He was the son of the musician Carlo Porsile, whose opera *Nerone* was produced, according to Burney, at Naples in 1686. Giuseppe was a pupil of Ursino, Giordano and Greco at the Conservatorio dei Poveri di Gesù Cristo in Naples. At first he held an appointment as vice-*maestro di cappella* at the Spanish chapel in Naples, but in 1695 he was called to Spain by Charles II (who died in 1700) to organize the music chapel at Barcelona. He remained there under Charles III, the Austrian contender to the Spanish throne, and served as singing-master to Charles's wife Elisabetta Cristina. To what extent he was also active as a teacher and composer in Naples before 1713 remains unclear, but his early opera *Il ritorno di Ulisse* was produced there in 1707.

At the end of 1711, Charles III returned to Vienna, becoming Charles VI, Holy Roman Emperor. Porsile remained at Barcelona in the service of Elisabetta until the end of 1713; then he went to Vienna, where he was granted an annual salary of 200 ducats and was appointed singing-master to the empress. The salary was not confirmed until 1717, and while being promised a more substantial appointment he served as *attuario di camera*. In a letter to the emperor dated 27 November 1720 (printed in La Mara, 1910), he complained of financial hardship, reminded the emperor of his long service and asked for a permanent position. On 17 December 1720 he succeeded Gregorio Genuesi as court composer with a salary of 1440 florins.

Between 1717 and 1737 Porsile produced at least 21 secular dramatic works and 13 oratorios for the Habsburg court. Only a few works received performances outside Austria, in cities such as Venice and Prague. During 1725–7 he was active as a member of the Viennese Caecilien-Bruderschaft, whose deans were Fux and Caldara. After the death of Charles VI in 1740 he continued to receive an honorary stipend, which was lowered to 1200 florins in 1741. He was awarded a final pension on 1 April 1749.

Burney indicated that Porsile's music was greatly admired by Zeno and by Hasse, whose wife, the celebrated soprano Faustina Bordoni, sang the role of Gianisbe in Porsile's *Spartaco* at Vienna in February 1726, shortly before she went to London. In a report to the emperor in 1715, Fux described Porsile as 'ein guter Virtuose von gutten Gusto'.

Porsile belongs to the first group of late Baroque Neapolitan composers. He was probably the only composer from Naples to receive a prominent post at Vienna during the Baroque era; the Habsburg court was largely dominated by the more conservative north Italian school. His melodic, harmonic and cadential patterns contain numerous examples of the formulae typical of his generation, but his arias also include some expressive cantabile writing and an avoidance of excessive coloratura. His ability to write in a strict contrapuntal style probably accounts in part for his acceptance at the Habsburg court. In his arias he included frequent imitative passages, and in his oratorios he produced some outstanding choruses at a time when choral music was generally in a state of decay. His adoption of the musical techniques preferred at Vienna is reflected by his use of the French overture. Subtle instrumental colouring is not characteristic of his serious dramatic works, but there are occasional unusual effects, such as the use of trombone solos in the oratorio *Il trionfo di Giuditta* (1723) and the concerto-like writing for two flutes in the cantata *Le sofferte amare*. Elsewhere there are frequent cello obbligatos. Although Porsile's music is overshadowed by that of his Viennese contemporaries, Fux and Caldara, its fusion of Neapolitan and north Italian elements was an important ingredient in the development of pre-Classical style in Vienna.

WORKS
DRAMATIC
(first performed in Vienna unless otherwise stated)

Il ritorno di Ulisse alla patria (G. A. Moniglia), Naples, S Giovanni de' Fiorentini, 1707, *I-Rn*, 40 arias and duets, *Nc*

Il giorno natalizio dell'imperatrice Amalia Wilhelmina (P. Pariati), 21 April 1717, *A-Wgm, D-Dlb*

La Virtù festeggiata (Pariati), 10 July 1717, *A-Wgm*

Alceste (festa teatrale, Pariati), 19 Nov 1718, *Wgm, Wn*

Meride e Selinunte (dramma per musica, Zeno), Neue Favorita, 28 Aug 1721, *Wgm, Wn, D-Dlb*

Il tempo fermato (componimento da camera), 15 Oct 1721, *A-Wn*

La Virtù e la Bellezza in lega (serenata), Grosses Hoftheater, 15 Oct 1722, *Wn*

Il giorno felice (componimento da camera, Pariati), 28 Aug 1723, *Wgm, Wn*

Componimento a due voci, Neue Favorita, 28 Aug 1725, ?*Wgm*

Spartaco (dramma per musica, G. C. Pasquini), Kleines Hoftheater, 21 Feb 1726, *Wgm, Wn*

Il tempio di Giano, chiuso da Cesare Augusto (componimento per musica, Pasquini), Neue Favorita, 1 Oct 1726, *Wgm, Wn*

La clemenza di Cesare (servizio di camera, Pasquini), Neue Favorita, 1 Oct 1727, *Wgm, Wn*

Telesilla (festa teatrale, Pasquini), 19 Nov 1729, *Wgm, Wn*

Scipione Africano, il maggiore (festa di camera, Pasquini), Neue Favorita, 1 Oct 1730, *Wgm, Wn*

Dialogo tra il Decoro e la Placidezza (festa di camera, Pasquini), 26 July 1732, *Wgm, Wn*

Dialogo pastorale a cinque voci, Neue Favorita, 28 Aug 1732, *Wn*

Dialogo tra la Prudenza e la Vivacità (festa di camera, Pasquini), 15 Oct 1732, *Wgm, Wn*

La Fama accresciuta dalla Virtù (festa di camera, Pasquini), 15 Oct 1735, *Wgm, Wn*

Sesostri, re d'Egitto, ovvero Le feste d'Iside (dramma per musica,

Pariati and Zeno), carn. 1737, *Wn*

Il giudizio rivocato (festa di camera, Pasquini), 15 Oct 1737, *Wgm, Wn*

Psiche (dramma per musica), *D-Dlb, US-Wc*

Doubtful: Osmeno e Fileno (dialoghetto), after 1712, *A-Wn*, attrib. Porsile or Caldara

ORATORIOS

(all performed at the imperial chapel, Vienna; MSS in A-Wgm, Wn)

Sisara (Zeno), 23 March 1719

Tobia (Zeno), 14 March 1720

Il zelo di Nathan (G. Velardi), 1721

L'anima immortale creata e redenta per il cielo (B. Maddali), 26 Feb 1722

Il trionfo di Giuditta (Maddali), 18 Feb 1723

Il sacrifizio di Gefte (G. Salio), 9 March 1724

Mosè liberato dal Nilo, 1 March 1725

Assalone nemico del padre amante, 14 March 1726

L'esaltazione de Salomone (Maddali), 6 March 1727

L'ubbidienza a Dio (A. M. Lucchini), 9 March 1730

Due re, Roboamo e Geroboamo (F. Fozio), 23 Feb 1731

Giuseppe riconosciuto (Metastasio), 12 March 1733

La madre de' Maccabei (F. Manzoni-Giusti), 14 March 1737

OTHER VOCAL

Mass, *A-KR*

Arias from operas and oratorios: 9 in *A-Wn*, 2 in *B-Bc*, 1 in *D-Dlb*, 1 in *F-Pn*, 3 in *GB-Lbm*, ?several in *I-Pca*, 1 in *US-CA*

Chamber cantatas, duets etc: 5 in *A-Wn*, 11 in *B-Bc*, 2 in *D-Bds*, 4 in *Dlb*, 1 in *DS*, 3 in *MEIr*, 1 in *GB-Lbm*, 7 in *I-Nc*, ?several in *Pca*

7 canzonette, S, bc, *D-Dlb*

INSTRUMENTAL

6 partite, 2 vn, bc, *D-MEIr*; 5 partite, 2 vn, vc, bc, *ROu*

Partie, solo lute, *A-Wn*; ed. in EDM, 2nd ser., *Landschaftsdenkmale*, i (1942)

2 sinfonie, 2 vn, 2 ob, va, bc, *D-Dlb*

Divertimento a 3, *A-Wgm*

Piece for fl, bc, *D-ROu*

BIBLIOGRAPHY

BurneyH; EitnerQ; FétisB; GerberL; GerberNL; SchmidlD; SchmidlDS

L. Allacci: *Drammaturgia* (Venice, enlarged 2/1755/R1961)

L. von Köchel: *Die kaiserliche Hof-Musikkapelle in Wien von 1543–1867* (Vienna, 1869)

La Mara [M. Lipsius]: 'Briefe alter Wiener Hofmusiker', *Musikbuch aus Österreich*, vii (1910), 3

A. Schering: *Geschichte des Oratoriums* (Leipzig, 1911/R1966)

E. Schmitz: *Geschichte der weltlichen Solokantate* (Leipzig, 1914/R1966, rev. 2/1955)

P. Nettl: 'Opernaufführung zu Znaim anno 1723', *Beiträge zur böhmischen und mährischen Musikgeschichte* (Brno, 1927), 14

U. Manferrari: *Dizionario universale delle opere melodrammatiche* (Florence, 1954–5)

F. Hadamowsky: 'Barocktheater am Wiener Kaiserhof', *Jb der Gesellschaft für Wiener Theaterforschung 1951–2* (1955)

U. Prota-Giurleo: 'Giuseppe Porsile e la Real cappella di Barcellona', *Gazzetta musicale di Napoli*, ii (1956), no.10

R. Brockpähler: *Handbuch zur Geschichte der Barockoper in Deutschland* (Emsdetten, 1964)

U. Kirkendale: *Antonio Caldara: sein Leben und seine venezianisch-römischen Oratorien* (Graz, 1966)

G. Henrotte: *The Ensemble Divertimento in Pre-classic Vienna* (diss., U. of North Carolina, 1967)

A. McCredie: 'Nicholas Matteis – English Composer at the Habsburg Court', *ML*, xlviii (1967), 127

O. E. Deutsch: 'Das Repertoire der höfischen Oper, der Hof- und der Staatsoper', *ÖMz*, xxiv (1969), 369–421

LAWRENCE E. BENNETT

Port. A term formerly used in Scotland for an instrumental composition or 'lesson', generally played on the harp. *Rory Dall's Port*, the best-known surviving example, was associated in the 17th century with a blind harpist of that name, but it was later adapted to Burns's song 'Ae fond kiss and then we sever'. There are several ports in the Straloch Lute Manuscript (1627), including *Jean Lindsay's Port*, and the 17th-century Skene Manuscript has a piece called *Port Ballangowne*. In the 18th century, Tytler (*Dissertation on Scotish Music*) described it as a particular genre of composition and wrote that 'every great family had its Port named after the family'.

FRANK KIDSON/R

Porta, Bernardo (*b* Rome, 1758; *d* Paris, 11 June 1829). Italian composer and conductor, active in France. A pupil of Magrini, he was at first *maestro di cappella* and director of the orchestra at Tivoli, and then in the service of the Prince of Salm, the prelate for Rome. In Italy he wrote masses, motets, two oratorios and an opera *La Principessa d'Amalfi*, produced with little success in Rome (1780). It has commonly been reported that he went to Paris in 1788 when his *Le diable à quatre*, an *opéra comique*, was badly received at the Comédie-Italienne. Eitner, however, suggested that the cantata performed in 1785 for the name day of Baron de Bagge was composed by Porta who must, therefore, have been in Paris by that time. He probably entertained hopes of following Anfossi's successful career as an opera composer in Rome but the Revolution kept him in Paris, where he remained. Among his many stage works performed there were *Les Horaces* (1800) and *Le connétable de Clisson* (1804); the latter had little success and earned its composer a satirical vengeful song. He taught harmony in various private establishments until 1822. Much of his instrumental music was intended for beginners.

WORKS

(printed works published in Paris unless otherwise stated)

STAGE

(first performed in Paris unless otherwise stated)

La Principessa d'Amalfi (opera), Rome, Argentina, 1780

Le diable à quatre (opéra comique, M.-J. Sedaine), Comédie-Italienne, 14 Feb 1788

Pagamin (opéra italien), Louvois, 1791

La blanche haquenée (opéra comique), Molière, 1793

Alexis et Rosette, ou Les Huhlans [Houlans] (opéra comique, 1, Desriaux), Théâtre Français Comique et Lyrique, 30 Aug 1793

La réunion du 10 août, ou L'inauguration de la République française (drame révolutionnaire, 5, Bouquier, P.-L. Moline), Opéra, 5 April 1794 (1794)

Agricol Viala, ou Le héros de 13 ans (opéra comique, Audouin), Opéra-Comique, 1 July 1794 (?1794)

La pauvre aveugle, ou La chanson savoyarde (1), Ambigu, 1797

L'oracle (1), Ambigu, 1797

Le prisonnier français, ou Le bienfait récompensé (drame historique, 1), Amis des Arts, 1 Sept 1798 (1798)

Deux morts qui se voient (1), Ambigu, 26 April 1800

Les deux statues (1), Ambigu, 29 April 1800

Les Horaces (opera, 3, N. F. Guillard), Opéra, 18 Oct 1800, *F-Po*

Le vieux de la montagne (opera), 1802, inc., unperf., *Po*

Le connétable de Clisson (opera, 3, Aignan), Arts, 9 or 10 Feb 1804 (1804)

Télémaque dans l'île de Calypso (incidental music, Bailly de Saint Paulin), unperf.

OTHER WORKS

Vocal: Cantate à Mr le Baron de Bagge ... pour le jour de sa fête (Moline), 1785 (n.d.); masses; motets; 2 oratorios

Inst: 4 sets of 3 qnts, 2 fl, vn, va, b (n.d.); 6 qts (?1786); Qts and trios, fl, vn, va, b (1780s); 2 sets of 3 trios, 3 fl (n.d.); 6 trios, 2 vn, b (n.d.); 3 duos pour commençants, 2 fl (n.d.); 6 duos, 2 vc (?1812); Sonate, vc, b, no.5 in Bononcini: 6 solos, 2 vc, ed. J. Simplon (London, n.d.); other works

BIBLIOGRAPHY

FétisB

M. Briquet: 'Porta, Bernardo', *MGG*

PAULETTE LETAILLEUR

Porta, Costanzo (*b* Cremona, 1528–9; *d* Padua, 19 May 1601). Italian composer and teacher. He was praised as an exceptionally skilful composer by fellow musicians and theorists alike. Artusi (*Delle imperfettioni*, 1600, p.70) extolled his mastery of contrapuntal complexity, while Zacconi (*Prattica di musica*, ii, 1622, p.130) named him first among the four most outstanding contrapuntists known to him. The extent and the consistently excellent quality of his music, sacred and secular, and his widespread influence as a teacher of many youn-

1. Costanzo Porta: portrait by an unknown artist in the Museo Civico, Padua

ger composers make him one of the major figures in Italian Renaissance music.

1. LIFE. The approximate date of his birth derives from a letter dated 1 April 1592, in which he stated that he was 63 years old. The Franciscan Minorite Conventuals, of which he eventually became a member, demanded a thorough training in classics, philosophy and theology. It may be assumed that he received his first schooling at their convent of Porta S Luca, Cremona. Somewhat later he moved to Casalmaggiore, perhaps to enter his novitiate; the year of his ordination is not recorded. In about 1549 he was transferred to S Maria Gloriosa dei Frari, Venice, though he did not, as Garbelotto stated, become choirmaster there (that position was held by Antonio Barges). Nor did he then study with Mauro Saraceni, as Franchini stressed, since Saraceni was born only in 1540. He did, however, become a pupil of Willaert, choirmaster of St Mark's; among his fellow pupils were Merulo and Zarlino. With Merulo he formed a lifelong friendship which is documented in terms of great affection in Merulo's edition of Porta's five-part introits of 1566; Zarlino unaccountably failed to mention Porta in any of his writings.

Porta took up his first professional position in 1552, as *maestro di cappella* of Osimo Cathedral, and he held the post for 13 years. This period proved to be significant, as it brought him under the patronage of the Della Rovere family, the ducal house of Urbino. Several of his publications, which began to appear in 1555, were dedicated to members of the family; Cardinal Giulio della Rovere, who was to be specially helpful in advancing his career, was twice honoured in this way.

On 9 January 1565 the Arca del Santo in Padua voted to resolve a conflict in the Cappella Antoniana by

offering the position of *maestro di cappella* to Porta. After some bargaining – he requested that his appointment be approved by the entire monastic community – he was ready on 14 April 1565 to assume his duties. On 12 May 1565 the minister-general of the order requested his services at the Pentecostal celebrations of the general chapter in Florence, where he met, among others, Duke Cosimo I de' Medici and his son Francesco and the cardinals Carlo Borromeo and Felice Peretti (later Pope Sixtus V). His 13-part *Missa Ducalis*, in which the 13th voice intones a cantus firmus throughout to the words 'protege Cosmum ducem principemque Franciscum', originated some time after this meeting and before 1569, when Cosimo was made grand duke.

Porta did not remain long at Padua. On 13 January 1567 Giulio della Rovere, as Archbishop of Ravenna, requested his transfer to that city. The development of the music at the basilica there, enthusiastically supported by Della Rovere, occupied Porta for the next seven years. His removal on 5 September 1574 to the Santa Casa at Loreto was again instigated by Della Rovere, who at the same time commissioned him to write masses in honour of the coming jubilee year, 1575, 'short and in a manner which would make the text easily comprehensible'. The resulting first book of masses was published in 1578, only a few weeks before the cardinal's death. Thereupon Cardinal Borromeo unsuccessfully attempted to win Porta's services for Milan Cathedral. Instead, on 30 June 1580, he returned to Ravenna, dedicating his important *Liber quinquaginta duorum motectorum* to the governor of Loreto as a parting gift.

During the following years Porta visited at least two important centres of musical activity: the Este court at Ferrara, where he was much taken with the famous 'concerti delle dame' and where he met Luzzaschi; and the Gonzaga court at Mantua, where he met Wert. In both places he was acclaimed for his madrigals. In 1585 he commemorated the election of his former protector Felice Peretti to the papacy as Sixtus V by dedicating to him his third book of six-part motets. By this time his fame was spreading far: in 1587 he was elected to membership in the Congregazione Romana dei Musici di S Cecilia, a group that included such illustrious figures as Palestrina, Lassus and Zacconi.

Porta apparently attracted pupils wherever he settled. Many of them later achieved some renown as composers, and the solid craftsmanship and control of contrapuntal writing exhibited in their works surely bear witness to Porta's gifts as a teacher. They include Lodovico Balbi, Valerio Bona, Oratio Colombani, Marsilio Cristoffori, Giulio Cesare Gabussi, Giovanni Ghizzolo, Tomaso Graziani, Giacomo Antonio Piccioli, Antonio Prandi, Bartolomeo Ratti, Alfonso Rossi and Pandolfo Zallamella. He may also have taught Diruta and Viadana.

In 1589 disunity arose in the chapel of Padua Cathedral, then under the direction of G. M. Mosto, and Porta was chosen on 1 May 1589 to replace him. In 1592 he was ordered peremptorily to move from his lodgings nearby to the Convento del Santo some distance away. His appeal against the order was rejected, and he moved to the monastery. In 1595 he once more became director of music at the Cappella Antoniana. For his many years of devoted service to his order he was honoured on 10 June 1596 by having the title of 'magister musicae' conferred upon him. In contrast to his previous term at the Cappella Antoniana, when he was actively protected by Cardinal della Rovere, his life now became increasingly difficult through lack of support. Several letters from him bewail the fact that he was not assigned enough musicians to fill all the existing vacancies. He spent his last years in a dwindling chapel, beset by failing health and by jealousy and intrigue on the part of his assistant and eventual successor, Bartolomeo Ratti. He died on 19 May 1601 (not on 26 May, as has sometimes been stated).

2. WORKS. Porta's lifelong service to the Minorite Friars is reflected in his music, the larger part of which consists of sacred works. Most of these are motets, seven books of which survive (a gap in the numbering indicates that one other is lost). Since they appeared at regular intervals throughout his career it is possible to trace through them the development of his great skills as a contrapuntist in the tradition of Gombert and Willaert. With few exceptions, the motets are relentlessly polyphonic. They are flexible structures unfolding through a succession of imitative points, the intensity of imitation being subject to great variety. This procedure normally results in entirely through-composed works, but several of the motets in two *partes* are cast in the familiar form of the responsory, *A–B–C–B*. These latter frequently include writing in double, and occasionally triple, invertible counterpoint in the repeated (*B*) sections. A noteworthy feature of the earlier motet publications is the frequency of paired imitation; the later books show an increasingly intense polyphonic complexity. The famous book of 1580 includes the often cited *Diffusa est gratia*, in which four of the seven voices are derived by various canonic means, as well as the six-part *Vidi speciosam*, with its mensuration canon. Even more consistently severe in their polyphony are the six-part motets of 1585, fully two-thirds of which involve the use of canon in three voices. Yet the same motets afford evidence that Porta was quite conversant with madrigalian devices; descriptive passages in the texts are often mirrored in appropriate rhythmic flexibility and melodic movement. Another feature, apparent in the later motets for a large number of voices, is the inclination towards polychoral treatment, in which vocal colours are managed with considerable brilliance – Porta had, after all, very close ties with Venice. The Marian litanies written for Loreto, the vesper psalms and *Magnificat* settings are other examples of his polychoral writing.

Porta wrote 15 masses, 12 of which were published in 1578. The print opens with six four-part masses named after the first six modes. They were long believed to be freely composed, but recent research has shown that the *Missa secundi toni* and *Missa tertii toni* are parodies based on Palestrina's madrigal *Vestiva i colli* and Rore's madrigal *Come havran fin* respectively. Stylistic features of the other four suggest that they too are parodies. Three other masses in the print are confirmed by their titles as parodies: the five-part *Missa 'Descendit angelus'* is based on a motet by Hilaire Penet and the six-part *Missa 'Audi filia'* on one by Gombert; the model for the six-part *Missa 'Quemadmodum'* is as yet unidentified. The remaining masses, both printed and manuscript, are cantus firmus works, some using Gregorian, some original melodies. The *Missa Ducalis* (whose 13 parts are disposed as three four-part choirs

and a tenor cantus firmus) and the eight-part *Missa 'Da pacem'* have several features in common: both have cantus firmi which retain their separate texts throughout; both introduce quite unusual textual troping in their final movements (the latter work includes similar troping at the beginning as well); and both were written for special purposes, rather than for general liturgical use, the one, as has been mentioned, pleading for Duke Cosimo I de' Medici and his son, the other commemorating the Battle of Lepanto (1571). Cantus firmus technique is also the basis of the five-part introits and the posthumously published *Hymnodia sacra*. The latter, with its 46 hymns, is among the largest vesper hymn cycles originating in the 16th century. Following the *alternatim* practice common at the time, Porta generally set the even-numbered stanzas of the hymn texts in an astounding variety of polyphonic treatments, leaving the odd-numbered stanzas to be chanted. As regards general stylistic features of the sacred music of the period – the nature of the melodic movement, highly regulated treatment of dissonance, modal usage, restraint in the use of chromaticism, rhythmic precision of the word-setting – he fully equalled the disciplined style of Palestrina; in polyphonic severity he exceeded it.

Porta's numerous secular works have not been exhaustively studied; three of the five madrigal books survive in incomplete form, many individual pieces are scattered in various anthologies, and others remain in manuscript. Porta followed the general trends of Italian madrigal composition during the second half of the 16th century: most of his settings are for five voices (the

2. *Opening of the cantus part of the motet 'Diffusa est gratia', for 7 voices, from Porta's 'Liber motectorum' (Venice: Angelo Gardano, 1580)*

single four-part book reflects the personal taste of the dedicatee); the texts are partly by classic poets, including Petrarch, Ariosto and Tasso, partly lightly amorous and frequently occasional. The occasional pieces highlight Porta's close ties with the house of Della Rovere, many of them celebrating weddings, births, departures and returns and other festivities in the family, as well as commemorating occasions on which Porta received some favour or bounty from them. His madrigals are much less contrapuntal than his church music. The madrigalian characteristic demanding that musical thought be matched to expressive content prompted him to be harmonically more adventurous, a trait beautifully exemplified by the five-part *Mentre nel tristo petto* in the 1569 book. Such a piece suggests that the high regard in which Guglielmo Gonzaga and Alfonso d'Este held Porta's madrigals was not misplaced.

WORKS

Edition: *C. Porta: Opera omnia*, ed. S. Cisilino (Padua, 1964–) [C]

SACRED VOCAL

Printed works, except anthologies, were published in Venice unless otherwise stated.

[37] Motectorum . . . liber primus, 5vv (1555); C ii
Liber primus [28] motectorum, 4vv (1559, rev. 2/1591); C i
Musica [44] introitus missarum . . . in diebus dominicis, 5vv (1566, rev. 2/1588); ed. in Musica liturgica, i/3–4 (Cincinnati, 1958–61)
Musica [40] introitus missarum . . . in solemnitatibus omnium sanctorum, 5vv (1566, rev. 2/1588); C xv
Musica [29] canenda . . . liber primus, 6vv (1571); C iv
Litaniae deiparae virginis Mariae, 8vv (1575)
[12] Missarum liber primus, 4–6vv (1578); Missa tertii toni, 4vv, ed. in Musica divina, v (Regensburg, 1950); Missa La sol fa re mi so, 6vv, ed. in Cw, xciii (1965)
Liber [52] motectorum, 4–8vv (1580); C v
Musica [29] canenda . . . liber tertius, 6vv (1585); C vi
[44] Hymnodia sacra totius per anni circulum, 4vv (1602); C xiii
Psalmodia vespertina omnium solemnitatem decantanda cum 4 canticis beatae virginis, 8, 16vv (Ravenna and Venice, 1605)
[23] Motectorum, 5vv (1605); C iii
Motets, psalms, litanies in 1563⁴, 1583², C. Merulo: Il primo libro de' motetti (Venice, 1583), 1588², 1590⁷, 1592³, 1596¹, 1596², 1601¹, Florilegii musici portensis . . . pars (Leipzig, 1603), 1607⁶, 1607⁹, 1609¹⁵, 1613², 1623²

Missa 'Da pacem', 8vv; Missa mortuorum, 4vv: *I-LT*; C x
Missa Ducalis, 13vv, ?holograph, *I-Fl*; C x
Antiphons, 4vv, *I-Ac, Bc, RA, TVca*; C xii
Other sacred works, incl. Magnificats, Te Deum, graduals, responsories, psalms, motets, Lamentations, hymns, antiphons: *D-As, F-Pn, I-Ac, Bc, MOd, Pc, RA, TVca* [many concordances]

SECULAR VOCAL

Printed works, except anthologies, were published in Venice unless otherwise stated.

Il primo libro de [29] madrigali, 4vv (1555); C xix
Il primo libro de [28] madrigali, 5vv (1559); C xx
Il secondo libro de [29] madrigali, 5vv (1569); C xxi
Il terzo libro de [29] madrigali, 5vv (1573)
Il quarto libro de [21] madrigali, 5vv (1586)
Madrigals in 1557¹⁶, 1559¹⁶, 1560¹⁷, 1562⁵, 1564¹⁶, 1567¹⁵, 1567¹⁶, V. Galilei: Il Fronimo (Venice, 1568, 2/1584¹⁵), 1570¹⁵, 1575¹², 1575¹⁵, 1576⁵, G. C. Gabussi: Il primo libro de madrigali (Venice, 1580), 1582⁵, 1583¹⁰, 1583¹², 1585¹⁷, 1586⁷, 1586¹⁰, 1586¹¹, 1588¹⁷, 1589¹², 1590¹¹, 1592¹¹, 1592¹⁵, 1593³, 1593¹¹, 1594⁶, 1595⁵, 1596², 1596¹¹, 1597¹⁵, 1598⁶, 1598⁷, 1598⁹, 1601¹⁰, 1604⁸
13 madrigals, 4vv, *I-Bc*
1 madrigal, 4vv, *F-Pn*; ed. in *Miscelánea en homenaje a Monseñor Higinio Anglés* (Barcelona, 1958–61), i, 169
Intabulations of all madrigals from 1559, 1569 and some from 1573 publications, *I-Fl*

INSTRUMENTAL

Fantasia, *F-Pn* Rés.Vma.851
Ricercar, a 4; Gerometta, a 8, *I-Bc* U 95

THEORETICAL WORKS

Trattato . . . ossia Instruzioni di contrappunto (MS, *I-Bc* B 140)

BIBLIOGRAPHY

G. Rossi: *Historiarum Ravennatum libri X* (Venice, 1589)
G. Franchini: *Bibliosofia e memorie letterarie di scrittori Francescani Conventuali* (Modena, 1693)
L. Busi: *Il Padre G. B. Martini* (Bologna, 1891/R1961)
G. Tebaldini: *L'archivio musicale della Cappella Antoniana* (Padua, 1895)
——: *L'archivio musicale della Cappella Lauretana* (Loreto, 1921)
R. Casadio: 'La cappella musicale della cattedrale di Ravenna', *NA*, xvi (1939), 136–85, 270
R. Casimiri: 'Musica e musicisti nella cattedrale di Padova', *NA*, xviii (1941), 114; xix (1942), 77
A. Einstein: *The Italian Madrigal* (Princeton, 1949/R1971)
F. Hafkemayer: *Costanzo Porta aus Cremona: Untersuchungen über seine kirchenmusikalischen Arbeiten* (diss., U. of Freiburg, 1953)
G. Reese: *Music in the Renaissance* (New York, 1954, rev. 2/1959)
A. Garbelotto: *Il P. Costanzo Porta da Cremona, OFM. Conv.* (Padua, 1955)
R. Lunelli: 'Nota complementare sul musicista Costanzo Porta', *Miscellanea Francescana*, lvi (1956), 282
E. E. Lowinsky: 'Early Scores in Manuscript', *JAMS*, xiii (1960), 121–73
L. P. Pruett: *The Masses and Hymns of Costanzo Porta* (diss., U. of N. Carolina, 1960)
——: 'Parody Technique in the Masses of Costanzo Porta', *Studies in Musicology: Essays . . . in Memory of Glen Haydon* (Chapel Hill, 1969), 210

LILIAN P. PRUETT

Porta, Ercole [Hercole] (*b* Bologna, 10 Sept 1585; *d* Carpi, 30 April 1630). Italian composer and organist. In 1609 he was organist at the collegiate church of S Giovanni, Persiceto, near Bologna, and directed the music there from 1612 until 1620. He was *maestro di cappella* at Carpi Cathedral from January 1622 until 1625 and from no later than 1628; in between he was organist at nearby Rubiera.

Apart from the *Hore di recreatione*, which is tentative in its adoption of the new monodic style, Porta's output consists of sacred music in the up-to-date concertato style for a few voices and continuo popular in the north Italian provinces where resources were limited. Thus much of the music in his 1609 and 1613 collections is for fewer than four voices. The 1613 book also contains a sonata for cornett, violin and two trombones in the same style. The presence of instruments is a particular feature of the *Sacro convito*, which includes a mass and two motets accompanied by a five-part church orchestra of two violins and three trombones, a scoring that became fairly common in larger-scale ceremonial music. This mass may be the first to include such an orchestra in a complete setting: it was probably intended for a major feast. Porta's music shows a good understanding of sonority and idiomatic vocal writing. Sometimes the voices have more ornate lines than the accompanying instruments, which here provide a sustained background; at other times they are doubled exactly – even the violins do not have independent parts. While this mass belongs to the long line of Venetian orchestral masses, Porta possibly learnt ways of combining voices and instruments from a Bolognese composer, Girolamo Giacobbi. The *Sacro convito* also contains a motet, *Corda Deo dabimus*, for soprano, alto and three trombones, the latter providing a richly sonorous accompaniment: such a combination is reminiscent of Giovanni Gabrieli, though it was not often specified by his successors. Porta also offered interesting advice to the organist in this publication: he should use his ear, since not all the dissonances are figured, and adopt a sparse texture when accompanying few voices, thickening it (without adding stops) in the fuller passages.

WORKS

Giardino di spirituali concerti, 2–4vv, bc (org) (Venice, 1609)
Hore di recreatione, 1, 2vv, bc (chit/other insts) (Venice, 1612)
Vaga ghirlanda di soavi et odorati fiori musicali, 1–5vv, bc, op.3 (Bologna, 1613)
Concerti, 1–4vv, bc, libri I–III (Venice, 1619) [lost; mentioned in A. Vincenti: *Indice di tutte le opere* (Venice, 1619)]

Motetti, 1–5vv, 2 trbn, 2 vn ad lib [lost; mentioned in Vincenti]
Sacro convito musicale . . . 1–6vv, 2 vn, 3 trbn, bc, op.7 (Venice, 1620)
Complectorium laetum, comodum et breve, 5vv, bc, op.8 (Venice, 1626)
Madrigali, 3vv (Venice, 1662) [lost; possibly the same as Lusinghe d'amore, canzonette, 3vv (Venice) mentioned in *WaltherML* and *FétisB*]
8 motets in 1613[5], 1622[2], 1623[2], 1627[2]; 8 motets in *PL-WRu*

Letter to Duke of Modena, *c*1627, *I-MOe*

BIBLIOGRAPHY

G. Gaspari: 'Dei musicisti bolognesi del XVII secolo', *Atti e memorie della RR. Deputazione di storia patria per le provincie dell'Emilia*, new ser., v/2 (1880), 37
A. G. Spinelli: *Notizie spettanti alla storia della musica in Carpi*, i (Carpi, 1900), 314f
J. L. A. Roche: *North Italian Liturgical Music in the Early 17th Century* (diss., U. of Cambridge, 1968)

JEROME ROCHE

Porta, Francesco della. *See* DELLA PORTA, FRANCESCO.

Porta, Gasparo della. *See* DELLA PORTA, GASPARO.

Porta, Giovanni (*b* Venice, ?*c*1690; *d* Munich, 21 June 1755). Italian composer. He may have been of noble birth. He is first heard of in 1706, when he was a member of Cardinal Ottoboni's *cappella* in Rome; later he became its *maestro*. In 1716 he returned to Venice, where he had operas performed that autumn and the next two. He is next heard of in London, where on 2 April 1720 his opera *Numitore* opened the new Royal Academy of Music. In its libretto he is called a virtuoso in the service of the Duke of Wharton; he may have spent the preceding period in the duke's service. He had an opera performed in Venice in autumn 1720, but did not resume his operatic career in Italy in earnest until spring 1722, producing a steady flow of works between the autumns of 1723 and 1726. Two performed in Naples in autumn 1725 and Carnival 1726 suggest a trip there; otherwise he worked mainly in Venice and Milan. On 24 May 1726 he was appointed *maestro di coro* at the Ospedale degli Incurabili in Venice. The duties of this important post were heavy, including teaching, conducting and composing (in 1729 alone he produced 32 motets and psalm settings). His production of operas became more intermittent; he had three staged in 1728 and six in 1730–33, all but one of the latter outside Venice. In 1736 he competed unsuccessfully for the post of *maestro di cappella* at St Mark's and in October 1737 became court Kapellmeister at Munich (he was officially installed in that post on 11 May 1738). He remained there until his death, composing a few stage works and a considerable quantity of church music.

Burney praised Porta as 'one of the most able masters of his time; uniting learning with invention and fire' and wrote of *Numitore* that its music 'seems superior to that of any preceding opera which we had from Italy'. Westerman's study of the operas makes plain that Porta followed the operatic conventions of the time with no special marks of originality. The mass by him in the British Library is effectively written, attaining at times a brilliant sound through orchestral passages reminiscent of the Venetian concerto style and sonorous choral textures with much doubling in 3rds and a minimum of contrapuntal intricacies. Handel 'borrowed' phrases from *Numitore* in *Samson* (1741–2, including 'Let the bright seraphim') and *Solomon* (1748, including the sinfonia called 'The Arrival of the Queen of Sheba').

WORKS
(music lost unless otherwise stated)

OPERAS
(all opere serie)

Amore e fortuna (F. Passarini), ?Rovigo, Campanella, aut. 1712, or Naples, S Bartolomeo, 1 Oct 1725; also as Amore di sangue
La costanza combattuta in amore (F. Silvani), Venice, S Moisè, 17 Oct 1716, *D-Dlb* (arias)
L'Argippo (D. Lalli), Venice, S Cassiano, aut. 1717, *Dlb*
L'amor di figlia (Lalli, after G. M. Moniglia), Venice, S Angelo, aut. 1718
Numitore (P. Rolli), London, Haymarket, 2 April 1720; ov., 36 vocal nos. (London, 1720); also as Rhea Silvia
Teodorico (A. Salvi), Venice, S Giovanni Grisostomo, aut. 1720
L'amor tirannico (Lalli), Venice, S Samuele, May 1722; Acts 1–2 by F. Chelleri, Act 3 by Porta
L'Arianna nell'isola di Nasso (N. Stampa), Milan, Ducale, 28 Aug 1723
La caduta de decemviri (S. Stampiglia), Milan, Ducale, 26 Dec 1723
Li sforzi d'ambizione e d'amore (A. M. Lucchini), Venice, S Moisè, carn. 1724
Antigono tutore di Filippo rè della Macedonia (G. Piazzon), Venice, S Moisè, carn. 1724, collab. T. Albinoni
La Mariane (Lalli), Venice, S Angelo, 15 Nov 1724, rev. of Albinoni's Gl'eccessi della gelosia, retaining at least 4 orig. arias
Ulisse (Lalli), Venice, S Angelo, carn. 1725
Agide rè di Sparta (L. Bergalli), Venice, S Moisè, ?carn. 1725
Aldiso (N. Stampa), Venice, S Giovanni Grisostomo, carn. 1726
Lucinda fedele (Zeno), Naples, S Bartolomeo, carn. 1726
Siroe rè di Persia (Metastasio), Florence, Cocomero, sum. 1726
Il trionfo di Flavio Olibrio (Zeno and Pariati), Venice, S Giovanni Grisostomo, 23 Nov 1726
Nel perdono la vendetta (C. Paganicesa), Venice, S Moisè, May 1728
La sorte nemica (Silvani), Vicenza, delle Grazie, May 1728
Doriclea ripudiata da Creso (G. B. Corte), Venice, S Moisè, 29 Dec 1728
Il gran Tamerlano (A. Piovene), Florence, Pergola, carn. 1730
Farnace (Lucchini), Bologna, Malvezzi, spr. 1731, *Dlb*
Gianguir (Zeno), Milan, Ducale, carn. 1732, rev. Munich, 1738, *Dlb*
Lucio Papirio dittatore (after Zeno), Rome, Dame, spr. 1732, *A-Wn* (arias)
L'Issipile (?Lalli, after Metastasio), Venice, S Giovanni Grisostomo, aut. 1732
Semiramide (Metastasio), Milan, Ducale, Jan 1733
Ifigenia in Aulide (Zeno), Munich, court, Jan 1738, *D-Dlb*
Artaserse (Metastasio), Munich, court, 1739

OTHER WORKS

Il ritratto dell'eroe (cantata, Lalli), Venice, S Giovanni Grisostomo, 1726
Caro padre, ah forse (cantata), 1732, *A-Wn*
Innocentiae triumphus, seu Genovefa (oratorio), Venice, Conservatorio della Pietà, 1736
Dafne (serenata), Munich, Nymphenburg, 10 July 1738
Der Traum des Scipio (azione teatrale, after Metastasio), Munich, late 1744
Apollo in Tempe (cantata), *Wn*
Sacred: at least 19 masses, *D-Dkh*, *Mbs*, *SWl*, *GB-Lbm*; 6 Magnificat, *D-Bds*, *LEt*, *Mbs*; 5 Credo, 3 Miserere, 3 litanies, Antiphon, Te Deum, Veni Sancte, 22 psalms, 2 Tantum ergo, Sub tuum, all *Mbs*; Nisi Dominus, *Bds*; Domine ad adiuvandum, *GB-Lcm*; De profundis, *D-SWl*; other works, *I-Vmc*
Miscellaneous arias, duets, cantatas, *A-Wgm*, *Wn*; *B-Bc*, *Br*; *D-Bds*, *Dlb*, *Mbs*, *SHs*, *F-Pn*, *GB-Cfm*, *Lbm*

BIBLIOGRAPHY

BurneyH
J. J. Maier: 'Archivalische Excerpte über die herzoglich bayerische Hofkapelle', *KJb*, vi (1891), 69, esp. 77
G. von Westerman: *Giovanni Porta als Opernkomponist* (diss., U. of Munich, 1921)
W. Dean: *Handel's Dramatic Oratorios and Masques* (London, 1959)
D. Arnold: 'Orphans and Ladies: the Venetian Conservatories (1680–1790)', *PRMA*, lxxxix (1962–3), 31

DENNIS LIBBY (text), JAMES L. JACKMAN (work-list)

Porta, Giovanni Battista (*b* Monza; *fl* 1616). Italian composer and organist. He was a pupil of G. C. Gabussi and seems to have remained at Monza all his life. His only known music is *Madrigali a cinque in laude di S Carlo* (Venice, 1616). He was probably one of an artistic group who met in the house of Gabrio Recalcati (to whom the collection is dedicated); their admiration for Carlo Borromeo may well have inspired the collection, the texts of which were written by G. P. Giussani.

BIBLIOGRAPHY
EitnerQ; SchmidlD

Portamento (It.). A smooth and rapid 'sliding' between two pitches, executed continuously without distinguishing the intervening tones or semitones. Portamento is characteristic of the voice, trombone and strings, especially the violin, as in shifting (but *see* GLISSANDO, a sliding in which intervening pitches are generally distinguishable). Portamento in the voice or in string playing is a legitimate effect but one whose use is easily subject to abuse. In modern string playing, an audible portamento in shifting from one position to another is generally avoided, but it was a common means of expression in the 19th century. For 'expressive portamento' and its execution in violin playing, see C. Flesch: *Die Kunst des Violin-Spiels* (Berlin, 1923, 2/1928; Eng. trans., 1924, 2/1930), i, pp.28ff. Portamento in the sense of *port de voix* is sometimes used as a synonym for appoggiatura. Carlo Tessarini (*Grammatica per i principianti di violini*, Rome, ?1745) used 'primo portamento' to mean '2nd position', 'secondo portamento' to mean 3rd position and 'terzo portamento' 7th position: this use is not common. Portamento is not to be confused with portato. *See also* SLIDE.

DAVID D. BOYDEN

Porta Rico. *See* PUERTO RICO.

Portative. Strictly the same as *organetto, organino,* i.e. in 14th- and 15th-century usage the name given to the little organ of treble flue pipes carried (Lat. *portare*) by a strap over the player's shoulder, played by the right hand (fingering 2-3-2-3 is implied in many paintings), its bellows blown by the left hand. It contained one, two or more octaves of pipes in single or multiple ranks, sometimes with one or two larger bass pipes like the Bourdons of larger POSITIVE organs. The keys are earlier shaped like buttons or typewriter keys. The sound no doubt was like a set of flutes played by a keyboard. Some composers, such as Landini and Dufay, are represented playing small organs, and the instrument was useful in the many 15th-century Italian paintings (especially Venetian ones) of angel choirs at the Virgin's Coronation, etc. French sources give the impression of not knowing the term (a bill from St-Maclou, Rouen, in 1519, refers to 'portaige d'une petites orgues'), while *portiff* was used in Germany (Frankfurt, 1434) and also *organi portatili* in Italy (Barcotto, MS *c*1650) and England (Roger North, MS *c*1715). Since in England 'positive organ' is a term very rarely used, such references as 'portatives' (poem of Gawin Douglas), 'payre of portatives' (1522 will), 'portatyffes' (St Andrew, Canterbury, *c*1520) are as likely to mean a small, movable organ as a portative proper, especially since some such organs evidently contained a regal stop (1536 contract). Often, as in Henry VIII's inventory of 1547, such a 'payre of portatives' in a privy chamber is contrasted with the larger 'organes' in the chapel.

PETER WILLIAMS

Portative organ with chromatic keys: detail from 'The Mystic Marriage of St Catherine' by Hans Memling (c1435–94), in the Hôpital St Jean, Bruges

Portato (It.). A type of bowstroke; *see* BOW, §II, 2(v).

Port de voix (Fr.: 'carrying of the voice'). (1) In Baroque vocal and instrumental music, an appoggiatura, particularly one that resolves upwards. Both the appoggiatura and its resolution were often repeated, and so the ornament was frequently interpreted as an appoggiatura followed by a mordent. *See* ORNAMENTS, §II, 2, and §V, 1.

(2) In modern French usage the term means the same as PORTAMENTO.

Portée (Fr.). STAFF.

Portenaro, Francesco. *See* PORTINARO, FRANCESCO.

Porter, Andrew (*b* Cape Town, 26 Aug 1928). British writer on music. While at school, at the Diocesan College, Rondebosch, he accompanied Albert Coates's rehearsals and played continuo at his performances. From 1947 to 1950 he was organ scholar at University College, Oxford, where he read English. He then embarked on a career in music criticism, in London, contributing to *The Times*, the *Daily Telegraph*, the *Daily Express* and other newspapers, before joining the *Financial Times* in 1952. There he eventually built up a distinctive tradition of criticism, with longer notices than were customary in other British daily papers, and based on his elegant, spacious and imaginative literary style – which however is always informed by a detailed knowledge of music history and the findings of textual scholarship as well as an exceptionally wide range of sympathies, with 19th-century opera and its interpretation as their focal point. Porter also established a reputation during the 1950s and 1960s as a sensitive critic of ballet and as a broadcaster. He wrote regularly for *Opera* (of which he was associate editor, 1953–6, and thereafter a member of the editorial board) and the *Gramophone*. In 1960 he was appointed editor of the

Musical Times; during his seven years in that position he substantially modernized the journal and widened its scope, particularly in the direction of new music and opera. In 1972–3 he spent a concert season in New York as critic of the *New Yorker*, where his extended and well-informed notices attracted considerable attention; after a year in England with a fellowship at All Souls College, Oxford, he returned for a longer-term appointment with the *New Yorker* in 1974, though not severing his links with London criticism. In the USA he undertook some teaching (notably at the City University of New York and the University of California at Berkeley, where he was Ernest Bloch lecturer, 1980–81) and broadcasting; he also became editor of the newsletter of the American Institute for Verdi Studies, founded in 1976, and a member of the editorial board of *19th Century Music*, founded in 1977. Porter has prepared singing translations of many operas, including works by Handel, Haydn, Mozart (*Lucio Silla*, *Die Zauberflöte* and others), Rossini, Verdi (including *La forza del destino*, *Don Carlos*, *Otello* and *Falstaff*), Wagner (the *Ring* and *Tristan*) and Strauss (*Intermezzo*); his English texts are always distinguished by the clarity of their language and their close attention to the line and rhythm of the music. As a scholar his work has centred on Verdi, and particularly *Don Carlos*, whose full original version he was principally responsible for rediscovering in the Paris Opéra library.

WRITINGS

'Britten's *Billy Budd*', *ML*, xxxiii (1952), 111
'Britten's *Gloriana*', *ML*, xxxiv (1953), 277
'Verdi and Schiller', *Opera Annual*, iii (London, 1956–7)
4 chaps. in *Chamber Music*, ed. A. Robertson (London, 1957)
5 chaps. in *Music and Western Man*, ed. P. Garvie (London, 1958)
'A Lost Opera by Rossini', *ML*, xlv (1964), 39
'Some New British Composers', *MQ*, li (1965), 12
'Verdi's Ballet Music, and *La Pérégrina*', *2° congresso internazionale di studi verdiani: Verona 1969*, 355
'A Sketch for *Don Carlos*', *MT*, cxi (1970), 882
'The Making of *Don Carlos*', *PRMA*, xcviii (1971–2), 73
'A Note on Princess Eboli', *MT*, cxiii (1972), 750
'*Don Carlos* and the Monk-Emperor', *Musical Newsletter*, ii/4 (1972), 9
A Musical Season (New York, 1974) [reviews from the *New Yorker*, 1972–3]
'Preamble to a New *Don Carlos*', *Opera*, xxv (1974), 665
Wagner: The Ring of the Nibelung (New York, 1976) [Eng. trans. of librettos]
Music of Three Seasons: 1974–1977 (New York, 1978)
STANLEY SADIE

Porter, Cole (Albert) (*b* Peru, Ind., 9 June 1891; *d* Santa Monica, Calif., 15 Oct 1964). American songwriter. His parents were wealthy, and his mother, Kate, an accomplished amateur pianist, arranged for him to learn the violin from the age of six and the piano from the age of eight at the Marion Conservatory, Indiana. Porter began writing melodies – *The Bobolink Waltz* (1902) for piano was his first published work – and contributed words and music for amateur shows at the Worcester Academy, Massachusetts (1905–9), and for the Dramatic Club at Yale University (1909–13). He sang with and conducted the university glee club and wrote two songs, *Bingo Eli Yale* and *Bulldog*, which remained popular as Yale's football songs. For a time he read law, but in 1915–16 studied harmony and counterpoint at Harvard University. In 1915 two of his songs were performed on Broadway ('Esmerelda' in *Hands Up*, and 'Two Big Eyes' in *Miss Information*) and in 1916 he had his first Broadway show, *See America First*, a 'patriotic comic opera' modelled on Gilbert and Sullivan; all these were failures.

Porter moved to Paris in 1917, and in a capricious act (not out of despondency) he joined the French Foreign Legion. For almost three years he served in Paris and Fontainebleau and after his discharge in 1919 remained in Paris, married a socialite, and gained a reputation for giving fashionable parties in Paris, Venice and on the Riviera, attended by the young, wealthy social élite. Meanwhile in 1919 he briefly studied counterpoint, composition, orchestration and harmony with d'Indy at the Schola Cantorum. He frequently performed his own songs at his parties; they matched the chic, esoteric mood of his social circle, but were slow to find acceptance in the theatre. However, a few appeared in revues such as *Hitchy-koo of 1919*, *Greenwich Village Follies* (1924) and *Paris* (1928). In 1923 he wrote music for a ballet, *Within the Quota*, introduced in Paris and New York by the Swedish Ballet (revised as *Times Past*, 1970) and one of the earliest examples of symphonic jazz. He first achieved popular success in 1929 with *Wake Up and Dream* in London, and *Fifty Million Frenchmen* in New York. There followed *Gay Divorce* (1932) with Fred Astaire, and *Anything Goes* (1934) and *Panama Hattie* (1940) with Ethel Merman; for these and other song-and-dance musicals (some of which were later filmed) he wrote songs combining witty, often cynical words with what were to become some of his best-known melodies – 'Let's do it', 'Night and Day', 'I get a kick out of you', 'Begin the Beguine', 'Just one of those things', 'You're the Top', 'It's De-lovely' etc. He also wrote songs for several films, notably *Born to Dance* (1936) and *Rosalie* (1937), and for revues.

In 1937 Porter was injured in a riding accident on Long Island, which cost him the use of his legs and eventual amputation of one, and caused him constant pain for the rest of his life. The demoralizing effect and the lack of any success with his songs for the next ten years gave rise to self-doubts and public speculation about his abilities as a songwriter, which were not stilled until 1948. That year he produced his masterpiece, *Kiss Me, Kate*; this musical play, based on Shakespeare's *The Taming of the Shrew*, was a departure from the song-and-dance musical comedies he had written, but it included some eight songs that became immensely popular. Of his later musicals only *Can-can* (1953) was successful. He also wrote songs for films in Hollywood, notably *High Society* (1956) in which Bing Crosby and Grace Kelly sang 'True Love'; a film biography with 14 of his songs, called *Night and Day*, was made in 1946. Porter's wife died in 1954 and he was a semi-recluse in New York for the last years of his life. Several of his shows were revived in the 1960s, and there have been revues based on his life and work.

Porter was musically one of the most thoroughly trained popular songwriters of the 20th century. He was perhaps better known however as a lyricist; his texts were in the height of fashion, seldom sentimental, and filled with *double-entendres* and witty rhymes, even referring directly to sex and drugs. At first his songs were too shocking for the theatre (but he never wrote for Tin Pan Alley) and they retain much of their freshness. Many of his melodies have chromatic descending lines (e.g. 'Let's do it'), or are slow with long lines spun from repetitions, sequences and variations of single motifs (e.g. 'What is this thing called love?'). Many have sections of repeated notes, chromatic figures or narrow ranges suggesting monotony (e.g. 'Ev'rytime we say goodbye'). Porter sometimes wrote for particular performers, first with 'Night and Day' for Fred Astaire. He experimented with harmony, used triplet figures within duple metres, and wrote in extended forms unusual in popular song ('Begin the Beguine' is 108 bars long). Wilder (1972) observed that after the mid-1950s the quality of Porter's songs deteriorated, but that until then he had created perhaps the most theatrically elegant, sophisticated and musically complex songs of American 20th-century popular music.

WORKS

Only professional musical comedies listed, with dates of first New York performance, unless otherwise stated; vocal scores or selections published. Book author in parentheses, lyrics by Porter. Lists of works in Eells and Kimball and Gill.

Collection: *The Cole Porter Song Book* (New York, 1959)

See America First (comic opera, T. L. Riggs and Porter), 28 March 1916
Hitchy-koo of 1919 (revue, G. V. Hobart), 6 Oct 1919
Hitchy-koo of 1922 (revue, H. Atteridge), Philadelphia, 19 Oct 1922
Greenwich Village Follies (revue, L. Fields and others), 16 Sept 1924
La revue des ambassadeurs (revue), 10 May 1928
Paris (M. Brown), 8 Oct 1928
Wake Up and Dream (J. H. Turner), London, 27 March 1929; New York, 30 Dec 1929
Fifty Million Frenchmen (H. Fields), 27 Nov 1929
The New Yorkers (H. Fields, after E. R. Goetz and P. Arno), 8 Dec 1930
Gay Divorce (D. Taylor), 29 Nov 1932, film as The Gay Divorcee, 1934
Nymph Errant (R. Brent, after J. Laver), London, 6 Oct 1933
Anything Goes (Bolton, P. G. Wodehouse, H. Lindsay and R. Crouse), 21 Nov 1934, film 1936
Jubilee (M. Hart), 12 Oct 1935
Red, Hot and Blue (Lindsay and Crouse), 29 Oct 1936, film 1949
You Never Know (R. Leigh), 21 Sept 1938
Leave it to me (B. and S. Spewack), 9 Nov 1938
DuBarry was a Lady (H. Fields and B. G. DeSylva), 6 Dec 1939, film 1943
Panama Hattie (H. Fields and DeSylva), 30 Oct 1940, film 1942
Let's face it (H. and D. Fields), 29 Oct 1941, film 1943
Something for the Boys (H. and D. Fields), 7 Jan 1943, film 1944
Mexican Hayride (H. and D. Fields), 28 Jan 1944, film 1948
Seven Lively Arts (revue, Hart, G. S. Kaufman and others), 7 Dec 1944
Around the World in Eighty Days (O. Welles, after J. Verne), 31 May 1946
Kiss Me, Kate (musical play, B. and S. Spewack, after Shakespeare: The Taming of the Shrew), 30 Dec 1948, film 1953
Out of this World (Taylor and R. Lawrence), 21 Dec 1950
Can-can (A. Burrows), 7 May 1953, film 1960
Silk Stockings (Kaufman, L. McGrath and A. Burrows), 24 Feb 1955, film 1957

Films: Born to Dance, 1936; Rosalie, 1937; Broadway Melody of 1940; You'll never get rich, 1941; Something to Shout About, 1943; Night and Day, 1946; The Pirate, 1948; High Society, 1956; Les Girls, 1957; Aladdin (for television), 1958; others
Other songs (some for shows): Bridget, 1910; Bingo Eli Yale, c1910; Bulldog, c1910; Esmerelda, 1915; Two Big Eyes, 1915; 3 for A Night Out (musical), London, 1920; 3 for Mayfair and Montmartre (revue), London, 1922; Let's Misbehave, c1925; The Laziest Gal in Town, 1927; 2 for The Battle of Paris (film), 1929; Miss Otis Regrets, c1931; Don't fence me in, 1934; Thank you so much, Mrs Lowsborough-Goodby, c1935; From this moment on, 1950

BIBLIOGRAPHY

F. Lounsberry, ed.: *103 Lyrics by Cole Porter* (New York, 1954)
D. Ewen: *The Cole Porter Story* (New York, 1965)
C. Porter and R. G. Hubler: *The Cole Porter Story* (Cleveland, 1965)
G. Eells: *The Life that Late he Led* (New York, 1967)
R. Kimball and B. Gill: *Cole* (New York, 1971)
L. Smit: 'The Classic Cole Porter', *Saturday Review* (25 Dec 1971)
A. Wilder: *American Popular Song* (New York, 1972)

DEANE L. ROOT

Porter, (William) Quincy (*b* New Haven, 7 Feb 1897; *d* Bethany, Conn., 12 Nov 1966). American composer, violist and educationist. He studied the violin as a child, and began composition early. At Yale University (BA 1919, MusB 1921) he studied composition with Parker and David Stanley Smith. In 1920 he took lessons in composition with d'Indy and the violin with Capet in

Paris. On returning to the USA in 1921, he studied with Bloch in New York, and later in Cleveland, where he joined the de Ribaupierre Quartet as violist in 1922, and the Cleveland Institute of Music faculty as a teacher of music theory in 1923. With the aid of a fellowship from the Guggenheim Foundation, Porter returned to Paris in 1928 for a three-year stay, this time not to study but to compose. During these years in Paris, Porter developed his personal style, and produced the works which first established his reputation – in particular, the Violin Sonata no.2 and the String Quartet no.3, both of which won awards of the Society for the Publication of American Music. In 1932 Porter was appointed professor of music at Vassar College, where he remained until called in 1938 to become dean of the faculty of the New England Conservatory, Boston. He succeeded Wallace Goodrich as director of the conservatory in 1942. Porter returned to Yale in 1946 as professor of music, and in 1958 he also became master of Pierson College, a post he held until his retirement in 1965. Among the larger works written at Yale were the Viola Concerto, first performed by Paul Doktor in New York in 1948, and the Concerto concertante, which won the Pulitzer Prize in 1954. In 1943, Porter was awarded the Elizabeth Sprague Coolidge Medal, and in the same year he was elected to the National Institute of Arts and Letters; in 1944 he was awarded an honorary doctorate by the University of Rochester.

Porter's personal style was characterized by smooth, scalic melodic movement in a sometimes highly chromatic, polyphonic texture. Although he wrote colourfully for the orchestra, his compositional technique was best adapted to chamber music, a medium in which he remained active as a player all his life. His nine string quartets, some of the most substantial contributions to that literature made by any American composer, reflect by their fluency and sensitivity the composer's intimate involvement with the genre.

WORKS

INCIDENTAL MUSIC

A Midsummer Night's Dream (Shakespeare), 1926; The Sunken Bell (Hauptmann), 1926; Sweeney Agonistes (Eliot), 1933; Antony and Cleopatra (Shakespeare), 1934; Song for a Broken Horn (H. M. Hill), 1952; The Merry Wives of Windsor (Shakespeare), 1954; Music for a Yale Library Film, 1956; The Mad Woman of Chaillot (Giraudoux), 1957; Music for an Elizabethan Masque at Yale, 1959

ORCHESTRAL

Ukrainian Suite, str, 1925; Suite, c, 1926; Poem and Dance, 1932; Sym. no.1, 1934; Dance in Three-time, chamber orch, 1937; 2 Dances for Radio, Four- and Five-time, 1938; Music for Str, 1941; Music on a Pastoral Theme, org, str, 1943; A Moving Tide, 1944; Va Conc., 1948
Fantasy, vc, orch, 1950; The Desolate City (Arabian, trans. W. S. Blunt), Bar, orch, 1950; Conc. concertante, 2 pf, orch, 1953; New England Episodes, 1958; Hpd Conc., 1959; Concertino for Wind Sym., 1959; Sym. no.2, 1962; Ohio, Ov. on 3 American Folktunes, 1963

CHAMBER AND INSTRUMENTAL

9 str qts: 1923, 1925, 1930, 1931, 1935, 1937, 1943, 1950, 1958
Vn Sonata, no.1, 1926; In Monasterio, str qt, 1927; Pf Qnt, 1927; Little Trio, fl, vn, va, 1928; Blues lointains, fl/va, pf, 1928; Vn Sonata no.2, 1929; Cl Qnt, 1929; Pf Sonata, 1930; Suite, va, 1930; Toccata, Andante and Finale, org, 1930; Qnt in 1 Movt on a Childhood Theme, fl, str, 1937, rev. 1960
Lonesome, pf, 1940; Canon and Fugue, org, 1941; 6 Miniatures, pf, 1943; Hn Sonata, 1946; Str Sextet on Slavic Folk Tunes, 1947; 4 Pieces, vn, pf, 1947; Divertimento, 2 vn, va, 1949; Juilliard Pieces for Str, 1949; Speed Etude, va, pf; Poem, vc/va/db, pf; Improvisation, vn, pf; Bagatelle, str qnt; Duo, vn, va, 1954; Duo, va, harp, 1957; Day Dreams, pf, 1957; Divertimento, wind qnt, 1960; Qnt, hpd, str, 1961; Variations, vn, pf, 1963; Ob Qnt, 1966

SONGS

To the Moon (Shelley), 1922; The Silent Voices (Tennyson), 1923; And, like a dying lady (Shelley), 1923; Music when soft voices die

(Shelley), 1924; 12 Songs for Helen on Nursery Rhymes, S, pf/chamber orch, 1931; This is the house that Jack built, S, pf/chamber orch, 1938

Introspections on The Banks O'Doon, S, fl, pf, 1955; 2 Songs (A. Porter), S/T, pf, 1956; The God of Love (3 Elizabethan Songs), S/T, pf, 1959; 7 Songs of Love (R. Graves), S, pf, 1961; 2 Songs (P. Colum), S, pf, 1966; 4 Shakespeare Songs, S/T, pf, 1966

MSS in *US-NH*

BIBLIOGRAPHY

H. Elwell: 'Quincy Porter', *MM*, xxiii (1946)

H. Boatwright: 'Quincy Porter', *Bulletin of the American Composers Alliance*, vi/3 (1957)

——: 'Quincy Porter (1897–1966)', *PNM*, v/2 (1967), 162

HOWARD BOATWRIGHT

Porter, Samuel (*b* Norwich, 1733; *d* Canterbury, 11 Dec 1810). English cathedral musician. He was a pupil of Maurice Greene and was organist of Canterbury Cathedral, 1757–1803. His posthumous *Cathedral Music* was published by his son, W. J. Porter, who owned, and perhaps inherited from his father, two sets of partbooks in the hand of John Gostling (now in *GB-T* 797–803 and 1176–82).

WATKINS SHAW

Porter, Walter (*b* probably *c*1587, or possibly *c*1595; *d* London, buried 30 Nov 1659). English composer, lutenist and tenor. Anthony Wood stated that he was the son of Henry Porter (BMus of Christ Church, Oxford), though it seems unlikely that this is the same Henry Porter listed among 'Lutes and others' at the funeral of Queen Elizabeth I and among King James I's sackbuts and hautboys (1603–17). The doubt about his date of birth arises from two conflicting pieces of evidence. In a petition to the governors of Westminster School dating from the last years of his life (probably 1658) he describes himself as 'being 70:tie and odd yeeres of age his strength and faculties decayed', whereas in a marriage licence dated 1630 – which, indeed, may not refer to this Walter Porter – his age is given as 35. His voice must have broken between 1603, when he was a Westminster Abbey chorister at Elizabeth I's funeral, and 1612, when, on 15 February, he sang tenor in a masque at Whitehall. It is perhaps more likely that these two events occurred when he was 16 and 25 years old respectively than when he was eight and 17.

On 5 January 1616 Porter was promised the next tenor vacancy among the Gentlemen of the Chapel Royal, and on 1 February 1617 he was sworn in. Shortly before this he must have written the madrigal *Wake, sorrow, wake*, an elegy on the death of Lady Arabella Stuart, who died on 25 September 1615; it is more likely to be the work of a composer of 28 who had already come into contact with Italian music than of one aged 20. If his self-proclaimed study with Monteverdi occurred at this stage in his life, the years between 1612 and 1615 seem the likeliest period for it. He published his *Madrigales and Ayres* (London, 1632, 2/?1639) with a dedication to the Earl of Bristol, whom he had attended in Spain, presumably in 1622, when the earl travelled there in connection with the ill-fated 'Spanish match' planned for Prince Charles. In 1633 Porter went with the Chapel Royal to Edinburgh for Charles I's coronation and in 1634 took part in Shirley's masque *The Triumph of Peace*, as both singer and theorbo player. He became Master of the Choristers of Westminster Abbey in 1639.

After musical church services were abandoned in the Civil War, Porter lived for a time (1644–56) in the household of Sir Edward Spencer. Looking around perhaps for a new protector he published his *Mottets of Two Voyces* in London in 1657 with a dedication to Edward Laurence. But he was living in poverty about 1658, when he petitioned the Westminster Abbey authorities several times for a pension, since he had never officially enjoyed a 'singing-man's' place and the remuneration that went with it. He added that 'the petitionr likewise intends (Being put into a Capacitie) to sett up a meeting for Musick once a fortnight and to traine up two or three boyes in the Art of Musick ... out of Westmr Schoole'.

The only specific indication that Porter was a pupil of Monteverdi is the MS addition of the name 'Monteverde' after the words 'my good Friend and Maestro' in the preface to the *Mottets* in copies at Christ Church, Oxford. But the style of the madrigals certainly supports Porter's claim. They are virtually the only English madrigals in concertato style. They include solo, duet and dialogue writing within the five-part texture, occasional recitative, virtuoso solo passages and the use of the *trillo*. A continuo ('Harpesechord, Lutes, Theorbos') is obligatory, the bass is copiously figured, there are introductory three-part 'toccatos, sinfonias and ritornellos' for two violins and bass, and these instruments sometimes play with the voices. Other pieces, consisting of two imitative upper parts over a bass, are in the style of chamber duets or trios, and there are also tuneful ayres or partsongs with verse and chorus sections. One (*O praise the Lord*) is a verse anthem including florid solo writing; another (*Farewell*) is a solo madrigal constructed over what seems to be a strophic bass related to the folia or *passamezzo antico*. The *Mottets*, which are settings of some of George Sandys's metrical psalm versions in a quasi-declamatory style, are comparatively uninteresting.

BIBLIOGRAPHY

G. E. P. Arkwright: 'An English Pupil of Monteverdi', *MA*, iv (1912–13), 236

C. W. Hughes: 'Porter, Pupil of Monteverdi', *MQ*, xx (1934), 278

E. Pine: *The Westminster Abbey Singers* (London, 1953), 115ff

I. Spink: 'Walter Porter and the Last Book of English Madrigals', *AcM*, xxvi (1954), 18

S. Boorman: 'Notari, Porter and the Lute', *LSJ*, xiii (1971), 28

IAN SPINK

Porte vente (Fr.). WIND TRUNK.

Portinaro [Pertinaro, Portenaro, Portinarius], **Francesco** (*b* Padua, *c*1520; *d* probably Padua, after 1578). Italian composer. He was from a noble Paduan family and spent most of his life contributing to the musical activities of the numerous cultural societies in and around Padua. Zacco stated, without supporting evidence, that he was born in 1516, but Casimiri suggested about 1525 as more plausible in the light of the date of his first publication. His first direct association with humanist academies began on 21 June 1555, when, together with four others from the same quarter of Padua, he formed a *societas musicorum*, but his membership there was short-lived, for in the following year he became *principe* of the Accademia dei Costanti, a Vicenzan group similarly devoted to the musical arts. On 3 March 1557 the Accademia degli Elevati Padoani was founded, of which he was appointed *maestro di musica*, and for three years he taught singing and playing, composed numerous pieces for them and directed their twice-weekly musical events. His *Il quarto libro de* *madrigali a cinque voci* (*RISM* 1560[20]) is a testimonial to his three years with the Elevati and includes pieces written for and by the members. During the following decade he sought to establish relationships with various noblemen, dedicating his publications to such famous patrons as Cardinals Scipione Gonzaga, Ippolito and Luigi d'Este and the Emperor Maximilian II. In 1565 he was a 'virtuoso' in the service of Cardinal Ippolito d'Este, but whether he was ever a member of Luigi d'Este's household in Tivoli, as stated by Radiciotti, is doubtful.

In August 1571 Portinaro was appointed interim *maestro di cappella* at Padua Cathedral while the authorities were negotiating to find a permanent replacement for Perisson. The records indicate that he had previously assisted there during Holy Week and on other high feast days; he had been proposed for the musical directorship 16 years earlier, but did not obtain it. He must have been considered by the governing board only as a last resort: in 1571 he was employed only temporarily (he returned to his former activities on 25 July 1573, as *maestro principale di musica* of the newly reorganized Accademia degli Rinascenti); and when in December 1576 the board, faced with the difficulties of attracting talent to the plague-ridden city, appointed him, a native, permanent *maestro di canto* and *magister capellae*, they referred to him only as 'persona sufficiente e de boni costumi'. Their reluctance to appoint him was presumably caused by his largely secular musical interests. He was replaced at Padua on 31 December 1578.

In addition to Portinaro's known published works, many occasional pieces were undoubtedly written for performance by the Paduan academies with which he was associated. His work was stylistically characteristic of their humanist milieu, combining impeccable literary taste with the textural and harmonic richness of the Venetian school. In his choice of texts he drew heavily on Bembo and set entire sestinas and canzoni by Petrarch. His *Mentre m'havesti cor* (Veniero's translation of Horace's *Donec gratus eram tibi*, settings of which were important in the development of the dramatic dialogue), is also noteworthy. He frequently suggested that in performance instruments might double the vocal parts.

WORKS
(all published in Venice)
SECULAR VOCAL

Il primo libro de madrigali, 5vv (1550)
Il secondo libro de madrigali, 5vv (1554)
Il terzo libro de madrigali, 5, 6vv, con tre dialoghi, 7vv, et uno, 8vv (1557)
Il quarto libro de madrigali, 5vv, con dui madrigali, vv, dui dialoghi, 7vv, et dui, 8vv (1560[20])
Il primo libro de madrigali, 4vv . . . con due madrigali, 6vv (1563[13])
Le vergini . . . 6vv, con alcuni madrigali, 5, 6vv, et duoi dialoghi, 7vv (1568, 2/1569 as Libro quinto de madrigali, slightly altered contents); dialogue ed. in DTÖ, lxxvii, Jg.xli (1960)

4 madrigals, 5vv, 1562[22], 1563[15], 1566[3], 1566[13]

SACRED VOCAL

Primi frutti de motetti . . . libro primo, 5vv (1548)
Il secondo libro de motetti, 6–8vv (1568)
Il terzo libro de motetti, 5–8vv (1572)

3 motets, 5vv, 1556[8], 1567[3]

Mass, 2 motets, *D-Mbs, Rp*

INSTRUMENTAL

4 lute intabulations: Fronimo dialogo di Vincentio Galilei fiorentino, nel quale si contengono le vere et necessarie regole del intavolare la musica nel liuto (Venice, 1568); La seconda parte del dialogo de Vincentio Galilei fiorentino, della intavolatura di liuto (Venice, 1569); 1584[15]

BIBLIOGRAPHY

G. O. Pitoni: *Notitia de contrapuntisti e de compositori di musica* (MS, *I-Rvat* C. G., I/1–2, c1725)
T. Zacco: *Cenni biografici di illustri scrittori e compositori di musica padoani: per le fautissime nozze Onesti-Piazzoni* (Padua, 1840 [*recte* 1850]), 20
N. Pietrucci: *Biografia degli artisti padovani* (Padua, 1858), 223
A. Solerti: *Ferrara e la corte Estense* (Città di Castello, 1900), 116
G. Radiciotti: *L'arte musicale in Tivoli nei secoli XVI, XVII, e XVIII* (Tivoli, 1907, enlarged 2/1921), 14
B. Brunelli: 'Francesco Portenari e le cantate degli accademici padovani', *Atti del R. istituto veneto di scienze, lettere, ed arti*, lxxix (1919–20), 595
R. Casimiri: 'Musica e musicisti nella catedrale di Padova', *NA*, xviii (1941), 107, 109ff, 128, 133, 204; xix (1942), 59, 64ff
E. M. Forin: 'Una "Societas musicorum" costituta a Padova nel 1555', *Memorie della Accademia patavina di Ss. Ll. Aa.: classe di scienze morali, lettere ed arti*, lxxviii (1965–6), 401

PATRICIA ANN MYERS

Portman, Richard (*d* ?London, *c*1655). English organist and composer. He succeeded Orlando Gibbons as organist of Westminster Abbey in 1625, having earlier been a chorister there under Gibbons. At Michaelmas 1638 he was sworn an episteler of the Chapel Royal, and within a month or so he succeeded John Tomkins, who had been an organist of the chapel. He retained his position at the abbey, and in a petition to parliament dated January 1654 he is still numbered among the former musicians of the church. A petition dated 29 February 1656, however, refers to Portman as 'deceased'. According to Rimbault, he spent some time in France during the Commonwealth with Dr Williams, Dean of Westminster and a generous patron of music, but he heads the list of London music teachers 'for Organ or Virginal' in John Playford's *Musicall Banquet* (London, 1652). His extant works include a book of meditations, *The Soules Life, Exercising itself in the Sweet Fields of Divine Meditation, Collected for the Comfort thereof, in these Sad Days of Distraction* (London, 1645, rev. 2/1660). His compositions, almost exclusively liturgical, reflect the current trend away from polyphony towards a simpler and more obviously harmonic idiom, and they have much in common with those of Adrian Batten.

WORKS
Short [Whole] Service (Ven, TeD, Bs, Ky, Cr, Mag, Nunc), full, *GB-Cfm, Cp, EL, LF, Lbm, Llp, Ob, Och, T, Y*
15 anthems (3 with text only), *GB-Ckc, Cp, DRc, Lbm, Lcm, LF, Llp, Ob, Och, Ojc, T, Y, US-NYp*
Saraband, hpd, *Och*; Verse, double org, *WB*

BIBLIOGRAPHY

E. F. Rimbault: *The Old Cheque-book, or Book of Remembrance of the Chapel Royal*, Camden Society, new ser., iii (London, 1872/*R*1966)
E. Pine: *The Westminster Abbey Singers* (London, 1953)
J. Steele: *English Organs and Organ Music from 1500 to 1650* (diss., U. of Cambridge, 1958–9)
P. le Huray: *Music and the Reformation in England, 1549–1660* (London, 1967)

PETER LE HURAY

Porto, Allegro (*fl* early 17th century). Italian composer. Pitoni said that he was a Jew 'di età giovine', which may mean that he died young. He may have spent some time in Germany and Austria, for his volume of 1619 is dedicated to a count at the Bavarian court and his 1625 publication to the Emperor Ferdinand II. His first three publications, including his first book of *musiche*, are lost, and none of his surviving works is complete. The title-page of his madrigals of 1622 is missing in the only known copy but was given by Pitoni, who also said that the dedication was dated in Trieste. The volume includes settings of two poems by Giovanni Sforza, Conte di Porzia, who may have been related to Conte Alfonso di Portia, to whom the 1619 book was dedicated. The 1625 book includes a madrigal scored for three voices, two cornetts and continuo.

WORKS

Nuove musiche, 3vv, bc (chit), libro secondo . . . op.4 (Venice, 1619), some ptbks lost
[Il primo libro di madrigali], 5vv, bc (Venice, 1622)
Madrigali, 5vv, bc (Venice, 1625)

BIBLIOGRAPHY

G. O. Pitoni: *Notitia de contrapuntisti e di compositori di musica* (MS, I-Rvat C.G., I/1–2, c1725)

COLIN TIMMS

Portogallo, Marcos Antônio. *See* PORTUGAL, MARCOS ANTÔNIO.

Portu, Francisco de Novo. *See* MERGOT, FRANCISCUS.

Portugal.

I. Art music. II. Folk music.

I. Art music. The first church musician known by name on the Spanish peninsula was a certain Andreas 'princeps cantorum' (489–525) at Mértola, 55 km south of Beja. Apringius, Bishop of Beja under the Visigothic King Theudis (531–48), wrote a commentary on *Revelations* mentioning musical instruments. The manuscript (dated 806) from which was copied the Mozarabic Antiphoner of León may also have come from Beja. An 11th-century fragment at Coimbra contains music written in Mozarabic neumes for the Third Sunday in Advent.

The first Council of Braga (561) forbade the singing of hymns or any other text 'of human composition' but this ban was lifted by the Council of Toledo in 633. Throughout the early Middle Ages, the Mozarabic liturgy (with minor local variants) prevailed in Christian Portugal as well as Spain until suppressed in favour of the Roman rite in the late 10th century. The oldest extant plainsong fragments from Braga (which can be dated c1140) are Roman chants copied on a one-line staff in heighted neumes.

Polyphony may have been known in Portugal as early as 959, in which year Muma Donna of Guimarães bequeathed several liturgical books to a convent which she had founded. Secular song must have flourished at the courts of Sancho I and Afonso III, for both employed jongleurs (according to documents dated 1193 and 1268 respectively). The Cancioneiro da Ajuda, a collection of 310 Portuguese song texts copied in about 1280 with blank music staves, contains pictures of instruments and specifies singers' names. The *trovador* Martin Codax, whose nationality has been disputed by Spanish and Portuguese, left seven love-songs in Galician dialect, probably written c1270. Six of these songs survive with music and have frequently been transcribed.

Leonor of Aragon, the Spanish princess who married Dom Duarte in 1428, delighted the Portuguese court with her singing and her polished playing of the *manicorde*. Excellent players were trained at Duarte's expense; one of them, Álvaro Fernandes, so pleased John II of Castile that Duarte had to ask sharply for his return. Throughout the 15th century, while Portugal pushed her explorations southward, the courts of Afonso V (1432–81) and John II (1455–95) attracted musicians from abroad, most notable of whom was Tristão de Silva, Afonso's *mestre de capela*, repeatedly

cited by theorists up to the 17th century. Portugal enjoyed a considerable musical interchange with Spain and Italy from the late 15th century, of which Silva, who came to Lisbon in the 1470s, is a product. The Portuguese Pedro do Porto (known in Spain as Pedro de Escobar), however, served as cantor at Isabella's court and was *maestro de capilla* at Seville Cathedral from 1507 to 1514; and the composer and theorist Vicente Lusitano made his career in Italy where in 1551, at Rome, he was the victor in the well-known dispute with Vicentino.

Among early 16th-century polyphonists were Fernão Gomes Correia and Vasco Pires, active at Coimbra; the former served as the bishop's cantor in 1515, the latter as *mestre de capela*. Other leading 16th-century polyphonists included Aires Fernandes, Heliodoro de Paiva, Pedro de Gamboa and António Carreira. None of these Renaissance Portuguese composers cultivated a musical style that can be called distinctively national. Aranda, a graduate of Alcalá de Henares University who published the first part-music in Portugal, included two- and four-part examples in his *Tractade de canto mēsurable* (Lisbon, 1535) that are considerably less learned than Vicente Lusitano's examples in his treatise on polyphony (published by Collet in 1913 from *F-Pn* fonds espagnols 219). On the other hand, Erasmus's Portuguese friend Damião de Goes is represented by an example in Glarean's *Dodecachordon* (1547) that has nothing of the conundrum about it. Excessive learning cannot, therefore, be called a hallmark of Portuguese style but rather an idiosyncrasy of Lusitano.

If some distinctive characteristics must be found in 16th-century Portuguese music, they will, therefore, have to be found outside musical style as such. One can point to the resentment of local musicians at seeing their best posts, such as the chair at Coimbra University, occasionally pre-empted by a royally appointed Spaniard such as Aranda. At the end of the century the Spaniard Hierónimo Román tried to encapsulate in his *Republicas del mundo* (Salamanca, 1595, f.252) what was then distinctive about Portuguese music: 'I will say in brief why the Portuguese exceed us, and that is because the lavishness of their instrumental music and singing during Divine Office gives them pride of place in the Catholic Church'.

The great sums that poured into the publication of Portuguese polyphony at the beginning of the 17th century confirm Román's views of Portuguese lavishness. Victoria's 1600 and 1605 publications at Madrid were considerably less luxurious than were the volumes of *Magnificat* settings and of masses published by Duarte Lobo in 1605, 1621 and 1639 at his own expense in Antwerp.

The true flowering of Portuguese polyphony began with the publication at Lisbon of a volume of *Magnificat* settings (1613), followed by three books of masses (1625, 1636, 1636) and a miscellany for Holy Week by Manuel Cardoso (1566–1650); a book of masses (1631) and a cycle of *Magnificat* settings (1636) by Filipe De Magalhães (c1570–1652); and the first collection of instrumental music on the Iberian peninsula not in tablature (1630) by the court organist Manuel Rodrigues Coelho.

Portuguese composers favoured the parody principle and often chose Palestrina as their model; all the parody masses in Cardoso's first book are based on Palestrina motets, and Duarte Lobo parodied only Palestrina and Francisco Guerrero. John IV was also an admirer of Palestrina; in 1655 he published an erudite 'reply' to criticism of the purity of Palestrina's *Missa 'Panis quem ego dabo'*. John IV was himself a composer and the collector of one of the best music libraries in Europe; he patronized every leading Portuguese and Spanish composer of the age, even leaving a bequest to pay for publication at Rome in 1657 of the *Psalmi pro Vesperi* of his lifelong musical companion João Lourenço Rabelo (*c*1616–61). Many Portuguese composers were active during the first half of the 17th century, among them the calced Carmelites Francisco de Santiago and Manuel Correa (*d* 1653), another Manuel Correa (*d* 1645), Nicolás Doizi de Velasco, Filipe de la Cruz, Filipe da Madre de Deos, Manuel de Tavares, Afonso Vaz da Costa, Estêvão de Brito and Manuel Leitão de Avilez. Portuguese music was also known in Latin America: works by Gonçalo Mendes Saldanha reached Cartagena and Bogotá; his works and those of Manuel de Tavarez and Manuel Mendès were sung at Puebla, Mexico. Other Portuguese composers active in the second half of the 17th century include Diogo Dias Melgaz and Pedro Vaz Rego at Évora; Francisco Martins at Elvas; and António Marques Lésbio (1639–1709), who was also a prominent author, at Lisbon.

Italian influence was evident in cantatas composed by André da Costa and Francisco José Coutinho to celebrate the arrival in 1708 of John V's Austrian bride. Italian style in 1708 meant recitatives for long narrative portions, whereas both Spanish and Portuguese style favoured short melodic incises repeated as often as need be during a long chain of *coplas*; Italian style in 1708 eschewed imitation as an outworn principle, whereas both Spanish and Portuguese middle Baroque style still clung to points of imitation, even in vernacular music; Italian style rigorously set the bounds of harmony within the walls of major and minor tonalities, whereas both Spanish and Portuguese composers as late as 1730 still wrote in the eight church modes or modifications thereof; Italians would have nothing to do with *chiavette*, but for vernacular music it still remained a favourite notation principle with the Spaniards and the Portuguese as late as 1730.

Domenico Scarlatti showed that he could be as repetitive of a catchy bar as the Spaniards and Portuguese with their interminable *coplas*. The charm of his later sonatas is enhanced by their echoes of Spanish and Portuguese modalities. However, all the Iberian traits that make his keyboard music vivid and set him apart from Pasquini and Zipoli were imbibed after years of Iberian residence. His church music is another matter. All that he wrote for the Portuguese royal chapel – and certainly all that of Giovanni Giorgi chosen as a model for aspiring composers in Solano's *Nova instrucção* (Lisbon, 1764) – is thoroughly Roman, and reflects John V's oft-expressed desire that Lisbon be more papal than the pope. It was John V in his zeal for Latinity who finally banished the *vilhancico* (villancico) from Portuguese court celebrations and who influenced his daughter Maria Bárbara (a pupil of Scarlatti) to do the same in Spain. Continuing in the tradition of John IV, John V dispatched both António Teixeira (1707–*c*1759) and Francisco António de Almeida to Italy in 1717 and *c*1720, respectively; both returned to compose operas and church music in the prevailing Neapolitan style. From 1720 to 1729 Domenico

Scarlatti was employed as *mestre de capela*. The Rococo age found piquant expression in the keyboard sonatas of Carlos de Seixas and Frei Jacinto.

Among Portuguese opera composers who flourished in the Classical era, João De Sousa Carvalho (1745–98) was the equal of the best Italians of his generation. Despite the competition of Italians such as Giovanni Giorgi and David Perez, other Portuguese opera composers won favour at the courts of José I and Maria I, notably Carvalho's pupils Marcos Antônio da Fonseca Portugal (1762–1830) and António Leal Moreira (1758–1819). Portugal's operas were sung in 104 cities, from St Petersburg to Rio de Janeiro, during his lifetime. Other Portuguese composers at the end of the 18th century included João José Baldi (1770–1816), Luciano Xavier dos Santos (1734–1808), António da Silva Leite (1759–1833) and José Maurício (1752–1815). The lasting worth of any of these 18th-century Portuguese composers cannot be measured only by their 18th-century reputations abroad; each must be judged as an individual speaking the musical *lingua franca* of the epoch. Almeida, Sousa Carvalho and Leal Moreira became more significant composers when judged as individuals and when not asked to speak a musical language different from that of Leo, Galuppi, Jommelli or Traetta.

The first director of the Conservatório Nacional in Lisbon, João Domingos Bomtempo (1775–1842), made concert tours in France and England during the Napoleonic era and published numerous large works in London and Paris. During the latter half of the century Alfredo Keil (1850–1907) composed operas and the Portuguese national anthem, José Vianna da Motta (1868–1948) became known internationally as a concert pianist, and Joaquim Casimiro Júnior (1802–62) composed religious music still heard in Lisbon.

20th-century Portuguese composers include Fernando Lopes Graça, Joly Braga Santos, Luis Filipe Pires, Alvaro Cassuto and Jorge Peixinho. Cláudio Carneyro (1895–1963) greatly influenced music in the north. Luís de Freitas Branco (1890–1955) was prominent both as a writer on musical subjects and as a composer. The publicity enjoyed by any one of these 20th-century composers depended on the shifting political scene at Lisbon. Throughout the 1960s it was only patronage such as the GULBENKIAN FOUNDATION could give that enabled orchestras in the capital to play the works of the junior composers. In 1970 Cassuto's international connections enabled him to find a haven in the USA.

João de Freitas Branco (*b* 1922), who became director of the São Carlos Theatre in 1970, was previously critic for *O globo*, editor of *A arte musical* and director of Juventudes Musicais. Maria Madalena de Azeredo Perdigão, director of the music service of the Gulbenkian Foundation, contributed to the development of musical education in the 1960s. Ivo Cruz (*b* 1901) became director of the National Conservatory in 1938. Among the small group of Portuguese musicologists in the 20th century, Macario Santiago Kastner has been the leading figure.

See also LISBON.

BIBLIOGRAPHY

DBP

F. Asenjo Barbieri: 'Estudio bibliográfico musical', *Revista de España*, xix (1871), 351

J. Vasconcellos: *El-Rey D. João o 4.º* (Oporto, 1905)

F. M. de Sousa Viterbo: *Subsídios para a história da música em Portugal* (Coimbra, 1933)

M. de Sampayo Ribeiro: *A música em Portugal nos séculos XVIII e XIX* (Lisbon, 1938)

J. Mazza: 'Dicionário biográfico de músicos portugueses', *Ocidente*, xxiii (1944), 193–200, 361; xxiv (1944), 249; xxv (1945), 17, 145; xxvi (1945), 43

A. Luper: 'Portuguese Polyphony in the Sixteenth and Early Seventeenth Centuries', *JAMS*, iii (1950), 93

S. Corbin: *Essai sur la musique religieuse portugaise au moyen âge 1100–1385* (Paris and Coimbra, 1952)

M. Joaquim: *Vinte livros de música polifónica do Paço ducal de Vila Viçosa* (Lisbon, 1953)

M. A. de L. Cruz: *História da música portuguesa* (Lisbon, 1955)

K. Speer: *A Portuguese Manuscript of Keyboard Music from the Late Seventeenth Century* (diss., Indiana U., 1956)

A. Carneiro: *A música em Braga* (Braga, 1959/R1964)

J. de Freitas Branco: *História de música portuguesa* (Lisbon, 1959)

R. Stevenson: 'Vicente Lusitano: New Light on his Career', *JAMS*, xv (1962), 72

A. Nobre de Gusmão: 'Cantores e músicos em Évora nos anos de 1542 a 1553', *Anais, Academia portuguesa da história*, xiv (1964), 95

E. Veiga de Oliveira: *Instrumentos musicais populares portugueses* (Lisbon, 1966)

M. de Sampayo Ribeiro: *Livraria de música de El-Rei D. Joao IV* (Lisbon, 1967 [vol.i is a facsimile of the *Primeira parte do index da livraria* (Lisbon, 1649)]

R. Stevenson: 'Portuguese Music: a Historical Résumé', *Journal of the American Portuguese Cultural Society*, iv (1970), 1, 49

II. Folk music

1. Introduction. 2. Vocal music. 3. Dances and instruments. 4. Continuity and change.

1. INTRODUCTION. The folk music and folkdances of Portugal are among the most thriving and abundant in Europe, and they also form a part of the folk traditions of Asia, Africa and the Americas. There are indications that Portuguese folk music was often classified as Spanish, just as the Portuguese themselves were considered Spanish wherever they settled in the New World, a tendency which still persists in certain places. One of the most interesting discoveries of Afro-Portuguese-Spanish folksongs was made by Robert Stevenson in Puebla and Oaxaca, Mexico: most of the songs date from the 16th and 17th centuries. The dispersal of Portuguese instruments is further evidence of the wide impact of Portuguese music. For instance, during the 15th century the four-course *cavaquinho* reached Africa, the Americas, and even Hawaii, where it became the four-string *ukelele* ('flea', alluding to the hopping of the fingers across the strings; see fig.2 below). In the northern areas of Latin America and in the West Indies it became known as the *cuatro*. The earliest transcriptions of Portuguese folk music date from 1872 (Das Neves e Melo) but most collections were made between 1930 and 1950. Most collectors specialized in particular regions and sometimes received small subsidies for publishing their collections, which reveal a multi-faceted music and dance tradition whose continued flexibility perhaps reflects a high capacity for assimilation. For instance, the same text may be associated with several different tunes (as in exx.1a–d, four variants of the ballad *Frei João*); and related tunes or variants of a single text may be used for different genres and styles.

2. VOCAL MUSIC.

(i) Ballads. Almeida Garrett's discovery of traditional ballads in the 1840s stimulated the first systematic collection of Portuguese folksong. His purpose was literary for he firmly believed that erudite or artistic literature should never lose sight of folk poetry. The romantic literary appreciation of folksong which he initiated in Portugal soon led to more systematic collections such as those by João Teixeira Soares de Sousa in the Azores (see Braga, 1869), Estácio da Veiga in the Algarve (1870), Rodrígues de Azevedo in Madeira (1880) and Leite de Vasconcellos (1886). Braga's and Leite de Vasconcellos's original collections were expanded and republished during the 20th century and are regarded as the most complete. Other important collections were made by D'Athaide Oliveira in the Algarve (1905), J. A. Tavares in Tras-os-Montes (1903–6) and Martins in Tras-os-Montes (1928). The Spanish scholar Ramón Menéndez Pidal contributed particularly to the international recognition of Portuguese ballads. He was impressed by their adherence to heroic, epic and Carolingian themes (see preface to Leite de Vascon-

Ex.1 Four variants of the ballad *Frei João* (Friar John)

(a) Tomás, 1913

Moderato

Le - van tou - se   Frei Jo - ão   Um dia___   de

madru - ga - da   Só para ir ver   a   Mo - re - na,

a   Mo - re - na   mal   fa - da - da

(b) Lopes Graça, 1964

Andante (♩ = 66)

Le - van - ta - se o   frei Jo - ão,___   Nu - ma ma -

- nhã   de ge - a - da,   Ba - teu ás   por - tas da Mo -

- re - na, *Oh tão   lin - da!*   Pe - la Mo - re - na bra -

- da - va.___

(c) Pico, Azores (Purcell, 1969)

Frei Jo - ão   s'al' - van - to - u   nu - ma ma - nhã de ge -

- a - da.   To - ma li - mão ver - de,   do - ce li - mo - ná.

(d) *fado* highly ornamented (Purcell, 1969)

Õ   Fe - liz,   a - bre-me a por - ta,   qu'eu 'stou c'os pés   na

g ea - da;   Õ   Fe - liz,   a bre-me a por - ta,   qu'ea

etc to complete the quatrain

'stou c'os pés na   g eada;

1. *Two desafio singers accompanying themselves on violão (six-string guitar, left) and guitarra (long-necked lute), Ponta Delgada, Azores*

2. *Cavaquinho (four-string ukelele)*

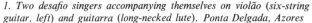

cellos, 2/1958–60). Of the Carolingian *Chansons de geste*, for example, survivals of *Floresvento* (*Floovent*) were found in Portugal but not in Spain. S. G. Armistead and J. H. Silverman, specialists in Judeo-Spanish ballads, published in 1971 the most comprehensive Portuguese ballad bibliography.

The wealth of ballads in Portugal with archaic themes and verses is important in the study of Pan-Hispanic and Pan-European ballads. For example, the ballad *A vingança de Rodrígues* is derived from the Spanish epic song *Las mocedades del Cid*. There are also fragments of a ballad on the death of the Castilian and Leonese King Don Fernando I: *A morte do Rei Dom Fernando* and *As Queixas de Dona Urraca*, which derived from a medieval epic song and served as a prologue to the *Cantar del Cerco de Zamora*. Historical ballads concerning the death of Prince Don Juan or of Prince Don Alfonso (who is virtually absent from the present-day Spanish ballad tradition) and dating from the reign of the Spanish Catholic monarchs are still found in the Portuguese ballad tradition. Occasionally Carolingian themes such as the Spanish *La muerte de Don Beltrán*, *Belardo y Valdovinos*, *Conde Claros fraile*, *Gaiferos jugador*, *Miselda y Don Gaiferos* and *El conde preso* have been collected. Biblical themes such as the *Samaritana*, *Tamar y Amnón* and the apocryphal *Fé del ciego*, which existed in oral tradition a century ago, have disappeared. There is, however, a profusion of religious themes such as *Santa Catarina*, *Jesús Peregrino* and *Santa Bárbara*. Rare classical ballads are still being discovered, such as *Hero y Leandro*, *Virgilios* and *Blancaflor y Filomena*. Other ballad themes concern captives, the vicissitudes of love, feminine revenge and deception, the husband's return, the unfortunate wife, incest, daring women, animals etc. Most of these themes are pan-Hispanic and in some cases have pan-European analogues. The ballad *Rico Franco*, for example, is analogous to the British *Lady Isabel and the Elf-knight* and the Dutch *Heer Halewijn*. *The Wedding of the Rooster's Daughter* (Portuguese) or *The Louse and Flea* (Spanish) is related to the *Frog's Courtship* in the Anglo-American tradition. *Jesús Peregrino* is known in France as *Mauvais riche*, in England as *Dives and Lazarus* and

in Italy as *El ricco epulone*. Some Portuguese ballads apparently lack counterparts in pan-Hispanic and pan-European balladry (*O raminho da Nossa Senhora*, *Quem morre sem sacramentos*, *Santa Iria*, *A Febre Amarela*, *O Castigo do Sacristão*). With the aid of a computer, Suzanne Petersen showed that the Portuguese ballad tradition is the most innovatory in the Hispanic world in its treatment of traditional narrative themes. The use of computers in comparative ballad scholarship has been developed by Diego Catalán.

(*ii*) *Fado* (from Lat. *fatum*: 'fate'). Text, musical structure and performing style distinguish this genre, the typical urban vocal music of cafés, cabarets and night clubs. Theories about its origin conflict. Pinto de Carvalho maintained that it was originally a maritime song style before becoming popular during the 19th century in the Alfama sector of Lisbon. According to Braga, its roots were in Moorish or Arabic tradition. Luís Moita and Alberto Pimental suggested South African influences as in the case of the *lundum* dance-song (see §4). Rural *fado* perhaps predated the now distinct styles of Lisbon and Coimbra; on the other hand the urban styles with their nostalgic reverence for the past could have been readily adapted in rural areas, since research has shown that many rural singers of *fado* learnt songs during visits to Lisbon. Some urban singers of *fado* consider that the term simply means 'solo song': indeed the style of *fado* is similar to that of the *desgarradas*, *despiques* and *desafios*, challenge or duel songs popular throughout rural Portugal but particularly prevalent in the Minho area of continental Portugal, and in the Azores (see fig.1).

The rhyme, metre and themes of *fado* texts often resemble the *literatura de cordel* (broadside literature). On the other hand, *fado* may contain some improvised material in the form of couplets or quatrains (as do the *desgarradas* and *despiques*). The form of the *fado* is strophic, both major and minor tonalities are used, and it is accompanied by simple triadic instrumental harmonies (chords of I, IV and V^7 with occasional secondary dominants). Accompanying instruments are the *viola* (four- or five-string guitar) and *guitarra portuguesa* (a long-necked lute, related to the English cittern and pandora of the Renaissance). The *viola* provides harmony and bass line while the *guitarra* plays improvisatory passages against the singer's line. Most *fado* is in duple time, with the instruments playing cross-rhythms against the vocal melody.

(*iii*) *Lyric songs*. Most lyric songs of Portugal are four-line strophic forms performed on festive occasions such as corn husking or grape gathering, public singing-duels, pilgrimages, St John's Day, the Holy Ghost Festival at Pentecost and various other folk festivities and dances throughout Portugal. A number of the qua-train lyrics remembered by the country singers have been handed down by oral tradition, but the quatrain form is commonly treated with inventiveness and spon-taneity and new lyrics constantly appear. Song genres deal with almost all aspects of life: weddings, prisoners, wakes, nature, the seamstress, weavers, bakers, rowing, fishing, young ladies, love, rivalry, family tragedies, political events, accidents, reaping, sowing and harvesting. Two song types considered most characteristic of the Portuguese are *despedidas* (farewell songs) and *saudades* (songs of longing). During Epiphany, quatrains sung as *janeiras* (New Year songs; see ex.2) and the ballad *Os Três Reis do Oriente* (ex.3) show a definite tendency towards responsorial structure, the choral response giving time for the soloist to invent the next verse.

Ex.2 *Janeira* (Marvão, 1955)

Ex.3 *Os Três Reis do Oriente*, ballad of the Three Kings (Marvão, 1955)

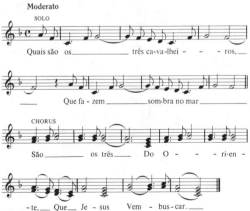

Of special interest are the cries of the vendors of fish, fruit or vegetables and work songs such as those of the ploughman half speaking and half chanting encourage-ment to his oxen (ex.4), the fishermen pulling in their nets, and the stone masons whom the singer often encourages individually by name (ex.5). Like work songs throughout the world, those of Portugal reflect the nature of the particular task in their rhythms and pitch

Ex.4 *Lavra, boi, lavra* ('Plough, ox, plough'), Ponte da Barca, Minho (Lopes Graça, 1953)

Ex.5 *Oh Pedra*, stone mason's work song (R. Gallop: *Portugal: a Book of Folk Ways*, Cambridge, 1961)

contours. In monotonous back-breaking work, specific pitch levels often mark the beginning and end of phy-sical movement. In ex.4, oxen are moved through their task with dirge-like march rhythm. In ex.5, the flexible rhythm is possibly related to indeterminate heaving movements at a large stone.

3. *Viola de arame (metal-string guitar) played by a dancing-master, Pico, Azores*

Ex.6 Two variants of *A Condessa*, game song (Purcell, 1969)

(a) from Madeira

Con - den - sia, oh Con-den-sin - ha, Con - den - sia do A - ra -

- gã - o, que - ro ped-ir as su - as fil - has des -

- tas tu - das que a - qui 'stã - o.

(b) from Goa

A - qui mo - ra Vis - con - des - sa, so - mos fil - has

de fran - ce - sa. A - qui lhas vi - mos pe - dir

pa - ra com e - las ca - sar.

3. DANCES AND INSTRUMENTS. Certain games and circle-dances such as *O Ladrão, Ladrão, O Ceguinho, A Condessa* and *A Ciranda* are accompanied by songs and occasionally instruments, commonly *guitarras* and *violas*. The Portuguese tradition is also rich in *canções de berço* (cradle songs), although few have been collected. Within a single geographical area the tunes of similar cradle, game or circle-dance songs may be alike but they usually differ radically between separate regions. Exx.6*a* and *b* show a considerable difference between the Goan and Madeiran variants of *A Condessa*.

Portuguese *danças* are composed and rehearsed by a country or village dancing-master for a particular festival or occasion, for example, Carnival. *Bailes* are country or circle-dances, generally unrehearsed, familiar to most people in the region. *Danças* or *bailes* may be lively or serious. As a sign of modesty the women used to keep their eyes down and never smiled when dancing, but such a serious demeanour has been gradually abandoned for a gayer one, partly through the influence of tourism. Liveliest and most varied of all the dances is the *vira* (rural waltz form) from the Minho area. The *corridinho* ('running step', a fast polka) is characteristic of the Algarve: fast spinning and fancy footwork reminiscent of Spanish flamenco are displayed by individual couples as they compete with each other. The different types of *viras* and *corridinhos* include formation-dances for couples with one or more singers and callers. They are usually accompanied by village musicians playing accordions or concertinas, *violas* or *violãos* (six-string guitar), *cavaquinhos* and *guitarras* (see figs.1 and 2). Formation-dancing of couples also occurs in the Azores, where it is called *chamarrita*. It is accompanied by *violas, violãos, guitarras* and violins. The singers, callers, dancers and instrumentalists often take turns in each of these roles, for many participants have at least two or three of these talents. The village dancing-master has been known to call, sing and play the *violão* simultaneously while dancing, in a display of multiple abilities reminiscent of the 16th-century *cortesano* (courtier). The *chamarrita* often shows the influence of instrumental technique in its melodic range and contour (ex.7). Dances related to an ancient sword dance tradition persist in Miranda do Douro where the *pauliteiros* or *paulitos* use sticks in place of swords (fig.5). The *charamba* (basically a circle-dance performed by couples) seems to have developed from an

4. Pauliteiros performing a stick dance, accompanied by tambores *(drums) and* gaita de foles *(bagpipe)*

old *bassa dança* style, to judge from its guitar harmonies. The accompaniment is percussive, using *tambores* (drums) or *adufes* (frame drums; fig.5) with *violas* and *guitarras*. The *charamba* is also sung in old *desafio* style in the islands of Terceira (Azores) and Madeira. Santos (1937) considered it to be an old slave lament of Arab origin.

The Portuguese not only disseminated their dances to other parts of the world but also assimilated foreign types. The *cana-verde*, a circle-dance for men and women associated with sugar-cane harvest festivities, shows African influences (ex.8). The *seguidilhas* in the Algarve is believed to have come from Spain, and the fandango may have come to Portugal via the Caribbean. The fandango, a couple-dance performed in line or circle formations, is still popular in the Minho region, accompanied by *guitarras*, *violas*, violin and accordions. In the Alentejo the accompaniment is *gaita de foles* (bagpipe; fig.6 below), *pífaro* (fife) and castanets; in the Beiras, harmonica, drum and triangles; in the Algarve, *guitarra*, *pífaro*, castanets and sometimes the *bandolim* (mandolin). Dances such as the *schottische*, mazurka

5. *Adufe (frame drum)*

Ex.7 *Chamarrita*, square-dance song (Andrade, 1960)

Sen-ho- ra San-ta Ca- t'ri - na,_ Mo-ra
em Cas - te - lo Branco._ Sen-ho - ra San - ta Ca -
- t'ri - na,_ Mo-ra em Cas - te - lo Branco. Mais a -
-bai - xo_ na Fe - teira,_____ O Di-vi-no Es-p'ri-to
Santo. Mais a - bai - xo__ na Fe - tei - ra,_ O Di-
- vi - no Es - p'ri-to Santo.

and polka from other parts of Europe also occur, and marches are probably the result of French influence during the 19th century.

Some of the dances in the Minho area, such as the *malhão*, *cana-verde*, *vira* and *chula*, may be accompanied by a small dance band (*ronda minhota*) composed of harmonicas, concertinas, violins, *cavaquinhos*, *violas*, *violãos*, drums, triangles and wind instruments. A similar instrumentation is found in Madeiran dances. Some dances have heel-tapping (the fandango and *bailarico*) which creates a rhythmic contrast with the musicians. Marine shells are used as rattles or castanets along the coast of the Minho, but in the interior of the

Minho, dancers' castanets are of wood. Of particular interest are the *adufes* (small hand-beaten frame drums played by women throughout the country), *pipas* (clay flutes), *gaitas* (bagpipes of northern Portugal) and *rebeccas* (folk violins). Chain-dances such as the *verde-gaio* are prevalent in central and northern Portugal. One of the older dances, *a farrapeira*, is accompanied by the *pífaro* and *gaita de foles*.

One of the most popular instruments used in accompanying folksongs and folkdances is the *viola*, a four- or five-string guitar. During the 18th century it had as many as three strings in a lower course. The Portuguese term 'viola', like the Spanish 'vihuela', was used generically during the Renaissance to denote any stringed instrument. The term is qualified according to

Ex.8 *Cana-verde* (Neves e Melo, 1872)

Oh mi-nha can - ni - nha ver - de Oh meu
Se - nhor do Bom - fim___ Oh mi-nha can - ni - nha
ver - de Oh meu Se - nhor do Bom - fim Lin - da
cara Lin - da ca - ra lin - dos o - lhos Vi - rem
se vi - rem se cá pa - ra mim Vi - ra t'a-
- go - ra Vi - rem se cá pa - ra mim__ lin-dos o-lhos Lin-da
ca - ra Oh meu Se - nhor do Bom - fim.

6. Gaita de foles (bagpipe)

how it is played or by its physical attributes, as in the *viola de mano* (plucked with the right hand), *viola de arco* (bowed with the right hand) or *viola de arame* (with metal strings; fig.3 above). The earliest publications which include accompaniments to Portuguese songs are instrumental method books: for instance Luis de Milán in 1536 included six Portuguese villancicos in his *Libro de música de vihuela de mano intitulado El Maestro*. In the *Documentos das chancelarias* (see Azevedo, 1934) the accompanying role can be found in references not only to the *viola* but also to *alaudes* (lutes) and the *guitarra* before 1450. It has not yet been determined whether these early melodies, those in the late medieval and early Renaissance songbooks such as the Cantigas de Santa María, Cancioneiro de Ajuda, Cancioneiro Vaticana (Colucci-Brancuti; now in *P-Lc*) and the Martin Codax, as well as those in the early instrument method books, were versions of the folktunes of the day. With their refined style and courtly purposes, what are presented as traditional melodies are more likely to have been artistic reworkings of folk material.

4. CONTINUITY AND CHANGE. Despite the long gap between the medieval collections and those of the 19th and 20th centuries, evidence of some continuity in song types is provided by references in literature as well as by the presence today of such songs as *villancetes* (carols), *romances*, *cantigas de berço*, *marítimas*, *loas*, *cantigas de romaria*, *as maias* (May songs), *as janeiras*, *os reis* (songs of the Three Kings), *desafios* or *despiques* and *desgarradas* (the last three are ultimately related to the ancient *cantigas de escarnio e maldizer*). Modern song

collections reveal medieval aspects, such as the modality and free rhythms of plainsong, co-existing with major (the commonest) and minor tonalities (see ex.1). Ancient and modern treatments of the same song may be observed among contemporary singers. For instance, the D and G modes are still found side by side with major and minor tonalities in such folksongs as the *romarias* (pilgrim songs), *folias* (processional and festive songs sung by the *foliões*, folk equivalents of the court jesters) and *romances* (ballads). The ornate influences of the East can still be seen in instrumentation and singing styles, especially in the most isolated mountainous regions and in the islands.

African rhythms and instrumentation were also a feature of Portuguese folk music apparently since the beginning of the 16th century. The following genres were once particularly popular. The *guineos* and *negros*, sung in Spain, Portugal and Latin America, are usually responsorial and feature hemiola shifts to 3/4 within a 6/8 metre; their texts, usually on the Christmas theme, mention African place names and African as well as European instruments, and use vocables such as 'gulugá, gulugué'. The dance-song called *lundum* (*londum, lundu*), originating from Africa (Angola or Zaïre), came to Portugal via Brazil where it was seen as a type of indecent samba. In Portugal it became a type of burlesque *modinha*. With the 'lascivious' *fôfa* dance it is perhaps one source of the *fado* (C. M. Dias, *Cartas de Lisboa*, Lisbon, 1905). The *canarios* are found in numerous 17th- and 18th-century guitar tutors in triple time, as opposed to Arbeau's notation in duple time. Lastly, the *arrombas* (from the Cuban rumba) appeared in notations in Portugal around 1700 (J. C. T. Lamaunce, *Cifras de viola por varios autores* in *P-Cug*). In 20th-century Portugal African traces survive in such dances as the *cana-verde*, the *bailes de escravos* (a shuffling chain-dance in imitation of slaves) and the *bailes dos pretos*, a circle-dance featuring a solo imitation of black African dancing, with appropriate costume, make-up and instruments providing 'African' rhythms; but the impact of Afro-Portuguese music and dance has been greater in the New World.

BIBLIOGRAPHY

GENERAL

T. Braga: *História da poesia popular portugueza* (Oporto, 1867, 3/1902)
J. Leite de Vasconcellos: *Tradições populares de Portugal* (Oporto, 1882)
C. Michaelis de Vasconcellos: 'Estudos sobre o romanceiro peninsular', *Revista lusitana*, ii (1890–92), 156–240; pubd separately (Coimbra, 1907–9, 2/1934)
J. do Rio [pseud. of P. Barreto]: *Fados, canções e dansas de Portugal* (Rio de Janeiro and Paris, 1909)
A. C. Pires de Lima: 'Tradiçoes populares de Santo Tirso', *Revista lusitana*, xvii (1914), 282–337; xx (1917), 1–39
S. Costa: 'Auto do Natal', *Terra portuguesa*, ii (1916), 97
M. A. Lambertini: *Bibliophilie musicale* (Lisbon, 1918)
F. A. Coelho: *Jogos e rimas infantis* (Oporto, 2/1919)
F. A. Martins: *Folclore do concelho de Vinhais* (Coimbra, 1928)
P. de Azevedo, ed.: *Documentos das chancelarias reais anteriores a 1531 relativos a Marrocos* (Lisbon, 1934)
J. Lopes Dias: *A Beira Baixa da microfone da Emissora nacional de radiodifusão* (Lisbon, 1936)
C. M. Santos: *Tocares e cantares da ilha: estudo do folklore da Madeira* (Funchal, 1937)
W. J. Entwistle: *European Balladry* (Oxford, 1939/R1951)
E. Ferreira: 'Reminiscências do Teatro Vincentino nos Açores', *Revista açoriana*, ii (1940), 152
G. Chase: 'The Music of Portugal', *The Music of Spain* (New York, 1941, 2/1959), 273ff
C. M. Santos: *Trovas e bailados da ilha: estudo do folclore musical da Madeira* (Funchal, 1942)
A. C. Pires de Lima: *Jogos e canções infantis* (Oporto, enlarged 2/1943)

J. A. and F. de C. Pires de Lima: *Contribuição para o estudo do romanceiro minhoto* (Oporto, 1943)

B. D. Rocha da Silva Guimarães: *Primeiro esboço duma bibliografia musical portuguesa* (Oporto, 1947)

A. C. Pires de Lima: *Estudos etnográficos, filológicos e históricos*, iii–iv (Oporto, 1948–9)

A. C. Pires de Lima and A. Lima Carneiro: *Romanceiro para o povo e para as escolas* (Oporto, n.d.)

R. Menéndez Pidal: *Romancero hispánico (hispano-português, americano y sefardí)* (Madrid, 1953)

A. Mourinho: 'Teatro rural em Trás-os-Montes', *Revista ocidente*, li (1956), 181

J. Andrade: *Bailhos, rodas e cantorias* (Horta, 1960)

F. Lopes Graça, M. Kiel and A. Redol: *Romanceiro geral do povo português* (Lisbon, 1964)

B. E. Pereira: *Bibliografia analítica de etnografia portuguesa* (Lisbon, 1965)

M. de Sampayo Ribeiro: *Livraria de música de El-Rei D. João IV* (Lisbon, 1967) [i: *Primeira parte do index da livraria*, Lisbon, 1649, facs.]

R. Stevenson: 'The Afro-American Musical Legacy to 1800', *MQ*, liv (1968), 475

J. B. Purcell: 'Traditional Ballads among the Portuguese in California', *Western Folklore*, xxviii (1969), 1, 77

——: 'A riqueza do romanceiro e outras tradições orais nas ilhas dos Açores', *Atlântida*, xiv (1970), 223

J. Sasportes: *História da dança em Portugal* (Lisbon, 1970)

S. G. Armistead and J. H. Silverman: *Folk Literature of the Sephardic Jews*, i: *The Judeo-Spanish Ballad Chapbooks of Yacob Abraham Yoná* (Berkeley, 1971) [with extensive bibliography]

S. Petersen: 'Cambios estructurales en el romancero tradicional', *El romancero en la tradición oral moderna*, ed. D. Catalan, S. G. Armistead and A. Sánchez Romeralo (Madrid, 1972), 167ff

J. B. Purcell: 'Sobre o romanceiro português: continental, insular e transatlântico: uma recolha recente', *El romancero en la tradición oral moderna*, ed. D. Catalan, S. G. Armistead and A. Sánchez Romeralo (Madrid, 1972), 55ff

BALLADS AND SONGS

J. B. Almeida Garrett: *Romanceiro e cancioneiro geral* (Lisbon, 1843–51, 3/1900–01)

C. F. Bellerman: *Portugiesische Volkslieder und Romanzen* (Leipzig, 1864)

T. Braga: *Cancioneiro e romanceiro geral português* (Coimbra, 1867–9, rev. and enlarged 2/1906–09)

——: *Cantos populares do archipélago açoriano* (Oporto, 1869)

S. P. M. Estácio da Veiga: *Romanceiro do Algarve* (Lisbon, 1870)

A. A. das Neves e Melo: *Músicas e canções populares coligidas da tradição* (Lisbon, 1872)

A. Rodrígues de Azevedo: *Romanceiro do archipélago da Madeira* (Funchal, 1880)

J. Leite de Vasconcellos: *Romanceiro português* (Lisbon, 1886, enlarged 2/1958–60)

T. Braga: 'Ampliações ao romanceiro das ilhas dos Açores', *Revista lusitana*, i (1887–9), 99

P. F. Tomás: *Canções populares da Beira* (Figueira da Foz, 1896, 2/1923)

P. de Carvalho: *História do fado* (Lisbon, 1903)

A. Pimentel: *A triste canção do sul* (Lisbon, 1904)

F. X. d'Athaide Oliveira: *Romanceiro e cancioneiro de Algarve (Lição de Loulé)* (Oporto, 1905)

P. F. Tomás: *Velhas canções e romances populares portugueses* (Coimbra, 1913)

C. Basto: 'Falas e tradições do distrito de Viana-do-Castelo', *Revista lusitana*, xiv (1914), 55

P. F. Tomás: *Cantares do povo* (Coimbra, 1919)

J. L. Dias: *Etnografia da Beira*, i (Lisbon, 1927)

F. A. Martins: *Folklore do concelho de Vinhais* (Coimbra, 1928)

P. F. Tomás: *Canções portuguesas* (Coimbra, 1934)

L. Moita: *O fado: canção de vencidos* (Lisbon, 1936)

J. L. Dias: *Etnografia da Beira*, iv: *O que a nossa gente canta* (Lisbon, 1937)

C. M. Santos: *Tocares e cantares da ilha: estudo do folclore da Madeira* (Funchal, 1937)

J. Diogo Correia: *Cantares da Malpica (Beira Baixa)* (Lisbon, 1938)

M. Maria de Melo: 'Música regional acoreana', *Portucale*, xi (1938), 142

A. Avelino Joyce: 'Acerca das canções populares de Monsanto e Paul', *Revista ocidente*, iv (1939), 276, 445

——: 'Relatorio do juri provincial da Beira Baixa', *Revista ocidente*, iv (1939), 99

A. Leça: 'Músico caminheiro', *Revista ocidente*, iv (1939), 25, 86, 241; v (1939), 86, 370; xii (1941), 418; xiii (1941), 97, 320; xiv (1941), 109, 249

A. Lima Carneiro: 'Cancioneiro musical de Monte Córdova', *Douro-Litoral*, i (1940–44), nos.1–3

A. Leça: *Da música popular do Baixo Alentejo* (Beja, 1941, 2/1942)

——: *Música popular portuguesa* (Oporto, n.d.)

K. Schindler: *Folk Music and Poetry of Spain and Portugal* (New York, 1941)

C. M. Santos: *Trovas e bailados da ilha: estudo de folclore musical da Madeira* (Funchal, 1942)

A. C. Pires de Lima: 'A linguagem e o folclore de entre Douro e Minho', *Douro-Litoral*, vi (1943), 40

J. A. and F. de C. Pires de Lima: *Romanceiro minhoto* (Oporto, 1943)

M. V. Diniz: 'Canções de Roda', *Douro-Litoral*, 2nd ser., ii (1944), 37

G. Sampaio: *Cancioneiro minhoto* (Oporto, 1944)

A. Lima Carneiro: 'Canções e danças do Monte Córdova', *Douro-Litoral*, 3rd ser., vi (1949), 51

J. Nunes de Oliveira: 'Cantaréus em Abragão (Penafiel)', *Douro-Litoral*, 3rd ser., vii (1949), 32

A. Lima Carneiro: 'Canções populares', *Douro-Litoral*, 3rd ser., viii (1950), 66

J. Carlos da Costa Moniz: *Doze canções populares da ilha Terceira, Açores* (Lisbon, n.d.)

V. Pereira: *Cancioneiro de Cinfães* (Oporto, 1950)

A. de Sousa: *Cancioneiro de entre Douro e Mondego* (Lisbon, n.d.)

F. Lopes Graça: *A canção popular portuguesa* (Lisbon, 1953)

A. Marvão: *Cancioneiro alentejano* (Beringel, 1955)

M. J. P. Ferreira: *O natal na Madeira: estudo folclorico* (Funchal, 1956)

A. Marvão: *O Alentejo canta* (Braga, 1956)

J. de Figueiredo: *Impérios marienses: folclore açoriano* (Lisbon, 1957)

V. Pereira: *Cancioneiro de Resende* (Oporto, 1957)

——: 'Subsídios para o cancioneiro raiano', *Douro-Litoral*, 8th ser., iii–iv (1957), 185

A. Lima Carneiro: *Cancioneiro de Monte Córdova* (Oporto, 1958)

J. L. de Fraga: 'Cantares açorianos', *Atlântida*, ii (1958), 325; iii (1959), 109, 212; iv (1960), 47, 238; v (1961), 32, 125; pubd separately (Angra, 1963)

F. Lopes Graça: *A música portuguesa e os seus problemas: ensaios* (Lisbon, 1959)

V. Pereira: *Cancioneiro de Arouca* (Oporto, 1959)

——: 'Corais mirandeses: novos subsídios para o cancioneiro raiano', *Douro-Litoral*, 9th ser., i (1959), 5

J. B. Soares: 'Subsídios para o futuro cancioneiro penafidelense', *Douro-Litoral*, 9th ser., iv (1959), 729

DANCES

A. Pimentel: *A dança em Portugal* (Esposende, 1892)

F. M. Sousa Viterbo: *Artes e artistas em Portugal* (Lisbon, 1892, rev. 2/1920)

A. J. de Morais Ferreira: *Dialecto mirandês* (Lisbon, 1898)

J. Leite de Vasconcellos: *Estudos de filologia mirandesa*, i (Lisbon, 1900), 43ff

M. Lopes: 'Da minha terra', *Revista lusitana*, xxxi (1933), 138

L. Chaves: 'Pantomimas, danças e bailados populares', *Revista lusitana*, xxxv (1937), 140; xxxvi (1938), 218

A. Leça: 'Danças e cantigas', *Vida e arte do povo português* (1940), 185

A. Miranda: 'Folclore de Penafiel, I: a Mourisca; II: o baile dos ferreiros de Penafiel e a dos paulileiros de Miranda', *Douro-Litoral*, ii (1940), 2

P. Homem de Mello: *A poesia na dança e nos cantares do povo português (Alto Minho)* (Oporto, 1941)

A. Miranda: *O baile das regateiras nas festas de Corpus Christi* (Penafiel, 1942)

——: *O baile dos alfaiates nas festas de Corpus Christi* (Penafiel, 1942)

——: *O baile dos pretos nas festas de Corpus Christi* (Penafiel, 1942)

——: *O baile dos sapateiros nas festas de Corpus Christi* (Penafiel, 1942)

L. Chaves: *Danças e bailados: notas de coreografia popular portuguesa* (Lisbon, 1944)

G. das Neves: 'Azurara (Concelho de Vila do Conde): algumas notas etnograficas', *Douro-Litoral*, 2nd ser., iv (1946), 60

L. Chaves: 'Nos domínios da etnografia e do folclore', *Revista ocidente*, xxxiv (1948), 249

L. Armstrong: *Dances of Portugal* (London, 1948, rev. 2/1950)

B. Daciano: 'A dança dos ferreiros e as festas de Penafiel (1959): relatório', *Douro-Litoral*, 3rd ser., viii (1950), 27

F. Lopes Júnior: 'As danças do entrudo', *Boletim do Instituto histórico da Ilha Terceira*, xi (1953), 143

A. Valentim, A. Mourinho and S. Júnior: 'Coreografia popular trasmontana: o galandum', *Douro-Litoral*, 5th ser., vii–viii (1953), 3

R. Bonito: 'O galandum e os seus problemas: considerações a propósito de uma dança popular trasmontana', *Douro-Litoral*, 6th ser., iii–iv (1954), 3

L. F. Machado Drumond: 'O baile popular terceirense: estudo do folclore regional', *Boletim do Instituto histórico da Ilha Terceira*, xiii (1955), 118–95

L. M. da Camara Almeida Mattos: 'Danças populares micaelenses', *Revista insulana*, xi (1955), 134–46

B. Bessa, A. Mourinho and S. Júnior: 'Coreografia popular trasmontana: o pingacho', *Douro-Litoral*, 8th ser., i–ii (1957), 5

A. Mourinho: 'A dança dos paulitos', *Revista ocidente*, liii (1957), 153
J. L. de Fraga: 'Cantares açorianos', *Atlântida*, ii (1958), 325; iii (1959), 109, 212; iv (1960), 47, 238; v (1961), 32, 125; pubd separately (Angra, 1963)
E. Amorim: *As danças e cantos populares nas romanarias do Minho* (Arcos de Valdevez, 1960)
T. Ribas: *Danças do povo português* (Lisbon, 1961)
J. Sasportes: *História da dança em Portugal* (Lisbon, 1970)
P. Homem de Mello: *Folclore* (Lisbon, 1971)

INSTRUMENTS

A. F. Maia and O. L. Vieira: *Apontamentos para um methodo de guitarra* (Leiriense, 1875)
F. Ferraz de Macedo: 'Cerâmica popular portuguesa: assobios de água', *Revista lusitana*, iii (1893–5), 82
I.L.L.P.: *A guitarra sem professor* (Lisbon, 1896)
M. A. Lambertini: *Indústria instrumental portuguesa* (Lisbon, 1914)
——: *Museu instrumental em Lisboa* (Lisbon, 1914)
——: *Primeiro núcleo de um Museu instrumental* (Lisbon, 1914)
M. L. de Sampayo Ribeiro: *As 'guitarras de Alcácer' e a 'guitarra portuguesa'* (Lisbon, 1936)
L. B. Leite d'Athaide: 'Viola de arame ou viola da terra', *Revista insulana*, iii (1947), 386
L. da Silva Ribeiro: 'Notas de etnografia de Terceira', *Revista lusitana*, xxxvi (1950), 107
F. Gonçalves: 'As trambonelas de Fão', *Douro-Litoral*, 3rd ser., viii (1950), 7
J. Nava: *Pequeno methodo de viola franceza* (Lisbon, n.d.)
F. Nunes: 'Reque-Reques e matracas de Fão', *Douro-Litoral*, 4th ser., i–ii (1950), 107
F. Gonçalves: 'Assobios onomatopaicos dos barristas de Barcelos', *Revista de dialectologia y tradiciones populares*, vii (1951), 327
F. Lopes Júnior: 'A viola de arame na vida, no folclore e no cancioneiro das ilhas', *Atlântida*, ii (1958), 116
L. Chaves: 'Nos domínios da etnografia portuguesa', *Revista ocidente*, lix (1960), 116, 237, 339
E. Veiga de Oliveira: *Instrumentos musicais populares portugueses* (Lisbon, 1966)
J. Dias: 'O cavaquinho', *Revista de etnografia*, viii/2 (1967), 337
ROBERT STEVENSON (I)
JOANNE B. PURCELL, RONALD C. PURCELL (II)

Portugal [Portogallo], Marcos Antônio (da Fonseca) (*b* Lisbon, 24 March 1762; *d* Rio de Janeiro, 7 Feb 1830). Portuguese composer and conductor. The son of Manuel Antônio da Ascenção (or Assumpção), he assumed the high-sounding name of Fonseca Portugal about 1785, taking it from his godfather, Captain José Correia da Fonseca Portugal. Previously he had used only his Christian names and continued to be known as Marcos Antônio in Portuguese musical circles throughout the 19th century. On 6 August 1771 he was admitted to the Seminário Patriarchal of Lisbon, where he received his first musical training. He studied composition under João de Souza Carvalho and wrote his first work (a *Miserere*) at the age of 14. There is no trace of Orao, the teacher who is credited by Fétis with having taught him counterpoint, or Borselli, the Italian singer who is said to have given him singing lessons. Nor is there evidence that he was ever accompanist at the Madrid Opera or that the Portuguese ambassador there sent him to Italy in 1787. On 23 July 1783 he was admitted to the celebrated brotherhood of S Cecilia, in whose records he is described as singer and organist of the chapel of the Seminário Patriarchal. In 1785 he was appointed conductor at the Teatro do Salitre, where he produced (25 July 1787) a *Licença pastoril* for the birthday of the Princess Maria Benedicta. His fame as a composer grew rapidly between 1785 and 1792. During that time he produced six Portuguese comic operas, which brought him wide popularity, especially *A castanheira*. He also contributed (under the name Marcos Antônio) several *modinhas* to the *Jornal de modinhas*, published at Lisbon.

In 1792, with royal protection and a government pension, Portugal went to Naples for further study. It is doubtful, however, that he actually studied there. Rather, he immediately began the series of 21 operas, both *seria* and *buffa*, that he produced with great success in all the major Italian centres during the next eight years. One of the most successful, *Le confusioni della somiglianza* (Florence, 1793), was repeated at Dresden, Milan, Vienna and Berlin in the next few years. Portugal returned to Lisbon in 1800 and was appointed *mestre de capela* of the royal chapel and director of the Opera, the prestigious S Carlos, where he produced a long series of new operas. In 1807 the French invasion forced the court to transfer to Rio de Janeiro, but Portugal remained at Lisbon directing the S Carlos. The finale of his cantata *La speranza* (1809) was adopted as the national anthem until 1834. In 1811, with his brother Simão, a church composer, he joined the court of the future John VI at Rio de Janeiro, where he was *mestre* of the royal chapel, master of music and director of the court spectacles. His presence there was influential in the quick adoption by local composers such as José Maurício Nunes Garcia of an operatic style of church music. Although Portugal exercised a musical dictatorship in Rio de Janeiro, often to the detriment of local composers, until about 1820 he also contributed to the city's musical splendour, particularly in his activities in the royal chapel. During his first two years in Brazil he produced revivals of old operas (*L'oro non compra amore*, 1811; *Artaserse*, 1812), as well as new ones (*A saloia namorada*, 1812, to a text by the Brazilian poet Domingos Caldas Barbosa). In 1811 he suffered an apoplectic fit; a second occurred in 1817. In that year he composed the hymn of acclamation for John VI, presented his serenata *Augurio di felicità* and a revival of his opera *Merope*. Unable to return to Lisbon with the court in 1821, he witnessed Brazilian independence and composed the *Hino da independência*, first performed on 12 October 1822.

In a list of his works begun in 1809 and afterwards kept up to date, Portugal enumerated 35 Italian operas, 21 Portuguese comic operas and over 100 pieces of church music. In his operas he cultivated an authentically Neapolitan style and was strongly influenced by the music of Perez and Cimarosa. The success of his operas in all the major European centres is indicative of his creative power within the established style. His sacred music is also in the fashionable Italian moulds of the time, with a marked emphasis on bel canto vocal writing and other features of dramatic music.

WORKS

LS – *Lisbon, Salitre*   VM – *Venice, S Moisè*
LC – *Lisbon, S Carlos*   FP – *Florence, Pallacorda*

OPERAS

Le confusioni della somiglianza, o siano I due gobbi (2, C. Mazzini), FP, 1793, *D-?Bds, Dlb, F-Pc, GB-Lbm, I-Fc, Mr*, rev. LC, 1804; Il Cinna (2, A. Anelli), Florence, Pergola, 1793, *Fc*; Lo spazzacamino principe (1, G. Foppa), VM, 1794, *Fc, Mr, PAc*; La vedova raggiatrice, o siano I due sciocchi delusi (2), Florence, Pergola, 1794, *Fc*; Demofoonte (3, Metastasio), Milan, La Scala, 1794, autograph *Mr*, copy *B-Bc*, rev. LC, 1808, ? autograph *US-Wc*
L'avventuriere (1, C. Mazzolà), Florence, private perf., 1795; Zulima (2, G. Gonella), FP, 1796, *I-Fc, Mc*; L'inganno poco dura (2, S. Zini), Naples, Fiorentini, 1796, *Nc*; La donna di genio volubile (La donna bizzarra) (2, G. Bertati), VM, 1796, *A-Wgm, I-Fc, Mr, US-Bb*; Il ritorno di Serse (2, F. G. Ferrari), FP, 1797, *Fc, Mr, PAc*, rev. as L'Argenide, LC, 1804; Le donne cambiate (1, Foppa), VM, 1797, *Fc*; Gli Orazi e i Curiazi (A. S. Sografi), Ferrara, Comunale, 1798; Fernando nel Messico (3, F. Tarducci), Venice, S Benedetto, 1799, *GB-Lbm, I-Fc*, rev. LC, 1805, *P-La*
La maschera fortunata (19 scenes, Foppa), VM, 1798, *I-Fc, Mr*; Alceste (3, Sografi), Venice, La Fenice, 1798, *Mr*; Non irritare le donne (1, Foppa), VM, 1798; La pazza giornata, ovvero Il matrimonio di Figaro (2, G. Rossi), Venice, S Benedetto, 1799, *Fc*; Idante, ovvero I

sagrifizi d'Ecate (2, G. Schmidt), Milan, La Scala, 1800, autograph *Mr*; Adrasto re d'Eggito (3, G. De Gamerra), LC, 1800; La morte di Semiramide (3), LC, 1801, *P-La*, *Ln*; Zaira (2, M. Buttarini), LC, 1802, *La*

Il trionfo di Clelia (2, Sografi), LC, 1802; La Sofonisba (2, G. Caravita and Del Mare), LC, 1803; L'oro non compra amore (2, A. Anelli), LC, 1804, *I-Mr*, *Nc*; Merope, LC, 1804, *P-La*; Il duca di Foix (2, Caravita), LC, 1805; Ginevra di Scozia (2, G. Rossi), LC, 1805; La morte di Mitridate (2, Sografi), LC, 1806, *La*; Artaserse (3, Metastasio), LC, 1806; Tito Vespasiano (3, after Metastasio: La clemenza di Tito), Livorno, Carlo Ludovico, 1807, *PAc*; Amor non si cela (2), Pesaro, Sole, 1808

Omar re di Termagene, Modena, Emilia, 1810; Inès de Castro (scena lirica, G. Ferretti), Rome, Valle, 1810, collab. V. Migliorucci [perhaps a pasticcio]; Il muto per astuzia (2, Foppa), Rio de Janeiro, S João, 1811, *I-Mr*; Adriano in Siria (3, Metastasio), Padua, Nuovo, 1813; Il trionfo di Gusmano (2, Rossi), LC, 1816; Penelope (2), St Petersburg, Michailov, 1818 [perhaps a pasticcio or an earlier work with new title]; others

At least 21 Port. comic operas, incl.: A casa de pasto (1), LS, 1784; Os bons amigos (1), LS, 1786; A castanheira, ou Brites papagaia (1), LS, 1787; O amor conjugal (1), LS, 1789; A noiva fingida (2, after G. M. Diodati), LS, 1790; A amantar militar (1), LS, 1791; O lunático iludido (O mundo da lua) (3, after Goldoni), LC, 1792; A saloia namorada (1, D. Caldas Barbosa), Rio de Janeiro, Court, 1812

OTHER WORKS

Cantatas and occasional works: Licença pastoril, LS, 1787, *P-La*; Pequeno drama, LS, 1787, *La*; La purissima concezione di Maria Santissima, cantata, 1788; O genio americano, cantata, Bahia, 1806; La speranza (cantata, G. Caravita), LC, 1809; Augurio di felicità (serenata, after Metastasio), Rio de Janeiro, Real Quinta da Boa Vista, 1817

Sacred: numerous masses, Credos, Glorias, hymns, matins, psalms, Te Deums, sequences, litanies, antiphons, Lamentations, canticles, etc, *P-La*, *Ln*, *Mp*

BIBLIOGRAPHY

DBP

M. Pereira Peixoto d'Almeida Carvalhães: *Marcos Portugal na sua música dramática* (Lisbon, 1910, suppl. 1916) [incl. catalogue of operas, cantatas etc]

G. Chase: *The Music of Spain* (New York, 1941, rev. 2/1959)

J. de Freitas Branco: *História da música portuguesa* (Lisbon, 1959)

Ayres de Andrade: *Francisco Manuel da Silva e seu tempo* (Rio de Janeiro, 1967)

GERARD BÉHAGUE

Portugal, Simão Victorino (*b* 1774; *d* Rio de Janeiro, ?1842). Portuguese organist and composer, brother of Marcos Antônio Portugal. He became a student at the Patriarchal Seminary in 1782 and was later the church organist there. He was principally a teacher of singing and the piano. By 1811 he had emigrated with his elder brother to Brazil, where he was appointed organist of the royal chapel; in 1842 Francisco Manoel was named *mestre de capela* in place of 'Simeao Portugal', who may have died about that time. Some of Simão Portugal's sacred compositions are in the cathedral archives in Lisbon and Évora; one psalm is catalogued in the Ajuda library.

BIBLIOGRAPHY

DBP, ii, 210f, 230, 473; *LaborD*

R. Almeida: *História da música brasileira* (Rio de Janeiro, 1942), 310ff

R. Stevenson: 'Some Portuguese Sources for Early Brazilian Music History', *Yearbook, Inter-American Institute for Musical Research*, iv (1968), 24

J. A. Alegria: *Arquivo das músicas da Sé de Évora: catálogo* (Lisbon, 1973), 23, 26, 36, 123

ELEANOR RUSSELL

Portunal [Portunalflöte] (Ger.). An ORGAN STOP.

Porumbescu, Ciprian (*b* Şipote [now Şipotele-Sucevei], nr. Suceava, 14 Oct 1853; *d* Stupca, nr. Suceava, 6 June 1883). Romanian composer, choirmaster and teacher. He began his musical education in his family circle, his father being a folksong collector and a friend of Carol Miculi, who visited them during the summer holidays.

After some instruction in the violin he became a pupil of Vorobchievici in Czernowitz, and at the Vienna Conservatory he was a pupil of Franz Krenn and Bruckner. Porumbescu was an enthusiastic organizer of musical life, conducting choirs and orchestras, writing songs, founding festivals and even acting on the stage. He became the president of Arboroasa ('Wooded Land', the ancient name of Bukovina), a student cultural society, in his own district, where he was confined for political reasons. Subsequently he became conductor of the România Jună ('Young Romania'), a Viennese student society. In Vienna his tunes were taken up as freedom songs by young Romanians, and his waltzes were played by the popular orchestras of the capital. He settled in Braşov as a music teacher and choirmaster of the Romanian Society and of St Nicholas's Church, and was more active as a composer in his last years. His *Crai nou* ('New moon') written in 1882, had become one of the most popular Romanian operettas by 1900. As he declared after its première, the model of his style was popular music. He also based many of his choruses on folk-music, with its modes and free rhythms. Porumbescu was one of the founders of the Romanian school of instrumental and vocal music with his Ballad for violin and piano, his *Rapsodia română*, folkdances and salon pieces for piano, and his songs on Romanian or German texts. The Bucharest Conservatory now bears his name.

WORKS

Edition: *Opere alese de Ciprian Porumbescu*, ed. V. Cosma, i–ii (Bucharest, 1954–8) [C]

STAGE

Candidatul Linte sau Rigorosul teologic [The candidate Linte, or The theological rigorist] (vaudeville, 2, Porumbescu), 1877, C ii

Crai nou [New moon] (operetta, 2, V. Alecsandri), 1882; excerpts in C i

SACRED CHORAL

Altarul Mânăstirii Putna [The altar of the monastery of Putna], cantata (Alecsandri), solo vv, male chorus, pf, 1877 (Leipzig, 1913)

Hymns and liturgical songs, most for male vv

SECULAR VOCAL

Tabăra română [Romanian camp] (Alecsandri), solo vv, male chorus, 1876

La malurile Prutului [On the banks of the Prut], waltz (Porumbescu), solo vv, male chorus, pf, 1877 (Leipzig, 1911)

Colecţia de [21] cîntece sociale pentru studenţii români [Social songs for Romanian students], unison vv, 1879 (Vienna, 1880)

Cît îi ţara românească [All through the Romanian countryside] (Porumbescu), chorus, pf, 1882 (Leipzig, 1911); Ger. and Rom. texts

Serenada (Dormi uşor) [Sleep gently], S, chorus (Leipzig, 1911)

Other choral works (most for male vv) on texts of Porumbescu, Alecsandri, etc

Solo songs on Rom. and Ger. texts

INSTRUMENTAL

Paraphrase sur un thème roumain, orch, 1882

Qnt, fl, str, 1875; Str Qnt, 1875; Arie română, fl, 2 vn, pf, 1877

Balada, vn, pf, op.29, 1880 (Bucharest, c1880); Rêverie, vn, pf, 1880 (Cluj, c1880); Rapsodia română, pf, 1882, C i; numerous other folkdances and salon pieces for vn, pf, and pf solo

WRITINGS

Elementele musicei vocale pentru şcoalele poporale şi normale [Elements of vocal music for grammar and normal schools] (MS, 1878)

BIBLIOGRAPHY

L. Morariu: *La semicentenarul Ciprian Porumbescu* (Suceava, 1933)

S. Parlescu: *Viaţa lui Ciprian Porumbescu* [Life of Porumbescu] (Suceava, 1940)

V. Cosma: *Ciprian Porumbescu* (Bucharest, 1957)

——: 'Porumbescu, Ciprian', *Muzicieni români: lexicon* (Bucharest, 1970)

ROMEO GHIRCOIAŞIU

Posaune (Ger.). (1) TROMBONE.

(2) An ORGAN STOP.

Posch (Ger.). KIT.

Posch, Isaac (*d* in Carinthia or Carniola, perhaps at Klagenfurt, 1622 or early 1623). Austrian composer, organist and organ builder. From 1614 at the latest he worked as provincial organist in Carinthia and as such was probably active in a general musical capacity among the Protestant nobility. There is evidence that he himself became a Protestant. By 1617–18 he appears to have settled in the neighbouring province of Carniola. He built an organ then at Oberburg, the residence of the bishops of Laibach (now Ljubljana). He signed the dedication of his 1618 volume from Laibach and dedicated the 1621 volume to the province of Carniola. In 1621 he built an organ for the Franciscan church at Laibach.

Like his contemporary Paul Peuerl, he made an important contribution to the development of the early Baroque variation suite. His 1618 volume consists mainly of 15 three-movement works of a highly individual kind, comprising variation, principal movement and *proportio tripla*. The ordering and character of the movements in the 1621 volume are equally individual; the nine pairs of five-part pavans and galliards are specially interesting. Posch's *Cantiones sacrae* also contains some notable music. It comprises 42 sacred concertos for various groupings of voices, five of which have parts for obbligato instruments; most are settings of words from the *Psalms* or the *Song of Songs*. With these pieces Posch appears as an immediate successor of Viadana, to whom he referred in his preface; he goes some way beyond his model, however, in both the structure and expressive qualities of his music.

WORKS

Musicalische Ehrenfreudt, das ist Allerley neuer Balleten, Gagliarden, Couranten und Täntzen teutscher Arth, a 4 (Regensburg, 1618); excerpts ed. in DTÖ, lxx, Jg.xxxvi/2 (1929/*R*)

Musicalische Tafelfreudt, das ist Allerley neuer Paduanen und Gagliarden, a 5, desgleichen Intraden und Couranten, a 4 (Nuremberg, 1621); (repr. with above vol., Nuremberg, 1626); ed. in DTÖ, lxx, Jg.xxxvi/2 (1929/*R*)

Harmonia concertans, id est Cantiones sacrae, 1–4vv, bc (Nuremberg, 1623); ed. in SEM, i, iv, vi (1968–72)

BIBLIOGRAPHY

K. Geiringer: 'Isaac Posch', *SMw*, xvii (1930), 53

A. Adrio: *Die Anfänge des geistlichen Konzerts* (Berlin, 1935)

H. J. Moser: *Die Musik in frühevangelischen Österreich* (Kassel, 1954)

D. Cvetko: *Zgodovina glasbene umetnosti na Slovenskem* [The history of music in Slovenia] (Ljubljana, 1958)

H. Federhofer: 'Unbekannte Dokumente zur Lebensgeschichte von Isaac Posch', *AcM*, xxxiv (1962), 78

WALTER BLANKENBURG

Posen (Ger.). POZNAŃ.

Poser, Hans (*b* Tannenbergsthal, Vogtland, 8 Oct 1917; *d* Hamburg, 1 Oct 1970). German composer and teacher. As a prisoner of war in Canada, he was helped by the Red Cross from 1940 to pursue his musical studies at a distance, his teachers being Hindemith and Grabner. After the war he moved to Hamburg and took lessons with E. G. Klussmann. In 1947 he was appointed to teach harmony and aural training at the institution which later became the Hamburg Hochschule für Musik, becoming professor in 1962. He was made an ordinary member of the Hamburg Free Academy of Arts in 1953. His most widespread success was with his television chamber opera *Die Auszeichnung* and the cantata *Till Eulenspiegel*, but in the German-speaking world he had most influence through his educational music.

WORKS
(selective list)

2 television chamber operas, incl. Die Auszeichnung (Poser, after Maupassant), 1959

Many choral works, incl. Till Eulenspiegel, op.35, 3 solo vv, chorus, orch, 1956

Inst pieces, songs, educational music

Principal publisher: Möseler

BIBLIOGRAPHY

S. Scheffler: 'Hans Poser', *Das Einhorn* [Yearbook of the Hamburg Free Academy of Arts] (1957–8), 135

E. Funck: 'Hans Poser', *Intervalle*, iii/5 (1970)

H. Wagner, ed.: *Hans Poser: 1917–1970* (n.p., 1972) [incl. list of works]

KLAUS L. NEUMANN

Posford, (Benjamin) George (Ashwell) (*b* Folkestone, 23 March 1906). British composer. After he had studied law at Christ's College, Cambridge, his musical career began in 1930; he wrote music for radio productions, and subsequently composed for the stage and for films. His orchestral compositions include *Broadcasting House* (1933, a rhapsody for orchestra with piano) and several symphonic poems. Musical plays and films for which he wrote music include *Goodnight Vienna* (1932), *The Gay Desperado* (1935), *Balalaika* (with Bernard Grun, 1936), *Magyar Melody* (originally *Paprika*, with Bernard Grun, 1938), *Full Swing* (1942), *Evangeline* (1946), *Masquerade* (1949), *Zip Goes a Million* (1951) and *Happy Holiday* (1955). Of these, *Balalaika* also achieved popularity in France, with additional numbers by Robert Stolz.

ANDREW LAMB

Position. A term applied to playing positions on string instruments and on the trombone. (For its application to harmony, *see* SPACING.) On a string instrument it indicates the placing of the left hand on the fingerboard so that the fingers can play from 1 on the lowest string to 4 on the highest without a SHIFT. On the trombone it refers to the degree of extension of the slide: first position is the 'home' position, and each successive position down to the seventh lowers the pitch by a semitone. (For a fuller discussion *see* TROMBONE.)

Position changes on string instruments are usually indicated by composers and theorists by fingerings, with the roman numerals I, II, III, IV designating the four strings (from highest to lowest). Unless some special effect is desired, however, composers usually leave the choice of positions to players.

On the violin the 1st position covers *a* to *d'* on the *g* string, *e'* to *a'* on the *d'* string, and so on. Thus the violin can be played in a range from (open) *g* to *b''* (on the *e''* string) without leaving 1st position. The 2nd position is achieved by moving a semitone or tone up, so that the first finger on the *g* string plays *b♭* or *b* and the fourth finger on the *e''* string plays *c'''* or *c♯'''* and so on. 'Half' position lies between the nut and first position. Leopold Mozart called the 2nd, 4th and 6th positions collectively 'halb Applicatur', the 3rd, 5th and 7th 'ganz Applicatur'; the French 18th-century word was 'ordre'; the English called 2nd position the 'half' shift, 3rd position the 'whole' or 'full' shift, 6th position the 'double' shift and 7th position the 'last' shift.

On the cello only the 1st position permits a diatonic scale of two octaves without shifts, by using the open strings; two complete octaves of C major, D major, D melodic minor and C melodic minor (ascending) can be played, the last three using the 'extended' position (a whole tone between first and second fingers). All others in two octaves require shifts or the use of the thumb. Corrette's cello *Méthode* (1741) described the 4th position as 'thumb position', although the *Méthode* (1772) of François Cupis *le jeune* made no mention of this. Tillière's *Méthode* (1774) followed Corrette's in calling the 4th a 'thumb' position and also indicated the use of the fourth finger in thumb-position arpeggios. In modern terminology all positions on the cello above 4th are called thumb position.

Because of its size the double bass has been the subject of many different fingering systems. Nearly all advocate the use of only the first, second and fourth fingers in the low positions; the third finger, being weaker, serves only as a support to the fourth, a tone lying comfortably between 1 and 4. Some players prefer the use of all fingers in all positions, although the stretch of a semitone – the double bass's 'extended' fingering – between each finger is frequently impossible. French schools of playing use the term 'first degree' to signify the position of the left hand when the first finger is placed a semitone above the nut; the next position, a semitone higher, is called 'second degree' and so on (according to the methods of Nanny and Cruft). The Austrian and German schools call first degree the 'half position', second degree is called 'first position', the positions being denoted by Roman numerals. Confusion arises higher up the instrument when sixth degree is equivalent to III/IV (Simandl, Montag) and to II MP, second 'medium position' (Lotter). On the double bass thumb positions are generally used from exactly halfway up the string, when the third finger, being longer, replaces the fourth. In passages of great rapidity or technical difficulty, the thumb may be used to advantage in any part of the instrument.

Before 1600 evidence of playing above 1st position is slight. Some viol treatises (particularly Ganassi's *Regola rubertina*, 1542–3) mention the possibility, and higher positions are shown in some paintings. In the early 17th century, Monteverdi's music implies shifts to 3rd and 4th positions, and in 1636 Mersenne wrote that the best violin players could reach an octave above the open strings, that is, 4th position. Music by the virtuoso violinist-composers of the late 17th century, such as Biber and Walther, requires the player to reach as high as the 7th position.

Gradually the use of high positions, even on the lower strings, became normal. Both Leopold Mozart and Geminiani expected good violinists to be able to play up to the 7th position on all strings. Cello sonatas by Dall'Abaco, Lanzetti and Porpora and Haydn's concertos explore the upper positions of the instrument; the sonatas and concertos of Boccherini exploit fully this extended compass.

BIBLIOGRAPHY
S. Babitz: *Principles of Extensions in Violin Fingering* (Los Angeles, 1947)
D. D. Boyden: *The History of Violin Playing from its Origins to 1761* (London, 1965)
For further bibliography *see* FINGERING and articles on individual instruments.

SONYA MONOSOFF

Positive. In current organ usage, strongly influenced by German terminology, a positive is (1) a movable organ as distinct from a PORTATIVE or portable organ, and (2) that manual of a larger organ that resembles (and perhaps historically originated in) such a smaller organ. The English 'chamber organ' is a positive; so are the

Positive organ, perhaps played by Paul Hofhaimer: woodcut by Hans Burgkmair from 'The Triumph of Maximilian I' (c1519); see also ORGAN, *figs.30, 31 and 32*

tall, shallow gothic instruments of two to three octaves and one to three ranks of flue pipes frequently represented in the 15th century as being played by one angel, blown by another (altar paintings of Van Eyck, Van der Goes). Henri Arnaut de Zwolle (MS, c1450) distinguished carefully between the small *portivus*, the larger *organum* or *opus* (cf *Werk*) and the *positivo*, especially the *positivo tergali* or RÜCKPOSITIV; the distinction was kept by Virdung (1511) and his plagiarizers. In England the term does not seem to have been used, while Schlick (1511) applied it to any small chest within a larger organ, such as the positive *zu Rück* or that *forn an die Brust* – as did some builders of the time (Van der Distelen at Antwerp Cathedral, 1505). In France, *le positif* usually means the CHAIR ORGAN in any source after c1520; previous to that it is unknown how many of the *petites orgues* were Chair organs or independent positive organs. Only from other sources is it clear that the *Posityff* at Zwolle (1447) and the *positif de la grande* at Angers (1513) were Chair organs. Later independent positives vary immensely, some with more than one manual, some with pedal stops, some blown by the player with a foot lever, some placed (Lat. *ponere*, *positum*) on tables, others too large to be easily movable, but most based on a Principal rank smaller than 8′.

PETER WILLIAMS

Pospíšil, Juraj (*b* Olomouc, 14 Jan 1931). Slovak composer. He studied at the Brno Academy and at the Bratislava High School for Musical Arts, graduating in 1955 and then joining the staff of the Bratislava Conservatory. A constructivist composer, he has drawn on the music of Janáček and on novel structural and notational techniques.

WORKS
(selective list)

Operas: Inter arma, 3 1-act operas, 1969

Orch: Hory a ľudia [Mountains and people], sym. poem, 1954; 3 syms., 1958, 1963, 1967; Pieseň o človeku [Song on man], sym. variations, 1961; Trbn Conc., 1962; Vn Conc., 1968; Cl Conc., 1972; Sym. Prelude, 1972; Hn Conc., 1973

Vocal: Margita a Besná, ballad, S, A, Bar, chorus, orch, 1955; Mikropoviedky [Micro-stories], S, fl, vn, vc, 1963; Bratislava, song cycle, Bar, pf, 1973

Chamber: Sonata, vc, pf, 1955; 2 nonets, 1960, 1962; 3 invencie, wind trio, 1961; Sonata, str, 1961; Hudba pre žeste [Music for brass], 1962; Glosy [Glosses], wind qnt, 1964; Protirečenia [Contradictions], cl qnt, 1964; Sonata, db, pf, 1964; Music for 12 Str, 1965; Sonata, vn, 1965; Villonská balada, cl, pf, 1966; Trojveršia [Triple verses (poetic form)], 9 insts, 1966; Sonata, db,

1967; Str Qt, 1970; Wind Qt, 1971; Sonata, db, str qt, 1971
Kbd: Pf Sonatina, 1953; Monológy, pf, 1959; Malá fantázia na husitské motívy [Little fantasia on Hussite motifs], org, 1960; Passacaglia and Fugue, org, 1963; Org Sonata, 1965
Elec: Médiation électronique, 1970
Principal publisher: Slovenský Hudobní Fond

LADISLAV BURLAS

Poss, Georg (*b* Franconia, *c*1570; *d* Rothwaltersdorf [now Czerwienczyce, Poland], after 1633). German composer and trumpet and cornett player. He spent his life serving the Habsburgs, probably starting as a chorister. In 1594 he is recorded as a trumpeter in the employment of Archduke Maximilian who, as Master of the Catholic Teutonic Knights at Mergentheim, Franconia, maintained a Kapelle under Aegidius Bassengius, and sent Poss to Venice to study music for three years. Poss then went to the court of Archduke Ferdinand at Graz, through the influence of the Hofkapellmeister, P. A. Bianco, and for 21 years pursued an exemplary career there as cornett player, first court trumpeter, composer and teacher. In 1618 he became Kapellmeister to Archduke Karl, Bishop of Brixen and Breslau and a brother of Archduke Ferdinand, at his court in Neisse, Silesia. He held the post for only four years, for Stefano Bernardi succeeded him in 1622. He was well rewarded for his services and was still mentioned in the archives of the court at Vienna in 1629 and 1633 as 'former Kapellmeister to Archduke Karl'. Poss was one of the composers – Annibale Perini, Francesco Stivori and Alessandro Tadei were others – who imported the style of Giovanni Gabrieli and other Venetians into Austria. His surviving music is all sacred and mostly polychoral. His parody masses, nine of which appeared in the *Liber primus missarum* in 1607, are based on works by Annibale Padovano, Giovanni Ferretti, Marenzio, P. A. Bianco, G. B. Boschetti, Ruggiero Giovannelli, Orazio Vecchi, Costanzo Porta and Giovanni Gabrieli – a choice determined by the repertory of the Graz Hofkapelle. The parody technique is reminiscent of Palestrina's in allowing for plentiful use of assonance and alliteration between the texts of the model and the mass. Two settings of Psalm l for soloists, chorus and instruments in particular display parallels to the pieces with instrumental accompaniment in Gabrieli's second set of *Symphoniae sacrae* (1615). The two motets published in 1615 are not modern in style but demonstrate solid compositional technique, harmonic logic and convincing formal structures.

WORKS
Liber primus missarum, 6, 8vv (Graz, 1607)
Orpheus mixtus, liber primus, 8–16vv (Graz, 1607) [motets]; 3 ed. in MAM, xv (1962)
2 motets, 2, 4vv, bc, 1615[13]
2 masses, 13, 16vv; Missa 'Hoc tegitur', 17vv; Missa 'In ecco', 26vv; Crux fidelis, 4vv; 2 Magnificat, 12, 18vv: *A-Wn*; 2 Miserere, 6, 8vv, *KR*
Lamentationes, 12vv; Miserere, 20vv: lost

BIBLIOGRAPHY
H. Federhofer: 'Graz Court Musicians and their Contributions to the *Parnassus musicus Ferdinandaeus* (1615)', *MD*, ix (1955), 179
——: *Musikpflege und Musiker am Grazer Habsburger Hof der Erzherzöge Karl und Ferdinand von Innerösterreich (1564–1619)* (Mainz, 1967), 195ff
H. J. Busch: *Georg Poss, Leben und Werk: ein Beitrag zur Geschichte der deutsch-venezianischen Schule in Österreich am Beginn des 17. Jahrhunderts*, Schriften zur Musik, xvii (Munich, 1972)

HELLMUT FEDERHOFER

Posse (Ger.: 'farce', 'broad comedy'). The noun *Bosse* (from the French *bosse*) or *Posse* denoted in 15th-century usage a decorative figure, especially a grotesque one, or ornamental masonry or sculpture such as a well-head or fountain. By the 16th century the term usually denoted a prank or trick, and by the middle of the 17th the term *Possenspil* (or *Possenspiel*) was in use to denote a type of broad comedy, sometimes specifically including music. *Possenspiel* was commonly used until the beginning of the 19th century (e.g. by Goethe and Schiller), but thereafter the shortened form *Posse* was normal, especially in Vienna, for popular comic entertainments. Apart from the non-theatrical *Possenreisser* (a joker, buffoon), various compound nouns specify types of farce, for example *Charakterposse* (a farce which lays emphasis on the characterization), *Lokalposse* (a farce rich in local allusions and dialect), *Situationsposse* (farce of situation) and *Zauberposse* (a farce in which magic and machinery play an important part; *see* ZAUBEROPER).

In Vienna the term *Posse mit Gesang* became the normal appellation for a farce with songs; much the same phenomenon had earlier been known under a variety of names: *Haupt- und Staats-Aktion, Musica bernesca, Maschinen-Comödie, Opera comique* etc. The borderline between *Posse* and other kinds of comedy, with and without music, cannot be clearly drawn. In the 19th century, however, the term *Posse mit Gesang* was the most widely used to describe a comic play that, while it contained fewer and shorter musical numbers than would have justified the sub-title Singspiel, nevertheless made extensive use of solo songs, with occasional rather rudimentary ensembles, incidental music and (roughly until the early 1840s) a number of short choruses. The leading authors of *Possen*, whether or not they preferred to use more pretentious sub-titles, were Joseph Alois Gleich (1772–1841), Karl Meisl (1775–1853), Adolf Bäuerle (1786–1859), FERDINAND RAIMUND and JOHANN NEPOMUK NESTROY. The most important musicians who furnished them with scores were Wenzel Müller, Ferdinand Kauer, Adolf Müller and Franz von Suppé.

PETER BRANSCOMBE

Posse, Wilhelm (*b* Bromberg, 15 Oct 1852; *d* Berlin, 20 June 1925). German harpist and composer. He received his early training from his father, a flautist and military musician, but taught himself the harp and appeared in 1860 at the Italian Opera in Berlin accompanying Adelina Patti. After a concert tour in southern Russia (1863–4) with his father, he studied at Kullak's academy in Berlin (1864–72) under Louis Grimm. He was solo harpist of the Berlin PO and Opera from 1872 to 1903 and taught at the Berlin Hochschule für Musik from 1890 to 1923, becoming professor in 1910. He was one of the first to adopt the Lyon–Healy harp, demonstrating it in Brunswick in 1895 (it had been seen only once before in Europe, in Amsterdam the previous year).

Liszt considered Posse the greatest harpist after Parish Alvars, consulted him on the harp parts of his later orchestral works and suggested several of his own piano pieces for transcription. The *Angelus* from *Années de pèlerinage*, *Drei Notturnos* (the *Liebesträume*) and *Consolations*, as well as three Chopin studies (op.10 nos.5 and 11, op.25 no.1), the *Fantaisie-impromptu* op.66 and the Mazurka op.24 no.1 were all published in transcriptions for the harp by Posse. Strauss also consulted Posse's *Acht grosse Konzert-Etüden* (Leipzig, n.d.) and the work was adopted by the Paris Conservatoire. Posse's other pedagogical works include *Sechs kleine Stücke*, *Drei Etüden* and *Sechs kleine Etüden*, all published in Leipzig. Posse composed some solo works for harp, but his greatest renown was as a teacher who stressed a full tone and well-grounded technique; his performance style has been carried on by Alexander Sleypuskin, Maria Korchinska and Vera Dulova.

BIBLIOGRAPHY

La Mara [pseud. of M. Lipsius], ed.: *Franz Liszt's Briefe* (Leipzig, 1893–1902), vii, 415; viii, 411

M. G. Scimeca: *L'arpa nella storia* (Bari, 1938), 165

H. J. Zingel: 'Posse, Wilhelm', *MGG*

H. Atterbury: 'Wilhelm Posse of Berlin', *Harp News*, iii/7 (1960–64), 6

A. N. Schirinzi: *L'arpa* (Milan, 1961), 128

ALICE LAWSON ABER

Possenti, Pellegrino (*fl* 1623–8). Italian composer. He lived at one time in Venice but had left by 1625: this is clear from the dedication of his *Accenti pietosi d'Armillo* of that year, and since the dedication is addressed to the mayor of Vicenza he may have been living there. He may have been an amateur composer. He was a fervent admirer of Monteverdi, as he proclaimed in the dedication of his *Canora sampogna*. Even without this testimony one might guess as much from the nature of his best music. The recitative and arioso of the two long laments in his 1623 book and of the two extended ottava settings in the book of 1625 are pliable and expressive, imaginative in word-setting and in the handling of dissonance and varied enough to sustain interest over a long span: this surely is music written under the impact of Monteverdi's – especially his already famous lament of Ariadne (1608) – and it is probably no accident that one of the laments in his 1623 book is a setting of Marino's *Lamento d'Ariana*, which itself had probably been written in response to Monteverdi's setting of Rinuccini's lament. Several of the 22 duets and four trios that comprise the rest of the 1623 volume display equal resource, and the same is true of the eight strophic songs of the 1625 book, a number of which are in the up-to-date Venetian manner: the most interesting is *Da grave incendio oppresso*, which in form and in some details of the melodic shape may have inspired Berti's even finer setting published two years later. The remaining work in this book is perhaps the most important of all, *Ecco Filli, o pastori* (in Fortune, appendix iv, 34ff), called simply 'canzonetta' but in fact a strophic-bass cantata; it is exceptional in that the fourth of the six variations is in triple time and thus shows the influence of the variation suite. This is an influence that recurs in Possenti's volume of instrumental music, which consists of 18 one-movement sonatas. They include tremolos and a very early use of the directions 'da capo' and 'sino al fine'.

WORKS

Canora sampogna composta di sette canne musicali, prima canna, dalla quale escono madrigali, 2, 3vv, canzonette, 2vv, Li sospiri d'Ergasto e Il lamento d'Ariana del Cavalier Marino, 1–3vv, [bc] (Venice, 1623, inc.; 2/1628)

Accenti pietosi d'Armillo, canzonette & arie, 1v, [bc] (Venice, 1625)

Concentus armonici, a 2–4 (Venice, 1628)

2 madrigals, 2vv, 4vv, both with bc, in 1624[11]

BIBLIOGRAPHY

L. Torchi: 'La musica istrumentale in Italia nei secoli XVI, XVII e XVIII', *RMI*, iv (1897), 621

N. Fortune: *Italian Secular Song from 1600 to 1635: the Origins and Development of Accompanied Monody* (diss., U. of Cambridge, 1954)

J. Racek: *Stilprobleme der italienischen Monodie* (Prague, 1965), 13, 101, 191, 197, 209

D. Arnold and N. Fortune, eds.: *The Monteverdi Companion* (London, 1968), 203

NIGEL FORTUNE

Post, Joseph (Mozart) (*b* Sydney, 10 April 1906; *d* Broadbeach, Queensland, 27 Dec 1972). Australian conductor and administrator. His second name indicates his family's regard for music. He was among the first students at the New South Wales Conservatorium of Music, where he graduated with teaching and performing diplomas for both the piano and the oboe; at the age of 21 he joined the teaching staff. In 1933 he became conductor at the Australian Broadcasting Commission and remained with the organization (with two intermissions) until 1965, when he was appointed assistant director of music. In that year he became director of his former school, the NSW Conservatorium. In 1966 he received the OBE for services to music.

Post's major interest, which few Australian musicians of his generation shared, was opera. He was associated with visiting Italian opera companies (1932–4), became musical director of the National Theatre Company in Melbourne (1947–54) and of the Elizabethan Theatre Trust, the forerunner of a national Australian Opera. He conducted a concert version of *Der Rosenkavalier* (1956) and during the Adelaide Festival of Arts (1964) a stage performance of Walton's *Troilus and Cressida*. He was also an excellent conductor of operas specially produced for television.

WERNER GALLUSSER

Postel, Christian Heinrich (*b* Freiburg, nr. Stade, 11 Oct 1658; *d* Hamburg, 22 March 1705). German poet, librettist and lawyer. His father was a Protestant minister and writer who left Freiburg with his family in 1676 to become pastor at the Heilige Geist-Kirche, Hamburg. His friendship with Gerhard Schott, founder and first director of the Hamburg Opera, undoubtedly led to Postel's later association with the Opera. He received his early education from his father and later attended the Johanneum school, Hamburg. In 1680 he went to Leipzig University to study law but was forced by an outbreak of the plague to move to Rostock University, from which he received a licentiate in law in 1683. He then undertook extended educational tours of Holland, Flanders, England and France, which enabled him to cultivate a lifelong interest in languages and literature. In about 1688, if not sooner, he returned to Hamburg and began an illustrious career as a lawyer. In 1700 he spent the summer in Switzerland and Italy; at this time he became acquainted with the Arcadian movement in Italy, and in Milan he met L. A. Muratori, an exponent of Italian neo-classicism.

Postel was the most important and prolific writer of librettos for the Hamburg Opera towards the end of the 17th century. He wrote texts for the major composers there, including Conradi, Förtsch, Keiser and Kusser; he did so only while the Opera was directed by Schott, upon whose death in 1702 he apparently severed his association with the Opera. His librettos are fine examples of dramatic poetry, generally patterned on conventional Italian models and full of somewhat complex German Baroque imagery. He naturally based his operatic dramas on the standard Baroque concept of alternating affective states. However, many of them, such as *Die schöne und getreue Ariadne* (set by Conradi), do not present simply a pastiche of contrasting emotional statements; rather, within the limitations of a fairly stereotyped plot, the characters are permitted distinctive, dramatic development as personalities. He was frequently criticized in the 19th century for being a typical representative of the Second Silesian School which was overfond of Marinism, but this view is not substantiated by his texts. He was a transitional figure in German libretto writing, standing between such writers as LUCAS VON BOSTEL and FRIEDRICH CHRISTIAN BRESSAND on the one hand and BARTHOLD FEIND on the other. As such he strove for a simpler poetic language, abandoned the previously favoured Alexandrine metre for the simpler, more effective iambic in recitatives, and successfully varied his metres in the arias for affective purposes. His poetry is highly expressive and colourful in the Baroque sense but without an excessive amount of bombast. His intensely dramatic works were the perfect vehicles for the music of composers such as Conradi, Förtsch and Keiser. As all his librettos survive (in D-

WRtl), it is to be hoped that a long-needed comprehensive study of his poetry and of his contribution to German Baroque opera will be undertaken.

BIBLIOGRAPHY
N. Wilckens: *Hamburgischer Ehrentempel* (Hamburg, 1770)
W. Flemming: *Die Oper*, Deutsche Literatur: Sammlung literarischer Kunst- und Kulturdenkmäler in Entwicklungsreihen, ser. 13*b*: *Das Barockdrama*, v (Leipzig, 1933)
H. C. Wolff: *Die Barockoper in Hamburg* (Wolfenbüttel, 1957)
D. I. Lindberg: *Literary Aspects of German Baroque Opera: History, Theory, and Practice* (diss., U. of California, Los Angeles, 1964)
GEORGE J. BUELOW

Posthius, Johannes (*b* Germersheim, Pfalz, 1537; *d* Mosbach, Baden, 24 June 1597). German poet. He was a royal physician at Heidelberg. His literary importance derives from the *Sonntags-Evangelia gesangsweise componirt, samt etlichen Psalmen und Kirchengesängen von D. Martin Luther und anderen Gottseligen Männern* (Amberg, 1608), for which he wrote the texts. It was reprinted as *Psalmen und geistliche Lieder . . . auff vier Stimmen* in Neustadt an der Haardt in 1619. The work which became widely known in southern Germany belongs to the genre established by Martin Agricola and Nicolaus Herman of lied-form translations of the Sunday Gospel texts. Posthius apparently used the Genevan metrical psalm as a model.

BIBLIOGRAPHY
P. Wackernagel: *Das deutsche Kirchenlied . . . bis zu Anfang des XVII. Jahrhunderts* (Leipzig, 1864–77), i, 645f [text]; v, 300ff [examples]
R. von Liliencron: *Liturgisch-musikalische Geschichte der evangelischen Gottesdienste von 1523 bis 1700* (Schleswig, 1893)
G. Pietzsch: *Quellen und Forschungen zur Geschichte der Musik am kurpfälzischen Hof zu Heidelberg bis 1622* (Wiesbaden, 1963)
WALTER BLANKENBURG

Post horn (Fr. *cornet de poste*; Ger. *Posthorn*; It. *cornetta di postiglione*). A small brass instrument used in the past by postillions and guards on mail coaches to announce the arrivals and departures and to call attention en route. Small arcuate horns were so used in France, England and Germany up to the early 17th century when instruments began to be constructed in one very small coil barely 7 cm across with a fundamental about *bb'*. In Johann Beer's *Concerto a 4* (MS, *D-SWl*) it plays brisk figures on this note and its octave, similar to the references of Bach (*Capriccio sopra la lontananza*, 1704) and Telemann ('Postillons', *Musique de table*, 1733; borrowed by Handel in *Belshazzar*). Later in the 18th century German post horns were made with three turns and calls rose to the 6th or 8th harmonic, still including the octave leap, now at a slower tempo. The character of these calls is perhaps best known through those works of Mozart which require a horn player to take up the post horn: the Serenade K320, and the *Deutsche Tanz* K605 no.3, which calls for a post horn in Bb and a second, lower instrument in F. In *Werkstäte der heutigen Künste* (Leipzig, 1764), J. Samuel Halle mentioned three-coil post horns built in different keys: C and A (equivalent to modern cornet pitches) in Saxony, but higher in Prussia.

By 1820 such post horns were procurable with crooks and tuning-slide for band music solos, and their use had spread to France (see fig.1). The pitch most used in Germany was F, but C was employed by Beethoven in *Deutsche Tanz* WoO8 no.12, and Eb was quoted by Schubert in *Winterreise*. The post horn is allotted a short solo (in F) in Spohr's *Notturno* op.34 for military band. Although some models were shaped like a trumpet, circular form remained the favourite; its continued

1. Post horn by Courtois frères, Paris, c1820 (Conservatoire National Supérieur de Musique, Paris)

2. Post horn (keyed), German, c1830 (Leslie Lindsey Mason Collection, Museum of Fine Arts, Boston, Mass.)

3. Post horn (valved), German, 2nd half of the 19th century (Leslie Lindsey Mason Collection, Museum of Fine Arts, Boston, Mass.)

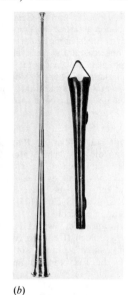

(a)   (b)

4. (a) 'The Mail Arriving at Temple Bar': engraving (published, 1834); (b) coach horn (with case) by Köhler & Son, London, c1870 (Spencer Collection, Brighton Museum)

appearance today as a post office emblem in so many European countries testifies to the breadth of its former use. From about 1825 post horns were also made with keys (see fig.2) to increase their ability to play tunes, and by the mid-19th century in both France and Germany with valves, as required in Mahler's Third Symphony (see fig.3). In Germany they might instead have a finger-hole ('transposing hole') placed three-quarters of the way along the tube from the mouthpiece and uncovered to raise the harmonic series from F to B♭. A diatonic 6th or more is available by opening and closing the hole; the horn held in one hand can be sounded only in the old manner.

In England a straight-built post horn came into use during the early 19th century and was adopted as the regulation horn for Royal Mail coaches (even if the guard liked to enliven the journey with tunes on the keyed bugle). This straight horn is of brass, 70 to 80 cm long, in A or A♭ an octave above the German post horn in A and sounded only up to the 4th or 5th harmonic. It is still made, and is used in performances of Koenig's famous Post Horn Galop (1844); it has a sliding joint midway along the tube for tuning. Koenig, Jullien's star cornettist, had come from Paris and preferred the continental pitches an octave lower for their better compass. He also recommended cornet beginners to practise on this 'proper' post horn.

Another characteristic English instrument is the coach horn, used exclusively with four-in-hand teams. It is also straight but is made of copper and differs from the post horn in having a conical bore and a narrow funnel-shaped bell which recalls the medieval buisine (see fig.4). It is also longer; the standard length was 90 cm, but it tended to become longer still, and John Augustus Köhler's 'heavy mail horn' measured 115 cm. The coach horn sounds the same series of notes as an army bugle, the actual pitch depending upon its length (a 107 cm horn is in D). The coach horn was still in use up to 1914 on the London to Oxford mail, which was conveyed by road on Sundays. Today only imitation

coach horns are made as hotel decorations. A number of tutors remain which give the calls sounded on the post horn and the coach horn, such as (John A.) Turner's Complete Tutor for the Coach Horn, Post or Tandem Horn, Bugle and Cavalry Trumpet (London, 1898), which is perhaps the best known though it is erratic and unsatisfactory over the matter of the post horn calls.

BIBLIOGRAPHY
E. Teuchert and E. W. Haupt: Musik-Instrumentenkunde in Wort und Bild (Leipzig, 1911)
A. B. Shone: 'Coaching Calls', MT, xcii (1951), 256
H. Walter: 'Das Posthornsignal bei Haydn und anderen Komponisten des 18. Jahrhunderts', Haydn-Studien, iv (1976), 21
                                              ANTHONY C. BAINES

Postlude (Lat. *postludium*; Ger. *Nachspiel*). A move-ment or section of a movement concluding a com-position (especially for organ), hence the equivalent of a coda, conclusion or epilogue. Hindemith's *Ludus tonalis* for piano (1943) ends with a postludium which is an exact reversion and inversion of the opening prae-ludium. Specifically the term is sometimes given to the organ piece, frequently improvised, which is played at the end of a service during the exit of the con-gregation, i.e. the concluding voluntary.

                                              MICHAEL TILMOUTH

Postnikova, Victoria [Viktoria] **(Valentinovna)** (*b* Moscow, 12 Jan 1944). Soviet pianist. Born into a family of musicians, she entered the Moscow Central Music School at the age of six and studied with E. B. Musaelian. In 1962 she joined Yakov Fliyer's class at the Moscow Conservatory. While still a student (she graduated, after the start of her international career, in June 1967), she attained laureate status at the 1965 Warsaw International Chopin Competition. She shared second prize in the 1966 Leeds Piano Competition, but several critics wrote that in musical sensitivity and maturity she far surpassed the other prizewinners. At her London début – on 31 July 1967, at the Proms, in

Chopin's E minor Concerto – and at subsequent London appearances, there was no doubt of her remarkable talents; in particular, a performance of Schumann's Concerto, at the Festival Hall in October that year, demonstrated vividly the communicative freshness and spontaneity of her phrasing (carried at times to the point of waywardness) and the luminous delicacy of her tone. She married the conductor Rozhdestvensky in 1969.

MAX LOPPERT

Poštolka, Milan (*b* Prague, 29 Sept 1932). Czech musicologist. While attending the Prague English Grammar School he studied the piano with Ilona Štěpánová-Kurzová and music theory with František Spilka. At Prague University he studied musicology with Očadlik and Sychra (1951–6), passing the state examination in musicology (1956); he took the CSc (1966) and doctorate (1967) with a dissertation on the life and work of Kozeluch. (He prepared the catalogues of Kozeluch's and Vanhal's printed works for *RISM*.) After working for the Encyclopedic Institute of the Czechoslovak Academy of Sciences in Prague, he joined the music department of the Prague National Museum, as a research assistant (1958–66), a research fellow (1966–72), senior research fellow (from 1972) and deputy director of the department (1964–72), where he is also curator of the collection of 18th- to 20th-century musicians' letters and other writings. In 1966 he was appointed lecturer in Baroque and Classical music history at Prague University; in 1972 he became director of a research team working on Czech 17th- and 18th-century music history at the Czechoslovak Academy of Sciences. In his research Poštolka has been primarily concerned with Czech 17th- and 18th-century music history, in particular the emigration of Czech musicians, and with musical semantics in music psychology. In his historical works, based on a thorough, comprehensive study of the source material, a logically thought-out assessment invariably leads to sound results.

WRITINGS
'Leopold Koželuh, ein Zeitgenosse Mozarts', *Internationale Mozartkonferenz: Praha 1956*, 135
'Joseph Haydn und Leopold Koželuh', *Internationale Konferenz zum Andenken Joseph Haydns: Budapest 1959*, 109
Joseph Haydn a naše hudba 18. století [Joseph Haydn and Czech music in the 18th century] (Prague, 1961)
'Hudební památky Morawtzovy sbírky' [Musical memorials of Morawetz], *Časopis Národního musea*, cxxxi (1962), 89
'Liszts Beziehungen zu Böhmen im Spiegel der Korrespondenz', *Franz Liszt in Böhmen*, ed. A. Buchner (Prague, 1962), 186; see also *SM*, v (1963), 255
Leopold Koželuh: život a dílo [Leopold Kozeluch: life and work] (diss., U. of Prague, 1967; Prague, 1964) [with thematic catalogue]
with F. Knobloch and J. Srnec: 'Musical Experience as Interpersonal Process: a Contribution to the Semantics of Music', *Psychiatry*, xxvii (Washington, DC, 1964), 259
'Bohemika 18. století v Maďarsku' [Bohemica of the 18th century in Hungary], *HV*, ii (1965), 683; iii (1966), 151
'Thematisches Verzeichnis der Sinfonien Pavel Vranický's', *MMC*, no.20 (1967), 101
'Die "Odae Sacrae" des Campanus und des Tranoscius: ein Vergleich', *MMC*, nos.21–3 (1970), 107–52
'Libreta strahovské hudební sbírky', *MMC*, nos.25–6 (1973), 79–149
'Musikerbriefe in der Musikabteilung des Nationalmuseums in Prag', *Beiträge zur Musikdokumentation: Franz Grasberger zum 60. Geburtstag* (Tutzing, 1975), 363 [with catalogue]
'18th-century Bohemia: Styles and Currents in Sacred Music'; 'Two Little Known Pupils of Haydn and Two Unknown Haydn Sources from Bohemia', *Haydn Conference: Washington 1975*
Joseph Haydn (in preparation)
Articles on 18th-century Czech composers in *Příruční slovník naučný* (Prague, 1962–7), *MGG* and *Grove 6* [incl. 'Kozeluch, Leopold', 'Vanhal, Johann Baptist']

EDITIONS
L. Kozeluch: 5 Sonáty (Prague, 1959) [with D. Šetková-Zahn]; *Tre sinfonie*, MAB, lxxii (1969)
with O. Pulkert: *Písně* (Prague, 1961–2) [songs by Dušek, Voříšek, Reicha and others]

RUTH BLUME

Poston, Elizabeth (*b* nr. Walkern, Herts., 24 Oct 1905). English composer, writer and pianist. She received her musical education at the RAM and on the Continent, and also studied the piano with Harold Samuel. She emerged as a composer in 1925, when seven of her songs were published (her popular early setting of *Sweet Suffolk Owl* was one of these). Her first work to be broadcast, from the BBC at Savoy Hill, was an RAM prize-winning violin sonata. In 1928 she published five songs in a more personal style. From 1930 to 1939 most of her time was spent abroad where, among other studies, she collected folksong. On returning to England she joined the BBC's music staff, and her war service was thus a period of intensive broadcasting which included the direction of music in the European Service. She resigned in 1945, but after a period in the USA and Canada returned to the BBC in 1947 to broadcast and advise for a year at the inception of the Third Programme. She was elected president of the Society of Women Musicians (1955–61).

Poston has distinguished herself in a wide field of musical activities. In collaboration with David Jones, Terence Tiller, Dylan Thomas, C. S. Lewis and others, she has produced many important scores for radio productions. Outstanding among her film scores is that for *Howards End* (1970); she lives in the house which was the subject of E. M. Forster's novel. Her extended choral works include *An English Kalendar* (1969) for female voices and harp and *An English Day Book* (1971) for mixed voices and piano, both commissioned by the Farnham Festival. A *Concertino da camera for Ancient Instruments* (1950) and a Trio (1958) for flute, clarinet (or viola) and harp (or piano) are her most significant chamber works.

Although her output is modest, Poston has evolved a personal style which stems from the neo-classical tradition and lays great emphasis on clean craftsmanship and melodic fluency. She has won particular respect as the editor of folksong, carol and hymn collections. Her association with Peter Warlock has made her a unique authority on the subject of the man and his music. Her publishers include Boosey & Hawkes, Oxford University Press, Novello, Chester and Elkin.

EDITIONS
Penguin Book of American Folksongs (Harmondsworth, 1964)
Penguin Book of Christmas Carols (Harmondsworth, 1965)
The Cambridge Hymnal (London, 1967)
Second Penguin Book of Christmas Carols (Harmondsworth, 1970)
The Faber Book of French Folksongs (London, 1972)

MICHAEL HURD

Potenzierung (Ger.). Term used by A. Lorenz to denote the building up of larger-scale structures hierarchically out of smaller-scale structural units; *see* ANALYSIS, §§II, 6; III, 4.

Pothier, Joseph (*b* Bouzemont, Vosges, 7 Dec 1835; *d* Conques, Belgium, 8 Dec 1923). French scholar and editor of plainchant. He was ordained priest on 18 December 1858 and took his vows as a Benedictine monk at Solesmes on 1 November 1860. He became prior of Ligugé in 1893 and abbot at St Wandrille in 1898. In

1860 Guéranger sent him as an assistant to Jausions to help him prepare a new edition of liturgical chant books for use in the monastic community. After Jausions' death Pothier completed and published the whole work himself, bringing out the first part, *Mélodies grégoriennes d'après la tradition* in 1880. This publication contributed greatly to the success of the teaching of the Solesmes school (Congress of Arezzo, 1882). In 1883, the second part gave rise to a long controversy with the supporters of the 'Medicean' edition (Pustet, Regensburg), at that time enjoying a special privilege given by the Holy See. When in 1904 Pope Pius X decided to publish an official 'Vatican' edition, Pothier headed the commission. From 1905 he was in complete charge up to 1913. His editions produced at Solesmes between 1883 and 1895 served as a basis for the following official books: *Kyriale* and *Missa pro defunctis* (1905); *Cantus missae* – those contained in the *Missale romanum* – (1907); *Graduale* (1908); *Officium pro defunctis* (1909); *Cantorinus seu toni communes* (1911–12); *Antiphonale* (1912, 2/1919).

Pothier is justly considered to have initiated the revival of Gregorian chant. His editions were so much better than earlier ones that many considered them definitive. Although their musical notation based on that of 14th-century MSS and designed by Pothier himself allows one to respect most of the traditional groupings of neumes, the square and awkward shape of the notes fails to convey the suppleness of the chant and the differentiation in rhythmic values: bars and 'white spaces' are inadequate to represent such variety. The melodic line is presented better, although it is often necessary to correct the use of semitones to restore the modal character. On the other hand the principles put forward in *Mélodies grégoriennes* based on Latin word accentuation well suits the practice of chant, which Guéranger had instituted on the founding of the Solesmes monastery. These principles, together with careful study of the neumes themselves, were able to give an adequate basis for the understanding of authentic plainsong performance. He contributed articles to the *Revue du chant grégorien*.

EDITIONS

Les mélodies grégoriennes d'après la tradition (Tournai, 1880, 2/1890)
Liber gradualis (Tournai, 1883, 2/1895)
Processionale monasticum (Solesmes, 1888)
Variae preces (Solesmes, 1888)
Liber antiphonarius (Solesmes, 1891)
Liber responsorialis (Solesmes, 1895)
Cantus mariales (Paris, 1903, 3/1924)

BIBLIOGRAPHY

R. Biron: *Bibliographie des Bénédictins de la congrégation de France* (Paris, 1906), 138ff
L. David: *Dom Joseph Pothier, abbé de Saint-Wandrille, et la restauration grégorienne* (St Wandrille, 1943)
P. Combe: *Histoire de la restauration du chant grégorien d'après des documents inédits* (Solesmes, 1969)

EUGÈNE CARDINE

Pothodion. *See* PROSODION.

Potier [Potiers], **Matthias.** *See* POTTIER, MATTHIAS.

Potiron, Henri (*b* Rezé-lès-Nantes, Loire-Atlantique, 13 Sept 1882; *d* Roye, Somme, 12 April 1972). French composer and musicologist. For more than 50 years he was music director at Sacré-Coeur de Montmartre and taught Gregorian modes and accompaniment at the Institut Grégorien in Paris from its foundation in 1923. He wrote nine polyphonic masses (some based on

Gregorian modes), numerous motets, pieces for organ, and organ accompaniments for parish use to all the plainsong repertory. In 1954 he took his doctorate at the Sorbonne with a thesis on Boethius in which he sought to clear Boethius of the accusations made against him by Westphal and many others of misunderstanding Greek musical theory and causing subsequent confusion among medieval theorists.

WRITINGS

Cours d'accompagnement du chant grégorien (Paris, 1925, rev. 2/1927; Eng. trans., 1933)
Leçons pratiques d'accompagnement du chant grégorien (Tournai, 1938; Eng. trans., 1949)
L'origine des modes grégoriens (Tournai, 1948)
L'analyse modale du chant grégorien (Tournai, 1948)
Les modes grecs antiques (Tournai, 1950)
La notation grecque et Boèce: petite histoire de la notation antique (Tournai, 1951)
Petit traité de contrepoint (Tournai, 1951)
La composition des modes grégoriens (Tournai, 1953)
Boèce, théoricien de la musique grecque (diss., U. of Paris, Sorbonne, 1954; Paris, 1954)
L'accompagnement du chant grégorien suivant les types modaux (Paris, 1960)

Articles in *Monographies grégoriennes, Revue grégorienne, Etudes grégoriennes*

EUGÈNE CARDINE

Potpourri (Fr.). From its original application to a jar, literally a 'rotten pot', in which were kept miscellaneous spices, vegetables and so on, the term came to be applied to a musical composition which was a similar hotchpotch of tunes from a pre-existing source or sources. During the 18th century the term was used in France for collections of songs which, with a thematic link, were sometimes given stage presentation. Later the term was used for instrumental collections, such as the *Potpourry français*, which was a collection of originally unconnected dance pieces issued by the publisher Bouïn. Still in the 18th century, the term was used by the publisher Breitkopf for a collection of new compositions by various composers, and around the end of the century it came to be applied to a string of melodies from an opera or operas, as in the *Potpourri tiré des airs de 'Zauberflöte', 'Domjuan' et 'Figaro' pour le piano-forte* by Josef Gelinek.

Others to produce potpourris were Daniel Steibelt, Czerny (e.g. *Potpourri brillant sur les motifs le plus favoris de l'opéra 'Faust' de Spohr* op.218) and Diabelli (*Potpourri tiré des oeuvres de Beethoven*). Often a potpourri included a set of variations on a selected theme. However, the term is extended only in a somewhat derogatory sense to the technically more ambitious and artistically more meritorious fantasies exemplified by many works of Czerny, the opera transcriptions and fantasies of Liszt, or the *Carmen* fantasy of Busoni. In just such a sense Chopin himself described his Fantasy on Polish Airs op.13 as a 'potpourri' in one of his letters. In England the term was apparently first used by J. B. Cramer, but subsequently the expressions 'selection' or 'fantasia' were more commonly used – the latter term, misleadingly, even for straightforward selections from operas or operettas. The term 'potpourri' is often used to indicate that a piece in a more precisely defined form is based on themes which are not original, for example an overture based on themes from the work it precedes (*see* MEDLEY).

During the 19th century selections from currently popular stage works were always in demand, and the task of producing them was often hack-work for the amateur or impoverished musician. The potpourri became a standard constituent of 19th-century orchestral and military band concerts of light music and often denoted more than a straightforward selection. By using themes familiar to their audiences the bandmasters were able to retain their attention for as much as 30 to 45 minutes and to exploit the allusions of particular pieces for programmatic purposes and for orchestral display. Such works are the elder Johann Strauss's *Der unzusammenhängende Zusammenhang* ('The incohesive cohesion', 1829) and most notably his *Ein Strauss von Strauss* ('A bouquet of Strauss', 1832). The latter work, introduced to Britain (as *Le bouquet des dames*) during Queen Victoria's coronation season, performed by Jullien at his promenade concerts and revived in Vienna as late as 1873, used music by Beethoven, Auber, Hérold, Bellini, Haydn and others, and included such effects as 'Chinese chimes, sledge party, post horn, cracking of whips, description of an earthquake, coronation procession, firing of cannon, ringing of bells, and shouts of thousands of spectators'. Other potpourris used links such as the chronological, as in C. M. Ziehrer's *Wiens Tanzmusik seit fünfzig Jahren* and the alphabetical, as in the *ABC-Potpourri* of Karl Komzák (1850–1905), in which each letter is used in turn to represent a different composer. In Germany the term potpourri is used for popular selections to the present day. *See also* QUODLIBET.

BIBLIOGRAPHY

M. Schönherr and K. Reinöhl: *Johann Strauss Vater* (London, 1954)

H. Engel: 'Potpourri', *MGG*

G. Birkner, ed.: 'Pot-pourry français' *Tanzmeister-Weisen des 18tes Jahrhundert* (Mainz, 1967)

ANDREW LAMB

Pott, August Friedrich (*b* Nordheim, 7 Nov 1806; *d* Graz, 27 Aug 1883). German violinist and composer. He studied the violin with Karl Kiesewetter in Hanover and joined the court orchestra in February 1822. His patron, the Duke of Cambridge, then sent him to Kassel for a year to study the violin with Spohr and composition with Hauptmann; in January 1827 he was made *Kammermusicus* at Hanover. His first tour (1829) took him to western and southern Germany, and possibly to Paris, but it was his Scandinavian tour, in 1831, which established him as a virtuoso; he dedicated his concerto *Les adieux de Copenhague* to King Frederick VI of Denmark, who named him professor of music at the University of Copenhagen. In February 1832 he gave a concert at Oldenburg, which won him the position of Hofkapellmeister there. He performed in Dresden, Berlin and Vienna (where a critic praised both his playing and his instrument, a Stradivari) in 1834, and two years later in Vienna and Salzburg, where he gave the first of his concerts to raise funds for a Mozart memorial. In London he played Lipinski's Concerto in B minor at the Philharmonic Society (21 May 1838); a critic for the *Musical World* wrote enthusiastically of the extraordinary power of his tone, his grandiose execution and the purity of his style.

The highpoint of Pott's career was the unveiling ceremony for the Mozart memorial in Salzburg in September 1842, the result of six years of tireless efforts to raise money for the project, through benefit concerts of his own and by other artists and from the proceeds of a Mozart album which he had edited. In later years his concert appearances were infrequent. Difficulties with orchestral and administrative personnel during the

political unrest of 1848 resulted in a two-year suspension of concerts at Oldenburg. After a reconciliation he resumed his duties until pensioned in 1861.

Pott's wife, born Aloyse Winkler von Foracest, was a gifted musician who studied the piano with Czerny and composition with Gyrowetz.

BIBLIOGRAPHY

G. Linnemann: 'A. Pott', *Musikgeschichte der Stadt Oldenburg* (Oldenburg, 1956), 189–227 [with complete list of works]

ALBERT MELL

Potter. English family of musical instrument makers and musicians.

(1) **Richard Potter** (*b* Mitcham, Surrey, baptized 21 April 1726; *d* London, buried Mitcham, 3 Dec 1806). Flute maker. He first set up shop about 1745 at Green Dragon Court, Foster Lane, Cheapside, subsequently moving to 5 Pemberton Row (then New Street) near Fleet Street about 1764. The latter address was kept as the family home and the business was transferred nearby to 5 Johnson's Court some time before 1786.

In 1785 Potter applied for a patent on an improved flute, a high-quality instrument with the latest features. The enrolled drawing shows four keys: D♯, F♮, G♯ and B♮, all in general use at the time. Potter's improvement lay not in the addition of these keys but in their construction, the closing being effected by rounded valves of soft metal instead of the usual soft leather. The holes were lined with silver tubes and the keys closed on the countersunk outer ends. Another innovation was the use of a metal tuning-slide with an attractive outer tube of wood, a slide or 'register' at the extreme end of the foot joint, and a screw-cork in the head joint with a projecting, graduating ivory pin. When these were made to correspond the instrument was in tune. Another advance often found on the Potter flutes was the addition of about 5 cm to the length to produce *c♯'* and *c♮'* at the lower end of the range with one or two foot keys. The earliest extant flute with a foot key is by Richard Potter; it dates from 1776 and is in the Chicago Historical Society collection, having once belonged to a bandsman in Cornwallis's army at Yorktown.

(2) **Richard Huddleston Potter** (*b* London, 10 Dec 1755; *d* London, buried 3 June 1821). Flautist, violist and teacher, the eldest son of (1) Richard Potter. Though he was apprenticed to his father, there is no evidence that he worked in the flute-making business. He taught the piano and was organist of St Bride's, Fleet Street, from 1785. He played the flute in the Handel festivals in Westminster Abbey and also at Crosdale's and other private concerts, and he was listed in Doane's directory as an oboist. He was among the elder professors that formed the 30 original members of the Philharmonic Society in 1813, and played the viola in its orchestra; he often audited the society's accounts and was its treasurer in 1818 and 1819. On 28 January 1783 he married Charlotte Baumgarten, daughter of the bassoonist Samuel Christian Baumgarten.

(3) **William Henry Potter** (*b* London, 7 Aug 1760; *d* Bromley, 19 March 1848). Flute maker, son of (1) Richard Potter. After completing his apprenticeship under his father he joined the firm which was first listed as Potter & Son about 1801. After his father's death he continued the business, giving up the 5 Johnson's Court address after 1817 and working from the family home until he retired to Bromley some time in the 1830s. In 1808 he was granted a patent for a device for the flute keys which produced an effect called the 'glide' which

enjoyed only temporary popularity. He continued in the style of manufacture begun by his father, though he sometimes omitted the inset into the tone holes. Generally, the Potters were esteemed for their craftsmanship. Their instruments were considered expensive and, like those of other high-quality builders, were often faked ('bastard Potters').

(4) (Philip) Cipriani (Hambly) [Hambley] **Potter** (*b* London, 3 Oct 1792; *d* London, 26 Sept 1871). Composer, pianist and teacher, son of (2) Richard Huddleston Potter and the most celebrated member of the family. Cipriani was the family name of his godmother, who was said to have been a sister of the painter Giovanni Baptista Cipriani, himself an intimate member of musical circles through his friendship with J. C. Bach and C. F. Abel. The name Philip was taken from a son of the painter, Edward Robert Philip Cipriani, a clerk in the Treasury through the support of Lord Lansdowne. 'Cip' or 'Little Chip', as he was known throughout his life because of his small size, was widely read, was a mathematician and spoke four languages. After musical instruction from his father, he was given over to a series of distinguished masters, and first studied counterpoint with Thomas Attwood. He worked with Crotch in 1808–9 and may have had lessons with John Wall Callcott. Potter, however, attributed his greatest advances to a five-year period of lessons from May 1805 with Joseph Woelfl, under whom he perfected his technique, memorized Bach's *Das wohltemperirte Clavier*, and learnt the principles of form in instrumental music which were then little known in England. On attaining his majority he was named an associate of the Philharmonic Society, and he became a member on 29 May 1815. In 1816 he was honoured with the commission of two works by the society, noteworthy since so few works by English composers were played at those concerts. Potter made his début as a pianist at the Philharmonic Concerts at the performance of his Sextet for piano, flute and strings op.11 on 29 April 1816.

Despite acclaim as a pianist, the lack of success of the commissioned works caused Potter to go to the Continent to study composition. He left England towards the end of 1817 and was drawn to Vienna by the presence of Beethoven, whose music he had admired despite discouragement from it by his elders. Although he carried letters of introduction, warnings that Beethoven was mad caused Potter to delay approaching him until urged to do so by the piano maker Streicher. Potter was well received at what was an especially troubled time for Beethoven, and he made a good impression which Beethoven conveyed to Ries in a letter of 5 May 1818: 'Botter [sic] has visited me a few times, he seems to be a good fellow and has talent for composition'. At Beethoven's suggestion Potter studied counterpoint with Aloys Förster, and Beethoven advised Potter on his scores. After about eight months in Vienna and other Austrian and German cities and a sojourn of similar length in Italy, Potter returned to England in the spring of 1819. From that time until 1836 he appeared often as a soloist, giving the English premières of many Mozart concertos, in which he embellished the printed solo part, and of the First, Third and Fourth Concertos by Beethoven. His piano playing was much admired for its brilliance, though it was not powerful, doubtless because of his small size. He appeared as a conductor of the Philharmonic Concerts until 1844 and won considerable acclaim, always conducting standing, and

without a baton. He served as a director of the society a number of times, though it was said that his opinions were often passed over in favour of those of less knowledgeable men.

In 1822 Potter was made the first piano teacher for the male division of the newly founded Academy of Music and he continued to teach the piano during his long association with the school. When Bochsa was dismissed in 1827 he was made the director of orchestra practice; it was his custom to insist that all male students play in the orchestra even if they could manage only a few notes. In 1832, on the dismissal of Crotch, Potter became the principal, a position he held until 1859 during a trying period of domination by the president, Lord Burghersh. Potter's influence as a teacher was great; a man of ready wit and generosity, he was much admired and loved.

Potter's own concerts, given almost yearly between 1828 and 1846, were among the finest of the season because of his insistence on a 'full band' when others would skimp, and the substantial music played. In the later concerts Potter included only a single work of his own, perhaps evidence of a lessening interest in his own music. He was elected to the Royal Society of Musicians in 1817, and served several times as an officer and as accompanist or conductor. He was also a member of the Society of British Musicians from its founding in 1834, and its concerts included performances of his compositions. He was a member of the Bach Society from its inception in 1849 and served as musical director of the Madrigal Society from July 1854 until his death.

Potter was said to have begun composing in his 14th year, though nothing exists before the two commissioned scores and several published works of 1816. After 1837 he almost ceased composing, though he revised a number of works including the E minor Overture and the Symphony no.8 in E♭ (for which he wrote a new slow movement). It is to be regretted that he gave up composition so early since the last symphonies, the G major String Quartet, the Sextet for flute, clarinet, viola, cello, double bass and piano and the three overtures to plays by Shakespeare are masterly. Duties at the academy, the lack of a ready outlet for performances, and his too great admiration for the music of others (he was among the first to admire warmly the music of Schumann and, in his last years, Brahms) caused him to give up writing; he turned instead to the preparation of editions of the music of others, including the complete piano music of Mozart which Coventry began to publish in 1836 and which was reissued by Novello in 1851.

With the exception of a few negligible songs and one substantial cantata *Medora e Corrado*, for the libretto of which he paid his impoverished friend Gabriele Rossetti a generous sum, Potter confined himself to instrumental music. His greatest achievement is the nine extant symphonies, the numbering and dating of which suggest missing works in the genre. All except one, are in Bb, are in four movements of moderate length. While they are uniform in instrumentation, there are many telling moments in the orchestration including numerous solo passages for wind and, in one instance, the use of a violin solo for colour. All have a forward drive, harmonic ingenuity and playful use of dissonance, and much counterpoint and strict imitation. Indeed, Wagner, who carefully conducted Potter's G minor Symphony (known variously as no.2 and no.10) in 1855, referred to the composer as an 'amiable elderly contrapuntist'. There are eight concerted works, the five earliest of which are less formal preparations for the composition of the three extant piano concertos. Again, the numbering and dating of these latter, together with a remark of Potter's pupil G. A. Macfarren, suggest that Potter actually wrote four. The Concerto in E♭ begins unusually with a movement in 6/4 metre. Other works of interest are the Piano Sonata in D op.3; the 'Enigma' Variations op.5, a preposterous satiric composition 'in the style of five eminent artists'; the Three Grand Trios op.12, the last of which is dedicated to Beethoven; the Horn Sonata op.13; and the Studies in All the Major and Minor Keys op.19, which include expressive as well as virtuoso pieces.

WORKS

Printed works published in London, MSS of unpublished works in *GB-Lbm*, unless otherwise stated

ORCHESTRAL

9 syms.: no.1, g, 1819, rev. 1826; B♭, 1821, rev. 1839, *Lam*; no.6, c, 1826; no.7, F, 1826; no.8, E♭, 1828, rev. 1846, *Lam*; no.10, g, 1832; 'no.2', D, 1833; c, 1834; 'no.4', D, 1834, arr. pf 4 hands as op.29 (c1851); at least 1 other, lost
For pf, orch: Introduction and Rondo, 'alla militaire', 1827; Bravura Variations, on a theme by Rossini, 1829; Ricercata, 'on a favorite French theme', 1830, op.24 (1835); at least 3 concs., d ('no.2'), 1832, E♭, 1833, E, 1835
Other: Ov., e, 1815, rev. 1848; Duo concertant, pf, vn, orch, op.14 (Bonn, ?1827); Concertante, on 'Les folies d'Espagne', vn, vc, db, pf, orch, 1829; Ov. 'Antony and Cleopatra', 1835; Ov. 'Cymbeline', 1836; Ov. 'The Tempest', 1837; March, 1854, *Lsm*

CHAMBER

3 Grand Trios, pf trio, E♭, D, b♭, op.12 (Bonn, c1824), no.1 arr. cl, bn, pf; Sonata di bravura, hn/bn/vc, pf, op.13 (Bonn, c1824); Sextet, fl, str qt, pf, op.11 (Bonn, ?1827); Sextet, E♭, fl, cl, va, vc, db, pf, 1836; Str Qt, G, *Lam*

PIANO
(solo except where stated)

op.
— Three Waltzes in German Style (1816)
— Recueil de valzers (1816)
— Trio, pf 5 hands (?1816)
— Andante 'La placidità' (Bonn, 1817)
1 Sonata, C (1818)
2 Variations, on Mozart's 'Fin ch'han dal vino' (Leipzig, 1818) [pubd without op.no. (1816)]
3 Sonata, D (Leipzig, 1818)
4 Sonata, e (Leipzig, 1818)
— Polonaise (Vienna, 1818)
— Rondeau (Leipzig, 1818)
— Thirteen Variations, on 'Bekränzt mit Laub' (Bonn, c1818)
— Rondeau brillant [no.1] (Vienna, ?1818)
— Fantasia, March and Trio (Vienna, ?1820)
6 Grand duo, pf 4 hands (Vienna, ?1821)
— Fantasia on 'Chi dice mal d'amore' (c1822)
— Mes rêveries (c1823)
— Le départ de Vienne, in *Harmonicon*, ii (1824), 81
15 Pezzi di bravura (Bonn, c1824)
16 Andante and Allegretto 'Il compiacente' (?1824)
17 The Parade, military divertimento (?c1824)
8 Impromptu, on the Scottish air 'Auld Robin Gray' (1825)
5 'Enigma' Variations (c1825)
9 Three Toccatas (Leipzig, ?1825) [no.1 pubd without op. no. (?1816); no.2 pubd without op. no. (Leipzig, 1818)]
19 Studies in All the Major and Minor Keys (1826)
20 Introduction and Rondo giocoso (?1826)
— Introduction and Variations, with coda and cadenza (Leipzig, ?1826)
— Allegro di bravura 'Il vispo e la fuggita' (before 1827)
21 Rondeau brillant no.2 (1827)
— Fugue, E, 3 pf, 1827, *Lam*
27 Fantasia and Fugue, 2 pf, c, 1818, *Lam* (?Bonn, c1830)
22 Fifty-four Impromptus (1832)
— Celebrated Octave Lesson (1834–48)
— Introduction and Variations, on 'Alice Gray' (before 1837)
— Impromptu, B♭, 1841
28 Trois amusements (?1848–51)
— Impromptu, D, in J. Benedict: *Select Practice for the Piano Forte* (?1850)

23 Introduction and Rondoletto (?1851)
— Impromptu, G/g, ?1852, *Lam*
— Eine Grille, 1868, *Lam*, facs. in *RAM Magazine* (1901), no.1
— Rondo scherzando 'Il sollievo' (n.d.)

Transcrs., arrs. and edns. of works by Mozart, Dragonetti, Beethoven and others

VOCAL

When evening draws her curtain round, 1v, pf (c1817)
No More, canzonet, 1v, pf, in *Harmonicon*, iii (1825), 21
Medora e Corrado (G. Rossetti), cantata, solo vv, chorus, orch, 1830, *Lam*
Wer unter eines Mädchens Hand, B, small orch, 1847, lost except for pp.1–3

WRITINGS

'Companion to the Orchestra', *Musical World*, iii/33 (1836), 97; iv/41 (1836), 1; iv/52 (1837), 177; v/61 (1837), 129
'Recollections of Beethoven, with Remarks on his Style', *Musical World*, i/7 (1836), 101; repr. in *MT*, x (1861), 150

BIBLIOGRAPHY

G. A. Macfarren: 'Cipriani Potter: his Life and Work', *PMA*, x (1884), 41
——: 'Cipriani Potter', *RAM Magazine* (1901), no.1, p.5
W. H. Holmes: *Notes upon Notes* (London, 1885)
C. B. Oldman: 'Cipriani Potter's Edition of Mozart's Pianoforte Works', *Festschrift Otto Erich Deutsch* (Kassel, 1963), 120
P. H. Peter: *The Life and Work of Cipriani Potter (1792–1871)* (diss., Northwestern U., 1972)

PHILIP H. PETER

Potter, A(rchibald) J(ames) (*b* Belfast, 22 Sept 1918; *d* Greystones, 5 July 1980). Irish composer. At the choir school of All Saints, Margaret Street, London, he studied under W. S. Vale (1929–33). Between 1933 and 1936 he studied at Clifton College, Bristol, under D. G. A. Fox, and his studies were completed at the Royal College of Music, London, where he was a pupil of Vaughan Williams from 1936 to 1938. He received his DMus from Dublin University in 1953. Awarded Carolan Prizes by Radio Éireann in 1951 and 1952, in 1968 he received the Jacobs Award for an outstanding contribution to Irish radio. He was appointed professor of composition at the Royal Irish Academy of Music, Dublin, in 1955, and was also active as a music journalist and broadcaster.

Potter was one of the most prolific of contemporary Irish composers; apart from his original music, he made many Irish folksong arrangements for broadcasting. All of his music is characterized by an effective, if conventional, use of instruments, designed to give clear expression to the melodic content. His uncomplicated style recalls Vaughan Williams in its use of block harmonies. The music is often broadly romantic, as, for example, in the sweeping melodic line of parts of the Variations on a Popular Tune, the idealistic ending of *Patrick* (the first Irish television opera) and the dramatic conflict of the *Sinfonia de profundis*. The character themes of the ballet *Careless Love* exemplify his facility in producing simple, but striking, melodic ideas ranging from modal motifs to 12-note themes in some of the ballet scores. These 12-note themes are not used serially, but as an overlay to music that is harmonically conventional. Of his many concertante works, the Elegy is one of the most moving. His *Concerto da chiesa* shows quite a different approach: the material grows largely from a chorale melody, and a Baroque-like style is used. The result is a work of much excitement and spontaneity. Most striking of his later works is the *Sinfonia de profundis*, first performed in 1969 in Dublin. Its conventional style and great emotional impact have made it one of the most popular of Irish orchestral works.

WORKS
(selective list)

ORCHESTRAL

Ov. to a Kitchen Comedy, 1950; Rhapsody under a High Sky, 1950; Overture to an Irish Occasion, 1951; Conc. da chiesa, pf, orch, 1952; Variations on a Popular Tune, 1955; Phantasmoraggia, 1956; Elegy, cl, harp, str, 1956; Caoine [Dirge], 1956; Fox and Geese, 1957; Finnegans Wake, 1957; Fantasia Gaelach, 1957; Under the Lilacs, 1958; Fantasie concertante, vn, vc, orch, 1959; The Scatterin, 1959; Capriccio, 1962; Irish Rhapsody, 1963; Concertino, 1963; Caprice, vc, orch, 1964; Hunter's Holiday, 1965
Sound the Sackbuts, 3 trbn, orch, 1965; Fantasie, cl, orch, 1965; Spanish Point, gui, orch, 1965; Concertino, tpt, orch, 1966; Concerto for Orchestra, 1966; Rapsóid deire lae [Rhapsody at the End of the Day], 1966; Dance Fantasie, 1967; Concertino benino, tpt, orch, 1967; Concertino, fl, orch, 1967; Binneadán Béal, harmonica, orch, 1967; Sinfonia de profundis, 1968; Planxty Louis, 1969; Fonn agus port [Melody and dance-tune], 1969; March 'The Phoenix', band, 1969; Máirseail an chriadóra [The potter's march], 1969

OTHER WORKS

Patrick (television opera, D. McDonagh), 1963
Ballets: Careless Love, 1961; Gamble no Gamble, 1962; Caitlín bhocht [Poor Cathleen], 1963; Full Moon for the Bride, 1964
Choral works incl. Missa brevis, SSATB, semichorus, 1949; 3 Songs of Hilaire Belloc, SATB, 1951; The Classiad (L. McMaster), SSA, orch, 1964; Lúireach Pháraig [St Patrick's breastplate], TTBB, orch, 1966; Hail Mary, A, T, SSATBB, orch, 1966; 10 Epigrams by Hilaire Belloc, SATB, 1967; Stabat Mater, 1973
Chamber music incl. 2 Fantasies, str qt, 1937, 1938; A Full House of Harpers, 2 harps, 12 Irish harps, 1963
Songs incl. 6 Songs from the Glens of Antrim (M. O'Neill), 1949; Ode to Dives (Belloc), 1956; Song Suite (S. Bell), 1963
Folksong arrangements, incidental music for radio and television
Principal publisher: Segway

BIBLIOGRAPHY

Catalogue of Contemporary Irish Composers (Dublin, 1968)
K. Fadlu-Deen: *Contemporary Music in Ireland* (diss., University College, Dublin, 1968)
C. Acton: 'Interview with A. J. Potter', *Éire-Ireland*, v/2 (St Paul, Minn., 1970), 115

SEÓIRSE BODLEY

Potter, John (*b* c1734; *d* after 1813). English writer and composer. He is said to have received a classical education, after which he studied mathematics and medicine. In 1761 he delivered the Gresham lectures on music, but was not appointed professor. The substance of these lectures was printed in Potter's *Observations on the Present State of Music and Musicians* (London, 1762), a work of considerable interest for its early proposal to establish a national academy for the training of professional musicians. The *Critical Review* responded favourably to the proposal but unfavourably to the rest of the book.

From about 1764 Potter was connected with Jonathan Tyers, proprietor of Vauxhall Gardens, whom he had met through David Garrick. Garrick's patronage of Potter ended in 1766, when he discovered that Potter was the author of anonymous reviews in the *Public Ledger* critical of the management of Drury Lane Theatre. Potter published a 'state of the case' of their controversy, a verse satire, *The Hobby Horse* (London, 1766). His reviews were collected and reprinted 'by a society of gentlemen, independent of managerial influence' (i.e. Potter himself) as *The Theatrical Review* (London, 1772). Potter feared that his controversy with Garrick would jeopardize his position at Vauxhall, but his dismissal in 1777 seems to have been on other grounds. Until then, however, Potter acted as assistant to the Tyers family and wrote music for their entertainments. Each year until about 1774, Potter published collections of his songs for Vauxhall. While at Vauxhall, he also advised the musician R. J. S. Stevens, the son of a friend and schoolfellow.

In 1765 and 1777 respectively Potter provided the texts for William Yates's serenata, *The Choice of Apollo*,

and J. A. Fisher's oratorio, *Providence*. A quarrel arose between Potter and Fisher over the merits and demerits of the music, and Potter published another verse satire, directed at Fisher, *Musick in Mourning* (London, 1780). In 1780 Potter left for the Continent, presumably because of financial difficulties. He had become a member of the Royal Society of Musicians in 1771 but was expelled probably about 1779 for not paying his annual subscription. Potter returned to England about 1784 and practised medicine; his chief support, however, seems to have been literature. Besides songs for Vauxhall, various single songs appeared in the *Gentleman's Magazine*, *The Spinnet or Musical Miscellany* and *Polyhymnia: or, The Complete Song Book*, the last of which Potter edited.

BIBLIOGRAPHY

J. Potter and D. Garrick: correspondence, Victoria and Albert Museum, London
R. J. S. Stevens: *Recollections of the Life of Richard John Samuel Stevens both Professional and Domestic* (MS, *GB-Cpl*)
European Magazine, vii (1785), 38, 283
The London Stage, 1660–1800 (Carbondale, Ill., 1960–68)

JAMIE CROY KASSLER

Pottgiesser, Heinrich Wilhelm Theodor (*b* Voerde, nr. Schwelm, 1766; *d* Elberfeld, 1829). German physician and flute designer. He studied at Dortmund, Halle and Berlin, and in 1787 qualified as a physician and surgeon in Duisburg. In addition to practising as a physician in Lünen (1788), Mülheim (1790) and Elberfeld (1795) he was interested in astronomical and musical matters and devised some important improvements for the flute.

WRITINGS

'Ueber die Fehler der bisherigen Flöten', *AMZ*, v (1802–3), cols.609, 625, 644, 673
'Nachtrag zu der Abhandlung: "Ueber die Fehler der Flöte, nebst einem Vorschlage etc." ', *AMZ*, xxvi (1824), col.265

KARL VENTZKE

Pottier [Potier, Potiers, Pottiers], **Matthias** [Mathieu] (*b* c1553; *d* Bruges, 4 Dec 1629). Flemish composer and priest. After being a chorister in St Donaas, Bruges, he entered the Bruges seminary on 23 June 1571 and was ordained priest on 16 June 1576. On 12 January 1577 he became *kapelmeester* of St Salvator's Cathedral, where only four months later (22 May 1577) he was appointed a prebendary canon. From 1584 to 1586 he stayed at St Omer and later became *kapelmeester* at Dunkirk. Early in January 1592 he succeeded Pevernage as *kapelmeester* at the Cathedral of Our Lady, Antwerp. He resigned from this post on 17 May 1615 on being made canon at St Donaas, Bruges (an appointment he took up on 2 September 1615); he was buried there.

Two collections edited by him were published by Phalèse: *Selectissimarum missarum flores* (*RISM* 1599[1]), containing a five-part mass by Pottier himself, and *Missae septem ex praestantissimis Italiae musicis octonis vocibus* (Antwerp, 1611).

BIBLIOGRAPHY

FétisB ('Pollier')
J. F. Foppens: *Compendium chronologicum episcoporum brugensium* (Bruges, 1731), 111
J. Gaillard: *Inscriptions funéraires et monumentales de la Flandre occidentale*, i (Bruges, 1861), 166; ii (1866), 250
D. van de Casteele: *Maîtres de chant et organistes de Saint-Donatien et de Saint-Sauveur à Bruges* (Bruges, 1870), 55
E. vander Straeten: *La musique aux Pays-Bas avant le XIXe siècle*, ii (Brussels, 1872/R1969), 275; iii (1875/R1969), 5
A. Goovaerts: *Histoire et bibliographie de la typographie musicale dans les Pays-Bas* (Antwerp, 1880/R1963)
L. de Burbure: *Notes* (MSS, *B-Aa*)

A. C. de Schrevel: *Histoire du séminaire de Bruges* (Bruges, 1895)
R. Vannes: *Dictionnaire des musiciens* (*compositeurs*) (Brussels, 1947)
A. Dewitte: 'De kapittelschool van de collegiale Sint-Salvator te Brugge 1516–1594', *Handelingen van het genootschap voor geschiedenis gesticht onder de benaming Société d'émulation te Brugge*, civ (1967), 25, 47, 57

GODELIEVE SPIESSENS

Potúček, Jura (*b* Bratislava, 20 June 1923). Slovak music bibliographer. After graduating from business school in Bratislava (1941) he worked in business (1941–53) and concurrently studied in the church music department of the Bratislava Conservatory (1947–9). Later he studied librarianship at Bratislava University (1959–64) while working as a librarian and bibliographer in the Musicology Institute of the Slovak Academy of Sciences (1954–74). In 1975 he became director of the music archive of the Slovak Music Foundation. His main areas of study have been music bibliography, lexicography and documentation (of which he is the leading Slovak exponent), and Slovak musical life and foreign musical contacts. Of his two standard bibliographies, the first (1952) lists Slovak printed music and literature about musicians active in Slovakia to 1949; the second (1955), its continuation, lists literary and theoretical writings on Slovak music. He has contributed the Slovak sections to the *Annual Bibliography of European Ethnomusicology* (Bratislava, 1967–) and wrote some 400 articles for the *Československý hudební slovník* (Prague, 1963–6); his major publication, the product of 25 years' work, was a biblical concordance (1970).

WRITINGS
Súpis slovenských hudobnin a literatúry o hudobníkoch [A catalogue of Slovak printed music and literature on musicians] (Bratislava, 1952, 2/1967)
'Bibliografia tlačených diel J. L. Bellu' [A bibliography of the printed works of J. L. Bella], *Hudobnovedný zborník*, i (1953), 132
Súpis slovenských hudobnoteoretických prac [A catalogue of Slovak writings on music] (Bratislava, 1955)
'Doplnky k hudobnej bibliografii' [Additions to music bibliography], *Hudobnovedné štúdie*, iii (1959), 205–75
'Súpis literatúry o súčasnej slovenskej hudbe' [List of writings on contemporary Slovak music], *K problematike súčasnej hudby* (Bratislava, 1963), 193
ed.: *Dokumenty k dejinám slovenskej hudby* [Documents on the history of Slovak music] (Bratislava, 1964–75)
'Slovenská hudobnofolkloristicá literatúra 1823–1961' [Slovak folk music literature], *Hudobnovedné štúdie*, vii (1966), 201
Súpis slovenských nenotovaných spevníkov 1585–1965 [Catalogue of Slovak songbooks without music] (Martin, 1967)
'Slovenské hudobniny v 1. tretine 19. storočia' [Slovak printed music in the first third of the 19th century], *Musicologica slovaca*, ii (1970), 181
'Hudobná priloha Hlahol z rokov 1862–1863' [The musical supplement Hlahol from 1862 to 1863], *Musicologica slovaca*, iii (1971), 227
J. Potúček: autobibliografia 1945–1970 (Bratislava, 1971)
with M. Svobodová: 'Music Journals in Slovakia 1871–1970', *FAM*, xxi (1974), 32
'Bibliografia slowackiego piśmienstwa o Chopine w wieku XX' [A bibliography of 20th-century Slovak writings about Chopin], *Rocznik chopinowski*, ix (1975), 179

Poueigh, (Marie Octave Géraud) Jean (*b* Toulouse, 24 Feb 1876; *d* Olivet, Loiret, 14 Oct 1958). French critic and composer. While a law student in 1895, Poueigh studied harmony privately with Hugounenc of the Toulouse Conservatory. In 1898 he left for Paris where he worked with Caussade and Lenepveu, and attended Fauré's classes at the Conservatoire without actually enrolling there. D'Indy, too, taught him between 1898 and 1902. From 1907 to 1909 he edited the folksong journal *Les chansons de France* founded by Bordes. Under the pseudonym Octave Séré, Poueigh contributed articles to *Ere nouvelle*, *Mercure musical*, *Mercure de France*, *Musica*, *Revue musicale S.I.M.*, and *Courrier musical* and wrote *Musiciens français d'aujourd'hui*, a collection of biographical and bibliographical essays on 27 French composers (including himself).

WORKS
Le meneur de louves, opera, n.d.; *Perkain*, opera, 1931
Fünn, ballet, 1900–02; *Frivolant*, ballet, 1914
Cantatas, folksong arrangements, instrumental pieces

Principal publishers: Choudens, Rouart

WRITINGS
Musiciens français d'aujourd'hui (Paris, 1911, rev. 2/1921)
Chansons populaires des Pyrénées françaises: traditions, moeurs, usages, i (Paris, 1926)

BIBLIOGRAPHY
S. Wallon: 'Poueigh, Marie Octave Gérard Jean', *MGG*

ELAINE BRODY

Pougin [Paroisse-Pougin], **(François-Auguste-)Arthur** (*b* Châteauroux, 6 Aug 1834; *d* Paris, 8 Aug 1921). French writer on music and violinist. As the son of itinerant actors he had few educational advantages, and his literary attainments were mainly due to his own efforts. He was educated in music at the Paris Conservatoire, where he studied the violin with Alard and harmony with Reber. A violinist in theatres from the age of 13, he became conductor at the Théâtre Beaumarchais in 1855, played in the Musard orchestra, and at the Opéra-Comique (1860–63). From 1856 to 1859 he was assistant conductor and répétiteur at the Folies-Nouvelles.

Pougin began as a writer on music with biographical articles in the *Revue et gazette musicale*. Early in his career he gave up teaching and playing at the Opéra-Comique in order to carry out his literary projects. Besides his frequent contributions to *Le ménestrel*, *La France musicale*, *L'art musical*, *Le théâtre*, *Chronique musicale* and other music periodicals, he edited the music articles in the Larousse *Dictionnaire universel* and was successively musical feuilletonist to *Le soir*, *La tribune*, *L'événement* and, from 1878, to the *Journal officiel*, where he succeeded Eugène Gautier. In 1885 he became chief editor of *Le ménestrel*.

With his early series of six biographies of French musicians of the second half of the 18th century (1861–4), Pougin was, with Ernest Thoinan, one of the pioneers of French musicology, although he was unable to make use of the unpublished documents now accessible. His main interest was always the musical theatre and his most important single work, on the life of Verdi, was published in Italian (1881) with additions by Folchetto (Jacopo Caponi) and illustrations by A. Formis. He later produced a revision in French of his own and Folchetto's versions (1886) but, being written some 20 years before Verdi's death, it is incomplete. He also edited the supplement to Fétis's *Biographie universelle* (1878–80) and a revision of Clément and Larousse's *Dictionnaire lyrique* (1898–1904). He wrote a comic opera *Le cabaret de Ramponneau* and an operetta *Perrina*, both unpublished. In 1905 he was decorated with the order of the Crown of Italy.

WRITINGS
André Campra (Paris, 1861, 2/1881) [orig. serialized in *Revue et gazette musicale*, xxviii (1861)]
Gresnick (Paris, 1862) [orig. serialized in *Revue et gazette musicale*, xxix (1862)]
Dezèdes (Paris, 1862) [orig. serialized in *Revue et gazette musicale*, xxix (1862)]
Floquet (Paris, 1863) [orig. serialized in *Revue et gazette musicale*, xxx (1863)]
Martini (Paris, 1864) [orig. serialized in *Revue et gazette musicale*, xxxi

(1864)]
Devienne (Paris, 1864) [orig. serialized in *Revue et gazette musicale*, xxxi (1864)]
Musiciens français du XVIIIᵉ siècle (Paris, 1864) [preceding 6 essays]
Meyerbeer: notes biographiques (Paris, 1864)
F. Halévy, écrivain (Paris, 1865)
Almanach de la musique (Paris, 1866–8)
William-Vincent Wallace: étude biographique et critique (Paris, 1866)
De la littérature musicale en France (Paris, 1867)
De la situation des compositeurs de musique et de l'avenir de l'art musical en France (Paris, 1867)
Bellini: sa vie, ses oeuvres (Paris, 1868)
Léon Kreutzer (Paris, 1868)
Albert Grisar: étude artistique (Paris, 1870)
Rossini: notes, impressions, souvenirs, commentaires (Paris, 1871)
A propos de l'exécution du 'Messie' de Haendel (Paris, 1873)
Auber: ses commencements, les origines de sa carrière (Paris, 1873)
Boïeldieu: sa vie, ses oeuvres, son caractère, sa correspondance (Paris, 1875)
Figures d'opéra comique: Madame Dugazon, Elleviou, les Gavaudan (Paris, 1875)
Adolphe Adam: sa vie, sa carrière, ses mémoires artistiques (Paris, 1876)
Rameau: essai sur sa vie et ses oeuvres (Paris, 1876)
Les vrais créateurs de l'opéra français: Perrin et Cambert (Paris, 1881)
Verdi: vita aneddotica (Milan, 1881 [annotated by Folchetto, pseud. of J. Caponi]; Fr. orig., 1886; Eng. trans., 1887)
Molière et l'opéra comique (Paris, 1882)
Viotti et l'école moderne de violon (Paris, 1888) [with catalogue of works]
Méhul: sa vie, son génie, son caractère (Paris, 1889, 2/1893)
L'opéra comique pendant la Révolution (Paris, 1891)
Acteurs et actrices d'autrefois: histoire anecdotique des théâtres de Paris depuis trois cents ans (Paris, 1896)
Essai historique sur la musique en Russie (Paris, 1897, 2/1904; Eng. trans., 1915)
La jeunesse de Mme Desbordes-Valmore (Paris, 1898)
Jean-Jacques Rousseau musicien (Paris, 1901)
La Comédie-Française et la Révolution (Paris, 1902)
Un ténor de l'Opéra au XVIIIᵉ siècle: Pierre Jélyotte (Paris, 1905)
Hérold: biographie critique (Paris, 1906)
Monsigny et son temps: l'Opéra-Comique et la Comédie-Italienne (Paris, 1908)
Marie Malibran: histoire d'une cantatrice (Paris, 1911; Eng. trans., 1911)
Madame Favart: étude théâtrale, 1727–1772 (Paris, 1912)
Marietta Alboni (Paris, 1912)
Massenet (Paris, 1914)
Un directeur d'Opéra au XVIIIᵉ siècle (A. P. J. de Vismes): l'Opéra sous l'ancien régime: l'Opéra sous la Révolution (Paris, 1914)
Une cantatrice 'amie' de Napoléon: Giuseppina Grassini 1773–1850 (Paris, 1920)
Le violon: les violonistes et la musique de violon du XVIᵉ au XVIIIᵉ siècle (Paris, 1924)

NORBERT DUFOURCQ

Pougnet, Jean (*b* Mauritius, 20 July 1907; *d* Ferring, Sussex, 14 July 1968). English violinist of Anglo-French parentage. He studied the violin with Rowsby Woof at the RAM, London, from 1918 to 1925, gaining many scholarships and prizes. Throughout his career he pursued the double life of a concert violinist and a leader of light music orchestras. His tone, never very large, was sweet and his style elegant, so that he excelled in chamber music (he played in trios with Angus Morrison and Anthony Pini, and in the London String Trio). Pougnet led the LPO (1942–5) and the BBC Palm Court Orchestra after World War II, but had to retire because of ill-health. His performances of the concertos of Bloch, Elgar and Delius are still remembered.

BIBLIOGRAPHY
J. Creighton: *Discopaedia of the Violin, 1889–1971* (Toronto, 1974)
WATSON FORBES

Pouishnov [Puishnov, Pouishnoff], **Lev** (*b* Odessa, 11 Oct 1891; *d* London, 28 May 1959). Ukrainian pianist. He studied at Kiev, and at the St Petersburg Conservatory, winning the gold medal and the Rubinstein Prize. From 1913 to 1917 he taught at Tbilisi; for the greater part of his life, however, he devoted his main energies to public performance. His first recital was given at the age of five; in 1911 he made his first concert tour with Leopold Auer. His London début in 1912 was followed in 1923 by his first appearance in the USA. In 1934 he toured Australasia and the East and he was the first professional pianist to give concerts in Iran. Pouishnov, who settled in London in the 1920s, was particularly well known for his interpretations of the Romantic piano literature.

RONALD KINLOCH ANDERSON

Poul, Anthony. *See* POOLE, ANTHONY.

Poulenc, Francis (Jean Marcel) (*b* Paris, 7 Jan 1899; *d* Paris, 30 Jan 1963). French composer and pianist. During the first half of his career the simplicity and directness of his writing led many critics away from any thought of him as a serious composer. Gradually since World War II it has become clear that the absence from his music of linguistic complexity in no way argues a corresponding absence of feeling or technique; and that while, in the field of French religious music, he disputes supremacy with Messiaen, in that of the *mélodie* he is the most distinguished master since the death of Fauré.

1. Life. 2. Piano music. 3. Chamber music. 4. Orchestral music. 5. Music for the stage. 6. Choral music. 7. Songs and other works for solo voice. 8. Summary.

1. LIFE. Born into a wealthy family of pharmaceutical manufacturers, Poulenc received a thorough academic training at the Lycée Condorcet and made his first musical contacts largely through his mother, herself an excellent pianist. Her brother, 'Oncle Papoum', gave his nephew an early familiarity with the less prim manifestations of Parisian theatrical life. He began learning the piano with his mother at the age of five, knew some of Mallarmé's poetry by heart when he was ten, and at 14 shared in the general amazement at *The Rite of Spring*. Two years later he began taking piano lessons from Ricardo Viñes, the friend and interpreter of Debussy and Ravel; and in 1917 and 1918 met Auric, Honegger, Milhaud and Satie, to whom he dedicated his first published composition, the *Rapsodie nègre*. He went on composing during his statutory period of military service (1918–21) but began to feel the need of some formal instruction. He tried both Paul Vidal and Ravel without getting beyond the first encounter and had already been dubbed a member of Les Six before finding a sympathetic teacher in Koechlin, with whom he studied from 1921 to 1924. By mutual consent Poulenc's involvement with counterpoint went no further than Bach chorales, but it is typical of his open-mindedness that, with Milhaud, he should have travelled to Vienna in 1921 to talk to Schoenberg and his pupils, and to Italy the following year to visit Casella. His reputation spread beyond Paris with Dyagilev's triumphant production of *Les biches* in 1924, although six years earlier the *Trois mouvements perpétuels* had enjoyed a vogue among the amateur pianists of Europe. However, over the next ten years natural ebullience was barely enough to conceal uncertainties of aesthetic and of technique. He reached a new maturity around 1935, precipitated by his reacquaintance with the singer Pierre Bernac and by the death of his friend Pierre-Octave Ferroud in a car accident. This tragedy, and a consequent visit to Notre Dame de Rocamadour, restored him to his paternal Roman Catholic faith, of which the first fruits were the *Litanies à la vierge noire* (1936).

During the war Poulenc remained in occupied France and demonstrated his 'resistance' by musical means, dedicating his Violin Sonata to the memory of Lorca and setting poems by Aragon and Eluard ('*C*' and *Figure humaine*), all during the black year of 1943. After the war he was concerned to resume his place in the new musical environment of Paris, defending the 'classical' Stravinsky against the 'Messiaenistes' and achieving a brilliant success with his first opera *Les mamelles de Tirésias* in 1947. The following year he and Bernac received an enthusiastic welcome on the first of several visits to the USA. In autumn 1954 trouble over the rights of *Dialogues des carmélites* put him under great nervous strain, but he made a complete recovery and in 1960 made another successful tour of North America with Denise Duval. He was working on a fourth opera based on Cocteau's *La machine infernale* when he died suddenly of a heart attack, some three weeks after his 64th birthday.

Between 1945 and his death he spent most of his time composing, accompanying Bernac and making records, of the music of Satie and Chabrier as well as his own. He never married but depended greatly on the support and advice of his friends, particularly Auric. He lived either in Paris or in his spacious country house Le Grand Coteau, at Noizay in Touraine; here, resisting the attempts of the villagers to make him mayor, he sought his ideal mode of life, 'une solitude coupée de visites d'amis'.

2. PIANO MUSIC. From Viñes Poulenc learnt a clear but colourful style of piano playing, based on a subtle use of the sustaining pedal, and in his own piano music he was insistent on there being 'beaucoup de pédale'. In his earlier pieces such a style gives body to the often arrogantly 'popular' tunes that abound, softening the ostinatos in the Sonata for piano duet (1918) and the quasi-Alberti bass in *Trois mouvements perpétuels* (1918). In *Promenades* (1921), written for Artur Rubinstein, a tougher harmonic language appears based on 4ths and 7ths, and the texture is thicker than in any of his other works for the instrument.

The bulk of his piano music dates from the early 1930s, a time when he was reappraising the materials of his art. He later admitted that his reliance on past formulae (long pedal notes, arpeggios, repeated chords) was not always free of routine and that in this regard his familiarity with the piano could be a hindrance; his most inventive piano writing, he claimed, was to be found in his song accompaniments. Even so, a piece such as the Second Nocturne, *Bal de jeunes filles*, of 1933 is charming enough not to need supporting with claims of originality; it is in the manner of Chabrier but still unmistakably Poulenc. His own favourite pieces were the 15 *Improvisations*, ranging in date from 1932 to 1959 and in dedicatee from Marguerite Long to Edith Piaf. This confirms that the piano was not a vehicle for his deepest thoughts; he called the *Thème varié* (1951) an 'oeuvre sérieuse' and included a retrograde version of the theme in the coda to show that he was up with the latest serial ideas, but it is hardly the best of him. Inexplicably, he loathed what many would regard as his best piano work, *Les soirées de Nazelles* (1930–36), a suite of eight variations enclosed by a 'Préambule' and a 'Final' which might be described as the fusion of eclectic ideas in a glow of friendship and nostalgia. Ex.1 is typical of the suite and of Poulenc in the use of the dominant 13th, the

Ex.1 *Les soirées de Nazelles* III

(Presto ♩ = 104)

Cédez, à peine

Au mouvement

etc

pause after the end of the first phrase, the barely disguised sequence of 4ths in the bass and the circuitous route taken in bars 3–5 between the closely related keys of E minor and G major, a characteristically impertinent blend of the preceding and succeeding harmonic areas.

3. CHAMBER MUSIC. Poulenc's output in this genre falls conveniently into three chronological groups. The four works of the first period (1918–26), each under ten minutes in length, are acidly witty, garnishing plain triadic and scalic themes with spicy dissonances. No doubt they share something of the spirit of the 18th-century divertissement, but the proprieties of harmonic and syntactical behaviour are not unfailingly observed. In the Sonata for clarinet and bassoon (1922) there are passages of jazz and bitonality, often leading to a mischievous cadence; in the Sonata for horn, trumpet and trombone (1922) the opening trumpet theme is one of Poulenc's 'folksongs', clearly a relation of many in *Les biches*, which needs the correction of only three 'wrong' notes in the first four bars for it to conform with 18th-century harmonic practice – as it were, Pergolesi with his wig awry. The central group comprises the Sextet for piano and wind (1932–9), one of his most popular works, and the Sonatas for violin and piano (1942–3) and for cello and piano (1948). Poulenc admitted to being unhappy writing for solo strings and had written and destroyed two violin sonatas (1919 and 1924) before the surviving example, dedicated to Ginette Neveu. A string quartet (1947) ended up in the Paris sewers, Poulenc rescuing three themes from it for his Sinfonietta. He was unable to negotiate the great gulf fixed between strings and the human voice, essentially his inspiration, and many sections of the Cello Sonata would sound better on a bassoon. The final three sonatas for woodwind, like the last three chamber works of Debussy, form part of a set that Poulenc did not live to complete. They have already entered their appropriate repertories by virtue both of their technical expertise and of their profound beauties. In the Sonata for oboe and piano (1962), Poulenc's last important work, dedicated to the memory of Prokofiev, his usual fast–slow–fast pattern of movements is altered to slow–fast–slow, in which the final 'déploration' fulfils both affective and instrumental requirements.

4. ORCHESTRAL MUSIC. The best of Poulenc's orchestral music dates from before World War II. The two postwar productions – the Sinfonietta (1947), commis-

Francis Poulenc

sioned to celebrate the first anniversary of the BBC Third Programme, and the Piano Concerto (1949), written for himself to play – demonstrate the dangers of sectional, 'surrealist' techniques of composition: they are garrulous, uncoordinated and unmemorable. The first of the pre-war works was the *Concert champêtre* (1927–8), inspired by the playing and character of Wanda Landowska. The countryside evoked is nothing more savage than a Parisian suburb and the fanfares in the last movement emanate from nothing more exotic than the bugles in the barracks of Vincennes, but for all that it is an enchanting work. Finer still are the two concertos commissioned by the Princess Edmond de Polignac, for two pianos (1932) and for organ, strings and timpani (1938). The earlier of the two, first performed by the composer and his friend Jacques Février, has no aim beyond entertainment, in which it succeeds completely; written in the period of 'back to X' initiated by Stravinsky, its models range from Balinese gamelan at the end of the first movement to Mozart at the beginning of the second, but as in the case of the Sonata for horn, trumpet and trombone, Poulenc's 18th-century style affords a number of calculated inelegances before branching off in a quite different direction. The Organ Concerto is altogether more ambivalent in emotional character. Recognizably a product of 'Janus-Poulenc', it leads the solo instrument from Bach's G minor Fantasia to the fairground and back again. Poulenc placed it 'on the outskirts' of his religious music.

5. MUSIC FOR THE STAGE. A number of Poulenc's dramatic works deal with the inconsequential, if not the downright absurd. His first effort was incidental music to *Le gendarme incompris* (1921), a nonsense play by Cocteau and Raymond Radiguet in which the policeman delivers himself of lines by Mallarmé; despite Milhaud's

enthusiasm, Poulenc withdrew the material soon afterwards. A month later, in June 1921, came the première of the ballet *Les mariés de la Tour Eiffel* incorporating two movements by Poulenc. This joint production by all the members of Les Six except Durey achieved no more than a brief *succès de scandale*. By contrast, *Les biches*, first performed in 1924, is still one of his best-known works. The absence of deep, or even shallow, symbolism was only accentuated by a tiny passage of mock-Wagnerian brass, complete with emotive minor 9ths, in a score which is above all clear and tuneful, matching the white and pale blue of Marie Laurencin's décor. Apart from the ballet *Les animaux modèles* (1940–41), based on eight fables from La Fontaine, Poulenc was occupied for the next 20 years by film music and incidental music to plays, until in 1944 he happened to reread Apollinaire's *Les mamelles de Tirésias* which he then set as his first opera. Described as an *opéra bouffe*, it includes a variety of scenes both inconsequential and absurd, but Apollinaire's underlying message, the need for more French babies and a corresponding distaste for incipient 'women's lib', has been a national preoccupation since Napoleon's time. The musical tone can therefore be either noble or popular, often both as in ex.2. Poulenc himself pointed out that the vocal phrase

Ex.2 *Les mamelles de Tirésias*, Act 1 scene v

(where Thérèse/Tirésias is reading in a newspaper of the death of two characters in a duel) would not disgrace a religious work; the three introductory bars confirm the continuity of Stravinsky's influence. *Les mamelles* is emphatically not an operetta – knowing winks, like smut, were anathema to Poulenc – but accommodates a host of musical techniques, lyrical solos, patter duets, chorales, falsetto lines for tenor and bass babies and, like Denise Duval whose Folies Bergères training was invaluable in the title role, it succeeds in being both funny and beautiful.

Poulenc's last two operas treat serious subjects seriously. In *Dialogues des carmélites* (1953–6) he charted the delicate vagaries of character and emotion among a group of nuns condemned to death in the French Revolution. The text, originally a film scenario, is built up from a number of short scenes whose brevity forced the composer to discriminate painstakingly between types of vocal line, of rhythm, even of vowel sound; the immediate success of this two-and-a-half-hour opera with an almost entirely female cast reveals Poulenc as a technician of the first order. He confronted similar problems in *La voix humaine* (1958) and enriched this 40-minute solo scena, one side of the telephone conversation between a young woman and the lover who is abandoning her, with non-referential 'motifs conducteurs', with a wide range of musical language mirroring both her manic condition and the perpetual interruptions of French telephonic life, with terrifying silences (as her lover is saying what the audience never hears), and with a long-term aim for A minor as the tragic goal of the harmony. The result is a powerful study of human despair.

6. CHORAL MUSIC. Several minor secular works such as the *Chansons françaises* (1945–6) continue the French tradition of Janequin and Sermisy, but Poulenc's early study of Bach chorales also left its mark. His masterpiece in the genre, *Figure humaine* (1943), is a highly complex setting of words by Eluard; although instrumental support would have reduced the performers' troubles, the composer wanted a pure choral tone in order to capture the mood of supplication.

After his return to Roman Catholicism in 1935 Poulenc produced a steady flow of religious choral works. Stretching over a quarter of a century they display a remarkable unity of tone as well as an increasing complexity in language and resources. The *Litanies à la vierge noire* (1936), written in the week after his visit to Rocamadour, are for three-part female chorus in a conventionally modal style that avoids conventional cadences, the organ punctuating the discourse with fervently chromatic chords. The difficult Mass in G (1937) is nevertheless 'more sober, more Romanesque' than his next major work in the genre, the *Stabat mater* (1950) for soprano, mixed chorus and orchestra, a powerful and profoundly moving work whose choral writing enlarges on the serious implications in that of *Les mamelles*. In the *Gloria* (1959) the choral writing is unsanctimonious to the point of wilfulness, as in the stressing of the phrase 'Gloria in *excelsis* Deo', while the ostinatos, the soaring soprano and the matchless tunes proclaim Poulenc a believer who had, in Tippett's phrase, 'contracted in to abundance'. Finally, the *Sept répons des ténèbres* (1961) pursue the same lush orchestral path but with a new concentration of thought, epitomized in the minute but spine-chilling codetta to 'Caligaverunt oculi mei' where Poulenc showed that his recognition of Webern was neither a matter of distant respect nor a piece of time-serving diplomacy.

7. SONGS AND OTHER WORKS FOR SOLO VOICE. In the *Rapsodie nègre* (1917) Poulenc showed a marked affinity with words which were less than explicit, but his setting of six poems from Apollinaire's *Le bestiaire* (1918–19) is an extraordinarily individual and competent piece of work for a young man of 20, in which he

captured the mood of the tiny, elusive poems, often by simple yet surprising means such as abnormal word-setting (as with 'mélancolie', the last word of all). The scoring is at once economical and faintly 'impressionist', but in *Cocardes* (1919) he imitated the sound of a street band, and Stravinsky's *The Soldier's Tale* was also surely in his mind. There followed a period of 12 years before Poulenc again wrote songs by which he set any store, the *Trois poèmes de Louise Lalanne* (1931) – a fictitious poet born of Apollinaire's lively imagination; the second poem is by him, the others by his mistress Marie Laurencin. Apollinaire and Max Jacob provided the texts for the other vocal works of 1931–2. Poulenc's favourite was *Le bal masqué*, a nostalgic romp in which the 'côté paysan' of his nature is uncluttered by any kind of chic.

On 3 April 1935 Poulenc and Bernac gave their first public recital, including the first performance of the *Cinq poèmes d'Eluard*. Poulenc had been attracted by Eluard's poetry since adolescence but there was 'a stillness about it which I did not understand'. In the *Cinq poèmes* 'for the first time, the key is grating in the lock', and the door opened wide the following year in the cycle of love-songs *Tel jour, telle nuit*, a masterpiece worthy to stand beside Fauré's *La bonne chanson*. It lacks the common touch of some other Poulenc songs, the sentimentality of *Hôtel* or the earthiness of the *Chansons villageoises*, but otherwise it is highly characteristic. Where a single song contains more than one tempo, Poulenc followed Satie's lead in making them 'successive' rather than 'progressive'; there is only one rallentando in the whole cycle; five of the nine songs move at a single, inexorable speed. However, Poulenc planned at least three of them (nos.3, 5 and 8) as transitions between their more important neighbours; in particular he intended the final climax of no.8, *Figure de force*, 'to make more keenly perceptible the kind of silence that marks the beginning of "Nous avons fait la nuit" '. Often piano and voice work on independent dynamic levels, a dimension of songwriting not widely explored before his time. The texture of the accompaniment is never complex but there must always be 'beaucoup de pédale'.

From this point there was little change in the technique of his songwriting, rather a continual refinement of means, an attempt to say more and more with less and less, a search for the pure line he admired so much in Matisse. This tendency reached its utmost point with *La fraîcheur et le feu* (1950), 'the most carefully wrought' of his songs, being a setting of a single Eluard poem in seven sections, in which two contrasted tempos (mostly crotchet = 120 and crotchet = 66–9) are treated as structural elements. Poulenc's last important setting of Eluard was of texts he commissioned from the poet to form *Le travail du peintre* (1956), a homage to seven contemporary painters. His last set of songs was *La courte paille* (1960), written for Denise Duval to sing to her young son and containing the hilarious patter song 'Ba, be, bi, bo, bu', but his last significant work for solo voice, *La dame de Monte Carlo* (1961), a monologue for soprano and orchestra to words by Cocteau, shows, like *La voix humaine*, that Poulenc understood all too well the terrors of mental depression.

In general, the sections that make up a Poulenc song are quite short and often built of two- or four-bar phrases. His technique has much in common with the 'surrealist' poets whom he set, in the value he placed on the resonance of the individual elements. He rarely began his songs with the beginning. Usually a line or two would come at a time, and in the case of *Montparnasse* (a song of 20 lines) the process was spread over a period of four years. Furthermore, ideas always came to him in particular keys and he never transposed them; for example, D♭ major seems to have been a key of relaxation and in it the fourth degree tends to be sharpened. Towards the end of the compositional process, therefore, he might be confronted with a collection of quite disparate tonal areas which he then had to combine to reach the listener as a single experience. Much though it annoyed him, the legend of Poulenc the rich playboy of music, from whom *mélodies* flowed with every exhalation of breath, is the perfect compliment to this most scrupulous of craftsmen.

8. SUMMARY. Poulenc never questioned the supremacy of the tonal–modal system. Chromaticism in his music is never more than passing, even if he used the diminished 7th more than any leading composer since Verdi. Texturally, rhythmically, harmonically, he was not particularly inventive. For him the most important element of all was melody and he found his way to a vast treasury of undiscovered tunes within an area that had, according to the most up-to-date musical maps, been surveyed, worked and exhausted. His standing in the world of contemporary music mattered to him and he kept alive to the best around him; in 1961 he wrote 'I'm truly sorry to miss [Boulez's] *Pli selon pli*, because I'm sure it's well worth hearing [plus que valable]'. His definitive statement came perhaps in a letter of 1942: 'I know perfectly well that I'm not one of those composers who have made harmonic innovations like Igor [Stravinsky], Ravel or Debussy, but I think there's room for *new* music which doesn't mind using other people's chords. Wasn't that the case with Mozart–Schubert?'. And if Poulenc was not quite a Schubert, he is so far the 20th century's most eligible candidate for the succession.

WORKS

DRAMATIC

(operas)
Les mamelles de Tirésias (opéra bouffe, prol, 2, Apollinaire), 1944; Paris, Opéra-Comique, 3 June 1947
Dialogues des carmélites (opera, 3, Bernanos), 1953–6; Milan, La Scala, 26 Jan 1957
La voix humaine (tragédie lyrique, 1, Cocteau), 1958; Paris, Opéra-Comique, 6 Feb 1959
Recits for Gounod: La colombe, 1923, unpubd

(ballets)
La baigneuse de Trouville and Discours du général for 'Les mariés de la Tour Eiffel' (1, Cocteau), 1921, unpubd, other nos. by Auric, Honegger, Milhaud and Tailleferre; Paris, Champs-Elysées, 18 June 1921
Les biches (1, 17th-century text), chorus, orch, 1923; Monte Carlo, 6 Jan 1924
Pastourelle for L'éventail de Jeanne (1, Y. Franck, A. Bourgat), 1927; Paris, 16 June 1927
Aubade (choreographic conc.), pf, 18 insts, 1929; Paris, 18 June 1929
Les animaux modèles (ballet, after La Fontaine), 1940–41; Paris, Opéra, 8 Aug 1942

(incidental music)
Le gendarme incompris (Cocteau, Radiguet), 1921, unpubd; Paris, Mathurins, May 1921
Esquisse d'un fanfare, ov. for Act 5 of Romeo and Juliet (Shakespéare), 1921
Intermezzo (Giraudoux), 1933, unpubd; Paris, Comédie des Champs-Elysées, March 1933
La reine Margot (Bourdet), 1935, unpubd, collab. Auric
Léocadia (Anouilh), 1940, unpubd except for song Les chemins de l'amour
La fille du jardinier (Exbrayat), 1941, unpubd

Le voyageur sans bagages (Anouilh), 1944, unpubd
La nuit de la Saint-Jean (Barrie), 1944, unpubd
Le soldat et la sorcière (A. Salacrou), 1945, unpubd
Amphitryon (Molière), 1947, unpubd; Paris, Marigny, 5 Dec 1947
Renaud et Armide (Cocteau), 1962, unpubd

(film scores)
La belle au bois dormant, 1935
La duchesse de Langeais (Baroncelli), 1942
Le voyageur sans bagages (Anouilh), 1944
Ce siècle a 50 ans, 1950, collab. Auric
Le voyage en Amérique (Lavorel), 1951; Cannes, Etoiles, 14 Aug 1951

ORCHESTRAL
Trois mouvements perpétuels [arr. of pf work], before 1927, unpubd
Concert champêtre, hpd, orch, 1927–8
Concerto, d, 2 pf, orch, 1932
Deux marches et un intermède, chamber orch, 1937; composed for entertainment at the Paris Exhibition, other nos. by Auric
Concerto, g, org, str, timp, 1938
Suite from 'Les biches', 1939–40
Suite from 'Les animaux modèles', 1942
Sinfonietta, 1947
Piano Concerto, 1949
Matelote provençale for 'La guirlande de Campra', 1952
Bucolique for 'Variations sur le nom de Marguerite Long', 1954
Orchestration of Satie: Deux préludes posthumes et une gnossienne, 1939

CHORAL
Chanson à boire (17th-century), TTBB, 1922
Sept chansons, unacc., 1936: Blanche neige (Apollinaire), A peine défigurée (Eluard), Pour une nuit nouvelle (Eluard), Tous les droits (Eluard), Belle et ressemblante (Eluard), Marie (Apollinaire), Luire (Eluard) [Blanche neige replaced La reine de Saba (J. Legrand), sung at 1st perf. but later rejected]
Litanies à la vierge noire, SSA, org, 1936
Petites voix (M. Ley), SSA, 1936: La petite fille sage, Le chien perdu, En rentrant de l'école, Le petit garçon malade, Le hérisson
Mass, G, SATB, 1937
Sécheresses (E. James), cantata, chorus, orch, 1937
Quatre motets pour un temps de pénitence, SATB: Timor et tremor, 1939; Vinea mea electa, 1938; Tenebrae factae sunt, 1938; Tristis est anima mea, 1938
Exultate Deo, SATB, 1941
Salve regina, SATB, 1941
Figure humaine (Eluard), cantata, 12vv, 1943
Un soir de neige (Eluard), chamber cantata, 6vv, 1944
Chansons françaises: Margoton va t'a l'iau, SATB, 1945; La belle se siet au pied de la tour, SATBarB, 1945; Pilons l'orge, SATBarB, 1945; Clic, clac, dansez sabots, TBB, 1945; C'est la petit' fill' du prince, SATBarB, 1946; La belle si nous étions, TBB, 1946; Ah! mon beau laboureau, SATB, 1945; Les tisserands, SATBarB, 1946
Quatre petites prières de Saint François d'Assise, male vv, 1948
Stabat mater, S, SATBarB, orch, 1950
Quatre motets pour le temps de Noël, unacc.: O magnum mysterium, 1952; Quem vidistis pastores, 1951; Videntes stellam, 1951; Hodie Christus natus est, 1952
Ave verum corpus, SMezA, 1952
Laudes de Saint Antoine de Padoue, male vv: O Jésu, 1957; O proles, 1958; Laus regi, 1959; Si quaeris, 1959
Gloria, S, chorus, orch, 1959
Sept répons des ténèbres, child S, male vv, boys' vv, orch, 1961

SOLO VOCAL

(with ens or orch)
Rapsodie nègre, Bar, fl, cl, str qt, pf, 1917, rev. 1933: Prélude, Ronde, Honoloulou, Pastorale, Final
Le bestiaire (Apollinaire), 1v, fl, cl, bn, str qt, 1918–19, orchd before 1922: Le dromadaire, La chèvre du Thibet, La sauterelle, Le dauphin, L'écrevisse, La carpe
Cocardes (Cocteau), 1v, cornet, trbn, b drum, triangle, vn, 1919: Miel de Narbonne, Bonne d'enfant, Enfant de troupe
Le bal masqué (Jacob), cantata, Bar/Mez, ob, cl, bn, pf, perc, vn, vc, 1932: Préambule et air de bravoure, Intermède, Malvina, Bagatelle, La dame aveugle, Finale
Poèmes de Ronsard [arr. of song cycle], 1v, orch, before 1934, unpubd
Chansons villageoises [arr. of song cycle], 1v, chamber orch, 1943
La dame de Monte Carlo (Cocteau), S, orch, 1961

(songs for 1v, pf)
Toréador (Cocteau), 1918, rev. 1932
Le bestiaire [arr. of work with ens], 1919
Cocardes [arr. of work with ens], 1919
Poèmes de Ronsard, 1924–5: Attributs, 1924; Le tombeau, 1924; Ballet, 1924; Je n'ai plus que les os, 1925; A son page, 1925
Chansons gaillardes (17th-century), 1925–6: La maîtresse volage, Chanson à boire, Madrigal, Invocation aux parques, Couplets bachiques, L'offrande, La belle jeunesse, Sérénade

Vocalise, 1927
Airs chantés (Moréas), 1927–8: Air romantique, Air champêtre, Air grave, Air vif
Epitaphe (Malherbe), 1930
Trois poèmes de Louise Lalanne, 1931: Le présent (Laurencin), Chanson (Apollinaire), Hier (Laurencin)
Quatre poèmes (Apollinaire), 1931: L'anguille, Carte postale, Avant le cinéma, 1904
Cinq poèmes (Jacob), 1931: Chanson, Cimetière, La petite servante, Berceuse, Souric et Mouric
Huit chansons polonaises, 1934: La couronne (Wianek), Le départ (Odjazd), Les gars polonais (Polska młodzież), Le dernier mazour (Ostatni mazur), L'adieu (Pożegnanie), Le drapeau blanc (Biala chorągiewka), La vistule (Wisła), Le lac (Jezioro)
Quatre chansons pour enfants, 1934: Nous voulons une petite soeur (J. Nohain), La tragique histoire du petit René (Jaboune), Le petit garçon trop bien portant (Jaboune), Monsieur Sans Souci (Jaboune)
Cinq poèmes (Eluard), 1935: Peut-il se reposer?, Il la prend dans ses bras, Plume d'eau claire, Rôdeuse au front de verre, Amoureuses
A sa guitare (Ronsard), 1935, alternatively with harp
Tel jour, telle nuit (Eluard): Bonne journée, 1937; Une ruine coquille vide, 1936; Le front comme un drapeau perdu, 1937; Une roulotte couverte en tuiles, 1936; A toutes brides, 1937; Une herbe pauvre, 1936; Je n'ai envie que de t'aimer, 1936; Figure de force brûlante et farouche, 1937; Nous avons fait la nuit, 1937
Trois poèmes (L. de Vilmorin), 1937: Le garçon de Liège, Au-delà, Aux officiers de la garde blanche
Le portrait (Colette), 1938
Deux poèmes (Apollinaire), 1938: Dans le jardin d'Anna, Allons plus vite
La grenouillère (Apollinaire), 1938
Priez pour paix (d'Orléans), 1938
Miroirs brûlants (Eluard): Tu vois le feu du soir, 1938; Je nommerai ton front, 1939
Ce doux petit visage (Eluard), 1939
Fiançailles pour rire (de Vilmorin), 1939: La dame d'André, Dans l'herbe, Il vole, Mon cadavre est doux comme un gant, Violon, Fleurs
Bleuet (Apollinaire), 1939
Banalités (Apollinaire), 1940: Chansons d'Orkenise, Hôtel, Fagnes de Wallonies, Voyage à Paris, Sanglots
Les chemins de l'amour (Anouilh: Léocadia), 1940
Chansons villageoises (M. Fombeure), 1942: Chanson du clair tamis, Les gars qui vont à la fête, C'est le joli printemps, Le mendiant, Chanson de la fille frivole, Le retour du sergent
Métamorphoses (de Vilmorin), 1943: Reine des mouettes, C'est ainsi que tu es, Paganini
Deux poèmes (Aragon), 1943: 'C', Fêtes galantes
Montparnasse (Apollinaire), 1941–5
Hyde Park (Apollinaire), 1945
Deux mélodies (Apollinaire), 1946: Le pont, Un poème
Paul et Virginie (Radiguet), 1946
Hymne (Racine), 1947
Le disparu (Desnos), 1947
Main dominée par le coeur (Eluard), 1947
Trois chansons (Lorca), 1947: L'enfant muet, Adelina à la promenade, Chanson de l'oranger sec
. . . Mais mourir (Eluard), 1947
Calligrammes (Apollinaire), 1948: L'espionne, Mutation, Vers le sud, Il pleut, La grâce exilée, Aussi bien que les cigales, Voyage
Mazurka (de Vilmorin), 1949
La fraîcheur et le feu (Eluard), 1950: Rayon des yeux, Le matin les branches attisent, Tout disparut, Dans les ténèbres du jardin, Unis la fraîcheur et le feu, Homme au sourir tendre, La grande rivière qui va
Parisiana (Jacob), 1954: Joueur du bugle, Vous n'écrivez plus?
Rosemonde (Apollinaire), 1954
Le travail du peintre (Eluard), 1956: Pablo Picasso, Marc Chagall, Georges Braque, Juan Gris, Paul Klee, Joan Miró, Jacques Villon
Deux mélodies 1956, 1956: La souris (Apollinaire), Nuage (L. de Beylie)
Dernier poème (Desnos), 1956
Une chanson de porcelaine (Eluard), 1958
La courte paille (M. Carême), 1960: Le sommeil, Quelle aventure!, La reine de coeur, Ba, be, bi, bo, bu, Les anges musiciens, Le carafon, Lune d'avril
Fancy (Shakespeare), ?1962

(melodrama)

L'histoire de Babar (J. de Brunhoff), reciter, pf, 1940–45

CHAMBER AND INSTRUMENTAL

Sonata, 2 cl, 1918, rev. 1945
Sonata, cl, bn, 1922
Sonata, hn, tpt, trbn, 1922, rev. 1945
Trio, ob, bn, pf, 1926
Villanelle, pipe, pf, 1934
Suite française [after Gervaise], 2 ob, 2 bn, 2 tpt, 3 trbn, perc, hpd, 1935

Sextet, wind qnt, pf, 1932–9
Sonata, vn, pf, 1942–3, rev. 1949
Sonata, vc, pf, 1948
Sonata, fl, pf, 1956
Elégie, hn, pf, 1957
Sarabande, gui, 1960
Sonata, cl, pf, 1962
Sonata, ob, pf, 1962

PIANO

Préludes, 1916, unpubd
Trois pastorales, 1918, unpubd, no.1 rev. as no.1 of Trois pièces
Sonata, duet, 1918
Trois mouvements perpétuels, 1918
Valse, 1919
Suite, C, 1920
Six impromptus, 1920
Promenades, 1921: A pied, En auto, A cheval, En bateau, En avion, En autobus, En voiture, En chemin de fer, A bicyclette, En diligence
Napoli, 1925: Barcarolle, Nocturne, Caprice italien
Pastourelle [arr. of ballet]
Deux novelettes, C, 1927, b♭, 1928
Trois pièces, 1928: Pastorale, Toccata, Hymne
Pièce brève sur le nom d'Albert Roussel, 1929
Nocturne no.1, C, 1929; no.2 (Bal de jeunes filles), A, 1933; no.3, F, 1934; no.4, c, 1934; no.5, d, 1934; no.6, G, 1934; no.7, E♭, 1935; no.8, 1938
Caprice [after finale of Le bal masqué], 1932
Valse-improvisation sur le nom de Bach, 1932
Improvisations nos.1–6, b, A♭, b, A♭, a, B♭, 1932; no.7, C, 1933; no.8, a, 1934; no.9, D, 1934; no.10 (Eloge des gammes), F, 1934; no.11, g, 1941; no.12 (Hommage à Schubert), E♭, 1941; no.13, a, 1958; no.14, D♭, 1958; no.15 (Hommage à Edith Piaf), c, 1959
Villageoises, 1933: Valse tyrolienne, Staccato, Rustique, Polka, Petite ronde, Coda
Feuillets d'album, 1933: Ariette, Rêve, Gigue
Presto, 1934
Intermezzi, C, D♭, 1934
Badinage, 1934
Humoresque, 1934
Suite française [after chamber work], 1936
Les soirées de Nazelles, 1930–36: Préambule, Variations, Cadence, Final
Bourrée au pavillon d'Auvergne, 1937
Mélancolie, 1940
Intermezzo, A♭, 1943
L'embarquement pour Cythère, valse-musette, 2 pf, 1951
Thème varié, 1951
Capriccio [after Le bal masqué], 2 pf, 1952
Sonata, 2 pf, 1952–3
Elégie, 2 pf, 1959
Novelette sur un thème de M. de Falla, e, 1959

Principal publishers: Chester, Durand, Eschig, Heugel, Ricordi, Rouart–Lerolle, Salabert

WRITINGS

BOOKS

Emmanuel Chabrier (Paris, 1961)
Moi et mes amis, ed. S. Audel (Paris, 1963)
Journal de mes mélodies (Paris, 1964)
Correspondance, 1915–1963, ed. H. de Wendel (Paris, 1967)
Pisma [Letters], ed. G. Filenko (Leningrad, 1970)

ARTICLES AND INTERVIEWS

'Entretien avec Francis Poulenc', *Guide du concert* (1929), April–May
'A propos de Mavra', *Feuilles libres* (1932), June–July
'Igor Stravinsky', *Information musicale* (3 Jan 1941), 195
'Le coeur de Maurice Ravel', *Nouvelle revue française* (1941), no.323, p.237
'Centenaire de Chabrier', *Nouvelle revue française* (1941), no.329, p.110
'La leçon de Claude Debussy', *Catalogue de l'exposition Claude Debussy*, ed. A. Martin (Paris, 1942), p.xii
'Oeuvres récentes de Darius Milhaud', *Contrepoints* (1946), no.1, p.59
'Francis Poulenc on his Ballets', *Ballet* (1946), Sept, 57
'Mes mélodies et leurs poètes', *Les annales* (1947)
Tribute to Christian Berard, *Ballet* (1949), April, 30
Contribution to 'Opera Forum', *Music Today* (London, 1949), 137
'Extrait d'un journal de voyage aux USA', *Table ronde* (1950), no.30, p.66
'La musique de piano d'Erik Satie', *ReM* (1952), no.214, p.23
'La musique de piano de Prokofieff', *Musique russe*, ii (Paris, 1953), 269
'Souvenirs: à propos de la musique de scène d'Intermezzo de Jean Giraudoux', *Jean Giraudoux et 'Pour Lucrèce'* (Paris, 1953)
Francis Poulenc: entretiens avec Claude Rostand (Paris, 1954)
'Hommage à Béla Bartók', *ReM* (1955), no.224, p.18

'Lorsque je suis mélancolique', *Mercure de France* (1 Jan 1956)
'Inventur der modernen französischen Musik', *Melos*, xxiii (1956), 35
Preface to G. Laplane: *Albéniz: sa vie, son oeuvre* (Paris, 1956)
'Comment j'ai composé les Dialogues des carmélites', *Opéra de Paris* (1957)
'La musique et les Ballets Russes de Serge de Diaghilev', *Histoire de la musique*, ed. Roland-Manuel (Paris, 1960), 985
'Opera in the Cinema Era', *Opera*, xii (1961), 11
'A propos d'une lettre d'Arthur Honegger', *SMz*, cii (1962), 160
'Hommage à Benjamin Britten', *Tribute to Benjamin Britten on his Fiftieth Birthday* (London, 1963), 13

BIBLIOGRAPHY
MONOGRAPHS AND CATALOGUES

H. Hell: *Francis Poulenc, musicien français* (Paris, 1958; Eng. trans., 1959)
Discographie des oeuvres de Francis Poulenc (Paris, 1963)
J. Roy: *Francis Poulenc* (Paris, 1964)
W. K. Werner: *The Harmonic Style of Francis Poulenc* (diss., U. of Michigan, Ann Arbor, 1966)
I. Medvedeva: *Fransis Pulank* (Moscow, 1970)
Catalogue de l'exposition à Tours: Georges Bernanos, Francis Poulenc et les 'Dialogues des carmélites' (Paris, 1970)
P. Bernac: *Francis Poulenc* (Paris, 1977; Eng. trans., 1977)

OTHER LITERATURE

L. Durey: 'Francis Poulenc', *The Chesterian* (1922), no.25, p.1
J. Cocteau: 'Les biches . . . notes de Monte Carlo', *Nouvelle revue française* (1924), no.126, p.275
D. Milhaud: 'Francis Poulenc et Les biches', *Etudes* (Paris, 1927), 61
R. H. Myers: 'Francis Poulenc', *MMR*, lx (1931), 129
G. Pitteluga: 'Francis Poulenc and the Praise of Paradox in Art', *The Chesterian* (1935), no.124, p.37
E. Lockspeiser: 'Francis Poulenc and Modern French Poets', *MMR*, lxx (1940), 29
A. Schaeffner: 'Francis Poulenc, musicien français', *Contrepoints* (1946), no.1, p.50
C. Rostand: *La musique française contemporaine* (Paris, 1952)
H. Jourdan-Morhange: *Mes amis musiciens* (Paris, 1955)
G. Favre: 'Francis Poulenc: Sécheresses', *Musiciens français contemporains*, ii (Paris, 1956), 122
D. Drew: 'The Simplicity of Poulenc', *The Listener* (16 Jan 1958), 137
P. Bernac: 'Notes sur l'interprétation des mélodies de Francis Poulenc', *Feuilles musicales* (1961), May–June, 68
H. Jourdan-Morhange: 'Francis Poulenc et ses poètes', *Feuilles musicales* (1961), May–June, 76
D. Cox: 'Poulenc and Surrealism', *The Listener* (11 July 1963), 69
R. H. Myers: 'Hommage à Poulenc', *Music and Musicians*, xi/7 (1963), 8
A. Payne: 'Tribute to Poulenc', *Music and Musicians*, xi/10 (1963), 44
N. Rorem: 'Poulenc: a Memoir', *Tempo* (1963), no.64, p.28
J. Bellas: 'Francis Poulenc ou le "son de voix de Guillaume" ', *Guillaume Apollinaire*, iii (1964), 130
M. Houdin: 'La jeunesse nogentaise de Francis Poulenc', *Bulletin de la Société historique et archéologique de Nogent-sur-Marne*, iv (1964)
J. Bellas: 'Les mamelles de Tirésias en habit d'Arlequin', *Guillaume Apollinaire*, iv (1965), 30
J. Amis: 'In Search of Poulenc', *Music and Musicians*, xxii/3 (1973), 44
ROGER NICHOLS

Poulet, Gaston (*b* Paris, 10 April 1892; *d* Paris, 14 April 1974). French violinist and conductor. After studying at the Paris Conservatoire, where he won a *premier prix* for violin playing in 1910, he made his début at Brussels in 1911 in Beethoven's Violin Concerto, with Ysaÿe conducting. In 1912 he founded the Gaston Poulet Quartet with Victor Ocutil, Amable Massis and Louis Ruyssen. In 1927 he initiated the Concerts Poulet, which took place in the Sarah Bernhardt theatre in Paris until they were merged with the Concerts Siohan in 1935. From 1932 to 1944 he was director of the Bordeaux Conservatory and conductor of the Bordeaux PO, and from 1940 to 1945 he also conducted the Concerts Colonne in Paris. He was appointed professor of chamber music at the Paris Conservatoire in 1944, and taught there until his retirement in 1962. He founded the Besançon Festival in 1948.

Poulet followed a dual career as violinist and conductor. He gave the first performance of Debussy's Violin Sonata with the composer (Paris, 1917). As a conductor, he had a very wide repertory, and received invitations to appear both in Europe and in South America – he gave the first performance in Buenos Aires of Debussy's *Le Martyre de Saint Sébastien* in 1928. His style of conducting was greatly influenced by his teacher, Toscanini.

CHRISTIANE SPIETH-WEISSENBACHER

Poulton, (Edith Eleanor) Diana (Chloe) (*b* Storrington, Sussex, 18 April 1903). English lutenist. She studied at the Slade School of Fine Art (1919–23) and was taught the lute by Arnold Dolmetsch (1922–5). From 1927 she often performed at the Haslemere Festival as soloist and in lute ensembles. She was one of the first professional English lutenists in the 20th century, and on the formation of the Lute Society in 1956 was elected its chairman, and subsequently (1973) its president. In 1971 she was appointed the first professor of the lute at the RCM. Her chief preoccupations have been the history of lute technique and the music of Dowland. Her book on Dowland, and her edition (with Basil Lam) of his music, provided for the first time material for a full assessment of the composer.

WRITINGS
'The Favourite Singer of Queen Elizabeth I', *The Consort*, xiv (1957), 24
'La technique du jeu du luth en France et en Angleterre', *Le luth et sa musique: CNRS Neuilly-sur-Seine 1957*, 107
'Some Changes in the Technique of Lute Playing from Le Roy to Mace', *LSJ*, i (1959), 7
'Notes on the Spanish Pavan', *LSJ*, iii (1961), 5
An Introduction to Lute Playing (London, 1961)
'Captaine Digorie Piper of the "Sweepstake" ', *LSJ*, iv (1962), 17
'Lute Stringing in the Light of Surviving Tablatures', *LSJ*, vi (1964), 14
'How to Play with Good Style by Thomas de Sancte Maria', *LSJ*, xii (1970), 23
John Dowland (London, 1972) [bibliography includes all her important Dowland articles]
'Dowland Rehabilitated', *MT*, cxviii (1977), 25
'Dowland, John', 'Lute', §§3–7, *Grove 6*

EDITIONS

English Ballad Tunes for the Lute (Cambridge, 1965)
John Dowland: Psalms (London, 1973)
with B. Lam: *John Dowland: Collected Lute Music* (London, 1973)

BIBLIOGRAPHY

S. Bloch: 'Saga of a Twentieth-century Lute Pioneer', *Journal of the Lute Society of America*, ii (1969), 37
DAVID SCOTT

Pound, Ezra (Loomis) (*b* Hailey, Idaho, 30 Oct 1885; *d* Venice, 1 Nov 1972). American poet and amateur composer. His musical achievements include an unorthodox *Treatise on Harmony*, a body of criticism, a role in the revival of older music and, most notably, music for two 'operas', *The Testament of François Villon* (1923) and *Cavalcanti* (1932). As a student Pound formed his taste on the Provençal troubadours, with their ideal union of composer and poet. Acquaintance with Arnold Dolmetsch deepened his love for early music, while other friendships broadened his experience. In 1913 the pianist Walter Rummel and Pound published arrangements of nine troubadour songs. From this unorthodox base, Pound, as 'William Atheling', reviewed London concerts from 1917 to 1920 in the *New Age*, attacking current repertory and performing practice. In the 1930s local concerts sponsored by Pound in Rapallo formed a model for the 1939 Settimana Vivaldiana at Siena, which helped to establish Vivaldi's modern reputation.

Villon, composed with help from Antheil, illustrates Pound's theories of song, combining troubadour monody with rhythmic notation intended to reproduce asymmetrical word rhythms with scientific precision. Such complex metres as 7/16 or 19/32 are frequent. Harmony is minimal, instrumentation pointillist, dialogue perfunctory, staging stylized, the performer's personality effaced – all operatic resources are subordinated to the rhythmic-melodic verse line. Pound's style is possibly the most original devised by an amateur. *Villon*, first performed in 1926, has been produced twice by the BBC, staged by the Western Opera Theatre (1971) and recorded by Fantasy Records of Berkeley, California (1972). *Cavalcanti*, a similar work, slightly more ambitious, was composed without assistance; it has remained unperformed.

Pound's *Treatise on Harmony*, in his *Antheil and the Treatise on Harmony* (Paris, 1924, 2/1927/R1968), is a somewhat obscure attempt to substitute rhythmic organization for textbook harmony or the vertical sonorities of impressionism. It is best understood against the background of Antheil's *Ballet mécanique*, Stravinsky's hold on the Paris of the 1920s and the general revolt against tonality.

BIBLIOGRAPHY
S. J. Adams: *Ezra Pound and Music* (diss., U. of Toronto, 1974)
R. M. Schafer, ed.: *Ezra Pound and Music* (New York, 1977)
STEPHEN J. ADAMS

Poupard, Henri-Pierre. *See* SAUGUET, HENRI.

Pourtalès, Guy [Guido James] **de** (*b* Berlin, 4 Aug 1881; *d* Lausanne, 12 June 1940). French music critic and writer. He studied literature in Geneva and Neuchâtel and at the universities of Berlin, Bonn and Paris, and music education in Karlsruhe with Mottl, under whose influence he became an ardent Wagnerite. For many years he was the music critic of *Marianne*, *La presse* and *Echo de Paris*, and on the occasion of the opening of the Wagner Museum at Triebschen in 1933 he gave the inaugural address. In his many novels about Romantic composers he was more concerned with the characters of the heroes than with the precise details of their careers. He received several literary prizes and was created an officer of the Légion d'honneur.

WRITINGS
La vie de Franz Liszt (Paris, 1925)
Chopin, ou le poète (Paris, 1927)
Louis II de Bavière ou Hamlet-roi (Paris, 1928)
Nietzsche en Italie (Paris, 1929)
Wagner, histoire d'un artiste (Paris, 1932)
La pêche miraculeuse (Paris, 1937)
Berlioz et l'Europe romantique (Paris, 1939)
ARNO HUTH/R

Poussé (Fr.). In string playing, up-bow; *see* BOW, §II.

Pousseur, Henri (Léon Marie Thérèse) (*b* Malmédy, 23 June 1929). Belgian composer, theorist and teacher.

1. LIFE. He studied at the Liège Conservatory (1947–52), where he took a *premier prix* for harmony and a *second prix* for organ, and then at the Brussels Conservatory, from which he graduated in 1953 with a *premier prix* in fugue (Absil's class). In Liège he was associated with the 'Variations' group around Froidebise, who introduced the music of Webern to him; in Brussels he had contact with Souris. While working as an organist (1949–52) and secondary school music teacher (1950–58) Pousseur quickly established a position in the avant garde. In 1951 he met Boulez in Royaumont, and three years later he was in Cologne to observe Stockhausen's work on the first electronic music created from sine-waves alone. He worked with

Berio and Maderna at the Milan studios for two months in 1957, and in 1958 he founded the Studio de Musique Electronique (SME) in Brussels. Pousseur's frequent and close cooperation with Butor began in 1960. He directed seminars at the Darmstadt summer courses (1957–67) and taught at the Cologne new music courses (1963–8); in addition, he was professor of composition at the Basle Conservatory (1963–4) and at the Boston Academy of Music (1964), and from this period he began to appear widely as a lecturer, in the USA and Europe. In 1965 he worked at the electronic music studios of Ghent University, and then he went to teach at the State University of New York at Buffalo (1966–8). Back in Belgium he was appointed lecturer at Liège University (1970), director of the Centre de Recherches Musicales de Wallonie, Liège (1970), and professor of composition at the Liège Conservatory (1971).

2. WORKS. Pousseur's earliest works, such as the *Trois chants sacrés*, show the extent of his admiration for Webern. In *Prospections* (1952) he was already investigating new applications of serialism, in this case to sixth-tones. The *Seismogrammes*, Pousseur's first electronic pieces, were composed entirely from sine-waves at the Cologne studios in 1954; like the following *Symphonies*, they owe a great deal to Stockhausen. The *Symphonies*, for 15 instruments, constitute one of the most complex contemporary attempts at 'total serialism'; and Pousseur took a leading part in the development of aleatory procedures, which remain a central concern. His *Scambi* (1957) – a tape piece created from maximally 'asymmetric' material: filtered white noise – consists of 16 sections which may be assembled in various orders. *Répons* (1960) was conceived for seven instrumentalists with rules to assign various roles (conductor, soloist, duo player, etc) and forms of play for the short sections of the piece. In this state the work posed difficulties for the players in performing their music and at the same time demonstrating the mobile structure, so a new version was prepared (1965) with the addition of a text by Butor, spoken by an actor as coordinator and as intermediary between the musicians and the audience. *Répons* is a game, but a game without competition, and its involvement of collective decision is important within the context of Pousseur's view of music as a model of social structure.

From 1960 Pousseur became increasingly concerned with wider, extra-musical materials. The sounds for the electronic ballet *Electre* (Italia Prize 1960), for example, are derived directly from the speaking voice. This interest, and the concern with mobile form, reached a high development in the 'fantaisie variable genre opéra' *Votre Faust*. Stimulated by Butor's use of literary excerpts, Pousseur saw in quotation a means of reintroducing all that had been proscribed by classical serial theory. His quotations, ranging from Monteverdi to his own music, necessitated, above all, a new approach to harmonic organization. The simplest means of integration was to present the *objets trouvés* in chronological order ('La chevauchée fantastique'), but elsewhere the assimilation is more sophisticated. For instance, the 'Prologue dans le ciel', an instrumental piece, is formed from nine series (taken from Schoenberg, Webern, Stravinsky, Boulez, Stockhausen and Pousseur), in each of which every pitch class has an unchanging duration different from that in all the other series, except that one 'pivotal' pitch class always has the same duration; the Webern series is heard in three versions, the original, a quasi-diatonic

A page from Pousseur's electronic ballet 'Electre' (1960)

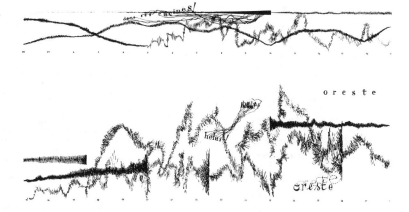

transformation and a whole-tone transformation. Similarly, in 'Le tarot d'Henri' each double page in the variable form has a specific harmonic character in a scale from diatonic to chromatic, by way of whole-tone harmony and a mode from the *Faust Symphony*. The same sort of mobility is used to integrate noises demanded by dramatic situation. *Votre Faust* can, indeed, be seen as centred on serialism, but capable of continuous extension in any direction away from that centre. Its course is determined in general, but choice operates at several levels: on the largest scale the form allows for audience intervention, by ballot or more vocally.

Working with quotations in *Votre Faust* left a permanent mark on Pousseur's music, in that the exploitation of the 'harmonic energy thrown out' by earlier serial music became a principal interest. The orchestral *Couleurs croisées* (1967), commissioned by the Koussevitzky Foundation, finds its starting material in the song *We shall overcome*, transformed harmonically and melodically in the six main sections of the work, each of them distinct in harmony so that the music moves from expressionist chromaticism to diatonic appeasement. This provision of an integrated framework for diverse elements (again intended as an analogue of a 'utopian' social organization) recurs in *Mnemosyne I* (1968) with different melodic structures, in *Les éphémérides d'Icare II* (1970) with the introduction of collective improvisation on given intervals and rhythms, in *Invitation à l'utopie* (1970) with the spectrum spoken language–sung language–sung phonemes–instrumental sound, and in the *Système des paraboles* (1972) with periodicity and aperiodicity.

The development of Pousseur's work towards 'a richer, more complex musical expression, better adapted to today's relativist and pluralist reality' (*Fragments théoriques*, 1970, p.247) has been explained and discussed in several of his essays. Others have taken up problems which have been of closest concern to him as a composer: harmony and the function of music in society. 'Stravinsky selon Webern selon Stravinsky' deals with the harmony of *Agon* and *The Rite of Spring*, in pointed contradiction to Boulez's negative approach. Pousseur's philosophy of music is treated in the collection *Musique, sémantique, société*, where he draws parallels between musical and social structures, finding in certain contemporary works a model for a control of complexity, such as man has lost in the political and economic spheres, and a prefiguring of a state of har-mony among men and between man and nature.

WORKS

Sept versets des psaumes de la pénitence, chorus 4vv, 1950
Trois chants sacrés, S, vn, va, vc, 1951; Steingruber, Trio Schneiderhan, Salzburg, 1952
Prospections, 3 pf in sixth-tones, 1952, unpubd
Seismogrammes I–II, 1-track tape [WDR, Cologne], 1954, unpubd
Symphonies à 15 solistes, 1954–5
Quintette à la mémoire d'Anton Webern, cl, b cl, vn, vc, pf, 1955; cond. Rosbaud, Donaueschingen, Oct 1955
Exercices, pf, 1956: Variations I, Tudor, Cologne, 1957; Impromptu et Variations II, Tudor, New York, 1957
Scambi, 2-track tape [RAI, Milan], 1957; broadcast, Milan, 1957
Mobile, 2 pf, 1956–8; Kontarsky Duo, Darmstadt, 1958
Madrigal I, cl, 1958
Liège, cité ardente, 1958; Sémaphore, 1958; Deux poèmes de Henri Michaux, 1959; Préhistoire du cinéma, 1959; Interlude pour les contes d'Hoffmann, 1961; Les perses, 1961; Prospective, 1961; all 1-track tape [SME, Brussels], all unpubd
Etude pour Rimes II, 2-track tape [SME, Brussels], 1958, unpubd
Rimes pour différentes sources sonores, 3 orch groups, 2-track tape [SME, Brussels], 1958–9; South West German RSO, cond. Boulez, Donaueschingen, 17 Oct 1959
Electre (ballet, P. Rhallys, after Sophocles), 2-track disc [SME, Brussels], 1960
Répons, fl, harp, 2 pf, perc, vn, vc, 1960; new version with actor (Butor), 1965; new version as Répons avec son paysage (Butor)
Ode, str qt, 1960–61
Caractères, pf, 1961
Madrigal II, fl, vn, va da gamba, hpd, 1961
Trois visages de Liège, 2-track tape [SME, Brussels], 1961
Madrigal III, cl, 2 perc, pf, vn, vc, 1962
Trait, 5 vn I, 4 vn II, 3 va, 2 vc, db, 1962
Votre Faust (fantaisie variable genre opéra, Butor), S, A, T, B, 5 actors, 12 insts, tape, 1960–67; Milan, Piccola Scala, 15 Jan 1969
Miroir de Votre Faust (Caractères II): Le tarot d'Henri, pf; La chevauchée fantastique, S ad lib, pf; Souvenirs d'une marionette, pf; 1964–5; Rzewski, Berlin, 1965
Portail de Votre Faust, S, A, T, B, 12 insts, tape, 1960–66; Ens Musiques Nouvelles, cond. Markowski, Brussels, Résidence, 12 Dec 1966
Jeu de miroirs de Votre Faust, 2-track tape [SME, Ghent, Brussels], 1967
Echos de Votre Faust: I, vc, 1967; II, Mez, fl, pf, vc, 1969
Ombres de Votre Faust, tape, may be combined with Miroir and/or Echos
Fresques de Votre Faust, org, vn, 2 amp insts, collab. J.-Y. Bosseur
Caractères madrigalesques (Caractères III, Madrigal IV), ob, 1965
Apostrophe et six réflexions, pf, 1964–6
Phonèmes pour Cathy (Madrigal V) (after Claudel), 1v, 1966
Couleurs croisées, orch, 1967; Belgian RSO, cond. Boulez, Brussels, Palais des Beaux-Arts, 26 Dec 1968
Mnemosyne I (Hölderlin), 1v/chorus 1v/1 inst, 1968
Mnemosyne II, systems of improvisation, 1 or more performers, 1969; M. Bekkelund (Mez), cond. Pousseur, Bonn, Beethovenhalle, 1970
Crosses of Crossed Colors, amp female v, 2–5 pf, 2 radios, 2 tape recs, 2 disc players, 1970; J. Blackett, cond. Pousseur, New York, 19 Nov 1970
Les éphémérides d'Icare II, pf, 18 insts, 1970; Ens Musiques Nouvelles, cond. Bartholomée, Madrid, 20 April 1970
Icare apprenti, any insts, 1970; Ens Musiques Nouvelles, cond. Bartholomée, Paris, Oct 1971

Invitation à l'utopie [= Les éphémérides d'Icare II + vv] (Butor), speaker, S, Mez, chorus 4vv, pf, 18 insts, 1970; T. Clais, L. Jespers, J. Nendick, RTB Chorus, Mercenier, Ens Musiques Nouvelles, cond. Bartholomée, Brussels, RTB Auditorium, 25 Jan 1971

Midi-minuit, orch, pf, jazz group, pop group, chorus, children's chorus, folksinger, 1970, collab. Bartholomée and others; Ens Alarius, Ens Musiques Nouvelles, Mercenier, Les Jelly-Fish, Chorale A Coeur Joie and others, Liège, Palais des Congrès, 16 Jan 1971

Ex-dei in machinam memoria, melody inst, elec ens, 1971; E. van Tright (ob), Warsaw, 25 Sept 1971

L'effacement du Prince Igor, orch, 1971; Belgian National Orch, cond. Gielen, Brussels, Dec 1971

Stravinsky au futur, 1v, inst, ens, elec, 1971, collab. Bartholomée, Boesmans, César, S. Kuijken; C. Lombard, E. van Tright, Ens Musiques Nouvelles, Centre de Recherches Musicales de Wallonie, Liège, 1972

Système des paraboles, 7 tape studies, 1972 [may be mixed freely to produce Parabole Mix]

Parabol Mix I–III [mixtures from Système] [WDR, Cologne], 1973; Düsseldorf, WDR, 4, 6, 7 Oct 1973

Vue sur les jardins interdits, 1973; B. Foccroulle (org), Royan, 27 March 1974

Schönbergs Gegenwart, actors, singers, insts, 1974; Ens Musiques Nouvelles, cond. Bartholomée, Berlin, 12 Sept 1974

Deuxieme vue sur les jardins interdits, org, 1973–4

L'ibericare, gui, 1975

Chronique berlinoise, Bar, pf qnt

Chronique illustrée, Bar, orch, 1976

19 × √8/4. vc, 1977

Principal publishers: Suvini Zerboni, Universal

WRITINGS

'L'impossible objet', *Propositions* (1953), no.1, p.16

'Domaines à venir', *Cahiers de la compagnie Renaud-Barrault* (1954), no.3, p.86

'Struktur des Baustoffes', *Die Reihe* (1955), no.1, p.42; Eng. trans. in *Die Reihe* (1958), no.1, p.30

'Anton Weberns organische Chromatik', *Die Reihe* (1956), no.2, p.56; Eng. trans. in *Die Reihe* (1958), no.2, p.51

'Da Schönberg a Webern: una mutazione', *Incontri musicali*, i (1956), 3–39

Ecrits d'Alban Berg, choisis, traduits et commentés (Monaco, 1957)

'Zur Methodik', *Die Reihe* (1957), no.3, pp.46–88; Eng. trans. in *Die Reihe* (1959), no.3, pp.44–88 [on Quintette]

'Filmarbeit im elektronischen Studio', *Musik der Zeit*, ii (1958), 17

'La nuova sensibilità musicale', *Incontri musicali*, ii (1958), 3–37; Fr. trans. in *Esprit* (1960), no.28, p.52; Ger. trans. in *Kommentare zur neuen Musik* (1961–2), 72

'Webern und die Theorie', *Darmstädter Beiträge zur neuen Musik* (1958), no.1, p.38

'Forme et pratique musicales', *RBM*, xiii (1959), 98; Ger. trans. in *Die Reihe* (1960), no.6; Eng. trans. in *Die Reihe* (1964), no.6, p.77

'Scambi', *Gravesaner Blätter*, iv (1959), 36

'Theorie und Praxis in der neuesten Musik', *Darmstädter Beiträge zur neuen Musik* (1959), no.2, p.15

'Caso e musica', *Incontri musicali*, iv (1960), 9–39

'Textes sur l'expression', *Cahiers de la compagnie Renaud-Barrault* (1961), no.41, pp.169–202

Reconnaissance des musiques modernes (Brussels, 1964)

'Notes pour une réforme de l'enseignement musical', *Revue nouvelle*, xlii (1965), 553

'Pour une périodicité généralisée', *Preuves*, xv (1965), 34

'La question de l'ordre dans la musique nouvelle', *RBM*, xx (1966), 136; Eng. trans. in *PNM*, v/1 (1966), 93; orig. repr. in *Musique, sémantique, société* (Tournai, 1972)

'Realistische Elemente in der elektronischen Musik', *Collage* (1966), no.6

'L'apothéose de Rameau (essai sur la question harmonique)', *Revue d'esthétique*, xxi (1968), 105–72

'Calculation and Imagination in Electronic Music', *Electronic Music Review* (1968), no.5, p.21; Fr. trans. in *Musique en jeu* (1970), no.1, p.34

Mort de Dieu et crise de l'art (Huy, 1968); repr. in *Musique, sémantique, société* (Tournai, 1972)

'Der Jahrmarkt von Votre Faust', *Beiträge 1968/69* (1969), 25

'Period', 'Serial Music', *Harvard Dictionary of Music*, ed. W. Apel (Cambridge, Mass., 2/1969)

'La polyphonie en question (à propos de Schoenberg, opus 31)', *Jaarboek IPEM*, v (1969), 47–80; repr. in *Musique, sémantique, société* (Tournai, 1972)

'Esquisse pour une rhapsodie pathétique', *L'arc* (1970), no.40, p.65 [on Beethoven]

Fragments théoriques I sur la musique expérimentale (Brussels, 1970)

'Henri Pousseur: Jeu de miroirs de Votre Faust', 'Pierre Bartholomée: Le tombeau de Marin Marais', WER 60039 (1970) [disc notes]

'Aveu', *PNM*, ix/2–x/1 (1971), 135 [poem on Stravinsky]

'Ecoute d'un dialogue', *Musique en jeu* (1971), no.4, p.73 [on Butor's Dialogue on the Diabelli Variations]

'Pierre Boulez', *VH 101* (1971), no.4, p.6 [interview]

'Stravinsky selon Webern selon Stravinsky', *Musique en jeu* (1971), no.4, p.21; no.5, p.107; Eng. trans. in *PNM*, x/2 (1972), 13–51; xi/1 (1972), 112–45

Musique, sémantique, société (Paris, 1972; It. trans., 1974)

BIBLIOGRAPHY

G. M. Koenig: 'Henri Pousseur', *Die Reihe* (1958), no.4, p.18; Eng. trans. in *Die Reihe* (1960), no.4, p.13

M. Faure: 'Entretien avec Henri Pousseur', *Lettres nouvelles*, x (1962), 111

P. Castaldi: 'Luciano Berio ed Henri Pousseur: l'aspirazione a una libertà integrale', *La musica moderna*, iii (1969), 65

J.-Y. Bosseur: 'Votre Faust: fantaisie variable genre opéra', *Cahiers du Centre d'études et de recherches marxistes* (1968), no.62

L. Berio: 'Notre Faust', *NRMI*, iii (1969), 275

K. Hupfer: 'Gemeinsame Kompositionsaspekte bei Stockhausen, Pousseur und Ligeti', *Melos*, xxxvii (1970), 236

D. Bosseur: 'Midi-minuit', *Musique en jeu* (1971), no.3, p.52

D. and J.-Y. Bosseur: 'Collaboration Butor/Pousseur', *Musique en jeu* (1971), no.4, p.83

J.-Y. Bosseur: 'Henri Pousseur', *Musique de notre temps*, ed. G. Kadar (Tournai, 1973), 185

J.-Y. Bosseur: 'Les scènes de foire dans *Votre Faust*', *Obliques*, iv (1974), 135

R. Witts: 'Report on Henri Pousseur', *Contact* (1976), no.13, p.13

HENRI VANHULST

Pouteau, Joseph (*b* Chaumes-en-Brie, 7 Feb 1739; *d* Paris, 3 Dec 1823). French organist and composer. He went to Paris about 1743–4 and studied the organ with his great-uncle Michel Forqueray, organist at St Martin des Champs, and composition with L.-C. Bordier, choirmaster at Saints Innocents. In 1753 he won a competition for the reversion to the post of organist at St Martin des Champs and in 1756 he became organist at St Jacques de la Boucherie. On Forqueray's death in 1757, Pouteau inherited his library and position as organist at the Filles-Dieu convent. He supported the Revolution and arranged *Le serment civique, ou Pot pouri national* for piano or harpsichord; later, however, the Revolutionary movement turned against the church and deprived him of his wealthy students. From about 1811 he taught the piano at the Ursulines convent school and was organist at St Merry. His compositions include motets, *ariettes*, harpsichord sonatas and an *intermède*, *Alain et Rosette* (1777).

WORKS

Stage: Alain et Rosette (intermède, 1, M. J. Boutillier), Paris, Opéra, 10 Jan 1777

Vocal: Motets, chorus, insts; 2 cantatilles, 1v, insts (1764–5); Ariettes with insts; ariettes in contemporary anthologies

Kbd: Sonates en pièces de clavecin, vn ad lib (Paris, Lyons, n.d.); Recueil périodique d'ariettes d'opéra comique et autres, arr. pf/hpd, vn ad lib (Paris, 1772–5); Le serment civique, ou Pot pouri national, arr. pf/hpd (Paris, c1790)

BIBLIOGRAPHY

FétisB

A. Choron and F. Fayolle: *Dictionnaire historique des musiciens* (Paris, 1810–11/R1971)

G. Servières: *Documents inédits sur les organistes français* (Paris, ?1922)

J. Bonfils: 'Pouteau, Joseph', *MGG*

M. Benoit and N. Dufourcq: 'A propos des Forqueray', *RMFC*, viii (1968), 229

FRÉDÉRIC ROBERT

Powell, Bud [Earl] (*b* New York, 27 Sept 1924; *d* New York, 1 Aug 1966). Black American jazz pianist. In the early 1940s he took part in the jam sessions at Minton's Playhouse, New York, where Charlie Parker, Dizzy Gillespie and others experimented in the new 'bop' idiom, and soon developed a jazz piano style suited to their innovations. He played in Cootie Williams's band in 1943–4, already showing an advanced style, but in 1945 he suffered the first of many nervous collapses.

His subsequent career was spent alternately in sanatoriums and performing in various small bop groups in New York and, from 1959 to 1964, in Paris.

Powell was the first and most important jazz pianist in the bop style, and his innovations transformed most jazz pianism of his time. He was at first influenced by Teddy Wilson and Art Tatum, whose technically demanding styles he commanded at will; however, he developed a novel approach to his instrument by assigning long single lines to the right hand in rapid, detached quavers, punctuated by spare, complex chords in the left. To this basic technique he brought a brittle, precise touch and enormous creative intensity, though this flagged in later years as his illness progressed. The uniform sonority of his playing was compensated for by its rhythmic and melodic mobility, and his best performances, almost always variations at fast tempos over the harmonic structures of popular songs, sustained themselves by rapid and unpredictable invention. Powell also composed a few excellent jazz tunes such as *Hallucinations* (*Budo*), *Tempus Fugue it* and *Bouncing with Bud*.

BIBLIOGRAPHY
S. Pease: 'Bud Powell's Style', *Down Beat*, xviii (15 June 1951), 16
M. James: *Ten Modern Jazzmen* (London, 1960), 125ff
M. Harrison: 'Bud Powell', *Jazz Era: the 40s*, ed. S. Dance (London, 1961), 200f
I. Gitler: *Jazz Masters of the 40s* (New York, 1966), 110ff
D. Ioakimidis: 'Bud Powell', *Jazz Hot* (1966), Oct
V. Schonfield: 'Bud Powell', *Jazz Journal*, xvii (1966), Oct, 18
J. Grunnet Jepsen: *A Discography of Thelonious Monk and Bud Powell* (Copenhagen, 1969)
R. Johnson: 'Powell on Blue Note', *Jazz Monthly*, xvi (1970), Oct, 8
BRADFORD ROBINSON

Powell, John (*b* Richmond, Virginia, 6 Sept 1882; *d* Richmond, 15 Aug 1963). American pianist and composer. After graduating from the University of Virginia in 1901, he studied in Vienna with Leschetizky (piano, 1902–7) and Navrátil (composition, 1906–7). He made his début as a pianist in Berlin in December 1907, and he performed widely in Europe before World War I and in the USA thereafter. From the late 1920s until World War II he was prominent in Virginian musical life, being particularly active in the White Top folk music festivals and the Virginia state choral festivals. He was also closely identified with the Virginia Federation of Music Clubs. His early works are in a late-Romantic style; the later pieces use Anglo-American folk idioms.

WORKS
(*selective list*)

Orch: Rhapsodie nègre, pf, orch, 1918; In Old Virginia, 1921; Natchez-on-the-Hill, 3 Virginian country dances, 1932; A Set of Three, 1935; Sym., A, 1945; Virginia Sym., 1951
Vocal: The Babe of Bethlehem, SATB, 1934; The Deaf Woman's Courtship, S, Bar, SATB, 1934; 5 Virginian Folk Songs, Bar, pf, 1938; Judith and Holofernes (opera)
Inst: Sonata Virginianesque, vn, pf, ?1906; Sonata, vn, pf, 1918
Pf: In the South, suite, 1906; Variations and Double-fugue on a Theme of F. C. Hahr, 1906; At the Fair, suite, 1907; Sonate noble, 1907; Sonata teutonica, 1913

R. D. WARD

Powell, Mel (*b* New York, 12 Feb 1923). American composer and teacher. Powell studied the piano with Nadia Reisenberg and was for some years a noted jazz pianist. After service in the US Army Air Force, he attended the Yale University School of Music, where he studied composition with Hindemith; he was awarded the degree of BM in 1952. He taught at Mannes School and Queens University in New York, and at Yale University (1958–69), where he became chairman of the composition faculty and director of the electronic studio. In 1969, he became dean of the school of music at the California Institute of the Arts. He has received many awards, from Sigma Alpha Iota (1956), the Guggenheim Foundation (1960) and the American Academy of Arts and Letters (1963), and has served as president of the American Music Center (1961–3) and on the editorial board of *Perspectives of New Music* and the *Journal of Music Theory*. In 1972 he was guest composer at the University of Wisconsin at River Falls.

Powell's use of 12-note technique makes possible the density of interval relations and of duration, registral distribution and local pitch contours that are characteristic of his music. In some works, such as *Filigree Setting* (1958), he employs quasi-improvisational techniques that permit the performer some choice of pitch succession or contour within an otherwise rigorously controlled general context. In other compositions, interval relations derived from pitch sets take precedence over serial pitch succession, as in *Haiku Setting*, to frame the subtle lyricism of the vocal part. Similar use of pitch sets and interval relations are employed in his electronically synthesized music, which takes into account the non-tempered nature of the electronic medium. He has also used sounds, such as speech, modified electronically, and in *Immobile* various light sources are also required.

WORKS
(*selective list*)

Six Love Songs, chorus, 1950
Sweet Lovers Love the Spring (Shakespeare), female chorus, pf, 1953
Divertimento, vn, hpd, 1954
Divertimento, wind qnt, 1957
Miniatures, fl, ob, vn, va, vc, hpd, 1957
Etude, pf, 1957
Filigree Setting, 2 vn, va, vc, 1958
Haiku Setting, S, pf, 1960
Electronic Setting, tape, 1961
Second Electronic Setting, tape, 1962
Improvisation, cl, va, pf, 1962
Two Prayer Settings (Goodman, Gregory), T, ob, vn, va, vc, 1962
Events (H. Crane), tape, 1963
Stanzas, orch, 1965
Analogs I–IV, tape, 1966
Immobiles 1–4, tape and/or orch, 1967
Immobile 5, tape, ens, *c*1967
Cantilena, S, vn, tape, 1970
Setting, vn, tape, wind, 1972

Principal publisher: G. Schirmer

WRITINGS
'A Note on Rigor', *PNM*, i/2 (1962–3), 121
'In Memoriam Paul Hindemith', *PNM*, ii/2 (1963–4), 1
Article on Stravinsky, *PNM*, ix/2 (1970–71), 130

BIBLIOGRAPHY
H. Sollberger: 'Mel Powell's *Haiku Setting*', *PNM*, iii/1 (1964–5), 147
L. Thimmig: 'The Music of Mel Powell', *MQ*, lv (1969), 31
RICHARD SWIFT

Powell, Verne Q (*b* Danville, Ind., 7 April 1879; *d* Boston, Mass., 3 Feb 1968). American maker of Boehm flutes and piccolos. He grew up in Kansas, and was largely self-taught. At an early age he learned to play both the flute and the piccolo; he made a fife when only seven, and a little later he collected enough money to buy himself a piccolo. He performed regularly with bands in Fort Scott, Kansas, while he trained with his brothers as a jeweller. When he was 16 he was an expert engraver. In 1904 he started his own jewellery business in Fort Scott.

In 1910 Powell went to hear Georges Barrère playing on a silver flute in Chicago; this inspired him to make a silver flute by melting down old spoons, watch cases, etc. WILLIAM S. HAYNES, who had been making wooden flutes, heard about this and asked Powell to join his firm in Boston. Powell worked with Haynes, mainly supervising the production of silver flutes, until 1926, in which year he started his own business. In 1927 he set up his shop at 295 Huntington Avenue, opposite the New England Conservatory of Music and one block from Symphony Hall.

Besides silver flutes, Powell made piccolos in wood and silver, alto flutes in silver, and concert flutes in gold and platinum. One platinum flute was made for the New York World's Fair in 1939, and is engraved with the trylon and perisphere, the symbol of the fair. This instrument was later purchased by William Kincaid, who bequeathed it to the flautist Elaine Shaffer.

Powell, while foreman at the Haynes factory, was responsible for introducing French-model silver flute making to the USA. Later, as an independent maker, he changed the scale of his flutes, which were formerly patterned after the then famous Louis Lot flutes, thereby perfecting the design of his own instruments. He gained the respect and friendship of many of the finest flautists in the USA and Europe, and he made Boston a leading centre of flute making.

In 1961 Powell sold his business to four of his former employees, under whose management the firm expanded and moved to 70 Bow Street, Arlington, Massachusetts.

FRIEDRICH VON HUENE

Powell, Walter (*b* Oxford, 1697; *d* Oxford, 6 Nov 1744). English countertenor. He was a chorister and from 1714 a lay clerk at Magdalen College, and a member of the choirs of Christ Church and St John's. On 16 April 1718 he was elected Yeoman Bedell of Divinity, and on 26 January 1732 promoted to Esquire Bedell. The Jacobite Thomas Hearne described him on this occasion as 'a good natured man, & a good singer'. When Handel visited Oxford for the Public Act in July 1733, Powell took a principal part in all the music he performed there, probably as a late substitute for Senesino. Besides anthems in St Mary's Church on 8 July, he sang in the oratorios at the Sheldonian Theatre (Ahasuerus and some of Mordecai's part in *Esther* on 5 and 7 July, Joad in the first performances of the new *Athalia* on 10 and 11, Barak in *Deborah* on 12) and Acis in the bilingual *Acis and Galatea* at Christ Church on the morning of 11 July. These were all in versions arranged or composed for Senesino. Powell sang at the Gloucester Three Choirs Festival in September the same year. In a letter of 29 April 1743 Jennens wrote of his attending Handel's oratorios at Covent Garden that spring, but it is not clear in what capacity. He is said to have sung an anthem on his deathbed 'with the full powers of his fine voice, and with the most animated enthusiasm'.

WINTON DEAN

Power, James (*b* Galway, 1766; *d* London, 26 Aug 1836). Irish music publisher and instrument maker. After starting out as an apprentice pewterer he entered the military instrument trade, and set up with his brother William in Dublin about 1802 as William Power & Co. Towards the end of 1807 he moved to London, where he established himself as a military instrument maker and music publisher. William continued the Dublin business until 1831, but the partnership with his brother ceased about 1810, although many publications were issued jointly by them up to 1820.

The brothers' major publishing venture was Moore's *Irish Melodies*. For this project they commissioned the poet Thomas Moore to provide original verses to be set to traditional melodies arranged by John Stevenson (a plan similar to the *Scottish Melodies* then being issued by the Edinburgh publisher George Thomson). The first two parts were published in London and Dublin in 1808 (not 1807 as often stated), and were an immediate success. After the sixth number (1815) a quarrel arose between the brothers, and part vii (1818) was issued by each separately. From part viii (1821) James employed Henry Bishop as arranger, though William also issued part viii, with arrangements by Stevenson. James, however, brought a successful action for breach of copyright, and the remaining two parts (1824–34) and a supplement (1834) were published by James alone.

Power also issued several other volumes of settings of Moore's poetry, including *Sacred Songs* (1816–24), *National Airs* (1818–28) and *Evenings in Greece* (1826–32). He maintained a very close relationship with the poet and paid a substantial annuity for his verses. Power's other publications included *A Selection of Scottish Melodies* (Bishop and Twiss, 1812), *Indian Melodies* (1813), *A Selection of Welsh Melodies* (John Parry, 1822) and similar works, besides many single songs, duets and glees by Stevenson, Horn, Attwood, Matthew King and others. His widow carried on the business until about 1838. The plates of the *Irish Melodies* were bought by Addison & Hodson, who reissued them in 1844, and their popularity continued well into the second half of the century.

BIBLIOGRAPHY

Catalogue of the Music Plates and of the Printed Copies being the Remaining Stock in Trade of . . . J. Power (London, 1840)

J. Power: *Notes from the Letters of Thomas Moore to his Music-publisher* (New York, 1854)

P. H. Muir: 'Thomas Moore's Irish Melodies 1808–1834', *The Colophon* (1933), no.15

C. Humphries and W. C. Smith: *Music Publishing in the British Isles* (London, 1954, 2/1970)

PETER WARD JONES

Power, Leonel [Lionel, Lyonel, Leonellus, Leonelle; Polbero] (*d* Canterbury, 5 June 1445). English composer and theorist. He shared with Dunstable the leadership of English style in the influential decades between 1410 and 1440. Somewhat overshadowed in reputation by his probably younger contemporary, Leonel (as the sources usually name him) shows a similarly high level of musical craftsmanship and originality in an output only slightly smaller.

1. Life. 2. Works. 3. Style.

1. LIFE. The first dated reference to Power (see Bowers, 1975) records him as instructor of the choristers and second in the list of clerks of the household chapel of Thomas, Duke of Clarence (*d* 1421), brother of Henry V and heir apparent. The next records his admission to the fraternity of Christ Church, Canterbury, on 14 May 1423. This fraternity included distinguished lay friends of the priory as well as regulars and other ecclesiastics. The suggestion (in *MGG*) that Power may have been master of the choir that was maintained to sing services outside the monastic liturgy in the nave or Lady Chapel has been confirmed by the discovery of his name in this context between 1439 (when the post may have been created for him) and his death. There is reference to 'Lionel Power of Canterbury esquire' on 20 September 1438 (a 'release of all personal actions' to one Thomas Ragon), with a memorandum of acknowledgment dated 19 April 1444. 'Lyonell Power' is listed as a recipient of livery from Christmas 1439 to Christmas 1444: when-

ever a distinction is made he is cited as a Kent man rather than a Londoner. He is listed among the esquires or gentlemen (*armigeri*, later *generosi*): that he was a layman therefore seems certain.

Three notices of his death survive. In a Canterbury calendar (*GB-Lbm* Cotton Tib.B.III, 4*v*) both date and year are given. The fraternity registers (*Lbm* Arundel 68 and *Llp* 20) record his obit on 6 June, the date given for his burial by the chronicler monk John Stone, possibly himself a composer.

On stylistic grounds (discussed in §3, below), Power's birthdate must lie between about 1370 and 1385. The notoriously unreliable historian Grattan Flood, without knowledge of any of the above information, claimed that he came from County Waterford, Ireland, was related to Bishop Milo Power and Sir Maurice Power and that, as a younger son of a wealthy Anglo-Irish family, he probably studied at Oxford. Why Flood confidently dated Power's musical works between 1380 and 1395 is not vouchsafed, for in his day Power's deathdate was not known, and the possibility had not yet been raised that the OLD HALL MS, in which he is well represented, might contain 14th-century music. Flood knew Power's treatise, which he dated about 1390, and referred tantalizingly to an Anglo-Irish contemporary who styled him 'noster Lionel'.

2. WORKS. The problems in determining the authentic works of Power are so great that a work-list cannot be left to stand without some discussion. For the nucleus we are dependent on the 40 works that bear undisputed ascriptions to him. Five more anonymous works, all mass movements, can be added by virtue of their musical relationship to movements ascribed to him. A further 12 items have conflicting ascriptions or belong to mass cycles with conflicting ascriptions. Altogether these comprise related and individual mass movements, and settings of Marian liturgical texts. No secular works or isorhythmic motets are anywhere ascribed to Power, nor any canonic compositions. There is no case for rejecting any of the unique or unanimous ascriptions, from which Power's personal style emerges as marginally more definable than Dunstable's and more easily extricable from the characteristics of English music in general. It should prove possible to add further anonymous works to those tentatively assigned to him by Hamm and others. But there is a real danger of confusion with works by other composers showing Power's influence – of which the anonymous Credo Old Hall no.82 is probably an example. The survival of an elementary discant treatise in his name supports the idea that he may have been a teacher, as does his musical primacy in Old Hall.

Together with Dunstable, Power was a pioneer of the unified mass cycle, though the extent of their individual responsibilities cannot be fully established because of uncertain chronology and conflicting attributions in crucial works. Power appears to have taken the initiative in pairing movements of the Ordinary. His four pairs in the Old Hall Manuscript are unified respectively by closely parallel style, structure and motifs (including an anticipation of head-motif technique), by the use of related chants but separate isorhythmic construction, by parallel structure and the appropriate Ordinary chants in the top voice, and by use of appropriate Ordinary chants in the tenor. In all cases, ranges and signatures support the pairing, although the movements are physically separated according to the organization of the

manuscript. The only Ordinary cycle ascribed to Power without contradiction is *Alma Redemptoris mater*, in which the tenor (the first half of the plainsong antiphon) is presented in identical, unornamented form in each movement, although there is no internal isorhythm within each movement. The four surviving movements (the cycle probably once had a troped Kyrie) vary in length according to the length of the introductory and interpolated duet sections. Many technical and stylistic features support Power's authorship (use of pseudo-augmentation, proportional passages and conflicting time signatures; see §3 below).

Power's claim to the Mass *Rex seculorum* is shared with Dunstable, and that to the Mass *Sine nomine* with Dunstable and Benet. Both of these are free tenor masses, the latter so free as almost to impair its unity. Stylistic evidence as to authorship is not fully conclusive, although certain rhythmic peculiarities, some wayward dissonances and the downward thrust of many melodic phrases suggest Power rather than Dunstable as the composer of *Rex seculorum* (Power used the rising triadic opening less than Dunstable). The tenor is an antiphon for St Benedict; Power has clearer Benedictine associations than Dunstable, and it would be Dunstable's only use of a non-Sarum chant. The majority ascription to Power in the sources is not decisive but cannot be wholly overlooked. *Sine nomine* is altogether less characteristic of Dunstable, and Bukofzer was inclined to favour Benet as the composer. The discovery in Milan of a source ascribing the mass to Power must revive Power's claim to the work: neither mass, however, shows sufficiently strong personal characteristics to permit any final decision.

3. STYLE. It is easier to attempt an approximate chronology for Power's more definitely authentic works than it is for Dunstable's. His composing career was probably more extended, and the early part of it is well defined and characterized in his substantial contribution to the Old Hall Manuscript. His 23 compositions in the original layer (which contains nothing by Dunstable) amount to more than three times the total for any other composer, perhaps indicating some degree of seniority, or a close connection with the compilation. By about 1410–15 he had mastered all the styles of the generation in which he presumably grew up, whereas Dunstable left little evidence of activity earlier than this date. This could be a distortion occasioned by the accidents of survival, which may in turn have deprived us of any isorhythmic motets that Power may have written. Otherwise it would seem to indicate that he was older than Dunstable, or earlier to mature as a composer. His later works are at present known exclusively from continental sources.

Power's Old Hall music includes the simplest of descant settings, with the chant in the middle voice (sometimes migrant, with very little elaboration), freely composed pieces of lush sonority for four and five voices (the Gloria–Credo pair Old Hall nos.21, 77), isorhythmic mass movements (the Gloria–Credo pair Old Hall nos.24, 84, and the Gloria no.23), four-part compositions with Ars Nova rhythms in ¢ time (the Sanctus–Agnus pair Old Hall nos.118, 141) and settings of an elaborately figured and rhythmically complex upper part supported by slower-moving lower parts (Gloria Old Hall no.22, Credo settings nos.81, 83). His style at this period could be seen as a fusion of the English love of full sonorities, a sensuous Italianate melodic instinct, the syncopated rhythms of the French Ars Nova and the proportional ingenuity of the Ars Subtilior (ex.1). It would be invidious to place simplicity earlier than complexity within this range, although surviving English manuscripts of the late 14th century present no evidence of even mild proportional usage nor, before the Fountains fragment (*GB-Lbm* Add.40011*B*), of combinations of the four prolations of the French Ars Nova and use of syncopation, all of which are present in Power's Old Hall works.

Ex.1 Gloria (Old Hall no. 22)

The Old Hall styles, particularly in the case of Power's paired mass movements, overlap with the next stratum, comprising his one contribution to the second layer of that manuscript, the cyclic mass or masses, and most of the motets surviving in continental sources; these later pieces are usually in ○ time (with use of ℂ) rather than ℂ, and with the treble dominating in the manner of the French chanson. The final stage of this approximate chronology consists of the last four motets of Hamm's edition, which clearly anticipate the smooth discant writing of Frye's generation, with their well-integrated duets and increasing participation of the lower parts in the evolution of a more homogeneous texture.

Power's melodic style is not always distinct from Dunstable's, though the rising triadic opening (*see* DUNSTABLE, JOHN, ex.2*d*) is much less common, except where the opening is based on a chant with this feature, such as *Alma Redemptoris mater*. Sequential passages, sometimes based on standard cadential figures, are increasingly common in the middle-to-late works (e.g. the Credo from the *Alma Redemptoris* cycle and *Mater ora filium*). Power was often explicit in his *ficta* indications, writing bold but logical progressions such as in ex.2. It has been suggested that he abandoned the use of plainsong in his later motets, but chant paraphrase is in many cases unmistakable and cannot be overlooked in assessing his melodic style. In some cases there are clear allusions to the relevant chant, especially in the top part and at beginnings of sections, but consistent use of the chant throughout the composition cannot be claimed. Examples of this include the duets in *Regina celi* (LP i, 19), and *Alma Redemptoris mater*, where the chant appears after an eight-bar introduction in migrant form, and intermittently thereafter. In other cases the chant can indeed be traced throughout the composition though, admittedly, portions of the melody may be elided, overlapped or compressed; migration or trans-

position may obscure the outlines; and the melody may get out of step with the words; yet all these features are found in less extreme form in simple descant pieces where the presence of chant is not in doubt (e.g. Byttering's *Nesciens mater*).

With regard to cantus firmus treatment in general, the Old Hall descant settings present the chant in the middle voice with occasional migration to the lowest. The underlay does not always correspond to that of the chant (e.g. *Ave regina* Old Hall no.43, and see above).

Ex.2 Gloria (Aosta)

Increased melodic freedom is found in *Beata viscera*, where it is still in the middle part; and most of the subsequent motets that use chant paraphrase it in the treble (*Salve regina*, LP i, 10, uses the *Alma Redemptoris* plainsong in the treble, an unusual technique at this date). Of his earlier mass movements, most of those whose tenor cantus firmi can be traced use appropriate chants for the Ordinary (one Sanctus–Agnus pair unusually has them in the treble), the exceptions being the Gloria–Credo pair Old Hall nos.24, 84.

Isorhythm in Power's surviving works is confined to mass settings: the Gloria–Credo Old Hall nos.24, 84, the Glorias no.23 and LP ii, 17 (his strictest and most ambitious isorhythmic construction), and the doubtful Credo for three voices. All except the last are isorhythmic in all parts, and this technique seems to be confined to relatively early works. The Old Hall Gloria–Credo pair show some non-coincidence of color and talea (*see* ISORHYTHM).

It is perhaps in features of rhythm that Power's personal style is most evident. The simultaneous use of conflicting time signatures for limited passages is common in early-to-middle works (e.g. the Agnus and Benedictus of the Mass *Alma Redemptoris*; see also ex.2), and at the same period the notation of one or more parts requiring to be read in augmentation to correspond with the others is found, in, for example, the Mass *Alma Redemptoris*, LP ii, 17, the Credos Old Hall nos.81, 83 and the Sanctus Old Hall no.115. These features are not confined to Power, though both are more common in his works than in those of other composers. Nor was he the only composer to incorporate very elaborate syncopations and proportional passages, especially in upper parts of his early works, though the complexity of the Gloria Old Hall no.22 and the Credos nos.81 and 83, the last of which uses blue coloration in addition to void and full red and black notes, as well as numerical and graphic signatures, is rarely surpassed (see ex.1). Short passages of this kind recur with diminishing frequency up to the midpoint of his output (as in ex.2). An individual feature of rhythm found throughout his career is a calculated disregard of regular mensuration. This is reflected by fluctuating bar lengths in modern transcription, as in exx.3 and 6 (early and late works respectively), and also ex.4, though shown here with regular barring. Together with this goes a predilection for asymmetry, especially in melodic and rhythmic sequences and imitation (see ex.4). His use of sequences is more extensive than Dunstable's; they are often closely packed, sometimes occurring on different beats of the bar – a stretto effect which is sometimes achieved by rhythmic inexactitude in the limbs of the sequence. There is also a little more imitation (see especially ex.6, but also exx.4 and 5).

Ex.3 Gloria (Old Hall no. 21)

Ex.4 *Anima mea liquefacta est (I-MOe α.X.1.11)*

Ex.5 Credo from Mass *Alma Redemptoris mater*

A constant refinement of harmony and texture can be traced in Power's development. His love of full sonorities is evident in his Old Hall compositions (no.15, exceptionally, has a 3rd in the final chord), and he often luxuriates freely over a single note or chord with free-wheeling imitations, as in ex.5 which also demonstrates the asymmetrical rhythms mentioned above. He shows a preference for relatively low tessituras (ex.6). Dissonances are prepared with increasing care, and the final motets are completely pan-consonant. Leaps of 4ths and 5ths are common in the early duets (ex.3); simultaneously sounded dissonances are not avoided, though simultaneous leaps are quite rare. Power's late duet writing has greater poise and fluency and is largely conjunct, with a few leaps of 3rds as well as carefully placed larger intervals (see exx.4 and 6). Early works in three or four parts gradually give way to three-part compositions with extensive duets; in the very last works the duets are shorter again, but more integrated (as in ex.6).

Power shows little awareness of text declamation, except on the occasional isolated word. None of his compositions is as consistently declamatory as Dunstable's *Quam pulchra es*, though his setting of this text contains more careful declamation than any of his other works (ex.6). A few distinct habits in early mass settings, though not confined to Power, include the telescoping of the Credo text (Old Hall nos.73, 77, 83, and the anonymous three-voice setting), and perhaps the commencement of polyphony not at 'Patrem' but at 'factorem' (no.73, also the anonymous three-voice setting; similarly the anonymous Gloria printed as no.10 in the complete works of Dunstable).

The treatise (*GB-Lbm* Lansdowne 763) is headed 'This tretis is contrivid upon the Gamme for hem that wil be syngers or makers or techers' and concludes 'Quod Lyonel Power'. It precedes an anonymous treatise on faburden and one on proportions ascribed to Chilston. The volume was copied by JOHN WYLDE, a 15th-century precentor of Waltham Abbey, and contains 20 musical treatises of which the three mentioned above are in English, the remainder in Latin. Power's treatise deals with the sights of DISCANT, naming them mean, treble and quatreble. 'To enforme a childe in his counterpoynt', Power gave exhaustive permutations for the two last-named (the highest; as master of the Lady Chapel at Canterbury, he would have been concerned primarily with training boys). In advocating contrary motion, he expressly forbade parallel perfect intervals, although there are some instances of such parallels in his own music, mainly in early works.

For a page of Power's treatise, *see* DISCANT.

Ex.6 *Quam pulchra es*
Antiphonale sarisburiense, 528

WORKS

Editions: *L. Power: Complete Works*, ed. C. Hamm, CMM, 1 (1969–76) [LP]
J. Dunstable: Complete Works, ed. M. F. Bukofzer, MB, viii (1953, rev. 2/1970) [JD]
The Old Hall Manuscript, ed. A. Hughes and M. Bent, CMM, xlvi (1969–72) [OH]

Title/Incipit	Voices	No. in edns.	Remarks
MASS CYCLES AND INTERRELATED MASS MOVEMENTS			
Gloria, Credo, Sanctus, Agnus	3	LP ii, 18	isorhythmic; on Alma Redemptoris mater
Kyrie, Gloria, Credo, Sanctus, Agnus	3	LP ii, 22; JD 70, 19–22	on Rex seculorum; also attrib. Dunstable
Kyrie, Gloria, Credo, Sanctus, Agnus	3	LP ii, 26; JD 71, 56–9	[Sine nomine]; also attrib. Dunstable and Benet
Gloria, Credo	4/5	LP ii, 8; OH 21, 77	
Gloria, Credo	3	LP ii, 11; OH 24, 84	isorhythmic; on lauds antiphons for St Thomas of Canterbury
Sanctus, Agnus	3	LP ii, 20; OH 116, 140	on Sarum Sanctus II, Agnus VII
Sanctus, Agnus	4	LP ii, 7; OH 118, 141	on Sarum Sanctus III, Agnus XII
SINGLE MASS MOVEMENTS			
Kyrie	3		bottom voice survives in *GB-Lbm* Lansdowne 462, f.152; frag. of 3vv setting *Lpro* E/163/22/1/3
Kyrie 'Lux et origo'	3		on Sarum chant; *I-AO*, ff.11*v*–12; *GB-Ob* Linc. lat.89, f.31*v* (top voice only)
Gloria	3	LP ii, 16; OH 22	
Gloria	4	LP ii, 9; OH 23	isorhythmic
Gloria	3	LP ii, 10; OH 25	
Gloria	3	LP ii, 25	also attrib. Benet
Gloria	3	LP ii, 4; JD 3	also attrib. Dunstable
Gloria	3	LP ii, 17	isorhythmic; on Sarum Gloria V; scribally paired with anon. Credo, 3vv, see 'Works of doubtful authenticity'
Credo	3	LP ii, 19; OH 73	on Sarum Credo (opening)
Credo	3	LP ii, 13; OH 81	
Credo	3	LP ii, 14; OH 83	
Sanctus	3	LP ii, 1; OH 96	on Sarum Sanctus I
Sanctus	3	LP ii, 2; OH 99	on Sarum Sanctus III
Sanctus	3	LP ii, 3; OH 109	on Sarum Sanctus X
Sanctus	3	LP ii, 15*a*; OH 115	Hamm suggested pairing with anon. Agnus, see 'Works of doubtful authenticity'
Sanctus	4	LP ii, 21; OH 117	on Sarum Sanctus III
Agnus	3	LP ii, 4; OH 133	on Sarum Agnus XII
Agnus	3	LP ii, 5; OH 137	on Sarum Agnus VII
Agnus	3	LP ii, 6; OH 138	on Sarum Agnus X
OTHER SETTINGS OF SACRED LATIN TEXTS			
Alma Redemptoris mater	3	LP i, 16; JD 40	? by Dunstable; free use of plainsong
Alma Redemptoris mater	3	LP i, 21; JD 60	also attrib. Dunstable; free use of plainsong
Anima mea liquefacta est [=Christus resurgens]	2/3	LP i, 18, 18*bis*	paraphrase of plainsong
Anima mea liquefacta est	3	LP i, 25	
Ave regina celorum, ave	3	LP i, 2; OH 43	on plainsong
Ave regina celorum, ave	4	LP i, 7	paraphrase of plainsong
Beata progenies	3	LP i, 1; OH, 49	on plainsong
Beata viscera	3	LP i, 5	on plainsong

Title/Incipit	Voices	No. in edns.	Remarks
Christus resurgens [=Anima mea liquefacta est]			
Gloriose virginis	4	LP i, 12	free use of plainsong
Ibo michi admontem	3	LP i, 24	
Mater ora filium	3	LP i, 23	
Quam pulchra es	3	LP i, 26	free use of plainsong
Regina celi	3	LP i, 19	free use of plainsong
Salve mater Salvatoris	3	LP i, 17; JD 62	also attrib. Dunstable
Salve regina	3	LP i, 10	paraphrase of plainsong Alma Redemptoris
Salve regina	3	LP i, 22; JD 63	also attrib. Dunstable; plainsong for invocations only
Salve sancta parens [=Virgo prudentissima]	3	LP i, 14	
		WORKS OF DOUBTFUL AUTHENTICITY (all anon.)	
Credo	3		isorhythmic; on Sarum Credo; scribally paired with Gloria in LP ii, 17
Credo	4/5	LP ii, 12; OH 82	probably by Cooke, on palaeographic grounds
Agnus	3	LP ii, 15b	Hamm suggested pairing with Sanctus in LP ii, 15a
Angelorum esca	3	LP i, 20	
Ave maris stella	3	LP i, 4	?attrib. based on misreading of folio no. in Castello del Buon Consiglio, Trent, 92 as 'Leonel'
Ave regina celorum, mater	3	LP i, 6	
Benedicta es celorum regina	3	LP i, 15	paraphrase of plainsong
Descendi in ortum meum	3	LP i, 13	
Regina celi	3	LP i, 2; OH 44	on plainsong
Regina celi	3	LP i, 11	paraphrase of plainsong
Sancta Maria	3	LP i, 8	
Spes nostra	3	LP i, 9	

BIBLIOGRAPHY

W. G. Searle, ed.: *The Chronicle of John Stone, Monk of Christ Church 1415–71* (Cambridge, 1902)

W. H. G. Flood: *A History of Irish Music* (Dublin, 1905, 3/1913/R1970, 4/1927)

S. B. Meech: 'Three Fifteenth-century English Musical Treatises', *Speculum*, x (1935), 242 [incl. edn. of treatise]

M. F. Bukofzer: *Geschichte des englischen Diskants und des Fauxbourdons nach den theoretischen Quellen* (Strasbourg, 1936)

T. Georgiades: *Englische Diskanttraktate aus der ersten Hälfte des 15. Jahrhunderts* (Munich, 1937)

F. Ll. Harrison: *Music in Medieval Britain* (London, 1958, 2/1963)

M. F. Bukofzer: 'English Church Music of the Fifteenth Century', *NOHM*, iii (1960), 165–213

N. Bridgman: 'Un manuscrit milanais (Biblioteca Nazionale Braidense Cod. AD. XIV.49)', *RIM*, i (1966), 237

C. Hamm: 'The Motets of Lionel Power', *Studies in Music History: Essays for Oliver Strunk* (Princeton, 1968), 126

M. Bent: *The Old Hall Manuscript: a Paleographical Study* (diss., U. of Cambridge, 1969)

R. D. Bowers: *Choral Institutions within the English Church, 1340–1500* (diss., U. of East Anglia, 1975), esp. 4033, 5036ff

——: 'Some Observations on the Life and Career of Lionel Power', *PRMA*, cii (1975–6), 103

A. M. Seaman: 'The Music of Lincoln College MS Latin 89: a Postscript', *RMARC*, xiv (in preparation)

For further bibliography see OLD HALL MS; DUNSTABLE, JOHN; ENGLAND: BIBLIOGRAPHY OF MUSIC TO 1600.

MARGARET BENT

Power, William. Irish music publisher, brother and sometime partner of JAMES POWER.

Powers, Harold S(tone) (*b* New York, 5 Aug 1928). American musicologist. He attended Stanford University and received the BMus from Syracuse University (1950). He then studied at Princeton University under Milton Babbitt and Edward T. Cone (theory) and Oliver Strunk and Arthur Mendel (musicology); he took the MFA there in 1952 and the PhD in 1959 with a dissertation on the raga system. He taught at Princeton (1955–8) and Harvard (1958–60) and then moved to the University of Pennsylvania, where he was appointed (1971) professor of music and South Asian regional studies. In 1973 he became professor of music at Princeton.

Powers's interests include theory, Italian opera and Indian music. His operatic studies are centred on later 17th-century Italian compositions and the ways in which these works show the development of formal organization for dramatic purposes; his comparative examinations of different settings of the same libretto reveal both progressive and conservative techniques employed by composers of the time. Powers's knowledge of Indian music was aided by study in India as a Fulbright fellow and a Rockefeller scholar (1952–4, 1960–61, 1967–8). His Indian teachers include Rangaramanuja Ayyangar, Balwant Ray Bhatt and Prem Lata Sharma. He is aware of the problems of a Westerner approaching non-Western music; in his writings, for example, he cautions the reader about making unjustified comparisons between Western mode and Indian raga, or attempting to consider present-day Indian practice in the light of early Indian theory. His historical and analytical study of raga classifications is a lucid exposition of one approach to this music, and the musical and historical methods employed should be equally applicable to any body of music, Eastern or Western.

WRITINGS

'Mode and Raga', *MQ*, xliv (1958), 448

The Background of the South Indian Rāga-System (diss., Princeton U., 1959)

Review of M. Hood: *The Nuclear Theme as a Determinant of Patet in Javanese Music* (Groningen, 1954), *JAMS*, xii (1959), 65

'Il Serse trasformato', *MQ*, xlvii (1961), 481; xlviii (1962), 73

Review of M. Kolinski, ed.: *Studies in Ethnomusicology* (New York, 1961), *EM*, vi (1962), 220; vii (1963), 149

'Indian Music and the English Language: a Review Essay', *EM*, ix (1965), 1

Review of A. Merriam: *The Anthropology of Music* (Evanston, Ill., 1964), *PNM*, iv/2 (1966), 161

ed.: *Studies in Music History: Essays for Oliver Strunk* (Princeton, 1968) [incl. 'L'Erismena travestita', 259–324]

'Sangīta-śāstra and śāstriya-sangīta', *Indian Music Journal*, ix (1968), 52

Review of W. Kaufman: *The Ragas of North India* (Bloomington, Ind., 1968), *EM*, xiii (1969), 350

'An Historical and Comparative Approach to the Classification of Ragas (with an Appendix on Ancient Indian Tunings)', *Selected Reports*, i/3 (1970), 1–78

'Ritigaula: a Case Study of Improvisation in Indian Music (with an Appendix on the South Indian Ornament System)', *Improvisation East and West*, ed. L. Meyer and E. Zonis (Chicago, 1973)

'The Modality of "Vestiva i colli" ', *Studies in Renaissance and Baroque Music in Honor of Arthur Mendel* (Kassel and Hackensack, 1974), 31
'The Structure of Musical Meaning: a View from Banaras', *PNM*, xiv/2–xv/1 (1976), 308
'India, subcontinent of', §§I–II, 'Mode', *Grove 6*

PAULA MORGAN

Powwow. A pan-Indian festivity, *see* NORTH AMERICA, §II, 2(iv).

Poynt [Poynte, Poynts, Poyntz] (*fl* 1555–84). English composer. He is probably to be identified with the Robert Poyntz (*b* Winchester, *c*1535) who belonged to a well-known Essex family and became a perpetual Fellow of New College, Oxford, on 26 August 1554, and graduated BA on 5 June 1556 and MA on 27 May 1560. As a Catholic divine Poynt emigrated to Louvain early in the reign of Elizabeth. Poynt wrote a fine five-part In Nomine (*GB-Lbm*, *Lcm*), one in four parts (*Ob*) and a full anthem *Blessed are all they that fear the Lord* (*Lbm*, cantus only).

NORMAN JOSEPHS

Poznań (Ger. Posen). City in central Poland, the earliest capital of the Polish state (until *c*1038). The musical tradition of Poznań, into which there has been little research, dates from the foundation there of the oldest bishopric in Poland in 968. At that time it was the first centre in the region to cultivate Gregorian chant, which was of the Benedictine type until the 12th century. The bishops of Poznań included Jan Łodzia z Kępy (*d* 1346), creator of the Polish sequence. The first mention of an organ in Poznań dates from 1400, and from the 15th century there are records of the performance of mystery plays in the church of Boże Ciało (Corpus Christi). In the 16th century the cathedral and the collegiate church of St Maria Magdalena (burnt down in the 18th century) were the main musical centres; music was also cultivated at the court of the Górka family, who patronized Hermann Finck and to whom the latter dedicated his treatise *Musica practica* (1556). Music-making among the middle classes in Renaissance Poznań is indicated by the musical items mentioned in wills of the period. An outstanding 16th-century composer from Poznań was Jan Brant, known as Posnaniensis. A permanent cathedral chapel was founded before 1650, when it numbered five singers and eight instrumentalists. During the Baroque period chapels also existed at other Poznań churches; in 1774 the collegiate chapel numbered 12 members.

In 1793 Poznań was annexed to Prussia, and until Poland regained its independence in 1918 the cultural life of the city was dominated by Polish–German struggles, which were unfavourable to artistic development. Poznań's symphonic music was provincial in character, although the city's position on the route from Berlin to Warsaw and St Petersburg took many famous virtuosos there, including Chopin and Liszt. In 1875 Ladegast built an organ of 43 stops in the collegiate church; it survives, and is one of the best Romantic instruments in Poland. At the beginning of the 19th century the music publishing house of A. Simon was based in Poznań; the publishing tradition was continued until the early 20th century by K. T. Barwicki (1871–1931), who was connected with the Polish nationalistic choral movement which developed at that time. Józef Surzyński, an editor of early Polish music, worked in

Poznań (1881–94), as did the composer Feliks Nowowiejski between 1919 and his death in 1946.

Poznań is one of the main centres of 20th-century Polish musical culture. Among the active musical institutions are the Opera (1919), named after Stanisław Moniuszko; the Filharmonia (1947), with which the famous Chór Chłopięco-Męski S. Stuligrosza works, continuing the tradition of the cathedral choir of Wacław Gieburowski; the only museum of instruments in Poland (a department of the National Museum); and the State Music High School (a conservatory from 1920). From 1953 the H. Wieniawski International Violin Competition has taken place in Poznań. At Poznań University (1919, named after Adam Mickiewicz) the professors of musicology have included Lucjan Kamieński (1922–39) and Adolf Chybiński (1945–52); their colleagues have included Wacław Gieburowski, Marian Sobieski and Maria Szczepańska.

Poznań libraries possess a number of music sources, notably the Chybiński collection (in *PL-Pu*), which includes parchment fragments with neumatic notation, 13th-century Notre Dame motets, polyphony of the late Ars Nova, choral parts (*c*1500) of works by Dufay and Josquin, partbooks from the Kraków Capella Rorantistarum and the most important source of Polish *kolędy* (carols). Other libraries contain a valuable fragment of choral parts (*c*1500, in *PL-Pr*), medieval liturgical manuscripts and a fragment of an early 16th-century theoretical treatise (in *PL-Pa*). The local Franciscan library possesses the manuscript of the musical treatise of Marek z Płocka (1518).

BIBLIOGRAPHY

H. Ehrenberg: *Geschichte des Theaters in Posen* (Poznań, 1889)
G. Chmarzyński, W. Kamiński, Z. Sitowski and T. Szulc: Chapters on music in *Dziesięć wieków Poznania* [Ten centuries of Poznań], ii (Poznań, 1956), 250–87
J. Klawitter, J. Młodziejowski and others: *Filharmonia poznańska* (Poznań, 1957)
M. Perz: 'Handschrift Nr. 1361 der Öffentlichen Städtischen Raczyński-Bibliothek in Poznań', *Chopin Congress: Warszawa 1960*, 588
F. Dąbrowski, ed.: *Państwowa wyższa szkoła muzyczna w Poznaniu* [The state music high school in Poznań] (Poznań, 1962)
N. Karaśkiewicz: *Chór chłopięcy i męski Państwowej filharmonii w Poznaniu* (Poznań, 1962)
M. Perz: 'Starosądecki urywek motetów średniowiecznych w Bibliotece Uniwersyteckiej w Poznaniu' [Fragments of medieval motets from Stary Sącz in Poznań University library], *Muzyka*, xxv/1 (1971), 77
T. Świtała: *Opera poznańska 1919–1969* (Poznań, 1973)

MIROSŁAW PERZ

Poźniak, Włodzimierz (*b* Kraków, 28 June 1904; *d* Kraków, 29 Jan 1967). Polish musicologist and composer. He studied musicology with Jachimecki at Kraków University until 1930 and composition in Kraków (1929–32) with M. Piotrowski, B. Wallek-Walewski and B. Rizzi. In 1932 he took the doctorate at Kraków with a dissertation on Eugeniusz Pankiewicz. He continued his musicological studies in Berlin (1934–5) with Schering, Schmitz, Schünemann and Ernst Pepping. He held posts as lecturer in the musicology department at Kraków University (1930–39), and lecturer in theoretical subjects at Kraków Conservatory (1930–37) and at the Moniuszko School of Music in Kraków (1937–9). He spent the war years as a POW in Germany, and then returned to his university post at Kraków, where he completed his *Habilitation* in 1947 with a work on the chorale Passion in Poland; he became reader in 1956 and head of the department in 1963. He also lectured at the State Music School in Katowice (1952–3), directed the collecting of folk music in southern Poland (1950–55) and from 1962 was the head of the folk music institute attached to the musicology department at Kraków University. His compositions include orchestral, chamber and vocal works, and he has edited folksong collections, and songs by Pankiewicz, Żelenski, Melcer and Kurpiński.

WRITINGS

Eugeniusz Pankiewicz (diss., U. of Kraków, 1932; Kraków, 1958)

Romans wokalny w twórczości M. Kl. Ogińskiego [Ogiński's solo songs] (Kraków, 1934)

Do genezy polskiego hymnu narodowego [The genesis of the Polish national anthem] (Katowice, 1939)

Pasja choralowa w Polsce [The chorale Passion in Poland] (Habilitationsschrift, U. of Kraków, 1947; Kraków, 1947)

'Niezrealizowane projekty operowe Moniuszki' [Moniuszko's unrealized operatic projects], KM, xxi–xxii (1948), 234

'Opera polska przed Moniuszką' [Polish opera before Moniuszko], Muzyka, ii/12 (1951), 30

Cyrulik sewilski J. Rossiniego [Rossini's Barber of Seville] (Kraków, 1955, 2/1957)

Paleografia muzyczna (Łódź, 1955) [manual]

Wesele Figara W. A. Mozarta [Mozart's Marriage of Figaro] (Kraków, 1956)

Historia instrumentacji (Kraków, 1965)

Echo muzyczne 1877–1882; Echo muzyczne, teatralne i artystyczne 1883–1907 (Kraków, 1965–73)

'Główne gatunki i formy muzyki polskiej XIX wieku' [Principal categories and forms in 19th-century Polish music], Z dziejów polskiej kultury muzycznej [A history of Polish musical culture], ii (Kraków, 1966), 265–400, 463–552

'Elementy muzyki ludowej w profesjonalnej muzyce drugiej połowy XIX wieku' [Folk music elements in professional music in the second half of the 19th century], Muzyka, xii/4 (1967), 8

'Ogólna charakterystyka skal na terenie Wielkopolski i Małopolski' [The general characteristics of the scales in the Wielkopolska and Małopolska regions], Studia Hieronymo Feicht septuagenario dedicata (Kraków, 1967), 37

FOLKSONG EDITIONS

Piosenki z żywieckiego [Folksongs from the Żywiec region] (Kraków, 1955)

Piosenki z krakowskiego [Folksongs from the Kraków region] (Kraków, 1955)

Pieśni ludu krakowskiego [Popular songs from Kraków] (Kraków, 1956)

BIBLIOGRAPHY

J. Parzyński: 'Włodzimierz Poźniak 1904–1967', Ruch muzyczny, vii (1967), 5

T. Przybylski: 'Włodzimierz Poźniak 28 VI 1904–29 I 1967', Kronika Uniwersytetu Jagiellońskiego za rok akademicki 1966–7 (Kraków, 1970)

ZOFIA HELMAN

Pozsony (Hung.). BRATISLAVA.

Pozzi, Luigi (b Venzone, nr. Udine, fl 1638–56). Italian composer. He received a degree in theology from the University of Padua in 1638. His publications describe him as 'Don', 'Dottore' and 'Academico sventato'. The first title implies that he was a cleric; the last suggests an association with Udine. The inclusion of a 'canzonetta furlana' in his third print also points to his origins in the Friuli region. Except for a single duet all his surviving compositions are sacred and secular songs for solo voice with continuo accompaniment. One song employs an extravagant and artificial chromatic notation.

WORKS

Arie . . . a 1, 2, mentioned in 1649 Vincenti catalogue

Zodiaco celeste in cui vegonsi dodici segni di spirituali concenti, 1v, bc (Venice, 1650)

La cerva savorgnana stridatrice di spirituali concenti, 1v, bc, op.3, (Venice, 1652)

L'innocenza dei Ciclopi, overo Concenti diatonici, cromatici ed henarmonici, 1, 2vv, bc (Venice, 1654)

1 song in 1656[4]

BIBLIOGRAPHY

L. Sereni: 'Passeggiate venzonesi: storie di stemmi e di famiglie nobili', Società filologica friulana (1971), 454

THOMAS WALKER

Pozzi Escot, (Olga) (b Lima, 1 Oct 1931). Peruvian composer, theorist and teacher. She received her musical education at the Sas-Rosay Academy of Music in Lima, the Juilliard School and the Hamburg Hochschule für Musik. She has taught theory and composition at the New England Conservatory, has been a fellow of the Radcliffe Institute, and has lectured in Europe and the Americas. Together with her husband, the American composer and musicologist Robert Cogan, she received a grant from the Ford Foundation and the Music Educators National Conference to write Sonic Design (1972), a new approach to the understanding and teaching of music from diverse cultures and periods. She became lecturer in contemporary music and director of the electronic studio at Wheaton College.

While living in the USA, she has maintained close contact with her native country, her external position permitting her a balanced view of the changing ideas in South America – ideas which have stimulated her musicological, teaching and compositional work. Works have been commissioned from her by the Organization of American States, the Venezuelan Government and the Hartt Chamber Players; her music has been performed by noted players throughout the Americas and Europe. A pursuit of unusual sonorities is a general characteristic of Pozzi Escot's work (the wide range of vocal effects in Lamentos provides a good example) and she has often written for highly individual combinations of voices and instruments, though also for conventional orchestra. Sessions has praised her study of his work as 'the best introduction to my music that I know'.

WORKS
(selective list)

VOCAL

Two Lamentations (Pozzi Escot), v, pf, 1950; Songs of my Country (trad.), v, pf, 1954; Songs of Wisdom (S. Crane), v, pf, 1955; Sands I (Pozzi Escot), A, orch, 1958; Credo (Hopkins), S, str qt, 1958; 3 Poems of Rilke, speaker, str qt, 1958; Lamentos (Pozzi Escot), S, 2 vn, 2 vc, pf, perc, 1962; Visione (Pozzi Escot), S, speaker, fl, a sax, db, 1964; Ainu (Pozzi Escot), 4 ens of 5vv, 1969

PIANO

Children's Pieces, 2 sets, 1942–6, 1947; 6 Portraits, 1949; 3 Sonatinas, 1950, 1951, 1952; Diferencias I, 1961; Diferencias II, 1963; Interra, pf, tape, 1968

OTHER WORKS

3 str qts, 1951, 1954, 1956; Metamorphosis, ballet, 1951; 3 symphonies, 1953, 1955, 1957; Cristos, a fl, dbn, perc, 3 vn, 1963; Sands II, 5 sax, elec gui, 4 b drums, 17 vn, 1966

WRITINGS

'Roger Sessions', Inter-American Music Bulletin, no.17 (1963)

'Contemporary Music and the Concert Repertory', Music of the Americas (Bloomington, Ind., 1965)

with R. Cogan: Sonic Design: the Nature of Sound and Music (Cambridge, Mass., 1972)

CÉSAR ARRÓSPIDE DE LA FLOR

Pozzoli, Ettore (b Seregno, nr. Milan, 22 July 1873; d Seregno, 9 Sept 1957). Italian pianist, composer and teacher. A pupil of Ferroni, Appiani and Polibio Fumagalli at the Milan Conservatory, he became a concert pianist for a short time, then a highly esteemed teacher. In 1899 he returned to the Milan Conservatory, where he taught solfeggio and theory. He published useful methods for these subjects and for the piano, as well as piano studies, transcriptions and editions of piano works by Bach, Beethoven, Liszt, Weber and others. He also contributed articles to music magazines. His compositions include an oratorio, La figlia di Jefte, an organ mass, motets, a set of orchestral variations, a piano concerto, a concert allegro for piano and orchestra, a quartet, a trio, pieces for violin and piano and some well-written piano pieces (for which he was best known).

BIBLIOGRAPHY

G. Confalonieri: 'In memoria di Ettore Pozzoli', *Ricordiana*, iii (1957), 547

——: 'Ettore Pozzoli', *I grandi anniversari del 1960 e la musica sinfonica e da camera nell' Ottocento in Italia*, Chigiana, xvii (1960), 145

S. Martinotti: *Ottocento strumentale italiano* (Bologna, 1972)

SERGIO MARTINOTTI

pp. *Pianissimo* (It.: 'very soft'); *see* PIANO.

Práč, Jan Bohumir [Prach, Ivan]. *See* PRATSCH, JOHANN GOTTFRIED.

Practice chanter. A double-reed wind-cap instrument, used by Scottish highland bagpipers, with tuning and fingering equivalent to that of an actual bagpipe chanter. Because of its narrow cylindrical bore and longer, less stiff reed, it sounds an octave lower than the bagpipe chanter and has a much softer tone.

Pradas Gallen, José (*b* Villahermosa del Río, Castellón, 21 Aug 1689; *d* Villahermosa del Río, 11 Aug 1757). Spanish composer. In 1700 he entered Valencia Cathedral as a chorister, where he had Teodoro Ortells as a teacher of theory and probably Cabanilles for organ. In 1712 he obtained after public competition the post of choirmaster and organist at the parish church at Algemesí, where he now began systematically to compose. In 1714 he seems to have competed unsuccessfully for the position of choirmaster at Valencia Cathedral (the post went to Pedro Rabassa). In June 1717, again after a competition, he secured a similar post at the cathedral in Castellón de la Plana, where he continued to compose prolifically. Finally, on 2 March 1728, on the strength of his reputation, and without the usual competition, he obtained the post of choirmaster at Valencia Cathedral. After nearly 30 years' service there he retired on 22 February 1757 and, freed of his obligations in Valencia, he returned to his native village where he died a few months later.

Many of Pradas Gallen's works are extant, including some he composed in Algemesí and Castellón: seven masses and a requiem, 60 psalms (including 34 *Miserere* settings, which make their composer probably the most prolific in this genre in Spain), 22 motets, 279 villancicos, some *gozos*, a cantata and an *Opera a San José* (mostly in *E-VAc*, also *E*, *Mn*).

BIBLIOGRAPHY

LaborD

J. Ruiz de Lihory: *La música en Valencia* (Valencia, 1903)

V. Ripollés: *El villancico i la cantata del segle XVIII a València* (Valencia, 1935) [incl. cantata *Ah del célebre confín* and aria *Ya, Señor*]

J. Piedra: 'Maestros de capilla del Real Colegio de Corpus Christi (Patriarca) (1662–1822)', *AnM*, xxiii (1968), 61–127

J. Climent: 'José Pradas (1689–1757)', *Tesoro sacro musical*, lvii (1974), 116 [incl. 5 arias]

JOSÉ LÓPEZ-CALO

Prades Festival. An annual festival held in Prades, a small French village 40 km from Perpignan, to which Pablo Casals chose to exile himself as a protest against General Franco's regime in Spain. In 1949 Casals was visited by the violinist Alexander Schneider, who was commissioned to offer him substantial contracts to play in the USA; Casals refused, but Schneider conceived the idea, to which Casals agreed, of inviting musicians to Prades to perform with him. The first festival (1950) coincided with the bicentenary of Bach's death, but its success led to the event being repeated annually during July and August as the Prades Festival. In 1968 management of the festival was taken over by the town, with the mayor as president; it is directed by a committee of Casals's associates and financially supported by the departmental government. Artists invited have included Rudolf Serkin, Isaac Stern, Clara Haskil, William Primrose, Marcel Dupré and Alexander Schneider, and (in the 1970s) Pierre Fournier, Alexis Weissenberg, Henryk Szeryng, Christoph Eschenbach, Josef Suk, the Academy of St Martin-in-the-Fields and the Deller Consort. The programmes, given in the small church of the abbey of St Michael of Cuxa, consist chiefly of works by Bach, Beethoven, Mozart, Brahms, Vivaldi and earlier composers.

CLAUDE SAMUEL

Prado, José (Antonio) de Almeida (*b* Santos, 8 Feb 1943). Brazilian composer. He studied the piano with Dinorah de Carvalho and composition with Lacerda and Guarnieri in Santos. In 1963 he graduated from the Santos Conservatory, where he taught the piano from 1965 to 1969. He then studied in Santiago de Compostela with Clemente Terni (1967) and in Paris with Boulanger and Messiaen (1969–73). Back in Brazil he directed the Municipal Conservatory of Cubatão, São Paulo (1973–4), took part in the Seventh Paraná Music Festival (1974) and was appointed professor of composition at the State University of Campinas (1974). He has also given piano recitals of his own and other Brazilian music.

Prado's early works, such as the *Variações sobre um tema do Rio Grande do Norte* for piano (1963), reveal the nationalist influence of Guarnieri. In this particular work, for example, the folk theme is varied with the use of typical features from folk genres such as the *tonada*, the *modinha* and the *moda de viola*, though the music is atonal. Prado quickly freed himself from this sphere, however, and began in the mid-1960s to cultivate a style in which post-Webernian serialism is found together with highly individual harmonic and timbre effects (the voice having an important part in the latter) and rigorous structures. His oratorio *Thérèse: l'amour de Dieu* displays a kinship with the mysticism of Messiaen's *Transfiguration*.

WORKS
(selective list)

Orch: Estações, 1964; Variações, pf, orch, 1964; Sym. no.1, 1969; Cerimonial, bn, orch, 1973; Exoflora, pf, orch, 1974; Aurora, pf, wind qnt, orch, 1975

Vocal: Missa da paz, chorus, 1965; Paixão segundo São Marcos, S, A, T, B, 3 choruses, org, pf, 1967; Pequenos funerais cantantes, Mez, Bar, chorus, orch, 1969; Villegagnon, ou Les isles fortunées, S, chorus, orch, 1973; Thérèse: l'amour de Dieu, S, A, chorus, orch, 1975

Ens: Letter from Patmos, ?1970; Letter de Jerusalem, perc, ?1971

Pf: Variações sobre um tema do Rio Grande do Norte, 1963; Toccata, 1964; Sonata, 1965; Variações, recitative e fuga, 1968; Taaroa, 1971; Momentos, 1973; Ilhas, 1973; Mapas celestes, 1974

Principal publishers: Tonos, Vitale

BIBLIOGRAPHY

Caldeira Filho: *A aventura da música* (São Paulo, 1969)

GERARD BÉHAGUE

Prado Peraita, Germán (*b* Barbadillo del Pez, nr. Burgos, 8 Oct 1891). Spanish scholar of plainchant. A Benedictine monk at Santo Domingo de Silos since 1909, he completed all his studies there and in 1915 was ordained priest. He was choirmaster of Silos Abbey from 1922 to 1948 and edited the *Revista* *eclesiástica* from 1924 to 1932. He is a specialist in Mozarabic rite in all its aspects, historical, textual and musical, and has lectured on Mozarabic and Gregorian chant in schools and seminaries throughout Spain.

WRITINGS

Textos inéditos de la liturgia mozárabe (Madrid, 1926)
Manual de liturgia hispano-visigótica o mozárabe (Madrid, 1927)
Historia del rito mozárabe y toledano (Silos, 1928)
'Mozarabic Melodies', *Speculum*, iii (1928), 218
with C. Rojo: *El canto mozárabe* (Barcelona, 1929)
Supplementum ad Kyriale: ex codicibus hispanicis excerptum (Tournai, 1934)
Cantus Lamentationum (Tournai, 1934)
El canto gregoriano (Barcelona, 1945)

EDITIONS

with W. M. Whitehill: *Liber Beati Jacobi: Codex Calixtinus* (Santiago de Compostela, 1944)
FRANCISCO LARA

Praeambulum (Lat.). PRELUDE.

Praeconium paschale. *See* EXULTET.

Praeger, Ferdinand (Christian Wilhelm) (*b* Leipzig, 22 Jan 1815; *d* London, 2 Sept 1891). German composer, pianist and writer. He was the son of Heinrich Aloys Praeger (*b* Amsterdam, 23 Dec 1783; *d* Magdeburg, 7 Aug 1854), a violinist, guitarist and composer (especially of chamber music), and opera director in Leipzig (1818–28), Magdeburg and Hanover. Ferdinand developed his gifts early, playing the cello well at the age of nine but transferring to the piano on Hummel's advice. In 1831 he taught at The Hague, also continuing his piano, violin and composition studies. In 1834 he settled in London, where he was much in demand as a teacher, and from 1842 he acted as London correspondent of the *Neue Zeitschrift für Musik*. He gave a successful concert of his compositions at Paris in January 1851, and in 1852 he played at Leipzig, Berlin and Hamburg. His overture *Abellino* was conducted by Berlioz in July 1855, and in 1867 his Piano Trio was chosen for performance at Meiningen. He also composed a symphonic prelude to Byron's *Manfred* (1880), piano pieces and songs. A concert of his works was organized by his pupils on 10 July 1879 in London.

An early enthusiast for Wagner, Praeger was partly (not, as he claimed, primarily) responsible for the invitation to Wagner to conduct eight of the Philharmonic Society's concerts in London in 1855. Wagner stayed with him; and they had further contacts in 1877, and at other times and places. Nevertheless, he greatly exaggerated his closeness to Wagner, and in *Wagner as I Knew him* (London, 1855; Ger. trans., Leipzig, 1892 as *Wagner, wie ich ihn kannte*) he went so far as to falsify evidence, inventing stories and altering letters (differently in the English and German editions) so as to exalt his role in Wagner's career. This distortion was exposed by various biographers, chiefly Ashton Ellis, and in 1893 Houston Stewart Chamberlain obtained the original letters from the Earl of Dysart as evidence for his exposure. This proved so devastating that the German publishers withdrew Praeger's book. Though now totally discredited, the book retains a certain interest for some personal impressions of Wagner, not all of which are as mendacious as was once thought. Praeger was in turn described by Wagner as, 'an unusually good-natured man, though one too excitable for his standard of culture' (*Mein Leben*).

BIBLIOGRAPHY

H. S. Chamberlain: *Richard Wagners echte Briefe an Ferdinand Praeger: Kritik der Praeger'schen Veröffentlichungen* (Bayreuth, 1894, rev. 2/1908)
W. A. Ellis: *The Life of Wagner* (London, 1906–8)
P. Pretzsch, ed.: *Cosima Wagner und Houston Stewart Chamberlain im Briefwechsel, 1888–1908* (Leipzig, 1934)
M. Gregor-Dellin, ed.: *Richard Wagner: Mein Leben* (Munich, 1963)
GEORGE GROVE/JOHN WARRACK

Praelegenda. *See* MOZARABIC RITE, MUSIC OF THE, §4(i).

Praelisauer. Family of south German monastic composers and organists, consisting of five brothers.

(1) **Anton Simon Ignaz Praelisauer** (baptized Kötzting, Bavaria, 13 Aug 1692; *d* Augsburg, 5 Jan 1746). His father, Josef Praelisauer, was Swiss (from canton Appenzell) and spent 20 years as sacristan in Kötzting. From 1718 Anton Praelisauer was organist at St Michael's Church and vice-prefect of St Gregory's seminary in Munich. In 1725 he became organist and in 1736 Kapellmeister of Augsburg Cathedral. Although he was a prolific composer, he published nothing, and none of his works is known. In 1743 the Augsburg Cathedral chapter commissioned him to compose choral antiphons, hymns and responsories for the feasts of St John Nepomuk and St Elizabeth of Portugal. He wrote, for the Jesuit theatre, music to 12 Latin school plays, of which only textual material is extant (*D-As, DI, Mbs, MT, Rs*; they include *Philalelia seu Mutus amicitia* and *Ruina imperii Macedonici*, given at Munich in 1718 and 1719 respectively, in addition to those listed in *MGG*).

(2) **Coelestin** [Franz Idelfons] **Praelisauer** (baptized Kötzting, 7 April 1694; *d* Tegernsee, 5 Feb 1745). He was educated in the seminary at Tegernsee, where he eventually entered the Benedictine order and became director of music. According to his contemporaries, he was an outstanding organist, teacher and composer. He made a detailed study of the works of Lassus and used them as models for his own compositions, most of which were written for the church and the school theatre. His responsories for the Vigil for the Dead were famous for their gravity and sensitivity, and his sacred folk play *Ecce Agnus Dei* was much admired.

(3) **Andreas Benedikt Praelisauer** (baptized Kötzting, 7 April 1699; *d* Polling, 5 Nov 1743). He entered the Augustinian prebendary college at Polling, near Weilheim in Upper Bavaria, in 1720; he was a canon, and held office as choirmaster for many years. He bequeathed musical material, partly his own work and partly that of his family, to the foundation. He wrote incidental music for two plays, *Jakob jubiläus sacerdos* (1738) and *Sacrae scripturae studium, angeli custodis gaudium*, whose texts were published at Tegernsee.

(4) **Columban** [Josef Bernhard] **Praelisauer** (baptized Kötzting, 11 Jan 1703; *d* Rott am Inn, 23 Oct 1753). He went to the Jesuit school in Munich and in 1720 entered the Benedictine monastery at Rott am Inn where he became *rector chori* and librarian. He is notable not only as a composer but also for his research into choral singing; his *Principia cantus choralis*, however, have not survived, and only the text remains of his *Actio scenica in annum millesimum*, which he wrote in place of his late brother (2) Coelestin Praelisauer, to mark the 1000th anniversary of the Tegernsee foundation.

(5) **Robert** [Martin Aemilianus] **Praelisauer** (baptized Kötzting, 4 Nov 1708; *d* Reinstetten, Württemberg, 18 Oct 1771). He went to the Jesuit school in Munich, where in 1725 he appeared as a singer in religious dramatic performances. In 1729 he took his vows at the

Benedictine abbey of Ochsenhausen, Württemberg, and became a priest in 1734; thereafter he served his monastery for a time as *rector chori* and as priest of various parishes, the last being Reinstetten. A set of *Compositiones piarum cantionum* and three arias for soprano with instrumental accompaniment survive (*Amor patientiae*, 1731, and two *Pro adventu*, both 1762; all in *D-B*).

BIBLIOGRAPHY

EitnerQ
F. J. Lipowsky: *Baierisches Musik-Lexikon* (Munich, 1811/*R*1971), 252f
D. Mettenleiter: *Musikgeschichte der Stadt Regensburg* (Regensburg, 1866), 251
Studien und Mittheilungen aus dem Benedictiner-Orden, vi/1 (1885), 98f
P. Lindner: 'Familia S. Quirini in Tegernsee: die Äbte und Mönche der Benediktinerabtei Tegernsee', *Oberbayerische Archiv für vaterländische Geschichte*, 1 (1897–8), suppl., 138ff
L. Söhner: 'Ein Choralforscher aus dem 18. Jahrhundert', *KJb*, xxvii (1932), 120
G. Rückert: 'Pflege der Musik im ehemaligen Kloster Polling', *Zeitschrift für bayerische Landesgeschichte*, vi (1933), 114
A. Layer: 'Praelisauer', *MGG*   ADOLF LAYER

Praeludium (Lat.). PRELUDE.

Praepunctus. An adjective used in medieval neume tables to describe a neume preceded by a PUNCTUM (single note) lower than the first note of the neume. The resulting group is usually known as a compound neume (for illustration *see* NEUMATIC NOTATIONS, Table 1).

BIBLIOGRAPHY

M. Huglo: 'Les noms des neumes et leur origine', *Etudes grégoriennes*, i (1954), 53

Praestant (Lat.). An ORGAN STOP.

Praesto (Lat.: 'quick'). *See* PRESTO.

Praetorius [Schulz, Schulze, Schultz, Schultze]. German family of musicians.

(1) Jacob Praetorius (i) (*b* Magdeburg, *c*1530; *d* Hamburg, 1586). Organist, copyist and composer, father of (2) Hieronymus Praetorius. He possibly studied with Martin Agricola at Magdeburg. After being converted to the Protestant faith he moved to Hamburg, where in 1550 he is recorded as clerk at St Jacobi (with the chapel of St Gertrud). In 1554 he became assistant organist, and from 1558 until his death he was first organist. In 1554 he compiled a set of monophonic liturgical chants and German chorales (*DK-Kk* Thott 151). In 1566 he compiled in six folio partbooks a collection of 204 sacred works for four, five, six and eight voices by German and Netherlands composers, *Opus musicum excellens et novum* (*D-ROu* Mus.Saec.XVI-49); it was evidently intended as the first of two such collections, but the second is lost. Most of the works for four to six voices were copied from works published by Georg Rhau, but 15 exist in no other source. The collection contains Praetorius's only known composition, a *Te Deum* for four voices.

BIBLIOGRAPHY

J. Bolte: 'Eine Choralsammlung des Jakob Praetorius', *MMg*, xxv (1893), 37
H. Leichsenring: *Hamburgische Kirchenmusik im Reformationszeitalter* (Berlin, 1922)
B. Friederich: *Der Vokalstil des Hieronymus Praetorius* (Hamburg, 1932)
L. Krüger: *Die Hamburgische Musikorganisation im XVII. Jahrhundert* (Strasbourg, 1933)

L. Hoffmann-Erbrecht: 'Das *Opus musicum* des Jacob Praetorius von 1566', *AcM*, xxviii (1956), 96 [incl. thematic index and facs.]

(2) Hieronymus Praetorius (*b* Hamburg, 10 Aug 1560; *d* Hamburg, 27 Jan 1629). Composer, organist, copyist and music editor, son of (1) Jacob Praetorius (i) and father of (3) Jacob (ii) and (4) Johannes Praetorius. After receiving his first organ instruction from his father, he studied at Hamburg with Hinrich thor Molen during 1573 and at Cologne with Albinus Walran from 1574 to 1576. His first position was as organist at Erfurt from 1580 to 1582, when he returned to Hamburg as assistant organist to his father at St Jacobi (with the chapel of St Gertrud); on his father's death in 1586 he became first organist, and he held this post until his death. He took part in the Gröningen organ trial of 1596, which Hans Leo Hassler and Michael Praetorius also attended; this was probably his only personal contact with other composers of polychoral works. Three of his four sons were musicians too: for the two most important ones see (3) and (4) below; the third son, Michael, published a five-part wedding motet at Hamburg in 1619 and died at Antwerp at an early age (the date is not known).

All but five of Praetorius's masses, motets and vocal *Magnificat* settings were published between 1616 and 1625 in Hamburg as a five-volume collected edition; all the volumes were published in other editions, and a number of works appeared in other publications. All of Praetorius's masses are parody masses, four based on his own motets; the other two, *Non auferetur sceptrum* and *Paratum cor meum*, are based on motets by Jacob Meiland and Stefano Felis respectively. He took most of his texts from the psalms and from antiphons; he also set some non-liturgical Latin texts as wedding motets. Of the six motets with German texts two incorporate traditional melodies, *Ein Kindelein so löbelich* and *Herr Gott dich loben wir* (the German *Te Deum*). 50 of the motets are polychoral compositions for eight to 20 voices divided into two, three or four choirs. They were among the earliest Venetian-inspired music to be published in north Germany and are Praetorius's most progressive and important works. They are similar in style to the polychoral motets of Hassler, but the expression of the text is more vivid because Praetorius introduced greater contrasts of texture, harmony and rhythm. They are less homophonic than such works by many other composers because of the extensive use of imitation and the breaking up of basically chordal structures by rhythmically and motivically active inner parts. The total vocal range frequently spans more than three octaves, and there are frequent contrasts of high and low vocal groupings. Apart from an optional *basso seguente*, no parts are prescribed for instruments, but contemporary documents from Hamburg describe performances of Praetorius's motets with instruments supporting or replacing voices. His finest polychoral motets are *Cantate Domino*, *Decantabat populus Israel*, *Ein Kindelein so löbelich* and *Herr Gott dich loben wir*. Embellished versions of his motets by Heinrich Scheidemann and other organists are in organ tablatures at Lüneburg, Munich, Pelplin and Regensburg. The nine eight-voice *Magnificat* settings, one in each tone and an additional one in the fifth tone, provide music for the even-numbered verses; the imitative textures are derived from the tone formulae. The second *Magnificat* in the fifth tone concludes with settings of the Christmas carols *Joseph, lieber Joseph mein* and *In dulci jubilo*.

In 1587 Praetorius compiled and copied a collection of monophonic German and Latin service music for the Hamburg churches, containing the chants for Matins, Mass and Vespers for the Sundays and feast days of the church year. It may have served as the model for Franz Eler's *Cantica sacra* (Hamburg, 1588), the contents of which are similar but not identical. Praetorius was also the chief compiler of the *Melodeyen Gesangbuch* (Hamburg, 1604), a collection of 88 four-part German chorale settings by the organists of the four largest Hamburg churches. It is the first German collection to specify organ accompaniment to congregational singing of chorales. It includes 21 of his own settings, and the other three composers represented are Joachim Decker, Jacob Praetorius (ii) and David Scheidemann, father of Heinrich Scheidemann.

The only organ works definitely by Praetorius are a complete set of eight *Magnificat* settings in the Visby (Petri) Tablature, which were composed by 1611, and an additional *Magnificat* in the first tone in the Clausthal-Zellerfeld Tablature. The modified cantus firmus technique employed in these works presents the notes of the tone in the tenor, cantus and bass parts, separated by freely contrapuntal and figurative interludes and imitative fugatos on motifs from the tones. They are full-textured works, often in five real parts, and were certainly designed for a large organ, including pedal (the organ that Praetorius played at St Jacobi, Hamburg, is described by Michael Praetorius in *Syntagma musicum*, ii, Wolfenbüttel, 1618, 2/1619/ R1958). The eight settings in the Visby Tablature are the earliest unified set of organ works by a north German composer. On stylistic grounds it is highly probable that Praetorius composed almost all of the anonymous organ pieces – settings of hymns, sequences and Mass items – in the Visby Tablature. The case for his authorship is convincingly argued by Kite-Powell. If this music is indeed by him he stands as the leading north German composer in the first two decades of the 17th century.

WORKS

Editions: *H. Praetorius: Ausgewählte Werke*, ed. H. Leichtentritt, DDT, xxiii (1905/*R*) [L]

The Polychoral Motets of Hieronymus Praetorius, ii, ed. F. K. Gable (diss., Iowa U., 1966) [G]

H. Praetorius: Polychoral Motets, i, ed. F. K. Gable, RRMR, xviii (1974) [RRMR xviii]

H. Praetorius: Polychoral Motets, ii, ed. F. K. Gable, RRMR, xix (1974) [RRMR xix]

(all printed works published in Hamburg)

MASSES

Liber missarum, 5, 6, 8vv (1616; = Opus musicum, iii): Missa 'Angelus ad pastores', 8vv, L; Missa 'Benedicam Dominum', 6vv; Missa 'Factum est silentium', 8vv; Missa 'Non auferetur sceptrum', 6vv (on Meiland's motet); Missa 'Paratum cor meum', 5vv (on Felis's motet); Missa 'Tulerunt Dominum meum', 8vv

MAGNIFICAT

Canticum Beatae Mariae Virginis seu Magnificat, 8, 10, 12vv (1602; 2/1622 = Opus musicum, ii): 8 Magnificat, tones 1–8; Magnificat alio modi, tone 5, L

MOTETS

[47] Cantiones sacrae de festis praecipuis totius anni, 5–8, 10, 12vv (1599, 2/1607⁵ [incl. 3 motets by Jacob Praetorius (ii)]; 3/1622 = Opus musicum, i) [1599]

Canticum Beatae Mariae Virginis seu Magnificat, 8, 10, 12vv (1602; 2/1622 = Opus musicum, ii) [1602]

Cantiones variae, 5–8, 10, 12, 16, 20vv (1618 = Opus musicum, iv) [1618a]

Cantiones novae officiosae, 5–8, 10, 15vv (1618; 3/1625 = Opus musicum, v) [1618b]

(Latin)

Ab oriente venerunt Magi, 5vv, 1599; L

Adesto unus Deus, 5vv, 1599
Angelus ad pastores ait, 8vv, 1599
Angelus ad pastores ait, 12vv, 1618a; G, RRMR xix
Ascendo ad patrem meum, 6vv, 1599
Beati omnes, 8vv, 1599; G
Beatus autor seculi, 6vv, 1618a; L
Beatus vir qui non abiit, 5vv, 1618a
Benedicam Dominum, 6vv, 1599
Canite tuba in Sion, 5vv, 1618a
Cantate Domino, 8vv, 1602; G, RRMR xviii
Confitemini Domino, 8vv, 1599; G
Cum nova conjugii, 8vv, 1618b; G
Decantabat populus Israel, 20vv, 1618a; L
Deus misereatur nostri, 10vv, 1618b; G
Dilectus meus mihi, 8vv, 1618a
Diligam te, Domine, 5vv, 1618b
Dixit Dominus, 12vv, 1602; G, RRMR xix
Domine Deus, benedic nos, 8vv, 1599; G
Domine, Dominus noster, 8vv, 1602
Domine, probasti me, 15vv, 1618b; G, RRMR xix
Domini est terra, 7vv, 1618b
Dum proeliaretur, 5vv, 1599
Ecce dies celebris, 8vv, 1618a
Ecce Dominus veniet, 8vv, 1599; G, RRMR xviii
Ecce Maria genuit, 8vv, 1618a
Ecce novus sanctam, 6vv, 1618a
Ecce nunc benedicte Domine, 8vv, 1618b
Ecce prandium meum, 7vv, 1599
Ecce quam bonum, 8vv, 1618b; G, RRMR xviii
Ego flos campi, 5vv, pubd separately (1627)
Ego sum ipse, 5vv, 1618a; ed. in Sammlung älterer Musik, vii (Berlin, 1837)
Exaltabo te Deus meus, 6vv, 1618b
Exultate Deo, 6vv, 1599
Exultate justi, 16vv, 1618a; L
Factum est silentium, 8vv, 1599
Firmetur manus tua, 8vv, pubd separately (1614), 1618a
Fuit homo missus, 5vv, 1599
Gaudete omnes, 6vv, 1599; ed. G. Dodd (London, 1970)
Gloria tibi, Domine, 7vv, 1599
Gratias agimus tibi, 8vv, 1599; G
Herculeum dulci modulo, 8vv, 1618a
Hoc pro certo habet, 8vv, 1618b
Hodie Christus natus est, 6vv, 1618b
Hodie completi sunt, 8vv, 1599
In convertendo Dominus, 10vv, 1618a; G
Indica mihi quem diligit, 8vv, pubd separately (1628)
In hoc festo, 8vv, 1599
In te, Domine, speravi, 6vv, 1618b
Jubilate Deo, 6vv, 1618a
Jubilate Deo, 12vv, 1599; G, RRMR xix
Laeto dum coelo socii, 8vv, pubd separately (1615), 1618a
Laudate Dominum in sanctis eius, 8vv, 1599
Laudate Dominum omnes gentes, 7vv, 1618a; L
Laudate Dominum omnes gentes, 8vv, 1618b; G, RRMR xviii
Laudate pueri Dominum, 10vv, 1599; G
Levavi oculos meos, 10vv, 1602; L
Mane nobiscum Domine, 6vv, 1599
Miserere mei Deus, 5vv, 1599
Musica est divinum donum, 5vv, 1618a; ed. in Sammlung älterer Musik, vii (Berlin, 1837)
Ne projicias me, 6vv, 1618a
Non est bonum hominem, 5vv, 1599
Non ex virile semine, 6vv, 1618a
Non moriar, 6vv, 1618b
Non nobis Domine, 6vv, 1618b
Nunc dimittis, 8vv, 1599; G, RRMR xviii
O admirabile commercium, 10vv, 1599; G
O bone Jesu, 6vv, 1599; L
Oculi omnium, 8vv, 1599; L
O lux beata Trinitas, 8vv, 1618a
Omne quodcunque facitis, 5vv, 1618b
Omnes gentes, 8vv, 1599
Omni tempore benedic Deum, 5vv, 1618b
O quam pulchra, 6vv, 1618b
O vos omnes, 5vv, 1599; L, ed. in Cw, xiv (1931, 2/1954)
Pater noster, 8vv, 1599; L
Peccavi quid faciam miser, 6vv, 1599
Puer natus est, 6vv, 1599
Puer qui natus est, 8vv, 1599; G
Quam pulchra es, 8vv, 1618a; G
Sic Deus dilexit mundum, 6vv, 1599
Surge illuminare Jerusalem, 8vv, 1599
Surge propera amica mea, 8vv, 1599; G
Surrexit pastor bonus, 5vv, 1599
Suscipe verbum, 8vv, 1599

Te Deum laudamus, 16vv, pubd separately (1613) [music as Herr Gott dich loben wir]
Te Deum patrem ingenitum, 8vv, 1599; G, ed. F. K. Gable (Minneapolis, 1969)
Tota pulchra es, 12vv, 1618a; G, RRMR xix
Tulerunt Dominum meum, 8vv, 1599
Veni puella, 6vv, 1618a
Venite exultemus Domino, 8vv, 1602
Verbum caro factum est, 7vv, 1599
Videns Dominus, 8vv, 1599; L
Vidi Dominum facie ad faciem, 5vv, 1618a
Vitam beatam, 6vv, 1618b
Vulnerasti cor meum, 5vv, 1618b

(*others*)

Also hat Gott die Welt geliebt, 6vv, 1618b; L
Das ist mir lieb, 6vv, 1618b; L
Ehre sey dem Vater, 6vv, 1642[4]
Ein Kindelein so löbelich, 8vv, pubd separately (1613), 1618a; G, RRMR xviii
Herr Gott dich loben wir, 16vv, pubd separately (1613), 1618a; G
Jeg Messias den Höystes Sön, 4vv, 1640[1]
Stat opr min Brud, min venniste, 4vv, 1640[1]
Wie lang, O Gott, 5vv, 1618b; L, ed. in Cw, xiv (1931, 2/1954)

ORGAN

8 Magnificat, tones 1–8, 1611 or earlier, *S-VII*; ed. in Kite-Powell, ed. in CEKM, iv (1963)
Magnificat, tone 1, *D-CZ*; ed. in Kite-Powell
Some anon. works, possibly by Praetorius, in *S-VII*; ed. in Kite-Powell

EDITIONS

Cantiones sacrae chorales, collection of Lat. and Ger. service music, 1587, *D-Ha*
Melodeyen Gesangbuch, 4vv (1604) [incl. 21 settings by H. Praetorius; 3 ed. in Winterfeld, 8 ed. in Organum, i/25–7 (Lippstadt, 1950)]

BIBLIOGRAPHY

J. Mattheson: *Grundlage einer Ehren-Pforte* (Hamburg, 1740); ed. M. Schneider (Berlin, 1910/*R*1969)
C. von Winterfeld: *Der evangelische Kirchengesang*, i–ii (Leipzig, 1843–5/*R*1966)
R. Eitner: 'Jacob Praetorius und seine Familie', *MMg*, iii (1871), 65
H. Leichtentritt: introduction to DDT, xxiii (1905/*R*1959)
———: *Geschichte der Motette* (Leipzig, 1908)
H. Leichsenring: *Hamburgische Kirchenmusik im Reformationszeitalter* (Berlin, 1922)
F. Dietrich: *Geschichte des deutschen Orgelchorals im 17. Jahrhundert* (Kassel, 1932)
B. Friederich: *Der Vokalstil des Hieronymus Praetorius* (Hamburg, 1932)
L. Krüger: *Die Hamburgische Musikorganisation im XVII. Jahrhundert* (Strasbourg, 1933)
———: 'Eine Quelle zur Hamburgischen Musikgeschichte', *Zeitschrift des Vereins für hamburgische Geschichte*, xxxiii (1933), 188
H. J. Moser: *Die evangelische Kirchenmusik in Deutschland* (Berlin, 1953)
F. K. Gable: *The Polychoral Motets of Hieronymus Praetorius*, i–ii (diss., Iowa U., 1966)
W. Apel: *Geschichte der Orgel- und Klaviermusik bis 1700* (Kassel, 1967; Eng. trans., rev. 1972)
F. K. Gable: introduction to RRMR, xviii (1974)
H. Glahn and S. Sørensen, eds.: *The Clausholm Music Fragments* (Copenhagen, 1974) [incl. preface]
J. Kite-Powell: *The Visby (Petri) Organ Tablature: Investigation and Critical Edition* (Wilhelmshaven, 1977)

(3) Jacob Praetorius (ii) (*b* Hamburg, 8 Feb 1586; *d* Hamburg, 21 or 22 Oct 1651). Composer, organist and organ teacher, second son of (2) Hieronymus Praetorius. He studied the organ in Amsterdam with Sweelinck, who in 1608 wrote a motet for his wedding. From 1603 until his death he was organist of St Petri, Hamburg. He was specially known as an excellent organ teacher. Matthias Weckmann was one of those who studied with him, and Berendt Petri, who was his pupil from 1609 to 1611, compiled about that time a notable manuscript of organ music, the Visby (Petri) Tablature, containing works by Praetorius and his father, among others. Praetorius contributed 19 four-part chorale settings to the *Melodeyen Gesangbuch* (1604) – see §2 above – and ten simple settings for voice and figured bass to one of Johann Rist's collections of sacred verses (1651). His three sacred motets and the wedding motets

are similar in style to comparable works by his father but have more expressive harmonies; the original prints of the wedding motets were destroyed in World War II. His surviving organ works require a large instrument and frequently specify two or three keyboards, including pedal. The three preludes are embryonic preludes and fugues: a full-organ introduction (prelude) is followed by a strict four-part imitative section (fugue or ricercare) with occasional motivic imitation and cadential flourishes. The recently discovered Clausholm *Magnificat* settings are paraphrases of some of his father's organ *Magnificat* settings in the Visby (Petri) Tablature. They and the remaining organ works employ a varied cantus firmus technique in their treatment of the borrowed melodic material. The most impressive work is the setting of *Durch Adams Fall* (unfortunately incomplete), which, because of its length, motivic interplay, virtuoso passages and contrasts of texture and rhythm, approaches the style of the chorale fantasia.

WORKS

Editions: *46 Choräle für Orgel von J. P. Sweelinck und seinen deutschen Schülern*, ed. G. Gerdes, Musikalische Denkmäler, iii (Mainz, 1957) [G]
    J. Praetorius: Choralbearbeitungen für Orgel, ed. W. Breig (Kassel, 1974) [B]

SACRED VOCAL

Gaudete omnes, 6vv; Surge propera, 5vv; Veni in hortum meum, 8vv: 1607[5]
In te, Domine speravi, canon, 6vv, 1648, *D-B*; facs. in *MGG*
19 chorale settings, 4vv, in Melodeyen Gesangbuch, ed. H. Praetorius (Hamburg, 1604); 1 ed. L. Erk and F. Filitz, *Vierstimmiger Choralsätze*, i (Essen, 1845); 1 ed. in Winterfeld; 4 ed. in Organum, i/25–7 (Lippstadt, 1950)
10 chorale settings, 1v, bc, in J. Rist: Neuer Himlischer Lieder Sonderbahres Buch, iv (Lüneburg, 1651); 2 ed. in Winterfeld

WEDDING MOTETS

(*lost; transcriptions extant, mostly in private collections*)

Caecilia virgo gloriosa ... in honorem nuptiarum ... Johannis Eggerdes, 6vv (Hamburg, 1601)
Carissima in delitiis [Epithalamion in solennitatem nuptiarum ... H. Bekemanni], 5vv (Hamburg, 1606)
Vidi speciosum, 8vv, in Tres cantiones sacrae (Hamburg, 1615)
Sponse musarum [Epithalamium harmonicum], 6vv (Hamburg, 1617), transcr. in *D-Bds*
Forti animo esto [Post nubila Phoebus], 8vv (Hamburg, 1619)
Quis novus hic [Ode gamica], 6vv (n.p., ?1628)
Indica mihi, [Hymenaeus ex sacro ecclesiae hymenaeo], 6vv (Hamburg, 1635)
Ich freue mich im Herrn ... Brautmesse ... H. von Petkun, 2vv, bc (Hamburg, 1640)

OTHER SECULAR VOCAL

Qui habitas in hortis, 1v, bc, *D-Hs* (inc.)
Viva la bella musica, canon, 4vv, 1614, lost, formerly Lübeck Stadtbibliothek; facs. in *Stammbuch von David von Mandelsloh*, ed. W. L. von Lutgendorff (Hamburg, 1893); ed. in Stiehl

ORGAN

Christum wir sollen loben schon, *D-Lr*; G, B
Durch Adams Fall ist ganz verderbt, *Bds* (inc.); G, B
Grates nunc omnes, *S-VII*; G, ed. in Kite-Powell
Herr Gott dich loben wir, 1636, *D-Lr*; G, B
Vater unser im Himmelreich, *CZ*; B
Was kan uns komen an für Noth, *CZ*; B

6 Magnificat, *DK-Kk*; ed. in Glahn and Sørensen
Magnificat germanicae, *S-VII*; G, ed. in Kite-Powell
3 preludes, C, D, F, *D-Lr*; ed. in Organum, iv/2 (Leipzig, 1925)

OTHER INSTRUMENTAL

2 galliards, a 5, 1607[28] (? by Jacob Schultz); ed. B. Engelke, *Musik und Musiker am Gottorfer Hofe*, i (Breslau, 1930)

BIBLIOGRAPHY

J. Mattheson: *Grundlage einer Ehren-Pforte* (Hamburg, 1740); ed. M. Schneider (Berlin, 1910/*R*1969)
C. von Winterfeld: *Der evangelische Kirchengesang*, i–ii (Leipzig, 1843–5/*R*1966)
R. Eitner: 'Jacob Praetorius und seine Familie', *MMg*, iii (1871), 65
M. Seiffert: 'J. P. Sweelinck und seine direkten deutschen Schüler', *VMw*, vii (1891), 145–260

C. Stiehl: 'Stammbuchblätter von Jakob Praetorius und Walter Rowe', *MMg*, xxvi (1894), 157; xxvii (1895), 43
H. Leichsenring: *Hamburgische Kirchenmusik im Reformationszeitalter* (Berlin, 1922)
F. Dietrich: *Geschichte des deutschen Orgelchorals im 17. Jahrhundert* (Kassel, 1932)
B. Friederich: *Der Vokalstil des Hieronymus Praetorius* (Hamburg, 1932)
L. Krüger: *Die Hamburgische Musikorganisation im XVII. Jahrhundert* (Strasbourg, 1933)
G. Frotscher: *Geschichte des Orgel-Spiels und der Orgel-Komposition*, i (Berlin, 1935, enlarged 3/1966)
H. J. Moser: *Die evangelische Kirchenmusik in Deutschland* (Berlin, 1953)
L. Schierning: *Die Überlieferung der deutschen Orgel- und Klaviermusik* (Kassel, 1961)
W. Apel: *Geschichte der Orgel- und Klaviermusik bis 1700* (Kassel, 1967; Eng. trans., rev., 1972)
H. Glahn and S. Sørensen, eds.: *The Clausholm Music Fragments* (Copenhagen, 1974)
J. Kite-Powell: *The Visby (Petri) Organ Tablature: Investigation and Critical Edition* (Wilhelmshaven, 1977)

(4) Johannes Praetorius (*b* Hamburg, *c*1595; *d* Hamburg, 25 July 1660). Organist and composer, fourth and youngest son of (2) Hieronymus Praetorius. He studied the organ with Sweelinck in Amsterdam between 1608 and 1611 and was organist of the Nikolaikirche, Hamburg, from 1612 until his death. He published six wedding motets for five, six and eight voices at Hamburg between 1615 and 1635.

FREDERICK K. GABLE

Praetorius, Abraham (*b* Mecklenburg; *fl* 1587–92). German composer. From 1587 (or 1588) to 1592 he was a singer at the Danish royal chapel. He is known for two works only: *Harmonia gratulatoria nuptiis et honori Sermi Domini Jacobi VI. Scotorum regi et Sermi Principis D. Friderici II. Daniae ... filiae Annae Illmae Scotiae reginae* for six voices (Copenhagen, 1590), and *Newe geistliche teutsche des königlichen Propheten Davidis Psalmen ganz lieblich zu singen und auff allerley Instrumenten zu gebrauchen* for five voices (Greifswald, 1592). The latter is a collection of chanson motets of considerable artistic merit. The individual compositions show the influence of Lassus's style in their frequent use of expressive musical symbolism. Apart from Psalm x the texts are based on psalm paraphrases by Kaspar Ulenberg (Cologne, 1582), which evidently had a wide circulation beyond denominational frontiers. Praetorius also made use of melodic material from Ulenberg's psalter. The motets are settings of only the first strophe of each psalm.

BIBLIOGRAPHY
O. Kade: 'Abraham Praetorius', *MMg*, xxxiii (1901), 1
WALTER BLANKENBURG

Praetorius, Bartholomaeus [Bartholomäus] [Schultz, Bartold, Bertil] (*b* Marienburg [now Malbork, Poland]; *c*1590; *d* Stockholm, buried 3 Aug 1623). German composer and cornettist partly resident in Sweden. He matriculated at Königsberg University in June 1608. He was a cornettist at the court of the Elector Johann Sigismund of Brandenburg from 1613 to 1620, when he moved to Stockholm to lead the new royal chapel that Gustavus II Adolphus engaged from Germany at the time of his marriage. His only known collection of music is the five-part *Newe liebliche Paduanen und Galliarden* (Berlin, 1616; one partbook now lost but two dances printed complete in Sachs, 260ff); the title and preface are modelled on those of William Brade's *Newe ausserlesene Paduanen und Galliarden* (1614). The 26 dances, each of which is in three sections, are all paired; the

dances in each pair are in the same key and form a suite. There are six more such dances by Praetorius in David Oberndörffer's *Allegrezza musicale* (1620), and there are also extant a four-part 'fugue' (actually a canon, in Thomas Rosa's *Hymnus sacra*, 1617) and a polychoral motet from his Swedish period (in *S-V*, inc.). A four-part wedding song (Königsberg, 1617) is lost.

BIBLIOGRAPHY
G. Erler, ed.: *Die Matrikel der Universität Königsberg in Preussen*, i (Leipzig, 1908), 181
C. Sachs: *Musik und Oper am kurbrandenburgischen Hof* (Berlin, 1910)
BENGT KYHLBERG

Praetorius, Christian Andreas. *See* SCHULZE, CHRISTIAN ANDREAS.

Praetorius, Christoph (*b* Bunzlau, Silesia; *d* Lüneburg, 1609). German composer. He was the uncle of Michael Praetorius. He matriculated at Wittenberg University in 1551. In 1560 he printed a funeral motet on the death of Melanchthon. In 1563 he became Kantor at the Johanneum at Lüneburg, where he taught music to the senior classes, while the third class was taught music by Lossius, the deputy headmaster. Praetorius was obliged to retire in 1581 because of deafness, and in the same year he composed a wedding motet for his successor Euricius Dedekind.

As a composer Praetorius produced no outstanding works, but he was one of the first well-known musical personalities active in north Germany. Both parts of his German *Ehrnlieder* begin with chorale motets (on the melodies *Vater unser im Himmelreich* and *Erhalt uns Herr bei deinem Wort*, but with different texts), and end with two settings of biblical texts. The 11 other pieces in each part are occasional works mostly intended for weddings. One of the texts was reprinted in 1582 in Lechner's *Neue teutsche Lieder* (see U. Martin, *AMw*, xi, 1954, p.315). In the foreword to the *Ehrnlieder* Praetorius explained that he had already composed many German and Latin hymns. He also edited a textbook in which he rejected antiquated mensural theory and dealt with the 12 modes of Glarean instead of the eight ecclesiastical modes. He thus reduced the amount of teaching material, but added noteworthy comments on the training of coloraturas, the ornamentation of cadences, text underlay and the use of 'voces fictae' in expressing the text and its emotions. Henning Dedekind and Joachim Burmeister, who both attended the Lüneburg school, quoted from his textbook and Dedekind reprinted several exercises from it.

WORKS
SACRED VOCAL
De obitu ... Domini Ph. Melanchthonis, 4vv (Wittenberg, 1560)
Fröliche und liebliche Ehrnlieder, 4vv (Wittenberg, 1581)
Der ander Teil frölicher und lieblicher Ehrnlieder, 4vv (Wittenberg, 1581)
Carmen nuptiale in honorem ... E. Dedekindi (Ülzen, 1581), lost (mentioned in *EitnerQ*, see also Onkelbach)

5 Lat. motets, 4, 5vv; 2 Ger. hymns, 4vv: *D-Lr*, *PL-WRu*

THEORETICAL WORKS
Erotemata musices (Wittenberg, 1574); canon ed. F. Jöde, *Der Kanon*, i (Wolfenbüttel and Berlin, 1943)
Erotemata renovatae musices (Ülzen, 1581)

BIBLIOGRAPHY
R. Molitor: *Die Nachtridentinische Choralreform*, i (Leipzig, 1901), 173
W. Gurlitt: *Michael Praetorius (Creuzburgensis): sein Leben und seine Werke* (Leipzig, 1915/R1968), 73ff
E. Preussner: 'Die Methodik im Schulgesang der evangelischen Lateinschulen des 17. Jahrhunderts', *AMw*, vi (1924), 407–49

M. Ruhnke: *Joachim Burmeister* (Kassel, 1955)
F. Blume and M. Ruhnke: 'Aus der Musikgeschichte der Stadt Lüneburg', *Festschrift aus Lüneburgs tausendjähriger Vergangenheit*, ed. U. Wendland (Lüneburg, 1956), 119
F. Onkelbach: *Lucas Lossius und seine Musiklehre* (Regensburg, 1960)
H. Walter: *Musikgeschichte der Stadt Lüneburg* (Tutzing, 1967)

reprinted from *MGG* (x, 1554) by permission of Bärenreiter
MARTIN RUHNKE

Praetorius [Pretorius, Ammon], **Conrad** [Konrad] (*b* Windsheim, Bavaria, *c*1515; *d* Alerheim, nr. Nördlingen, 30 Dec 1555). German poet and composer. He probably studied at Ansbach, at an advanced Lateinschule founded in 1529. After some years as Kantor at Windsheim, he was from 1549 to 1555 Rektor of the Lateinschule at Ansbach, where he became a member of the circle round Caspar Othmayr. His only known piece of music is a motet published in a commemorative volume that these friends produced after Othmayr's death in 1553, *In epitaphiis Gaspari Othmari* (only the bass partbook survives: n.p., n.d., probably Nuremberg, 1554[30]). Praetorius's motet is a setting of two distichs, the first of which runs: 'Harmonicae decus et columen lumenque camoenae/ Othmar et ingenio clarus et arte potens'. He also became well known as a poet and established close contacts with the University of Wittenberg. His particular contribution to Ansbach was to build up an educational system consistent with the ideals of the Reformation, with particular emphasis on music. He was also tutor to Margrave Georg Friedrich the Elder of Brandenburg-Ansbach. In 1555 he became preacher at Alerheim but died at the end of that year.

BIBLIOGRAPHY

O. Kade: 'Nachtrag zu Caspar Othmayr', *MMg*, viii (1876), 11
H. Albrecht: *Caspar Othmayr: Leben und Werk* (Kassel, 1950)
G. Schmidt: *Die Musik am Hofe der Markgrafen von Brandenburg-Ansbach* (Kassel, 1956)
W. Brennecke: 'Zu Caspar Othmayrs Epitaph', *Mf*, xiv (1961), 185
F. Krautwurst: 'Praetorius, Konrad', *MGG*
WALTER BLANKENBURG

Praetorius, Hieronymus. *See* PRAETORIUS family.

Praetorius, Jacob. *See* PRAETORIUS family, (1) Jacob (i) or (3) Jacob (ii).

Praetorius, Johannes. *See* PRAETORIUS family.

Praetorius [Schultheiss, Schultze], **Michael** (*b* Creuzburg an der Werra, nr. Eisenach, 15 Feb 1571 or in 1572–3, possibly in 1569; *d* Wolfenbüttel, 15 Feb 1621). German composer, theorist and organist. He was the most versatile and wide-ranging German composer of his generation and one of the most prolific, especially of works based on Protestant hymns. He is also important as a theorist, notably through his *Syntagma musicum*.

1. Life. 2. Music. 3. Writings. 4. Conclusion.

1. LIFE. Wetzel and Walther both stated that Praetorius was born on 15 February 1571 and died on his 50th birthday, but this could be a mistake, since according to a poem appended to his funeral sermon he was only in his 49th year when he died. Yet another date is suggested by the statement 'Aō. aetat. XXXV' in the legend round the woodcut portrait of 1604 (see fig.1) in the first part of *Musae Sioniae* (1605), in conjunction with the fact that his family moved to Creuzburg an der Werra in 1569. But 1571 is the most commonly accepted year of his birth. His father, who was also called

1. Michael Praetorius: woodcut (1604) from his 'Musae Sioniae' (1605)

Michael and came from Bunzlau, Silesia, was from 1534 at the latest a colleague of Johann Walter (i) at the Lateinschule at Torgau. In the Protestant infighting that broke out after the Augsburg Interim (1549) he was among the strict Lutherans, which led to his losing office more than once and having to move. His son Michael was born during a second period of service at Creuzburg that began in 1569, but in 1573 the family moved to Torgau, the mother's home, because of renewed banishment. At the Lateinschule there Praetorius was taught music by Michael Voigt, Walter's successor as Kantor. In 1582 he matriculated at the University of Frankfurt an der Oder, where his brother Andreas was professor of theology. In 1584 he attended the Lateinschule at Zerbst, Anhalt, the home of two of his sisters, and from there he returned to Frankfurt an der Oder, probably in the spring of 1585. Although he probably had no musical education after leaving school, it is certain that at Frankfurt he became acquainted with Bartholomäus Gesius, with whom he shared a strong interest in Protestant hymns and their melodies as well as in *alternatim* practice. After the early death of his brother, who had been keeping him, he was appointed, probably at the beginning of 1587, organist of St Marien, Frankfurt. By his own account he held this post for three years, but it is not known why he gave it up or where he went in 1590.

According to a later report Praetorius settled at Wolfenbüttel in about 1592–3, but to judge from his own testimony in his *Motectae et psalmi* (1607) and *Polyhymnia caduceatrix* (1619) it was not until 1595 that he entered the service, as an organist, of Duke Heinrich Julius of Brunswick-Wolfenbüttel, who had his residence there. In 1596 he took part with the most famous German organists of the day in the consecration of the organ in the castle chapel at Gröningen, near Halberstadt, a castle that Heinrich Julius had had built in his capacity as postulated Bishop of Halberstadt after introducing the Reformation there in 1591. In 1602 he stayed at Regensburg 'on his own business'. It is not known what this was, but Regensburg was where the strictest Lutherans gathered, so he may have had connections there through his father. In any case he made close personal friends there – dedicatory poems by the Regensburg pastor Christoph Donaverus appear in ten of his printed works; moreover, the first part of *Musae Sioniae* was published there in 1605. On his return to Wolfenbüttel towards the end of 1602 he was given a new appointment with a considerable increase in salary, so that he could now afford to set up his own household. In September 1603 he married Anna Lakemacher, who bore him two sons.

Praetorius had won such esteem by 1604 that, while retaining the post of organist, he was appointed court Kapellmeister on the retirement of Thomas Mancinus. The Kapelle, which at the time he took over consisted of six to eight singers and about the same number of instrumentalists, was modest, but evidently sufficient for his wishes, which he expressed in the dedication to the *Motectae et psalmi* (1607). It was well supported by the duke, who must have taken it with him on at least some of his journeys; one city he went to was Prague, which Praetorius certainly seems to have visited. There is evidence that in 1605 and 1609 he stayed at the court of the music-loving Landgrave Moritz of Hesse at Kassel. This was an extremely busy period for him: most of his collections of music appeared between 1605 and 1613. Between 1606 and 1612 he collaborated with the most famous organ builder of his day, Esaias Compenius, who was engaged by the Wolfenbüttel court at Praetorius's instigation and with whom he wrote the *Orgeln Verdingnis* mentioned in the second and third volumes of *Syntagma musicum*.

The sudden death of Duke Heinrich Julius in Prague in 1613 was a turning-point in Praetorius's life. The Elector Johann Georg of Saxony immediately asked the duke's successor, Friedrich Ulrich, to let Praetorius spend his year of mourning as deputy for the aging Rogier Michael, Kapellmeister of the electoral court. The year eventually became two and a half years, which Praetorius spent mostly at Dresden. He not only had responsibility for the music at the Assembly of Electors at Naumburg in 1614 and met Schütz in Dresden but also, more importantly, got to know there the latest Italian music, which influenced his later work in significant ways; he must also have devoted more and more time to his theoretical work. The fact that he did not return to Wolfenbüttel after one year may have been due not least to the scant attention that the young Duke Friedrich Ulrich paid to a memorandum he had submitted to him about the reorganization of the Hofkapelle. Even after his period in Dresden officially ended in 1616, he continued to receive an honorarium from there until at least 1618 and was often away from Wolfenbüttel. From 1614 he was also Kapellmeister to the administrator of the bishopric of Magdeburg. At Easter 1616 he was working at Halle, and in 1617 he built up the Hofkapelle of the counts of Schwarzburg at Sondershausen and also stayed once more with Landgrave Moritz of Hesse at Kassel, this time for a baptismal celebration, for which he wrote a

Concertgesang. In 1618 he was summoned, along with Schütz and Scheidt, to Magdeburg Cathedral to mark the reorganization of the music there, and he is known to have visited Leipzig, Nuremberg and Bayreuth (again with Schütz and Scheidt) in 1619. No wonder the efficiency of the Wolfenbüttel Hofkapelle declined when its Kapellmeister was away so much. Moreover, on his eventual return it continued to suffer, because of his ill-health – probably brought on by overwork – and at Trinity 1620 he was not reappointed. He had been appointed prior of the monastery at Ringelheim, near Goslar, in 1614, and he no doubt continued to draw an income from this position. He left an impressive fortune, most of which was to be used to set up a foundation for the poor. As the son and grandson of theologians he was a firm Christian all his life (in the words of his funeral sermon he 'often regretted that he never took holy orders'). This is borne out by the titles (listed in *Syntagma musicum*, iii, 225ff) of a number of theological tracts he wrote, all of which are lost. His initials, M.P.C. (= Michael Praetorius Creuzburgensis), also meant for him 'Mihi Patria Coelum'.

2. MUSIC. The most immediately impressive facts about Praetorius are his enormous creative power and, considering his relatively short life, his astonishing output of works. He took 28 pages of *Syntagma musicum* (iii, 199ff) to give a complete list of works he had already written as well as those he had still only planned; he later had more ambitious plans, which, however, were largely unrealized. Some of his works are lost. The fourth part of *Polyhymnia*, marking the centenary of the Reformation in 1617, must have existed in manuscript. Of his secular works only the single collection of instrumental French dances, *Terpsichore* (1612), is extant, yet according to *Syntagma musicum* (iii, 220f) he planned this in eight parts, some vocal, some instrumental, and he remarked that these were 'almost ready but not yet in print'. A conspicuous feature of his output is his extraordinarily systematic approach to his works, including a thorough grasp of their texts as well as an exhaustive consideration of their practical application. All this goes hand in hand with an urge to collect and with a sense of pedagogic responsibility. The method in Praetorius's approach to his work explains why his music appeared almost without exception in personal prints, several of which he published himself (sometimes he managed to prepare them only by keeping a special office to work in).

Despite this urge towards universality, Praetorius nevertheless confined himself in his sacred music to works – over 1000 of them – based on Protestant hymns and, to a lesser extent, to the Latin liturgy of the Lutheran service of his time. The only exceptions among his published works are *Motectae et psalmi* (1607) and *Polyhymnia exercitatrix* (1619–20), based mainly on psalm texts, and a few other pieces. Within the limited sphere of hymn-based works, however, he continued to work on a comprehensive scale in that he assembled a great many hymn texts as well as melodies (the latter often in versions varying from province to province). Thus parts iv–viii of *Musae Sioniae* are specially rich sources for hymnology that have not yet been fully studied. Praetorius's works are also important for knowledge of liturgical practice at the time, for instance concerning the interpolation into the Latin *Magnificat* at Christmas and Easter of German songs called *Laudes* (see *Megalynodia Sionia*, 1611). Moreover, his work clearly forms the climax in the history of Protestant church music of *alternatim* practice, for which he gave new instructions from work to work, most completely in the 'Introductio pro cantore' in *Urania* (1613). A peculiarity here is the inclusion of a congregational hymn or chorale in a polychoral work, an idea he derived from his visits to Kassel in 1605 and 1609.

According to Blume, Praetorius's church music, as well as his theoretical works, can be assigned to five periods, which partly overlap. The first embraces *Motectae et psalmi* (1607) and *Megalynodia Sionia* (1611), which, according to Praetorius's preface, originated at Regensburg in 1602. In the second period come the nine parts of *Musae Sioniae*, in the third the Latin liturgical works of *Missodia Sionia*, *Hymnodia Sionia* and *Eulogodia Sionia* (all 1611), as well as *Urania* and *Kleine und Grosse Litaney* (both 1613), which are linked in content to *Musae Sioniae*. To the fourth period belongs principally his work on *Syntagma musicum*, and in the last period there are the *Puericinium*, two parts of *Polyhymnia* and Psalm cxvi (*RISM* 1623[14]).

Megalynodia Sionia contains parodies, based mainly on madrigals by Lassus and Marenzio, and can probably be regarded as a prentice work, while in *Motectae et psalmi* Praetorius contributed to the repertory of the Latin motet, obviously without intending to offer anything particularly individual; a much more characteristic feature here is his appropriation of works by other composers, among them Aichinger, Hassler and Palestrina, a practice that recurs occasionally in his later works. In the second period, at least two stages in his development can be seen in the nine parts of *Musae Sioniae*. Parts i–iv consist mainly of eight-part works for two choirs (part ii also contains, with somewhat greater relevance to the ecclesiastical year, five 12-part pieces, and part iii two nine- and three 12-part pieces), with a somewhat random choice of hymns. In part v, however, Praetorius began to arrange systematically the complete repertory of German hymns, in this case those of the Ordinary for Matins, Mass and Vespers, as well as those of the ecclesiastical year, in arrangements for two to seven voices, some of them in motet style. Parts vi–viii consist almost entirely of simple, homophonic settings: in part vi the hymns of the ecclesiastical year are once more to be found; in part vii, among other pieces, catechistic, penitential and communion hymns as well as those 'of the Christian life'; and in part viii, hymns of the cross, solace and death, and Tischlieder. Part ix again presents the core of the Lutheran repertory, but here arranged predominantly for two and three voices. Compared with the imitative four-part works of Melchior Franck (1602) and Hassler (1607), the eight-part motets of parts i–iv are less linear and with their frequent dialogues between short homophonic phrases – an essential feature of polychoral music – far more expressive of their texts and thus more indicative of future developments. There is no continuous cantus firmus: in the Protestant motet of about 1600 hymn melodies appear in all parts. In his pieces for two to four voices too Praetorius stands out from his contemporaries by virtue of the attractive qualities of his music, to which his well-known four-part arrangement of the carol *Es ist ein Ros entsprungen* bears witness.

The three collections from Praetorius's third period, comprising arrangements from the Latin liturgy, are on the whole similar to *Musae Sioniae*, above all part ix; but the musical character of the borrowed material obviously induced in him a stronger feeling for older stylistic elements arising from 16th-century Netherlands polyphony. For example, in no other volume does canonic technique play as prominent a role as in *Hymnodia Sionia*. Yet the works in the collections of this period are also very harmonically orientated and are thus not at all archaic. *Hymnodia Sionia* also includes four organ arrangements, in which the cantus firmus appears in long note values in the bass. Although Praetorius was active throughout his life as an organist, these pieces, together with four other organ chorales at the end of part vii of *Musae Sioniae*, which are more strongly influenced by the motet, were his only contribution, though an important one, to the early history of the German organ chorale. *Urania*, which also belongs to the third period, consists of hymns for two to four choirs with the cantus firmus always in the highest part so that the congregation could join in at any time. The same treatment is to be found in most of the pieces in the litany volume and in the *Epithalamium* for Duke Friedrich Ulrich (1614).

The last two periods of Praetorius's work show further new developments. After the death of Duke Heinrich Julius he carried out a conscious reorientation: he introduced the continuo more systematically (he had already added an optional continuo part to some of his bicinia) and also, more significantly, assimilated elements from the most recent Italian vocal music, frequently notating a vocal line not only in its simple, basic form but also in an embellished version. There are other new elements too: the massive sound of 16 and more parts, the fruitful contrast of tutti and concertato

2. *Title-page of Praetorius's 'Theatrum instrumentorum'* (1620)

sections, the liberal use of echo effects, and not least the skilful introduction of connecting instrumental ritornellos. The resulting richness and variety give an added dimension to Praetorius's later works. His *Polyhymnia caduceatrix* (1619), in which he indulged in all the possibilities open to an early Baroque composer of choral music, seems far more daring than Schütz's *Psalmen Davids*, published in the same year; it is the most valid counterpart in Protestant Germany to Monteverdi's Vespers (1610). Nevertheless there was no fundamental break in Praetorius's development, for characteristically he still concentrated, though not exclusively, on the hymn. His last work, the fine five-part setting of Psalm cxvi (published in *RISM* 1623¹⁴), which he wrote in anticipation of his approaching death 'as a farewell to myself', shows almost all his new advances – only a continuo part is lacking, because of a request from the editor who commissioned it.

3. WRITINGS. *Syntagma musicum* also belongs to Praetorius's last years. The three parts that appeared (the fourth was to have contained instruction in composition) display a tendency typical of him, towards an encyclopedic, systematic approach to the theory and practice of music. The first volume deals with religious music, its principles and its liturgical constituents. It is of real value only in its wealth of quotations from every period. Of particular importance among these is the unique, full account from Johann Walter of his collaboration with Luther and of the musical reforms that Luther sought. In the second volume, 'De organographia', Praetorius gave, in combination with the instructive illustrated section 'Theatrum instrumentorum' (also issued 1620), detailed information about the instruments of his day, with a particularly thorough treatment of the organ. The third volume deals with the musical forms of Praetorius's own day, with a detailed consideration of technical manners such as notation, proportions, solmization, transposition and polychoral writing. The importance of *Syntagma musicum* lies less in its influence on the succeeding generation of composers (because of new developments at the beginning of the 17th century, in particular the rise of continuo) than in its high documentary value. It reflects the extraordinary diffuseness of instrumentation in the early Baroque period, the numerous families of instruments and the prominent position of the organ, and consequently the enormous variety of tone colour available in the performance of polyphonic and *alternatim* music which reached a highpoint in Germany in Praetorius's lifetime.

4. CONCLUSION. When making a general evaluation of Praetorius's life and work one must bear in mind that he was largely self-taught, though he made up through his immense efficiency and self-discipline for everything that had been denied him in his education. The much debated thesis that his work was more retrospective than forward-looking is disproved by a close study of the works from the last years of his life, when he combined with his manifest commitment to the heritage of the Reformation a great receptiveness to recent changes in musical style. His character cannot be understood unless one first sees in it the academically cultivated Lutheran Kantor with pronounced theological leanings. The central connection of his life's work with divine service, especially with the hymn, is fundamental, as also is his aspiration to a universality incorporating all

aspects of music into his ideas and practice. His play on words in the preface to *Polyhymnia caduceatrix*, that the 'Concio' (a 'good sermon') should also include the 'Cantio' ('good music and singing', with abundant use of instruments), is virtually his manifesto. He obviously saw himself as a mediator for the tradition of Lutheran church music, not least because of his upbringing at Torgau: his inclusion at the beginning of *Musae Sioniae* of Walter's translation of Luther's 'Encomion musices' in a form that he himself had probably corrected, the inclusion of a number of pieces by Walter in parts v and vii of *Musae Sioniae* and the publication of Walter's own words in *Leiturgodia Sionia latina* and in *Syntagma musicum*, i, are clear signs of this. But he further developed the theological understanding of music, which culminated in the eschatological concept of the heavenly choir (cf Walter's *Lob und Preis der löblichen Kunst Musica*, 1538), saying (in the 'Commefactio' of *Urania*), with reference to Isaiah: 'Musica per Choros Caelestia canens ... because the art of choral singing is truly the correct, heavenly way of making music'. In its theoretical foundations and practical aims and in its realization through composition, Praetorius's work thus displays an unusual degree of uniformity at a time of great change in musical history.

WORKS

Editions: *M. Praetorius: Gesamtausgabe der musikalischen Werke*, ed. F. Blume and others (Wolfenbüttel, 1928–40, 1960) [B]

M. Praetorius: Sämtliche Orgelwerke, ed. K. Matthaei (Wolfenbüttel, 1930) [M]

(printed works published at Wolfenbüttel unless otherwise stated)

SACRED VOCAL

Musae Sioniae ... geistliche Concert Gesänge über die fürnembste deutsche Psalmen und Lieder ... erster Theil, 8vv (Regensburg, 1605); B i

Sacrarum motectarum primitiae, 4–16vv (Magdeburg, 1606), lost

Musarum Sioniarum motectae et psalmi latini, 4–16vv (Nuremberg, 1607⁶, possibly 2nd edn. of Sacrarum motectarum primitiae); B x

Musae Sioniae ... geistliche Concert Gesänge über die fürnembste deutsche Psalmen und Lieder ... ander Theil, 8, 12vv (Jena, 1607); B ii

Musae Sioniae ... geistliche Concert Gesänge ... dritter Theil, 8, 9, 12vv (Helmstedt, 1607); B iii

Musae Sioniae ... geistliche Concert Gesänge ... vierdter Theil, 8vv (Helmstedt, 1607); B iv

Musae Sioniae ... geistlicher deutscher ... üblicher Lieder und Psalmen ... fünffter Theil, 2–8vv (1607¹²); B v

Musae Sioniae ... deutscher geistlicher ... üblicher Psalmen und Lieder ... sechster Theil, 4vv (1609⁹, abridged ?2/1611⁵ as 134 geistliche Lieder und Psalmen auf die Fest-Tage ... in Contrapuncto simplici); B vi

Musae Sioniae ... deutscher geistlicher ... üblicher Psalmen und Lieder ... siebender Theil, 4vv (1609¹⁰) [incl. 4 org works]; B vii

Musae Sioniae ... deutscher geistlicher ... Lieder und Psalmen ... in Contrapuncto simplici ... gesetzet ... achter Theil, 4vv (1610¹², 2/1612⁶ as Ferner Continuierung der geistlichen Lieder und Psalmen); B viii

Musae Sioniae ... deutscher geistlicher ... Psalmen und Lieder ... auf Muteten, Madrigalische und sonsten eine andere ... Art ... gesetzet ... neundter Theil, 2, 3vv (1610, 2/1611 as Bicinia und Tricinia); B ix

Eulogodia Sionia, 2–8vv (1611); B xiii

Hymnodia Sionia, 3–8vv (1611) [incl. 4 org works]; B xii

Megalynodia Sionia, 5–8vv (1611); B xiv

Missodia Sionia, 2–8vv (1611); B ix

Kleine und Grosse Litaney, 5–8vv (1613); B xx

Urania, oder Urano-Chorodia, 2–4 choirs (1613); B xvi

Epithalamium: dem ... Fürsten ... Friedrich Ulrichen, Herzogen zu Braunschweig, 17vv, bc, perf. 4 Sept 1614 (1614); B xx

Concertgesang ... dem ... Fürsten ... Mauritio, Landgrafen zu Hessen, 2–16vv, bc, perf. 26 June 1617 (1617, repr. in Polyhymnia caduceatrix); B xx

Polyhymnia caduceatrix et panegyrica, 1–21vv, bc (1619); B xvii

Polyhymnia exercitatrix seu tyrocinium, 2–8vv, bc (Frankfurt am Main, 1619, bc 1620); B xviii

Puericinium ... darinnen 14 teutsche Kirchenlieder und andere Concert-Gesänge, 3–14vv (Frankfurt, 1621) [= pt.iii of Polyhymnia]; B xix

(printed works without title-page, place or date)
Ich suchte des Nachts; B xx
Wie schön leuchtet der Morgenstern; B xx
Attollite portae capita vestra; B xx
Quis est iste qui venit; B xx
Venite ad sanctuarium Domini; B xx

2 Ger., 1 Lat. works: 1618[1], 1623[14], Cantionale sacrum, i (Gotha, 1646)

Euphemia harmonica, 1610, *D-Dlb*

INSTRUMENTAL

Terpsichore, musarum aoniarum quinta, a 4–6 (1612[16]); B xv
8 chorales, org, in Musae Sioniae ... siebender Theil (1609[10]) and Hymnodia Sionia (1611); M

WRITINGS

Leiturgodia Sionia latina (Wolfenbüttel, 1612)
Syntagmatis musici tomus primus (Wittenberg and Wolfenbüttel, 1614–15)/*R*1959)
Syntagmatis musici tomus secundus (Wolfenbüttel, 1618, 2/1619/*R*1958); with *Theatrum instrumentorum* (Wolfenbüttel, 1620/*R*1958)
Syntagmatis musici tomus tertius (Wolfenbüttel, 1618, 2/1619/*R*1958)
Kurtzer Bericht wass bei uberlieffergung einer klein und grosverfertigten Orgell zu observiren, *D-W* [collab. E. Compenius; mentioned in *Syntagmatis musici tomus secundus* and *tomus tertius* as *Orgeln Verdingnis*]; ed. F. Blume, *Michael Praetorius und Esaias Compenius, Orgeln Verdingnis* (Wolfenbüttel, 1936)

For other works, lost or only projected, see B xx

EDITION

L. de Sayve: Teutsche Liedlein, 4vv (Wolfenbüttel, 2/1611)

BIBLIOGRAPHY

WaltherML
J. C. Wetzel: *Hymnopoeographia*, ii (Herrnstadt, 1721)
A. Göhler: *Verzeichnis der in den Frankfurter und Leipziger Messkatalogen der Jahre 1564 bis 1759 angezeigten Musikalien* (Leipzig, 1902/*R*1965)
W. Gurlitt: *Michael Praetorius (Creuzburgensis): sein Leben und seine Werke* (Leipzig, 1915/*R*1968)
F. Blume: *Das monodische Prinzip in der protestantischen Kirchenmusik* (Leipzig, 1925)
P. Zimmermann: 'Zur Biographie des Kapellmeisters Michael Praetorius', *Jb des Braunschweigischen Geschichtsvereins*, 2nd ser., iii (1930)
F. Blume: 'Das Werk des Michael Praetorius', *ZMw*, xvii (1934–5), 321–31, 482–502; repr. in F. Blume: *Syntagma musicologicum: gesammelte Reden und Schriften*, ed. M. Ruhnke, i (Kassel, 1963), 229–64
R. Unger: *Die mehrchörige Aufführungspraxis bei Michael Praetorius* (Wolfenbüttel, 1941)
H. Grimm: *Meister der Renaissancemusik an der Viadrina* (Frankfurt an der Oder, 1942)
R. V. Fay: *The Vocal Style of Michael Praetorius* (diss., U. of Rochester, NY, 1946)
F. Lesure: 'Die "Terpsichore" von Michael Praetorius und die französische Instrumentalmusik unter Heinrich IV', *Mf*, v (1952), 7
G. von Dadelsen: 'Zu den Vorreden des Michael Praetorius', *Kongressbericht: Wien Mozartjahr 1956*, 107
A. Forchert: *Das Spätwerk des Michael Praetorius* (Berlin, 1959)
F. Blume: Afterword to *Michael Praetorius: Gesamtausgabe der musikalischen Werke*, xx (Wolfenbüttel, 1960); repr. in F. Blume: *Syntagma musicologicum: gesammelte Reden und Schriften*, ed. M. Ruhnke, i (Kassel, 1963), 265
L. U. Abraham: *Der Generalbass im Schaffen des Michael Praetorius* (Berlin, 1961)
A. Forchert: 'Praetorius, Michael', *MGG*
M. Ruhnke: *Beiträge zu einer Geschichte der deutschen Hofmusikkollegien im 16. Jahrhundert* (Berlin, 1963)
K. Gudewill: 'Heinrich Schütz und Michael Praetorius: Gegensatz und Ergänzung', *Musik und Kirche*, xxxiv (1964), 253; also in *Acta Sagittariana* (1964), no.5, p.47
P. Winter: *Der mehrchörige Stil: historische Hinweise für die heutige Praxis* (Frankfurt am Main, 1964)
H. E. Samuel: 'Michael Praetorius on Concertato Style', *Cantors at the Crossroads: Essays on Church Music in Honor of Walter E. Buszin* (St Louis, Missouri, 1967), 95
F. Blume: 'Michael Praetorius Creuzburgensis: Rückblick auf einen ausserordentlichen Musiker', *Neue Zürcher Zeitung* (21 Sept 1971); repr. in F. Blume: *Syntagma musicologicum: gesammelte Reden und Schriften*, ii, ed. M. Ruhnke (Kassel, 1973), 129
W. Deeters: 'Alte und neue Aktenfunde über Michael Praetorius', *Braunschweigisches Jb*, lii (1971), 102
K. Gudewill and H. Haase: *Michael Praetorius Creutzbergensis 1571 (?–1621): zwei Beiträge zu seinem und seiner Kapelle Jubilaumsjahr* (Wolfenbüttel, 1971)
M. Ruhnke: 'Michael Praetorius', *Musik und Kirche*, xli (1971), 229
W. Blankenburg: 'Überlieferung und Textgeschichte von Martin Luthers "Encomion musices" ', *Luther-Jb 1972*, 80
W. Deeters: 'Das Lehen der Familie Praetorius', *Braunschweigisches Jb*, liii (1972), 112
A. Forchert: 'Michael Praetorius: Werk und Wirkung', *Sagittarius*, iv (1973), 98
C. Dahlhaus: 'Über den Motettenbegriff des Michael Praetorius', *Beiträge zur Musikgeschichte Nordeuropas: Kurt Gudewill zum 65. Geburtstag* (Wolfenbüttel, 1978)

WALTER BLANKENBURG

Prague (Cz. Praha). City on the River Vltava (Moldau), capital of the Republic of Czechoslovakia from 1918 and formerly capital of Bohemia. Because of its strategic position it has fallen repeatedly under foreign domination and its musical life has been extensively influenced by ideas from other countries. A long history of musical education has also led to Prague composers and, particularly latterly, performers, achieving international fame. The reputation of the citizens as music lovers is firmly established, and for its size the city has a greater degree of musical activity than almost any other European city.

1. To 1620. 2. 1620–1830. 3. 1830–1918. 4. From 1918.

1. TO 1620. Prague did not attain importance until it became the political headquarters of the Přemyslid dynasty (probably in the 9th century). In time the Přemyslid princes asserted their independence and built up an economically and politically important kingdom which, although bounded by German tribes of the Holy Roman Empire, managed to remain autonomous. The Přemyslids appear to have owed allegiance to the Holy Roman Emperor; this was formally recognized in the Golden Sicilian Bull of 1212 in which Frederick II granted the rights of the Kingdom of Bohemia in perpetuity and guaranteed its borders. The Bohemians were empowered to take part in the election of the emperor but their obligations to him were minimal, which gave them a unique position.

The earliest cultural developments were associated with the introduction of Christianity. Most surviving medieval sources relate to the Church, the earliest containing neumes (of the St Gall type) dating from the 11th century (see Plocek). The earliest records of vernacular (Czech) religious songs date from the same period. A troper of 1235 casts lights on the practice of plainchant at the cathedral. At the church of St Jiři liturgical dramas for Holy Week and Easter are known to have been performed from the 13th century; this practice developed in the 14th century and was adopted in other Prague churches. Monodic *planctus* (laments, for example of the Virgin and Mary Magdalen beneath the cross) are attested from the 14th century.

Secular music is less well documented. The court was a leading patron, and epics, sung by *jongleurs* and wandering minstrels, were popular there until the end of the 12th century. Subsequently Minnelied appears to have been encouraged at court. A number of important Minnesinger spent time in Prague, including Reinmar von Zweter, Frauenlob and Heinrich von Mügeln. King Václav II, whose coronation in 1297 occasioned great musical festivities, composed Minnelieder; the texts of three of his songs survive in the Manesse manuscript. Mülich von Prag belongs to the transition period from Minnelied to Meisterlied at the beginning of the 14th century; some of his work is in the 15th-century Colmar manuscript.

The last Přemyslid died in 1306 and by 1310 John of Luxembourg was king. The Luxembourgs were orientated towards France both politically and culturally; Machaut was in John of Luxembourg's service from about 1323 and possibly spent some time in Prague. Nevertheless the importance of the alliance with the Holy Roman Empire was realized and this culminated in the election of Charles of Bohemia as Emperor Charles IV in 1356. In 1346 the bishopric of Prague was elevated to an archbishopric, thereby achieving increased independence; from this period the Ambrosian and Old Slavonic rites were cultivated alongside the ubiquitous Roman rite. In the vernacular sacred songs of this period a folksong element is sometimes detectable, for instance in the *koleda* (Christmas song). There is early evidence of the importance of instrumental music; drums, trumpets and strings were played at the coronation of John of Luxembourg in 1311 and there was a court band. Town trumpeters are mentioned as early as 1409 and were obviously men of some stature since one, Aleš, became a councillor in 1414–15. Two secular instrumental melodies survive from the end of the 14th century, but most instrumental music was improvised. The organ was probably in use quite early but the first clear reference is to its use at the 1311 coronation. A new organ was built at the cathedral in 1369.

Prague's elevation to imperial capital brought great wealth to the city. In 1348 Charles IV founded Prague University, later named the Charles-Ferdinand University after him. The first university in central Europe, it was modelled on that of Paris. The *Musica* of Jehan des Murs was evidently used there as commentaries on it, together with treatises by those connected with the university, survive; the earliest treatise preserved in Prague that deals with polyphony is *Tractatus de cantu perfecto et imperfecto* by Henricus de Zeelandia (late 14th century). At that time Prague was essentially a centre of serious learning and conflicts arose between the intellectual leaders of the city and those who came seeking favours from the court; among the latter churchmen were prominent. There was much antagonism to the moral laxity of the Church and demands were made for services in the vernacular. In 1391 the Bethlehem Chapel was founded expressly for vernacular preaching to the common people; Jan Hus became a preacher there in 1403, aiming to abolish church abuses and return to the simplicity of early Christianity; he was initially supported by the Archbishop of Prague. The Hussite movement had far-reaching effects on music and led in particular to an increased cultivation of vernacular religious songs. The use of instruments was forbidden, and polyphony, secular music and dancing were discouraged. The continuing development of vernacular hymnody during the 16th and early 17th centuries stimulated the publication of many hymnbooks, some including music (*see* CANTIONAL). The best known printing house in Prague was that of Georg Nigrin, active around 1600.

Under the Jagellon dynasty (1471–1526) a considerable flowering of music took place. The Jagellons reestablished religious tolerance and under their patronage a school of composition grew up influenced by Netherlands polyphony. Much church music was written, especially for the Utraquists who had their own form of Mass which used Latin and Czech, omitted the Agnus Dei and had other variants. Polyphonic music

and Czech vernacular songs were cultivated in literary brotherhoods, guilds of leading citizens who met in many of the Prague churches to perform music; these groups flourished all over Bohemia and each had its own songbook. The Prague Collegium Musicum (founded 1616) was the most famous. In the schools and university polyphonic odes with humanistic texts were cultivated.

A Habsburg, Ferdinand, younger brother of Emperor Charles V, was elected king in 1526 and became emperor on his brother's abdication in 1556. He made Prague an important musical centre, albeit at the expense of native composers and performers; he founded a Hofkapelle in 1564 and engaged foreign musicians, and many noble families followed his example. His successor Rudolf II (1576–1612) was served by such outstanding musicians as Monte, Regnart, Kerle and Luython. Handl worked as an organist in Prague at this period. The concern of the Habsburgs was to secure the imperial succession; they ceased to respect Bohemian rights and liberties and as Catholics they felt antagonism towards the Protestants. The struggle for political and religious liberty became outright war in 1618 when an attempt was launched to make the Protestant Frederick V, Elector Palatine, King of Bohemia. The Czechs were finally defeated by imperial troops at White Mountain near Prague in 1620.

2. 1620–1830. The events of 1620 wrought a considerable change in Prague's cultural life. With the firm establishment of Habsburg domination it was no longer capital of an independent state but merely a provincial capital. The nobility of Bohemia were dispossessed to make way for foreign appointees, many of whom were responsible for the city's beautiful Baroque palaces, but few of whom spent much time there, preferring to stay close to Vienna, the centre of political power. For musicians an absentee nobility meant a lack of patrons. Another factor was the persecution of the population, and this allied to lack of patronage caused an unprecedented emigration of musicians in the 17th and 18th centuries to obtain better positions and greater artistic opportunities in other parts of Europe. The leading composers resident in Prague during these two centuries were worthy and talented but tended to be inferior to their compatriots who sought fame abroad. Apart from the lack of employment for the many musicians that Prague produced, the Habsburg domination had other effects, including the almost complete obliteration of the Czech language as a vehicle for culture. As late as the 1820s opera was given in German and even the art songs proposed by nationalistically inclined composers such as V. J. Tomášek were settings of German poetry. But although the Habsburg influence in Prague was not generally favourable to native composers and musicians, it fostered a varied musical life: oratorio in particular flourished, and works by Hasse, Caldara, Fux, Lotti, Leo and other widely known composers were often heard.

The most notable resident composer in the Baroque era (though he also spent much time in Italy) was B. M. Černohorský, choirmaster of St Jakub and a composer of organ music who attracted many pupils from outside Prague and in effect founded the city's strong tradition of organ playing. František Tůma and Joseph Seger continued his work: Seger was renowned for his church and organ music and Tůma wrote orchestral partitas and chamber music. F. X. Brixi and J. E. Koželuch

1. Arena of Prague castle during the première of Fux's opera 'Costanza e Fortezza', given as part of the festivities in celebration of the coronation of Emperor Charles VI as King of Bohemia in 1723: engraving by Birckart after Giuseppe Galli-Bibiena

were other noteworthy mid-18th-century composers of church music; the former also wrote delightful organ concertos. The 18th century also saw the publication, by T. B. Janovka, of the first music dictionary in the Czech lands, *Clavis ad thesaurum magnae artis musicae* (Prague, 1701).

The growth of opera in the 17th and 18th centuries was one of the most important musical developments in Prague. The taste of the new aristocracy was for Italian opera but, with little native tradition to build on, the early exponents were mainly musicians from abroad. Initially performances were irregular, given during the visits of the Viennese court by touring Italian companies. These occasionally introduced works on Czech subjects, such as Bartolomeo Bernardi's *La Libussa*, performed in Prague in about 1703–5. The coronation of Emperor Charles VI as King of Bohemia (1723) stimulated operatic enterprise; the première of Fux's *Costanza e Fortezza*, conducted by Caldara, was given as part of the festivities and among those taking part were C. H. Graun, J. J. Quantz, S. L. Weiss and J. D. Zelenka (see fig.1). Subsequently Count Sporck (1662–1738) engaged an Italian company, directed by Antonio Denzio, which gave its first performance on 24 October 1724 (Bioni's *Orlando furioso*) and continued on a regular basis at his Prague residence and his summer palace, Kuks, until Sporck's death; the repertory of this company included works by Vivaldi, among them sev-

eral that received their premières in Prague. After 1738 operas were given in various Prague theatres and visiting companies, run by skilful Italian managers such as A. and P. Mingotti and Pasquale Bondini, continued to be popular. Important premières were those of Gluck's *Ezio* (1750) and *Issipile* (1752).

One pressing need was that for a real opera house. This was fulfilled by Count Nostitz (1725–94), who founded a new theatre with a company directed by Bondini in 1783, which became known as the Stavovské Divadlo (Estates Theatre, financed by the Bohemian Estates, 1798) and subsequently as the Královské Zemské Divadlo (Royal Provincial Theatre, 1861) and the Tylovo Divadlo (Tyl Theatre, 1945). At first Sunday afternoon performances were given in Czech and after 1861 two more weekly Czech performances were added. Following the success of *Die Entführung aus dem Serail* (1783) and *Le nozze di Figaro* (1786) Mozart was invited to Prague at the beginning of 1787, when he conducted the new Prague Symphony and a performance of *Figaro*; his success there led to Bondini's commissioning a new opera, to be given the following autumn at royal wedding celebrations. This was *Don Giovanni*, which Mozart conducted on 29 October. He visited Prague twice more, briefly in 1789 when travelling between Dresden and Berlin, and in the last weeks of his life, when he conducted the première of *La clemenza di Tito*, commissioned by the impresario

Domenico Guardasoni on behalf of the Bohemian Estates for the festivities surrounding the coronation of Leopold II as King of Bohemia, and given on 6 September 1791 (at first with only limited success). Although Italian opera continued to predominate, the repertory of the Estates Theatre after 1790 reveals an increasing number of German works and even one or two French operas. The ousting of Italian opera was completed under Karl Leibich's direction (1808–16); he engaged as conductor first Wenzel Müller (1808–13) and then C. M. von Weber (1813–16), together with whom he broadened the repertory to include operas by several French composers, Beethoven and Spohr, raised performance standards and worked to dispel some of the apathy engendered in the city's musicians by the popularity of Mozart resulting from the success of *Figaro* and *Don Giovanni*. Nevertheless the main establishment figures at the beginning of the 19th century, B. D. Weber, first director of the Prague Conservatory (founded 1811), and Jan Vitásek, first director of the Varhanická Škola v Praze (Prague Organ School, 1830), were firm Mozartians and strongly resisted the introduction of a more modern idiom.

The development of instrumental concerts in Prague was a disorganized process. Although the nobility (e.g. the Kinsky, Lobkowitz, Hartig, Pachta and Černin families) had their own bands, these were seldom resident in Prague, and the only orchestral tradition was that of the opera orchestras. A wealthy merchant, Jan Ratzenbeck, offered refreshments and instrumental music at a house in the New Town district from 1754, but the first regular series of concerts were those of the musical academy organized by Antonio Duni in 1767 and given once or twice weekly; how long these continued is not recorded. The numerous synagogues, some equipped with organs, were important centres of orchestral music throughout the 18th century. Many travelling virtuosos visited Prague in the second half of the 18th century; the first licence for a public performance of this kind was granted to two Italian lutenists on 7 November 1764. Touring instrumentalists apparently found Prague audiences eager and undiscriminating and few of these visitors were artists of the first rank, though there were exceptions, such as the clarinettist Stadler in 1791 and Beethoven, who visited the city six times between 1796 and 1812. The most prominent Czech composers working in Prague in the later 18th century were F. X. Dušek, a fine pianist and composer who was host to Mozart on his visits to the city, and Tomášek, a pioneer of the Romantic piano piece and famous as a piano teacher. During the 17th, 18th, and 19th centuries instrument making flourished in Prague; organ builders and violin makers were particularly active.

The Church, and particularly the Jesuits, played a leading role in Prague's musical life in the 17th and 18th centuries. Catholicism was reintroduced; the monasteries, mostly in ruins since the Hussite wars, were rebuilt, and churches were refurbished and new ones built in Baroque style. These became important musical centres until most of the monasteries were secularized under Joseph II. The Jesuit colleges emphasized music and trained boys as church musicians as well as providing opportunities for composers of choral and organ music. Prague's Jesuit College was founded in 1556. The Clementinum, later the home of the State and University Library, was originally a Jesuit monastery; among its pupils in the 18th century were Gluck,

Johann Stamitz, J. D. Zelenka, Franz Benda and Josef Mysliveček. The Clementinum had its own music printing press (the only other notable music publisher in 18th-century Prague was Georg Labaun, who published the works of Černohorský). The great Baroque church of St Mikuláš in the Little Quarter, which was rebuilt from 1703, was the venue for lavish performances of oratorios and other ecclesiastical choral music. Another important church was that of St František built in 1688 and run by the Knights of the Cross; the post of organist and choirmaster there was one of the most coveted in Prague and the choirboys were renowned for their performances of school and sepulchre dramas with music. The Loreto Church (1694), the minorite church of St Jakub (rebuilt in 1702) and the Premonstratensian Monastery of Strahov (founded 1148 but much altered during the Baroque period) were also important.

During the period of the Mozart cult there were a number of political changes that were to create the opportunity and impetus for the growth of Czech nationalism. The reign of Joseph II (1780–90) – the so-called 'period of enlightenment' – saw a number of important reforms in the Czech lands, including the abolition of serfdom and the reintroduction of religious freedom, as well as the abolition of the fraternities of *literati* (though their musical importance was no longer great). Administratively, however, Habsburg control was not weakened and this was to prove a spur to nationalist ambitions. Even before the reforms there had been agitation for the use of Czech in schools and scholars had begun to rediscover the country's independent past. A Piarist priest, M. A. Voight (1733–87), wrote *Von dem Alterthume und Gebrauche des Kirchengesanges in Böhmen* (1775), which heralded a number of antiquarian publications on music culminating in the three-volume *Allgemeines historisches Künstler-Lexikon für Böhmen und zum Theil auch für Mähren und Schlesien* (1815) by the organist and choirmaster of Strahov, B. J. Dlabač. The Royal Bohemian Academy of Sciences was founded in 1784 and in 1791 a chair of Czech language and literature was created at Charles University.

Just as opera had reflected the demand for things foreign after 1620, so it quickly came to reflect the growing tide of national feeling. An enterprising Italian company performed *Die Zauberflöte* in a Czech translation in the 1794–5 season and subsequently many more works were given in Czech. A society for the promotion of music in Bohemia was set up in 1808 and was instrumental in establishing the Prague Conservatory in 1811. However, the conservatory's function was to train performers (composition did not become part of the curriculum until the late 19th century) and as much for this reason as for the conservatism of B. D. Weber, its director, it played no role in the creation of a national musical idiom. Similarly Societa, established as a musicians' benevolent society in 1803, sponsored regular concerts but concentrated on the works of foreign composers. There were no composers of sufficient calibre in Prague at the beginning of the 19th century to fulfil the dearest wish of the nationalists, the creation of an authentic Czech opera. František Škroup's *Dráteník* ('The tinker'), first performed on 2 February 1826, was a Czech opera of the Singspiel type and a great success, but his subsequent works failed; the Singspiel was too slight a medium to satisfy a public familiar with C. M. von Weber and his contemporaries. Škroup's failure

2. Stavovské Divadlo (Estates Theatre), Prague, now the Tyl Theatre: wash drawing (c1830) by Vincenz Marstadt

caused a temporary reversion to a repertory dominated by foreign works.

3. 1830–1918. The Varhanická Škola v Praze (Prague Organ School) was founded by the Spolek pro Pěstování Církevní Hudby v Čechách (Society for the Encouragement of Church Music in Bohemia) in 1830, and the most important directors before its amalgamation with the Prague Conservatory in 1890 were J. N. Vitásek (1830–39) and F. Z. Skuherský (1865–90). In the mid-1830s the spark of musical nationalism was rekindled, initially in response to the publication of a number of folksong collections. Composers attempted to incorporate folk material into modest choral compositions, while traditional dances and the polka, a new dance based on traditional models, became popular in the salons. Polka composers such as Josef Labitzky and F. M. Hilmar were regarded as nationalist pioneers. In the years 1835–9 and 1844 the six volumes of *Věnec* ('Garland of patriotic songs') were published in a largely successful attempt to create Czech art song. Political encouragement was given by the ideas and aftermath of 1848, the 'year of revolutions', and by the Habsburg defeats in Lombardy in 1859. In the 1860s two important institutions were founded: the Prague Hlahol (male-voice choir, 1861) and the Umělecká Beseda (Artistic Society, 1863), an association of leading figures in all the arts which remained in existence until 1973; it founded the Hudební Matice publishing company (1871) and the influential journal *Hudební revue* (1908–20).

Standards of performance continued to rise. In 1840 two concert-giving societies were inaugurated, the Cecilská Jednota or Cecilienverein (to c1864) and the Žofín Academy (Žofínská Akademie or Sophien Akademie, to 1899); orchestral music was thus put on a more professional basis. The expensive but excellently prepared concerts of the Žofín Philharmonic were particularly notable. The German-dominated opera at the Estates Theatre continued to command respect; under Škroup a series of Wagner productions showed the level of improvement achieved: *Tannhäuser* (1854), *Lohengrin* (1856) and *Der fliegende Holländer* (1856) were resounding successes. However, it was important to Czech citizens that they should have their own opera house. Plans were made for a theatre for Czech opera and drama; when it opened in 1862 as the Provisional Theatre there was still no suitable Czech opera to perform and its first opera production under J. N. Maýr (1862–6 and 1874–81) was of Cherubini's *Les deux journées*.

In 1861 Count Jan Harrach (1828–99) offered prizes for the best opera and libretto on a Czech theme. In response to this competition Smetana, already established as a conductor of the Hlahol and with the Žofín Academy, wrote his first opera *Braniboři v Čechách* ('The Brandenburgers in Bohemia'). After some disagreement (Smetana had made enemies in the Prague establishment by his criticism of their standards), his opera was declared the winner and he conducted the first performance at the Provisional Theatre on 5 January 1866 with tremendous success, and that year he became the theatre's principal conductor until Maýr resumed the post in 1874. Some additional buildings were occupied by the opera during this period, notably the Nové České Divadlo (New Czech Theatre, 1869–75) and the Novoměstské Divadlo (New Town Theatre, 1857–85, capacity c3000), both wooden structures suitable only for summer performances. Smetana composed a series of operas on nationalistic subjects which were received with varying degrees of critical acclaim (*The Bartered Bride* failed at its first performance on 30 May 1866). He demonstrated the possibility of genuine Czech opera and so encouraged other composers. During his period at the Provisional Theatre he introduced operas by Karel Bendl, Vilém Blodek, L. E. Měchura, Karel Šebor and J. R. Rozkošný. From the 1870s to the 1890s opera was also performed on other Prague stages: in the New Town Theatre, the New Czech Theatre and the Aréna Na Hradbách (Arena on the Ramparts, 1869–75, on the site of the present National Museum), which was replaced by the Národní Aréna Na Hradbách (National Arena on the Ramparts, 1876–80).

Smetana's most politically effective opera was *Libuše*, a festival opera which deals with the legendary founder of Prague and emphasizes the historic achievements of the Czech nation. It was written for the opening on 11 June 1881 of the new Národní Divadlo (National Theatre), which grew out of the Provisional Theatre. It burnt down a few nights later and Czech Prague music lovers united in the effort to rebuild it; it was reopened on 18 November 1883, again with *Libuše*. During the 19th century the premières of a number of important Czech works were given there, including Dvořák's *Čert a Káča* ('The Devil and Kate', 1889) and *Rusalka* (1901), Fibich's *Nevěsta Messinská* ('The Bride of Messina', 1884) and his trilogy of stage melodramas *Hippodamia* (1890). Works from abroad were not neg-

lected; a balance was struck between Italian, French and German operas and a number of Polish and Russian works were also performed. A highlight was Tchaikovsky's visit in February 1888 to conduct *Eugene Onegin*.

After the opening of the Provisional Theatre, the Estates Theatre, with Škroup as conductor (1827–57), had been slightly eclipsed and became exclusively a German theatre. It was no match, however, for the National Theatre despite extensive renovation, and the Neues Deutsches Theater was subsequently opened in 1888 (it was renamed the Smetana Theatre in 1949) on the site of the former New Town Theatre. The German company had an outstanding director in Angelo Neumann (1885–1910) while important figures at the National Theatre were Adolf Čech (1876–1900) and Karel Kovařovic (1900–20), who was one of the great figures in Czech music culture and was responsible for firmly establishing the company. Kovařovic gave the Prague première of Janáček's *Jenůfa* (but with his own alterations to the orchestration), which established the composer's reputation. There was a pact whereby the National Theatre generally gave the Prague premières of new French works and the Neues Deutsches Theater those of German operas (e.g. *Salome* in 1906); however, the Neues Deutsches Theater mounted the Prague première of *Pélléas et Mélisande* (1908), the National Theatre that of *Elektra* (1910), and *Parsifal* received its first two performances in the city (in Czech and German) at the rival theatres on the same night, 1 January 1914. The Czech–German rivalry which permeated Prague musical life at the end of the century was reflected at first in these two theatres, though some degree of cooperation was necessary over performing

3. *Národní Divadlo* (*National Theatre*), *Prague: steel engraving, late 19th century*

rights, and the exchange of orchestra players and singers. Less important was the Vinohrady Theatre, which was built outside Prague in 1907 mainly as a dramatic theatre, but it also mounted operas until 1919 and was especially outstanding during the period 1914–19 when it was under the direction of Ostrčil.

The foundation of the Kammermusikverein in 1876 marked the beginning of what has become Prague's main musical achievement. Chamber groups soon began to be established, most notably the Czech Quartet (1891). The Český Spolek pro Komorní Hudbu (Czech Society for Chamber Music) was formed in 1894 as a Czech rival to the Kammermusikverein; between 1894 and 1918 it gave 208 concerts and has continued to be active. While the Czech society boasted the best performers the Germans caused the greatest furore when Schoenberg conducted his *Pierrot lunaire* in 1913. The same division by nationality was evident in the sphere of musicology which was first taught at the bilingual Charles University in 1869 when Ambros was appointed extraordinarius in music history. The university was divided nationally in 1883: the aesthetician Otakar Hostinský lectured on musical subjects in the Czech section from 1883 and Zdeněk Nejedlý lectured in music history from 1905 until World War II. From 1885 to 1896 Adler was extraordinarius in musicology at the German section, and was followed by Heinrich Rietsch (1900–27). The Prague Conservatory grew in importance through the century, especially after the Prague Organ School was amalgamated with it in 1890. It produced many virtuosos, including the internationally known violinists, Josef Slavík, František Ondříček, Otakar Ševčík and Jan Kobelík. Three composers closely connected with it were Bendl, Karel Knittl and Dvořák; the last was appointed professor of composition, harmony and form in 1890. His master class produced the leading Prague composers of the post-World War I period, including Vitězslav Novák and Josef Suk (i), and his international stature as a composer was also a factor in maintaining the morale of Czech musicians in the city during the difficult period at the turn of the century, when pressure for freedom from Habsburg domination reached its zenith.

In the course of the 19th century Prague became a first-rate musical centre. Throughout the century it was popular with touring virtuosos and the rise in performance standards and the discrimination of its musicians were reflected in its attracting the best performers and many distinguished composers. Paganini visited the city in 1828 and 1829, Chopin in 1829 and 1830, and Wagner as early as 1832; when Berlioz went in 1846 he conducted two concerts and was impressed by the capabilities of the Žofín Philharmonic in excerpts from his *Roméo et Juliette*. Liszt visited several times in the 1840s, and conducted his *Hungarian Coronation Mass* in the Cathedral of St Vít in 1856. Mahler conducted at the Neues Deutsches Theater during the 1885–6 season and gave the first performance of his Seventh Symphony on 19 September 1908 with the Czech PO. In 1894 the orchestra of the National Theatre had organized four concerts as the Česká Filharmonie (Czech Philharmonic), the first of which was given in 1896 under the direction of Dvořák, to raise money for their pension fund. The Czech PO became an independent orchestra in February 1901, after a strike by the members of the National Theatre orchestra, and gave its first concert under Čelansky. Other conductors before

1918 were Oskar Nedbal (1896–1906) and Vilém Zemánek (1902–6).

A number of music publishers flourished: Marco Berra, an Italian immigrant, started his publishing house in 1811 and was particularly associated with the early nationalist composers. Other publishers included Christoph & Kuhé, Jan Hoffman (1814–49), who collaborated with Berra in the publication of *Věnec*, the Umělecká Beseda and the Hudební Matice. The firm of Urbánek, founded by F. A. Urbánek (i) dominated the later 19th century and was active until the nationalization of the publishing industry after 1948. A number of periodicals devoted to music also appeared: *Dalibor*, which began in 1858 and was twice revived, finally ceasing in 1927; *Hudební listy*, which published also with interruptions, over the period 1873–1935; *Hudební revue*; and *Cyril* (1874–1948).

4. FROM 1918. On 28 October 1918, with the end of World War I and the Habsburg Empire disintegrating, Prague became capital of the new Republic of Czechoslovakia. The city's return to political importance coincided with a slight decline in musical status. The great composers and conductors who had shaped Prague's musical life at the end of the 19th century were either dead or died within a few years of the Republic's foundation. The second generation of post-Smetana Romantic nationalists, mostly products of the Dvořák master class at Prague Conservatory, became dominant. Particularly notable were J. B. Foerster, Novák, Suk and Otakar Ostrčil; however, none of these gained the international repute that was accorded Leoš Janáček, whose success drew post-war attention away from Prague to the Moravian capital of Brno. Moreover, although Foerster, Novák and Suk all taught at the conservatory master class, they had surprisingly little influence on the course of Prague's musical life. Foerster was a recluse, Suk more interested in his performing career and Novák, although a passionate innovator and a very important teacher, was too stormy and undiplomatic a figure to be an effective leader of a more progressive style of musical life. Only Ostrčil can be said to have played an important role, as chief conductor of the National Theatre from 1920 to 1935; although not an innovatory composer himself, he made considerable efforts to include modern works in the operatic repertory and caused a riot with his production of Berg's *Wozzeck* (11 November 1926).

In 1920 the small Royal Provincial Theatre (formerly the Estates Theatre) became part of the National Theatre complex and only reverted to a German theatre during the Nazi occupation (1939–45); it was renamed the Tyl Theatre in 1945 and is most suitable for Mozart and other small-scale works. The Neues Deutsches Theater continued to compete with the National Theatre: Zemlinsky was director from 1911 to 1927, when he was succeeded by Szell, under whom the theatre's repertory included works by Schoenberg, Shostakovich, Krenek, Milhaud, Hindemith, Weill and Ravel. At the National Theatre Talich succeeded Ostrčil in 1935, and was chief conductor there until 1944 and for the 1947–8 season. After the liberation in 1945 a new experimental Czech theatre, called the Theatre of 5 May, was established in the former Neues Deutsches Theater under the direction of Alois Hába. In 1948 it was also incorporated into the National Theatre complex and renamed the Smetana Theatre; it was renovated in the 1970s as were many important historic buildings in Prague. Musicians of German origin were still numerous in Prague between the wars, and the Verein für Musikalischen Privataufführungen, a group of German composers who followed the Second Viennese School, were active from about 1922 and had considerable influence through their journal *Der Auftakt*.

The inter-war period was notable for the founding and development of a number of musical institutions. After 1918 the Czech PO became an important ensemble under Talich (1919–39), Kubelik (1936–48), Ančerl (1950–68) and Neumann (1968–). Czechoslovak Radio began in Prague in 1923 and a radio orchestra, Symfonický Orchestr Československého Rozhlasu, conducted by K. B. Jirák and Otakar Jeremiáš among others, was formed the following year. Pride in the achievements of the two pioneering nationalist composers was marked by the establishment of the Smetana Museum (1928) and the Dvořák Museum (1932). The Spolek pro Moderní Hudbu (Society for Modern Music) flourished between 1920 and 1939, while many 19th-century musical institutions, such as the amateur choral societies and the Umělecká Beseda, remained active. Avant-garde composition was centred on Alois Hába, who pioneered a microintervallic system of composition that was influential for many years and attracted composers from abroad to his composition class at the conservatory, which began in 1923. Other prominent composers resident in Prague in the 1920s were Bohuslav Martinů and Ladislav Vycpálek. Gustav Becking (1930–45) and Paul Nettl were notable musicologists at the German section of the university.

The Symfonický Orchestr Hlavního Města Prahy FOK [Film-oper-koncert] (Symphony Orchestra of the Capital of Prague, Film-Opera-Concert) was founded in 1934 under Rudolf Pekárek: other conductors have included Smetáček (1942–56) and Neumann (1956–63). In 1935 a contemporary music society known as Přítomnost (The Present) was founded under Hába's aegis and attracted not only his disciples but composers of other orientations, including those associated with the Soviet-aligned Union of Workers (Svaz DDOČ) led by Ervín Schulhoff and Vít Nejedlý, and the neo-classical group allied to the Society of Graphic Artists (Mánes), who included Pavel Bořkovec and Iša Krejčí; independent composers such as the jazz-inspired Jaroslav Ježek and E. F. Burian were also associated with Přítomnost, which had its own journal, *Rytmus*. Ježek and Burian collaborated with the poets and actors Voskovec and Werich in the popular satirical revue theatre Osvobozené Divadlo (Liberation Theatre) which ran from 1925 to 1938. In the 1920s and 1930s Prague re-established its position as the musical capital of the country: the second, third and 13th festivals of the ISCM were staged there, and at the second in 1924 Schoenberg's *Erwartung* had its world première and Bartók's Dance Suite its Prague première.

The independent Czechoslovak Republic was short-lived; by 1939 it had been incorporated into Hitler's Grossdeutsches Reich and until 1945 the city was isolated from musical trends elsewhere. The German occupation broke up musical institutions: Charles University was closed, as was the National Theatre (in 1944), and even the Neues Deutsches Theater ceased to function. Many musicians fled in time and several died in the allied forces; a significant number of those remaining were imprisoned or sent to concentration camps. The Jewish community in Prague, one of the largest and best established in central Europe, and its important musical tradition were almost entirely obliterated. In May 1945 the Soviet Army entered Prague. Cultural life was quickly re-established and musicians lost little time in reopening international contacts and reorganizing themselves. Among the first events were the creation of the Syndikát Československých Skladatelů (Syndicate of Czechoslovak Composers, 1946–9) and the inception of the Pražské Jaro (Prague Spring) festival in 1946. The festival was intended as a means of attracting visiting artists to the city for the first time since 1939; from 1946 the Prague Spring became a three-week annual festival of considerable repute. After the war the German language ceased to be used in public; since then German-speaking musicians and German musical culture have played no more important a part in Prague's cultural life than any other foreign import.

After 1945 Czechoslovakia became a socialist state and gradually all musical institutions were nationalized; for example, responsibility for music education was transferred to the state. New specialist primary schools for the musically gifted were set up, and a new Academy of Musical Arts (AMU) replaced the Prague Conservatory master school in 1946. Many organizations were founded to cover various aspects of musical activity. These were mostly based in Prague and included organizations replacing a number of previously independent firms. The state gramophone record company Supraphon (1946), the state film industry with its own symphony orchestra based at Prague-Barrandov (1945), the Státní Nakladatelství Krásné Literatury Hudby a Umění (State Publishers of Fiction, Music and Art, 1953), known from 1961 as Státní Hudební Vydavatelství (State Music Publishers), and the state concert agency Pragokoncert (1962) are typical examples. Such institutionalization produced benefits for musicians in the form of state support and encouragement. The Svaz Československých Skladatelů (Union of Czechoslovak Composers, 1949–70) was not only an ideological organization but a benevolent society providing pensions, grants and health camps; it took a leading part in propagating new Czech music through radio and television (Czech Television began in Prague in 1953), through its journal *Hudební rozhledy* ('Musical views'), which it took over from the Syndicate of Czechoslovak Composers, and through two subsidiary institutions, the Český Hudební Fond (Czech Music Fund, 1953) and Panton (1958). The music fund encourages performances of new Czech music abroad and publishes a bulletin, *Music News from Prague*, in several languages. It also promotes concerts in Prague including the important Týden Nové Tvorby (Week of New Works), an annual festival of new Czech compositions in all media which began in 1956. The publishing company Panton produces scores, books and records of contemporary music.

Musicological study also received state encouragement; an important factor was the systematic removal of musical archives and other items from private hands to central locations. Much of the wealth of castle and monastic libraries, including some medieval and many 18th- and 19th-century music manuscripts, has been placed in the music division of the National Museum in Prague, where it is being catalogued. A fine collection of historic instruments has also been created there. Another important manuscript collection is in the library of Charles University. Apart from the musicological items contained in *Hudební rozhledy* two important musicological journals are produced in Prague: *Miscellanea musicologica* (1956–), edited at the Music Department of Charles University and *Hudební věda* (1964–), which stems from the music section of the Czech Academy of Sciences. Musicologists at Charles University included Josef Hutter (1934–9 and 1945–8), Antonín Sychra (1948–69) and Očadlík (1951–64).

The logical conclusion of this state control of musical activities was the centralization of all musicians – performers, composers, historians and critics – under one organization, the Svaz Českých Skladatelů a Koncertních Umělců (Union of Czech Composers and Concert Artists), with its headquarters in Prague, in 1972. The basing of so many of the national organizations in Prague has naturally made it dominant in musical politics, but it has to some extent lost its leadership in performance with the creation of symphony orchestras, opera companies and other ensembles in provincial cities. Perhaps because it has been so closely associated with the musical establishment Prague has tended to lag behind in the exploration of contemporary trends of composition. However, in the 1960s new groups began to form. The Pražská Skupina Nové Hudby (Prague New Music Group, 1965) included the composers Zbyněk Vostřák and Marek Kopelent. A number of performing ensembles for new music were formed – Komorní Harmonie (Chamber Harmony, 1960), Musica Viva Pragensis (1961), Sonatori di Praga (1964), Due Boemi di Praga (1964), and others. A number of composers, such as Miloslav Kabeláč, began to cultivate electronic and aleatory techniques. In addition to the composers already mentioned other progressive younger composers working in the city include Jan Klusák, Luboš Fišer and others. An annual jazz festival began in 1964, while the jazz–pop world of the satirical revue started at the Semafor Theatre in 1959 with the poet Jiří Suchý and the composer Jiří Šlitr.

The musical life of Prague in the 1970s is rich and varied. A great deal of contemporary Czech music is heard, although there is a degree of isolation from trends abroad. However, leading ensembles and performers are regularly invited to the Prague Spring, a highpoint of the musical year. Opera and ballet are performed by the National Theatre Company at the Smetana Theatre (which became part of the National Theatre Company after World War II), Tyl Theatre and National Theatre. Czechoslovak Radio plays a leading role through the concert performances of the Radio SO and the annual Concertino Praga started in 1955 as an international competition for young musicians featuring a different instrument each year. Supraphon presents record programmes and occasional live musical events at its own theatre, and the Czech PO gives a number of concerts, though it spends much time touring, as do the many internationally known ensembles originating in Prague. Notable groups include the Czech Quartet (founded 1891), Prague Quartet (1919), Czech Nonet (1924), Prague Wind Quintet (1928), Czech Piano Quartet (1941), Czech Philharmonic Wind Quintet (1944), Smetana Quartet (1945), Vlach Quartet (1950), Ars Rediviva (1951), Dvořák Quartet (1951), Prague Chamber Orchestra (1951), Suk Trio (1951), Foerster Trio (1955), Novák Quartet (1955), Prague String Quartet (1955),

Prague Madrigalists (1956), Czech Chamber Orchestra (1957), Prague Chamber Soloists (1961) and Musici Pragenses (1962). Many of these groups have a continuous history of distinction through many changes of personnel, and effectively make the city one of Europe's leading centres of chamber music. More important, however, in Prague's everyday musical life are the annual subscription concert series of the Prague SO FOK, and the summer concert series which emphasizes chamber music and is presented between June and September in the historic buildings and gardens of the city. Frequent concerts are given in the Smetana Museum, the villa Bertramka (formerly the home of Dušek) and Smetana Hall (built 1905–11). The Prague Madrigalists organize a series of concerts of both early and contemporary music on the steps of the grand staircase of the National Museum. Two of the city's churches play a leading role in musical life: St Jakub is renowned for its organ concerts, while St Mikuláš in the Little Quarter features choral works. Allied to this regular activity are the occasional promotions by ad hoc groups, student ensembles and the numerous fine solo artists working in Prague, as well as concerts by visiting performers.

BIBLIOGRAPHY

O. Teuber: *Geschichte des Prager Theaters* (Prague, 1883–7)

R. von Procházka: *Mozart in Prag* (Prague, 1892; 4/1938, ed. P. Nettl as *Mozart in Böhmen*; 5/1955)

J. Branberger: *Konservatoř hudby v Praze* [Prague Conservatory] (Prague, 1911; Ger. trans., 1911)

R. Perlík: *K dějinám hudby a zpěvu na Strahově* [History of music and song in the Strahov Monastery] (Prague, 1925)

A. Z. Idelsohn: *Jewish Music in its Historical Development* (New York, 1929), esp. 205, 380, 382, 438ff, 457

E. Trolda: *Prager Kirchenmusik im Zeitalter des Barocks* (Prague, 1929)

Z. Nejedlý: *Dějiny opery Národního divadla* [A history of opera at the National Theatre] (Prague, 1936, 2/1949)

J. Bartoš: *Prozatímní divadlo a jeho opera* [The Provisional Theatre and its opera] (Prague, 1938)

O. Kamper: *Hudební Praha v XVIII. věku* [Musical Prague in the 18th century] (Prague, 1938)

L. Novák: *Opera a balet staré gardy Národního divadla* [Opera and ballet of the old guard at the National Theatre] (Prague, 1938)

R. Rosenheim: *Die Geschichte des deutschen Bühnen in Prag 1883–1918: mit einem Rückblick 1783–1883* (Dresden, 1938)

H. Doležil and A. Piša: *Soupis repertoáru Národního divadla v Praze 1881 až 1935* [The National Theatre's repertory, 1881–1935] (Prague, 1939)

Z. Němec: *Weberova pražská léta* [Weber's years in Prague] (Prague, 1943)

V. Němec: *Pražské varhany* [Prague organs] (Prague, 1944)

L. Veselý: *Soupis repertoáru Národního divadla 1945–50* [The National Theatre's repertory, 1945–50] (Prague, 1951)

Z. Nejedlý: *Dějiny husitského zpěvu* [A history of Hussite song] (Prague, 1954–6 [orig. pubd 1904–7])

T. Volek: 'Hudebníci Starého a Nového města pražského v roce 1770' [Musicians of Prague's old and new town districts in 1770], *MMC*, no.1 (1956), 43

V. Holzknecht: *Jaroslav Ježek a Osvobozené divadlo* [Jaroslav Ježek and the Liberation Theatre] (Prague, 1957)

P. Nettl: *Das Prager Quartierbuch des Personals der Krönungsoper 1723* (Vienna, 1957)

T. Volek: 'Čtyři studie k dějinám české hudby 18. století' [Four studies in 18th-century Czech music history], *MMC*, no.6 (1958), 39–135

M. Očadlík: '75 let opery Národního divadla' [75 years of opera at the National Theatre], *MMC*, no.9 (1959), 31–77

K. M. Komma: *Das böhmische Musikantentum* (Kassel, 1960)

V. Holzknecht, ed.: *150 let pražské konservatoře* [150 years of the Prague Conservatory] (Prague, 1961)

T. Volek: 'Repertoir Nosticovského divadla v Praze z let 1794, 1796–8' [The repertory of the Nostitz Theatre in Prague in the years 1794 and 1796–8], *MMC*, no.16 (1961), 5–191

F. Pala: *Opera Národního divadla v období Otakara Ostrčila* [Opera at the National Theatre under Otakar Ostrčil] (Prague, 1962–70)

V. Holzknecht: *Česká filharmonie, příběh orchestru* [The history of the Czech PO] (Prague, 1963)

V. Müller: *Vyprávění o Narodním divadle* [Stories of the National

Theatre] (Prague, 1963)
J. Fukač: 'Archaische Tendenzen in der Prager Barockmusik', *Sborník prací filosofické fakulty brněnské university*, F9 (1965), 93–105
F. Mužík: 'Zavišova píseň [Záviš's song], *Sborník prací filosofické fakulty brněnské university*, F9 (1965), 167
J. Kotek: 'K historii stavovských organizací českých hudebníků' [A contribution to the history of professional organizations of Czech musicians], *HV*, iii (1966), 133
J. Němeček: 'Komentář k premiérám Wagnerových oper na Národním divadle' [A commentary on the premières of Wagner's operas at the National Theatre], *HV*, iii (1966), 676
T. Volek: 'Obrozenský zájem o českou hudební minulost' [The national revivalists' interest in the Czech musical past], *HV*, iii (1966), 599
J. Bužga: 'Die Gattungen des Musiktheaters in den böhmischen Ländern im 17. Jahrhundert', *IMSCR*, x *Ljubljana 1967*, 126
L. Hrdý: 'Pražské koncerty a statistika 1925–39' [Prague concert statistics, 1925–39], *HV*, iv (1967), 339
V. Lebl: 'Český hudební život 1890–1918' [Czech musical life, 1890–1918], *HV*, iv (1967), 192–242
T. Volek and M. Skalická: 'Vivaldis Beziehungen zu den böhmischen Ländern', *AcM*, xxxix (1967), 64
J. Berkovec and V. Petrovský: *Streifzüge durch das musikalische Prag* (Prague, 1968)
J. Němeček: *Opera Národního divadla v období Karla Kovařovice* [Opera at the National Theatre under Kovařovic] (Prague, 1968–9)
Z. Pilková: 'Populární koncerty Umělecké besedy v letech 1886–1903' [The popular concerts of the Umělecká Beseda in the years 1886–1903], *HV*, v (1968), 210
J. Wenig: *Sie waren in Prag* (Prague, 1971)
J. Bužga: 'Einige Quellen zur Geschichte der Osteroratorien in Prag und Brno (Brünn)', *De musica disputationes Pragenses* (Prague, 1972)
Z. Pilková: 'K dějinám českých reprodukčních těles v 19. století' [The history of Czech performing bodies in the 19th century], *HV*, x (1973), 146
V. Plocek: *Catalogus codicum notis musicis instructorum qui ... in Bibliotheca universitatis Pragensis servantur* (Prague, 1973)
M. Tarantová: 'Altprager musikalische Salons im Vormärz', *Sborník prací filosofické fakulty brněnské university*, H8 (1973), 145
J. Bužga: 'Musiker und musikalische Institutionen im Zeitalter des Barocks in den böhmischen Ländern', *Beiträge zur Musikgeschichte Osteuropas*, ed. E. Arro (Wiesbaden, 1977)
T. Volek and S. Jareš: *Dějiny české hudby v obrazech* [History of Czech music in pictures] (Prague, 1977)

For further bibliography *see* CZECHOSLOVAKIA, §I, I, and *Dějiny české hudební kultury 1890–1945* [History of Czech music culture 1890–1945] (Prague, 1972–) [incl. extensive bibliography and discussion of sources].

J. BUŽGA, ADRIENNE SIMPSON

Prague String Quartet. Czech string quartet. It was founded in 1955. Its members are Bretislav Novotný (*b* Vsetín, 10 Jan 1924), violin; Karel Přibyl (*b* Rtyně, 26 March 1931), violin, who succeeded Miroslav Richter in 1957; Lubomír Malý (*b* Prague, 6 March 1938), violin, whose predecessors were Hubert Šimáček (until 1957) and Jaroslav Karlovský (until 1968); and the cellist Jan Širc (*b* Kosmonosy, 3 May 1934), who succeeded Zdeněk Koníček in 1968. Novotný studied at the Prague Conservatory with Voldan and made his début as a soloist in Prague in 1949. He has continued his solo career alongside his work with the quartet, and was named Artist of Merit in 1974. Přibyl studied with Voldan and Pekelský in Prague and was leader of the orchestra at the National Theatre until 1957. Malý was a pupil of Zahradník at the Prague Conservatory and is active as a soloist as well as in chamber music. Novotný teaches at the Prague Conservatory, Přibyl and Malý at the Academy of Music. Širc studied with Jaroš and Zelenka in Prague. He was formerly principal cellist with the Prague Radio SO.

The quartet, which succeeded another organization of the same name, made its début in Prague in 1956. In 1958 it won the International Quartet Competition in Liège and thereafter started on a career that has taken it round the world several times. In 1961 the ensemble was given the status of an independent chamber music organization of the Prague SO, enabling its members to devote themselves exclusively to chamber music.

Besides the standard German Classical repertory (with particular emphasis on the Beethoven quartets), they play works by many later Russian, French, Hungarian and German composers, but their especial interest is Czech music. They play the complete quartets of Dvořák, Smetana and Janáček, as well as many works by Suk, Novák and Martinů, and encourage the works of young Czech composers. They have recorded much of their repertory. In 1967 the Prize of the City of Prague was awarded to the quartet for its services to Czech music and to the city.

RONALD KINLOCH ANDERSON

Praha (Cz.). PRAGUE.

Prahács, Margit (*b* Budapest, 12 April 1893; *d* Budapest, 1 July 1974). Hungarian musicologist. After studying piano with Emánuel Hegyi at the Budapest Academy (diploma 1917), she enrolled in the faculty of philosophy and aesthetics at Budapest University, where she took a doctorate in 1924 with a dissertation on the psychology of music. She also taught at the Fodor Music School (1917–27). A scholarship enabled her to continue her studies in Berlin from 1926 to 1927 with Abert, Sachs and Schünemann. In 1928 she was appointed librarian at the Budapest Academy, a position she retained until her retirement in 1961. She became lecturer in musical aesthetics in Budapest at the university in 1937; in 1936 she received the Baumgarten Prize for her work in aesthetics and visited Italy. She remained at the university until 1947, during which time she founded a collegium musicum for the performance of early music. She also took part in organizing the Liszt Museum at the Academy. She was a corresponding member for Hungary at the European Liszt Centre from 1970, and in 1971 she was elected an honorary member of the American Liszt Society. As a critic Prahács contributed to numerous Hungarian periodicals. Most of her writings are devoted to Hungarian music, particularly that of Liszt, but she contributed several valuable studies in her special field of musical aesthetics.

WRITINGS

A muzikalitás lelki feltételei [Psychological conditions of musicianship] (diss., U. of Budapest, 1925)
'Stílusanalógiák a zene és a képzőművészetek között' [Style analogies between music and visual arts], *Magyar művészet* (1926), 439, 568
'A cigányzene és a magyar népzene' [Gypsy music and Hungarian folk music], *Napkelet*, viii (1930), 47
'A magyar népzene vitás kérdéseiről' [Debatable questions about Hungarian folk music], *Napkelet*, viii (1930), 505
'Forma és kifejezés a zenében' [Form and expression in music], *Athenaeum*, xviii (1932), 48
A zeneesztétika alapproblémái [Basic problems of musical aesthetics] (Budapest, 1935)
'Die ästhetischen Probleme Paulers', *Gedenkschrift für Ákos von Pauler* (Berlin, 1936), 186
'Liszt Ferenc és a magyar műveltség' [Franz Liszt and Hungarian intellectuals], *Magyar szemle* (1936), no.26, p.57
'Liszt Ferenc idealizmusa' [The idealism of Franz Liszt], *Athenaeum*, xxii (1936), 191
'A XIX. század magyar zenéje' [Hungarian music of the 19th century], *Magyar művelő déstörtenet*, v (1939), 641
'A nemzeti kórusstílus kibontakozása' [The development of the national choral style], *Emlékkönyv Kodály Zoltán hatvanadik születésnapjára* (Budapest, 1943), 72
'Claudio Monteverdi: halálának 100 évfordulója alkalmából' [Claudio Monteverdi: the 100th anniversary of his death], *Magyar zenei szemle*, iii (1943), 273
Magyar témák a külföldi zenében [Hungarian themes in non-Hungarian music] (Budapest, 1943) [with foreword by Z. Kodály]
'François Liszt épistolier', *Nouvelle revue de Hongrie* (Budapest, 1944), 63
'Bartók bibliográfia', *Zenei szemle* (1948), no.8, p.432
'Bartók Bibliography', *Tempo* (1949–50), no.14, p.39

'Zene a régi óvodában' [Music in the ancient nursery], *Emlékkönyv Kodály Zoltán 70. születésnapjára* (Budapest, 1953), 515–65
'A Zeneművészeti Főiskola Liszt hagyatéka' [The Liszt Museum of the Academy], *Zenetudományi tanulmányok*, vii (1959), 427–582, 692
'Liszts letztes Klavierkonzert', *SM*, iv (1963), 195
Franz Liszts Briefe aus ungarischen Sammlungen 1835–1886 (Budapest and Kassel, 1966) [with catalogue and chronological table]
JOHN S. WEISSMANN

Prant, Jobst vom. *See* BRANDT, JOBST VOM.

Pratella, Francesco Balilla (*b* Lugo di Romagna, 1 Feb 1880; *d* Ravenna, 17 May 1955). Italian composer, critic and musicologist. He studied at the Pesaro Liceo Musicale, where he had a few lessons from Mascagni. Later he directed the Licei Musicali of Lugo di Romagna (1910–29) and Ravenna (1927–45). In 1910 he had become associated with Marinetti's futurist movement, and he drew up a *Manifesto dei musicisti futuristi* (1910), followed by the *Manifesto tecnico della musica futurista* (1911) and *La distruzione della quadratura* (1912). In the first of these polemics, naively belligerent rhetoric (some of it apparently inserted by Marinetti) alternates with sound criticism of the state of music in Italy. The other two advocate atonality, microtones, rhythmic irregularity, etc; they are of mainly theoretical interest, as neither Pratella nor any other futurist realized their full implications in practice. Basically, indeed, Pratella was halfhearted in his futurism, gradually withdrawing from the movement after World War I. Later, in addition to composing, writing criticism, teaching, and editing early music, he became increasingly absorbed in the study of Italian (particularly Romagnan) folk music, which had already influenced such pre-futurist works as *Romagna* and *La Sina 'd Vargöun*.

Despite an insecure technique, Pratella's melodic invention has, at its best, an airy, free-ranging lyricism, with modal arabesques that recall both Pizzetti and Romagnan folktunes. His most convincing achievements are in small-scale lyrical pieces that have nothing to do with futurism: the song collection *I canti del cammino* is a good example. The once notorious *Musica futurista* represents him far less favourably; with its constant repetition of short phrases, its over-reliance on the whole-tone scale and its amorphous shape, it is a mere historical curiosity. Pratella's most substantial futurist work, *L'aviatore Dro*, though uneven and very dated, deserves more serious attention. Here his futurist and folkloristic sides sometimes interact creatively.

WORKS
(selective list)

DRAMATIC

Lilia, op.15 (opera, Pratella), 1903; Lugo, 1905; expanded as Il regno lontano, c1905
La Sina 'd Vargöun, op.22 (scene della Romagna bassa, Pratella), 1906–8; Bologna, 1909
L'aviatore Dro, op.33 (opera, Pratella), 1911–14; Lugo, 1920
Dono primaverile, op.48 (incidental music, Pratella), 1916–21; Bologna, 1923; rev. as Il principe malinconico
La ninna nanna della bambola, op.44 (children's opera, Pratella, after L. de Nardis), 1920–22, some music from 1901–2; Milan, 1923
La leggenda di San Fabiano, op.54 (sacra rappresentazione, A. Beltramelli, Pratella), 1928–32; Bologna, 1939
L'uomo, op.59 (opera, Pratella), 1934–49, unperf.
Nòstra médar Rumagna, op.61 (incidental music, Pratella), 1952–4
Operettas, other incidental music, film scores

OTHER WORKS

Orch: Romagna, opp.17–21, 5 sym. poems, 1903–4; Musica futurista, op.30, 1912, soon renamed Inno alla vita, rev. 1933; La guerra, op.32, 3 dances, 1913, rev. as Il rondò della vittoria, 1932
Choral: La chiesa di Polenta, op.10 (Carducci), 1v, chorus, orch, 1903; Laudes creaturarum (Il cantico di frate sole di Sancto Francesco), op.50, chorus, org, str, 1927; other pieces

Inst: Pf Trio, op.28, 1911; Sonata seconda, op.37, vn, pf, c1920; Giallo pallido, op.39, str qt, 1923; Per un dramma orientale, op.40 [adapted, probably c1934, from unpubd intermezzos of 1922 for Marinetti: Il tamburo di fuoco], wind qnt, pf, str qt (1938); Sonata terza, op.55, pf qnt, 1937; Sonata quarta da conc., op.58, vc, pf, 1940s; several early pieces, vn, pf; kbd music, etc
Songs: Le canzoni del niente, op.36, 1v, pf, 1917–18; I canti del cammino, op.52, 1v, pf trio, 1928; many others, folksong arrs., edns. and arrs. of works by Carissimi, Sacchini, Viadana, etc.

Principal publishers: Bongiovanni (Bologna), Carisch, Fantuzzi (Milan), Ricordi, Sonzogno (Milan)

WRITINGS

Manifesto dei musicisti futuristi (Milan, 1910); repr. in *RMI*, xvii (1910), 1007, also in *I manifesti del futurismo* (Florence, 1914) and Pratella (1918–19), (1933) and (1971); Eng. trans. in N. Slonimsky: *Music since 1900* (New York, 4/1971), 1294, and in U. Apollonio, ed.: *Futurist Manifestos* (London, 1973), 31
Manifesto tecnico della musica futurista (Milan, 1911) [title variants exist]; repr. in *RMI*, xviii (1911), 486, also in *I manifesti del futurismo* (Florence, 1914) and Pratella (1918–19), (1933) and (1971); Eng. trans. in N. Slonimsky: *Music since 1900* (New York, 4/1971), 1926
La distruzione della quadratura (Bologna, 1912) [pubd with 2 previous manifestos as preface to pf red. of *Musica futurista*]; repr. in *I manifesti del futurismo* (Florence, 1914) and Pratella (1918–19), (1933) and (1971)
Teoria della musica (Bologna, 1912, enlarged 2/1919)
Musica italiana (Bologna, 1915)
Cronache e critiche dal 1905 al 1917 (Bologna, 1918)
L'evoluzione della musica: dal 1910 al 1917 (Milan, 1918–19)
Saggio di gridi, canzoni, cori e danze del popolo italiano (Bologna, 1919)
Luci ed ombre: per un musicista italiano ignorato in Italia (Rome, 1933) [on Gnecchi]
Scritti vari di pensiero, di arte, di storia musicale (Bologna, 1933)
Etnofonia di Romagna (Udine, 1938)
Primo documentario per la storia dell'etnofonia in Italia (Udine, 1941)
Autobiografia, written 1947–55 (Milan, 1971) [apparently abbreviated; incl. list of works and writings]

BIBLIOGRAPHY
A. Toni: 'La Sina 'd Vargöun di F. B. Pratella', *RMI*, xvii (1910), 195
G. Barini: 'Musica futurista', *Nuova antologia*, ccxlviii (1913), 152
F. Torrefranca: 'Futurismo passatistico', *Il marzocco*, xviii/28 (1913), 4
G. Bastianelli: 'La musica futurista', *Musicisti d'oggi e di ieri* (Milan, 1914), 59
——: 'Ancora a proposito della musica futurista', *Musicisti d'oggi e di ieri* (Milan, 1914), 67
G. M. Gatti: 'F. Balilla Pratella', *Musicisti moderni d'Italia e di fuori* (Bologna, 1920, 2/1925), 127
A. Ghigi: *Francesco Balilla Pratella* (Ravenna, 1930) [incl. list of works, writings and bibliography]
M. Saint-Cyr: 'Francesco Balilla Pratella', *Rassegna dorica*, iii (Rome, 1931–2), 165
C. Marabini: 'Balilla Pratella: musica e futurismo', *Nuova antologia*, cdlxxxix (1963), 67
A. Gentilucci: 'Il futurismo e lo sperimentalismo musicale d'oggi', *Convegno musicale*, i (Turin, 1964), 275
Discoteca alta fedeltà, xii (Milan, 1971), Jan–Feb [futurist-music number, incl. M. Morini: 'Futurismo e musica: cronologia', G. Tintori: 'Un opera futurista: L'aviatore Dro', and articles by L. Pestalozza, A. Gentilucci and others]
R. J. Payton: *The Futurist Musicians: Francesco Balilla Pratella and Luigi Russolo* (diss., U. of Chicago, 1974)
——: 'The Music of Futurism: Concerts and Polemics', *MQ*, lxii (1976), 25
JOHN C. G. WATERHOUSE

Pratensis, Jodocus. *See* JOSQUIN DESPREZ.

Prati, Alessio (*b* Ferrara, 19 July 1750; *d* Ferrara, 17 Jan 1788). Italian composer. He had lessons from Pietro Marzola, *maestro di cappella* of Ferrara Cathedral, and in 1768, encouraged by Piccinni, went to study in Naples (Florimo incorrectly supposed that he entered Piccinni's conservatory, S Maria di Loreto). In 1774–5 he had ten months' study in Rome with Abate Speranza, a contrapuntist in the strict style, returning then to Naples. Unable to establish himself there, he went to France, where he is said to have taught singing and the harpsichord for two years at Marseilles and later to have been in the service of the Duke of

Penthièvre in Paris (he seems also to have been living at Lyons when his first set of sonatas was published there). Music by him was first performed at the Concert Spirituel at the end of 1776, and in 1779 his first opera, *L'école de la jeunesse* was successful at the Théâtre-Italien. The published score is dedicated to Mme de Genlis, the celebrated writer and governess of the children of the Duke of Chartres, Penthièvre's son-in-law. If, as has been stated, Prati taught music in Paris to some royal princes, these were probably the ones (among them the future king, Louis-Philippe).

In 1782 the Grand Duke Paul Petrovich and his wife visited Paris; Prati ingratiated himself with them and at the end of that year went to St Petersburg, probably by way of Berlin and Warsaw. In March 1783 he gave three concerts there, including an oratorio *Giuseppe riconosciuto*. Any hopes he may have had of an appointment were disappointed, and in the summer he left, passing through Vienna. In 1784 he was in Ferrara, which he is said to have had to leave because of a controversy (he may have wanted to succeed Marzola who died that year; he eventually returned to Ferrara as coadjutor to the new *maestro*, Petrucci). He now began to be in demand as an opera composer and fell in love with the prima donna Cecilia Giuliani (née Bianchi), but he produced only a few operas before his early death.

Prati seems to have had difficulty in achieving the success that his talent deserved, perhaps partly because of his personality. He is said to have been of melancholic temperament, and all his operas are serious, including the *opéra comique*, a very moral *drame bourgeois*. His talent is more evident in these, with their generally excellent craftsmanship (even his contrapuntal training is occasionally apparent), than in his instrumental music. The first set of sonatas makes excessive use of Alberti basses, while the later ones aim at brilliance, with more varied textures and expansive (though not difficult) passage-work.

WORKS

OPERAS

L'école de la jeunesse, ou Le Barnevelt français (opéra comique, 3, L. Anseaume), Paris, Théâtre-Italien, 11 Oct 1779 (Paris, 1779)

L'Ifigenia in Aulide (dramma per musica, 3, L. Serio), Florence, Pergola, aut. 1784; *US-Wc*

Armida abbandonata (opera seria, 2, G. Sertor), Munich, Court, carn. 1785

La vendetta di Nino (melodramma tragico, 2, F. Moretti), Florence, Pergola, carn. 1786; *GB-T, I-Bc, Fc*

Olimpia (dramma per musica, 2, A. L. Tottola), Naples, S Carlo, 6 June 1786; *I-Nc, P-La, US-Wc*

Demofoonte (dramma per musica, 3, Metastasio), Venice, S Benedetto, 26 Dec 1786; *?D-Bds, P-La*

L'Aminta (azione pastorale, G. Muzzarelli Brusantini), Ferrara, for entrance of papal legate Cardinal Spinelli, ?1787

Doubtful: Semiramide (Metastasio), Paris, 1780; Didone abbandonata (Metastasio), Munich, 1783

OTHER WORKS

Inst: Fl Conc. (Paris, ?1786); Ob Conc., perf. Paris, 1777 (n.p., *c*1950); 2 hpd concs., *I-Nc*; 6 Sonatas, hpd/pf, vn, op.1 (Lyons, n.d.; London, n.d.), 3 rev. as 3 Sonatas, harp/pf, vn, op.6 (Paris, ?1781); 3 Sonatas, harp/hpd, vn, op.2 (Berlin and Amsterdam, 1782) [described as trios in score]; 3 Sonatas, harp/hpd, vn, op.3 (Berlin and Amsterdam, 1782) [described as trios in score]; 6 Sonatas, hpd/pf, vn (Paris, 1782 or later); Duo, 2 harps (Paris, ?1786); Duo, 2 vc, *?D-Bds*; Sinfonia, D, org, *I-Bsf*

Vocal: Giuseppe riconosciuto (oratorio, Metastasio); 3 rondeaux italiens traduits en français (Paris, *c*1781); Recueil de romances italiennes et françaises (Berlin, 1782); 6 romanzi in lingua italiana e francese (Metastasio) (Venice, *c*1782); Sarete alfin contenti (Metastasio: Demetrio), recit, Agitata in tanti affanni (not by Metastasio), aria, *Journal des ariettes italiennes* (1782), Oct, no.91; Scène italienne d'Armide (Son pur giunta, recit, Infelice in tanto orrore, rondò) (Paris, 1784) [possibly from Armida abbandonata, although pubd earlier]

BIBLIOGRAPHY

EitnerQ; GerberL; GerberNL

C. Laderchi: *Notizie biografiche intorno ad Alessio Prati* (Ferrara, 1825)

F. Florimo: *La scuola musicale di Napoli e i suoi conservatorii*, ii (1882/*R*1969), 401

R. A. Mooser: *Annales de la musique et des musiciens en Russie* (Geneva, 1948–51)

DENNIS LIBBY

Pratinas of Phlius (*fl* Athens, *c*500 BC). Greek tragic and (probably) dithyrambic poet. He wrote 50 plays, 32 being satyr plays, a form of which he was one of the first exponents. Four fragments of his lyric writing have survived. One of these (5, ed. Edmonds) is an exhortation to pursue 'neither tense [*syntonon*] music nor the relaxed [*aneimenan*] Iastian' but instead to 'plough the middle [*mesan*: 'mean'] furrow and Aeolize ['compose in the Aeolian *harmonia*'] in your melody', since the *Aiolis harmonia* 'is certainly suited to all song-braggarts'. Pratinas's reference was probably to the central concept of Hellenic ethos theory – the mimesis of character traits. The *Aiolis harmonia* was thought to express the blithe, free-spoken nature of the Aeolian peoples; it was a mean between such 'tense' modes as the Mixolydian and the serenity of the 'relaxed' Iastian (renamed Hypophrygian).

In a long fragment (1, ed. Edmonds), probably from a dithyramb, Pratinas complained of the abuses to which the dithyramb (the choral hymn to Dionysus) had been subjected. 'The Muse', he asserted, 'has made song queen: the aulos must dance second, as a servitor should – or take the lead in revels [*kōmois*]'. (This may be the source of Monteverdi's guiding principle, 'L'orazione sia padrona dell'armonia e non serva'.) While he felt outraged by virtuoso displays on the aulos at the expense of the text, Pratinas was presumably not condemning the instrument itself. The abuses he condemned eventually had their most obvious effects on the dithyramb (*see* TIMOTHEUS); but tragic dramas of the late 5th century BC also show clear traces of such libretto writing, and line 12 of this fragment is thought to contain a punning reference (*phryneou*: 'toad') to the early tragic poet Phrynichus ('little toad'). Pratinas, who seems to have been strongly didactic and prone to theorize in his poetry, was a reactionary many decades before Aristophanes attacked the 'new music' associated with Euripides and the dithyrambists.

See also GREECE, §I.

BIBLIOGRAPHY

H. W. Smyth, ed.: *Greek Melic Poets* (London and New York, 1904/*R*1963), 70ff, 341ff

H. W. Garrod: 'The Hyporcheme of Pratinas', *Classical Review*, xxxiv (1920), 129

E. Diehl, ed.: *Anthologia lyrica graeca* (Leipzig, 1925, rev. 3/1949 by R. Beutler, 4/1954), v, 154ff

J. M. Edmonds, ed. and trans.: *Lyra graeca*, iii (London and Cambridge, Mass., 1927, rev. 2/1940/*R*1967), 46ff

A. W. Pickard-Cambridge: *Dithyramb Tragedy and Comedy* (Oxford, 1927, rev. 2/1962), 14ff, 65ff, 92ff

M. Pohlenz: 'Das Satyrspiel und Pratinas von Phleious', *Göttingen gelehrten Nachrichten* (Berlin, 1927), 298

K. Ziegler: 'Tragoedia', *Paulys Realencyclopädie der klassischen Altertumswissenschaft*, vi/A/2 (Stuttgart, 1937), 1899–2075

F. Stoessl: 'Pratinas', *Paulys Realencyclopädie der klassischen Altertumswissenschaft*, xxii/2 (Stuttgart, 1954), 1721

D. L. Page, ed.: *Poetae melici graeci* (Oxford, 1962), 367ff

W. D. Anderson: *Ethos and Education in Greek Music* (Cambridge, Mass., 1966, 2/1968), 47f

D. A. Campbell, ed.: *Greek Lyric Poetry* (London and New York, 1967), 100f, 403ff

WARREN ANDERSON

Prato, Johannes de. *See* STOKEM, JOHANNES DE.

Prato, Lorenzo da (*b* Prato; *fl* Bologna, 1470–75). Italian organ builder. The son of Giacomo da Prato, he was the leader of the important 15th-century Tuscan school of organ building centred in Prato (its other notable member was Matteo da Prato). He is known principally as the builder of the organ *in cornu Epistolae* of the Basilica of S Petronio in Bologna, commissioned on 2 June 1470 and completed in 1475. The original gilded case of 1474–83 survives, enclosed in a monumental Baroque stone outer case of 1661–75. In 1528 the organ was lowered in pitch by G. B. Fachetti, and in 1686 was moved to its present position. It is thought that the original specification was probably eight chorus or ripieno ranks with the longest pipe about 6·5 m long and a 4′ flute. The organ still has only one manual, and is playable; it has pedal pull-downs. It is uncertain whether its spring-chest is original or to which early period its present quality really belongs. However, it certainly rates as one of the most important surviving early organs. The nicking on some of the pipes is thought to be original.

BIBLIOGRAPHY
A. G. Hill: *The Organ Cases and Organs of the Middle Ages and Renaissance*, ii (London, 1891)
R. Lunelli: *Der Orgelbau in Italien in seinen Meisterwerken* (Mainz, 1956), 6
——: *S. Petronio Bologna* (Mainz, 1956)
J. A. Burns: 'The Organs of San Petronio, Bologna', *The Organ*, xi (1960–61), 191
P. Williams: *The European Organ 1450–1850* (London, 1966), 206f, 213

GUY OLDHAM

Pratoneri, Gaspero [Spirito da Reggio] (*fl* 1566–*c*1595). Italian composer. He has been confused in many sources with the earlier Hoste da Reggio. In the dedication of Vincenzo Spada's *Primo libro delle canzoni a sei voci* (1592), addressed to the 'virtuosissimi signori del ridutto del Sgr. Spirito Pratoneri', he is referred to as 'canonico di Reggio'; in about 1569 he was *maestro di cappella* at S Prospero, Reggio. The title-pages of three of his publications show that he was called 'Spirito' or 'Spirito da Reggio'; he appears as the latter in madrigal anthologies and in his own first volume of madrigals. He was never called 'Spirito l'Hoste', however; this seems to be an invention of Fétis. His two volumes of madrigals are full of occasional pieces celebrating the weddings and the comings and goings of the gentry of Reggio. The music is undistinguished, perhaps reflecting amateur or provincial taste.

WORKS
(all except anthologies published in Venice)
Il primo libro de madrigali, 5vv, con doi, 6vv (1568)
Harmonia super aliquos Davidis psalmos . . . ad Vesperas, 6vv (1569)
Panegirica, 8vv/insts (1584)
Madrigali ariosi . . . 4vv, con un dialogo, 8vv (1587)
Madrigals in 1566², 1568¹², 1583¹⁰, 1587⁶, 1588¹⁶, 1588²⁰, 1591⁸, 1604¹³

BIBLIOGRAPHY
FétisB
G. Gaspari: *Catalogo della Biblioteca del Liceo Musicale di Bologna*, ii (Bologna, 1892/*R*1961), 298

JAMES HAAR

Pratsch, Johann Gottfried [Prach, Ivan; Práč, Jan Bohumir] (*b* Silesia, *c*1750; *d* ?St Petersburg, *c*1818). Czech composer, teacher and folksong collector. Much of his life was spent in Russia. From 1780 until 1795 he taught music at the Smolnïy Institute, and in 1784 he was appointed harpsichord teacher at the St Petersburg Theatre School. His keyboard compositions include a

Sonata in C (1787), six variations on an Allemande by Martín y Soler (1794), Fandango (1795), 12 variations (1802), a Sonata based on Russian themes (1806), eight variations on the folktune *Tï podi, moya korovushka, domoy* ('Be off home with you, my little cow!', 1815) and an unpublished Rondo. He also made a keyboard arrangement of the music from Martín y Soler's opera *Gore-bogatïr Kosometovich* ('The good-for-nothing Bogatïr Kosometovich') and Pashkevich's *Fevey* (both 1789). His most important work, however, was the *Sobraniye narodnïkh russkikh pesen s ikh golosami* ('Collection of Russian folksongs with vocal parts'), one of the earliest collections of Russian folktunes, which he made in collaboration with N. A. L'vov. In its first edition (1790) this comprised 100 songs; larger revised editions were published in 1806 and 1815.

BIBLIOGRAPHY
N. Findeyzen: *Ocherki po istorii muzïki v rossii* [Essays on the history of music in Russia], ii (Moscow and Leningrad, 1929)
R. A. Mooser: *Annales de la musique et des musiciens en Russie au XVIIIe siècle*, ii (Geneva, 1951)

GEOFFREY NORRIS

Pratt, Carroll C(ornelius) (*b* North Brookfield, Mass., 27 April 1894). American psychologist and musicologist. He studied at Clark College (AB 1915), Clark University (PhD 1921), the University of Cambridge (1919) and the University of Berlin (1931). He was instructor and assistant professor of psychology at Harvard University (1923–37), where he also served briefly as an organist and choir director; he then moved to Rutgers University, serving as professor and chairman of the department of psychology. He directed the Institute of Psychology and Philosophy at Ankara University (1945–7) before being appointed chairman and professor of psychology at Princeton University (1947–62) and then at Rider College (1962–71). He has served as editor of the *Psychological Review*, and as president of the American Society for Aesthetics (1950–52). Clark University awarded him an honorary DSc in 1948.

Pratt has studied and written about various aspects of aesthetics and of the psychology of music. Examining objective and subjective musical experience, he concluded that the hearer responds primarily to the inherent tonal design of the music rather than to its symbolic references, and that therefore some important aspects of musical response are not culturally determined.

WRITINGS
'Some Qualitative Aspects of Bitonal Complexes', *American Journal of Psychology*, xxxii (1921), 490
'Bisection of Tonal Intervals Smaller than an Octave', *Journal of Experimental Psychology*, vi (1923), 211
'Variability of Judgments on Musical Intervals', *Journal of Experimental Psychology*, ix (1926), 492
'Bisection of Tonal Intervals Larger than an Octave', *Journal of Experimental Psychology*, xi (1928), 17
'Comparison of Tonal Distances', *Journal of Experimental Psychology*, xi (1928), 77
'Quarter-tone Music', *Journal of Genetic Psychology*, xxxv (1928), 286
The Meaning of Music (New York, 1931/*R*1968 with extensive new introduction)
'Aesthetische Gemütsbewegung', *Zeitschrift für Psychologie*, cxxxi (1934), 376
'Structural versus Expressive Form in Music', *Journal of Psychology*, v (1938), 149
Music as the Language of Emotion (Washington, DC, 1952) [1950 Elson Lecture at the Library of Congress]
'The Stability of Esthetic Judgments', *Journal of Aesthetics and Art Criticism*, xv (1956–7), 1
'Musicology and Related Disciplines', in A. Mendel, C. C. Pratt and C. Sachs: *Some Aspects of Musicology: Three Essays* (New York, 1957)

RAMONA H. MATTHEWS

Pratt, Silas G(amaliel) (*b* Addison, Vermont, 4 Aug 1846; *d* Pittsburgh, 30 Oct 1916). American composer and author. He left school at the age of 12, and while working in three Chicago music stores he saved enough money to spend 1868–71 in Germany studying with Franz Bendel, Theodor Kullak and others. A wrist injury caused by too-strenuous practice prevented his career as a concert pianist. Upon returning to Chicago he became organist of the Church of the Messiah, and with George P. Upton organized the Apollo Club. During his next trip to Germany (1875–7) Liszt gave him some lessons, and he conducted his own *Centennial Overture* at Berlin (4 July 1876). From 1877 to 1888 he again lived in Chicago, where in June 1882 his second opera, *Zenobia, Queen of Palmyra*, was produced in concert form at Central Music Hall and staged the following March at McVicker's Theater. His first opera, titled *Antonio* when begun in 1870 but retitled *Lucille*, had a three-week run at the Columbia Theater in Chicago during March 1887. His third opera *Ollanta*, on an Inca subject, was never produced. In 1888 Pratt moved to New York, where in 1895 he became principal of the West End School of Music. In 1906 he founded the Pratt Institute of Music and Art in Pittsburgh, and was its president until his death. He wrote *Lincoln in Story* (New York, 1901) and *The Pianist's Mental Velocity* (New York, 1905).

WORKS

OPERAS
Antonio, 1870–71, selections perf. Chicago, Farwell Hall, 1874; rev. as Lucille, Chicago, Columbia Theater, 1887
Zenobia, Queen of Palmyra (4, Pratt), concert perf. Chicago, Central Music Hall, 15 June 1882, staged Chicago, McVicker's Theater, 26 March 1883, vocal score (Boston, Mass., 1882)
The Musical Metempsychosis (musical entertainment), 1888
Ollanta (Pratt), not produced

OTHER WORKS
A Columbian Festival Allegory: the Triumph of Columbus, New York, Metropolitan Opera, 10 Oct 1892, vocal score (New York, 1892)
The Inca's Farewell, cantata, Bar, chorus, vocal score (Boston, Mass., 1891)
?3 syms., incl: no.1, perf. Chicago, 1871; 'Prodigal Son', 1875; Lincoln Sym.
3 sym. poems: Magdalene's Lament, c1870; Sandalphon; A Tragedy of the Deep [on the sinking of the Titanic], c1912
Centennial Ov., perf. Berlin, 4 July 1876
c50 pf pieces
Choruses, songs, incl. The [Civil] War in Song: a Military and Musical Allegory (New York, 1891)

BIBLIOGRAPHY
W. S. B. Mathews, ed.: *A Hundred Years of Music in America* (Chicago, 1889), 688ff
E. E. Hipsher: *American Opera* (Philadelphia, 1927), 361ff
F. L. G. Cole: 'Pratt, Silas Gamaliel', *DAB*
ROBERT STEVENSON

Pratt, Waldo Selden (*b* Philadelphia, 10 Nov 1857; *d* Hartford, Conn., 29 July 1939). American musical scholar. He was educated at Williams College (BA 1878, MA 1881), and at Johns Hopkins University, where he studied Greek, archaeology and aesthetics. He was largely self-taught in music. After two years with the Metropolitan Museum of Art in New York, he went to the Hartford Theological Seminary in 1882 as professor of ecclesiastical music and hymnology, a position he retained until his retirement in 1925. Concurrently he taught at several other colleges, including the Institute of Musical Art in New York, and served as a church organist and a choral conductor. He was president of the Music Teachers National Association (1906–8), an editor of its *Proceedings*, and president of the American section of the International Musical Association (1911–16). He wrote a standard history of music and several books on the use of music in the church, and edited the American supplement to *Grove 2*, a book of children's songs and a Sunday school hymn-book. He was awarded honorary degrees by Syracuse University (MusD 1898) and Williams College (LHD 1929).

WRITINGS
The History of English Hymnody (Hartford, 1895) [reference list in pamphlet form]
Musical Ministries in the Church (New York, 1901, rev. 4/1915)
The History of Music (New York, 1907, repr. 1919 with supplementary death dates, enlarged 3/1935, with chap. on early 20th century by A. Mendel)
Class Notes in Music History (New York, 1908, rev. 5/1938)
ed.: Grove's Dictionary of Music and Musicians: American Supplement (New York, 1920, rev. 2/1928)
The Music of the Pilgrims (Boston, 1921/R1971) [on the Ainsworth Psalter]
The New Encyclopedia of Music and Musicians (New York, 1924, rev. 2/1929)
The Problem of Music in the Church (Chicago, 1930)
The Music of the French Psalter of 1562 (New York, 1939)

BIBLIOGRAPHY
F. H. Johnson: *Musical Memories of Hartford* (Hartford, 1931), 71ff
O. Kinkeldey: 'Waldo Selden Pratt', *MQ*, xxvi (1940), 162
RAMONA H. MATTHEWS

Praupner [Braupner, Brautmer, Brautner, Prautner], **Jan (Josef)** (*b* Litoměřice, 9 Jan 1751; *d* Prague, after 1824). Bohemian violinist, choirmaster and composer, brother of Václav Praupner. He studied music at Litoměřice, where he attended the grammar school, and in about 1770 he studied philosophy at Prague. As a violinist he was active in the Prague Theatre orchestra (as early as 1778), at the Týn and Crusaders' churches and at the metropolitan cathedral (from about 1790; he was still listed there in 1824). In 1807 he succeeded his brother as the choirmaster of the Crusaders' Church. He was renowned as a violinist and music teacher. His extant compositions, all sacred works in a high Classical style similar to that of Michael Haydn, comprise two masses, a Requiem, a *Te Deum* and eight lesser works (all in *CS-Pnm*).

BIBLIOGRAPHY
O. Teuber: *Geschichte des Prager Theaters*, i (Prague, 1883), 342
For further bibliography *see* PRAUPNER, VÁCLAV.
MILAN POŠTOLKA

Praupner [Braupner, Brautmer, Brautner, Prautner], **Václav** [Venceslaus] **(Josef Bartoloměj)** (*b* Litoměřice, 18 Aug 1745; *d* Prague, 1 April 1807). Bohemian composer, violinist and organist, brother of Jan Praupner. He studied music at the Jesuit Gymnasium in Litoměřice, and before 1770 went to Prague, where he studied philosophy and theology. He became a church musician and music teacher for noble families; from 1783, with interruptions, he was orchestra director of several Prague theatres and choirmaster of various churches, including the Týn and the Crusaders' churches from 1794 until his death. He was one of Mozart's adherents in Prague, and met Mozart in 1787. Esteemed as a violinist, violin and singing teacher and orchestra director, he was elected the first director of the Prague Tonkünstler-Sozietät in 1803.

Praupner's most notable composition is the scenic melodrama *Circe* (1789). Developing J. A. Benda's model, he wrote music that abounds in abrupt modulations and chromaticism, and the orchestration reflects the dramatic situations of the text. Retrospective traits, such as *a cappella* writing and the use of a double chorus, occur in his sacred compositions.

WORKS

(*MSS, some autograph, in CS-Pnm, unless otherwise indicated*)

Circe (melodrama, 1), 1789, Prague, Thun Theatre, 1794

Sacred: 2 solemn masses, F, C; Credo solenne, g, 2 choirs, orch, 1781; 4 introits; 2 motets, c, D; Solemn motet, B♭, 1806; 2 alleluias, C, D; 2 litanies, E, B♭; 2 responsories, a, C, for Holy Week, Nativity; Te Deum, C; Domine ad adiuvandum, ps; Trauert, ihr englischen Chöre, Lied vor der Fastenpredigt, *D-Bds*; Vespers, 3 choirs, lost

Inst works, incl. syms., concs., all lost

BIBLIOGRAPHY

ČSHS

Jb der Tonkunst von Wien und Prag (Prague, 1796), 110f, 145, 148, 151

AMZ, ii–xxii (1799–1820)

G. J. Dlabacž: *Allgemeines historisches Künstler-Lexikon*, ii (Prague, 1815/*R*1973), cols.497ff

O. Teuber: *Geschichte des Prager Theaters*, ii (Prague, 1885), 117f, 254

A. Podlaha: *Catalogus collectionis operum artis musicae quae in bibliotheca capituli metropolitani pragensis asservantur* (Prague, 1926), pp.xxxv, xxxvii

O. Kamper: *Hudební Praha v xviii. věku* [18th-century musical Prague] (Prague, 1936), 39, 208ff

V. Němec: *Pražské varhany* [Prague organs] (Prague, 1944), 133, 135f, 138f, 142f, 248

J. Němeček: *Nástin české hudby xviii. století* [Outline of 18th-century Czech music] (Prague, 1955), 199, 271f, 300f

J. Berkovec: *Jiráskův F. L. Věk skladatel: hudební portrét F. V. Heka* [Jirásek's novel *F. L. Věk* as *Composer*: a musical portrait of F. V. Hek] (Prague, 1958), 10, 23ff, 40, 72, 82f

T. Volek: 'Repertoir Nosticovského divadla v Praze z let 1794, 1796–98' [The repertory of the Nostic Theatre in Prague from 1794, 1796–8], *MMC*, xvi (1961), 186

J. Bužga: 'Praupner, Václav', *MGG*

MILAN POŠTOLKA

Prausnitz, Frederik [Frederick] **(William)** (*b* Cologne, 26 Aug 1920). American conductor of German birth. After emigration to the USA as a youth, he was trained at the Juilliard School, New York, where he stayed on as a member of the conducting staff and faculty. He conducted the New England Conservatory SO, Boston (1961–9) and in 1971 became music director of the Syracuse (New York) SO. The education of young professionals has been one of his particular interests, and he has served as visiting lecturer or consultant at Harvard, the University of Michigan and Sussex University.

Prausnitz is a dedicated champion of contemporary music, giving the first American performances of works by, among others, Dallapiccola, Gerhard, Goehr, Lutyens, Petrassi, Schoenberg, Stockhausen, Varèse and Webern. Conversely, he has introduced American composers such as Carter, Schuman, Sessions and Wolpe, to European audiences. He has made a number of recordings of 20th-century music, beginning with the first complete recording of Walton's *Façade* with Dame Edith Sitwell. He conducts the music of late 19th- and early 20th-century composers – Mahler, for example, early Schoenberg, and, notably, Elgar – with a special sense of identification and communicative power. By virtue both of technique and temperament, Prausnitz is most effective in music whose expressive gestures are sweeping and grand, but all his work is marked by the imprint of a probing and original mind. For the unusual spelling of his first name, he is indebted to an Italian poster printer, who omitted the penultimate 'c' on the occasion of his Rome début.

MICHAEL STEINBERG

Prautner, Jan. *See* PRAUPNER, JAN.

Prautner, Václav [Venceslaus] **(Josef Bartoloměj).** *See* PRAUPNER, VÁCLAV.

Praxeis [praxis] (Coptic, from Gk.: 'acts'). Lesson from the book of *Acts* in the Coptic Church; *see* COPTIC RITE, MUSIC OF THE.

Pražák, Přemysl (*b* Prague, 19 March 1908; *d* Prague, 27 Oct 1966). Czech writer on music. He studied law (LLD 1931) and literature at Prague University, where he also attended Nejedlý's musicology lectures; he studied music privately. His principal published work is a minutely detailed account of Smetana's operas in four volumes, *Smetanovy zpěvohry*. He also wrote on Smetana's relationship to Neruda and to Czech literature in general. He edited symposia on Mařák, Kaprálová and Foerster and wrote reviews and lectures for Czechoslovak radio. At his death he left unpublished studies of operas by Fibich and Dvořák.

WRITINGS

ed.: *Otakar Mařák: sborník statí a vzpominek* [Collection of essays and reminiscences] (Turnov, 1937)

Bedřich Smetana v české literatuře [Smetana in Czech literature] (Brno, 1939)

Neruda o hudbě [Neruda on music] (Prague, 1941)

Neruda a Smetana (Prague, 1942)

Smetanovy zpěvohry [Smetana's operas] (Prague, 1948)

ed.: *Vítězslava Kaprálová: studie a vzpominky* [Studies and reminiscences] (Prague, 1949)

ed. with J. Bartoš and J. Plavec: *J. B. Foerster: jeho životní pout' a tvorba 1859–1949* [His life and works 1859–1949] (Prague, 1949)

Bedřich Smetana (Martin, 1956)

Světoví mistři hudby v naši vlasti [World-famous composers in our country] (Prague, 1958)

GRACIAN ČERNUŠÁK/R

Precentor. In a general sense, one who leads the singing in church (the cantor in a synagogue). More specifically, in the English dissenting churches and in Scottish Presbyterianism, the minister or layman who strikes up the tune for the congregation in the absence of an instrument; in cathedrals, an important musical officer among the clergy: *see* CATHEDRAL MUSIC AND MUSICIANS, ANGLICAN.

WATKINS SHAW

Preces (Lat.: 'prayers'). In the Western rites, the name for a series of short petitions in the form of versicles and responses. They form a specific category of chant in the Gallican and Mozarabic liturgies (*see* GALLICAN RITE, MUSIC OF THE, §13; MOZARABIC RITE, MUSIC OF THE, §3, x), but in the Roman rite they are confined to the Office of Prime for ferial Sundays (but *see also* LITANY, for the same type of chant). For the use of the term in the Anglican services of Matins and Evensong *see* VERSICLE.

Prechtel, Franz Joachim. See BRECHTEL, FRANZ JOACHIM.

Pre-Classical. A term applied to what came before and led up to the 'classical' synthesis achieved by Mozart and Haydn; more loosely it has been used to signify any music before the late 18th century. It is applied most aptly to the Arcadian classicism represented by Vinci, Pergolesi and Hasse (*see* CLASSICAL, §2) and thus to a musical style more appropriately called 'galant'. From the critical standpoint of the later 18th century, the virtues of the earlier Italian operatic style were simplicity, directness and boldness. The question was often raised whether the subsequent evolution of the Italian style represented an improvement or a dilution. With respect to Pergolesi in particular, Vogler (1778) posed the question 'whether through later additions dryness was avoided or instead simplicity was spoilt'. In a lengthy analysis and recomposition of Pergolesi's *Stabat mater*, he pointed out the essential differences between his generation and that of the 1730s. He regularized all the musical periods, balanced the weight of tonic and dominant, filled out the harmony to four parts, thickened the orchestration, and corrected what appeared to him as cavalier part-writing. He did all this while maintaining that the origins of 'modern' musical style were to be sought nowhere else but in the breakthrough to true melody achieved by Pergolesi and his generation. 'Facile inventis addere.'

DANIEL HEARTZ

Preconium paschale. *See* EXULTET.

Predieri. Italian family of musicians active mainly in Bologna. They included the singer Giuseppe Predieri (*b* Bologna, *c*1650; *d* Bologna, 1722) and the six members of the family discussed below; some of the family relationships are unclear.

(1) **Giacomo (Maria) Predieri** (*b* Bologna, 9 April 1611; *d* Bologna, 1695). Organist, cornettist and composer. He was a cornettist in Bologna's civic instrumental group and a singer at S Petronio there from October 1636 to December 1657, serving as vice-*maestro di cappella* from 1650 to 1657. He was organist at the cathedral of S Pietro from 1679 to 1693; simultaneously he served as *maestro di cappella* to the Confraternità de' Poveri di S Maria Regina Coeli around 1681. He was among the founder-members of the Accademia Filarmonica in 1666 and in 1693 was chosen *principe*, a position he could not fill because of an apoplectic stroke. His oratorio *Il valore della povertà*, the music of which is lost, was given at Bologna in 1681.

(2) **Antonio Predieri** (*b* Bologna, *c*1650; *d* Bologna, 1710). Singer, nephew and pupil of (1) Giacomo Predieri. He first appeared as a tenor in *L'inganno trionfato* by F. M. Bassani (1673). From 1684 to 1687 he was in the service of the Duke of Mantua and from 1687 until at least 1699 served the Duke of Parma, performing in operas at Milan, Modena, Naples and Rome, as well as at Parma and Piacenza. He specialized in comic roles and many *vecchia* parts were created for him. From 1689 to 1696 he sang at the church of the Steccata in Parma and on festive occasions at the cathedral. In 1685 he was admitted to the Accademia Filarmonica of Bologna; he later appeared as a singer at Genoa (1699), Milan (1704), Florence (1707) and Forli (1710).

(3) **Angelo [Tommaso] Predieri** (*b* Bologna, 14 Jan 1655; *d* Bologna, 27 Feb 1731). Teacher, singer and composer, son of Marco Filippo and Virginia Vignoli. He studied music with Camillo Cevenini and Agostino Filipucci. In 1671 he was admitted to the Accademia Filarmonica as a tenor singer. He entered the Third Order of Franciscans on 3 January 1672, taking the religious name Angelo. In 1673 he was elected *maestro di cappella* at the church of S Maria della Carità. Among his pupils was G. B. Martini, who praised him as having a rare talent for teaching and held him in great esteem as his first mentor. He is known to have written a Kyrie, for five voices and instruments, and a 'Christe eleison', for soprano, alto and instruments; 'Et in saecula saeculorum' from an otherwise lost psalm *Dixit*

Dominus was published in Martini's *Esemplare, o sia Saggio fondamentale pratico di contrappunto fugato*, ii (Bologna, 1775), 135.

(4) **Giacomo Cesare Predieri** (*b* Bologna, 26 March 1671; *d* Bologna, 1753). Composer and singer, son of Carlo and Vittoria Torri. He was a pupil of his uncle (1) Giacomo Predieri and G. P. Colonna. Admitted to the Accademia Filarmonica as a singer on 13 May 1688, he advanced to the rank of composer on 29 November 1690, and was named *principe* in 1698, 1707 and 1711. He was *maestro di cappella* at six institutions in Bologna: the cathedral of S Pietro (1696–1742), the Congregazione di S Gabriele (*c*1681), the churches of S Salvatore (*c*1700), S Paolo and S Bartolomeo and the Arciconfraternità della Vita (*c*1705–21). He wrote a good deal of sacred music, including 11 oratorios, of which only one survives.

WORKS
ORATORIOS
(*all lost unless otherwise stated*)

Mosè bambino esposto al Nilo, Bologna, Palm Sunday, 1698
Davide perseguitato, Bologna, 1702
Il trionfo della croce (G. B. Taroni), Cento, 14 Sept 1702, *D-Bds*
La sepoltura di Cristo, Bologna, 1704
La fiamma della carità, Bologna, 1705
Il Gefte, Bologna, 11 March 1706
La martire d'Alessandria S Catterina (G. B. Taroni), Bologna, Lent 1709
Maria e Giuseppe in traccia di Gesù (L. A. Mescoli), Bologna, 30 March 1713
La purificazione di Maria Vergine, Bologna, 28 March 1715
Jezabelle, Bologna, 25 March 1719 [collab. F. Arresti]
La decollazione di S Giovanni Battista, Bologna, 3 April 1721

OTHER WORKS

Cantate morali e spirituali, 2, 3vv, some with vns, op.1 (Bologna, 1696)
1 canzone sacra in La ricreazione spirituale nella musica delle sagre canzoni (Bologna, 1730)
1 sonata, g, vn, vc, in Sonate a violino e violoncello di vari autori (Bologna, *c*1700)
Credo, 4, 5vv, insts, *I-Bc*
Salmi, 8vv, 1690, *Bam*, *Bc*
Fuga, 8vv, 1690, *Baf*
Laudate Dominum, 8vv, *I-Fc*
Astra coeli cari ardores, A, org, 1745, *Bc*

(5) **Luca Antonio Predieri** (*b* Bologna, 13 Sept 1688; *d* Bologna, 1767). Composer and violinist, son of Vitale and Maria Menzani. He studied the violin with Abondio Bini and Tommaso Vitali, counterpoint with his uncle (4) Giacomo Cesare Predieri, (3) Angelo Predieri and Giacomo Antonio Perti. He was among the instrumentalists at the church of S Petronio for the patronal feast in 1704, 1705 as a violist and 1706–11 as a violinist. On 25 June 1716 he was admitted to the Accademia Filarmonica as a composer, and in 1723 served as *principe*. He was *maestro di cappella* in several Bolognese churches: S Paolo (1725–9), Madonna della Galliera (1726), Arciconfraternità della Vita (1727) and the cathedral of S Pietro (1728–31). In addition to sacred music, he wrote numerous operas, among which his *Partenope* inaugurated the Teatro Marsigli-Rossi in 1710.

At the end of 1737 he went to Vienna, and after two years was made vice-*maestro* of the court chapel. A series of letters written to Padre Martini reveals his cordial relationship with Fux, his successes at court and his favour with the emperor, who found in him a worthy successor to Caldara. In 1741, at the death of Fux, he assumed the direction of the court chapel, although he used the title of first *maestro* only in 1746. He retired in 1751, keeping his title and stipend until 1765 when he returned to Bologna.

His sacred works exhibit a mastery of vocal polyphony and polychoral writing. His operas and oratorios are characterized by careful word setting in the recitatives and effective use of dynamic colours in the arias.

WORKS

OPERAS
(all lost unless otherwise stated)

La Partenope (S. Stampiglia), Bologna, Teatro Marsigli Rossi, 28 Oct 1710

La virtù in trionfo o sia La Griselda (A. Zeno, T. Stanzani), Bologna, Teatro Marsigli Rossi, 18 Oct 1711; 1 aria, *I-Bc*

Lucio Papirio (A. Salvi), Pratolino, Villa Medici, 1714; 4 arias, *GB-Lbm*

Astarte (Zeno, P. Pariati), Rome, Capranica, 1715

Il pazzo per politica (G. B. Gianoli), Livorno, S Sebastiano, 1717

La fede ne' tradimenti (G. Gigli), Florence, Pergola, 1718

Merope (Zeno), Livorno, S Sebastiano, 1718

Il duello d'amore e di vendetta, Livorno, S Sebastiano, 1718

Il trionfo della virtù (F. Pecori), Florence, Pergola, 1719

Il trionfo di Solimano, ovvero Il trionfo maggiore è vincere se stesso, Florence, Pergola, 1719

La finta pazzia di Diana, Florence, Pergola, 1719

Anagilda (Gigli), Turin, Court theatre, 1719

Tito Manlio (M. Noris), Florence, Pergola, 1721

Sofonisba (F. Silvani), Rome, Alibert, 1722

Scipione, Rome, Alibert 1724

Cesare in Egitto (G. F. Bussani), Rome, Capranica, 1728

Eurene (C. Stampa), Milan, court theatre, 1729

Sirbace, Pistoia, Accademici Risvegliati, 2 July 1730 [later version of Eurene]

Scipione il giovane (G. F. Bortolotti), Venice, S Giovanni Grisostomo, 1731

Alessandro nell'Indie (P. Metastasio), Milan, court theatre, 1731

Amor prigionero, Vienna, 1732, *A-Wn*

La serva padrona (G. A. Federico), Florence, Pergola, 1732

Il sogno di Scipione (Metastasio), Vienna, 1 Oct 1735

Zoe (Silvani), Venice, S Cassiano, 1736

Gli auguri spiegati (G. C. Pasquini), Laxenburg, 3 May 1738, *Wgm*

La pace tra la virtù e la bellezza (Metastasio), Vienna, 15 Oct 1738, *Wgm*

Perseo, Vienna, 4 Nov 1738, *Wgm*

Astrea placata, ossia La felicità della terra (Metastasio), Vienna, 28 Aug 1739, *Wgm*

Zenobia (Metastasio), Vienna, 28 Aug 1740, *Wgm*

Ipermestra (Metastasio), Vienna, court theatre, 1744; collab. J. Hasse

Armida placata (Pasquini), Vienna, Burgtheater, 1750; collab. C. Wagenseil, J. Hasse, G. Bonno, G. Abos

ORATORIOS
(all lost unless otherwise stated)

S Cipriano e Giustina martiri, Bologna, Oratorio della Vita, 17 March 1712

L'Adamo (G. Melani), Bologna, Madonna di Galliera, 1723

La caduta di Gerusalemme, Bologna, Oratorio della Vita, 1st Thursday of Lent, 1727

S Pellegrino Laziosi, Bologna, Madonna di Galliera, 1729 [as I prodigi del crocifisso nella conversione di S Pellegrino Laziosi, Cento, 1734]

Gesù nel tempio, Bologna, Oratorio della Vita, 31 March 1735

Il sacrificio d'Abramo (F. Menzoni-Giusti), Vienna, 1738, *A-Wgm, Wn*

Isacco figura del Redentore, Vienna, 12 Feb 1740, *Wgm, D-MEIl*

SACRED VOCAL

Masses, mass movements, 4, 5vv, insts, *A-Wn, D-Dlb, MÜs*

Antiphons, litanies, psalms, *KR, I-Baf, Fc*

Stabat Mater, 4vv, *Fc*

Super astra in corde meo, motet, A, org, *Bc*

Several other motets, *Baf, Bc, Fc*

1 canzona in La ricreazione spirituale nella musica delle sagre canzoni (Bologna, 1730)

OTHER WORKS

1 cantata, in Recueil d'airs sérieux et à boire de différents autheurs (Amsterdam, 1711)

Quel ruscel che tra sassi si frange, cantata, *Bc*

Individual arias, *B-Bc, GB-Lbm, F-Pn*

1 concerto, in 6 concerti a 5 (Amsterdam, *c*1717)

1 sinfonia, Bb, *I-Bsp*

(6) Giovanni Battista Predieri (*fl* 1730–55). Composer. He studied law and was a canon at the church of S Maria Maggiore in Bologna. On 1 July 1749 he was admitted to the Accademia Filarmonica. From about 1748 to 1753 he was *maestro di cappella* at the church of S Paolo in Bologna. Some of his instrumental works

are set in Baroque forms such as the concerto grosso but reveal transitional characteristics in their *galant* style, especially in the harpsichord parts. Others are sonatas in binary, three-movement form with Rococo elegance in the keyboard figurations.

WORKS

ORATORIOS

La fuga di Lotte, Bologna, Madonna di Galliera, 1746; listed in catalogue *I-Bc*

Giuseppe riconosciuto, Fermo, 1755, lost

Danielle liberato dal lago de' lioni, Bologna, Madonna di Galliera, 1764; listed in catalogue *Bc*

INSTRUMENTAL
(all in I-Bc)

3 concertos, hpd, str

2 sonatas, hpd; 1 sonata, 2 hpd; 1 sonata, vn, hpd

2 sonate per l'Offertorio

BIBLIOGRAPHY

G. B. Martini: *Scrittori di musica: notizie storiche e loro opere*, iii (MS, *I-Bsf*)

G. Gaspari: *Miscellanea storico-musicale*, i-iv (MS, *Bc* UU/12)

L. von Köchel: *Die kaiserliche Hofmusikkapelle in Wien von 1543 bis 1867* (Vienna, 1869)

C. Ricci: *I teatri di Bologna nei secoli XVII e XVIII* (Bologna, 1888/*R*1965)

A. Bertolotti: *Musici alla corte dei Gonzaga in Mantova nel secolo XV al XVIII* (Milan, 1890/*R*1969)

G. Gaspari: *Catalogo della Biblioteca del Liceo musicale di Bologna* (Bologna, 1890–1943/*R*1961)

L. Busi: *Il Padre G. B. Martini* (Bologna, 1891/*R*1961)

A. Schering: *Die Geschichte des Instrumental-Konzerts* (Leipzig, 1905, 2/1927/*R*1965)

——: *Geschichte des Oratoriums* (Leipzig, 1911/*R*1966)

L. Torchi: 'La musica strumentale in Italia nei secoli XVI–XVIII', *RMI*, viii (1920), 10

N. Morini: *La R. accademia filarmonica di Bologna* (Bologna, 1930)

N. Pelicelli: 'Musicisti in Parma nel secolo XVII', *NA*, x (1933), 248

U. Manferrari: *Dizionario universale delle opere melodrammatiche*, iii (Florence, 1955)

A. Damerini: 'L. A. Predieri e il suo "Stabat" ', *Musicisti della scuola emiliana*, Chigiana, xiii (1956)

——: 'Musicista sconosciuto', *La scala* (1957), 52

Catalogo degli aggregati dell'Accademia filarmonica di Bologna, Monumenta bononiensia (Bologna, 1971)

R. Ortner: *Luca Antonio Predieri und sein Wiener Opernschaffen* (Vienna, 1971)

ANNE SCHNOEBELEN

Preface. The introductory part of the Canon of the Mass. It is followed by the singing or recitation of the Sanctus, after which the Canon, the central prayer of oblation which includes the words of consecration, is resumed. Despite a certain rigidity of pattern, the Preface was at one time highly varied. (The Leonine Sacramentary, for example, a 6th-century private compilation drawn from Roman sources, had 267 formulae; some medieval books contain even more.) The missal approved by Pope Pius V in 1570 contained only 11; that approved by Pope John XXIII in 1960 contained 15; but the missal of Pope Paul VI (1965), with 83 prefaces, represents a return to earlier practice.

The Preface begins with the words 'Vere dignum', usually appearing in MSS as a monogram, VD. It is most frequently one sentence, of which the main clause ends with the words 'per Christum Dominum nostrum'. This is followed by a relative clause beginning 'per quem', which leads directly into the Sanctus. In some cases the opening vocatives, ending 'aeterne Deus', are immediately followed by a relative or causal clause, which ends 'per Christum Dominum nostrum', and which is followed by a relative clause, or by a concluding sentence, beginning 'et ideo', ending with the Sanctus.

The music for the Preface must thus be capable of accommodating texts of different lengths, whose phrase structure may also differ. There are three Preface melodies in the Vatican edition (see Johner or Stäblein), for weekdays, Sundays and special feasts. The ferial and Sunday melodies have been in general use since the 13th century at latest; the ferial melody first appears in Cistercian and Carthusian MSS of the 12th century. The solemn melody may have a more complex tradition than the others. Wagner (p.90) published it as it appears in the 11th-century sacramentary *I-MC* 339 and commented on its prolonged use (until the 19th century) in Germany. However, the number of points at which versions of this melody differ seems considerable: compare Wagner's Monte Cassino melody with the other 11th-century readings of it given in *I-BV* VI. 40 (Jammers, Tafel 18) and in the Subiaco Sacramentary (PalMus, ii, pl.25). Further study is needed of the melodies for the Preface in medieval sacramentaries and missals.

BIBLIOGRAPHY

P. Wagner: *Einführung in die gregorianischen Melodien*, iii (Leipzig, 1921/*R*1962), 69ff
D. Johner: *Cantus ecclesiastici* (Regensburg, 5/1926)
M. Righetti: *Manuale di storia liturgica*, i (Milan, 1945, 3/1964), 276ff, 295ff, iii (Milan, 1948, 3/1966), 356ff
The Liber usualis with Introduction and Rubrics in English (Tournai, 1950)
B. Stäblein: 'Präfation', *MGG*
E. Jammers: *Tafeln zur Neumenschrift* (Tutzing, 1965)
RUTH STEINER

Prefatory staff. A notational device used in many scholarly editions to show the original pitch and note values of the piece edited, together with certain other information. It ideally consists of a portion of staff (with the original number of lines) preceding the opening of each part, with the original clef, key signature, time signature and initial note(s) and rest(s); or, in music for the lute etc., the beginning of the tablature. *See* EDITING, §3.

Preghiera (It.: 'prayer'). A term used of the number common in 19th-century opera in which a character prays for divine assistance in his plight. Moses's 'Dal tuo stellato soglio' in Rossini's *Mosè in Egitto* (1818) is perhaps the best-known *preghiera* actually so titled in early editions of an opera. Desdemona's 'Ave Maria' in Verdi's *Otello* is a late example of the traditional gentle *preghiera*, and Tosca's 'Vissi d'arte' may be considered a *verismo* development of the tradition. Elisabeth's air in Act 5 of *Don Carlos*, being addressed not to God but to the spirit of Charles V, is a *preghiera* with a difference.

ANDREW PORTER

Preindl, Josef (*b* Marbach, Lower Austria, 30 Jan 1756; *d* Vienna, 26 Oct 1823). Austrian composer, organist and theorist. After early music instruction from his father, who was organist at Marbach, he was, from 1763, a choirboy at Mariazell, Styria. In 1772 he was appointed organist at the orphanage in Vienna by Propst Ignaz Parhamer. He completed his training in Vienna under Albrechtsberger, the influence of whose teaching method is apparent in Preindl's important theoretical work, the posthumously published *Wiener Tonschule* (1827). In 1775 he became organist at the church of Maria am Gestade; in 1783 he was organist of the Carmelite church in Vienna-Leopoldstadt where Albrechtsberger was *regens chori*. In 1787 he moved to St Michael's where he remained until 1793 when he became Kapellmeister at St Peter's. From 1795 he was also vice-Kapellmeister at St Stephen's and from 1809

(after the death of Albrechtsberger) Kapellmeister.

Preindl was a popular piano teacher and probably gave lessons to members of the noble family of Fürstenberg-Weitra. His music has not been thoroughly studied (many works were destroyed in World War II), but in his lifetime it was widely circulated and continued to be known for some time after his death. He was among the favourite composers of Prince Nikolaus Esterházy (the younger). When Bruckner sat for the *Oberlehrer* examination in Linz in 1845 he was given a theme by Preindl on which to write a strict fugue.

WORKS

(all printed works published in Vienna)

Liturgical: *c*14 masses, 4vv, orch, incl. opp.7–8, 10–12 (n.d.), *A-KN, KR, Wgm, D-Dlb*; 2 Requiem with orch, E♭, *A-KR*, op.50 (n.d.); Te Deum, 4vv, orch, op.51 (n.d.); several graduals and offertories, incl. opp.13–18 (n.d.), *KN, Wgm, D-Mbs*; Lamentatio Jeremiae Prophetae, vv, org (n.d.); other works, incl. vespers, litanies, psalms, motets, *A-GÖ, Wgm, Wn, Wsp*

Songs: Melodien von allen deutschen Kirchen-Liedern samt dazu verfassten neuen Kadenzen und Präambuln, acc. org/pf. (n.d.) ['Preindl-Gesangbuch']; other sacred songs, 4vv, and occasional works, pubd separately (n.d.)

Pf: 2 concs., op.1 (1797), op.2 (n.d.); Sonatas (n.d.); variations, op.3 (n.d.), op.4 (1798), op.6 (n.d.); 3 fantasias, op.5 (1800), op.7 (1803), op.25 (n.d.); Et incarnatus est, org, autograph, *Wn*

THEORETICAL WORKS

Gesang-Lehre, op.33 (Vienna, 2/1833)
Wiener Tonschule, oder Elementarbuch zum Studium des Generalbasses, des Contrapunktes, der Harmonie- und Fugen-Lehre, ed. I. von Seyfried (Vienna, 1827, 2/1832 as *Anweisung zum Generalbasse*)

BIBLIOGRAPHY

EitnerQ; *FétisB*
AMZ, ciii (1823), 24
H. Brunner: 'Die Kantorei bei St. Stephan in Wien', *Beiträge zur Geschichte der Wiener Dommusik* (1948), 19
E. Tittel: 'Preindl, Joseph', *MGG*
UWE HARTEN

Preiner, Johann Jacob. *See* PRINNER, JOHANN JACOB.

Prelleur, Peter [Pierre] (*fl* 1728–*c*1755). English organist, harpsichordist and composer, probably of French extraction. He began his career as a writing master at Spitalfields. He played the harpsichord at the Angel and Crown tavern in Whitechapel and his musical talent led to his election in 1728 as organist at St Alban's, Wood Street, London. About 1730, according to Hawkins, he was commissioned by Cluer and Dicey to write his *Introduction to Singing* (London, 1735). This was first published in 1731 as Part 1 of a much larger work entitled *The Modern Musick-master, or The Universal Musician*, a beautifully printed book which contains, as well as the introduction to singing, instructions for playing the recorder, German flute, hautboy, violin and harpsichord (facsimile edition, Kassel, 1965; for illustration, *see* EDUCATION IN MUSIC, fig.8). There are many good tunes provided for each instrument, as well as a brief history of music (condensed from Bontempi's *Historia*, 1695) and a musical dictionary.

In 1732, with a B. Smith, Prelleur edited *The Harmonious Companion, or The Psalm Singer's Magazine* (London, 1732), and in 1735 he was elected the first organist of Christ Church, Spitalfields, triumphing over stiff competition and intrigue. Since about 1728 he had also been harpsichordist and composer for the Goodman's Fields Theatre. He remained there until the theatre was closed under the Licensing Act of 1737, whereupon he transferred to the New Wells (or Goodman's Fields Wells) theatre in nearby Leman Street. For the New Wells he wrote much music, especially songs, pantomimes and overtures, and also the delightful interlude *Baucis and Philemon*, which includes an overture (laid out like a trio sonata) for strings, obbligato oboes and continuo, as well as songs and duets. He died before 1758, according to a report in *Divine Melody*.

WORKS

STAGE WORKS

Harlequin Hermit, or The Arabian Courtezan (pantomime), London, New Wells, 1739; some songs pubd singly

Baucis and Philemon (interlude), London, New Wells, 1740; ov. and songs pubd (London, c1740)

Harlequin Student, or The Fall of Pantomime (pantomime), London, New Wells, 1741; some songs pubd singly

OTHER WORKS

The Medley, ov. for insts (Dublin, 1736)

15 hymns in Moze, ed., Divine Melody in 24 Choice Hymns (London, 1758)

1 ov. in 6 Medley or Comic Ovs. in 7 parts (London, 1763)

Concerti Grossi, *GB-Cfm*

Numerous songs pubd singly and in 18th-century anthologies

BIBLIOGRAPHY

EitnerQ; *GerberL*; *HawkinsH*

PETER PLATT

Prelude (Fr. *prélude*; Ger. *Vorspiel*; It. *preludio*; Lat. *praeludium, praeambulum*). An instrumental movement intended to precede another movement, a group of movements or a large-scale work. Its form is unpredictable, though generally self-contained (except where the prelude to an opera, for example Wagner's *Die Meistersinger*, leads directly into the stage action; for separate concert performance a special ending will be required). From the 19th century onwards, particularly, the term has been illogically applied to short pieces with no prefatory function, usually exploring a single motif or mood (*see* CHARACTERISTIC PIECE). Moreover, movements that are genuinely preludial often have other titles, such as overture, *intonazione* or intrada. The 'introduction' that sometimes opens a symphony or sonata in the 18th and 19th centuries is not preludial in the sense defined above, as it is incomplete without the rest of the movement (*see* INTRODUCTION).

Preludes evolved from the short improvisations made by lutenists checking the tuning of their instruments, keyboard players testing the touch and tone of theirs, or church organists establishing the pitch and mode of the music to be sung during the liturgy (for contemporary statements about the practical uses of preludes, see M. Praetorius, *Syntagma musicum*, iii, 1618, p.21; F. Couperin, *L'art de toucher le clavecin*, 1716; and J. G. Walther, *Musicalisches Lexicon*, 1732, 'Tastatura'). There are three basic types: the unattached prelude, which has no prescribed sequel but may precede any piece or group of pieces in the same mode or key; the attached prelude, which has one specific sequel; and the independent prelude, which has no sequel. The so-called chorale prelude is a special kind of attached prelude originally meant to preface congregational singing of the hymn on which it is based (*see* CHORALE SETTINGS).

Most early preludes are of the unattached type, the oldest to survive being the five short praeambula for organ in Adam Ileborgh's tablature of 1448, where they are grouped together in a section headed 'Incipiunt praeludia diversarum notarum'. Each consists of a florid, quasi-improvisatory right-hand part accompanied by one or two slower-moving parts in the bass. Other 15th-century German sources, notably Conrad Paumann's *Fundamentum organisandi* (1452; CEKM, i) and the Buxheimer Orgelbuch (1460–70; EDM, 1st

ser., xxxvii–xxxix), introduce an additional element by juxtaposing florid passages and sustained chords.

Many more preludes are known from 16th-century sources. Examples from Germany are found in the keyboard tablatures of Leonhard Kleber (c1524) and Hans Kotter (before 1535); they are not significantly longer than their 15th-century predecessors (15–20 bars), have rapid passage-work in the hands alternately and show a clear sense of harmonic direction (see HAM, no.84). Among the few French examples are the preludes in Attaingnant's *Magnificat sur les huit tons avec Te Deum Laudamus, et deux préludes* (1530) and his *Treize motets et un prélude* (1531). From Poland come unattached preludes in the German-influenced Lublin tablature (CEKM, vi), in a four-part chordal texture enlivened by quasi-polyphonic motivic play. In Italy prelude-like keyboard pieces generally bore other titles (*see* INTONAZIONE; RICERCARE; TOCCATA); the best-known source is *Intonationi d'organo composti sopra tutti li dodici toni* (1593), containing works by Andrea and Giovanni Gabrieli which characteristically begin with sustained chords and then alternate such chords with rapid passage-work (see HAM, no.135). In Spanish sources, like Luis Venegas de Henestrosa's *Libro de cifra nueva* (1557), preludes are often entitled 'entrada'. Examples from England are found in the works of the virginalists, including Byrd and Bull; those of the latter show an expanded repertory of virtuoso techniques (see the Fitzwilliam Virginal Book, ii, nos.22, 259, 274).

Although pieces like the unattached keyboard prelude are often found in 16th-century lute, guitar and cittern anthologies, use of the word 'prelude' or 'praeambulum' was apparently limited to northern Europe and was principally used in the publications of Phalèse and Le Roy. Preludial pieces were generally grouped together, and their titles indicated the mode or key they were intended to establish (e.g. 'Praeludium super D la sol re'). The less common attached prelude appeared side by side with the unattached type in Francesco Spinacino's *Intabulatura de lauto* of 1507, where the sequel to each is indicated by name alone – for example *Recercar de tous bien*, as prelude for Hayne van Ghizeghem's chanson *De tous bien plaine*, an arrangement of which appears earlier in the collection (there is no musical relationship between the two works). But in four bipartite pieces in Joan Ambrosio Dalza's *Intabulatura de lauto, libro quarto* (1508), the prelude, headed 'Tastar de corde' (touching of the strings), is followed by the full text of its sequel (see HAM, no.99).

Brief unattached preludes in an improvisatory style continued to be written in the 17th century; there are examples in J. E. Kindermann's *Harmonia organica* (1645), in an anonymous French organ manuscript (*GB-Lbm* Add.29486), the toccatas to be played before Mass in Frescobaldi's *Fiori musicali* (1635), and in the works of Kerll and Pachelbel. But during the 17th century and the first half of the 18th the attached prelude, followed by either a fugue or a suite of dances, became the predominant type. Three praeambula by the younger Jacob Praetorius are rudimentary examples of the paired prelude and fugue, one of the most important German Baroque keyboard forms: in each, a short chordal section is followed by a fugue on a single subject. This bipartite plan was extended in some preludes by north German composers like Scheidemann and Tunder by the addition of a short chordal postlude after the fugal section (see HAM, nos.195 and 215). Later in the century Buxtehude enlarged the single-movement prelude and fugue form by multiplying the number of alternate free and fugal sections (see HAM, no.234), creating what is virtually a full-scale toccata. Buxtehude's combined prelude–fugue form was also cultivated by F. X. Murschhauser, F. T. Richter, Georg Böhm and Johann Krieger. A less unwieldy and more usual plan in two distinct movements was preferred by J. C. F. Fischer (*Ariadne musica*, c1702; see HAM, no.247) and J. S. Bach, whose finest preludes and fugues, including many from *Das wohltemperirte Clavier* (1722) and from the various sets for organ, reach heights that have never been surpassed.

The prelude joined to a suite of dances is less exclusively German. Many can be found, such as those for lute by Esaias Reusner (ii) in *Deliciae testudinis* (1667; see HAM, no.233); for strings in the sonatas of Corelli and the unaccompanied suites of J. S. Bach; and for keyboard in J. C. F. Fischer's *Pièces de clavessin* (1696), Purcell's posthumous *Choice Collection of Lessons* (1696), Handel's *Suites de pièces* (1720) and Bach's six English Suites. Except for Bach's, suite preludes tend to be lighter than preludes paired with fugues. The improvisatory origin of the form is not reflected in all of these examples. It is totally absent, for instance, from the preludes to Bach's English Suites nos.2–6, which are highly organized movements in ritornello form; on the other hand, it can be felt in the short flourish that opens English Suite no.1, and in the florid passages and structural freedom of countless other preludes.

The heritage of improvisation is most obvious in the French 'unmeasured' preludes of the second half of the 17th century (*see* PRÉLUDE NON MESURÉ). In their simplest form these odd-looking pieces consist of a string of unbarred semibreves whose rhythmic interpretation is left to the taste of the performer. Unmeasured preludes first appeared in Denis Gaultier's lute collection *La rhétorique des dieux* (c1655; PSFM, vi), and they were widely imitated both by other lutenists and by harpsichord composers such as Louis Couperin, Lebègue, D'Anglebert (see HAM, no.232), Le Roux and Rameau. None was written by François Couperin; the eight preludes in *L'art de toucher le clavecin* are all in normally barred rhythms. It is clear, however, that Couperin intended several of his preludes to have an improvisatory effect, for he directed that they should be played in a free style unless marked 'mesuré'. He also remarked that his preludes could be played either with or without a sequel, and thus was among the first to recognize the independent prelude. Another was J. S. Bach, whose 15 praeambula from the *Clavier-Büchlein vor Wilhelm Friedemann Bach* (1720) are early versions of the familiar and indisputably independent Two-part Inventions BWV772–86.

Few preludes of any description were written during the second half of the 18th century, for the Classical period had little use for the fugues and suites to which attached preludes could have belonged, and the independent type was not yet fully established. Nevertheless, keyboard players continued the traditional practice of prefacing their items with a short improvised prelude to prepare the listener for the music that followed. A number of short introductory movements to fugues, for string ensemble, were written in the late 18th century by J. G. Hintereder, Franz Tuma, G. M. Monn, Karl Kohant and others, apparently for use in church, as well

as the preludes to fugues by J. S. and W. F. Bach written by Mozart. Albrechtsberger was among those to have written preludes and fugues for organ. Although improvised preludes were inevitably ephemeral, some idea of their character can be gained from Ignaz Moscheles's dual-purpose publication *50 Praeludien* op.73 of 1837 ('50 preludes in major and minor keys intended as short introductions to any movement, and as preparatory exercises to the author's studies'). Beethoven's *Zwei Praeludien durch alle Dur-Tonarten* op.39 are no more than student exercises in modulation.

The 19th century's awakening interest in music of earlier times encouraged a revival of forms that had fallen into disuse. The attached prelude reappeared in a number of Bach-influenced works, such as Mendelssohn's Six Preludes and Fugues for piano op.35 (1832–7), Liszt's Prelude and Fugue on B–A–C–H, Brahms's two preludes and fugues for organ (1856–7), Franck's *Prélude, choral et fugue* for piano (1884) and Reger's Prelude and Fugue for violin op.117.

More typical of the Romantic period and its aftermath, however, are the many independent preludes for piano, whose prototype was Chopin's matchless set of 24 Preludes op.28 of 1836–9. (They were not the first: J. N. Hummel had published a set of 24 preludes 'in the major and minor keys', op.67.) Although some of his preludes are epigrammatically short, others are so large in scale and so dramatic in content that they would overshadow any alien sequel to which they might be attached. It seems likely, therefore, that they were always intended either to be played as a complete cycle or to serve as a quarry from which shorter homogeneous groups could be made up. Chopin's collection was the model for those of Stephen Heller (op.81), Alkan (op.31, 1847), Cui (op.64) and Busoni (op.37), each of which contains 24 independent preludes in the major and minor keys (Alkan's set includes two in C major), and seems to have established the prelude as an important kind of non-programmatic characteristic piece, subsequently exploited by such composers as Skryabin, Szymanowski, Rakhmaninov, Debussy, Shostakovich, Gershwin, Messiaen, Ginastera and Martinů. These preludes have no prefatory function and are simply collections of short pieces exploring particular moods, musical figures or technical problems. Debussy's have programmatic titles, which are otherwise rare. His *Prélude à l'après-midi d'un faune* is an orchestral tone poem.

Schoenberg's Prelude op.44 for chorus and orchestra is one of the few attached preludes written in the 20th century which was not intended as an evocation of the Baroque type. It was composed as the first movement of a suite commissioned from several composers by the American publisher Nathaniel Shilkret; his section was to precede a depiction of the Creation, and its mood is skilfully conveyed both by orchestral effects and by the restriction of the choral part to vowel sounds rather than words.

Liszt's symphonic poem *Les préludes* is unrelated to the musical genre, as it took its name (as well as its programme) from a poem by Lamartine.

BIBLIOGRAPHY

BrownI

O. Kinkeldey: *Orgel und Klavier in der Musik des 16. Jahrhunderts* (Leipzig, 1910/R1968)

W. Merian: *Der Tanz in den deutschen Tabulaturbüchern* (Leipzig, 1916/R1968)

L. Hibberd: *The Early Keyboard Prelude: a Study in Musical Style*

(diss., Harvard U., 1941)
J. M. Chomiński: *Preludia* (Kraków, 1950)
A. Curtis: *Unmeasured Preludes in French Baroque Instrumental Music* (diss., U. of Illinois, 1956)
W. Apel: 'Der Anfang des Präludiums in Deutschland und Polen', *Chopin Congress: Warszawa 1960*, 495
Y. Rokseth: 'The Instrumental Music of the Middle Ages and early 16th Century', *NOHM*, iii (1960), 406–65
H. Hering: 'Präludium', *MGG*
W. Apel: *Geschichte der Orgel- und Klaviermusik bis 1700* (Kassel, 1967; Eng. trans., rev., 1972)
——: 'Solo Instrumental Music', *NOHM*, iv (1968), 602–701

HOWARD FERGUSON

Prélude non mesuré (Fr.). A term usually reserved for a body of 17th-century harpsichord preludes written without orthodox indications of rhythm and metre. Various methods of notating such works can be seen in the manuscripts and early printed editions of Louis Couperin, Nicolas Lebègue, J.-H. d'Anglebert and Gaspard Le Roux. In the early 18th century unmeasured notations were largely abandoned, some publishers even omitting the unmeasured preludes altogether when republishing harpsichord music. The interpretation of these extraordinary-looking pieces has caused confusion for players and scholars.

1. Origins and background. 2. Styles. 3. Notation and interpretation.

1. ORIGINS AND BACKGROUND. Rhythmically free preludial pieces were common before the 17th century (under such titles as *intonazione*, toccata, ricercare and PRELUDE), but the usual notation of these pieces was rhythmically precise even if the notes did not fall into regular patterns. Although it seems likely that 17th-century harpsichordists adopted elements of the French lute prelude, the earlier tradition of keyboard pieces that did not conform to regular rhythmic groupings but were written in measured notation is a main line of descent for the *prélude non mesuré*.

Rhythmically unmeasured notation for preludes originated in lute preludes designed to test the tuning of the instrument before playing, at about the same time as the *nouveau ton* triadic tuning was introduced for that instrument. The earliest examples date from about 1630. The five short unmeasured preludes in the lute manuscript of Virginia Renata (*D-Bds* 40264) are in various tunings; four include the normal rhythmic signs above the tablature, while one does not indicate any rhythm but includes a series of slurs to group the notes. A generation later Denis Gaultier wrote similar preludes. Although they are generally playable in free rhythm, they include sections which fall naturally into regular groups. Thus the genuinely unmeasured lute pieces represent a style in which notes cannot satisfactorily be grouped into regular rhythmic and harmonic patterns, independent of the presence or absence of

notated rhythm; numerous pieces written without rhythmic notation, particularly in the late 17th-century lute repertory, clearly fall into regular patterns and thus are not really unmeasured. Unmeasured music was also written for the viol: de Machy included eight such preludes in his *Pieces de violle* (1685) and Sainte-Colombe wrote many unmeasured movements for one and two viols together, surviving with titles such as *La volontaire ... parce qu'estant sans mesure, on joue comme on veut* ('because it is unmeasured one plays it how one wishes') and *L'aureille ... parce qu'il se joue sans mesure et seulement il faut jouer d'aureille* ('because it is played unmeasured, only by ear'). Wholly unmeasured notation for these instruments is normally found only in manuscript books. Despite superficial similarities, however, the harpsichord preludes are really a separate phenomenon from the lute and viol examples, and in the past too much has been made of their connection with the lute pieces. The surviving repertory of *préludes non mesurés* for harpsichord comprises over 50 works.

2. STYLES. Most unmeasured preludes fall into one of two main groups: toccatas and *tombeaux*, relating to the Italian toccatas of Frescobaldi and Froberger and to the elegiac *tombeaux* composed, mostly by the French, in honour of dead teachers, patrons or friends. (Many such laments occur in the works of Froberger, often disguised as allemandes, as in Suites nos.12 and 30; see also the *Tombeau ... de M. Blancheroche, lequel se joue fort lentement à la discretion sans observer aucune mesure*.)

The toccata style is recognizable in four of the preludes of Louis Couperin (nos.1, 3, 6 and 12 in *Pièces de clavecin*, ed. P. Brunold, rev. T. Dart, 1959). These are in three sections, the outer two freer and the central one strictly fugal. One (no.6), occurring in both the Bauyn (*F-Pn* Rés.Vm⁷674–5) and Parville (*US-BE* 778) manuscripts, bears the title 'Prelude ... a l'imitation de Mr. Froberger' in the latter source. The fact that it is almost certainly derived from Froberger's first organ toccata confirms the connection between the two forms. Furthermore, its interpretation of the opening chord of Froberger's toccata is instructive: Couperin's notation (ex.1) elaborates the chord into a series of arpeggios, recalling Lebègue's remark that in harpsichord playing the 'manner is to break and re-strike the chords quickly rather than play them as on the organ' (*see* KEYBOARD MUSIC, §1, ex.4, for the toccata).

The *tombeau–allemande* style in normal measured notation is characterized by a slow tempo, a freedom of rhythm and a characteristic opening motif of an anacrusic melodic scale rising a 4th (usually from the leading note to the mediant). Three of Couperin's

Ex.1 Louis Couperin: Prelude no. 6

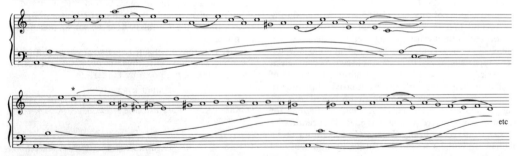

etc

preludes (nos.2, 4 and 13 in the Brunold and Dart edn.) relate to this style (ex.2a). Couperin's *Tombeau de Mr Blancrocher* (ex.2b) might as well have been written in the same unmeasured notation, for the musical style is almost identical.

Ex.2

(a) Louis Couperin: opening of Prelude no. 13

(b) Louis Couperin: *Tombeau de M. Blancrocher*

3. NOTATION AND INTERPRETATION. The basic unmeasured notation as devised by Louis Couperin consists of a succession of slurred semibreves. Playing it depends mainly on understanding the several meanings of the slurs, distinguishable by their context. Firstly, slurs can indicate sustained notes, as in ex.1, when notes in immediate succession form a chord. The combined factors of sustained sound and chordal cohesion tend to give such notes the rhythmic weight of a strong beat. Secondly, slurs can indicate that a group of notes has ornamental significance (ex.3) or melodic importance

Ex.3 Louis Couperin: Prelude no. 1

(ex.1, at asterisk). Thirdly, slurs can isolate notes from what precedes or follows. These last slurs are sometimes not attached to any note at all, and usually extend from the lower staff to the upper one. In ex.4 the slurs indicate a chord sequence quite at variance with the vertical alignment on the page. Thus a manner of arpeggiating is suggested by an exceedingly elegant and economical notation.

In the preface to his *Les pièces de clavessin* (1677) Lebègue commented on the difficulty of notating

Ex.4 Louis Couperin: Prelude no. 4, ending

Harmony from★

preludes intelligibly, and he devised a modified notation which was the basis of most later published *préludes non mesurés*. His notation uses normal note values from semibreve to semiquaver (including dotted notes) and bar-lines, but the bar-lines (usually sloping) indicate chord changes; thus they appear to have a meaning like that of the third kind of slur mentioned above, in that they are lines unattached to any note, sloping from the lower staff to the upper one, designed to clarify the harmonies.

Lebègue's semi-measured notation was not universally adopted; indeed, no other composer used such a precise notation. Louis Marchand, Clérambault and Rameau all used a notation first adopted by D'Anglebert for the printed preludes of 1689. (These preludes survive in his own handwriting, written entirely in semibreves, in *F-Pn* Rés.89*ter*.) D'Anglebert's system is perhaps the closest any composer came to an acceptable solution to the problems of unmeasured preludes. Semibreves are used for the basic notation, but fragments of melodic importance are identified by being notated in quavers. The sequence of notes from left to right indicates conventionally the sounding sequence of notes in time, and the occasional barlines indicate the end of a significant musical sentence. In ex.5 the use of quavers for the arpeggio shows that it is not to be played fast but rather melodically, and the bar-line indicates a pause to mark the arrival on the dominant.

Ex.5 D'Anglebert: Prelude no.2

D'Anglebert's notation, unlike Lebègue's, is not in any real way more measured than the semibreve notation used by D'Anglebert in his manuscript preludes or by Louis Couperin. It simply uses white notes for harmonic pitches and black ones for melodic passages. The black notes are quavers (semiquavers for ornamental notes) because these can be ligatured into melodic groupings which are more easily assimilated by the player. The visual aspect of this notation is a parallel with the kind of notation used by Italian toccata composers, where shorter notes do not always imply an increase in speed, but may show a distinction between harmonic and melodic passages (*see* KEYBOARD MUSIC, §1, ex.4).

Many of these preludes are highly organized works, cogently and coherently planned, with a powerful harmonic structure and a careful use of motivically developed melodic elements. Continued performance from the original unmeasured notations brings a musical insight and freedom not to be obtained from any other notation.

BIBLIOGRAPHY

A. Curtis: *Unmeasured Preludes in French Baroque Instrumental Music* (diss., U. of Illinois, 1956)

——: 'Musique classique française à Berkeley', *RdM*, lvi (1970), 123–64

D. Moroney: 'The Performance of Unmeasured Harpsichord Preludes', *Early Music*, iv (1976), 143

DAVITT MORONEY

Premium (Lat.). PROOIMION.

Premonstratensian canons. In the Western Christian church, the order of canons regular of Prémontré (O. Praem.), also known as 'White Canons' from the colour of their habit, or 'Norbertines' from the name of their founder, St Norbert (*c*1080–1134). The name of Prémontré comes from the place near Laon where Norbert and his first disciples established themselves in 1120. The early Premonstratensian Statutes (1131–4), based on the Rule of St Augustine, were monastic and largely modelled on the *carta caritatis* of the Cistercians. A certain degree of centralization was also reminiscent of Cîteaux. As the order developed, the individual houses ('canonries') were grouped into 'circaries' according to regional or (later) linguistic affinities. The order, greatly reduced by the Reformation and the French Revolution, is now organized into six circaries; extending from Europe to India, Brazil and North America, there are some 1645 Premonstratensians, including priests, lay brothers, nuns, novices and postulants.

The *Constitutions* (1971) stress community and pastoral activities, whereas previously the emphasis was on contemplation and liturgy: the White Canons used to sing each day in choir the full daily Office and conventual sung Mass, according to their own rite. The Premonstratensian rite dates from the 12th century, and from that time onwards has had a constant struggle for existence. It was approved by Pope Alexander III in his bull *In apostolicae sedis* (1177), and by Alexander IV in *Felicis recordationis* (1256). The early *Statutes*, those of 1505 and of 1630, and visitation injunctions such as those of Bishop Redman in England during the 15th century, stressed the need for uniformity in the books of the rite, and for the preservation of the traditional forms of worship. The rite has had to contend with the rival claims of the Roman rite in the 16th and 17th centuries, and twice in the 20th century.

The medieval Premonstratensian rite contained many sequences of which only a handful were retained in later centuries, including, however, the Christmas sequence *Laetabundus*. Another feature of it was the series of rhymed and historiated antiphons. Many Premonstratensian chant melodies are fairly close to their Roman counterparts, but there are also notable differences: the opening of the offertory *Jubilate Deo universa terra*, for example, has no repeat and no melisma, and there is a slightly different tone for the Lamentations and also for the litany of the saints. Some *Venite* tones contain a B♭ in places where the Roman equivalents use a B♮. Sometimes the differences are textual as well as musical: for example, the sequence *Victimae paschali laudes* includes the original line now missing in the Roman version, and the alleluia for Easter Day has two verses ('Pascha' and 'Epulemur') instead of one.

After a period of decadence following the Council of Trent, and of increasing Romanization, which lasted until Pius X's *Moto proprio* of 1903, a commission for sacred music was set up under Lambert Wendelen of Tongerloo, charged with re-editing the service books according to the earliest and best traditions of the order. In 1908 the new gradual was accepted by the general chapter and published two years later in 1910; the processional followed in 1932 and the antiphoner in 1934, but these books and indeed the rite itself were discarded some 40 years later when Latin was replaced by the vernacular in many canonries.

Music other than chant does not appear to have been extensively cultivated among the Premonstratensians. The minutely detailed 17th-century *Statutes* banned certain musical instruments ('violas, citharas aliaque instrumenta'). The organ was a notable exception, for organ *alternatim* performance was used to add solemnity to the services on Sundays and festivals. The *Ordo* of 1635 gave full instructions as to its use, during both Mass and the Divine Office.

See also ANTIPHONER, §3(iv); GRADUAL (II), §4(iii).

BIBLIOGRAPHY

Ordinarius sive liber caeremoniarum: ad usum candidissimi et canonici ordinis Praemonstratensis renovatus (Paris, 1635)

Statuta candidi et canonici ordinis praemonstratensis renovata, ac anno 1630 . . . plene resuluta (Averbode, 1898)

Graduale ad usum canonici Praemonstratensis ordinis (Paris, 1910)

F. Petit: *L'ordre de Prémontré* (Paris, 1927)

Processionale ad usum sacri et canonici ordinis Praemonstratensis (Paris, 1932)

Antiphonarium ad usum sacri et canonici ordinis Praemonstratensis (Paris, 1934)

P. Lefèvre: *L'ordinaire de Prémontré d'après les manuscrits du 12e et 13e siècle* (Louvain, 1941)

B. Lerykx: 'Essai sur les sources de "l'Ordo Missae" prémontré', *Analecta praemonstratensia*, xxii (1946), 35–90

H. M. Colvin: *The White Canons in England* (Oxford, 1951)

P. Lefèvre: *La liturgie de Prémontré* (Louvain, 1957)

J. B. Valvekens, ed.: 'Acta et decreta capitulorum generalium ordinis Praemonstratensis', i–iii, *Analecta praemonstratensia*, xlii, xliv, xlv (1966–73)

N. J. Weyns: 'Le missel prémontré', *Analecta praemonstratensia*, xliii (1967), 203

P. Lefèvre: 'L'antiphonale psalterii d'après le rite de Prémontré', *Analecta praemonstratensia*, xlix (1968), 247

——: 'L'Office de Noël et de son octave dans la liturgie de Prémontré', *Analecta praemonstratensia*, xlvi (1970), 179–219

The Day of Pentecost: Constitutions of the Canons Regular of Prémontré (De Pere, Wisc., 1971)

P. Lefèvre: 'Les antiennes empruntées aux livres des rois dans la liturgie de Prémontré', *Analecta praemonstratensia*, xlvii (1971), 24

——: 'Les répons prolixes: les heures diurnes du "triduum sacrum" dans la liturgie canoniale', *Analecta praemonstratensia*, xlviii (1972), 5

N. J. Weyms, ed.: *Antiphonale missarum praemonstratense* (Averbode, 1973)

MARY BERRY

Prendcourt [Prencourt], 'Captain' ?F. de (*fl* 1686–1705). Keyboard player and composer of Saxon or French origin resident in England. James II's Roman Catholic Chapel Royal was opened on Christmas Day 1686. The king summoned a number of foreign musicians to England to serve in it, including 'Sig.

Fede', Gottfried Finger and Prendcourt, who styled himself 'Captain'. Nearly everything that is known about Prendcourt is derived from the account of Roger North who, as Attorney General in James II's administration, could have known him well. North stated, however, that he was 'Master of the Chappell', but this must be a mistake, since Fede is known to have held that office. Secret Service documents of January and March 1687 record payments 'for linens for the children of the chappell delivered to Mr Bradcourt' and to 'Mr Brancourt' for 'the dyet of the boys'. In spite of the misspellings these must refer to Prendcourt, who must thus have been Master of the Children rather than of the chapel itself.

Prendcourt was a page of honour to the Elector of Saxony before coming to England. He was an excellent organist and harpsichordist and apparently a prolific composer, but in manner he was arrogant, and he would play only his own music. When James II fled the country in December 1688 Prendcourt was thrown on his own resources and taught the harpsichord. He was given hospitality in several households but acquired a bad reputation by selling the furnishings of the rooms he occupied to relieve his financial distress. He declared himself to be a Protestant, but North believed him to be a Jesuit and stated that he never took the sacrament in the English church and would not compose for its services. Letters of 1705 show that he was then engaged in making arrangements of music for Thomas Coke of Melbourne Hall, Derbyshire, and that he acted as go-between in Coke's contacts with Marshal Tallard, the French Marshal of Horse taken prisoner at Blenheim.

Prendcourt was a good teacher and left a treatise on harpsichord playing and thoroughbass which was transcribed and annotated by North (*GB-Lbm* Add.32531 and 32549). It contains useful remarks on fingering and ornamentation (*see* FINGERING, §I, 3(iii)). Prendcourt's style of notation was so individual in certain respects that a manuscript of four harpsichord suites (*GB-Y* M.16(s)) notated in this manner and containing handwriting much the same as that in the letters to Coke may with some certainty be attributed to him. The suites seem to be his only surviving music. North considered his sacred music his best, but his compositions for the Chapel Royal have disappeared, together with nearly all traces of the activity of the chapel.

BIBLIOGRAPHY
M. C. Burton: 'Mr Prencourt and Roger North on Teaching Music', *MQ*, xliv (1958), 32
J. Wilson, ed.: *Roger North on Music* (London, 1959), 49ff
J. Harley: 'Ornaments in English Keyboard Music of the Seventeenth and Early Eighteenth Centuries', *MR*, xxxi (1970), 177ff
M. Tilmouth: 'York Minster MS. M.16(s) and Captain Prendcourt', *ML*, liv (1973), 302

MICHAEL TILMOUTH

Prenestino, Giovanni Pierluigi da. *See* PALESTRINA, GIOVANNI PIERLUIGI DA.

Prenner [Brenner, Pyrenaeus], Georg (*b* Laibach [now Ljubljana]; *d* St Pölten, 4 Feb 1590). Austrian composer of Slovenian birth. In 1554 and 1560 he is recorded as a copyist in the Kapelle at Prague of Archduke Maximilian, whom he later served as court chaplain and almoner after the archduke had become emperor as Maximilian II. He left imperial service on 20 August 1572 on being appointed abbot of the monastery of St Dorothea, Vienna. In 1578 he took up a similar appointment at the monastery of Herzogenburg, near St Pölten. On 5 March 1587 the Emperor Rudolf II nominated him an imperial councillor. He appears to have been active as a composer only in the 1560s, and his output is almost exclusively sacred. His published works appeared only in anthologies, some of them among the most popular of the time: 17 motets in *RISM* 1564²⁻⁵, five in 1567², 16 in 1568²⁻⁶ (*Hodie natus est*, *Beata Virgo Maria* and *Conceptio est hodie*, from 1568², ed. in TM, xxviii, xxxi, 1974) and three in 1569⁴⁻⁶. *Carole, plena tui spe* (in 1568²; ed. in MAM, xxi–xxii, 1971), composed in honour of Archduke Karl of Styria, is representative of the late Netherlands motet style; a solmization theme, reminiscent of the Josquin period, is repeated in canon within an up-to-date contrapuntal framework. Over 40 works by Prenner survive in manuscript, some of which are copies of works in printed anthologies: their sources are given by Eitner, and to them should be added a few others (in *A-Gu* and *D-Dlb*).

BIBLIOGRAPHY
EitnerQ
H. Federhofer: 'Etats de la chapelle musicale de Charles-Quint (1528) et de Maximilien (1554)', *RBM*, iv (1950), 180
W. Boetticher: *Orlando di Lasso und seine Zeit* (Kassel, 1958)
A. Dunning: Introduction to MAM, xxi–xxii (1971)
W. Pass: 'Jacob Vaets and Georg Prenners Vertonungen des "Salve regina" in Joandlus' Sammelwerk von 1568', *De ratione in musica: Festschrift Erich Schenk* (Kassel, 1975), 29
A. Dunning: *The Fifth Volume of Pietro Giovanelli's 'Thesaurus musicus' (1568)*, MSD (in preparation)

ALBERT DUNNING

Prentner, Johann Joseph Ignaz. *See* BRENTNER, JOHANN JOSEPH IGNAZ.

Prentyce [Prentes], Henry (*b* mid-15th century; *d*? London, 1514). English composer. He is recorded as a clerk of the Fraternity of St Nicholas, London, in 1502. In 1508 his wife also obtained membership. By 1511 he was a Gentleman of the Chapel Royal, and the church-warden's accounts of St Mary-at-Hill mention him, along with Cornysh and others, as a visiting singer engaged at the church during 1510–11. His only extant composition is a five-voice *Magnificat* in an early 16th-century choirbook (*GB-Cgc* 667; ed. in EECM, iv, 1962). This work is grandiose and elaborate and displays the structural features that had become standard to the genre in England by the late 15th century. Prentyce frequently used decorative imitation and occasionally developed a point through all voices at verse openings. His part-writing, especially in the agile solo sections, is graceful and fluent. Other works by him were probably destroyed during the Reformation.

BIBLIOGRAPHY
F. Ll. Harrison: *Music in Medieval Britain* (London, 1958, 2/1963), 24, 461f
H. Baillie: 'Some Biographical Notes on English Church Musicians, Chiefly Working in London (1485–1569)', *RMARC*, ii (1962), 18–57, esp.49

S. DIANNE BISHOP

Preobrazhensky, Anatoly Viktorovich (*b* Sïzrani, 28 Feb 1870; *d* Leningrad, 17 Feb 1929). Russian musicologist. He graduated from the ecclesiastical academies at Ekaterinoslav (1889) and Kazan (1894), then taught Russian language and literature at various educational institutions in Taganor and Bakhmut. From 1898 he taught at the Moscow Synodal School. In 1902 he moved to St Petersburg to become lecturer and librarian at the court chapel, of which he was assistant director in the last years of his life; while there he wrote a book on one of the chapel's distinguished former directors, Alexey Lvov. From 1920 Preobrazhensky was also a professor in the Russian music department of the Russian Institute for the History of the Arts, and from 1921 at the Petrograd/Leningrad Conservatory. His research interests centred on Russian sacred music, on which he wrote several generalized surveys; he also made valuable studies of individual composers, notably Turchaninov and Bortnyansky.

WRITINGS

Slovar' russkovo tserkovnovo peniya [Dictionary of Russian church chant] (Moscow, 1896)

Po tserkovnomu peniyu [On church chant] (Ekaterinoslav, 1897, 2/1900)

'D. S. Bortnyansky', *RMG* (1900)

Vopros o edinoglasnom penii v russkoy tserkvi XVII veka [The question of monodic chant in the Russian church of the 17th century] (St Petersburg, 1904)

Alexey Fyodorovich L'vov: evo zhizn' i deyatel'nost' [Life and works] (St Petersburg, 1908)

Kratkiy ocherk istorii tserkovnovo peniya v Rossii [Concise survey of the history of church chant in Russia] (St Petersburg, 2/1910)

Protoiyerey P. I. Turchaninov [Archpriest Turchaninov] (St Petersburg, 1910)

Kul'tovaya muzïka v Rossii [Sacred music in Russia] (Leningrad, 1914)

BIBLIOGRAPHY

G. B. Bernandt and I. M. Yampol'sky: *Kto pisal o muzïke* [Writers on music], ii (Moscow, 1974) [incl. complete list of writings]

Preparation. In part-writing, the 'softening' of the dissonant effect of an accented NON-HARMONIC NOTE (i.e. an appoggiatura) by presenting it as a consonant note in the previous chord; the result is called a 'prepared appoggiatura'. The dissonance is softened further if the preparation note is tied to the appoggiatura, creating a suspension.

Prepared piano. A piano in which the pitches, timbres and dynamic responses of individual notes have been altered by means of bolts, screws, mutes, rubber erasers and/or other objects inserted at particular points between the strings. The technique of altering the tone of a piano in this way was developed by Cage for his *Bacchanale* (1938), and the prepared piano is used in a number of his subsequent compositions, as well as in works by Lou Harrison, Toshiro Mayuzumi and Christian Wolff. Since the tonal alteration desired varies from one piece to another and depends on the nature and placement of the objects used to effect it, these have to be indicated in the score, as shown in the Table, p.217, which reproduces the table of preparations for Cage's *Sonatas and Interludes* (1946–8).

EDWIN M. RIPIN

Prepositus Brixiensis [Melchior de Brissia; Preponitus Brisiensis] (*b* ?Brescia; *fl* Padua, 1411–25). Italian composer. He has often been incorrectly identified with MATHEUS DE BRIXIA (Gallo and Mantese, p.24, note 3). He was a singer at Padua Cathedral from 1411 to 1425. His four ballate (in the second fascicle of *GB-Ob* 213, copied about 1428) follow the normal formal scheme; they all have refrains of only two lines. Both voices in the two-voice ballate are provided with text. The upper voices – mostly very melismatic – contain word repetitions as occur also in the works of Ciconia. These works may originally have been written in 14th-century Italian notation, since they lack syncopation, and there are rhythmic changes from bar to bar. Accidentals are often provided at the beginnings of sections. The form of the ballata is recalled also in his small homophonic rondeau

Desgardés vous: a second line of text, under the first, is provided in the upper voice. This work occurs in a part of *I-Bu* 2216 which (according to Gallo) originated at Brescia after 1440.

WORKS

Edition: *Early Fifteenth-century Music*, ed. G. Reaney, CMM, xi/5 (1975) [complete]

BALLATE

I occhi d'una ançolleta, 3vv
I pensieri dolçe amor, 2vv
Orsa vanta, 3vv
O spirito gentil, 2vv

RONDEAU

Desgardés vous, 2vv

BIBLIOGRAPHY

W. Korte: *Studien zur Geschichte der Musik in Italien im 1. Viertel des 15. Jahrhunderts* (Kassel, 1933)

G. Reaney: 'The Manuscript Oxford, Bodleian Library, Canonici Misc. 213', *MD*, ix (1955), 73–104

A. Gallo and G. Mantese: *Ricerche sulle origini della capella musicale del duomo di Vicenza* (Venice, 1964)

F. A. Gallo: *Il codice musicale 2216 della Biblioteca universitaria di Bologna* (Bologna, 1968–70)

G. Reaney: 'The Italian Contribution to the Manuscript Oxford, Bodleian Library, Canonici Misc.213', *L'ars nova italiana del trecento II: Certaldo 1969*, 443

H. Schoop: *Entstehung und Verwendung der Handschrift Oxford, Bodleian Library, Can. misc. 213* (Berne, 1971)

HANS SCHOOP

Prés, Josquin des. *See* JOSQUIN DESPREZ.

Presa (i) (It.: 'handle', 'catch'). A sign used in a canon to indicate the places at which the *guida* (subject) of the canon is to be taken up by other voices. *See* CANON (i).

Presa (ii) (Lat.). A response sung, originally by the congregation, in the Preces of the Gallican rite; *see* GALLICAN RITE, MUSIC OF THE, §13.

Preschner, Paul (*fl* late 16th century). German composer. Rühling's *Tabulaturbuch auff Orgeln und Instrument* (Leipzig, 1583[24]) includes a transcription of Preschner's five-part motet, *Also hat Gott die Welt geliebt*. Two MS sources of this motet were apparently destroyed at Liegnitz (now Legnica) during World War II; Bohn's catalogue lists a five-part mass and two five-part motets by the composer, which were also destroyed.

BIBLIOGRAPHY

E. Bohn: *Die musikalischen Handschriften des XVI. und XVII. Jahrhunderts in der Stadtbibliothek zu Breslau* (Breslau, 1890)

RICHARD MARLOW

Prescott, Abraham (*b* Deerfield, New Hampshire, 5 July 1789; *d* Concord, New Hampshire, 6 May 1858). American maker of bowed string and keyboard instruments. He learnt cabinet making from his uncle, and made his first instrument, a 'bass viol' or 'church bass' (in fact a large cello), in 1809 in Deerfield. The instrument, bought by a local musician for use in church services, was the first of several hundreds made and sold by Prescott by the 1840s. He played the 'bass viol' (again, probably the cello) while attending Atkinson Academy, served as fife major in the 1812 war and later gave occasional singing lessons. Prescott combined commercial acumen with his musical and religious associations (he was a deacon of the Baptist Church) and built a thriving music business. While still in Deerfield he continued to farm and had several apprentices (including David and Andrew Dearborn) to assist with

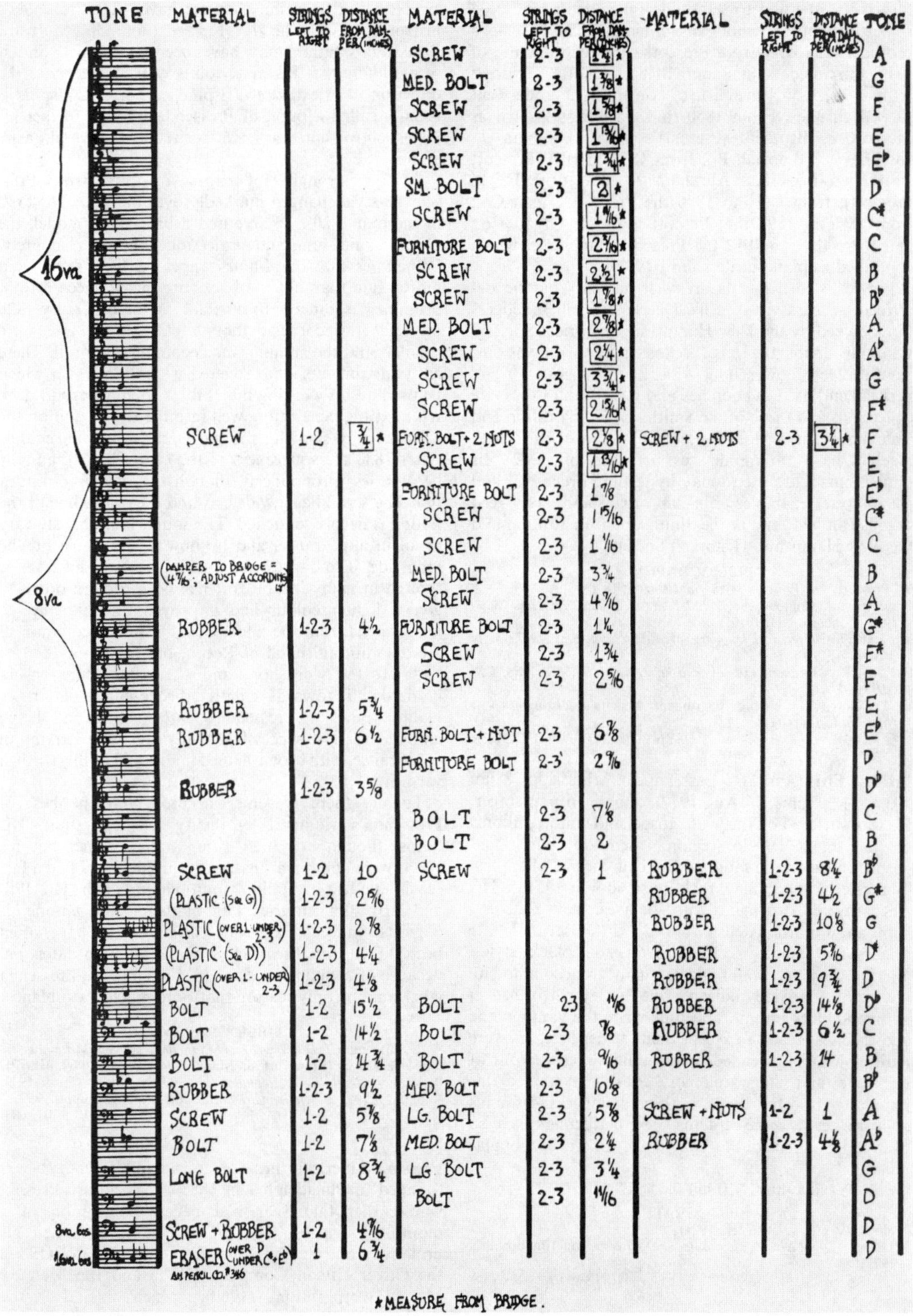

Material	Strings left to right	Distance from damper (inches)	Material	Strings left to right	Distance from damper (inches)	Material	Strings left to right	Distance from damper (inches)	Tone
			SCREW	2-3	1¼*				A
			MED. BOLT	2-3	1⅜*				G
			SCREW	2-3	1⅝*				F
			SCREW	2-3	1 13/16*				E
			SCREW	2-3	1¾*				E♭
			SM. BOLT	2-3	2*				D
			SCREW	2-3	1 9/16*				C♯
			FURNITURE BOLT	2-3	2 3/16*				C
			SCREW	2-3	2½*				B
			SCREW	2-3	1⅞*				B♭
			MED. BOLT	2-3	2⅞*				A
			SCREW	2-3	2¼*				A♭
			SCREW	2-3	3¾*				G
			SCREW	2-3	2 15/16*				F♯
SCREW	1-2	¾*	FURN. BOLT + 2 NUTS	2-3	2⅛*	SCREW + 2 NUTS	2-3	3¼*	F
			SCREW	2-3	1 13/16*				E
			FURNITURE BOLT	2-3	1⅞				E♭
			SCREW	2-3	1 15/16				C♯
			SCREW	2-3	1 1/16				C
(DAMPER TO BRIDGE = 4 7/16; ADJUST ACCORDINGLY)			MED. BOLT	2-3	3¾				B
			SCREW	2-3	4 7/16				A
RUBBER	1-2-3	4½	FURNITURE BOLT	2-3	1¼				G♯
			SCREW	2-3	1¾				F♯
			SCREW	2-3	2 5/16				F
RUBBER	1-2-3	5¾							E
RUBBER	1-2-3	6½	FURN. BOLT + NUT	2-3	6⅞				E♭
			FURNITURE BOLT	2-3	2 9/16				D
RUBBER	1-2-3	3⅝							D♭
			BOLT	2-3	7⅛				C
			BOLT	2-3	2				B
SCREW	1-2	10	SCREW	2-3	1	RUBBER	1-2-3	8¼	B♭
(PLASTIC (See G))	1-2-3	2 5/16				RUBBER	1-2-3	4½	G♯
PLASTIC (OVER 1: UNDER 2-3)	1-2-3	2⅞				RUBBER	1-2-3	10⅛	G
(PLASTIC (See D))	1-2-3	4¼				RUBBER	1-2-3	5 7/16	D♯
PLASTIC (OVER 1 - UNDER 2-3)	1-2-3	4⅛				RUBBER	1-2-3	9¾	D
BOLT	1-2	15½	BOLT	2-3	1 1/16	RUBBER	1-2-3	14⅛	D♭
BOLT	1-2	14½	BOLT	2-3	7/8	RUBBER	1-2-3	6½	C
BOLT	1-2	14¾	BOLT	2-3	9/16	RUBBER	1-2-3	14	B
RUBBER	1-2-3	9½	MED. BOLT	2-3	10⅛				B♭
SCREW	1-2	5⅞	LG. BOLT	2-3	5⅞	SCREW + NUTS	1-2	1	A
BOLT	1-2	7⅛	MED. BOLT	2-3	2¼	RUBBER	1-2-3	4⅛	A♭
LONG BOLT	1-2	8¾	LG. BOLT	2-3	3¼				G
			BOLT	2-3	1 1/16				D
SCREW + RUBBER	1-2	4 7/16							D
ERASER (OVER D UNDER C♯ + E♭) AM. PENCIL CO. #346	1	6¾							D

*MEASURE FROM BRIDGE.

Prepared piano: table of preparations from Cage's 'Sonatas and Interludes' (*1946–8*)

instrument building.

In 1831 he opened a music store in Concord, New Hampshire; by 1833 he moved the whole of his business there for better trade and shipping facilities with Boston. By the late 1830s, he had begun the manufacture of small reed organs (known as 'lap organs' or 'rocking melodeons'). In 1845 the Prescott firm, now Abraham Prescott & Son (his son was Abraham J. Prescott) turned its attention to seraphines, melodeons and reed organs for church, school and home use. The Dearborn brothers took over from Prescott's the manufacture of string instruments in about 1848, and after Prescott retired in 1850, the firm's constitution underwent several changes. From 1850 to 1852 it was known as Prescott & Brothers (Prescott's sons: Abraham J., Joseph W. and Josiah B.); from 1852 to 1870 Prescott Brothers (after 1858 Abraham J. & George D. B. Prescott); from 1871 to 1886 the Prescott Organ Co.; from 1887 to 1891 the Prescott Piano & Organ Co.; and from 1891 to 1912 the Prescott Piano Co. (which continued as piano dealers until 1917).

Prescott's instruments are well made. What he described as 'bass viols' in his Deerfield business ledgers (now owned by the New Hampshire Historical Society) were no doubt the large cellos (typical dimensions: length 82 cm, lower bout 51 cm, upper bout 40 cm, neck 25 cm) used in churches and now found in private collections and those of the Smithsonian Institution and Yale University. Most Prescott basses are fitted with machine-head tuning devices in place of pegs. His double basses are used today by leading orchestral and jazz players. Examples of his lap organs and larger reed organs can be found at the Smithsonian Institution and the New Hampshire Historical Society.

BIBLIOGRAPHY
W. Prescott: *The Prescott Memorial* (Boston, 1870)
Prescott Piano Company: *Over 100 Years of Musical Progress 1809–1910* (Concord, NH, 1910)
W. Henley: *Universal Dictionary of Violin and Bow Makers*, iv (Brighton, 1960), 167
S. R. Ogden: *Abraham Prescott and his Bass Viols* (MS, 1966, *US-CDhs*)
B. D. Turcott: 'Concord Instrument Makers', *Historical New Hampshire*, xxii/1 (1967), 18
CYNTHIA ADAMS HOOVER

Presley, Elvis (Aaron) (*b* East Tupelo, Mississippi, 8 Jan 1935; *d* Memphis, 16 Aug 1977). American pop singer. He was nurtured on the white gospel and country idioms of the East Tupelo region, then on blues and gospel music on the radio and in churches in Memphis, Tennessee. He became a rock music idol in 1954–5. His voice covered two and a third octaves, from *G* to *b''*, with an upward extension to *d'''* in falsetto. White singers had made records drawing on black styles, altering them musically and textually to accommodate the tastes of a wide audience, but Presley performed in authentic black idioms, at a time when the young white audience was ready to accept them. Older listeners were initially hostile, offended by the uninhibited fervour of his style and stage manner. Presley sustained his popularity into the 1970s, both as a singer and for his appearances in some 30 films. Few performers have so thoroughly affected the course of American popular music.

See also POPULAR MUSIC, §III, 4(ii) and fig.17.

BIBLIOGRAPHY
J. Hopkins: *Elvis* (New York, 1971)
R. Barry: *The Elvis Presley American Discography* (Phillipsburg, 1977)
HENRY PLEASANTS

Pressburg (Ger.). BRATISLAVA.

Pressenda, Joannes Franciscus (*b* ?1777; *d* Turin, 1854). Italian violin maker. Pressenda and his pupil Joseph Rocca are regarded as the finest Italian violin makers of the 19th century, although it is certainly an exaggeration to claim, as some have, that Pressenda's instruments will one day replace those of Stradivari. Pressenda's father may have been a violinist, and it seems likely that his first violins were made under the direction of Alexandre d'Espine in Turin. D'Espine is usually called a pupil of Pressenda, though in fact his labels show him to have been active several years earlier.

Always strongly influenced by Stradivari, Pressenda's style changed markedly over the years. At first, in the mid 1820s, he favoured a broad, flat model, the corners quite long and projecting out rather squarely. Sometimes the sound-holes appear a little small, and more often than not the backs are in one piece, with a prominent sap-mark to one side or the other. By 1828 or 1829 the corners, though still set square, were smaller, and the arching was becoming quite full. These early instruments were covered with the varnish which he used all his working life, a thick, rich orange to deep red mixture, penetrating well into the wood, and on the table usually showing the hard grains light in colour. After 1830 the squareness of the centre bout gradually became less pronounced, though the model continued full. The scroll has a wide ear, and the centre line of the fluting is deeply scratched. The sound-holes hardly vary at all in appearance, and by now seem almost on the long side. The darkest red varnish is from these years, though in many instances it has been ground down to give a lighter colour and improved transparency. In instruments from the late 1830s it is not uncommon to see the youthful hand of Rocca, but by about 1840 he had left the workshop, and thereafter there was a gradual shift towards a flatter, broad-edged pattern of violin, some of Pressenda's late instruments being among the most successful. Many are quite striking in appearance, with broad-flamed maple and orange-brown varnish.

Tonally there is some variation, but the best of Pressenda's violins fully justify his reputation. His cellos, though extremely rare, are also fine, but his violas were built on a small pattern. Pressenda had a far-reaching effect on Italian violin making of the late 19th and early 20th centuries, Fagnola being chief among his copyists. Indeed, Fagnola's earlier copies have often been taken for Pressenda's work, though later on, because of commercial demand, the facsimile Pressenda label was the only feature that bore much resemblance.

BIBLIOGRAPHY
W. L. Lütgendorff: *Die Geigen- und Lautenmacher vom Mittelalter bis zur Gegenwart* (Frankfurt am Main, 1904, 3/1922/R1969, 6/1922)
R. Vannes: *Essai d'un dictionnaire universel des luthiers* (Paris, 1932, 2/1951/R1972 as *Dictionnaire universel des luthiers*, suppl. 1959)
CHARLES BEARE

Presser. American firm of music publishers. It was founded in Philadelphia in 1883 by Theodore Presser, who earlier that year had begun publication of a monthly magazine, *The Etude*. Presser expanded his firm by acquiring the John Church Company (1930), the Oliver Ditson Company (1931) and the Mercury Music Corporation (1969), which included the catalogues of Beekman Music and Merrymount Music. In 1970 Elkan-Vogel also became a subsidiary.

The Presser Company is the sole agent in the USA for Gentry Publications, Columbia Music, Mowbray Music, New Music Editions, Society for the Publication of American Music and Tritone–Tenuto Publications, as well as for foreign firms such as Berbèn (Ancona), Billaudot, Editions Musicales Transatlantiques and Heugel (Paris); Impero (Wilhelmshaven); and Universal Edition (London, Vienna and Zurich). The company serves the needs of dealers, teachers and musicians, drawing from a huge stock of classical, educational and light music. It also maintains a large library of works for rental, including opera, ballet and orchestral music. Among the many American composers represented by Presser are George Antheil, Babbitt, Arthur Berger, Carter, Cowell, Kenneth Gaburo, Hovhaness, Ives, Harrison Kerr, Luening, Piston, Riegger, Siegmeister and Strang. In 1949 the company's main office was moved to Bryn Mawr, Pennsylvania.

W. THOMAS MARROCCO, MARK JACOBS

Presser, Theodore (*b* Pittsburgh, 3 July 1848; *d* Philadelphia, 27 Oct 1925). American publisher and musical philanthropist. He studied at the New England Conservatory in Boston and later spent two years at Leipzig. In 1883 he founded at Lynchburg, Virginia, *The Etude* (moved a few months later to Philadelphia), a monthly magazine devoted to the interests of music teachers and students; later that year he established a music publishing business which, as the Theodore PRESSER Company, became an important firm. In 1906 he opened at Philadelphia the Presser Home for Retired Music Teachers, the only such institution in the USA. In 1916 the Presser Foundation was established, with funds of over $1,000,000, for the support of the home, a department of scholarships (given directly to institutions and not to individuals), and a department for the relief of deserving musicians.

WARREN STOREY SMITH

Pressus (? from Lat. *pressim*: 'compactly'). In Western chant notations, an ornamental neume, usually consisting of a neume with added ORISCUS and a final PUNCTUM. If the initial neume is a VIRGA with *oriscus* (also known as a *virga strata* or a FRANCULUS), a three-note group results; if the initial neume is a *pes* (*see* PES (ii)) with *oriscus* (*pes stratus*), a four-note group results, and so on. Suñol and Cardine, among others, distinguished a *pressus minor*, where a foreshortened form of the *franculus* and *punctum* are added to other neumes. As with all neumes that include the *oriscus*, the exact significance of the *pressus* is unclear. The *oriscus* was usually represented as a note of the same pitch as the preceding one when the change to staff notation came. Mocquereau originally believed that the unison notes should be sung with special emphasis, but later renounced this view (for illustration *see* NEUMATIC NOTATIONS, Table 1).

BIBLIOGRAPHY
P. Wagner: *Einführung in die gregorianischen Melodien*, ii: *Neumenkunde: Paläographie des liturgischen Gesanges* (Leipzig, 1905, rev., enlarged 2/1913/*R*1962)
A. Mocquereau: *Le nombre musical grégorien ou rythmique grégorienne* (Rome and Tournai, 1908–27)
H. M. Bannister: *Codices e vaticani selecti, phototypice expressi*, Monumenti vaticani di paleografia musicale latina, xii (Leipzig, 1913/*R*1969)
G. M. Suñol: *Introducció a la paleografia musical gregoriana* (Montserrat, 1925; Fr. trans., rev., enlarged 2/1935)
M. Huglo: 'Les noms des neumes et leur origine', *Etudes grégoriennes*, i (1954), 53
E. Jammers: *Tafeln zur Neumenkunde* (Tutzing, 1965)
E. Cardine: 'Sémiologie grégorienne', *Etudes grégoriennes*, xi (1970), 1–158

Prestant (Fr., Ger.). An ORGAN STOP (*Octave, Praestant*).

Presten [Preston], **Jørgen** [Jörgen, Georgio] (*d* Copenhagen, before 28 Nov 1553). Composer, presumably of Netherlands origin, active in Denmark. He was leader of the *kantori*, the choir of the royal chapel of Christian III, in 1551, and two years later died of the plague. According to an entry in *Kancelliets brevbøger* dated 28 November 1553, negotiations were started with his widow for the sale to the king of a set of 'songbooks' owned by Presten; these apparently have not survived. His works are known from another, perhaps corresponding, set of manuscript partbooks prepared under the direction of the chief trumpeter, Jørgen Heyde (or Georg Hayd), for the instrumentalists of the royal chapel, the copying of which was begun in 1541. Two of the eight-part pieces, *Nun bitten wir den heiligen Geist* and *Ach Herr seh uns genädig an*, were sent by Heyde from Copenhagen to his former master Duke Albrecht of Prussia on 30 May 1545. Since the second of these is based on Christian III's motto 'Ach Gott schaff deinen Willen', which appears both as an acrostic and as a refrain, it seems likely that Presten was by then employed at the Danish court. A motet *Commoda res*, inscribed in the manuscript 'a Georgio P . . . anno XLIII redditum' and therefore also attributed to Presten, is a five-part canon on Duke Albrecht's motto 'Vertrau Gott allein'; this has been taken to suggest that Presten, like a number of other musicians such as Heyde and Adrianus Petit Coclico, had been in the service of Duke Albrecht before going to Denmark. However, the Königsberg and Copenhagen courts were so closely related at this period that it cannot be taken as certain. On the other hand, the presence of five of Presten's pieces in the incomplete set of Swedish partbooks from about 1560, the only other known source of his music, can probably be attributed to the migration of musicians such as Heyde and Johan Paston (? Josquin Baston) who went, in 1556 and 1559 respectively, from service with Christian III to the court of Erik XIV.

Presten was the most productive of the foreign composers at the Danish court: 19 works attributed to him survive, comprising six Latin motets, ten German hymns and three instrumental *fugae* or canons. In the Copenhagen source all the vocal pieces are untexted except *Peccavimus tibi*, which has the text in the bass. Ten of the pieces are cantus firmus settings, with the cantus firmus in short phrases, without ornamentation, in the tenor. Imitation is sometimes used at the beginnings of phrases but is not pursued, and there is rarely any overall sense of structure. In the eight-voice *Christ ist erstanden* the melody is sung by the two highest voices in canon while the other voices accompany them with free counterpoint. The three instrumental canons, with their lively rhythms and wider ranges, are musically more interesting.

WORKS

All in *DK-Kk* Gl.Kgl.Saml.1872, 4; those marked * are also in *S-Sk* S229 and *Skma* Ty.Ky.45

Edition: *Music from the Time of Christian III: Selected Compositions from the Partbooks of the Chapel Royal (1541)*, ed. H. Glahn, Dania sonans, iv–vi (1978–)

*Appropinquet, 7vv; Dies est leticiae, 7vv; Peccavimus tibi, 6vv; Veni Creator, 6vv; Surge illuminare, 6vv

Ach Herr sehe uns genedig an, 5vv; *Ach Herr sehe uns genedic an, 7vv; *Ach Herr sehe uns gnaedig an, 8vv; *Christ bet und wach, 8vv; Christ ist erstanden, 6vv; Christ ist erstanden, 8vv; Der gottlose Hauff, 6vv; *Erhalt uns Herr, 7vv; Nun bitten wir den heiligen Geyst, 8vv; Vater unser in Himmelreich, 6vv

3 fugae, a 5, 6

Commoda res/Vertrau Gott allein, motet, 5vv; attrib. 'Georgio P.', ? by Presten

BIBLIOGRAPHY
C. Ravn: *Koncerter og musikalske selskaber i aeldre tid* (Copenhagen, 1886), 7
J. Foss: 'Det Kgl. Cantoris Stemmebøger A.D. 1541', *Aarbog for musik* (1923), 22
M. van Crevel: *Adrianus Petit Coclico: Leben und Beziehungen eines nach Deutschland emigrierten Josquinschülers* (The Hague, 1940)
H. Glahn: 'En ny kilde til belysning af det preussiske hofkapels repertoire på Hertug Albrechts tid', *STMf*, xliii (1961), 145
——: ' "Det Kongelige Kantoris Stemmebøger" – Trompeterkorpsets Stemmebøger', *DAM*, viii (1977), 137
MARGARET MUNCK (with JOHN BERGSAGEL)

Prestissimo (It.: 'very fast'). *See* PRESTO.

Presto (It.: 'ready', 'prompt'). Quick, fast; one of the earliest tempo designations in music. Nicola Vicentino (1555) gave it as the speed of a crotchet; and Banchieri used it specifically as a tempo mark in 'La battaglia' (from *L'organo suonarino*, 1611) along with *adagio*, *allegro* and *veloce*. But on the whole it appears in other sources from the first half of the 17th century as the single alternative to the slow tempo, be it *adagio*, *tardo* or *lento*. In Giovanni Priuli's *Sacrorum concentuum pars prima* (Venice, 1618) there are no tempo marks for the motets nor for the two instrumental sonatas (nos.35 and 36); but all the instrumental canzonas are marked *presto* at the beginning, and most have the subsequent contrasting instruction *tardo*. This is typical and is very similar to the pattern of its uses by Michael Praetorius (*Polyhymnia caduceatrix*, 1619; *Puericinium*, 1621), by Monteverdi, whose 'Chiome d'oro' (1619) includes the marking *presto honestamente*, by Schütz, who preferred the form *praesto*, and by other early 17th-century composers. In practically all such cases *presto* may be taken as the equivalent of *tempo giusto*, against which the *adagio* or *tardo* could be inserted as deviations, just as *forte* was often the normal dynamic against which *piano* and *pianissimo* could provide echoes and contrasts. So *presto* did not necessarily imply any particular hurry in the 17th century. As late as the middle of the 18th century it was often used interchangeably with *allegro*: three different versions of the first movement of J. S. Bach's Sixth Violin Sonata are marked respectively *presto*, *vivace* and *allegro*; and Grassineau (1740) defined *presto* as 'fast or quick, gayly yet not with rapidity'.

But the tradition by which *presto* became a faster tempo than *allegro* grew alongside the older tradition, in which it was merely a moderately fast tempo. Brossard (1703) said 'the speed must be pressed on, making the beats very short'; and the anonymous *A Short Explication* (London, 1724) placed it faster than *allegro* or even *più allegro*. All early examples of *presto* must be approached with caution: as the 18th century progressed *presto* became more and more the accepted word for the fastest of all tempos except *prestissimo*. But Mozart, for instance, tended to avoid *prestissimo*, and in his letter about the Haffner Symphony (7 August 1782) stated that its finale, marked *presto*, should go as fast as possible.

Prestissimo, the superlative form ('very fast', 'as fast as possible'), logically appeared at about the same time as *presto*: it occurs in J. Vierdanck's *Pavanen* (1637) and in Schütz's *St John Passion* (1665); and it is even used as the tempo designation for sarabands in the manuscript *GB-Lbm* Add.31424. But even though it is defined in most dictionaries from Brossard on, the word was never very often used. Handel used it occasionally, as in the section 'For he is like a refiner's fire' from *Messiah*, and Beethoven for the finale of his Piano Sonata in C minor op.10 no.1 and the second movement of his Sonata in E op.109. There seems always to have been a feeling that too frequent use would lead to a cheapening of the extreme effect implied. Schumann was surely a little less than serious, from this point of view, when he marked the first movement of his G minor Piano Sonata *il più presto possibile* (*so rasch wie möglich*), but later in the movement gave the indication *più presto schneller*) and shortly before the end *ancora più vivo* (*noch schneller*). The point here, of course, is that changes of figuration on each occasion make faster tempos possible: there is no absolute fastest possible tempo, because not only the abilities of the performer change but also the nature of the music. And most composers have accordingly been content with *presto*.

Presto and *prestissimo* also occur as marks of expression or mood. Thus Verdi, for instance, rarely used them as tempo marks except in his last opera, *Falstaff*: otherwise he confined them to such formulations as *allegro prestissimo* (just before the end of Act 1 of *I due Foscari*) or *tutto questo recitativo molto presto* (*Il trovatore*). His fast tempos were *velocissimo*, *allegro agitato* or *allegro assai mosso*.

For bibliography *see* TEMPO AND EXPRESSION MARKS.

DAVID FALLOWS

Preston, Christopher (*fl c*1665–85). English keyboard player and composer. On 7 January 1668 he was appointed to the royal household as a musician-in-ordinary for the virginals with the right of succession to Christopher Gibbons's place and fee on the latter's death; his succession was ratified on 25 October 1676 after Gibbons's death. Preston himself died probably before 1685, as on 1 January 1690 a reference to his widow, 'Mary Preston of York', describes him as 'late musician to King Charles II'. His extant compositions amount to five short keyboard pieces in Locke's *Melothesia* (1673).

PETER DENNISON

Preston, Jørgen. *See* PRESTEN, JØRGEN.

Preston, Simon (John) (*b* Bournemouth, 4 Aug 1938). English organist. He studied with C. H. Trevor at the Royal Academy of Music from 1956 to 1958 and then became organ scholar of King's College, Cambridge, where he took his MusB degree. He made an outstanding début at the Festival Hall in 1962 in Janáček's Glagolitic Mass. He was sub-organist at Westminster Abbey from 1962 to 1967; after that his recitals took him all over Europe and North America. At the same time, under the influence of George Malcolm, he established a reputation as a harpsichordist.

Preston is a fastidious perfectionist: his virtuosity as a solo organist is solidly based on intellectual resources which give him an insight into music ranging from the Baroque to the present day. His instinct for colour in registration has made him the leading English interpreter of the organ music of Liszt and Messiaen (to whose mysticism he is particularly attracted). He has, however, also made a much admired recording (with Menuhin and the Bath Festival Orchestra) of Handel's organ concertos, and given first performances of new English organ works. Since his appointment in 1970 as organist and lecturer in music at Christ Church, Oxford, he has raised the choir's standards, as was shown by his distinguished recording in 1972 of choral music by Walton (including a new *Jubilate* which Preston conducted at the English Bach Festival in that year). In the late 1970s he directed some admired recordings, notably of masses by Haydn, with his choir and the Academy of Ancient Music. He was appointed organist of Westminster Abbey from 1981.

STANLEY WEBB

Preston, Stephen (John) (*b* Skipton, Yorks., 24 May 1945). English flautist. He studied with John Francis and Geoffrey Gilbert at the GSM and in 1972 won the Dame Myra Hess Award. He has specialized in the Baroque and Classical flutes and plays in various ensembles including L'Ecole d'Orphée, the English Concert and the Academy of Ancient Music. While observant of the letter and spirit of early performing practices, he has a personal style marked by a certain vivacity and sweetness of tone, evident in his numerous recordings. He teaches the Baroque flute at the GSM.

Preston, Thomas (*d* ?Windsor, after 1559). English composer. It is possible that he is the Preston recorded in 1543 as organist and instructor of the choristers at Magdalen College, Oxford. A Preston, again without christian name, is recorded in the archives of Trinity College, Cambridge, as an organist and choirmaster between 1548 and 1552, and again from 1554 to 1559. The payments of 1558 and 1559 are of allowances due to absent Fellows, and are consistent with his presence as organist at St George's, Windsor, in those years. Preston of Windsor is listed, with Sebastian Westcott of St Paul's and Thorne of York, as a musician deprived of his office because of his faith, in Nicholas Sanders's *De visibilia monarchia* (Louvain, 1571, p.702). It is just possible that he wrote the play *Cambises* (produced *c*1560 and published *c*1569); other London musicians such as Redford, John Heywood, John Taylor and Westcott himself were all at some time concerned with dramatic productions.

The style of Preston's organ music is consistent with a creative career centred around the reign of Mary. All the authenticated keyboard compositions are for the Latin liturgy. The oldest of them, the offertory *Reges Tharsis*, is found in the earliest (pre-1549) section of *GB-Lbm* Add.29996, though this may be the work of John Preston, organist of St Dunstan-in-the-West in 1544–5. The rest are from a section of Add.29996 entirely devoted to Thomas Preston's music. Its characteristics include a command of flowing counterpoint in four parts, the use of rhythmic intricacy and the exploitation of a virtuoso keyboard technique. His most significant work is the setting of the Mass for Easter Day, which unfortunately breaks off in the manuscript in the middle of the sequence. The one anonymous piece in this section of Add.29996, the ground *Uppon la mi re*, may be by him; and the series of hymns based on faburdens on ff.158–178*v* may also be by him.

WORKS

Editions: *Early Tudor Organ Music I: Music for the Office*, ed. J. Caldwell, EECM, vi (London, 1966) [C]
  Early Tudor Organ Music II: Music for the Mass, ed. D. Stevens, EECM, x (London, 1969) [S]

ORGAN

Resurrexi (int), Haec dies (grad), Alleluia, Pascha nostrum (all), Fulgens praeclara (seq), S no.5 (Proper for Easter)
Beatus Laurentius (ant), C no.5
Benedictus sit (off), S no.6

Confessio et pulchritudo (off), S no.7
Diffusa est gratia (off), S no.8
Felix namque (off) (8 settings), S nos.12–19
Reges Tharsis (off), S no.26

OTHER INSTRUMENTAL

In nomine, 4 parts, *GB-Ob* Mus.Sch.D. 212–16
O lux beata Trinitas, 3 parts, *Lbm* R.M.24.D.2

BIBLIOGRAPHY

E. H. Fellowes: *Organists and Masters of the Choristers of St. George's Chapel in Windsor Castle* (London, 1939)
F. Ll. Harrison: *Music in Medieval Britain* (London, 1958, 2/1963)
D. Stevens: 'Thomas Preston's Organ Mass', *ML*, xxxix (1958), 29
H. Baillie: 'Some Biographical Notes on English Church Musicians, Chiefly Working in London (1485–1560)', *RMARC*, ii (1965), 18
J. Caldwell: 'Keyboard Plainsong Settings in England, 1500–1660', *MD*, xix (1965), 129
D. Mateer: 'Further Light on Preston and Whyte', *MT*, cxv (1974), 1074

JOHN CALDWELL

Preston & Son. English family of music publishers. The firm was started by John Preston (*d* Jan 1798), who by about 1774 was established as a guitar and violin maker in London. In 1789 his son Thomas entered the business, and continued it alone after his father's death until about 1834, when it was acquired by COVENTRY & HOLLIER.

The Preston firm rapidly rose to become one of the most flourishing in the trade. Its publications covered music of every kind, and included a long annual series of country dances begun in 1786, popular operas by Arnold, Hook and Reeve, and works such as Bunting's *General Collection of the Ancient Irish Music* (1796) and J. S. Smith's collection *Musica antiqua* (1812). It was also the printer of George Thomson's collections of national songs from 1793. In addition the Preston firm bought the plates and stock of several other firms, including ROBERT BREMNER (1789), Thomas Skillern the elder (*c*1803), H. Wright (*c*1803), and Wilkinson & Co. (*c*1810). From these it did a vast reprint business, the most notable items of which were oratorios and other works of Handel acquired from H. Wright (formerly WRIGHT & WILKINSON), the successor of Walsh and Randall.

BIBLIOGRAPHY

F. Kidson: *British Music Publishers, Printers and Engravers* (London, 1900/R1974)
C. Hopkinson and C. B. Oldman: 'Thomson's Collections of National Song', *Edinburgh Bibliographical Society Transactions*, ii (1940), 1–64
C. Humphries and W. C. Smith: *Music Publishing in the British Isles* (London, 1954, 2/1970)

FRANK KIDSON/WILLIAM C. SMITH/
PETER WARD JONES

Preti, Alfonso (*b* ?Mantua; *fl* 1586–92). Italian composer. According to Eitner he was 'a nobleman at Mantua and a virtuoso'. His active career as a published composer began in 1586 with his *Primo libro de madrigali* for five voices (Venice, 1587), described in the dedication to the Duke of Mantua as 'the first offspring of my weak and sterile imagination'. This publication contains 15 madrigals, one of which is an extended cycle in five sections. Preti fostered madrigal composition in his own works and in the organization of a circle of madrigal composers, consisting of both enthusiastic amateurs and professionals, and in the publication of a collection of madrigals assembled from the members of this group. The anthology, *L'amoroso caccia* (*RISM* 1588¹⁴), contains, as its title-page proclaims, works 'by native Mantuan composers', including Preti himself, dedicated to 'the most excellent musicians of Rome'. There is no evidence to indicate a specific relationship between these 24 Mantuans and any Roman composers, but it is quite possible that the reference is to the circle around Marenzio, since he had been known in Mantua since his visit there in 1580 and may have lived and worked in the service of Guglielmo Gonzaga there in the 1570s. Pallavicino, a long-time resident of Mantua, must have known Preti well and he clearly thought sufficiently highly of him to include one madrigal, *Tra mille fior*, in his fourth book of madrigals for five voices (*RISM* 1588[28]). It is a well-wrought, thoroughly imitative work, with little concession to the 'modern' chordal style of Andrea Gabrieli or the lighter works of Marenzio. Preti's last known composition, *Ninfe a danzar venite*, appeared in *Il trionfo di Dori* (*RISM* 1592[11]).

BIBLIOGRAPHY
I. Fenlon: *Patterns of Style and Patronage: Music at the Mantuan Court c1565–1600* (diss., U. of Cambridge, 1977)

STEVEN LEDBETTER

Pretorius, Conrad. *See* PRAETORIUS, CONRAD.

Prêtre, Georges (*b* Waziers, 14 Aug 1924). French conductor. He studied the trumpet and composition at the Paris Conservatoire, and conducting under Cluytens. In 1946 he conducted Lalo's *Le roi d'Ys* at the Marseilles Opera, and spent the next ten years working in provincial opera houses. He made his Paris début in 1956 with Strauss's *Capriccio* at the Opéra-Comique (the first Paris performance), and was then engaged there until 1959. In 1960 he appeared at the Paris Opéra, and then conducted widely in Europe and the USA.

Although he conducts concerts, Prêtre is most successful in opera. He often worked with Callas, and recorded *Tosca* and *Carmen* with her. A dedicated interpreter of Poulenc's music, he was responsible for the first performances of *La voix humaine* and *Gloria*, among other works, and has recorded most of Poulenc's orchestral music. His wide experience of the theatre and his dynamic personality give him a natural sense of authority. He has nevertheless been criticized for placing too much emphasis on personal triumph, sometimes sacrificing precision and detail to a striking overall effect.

CHRISTIANE SPIETH-WEISSENBACHER

Preumayr. German family of musicians active in Sweden.

(1) **Johan Conrad Preumayr** (*b* Koblenz, Dec 1775; *d* Stockholm, 20 March 1819). Bassoonist, son of Severin Preumaier. He settled in Stockholm and played in the royal orchestra from 1811 until his death.

(2) **Carl Josef Preumayr** (*b* Koblenz, 2 July 1780; *d* Stockholm, 20 July 1849). Singer, cellist and bassoonist, brother of (1) Johan Conrad Preumayr. He played the cello and the bassoon in the royal orchestra in Stockholm, and also appeared there as an actor and a bass; his operatic roles included Sarastro in *Die Zauberflöte*, Osmin in *Die Entführung aus dem Serail* and the Commendatore in *Don Giovanni*. He was a member of the literary and musical society Par Bricole, and was elected a member of the Swedish Academy of Music in 1841.

(3) **Frans Carl Preumayr** (*b* Ehrenbreitstein, 24 April 1782; *d* Stockholm, 15 Feb 1853). Bassoonist, brother of (1) Johan Conrad Preumayr and the most celebrated

member of the family. He was the leading bassoonist in the royal orchestra from 1811 to 1835, and was director of music to the Swedish Lifeguards and to the Kalmar Regiment. In 1830 he toured Europe, giving concerts in France, Germany and England, where his playing was praised enthusiastically. He was also a member of Par Bricole.

BIBLIOGRAPHY
F. O. Baeckström: *Minnestal hållne uti Frimurareordens stora landtloge i Stockholm* (Stockholm, 1855)
F. A. Dahlgren: *Förteckning öfver Stockholms teatrar* (Stockholm, 1866)
E. Åkerberg: *Musiklivet inom Par Bricole, 1779–1890* (Stockholm, 1910)
——: *Sällskapet Par Bricole, historik* (Stockholm, 1946)
F. Rudelius: *Kalmar regementes personhistoria 1623–1927* (Norrköping, 1955)

WILLIAM WATERHOUSE

Preussner, Eberhard (*b* Stolp, Pomerania, 22 May 1899; *d* Salzburg, 15 Aug 1964). German educationist and writer on music. He studied at the Berlin Hochschule für Musik and concurrently studied musicology with Wolf, Schünemann and Abert at Berlin University. He took the doctorate in 1924 with a dissertation on singing in Protestant *Lateinschulen* in the 17th century. He then worked under Leo Kestenberg at the Berlin Central Institute for Education until 1934, when he took over the organization of German choral singing, for which he was responsible until 1938. He was subsequently (1939) appointed executive director and lecturer in music education at the Salzburg Mozarteum, succeeding Paumgartner as its president (1959); he revived and directed its annual summer academy held at the time of the Salzburg Festival. He was a member of the directorate of the Salzburg Festival and of many international committees, and was a visiting professor at the University of Michigan, Ann Arbor (1952), and Oberlin College, Ohio (1960). He edited the periodical *Die Musikpflege* (1930–43) and *Die musikpädagogische Bibliothek* (1959–64), which had been founded by Kestenberg in 1928. As a writer he produced a book on the sociology of music and a biography of Hindemith, both unpublished, and many music textbooks.

WRITINGS
Die Methodik im Schulgesang der evangelischen Lateinschulen des 17. Jahrhunderts (diss., U. of Berlin, 1924; *AMw*, vi, 1924, 407)
Allgemeine Pädagogik und Musikpädagogik (Leipzig, 1929)
'Das Musikleben der Gegenwart', *Atlantis-Buch der Musik*, ed. F. Hamel (Zurich and Freiburg, 1934–5)
Die bürgerliche Musikkultur (Hamburg, 1935, 2/1950)
Musikgeschichte des Abendlandes (Vienna, 1951–2, 2/1958)
'Paul Hindemith', *ÖMz*, x (1955), 285
'Bild einer neuen Musikschule', *Musikerkenntnis und Musikerziehung: Dankesgaben für Hans Mersmann* (Kassel and Basle, 1957), 100
'Musik und Menschenerziehung', *Wissenschaft und Praxis: eine Festschrift . . . Bernhard Paumgartner* (Zurich and Freiburg, 1957), 87
Allgemeine Musikerziehung (Heidelberg, 1959)
Wie studiere ich Musik? (Heidelberg, 1962)
ed. C. Bresgen: *Schriften, Reden, Gedanken* (Salzburg, 1969)
'Hindemith, Paul', *MGG*

BIBLIOGRAPHY
H. Scholz: 'Eberhard Preussner zum Gedächtnis', *ÖMz*, xix (1964), 452
C. Bresgen: 'Eberhard Preussner', *Schriften, Reden, Gedanken* (Salzburg, 1969) [incl. complete list of writings]

RUDOLF KLEIN

Previn, André (George) [Priwin, Andreas Ludwig] (*b* Berlin, 6 April 1929). American conductor, pianist and composer of German birth. He studied the piano as a child at the Berlin Hochschule für Musik and at the Paris Conservatoire. The Nazi regime prompted the emigration of his family (of Russian-Jewish origin) to the USA in 1939, where his great-uncle, Charles Previn, was musical director for Universal studios in Hollywood. The family settled in Los Angeles, where Previn studied composition with Castelnuovo-Tedesco, also taking lessons from Toch. He obtained American nationality in 1943. He became a professional jazz pianist and an orchestrator for MGM studios before leaving school, and was soon appointed MGM's musical director. His first original film score was for *The Sun Comes Up* (1949), and his records as a jazz pianist were notably successful. In 1951, during army service, he began to study conducting with Monteux in San Francisco. He left MGM, but continued freelance film work (winning 'Oscar' awards four times between 1959 and 1963), and began to develop a career as a concert pianist and conductor. His conducting début was with the St Louis SO in 1963, and he was conductor-in-chief of the Houston SO, 1967–70, succeeding Barbirolli. In 1965 he began, in the recording studio, an association with the London Symphony Orchestra that led to his appointment as its principal conductor (1969–79); thereafter Conductor Emeritus.

Previn has continued to make occasional appearances as a pianist (sometimes combining the role with that of conductor in a Mozart concerto), and as a composer, and also established a reputation as an engaging and fluent talker about music on the television screen. Conversations with another verbal expositor, Antony Hopkins, resulted in an anecdotal book, *Music Face to Face* (1971). His musical versatility and his winning public manner gave him a following (even among non-concertgoers) comparable to Leonard Bernstein's in the USA, unparalleled in Britain since Sir Malcolm Sargent. Musically his acclimatization on the British scene was confirmed by his success as a conductor of Vaughan Williams (he recorded all nine symphonies with the LSO) and Walton. From his earliest professional years he became a master of the problems of timing and tact in the recording studio, and under his direction the LSO fulfilled an extensive and profitable recording programme, including much music by Rakhmaninov.

Previn has a declared predilection for nationalistic or otherwise strongly coloured orchestral music. His repertory has generally not gone further back than Mozart, nor much forward from Bernstein and Britten, and in his early years in London there was an impression that, precipitated from a brilliant career in a different field, he was not wholly familiar with the symphonic repertory. He successfully toured with the LSO in western Europe and the USA on numerous occasions, in 1971 and 1975 to the Far East. In London, as pianist and chamber musician rather than conductor, he was the artistic director for South Bank Summer Music, 1972–4, and he has been guest conductor with leading orchestras in New York, Paris, Amsterdam and elsewhere. In 1975 he was appointed principal conductor of the Pittsburgh SO from 1976, in addition to his other commitments. His Covent Garden début was announced for November 1976, but he withdrew.

Previn has been bold enough not to repress his flair for popular music, composing the scores for the musicals *Coco* (1969) and *The Good Companions* (1974). Among his other compositions are a Symphony for strings (1962), concertos for cello (1968) and guitar (1971), and chamber and piano works including *Four Outings* for brass quintet (1974). A piece for actors and orchestra, *Every Good Boy Deserves Favour* (to words by Tom Stoppard), was performed at the Festival Hall in 1977.

BIBLIOGRAPHY

E. Greenfield: *André Previn* (London, 1973) [with discography by M. Walker]

ARTHUR JACOBS

Previtali, Fernando (*b* Adria, 16 Feb 1907). Italian conductor and composer. He studied at the Turin Conservatory with Alfano (composition), Matthey (organ) and Grossi (cello), and joined the orchestra of the Teatro Regio, Turin, as a cellist. In 1928 he moved to Florence to work with Gui at the Teatro Comunale, and helped to establish the orchestra of the Maggio Musicale Fiorentino. Gui encouraged Previtali's interest in contemporary music, and he became a leading interpreter of Busoni's music, as well as conducting the premières of many works including Ghedini's *Re Hassan* (1939) and Dallapiccola's *Volo di notte* (1940). He was chief conductor of the Rome RSO from 1936 to 1953 (except during 1943–5), and was responsible for many fine opera broadcasts and recordings. In 1953 he was appointed conductor and artistic adviser to the Accademia di S Cecilia (of which he had been a member since 1943), and he has made several tours abroad with the S Cecilia Orchestra in Europe and the USA, where he made his début with the Cleveland Orchestra in 1957. He conducted opera frequently at Buenos Aires from 1959; was appointed principal conductor at the Teatro San Carlo, Naples, in 1972; and subsequently became artistic director of the Turin Teatro Regio and the Teatro Comunale, Genoa. He made his American opera début at Dallas in 1975 (with Donizetti's *Anna Bolena*). An accurate interpreter, an authoritative orchestral trainer and a skilled teacher of conducting, he has contributed to music journals and published editions of early music. His own works include a ballet, *Allucinazioni* (Rome, 1945), *Gloria victis* for choir and orchestra, and chamber music; he has published *Guida allo studio della direzione d'orchestra* (Rome, 1951).

LEONARDO PINZAUTI

Prévost, André (*b* St Jérôme, Quebec, 30 July 1934). Canadian composer and teacher. He studied composition with Pépin at the Montreal Conservatory, where in 1960 he received a first prize in composition, the first to be awarded there. In the same year he went to Paris for further study with Messiaen and Dutilleux. He returned to Montreal in 1963, and in the following year he was appointed professor of composition and analysis in the music faculty of Montreal University. Prévost quickly established himself as an important and lively force in Canadian music, most notably with a series of impressive orchestral scores. *Fantasmes* (1963) was commissioned by the Montreal SO, which recorded it and in 1964 awarded it the annual prize; *Pyknon* for violin and orchestra was written as a test piece for the Montreal International Violin Competition of 1966. The success of these and other works led to the composition of his most ambitious work, *Terre des hommes*, a lengthy cantata performed at the opening of Expo 67. Prévost avoids dogmatic adherence to any particular system, drawing freely, as he has stated, on 'atonality, modes, serial techniques and mathematical hypotheses' within a style that is essentially intuitive, expressive and forthright. The structure and character of a work are sometimes shaped by an underlying, even programmatic idea; *Fantasmes*, for instance, has an explicit, Messiaen-like preface. The harsh colours, dissonances and strident themes of this work attempt to depict a nightmarish, hallucinatory vision of a violent, tension-ridden world. Its first performance took place on 22 November 1963, the day of President Kennedy's assassination, and the score carries a posthumous dedication to him, the 'victim of a world which I have sought to describe in my music'.

WORKS
(*selective list*)

Orch: Scherzo, str, 1960; Fantasmes, sym. movt, 1963; Pyknon, pièce concertante, vn, orch, 1966; Diallèle, 1968; Evanescence, 1970; Hommage [to Beethoven], chamber orch, 1971
Choral: Terre des hommes (cantata, M. Lalonde), solo vv, 3 choruses, 2 orchs, 1967; Psalm cxlviii, 200vv, 4 tpt, 4 trbn, org, 1971
Chamber: Mobiles, fl, str trio, 1960; Sonata, vn, pf, 1961; Sonata, vc, pf, 1962; Tryptique, fl, ob, pf, 1962; Suite, str qt, 1968; Str Qt no.2 'Ad pacem', 1972

Principal publishers: Berandol, BMI Canada, Ricordi Canada

BIBLIOGRAPHY
A. Prévost: 'Propos sur la création', *Vie musicale* (1967), no.7, p.14
Z. Heller: 'André Prévost', *Music Scene* (1968), Nov–Dec, 36
A. Prévost: 'Formulation et consequence d'une hypothèse', *Cahiers canadiens de la musique*, i (1970), 67
M. Lalonde: 'Le poème en tant que composition musicale', *Musiques du Kébèk*, ed. R. Duguay (Montreal, 1971), 73
A. Prévost: 'L'atonalisme naturel', *Musiques du Kébèk*, ed. R. Duguay (Montreal, 1971), 167

WARREN DRAKE

Prévost, Eugène-Prosper (*b* Paris, 23 April 1809; *d* New Orleans, 19 Aug 1872). French composer. He entered the Paris Conservatoire in 1827, studying composition with Le Sueur; Berlioz was a colleague of his there. He wrote two *opéras comiques* during his student days, *Le grenadier de Wagram* and *L'hôtel des princes*, both of which were produced in Paris in 1831. He won the second prize in the Prix de Rome in 1829 with his cantata *La mort de Cléopâtre*, and first prize in 1831 with *Bianca Capello*. On his return from Italy in 1835, his *Cosimo* was produced at the Opéra-Comique and was very well received. He became the conductor at the theatre in Le Havre, where his wife, Eléonore Colon, was a singer. His conducting career took him to New Orleans, though his operas continued to be staged in Paris as well as in the USA. He returned to Paris to manage the Bouffes Parisiens for a short time before settling permanently in New Orleans in 1867.

Prévost wrote about ten comic operas, most of which remained unpublished. The critic Gasperini, in his review of Prévost's last work *L'illustre Gaspard* (1863), made the reasonable judgment: 'It is all clever, light, totally unpretentious; yet it is all written in a masterly fashion'. He also composed a few pieces for orchestra and a mass for chorus and orchestra. The latter shows the influence of his older contemporaries Cherubini, Le Sueur and Charles-Henri Plantade; it contains many choruses in syllabic style and its melodies are charming and expressive, though there is a total absence of fugue and a strictly limited use of counterpoint. Prévost is also often credited with three settings of the *Te Deum*, works by his teacher Le Sueur which he arranged in a piano reduction in 1829, in collaboration with Ermel, a fellow pupil at the Conservatoire.

WORKS

OPERAS
(*first performed in Paris unless otherwise stated*)

L'hôtel des princes (opéra comique, 1, Ferrières and Marconay), Théâtre Ambigu, April 1831
Le grenadier de Wagram (opéra comique, 1, H. Lefebvre and St Amans), Théâtre Ambigu, 14 May 1831
Cosimo (opéra bouffe, 2, St Hilaire and P. Duport), Opéra-Comique, 13 Oct 1835, vocal score (Paris, ?1835)
Les pontons de Cadix (opéra comique, 1, Duport and Ancelot), Opéra-Comique, Nov 1836
Le bon garçon (opéra comique, 1, A. Bourgeois and Lockroy), Opéra-Comique, 22 Sept 1837
Alice Clari (opera, 3), New York, 1846
Blanche et René (opéra comique, 2), New Orleans, 1861
L'illustre Gaspard (opéra comique, 1, Duvert and Lausanne), Opéra-Comique, 11 Feb 1863

OTHER WORKS
Cantatas: La mort de Cléopâtre, 1829, *F-Pn*; Bianca Capello, 1831, *Pn*
Mass, chorus, orch
Several pieces, orch, *Pn*

JEAN MONGRÉDIEN

Prévost, François (1680–1741). French dancer; *see* DANCE, §V, 1.

Prey, Claude (*b* Fleury sur Andelle, 30 May 1925). French composer. An arts graduate of the universities of Paris and Quebec, he engaged in anthropological research in Brazil and Canada before studying at the Paris Conservatoire with Messiaen and Milhaud. Prey is principally concerned with renewing opera and with breaking the barrier between the theatre and the concert hall; his vocal works are to his own texts, except for *Le coeur révélateur* which won the Italia Prize in 1963.

WORKS
(*selective list*)

Lettres perdues, opéra épistolaire, 1960; Le coeur révélateur, chamber opera, 1962; Jonas, opera-oratorio, 1963; Métamorphose d'Echo, mono-mimo-micro-opera, Mez, 24 str, 1965; Mots croisés, A, T, 2 orch, 1965; Donna mobile, television opéra d'appartement, 1965; La noirceur du lait, opéra-test, 1967; On veut la lumière? Allons-y!, opéra comique mêlé de complaintes, 1967; Fêtes de la faim, opera, 1969

Principal publisher: Amphion

ANNE GIRARDOT

Prey, Hermann (*b* Berlin, 11 July 1929). German baritone. As a boy he sang in the Berlin Mozart Choir before going to study at the Berlin Music Academy. After winning a singing competition organized by the Hesse State Radio in 1951, he made his stage début at the Wiesbaden State Theatre in 1952. The following year Günther Rennert, then administrator of the Hamburg Staatsoper, engaged him as a leading baritone. In 1957 he made his first appearance with the Vienna Staatsoper (where he has since been a regular guest), and in 1959 with the Bavarian Staatsoper in Munich. He continued to visit that house, making many notable appearances during the summer festival. His début at the Metropolitan was in 1960, as Wolfram. In 1965 he sang the same role, one of his best, at the Bayreuth Festival. Since 1959 he has appeared regularly at the Salzburg Festival; among his most notable roles there have been Figaro (*Il barbiere di Siviglia*), Guglielmo and Papageno. He made his Covent Garden début as Figaro (Rossini) in 1973.

Prey is a notable lieder singer whose readings have grown considerably over the years in interpretative depth. On the stage his genial and relaxed manner are seen to advantage in Mozart, where his mellifluous tone and keen phrasing are splendidly apt. He has made many recordings, outstanding among them his Figaro in Karl Böhm's *Le nozze di Figaro*, although his usual role on the stage is that of the Count.

ALAN BLYTH

Přibyl, Vilém (*b* Náchod, 10 April 1925). Czech tenor. He was originally a technician but made his début with an amateur group in 1952 in Hradec Králové and took singing lessons with Jakoubková there (1952–62). He joined the opera in Ústí nad Labem in 1960 and the Janáček Opera in Brno in 1961 (where he took further lessons with Vavrdová at the academy). He was given the main heroic tenor parts for which his ringing yet tender voice and strong temperament were valuable; he inclines towards a psychological interpretation of character by subtle acting and vocal methods. Apart from such roles as Radamès, Othello, Don José and Lohengrin, he has achieved his greatest success with Smetana's Dalibor and Laca in *Jenůfa*. He has also taken the leading roles in Martinů's *The Greek Passion*, Prokofiev's *War and Peace* and *The Fiery Angel*, Shostakovich's *Katerina Ismaylova* and *The Nose*. He has sung at the Holland, Vienna, Salzburg, Edinburgh and other festivals and in London at Covent Garden (Florestan) and the Festival Hall. In 1969 he joined the staff of the Janáček Academy of Arts, Brno. He was made Artist of Merit in 1969 and National Artist in 1977.

ALENA NĚMCOVÁ

Price, John (*fl c*1605; *d* Vienna, June 1641). English instrumentalist. He was resident at the Württemberg court in Stuttgart from 1605 to at least 1625 (and possibly until 1629), at the Saxon court in Dresden from 29 April 1629 to 1633, at the Danish court in Copenhagen in 1634 and at the imperial court in Vienna (probably in the service of the empress) from 1637 until his death. His son Johann (who was Imperial Kammermusikus in Vienna) sought, as late as 1650, payments due to his father from Prince Johann Georg I of Saxony.

Mersenne admired Price's skill in securing a range of three octaves from a three-hole flute, and Price impressed Philipp Hainhofer of Dresden by playing the viola da gamba with one hand and an 'English *pfeifflin*' (perhaps a flageolet) with the other. His performances in 1611 on the cornett and the viola bastarda won him extravagant praise and a salary much greater than that of B. Froberger, the Kapellmeister. In 1629, in Dresden, Schütz much resented the fact that Price received a salary of 300 *Talern*, considering him no more than a charlatan. Price, however, knew the French, English and Italian styles of the day and performed music not only for the prince elector's court but at plays, masques and on other occasions. None of his own compositions survives.

BIBLIOGRAPHY
M. Mersenne: *Harmonie universelle* (Paris, 1636–7/*R*1963), book 5, 231f
M. Fürstenau: *Zur Geschichte der Musik und des Theaters am Hofe der Kurfürsten von Sachsen* (Dresden, 1861)
A. Sittard: *Geschichte der Oper am Hofe zu Stuttgart* (Stuttgart, 1890–9i)
H. J. Moser: *Heinrich Schütz, sein Leben und Werk* (Kassel, 1936; Eng. trans., 1959)

E. FRED FLINDELL

Price, Jorge Wilson (*b* Bogotá, 20 May 1853; *d* Bogotá, 9 Oct 1953). Colombian music educator. His father, Henry Price (*b* London, 5 March 1819; *d* New York, 12 Dec 1863), a composer and painter, took him to New York in 1855; after Henry's death the boy's mother took Jorge back to Bogotá in 1864. Having completed his college studies there Price divided his time between a business career (1869–89) and music. Aided by a grant from President Rafael Núñez he founded on 22 February 1882 the Academia Nacional de Música (Conservatorio Nacional de Música from 1910). While he was its director (1882–99, 1909–10) he translated seven texts by Stainer, Cummings, Pauer and Ridley Prentice, and in 1889 inaugurated the degree of Maestro en Música. After his retirement he published a valuable monograph including his autobiography: 'Datos sobre la historia de la música en Colombia', *Boletín de historia y antigüedades*, xxii (1935), 623, 803.

ROBERT STEVENSON

Price, (Mary Violet) Leontyne (*b* Laurel, Mississippi, 10 Feb 1927). Black American soprano. While training as a teacher, she sang with her college glee club. In 1949 she won a scholarship to the Juilliard School, New York, where she sang Alice Ford. In 1952 Virgil Thomson chose her for a Broadway revival of his opera *Four Saints in Three Acts*; thereafter she was immediately engaged as Bess in a new production of Gershwin's opera, which later made a world tour, and in which she remained for two years. A concert career (including first performances of works by Barber and Sauguet) was interrupted by a highly successful television appearance as Tosca (1955). This, and appearances at San Francisco in 1957 (as Madame Lidoine in Poulenc's *Dialogues des Carmélites* and as Aida), decided the course of her career. At her débuts at the Verona Arena, Vienna and Covent Garden (all 1958) and La Scala (1960), she had further triumphs as Aida. In 1960 she first appeared at the Salzburg Festival as Donna Anna, returning there in 1962–3 as Leonora in *Il trovatore*; in the latter role she had made an acclaimed Metropolitan début (27 January 1961). A notable appearance among many in New York was as Cleopatra in Barber's *Antony and Cleopatra*, commis-

Leontyne Price in the title role of Verdi's 'Aida'

sioned for the opening of the new Metropolitan (1966); in 1975 she played Puccini's Manon there. Though her repertory has embraced Poppaea, Handel's Cleopatra, Tatyana, and Mozart and Puccini roles, it is principally in Verdi that she has achieved fame as one of the world's foremost sopranos. Her voice is a true *lirico-spinto*, able to fill Verdi's phrases with clean, full, dusky tone. Musically she is a subtle interpreter, though her acting does not always show great dramatic involvement. Many recordings, of Mozart, Puccini and especially Verdi operas, have faithfully documented her career.

She was married, 1952–72, to the American bass-baritone William Warfield (*b* 1920).

BIBLIOGRAPHY
A. Blyth: 'Leontyne Price talks', *Gramophone*, xlix (1971), 303
J. B. Steane: *The Grand Tradition* (London, 1974), 407ff
ALAN BLYTH

Price, Margaret (Berenice) (*b* Blackwood, Mon., 13 April 1941). Welsh soprano. As a student at Trinity College of Music she won several prizes. Soon after completing her studies she made her début with the Welsh National Opera in 1962, as Cherubino; the following year she replaced the indisposed Teresa Berganza in the same role at Covent Garden. At this time the conductor and pianist James Lockhart became her coach, accompanist and mentor; as a duo they gave many recitals, which included songs in five languages from a wide repertory (among them Musorgsky's *The Nursery* and Schoenberg's *Das Buch der hängenden Gärten*). In 1967 she appeared with the English Opera Group in *The Impresario*, as Titania (*A Midsummer Night's Dream*) and Galatea (*Acis and Galatea*). The next year she made an auspicious Glyndebourne début as Constanze; in later seasons she repeated the role there and played Fiordiligi. At Covent Garden she has appeared as Pamina, Marzelline (under Klemperer), Fiordiligi, Donna Anna and the Countess. Her German opera début in 1971 (Cologne, *Don Giovanni*) was highly successful, and led to many other European appearances. She first appeared in the USA at San Francisco in 1969 (Pamina), and at the Paris Opéra in 1973; there she also sang a much-praised Desdemona in 1976. Her television roles include Salud (*La vida breve*) and a remarkable Tatyana. Her voice is a full, round, warm lyric soprano capable of dramatic power and utterance. In all her Mozart roles her singing is admirably clean, shapely in phrase, both sweet and brilliant of tone, with fluent runs and immaculately negotiated intervals.

ALAN BLYTH

Price, Robert (*d* Herefordshire, 2 Nov 1761). English painter and musician. He was the son of Uvedale Price (1685–1761). About 1737 he travelled to Rome, where he studied painting, and music under Andrea Basili. He took part in amateur theatricals in Geneva, where he superintended the orchestra, painted the scenes, composed airs for the pantomimes and acted. After his return to England he married Sarah (*d* 1759), sister of the Hon. Daines Barrington. The couple were patrons of several musicians, including J. B. Malchair and J. C. Smith. According to his friend Benjamin Stillingfleet, Price had been impressed by Rameau's *Démonstration du principe de l'harmonie* (Paris, 1750) but perplexed by its arrangement and style. He consequently drew up a concise treatise in two parts: a scientific investigation of the principles of harmony, and an application of those

principles to the practice of composition. The MS is now lost. Price also composed music, and in 1759 was a steward at the meeting of the three choirs in Hereford.

WORKS
(*all first performed at King's Theatre, London*)
Arias: Aspri rimorsi, for N. Porpora's opera Temistocle (Zeno), 22 Feb 1743; La destra ti chiede, for N. Jommelli's opera Demofoonte (Metastasio), 9 Dec 1755; Se mai turbo, for pasticcio Alessandro nel India (Metastasio), 11 Dec 1755
6 sonatas, 2 vn, bc (London, *c*1760)

WRITINGS
'A Comparison of German and Italian Music', in J. Mainwaring: *Memoirs of the Life of the Late George Frederic Handel* (London, 1760/*R*1964, 1967)

BIBLIOGRAPHY
W. Coxe: *Literary Life and Select Works of Benjamin Stillingfleet* (London, 1811) [includes essays on Price by Stillingfleet and R. N. A. Neville]
JAMIE CROY KASSLER

Prick-song. A term current during the late 15th-century and the 16th to signify the notation of mensural music, and hence by association polyphonic music itself (as distinct from plainchant). Shakespeare (*Romeo and Juliet*, Act 2 scene iv) had Mercutio describe Tybalt as one who 'fights as you sing prick-song, keeps time, distance, and proportion; rests me his minim rest, one, two, and the third in your bosom'. The term 'pricking of musick bookes' was used to denote the writing of them. Details of payment for such work are often found in the accounts of cathedral and college choirs.

The word 'prick' was also used to denote the dot of addition and possibly other early uses of the dot, as described in Dowland's translation of Ornithoparchus's *Musicae activae micrologus* (London, 1609): 'A *Pricke* is a certaine indivisible quantity, added to the notes, either for *Division*, or for *Augmentation*, or for *Certainty* sake. Or it is a certaine Signe lesser than any other accidentally set either before, or after, or betweene notes'.

Priest, Josias [Josiah, Joseph] (?buried Chelsea, 20 April 1734). English dancing-master and dancer. The beginning of Priest's career is obscure. He was dancing on the London stage by 1667 and was in trouble for 'teaching, practising and executing music' without a licence in 1669. He arranged the witches' dances for Davenant's *Macbeth* with Locke's music in 1672 or 1673 and for Crowne's court masque *Calisto* in 1675. Priest also ran a boarding-school for young ladies, which moved from Leicester Fields to Chelsea in 1680. He commissioned Purcell's *Dido and Aeneas* for performance at his school in 1689 and must have arranged its 17 dances himself. His partnership with Purcell then moved on to the public stage, and his arrangements of the numerous and important dances for *The Prophetess* (*Dioclesian*) (1690), *King Arthur* (1691) and *The Fairy Queen* (1692) were highly praised. Priest can be traced in the Chelsea rate-books until 1714 and apparently died in 1734.

OLIVE BALDWIN, THELMA WILSON

Priestman, Brian (*b* Birmingham, 10 Feb 1927). English conductor. After studying at the University of Birmingham and at the Brussels Conservatory, he founded the Orchestra da Camera, Birmingham, and performed an enterprising repertory. He was music director of the Royal Shakespeare Theatre, Stratford-on-Avon, from 1960 to 1963, music director of the Edmonton SO, Canada, 1964–8, resident conductor of the

Baltimore SO, 1968–9, and music director of the Denver SO, 1970–78. In 1973 he became principal conductor of the New Zealand Broadcasting Corporation SO, and music director of the Miami Philharmonic, 1978–80. He was appointed professor of the University of Cape Town College of Music from 1981.

Priestman combines a sound classical style with a strong interest in contemporary music and a scholarly grasp of Baroque performance. He has given the premières of works by Gerhard, Ginastera, Joubert, Josephs and others. His recordings include three major Handel works – *Hercules*, *Rodelinda* and *Serse* – and he has published useful performing editions of *Messiah* and the *Water Music*.

BERNARD JACOBSON

Priest vicar. A member of the Anglican Church clergy; *see* CATHEDRAL MUSIC AND MUSICIANS, ANGLICAN.

Prieto, Claudio (*b* Muñeca de la Peña, Palencia, 24 Nov 1934). Spanish composer. He studied first in Madrid, with Ricardo Dorado and at the Escorial with Rubio; later he was a pupil of Petrassi in Rome. In 1964, the year in which he won the National Prize of the Sindicato Español Universitario, he settled in Madrid as a freelance composer. His technique extends from serialism to more experimental practices, with particular emphasis on new timbres, means of articulation and forms. Abstract in conception, the music has great constructive and expressive severity.

WORKS
(selective list)

3 movimientos, vn, ens, 1962; 3 piezas, str qt, 1963; Contrastes, orch, 1967; Oda XIV (Horace), S, ens, 1967; Sonidos, str qt, 1968; Solo a solo, fl, gui, 1969; Algemara, orch, 1970; Círculos, ens, 1970; Primera palabra, ens, 1971; El juego de la música, wind qnt, 1972; Nebulosa, orch, 1972; Catedral de Toledo, nuevos conceptos, orch, 1973; Reflejos, 4 cl, 1973

BIBLIOGRAPHY
T. Marco: *Música española de vanguardia* (Madrid, 1970)
TOMÁS MARCO

Prieto Arrizubieta, José Ignacio (*b* Gijón, 12 Aug 1900). Spanish composer and conductor. He studied the piano and harmony with Pedro Martínez in Bilbao. From 1924 until its disbandment in 1969 he was director of the schola cantorum of the Pontifical Seminary in Comillas, apart from a period (1927–30) when he undertook further studies with Lamote de Grignon, Lambert and Zamacois in Barcelona. He raised the schola to a high standard, continuing the work of its founder Otaño; he took them on tour to most European countries. In 1954 he made a long tour of Japan as a choral and orchestral conductor, and in the same year was appointed to teach harmony at the Pontificio Istituto di Musica Sacra in Rome, a post he held until 1960. He also conducted the Madrid University Chorus (1969–73). His works, which make use of advanced harmony and techniques of scoring, establish him as perhaps the leading Spanish composer of religious music of his time.

WORKS
(selective list)

Sacred: Misa jubilar, chorus, orch, 1943; Missa nova, unacc. chorus; Missa novissima, unacc. chorus; 3 Responsories, chorus; Eucarísticas, 1v, org; motets, etc

Secular: 3 coros en estilo madrigalesco, 1940; Sinfonía cántabra, orch, unpubd; Suite, E, orch, unpubd; Xavier (mystery-ballet), unpubd; other choral pieces

JOSÉ LÓPEZ-CALO

Prigozhin, Lyutsian Abramovich (*b* Tashkent, 15 Aug 1926). Soviet composer and teacher. He studied at the Tashkent Music School from the age of ten and then at the music school of the Leningrad Conservatory, which was evacuated to Tashkent during World War II. In 1945 he graduated in piano from the music college of the Leningrad Conservatory and entered Shcherbachov's composition class at the conservatory; he was a pupil of Kochurov from 1949 until his graduation. He joined the Composers' Union in 1950, and in 1964 he was appointed a board member of the Leningrad branch, whose chamber orchestral section he headed between 1969 and 1972. In 1967 he was appointed to teach theory and composition at the Leningrad Conservatory.

Prigozhin's mature works begin with the cantata *Sten'ka Razin* (1949–50), presented as a graduation piece; it clearly reveals his inclination towards epic and dramatic subjects, besides showing signs of important aspects of his individual style. During the following decade he composed in the most varied genres: instrumental (the Sinfonietta and the two symphonies met with great public success), vocal and 'applied'. The oratorio *Nepokorenniy Prometey* ('Prometheus unsubdued', 1960) was the first major work to display his distinctive style, which is exhibited in more concentrated form in the oratorio *Slovo o polku Igoreve* ('Lay of the host of Igor', 1966). In this piece, on an ancient Russian literary classic, Prigozhin brought life to myth and epic by means of a laconic thematicism absorbing *znamenniy* chant, the lyrical 'protracted' song, choral psalmody and ritual laments. The chamber oratorio *V'yuga* ('The snowstorm') and the chamber cantata *Predtechi* ('The precursors') continued in this direction. Emotional restraint, concentration, severity of colour and sharpness of rhythmic–melodic outline are also characteristic of Prigozhin's chamber pieces, among which the two violin sonatas and the String Quartet are outstanding.

WORKS
(selective list)

STAGE AND ORCHESTRAL

Operas: Ya sïn trudovovo naroda [I am a son of the working people] (after V. Katayev), 1951, unpubd; Doktor Aybolit (radio opera for children, Prigozhin, after K. Chukovsky), 1965, unpubd; Mal'chish-Kibal'chish (radio opera for children, S. Tikhaya, T. Svirina, after A. Gaydr), 1969, unpubd; Robin Gud (Yu. Dimitrin, after Eng. folk ballads), 1972, unpubd

Ballet: Krug ada [Circle of hell] (G. Glikman, M. Likhnitskaya, L. Ankudinova), 1964, unpubd, orch suite, 1964

Orch: Sinfonietta, 1953; Sym. no.1, 1955; Sym. no.2, 1957, rev. 1960

ORATORIOS AND CANTATAS

Oratorios: Nepokorenniy Prometey [Prometheus unsubdued] (after Aeschylus), chorus, orch, 1960; Slovo o polku Igoreve [Lay of the host of Igor] (old Russ., trans. Prigozhin), 2 solo vv, chorus, orch, 1966; V'yuga [The snowstorm] (after Blok: The Twelve), chamber oratorio, 2 solo vv, chamber chorus, cl, pf, perc, 1968

Cantatas: Sten'ka Razin (Pushkin, trad.), solo vv, chorus, orch, 1949, unpubd; Pesn'o khlebe [Song about bread] (A. Poperechnïy), chorus, orch, 1959; Predtechi [The precursors] (Aesop, Li Po, Wisdom of Solomon, Basho, Father-Superior Feodosy of Kiev), chamber cantata, 2 solo vv, ens, 1971, unpubd

OTHER WORKS

Choral: Krugovorot [Rotation] (Blok), 1973, unpubd; folksong arr.

Chamber: Music for Str and Fl, 1961; 2 sonatas, vn, pf, 1967, 1969; Str Qt, 1970; Musica rustica, wind qnt, 1973, unpubd

Songs for 1v, pf: 2 Songs (Burns), 1955; 3 Songs (Shakespeare, Burns), 1955; 2 songs from show 'Ostrov sokrovishch' [Treasure island], 1956; Pesnya matrosa [Sailor's song] (A. Cunningham) (1956); 2 Children's Songs (S. Morshak), 1956; 5 Songs (Svetlov), 1961; 3 English Ballads (trad.), 1966, unpubd

Pf: Kalendar' prirodï [Nature's calendar], 1962; Sonata, 1973; Sonatina, 1973

Music for the theatre, cinema and radio

Principal publishers: Muzgiz, Muzïka, Sovetskiy kompozitor

BIBLIOGRAPHY
M. Aranovsky: *L. Prigozhin: Simfon'yetta* (Leningrad, 1958)
A. Uteshev: *Lyutsian Prigozhin* (Moscow, 1959)
G. Orlov: 'Lyutsian Prigozhin', *Sovetskaya muzïka: stat'i i materialï*, ii (Moscow, 1966)
E. Ruch'yevskaya: 'Khudozhnik temperamentnïy, ishchushchiy' [A temperamental, searching artist], *SovM* (1970), no.11

A. KLIMOVITSKY

Příhoda, Váša (*b* Vodňany, 22 Aug 1900; *d* Vienna, 26 July 1960). Czech violinist. He was given childhood lessons by his father, who ran a music school, and at the age of ten he became a private pupil of Jan Mařák, professor at the Prague Conservatory. He began giving public concerts when he was 12, appeared at the Prague Mozarteum in 1913, and made his début with the Czech PO in 1915. He appeared in Switzerland, Yugoslavia and Italy in 1919, but the tour failed financially, and he was obliged to join a Milan café orchestra. A subscription concert brought him to the attention of Toscanini, whose praise opened the way to a successful tour of Italy early in 1920, followed by appearances in the USA, South Africa, South America and Europe. He also began teaching privately in Prague, and from 1936 at the Salzburg Mozarteum. During World War II he continued to give concerts in Germany, Austria and Bohemia, and taught at the Munich Academy of Music in 1944.

After being charged with collaboration with the Nazis, Příhoda left Czechoslovakia in 1946 and settled in Rapallo. In 1950 he took Turkish nationality; he moved to St Gilgen, and became a professor at the Vienna Academy of Music where he taught until his death. He returned to Czechoslovakia in 1956 for concerts at the Prague Spring Festival and elsewhere, and shortly before his death he sold his Stradivari violin, the 'Camposelice' dated 1710, to the Czechoslovak state. Příhoda was a romantic virtuoso whose subjective approach to music sometimes went beyond good taste and was not always completely in harmony with a work's stylistic demands, but his vibrantly expressive phrasing communicated spontaneous and passionate feeling. His excellent technique was best displayed in the works of Paganini. He made a number of gramophone records from the 1930s onwards, and composed several works for violin.

BIBLIOGRAPHY
ČSHS
O. Pičman: 'Váša Příhoda', *Za hudebním vzděláním* [For musical education], iv (1928–9), 65
B. Voldan: 'Náčrtek životopisu Váši Příhody od jeho učitele prof. Jana Mařáka' [Sketch of Váša Příhoda's life by his teacher Professor Jan Mařák], *Hudební výchova*, ix (1930), 75
B. Štědroň: 'Za Vášom Příhodom' [After Váša Příhoda], *SH*, iv (1960), 515 [obituary]
J. Vratislavský: *Váša Příhoda* (Prague, 1970) [incl. list of works and discography]
J. Creighton: *Discopaedia of the Violin, 1889–1971* (Toronto, 1974), 601ff

ALENA NEMCOVÁ

Prima (It.). (1) UNISON.
    (2) PRIME.

Prima donna (It.: 'first lady'). The principal female singer in the cast of an opera or in the roster of an opera company. In the documents reporting even the earliest opera productions special attention was focussed on the leading soprano, but the expression 'prima donna' seems to have come into common use only around the middle of the 17th century, with the opening of public opera houses. In Venice, where in any season several theatres were operating in competition, the ability of a famous leading lady to attract audiences became a matter of economic importance, and this served to feed the vanity of singers (not in any case among the least egotistical of beings) and led to the 18th-century cult of the prima donna, which has lasted ever since. The nature of the cult is evident from 18th-century terminology. Virtually every singer who gained the status of prima donna insisted on keeping that title, and any other female singer in the cast could at best be called 'seconda donna'. When conflicts arose managerial ingenuity devised such expressions as 'altra prima donna', 'prima donna assoluta', and even 'prima donna assoluta e sola'.

In some cases prima donnas made it a point of status to be difficult. For example, into the contracts of Adelina Patti (1843–1919) at the height of her career went not only the stipulation that her name appear on posters in letters at least one-third larger than those used for other singers' names, but also a clause excusing her from attending rehearsals. As a result of the notoriety that many female singers acquired, the term 'prima donna' entered the vocabulary as an expression for anyone (not necessarily a singer) who carries on in an outrageously egotistical manner. The abuses of the prima donna cult understandably inspired an outpouring of satirical writing, for example Benedetto Marcello's *Il teatro alla moda* (c1720) and librettos by Metastasio (*La cantante e l'impresario*, 1724), Calzabigi (*La critica teatrale*, 1769) and Casti (*Prima la musica, poi le parole*, 1786). The need to meet a prima donna's demands, however, shaped many librettos and opera scores, particularly because her status was reflected in the number and character of the arias allotted to her.

BIBLIOGRAPHY
H. Sutherland Edwards: *The Prima Donna: her History and Surroundings from the Seventeenth to the Nineteenth Century* (London, 1888/R1978)

OWEN JANDER

Prima prattica. The terms *prima prattica* and *seconda prattica* (then spelled *pratica*) arose during the controversy between Claudio Monteverdi and Giovanni Maria Artusi in the early years of the 17th century.

The expression *seconda prattica* first appeared in print in a letter which must have been written c1601 signed 'L'Ottuso Academico', reproduced by Artusi in *Seconda parte dell'Artusi* (1603). The term occurs in reference to the practice of rising after a flattened note and descending after a sharpened one, which l'Ottuso defends, saying that all the moderns are doing it, 'most of all those who have embraced this new second practice'. Artusi had criticized this and other melodic licences as well as the free introduction of dissonances in *L'Artusi, overo Delle imperfettioni della moderna musica* (1600). Only in 1605 did Monteverdi reply briefly to this public attack; in a prefatory letter to his fifth book of madrigals he promised to defend his new practices by considerations based on both the reason and the senses in an essay he would entitle *Seconda pratica overo Perfettione della musica moderna*. The second part of the title parodies Artusi's; the phrase *seconda pratica*, on the other hand, may have originated in the circles around Monteverdi or in Ferrara as a designation of the modern madrigal style.

Giulio Cesare Monteverdi, the composer's brother, attributed the term to Monteverdi in an explication ('Dichiaratione' in *Scherzi musicali*, 1607) of Claudio's brief preface which is a veritable manifesto for the new style. Giulio Cesare stated that in the first practice, for which Gioseffo Zarlino codified the rules, the paramount consideration for the composer was the 'harmony', or beauty of the contrapuntal part-writing, whereas in the second practice, for which Claudio hoped to sum up the rules, it is the text that reigns, and this obeys the precept of Plato, who proclaimed that in a song (*melos*), the *harmonia* (agreement or relation of sounds) and the *rhythmos* (time and rhythm) should follow the *logos* (word or thought) (*Republic* 398D). Giulio Cesare interpreted these words to mean that counterpoint and rhythm should be subordinated to the text. Thus, if the text demands certain crudities of harmony and melody or irregularities of rhythm, these departures from the correct usages of the first practice are justified for the sake of expressing the meaning and rhythm of the text.

Giulio Cesare named as masters of the first practice Ockeghem, Josquin, Pierre de La Rue, Jean Mouton, Crecquillon, Clemens non Papa and Gombert, and he considered it to have reached its perfection with Adrian Willaert. According to Giulio Cesare the second practice was 'revived' from that of the ancient Greeks by Cipriano de Rore, who then was emulated by Gesualdo, Emilio de' Cavalieri, Fontanelli, Bardi, Giovanni del Turco, Tomaso Pecci, Ingegneri, Marenzio, Wert, Luzzaschi, Jacopo Peri and Giulio Caccini.

Although these terms for the two practices were new, recognition of two diverse approaches to composition was apparently current when the controversy began. Girolamo Diruta (1609) distinguished between *contrapunto osservato*, strict counterpoint, and *contrapunto commune*, a freer modern style; Adriano Banchieri followed suit in *Cartella musicale* (1614). Both authors treated the two styles as if they existed side by side. The Monteverdi brothers, on the other hand, implied that the *seconda prattica* replaced the *prima*, although in fact a number of Monteverdi's sacred works are written in an idiom adapted from and adhering to the rules of the latter.

Marco Scacchi later pointed out (1649) that unlike the composers of *musica antica*, who had available only one practice and style, modern composers could choose between two practices – the first, *ut harmonia sit domina orationis* (in which harmony is mistress of the word), and the second, *ut oratio sit domina harmoniae* (in which the word is mistress of harmony) – and three styles, the church (*ecclesiasticus*), the chamber (*cubicularis*) and the stage (*scenicus*) or theatrical (*theatralis*). Scacchi's classification was further developed by his pupil Angelo Berardi and by Christoph Bernhard and J. J. Fux. It eventually served Johann Mattheson as the basis for a comprehensive classification of musical styles in *Der vollkommene Capellmeister* (1739/R1954).

BIBLIOGRAPHY

G. M. Artusi: *L'Artusi, overo Delle imperfettioni della moderna musica* (Venice, 1600)
——: *Seconda parte dell'Artusi* (Venice, 1603)
C. Monteverdi: *Il quinto libro de' madrigali* (Venice, 1605)
——: *Scherzi musicali* (Venice, 1607)
G. Diruta: *Seconda parte del Transilvano dialogo* (Venice, 1609)
A. Banchieri: *Cartella musicale nel canto figurato, fermo & contrapunto* (Venice, 1614)
M. Scacchi: *Breve discorso sopra la musica moderna* (Warsaw, 1649)
A. Tessier: 'Les deux styles de Monteverdi', *ReM*, iii (1922), 223–54
E. Katz: *Die musikalischen Stilbegriffe des 17. Jahrhunderts* (Freiburg, 1926), 83 ff [letter of M. Scacchi to Christoph Werner]
O. Strunk: *Source Readings in Music History* (New York, 1950), 383ff [translated extracts from Artusi (1600) and Monteverdi (1605, 1607)]
D. Arnold: ' "Seconda Pratica": a Background to Monteverdi's Madrigals', *ML*, xxxviii (1957), 341
W. Witzenmann: 'Stile antico e stile nuovo nella musica sacra di Claudio Monteverdi', *RIM*, ii (1967), 372
C. Palisca: 'The Artusi-Monteverdi Controversy', *The Monteverdi Companion*, ed. D. Arnold and N. Fortune (London, 1968), 133–66
J. Roche: 'Monteverdi and the *Prima Prattica*', ibid, 167
A. Gianuario: 'Proemio all' "oratione" di Monteverdi', *RIM*, iv (1969), 32
C. Palisca: 'Marco Scacchi's Defense of Modern Music (1649)', *Words and Music: the Scholar's View . . . in Honor of A. Tillman Merritt* (Cambridge, Mass., 1972), 189–235 [incl. Eng. trans. of Scacchi's *Breve discorso*]

CLAUDE V. PALISCA

Primas, Hugh. See HUGH PRIMAS OF ORLEANS.

Primavera, Giovan Leonardo (*b* Barletta, *c*1540–45; *d* ?Naples, after 1585). Italian composer and poet. He left Barletta for Naples where in about 1560 he was serving Fabrizio Gesualdo, to whom he dedicated his earliest madrigals. He lived in northern Italy from about 1565 to about 1578; his publications from this period were signed in Venice and many were addressed to northern patrons. According to the title-page of his fourth book of madrigals, *I frutti*, he was *maestro di cappella* for the Spanish governor of Milan, Luis de Requesens, who ruled from April 1572 to September 1573. This book was dedicated to Nicola Antonio Caracciolo, Primavera's former employer in Naples, who had moved to Venice in about 1571. Primavera included works by northern composers and poets in his publications. He wrote several *napolitane* expressly for northern audiences: four have texts which recall the villotta, and five contain specific references to Venice. Although there is no evidence that Primavera and Carlo Gesualdo founded a *Camerata di propaganda per l'affinamento del gusto musicale* in Naples, he had, however, returned to Naples by 1585 and was on good terms with Gesualdo, to whom he dedicated his seventh book of madrigals in that year.

Primavera's *napolitane* show in both poetry and music the influence of popular traditions. Like those of his southern contemporaries Troiano and Dell'Arpa, they proceed in short compact phrases with syllabic declamation on short note values. Homorhythmic textures with long chains of parallel 5ths predominate, although there are some imitative canzoni in book 3. The three voices, disposed in close position, move within a range which seldom exceeds a 10th. Strophes of changing rhymed couplets (e.g. *ABB, CDD, EFF, GHH*) in tripartite musical forms are common. The first two madrigal books consist mainly of settings of Petrarch's sonnets in the customary two parts; there is a complete sestina in book 7 (*Chi è fermato*). The other books contain poems by Primavera himself (who apologized for his 'little and badly composed rhymes'), Sannazaro, Tasso and Tansillo (*A cas'un giorno*). There are laments for Anna of Aragon and John of Austria, and madrigals as homage to Chiara Pisana, Vincenzo Gonzaga and Caracciolo. In the earlier madrigals, the music of the final line is often repeated; word-painting devices are used sparingly, although words signifying darkness are often symbolized by black notation.

WORKS

Il primo et secondo libro de madrigali, 5, 6vv (Venice, 1565[16])
Il primo libro de canzone napolitane, 3vv (Venice, 1565[17])
Il secondo libro de canzon napolitane, 3vv (Venice, 1566[15])
Il terzo libro de madrigali, 5, 6vv (Venice, 1566[13])
Il primo libro delle napolitane, 4vv (Venice, 1569[31])
Il terzo libro delle villotte alla napolitana, 3vv (Venice, 1570[31])
Il turturino: il primo libro delle [5] napolitane ariose da cantare et sonare nel leuto (Venice, 1570)
I frutti . . . libro quarto, 5, 10vv (Venice, 1573)
Il quarto libro de le canzoni napolitane, 3vv (Venice, 1574)
Il quinto libro di madrigali, 5vv (Venice, 1578)
Il sesto libro de madrigali, 5vv; lost, cited in Pitoni
Il settimo libro de madrigali, 5vv (Venice, 1585[31])
1 work, 4vv, 1566[2]; 1 work, 6vv, 1584[15]
2 works, Tarasconi Codex, nos.185, 200, I-Mc

BIBLIOGRAPHY

G. O. Pitoni: Notitia de contrapuntisti e de compositori di musica (MS, I-Rvat, C.G.I/1–2, c1725)
G. M. Monti: Le villanelle alla napoletana e l'antica lirica dialettale a Napoli (Città di Castello, 1925)
A. Einstein: The Italian Madrigal (Princeton, 1949/R1971)
B. M. Galanti: Le villanelle alla napolitana, Biblioteca dell' Archivum Romanicum, 1st ser., xxxix (Florence, 1954)
P. Sorrenti: I musicisti di Puglia (Bari, 1966)
D. G. Cardamone: The Canzone villanesca alla napolitana and Related Italian Vocal Part Music: 1537 to 1570 (diss., Harvard U., 1972)

DONNA G. CARDAMONE

Prima volta (It.: 'first time'). See VOLTA (iii).

Prime (Lat. prima, hora prima, ad primam). (1) The first of the LITTLE HOURS of the DIVINE OFFICE, recited at sunrise. It is combined with the monastic officium capituli, or prayers for God's blessing on the day's work. The martyrology is read at Prime. See also LITURGY OF THE HOURS.

(2) Another name for UNISON.

Primo (It.: 'first', 'principal'). In piano duets, the part for the player seated on the right and playing the upper parts of the piece.

Primo musico (It.: 'first musician'). A term used in the 17th and 18th centuries for the leading castrato in an opera or in an opera company (see MUSICO).

Primo uomo (It.: 'first man'). The principal male singer in the cast of an opera or in the roster of an opera company. Whereas in the first half of the 17th century there was a strong tendency in opera to focus attention on female protagonists (Eurydice, Ariadne, Poppaea, Dido, Helen of Troy etc), after about 1650 a trend developed towards opera plots in which the protagonists were historical heroes (Xerxes, Scipio Africanus, Alexander the Great etc). This new emphasis was due partly to papal decrees forbidding women performers in the theatre and also to the appearance of a large number of excellent castrato singers. Just as a leading lady had been given the title 'PRIMA DONNA', so a famous castrato now claimed the title 'primo uomo'. His importance is evident in the roles he sang, which were occasionally as extensive as those created for the prima donna herself. For example, in Handel's Giulio Cesare (1724) Cleopatra and Julius Caesar (first sung by Cuzzoni and Senesino respectively) each have eight arias. At first the term 'primo uomo' normally referred to a castrato, but during the 18th century it applied to leading tenors as well.

OWEN JANDER

Primrose (fl c1650). English composer. He was possibly employed as a household musician. From the muniments of Sir William Boteler (Butler) of Biddenham, Bedfordshire (d 1656), an eminent local patron, a prominent parliamentarian and apparently a keen musician, comes an MS partbook containing the bass parts of over 60 consort pieces for three viols by Jenkins, William Lawes, Hingeston, Blondill and 'Mr Primrose' (GB-BEcr TW 1172). The 11 consecutive Primrose pieces, all binary dances, are grouped into three-movement suites comprising Allmaine-Corant-Saraband, the final suite lacking a saraband (completed in the MS by a matching saraband by Jenkins). One of the complete suites also survives in full score, on three staves, on an accompanying sheet of paper, apparently in the same hand (TW 1173). This D minor suite, simple in harmony and texture, is less tautly constructed than Jenkins's work and is noteworthy only for some interesting hemiola rhythms in the corant.

An almande and some 'brandes' by Primrose are included, with music by other English composers, in the Dutch dance collection 'T uitnement kabinet (Amsterdam, 1646).

RICHARD MARLOW

Primrose, William (b Glasgow, 23 Aug 1903). Scottish violist. He studied the violin in Glasgow with Camillo Ritter then at the Guildhall School of Music, London, and in Belgium under Ysaÿe (1925–7), who advised him to change to the viola. He toured as a soloist and in the London String Quartet (1930–35). Toscanini chose him as principal viola in the NBC Orchestra (1937–42). He appeared as a soloist with orchestras in Europe and the USA, becoming the foremost viola virtuoso. Playing on a viola of moderate size, he produced a tone of rare sweetness and beauty.

In 1939 he formed the Primrose Quartet. In 1944 he commissioned Bartók to write a viola concerto, and gave the first performance of the work which was completed by Tibor Serly after Bartók's death. Among other composers inspired to write for him were Rubbra, Fricker and Hamilton. He formed the Festival Quartet (1955–62) from the faculty of the Aspen Music Festival. In 1962 the University of California at Los Angeles invited Heifetz, Piatigorsky and Primrose to teach their respective instruments and chamber music. In 1963 Primrose suffered a heart attack and, although he returned to the concert platform, in 1965 he joined the faculty of the school of music at Indiana University in Bloomington. In 1972 the Japanese Ministry of Education invited him to teach at the Tokyo University of Fine Arts and Music, and with this came an invitation to teach at Toho Gakuen in Tokyo and Suzuki's institute in Mutsumoto. In 1968 Primrose returned briefly to Glasgow to judge the finals of the BBC Viola Competition. In 1953 he was appointed CBE. His memoirs, Walk on the North Side, were published in 1978.

WATSON FORBES

Prin, Jean-Baptiste (b England, c1669; d Strasbourg, after 1742). French performer, composer, teacher and dancing-master. He was taught the trumpet marine by an English teacher and by his father, a French émigré bookdealer in England. His father must have been the M Prin that Samuel Pepys mentioned having heard at Charing Cross on 24 October 1667.

He is known to have been married in Lyons in January 1689. After 1698 he was a dancer in Paris as well as a performer on the trumpet marine. In 1704 he returned to Lyons, where he married again. Until his retirement to Strasbourg in 1737 he found employment as a teacher and player of the trumpet marine in Lyons, noting in his memoirs that he had caused more than 150 of the instruments to be constructed during these years. Church records show the baptism of a child of his third marriage in July 1735. One of his sons achieved some fame as a dancer and actor in Paris early in the century, and another became the director of the Comédie in Bordeaux in 1755.

In 1742 Prin donated his trumpet marine and his manuscripts to the academy at Lyons. The instrument was sold in 1792, but the manuscripts were deposited in the municipal library, where they still remain. In all they contain 216 different works for the trumpet marine. Of these, seven are attributed specifically to Prin, 56 to J. B. Lully, and one each to Hotteterre and Philidor. Those remaining, whether original or arrangements, are presumably by Prin. Altogether the manuscripts represent about 85% of the known literature for the instrument. His *Traité sur la trompette marine* treats its history, construction and performance.

Prin's music, much in the vein of the simpler instrumental pieces of the period, is written idiomatically for the trumpet marine. His melodies basically move stepwise; the few skips are harmonically orientated and are restricted to crotchet or longer rhythms because of the difficulty of performance. Similarly the slurs, carefully notated in the manuscripts, are restricted to two-note patterns. The only ornament discussed and employed by Prin is the trill, which is always indicated by a small cross.

About 80% of his music is cast in a binary dance form; about half of these works are non-modulating. Prin was particularly fond of the rounded binary form and the rondeau. In the latter form the trumpet marine does not play during the episodes, which are in other keys. In the former, however, modulations are made either to the dominant or subdominant, both of which are possible on the instrument.

WORKS

Livre de la musique du roy, 1702, *F-LYm* Res.133651 (165 pieces including 17 duets and Prin's 4 concerts)

Airs de trompette et viollons, 1718, *LYm* Res.133934 (75 pieces; vn 2 part missing)

Concert de trompette, haubois et viollons, 1724, *LYm* Res.133671 (4 vols. containing the accompaniment for the concerts)

Traité sur la trompette marine, 1742, *LYm* Res.133670 (includes 86 pieces, of which 16 are duets)

BIBLIOGRAPHY

L. Vallas: 'J.-B. Prin et sa méthode de trompette marine', *Revue musicale de Lyon*, ix (1911–12), 378

F. W. Galpin: 'Mr Prin and his Trompette Marine', *ML*, xiv (1933), 18

CECIL ADKINS

Prince. American melodeon manufacturers. About 1840 George A. Prince (*b* Boston, 17 Feb 1818; *d* Buffalo, 3 March 1890) established the firm George A.

Prince & Co. in Buffalo, New York; it was one of the first to attempt large-scale production of reed organs in the USA, employing 150 men and producing 75 instruments a week by 1846. Prince took out several patents in 1876 for improvements in melodeons. In 1847 Emmons Hamlin, then working for Prince, discovered a method of improving the tone of reeds by slightly bending and twisting the tongue. In 1854 Hamlin left Prince, and, with Henry Mason, son of Lowell Mason, founded the Mason & Hamlin Organ & Piano Co., which dominated reed organ manufacturing in the USA in the late 19th century. Hamlin also introduced the double bellows during the 1850s while in Prince's employ. In the 1860s Prince began making larger reed organs, including the 'New Organ Melodeon', which had two manuals, four sets of reeds, and one and a half octaves of pedals. The firm went into bankruptcy in 1875.

BIBLIOGRAPHY

R. F. Gellerman: *The American Reed Organ* (Vestal, NY, 1973)

BARBARA OWEN

Princess's Theatre. London theatre opened in 1840; *see* LONDON, §IV, 3.

Princes Theatre. London theatre built in 1911; *see* LONDON, §IV, 3.

Principal. An ORGAN STOP; *see also* PRINCIPALE.

Principale [Principal, Prinzipal, Prinzipale]. A trumpet register and a style of playing from the 16th century to the 18th. In its widest sense, principale refers to the low register of the natural trumpet from C to *c''*, as opposed to clarino, from *c''* upwards. The terms 'Principale' (the register) and 'Principalblasen' (playing in the principale register) were German, and were not used in other countries. Ex.1 shows the range of the natural trumpet, together with the Italian and German designations both of the individual notes and also of the various registers of the instrument, each centred on a certain note.

The natural trumpet was used in two ways: as a solo instrument for signalling purposes, it was played in the principale register (*see* SIGNAL); and for ceremonial purposes several players banded together in a 'corps'. From about 1585 to 1685, according to Bendinelli, Monteverdi, Fantini, Praetorius, Schütz and Speer, the trumpet corps consisted of from five to seven players, who improvised in specific registers of their instrument, termed – from top to bottom – clarino, quinta, alto e basso, volgano and basso (to use the Italian terminology). From about 1685 to 1800 three parts, two clarinos and one principale, became common; the best example of this kind of writing is Handel's 'Dettingen' *Te Deum*. If a fourth part was added, it had the same

Ex.1 The registers of the natural trumpet

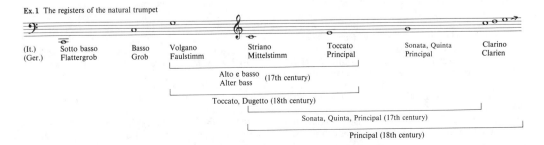

(It.)	Sotto basso	Basso	Volgano	Striano	Toccato		Sonata, Quinta	Clarino
(Ger.)	Flattergrob	Grob	Faulstimm	Mittelstimm	Principal		Principal	Clarien

Alto e basso / Alter bass (17th century)

Toccato, Dugetto (18th century)

Sonata, Quinta, Principal (17th century)

Principal (18th century)

notes as the kettledrums and was called toccato, dugetto or the like. (Or, in the writing of Austrian composers, the two lower parts were called tromba 1 and 2 and the two upper parts clarino 1 and 2.)

The principale player had to develop a strong and blasting tone (Ger. *schmettern*, to blast). He also had to excel in the use of double and triple tonguing, regarded by many as the noblest aspect of trumpet playing. In the field, where he was used for signalling purposes, the trumpeter was also entrusted with courier duties, carrying messages to the enemy; the dangers of such assignments are vividly recounted by J. E. Altenburg: *Versuch einer Anleitung zur heroisch-musikalischen Trompeter- und Pauker-Kunst* (Halle, 1795/R1968), pp.41ff.

REINE DAHLQVIST, EDWARD H. TARR

Pring, Katherine (*b* Brighton, 4 June 1940). English mezzo-soprano. She studied at the RCM, London, and at the Geneva Conservatory, joining Sadler's Wells Opera in 1968. She made her Covent Garden début in 1972 as Thea in Tippett's *The Knot Garden*, and first sang at Bayreuth the same year. Her wide repertory includes Dorabella, Azucena, Preziosilla, Eboli, Carmen, Santuzza, and both Waltraute and Fricka in the English National Opera's *Ring* cycle. An intelligent and highly dramatic artist, she has also appeared in many 20th-century operas, as Jocasta (*Oedipus rex*), Kate (Britten's *Owen Wingrave*) and Agave, which she sang with great success in the first British performances of Henze's *The Bassarids* at the Coliseum (1974). Her voice is of lyrical quality and weight, but excellent projection and fine diction enable her to sing the heavier roles in the German and Italian repertories without difficulty.

ELIZABETH FORBES

Prinner [Preiner], **Johann Jacob** (*b* ?Münzbach, 1624; *d* Vienna, 18 March 1694). Austrian composer, organist, poet and music theorist. He was educated partly in Italy, studying in Siena in 1651. He appears to be identical with the J. J. Preiner who was organist at the abbey church at Kremsmünster, Upper Austria, from 1 July 1652 to 1 September 1659. At the end of 1670 J. H. Schmelzer, praising Prinner as composer, organist and poet, described him as Kapellmeister at the court of Prince Eggenberg at Graz. The latter was dismissing his musicians at the time, so Schmelzer recommended Prinner for the post left vacant by Biber at the court of the Prince-Bishop of Olomouc at Kroměříž, but P. J. Vejvanovský was appointed; since, however, some suites by Prinner, one dated 1676, survive at Kroměříž, he may nevertheless have lived there for a time. The petition he addressed to the Emperor Leopold I on 7 November 1680, asking to be made chamberlain to Archduchess Maria Antonia, in Vienna, discloses that he taught her the harpsichord. The petition was granted, but when in 1685 the archduchess moved to Bavaria on her marriage to the Elector Maximilian Emanuel, Prinner remained in Vienna. He drew an annual pension of 420 florins from the imperial court until his death.

Prinner's 47 arias for soprano and continuo are settings of verses in several stanzas; he himself probably wrote the texts, some of which are in dialect. They are unpretentious songs in the popular Viennese style, similar to the German songs of Leopold I and Schmelzer. Some of the melodies may have originated in Viennese dance music and street songs and have been provided with new texts. The influence of French instrumental music is also discernible. In his suites Prinner added to the standard movements introductory and closing movements as well as a gavotte or aria between the saraband and gigue.

Prinner's *Musicalischer Schlissl* (autograph, 1677, *US-Wc*) presents the fundamental principles of his teaching of theory. The treatise contains an outline of the rudiments of music and thoroughbass, but this is unimportant compared with the contemporary treatises on the latter subject by Poglietti and Georg Muffat. The most valuable section of the volume is that containing detailed instructions for the technique of playing string instruments. The most notable of these is Prinner's recommendation that the violin should be held by the chin as the only means of leaving the left hand free to execute the fingering correctly without needing also to support the instrument. He expressly condemned players who rest their violins on the chest. He followed French practice in the technique of bowing, but was acquainted only with Italian ondeggiando technique and not with its French equivalent. The sections on counterpoint and rhetorical figures follow closely – often word for word and with the same examples – Christoph Bernhard's *Ausführlicher Bericht vom Gebrauche der Con- und Dissonantien*. Prinner condemned as fashionable folly the preference shown in Austria for foreign artists (that the Emperor Leopold I shared this view is illustrated by his appointment of Fux as composer to the imperial court in 1698 despite the opposition of the Italian musicians there).

WORKS

Suites in *CS-KRa*: Serenata canicularis, a 4; 2 balleti francesi, a 4 (inc.); balletti, a 4 (dated March 1676)

47 arias, S, bc, autograph *c*1680–85, *D-Mbs*; 13, ed. W. Vetter, *Das frühdeutsche Lied*, ii (Münster, 1928); 3 in Nettl (1934); 1, ed.in Mw, xv (1957; Eng. trans., 1958)

Suites, str, lost

BIBLIOGRAPHY

P. Nettl: 'Die Wiener Tanzkomposition in der 2. Hälfte des 17. Jahrhunderts', *SMw*, viii (1921), 158

——: 'Zur Geschichte der Musikkapelle des Fürstbischofs Karl Liechtenstein-Kastelkorn von Olmütz', *ZMw*, vi (1921–2), 487

——: *Das Wiener Lied in Zeitalter des Barock* (Vienna and Leipzig, 1934), 22ff; appx, 6ff

H. Federhofer: 'Eine Musiklehre von J. J. Prinner', *Festschrift Alfred Orel zum 70. Geburtstag* (Vienna and Wiesbaden, 1960), 47

——: *An Essay on Thoroughbass by Georg Muffat* (1699), MSD, iv (1961), 13ff

R. Flotzinger and G. Gruber, eds.: *Musikgeschichte Österreichs*, i (Graz, 1977), 335

HELLMUT FEDERHOFER

Printing and publishing of music.

I. Printing. II. Publishing.

I. Printing. Printing is a technique for producing many identical copies taken from raised, incised or plane surfaces: that is, from type or from wood or metal blocks cut in relief; from copper, pewter or other metals engraved and punched; from stone or metal plates bearing an image imperceptibly raised. These, generally called letterpress, intaglio and lithographic printing, have each been used for printing music, and each has enjoyed a period of pre-eminence. This waxing and waning was not in the lineal order of a successor taking the place of its antecedent: over long periods the processes were in use side by side, the unique qualities of each employed for some particular purpose. At the beginning of the 19th century, for example, Breitkopf & Härtel were printing music from type, from engraved plates and from lithographic stones concurrently; and it is only since about the 1960s that music type has all but disappeared from the case rooms of printing offices.

1. Early stages and woodblock printing. 2. Printing music from type. 3. Engraving. 4. Lithography and more recent processes.

1. EARLY STAGES AND WOODBLOCK PRINTING. Before the technique of printing was established and exploited widely, music was preserved and circulated in manuscript, or survived as a repertory carried in oral tradition among priests and professional lay musicians. During the latter part of the 15th century and the 16th printing became the accepted means by which works of literature, history, philosophy and scientific speculation were multiplied and disseminated in hundreds of copies – school primers by the thousand; but vocal and instrumental music was still circulated in handwritten form. Manuscripts were prepared for sale in this way at least until the beginning of the 19th century: the names of Foucault in Paris, Traeg in Vienna, Breitkopf in Leipzig and Ricordi in Milan recall the continuity and significance of this tradition. The dichotomy between the means chosen to perpetuate the 'word' on the one hand and the 'note' on the other arises no less from social and economic factors than from technological ones: and it raises questions about the spread of musical literacy, about the regulation of printing by state institutions, about the size and nature of the musical public and the scale of the market – national and international – at any given time. These issues have to be borne in mind, for each was one of the forces influencing, and reacting with, changes in technology.

The early stages of music printing show a diversity of technical solutions, for it cannot be claimed that music adapted itself immediately to the printed page. It first appeared, albeit in manuscript, in the *Codex spalmorum* signed by Fust and Schoeffer in Mainz in August 1457. Sir Irvine Masson in his study of the surviving copies of this superb book found evidence that 'although no music was printed the compositors made the most careful provision for its being added by hand', and after citing examples suggested that 'no doubt the compositors of the psalter worked from manuscript which was musically complete'. If that is so, then those who subsequently wrote the music – using different styles of notation – were very careless. For example in the exceptionally fine copy in the library of the queen at Windsor a splendid red printed initial on folio 29*b* driven well into the vellum has been unskilfully erased to accommodate a melody notated in Gothic style: in the British Library copy the corresponding initial has been written over.

This pattern with its resulting infelicities was characteristic of many liturgical books printed during the 15th century and even into the 16th. Sometimes space for music was left blank on the page, sometimes the staff lines were printed (in red, only exceptionally in black). Presumably the music necessary to complete the text was added by professional scribes attached to the court, cathedral or monastery where the books were to be used, but however well written, the result is generally unsatisfying to the eye. The notes and the staves have to be scaled to the space left by the printer. The ink is dull and the music as a whole cannot hold its own against the strength, and in some cases the nobility, of the letter forms in which the text is printed.

The principal reason for the survival of this makeshift technique has often been assumed to be that liturgical usage in music, even in the words of the Offices, was not uniform throughout the Western church in the 15th century. Dioceses and monastic establishments introduced variants of the accepted text of Rome and the musical expression of the different uses diverged even more. It was common sense for the printer, therefore, to omit from his books – expensive as they were to produce – those elements that would restrict his sale to one market. Even though many titles exist which suggest that only one diocese could use them, they were in fact often suitable for sale elsewhere, if the music were not printed. Martin Morin of Rouen signed a *Missale ad usum Sarum* 12 October 1492 in which a space was left for music and for the English in the marriage service to be added; in about 1500 he printed another *Missale ad usum Sarum* where blanks were left for the music but the responses in the marriage service were printed in English (both in *GB-Lbm*).

The basic problems of music printing using wholly typographic means had been solved by about 1473, for a gradual which has survived in a single copy (*GB-Lbm*) has notes, staves, clefs (F and C), two vertical lines that abut on to the staves at each end, and text, all printed in black at two impressions (see fig.1). Large initials for which the printer left space have been rubricated by hand and an additional red line has been drawn on the staves to indicate the position of F. Unfortunately the book does not bear a date, nor is the printer or the place of printing known, but the pages themselves are eloquent: they have been planned and achieved by a rational mind thinking in typographic terms. The relationship between the depth of the type area and the measure between the vertical lines that extend above and below the seven five-line systems is nicely judged; so is the interval between the individual staff lines in relation to the size of the Gothic notes and the size and the visual 'weight' of the text type, although it appears from the irregularity of the fount that the matrices were not well struck and justified.

A passage on leaf vii*a* of Jean Charlier de Gerson's *Collectorium super Magnificat* (Esslingen: Conrad Fyner, 1473) where five identical black squares are shown descending in regular steps above the names of the principal notes of a scale hardly qualifies as music printing. The true successor to the 1473 gradual appeared in Rome where on 12 October 1476 Ulrich Hahn completed *Missale secundum consuetudinem curie romane* and in the colophon claimed to have been the first to print music 'non calamo ereove stilo: sed novo artis ac solerti industrie genere Rome conflatum impressumque unacum cantu: quod numquam factum extitit'. Hahn's work is outstanding in quality. The text of the Office is printed in red and black with a superb type in two columns. The notes in Roman notation are printed in black on red staff lines made up from pieces of rule the length of the column measure. Initials in red or blue, with touches of yellow in some capitals, are added by hand. As in the gradual of 1473, but here in a masterly way, the relationship of the parts is calculated to achieve a unity that satisfies, and one which is wholly efficient.

The missal was Hahn's only book containing music, but his methods were copied – though at an interval of five years – throughout Europe. Richel printed a *Missale constantiensis* in Basle before 1481; Reyser printed a *Missale herbipolense* at Würzburg in 1481;

1. *Page from the Constance Gradual (GB-Lbm IB 15154, f.1r), the first printed music (? southern Germany, c1473)* [*73% of actual size*]

Scotus printed two missals in Venice in 1482, and in the same year at Milan Valdarfer printed a *Missale ambrosianum*. In 1489 in Paris Higman and Hopyl printed a *Missale andegavense*; two years later the Compañeros Alemanes produced an *Antiphonarium Ord. S Hieronymi* in Seville. It was not until 1500 that Hahn's technique reached England, but the *Missale Sarum* printed by Pynson in London in that year was a splendid book worthy to be set alongside its exemplar.

Altogether, liturgical books with music – notes and staves – printed at two impressions were produced in at least 25 towns by 66 printers between 1476 and 1500. Most of the printers are represented by only one or two books, but others clearly were specialists: Ratdolt, the splendid printer of Augsburg, was responsible for 13; Higman, a most refined craftsman, produced 12 in Paris; Johannes Emericus de Spira in Venice printed no fewer than ten in seven years; Sensenschmidt of Bamberg produced seven; and Wenssler of Basle produced five.

Those who needed printed books for the celebration of religious Offices were well served, as were the authors of works on the theory of music, though by different technical methods. For historical reasons, discussions of music theory during the Middle Ages and early Renaissance were built on an arithmetical basis: thus manuscripts contain diagrams of ratios and relationships as well as notes. When these treatises and polemical discourses were printed, the diagrams and sometimes simple arithmetic were reproduced by woodcuts. (The tradition of block cutting was already well established throughout Europe in the 15th century and many early printed books had been decorated with splendid woodcut initials and borders, and with representations of buildings, animals and people.) It was therefore easy to extend the practice to the music, though in some texts spaces were left in the printed page for the notes and staves to be written in. The technique offered great advantages. The musical material was not complicated and the examples were usually short; many models of the required notation were available. Unless musical types and the knowledge of how to use them were available locally it was natural that the printer should turn to a woodcutter, a craftsman more likely to be within call than a typesetter.

It is nevertheless difficult to account for the poor quality of much of early woodcut music. The technique was essentially simple. But it demanded judgment and manual dexterity and control from the operator to produce a block with the text and music reading from right to left, precise in every detail on a flat surface with everything else cut away. The graphic nature of music – a system of horizontal and vertical lines crossing at right angles with associated elements, notes, clefs and other signs, imposing shapes and angles of their own – presented difficulties. Unless the point of intersection of staff and note stem were cut very clean, and subsequently inked and printed with care, the ink tended to blob or spread at the junction. To avoid this some cutters left a small nick breaking the surface at the intersection, to reduce the density of the film of ink at this point. For the same reason it was not easy to cut open (white) notes with a staff line at its proper thickness running through.

Woodcut music from the 15th and 16th centuries varies enormously in extent and quality: this is to be expected, taking into consideration the large amount

that was produced. From 1500 to 1600, 326 separate works on the theory of music were issued in a total of 611 editions by 225 printers in 75 towns throughout Europe (see Davidsson, 1965). Some of the texts were remarkably popular, running through 30 editions in 49 years, or 40 editions in 63 years, repeated sometimes in the same form by the first printer, sometimes with new blocks for the music, sometimes with the originals, and sometimes by a different printer in the same town or elsewhere.

The following well-known early examples of music printed from blocks may be cited. The *Grammatica brevis* of Franciscus Niger, in its second edition printed in Basle (*c*1485) has a few pages with four lines of notes without staves (but with a clef) to illustrate the rhythms of five different poetic metres using verses from Virgil, Lucan, Ovid and Horace. This was followed by the *Musices opusculum* of Nicolaus Burtius, printed in Bologna by Ugo de Rugeriis for Benedictus Hectoris in 1487 (see fig.2*a*). Woodcuts were used to show the hymn *Ut quaeant laxis*, specimens of note forms and ligatures and, in the section on counterpoint, a short complete composition for three voices, all with staves. The cutting is thick and unskilful. In contrast to this hesitant performance the treatment of the music in *Flores musice omnis cantus Gregoriani* by Hugo Spechtshart of Reutlingen, printed in Strasbourg by Johann Prüss in 1488, is accomplished. As its title suggests, the practice of plainchant is treated in detail: the music, in Gothic notation on five lines with clef and directs, appears on 67 pages mostly occupying the whole panel. The second edition (*c*1490) is usually overlooked, but the cutting and printing of new blocks for the music in quite different notation is equally accomplished. The last two pages of *Historica beatica* (a play by Carolus Veradrus) printed by Eucharius Silber (Rome, 1493) are followed by a four-part song, which is the first printing of dramatic music, although the cutting of the block is not good. As King wrote, 'this is probably the earliest German secular song, found in *Von sant Ursulen schifflin* (Strasbourg, 1497) is also reproduced by an unusual use of this process – the notes (in Gothic form), the staves, and the text all being cut on wood'. Perhaps Andrea Antico was unaware of this when in *Liber quindecim missarum* (*RISM* 1516[1]) he said that he cut the notes in wood which nobody before him had done. This splendid folio of 161 pages is set off with fine initial letters and the work is a remarkable technical achievement, though the impression is rather flat and heavy (fig.2*b*). Antico had no imitators in printing large-scale collections of music from woodblocks, though woodcutting of the highest artistry may be seen in Luther's *Geistliche Lieder* printed by Valentin Bapst (Leipzig, 1545). Although these books are outstanding, there is much to admire in the decorative touches that enliven many more workaday theoretical treatises, for example, the illustration showing a priest playing an organ in the *Theorica musicae* of Gaffurius (Milan, 1492). In Gregor Reisch's *Margarita philosophica*, a full-page cut is printed as a part title before the main divisions. The section devoted to arithmetic, music, geometry and astronomy is prefaced with a woodcut showing among other features a group of musicians. The composition and cutting of the block in the first edition of 1503 (Freiburg: Johann Schott) is somewhat rudimentary but the corresponding block in the edition of 1504 (Strasbourg: J. Grüninger) is finer both in design and in execution.

2. Two examples of music printed from woodblocks: (a) page showing note forms and ligatures from the 'Musices opusculum' of Nicolaus Burtius, printed by Ugo de Rugeriis for Benedictus Hectoris (Bologna, 1487); (b) beginning of the Kyrie from Pipelare's 'Missa L'homme armé', part of a page from the 'Liber quindecim missarum' printed by Andrea Antico (Rome, 1516), exemplifying woodcutting of the highest technical and artistic achievement [(a) 47%, (b) 27% of actual size]

It is normally stated of such works that the blocks were cut in wood. It might be more precise to say 'wood or perhaps metal'. It is very difficult to resolve which is used by inspecting a well-printed page. It is feasible that an ill-prepared woodblock, inadequately inked, might show grain, though no examples are known. Nor is evidence for the use of metal easier to come by. Comparison of numerous copies of a book in a single edition, or of copies in different editions, sometimes yields results. In the first edition of *Practica musicae* by Gaffurius, printed by Guillermus Le Signerre for Johannes Petrus de Lomatio (Milan, 1496), the examples of plainchant and mensural notation are well cut and printed without blemish. The edition of 1508 (Brescia: Angelo Britannico) was printed using the same blocks, but small circles appear in association with music on two folios. This suggests that the music was cut on a plate nailed to a wooden mount, and that a careless beater inked the heads of the nails, which printed. In the edition of 1512 (Venice: Agostino Zani) some musical examples are slanting, which again suggests that the printing surface was mounted – and carelessly – because the forme could not have been locked up unless all the type, furniture and associated material were properly squared: this again suggests a metal plate rather than a woodblock. Such plates for illustrations in 16th-century books have survived with flanges pierced to take mounting nails.

However this may be, the use of wood or metal blocks to print music, usually in small books, librettos and similar volumes, continued into the 19th century.

The first music to be printed in America, the ninth edition of the *Bay Psalm Book* (Boston: B. Green and J. Allen, 1698), was taken from woodblocks (*see* PSALMS, METRICAL, ex.28).

2. PRINTING MUSIC FROM TYPE. The processes used to print music from type are the same as those used for literary texts (see fig.3). The type has to be made in the normal manner – cutting the design on a punch, using the punch to strike a matrix and then casting as many copies of the pattern as needed (more minims than breves, for example). Spaces of varying widths are also cast so that notes can be separated as required by the music. The type is set up by a compositor working from a copy manuscript that has been marked to show line-ends and other details of layout. A manuscript for Christopher Simpson's *Principles of Practical Musick* (1665) has survived and is marked in this way (*GB-T*). The actual printing of the prepared copy is not affected by the material to be printed – text, pictures or music – and the normal press was used.

The techniques of printing plainchant were highly developed by 1500, but there was no corresponding evolution in the printing of mensural music from type during the same period: attempts were isolated and restricted in scope. The first example, four lines on a single page, appeared in the first edition of Franciscus Niger's *Grammaticus* (Venice: Theodor of Würzburg, 1480): only the notes and clef were printed, accurately aligned for anybody to rule the staves. Other examples appear in two books printed by Michel de Toulouse in

Paris, both undated and assigned to about 1496. One was an edition of *Utilissime musicales regule* by Guillermus Guerson and the other an anonymous treatise *L'art et instruction de bien danser* (a unique copy is in the Library of the Royal College of Physicians, London). Music appears on 18 pages of the latter, mostly in chant notation, printed black on four red lines, but there are almost two pages of music in mensural notation. At first glance the achievement is not impressive but closer examination shows that, although the type from which the notes are printed has been badly cast, their typographical arrangement was workmanlike.

In Venice there were moves that transformed music printing and made polyphonic music generally available in greater quantity and over wider areas than ever before. The innovator was Ottaviano dei Petrucci of Fossombrone. In about 1490 he went to Venice apparently to study the technique of printing in order to devise a method for printing music from movable type. In 1498 he obtained from the Signoria of Venice an exclusive 20-year privilege for printing and selling music for voices, organ and lute throughout the Venetian Republic. His first book was published in 1501: *Harmonice musices odhecaton A* (*RISM* 1501), a collection of 96 pieces arranged as partsongs with the cantus and tenor on the left-hand page of an opening and the altus and bassus on the right – a layout modified satisfactorily for three-part items. A second edition appeared in 1502/3 and a third in 1503/4. Altogether he printed at least 43 musical titles in Venice, the latest in 1509. He returned to Fossombrone in 1511 and printed there until 1520. His later music printing deteriorated in appearance: the type looks worn and the system less well organized.

Petrucci's music printing was splendid. His note forms were abundant and with their equivalent rests varied enough to set the most elaborate works of the composers of his day. The characters were elegant, the punch-cutting, justification of the matrices and typecasting were accomplished. The presswork was so meticulous that he was consistently able to achieve perfect register of notes, staves and text though (at least

initially) three impressions were required: first for the staves, second for the notes, and third for the text, initial letters, signatures and page numbers. The whole achievement immediately conveys typographical conviction which on analysis is found to derive from a skilful choice of size for individual elements – notes, key signatures, the staff system, clefs etc – and from the manner in which they are related. For example, the length of a note stem is the depth of four spaces on the staff, a relationship that has persisted to our own day: the stem of the B♭ key signature is longer than the stem of a note and in this way maintains its role as a flag. The directs are very noticeable, serve their purpose and balance the large initials and other display material at the left of the staves. Only by the use of notes, letters and spaces, all casts in sizes that worked exactly together without bodging, could such results be achieved. (Petrucci had equal success with his system of tablature, the first to be printed from movable type; see fig.4.) It is not known who cut the punches for these founts and justified the matrices. Francesco Griffo of Bologna, a brilliant punch-cutter, who was the first to cut 'littera cursiva' (italic) types, under commission from the printers Soncino and Aldus Manutius, worked with Petrucci in Fossombrone in 1511, but there is no evidence that they had collaborated earlier in Venice.

The shining example of Petrucci encouraged other printers into imitation. The first was Erhard Oeglin of Augsburg who issued *Melopoeiae sive Harmoniae* (1507: settings by Petrus Tritonius and others of Horace's odes) and a few later titles. The books do not achieve the elegance of Petrucci but Oeglin made good register with his two workings. His staff lines are assembled from short pieces of type. A book on the grand scale (folio: $44 \times 28 \cdot 5$ cm) which approaches Petrucci's quality is the *Liber selectarum cantionum quas vulgo mutetas appellant, sex quinque et quatuor vocum* (Augsburg: Grimm and Wirsung, 1520[4]). The hand of a master is seen in *Rerum musicarum*, a treatise by Johannes Frosch (Strasbourg: Peter Schoeffer jr and Mathias Apiarius, 1535): the scale of the work is much along the lines of Petrucci's and the achievement, by two impressions, is comparable. The sole surviving part (trip-

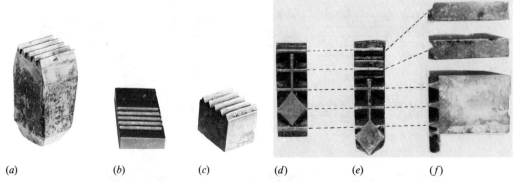

(a)   (b)   (c)   (d)   (e)   (f)

3. Steps in making music type illustrated by material from the 'grande musicque' cut by Hendrik van den Keere for Christopher Plantin (1577): (a) steel punch with a five-line staff system engraved in relief on its end; (b) matrix produced by striking the punch into a billet of copper (here c20 mm wide) to leave the staff lines recessed; (c) type cast from the matrix; (d) type cast with the matrix in 'normal' position in the mould; (e) note head from the same matrix projecting below the normal position of the lowest staff line; (f) type shown in (e) turned on its side to show that the projecting note head was cast with only three lines attached and completed by two additional types, each carrying a separately cast segment of staff line; (d), (e) and (f) illustrate the principle of 'kerning' or overhang

4. *Part of a page from Joan Ambrosio Dalza's 'Intabolatura de lauto' (f.3v) printed by Petrucci (Venice, 1508); the decorative initial and unbroken staff lines indicate that the sheet was passed through the press at least twice, as in the method devised by Petrucci for printing mensural music*

5. *Part of a page from 'XX Songes' (London, 1530), showing the beginning of Taverner's 'Love wyll I' [67% of actual size]*

6. *Part of a page from the 'Liber primus missarum' of Carpentras (signature A2), the first printed music with oval note heads (Avignon, 1532; cut by Etienne Briard, printed by Jean de Channey)*

lex) of *XX Songes* printed 'at the sign of the Black Morens' in London in 1530 (*RISM* 1530⁶) is equally elegant and well printed (see fig.5).

In 1532 Jean de Channey printed at Avignon, at the composer's expense, the first of four volumes of sacred music by Carpentras. Although oval note heads had appeared in the woodcut music of J. F. Locher's *Historia de rege frantie* (Freiburg: F. Riederer, 1495; copy in *GB-En*), the Carpentras books are remarkable as the first to use type cast with a rounded, almost oval note form instead of the traditional lozenge and square. Cut by Etienne Briard of Bar-le-Duc, the open notes have stems with a strong downward stroke followed through with a splendid calligraphic swing, swelling and diminishing to reconnect with the stem. The black notes are rather lifeless by comparison. Briard not only abandoned the accepted note forms but cast aside the whole system of proportional notation and replaced complicated ligatures with single notes. The music was printed in two impressions (see fig.6).

By this time a great step forward had been taken elsewhere, marked by the survival of fragments of two anonymous pieces printed by John Rastell in London (perhaps in 1526, or earlier) each of which survives in a unique copy (*GB-Lbm*). One, printed on part of a broadside, is an incomplete song for one voice; the other is a three-part song 'Tyme to pas with goodly sport' which is in Rastell's play *A New Interlude and a Mery of the Nature of the iiii Elements* (for illustration *see* RASTELL, JOHN). The fragments are remarkable because the music – notes and staves – the clefs, indications of key, and the words were all printed together at one impression. This was made possible by casting the note and a fragment of a complete set of staff lines on the same type body. Spacing-pieces of various widths bearing only fragments of staff lines were used to maintain continuous systems between notes. The type, not undistinguished in design, looks rather shaky on the page, and as far as is known was used only once more – in Coverdale's *Goostly Psalmes* (c1538); but if the date assigned to it by King is accepted – and his argument is close-knit and dispassionate – Rastell 'can be credited with several achievements: the earliest mensural music printed in England; the earliest broadside with music printed from type anywhere in Europe; the earliest song printed in an English dramatic work. Rastell also made the first attempt at printing a score, by any process in any country'.

If this survival is regarded as a freak with no known progenitor and without issue the same cannot be said of the work of Pierre Attaingnant in Paris, who was often held to be the first to devise and use the technique of printing music from type at one impression. He issued his first book, *Chansons nouvelles en musique a quatre parties: naguere imprimees a Paris*, on 4 April 1527/8; (*RISM* 1528³) and until 1551 maintained a steady output of music from the collections of the finest composers of the late 15th century and of his own day. His typographical apparatus was accomplished in design and finish, and he used it with neat authority, demonstrating his powers as a publisher as well as a printer who gave to posterity a system that was to survive, little altered, for more than 200 years (see fig.7).

The techniques of Attaingnant were much imitated, and his repertory of music was raided. The high estimation in which both were held can be measured by the speed with which printers inside and outside France

procured types for single-impression music. Jacques Moderne, in Lyons, produced his *Motetti del fiore* in 1532 (*RISM* 1532¹⁰, 1532¹¹), printed in elegant note forms based on those of Petrucci rather than upon the squatter types of Attaingnant (for illustration *see* MODERNE, JACQUES). The enterprising Christian Egenolff of Frankfurt am Main printed at one impression *Melodide in odas Horatij: et quaedam alia carminum genera*, by Petrus Tritonius, in 1532. In Nuremberg Hieronymous Formschneider ('Grapheus') issued Senfl's *Varia carminum genera* in 1534. Georg Rhau of Wittenberg printed more than 60 primers and works of musical theory with examples cut in woodblock, and also music at single impression from 1538. Joanne de Colonia, in Naples, is said to have been the first (in 1537) to print music at one impression in Italy, but it was Antonio Gardane and the Scotto family in Venice who established that city as the pre-eminent centre of Italian music printing. Though the printing of music at one impression was not practised in the Low Countries until 1540 (by Willem van Vissenaecken at Antwerp), the process flourished in the hands of Tylman Susato (for illustration *see* SUSATO, TYLMAN). Susato used a splendid character which aligned very well with the staves and may be seen to advantage in his *Premier livre des chansons a quatre parties* (*RISM* 1543¹⁶). He was soon joined by Pierre Phalèse at Louvain and Christopher Plantin who published important partbooks in the 1570s at Antwerp.

There were capable and energetic followers in France, of whom Robert Granjon and Philippe Danfrie were historically the most important. In 1549 Granjon, one of the great French punch-cutters, obtained a privilege to print music, but it was not until ten years later that he took advantage of it to print, at Lyons, some compositions by Barthélemy Beaulaigue (see fig.8). He used a music type that follows generally the style of the notes used for Carpentras' music at Avignon, though scaled down: the open notes are freely cut and calligraphic, the black notes rounded. Granjon's refined and elegant types match very well his *civilité* letter ('lettre françoise d'art de main') in which he set the words of Beaulaigue's songs. In 1558 Philippe Danfrie, an accomplished engraver, copied Granjon's music fount and called his version 'musique en copie' or 'musique d'escriture'. His notes too are rounded, but lack authority.

In 1559 the elder Guillaume Le Bé started to cut a system with rounded notes, large and small, for a 'tablature d'espinette', but designed for double impression. They were used for two tablatures by Adrien Le Roy and Ballard, founders of a dynasty of French music printers. Towards the end of the 17th century Pierre Ballard had a character engraved in which the points at the corners of the lozenge and the open notes were rounded and the black notes were completely circular, with the stem central (*see* GANDO, illustration, F). With these exceptions the typographical music of France and the rest of Europe was published in the square and lozenge notation of Attaingnant, however distant in quality and style from its exemplar, and continued to be so for a century – in France until the last decade of the 18th century.

So far it has been assumed that (in general) the methods of setting and printing the type in music volumes were the same as those used for text, always bearing in mind that the nature of music might well call for modifications in detail. Books are set vertically because the reading eye is more efficient in dealing with short lines (10 to 12 cm according to the size of character) than with long ones. For aesthetic and practical reasons musicians have generally liked their music lines long, with the depth of the page less than its width. Because of these preferences, 'special layout patterns have been found desirable for musical notation. These in turn have called for peculiar formats requiring appropriate imposition schemes' (Krummel, 1971). This practice, adopted for music books in the 16th and 17th centuries, prevailed for many years. In the first edition of *The Letter-press Printer* (London, 1876), Joseph Gould showed among his schemes of imposition 'A sheet of Quarto the Broad Way commonly used in Works of Music'; in the second edition (1881) a sheet of octavo was shown arranged the broad way to meet the same need.

Evidence of the technical processes involved in printing music can often be discovered from examination of surviving copies. Some printed music shows the importance of the frisket. For example, on f.59v of the *Liber*

selectarum cantionum (1520[4]), some short printed staves at the left of the page break off sharply, leaving a blank on the right. Inspection shows that the staves are continuous across the whole page but beyond the short pieces printed with notes they appear as blind impressions. Clearly the short pieces of the staff system needed for the few notes of music were inked just beyond the desired limit, and the frisket cover was cut to act as a mask, allowing the required staves to print through with a crisp vertical edge. The remaining length of the staff, uninked, and acting as bearers, supported the frisket and tympan and so prevented the paper from sagging into an otherwise empty space in the forme. Similar support may have been provided when the notes in the music forme were printed. In Oeglin's *Harmonie Petri Tritonii super odis Horatii Flacci* (1507; *GB-Lbm*) there is a blind impression of uninterrupted rows of notes, of a different character from any used in the book, which were no doubt acting in this way (for example f.cvr). Finally, on the title-page of *Processionarum ordinis praedicatorum* (Seville: Meinardus Ungut and Stanislaus Polonus, 1494) there is a blind stamped

7. *Two examples of music printed by one pass through the press: extract from Janequin's 'Fyez vous' (above), in the 'Tiers livre contenant XXI chansons musicales a quatre parties' (F-Pm MS 20, f.152v), printed and published by Pierre Attaingnant (Paris, 1536); part of the discantus of Byrd's 'Miserere mihi, Domine' (below), from 'Cantiones sacrae' (with Tallis; London, 1575), printed by Thomas Vautrollier with type imported from France; both demonstrate the simplicity and logic, but also the shortcomings, of the one-note-one-type system with note head and stem cast on a single type containing segments of a complete staff system: observe also Attaingnant's use of an alternative, 'squatter' type to print notes one above the other [(above) 85%, (below) 80% of actual size]*

8. *Granjon's types for words and music in Beaulaigue's 'Chansons nouvelles'* (Lyons, 1558) [95% of actual size]

frame composed entirely of capital letters P, marking the type area of a normal page, and perhaps arranged to support the sheet in the printing of an otherwise empty red forme.

It is clear from the impression of spaces that have risen in the forme and been inked, as well as from the nature of the damage that type sustains, that normal spacing quads in various sizes were used and that notes were cast full on their body. Such traces often show how well the red and black formes were imposed to register accurately. This is clear, for example, in *L'art et instruction de bien danser* (B iv and B iir and elsewhere), a book that is often dismissed as rough, or interesting as a curio only. The very close approach and overlapping of characters in the same forme show how freely kerning was used: Ratdolt's *Graduale* (1494, *GB-Cu*) provides splendid examples, as does *Rerum musicarum* by Johannes Frosch, printed in 1535 by Peter Schoeffer and Mathias Apiarius.

The introduction of single-impression music type was welcomed and imitated; but the advantage of being able to build up a musical phrase, notes and staff complete, by the gathering of single types in the order they appeared in the copy was purchased at a price. Compared with the complexity of some text letters there was nothing intrinsically difficult about cutting a punch for a note designed for double-impression printing. Such a note was economical, too: few note forms were required; they could be cast in quantity; and they were of universal application, appropriate to any degree of any scale. To cut a punch for a note designed for single-impression printing was much more difficult. The note had to be given a fixed place in relation to fractional parts of staff lines worked with it on the same punch. The staff lines had to appear at exactly the same intervals on every punch, so that when the matrices were struck and type was cast from them, the staffs made continuous and parallel lines. Fournier, a virtuoso punch-cutter, commented on the difficulty of achieving this and described how he made patterns for laying parallel, evenly spaced lines on the surface of the end of the punch before he started to work the metal. Matrices

were struck and justified with extreme care and then cast to their full width so that the staff lines extended right across the character, special attention being paid to the cleaning and finishing of their ends. Not many types achieved the perfection that the system called for, and in use they quickly lost their pristine excellence: the edges of the traversing lines were often damaged and caused breaks in the printed image. Making every allowance for chance damage, it is clear that many founts were not skilfully cut. Some writers have suggested that the primitive appearance of some founts, for example Rastell's, may be due to the use of a technique in which matrices were struck twice, once for the note and once for the staves; an attempt to strike a matrix in this way may produce a much deformed character, and better results are obtained by casting in a matrix that has been engraved with a burin wholly without the use of punches.

Although it was difficult to make satisfactory punches, the number required was limited by the character of the music for which they were prepared. The range of pitches and of note values was still relatively small. The 'grande musicque' cut for Plantin by Hendrik van den Keere in 1577 had notes for values ranging from the breve to the quaver (*fusa*) and cast with fragments of a five-line staff, but the number of each form was limited (for illustration *see* PLANTIN, CHRISTOPHER). Assuming a G clef, there were three minims, three crotchets and three quavers cast as g', a' and b'. If they were turned top to bottom the same types would serve for d'', c'' and b'. But if d' or f'' were required, some method would have to be found to change the disposition of the staff lines.

In Van den Keere's 'moyenne musicque' (which survives at the Plantin Moretus Museum, Inventory 237) some of the punches show five staff lines, some six; and some of the punches for Granjon's 'moyenne music' (Inventory 241) show seven. The matrices struck by these punches could be placed in a number of alternative positions in the mould to cast a note in a chosen position on the staves. Thus relatively few punches and matrices could be manipulated, to produce a wide variety of

9. Two printed versions of a Purcell song in 'Orpheus Britannicus': (above) from the first edition (London, 1698), printed by John Heptinstall, and (below) from the second (London, 1706), printed by William Pearson; in both systems the stems of quavers occurring in groups of two or more are 'tied' with a beam, but there are great differences in the structure of the notes – in the Heptinstall character the quavers are cast in two parts, looking forward to the 'mosaic' music types of the 1750s [both 86% of actual size]

notes. This versatility must have saved the printer a great deal of money and time. On the other hand, the printed image was not wholly satisfactory: slightly imperfect casting or other faults left minute gaps between the individual types in the line which the ink could not fill, and as a result white space showed: this was even more noticeable as the types became worn. To prevent this as far as possible, a system of 'bonding' or fitting was developed, using longer pieces of single or double staff line above or below a note cast on fewer staff lines. This was widely used, for example, in *Kirchengesang darinnen die Heubtartickel* (1566) and *Selectae cantiones quinque et sex vocum* by Jacob Meiland (Nuremberg: Dietrich Gerlach, 1572).

Apart from the examples of Channey, Granjon and Danfrie mentioned earlier, note heads were cut as lozenges or squares and stems were centred: this style persisted almost to the end of the 17th century, but by that time it was so at variance with the taste of the day that punches were cut in the pattern of written notes,

with the heads oval or roundish with stems to the left or right. The innovator of this style was the London printer John Heptinstall, who first used the face in John Carr's *Vinculum societatis* (*RISM* 1687[6]). The notes were cast with fractions of staves (for illustration *see* NOTATION, fig.52). Fractions of beam cut at a suitable angle – sometimes with a fragment of stem attached, sometimes not – were also provided to join successive quavers and semiquavers moving upwards and downwards. This feature gave the character its name 'the new tied note'. The note heads are over-large and the type ill-fitted, but it continued in use until at least 1699.

Alternative types soon became available: Peter de Walpergen in Oxford cut two splendid examples which were used only once or twice. In 1699 William Pearson published *Twelve New Songs* (*RISM* 1699[5]), a collection of pieces by various composers, issued chiefly to encourage his 'new London character'. Smaller in scale than Heptinstall's, the type was better fitted and better cast and was used extensively by Pearson, most notably perhaps in *Orpheus Britannicus* (2/1706), and by his successors into the mid-18th century (see fig. 9).

By this time, however, the mainstream of music printing was served by the engraver and the offerings of the type printer were found in the backwaters of hymn-books, small songbooks and the like: but not for very long. In 1749/50 Jacques-François Rosart cut a series of punches for a revolutionary method of music printing which he offered to Johannes Enschedé at Haarlem. He received no encouragement and it was J. G. I. Breitkopf, working to the same principles as Rosart, who took the credit for the innovation and brought the system to fruition. In 1754 Breitkopf started to have his punches cut and in February 1755 he published a *Sonnet* to demonstrate the quality of his system. In a preface to the *Sonnet* he commended his work to 'lovers of the musical art' and to printers. He continued:

the method used until now has fallen somewhat into disrepute, since it possesses neither the beauty demanded nowadays nor is it adequate to meet the needs of the art of music which has been brought to a state of perfection. The printers themselves are not very satisfied with the old method, partly because its intricacy is burdensome, but mainly because the typesetting is not so regular that it can be achieved without a lot of ingenious devices and botching which the compositor first of all has to work out for himself.

Breitkopf did not explain the theoretical basis of his system, but P.-S. Fournier (Fournier *le jeune*), who enjoyed Breitkopf's confidence, described the essentials in his *Traité historique et critique sur l'origine et les progrès des caractères de fonte pour l'impression de la musique, avec des épreuves de nouveaux caractères de musique présentés aux imprimeurs de France* (1765). All the types were cast on the same-sized body, 'being the fifth part of the body of each line of music' (i.e. the size of only one staff line). All the symbols used were formed to this dimension, so that the clefs, notes and other characters which were necessarily larger than the body were made up of several pieces 'set skilfully one above the other. A note, for example, is made up of three and four pieces; a clef of two, the upper part formed by one punch, the lower part formed by another punch, and these parts joined together form the character of the complete clef'. Such founts are now called 'mosaic types' (see figs.10 and 11 below).

In 1756 Fournier published an *Essai d'un nouveau caractère de fonte pour l'impression de la musique, inventé et exécuté dans toutes les parties typographiques* as a specimen of a new character which aimed at rendering music from type as if it had been printed by copper-plate engraving. It offered short dance movements, printed at two impressions to demonstrate the elegance and logic of the system. Fournier later developed this experimental character into a second music fount, this time for single-impression printing. It was based on a different system from that perfected by Breitkopf. While Breitkopf's type was designed on one body size and could be assembled into composite pieces as required, in Fournier's system the symbols were cut for casting on five different bodies, according to size. The minims, crotchets and simple quavers, key signatures, measures and other symbols of the same height were made in one piece (with segments of three or four staff lines incorporated), instead of in the three or four pieces that other systems required. In addition Fournier provided a wide range of characters which worked with the composite pieces. Fournier claimed that this arrangement made typesetting simpler, more reliable and quicker. The

number of types required was reduced by half: as he wrote, his 'character being only about 160 matrices instead of at least 300 that other systems carry'. A third type for single impression was cut by J. M. Fleischman for Izaac Enschedé – founder of a great dynasty of printers in Haarlem, in the Netherlands – as a reply to Breitkopf's. It was a superlative achievement. By 1760 he had cut 226 punches and struck and justified 240 matrices so skilfully that the music printed from his type approached the clarity of engraved music (see fig.10*b*).

Three other systems of mosaic music are worthy of note. First W. Caslon & Son of London showed a music type in two sizes in a specimen book of 1763. It is not known who cut the punches, but the character offers a wide range of sorts and fits agreeably. The second appeared in a *Manifesto d'una nuova impressa di stampare la musica in caratteri gettati nel modo stesso come si scrive* published by Antonio de Castro (Venice, 1765). To show the capabilities of his type he printed a *Duetto* by Giuseppe Paolucci. The 'manifesto' type 'Inciso et Gettato dal M. Rev. Sig D. Giacomo Falconi' is ramshackle and loose but it holds together well enough to be read without confusion; it was used for extensive works – Paolucci's *Preces octo vocibus* (Venice, 1767), for example, and his *Arte pratica di contrappunto* (1765).

The third system of this group was offered by Henric Fougt, a native of Lapland working in Sweden in 1766; the next year he went to England and obtained a patent. Although his technique was basically the same as Breitkopf's, it was simpler and called for fewer punches; and it proved robustly effective. In his patent he described the analysis by which he arrived at his system and, as the only account of its kind, it is worth study (Poole, 1965–6).

The first major work in which Breitkopf used his type was *Il trionfo della fedeltà* by the Electress Maria Anna Walpurgis of Bavaria, issued in score in three volumes in 1756. In the same year he published a *Recueil d'airs à danser*, and thenceforth his output was extensive: according to Fournier, Breitkopf issued 51 musical works including operas, keyboard works and songs between 1755 and 1761. This output continued in bulk and variety well into the 19th century.

Fournier's small music is elegantly shown in the *Anthologie françoise* (1765; for illustration *see* FOURNIER, PIERRE-SIMON); Fleischman's types are best studied, for themselves and in relation to Breitkopf's, in the *Haerlemse zangen* that Izaac and Johannes Enschedé published in 1761. The poems were translations into Dutch of the texts that appeared in High German in the *Berlinische Oden und Lieder* (1756), and the settings were to the same music that Breitkopf had used (see figs.10*a* and *b*). A comparison between the work of Fleischman and the type used by Johann Jacob Lotter of Augsburg, one of Breitkopf's earliest imitators, is offered by editions of Leopold Mozart's violin method: Lotter's *Versuch einer gründlichen Violinschule* (1756) and Johannes Enschedé's *Grondig onderwys in het behandelen der viool* (1766).

Fougt printed extensively. His first work was an edition of *Six Sonatas for Two Violins and Bass* by Francesco Uttini, and he issued seven other important works principally of chamber music. He issued a large number of single sheets (82 have survived), mostly songs, before he left England to return to Sweden in 1770. His equipment is said to have been purchased by R. Falkener and used, with technical improvements, to produce songsheets.

The Caslon type, sturdy and economical, was used widely during the latter part of the 18th century, notably on songsheets, and is well represented on inserts in the *Lady's Magazine*, the *Hibernian Magazine* and elsewhere. Caslon's types were much used in America. Christopher Saur of Germanstown, Pennsylvania, was the first to print music from movable type in America with his *Geistreiche Lieder*, a collection of 40 tunes that he printed in 1752 from types he had cast himself. In October 1783 the *Boston Magazine*, printed and published by Norman & White, issued 'A New Song', *Throw an apple*, set to music by A. Hawkins. According to Isaiah Thomas, the famous Massachusetts printer, 'Norman cut the punches and made every tool to complete the ... types': he also cast them. Thomas himself

had a complete series of the Caslon founts, including music, for in 1786 he issued *The Worcester Collection of Sacred Harmony*, 'printed typographically at Worcester, Massachusetts'. In addition to hymns and psalm tunes the collection includes the four-part vocal lines of the 'Hallelujah' chorus from Handel's *Messiah* very competently set in score, eight lines to the oblong page.

Given a knowledge of music and the advice of an editor, the compositor setting types with note and staff incorporated would have few major difficulties, though the fitting of sorts cast on different bodies would have been time-consuming. The compositor setting mosaic music was faced with other and more searching problems. Some of them were examined by Christian Gottlob Taubel, a Leipzig printer, in his *Praktisches*

(a)

(b)

10. *Two approaches to the same music: (a) German original published by Breitkopf (Leipzig, 1756), and (b) Dutch copy published by Enschedé (Haarlem, 1761) using Fleischman's types [(a) 49%, (b) 55% of actual size]*

Handbuch der Buchdruckerkunst für Anfänger (Leipzig, 1791). The setting of music, he warned, is much more difficult and needs more care than the setting of ordinary text; anybody proposing to become a music compositor must not have an irascible temperament or be in too much of a hurry; if he is too eager to get on he will overlook detail; music typesetting calls for the tedious and painstaking construction of involved pieces of music using only very small units; the compositor must be able to reproduce in type exactly what the author has drawn with his pen. Caution against hasty work runs through his advice about casting off copy, maintaining optical and musically even spacing, ensuring good underlay of words and arranging convenient turn-over breaks.

Whereas music type before Breitkopf was set line by line as ordinary text, mosaic music had to be set in blocks across the staff systems and the compositor needed cool judgment and an intimate knowledge of his cases, fitted as they were with hundreds of different characters, to build his musical jigsaw accurately. Taubel provided general advice and illustrative examples, but the beginner would have needed much practice under an experienced overseer before he could have carried on unsupervised.

Mosaic type was expensive and used large quantities of metal. Even with careful handling, the fine-cut pieces of note, stem and staff line – coming as they did to the edge of the type body – were easily damaged and the types seldom looked convincing and unbroken across even a narrow page. There was a great deal of experiment in the early 19th century to counter these difficulties. Many of these trials used notes with head and tail complete. In 1802 François Olivier obtained a patent for ten years to protect the development of a system which contained new features. The punches were cut in steel without fragments of staff lines, tempered, struck into copper matrices, and justified. The staff lines were engraved in a chosen position in the matrices by means of a burin and were then cut to a predetermined depth by a special steel saw. The types were cast in the usual way, using one of seven moulds. The advantage of the method was that few punches were required – a quaver or a semibreve could be struck with the same punch into a number of matrices and defined as a particular note by the position in which the staves were engraved. In spite of all precautions the alignment of the staff lines was not smooth, and although Olivier and his partner Godefroi published albums and methods, success escaped them; Olivier died, a disappointed man, in 1812.

In 1820 Eugène Duverger of Paris obtained a 15-year patent for a system which among other desiderata would ensure that the staves were parallel and unbroken. In October 1834 an account of his process, including a specimen showing his characters in three sizes, appeared in the *Bulletin* of the Société d'Encouragement pour l'Industrie Nationale. His types did not incorporate fragments of the staves. Using a setting stick engraved with staff lines as a guide and with spaces similarly marked, he set his types, sometimes using notes with complete stems, sometimes with part only, in their correct positions vertically and horizontally. The other signs – words, key signature and the like – were also set. Long slurs were made of very narrow strips of copper, bent and cut to the length required: bars tying the tails of successive quavers were made of pieces of pewter slipped into kerns made across the stems of the notes.

The matter was proofed and corrected. The whole was then brushed over with oil and covered with fine plaster which was allowed to set. When it was sufficiently firm the plaster was carefully removed from the type. A plane, fitted with a cutting iron bearing five sharp points at intervals corresponding with those engraved on the setting stick, was passed over the face of the plaster in accurately marked positions to make a trace of five lines, thus leaving the music with its staffs complete. The plaster mould was baked in an oven, put into a casting box and type metal alloy poured in. When the metal was solid and cool enough to handle, the casting was removed from the box and separated from the plaster. Any defects were corrected by hand and the plate was squared up and planed over the back to a uniform thickness, mounted and imposed with other plates in a chase, ready for printing at one impression. The system, which received a 'Brevet d'addition et de perfectionnement' in October 1838, was widely used, and when skilfully manipulated produced very satisfactory results; but it was found costly and suitable only for editions in large numbers.

Many other systems were developed in France, some purely typographical, others combining type with plaster moulding. The typographical systems include those of Derriey – a tour de force of cutting and founding, but used only in a specimen sheet – and of T. Beaudoire, which was used in books and periodicals. Of the mixed methods those of Tantestein, Curmer and Reinhard of Strasbourg were the most successful.

In England, Edward Cowper, a prolific inventor of machinery and processes in printing technology, patented in 1827 a revolutionary method of music printing. The printing surface consisted mainly of the ends of pieces of copper wire passed through a three-ply block of wood and made to stand 1·6 mm above the surface of the block. The ends of the wire formed the black notes; the white notes were made up from two curved pieces, which were pushed into the surface of the wood to form the elliptical character. Other characters were created from curved shapes which had been drawn through holes in a steel plate in long pieces and then cut into units about 8 mm long. The edges of small pieces of brass printed the stems of notes, slurs, beams and the like, and were tapped into the wooden block to stand at the same height as the notes. If the words of a song were to be printed they were set in type, moulded in plaster and cast into lines which were cut up and underlaid in grooves cut into the wood. The staves, with their clefs, were made on separate blocks (each system on its own narrow strip of wood) which were arranged in a chase to register accurately with the note blocks. The second part of the invention was centred on a revolving tympan. When taking impressions the note blocks were locked up in one chase and the staff blocks in another, and both were put in one forme, head to head, adjusted so that the staves would fall correctly on the notes if one chase had been folded over on to the other. Two sheets of paper were laid on the tympan and buttoned down by separate friskets. The forme was inked all over and an impression was taken. The tympan was lifted and as a result of a special mechanism the surface holding the paper and the friskets was turned through 180°. A second impression was taken, the notes and staves neatly overprinting to complete the music. This method was much used in the 1830s.

A second patent from which much was expected was

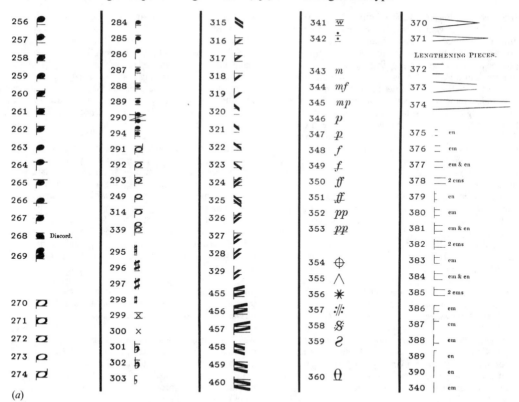

(a)

(b)

11. By the 19th century 'mosaic' music type systems had reached their maximum complexity: (a) part of the specimen sheet of Diamond Music, offered by V. & J. Figgins in London, containing 452 separate types in the fount which had to be supplemented by a large supply of specially cast spacing material; (b) Diamond no.3 music type offered by Stevens, Shanks & Sons, London [(a) 103%, (b) 82% of actual size]

taken out in 1856 by Gustav Scheurmann, a music seller and publisher of Newgate Street, London. It was designed to separate the staves from the notes and other necessary symbols and words into two formes, printed one after the other by a specially adapted press. The characters were cut and cast in the usual way but special attention was given to the casting of beams for joining the tails of successive quavers and the like. For this feature he devised a special mould that would cast bars at any angle on a body which mounted in steps from left to right and on which the kerned stems of the notes rested. From the short example given in *Grove 1* (iii,

248), the method produced excellent results, but the inventor was not satisfied until his music could be printed in one impression; and on this ultimate he foundered. It is a great pity that Scheurmann did not persist with his two-impression technique because, as he demonstrated, he could overprint his two formes accurately on lead and from this create an electrotype which, backed with metal, could be imposed as a plate for letterpress printing at one impression.

Although these various methods (and there were many more) had something to offer in technical ingenuity to improve various features of the earliest mosaic music types, it was the descendants of Breitkopf who won the day. It was remarkable how many different complete systems of type in different sizes were offered during the 19th century, in England, Germany and America, most of them demonstrating in the accuracy of their fit the superb quality of the punch-cutting, matrix-striking and letter-founding of their day. These types, however, were not created merely to demonstrate technical brilliance: they were made to serve a market.

The relationship between the improvements in the processes of music printing and market demand may be illustrated by short quotations from sources published in 1834. In the preface to the first volume, 'Instrumental', of the *Musical Library*, it is stated:

the Musical Library was commenced with a view to afford the same aid in the progress of the musical art that literature has so undeniably received from the cheap publications of the day . . . before this work appeared, the exhorbitant sums demanded for engraved music amounted to a prohibition of its free circulation among the middle classes; at a time too when the most enlightened statesmen saw distinctly the policy of promoting the cultivation of the art in almost every class of society.

In an account of the 'various processes applied to printing music' on the first four pages of the first 'monthly supplement' to the *Musical Library* (April 1834) the writer said:

In each process [intaglio and lithography], the manual labour of printing off the copies involving considerable nicety and attention, is a source of constant recurring expense. In printing music from the *surface* of moveable types, or stereotype plates, either by the printing press or printing machine, the operation is rapid and certain; the market may be supplied at once to the extent of the demand; and the consumer may receive the full benefit of mechanical improvements, in the diminished cost of the article produced. Such a work as the 'Musical Library' could only be undertaken with the aid of musical typography.

The system that the publisher of the *Musical Library* had adopted was 'a secret process of music printing invented by M. Duverger of Paris'.

The wisdom of the commercial argument summarized above, brilliantly demonstrated in practice by Alfred Novello some years later, was well served by the type founders. In 1820 William Clowes, printer of the *Harmonicon* and other music, imported from Germany punches and matrices for music type and developed the technique they offered to real excellence in his own foundry. In the 1830s Hugh Hughes of Dean Street, London, offered two sizes of music type and V. Figgins, the Patent Letter Foundry and Miller & Richard all had founts to offer the music publisher (see figs.11*a* and *b*), in such variety that by 1876 manuals of instruction could give no reliable general information about typesetting. There was so much music printed from type in London during the latter half of the 19th century that the compositors engaged exclusively in music typesetting were numerous enough to establish and maintain their own trade union, the London Society of Music Compositors (1872).

John Southward indicated something of the market in his handbook *Practical Printing* (1882):

In many of the large offices in London and the country, music composition is regularly done, but in the metropolis it has been made into an independent department of the printing business. There are offices which undertake hardly any other kind of work. If the manager of a periodical desires to give a page of music, he sends the copy to one of the music-printing establishments, and in due time receives back a stereo or electro plate which he can work with the rest of his pages . . . the fact of the demand for music work being altogether beyond the means of supply, originally called this trade into existence.

He treated of the principles of music typesetting in general terms because although 'most of the letter-founders supply music types their systems, unfortunately, differ somewhat'. He used the type of the Patent Letter Foundry for his illustrations as this system was 'the most complete'.

The demand for typographical music was not a wholly British phenomenon. The publication of manuals of instruction, taking the beginner step by step through the rudiments of notation to the setting of scores and other intricacies, much more thoroughly than Taubel had done in 1791, provides some evidence of this. In Germany there were three such books, one in two editions, between 1844 and 1875. Type founders provided founts of type, each being offered as better than the last, not only during the 19th century but well into the 20th.

In America Thomas Adams (*Typographia*, 1856), devoted a page to music, with examples set in the type of L. Johnson & Co., Philadelphia. Thomas MacKellar (*The American Printer*, 1873 and 1879), was much more thorough, using the types of MacKellar, Smiths & Jordan of Philadelphia, and as late as 1904 Theodore Low de Vinne devoted 18 pages of his treatise *Modern Methods of Book Composition* to music.

This account of the development of music printing from type has been concerned largely with method: even with the same techniques, standards achieved varied enormously. This was particularly true during the 16th and 17th centuries, when the punch-cutter (who made the moulds, struck and justified the matrices) and the founder (who cast the types) had to be remarkably skilful to manipulate current engineering techniques if type of sufficient merit and versatility was to give acceptable printed results. For every outstanding printer using type of good quality with skill – Attaingnant, Moderne, Ballard (sometimes), Petrucci, Gardane, Scotto, Susato, Vautrollier and Day – there were others whose work left much to be desired, who used types that were badly fitted, indifferently cast and with only a limited range of characters. Some founts produced such broken staff-line systems that the page almost defied reading at the required speed of performance; others were so inadequate that the printer had to set a special warning between the staff lines to instruct the performer that a quaver with an asterisk above it should be read as a semiquaver.

3. ENGRAVING. The polyphonic music of the 16th and 17th centuries was printed in partbooks, or in books showing all parts on facing pages, or in score. Attaingnant arranged moving parts together on the same set of staves in some of his keyboard volumes, the unknown German printer of an early collection of *Kirchengeseng* of the Bohemian Brethren (1566) used the same technique and William Godbid managed to print Thomas Tomkins's *Musica Deo sacra* (1668) in four parts on a

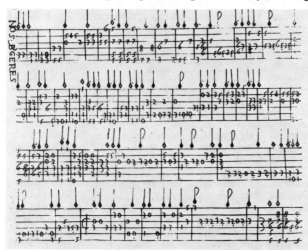

12. *Part of a page of 'Intabolatura da leuto del divino Francesco da Milano', said to be the first music printed from engraved plates (before 1536)*

two-staff system. The ingenuity shown by the printers of these pieces draws attention to the limitations of their type (carrying integrated notes and staff segments), and to its clumsy inability to show, confidently, more than one part on one set of staves. The inadequacy of the system to reproduce elaborate keyboard music with its rapid succession of short notes and dense chords, to render satisfactorily solo and concerted string and wind music extended in tonal range and scalar agility, or to notate florid song, became increasingly obvious. The hand equipped with the nimble and flexible pen was able to meet all these challenges in manuscript, and it was the hand-driven line engraved in copper that furnished the needs of the composer and the connoisseur from the latter part of the 16th century onwards.

The earliest date known on any intaglio engraving is 1446 although there is evidence that plates were being produced at least ten years earlier. It is not known how they were printed. The first mention of a copper-plate printing press is probably that in a document of 1540 in the Antwerp archives, cited by Goovaerts (1880); but the hand mangle had been developed commercially in the 14th century. The maps for editions of Claudius Ptolemy's *Geographia* issued in Bologna (1477), Rome (1478) and Florence (1482) were printed from copper plates and show place names splendidly cut in various sizes of Roman capital. It seems curious that music was not prepared for printing from incised copper plates, too: perhaps the techniques of copper-plate engraving and, particularly, printing were not widely known, for, after the editions of Ptolemy's *Geographia* and a map of central Europe printed in 1491, very few maps were produced from engraved plates until about 1540. The earliest known practical music to be produced by copper-plate engraving seems to be *Intabolatura da leuto del divino Francesco da Milano novamenta stampada* (fig.12), published without printer or date but attributed by A. J. Ness in his edition to some time before 1536, when Marcolini da Forlì issued *Intabolatura di liuto de diversi, con la bataglia, et altre cose bellissime, di M. Francesco da Milano, stampata nuovamente.* Ness suggested that Francesco Marcolini (the publisher of the latter volume) may have been responsible for the other title too, because in his preface he claimed that he had been experimenting with

'engraving on wood and metal' (perhaps copper) in seeking Petrucci's 'secrets' of printing lute tablature. After this, there was a gap of some decades before music was again engraved.

The table showing the finals and dominants of the 12 modes in Vincenzo Galilei's *Dialogo ... della musica antica e della moderna* (Florence: Giorgio Marescotti, 1581) is not fully mensural music. Otherwise, engraved music is next found in a number of devotional prints made after paintings or drawings by Marten de Vos and other Flemish artists. In some of the engravings a whole score is shown as an open book; in others the separate vocal parts – nine in one case – are disposed about the picture on scrolls or on tablets held by angels. The engravings contain complete works, some of them by known composers such as Andreas Pevernage, Cornelis Verdonck and Cornelis Schuyt, some by composers otherwise unknown, such as D. Raymundi. The first print, the Virgin and St Anne with Jesus, engraved in masterly style by Johann Sadeler after de Vos, appeared in Antwerp in 1584 (for illustration *see* SADELER, JOHANN) and was reprinted in Rome (1586) and in Antwerp (1587). Others (all but one by the same engraver) were published in Mainz (1587) or Frankfurt am Main (undated). The engravings are superb as pictorial compositions, and the notation of the music, though small, is clear and accurately reproduced. In the same vein is *Encomium musices*, a book made up of 18 plates, each illustrating a different scene from the Bible (Antwerp: Philip Galle, c1590). The designs by Jaen von de Straet provide a mass of information about musical instruments of the day which the brilliant engraving of Adriaen Collaert and others has preserved in the copper. The title-page shows three female figures, Harmonia, Musica and Mensura, framed by a fine show of musical instruments and supporting an open score of a motet for six voices by Pevernage (for illustration *see* PEVERNAGE, ANDREAS).

By this time Simone Verovio, a calligrapher and engraver, had issued in Rome two collections of pieces printed from engraved copper plates. The first was *Diletto spirituale: canzonette a tre et a quattro voci composte da diversi ecc.mi musici, raccolte da Simone Verovio, intagliate et stampate dal medesimo: con l'intavolatura del cimbalo et liuto* (*RISM* 1586³), a folio of

23 leaves (for illustration see VEROVIO, SIMONE). The title describes the nature of the work. Each two-page opening shows the separate vocal parts with words, a version for keyboard in three or four parts and another for lute in Italian tablature, all elegantly engraved and skilfully printed. Verovio produced similar works until 1608, sometimes entirely on his own, sometimes with the assistance of a compatriot engraver Martin van Buyten. His methods were adopted by his successors in Rome, some anonymous (as was the printer of J. H. Kapsberger's *Libro primo di mottetti* of 1612), but one of whom, Nicolò Borboni, was as accomplished as Verovio himself. He is best known for his *Musicale concenti a una, et due voci . . . libro primo* (1618), which he composed and engraved, and for the editions of Frescobaldi's keyboard works, superbly engraved by Christopherus Blancus (from 1615), which he published.

Meanwhile, music printed from engraved copper plates had appeared in England (1612–13) and the Netherlands (1615), but it was not known for about another 40 years in France (c1660) and in Germany not until 1689 (though engraved music appeared in typeset books in France and Germany in the 1620s and 1630s). The English work was *Parthenia or The Maydenhead of the First Musicke that Ever was Printed for the Virginalls: composed by Three Famous Masters: William Byrd, Dr John Bull and Orlando Gibbons* (*RISM* 1613¹⁴) engraved by William Hole for Dorothy Evans, and printed by G. Lowe. It is an accomplished piece of engraving showing a command equal to Verovio's, but with the parts so condensed that the music would have been extremely difficult to play. The first Dutch example was issued by Joannes Janssen in Amsterdam: *Paradisus musicus testudinis* by Nicolas Vallet, engraved by Joannes Berwinckel (*RISM* 1618¹⁶). The Ballard monopoly of typographic music printing in France did not extend to printing from copper plates, and composers who did not wish to entrust their music to Ballard published it on their own account or through a music seller. The first of these was Michel Lambert who, before 1660, published in Paris *Les airs de Monsieur Lambert* engraved by Richers. Eventually the technique spread across the Atlantic where it was used in 1721 for *An Introduction to the Singing of Psalm Tunes* by John Tufts, published by Samuel Gerrish in Boston, and for *The Grounds and Rules of Music Explained* by Thomas Walter (Boston: F. Franklin).

In England, Roger North described (c1695) how he bought a copper plate 'polish't and grounded' and etched some music on it. He used the acid too strong and the result was not satisfactory. Later (c1715–20) he related how 'etching, with a litle graving (and perhaps worse ways) have been used' to meet the demand for printed music. He refers to the work of 'Stephen Rogers in Holland' whose music was 'wonderfull fair'. In a well-known passage from his *History of the Science and Practice of Music*, Hawkins also referred to Roger and those Dutch artificers who found a means to soften copper so as 'to render it susceptible of an impression from the stroke of a hammer or a punch, the point whereof had the form of a musical note'. Certainly in 1686 Johannes Stichter, a printer and publisher in Amsterdam, announced that he sold various sorts of music 'printed in a newly invented way'. There is no ambiguity in the claims of Thomas Cross (see fig.13)

who in *Dear Sally, a New Song* (c1690) said of himself that he:

arriv'd to such perfection in musick that Gent may have their works fairly engraved, as cheap as Punct & Sooner; he having good hands to assist him, covenanted for a term of years; he can cut miniture, without having it writ with ungum'd ink, to take off upon the plate as they do for other people.

However elusive these flickers of information may be, they are given substance in the first account of the methods of music engraving to be written by a practitioner. It occurs in *L'encyclopédie*, where Mme Delusse provided a commentary on the second of two plates concerned with 'Gravure en lettres, en géographie et en musique' (fig.14). She said that when music was first engraved on copper the notes were drawn with a steel point – sometimes in their ordinary written form, sometimes as lozenges – and were then bitten in with acid. She cited collections of organ music (perhaps Guillaume-Gabriel Nivers'), a large proportion of the operas of Lully and Mouret, the motets of Campra and Lalande, and the cantatas of Bernier and Clérambault as examples of music engraved in this manner. The notes, she wrote, were not as regular in form as those later produced by punches. By correcting this irregularity and bringing the characteristics to conform as closely as possible with the written notes, the style of music engraving had come gradually to the state of perfection in which it existed at the time of her writing.

At the outset of her description of the current technique Mme Delusse stated that the aim of the engraver was to reproduce the manuscript copy exactly, on a copper or pewter plate, freehand; and she went on to summarize methods that have persisted, with slight modification, to the 20th century. The plate was first squared up and a rectangle drawn with a point and ruler close to the four edges of the metal. The area was then scaled against the copy to determine how the music was to be laid out. She described this important stage in the process inadequately. Fortunately, manuscripts that have been through the engraver's hands during the 18th century have survived, and much can be learnt from them. The number of notes seems to have been counted, to determine how much space a work would take. In scores, consideration was given to the relative movement of the parts and to the ranges which determined the number of leger lines required. The engraver knew the size of the punches and of the plates used for certain kinds of music – keyboard, vocal, orchestral and so on. With this information he could calculate how many lines the music would occupy, making necessary provision for clefs, key and time signatures, and the titles to the whole work and to the individual movements. He then decided how many lines could be accommodated on a plate, and worked through the piece marking the places for line breaks. This was not a simple mechanical count because the planning had to take account of the logic of the music, allowing space, as far as possible, in proportion to the value of the notes. This proved relatively simple in the quicker movements, but there are many indications in the manuscripts of second thoughts and recalculation in the slower movements. With his estimates made, the engraver was ready to work his plate. He set his compass to the calculated interval between the top lines of each staff system and scribed these positions on each long edge of the rectangle. He then used a five-pointed marker to make five equidistant scratches at each edge: these were

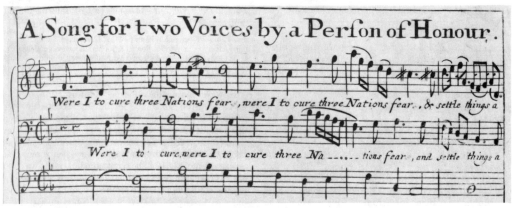

13. *Engraving by Thomas Cross of London of a song by Purcell (Z517); the small note heads and compressed writing of the underlay are characteristic of the songsheets which Cross and others produced to be sold cheaply and in quantity [86% of actual size]*

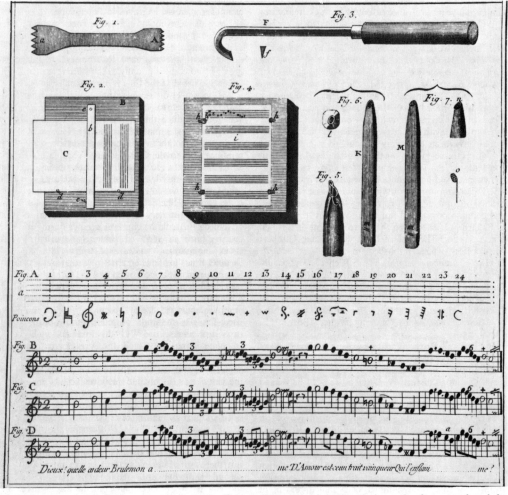

14. *18th-century music engravers' tools, reproduced from 'L'encyclopédie': 'Fig.1' shows the five-pointed tool for pricking the position of staff systems (in two sizes) on the metal engraving plates; in 'Fig.2' a squared-up plate rests flat on a stone under a straight edge (b), with two systems already cut by a scorer ('Fig.3'); 'Fig.4' shows the plate completely scored, with some characters (made by the punches indicated in 'Figs.6–7') already in position; 'Figs.A–D' show a variety of punches; the text in the last line was engraved with a burin*

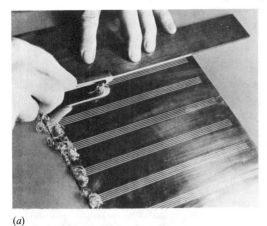

(*a*)

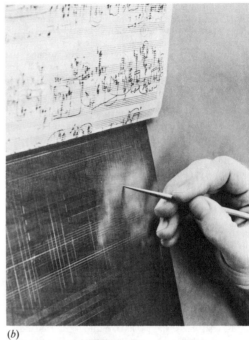

(*b*)

15. The basic processes used in engraving from the 18th century to the present (showing the German practice, with punches); (*a*) cutting the staff lines on the metal plate, (*b*) translating the music from manuscript on to a spaced plate (working from right to left), (*c*) striking punches (music or lettering) into the plate, (*d*) cutting a slur, (*e*) pulling a proof

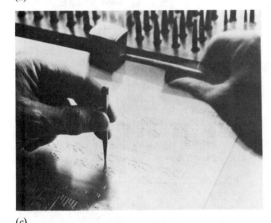

(*c*)

(*d*)

(*e*)

used to align the staff lines, which were drawn with the sharp tooth of a scorer. The single-tooth scorer was later superseded by a five-point scorer which could engrave a system of staff lines in one operation; this is now universally employed by engravers, though the single-tooth scorer is retained by some practitioners for cutting bar-lines.

When the ruling was finished, the burr raised by the cutting tools was removed with a scraper, working across the lines with a light hand. This done (Mme Delusse wrote), everything on the manuscript was lightly drawn on the plate with a steel point, working from right to left so that all would appear the correct way round when printed. If a song were being set, the words and music had to be indicated in their correct relationship. The marking would have to observe the same logic that dictated the cast-off, so that the relationship of the parts could be grasped as a whole at sight, and to achieve this the engraver might well have had to modify some of the detail written on the manuscript at the planning stage. The pitch and the value of each note were shown by conventional signs at the end of the mark indicating the position of their stems.

Once the plate was completely marked, the copy was laid aside. Apparently the favoured practice in France in the late 18th century was to engrave any words below the music first with a burin, and then to stamp the note heads, rests, clefs, sharps, flats, naturals, directs and so on, using punches driven by a hammer with a flat face. This done, the plate was transferred from the thick, smooth stone that supported it during the punching and laid on an anvil, where it was planished or flattened

using a hammer with a slightly convex face, to remove the distortions and bulges in the metal caused by the action of the punches. The plate was then laid on a smooth surface to be finished. The note stems, bar-lines, slurs, tails to single quavers, the beams connecting the stems of groups of quavers, and subdivisions of quavers, were put in with a burin or with a scorper (a burin with a wide cutting edge). To enable all cutting to be done from right to left the plate had to be turned around and about; indeed to cut slurs the engraver often held his graver still and turned the plate on to it. When the cutting was finished the scores were drawn through the staves again to open any lines that might have been closed up during punching. The plate was examined carefully, touched up as necessary, burrs scraped, and unrequired scratches and dots burnished away. A proof copy was pulled and any errors noticed by the composer and the printer's reader were marked for amendment. For correction, the plate was rested on the edge of the bench, between the arms of correcting callipers, each of which carried a point turned inwards at its end. The point of the arm over the face of the plate was placed on the character to be changed and pressed down; the point of the arm resting on the bench under the plate met it and located the position of the fault through the metal. The mark on the back was ringed, the plate was turned over face down on the stone and the area around the error was struck with a dot punch. The plate was turned over again, and the metal raised on the surface was burnished to obliterate the defective work. The back was also gently tapped with a hammer over the same area. Once the surface was smooth and flat, the corrections

16. Part of a song from La Borde's 'Choix de chansons' (Paris, 1773), the music engraved without punches, with the full-page engraving by Saint-Quentin that illustrates it [68% of actual size]

were made; care was taken not to disturb the original work around it. The plate was then ready for printing at the rolling press (see also fig.15).

The first comprehensive account of the printing of music from engraved plates is in *Nouvel manuel complet de l'imprimeur en taille douce* by Berthiaud, revised by P. Boitard (1837), in which a whole section is devoted to music. According to them, music was rarely engraved on copper with a burin but was usually worked on pewter with a hammer and punches. If music came to the printer on copper plates then it was printed as any other copper-plate engraving, but the printing of music from pewter plates required procedures different from those usual with copper. The preliminary cleaning was modified, the inking was carried out cold with specially formulated ink, the force of the press was reduced, and the top roller had to be of sufficient diameter to prevent the plate from bowing as it passed through the press and curving upwards to take the shape of the roller.

It is not always easy to discover the methods used by printers and publishers to impose music printed from engraved plates, because much of the evidence is bound up tightly in the spines of library volumes. But it is possible to notice trends from broken-down and incomplete pieces and from superlative copies specially retained in their original condition. It seems that Roger engraved his vertical folios on large plates (278 mm deep × 516 mm wide, for example) with two pages to view, to provide a fold down the middle; his oblong music is usually printed on a single plate to a page (for an example of his engraving *see* ROGER, ESTIENNE). Walsh followed no fixed practice, as W. C. Smith found: 'Any attempt to apply to Walsh's music the usual rules based on the foldings of the paper, direction of lines, or position of watermarks is out of the question, as it is clear that he used to cut his paper without regard to such, and as it suited his purpose at the time'; later 'It can be added that at times he used paper folded once, giving 4 pp. folio stitched through the folds ... but this was not always the case and he appears to have used cut single sheets sewn together'.

Berthiaud and Boitard said that it was rare for music to be printed in single plates; more often two or four plates were printed on a sheet of paper which, when it was folded down the middle, showed the impressions paged in correctly numbered order. This was achieved by printing the first page, turning the paper over and then printing the third page, imposed as the first but in the other half of the sheet. After allowing the sheet to dry for 24 hours, the second and fourth pages were printed in the same way.

The printing quality of pewter plates depended on the alloy from which they were made. Generally the alloys were more brittle as the proportion of antimony was greater. This, taken with the reaction of the metal to the punch and working at the press, may explain the cracks that disfigure some music printed direct from plates, particularly during the 19th century. Some runs were considerable: on the evidence of R. J. S. Stevens (1778; MS, *GB-Cpl*) 4000 copies were taken by Thomas Straight from a pewter plate before it was worn out. Cracks rarely appear in copper plates; wear can be attributed to other causes: 'the abrasive action of the plate printers' wiping canvasses ... could break down fine work on a copper plate within a hundred impressions, and during a long run the cost of rebiting and repairs could absorb almost as much as the expenditure

on the original work' (Bain, quoting Pye). This experience related to book illustration where detail was much finer than in music printing, but the points are valid for copper-plate printing generally.

These imperfections give rise to bibliographical distractions, because cracks, missing or damaged notes and faint copies suggest late impressions taken from worn metal or new editions taken from 'the original plates'. Instead, many faults arose from causes intrinsic in metals and processes, and might have declared themselves early as well as late or arisen too from human shortcomings. Cracks may be attributable to any one of several causes: they might have been in the blank plate before working, they might have been opened by a burin where the metal was weak, or they might have spread under machine pressure at any stage of the printing run. Discrepancies in engraving style that occur through the parts of an instrumental work might stir thoughts of cancelled and re-engraved plates, but, since other evidence is lacking, it is safer to attribute such differences to trade practices. It is not always safe to accept 'T. Cross *sculp.*' as proof that all, or even most, of the music in a work has been engraved by Thomas Cross: he had 'good hands' to assist him. William Forster shared between engravers the work of punching his edition of certain Haydn symphonies, as the surviving manuscripts show and as the printed copies betray.

In France the subdivisions of labour followed another pattern. Three first-class engravers were called on to present the *Pièces de clavecin composées par M. Couperin* (1713), though only one, Du Plessy, seems to have been responsible for the music. The title-page of *Pièces de clavecin avec voix ou violon ... par Mr Mondonville oeuvre V* (c1745) shows the names of F. Baillieul (*scripsit*), Hué (*sculpsit*), Rigaud (*inventit*) and Aubert (*sculpsit*). The *fermier-général* composer Jean-Benjamin de La Borde was rich enough to be able to commission Mlle Vendôme (the most famous of a group of outstanding music engravers) and Mora to engrave his insipid *Choix de chansons* (1773; fig.16) and Moreau le Jeune, Le Bouteux, Le Barbier and Saint-Quentin, the leading illustrators of the day, to create one of the most superbly decorated books of the century. This work's unique technical excellence shows only the best of a great deal of very good engraving which set the standard for the rest of Europe.

The critics of engraving in England, France and elsewhere said that the process, although elegant, fluent and suited to music, was slow and expensive. Some offered a new typography as a means of capturing the charms of engraving without its disadvantages, but this proved a not very satisfactory alternative; others, later, adopted lithography to achieve the same ends.

4. LITHOGRAPHY AND MORE RECENT PROCESSES. Lithography is defined in the *Oxford English Dictionary* as 'the art or process of making a drawing, design or writing on a special kind of stone (called a "lithographic stone") so that impressions in ink can be taken from it'. The practice is based on the phenomenon that one greasy substance will receive another but any greasy substance will repel water. The man who used this principle to develop a quite novel method of printing was Alois Senefelder. He wanted to be a playwright but could not afford to publish at his own expense through the trade; he accordingly took up the study of printing techniques. He found the most promising was that of

17. Part of Gleissner's 'Feldmarsch der Churpfalzbayer'schen Truppen' (1796), traditionally accepted as the first piece of music successfully reproduced by Senefelder from etched stone [54% of actual size]

etching on a copper plate. He later substituted a piece of kellheim limestone and found that he could write with more command and more distinctly on the stone than on the copper plates. He used his own ink prepared with wax, soap and lampblack and decided to try the effect of biting the stone with 'aqua fortis' (nitric acid), wondering 'whether, perhaps, it might not be possible to apply printing ink to it, in the same way as wood engravings, and so to take impressions from it'. After pouring off the acid he found the writing 'elevated about a tenth part of a line', or about 2 mm, and that satisfactory impressions could be taken.

A page of poorly printed music in a prayer book that he saw at Ingolstadt persuaded him that his 'new method of printing would be particularly applicable to music printing' and he began with the work of a friend, Franz Gleissner. It is usually accepted that the first of Gleissner's compositions to be printed was the *Feldmarsch der Churpfalzbayer'schen Truppen* (1796; fig.17), but in the first part of his *Complete Course of Lithography* (1818; Eng. trans., 1819 – from which the above quotations are taken), Senefelder gave primacy to *12 neue Lieder für's Klavier* (1796). He copied the music on stone and, using a copper-plate printing press, with the assistance of one printer, took 120 copies. The composing of the songs, the writing, engraving and printing took less than two weeks.

These techniques of relief etching and printing from stone, refined and developed by Senefelder, were much used for music printing up to at least the first decade of the 19th century. In his study of Senefelder's life and work (1914), Carl Wagner showed a stone plate with music etched in high relief from the printing office of H. Gombart of Augsburg, dating from about 1800 (fig.18a).

Music printed by this method can sometimes be identified by the impression left in the paper by the raised characters, for example in *Sonate à quatre mains pour le pianoforte ... Oeuvre II* by Franz Danzi (Munich: Falter, *c*1797).

Senefelder continued to experiment, observing the chemical and physical affinities between different substances. He noticed that gum-water prevented the chemical writing ink made of soap and wax from adhering to the stone; he drew lines with soap on a polished stone, moistened the whole surface with gum water and applied oil-based ink which adhered only to the soap lines. He described his experiments:

In trying to write music on the stone, with a view to print it in this way, I found that the ink ran on the polished surface; this I obviated by washing the stone with soap water, or linseed-oil before I began to write; but in order to remove again this cover of grease which extended over the whole surface (so that the whole stone would have been black on the application of the colour [printing ink]) after I had written or drawn on the stone, it was necessary to apply aqua fortis, which took it entirely away, and left the characters or drawings untouched.

Out of these principles, rationalized in 1798, Senefelder developed the 'chemical printing' of true lithography, which allowed impressions to be taken from lines barely raised above the flat surface of a stone. He quickly extended the range of his procedures, or 'manners' as he called them. With the engraved manner the drawing was engraved in the surface of the stone with needles without being etched; this was used in the first work he produced after his discovery of chemical printing, *Eine Symphonie von vier obligaten Stimmen* by Gleissner, where, to make the title-page as neat as possible, the engraved manner was used. It was possible to combine the engraved manner with the elevated (surface) manner. In his *Rapport sur la lithographie ...*

adressé a la Société d'encouragement de Paris (20
October 1815, p.3), G. Engelmann showed a piece of
music in which the notes had been written in ink and the
staff lines engraved; and Senefelder combined the
methods in title-pages, 'where the finest hair strokes
[were] drawn in first with the needle, and the thicker,
or shade lines, added with the pen'. By 1800 Senefelder
had demonstrated that the chemical printing process
was not limited to stone; other substances 'as wood,
metal, paper, even fat substances, as wax, shellac and
rosin' could be used under certain circumstances. He

did not cease to refine the techniques of his earlier
discoveries such as 'transferring from paper, upon
which drawing or writing is previously executed with
prepared ink'.

Senefelder regarded his process as of universal application – apt for quick reproduction, in any quantity,
of originals as various as orders of the day struck off on
the battlefield, bill heads, advertising copy and works of
art. The early development of lithography was very
much associated, however, with the printing of music,
largely because of Senefelder's own interests and needs,

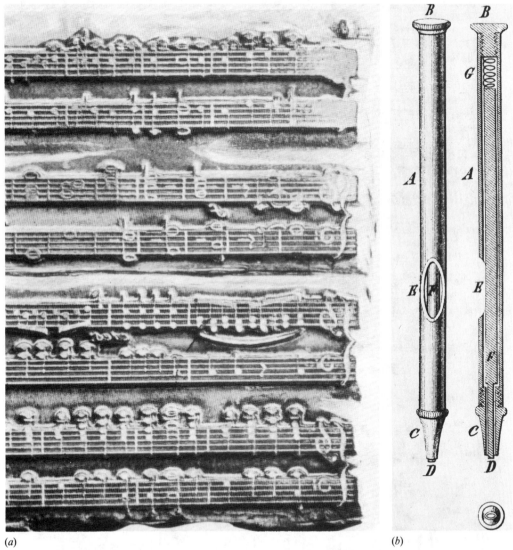

(a)   *(b)*

*18. (a) Part of a stone plate etched with music in high relief, from the printing office of H. Gombart in Augsburg; (b)
device for laying down identical note heads in succession (from G. Engelmann's 'Traité théorique et pratique de
lithographie', Mulhouse, 1839–40), which consisted of a metal tube through which a rod (F) passed, enclosing at G
a small spring: at the lower extremity of the rod a note head was engraved in relief, with lithographic ink being
introduced round the rod through an aperture (E) in the outer case; a step cut in the rod blocked the flow of ink to the
nozzle (C) until the end of the rod (D) was pressed against the stone, raising the rod (F) and allowing the ink to be
moved by capillary attraction down the nozzle on to the note head; when the pressure was released the spring (G)
forced the rod down and cut off the ink supply, leaving enough in the nozzle to keep the note head covered for the
next application*

19. Beginning of Act 1 of 'Tannhäuser', printed from the composer's autograph; Wagner wrote the score on lithographic transfer paper which was then laid down on to the stone

and because of his association with Gleissner (and Gleissner's wife, a remarkable woman), Falter, J. A. André and Steiner at critical points in his career.

During his experiments Senefelder laid out his music complete and in detail direct on the stone, working from right to left with a sharp black-lead pencil; pen-work remained the basis of the technique in its commercial development. It may well be that the early lithographers followed the procedures of the pewter-plate engravers: ruled their staff systems first (line by line), established clefs, key signatures and indications of pulse, laid the note heads in position and, aided by drawing instruments, completed stems, beams, slurs, binds, indications of dynamics and the like as required. The note heads in early lithographic music are often circular, and it is known from a well-informed writer, Marcel de Serres, who visited Munich and Vienna to study lithography, that in order to draw round and uniform note heads a special former had to be used. Similarly, for the same purpose, a resinous tampon was introduced, cut at one end to the size and shape of a note head, which was inked and stamped where required on the stone. Engelmann, one of the most important innovators of the lithographic science, reported that as it was time-consuming to form the note heads with a pen and difficult to make them uniform, German lithographers had developed a tool which under the pressure of a plunger and spring delivered a measured amount of chemical ink down a tube of circular or oval section, and at the end of the tube in contact with the stone formed a note head (see fig.18*b* above). With the aid of this pen it was possible to lay quickly a large number of identical note heads. Considerable skill was required to manage the pen where lines crossed: if both lines were wet the ink might 'blob' at the intersection.

The procedures required for writing direct on the stone, however, were arduous: it is not surprising that once the so-called transfer process was understood it was much used, particularly for ephemera. In this, the writing or drawing was copied from left to right with a flexible pen, a common goose-quill for want of a steel pen of comparable elasticity, using chemical ink on transfer paper, which had a specially prepared surface on one side. When the work was finished and the ink dry, the back of the paper was sponged with very weak nitric acid and the leaf put between sheets of dry blotting paper to absorb superfluous liquid and ensure that the paper was uniformly damp. While still moist the sheet was laid on the surface of a highly polished stone face down and, protected with backing sheets, was passed two or three times through the press. The stone was then removed from the press and bitten in, and pure water was poured over it until the paper was disengaged, leaving an exact image, reversed right to left in the correct sense for printing. The stone was then prepared for printing in the manner used for stones on which the writing had been applied direct.

Although Senefelder acquired a British patent in 1801, he was still writing in the future tense, urging its adoption for music printing, in his *Complete Course* in 1818. It is impossible to judge by looking at printed sheets to what extent, and when, the process of transfer to stone from originals written on prepared paper in chemical ink became an accepted practice for music. The process was increasingly used in commerce and law from the 1820s onwards, and certainly Wagner's writing of the full score of *Tannhäuser* in 1845 (see fig.19)

shows that the technique had by this time become reliable even in the hands of amateurs. In the same year, he wrote, he had 25 copies made of the scores of *Der fliegende Holländer* and *Rienzi*, 'by means of the so-called autographic transfer process, although only from the writing of copyists'.

Traditionally, music was laid direct on the stone with pen, brush and, sometimes, graver, or at one remove via transfer paper. In his British patent Senefelder described how 'plates of copper, tin, pewter, and various metallic compounds already etched or engraved' could be charged with a specially prepared ink and passed through a rolling press to yield impressions which could be readily transferred to stone. It is not known who was the first to compound the qualities and defects of engraving and lithographic techniques by transferring a proof taken from a punched and engraved plate to a lithographic stone for printing; nor is it known when that was first done. But it was a crucial development, and it set a pattern which has persisted in some guise or other.

Dans le temple d'industrie, a song dedicated to Louis XVIII on the Exhibition of the products of French industry, 'drawn, written and printed on the lithographic plates of A. Senefelder & Co., rue Servandoni no.13' (Paris, *c*1820) shows a splendid portrait and some accomplished writing, but the music 'engraved by Madame Pannetier' was printed from intaglio plates in a rolling press. In France the 1830s and 1840s produced some examples that seem to have been transferred from intaglio plates to stone for printing. In 1848 it was stated that D'Almaine & Co. had 'recently introduced a new and very superior mode of printing music at a charge infinitely lower than by the old processes, whilst the notation is rendered beautiful and agreeable to the eye'. This company had facilities for printing by letterpress, intaglio and lithography, and the new process might well have been derived from a combination of the intaglio and lithographic methods. *The Official and Descriptive Catalogue* of the Great Exhibition provides clear evidence that such a combination was being worked in London in 1851, for it is recorded in Class 30 that Jullien & Co. of 214 Regent Street exhibited 'specimens of ornamental printed music: three of the titles are printed in oil colours, and three printed in colours from stone. The music was engraved on pewter, and afterwards transferred and printed from stone'. During the 19th century developments in the design of printing machinery led to experiments with metal plates treated to give the same results as lithographic stone. Although zinc, for example, offered satisfactory properties for lithography, its adoption for music printing was belated. Lowe & Brydone, one of the largest British music printers, used stone until 1895, when they started to print from zinc.

The paper size of the earliest lithographic music was not at all uniform; some works were printed with two or more pages on a stone, others with one page on each stone. In 1797 Senefelder was using stones of about 2500 square cm in surface area for his music, but as presses improved it was possible to use larger stones and by the latter part of the 19th century stones and zinc plates were giving 16 pages in full music size or 64 pages in octavo, imposed in accord with the same principles as those governing imposition in letterpress printing.

The next great step forward came with the introduc-

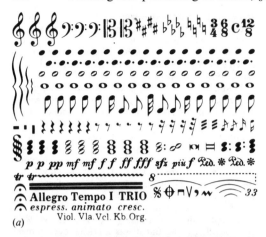

(b)

20. (a) Specimen Notaset transfer sheet; (b) characters being rubbed down on to pre-determined positions

21. (a) The Musicomp, designed by Armando dal Molin (1977): the keys on the left set the pitch (7 notes, 4 octaves, with 2 more octaves available) and the keys on the right select, from a comprehensive range, the required musical and plain-language symbols, with the notes disposed according to their value by a space bar; the music is displayed on the screen by keyboard command through computer coding and stored in a microcassette (capable of storing 30 pages of music) before passing on to print-out in a complete form

tion of the camera into the field of the reproductive graphic arts. As soon as photography had become a practical process in 1839 as a result of the work of Louis Daguerre and W. H. Fox Talbot, attempts were made to apply it to lithography; but it was not until 1852 that R. J. Lemercier and his colleagues succeeded in devising a process – difficult and hazardous in its operation – which they described in *Lithophotographie: ou, Impressions obtenues sur pierre à l'aide de la photographie*. Alphonse Poitevin's process, in which the lithographic stone was sensitized with bichromated albumen, was perfected in 1855 and won general acceptance; it still persists in certain applications. In 1857 Eduard I. Asser of Amsterdam succeeded in making transfers from photographic prints on to a non-sensitized stone and in 1859 Henry James was the first to make photographic transfers on to grained zinc. Instead of being written on stone or on transfer paper and then chemically 'fixed', music could now be derived from any original that could be photographed, the negative printed down on to stone or zinc and subsequently treated to yield a printing surface.

It is not surprising that this technology gave tremendous impetus to the development of new methods – or old methods in new guises – in the origination of music for printing. Instead of writing and drawing in reverse on stone or from left to right on special paper it was now possible to write from left to right on ordinary smooth paper, photograph the result and transfer it on to the stone or zinc plate for printing. Instead of punching and engraving metal plates it was possible to adapt traditional practices to paper, using, instead of gravers, pens and drawing instruments, and special punches carrying note heads, clefs, letters and even complete, frequently used words (for example *piano*, *accel.*, *ped.*). This process was worked either on lithographic transfer paper for direct transfer to stone or metal; or on ordinary papers for the camera and subsequent printing down for lithography; or for line engraving in relief. In the 1920s and 1930s the process was much used in France, where it was known as *similigravure*: its late developments are represented in the work of the Grafische Industrie, Haarlem, Netherlands, and Caligraving of Thetford, England.

The Halstan process, by which the music examples in this dictionary are reproduced, is also graphical in essence. It was devised by Harold Smith, a master music engraver, and developed from 1919 onwards by him and his brother Stanley, a photographer and engraver. The method is based on a meticulously planned original, drafted in pencil by a musician and then realized by processors using a variety of flexible stencils, standard drawing instruments and pens, all worked with dense black ink. Any underlay of words is proofed in type and then laid down in position. The finished sheet is reduced by photography (3:2) and printed on to a lithographic zinc plate. Emphasis on quality and technical innovation has ensured a strong following for the process, exemplified at its best by the Britten scores printed for Faber Music.

These graphical processes all require particular tools for making note heads, clefs and other musical symbols, whereas the equipment for ruling staves, stems, beams, slurs and the like is common to them all. Traditional procedures, however, have been strongly challenged by a system based on the technique of dry transfer, in which punches, stencils and other similar hand tools are not required. Instead, multiple copies of individual

21. (b) A reproduction of part of a line of music originated on the Musicomp: the tempo, beams, slurs, crescendos and bar-lines, normally added by hand in other systems, are here all an integrated part of the whole

music symbols are printed in a dense black substance (plastic 'ink') on one side of a thin transparent film. When the face of the sheet is turned down on to paper and the form of any character is rubbed from the back, the 'ink' leaves the sheet and adheres to the paper. In this way a succession of note heads, clefs, rests and a wide range of other units in any quantity – each individual character in every respect uniform with its fellow – can be rubbed down in any position. Letraset in Great Britain offer music sheets, but the most comprehensive system has been developed in the Netherlands as Notaset, and is much used (see fig.20); such systems are also extensively used by Bärenreiter. Basically simple, the technique demands care in practice. Each work starts as a detailed layout made on previously ruled paper by a musically trained planner and is then developed by operators using transfer sheets, rubbing down the necessary characters in place as they appear. The whole is finished with a pen as required, after which it is photographed and printed down on to a zinc plate.

All the processes described in this section are relatively slow, and call for the work of many hands: yet they and variants of them have survived and sometimes prospered, while the amount of work done by the engravers of pewter plates has declined catastrophically. The shift from punching and engraving has been much accelerated by the rapid development of efficient music typewriters. Attempts were made in the 18th century to use the action of a piano to record on paper notes as they were struck, but it was not until 1833 that the first practical typewriter for music was described in a French patent (no.3748) awarded to Xavier Progin of Marseilles for what he called 'une machine ou plume ktypographique'. Other machines followed, by Berry (1837) and Guillemot (1859), but 'the first serious, commercially distributed machine was the Tachigrafo Musicale introduced by Angelo Tessaro in 1887' (Adler, 1973) and marketed in Italy by Ricordi. During the next 60 years there were literally hundreds of patents granted throughout the world, particularly in America, for music typewriters. Most, for one reason or another, fell by the wayside; some were developed; a few succeeded, as for example the machine patented by Lily Salmon (later Pavey) which was manufactured for a time by the Imperial Typewriter Co. in England. Two or three types of machine have enjoyed wide and continuing use over a long period. One of these is the Keaton Music Typewriter, invented and developed by Robert H. Keaton of San Francisco, formerly a professional violinist. Intended for the individual musician and the small publisher, it has been highly successful throughout the USA: the makers have made no attempt to promote sales elsewhere, though one or two machines have found their way to Europe.

If Keaton's machine has served a domestic market only, the typewriters invented and developed by Armando Dal Molin and Cecil Effinger have each at-

22. Musicwriter (1973 model) designed by Cecil Effinger

tained wide international fame and influence. Armando Dal Molin, born in Italy but a US citizen since 1952, an engineer in Milan and an amateur musician, first devised a music typewriter for his own use in 1945, and in 1946 obtained an Italian patent for it. In the same year he went to the USA to develop his machine further, and in 1948 he exhibited his Music Writer at the New York World's Fair of Music. It was a great success and the Remington Typewriter Company obtained an option on the manufacturing rights (1949); but this option was not taken up. Dal Molin and his friends decided to manufacture and sell the typewriter themselves, and at the same time set up a music typing studio to demonstrate the machine's capacity. This was so successful that in the late 1950s they decided to stop the manufacture of the machine for sale and to concentrate on the origination of music for publishers and their printers. Refinements were incorporated in the machine in 1955; Dal Molin wrote in 1973: 'by 1956 the process had taken over the New York area and by the early '60s it had spread to the whole country where it now accounts for 90% of today's market'. It has been estimated that by 1972 the undertaking had produced 400,000 pages. By 1953 Dal Molin was convinced that the best way to lay out a page of music was by using a computer; he designed and built a system of origination, computerized from keyboard to photon-generated negatives, showing music complete except for the slanted beams and slurs (see fig.21). The installation has been working commercially since 1970 and in the first five years it produced 25,000 pages with only an occasional error. Examples show that the work is of the highest quality, and a great deal of origination is flowing from Europe to Music Reprographics (Dal Molin's company).

Cecil Effinger, a composer and professor of music at the University of Colorado (1956), conceived the idea of a music typewriter in Paris in 1945 (see fig.22). He had made his first model the 'size of a large table – not functional' by November 1947, and developed it through subsequent forms to the fifth, shown first at Denver, Colorado, in July 1955. The first Musicwriter was exported in November the same year, and the model has since been in demand throughout the world. It is simple and rugged in construction and engineered to fine limits. The dies for the note heads and other characters are well designed and cut to give a clear, dense, black impression through the ribbon. The machine is best used by professionals working to previously planned copy, but it can be operated by amateurs, and will cut stencils. Special papers are manufactured for diazo reproduction as well as for the camera and transfer to lithographic plates. Computer applications have also been developed (1960, 1972).

II. Publishing

1. Introduction. 2. The age of letterpress printing, 1501–1700. 3. The age of engraving, 1700–1860. 4. The age of offset printing, after 1860.

1. INTRODUCTION. The music publisher issues musical editions which consist primarily of musical notation; a publisher who issues books about music, methods, librettos and other primarily verbal texts, but does not also issue musical editions, is not generally regarded as a music publisher. The music publisher's activities involve obtaining a text and working with the composer or editor, financing the printing, promoting, advertising and distributing the copies.

A survey of music publishing comes close to describing in summary the cultural history of music from the special perspective of the student of musical documents. Music publishing is part of the history of society and of commerce. It owes its existence to three phenomena that appeared in Western civilization during the Renaissance: the invention of printing; the growth of modern capitalism, which provided the publisher with a framework for his economic and promotional activities; and the rise of the professional composer, who needed the services of the music publisher. Music printing – which preceded music publishing – is part of the history of technology; but the two are closely related, as most publishers did their own printing.

Musical texts may be printed but not published. Luxurious editions were often prepared as keepsakes for private and limited circulation, as, for example, were the earliest copies of *Parthenia* (London, c1613[14]); later impressions of this book, however, were intended for sale and should therefore be regarded as having been published. Other music was printed but not published in order to ensure control over performances. Ten part-books make up John Barnard's *Selected Church Musick* (*RISM* 1641[5]), but there is no extant continuo part; apparently the vocal parts were printed so that the singers could learn the music, but no performance could take place without a continuo. In the 19th century full scores and instrumental parts for operas and large symphonic works were often printed but not published, so the owner could more effectively demand royalties or specify conditions of performance. Vocal scores, which were both printed and published, could be used to familiarize the public with a work and to train singers, but full-scale performances with orchestra could not be given until arrangements were made with the publisher to rent the parts and the conductor's score.

The opposite condition can also exist: a work may be published but not printed. Through history there have been music copyists whose manuscripts were presumably intended to be equivalent to a printed copy (*see* SOURCES, MS, §I). It has been suggested that, when William Byrd and Thomas Tallis secured rights not only to music printing but also to music paper in their patent of 1575, they had some connection with copyists. Reports indicate that the money they made came mostly from the paper; and when Thomas Morley re-negotiated the patent in 1599 he took pains to retain the coverage of music paper. In the early 18th century, Italian opera was rarely printed; yet, through manuscripts, it came to dominate European musical taste. Provincial newspaper announcements of the 18th and 19th centuries tell of men who made a living by copying music 'cheaper and more accurately' than printed editions. In modern times, through photography and lithography, any manuscript can be duplicated, and hence can become the basis for a published edition. Various blueprint processes have also been widely used, especially from 1920 to 1960, to copy and circulate contemporary music. The manuscript is an appropriate means of publishing a musical text when few copies are likely to be needed.

Before Gutenberg's invention of printing, books were extensively distributed in manuscript; and the origins of book publishing are commonly seen as beginning well before that time. There is no evidence, however, of copyists who specialized in music. There were music scribes attached to courts and chapels, such as those at Mechlin or Ferrara: the music they copied was often widely circulated and much used, but this is distinct from the processes of publication.

During the period of incunabula several dozen printers issued theoretical treatises, but few ever issued more than one such book. The printers of liturgical music, on the other hand, usually issued more than one book, perhaps because they had made an initial investment in music type. By 1480 liturgical books containing music in plainchant notation were being issued throughout Europe at the rate of several dozen a year. Books for service use in Germany and central Europe were produced by Johann Sensenschmidt and later by Johann Pfeyl in Bamberg, Georg Reyser in Würzburg and Georg Stuchs in Nuremberg. For a few years just before 1490 about a dozen books a year came from the press of Michael Wenssler in Basle. The most prolific German printer was Erhard Ratdolt in Augsburg. In Paris in the 1480s several dozen missals were printed for various French bishoprics by Jean Dupré, who left space for manuscript music; in the 1490s Johannes Higman issued such books, using music type. These men were still essentially printers. The stimuli to a separation between printing and publishing were twofold: first, printers had to sub-contract work to other printers; second, financial support was sought outside the trade. The first music publishers who were not also their own printers appeared after 1480, when Venetian merchants like Lucantonio Giunta and Ottaviano Scotto called on printers like Johannes Emericus de Spira and Johannes Hamman to print music books, mostly Roman missals. The Giunta family was to become the major Italian publisher of liturgical music books throughout the 16th century.

The 16th-century history of liturgical books has yet to be studied in detail, but it appears that the output in the Netherlands and Germany declined sharply about 1515; in France it flourished longer and did not disappear until after 1550. England produced liturgical books for a few years around 1500 and again during the reign of Mary Tudor. Even so, more 16th-century liturgical music books probably came from the Giuntas than from all other publishers combined.

2. THE AGE OF LETTERPRESS PRINTING, 1501–1700. Petrucci has been called the Gutenberg of music printing. The comparison is not quite appropriate, since he was not the first to print music; but in matters of artistry the comparison is apt. Besides being the first printer to use multiple-impression movable type, he deserves to be recognized as the first publisher of polyphony. Between 1501 and 1509 in Venice he issued the three *Canti* volumes of the *Odhecaton*, five books of *Motetti*, 16 mass books, 11 collections of popular frottolas and six lutebooks. In 1511 he resumed printing in his native Fossombrone, with less exceptional results. His 61 known publications, the last dated 1520, provide an invaluable record of the musical works of Franco-Flemish polyphony and a testimony to their contemporary reputation.

Although Petrucci's success seems to have stimulated other printers to attempt music (Caneto, Sambonetto and particularly Dorico, as well as Oeglin and Schoeffer in Germany), his main successor, Andrea Antico, was neither a printer nor a publisher, but a woodcutter or engraver whose blocks were used by music printers in editions sponsored by others. The blocks have been identified in about a dozen books, most of them vocal canzonas, first issued when Antico was in Rome between 1510 and 1518. From 1520 to 1538 he worked in Venice, after 1532 in partnership with Ottaviano Scotto. About two dozen more music books were issued during this period, using his music blocks.

The next flourishing music publishing concern was established in Paris, during the reign of François I, at the time of the so-called 'scholar printers', by Pierre Attaingnant, whose first anthology dates from 1527/8. Attaingnant's several music typefaces, if not unprecedented, are very important; but it remained for Attaingnant to realize their usefulness and through them to compromise the artistry of Petrucci in the interests of commerce. Whereas Petrucci enjoyed a modest success, Attaingnant flourished for a quarter of a century. His books follow formulae of many kinds, in their appearance, their content and even their titles. His speciality was the early French chanson, which he issued in oblong partbooks, at first octavo and later quarto. But he also issued several tablature books and folio mass collections, for which other music type was made.

Venetian music publishing after Petrucci and Antico is the story of two great names, Gardane and Scotto. Their output, devoted almost entirely to sacred and secular partbooks, is prodigious: around 1590, after Amadino and Vincenti had entered the picture, Venice was publishing more music than all of the rest of Europe. Antonio Gardane, originally from southern France, began printing in Venice in 1538, specializing in the music of Arcadelt and featuring the series of *Motetti del frutto*. By 1545 he was issuing a dozen or more new titles every year, a total which reached 30 just before 1600. His heirs continued to publish music up to

23. Title-page of Banchieri's 'Il metamorfosi musicale'; published by Ricciardo Amadino (Venice, 1601)

1685, sometimes retaining the name of Gardane, else-where using that of Magni, the founder's grandson-in-law. Over its long history the Gardane dynasty issued about 3000 musical editions. The firm begun by Girolamo Scotto produced perhaps half this total. It began in 1539, and for a time rivalled Gardane in the quantity and quality of its output. But before 1570 the firm had waned, and after 1590 its occasional publications were mostly reprints of Palestrina masses.

The innovatory music of the 'nuove musiche' was favoured by two younger Venetians, Ricciardo Amadino and Giacomo Vincenti, who were partners between 1583 and 1586 but worked separately thereafter. Amadino's firm perished during the decline of Venice, and is last heard of in 1617; but the name of Vincenti persisted until 1667, and appeared on well over 1000 musical editions. Lesser Venetian publishers included Francesco Rampazetto, who issued reprints in the 1560s; the composer Merulo ('Claudio da Correggio'), whose editions also dated from the 1560s, and were regarded as models of editorial accuracy; and Alessandro Raverio, who printed over a dozen music books a year during his short career, 1606–9. Venetian commerce enjoyed its last great prosperity between 1540 and 1610, and the book trade was extremely prolific: it was almost inevitable that its music publishers would also be important, and their fecundity is astonishing. The prolific output of Venice probably helped significantly in the spread of the polychoral and monodic styles.

The centre of early German music publishing was Nuremberg. Activity began with two type-cutters who also used their own type as printers: Hieronymus Formschneider ('Grapheus') and Johann Petreius. Formschneider issued several treatises, beginning in 1532, using woodcuts. He then cut a music face, and used it in about a dozen music books which he printed between 1534 and 1539. (His name also appears in the imprint of Heinrich Isaac's *Choralis constantinus*, dated 1550–55.) Formschneider is important mainly because his music type was used by so many of the Lutheran printers of northern Germany later in the century. Petreius issued several dozen music books between 1536 and 1553; but he too is important mainly as a designer of music type, which was used in southern Germany, central Europe, and as far away as Antwerp and Paris. His two music faces are particularly attractive and complex in their construction. The most prolific of the Nuremberg houses, however, was the partnership of Johann Berg ('Montanus') and Ulrich Neuber. These men issued about 100 editions, mostly partbooks and vernacular song collections, using Petreius type (1540–71), while their successors, Dietrich Gerlach (1567–93) and Paul Kauffmann (1594–1618), issued several hundred more.

Other music publishers arose in Paris after the death of Attaingnant. Of these, Nicolas Du Chemin issued about 200 music books (1549–76), including two series of chansons in the style of Attaingnant and about 30 folio mass books. Michel Fezandat issued several Calvinist psalm books and tablature books (1550–58). But it was Adrian Le Roy and Robert Ballard, partners in publishing from 1551, who in 1553 obtained the exclusive royal monopoly for music printing, which was to remain in force for over two centuries. Their earliest editions were mostly tablature books and psalters; in 1557–9, 22 folio choirbooks appeared. Thereafter

secular partbook anthologies predominated in their catalogue. At first, type from Petreius in Nuremberg was used, but just before 1560 they used new music founts, commissioned from the great punch-cutter, the younger Guillaume Le Bé. These Le Bé fonts were to be used in the firm's music for the rest of its long career. After the death of Le Roy in 1598, the Ballard name was used alone.

The fourth music publishing centre at that time was Antwerp. Printing began there with a privilege issued in 1540 to Willem van Vissenaecken, who had music type specially cut for him, but issued only one collection. His competitor and successor was Tylman Susato, who issued about 60 music books (1543–64) devoted mostly to chansons and motets in reprint, also some Flemish songbooks and psalm books. Jean de Laet and Hubert Waelrant also issued about 20 attractive vocal collections (1554–65). The major music publisher of the Low Countries was Pierre Phalèse (i), who worked in Louvain and issued nearly 200 chanson, motet and lute collections between 1545 and his death in about 1575. As early as 1570 he had as his partner Jean Bellère in Antwerp; and after the death of the elder Phalèse, his son Pierre Phalèse (ii) moved to Antwerp, where the family continued to publish music up to 1691. The several editions issued in Antwerp by Christopher Plantin and his heirs (1580–1606) should also be cited for their musical and visual interest.

Like book publishing, music publishing favoured commercial centres in preference to university towns. In addition to the four cities discussed above, Lyons, Augsburg and Frankfurt also housed music publishing firms, mostly in the 1530s. In 1532 Jacques Moderne began printing in Lyons with a folio missal and three motet collections. After five years of inactivity, he resumed with a series in the style of Attaingnant, entitled *Le parangon des chansons* (beginning *RISM* 1538[15]); in addition to the 18 books which made up the series, 'Grand Jacques' (as Moderne called himself) issued about a dozen other music books. Although he was active as late as 1556, most of his music after 1541 was reprinted from Paris or Venice editions. In Augsburg the anthologies printed by Melchior Kriesstein (1540–49) and Philipp Ulhart (1537–79) also consisted mostly of music taken from other publishers' books. The Frankfurt printer Christian Egenolff, on the other hand, issued several original works, consisting of German folksongs and Horatian odes. By 1560 all of these men had ceased publishing music, and thereafter their cities were of minor importance.

The commercial centres, in the mainstream of activity, could be expected to produce editions of a musical repertory that was stylish and distinguished but essentially conservative. The character of the music produced at each was distinctive, but activity elsewhere varied much more widely in character and in quality, in different countries, cities and periods. Because of religious conflict and the political decentralization of the country, German publishing was particularly diversified in style and scattered geographically. Nuremberg produced attractive editions of the music of the well-known composers, and never completely abandoned its leadership. But music was also issued between 1550 and 1700 by over 1000 different music printers in nearly 200 other German cities. Of these Wittenberg was the earliest important centre. Georg Rhau, who had printed some musical treatises as early as 1517, obtained a fount of music type from Formschneider in Nuremberg and several dozen Lutheran service books were issued from his press (1538–65). His work was carried on by such men as Johann and Andreas Eichhorn in Frankfurt an der Oder (1556–1615), Andreas Hantzsch in Mühlhausen (1566–99), Johann Schwertel (1565–80) and Matthäus Welak (1581–96) in Wittenberg, Georg Baumann in Erfurt (1557–97) and Breslau (1590–1618) and Gimel Berg in Dresden (1570–97, his heirs to 1687). In the south the major publisher was Adam Berg in Munich (1566–1626), whose many editions of Lassus culminated in the magnificent folio *Patrocinium musices* (1573–87), one of the most sumptuous musical editions ever produced. Important musical editions were also issued by Kraków printers, active as early as 1550, and by Nigrin in Prague (1579–1604).

In the years around 1600 courtly patronage supported extensive, but often temporary, music publishing activity by Justus Hauck (1604–18) and Johann Forkel (1621–34) in Coburg and by Johann Weidner in Jena (1605–28), and to the north by the Fürstliche Druckerey in Wolfenbüttel (1607–13) as well as Philippe von Ohr (1597–1609) and Heinrich Carstens (1615–22) in Hamburg. From about 1600 also come the earliest of the printers who specialized in 'occasional' works (*Gelegenheitskompositionen*), music for events such as weddings, funerals and baptisms. Leipzig was the centre for such publishing around 1625; a few years later the Hamburg press of Jacob Reberlein (1630–62, his heirs to 1690) was particularly important. By far the most prolific publishing centres for occasional music, however, were those near the Baltic Sea, in Lübeck, Rostock, Greifswald, Stettin (Szczecin), Danzig (Gdańsk) and above all in Königsberg (Kaliningrad), which included among its printers Georg Osterberger (1577–1612), Lorenz Segebad (1623–42), Paschen Mense (1642–51) and Johann and Friedrich Reussner (1644–93). Publishers of Lutheran hymnbooks included Georg Runge in Berlin (1616–39, his heirs to 1685), who issued many editions of Johannes Crüger's *Praxis pietatis melica*, Balthasar Wust in Frankfurt am Main (1656–1702) and the Endter family in Nuremberg (1617–99). Major printers of the Catholic south included Georg Widmanstetter in Graz (1587–1614), Adam Meltzer in Dillingen (1603–10) and Michael Wagner in Innsbruck (1640–68). In general, however, the large German publishers declined after 1600. During the years just before the Thirty Years War, Leipzig printers such as Johann Lanckisch (1619–56) and Johann Glück (1618–24) issued many of the occasional works of J. H. Schein. But Leipzig remained at best a secondary music publishing centre, in spite of its book fairs and musical life. The same is true of Frankfurt, where several Catholic service books were issued in competition with such books from Cologne.

German music publishing declined during the Thirty Years War; but the disappearance of a number of large firms around 1600, particularly in Nuremberg, suggests that the war hastened rather than caused the decline. Decentralized as they were, German music publishers were also book publishers, to a greater extent than those of Italy or France: one also finds, particularly after 1630, imprints which name two men – a printer and a publisher – occasionally in different cities. From Germany, Lutheran music publishing spread to the east and north, to Prussia and Poland with Georg Rhetus in Danzig and Thorn (1634–43, his heirs to 1664), and

Andreas Hünefeld in Danzig (1608–47); to Copenhagen in 1537, the main press being that of Henrik Waldkirch (1602–40); and to Stockholm in 1586 and Iceland in 1594.

Calvinist psalm books were also printed in great quantities. Those before 1560 are modelled largely on Lutheran service books. In 1560, at Calvin's request, Antoine Vincent of Lyons arranged for various printers to issue 20,000 psalm books for service use. The editions of the Marot and de Bèze versions, which appeared from Paris, Lyons, Geneva and elsewhere, are on a modest scale. Several hundred French psalters, many with music, were issued over the next two centuries, at first by small, provincial French printers, throughout the period in Geneva, and frequently around 1650 in Charenton, near Paris. Geneva also produced a number of Italian psalm books for use by Piedmontese Calvinist congregations. Dutch psalm books, mostly in the Dathenius versions, were issued in the 17th century, usually in small format and with painfully tiny and ill-printed musical notation. The leading German printer of psalm books was Christopher Corvinus at Herborn in Nassau, who in the years around 1600 issued not only Lobwasser's German versions but also George Buchanan's Latin paraphrases and at least one Hungarian psalm book. In England, the psalms of Sternhold and Hopkins, which had first been printed in Geneva, went through many editions, apparently modelled on Dutch patterns. John Day, apparently exiled to Emden during the reign of Queen Mary, returned to London and in 1559 received a royal patent which came to include psalm books. Day printed nearly 40 editions of Sternhold and Hopkins before his death in 1584; his son Richard inherited the patent and worked with several London printers in issuing nearly 50 more. In 1603 the Company of Stationers bought up the Day patent and used it to provide work for their printers. Between 1603 and 1650 several hundred more editions of the psalm book were printed with musical notation. John Playford later attempted to revive and revitalize the music of the psalm book.

In Italy most of the activity before 1600 took place in Venice. In Rome the brothers Dorico, partners with Antico as early as 1524, issued several dozen music books of their own (1533–72). Antonio Blado (1551–80) and Antonio Barré (1555–64) also printed some music. Later some rather interesting madrigal partbooks came from Sabbio in Brescia (1579–88), Baldini in Ferrara (1582–1614), the Marescotti family in Florence (1580–1611) and Tradate in Milan (1598–1612). In the quantity of musical editions issued between 1570 and 1640, Milan was a remote second to Venice among the Italian cities. Its most prolific publisher was the firm begun by the heirs of Simone Tini, which eventually came to be managed by Filippo Lomazzo (1583–1628). Other printers were active at this time in Naples and Palermo. As Venice waned, Rome became a centre for editions of the elaborate concerted music of the Counter-Reformation. Bartolomeo Zannetti (1602–21), L. A. Soldi (1604–35), G. B. Robletti (1609–50), Andrea and Girolamo Fei (1615–85) and Paolo Masotti (1621–37) were among the most important publishers. After 1650 Bologna slowly became a printing centre (particularly for instrumental music), displacing Rome as Rome had displaced Venice. Giacomo Monti printed music there as early as 1636. His successors issued large amounts of

24. Daman's 'The Psalmes of David in English Meter': title-page of the tenor partbook; published by John Day (London, 1579)

music from 1668 to 1709, often in partnership with the publisher Marino Silvani (1665–1727). Venice re-entered the scene with Giuseppe Salà (1675–1715), also mainly a publisher of instrumental music.

English secular music publishing began with Thomas Vautrollier, who in 1570 printed a Lassus anthology (which was commercially unsuccessful). Five years later Tallis and Byrd received a royal patent, covering music printing and music paper. Their own *Cantiones sacrae* (*RISM* 1575³), also printed by Vautrollier, sold badly too. A hiatus of 12 years followed; by 1587 Tallis was dead, and Vautrollier's music type had been acquired by the printer Thomas East. Between 1588 and 1596 East printed for Byrd well over a dozen important early partbook collections, mostly of madrigals. Byrd's patent expired in 1596, and Peter Short then began printing music; William Barley also sponsored several other music books. In 1598 Thomas Morley became the successor to Tallis and Byrd, by obtaining another royal patent (although psalm books were excluded). Barley became his associate, and East and Short were forbidden to print music. But in 1599 Morley failed in an attempt to take over part of Richard Day's psalm book patent, and about 1602 he died. Once again other printers became active, including Short, East and John Windet. Their respective successors were Humfrey Lownes (1604–13), Thomas Snodham (1609–24) and William Stansby (1609–38), all of whom printed madrigal partbooks, though Barley had acquired the patent for its last few years. Folio lute tablature books appeared as well as madrigal partbooks after 1600; but by 1610 interest in secular music was waning, and by 1620 new music was rarely published in England.

In northern and western Europe in the 17th century there arose a new kind of 'gentleman's music edition'. French *airs de cour*, issued by the Ballards in annual

numbered series, were profitable enough to dominate the firm's production throughout the century, although they also issued many tall folio scores of Lully operas after 1670. In Germany, illustrated poetical–musical anthologies, in the style of contemporary 'emblem books', were popular after 1650. Many of these were issued by the Stern family in Lüneburg and involved the poet Johann Rist and his circle of friends of the Elbschwanenorden. In much the same spirit is Adriaen Valerius's *Neder-landtsche gedenck-clanck*, the famous Dutch folksong collection published in Haarlem in 1626 (*RISM* 1626¹⁴).

John Playford (i) in London also served the tastes of the gentleman. Between 1651 and his death in 1684, he published about 100 music books, most of them printed by Thomas Harper or (later) by William Godbid. Playford's output ranged widely, to include anthologies of Restoration songs, his own much reprinted instruction book, psalms and instrumental pieces. Among music publishers Playford must be considered as the first great promoter; and, judging from the quantity of his output and the extent to which many of the volumes seemed to be directed at a new musical market, he was one of the most successful. On his death his son Henry continued his work, but with notably less success. Whereas John Playford had very few competitors, Henry had to share his audience with such men as John Heptinstall (1686–1717) and William Pearson (1699–1735). Other minor printers emerged in London around 1680 (during the days of the Popish Plots and conflicts over the succession) to fill a passing demand for broadside ballads with music.

Simone Verovio deserves credit as the first publisher to use engraving successfully. Verovio, working in Rome, issued only about 20 editions (1586–1608). Although some were reprinted, there is no evidence that he understood the advantages of the process. Before the 18th century, music engraving was largely a luxury, useful because it conveyed better than letterpress printing the peculiarities of manuscript music notation; its use also reflected the elegance of distinguished patronage. Not until the end of the century did men like Estienne Roger in Amsterdam, and John Walsh and Thomas Cross in London, come to appreciate the commercial advantages of engraving.

In summary, the history of music publishing before 1700 is one of early brilliance and extended decline. The peak was reached before 1580, in Venice, Nuremberg, Paris and Antwerp. The decline was apparent by 1600 and is reflected in a diminished output, in printing that is less spacious, less craftsmanlike and less original; few new music typefaces were cut after 1580. Petrucci and his many followers had shown that music could be published; it remained for the publishers of the 18th century to learn how it could be published most advantageously.

3. THE AGE OF ENGRAVING, 1700–1860. Music publishing during the next period – beginning with the extensive commercial use of engraving and continuing up to the first extensive use of offset lithography – is a story of four cities: London from around 1700; Paris between 1740 and 1760; Vienna just before 1780; and Leipzig around 1800. The activity in each city continued after the next rose to prominence; the quantity of published music became cumulatively greater, as did the competition between publishers and the stimulation of general public interest in music.

In spite of the development of engraving, letterpress printing and manuscript copying continued to be used extensively throughout the 18th century. As late as the 1730s, Francesco Moücke in Florence was still issuing oblong anthologies of Italian cantatas badly printed from movable type. German publishers, chief among them J. J. Lotter in Augsburg, issued a variety of musical editions, most notably treatises but also a few instrumental collections and songbooks, using crude but complicated movable type, most of which had been cut around 1680 for use in Nuremberg. Throughout the 18th century and into the 19th, in France, Spain and Italy, typeset liturgical books and treatises on plainchant were still printed from movable type, as were the many Dutch and Genevan psalm books and German and Scandinavian hymnbooks. Letterpress printing remained the most desirable method when the musical notation was simple (or in some cases, complicated but not requiring speed in performance), when fixed and generally large press runs were involved, or when most of the volume comprised text, as in treatises. After 1700 the publishing of typeset music came to be associated therefore largely with pedagogic and amateur music, and to a degree with the provincial more than with the cosmopolitan press. Typography was also revived and refined around 1750, by four men; of the four, however, Fournier and Enschedé as publishers produced little, while the editions of Fougt and of his successor, Robert Falkener, were mostly imitations of those of Leipzig engravers. The impact of Breitkopf was much greater.

One of the chief virtues of music 'publishing' in manuscript form, such as was used for 18th-century Italian opera, was that the use of manuscript offered the opera house or the composer a measure of control over the text unavailable when copies were printed and widely distributed. Before any forms of copyright were established, such a system of limited distribution seemed highly desirable. Furthermore, an opera house considering performance of a work could alter a neatly assembled typeset edition only with some difficulty; and because of the needs of singers and others involved in opera production, changes were always being called for. Instrumental music also came to appear often in manuscript rather than in typeset form, but for notational reasons. Type was harder to read than handwriting – short note values were particularly troublesome, since the beams were seldom continuous, and chords were impossible without breaking individual sorts of type; this problem might be solved either by manuscript or by engraving. By 1700 most of the current musical repertory had moved outside the world of music publishing as it involved letterpress printing. Italian music, if it was printed at all, was printed abroad. J. S. Bach saw little of his music printed, almost all of it instrumental, with utilitarian titles such as 'Übung'. Nevertheless two musical styles were spread widely throughout 18th-century Europe – 'Neapolitan' opera at the beginning and 'Viennese Classicism' at the end – and it is evident that manuscripts of this music served the purposes of publication (in its widest functional sense) very effectively.

The origins of 18th-century music publishing from engraving took place in London and Amsterdam. Estienne Roger set up his shop in Amsterdam around 1690 and was soon engraving small oblong quarto piracies of Bolognese instrumental music. By 1700 his editions were large oblong folios, well executed with hand-drawn music on copper plates. His emphasis on Italian music suggests an international distribution of copies through northern and western Europe. After Roger's death in 1722 his widow and his son-in-law, Michel-Charles Le Cène, continued to publish until 1743.

London music publishers, inspired by the success of John Playford, experimented with new ways of printing and distributing music. While the nationalistic vocal music was favoured by letterpress printers and their associates in London, engravers were attracted to Italianate instrumental music. Thomas Cross, who engraved Henry Purcell's *Sonnata's* in 1683, also prepared many single songsheets, undated but probably almost all from the last decade of the century. He apparently used hard copper plates on which the signs were drawn by hand; in contrast the elder John Walsh, who began publishing in 1696, apparently used soft plates of pewter or lead, on which the signs were impressed with punches. The firm of Walsh was one of those that established the pattern of modern music publishing. Although his catalogue consisted at first of songsheets (sometimes collected into periodical series) and works of other publishers which he sold at his shop, Walsh soon began to issue instrumental music, much of it taken from continental sources. His speciality, however, was the anthology of 'Favourite Songs' from the London stage; and he became the principal publisher of Handel's music. By 1736, when the elder Walsh died, London music publishing was well established.

Few competitors challenged Walsh during his lifetime. John Cluer issued some handsome scores of Handel operas, neatly engraved by hand rather than punched, and in small format. English letterpress printers, such as John Watts, also issued ballad opera librettos and song anthologies that included crude

CATALOGUE
de Musique vocale & instrumentale
Mise au jour par IMBAULT Professeur et Marchand de Musique
au Mont d'or, rue St Honoré entre l'hôtel d'Aligre et la rue des Poulies N° 627

Sinfonies en Œuvre		Quatuors		Duos		Concertos	
Pierlot Œuvre 1er	9	Fodor 2 Liv	9	Michel Airs variés p. Clarin	6	Devienne pour Flute N° 2	
Borghi 1er	9	Hoffmeister 7	9	Blasius 8 p. Violon	7.4		4.4
Ditto 2e	9	Cambini 22 Liv	9	Michel 5 p. Clarinette	7.4	Michel pour Clarinette	
		Pirlinger	9	Fodor 7 p. Violon	7.4	N° 7.8 Chaque	4.4
		Bruni 6	9	Jarnowich Violon et Basse	1.10	Fodor pour Violon	
		Kreutzer 1er	9	Guthman p. Violon	7.4	N° 7.10 Chaque	4.4
		Flad 1er pour Flute	6	Cambini 6 p. Flute	7.4	Reicha pour Violoncelle	4.4
		Pleyel 5 Quintetti	6	Fodor 8 p. Violon	7.4		
		Ditto 1re Livraison	6	Michel 6 p. Clarinette	7.4	Triklir pour Violoncelle	
		Ditto 2e id	6	Beauvalet p. Chant	6	N° 4.5.6.7 Chaque	4.4
Sinfonies Périodiques		Ditto 3e id	6	Amon 2e pour Violon et Alto	7.4	Duport pour Violoncelle	
Haydn N° 11.13.14.15.17.18		Ditto 4e id	6	Reinhard petits et aisés	3	N° 1.2.3 Chaque	4.4
chaque	4.4	Ditto arrange p. flute	9	Schwind id	3		
Schaffer Ouv de Didon	3	D° 7e Q. p. Violon	9	Juliano	1.10	Viotty pour Violon	
Pleyel N° 1.2.3.4.5.6				Fodor 9e p. 2 V.	7.4	N° 11.12 chaque	6
7.8.9.10.11.12 chaque	4.4			Gebauer pour V. et A.	7.4		
Clementi N° 1.2	4.4					Borghi p. Violoncelle	4.4

Sinfonies Concertantes		Ouvertures en Quatuor		Ouvertures en Duo		Clavecin	
Pierlot N° 1.2		Tarare	2.8	Tarare p. 2 V.	1.4	Mozart 6 Sonates	7.4
chaque	4.4	Les Dettes	2.8	Ditto p. 2 Flut	1.4	Kozeluch 6 id	7.4
Devienne p. Cor et Basson	4.4	Les Curieux punis	2.8	Les Curieux punis p. V.	1.4	Clementi 10 id	4.4
Devienne 2 p. Oboe et Basson	4.4	Les promesses de mariage	2.8	Les Dettes	1.4		
Viotti 1er p. 2 V.	6	La Negresse	2.8	Les Promesses de mariage	1.4	Bruni id	7.4
		La Fête de l'arquebuse	2.8	La Fête de l'arquebuse	1.4		
		Œdipe à Colonne	2.8	Œdipe à Colonne	1.4	Fion 1er Concerto	6
		Celestine	2.8	Celestine	1.4	Kozeluch 1er id	4.4
		Berthe et Pepin	2.8	Berthe et Pepin	1.4	Clementi 13 Sonates	7.4
		La Noce Béarnoise	2.8	La Noce Béarnoise	1.4	Clementi 14 id	7.4
Partitions		Trios		Sonates		Hoffmeister id	7.6
Tarare Gd Opera	30	Weiss p. Flute	2.8	Triklir p. Vlle	7.4	Viotty Concerto N° 1.2 chaq	
Les Promesses de mariage		Rousseau Airs variés				Haydn petites Pièces	8
Œdipe à Colonne Gd Op	24	Œuvre 1 et 2 chaque	6			Clementi 19. Prélude	7.4
La Negresse avec Parties	12	Ouverture de Tarare	1.10			Pleyel 1re Suite	9
Les Parties Séparées seules	6	id. des Dettes	1.10	Airs Variés		ditto 2e idem	9
		Id. des Curieux punis	1.10			ditto 3e idem	9
				Cartier 3 p. Violon	3	Mazzinghi Son	9
				Henry id	3		
				Alday id	3		
				Fodor Pot pouri	4.10		
Ouvertures et Suites pour Harmonie		Airs avec accomp. de Harpe		ditto 2e et prélude	4.4	Ouvert. pour Clavecin	
Ouv. de Tarare	1.10	Burkhoffer 22		ditto Airs de Tarare p. V.	12	Les Dettes	3
ditto des Dettes	1.10	Airs de Richard Cœur de Lion	4.4	Alday, id. p. V. et A.	12	Les Curieux punis	2.8
ditto des Curieux punis	1.10	Rosteme 3 p. Guittare	6	Cartier, idem p. V. et A.	12	Les Promesses de mariage	2.8
pre Suite d'Airs de Tarare	6	Airs de Tarare	1.10	Devienne, id. p. Fl.	12	Ouver. et Airs de Tarare	9
Ouv. des Promesses de mariage	1.10	Airs des Dettes	2.8	Le Fevre, id. p. Clarin	12	Airs des Dettes	2.8
						des Esclaves par Amour	1.4
						del Marchese Tulipano	1.10
						Œdipe à Colonne	2.8
						Celestine	2.8
						Berthe et Pepin	2.8

25. Imbault catalogue, taken from a copy of Sacchini's 'Oedipe à Colone' (Paris, 1787) woodcuts of the tunes. There also appeared a multitude of songsheets naming no printer or publisher, which must have been sold casually at music shops, much like the earlier broadside ballads of England.

After Walsh's death his son John maintained the firm for another 30 years. Other publishers came into prominence, notably John Johnson (c1740–1762, his widow to 1777); the Thompson family, including Ann, Peter, Charles, Samuel and Henry (c1750–1805); Robert Bremner (c1760–1789), a Scotsman; Peter Welcker and his heirs (1762–85); William Randall, the heir to Walsh (1766–83); William Napier (c1772–1791); John Preston (c1774–98), who was succeeded by his son Thomas for the next 36 years; John Longman (beginning c1767) with various partners, notably Francis Broderip (1776–98); and John Bland (c1776–95). Their editions consisted of instrumental music in imitation of the editions which were appearing at this time from Paris and Amsterdam (including, for example, series of 'Periodical Ouvertures') and songs from English comic operas and from the summer gardens.

The English music publishing industry, flourishing by 1775, continued to grow in the 19th century. Firms sprang up, dissolved, merged and separated, sold their titles, plates and stocks. Among the firms that began about 1800 are several that are still active, notably Chappell (1811), Novello (1811), Boosey (active in music after c1816) and Cramer (alone after 1824). Cramer, established by the virtuoso pianist Johann Baptist Cramer, was one of several firms in London to claim such a founder, the most important earlier one being that of Muzio Clementi; the Corri family and J. L. Dussek are among other composer–publishers. The early 19th century also marked a highpoint of music publishing in other British cities. In Edinburgh the London firms of Bremner and Corri maintained offices which often did their own publishing. The family of Hime (c1790–c1835), active in Liverpool, Dublin and Manchester, specialized in songsheets, many of which were piracies of London editions. William Power in Dublin, with his brother James in London, was responsible for two of the most famous editions of folk music, the *Irish Melodies* (1807–34) and *National Melodies* (1818–28) of Thomas Moore. Equally important were the editions of national songs by George Thomson in Edinburgh (1793–1845), to which Pleyel, Haydn, Beethoven, Weber and Hummel contributed.

British music publishing never forgot its origins in the popular songsheet. The annual output of several hundred such editions a year, a level established soon after 1700, appears to have persisted throughout the 18th century and into the 19th. Gradually the single sheet, printed on one side, was expanded into two sheets, printed on inside pages. A cover was often added; later, especially with the advent of lithography, a picture was often included. Most publishers were happy to include in their catalogues both songsheets and other popular forms, as well as more ambitious sonatas and symphonies. Through agreements for simultaneous publication between British publishers and continental publishers or composers, a kind of international copyright was effected. British music publishers remained largely committed to the process of engraving, and thus they tended to maintain their identity (apart from the publishers of religious service books and song anthologies issued in small format and in large press runs with

movable type). Three 19th-century uses of movable music type by music publishers, however, deserve mention. Editions using solfège notation promoted by such firms as Curwen (founded 1863) were printed with type: they played a large part in the rise of the English choral tradition. William Clowes in London, later in Beccles, also used type for such popular publications as Charles Knight's *Musical Library* (1834–7). Novello used type for its 'cheap music' programme begun in 1847, through which major vocal works were widely circulated for many years. Other firms from the mid-19th century included Wessel, who specialized in foreign music (c1823–60) and Augener (founded 1853), who at first issued only lithographed editions.

In 18th-century France the Ballard family continued to hold its royal monopoly for music printing up to the Revolution. But the output of its press was neither particularly large nor central to Paris music, consisting mainly of popular songs and treatises. A music publishing industry was again established in Paris, using engravings (which were exempt from the control of the monopoly). The operas of Lully, first issued by the Ballards in typeset editions during the composer's lifetime, were reissued around 1710 in new editions, most of them engraved by H. de Baussen. There was more extensive activity in the second quarter of the century, when some composers arranged for their music to be issued by Charles-Nicolas Le Clerc, a publisher, and distributed by the family of Boivin, music dealers. These editions are typically small oblong folios, devoted to anthologies of dances, *airs* and cantatas and to current dramatic music.

The 'classical' period of Parisian music publishing, which began well before 1750, reached its fullness in the next two or three decades. The main early operatic publisher was La Chevardière; other publishers, such as LeMenu, Bailleux, Venier and the Bureau d'Abonnement Musical, specialized in instrumental chamber music. This was often issued serially, in annual cumulations, or as 'periodical' symphonies or overtures. Editions from this period are mostly in large folio format, usually upright for operas but oblong for instrumental music. Many of the leading engravers of the period were women. This was the time when publishers' catalogues were commonly added to their editions – expandable lists engraved on separate plates which called attention to other available titles.

Parisian classical editions proved successful enough to be widely imitated in London, Amsterdam and eventually in Germany. In Lyons, Guera and Castaud were active; through Antoine Huberty, Parisian music publishing practices were transplanted to Vienna. In Paris, the classical style persisted until the Revolution, after which three changes gradually took place: single songsheets came to be issued more frequently; the slender and well-spaced pre-Revolution opera score, with few instruments and on large staves, was replaced by a full score, thicker and with more parts exactly specified; and the method book, usually for specific instruments but also for singing and solfège, gained importance while the editions of chamber music parts slowly declined. Important firms of this period include LeDuc, Sieber, Naderman, Pleyel, the Gaveaux and Imbault.

Among the important new names in 19th-century Paris were Richault, Pacini, Carli, Janet & Cotelle, Frey, Maurice Schlesinger, Troupenas and Brandus & Dufour, mostly successors to established firms. The musical repertory of Parisian publishing broadened considerably, although the three basic forms persisted. Single songs, for instance, enjoyed a vogue after 1830 with the rise of lithography. As in England, the simple song with rudimentary accompaniment, printed on a single sheet, was replaced by the song with a florid vocal line and sentimental text, heavily accompanied by piano or often guitar, printed in an edition of several pages with an illustrated, decorative cover. The Paris Conservatoire was enjoying a prosperous period, and for a time it served as its own publisher; this being a time of emphasis on music pedagogy, the method book maintained its popularity. The opera full score, on the other hand, proved unfeasible as a publication, and declined during the first quarter of the century. About 1840 it was succeeded by the smaller vocal score in so-called 'Parisian format', which served to circulate the music of French and Italian Romantic grand opera.

Very soon after 1750, when Parisian music publishing was first being established, the firm of Breitkopf in Leipzig began to show an interest in music. Quite apart from his importance in music typography, Breitkopf deserves to be mentioned for his particular strategy for music publishing. His remarkable plan involved the three major methods used at the time of committing music to paper: manuscript copying, engraving and letterpress printing. Breitkopf chose not to join the engravers, who were now well established in London and Paris and were beginning to appear in Amsterdam and various German cities. He used the other two graphic processes instead. His typeset music had the disadvantages and advantages of typeset books: the size of the edition needed to be determined in advance before copies were sold, and internal changes were difficult; but presswork was likely to be much cheaper once the type was set, and thus Breitkopf could print editions in large numbers and distribute them widely at a low price, creating his own market. His contribution to the rise of the sentimental German song of the *Sturm und Drang* period is probably considerable. Breitkopf was also willing to sell his type to other printers and to print music for other publishers – among them Schwickert in Leipzig, Rellstab in Berlin and Hartknoch in Riga – thus increasing the use of his kind of musical edition. He developed his own copying programme, through which he provided on demand a very wide repertory of music that would not have justified large, typeset editions; his great thematic catalogues were issued for these manuscript copies. Breitkopf thus attempted, in effect, to encircle the music engravers: with his popular editions, set in type, he undersold them, and with his manuscript copies he circulated a larger repertory than they could afford. This strategy apparently succeeded for a time. Its effectiveness had declined by 1800, probably because the music engraving industry had become too extensive, and so much closer than Breitkopf to the musicians themselves in Paris, England, the Netherlands and Italy. Even so, the firm was now well established as a music publisher, and much of the groundwork was laid for Leipzig to become the centre of European music publishing a few years later.

During the second half of the 18th century music publishing spread from Paris and London to Amsterdam and various German cities. The two Nuremberg publishers around mid-century, Balthasar Schmid (1725–c1786) and Johann Ulrich Haffner (1740–70), each produced only a few editions, but with interesting music and distinctive appearance. The Dutch firm of Hummel, established in Amsterdam about 1754, in The Hague by 1756 and in Berlin in 1774, competed strongly with Paris and London for many years, especially through its extensive chamber music catalogue. Particularly important about 1780, the firm declined by 1800, and Amsterdam ceased to be an important publishing centre. In several German cities music publishing was established before 1800, based on practices derived from Parisian engraving rather than from Breitkopf's typography. Among the important men who began their work at this time were Bernhard Schott in Mainz (1770), J. M. Götz, mostly in Mannheim (1773), Johann André in Offenbach (1774), H. P. Bossler, mostly in Speyer (1781), Macario Falter in Munich (1787), Nicolaus Simrock in Bonn (c1790), J. A. Böhme in Hamburg (1794), J. P. Spehr in Brunswick (c1794) and G. Gombart in Augsburg (1795). Of these, André and Falter were additionally important in the first years of the 19th century as early users of the lithographic process.

Vienna, the earliest major centre of German music publishing, was the third important European centre. The industry was late in establishing itself there: the demand for music had probably been well enough satisfied by manuscripts from Italy, engravings from Paris, and typeset editions from Leipzig. Viennese music shops had been affiliated more closely with art dealers than with booksellers. Not until the 1770s did Parisian-style engravings come to be published in Vienna, possibly through the efforts of Huberty, the Parisian publisher who settled there. The most important early engraver, however, was an Italian, Christoph Torricella, and through the efforts of two other Italians, Carlo and Francesco Artaria, Viennese music publishing began in 1778. Artaria's editions were immediately successful, and this firm dominated Viennese music publishing until the end of the century. Among the few competitors was Joseph Traeg, who started as a dealer in 1781, then later published music of his own and became Breitkopf's agent (he also traded in manuscript material). The composer F. A. Hoffmeister began in business in 1784. He issued some very important and ambitious editions for a few years, then sold his stock to Artaria, and finally re-established himself as the partner of Ambrosius Kühnel in Leipzig. Less important Viennese music publishers included the composer Leopold Kozeluch, manager of the Musikalisches Magazin (1784–1802); Josef Eder, later succeeded by his son-in-law, Jeremias Bermann (1789–c1840); the several partners of the Hoftheater-Musik-Verlag (1796–1822); Ignaz Sauer, later in partnership with Max Josef Leidesdorf (1798–1835); and Carlo Mechetti and later his nephew Pietro (1799–1855).

In 1798 Tranquillo Mollo, formerly at Artaria, set up his own shop; three years later Giovanni Cappi, also from Artaria, did so too. In 1801 the Kunst und Industrie Comptoir (or Bureau d'Arts et d'Industrie) opened, managed by five men including Joseph Sonnleithner, the librettist of Beethoven's *Leonore* (1805). In 1803 the inventor of lithography, Alois Senefelder, moved to Vienna and established his Chemische Druckerei, in competition with the engravers. Thus the period of diversification in Viennese music publishing began. New firms from the next few years include Thaddäus Weigl (1803–31) and Pietro Cappi (founded 1816). Not until after 1820 did clear leaders emerge in Vienna. Anton Diabelli, successor to Pietro Cappi and later Weigl, is also known for the famous piano variations by Beethoven and others. Sigmund Anton Steiner acquired Senefelder's lithography shop in 1812, but soon chose instead to issue engraved editions. The two main publishers by the mid-19th century were S. A. Spina, successor to Diabelli, and Tobias Haslinger, successor to Steiner. Viennese publishing owed much to composers in the local community, notably Mozart, Beethoven and Schubert, but also the many Kleinmeister whose efforts were devoted to amateur instrumental music more than to the songs so popular in Paris and London. In appearance the Viennese editions – clumsily punched with crudely designed signs, and printed from plates that were frequently cracked and seldom wiped completely clean – recall the 18th century, and contrast with the handsome, well-executed editions from London and Paris. As the centre of music publishing moved to Leipzig, Viennese editions improved in appearance, at a time when their repertory was moving in the direction of virtuoso keyboard music and Strauss waltzes.

In the early 19th century Leipzig became the fourth centre of music publishing, and in due course the greatest. Breitkopf's firm, now Breitkopf & Härtel (and managed by G. C. Härtel), still experimented with different methods of printing, including lithography, but finally settled on engraving around 1811. As early as 1800 the Viennese publisher Hoffmeister had set up his partnership with Kühnel. Their Bureau de Musique proved highly successful, and in 1814 it was acquired by C. F. Peters. In 1807 Friedrich Hofmeister (not to be confused with Hoffmeister) began his activity as a publisher; he later acquired and prepared the great German national bibliography of printed music now known by his name. Other important Leipzig firms founded before 1860 include H. A. Probst (1823, later Probst–Kistner), Bartholf Senff (1844), Siegel & Stoll (1846, later C. F. W. Siegel) and C. F. Kahnt (1851). Leipzig, drawing its support from the local book-publishing industry and from the Gewandhaus and the conservatory, inevitably became the centre of German music publishing, at a time when German tastes prevailed in most of the Western world. Music publishing involved both the music of famous composers like Schumann, Mendelssohn and Liszt, and a vast output of 'Trivialmusik', including salon orchestrations, arrangements of operatic favourites, sentimental songs (singly and in series) and children's instructional pieces. Outside Leipzig established German firms like André, Schott and Simrock continued to flourish, as did Spina and Haslinger in Vienna. Berlin challenged the primacy of Leipzig through such important new firms as A. M. Schlesinger (1810), Traugott Trautwein (1820) and Bote & Bock (1838). Also important were firms founded by A. H. Cranz in Hamburg (1814), A. Benjamin in Altona (1818), Adolf Nagel in Hanover (1819), Josef Aibl in Munich (1825), Julius Schuberth in Hamburg (1826, with branches later in Leipzig and New York), F. Pustet in Regensburg (1826), K. F. Heckel in Mannheim (1828) and Henri Litolff in Brunswick (1828).

Among 19th-century music publishers in other countries, the most important was Ricordi, established in 1808 in Milan. This firm was one of several that issued the operatic music of Rossini and his contemporaries, but its dominance was not assured until Tito Ricordi, and his most successful composer, Giuseppe Verdi, entered the picture; since then the name of Ricordi has been virtually synonymous with Italian opera. In Switzerland the firms of Hans-Georg Nägeli in Zurich (founded 1791) and Rieter-Biedermann in Winterthur (1849–84, later in Leipzig) were comparable to the German and Viennese publishers of their day. Germans were also responsible for the important early work in countries to the east. In Hungary the firm of József Wagner (founded 1839), taken over by József Treichlinger, was passed to Julius Rosenthaler (Gyula Rószavölgyi) in 1858, under whose name it continued for many years. Gustaw Sennewald (his firm active 1832–1905) was the largest early publisher in Warsaw; in St Petersburg J. D. Gerstenberg (1793–9) was noteworthy. Lissner (1795–1824), Dalmas (c1800–1829) and Paez (1810–26) were also productive there; then Feodor Stellovsky (1840–76) acquired the stock of several small firms and became the leading publisher before the founding of the house of Bessel in 1869. In Moscow the firm of Gutheil dates from 1859 and that of Jürgenson from 1861. Marco Berra (founded c1815) was the most important early publisher in Prague. Of several early Swedish publishers the most important seems to have been J. C. Hedbom (1827–52). In Copenhagen, Søren Sønnichsen (1783–1826) was particularly prolific, as was the composer C. C. Lose with his various associates (1802–79). Outside western Europe and the USA music publishing was slow to be established. Latin America had several publishers of local popular music, in Havana, Mexico City, Buenos Aires and above all in Rio de Janeiro, where Pedro

26. Haydn's 'The Seasons': title-page of the first edition with engraving by Amadeus Wenzel; published by Breitkopf & Härtel (Leipzig, 1802)

Laforge (1834–69) and Filippone & Cia (1847–c1884) each issued several hundred editions.

In the American colonies several dozen religious music books, engraved or typeset, were issued from east coast cities. Not until 1785, however, did Isaiah Thomas in Massachusetts import a font of Caslon music type from London and become a recognized publisher of religious 'tune books'. The beginnings of American sheet-music publishing came in 1793, when music shops in imitation of London firms were established by Moller and Capron in Philadelphia, and later by Joseph Carr in Baltimore, George Gilfert and James Hewitt in New York, George Willig in Philadelphia and P. A. von Hagen in Boston. Shortly after 1800 George Blake in Philadelphia and Gottlieb Graupner in Boston were, with Carr and Willig, the country's leading publishers. Their output consisted almost entirely of songsheets, a few devoted to music by native composers but mostly reprints of popular London editions. Towards mid-century the firms of Oliver Ditson in Boston, and Firth, Hall & Pond in New York, rose to prominence. After 1830 a shift can be seen from the eastern seaboard to the west and south; the main publishers included Silas Brainard in Cleveland, F. D. Benteen in Baltimore, F. W. Peters and other members of his family in Cincinnati, Louisville and elsewhere, Root & Cady in Chicago and Balmer & Weber in St Louis. With this geographical shift, there arose around 1830 – about the time of the advent of lithography – a new emphasis on music which reflected local interests. London comic opera songs began to be replaced in the catalogues by minstrel show tunes, although the fashions of guitar accompaniments, sentimental texts and illustrated covers show that the industry in America still generally retained its London models. The American publishers of classical music were established somewhat later, mostly by immigrant Germans, among them Gustave Schirmer in New York (1861), Jno. Fischer in Dayton, Ohio (1864), and later in New York, Carl Fischer in New York (1872), Theodore Presser in Philadelphia (1884) and E. C. Schirmer in Boston (1891). The firm of Oliver Ditson also came to specialize in this area.

4. THE AGE OF OFFSET PRINTING, AFTER 1860. The third main era in the history of music publishing began with the development of offset lithography. Leipzig, the established centre of music publishing, quickly converted its equipment. The firm of C. G. Röder, specialists in music engraving and printing from 1846, successfully used a lithographic steam press as early as 1863, and by 1867 were engraving and printing music for Peters as well as other publishers in Leipzig and throughout Europe. Music publishers were prospering everywhere in the late 19th and early 20th centuries. Whether in Paris, London, Milan or New York, their affluence is evident from the vast quantity of their production, although their editions had come to be fixed in appearance, and in content mostly devoted to salon music, works which would sell, and what we now see as musical trivia.

Before 1860 music was published mostly for performance. Editions were intended for musicians, and thus were (as they still are) likely to be sold at shops which also sold violin strings, piano-tuning supplies, music stands, guitars, small instruments and the like, rather than at book shops. Music designed for study purposes first appeared in the late 19th century, as a result of the rise of public concerts and (later) sound recordings, and the growth of the academic study of music and the rise of musicology. Public concerts and recordings have contributed to the popularity of the miniature score, while musicology has fostered historical and critical editions.

Miniature scores were occasionally printed earlier in the 19th century, but the first publisher to specialize in them was Albert Payne. Working in his father's music shop in Leipzig, Payne began issuing his Kleine Kammermusik Partiturausgabe in 1886. Six years later he sold his series to Ernst Eulenburg, whose editions have dominated the market ever since. Most of the small scores – variously designated as 'study', 'miniature', 'pocket' or 'reading' scores – are photographic reductions of conductor's scores; but in modern times some contain original material, such as analytical notes and scholarly corrections which are not found in print elsewhere. Other publishers slowly entered the market, including Donajowski in Leipzig (later Wiener Philharmonischer Verlag) and Hawkes in London, publishing the standard classics; by the mid-20th century virtually every publisher issued 'study scores' of the most important of its copyright works.

The historical edition has many ancestors, such as Arnold's Handel edition (1787–97) and, around 1800, Breitkopf's 'Oeuvres complettes'. Its modern beginnings derive from the mid-19th century and the collected editions by Breitkopf & Härtel of Beethoven, Mozart and other master composers. The same firm acted as publisher of the Bach Gesellschaft edition. Other auspicious series also appeared about this time, some of them not sponsored by either a commercial publisher or government patronage; Friedrich Chrysander's great Handel edition, produced largely in the editor's home, is an example; another is represented by the Musical Antiquarian Society editions in London. The publication of scholarly editions was well established throughout Europe by the end of the 19th century. (For a fuller account see EDITIONS, HISTORICAL.)

The impact of scholarship may also be seen in the 'scholarly performing' edition, which reflects the publisher's scrupulous concern for accuracy of detail and respect for the composer's intentions. The Leipzig firm of Steingräber was long respected in this work, particularly for its variorum edition of Bach's keyboard music prepared by Hans Bischoff. In recent years Bärenreiter has been pre-eminent in the production of scholarly performing editions. Also noteworthy are Henle, of Munich and Duisburg, for its classical 'Urtexts', the private press of L'Oiseau-Lyre in Monaco, which has issued attractive and well-edited publications, and the American Institute of Musicology, which has undertaken an ambitious publishing programme of scholarly editions of early music.

Other publishers adapted the device of the 'publisher's series' to publicize their editions of the standard classics. Such series were created mainly as a convenience, both in design and in distribution – the distinctive appearance and numbering of editions proved convenient in publicizing the name of the firm and for ordering purposes. The editions in such series usually varied considerably in their quality and objectives: some were important for the phrasings, fingerings and other nuances used by a famous performer rather than for the accuracy of the text; others attempted to combine both, often with considerable success. The best-known of the early series was the Edition Peters, begun in 1867. Other famous series include Schirmer's Library of Musical Classics, Novello's Standard Edition, and the Edition series of such firms as Litolff and Ricordi as well as Bote & Bock, Carl Fischer, Augener and Presser. Sometimes a publisher gathered a number of works for a particular group of users in one series, such as Moecks Kammermusik, Archives des Maîtres de l'Orgue or Diletto Musicale. Special series vary in policy from publisher to publisher and from time to time. Such designations are in some cases reserved for particularly important editions, and constitute a special endorsement, while in others they appear on all or nearly all of the publisher's issues.

Leipzig maintained its domination of music publishing until the end of the 19th century. Even the early nationalist composers promoted the cause of their country's distinctive music through German editions: Smetana may have published most of his music through Urbánek in Prague, but Dvořák worked exclusively with Simrock; Grieg saw much of his music published with the support of Peters; Sibelius was issued by Breitkopf & Härtel. The Russian nationalists worked at first with local publishers, Tchaikovsky with Jürgenson and Musorgsky with Bessel. Their music, however, which was becoming increasingly popular, could claim no copyright protection beyond the boundaries of Russia. M. P. Belyayev, originally from St Petersburg, established his firm in Leipzig in 1885 as a specialist in Russian music, calling on advice from Rimsky-Korsakov, Lyadov and Glazunov. In the USA Arthur P. Schmidt, active for a time in Leipzig, worked in Boston as the publisher of music by American composers, the New England School in particular.

Forward-looking composers of the early 20th century, on the other hand, usually found their publishers outside Leipzig. The most important early proponent of new music in the German-speaking world was the Viennese firm of Universal Edition, founded in 1901 through the efforts of Emil Hertzka. Most of the music of Schoenberg and his circle appeared under its imprint, as did many editions of Mahler, Richard Strauss and Bartók. Koussevitzky, before his conducting career, left Russia and with his wife Natalie founded in Paris the Editions Russes de Musique, which first issued many of the works of Stravinsky, Prokofiev and other Russians. Debussy and Ravel worked mainly through the Paris firm of Durand. In Great Britain Vaughan Williams and Walton worked mainly through Oxford University Press, Britten through Boosey & Hawkes (later through Faber), Bax through Murdoch and Chappell, Elgar through Novello, others through such firms as Augener, Stainer & Bell and Chester.

In the United States of America the composer Arthur Farwell managed the Wa-Wan Press in Newton Center, Massachusetts (1901–9), for the announced purpose of encouraging a distinctive national style based on American Indian music. Among other firms Schirmer in New York was long known for publishing art songs by native American composers; the Cos Cob Press, Arrow and Southern Music also published significant works by American composers. After about 1940 Boosey & Hawkes, with several offices outside London, was particularly active in its work with contemporary composers of all countries. Since World War II Schott of Mainz and its London sister firm have been specially active in contemporary music, publishing (for example)

27. Title-page of Mahler's Ninth Symphony; published by Universal Edition (Vienna and Leipzig, 1912)

Hindemith, Tippett and Henze as well as many younger composers.

Popular music publishing enjoyed a quiet but prosperous career since the days of John Walsh; it flourished in England, France and the USA in particular, especially in the great age of illustrated covers in the mid-19th century. In London Chappell enjoyed great success with Gilbert and Sullivan; other firms were active with music-hall ballads and show tunes, especially Francis, Day & Hunter. Chappell returned to prominence with the leadership of the Dreyfuss brothers, Louis and Max, one in London and the other in New York, thereby effectively controlling much of the music of the London and Broadway stages. The basic edition of these publishers was the songsheet, although published arrangements for salon orchestra or dance band became very popular. Salon arrangements also spread to central Europe. World War I stimulated the publication of patriotic songs, especially in the large nations. In Germany the output of 'Schlager' tunes amounts to about as high a proportion of the total current music publication as it does in the English-speaking world.

In the USA the early years of the 20th century saw the great day of Tin Pan Alley, with a host of prolific and profitable New York firms including Belwin, Irving Berlin, Famous Music, Leo Feist, Sam Fox, Galaxy, T. B. Harms, E. B. Marks, Mills, Robbins, Shapiro-Bernstein, Harry Von Tilzer and M. Witmark. The most important firm outside New York was Jerome H. Remick in Detroit. John Stillwell Stark, a small publisher in Sedalia, Missouri, gained an enviable reputation as the publisher for the master of ragtime, Scott Joplin. The early 20th century was a great period of local music publishing in America; through the assistance of music engravers in the large cities, shops in the small towns arranged for publication of the compositions of local amateurs. In time this regional activity disappeared, or largely degenerated into 'song-shark' publishing, which extracts large sums of money from the gullible novice in return for a few printed copies and promises to 'plug' (i.e. promote) the song with famous performers and other influential parties.

Last among the kinds of music publishers which appeared early in the 20th century was the educational specialist. They issue a great variety of musical materials including books for class use by children in schools, band parts, music for large choruses, collections of favourite songs for amateur use, charts and other supplies for pedagogical purposes and children's instructional music. Some such firms are affiliated more with the world of textbook publishing than with that of music publishing.

Since the 1930s three trends in music publishing have been significant. With World War II publishers in Germany and, most notably, from the Vienna firm of Universal, moved to England or America, sometimes founding new firms but usually contributing to established ones. The bombing of German cities (Leipzig in particular) took a heavy toll in publishers' stocks and plates. After the war some of the Leipzig firms re-established their offices there; others moved to the West, while still others set up offices in both East and West Germany. From the war also came the significant rise in music reprinting. German musical editions were generally unavailable in England and America, and the technology of offset lithography was used to reissue the standard editions. Music reprinting was well established by the 1960s, when numerous firms began to produce small editions of important out-of-print texts for libraries and for scholars, including many of the 19th-century complete editions in reduced format.

Second, there was a serious decline in the number of music engravers. This was not a new problem (William Gamble's treatise on engraving had been written because the situation had been so serious in England during World War I); but after World War II the music engraver almost became extinct. It would appear that fewer than half the new musical editions produced since the 1950s in the USA and the 1960s in Europe involved engraving. The great pity is that with the music engravers will also die a complicated and important skill in organizing the symbols on a page of music so as to convey the composer's text to the performer as clearly as possible. Many publishers prefer to issue reproductions of a composer's, or a copyist's, manuscript, which represents a substantial economy in the age of photolithography and is in any case the only possibility for scores using modern graphical notations.

Third, the role of the publisher has been influenced by the rise of the recording industry and performing rights organizations. Conceding that many varieties of music publisher are still active, it is still generally true that the publisher is now less concerned with the printed documents he produces, promotes and distributes, and more concerned with the various legal ownership rights to 'artistic property' which he shares with or manages for the creator. The implications of music copyright – of the performance and the so-called 'mechanical' rights – bring the publisher into the world of law more closely than before, as they take him further from the world of printing. The possibilities of coordinating a music publishing programme with the related activities of a recording company, a sound-equipment manufacturer, a film producer or the entertainment industry, have resulted in many music publishers' being absorbed into the giant conglomerate corporations. While to many qualified observers the future of music publishing looked bleak in the 1970s, it is difficult, reflecting on the history of the industry, to see the state of publishing as being less secure than at many times in the past. So long as music depends on the creative efforts of composers, it seems safe to predict, music publishers will be needed to work out the complicated problems of issuing, distributing and promoting their works.

BIBLIOGRAPHY

REFERENCE AND BIBLIOGRAPHICAL SOURCES

R. Eitner: *Buch- und Musikalien-Händler, Buch- und Musikalien-drucker nebst Notenstecher* (Leipzig, 1904)

O. E. Deutsch: *Music Publishers' Numbers* (London, 1946; Ger. trans., rev., 1961 as *Musikverlagsnummern*)

G. A. Marco: *The Earliest Music Printers of Continental Europe: a Checklist of Facsimiles Illustrating their Work* (Charlottesville, Virginia, 1962)

Å. Davidsson: *Bibliographie zur Geschichte des Musikdrucks* (Uppsala, 1965)

J. J. Fuld: *The Book of World-famous Music* (New York, 1966, rev. 2/1971)

H.-M. Plesske: 'Bibliographie des Schrifttums zur Geschichte deutscher und österreichischer Musikverlage', *Beiträge zur Geschichte des Buchwesens*, iii (1968), 135–222

D. W. Krummel: *Guide for Dating Early Published Music* (Kassel, 1974)

——: 'Musical Functions and Bibliographical Forms', *The Library*, 5th ser., xxxii (1976), 317

GENERAL HISTORIES

J. A. Novello: *Some Account of the Methods of Musick Printing, with Specimens of the Various Sizes of Moveable Types, and of Other Matters* (London, 1847)

F. Chrysander: 'A Sketch of the History of Music-printing, from the 15th to the 18th Century', *MT*, xviii (1877), 265, 324, 375, 470, 524, 584

H. Riemann: *Notenschrift und Notendruck: bibliographisch-typographische Studie* (Leipzig, 1896)

W. B. Squire: 'Notes on Early Music Printing', *Bibliographica*, iii (1897), 99

K. Meyer and E. J. O'Meara: 'The Printing of Music, 1473–1934', *The Dolphin*, ii (1935), 171–207

B. Pattison: 'Notes on Early Music Printing', *The Library*, 4th ser., xix (1939), 389–421

E. Laaff: *Musik mit Fleiss gedrucket* (Eltville, nr. Wiesbaden, 1956)

A. B. Barksdale: *The Printed Note: 500 Years of Music Printing and Engraving* (Toledo, Ohio, 1957) [exhibition catalogue, Toledo Museum of Art]

A. H. King: *Four Hundred Years of Music Printing* (London, 1964)

TECHNICAL ACCOUNTS: GENERAL

A. Senefelder: *Vollständiges Lehrbuch der Steindruckerey* (Munich, 1818; Eng. trans., 1819/R1968 as *A Complete Course of Lithography*)

W. D. Richmond: *The Grammar of Lithography* (London, 1878, 12/1912)

Berthiaud and P. Boitard: *Imprimeur en taille-douce* (Paris, ?1892)

American Dictionary of Printing and Bookmaking (New York, 1894)

F. Thibaudeau: *La lettre d'imprimerie* (Paris, 1921)

G. A. Glaister: *Glossary of the Book* (London, 1960)

W. T. Berry and H. E. Poole: *Annals of Printing: a Chronological Encyclopedia from the Earliest Times to 1950* (London and Toronto, 1966)

M. Twyman: *Lithography 1800–1850* (Oxford, 1970)

M. Adler: *The Writing Machine: a History of the Typewriter* (London, 1973)

I. Bain: 'Gift and Annual Illustrations: some Notes on their Production', in F. W. Faxon: *Literary Annuals and Gift Books: a Bibliography 1823–1903* (London, 1973), 19

TECHNICAL ACCOUNTS: MUSIC

R. Dietrich: *Anleitung zum Satz der Musiknoten-Typen* (Leipzig, 1872)

T. Beaudoire: *Manuel de typographie musicale* (Paris, 1891)

H. Robert: *Traité de gravure de musique sur planches d'étain et des divers procédés de simili gravure de musique* (Paris, 1902, 2/1926 as *Gravure de musique et similigravure*)

W. Gamble: *Music Engraving and Printing: Historical and Technical Treatise* (London, 1923/R1971)

D. Flower: 'On Music Printing, 1473–1701', *Book-collector's Quarterly*, iv (1931), 76

H. J. Foss: 'The Printing of Music: some Problems of Today', *Gutenberg Jb 1931*, 293

K. Hader: *Aus der Werkstatt eines Notenstechers* (Vienna, 1948)

T. Ross: *The Art of Music Engraving and Processing* (Miami, 1971)

SPECIAL STUDIES

O. Kinkeldey: 'Music and Music Printing in Incunabula', *Papers of the Bibliographical Society of America*, xxvi (1932), 89–118

G. Kinsky: *Erstlingsdrucke der deutschen Tonmeister der Klassik und Romantik* (Vienna, 1934)

C. B. Oldman: *Collecting Musical First Editions* (London, 1934); also in J. Carter: *New Paths in Book Collecting* (London, 1934), 95

D. W. Krummel: 'Graphic Analysis: its Application to Early American Engraved Music', *Notes*, xvi (1958–9), 213

Å. Davidsson: 'Das Typenmaterial des älteren nordischen Musikdrucks', *Annales Academiae regiae scientiarum upsaliensis*, vi (1962), 76

K. Meyer-Baer: *Liturgical Music Incunabula: a Descriptive Catalogue* (London, 1962)

A. Tyson: *The Authentic English Editions of Beethoven* (London, 1963)

H. E. Poole: 'New Music Types in the Eighteenth Century', *Journal of the Printing Historical Society*, i (1965), 21; ii (1966), 23

Å. Davidsson: 'Korrektur till ett dansk musiktryck år 1620', *Nordisk tidskrift för bok- och biblioteksväsen*, liii (1966), 92

D. W. Krummel: 'Oblong Format in Early Music Books', *The Library*, 5th ser., xxvi (1971), 312

A. H. King: 'The 500th Anniversary of Music Printing', *MT*, cxiv (1973), 1220

NATIONAL STUDIES

A. Goovaerts: *Histoire et bibliographie de la typographie musicale dans les anciens Pays-Bas* (Antwerp, 1880/R1963)

American Dictionary of Printing and Bookmaking (New York, 1894)

F. Kidson: *British Music Publishers, Printers and Engravers* (London, 1900/R1967)

A. Göhler: *Die Messkataloge im Dienste der musikalischen Geschichtsforschung* (Leipzig, 1901/R1965)

R. Steele: *The Earliest English Music Printing* (London, 1903/R1965)

M. Brenet: 'La librairie musicale en France de 1653 à 1790, d'après les registres de privilèges', *SIMG*, viii (1906–7), 401–66

G. Cucuel: 'Quelques documents sur la librairie musicale au XVIIIe siècle', *SIMG*, xiii (1911–12), 385

——: 'Notes sur quelques musiciens, luthiers, éditeurs et graveurs de musique au XVIIIe siècle', *SIMG*, xiv (1912–13), 243

P. Cohen: *Die Nürnberger Musikdrucker im sechzehnten Jahrhundert* (Erlangen, 1927)

P. Bergmans: 'La typographie musicale en Belgique au XVIe siècle', *Histoire du livre et de l'imprimerie en Belgique des origines à nos jours*, v (Brussels, 1929), 47

W. A. Fisher: *150 Years of Music Publishing in the U.S.: an Historical Sketch* (Boston, 1934)

H. Dichter and E. Shapiro: *Early American Sheet Music: its Lure and its Lore, 1768–1889* (New York, 1941)

A. Weinmann: *Beiträge zur Geschichte des alt-Wiener Musikverlages* (Vienna, 1948–)

C. Hopkinson: *A Dictionary of Parisian Music Publishers, 1700–1950* (London, 1954)

C. Humphries and W. C. Smith: *Music Publishing in the British Isles* (London, 1954, rev. 2/1970)

C. Johansson: *French Music Publishers' Catalogues of the Second Half of the Eighteenth Century* (Stockholm, 1955)

A. Weinmann: *Wiener Musikverleger und Musikalienhändler von Mozarts Zeit bis gegen 1850* (Vienna, 1956)

B. Vol'man: *Russkiye pechatniye noti XVIII veka* [18th-century printed Russian music] (Leningrad, 1957)

C. Sartori: *Dizionario degli editori musicali italiani* (Florence, 1958)

C. Hopkinson: *Notes on Russian Music Publishers* (London, 1959)

H. Gericke: *Der Wiener Musikalienhandel von 1700 bis 1778* (Graz, 1960)

M. Donà: *La stampa musicale a Milano fino all'anno 1700* (Florence, 1961)

Å. Davidsson: 'Das Typenmaterial des älteren nordischen Musikdrucks', *Annales Academiae regiae scientiarum upsaliensis*, vi (1962), 76

R. Elvers: 'Musikdrucker, Musikalienhändler und Musikverleger in Berlin 1750–1850', *Festschrift Walter Gerstenberg* (Wolfenbüttel, 1964), 37

O. W. Neighbour and A. Tyson: *English Music Publishers' Plate Numbers in the First Half of the 19th Century* (London, 1965)

Å. Davidsson: 'Korrektur till ett dansk musiktryck år 1620', *Nordisk tidskrift för bok- och biblioteksväsen*, liii (1966), 92

K. Hortschansky: 'Pränumerations- und Subskriptionsliste im Notendrucken deutscher Musiker des 18. Jahrhunderts', *AcM*, xl (1968), 154

H.-M. Plesske: 'Bibliographie des Schrifttums zur Geschichte deutscher

und österreichischer Musikverlage', *Beiträge zur Geschichte des Buchwesens*, iii (1968), 135–222

A. Helmer: 'Nagot om musikaliedatering', *Svenskt musikhistoriskt arkiv bulletin*, iv (1969), 6

M. Przywecka-Samecka: *Drukarstwo muzyczne w Polsce do końca XVIII wieku* [Music printing in Poland until the end of the 18th century] (Kraków, 1969)

E. L. Berz: *Die Notendrucker und ihre Verleger in Frankfurt am Main von den Anfängen bis etwa 1630* (Kassel, 1970)

B. Vol'man: *Russkiye notnïye izdaniya XIX – nachala XX veka* [Russian music printing in the 19th and early 20th centuries] (Leningrad, 1970)

D. Fog: *Dänische Musikverlage und Notendruckereien* (Copenhagen, 1972)

J. Stenzl: 'L'imprimerie musicale fribourgeoise à l'époque baroque', *Revue musicale suisse*, cxiv (1974), 160

D. W. Krummel: *English Music Printing, 1553–1700* (London, 1975)

H. Schaefer: *Die Notendrucker und Musikverleger in Frankfurt am Main von 1630 bis um 1720* (Kassel, 1975)

D. Fog and K. Michelsen: *Norwegian Music Publication since 1800* (Copenhagen, 1976)

H. Kellman: 'Book Production and Book Distribution at the Netherlands Court', *Formen und Probleme der Überlieferung mehrstimmiger Musik im Zeitalter Josquins Desprez: Wolfenbüttel 1976*

PUBLISHERS

O. von Hase: *Breitkopf & Härtel: Gedenkschrift und Arbeitsbericht* (Leipzig, 1917–19)

R. S. Hill: 'The Plate Numbers of C. F. Peters' Predecessors', *PAMS 1938*, 113

C. Sartori: *Bibliografia delle opere musicali stampate de Ottaviano de Petrucci* (Florence, 1948)

W. C. Smith: *A Bibliography of the Musical Works Published by John Walsh during the Years 1695–1720* (London, 1948, enlarged 2/1968)

A. Weinmann: *Beiträge zur Geschichte des alt-Wiener Musikverlages* (Vienna, 1948–)

J. A. Stellfeld: *Bibliographie des éditions musicales plantiniennes* (Brussels, 1949)

F. Lesure and G. Thibault: 'Bibliographie des éditions musicales publiées par Nicolas du Chemin', *AnnM*, i (1953), 269–373; iv (1956), 251; vi (1958–63), 403

F. Lesure and G. Thibault: *Bibliographie des éditions d'Adrian Le Roy et Robert Ballard, 1551–1598* (Paris, 1955)

C. Sartori: 'Una dinastia di editori musicali: documenti inediti sui Gardano e i loro congiunti Stefano Bindoni e Alessandro Raverii', *La bibliofilia*, lxviii (1956), 176–208

——: *Casa Ricordi: profilo storico* (Milan, 1958)

Novello & Co. Ltd: *A Century and a Half in Soho* (London, 1961)

A. Dunning: *Joseph Schmitt* (Amsterdam, 1962)

B. S. Brook, ed.: *The Breitkopf Thematic Catalogue, 1762–1787* (New York, 1966)

U. Meissner: *Der Antwerpener Notendrucker Tylman Susato* (Berlin, 1967)

W. C. Smith and C. Humphries: *A Bibliography of the Musical Works Published by the Firm of John Walsh during the Years 1721–1766* (London, 1968)

D. Epstein: *Music Publishing in Chicago before 1871: the Firm of Root & Cady, 1858–1871* (Detroit, 1969)

D. Heartz: *Pierre Attaingnant, Royal Printer of Music* (Berkeley, 1969)

F. Lesure: *Bibliographie des éditions musicales publiées par Estienne Roger et Michel-Charles Le Cène* (Paris, 1969)

S. Pogue: *Jacques Moderne: Lyons Music Printer of the Sixteenth Century* (Geneva, 1969)

E. Roth: *The Business of Music: Reflections of a Music Publisher* (London, 1969)

C. Johansson: *J. J. & B. Hummel: Music Publishing and Thematic Catalogues* (Stockholm, 1972)

W. Matthäus: *Johann André, Musikverlag zu Offenbach am Main* (Tutzing, 1973)

S. Boorman: 'On Petrucci's Sources and Printing Techniques', *Formen und Probleme der Überlieferung mehrstimmiger Musik im Zeitalter Josquins Desprez: Wolfenbüttel 1976*

A. Devriès: *Edition et commerce de la musique gravée à Paris dans la première moitié du XVIIIe siècle: les Boivin, les Leclerc* (Geneva, 1976)

H. E. Poole: 'Jacques-François Rosart: a Neglected Pioneer of Music', *Early Music*, v (1977), 352

A. Devriès and F. Lesure: *Dictionnaire des éditeurs de musique français* (Geneva, 1979–)

MUSIC TITLES AND ILLUSTRATIONS

J. Grand Carteret: *Les titres illustrés et l'image au service de la musique* (Turin, 1904)

W. E. Imeson: *Illustrated Music-titles* (London, n.d. [?1912])

W. von Zur Westen: *Musiktitel aus vier Jahrhunderten* (Leipzig, 1921)

A. H. King: 'English Pictorial Music Title-pages, 1820–1885', *The Library*, 5th ser., iv (1949–50), 262

G. Fraenkel: *Decorative Music Title Pages: 201 Examples from 1500 to 1800* (New York, 1969)

R. Schaal: *Musiktitel aus fünf Jahrhunderten* (Wilhelmshaven, 1972)

For further bibliography *see* BIBLIOGRAPHY OF MUSIC and LIBRARIES.

H. EDMUND POOLE (I), DONALD W. KRUMMEL (II)

Printz, Wolfgang Caspar (*b* Waldthurn, Upper Palatinate, 10 Oct 1641; *d* Sorau, Lower Lusatia [now Żary, Poland], 13 Oct 1717). German music theorist, historian, composer and ?novelist. He was an important figure in late 17th-century German music, whose several books contain prolific documentation of the theory and practice of music during his lifetime.

1. LIFE. Printz left two autobiographical sketches, one in his *Historische Beschreibung* (1690), the other a more extensive essay completed by his son after his death and published in Mattheson. After early schooling at Waldthurn, he moved with his parents to nearby Vohenstrauss, where he entered the Lateinschule. His music teacher, Kilian Hammer, taught him the use of a seventh solmization syllable, *si*, which was at that time a progressive step in music education. He also learnt to play the violin and keyboard instruments. In 1654 he was sent to Weiden to continue his education; there he studied with the Kantor Wolfgang Altus and the organist Johann Conrad Merz, and he also learnt instruments from Hans Christoph Schaber. In 1659 he went to the University of Altdorf as a theology student. His musical activities there revolved around a Stadtpfeifer (whom he called simply Christoph), who gave him free board for a half-year in return for instruction in music that he gave to his two children. Printz also belonged to the university collegium musicum (led by a jurist, Nicolaus Ritterhusius): he played the violin and learnt the bass violin. He was forced to return home at the beginning of 1661 because his father was unable to continue paying for his education. He set out on a career as a Lutheran minister but soon found that political conditions resulting from the conversion of the local aristocracy to Catholicism made it impossible for him to continue. Having earlier preached against Catholicism, he was placed under house arrest for eight days. This experience, he said, led him to become a professional musician.

Later in 1661 Printz became a tenor in the court chapel at Heidelberg, but he soon left, and as a companion to a certain Dutch nobleman, who employed him as his chamber valet, he made a lengthy and significant journey through Italy. His experiences in most of the major Italian cities provided much material for his later writings, for example the narrative sections of *Phrynis Mitilenaeus*. In Rome he met Kircher, who was a major influence on his theoretical writing and whose famous museum of musical curiosities he visited. He began to collect music books and to study music theory seriously. On his way back to Germany he fell ill at Innsbruck, where he was left by his employer. Later he wandered back on foot to his home at Vohenstrauss by way of Munich, Ingolstadt, Bayreuth, Gera, Altenburg and other places. After a brief stay at home he went to Dresden, where he introduced himself to Francesco Santi, a musician in the electoral chapel, whose brother he had met in Rome. Santi gave him documents of recommendation to Count Leopold of Promnitz, who resided at Sorau and who immediately employed him as

court composer and music director. This position was dissolved after the count's death in January 1664, whereupon Printz became Kantor at Triebel. In 1665 he returned to Sorau as Kantor, and in 1682 he also became director of music to Count Balthasar Erdmann of Promnitz. His life was exceedingly productive, though largely uneventful, except for the tragic loss of his entire library in the fire that destroyed Sorau in May 1684; he also reported that in 1688 an attempt was made to poison him. These and many other colourful events are described in rich detail in his autobiographical essay in Mattheson.

2. WORKS. Although Printz said that he composed 150 'largely full-voiced concertos' and 48 seven-part canzonettas, none of them exists, perhaps not even the canzonettas mentioned by Eitner. He is important solely for his writings, which according to his autobiography included 22 treatises, although only six are extant. They are unquestionably of great value as documents of music theory and history, but they have yet to be fully evaluated. Heckmann has shown, however, that Printz was responsible for original and influential concepts of rhythm and metre. In his early *Compendium musicae* (1668) – which must not be confused with the totally different work of 1689 that shares this initial title – he developed the concept of intrinsic values of stress within metres, i.e. *quantitas intrinseca*. According to this familiar doctrine, which replaces the old concept of *tactus*, beats within a bar have intrinsic strong or weak stresses that not only determine the correct placing of texts according to their poetic metre but also provide the principle by which dissonances are prepared and resolved. Printz is best known generally for his *Historische Beschreibung*, the first major German history of music. It clearly reveals his extensive knowledge of the literature of previous centuries, not only in music but also in philosophy, classical studies and other related subjects. Though some of his information is inaccurate and he had certainly borrowed a great deal without acknowledgment from other sources, the book is still an impressive achievement, which authors throughout the 18th century continually used as a source of information.

Printz's most important work, *Phrynis Mitilenaeus, oder Satyrischer Componist*, is generally underrated, even though it is one of the most extensive summaries of music theory written in Germany in the 17th century. It is in three volumes (a fourth volume, though referred to, was apparently never published) and is cast in the unusual form of partly satirical narratives and dialogues, which tell much of importance about music and musicians of the period, especially about the musical culture of the peasant class. Large portions explore in depth such subjects as a theory of intervals, rhythm and metre, modes and their affections, transposition, counterpoint, text-setting, proportions, tuning and temperament, the thoroughbass and the concept of melodic figuration and variation; there is a specially significant discussion of musical invention. Printz may justifiably be considered the first German theorist to attempt a codification and encyclopedic presentation of musical knowledge, and as such he is a true predecessor of 18th-century German writers such as Mattheson and Walther, whom he influenced considerably.

WRITINGS

Compendium musicae in quo . . . explicantur . . . omnia ea quae ad Oden artificiose componendam requiruntur (Guben, 1668)

Anweisung zur Singe-Kunst oder Kurtzer Bericht wie man einen Knaben . . . könne singen lehren (Guben, 1671) [1666 edn. mentioned in *EitnerQ*]

Phrynis Mitilenaeus, oder Satyrischer Componist (Dresden and Leipzig, 1696); also pubd separately in 3 vols.: i–ii (Quedlinburg, 1676–7), iii (1679) [incl. *Declaration oder Weitere Erklärung*]

Musica modulatoria vocalis oder Manierliche und zierliche Sing-Kunst (Schweidnitz, 1678)

Declaration oder Weitere Erklärung der Refutation des Satyrischen Componistens (n.p., 1679) [response to essay against *Phrynis*, pubd anon. 1678]

Compendium musicae signatoriae et modulatoriae vocalis, das ist Kurtzer Begriff aller derjenigen Sachen, so einem, der die Vocal-Music lernen will, zu wissen von nöthen seyn (Dresden, 1689/R1974, 2/1714)

Exercitationes musicae theoretico-practicae curiosae de concordantiis singulis, das ist Musicalische Wissenschaft und Kunst-Übungen, i–iii (Dresden, 1687); iv–vi (Dresden, 1688); vii–viii (Dresden, 1689)

Historische Beschreibung der edelen Sing- und Kling-Kunst (Dresden, 1690/R1964)

NOVELS
(authorship uncertain, formerly attrib. J. Kuhnau)

Musicus vexatus oder Der wohlgeplagte doch nichtverzagte, sondern jederzeit lustige Musicus instrumentalis (Freiberg, 1690)

Musicus magnanimus, oder Pancalus, der grossmüthige Musicant (Freiberg, 1691)

Musicus curiosus, oder Battalus, der vorwitzige Musicant (Freiberg, 1691)

WORKS
Canzonette d'avanti . . . in una opera cantata . . . con ritornelli, sonatine e sinfonie . . . con 5 viole ornate, 1679, formerly in Soran, Kirchenbibliothek [incl. *Musica Caesarea sive Melothesia ab augustissimo imperatore Ferdinando III composita*]
150 concs. and 48 canzonettas, a 7, lost

BIBLIOGRAPHY
EitnerQ; *WaltherML*

J. Mattheson: *Grundlage einer Ehren-Pforte* (Hamburg, 1740); ed. M. Schneider (Berlin, 1910/R1969)

E. Schmitz: 'Studien über W. C. Printz als Musikschriftsteller', *MMg*, xxxvi (1904), 100

R. Alewyn: *Johann Beer: Studien zum Roman des 17. Jahrhundert* (Leipzig, 1932)

H. Heckmann: *W. C. Printz und seine Rhythmuslehre* (diss., U. of Freiburg, 1952)

——: 'Der Takt in der Musiklehre des siebzehnten Jahrhunderts', *AMw*, x (1953), 116

H. Riedel: *Die Darstellung von Musik und Musikerlebnis in der erzählenden deutschen Dichtung* (diss., U. of Bonn, 1959)
GEORGE J. BUELOW

Prinzipal (Ger.). An ORGAN STOP (*Principal*); *see also* PRINCIPALE.

Prioli, Giovanni. *See* PRIULI, GIOVANNI.

Prioli, Marieta Morosina. *See* PRIULI, MARIETA MOROSINA.

Prior imitation. *See* VORIMITATION.

Prioris, Johannes (*b* ?Brabant, *c*1460; *d* *c*1514). Franco-Netherlands composer. Vander Straeten surmised that the Flemish version of his name might have been 'De Veurste' or 'De Vorste'. Archives of the town of Vorst near Brussels cite in 1536 an individual named 'Prioirs' who may have been a descendant or a relative. Possibly he is identifiable with the 'D. Priori organistae cum famulo suo' who received two ducats for services rendered at St Peter's, Rome, in 1491. However, 'D[ominus] Prioris' occupied a post among native Italian singers in the relatively unimportant choir of St Peter's while the noteworthy Franco-Netherlanders in the employ of the Vatican usually served in the Sistine Chapel. Although works of his appear in seven Vatican MSS – a fact which seems to support the hypothesis that he lived in Rome – it should be pointed out that five of these sources were written after he was well established in France.

In 1503 the Ferrarese ambassador to the court of Louis XII wrote to Duke Ercole I stating that he had obtained a mass from 'Prioris, suo [i.e., the king's] maystro de capella' and Jean d'Auton mentioned that he was *maître de chapelle* in 1507. Crétin included him among the followers of Ockeghem in the well-known *Deploration*, and also referred to him as 'nostre bon père et maistre' in an epitaph for Jean Braconnier (*d* 1512). Presumably Prioris died some time after Braconnier but before Louis XII, since an account of the king's obsequies (January 1515) indicates that 'Conrard' was by then *maître de chapelle*. He was also named in the company of some of the best-known musicians of his time by Eloy d'Amerval, Jean Daniel and Rabelais and in Pierre Moulu's motet *Mater floreat florescat*. As late as 1545, a singer of the French royal chapel, Pernot Vermont (*d* 1558), stipulated in his will that his funeral service should include a performance of Prioris's Requiem, which may have been composed to commemorate the death of Anne of Brittany (*d* 9 Jan 1514).

Prioris was a highly polished musician capable of utilizing the wide variety of current compositional techniques. His chansons are mainly settings of rondeaux in the manner of Busnois and Hayne van Ghizeghem, while the influence of Ockeghem's contrapuntal style is strong in the longer motets and masses. He was one of a small group of composers, along with Agricola, Compère, Josquin and La Rue, who cultivated the motet-chanson. He also wrote several short song-motets, including the popular *Dulcis amica Dei*. The more chordal Italianate style is evident in his setting of *Consomo la vita mya*, in substantial portions of his *Missa 'Allez regrets'* and in his Requiem, one of the earliest known polyphonic settings of the Mass for the Dead.

WORKS
MASSES

Missa 'Allez regrets', 4vv, *I-Rvat* C.S.35 (based on Hayne van Ghizeghem's chanson)

Missa de angelis, 4vv, *A-Wn* 11883, *Wn* 15497, *I-CMac* D (M), *Rvat* C.S.23, *VEcap* 761

Missa de venerabili sacramento, 6vv, *D-Ju* 7, *I-Rvat* Pal.lat.1982 (T of Kyrie I missing)

Missa 'Je ne demande', ?vv (listed in Eitner but no longer extant)

Missa 'Tant bel mi sont pensade', 6vv, *F-CA* 18, *I-Rvat* C.S.23, *Fr* 2356 (based on anon. chanson in *Bc* Q17, *Fn* Magl.XIX.107bis and other sources)

Requiem, 4vv, *CMac* N(4), 1532⁵, 1553¹

OTHER SACRED

Alleluia O filii, O filiae, 4vv, *Rvat* C.S.42

Ave Maria, 3vv, *GB-Cmc* Pepys 1760

Ave Maria, 8vv, *D-Ek* Lit.O No.38, no.1, 1520³, 1545⁷ (canon, 8vv derived from 4)

Benedicta es caelorum regina, 5vv, *I-Rvat* C.S.45

Da pacem Domine, 6vv, 1520³, 1545⁷ (canon, 6vv derived from 3)

Dei genitrix, 4vv, *GB-Cmc* Pepys 1760

Domine non secundum, 4vv, *I-Rvat* C.S.63

Dulcis amica Dei, 3/4vv; ed. in *SMd*, v (1967), 3; *MB*, xviii (1962, rev.2/1969), 64

Factum est cum baptizaretur, 4vv, *I-Rvat* C.S.42

In principio erat verbum, 4vv, *Rvat* C.S.42, *Rvat* Pal.lat.1982

Magnificat primi toni, 3, 4vv, *Rvat* C.S.44

Magnificat terzi toni, 2, 4vv, *Rvat* C.S.44

Magnificat quarti toni, 4, 5vv, *D-Ju* 20

Magnificat quinti toni, 3, 4, 5vv, *Bds* 40013, *Ju* 20, *Ngm* 83795 (*Ju* 20 contains an alternative setting of verse 8 in the hand of J. Walter)

Magnificat octavi toni, 4, 6vv, *Bds* 40013, *Ju* 20, *Ju* Weimar B, *Ngm* 83795

Magnificat [octavi toni], 2–4vv, *I-Fd* II.27 (probably not by Prioris on stylistic grounds)

Quam pulchra es, 4vv, *GB-Cmc* Pepys 1760

Regina caeli, 4vv, *I-Rvat* C.S.42

Deuil et ennuy/Quoniam tribulatio, 4vv; ed. M. Picker, *The Chanson Albums of Marguerite of Austria* (Berkeley, 1965), 253

Royne du ciel/Regina caeli, 4vv, *I-Bc* Q17, *Fc* Basevi 2439

SECULAR

C'est pour aymer, 3vv, *F-Pn* fr.1596, *US-Wc* Laborde

Elle l'a pris, 3vv, *F-Pn* fr.1596, 1538[9]

Entre je suis [= Par vous je suis], 5vv, *A-Wn* 18746; ed. M. Picker, *The Chanson Albums of Marguerite of Austria* (Berkeley, 1965), 253

Gentils galans, 4vv, *D-Rp* C.120, 1504[3] (attrib. C. van Stappen in 1504[3]; probably not by Prioris)

Je ne demando, 3vv, *I-Bc* Q16 (attrib. 'J.p:' in source; probably not by Prioris)

Mon cueur a demy, 3vv; ed. E. Droz and G. Thibault, *Trois chansonniers français du XVᵉ siècle* (Paris, 1927), 74 (anon. in all sources; erroneously attrib. Prioris in modern literature)

Mon cueur et moi, 3vv; ed. K. Jeppesen, *Der Kopenhagener Chansonnier* (Copenhagen, 1927/R); H. E. Bush, 73

Mon plus que riens, 3vv, *I-Fc* Basevi 2439

Par vous je suis [= Entre je suis], 5vv, *Fc* Basevi 2439 (incorporates the popular Flemish melody 'In minen sin')

Par vous sermens, 3vv, *Bc* Q17, *Fc* Basevi 2439, c1535[14]

Plus que aultre, 3vv, *F-Pn* fr.1597, *US-Wc* Laborde

Riens ne me plaist, 3vv, *I-Fc* Basevi 2439

Vostre oeul s'est bien, 3vv, *DK-Kk* Ny Smlg.1848, *F-Pn* fr.2245, *I-Bc* Q17, *Fr* 2794

Consomo la vita mya, 3/4vv, *CH-SGs* 462, 463, *F-Pn* fr.1597, *GB-Cmc* Pepys 1760, *Lbm* 35087, *I-Fn* Magl. XIX.117, *US-Wc* Laborde; ed. in SMd, v (1967), 3; M. Bukofzer (1950), 211 (3vv setting possibly by Serafino dall'Aquila who wrote the poem. The unique attribution to Prioris in *GB-Cmc* may apply only to the additional part that appears there and in *US-Wc*)

BIBLIOGRAPHY

EitnerQ

E. vander Straeten: *La musique aux Pays-Bas avant le XIXᵉ siècle* (Brussels, 1867–88/R1969)

F. X. Haberl: 'Die römische "Schola cantorum" und die päpstlichen Kapellsänger bis zur Mitte des 16. Jahrhunderts', *VMw*, iii (1887), 239

R. de Maulde la Clavière, ed.: *Chronique de Louis XII par Jean d'Auton*, iv (Paris, 1895), 244

A. Pirro: 'Notes sur Jean Braconnier, dit Lourdault', *ReM*, ix (1928), 252

H. E. Bush: 'The Laborde Chansonnier', *PAMS 1940*, 73

M. Bukofzer: *Studies in Medieval and Renaissance Music* (New York, 1950), 211

T. H. Keahey: *The Masses of Johannes Prioris* (diss., U. of Texas, 1968)

C. Douglas: *The Motets of Johannes Prioris with a Prefatory Bio-bibliographical Study* (diss., U. of Illinois, 1969)

L. Lockwood: 'Josquin at Ferrara: New Documents and Letters', *Josquin des Prez: New York 1971*, 103

R. Wexler: *The Complete Works of Johannes Prioris* (diss., New York U., 1974)

RICHARD WEXLER

Pritchard, John (Michael) (*b* London, 5 Feb 1921). English conductor. The son of a professional violinist, he was taught privately by his father, later studying the piano, the viola and conducting in Italy. After his war service had ended in ill-health, he conducted the semi-professional Derby String Orchestra (1943–5). In 1947 he joined the re-formed Glyndebourne Festival Opera as répétiteur for its appearance at the first Edinburgh Festival. The next year he became chorus master and assistant to Fritz Busch, whose sudden indisposition during *Don Giovanni* at the 1949 festival led to Pritchard's conducting début there in mid-performance. He remained associated with Glyndebourne as conductor, music counsellor (from 1963) and musical director (1969–78).

His career, divided between opera and concerts, steadily developed in the 1950s after a three-month engagement with the Vienna Staatsoper in the 1951–2 season, followed by his Covent Garden début in the autumn of 1952 (conducting Verdi's *Un ballo in maschera*). The next year he first conducted in the USA (Pittsburgh SO), and successive international tours included his South American début in 1966 at Buenos Aires (Teatro Colón), and his first opera performance in the USA at Chicago (Lyric Theater) in 1969. He has generally preferred to pursue a freelance career, but he has spent influential periods as musical director of the Royal Liverpool PO, 1957–63, and of the LPO, 1962–6. He was appointed musical director of the Huddersfield Choral Society in 1973, principal conductor of the Cologne Opera in 1978 and chief guest conductor of the BBC SO in 1979.

Pritchard's Liverpool engagement was distinguished by his introduction there (and later in London) of contemporary music concerts on the 'Musica Viva' model pioneered at Munich, in which performances were preceded by verbal introduction and music examples. A consistent champion of a wide range of new music, he conducted the premières of Britten's *Gloriana* and Tippett's *The Midsummer Marriage* and *King Priam*, all at Covent Garden, and the British première of Henze's *Elegy for Young Lovers* at Glyndebourne. His performances in a comprehensive repertory of major orchestral classics are characterized by reliability rather than by special distinction, although individual occasions or works have afforded memorable experiences. He was made a CBE in 1962 and received the Shakespeare Prize of the FVS Foundation of Hamburg in 1975.

BIBLIOGRAPHY

H. Rosenthal: 'John Pritchard', *Opera*, xxii (1971), 870

NOËL GOODWIN

Priuli [Prioli], Giovanni (*b* Venice, c1575; *d* Vienna, 1629). Italian composer and organist. His first madrigal book (1604) describes him as being in the service of the Duchess of Urbino, but he was also in Venice during the 1600s: he studied there under Giovanni Gabrieli, occasionally substituted for him as an organist at St Mark's and was involved with musical activities at the Scuola di S Rocco in 1609 and 1612. In 1614 or 1615 he became Hofkapellmeister to Archduke Ferdinand at Graz and continued to serve him in the same capacity in Vienna when he became emperor as Ferdinand II in 1619. In 1622 Priuli was succeeded by Giovanni Valentini and may subsequently have worked for a time in Mantua.

Priuli's output is divided equally between sacred and secular music: he published five volumes of each. His madrigals show the move from the customary five-part texture to a concertato style characteristic of the period; *Presso un fiume tranquillo* (1625) is an opulent work comparable to Monteverdi's setting of the same text in his sixth book of madrigals (1614).

The sacred music is mostly for large numbers of voices, which are not always divided into separated choirs. For instance, the ten-part *Bonum est confiteri* (1619) uses freely changing concertato textures, melodic elaboration is subservient to polyphony, and the tuttis contain individual rhythms that move against block chords: this is very like early Gabrieli. There is a preference for numerous lower voices, and this sonority is sometimes exploited for word-painting. When writing for double choir Priuli makes the tuttis as interesting rhythmically as the thinner textures, as in the *Missa Sancti Benedicti* (in the second 1624 volume). By contrast he contributed two attractive solo motets to Leonardo Simonetti's *Ghirlanda sacra* (Venice, 1625[2]), one of which exploits for expressive purposes a contrast between long-drawn-out held notes and rapid semiquaver divisions.

Priuli had a considerable talent for writing instrumental works for church use after the manner of his teacher Gabrieli: there are 16 such works in the two volumes of 1618–19. They are not as elaborate contrapuntally as similar works by Gabrieli; there is careful thematic integration between various sections. The 12-part *Canzone in echo* (1619) has extended passages for the three topmost instruments echoing one another (the echoes are indicated by dynamic markings).

WORKS
(all except anthologies published in Venice)

SACRED
Sacrorum concentuum . . . pars I, a 5–8 (1618); ed. in Concentus musicus, ii (Cologne, 1973)
Sacrorum concentuum . . . pars altera, a 10, 12 (1619)
Psalmi Davidis regis, 8vv (1621)
Missae 4, 6, 8vv, bc (org) ad lib (1624)
Missae 8, 9vv, vn, vle, cornett, bc (1624)
8 motets in 1615³, 1624¹, 1625², 1641³, 1646⁴, 1672²; 4 motets in 1615¹³, ed. in MAM, xxiii (1970); 4 psalms in 1646³
Sacred works in *A-Wn*; *D-Bds*, *Rp*; *GB-T*; *USSR-KA*

SECULAR
Il primo libro de madrigali, 5vv (1604)
Il secondo libro de madrigali, 5vv (1607)
Il terzo libro de madrigali, 5vv, di due maniere, l'una per voci sole, l'altra per vv, insts (1612)
Musiche concertate, 3, 5–9vv, insts, libro IV (1622)
Delicie musicali, 2–10vv, some with insts (1625); 2 pieces ed. in DTÖ, ixxvii, Jg.xli (1934); some ed. in MAM, xlv (1977)
1 madrigal in 1610¹⁴

BIBLIOGRAPHY
L. von Köchel: *Die kaiserliche Hofmusikkapelle in Wien von 1543 bis 1867* (Vienna, 1869), 56ff
A. Einstein: 'Italienische Musik und italienische Musiker am Kaiserhof und an den erzherzoglichen Höfen in Innsbruck und Graz', *SMw*, xxi (1934), 48
———: *The Italian Madrigal* (Princeton, 1949/*R*1971), 762, 859f
H. Federhofer: 'Graz Court Musicians and their Contributions to the *Parnassus musicus Ferdinandaeus* (1615)', *MD*, ix (1955), 185ff
D. Arnold: 'Music at the Scuola di San Rocco', *ML*, xl (1959), 229
H. Federhofer: *Musikpflege und Musiker am Grazer Habsburgerhof 1564–1619* (Mainz, 1967)
J. L. A. Roche: *North Italian Liturgical Music in the Early 17th Century* (diss., U. of Cambridge, 1968)
A. Biales: 'Giovanni Priuli's *Sacrorum concentuum pars prima* (1618)', *AnMc*, no.12 (1973), 97
E. Selfridge-Field: *Venetian Instrumental Music from Gabrieli to Vivaldi* (Oxford, 1975)

JEROME ROCHE

Priuli [Prioli], **Marieta Morosina** (*fl* 1665). Italian noblewoman, from the distinguished Venetian Morosina family; she was almost certainly related by marriage to GIOVANNI PRIULI. She dedicated a volume of *Balletti e correnti* (Venice, 1665) for three string instruments and harpsichord continuo to the Habsburg Empress Mother Eleonora. The volume contains five sets of pieces paired by key, though not by theme, and eight independent *correnti*. They are conservative in style.

ELEANOR SELFRIDGE-FIELD

Prix de Rome. Annual award given by the Académie des Beaux-Arts in Paris from 1803 to 1968; *see* PARIS, §VI, 2. For a list of its recipients up to 1951 and further information, see *Grove 5*, 'Prix de Rome'.

Pro, Serafín (*b* Havana, 30 July 1906). Cuban composer. He received his training in music at the Havana Municipal Conservatory with Chartrand (piano) and Ardévol (theory). He took part in the Havana Choral Society and the University Chorale, of which he was assistant director; he also served as editor of the bulletin of the Grupo de Renovación Musical, a musical youth movement of the 1940s made up of followers of Ardévol. A strong proponent of the importance of form, Pro has written in a more expressive musical language than some of his more academically orientated colleagues in the Grupo. He taught composition and theory

at the Amadeo Roldán Conservatory from 1936 to 1962 and at the Alejandro García-Caturla Conservatory from 1962 to 1967, as well as establishing and conducting several choirs and editing a number of journals.

WORKS
(selective list)
Orch: Sonata, Chorale and Fugue, str, timp, 1951
Choral: Las siete doncellas (Lorca), 1940; Estar Así (E. Florit), 1940; Canción de Cuna Junto al Pesebre, S, female vv, 1941; Aspiración (R. R. Vidal), 1943; Monumental, Lago del alma, La canción del viento (Vidal), 1967
Chamber: Sonata, vn, pf, 1944; Ricercar, 2 tpt, 2 trbn, 1949; Capriccio, fl, ob, cl, bn, 1955
Pf: Sonata, E, 1942; Suite clásica en modo frigio, 1943

JOHN M. SCHECHTER

Proagōn. In ancient Athens, a ceremonial parade of the *choregoi* (*see* CHORĒGIA), poets, actors and choruses a few days before the dramatic festivals (Great Dionysia and Lenaia), at which the names and subjects of the plays were probably announced.

BIBLIOGRAPHY
A. Pickard-Cambridge: *The Dramatic Festivals of Athens* (Oxford, rev. 2/1968), 67ff

Pro Arte Quartet. Belgian string quartet. It was founded in 1912, and its members all studied at the Brussels Conservatory. The leader, Alphonse Onnou (*b* Dolhain-Limbourg, 29 Dec 1893; *d* Madison, Wisc., 20 Nov 1940), was a pupil of Cornelis. The other members were Laurent Halleux (*b* Hodimont-Verviers, 24 Jan 1897), a pupil of César Thomson; Germain Prévost (*b* Tournai, 23 Aug 1891), and Robert Maas (*b* Linkebeek, nr. Brussels, 24 June 1901; *d* Oakland, Calif., 7 July 1948), a pupil of Jacobs. The quartet made its début in Brussels in 1913 and soon became known as an exponent of modern music, achieving its greatest fame during the 1920s and 1930s. In 1921, with the aid of Paul Collaer and Arthur Prévost, the Pro Arte Concerts began, in which performances were given of new works by, among others, Bartók, Casella, Honegger, Martinů, Milhaud and Rieti. The quartet performed with great success at the 1923 ISCM Festival in Salzburg, and the same year played new works commissioned by Elizabeth Sprague Coolidge at a concert in Rome. After touring Europe the quartet visited England for the first time in 1925, and the following year played at the inauguration of the Hall of Music in the Library of Congress, Washington, DC. This was followed by the first of several tours of the USA, and a tour of Canada. Subsequent visits to England included annual series of a week's performances in Cambridge (1932–8). In 1932 the quartet was granted the title Quatuor de la Cour de Belgique, in recognition of its services to Belgian music. Onnou, Halleux and Prévost moved to the USA in 1940, and Onnou died the same year, but the quartet continued until 1947, as quartet-in-residence at Wisconsin University, led first by Antonio Brosa, and from 1944 by Rudolf Kolisch. Since then the title Pro Arte Quartet has been taken by the faculty quartet of the University of Wisconsin at Madison, led first by Kolisch and then, from 1967, by Norman Paulu.

At first the Pro Arte Quartet was less consistently successful with the classical repertory than with modern works, to which it brought exceptional polish and ease; but in time it came to be equally highly regarded in Mozart, Haydn and Schubert. Its style was without either the intensity of the Busch Quartet or the rich warmth of the Léner, but concentrated on finesse, lucidity of texture and rhythmic buoyancy. Among its gramophone records were many of Haydn's quartets, several of which had not previously been recorded, as well as works by Mozart, Schubert, Brahms and Dvořák and the Debussy and Ravel quartets. An Austrian quartet of the same name was founded in Salzburg in 1973.

ROBERT PHILIP

Pro Cantione Antiqua. English vocal ensemble. It was formed in 1968 by Mark Brown, Paul Esswood and James Griffett to sing the repertory of the medieval, Renaissance and Baroque periods. Its début took place that year, in Westminster Cathedral, conducted by Colin Mawby; the ensemble has also been directed by Bruno Turner, who prepared editions of music by several Renaissance composers for the group, as well as Philip Ledger, Henry Washington and others. Usually the group consists of six to nine male singers, including countertenors. Its recordings include an extensive anthology of the Franco-Flemish school, Italian motets, and other music by Morales, Victoria, Lassus, Palestrina, Tallis and Byrd. It has been much praised for the accuracy and the intensity of its singing.

Processional (from Lat. *liber processionalis, processionale, processionarium*). A small liturgical book of the Western Christian Church, containing the chants, rubrics and collects appropriate to liturgical processions. It is of particular musical interest since it contains antiphons, verses, rhymed Preces and even polyphonic chants that do not occur in other liturgical books. Like the pontifical, it was a comparatively late addition to the repertory of official liturgical books, originating in the 11th and 12th centuries; the processional antiphons are much older, and formerly occurred in the gradual.

1. Sources of processional chants. 2. Categories of noted processionals. 3. Musical repertory.

1. SOURCES OF PROCESSIONAL CHANTS. Processions occur in most ancient religions. Essentially, they comprise a communal progress on foot for the purpose of petition, penitence or even protocol (as in the processions of the Byzantine court), and the singing of chants. The latter may be very diverse in style – syllabic, melismatic or in litany form (i.e. comprising a series of invocations or petitions, to each of which the congregation makes a brief response).

The oldest known processionals (books containing the processional chants) date from the 12th century, although a book of the chants for the Rogationtide procession at Metz Cathedral (now in *F-MZ*) was copied in the second half of the 11th century; certain other books derived from the Romano-Germanic pontifical of Mainz, and containing important elements of the ritual and processional, may date from the 11th century (*A-Wn* 1888) or even the late 10th century (*I-Rvat* Palat.489).

Earlier – from the late 8th century – processional antiphons often occurred in the gradual. This is true of antiphons for processions immediately following the blessing of candles (Candlemas), ashes (Ash Wednesday) or palms (Palm Sunday), which were copied before the introit of the day; it is also true of the processional antiphons for the Major Litanies, copied at the end of the graduals (see R.-J. Hesbert, ed., *Antiphonale missarum sextuplex*, Brussels, 1935, pp.cxxiff, nos.200–214). (In the tradition of southern French graduals with Aquitanian notation, the relationship between the processional antiphons and introits later extended to all festivals; elsewhere, processional antiphons came to be grouped around the ancient antiphons of the Major Litanies.)

The procession of the Major Litanies ('St Mark's Procession', though unrelated to the festival of St Mark) was introduced at Rome under St Gregory the Great in 592. It took place on 25 April between St Lawrence in Lucina and St Peter, and represented the christianizing of an old pagan procession held on the same day, the *robigalia*, which had persisted at Rome until the Late Empire. Another distinct procession, that of the Minor Litanies (or rogations) was instituted in Gaul in 469 by St Mamertus, Bishop of Vienne, on the three days before Ascension. Both processions were in due course adopted into the Roman liturgy: the Gallican Minor Litanies continued to survive even after the introduction into Gaul of the Roman liturgy and its Major Litanies of 25 April; on the other hand, the Gallican Minor Litanies were adopted at Rome in 816, under Leo III, and the same chants were specified for them as for the Litanies of 25 April.

The chants for the Litanies occur in Gregorian graduals written and noted in France, assigned sometimes to 25 April and sometimes to the three days before Ascension, and to them are appended Preces that are remnants of the ancient Gallican liturgy abolished at the Carolingian reform (see P. de Clerck: *La prière universelle dans les liturgies latines anciennes*, diss., Institut Catholique de Paris, 1970). In consequence, a study of the chants of the Major and Minor Litanies must begin with an examination of the oldest graduals (listed in *Le graduel romain, ii: Les sources*, Solesmes, 1957), in particular those of the 10th and 11th centuries noted with neumes.

The inconsistency between the graduals in which the chants were assigned 'according to the Romans' ('secundum Romanos') to April 25, and those where the chants were assigned 'following the custom of the Gallican church' ('juxta morem gallicanae ecclesiae') to the three days before Ascension, was not eliminated: an attempt at codification, in the Ordo XXXI (following the numbering of M. Andrieu: *Les ordines romani du haut moyen-âge*, Louvain, 1931–56) entitled 'Quando letania major debet fieri', did not win acceptance. Nevertheless, the *Ordo romanus antiquus* (following the appellation of Melchior Hittorp, i.e. Andrieu's Ordo L), which was drafted at St Alban in Mainz in about 950, seems to have influenced the processional tradition in several churches of south Germany.

As mentioned above, the graduals of south-west France noted with diastematic Aquitanian neumes generally contain processional chants before the introit of the Mass of the day. These Aquitanian graduals generally contain more processional chants than the other French graduals with chants of Gallican origin pressed into service as processional chants. Moreover, they contain the earliest evidence of the melodies, from the early 11th century, owing to the precise diastematic Aquitanian notation they use. No single archetype has been discovered for the Aquitanian processional chants despite a complete study of the processional chants in Aquitanian graduals and in processionals proper, except perhaps in the case of the antiphons of the Litanies. Useful comparisons are possible, nevertheless, between graduals and processionals of the same tradition.

Precursors of the processional – besides the gradual

– also include the antiphoner or breviary. Some noted antiphoners, for instance that of Hartker (*CH-SGs* 390–91: PalMus, 2nd ser., i, 1900), or the Codex Albensis (*A-Gu* 211; ed. Z. Falvy and L. Mezey: *Codex Albensis: ein Antiphonar aus dem 12. Jahrhundert*, Monumenta Hungariae musicae, i, Budapest, 1963), contain the Maundy antiphons. These antiphons, sung weekly in monasteries and annually in other churches on the evening of Maundy Thursday during the Washing of the Feet (see T. Schäfer: *Die Fusswaschung*, Texte und Arbeiten, xlvii, Beuron, 1956), appear in many processionals and graduals, although they do not accompany a procession and were omitted from a number of manuscript processionals.

Some breviaries contain processional chants proper, however. A fragmentary breviary with neumes, *CH-Bu* N I 6 (ed. A. Dold, Texte und Arbeiten, xliv, 1954, pp.19ff), contains the antiphons for the Palm Sunday procession; a 14th-century noted breviary from Lyons (*F-C* 43, ff.249*v*–260) contains the penitential processional chants of the Major Litanies.

Some manuscripts present the various categories of chant (for Mass, Offices, processions and other miscellaneous rites) either in separate volumes (e.g. *F-Pn* lat.12584, of the 11th century, or *GB-WO* F 160, of the 13th century) or in a single volume, with the chants in the order in which they are performed, the processional chants occurring between Terce and the introit at Mass (e.g. *I-Rvat* lat.7018, of the 11th century, or *I-BV* V 19–20, of the 12th century). Some other manuscripts contain processional antiphons on flyleaves; some contain the texts of the processional chants without musical notation (e.g. *F-Pn* lat.2819, of the 11th or 12th century). Processional chants occur also in tropers and prosers, such as those of St Martial at Limoges (*F-Pn* lat.909, 1136 and 1240). Husmann, in his catalogue of these manuscripts (RISM, B/V/1, 1964), gave an account of processional chants where they occur.

Some processionals (in the strict sense) that were carried in procession do not contain the processional chants but only the rubrics and the collects recited at each station during the procession (e.g. *F-AI* 17, of the 15th century, from Albi Cathedral; *D-Mbs* clm.3905, of the 12th century, from St Afra at Augsburg; *GB-SB* 148, of the 15th century; and the Sarum processional edited by C. Wordsworth: *Ceremonies and Processions of the Cathedral Church of Salisbury*, Cambridge, 1901). The incipits of the chants are given in these manuscripts, however, and it is possible, in the absence of a complete processional, to reconstruct the repertory of the church in question.

Chant incipits appear also in the ordinal (Ordo), a liturgical book with rubrics, collects and lessons, which is another valuable source for the study of processional chants. Manuscript ordinals are listed in *Le graduel romain*, ii: *Les sources* (Solesmes, 1957), pp.189ff; printed ordinals are listed by A. Hänggi (*Der Rheinauer Liber ordinarius*, Fribourg, 1957, pp.xxvff); and more recently discovered ordinals are listed by A. Jacob (*Revue d'histoire ecclésiastique*, lxv, 1970, pp.789ff). The manuscript ordinals of the Bibliothèque Nationale in Paris have been analysed by J. Dufrasne (*Les ordinaires manuscrits des églises séculières conservés à la Bibliothèque nationale de Paris*, diss., Institut Catholique de Paris, 1959; available in microfiche from CIPOL – International Committee for Ecumenical Liturgical Publications).

2. CATEGORIES OF NOTED PROCESSIONALS. Manuscript processionals are to be listed and described by Huglo in a forthcoming volume of *RISM*. They fall into a number of categories. The majority are of small portable format and serve for all the processions of the liturgical year. They generally begin with the Sundays and festivals of the Proper of Time, including those of the Christmas cycle, followed by the festivals of the Proper of the Saints (generally beginning with 24 June – St John the Baptist), and they generally conclude with the chants for various processions to pray for rain, fine weather, etc.

Many, though not all, processionals include after the chants for Palm Sunday the Maundy antiphons, those for the Veneration of the Cross on Good Friday, and sometimes also the chants for the Easter Vigil, such as the EXULTET and the hymn *Inventor rutili* (see G. M. Dreves, Analecta hymnica medii aevi, l, Leipzig, 1907, pp.30f). These non-processional chants were included in the processional for the sake of convenience.

A very complete type of processional was established in England in 1197 at the revision of the Sarum liturgy; this later spread to all the churches in England (see Bailey, 1971).

Some manuscript processionals contain only the chants and rubrics for the stations of the processions of the Major and Minor Litanies. Such books would have been used only four times a year; they are of very limited distribution and are found most often in Italy. They seem to have originated in imitation of the Ambrosian processional, which contains only the chants, collects and lessons for the three days before the vigil of Pentecost. The Ambrosian processionals contain the antiphon texts encountered elsewhere but with distinct Ambrosian melodies: *D-F* Mus.Hds. in 4° 1 (olim 5192), copied about 1400, which belonged to Cardinal Francesco Piccolpasso; Milan, Biblioteca dell' Università Cattolica del S Cuore, kept until 1970 at the Collegio degli Oblati at Rho (described by G. Tibiletti, *Ephemerides liturgicae*, lxxxvii, 1973, pp.145ff); *F-SO* réserve 64, of the 15th or 16th century (described by M. Huglo: *Fonti e paleografia del canto ambrosiano*, Archivio ambrosiano, vii, Milan, 1956, p.75).

The oldest Gregorian processional containing only the chants of the Major and Minor Litanies dates from the 12th century: *I-PCc* 191(28). This processional must be studied in conjunction with *PCd* 9 (26 ff.), which contains only the lessons for the stations of the rogation processions. A similar division occurred at times outside Italy, e.g. in nine manuscripts at *D-AAm*, *F-CA* 68(69) and 80(81), *F-CHR* 353 (burnt in 1944) and in *F-VN* 139.

The Corpus Christi procession at times occurred in its own book, e.g. *D-AAm* 57(LV) and 58 (see O. Gatzweiler: *Die liturgischen Handschriften des Aachener Münsterstifts*, Münster, 1926, pp.170f). Various unofficial popular customs often came to be associated with this procession, for instance at Angers, Effeltrich near Erlangen and Prague; for a study of these customs – occasionally including the use of musical instruments – it is necessary to consult sources other than manuscript processionals (see Bowles, 1964; J. Torsy, 1972). The same applies also to the popular customs associated with pilgrimage processions and other popular processions such as that of St Josse at Montreuil-sur-Mer, of St Guy (Veit) in the Rhineland, and of St Willibrord on the Tuesday after Whit Sunday at Echternach.

Some processionals conclude with the chants for burial rites, which included a procession to the graveside according to the requirements of the ritual. Because of this, some manuscripts of the funeral rites with notation (e.g. *F-Pn* lat.14825 and various manuscripts at Karlsruhe, described by H. Ehrensberger: *Bibliotheca liturgica manuscripta*, Karlsruhe, 1889), and noted manuscripts of the Office of the Dead (e.g. *A-Ssp* a V 10) have been wrongly termed processionals. (They are to be described in a forthcoming catalogue of manuscript rituals by P. M. Gy.)

Each of the religious orders imposed a processional of its own, and these were propagated through manuscripts and subsequently in printed editions. The processionals of most of the orders have remained substantially identical with the originals through the history of each order.

The processionals of the various regular canons subscribing to the Rule of St Augustine, particularly the Premonstratensians, follow the pattern of the *Ordinaire prémontré d'après les manuscrits du XIIe et du XIIIe siècles* (ed. P. Lefèvre, Louvain, 1941). They are characterized by the festivals of St Augustine, patron of the orders: principal festival, 28 August, festivals of the translation of his relics to Pavia (*translatio prima*, 28 February; *translatio secunda*, 11 October) and the festival of his conversion (5 May). About ten Premonstratensian processionals survive in manuscript, and there are several printed editions, including those of 1584 and 1666. That of 1727 is neo-Gallican, and has no link with the ancient tradition (*see* NEO-GALLICAN CHANT).

No unifying factor links the processionals of the Benedictines. A standard Cluniac processional was, however, approximately followed, in the abbeys affiliated to Cluny: *F-Pn* lat.12584, of the 11th century, the antiphoner, processional and gradual of St Maur-des-Fossés (see R.-J. Hesbert: *Manuscripti 'cursus monasticus'*, Corpus antiphonalium officii, ii, Rome, 1965, pp.xvff and plate X); *B-Br* II 3823 (Fétis 1172), an early 12th-century Auvergne gradual (*Le graduel romain*, ii, p.38); and *F-SO* réserve 28, of the 15th century, from Cluny (see J. Hourlier, *Revue grégorienne*, xxx, 1951, p.233).

No Carthusian processional exists: in their simplified liturgy the Carthusians retained only the processions of Candlemas, Ash Wednesday and Palm Sunday, and the chants for these were copied in the standard gradual drawn up after the first Carthusian Chapter General of 1140.

In the liturgy and chant reform undertaken by the Cistercians in the early 12th century, the number of processions was considerably reduced. The noted books had been lost before 1480 from the standard exemplar of the liturgical books of the order (*F-Dm* 114(82) drawn up at Cîteaux between 1185 and 1191); the earliest surviving Cistercian processional is, therefore, a copy, and is from the abbey of Pairis in Alsace (*F-CO* 442, of the 12th century; published as the second part of the *Hymnarium parisiense* by K. Weinmann, Regensburg, 1905). Cistercian processionals generally begin with the antiphon *Lumen ad revelationem* for 2 February. The Cistercian processional must have been printed at about the same time as the antiphoner (1545), but no edition except that of 1689 is known.

The Dominican processional drawn up in 1254 constitutes the fourth volume of the standard exemplar of Humbert of Romans (*I-Rss* XIV lit.1, ff.58v–66r). It begins with the rubric 'De processionibus in genere: Cum imminet aliqua processio'; this was sometimes omitted in manuscript processionals, but was retained in printed Dominican processionals, and still appears in the edition of 1913. Dominican processionals commence with the Palm Sunday antiphon *Pueri hebreorum*. The only variable section is that concerning the Washing of the Altars on Maundy Thursday, since the antiphons, verses and collects were chosen according to the patrons of the altars being washed. Between the Maundy Thursday responsories (*In monte Oliveti*, etc) were inserted an antiphon with verse, and a collect, in honour of the patron of the altar then being washed. The degree of precision of the manuscripts varies: some present only the standard responsories; some give the general rubric from the standard exemplar, 'Here should be placed antiphons, verses and collects of the saints according to the disposition of the altars in any convent'; some (rather fewer) give the list of antiphons, verses and collects proper to the church in question, either within the manuscript (e.g. *F-CO* 412) or as a supplement at the end. This pattern for the Washing of the Altars is rarely found other than in Augustinian and Dominican manuscripts.

Almost 140 manuscript Dominican processionals survive; the Dominican processional was printed by Spira at Venice as early as 1493, and has since gone through many editions. To study it, it is necessary only to refer either to the standard exemplar from the Dominican house in Paris (*I-Rss* XIV lit.1, mentioned above), or to the small portable copy of the Master General of the Order (*GB-Lbm* Add.23935, ff.98v–106v) used by him on his visitations to check that the liturgy and chant were being accurately maintained. (The content of this small portable copy has been edited by C. Allworth, *Ephemerides liturgicae*, lxxxiv, 1970, pp.182ff and table 1.) The study of each Dominican processional thus amounts only to the study of the peculiarities distinguishing the copy from the exemplar, and notably of the particular chants sung during the Washing of the Altars, or of the various supplements, such as polyphonic pieces, which were sung despite their prohibition by the Chapter General.

The Franciscan processional is identical with the standard Roman processional. It contains the chants for the processions of the Roman missal, Candlemas, Ash Wednesday and Palm Sunday, according to the rubrics of the missal. It was frequently printed in the 16th century, one of the earliest editions being that of H. Estienne (Paris, 1507).

3. MUSICAL REPERTORY. In analysing the processional chants, the earlier period, in which the processional chants appeared in the gradual, etc, should be studied separately from the later period when they were collected into a volume of their own.

In the earlier period, the repertory consisted above all of the great processional antiphons, and also (according to region) of *versus*, or hymns with refrains, composed in the 9th century (see G. M. Dreves, Analecta hymnica medii aevi, l, Leipzig, 1907, pp.237, 250ff), and rhymed Preces for the rogations (see M. Huglo, *Hispania sacra*, viii, 1955, pp.361ff). The great processional antiphons sometimes included verses, and were often in consequence termed *responsoria*. They make up a group of their own within the category of the antiphon (*see* ANTIPHON, §4). Many of them are remnants of the liturgical and musical repertory of the ancient Gallican liturgy and were changed into processional chants during the Carolingian reform when Gregorian chant was imposed on the Frankish Empire (*see* GALLICAN RITE, MUSIC OF THE).

Some of the earliest specimens of organum are processional antiphons (e.g. in the Winchester Troper: see A. Holschneider: *Die Organa von Winchester*, Hildesheim, 1968) or verses of responsories which occur in the processional. The Sarum processional contains a number of examples of faburden in chants such as the *Salve festa dies*, or those for the Litany of the Saints (*GB-Llp* 438); according to the London chronicle for the year 1531, 'after came Paul's choir . . . singing the litany with faburden'.

The later period, in which separate manuscript processionals are found, begins according to region from the 12th century. During this period, the processional antiphons were almost everywhere replaced by greater responsories from the antiphoner, except for litanies and at rogationtide. This development did not occur uniformly everywhere, however, and the distribution of the Matins responsories over the various festivals of the church year differed from place to place: each church had a list of its own. The practice of this later period – with its use of responsories – is mostly reflected in printed processionals.

Macé, in his *Instruction pour apprendre à chanter à quatre parties selon le plain-chant* (Caen, 1582), included a harmonization, in four voices, of the Candlemas processional antiphon *Lumen ad revelationem*.

BIBLIOGRAPHY
PROCESSIONS AND PROCESSIONAL CHANTS

P. M. Quarti: *Biga Aetherea duplici sacro tractatu rapiens in coelum animo: in primo agitur de processionibus ecclesiasticis et de litaniis sanctorum* (Venice, 1665), 1–80
J. Pothier: 'Prières litaniales ou processionelles', *Revue du chant grégorien*, ix (1901), 113
C. Maydeston: *Ordinale Sarum, transcribed by W. Cook*, Henry Bradshaw Society, xxii (London, 1902)
A. Franz: *Die kirchlichen Benediktionen im Mittelalter* (Freiburg, 1909), 444ff
D. de Bruyne: 'L'origine des processions de la chandeleur et des rogations à propos d'un sermon inédit', *Revue bénédictine*, xxxiv (1922), 14
K. Young: *The Drama of the Medieval Church* (Oxford, 1933, 2/1962)
H. Leclercq: 'Procession', 'Processionnal', *Dictionnaire d'archéologie chrétienne et de liturgie*, xiv/2 (Paris, 1948), 1895
F. A. Yates: 'Dramatic Religious Processions in Paris in the Late Sixteenth Century', *AnnM*, ii (1954), 215–70
R. B. Donovan: *The Liturgical Drama in Medieval Spain*, Studies and Texts, iv (Toronto, 1958)
H. J. Graef: *Palmweihe und Palmprozession in der lateinischen Liturgie* (Kaltenkirchen, 1959)
G. Kiesel: 'Die Springprozession des heiligen Willibrord in geschichtlicher und volkskundlicher Sicht', *Saarbrücker Hefte*, xvi (1962), 35
T. Klein: *Die Prozessionsgesänge der Mainzerkirche aus dem 14. bis 18. Jahrhundert*, Quellen und Abhandlungen zur mittelalterlichen Kirchengeschichte, vii (Speyer, 1962)
M. Gushee: 'A Polyphonic Ghost', *JAMS*, xvi (1963), 205
J. Hoffmann: 'Die Fronleichnamprozession in Aschaffenburg nach den Prozessionsbüchern des 14. bis 16. Jahrhunderts', *Würzburger Diözesangeschichtsblätter*, xxvi (1964), 109
E. A. Bowles: 'Musical Instruments in the Medieval Corpus Christi Procession', *JAMS*, xvii (1964), 254
F. Pauly: 'Die Tholeyer Prozessionsliste von 1454', *Rheinische Vierteljahrblätter*, xxix (1964), 331
R. Janin: 'Les processions religieuses à Byzance', *Revue des études byzantines*, xxiv (1966), 69
E. J. Lengeling: 'Die Bittprozessionen des Domkapitels und der Pfarreien der Stadt Münster vor dem Fest Christi Himmelfahrt', *Monasterium* (Münster, 1966), 151–220
M. Bouille: 'Les anciennes processions du jeudi-saint et du vendredi-saint', *Cahiers d'études et de recherches catalanes*, xxxiv–xxxviii (1967), 133

A. Kurzeja: *Der älteste Liber ordinarius der Trierer Domkirche*, Liturgiegeschichtliche Quellen und Forschungen, lii (Münster, 1970)
H. Hofmann-Brandt: *Die Tropen zu den Responsorien des Offiziums* (diss., U. of Erlangen, 1971)
J. Torsy: 'Zur Verehrung der Eucharistie im Spätmittelalter: eine Fronleichnamprozession in Wittlar im Jahre 1436', *Von Konstanz nach Trient: Festgabe für August Franzen* (Paderborn, 1972), 335

EDITIONS AND DESCRIPTIONS OF MANUSCRIPT PROCESSIONALS

W. G. Henderson, ed.: *Manuale et processionale ad usum insignis ecclesiae eboracensis*, Surtees Society, lxiii (Durham and London, 1875)
——: *Processionale ad usum insignis et preclarae ecclesiae Sarum* (Leeds, 1882)
X. B. de Montault: 'Processionnal de l'abbaye St Aubin à Angers', *Bulletin historique et philologique du comité des travaux historiques et scientifiques*, i (1885), 132
J. W. Legg: *The Processional of the Nuns of Chester*, Henry Bradshaw Society, xviii (London, 1899)
C. Wordsworth: *Ceremonies and Processions of the Cathedral Church of Salisbury, edited from the Fifteenth-century Manuscript No.148* (Cambridge, 1901)
F. Ghisi: 'Un processionale inedito per la settimana santa nel opera del Duomo di Firenze', *RMI*, lv (1953), 362
P. M. Gy: 'Collectaire, rituel, processionnal', *Revue des sciences philosophiques et théologiques*, xliv (1960), 441
G. Benoit-Castelli: 'Un processionnal anglais du XIVe siècle: le processionnal dit "de Rollington" ', *Ephemerides liturgicae*, lxxv (1961), 281–326
H. Husmann: *Tropen und Sequenzerhandschriften*, RISM, B/V/1 (1964)
A. Leroy: 'Le processionnal et l'office de St Josse', *Bulletin de la Commission départementale des monuments historiques du Pas-de-Calais*, viii (1967), 298
C. Allworth: 'The Medieval Processional, Donaueschingen MS 882', *Ephemerides liturgicae*, lxxxiv (1970), 169
Sister Jane Patricia: 'Un processional cistercien du XVe siècle', *Etudes grégoriennes*, xi (1970), 193
T. Bailey: *The Processions of Sarum and the Western Church*, Studies and Texts, xxi (Toronto, 1971)
A. Canellas: 'Un processionnal de Saragosse (Bruxelles, Bibliothèque royale, IV 473)', *Texts and Manuscripts: Essays Presented to G. I. Lieftinck*, ii (Amsterdam, 1972), 34 [with 6 figs. and plates]
F. Wormald: 'A Medieval Processional (S. Giles, Norwich) and its Diagrams', *Kunsthistorische Forschungen Otto Pächt* (Salzburg, 1972), 129 [with 9 illustrations]
P. Gleeson: 'Dominican Liturgical Manuscripts from before 1254', *Archivium Fratrum Praedicatorum*, xlii (1972), 81–135
G. Tibiletti: 'Antifonario processionale delle litanie triduane (manoscritto del 1492)', *Ephemerides liturgicae*, lxxxvii (1973), 145

MICHEL HUGLO

Processo [processus] (Lat.). Synonym for AMBITUS in medieval and Renaissance theory.

Procopius von Templin (*b* Templin, 1607; *d* Linz, 22 Nov 1690). German friar, preacher and hymn writer, active principally in Austria. He came from a Protestant family. He went as a soldier to Bohemia, where in 1625 he became a Catholic, and he entered the Capuchin order in Vienna on 3 June 1627. He then worked as a preacher in Prague, Passau (in 1642), Vienna, Salzburg and elsewhere. In 1651 he was working for his order in Rome. Later he worked in Linz and again in Passau (in 1659), and from 1669 he was a member of the Capuchin community in Salzburg, where most of his collected sermons were published. He produced several collections of hymns, for which the music was provided by Georg Kopp, F. Berenger (1632–95), a Benedictine monk from the monastery of Formbach, and a Capuchin monk, Father Albinus.

WORKS

Mariae Hülff Ehren Kräntzel, das ist himmelische Lobgesänger (Passau, 1642) [music by G. Kopp]
Hertzenfreud und Seelentrost, das ist himmelische Betrachtungen und . . . Lobgesänger, erste Teil (Passau, 1660) [music by F. Berenger]
Hertzenfreud und Seelentrost . . . ander Teil (Passau, 1661) [music by Albinus]
Eucharistiale . . . opusculum I (Passau, 1661) [music by Kopp]
Poenitentiale . . . opusculum II (Passau, 1662)

BIBLIOGRAPHY

W. Bäumker: *Das katholische deutsche Kirchenlied in seinen Singweisen*, iii (Freiburg, 1891/*R*1962), 356

V. Gadient: 'Procop von Templin', *Deutsche Quellen und Studien*, iii (1912)

A. Kober: *Die Mariengedichte des Procopius von Templin* (diss., U. of Münster, 1925)

N. Tschulik: 'Procopius von Templin und das deutsche Lied im 17. Jahrhundert', *Mf*, vi (1953), 320

WALTHER LIPPHARDT

Procter, (Mary) Norma (*b* Cleethorpes, 15 Feb 1928). English contralto. She studied with Roy Henderson and Alec Redshaw, making her début in 1948 at Southwark Cathedral in *Messiah*. Her busy career has consisted mainly of oratorio, concert and recital appearances, throughout Britain and the Continent; but in 1958 she sang the title role in Britten's *The Rape of Lucretia* at Aldeburgh, and in 1961 Gluck's *Orpheus* at Covent Garden. She has worked with many leading conductors, from Walter to Boulez, and her extensive repertory includes Bach cantatas, Handel oratorios, Beethoven's Ninth Symphony, *Elijah* and several works by Mahler, including *Das klagende Lied* and the Second, Third and Eighth Symphonies. Her full-toned, vibrant voice is securely managed and expressive, without the hollow, hooting quality associated with English oratorio style. Her operatic appearances were dignified and vocally well characterized.

ELIZABETH FORBES

Prod'homme, J(acques) G(abriel) (*b* Paris, 28 Nov 1871; *d* Neuilly-sur-Seine, nr. Paris, 18 June 1956). French musicologist, music historian and writer on music. After schooling at the Lycée Condorcet (until 1887) and a year's training in the merchant marine at Guadeloupe he studied music history and philology at the Ecole des Hautes Etudes, Paris (1890–94), and later continued his studies in Germany (1899–1910), Belgium and Holland (1912, 1913). His career as a music journalist began in 1895 with contributions to *Revue socialiste*, *Enclos* and other journals; in Munich, where he lived from 1897 to 1900, he founded and edited the *Deutsche-französische Rundschau* (1899–1902). On his return to Paris he founded (with Dauriac and Ecorcheville) the French section of the International Musical Society (1902), of which he was secretary from 1903 to 1913; he was also a founder (with La Laurencie, 1917), secretary (1917–20), vice-president (1929–36) and later honorary president of the French Musicological Society. In 1931 he succeeded Bouvet as curator of the Paris Opéra library and archivist of its museum, and in 1934 he became librarian of the Paris Conservatoire in succession to Henri Expert; he held both posts until 1940. As a music critic he wrote for many French and foreign journals including *Le ménestrel*, *Revue musicale*, *Revue Pleyel*, *Signal* and *Mesidor*, and in 1921 he joined the committee of La Critique Dramatique et Musicale.

Prod'homme's stature as one of the leading French music historians of his generation was largely due to the diversity of his career and the energy he devoted to it and to his writings, which were informed by his independence of mind and enthusiasm for the subject. Besides his many biographies of composers (including Gluck, Gossec, Paganini, Liszt and Berlioz) he produced translations of Wagner's complete prose works (13 volumes) and operas, Beethoven's conversation books and operas by Haydn and Mozart. He was

made a Chevalier of the Légion d'honneur in 1928 and was a member of the Académie Française, the Académie des Beaux-Arts and the Académie Royale de Belgique.

WRITINGS

Le cycle Berlioz, i: *La damnation de Faust*; ii: *L'enfance du Christ* (Paris, 1896–9)

'Marie Fel (1713–1794)', *SIMG*, iv (1902–3), 485–518

with C. Bertrand: *Guides analytiques de l'Anneau du Nibelung, Crépuscule des dieux* (Paris, 1902)

Hector Berlioz 1803–1869: sa vie et ses oeuvres (Paris, 1905, rev. 2/1913; Ger. trans., 1906)

Les symphonies de Beethoven (1800–1827) (Paris, 1906/*R*1977)

trans. with F. Holl and others: *Oeuvres en prose de Richard Wagner* (Paris, 1907–25)

Paganini (Paris, 1907, 2/1927; Eng. trans., 1911/*R*1977)

Franz Liszt (Paris, 1910)

with A. Dandelot: *Gounod, 1818–93: sa vie et ses oeuvres* (Paris, 1911/*R*1973)

Ecrits de musiciens (XVe–XVIIIe siècles) (Paris, 1912) [Palestrina, Lassus, Lully etc]

Richard Wagner et la France (Paris, 1921)

La jeunesse de Beethoven, 1770–1800 (Paris, 1921, 2/1927) [index by D. W. MacArdle, 1945]

trans.: *R. Wagner: Drames musicaux* (Paris, 1922–7)

L'Opéra, 1669–1925: description, histoire, répertoire, principaux artistes, bibliographie (Paris, 1925/*R*1972)

W. A. Mozart (Paris, 1925, 2/1943) [trans. of A. Schurig: *W. A. Mozart: sein Leben und seine Werke*, Leipzig, 1913]

Pensées sur la musique et les musiciens (Paris, 1926)

Beethoven raconté par ceux qui l'ont vu (Paris, 1927)

'Les débuts de Beethoven en France', *Beethoven-Zentenarfeier: Wien 1927*, 116

'Les oeuvres de Schubert en France', *Internationaler Kongress für Schubertforschung: Wien 1928*, 87

Mozart raconté par ceux qui l'ont vu 1756–1791 (Paris, 1928)

Schubert raconté par ceux qui l'ont vu (Paris, 1928)

with E. Crauzat: *Paris qui disparaît: Les menus plaisirs du roi, L'Ecole royale et le Conservatoire de Paris* (Paris, 1929)

Wagner raconté par ceux qui l'ont vu (Paris, 1929)

'Beethoven et Pleyel', *Studien zur Musikgeschichte: Festschrift für Guido Adler* (Vienna, 1930/*R*1971), 190

'Trois lettres inédites de Cosima Wagner', *Mélanges de musicologie offerts à M. Lionel de la Laurencie* (Paris, 1933), 282

Les sonates pour piano de Beethoven, 1782–1823 (Paris, 1937, rev. 2/1950)

trans.: *Cahiers de conversation de Beethoven, 1819–1827* (Paris, 1946)

L'immortelle bien-aimée de Beethoven (Paris, 1946)

Les écrits divers sur la musique et les musiciens (Paris, 1946) [trans. of R. Schumann: *Gesammelte Schriften über Musik und Musiker*, Leipzig, 1854]

Gluck (Paris, 1948/*R*1977)

François-Joseph Gossec, 1734–1829 (Paris, 1949)

with F. Goldbeck: *Entretiens sur la musique* (Paris, 1953) [trans. of W. Furtwängler: *Gespräche über Musik*, Zurich, 1948]

'Bibliographie berliozienne', *ReM*, special no. (1956), 97–147

BIBLIOGRAPHY

M. Garros: 'Jacques-Gabriel Prod'homme (1871–1956)', *RdM*, xxxvi (1957), 3

Proemium (Lat.). PROOIMION.

Profe [Profius], **Ambrosius** (*b* Breslau [now Wrocław], 12 Feb 1589; *d* Breslau, 27 Dec 1661). German organist, teacher, publisher, music editor, composer and theorist. After studying theology at Wittenberg, he became a teacher at the Elisabeth Gymnasium at Breslau in 1617 and in the same year was appointed Lutheran Kantor and schoolmaster at Jauer (Jawor), Silesia. In 1629 Lutheranism was suppressed there and Catholic worship re-established, so he was obliged to return to Breslau, where he set up as a merchant. In 1633 he was appointed organist of St Elisabeth there, without, however, giving up his commercial activities. His organist's post came to an end in 1649, when part of the church fell in and destroyed the organ; but he continued his business career and died prosperous.

It is not as a composer but as an assiduous editor and collector that Profe particularly deserves mention. His principal collection is the *Geistliche Concerten und Harmonien* in four volumes (1641–6), completed by the *Corollarium* of 1649. His aim was to introduce Italian vocal works, mainly in motet style, to church musicians in eastern and central Germany: he included works by 31 composers mainly of the Venetian school, whose polychoral writing had long been popular in Silesia, in particular 27 works by Giovanni Rovetta. Profe's texts have not yet been compared with the original Italian editions. (It is interesting that 11 original Venetian editions of Rovetta, published between 1636 and 1650, were kept at Breslau and could thus have come from Profe's own library.) He also included pieces by a few composers from eastern Germany and three unique works by Schütz, among them the seven-part dialogue *Ich beschwöre euch*, which concludes the second book (1641). In 1644 he issued Scheidt's *LXX Symphonien auff Concerten manir*. With the 31 Christmas pieces of *Cunis solennibus* (1646) Profe sought to rescue from oblivion songs from the past that 'were called rotulas, or lullabies for the Christ-child, and were sung in the middle of the *Magnificat*, and can still be used devotionally by us and our successors'; 18 of the pieces have German words, ten are in Latin, and three have mixed texts. Profe also took steps to make known the songs with continuo of Heinrich Albert, from north Germany. These were certainly known and loved in Breslau, but the original folio editions were out of print, and in 1657 Profe brought out a selection of 134 of them in two volumes in a more convenient smaller format.

Of Profe's own works, the most important is the school music textbook *Compendium musicum, das ist, Kurtze Anleitung wie ein junger Mensch . . . möge singen lernen* (Leipzig, 1641). In this little work he attacked the old solmization system based on the hexachord, for which Mattheson warmly commended him in 1717 and 1740. But praise from a modern musician such as Mattheson was not always Profe's lot in his own time: Otto Gibelius complained in his *Kurtzer . . . Bericht von den Vocibus musicalibus* (1659) that, instead of singable syllables such as *do-re-mi*, Profe used letter names ('abcedieren'), which sounded appalling. Apart from this textbook only a few pieces of music by Profe survive.

WORKS

Rhum und Danck-Liedlein, Die Gütte des Herren, 7vv, bc (Breslau, 1634)

2 works, 5vv, vn, 1646³

Spiritus sancti gratia, 6vv, formerly in the Breslau Stadtbibliothek, probably now in *PL-WRu*

ed.: 1627⁸, 1641², 1641³, 1642⁴, 1646³, 1646⁴, 1649⁶, Heinrich Alberts Arien . . . als ein Vade mecum verleget (Leipzig, 1657), Heinrich Alberts Arien ander Theil (Brieg, 1657), M. H. Schacht: Musicus danicus (1687), lost, cited in *GerberNL*

BIBLIOGRAPHY

EitnerQ; *FétisB*; *GerberNL*; *WaltherML*

J. Mattheson: *Das beschützte Orchestre* (Hamburg, 1717)

——: *Grundlage einer Ehren-Pforte* (Hamburg, 1740); ed. M. Schneider (Berlin, 1910/*R*1969)

C. J. A. Hoffmann: *Die Tonkünstler Schlesiens* (Breslau, 1830)

Postler: 'Ein noch unbekanntes Sammelwerk von Ambrosius Profe', *MMg*, xiv (1882), 12

R. Starke: 'Ambrosius Profe', *MMg*, xxxiv (1902), 189, 199

H. Kretzschmar: *Geschichte des neuen deutschen Liedes* (Leipzig, 1911/*R*1966)

G. Schünemann: *Geschichte der deutschen Schulmusik* (Leipzig, 1931), 180ff

H. J. Moser: *Heinrich Schütz: sein Leben und Werk* (Kassel, 1936, rev. 2/1954; Eng. trans., 1959)

A. Adrio: 'Ambrosius Profe (1589–1661) als Herausgeber italienischer Musik seiner Zeit', *Festschrift Karl Gustav Fellerer* (Regensburg, 1962), 20

I. Schubert: *Wolfgang Hase als Musiktheoretiker* (diss., U. of Graz, 1969)

J. Roche: 'Anthologies and the Dissemination of Early Baroque Italian Sacred Music', *Soundings*, iv (1974), 6

FRITZ FELDMANN

Professional Concerts. London concert series established in 1783; *see* LONDON, §VI, 4(ii).

Profeta, Laurenţiu (*b* Bucharest, 12 Jan 1925). Romanian composer. He studied with Chirescu (theory and solfège), Constantinescu (harmony) and Mendelsohn (composition) at the Bucharest Conservatory (1945–9), and with Mesner (composition), Golubyev (counterpoint) and Berkov (harmony) at the Moscow Conservatory (1954–6). His appointments have included those of deputy manager of Romanian broadcasting (1948–52) and music director in the ministry of culture (1952–60); in 1968 he became secretary to the Composers' Union in Bucharest. As a composer he has worked in all fields, including music for children and light music. Melody is paramount in his work, which may explain the preponderance of vocal pieces.

WORKS
(*selective list*)

Ballets: Soţia căpitanului [The captain's wife] (3, O. Danovschi), 1946, Bucharest, 1947; Prinţ şi cerşetor (3, I. Hristea, Danovschi, after Twain), 1967, Bucharest, 1968; Marinarul visător [Dreaming sailor] (3, N. Itu), Constanţa, 1972

Orch: Imagini din lumea copilăriei [Images from the realm of childhood], 1945; Poemul patriei, 1952; Zile de vacanţă [Holidays], sym. suite, 1956

Choral: Cîntece de tabără [Children's camp songs], solo vv, children's vv, orch, 1957; Intîmplarea din grădina [Adventure in the garden], oratorio, narrator, Bar, solo vv, children's vv, orch, 1958; Cantata patriei, 1959; Brăduţul singuratic [The lonely fir tree], sym. story for children, 1960; 6 piese umoristice, solo vv, children's vv, tape, 1966; Madrigal '75, cantata, vv, small orch, 1975

Songs: Cîntece de ieri şi de azi [Songs of yesterday and today], Bar, pf, 1960; Cîntice ţigăneşti [Gypsy songs], 1v, pf, 1968

Principal publishers: Muzgiz, Muzicală

VIOREL COSMA

Profius, Ambrosius. *See* PROFE, AMBROSIUS.

Programme music. Music of a narrative or descriptive kind; the term is often extended to all music that attempts to represent extra-musical concepts without resort to sung words.

1. The term and its meaning. 2. History of the concept.

1. THE TERM AND ITS MEANING. The term 'programme music' was introduced by Liszt, who also invented the expression SYMPHONIC POEM to describe what is perhaps the most characteristic instance of it. He defined a programme as a 'preface added to a piece of instrumental music, by means of which the composer intends to guard the listener against a wrong poetical interpretation, and to direct his attention to the poetical idea of the whole or to a particular part of it'. Very few of the programmes of Liszt's own symphonic poems are of a narrative character. He did not regard music as a direct means of describing objects; rather he thought that music could put the listener in the same frame of mind as could the objects themselves. In this way, by suggesting the emotional reality of things, music could indirectly represent them. Such an idea – already familiar in the writings of Rousseau – was also expressed by Beethoven when he described the Pastoral Symphony as 'mehr Empfindung als Malerey' ('more the expression of feeling than painting').

The close connection in some of Liszt's thinking between

'narrative' and 'emotional' depiction has led to confusion over the use of the term 'programme music'. Some prefer to attach the term purely to instrumental music with a narrative or descriptive 'meaning' (for example, music that purports to depict a scene or a story). Others have so broadened its application as to use the term for all music that contains an extra-musical reference, whether to objective events or to subjective feelings. The responsibility for this broadening of the term lies partly with Friedrich Niecks, whose romantic enthusiasm caused him to overlook, in his influential work on the subject (1956), the vital aesthetic distinction between representation and expression. It is the narrow sense of the term which is the legitimate one. The other sense is not only so wide as to be virtually meaningless; it also fails to correspond to the actual usage of composers and critics since Liszt's invention of the term.

Programme music, which has been contrasted with ABSOLUTE MUSIC, is distinguished by its attempt to depict objects and events. Furthermore, it claims to derive its logic from that attempt. It does not merely echo or imitate things which have an independent reality; the development of programme music is determined by the development of its theme. The music moves in time according to the logic of its subject and not according to autonomous principles of its own. As Liszt wrote: 'In programme music. . .the return, change, modification, and modulation of the motifs are conditioned by their relation to a poetic idea. . .All exclusively musical considerations, though they should not be neglected, have to be subordinated to the action of the given subject' (*Schriften*, iv, 69).

Liszt thought of himself as putting forward a new ideal for symphonic music, an ideal that had been foreshadowed in Beethoven's Pastoral Symphony and in certain works of Mendelssohn, Schumann and Berlioz, but which he nevertheless thought to be absent from the body of classical music. He considered the idea of exalting the narrative associations of music into a principle of composition to be incompatible with the continuance of traditional symphonic forms. The term 'programme music' came to be applied not only to music with a story but also music designed to represent a character (Strauss's *Don Juan* and *Don Quixote*) or to describe a scene or phenomenon (Debussy's *La mer*). What is common to all these is the attempt to 'represent' objects in music; but a certain confusion has entered the use of the term by its application to any form of musical 'depiction', whether instrumental, or vocal, or incidental to an action on the stage. Properly speaking, however, programme music is music with a programme. Further, to follow Liszt's conception, programme music is music that seeks to be understood in terms of its programme; it derives its movement and its logic from the subject it attempts to describe. On that view it would be wrong to call, for example, Couperin's *Le tic-toc-choc* a piece of programme music. The logic of Couperin's piece is purely musical, even if its thematic material is derived from the imitation of a clock. By contrast, the logic of Liszt's symphonic poem *Tasso* is (according to the composer) derived from the events of Tasso's life: it is the sequence of those events, and their intrinsic nature, that dictate the development of the music. (But it should be said that Liszt's own programme music did not always follow his own theoretical precepts.)

However the term is used, it is clear that the idea of music's representing something is essential to the concept of programme music. It is important to understand, therefore, what might be meant by 'representation' in music. The first distinction to make is that between representation and EXPRESSION. It is only recently that attempts have been made to formulate the distinction with any precision, and there is no agreement as to the relation between the terms. But that a distinction exists seems obvious to any lover of the arts. A painting may represent a subject (the Crucifixion, say) and it may also express an emotion towards that subject. To represent a subject is to give a description or characterization of it: it is to say (in words or in images) what the subject is like. Such a description may or may not be accompanied by an expression of feeling. Furthermore, there can be expressions of emotion that are not accompanied by representation. Mozart's *Masonic Funeral Music* is certainly an expression of grief, but it contains no attempt to represent or describe the object of grief. It has been argued that all music expresses emotion. If that is so, then, unless some distinction can be made between representation and expression, all music would have to be regarded as representational. To say that would lead to the conclusion that there was no essential distinction between music and painting in their relation to the world.

It is a matter of dispute whether music is capable of literally representing its subject, in the way that painting and literature represent theirs. What passes for representation might often be more accurately described as 'imitation', as when a piece of music mimics the sound of a cuckoo. That there is a difference between representation and imitation is clear. An architectural detail can imitate the curve of a seashell without becoming a representation; or a man can imitate another's manner without representing it. Representation is essentially descriptive: it involves a reference to objects in the world and an attempt to describe them. Imitation is merely copying, and its intention may be no more than decorative. Examples of musical imitation have abounded from the very beginning of music. Indeed, both Plato and Aristotle ascribed an imitative character to the music of their time. It is nonetheless debatable whether music is made representational by imitation alone. Certainly Liszt had more than mere imitation in mind when he introduced the concept of programme music.

It is seldom clear what is meant when it is said that music can represent things. The question arises whether music can actually describe the world or whether it is merely evocative. If representation in music were merely a matter of evocation, it would be misleading to class it as representation, for that would imply an unwarranted analogy with the descriptive arts of literature and painting. That is why Liszt insisted that true programme music had a narrative or descriptive element which was essential to the understanding of it. In other words, for Liszt the subject has become part of the meaning of the music; to listen to the music with false associations was, in Liszt's view, actually to misunderstand it. Whether or not there is 'programme music' in Liszt's sense, it is clear that it would provide the most plausible example of representation in music. It is further clear that in its strictest sense programme music does not include music that is merely expressive, imitative or evocative. It is doubtful even whether Debussy's *La mer* is a description rather than an evocation of its subject, although the titles of the movements seem to suggest a certain 'narrative' component to its meaning (for example, one of the movements is entitled 'De l'aube à midi sur la mer', which prompted Satie to remark that he particularly liked the moment at 11.15).

Programme music must further be distinguished from the 'representational' music that accompanies words, whether in lieder, in oratorio or on the stage. While all these share devices with programme music and have influenced it continuously throughout the history of music, it is still necessary to distinguish music which purports to carry its narrative meaning within itself from music which is attached to a narrative arising independently, whether through the words of a song or through the action of a dramatic work. The distinction is not absolute, but, unless it is made, the idea of programme music as a separate genre must remain entirely illegitimate.

2. HISTORY OF THE CONCEPT. When Liszt invented the term 'programme music' he was aware that he had not invented the thing that he sought to describe. Berlioz's symphonies are essentially narrative in conception; so too is Weber's *Concertstück* for piano and orchestra, a descriptive work in one continuous movement (made up of several sections in different tempos) which was one of the first Romantic examples of the symphonic poem. One of the difficulties involved in tracing the history of programme music lies in the elusiveness of the distinctions discussed above: whether all representational music should be considered programme music; whether 'imitation' should be counted as a species of representation; and whether a deliberate expressive character is sufficient to rank as a 'programme' in Liszt's sense. Clearly there are many different ways of deriving a history according to the way in which those fundamental critical (and philosophical) questions are answered. For example, the French harpsichord composers of the 17th and 18th centuries were in the habit of giving titles to their pieces. To some writers on this subject the presence of a title is sufficient to bring a piece under the rubric 'programme music'. But to others that way of thought involves a confusion, for it seems not to distinguish a piece that expresses some emotion suggested by the title from another that either evokes its subject or (in some more concrete sense) actually attempts to describe it. Many critics of Couperin's music, for example, would prefer to speak of the relation between his keyboard pieces and their ostensible 'subjects' as one of expression and not one of representation. The borderline between expression and representation is a hazy one, and it is often impossible to say of a piece by Rameau or Couperin on which side of the borderline it might lie.

If mere imitation is not regarded as a sufficient criterion of programme music, it must be concluded that the history of the genre is considerably shorter than might otherwise appear. It seems to have no medieval examples. Even Janequin's famous chanson *La bataille* or *La guerre* (published in 1529 and thought to refer to the Battle of Marignan of 1515), is hardly to be considered true programme music: while it imitates the sounds of battle, there is no narrative sequence to those sounds and no attempt to subordinate the musical structure to the evolution of an extra-musical theme. Less certain cases are provided by suites in which the titles of each piece form a narrative sequence. Byrd's *Battel*, a suite for keyboard of 15 pieces – entitled (for example) 'The Marche to the Fight', 'The Retraite' and 'The Burying of the Dead' – does, in a sense, have a programme, but the programme serves to unite the separate musical units and to explain their expressive characters; only in a very limited sense do the pieces attempt also to describe the scenes referred to.

Other puzzling cases are those in which a composer declares himself to have been inspired by some literary or artistic source. Again there are Renaissance and Baroque examples of composers who have written pieces under the inspiration of pictures. Biber, for example, wrote in about 1671 a set of 15 mysteries for violin and keyboard after copperplate engravings of Bible themes; there is an earlier instance by Froberger. Such cross-fertilization between a representational art (such as engraving) and music is a familiar feature of more recent music. Musorgsky's *Pictures at an Exhibition* provides a Romantic example of the same kind of musical device. Here, though, there is the added representational refinement of a 'Promenade' linking some of the pieces, indicating the presence of a 'narrator' in the music, a kind of 'reflector' in Henry James's sense, who remains the true subject matter of the narrative. By that device Musorgsky's work comes nearer to the central examples of programme music such as the symphonic poems of Liszt. An even more remarkable example of cross-fertilization is the quartet by Janáček composed after reading Tolstoy's nouvelle *The Kreutzer Sonata*, itself inspired by Beethoven's violin sonata. The mere fact that Janáček's quartet was so inspired no more makes it into a programmatic narrative of the events in Tolstoy's story than it makes Tolstoy's story into a 'representation' of Beethoven's sonata. Inspiration, even when consciously referred to, cannot suffice to make music into programme music.

There is no doubt that programme music was established by 1700, when Johann Kuhnau published his six Bible sonatas. Each of them is preceded by a summary of the story that the music is meant to convey, and each is divided into recognizable parts, corresponding to the events of the narrative. The pictorialism is naive compared with the symphonic poems of Liszt and Strauss, but there is no doubt that the music lays claim to a narrative significance or that the composer intended that significance to be a proper part of the understanding of the music. Later examples of similar narrative music are Vivaldi's concertos the 'Four Seasons', which are prefaced by short 'programmes' in verse, and Couperin's *Apothéoses*, extended representations of Lully and Corelli ascending to find their proper places of rest upon Parnassus, in which each section refers to a separate episode in their apotheosis. Comparable pieces were written by Telemann and other French-influenced composers. The development of such programme music was affected by the French *ballet de cour*, which required just such pictorial accompaniments to its solemn and dramatic performances; but there is no doubt that by the mid-18th century programme music had emancipated itself from any suggestion of a balletic meaning. A notable example is the long orchestral work by Ignazio Raimondi called *Les aventures de Télémaque dans l'isle de Calypso*, based on Fénelon's epic poem. This, published in 1777, includes one of the first attempts to diversify the 'narrative' by representing its several characters in different ways: Calypso, for example, is represented by a flute, and Telemachus by a solo violin.

By the time of Beethoven even the most abstract and

classical of musical forms had become capable of bearing a programmatic meaning. The Pastoral Symphony is but one example of a piece that seems to be straining to break free of the constraints imposed by its Classical format in the interests of a pictorial idea. The 'Lebewohl' Sonata op.81*a* is another. Both have precedents, in the 18th-century depictions of Nature and in Bach's capriccio for his departing brother. Like Vivaldi's 'Four Seasons' and Dittersdorf's symphonies based on Ovid's *Metamorphoses*, they attempt to combine a narrative depiction with a rigorous musical form. This led Beethoven's admirers to suppose that the idea of a 'purely musical' structure was after all an illusion, and that the greatness of Beethoven's symphony, in particular its architectural perfection, was of a piece with its profound extra-musical meaning, and that great symphonic writing was but the expression of an independent poetic idea. This impression was enhanced by Beethoven's hint that an understanding of his sonata op.31 no.2 could be induced by a reading of Shakespeare's *The Tempest*. Schering (1936) attempted to explain Beethoven's entire output as programmatic reflections on themes from Shakespeare and Goethe.

Whatever one thinks of those speculations, which have been further extended to the symphonies of Haydn and Mozart (the French theorist Momigny even set a verbal text to a Mozart quartet movement as an interpretation of it), there is no doubt that the greatest step towards true programme music in the Romantic sense was made not by Beethoven but by Berlioz, who introduced into musical representation for the first time a distinction vital to any true narrative portrayal of things in the world, the distinction between subject and object. By his use of the solo viola in his symphony *Harold en Italie* and by his exploitation of its deeply subjective tones he was able to create a sharp division between the individual protagonist – the feeling, suffering and rejoicing being at the centre of the narrative – and the external circumstances of his experience. Berlioz also introduced the device of the IDÉE FIXE, a melody representative of a character or feeling, which reappears in a variety of forms and develops with the changing circumstances. This was a substantial step towards the Wagnerian LEITMOTIF, through which device the narrative pretensions of music were to receive their most striking confirmation. The leitmotif, a theme which is associated with a character, a circumstance or an idea, and which develops sometimes out of all recognition in order to convey the evolution of its narrative theme, permitted representation in music without a hint of imitation. By means of this device later composers, in particular Liszt and Richard Strauss, were able to associate specific themes with a fixed representational meaning. The traditional devices survived, and with Strauss imitation was carried to extremes never previously envisaged. But it was through the leitmotif above all that music was able to emulate the descriptive range of language and that Liszt was able to approach the ideal he had set himself, the ideal of a music that could not be understood even as music unless the correct poetic conception was invoked in the hearer's mind.

It is possible to doubt that Liszt ever realized that ideal, or indeed that it is capable of realization, because the conception of musical understanding underlying the theory of programme music may not be a coherent one (for further discussion, *see* ABSOLUTE MUSIC). Nonetheless, once the theoretical foundations of the genre

had been laid, programme music became highly important. Indeed the 'programme' survived as a basic determining idea in symphonic music until well into the 20th century, receiving no serious intellectual setback until the reaction led by Schoenberg in Vienna, by Bartók in Hungary, and by the cosmopolitan Stravinsky. It gave rise to many of the great works of Czech and Russian nationalism, to the symphonies of Mahler and to the French school of orchestral writing.

There is no doubt too that the concept of programme music led to the IMPRESSIONISM of Ravel and Debussy. But it is doubtful that their music should be regarded as truly programmatic in the Romantics' sense; impressionism may rather have constituted a partial reaction against the narrative pretensions of the symphonic poem – it was another attempt to put evocation in the place of narrative. In that sense it would be better to compare Debussy's *Préludes* with the *ordres* of Couperin and to consider that the titles (which Debussy was at pains to put not at the beginning but at the end of the pieces) serve to indicate an expressive atmosphere rather than a definite descriptive significance. Indeed, it seems that Debussy did not intend a knowledge of the subject to be essential to an understanding of his music. It is from Debussy's pure style and clean textures that much of the most abstract of modern music has taken its inspiration.

By the end of the 19th century the increasing afflatus of Romanticism had served once again to destroy the distinction between representational and expressive intentions in music. So long as music aims to capture a particular episode, a particular sequence of events or a particular human character, then its representational claims are not in doubt. When, however, it attaches itself to a programme phrased entirely in emotional or quasi-religious abstractions, it is doubtful that it can be considered to be a depiction rather than an expression of its subject matter. For example Tatyana Schloezer wrote a programme for the Symphony no.3 'Le divin poème' by Skryabin (whose mistress she was) beginning:

The Divine Poem represents the evolution of the human spirit, which, torn from an entire past of beliefs and mysteries which it surmounts and overturns, passes through Pantheism and attains to a joyous and intoxicated affirmation of its liberty and its unity with the universe (the divine 'Ego').

That is an example of the 'programme' at its most self-important. It is also an example of the degeneration of the concept from something relatively precise to something entirely vaporous. For Skryabin, Mahler and their contemporaries the 'programme' was on the verge of becoming irrelevant to an understanding of the music. The entire burden of the musical movement lay now in expression; representation had been cast aside. In so far as the programme continued to exist it was a source of exasperating literary preciosities rather than of genuine musical ideas. It is hardly surprising that composers soon began to turn their backs on programme music and find their way to expression through more abstract musical means; but in the 1960s and 1970s some revival of programmatic or semi-programmatic devices could be noted, for example in the works of Maxwell Davies, Leeuw, Norby and Schafer.

BIBLIOGRAPHY

J. J. Engel: 'Über die musikalische Malerei', *J. J. Engel's Schriften*, iv (Berlin, 1806), 297–342

A. B. Marx: *Über Malerei in der Tonkunst* (Berlin, 1828)

H. Berlioz: 'De l'imitation musicale', *Revue et gazette musicale*, iv (1837), 9, 15

A. Elwart: 'De la musique imitative', *Revue et gazette musicale*, xiii (1846), 340

A. W. Ambros: *Die Grenzen der Musik und der Poesie* (Prague, 1856)

O. Hostinsky: 'O hudbe "programni" ' [About musical 'programmes'], *Dalibor*, i (1873)

——: 'Jak se vykládajé skladby instrumentální' [How we interpret instrumental music], *Dalibor*, ii (1874)

M. Brenet: 'Les batailles en musique', *Guide musical* (23 Feb 1888)

W. Wallace: 'The Scope of Programme Music', *PMA*, xxv (1898–9), 139

R. Hohenemser: 'Über die Programmusik', *SIMG*, i (1899–1900), 307

H. Leichtentritt: 'Vorläufer und Anfänge der Programm', *AMz*, xxx (1903)

K. Nef: 'Schlachtendarstellungen in der Musik', *Grenzboten*, iii (1904), 280

W. Klatte: *Zur Geschichte der Program-Musik* (Berlin, 1905)

E. Newman: 'Programme Music', *Musical Studies* (London, 1905), 103–86

F. Niecks: *Programme Music in the Last Four Centuries* (London, 1906)

E. Bienenfeld: 'Über ein bestimmtes Problem der Programmusik', *SIMG*, viii (1906–7), 163

M. D. Calvocoressi: 'Esquisse d'une esthétique de la musique à programme', *SIMG*, ix (1907–8), 424

O. Klauwell: *Geschichte der Programmusik von ihren Anfängen bis zur Gegenwart* (Leipzig, 1910)

H. Antcliffe: 'The Sense of Programme', *PMA*, xxxvii (1910–11), 103

M. Brenet: 'Essai sur les origines de la musique descriptive', *Musique et musiciens de la vieille France* (Paris, 1911), 83

W. P. James: 'Music Pure and Applied', *ML*, ii (1921), 373

R. W. S. Mendl: 'The Art of the Symphonic Poem', *MQ*, xviii (1923), 443

A. Wellek: *Doppelempfinden und Programmusik* (diss., U. of Vienna, 1928)

K. Schubert: *Programm-Musik*, Musikalische Formen in historischen Reihen, xiii, ed. H. Martens (Berlin and Wolfenbüttel, 1934, 2/1961)

A. Schering: *Beethoven und die Dichtung* (Berlin, 1936)

D. F. Tovey: *Essays in Musical Analysis*, iv: *Illustrative Music* (London, 1937/R)

A. Schering: *Das Symbol in der Musik* (Leipzig, 1941)

A. Carapetyan: 'The Concept of the "imitazione della natura" in the 16th Century', *JRBM*, i (1946), 47

R. Raffalt: *Über die Problematik der Programm-Musik* (Passau, 1949)

P. Tchaikovsky: *P. I. Chaykovsky o programmnoy muzïke* (Moscow, 1952)

Z. Lissa: *O specyfice muzyki* [On the specific qualities of music] (Warsaw, 1953; Ger. trans., 1957)

H. Unverricht: *Hörbare Vorbilder in der Instrumentalmusik bis 1750: Untersuchung zur Vorgeschichte der Programmusik* (Berlin, 1953)

H. Searle: *The Music of Liszt* (London, 1954, rev. 2/1966)

N.-E. Ringbom: *Über die Deutbarkeit der Tonkunst* (Turku and Helsinki, 1955)

F. Howes: *Music and its Meanings* (London, 1958)

A. Copland: *Music and Imagination* (New York, 1959)

D. Cooke: *The Language of Music* (London, 1959/R1962)

A. Sychra: 'Die Einheit von "absoluter" Musik und Programmusik', *BMw*, i/3 (1959), 2

R. Negreanu: *Despre muzika cu program* (Bucharest, 1960)

E. Shishova-Gorskaya: *Programmnaya muzïka* (Moscow, 1961)

A. Wellek: 'Über das Verhältnis von Musik und Poesie', *SMw*, xxv (1962), 574

A. Palm: 'Mozarts Streichquartett d-moll, KV 421, in der Interpretation Momignys', *MJb 1962–3*, 256

W. Wiora: 'Zwischen absoluter und Programmusik', *Festschrift Friedrich Blume* (Kassel, 1963), 381

A. Damerini: 'Musica a programma', *La MusicaE*

K. P. Bernet Kempers: 'Die Instrumentalmusik im Banne der Literatur', *Colloquium amicorum: Joseph Schmidt-Görg zum 70. Geburtstag* (Bonn, 1967), 11

M. Butor: 'Musik, eine realistische Kunst', *Melos*, xxxiv (Feb 1967), 37

W. Stockmeier: *Die Programmusik* (Cologne, 1970)

E. Lockspeiser: *Music and Painting* (London, 1973)

L. Orrey: *Programme Music* (London, 1975)

R. Scruton: 'Representation in Music', *Philosophy* (1976)

ROGER SCRUTON

Progression. A succession of chords or chord-like constructions having a coherence as an expression of harmony ('chord progression', 'harmonic progression'), especially one which is based on a familiar pattern ('blues progression'). Some writers use 'progression' as a translation of the Schenkerian concept of *Zug* (*see* ZUG (i)).

Progressive jazz. A term applied to attempts, chiefly in the 1940s and 1950s, to renew the big band tradition of the 1930s; it is generally associated with the work of Stan Kenton. The movement sought more complex goals for the large jazz ensemble and especially a more advanced vocabulary; in the work of Kenton and his arrangers, like Pete Rugolo and Bob Graettinger, this was expressed almost solely in terms of extreme loudness and dissonant, often illogical harmonies. More successful in the 1940s was the work of Earle Spencer and Boyd Raeburn who produced several orchestral pieces (particularly those by George Handy, a pupil of Aaron Copland) that were fairly modern in temper and quite adventurous in their resources, though with an increasing tendency to densely overcrowded scores. Improvisation usually had little place in progressive jazz; its exponents produced much overtly commercial material and the contradiction between it and the more ambitious music was never resolved.

BIBLIOGRAPHY
A. Jackson: 'Boyd Raeburn', *Jazz Monthly*, xii (1966), Nov, 5
M. Sparks: *Kenton on Capitol* (Hounslow, 1966)
A. Morgan: 'The Progressives', *Jazz on Record*, ed. A. McCarthy (London, 1968), 361

MAX HARRISON

Prohaska, Felix (*b* Vienna, 16 May 1912). Austrian conductor, son of Karl Prohaska. He studied the piano with Friedrich Wührer and Eduard Steuermann, the violin with Gottfried Faist and Oskar Fitz, and theory with Egon Kornauth, Hans Gál, Joseph Polnauer, Felix Salzer and Oswald Jonas. He taught at the Graz Conservatory (1936–9) and was also active as the co-répétiteur at the opera there. From 1939 to 1941 he conducted at the opera in Duisburg, and from 1941 to 1943, at the German Opera in Strasbourg, at the same time directing the opera class at the Strasbourg Conservatory; from 1943 to 1945 he conducted the German Opera in Prague. He taught at the Vienna Academy (1945–6) and was a conductor of the Staatsoper in der Volksoper (1946–55); he was also a professor in the conducting class of the Vienna Conservatory from 1947 to 1950. Prohaska was Generalmusikdirektor of Frankfurt am Main from 1955 to 1961, and has since directed the Hochschule für Musik in Hanover. Guest appearances as a conductor have taken him to Salzburg (1945–6), Perugia (1951), Copenhagen (1952 and 1956) and South America; he has made many recordings.

BIBLIOGRAPHY
P. Lafite: 'Felix Prohaska', *ÖMz*, i (1946), 279

OTHMAR WESSELY

Prohaska, Jaro(slav) (*b* Vienna, 24 Jan 1891; *d* Munich, 28 Sept 1965). Austrian bass-baritone. From 1898 to 1906 he was a member of the Vienna Sängerknaben, with which he was an alto soloist, and in 1907 he began a career as an organist at St Thekla's Church, Vienna, where he later became a choirmaster and conductor. During World War I he was taken prisoner on the Russian front; he then studied music in Vienna under Otto Mueller, and singing at the Vienna Academy of Music, 1919–23. He made his début as a concert singer in 1920 and his stage début in 1922 at Lübeck. After an engagement at Nuremberg (1925–31) he joined the Berlin Staatsoper, of which he remained a member until 1952. He sang regularly at Bayreuth, 1933–44, as Hans Sachs, Wotan, Gunther, Telramund, Amfortas and the Dutchman. He appeared at the Teatro Colón, Buenos

Aires, in 1935 and 1937; although announced to appear at Covent Garden in 1938 he did not do so. In addition to Wagner roles his repertory included Baron Ochs, which he sang at the 1949 Salzburg Festival. In 1947 he was appointed head of the West Berlin Musikhochschule, and in 1952 became director of its opera school. When he retired in 1959 he was made a professor emeritus. Herman Prey was one of his many pupils.

HAROLD ROSENTHAL

Prohaska, Karl (*b* Mödling, nr. Vienna, 25 April 1869; *d* Vienna, 28 March 1927). Austrian composer. He studied the piano with Anna Assmayer and Eugen d'Albert and theory with Franz Krenn, Eusebius Mandyczewski and Heinrich von Herzogenburg; Brahms also showed an interest in his musical development. In 1894–5 he taught at the Strasbourg Conservatory and was also a stage assistant at the Bayreuth Festival. From 1901 to 1905 he conducted the Warsaw PO. He taught the piano from 1908, and later also theory at the conservatory of the Gesellschaft der Musikfreunde in Vienna; he remained on its staff when it was established as the Staatsakademie für Musik und darstellende Kunst. The new status of the school as the Hochschule für Musik in Vienna (1924) was largely due to Prohaska's efforts, but a disease of the eyes soon made it impossible for him to teach.

Prohaska was in great demand as a teacher. As a composer he took the Romantic styles of Schumann and Brahms as a point of departure, but also drew on the harmonic techniques of his own time. Full-bodied melodies and a strong attraction to polyphony are further characteristics of his works.

WORKS
Madeleine Guinard (opera, L. Braun), Breslau, 28 May 1930, lib (Vienna, 1930)
Vocal: Fruhlingsfeier (Klopstock), solo vv, chorus, orch, org, op.13; Christmas songs, 4 female vv, pf, op.10; Aus dem Buche Hiob, motet, 8vv, org, op.11; unacc. partsongs, opp.2, 8, 9, 12; solo songs, opp.3, 7, 14, 17, 18 (all pf acc.), 21 (str qt acc.), 24 (orch acc.)
Instrumental: Sonata, vn, pf, op.1; Str Qt, op.4; Pf Trio, op.15; Str Qnt, op.16; Variations and Fugue, pf, op.19; Serenade, small orch, op.20; Passacaglia, orch, op.22; Prelude and Fugue, org, op.23

BIBLIOGRAPHY
N. Schnoor: 'Carl Prohaska', *Die Musikwelt*, ix (1927), 6
A. Aber: 'Karl Prohaska und seine Chorwerke', *Rheinische Musik- und Theaterzeitung*, xxix (1928), 15
N. Latzko: 'Madeleine Guimard in Aussig', *Rheinische Musik- und Theaterzeitung*, xxx (1929), 15

OTHMAR WESSELY

Prohemium [proimion]. *See* PROOIMION.

Prokeimenon. A verse usually taken from the psalms which, in Orthodox services, is announced by the ANAGNŌSTĒS before the reading of a lesson. This is usually followed by a STICHOS.

Prokofiev, Sergey (Sergeyevich) (*b* Sontsovka, Ekaterinoslav district, Ukraine, 23 April 1891; *d* Moscow, 5 March 1953). Russian composer and pianist. He established himself as a composer of heavily ironic, often wilful and unconventional music in the last years of tsarist Russia. After the Revolution he lived mainly in the USA, then Paris, and his style gradually became smoother and more settled. The last 17 years of his life he spent in the USSR, both stimulated and restricted by the cultural policies prevailing under Stalin. At all periods he concerned himself with music for the stage, having a sharp sense of drama and character; but he was also one of the most notable 20th-century contributors to the genres of symphony, concerto and piano sonata.

1. Russia: 1891–1918. 2. USA: 1918–22. 3. Paris: 1922–36. 4. USSR: 1936–53.

1. RUSSIA: 1891–1918. Prokofiev was born into an affluent and cultured household. His father was an agricultural engineer, who managed a large estate in the Ukrainian steppe. His mother was a well-educated, sociable woman and a good pianist, whose devotion to music, especially to the works of Rubinstein, Chopin and Beethoven, had the greatest influence in his early years. An adored only child, Prokofiev was musically precocious. He wrote his first piano piece at the age of five; at nine he was playing the easier Beethoven sonatas; and by summer 1902, when Glier went to Sontsovka to tutor the boy, he was already the composer of two operas and numerous short piano pieces.

From Glier he learned the rudiments of harmony, form and orchestration and, with help, he soon completed a four-movement symphony. The first of the Little Songs date from that summer, too. Over the next five years he was to compose 60 of these short mood pieces for piano, most of them in simple three-part form, and of all the music of Prokofiev's childhood these pieces most clearly contain the seeds of future developments. The earliest of them are still childish and imitative, but increasingly they form a diary of his musical experiments. By 1904 he was writing scherzos and marches with unusual metres and uncommon tonalities, dance movements with wild and capricious rhythms, and many of the later pieces are full of his distinctive brand of musical humour.

Sontsovka may have been musically as well as geographically isolated, but Prokofiev was kept in touch with the current musical repertory through both Glier's teaching, which continued spasmodically until 1904, and annual winter visits with his mother to Moscow. On these visits he played his latest pieces to Taneyev; by 1903 his impressive list of works included a violin sonata, part of a piano sonata and a new opera, *Pir vo vremya chumï* ('A feast in time of plague'). It was now necessary to his development as a composer that he should have more continuous contact with the professional musical world, and also that his general education should become formal. The matter hung in the air for some time: the Prokofievs were loath to commit him so early to a musical career. In spring 1904, however, he was taken to St Petersburg and, on the advice of Glazunov, he applied for entrance to the conservatory.

The following September Prokofiev passed the entrance examination. He was to spend the next ten years at the St Petersburg Conservatory, and was to prove one of its most unruly students. The conservatory itself was far from settled in those years. 'Bloody Sunday' and the first rumblings of revolution in January 1905 had immediate repercussions among the musical intelligentsia in the city. Rimsky-Korsakov was dismissed from his conservatory post for anti-government activities, and several of his colleagues, including Glazunov and Lyadov, resigned in sympathy. The building was closed completely for six months, and the following session, 1905–6, was repeatedly disrupted by staffing problems. But the lack of continuous teaching was not the sole cause of Prokofiev's unhappiness. A self-willed and arrogant boy, much younger than his classmates, he made few friends. More than that, he was sadly disillusioned with the teaching. Lyadov's harmony class he found dull and creatively inhibiting, and his relationship with him often developed into open clashes. His later lessons in orchestration with Rimsky-Korsakov he found equally tiresome; he was clearly too young to derive much benefit from Rimsky's experience. It was as well, then, that Lyadov's counterpoint class of 1906 introduced him to two men whose friendship – which was to be lifelong – more than compensated for the general lack of attention accorded his talent. They were Boris Asaf'yev and Nikolay Myaskovsky.

Myaskovsky, who was then 25, had a profound influence on Prokofiev over the next few years. Most of all he gave him encouragement, and it was to Myaskovsky, rather than Lyadov, that Prokofiev showed his latest pieces, the opera *Undina* and a series of piano sonatas (two of which were later remodelled into the sonatas opp.1 and 28). His friendship with Myaskovsky also marked the beginning of his regular contact with new music in St Petersburg. Together they explored the works of Skryabin (whose influence it was difficult for any young Russian composer to escape), Reger, Strauss and Debussy. They procured an introduction to the Evenings of Contemporary Music, the rallying ground of the St Petersburg musical avant garde. These concerts were established under the auspices of some of the leaders of Dyagilev's 'World of Art' movement, Karatïgin, Alfred Nurok and Walter Nuvel; here the works of Schoenberg, Strauss and Stravinsky had their first performances in Russia, and here too, on 31 December 1908, Prokofiev made his public début as a composer–pianist. He played some of his short piano pieces of 1907–8, among them the fiery *Navazhdeniye*, or *Suggestion diabolique*, and took the audience by storm. The press pronounced his music 'unintelligible' and 'ultra-modern'; and in the next few years he did his best to maintain this image of the 'enfant terrible'.

At the end of the 1908–9 session Prokofiev graduated from the composition course at the conservatory. He had enjoyed little enough of it, and his grades were far from brilliant. In his disillusionment with the composition teaching he had become interested in piano performance, and his first public appearances made him realize that it was as an exponent of his own piano music that he might become better known. And so he decided, for the time being, to continue at the conservatory in the piano and conducting courses.

Prokofiev spent summer 1909, as usual in Sontsovka, composing; his method of working and his attitude to his music were already established. He repeatedly revised and rearranged his scores. Not only did he make substantial revisions to earlier works, but he would frequently adapt movements and whole pieces for new combinations of instruments; piano and orchestral suites appeared from ballet and opera scores, orchestral movements from chamber pieces, and vocal lines were adapted for violin, mostly to attract performances, but also because, for him, a musical idea did not necessarily have a specific context. Moreover, completely new works were composed using thematic ideas from earlier scores. The music of an unfinished string quartet went into the opera *Ognennïy angel* ('The fiery angel') before being rewritten as the Third Symphony; the main musical ideas of the Fourth Symphony had their origins

in the ballet *Bludnïy sïn* ('The prodigal son'). Of the three works written in summer 1909 only one, the Four Etudes op.2, achieved its final form at once. The First Piano Sonata op.1 was a revision of an earlier work (it was to receive short shrift from the new music circles because it sounded like Rakhmaninov), and the Sinfonietta op.5 was to go through two more versions before its eventual publication in 1931.

Prokofiev began his piano course with Anna Esipova in autumn 1909 and, as ever, differences soon developed between pupil and teacher. Prokofiev's training as a pianist had been a haphazard business. From his early lessons with his mother, and later with Alexander Winkler, he had acquired remarkable dexterity and panache, but no sense of discipline. He disdained the Classical repertory, and if he played Mozart or Schubert at all it was with his own doublings and 'improvements'. Only when faced with expulsion from the course did Prokofiev accept the rigours of Esipova's methods, and much to his benefit; these four years were decisive to his later career as a pianist, and also to the evolution of certain aspects of his compositional style. The strength of his playing, its precision and steely brilliance – these were his own assets; Esipova developed its lyrical aspects and his awareness of tone quality. He even grew to appreciate Mozart and Schubert.

Nikolay Tcherepnin's conducting course was of tremendous importance to Prokofiev, not because he was ever more than a competent conductor, even of his own music, but because Tcherepnin, the 'modernist' on the conservatory staff, further promoted his urge to experiment with musical sounds. It was an influence not superseded until Prokofiev's introduction to the heady world of Dyagilev's Ballets Russes in 1914. Tcherepnin himself composed in a style that owed much to both Debussy and late Skryabin; the sensuousness of such sounds, mixed with his current attraction to the poems of the symbolist writers Bal'mont and Blok – their mysteriousness, above all – led Prokofiev to compose a series of intense and atmospheric works, which contrast strongly with most of his pieces hitherto. The highly charged Romanticism of late Skryabin and early Strauss is not a quality one readily associates with Prokofiev, but in fact it is strongly in evidence in certain works written over these ten years or so, works like the symphonic poems *Snï* ('Dreams') and *Osenneye* ('Autumnal sketch'), both of 1910, the cello Ballade (1912), the one-act opera *Maddalena* (1911–13) – strongly influenced by Strauss's *Elektra* and *Salome* – the songs of opp.9, 23 and 27, and much of *The Fiery Angel*.

In 1910 Prokofiev's father died, and the circumstances of the 19-year-old composer's life were drastically changed. The estate at Sontsovka had to be given up; his mother gave him a home in St Petersburg and continued to support him as best she could, but the young man who had known no financial hardship was now faced with making his own way in life. The tragedy coincided with the beginnings of his recognition as a composer: 1911 was something of a landmark in his career. He had his first public symphony concert, when *Dreams* and *Autumnal Sketch* were performed in Moscow that July; his works appeared in print for the first time when Jürgenson issued the First Piano Sonata and the pieces of op.3; and he began his first 'more or less mature composition, both as regards the conception and its fulfilment' (as he later wrote), the First Piano Concerto. This was also to be his first truly controversial work, bringing him to the forefront of critical opinion in musical circles in both St Petersburg and Moscow. His initial notion was to write a short concertino for piano and orchestra which he could perform himself, and which might also be a reasonable financial proposition. It was to be expanded into a long, continuous and brilliant movement with an incisive and virtuoso part for the soloist.

The première of the First Piano Concerto in Moscow caused something of a furore, and it was most probably the violent reactions of some of its critics, along with his own love of pianistic bravura, that urged Prokofiev to compose some of the boldest piano pieces of his youth in 1912, among them the Toccata op.11, the Humoresque Scherzo of op.12 and the first of the Sarcasms op.17. And if the First Piano Concerto caused a sensation, the Second (completed early in 1913) left its listeners, according to the critic Karatïgin, 'frozen with fright, hair standing on end'. It was his most complex and serious work to date; and, despite its physical excitement, it is a difficult, rather perverse work, which has never become as popular as the First and Third Concertos. To the audience at its first performance in St Petersburg it must have seemed like a futurist impertinence. Prokofiev had created a major scandal; most critics could hardly find strong enough terms for condemnation.

The year 1913–14 was Prokofiev's last at the conservatory, and he was to leave with characteristic aplomb. He coveted the Rubinstein Prize, the highest award offered to a student pianist, and he set out to attain it by unorthodox means. Instead of the customary classical concerto, he offered his own First Concerto and had Jürgenson print it for the occasion. His gambit succeeded and, although his examiners, Glazunov among them, were far from unanimous, he won the prize, a grand piano.

Immediately after his graduation, in June 1914, Prokofiev made a trip to London, in the company of Walter Nuvel. He was by then 23, and clearly on the threshold of fame in Russia, as both pianist and composer. Admired in new-music circles, he was also beginning to find acceptance by the musical establishment: he had recently performed his First Concerto at one of Koussevitzky's subscription matinées. His compositional style was already distinctive and well formed. But he now came into contact with the fashionable musical set, not of Russia but of all Europe: Dyagilev, Stravinsky and the Ballets Russes. Dyagilev's charisma he found irresistible, and musically he fell under the spell of Stravinsky's stage works. In London he saw The Nightingale, The Firebird and Petrushka, but it was, not surprisingly, The Rite of Spring which had most impact on his works of the following years. Stravinsky was possibly the only contemporary composer to have a direct influence on Prokofiev's music, on works like Ala i Lolli, Skazka pro shuta ('The tale of the buffoon'), the cantata Semero ikh ('They are seven') and the Second Symphony, though it was one Prokofiev was curiously unwilling to acknowledge. He admired Stravinsky, but there were obviously personal rivalries between them.

Prokofiev met Dyagilev in London and played him his Second Piano Concerto. Ever on the lookout for new Russian exotica, Dyagilev thought of presenting the work as a ballet but then decided to commission a new score from Prokofiev, for a ballet on a prehistoric theme. Prokofiev's relations with the Ballets Russes were to be unproductive for some time to come; it was not until 1921 that one of his ballets was staged by the company. Ala i Lolli, begun in 1914, was doomed from the start. Both Prokofiev and Gorodetsky, who wrote the scenario, were totally inexperienced in writing for the ballet stage, and Stravinsky's 'paganism' in The Rite of Spring was not easy to match. Dyagilev arranged a concert in Rome for Prokofiev in March 1915, but he rejected his score. A second ballet was commissioned; The Tale of the Buffoon, or Chout, begun in 1915, was to be one of Prokofiev's brightest and wittiest works, but war prevented its immediate performance.

Most of the war period Prokofiev spent in Petrograd, avoiding conscription by enrolling once more as a student at the conservatory, this time in the organ class. Since his contact with Dyagilev he had become something of a fashionable figure in musical Petrograd, and his recent works had several performances. With the première of The Tale of the Buffoon postponed, he took up an idea that had been in his mind for some time, to compose an opera based on Dostoyevsky's The Gambler. Since Dyagilev's departure from Russia the younger members of the Mariinsky Theatre directorate were keen to match his successes on home ground, and the new conductor of the theatre orchestra, Albert Coates, promised to perform Prokofiev's opera. Aware that a sensation was expected of him, Prokofiev allowed his imagination free play; in its original form Igrok ('The gambler') is his most violent and impulsive score. He worked quickly, and rehearsals began in January 1917. There were difficulties almost at once; the singers were unhappy in their roles, the director resigned, the orchestra revolted, and with the first Revolution at the end of February 1917 the performance had to be cancelled.

The February Revolution caused no major disruptions in the musical life of Petrograd, however; the theatres remained open and concerts continued. Prokofiev spent that summer in a village on the outskirts of the city at work on the First Violin Concerto and the Classical Symphony. The latter began as an experiment in composing without the piano; it was deliberately close to Haydn in style, with the addition of 'something new'. The title is the composer's own, chosen partly to 'tease the geese', but also in the hope that the work would become a classic. His hopes were fulfilled: it was among the first of his works to gain international recognition.

Meanwhile Petrograd was reaching a state of crisis. In September it was rumoured that the city was about to fall to the Germans, and Prokofiev left to join his mother in the Caucasus. On 7 November 1917 the Bolsheviks under Lenin seized power from the provisional government. In the wake of revolution came civil war, dividing the country into several fronts on which the Red Army fought the Whites. Kislovodsk in the Caucasus, where Prokofiev was staying, remained in White hands until March 1918, when it was occupied by the Red Army. Prokofiev then returned north, first to Moscow then to Petrograd. He gave some concerts, including the first performances of the Classical Symphony and the Third and Fourth Piano Sonatas, but by this time he had decided to go abroad. It seemed to him that Russia, in its present unsettled state, had little use for new music. In May 1918 he left for the USA, apparently with the intention of returning after a few months.

2. USA: 1918–22. As a composer of 27, Prokofiev was well justified in regarding his immediate future with optimism. Within Russia his career had been strikingly successful. He had been able to compose almost entirely on his own impulse, with few financial difficulties and no more than an encouraging amount of opposition from his critics. His contacts with western Europe, if not yet productive, were at least encouraging. A performance of *The Tale of the Buffoon* was still promised by Dyagilev, and Prokofiev hoped, now that the work was completed, that *The Gambler*, too, might be staged. America, with its reputation for artistic open-mindedness, must have seemed to offer exciting prospects in his present situation.

The journey to New York, by way of Vladivostok, Tokyo and San Francisco, took over four months. On board ship he occupied himself with fresh compositional plans. A libretto for a new opera, *Lyubov k tryom apelsinam* ('The love for three oranges'), was sketched out; a two-movement string quartet was begun (and soon discarded). His reputation, he found, had indeed arrived before him, but he was soon to encounter the attendant pressures. As a composer and as a phenomenon from 'Godless Russia' he was expected to outdo the novelty value of a Stravinsky, to satisfy the critics; and as a performer he would have to compete in technical virtuosity with artists like Rakhmaninov, to satisfy his promoters and audiences.

Prokofiev began well enough. His first solo recital, in the Aeolian Hall, New York, on 20 November, created an appropriate sensation; the manufacturers of Steinway–Duo-art player pianos immediately requested recordings from him, and a New York publishing house commissioned some new piano pieces, *Skazki staroy babushki* ('The tales of an old grandmother') op.31 and the Four Pieces op.32. Two concerts given by Frederick Stock in Chicago, including the First Piano Concerto and the *Scythian Suite* (from *Ala i Lolli*), were so successful that the directors of the Chicago Opera offered to produce one of his stage works. They approved the plans for his new opera, and a contract for *The Love for Three Oranges* was signed in January 1919; the work was to be completed by October for inclusion in the winter season.

The prospect of a performance must have filled Prokofiev with elation, but in the event it was to be short-lived. Despite his lifelong attraction to opera, uncomplicated success in this medium continually eluded him. He spent long periods, often against all creative and financial odds, at work on at least ten opera scores; the disappointments he encountered in trying to have them staged must have been among the saddest blows in his composing career. Three of the ten, *Maddalena* (1911–13), *Khan Buzay* (1942) and *Dalyokiye morya* ('Distant seas', 1948), had to be abandoned for lack of support before they were finished. Three more, *The Fiery Angel* (1919–27), *Voyna i mir* ('War and peace', 1941–52) and *Povest' o nastoyashchem cheloveke* ('The story of a real man', 1947–8), had no complete staged performances in his lifetime. *Semyon Kotko* (1939), his first Soviet opera, survived initial production difficulties and reached the stage in 1940, but was soon dropped because of its 'inappropriate' subject matter. Only *The Love for Three Oranges*, one

of his best scores, gained truly international acclaim for Prokofiev, and even with this work there were initial complications. Despite a near-fatal illness in spring 1919 Prokofiev completed the work in time, and by December rehearsals were well under way; then the conductor Campanini died and the première was postponed until the following season. A wrangle over financial compensation resulted, along with another postponement, and the opera was not performed until December 1921.

In the process Prokofiev's American career had reached a low ebb. By devoting all his energies to the opera he had sacrificed his contacts in the performing world, and in any case his promoters were unwilling to risk the bad publicity he might gain by performing too much of his own music. He was in financial difficulty. His decision to leave the USA was becoming inevitable, but having no desire to return to Russia with a sense of failure, he set his sights on Paris, where Dyagilev's Ballets Russes had now resumed their seasons of opera and ballet. Even in the middle of this disillusionment, however, he began work on another opera, *The Fiery Angel*, uncommissioned and in any light an unwise proposition, may well have been sheer escapism. This strange, though musically powerful work seems certainly to have fulfilled a strong inner need in Prokofiev; on only one other score, *War and Peace*, did he ever lavish so much time and care.

In April 1920 Prokofiev went to Paris. His contact with the USA continued; in the short term, he had still to attend to the production of *The Love for Three Oranges*, and until 1938 he gave prolonged concert tours throughout North America. As a composer, however, he was to meet with much more ready acceptance in Europe, and it was in France that he wrote most of his music over the next 16 years. Straight away he renewed his association with Dyagilev and Stravinsky, and as a result spent summer 1920 in Mantes-la-Jolie revising the ballet *The Tale of the Buffoon* for its inclusion in the company's next summer season. In December he made a long concert tour of California, which he found delightful; there he wrote the Five Songs without Words op.35 for the soprano Nina Koshits.

The Tale of the Buffoon opened in Paris on 17 May 1921 as the novelty of the season. It was a lavish production, which pleased the Parisian audiences, but soon shocked the London critics. Well pleased with the excitement he had created, Prokofiev retired for the summer to Etretât on the coast of Brittany to work on the Third Piano Concerto. The idea of composing a large virtuoso concerto, for his own performance, had been in his mind for several years, and many of the main themes were already sketched out. Part of the first movement dates from 1911; the main melody of the second movement was written in 1913; the two main first-movement themes and two of the central variations date from 1916–17; and part of the finale came from his discarded string quartet of 1918. But in spite of its diverse origins, this was to be one of Prokofiev's most attractive and satisfying scores; it is still the most popular of his five piano concertos.

In Brittany Prokofiev renewed his friendship with Bal'mont, who had emigrated to France. He had been captivated by Bal'mont's 'cosmic and barbarous exotic images' at the height of the symbolist vogue in pre-war St Petersburg, and had set several of his poems, both then and later, in his songs of opp.7, 9 and 23, and in the dramatic cantata *They are Seven* op.30. In the course of the summer of 1921 he set five new poems in his cycle of op.36; Bal'mont reciprocated with a sonnet on the Third Piano Concerto.

At the end of October Prokofiev was back in Chicago for the rehearsals of *The Love for Three Oranges*. The première, given in French, was warmly received in Chicago, perhaps simply from civic pride, but it was by no means appreciated by the critics in New York, who heard it a few weeks later. There were similar responses from the two cities to the Third Piano Concerto, given by the composer in December and January. Indeed, his American season, which had begun promisingly enough, had collapsed completely by spring 1922, when Mary Garden, his supporter with the Chicago Opera, resigned her directorship. With this his hopes for a performance of *The Fiery Angel* faded, and he had once more to retreat from the American scene, 'with a thousand dollars in my pocket and an aching head'.

3. PARIS: 1922–36. Prokofiev returned to Europe in March 1922, with a fervent desire for peace, quiet and time to compose. He went first to Paris to join his mother, who had left Russia in spring 1920. Then, along with her and the poet Boris Verin, he rented a house in the village of Ettal, near Oberammergau in the Bavarian Alps. This was to be his first real home after four years of travelling, and the 18 months he spent there were in many ways of crucial importance to his future. Financed by the proceeds of his American trip and the concerts he continued to give throughout the European centres, he was for a time able to devote most of his energies to composition. Some of this activity was directed towards profitable ends – he arranged the piano scores of *The Love for Three Oranges* and *The Tale of the Buffoon* for publication and extracted a symphonic suite from the ballet – but mainly he worked on *The Fiery Angel*. The atmosphere of the surrounding countryside was conducive to work – the witches' sabbaths portrayed in *The Fiery Angel* must have happened thereabouts – and by the beginning of 1923 he had completed the opera in piano score. He then revised the Second Piano Concerto, the original score having been lost, and began the Fifth Piano Sonata.

In spring 1923 Prokofiev received his first official invitation to return to Russia, when the Leningrad PO offered him a series of concert engagements. Over the preceding five years he had kept in touch with musical affairs in the USSR through his correspondence with personal friends. He was in contact with Myaskovsky and Meyerhold, who loyally defended his decision to stay abroad to the Soviet musical establishment. In May 1923 a report on his activities appeared in the journal *K novïm beregam*, and around the same time some of his recent works were performed in Leningrad and Moscow. Three of the songs of op.36 had their première in Moscow in October 1923; the Third Piano Concerto and the *Scythian Suite* were both given there in 1925; and in February 1926 *The Love for Three Oranges* opened in Leningrad, where it ran for 49 performances. But in 1923 Prokofiev was not yet ready to return to Russia. His career in western Europe was just beginning, and the future looked promising. He had strong family ties there; his mother was ill and largely dependent on him (she died in December 1924). In September 1923 he married the Spanish-born singer Lina Llubera, and in 1924 his son Svyatoslav was born; his second

son, Oleg, was born in 1928. So he declined the offer from Leningrad, and a similar invitation the following year, but he kept the possibility open for the future.

After his marriage Prokofiev moved with his family to Paris. Over the next few months several of his works had their first performances there – the First Violin Concerto, the Fifth Piano Sonata, the revised Second Piano Concerto and *They are Seven* – but with mixed success. Perhaps because of certain anomalies in the idiom of his music, its mixture of sophisticated elements with a sort of home-grown innocence, of steely dissonance with almost tender lyricism, perhaps also because of his personality, Prokofiev must have found the Paris of the early 1920s a difficult world to conquer, to shock or to amuse. To be Russian was in itself no longer chic. Stravinsky may still have been a fashionable figure in musical circles, but he was by now truly Parisian, and Prokofiev could not approve of his recent music, his 'pseudo-Bachism', as Prokofiev later described it. Milhaud, Poulenc and the other members of Les Six were very much in vogue, and although Prokofiev was personally friendly with the group he could not share their musical attitudes. However, in summer 1924, the year of Honegger's *Pacific 231*, he set out to write his own work 'of iron and steel'.

This was the Second Symphony, perhaps his most startling and certainly his most complicated score. Its composition, which he found an unusually difficult process, occupied him throughout the following autumn and winter and even then, again untypically, he had doubts about the result. The première of the symphony in June 1925 did nothing to dispel his doubts. The work was far from successful; and Prokofiev would have been thrown into deep despair had not Dyagilev just then approached him with a new, and most surprising, commission.

With its formal recognition by most of the major countries of western Europe, Soviet Russia and the life of its people had suddenly become topical, and Dyagilev now proposed to stage a ballet on a Soviet theme. The constructivist painter Yakulov, who had only recently left Russia, was to write the scenario. The theme of the new work was to be industrialization; it was to be a ballet of construction, with a 'wielding of hammers big and small . . . and a flashing of light signals'. Prokofiev was delighted by the idea, and began work on *Stal'noy skok* ('The steel step'), or *Le pas d'acier*, Dyagilev's title, with great enthusiasm. Most of the music was composed over a two-month period, in August and September 1925.

Towards the end of that year Prokofiev and his wife left Europe for a concert tour of the USA. It was his first visit for almost four years, and by comparison with his last it was comfortably successful. The following spring the couple gave a recital tour in Italy. It was on his travels at this time that Prokofiev devised a new system of orchestrating his scores that allowed him to carry out the process even on rough train journeys. With practice he found it possible to indicate not only the instrumentation, but also details of accent and bowing by expanding his original piano score on to one or more additional staves. Most of his later works were notated in this way, with the transcription into full score left to an amanuensis.

The orchestration of *The Steel Step* was completed by spring 1926. Its première was postponed until the following year, but in the meantime Bruno Walter had accepted *The Fiery Angel* for performance in Berlin. Prokofiev accordingly spent summer 1926 revising the music and reorganizing the dramatic structure of the opera. At the same time he worked on the 'American' Overture op.42. In the autumn he was once more in correspondence with concert authorities in the USSR; this time he accepted their invitation to make an extensive tour in western Russia.

On 18 January 1927 Prokofiev arrived in the USSR after an absence of almost nine years. His tour lasted for

1. Sergey Prokofiev with his wife, Lina

three months, during which he gave 21 concerts in Moscow, Leningrad, Khar'kov, Kiev and Odessa. He conducted or performed most of his recent works, among them the suites from *The Love for Three Oranges* and *The Tale of the Buffoon*, the Second and Third Piano Concertos and his piano sonatas and songs. The 'American' Overture and the Quintet op.39 had their premières in Moscow, and Prokofiev attended the Leningrad production of *The Love for Three Oranges*. Everywhere he was received as a celebrity; indeed the great success of the tour, along with his renewal of personal friendships, must have made the prospect of a permanent return very attractive.

Rehearsals for *The Steel Step* had already begun in Paris, however, and its successful première was on 7 June 1927. Dyagilev had spared no expense; the production played up the Bolshevik subject matter to the full, and Prokofiev's music sounded authentically 'constructivist'. In fact the ballet owes more to the influence of *The Rite of Spring* and to the machine music of Les Six than to anything specifically Soviet, a fact not lost on the Russian Association of Proletarian Musicians (RAPM) when they auditioned, and rejected, the ballet in Moscow in 1929. But the novelty value of the whole spectacle was considerable, and its success was repeated a month later in London.

With the orchestration of *The Fiery Angel* completed, and its Berlin performance postponed indefinitely,

Prokofiev began a similar process of revision on his early opera *The Gambler*. Meyerhold had long been eager to stage the première of the work, and in the course of 1926 and 1927 he came to Paris to discuss the possibility of producing it as a follow-up to the Leningrad production of *The Love for Three Oranges*. Prokofiev's revisions, carried out over the winter of 1927–8, were extensive; the opera was more or less rewritten. *The Gambler* had its first performance in April 1929, but this was in Brussels; in Leningrad 'interest in the project had gradually waned' in the light of the RAPM's disapproval of the opera.

Two large and important works occupied Prokofiev throughout the remainder of 1928: the Third Symphony and the ballet *The Prodigal Son* (*L'enfant prodigue*). The symphony was a product of Prokofiev's unshakable faith in the worth of *The Fiery Angel*. In June 1928 the second act of the opera was given a concert performance under Koussevitzky in Paris, and Prokofiev decided that, rather than make an orchestral suite from the music, he might develop its thematic material symphonically. The drama and intensity of the resultant Third Symphony op.44 are the only hints to the listener of its operatic origins. Prokofiev rightly considered it one of his best scores.

Dyagilev's request for a ballet on the biblical theme of the prodigal son was as surprising to Prokofiev as his last commission, but it was a task he found 'both easy and pleasant'. Aided by a strong, dramatic plot, he wrote and orchestrated the music in the space of three months (November 1928 to February 1929). The two new works had their first performances within four days in the middle of May 1929 – the ballet not without problems. Dyagilev was already ill (he died only two months later) and had lost enthusiasm for the work; Lifar, in a fit of pique, did not wish to perform the title role. It was only at the last minute that all was made well, and Prokofiev's ballet, given in a programme with Stravinsky's *Renard*, was warmly received.

In strong contrast with the Third Symphony, *The Prodigal Son* is a cool, transparent score, closer in spirit to some of Prokofiev's Soviet-period works – *Zolushka* ('Cinderella') or the Sixth Symphony, for instance – than to his earlier ballets. When he received a commission in summer 1929 for a symphonic work to commemorate the 50th anniversary of the Boston SO, Prokofiev again thought of re-using material from his theatrical music. The Fourth Symphony, extracted partly from the music of *The Prodigal Son* and partly from music he had written for the ballet but not included in it, is less of a success than the Third, however. Its material, though often strikingly beautiful, is more tuneful, less symphonic, and the work seems to lack momentum.

In October 1929 Prokofiev was involved in a motor-car accident, which temporarily injured his hands, so that his visit to Moscow in November was without concert engagements. He was able on this occasion to hear much new Soviet music and to become acquainted with some of the workings of the musical establishment, though still as an outsider. More or less recovered from his accident, he undertook an extensive concert tour of the USA, Canada and Cuba early in 1930. Since his success in Europe, respect for Prokofiev's music had increased immeasurably in the USA, and his reception both by the public and by the press 'was quite serious this time'. A string quartet was commissioned by the

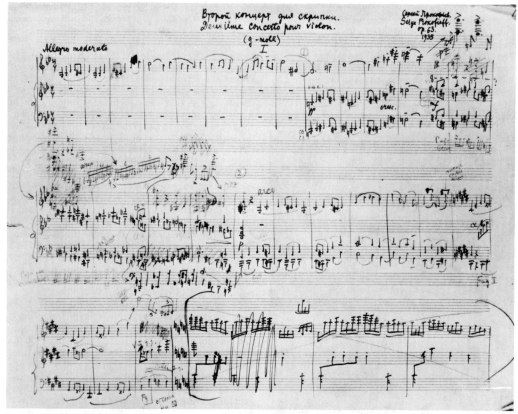

2. Autograph sketches for the opening of Prokofiev's Violin Concerto no.2, composed 1935 (USSR-Mcm)

Library of Congress, and the Metropolitan Opera in New York showed interest in staging *The Fiery Angel*. His hopes raised, yet again, Prokofiev began a second revision of the opera's dramatic structure; Act 2 was broken up into a number of short, dynamic scenes. But, once more, the production failed to materialize, and the planned revision was never completed.

On his return to Europe, Prokofiev gave a series of concerts in Brussels, Turin, Monte Carlo and Milan before returning to Paris to work on the string quartet, and on a new ballet, commissioned by the Paris Opéra. The ballet, *Na Dnepre* ('On the Dnieper'), or *Sur le Borysthène*, written in collaboration with Lifar, was to be the least memorable of his theatrical works. Its plot, set among the peasants of the Ukraine, was far from gripping. Its music was written as an abstract piece and, though not unlike *The Prodigal Son* in idiom, it is loosely constructed and rather pallid. It survived no more than a few performances at the Opéra in 1932.

Apart from the Fifth Sonata, Prokofiev composed practically nothing for the piano in the 1920s. Then in 1931 he received a commission for a new piano concerto, for the left hand alone, from the Austrian pianist Paul Wittgenstein. It was a project that seized his imagination, and over the summer months he produced an energetic four-movement work, modest in scale, but of considerable virtuosity for the soloist. It was received by Wittgenstein with politeness, but a total lack of understanding, and he never performed it. The score remained in his possession, however, and it was not until

1956 that the Fourth Piano Concerto had its première. It is regrettable that Wittgenstein's cool response to the concerto deterred Prokofiev from making a two-hand version of the score. Instead, he wrote the Fifth Piano Concerto. This he planned as a non-virtuoso work which he would call 'Music for Piano' to separate it from his other concertos. In the event, however, the performer in him took over, and in winter 1931–2 the piece grew, both in length and in stature. The Fifth Concerto is no less a virtuoso piece than its predecessors; its unconventional structure is nonetheless evidence of the composer's original intentions. Its five movements are arranged in the manner of a suite, full of vivid moods and sharp contrasts. Perhaps because of a certain lack of cohesion, it has never been as widely performed as the First and Third Concertos.

The years 1932–6, like the period 1918–22, saw great flux and change in Prokofiev's life. It was a time of decision for him: whether to return to the USSR and become a Soviet citizen, or to remain, as Stravinsky and Rakhmaninov had done, in the West as an emigré. Exactly when he made his decision, or even if he formulated it as such, is unclear; Victor Seroff in his biography of Prokofiev describes a conversation with him in Paris in 1932 which implied that his mind was already made up; other sources disagree. It is easier to speculate on the reasons why he decided to return. Certainly, perhaps naively, he disregarded the political implications of such a move. Prokofiev had never held any strong political views; he may well have assumed that the Soviet authorities would respect this, and that if any pressures were being brought to bear on composers, of all people, they somehow would not apply to him. Quite simply, he wanted to go home. Throughout his stay in the West he had never ceased to be, above all, a Russian. He had made many close acquaintances, but his real friends were Russians, and most of them, Myaskovsky, Derzhanovsky, Meyerhold and Asaf'yev, were in the USSR. He missed the support and confidence of these people; most of all he missed the vital stimulus of being in the company of Russians in Russia.

The process of his return was a gradual one; it was not until spring 1936 that he was permanently resident in Moscow. Until then both he and his wife held Nansen passports. Although his trips to the USSR became increasingly frequent after 1932, and from 1933 he had the use of an apartment in Moscow, his home was still in Paris. His family lived there, all his belongings were there, and most of the music he wrote between 1932 and 1936 was composed in Paris.

Gradually the sources of Prokofiev's commissions changed. Of the works of this period only two had their origins in France: the Sonata for two violins (1932) was written for the Triton chamber concerts in Paris, and the Second Violin Concerto (1935) was a commission from the French violinist Robert Soetans. The concerto had its first performance in Madrid on a tour Soetans made with Prokofiev to Spain, Portugal and north Africa at the end of 1935. Two more works, the *Symphonic Song* op.57 and the Cello Concerto in E minor op.58, though written for performance in Paris, had their premières in Moscow, in 1934 and 1938. The remainder, all large-scale pieces, were written for Soviet performance.

Prokofiev's first Soviet commissions came in 1933. That year he made two trips to the USSR, to Moscow in April and to the Caucasus for an extensive concert tour in the autumn. In the spring the Leningrad film director Feinzimmer approached him with the request for music for his film *Poruchik Kizhe* ('Lieutenant Kijé'). This satirical tale, of the soldier who never was, perfectly matched Prokofiev's sense of humour, and he spent that summer in Paris working on the delightfully frivolous score which was to become perhaps his most popular work. Then he received a commission from the Moscow Kamerniy Theatre for music for a dramatic extravaganza in which it was planned to combine extracts from Shaw's *Caesar and Cleopatra*, Shakespeare's *Antony and Cleopatra* and Pushkin's *Egyptian Nights*. Less inspired by this idea, Prokofiev wrote some rather undistinguished music for chamber orchestra, which accompanied the play in its short run in April 1935. The best of the music he included in the orchestral suite *Evipetskiye nochi* ('Egyptian nights') op.61.

Towards the end of 1934 a suggestion came from the Kirov Theatre in Leningrad to stage a new ballet by Prokofiev. The choice of subject, *Romeo and Juliet*, was controversial from the start, and soon the project was taken over by the Bol'shoy Theatre in Moscow. The problem was the ending to the story; as Prokofiev later put it, 'living people can dance, the dying cannot'. A happy ending, with Romeo arriving in the nick of time, seemed the only solution, and it was with this dénouement that the first version of the score was composed. It was the longest ballet Prokofiev had ever written, and the most intensely dramatic. Even so, its composition took him only four months, and at the end of summer 1935 his piano score was heard by the theatre directorate. The work was rejected out of hand as being unsuitable for dancing. Prokofiev carried out large-scale revisions to the music in the months that followed. The choreographers found a way of restoring the original tragic ending to the drama. But it was to be some years before *Romeo i Dzhuletta* was seen in Moscow.

4. USSR: 1936–53. With the arrival of his wife and family in Moscow in spring 1936, Prokofiev took up permanent residence in the USSR. His move there coincided with a critical period for Soviet music. With the dissolution of the RAPM in 1932 and the subsequent establishment of the Union of Soviet Composers, the administration of musical affairs throughout the country was, in effect, subject to government control. The Party Central Committee had also recommended general guidelines for composers and these, on the surface at least, probably seemed not unreasonable to Prokofiev. Composers were advised to pay heed to the social content of their music and its appeal to the people at large; as a basis for their idiom they might look to the traditions of the past and to folk resources within the countries of the USSR.

In practice, however, this was the beginning of Russia's artistic isolation from western Europe, as one important result was the disappearance from concert programmes within the USSR of much recent music by progressive composers in the West. None of this as yet directly affected Prokofiev, although he had already felt the effects of censorship with *The Steel Step* and *The Gambler*. In January, only months before his family moved to Moscow, came *Pravda*'s overt condemnation of Shostakovich. Again, while Prokofiev was not directly involved, the implications of such an attack could not have escaped him. Whether as a reaction to such events, or because of his disappointment over *Romeo and Juliet*, or simply as a change from the scale of his recent scores, he concentrated his attention in the meantime on a number of short pieces, many of them written for children. From this period date the Music for Children, a series of easy pieces for piano, the Three Children's Songs op.68 and *Petya i volk* ('Peter and the wolf').

By the middle of 1936 preparations were being made for two important jubilees the following year, the 20th anniversary of the Revolution and the centenary of Pushkin's death. Prokofiev wrote his Three Romances op.73 to texts by Pushkin during summer 1936, and at the same time he worked on three separate commissions he had received in connection with the Pushkin celebrations. He had been asked by the director Romm to provide music for a film version of *The Queen of Spades*; Meyerhold had commissioned a 'stormy background' for his projected experimental production of *Boris Godunov*; and from the Kamerniy Theatre came the request for incidental music to a new stage adaptation of *Evgeny Onegin*. Since all three had famous operatic settings, Prokofiev regarded the task as a challenge, and it is clear from his manuscripts that he took great care in composing the music. He was prompted to write an article on the question of combining music with spoken dialogue, and he was concerned, as he was in his later operas, to find musical equivalents for the characters as they develop dramatically. For various reasons, however, none of the Pushkin productions materialized. Prokofiev was to re-use many of his thematic ideas in later scores, notably in *Semyon Kotko* and *War and Peace*.

For the other celebrations he composed his mammoth *Cantata for the Twentieth Anniversary of the October Revolution*, to texts by Marx, Lenin and Stalin, and for a total of 500 performers. It was a sincere attempt to approach the concept of socialist realism, and in fact its performance calls for such 'realistic' sound-effects as gun shots, machine-gun fire and sirens. Prokofiev had begun the work early in 1936 in Paris, though some of its themes date from years earlier; its orchestration occupied him through summer 1937. Once again, however, its hoped-for performance never took place. Its critics suspected Prokofiev's motives in writing such a work, and there were accusations of vulgarity. The première of the cantata was not until 1966, long after Prokofiev's death, and proved it an immensely gripping and dramatic score, comparable with the composer's best music of the 1930s.

Prokofiev made two concert tours abroad during this period, the first in December 1936 through western Europe and the USA, and the second at the beginning of 1938 to Czechoslovakia, France, Britain and the USA. These were his last tours outside the USSR – a further trip, planned for 1940, was cancelled – and in the course of his stay in the USA he visited the studios in Hollywood to study film music techniques. He was able to apply his findings in his next important commission, to work with Sergey Eisenstein on the music for *Alexander Nevsky*. It was an ideal collaboration; from the start the two men were able to combine their talents and deal intuitively with each other's art. The result needs no description here: *Alexander Nevsky* is now a film classic, and in 1939 Prokofiev rearranged the music in the form of a cantata.

The film score occupied most of Prokofiev's time between May and October 1938, but in the course of the summer he found a subject for a new opera. It was Valentin Katayev's civil war story *I am the Son of the Working People*. The idea of writing a specifically Soviet opera, with relevance to everyday life, had attracted Prokofiev for some time, but he realized that there were problems involved. As he put it, 'a recitative for a commisar trying to dial a telephone could cause the raising of eyebrows'. Indeed, in *Semyon Kotko* he did not entirely overcome such problems, and although the score contains quantities of fine music, the drama as a whole rarely raises itself above the level of a bad western.

There were more problems over the production of the work. Its première was planned for the 1939–40 season at the Stanislavsky Theatre, where Meyerhold was the principal producer. But this collaboration between Prokofiev and Meyerhold was to prove as abortive as the others, and it was to be Meyerhold's last project. In June 1939, before the opera was finished, he was arrested and later executed 'as a result of a slanderous report'. After several postponements *Semyon Kotko* had its first performance in June 1940. Both the plot and the music of the opera were found to be suspect, however, and the following year it was dropped from the repertory.

In 1939, besides his work on the opera, Prokofiev began three new piano sonatas and composed the cantata *Zdravitsa* ('Hail to Stalin') op.85. He worked on all these pieces, and even on their separate parts, simultaneously, to avoid losing time. The Sixth Sonata was completed in spring 1940; the others he continued to compose spasmodically during the years of the war. The following May, before *Semyon Kotko* had had its première, he started on two new stage works, the ballet *Zolushka* ('Cinderella') and opera *Obrucheniye v monastïre* ('Betrothal in a monastery'), or *The Duenna*. *Cinderella* was to be a long-term project; the outbreak of war in June 1941 interrupted its composition, and other commissions then took precedence. *The Duenna* he finished by the beginning of 1941. Sheridan's play, with its heady mixture of humour and romance, had fired his imagination, and he planned a bright, lyrical work in the manner of Mozart or Rossini. In this he completely succeeded. *The Duenna* is in many respects the Soviet counterpart to *The Love for Three Oranges*, though its musical idiom is much simpler, its humour more restrained.

The events of 1941 altered the circumstances of both Prokofiev's career and his personal life. That spring he suffered the first of a series of heart attacks which badly affected his health over the next few years. With the outbreak of war the Soviet government evacuated large numbers of artists, Prokofiev among them, away from the capital to the comparative safety of the southern republics. He spent varying periods of time over the next year or two in the Caucasus, in Georgia and in Kazakhstan. His family life in Moscow was completely disrupted, though there were other reasons for this, too.

Prokofiev had become acquainted with Mira Mendelson, who was then 25 years old and a recent

3. *Sergey Prokofiev, 1951*

graduate from the Moscow Literary Institute, in spring 1940. Their friendship led to the break-up of his marriage. The details of the matter are complicated, and it has been suggested that political dealings were involved. Lina Prokofiev, as a foreigner, was certainly by that time *persona non grata* in Moscow; some years later she was arrested on charges of espionage and committed to a labour camp. Mira Mendelson had strong party ties and, as Seroff has aptly put it, the years 1939–41 were 'less conducive to romance than they were to survival'. What is clear about the affair is that until his wife's arrest Prokofiev was never completely estranged from her, and Mira Mendelson, though she lived with the composer until his death, was not, as Soviet sources state, his second wife.

The outbreak of war gave impetus to a project Prokofiev had sketched out in spring 1941, for an opera based on *War and Peace*. His initial plan for a small-scale, intimate opera which would highlight the personal dramas in the novel was expanded, and on his arrival in Nalchik in August 1941 he began the music. At the same time he completed the symphonic suite *1941-y god* ('The year 1941') and composed the Second String Quartet, in which he used, to wonderful effect, material drawn from local Kabardian folksongs and folkdances. The quartet was the first of his wartime compositions to reach performance, in September 1942.

In November Prokofiev was moved from Nalchik to Tbilisi. There, the following April, he finished *War and Peace* in piano score and also completed his Seventh Piano Sonata. He sent the score of the opera to Moscow for approval, and in the meantime began its orchestration. In May 1942 he travelled to Alma-Ata at Eisenstein's invitation to work on the music for the film *Ivan Groznïy* ('Ivan the Terrible'). Eisenstein's wartime studios were elaborate, and Prokofiev found the environment stimulating. During his year's stay there he worked on several very different projects. The music for Part I of the film was composed between June and November; he wrote the *Ballada o malchike, ostavshemsya neizvestnïm* ('Ballad of an unknown boy') and made extensive sketches, including a complete libretto, for a new opera, *Khan Buzay*, which, like his recent quartet, was to use local folk material; and in March 1943 he completed the orchestration of *War and Peace*.

Following the advice of the Committee on the Arts in Moscow, Prokofiev had drastically revised the opera in the process; the war scenes had been extended and the patriotic elements strengthened. It was no longer an intimate opera but an epic and heroic work. Prokofiev's incentive in revising the score was the promise of a production of the opera at the Bol'shoy at the end of 1943, for which Eisenstein was to design the sets. After a summer spent in Perm, in the Urals, working on *Cinderella* and the Flute Sonata op.94, he returned to Moscow for the rehearsals. But, as had happened so often, the performance was first cancelled, then postponed indefinitely. Throughout the rest of his life Prokofiev continually made revisions and additions to *War and Peace*, including the composition of two new scenes, in a series of attempts to secure performances. It was only in 1957, however, after his death, that anything like a complete version of the opera was staged.

During spring 1944 the orchestration of *Cinderella* was at last completed and for the summer Prokofiev moved to the large country house run by the Union of Composers on Ivanovo estate, some 80 km west of Moscow. There he finished the Eighth Piano Sonata, begun as long ago as 1939, and composed the Fifth Symphony. It was 15 years since his last essay in symphonic form, and even longer – the Second Symphony was composed in the mid-1920s – since he had written a completely abstract work of these dimensions; his orchestral works of the intervening years had consisted mainly of suites from his stage pieces. He now saw his new symphony as 'the culmination of a long period of my creative life ... a symphony of the grandeur of the human spirit'. He had long planned the work – some of its themes date back to the 1930s – and in Moscow much was expected of it. The Fifth Symphony is a work of stature and dignity, from its majestic opening to its exuberant finale. There are moments of humour and bright lyricism, but most of all it impresses one as an essentially sombre and introspective score. It is thought by many to be his greatest symphony, and it is probably his most frequently performed. Certainly, it is his most conventional, and on that count alone it is not his most characteristic work.

On 13 January 1945 Prokofiev conducted the première of the symphony in Moscow, to a rapturous reception. This was to be his last public appearance on the concert platform. Shortly afterwards he had a bad fall and suffered concussion. His doctors prescribed complete rest, and he spent the next four months in a sanatorium near Moscow; but the repercussions of the accident affected him, often severely, until his death. He was forced to ration his energies and gradually, in the late 1940s, his prodigious rate of composition slowed down. In the short term, however, Prokofiev recovered his spirits, and during the summer, which he again spent at Ivanovo, he worked on a typically wide range of compositional projects. He finished his experimental (and unsuccessful) *Ode to the End of the War*, scored for eight harps, four pianos and a variety of wind and percussion instruments. He composed a number of themes for use in his future Ninth Piano Sonata, and sketched out a Sixth Symphony. Between June and November the music for Part 2 of *Ivan the Terrible* was assembled. His health deteriorated again during the winter, and another period in hospital left him weak. He wrote little new music in the months that followed, but he arranged the music of his ballet *Cinderella* into three separate symphonic suites.

In spring 1946 he was advised, for the sake of his health, to leave Moscow, and in June he moved with Mira Mendelson to the village of Nikolina Gora, to the west of the city. There he occupied a villa in the middle of the country, and for the rest of his life this virtually became his home. During winter 1946–7 he finished the Sixth Symphony, one of his most poignant scores. By comparison with the Fifth it is modest in scale, purer in tone, and totally devoid of pretentiousness. It represents the best of his late music, in its tunefulness, the simplicity of its idiom, its easy pace and its mellowness. Nothing could contrast more strongly with the characteristic music of his youth, but comparisons are invalid here; in 1947 the quality of his creative thought was unimpaired.

The Sixth Symphony and the Ninth and last Piano Sonata had their premières in autumn 1947, and for the 30th anniversary of the Revolution Prokofiev wrote the 'festive poem' *Tridtsat' let* ('30 Years') op.113 and the cantata *Rastsvetay, moguchiy kray* ('Flourish, mighty homeland') op.114. The official response to these works was subdued: it was the calm before the furious storm which broke on the Soviet musical world at the beginning of 1948. During the war, in the face of more pressing matters, the party's concern for the arts had been relaxed; now state intervention was felt necessary to rectify the unhealthy state of musical affairs. A decree of the party central committee was published on 10 February which declared the works of most prominent Soviet composers, Prokofiev among them, 'marked with formalist perversions ... alien to the Soviet people'. *War and Peace* came under special fire, and many of Prokofiev's earlier works were banned from performance.

At the time Prokofiev was working on a new opera, *Povest' o nastoyashchem cheloveke* ('The story of a real man'), about the heroism of the World War II pilot Alexey Meres'yev; this, he was confident, would restore the balance. The opera was given a 'closed preview' to party and Union of Composers officials in the Kirov Theatre in Leningrad on 3 December 1948; it was presented without sets, costumes or props. The reaction was almost unanimously unfavourable, and though Prokofiev strongly defended his opera it was withdrawn from the Kirov's programme; it was not staged publicly until the years of ideological 'thaw' after Stalin's death.

After 1948, and doubtless partly as a result of its events, Prokofiev's health failed rapidly. More and more he sought the seclusion of Nikolina Gora, venturing into Moscow only for occasional performances of his music. His detachment increased with the deaths of his closest friends – Asaf'yev died in 1949, Myaskovsky in 1950 and Pavel Lamm in 1951 – and his creative spirit seemed broken. Many of the works of these last years were in response to official commissions: for the children's radio division he wrote the choral suite *Zimniy koster* ('Winter bonfire', 1949–50), the oratorio *Na strazhe mira* ('On guard of peace', 1950) and the Seventh Symphony (1951–2); the symphonic poem *Vstrecha Volgi s Donom* ('The meeting of the Volga and the Don', 1951) was composed for the opening of the Volga-Don canal. All these works are a sad reflection of his talent.

Prokofiev's last ballet, *Skaz o kammenom tsvetke* ('The tale of the stone flower'), begun in autumn 1948, was an exotic fantasy, based on Bazhov's collection of legends from the Urals. In this something of his characteristic enthusiasm was revived, and he created a rich, colourful and energetic score, which makes much of the scenario's outlandish setting. The strongest work of his last years, however, is unquestionably the Symphony-Concerto for cello and orchestra, which he wrote in close collaboration with Mstislav Rostropovich, and which incorporated much of the best music from his Cello Concerto op.58.

During his last winters Prokofiev lived in Moscow so that he might keep in daily contact with his doctors. In October 1952 he attended his last concert, for the première of his Seventh Symphony, and five months later he died of a brain haemorrhage on the day of Stalin's death. The irony of the coincidence would not have escaped him.

WORKS

OPERAS

op.

— Velikan [The giant] (3), vocal score, 1900, unpubd
— Na pustïnnïkh ostrovakh [Desert islands], ov. and 3 scenes of Act 1, 1900–02, unpubd
— Pir vo vremya chumï [A feast in time of plague] (1, after Pushkin), vocal score, 1903, 1 scene rev. 1908–9, unpubd

— Undina (4, M. Kilstett, after de la Motte Fouqué), 1904–7, unpubd
13 Maddalena (1, after M. Lieven), 1911–13, inc., unpubd; BBC, London, 25 March 1979 [orchd E. Downes]
24 Igrok [The gambler] (4, Prokofiev, after Dostoyevsky), 1915–17, rev. 1927–8; Brussels, Monnaie, cond. M. Corneil de Thoran, 29 April 1929; see orch works, op.49
33 Lyubov k tryom apelsinam [The love for three oranges] (prol, 4, after Gozzi), 1919; Chicago, Auditorium, cond. Prokofiev, 30 Dec 1921; see orch works, opp.33bis, 109, pf works, op.33ter
37 Ognennïy angel [The fiery angel] (5, after Bryusov), 1919–23, rev. 1926–7; Act 2 in concert perf., Paris, cond. Koussevitzky, 14 June 1928; complete, Paris, Champs Elysées, cond. Bruch, 25 Nov 1954; see orch works, op.44, vocal orch works, op.37bis
81 Semyon Kotko (5, V. Katayev, Prokofiev, after Katayev), 1939; Moscow, Stanislavsky, cond. M. N. Zhukov, 23 June 1940; see orch works, op.81bis
86 Obrucheniye v monastïre [Betrothal in a monastery] (The Duenna) (4, Prokofiev, M. Mendelson, after Sheridan), 1940–41; Leningrad, Kirov, cond. B. Khaikin, 3 Nov 1946; see orch works, op.123
— Khan Buzay, 1942–, inc., unpubd
91 Voyna i mir [War and peace] (5, epigraph, Prokofiev, after Tolstoy), 1941–3, rev. 1946–52; concert perf., Moscow, 16 Oct 1944; 8 scenes, Leningrad, Malïy, cond. S. A. Samosud, 12 June 1946; complete, with cuts, Moscow, Stanislavsky, cond. A. Shaverdov, 8 Nov 1957; see orch works, op.110, pf works, op.96
117 Povest' o nastoyashchem cheloveke [The story of a real man] (4, Prokofiev, Mendelson, after B. Polevoy), 1947–8; private concert perf., Leningrad, Kirov, cond. Khaikin, 3 Dec 1948; staged, Moscow, Bol'shoy, cond. M. F. Ermler, 8 Oct 1960
— Dalyokiye morya [Distant seas] (Prokofiev, after V. A. Dïkhovichnï), 1948–, inc., unpubd; planned as op.118

BALLETS

20 Ala i Lolli (Gorodetsky, Prokofiev), 1914–15, withdrawn, unpubd; see orch works, op.20
21 Skazka pro shuta [The tale of the buffoon] (Chout) (6 scenes, Prokofiev, after Afanasyev), 1915, rev. 1920; Paris, Gaîté Lyrique, cond. Prokofiev, 17 May 1921; see orch works, op.21bis
39 Trapetsiya [Trapeze] (1), 1924; Berlin, Romanov Company, late 1925; music also as Quintet, op.39
41 Stal'noy skok [The steel step] (Le pas d'acier) (2 scenes, Prokofiev, G. Yakulov), 1925–6; Paris, Sarah Bernhardt, cond. Désormière, 7 June 1927; see orch works, op.41bis
46 Bludnïy sïn [The prodigal son] (L'enfant prodigue) (3, Kochno), 1928–9; Paris, Sarah Bernhardt, cond. Prokofiev, 21 May 1929; see orch works, opp.46bis, 47
51 Na Dnepre [On the Dnieper] (Sur le Borysthène) (2 scenes, Lifar, Prokofiev), 1930–31; Paris, Opéra, cond. P. Gaubert, 16 Dec 1932; see orch works, op.51bis
64 Romeo i Dzhuletta [Romeo and Juliet] (4, Prokofiev, others, after Shakespeare), 1935–6; Brno, cond. Q. Arnoldi, 30 Dec 1938; see orch works, opp.64bis, 64ter, 101, pf works, op.75
87 Zolushka [Cinderella] (3, N. D. Volkov), 1940–44; Moscow, Bol'shoy, cond. Y. Fayer, 21 Nov 1945; see orch works, opp.107–10, chamber works, op.97bis, pf works, opp.95, 97, 102
118 Skaz o kammenom tsvetke [The tale of the stone flower] (4, L. Lavrovsky, Mendelson, after P. Bazhov), 1948–53; Moscow, Bol'shoy, cond. Fayer, 12 Feb 1954; see orch works, opp.126–9

OTHER DRAMATIC WORKS

(incidental music)

— Evipetskiye nochi [Egyptian nights] (Pushkin, Shakespeare, Shaw), 1934; Moscow, Kamernïy, April 1935; see orch works, op.61
70bis Boris Godunov (Pushkin, produced Meyergold), 1936; Moscow, Central Children's Theatre, April 1957; selected nos. from opp.70, 70bis and 71 arr. as Pushkiniana by Rozhdestvensky (1962)
71 Evgeny Onegin (Pushkin), 1936, unpubd; BBC, London, 1 April 1980
77 Hamlet (Shakespeare), 1937–8; Leningrad, 15 May 1939; see pf works, op.77bis

(film scores)

— Poruchik Kizhe [Lieutenant Kijé], 1933, unpubd; film unrealized; see orch works, op.60, other vocal works, op.60bis
70 Pikovaya dama [The queen of spades] (after Pushkin), 1936; film unrealized
— Alexander Nevsky (dir. Eisenstein), Mez, chorus, orch, 1938, unpubd; see vocal orch works, op.78, other vocal works, op.78bis
— Lermontov, 1941, unpubd; see orch works, op.110, pf works, op.96

—   Kotovsky, 1942, unpubd

—   Partizani v stepyakh ukraini [The partisans in the Ukrainian steppes], 1942, unpubd

—   Tonya, 1942, unpubd; film unrealized

116   Ivan Grozniy [Ivan the Terrible] (dir. Eisenstein), part 1, 1942–4, part 2, 1945, unpubd; arr. as oratorio by A. Stasevich, 1961

ORCHESTRAL

—   Symphony, G, 1902, unpubd

—   Symphony no.2, e, 1908, unpubd, reworked in Piano Sonata no.4

5   Sinfonietta, A, 1909, rev. 1914–15, unpubd; rev. as op.48

6   Sni [Dreams], sym. tableau, 1910, unpubd

8   Osenneye [Autumnal sketch], small orch, 1910, rev. 1915, 1934

10   Piano Concerto no.1, Db, 1911–12

16   Piano Concerto no.2, g, 1912–13, unpubd; rev. 1923

19   Violin Concerto no.1, D, 1916–17

20   Suite from Ala i Lolli (Scythian Suite), 1915

21bis Suite from The Tale of the Buffoon, 1920

25   Symphony no.1 'Classical', D, 1916–17

26   Piano Concerto no.3, C, 1917–21

29bis Andante from Piano Sonata no.4, 1934

33bis Suite from The Love for Three Oranges, 1919, rev. 1924

34bis Overture on Hebrew Themes [after chamber work], 1934

40   Symphony no.2, d, 1924–5; see also op.136

41bis Suite from The Steel Step, 1926

42   'American' Overture, Bb, chamber orch, 1926, unpubd

42bis 'American' Overture, Bb, full orch, 1928

43   Divertissement, 1925–9; see pf works, op.43bis

44   Symphony no.3, c [material from The Fiery Angel], 1928

46bis Suite from The Prodigal Son, 1929

47   Symphony no.4, C [material from The Prodigal Son], 1929–30, unpubd; rev. as op.112

48   Sinfonietta, A [rev. of op.5], 1929; see pf works, op.52

49   Four Portraits and Dénouement from The Gambler, 1931

50bis Andante from String Quartet no.1, str, ?1930, unpubd

51bis Suite from On the Dnieper, 1933

53   Piano Concerto no.4, Bb, left hand, 1931

55   Piano Concerto no.5, G, 1931–2

57   Symphonic Song, 1933, unpubd

58   Cello Concerto, e, 1933–8

60   Suite from Lieutenant Kijé, with Bar ad lib, 1934

61   Suite from Egyptian Nights, 1934

63   Violin Concerto no.2, g, 1935

64bis Suite no.1 from Romeo and Juliet, 1936

64ter Suite no.2 from Romeo and Juliet, 1936

65bis Letniy den [Summer day], children's suite [after nos.1, 9, 6, 5, 10–12 of pf work op.65], small orch 1941

69   Four Marches, military band, 1935–7

72   Russian Overture, with quadruple ww, 1936; rev. with triple ww, 1937, unpubd

81bis Suite from Semyon Kotko, 1941

88   Symphonic March, Bb, 1941, unpubd

89bis March, Ab, military band [after no.2 of 7 Songs, op.79], ?1941

90   1941-y god [The year 1941], suite, 1941

99   March, Bb, military band, 1943–4

100 Symphony no.5, Bb, 1944

101 Suite no.3 from Romeo and Juliet, 1946

105 Ode to the End of the War, wind, 8 harps, 4 pf, perc, dbs, 1945

107 Suite no.1 from Cinderella, 1946

108 Suite no.2 from Cinderella, 1946

109 Suite no.3 from Cinderella [3rd no. from The Love for Three Oranges], 1946

110 Waltz Suite [from Cinderella, War and Peace and Lermontov], 1946

111 Symphony no.6, eb, 1945–7

112 Symphony no.4, C [rev. of op.47], 1947

113 Tridtsat' let [30 years], festive poem, 1947

120 Pushkin Waltzes, 1949, unpubd

123 Letnyaya noch [Summer night], suite from The Duenna, 1950

125 Symphony-Concerto, e, vc, orch, 1950–51, rev. 1952 [after op.58]

126 Wedding Suite from The Tale of the Stone Flower, 1951

127 Gypsy Fantasy from The Tale of the Stone Flower, 1951, unpubd

128 Urals Rhapsody from The Tale of the Stone Flower, 1951, unpubd

129 Khozyayka mednoy gori [Lord of the copper mountain], suite from The Tale of the Stone Flower, unrealized

130 Vstrecha Volgi s Donom [The meeting of the Volga and the Don], festive poem, 1951

131 Symphony no.7, c♯, 1951–2

132 Cello Concerto, g, 1952, completed by Rostropovich and Kabalevsky

133 Piano Concerto no.6, 2 pf, str, 1952, inc.

136 Symphony no.2, d [rev. of op.40], unrealized

VOCAL ORCHESTRAL

7   Two Poems (Bal'mont), female chorus, orch, 1909–10, unpubd: Beliy lebed [The white swan], Volna [The wave]

18   Gadkiy utenok [The ugly duckling] [after song op.18], 1v, orch

30   Semero ikh [They are seven] (after Bal'mont), cantata, T, chorus, orch, 1917–18, rev. 1933

35bis Mélodie [no.2 from 5 Songs, op.35], 1v, orch, ?1920

37bis Ognenniy angel [The fiery angel], vocal suite from opera, 1v, orch, 1923, inc., unpubd

67   Petya i volk [Peter and the wolf] (Prokofiev), tale for children, narrator, orch, 1936

74   Cantata for the 20th Anniversary of the October Revolution (Marx, Lenin, Stalin), 2 choruses, orch, military band, accordion band, perc band, 1936–7, unpubd

76   Pesni nashikh dney [Songs of our times], solo vv, chorus, orch, 1937: Marsh [March], Cherez mostik [Over the bridge], Budte zdorovi [Good luck], Zolotaya Ukraina [Golden Ukraine], Brat za brata [Brother for brother], Devyshki [Maidens], Dvadtsatiletniy [The 20-year-old], Kolibelnaya [Lullaby], Ot kraya do kraya [From shore to shore]

78   Alexander Nevsky (V. Lugorsky, Prokofiev), cantata [from film score], Mez, chorus, orch, 1939

85   Zdravitsa [Hail to Stalin], chorus, orch, 1939

93   Ballada o malchike, ostavshemsya neizvestnim [Ballad of an unknown boy] (P. Antokolsky), S, T, chorus, orch, 1942–3, unpubd

114 Rastsvetay, moguchiy kray [Flourish, mighty homeland] (E. Dolmatovsky), cantata for the 30th anniversary of the October Revolution, 1947

122 Zimniy koster [Winter bonfire] (S. Marshak), suite, reciters, boys' chorus, orch, 1949–50

124 Na strazhe mira [On guard of peace] (Marshak), oratorio, Mez, reciters, chorus, boys' chorus, orch, 1950

OTHER VOCAL WORKS
(choral)

66a Two Choruses, vv, pf, 1935: Partizan Zheleznyak, Anyutka

66b Four Songs, 1v/vv, pf, 1935: Rastet strana [The fatherland awakens], Skvoz snega i tumani [Through snow and fog], Za goroyu [Beyond the hill], Pesnya o Voroshilove [Song of Voroshilov]

89   Seven Songs and a March in A, vv, pf, 1941–2: Pesnya [Song], Pesnya smelikh [Song of the brave], Klyatve tankista [The tankman's vow], Sin Kabardi [Son of Kabarda], Podruga boytsa [The soldier's sweetheart], Frits [Fritz], Lyubov voyna [Love of war]; nos.1–2 and 7 unpubd

98   National Anthem (S. V. Mikhalkov, El-Registan), 1943, All-Union Hymn (S. P. Shchipanchev), 1946; both in sketches, unpubd

121 Soldiers' Marching Song (Lugovsky), 1950

(songs, 1v, pf)

—   Juvenilia, unpubd: Skazhi mne [Tell me] (Lermontov), 1903; O, net, ne Figner [Oh, no, not Figner], 1903; Smotri, pushinki [Look, the down] (Prokofiev), 1903; Uzh ya ne tot [I am no longer the same] (Pushkin), 1903; Mastitiye, vetvistiye, dubi [Ancient, gnarled oaks] (A. Maykov), 1906–7

9   Two Poems, 1910–11: Est' drugiye planeti [It is of other planets] (Bal'mont), Otchalila lodka [The drifting boat] (A. Apukhtin)

18   Gadkiy utenok [The ugly duckling] (after Andersen), 1914, orchd; see vocal orch works, op.18

23   Five Poems (Bal'mont), 1915: Pod krishey [Under the roof], Seroe platitse [The little grey dress], Doversya mne [Follow me], V moyem sadu [In my garden], Kudesnik [The prophet]

27   Five Poems (Akhmatova), 1916: Solntse komnatu napolnilo [The sun has filled my room], Nastoyashchuyn nezhnost' [True tenderness], Pamyat' o solntse [Memory of the sun], Zdravstvuy [Greetings], Seroglaziy korol [The king with grey eyes]

35   Five Songs without Words, 1920; see vocal orch works, op.35bis, chamber works, op.35bis, pf works, op.52

36   Five Poems (Bal'mont), 1921: Zaklinaniye vodi i ognya [Incantation, fire and water], Golos ptits [Birdsong], Babochka [The butterfly], Pomni menya [Remember me], Stolbi [The pylons]

—   Five Kazakh Popular Songs, 1927

60bis Two Songs from Lieutenant Kijé, 1934: Stonet siziy golubochek [Moans the little grey dove], Troika

68   Three Children's Songs, 1936: Boltunya [Chatterbox], Sladkaya pesenka [Sweet song], Porosyata [The little pig]

73   Three Romances (Pushkin), 1936: Sosni [Pine trees], Pumyanoy zareyu [With a blush], V tvoyu svetlitsu [In your brightness]

78bis Three Songs from Alexander Nevsky (Lugovsky), 1939: Vstavayte, lyudi russkiye [Arise, men of Russia], Otzovitesya, yasni sokoli [Mark, ye bright falcons], A i bilo delo na Neve-reke [And it happened on the Neva banks]

79   Seven Songs, 1939: Pesnya o rodine [Song about the fatherland],

Stakhanovka, Nad polyarnïm morem [On the polar seas], Provodï [Send-off], Smelo vpered [Forward], Shol stanitseyu Kazak [Through the village came a Cossack], Hey, po doroge [Hey, to the road]; see orch works, op.89bis

104   Twelve Russian Folksongs, 1944
106   Two Duets, Russian folksong arrs., T, B, pf, 1945
—   Pro soma [Broad and deep the river flows] (Mikhalkov), inc., unpubd

CHAMBER AND INSTRUMENTAL

—   Juvenilia, vn, pf, unpubd; Sonata, c, 1903; Little Song, d, 1903; Little Song no.2, c, 1904
12bis   Humoresque Scherzo, 4 bn [after no.9 of 10 pf Pieces, op.12], 1915
15   Ballade, c, vc, pf, 1912
34   Overture on Hebrew Themes, c, cl, str qt, pf, 1919; see orch works, op.34bis
35bis   Five Melodies, vn, pf [after 5 Songs, op.35], 1925
39   Quintet, g, ob, cl, vn, va, db, 1924; see ballets, op.39
50   String Quartet no.1, b, 1930; see orch works, op.50bis, pf works, op.52
56   Sonata, C, 2 vn, 1932
80   Sonata no.1, f, vn, pf, 1938–46
92   String Quartet no.2 (on Kabardinian themes), F, 1941
94   Sonata, D, fl, pf, 1943; arr. as op.94bis for vn, pf, 1944
97bis   Adagio, vc, pf [from Cinderella], 1944
115   Sonata, D, unison vns/vn, 1947
119   Sonata, C, vc, pf, 1949
134   Sonata, c♯, vc, inc., unpubd

PIANO
(juvenilia)

Indian Galop, F, 1896; March, C, 1896; Waltz, C, 1896; Rondo, C, 1896; March, b–D, 1897; Polka, G, 1899; Waltz, G, 1899; Waltz, C–G, 1899; March, 1900; [untitled work], 7 pieces, 1901; Little Songs, 1st ser., 12 pieces, 1902; Bagatelle no.2, a, 1902; Little Songs, 2nd ser., 12 pieces, 1903; Sonata, B♭, 1903–4; Little Songs, 3rd ser., 12 pieces, 1903–4; Variations on 'Chizhika', 1904; Little Songs, 4th ser., 12 pieces, 1905; Polka mélancolique, f♯, 1905

Little Songs, 5th ser., 12 pieces, 1906; Song without Words, D♭, 1907; Intermezzo, A, 1907; Humoresque, f, 1907; [untitled work] b♭, 1907; Oriental Piece, g, 1907; [untitled work], c, 1907; Sonata no.2, f, 1907, reworked in op.1; Sonata no.3, a, 1907, reworked in op.28; 4 Pieces, 1907–8, rev. as op.3; Sonata no.4, ?1907–8, lost; 4 Pieces, 1908, rev. as op.4; Sonata no.5, 1908, reworked in op.29; Examination Fugue, 1908; Andante, c, 1908, inc.; 2 Pieces, 1908; Study, c, 1908; Piece on Es–C–H–E, 1908; Sonata no.6, ?1908–9, lost

For 4 hands: March, C, 1897; March, C, 1899; March, F, 1899; Piece, F, 1899; Piece, d, 1900; Piece, with zither, 1900, inc.; Bagatelle no.1, c, 1901

(mature works)

1   Sonata no.1, f [after Sonata no.2, 1907], 1909
2   Four Etudes, 1909
3   Four Pieces [rev. of 4 Pieces, 1907–8], 1911: Skazka [Story], Shutka [Jest], Marsh [March], Prizrak [Phantom]
4   Four Pieces [rev. of 4 Pieces, 1908], 1910–12: Vospominaniya [Reminiscences], Porïv [Elan], Otchayanie [Despair], Navazhdeniye (Suggestion diabolique)
11   Toccata, d, 1912
12   Ten Pieces, 1906–13: March [after Little Songs, 5th ser., no.6], Gavotte, Rigaudon, Mazurka, Capriccio, Legenda, Prelude, Allemande, Humoresque Scherzo, Scherzo; see chamber works, op.12bis
14   Sonata no.2, d, 1912
17   Sarcasms, 5 pieces, 1912–14
22   Mimoletnosti (Visions fugitives), 20 pieces, 1915–17
28   Sonata no.3 (from old notebooks), a [after Sonata no.3, 1907], 1917
29   Sonata no.4 (from old notebooks), c [after Sonata no.5, 1908 and Sym., 1908], 1917
31   Skazki staroy babushki [The tales of an old grandmother], 4 pieces, 1918
32   Four Pieces, 1918: Dance, Minuet, Gavotte, Waltz
33ter   March and Scherzo from The Love for Three Oranges, 1922
38   Sonata no.5, C, 1923, rev. as op.135
43bis   Divertissement [after orch work], 1938
45   Veshchi v sebe [Things in themselves], 2 pieces, 1928
52   Six Pieces, 1930–31: Intermezzo, Rondo, Etude [all from The Prodigal Son], Scherzino [from 5 Songs, op.35], Andante [from Str Qt no.1, op.50], Scherzo [from Sinfonietta, op.48]
54   Two Sonatinas, e, G, 1931–2
59   Three Pieces, 1933–44: Progulka [Promenade], Peyzazh [Landscape], Pastoral Sonatina, C
62   Mïsli (Pensées), 3 pieces, 1933–4
65   Music for Children, 12 pieces, 1935; see orch works, op.65bis

75   Ten Pieces from Romeo and Juliet, 1937
77bis   Gavotte [from Hamlet], 1938
82   Sonata no.6, A, 1939–40
83   Sonata no.7, B♭, 1939–42
84   Sonata no.8, B♭, 1939–44
95   Three Pieces from Cinderella, 1942
96   Three Pieces, 1941–2: Waltz [from War and Peace], Contredanse, Mephisto-waltz [both from Lermontov]
97   Ten Pieces from Cinderella, 1943
102   Six Pieces from Cinderella, 1944
103   Sonata no.9, C, 1947
135   Sonata no.5, C [rev. of op.38], 1952–3
137   Sonata no.10, c, inc., unpubd
138   Sonata no.11, unrealized
—   Dumka, after 1933, unpubd

OTHER WORKS

Music for gymnastic exercises, ?1936, inc., unpubd
Arrs.: D. Buxtehude: Organ Prelude and Fugue, pf, 1920/?1918; F. Schubert: Waltzes, suite, pf, 1920/?1918, pf 4 hands, 1923

Principal publishers: Boosey & Hawkes, Editions Russes de Musique, Gutheil, Jürgenson, Muzgiz

BIBLIOGRAPHY

MONOGRAPHS AND COLLECTIONS OF ESSAYS

I. V. Nest'yev: Prokofiev: his Musical Life (New York, 1946)
Tempo, no.20 (1949) [special no.]
S. I. Shlifshteyn, ed.: S. S. Prokof'yev: materialï, dokumentï, vospominaniya [Materials, documents, reminiscences] (Moscow, 1956, 2/1961; Eng. trans., 1960, 2/1968; Ger. trans., 1965)
M. Sabinina: Sergey Prokof'yev (Moscow, 1956)
I. V. Nest'yev: Prokof'yev (Moscow, 1957, enlarged 2/1973; Eng. trans., 1961)
I. Martïnov: Lavreat leninskoy premii Sergey Prokof'yev (Moscow, 1958)
L. Gakkel: Fortep'yannoye tvorchestvo S. S. Prokof'yeva [Prokofiev's piano works] (Moscow, 1960)
L. Polyakova: 'Voyna i mir' Prokof'yeva (Moscow, 1960, rev. 2/1971)
C. Samuel: Prokofiev (Paris, 1960; Eng. trans., 1971)
T. Boganova: Natsional'no-russkiye traditsii v muzïke S. S. Prokof'yeva (Moscow, 1961)
A. Klimovitsky: Opera Prokof'yeva 'Semyon Kotko' (Moscow, 1961)
L. Berger, ed.: Chertï stilya S. Prokof'yeva [Aspects of Prokofiev's style] (Moscow, 1962)
S. Katanova: Baletï S. Prokof'yeva (Moscow, 1962)
G. Ordzhenikidze: Fortep'yanne sonatï Prokof'yeva (Moscow, 1962)
S. I. Shlifshteyn, ed.: Notograficheskiy spravochnik S. S. Prokof'yeva [Reference list of Prokofiev's works] (Moscow, 1962)
P. R. Ashley: Prokofiev's Piano Music: Line, Chord, Key (diss., Rochester U., 1963)
L. Danko: Operï S. Prokof'yeva (Moscow, 1963)
M. R. Hofmann: Serge Prokofiev (Paris, 1963)
Y. Soroker: Kamerno-instrumental'noye ansambli S. Prokof'yeva (Moscow, 1963)
H. A. Brockhaus: Sergej Prokofjew (Leipzig, 1964)
L. and E. Hanson: Prokofiev (London, 1964)
M. Rayment: Prokofiev (London, 1965)
I. V. Nest'yev and G. Y. Edelman, ed.: Sergey Prokof'yev: stat'i i materialï [Articles and materials] (Moscow, 1965)
S. I. Shlifshteyn, ed.: Sergey Prokof'yev/Sergei Prokofiev (Moscow, 1965)
L. Danko: S. S. Prokof'yev (Moscow and Leningrad, 1966)
Yu. Kremlyov: Esteticheskiye vsglyadï S. Prokof'yeva [Prokofiev's aesthetic standpoint] (Moscow, 1966)
T. Ter-Martirosyan: Nekotorïye osobennosti garmonii Prokof'yeva [Features of Prokofiev's harmony] (Moscow and Leningrad, 1966)
M. H. Brown: The Symphonies of Prokofiev (diss., Florida State U., 1967)
Ya. Kholopov: Sovremennïye chertï garmoniya Prokof'yeva [Contemporary aspects of Prokofiev's harmony] (Moscow, 1967)
S. Morozov: Prokof'yev (Moscow, 1967)
V. Seroff: Sergei Prokofiev: a Soviet Tragedy (New York, 1968)
M. Tarakanov: Stil simfoniy Prokof'yeva [Prokofiev's symphonic style] (Moscow, 1968)
M. Aranovsky: Melodika S. Prokof'yeva (Leningrad, 1969)
R. McAllister: The Operas of Sergei Prokofiev (diss., U. of Cambridge, 1970)
V. Blok, ed.: S. S. Prokof'yev: stat'i i issledovaniya [Articles and researches] (Moscow, 1972)
V. Blok: Violonchel'noye tvorchestvo Prokof'yev (Moscow, 1973)
S. Prokofiev: Autobiografiya, ed. M. G. Kozlova (Moscow, 1973)
S. Moisson-Franckhauser: Serge Prokofiev et les courants esthétiques de son temps (Paris, 1974)
V. Blok: Metod tvorcheskoy rabotï S. Prokof'yeva [The working methods of Prokofiev] (Moscow, 1979)
R. McAllister: Prokofiev (London, in preparation)

ARTICLES ON PARTICULAR WORKS
(operas)

M. Sabinina: ' "Voyna i mir" ', *SovM* (1953), no.12

C. Bruch: ' "Ognennïy angel" v Parizhe', *SovM* (1955), no.7

Ya. Keldïsh: 'Eshcho ob opere "Voyna i mir" ' [More about the opera 'War and Peace'], *SovM* (1955), no.7

D. Mitchell: 'Prokofiev's "Three Oranges": a Note on its Musical-dramatic Organisation', *Tempo*, no.41 (1956), 20

H. Swarsenski: 'Prokofieff's "The Flaming Angel" ', *Tempo*, no.39 (1956), 16

A. Zolotov: 'Ode to Heroism: "The Story of a Real Man" at the Bolshoy Theatre', *Current Digest of the Soviet Press* (1960), no.48

J. Renate: 'Von "Spieler" zur "Erzählung von Wahren Menschen"', *Musik und Gesellschaft*, xi (1961)

D. Lloyd-Jones: 'Prokofiev and the Opera', *Opera*, xiii (1962), 513

A. Porter: 'Prokofiev's Early Operas', *MT*, ciii (1962), 528

M. Sabinina: 'Ob opere kotoraya ne bïla napisana' [On the opera that was never written], *SovM* (1962), no.8 [on *Khan Buzay*]

L. Polyakova: 'O poslednem opernom zamïsle S. Prokof'yeva "Dalekie morya" ' [On Prokofiev's last operatic creation 'Distant seas'], *SovM* (1963), no.3

A. Jefferson: ' "The Angel of Fire" ', *Music and Musicians*, xiii/12 (1965), 32

E. Mnatsakanova: 'Neskol'ko zametok ob opere "Igrok" ' [Some notes on the opera 'The Gambler'], *Muzïka i sovremennost*, iii (1965), 122

——: 'Prokof'yev i Tolstoy', *Muzïka i sovremennost*, iv (1966)

G. Pugliese: 'The Unknown World of Prokofiev's Operas', *High Fidelity*, xvi (1966), 44

A. Porter: 'Prokofiev's Late Operas', *MT*, cviii (1967), 312

R. McAllister: 'Prokofiev's Early Opera "Maddalena" ', *PRMA*, xcvi (1969–70), 137

——: 'Natural and Supernatural in "The Fiery Angel" ', *MT*, cxi (1970), 785

——: 'Prokofiev's Tolstoy Epic', *MT*, cxiii (1972), 851

M. H. Brown: 'Prokofiev's *War and Peace*: a Chronicle', *MQ*, lxiii (1977), 297–326

(other dramatic works)

P.-O. Ferroud: 'The Ballets of Sergei Prokofiev', *The Chesterian*, xv (1933–4), 89

P. Hope-Wallace: 'Prokofiev's Music for "Cinderella" ', *Ballet* (1949), 34

U. Seelmann-Eggebert: 'Prokofjew und die Filmmusik', *NZM*, Jg.125 (1964), 522

(orchestral works)

M. Montagu-Nathan: 'Prokofiev's First Piano Concerto', *MT*, lviii (1917), 12

A. Frank: 'Piano Concerto no.3', *The Concerto*, ed. R. Hill (Harmondsworth, 1952), 382

E. Lockspeiser: 'Prokofieff's Seventh Symphony', *Tempo*, no.37 (1955), 24

W. W. Austin: 'Prokofiev's Fifth Symphony', *MR*, xvii (1956), 205

I. Yampol'sky: 'Prokofiev's Third Symphony', *Musical Events* (1962), Sept, 22

R. Layton: 'Sergei Prokofiev', *The Symphony*, ed. R. Simpson (Harmondsworth, 1967), 166

A. Shitke: 'Osobennosti orkestrovovo golosovedeniya S. Prokof'yeva' [Features of orchestral part-writing in Prokofiev], *Muzïka i sovremennost*, vii (1974)

(piano sonatas)

F. Merrick: 'Serge Prokofiev's Sixth Piano Sonata', *MT*, lxxxv (1944), 9

——'Prokofiev's Piano Sonatas 1–5', *MT*, lxxxvi (1945), 9

——: 'Prokofiev's Seventh and Eighth Piano Sonatas', *MT*, lxxxix (1948), 234

——: 'Prokofiev's Piano Sonatas', *PRMA*, lxxv (1948–9), 13

——: 'Prokofiev's Ninth Piano Sonata', *MT*, xcvii (1956), 649

M. H. Brown: 'Prokofiev's Eighth Piano Sonata', *Tempo*, no.70 (1964), 9

E. Roseberry: 'Prokofiev's Piano Sonatas', *Music and Musicians*, xxi/7 (1971), 38

OTHER LITERATURE

M. Calvocoressi: 'Sergej Prokofjew', *Musikblätter des Anbruch* (1922), 172

B. de Schloezer: 'Igor Strawinsky und Sergej Prokofjew', *Melos*, iv (1924–5)

G. Abraham: 'Prokofiev as a Soviet Composer', *MR*, iii (1942), 241

N. Nabokov: 'Prokofiev, Russian Musician', *Atlantic Monthly* (1942), July, 62

G. Abraham: *Eight Soviet Composers* (London, 1943)

H. Ottaway: 'Sergei Prokofiev and Benjamin Britten', *MO*, lxiii (1949–50), 576

A. Werth: 'The Real Prokofiev', *The Nation*, clxxvi (1953), 285

H. Swarsenski: 'Prokofieff: Unknown Works with a New Aspect', *Tempo*, no.30 (1953–4), 14

M. Prokofieva: 'Iz vospominaniy' [From reminiscences], *SovM* (1961), no.4

S. Prokofiev: Correspondence with V. Alpers, *Muzïkal'noye nasledstvo*, i (1962)

J. Szigeti: 'The Prokofiev I Knew', *Music and Musicians*, xiii/9 (1963), 10

A. Jacobs: 'A Prokofiev Problem', *Opera*, xvi (1965), 31

R. Zanetti: 'Prokofjew und Diagilew', *Melos*, xxxii (1965), 443

S. Prokofiev: Correspondence with V. Meyerhold, *Muzïkal'noye nasledstvo*, ii (1968)

K. Kh. Adzhemov: *Nezabïvaemoye* [Memoirs] (Moscow, 1972)

D. S. Kabalevsky and others, eds.: *S. S. Prokof'yev i N. Y. Myaskovsky: perepiska* [correspondence] (Moscow, 1977)

RITA McALLISTER

Prokopiev, Trajko (*b* Kumanovo, 6 Nov 1909). Yugoslav composer and conductor. He completed his studies in composition with Milojević and Slavenski at the Belgrade Academy of Music in 1934, and in conducting at the Prague Conservatory with Dědeček in 1947. Before World War II he was a music teacher and choirmaster in several Yugoslav towns; he then worked in Skopje as conductor of the Skopje SO and chief radio music editor (1947–50) and as conductor of the opera (1950–73). His music is lyrical and markedly national in its dependence on Macedonian folk music.

WORKS
(selective list)

Stage: Labin i Dojrana, ballet, 1958; Rastanak [Separation], opera, 1972

Other works: choral cycles, incl. Kumanovke, Lenka; solo songs, chamber and pf pieces

Principal publisher: Društvo na Kompozitorite na Makedonija

STANA ĐURIĆ-KLAJN

Proksch [Prokš], **Joseph** [Josef] (*b* Reichenberg [now Liberec], Bohemia, 4 Aug 1794; *d* Prague, 20 Dec 1864). Czech-Austrian teacher. Blind from the age of 17, he studied at the Prague Institute for the Blind (1809–16) with Johann Kozeluch (piano) and Václav Farník (clarinet) and, after touring the Austrian Empire, returned to teach in Reichenberg; he also studied briefly in Berlin (1825) with J. B. Logier, a fashionable exponent of a method of teaching by simultaneous group-performances on a number of pianos. From this Proksch evolved his own teaching method and in 1830 opened his *Musikbildungsanstalt* in Prague, a progressive institution which offered a comprehensive musical education and which, with its public examinations and concerts, contributed much to Prague's musical life, attracting the attention of visiting celebrities such as Liszt and Berlioz. Its pupils included Jindřich Kàan, Wilhelmine Clauss-Szavardy and Smetana, whose years at the institute (1843–7) and as a private harmony and composition pupil of Proksch, had a far-reaching influence on his career as a virtuoso pianist and composer. Proksch published several books explaining his methods together with volumes of teaching material. He composed several masses and other church music, a Singspiel, incidental music, a ballet, a string quartet, orchestral music, much piano music and many piano arrangements. After his death the work of the institute was carried on by his son Theodor (*d* 1876), his daughter Marie (*d* 1900) and his great-nephew Robert Franz Proksch (*d* 1933).

WRITINGS

Versuch einer rationellen Lehrmethode im Pianoforte-Spiel (Prague, 1841–64, 2/1894)

Allgemeine Musiklehre (Prague, 1857)

Aphorismen über katholische Kirchenmusik (Prague, 1858)

Die Kunst des Ensembles im Pianoforte-Spiel (Prague, 1859) [a collection of pieces for 2–4 pianos, both original and arrangements, for use with the *Lehrmethode*]

BIBLIOGRAPHY
R. Müller: *Joseph Proksch* (Prague, 1874)
Z. Nejedlý: *Bedřich Smetana* (Prague, 1924–33, 2/1950–53), v, 297ff, 324ff
V. Helfert: *Tvůrčí rozvoj B. Smetany* [Smetana's creative development] (Prague, 1924), 66ff
H. P. Kraus: *Musikbibliothek Joseph Proksch* (Vienna, 1934) [catalogue of the Proksch library, offered for sale by H. P. Kraus]
M. Rejchlová: *Josef Proksch a jeho Hudebně vzdělávací ústav v Praze* [Proksch and his teaching institute in Prague] (diss., U. of Prague, 1952)
F. Bartoš, ed.: *Bedřich Smetana: Letters and Reminiscences* (Prague, 1955), 19f, 22
R. Budiš: *Smetanův učitel Josef Proksch* [Smetana's teacher Joseph Proksch] (Liberec, 1962)
F. Plíva: 'Neznámé originály z pozůstalosti Josefa Proksche' [Unknown original works from Proksch's Nachlass], *HRo*, xviii (1965), 781
B. Large: *Smetana* (London, 1970), 23ff
J. Clapham: *Smetana* (London, 1972), 17ff
R. Budiš: 'Die Prager Jahre des Josef Proksch', *Sborník prací filosofické fakulty brněnské university*, H8 (1973), 73
E. Slavická-Háchová: 'Ke Smetanovým studiím u Josefa Proksche' [Smetana's studies with Proksch], *HV*, xi (1974), 147

JOHN TYRRELL

Prolatio (Lat.: 'prolation'). In the system of mensural notation of the late Middle Ages, the relationship between semibreve and minim; *see* NOTATION, §III.

Prologos. In a Byzantine KALOPHONIC CHANT, that part which precedes the KRATĒMA.

Prologue. The introductory scene to a dramatic work, in which the author explains, either directly or indirectly, the context and meaning of the work to follow. Less commonly, the prologue may simply pay homage to the author's patron.

Prologues were a usual feature of Baroque opera, the idea apparently having been adopted partly from the first INTERMEDIO that often preceded spoken comedies and pastorales in the late 16th century, and partly from the prologues to pastoral plays like Tasso's *Aminta* (1573) or Guarini's *Il pastor fido* (1581–4). Prologues were also characteristic of Italian neo-Senecan drama, and were defended by the 16th-century dramatic theorist G. B. Giraldi Cinthio as necessary to provide the intellectual background to the plot and to create the appropriate emotional tension in the audience.

Opera prologues were generally either literary or topical in content. Literary prologues reflected the neoclassical aims of Renaissance drama, showing mythological figures whose relationships and potential conflicts constituted an allegory of the action to follow. The first opera prologues derived their form from those of pastoral drama, and consisted of a series of hendecasyllabic quatrains rhyming *abba*, usually set strophically to music. At first these were for only one character, usually Tragedia (Rinuccini's *Euridice*) or Musica (*L'Orfeo*). By the middle third of the 17th century, particularly at Venice, it became customary for several allegorical characters to appear. At first they declaimed the traditional quatrains in dialogue, but with increasing dramatization the poetic form of the prologue was diluted. The allegorical characters normally represented forces at work in the ensuing drama; thus Fortuna, Virtù and Amor dispute their respective powers over men's fates in the prologue to Monteverdi's *L'incoronazione di Poppea* (1642), Amor's self-declared triumph being subsequently mirrored in the opera. With the growing complexity of opera plots and increasing interest in cleverness of the action, prologues came to be integrated ingeniously into the main opera; thus the prologue to *Pompeo Magno* (text by Minato and music by Cavalli, 1666) ends with Fama hearing the crowd chorus 'Viva Pompeo', which begins the action.

Topical prologues were most often political allegories designed to show the ruler's actions in a favourable light. Quinault's prologue for Lully's *Alceste* (1674), for example, depicts the nymphs of the Seine and the Marne being consoled by La Gloire, who brings news of Louis XIV's defeat of a rival river, the Rhine (in reality his recent military victory over the Netherlands). New topical prologues were normally added to revivals of operas in the 17th century, usually incorporating references to the new production's patrons or venue. Thus Stradella's prologue 'Questo è il giorno prefisso' for the Roman production of Cavalli's *Giasone* in 1671, while textually parodying the original, is really a vehicle for display of the elaborate stage machines of the newly opened Teatro Tordinona.

Whether literary or topical in function, prologues became less common in the 18th century, partly because of the libretto reforms introduced by Zeno and the Arcadians, partly perhaps because fewer operas were performed strictly at court. Naples had an important tradition of operatic prologues during the monarchy (1734–82); these were usually written for three characters, whose parts were sung by the prima donna, primo uomo and tenor of the opera, and used allegory to praise the ruler or to refer to the particular festivity for which the opera was commissioned. Handel wrote only one prologue for an opera – a ballet for the 1734 revival of *Il pastor fido* that represents Terpsichore required to depict human emotions (later integral to the plot) in dance to qualify as a muse. In the late 18th century and early 19th, operatic prologues were rare. Wagner's *Das Rheingold* is properly considered the literary prologue to the rest of the *Ring*, as it presents the necessary musical and mythological background to the plot. The prologue to Gounod's *Roméo et Juliette* (1867) is similarly literary in purpose; a chorus at the end of the overture gives a short synopsis of the Capulet–Montague tale. Boito's *Mefistofele* (1868) was originally introduced by a 'Prologo in cielo' conceived as a four-movement symphony for orchestra and chorus (song of the penitents and choir of the blessed; instrumental scherzo and entry of Mephistopheles; chorus of seraphim; combined chorus of penitents, blessed and seraphim); for the 1875 revival he wrote a 'Prologo in teatro', a dialogue between a critic, a member of the audience and Boito himself, but eventually returned to the more popular 'Prologo in cielo'. Leoncavallo's *Pagliacci* opens with a prologue explicitly modelled on those of ancient drama; Tonio, having declared himself to be 'Prologo', addresses the audience with an exposition of the dramatic theory of *verismo*. In the 20th century various kinds of literary prologues have preceded operas, ranging from the brief spoken prologue of Stravinsky's *Oedipus rex*, through the allegorical competition for theatrical supremacy among 'tragedies', 'comedies', 'lyrics', 'empty heads' and 'ridiculousnesses' that precedes Prokofiev's *Love of Three Oranges*, to the famous lion-taming scene that sets the horrific tone for Berg's *Lulu*.

BIBLIOGRAPHY
H. Leichtentritt: 'On the Prologue in Early Opera', *PAMS 1936*, 88
R. Allorto: 'Il prologo dell'*Orfeo*: note sulla formazione del recitativo monteverdiano', *Congresso internazionale sul tema Claudio Monteverdi e il suo tempo: Venezia, Mantova e Cremona 1968*, 157
O. Jander: 'The Prologues and Intermezzos of Alessandro Stradella', *AnMc*, no.7 (1969), 87

B. R. Hanning: 'Apologia pro Ottavio Rinuccini', *JAMS*, xxvi (1973), 240

SUZANNE G. CUSICK

Prolongation. In Schenkerian analysis (*see* ANALYSIS, §III) the generation of the substance of a tonal piece or movement by a linear elaboration of its URSATZ, the basic two-part contrapuntal unit underlying its structure. Prolongation may be applied to the melodic line or to the bass, or to one of the middle parts of the composition; it may also link a middle part to an outer part or, in some instances, the outer parts to each other. The simplest forms of prolongation involve either conjunct elaboration of melodic notes or chordal elaboration of harmonic degrees. A conjunct elaboration, called a *Zug* (*see* ZUG (i)), is a linear progression upwards or downwards encompassing an interval that is usually specified in its name (thus, for instance, a *Terzzug* is a linear progression encompassing a 3rd, e.g. $f''-e''-d'$, $b\flat-c'-d'$). A chordal elaboration is called an ARPEGGIATION – Schenker used the term *Brechung*, the 18th-century German name for arpeggio – and this form of prolongation is especially common in the bass part. In the analysis of the beginning of the Menuetto from Mozart's String Quartet K421/417b (ex.1), there is an arpeggia-

Ex.1 Mozart: String Quartet in D minor K421/417b, Menuetto

tion to the first note of the fundamental melodic line (the *Urlinie*) and one from the first note of the bass; a descending *Terzzug* 'prolongs' the descent of the *Urlinie* from 3 to 2. These prolongations are all illustrated in the first middleground layer of the analysis. There is one method of prolongation, called UNTERBRECHUNG, which is applied not to the individual parts of a composition but to the *Ursatz* as a whole, dividing it into an imperfect cadence and an authentic perfect cadence.

Arpeggiation, *Unterbrechung* and the use of *Züge* were first described thoroughly in Schenker's principal writing on musical analysis, *Der freie Satz* (1935). Among other important methods of prolongation described in it are ÜBERGREIFEN, UNTERGREIFEN, AUSFALTUNG, HÖHERLEGUNG, TIEFERLEGUNG and KOPPELUNG.

WILLIAM DRABKIN

Promenade concerts. Informal concerts at which inexpensive tickets are sold for standing room or floor space (although not actually for 'promenading' in the manner of the 18th- and 19th-century London pleasure-garden concerts; *see* LONDON, §V). The most famous, the London Henry Wood Promenade Concerts, started in 1895 and have been given in the Royal Albert Hall since World War II. They were anticipated by other informal concerts given from 1838, themselves modelled on those given in Paris by Philippe Musard from 1833 (*see* LONDON, §VI, 4, ii). 'Proms' have been given elsewhere in Britain, notably in Manchester by the Hallé Orchestra. From 1972 opera and ballet proms were given at Covent Garden, and in 1976 they were introduced at the Scottish Opera in Glasgow. Similar informal concerts are given in the USA, sometimes with refreshments served to the audience; they include the 'Boston Pops' and, in New York, proms and the 'Rug Concerts' initiated by Boulez.

Promethean chord. *See* MYSTIC CHORD.

Pro-Musica. American society, one of several formed in the 1920s to promote new and unfamiliar music. Founded and directed by the French pianist E. Robert Schmitz in New York in April 1920, it was known as the Franco-American Musical Society during its first few years, when its aim was to internationalize music by an exchange between France and the USA. A broader base was sought, the name was changed to Pro-Musica Inc, and chapters were activated, some in the west and mid-west of the USA, others in Canada, Europe and the Far East. During the 12 years of its existence Pro-Musica established over 40 chapters in, for instance, Boston, New York, Cincinnati, Cleveland, Chicago, Minneapolis, St Paul, Salt Lake City, Seattle, Kansas City, Denver, Berkeley, San Francisco, Los Angeles, Montreal, London, Paris, Tokyo, Honolulu and Moscow. Schmitz sought support from socially and financially prominent patrons for his advisory board and for each chapter in order to achieve his aim for Pro-Musica, as stated in the articles of incorporation of the society: 'Its objective is to stimulate and promote a better understanding, relationship and co-operation between nations, races, societies and classes by making available the best of the past, present and future artistic compositions in the field of music and allied arts'.

Schmitz had contacts with many musicians in Europe. He had studied at the Paris Conservatoire and with Debussy, had toured Europe extensively as a soloist and accompanist for singers, and had conducted his own orchestra in Paris before World War I. He was able to arrange appearances and tours for many of the most important composers of the century; he introduced (often for the first time) the music and the composers themselves to audiences in big cities and in remote areas which would not otherwise have had the opportunity to hear them. Pro-Musica chapters became part of the established musical life in each city, with concerts by local performers interspersed with appearances by guest composers on tour. In 1928 Ravel's first appearance in the USA was sponsored by Pro-Musica, and was followed by a tour of lecture-recitals for 30 chapters. During the same year Bartók and Respighi were introduced and made extensive tours of the USA and Canada, American works were heard by the Paris chapter, and the American tenor Roland Hayes sang in Moscow and Leningrad. Among the many artists to appear for Pro-Musica were Hindemith, Schoenberg, Honegger, Milhaud, Roussel, Tansman, Prokofiev, Casella, Bliss, Tailleferre, Schmitt, Kodály, Stravinsky, Webern, Tcherepnin and Toch.

From 1923 Pro-Musica sponsored International Referendum Concerts with programmes suggested by their international advisory board. Several important premières were given, such as two of Ives's *Three Quarter-tone Pieces* in February 1925. *Pro-Musica Quarterly*, published four times a year by the society, was edited by Germaine Schmitz (wife of the founder) under the name of Ely Jade. It featured articles on music and news of the activities of the organization.

VIVIAN PERLIS

Pro Musica, New York. American ensemble founded in 1952 by NOAH GREENBERG.

Pro Musica Antiqua. Belgian ensemble of singers and instrumentalists. It was formed in 1933 by the conductor Safford Cape and specialized in 13th- to 16th-century music. Van den Borren served as the group's musicological adviser. After the success of its initial concerts in the Netherlands and Belgium Pro Musica Antiqua performed throughout Europe and later in both North and South America. The ensemble was praised for its efforts to attain an ever-higher standard of historical authenticity, using reproductions of rare historical instruments, and for its tasteful and poetic musical interpretations. Soon after its formation the group began recording for L'Anthologie Sonore, directed by Curt Sachs, and the History of European Music in Sound. In 1939 it made soundtracks of music by Dufay and Obrecht for the exhibition of Belgian art of the period at the New York World's Fair. After a five-year interruption during the war, the ensemble resumed its concert and recording activity in 1946 and made a large number of long-playing records of early music. Franz Mertens, a member from 1936, succeeded Cape as director in 1967. The group retired after a farewell concert on Belgian radio in 1974.

HOWARD SCHOTT

Pronomus [Pronomos] (*fl c*440 BC). Greek poet and musician, the most famous of the Theban school of auletes. An epigram (*Greek Anthology*, xvi, no.28), perhaps early in date, celebrates their skill and the special pre-eminence of Pronomus. His renown was such that

he gave lessons to Alcibiades (Athenaeus, iv, p.184*d*); Aristophanes (*Ecclesiazusae*, l.102) mentions him in passing, not unfavourably. Both Pausanias (ix, 12, 5; cf 6) and Athenaeus (xiv, 631*e*) state that he was the first to play a number of modes (*harmoniai*) on one double-aulos. The former specified these as the familiar basic group consisting of Dorian, Phrygian and Lydian; Athenaeus referred simply to 'the modes' (the emendation 'all the modes' comes from a 19th-century editor). K. Schlesinger suggested that Pronomus might have achieved his feat by extending the straw mouthpiece, thus obtaining Phrygian and Lydian as species (*eidē*) of Dorian; this has been disputed. With the help of rotating bands, however, he could have produced true modes. Such fittings are known to have been in use from the middle of the 5th century BC; they served to cover or expose auxiliary finger holes. Alternatively, his auloi may have had the finger holes arranged in staggered rows, although Pollux (iv, §80) states that Diodorus of Thebes introduced this modification. However perfected, the aulos of Pronomus's period was undoubtedly the instrument banned from Plato's ideal state because of its 'panharmonic' capacities (*Republic*, 399*d*, ll.3–4).

When the Peloponnesian city of Messene was founded in 369 BC, the builders worked to the rival aulos melodies of Pronomus and the composer Sacadas of Argos (Pausanias, iv, 27, 7). A well-known vase of the late 5th century BC probably shows Pronomus (rather than his son, also named Pronomus), accompanying the performance of a satyr-play (*see* GREECE, fig.3). He would have been responsible for the music; by this time, any such setting would have been composed by the aulete, not by the dramatic poet.

BIBLIOGRAPHY
F. Greif: 'Etudes sur la musique antique', *Revue des études grecques*, xxiii (1910), 1–48, esp. 33–41
J. M. Edmonds, ed. and trans.: *Lyra graeca*, iii (London and Cambridge, Mass., 1927, 6/1967), 268ff
A. W. Pickard-Cambridge: *Dithyramb Tragedy and Comedy* (Oxford, 1927, 2/1962 rev. T. B. L. Webster), 55, 312, pl.xiii
K. Schlesinger: *The Greek Aulos* (London, 1939/R1970), 70ff
D. L. Page, ed.: *Poetae melici graeci* (Oxford, 1962), 396
WARREN ANDERSON

Prooimion [proimion] (Gk.: 'proem', 'introduction'; Lat. *prooemium*, *proemium*, *premium*, *prohemium* etc). A term used, like *anabolē*, in various musical contexts since antiquity, signifying some sense of the word 'prelude'. TERPANDER (*fl* 7th century BC) is said to have made lyric *prooimia* as prefaces to the public recitation of Homeric epics; the Homeric Hymns were likewise termed *prooimia* in antiquity, though the longer hymns may well have constituted independent pieces (Sikes and Allen, 2/1936, esp. pp.lxv, xciiiff). Three settings of *prooimia* survive from late antiquity (*see* MESOMEDES). For further references to the *prooimion* in antiquity, *see* ALCMAN; SACADAS OF ARGOS; STESICHORUS.

In Byzantine chant the *prooimion* (also termed *koukoulion*, with alternative English spellings *cuculion*, *kukulion* etc) is the introductory strophe of a kontakion, which differs metrically from the succeeding stanzas (*see* BYZANTINE RITE, MUSIC OF THE, §10). The 'prooimiac psalm' (*ho prooimiakos psalmos*) is the introductory psalm at Hesperinos, or Byzantine Vespers, Psalm ciii in the Septuagint. The simple refrains customary in the prooimiac psalm were greatly extended and elaborated from the 14th century (*see* HESPERINOS; KOUKOUZELES, JOANNES; LAMPADARIOS, JOANNES).

16th-century Latin humanists revived the terms *anabolē* and *prooemium*: HANS KOTTER used the latter term to mean 'prelude' in his keyboard tablatures.

BIBLIOGRAPHY

E. E. Sikes and T. W. Allen, eds.: *The Homeric Hymns* (London, 1904, 2/1936 rev. T. W. Allen, W. R. Halliday and E. E. Sikes)

R. Böhme: *Das Prooimion: eine Form sakraler Dichtung der Griechen* (Bühl, 1937)

H. Koller: 'Das kitharodische Prooimion', *Philologus*, c (1956), 159–206

Proper chants (from Lat. *Proprium* [*missae et officii*]). Chants whose texts vary from day to day, as distinct from those whose texts remain constant (ORDINARY CHANTS). Strictly the term applies to chants from both Mass and Office, but it is customary to use the term chiefly to refer to Mass chants, owing to the need for terms that distinguish between those parts of the Mass most often set polyphonically from the second half of the 14th century onwards (the Ordinary), and those usually sung as plainchant. Nevertheless, there are settings of cycles of Proper chants by, for example, composers of the Notre Dame School (*see* MAGNUS LIBER), Isaac and Byrd.

The Proper chants of the Mass are the introit, gradual, alleluia, tract, offertory and communion. The sequence, sung throughout the Middle Ages on important feast days, may also be included in this category, as may also tropes, adjuncts to the above group of chants, which were always Proper to a particular feast. The principle of varying chants for reasons of liturgical propriety also affects the unvarying texts of the Ordinary (Kyrie, Gloria etc) in that they may be sung to a small corpus of different melodies, each one for use on a different occasion (double feasts, single feasts, feasts of the BVM etc).

See also MASS, §I, 2.

Proper of the Saints (from Lat. *Sanctorale*). The collective name for the year's cycle of services of the Western Church in commemoration of saints (apostles, evangelists, martyrs, doctors, bishops, confessors, virgins etc), including the Blessed Virgin Mary; hence also the name for the part of a liturgical book containing the services. Only those services with individual formularies (usually for the most revered saints, but this varies from church to church) are said to be 'Proper'; formularies where the saint's name is not specified and may be supplied as required are gathered elsewhere in liturgical books, forming the COMMON OF SAINTS. The separation of the saints' services from the PROPER OF THE TIME in liturgical books occurred from the 11th and 12th centuries, when formularies for the Sundays after Epiphany (until Septuagesima), Easter and Whitsun (less ancient than other parts of the Proper of the Time) displaced the saints' services which had formerly appeared in blocks during the year's cycle. The separation happened in different ways and periods in different parts of Europe.

For more details *see* SOURCES, MS, §II; *see also* LITURGY AND LITURGICAL BOOKS.

Proper of the Time (from Lat. *Temporale*). The collective name for the year's cycle of services of the Western Church, except nearly all those in commemoration of saints; hence, also, that part of a liturgical book containing the services. The cycle revolves elliptically round Christmas Day (25 December), its Octave (1 January,

Feast of Circumcision) and Epiphany (6 January), whose dates are constant; and Easter and Whitsun (Pentecost), and, from the 11th century, Trinity, whose dates vary from year to year. All Sundays are named in relation to these high feasts. Early liturgical books included the services for saints side by side with the other formularies at their appropriate place in the church year, but from the 11th and 12th centuries these were increasingly written in a separate part of a liturgical book (the PROPER OF THE SAINTS and COMMON OF SAINTS). Several of the saints' days in the Christmas season, however (e.g. St Stephen, 26 December, St John the Evangelist, 27 December, Holy Innocents, 28 December), have remained, anomalously, in their ancient place within the Proper of the Time.

For more details *see* SOURCES, MS, §II; *see also* LITURGY AND LITURGICAL BOOKS.

Prophecies. Lessons from the Books of the Prophets, replacing the Epistle at Mass at various times during the year such as Epiphany, the Monday, Tuesday and Wednesday of Holy Week, and used above all on Holy Saturday, the liturgy for which includes a set of nine (formerly 12) readings (not all from the Book of the Prophets, however). A further group of ancient writings was widely regarded as prophetic of Christ in the Middle Ages and Renaissance, even though it was noncanonical and not admitted to the liturgy; this was the Sibylline Oracles. Music concerned with the Sibyls includes Lassus's *Prophetiae Sibyllarum*, a motet cycle for four voices representing the sayings of 12 Sibyls. *See* SIBYL, SONG OF THE.

RICHARD SHERR

Prophetarum, ordo (Lat.: 'ceremony of the prophets'). A title given to a dramatic or semi-dramatic presentation of prophecies of the Coming of Christ. The text originated in the Pseudo-Augustinian sermon 'Contra Judaeos' (*PL*, xlii, p.1117); Old Testament prophecies, and others by Virgil and the Sibyl (*see* SIBYL, SONG OF THE), were included. An early versified *ordo prophetarum* is found, with musical notation, in a St Martial troper (*F-Pn* lat.1139, 11th–12th centuries). A 14th-century version without music, from Rouen (*F-Rm* 384), is headed *Ordo processionis asinorum* ('Ceremony of the procession of the asses') and may be related to the liturgical revels known as the Feast of Fools. The ass is that of the prophet Balaam (*Numbers* xxii.21).

See also MEDIEVAL DRAMA, §II, 2; FEAST OF FOOLS; ADAM, PLAY OF.

JOHN STEVENS

Prophetia (Lat.: 'prophecy'). A name given to the *Benedictus* as a chant of the ancient Gallican Mass; *see* GALLICAN RITE, MUSIC OF THE, §7(iv).

Prophetologion (Gk.). A lectionary of the Byzantine rite; *see* LECTIONARY and BYZANTINE RITE, MUSIC OF THE, §2.

Propiac, (Catherine Joseph Ferdinand) Girard de (*b* Dijon, 1759; *d* Paris, 31 Oct 1823). French man of letters and composer. He began composing at an early age and made his début in 1787 at the Comédie-Italienne with *Isabelle et Rosalvo* and *Les deux morts*, both *opéras comiques*. Between 1787 and 1790 he composed three more, which had some success. He emigrated in 1791, served in Condé's anti-Revolutionary army and stayed for a time in Hamburg. He returned to

Paris after Napoleon came to power in November 1799 and under the Consulate (1799–1802) obtained a post as archivist to the Prefecture of the Seine. Thereafter he devoted himself almost exclusively to literature, though he composed two minor *opéras comiques*; these were probably occasional works, performed in small theatres. His literary works include several translations.

WORKS

All stage works were first performed at the Comédie-Italienne, Paris, unless otherwise stated.

Isabelle et Rosalvo (comédie with ariettes, 1, M.-V. Patrat), 18 June 1787 (Brussels and Paris, 1788), excerpts pubd separately
Les deux morts (opéra comique), 20 June 1787 (Brussels, 1788)
Les trois déesses rivales, ou Le double jugement de Paris (comédie lyrique, 1, J. de Piis), 28 July 1788 (Paris, ?1788), excerpts pubd separately
La fausse paysanne, ou L'heureuse inconséquence (comédie, 3, de Piis), 26 March 1789 (Paris, ?1789), excerpts pubd separately
Les savoyards, ou La continence de Bayard (comédie, 1), 30 May 1789
La double apothéose (opéra comique, 2), Paris, Théâtre des Troubadours, 1800
La pension des jeunes garçons (opéra comique, 1), Paris, Théâtre des Jeunes Artistes, 1801
Romances on poems by Patrat; many romances in contemporary anthologies

BIBLIOGRAPHY
FétisB
M. Briquet: 'Propiac, Catherine Joseph Ferdinand, Chevalier Girard de', *MGG*

PAULETTE LETAILLEUR

Proportions (from Lat. *proportio*). As applied to music, the relationships between numbers, deduced in the form of a ratio, for both pitches and time-units in Western music. Proportions in the sense of relationships between note values became the subject of speculation and controversy in theoretical writing of the late 15th century. Signatures indicating proportional alteration of note values were widely used in 15th- and 16th-century music.

1. General. 2. Renaissance theory and practice.

1. GENERAL. It was natural for medieval scholars trained in the Boethian Quadrivium, where music was juxtaposed with the three sciences of arithmetic, astronomy and geometry, to give mathematical expression to the essence of music. That intervals between notes, for instance, could be expressed as mathematical ratios meant that they could also easily be related to other natural phenomena susceptible to mathematical interpretation, and ultimately to abstract and speculative concepts and ideals – the harmony of the spheres, and divine and universal principles of form. 'The body of the universe was created to be at unity owing to proportion; in consequence it acquired concord' (Plato: *Timaeus*, trans. H. D. P. Lee, 1965, p.44).

Since Pythagoras's famous observations on the sounds produced when hammers of different sizes struck an anvil, intervals between notes had usually been expressed as numerical ratios. In the Middle Ages the ratio was reckoned in terms of the lengths of the string of the monochord required to produce the notes. Thus the interval of the 4th, the *diatessaron* (literally: 'through four [notes]'), was formed by two notes whose respective lengths on the monochord were in the ratio 4:3. The 5th (*diapente*: literally: 'through five [notes]') was expressed as the ratio 3:2; and the octave (*diapason*: literally: 'through all [notes]') was 2:1.

Some metric changes in the music of the late Middle Ages and Renaissance, those outside the normal scope of the mensural system, were effected by a system of proportions: a proportional signature indicated a differ-

ent value for the notes of a piece, relative to their previous value (or 'normal' value, however that might be understood). The proportion might affect a passage within one voice of a piece; might distinguish one or more voices from the others throughout the piece; or might affect all voices simultaneously in the course of a piece. While the first two cases present no ambiguities, the third is open to misunderstanding, since the relationship between note values is indicated only by the signature, and this may be interpreted differently by different composers and theorists. The interpretation of signatures in this case must take into account the consensus of opinion at the time and place relevant to the composition, since a minority of theorists might disagree and a minority of compositions might use the signature in a different way. An ideal situation, from the modern interpreter's point of view, exists where each composer's favoured practice is known, as for Dufay (see Hamm) and Isaac (see Gossett), despite inevitable minor points of controversy. Mendel highlighted elements of conflict and suggested the criteria that the ideal should satisfy.

A further ambiguity concerns the use of a signature normally indicating a proportion as the initial signature of a piece. Since there is disagreement among both ancient and modern theorists as to the place and the effect of the *tactus*, or pulse, in a given mensuration, it is occasionally unclear how this use of signature should be interpreted in terms of pulse. The interpretation will affect the modern editor's choice of note values in transcription and the modern performers' choice of speed. This may often be resolved with reasonable success by computing the frequency with which notes of a particular value are used and relating this to a composer's normal practice (as Hamm did for Dufay).

2. RENAISSANCE THEORY AND PRACTICE. For an introduction to the complexities and confusions which the system of proportions involved both in theory and practice, see the standard textbooks on notation by Wolf and Apel. Ex.1 (also cited in Hamm, p.29) shows the principle on which the system was based: a sign indicates that the value of the minim decreases in the ratio 4:3; each minim loses a quarter of its value. It is characteristic that a sign derived from one of the common mensuration signs should have been used to effect the diminution of value. Composers appear to have felt it desirable to use a sign that expressed the mensural relations between the different levels of note values. Thus in ex.1, the reversed C has two semibreves to the breve and two minims to the semibreve, just as C would have. But to have used C in this case would have implied no diminution in the value of the minim, which in this period remained constant through a change of mensuration. A modified mensuration sign indicated a proportional change rather than a simple mensural one.

Following Boethius, theorists of the late 15th century classed the proportions into species or genera. Proportions of the type n:1 (2:1, 3:1, 4:1 etc) had the quality of the *genus multiplex* and were called simply *dupla*, *tripla*, *quadrupla* and so on. Proportions of the type $n + 1$:n (3:2, 4:3 etc) belonged to the *genus superparticularis* and their names all contained the prefix *sesqui-* (originally *semique-*: 'and a half'), as in *sesquialtera*, *sesquitertia*, *sesquiquarta* and so on. Proportions of the type $n + 2$:n, $n + 3$:n, $n + 4$:n and so on belonged to the *genus superpartiens*; their names ended with the value of

Ex.1 from Dufay: *Alma redemptoris mater*

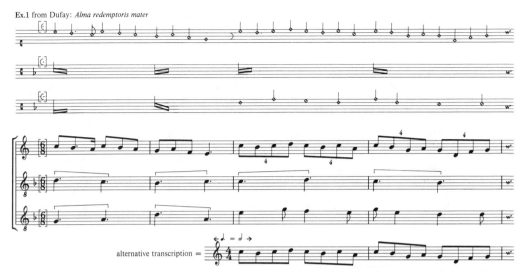

alternative transcription =

n, and the value of the added number was indicated within the adjective *super . . . partiente*; so that the *proportio supertripartiente quintas*, for instance, was $n + 3:n = 5 + 3:5 = 8:5$. Even more impractical proportions were of the *genus multiplex superparticulare*, of the type $n \times m + 1:n$; thus the *proportio tripla sesquiquarta* was $n \times 3 + 1:n = 4 \times 3 + 1:4 = 13:4$. Crowning the rest came the fifth species, the *genus multiplex superpartiens*, proportions of the type $n \times m + 2:n$, $n \times m + 3:n$, $n \times m + 4:n$ and so on; the *proportio quadrupla supertripartiente quintas* was $5 \times 4 + 3:5 = 23:5$. To reverse the whole ratio (for indicating an augmentation rather than a diminution of value) the prefix *sub*- was added to the name. Thus the *proportio subtripla* was $1:3$.

The *dupla* proportion was known to Jehan des Murs at the beginning of the 14th century (under the name *diminutio*). The system was described in increasing detail by theorists from Prosdocimus de Beldemandis (1404), through Guillelmus Monachus (c1460) and Tinctoris (c1473–5) to Gaffurius (1496), by which time the theoretical possibilities described far exceeded the needs of actual performance. Morley gave a detailed description of the system in *A Plaine and Easie Introduction to Practicall Musicke* (1597; ed. Harman, p.214) but lampooned it later in his treatise:

it was a world to hear them wrangle, every one defending his own [Proportions] for the best. 'What?' saith one, 'you keep not time in your Proportions.' 'You sing them false,' saith the other. 'What Proportion is this?' saith he. 'Sesquipaltry,' saith the other. 'Nay,' would the other say, 'you sing you know not what; it should seem you came lately from a barber's shop where you had "Gregory Walker" or a Curranta played in the new Proportions by them lately found out, called "Sesquiblinda" and "Sesquihearkenafter'.

Although controversy surrounds another aspect of time in Renaissance polyphony, the *tactus*, as a general rule the downbeat–upbeat unit comprising the *tactus* may be said usually to have occupied a semibreve, outside proportional time. Italian theorists of the 16th century referred to music in normal or whole values (*integer valor*) as being written 'alla semibreve'. *Proportio dupla*, where the value of each note was halved, did not alter the time occupied by the *tactus* unit, but in the proportion it would be equivalent to a breve (*alla breve*); *proportio quadrupla* resulted in music *alla longa*. The term 'alla breve' with the signature ¢ has survived until today, still implying relatively quick tempo because the strong beat falls on a larger note value than in C (or 4/4) time.

See also NOTATION, §III, 3(vii), 4(iii), and THEORY, THEORISTS.

BIBLIOGRAPHY

J. Wolf: *Geschichte der Mensuralnotation von 1250 bis 1460* (Leipzig, 1904)
——: *Handbuch der Notationskunde* (Leipzig, 1913–19)
W. Apel: *The Notation of Polyphonic Music, 900–1600* (Cambridge, Mass., 1942, rev. 5/1953)
H. Hewitt: 'A Study in Proportions', *Essays on Music in Honor of Archibald Thompson Davison* (Cambridge, Mass., 1957), 69
C. Dahlhaus: 'Zur Theorie des Tactus im 16. Jahrhundert', *AMw*, xvii (1960)
U. Günther: 'Die Anwendung der Diminution in der Handschrift Chantilly 1047', *AMw*, xvii (1960), 1
——: 'Der Gebrauch des *tempus perfectum diminutum* in der Handschrift Chantilly 1047', *AMw*, xvii (1960), 277
C. Hamm: *A Chronology of the Works of Guillaume Dufay based on a Study of Mensural Practice* (Princeton, 1964)
A. Hughes: 'Mensuration and Proportion in Early 15th Century English Music', *AcM*, xxvii (1965), 48
A. Mendel: 'Some Ambiguities of the Mensural System', *Studies in Music History: Essays for Oliver Strunk* (Princeton, 1968), 137
P. Gossett: 'The Mensural System and the "Choralis Constantinus" ', *Studies in Renaissance and Baroque Music in Honor of Arthur Mendel* (Kassel and Hackensack, 1974), 71–107

Proportz (Ger.: 'proportion'). A term used in 16th- and 17th-century Germany for an after-dance derived from a duple-metre dance (e.g. allemande or pavan) by the application of *proportio sesquialtera* to the melody of the first dance, that is, three notes of the after-dance in the time of two notes in the model. Sometimes such after-dances were incorrectly labelled 'Proportz tripla', meaning that three notes of the after-dance took the time of one in the model (*see* NACHTANZ).

Proposta (It.: 'proposal'). In FUGUE, the SUBJECT, as opposed to the answer. The term gained currency in the writings on fugue of Italian theorists in the Baroque period; the term for the answer is *risposta*.

Proprietas (Lat.: 'propriety'). In mensural music of the late 13th century, a quality of ligatures that depended on the value of the first note of the ligature. The first note was normally assumed to be a breve unless its normal shape was modified. If the first note was of normal shape (for an ascending ligature this meant without tail, for a descending ligature this meant with a tail descending to the left) then the ligature had propriety and the first note was a breve. If the ascending ligature began with a note with a tail descending to the right, or if the descending ligature began with a note without a tail, then the ligature had no propriety and the first note was a long. Ligatures *cum opposita proprietate* were a special case, written with a tail ascending to the left, where the first two notes of the ligature were always understood to be semibreves. A quality of ligatures that depended on the value of the final note of the ligature, *perfectio* ('perfection'), was governed by similar rules. For the usual shapes for two-note ligatures *see* PERFECTIO, Table 1. Ligatures of three, four and more notes were governed by the same rules, with all but the first and last notes understood to be breves (except in the case of opposite propriety, when the second note was always a semibreve).

See also LIGATURE; NOTATION, §III, 2(vii), 3(ii); and RHYTHMIC MODES.

BIBLIOGRAPHY
F. Reckow: 'Proprietas', *HMT*

Prosa [prose]. A text for a sequence (*see* SEQUENCE (i)). The term was sometimes used loosely in medieval sources to apply to texts of other kinds of chants, for example Kyries, or to text underlay for melismas (a phenomenon better referred to as PROSULA).

A *prosa* in the restricted sense is a Latin text constructed largely in 'couplets': two lines of text set syllabically to the same phrase of music, hence having the same (or almost the same) syllable count. Successive couplets are of varying lengths, however, so that the line structure of the whole is not regular, like verse, but irregular. In the early repertory (written *c*850–1000) *prosae* neither scanned nor rhymed, but later they did both, becoming almost indistinguishable from verse.

Frequently a number of *prosae* were written to one sequence melody, but (in the early repertory, at least) any given *prosa* could be sung to only one melody. *Prosae* were sung at Mass after the alleluia. Usually they were proper to a holy day or saint's day. The entire repertory consists of several thousand items, as published in *Analecta hymnica medii aevi*. Volume liii contains most of the early repertory.

The term *prosa* is a late Latin contraction of the expression *prorsus oratio* ('straightforward discourse') being the classical circumlocution for language not cast in verse. During the early medieval period, however, the term was used particularly for 'art prose', i.e. prose that was elevated in style by careful attention to rhythm (for example, use of the so-called cursus) including the construction of clauses (*cola*) and periods; and to diction, especially assonance and eventually rhyme. 'Rhymed prose' was a striking development of the 9th and 10th centuries. The couplets used in this prose (or sequence) can be viewed as a systematic application of *bicola* or pairs of clauses, as described by late Latin rhetoricians.

The term *prosa* is first applied regularly to the texts of sequences in 10th-century manuscripts. One of the earliest such appearances is in *F-Pn* lat.1240 (923–4), as *congregatio prosarum* ('collection of *prosae*' – which, however, also includes some prosulas). NOTKER of St Gall (*c*840–912) published his *prosae* under the title *Liber hymnorum* (884). There is no information concerning terminology used for the West Frankish repertory of the 9th century. *Prosae* were regularly sung (rather than recited or read silently), and the melodies – the sequences – were in the first instance to be sung with their *prosae* (although some scholars feel that sequences

were originally – or also – sung without text, as melismas, or played on instruments); therefore 'prosa' and 'sequence' came to be virtually interchangeable terms, each referring to melody plus text.

Prosae were composed in a wide variety of styles. Early West Frankish examples sometimes betray their descent from the tradition of highly rhythmic, sonorous, colourful but non-classical Latin cultivated particularly by Irish monks. Notker's *prosae*, on the other hand, are distinguished by their careful observance of classical canons of taste; beyond that, Notker's texts have a superior poetic quality, but they are not as musical as the West Frankish ones. During the 10th and 11th centuries, *prosae* often became *poesia per musica*, less interesting in their own right than the melodies they served; but sometimes they were vehicles for elaborate rhetorical conceits and inventions. In the hands of ADAM OF ST VICTOR in the 12th century they became exquisite meditations on sacred subjects, now cast entirely in rhyme and scansion, using the highly developed poetic-religious diction of the later Middle Ages.

BIBLIOGRAPHY
G. M. Dreves and [later] C. Blume, eds.: *Analecta hymnica medii aevi* (Leipzig, 1886–1922), vii–x, xxxiv, xxxvii, xxxix, xl, xlii, xliv, liii–lv
T. F. Kelly: 'New Music from Old: the Structuring of Responsory Prosas', *JAMS*, xxx (1977), 366

RICHARD L. CROCKER

Proscaenium (Lat.). PROSKĒNION.

Prosdocimus de Beldemandis (*b* ?Padua; *d* Padua, 1428). Italian theorist in the fields of mathematics, astronomy and music. After studying at the universities of Bologna and Padua, he taught at the University of Padua. His first musical treatise, written in 1404 and entitled *Exposiciones tractatus pratice cantus mensurabilis magistri Johannis de Muris*, is an extensive commentary on the work of that French theorist. In 1408 Prosdocimus considerably abridged the work, changing it so that it was no longer a commentary, as the *Tractatus pratice cantus mensurabilis*; only the first and last pages of this version of the work survive. In 1409 he compiled a *Brevis summula proporcionum quantum ad musicam pertinet* (*CS*, iii, 258–61); in this work traditional commonplaces regarding intervallic proportions are expounded, although in other works he applied the terminology and notation of mathematical proportions also to ratios between rhythmic values, thus placing himself among the pioneers of a new department of musical theory.

On 15 May 1409 Prosdocimus proceeded to the degree of doctor *in artibus* at the University of Padua; his sponsor was Biagio Pelacani, a famous scientist, who attended the literary and musical meetings described by GIOVANNI DA PRATO. A new period in Prosdocimus's activity as a theorist, in which he revised earlier works, began after he had proceeded to the degree of doctor in medicine (15 April 1411, also at Padua). At this time he produced second versions of his *Exposiciones . . . Johannis de Muris* (ed. F. A. Gallo) and the *Tractatus pratice cantus mensurabilis* (*CS*, iii, 200–28) and three new works, all written at Montagnana in 1412: a *Contrapunctus* (*CS*, iii, 193–9) containing rules for note-against-note two-voice counterpoint, a *Tractatus plane musice*, a compilation of received theory concerning plainsong, with examples of the psalm tones, and a *Tractatus pratice cantus mensurabilis ad modum ytalicorum* (*CS*, iii, 228–48) in which are expounded the original features of 14th-century Italian notation which had by then become quite submerged in those of France. Then, at Padua in 1413, Prosdocimus wrote the *Parvus tractatulus de modo monocordum dividendi* (*CS*, iii, 248–58), in which he described three different ways of dividing the monochord. This work was dedicated to Nicolaus de Collo da Conegliano, a university colleague.

With this treatise, Prosdocimus had exhausted the topics of contemporary music theory, and for several years he wrote nothing. In 1425, however, he produced his *Tractatus musicae speculative* as a polemic against part of the *Lucidarium* of Marchetto da Padova. This work was dedicated to a close friend of Prosdocimus, Luca de Lendenaria, who had died in September 1424: Luca had been a singer at Padua Cathedral and had studied music with Prosdocimus in their youth (*see* LUCA, D.). In the work, Prosdocimus particularly attacked Marchetto's division of the whole tone into five equal parts called *dieses* (singular *diesis*). This treatise seems to have revived Prosdocimus's interest in music theory. He revised practically all his earlier works, producing a third version of the *Tractatus pratice cantus mensurabilis* and second versions of the *Contrapunctus*, the *Tractatus plane musice*, the *Tractatus pratice cantus mensurabilis ad modum ytalicorum* (ed. C. Sartori) and the *Parvus tractatulus de modo monocordum dividendi*. These revisions were accomplished mainly by adding material related to his arguments against Marchetto's fivefold division of the whole tone; he expressly cited arguments developed at greater length in the *Tractatus musicae speculative*.

Prosdocimus's fundamental bias was towards older theorists and practice. He cited Franco with approval; his only polyphonic examples are two 14th-century French motets; Jehan des Murs was undoubtedly the theorist with the greatest influence on him. He adopted a rather polemical attitude towards contemporary music: he expressly denied an assertion of Egidius de Murino, and repeatedly criticized contemporary musicians. Prosdocimus's opposition to modernity was not absolute, however, nor unreasoned – he even suggested notational innovations; but he thought it indispensable that new ideas should be tested by both reason and tradition. For the modern reader the polemical observations which enliven most of his writings offer much valuable information about Italian music in the early 15th century, and reveal an original and individual personality.

BIBLIOGRAPHY
A. Favaro: 'Intorno alla vita ed alle opere di Prosdocimo de Beldomandi matematico padovano del secolo XV', *Bullettino di bibliografia e di storia delle scienze matematiche e fisiche*, xii (1879), 1–74, 115–251
——: 'Appendice agli studi intorno alla vita ed alle opere di Prosdocimo de Beldomandi matematico padovano del secolo XV', *Bullettino di bibliografia e di storia delle scienze matematiche e fisiche*, xviii (1885), 405
D. R. Baralli and L. Torri: 'Il *Trattato* di Prosdocimo de' Beldomandi contro il *Lucidario* di Marchetto da Padova', *RMI*, xx (1913), 707–62
C. Sartori: *La notazione italiana del trecento in una redazione inedita del Tractatus pratice cantus mensurabilis di Prosdocimo de Beldemandis* (Florence, 1938)
F. A. Gallo: 'La tradizione dei trattati musicali di Prosdocimo de Beldemandis', *Quadrivium*, vi (1964), 57
——: *La teoria della notazione in Italia dalla fine del XIII all'inizio del XV secolo* (Bologna, 1966), 87ff
——, ed.: *Prosdocimi de Beldemandis 'Expositiones tractatus pratice cantus mensurabilis magistri Johannis de Muris'* (Bologna, 1966)
——: 'Citazioni di teorici medievali nelle lettere di Giovanni del Lago', *Quadrivium*, xiv (1973), 171
——: 'La trattatistica musicale', *Storia della cultura veneta*, ii, ed. G. Folena (Venice, 1976)

F. ALBERTO GALLO

Prose. *See* PROSA.

Prošev, Toma (*b* Skopje, 10 Nov 1931). Yugoslav composer and conductor. After completing studies at the Zagreb Academy of Music in 1957, he studied composition at the Ljubljana Academy under Škerjanc (until 1960) and later in Paris with Boulanger. He was music editor with Radio-Televizije Zagreb (1957–60) and a lecturer at the Lisinski Music School in Zagreb (1960–67), while also conducting the Musica Viva ensemble. Returning to Skopje in 1967 as a lecturer at the Visoki Music School, he continued his conducting activities with the Sveta Sofija Ensemble, as well as in opera and ballet.

Prošev's early works, written between 1950 and 1957, employ a moderately advanced European mainstream style influenced by Hindemith and making much use of folksong. From 1957 to 1963, influenced by his further studies and contacts, he made considerable use of 12-note procedures. After 1963 he composed works using free atonal methods with some debt to serial techniques, great formal freedom, frequent though clearly circumscribed aleatory coordination and occasional employment of electronic sounds.

WORKS
(*selective list*)

DRAMATIC AND VOCAL
Operas: Paučina [The spider's web], 1958; Mali princ [The little prince], 1966
Ballets: Okviri i odjeci [Frames and echoes], 1961; Pesma nad pesmama, 1967; Relacije [Relaxations], 1969
Oratorios: Jama [The pit] (I. G. Kovačić), 1961; Skopje (A. Popovski), 1965; Sunce prastare zemlje [The sun of the ancient earth] (Popovski), 1966; Poruka [The message] (G. Todoroski), 1968
Cantatas: U zbegu, 1959; Epitaf, 1v, orch, 1961; Car Samuil [Tsar Samuel], 1965; Dnevnik jednog malenog [Diary of a little man], 1967; Canticum canticorum, chamber cantata, 1967; Jedan Čovek [One man] (C. Janevski), 1968
Other works: Mali ptići [Little bird], suite, chorus, orch, 1964; Sveta Sofija ohridska, 1v, str, 1966; Boje [Colours] (E. Čolaković), S, A, T, B, 2 speakers, chorus, ens, tape, 1967; Čovek [Man], 3 choruses, 1968; Nebo [The sky], 1v, chamber orch, 1968; Luzna [The scar] (Ožiljak), 1v, pf, 1968; Tempera IX, speaker, 1v, chorus, ens, 1974

INSTRUMENTAL
Orch: Pf Concertino, 1958; Makete [Models], 1960; Koncertantna muzika, vc, str, 1960; Sym., 1962; Koncertantne improvizacije, vn, str, 1962; 2 vn concs., 1963, 1969; Ondes Martenot Conc., 1964; Relacije, 1964; 3 kompozicije, cl, str, 1966; Tempera II, str, 1966; Koncertantna muzika, gui, str, 1968; Tempera III, perc, str, 1968; Concertino, ob, str, 1968; Tempera IV, 1969; Svečani preludij [Ceremonial prelude], 1969; Pf Conc., 1969; Tempera V, 1970; Simfonia 2, str, 1971; Tempera VI, str qt, str, 1971; Tempera VII, perc, str, 1972; Simfonijski stav, 1973; Tempera VIII, 3 fl, str, 1973; 3 lirski slike [3 lyrical sketches], 3 fl, str, 1973; Tempera X, chamber orch, 1974
Chamber: Sonata, vn, pf, 1953; Str Qt, 1959; 4 Preludes, str qnt, 1962; La Fontainove basne, str qnt, 1962; Tempera I, hn, str qt, 1963; Radianti, ens, 1963; Wind Qnt, 1963; Str Trio, 1964; Metastaza, ens, 1964; Morphographie, ens, 1965; Diametrija, ens, 1965; 10 Miniatures, vn, pf, 1966; Adagio, eng hn, str qnt, 1968; Oscilacije, str qt, 1968; Kamerna muzika I, bn, ens, 1969; Kamerna muzika II, vc, ens, 1971; Integrali, pf, ens, 1972; Intimni dijalozi, 2 vn, 1972; Musandra 3, brass qnt, 1974
Pf: Klasična sonata, 1953; Intima, 1962; Klasična svita, 1963; Muzička slikovnica [Musical sketchbook], 1965; 5 aforizama, 1965

Principal publishers: Udruženje kompozitora Makedonije, Zimmermann

NIALL O'LOUGHLIN

Proske, Carl [Karl] (*b* Gröbnig, Upper Silesia, 11 Feb 1794; *d* Regensburg, 20 Dec 1861). German music scholar and editor. He was a medical doctor before settling in 1823 in Regensburg, where he turned to the study of theology and was ordained on 11 April 1826. In 1827 he was appointed vicar-choral at the collegiate monastery of the Alte Kapelle in Regensburg; he was made a canon there in 1830. From that time he devoted himself entirely to church music reform, in which he was a highly influential figure. His publishing activities began with the Denkschrift *Die Verbesserung der Domkirchenmusik* (1829–30). Between 1834 and 1838 he made three extended visits to Italy to collect liturgical vocal works; his library (left after his death to the Regensburg bishopric; now *D-Rp*) eventually contained over 3000 examples of 15th- and 16th-century church music. He began publication of the collection *Musica divina* in 1853, completing three volumes in 1859 (a fourth appeared in 1864), and a second selected edition, *Selectus novus missarum*, appeared between 1856 and 1861. Fétis praised these as the most significant such publications of the time. Proske also edited works by Palestrina and A. Scarlatti.

BIBLIOGRAPHY
D. Mettenleiter: *Carl Proske* (Regensburg, 1868, 2/1895)
G. Jakob: 'Dr. Carl Proske', *Caecilienkalender*, ii (1877), 31
F. X. Haberl: 'Zum 100. Geburtstag von Dr. Carl Proske', *KJb*, xix (1894), 22
K. Weinmann: *Carl Proske: der Restaurator der katholischen Kirchenmusik* (Regensburg, 1909)
——: 'Die Proskesche Musikbibliothek in Regensburg', *Festschrift . . . Rochus Freiherrn von Liliencron* (Leipzig, 1910/R1970), 387
O. Ursprung: *Restauration und Palestrina-Renaissance in der katholischen Kirchenmusik* (Augsburg, 1924)
A. Scharnagl: 'Proske als Lasso-Forscher', *KJb*, xli (1957), 147
——: 'Carl Proske zum 100. Todestag', *Musica sacra*, lxxxii (1962), 90
——: 'Dr. Carl Proske: Leben und Werk', *Der Zwiebelturm*, xvii (1962), 2
based on *MGG* (x, 1655–6) by permission of Bärenreiter
AUGUST SCHARNAGL

Proskēnion [proscaenium]. A high platform on a row of columns in front of the SKĒNE, which was used as a raised stage in Greek theatres from the late 4th century BC.

Prosodion [pothodion]. In ancient Greece, a processional dancing song accompanied by the aulos and sung by youths or young girls at a *prosodos* or religious procession to a temple or altar; ancient authors distinguished it from the HYMN. It is attested as early as the 7th century BC but declined from the 5th century BC, although there is evidence that *prosodia* were composed as late as the 2nd century AD. The *prosodion* should be distinguished from the *prosōdia*, meaning a song sung to the accompaniment of the kithara.

BIBLIOGRAPHY
R. Muth: 'Prosodion', *Paulys Real-Encyclopädie der classischen Altertumswissenschaft*, xxiii (Stuttgart, 1957), 856
GEOFFREY CHEW

Prosomoion. A Byzantine TROPARION which is modelled on another hymn and which adopts its melody. *See* AUTOMELON and STICHĒRON.

Prosperi, Carlo (*b* Florence, 13 March 1921). Italian composer. He studied in Florence under, among others, Frazzi and Dallapiccola, obtaining diplomas in the horn (1940) and composition (1949). After eight years in the programme department of RAI in Rome, he returned to the Florence Conservatory as a composition teacher in 1958. He is a member of the Cherubini Academy, Florence.

By turning from the conservative idiom of his early works to a free use of 12-note serialism, Prosperi gained an advantage over many Italian composers of his generation, making a promising début at the 1956 Venice Biennale with *Toccata e fanfara*. The promise was disappointed, however, by the succeeding *Concerto d'infanzia*, a homage to the world of childhood even involving the realistic setting of nursery rhymes. It inaugurated a number of vocal works (*Marezzo*, *Noi solda'* and *Tre canti di Betocchi*), where a problem-free compositional attitude is coupled with poetic contents gradually outlining an intellectual backwater, whose features recall the 'Strapaese' movement of the 1930s. In instrumental works his substantial disengagement from new techniques is first exemplified in *Filigrane*, a disarming contribution to the flute literature, strikingly contrasting with those of the contemporary avant garde. Its simplicity of form and texture and the naivety of its tonal recoveries and instrumental writing recur in later compositions, notably *Incanti*, which seemingly pursue an unconcerned poetry of sound but actually end in a voluntary regression to childlike academicism. Significantly foreshadowed in the youthful *Intervalli*, the hushed atmospheric power of *In nocte secunda*, *Constellazioni* and *Stellae inerrantes* thus may suggest only a tardy 'crepuscolarismo' and not the impressionist revival supposed by some critics.

WORKS
(selective list)

Orch: Variazioni, 1951; Toccata e fanfara, tpts, perc, str, 1955; Rondò-ragtime, 1961; Conc. dell'arcobalens, pf, mar, str, 1972–3
Choral: Marezzo (Montale), speaker, chorus, orch, 1961; Noi solda' (Betocchi, Bedeschi), S, speaker, male vv, orch, 1966; 3 canti di Betocchi, chorus, 3 fl, 1969
Solo vocal· 3 frammenti di Saffo, 1v, pf, 1944; 5 strofe dal greco, S, chamber orch, 1950; Conc. d'infanzia (anon.), female v, orch, 1957; Incanti (Valéry), S, solo insts, orch, 1963
Inst: Sonatina profana, pf, 1943; Introduzione, caccia e ripresa, 3 hn, 1944; Intervalli, pf, 1953; 4 invenzioni, cl, harp, vn, va, 1953; Fantasia, pf, 1955; Filigrane, fl, 1958; White Jazz, vn, 1959; In nocte, vn, gui, 1964; In nocte secunda, gui, hpd, 6 vn, 1968; Stellae inerrantes, 3 gui, 1970; Costellazioni, hpd, 1971; Tityrus, 4 rec (1 player), 1973; Canto dell'arpeggione, gui, 1974; Chant, vn, pf, 1975; Melody for Mavi and Michael, vn, harmonium, 1975; Toccata, str, 1975

Principal publishers: Ricordi, Suvini Zerboni

WRITINGS
L'atonalità nella musica contemporanea (Caltanissetta and Rome, 1957)

BIBLIOGRAPHY
R. Vlad: *Storia della dodecafonia* (Milan, 1958), 252f
G. Cogni: 'A proposito di *In nocte secunda* di Carlo Prosperi', *Chigiana*, xxv (1968), 305
CLAUDIO ANNIBALDI

Prosula. A prosula is a text created to fit a melisma in Gregorian chant. Alternative terms similarly employed in the medieval MSS include 'prosa', 'tropus' and 'verba' (*see* PROSA and TROPE (i)).

There are prosulas for chants of both the Mass and the Office, and, within the Mass, for both the Ordinary and the Proper. Best known are those for the Kyrie eleison; but more numerous than these in 10th- and 11th-century sources are those for offertory verses and alleluias. The prosula is nearly always in strictly syllabic style, with one syllable for each note of the melisma. As a rule, the contours, phrasing and articulation of the melody were carefully observed by the prosula writer, so that the phrases of text match those of the melody and accented syllables fall on appropriate notes. The beginnings and endings of words in the text often coincide with the beginnings and endings of neumes in the melisma.

The prosula seems to have served two purposes: to enrich the liturgy with new devotional texts and to make it easier for singers to memorize the melodies. The offertories of Gregorian chant, when their verses are

Ex.1 Offertory. Prosulas 1 and 2; *F-Pn* lat.776, f.33. Prosula 3; *F-Pn* n.a.lat.1535, f.89*v*

considered, have relatively long texts, and the prosulas written for them can be properly appreciated only in this full context. Most of them restate in new words, sometimes in striking phraseology, the subject matter of the offertory; a few add new images and ideas. In one respect, however, the existence of prosulas signals a decline. The apparently subtle rhythmic distinctions represented in the notation of melismas in MSS such as those of St Gall must have been lost when words were applied to these melodies.

Among the offertories for which prosulas were provided is that for Quinquagesima, *Benedictus es*. (It is noteworthy that offertory prosulas were sung frequently on days when, because of the liturgical season in which they occur, there are no tropes, and perhaps no Gloria or *prosa*.) The long melisma on the syllable 'me-' of 'cor meum' at the end of the third verse of this offertory is given a prosula in various sources; it is shown with two prosulas from the 11th-century Aquitanian gradual *F-Pn* lat.776 in ex.1. Occasionally the prosulas use more or fewer notes than the melisma, making it evident that the melismatic and texted versions could not have been sung simultaneously. The third text in the example appears with this melody when it is borrowed for use in the Responsory *Petre amas me* in the 13th-century Sens Antiphonary *F-Pn* n.a.lat.1535; in it the structure depends rather less than usual on that of the melisma, and more on the principle of having several phrases in succession, wherever possible containing the same number of syllables, having the same pattern of accents and ending in the same sound.

Alleluia prosulas were written to fit the music for the word 'Alleluia' and the jubilus that followed, and often also for one or more melismas in the alleluia verse. Occasionally the prosula was made to cover the entire verse, incorporating all or most of the existing text, as in this alleluia from *F-Pn* lat.776:

Alleluia. V. Letabitur iustus in domino et sperabit in eo et laudabuntur omnes recti corde.

[Prosula] *Alle*viata christe *lu*mine clara illustra corpora nostra munda hac animas gau*di*a sanctorum coniungas splendore in aeterna requie. V. *Leta*ndo sublima*bitur iustus* fulgidus nec non et fide actus *in* dominico populo fervens *domino et sperat* ut sua capiat regni premia christus cum regnaverit ad iuditium micans gaudebit et rutila*bit in eo et laude* dignissima tunc gloria*buntur* florigero solio sedentes *omnes recti* probi et casti corpora simul *corda* cum quibus redemptor te gaudent te alme pneumate feliciter congaudenter una protecti tuo iuvamina.

Texts for the Kyrie eleison of the Mass, on the other hand, often omit the word 'Kyrie'; they are not regarded as prosulas by some writers, who believe that in these works the music was written after the text, to fit the expanded version.

The MSS in which prosulas appear vary in character (*see* SOURCES, MS). Some are graduals, in which the prosulas follow immediately the melismas to which they are set (*F-Pn* lat.776, 903, n.a.lat.1235; Benevento VI-34). Others are tropers. In some of these the prosulas appear together, in the order in which they fall in the liturgical year (lat.1084, 1118, 1338, n.a.lat.1871; *D-Mbs* clm.14322). In others, each of them stands with the tropes and *prosae* for its day, in the order in which they appear in the service (*F-Pn* lat.9449; *I-Rc* 1741; *Rn* 1343; the troper of *Ra* 123). It must be added that when the melodies are not notated, or are written imprecisely, sorting the prosulas out and identifying the melodies that underlie them can be difficult.

When prosulas for the Office are found, they are for the responsories of Matins or Vespers; such texts are usually given in antiphonaries and breviaries, though a few do appear in tropers. Prosulas may appear at two points in a responsory: in a melisma towards the end of that part of the responsory that serves as a refrain after the verse (itself sometimes a later addition to the work), or in the verse, where the prosula is fitted in around the existing text. *Descendit de celis*, an old responsory for Christmas, is the one most frequently given prosulas; it has a full complement of them in, for example, the 11th-century Nevers Troper *F-Pn* lat.9449. Another instance where prosulas are written for a melody that is a later addition to a chant occurs in troped versions of the Gloria in excelsis, where various texts, known as 'Regnum prosulae', are set to a melody interposed between the phrases 'Jesu Christe' and 'Cum Sancto Spiritu'.

BIBLIOGRAPHY

L. Gautier: *Histoire de la poésie liturgique au moyen âge*, i: *Les tropes* (Paris, 1886/R1966)
P. Wagner: *Introduction to the Gregorian Melodies* (London, 1907), 243ff [Eng. trans. of pt.i of *Einführung in die gregorianischen Melodien* (Fribourg, 1895, 3/1911)]
B. Stäblein: 'Tropus', *MGG*
R. L. Crocker: 'The Troping Hypothesis', *MQ*, lii (1966), 183
K. Rönnau: 'Regnum tuum solidum', *Festschrift Bruno Stäblein* (Kassel, 1967), 195
R. Steiner: 'The Prosulae of the Manuscript Paris, Bibliothèque nationale, f.lat.1118', *JAMS*, xxii (1969), 367
——: 'The Responsories and Prosa for St Stephen's Day at Salisbury', *MQ*, lvi (1970), 162
P. Evans: *The Early Trope Repertory of Saint Martial de Limoges* (Princeton, 1970)

RUTH STEINER

Prot, Félix-Jean (*b* Senlis, Oise, 1747; *d* Paris, early 1823). French composer, violinist and violist. He studied the violin with Desmarets and composition with Gianotti. When he was 14, his one-act *opéra comique Le bal bourgeois*, for which Favart wrote some music, was performed with great success at the Foire de St Laurent. He joined the orchestra of the Comédie-Française as a violist in 1775 and remained there for 47 years. In 1779 his *Les rêveries renouvelées des grecs*, a parody of Gluck's *Iphigénie* operas, was performed at the Théâtre-Italien. Two more operas followed in the 1780s, but in spite of the support of Favart, Prot could not compete with Grétry, Duni, Philidor and Monsigny during a period in which French musical theatre received poor support; therefore he turned to teaching and the composition of chamber music.

Prot's early duos and trios were didactic and the duos were often provided with an optional bass line. Most of the early works have only two movements, but beginning with the *Duos nouveaux* (1797–8) the three-movement form and a freer concertante style become more common, reflecting Italian influence. His *Symphonie concertante* for two solo violas and orchestra is the earliest known work with this instrumentation.

WORKS
(all printed works published in Paris)

STAGE

Le bal bourgeois (opéra comique, 1, C. S. Favart), Paris, Foire St Laurent, Aug 1761 (1762), collab. Favart
Les rêveries renouvelées des grecs (parodie in verse and vaudevilles, 3, Favart, C. H. F. de Voisenon, J. N. Guérin de Frémicourt), Paris, Théâtre-Italien, 26 June 1779 (1779)
Le printemps (divertissement pastoral, 1, A. P. A. de Piis, P. Y. Barré), Marly, 19 May 1781 (1781)
L'amour à l'épreuve (opéra comique, 1, L.-F. Faur), Paris, Théâtre-Italien, 13 Aug 1784 (1784)

Vocal: L'amant malheureux, ariette, with insts (1774); Dors mon enfant, ariette (n.d.)

Duos: 6 duo, va, vn, op.1 (1776); 6 duo dialogués et concertants, vn, va, op.2 (1780); 6 duos. . .pour les jeunes élèves et amateurs, 2 vn (1781, 2/1788); 6 duo nouveaux, 2 vn, op.4 (1782, 2/1788); 6 duo, 2 vn, op.5 (1783, 2/1788); 6 duo, 2 vn, op.6 (1785, 2/1788); 6 duos, 2 vn, no op. (n.d.); 6 duo, 2 va, op.9 (n.d.); 6 duos nouveaux, 2 vn, op.13 (n.d.); 3 simphonies en duos, 2 vn, op.14 (n.d.); 6 duos nouveaux, 2 vn, op.17 (n.d.); 3 simphonies en duos, 2 vn, no op. (n.d.); other pubd collections listed by Briquet

Other inst: Simphonie concertante, 2 va, orch (1786); 3 simphonies en trio, 2 vn, bc, no op. (n.d.); 3 simphonies en trio, 2 vn, bc, op.15 (n.d.); other pubd collections listed by Briquet

Pedagogical: Méthode pour le violin (Paris, c1780–82), lost

BIBLIOGRAPHY

FétisB

E. van der Straeten: *The History of the Violin* (London, 1933)

M. Briquet: 'Prot, Félix-Jean', *MGG*

B. S. Brook: *La symphonie française, dans la seconde moitié du XVIIIe siècle* (Paris, 1962)

ARISTIDE WIRSTA

Prota. Italian family of musicians, active in Naples in the 18th and early 19th centuries.

(1) Ignazio Prota (*b* Naples, 15 Sept 1690; *d* Naples, Jan 1748). Teacher and composer. As a child he received musical instruction from his uncle, the priest Filippo Prota (*d* Naples, 1 Jan 1740), *maestro di cappella* of S Giorgio Maggiore, Naples, of whose works only a *Lectio III primi nocturni sabati sancti* for contralto survives (*I-Nf*). In 1706 Ignazio entered the Neapolitan conservatory S Maria di Loreto, where he completed his musical training under *primo maestro* Gaetano Veneziano and *secondo maestro* Giuliano Perugino. On 9 March 1713 he married the 14-year-old Caterina d'Ambrosio. Of their descendants, two sons, (2) Tommaso and (3) Giuseppe, two grandsons, Ignazio and (4) Gabriele, and a greatgrandson, (5) Giovanni, became musicians. The relationship of a Gaetano Prota, an oboist in the Teatro S Carlo orchestra in Naples with (3) Giuseppe during the 1786 season, is not known.

Ignazio contributed a prologue, several arias and three *buffo* scenes to a performance of C. F. Pollarolo's *Tito Manlio* at the Teatro S Bartolomeo in Naples in 1720. The following year he composed his first *opera buffa*, in Neapolitan dialect, *La fenta fattucchiera*, for the Teatro dei Fiorentini. After his appointment as a *maestro* of the Neapolitan conservatory S Onofrio a Capuana, in June 1722, Ignazio curtailed his promising career as an operatic composer in favour of teaching. He served S Onofrio for 26 years until his death, first with *maestro* Francesco Feo (1723), then Leonardo Leo (1739), and finally Francesco Durante (1745). He never attained the first position, but was highly respected by his students, among them Gennaro Manna, Jommelli, Latilla and Domenico Fischietti. His successor at S Onofrio was Girolamo Abos, who had assisted him since 1742. In 19th-century literature (Fétis, Florimo, Eitner) various members of the Prota family are confused, and Ignazio's biography is discussed under the name of his son (3) Giuseppe.

WORKS
STAGE WORKS

(all performed in Naples; music lost unless otherwise indicated)

Prologue, arias, and 3 buffo scenes for Tito Manlio (opera seria), by C. F. Pollarolo, S Bartolomeo, 1720, 1 aria, Vaghe luci, *I-Nc*

La fenta fattucchiera (opera buffa, A. Birini), Fiorentini, spr. 1721

La vedova ingegnosa (intermezzo, T. Mariani), in Emira by L. Leo, S Bartolomeo, 12 July 1735

La Camilla (opera buffa, A. Palomba), Nuovo, wint. 1737

(2) Tommaso Prota (*b* Naples; *d* after 1768). Composer, son of (1) Ignazio Prota. In a legal document of 1750, Tommaso Prota, Tommaso Traetta, Gennaro Piano, Antonio Cherubino and others are referred to as having been students of the conservatory S Maria di Loreto; it has therefore been assumed that Prota and Traetta (*b* 1727) were approximate contemporaries. In 1748 Tommaso presented himself to the Neapolitan public with an *opera buffa*, *La moglie padrone*, at the Teatro Nuovo. From existing manuscripts, performance records, and publications of his works it seems that Tommaso left Naples for Malta, worked in various Italian cities and perhaps also in Paris and London.

WORKS
STAGE

(all lost)

La moglie padrona (opera buffa, 'Lantino Liviano' [A. Villano]), Naples, Nuovo, 1748

L'abate ossia Il poeta moderno (opera buffa), Malta, Manoel, 1752

Il cicisbeo burlato (intermezzo), Bologna, Marsigli-Rossi, Jan 1764

OTHER VOCAL

Cantata (Tirsi e Doralice), 2vv, insts, *F-Pc*

Prologo (Marte, Tebo, e Minerva), 3vv, insts, *Pc*

Meditazione del Giudizio, dell'inferno, e del paradiso, 3vv, vns, bc, *GB-Lbm*

Salve regina, B, vns, bc, *Lbm*

Vespere autem sabathi, 3vv, vns, bc (1768), *I-Nc*

INSTRUMENTAL

6 sonate, 2 fl, bc, op.1 (Paris, n.d.)

6 sonate ovvero divertimenti da camera, 2 fl/vn, bc (London, n.d.)

Sinfonia, 2 vn, mand obbl, bc; sonata, mand, bc: *F-Pc*

Sinfonia, vn, bc, Pisa, 1756; sonata, 2 fl, bc: *GB-Er*

Concerto, fl, vns, bc: *I-Nc*

(3) Giuseppe Prota (*b* Naples, 3 Dec 1737; *d* Naples, 21 July 1807). Oboist and teacher, son of (1) Ignazio Prota. In 1748, after his father's death, he entered the conservatory S Maria di Loreto, where he studied wind instruments under Cherubino Corona. He was soon recognized as an outstanding player, and in 1762, when only 24, succeeded Corona as teacher of the oboe, bassoon and flute at the Loreto Conservatory. When the Mozarts visited Naples in 1770, Leopold listed 'Sgr Broda suonatore del'oboe' in his travel notes among the prominent Neapolitan musicians. On 8 June 1778 Giuseppe became oboist of the royal chapel, and in the following year teacher of wind instruments at the conservatory Della Pietà dei Turchini; he held these positions until his death. His son Ignazio was also an instrumentalist, and in 1813 was first oboe at the Teatro S Cecilia in Palermo.

(4) Gabriele Prota (*b* Naples, 19 May 1755; *d* Naples, 22 June 1843). Composer, son of Giovanni Prota, a son of (1) Ignazio Prota. In 1780 he was *maestro* of the Ss Annunziata church in Naples, and later of the monastery church S Chiara. In 1785, according to Prota-Giurleo, he married a young Parisian, Rosalie Laurent, who had been educated in Naples. During the 1790s he composed several successful *opere buffe*, among them *Gli studenti*, for Neapolitan theatres. Gabriele and his wife became politically associated with the Jacobinian cause and the 1799 republican uprising, and were incarcerated after the Bourbons had crushed the revolution. In 1806, when the French began to rule Naples, the king Joseph Buonaparte appointed Mme Prota director of the newly formed music school for women, the Collegio delle Donzelle, and Gabriele became *maestro di cap-*

pella and singing teacher there. Because of the success of the institution, both were allowed to retain their positions after the Bourbons returned to power in Naples in 1815.

WORKS
OPERAS
Ezio (opera seria, Metastasio), Perugia, Civico de' Verzaro, carn. 1784
Le furberie (opera buffa, G. Palomba), Naples, Nuovo, carn. 1793
Le donne dispettose (opera buffa, G. Palomba), Naples, Fondo, carn. 1793
Gli studenti (opera buffa, G. Palomba), Naples, Fondo, May 1796, *I-Nc*

SACRED VOCAL
Kyrie, 4 S, vns, b; Litanie, 4vv, vns, b; Miserere (per la Settimana Santa), 4vv, vns, b: all *I-Nc*
Stabat mater, Naples, April 1819, lost

(5) **Giovanni Prota** (*b* Naples, *c*1786; *d* Naples, ? 13 June 1843). Composer and teacher, son of (4) Gabriele Prota and Rosalie Laurent. His approximate date of birth is based on Prota-Giurleo's claim that the parents were married in 1785. A *Missa di requiem a due cori con più stromenti* dated 20 December 1798, attributed to Giovanni (held in Naples) would therefore represent the efforts of a 12-year-old. His first opera, *Il servo furbo* (*astuto*), was staged at the Teatro dei Fiorentini in Naples in 1803, and an *opera buffa*, *Amor dal naufragio*, was given at the Teatro Nuovo in 1810, when the *Corriere di Napoli* praised 'Sig Prota, giovine maestro di cappella' for his accomplishments in the genre. About 1820, Giovanni became voice teacher and *maestro e compositore* at the Real Casa d'Educazione Miracoli, the Regina Isabella Borbone school for young noblewomen in Naples. Much of his church music (the manuscripts are dated) was written when he was at this institution, and scorings for one to three sopranos, organ or orchestra, are noticeable.

WORKS
SACRED VOCAL
(*in I-Mc, Nc, unless otherwise stated*)
Mass (Ky–Gl–Cr), 2vv, org; 8 masses (Ky–Gl), 2–7vv, org/orch [2 dated: June 1821 and 10 April 1825]; 4 Pastoral masses [1 dated 1824]; 1 Kyrie, 4vv, orch; 3 Credo; 6 Requiem masses, 3–8vv, org/orch [1 dated 20 Dec 1798]
14 lessons for the nocturnes of Holy Week, 1–2vv org; 7 Domine salvum fac, 1–3vv, chorus, b/org; 6 lessons for the nocturnes De'morti, 1v, orch; 5 litanies, 1–3vv, org/orch, incl. Litanie pastorali; 3 Dixit Dominus, 2–3vv, org/orch; 3 Magnificat, 3vv, org, *F-Pc*; Miserere, 2vv, org; Miserere, 3vv, org, 20 Feb 1813; Ecce sacerdos, 3vv, org; Ecce sacerdos, 5vv, orch; Salve regina, S, org; Salve regina, S, orch; Tantum ergo, 1v, org; Tantum ergo, 2vv, org; Tota pulchra es, 1v, org, *F-Pc*; Tota pulchra es, 3vv, org
Ave maris stella, 3vv, org; Libera me, 3vv, org; Mottetto pastorale, 15 Dec 1825; Nonna volgarizzato, S/T, org; Responsorium S. P. Francisci, 3vv, orch; Rorate coeli, 3vv, org; Sette stazioni della Vergine addolorata, 2vv, org; Sette stazioni della Vergine addolorata, 3vv, org; Tre ore d'agonia di Nostro Signore, 2vv, vns; Tre ore d'agonia di Nostro Signore, 3vv, bc; Turba (Passio del Venerdi Santo), 4vv, org; Veni Creator, 4vv, orch; Veni dilecta mea, S, orch; Veni sponsa, 3vv, org

OPERAS
(*all performed in Naples*)
Il servo furbo (opera buffa, G. Palomba), Fiorentini, carn. 1803, *I-Nc*
Amor dal naufragio (opera buffa, A. L. Tottola), Nuovo, Jan 1810, *Nc*
Il cimento felice (opera semiseria, M. Cimorelli), Fiorentini, aut. 1815, *Nc*

OTHER SECULAR VOCAL
Solfeggi for various voices and bc, *I-Mc*
Sonetto 'Scioglie Eurilla dal lido', S, pf, *Mc*
Il baciamente (cantata), 5vv, 1831, music lost, lib,

INSTRUMENTAL
2 pastorales, org; 5 trattenimenti, org; Trattenimento, G, org: all *I-Mc*
Sonata di cembalo, *GB-Lbm*
Sinfonia, B♭, orch; Sinfonia 'Giuseppe Riconosciuto', pf arr.; Sinfonia 'Armida e Rinaldo', pf arr.; Sinfonia 'Amor dal naufragio', pf: all *I-Nc*

WRITINGS
Principii della musica a dialogo (Naples, 1829)

BIBLIOGRAPHY
S. di Giacomo: *I quattro antichi conservatorii musicali di Napoli* (Milan and Naples, 1924–8)
B. Croce: *La rivoluzione napoletana del 1799* (Bari, 1926)
U. Rolandi: *Musica e musicisti in Malta* (Livorno, 1932)
U. Prota-Giurleo: *La famiglia napoletana dei Prota nella storia della musica* (Milan, 1957)

HANNS-BERTOLD DIETZ

Prota-Giurleo, Ulisse (*b* Naples, 13 March 1886; *d* Perugia, 9 Feb 1966). Italian musicologist. He spent most of his life in Naples and dedicated himself to the history of Neapolitan music and theatre. He began work in this field in 1912 on the encouragement of his teacher Salvatore di Giacomo, whom he assisted in compiling a music catalogue of the Oratorio dei Filippini (1918) and two volumes on the four conservatories in Naples (1924–8). From 1920 to 1930 he gathered information on the history of music in Naples and on Neapolitan theatrical and artistic life (with special reference to the 17th and 18th centuries), making important contributions to knowledge of the Scarlatti family, Logroscino and the early history of *opera buffa*, Sacchini, Cimarosa, Porpora, Piccinni, Provenzale and others, and to the history of Neapolitan organists of the 17th and 18th centuries. His aim to publish a lengthy history of music in Naples was thwarted by the lack of an interested publisher; instead, part of his research appeared as 'Breve storia del teatro di corte e della musica a Napoli nei secoli XVII e XVIII' (1952). It bears comparison with the work of Croce, Di Giacomo and Pannain as one of the most important 20th-century essays on the history of Neapolitan music.

WRITINGS
Musicisti napoletani in Russia (Naples, 1923)
La prima calcografia musicale a Napoli (Naples, 1923)
Musicisti napoletani alla corte di Portogallo (Naples, 1924)
Alessandro Scarlatti 'il Palermitano' (Naples, 1926)
La grande orchestra del Teatro San Carlo nel '700 (Naples, 1927)
Nicola Logroscino 'il dio dell'opera buffa' (Naples, 1927)
'Notizie sul musicista belga Jean Macque', *IMSCR*, i *Liège 1930*, 191
'Breve storia del teatro di corte e della musica a Napoli nei secoli XVII e XVIII', *Il teatro di corte del Palazzo reale di Napoli* (Naples, 1952), 19–146
Francesco Cirillo e l'introduzione del melodramma a Napoli (Grumo Nevano, 1952)
Francesco Durante nel 2° centenario della sua morte (Frattamaggiore, 1955)
La famiglia napoletana dei Prota nella storia della musica (Milan, 1957)
Miserere, tradotto in dialetto napoletano da Nicola Valletta (Naples, 1960)
I teatri di Napoli nel '600: la commedia e le maschere (Naples, 1962)
Gian Leonardo dell'Arpa nella storia della musica (Naples, 1964)
'Notizie biografiche intorno ad alcuni musicisti, d'oltralpe a Napoli nel Settecento', *AnMc*, no.2 (1965), 112–43
with A. Giovine: *Giacomo Insanguine detto Monopoli, musicista monopolitano: cenni biografici, elenco di rappresentazioni, bibliografia, indice vari e iconografia* (Bari, 1969)
Further articles in *Nostro tempo*, *La scala*, *Gazzetta musicale di Napoli*, *Archivi*, *L'organo* and in other journals and encyclopedias

BIBLIOGRAPHY
A. Giovine: *Ulisse Prota-Giurleo: ricordo di un mio maestro* (Bari, 1968)
F. Degrada: 'In memoria di Ulisse Prota-Giurleo', *RIM*, i (1966), 295

CAROLYN M. GIANTURCO

Protheroe, Daniel (*b* Cwmgiedd, nr. Ystradgynlais, 5 Nov 1866; *d* Chicago, 25 Feb 1934). Welsh conductor and composer. Before his voice broke, he won at the National Eisteddfod in 1880 and 1881. He was briefly conductor of the Ystradgynlais Choir before he emigrated at 19 to Scranton, Pennsylvania. His first music teachers in Wales had included J. T. Rees, and he continued his studies, gaining the BMus (Toronto) in 1890 and later DMus there. At Scranton he was conductor of the Cymmrodorion Choral Society for eight years, and on moving to Milwaukee in 1894 and subsequently to Chicago he conducted a number of flourishing choirs. In Chicago he was also on the staff of Sherwood Music School and director of music at the Central Church. The foremost musician in the Welsh community in the USA, Protheroe frequently visited Wales, where he was also admired as a conductor (e.g. at the Harlech Festival, 1931), eisteddfod adjudicator and composer. Of his compositions, those for male-voice choir have enjoyed lasting popularity (*Invictus*, *Nidaros*, *Bryn Calfaria*, *Jesu, lover of my soul*), as have a number of his hymn tunes ('Milwaukee', 'Wilkesbarre', 'Hiraeth', 'Cwmgiedd'). He edited *Can a Mawl* (Chicago, 1918), the hymnbook of the Welsh Calvinistic Methodists in the USA and published *Arwain corau* (1914) and *Nodau damweiniol a d'rawyd* (1924).

BIBLIOGRAPHY
R. D. Griffith: 'Protheroe, Daniel', *Dictionary of Welsh Biography* (London, 1959)

OWAIN EDWARDS

Protopopov, Vladimir Vasil'yevich (*b* Moscow, 13 July 1908). Soviet musicologist. He qualified in 1930 at the Moscow District Music Technical College, where he had studied composition with Iosif Dubovsky, and in 1938 he graduated from Lev Mazel''s theory and musicology class at the Moscow Conservatory. He took his *kandidat* degree in 1942 with a dissertation on Taneyev's chamber music, and in 1960 was awarded a doctorate for his work on Glinka's operas. In 1938 he joined the teaching staff of the Moscow Conservatory, in 1943 was appointed senior lecturer and in 1962 professor. From 1948 to 1960 he was also a senior research fellow at the Institute for the History of the Arts in Moscow. Protopopov has made important studies of the history of polyphony and musical form; he has also written on 19th-century and Soviet Russian music, and has been responsible for editing several volumes of the complete works of Glinka, Tchaikovsky and Rimsky-Korsakov. He has taken part in a number of international musicological conferences and in 1960 was awarded a prize at the Warsaw International Competition for research on Chopin.

WRITINGS
'O muzïkal'nom yazïke Zolotovo petushka' [The musical language of The Golden Cockerel], *SovM* (1938), no.6, p.20
'O tematizme i melodike S. I. Taneyeva' [Taneyev's themes and melodies], *SovM* (1940), no.7, p.49
'Nekotorïye osobennosti opernoy formï Rimskovo-Korsakova' [Some features of Rimsky-Korsakov's opera forms], *SovM sbornik*, iii (1945), 87
ed.: *Pamyati Sergeya Ivanovicha Taneyeva 1856–1946* [In memory of Taneyev] (Moscow and Leningrad, 1947) [incl. 'Tvorcheskiy put' S. I. Taneyeva' [The creative path of Taneyev], pp.60–101]
'Ob odnom vazhnom printsipe muzïkal'noy formï D. D. Shostakovicha' [An important principle in Shostakovich's musical form], *Soobshcheniya Instituta istorii iskusstv*, ix (Moscow, 1956), 36
'Variatsionnïy metod razvitiya tematizma v muzïke Shopena' [Variation technique in the development of themes in Chopin's music], *Friderik Shopen*, ed. G. Ya. Edel'man (Moscow, 1960), 232–95
Printsipï opernoy formï Glinka [The principles of Glinka's opera forms] (diss., Institut istorii iskusstv, Moscow)
Ivan Susanin Glinki [Glinka's Ivan Susanin] (Moscow, 1961)
'Kontrastno-sostavnïye formï' [Contrasting structural forms], *SovM* (1962), no.9, p.33

'Voprosï muzïkal'noy formï v proizvedeniyakh D. Shostakovicha' [Questions of musical form in Shostakovich's compositions], *Chertï stilya D. Shostakovicha*, ed. L. Berger (Moscow, 1962), 87–125
Istoriya polifonii: russkaya klassicheskaya i sovetskaya muzïka [The history of polyphony: Russian Classical and Soviet music] (Moscow, 1962)
ed.: *Vospominaniya o P. I. Chaykovskom* (Moscow, 1962, rev. and enlarged 2/1973)
Istoriya polifonii: zapadno-evropeyskaya klassika XVIII–XIX vv. [The history of polyphony: west European classics of the 18th and 19th centuries] (Moscow, 1965)
Variatsionnïye protsessi v muzïkal'noy forme [Processes of variation in musical form] (Moscow, 1967)
ed., with I. F. Bel'za: *V. Ya. Shebalin* (Moscow, 1970) [incl. 'O variatsionnosti v muzïke Shebalina' [Variation technique in Shebalin's music], p.181]
Printsipï muzïkal'noy formï Betkhoven: sonatno-simfonicheskiye tsiklï opp.1–81 [Principles of Beethoven's musical form: the cycles of sonatas and symphonies, opp.1–81] (Moscow, 1970)
'Muzïka petrovskovo vremeni o pobede pod Poltavoy' [Music of the Petrine era on the victory at Poltava], *SovM* (1971), no.12, p.97
ed.: *Muzïka na Poltavskuyu pobedu* [Music on the victory at Poltava] (Moscow, 1973)
'Nikolay Diletsky i evo russkiye sovremenniki' [Nikolay Diletsky and his Russian contemporaries], *SovM* (1973), no.12, p.82
ed.: S. Skrebkov: *Khudozhestvennïye printsipï muzïkal'nïkh stiley* [Artistic principles of musical style] (Moscow, 1973)
LEV GINZBURG

Prōtopsaltēs. The lead chanter on the right-hand choir of a Byzantine church.

Prototype melody. A term used in literature on Gregorian chant to describe melodies adapted to new texts; *see* CENTONIZATION.

Prout, Ebenezer (*b* Oundle, 1 March 1835; *d* Hackney, 5 Dec 1909). English musical scholar and editor. The son of a Congregationalist minister, Prout worked as a schoolmaster from 1852, taking the degree of BA (London) in 1854. He turned to the musical profession in 1859 and taught at the National Training School for Music from 1876 to 1882 and at the RAM from 1879 till his death; he also taught for some years at the GSM. Though almost entirely self-educated in music, he rose by his gifts and methodical industry to a position of distinguished authority in the technique of composition, in which field he published a series of solid works which led to his appointment in 1894 as professor of music in Trinity College, Dublin, then a non-resident post. He received the honoorary degree of MusD from Dublin in 1895. From 1871 to 1875 he was the first editor of the *Monthly Musical Record*, to which he contributed, among much else, analyses of the later works of Wagner; he was also music critic of *The Academy* (1874–9) and *The Athenaeum* (1879–89).

His name is most widely known through his edition of Handel's *Messiah* (1902), in which he succeeded to a large extent in eliminating textual errors which had been current for several generations. He correctly assigned the 'Guadagni' version of 'But who may abide?' to the alto voice, and grasped something of the principle of 'over-dotting'. But he was unsympathetic to reviving ornamentation, and he remained wedded to the idea of additional accompaniments, himself adding to those of Mozart. Further, he failed to understand, or take account of, the complex history of the work with its numerous variant movements. He also edited *Samson* (1880) and a series of arias from Bach's cantatas and Handel's operas. As a composer he was industrious, though not original. Among his larger works are four symphonies, several cantatas (including *Alfred*), a concerto for organ and orchestra in E minor, and a duet-sonata in A for pianoforte and harmonium.

His reputation rests on his treatises. Those on harmony, counterpoint and double counterpoint, though remarkably thorough and independent, are based on an approach now outmoded. But his works on fugue and form (both translated into Russian), and, especially, on the orchestra (translated into German), results of intense study of a wide range of music, retain a great deal of value. His library was acquired by Trinity College, Dublin.

For Prout's place in the history of analysis see ANALYSIS, §II, 3(ii).

WRITINGS

(most with numerous re-editions)

Instrumentation (London, 1876)
with E. Holmes: The Life of Mozart (London, 1878)
Harmony: its Theory and Practice (London, 1889; largely rewritten 20/1903)
Counterpoint, Strict and Free (London, 1890)
Double Counterpoint and Canon (London, 1891)
Fugue (London, 1891)
Fugal Analysis (London, 1892)
Musical Form (London, 1893)
Applied Forms (London, 1895)
The Orchestra (London, 1897)

BIBLIOGRAPHY

H. Davey: 'Prout, Ebenezer', DNB
'Ebenezer Prout', MT, xl (1899), 225
J. A. Westrup: 'Ebenezer Prout (1835–1909)', MMR, lxv (1935), 53
E. Lomax: 'Dr. Ebenezer Prout – and Bach', Music in Education, xxiii (1959), 76

WATKINS SHAW

Provedi, Francesco (b Siena, c1710; d ?Siena, after 1755). Italian music theorist. He was a knife maker by profession who had an interest in music history and theory; according to Schmidl he was also a chapel singer in Provenzano. He published two treatises. His *Lettera* (dated 4 October 1743) argues in favour of Guido of Arezzo's more complicated method of sight-singing as opposed to the French one of Anselmo then recently introduced by F. Frittelli as *maestro di cappella* at the Siena Cathedral. Provedi's *Paragone* (1752) purports to establish continuity between the music of the Greeks and Gregorian chant. Correspondence between Padre Martini and Provedi on the latter's writings continued up to 1755.

WRITINGS

Lettera di Francesco Provedi Coltellinajo Sanese ad un suo amico in Roma, in cui si esamina qual sistema di musica sia più perfetto, o quello di Guido Aretino, o quello di Anselmo Fiammingo (Siena, 1744)
Paragone della musica antica e della moderna. Ragionamenti IV (Siena, 1752); ed. S. Occhi: Raccolta d'opuscoli scientifici et fiologici, i (Venice, 1974)

BIBLIOGRAPHY

EitnerQ; SchmidlDS
F. Frittelli: Il modo di solfeggiare all'uso francese (Siena, 1744)
Correspondence between Padre Martini and Provedi, I-Bc
M. Casamorata: 'Studi bibliografico-biografici su musicisti toscani', Gazzetta musicale di Milano, vi/32 (1847), 253

CAROLYN M. GIANTURCO

Provenzale, Francesco (b Naples, c1626; d Naples, 6 Sept 1704). Italian composer and teacher. He was the first prominent Neapolitan musician to compose opera, and he is now recognized as the forerunner of the long line of Neapolitan composers of opera and other forms of vocal music, sometimes called the Neapolitan school, active in the 18th century.

1. LIFE AND MUSICAL ACTIVITIES. Some indication of Provenzale's date of birth comes from the records of his marriage banns, which are dated 5 January 1660 and state that he was at the time 'about 33 years old'. It is known that he became associated with the opera com-

pany in Naples around 1652–3 and that this company presented his first opera, *Il Ciro*, probably in 1653. The total extent of his composition for the Neapolitan operatic stage in the 1650s remains a matter for conjecture. But the preface to the libretto of his *Il Theseo, o vero L'incostanza trionfante* (Naples, 1658) testifies that he had a hand in at least four operas during that decade:

This time you have a drama that cannot fail to please you. The poet is able, and much more so is the composer of the music, your Neapolitan Sig. Francesco Provenzale, who, if he knew how to satisfy you in Ciro, Xerse and Artemisia, certainly knows how to please you even more in this one, in which he has managed to demonstrate the vivacity of his spirit to better advantage.

An opera with the title 'Il Ciro' and with music by an unstated Neapolitan composer was presented at the Teatro SS Giovanni e Paolo, Venice, in 1654, with additional music by Cavalli. There seems no doubt that this opera was Provenzale's. Provenzale may afterwards have returned the compliment that Cavalli paid him by adapting his *Il Ciro*. Cavalli wrote two original operas called *Xerse* and *Artemisia* for Venice, in 1654 and 1656 respectively. Since the operatic company then in Naples was in the habit of borrowing extensively from the Venetian repertory, it is possible that Provenzale's *Xerse* and *Artemisia* were arrangements of Cavalli's operas rather than compositions totally his own. Equal uncertainty surrounds Provenzale's work for the professional theatre in the 1660s. Prota-Giurleo has used circumstantial evidence to ascribe to him two operas to which no contemporary document of the 1660s puts a composer's name. These are *La Cloridea* (Naples, 1660) and *La Bisalva, ovvero Offendere chi più s'ama* (Naples, 1667–8), credited to Provenzale on the grounds that the librettist, Pedro Sanz Palomera y Velasco, was witness at his wedding and was evidently a friend of his. As regards his next operas, *Il schiavo di sua moglie* and *La Stellidaura vendicata*, there is no doubt either about dates or about attribution. The music of both these works has survived. The score of the first gives the year of composition as 1671; the second was, according to documentary evidence, first performed in the Naples suburb of Mergellina in September 1674. Some authorities have expressed the view that Provenzale was involved in another opera presented in Naples in 1678, *Chi tal nasce tal vive, o vero L'Alessandro Bala*, but this has not been proved. There is no evidence that he was engaged in opera for the professional stage after 1678.

Provenzale's dissociation from opera at Naples in his later years is a fact of some interest. It may partly be explained by the increasing competition created by other, non-Neapolitan opera composers, notably P. A. Ziani and Alessandro Scarlatti, who came to work in Naples at one time or another during the last quarter of the century. It may also be accounted for by the growing scope of his other activities. These included composing and directing music in his capacity as *maestro di cappella* to the city of Naples, a post he gained on 17 September 1665. Since 1663 he had also been busy as a teacher, having been appointed chief *maestro* at the Neapolitan Conservatorio S Maria di Loreto that year (he was paid from 1 March). This latter appointment was an important one. It helped to establish a tradition in the Neapolitan conservatories (of which there were four) that the music teachers should be men of competence and high standing. In fact it was during his years as a teacher that the conservatories first began to produce graduate composers and performers of such quality as to bring Naples and its music an international reputation. Provenzale's teaching methods included making his pupils perform operas on sacred subjects in the conservatory, a good way of training them for the professional theatre. He himself composed one such work, *La fenice d'Avila Teresa di Giesù* (1672), and he probably composed others too. The libretto of another sacred opera with music by Provenzale, *La colomba ferita* was published in Naples in 1672 and dedicated to a nun at the convent of Donna Regina. He left the Loreto at the end of October 1675, having undertaken to head the music staff at another conservatory, the S Maria della Pietà dei Turchini. Here he taught until old age forced his retirement in April 1701.

In July 1686 he gained the additional post of *maestro di cappella* to the treasury of S Gennaro. He held this appointment until October 1699, when he was dismissed on the grounds that his style of composition was then out of date. The other official position in Naples in which he was interested was that of *maestro di cappella* to the viceregal court, but he never succeeded in obtaining this. Shortly after the court had elected P. A. Ziani *maestro di cappella* on 12 March 1680, it appointed Provenzale *maestro onorario* without salary on the tacit understanding, it seems, that he was to be Ziani's successor. But when Ziani died on 12 February 1684 his job was given not to Provenzale but to the 23-year-old Alessandro Scarlatti, who had arrived in Naples the previous year. Provenzale at once resigned in protest. He returned to court service between 24 January and 11 March 1688 as *maestro di cappella di camera* (at 19 ducats monthly) at the time when Scarlatti had temporarily lost the court's favour. Finally, on 27 June 1690 he was reinstated *maestro onorario* (with a salary of 19 ducats monthly) with the task of 'serving during the absences and illnesses of Alessandro Scarlatti'.

2. WORKS. The music of the two surviving operas whose music is entirely by Provenzale, *Il schiavo di sua moglie* and *La Stellidaura vendicata*, consists of a free alternation of recitatives, ariosos, arias and ensembles such as is found in other Italian operas of the period. His lyrical items are variously structured, only a minority being in the da capo form that later, 18th-century Neapolitan composers used so often. The chromatic, highly expressive style he adopted in certain laments has been praised by historians ever since Rolland first drew attention to them. However, his style is generally more lively and genial than this. Although it is often modelled on that of Cesti and other Venetian contemporaries, he was capable of producing melodies with a warm individuality of their own, and some of his songs too have a dance-like, popular flavour that recent commentators have claimed is akin to southern Italian folk music (see ex.1). His religious compositions, mostly written in pursuance of his duties as *maestro di cappella* to the city of Naples or to one or other of the conservatories there, possess the same pleasant features. These compositions are of two basic kinds, the one choral (with sections of mixed polyphonic and homophonic writing) and the other for vocal soloists with or without choral interludes. The solo parts require singers of technical proficiency. Much of the choral writing on the other hand is comparatively easy to sing, perhaps because Provenzale originally intended it for his pupils or other young performers.

WORKS

DRAMATIC

Il Ciro (G. C. Sorrentino), Naples, S Bartolomeo, 1653; with musical additions by F. Cavalli, Venice, SS Giovanni e Paolo, 1654; further musical additions by A. Mattioli, Venice, 1665, *I-Vnm*

Xerse (N. Minato), Naples, S Bartolomeo, ?1655; ?adaptation of F. Cavalli opera

Artemisia (Minato), Naples, S Bartolomeo, ?1657; ?adaptation of F. Cavalli opera

Il Theseo, o vero L'incostanza trionfante (G. delle Chiavi), Naples, S. Bartolomeo, 1658

Il schiavo di sua moglie (A. Perrucci), Naples, S. Bartolomeo, 1671, *I-Rsc*

La colomba ferita (sacred opera, G. Castaldo), Naples, ? Convent of Donna Regina, 18 Sept 1672

La fenice d'Avila Teresa di Giesù (sacred opera, Castaldo), Naples, Conservatory S Maria di Loreto, 6 Nov 1672

La Stellidaura vendicata (Perrucci), Naples, Villa Cursi Cicinelli, Mergellina, 2 Sept 1674, *I-Rsc*, some arias also in *Nc*; also perf. with title Difendere l'offensore, ovvero La Stellidaura vendicata; 1 aria, ed. L. Landshoff, *Alte Meister des Bel Canto*, i (Leipzig, 1912)

Il martirio di S Gennaro (G. Paolella), Naples, Royal Palace, 6 Nov 1664, possibly by Provenzale

Cantatas, S, bc, *I-Nc*: A che mirarmi, o stelle; Giunto il fatal dì; La mia speme; Sdegnosetta, che vuoi tu; Sui palchi delle stelle [sacred]; Squarciato appena avea

Cantata, S, T, bc, *Nc*: Voi ombre notturne

SACRED

Missa defunctorum, 4vv, 2 vn, bc, *I-Mc*, *Nc*

Pange lingua, 9vv, 2 vn, bc, *Bc*, *Mc*, *Nc*, *Nf*; Pange lingua, 8vv, vn, bc, *Mc*, *Nc*, another version, 4vv, *Mc*; Pange lingua, 2vv, insts, *Mc*, *Nc*

Beatus vir, S, insts; In conspectu angelorum, 2vv, insts; Vespro breve, 9vv, insts; Dialogo per la passione del Signor, 5vv, 2vn, bc, 1686: all *Nf*

Mottetti, 2vv, bc (Naples, 1689)

BIBLIOGRAPHY

R. Roland: *Les origines du théâtre lyrique moderne: l'histoire de l'opéra en Europe avant Lully et Scarlatti* (Paris, 1895, 4/1936)

H. Goldschmidt: 'Francesco Provenzale als Dramatiker', *SIMG*, vii (1905–6), 608

S. di Giacomo: *Maestri di cappella, musici ed istromenti al Tesoro di S. Gennaro* (Naples, 1920)

——: *I quattro antichi conservatorii musicali di Napoli* (Milan and Naples, 1924–8)

G. Pannain: 'Francesco Provenzale e la lirica del suo tempo', *RMI*, xxxii (1925), 497

U. Prota-Giurleo: 'Francesco Provenzale', *Archivi*, xxv (1958), 53

W. Stalnaker: 'Provenzale, Francesco', *ES*

A. Mondolfi Bossarelli: 'Vita e stile di Francesco Provenzale: la questione di "Alessandro Bala" ', *Annuario del Conservatorio S. Pietro a Maiella, Naples*, x (1962–3), 15

M. F. Robinson: 'The Governors' Minutes of the Conservatory S. Maria di Loreto, Naples', *RMARC*, x (1972), 37, 49

L. Bianconi: 'Funktionen des Opernthaters in Neapel bis 1700 und die Rolle Alessandro Scarlattis', *Colloquium Alessandro Scarlatti Würzburg 1975*

MICHAEL F. ROBINSON

Ex.1 *Il schiavo di sua moglie*, Act 1

LUCILLO
Quan-te di queste   da-me si tro - va-no co-
- sì,   quan-te di ques-te   da-me   si tro - va-no co-
- sì   che di ma - ri - to han' fa - me.
che di ma-ri-to han' fa - me   e'l cer - ca-no o-gni
di,   che di ma - ri-to han' fa - me
che di ma-ri-to han'fa - me   e'l cer - ca-no o-gni   di.

Prowett, Stephen (*b* c1495; *d* Norwich, 1560). English composer. Two parts of his five-part settings of the Jesus antiphon *O bone Jesu* and a Marian antiphon *Plaude potentissima parens plasmatoris* survive in a pair of partbooks dating from about 1530: *GB-Cu* Dd.xiii.27 and *Cjc* K31 (James 234). The latter composition is chiefly remarkable for the unrelievedly alliterative nature of its text.

A plausible candidate for identification with the composer (given the title 'dom' in the sources) is the Stephen Prowett, priest of Norwich, to whom a reference occurs in the accounts of the churchwardens of St Mary's, Bungay, Suffolk, in 1526. Probably he was then associated with either the parish church of St Peter Mancroft, Norwich, or the nearby collegiate church of St Mary de Campis – both institutions maintained choirs, and probably expert ones. In 1547 he was one of the stipendiary priests at St Peter Mancroft; subsequently he became the parish chaplain, and in 1556 became rector of the church. His will was proved in March 1560, and among his effects was 'a payer of Clavycords'.

ROGER BOWERS

Prowo, Pierre (*b* Altona, 8 April 1697; *d* Altona, 8 Nov 1757). German organist and composer. He came from a family of good standing and sympathetic towards music. He is known to have been organist of the Altona Reformierten Kirche from 1738. A large number of his instrumental works survive, and show competence as a secondary master in the development between suite and sonata.

WORKS
(all surviving works in D-SWl)

Jahrmarkt von St Germain (opera), Hamburg, 1738, recits only; lost
Die Vereinigung der Vier Temperamenten (cantata), S, S, S, B, chorus, orch, 16 June 1736; lost
Concerto, fl, 2 vn, bc; 6 concertos, 3 ob, 2 bn, 1 ed. R. J. Koch (Wolfenbüttel, 1959); 6 concertos, 2 rec, 2 ob, 2 bn, bc, 1 ed. in EDM, xiv (1941)
13 sonatas, 2 rec, bc; 7 sonatas, fl, vn, bc; sonata, rec, fl, bc; sonata, fl, va da gamba, bc; 12 sonatas, fl, bc; sonata, ob, bc

BIBLIOGRAPHY

EitnerQ
O. Kade: *Die Musikalien-Sammlung des grossherzoglichen Mecklenburg-Schweriner Fürstenhauses aus den letzten zwei Jahrhunderten* (Schwerin, 1893–9)
H. Schultz: Preface to *Deutsche Bläsermusik vom Barock bis zur Klassik*, EDM, xiv (1941)
H. C. Wolff: *Die Barockoper in Hamburg (1678–1738)* (Wolfenbüttel, 1957)
R. J. Koch: Preface to P. Prowo: *Concerto a 5* (Wolfenbüttel, 1959)

KURT STEPHENSON

PRS. Performing Right Society; *see* COPYRIGHT COLLECTING SOCIETIES, §II.

Pruck, Arnold de. *See* BRUCK, ARNOLD VON.

Pruden, Larry (*b* New Plymouth, 28 July 1925). New Zealand composer. He began composing at the age of 12 and was self-taught until he won a government bursary to study composition, conducting and percussion at the Guildhall School of Music, London (1951–4). There he was, like his compatriots Carr and Farquhar, a member of Frankel's composition class. In 1955 he joined the staff of the NZBC, and in 1975 he received the Mozart Fellowship at the University of Otago. Most of his colourful, highly professional and approachable works have related to places; examples include the overture *The Antipodes* (1950), the *Harbour Nocturne* (1956), *Dances of Brittany* (1956), the *Back Country Overture* (1961) and *Taranaki, a Provincial Overture* (1976). His other compositions include a lyrical *Soliloquy* for strings (1952), a String Trio (1954) and *Haast Highway*, which won first prize in the 1975 New Zealand Brass Bands Association competition.

J. M. THOMSON

Prudent [first name unknown] (*d* Paris, ?c1780). French composer. He lived in Paris, published his own works and became known as a *maître de musique et d'instruments*. His most important composition is an *opéra comique*, *Les jardiniers* (1771); it was later performed in Germany. He also wrote several *cantatilles* and some instrumental works.

WORKS
(all printed works published in Paris)

Les jardiniers (comédie with ariettes, 2, Davesnes), Paris, Comédie-Italienne, 15 July 1771 (?1771), excerpts pubd separately
Vocal: Diligite justitiam, motet, chorus, 1766; Cantatilles, with insts, incl. Les quatre saisons du coeur (1745), La fierté inutile (1745), L'heureux caprice (1745), L'aurore de l'amour (n.d.), L'innocence (n.d.), La sérénade (n.d.), others, lost
Inst: Les bouquets de Chassenay, hurdy-gurdy, bagpipe, tr viol, vn, b (n.d.); ?other works

PAULETTE LETAILLEUR

Prudent, Emile (Racine Gauthier) (*b* Angoulême, 3 Feb 1817; *d* Paris, 14 May 1863). French pianist, composer and teacher. Entering the Paris Conservatoire at the age of ten, he won the first piano prize in 1833 and the second harmony prize the following year. He did not find his studies easy and remained undistinguished until inspired by Thalberg's pianistic style, which created a furore in Paris in 1836. This style he imitated in works such as the fantasy on *Lucia di Lammermoor* (op.8), of which Thalberg himself was the dedicatee. His provincial and international reputation now began to grow, though he did not make his Paris début until 1842. Here the neatness, warmth and delicacy of his playing was much appreciated, though a lack of originality and real depth of feeling was noticed by the critics. During his many foreign tours Prudent made a reputation both as a performer and a teacher. He had less standing as a composer, however, as his many operatic fantasias suffered in comparison with those of Liszt and Thalberg. He died suddenly in the summer of 1863 at a time when the rapid fingerwork for which he had been famed was beginning to decline.

Prudent's compositional style lacks originality and depth. Although at the time it fulfilled its function – the salon and concert hall – its interest today is purely historical. It exhibits all the characteristics of its time – emphasis on triple metres, sentimental rather than colourful chromaticism, arpeggiated figurations for the left hand and delicate filigree work for the right. Prudent's idea of the variation principle was one of increasingly elaborate decorations above a constant harmonic pattern and most of his work suffers from his pursuit of this particular *idée fixe*. His harmonic vocabulary rarely moves beyond the diminished 7th and the dominant 13th, while his most adventurous tonal contrasts are made by the flattened submediant or changes of mode on the tonic. The one personal characteristic which remains to intrigue the modern scholar, and which gives some indication of Prudent's performing style, is the enormous number of tempo and stylistic directions used, suggesting a determination to evoke every delicate tint of which the instrument was capable.

BRIAN PRIMMER

Prudenzani, Simone [Simone di Golino di Prudenzano] (*b* Prodo, nr. Orvieto, 2nd half of 14th century; *d* c1440). Italian poet. He wrote a long poem, made up of sonnets, entitled *Saporetto* or *Liber saporecti*; this is divided into four parts (*Mundus placidus, blandus, tranquillus* and *meritorius*), and is linked with a group of 18 *novelle* in ballata metre, entitled *Sollazzo* or *Liber solatii*. These works describe life at the fictitious court of Pierbaldo, Lord of Buongoverno, who begs his friend Bonare to send his son Sollazzo to sing and play for the amusement of Pierbaldo's court. They provide valuable evidence of the musical repertory then in vogue by specifying the compositions performed (by incipit). Some of the identifiable compositions were written by the most famous composers of the late 14th and the early 15th centuries. Prudenzani also gives interesting information about dances, musical instruments and performing practice.

BIBLIOGRAPHY

S. Debenedetti: 'Il "Sollazzo" e il "Saporetto" con altre rime di Simone Prudenzani d'Orvieto', *Giornale storico della letteratura italiana*, suppl.xv (1913), iv
——: *Il 'Sollazzo': contributi alla storia della novella, della poesia musicale e del costume nel trecento* (Turin, 1922)

F. ALBERTO GALLO

Prugg, Jacob de. *See* BROUCK, JACOB DE.

Prumier, Antoine (*b* Paris, 2 July 1794; *d* Paris, 20 July 1868). French harpist and composer. He studied the harp with his mother and showed an early talent for both music and mathematics. In 1810, after taking first prize in mathematics at the Lycée Bonaparte, he entered the Conservatoire, where he studied the harp under Naderman and took *second prix* in Catel's harmony class (1812). He took the licencié ès lettres at the Ecole Polytechnique and the licencié ès sciences at the Ecole Normale, then re-entered the Conservatoire and studied counterpoint under Eler. He became harpist at the Théâtre-Italien, but moved to the Opéra-Comique in 1835 when he became professor at the Conservatoire, succeeding Naderman. Within a month he had persuaded the authorities to allow him to teach the double-action harp. He retired in 1867. Not a highly regarded performer, Prumier was nevertheless a good teacher; among his pupils were Josef Hasselmans and Samuele Merlow. He was a captain in the National Guard, was decorated by the Légion d'honneur in 1845, and was a vice-president of the Association des Artistes Musiciens for 17 years and received its award in 1850. He wrote a number of examination pieces for use at the Conservatoire, a *Méthode pour harpe à double mouvement* op.76 (Paris, 1865) and about 75 forgotten works for harp.

Prumier's son Ange-Conrad (*b* Paris, 5 Jan 1820; *d* Paris, 3 April 1884) studied with his father at the Conservatoire (where he took the *premier prix* for the harp in 1838 and for counterpoint and fugue in 1845) and succeeded him at the Opéra-Comique in 1840. He also played at the Opéra and the Pasdeloup and Conservatoire concerts. He was tutor of preparatory harp classes at the Conservatoire from 1838 to 1851, and in 1870 succeeded Labarre as professor. His *Etudes spéciales pour la harpe* (Paris, 1866), a continuation of his father's *Méthode*, advocated holding the harp on either shoulder, but the practice was not generally accepted.

BIBLIOGRAPHY

FétisB
B. Bagatti: *Arpa e arpisti* (Piacenza, 1932), 48
M. G. Scimeca: *L'arpa nella storia* (Bari, 1938), 166
M. Tournier: *La harpe* (Paris, 1959; Eng. trans., 1959), 39
A. N. Schirinzi: *L'arpa* (Milan, 1961), 129
H. Charnassé and F. Vernillat: *Les instruments à cordes pincées* (Paris, 1970), 45f

ALICE LAWSON ABER

Prumion. A category of chant in SYRIAN CHURCH MUSIC.

Prunet. *See* PERRINET.

Prunières, Henry (*b* Paris, 24 May 1886; *d* Nanterre, 11 April 1942). French musicologist. He was a pupil of Rolland at the Sorbonne from 1906, taking the doctorat ès lettres there in 1913 with dissertations on Italian opera in France before Lully and the *ballet de cour* in France before Benserade and Lully; later he also took the diploma of advanced librarianship (1935). After compiling a catalogue of the music in the Biblioteca Laurenziana, Florence (1908), he taught at the Ecole des Hautes Etudes Sociales (1909–14). In 1920 he founded and directed (until 1939) the *Revue musicale* and from 1921 its series of concerts, largely of contemporary music, given in the Théâtre du Vieux Colombier; at these, he ardently promoted the music of Bartók, Malipiero, Pizzetti and Casella. Concurrently he worked as Paris music correspondent of the *New York Times* (1924–35) and general secretary and chairman of the French section of the International Music Society, of which he was a co-founder.

Prunières' writings are largely centred on French music of the 17th century. Above all, he was responsible, almost single-handed, for rediscovering Lully and identifying him as the founder of French music and the creator of a style which dominated French music until the Revolution. The background to his Lully studies is admirably covered in the doctoral dissertations, and he returned repeatedly to the period in articles published throughout his life. One of his last enterprises was a collected edition of Lully's music, sadly left incomplete. Of these volumes, the most useful is *Alceste* since there is no complete full score of this work dating from Lully's lifetime; Prunières' collation of librettos, part-books and incomplete versions is masterly. Nothing that Prunières wrote later is as enduringly valuable as the two dissertations. His short books, *Lully* (1910) and *Monteverdi* (1924), are hampered by the limitations of the series to which they belong, and they may appear simplistic or facile because Prunières was constrained to present only the conclusions of his studies and not the research itself. In *Cavalli et l'opéra vénitien* (1931), however, he overcame these restraints. This is probably his most successful book for the general reader, combining something of the breadth of scope of his scholarly writing with the lively anecdotal style in which it came naturally to him to communicate his passion for the 17th century.

WRITINGS

'Lecerf de la Viéville', *BSIM*, iv (1908), 619
with L. de La Laurencie: 'La jeunesse de Lully', *BSIM*, v (1909), 234, 329
Lully (Paris, 1910, 2/1927)
'Recherches sur les années de jeunesse de Lully', *RMI*, xvii (1910), 646
'Notes sur la vie de L. Rossi', *SIMG*, xii (1910–11), 12
'Notes sur les origines de l'ouverture française', *SIMG*, xii (1910–11), 565; also in *IMusSCR*, iv *London 1911*, 149
'Lully à l'Odéon', *BSIM*, vii/12 (1911), 70
'Jean de Cambrefort', *Année musicale*, ii (1912), 205
La musique de la chambre et l'écurie (Paris, 1912)
'Lully, fils de meunier', *BSIM*, viii/6 (1912), 57
'Les représentations du Palazzo d'Atlante à Rome (1692)', *SIMG*, xiv

(1912–13), 218

'Notes bibliographiques sur les cantates de L. Rossi au Cons. de Naples', *ZIMG*, xiv (1912–13), 109

L'opéra italien en France avant Lulli (diss., U. of Paris, 1913; Paris, 1913/*R*1975)

Le ballet de cour en France avant Benserade et Lully (supplementary diss., U. of Paris, 1913; Paris, 1914/*R*1970)

'Documents pour servir à la biographie des luthistes R. Ballard et F. Pinel', *ZIMG*, xv (1913–14), 587

'Le ballet sous Louis XIII', *BSIM*, x/2 (1914), 1

'Notes sur un musicien oublié, Louis Maurice de la Pierre', *RdM*, ii/6–10 (1920–21), 71

'La Fontaine et Lully', *ReM*, ii/10 (1921), 98

'Une chanson de Molière', *ReM*, ii/4 (1921), 151

'Un opéra de Paolo Lorenzani', *Congrès d'histoire de l'art: Paris 1921*, 867

'Paolo Lorenzani à la Cour de France (1678–1694)', *ReM*, iii/10 (1922), 97

'Un portrait de Hobrecht et de Verdelot par Sebastiano del Piombo', *ReM*, iii/8 (1922), 193

ed.: Stendhal: *Vie de Rossini* (Paris, 1923)

'Wagner et Renoir', *ReM* (1923), 189 [special issue]

Claudio Monteverdi (Paris, 1924)

'Die Moderne: Franzosen', *Handbuch der Musikgeschichte*, ed. G. Adler (Frankfurt am Main, 1924, rev. 2/1930/*R*1961), 948

'L'Academie Royale de Musique et de Danse', *ReM*, vi/3 (1925), 3

'Lully and the Académie de Musique et de Danse', *MQ*, xi (1925), 528

'Portraits et médaillons', *Cinquante ans de musique française*, ii, ed. L. Rohozinski (Paris, 1925), 359–420

La vie et l'oeuvre de Claudio Monteverdi (Paris, 1926; Eng. trans., 1926/*R*1973)

La vie illustre et libertine de Jean-Baptiste Lully (Paris, 1929/*R*1977)

'La cantate italienne à voix seule', *EMDC*, II/v (1930), 3390

'Le Page de Dassoucy: contribution à l'histoire des moeurs musicales au XVIIᵉ siècle', *Studien zur Musikgeschichte: Festschrift für Guido Adler* (Vienna, 1930/*R*1971), 153

Cavalli et l'opéra vénitien au XVIIe siècle (Paris, 1931)

'Des rapports artistiques internationaux considérés du point de vue de la musique, de la musicologie et des musiciens', *I° congresso internazionale di musica: Firenze 1933*, 233

'Les musiciens du Cardinal Antonio Barberini', *Mélanges de musicologie offerts à M. Lionel de la Laurencie* (Paris, 1933), 119

Nouvelle histoire de la musique (Paris, 1934–6; Eng. trans., 1943/*R*1972)

'Les tendances actuelles de la musique', *Encyclopédie française*, xvii/2, ed. L. Febvre (Paris, 1935)

'Le symbolisme dans la création musicale', *2e congrès international d'esthétique et de science de l'art: Paris 1937*, 232

EDITIONS

Maîtres du chant (Paris, 1924–7)

J.-B. Lully: Oeuvres complètes (Paris, 1930–39, inc.)

BIBLIOGRAPHY

'Hommage à Henry Prunières', *ReM* (1952), no.213 [special issue, incl. tributes by Rolland, Chailley, Cocteau, Dufourcq, G. M. Gatti, Jolivet, Lifar, Malipiero, Malraux, Milhaud, Pincherle and others]

C. van den Borren: 'Henry Prunières', *RBM*, i (1946–7), 179

PATRICIA HOWARD

Psali (from Gk. *psallein*: 'praise'). A category of hymn in the MUSIC OF THE COPTIC RITE.

Psalinīs, Ubertus de. *See* HYMBERT DE SALINIS.

Psalm (from Gk. *psalmos*; Lat. *psalmus*). An ancient Greek term which, though originally meaning a 'striking' or 'plucking', especially of the strings of a musical instrument, was applied to the poems of the Hebrew 'Book of Praises' (*séfer t'hilím*), in other words the biblical *Psalms*, by the Jewish translators of the Septuagint (the Greek version of the Old Testament) in the 2nd century BC. It was also later applied to certain apocryphal religious poems, and also to non-Hebrew poems of the early Christian Church, such as the so-called *psalmi idiotici* and the psalm against the Donatists by St Augustine. This article is concerned with the musical settings of the biblical *Psalms*, and of texts, such as the biblical canticles, whose settings are similar to those of the psalms, in Judaism, early Christianity and the traditions springing from Latin Christianity. (For accounts of psalmody

in the Eastern Churches, see the articles on the various rites.) No detailed account is given here of the various independent musical forms which originated ultimately in psalmody, even though these often retained psalmodic texts; for these *see* ANTIPHON; COMMUNION; GRADUAL (i); INTROIT (i); OFFERTORY etc. For metrical psalm settings, *see* PSALMS, METRICAL.

I. Antiquity and early Christianity. II. Latin monophonic psalmody. III. Polyphonic psalms.

I. Antiquity and early Christianity

1. Transmission of texts; numeration. 2. Age; authorship. 3. Poetic structure and metre. 4. Categories of psalm. 5. Performing practice. 6. Liturgical functions.

1. TRANSMISSION OF TEXTS; NUMERATION. The main translations of the psalter from the Hebrew were those of the Greek Septuagint and the Syriac *p'shitta*, besides the Latin versions. Of the latter, the oldest was the *Vetus Itala*, of which only fragments survive (mainly in the texts of Gregorian chants). St JEROME later made three translations, which are known as the *psalterium romanum*, the *psalterium gallicanum* and the *psalterium juxta Hebraeos*; of these the first two were taken over into the Vulgate Latin translation of the Bible, although the third is the most important for the student of the biblical text.

These translations differ not only in textual detail but also in their numbering of the psalms. The Vulgate and the Syriac text (and following the Vulgate, the older Roman Catholic versions of the English Bible) follow the numeration of the Septuagint; this differs from the numeration of the Hebrew (Masoretic) text, which was followed in the Authorized Version and most other Protestant versions of the Bible including the Revised Standard Version. The differences are shown in Table 1.

The psalter came to be divided for liturgical use into five books, analogous to those of the Pentateuch, comprising (according to the Masoretic numeration) 1–41, 42–72, 73–89, 90–106 and 106–50. The numbering used in this article is that of the Revised Standard Version unless otherwise stated.

TABLE 1

Masoretic, Protestant	Septuagint, Vulgate, Roman Catholic
1–8	1–8
9–10	9
11–113	10–112
114–15	113
116 vv. 1–9	114
116 vv. 10–19	115
117–46	116–45
147 vv. 1–11	146
147 vv. 12–29	147
148–50	148–50

2. AGE; AUTHORSHIP. Besides the psalms, there are other collections of ancient Near Eastern hymns and poems which to some extent resemble them: poems for cultic or royal ceremonies from Sumerian, Akkadian, Ugaritic and Egyptian literature. These resemble the psalms notably in their parallelistic structure – the so-called *parallelismus membrorum*, or structure comprising pairs of balanced half-verses. Nevertheless, the psalms are more impressive as poetry and range over a wider scope of subject matter: praise, thanksgiving, profession of faith, cries for help, complaints, supplications, expressions of penitence, community hymns, cultic songs and even polemics (Psalm cxxxvii) and oracles

(e.g. Psalms ii, xxix). Through the Septuagint and Vulgate, the parallelistic structure of the psalms entered Greek and Latin literature.

The traditionally accepted Davidic authorship of the psalter (*see* DAVID) is not asserted in the psalter itself but appeared first in the Apocrypha (*Ecclesiasticus* xlvii.8ff). In the psalter only 73 psalms are ascribed to David, with others ascribed to Asaph, Jeduthun, Heman, the Korahites and even Moses. W. F. Albright recognized only Psalm xviii as Davidic.

Modern biblical scholars, such as H. Gunkel, S. Mowinckel, H. H. Rowley, T. H. Robinson, J. Kraus and W. F. Albright, have sought to date the psalms by comparative philology, using the evidence of Ugaritic and Mesopotamian parallels. Though differing in many details, they broadly agree that the psalms were composed by priests, singers or prophets in the service of the Temple. Such a hypothesis would explain the unity of the style of the psalms as well as their rich diversity.

3. POETIC STRUCTURE AND METRE. The device of parallelistic structure occurs in the psalter in a variety of ways – synonymic (two half-verses stating the same thing in two different ways), antithetic (using the half-verses to oppose contrasting statements), synthetic (the second half-verse completes the statement) and climactic, as in the following, from Psalm xxix:

Ascribe to the Lord, O heavenly beings: ascribe to the Lord glory and strength!
Ascribe to the Lord the glory of his name: worship the Lord in holy array!

Monumental climaxes could be created in this way, as in Psalm xliv.4–12, and they suggest an analogous musical structure.

In some of the oldest canticles, words *in pausa* (at a caesura or at the end of a verse or important subdivision) are frequently lengthened. This poetic device originated at a very early date, probably before the kingdom of Israel, that is, before *c*1000 BC. This poetic device is similar to the lengthening of the final mute 'e' in French poetry when it is sung, and may have been the origin of the so-called 'punctuating melismas' of all later psalmody, for both parallelistic structure and the lengthening of words *in pausa* are characteristic of all psalmody, not merely Hebrew psalmody. Modern metrical theory generally supposes that the poetic stress of a Hebrew word coincided with its stress in normal usage; this was not the case in Greek and Latin poetry. Most modern scholars assume that each word had a single accent, and that each half-verse contained two, three or four accents, and a theory of pairs of half-verses with two or three accents in each member has been constructed, but with numerous exceptions. Since the Hebrew language is mainly iambic and anapaestic in metre, the verses have a rising rhythm, as in Psalm xix.1:

Ha-shamáyim m'saprím k'vód Él: uma'assé yadáv magíd harakíah.
(The heavens are telling the glory of God: and the firmament proclaims his handiwork.)

Each half-verse here contains four accented syllables and in each only one word is not accented on the final syllable.

4. CATEGORIES OF PSALM. The psalter contains poems from many different centuries, but successive editing has imposed a certain stylistic unity on them. Psalms cxxii, cxxvi, cxxxiv and cxxxvii clearly betray their exilic or post-exilic origin, and other uniform groups of psalms may be discerned. Psalms iii to xli are almost all ascribed to David. Psalms cxx to cxxxiv are termed 'songs of pilgrimage' (i.e. to Jerusalem), rendered in the Vulgate as *cantus graduum* ('songs of degrees' in the Authorized Version). Even in pre-Christian times, Psalms cxiii to cxviii were known collectively as the Hallel.

Scholars have assumed, and with some justification, that these groups of psalms may be distinguished by their distinctive subject matter; but the groups that they have attempted to distinguish (such as those glorifying Yahweh's accession to the throne, those celebrating Yahweh as king of the world on New Year's Day, or those dealing with creation) in the absence of ancient titles can be at best hypothetical. The search for these categories, suggested in the first place by the headings of some of the psalms (see below), was stimulated also by the theory of H. Gunkel concerning the 'practical function' (*Sitz im Leben*) of the psalms, so that scholars have attempted to assign a precise function to all the psalms – cultic, royal, autobiographical on the part of the psalmist and so on.

The headings of some psalms are notable. These vary from simple descriptions ('a psalm', 'a song', 'by David') to puzzling metaphors ('according to The Hind of the Dawn', Psalm xxii; 'according to The Dove on Far-off Terebinths', Psalm lvi). The frequent 'lamnatzeah', generally mistranslated 'to the choirmaster', probably signifies a type of victory song to be arranged by the master of ceremonies. Some of the headings remain unexplained. The term 'higgaion' (e.g. in Psalm ix.16) seems to signify a murmur on the lyre (b'kinnor). The 'poetic' and metaphorical titles are generally understood today as incipits of secular songs, to whose melodies the psalms were sung; some of the apocryphal psalms also bear headings of this type.

The Dead Sea Scrolls also contain some non-canonical psalms, apparently composed in the 2nd and 1st centuries BC (the best edition is that by J. A. Sanders, New York, 1965).

5. PERFORMING PRACTICE. Temple psalmody must be distinguished from that of the ancient synagogue and that of the early Christian Church, especially since it was executed by professional singers (Levites), accompanied by various instruments. In later psalmody, each verse was chanted to a fairly rigid formula; yet the diversity of the psalm headings seems to exclude a simple rigid psalmodic structure in the Temple and in consequence to deny a direct connection between the chant of primitive Christianity and that of the Temple. As early as 150 years after the destruction of the Temple, however, the rabbis were unable to agree on the manner in which the Hallel psalms had been sung in the Temple.

Synagogal psalmody seems to have been simple and to have been adopted by the early Christian Church; the Talmud offers evidence of the existence of antiphonal, direct and responsorial psalmody in late antiquity (see below, §II). Of the various Jewish psalmodic traditions that survive, that of the Yemenites seems to be the oldest, and its simple formulae resemble those of the earliest corpus of Gregorian psalmody.

6. LITURGICAL FUNCTIONS. In the Temple the psalms were regularly chanted daily by the chorus of Levites, accompanied by instruments. Each weekday had a Proper psalm, and the Hallel was sung at the New Moon and festivals. In the synagogue liturgy about 50 psalms are recited each day of the week in services in the morning, afternoon and evening, with further psalms added on Sabbaths and holy days. The penitential and

supplicatory psalms are chanted at certain times, including fast days. Outside the synagogue a pious orthodox Jew normally recites the entire psalter during the course of a week. In the ancient synagogue Proper psalms were prescribed for each Sabbath, varying with the pericopes from the Pentateuch; these Proper psalms were probably the model for Christian Mass psalmody, especially the gradual.

The psalter is used rather differently in the various Christian rites. In the Eastern Churches psalms are seldom sung entire: they are varied and associated with non-biblical poetry, verses from other parts of the Bible and so on (for some details *see* SYRIAN CHURCH MUSIC). The Western Churches, on the other hand, generally leave the psalm texts untouched when complete psalms are sung; or, as in the Mass, a few verses of a psalm are sung as part of an antiphonal or responsorial chant. In the Divine Office the psalms are the basis of the service, with canticles imparting a characteristic flavour to individual services such as Vespers.

Doxologies are closely linked with psalms in the liturgy in Judaism as in Christianity (*see* DOXOLOGY); the Hebrew psalter contains doxologies at the close of each of the first four books (Psalms xli.13, lxxii.18f, lxxxix.52, cvi.48). Psalm cl is considered in its entirety as a doxology.

See also JEWISH MUSIC, §I; CHRISTIAN CHURCH, MUSIC OF THE EARLY.

II. Latin monophonic psalmody

1. Development of psalmodic forms. 2. Common tones for the Office psalms and canticles and the introits. 3. Invitatory tones. 4. Tones of the great responsories.

1. DEVELOPMENT OF PSALMODIC FORMS. The history of psalmody is incomplete before the 9th century, for no musical notation survives from before AD 800, the date of the earliest Frankish chant books. We are thus dependent on literary-historical reports to describe much more than half of the time during which psalms have been sung. The oldest surviving notation (apart from the few relics of antiquity) is from about the 9th century, and was developed specifically for psalmody, since the whole repertory of Western chant that it transmits was founded on the psalms. Previously psalmody was an oral tradition and it is therefore impossible to describe it precisely.

Comparisons of chant dialects, such as Old Roman and Gregorian, on the theory that what they share is most probably ancient, and researches into the psychology of memory as it applies to oral traditions are the most promising lines of inquiry. Comparative studies of the psalmodic traditions of the Jewish diaspora which, though widely scattered and long out of touch, still show resemblances to one another and to ancient Christian psalmody, have provided some proof of the strength of these traditions, although their conclusions about points of melodic detail should be treated with care (Idelsohn, Werner).

Medieval Jewish psalmody is especially inaccessible through the absence of sources (*see* JEWISH MUSIC, §I). Musical remains of the psalmody of the Eastern Churches are likewise quite late, but its development was different from that of the West. In Byzantine chant particularly psalm singing did not develop so extensively; composers devoted their creative energies to hymn composition (e.g. troparia, kontakia etc; *see* BYZANTINE RITE, MUSIC OF THE).

The critical period for the dependence of Christian on Jewish psalmody was the time when Christianity was perceived as a Jewish sect, and when the influence of Jewish Christians and of their traditions was still strong. Jewish singers within the Christian communities continued the practice of the synagogue and helped establish the framework of early Christian liturgy and song, especially the psalmody of the synaxis, the service of readings and prayers which preceded the Eucharist proper (*see* MASS, §I). In Syria, especially, Jewish Christians maintained links with the synagogue for several centuries, though they had become a little-noticed minority in the church. The earliest church of the Near East of which there are still remains, at Dura-Europos, had still, in the early 3rd century, an ambo shaped like the synagogal *bēma* from which cantor and lector chanted.

Though the melodic substance of the psalmody passed from synagogue to church is now beyond recall, there are precise descriptions of its formal structure in Talmudic literature. Seven different types have been distinguished, all responsorial and based on the formal principle of the 'confrontation of soloist and choir' (see Avenary, 1953). These are: (1) repetition of each phrase or verse by the people in response to the soloist; (2) intonation of the incipit by the soloist; (3) repetition of a phrase from the first verse as a refrain, on the model of Psalm cxxxvi; (4) use of 'Hallelujah' as a response; (5) alternate singing of half-verses by soloist and people; (6) repetition of verses; (7) use of textual additions as responses.

Fragmentary and brief though these Talmudic descriptions are, the formal structures and psalmodic practice of medieval Christian chant can be discerned in them. All are responsorial; nos.3 and 5 have the seeds of Western antiphony; and the different direction of Eastern chant, which developed the chanting of texts modelled after psalms and added to them, rather than using strict psalmody, is presaged in no.7. Several of them presuppose a knowledge of the text, and this suggests a difficulty in the use of such psalmody among non-Jewish Christians unfamiliar with the scriptures. Difference of language presented a further difficulty, for most churches soon adopted a vernacular text, and were forced to adapt the Hebrew melodic tradition, thus giving rise to the subsequent divergence of Jewish and Christian psalmody.

From its beginning in Judaism, the history of Western psalmody can be traced in three broad stages, separated by the Edict of Milan (AD 313) and the age of Pope Gregory I (*c*600). In the first stage the liturgy was still mostly improvised, with variability in the choice of texts for readings and psalmody; local tradition was the guide, hierarchical authority not yet having arrogated to itself the right to regulate worship with the precision and insistence of later centuries. The chief use of psalmody was in the synaxis, at which psalms were interspersed in the lessons. This association of psalm with lesson was perhaps a Christian invention, for it is not found in the synagogue before the 8th century, but the manner of performance and the melodic tradition were probably still close to their Jewish antecedents. Tertullian (*c*200) mentioned this *cantus responsorius*, in which the gradual can be seen, and a solo psalm without response, the later tract, was probably then being sung (*De oratione*, chap.27; *PL*, i, 1301).

St Augustine, some 200 years later, reported that the responsorial psalmody of the Mass required a longer text than the later gradual (evidently a whole psalm) and that its melody was less florid, for the response was sung by the congregation, not by a trained choir (*PL*, xxxvii, 950, 1596, 1784). The adoption of Latin for Roman worship (*c*250) must have caused difficulties in psalmody, as on the change from Hebrew to Greek, but nothing is known of them. There were of course ready models in the psalmody of the African Church which had been Latin from its beginnings, and in that of rural Italy. The text of Latin psalmody in these early centuries was drawn from the Old Latin version of the psalter (*Vetus Itala*), but from the late 4th century there was widespread acceptance in the West of the second of St Jerome's translations, which because of its rapid penetration into Gaul became known as the Gallican psalter. Until the late Middle Ages the church throughout most of Italy continued to use a psalter of the ancient type (perhaps Jerome's first translation, a very cursory revision of the Old Latin), which came to be called the Roman psalter.

The emancipation of the church under Constantine in 313, and the subsequent acceptance of Christianity as the state religion, moved the liturgy from its variable and still improvisatory condition to one of fixity by the reign of Gregory the Great (590–604). Within this period both Mass and Office assumed the shapes that have endured with little significant change to modern times. In the 4th century the bishop became a civic as well as a religious official and the worship over which he presided took on aspects of civic as well as religious celebration. It was probably his new rank that led to his being greeted with music, a new kind of psalmody, at his processional entry to celebrate the Eucharist. The antiphonal psalmody of this entrance rite became the *antiphona ad introitum* of early manuscript sources – the later introit – and antiphonal psalmody developed around the other processions of the Eucharist as well, at the offertory and the Communion. But the nature of the music of these rites in their early stages is unknown. By the time it was written down the offertory psalmody was quite distinctive, and stylistically remote from that of the introit and Communion. The antiphons of the latter were more neumatic than melismatic, and their verses were sung to fixed psalm tones, but the offertory was highly melismatic throughout, even in the earliest manuscripts, and its verses were sung by a soloist, so that it resembled the responsorial chants rather than the antiphonal. Like the Communion, the offertory later lost its verses and was reduced to antiphon alone. Only the introit maintained its antiphonal character throughout the Middle Ages, though even by the time of the first sources it had been reduced to antiphon, psalm verse, doxology and an additional verse *ad repetendum*.

The years between Constantine and Gregory I also saw the rise of monasticism, which gave the chief impetus to the growth of the daily round of psalmody that came to make up the Office Hours. Beginning in Egypt (*c*300), the monastic movement spread within a century throughout East and West. Its psalmody was institutionalized in the West in the *Regula magistri* (*c*540), the forerunner of the Rule of St Benedict. Benedict's model for the ordering of the Office, however, was rather the liturgy of the Roman basilicas (*see* BENEDICT OF NURSIA). Psalmody had undoubtedly been practised before this in non-eucharistic services as well as at Mass, but was reduced to uniformity and system by the monastic Rule. The vigils of the early Christians became the Nocturns (Matins) and Lauds of the Western Office, evening psalmody became Vespers, and later Compline, and the other periods of the day were consecrated by

fixed times for psalmody – Prime, Terce, Sext and None (*see* DIVINE OFFICE and articles on individual Offices). A monk of Benedict's day would spend about four hours at this *opus Dei*; this increased considerably, until, some five centuries later, the *horarium* drawn up by Lanfranc required monks to spend eight hours daily at religious services. At Matins responsorial psalmody took root as it had at Mass, a psalm sung by a cantor with the community responding after the reading of a lesson. This became the great responsory of the later Office, a chant which in liturgical function, and to a degree in style, resembles the gradual. Like the gradual, it comprises solo verses and choral responds, but its repetition patterns are more complicated and the verses are sung to reciting tones similar to, but more elaborate than, those of antiphonal psalmody. But the greater part of Office psalmody was antiphonal, probably even in these early years sung to psalm tones by alternating sides of the choir. The monastic ideal called for the chanting of the whole psalter each week, and was established also in secular churches, where bodies of clergy (canons etc) performed the *opus Dei*.

The Roman liturgy had by the time of Gregory the Great assumed a stable and familiar shape; the assumption that the melodic shape of its psalmody would also be familiar in some degree is not implausible. It was at any rate a Roman liturgy and its chant which superseded the local liturgies and dialects of chant under the Carolingians in the 8th and 9th centuries, and established firmly the common psalmodic language that is found uniformly in surviving Western manuscripts. The stabilization of psalmody in the third broad stage of its history, following the age of Gregory, was achieved between this time and the 11th century, and is known from three main sources: service books for Mass and Office, the writings of theorists and the lists known as tonaries, which categorized chants according to mode and specified the ending (*differentia*) of a psalm tone to be used with a given antiphon. Important medieval theoretical works on psalmody include the *Commemoratio brevis de tonis et psalmis modulandis* (*c*900; *GS*, i, 213), the *Musica disciplina* of Aurelian of Réôme (*c*850; *GS*, i, 27), and the *Instituta patrum de modo psallendi* (13th century; *GS*, i, 5). The tonaries have been exhaustively studied by Michel Huglo (1971; *see* TONARY).

The most common classification of psalmody is the division into DIRECT PSALMODY, ANTIPHONAL PSALMODY and RESPONSORIAL PSALMODY, terms that can denote both structure and performing practice, but which lost much of their original meaning because the historical development of psalmodic chanting altered the character of the chants they describe. Thus the *cantus responsorius*, originally a whole psalm sung by a cantor to which the congregation made repeated response, became reduced in the later Middle Ages to a single ornate response followed by a verse, but with the choir joining in for the last words of the verse rather than repeating the response; and the antiphonal psalmody, by its admission of the refrain-like antiphon, moved very close to the responsorial type.

The fully developed Western psalmodies can also be categorized by liturgical genre, but such classification is not valid for their stylistic character. This character ranges from the simple and rigid formula of the psalm tones to the great freedom of many Mass antiphons (introits, offertories and communions), while between these extremes lie psalmodies that make varying use of the principles of CENTONIZATION (formulaic composition) and melody-type. The most obvious use of centonization occurs in the tracts, all of which are built on the recurrent and systematic use of standard phrases (and which constitute the most significant surviving examples of direct psalmody). The graduals and the great responsories make less use of centonization.

All these musical techniques are found, in varying degrees, in a variety of liturgical genres of psalmody. Psalm tones are found in the solo sections of the Office responsories, though the responsories are otherwise formulaic like the graduals; and some Office antiphons, and a few introit antiphons, have a formulaic appearance, though the former are more usually based on melody-types and the latter are more usually free in style. There is some doubt, however, as to whether centonization and melody-type should be regarded as deliberately chosen techniques of composition, or as evidence of the little-understood processes in purely oral traditions, in which all performing is composition (or perhaps recomposition), and calls upon the performer's memorized store of familiar phrases and the peculiar ability of the memory to apply them in varying patterns to different situations. It may be that the 'techniques' of psalmody so carefully categorized by modern scholars all derive from the homogeneous processes common to the music of oral traditions.

An example of such processes may be found in the introits of the Friday and Saturday of Easter week, *Eduxit eos Dominus* and *Eduxit Dominus populum*. The incipits of these two melodies are the same in the Gregorian version, though the subsequent melodies differ. But when they are compared with the versions in the Old Roman tradition (see ex.1) it can be seen that the Old Roman melodies are practically the same; that the two texts are set to a single melody-type; and that the dissimilar Gregorian versions bear resemblances to the Old Roman type melody, as if they were distant variations of it. The rigid Old Roman formula has been relaxed in the course of the formation of the Gregorian melodies, until only the incipit remains to show that the two Gregorian melodies are closely related.

Ex.1

Old Roman (*I-Rvat* lat. 5319, f. 93*v*)

E - du - xit e - os   Do - mi - nus in   spe...

Gregorian (*GR*, p. 235)

E - du - xit e - os   Do - mi-nus in   spe...

Old Roman (*I-Rvat* lat. 5319, f. 95)

E - du - xit Do- mi - nus po -pu - lum su - um...

Gregorian (*GR*, p.238)

E - du - xit Do- mi - nus po - pu -lum su - um...

2. COMMON TONES FOR THE OFFICE PSALMS AND CANTICLES AND THE INTROITS.

(i) *Description and structure of tones.* The antiphonal psalmody of the Office contains the most complete and systematic form of the monophonic psalm. The Benedictine Office, and the ancient Roman Office that preceded it, specified that the whole psalter should be chanted once a week. The psalms were thus distributed over the Office Hours of the seven days, in somewhat different patterns according to local or monastic use, and were sung antiphonally to the rigidly formulaic melodies known as psalm tones. There are various series of these, one for each of several liturgical genres: antiphonal psalmody of the Office, antiphonal psalmody of the Mass (introit verse and doxology, and formerly communion verse) and Office canticles. Psalm tones are used also for the solo verses of the great responsories and the invitatory psalm of Matins (Psalm xcv), but these should be considered separately, the former because of their great complexity, the latter because of their unusual construction and because they do not constitute a series as do the common tones.

Each series of common psalm tones comprises eight tones, one appropriate to each of the church modes, the choice of tone being determined by the mode of the accompanying antiphon. Within a series each tone is a single melodic formula which is adapted and repeated for every verse of the psalm or canticle, and for the lesser doxology (*Gloria Patri*) which, by ancient tradition, has almost always been added to them. All the tones are inflected recitatives (*see* INFLECTION) and follow the same basic plan. The reciting note (*tenor, tuba*) is inflected at its beginning (intonation, *intonatio*), its midpoint (mediant, mediation, *mediatio*) and its end (*terminatio, differentia, distinctio*). If the first half-verse is specially long, it may be further divided by a slight inflection (flex, *flexa*). The introit tones have in addition a second intonation for the second part of the verse, immediately following the mediation. This plan may be represented schematically thus: intonation – reciting note – [flex – reciting note] – mediation: [second intonation] – reciting note – ending.

An exception must be made for the doxology of the introit tones, which is tripartite, the middle section being a repeat of the first but with the second rather than the first intonation (i.e. second intonation – reciting note – mediation). This unusual construction resembles that of the invitatory tones (see below, §3), and probably belongs to the more ancient strata of psalmody. The introit, it should be noted, has an invitatory function at Mass.

The most variable element in this scheme is the ending. Since each psalm was framed by an antiphon, there had to be a smooth transition from the last cadence of the psalm (the termination of the doxology) to the incipit of the antiphon. Though antiphons are frequently constructed from melody-types, they begin on almost any note, even within a single mode, and this variety would in many cases yield an awkward transition if there were but one cadence for the conclusion of each tone. To prevent this, a variety of endings (*differentiae, distinctiones* etc) were devised for each tone. There was a great number of these, with considerable variation from one source to another. The 9th-century tonary of Metz, for instance, has as many as 13 endings for the 7th tone for Office psalmody (ed. W. Lipphardt, *Der karolingische Tonar von Metz*, Münster, 1965; *see also* TONARY, §3).

The principles governing this most strictly formulaic of psalmody styles are best demonstrated by setting out the three systems of tones, for the common Office psalms, the introits and the canticles. This is shown in ex.2, following the Vatican editions (here abbreviated

Ex.2

(a) Tone 1: D-authentic

(b) Tone 2: D-plagal

(c) Tone 3: E-authentic

(d) Tone 4: E-plagal

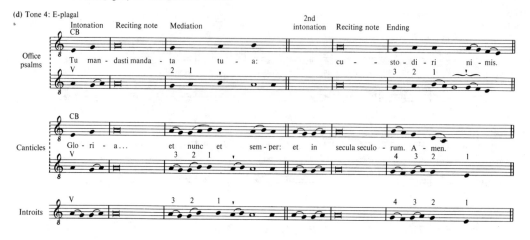

(e) Tone 5: F-authentic

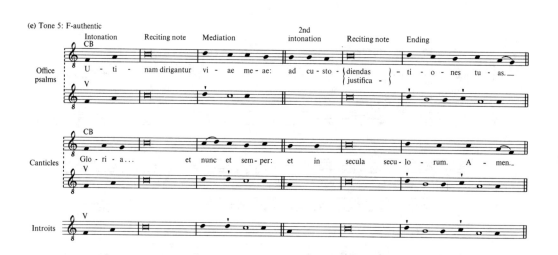

(f) Tone 6: F-plagal

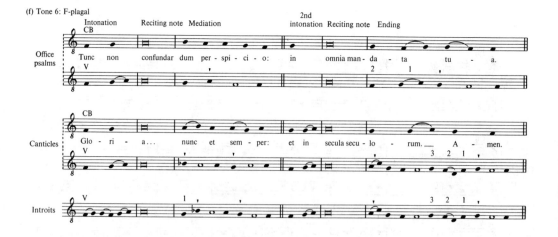

V), and also including the common tones and canticle tones of the earliest source, the *Commemoratio brevis* (here abbreviated CB). The component elements of the tones are discussed separately.

(*ii*) *Reciting note.* The tones are not 'modal melodies' and often do not end on the final of the mode; they are formulas adapted to the characteristics of the mode of the antiphon. The most characteristic element of the tone is its reciting note. There was an inherent tendency, sometimes stated as a rule, to recite a 5th above the modal final in authentic modes and a 3rd above in plagal modes. This does not accord with medieval custom (universal after the early 12th-century *De musica* of Johannes Afflighemensis) for the 3rd, 4th and 8th tones, but is attested in several ancient sources, including the *Commemoratio brevis* (for the 3rd tone). The situation is summed up in Table 2.

There is considerable evidence that *b* was used in

TABLE 2

mode	1	2	3	4	5	6	7	8
final	D	D	E	E	F	F	G	G
normal reciting note	A	F	C	A	C	A	D	C
possible primitive reciting note			B	G				B

early times as a reciting note in the 3rd and 8th tones, chiefly in Beneventan, Aquitanian and St Gall sources (as well as in the *Commemoratio brevis*). Its substitution by *c'* in later manuscripts is often attributed to a growing distaste for reciting on the lower note of a minor 2nd, although it may also have been a matter of early local preference – 'dialect'. The *Commemoratio brevis* specifies *b'* as the reciting note in both its versions of the 3rd tone. The comparison of reciting passages within the antiphons of Beneventan and Aquitanian 3rd-mode introits with corresponding passages in other sources shows a similar preference for *b* (see Gajard, 1954). B was the reciting note for the 3rd tone in neumatic (staffless) St Gall sources, as is shown by the use of the *virga strata* – a neume that usually indicates a rising minor 2nd – as an inflection within the reciting line. This suggests *b*, not *c'*, as the reciting note, and *b–c'*, not *c'–d'*, as the inflection (see Cardine, 1954).

Evidence for a primitive recitation on *b* in the 8th tone is more oblique. There are Old Roman G-mode introits whose Gregorian versions are in the 8th mode and which have a preference for *b* within the antiphon as well as *b* as a reciting note, such as *Invocavit me* (I-Rvat F22, f.20). Beneventan 8th-mode tracts often also have passages of recitation on *b* where corresponding versions in other traditions have *c'*.

Some tones do not fit this eightfold system neatly because the two halves of their verse structure use different reciting notes. Of these, the 6th introit tone and an idiosyncratic tone known as the *tonus peregrinus* were the most common. The former had *a* and *f* as reciting notes, the latter *a* and *g*. The *tonus peregrinus* was much discussed by medieval theorists, posing a problem for them not so much because of its unstable reciting note but because it was associated with a group of unusual antiphons which defied modal classification. It was customarily regarded as less ancient than the regular tones, and as somewhat suspect for liturgical use. Some modern scholars (e.g. E. Werner in *The Sacred Bridge*, p. 419) have suggested, on the basis of melodic comparisons, that it may be Jewish in origin (*see* ANTIPHON, §5(i); GALLICAN RITE, MUSIC OF THE, §10).

(*iii*) *Ending*. Two concerns are evident in the systems of endings, or cadence formulae, for the various tones: the relationship between textual and musical accentuation, and the melodic transition from the final cadence to the repeated antiphon. The first results in two broad classifications of cadences, tonic and cursive (*see* CURSUS), of which the former are adapted by the inclusion or omission of notes to the changing accent patterns at the end of the psalm verses, while the latter disregard textual accent and apply an unchanging melodic ending to the last few syllables of each verse. The cadences of the Office psalms and the canticles are tonic; those of the introits and the responsories are cursive. Ex.3 illustrates the various changes in accentuation in the two types. The 7th tone of the Office psalmody has here a cadence of two accents, which always fall on the notes *e'* and *c'*, the void notes being added for dactyls. The other example, from the 2nd introit tone, with an ending on *d'*, is shown with three differently accented endings.

The other concern evident in the cadence formulae for the transition from ending to antiphon was perhaps the major preoccupation of medieval theorists writing about psalmody. A developed system of endings already existed in Aurelian's day (*c*850), but his description of them, given in terms of grammatical accents, yields only an imprecise idea of their melodic shape. The *Commemoratio brevis* of 50 years later contains the endings, precisely notated in Daseian notation, and for several centuries thereafter they appeared unambiguously in countless tonaries, albeit with some disagreement and confusion.

The number and the melodic structure of the endings

differ somewhat from source to source; there are always more endings for the Office tones than for those of the introits, some of which often have only one ending. The proportional distribution of endings among the various tones, however, remained fairly constant throughout the Middle Ages, those with fewest being the 5th and 6th. Since these are the modes with the smallest number of antiphons, it might be suspected that endings multiplied in proportion to demand. As early as *c*900, Regino of Prüm complained that there were too many and superfluous *divisiones*, and reduced their number in his own tonary. The endings were recorded in the lists in tonaries, and in medieval service books, where they represent the most distinctive element for identifying the correct psalmody. Psalms were normally indicated after antiphons by their textual incipits, their melodic intonations and the endings, over the vowels e u o u a e – from the last words of the doxology, *seculorum amen* (*see* EVOVAE).

The easy assertion that the endings were designed as transitions from psalms to antiphons poses a problem, for there is no easily recognizable way in which this was done. One might expect that the last note of the ending would be the same as the first note of the antiphon, but this occurs only haphazardly. The *Alia musica*, a treatise from about 900, refers to transition not through unison link but by suitable interval; this may seem confusing, but may reflect an ancient tradition. A more comprehensible approach is found in tonaries; the antiphons within a mode are divided into groups, and each group is assigned to a particular ending. Since most antiphons are based on melody-types and can be classified to some degree by incipit, such sub-grouping does produce a satisfying conjunction of psalm and antiphon.

Ex.4 Psalm tone ending and antiphon from the Old Roman introit *Eduxit Dominus* (CH-CObodmer, f.lxxxvi *v*)

Some Old Roman antiphons have a type of psalm–antiphon link in which the ending is the same, note for note, as the incipit of the antiphon. If these cases are closer to the earlier practice in oral tradition, they may illustrate widespread ancient practice. An instance of this is given in ex.4, from the introit *Eduxit eos* in the gradual of S Cecilia in Trastevere (*CH-CObodmer*, without shelf-number, f.lxxxvi *v*). This ending–incipit pattern coincides also with the intonation of the 7th Gregorian psalm tone and 7th introit tone (this is also the mode of the corresponding Gregorian melody); the melodic content of the tones may thus have been deeply embedded in the antiphons themselves in earlier times, as is suggested

Ex.3

(a) 7th psalm tone

by many Old Roman introit antiphons.

The extent and variety of the systems of endings for the common Office psalms may be seen in ex.5, which reproduces those from a 13th-century English antiphoner (*GB-WO* F.160; PalMus, xii). Here the distribution of endings and final notes among the eight tones is as follows: 1st tone, 13 endings and 5 finals (*d*, *e*, *f*, *g*, *a*); 2nd tone, 1 and 1 (*d*); 3rd tone, 5 and 4 (*g*, *a*, *b*, *c'*); 4th tone, 8 and 7 (*d*, *e*, *f*, *g*, *a*, *b*, *d'*); 5th tone, 2 and 2 (*c'*, *a*); 6th tone, 1 and 1 (*f*); 7th tone, 6 and 3 (*a*, *c'*, *d'*); 8th tone, 3 and 2 (*g*, *c'*). The distribution of cadence formulae among the tones is here in about the average proportion found in medieval sources, with the first tone having the most. The 4th tone has the most finals, but this is partly because it is often found, as here, transposed up a 4th as well as at its customary reciting position on *a*, to accommodate the peculiar class of antiphons whose final is *a*. The Old Roman antiphoners far exceed the Gregorian books in the number and variety of their endings, with more than 20, for example, for both the 1st and 8th tones.

(*iv*) *Intonation.* The opening formula of the psalm tone must make a smooth junction with the end of the preceding antiphon, as the cadence must with the beginning of the subsequent antiphon. As the antiphon's final note is always the same in a given tone, however, there is no problem like that of linking ending to antiphon. The intonations of the tones never display the elaboration found in some endings (see ex.2). Those for the common Office psalmody, canticles and introits are all cursive, containing the same formula applied without adjustment to every textual incipit, no matter what its accentual pattern – unlike the intonations of the responsory tones. Those for the 1st, 3rd, 4th, 6th and 7th tones cover two syllables; those for the 2nd, 5th and 8th cover three. In Office psalmody, the intonation was commonly sung only for the first verse, with subsequent verses starting immediately on the reciting note. A notable variety is seen in the contrasting versions in early sources of the 4th-tone intonation. The usual form is *a–g–a*, with the reciting note continuing on *a*, but *e–g–a* also occurs, and may be older. Both 4th tones in the *Commemoratio brevis* have *e–g–a*, which is also the incipit for reciting psalmodic lines in a number of ancient chants, including the *Te Deum*, some melodies of the Gloria in excelsis (see Gloria XV of the Vatican editions, *LU*, p.57), and tones of the 4th mode for the invitatory psalm.

3. INVITATORY TONES. Since the time of St Benedict at the latest, Psalm xcv has been the opening psalm of daily Matins in the Western Church. It still has a place among the Sabbath morning prayers of the synagogue, and the Christian use of it may be primitive. Benedict called for Psalm iii as the first prayer of the day, with Psalm xcv to follow it immediately. Both have very apt texts, the former including the verse 'I lie down and sleep; I wake again, for the Lord sustains me'.

It was probably the direct call of Psalm xcv to worship and praise that gained it its eventual unique position: 'O come, let us sing to the Lord ... let us come into his presence with thanksgiving ... let us worship and bow down'. Such a call accords perfectly with, and may be partly the inspiration for, the Benedictine monastic spirit that placed daily psalmody as a monk's chief task. The many musical settings given it in medieval sources, together with the unique and ancient structure maintained in these settings, demonstrate its popularity and

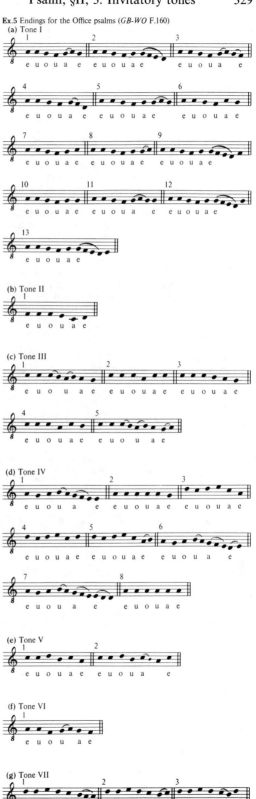

Ex.5 Endings for the Office psalms (*GB-WO* F.160)

(h) Tone VIII

the strength of its tradition. It ranks alongside those parts of the liturgy whose conservative character testifies to their antiquity. For the invitatory psalm, this antiquity is seen first in its text, which continued to follow the Roman psalter even in those churches that adopted the Gallican psalter for common psalmody. Its structure, too, is unlike that of the common Office psalms. Instead of the customary 11 verses that it has, for instance, in the psalter, it is divided into five verses only plus the doxology when it serves as invitatory, and these five are subdivided into three rather than two parts, like the doxology of the introit with its two internal intonations and two mediations. Many of the invitatory tones use different reciting notes for these three sections. The tones for the invitatory were never arranged into the eightfold system of the common Office psalmody and the introits.

Ex.6

Medieval sources sometimes have a considerable number of melodies for the invitatory, some unique, others repeated for different feasts and with different antiphons. Some books have a section devoted com-

pletely to invitatory tones, to which reference can be made from any feast, but with no attempt to arrange them by mode. The proper antiphon appears under the feast with the incipit of the tone that is to accompany it. Other books give each invitatory tone in full at the first feast for which it is to be used, while others again do not include them at all but depend on a separate source. Steiner has studied a manuscript with 22 notated tones, *E-Tc* 44.2. The proper invitatory antiphons also appear in large numbers, the Worcester antiphoner (PalMus, xii), for instance, having nearly 100.

The 4th mode is most commonly used for the invitatory, while the 1st and 8th are not used at all, although in the Sarum rite a group was classified as 1st mode that is elsewhere assigned to the 4th. Most of the many invitatory antiphons had only a regional popularity; only a few are spread through a large number of sources, including the antiphons for Christmas and Palm Sunday.

Alone among antiphonal chants, the invitatory psalm retains the ancient practice of singing the antiphon between the verses of the psalm. Later, however, a cantor (or cantors) sang the verses, and the antiphon was divided so that it was sung entire after one verse, with only its second part being sung after the next verse; this practice moved it closer to responsorial chanting. Ex.6 shows the 3rd verse of the invitatory psalm set to the tone for the 5th mode from the Vatican editions. Here the tripartite structure is seen, with a different intonation and cadence for each section. In this tone, unlike many others, a single reciting note is maintained throughout, but with a number of inflections where common psalmody would keep to a monotone. Other tones may have different reciting notes in different sections, and may use the same intonation, and almost always the same mediation, or, as here, a variant of it.

See also INVITATORY.

4. TONES OF THE GREAT RESPONSORIES. Each nocturn of Matins comprises a group of psalms sung antiphonally, followed by a group of lessons, each of which is followed by responsorial psalmody – one of the great responsories. Thus the responsories resemble the graduals of the Mass in their liturgical function (being postludes to a reading, and perhaps intended as reflections on it) and to some degree in their style. Like the graduals, they may originally have been complete psalms, but appear in extant sources with no more than a few verses of a psalm – or of another text, such as an extract from the *acta* of the saint for the day – arranged in a basic pattern, comprising a choral respond, a psalm verse sung by a cantor or cantors and a respond repeated in whole or in part. There may be additional verses, each followed by the respond; in the last responsory of each nocturn the doxology appears as the last of these verses.

The responds are largely free, though formulaic, but the verses are usually sung to a system of tones like those of common psalmody and introits, except that they are far more elaborate. Responsories are found in every mode, and the system of tones is thus eightfold. In structure these tones are closer to introit tones than to those of Office psalmody, since they include a second intonation. But each component – intonation, mediation, second intonation and ending – is much more complex than its counterpart in other categories of psalm tone, and the components themselves may be adapted to fit the text by

Ex.7

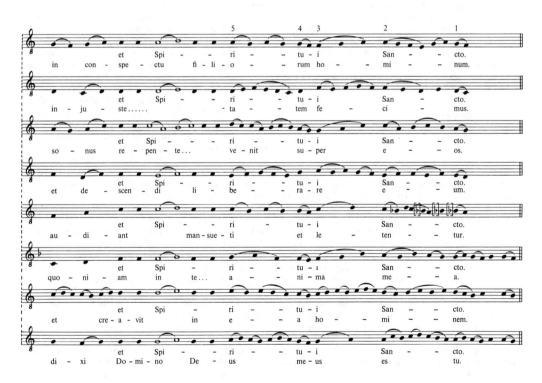

the omission or addition of notes. Responsory tones thus vary considerably from one verse to another. The eight tones of the Gregorian responsories are set out in ex.7, each to the text of the doxology as well as a Psalm verse.

The reciting note of the 5th tone is *c'* in both sections, whereas the other tones all have different reciting notes for the two sections, as follows. 1st: *g*, *a*; 2nd: *f*, *d*; 3rd:

a, *c'*; 4th: *g*, *f*; 6th: *c'*, *f*; 7th: *c'*, *d'*; 8th: *c'*, *g*. As with common psalmody, there was some early preference for *b* rather than *c'* as the reciting note of the second member of the 3rd tone, and of the first member of the 8th. Thus recitation in the Gregorian responsories generally occurred in the authentic tones on the notes a 4th and 5th above the final of the mode, and in the plagal on the note a 3rd above the final, and on the final itself; this is sometimes stated as a 'rule'. Even more than in the invitatory tones, however, the reciting notes in responsories tend to become lost in decoration, mostly through ascents to the note a degree higher at accented syllables. Owing to the extension of intonation and cadence there is no recitation at all in shorter verses, however, the intonation and cadence being linked directly. The intonations are adjusted to the textual accentuation, the adjustment being made around the first principal accent of the verse. This accent may be in the second rather than the first word, especially if the first word is a monosyllable, and is in some instances delayed even to the third word, as in the verse *Et intrantes dómum*. In such cases, a kind of secondary recitation is set up for several syllables before the intonation proper begins. Another idiosyncratic feature of the intonations is the melisma which concludes the formula in most tones.

The mediation is in every case tonic and always begins at the third syllable before the final accent. Each mediant has five melodic units, represented by arabic numerals in ex.7. These five units match the last syllables exactly unless the last accent introduces a dactyl, in which case an extra note must be used (see the void notes in ex.7). The dactylic mediation ending is illustrated for each tone by the text of the doxology. The final termination, unlike the mediation, is cursive, in every case comprising the last five syllables of the verse. The melodic formula has five units, like the mediation, and these are again represented by arabic numerals in ex.7.

III. Polyphonic psalms

1. Up to 1600   2. After 1600.

1. UP TO 1600.

(*i*) *Use in worship*. The ancient Hebrew psalms were adopted as the basis of formal worship in the Christian Church, whose earliest services consisted almost entirely of psalm singing. In the Roman Church this feature survived most clearly in the Office of Vespers, which included the recitation of five psalms. In the Mass, however, the expansion of the liturgy throughout the Middle Ages and the increasing elaboration of antiphons and responsorial material, led to an early shortening of the original psalms, so that eventually the introit, gradual and other parts of the Proper seldom contained more than a single psalm verse (indicated by ℣ in liturgical books). Complete psalms thus became characteristic of the Offices, and of certain ceremonies and processions. For most of its history the Roman psalter has used the 'poetic prose' of the Vulgate translation of the Bible, each psalm being sung to one of the eight melodic formulae ('tones') which could easily be adapted to succeeding verses of different length.

In the 16th century, however, most Protestant churches sought to return to a form of worship based largely on psalms in the vernacular, and prose translations were sung in several languages, including German and English. But to encourage congregational singing,

many Protestants adopted metrical versions in preference to biblical prose, using strophic melodies analogous to hymn tunes. The need for adaptability in the prose types, and the effect of doctrinal pressures on Protestant metrical forms, meant that polyphonic treatment of liturgical psalms seldom amounted to more than simple chordal harmonization. Their functional character, and particularly the use of recurrent music for each verse or pair of verses, kept them distinct from the repertory of through-composed psalm settings used as occasional motets or anthems.

(*ii*) *Settings based on Gregorian tones*. In the Roman Church the Gregorian tones may, in the late Middle Ages, have attracted improvised polyphony of the fauxbourdon type: there are very few written examples and they are nearly always for the psalms of Sunday Vespers, such as Binchois' *In exitu Israel* and the anonymous cycle of five in *I-MC* 871. Even in the 16th century only Italy, and to a lesser extent Spain, had any strong tradition of written psalm polyphony, mostly using the technique of *falsobordone* in which the chant was the highest of three or four voices. Polyphony might be used only in alternate verses ('salmi a versi senza risposte') or the psalm could be sung by two alternating polyphonic choirs ('salmi a versi con le risposte'). Such settings rely heavily on root-position triads as a basis for recitation, although by the end of the century they were occasionally subjected to florid embellishment, as in collections entitled *Salmi passeggiati* or *Falsobordoni concertati*.

The use of two alternating choirs in psalm settings can be traced to Ferrara in the 1470s, whence comes a large manuscript *Libro de canto da vespero* (*I-MOe* αM.1, 11–12), containing double-choir psalms by Giovanni Brebis and Johannes Martini. This technique was cultivated in a more elaborate form in the 16th century in the double-choir psalms of Gasparo Alberti, Francesco Santa Croce, Jacquet of Mantua, Willaert and several others. Their works were distinguished by the term 'salmi spezzati' (apparently first used by Aaron in 1536) and were in principle through-composed, permitting a more varied and flexible texture and layout than in *falsobordone* settings. The original psalm tones, largely preserved by Willaert, were generally abandoned by the native Italians, and the two four-part choirs began increasingly to depart from the verse structure of the psalm and to overlap or even combine into eight real parts, especially in the doxology. These techniques undoubtedly contributed to the rise of the polychoral motet in the second half of the 16th century, although the liturgical function of the Office psalms kept them a distinct category.

Polyphonic adornment of the Gregorian tones achieved only limited popularity in northern Europe. For example, in England before the Reformation faburden techniques were applied to the *Magnificat* and, on occasion, to certain processional psalms, but scarcely if ever to the Office psalms. In Germany Georg Rhau published a collection of Vespers psalms (*RISM* 1540⁵), in which the polyphony is for alternate verses, with the chant in the tenor, and an earlier, manuscript collection is in Jena (*D-Ju* 34). Several composers, including Johann Walter (i), Vulpius and Calvisius published polyphony of the *falsobordone* type for the German vernacular psalms in Luther's translation. After the English Reformation the prayer book psalms evidently continued to be sung to some form of the old Gregorian tones. Those for major feasts were occasionally set, with the chant in the tenor, to a harmonic formula adapted for each succeeding verse by the composer himself: the best-known of these 'festal' psalms are those in five parts by Tallis.

(iii) *Protestant metrical psalms.* In some parts of northern Europe, metrical psalms in the vernacular became a central feature of religious life and worship from about 1520 onwards. One of the earliest and most important translations of the psalms was that by Clément Marot, which became the basis of the official Calvinist psalter. A repertory of tunes, to some extent international, was assembled or adapted from plainchant, secular and popular sources, with a small number that were probably newly composed. Polyphony was banned in Calvinist churches, so that many of the published polyphonic settings must have been intended for domestic devotions or recreation, and were sometimes even advertised as 'biens convenables aux instruments'. Many were in a simple chordal style, including Loys Bourgeois' influential *Vingt-quatre psaumes à 4 voix* (Lyons, 1547), and Goudimel's complete psalter of 1563, which achieved widespread recognition as a standard polyphonic version. Some collections included settings in a more contrapuntal or partially imitative texture, particularly those published in France where the Marot psalter was used by Catholic as well as Protestant communities. The more important were those of Certon (1546), Mornable (1546), Janequin (1548 and 1549) and the later publications of Bourgeois. A few composers, notably Claude Le Jeune (1564), dropped the tunes altogether and composed what amounted to free motet settings. At about the same time, studied contrapuntal treatments of the psalm tunes, probably for didactic use, began to appear in the *tricinia* of Lassus, Crecquillon and others.

Metrical psalms became widely popular in England after the accession of Elizabeth I in 1558, partly through the agency of Protestants who had been exiled abroad during the reign of the Catholic Mary Tudor (1553–8). The standard metrical psalter was that of Sternhold and Hopkins, completed by 1562 and published in that year with 65 tunes taken from the Genevan psalter and other sources. A year later there appeared *The Whole Psalmes in Foure Parts* (*RISM* 1563[8]) in which the same tunes were provided with simple harmonizations. Other metrical psalters also appeared, notably that of Archbishop Parker (1567), for which Tallis provided several harmonized tunes. Polyphonic collections later in the century included those of William Daman (1579), and an anthology of works by various composers published by Thomas East in 1592.

See also PSALMS, METRICAL.

(iv) *Independent psalm motets.* The personal and symbolic qualities of many of the psalms made them especially attractive to 16th-century composers, who used them extensively as texts for the new repertory of motets evolved by Josquin and his contemporaries about 1500. Josquin wrote over 20 such psalm motets, clearly endeavouring to match the musical speech as closely as possible to the expressive elements of the text. A psalm tone cantus firmus was rarely used, and then only as an expressive element in itself. Many settings omit the doxology, and some composers treated the main texts with considerable freedom, for example by using extracts, assembling verses from different psalms and incorporating paraphrased or even non-biblical texts. These motet settings, therefore, cannot have been used as liturgical psalms: if sung in church at all, they must have served a votive or ceremonial function outside the formal liturgy. Many collections, including the cycles of penitential psalms by Lassus and others were probably published as sacred madrigals for domestic singing.

The Netherlands composers introduced and firmly established psalm setting in Italy, where it contributed to the wider motet repertories of Rome, Venice and most other major cities. The genre became especially significant in Germany, where it was cultivated by all the leading composers of Latin polyphony, as a result of the renewed interest in the psalms engendered by the Reformation. Thomas Stoltzer was one of the first to set both Latin and German psalm texts in motet form, and some later published collections mixed Latin and German settings, with little or no stylistic distinction between them. In France, Latin psalms were relatively neglected after Attaingnant's anthology of 1535. English composers, however, took some interest in the form in the third quarter of the 16th century. Some 70 settings survive, by William Mundy, Robert White and others, but it is not clear whether they were intended for occasional church use as anthems, for public ceremonies or for private devotions.

2. AFTER 1600. To trace the development of psalm composition during the 17th and 18th centuries is largely to trace the history of the motet and the anthem during the same period. The book of *Psalms* continued to provide a main source for Latin motet texts (as it had done before 1600), though the compositional techniques available to the composer now ranged from those associated with unaccompanied vocal polyphony to those of the latest concertato styles. The psalm settings of Monteverdi's *Vespro della Beata Vergine* (1610), *Selva morale* (1640) and *Salmi a . . . voci concertati* (1651) bring together elements of 16th-century choral polyphony, Venetian *cori spezzati*, and the monodic style of early 17th-century opera and the continuo madrigal; the Vespers especially apply both *falsobordone* and cantus firmus techniques to Gregorian psalm tones. It was a time of great activity in psalm composition, particularly at Venice and Rome; other composers include Tullio Cima, Simone Molinaro, Antonio Mortaro, Giovanni Rovetta and Lodovico Viadana. Later Alessandro Scarlatti's motets, most of which date from between 1680 and 1720, exemplify further both the ubiquity of psalm texts and the variety of their treatment. Of some 40 motets on biblical texts, all but three are settings of verses from the psalms, and the forces they require range from an unaccompanied four-part chorus (*Exaltabo te Domine*, Psalm xxx) or a chamber ensemble with solo voices (*Diligam te Domine*, Psalm xviii) to large-scale choral and string orchestral forces with solo voices and continuo (one of two settings of *Nisi Dominus aedificaverit*, Psalm cxxvii). Noteworthy is Scarlatti's frequent, and by this time archaic, use of Gregorian psalm tones as cantus firmi (often in long notes) in both *stile antico* and *stile moderno* settings.

A similar reliance on psalm texts (though seldom to such an extent on psalm tones) is found in Latin motets by other 18th-century composers, both in Italy and elsewhere. The words of English anthems, too, are mostly from the book of *Psalms*, as a glance at the anthems of such composers as Pelham Humfrey, Blow and Purcell confirms. Three of Handel's Coronation Anthems and all 11 Chandos Anthems are settings of psalm texts, in either translation or paraphrase. The prevalence of binary structures in the ninth Chandos Anthem, *O praise the Lord with one consent* (a setting of verses from Psalms cxvii, cxxxv and cxlviii in the metrical version of Tate and Brady), illustrates the extent to which musical form in these works is determined by the tendency for each verse of a psalm to divide into two complementary statements (*parallelismus membrorum*). Psalm texts are much less important in the Lutheran church cantata, where the chorale is a more fruitful source for both words and music. Most of Buxtehude's psalm settings, though called cantatas, are to Latin texts, and while Bach's cantatas contain frequent quotations from the psalms, only a few (e.g. *Der Herr denket an uns* BWV196) have texts drawn entirely from a single psalm. Probably the best known of Bach's psalm settings are the motets, *Singet dem Herrn* (BWV225) and *Lobet den Herrn* (BWV230).

While most psalm settings originated as separate pieces (chiefly motets and anthems) for specific church or ceremonial occasions, the practice of publishing collections of psalm compositions by a single composer also continued after 1600. Among the finest are the four volumes by Sweelinck comprising all 150 psalms (three of them set twice) in the French metrical versions of Clément Marot and Théodore de Bèze, published at Amsterdam between 1603 and 1621. These take the form of unaccompanied motets for between three and eight voices, in most of which Sweelinck treated the appropriate melody from the Genevan psalter as a free cantus firmus. Schütz also set the complete psalter in the German metrical version of Cornelius Becker, but it was his more elaborate settings of some 26 psalms in Luther's version (*Psalmen Davids*, 1619) that established his reputation as the foremost German composer of church music. These are multi-choral works supported by continuo, and sometimes by other instruments also, in the tradition of Andrea Gabrieli's *Psalmi Davidici* (1583) and Viadana's *Salmi . . . per cantare e concertare nella gran solennità di tutto l'anno* (1612).

Later in the century G. B. Bassani issued the first of his five volumes of psalms, *Armonici entusiasmi di Davidde ovvero salmi concertati* (Venice, 1690). In some of Bassani's psalms, especially perhaps the *Salmi per tutto l'anno* (1704) for double chorus and continuo, the *stile antico* continues to exert its influence, but others are stylistically closer to the chamber cantata, a genre in which he excelled. In the same tradition were the popular and influential settings by Benedetto Marcello of the first 50 psalms in the Italian paraphrased version of G. A. Giustiniani, published under the title *Estro poetico-armonico* (Venice, 1724–6). Several other editions followed, and an English version by John Garth was published in London in 1757. Scored for one to four voices with continuo (and in some cases strings), they were designed, like many similar pieces, for private rather than church use. An interesting and perhaps unique feature of Marcello's settings is the use they make, as cantus firmi, of certain Jewish liturgical melodies dating from the 12th–14th centuries.

Despite the comprehensiveness of such volumes, certain psalms (e.g. nos. li, c, cx, cxxx and cl) were favoured more than others for elaborate musical setting, and this is even more marked after 1800. With the greater proliferation of public concerts in the 19th century and the decline of the church as a main focal point of compositional activity, the subsequent history of psalm composition is largely traced through isolated works written for concert use and scored for full orchestra and chorus, often with solo voices. Noteworthy examples of the genre are Mendelssohn's settings (in German) of Psalms xlii, xcv, xcviii and cxiv, Schumann's of Psalm cl, Dvořák's of Psalm cxlix and Liszt's of Psalm xix. Bruckner represents what is perhaps the ultimate stage in this development by his large-scale settings of Psalms cxii and cl, though both he and Liszt, motivated by the spirit of 19th-century liturgical reforms, also wrote more modest and devotional settings suitable for church use. Also more intimate in style (though designed for choral societies rather than for church choirs) are such settings as Schubert's, for women's voices and piano, of Psalm xxiii in the German version of Moses Mendelssohn, and Brahms's, for similar forces (with strings ad lib), of Psalm xiii. The second of Brahms's two motets op.29 is a setting of Psalm li.

Among the most impressive 20th-century psalm compositions are Kodály's *Psalmus hungaricus* (1923) and Stravinsky's *Symphony of Psalms* (1930). The first is a setting of Psalm lv in the 16th-century paraphrased version of Mihály Kecskeméti Vég. It was written to celebrate the 50th anniversary of the merging of Buda with Pest to form the Hungarian capital, and embodies nationalistic as well as religious feeling. Stravinsky selected the Latin text of his *Symphony of Psalms* from Psalms xxxix, xl and cl to form a logical progression from contrition to jubilation in a three-movement work scored for chorus and orchestra without upper strings. Strongly influenced by Stravinsky's work is Krzysztof Penderecki's *Psalmy Dawida*, a four-movement work for chorus, percussion and double basses to Latin words (some of them recalling Stravinsky's) from Psalms xxvii, xxx, xliii and cxliii. Schoenberg found expression for his Jewish faith in *De profundis* (1949), a setting for six-part chorus of the Hebrew version of Psalm cxxx. His *Moderner Psalm* op.50c is an unfinished work in a projected series of religious compositions to words by Schoenberg himself.

Some of the best-known settings of verses from the psalms are contained in oratorios or other large-scale choral works, among them Handel's *Messiah*, Mendelssohn's *Elijah*, Brahms's *German Requiem*, Honegger's *Le roi David* and Walton's *Belshazzar's Feast*. Psalm texts have occasionally been used for solo songs with piano accompaniment, for example Dvořák's ten *Biblické písně* ('Biblical songs') and Edmund Rubbra's settings of Psalms vi, xxiii and cl, but such works are not common. Also rare are purely instrumental compositions based on, or inspired by, the psalms. Some 17th-century composers, including Sweelinck and Henderick Speuy, wrote keyboard pieces (mainly variations) on psalm melodies, and Julius Reubke's organ sonata *Der 94. Psalm*, and Herbert Howells's *Three Psalm Preludes* (also for organ) are among more recent examples. Justin Connolly's *Anima* (1975) is an orchestral piece prefaced by the sixth verse of Psalm cxxiv (which begins with the word 'anima' in the Vulgate version); Penderecki's *Psalmus* (1961) is an electronic piece for tape.

See also PSALMS, METRICAL.

BIBLIOGRAPHY

ANTIQUITY AND EARLY CHRISTIANITY

P. Wagner: *Einführung in die gregorianischen Melodien: ein Handbuch der Choralwissenschaft*, i: *Ursprung und Entwicklung der liturgischen Gesangsformen bis zum Ausange des Mittelalters* (Fribourg, 1895, 3/1911/R1962; Eng. trans., 1907)

Patrologia orientalis, ed. R. Graffin and F. Nau, vii (Paris and Fribourg, 1911), 180

S. Mowinckel: *Psalmenstudien*, i (Oslo, 1921–4/R1961)

H. Gunkel and J. Begrich: *Einleitung in die Psalmen* (Göttingen, 1928–33, 2/1966)

O. Eissfeldt: *Einleitung in das Alte Testament* (Tübingen, 1934, 2/1955; Eng. trans., 1964)

W. F. Albright: *Archeology and the Religion of Israel* (New York, 1942)

J. Coppens: 'Les parallèles du psautier avec les textes des Ras Shamra Ougarit', *Le Muséon*, lix (Louvain, 1946), 113–42

E. Werner: 'The Origin of the Eight Modes of Music (Octoechos)', *Hebrew Union College Annual*, xxi (1948), 211–55

J. Muilenberg: 'A Study in Hebrew Rhetoric: Repetition and Style', *Vetus testamentum*, suppl. i (Leiden, 1953)

E. Werner: 'The Origins of Psalmody', *Hebrew Union College Annual*, xxv (1954), 327

M. Tsevat: *A Study of the Language of the Biblical Psalms* (Philadelphia, 1955)

C. H. Kraeling and L. Mowry: 'Music in the Bible', *NOHM*, i (1957), 283

R. E. Murphy: 'A New Classification of Literary Forms in the Psalms', *Catholic Biblical Quarterly*, xxi (1959), 83

H. Preuss: 'Die Psalmenüberschriften in Targum und Midrasch', *Zeitschrift für die Alttestamentliche Wissenschaft*, lxxi (1959), 44

E. Werner: *The Sacred Bridge* (London and New York, 1959/R1970; ii, in preparation)

S. Mowinckel: *The Psalms in Israel's Worship* (Oxford, 1962)

'Music', *The Interpreter's Dictionary of the Bible*, ed. G. A. Buttrick (New York, 1962)

H. Avenary: 'A Genizah Find of Saadya's Psalm-preface and its Musical Aspects', *Hebrew Union College Annual*, xxxix (1968), 145

LATIN MONOPHONIC PSALMODY

'Le cursus et la psalmodie', *Le codex 121 de la Bibliothèque d'Einsiedeln (Xe–XIe siècle): Antiphonale missarum sancti Gregorii*, PalMus, 1st ser., iv (1894)

P. Wagner: *Einführung in die gregorianischen Melodien: ein Handbuch der Choralwissenschaft*, i: *Ursprung und Entwicklung der liturgischen Gesangsformen bis zum Ausgange des Mittelalters* (Fribourg, 1895, 3/1911/R1962; Eng. trans., 1907); ii: *Neumenkunde: Paläographie des liturgischen Gesanges* (Leipzig, 1905, 2/1912/R1962); iii: *Gregorianische Formenlehre: eine choralische Stilkunde* (Leipzig, 1921/R1962)

E. Garbagnati: 'Ricerche sull'antica salmodia ambrosiana', *Rassegna gregoriana*, x (1911), 361

A. Z. Idelsohn: 'Parallelen zwischen gregorianischen und hebraïsch-orientalischen Gesangsweisen', *ZMw*, iv (1921–2), 515

A. Auda: *Les modes et les tons de la musique et spécialement de la musique mediévale* (Brussels, 1930)

P. Wagner: 'Untersuchungen zu den Gesangstexten und zur responsorialen Psalmodie der altspanischen Liturgie', *Spanische Forschungen der Görres-Gesellschaft: gesammelte Aufsätze zur Kulturgeschichte Spaniens*, ii, ed. H. Finke (Münster, 1930), 67–113

A. Gastoué: 'Chant juif et chant grégorien, iii: psaumes et cantiques', *Revue grégorienne*, iii (1931), 70

P. Ferretti: *Estetica gregoriana ossia Trattato delle forme musicali del canto gregoriano*, i (Rome, 1934; Fr. trans., 1938); ii completed and ed. by P. Ernetti as *Estetica gregoriana dei recitativi liturgici* (Venice, 1964)

E. Cardine: 'La psalmodie des introïts', *Revue grégorienne*, xxvi (1947), 142, 229; xxvii (1948), 16

J. Smits van Waesberghe: 'L'évolution des tons psalmodiques au Moyen-Age', *1° congresso internazionale di musica sacra: Roma 1950*, 267

S. Van Dijk: 'Medieval Terminology and Methods of Psalm Singing', *MD*, vi (1952), 7

H. Avenary: 'Formal Structure of Psalms and Canticles in Early Jewish and Christian Chant', *MD*, vii (1953), 1

C. Gindele: 'Doppelchor und Psalmvortrag im Frühmittelalter', *Mf*, vi (1953), 296

E. Cardine: 'La corde récitative du 3e ton psalmodique', *Etudes grégoriennes*, i (1954), 47

J. Gajard: 'Les récitations modales des 3e et 4e modes et les manuscrits bénéventains et aquitains', *Etudes grégoriennes*, i (1954), 9–45

W. Apel: *Gregorian Chant* (Bloomington, Ind., 1958, 3/1966)

S. Corbin: 'La cantillation des rituels chrétiens', *RdM*, xlvii (1961), 3–36

O. Heiming: 'Zum monastischen Offizium von Kassianus bis Kolumbanus', *Archiv für Liturgiewissenschaft*, vii (1961), 89–156

Z. Falvy: 'Zur Frage von Differenzen der Psalmodie', *SMw*, xxv (1962), 160

E. Jammers: 'Der Choral als Rezitativ', *AMw*, xxii (1965), 143

H. Berger: *Untersuchungen zu den Psalmdifferenzen* (Regensburg, 1966)

H. Leeb: *Die Psalmodie bei Ambrosius* (Vienna, 1967)

A. Herzog and A. Hajdu: 'A la recherche du *tonus peregrinus* dans la tradition musicale juive', *Yuval*, i (Jerusalem, 1968), 194

D. Randel: 'Responsorial Psalmody in the Mozarabic Rite', *Etudes grégoriennes*, x (1969), 87

——: *The Responsorial Psalm Tones for the Mozarabic Office* (Princeton, 1969)

A. Sendrey: *Music in Ancient Israel* (New York, 1969; Ger. trans., 1970) [see review by E. Werner in *JAMS*, xxiii (1970), 529]

R. Erbacher: *'Tonus peregrinus': aus der Geschichte eines Psalmtons* (Münsterschwarzach, 1971)

M. Huglo: *Les Tonaires: inventaire, analyse, comparaison* (Paris, 1971)

J. Dyer: 'The Office Psalmody of the Old-Roman Chant', unpubd paper read for the AMS annual meeting, Chicago, 1973

R. Steiner: 'Tones for the Palm Sunday Invitatory', unpubd paper for the AMS annual meeting, Washington, DC, 1976

POLYPHONIC PSALMS TO 1600

L. Ellinwood: 'Tallis' Tunes and Tudor Psalmody', *MD*, ii (1948), 189

G. d'Alessi: 'Precursors of Adriano Willaert in the Practice of Coro Spezzato', *JAMS*, v (1952), 187

L. Finscher: 'Zur Cantus-Firmus-Behandlung in der Psalm-Motette der Josquinzeit', *Hans Albrecht in Memoriam* (Kassel, 1962), 55

K. Fischer: *Die Psalmkompositionen in Rom im ausgehenden 16. und beginnenden 17. Jahrhundert* (diss., U. of Cologne, 1970; rev. Regensburg, 1979)

A. F. Carver: 'The Psalms of Willaert and his North Italian Contemporaries', *AcM*, xlvii (1975), 270

For further bibliography *see* PSALMS, METRICAL.

POLYPHONIC PSALMS AFTER 1600

J. W. Enschedé: 'Vier Psalm-orgelboeken (1775–1778)', *TVNM*, viii/1 (1905), 62–83

L. Hirschberg: 'Moses Mendelssohns Psalmen in der klassischen Musik', *Gedenkbuch für Moses Mendelssohn* (Berlin, 1929), 115

A. Röseler: *Studien zum Instrumentarium in den Vokalwerken von Heinrich Schütz: die obligaten Instrumente in den Psalmen Davids* (Berlin, 1957, 2/1958)

C. Engelbrecht: 'Die Psalmvertonung im 20. Jahrhundert', *Gestalt und Glaube: Festschrift Oskar Söhngen* (Witten and Berlin, 1960), 153

L. Finscher: 'Psalm', §C, *MGG*

K. L. Jennings: *English Festal Psalms of the Sixteenth and Seventeenth Centuries* (diss., U. of Illinois, 1966)

A.-M. Bergin: *The Salmi concertati (1626) of Giovanni Rovetta: a Complete Transcription with a General Commentary* (diss., Otago U., 1967)

M. D. Cordovana: *An Analytical Survey and Evaluation of the 'Estro poetico-armonico' of Benedetto Marcello (1686–1739)* (diss., Catholic U., Washington, DC, 1967)

D. Hermany: 'Anthems based on Psalms', *Journal of Church Music*, ix (Nov 1967), 12; x (Feb 1968), 12; x (March 1968), 12

C. R. Timms: *A Transcription and Critical Study of Francesco Severi's 'Salmi passaggiati'* (diss., U. of London, 1967)

D. Hermany: 'Organ Music based on Psalms', *Journal of Church Music*, xi (March 1969), 11

B. Newman: 'Psalms in Concert', *Church Music*, ii/32 (1969), 13

V. Schultz: *Choral Psalm-settings of the 20th Century in the B. C. M.* (diss., Kent State U., 1969)

J. E. Shaffer: *The Cantus Firmus in Alessandro Scarlatti's Motets* (diss., George Peabody College, Nashville, 1970)

K. Fischer: *Die Psalmkompositionen in Rom im ausgehenden 16. und beginnenden 17. Jahrhundert* (diss., U. of Cologne, 1970; rev. Regensburg, 1979)

R. Leavis: 'Bach's Setting of Psalm CXVII (BWV230)', *ML*, lii (1971), 19

J. M. Zimmerman: *The Psalm Settings and Anthems of William Child (1606–1697)* (diss., Indiana U., 1971)

D. Arnold: 'Schütz's "Venetian" Psalms', *MT*, cxiii (1972), 1071

M. Salevic: *Die Vertonung der Psalmen Davids im 20 Jahrhundert: Studien im deutschen Sprachbereich* (Regensburg, 1976)

ERIC WERNER (I), THOMAS H. CONNOLLY (II),
PAUL DOE (III, 1), MALCOLM BOYD (III, 2)

Psalm book, metrical. *See* PSALMS, METRICAL, and PSALMODY (ii).

Psalm interlude. A passage of organ music played between the stanzas, or even between the lines, of a metrical psalm. After the Restoration, metrical psalms were commonly accompanied on the organ in England (though not in Presbyterian Scotland). John Playford provided plain keyboard harmonizations of four psalm tunes in the first and second editions of *Musick's Hand-maide* (1663 and *c*1668). John Blow merely provided little flourishes between the lines of the tunes (*The Psalms . . . Set Full for the Organ or Harpsichord*, *c*1731). His younger contemporaries were more ambitious; interludes were written by John Reading (iii) (MSS at *GB-Ldc*) and Daniel Purcell (in *The Harpsichord Master Improved* (1718) and in a publication devoted to his own music brought out in the same year and reissued *c*1730); an example on the 'Old Hundredth' is printed in *MT*, xlvi, 1905, p.162. Later 18th-century publications included *Eighteen Preludes or Short Fugues for the Organ or Harpsichord Proper for Interludes to Psalm Tunes* (*c*1770) and *Forty Interludes to be Played between the Verses of the Psalms: twenty five . . . by Mr. J. Keeble, & fifteen by Mr. J. Kirkman* (*c*1787). Samuel Wesley published a collection of *Parochial Psalm Tunes and Interludes* (n.d.) and *A Book of Interludes for Young Organists* (n.d.). S. S. Wesley in *A Selection of Psalm Tunes* (*c*1860) provided an introductory playing-over of each tune (sometimes in elaborate counterpoint) with a separate harmonization for, and interlude between, each stanza. The interlude by Wesley shown in ex.1, which is for the tune known

Ex. 1

as 'St Mary', illustrates the degree of harmonic extravagance apparently considered permissible. Later in the 19th century, however, with the increasing importance of the harmonized singing of hymns and psalms by the choir, the old methods of accompaniment, including the playing of interludes, fell gradually into disuse.

JOHN CALDWELL

Psalmodeya. Office of the Coptic Church; *see* COPTIC RITE, MUSIC OF THE.

Psalmodikon. An instrument of the 'bowed zither' category, used at one time in Scandinavian countries to regulate choral singing. There is some divergence of opinion as to its origin. Several reference works treat it (albeit with some reserve) as the invention of a Swedish pastor, Johann Dillner (1785–1862), who is known to have submitted it to and had it approved by the Swedish Academy in 1829. Recent Norwegian scholars, however, have tended to claim that it was introduced somewhat earlier in Norway by a cantor, Lars Roverud, who in turn seems to have got his inspiration from Denmark. Yet it seems to have found little favour in Denmark in spite of its use in some schools. There is at present no evidence of any contact between Dillner and Roverud.

In its earliest form the psalmodikon consisted of a flat, rather shallow soundbox, in plan a tall trapezium, with a single (bowed) string of gut supported by a nut at each end and passing over a bridge. Beneath and parallel to this string was a strip or 'rule' of wood transversely ridged to form frets, with the stopping positions marked by letters (see illustration). Thus the player could follow a printed cue-sheet instead of formal music notation. There were also a number of wire drone strings which passed over sections of the bridge that were cut lower so as not to impede free bowing. In some early instruments further clearance was provided by cutting the soundboard away in a concave 'bout' on the near side of the bridge. Additionally the more sophisticated examples were provided with several alternative rules differently marked so that the instrument could be played in several keys.

The presence of a bowed string associated with a fretted and lettered fingerboard recalls John Playford's 17th-century PSALTERER (though there is no evidence that either Dillner or Roverud had any knowledge of Playford's work). Both instruments were designed expressly to support choral singing in lieu of an organ or other skilled instrumental accompaniment.

The psalmodikon enjoyed great popularity in Norwegian and particularly Swedish schools until about 1860, and in a number of different versions, some with as many as four bowed strings, and with a variable number of drones. Such instruments were professionally made, but certain museum collections have examples of rustic copies of varying sophistication. Probably the most singular of these is one colloquially called *notstok*,

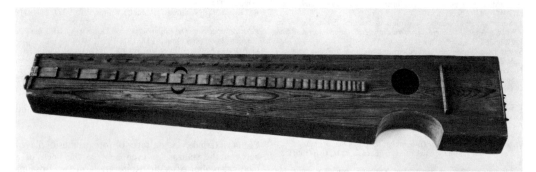

Psalmodikon with 14 sympathetic strings, Swedish, 19th century (*Musikhistorisk Museum, Copenhagen*)

in which the body was boat-shaped (sometimes not even hollowed out) while the fingerboard resembled a long handle passing through it. A keyed psalmodikon was also known at one time; all forms of the instrument, however, except perhaps the rural ones, seem to have gone out of use with the introduction of the harmonium in Scandinavian schools.

BIBLIOGRAPHY

A. Hammerich: *Das Musikhistorische Museum in Kopenhagen: beschreibender Katalog* (Copenhagen, 1911), 105

O. Anderssen: *The Bowed Harp: a Study in the History of Early Musical Instruments*, ed. K. Schlesinger (London, 1930)

L. Løchen: 'Kantor Lars Roverud og hans salmodikon', *By og bygd*, xi (1958), 85

——: 'Mer om salmodikon', *By og bygd*, xiii (1960), 159

PHILIP BATE

Psalmody (i) (from Gk. *psalmōdia*). The singing of psalms. The Greek term originally meant singing with a string instrument, but has been used since early Christian times (e.g. by Eusebius) to refer to the singing or composition of psalms; a comparable change occurred in the meaning of *psalmos* (see PSALM, §I). For a discussion of psalmody in Jewish and Christian antiquity and the Middle Ages, *see* PSALM, §§I, II; ANTIPHONAL PSALMODY; DIRECT PSALMODY; INFLECTION; RESPONSORIAL PSALMODY.

Psalmody (ii). A general term for music sung in Protestant churches in England and America from the 17th century to the early 19th. Following traditional practices of the Roman Church, the term was first associated with the chanting of psalms and later with the singing of metrical psalms, but as these were gradually replaced by hymns the term was retained to cover all kinds of music sung by amateur choirs. With the decline of the older type of parish choir in England the term fell into disuse, but it survived in America. It is now the most appropriate term to describe a body of music that, after long neglect, has recently attracted musicological attention.

I. England. II. North America.

I. England. Psalmody in England began with the rise of parish church choirs towards the end of the 17th century. It was a type of music specifically designed to allow such choirs to dominate or replace congregational psalm singing. Two categories of psalmody can be sharply distinguished: that of the country parish church without an organ, sung by a predominantly male choir to which instruments were later added; and that of the town church, sung by children accompanied by an organ. Both types were eventually taken up in dissenting bodies and spread also to America, Scotland and Wales. Country choirs also sang psalmody outside church and often combined to form choral societies, which aspired to the performance of oratorios; smaller groups sang psalmody in the home for recreation. Psalmody of the country type was reformed out of existence during the 19th century as a result of urbanization and various religious movements.

1. Country parish psalmody: (i) The country parish choir (ii) The music of country parish choirs. 2. Town psalmody. 3. The psalmody of dissenters.

1. COUNTRY PARISH PSALMODY.

(i) *The country parish choir.* The only kind of church choir heard in England during most of the 17th century was the kind that sang in the royal chapels, in cathedrals and in half a dozen collegiate parish churches. These professional choirs chanted the liturgy and prose

psalms, and sang polyphonic anthems and canticle settings with organ accompaniment. In contrast the music of the ordinary parish church consisted of metrical psalms, sung unaccompanied by the whole congregation, led only by a parish clerk who was often incompetent. Over several generations a traditional manner of singing the psalms had grown up which may be described as 'discordant heterophony' (*see* PSALMS, METRICAL, §III, 1(iv)).

Those who began to encourage the formation of parish choirs towards the end of the 17th century had not the remotest idea of imitating cathedral music. Their sole aim was to improve the singing of metrical psalms by training a few people to lead it. The earliest known reference to a 'choir' in this sense is found in *A New and Easie Method to Learn to Sing by Book*, published in 1686. The anonymous compiler said in his preface:

I have added several Psalm Tunes in Three Parts, with Directions how to sing them . . . This requires somewhat more Skill than the Common Way, yet is easie enough, at least for a sober Company of Persons with good Voices, to attain unto. It would therefore be a commendable thing, if Six, Eight, or more, sober young Men that have good Voices, would associate and form themselves into a Quire, seriously and concordantly to sing the Praises of their Creator: A few such in a Congregation (especially if the Clark make one to lead) might in a little time bring into the Church better Singing than is common, and with more variety of good Tunes, as I have known done.

It will be noticed that a male choir only is proposed. The three-part harmonization of psalm tunes (two tenors and bass, with the melody in the top part) had been the invention of John Playford, who also probably had male voices chiefly in view, though he pointed out that women or children could sing all three parts an octave higher. *The Whole Book of Psalms in Three Parts* (1677) was probably the first harmonized psalmbook intended primarily for parish church use. Yet Playford, though he may have directed a choir at the Temple Church (not a parish church), where he was clerk, stopped short of actually proposing the formation of a parish choir – perhaps because he was afraid of being accused of 'popery'. His book sold only 1000 copies in its first 18 years, but when it was reprinted by his son Henry in 1695 it became an immediate success: there were seven editions in seven years for a total sale of at least 14,500 copies. Clearly parish choirs had blossomed between 1677 and 1695.

The rise of the parish choir seems to have been closely associated with the formation of high-church religious societies, which were founded mostly to encourage Christian morality among young men (the first London societies were established in 1678; outside London, the first was at Romney, Kent, in 1692). They met under the direction of the vicar or rector of the parish for prayers, religious discussion and the singing of metrical psalms. Josiah Woodward, one of the leaders of the movement, was convinced that psalm singing and moral self-improvement were mutually conducive, and the societies were called on to lead the services in some churches. The psalm tunes they practised at their private meetings were at first sung from within the congregation, but the societies soon wanted a special place in church where they could sing as a body: the earliest recorded instance was at St Nicholas, Liverpool, in 1695. Not unnaturally they also began to sing on their own and to seek more interesting music than plain psalm tunes. Henry Playford was quick to cater for this new demand with his *Divine Companion* (1701), which was copied by many others, especially in the north of

England. It was one thing, however, for the 'singers' to sing an anthem before or after service, but when they took over the metrical psalms with new and difficult tunes they ran into opposition from people who clung to their old ways. 'What terrible outcries do they make . . . against any alterations; and if their understanding does not help 'em to any arguments against the thing itself, they immediately cry out Popery' (Chetham, *A Book of Psalmody*, 1718). In a matter of two decades, choirs which had been first intended to promote the singing of the congregation were now bent on arrogating the music entirely to themselves, and even to imitating cathedral music. They were abetted in these efforts by country singing teachers, who often travelled from village to village training choirs and selling books of their own compiling.

It is hardly surprising that many of the clergy now turned against the parish choirs. Edmund Gibson, Bishop of London, thundered in 1724 against

the inviting or encouraging those idle Instructors, who of late years have gone about the several counties to teach tunes uncommon and out of the way (which very often are as ridiculous as they are new; and the consequence of which is, that the greatest part of the congregation being unaccustom'd to them are silenc'd.).

In some cases bishops refused to grant facilities for the building of galleries or pews for the singers, or stipulated that 'some of the singers . . . do sometimes disperse themselves into the body of the said church for the direction and assistance of such persons as shall have a pious intention of learning to sing'. Positive

1. *An 18th-century church choir: engraving from 'The Psalm Singer's Necessary Companion' (1700)*

clerical support for the singers was rare. A musical clergyman was more likely to want to 'reform' the singing, as at Aston, Yorkshire, where William Mason 'taught the blacksmith to sing Marcello's Psalms like an angel'. At the other extreme, parsons banned the singers altogether or restricted their music; in revenge the choir sometimes moved over in a body to the local Methodist or dissenting chapel. But the typical Georgian parson's attitude was one of laissez-faire, and the choir soon became a recognized institution in country churches that had no organ. Indeed, apart from secular folksongs and dances, psalmody was the only communal music enjoyed by rural Englishmen in this period.

The heyday of the country choirs was from about 1760 to 1820. A typical group of singers near the beginning of this period was that described by Parson Woodforde at Castle Cary, Somerset, in 1769:

The Singers in the Gallery were, John Coleman, the Baker; Jonathan Croker; Willm Pew Junr.; Thos Penny; Willm Ashford; Hooper the Singing Master; James Lucas; Peter, Mr. Francis's man; Mr. Mellian's man James; Farmer Hix's son; Robert Sweete; and the two young Durnfords.

A broad spectrum of rural society was thus represented, including tradesmen, farm people and domestic servants, many of whom were probably illiterate and learnt their words, at least, by rote. They received no pay from the parish, except perhaps a small gratuity at Christmas or an annual choir feast, but some choirs offered their services at neighbouring parish churches, in which case a payment was often made out of the funds of the host parish. The churchwardens' accounts at Caddington (Bedfordshire), for example, record in 1779 the purchase of 2½ quarts of beer to reward the Luton singers. Some parish accounts record payments for books for the choir, others for the singing teacher's fees, but occasionally the vestry refused to make any payments for church music; this might have been because of the strength of nonconformity in the parish, for all ratepayers could vote in a general vestry even if they did not attend the parish church.

The country choirs were at first either entirely unaccompanied, or were supported only by a 'bass viol' (i.e. a viola da gamba, cello or hybrid instrument of similar compass). Hely's *Compleat Violist* (1699) tells how to accompany psalm tunes. In the same year Henry Playford published directions for playing the 'psalterer', a one-string instrument with frets labelled with letters; he claimed that it was the invention of his father, John Playford. In 1761 John Arnold recommended the bassoon as 'now in great Request in many Country Churches . . . as most of the Bass Notes may be played on it, in the Octave below the Bass Voices'; by the end of the 18th century a small band of instrumentalists had become a common addition to the parish choir. At Swalcliffe (Oxfordshire) 66 subscribers contributed to the purchase in 1783 of an oboe, a vox humana and a bassoon; a bass viol was added in 1785. This band played until it was replaced by an organ in the west gallery in 1842. The exact composition varied greatly from parish to parish: the 'bass viol' or bassoon was almost always present to support the bass; a clarinet often took the 'counter' or alto part an octave above pitch, and a flute or violin often doubled the tenors an octave higher, or the sopranos at pitch. In some churches the vicar banished the violin because of its association with tavern revelry. Less frequently may be found oboes, trumpets, serpents, horns, drums and a

2. A 19th-century village church choir: painting (1847) by Thomas Webster in the Victoria and Albert Museum, London

specially devised instrument called the 'vamphorn' through which the player half sang, half blew. Instruments of tenor register are rarely heard of: the tune, sung by the tenors, was doubled (if at all) in the higher octave. Stringed keyboard instruments were also rarely used. From about 1790 some psalmody books contained separate instrumental parts, particularly for 'symphonies' (introductions and interludes); but the primary function of the instruments was still to double voices, keeping them together and on pitch. One of the largest country choirs reported was at Winterborne St Martin (Dorset). In 1820 it contained 20 singers, including two 'counters'; they were supported by two clarinets playing the tune, two for the countertenor, an hautboy for the tenor (which by this time had yielded the tune to the treble voices) and a cello for the bass.

For most of the 18th century the majority of choirs continued to be made up only of men, and hence the basic harmony was tenor and bass, two tenors and bass, or alto, tenor and bass, with the tune in the tenor. An increasing number of psalmody books included treble (soprano) parts as well, but they are frequently inessential to the music or even anomalous, and were apparently not much used. Gradually, however, children and then women were allowed to join the singers, and after a generation of uncertainty the modern soprano, alto, tenor and bass arrangement, with the tune in the soprano, had become widespread by about 1810. Choirs sang metrical psalms and hymns with elaborate tunes, anthems and set-pieces with metrical hymn texts; the more ambitious ones, especially in Yorkshire and the north Midlands, sang settings of the canticles and chanted psalms, and even chanted the whole service.

The congregation had to turn round to 'face the music' when, as was most common, the choir was in the west gallery at the back of the church. Inevitably, this created a 'concert hall' atmosphere, and parsons frequently had to complain of tuning up during prayers or sermon, over-long anthems dwarfing the rest of the service, and other abuses. With the coming of more earnest religion in the Evangelical and Tractarian movements, criticism of parochial psalmody (which had always been present) became more and more insistent, and energetic efforts were made to get rid of it. There were always those, however, who saw virtue in the heartfelt singing of the choirs, however unpolished it might be. Sympathetic descriptions have been left by Thomas Hardy, whose father and grandfather had sung in church choirs, and by George Eliot. John Eden, in a sermon at Bristol in 1822, made an eloquent plea against the growing tendency to disband the singers:

Let it be remembered . . . that music, harsh, imperfect, and discordant as it may be in a country choir, is nevertheless a source of innocent and rational amusement to the performers; it occupies their hours of leisure; it is a grateful recreation, when the labour of the day is past; it solaces them in affliction; and it sheds an increase of pleasure on their hours of happiness: if this fail to prove its virtue and value, let me add that it keeps them from seeking amusement in the alehouse, and from the long train of evils commonly incident on such a practice.

But the spread of education and urbanization produced an intolerance for this rough music, a desire for a kind of music that would reflect the improved wealth and standing of the congregation. Reforming Evangelicals wanted to restore the singing to the people, while romantic antiquarians and Tractarians wanted to revive the music of the remote past. More and more clergymen were determined to suppress the singers and their psalmody, and the simplest way to do it was to introduce an organ. This was still beyond the means of most villages, however, and a useful compromise was found in the barrel organ – merely a curiosity before 1790, but a normal feature in country churches during the first half of the 19th century. With it came a roll of tunes prepared by trained musicians, usually in London, and so the psalmody of the towns was quickly introduced into the country churches. The seraphine or harmonium was a slightly later development. Sometimes the singers and instrumentalists were permitted to perform along with the new organ or harmonium, but more often they retired at once, realizing that their day had passed. Indeed, few country choirs of the old kind survived after the mid-19th century: the west of England was their last home, and the last choir of all, at Winterborne Abbas (Dorset), continued just long enough to be described by a musicologist (Canon Galpin gave a detailed description of its performance in 1896); it was disbanded shortly afterwards. The psalmody that the old choirs had sung usually disappeared with them, and in Victorian times an entirely different kind of parish church music arose, based on the surpliced choir in the chancel, the diocesan festival, *Hymns Ancient and Modern*, the *Cathedral Psalter* and Novello's octavo series of church music.

(ii) *The music of country parish choirs.* Henry Playford was the first to provide music for country choirs that went beyond simple harmonized psalm tunes. *The Divine Companion* (1701) was 'fitted for the use of those who already understand Mr. John Playford's Psalms in three parts. To be used in Churches or Private Families for their Greater Advancement in Divine Musick'. As well as some new psalm tunes in a lively and up-to-date style, the collection contained hymns and anthems. The hymns, most of them strophic songs for voice and bass, were no doubt for 'Private Families'. Of the anthems Playford wrote in his preface:

We have, 'tis true, had Anthems long since sung, and continued in our Cathedrals and Chapels ... But our Parochial Churches, which are equally dedicated to Gods Glory, and innumerable, in respect of those before mention'd, have been altogether destitute of such necessary assistances to Praise their Maker by ... This has made me importunate with my Friends to compile such a set of short and easy Anthems as may be proper for the Places they are designed for, and from such little beginnings in the practice of Musick, endeavour to persuade them into a knowledge of things of a Higher Nature, as Harmonia Sacra, &c.

The 19 anthems are the work of some of the most accomplished professional composers of the day, mostly cathedral musicians: Akeroyde, Church, Clarke, Croft, King, Turner and Weldon. In style they are remarkably similar: all are in two or three parts (tenor and bass, or alto, tenor and bass; in either case the tenor part could be sung an octave higher as a treble), simple and short, and entirely homophonic (ex.1). Evidently the composers were writing to instructions from Playford, in a style that was conceived as appropriate for country musicians. There is no doubt that these anthems were used, for every country psalmody collection until 1715 borrowed some anthems from *The Divine Companion*. John Bishop, another professional, provided further materials in his *Set of New Psalm Tunes* (1710), which was 'design'd for the use of St. Laurence Church in Reading; and are taught by Tho. Batten'. This too was a source for country collections, as were John Church's *Introduction to Psalmody* (1723) and Pearson's *Second Book of the Divine Companion* (c1725), a sequel to Playford's.

Ex.1 Anthem, Jeremiah Clarke: *Praise the Lord, O my soul*
(a) Original version, from Henry Playford: *The Divine Companion*
(London, 1701)

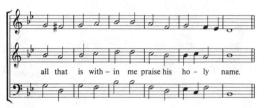

Praise ___ the Lord, O my soul, and

all that is with – in me praise his ho - ly name.

(b) A later version, from William Tans'ur: *The Royal Melody Compleat*
(London, 1755)

Praise the Lord, O my soul, and all that
2. God is gra - cious and good, his mer - cy
3. Bless the Lord, an - gels all, ye that ex -

is with – in me praise his ho - ly name.
is e - ter - nal to them that fear him.
- cel in strength, and do his com - mand-ments.

At first country musicians merely borrowed materials from their professional models, sometimes simplifying or adapting in the process, but they soon began to produce their own music. The earliest known parochial anthem of country provenance is 'Hear my pray'r, O Lord' from *A Book of Psalmody* (2/1713) by John and James Green (the Greens were from Wombwell, near Darfield, Yorkshire). The contrast between this anthem, with its unusual harmonies and artless prosody, and those put out by Playford is obvious and striking (ex.2). In some cases there are notable archaisms, such as the organum-like cadence in James Green's *O God my heart is ready* (1715) (ex.3). The early anthems follow Playford's lead in one respect: they are largely homophonic, the only contrasts in texture occurring when one part rests.

Many other country composers followed the Greens in publishing collections that included anthems of their own composition. The West Riding gained an early lead, but in the course of the century every part of England except the extreme north and south-west was represented by at least one local collection. The compilers were generally either singing teachers or booksellers, in some cases both; a few, such as William Knapp of Poole (Dorset), were parish clerks. They can be clearly distinguished from professional musicians and London publishers who from time to time published a book intended to bring country psalmody back into the mainstream of art music: examples of the latter, besides those already mentioned, are Alcock (1745), Broderip (1750, 1764), Bremner (1756), Langdon (1774), Billington (1784), Arnold and Callcott (1791), Hellendaal (1793) and Bond (1796).

The most successful of all country psalmodies, John Chetham's *Book of Psalmody* (1718), was perhaps a compromise between the two types. Chetham himself was an educated man, schoolmaster and curate of Skipton (Yorkshire), and there are signs that he had links with the cathedral tradition: his was the first country psalmody book to include 'chanting-tunes' that were clearly derived from cathedral chants and set to the

Ex.2 Anonymous anthem, *Hear my pray'r O Lord*;
John and James Green: *A Book of Psalmody* (London, 2/1713)

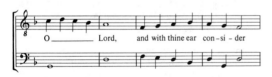

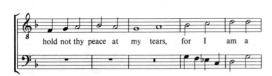

Ex.3 James Green: *O God my heart is ready*;
John and James Green: *A Collection of Choice Psalm-Tunes* (London, 3/1715)

canticles – a feature borrowed in many later collections. Chetham's book went through 11 editions in the 18th century, and was used all over the north of England, particularly at Halifax parish church. There it became so venerated that 19th-century organists were obliged to present their own work in the form of additions or revisions to Chetham's – as, for instance, in *Pohlmann's National Psalmody, or New Appendix to Houldsworth's Cheetham's Psalmody, for Home and Congregational Use*, edited by H. J. Gauntlett (Halifax: Pohlmann & Son, 1878).

From the 1720s anthems became longer, more elaborate and in some cases contrapuntal; they grew from two to three, and ultimately to four and even more voices, though the tenor remained clearly the 'leading' part. Indeed in many anthems the tenor and bass seem musically satisfying by themselves, more so than with the upper parts added, which suggests that the others may have been more or less optional. The same anthem often appears in drastically altered forms in different books, or the tenor may be nearly identical in two versions, while the other parts are entirely different, perhaps as a result of the oral transmission of the tenor. Some of the anthems from Playford and Bishop became so transformed in several stages that by the later 18th century they had become barely identifiable (ex.1b).

The development of elaborate psalm tunes, though equally characteristic of country psalmody, tended to follow after the development of anthems. One reason for this was that the singers could do as they pleased with the anthem, but in metrical psalms they had to reckon with opposition from both clergy and congregation. Another was that psalm tunes had to be repeated with each verse of the psalm, which hindered any anthem-like elaboration in the setting. One solution was to have an elaborate refrain, repeated with every verse. Only one of the 150 psalms actually has such a refrain – Psalm cxxxvi – and this was, in fact, one of the first to be treated in extended settings with word repetitions. Psalm xxiv.7–10 also has a refrain-like repetition, and this was the text of the first FUGING-TUNE, in the second edition of Chetham's *Book of Psalmody* (1722). This piece, judging by its style and effective structure, was the work of a professional composer. It was very popular and was reprinted (though often in debased form) in many later collections. Apart from these two examples, fuging-tunes are not found before about 1750, though there are increasing numbers of tunes with solos, duets, word repetitions and extended melismas and ornaments.

William East's collections of about 1750–55 show a new trend. They contain services and anthems 'as sung in Cathedrals', including examples by Lawes, Blow, Purcell, Tudway and Maurice Greene as well as some of parochial origin. But they are clearly for local parish church use, being sold by various booksellers at Midland towns 'and by Mr. John Harrot, teacher of

Ex.4 Fuging tune, set to Psalm xci. 1, 2, 9, 10;
W. East: *The Voice of Melody* (Waltham, 2/1750)

1. He that __with-in the se - cret place

Of God most high__doth dwell, Un - der__ the
- der__ the sha-dow of_ his grace
Un · -

sha - dow of__ his grace He shall,__
He shall,__ he shall__

he shall__
He shall,__ he shall__

be safe and well.
be safe and well.

Psalmody at Great Bowden [Leicestershire]'. One is called *Collection of Church Musick for the Use of his Schools Waltham Leicestershire*. It contains a 'Tribute' to the author, signed 'John Stanley':

> Accept my Friend what Justice makes me do,
> And your Harmonick Notes compels me to:
> Great Playford's Works Immortaliz'd his Name,
> And Tansur's stretch'd the blowing Cheeks of Fame;
> Green, Barber, Chetham, Smith, &c in thought was best,
> Yet all these Worthies are Reviv'd in East . . .

The development of country psalmody, from Playford to East, is thus clearly outlined. East's psalm tunes are all 'in the Fugeing, Syncopating and binding taste'; about half of them are attributed to John Everet, of Grantham, whose own collection was published by East in 1757. They show little concern for the problems of strophic repetition; the first verse only is set to music, word repetitions and overlaps included, and the other verses are left to take care of themselves (ex.4). This 'extreme' type of fuging-tune was popular in the remoter country collections in the later 18th century, and was imitated in American psalmody books. More than other elaborate tunes it obscured or vitiated the sense of the words and on these grounds was criticized by such clergymen as John Wesley and such country musicians as John Arnold, who deplored 'these new-fashioned fuguing Psalm-Tunes' in the prefaces of his collections. In more 'moderate' fuging-tunes, such as those of William Tans'ur, the 'fuging' section is in most cases either a repetition of the last line after a full cadence, or an Alleluia or Amen; hence the tune can be sung without it.

Towards the end of the 18th century increasingly strident objections to country psalmody, particularly on the part of Evangelical clergymen, generated a new type of 'reforming' psalmody collection, which not only tried to impose professional musical standards but also was designed to re-establish congregational singing in country churches, led but not replaced by a choir. Among these were the collections of Newton (1775), Cecil (1785), Jones of Nayland (1789, 1795) and Tattersall (1794), all incumbents of country churches, and Gresham (1797), a church organist and schoolmaster. Comprehensive books of psalms and hymns, intended for both town and country use, also became popular, Miller's *Psalms of David* (1790) being the first in a long series which included collections by Benjamin Jacob (1819), Greatorex (c1825) and Hackett (1840). In many parishes the vicar and organist combined to compile a local selection whose music was that of the town psalmody. Under Methodist influence, such elaborate music as remained in these collections was often of the set-piece type, settings of metrical psalm or hymn texts in a style derived, or in music actually adapted, from secular and operatic sources. Those few country choirs that survived in Victorian times chiefly sang hymn tunes of the ornate type, until the bands were replaced by the harmonium.

2. TOWN PSALMODY.
John Arnold, in *Church Music Reformed* (1765), pointed out that

in the Churches of *London* and *Westminster*, which abound chiefly with large Congregations, it is customary for the People, who chiefly sing by the Ear, to follow the Organ . . .; but, in Churches where there is no Organ, they generally follow the Clerk, who sings the Melody of the Tune . . . In most Country Churches the Psalms used to be sung formerly much after the same Manner as is now used in the Churches of *London*, &c . . . till about half a Century ago, when several Books of Psalmody were printed and published, containing some very good Psalm

Tunes and Anthems in four Parts; of which the People in the Country soon became particularly fond.

There is a clear distinction between the two traditions; the London churches generally continued to sing psalm tunes of the old type in the old way. What was true of the churches of London and Westminster was also generally true of the larger provincial town churches, particularly those in cathedral cities, where one of the cathedral musicians was frequently organist. Other large cities, such as Newcastle, Nottingham, Birmingham, Leeds and Bath, had more than one church with an organ, and in general organs became more widespread during the 18th century.

Ex.5 Henry Heron: 'An anthem Sung by the Charity Children of Lime Str[ee]t Ward before the Right Honble. S[ir] Wat[ki]n Lewis Kt. Lord Mayor (and the Sherriffs) of the City of London, on Sunday the 13th of May 1781, at the Parish Church of St. Andrew Undershaft, Leadenhall Street'; William Gawler: *Harmonia sacra* (London, 1781)

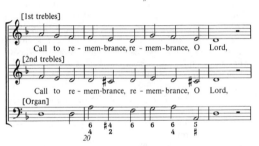

Another factor in many town churches was the presence of the 'charity children', also mentioned by Arnold. From early Elizabethan times the statutes of many grammar schools contained a provision for teaching the psalm tunes to the children and taking them to the parish church to lead the singing every Sunday. They wore uniforms, provided by the parish if there was no endowment to clothe them, and they often assembled on either side of the organ in the church's west gallery, providing a strong if at times rather shrill rendering of the psalm tunes. Thus in town church music, unlike that of the country, the emphasis was on the highest voice. Organ settings also had the tunes in the treble, with interludes and elaborate 'givings-out' for playing the tune through (see PSALMS, METRICAL, §III, 1(iv)). Until well into the 18th century the charity children had no special music, but their presence is indicated in such collections as Thomas Wanless's *The Metre Psalm Tunes ... for the Use of the Parish-church of St. Michael's of Belfrey's in York* (York, 1702), which has settings for soprano, alto, tenor and bass with the tune in the treble. The children of the Bluecoat School sang at this church, where Wanless (organist of the minster) played the organ.

The phrase 'town psalmody' may be properly applied to elaborate music specifically written for the charity children or other choirs. The custom grew up during the 18th century of using the occasion of the annual 'charity sermon', at which alms were solicited for the benefit of the school, to display the singing of the children. Charity hymns were specially written for the purpose and set to music for one or two treble parts and figured bass; anthems, with suitably selected texts, were written in similar fashion (ex.5). The first book to contain this kind of music was Pearson's *The Second Book of Divine Companion* (c1725).

About the middle of the 18th century several charities with strong Methodist connections were founded in London – the Foundling, Lock, and Magdalen hospitals were the most important – and their inmates provided music for their chapels (*see* LONDON, §I, 5). This music was also treble-dominated, consisting of women's or children's voices supported by the organ, and the printed collections of their psalms, hymns, anthems and set-pieces were widely used, first in other private chapels and later in town parish churches. In the 19th century many town churches employed a professional quartet at parish expense; a red velvet curtain was drawn back to reveal the fashionably dressed singers, who then provided a concert of hymns or anthems with organ accompaniment. Other churches had a surpliced choir of men and boys in the chancel. Despite the efforts of both Evangelicals and Tractarians, choirs in most churches continued to replace the congregation more than to lead it, and the music they sang was increasingly modelled on that of the cathedrals, simplified where necessary.

3. THE PSALMODY OF DISSENTERS. Independent and Presbyterian churches, especially in London and the south of England, were musically conservative during most of the 18th century. Organs were excluded, and the tune supplements to Watts and other collections of psalms and hymns generally contained only tunes of the older type. Gawthorn's *Harmonia perfecta*, dedicated 'to the Gentlemen who support the Friday Lecture in Eastcheap', continued the Presbyterian psalm-singing

movement begun earlier by William Lawrence (*see* PSALMS, METRICAL, §III, 2(i). It included four anthems and a metrical 'Dialogue on Death', but these were more probably used at the Friday meetings than as an accompaniment to Sunday worship.

The first signs of elaborate psalmody in dissenting meetings came from the north, shortly after parish churches there had begun to sing anthems. Alverey Jackson led a new movement in Baptist circles in Yorkshire and Lancashire from about 1717. At Rossendale (Lancashire) about 1720, elaborate tunes began to be sung and choirs formed to lead them; bands followed later in the century. The 'Deighn Layrocks' (i.e. Larks), the singing society that led this music, became a famous choir which for more than a century was much in demand at local festivals of choral music. Caleb Ashworth, a Baptist minister, began his career at Rossendale and later moved south to the Midlands. His *Collection of Tunes* (*c*1760) is outwardly similar to parish church psalmody books, and was no doubt partly intended for Anglican use: but it has some differences. The anthems in it are 'more proper to entertain and improve those who have made some proficiency in the Art of Singing, than to be introduced into public Worship'. The psalm tunes are printed in one key but directed to be sung in another, indicating unaccompanied singing. There are also two selections from Handel oratorios, at this date unheard of in Anglican cathedrals or parish churches. (Newbigging described the effect produced by 'the weird exultant music of *Glad Tidings* or the *Hallelujah Chorus* sung by the majority of the congregation'.) Stephen Addington, an Independent minister, published a similar *Collection of Psalm Tunes* in 1780 which was many times reprinted. Rippon's *Selection of Psalm and Hymn Tunes* (*c*1791) was even more popular.

The Methodist movement initiated a new style of singing and brought in music originating in the theatre or the concert hall, at first in open-air meetings and eventually in churches and meeting-houses. Under John Wesley's authoritarian rule Methodist meetings excluded organs and elaborate polyphony, and whole congregations were taught to sing in four-part harmony. Thomas Williams wrote in 1789:

The method of singing in the congregations, commonly termed *methodistical*, has been often charged with levity . . . But the use of song tunes, and trifling airs, . . . has almost entirely ceased since they have been supplied with a variety of better compositions, and many of their chapels are remarked for good singing. One custom, which seems to have originated among them, has certainly a very agreeable effect, namely, that of the women singing certain passages by themselves, which are frequently repeated in full chorus.

This innovation was actually first proposed by George Whitefield, leader of the Calvinistic Methodists, in his *Selection for the Tabernacle* (1753). Methodist practices were soon introduced in other dissenting bodies, particularly in the north of England, where there was a growing enthusiasm for choral singing. When the spinners and weavers of Lancashire and Yorkshire met with their families for many hours of psalmody, with bands of instruments for accompaniment:

some devoted themselves to oratorios, then composed anthems, and then transferred their talents to Nonconformist meeting-houses. Many old records refer to the innovation, and show how the deacons would tolerate at first only the [string] bass, then admitted a string quartet, and gradually winked at the table-pew or the gallery housing a miscellaneous band.

The connection between choirs (both of parish churches and dissenting bodies) and oratorio performances is reported in full detail in Millington's *Sketches*, relating to the Eccles area but touching on musical activities over a wide area of Lancashire, Yorkshire and the north Midlands. Groups of singers and instrumentalists met in cottages to practise music for church and chapel, and combined for larger monthly meetings to sing Handel, Haydn, and cathedral music by Greene, Nares, Boyce and others; the musicians of several such local societies gathered for a quarterly assembly, even if it meant walking 20 miles with their instruments. It was on such foundations that the provincial festivals, great and small, were built, with professionals from London providing only the principal parts. Even the London oratorios at Covent Garden and Drury Lane frequently had recourse to choirs from Lancashire and Yorkshire, who often knew their Handel better than any in London.

Another area where nonconformity was particularly strong was south-west England. At Wellington (Somerset), the Baptist meeting-house, enlarged in 1765, had a singing gallery opposite the pulpit, in which a large choir performed psalmody, led by a precentor equipped with a pitchpipe. When a new chapel was erected in 1833 provision was made for an 'orchestra' as well as a choir: the gallery held about 30 people. The orchestra consisted of a double bass played by John Stradling, grocer; cello by Charles Fry, wool sorter; flutes by William Beall, wool worker, and Thomas Slade, factory foreman and also a deacon of the chapel; violins by W. Stuttaford and James Bragg; serpent by George Viney. The hymns were 'lined out' (a practice whereby each line was read out before being sung) by William Horsey, 'formerly draper and grocer, latterly gentleman', until the custom lapsed in 1864. In 1870 a harmonium was purchased and the old singing gallery closed.

Psalmody in worship varied greatly in the 19th century: some ministers disapproved of organs and preferred the bands, while others followed the more fashionable move in the high-church direction, introducing organs, and then anthems and chanted psalms. The representative Victorian collection was Allon and Gauntlett's *Congregational Psalmist* (1858). It contained hymns with tunes both plain and ornate, including some translated medieval hymns, simple 'congregational anthems', and chants, Sanctus settings and sentences. It was adapted for Baptist use in *The Baptist Tune-book* (1860). The organ or harmonium increasingly replaced the orchestra in chapels and by 1886 Minshall was advocating 'a return to the old custom of having orchestral instruments used regularly in our services'. In many churches at this date for Sunday morning a simple anthem was chosen, which the congregation joined in; in the evening a more elaborate composition was sung by the choir, 'such as a chorus and solo from the oratorios'. The spread of Tonic Sol-fa singing classes, and the publication of music in Sol-fa notation, made this congregational participation a possibility.

BIBLIOGRAPHY

[J. Woodward]: *An Account of the Rise and Progress of the Religious Societies* (London, 1701)

N. Tate: *An Essay for Promoting of Psalmody* (London, 1710)

E. Gibson: *The Excellent Use of Psalmody* (London, 1724)

A. Bedford: *The Excellency of Divine Music* (London, 1733)

W. Tans'ur: *A New Musical Grammar* (London, 3/1756)

W. Riley: *Parochial Music Corrected* (London, 1762)

J. Arnold: Preface to *Church Music Reformed* (London, 1765)

W. Vincent: *Considerations on Parochial Music* (London, 1787)

E. Miller: *Thoughts on the Present Performance of Psalmody in the Established Church in England* (London, 1791)

Free Remarks on the Public Psalmody of Dissenters (Hull, 1814)

W. Cole: *A View of Modern Psalmody* (Colchester, 1819)

J. Eden: *Church Music: a Sermon* (Bristol, 1822)

[D. E. Ford]: *Observations on Psalmody, by a Composer* (London, 1827)

J. A. Latrobe: *The Music of the Church* (London, 1831)

The Church-goer: Rural Rides (Bristol, 1847, 2/1850)

G. Eliot: *Adam Bede* (London, 1859)

'Congregational Psalmody', *British Quarterly Review*, lxx (1862), 366 [review]

T. Newbigging: *History of the Forest of Rossendale* (London, 1868)

T. Hardy: *Under the Greenwood Tree* (London, 1872)

J. S. Curwen: *Studies in Worship Music* (London, 1880–85)

W. Millington: *Sketches of Local Musicians and Musical Societies* (Pendlebury, 1884)

E. Minshall: *Organs, Organists, and Choirs* (London, 1886)

F. W. Galpin: 'An Interesting Survival', *Musical News*, v (1893), 31, 56

J. S. Curwen: 'The Old Village Musicians', *Strand Musical Magazine* (1897), 137

F. W. Galpin: 'Notes on the Old Church Bands and Village Choirs of the Past Century', *The Antiquary*, xlii (1906), 101

A. L. Humphreys: *Materials for the History of the Town and Parish of Wellington in the County of Somerset* (London, 1908–14)

G. V. Portus: *Caritas Anglicana, or, an Historical Enquiry into those Religious ... Societies ... in England between the years 1678 and 1740* (London, 1912)

J. W. Legg: *English Church Life from the Restoration to the Tractarian Movement* (London, 1914)

C. W. Pearce: 'English Sacred Folk Song of the West Gallery Period (circa 1695–1820)', *PMA*, xlviii (1921–2), 1–47

K. H. Macdermott: *Sussex Church Music in the Past* (Chichester, 1922)

[J. Woodforde]: *The Diary of a Country Parson*, ed. J. Beresford, i (London, 1924), 92

J. T. Lightwood: *Methodist Music in the Eighteenth Century* (London, 1927)

W. T. Whitley: *Congregational Hymn-singing* (London, 1933)

K. H. Macdermott: *The Old Church Gallery Minstrels* (London, 1948)

M. Byrne: 'The Church Band at Swalcliffe', *GSJ*, xvii (1964), 89

N. Temperley: 'John Playford and the Metrical Psalms', *JAMS*, xxv (1972), 331–78

F. Hudson: 'The New Bedford Manuscript Part-books of Handel's Setting of "L'Allegro" ', *Notes*, xxxiii (1976–7), 531

N. Temperley: *The Music of the English Parish Church* (Cambridge, 1979), i, chap. 6

II. North America. The following discussion of North American psalmody covers the practice of Protestant vocal music in general, including hymns and anthems, in the two centuries after the English settlement of Massachusetts (*c*1620–1820).

1. Early psalmbooks and tracts. 2. Mid-18th-century tune books and elaborate psalmody. 3. Musical style. 4. Reform.

1. EARLY PSALMBOOKS AND TRACTS. When the Pilgrims landed at Plymouth in 1620 they carried with them Henry Ainsworth's *Book of Psalmes: Englished both in Prose and Metre* (Amsterdam, 1612), which included a supplement of 39 monophonic tunes. Sternhold and Hopkins's *Whole Booke of Psalmes* (London, 1562), later called the 'Old Version', also circulated in America during the 17th and 18th centuries, as well as Thomas Ravenscroft's *Whole Booke of Psalmes* (London, 1621), containing four-part settings of the British psalm tune repertory for recreational use. The earliest American psalmody was thus rooted in a European tradition of considerable musical power. The tunes in Ainsworth's psalter, many of them traceable to French and Dutch folk sources, were generally rather long (eight lines is typical) and often enlivened by syncopation. Ravenscroft's harmonizations, set mostly in block chords, still contained elements of the contrapuntal tradition.

In time the musical skills of New Englanders declined, a trend influenced by the difficulty of survival in an unsettled country far from an established tradition of polyphonic music-making. Psalmody nevertheless remained important to the settlers; it is not accidental that the earliest book printed in the English-speaking New World was a metrical psalter, the *Whole Booke of Psalmes* (Cambridge, 1640), known as the 'Bay Psalm Book'. The clergymen who assembled it aimed at textural accuracy. They also simplified the tradition by using fewer metres than either Ainsworth or Sternhold and Hopkins. Congregations throughout Massachusetts Bay Colony immediately adopted the Bay Psalm Book (*see* PSALMS, METRICAL, §V).

By the beginning of the 18th century musical literacy in the American colonies had declined, and the repertory had shrunk to a handful of tunes – fewer than six in some congregations. The clergy reacted, and from 1720 polemical tracts began to appear in Boston deploring the state of psalmody and recommending improvements, specifically advocating the formation of singing schools – instructional sessions devoted to teaching note-reading. Tune books were also published – collections of psalm tunes with instructional prefaces, designed for use in the singing schools. Among the leaders of this first group of musical reformers were Thomas Symmes, whose writings on the advantages of 'Regular Singing' (singing from notation and observing uniformity of rhythm and pitch) are powerful and persuasive; John Tufts, whose *Introduction to the Art of Singing Psalm-tunes* went through 11 editions between 1721 and 1744; and Thomas Walter, whose *Grounds and Rules of Musick*, first issued in 1721, was still in print nearly half a century later as part of Daniel Bayley's *New and Complete Introduction to the Grounds and Rules of Music* (Newburyport, 1768).

The reformers' tracts leave no doubt that they encountered strong resistance. Many colonial Protestants did not share the conviction that the 'Usual Way' of singing – by rote, at a slow tempo, in a freely embellished style – represented a corruption of psalmody. Sanctioned by use, and gratifying in the relaxed freedom it allowed the singer, the 'Usual Way' was set aside only with great reluctance and continued in rural areas throughout the century and later. No notated versions of singing in the 'Usual Way' have come down from early 18th-century New England, and the only detailed descriptions of the style survive in the writings of its opponents, the reformers. The style has been suggested as evidence of the existence of an indigenous folk tradition, existing side by side with 'Regular Singing', the better-recorded written practice.

2. MID-18TH-CENTURY TUNE BOOKS AND ELABORATE PSALMODY. Early in the century, when the written tradition was moribund, psalmody was renewed by the singing school, which did more than merely teach the skills of singing and note-reading. As well as stimulating the publication of tune books and, eventually, the composition of music to fill them, the singing school was the only American institution of its time which gave native musicians the opportunity to earn their living as musicians. An examination of the tune books published in America during the 18th century provides a reliable measure of the singing school's influence on the psalm tune repertory. Before 1760 more than 30 separate publications containing sacred music appeared in the American colonies, including various editions of the Bay Psalm Book and the many issues of Tufts's and Walter's collections. All these issues, however, covered no more than 75 different tunes, almost exclusively British and harmonized in block chords – a repertory small and uniform in style.

During the second third of the 18th century the stylistic uniformity of Anglo-American psalmody began to give way. Together with the traditional tunes set simply in block chords, there was a growing tendency towards texture changes, melismas and fuging-tunes, with their brief imitative sections. This new, more elaborate style, cultivated by British psalmodists of the period, including William Tans'ur, William Knapp and John Arnold, slowly gained favour in the American colonies. Collections by these composers and others circulated in America during the 1750s and 1760s; moreover, their music began to appear in tune books printed in the colonies during the latter decade. *Urania* (Philadelphia, 1761), compiled by James Lyon, is the earliest sign of the increase in the size and stylistic range of the printed repertory of psalmody in the 1760s. 198 pages in length, it dwarfed all previous American musical publications, and its inclusion of elaborate, modern British music (more than a dozen anthems and set-pieces, several hymn tunes, as well as a selection of psalm tunes), most of it never before published in America, make it a landmark in American psalmody. Two publications by Josiah Flagg, the *Collection of the Best Psalm Tunes* (Boston, 1764) and *Sixteen Anthems* (Boston, 1766), further established the American tune book as a forum for the publication of 'modern' music. Finally, the American editions of Tans'ur's *Royal Melody Complete* (Boston, 1767, with many later editions) and Aaron Williams's *Universal Psalmodist* (Newburyport, 1769, published by Daniel Bayley with Tans'ur's work as the *American Harmony*) were another step towards broadening American psalmody's stylistic framework. Between 1760 and 1770 some 300 tunes had been added to the colonial store of psalm tunes; in less than a decade the printed repertory had eclipsed oral command.

It is difficult to imagine the American tune books of the 1760s without singing schools. The increase in the printed repertory indicates that reading music was no longer a rare skill, a tribute to the effectiveness of the singing school. Though slowed down by the war (1775–81), the repertory of American psalmody continued to grow throughout the rest of the century. By 1800 more than 1000 different compositions had been printed in American tune books. When that figure is compared with the few tunes used by colonial Christians early in the century (70 tunes available in American tune books by 1760; 400 tunes printed before 1770) it is clear that the tradition was transformed by the impact of musical literacy, and that the decade of the 1760s was a crucial time in that transformation.

From 1770 the contributions of native composers increased. Much of the music in American tune books was still taken from British sources, but more was composed by American singing teachers, tradesmen and citizens, who had picked up their musical training as singing school scholars or from tune book prefaces. The most prominent and prolific of them and the first American psalmodist composer of real consequence was William Billings, whose *New-England Psalm-singer* (Boston, 1770) is another landmark. Published at a time when only a dozen or so American tunes had appeared in print, Billings's work, made up entirely of his own compositions, increased the figure tenfold. Moreover, the patriotic overtones of his prefatory remarks (and of some of the texts he set) and his unabashed confession of his own inexperience and unwillingness to follow established compositional rules provided musical Americans with a bold example of a native composer.

Billings's example was not ignored. By the end of 1782 compositions by at least 19 different Americans had appeared in print. The sudden increase can be traced to two Connecticut collections, *Select Harmony* (Cheshire, 1779) by Andrew Law and *Chorister's Companion* (New Haven, 1782) by Simeon Jocelyn and Amos Doolittle. Like Lyon, Flagg and Bayley before them, Law and Jocelyn were compilers rather than composers; many of the tunes introduced into print in either *Select Harmony* or *Chorister's Companion* soon became part of the central American repertory. The two works also changed the content of American tune books. Earlier collections had generally been either assortments of British music or entirely original, such as Billings's publications. *Select Harmony* and *Chorister's Companion* were eclectic compilations in which British tunes, many of them established favourites, and newly composed American tunes both appeared. It is noteworthy that later tune books which enjoyed many editions displayed similar components of European and American music, among them the *Worcester Collection* (Worcester, 1786, 8/1803); Andrew Adgate's *Philadelphia Harmony* (Philadelphia, 1789, 9/1807); and the *Village Harmony* (Exeter, New Hampshire, 1795, 17/1821).

3. MUSICAL STYLE. Written for singing schools, recreational use and worship, the music of 18th-century Americans answered specific needs and represented a true community practice. Composed by self-trained musicians, mostly without keyboard skill or knowledge of 18th-century European harmonic practice, the music often lacks harmonic direction and creates an impression of crudeness. It is precisely that harmonic roughness, coupled with an often powerful, folklike melodic inspiration, which to modern ears gives the music a freshness and unhackneyed charm. Most American tunes of the time set only a single stanza of metrical text. Plain tunes (settings in block-chord texture in which the phrase structure reflects the textual metre exactly) are in the majority. Sometimes, however, the composer transcends the metre by repeating or extending certain words. In fuging-tunes, particular demands upon the composer's ability to extend his material are made. Set-pieces (through-composed settings of several stanzas of verse) and anthems (through-composed settings of prose texts) constitute only a small proportion of the American-composed repertory. Lack of skill is most apt to show up as a defect rather than an asset in these larger-scale works; many founder for lack of tonal variety. Billings's description of his method of composition helps to explain some of the irregularities of 18th-century psalmody. In his *Continental Harmony* (Boston, 1794), he wrote of composing the tenor part, the 'air', first, then of adding the other voices in turn. The 'grand difficulty in composition', writes the composer, 'is to preserve the air through each part separately, and yet cause them to harmonize with each other at the same time' (p.xxxi).

Stylistic differences among American psalmodists can be observed. Billings himself moved towards a more standard harmonic practice than can be found in his earlier pieces. Connecticut composers including Daniel Read, Lewis Edson, Asahel Benham and Oliver Brownson shared a stylistic framework both relatively uniform and influential. Others, for example Timothy Swan, Justin Morgan, Jacob French and Supply

Belcher, as well as Jeremiah Ingalls, Daniel Belknap and Stephen Jenks, composed pieces which resemble the music of Billings and the Connecticut composers closely enough for one to be able to speak of a unique American musical idiom.

From the 1760s American psalmody had evolved without reference to any stylistic standard or ideal. By the end of the century it was common to see printed side by side in American collections tunes almost as old as Calvinism itself, recent tunes by Yankee singing teachers and the newly popular florid British hymn tunes – most of them drawn from Thomas Butts's *Harmonia sacra* (London, *c*1760) and Martin Madan's 'Lock Hospital Collection' (London, 1769) – which in style resembled the Italianate solo songs favoured in mid-18th-century British drawing rooms. Andrew Law was apparently the first to see any incongruity in this musical mixture when he attacked native composers in the preface to his *Musical Primer* (Cheshire, 1793). Law's attack, and similar comments by others, were more than a statement of preference for one kind of music over another. They recognized that American psalmody had drawn upon sharply differing musical repertories and that these repertories might not be of equal value. During the last part of the 18th century and the first two decades of the 19th, a standard of musical taste imported from Great Britain gradually came to be imposed on American psalmody.

4. REFORM. Reform took on a variety of guises. American composers began in the 1790s to follow European models more closely. The music of Samuel Holyoke, Oliver Holden and Jacob Kimball shows some command of European thoroughbass practice. Holyoke and Holden, in fact, joined with Hans Gram to produce the *Massachusetts Compiler* (Boston, 1795), a reform landmark which prefaced an assortment of European compositions by a lengthy digest from prominent European thoroughbass manuals and instructional treatises. European music occupied an increasingly large proportion of the repertory in collections published after the turn of the century, and particularly in collections issued in larger cities after 1810. The American tunes that did survive were likely to be purged of at least some of their crudities, as in William Cooper's *Beauties of Church Music* (Boston, 1804). Denunciations of American compositional style became increasingly frequent, and fuging-tunes came in for special attack for their supposed textural obfuscation, for example in John Hubbard's *Essay on Music* (Boston, 1808). Some reformers sought to encourage the cultivation of music by European masters; others, viewing psalmody as a practice in which solemnity and decorum should outweigh all other qualities, advocated a return to the ancient psalm tunes in use before the War of Independence. The former led to the establishment of musical organizations such as the Boston Handel and Haydn Society (1815), of which the psalmodist Bartholomew Brown was an original member; the latter led to the discarding of all musical elaboration and eventually to the formulation of a strictly circumscribed, devotional musical style favoured by Thomas Hastings, Lowell Mason and their followers. However divergent these two approaches may have been, they had one thing in common: a rejection of the native composer and of the American idiom developed about the time of the War of Independence.

The success of the reform movement marked the end of the indigenous New England compositional style. It did not, however, consign the repertory entirely to oblivion. Some New England tunes survived in shape-note collections published in the south, by 1820 the centre of its own unique, folklike tradition of polyphonic hymnody. And from 1829, when the *Stoughton Collection* appeared in Boston, the heart of the repertory was periodically reprinted in various tune books. Those collections carried the music in something like its original form, giving pleasure both to those who had grown up with native psalmody and to others who could see value in the long-discredited music of their forefathers.

BIBLIOGRAPHY

G. Hood: *A History of Music in New England* (Boston, 1846/*R*1970)
N. Gould: *Church Music in America* (Boston, 1853)
F. J. Metcalf: *American Writers and Compilers of Sacred Music* (New York, 1925/*R*1967)
A. P. Britton: *Theoretical Introductions in American Tune-books to 1800* (diss., U. of Michigan, 1949)
G. Chase: *America's Music* (New York, 1955, rev. 2/1966)
A. C. Buechner: *Yankee Singing Schools and the Golden Age of Choral Music in New England, 1760–1800* (diss., Harvard U., 1960)
M. Frost, ed.: *Historical Companion to Hymns Ancient & Modern* (London, 1962)
J. W. Thompson: *Music and Musical Activities in New England, 1800–1838* (diss., Peabody College for Teachers, 1962)
I. Lowens: *Music and Musicians in Early America* (New York, 1964)
R. T. Daniel: *The Anthem in New England before 1800* (Evanston, 1966)
R. Stevenson: *Protestant Church Music in America* (New York, 1966)
R. Crawford: *Andrew Law, American Psalmodist* (Evanston, 1968)
C. E. Lindsley: *Early Nineteenth-century American Collections of Sacred Choral Music, 1800–1810* (diss., U. of Iowa, 1968)
R. Crawford: 'Connecticut Sacred Music Imprints, 1778–1810, Part II', *Notes*, xxvii (1970–71), 671

NICHOLAS TEMPERLEY (I), RICHARD CRAWFORD (II)

Psalmody (iii). *See* PSALTERER.

Psalmos. A psalm verse with long melismas, introducing the recitation of the Gospel in the Divine Liturgy and Holy Week Offices of the Coptic Church; *see* COPTIC RITE, MUSIC OF THE.

Psalms, metrical. Paraphrases of the biblical psalms in verse, often designed for singing to tunes of a simple popular type (known today as hymn tunes).

I. Introduction. II. The European continent. III. England. IV. Scotland and Ireland. V. North America.

I. Introduction. Translation of the psalms into verse goes back to Apollinaris in the 4th century, and poetic paraphrases may have been made as early as the 2nd century for the so-called 'Gnostic psalter' of Bardesanes and Harmonius. It continued throughout the Middle Ages, chiefly for the purposes of edification and private devotion. Metrical versions of the seven 'penitential psalms' (vi, xxxii, xxxviii, li, cii, cxxx and cxliii) held a special place in the devotional life of the Roman Church, but in the 16th century a new motive was added – that of public worship. Hus and Luther acknowledged the power of congregational singing, which required texts in verse because prose could not easily be sung by the people at large. Thus the enormous increase in the quantity of metrical psalms after 1520 was a direct outgrowth of the Reformation. The first collections of Lutheran chorales (1524) included a number of psalm paraphrases among the freely composed hymns (*see* CHORALE, §4). The more radical reformers, however, believing that only the inspired words of the Bible were suitable for use in worship, sought to confine the texts to close translations of the psalms and a few other biblical lyrics. They used the verse forms of popular song, partly for ease of learning and partly in the hope that people would set aside the lewd or superstitious songs they knew and sing the psalms instead. Psalms were, in fact, sung in everyday situations as well as in church. They were enormously popular, and were an important element in 16th- and 17th-century music printing and publishing. The tunes were soon harmonized in both simple and elaborate settings.

The German Reformed sect, centred at Strasbourg, included 22 metrical psalms in its *Kirchenampt* of about 1524, and produced a complete psalter by 1538. Zwingli, the first leader of the Swiss Reformed Church, disallowed music in worship altogether, but Calvin threw his influence behind the psalm-singing movement, and between 1539 and 1562 supervised the development of the French metrical psalter. The movement then spread to Britain, the Low Countries, Scandinavia, Eastern Europe, and eventually- to the colonies in America and other parts of the world. Some metrical versions of the psalms, such as the American Bay Psalm Book, are extremely literal; others, such as those of Isaac Watts, are so freely paraphrased that a metrical psalm of this type cannot be clearly demarcated from a hymn (*see* HYMN, §IV).

For the music of the voluntary parish church choir in England, consisting of psalms, hymns and anthems, which began to appear about 1690 and continued through the 18th and 19th centuries, and for the general practice of amateur Protestant vocal music in North America from the 17th century to the 19th, *see* PSALMODY (ii).

II. The European continent

1. General. 2. France and Switzerland. 3. The Low Countries (French language). 4. The Low Countries (Dutch language). 5. Germany.

1. GENERAL. The creation of a metrical psalter in the vernacular, complete with melodies and attendant polyphonic settings, is the chief contribution of Calvinism to the music of western Europe. The origin, growth and distribution of the psalter form a short but intense episode in the history of music. In less than a century the poetry was written, the psalm melodies were composed and the main corpus of polyphonic music inspired by the psalter was created. This period of growth parallels the growth and spread of Calvinism in western Europe. The Calvinist doctrines and psalter found an especially receptive audience in France, Switzerland, the Low Countries and certain areas of Germany (*see* CALVIN, JEAN). The following discussion is organized into four categories, corresponding to the various geographical areas (and languages) in which the Calvinist psalter flourished. Discussed within each category are both the monophonic psalters and the polyphonic settings.

2. FRANCE AND SWITZERLAND.
(*i*) *Monophonic psalters*. The history of the Calvinist psalter begins in the Catholic court of France. In 1537 the poet Clément Marot, *valet de chambre* to King François I, completed rhymed translations of 30 psalms, taking the first 15 psalms in numerical order and then selecting the remainder at will. Marot's psalms were very popular at court. Chroniclers reported that monarch, courtiers and courtesans sang them to popular tunes. In 1540 Marot gave a manuscript of the *Trente pseaulmes* to Emperor Charles V, who urged the poet to continue his work.

Marot's *Trente pseaulmes* first appeared in print in Calvinist psalters. Jean Calvin, exiled from Geneva and leading a small congregation at Strasbourg, used Marot's psalms in his first psalter, *Aulcuns pseaulmes et cantiques mys en chant* (Strasbourg, 1539). This book contains 13 Marot psalms and six psalms and three canticles by Calvin, who wanted his congregation to sing scriptural songs only. *Aulcuns pseaulmes* is a psalter with melodies, but without preface or an appendix of liturgical texts. Several of the melodies were borrowed from earlier Strasbourg songbooks, and at least two tunes in Calvin's first psalter can be ascribed to the Strasbourg musician Matthias Greiter.

Calvin returned to Geneva in 1541, and in the following year brought out his second psalter, *La forme des prieres et chantz ecclesiastiques* (1542). This book contains Marot's *Trente pseaulmes*, two Marot canticles, and five psalms and two canticles by Calvin, each text with its own melody. *La forme des prieres* (see fig.1, which shows one of the most popular of the Genevan psalms, Marot's *Du fond de ma pensée*) begins with a lengthy preface by Calvin on the sacraments and on psalm singing. It concludes with liturgical texts (prayers to be read at worship and forms for the sacraments).

In 1542 Marot fled to Geneva to escape religious persecution. There he revised his first 30 psalms and added 25 new texts to the Calvinist repertory: 19 psalms, four canticles, and two table graces. The earliest extant publication of this material is *Cinquante pseaumes en francois par Clem. Marot* (1543). It is an edition without melodies, and bears no printer's name or place of publication. That same year Calvin published a Genevan edition of the *Cinquante pseaumes* with melodies. No copies of this book survive. In fact, not one Genevan edition of *Cinquante pseaumes* with melodies exists today, even though there is evidence that several were printed between 1543 and 1551, when *Pseaumes octantetrois* appeared.

Pseaumes octantetrois de David, mis en rime Francoise, a savoir, quaranteneuf par Clement Marot ... et trentequatre par Theodore de Besze, de Vezelay en Bourgongne (Geneva, 1551) is the first Calvinist psalter in which the work of poet and musician is acknowledged. Marot, who had died by that time, and Théodore de Bèze, the theologian who continued the work of versifying the psalms, are both mentioned in the title. The musician responsible for the melodies was Loys Bourgeois, who had been active as a music teacher in Geneva since 1545. Bourgeois explained his work on the melodies in a preface, claiming that he wrote new melodies for the 34 De Bèze psalms, rewrote 12 and revised 24 of the old melodies, and left only 15 untouched. Writers have often credited Loys Bourgeois for work on other Genevan psalters, but his role, though substantial, was confined to this publication. It is not known who wrote the melodies for the Calvinist psalters of 1542 and 1543, nor is it known who wrote the new melodies for the complete psalter of 1562. Bourgeois left Geneva in 1552.

Pseaumes octantetrois was published in Geneva each succeeding year until 1554. Six new psalms (without music) were added by De Bèze to the 1554 edition, though they were not acknowledged in the title until *Pseaumes octante-neuf* was published the following year. The 1556 edition of this book contains another preface by a Genevan musician, Pierre Vallette, who replaced Bourgeois as music teacher for a short time. His preface is a little treatise explaining how to read the musical notation of the psalter; he made no reference to writing or revising any psalm melodies.

The complete edition of the Calvinist psalter was published in Geneva in 1562 as *Les pseaumes mis en rime francoise, par Clément Marot, & Théodore de Bèze*. Antoine Vincent was the merchant printer in charge of producing the tens of thousands of copies that issued from printing presses in Geneva, Paris, Lyons, Caen, St Lo and elsewhere, each copy duly marked 'pour Antoine Vincent'. This extensive printing venture, involving 24 printers in Paris alone, shows the immense popularity of the Calvinist psalms. A bibliography compiled by Orentin Douen in 1879 lists 44 different editions of the psalter in 1562, 1563, and 1564. As hostile a commentator as Florimond de Raemond wrote in his *L'histoire de la naissance de ... l'hérésie* (1610) that the psalms of Marot and De Bèze 'were received and welcomed by everyone with as much favour as ever any book was, not only by those with Protestant sympathies, but also by Catholics; everyone enjoyed singing them'.

The complete Calvinist psalter contains 125 different melodies for 152 texts (150 psalms and two canticles). 85 melodies are repeated from the 1551 edition; 40 are new. The creator of the new melodies was a certain 'Maitre Pierre'. Since Pierre Dagues, Pierre Vallette, Pierre Davantes and Pierre du Buisson were active as musicians in Geneva at this time, the identity of 'Maitre Pierre' remains a mystery. But it is known that Loys Bourgeois and the other creators of the Calvinist melodies did not use the French chanson repertory as a

Ex.1 The melody for Psalm lxxii compared with the tenor of Josquin's chanson *Petite camusette*

1. Tes ju – ge – ments, Dieu ve – ri – ta – ble,
3. Veui – lle ta jus – tice e – qui – ta – ble,

Pe – – ti – te ca – mu – set – te,

2. Baille au Roy pour reg – ner.
4. Au fils du Roy don – ner.

à la mort m'a – vez mis

principal source of melodies for the psalter. Although there are reliable reports that Marot's psalms were sung to popular tunes, there is very little evidence that the psalter melodies themselves were derived from chansons. Ever since Orentin Douen (in his *Clément Marot et le psautier huguenot*, 1878–9) illustrated some similarities between a group of Genevan melodies and some chansons, writers have repeated his conclusion that many psalms are based on specific chansons. In Douen's work, however, the similarities shown are limited to short groups of notes here and there, and can more easily be described as idiomatic coincidences than as direct borrowings. For example, one of the psalm

Car, fauoriz estes & bien aimez,
Du grand Seigneur, qui les Cieulx a fermez,
Et terre confinee.

Dieu a les Cieulx vniuersellement,
Pour sa demeure: aux hommes, seulement,
La terre il a donnee.

O Seigneur Dieu, l'homme par mort transi,
Ne dit ton loz, ne quiconques aussi,
En la fosse deualle.

Mais, nous viuans, par tout, ou nous irons,
De bouche & coeur le Seigneur benirons,
Sans fin, sans interualle.

PSALME CXXX.

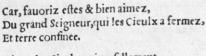

v fond de ma pense e Au

fond de tous ennuis, Dieu, ie t'ay addresse e

Ma clameur iours & nuictz. Entes ma voix plain-

ti ue, Seigneur, il est faison. Ton aureil-

I en ten ti ue, Soit à mon oraison.

Si ta rigueur expresse,
En noz pechez tu tiens:
Seigneur, Seigneur, qui est-ce,
Qui demourra des tiens?

Si n'es-tu point seuere:
Mais, propice à mercy.
C'est pourquoy on reuere,
Toy & ta Loy aussi.

En Dieu ie me console,
Mon ame s'y attend:
h ʒ

1. Marot's setting of Psalm cxxx, 'Du fond de ma pensée', from Calvin's second psalter 'La forme des prieres' (1542) melodies that Douen claimed was a remade chanson is Psalm lxxii, 'Tes jugements, Dieu veritable', which does indeed bear some similarity to the tenor of Josquin's *Petite camusette*. After the almost identical incipits (ex.1), however, the comparison becomes unconvincing.

Pierre Pidoux (1962) showed that several Genevan melodies are made from Gregorian chant. For example, the comparison of Psalm lxxx, 'O pasteur d'Israel escoute', with the Easter sequence, *Victimae paschali laudes*, reveals a much closer relationship than any displayed by Douen's chanson–psalm pairings (ex.2). Unlike the above chanson example, here very little of the older melody need be discarded in order to find the Genevan adaptation. The relationship is obvious enough to justify calling the sequence a model for the psalm tune. Moreover, comments by Loys Bourgeois in his psalter preface of 1551 imply that he used chant for two or three psalms.

Ex.2 The opening of the melody for Psalm lxxx compared with the Easter sequence *Victimae paschali laudes* (transposed up a 4th)

(ii) Polyphonic settings. The immense popularity of the Calvinist psalms led composers to use the texts for polyphonic composition. The first settings came soon after Calvin's first psalter of 1539. One year later Jacques Moderne of Lyons included the earliest known polyphonic setting of a Marot psalm in the sixth book of his series *Le parangon des chansons*. The piece is a complete setting of Psalm cxxxvii, *Estans assis aux rives aquatiques*, by a certain Abel, a composer of whom nothing is known. Abel's extended composition in three movements is not based on any known melody. In 1544 Moderne printed a second psalm by an obscure composer, Gentian, whose setting of Marot's Psalm cxxx appears in the second book of the series *Le difficile des chansons*. This composition is also in three movements and freely composed, without reference to the psalter melody.

Later in the decade French printers began issuing publications devoted exclusively to polyphonic settings of the 50 Marot psalms. The first of these was a collection of 31 settings in four parts by Pierre Certon, published in Paris by Pierre Attaingnant in 1546. Only a superius partbook without title-page remains, but it is enough to show that Certon used the Calvinist melodies.

No reference to the melodies is found in a second book, published that year by Attaingnant as a sequel to the Certon collection and containing 23 settings by Antoine de Mornable.

Loys Bourgeois' polyphonic settings of Marot's 50 psalms appeared in two Lyons publications in 1547. In *Pseaulmes cinquante de David*, Bourgeois wrote in a four-voice note-against-note style, with the unchanged psalm melody in the tenor. He labelled this simple polyphonic style and the syllabic text treatment 'a voix de contrepoinct egal consonante au verbe'. For the 24 settings in *Le premier livre des pseaulmes* Bourgeois used three styles, which he again labelled in the title: 'a voix pareille' (note-against-note, with psalm melody as tenor cantus firmus); 'familiere, ou vaudeville' (a freer note-against-note texture, with some ornamentation in the accompanying voices or even in the melody itself); and 'plus musicale' (imitative counterpoint, with each phrase of the psalm melody the basis of a point of imitation – see ex.3, which uses the melody shown in fig.1). Only 15 of the 24 settings, however, use known Calvinist melodies.

Other composers who filled single publications with settings of some or all of Marot's *Cinquante pseaumes*

Ex.3 Loys Bourgeois' setting of Psalm cxxx in imitative style, from *Le premier livre des pseaulmes* (Lyons, 1547)

(Note values halved)

are Clément Janequin (1549), Pierre Colin (1550), Claude Goudimel (1551, 1557, 1559, 1560), Pierre Certon, again (1555), Jacques Arcadelt (1559), and Michel Ferrier (1559). All of these composers except Colin used the Genevan tunes, although Goudimel sometimes composed without them.

Loys Bourgeois, the writer of many of the melodies in *Pseaumes octantetrois* (1551), was also the first composer to produce a polyphonic setting of this enlarged psalter. Only a bass partbook of *Pseaulmes LXXXIII de David* (1554) remains; it shows, however, that Bourgeois used the psalter melodies. Philibert Jambe de Fer also used the psalter melodies, setting only the De Bèze texts in his *Psalmodie de quarante et un pseaumes royaux* (1559). Both Marot and De Bèze texts from *Pseaumes octantetrois* form the basis for the polyphonic psalters by Janequin (1559), Thomas Champion (1561), and Claude Goudimel (1562). All three of these publications use the Calvinist melodies.

Soon after the publication of the complete Geneva psalter in 1562, composers began to write polyphonic settings of all 150 psalms. Four polyphonic psalters, each entitled *Les cent cinquante pseaumes de David*, appeared in 1564: one by Goudimel in Paris, two by Jambe de Fer in Lyons, and one by Richard Crassot in Lyons. All are in note-against-note style with the psalm

melody in the tenor. (See below, however, on Goudimel's style.) Other composers who set the complete psalter are Hugues Sureau (1565), Jean Servin (1565), Pierre Santerre (1567), Claude Goudimel, again (1568), Paschal de L'Estocart (1583), and Claude Le Jeune, twice (1601, and 1602–10 in three volumes). These settings are all based on the Genevan melodies. When composers set the entire psalter, they presented the psalm tune as cantus firmus, accompanied by either chordal texture or a more elaborate counterpoint. The given melody, however, was always clearly present. In their prefaces, the composers of the Calvinist repertory stated that they had retained 'the usual melody which is sung in church', because so many people enjoyed singing the psalms outside of the church 'in a more melodious setting, from the art of music'.

Claude Goudimel made the most substantial contribution to the Calvinist repertory with his three different settings of the psalter. Between 1551 and 1566 he produced eight books of psalm motets. For these compositions he used the entire text, grouping several stanzas into a single movement. Psalm cxix, for example (vol.iii, 1557), has 28 stanzas and is in five movements. Often the various movements, or even the stanzas, are set off from each other by contrasts in texture, cantus firmus treatment or number of voices used. Imitative counterpoint is the style of these works. In the earlier settings Goudimel did not build the points of imitation on the psalter tunes, but he did use them for the later psalm motets.

Goudimel's second setting of the Genevan melodies is his complete polyphonic psalter of 1564 (part published in 1562). Here he used the note-against-note style with the tune appearing in tenor or superius. There are, however, only 125 different melodies in the Geneva psalter, some of them being assigned to more than one psalm. When Goudimel set one of these melodies a second time in his 1564 psalter he wrote in a more ornate style. Tenor or superius still carry the unaltered psalm tune, so that, as in the simpler settings, the length of the given melody determines the length of the polyphonic composition. Here, however, the accompanying voices do not move with the melody to form a chordal texture. Instead, each voice is rhythmically independent and indulges in occasional short melismas, brief imitations and ornamental melodic figures. The setting of the text is still mainly syllabic, but the four voices no longer declaim the words together. Goudimel used this more ornate style exclusively in his third setting of the psalm tunes (another complete polyphonic psalter), published in 1568. For purposes of comparison, the openings of Goudimel's three settings of Psalm i are given in ex.4.

The most eloquent testimony to the popularity of the polyphonic settings is the large number of them that were printed. The publications listed above contain over 2000 settings of the Marot–De Bèze texts. Large as this number is, it represents only about two-thirds of the polyphonic repertory based on the Calvinist texts and tunes. More than 100 psalms appeared in instrumental publications like Le Roy's *Tiers livre de tabulature de luth* (1552), which contains 21 settings for voice and lute. With the polyphonic *chansons spirituelles* and the settings of psalms by Calvinist poets other than Marot and De Bèze, the total number of compositions swells to over 3000, which does not include what was published in countries other than France and Switzerland. Nor

Ex.4 The openings of Goudimel's three settings of Psalm i

(a) from the *Tiers livre contenant huit pseaumes de David* (Paris, 1557)

(b) from *Les cent cinquante pseaumes de David* (Paris, 1564)

(The cantus firmus is in the tenor)

(c) from *Les cent cinquante pseaumes de David* (Paris, 1568)

(The cantus firmus is in the top voice)

does this number include the motet and chanson contrafacta prepared by various Calvinist editors who substituted a Calvinist psalm or *chanson spirituelle* for the original text. The chansons of Lassus were a prime target. Simon Goulart, a minister and publisher of music in Geneva, issued a series of publications in which Lassus's texts were either adapted or completely replaced. In 1597, a certain Louis Mongart prepared a polyphonic psalter named *Cinquante pseaumes de David*. He explained his editing technique in the preface: 'I have accommodated the text of the psalms to French, Italian, and German chansons, and even to several Latin motets of Orland de Lassus, prince of musicians of our century'.

The complete polyphonic Calvinist repertory – psalm setting, instrumental arrangement, *chanson spirituelle* and contrafactum – rivals, in quantity at least, the Parisian chanson, the Italian madrigal and the polyphonic Lutheran chorale. Yet this huge repertory is barely mentioned in contemporary records: only three references are known.

The first is from *Histoire ecclésiastique des églises réformées*, a work formerly attributed to Théodore de Bèze. It tells of the Huguenot Anne de Bourg, who was a prisoner in the Bastille in 1560. Although 'confined in a cage where he suffered all the discomforts imaginable, he rejoiced always and glorified God, now taking up his lute to sing him psalms, now praising him with his voice'.

A second reference to the polyphonic performance of Calvinist psalms is in a letter by a certain Villemadon, courtier to Marguérite of Navarre. He wrote to Catherine de' Medici on 26 August 1559 telling her that when Charles V visited Paris in January 1540, the musicians of François I and the emperor, indeed all the musicians of France, outdid one another in setting Marot's psalms to music. Everyone in France was then singing psalms. The courtier described his visit to the sick-bed of the dauphin Henry, whom he found singing psalms, accompanied by lutes, guitars, viols, spinets, flutes, and the voices of his singers. Unfortunately very few of the earliest settings for Marot's psalms have survived. Perhaps most of them were contrafacta, as later writers like Florimond de Raemond suggested. The polyphonic psalters of the later 1540s do not contain the earliest settings, because these later publications are by composers not connected with the court from 1537 to 1542, the years when Marot's psalms were in high royal favour. Moreover, since all of these settings are based on melodies or texts printed in 1543 or later, they do not reflect the activity Villemadon described.

A third reference to the singing of polyphonic Calvinist psalms is in a chronicle by Marcus van Vaernewijck of Ghent (1566–8). In his description of the religious unrest in the Low Countries he commented on the popularity of the psalms among the Calvinists, adding that 'they were also sung in parts in the homes, in the shops, and similar establishments'. This is the only known reference to the actual singing of polyphony in the homes of the Calvinists, and agrees with statements and implications in the titles and prefaces of the polyphonic psalm collections: these compositions were not meant to be sung in church, where polyphony was frowned upon, but in the homes and in places where amateurs gathered to make music. Nevertheless, various writers have suggested that the polyphonic Calvinist psalms were, indeed, sung in church. Such conjectures ignore evidence presented by the publications themselves. Goudimel prefaced his chordal settings published in Geneva in 1565 with the instruction that these settings were not to be sung in church but in the home. As for the more difficult motet-like settings, they were frequently dedicated to collèges musicaux, which were groups of amateurs. The evidence from contemporary chronicles and from the publications shows that, in the 16th century at least, both the simple and complex settings of the Calvinist psalms were meant for amateur performance, not for the church.

3. THE LOW COUNTRIES (FRENCH LANGUAGE).

(i) Monophonic psalters. The earliest known edition of Marot's complete Trente pseaulmes appeared in the Low Countries in 1541, one year before they all appeared in Calvin's first Genevan psalter. In 1541 the Antwerp printer Antoine des Gois issued Psalmes de David, translatez de plusieurs Autheurs, & principallement de Cle. Marot. This is a psalter without music that contains the 30 psalms of Marot along with 15 by lesser-known poets, some of them identified by only an initial. Ten of the 45 psalms are headed by references to pre-existent melodies to which the texts could be sung. For example, Marot's Psalm x was to be sung 'sus Dont vient cela', a popular chanson. The book was approved for publication by Pierre Alexandre, confessor to Mary of Hungary, Regent of the Low Countries. Psalmes de David has been considered a Protestant publication because Alexandre was later proclaimed a heretic. And the references to melodies prompted some writers to consider the book an early Calvinist psalter designed for use in secret worship. There could have been no eager Protestant market for this publication, however, because Calvinism had barely penetrated the Low Countries in 1541. The Lutherans and Anabaptists active in Antwerp would have had little use for a French psalter, since these Protestants spoke German or Dutch. Although there are reasons for believing that Psalmes de David may have been Protestant in intent, it certainly is not a Calvinist psalter. It was, however, the first appearance in the Low Countries of Marot's Trente pseaulmes, texts that were to be used later by the Calvinists there.

All of the Calvinist texts and tunes were published by Christopher Plantin in Antwerp in 1564, two years after the psalter was completed in Geneva. Plantin took precautions because he evidently knew that the Geneva psalter might be considered a heretical publication. Before publication he requested and received permission to print this book from both the religious and secular authorities. After publication the psalter was again examined and approved by a priest. In spite of these safeguards, the book was condemned and Plantin was ordered to destroy his entire production. The authorities gave as their reason that, although the texts might be pure, the melodies were those used by the heretics.

The public singing of psalms was forbidden by royal decree, and if the Inquisition found psalters in homes they imprisoned the owners. In April 1566, however, the activities of the Inquisition were curtailed for a time, and there was a period of religious freedom. Refugees flocked back from England and Germany, singing psalms in their boats and wagons. In May the Protestants held their first open-air services, usually in the fields just outside the city walls. Thousands of people in Flanders, Holland and Zeeland forsook Mass to hear the preachers of the new religion. Several chroniclers have described the singing of psalms at these gatherings. Marcus van Vaernewijck wrote in Ghent in 1566: 'these psalms appealed to the members of the new religion so much that in the evening they would gather in groups of two to three hundred and sing them in different streets and alleys of the city. . . .One hardly heard any other songs. . . .Out in the fields, the preachers taught the people how to sing them, using simple tunes'. Psalm singing accompanied the frenzied outburst of image breaking in August 1566, which in turn led to strong repressive measures from ruling Spain. Immediately after the image breaking, however, there was even greater religious freedom for the Protestants. They quickly built churches in which, according to chroniclers, they spent the entire Sunday listening to sermons and singing psalms. Within a year the churches in the southern provinces of the Low Countries were torn down by the Duke of Alva and his Spanish troops, whose task it was to subjugate the rebellious Low Countries. Psalm singing once again became a heretical activity, punishable by death.

(ii) Polyphonic settings. Soon after the printed appearance of Marot's psalms in Antwerp (Psalmes de David, 1541) composers began using them as texts. The first polyphonic setting of a Marot psalm to appear in the Low Countries was by Benedictus Appenzeller, and was included in a collection of his chansons printed in 1542 by Henry Loys and Jean de Buys of Antwerp. In setting Marot's Psalm cxxx, Appenzeller simply wrote in the typical Netherlands style of his day, with no reference to the Calvinist melody.

In all, 33 settings of Marot's psalms, canticles and graces appeared in Netherland chanson collections in the 16th century. The earlier settings are all in the typical chanson style of that era and area, and are without reference to known melodies. In addition to Appenzeller, the composers are Manchicourt, Susato, Gerarde, Clemens non Papa, Crispel, Caulery, and Waelrant, all composers active in the Low Countries. Later in the century, five composers (Lassus, Noë Faignient, Philippe de Monte, Séverin Cornet, Andreas Pevernage) used the Calvinist tunes as well as texts, but the settings still appeared in chanson collections. These compositions range in style from the homophonic setting of Psalm cxxx by Lassus, to the four psalm motets for five voices by Pevernage which use imitation, expressive dissonance, text-painting, diminution and augmentation of the given melody, and even attempt musique mesurée. Pevernage's setting of Psalm xxxiii, Resveillez-

Ex.5 Pevernage's setting of Psalm xxxiii, from *Chansons d'Andre Pevernage, livre premier* (Antwerp, 1589)

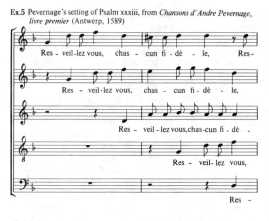

vous, chascun fidèle, with its short notes, animated motifs and high voices, is an excellent example of a polyphonic idiom in which text determines style. The bright sound and lively rhythmic quality of this piece is an appropriate setting for a text that urges the faithful to rise and praise the Lord with psaltery and harp (ex.5).

The only publications in the Low Countries exclusively devoted to polyphonic settings of the Marot–De Bèze texts are by the composers Jean Louys and Sweelinck. Louys set all the texts of Marot's *Cinquante pseaumes*, using the psalter melodies and the first stanza of each text. Entitled *Pseaulmes cinquante de David*, his collection appeared in three volumes, published in 1555 by Waelrant & Laet of Antwerp. Like most of the motets published in the Low Countries at this time, the psalms are for five voices. The motifs are often extended to form long, melismatic phrases, rather than being declamatory and brief as in the contemporaneous French motet style cultivated by Sermisy and Certon. Pervading imitation, a thick texture, an avoidance of clearcut phrase divisions and very little chordal writing are characteristics that place Louys' psalms squarely in the mid-century Netherlands tradition of Crecquillon, Clemens non Papa and Gombert.

Jan Pieterszoon Sweelinck was the only composer who finished the task of setting all of the Marot–De Bèze psalms in a florid motet style. Claude Le Jeune presented 12 elaborate settings in his *Dodécacorde* of 1598, and Claude Goudimel worked his way through almost half of the psalter in his eight books of psalm motets. Unlike Goudimel, Sweelinck did not set all the stanzas of each psalm, although he did use the complete texts of 32 of them. Sweelinck brought out his 153 compositions in four books, published in Amsterdam between 1604 and 1621. His work is the climax and crown of the Calvinist repertory. Into a rich fabric of late Renaissance polyphony, ranging from two to eight voices, Sweelinck wove the Genevan melodies in a variety of ways: as unembellished cantus firmus in one voice, as cantus firmus moving from voice to voice, or as basis for equal imitation in all voices. Ex.6 shows the openings of two psalm motets by Sweelinck, the first in cantus firmus style, the second using equal imitation. Chromaticism, word-painting, echo effects and double-chorus writing are also present. Sweelinck's psalms signal the end of an era in two respects. His vocal music in general is the 'brilliant and noble sunset' (Reese, 1954, p.518) of the great production of the Netherlanders in the field of vocal polyphony; his psalm settings mark the twilight era of the music of Calvinism. The Calvinist churches of western Europe continued to use the psalter, but the period of creative activity begun in Paris by Clément Marot ended in Amsterdam with Sweelinck's contrapuntal masterpieces.

4. THE LOW COUNTRIES (DUTCH LANGUAGE).

(i) *Monophonic psalters*. The first metrical Dutch psalter printed in the Low Countries was the SOUTERLIEDEKENS, a volume of rhymed psalms set to Dutch and French folktunes. Printed by Symon Cock of Antwerp in 1540, this psalter was the first publication in the Low Countries to use movable music type. The question of the confessional character of the *Souterliedekens* has occupied several scholars. Recent investigation has produced evidence of Lutheran

Ex.6 The openings of two psalm motets by Sweelinck, from *Cinquante pseaumes de David* (Amsterdam, 1604)

(a) Psalm xxiv, in cantus firmus style

(b) Psalm cxxx, using equal imitation

influence in the prologue, and has shown that many psalms take the Dutch Lutheran Bible of 1526 as a textual basis. In fact, several heretical expressions from the marginal glossary of this Bible found their way into the *Souterliedekens*.

The second Dutch psalter printed on Netherlands soil was the work of Lucas de Heere, a Ghent artist who was also a fervent Calvinist. His *Psalmen Davids na d'Ebreeusche waerhyt ... op de voysen en mate, van*

Clement Marots Psalmen was published in Ghent in 1565. As its title implies, this psalter contains translations of Huguenot psalms with their respective melodies retained. De Heere used the complete Geneva psalter of 1562 as his source, and although only Marot is acknowledged in his title, eight of De Heere's 36 translations are of De Bèze texts. He not only used the poetic structure of the French texts so that his psalms could be sung to the Genevan melodies, but in most cases translated literally from the French.

There is no evidence that De Heere's psalms were ever used by Dutch-speaking Calvinist congregations, which had been meeting secretly in the Low Countries for about a decade. The probable reason De Heere's psalter was not adopted is that Dutch Calvinists already had one. Since 1551, printers in London and Emden had issued 12 editions of the psalms of Jan Utenhove. Utenhove was of noble birth, but fled his home city of Ghent in 1544 because of his Protestant beliefs. His first psalms, published by Steven Mijerdman of London, were meant for the exiled Dutch Protestant church that Utenhove and others had founded in London.

In 1553 Mary Tudor's accession to the throne made England unsafe for Protestants; the young congregation fled to Denmark and thence to Germany, where they found a refuge in Emden. There Utenhove continued his work of rhyming the psalms, which were printed in Emden by Gillis van der Erven. Utenhove returned to England in 1559, soon after Protestantism was restored by Elizabeth, and his subsequent psalters were printed by John Day of London. He finished his work on the psalms in 1565, and a complete psalter was published the following year. Entitled *De psalmen Davidis, in Nederlandischer sangsryme*, most of its texts are translations of the Marot–De Bèze psalms, and the majority of its melodies are from the Geneva psalter.

The complete triumph of the Genevan tradition occurred when Petrus Dathenus issued his *De Psalmen Davids, ende ander lofsanghen, wt den Francoyschen dichte in Nederlandschen overghesett*, published in Rouen, Ghent and Heidelberg in 1566. This is simply the complete Geneva psalter in Dutch. Like De Heere, Dathenus translated the Marot–De Bèze texts, often literally, and fitted his translations to the Genevan melodies. His psalter was accepted by the Synod of Wesel in 1568 and remained the official songbook of the Dutch-speaking Calvinist Church for more than two centuries. The Dathenus texts were replaced by a more modern version in 1773. Although for this and subsequent revisions the Marot–De Bèze poems no longer served as models, the Genevan melodies were retained. They are still sung by Calvinist congregations in the Netherlands and Belgium.

(ii) Polyphonic settings. The *Souterliedekens* also provided the first texts and melodies for polyphonic settings of Dutch psalms. Clemens non Papa set all but ten of the *Souterliedekens*, and Tylman Susato published these as volumes iv–vii of his *Musyck boexken* series (1556–7), composing the ten missing psalms himself. All of Clemens's settings are for three voices, each in a partbook: superius, tenor and bassus. The tenor always carries the 1540 melody, and is usually a true tenor part with a soprano or alto written above it and a bass beneath. Occasionally, however, Clemens assigned the melody (always printed in the tenor partbook) to a high voice, and wrote an alto and bass beneath it. The

alto part then appears in the superius partbook, even though it is not the highest voice. Evidently Clemens wanted a variety in the cantus firmus texture, but he (or Susato) also wanted all the *Souterliedekens* melodies in one partbook.

Susato's next four volumes in the *Musyck boexken* series appeared in 1561 and contained 123 polyphonic settings of the *Souterliedekens*, set for four voices by Gherardus Mes. The first volume is labelled *Souterliedekens V*, implying that it is a continuation of the series that began with Clemens's four volumes. The title also labels Mes a 'discipel van Jacobus non Papa'. Two of the four partbooks are missing, making an assessment of this work extremely difficult.

The third composer to place the popular *Souterliedekens* in polyphonic setting was Cornelis Buscop. 50 of his settings were published in Düsseldorf in 1568 under the title *Psalmen David, vyfftich, mit vier partyen*. Buscop's preface indicates that he had composed others for five and for six voices. The published four-part psalms are in modest motet style, each phrase of the *Souterliedekens* melody being used to build one or two points of imitation. Buscop did not, however, use the given melody for each composition; some appear to be freely composed.

Polyphonic settings of early Dutch psalms other than the *Souterliedekens* are very scarce. The few that remain have texts by unknown authors. Although there is some evidence that the Dathenus texts were set polyphonically by Dutch composers in the 16th century, the music has not been found. The earliest known polyphonic publications containing the official Dutch texts are from the following century. These are Dutch editions of the note-against-note settings of the Geneva psalter by Claude Goudimel and Claude Le Jeune, in which the Dathenus texts are used as contrafacta.

5. GERMANY.

(i) Monophonic psalters. Metrical translations of psalms are prominent in the earliest Lutheran songbooks. The first published collection of Lutheran chorales, the so-called *Achtliederbuch* of 1524, contains three rhymed psalm translations by Luther himself. In the *Erfurt Enchiridion* of the same year, seven of the 26 songs are metrical psalms. The first publication devoted exclusively to metrical psalms is by the Meistersinger Hans Sachs, who worked very closely from Luther's prose translation of all the psalms, and published *Dreytzehn Psalmen zusingen, in den vier hernach genotirten Thonen* in 1526. In the following decades complete metrical psalters were published by other confessional groups in Germany. The first complete Lutheran psalter, however, did not appear until 1553. It was the work of Burkhard Waldis, and was published in Frankfurt under the title *Der Psalter, in newe Gesangs weise, und künstliche Reimen gebracht, durch Burcardum Waldis, mit ieder Psalmen besondern Melodien*. Waldis's texts and melodies did not find wide acceptance. Nor did the metrical psalms of later Lutheran poets gain the popularity in Germany that the Marot–De Bèze psalter did in France, Switzerland, the Low Countries and eventually in Germany itself.

A translation of the Marot–De Bèze psalms became by far the best-known psalter in Germany. In 1565 Ambrosius Lobwasser finished his translation of the entire French psalter into German. It was published in Leipzig in 1573, and entitled *Der Psalter dess königlichen Propheten Davids, in deutsche Reymen verstendiglich und deutlich gebracht*. The Lobwasser translation enjoyed immediate popularity, and was used by Lutheran congregations as well as Calvinist. As a result, several Calvinist melodies found a permanent place in the Lutheran repertory (e.g. Psalm xlii = 'Freu dich sehr, O meine Seele'; 'Les commandemens de Dieu' = 'Wenn wir in höchsten Nöten sein'). One of the reasons for the popularity of Lobwasser's work was that his texts were usually accompanied in print by the homophonic settings of Goudimel. (Part-singing of the psalms was introduced into the German Calvinist service long before it was permitted in Geneva or the Low Countries.)

Lobwasser had many imitators. They modelled their translations on the French psalms, and used either the Genevan melodies alone or the Goudimel settings. In 1588 Philipp von Winnenbergh published his translation with a new arrangement of the Goudimel four-part pieces: the melody was in the superius instead of the tenor. Other translator–arrangers were Paul Melissus Schede (1572), Martin Opitz (1637) and Hans von Bonneck (1634). None of these psalters, however, diminished the popularity of Lobwasser's version.

To counteract the spread of the Calvinist psalms, the Catholics and Lutherans created their own metrical psalters, often imitating the very psalms they were attempting to replace. A metrical psalter for Catholics was prepared by Kaspar Ulenberg and published in Cologne in 1582. *Die Psalmen Davids in allerlei teutsche Gesangreimen bracht* contains all 150 psalms fitted to 81 melodies, which are very like their Genevan prototypes. *Der Lutherische Lobwasser, das ist Der ganz Psalter Davids* is the work of Johann Wuestholtz, who claimed in his preface to have corrected Lobwasser's work. The melodies are Genevan. The Lutheran theologian Cornelius Becker, far from bringing out a 'Lutheran Lobwasser', or using the Genevan melodies, sharply criticized the Lobwasser psalter in the preface to his *Der Psalter Davids gesangweis, auff die in Lutherischen Kirchen gewöhnlichen Melodeyen zugerichtet* (Leipzig, 1602). Becker disliked the 'strange French melodies', which 'sounded sweet only to worldly ears'. As his title states, Becker used Lutheran melodies for his new translations.

The publication of metrical psalters in Germany continued to follow strict confessional lines. For Lutherans and Catholics, however, the metrical psalm never gained the dominating position that it held in the song repertory of the Calvinist church.

(ii) Polyphonic settings. The earliest polyphonic settings of metrical psalms in Germany were by Johann Walter (i) in his *Geystliches Gesangkbuchleyn* of 1524. In the same year that the first monophonic Lutheran songbooks appeared, Walter made polyphonic settings of the songs, which included Luther's rhymed psalms. Polyphonic settings of the entire psalter came somewhat later. Perhaps the earliest venture was by the Kassel Hofkapellmeister Johannes Heugel, who sometime between 1555 and 1570 set for four and five voices the entire psalter (tunes and texts) of Burkhard Waldis. These modest contrapuntal settings survive in a Kassel manuscript (*D-Kl* 4° Mus.94). The Stuttgart Hofkapellmeister Sigmund Hemmel did not limit his source to a single monophonic psalter, but selected psalm texts and tunes from various German songbooks, several of them from non-Lutheran centres like Strasbourg and Konstanz.

Hemmel used the given melody if there was one; if not, he chose an existing Lutheran melody that fitted the psalm text. He created his psalter between 1561 and 1564. It was published posthumous as *Der gantz Psalter Davids, wie derselbig in teutsche Gesänge verfasset, mit vier Stimmen kunstlich und lieblich von neuen gesetzt* (Tübingen, 1569).

The Lobwasser–Goudimel psalter appeared in 1573. Subsequent polyphonic metrical psalters in Germany were deeply influenced by this exceedingly popular publication. Other poets (e.g. those cited in 5 (i) above) fitted their metrical translations to the Goudimel settings. Other composers set other German metrical psalms in homophonic style. One of the earliest examples of this practice is David Wolkenstein's *Psalmen für Kirchen und Schulen auff die gemeine Melodeien syllaben weiss zu 4 Stimmen gesetzt* (Strasbourg, 1577 and 1583). German composers were also quick to set the monophonic psalters that had been produced to stop the spread of the Calvinist psalms. Ulenberg's Catholic psalter was set by Orlande and Rudolph de Lassus, Sigerus Pauli and Konrad Hagius. Cornelius Becker's Lutheran psalter was set by Sethus Calvisius and Heinrich Schütz. Composers connected with Calvinist centres made more elaborate settings of Lobwasser's texts and the Genevan melodies. Michael Praetorius included ten settings of Genevan psalm tunes in the fourth volume of his *Musae Sionae*, which he dedicated to Duke Frederick of Rhein-Pfalz, a Calvinist. 11 more Calvinist psalm settings are in other volumes of that gigantic work. Other composers who set more than a few of the German–Genevan psalms are Samuel Mareschall (Basle, 1606), Moritz, Landgrave of Hesse (Kassel, 1612), and Johannes Crüger (Berlin, 1658).

The most significant contribution of the Lobwasser–Goudimel psalter, however, is not the number or quality of the subsequent polyphonic psalm settings it engendered. Scholars of Lutheran church music agree that Goudimel's homophonic psalm settings greatly influenced the texture of the Lutheran chorale. The cantional style (chordal, melody in the soprano), first used in a Lutheran hymnal by Osiander in 1586, is the direct descendant of the simple Goudimel psalm setting. It is a style familiar to all who have sung a Protestant hymn.

BIBLIOGRAPHY

F. de Raemond: *L'histoire de la naissance, progrez et décadence de l'hérésie de ce siècle* (Paris, 1610)

F. Bovet: *Histoire du psautier des églises réformées* (Paris, 1872)

O. Douen: *Clément Marot et le psautier huguenot* (Paris, 1878–9)

A. Gastoué: *Le cantique populaire en France* (Lyons, 1924)

R. R. Terry: *Calvin's First Psalter* (London, 1932)

R. Lenaerts: *Het Nederlands polifonies lied in de 16de eeuw* (Mechelen and Amsterdam, 1933)

K. Ameln and P. Pidoux, eds.: *C. Goudimel: Les pseaumes mis en rime francoise, 1565* (Kassel, 1935) [facs. edn.]

W. S. Pratt: *The Music of the French Psalter of 1562* (New York, 1939)

B. van den Sigtenhorst Meyer: *De vocale muziek van Jan P. Sweelinck* (The Hague, 1948)

H. Bruinsma: *The 'Souterliedekens' and its Relation to Psalmody in the Netherlands* (diss., U. of Michigan, 1949)

K. P. Bernet Kempers: 'Meerstemmig psalmgezang in de Hervormde Kerk van Nederland', *TVNM*, xvii/3 (1951), 167

G. Reese: *Music in the Renaissance* (New York, 1954, rev. 2/1959)

E. Droz: 'Antoine Vincent: la propagande protestante par le psautier', *Travaux d'humanisme et renaissance*, xxviii (1957), 276

P. Pidoux: 'Les psaumes d'Antoine de Mornable, Guillaume Morlaye, et Pierre Certon', *AnnM*, v (1957), 179

'Notes sur quelques éditions des psaumes de Claude Goudimel', *RdM*, xlii (1958), 184

S. J. Lenselink: *De Nederlandse psalmberijmingen van de Souterliedekens tot Datheen* (Assen, 1959)

P. Pidoux, ed.: *La forme des prières et chantz ecclesiastiques, 1542* (Kassel, 1959) [facs. edn.]

L. Finscher: 'Psalm', §C, *MGG*

P. Pidoux: *Le psautier huguenot*, i–ii (Basle, 1962)

M. Honegger: 'La chanson spirituelle populaire huguenote', *Jb für Liturgik und Hymnologie*, viii (1963), 129

——: Review of P. Pidoux: *Le psautier huguenot*, *RdM*, xlix (1963), 237

W. Blankenburg: 'Die Kirchenmusik in den reformierten Gebieten des europäischen Kontinents', in F. Blume: *Geschichte der evangelischen Kirchenmusik* (Kassel, rev. 2/1965; Eng. trans., enlarged, 1974, as *Protestant Church Music: a History*), 341–400

M. Jenny: 'Weltlicher Ursprung der Genfer Psalmweisen?', *Musik und Gottesdienst*, xix (1965), 149

P. Pidoux: 'Vierhundert Jahre Goudimel-Psalmen', *Musik und Gottesdienst*, xix (1965), 141

H. Slenk: *The Huguenot Psalter in the Low Countries* (diss., Ohio State U., 1965)

P. Pidoux: 'Weltlicher Ursprung der Genfer Psalmweisen?', *Musik und Gottesdienst*, xx (1966), 167

H. Slenk: 'Christopher Plantin and the Genevan Psalter', *TVNM*, xx/4 (1967), 226

S. J. Lenselink: *Le psautier huguenot*, iii (Assen, 1969)

W. S. Pratt: *The Music of the French Psalter of 1562* (New York, 1969)

H. Slenk: 'Jan Utenhove's Psalms in the Low Countries', *Nederlands archief voor kerkgeschiedenis*, xlix (1969), 155

P. Pidoux: 'Loys Bourgeois' Anteil am Hugenotten-Psalter', *Jb für Liturgik und Hymnologie*, xv (1970), 123

G. Aeschbacher: 'Bemerkungen zur rhythmische Gestalt des Huguenotten Psalters', *Festschrift Arnold Geering* (Berne, 1972), 11

D. Gutknecht: *Untersuchungen zur Melodik des Hugenottenpsalters* (Cologne, 1972)

III. England.

The singing of metrical psalms was a feature of English Protestant worship from the time of the Reformation, and remained so until it was gradually replaced by hymn singing during the 18th and 19th centuries. For more than a century it was also a common form of domestic music. Some of the tunes composed for the metrical psalms have remained in continuous use for over 400 years, and thus represent one of the oldest English musical traditions still in existence.

1. The Church of England: (i) Introduction (ii) Texts (iii) Tunes (iv) Performing practice. 2. The dissenting churches: (i) Presbyterians (ii) Independents (iii) Baptists. 3. Domestic use. 4. Harmonized settings: (i) Harmonized chants (ii) 'Anthems' with metrical psalm texts (iii) Elaborate settings of psalm tunes (iv) Note-against-note harmonizations.

1. THE CHURCH OF ENGLAND.

(*i*) *Introduction*. The death of Henry VIII in 1547 opened the way for the Protestant reforming party to replace Latin services with English ones, and to introduce many other changes in the practice, discipline and official theology of the Church. Throughout the brief reign of Edward VI (1547–53) the trend moved steadily in favour of the Puritan party, as can be seen by comparing the first (1549) and second (1552) versions of the Book of Common Prayer. In music as in other matters, there was a tendency to get rid of anything associated with Romanism – the chanting of the liturgy, the office hymns (which at one time Cranmer had wanted to retain), the elaborate polyphony of the larger churches and the minor orders of clergy who had kept it up. The predominant influence was that of the Reformed churches of Germany, Switzerland and France. Unlike the Lutherans, the English reformers held the view that psalms, being divinely inspired, were preferable to any merely human composition; and they introduced metrical translations of the psalms so that the sacred texts could be sung by the people at large. The foreign Protestant Church, established in London in 1550 under the leadership of John à Lasco to accommodate the many exiles from the Continent, was probably a strong influence on English churches, especially in London. At à Lasco's church metrical psalms were sung unaccompanied, and it is not unlikely that the same practice was tried out in English churches. Several metrical translations were already available and others were quickly produced. But there is little information about the music used in parish churches at this time. Surviving settings of metrical psalms from the Edwardian period (see §4 below) are clearly for choirs, not congregations.

During the reign of Mary I (1553–8), when the Latin rites were restored, the tradition of English psalm singing was developed by exiles abroad, especially at Frankfurt, Geneva, Emden and Strasbourg. After Elizabeth I's accession, metrical psalm singing, though not included in the liturgy, was allowed by the Queen's Injunctions of 1559, and it very quickly became a normal and popular part of both cathedral and parish church practice. In a wave of Puritan feeling in the late 1560s, most surviving parochial choirs were swept away, organs were pulled down, plainsong and chanting were condemned in sermons, and metrical psalms became the only form of music generally used in church.

(*ii*) *Texts*. Verse translations of the psalms had circulated in private use in Henry VIII's time. Miles Coverdale's *Goostly Psalmes and Spirituall Songes* (*c*1538) included 15 psalm versions with tunes, based directly on Lutheran sources; but it had no lasting influence. Robert Crowley's *The Psalter of David Newely Translated into Englyshe Metre* (1549) is the first complete version surviving, though its preface refers to 'other translations'. Several other versions of selected psalms appeared in Edward's reign, but the only one that was to be of any lasting importance was that of Thomas Sternhold. Like Marot of the French psalter, Sternhold was a court poet, who described himself on the title page of *Certayne Psalmes* (*c*1549) as 'grome of the kynge's Majesties roobes'. The preface contains nothing to suggest that he intended the psalms for public use. After his death a larger collection appeared, containing 37 of his versions, all but two of them in the traditional English ballad metre, or common metre. This small beginning became the nucleus of both the English and Scottish psalm books.

In 1553 the Protestant leaders went into exile at Frankfurt; later they split into two parties, those who most disliked the Prayer Book and other compromises with tradition going to Geneva, where, of course, they came under the direct influence of Calvin. The next edition, published at Geneva in 1556, was an integral part of *The Forme of Prayers and Ministration of the Sacraments*, devised by John Knox and approved by Calvin, which was to become the prototype for Presbyterian worship. Seven new psalms and a metrical Ten Commandments were added by William Whittingham, a Puritan leader who became Calvin's brother-in-law. For the first time tunes were provided, and the new versions were mostly in metres that would fit the tunes in the French psalter. Further editions appeared both in Geneva and (after 1558) in London, gradually adding more versions – the bulk of them by John Hopkins – until by 1562 the entire psalter had been versified and was published by John Day. A few hymns and alternative versions were later added. The Elizabethan editions contain a number of concessions to the Anglican party in the form of metrical canticles and prayers arranged in an order that reflects the Book of

Common Prayer, and to the exiles from Strasbourg in the form of a group of original hymns, some of Lutheran origin. From 1560 the title-page claims that the psalms are 'newly set fourth and allowed, according to the order appointed in the Quenes Majesties Injunctions'. The Injunctions of 1559 had allowed that:

for the comforting of such that delight in music, it may be permitted that in the beginning, or in the end of common prayers, eyther at mornyng or evenyng, there may be sung an hymne, or such like songue, to the praise of almighty God, in the best sort of melody and musicke that may be conveniently devised, havyng respect that the sentence of the Hymne may be understanded and perceyved.

From 1566 onwards the passage on the title-page recited these specific times at which the psalms could be sung. It may be noted that the passage is vague about the kind of text and music to be sung, and it was in fact used to justify both anthem singing in cathedrals and metrical psalm singing in parish churches. But it was not long before the statements on the title-page came to

2. Setting of Psalm xliv, with sol-fa letters against the notes of the tune, from 'The Whole Booke of Psalmes, Collected into Englishe Meter by Thomas Sternhold, John Hopkins' (1569)

be regarded as evidence for the exclusive authority of Sternhold and Hopkins's version, especially since this was often bound up with Bible or Prayer Book.

The complete edition of Sternhold and Hopkins contained metrical versions of all 150 psalms, with alternative versions of Psalms xxiii, l, li, c, cxxv and cxxxvi. Of these 156 versions, 131 were in common metre (8:6: 8:6), six in short metre (6:6:8:6), three in long metre (8:8:8:8), two in the metre 6:6:6:6:4:4:4:4, and 14 in other 'peculiar metres' of which no two were alike. Before and after the psalms were 24 metrical songs of various kinds, including three metrical psalms used for special purposes, several canticles and other biblical texts and some original hymns; these were often known collectively as the 'Divine Hymns' (see CANTICLE, §4, and HYMN, §IV). The book was completed by 'A Treatise on the Use and Virtue of the Psalmes by Athanasius the great', a collection of prayers for private use and an index of first lines of the psalms. Some editions contained also an explanation of sol-fa notation. Each psalm was headed with a Latin title and a summary or annotation of its contents. The full edition provided tunes for 48 of the psalms and 18 of the hymns; in each case the first verse was underlaid. The other psalms had cross-references, such as 'Sing this as the 3rd psalm'. Some editions from 1569 onwards had sol-fa letters printed on the staves beside the notes (fig.2).

The great popularity of the collection, together with its supposed 'authority', left it without a serious rival for over a century. Over 470 editions with music were published. John Day's monopoly in the printing of the psalms passed to his heirs, and was acquired in 1603 by the Stationers' Company, who used it to prevent any other version from being printed, and to provide employment for the poorer London printers. Consequently the printing in later editions is often badly botched. The psalm and hymn texts varied little from one edition to another, though from 1621 onwards some small editions omitted four of the hymns and the annotations at the head of the psalms. From 1599 to 1649 some editions, known as 'Middelburg Psalms' because they were first printed by Schilders of Middelburg, had the prose psalms in the margin; they had many more tunes than the ordinary editions. Many editions omitted some tunes, some reducing the number as low as 29 for psalms and 17 for hymns. Only 18 psalms have tunes in every musical edition. After 1620 more and more editions appeared without tunes, and after 1687 no editions had tunes. The hymn supplement was further cut down and disappeared altogether from many 18th-century editions.

Criticism of the Sternhold and Hopkins translation had been growing almost from its first appearance, and in 1644 the Westminster Assembly of Divines debated the possibility of imposing a new version which would be closer in sense to the original Hebrew. Francis Rous's version was accepted, with revisions, but it did not please the House of Lords. William Barton's, favoured by the Lords, was rejected by the Commons. The result was that neither was officially adopted, and most people went on using the 'Old Version', as it now began to be called. In 1696, however, *A New Version of the Psalms of David, fitted to the Tunes used in Churches* was compiled by Nahum Tate and Nicholas Brady, published by the Stationers' Company, and 'allowed and permitted' by the king in council on 3 December 1696.

It contained the psalms only, almost all of them in the three commonest metres; it was never printed with tunes underlaid, but a supplement of tunes was issued with the 1698 edition, containing only nine tunes, all of them from the Old Version. In 1700 a *Supplement* appeared, containing metrical canticles and prayers, some new hymns, alternative versions of some of the psalms, and a much larger selection of the old tunes. The *Supplement* was authorized by the queen in council on 30 July 1703, but it was never treated, like the Old and New Versions, as an appendage to the Prayer Book.

The New Version met with bitter opposition, led by William Beveridge, Bishop of St Asaph (1637–1708), and was at first adopted in only a few London churches. The two 'authorized' versions continued side by side, and it was not until the early 19th century that Tate and Brady's became decidedly the more popular of the two. Even so, several London and many country churches were still using the Old Version after 1800, and the last edition was printed as late as 1861. Only one psalm text from it is still in common use: the Old Hundredth, *All people that on earth do dwell*, attributed to William Kethe and still sung to the French tune allotted to it in 1561. On the other hand, the New Version outlived even the appearance of *Hymns Ancient and Modern* (1861) and was still the only hymnbook in use at St Thomas, Southwark (with no organ), as late as 1879. Several of the metrical psalms from the New Version are still in use, notably *Through all the changing scenes of life* (Psalm xxxiv) and *As pants the hart* (Psalm xlii).

Less important versions, outside the main tradition, appeared as early as 1567 in Archbishop Parker's *The Whole Psalter translated into English Metre*. It was originally written for his own use, but was printed with Tallis's nine tunes, perhaps with the intention that it might be used in public worship: 'The Tenor of these partes be for people when they will syng alone, the other parts, put for greater queers [choirs], or to suche as will syng or play them privately'. However, there is little likelihood that Parker's version was ever widely used in church; indeed, the long hegemony of Sternhold and Hopkins had already begun. In 1660 a Latin translation based on the Old Version was published at Oxford for the use of colleges, under the title *Psalmi aliquot Davidici in metrum Latini traducti*. It was bound with the Latin Book of Common Prayer which was allowed to be used at Oxford and Cambridge colleges. A 1681 edition of the same book (not listed in Wing) contains ten tunes, all standard ones used with the English metrical psalms.

During the 18th century there was an increasing tendency for the more affluent parishes to have their own selections of psalms printed, choosing some from the Old Version, some from the New, and at times adding examples from other translations and even hymns. The earliest local collection of this kind was *The Psalms and Hymns, usually sung in the Churches and Tabernacles ... of St Martins in the Fields and St James's Westminster* (1688). By 1800 there were hundreds of them. Versions originating with the dissenters were increasingly drawn upon in these books, above all Watts's *Psalms of David* (1719). A popular version in the later 18th century was that of James Merrick (1765), in whose unctuous periods some found a pleasing contrast to the rough simplicity of the older translations. Tattersall's *Improved Psalmody* (1794), which had a considerable vogue, used Merrick's version alone,

providing music for every psalm (including six settings by Haydn). But most churches in the later Georgian period used an eclectic assortment of psalms and hymns. Some staunch high churchmen continued to believe that only the two 'authorized' versions could legally be used, but the judgement in the case of Holy and Ward versus Cotterill in the Consistory Court of York (1820) made it clear that any hymn or psalm was equally allowable. From that date there was nothing to impede the rise of the modern hymnbook, in which metrical psalms form an insignificant proportion.

(*iii*) *Tunes*. The first music printed for Sternhold and Hopkins's psalms was in the Geneva edition of 1556, where every psalm had its individual or 'proper' tune. 27 of these 52 tunes were dropped in the 1558 edition, and 17 new ones replaced them. The great majority of the tunes were necessarily in common metre, and were usually of eight lines, though some were of four or 12 lines. In contrast, several tunes were taken from the French Geneva psalter prepared by Bourgeois under Calvin's supervision. These had the variety of metre characteristic of the French psalms, and it is evident that some of the metrical versions added to Sternhold and Hopkins after the exiles had reached Geneva were specially written in these metres so that the French tunes could be sung to them. The French tunes were fresh, catching, and in some cases based on French popular songs; many of them became English favourites and have remained so (ex.7). By contrast the English

Ex.7 Psalm 1, first version (Whittingham), to the tune Frost no.69 (from the French psalter). Source: 1558 psalm book

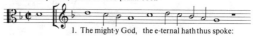
1. The might-y God, the e-ternal hath thus spoke:

And   all the world   he   will call and pro-voke:

Even   from the east   and   so forth to   the west.

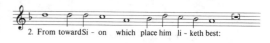
2. From toward Si - on   which place him   li - keth best:

God   will ap - pear   in   beau-ty   most ex - cel - lent.

3. Our   God will come   be - fore that long time be   spent.

tunes were dull and aimless, lacking any kind of popular appeal (ex.8). None of them appears to be drawn from English folksongs of the time, and very few were to enjoy a long life in English psalm singing: those that did (such as Frost, 1953, nos.17, 37, 63, 117, 157) generally had a strong 'modern' sense of tonality and some elements of repetition or sequence that made them easy to grasp.

The composer of these English tunes has not been

Ex.8 Psalm v (Sternhold), to the tune Frost no.20. Source: 1556 psalm book

In - cline thine ear   to   my re-quest,

O Lord   my plaint con-sider: 2. And   hear my

voice,   my King, my God,   to thee   I make my

prayer.   3. Hear   me be - time, Lord,   tar - ry not,

for   I   will have re - spect: My   pray-er ear —

- ly   in the morn   to thee   for to di - rect.

identified. They may have been already in use in Edward VI's time and may even have been the tunes which Sternhold himself had used when he sang his psalms to the young king. More probably they were the work of the best musicians that could be found in the small band of exiles. The community was made up of devout and learned men, who had given up much of what they had for their faith; they had no need of popular tunes, and they had leisure to learn unfamiliar music. These austere and graceless melodies aptly expressed their mood and ideals. But it was quite another matter when the time came to introduce psalm singing to the English people. We read that the singing spread like wildfire from one London church to another in the autumn of 1559. It is hard to imagine that such a blaze was set alight by the spiritless tunes of 1556. It seems far more likely that the Puritan leaders, following Calvin's example, used popular English ballad tunes at this critical time as the only sure way to get the congregations singing heartily. The queen and others called the new psalms 'Geneva jigs'. Wither in 1619 wrote of the impiety of using 'those roguish tunes, which have formerly served for prophane Jiggs' with psalms or hymns. William Slatyer, in his *Psalmes or Songs of Sion, turned into the Language, and set to the Tunes of a Strange Land* (1642), was bold enough to suggest singing the psalms with such popular tunes as 'Goe from my window', 'Barow Faustus dreame', 'The Queen of Love', and so on. For this he was severely reprimanded by the Court of High Commission.

But whatever tunes were sung, the printed psalm books show no trace of secular influences. Many of the dullest and most severely modal of the English tunes were allowed to drop, but others were retained. Many of the French tunes survived, and a few excellent German ones were added. The first folio edition of 1565 established a standard set of 48 tunes (the one to Psalm cxx was replaced in 1569) which remained the norm until 1661. However, from 1588 onwards some printers, presumably under the guidance of a musical editor

whose identity is now unknown, began cautiously introducing some of the popular 'short tunes' (see below), a tendency that became more marked under the influence of Ravenscroft's harmonized *Psalmes* (1621). For the 1661 folio edition Playford completely revised the selection and allocation of tunes, but still retained most of the old 'long tunes' with the psalms to which they had always been attached, and he did the same in his popular three-part *Psalms* of 1677, perhaps out of a feeling that they had official authority. By that time, however, only a handful of the old tunes were commonly used: those to the *Magnificat* and to Psalms l, lxxxi, c, cxiii, cxix and cxlviii (Frost, nos.4, 69, 99, 114, 125, 132, 174). Thomas Mathew's unique edition of 1688 repeated each tune throughout all the verses of the psalm, in imitation of French and Dutch psalm books; the tunes he selected were based largely on Ravenscroft.

The tunes printed in the psalm books, however, did not necessarily represent the tunes actually in common use. Ballad tunes apart, Thomas East in the index to the second edition of his *Psalmes* (1594) wrote: 'The Psalmes are song to these 4 tunes in most churches of this Realme'. The four tunes referred to (Frost, nos.19, 42, 45, 121) were all of the 'short' or four-line variety, three common metre and one short metre. None of them had been generally printed in the psalm books. All four were of similar character: simple, small in range, chiefly conjunct in motion, and easily learnt (ex.9). It is impossible to say when they were first introduced or where they came from. The earliest to be printed (in any surviving source) was Frost 121, named 'Oxford' by East, which had appeared in the Scottish psalter of 1564; three of them had appeared in Daman's *Psalmes* (1579), one as the first half of a long tune. Their style is closer to that of the ballad tune than had been that of the long tunes. They could be used for all the psalms in common metre and short metre (137 out of 156) and for many of the hymns as well. East in fact set 103 of the psalms to these four tunes.

Ex.9 Psalm viii (Sternhold), to the tune Frost no.19. Source: East's *Psalmes* (1592), harmonies omitted

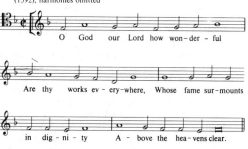

O   God   our Lord how won - der - ful

Are thy   works ev - ery-where,   Whose fame sur-mounts

in   dig - ni - ty   A - bove the   hea - vens clear.

The four-line tune gained still more in popularity: East added some new ones (including 'Winchester', to become one of the most popular of all), and Ravenscroft added a large number, including the very fine 'York' and 'Martyrs' (from the Scottish psalm book) and 'St Davids' (which he called 'Welch Tune'). Gradually were introduced in some editions of the psalm book, and they formed the majority of those provided as a supplement to Barton's *Psalms* (1644). In Playford's revision of the psalm book in 1661, ten short common metre and short metre tunes were printed, but by altering the cross-references he set 114 psalms to them. A similar balance is found in his three-part *Psalms* of tunes that incorporated solos, repeated last lines, and even fugal treatments of some lines (*see* PSALMODY (ii)). Tunes of this sort were seldom adopted in the larger town churches, however. (The later history of the psalm tune is discussed in HYMN, §IV, 3.)

(*iv*) *Performing practice.* Throughout the period that the metrical psalm was in use the normal occasions for singing psalms in parish churches were before Morning Prayer, before Ante-Communion, before the sermon (giving the parson an opportunity to change his surplice for gown and bands), and before and after Evening Prayer. The place provided for the anthem in the 1662 Prayer Book was not normally used for a metrical psalm. In many cathedrals it was the custom for people to come and hear the sermon after attending Morning

Ex.10 Psalm xxxvi (New Version), vv. 5–10, to the tune 'Wareham', by William Knapp (tenor part of a four-part setting in Knapp's *A Sett of New Psalm Tunes*, 1738)

3. *Five choirboys and two men singing from psalm books in an organ gallery: pen and ink drawing with wash, 'Obediah, the Psalm Singer' (1783), by John Nixon (private collection)*

1677, which had a few new short tunes apparently evolved from earlier ones. (In the oral tradition that governed the first hundred years of psalm singing many tunes became altered, most often by confusion between one tune and another.)

The later 17th century provided few newly composed tunes of any kind. A more creative period followed the publication of the New Version: 'St James' (first printed 1697), 'St Magnus' (1707) and 'St Anne' (1708) are in the best tradition of four-line tunes. Signs of an interest in greater variety of metre and character also began to appear. The only important tune for one of the psalms in 'peculiar metre' contributed by the 17th century was the one for Psalm civ, presumed to be Ravenscroft's (Frost 119), still popular as 'Old 104th'. A new tune in the same metre was printed in the *Supplement to the New Version* (1708 edition), later named 'Hanover' and attributed to Handel; today it is ascribed, but with little better evidence, to Croft. The new tune for Psalm cxlviii (6:6:6:6:4:4:4:4), printed in 1707, was certainly Croft's. Not many new tunes of the plain short variety date from after 1710.

By the end of the 17th century it had become common to ornament many of the old tunes (see (iv) below), and in the 18th century it became more and more usual to write ornaments into the tune from the start. Two or more notes were thus sung to one syllable, as in 'Easter Hymn' (1708). In many of the standard metres this often meant writing a tune in triple time, which indeed became very popular. More elaborate subdivisions of notes, often including dotted notes, became a standard usage: 'Wareham', by William Knapp, can be taken as typical (ex.10). In country churches where no organs were available, volunteer choirs began to prefer

Prayer in their parish churches. After the sermon they would sing a psalm, with organ accompaniment if the organist was still at his post. In Elizabethan times some Puritan ministers allowed metrical psalms and canticles to be substituted for the prose versions of the Prayer Book, but this was illegal and was eventually suppressed. (It was proposed again by a committee of the Long Parliament in 1641.)

The psalms were chosen and announced by the PARISH CLERK, who then led the singing while the congregation followed as best they could, or as much as they would. The practice of 'lining out' (see fig.4), whereby the clerk would read each line before it was sung (for the benefit of the illiterate), was first laid down in the *Directory for the Publique Worship of God* (1644), though it may have existed earlier. It turned into a kind of chanting in some places, but disappeared in England well before 1800.

The longer psalms were divided into sections in the psalm book, with little regard to sense, and it was common for only the first section to be sung; though on occasion a long psalm would be sung in its entirety (lasting over an hour, according to Pepys, on 6 January 1661), especially when alms were being collected. Bishop Gibson in 1724 charged his clergy to select a course of psalms for each Sunday in the year, and this advice was followed by many compilers.

At first psalms were sung at a brisk pace, as is evident from their early nickname 'Geneva jigs'. They had characteristic rhythms, often refusing to fit into regular measures. But in the course of generations of unaccompanied singing the pace slowed down considerably. The time signature C became more usual than ¢ after about 1620. By the late 17th century the usual tempo had dropped to the singularly slow rate of two or three seconds per note, and most of the rhythmic irregularities in the psalm tunes had been ironed out. This slow pace was maintained for the old tunes throughout the 18th century, despite the efforts of Methodists, Evangelicals and musicians to speed it up. It survives in metronomic indications in Benjamin Jacob's *National Psalmody* (1819): for instance 'Old Hundredth', written out in minims, is marked at crotchet = 60, 'Rather Slow'. For newer tunes, however, and particularly those of the Methodist type, a somewhat brisker tempo was thought proper.

As the tempo of psalm singing grew steadily slower during the 17th century, parish clerks and the more venturesome lay members began to fill in the long period between one note and the next with various kinds of embellishment. Since this practice was entirely uncontrolled the resulting heterophony must have been at times quite discordant. (In Scotland a similar practice survived long enough to be written down by Joseph Mainzer, while in the southern USA it can still be heard.) It was first recorded in *A New and Easie Method to Learn to Sing by Book* (1686), where the tune

4. Tune for Psalm iv from John Chetham's 'A Book of Psalmody' (1718); reference is made at the top to the practice of 'lining out', and the music is an attempt to represent the mode of singing psalm tunes known as the 'old way of singing'

Ex.11 Psalm xxv, to the tune 'Southwell' (Frost no.45), from *A New and Easie Method* (1686). (The plain version is given in up-stemmed notes.)

'Southwell' is printed first in the ordinary way, then in an ornamented version, with this explanation: 'The Notes of the foregoing Tunes are usually broken or divided, and they are better so sung, as is here prick'd' (ex.11). Later descriptions of this kind of ornamentation call it 'the Old Way of Singing', and it is generally associated with lining out (see fig.4). The practice seems to have come into conflict with the newer, though equally ornate, style associated with country choirs in the early 18th century, and to have died out by mid-century. A style of ornamentation closer to that of contemporary art music prevailed in later psalm singing.

Ex.12 'New Tune' (up-stemmed), from Playford's *Introduction* (1658 edn.) (Frost no.25) and 'Oxford' (down-stemmed), from Ravenscroft's *Psalmes* (1621) (Frost no.121)

The earliest source of 'Oxford' (*Scottish Psalter*, 1564) has no sharps to F.

Choirs may have performed harmonized settings of the tunes during the early years of Elizabeth's reign, but this was a short-lived phenomenon, except possibly in cathedrals. Though East and Ravenscroft published fully harmonized psalm books (see §4 below), psalm singing was basically monophonic in their day. However, improvised two-part harmonization was sometimes practised, and in a few cases gave rise to new tunes which then took on independent existence. This is almost certainly the origin of 'London Old', a short tune popular from about 1640 to 1760 (ex.12). John Playford was the first to make a sustained effort to restore harmony to the parish church, but it was not until the rise of the volunteer choirs in the 1690s that his work bore any fruit.

Many harmonized collections appeared in the 18th century, with the tune usually in the tenor. The essential harmony was two-part (TB), as in Playford's settings, with an optional alto and sometimes also a treble. Isaac Smith in 1770 explained that he had not provided a treble part in his collection 'because, except in choirs, proper voices are not easily found'. This reflected the

5. Gallery of Dorking Church, Surrey, with five singers accompanied by a flute, oboe and bassoon: pen and ink drawing with wash (1788) by John Nixon (private collection)

custom that women played only a modest role in church, and were not expected to sing loudly, if at all. It was for this reason that the tenor continued to sing the tune long after a treble-dominated texture had become normal in secular music. In towns with organs, on the other hand, the charity children led the singing, and a texture of SB or SSB was usual. For this medium a *galant* style of tune was evolved after about 1750. Congregational harmony, practised by the Methodists, was hardly heard in parish churches until Victorian times.

Church organs (outside cathedrals and collegiate churches) were rare from about 1570, non-existent between 1645 and 1660, and still rare after the Restoration; they gradually began to appear in the larger town churches. The bulk of metrical psalm singing, therefore, was entirely unaccompanied until late in the 17th century, when some churches adopted a 'bass viol' (actually a cello or gamba), or an instrument invented by Playford called the 'psalmody' or 'psalterer', which had a body like a cello but only one string with lettered frets. Gradually in the 18th century many village churches developed small bands of wind and string instruments which played with the singers in the west gallery (see fig.5). They played the voice parts (sometimes an octave higher, often with extra ornaments) and doubtless made it possible to perform elaborate settings which would have defeated an unaccompanied village choir. Gallery musicians of this kind were still playing and singing the Old and New Versions with ornate tunes into early Victorian times, until displaced by barrel organ or harmonium.

Organs did accompany psalm tunes from earliest times, however, especially in cathedrals, as Thomas Mace's famous account of the singing at York Minster during the siege of 1644 bears witness. Few organ settings of psalm tunes appear to have survived before 1668, when a page of them appeared in Tomkins's *Musica Deo sacra*. William Godbid also printed up a double sheet for binding in Playford's *Musick's Hand-*

maide (1663, 1678). It showed four tunes in a very full harmonization, including thick left-hand chords, but almost entirely unornamented (ex.13). The style of organ accompaniment changed a great deal in the next 50 years. Early 18th-century examples are thinner in layout, but crowded with ornaments; and there are interludes between the lines (ex.14). The singing of the psalm was usually preceded by an even more elaborate 'giving-out' of the tune by the organ alone, often on a solo cornet stop. Many critics complained that the tune became almost unrecognizable under the wealth of added ornament.

Ex.13 'The tune of the 25 Psalm' (Frost no.45), from Playford's *Musick's Hand-maide* (*RISM* 1663'); see also ex.14

2. THE DISSENTING CHURCHES.

(*i*) *Presbyterians*. The conforming Puritans, throughout the reigns of Elizabeth I, James I and Charles I, hoped to complete their work by making the Church of England a fully reformed state church on Calvinistic lines. From time to time the more ardent spirits grew impatient with delay, and either emigrated to the Continent or America, or formed clandestine meetings to conduct worship as they thought best. Meanwhile in some areas puritanical innovations were possible within the Church through the sympathy of the incumbent, or in some cases of the bishop.

With the triumph of the Parliamentary forces in the Civil War, success was at last within reach, and the Westminster Assembly of Divines met in 1643 to formulate the worship of the new national church. Their *Directory for the Publique Worship of God* (1644) became the basis for all subsequent Presbyterian worship. As far as music was concerned the Divines allowed for psalm singing before and after the sermon.

It is the duty of Christians to praise God publiquely, by singing of psalmes together in the Congregation, and also privately in the Family. In singing of psalmes, the voice is to be tunably and gravely ordered; but the chief care must be, to sing with understanding, and with grace in the heart, making melody unto the Lord.

To this end they proposed lining out 'where many in the congregation cannot read'. Singing was to be unaccompanied; and they wished the translations to be more literal than those of Sternhold and Hopkins, and revised Rous's version for the purpose.

After the Restoration, the Presbyterians at the Savoy Conference petitioned for similar concessions, among others; but these being refused, they declined to subscribe to the Act of Uniformity (1662). As a result 3000 Presbyterian ministers were ejected from their livings. From this time the Presbyterians formed a dissenting church. After a generation of persecution, they became free under the Toleration Act (1689) to organize their worship in licensed meeting-houses. In the following period they continued to sing largely metrical psalms, using first Rous's version or the American 'Bay Psalm Book', and later that of John Patrick (1679, completed 1691) which was 'fitted to the tunes used in parish-churches'. Singing in the meeting-houses was led by a precentor, who occupied a small desk beneath the great canopied pulpit; lining out was practised. The standard of singing was probably at least as low as it was under similar conditions in the established Church. In the early 18th century an interesting movement to improve it was started by the congregation of the King's Weigh House, Little Eastcheap. They employed a teacher of psalmody, William Lawrence, and established a course of Friday evening lectures which were followed by psalm-singing practices. The lectures, by Presbyterian ministers (and one Independent), were published in 1708 as *Practical Discourses in Singing in the Worship of God*; they enlarged on the duty of praising God in psalms, though some of the lecturers accepted hymns as well. Lawrence compiled a manuscript collection of tunes for the use of the society, consisting largely of standard tunes also in use in the Church of England. He published it in 1719 as *A Collection of Tunes suited to the Various Metres in Mr Watts's Imitation of Psalms of David or Dr Patrick's Version*. In that year the Independent Dr Watts's *Psalms* had appeared and was soon adopted in many Presbyterian congregations. Lawrence's successor as 'conductor of psalmody at the Friday lecture in Eastcheap' was Nathaniel Gawthorn, who published another tune collection, *Harmonia perfecta*, in 1730. It was designed to supplement Lawrence's book, and contained some entirely new tunes, and also several anthems – probably not for use in worship. This suggests that voluntary choirs had already begun to form, perhaps as a result of the Eastcheap Society; certainly they existed in many dissenting meeting-houses during the later 18th century, though they did not yet imitate the instrumental bands of the parish

Ex.14 'Southwell tune', from *The Psalms by Dr. Blow Set full for the Organ* (c 1731) (Frost no.45)

churches.

English Presbyterianism soon after this period ceased to have a distinctive existence. Its meeting-houses passed into the control of ministers of Arian theology and eventually drifted into Unitarianism; Watts's hymn texts were adapted to the changing beliefs, and metrical psalms dropped out of use. Other Presbyterian congregations joined forces with the Independents.

(ii) *Independents*. Those who did not believe in a state church, but wanted each congregation to govern itself, were known generally as Independents, or later as Congregationalists. Henry Ainsworth, one of their first leaders, left England with his congregation in 1593 for the greater freedom of the Netherlands. There, at Amsterdam, he brought out *The Book of Psalmes: Englished both in Prose and Metre* (1612) with learned disquisitions and annotations.

The Independents had the support of the army during the Civil War, and when Cromwell took over political control they enjoyed a period of supremacy. It produced no musical revolution; most people went on singing Sternhold and Hopkins. The Independents suffered the same persecution as the Presbyterians under Charles II. They, too, adopted Patrick's version when it came out, but moved more rapidly away from metrical psalms in the direction of hymns. Watts's *Hymns* appeared in 1707 and were quickly adopted by many Independent congregations. His *Psalms of David imitated in the Language of the New Testament* followed in 1719, and soon displaced other versions in the use of all but the most conservative groups. They were free paraphrases, omitting or modifying the many passages in the psalms that were thought inappropriate for Christian use. In a short preface Watts urged a change in the style of singing, which should be hearty and spirited; he deplored lining out and the slow pace that was then customary. Many Independent congregations put these ideas into practice, and their psalm singing often had a vitality that was lacking elsewhere until the Methodist revival had had its effect.

Watts's psalms were written in the standard metres, and the first tune books issued with them merely reprinted the Anglican tunes. Several collections later in the century, however, matched new music to Watts's psalms and hymns. One of the most popular was *A Collection of Psalm Tunes* (3/1780) by Stephen Addington, an Independent minister at Market Harborough, who provided a tune for each psalm and hymn. He wanted 'all who have Breath and Voice to praise the Lord; and therefore would be far from encouraging either Clerks or Choirs of Singers to introduce such Tunes as few can ever sing but Themselves'. The harmony was basically two-part (TB) with an optional alto part; the tunes came from many sources, and some were elaborate. Watts's *Psalms*, and other similarly free paraphrases of scripture, continued in use among Congregationalists, but in the 19th century they merged with hymns as the old disputes about the propriety of verses of human composition faded into the past.

(iii) *Baptists.* The Baptists began to form a distinct sect in 1608, when John Smyth, leader of a congregation of Separatists, baptized himself at Amsterdam. The General (Arminian) Baptists, like the Society of Friends, resisted any form of congregational singing, on the grounds that only a spontaneous song guided by direct inspiration was compatible with their interpretation of scriptural injunctions. They shifted from this position only in the later 18th century. The Particular (Calvinistic) Baptists, on the other hand, were more receptive to the notion of congregational singing. Benjamin Keach, pastor of a congregation at Horsleydown, Southwark, from about 1673 began gradually to introduce hymns and psalms into the services there. His *Spiritual Melody* (1691) is a collection of these, but without music. There was no lack of opposition, and a prolonged war of tracts and pamphlets was carried on in the 1690s on the propriety of 'singing in the public worship of God'. The dispute erupted again several times in the 18th century. Gradually, however, Keach's example was followed, and Baptist congregations accepted both psalms and hymns. Under Methodist influence, and especially in the North of England, many Baptist meetings began to elaborate their singing, and eventually adopted choirs and bands. They tended however to use hymns chiefly as a reflection on the sermon, and consequently needed a very large number to cover the possible range of subjects. John Rippon's *Selection of Hymns* (1787), containing 588 texts, filled this need and, with its tunes, became immensely popular. For the same reason metrical psalms dropped out of frequent use well before the end of the 18th century.

3. DOMESTIC USE. The tradition of using psalms for domestic or private devotions is far older than the Reformation, and many metrical versions, both English and Latin, had long been in existence. The versions of Sir Thomas Wyat the elder, the Earl of Surrey and Miles Coverdale are among the earliest produced in furtherance of the Reformation, and they too were for private use. Coverdale's *Goostly Psalmes* were published with tunes before 1539: both texts and music were closely modelled on Lutheran sources. He dedicated his book to 'the lovers of God's word', 'That they may thrust under the borde All other balletes of fylthynes'. This motive was perhaps even more important among the early reformers than that of congregational singing. Almost every 16th-century collection, including Sternhold and Hopkins, mentions in title or preface the idea that the psalms could replace frivolous or lewd secular ballads; the same was true of most French, Dutch and German publications. But it was not only in Puritan circles that sacred music was sung in the home. The *XX Songes* of 1530 was a set of partbooks containing Latin prayers and carols mixed with secular and instrumental music of various kinds. Le Huray (1967) listed 59 such publications between 1530 and 1657; the majority (not all) were undoubtedly designed for home use. Some were metrical psalms, some devotional or moral poems of various kinds; some were a mixture of either or both with secular pieces. Many were explicitly designed for singing with viols, lute, orpharion or virginals; some were even printed in table format, which made them wholly unsuitable for church use.

The tradition of private psalm singing continued in the 17th century, though the standard of devotion may not have been maintained. Wither wrote in 1619:

The little reverence that is used amongst us oftentimes in singing the *Psalms*, especially in some private families (I dare not say, in our Churches) is much to be blamed in many respects. S. *Chrysostom* . . . thought it scarce seemly to sit when we sing: But, had he seene with how many undecent gestures, and mixtures of other employments, we dare undertake so holy an exercise, he would have trembled at our presumption.

Those who kept up the custom had to put up with a certain amount of ridicule:

Such is our contrarietie to vertue and godlinesse, that should we heare a Familie so early gathered together in celebrating Gods praises; those, at their drunken Carols should not receive one reproofe, for every ten scoffes which are cast at these.

But the tradition persisted. Pepys, at home on a Sunday evening in 1664, sang 'Ravenscroft's 4-part psalms, most admirable music' with two other men and a boy. Playford continued to cater for this demand in some of his earlier psalm publications. Editions of his *Introduction to the Skill of Musick* from 1658 to 1670 contain 'the Tunes of the Psalms As they are commonly sung in Parish-Churches. With the Bass set under each Tune, By which they may be Played and Sung to the Organ, Virginals, Theorbo-Lute, or Bass-Viol'. From the 1672 edition onwards there is instead a reference to his *Psalms and Hymns in Solemn Musick* (1671) for those who wished to sing with these instruments. The 1671 book was intended chiefly for domestic use, though Playford also hoped that it might be adopted in churches, and presented a number of copies to the Company of Parish Clerks of London. It was not a successful book. Playford wrote that 'the only exception that ever I heard against it, was, that the largeness of the Volume, and the not having all the Psalms in their order, made it not so useful to carry to Church'. In his 1677

Psalms – described in §4 (iv) below – he corrected these defects, abandoned the 'domestic' market, and catered solely for parish church use. But the author of *A New and Easie Method to Learn to Sing by Book* (1686) was still providing for the pious private psalmist, and perhaps also for dissenters:

'Tis pity we have not a better Translation of the *Singing Psalms* publickly in use; however, for Private Families there are several well done, especially the last by Mr *Patrick*. . . . The promoting of this (as to the Tune and Melody) is the chief of my design in this Essay. If therefore any Reader come with no better ends, than to accomplish himself to bear a Part in a Drunken Catch, A Smutty or Atheistical Song, I assure him, there's not a Word here design'd for his service, 'till upon better thoughts a *Penitential Psalm* should seem more suitable.

In this book the psalms are set for two trebles or tenors (in the G clef) and bass.

With religious toleration and the advance of secular materialism, it is not surprising that family prayers and psalm singing declined. Dr Thomas Bray wrote in 1697 that the singing of psalms in families had fallen into 'disuse', and urged its revival, printing psalms (from the New Version) and tunes for this express purpose. At the same time he urged ministers to form religious societies in their parishes which would meet for private prayer and singing and would then by their example restore true devotion in the parish church. Many such societies were in fact established. The result was not a revival of domestic psalm singing, but the appearance of voluntary parish choirs, for whom 18th-century tune books were chiefly designed.

4. HARMONIZED SETTINGS. Various settings of the metrical psalms in harmony were printed from 1549 onwards, but their purpose is not always clear. In Edward VI's reign and the early years of Elizabeth's many parish churches still had choirs; but after about 1570 only cathedrals, chapels royal and a handful of collegiate parish churches could enjoy harmony. Domestic psalm singing was an established custom until at least the middle of the 17th century. Some publications may represent efforts to introduce harmonized singing in parish churches, but voluntary parish choirs did not exist until shortly before 1700.

(*i*) *Harmonized chants.* The earliest type of harmonized setting is found in Crowley's *Psalter* (1549), where all the psalms are set to the 7th Gregorian psalm tone, in the tenor, harmonized in four parts. Similarly one of the two compositions in Seager's *Psalms* (1553) is based on the 6th psalm tone. These are merely adaptations of the faburden practice which had long been in use for chanting the Latin psalms in churches that had choirs.

(*ii*) *'Anthems' with metrical psalm texts.* The metrical texts were frequently used for compositions of the motet or anthem type. In these settings there is no clearly defined tune for a congregation to sing. Hence they were either for choirs or for domestic use. Early models for these 'psalm anthems' are found in the second composition in Seager's *Psalms* and in Tye's *Acts of the Apostles*, both published in 1553, and in the Wanley and Lumley Partbooks; these were designed for strophic repetition. Through-composed settings of Sternhold and Hopkins's psalms and hymns are extant by Tallis, Farrant, Philip van Wilder, Byrd, Edmund Hooper, Nathaniel Giles, Thomas Tomkins and other leading composers of the day. The use of the Sternhold and Hopkins texts may have been regarded as authorizing these pieces for cathedral use, along with anthems taken from scripture or the liturgy. Especially popular texts were those of the

original hymns in the Sternhold and Hopkins supplement: for example, 'A Lamentation' (*O Lord, in thee is all my trust*) was set as an anthem by nine composers including Hooper, Giles, John Ravenscroft and Martin Peerson, in addition to the simple harmonization by Tallis. A curiosity is Thomas Caustun's adaptation of an instrumental In Nomine by Taverner, to Sternhold's Psalm xx (in Day's *Certaine Notes*, 1560).

Polyphonic settings of versions other than Sternhold and Hopkins were probably for domestic use. These include Croce's *Musica sacra*, adapted by East (1608); Leighton's *The Teares or Lamentacions of a Sorrowfull Soule* (1614); and Robert Tailour's *Fifti Select Psalms* (1615). Metrical psalm texts are also found here and there in sets of lute-songs and madrigals. A later type, influenced by the Italian cantata, is represented by William and Henry Lawes's *Choice Psalmes put into Musick* (1648) and Walter Porter's *Mottets of Two Voyces* (1657), both using Sandys's version, and three psalm settings for voice and figured bass in Playford's *Psalms and Hymns* (1671). This tradition was revived

Ex.15 Psalm cxiii, to the tune Frost no.125, in a five-part setting by Cosyn (1585)

Ye   child-ren which do   serve the   Lord,

praise   ye his   name with one   ac – cord,

yea,   bless – ed   be   al – ways his   name.

(*Cantus is editorial*)

in the later 18th century. John Travers's *The Whole Book of Psalms* (c1750) has settings of the first few verses of every psalm in the New Version, mostly for solo voice and figured bass, but some for several voices. There are also elaborate settings of metrical psalms by John Broderip (1769), William Hayes (c1775) and Hugh Bond (c1776).

(*iii*) *Elaborate settings of psalm tunes.* Day's *Psalmes in Foure Partes* (1563), discussed below, contains a few settings that are not entirely homophonic: some by Caustun even include brief points of imitation (see Frost, no.160), but these are always alternatives to homophonic settings. A further step was to apply contrapuntal treatment to the whole tune, with overlapping points of imitation. The tune then became in effect the cantus firmus for a polyphonic motet. It was in Scotland that this technique chiefly developed (as can be seen in MB, xv). An early English example is Parsons's second setting of Psalm xliv in Day's 1563 book (see Frost, 1962, p.48). The earliest fully worked-out English examples are the 14 five-part settings in Cosyn's *Musike of Six, and Five Parts* (1585) (ex.15); others are in Daman's collections of 1591. There is a single example in John Mundy's *Songs and Psalmes* (1594). This type of setting was well suited to domestic use by proficient amateurs, and could be sung as a consort song with viol accompaniment. In England it does not seem to have survived into the Jacobean period.

A unique set of compositions by William Lawes (1602–45) has survived in manuscript (*GB-Och* 768–70), entitled 'Psalmes for 1, 2 and 3 partes, to the comon tunes'. In these pieces Lawes alternated stanzas set to original music for voices and bass, in cantata style, with stanzas for 'Chorus' set to the common tunes in a plain two-part harmonization. There are nine of these 'Psalmes', using six psalms and three hymns from Sternhold and Hopkins.

(*iv*) *Note-against-note harmonizations.* The most serviceable type of harmonization was a homophonic one, allowing an occasional syncopation or passing note but otherwise preserving the rhythm of the tune in all parts. It could give pleasure to music lovers (as Ravenscroft's settings did to Pepys); it was also capable of being used in cathedral or church, while the congregation sang the tune in unison. Such settings of the French psalms by Goudimel and Le Jeune had proved immensely successful on the Continent, and John Day in 1563 brought out a large collection of them for English use. It was printed in the form of partbooks, entitled *The Whole Psalmes in Foure Parts, whiche may be song to al Musical Instrumentes, set forth for the Encrease of Vertue: and aboleshyng of other Vayne and Triflyng Ballades* (*RISM* 1563[8]). There was no reference to church performance, perhaps because of current Puritan mistrust of elaborate music. The production of the book was lavish, and the provision of music more generous than any ordinary church would require. The texts were those of Sternhold and Hopkins, with a few additions: the tunes of the common psalm book (which Day was also printing and publishing) were provided for the psalms that had tunes there, with eight new tunes as alternatives. The settings were for four voices, with the tune most often (not always) in the tenor (ex.16). Many of the tunes were set two or more times by different composers – Psalm xliv had as many as five settings – and the total number of compositions was 141, including a few prose

anthems. But this was not a complete psalm book. Only the first verse of each psalm was printed, and many psalms – those without proper tunes – did not appear at all. Thus, if used in church, it could only be used side by side with the psalm book. It was well suited to the choirs that had survived in some city churches, or to cathedral choirs, and may have been used by them, though there is little evidence. By far the largest number of settings are by William Parsons (who was probably organist of Wells Cathedral); for this reason it has sometimes been called 'Parsons's Psalter' on the assumption that he was the musical editor. The other names are not distinguished, apart from 'M. Talys', assumed to be Thomas Tallis, who provided a setting of 'A Lamentation', already printed in Day's *Certaine Notes*, and a short anthem. After Parsons the principal contributors were Caustun, Hake and Brimle.

Ex.16 Psalm c, to the tune Frost no.114, set by W. Parsons in Day's *The Whole Psalmes* (*RISM* 1563[8])

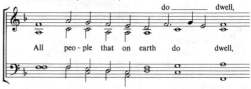

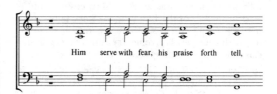

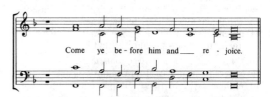

Day's collection was not reprinted, and it was 16 years before any similar publication appeared. Archbishop Parker's *Psalter* (c1567) is in quite a different class. It contains nine great tunes in four-part harmony by Tallis, including the celebrated 'Canon', and the well-known rhyme in which Parker characterized eight of the tunes. He was the first English compiler to say that a tune should be matched to the mood of the psalm.

In 1579 John Bull, a London goldsmith, sponsored the publication of a collection of four-part settings by William Daman, a Gentleman of the Chapel Royal, without the author's permission. It was similar in scope to Day's, and was also in the form of partbooks, with only the first stanza of each psalm and hymn printed, and only of those psalms for which there are tunes. Many of the tunes are the same as those in the psalm book, but there are ten new tunes, including four of the short tunes now printed for the first time. There are four new hymn texts, and two prose psalms set as anthems. Cosyn's 1585 collection, also in partbooks, includes 43 settings in six parts, using many of the proper tunes but also some of the short ones. Sometimes the tune is in the tenor, sometimes in another part. Cosyn took a more Puritan stance than Daman by including only psalms, ignoring the hymns and canticles. Both books are explicitly for domestic use – Daman's 'to the use of the godly Christians for recreatyng themselves', Cosyn's 'for the private use and comfort of the godlie'.

A very different kind of book is Thomas East's *The Whole Booke of Psalmes: with their Wonted Tunes, as they are song in the Churches, composed into Foure Parts: all of which are so placed that Foure may sing ech one a Several Part* (1592). As the title implies, this is a psalm book, containing the entire texts of all the psalms and hymns of the standard version. It is small and compact in volume, easy to carry between home and church, and all four parts are shown together at each page opening, with words of one verse underlaid to every part. East left most of the proper tunes with their usual psalms; but for the many psalms not provided with tunes in the common psalm book, instead of following the cross-references he provided new four-line tunes, using the same four tunes for the great majority of the psalms. (As already pointed out, he stated in the second (1594) edition that these four tunes were the only ones in use in most churches.) The settings were 'compiled by sundry authors, who have so laboured heerin, that the unskilfull with small practice may attaine to sing that part, which is fittest for their voice' (ex.17). Richard Alison, Dowland, Farmer and Michael Cavendish are among the musicians he called on: le Huray pointed out that none of these was a church musician. Nevertheless

Ex.17 Psalm cxlvi (Hopkins), to the tune Frost no.172a, set by J. Farmer in East's *Psalmes* (1592)

My soul praise thou the Lord   al-ways,   my God   I

will con-fess: While breath and life pro-long my days

My tongue no   time shall   cease.

it seems likely that East hoped that this book would be used in some churches as well as for recreation, else he would not have taken so much trouble to make it conform to parish church conventions. Even the most devout music lover would hardly have needed the whole of Psalm cxix, set to a single tune, for his evening diversion. Though evidence is lacking, East's *Psalmes* may have been tried out in some churches where enough educated musicians could be induced to form a choir. It ran to four editions, the last dated 1611.

East's book was the first complete, harmonized edition of Sternhold and Hopkins. It contained all that was in the psalm books, and more besides. It could thus be used by a choir while the ordinary psalm books were in the hands of the congregation. This was an important new departure, and it sets East apart from all the compilers of harmonized editions who had preceded him. East also initiated (in his 1594 edition) the colourful and peculiarly English practice of attaching place names to tunes. The names seem to have been distributed at random. The need was for any easily remembered label now that tunes were no longer connected uniquely with particular psalms.

Two publications of 1599 recognized the dominance of the same four short tunes that East had marked out as the most popular. Alison's *The Psalmes of David in Meter* continued the the domestic tradition, with only one verse underlaid; the tunes in this case are in the topmost voice, harmonized in four parts with optional accompaniments for lute and cittern, and arranged in table format. Barley's *The Whole Booke of Psalmes, with their Woonted Tunes, as they are sung in Churches, composed into Foure Parts* was a close copy of East, even to its appearance and the wording of its title, and with most of the same tunes. It contained, however, new settings by Morley and Bennet.

The next publication in this category was Thomas Ravenscroft's *The Whole Booke of Psalmes … Composed into 4 Parts by Sundry Authors* (1621) which was also closely modelled on East in design, format, and purpose. Its title shows that it was, like East's and Barley's books, a psalm book, planned for possible use in church as well as at home. But Ravenscroft departed from the practice of all his predecessors by introducing a large number of tunes foreign to the psalm book – no fewer than 33, all of the short variety except the splendid 'Old 104th', already referred to. The sources of many of these tunes are unknown. Eight came from the 'common tunes' in the Scottish psalm book of 1615; one was adapted from Tallis's 'Canon'. The others Ravenscroft called Welsh, French, German, Dutch, Italian etc, but none of his new tunes have been discovered in earlier sources from these countries. In allocating the tunes to the psalms he claimed in his preface to have taken special care to select tunes 'proper to the nature of each psalm', but a careful study reveals that in fact he used a largely random procedure. And he did not, as had East and Barley, allot the few popular tunes to a very large number of psalms, but portioned out popular and unfamiliar with a fairly even hand. For harmonizations he used some music from earlier books, including Day's, East's and Barley's, and new settings by a number of church musicians of the day as well as many of his own.

Ravenscroft's book was not as popular as East's – there was only one more edition in the 17th century (1633). Perhaps it was because, as Playford put it in

1677, he had been guilty of 'intruding among our *English* Tunes, many Outlandish [i.e. foreign] *Welsh* and *Scotch* Tunes, of neither good *form* nor *ayre*'. Barton in 1644 omitted 'multitudes of tunes [in Ravenscroft] as unnecessary and burdensome', but this at least suggests that Ravenscroft was a possible source for church use. There is other evidence that it was: from 1622, some editions of the psalm book contained five of Ravenscroft's new tunes and allocations that are not found elsewhere; others appear in a later revision of 1636.

Henry Lawes's *A Paraphrase upon the Psalmes of David . . . Set to New Tunes for Private Devotion: and a Thorow Base, for Voice, or Instrument* (1636) is somewhat outside the mainstream. The metres of Sandys's version are various and subtle: the tunes, all new, lack popular characteristics and seem designed for solo singing. They are set in two parts only, in block harmony. William Slatyer's *The Psalmes of David in 4 Languages and in 4 Parts* (1643) is eccentric. It consists of Psalms i–xxii in the Old Version, with texts in English and also translated into Greek, Hebrew and Latin, for purposes unknown; the settings are borrowed from various sources.

John Playford, having begun with tenor and bass only in his *Introduction* (1658), added two optional counter-tenor parts in his *Psalms and Hymns* (1671); the tunes he printed were chiefly the old ones, emended to bring them into conformity with contemporary practice. He provided alternative translations (which he hoped would be accepted by 'authority') and hymn texts, and printed only selected verses of the Sternhold and Hopkins texts – but in deference to the establishment printed them in black letter, while the other texts were in roman. The settings were his own. His *Whole Book of Psalms in Three Parts* (1677), in contrast, was a complete psalm book in the East–Ravenscroft tradition; every psalm had a tune printed with it, underlaid with the first verse, and the other verses printed below. Playford made some revisions in the text (not all judicious) and further modernized and reallocated the tunes. But there were few new tunes, and even these seem to have been derived from earlier ones. He gave a revised selection of hymns with several new texts, and four alternative versions of psalms (dropped from later editions). The preface gave an informative statement of his policy and of the state of psalm singing in his time. But his most significant innovation was to set the tunes in three parts throughout – cantus and medius (of nearly equal compass) and bassus. 'All *Three Parts* may be as properly sung by Men as by Boys or Women', and all were printed in G or F clefs (ex.18). Here was a book that could well serve a parish choir, with or without instrumental accompaniment; and eventually parish choirs took full advantage of it. After the second edition, brought out by Henry Playford in 1695, it outstripped all its predecessors in popularity, going into 19 editions with little alteration (one new tune was added in 1700), the last appearing in 1738. (The 20th edition (1757), revised by Joseph Fox, left out five tunes and added 15 new ones and three anthems.)

Playford's was the last harmonized Sternhold and Hopkins, and one of the last books that set out the complete psalms beneath the music. In the 18th century music was provided for organists, parish clerks and choirs, but not for congregations: not until the mid-19th century would the people again have the tunes printed in their hymnbooks. Selections of psalms and hymns in various versions were printed with music, often for the use of an individual church or chapel. The dissenting churches, where lining out continued to thrive, frequently printed their tunes in a supplement at the end of the psalm book, and the practice was followed with Tate and Brady's *New Version*, whose *Supplement* was designed for use with either the Old or the New Version. The tune book, published independently of the full text to be sung (though often with tunes underlaid with one verse), had existed in the 16th century chiefly for domestic or cathedral use. Playford's *Introduction*, from 1658 onwards, included a modest collection of tunes which was found increasingly useful as versions multiplied.

Adaptable tune books continued to appear throughout the 18th century for both Anglicans and dissenters. They show that many places of worship maintained the conservative tradition of plain old psalm tunes throughout the period of elaborate psalmody. In 1790 Dr Miller's *Psalms of David* was the first of a new type of book influenced by evangelical ideas. It was designed to embody the entire text and music needed for a parish church. The psalms were arranged in order throughout the year; settings were firmly congregational, with the tune in the treble and chords filled in for organ accompaniment. Several other books on the same lines appeared in rapid succession. Beginning with Sampson's *Ancient Church Music* (1799) and continuing with Crotch's *Tallis's Litany with a Collection of Old Psalm Tunes* (1803), an effort was made in some quarters to revive those of the ancient psalm tunes that had dropped out of knowledge.

Ex.18 Psalm xlvii, to the tune 'London New' (Frost no.222), set by Playford in his *Psalms* (1677)

Ye peo-ple all with one ac - cord Clap hands and much re-joice. Be glad and sing un - to the Lord With sweet and plea-sant voice.

★ B♭ in original

BIBLIOGRAPHY

HawkinsH

Injunctions given by the Queenes Majestie concerning both the Clergy and Laity of this Realme (London, 1559); repr. in *Visitation Articles and Injunctions of the Period of the Reformation*, ed. W. H. Frere, iii (London, 1910), 8

[W. Whittingham]: *A Brieff Discours of the Troubles Begonne at Frankfort* (? Geneva or Zurich, 1575, repr. London, 1908)

G. Wither: *A Preparation to the Psalter* (London, 1619)

Directory for the Publique Worship of God (London, 1644, repr. 1903)

T. Mace: *Musick's Monument* (London, 1676/R1958)

T. Bray: *A Short Discourse upon the Doctrine of our Baptismal Covenant* (London, 1697)

B. P[ayne]: *The Parish-clerk's Guide* (London, 1709)

N. Tate: *An Essay for Promoting of Psalmody* (London, 1710)

L. Milbourne: *Psalmody Recommended* (London, 1713)

E. Gibson: *A Method or Course of Singing in Church: the Excellent Use of Psalmody* (London, 1724)

W. Riley: *Parochial Music Corrected* (London, 1762)

W. Mason: *Essays on Church Music*, iii (London, 1795); repr. in *W. Mason: Works* (London, 1811)

W. Cole: *A View of Modern Psalmody* (Colchester, 1819)

J. Gray: *An Inquiry into Historical Facts Relative to Parochial Psalmody* (York, 1821)

J. S. Curwen: *Studies in Worship Music* (London, 1880–85)

J. Julian: *A Dictionary of Hymnology* (London, 1892, rev. 2/1907)

W. H. Frere: *A New History of the Book of Common Prayer with a Rationale of its Offices, on the Basis of the Former Work by F. Procter* (London, 1902)

R. Steele: *The Earliest English Music Printing* (London, 1903)

W. H. Frere: *The English Church in the Reigns of Elizabeth and James I* (London, 1904)

R. W. Dale: *A History of English Congregationalism* (London, 1907)

L. F. Benson: *The English Hymn* (Richmond, Virginia, 1915)

W. T. Whitley: *A History of British Baptists* (London, 1923)

——: *Congregational Hymn-singing* (London, 1933)

M. M. Knappen: *Tudor Puritanism* (Chicago, 1939/*R*1970)

W. S. Pratt: *The Music of the French Psalter of 1562* (New York, 1939)

M. Frost: *English and Scottish Psalm and Hymn Tunes c.1543–1677* (London, 1953)

H. Baillie: *London Churches, their Music and Musicians (1485–1560)* (diss., U. of Cambridge, 1958)

M. Frost, ed.: *Historical Companion to Hymns Ancient and Modern* (London, 1962)

P. le Huray, ed.: *The Treasury of English Church Music*, ii (London, 1965)

E. Parks: *The Hymns and Hymn Tunes found in the English Metrical Psalters* (New York, 1966)

P. le Huray: *Music and the Reformation in England, 1549–1660* (London, 1967)

A. Smith: *The Practice of Music in English Cathedrals and Churches in the Reign of Elizabeth I* (diss., U. of Birmingham, 1967)

R. Illing: *Est–Barley–Ravenscroft and the English Metrical Psalter* (Adelaide, 1969)

N. Temperley: 'The Adventures of a Hymn Tune', *MT*, cxii (1971), 375, 488

——: 'John Playford and the Metrical Psalms', *JAMS*, xxv (1972), 331–78

D. W. Krummel: *English Music Printing, 1553–1700* (London, 1974)

N. Temperley: 'Middleburg Psalms', *Studies in Bibliography*, xxx (1977), 162–9

——: *The Music of the English Parish Church* (Cambridge, 1979)

IV. Scotland and Ireland

1. Scotland: (i) Texts (ii) Music (iii) Performing practice. 2. Ireland.

1. SCOTLAND. Metrical psalms have retained an important position in the Scottish service since the Reformation in 1560. The Scottish Church was persuaded by Calvin's teaching that, first, praising God was the right of the whole congregation and not simply of priests and a select body of singers, and second, that only material from the Bible should be used. The psalms were translated into metre mainly for ease of recollection, but the fact that the original Hebrew psalms were also metrical was regarded as something of a divine injunction. Hymns were gradually introduced in the 19th century but they never supplanted the psalms. Efforts to introduce chanted prose psalms have met with little success.

(i) Texts. The earliest metrical psalms known in Scotland were 22 in *Ane Compendious Buik of Godlie Psalms and Spiritual Sangis* (?Dundee, 1542–6), brought out by the three Wedderburn brothers of Dundee. Commonly known as *The Gude and Godlie Ballatis*, they were Scots translations by John Wedderburn of psalms and hymns by Luther. Though never authorized for use in church, they were very popular for domestic use: the last edition was printed as late as 1621. Apparently they were intended to be sung

to common secular melodies, for no music was printed. In one instance the tune of *Exaudi Deus orationem meam* (Psalm lv) is indicated, possibly an adaptation of a Gregorian melody.

The early psalms of Sternhold and Hopkins also seem to have been known in Scotland. John Knox, leader of the Scottish Reformation, describing the death of Elizabeth Adamson in 1555, stated that she sang 'Psalm ciii', *My saule praise thou the Lord always* (this is actually Psalm cxlvi by Hopkins). According to the Protestant exiles in Frankfurt in 1554 the singing of metrical psalms 'in a plain tune' was the custom in Scottish churches, but there is no evidence that they formed a part of the service itself.

Although Knox knew the Wedderburn psalms he did not adopt them for the Reformed church, perhaps because he found the language too broadly Scots, but probably on account of their Lutheran origins. In 1555 he went to Geneva where he came under the influence of Calvinism, and in 1558 he was appointed one of the ministers of the English congregation there. The following year he took to Scotland their Book of Order, *The Forme of Prayers and Ministration of the Sacraments* (Geneva, 1556), which had been rejected in Frankfurt in favour of the Prayer Book. The 11th section contained *One and Fiftie Psalmes of David, in English Metre*, 37 of which were by Sternhold, seven by Hopkins and seven by Whittingham.

The first General Assembly of the Church of Scotland (1560) recognized the Geneva *Forme of Prayers* as its Book of Common Order, and in 1562 it was printed, without the psalms, by Robert Lekprevik of Edinburgh. By 1563 the number of psalms for the Anglo-Genevan Church had increased to 87 (the additional translations were by Pullain and Kethe). These were adopted by the Assembly as the basis for a complete metrical psalter, and new translations of the outstanding psalms were ordered. In fact most were borrowed from the English psalter, with only 21 by Scots (15 by John Craig and 6 by Robert Pont). All the versions were carefully revised and printed with music in 1564 by Lekprevik as an adjunct to the *Forme of Prayers*.

In 1579 an Act of Parliament ordained that 'all Gentlemen with 300 merks of yearlie rent, and all substantious yeomen, etc., worth 500 pounds [Scots] in land or goods, be holden to have ane bible and psalme booke', under specific penalties. 60 editions of the Book of Common Order together with the psalms were printed in the period 1564–1644. Many were printed abroad – in Middelburg, Dort, Geneva and London – probably because printing there was of a better quality without being more expensive. In 1575 Bassandine changed the title to *The CL Psalmes of David*; this was adopted and gave rise to the custom of calling the whole of the service book the Psalm Book.

At first the Assembly had the right to supervise the copy and the printing of the book, but later this vigilance was relaxed, perhaps owing to the Church's increasing involvement with politics. After the first edition of 1564, some of the spiritual songs from the Anglo-Genevan book had been appended, but Bassandine's 1575 edition included metrical versions of the Lord's Prayer (Coxe's), Whittingham's Ten Commandments with a responsory prayer, the first Lamentation, the *Veni Creator* from the English Prayer Book and a metrical doxology. Andro Hart, in his edition of 1615, added on his own initiative a metrical version of the Song of Moses.

Many of the editions from 1601 onwards printed the prose version of the psalms in the margin, probably to aid comprehension. Only Raban's edition (Aberdeen, 1633) and Tyler's edition (Edinburgh, 1644), the last of the 1564 psalter, used the Authorized Version; the rest all used the translation from the Geneva Bible of 1560.

The main drawback of the 1564 psalter was its variety of metres. 27 psalms were in metres other than common, long or short, and were not easy for an illiterate people to learn. Some had been created to fit French melodies and were more suited to the French language than the Scots (ex.19). The General Assembly of 1601 proposed a new translation of the Bible and a revision of the psalms. James VI (later James I of England), who had versified some psalms in *His Majesties Poeticale Exercises at Vacant Hours* (1591) supported the proposal enthusiastically. The Assembly, not wanting to encourage interference from the king but seeking to placate him, charged Robert Pont with the revision. Nothing further was done but James, far from forgetting the matter, set to work himself. Other writers such as Alexander Montgomerie, Mure of Rowallen (compiler of the Rowallen Lutebook), Drummond of Hawthornden and Alexander of Menstrie were also making new versions but, because of the king's declared purpose, could not do so openly.

Ex.19 Psalm lxxxi from the 1564 psalter; text by Pont

The strained relations between crown and church delayed any new version until the middle of the century. James's introduction of the Five Articles (concerning kneeling at Communion, the Christian calendar, private communion, private baptism and confirmation) in 1618 aroused much hostility. Although the Five Articles were widely disregarded in practice, such a storm had been raised that even moderate reforms were impossible. The church successfully resisted James's version of the psalms during his lifetime. Such was the king's industry that by the time he died in 1625 he had reached Psalm cxxx. Charles I believed it his duty to see his father's wishes carried out and instructed Menstrie to review them. The result, a substantial revision, was printed as *The Psalmes of King David translated by King James* (Oxford, 1631), commonly known as the 'Menstrie Psalms'. Another version, again thoroughly revised, appeared in 1636. There was considerable opposition to the 'Metaphrase', as James's version was called, although it appears that some congregations did use it. Charles's disastrous attempts to impose a version of the English Prayer Book on the Church of Scotland provoked the signing of the National Covenant in 1638. In the same year the General Assembly, controlled by Covenanters, rejected all Charles's innovations, including the royal psalter.

The Westminster Assembly of Divines of 1643–7 aimed to produce a new version of the psalms for use throughout England and Scotland. Rous's psalms were revised, first by the Westminster Assembly (which included Scottish commissioners) and subsequently by Scottish divines in Scotland. The Scottish Church as well as the English refused to accept it, and on 8 July 1647 the General Assembly recommended another complete revision. The revisers were permitted to draw on other versions as well as the Westminster one and the 1564 Scottish one. The revision was extensive: of a total of 8620 lines only 1588 are from the Westminster version. Other sources used include James's version, the Bay Psalm Book of 1640 and Rous's original translation. On 1 May 1650 the *Psalms of David in Meeter* came into use, and has remained unaltered as the official Scottish psalter (*see* PARAPHRASES, SCOTTISH).

Nearly all the psalms are in common metre. Including second versions, four are in short metre: Psalms xxv, xlv (2nd version), l, lxvii; four are in long metre: Psalms vi, c, cii (2nd version), cxlv (2nd version); and five are irregular: Psalms cxxiv (2nd version), cxxxvi, cxxxvi (2nd version), cxliii, cxlviii.

The first Gaelic translation of *The Forme of Prayers*, entitled *Foirmna nurrnuidheah* (Edinburgh, 1567) was printed without the psalms, which were not translated until the following century. In 1659 the Synod of Argyll issued the first 50 in *An ceud chaogad do Shalmaibh Dhaibhidh*. Robert Kirk, minister at Balquidder, made an independent translation of the complete psalter, *Psalma Dhaibhidh a nmeadrachd* (Edinburgh, 1684) but the one recommended by the Assembly was the completed Argyll version of 1694. An amended version by Alexander MacFarlane (Glasgow, 1753), containing fewer Irishisms, became popular in the north highlands; John Smith's translation of 1787 was more popular in the west. *Sailm Dhaibhidh* (Edinburgh, 1826), a revised version of the Argyll translation, was authorized by the Assembly, but Smith's version has remained in use, and is still bound with the Gaelic Bible issued by the National Bible Society of Scotland.

(*ii*) *Music*. Although the reformers believed that each psalm should be sung only to its own or 'proper' tune, this ideal was never fully realized, with the result that sometimes the same tune had to be used for two psalms. The first Scottish psalter of 1564 contained 105 tunes; 42 came from Geneva, of which 31 were French including some by Loys Bourgeois. A few were German and the rest were presumably by Scottish and English composers; it shared 16 tunes with Day's *Whole Booke of Psalmes* (1562). Out of 28 editions of the psalter printed by 1625 only three omitted the music.

The tunes were unbarred and written in C clefs. The majority were eight lines long. The first verse of the psalm was underlaid; only one note was allowed for each syllable, but long and short notes were interspersed to give a certain rhythmic flexibility. However, the rhythms varied slightly from edition to edition, gradually becoming more regular.

In 1562 the Earl of Moray, later Regent of Scotland, commissioned David Peebles to produce simple four-part harmonizations of the psalm tunes coming into Scotland from Geneva. By 1566 the completed psalter was copied into partbooks by Thomas Wood, vicar of St Andrews. (Two copies by Wood survive, five partbooks in *GB-Eu*, one in *EIRE-Dtc* and one in *GB-Lbm*; the contratenor is incomplete.) Most of the settings are by Peebles but other Scottish composers contributed, including John Angus, Andrew Blackall, John Black, John Buchan and Andrew Kemp. The harmonies are simple, with the melody in the tenor (see ex.21).

In spite of Moray's attempt to uphold the musical tradition threatened by the Reformation, standards seem to have declined rapidly. In 1579 an Act of Parliament provided money to revive the decaying 'sang schules' (song schools), but the austere psalm tunes could not revitalize institutions created to study the complexities of Renaissance polyphony. The churches had no musical instruments and choirs were rare, for past experience had shown that they tended to be used for display, thus supplanting congregational singing. Many of the proper tunes, particularly those of French origin, were too difficult for congregations to sing unaided and it appears that many were not sung at all. Editions of the psalter between 1599 and 1611 omitted some of the tunes altogether.

The Middelburg Psalter of 1602, which left out 61 proper tunes, was the first to introduce the principle of common tunes by printing three tunes for 22 psalms. One of these tunes, later called 'Common' (ex.20) was originally the proper for Psalm cviii; the others were 'London', from Daman's psalter of 1579, and 'English', from East's psalter of 1592. The 1615 edition contained 12 common tunes, grouped together at the beginning and distinguished by names after the English practice. In Raban's Aberdeen psalter of 1625 the common tunes, increased to 15, were harmonized, and the local tune 'Bon accord' in reports (i.e. with imitative entries; *see* REPORTS) was added. The harmonized psalter of 1635 contained 31 common tunes.

Ex.20 'Common'

Only six of the 31 editions printed after Raban's 1625 psalter contained music. One of these was the harmonized psalter of 1635, edited by Edward Millar. In the introduction he expressed his hope of standardizing the harmonies used in churches 'where sundrie Tribles, Bases and Counters set by diverse authors . . . do discordingly rub upon each other'. Some of the harmonizations appear to have been his own but he took most of them from Wood's psalter, sometimes modifying them. Not all the tunes from the 1564 psalter are included and some are used for different psalms. In all there are 104 proper tunes, 31 common tunes and eight

Ex.21 Psalm c from 1635 psalter

in reports. The harmonies are simple, and he took care to make each part move as melodically as possible (ex.21). The tune is in the tenor throughout except in two reports, Psalm xii ('Bon accord') and Psalm xxi ('Aberfeldy' from Raban's psalter of 1633). There is no evidence that the Church ever authorized this psalter or even that it was used in church. The common tunes are laid out with the tenor and contra on one page and the treble and bass upside down on the facing page, suggesting a domestic setting where the singers could gather round the book. It is possible that Millar was encouraged by those who supported Charles I's desire for a more elaborate service. Livingston suggested that the tunes in reports were sung as anthems in the Chapel Royal, Stirling, where Millar was appointed Master of Music shortly after the psalter's publication. According to the Records of the Privy Seal the English Service, with choristers and organs, had been in force there since 1617. It is possible that such royal and episcopal associations prevented the psalter from arresting the decline in the standards of church worship.

The 1650 psalter was published without music, a reflection on the state of psalm singing at that time. In 1645 the Synod of Lothian had stopped psalm singing and Scripture reading altogether (replacing them with 'lectures', presumably political); not until 1653 were they restored. In 1666 an edition was published in Aberdeen containing 12 of the old common tunes – 'Abbey', 'Common', 'Duke's', 'Dundee', 'Dunfermline', 'Elgin', 'English', 'French', 'King's', 'London' ('London New'), 'Martyrs' (ex.22) and 'Stilt' ('York') – and 'Bon accord' in reports. A later edition by John Forbes, also of Aberdeen, contained printed harmonized versions and in addition a short-metre tune, the old proper to Psalm xxv. By the end of the 17th century the 12 common tunes were firmly entrenched and no others were allowed.

Ex.22 'Martyrs'

The first attempt to improve this state of affairs was made in 1726, when Thomas Bruce challenged the sanctity of the common tunes with his *The Common Tunes, or Scotland's Church Music made Plain* (Edinburgh, 1726); in addition to 11 common tunes ('Common' was dropped) it contained 11 from the 1635 psalter and eight entirely new ones. These last were short-lived.

The turning-point came in the middle of the 18th century with the beginning of the choir movement in Aberdeenshire. In 1748 Sir Archibald Grant instructed the local schoolmaster to form a children's choir for the parish church of Monymusk. Five years later Grant appointed Thomas Channon, an English soldier stationed in Aberdeen and probably a Methodist, to improve the standard of psalm singing. Channon endeavoured to impose a simpler, more disciplined style of singing, without ornaments, and to encourage singing in parts, normally treble, tenor and bass. His innovations met with considerable opposition in the Aberdeen establishment, not only because he introduced new tunes but because he increased the speed of singing and used a pitchpipe. The choir movement spread, encouraging the production of such tutors as Robert Bremner's *The Rudiments of Music with Psalmody* (Edinburgh, 1756) and anthologies of tunes.

Among the first anthologies were Thomas Moore's various psalter 'companions', published between 1750 and 1761. They contained a number of English tunes adapted to the Scottish metres. A large number of tune books followed, reviving old Scottish psalm tunes, importing old English ones and introducing new ones. Similar 19th-century anthologies include R. A. Smith's *Sacred Harmony* (Edinburgh, 1825–8), T. L. Hateley's *Free Church Psalmody* (Edinburgh, 1844), G. and J. Cameron's *The Sacred Harp* (Glasgow, 1849) and William Carnie's *The Northern Psalter* (Aberdeen, 1872). The tune writers, many of whom were amateurs, enjoyed their new freedom to the full and included decorative runs, dotted rhythms and repeat lines (ex.23).

Ex.23 'Desert', first two lines

Tunes with a Scottish flavour using a pentatonic or six-note scale were popular; one of the best known is 'Kilmarnock' (ex.24). Melodies were also adapted from Handel, Haydn, Mozart, Beethoven and even Palestrina. Inevitably many of the Victorian tunes are cloyingly sentimental, such as the ubiquitous 'Crimond', popularized to Psalm xxiii by the Glasgow Orpheus Choir.

In 1899 the Church of Scotland issued a new hymnary and psalter, the latter containing 226 tunes of a generally higher standard. It was followed by *The Scottish Psalter* (London, 1929) which is currently in

use. Many of the 16th-century tunes have been restored: 14 tunes from the French and Anglo-Genevan psalters, 9 common tunes from the 1615 psalter and six more common tunes from the 1635 harmonized psalter. Its four tunes in reports include 'Bon accord' and 'Aberfeldy'. The music is printed in semibreves and minims, and many of the long notes ironed out in the preceding two centuries have been restored.

The reformed Scottish churches never adopted the practice of having proper psalms for the day. As a result some of the more obscure psalms are rarely, if ever, sung. *The Church Hymnary: Third Edition* (London, 1973), authorized by the Assemblies of the Church of Scotland and the Presbyterian Churches of England, Wales and Ireland recognized this by including only the most common psalms. In most cases only excerpts from the psalm texts are printed. Of the 57 psalms or psalm portions obtained, all but nine are taken from the 1650 psalter; two are from the psalter of the Presbyterian Church in Ireland and the remaining seven combine verses from each. The tunes printed for these psalms include 12 from the old Scottish psalters: 'Old 44th', 'Old 100th', 'Old 107th', 'Old 124th', and eight common tunes. However, this hymnary is not intended to replace the 1929 psalter. The Free Church of Scotland has retained its own psalter, *Scottish Psalmody*; a new edition is in preparation.

(*iii*) *Performing practice*. Few details survive concerning early performing practice. According to Walter Steuart of Pardovan's *Collections and Observations . . . concerning . . . the Church of Scotland* (Edinburgh, 1709, ii, 1, §26), the minister or the 'uptaker of the psalm' read over the whole of the intended portion, and then the singing followed without interruption. At the Westminster Assembly the Scots agreed only reluctantly, after some debate, to adopt the English practice of 'lining out' (intoning and singing the lines one by one). In 1746 the General Assembly recommended that this practice should cease but it continued in many churches until well into the 19th century, and can still occasionally be heard in the west highlands and islands.

To what extent conclusions and doxologies were sung is unclear. The first of these appeared to Psalm cxlviii in Bassandine's 1575 edition. Charteris's Edinburgh edition of 1596 includes 32. The 1635 psalter contains two conclusions and one doxology, all in common metre (which may have been added simply on the printer's initiative). The 1650 psalter contains none, but in 1661 the Synod of Lothian ordered them to be sung with the psalms. Bearing in mind Calvin's principle that all matter extraneous to the Bible should be rejected, it is unlikely that doxologies were ever very popular; in the 17th century the church may have been under some pressure to adopt them to conform with episcopal practices. The 1929 psalter contains seven in different metres at the end of the book, but they are not generally sung.

There is no information about the speeds at which the early psalms were sung. It is clear, however, that by the 18th century they were sung extremely slowly: as late as 1772 Bremner wrote, in his *Church Harmony, or Psalm-tunes in Four Parts* that the length of a semibreve in common time (¢) ought to be between three and four seconds, although for tunes in triple time, being of a 'more light and airy nature', the time of one second to a minim was sufficient. With the subsequent improvement

Ex.24 'Kilmarnock'

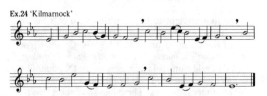

Ex.25 'French'

'French' as sung in Sutherland and Caithness, from T. L. Hately, *Seann Fhuinn nan Salm ... or the Old Gaelic Psalm Tunes* (Glasgow, 1845/*R*1931)

Ps cxxi Mo shuile tog – am suas a chum, Mo   shuil – – e   tog – am   suas
My eyes   lift   I   up   to   My   eyes   lift   I   up

a   chum,   Nam beann o'n d'thig mo   neart   Nam   beann
to   The hills from which comes my strength   The   hills

o'n   d'thig   mo   neart   O'n Dhia rinn tal- amh a – gus neamh   O'n
from   which comes   my   strength   From God who made earth   and heaven   From

Dhia   rinn   tal – amh   a – – gus   neamh   Tha m'furtachd ui – le   teachd
God   who made   earth   and   heaven   My   help all   comes

Tha   m'fur – tachd   uil – – e   teachd.
My   help   all   comes.

of church singing standards, the psalms were gradually taken faster. In the 1970s the speed was approximately semibreve = 60, triple-time tunes being rather faster. In those seceding churches that sing unaccompanied the speed was usually considerably slower.

The old slow speeds naturally encouraged the congregations to ornament the tunes with runs, turns and shakes. Bremner wrote in his *Rudiments of Music*:

Had these nonsensical graces been the same everywhere, it would have been the less matter, but every congregation, nay, every individual, had different graces to the same note, which were dragged by many to such immoderate length that one corner of the church, or the people in one seat, had sung out the line before another had half done: and from the whole there arose such a mass of confusion and discord as quite defaced this noblest part of Divine worship.

In the Gaelic-speaking congregations of the east coast of Ross, Sutherland and Caithness a highly ornamented style of singing was developed which may have originated in the melismas of plainchant. Only six tunes were sung: 'Dundee', 'Elgin', 'French', 'Martyrs', 'Old London' and 'Stilt'. In the middle of the 19th century T. L. Hately, the precentor to the Free Church General Assembly, attempted to notate these so-called 'long tunes' (ex.25). Joseph Mainzer also transcribed them (*Gaelic Psalm Tunes of Ross-shire*, 1844); his edition of 'French' is now sung at the close of the annual National Mod, but as he fitted it into regular bars of 4/4 and added a piano accompaniment it is a poor echo of the old manner. With the retreat of Gaelic from the east coast in the 20th century the long tunes died out. However, the practice of adding grace notes and slurs to the unaccompanied, unison melody still flourishes in some congregations in the west highlands and islands. They are rather simpler than the long tunes but the melody can only sometimes be identified. (*See* SCOTLAND, §II, 4.)

Although choirs were largely discarded at the time of the Reformation, there is some evidence that harmony was sung in centres that had sang schules. James

Melville wrote in his diary of 1574 that, as a student in St Andrews, he had learnt many of the trebles of the psalms (the melody being in the tenor); Calderwood claimed that in 1582 crowds in the streets of Edinburgh welcomed the returning minister Durie with Psalm cxxiv 'sung in such a pleasant tune in four parts'. There are a few exceptional references to choirs: in 1587 the Kirk Session of Glasgow ordered the music teacher, William Struthers, to choose four men to sing beside him in the church, and in 1621 Stirling Kirk Session decreed that the children of the sang schule should sit beside their master in the reader's place. These are isolated examples, however, and the members of the sang schules and others who could sing a part normally sat in the body of the congregation. The table-book format of the 1635 psalter suggests that harmony may have been used in private or family worship, which was strongly encouraged.

Choirs were not formed until the middle of the 18th century, when it was realized that they could assist the singing without taking the place of the congregation, but in the first decades of the 19th century in Paisley Abbey and St George's, Edinburgh, R. A. Smith and Andrew Thomson improved the choirs so much that the congregations felt discouraged. Later in the century Hately in the south and William Carnie in the north-east avoided this danger by teaching huge classes – from 500 to 1000 members – which were congregational rather than choir practices.

The use of instruments in church was banned altogether in accordance with Calvin's principles. Not until the beginning of the 19th century did organs and harmoniums begin to appear; some of the seceding churches still consider them inappropriate. With the advent of the organ the melody, for so long in the tenor, was transferred to the treble. However, the distinction is to some extent academic as the majority of the congregation sing in unison at their own pitch. The 1929

Scottish psalter has attempted to introduce a modified form of the old style, printing alternative settings known as 'faux-bourdons' in which the tune is in the tenor while the rest of the choir add the harmony (ex.26). In other, two-part versions, a descant is sung above a unison melody, the harmonies being provided only by the organ.

Ex.26 'Dunfermline': 'faux-bourdon' setting in 1929 psalter

The *Church Hymnary: Third Edition* includes a few prose psalms, some pointed for Anglican chant and some for Gregorian psalm tones. The latter are simpler for a congregation to sing, but in view of the continuing resistance of the average congregation to anything Roman, it will be a long time before they are accepted.

2. IRELAND. The Presbyterian Church in Ireland, like the mother church in Scotland, has a strong tradition of metrical psalm singing. The Church came into being when the General Synod of Ulster (founded in 1642) joined with the Secession Synod in the Union of 1840. Before the Union, Presbyterian practice had been to use the psalms alone in public worship, although the Scottish paraphrases (and, in a few congregations, hymns) had already come into use in the Synod of Ulster. One of the terms of the union, in fact, was that the paraphrases ought not to be authorized, even though they were not prohibited and thus continued to be used by some congregations.

In 1841, 1859, 1868 and 1887 the General Assembly of the Presbyterian Church in Ireland issued revisions of the Westminster *Directory for the Publique Worship of God* (1644). The last of these stated that 'the metrical version of the Book of Psalms, as published by this Church or as used by the Church in Scotland, is the only psalmody authorised by the General Assembly' (the first three had only approved the Psalter 'as used in the Church of Scotland'). The reason for the double approval was that following the Evangelical Revival of 1857 an attempt had been made to introduce hymns. There was strong opposition to this, for while many approved the use of hymns in mission services they were opposed to any such innovation in the 'House of God'. At the same time, some of the criticisms of the Scottish Psalter of 1650 were considered to have substance, so instead of approving the introduction of hymns it was agreed to revise the Psalter. The result was the publication in 1880 of *The Psalter in Metre, a Revised Version, Prepared and Published by the Authority of the Presbyterian Church in Ireland, with Tunes*. By removing a number of archaisms, by providing a considerable number of new alternative versions, and by introducing a greater variety of metres it was hoped to solve the hymnody problem. But this failed, and the *Church*

Hymnary (in cooperation with the Scottish Churches) was approved in 1899. The new psalter was primarily the work of Rev. John Moran and Professor J. G. Murphy. The revision had much to commend it and it is now used universally throughout the Church. A number of congregations still sing only psalms and paraphrases.

BIBLIOGRAPHY

D. Calderwood: *History of the Kirk of Scotland*, Wodrow Society (Edinburgh, 1842–9)
N. Livingston: *The Scottish Metrical Psalter of 1635: Reprint with Dissertations* (Glasgow, 1864)
J. W. MacMeeken: *History of the Scottish Metrical Psalms* (Glasgow, 1872)
W. Cowan: 'A Bibliography of the Book of Common Order and Psalm Book of the Church of Scotland: 1556–1644', *Edinburgh Bibliographical Society*, x (1913), 52–100
W. McMillan: *The Worship of the Scottish Reformed Church, 1550–1638* (London, 1931)
M. Patrick: *Four Centuries of Scottish Psalmody* (London, 1949)
J. H. S. Burleigh: *A Church History of Scotland* (London, 1960)
T. H. Keir: 'The Church Hymnary: Third Edition', *Liturgical Review*, iii/1 (1973), 26
E. A. MacLean: 'Gaelic Psalm-singing and the Lowland Connection', *Liturgical Review*, iii/2 (1973), 54

V. North America. In the early years of the Protestant settlements of North America, metrical psalm singing was often the only form of organized music. It occupied a most important place in the cultural life of the people, and was invested with the strong feelings of a struggling community far from home. The Puritans, in particular, treated the psalms and their tunes with veneration, and sang them in everyday situations as well as at church on Sundays. The tradition naturally followed very similar patterns to those of the parent countries in Europe. By the time a more assertively American school of psalmody had arisen in the late 18th century, metrical psalms were rapidly giving way to hymns in many churches.

1. History of psalm singing: (i) Episcopal churches (ii) Pilgrims (iii) Dutch Reformed Church (iv) Puritans (v) Presbyterian churches (vi) German Reformed Church. 2. Psalm books: (i) Function and character (ii) The Bay Psalm Book.

1. HISTORY OF PSALM SINGING.
(*i*) *Episcopal churches*. The psalms of Calvin's French psalter were sung in America as early as 1564–5 during the Huguenot expeditions to Florida and South Carolina, just as Sir Francis Drake's men sang psalms, to the delight of the Indians, while camping on the coast of California in 1579. However, the first Protestant church to establish itself permanently on the American continent was the Church of England: at Jamestown, Virginia, a church was built in 1607, the year that the colony was founded. Commercial enterprise rather than religious fervour was dominant in the minds of the early Virginian colonists. They were content to continue the traditions of the Anglican church, which was established there by law, as it was later in Maryland, North and South Carolina and Georgia. In the northern colonies Anglican churches were organized by the early 18th century.

The bibles and prayer books imported from England had the usual metrical psalms bound in the back – Sternhold and Hopkins, or later, Tate and Brady. The singing was very much as it was in English parish churches. In the larger town churches organs were gradually acquired: at King's Chapel, Boston, in 1714; at Trinity Church, Newport, Rhode Island, in 1733; at Trinity Church, New York, in 1737; at five Virginia churches between 1737 and 1767; at all three Anglican churches in Philadelphia in 1762–6. In smaller churches, parish clerks led the people in unaccompanied singing. Tate and Brady's psalms, the *New Version* of which was first published in America in New York in 1710, were very widely used by the mid-18th century.

After the Revolution authority over the congregations passed to the Protestant Episcopal Church, and for the first time, in 1790, a selection of psalms and hymns for use in the churches was laid down by authority, and annexed to the Book of Common Prayer. It consisted of the entire *New Version* of Tate and Brady, with 27 hymns. A revised selection was made in 1833, still including a large number of Tate and Brady's psalms, and continued in use until 1866. Thus the Episcopal Church was one of the last to sing metrical psalms as a regular part of its services.

The tunes sung with these psalms were at first the same as those used in England, as can be seen from a tune supplement bound in with a Boston edition of Tate and Brady in 1720; they were also the same as those used by the Puritan churches. A later tune supplement to Tate and Brady was engraved and probably compiled by Thomas Johnston, who was also one of the first American organ builders; Daniel Bayley's collections indicate a more florid taste. On the whole, however, Episcopal churches were musically more conservative than Congregational ones, avoiding the excesses of fuging-tunes and elaborate 'set pieces'. A most influential Anglican musician was Francis Hopkinson. His *Collection of Psalm Tunes . . . for the Use of the United Churches of Christ Church and St Peter's Church in Philadelphia* (Philadelphia, 1763) contains some fairly ornate tunes, including some of Hopkinson's own, but

Ex.27 Peter Valton (c1740–84): 'St Peters', in Eckhard's book of 1809, where it is allocated to 'Psalm 46' – i.e. Psalm cl (New Version), v.1 of which is underlaid here.

they are in the *galant* taste of the time, resembling the music of town rather than country churches in England. The prevalence of organs and the stronger links with the mother country tended to keep Anglican church music closer to the European art music of the time. The same tendency is shown in the tunes of *The Book of Common Prayer. . .Proposed to the Use of the Protestant Episcopal Church* (Philadelphia, 1786), and in Jacob Eckhard's Choirmaster's Book of 1809, used at St Michael, Charleston, South Carolina, together with a special *Selection of Psalms and Hymns* prepared by the rectors of the two principal Charleston churches in 1792 (see ex.27).

(*ii*) *Pilgrims.* The band of about 100 English Pilgrims who founded the colony at Plymouth, Massachusetts, in 1620 were members of a group of 'Separatists' who had gone into exile at Leyden, Holland, in 1609. They had rejected the worship of the Church of England, and so instead of Sternhold and Hopkins's psalms they adopted the version of Henry Ainsworth, pastor of a neighbouring Separatist community at Amsterdam. Ainsworth was one of the most cultivated biblical scholars of his day, and in *The Book of Psalmes: Englished both in Prose and Metre* (Amsterdam, 1612) he offered not only a complete new prose translation of the psalms accompanied by a pithy commentary, but also a new metrical version and an excellent selection of tunes. In variety of metres and in his choice of tunes, Ainsworth was as much influenced by the Franco-Dutch psalter as by Sternhold and Hopkins:

Tunes for the Psalms I find none set of God; so that each people is to use the most grave, decent and comfortable manner of singing that they know. . . .The singing-notes, therefore, I have most taken from our former Englished Psalms, when they will fit the measure of the verse. And for the other long verses I have also taken (for the most part) the gravest and easiest tunes of the French and Dutch Psalms.

Details of Ainsworth's tunes and their origins are provided by Pratt and Frost. The tunes, like the rest of the book, are learned rather than popular, and are not all easy to sing. However, Edward Winslow recalled 'there being many of our congregation very expert in music' at Leyden; some of these must have been on the momentous voyage of the *Mayflower*, for Ainsworth's *Psalmes* were used for many years in the Plymouth colony, in the total absence of instrumental or professional aid. Later generations lost their forefathers' skill. In 1681 Plymouth church decided to institute lining out, and in 1691, on the amalgamation of the Plymouth colony with the much larger and more successful settlement to the north, the church formally recognized the 'difficulties' of many of the Ainsworth tunes and allowed the substitution of easier ones used with the Bay Psalm Book. So Ainsworth's book was never to be widely popular in America, though it was used at Ipswich and Salem, both outside the Plymouth colony, until 1667. It was reprinted several times, but never in America.

(*iii*) *Dutch Reformed Church.* The Dutch colony of what is now New York was established in 1613, but the first church was not organized until 1628, when the Dutch and French Protestant settlers combined; they knew identical tunes, and each sang them in their own language. The Dutch psalter, prescribed by the Synod of Dort (1618), was used with strict invariance for a full 100 years after the English conquest of the colony in 1664. An organ was erected in the New York church in 1727. The first English psalm book for the Dutch Reformed Church was *The Psalms of David. . .for the*

Use of the Reformed Dutch Church of the City of New York (New York, 1767). Francis Hopkinson was the translator, and his job was the singular one of adapting the psalm versions of Tate and Brady to fit the tunes of varying metres in the old Dutch psalter. The music still remained unaltered.

The new book did not long satisfy the English-speaking congregations; many of the tunes in peculiar metres were unfamiliar through long disuse, and there was a demand to relax the strict confinement to psalms and to introduce some of the hymns popular in other American churches. The central Synod continued to maintain a strict control over the worship of individual congregations, but after the Revolution it authorized a new book (1789) that included 135 hymns selected by Dr John Livingston. The psalms in this book were selected largely from Tate and Brady's and Watts's versions, with only a few of Hopkinson's remaining; and the great majority were in common, short or long metre. No music was provided and no tunes suggested. Later editions increased the proportion of hymns, until in *Hymns of the Church* (New York, 1869) the remaining metrical psalms were mixed in with hymns.

Despite these updating procedures, congregational singing remained at a low ebb. In the parochial school system sponsored by the Church, the leader of the church psalmody was also the schoolmaster; but he did not generally use his position to teach the school children how to sing. As a result congregations were generally unable to take part in the psalm singing. Until the mid-19th century the schoolmaster and the organist often performed the music alone.

(iv) Puritans. The Massachusetts Bay colony was founded in 1629 by puritan members of the Church of England, who had at first no idea of seceding from the church, though they rejected its ritual. They brought with them Sternhold and Hopkins's psalms, and we may suppose that they sang them mainly to the handful of four-line tunes then in common use (see ex.9, above). They were not of a temper to concern themselves with artistic improvements in the singing. But they were unhappy with Sternhold and Hopkins because 'their variations of the sense, and alterations of the sacred text too frequently, may justly minister matter of offence'. Accordingly, a group of 30 divines assembled to prepare a still more literal translation, 'that as wee doe injoye other, soe (if it were the Lord's will) we might injoye this ordinance also in its native purity'. They published, in 1640, *The Whole Booke of Psalmes Faithfully Translated into English Metre* (see §2 (ii) below).

The Bay Psalm Book, or New England Psalm Book, as this collection became known, was at once adopted by almost every church in the colony. By means of lining out, which was in use in 1647 and perhaps earlier, the people could easily be taught to fit the new words to the old tunes. The compilers referred at the end of the book to 48 tunes to which the psalms might be sung, including 39 common-metre tunes 'as they are collected, out of our chief musicians, by Tho. Ravenscroft'. But it is highly unlikely that more than a handful of these were used in church. Copies of Ravenscroft's and Alison's harmonized settings are known to have been in the possession of early New England settlers, but, as in the old country, they would have been used domestically.

The Bay Psalm Book lasted for over a century, and spread to other American colonies and even to many dissenting churches in Britain. There is no doubt that the new psalms continued to be sung to the old tunes. When for the first time a musical supplement appeared, with the ninth edition of 1698, the 13 tunes in it were all standard ones from English sources (see fig.6 below). They were set for tenor and bass, with sol-fa letters below the staves, suggesting that the basses were sung, not played (see ex.28). In later editions the tunes were

Ex.28 'Low Dutch Tune', from the Bay Psalm Book (1698)

Psalm xxiii, as sung to the above tune (v.1)

The Lord to me a shepherd is,
Want therefore shall not I:
He in the folds of tender grass
Doth make me down to lie.

printed without basses. As in English country churches, the speed of singing had slowed to a drawl by this date. With no strong leadership of any kind, tunes were ornamented at will by individual members of a congregation, and the discordant heterophony that resulted was described by would-be reformers as 'indecent', 'like the braying of asses', 'tortured and twisted as every unskilful throat saw fit' and so on (see ex.11, above). Something of the chaos that often prevailed may be gathered from entries in Samuel Sewall's *Diary*, describing services at the South Meeting House, Boston:

1705, Dec. 28. Mr. Willard . . . spoke to me to set the Tune; I intended Windsor and fell into High-Dutch, and then essaying to set another Tune went into a key much too high. So I pray'd Mr. White to set it; which he did well, Litchf[ield] Tune.

1718, Feb. 2. In the Morning I set York Tune, and in the 2d going over, the Gallery carried irresistibly to St David's which discouraged me very much.

But the people liked this way of singing, and in some churches persisted with it despite efforts at reform. In the strongly individualistic, Congregational tradition of New England, every church was at liberty to govern its own practice.

Reform got under way in 1720, with the appearance of the Rev. Thomas Symmes's anonymous pamphlet, *The Reasonableness of Regular Singing, or Singing by Note*. In the following year two important singing methods were published by John Tufts and Thomas Walter. Each carried an appendix of psalm tunes, and Tufts introduced a new musical notation based on sol-fa letters. Walter's appendix presented the tunes in three-part harmony. (For discussion of the new era of American singing that resulted from these publications and from the formation of singing schools, *see* PSALMODY (ii), §II.) It is sufficient to point out here that the teaching of singing from notes naturally generated church choirs, which tended, as in England, to take the singing out of the hands of the people – where the people would let them. The attention which was thus focussed on singing led in turn to a desire for better literary and musical materials to sing. The Bay Psalm Book soon gave way in popularity to more elegant if less literal translations – the *New Version* of Tate and Brady, and (particularly among Congregationalists) Isaac Watts's *Psalms of David Imitated in the Language of the New Testament* (first American publication, Philadelphia, 1729). More conservative congregations stuck to the old book (revised in 1758) but the supplements attached to later editions show that the traditional psalms, as well as the newer ones, were sung to increasingly elaborate tunes.

Two tunes of this date appear to be the first printed compositions of American origin: 'Southwel New' (ex.29) from Walter (1721), and '100 Psalm New' from

Ex.29 'Southwel New Tune', from Walter (1721) [originally on three staves, ]

Ex.30 '136 Psalm Tune', from Johnston's tune supplement to Tate and Brady's *New Version* (1755), here underlaid with the first verse of Psalm cxxxvi

Tufts (1723). Some of the earliest tunes containing florid melismas ('Northampton', 'Isle of Wight', '24 Psalm') were drawn from English sources. But at the mid-century two tune supplements from New England, engraved (and possibly compiled) by James Turner and Thomas Johnston respectively, include some ornate tunes probably of American origin. One of them in the Johnston supplement (1755), called 'Psalm 136', comes near to being a fuging-tune, though for tenor and bass only (ex.30). In the latter part of the century, more especially after the Revolution, there was a burgeoning of elaborate psalmody in which the Congregational churches (descendants of the old Puritan bodies) were often in the vanguard (*see* PSALMODY (ii), §II, 2). It was perhaps partly for the purpose of countering this trend that organs were gradually introduced in Congregational churches towards the end of the 18th century. The first was at Providence, Rhode Island, in 1770; in 1798 Bentley had heard of only four Congregational churches with organs in America – three in Boston and one in Newburyport.

Under the influence of the 'Great Awakening' and subsequent evangelical movements, metrical psalms tended to be replaced by hymns, and by 1830 formed a small proportion of the verses in most Congregational hymnbooks (*see* HYMN, §IV, 4).

(*v*) *Presbyterian churches.* The Presbyterians also claimed descent from the Puritans, but retained a more authoritarian and centralized form of church government by Synod. From 1668, and especially in the 18th century, both in what is now the United States and in Canada, a constant influx of Scots and Scots-Irish

produced a distinctive brand of Presbyterianism – one that was strongly resistant to liberal trends. *The Psalms of David in Meeter*, in the Scottish version of 1650, was to Presbyterian minds almost a part of the Bible with which it was usually bound. The success of the Scots in colonizing the frontier outposts of the American and Canadian interiors left them often remote from acculturating influences, and they continued the 'old way' of singing long after it had been forgotten elsewhere. The 12 common tunes were lined out by a precentor, and sung by the people in the kind of slow heterophony described by Joseph Mainzer, which survived well into the 20th century in remote places. In urban centres such as Boston, Philadelphia and New York, there were schisms in the 18th century: 'New Side' synods welcomed the influence of the evangelical movement; 'Old Side' synods preferred to continue in the old ways. The psalm singing was, indeed, often the central issue in the fierce disputes that raged in Presbyterian circles at this date. James Lyon's *Urania* (Philadelphia, 1761) was subscribed to by a number of prominent Presbyterian clergymen; it must have represented the avant garde of Presbyterian singing. In 1774 John Adams, accustomed to the elaborate choir singing of New England, reported that the Old Presbyterian Society of New York was still 'in the *old way*, as we call it – all the drawling, quavering, discord in the world'. A revision of Watts's *Psalms* in a conservative direction, restoring those portions that Watts had deliberately omitted, was prepared by Joel Barlow in 1785, and the synods of Philadelphia and

New York left individual parishes to decide whether to use it or to continue to sing the old psalms in the old way. The *Directory for the Worship of God* (1788) at last substituted 'singing psalms or hymns' for the 1644 Westminster directory's 'singing of psalms', paving the way for the authorization of Watts's hymns in 1802. In town churches the sterner kind of Presbyterianism faded gradually; organs were purchased, choirs took over the psalms and hymns. Congregational singing survived only in the wild country places.

(*vi*) *German Reformed Church*. Of the various sects that flourished among the German communities in Pennsylvania during the 18th century, only the Reformed Church, with its Calvinist ancestry, sang metrical psalms. The first settlements were founded by Dutch Reformed ministers early in the century. They used the Marburg Collection of psalms in Lobwasser's version, and in 1753 this book was reprinted by Christopher Sauer at Germantown, Pennsylvania, as *Neu-vermehrt und vollständiges Gesang-Buch*, with all the traditional tunes. But the knowledge of the old chorale melodies was disappearing among the people; lining out had to be introduced, and by the end of the century it often happened that the minister and the organist were the only audible singers. At a synod held in Reading in 1794, it was resolved 'that a new hymn-book be prepared, of which the Psalms shall be taken from Lobwasser and Spreng's improved version, and the Palatine hymn-book shall form the basis of the hymns'. This, the first officially authorized book, was published in 1797. The psalm tunes had been greatly reduced in number, by the omission of little-used tunes. Between 1800 and 1850 there was a gradual change to the English language in many churches, and the first English collection, *Psalms and Hymns for the Use of the German Reformed Church in the United States of America*, appeared in 1830: all 150 psalms were still included, but they were largely in Watts's version and drew on Anglo-American sources for their tunes. A newly compiled German book appeared in 1842, and another, *Deutsches Gesangbuch* (edited by Philip Schaff), in 1861. By this time such metrical psalms as survived were embedded in a large collection of hymns, arranged by the church year. Tunes were no longer printed with the words; suggestions for tunes showed, however, an interest in reviving the traditional German chorale melodies.

2. PSALM BOOKS.
(*i*) *Function and character*. Of the psalm books printed in America only those for the Dutch and German Reformed Churches contained tunes printed with the psalms. In the Dutch version the tune was reprinted over each verse of the psalm; in the German, the first verse was underlaid and the rest printed beneath. These formats were modelled on European books that had been used with a tradition of accompanied singing. When an organ could not be obtained the congregation was at a loss and the knowledge of the tunes quickly faded. With the introduction of English psalms and hymns the older type of underlaid psalm book disappeared.

The great majority of psalm books in the English American tradition had no music at all (perhaps 80% of the surviving editions up to 1800). Before the era of the singing schools, there were so few tunes that they were known from memory, having been sung unaccompanied

for generations. After choirs were well established, they generally sang from their own books containing special selections of psalm and hymn tunes and through-composed set pieces and anthems. Most of the tune supplements date from the intermediate period (about 1720–75).

In the early days, when psalms were lined out, the congregation did not really need books at all in church. They knew the tunes, and they took the words from the parish clerk, elder, or minister. No doubt the Bay Psalm Book was designed, as much as anything, for domestic singing and private reading – as the title of the third edition suggests (see below). In the same way the early tune supplements were for the benefit of devout singers at home rather than for the church; bass parts were soon found unnecessary. With the singing school movement came the possibility of learning new music in parts, and for this Walter and Tufts prepared their instructional books. When the music was sung in church it was convenient for the singers to have it in the psalm book. The tune appendix of Tufts was itself used as a supplement for editions of psalm books; others had supplements of similar scope, usually (from 1737 onwards) in three parts. Tune supplements were only loosely attached to psalm books. The same supplement was used for different psalm books and vice versa, while most psalm books had no tunes at all. Evidently it was up to the purchaser to order whatever tunes he liked. Very probably the books with tunes were used by the members of the 'choir' – those who had rehearsed them in the singing school or psalmody society. The tunes attached to the 1774 Tate and Brady are entitled *A New Collection of Psalm Tunes Adapted to Congregational Worship*, which might seem to indicate an effort to prevent choirs from monopolizing the singing. But all the tunes in it are in four-part harmony, many are elaborate, and some are of the fully fuging variety. It seems that in some churches tunes of this sort were actually sung by congregations at large. With the disappearance of tune supplements and the flowering of psalmody books after the Revolution, choirs took over an increasing share of the music, singing anthems and set pieces in which nobody could take part without rehearsal. When evangelical hymn singing made its way into churches congregations could once more take their full part (*see* HYMN, §IV, 4). However, psalm books (without tunes) continued to appear until after the middle of the 19th century.

(*ii*) *The Bay Psalm Book*. The Bay Psalm Book (1640) was the first English book ever printed in America: 1700 copies were run off on a small press belonging to Harvard College. The compilers, like Barton and Rous in England, eliminated some of the more unusual metres found in the Old Version, thus allowing all 150 psalms to be sung to the few tunes that were at the command of congregations. The collection was thoroughly revised for the third edition of 1651, chiefly by Henry Dunster and Richard Lyon. They polished the versification somewhat and added alternative translations. They further reduced unusual metres, so that 125 (instead of 112) out of 150 psalms were now in common metre; and they added 36 other 'scripture-songs', still maintaining the Calvinistic principle that only inspired words were suitable for singing in worship. The new title was *The Psalms Hymns and Spiritual Songs of the Old and New Testament Faithfully Translated into English*

Metre for the Use, Edification, and Comfort of the Saints in Publick and Private, especially in New England. This proved to be the definitive edition. It was reprinted under this title, with scarcely any alterations in the verbal text, for over a century.

When for the first time a tune supplement, printed from wood blocks, was bound in with the ninth edition (1698), the 13 tunes in it, and their basses, were drawn from the 1679 edition of Playford's Introduction to the Skill of Musick, though the preface and the idea of using sol-fa letters probably come from the 1672 edition of the same book (see fig.6). Lowens has conjectured that the supplement was printed in England as part of a lost London edition of the Bay Psalm Book, but it does not resemble other English music printing of the time. The tunes are as set out in Table 1. It is a curious fact that the allocation of 'Lichfield' to Psalm lxix, like the rest, is copied from Playford, where it is actually a misprint for xcvi (through printing 69 for 96): the first verse of Psalm xcvi is printed under the tune in Playford. In New England, however, the tune (as a result of this misprint) came to be associated with the real Psalm lxix, the first

TABLE 1

Frost no.	Tune name	Metre	Key	Psalm
121	Oxford	C.M.	g	iv
25	Lichfield	C.M.	g	lxix
19	Low Dutch	C.M.	G	xxiii
205	York	C.M.	F	lxxiii
129	Windsor	C.M.	g	cxvi
154a	Cambridge Short	S.M.	g	lxx
234	St David's	C.M.	F	xcv
209	Martyrs	C.M.	g	xxxix
333a	Hackney	C.M.	d	lxi
132	Psalm cxix Second Meeter	D.C.M.	e	cxix
114	Psalm c First Meeter	L.M.	G	c
125	Psalm cxv [sic] First Meeter	8:8:8:8:8:8:8:8: 8:8:8:8	G	(cxiii)
174	Psalm cxlviii First Meeter	6:6:6:6:4:4:4:4	C	cxlviii

verse of which is printed with it in editions from 1705 to 1730. Other misprints closely follow Playford, proving the provenance of the tunes beyond doubt.

For the 1705 edition the music was completely reset in a different style, without basses or sol-fa letters but with the first verse of the allocated psalm underlaid. Many of the tunes are transposed up a tone ('Martyrs' down a 3rd), a somewhat pointless manoeuvre for unaccompanied singing. The reason was evidently that the 1705 tunes were copied from the 1694 or 1697 edition of Playford, where the same transpositions had been made to bring the tunes into line with Playford's Whole Book of Psalms (1677). The 13 tunes were reduced to 11 by omitting 'Hackney' and 'Psalm 115'. The printer evidently had little competence in music: there are no clefs, several misprints and 'Oxford' has a key-signature of one flat despite transposition to A minor. These mistakes were not corrected until 1726. The next few editions were closely similar to that of 1705, with one other tune, 'Ten Commandments' (Frost no.178), appearing in some editions and not others. The tune selection was evidently a standard one in New England, for the 1720 Boston edition of Tate and Brady had the very same 11 tunes in a different order. One British edition of the Bay Psalm Book (Glasgow, 1720) contains a similar selection, printed by James Duncan, printer to the city of Glasgow.

The 1737 edition carries an entirely different tune supplement of a much more ambitious kind, along the lines of Tufts's and Walter's books. It has 34 tunes in three-part harmony, with sol-fa letters underlaid. The selection of tunes owes far more to Tufts and Walter than to the previous supplements, reprinting some of their most 'advanced' and ornate tunes and such novelties as '100 Psalm New'.

Two copies of the 1744 edition are bound up with the Tufts supplement itself, printed from the plates of the 1738 edition. The 1758 edition has Turner's supplement, first printed with a psalm book of local use only, made by John Barnard, minister of a church in Marblehead. This edition has also a revised text, by Thomas Prince. But the days of the Bay Psalm Book were numbered. A few more editions were still to come, without music, but between 1761 and 1780 the New Version and Watts's Psalms each appeared in more than ten times as many editions.

6. The 'York' tune for Psalm lxxiii, with sol-fa letters, from the supplement to the ninth edition (1698) of the 'Bay Psalm Book'

BIBLIOGRAPHY

The Whole Booke of Psalmes Faithfully Translated into English Metre (Cambridge, Mass., 1640/R1956) [The Bay Psalm Book]
J. Cotton: Singing of Psalms a Gospel Ordinance (London, 1647)
T. Symmes: The Reasonableness of Regular Singing (Boston, 1720)

J. Tufts: *An Introduction to the Art of Singing Psalm-tunes* (Boston, 1721, 3/1723/*Rc*1966)
Das neue und verbesserte Gesang-buch (Philadelphia, 1797)
G. Hood: *History of Music in New England* (Boston, 1846)
J. S. Curwen: *Studies in Worship Music* (London, 1880–85), 57ff
C. W. Baird: *Huguenot Emigration to America*, i (New York, 1885), 65ff
J. Sabin: *Bibliotheca americana*, xvi (New York, 1886), 27ff
D. D. Demarest: *The* [Dutch] *Reformed Church in America* (New York, 4/1888)
O. Seidensticker: *The First Century of German Printing in America 1728–1830* (Philadelphia, 1893)
S. Lothrop Thorndike: 'The Psalmodies of Plymouth and Massachusetts Bay', *Colonial Society of Massachusetts Publications*, i (1895), 228
J. H. Dubbs: 'History of the Reformed Church, German', *American Church History*, viii (1902), 213–423
L. F. Benson: 'The American Revisions of Watts's Psalms', *Journal of the Presbyterian Historical Society*, ii (1903–4), 18
O. G. T. Sonneck: *Francis Hopkinson and James Lyon* (Washington, DC, 1905/*R*1967)
A. H. Messiter: *A History of the Choir and Music of Trinity Church, New York* (New York, 1906)
W. Bentley: *Diary*, ii (Salem, 1914), 259
L. F. Benson: *The English Hymn* (New York, 1915/*R*1962)
W. S. Pratt: *The Music of the Pilgrims* (New York, 1921/*R*1971)
M. van Doren, ed.: *Samuel Sewall: Diary* (New York, 1927)
W. S. Pratt: *The Music of the French Psalter of 1562* (New York, 1939)
H. C. Macdougall: *Early New England Psalmody: an Historical Appreciation, 1620–1820* (Brattleboro, 1940)
W. W. Sweet: *Religion in Colonial America* (New York, 1942)
D. Wing: *A Short-Title Catalogue of Books Printed in England, Scotland and Ireland...1641–1700* (New York, 1945–51, rev.2/1972)
H. B. Satcher: 'Music of the Episcopal Church in Pennsylvania in the Eighteenth Century', *Historical Magazine of the Protestant Episcopal Church*, xviii (1949), 372–413
A. P. Britton: *Theoretical Introductions in American Tune-books to 1800* (diss., U. of Michigan, 1949)
M. Frost: *English and Scottish Psalm and Hymn Tunes c.1543–1677* (London, 1953)
G. Chase: *America's Music from the Pilgrims to the Present* (New York, 1955)
L. Ellinwood, ed.: *The Charleston Hymnal of 1792* (Charleston, 1956)
T. W. Dean: *The Organ in Eighteenth Century English Colonial America* (diss., U. of Southern California, 1960)
I. Lowens: *Music and Musicians in Early America* (New York, 1964), 25ff
T. M. Finney: 'The Third Edition of Tufts' *Introduction* . . .', *JRME*, xiv (1966), 163
C. K. Shipton and J. E. Mooney: *National Index of American Imprints through 1800* (n.p., 1969)
D. K. Stigberg: *Congregational Psalmody in Eighteenth Century New England* (diss., U. of Illinois, Urbana, 1970)
G. W. Williams, ed.: *Jacob Eckhard's Choirmaster's Book of 1809* (Columbia, South Carolina, 1971)
N. Temperley: 'John Playford and the Metrical Psalms', *JAMS*, xxv (1972), 331–78
R. G. Appel: *The Music of the Bay Psalm Book* (Cambridge, Mass., 1975)

NICHOLAS TEMPERLEY (I, III, V), HOWARD SLENK (II), MARGARET MUNCK (IV,1), JOHN M. BARKLEY (IV,2)

Psalm tone. *See* PLAINCHANT; PSALM; *see also* MODE.

Psalmus (Lat.). PSALM.

Psalter [Psalterium] (Ger.). PSALTERY.

Psalter, Liturgical. At the heart of the DIVINE OFFICE lies the weekly chanting or reading of the entire book of *Psalms*, together with the biblical canticles. The arrangement of the psalms for the different days and the various parts of the Office has not always been the same everywhere; this is also true of the antiphons which introduce the individual psalms or groups of psalms. Two different ways of dividing the psalms can be briefly described here. One is outlined in the Rule of St Benedict (written *c*530, but thought to represent in many respects a codifying of earlier practice), which forms part of the monastic cursus. Psalms i–xix (Vulgate numbering) are said at Prime, from Monday to Saturday; xx–cviii at Matins (12 each day), and cix–cl at Vespers. In the monastic cursus some long psalms are divided into sections which are treated as separate psalms, and some short psalms are combined into one. Certain psalms of a distinctive character or with allusions to a particular time of day are omitted from the numerical series and given special places in the Divine Office. For example, Psalm iv is said at Compline; it ends with the verse 'In peace I will both lie down and sleep; for thou alone, O Lord, makest me dwell in safety'. In another arrangement of the Divine Office (followed by the secular clergy, and called the Roman cursus), Psalms i–cviii are said at Matins (i–xxv on Sunday and 12 each on the other days, with some omissions from the numerical series); and cix–cl at Vespers, again with some omissions. A variant of this, thought to reflect revisions made by Pope Gregory I (590–604), has Psalms i–xx for Sunday Matins, and xxi–xxv for Prime.

A liturgical psalter is an MS or printed edition of the book of Psalms modified (usually with additions) to adapt the text to a liturgical use. According to Righetti, the modifications fall into four main types: (1) the addition at the end of the psalter of such texts as the biblical canticles, the Creed, litany, *Te Deum* etc; (2) the insertion of marginal indications of the days of the week on which particular psalms are to be said, or of verses to be used as refrains; or at the end of each psalm either a doxology or a prayer; (3) the incorporation of invitatories, hymn incipits, antiphons (all of these sometimes with musical notation), versicles and short lessons (chapters) – this material provides a fairly complete picture of the Sunday and ferial Office; and (4) the rearrangement of a psalter of the preceding type, so that the psalms are presented in the order in which they are actually said, with account taken of the omissions referred to above.

The information contained in liturgical psalters of types 3 and 4 is fundamental to an understanding of the Sunday and ferial Office of a place; the Proper of the Time and of the Saints – often all that is given in an antiphoner – is essentially a more or less lengthy series of interruptions into that Office. Psalters are often separate books, but may commonly be incorporated in breviaries. Occasionally, however, antiphoners outline the liturgical psalter by giving the antiphons and psalm incipits for Matins, Lauds, Vespers and, rarely, the other hours as well for one full week. This is done after the first or the fifth Sunday after Epiphany. For examples, see *Corpus antiphonalium officii*, ed. R. Hesbert, i (Rome, 1963), nos.27–32 (Verona), and nos.36–42 (Ivrea); ii (Rome, 1965), nos.26–32 (Benevento), and nos.26–32⁹ (Silos); and *GB-WO* F.160 (published in PalMus, xii, 60ff).

BIBLIOGRAPHY
V. Leroquais: *Les bréviaires manuscrits des bibliothèques publiques de France* (Paris, 1934), i, x, xvff
——: *Les psautiers manuscrits latins des bibliothèques publiques de France* (Paris, 1940–41)
M. Righetti: *Manuale di storia liturgica*, i (Milan, 1945, 3/1964), 306ff
A. Frutaz and P. Siffrin: 'Salterio', *Enciclopedia cattolica*, x (Rome, 1953), 1702
J. Pascher: *Das Stundengebet der römischen Kirche* (Munich, 1954)
RUTH STEINER

Psalterer. A bowed string instrument of the late 17th century. It was intended for use in regulating choral singing in churches where neither organ nor other instrumental support was available, and it was adapted to the use of the musically untaught. Its invention is attributed to John Playford the elder (*d* 1686). No examples are known to survive, but the instrument appears to have had some currency during the early years of the 18th century. This is shown by a description in *The Psalmody* published by Henry Playford in 1699; by an advertisement in the 6th edition of John Playford's *The Whole Book of Psalms*, issued by Samuel and John Sprint and Henry Playford in 1700; and by a description published by James Leman in 1729. From these sources it is known that the psalterer (or 'psalmody', as it was evidently sometimes called) was similar in form to the bass viol of the period but had only two strings, tuned an octave apart and passing over a fretted fingerboard on which the stopping positions were marked by letters. By fingering the instrument according to a prepared letter sequence or code, the player could produce simple melodies for psalms or hymns and their appropriate basses; clearly these printed guides were supplied by certain music sellers.

A rather more advanced version of the instrument was suggested by Leman, who proposed the addition of a third or 'mean' string between the other two, tuned a 5th above the lower. He left the matter with the observation 'And this I suppose to be the utmost improvement that can be made upon this instrument'; in fact the idea of a marked and fretted fingerboard was to reappear in Sweden about 1829, with a more advanced instrument, the PSALMODIKON.

BIBLIOGRAPHY

W. Sherwin: *An Help to the Singing of Psalm-tunes, with Directions for Making an Instrument with One String* (London, 1725)
J. Leman: *A New Method of Learning Psalm-tunes with an Instrument of Music called the Psalterer* (London, 1729)
N. Temperley: 'John Playford and the Metrical Psalms', *JAMS*, xxv (1972), 331–78

PHILIP BATE

Psaltérion (Fr.). PSALTERY and DULCIMER.

Psaltērion. The psalter of the Greek Septuagint containing the 150 psalms divided into 20 kathismata. *See* KATHISMA.

Psalterium (Lat., from Gk. *psaltērion*). A term used in medieval texts for a variety of instruments, probably including the harp, crwth, PSALTERY and dulcimer. It is also the modern German term for the psaltery.

Psaltery [sawtry] (Fr. *psaltérion, saltere, sauterie*; Ger. *Psalterium, Psalter*; It. and Sp. *salterio*). An instrument of the zither family consisting of a raised piece of wood, or a wooden box with soundholes, with strings stretched parallel to the soundboard and attached at either side by wooden pegs or metal pins. Usually the strings are plucked, by the fingers or by plectra.

1. The ancient Greek and Latin terms. 2. The instrument.

1. THE ANCIENT GREEK AND LATIN TERMS. The Latin term 'psalterium' (Gk. *psaltērion*) was applied to a variety of ancient and medieval string instruments. It belongs to the category of words (like 'organum' and 'antiphona') that requires special study to trace frequent shifts in meaning. Tentatively the history of the term falls into three stages: its original usage, in its Greek form, as a term for the harp; as a term figuring prominently in ecclesiastical literature concerning the book of *Psalms*; and its eventual application to box zithers such as the psaltery and dulcimer.

The term was derived from the Greek 'psallein' ('to pluck with the fingers'); the related 'psaltria' might refer to female players of the more common kithara or lyre, but 'psaltērion' itself was reserved for the comparatively rare harp. Athenaeus (xiv, 636), for example, quoted Apollodorus identifying it with the MAGADIS, another term for harp; and Pseudo-Aristotle (*Problemata*, xix, 23) referred to the unequal strings of the triangular *psaltērion* (*see* TRIGŌNON).

The term entered Christian literature by way of the Septuagint, the translation of the Old Testament into Greek made in the 3rd century BC, which served as the basis for early Christian versions. The Septuagint in most cases rendered 'nebel', the Old Testament harp, by either 'nabla' or else (especially in the psalms) 'psaltērion'. At the same time it translated the Hebrew 'mizmōr', which occurs in the superscription of 57 psalms, as 'psalmos', a hymn sung with harp; this led Greek-speaking Jews to adopt for the entire book the name 'biblos psalmōn', ('book of psalms'), and eventually simply 'psaltērion' ('psalter'). Jerome corroborated these usages in the Vulgate by rendering 'nebel' as 'psalterium' with even greater consistency than the Septuagint.

These circumstances, that the book of *Psalms* as well as one of its most frequently mentioned instruments were both called 'psalterium', have assured for the term a rich existence in Christian literature. Its hundreds of occurrences in patristic and medieval commentary on the psalms serve mostly as starting-points for allegorical exegeses, but a number of passages have at least some organological significance. Eusebius of Caesarea established in his prologue to the psalter (*PG*, xxiii, 73) the notion that David stands in the midst of his four subordinate Levite musicians, Asaph, Ethan, Heman and Idithun, holding the *psalterium*. Later, Isidore of Seville (*GS*, i, 23) described the instrument as being shaped like the triangular Greek letter *delta*, a reference found in most subsequent psalter prologues. Meanwhile, commentary on Psalm xxxii.2, following the lead of Basil (*PG*, xxix, 328), regularly referred to the contrast between the kithara with its soundchest at the bottom of the instrument and the *psalterium* with its soundchest at the top, a feature corroborated by ancient depictions of harps (Wegner, plates 68, 70, 72). These references add little to present organological knowledge, but do at least suggest general unanimity among Christian, Jewish and Greek sources in their identification of 'psalterium' with the triangular harp. At the same time the Christians declare, rather too categorically, that the instrument had ten strings in imitation of the ten commandments, a concept deriving from occasional Septuagint phrases such as 'en decachordō psalteriō' (Psalm xcii.4).

In the Carolingian period a contradictory tradition arose when the *psalterium* was said to be 'quadratum' (rectangular). The earliest extant source for this notion, Rabanus Maurus's *De universo* (*PL*, cxi, 498), pronounced it in the same passage to be both 'quadratum' and 'ut alii volunt, in modum deltae literae' ('as others prefer, in the shape of the letter delta'). Subsequently the two conceptions of its shape co-existed: the triangular in the more conventional psalter commentaries (e.g. Honorius of Autun, *PL*, clxxii, 269), and the rectangular in the group of texts associated with the curious letter of Pseudo-Jerome to Dardanus. The former is illustrated chiefly by depictions of David holding a variety of string instruments, many of which bear resemblance to real instruments (both contemporary and classical); while the latter is illustrated with a schematic rectangular shape traversed by ten lines,

1. *Page from an early MS of the Pseudo-Jerome epistle to Dardanus, northern France, mid-9th century (F-AN 18, f.13r); King David holds the so-called 'psalterium decachordum' or 'psalterium quadratum' – several other schematic instruments appear, also inspired by the text*

suggesting a pseudo-instrument inspired by the text. It is this latter instrument which some organologists have singled out as the *psalterium decachordum* (see fig.1).

The precise steps leading to the last stage in the history of the term 'psalterium' – its application to box-zithers which came into the West by way of Moorish Spain and Byzantium – have not received definitive study. The underlying reason for the change in the term's meaning, however, may have been the general resemblance of the prevailing two-dimensional illustration (of the triangular or rectangular *psalterium*) in early medieval manuscript illumination and sculpture to the more complex yet equally flat shapes of contemporary zithers. Frequently the artist seems to have rendered a harp as a zither by failing to isolate one of its sides as a soundchest and by giving the impression of a solid board or bow behind the strings. This, together with the absence of a neck on either instrument, as well as the general fluidity of early medieval instrumental terminology, renders the final, contradictory application of the term not at all surprising.

2. THE INSTRUMENT. The early history of the psaltery is as yet unfathomed, as there is insufficient coincidence between verbal descriptions and visual representations. The *asor* referred to in *Psalms* and the *plinthion* of the Greeks may, for instance, have been psalteries, but suitable contemporary corroboration from the visual arts is lacking. A carved ivory box from Nimrud, dating from about 800 BC (now in the British Museum, no.118179), shows two instruments with rectangular frames with approximately ten parallel lines stretched across them. If these lines represent strings, the instruments could be classed as psalteries, but if not, they might be some form of percussion instrument.

The triangular and rectangular psalteries mentioned in the letter from Pseudo-Jerome to Dardanus may or may not have actually existed when this hoax was perpetrated in about the 9th century AD, but from that time onwards they appear more and more frequently in the visual arts, played generally by David and his musicians or by Elders of the Apocalypse. Some examples are fantasies which could never have worked, while others display a knowledge of craftsmanship that must have been based on fact. The words 'rote', 'rota' and 'rotta', much associated with the lyre family, were sometimes also applied to the triangular psaltery: in one piece of evidence, on an 11th-century capital in the cloister of the abbey of Moissac, a musician holding a triangular psaltery appears with a carved inscription naming the instrument as a *rota*. This carving is one of many that could be mistaken for a triangular harp, but other examples, particularly manuscript illustrations, show that the strings of the psaltery run parallel to the soundboard. The absence of soundholes for many of these representations may indicate that such psalteries were basically raised pieces of wood rather than hollow boxes. From the 12th century onwards, however, soundholes appear with greater frequency, suggesting the presence of such a box.

By this time the Eastern psaltery known as *qānūn* (from the Greek 'kanōn') had entered Spain with the Moors and influenced the development of the European psaltery. Its name was absorbed into other languages, becoming *canon* in Latin, *caño* in Spanish, etc., while smaller or 'half-shaped' versions of the instrument were known as *micanon* (Fr.), *Metzkanon* (Ger.), *mezzocan-*

2. Trapeziform psaltery with three strings to a note: detail from the altarpiece 'The Coronation of the Virgin, with Adoring Saints' (14th century), School of Orcagna, in the National Gallery, London; for a further illustration see CANON(ii)

3. Psaltery-harp: detail from 'The Coronation of the Virgin' (c1350), by an unknown German artist, in the Städelsches Kunstinstitut, Frankfurt am Main

(a)

(b)

4. (a) Pig's head psaltery: detail from the painting 'Musician angels' (1480) by Hans Memling in the Koninklijk Museum voor Schone Kunsten, Antwerp; (b) Bohemian wing: miniature from the 'Passional of Abbess Kunhuta' (1319–21) (CS-Pu)

one (It.), *medius canon*, *medium canale* and *medicinale* (Lat.), and *medio caño* (Sp.). Trapeziform instruments with three or four strings to a note, which were played mostly in southern Europe, were based on it (see fig.2). The preferred instrument in the north was one with incurved sides, later known as the 'pig's head psaltery' on account of its shape (see fig.4a). This was generally single- or double-strung. None of these types was restricted to any one district, however, and they all appear in the *Cantigas de Santa Maria* of Alfonso El Sabio of Castile (reigned 1252–84). (It is worth noting that in Italian manuscripts David is often depicted playing a psaltery, whereas in corresponding northern sources he plays a harp.) The Latin names 'ala' and 'medio ala', used sometimes for wing-shaped psalteries, have led to the application of the term 'Bohemian wing' to the varied shapes used in eastern Europe (see fig.4b). Also in eastern Europe there flourished the instrument now known as the psaltery-harp, which combined the basic features of both harp and psaltery and thus contained a double soundbox (see fig.3).

The strings of the later medieval psaltery were normally metal, but earlier ones may more often have been gut. They were plucked by the fingers or by plectra, or by a combination of both, as can be seen in the manuscript from 15th-century Piedmont (*GB-Lbm*

Add.27697, f.105v). When the player needed to move around he carried the instrument on a strap round his neck and played it, thus supported, in front of his chest; otherwise he sat with it on his lap or on a table.

The psaltery was widely used up to about 1500, being referred to frequently in lists of musicians such as that of the Feast of Westminster in 1306, where performers included 'Gillotin le Sautreour' and 'Janyn le Sautreour qui est ove Mons. de Percy'. Like most other medieval instruments it had no specific repertory but was used to play whatever music the occasion demanded. Its use as a solo instrument is well demonstrated by Chaucer's often-quoted passage from 'The Miller's Tale':

> And al above ther lay a gay sautrie,
> On which he made a-nyghtes melodie
> So swetely that all the chambre rong:
> And *Angelus ad virginem* he song;

later in the same poem there is another reference:

> He kiste hire sweete and taketh his sawtrie,
> And pleyeth faste, and maketh melodie.

As its strings had to be tuned within one scale before performance, the psaltery could not cope with Renaissance chromaticism, and from the late 15th century onwards it was used less than before, although it never became extinct. From the Baroque era there survive several examples of a double psaltery, known as 'arpanetta' in Italy and 'Spitzharfe' in Germany. Descended from the *qānūn*, which it resembled in shape, this instrument stood upright on a table and had strings on each side, the treble ones on the right and the bass on the left. It was used mainly for domestic music, as was also the BELL HARP (probably invented by John Simcock of Bath around 1700).

By the 18th century, however, the psaltery had evolved into several quite different instruments. When struck with hammers it had a quite separate existence as the dulcimer; provided with a keyboard mechanism, it had become the harpsichord; the application of frets produced the zither, which in its simplest form, the *Scheitholt*, can be seen among the 16th-century wall-paintings in the church at Rynkbye, Denmark. In the 20th century the psaltery has been revived for the performance of early music. It is used occasionally in schools, as is also, in Germany, a bowed psaltery in different sizes, promoted by Edgar Stahmer in the 1930s. As a folk and national instrument the psaltery has survived in such forms as the Russian *gusli* and the Finnish *kantele*, but these forms have been somewhat affected by innovations due to modern technology.

BIBLIOGRAPHY
S. Virdung: *Musica getutscht* (Basle, 1511/R1970)
M. Agricola: *Musica instrumentalis deudsch* (Wittenberg, 1528/R1969, enlarged 5/1545)
M. Praetorius: *Syntagma musicum*, ii (Wolfenbüttel, 1618, 2/1619/R1958), 76, pl.xxxvi
M. Mersenne: *Harmonie universelle* (Paris, 1636–7/R1963; Eng. trans., 1957), 224ff
F. W. Galpin: *Old English Instruments of Music* (London, 1910, rev. 4/1965 by T. Dart), 5, 21, 42ff, 228f
——: *A Textbook of European Musical Instruments* (London, 1937), 84ff
C. Sachs: *The History of Musical Instruments* (New York, 1940), 117f, 136, 262, 292f
A. J. Hipkins: 'Psaltery', *Grove 5*
A. Buchner: *Musical Instruments through the Ages* (Prague, 1956, 4/1962)
R. Hammerstein: 'Instrumenta Hieronymi', *AMw*, xvi (1959), 117
G. Hayes: 'Musical Instruments', *NOHM*, iii (1960), 466ff, 481ff, 491
J. La Rue and J. B. Holland: 'Stimmer's Women Musicians: a Unique Series of Woodcuts', *Bulletin of the New York Public Library*, lxiv (1960), 9f
R. Stevenson: *Spanish Music in the Age of Columbus* (The Hague, 1960, rev. 2/1964), 8, 22, 45f, 48
H. Avenary: 'Hieronymus' Epistel über die Musikinstrumente und ihre altöstlichen Quellen', *AnM*, no.16 (1961), 55
A. Baines, ed.: *Musical Instruments through the Ages* (Harmondsworth, 1961, rev. 1966), 204ff, 222
H. H. Carter: *A Dictionary of Middle English Musical Terms* (Bloomington, Indiana, 1961)
H. Steger: *David, Rex et Propheta* (Nuremberg, 1961)
H. H. Dräger and M. Wegner: 'Psalterium', *MGG*
M. Wegner: *Griechenland*, Musikgeschichte in Bildern, ii/4 (Leipzig, 1963)
F. Ll. Harrison and J. Rimmer: *European Musical Instruments* (London, 1964), 15f, 18, 27, 70
S. Marcuse: *Musical Instruments: a Comprehensive Dictionary* (New York, 1964)
R. Rastall: 'The Minstrels of the English Royal Households, 25 Edward I – 1 Henry VIII: an Inventory', *RMARC*, iv (1964), 1–41
A. C. Baines: *European and American Musical Instruments* (London, 1966), 60f
J. W. Mc Kinnon: 'Musical Instruments in Medieval Psalm Commentaries and Psalters', *JAMS*, xxi (1968), 3
J. Rimmer: *Ancient Musical Instruments of Western Asia in the British Museum* (London, 1969)
K. Kos: *Musikinstrumente im mittelalterlichen Kroatien* (Zagreb, 1972)
T. Seebass: *Musikdarstellung und Psalterillustration im früheren Mittelalter* (Berne, 1973)
W. Stauder: *Alte Musikinstrumente* (Brunswick, 1973)
S. Marcuse: *A Survey of Musical Instruments* (London, 1975), 209ff
J. Montagu: *The World of Medieval and Renaissance Musical Instruments* (Newton Abbot, 1976)
D. Munrow: *Instruments of the Middle Ages and Renaissance* (London, 1976)
C. Page: 'Musical Instruments in Medieval Latin Biblical Glosses', *Fellowship of Makers and Restorers of Historical Instruments: Bulletin and Communications* (April 1976), 28
——: 'References to String Materials in some Medieval Texts c.1050–c.1430: an Annotated Anthology', *Fellowship of Makers and Restorers of Historical Instruments: Bulletin and Communications* (April 1976), 33
M. Remnant: *Musical Instruments of the West* (London, 1978)
    JAMES W. Mc KINNON (1), MARY REMNANT (2)

Psaltēs. A chanter in a Byzantine choir.

Psaltikē. See AKOLOUTHIAI.

Psaltikē technē. The 'art of the psaltikē' – a new method of Byzantine chanting which coincided with the appearance of AKOLOUTHIAI in the 14th century. Essentially, it amplified traditional musical forms and subjected them to an exacting discipline in their interpretation and execution. At the same period there appeared a number of elaborate treatises and musical exercises which aimed at explaining the new art. Its new features were the introduction of the phthorai, of subsidiary neumes of ornamentation (called cheironomiai), and of TERETIS-MATA. See PHTHORA.

DIMITRI CONOMOS

Psantria (Aramaic). Ancient Jewish instrument, possibly a lyre or harp; *see* JEWISH MUSIC, §I, 4(iv).

Psellus [Psellos], Michael [Konstantin] (*b* Nicomedia or Constantinople, 1018; *d* before 1080, ?1078). Byzantine scholar, politician and philosopher. He began his career as a government official and eventually became imperial secretary and professor of philosophy at the University of Constantinople. He fell out of favour and retired to a monastery on Mt Olympus in Bithynia, but later returned to court service and finally attained the office of prime minister.

His encyclopedic knowledge and above all his revival of Platonism exerted an influence beyond that of Byzantine culture on western European humanism. Three of his letters are concerned with musical questions; one describes the essence and effect of the art in a discussion of ancient Greek music. His commentary on Plato's *Psychogony* is related to the *Timaeus* commentary of Proclus; his introduction to rhythm draws on the *Elements of Rhythm* of Aristoxenus. Elsewhere he touches on questions of acoustics, as in the description of an echo in a hall in Nicomedia.

A work on the four mathematical disciplines (*Syntagma eusynopton eis tas tessaras mathēmatikas epistēmas*) with an introduction to harmonics, printed several times since the Renaissance, was not written by Psellus but by an unknown author, possibly the monk Gregorius Solitarius, in about 1008. The method of investigation in the section on harmonics corresponds with that of the school of Aristoxenus: the names of the notes, intervals, systems, modes, scales and melopoeia are all discussed. In the theory of intervals, the focal point of the work, after the additive definition of the micro-interval, there is a consideration of harmony as numerical proportion following the traditions of Pythagoras and, above all, THEON OF SMYRNA. The more comprehensive treatises of GEORGIOS PACHYMERES and MANUEL BRYENNIUS depended largely on this compendium, the oldest known Byzantine musical treatise; their dependence is evident in the borrowings which they make in many places.

BIBLIOGRAPHY

K. Krumbacher: *Geschichte der byzantinischen Literatur*, ii (Munich, 1897), 433ff

H. Abert: 'Ein ungedruckter Brief des Michael Psellos über die Musik', *SIMG*, ii (1900–01), 333

C. Zervos: *Un philosophe néoplatonicien du XIe siècle: Michel Psellos* (Paris, 1920)

J. M. Hussey: *Church and Learning in the Byzantine Empire* (London, 1937), 37ff, 61ff, 73ff

G. Ostrogorsky: *Geschichte des byzantinischen Staates* (Munich, 2/1952), 261ff

H. G. Beck: *Kirche und theologische Literatur im byzantinischen Reich* (Munich, 1959), 538ff

L. Richter: 'Antike Überlieferungen in der byzantinischen Musiktheorie', *DJbM*, vi (1962), 90, 94

Cambridge Medieval History, iv/2 (Cambridge, 1967), esp. 281ff

L. Richter: 'Psellus' Treatise on Music in Mizler's *Bibliothek*', *Studies in Eastern Chant*, ii (London, 1971), 112

LUKAS RICHTER

Pseudo-Aristoteles. *See* LAMBERTUS.

Pseudo-Chilston. The name by which an anonymous treatise in *GB-Lbm* Lansdowne 763 on DISCANT is now generally cited. The treatise was wrongly attributed by Burney and Hawkins to the author of three treatises which follow it in the MS. *See* CHILSTON.

Pseudo-Guido Caroli loci. Name often given to the anonymous author of a 12th-century discant treatise; *see* GUY DE CHERLIEU, §3.

Psychoacoustics. *See* PSYCHOLOGY OF MUSIC, §II, 4(ii); *see also* HEARING, §4.

Psychoanalysis. *See* PSYCHOLOGY OF MUSIC, §I, 4.

Psychology of music.
I. Background and theories. II. Perception. III. Memory. IV. Assessment.

I. Background and theories

1. Introduction. 2. Up to World War I: (i) To 1850 (ii) 1850 to World War I. 3. Between the wars: (i) Mentalism (ii) Behaviourism (iii) Gestalt theory. 4. Psychoanalytic theory. 5. Recent developments: (i) Information theory (ii) Cybernetic theory (iii) Artificial intelligence.

1. INTRODUCTION. The psychology of music is an area within psychology directed to the study of all forms of musical behaviour from the most primitive to the most highly developed. Its methods are those of experimental psychology and it draws upon all findings of relevance within the larger discipline, including clinical and neurological studies. The scope of psychology itself is wide, ranging from biology, genetics and animal behaviour, through human perception, cognition and personality, to social and ethnic studies. Ultimately musical psychology must be concerned with the historical development of music, with the cognitive processes and emotional responses involved in music, with the exercise of musical skills, with the variety of musical personalities and processes of creation, with the role of music in healing mental or physical illness, and with the social psychology of collective music. The discipline is as yet in its infancy, despite its Pythagorean origins, and hitherto research has centred predominantly on perceptual studies of the attributes of sound and on surveys of musical aptitudes, leaving other equally important areas sparsely explored.

Advances in science come about by changes of metaphor or conceptual orientation which engender new lines of inquiry. The post-World War II conceptual innovations in psychology which gave new energy to research also brought experiments on the perceptual and cognitive aspects of musical psychology more within the realm of the possible. 'We do not know all about the human mind. But we have learned how to go about looking for what we do not know' (Lindsay and Norman, 1972). This observation well described the infancy of the psychology of music in the 1970s, a principal task being to discover how the human being makes sense of music.

Three postwar conceptual innovations in psychology offer a means of finding out about the musical mind. One is a rapprochement between the cognitive and the Freudian learning theories (Dollard and Miller, 1950; Pribram, 1968; Pribram and Hill, 1976); this enables the psychologist to relate emotional to cognitive memory. Musical memory accommodates not only harmonic and rhythmic elements of music but also a spectrum of qualitative differences in aesthetic and affective experience.

A second influential model in psychology is the cybernetic view of man as a purposeful self-regulating biological system, which is kept in balance by feedback in the cycle of perception (input) and action (output). This notion of homeostatic balance originated with Cannon and was shared by Freud in his constancy principle. But its adoption in the cybernetic view enables the psychologist to look at smooth, continuous perception–action sequences which contain variations in the information load, such as music, without regarding them as chains of aggregated segments of behaviour. The musical perception–action sequence maintains a balance of intellectual control and expressivity, and this is mediated by intrinsic feedback.

The third innovation in psychology particularly appropriate to music was the concept of 'information' and the limited human capacity to process it in the perception–action cycle. Interpreting music, whether classical or avant-garde, is a continuing endeavour to make its forms and diction apparent to the listener, who makes sense of it according to his experience. However, there may be more 'information' in the music than he may be able to take in while hearing it. Though information theory may not provide a method of measuring it, the concept of 'information' is important to the psychology of music.

Within psychology music has many affinities as an object of study. It shares with language the problem facing psycholinguistics, that of explaining the capacity to generate and comprehend syntactical utterances and to relate reception of acoustic properties to understanding. It shares with the visual arts the task of relating sensory and cognitive processes to creativity and aesthetic experience. Yet unlike both linguistic and visual skills, music does not serve to communicate the furniture and circumstances of life, though it does seem to communicate subjective states. Although (as far as we know) music is an essential attribute of the human species, it does not further that overriding biological priority of information exchange. Music, unlike speech, is not vital to the survival of the species, but it makes special and selective use of the bodily dispositions underlying speech and gesture.

Music, like language, develops within a culture, and the musical scales and rhythms of each culture have within them elements experienced by the members of that culture as expressive each of a certain communicable mood. Studies of indigenous music which relate style to culture, such as cantometrics (Lomax, 1968), are the concern of the psychology of music. Comparative musicology (studying musical systems of different cultures) provides evidence relevant to the nature of innate human receptivity to the sounds of music, to what extent it is morphology-dependent, to what extent a cultural skill. In fact, the psychology of music is engaged in bridging the gap between ethnomusicology and psychoacoustics.

There is a large body of research in psychoacoustics but there has not been a great deal that was specifically orientated towards music. The effect of musical experience on discriminatory powers has so far not been studied in detail, and musicians are often surprised at what psychoacousticians have to say about these powers. The important new development is that of relating psychoacoustic phenomena to the psychological processes of learning. This analysis of sensory and cognitive processes in learning music is a beginning, which in the future may lead to an understanding of the relations between early or primitive learning and the highly complex skills of the professional musician.

See also AMUSIA; ANALYSIS; CONSONANCE; HEARING; MUSIC THERAPY; PHYSICS OF MUSIC; SOUND.

2. UP TO WORLD WAR I.

(i) *To 1850.* The origins of the psychology of music may be traced back to the Greek philosophers of the 6th century BC who sought to integrate the laws of nature with theories of aesthetics. The correspondence between heard musical consonances (octave, 5th and 4th) and certain simple ratios of monochord string lengths was interpreted by the Pythagoreans as a manifestation of pleasure-in-proportion, which seems to have been due to a kind of super-sense above the baser ones. Plato's prescription of the study of harmony as conducive to the liberation of the soul from the tyranny of the senses implies a similar psychological distinction between mere perception (directly dependent on sense organs) and an inbuilt response to the rhythms of the universe and to proportion, leading to a state of being where the flux of the senses is resolved in an equilibrium. Today some psychologists regard aesthetic pleasure as measurable in terms of arousal of the autonomic nervous system as reflected in heart rate, respiration, electrical skin conductivity (the Galvanic Skin Reflex) or electrical waves in the brain as shown by electro-encephalograph recordings (EEG). But the classical notion of a more perfect state of being as an elevated level of quiescence or harmonic resolution has yielded to a homeostatic model which recognizes that it is essential to well-being that arousal should fluctuate around an optimal level. In prolonged periods of reduced and featureless sensory experience the integration of perception and thought breaks down into hallucination. The necessity for fluctuations in sensory input suggests that the tensions of harmonic progression have equal importance with its resolutions in achieving the optimal state of the musician's nervous system that characterizes his aesthetic pleasure.

Another implicit psychological assumption in Pythagorean theory was that of identical correspondence between a specific external property (string length) and the resulting sensation of tone. In Western thought such 'naive realism' began to be systematically modified only with the advent of experimental psychology and its methodical investigation of the relations between physical facts (e.g. wave frequency) and facts of sensation (e.g. pitch). Leibniz, for instance, held that the beauty of music consisted in 'the agreement of numbers and in the counting of the beats or vibrations of sounding bodies, which meet at certain intervals'. He seemed to grade degree of consonance with simplicity of the ratio of the interval even though he considered the 'soul' unaware of the counting it performs. (He distinguished between 'apperception' and perception without such awareness.)

Although 18th-century theorists such as Mattheson (see Lenneberg, 1958; Kivy, 1973), Rameau (1750) and Tartini (1754) emphasized sensation and the affects more than had their mathematically- and mechanistically-minded 17th-century predecessors (*see* PHYSICS OF MUSIC, §§1, 2), rationalism survived even as late as the argument of Delezenne (1826–7) that the sense of interval must be innate and not a product of convention because 'our scale . . . can be found in identical form throughout Europe'. But despite his anthropological parochialism (surprising so long after the Age of Discovery), Delezenne's experimental techniques were advanced in their scientific rigour. He devised adjustment tasks for tuning octaves, 5ths, 3rds and 6ths, in random order of presentation, with visual cues eliminated; and he correlated the accuracy of his subjects' performance with the differences in their musical training.

(ii) *1850 to World War I.* When psychology as a whole forsook the philosopher's armchair for the experimental laboratory – borrowing theoretical models from contemporary physics and combining empiricist interest in sensation with advances in physiology – research in the psychology of music was at first most energetically pursued in Germany. Both Helmholtz (1863) and Fechner (1860, 1876) were originally physicists and physiologists. Fechner continued the classical effort to link physical laws to aesthetics, but he used experimental methods which introduced some objectivity into the assessment of aesthetic preferences. The method of preference judgments for 'pleasingness' was regarded as appropriate to musical aesthetics and has survived until now (Valentine, 1962), but increasingly sophisticated methods of statistical correlation and multivariate analysis have enabled certain dimensions of artistic attributes to be more clearly defined, although the influence of cultural fashions and personal associations as confounding variables continues to impede progress. Fechner's own 16 principles of the psychology of aesthetics were the fruit not of his empirical findings but of his personal observations, and no scientific psychological theory of musical aesthetics has yet emerged.

Helmholtz concentrated on the psychoacoustic aspects of music and was not interested in individual differences of taste. From the structure of the basilar membrane (*see* HEARING) he deduced a model of pitch perception by resonance of the hair cells, using the attractive analogy of sympathetic vibration as exemplified by the strings of the piano. All modern 'place theories' are but modifications of his hypothesis that the frequency range is represented lengthwise on the basilar membrane, although his resonance principle is no longer tenable, nor is his explanation of combination tones.

Helmholtz's theory rested on Ohm's Law of Acoustics (which held that the ear in effect performs a Fourier analysis on a complex sound wave, discerning each partial tone in the harmonic series, for instance), and Muller's Law of Specific Nerve Energies (that each nerve fibre may react to but one point in a range of input), which he interpreted as meaning that there would be one nerve for each pitch that could be discriminated. But he saw that a crucial question – still unanswered – remained: why do we usually hear complex tones as unanalysed? Ohm's Law had in fact been founded on resonance experiments by Seebeck (1846) which showed that the sensations of each overtone did not correspond to their physical amplitudes, a problematic finding for Ohm and Helmholtz and one which they dismissed. Nevertheless, *Die Lehre von den Tonempfindungen* (Eng. version, *On the Sensations of Tone*) remains essential reading. It is a monumental synthesis of physics, physiology and musical psychology (although there have since been great advances in psychoacoustics).

Mach (1886), like Helmholtz, worked on the sensory psychology of vision and audition. Analysing the perception of temporal order and of musical rhythms, he anticipated the perceptual-moment hypothesis (of a central integrator based on very small units of time), somewhat foreshadowing current theories that attribute such a basic rhythmic integrator to the electrical rhythms of the nervous system. His view that recognizing the time ratios of two rhythms depends on their being simple ratios is essentially that underlying investigations of rhythm carried out 70 years later by Fraisse (1956). This phase in musical psychology, particularly the work of Stumpf and Mach, contained the seeds of later Gestalt approaches.

The study of individual differences in musical aptitude grew out of this early sensory psychology combined with the influence of Galton's anthropometric methods and his studies (1869) of the heredity of gifted people (including 120 musicians). Stumpf, himself a musician–scientist, devised tests which he administered to both musical and unmusical people (1883); and the late 19th century saw the first theoretical attempt to define musicality, that of Billroth (1895). Révész (1916) followed Stumpf's lead in devising tests, and made a detailed study of a child prodigy. Thus far tests were not standardized; the pioneer in objective testing and inventing apparatus for such tests was Carl Seashore, in the USA, whose work began in the early part of the 20th century.

3. BETWEEN THE WARS.

(*i*) *Mentalism.* Between the two world wars much experimental work was done by psychologists who adhered to the view of Wundt and Tichener that conscious experience could be analysed into atoms of mental feelings and sensations. Body and mind were viewed as distinct but parallel entities. The sensory registering (by the ear) of physical sound was seen as being presented for interpretation to that repository of musical talent, the mind. In present-day psychology distinctions between sensation and perception are difficult to maintain in those terms since information is known to be progressively integrated at all levels of the auditory pathway, and it would be logically impossible to draw a line between 'ear' and 'mind', or to define a 'raw' sense-datum. The notion that the ear conveys a sensation to the mind which the mind in turn listens to begs the question of how the mind might 'listen', and obscures the fact that the coded pattern of brain activity during perception represents the musical experience.

This period culminated in three books on the psychology of music, by Mursell (1937), Seashore (1938) and Schoen (1940). Schoen was principally concerned with the affective and aesthetic influence of music, Mursell with the elements of music and particularly rhythm. Seashore's main contribution was in mapping certain musical phenomena such as instrumental timbre and vibrato, and in measuring musical aptitudes. His mentalistic stance was to be much criticized by the behaviourists.

(*ii*) *Behaviourism.* The mid-20th-century antithesis between behaviourism and cognitive and personality theories has made it difficult in many respects to study music experimentally at all: there appears to have been a no-man's-land between psychophysical experiments on the basic elements of music and those aesthetic theories which draw largely upon Gestalt or Freudian principles. Behaviourists regard non-experimental Freudian theory as untestable, and Gestalt theory as wrong-headed; but at least the argument was joined over work by the Gestaltists on visual perception, whereas musical perception never became an area for debate.

Behaviourism influenced the experimental psychology of learning. But again few experiments were done specifically with musical material, and many conclusions were transferred from research on verbal learning, the assumption being that the memory processes of language and music would be strictly analogous. Behaviourism took over empiricist principles of association of ideas, applying them to the connection between environmental stimuli and responses. The Pavlovian conditioned reflex provided a model of an irreducible unit in a chain of learnt association responses. The choice of what constitutes an irreducible stimulus–response unit, however, is arbitrary (see Chomsky, 1959), and indeed the present lack of rapport between psychoacoustic and musical experiments may be partly due to insufficient regard for individual differences in musical education that confound the stimulus–response formulation. This formulation, allied to the total rejection of introspective evidence, minimized the possibility of regarding man as self-organizing, purposive or creative; thus originality in musical composition or performance would not be accounted for by the theory. Also, in regarding learning of stimulus–response links as the simplest principle of psychological explanation (the Law of Parsimony), it minimizes the attribution of musicality to innate or hereditary factors. In his behaviourist account of musical psychology (1953), Lundin said, for instance, that 'Physical structures are inherited, but no psychic "gifts" or "powers" are'. Thus the notion of an inherited element in musical intelligence is unacceptable to a behaviourist, who would recognize embouchure or shape of hand as physical structures while presumably rejecting 'ear' and brain, and who would regard a disposition to respond to music as being entirely a culturally acquired characteristic.

Most important, the theoretical framework of behaviourism makes it difficult to research or even consider the self-directed selectivity of attention and the complex integration of perceptual–motor skills which are basic to musical performance. To a behaviourist, learning comprises chains of responses linked by time-contiguity or associative factors and governed by reward, punishment or drive-reduction which occurs after the response. But musical learning often occurs through sensory effects during the response itself. Not until the advent of cybernetic psychology with its concept of feedback was the way open to a psychology of musical skills with an appropriate theoretical framework. Although little investigation has yet been carried out specifically of musical learning in cybernetic terms, the study of control and communication in self-steering systems introduces into psychology the possibility of dealing with the continuity of skilled behaviour, like music-making, for which the behaviourist reduction to discrete units is unsuited.

(iii) *Gestalt theory*. 'Gestalt' means form, entity or configuration, and Gestalt theory is antithetical to behaviourism in emphasizing the immediate perception of whole configurations as opposed to aggregates of separately perceived component elements. Although from the outset examples from music were cited, comparatively few experiments were devoted to it; the theory was predominantly worked out on experimental evidence of visual phenomena, and led to a proposed neurological model of free-floating electricity in the brain, acting analogously to magnetic field forces and somehow outside the system of neurons and synapses. This now discredited part of the theory was less appropriate to the temporal patterns of music than to the spatial ones of the visual field; and there may be no basis for a unitary theory of the perception of visual and musical forms, perception of temporal and spatial patterns making different demands upon the nervous system despite the sequential nature of eye movements in scanning. Gestaltists recognized from the first that there is a problem in the immediate perception of pattern in sequential sensory experience: 'in order to apprehend a melody it is not enough to have the impression of a momentarily sounding tone in consciousness, but – where the tone is not the first one – it is necessary to have at least a few of the preceding tones simultaneously presented in memory' (Von Ehrenfels, 1890). Today this paradox of simultaneous yet sequential musical perception is studied in terms of varying degrees of durability of short-term memory traces, current neurological theory distinguishing between short-term reverberation of neuronal circuits and long-term structural changes at synapses of nerve pathways, and memorability of musical passages being dependent upon the education and coding strategies of the individual.

As against the behaviourist principle of synthesis of separate atoms of perception, the Gestalt view is of a whole immediately perceived as such, though 'what is perceived depends on the significance of the object for the perceiving subject. What has no significance is generally overlooked' (Koffka, 1935). Then with continued experience the whole becomes increasingly articulated with perceptual details, again analogous to the increasingly finer detail visually perceptible as illumination is intensified. But in contrast to visual perception, a more articulate perception of the entire pattern of a piece of music can occur only through repeated hearings, a process different in kind from the scannings of an omnipresent display. Certainly the role of memory is more evident. Moreover Koffka's 'significance', the degree of articulation not overlooked at first hearing, depends on the particular musical education of the listener, stored in long-term memory. It is sometimes not clear in Gestalt theory whether the immediately perceived owes its im-

mediacy to innate properties of the nervous system or to learning. In harmonic perception, as in that of complex tones, Gestaltists regard a chord as an immediately perceived whole (rather than as the sum of its constituent notes), but whether such perception is innate or whether 'neural systems' or 'cell assemblies' (Hebb, 1949) have been built up in the brain by cultural learning is not always made clear. The apprehension of the Gestalten of larger musical forms, however, is accepted as dependent upon education.

Gestalt theory had its greatest impact in musical psychology on the study of rhythm in the sense of temporal patterning. Koffka studied the perceptual organization involved where trains of metronomic beats were subjectively perceived as grouped in either twos or threes, a phenomenon that Carl Seashore (1918) termed 'subjective rhythm'. Gestaltists would, unlike behaviourists, view this tendency as innate. Duple subjective rhythm seems more prevalent than triple, a finding congruent with Curt Sachs's historical survey of rhythm (1953) and often associated with the symmetry of the body. Of the six Gestalt principles of perceptual organization (invariably illustrated by visual rather than auditory examples in psychology textbooks), the principle of proximity seems the most directly relevant to musical rhythm where, for example, in hearing as in vision, the x grouping in ex.1 is more immediate than the y.

Ex.1

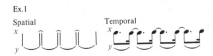

It is less easy to construe musically some of the other Gestalt principles, such as that of 'closure'. At one time Gestalt theory had a certain impact on musical teaching methods, increasing the advocacy of learning wholes rather than parts. But clearly the perception of wholes at different hierarchical levels of organization in a musical work differs in immediacy, and in any case involuntary perception of configurations at a lower level cannot in the musician's working life preclude analysis at all levels. The great merit of the Gestalt movement was, rather, to focus attention on the perception of temporal patterns, an area in musical psychology still overdue for experimental research.

4. PSYCHOANALYTIC THEORY. Perhaps because of the comparative neglect of music by Freud himself there is no single psychoanalytic theory of music; and the various contributions of psychoanalysts, whether studies of individual musicians or of music's role in personality structure, do not make a coherent whole. Before the rise of ego psychology the emphasis was upon music as sublimation, as an outlet for excessively strong excitation arising from sources of sexuality. The later ego psychologists often regard music as a mode of mastering anxiety by working through (Kohut, 1956), or as a defence against threat, or as an 'autonomous' ego activity freed from the exigencies of inner conflict.

An important aspect of music discussed by Bardas (1919) and, later, psychoanalysts (e.g. Pfeifer, 1923; Kohut, 1956) is that because of its presumed origins in infantile auditory experience and vocalization it is a non-referential language which facilitates benign regression by its power to express deep emotions while evading the dangers of verbal logic and articulation. Because it is in this way a 'safe' language, not explicitly involving the expression of relations to others and unlikely to be indiscreet, it has easier access to the unconscious (Coriat, 1945), a view important in the rise of music therapy. That music can express or evoke emotions not amenable to 'discursive projection' is widely accepted, though there are confusions in the literature between its relation to rhythms of life which are organic and to those complex patterns of sensitivity and defences which arise from an individual's life history and engender his particular response to music.

As to the individual's development of musicality, most writers stress the role of sound in the infant's autocentric primary organization of experience where 'sensing is extensive, primarily visceral, centred in the autonomic nervous system, and manifests itself in the form of emotion' (Spitz, 1965). At birth the infant is all id and no ego, with little or no sense of the boundary between self and external reality and, in particular, no sense of time by means of which to tolerate the delay of gratification. Mother–child pre-verbal communication initiates ego development, a sense of reality separate from self, and a capacity to understand moods expressed in the mother's voice and conveyed rather by such musical qualities as cadence, timbre and pace than by semantic content (of which she is probably more aware). The origins of musical experience in this pre-logical language are seen by psychoanalysts to explain why music resists definition in purely logical terms.

Some theorists stress the constitutional differences in sensitivity to auditory stimulation as possible determinants of musicality. Oversensitivity to noise might lead (Bregman and Escalona, 1949) to a selecting and focussing of attention to admit only pleasant sounds to consciousness, or might provoke attempts to master the anxiety associated with early auditory perception (Kohut and Levarie, 1950). It is emphasized that, while an infant can close his eyes, he cannot close his ears to escape frightening auditory experience, so that organizing this experience and searching for 'good' stimuli represents an attempt to control it. Adler (1917), on the other hand, suggested that overcompensation for hearing defects or inadequate auditory sensitivity could also take the form of musicianship. Other theorists emphasize early environment and the musicality of the mother, rather than sensitivity of hearing (Racker, 1951; Niederland, 1958; A. Freud, 1965). Gutheil (1954) traced music, as a mastery-type defence mechanism, back to the rhythm and time patterns of breast feeding, where maternal inadequacies might lead to faulty time control in the infant and subsequent musical activity as an attempt to redress this lack of control. Yates (1935) also saw in the cultivation of musical rhythm an attempt to establish the sureness and dependability of time. This aspect of music would be in Erikson's terms an adjunct in establishing the first stage of identity, the stage of trust versus mistrust.

More recent psychoanalytic theories of art associated with ego psychology take as their departure an expanded view of sublimation derived from certain observations of Freud's, notably in The Ego and the Id (1927). Sublimation takes place through the ego, but psychic energy is neutralized and does not remain inextricably associated with sexuality. As Kris (1952) noted, 'energy used in art creation is not only neutral but autonomous, that is, detached from the original conflict'.

This detaching of creative energy from sexuality significantly expanded a theory that postulated their original fused identity. But the Freudian concept of 'psychic energy' itself remains difficult to reconcile with the biological concept of energy taken in from the environment by metabolism and used in behaviour which maintains the equilibrium of the organism without any separation of psychic energy from the whole process. In regard to music, however, the essential question is whether sublimation as a source of musical activity can be accepted in its role as a mechanism of ego defence in spite of the unsatisfactory notion of psychic energy, and there seems no reason why it should be rejected, for creative activity may be seen as simply an impunitive way of dealing with frustration and conflict or the disturbances caused by traumatic memory.

A characteristic ego-psychology view of the arts is that they embody various forms of 'regression in the service of the ego' (Kris, 1952): the artist makes use of earlier modes of thought. These views raise in crucial form the question of how far music is to be assigned to primary, how far to secondary, process. Primary process, an unconscious id function based on the infantile pleasure principle, is the immediate discharge of tension through wish-fulfilling fantasy or dream, without structuring time and space or distinguishing between opposites. Secondary process, based on the reality principle, is an ego function where structural elements are sharply differentiated (the acquired knowledge of the regularities of the external world facilitating a tolerance of tension so that its resolution may be delayed), and is responsible for the design and organization of artistic creation. Some theorists lay predominant emphasis on primary process in music, seeing a strong parallel between art activity and dreams – and between 'dream work' and musical composition since both use mechanisms such as condensation, displacement, omission or reversal. To attribute to music the various psychoanalytic mechanisms of dreams, jokes or verbal errors is to imply that there is some common symbolism or representation in music upon which these mechanisms operate. In any case many theorists fail to distinguish clearly between a theory of musical appreciation and one of musical creativity. But others, notably Ehrenzweig (1953), draw a distinction between the craftsmanship of musical composition, which they see as an ego function, a conscious mode of formal organization, and the germinal creative process which occurs in the 'hidden layers of dangerous symbolism, in the unarticulated thought structures of the unconscious'.

Ehrenzweig also discerned a 'sharp distinction between articulate and inarticulate form elements, such as scale steps and scale-free tone steps, articulate and free rhythms' etc, which he said correspond to conscious and unconscious processes in musical composition. But to assign totally to unconscious processes the cognition of 'tone of voice', rhythmic suppleness, vibrato, glissando and so forth reckons without the trained musician's powers of conscious control over these musical elements. (Moreover, Freud's diagnosis identifying Mahler's traumatic memories of his parents' quarrels as underlying the intrusion of banal streetorgan themes at moments of high emotional intensity in his music suggests that 'unarticulated thought structures of the unconscious' are sometimes tied to articulated forms.) Ehrenzweig's distinction led him to the view that 'the primitive musician, like the child listening to a tale half understood, is able to bear long stretches of inarticulate material which would drive the civilized listener to distraction' – as if to imply that the civilized listener has been educated to feel unsafe without reassuring moments of articulation. Ehrenzweig's view raises the question, however, whether certain 20th-century musical idioms including electronic music might reflect a post-Freudian attitude of freer access in art to unconscious strata of perception as an enrichment of conscious experience.

Perhaps because psychoanalytic data is derived from patients, there is little consideration of what character a balanced aesthetic, emotional and intellectual enjoyment of music might have. Some psychoanalysts hold that listening to music induces an emotional response with intellectual processes attenuated or perhaps even totally suspended. Even though music structures time and tone, and therefore is a vehicle for the ego function of mastery, some theorists dwell on the capacity of music to facilitate regression to such primary experience as the 'magic of movement' (Sterba, 1939). In responding to this evocation of motion in music the listener may enjoy a reverberation of the primary state of boundlessness between self and outer reality. Kohut and Levarie (1950) characterized some musical enjoyment as inducing, in Freud's words, 'oceanic feelings' and a sense of 'magical omnipotence' and 'rhythm as mediating a kinaesthetic discharge of tension'. Yet they also emphasized the enjoyment of the effort involved in acquiring control of perceptual experience. The passive listener seeks in music the dissolution of his resistances, while the active one seeks order from evanescence. Psychoanalytic theory has not attended greatly to the possible desirability of a balance between these two functions.

Psychoanalytic interpretation lacks, moreover, a consistent gauge of 'meaning' in the paralinguistic role of music. Though music is valuable to the psychoanalytic process in evading verbal logic and gaining access to the unconscious, it yields idiosyncratic data for each individual because the absence of denotative meaning robs it of an objective measure of distortions such as exists in the psychopathology of jokes, slips of the tongue and dreams. Perhaps this is why music therapy remains an art akin to religious faith-healing, rooted in empathy, and little amenable as yet to theoretical organization. Psychoanalytic therapy is anchored in the power of objective verbal language to describe personal relationships; hence music therapy, lacking this dimension, functions mainly as a preparatory adjunct to establish accessibility and trust. (For an excellent critical review see Noy, 1966–8; also Noy, 1969, on primary and secondary process.)

5. RECENT DEVELOPMENTS.
(i) *Information theory*. Information theory was developed in communication engineering and is an approach to the efficiency of a communication channel in the number of different messages which can be transmitted in a unit of time. It is based on mathematical probability theory. Shannon and Weaver (1949) distinguished three levels of the theory. The 'technical' level is concerned with efficiency of transmission, the 'semantic' with the reception of the intended meaning, and the 'effective' with the influence of the message upon the receiver. The mathematical theory applies only to the technical level, and while Shannon and Weaver said it could be applied to the other levels they did not show

how this was to be done – how one might measure, for instance, whether the listener is influenced in the way the composer intended. Shannon would be regarded by many as misleading himself in supposing that the semantic aspects could be described by the theory. However, information theory stimulated psychological research by appearing to offer 'a methodology for quantifying organization or patterning' (Attneave, 1956).

'Information' is measured in terms of the reduction of 'uncertainty' (which is at a maximum for complete randomness), each event being assigned a numerical value according to the number of possible events from which it has been selected. The greater the number of possible messages from which it was selected, the higher its information value. According to this theory, a low-probability or surprising event is of high information value, so that the more random statistically a message is, the higher is its 'information' content, while a more predictable, repetitious or redundant message has a lower information value. On the face of it the elements of Western tonal music (or indeed other formal idioms) appear susceptible to this mode of analysis, according to which information is inversely related to the expectations of the listener; for instance, in a musical idiom abounding in perfect cadences an interrupted cadence does seem particularly informative. An entire corpus of music might be regarded as comprising a 'code' – a 'population' or 'alphabet' of symbols combined in sequence according to a system of rules or constraints; and a numerical value might be attached to each event in the sequence according to the probability of its occurrence – just as sampling procedures have been used to derive values assigned to each letter and word in the English language. Any fairly large verbal or musical sample is assumed to have the same statistical structure as the 'population' from which it is drawn.

Transmission of a message from sender to receiver involves a channel of communication where noise in the system interferes with the reception of the message, channel capacity (i.e. the speed at which the code can be efficiently transmitted) being systematically related to the signal-to-noise ratio. The message is recoded at transmitter level to suit the characteristics of the channel and to take account of the structural characteristics (probability) of the message source. Noise (i.e. extrinsic or intrinsic characteristics, which are confusable with true messages) changes the signal from more to less probable. In listening to music the signal-to-noise ratio involves not only doubtful intonation, faulty room acoustics, extraneous traffic noises and the like but also the fluctuating receptivity of the listener's nervous system. A constant error, however, such as consistently predictable bad intonation, would not affect transmission rates. Psychology, regarding the human perceiver as an information channel of limited capacity (see Broadbent, 1958), investigates the limits of what can be attentively registered at a given speed. 'Redundancy', the repetition of information already present in the message, is wasteful in a relatively noiseless channel but increases the likelihood, where noise has to be overcome, that the message will be conveyed. And in music, redundancy (for instance, repetitive textural configurations like an Alberti bass) may reduce the information load on the perceiver so that other aspects of the music can be more attentively monitored.

One may regard the source-to-receiver channel in music as in five stages: the composer's idea, the score, the performance (including noise), the listener's reception (including noise), and the listener's idea. Between each pair of stages certain remappings take place, each transition (from ideal to notational to physical to physiological and psychological to ideal) involving modifications of the message pattern; but the first and last stages are assumed to correspond in so far as the composer and listener have a common grammatical basis for discounting discrepancies during the transmission. The use of sign theory (Morris, 1946) to define this process, though legitimate for the intervening stages, is problematic for the first and last stages since their inaccessibility obliges one to take it on trust that a mental representation is a complete sign system. In regarding composer-to-listener as a communication channel the information theorist would regard the intervening stages as sources of noise. The score is seen as constructed from a finite set of possible imagined sounds (drawn from an infinite set, according to the theory) to which the composer restricts himself according to a so-called 'cultural alphabet', that is, a code analogous to the complete set of possible phonemes in a language. Western music might be assumed to involve about 100 pitch levels *times* about eight loudness levels (as indicated in musical notation) *times* all the possible durations *times* all the available ranges and blends of instrumental and vocal timbres. This already large set establishes the probabilities involved in the composer's choice of the first sound (which may be a chord or combination of different pitch levels, timbres and so on), and the alternatives increase exponentially with every subsequent choice – though the total possible increase is reduced by the constraints of tonal harmony and rhythmic organization and by the characteristic style of the composer in ordering these elements.

Information theory appeared attractive at first sight as a possible method of measuring the transmissibility of music (for an extended discussion of its aesthetic applications, see Moles, 1958). However, some music theorists did not relate their general assumptions to their method of applying Shannon's measure of information, the H formula. Is there a corpus of music susceptible to analysis in terms of information theory? Can information theory be used to measure the capacity of an individual to make sense of music? Psychologically the two questions are related because the individual's musical processes of cognition are developed in listening to the music of his culture, and the organization of his long-term memory must have some conformity to the grammatical structures of that culture.

One of the simplest mathematical descriptions of sequences of events is that of the Markov chain. In this model it is supposed that a random process is observed at certain time-intervals and that at each one it takes one of several states; the state in the current time-interval depends only on the immediately preceding state and not on the previous history of the sequence. In communication systems these constraints are taken into account in devising optimal codes. Language has been regarded by some theorists as a Markov chain though as one of a higher order to account for sequential dependencies in groupings of more than one word. Cohen (1962) critically analysed the validity of applying the Markov model and the mathematical assumptions of information theory to music.

One mathematical assumption is that all very large samples from an infinite sequence have the same statistical structure. But defining on non-mathematical grounds the infinite sequence (e.g. all possible sounds, all actually heard, or only those of Western tonal music) reduces the validity of applying information theory to music, while restricting the infinite sequence to a certain alphabet introduces circularity into the attempt to define a particular style by means of the theory. In a very large sample, even the works of one composer, a particular configuration might occur only once, and without its recurrence it would be difficult to relate the sample to the statistical structure of the infinite sequence (it could be a random event).

For language the Markov model has been shown to be inadequate since simple sequential dependencies cannot account for sentences containing 'embedded structures', that is, those necessitating reference to a higher order of grammatical organization. Thought is hierarchically organized in music perhaps even more than it is in spoken language, since the forms and devices of musical composition hold sway over the generation of phrases. Composers use not only 'embedded structures' analogous to those which make it impossible to regard verbal language as a Markov chain, they also use the overall structural schemata of composition which make the function of any single note significant in many schemata and on many different levels. The temporal locus of that note cannot be understood as the outcome only of probabilities attaching to the previous one. Indeed, a grammar of music based only on left-to-right dependencies could prove inadequate even to a brief musical utterance such as is found in primitive melody. For these reasons later models of the grammar of music have rejected the Markov chain in favour of one from linguistics (Winograd, 1968).

Whether the Markov process can describe the psychological processes of the listener is equally questionable. Information theory has been used in experiments where brief sets of stimuli are constructed by randomization and the musician's capacity to process information is calculated in bits (i.e. number of yes–no binary choices made in identifying an event from an array of possible events; Quastler, 1956, Attneave, 1956). Here the theory is inappropriate since the musician's grammatical knowledge of music enables him either to 'chunk' adjacent notes in a sequence or to identify single items by a hierarchically organized understanding of tonal and rhythmic relations. The measure in bits is contaminated by the fact that his internal grammar, derived from his total past experience of music, is not necessarily an equivalent statistical structure to every other sample drawn from the infinite sequence, nor is it governed only by the left-to-right dependencies of a Markov process.

An infinite memory capacity is another mathematical assumption of information theory, for the value of H is determined on the basis of an ideal observer with which the human information processor cannot validly be equated. The temporal limit of human short-term memory exerts its effect upon understanding music while it is being heard. Short-term capacity to retain input, particularly if further input is occurring, is seen by psychologists (Broadbent, 1958) as acting like a filter in the channel between sensory reception, perception and idea. Studies in psycholinguistics have shown the effect this limit on short-term memory has upon the understanding of 'embedded structures' (Miller and Isard, 1964).

A more radical objection to the use of information theory in musical psychology concerns the composer's use of redundancy. A work of art is not merely a message, nor is the composer merely a source. He uses redundancy not merely to ensure the retention of thematic material but for various aesthetic or emotional reasons, and the psychological impact upon the listener is more than simply a matter of a correct transduction yielding intelligibility. The distinction at the technical level – that information theory is concerned with the transmission, not the meaning of the message – is difficult to maintain where aesthetic comprehension rather than either pattern recognition or understanding denotative meaning is involved. Redundancy may be used to convey qualitatively different mood changes, a commonplace example being the simple repetition of a phrase which, even though the two phrases are identical in all attributes, may convey the energetic vehemence of reiteration or the pathos of an echo, depending on the particular phrase. In theory there may be interest for experimental psychology in discovering the optimal use of redundancy for evoking immediate perception of forms and their thematic transformations in music. For instance, symmetry is defined as highly redundant, but psychologically the symmetry of some temporal patterns in music may render them particularly difficult to monitor (see §III). Moreover, this optimum varies with the musical education of the listener, an average level of which cannot be assumed in the general population as it can for verbal communication.

If the composer's influence on the total response of the listener – intellectual, aesthetic and emotional – represents Shannon's 'effective level', then, in order to remap to this level the mathematical values developed at the 'technical' one, it would be necessary to include weightings for every psychological variable upon which the listener's selectivity of attention to the music is based. These variables would include not only the limits of the immediate memory span and the particular musical experience of the listener, but also the variety of cognitive styles and of personal dynamic values which he directs to the features of the music. These biasses upon perceptual processes in music present difficulties for the use of information theory.

The significant contribution of information theory to musical psychology has been to introduce the concepts of 'information', 'recording', 'uncertainty', 'noise' and 'redundancy', and of the individual listener as a channel of 'limited capacity', rather than in any direct application of the mathematical theory to various musical languages and idioms or to the measurement of musical perceptual processes.

(ii) Cybernetic theory. Cybernetics – 'the science of control and communication in the animal and the machine' (Wiener, 1948) – is concerned not with what a machine or a biological system is made of but with what it can do. This study of 'steersmanship' in self-regulating systems is of particular value to biology, neurophysiology and psychology; and in the last-mentioned discipline it is of particular importance to the study of skill-learning. Hence its potential value to the psychology of music.

Its first fundamental concept is that of 'difference': either that two states (say, present state and desired outcome) are demonstrably different or that one state changes with time. Although some varieties of change appear continuous (e.g. the smooth progress of a skilled muscular movement), theoretically the choice of very small time units at which discrete samples of the change are taken makes unit measurement possible. This measurement is defined by transformation rules governing the relation between something acted upon (the operand), that which acts upon it (the operator), and that which it becomes (the transform). Each state may consist of many elements, and different types of transform are defined. This basic method is expanded to study complex systems where dynamic interconnections are such that the alteration of one element has far-reaching consequences for very many others.

Its second essential concept, that of 'feedback', was influential in replacing, for many psychologists, the metaphor of the reflex arc. Behaviourists use this conditioned reflex metaphor as the basic stimulus–response unit, with a concomitant view of learning as motivated by subsequent reward, whereas cybernetic-orientated theorists stress that learning proceeds by the continuing correction of present action and that intrinsic sensory-motor feedback rather than subsequent reward is the directive factor in learning. The feedback unit essentially measures present state against some desired or optimal state; 'negative feedback' is an error-evaluating device to provide information upon which further action occurs to reduce the discrepancy between these two states. A servo-mechanism (e.g. a thermostat) is a negative feedback device which operates a transformation rule to convert a measure of output into the appropriate control upon further output (see the T–O–T–E units of Miller, Galanter and Pribram, 1960: 'Test, Operate, Test, Exit' is the prototypical feedback loop of human skill).

Homeostasis (the tendency in a biological system to restore and maintain its balance in a changing environment) is a form of servo-mechanism. When disturbed, the parts of the system react and interact until balance is regained; in sickness this includes the function of self-repair. Neurologically, the notion of hierarchies of feedback units and brain thermostats, which has inspired many brain models (Ashby, 1952; Young, 1964), is strongly supported and forms the background to the use of cybernetics in experimental psychology. Homeostasis includes not only intrinsic neural mechanisms but also the organism's outward action on the environment, action which is directed to maintaining the balance of the system through the varying load conditions imposed upon it. Thus the perception–action sequence forms part of the homeostatic process.

The third essential concept in cybernetics is that of 'quantity of variety'. Each element of perception or of action is selected from the total set of possible states of environment and organism. This total set is not random but is governed by constraints such as the laws of nature (e.g. there are only three dimensions in which objects can exist or movements occur, and present position is constrained by immediately preceding position). Any second-by-second account of an action or the process of learning exhibits the nature of the sequential constraints which can be expressed in terms of cybernetic transformations. The cybernetic principles of transmissibility of variety relate closely to those of information theory, and all homeostatic processes are seen as limited by the amount of information or variety the system is equipped to handle.

In the experimental psychology of learning, particularly that of skills, research has centred on different levels of feedback, distinguishing reactive (or intrinsic) feedback of neural circuits from the movement itself, as contrasted with operation (extrinsic or augmented) feedback, which is also called *KR* (knowledge of results – Smith and Sussmann, 1969; Fitts, 1964). *KR* also subdivides into dynamic sensory effects such as listening to the evenness of a sound one is producing or static effects such as seeing a line after one has drawn it. Various augmented feedback techniques, such as computer reproduction which the subject monitors as he performs, are used to investigate such skills as the breath control so necessary to vocal and some instrumental music (Smith, 1966). These have shown the basis of motor-skill learning to be a progressive change in regulation of response brought about by continuous self-generated activity. Practice gradually changes magnitude and frequency characteristics of movements. Automated extrinsic feedback devices also include programmed instruction. The systematic displacement of intrinsic feedback by delay or reversals of the visual field have demonstrated, by the consequent disruption of function, its essential role in learning.

It is easy to see the intuitive appeal of the cybernetic approach to the psychology of music. A performing musician is a biological homeostatic system. He has acquired the capacity to regulate the perception–action sequence through moment-to-moment variations in informational input as well as to regulate variations in the system itself – for instance, degree of alertness or relaxation necessary to certain music and to the control of fatigue. He is encoding and decoding in the input–output sequence and he operates a complex hierarchic organization of the components of his skill, subroutines being thoroughly integrated into the overall planned activity with varying degrees of autonomy governing the several aspects. He can control the direction of his attention towards certain aspects from moment to moment, depending on the degree of the information load and whether intrinsic or adventitious information is at that moment particularly important. His acquisition of skill is a gradual elimination of the degrees of freedom of involuntary muscular activity through the error-evaluation of feedback. In interpreting music his choices, both musical and consequently technical ones, are also akin to the cybernetic model of problem solving. His planned sequences, particularly improvisations, show the feedback and feedforward processes (which are apparent also in speaking) at a high level of complex integration.

(*iii*) *Artificial intelligence.* Though 'the language of music' is to some extent a metaphorical notion, the psychologist can study music in linguistic terms to investigate the nature and limits of the human capacity to process musical information. Despite the relative absence of explicit reference to the world of objects and events, the fact that music is both syntactic and communicative justifies a psycholinguistic approach to its comprehension. The morphology and neural mechanisms evolved to serve language are also basic to music, and indeed Darwin (1871) held that musical communication preceded speech in man's evolution.

In ordinary Western music two distinguishable language codes can be seen to exert pressure upon each other: that symbolizing utterance and gesture in the prosodic and choric elements of melodic line, and that

of the formal techniques and logical structures of harmony and composition. The listener enjoys not only the expressive elements of diction and movement in music but also the argument of its forms. He has acquired a matrix of expectancies, analogous to the internalized grammar that is shared by speakers of a language (even children) and by which they make sense of conversation. This grammar enables him often to recognize a wrong note in the performance of a tonal work he is hearing for the first time. The internalized grammar may operate without any capacity explicitly to state its rules. But as more composers come to favour invented rather than evolved idioms, corresponding to abstract rather than natural languages, the equilibrium between the two language codes is changed and the precise load which this places upon the listener's capacity to process information is a problem in cognitive psychology. Thus 'musical psycholinguistics' is faced with defining the syntax of music and showing how the listener makes sense of it.

New attacks on this problem take as point of departure the Chomskian revolution in linguistics and the computer-simulation approach to psychology, the computer programme embodying a formally precise model of those grammatical rules of music that may unconsciously be used by the ordinary listener. Longuet-Higgins and Steedman (1971) programmed a computer to assign correct key and time signatures to deadpan, pure-tone renderings of the 48 fugue subjects of Bach's *Das wohltemperirte Clavier*. The tonal basis of their algorithm for key is a matrix of perfect 5ths and major 3rds; and the rhythmic algorithm used to discover the natural stresses from an unaccented performance isolates the 'dactyl' (a long and two equally short notes, followed by a longer one) as strongly indicative of rhythmic boundaries. They suggest that the success of each algorithm is an indication of the possible role in musical perception of rhythmic patterns originating from poetic metre and of tonal relations based on the harmonic series. Of course there are interactive effects between tone and time elements, and Longuet-Higgins's subsequent models of possible cognitive processes may be expected to be progressively refined by building in rules of interaction, much as has happened with transformations in successive models of generative grammar. Winograd (1968) has adapted to the computer analysis of tonal harmony the systemic linguistic grammar of Halliday, having found its close connection between syntax and semantics to be appropriate to music. The computer produced relatively sophisticated parsings of Bach and Schubert, recognizing modulations, implied tonalities and complex tonality structures. Thus artificial intelligence provides powerful heuristics for the experimental investigation of musical grammars.

Several musical parallels to experimental psycholinguistics are only now beginning to be studied: dichotic listening where different messages are presented one to each ear and the principles of attentional capacity and continuity are explored; the strategies by which the individual can code adjacent items to enlarge the capacity of his immediate memory span; the effect of syntactic boundaries upon memorability, etc. But musical psycholinguistics will depend upon the work of grammarians of music and upon a closer rapprochement of disciplines, including ethnomusicology, than has existed hitherto. One important task is to bridge the gap between theoretical rules of practice and the perceptual capabilities that may be humanly expected of the listener but for the investigation of which purely psychoacoustic studies are not sufficient. A consequent of the absence of dictionary meaning is that musical psychology is concerned with coding rather than recoding strategies. It would make no sense to maintain that, as occurs with language, a listener could paraphrase a musical phrase, or abstract it and remember only its 'meaning'; for although both in language and in music the 'meaning' for some phrases might be a mental image, the musical image would be of the phrase itself.

II. Perception. Perception is a process of matching incoming sensory data against the memory store of experience, and thus depends partly upon elements that have been learnt as well as the structure and function of sensory transducers (ears, eyes, skin etc) and of the nervous system. It follows that a fundamental question in psychology is how far musical perception depends upon inbuilt structures, how far upon musical experience. There is hence a great need for studies which more accurately grade and control the degrees of musical education of the subjects used. In particular individual differences in musical training must be accounted for before attributing perceptual processes to the mechanics of the auditory system; but equally any psychological explanation of musical perception must be congruent with the precise nature of that system, as far as it is now known.

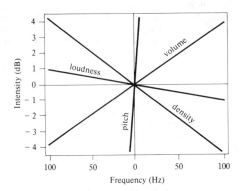

1. Contours of equal-pitch–loudness–volume density specific to 500 Hz and 60 dB (after Stevens, 1934)

The four attributes of tone basic to musical perception are pitch, loudness, timbre and time (hence rhythm), which depend respectively upon the frequency, amplitude, complexity and duration of the sound wave. Caution is needed when considering them separately, since so many studies have demonstrated their perceptual interdependence, loudness being also dependent on frequency (Fletcher and Munson, 1933), pitch dependent on amplitude (Snow, 1936), and timbre affected by frequency (Saldahna and Corso, 1964). Furthermore, Fletcher (1934) demonstrated that 'just noticeable differences' (j.n.d.s) for pitch as a function of intensity are five times greater for pure tones than those for five-partial tones of the same fundamental frequency. Stevens (1934) presented a diagram (fig.1) of equal-pitch–loudness–volume density functions over a small range of frequency and intensity. High-pitched tones seem subjectively denser and less voluminous than low-pitched ones, and Stevens, Guirao and Slawson (1965) suggested that density is loudness per unit volume which

in turn may be a function of timbre.

1. Pitch: (i) The ear and the brain (ii) Discrimination (iii) Scaling (iv) Improvement of discrimination (v) Critical bands (vi) Loudness (vii) Duration (viii) Satiation and masking effects. 2. Loudness: (i) General (ii) Discrimination, duration (iii) Masking. 3. Timbre and texture: (i) Timbre (ii) Vibrato (iii) The trill and stream segregation. 4. Rhythm, temporality, tempo: (i) General factors (ii) Psychoacoustics (iii) Memory (iv) Pulse and beat (v) Affective response. 5. Melody and harmony.

1. PITCH.

(i) The ear and the brain. A question much debated is exactly how and at what level the perception of pitch is integrated in the process (itself still imperfectly understood) of converting mechanical energy of sound waves into the electrical pattern of nerve impulses in the brain which constitute perception. This problem was originally couched in terms of ear versus brain, 'peripheral' versus 'central' function. 'Place theory' (Helmholtz, 1863) contended that the ear performed a frequency analysis, 'Telephone theory' (Rutherford, 1886) that the brain analysed the timing of nerve impulses. The latter was later refined into 'Periodicity theory' (on the ground that the timing was derived from the periodicity of the stimulating waveform; Ritoma, 1970). A significant corollary of the peripheral versus central distinction is that purely sensory (ear) function would be morphology-dependent and therefore innate whereas cortex function could be attributable at least in part to learning. But this basic distinction may be untenable since redistribution of coding occurs through synapses (nerve junctions), and descending nerve pathways can exert feedback control, modifying receptivity. There could thus be inbuilt structures favouring certain types of auditory input higher in the nervous system. In fact Békésy's view (1960) that the cochlea performs an approximate frequency analysis which is made more specific at each higher synaptic level has recently been strongly supported (Gulick, 1971). Since about one third of the cells in the animal primary cortex will not respond to pure tones at all, but only to clicks or bursts of noise (Whitfield, 1967), it is clear that neural sound analysis in the additive fashion envisaged by Helmholtz is far too simple an account of acoustic information processing in any mammalian species. The human system will have evolved with specialized sound detectors for dealing with speech, so that consonant and vowel detectors are likely to be well represented, and the relativity of pitch changes may be more primary in the nervous system than the absolute values.

This reappraisal of Helmholtz's attribution of pitch perception to the mechanical properties of the ear came through transduction problems. First, how can the nervous system, working on an all-or-none basis, code frequencies higher than the maximum speed at which a single nerve can fire? Hence 'Volley theory' (that above this frequency nerves in a bundle fire in rotation; Wever, 1949), which is supported by micro-electrode recordings from single nerves. Since the nervous system codes intensity as well as frequency by rates of firing, some at least of the relationship between perceived pitch and intensity also awaits explanation in terms of neural coding. Secondly, pitch perception is finer than could be accounted for by cochlear resonators, which supports the suggestion that refinement of tuning occurs at higher synaptic levels. Thirdly, there is the problem of combination tones: how is it that the fundamental note is heard when it is absent from the physical stimulus and only some of its harmonic series are present? Helmholtz attributed that phenomenon to difference-tone distortion in the cochlea, but that would apply only at high intensities (Zwicker, 1955). The perception of the fundamental tone in music is independent of timbre since it can be recognized whatever instrument is playing. Houtsma and Goldstein (1972) showed that, in the total absence of the fundamental, all harmonics below the tenth partial are effective conveyors of fundamental pitch, the strongest being a cluster of four to six adjacent ones; and since the perception of a melody at fundamental pitch can be obtained by presenting, one to each ear, pairs of harmonics whose numbering in their respective series is changed for each melody note, their integration into a sensation of the missing fundamental must be taking place in the nervous system at a point upstream from the separate pathways from each ear. This supports periodicity theory as against the Helmholtzian view. But it also shows the perceived change of pitch to be a property of the central pitch mechanism. Inharmonic partials, say 820, 1020 and 1220 Hz, evoke a perceived fundamental of 204 Hz where harmonics of 800, 1000 and 1200 would evoke one of 200 Hz. These findings are a problem for periodicity theory since the distance between peaks remains equal. They also have important implications for explanations of 'dissonance'. Again the Helmholtz view of dissonance as a sensation of interference patterns caused by unresolved beating effects in the cochlea is not satisfactory, since, as Mach (1886) pointed out, a similar sensation ensues from two slightly mistuned tuning-forks held one to each ear, suggesting that perception of dissonance is central rather than peripheral. That we have learnt through the evolution of musical styles to tolerate increasingly more dissonance may mean either that dissonance is central or that beats are not as unpleasant as some theorists have tacitly assumed. Certainly Plomp (1966) found that audible beats were judged less disagreeable than the dissonance associated with a great number of less audible beats.

(*ii*) *Discrimination.* What is the smallest just noticeable difference (j.n.d.), and what factors affect it? Shower and Biddulph (1931) showed that j.n.d.s vary with intensity. But even where intensity is held constant the fluctuations of the listener's transducer or auditory system may yield intensity differences between stimuli which influence pitch discrimination, particularly above 4000 Hz (the highest note on the piano), where difficulty in detecting or judging direction of pitch changes becomes much more pronounced. Henning (1966) attempted to control this factor by randomly varying intensity of signals to force his two musician subjects to attend to pitch only, yet found a steep increase in the size of j.n.d.s above 5000 Hz. In this connection Sergeant (1970) pointed out that results in many such tests carried out in schools using loudspeakers are confounded by the varying loss of signal intensity in different parts of the classroom (for instance, ranging from a loss of 0 dB to more than 25 dB in a lecture room of about 10 m × 7·5 m).

Pitch discrimination is also affected by timbre and, as indicated above (Fletcher, 1934; Henning and Grosberg, 1968), is greater with complex than with pure tones, again perhaps suggesting that more frequency information is integrated higher in the auditory pathway. Receptivity may be enhanced by learning and experience. Sergeant (1970) found that musicians were

much better than non-musicians at discriminating complex tones though not pure ones. The view that learning rather than auditory morphology governs discrimination is supported by a cross-cultural study (Tanner and Rivette, 1964) where Indian students were unable to detect the direction of pitch changes. So-called 'tone deafness' thus may be culturally induced or even the product of childhood resistances (see §I, 4).

(*iii*) *Scaling.* How does our experience of pitch relate to objective frequency? Stevens and Volkmann (1940) derived the 'mel' scale of pitch from experiments where subjects successively bisected the range of pitch whose upper limit was 1000 Hz, repeating the judgments using the previous one as standard, until the whole range had been mapped into 'mel' units. Even though pure tones were used, abolishing the effect of resemblances between the harmonics, the method took no account of the octave similarity as a possible influence in these judgments, though it is recognized even by animals (Blackwell and Schlosberg, 1943). Stevens imagined he avoided the difficulties of relative musicality of subjects by choosing this fractionation method, when it merely prevented him from assessing the implicit tonality effects. However, the 'mel' scale has come increasingly under attack. Attneave and Olson (1971) constructed subjective scales of pitch by transposition methods, which show 'the musical not the mel scale to describe the morphophoric function of pitch'. Révész (1913) did consider the octave in distinguishing 'tone height' (corresponding to frequency) from chroma (the cyclical resemblances of octaves). However, he assumed that octave perception was an accurate and built-in 1 : 2 frequency ratio detector, which is not supported by the evidence. The 'stretched octave' (i.e. the tendency to pitch an octave sharp) has been known since the Greeks. In modern times it has been demonstrated by Stumpf and Meyer (1898) and Ward (1954). Apparently the stretch increases by five per cent after 24 hours of sleeplessness (Elfner, 1954). Nevertheless the octave similarity in pitch perception is unlikely to be entirely culturally induced and any theory of hearing that fails to account for it cannot be satisfactory.

(*iv*) *Improvement of discrimination.* Carl Seashore (1938) took the view that pitch discrimination was an essential sign of innate musicality, that its improvement could not be attributed to better receptivity ('training probably does not modify the capacity of the sense organ') but that conscious recognition of the nature of pitch could be the result of training. There are numerous examples of experimental training being effective, even with children who at the outset could not discriminate octaves (Wolner and Pyle, 1933). Robert Seashore (1935) trained adults from a discriminatory power of 9·2 Hz to 4·6 Hz. Wyatt (1945) used a chromatic stroboscope in training subjects to match standard tones and to sing intervals. Here the average improvement for musicians was 7·75 points on the Seashore test and for non-musicians 4·50; there was also some improvement on notes and intervals an octave below or above those used in the training.

An early longitudinal study with tests of children aged from six to 19 showed an improvement from discrimination of three-eighths of a tone at the age of six to one-eighth at the age of nine; there was little corresponding progress thereafter. A telling feature of the improvement of pitch discrimination with age comes from the Russian National Conservatory for gifted musicians (Blagonadejina, quoted by Teplov, 1966), where violinists and cellists achieved thresholds of between 3 and 12 cents whereas pianists were between 12 and 21 cents. This suggests that the training for intonation with its intrinsic feedback had its effect on pitch discrimination. However, there is very little correlation between pitch discrimination and musicality (see Teplov, 1966, Table 4, p.130), and indeed Teplov took the view that specific instrumental training plays such a part that pitch discrimination has nothing to do with a musical ear, in the artistic sense of the phrase, but with the ear of a 'tuner of instruments'.

Studies of the intonation of proficient musicians show considerable variability, for in tuning an instrument to a standard pitch there can be a standard deviation of as much as 10 cents (Corso, 1954). Equally there is variability in the playing of intervals, and this has assumed importance in the debate as to which scale – Pythagorean, just intonation or equal temperament – is used by string players. When comparing the results between experimenters (Greene, 1937; Nickerson, 1948; Mason, 1960; Shackford, 1961–2) it is important to note whether they calculated intervals independently, or with reference to a key note, particularly where the same interval (e.g. the tritone) has different values according to its function in the scale. As Ward pointed out in a cogent analysis (1970), a theorist who identifies Pythagorean tuning rather than equal temperament plus a tendency to play sharp, should present evidence where the Pythagorean interval is smaller than the equal temperament one, as well as in those instances where it is larger.

(v) *Critical bands.* Phenomena originally demonstrated empirically by Fletcher (1940) led to the concept of the 'critical band'. A subject is presented with a stimulus tone which he must detect through a masking band of all frequencies in the spectrum (white noise). As the band is progressively narrowed the intensity at which the target tone is just audible does not alter until, at a narrow masking band round it, its audibility abruptly changes. Similar effects are observed in animals (cats, Watson, 1963; chinchillas, Miller, 1964; and rats, Gourevitch, 1965), which argues for a physiological and against a cultural or educational basis to the phenomenon.

Nevertheless Swets (1963) took the view that attentional processes are involved, and the question remains open. For all species studied the critical bandwidth seems to represent 70% of its central value and to correspond to the same distance of 1 to 2 mm on the basilar membrane; it may thus act as a filter, whether mechanically in the cochlea, or neurally, or both. It relates consistently to the mel scale of pitch and to the j.n.d. scale of frequency discrimination. Furthermore, it was invoked by Plomp and Levelt (1962, 1965) as governing our perception of musical consonance. Using musically naive subjects they correlated their judgments (scored on a seven-point scale) for pleasingness of two-tone intervals with the critical bandwidth. Mean judgments did not vary when the two tones were separated by more than the critical band (surprisingly enough), but if the two tones fell within a critical band their pleasingness rapidly diminished until a low point was reached when they were separated by only 0·2 of a critical band, after which the region where audible beats are heard seemed to reduce the unpleasant sensation.

Since aesthetic judgments are notoriously culture bound and dissonance tolerance seems related to musical sophistication, to base a theory of musical consonance on these sensory data would seem an oversimplification.

(vi) *Loudness.* Intensity does not affect the pitch of complex tones of musical instruments, nor with pure tones does it affect the middle frequencies so much as the extremes, where as a function of intensity low notes sound lower and high notes higher (Gulick, 1971). Fletcher (1934) attributed the relative constancy of pitch of complex musical tones to the effect of the upper partials, but it is also true to say that, at the range of intensity changes encountered in music, the degree of variation of pitch even for pure tones is not large.

(vii) *Duration.* Licklider (1951) explored the dimensions of pitch and duration. Pure tones of about two or three milliseconds are heard as clicks; even those of ten milliseconds sound like clicks, though with some pitch quality. Furthermore, the pitch of tones seems to fall as duration is decreased. Longer durations are required to perceive low tones, perhaps because fewer cycles of the sound wave occur in the same unit time. Below 1000 Hz, two or three cycles are required for pitch to be perceptible. The critical duration for pitch perception was defined by Gulick (1971), using data from several experiments, as related to a fixed number (6 ± 3) of cycles below 1000 Hz, whereas above 1000 Hz it is a fixed duration (ten milliseconds).

(viii) *Satiation and masking effects.* If a subject is exposed to a loud continuous tone (85 dB) which is near to the pitch of a subsequently presented test tone, the test pitch appears shifted away from the satiating tone. This effect varies with the interval between the two tones, diminishing as the interval lengthens (Christman and Williams, 1963). A similar effect occurs where a tone is masked by a band of frequencies, tones above that band appearing to shift upwards, those below shifting downwards (Egan and Meyer, 1950). All these psychophysical relations became more important to musical psychology with the advent of electronic music, in which more finely graded changes of pitch, intensity and duration are possible, though not necessarily perceptible. Conversely the exploitation of certain auditory effects may tax to the limits the auditory system of the listener.

2. LOUDNESS.

(i) *General.* Perception of loudness mainly correlates with sound intensity but is also affected by frequency, duration and waveform. Norman (1972), using data of Robinson and Dadson (1956), illustrated the relationship of frequency to loudness at various sound pressure levels: the equiloudness contours (fig.2) are produced by matching coupling tones at different frequencies with a standard (always of 1000 Hz). Fletcher and Munson (1933) did the early work on these contours. There is considerable variation at lower intensities, but if sounds are loud enough little difference is experienced between frequencies. The curve flattens as the pain threshold is approached. For most intensities (below 100 dB) a tone of a given frequency (say 500 Hz) will seem louder than a tone of lower frequency (say 400 Hz) which is of matched intensity.

Explanations of the relationship of loudness to pitch have invoked the possibility of a contraction of middle ear muscles at high intensities altering the resonance properties of the ear, or of a shift along the basilar

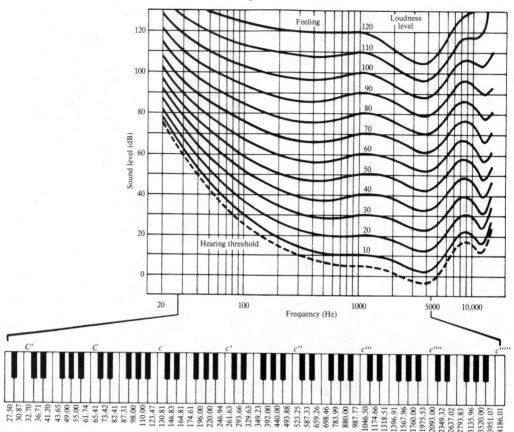

2. Equiloudness contours from 20 Hz to 10,000 Hz (after Robinson and Dadson, 1956)

membrane of the cochlear potential (Stevens and Davis, 1938). But this does not explain the differences at moderate intensities. Moreover, binaural effects of pitch changes with increasing loudness, by presenting the same tone to the other ear, show such effects as having a central component (Thurlow, 1963). The greater part of the range of orchestral instruments lies in the frequency range to which the perception of loudness is most sensitive. Thus if an orchestral recording is played at much lower than actual performance intensities, many frequencies become inaudible and the loudness relationships between instruments become distorted (unless the amplifiers used are equipped with loudness compensators).

(*ii*) *Discrimination, duration.* Loudness varies as to the logarithm of intensity, and the difference threshold increases as the signal becomes louder by a constant proportion within the logarithmic scale of intensity, according to Weber's Law. This difference threshold corresponds to the constant increase with loudness found in measurement of masking thresholds (Miller, 1947).

When the tone duration is less than 500 milliseconds the threshold of its audibility varies directly with its duration (Garner, 1947) and perceived loudness increases up to a duration of about a second (Littler, 1965). Below 500 milliseconds the threshold of audibility plotted against duration can vary according to the frequency used from 2 dB to even more than 36 dB

(Plomp and Bouman, 1959).

(*iii*) *Masking.* The presence of one sound at a certain frequency may render another inaudible. The relation between loudness and frequency is involved in this phenomenon, for each tone of a frequency near that of the signal is more effective in masking it than are those further away in the frequency spectrum. Where a single frequency is used as masking tone, the curves show notches in the frequency region of both fundamental and overtones of the signal tone, where the incidence of beats between the two tones renders the signal more audible. Masking by a narrow band rather than a single frequency avoids this effect. The 'critical band' concept arose from this practice in masking experiments and is sufficiently consistent for theorists to hypothesize that it represents equidistant areas of the basilar membrane where effects summate, and thus to attribute masking effects to morphological factors rather than learning. However, there is some indication that the trained listener or musician may improve his signal-detecting capacities by a superior retention of his image of the signal for which he is listening; attentional factors are also involved (Swets, 1963).

A masking tone has little effect upon a tone of lower frequency compared with its effect upon one of higher frequency. This is also true of forward masking, where the masking tone precedes the signal in time; the effectiveness of forward masking varies inversely with the time interval in linear fashion. In backward masking, where the masker follows the signal, the linear relation between masking and time interval does not hold, for the effectiveness of the masker decreases much more rapidly than the increase of the time interval.

The masking phenomenon indicates the degree to which the nervous system has limitations of function associated with time. Forward masking indicates that recently stimulated units are less sensitive than rested ones, while backward masking indicates the overtaking by subsequent stimulation of initial stimulation which is not yet complete. The importance of the parameters of masking to the professional knowledge of musicians is self-evident (for reviews see Elliott, 1962, and Jeffress, 1970). However, the theory of signal detectability which has provided a framework and methods for work on masking suggests the possible degree to which musical training might account for individual differences in performance in detection of weak signals through noise. Swets, Green and Tanner (1962) held that 'the possibility that the parameters of the mechanism of frequency selectivity vary from one task to another under intelligent control' makes it advisable to regard all these psychophysical relations as susceptible to modifications due to training.

3. TIMBRE AND TEXTURE.

(i) *Timbre.* Timbre 'is that attribute of auditory sensation in terms of which a listener can judge that two sounds similarly presented and having the same loudness and pitch are dissimilar' (American Standards Association, 1960; Plomp, 1970). This definition indicates the multi-dimensional role assigned to timbre when the unidimensional attributes of loudness and pitch are held constant. All other attributes of sound sensation contribute to timbre: those of the spectrum of overtones, of waveform, sound pressure, number and frequency of formants, and the transients (prefixes or starting noises) which play a large part in the recognition of instrumental timbre. The recent advance in multi-dimensional scaling techniques brings timbre research more into the realm of the possible. A study using these techniques (Howard and Silverman, 1976), varying fundamental frequency, waveform, formant frequency and number of formants, yielded three perceptual dimensions towards which musicians presented a more homogeneous response than did non-musicians, pitch being a more salient dimension than tone quality. Hitherto very few experiments have been done on timbre compared with other characteristics of sound sensation, for pure tones have been predominantly used in hearing research. Helmholtz's original work (1863) on the relation of timbre to waveform characterized tones in such subjective terms as 'sweet and pleasant' or 'sharp and penetrating'.

Research on timbre has been central to work on the perception of speech, and the simulation of vowel sounds on a musical instrument (vibrating reed plus organ plus piston: Willis, 1830) demonstrates the factors in common, for timbre differences between vowels correlate with peaks in the amplitude pattern or formants of sound waves. Slawson (1968) studied the relation of both vowel quality and musical timbre to the spectrum envelope of the waveform and to fundamental frequency. He found that for both vowel and musical timbre perception, when raising the test stimulus an octave above the standard in fundamental frequency, the least difference in perceived timbre quality was achieved when the lower two formants of the second stimulus

were increased by 10%, these small changes making large differences in quality. Only small differences in quality resulted from changing solely the fundamental frequency or solely the upper formants. This important study suggests that perceived invariance of timbre is a function of the acoustical features and that a biological auditory mechanism plays a greater part than learning.

The effects of phase differences in the harmonics upon perceived timbre have been demonstrated (Licklider, 1957; Schroeder, 1959). Changing the phase of a high overtone results in a greater difference in perceived quality than changing that of a low harmonic; and the presence or absence of large peaks in the waveform also has a great effect. Using the multi-dimensional scaling technique, Plomp and Steeneken (1969) compared timbre differences resulting from complex tones differing only in the phase patterns of harmonics. The greatest difference was perceived between a tone consisting of all sine (or all cosine) harmonic patterns and one consisting of alternating sine and cosine; it was also established that phase differences affected timbre independently of differences of amplitude or sound pressure level. Tones consisting of three harmonics and one slightly mistuned give rise to 'beats' which essentially give a complex tone of different timbre from that where all frequencies are related proportionally. Originally Helmholtz attributed this effect to non-linear distortion in the ear, but clearly it should rather be attributed to the ear's sensitivity to phase (Goldstein, 1967; Plomp, 1967). In general, these beats are much more evident at low frequencies. Plomp (1970) also found that timbre changes due to phase differences were more easily perceptible if the phase relation was changed gradually than by a jump from one phase pattern to another.

Saldahna and Corso (1964) demonstrated the salience of starting noises (or transients) in timbre recognition. 20 trained musicians identified recordings of tones played by ten musical instruments, with or without vibrato and with or without transients. Recognition was better with vibrato and, more importantly, with the initial transients; the offset transients did not affect recognition. Plomp (1970) took the view that 'the function of the cochlea has to be understood primarily in relation to timbre rather than to pitch perception', a view congruent with that of Slawson, that timbre perception is largely biologically determined; thus learning would play a smaller part than was supposed when the Helmholtzian view of the ear as a Fourier analyser assigned the unitary perception of complex tones to a higher function.

The research reported here marks only a beginning on the question of what features of the stimulus are salient in the identification of musical timbre. The further questions concerning the power of timbre in holding attention to a melodic line (i.e. as against the grammatical constraints of a particular musical idiom) have not yet become an object of experimental investigation. The dichotic listening experiment is an appropriate technique for further study.

(ii) *Vibrato.* Carl Seashore's laboratory was responsible for the early work on vibrato. His definition (1938) poses more questions than it answers: 'A good vibrato is a pulsation of pitch, usually accompanied with synchronous pulsations of loudness and timbre, of such extent and rate as to give a pleasing flexibility, tenderness, and richness to the tone'. But precisely what auditory perceptual factors give rise to these subjective impressions?

Harold Seashore's analyses of vocal vibrato (Seashore and Tiffen, 1932) and those of Small (1937) for violin vibrato showed a rate of six to seven pulsations per second to be usual, though the range was wider for the voice (averaging nearly a semitone) than for violin (half as much). Methods of calibration have improved since his conclusion that the perceived pitch of a vibrato tone is the mean pitch level of the oscillations; however, little further research has yet been undertaken. Fletcher, Blackham and Geertsen (1965) demonstrated that string players' vibrato Gs from 196 Hz to 1570 Hz had oscillations such that the peak pitch was 30 to 40 cents above the note while the lower unit was just on the note. This would make the mean 15–20 cents above the note and, as in the stretched octave, would show a tendency to play sharp – if such a mean is indeed the perceived note. Papich and Rainbow (1975) also found all oscillation to be above the conceived pitch and that vibrato is present in the initial attack on all tones. As in the case of pitch and timbre, studies are needed where vibrato tones are matched to pure tones to ascertain the perceived pitch of the vibrato tones, though the difficulty arises that different subjects making the same match may be choosing different single frequencies to compensate for the contrast between pure tones and 'flexible, rich and tender' ones.

That the lower oscillation coincides more or less with the principal note in vibrato suggests that vibrato is perceived as an expressive convention peculiar to Western culture and in that respect is akin to the trill, which is generally understood as representing the lower of the two tones. For instance, Indian ragas are preferred without vibrato; nevertheless, how far frequency interacts with texture to render a rapid oscillation as perceptually a single line seems to be a matter not only of cultural convention or preference but also one involving the resolution power of the nervous system, as becomes evident from work on stream segregation.

(iii) The trill and stream segregation. 'Stream segregation' is the name given (Bregman and Campbell, 1971) to a phenomenon otherwise described as 'rhythmic fission' (Dowling, 1968) or the 'trill threshold' (Miller and Heise, 1950). The phenomenon, well known to musicians, is employed in, for example, Bach's solo violin works where alternate notes in a passage contribute to two different interrelated melodies each of which is perceived as separately pursuing its own logic. The phenomenon depends upon a rapid presentation rate and a sufficient separation between the two frequency ranges.

Miller and Heise (1950) alternated two 100-millisecond sine wave tones at a rate of ten per second, gradually increasing the frequency interval between the two tones, using tones in different trials to cover the frequency range 150 to 7000 Hz. They found the point at which the alternating stimulus ceased to sound like a trill and resembled two separate simultaneous tones was at an inverval of at least three semitones. They then (1951) introduced a third tone into such an alternating pattern and required the subject to adjust its frequency to the point where it first seemed separate from the rest of the pattern. This point depended on the nature of the alternating pattern as well as on the absolute frequency differences.

Dowling (1973) studied melodic fission by presenting two familiar melodies intercalated, the subject having to name one melody as soon as possible and then the other. The trials started with maximum overlap of the two melodies and, as subjects found this impossible for the identification of melodies, one was transposed a semitone up on every fourth trial. The median separation needed was 1·2 semitones between the highest note of the lower tune, and the lowest of the higher, though there was considerable variability depending on the tunes used.

Norman (1967) followed up the experiment of Heise and Miller. He found that subjects could easily tell when an extraneous note occurred in a ten-note 'trill' (of not more than three-semitone separation) if the inserted note fell within the trill interval; but if the extraneous note was much higher or much lower they could not say whether it had followed an upper or lower note of the trill. Bregman and Campbell (1971) found that subjects could report the order of either upper or lower notes in a sequence of 100-millisecond notes divided by a certain critical interval into four upper and four lower but they could not report how the two streams were enmeshed.

Again the critical band is invoked as necessitating 'extra perceptual processing time' for switching attention between different bandwidths if a space of more than a critical bandwidth is to be spanned. This interpretation is in line with other work on memory and attention, for if an enmeshed list of digits is presented one to each ear then subjects find it easier to report ear by ear than in the order in which the digits were presented (Broadbent, 1958), retaining the report of the second ear in short-term memory storage, rather than switching attention alternately between the two ears.

This work has important implications for the perception of music, for it appears to indicate a neurological limit (the critical band) to the perceptibility of musical phrases. It suggests that there was intuitive wisdom in the rules of strict counterpoint whereby, if a voice made a leap of a large interval, it had subsequently to return by step within that interval, the wisdom being the recognition that extra 'perceptual processing time' was needed for jumps beyond the critical band, and the motion by step that followed gave the steadying time needed. However, auditory stream segregation is reduced and perceptibility improved when tones presented at a rapid rate are connected (by legato or rapid glissando), or even when they are semi-connected (Bregman and Dannenbring, 1973). This suggests a bias in receptivity in the human auditory system, similar to that for speech perception, where continuity is an important factor.

There is disagreement about whether stream segregation represents a preattentive phenomenon (Bregman and Campbell, 1971) or an attentive one (Dowling, 1973; Norman, 1967). These issues imply that, if preattentive, the phenomenon belongs to the perception of texture in music but, if attentive (i.e. memorable), then it belongs to learning and memory.

A further experiment (Idson and Massaro, 1976) set out to test the effects on perceptual memory of masking the three test notes A, C, D♯ arranged in six different orders by interleaved interpolations (B and C♯) where such interpolations were either in the same register or removed up or down an octave. Only those trials where the masker was in the same register were effectively masked. Again this suggests that focussing attention on one critical bandwidth can aid attenuation of the unwanted masking stimulation if it lies outside the bandwidth. It is not unlike the phenomenon in dichotic listening experiments whereby it is easy to attenuate the unwanted of the two messages if the timbre of that voice is different from the attended one. The difference between a man's voice and a child's, for instance, involves not only different spectral properties but different critical band levels. In musical psychology we are brought back to the question, as yet not investigated, of the relative salience of timbre versus the grammatical constraints of the melodic line in holding the listener's attention.

4. RHYTHM, TEMPORALITY, TEMPO.

(*i*) *General factors.* Definitions of rhythm are many and various (for a review discussion see Fraisse, 1956). Essentially, rhythm is temporal pattern. In music the term refers to durations of tones or silence structured by periodicity and accent; but it can also refer to series of events of equal duration and intensity structured by changes of another attribute, for instance pitch. Change of any attribute engenders perceptual grouping. This definition is neutral as between perception and muscular response; the reader's first move in placing any psychological use of the concept should be to distinguish which of these two aspects is in question. Practising musicians would probably prefer Tobias Matthay's definition (1932): 'Rhythm is musical motion; that is the sensing of a succession of sounds as movement, progression or growth'. It is widely held that rhythm is a concept based on motor function, that biological organisms have evolved with receptivity to environmental periodicities, and that the nervous system is constituted on a rhythmic basis which enables it to organize and control natural movement sequences and the sounds of speech or of music according to certain temporal constraints (Lashley, 1951).

In music, periodicity exists within the rhythmic structure at hierarchically organized levels, for just as one can analyse sentence structure first into noun-phrase and verb-phrase and then down to the level of each word, and acoustically to each phoneme, so musical phrase structure, particularly in its rhythmic aspect, can be regarded at various 'architectonic' levels (Cooper and Meyer, 1960). Periodicity may be basically regular or irregular (as in the rhythms of speech, simple recitative, and the music of some non-Western cultures). Where the beat is regular, to be musically 'rhythmic' involves a good correspondence between the intended actions of the performer, or the perceptual response and expectancies of the listener, and an arbitrary measure of clock or metronomic time. The experimental study of experience of durations can be conducted only against such an arbitrary measure, for time exists only in so far as it is mapped by the occurrence of events. There is no measurable sensory transduction such as exists for pitch, loudness or timbre.

Yet musicians would agree that minute deviations from exact metronomic subdivisions of the beat frequently enhance the sensation of rhythm. This may be an effect dependent on surprising the listener's implicit expectation of an exactly regular pattern; or metronomic rhythms may be 'dull' in so far as they do not correspond to the natural rhythms of movement dependent on biological structure; or deviations may be the product of accent which serves to group notes into complexes, each of a strong and one or more weak notes, the nature or duration of the strong beat influencing the durations of all other components of the group.

Indeed, sensitive musicianship includes the art of what Schnabel called 'acoustic illusion', whereby the manipulation of intensity or duration enhances the rhythmic articulation to give perceptually the correct values at the different levels of rhythmic structure (private communication to the author).

The role of accent in rhythmic structure is disputed, possibly owing to its origins in prosody, for according to their locus, accents may emphasize or contradict the regular metrical organization, and cross-accents may have their impact of perversity because rhythm is related to bodily gesture. Grouping by beats or bars and grouping by accent may overlap and introduce the ambivalence of co-existent alternative groupings of elements. However, accents do introduce minute metronomic irregularities, for in experiments where a subject imposes a subjective grouping on heard indistinctive metronome beats, it is evident which grouping has been imposed by the departures from strict synchrony in his tapping, though the subject is often unaware of a discrepancy (Stetson, 1905). The thwarting of implicit expectations of regularity may also underlie the pleasures of syncopation which depend (as do the pleasures of delayed harmonic resolution) on exploiting the tension tolerance of the listener. Clearly, in the Western idiom, it is desirable to integrate harmonic factors into the psychological study of rhythm since they have a qualitative effect upon rhythmic patterns and imply differences in gesture which any choreographer understands.

Four psychological aspects of the perception of rhythm may be distinguished as relevant research areas: psychoacoustics; the organization and use of memory in temporal pattern recognition; the time and beat factors; and the relation of affective response to rhythm and bodily movement. The empirical and theoretical work on four aspects is now considered in turn. It must however be stressed that the close integration and modifying effect of tonal or rhythmic factors in Western diatonic music makes such analytical separation yield only partial information as to the perceptibility of temporal patterns in music.

(*ii*) *Psychoacoustics.* All aspects of auditory perception, including those of pitch, loudness and timbre, are dependent on temporal factors. From the neurological point of view, hearing is the most temporally accurate of the senses, as vision is the most spatially accurate. The problem of how the nervous system organizes and integrates large amounts of perceptual information at a given speed has led to 'psychological moment' theories (Stroud, 1956; White, 1963) postulating a central timing mechanism whereby all that is processed in a single micro-unit of time is unchangeable, modification of perceived input having to be processed by the succession of subsequent units. A musician may understandably question this theory since a number of notes may be played in one tenth of a second; but this fact simply raises the question of how far we perceive in, as it were, preprogrammed groups. Whether or not perceptual sampling occurs by discrete units analogous to single frames in a filmed sequence, the powers of resolution of the nervous system set significant limits to rhythmic capabilities. A hypothesized 'perceptual moment' is long (100 milliseconds) compared to some acoustic parameters, and the relation between them needs to be understood. Musical rhythm psychology is therefore concerned with the perception of minimum audible duration and minimum temporal separation, with the perception of successiveness, temporal order and number.

Minimal audible duration is perhaps of greater interest in the hearing of identifiable pitch or timbre than in the recognition that each brief constituent of a rhythmic pattern has occurred – though the audibility of very short tones related to longer ones in a rhythmic sequence is dependent on these parameters. A tone of two milliseconds (one five-hundredth of a second) is perceptible, though only as a click; as duration increases up to 50 milliseconds tones increasingly acquire pitch quality (Licklider, 1951). Duration is in reciprocal relation to intensity up to about 100–200 milliseconds, briefer tones having to be of greater intensity to be perceptible (Zwislocki, 1960); different signals are equally perceptible if the product of their duration and intensity is held constant. This equal energy rule shows that the nervous system is integrating stimulation over a short period.

The more interesting question concerning perceptibility of rhythmic patterns arises when a plurality of signals is investigated, for it can be maintained that discrete events are essential to rhythm perception (though the speeding up or slowing down of a glissando or of the portamento of singers may contribute to rhythmic sensation).

In detecting differences of onset times (important to musical synchrony, particularly to the conductors of large ensembles), it might be thought, since duration and intensity summate in the nervous system up to 100–200 milliseconds, that information arriving within that interval might be difficult to distinguish. Yet that is not so. Hirsh (1957, 1966) established that two clicks delivered to the same ear were distinguishable as being two rather than one when onsets are only two milliseconds apart. Notably, he found that if two tones are separated by two milliseconds one can detect that there were two signals, but it takes a lag of at least 17 milliseconds to say which order they were in, even when the signals are bands of noise at different pitch levels rather than pure tones. The rise time of instrumental tone makes it difficult to investigate this effect with complex tones, and indeed rise time constitutes a margin of error in the perception of musical synchrony. Patterson and Green (1970), having improved methodology by eliminating cues of spectral differences, still found discrimination between two signals possible where the total time involved was two milliseconds, though the subjective impression was still qualitative, the clicks sounding like a 'tick' and a 'tock'. Leshowitz (1971) showed that the ear can reliably detect a gap of six milliseconds between two ten-millisecond clicks on the basis of slight differences in energy spectra associated with different frequencies. Green's review (1971) of temporal auditory acuity (i.e. the shortest time-interval within which the ear can discriminate the order of auditory events) supports Hirsh's view that the 'temporal grain' of the nervous system in this respect is two milliseconds.

Studies of the gaps between the cessation of one tone and the onset of another do show a frequency effect. Perrott and Williams (1971) asked listeners to judge time-intervals between two tone pulses and found that temporal resolution was inversely related to the size of the frequency differences between them; again this has implications for contemporary composers using electronic or similar idioms: to perceive large jumps in pitch requires extra processing time. Divenyi (1971)

pursued this question by asking subjects to adjust a time-interval between a pair of tone bursts to match the time-interval between a previous standard pair. When the fourth tone burst was different in frequency from the other three they set the time-interval shorter, and the degree of this discrepancy was related to the pitch difference up to an interval of three octaves. However, he could banish this frequency effect upon time-interval perception by altering the intensity of the fourth burst.

Auditory flutter (a regularly interrupted tone) and the stage at which it sounds continuous (auditory flutter fusion) was originally studied by Garner (1947), who found that the duration of brief stimuli (rather than repetition rate) effectively influenced perceptibility (i.e. the threshold of hearing). However, he used pure tones, and the periodicity of interruption may well have produced a modulating tone at the frequency of the interruption, so that it was the perceptibility of the resultant tone that was measured rather than the tone presented. To eliminate this, experiments now use bands of noise. This research borders upon that concerning timbre and texture according to the question asked, as Gerber (1974) pointed out. The subject can detect that an interruption occurs by a subjective impression of qualitative timbre differences at very high rates of interruption (1000 per second, or even higher). But by starting at a low value, increasing it, and asking when an interrupted sound becomes fused, which is about 50 per second (auditory flutter fusion threshold), a different rate is marked from that when decreasing the rate of interruption and asking when a fused sound becomes interrupted, which is about 100 per second (descending flutter threshold).

The preceding questions are directed to discrimination of durations. But temporal pattern recognition involves identification of many events, their number, durations and the structural relations between them. Research on stream segregation (§II, 3(iii)) has shown the importance of frequency relations to temporal order and therefore to rhythmic perceptibility (Bregman and Campbell, 1971). It also indicated the degree to which the detection of temporal factors engenders preattentive processing in terms of timbre and texture, whereas the identification of order engages attentive memory processing. To distinguish repetitions or differences in rhythmic patterns as they recur in music necessitates their having been coded into primary memory. This may contribute to an explanation for Hirsh's difference between the two-millisecond gaps needed to know that discrete temporal events have occurred and the 17-millisecond gaps needed to report what order they were in. Where a sequence exceeds the two events which can be judged in simple relational terms, like 'before–after', 'louder–softer', 'longer–shorter' etc (although psychoacoustic parameters are still involved), it would seem appropriate to begin the transition to the cognitive factors in rhythmic pattern perception, for even three events require from the listener the use of an ordinal labelling system which proliferates the simple relational judgment into complexes. A search of the short-term sensory memory trace is involved in applying these labels.

(iii) *Memory*. The perception of temporal patterning is dependent both on immediate memory and on expectancy: as William James expressed it (1890), 'the practically cognized present is not a knife-edge, but a saddleback, with a certain breadth of its own, on which we sit perched, and from which we look in two directions into time'. Temporal pattern recognition must occur in the order imposed by the stimulus (as contrasted with the subjective ordering in visual scanning of an omnipresent display).

The evolution of the human nervous system in the service of biological needs of information exchange suggests a closely-knit voice–ear neural organization including a strong feedback system. Research on speech perception favours the 'internal generation' model (Liberman and others, 1964), that we perceive speech by synthesis at some neural level of the voice–ear system; and this may very well be the appropriate model for musical perception. If so, then the rhythmic patterns of music are likely to be immediately perceptible in so far as they conform to the neural constraints upon the production of rhythm. It is increasingly thought that both perception and action in all serial ordered behaviour (speech, music, gesture, perceptual–motor skills) is hierarchically organized, that is, it involves different conceptual planning levels as opposed to simple grammatical chains. It is most likely that this hierarchical organization is rhythmically based, that the two concepts are highly related, and that the character of segmentation in planned sequences is dependent on neural organization. The perception of speech or music is bounded therefore not only by the powers of acoustic resolution but also by the rules governing the structure of language or of music, rules which underlie the structure of memory; thus the span of immediate memory (how much may be retained in a single 'now') is related to grammatical rules which are themselves rhythmically based, and by perceptual strategies developed in speaking, singing, playing music, or listening. What is regarded or retained as a pattern length is influenced both by its rhythmic structure (Garner, 1974) and by the degree to which immediately subsequent or preceding parts of the sequence interfere with memory processing. One's repertory of patterns which may each be regarded as a single rhythmic structure is extended with experience, so that the span of immediate memory is also expanded; but nevertheless memory imposes temporal constraints on the perception of rhythm.

The rhythms of some formal techniques in music are less readily perceptible than others; the hierarchical ordering imposed by the composer, though observing that of a shared 'language', may not easily be assimilable by the listener given the temporal constraints on both peripheral and central processing. The salience of forward temporal order and its resistance to mental reversal, although a vital feature of both speech and music, particularly concerns the perception of rhythm. In perceiving time-ordered sequences of more than a very few items there is no simple mental operation, analogous to spatial right–left reversal with visual pattern recognition, by which, for instance, a melody played backwards might be recognizable. The second aspect of rhythm psychology therefore comprises the particular memory processes involved in temporal pattern recognition. These are of two main kinds: number and duration. 'Temporal numerosity' is the name given to the perception of the number of events per unit time accomplished 'without counting'. Cheatham and White (1954) found accuracy to decline sharply above a rate of about ten events per second, as did Pieron (1945). Since the ear is able to monitor repetitive stimuli at a much faster rate than this when detecting only qualitative differences, a rate of ten per second suggests that the limitation occurs

in central processing, supporting Broadbent's (1958) and Sperling's (1960) view of sensory memory as a large capacity store with a quick decay, from which little can be coded into primary memory. Cheatham and White found roughly similar limits in the visual mode which also suggests limitations in the cortex, though there is a difference between vision and hearing in estimation of number during the first 300 milliseconds which argues for a peripheral rather than central limitation difference between vision and audition. There is an opportunity here for musical psychology to explore the effects of variables such as different types of rhythmically structured versus non-structured sequences upon temporal numerosity, and indeed whether trained musicians have better arhythmic numerosity perception, since ten or more unaccented events per second is hardly unknown in music. It has been pointed out that the consistent underestimation of the number of events has important implications for the upper limit of morse-code reception rate (Sanford, 1971) and the implications are equally significant for musical perception.

As to duration, one of the few studies conducted using experienced musicians as subjects and musical material is that of Divenyi (1971), who systematically related the subjects' ability to detect duration differences between the two time-intervals bounded by three tones (of which one was of a different frequency) to discover how this detection of temporal irregularity is affected by absolute distance, ratio, range or order of the two frequencies used and by different presentation rates (intervals of 300, 600 and 800 milliseconds). Detectability was adversely affected by absolute proximity below a major 3rd, for instance for the major 2nd ratio 9 : 10 (which may again suggest a critical band effect) and by simple ratios, i.e. for intervals of a perfect 4th (ratio 3 : 4), perfect 5th (2 : 3) and octave (1 : 2). The other interval evoking poorer performance was the major 7th; it is argued that this arises because of its proximity to the octave. Divenyi also included a subjective measure, subjects characterizing musical intervals on a tense–relaxed dimension, but concluded that its lack of correspondence with detection performance for the various frequency intervals suggests that the interaction between frequency and time estimation is 'exempt from voluntary control'. One notable conclusion he drew from his study is that a different perceptual process seems to be involved for perceiving time-intervals of less than 600 milliseconds than for those of more than that. This time-interval coincides with that in which Fraisse (1956) found least variability, where listeners imposed subjective ordering on featureless trains of pulses. Also it is in the vicinity of the 'indifference' interval, that is, the level which divides the overestimation of short time-intervals from the underestimation of long ones, though Woodrow (1934) pointed out that from all the experiments he reviewed this interval can only be arrived at by a statistical average.

Fraisse (1963) neatly delineated the parameters of time perception – the tempo range of particular interest to musicians – as that between the 'temporal grain' of the nervous system and the limit of the immediate memory span of an empty time-interval by saying: 'Between the lower limit, where we are first able to discern two distinct stimuli and the upper limit, where one stimulus is already part of one past when the next occurs, there is perception of true succession and of an increasing interval between successive stimuli'. The upper breaking-point between qualitatively different perceptual processes in duration perception, whether of empty or of filled intervals, is according to Fraisse one-and-a-half to two seconds; for in a longer span the two events no longer 'belong to the same present'. The experience of a rhythmic beat is thus not possible, since it depends on the previous beat having survived in memory.

Most of the studies on temporal order deal with events separated by very short intervals, yet even here the role of memory is to be reckoned with. There is a marked increase in the difficulty of reporting the order of even three events, as compared with two, and the difficulty increases with sequence length. This may be attributable to the interference which later items exert upon the processing of earlier ones, for 'echoic' memory is thought to be a rapidly fading trace (Neisser, 1967; see §III). If four sounds (not however conventional music sounds – e.g. a buzz, a hiss or a noise) are presented in continuous repetition (a 'loop'), the duration of each must be 700 milliseconds for inexperienced listeners efficiently to report their temporal order, or 300 for experienced ones to do so (Warren and others, 1969). But this value drops to 200 if a single presentation only is monitored (Warren, 1972) and to a mere 50 if only three sounds are presented (Peters and Wood, 1973). Contrast the 300 milliseconds per component with the speed of monitoring of speech and music, and the role that the existing structure of language and music memory stores has in perceptual processes is suggested, for compressed speech is intelligible at below 50 milliseconds per phoneme (Aaronson, 1967) and the rate for ordering musical notes is only marginally slower (Winckel, 1960). Warren and Obusek (1972), when intercalating two musical tones with a hiss and a buzz (again presented in a continuous loop), found order perception at only 200 milliseconds per item if the related musical items were contiguous, though it was more difficult if the lower frequency preceded the higher and not possible at that rate if the two tones were intercalated with the noises instead of being adjacent to each other. Divenyi and Hirsh (1975) found the performance in identifying temporal order of three-tone sequences was considerably poorer when a fourth stimulus (not to be reported) was added, again suggesting the interference effect upon memory of subsequent events. Though these studies of temporal order are not directly concerned with durational rhythmic patterns but with the rhythmic pattern imposed by the change of another attribute, they do show that duration perception is influenced by adjacent frequency relations and by the interference effects of continuing sequences.

Where sequences are presented in a loop, it is left to the subject to choose which event starts the pattern he perceives, and thus the nature of the whole problem is subjectively imposed, much as was subjective rhythm in the experiments by Stetson (1905) and Fraisse (1956). Garner's studies of temporal pattern perception (Royer and Garner, 1966; Garner and Gottwald, 1969; Garner, 1974) typically have subjects listening to (or watching) eight-item sequences composed of two distinguishable stimuli of equal durations arranged in different patterns and presented at five different rates, each in a continuous loop; as soon as he can identify it, the subject taps the rhythm. Although rates of presentation indicate qualitatively different processes, slow rates evoking an 'active intellectualized learning' and fast rates a more passive process of seemingly allowing the

Gestalt to impose itself, the main interest is in which of the eight possible starting-points (all correct ones) the subject selects from the continuous sequence. He tends to choose either the first of a run of the same stimulus or (less often) the first of a run of regular alternations; there was considerable consensus in the preferred pattern, which pertains at all presentation rates. If the pattern is coded into memory in terms of same versus different then, clearly, starting with the first of a run of the same or of a regular series of alternations is a more economical strategy, for both are less information-loaded than where such figures fall in the middle of a pattern. It is an interesting question how far change constitutes implicit accent in these otherwise equally timed 'deadpan' sequences. Given that duration, were the attribute changed (finite sequences of crotchets and quavers, say, presented in a continuous loop), then would there be a preferred perceptual organization? Which type of pattern is more easily coded? Would the first of a run of quavers still remain a preferred starting point or would implicit prosodic influences remove the locus of accent? Garner's approach to temporal pattern perception is an information theory one (therefore he sees difficulty of pattern perception as increasing with the number of perceived alternatives; see §I, 5, i). But this view considers only surface structure – the relation between adjacent items; it deals with succession and arbitrary numerical design, which certainly are elements in musical rhythmic structure, but it could hardly be expected to accommodate the ordered levels of rhythmic organization in syntactic music – the prosodic element.

How far can musical syntactic organization be considered in terms of a linguistic analysis that assumes similar underlying perceptual–motor processes? Such an assumption is implied in Cooper and Meyer's (1960) model of rhythmic structure based on the patterns of poetic metre at the phoneme and accent level of analysis. Martin (1972) proposed two simple rules for generating rhythmic behaviour sequences (whether speech, music, or other meaningful sound-patterns) that can accommodate durations between both adjacent and non-adjacent levels. In speech, altering the main emphasis (i.e. the accent at the highest level in the structure) will subtly re-order the time relations of each adjacent syllable in the whole phrase by altering all other hierarchical order values for the remaining accents, and this may very well be part of the reason for the subtle differences in rhythm between different musical performers. (Try speaking six versions of the same sentence emphasizing different words, e.g. 'I had already asked your help', observing the changes of rhythmic pattern; the locus of main accent may necessitate imposing a different subsidiary one if too many short syllables fall together.) It is central to this model that the rhythmic organization of speech requires accented syllables to fall roughly at equal time intervals, and the dominant influence of accents on the temporal organization of utterance entails their being in some sense planned first. The listener is equipped to foresee these focal points and his perceptual sampling is arranged accordingly, perception of initial elements of syntactic structures facilitating the anticipation of later elements. There are both feedback and feedforward processes in syntactic temporal pattern perception. How far the human disposition to perceive prosodic organization in music (itself dependent on the syntax of bodily movement, and on how much one can sing or say in one breath) either complements or outweighs the perception of arbitrary numerical design might become apparent by correlating a taxonomy of rhythmic patterns (e.g. Gordon, 1974) with their perceptual difficulties for music students at different levels of achievement, and further by observing what common principles underlie the individual differences in performing the same notation of a musical rhythm (Gabrielsson, 1973, a, b, c, f; Seashore, 1938, p.242).

The memory factors in perception of musical rhythm that determine the psychological length of a rhythmic pattern therefore include its syntactic structure, its symmetry (which reduces information load), the distribution of accents and how far the intervening events fall within the 'numerosity' span or are 'chunkable' (see §III) into groupings of smaller familiar patterns. A great many earlier researchers (Bolton, 1894; Wundt, 1896; Squire, 1901; MacDougall, 1903; Isaacs, 1920) used the concept of 'a wave of attention' as being the limiting factor in rhythm perception, this wave being seen as a reflex type of response. Whether or not it is applied to the basic beat or (more often) to the span of rhythmic pattern perceptible in 'a single row', it was subsuming the function which is here regarded as that of short-term memory. However the dependence of recognition upon long-term memory factors (i.e. upon grammatical comprehension and familiarity with rhythmic patterns which expand perceptual capabilities, and therefore the length of a 'single row') is not accommodated by the 'wave of attention' concept. (The concept of an immediately perceptible temporal Gestalt is also dependent on this relation between short-term memory capacity and the nature of the individual's long-term memory store.) One must be careful not to confuse the 'wave of attention' (Puffer, 1905; Dunlap, 1911) with some hypothesized periodicity in nervous discharge.

(iv) *Pulse and beat.* Another aspect of musical rhythm is the perception of accent, pulse and tempo. Accent is the emphasis, by added intensity or duration, of one tone which serves to group a number of weaker ones to it. Pulse perception is the recognition of that regular recurrence by which music is conceptually segmented into bars (measures) and which is related in origins to poetic metre, though distinguishable from conversational speech rhythms, for they are characterized by accent without pulse. The rhythms of recitative are significant according to their resemblance to conversational speech. Although language seems to be stored in the opposite cortical hemisphere of the brain from music and other pattern recognition processes, the musical forms using an irregular rhythmic basis akin to speech raise a problem about this distinction, for rhythm appears to be the one musical attribute which does not manifest this clearcut language–music distinction in the storage of music and speech in opposite hemispheres of the cortex (*see* AMUSIA).

Pulse regularity was introduced into music early in its history from the ritualistic marriage of song and dance, voice and gesture. The compelling force of this marriage lends point to Lashley's theory (1951) of a rhythmic neurological substrate closely connecting hierarchically ordered perceptual and motor activities. Evidence connecting a certain regular time interval with perceptual processes has led to alpha rhythm in the brain being invoked as the possible biological rhythmic substrate (Lenneberg, 1967). This alpha rhythm (around eight to ten per second) is lengthy compared to the temporal resolution powers of the nervous system

psychoacoustically, but musical psychology may eventually find some legitimate link between the two, to which the particular perceptual salience of certain poetic metres underlying musical rhythm may be related (see Cooper and Meyer, 1960; Longuet-Higgins and Steedman, 1971). The relation between gesture and voice in music has been the basis of many versions of the 'Motor theory of Rhythm' which interprets Plato's definition of rhythm – kineseōs taxis, or 'order in movement' – in the restricted sense of indicating that we perceive rhythm by an implicit muscular response. His definition has remained tenable, although the distinctions between 'mental' and 'muscular' or 'voluntary' and 'involuntary' remain problematic in contemporary terms.

How far biological rhythms underlie our perception of time is disputed, for perception of time-intervals is also influenced by the number of events which have occurred in them (Ornstein, 1969) and also (in music) by how these events are related to each other. Historically, the transition in music from the Platonic principle that the rhythm of music follows that of the words (*Republic*, iii, 398) to the metronomic pulse as the governing factor, introduced a time-based relationality between elements which may be understood either intellectually or by an implicit motor response, as any teacher of music will recognize, for an awareness of the fact that a triplet represents a division of the beat into three equal time-intervals is no guarantee of knowing just how to reproduce or tap them out equally. The Motor theory of Rhythm has often been used to explain subjective ordering of trains of equal unaccented pulses into two or fours rather than threes (Woodrow, 1951), an untestable theory in the absence of a race of three-legged humans, for perception of waltz rhythm depends on the analysis at a higher level of architectonic organization, alternate bars being strong and weak. But in trying to understand the response to, and the memorability of, different rhythms one is always dealing with two forms of organization, the metronomic and the prosodic.

The relation of pulse to tempo is the subject of research that seeks to distinguish pace as a determining influence in perceptibility of rhythm (Fraisse, 1956): the notion is that how much can be perceived 'in a single now' relates to the satisfactory nature of 'good Gestalt' of certain rhythmic patterns, but that this also depends upon the speed at which they are presented. It is difficult to consider time and pulse factors of rhythmic perception independently from memory ones, as temporal pattern perception depends upon the structural aspects of the language and the existence of a memory store arranged according to the rules of that language. Analysis of temporal rhythmic patterns according to hierarchically ordered linguistic rules (Martin, 1972) seems a more useful approach than a Gestalt one which often rests on a problematic analogy between visual and auditory pattern perception, problematic since the temporal factors in transduction differ between the two modalities.

In spite of the fact that there is no sensory transduction of time as a physical entity, the time experience has frequently been treated metaphorically as a sensory process; time is seen as an impingement of quanta: much as quanta of light fall upon the retina, sensations of time are seen as recorded in the nervous system in terms congruent with an internal 'biological clock'. The two theories mentioned earlier attempt to measure the time-base; 'perceptual moment' theories of White (1963) and of Stroud (1956) suggest 100 milliseconds, and those based on the division of time experience into qualitatively different zones evoking different processes choose the 'indifference interval' (600–700 milliseconds, according to Fraisse, 1963) as the point where 'real' time and the experience of time coincide. Unfortunately there are rival estimates of the indifference interval, from Fraisse's 700 milliseconds to Treisman's three seconds (1964). Fraisse based his distinction between 'temps long' and 'temps court' upon this time-interval. (For reviews of earlier estimates of the time-base see Woodrow, 1934, 1951.) An earlier theory identified heartbeat as the biological clock, this being the principle underlying eurhythmics (Jaques-Dalcroze, 1919) and it has been more recently studied (Ochberg, Pollak and Meyer, 1964). However, heart rate can be brought under voluntary control by sensory feedback and to this extent cannot be seen as an unmodifiable biological clock (Brener and Hothersall, 1971). Respiration has also been invoked as the time-base (Munsterberg, 1892) as an automatic bodily process nevertheless under some voluntary control, for changes in respiration occur with different musical tempos. However, rhythm need not always have this effect upon respiration and the argument is based, *a posteriori*, on synchronous responses related to motor responses. Moreover, since Neal Miller's experiments demonstrating control over the functions of the autonomic nervous system including heart (previously assumed to be involuntary), the distinction between voluntary and involuntary is not clearcut (*Biofeedback and Self-control*, 1970–).

The 'perceptual moment' interval of 100 milliseconds is close to the rhythm of alpha wave in the brain, also invoked as the biological clock. This theory was anticipated by MacDougall's claim (1902) that our rhythmic sense is mediated by the basic and primitive rate of nervous discharge. But alpha rhythm is not always present and, as Ornstein (1969) inquired, does the clock stop when alpha rhythm peters out? Furthermore, according to Kamiya (1971), people can learn either to suppress entirely or to change the frequency of their own alpha rhythm.

Although the biological clock is seen as independent of the stimulation by momentary environmental rhythms (an aspect essential to the musician's independent sense of tempo), certain conditions such as environmental temperature or infection which raise body temperature were seen to influence time and tempo sense (François, 1927; Hoagland, 1933, 1935). This view of the clock as a chemical or metabolic process has not been supported. Bell and Provins (1963) failed to replicate Hoagland's study, though Baddeley (1966) found that cold temperature shortened time experience. The range of individual variability (Bell, 1965) is also against the theory.

If the search for a biological clock is unsatisfactory there is nevertheless a concatenation of empirical evidence on the importance of certain short time-intervals which indicate that a rhythmic base to sequential organization probably does exist in the nervous system. For instance, the fact that delayed auditory feedback has its most disruptive effect on both speech (Black, 1951) and music (Gates, Bradshaw and Nettleton, 1974) at roughly one-sixth of a second is an indication of such a rhythmic base. But there is as yet no consistency between these various theories as to the time-interval concerned or the organic process which controls it.

The Motor theory of Rhythm, that rhythm is mediated by 'voluntary' muscles, puts greater emphasis on learning and the trained and disciplined character of these muscular responses. Appeal is sometimes made to the origins of music as an aid to rhythmic teamwork (Bucher, 1919), but song is an occasional adjunct rather than a necessity to work rhythms. Mainwaring (1933) has shown that very young children do not spontaneously show synchronous responses to music, thus emphasizing the element of training rather than involuntary muscular response. However, the lack of overt response does not preclude the possibility of implicit response, and the study of kinesics (Birdwhistell, 1970) indicates some degree of natural synchrony between voice and gesture. This is likely to be vaguely so compared with musical synchrony, though even in musical performances the asynchrony is quite considerable. Vernon (1936) found asynchronies of 30 milliseconds for chord playing, and Small (1936) found deviations from precise durations in melody playing of 10·31%.

Perception of rhythmic structures is seen to relate to bodily movement in so far as these structures are based upon poetic metres, although the poetic metres of various languages differ in the degree to which they are based on quantity or on stress. However, many writers (Stetson, 1905; Jackson, 1915–18; Wedge, 1927; Cooper and Meyer, 1960) identify the musical pattern of relative durations at the lowest level of structure (phoneme, as it were) with the shorts and longs of Greek poetic metre, and some Gestalt principles are invoked in conjunction with this view. For instance, a succession of iambs is held to be perceived as such rather than as trochees because the Gestalt principle of proximity operates as a determining factor in grouping (see §I, 3, iii, ex.1). This view depends upon beginnings rather than durations. Fraisse also saw rhythmic structures as a figure–ground phenomenon; we are very conscious of the tick-tock time-interval of the clock, but less so of the tock-tick. Where durations are equal the figure corresponds with y in ex.1, whereas the ground corresponds with x. Similarly, he said, we are less conscious of the spaces between phrases. This example does not give enough weight to the fact that the function of 'ground' here is to provide breathing spaces. After the rise of polyphony, the shift away from musical rhythm being determined by that of the words also removed the locus of breathing spaces, so that the carry-over of verbal sense in vocal music must in some degree obscure the figure–ground phenomenon. But in any case it is questionable how far visual figure–ground principles can apply to music, just as the Gestalt principle of closure is an entirely spatial concept (closure – that a broken circle is perceived as a circle because of the electric field forces in the visual cortex), for there is no doubting that a phrase is unfinished when an ostinato figure or a ground bass ends in mid-phrase. This Gestalt orientation of Fraisse, seen in conjunction with his experiments distinguishing qualitatively different time experience plus a homogeneity of the absolute durations which are most easily perceptible, suggests a biological basis rather than a learnt one for the perception of rhythm. Indeed, in emphasizing the resemblance between his results and the laws of rhythm of Aristoxenus, he is suggesting that these laws were the result of an intuitive recognition of the biological factors indicated by his experiments.

The shift in musical history engendered by the rise of polyphony and its regular rhythmic pulse, whereby accents could be either commetric or contrametric, introduced a problem as yet unconsidered by psychologists. It is the librettist's question of how it is possible to monitor two coexistent grammatically structured sequences which have rhythmic focal points at different moments, if in fact it is the case that the span of expectancy is rhythmically mapped on the basis of what has already been monitored, and if this rhythmic mapping has a neurological basis.

(v) *Affective response*. Finally, the affective response to rhythm is a growing research area. The enduring influence of the Motor theory of Rhythm probably owes its continuity to the intuitive recognition of the part rhythm plays, not only in perceptual–motor skills but also in emotional expression; indeed, the coordination of these two aspects is the basis of all artistic endeavour in music. The progress (from infancy onwards) from involuntary spontaneous rhythmic movements (which Freud described as the discharge of neural tension) towards voluntary muscular control, and its close relation to the perception and ordering of time, is recognized not only by cognitive psychologists (like Bruner) but also by clinical ones. The acquisition of voluntary control is part of the progress towards control by the 'reality principle' of Freud and its related secondary process. The vital role of rhythm in ordering the perception of reality is particularly recognized in MUSIC THERAPY.

Although the Motor theory of Rhythm cannot be a sufficient explanation of rhythm perception, the well-nigh universal capacity to respond to rhythmic music on occasion by some responsive gesture of hand or foot suggests that perception of rhythm is conducive to some optimal state of stimulation. 'Metrical accentuation means a rise in arousal potential' (Berlyne, 1971), though it must be remembered that regular rhythm can also have the de-arousing or soporific effect of a lullaby. The regular beat itself is the stable measure against which diversity or complexity is experienced and is only one aspect of the arousal effect. Rhythm, by ordering a vista of expectancy, can provide for the neurologically arousing surprise or complexity of pattern within the control and dependability of a regular beat. That surprise is neurologically arousing is evident even in studies of perception in infants (Schaeffer and Parry, 1970); indeed the orientating reflex of animals is a state of neurological arousal to environmental stimuli which are surprising or informative. As yet there is no specific research on the effects of responding to various rhythms upon the arousal system in the brain-stem which mediates the general level of alertness, and which can be stimulated either by sensory experience or by cognitive processes.

An early study (Husband, 1934) on the effects of musical rhythms upon bodily sway (which is an indication of muscle tone and which is at its greatest when standing with closed eyes) showed that there was three times as much sway to musical rhythm as to pure rhythm, and most of all to jazz. The obvious objection, that subjective autosuggestion possibly exaggerated responses, does not alter the fact that intensity of responses was consistently correlated to the type of musical or non-musical rhythm.

A common element in the attitudes of motor theorists is that of the role of affect or emotion. MacDougall (1903) saw 'emotional tone' as a concomitant of rhythm experience, and Stetson (1905) saw 'imagery or mental

beats' as only auxiliary to the (explicit or implicit) organized muscular movements. Affect and muscular response, both aspects of arousal, were in the earlier theorists' view seen as causal explanations of the perception of rhythm. But the present view of emotion as a high activation level (Duffy, 1957) and this neurological arousal ensuing from perceptual processes is much more in line with that of Ruckmick (1913) in which kinaesthesis forms only part of a complex state of consciousness which typifies the experience of rhythm. The emotional response (i.e. the high arousal level) evoked by jazz, North Indian and Afro-Cuban music must be due to the increment of arousal that accompanies the thwarting of expectation characteristic of syncopation and jazz breaks. Weaver's study (1939) of the intensity of muscular response to syncopation concludes that syncopic accents increase the experienced intensity of the adjacent time-keeping beat (and presumably the more so where the latter is silent). It is possible that a Gestalt orientated psychologist would see the inverted arsis–thesis or agonist–antagonist relations in syncopation as an ambivalent perceptual process analogous to visual figure–ground reversal. Musical examples abound (e.g. Beethoven's Piano Sonata op.110, repeated G major chords in the last movement) where the protracted use of syncopation makes it extremely hard to convey the relation to an implicit time-keeping beat, and the inverted figure–ground ambiguity of perception taxes the conflict tolerance of the listener as well as the short-term memory capacity of the 'single now'. In practice it is clear that the implicit beat is harder to retain the longer a series of syncopes is continued.

A major effect of perceptual structures is to minimize the conflict engendered by the ambiguity of coexistent alternative structures. Syncopation and rhythmic ambiguities are ways of exploiting conflict feelings within a controlled structure. The control of an established rhythmic structure must survive, for if the structure disintegrates there is no longer the ambiguity or conflict, but rather the absence of perceptible form. Psychoanalytic attitudes to rhythm are based on this view, which is related to that of Berlyne (1971) if his concept of 'conflict' can be seen as psychoanalytic 'tension' and his concept of 'arousal' can be related to the psychoanalytic libidinal or instinctive energy. Haish (1953), for instance, pointed out the effects of rhythm upon brain-stem and muscle tone; he saw rhythm as the periodic discharge of tension and therefore as the most primitive component of music. Hanson (1944–5) reviewed the changes in rhythmic patterns through the history of Western music as a development of techniques that intensify emotional tension. Gutheil (1954) also saw syncopation or changes of rhythm as effecting an increase of tension. On the other hand rhythm as a structuring or organizing principle is seen as a form of mastery of the conflict engendered by instinctual urges; fears of lack of control can be held at bay by temporal structure. Thus temporal structure, as for instance in musical games with their regularity of rhythm, plays a great part in educating the growing child to an understanding of the temporal map of the immediate future. The new-born infant's primitive inability to tolerate delay is gradually transformed by learning time-control.

The lack of empirical evidence of any precision on the effects of musical rhythmic patterns and tempos in terms of arousal serves to keep the subject in a stage of more speculative theory. There is a growing body of evidence in music therapy that the time structure of rhythmic patterning is particularly effective in treating the pathology of attention found in the mentally ill or the mentally handicapped; but this also awaits more precise empirical work. Finally, the nature of coding processes in musical memory, particularly for rhythmic patterns, calls for purely musical experiments. Perhaps, as with many other aspects of psychology, a systematic study of dysfunction in clinical cases combined with evidence of coding processes and the arousal effects of certain rhythms will illuminate the way in which biological rhythms are the basis of integration in sequential activities, which in turn include the perception of rhythms.

5. MELODY AND HARMONY. At the point at which melody and harmony enter into psychological discussion, there is a shift from psychoacoustic to cognitive factors which is both significant and problematic. The enduring and fundamental problem of receptivity to certain musical systems is the degree to which those systems have evolved according to certain psychoacoustic facts; how far, for instance, Western tonal harmony is dependent upon culture or upon morphology (*see* CONSONANCE; INTERVALS). This problem is often tacitly left in abeyance by researchers into 'melodic sense' or 'harmonic sense', but in considering how such a sense develops the implicit question of whether there is any innate disposition to clothe musical thought in a certain musical system is always present. Hence the most pertinent area of research is that of the development of cognitive structures from birth to maturity.

Generally perception of melody is discussed in terms of recognition or recall, as a manifestation of tonal memory; indeed perception is an aspect of memory. But the stages of its acquisition reveal three aspects. Melody perception is not only the recognition of the direction of melodic movement (up or down), nor yet only of precise size of interval steps; it is also the sense of the tonal centre of gravity of a phrase, or the sense that this focal basis has moved, as it does in modulation into a new key. Thus appropriate tests include not only those of recall or recognition (the memory component), but also those of the ability to predict, for instance, the most suitable end-note to a phrase according to its idiom, or to detect a 'wrong note', i.e. one that in a particular idiom makes no 'sense'. In this respect musicality is the implicit grasp of the grammar of one musical language, which an education in that music serves to make explicit. Given the task of choosing, out of four given alternatives, a suitable end-note to an eight-bar phrase, the majority of seven-year-old children will choose a note of harmonic stability, particularly, if indicated, the tonic (Reimers, 1927; Teplov, 1966). This applies equally to children with and without musical instruction. However, a child may choose (say) the supertonic either through a lack of comprehension of the idiom, or because he knowingly wishes the inconclusive end suggested by an implicit imperfect cadence to convey that the tune will continue. In short, a less obvious solution may indicate either less 'musicality', or much more musical sophistication manifest in the comparative enjoyment of tonal ambiguity. Devising tests for 'melodic sense' is therefore no simple matter and is resistant to any conceptual separation from 'harmonic sense'.

Studies of the spontaneous chant of very young children (Moorhead and Pond, 1941; Révész, 1944) show a preponderance of simple musical intervals, particularly 3rds, also octaves, perfect 5ths and 4ths. The importance of tonal factors in memory for melody is even more apparent in the six to 14 age group (Brehmer, 1925). In melodic recognition tests, alterations in melodies are more easily detected when they include tonally extraneous notes or do not provide a 'satisfying ending' rather than those which do not modify tonal structure.

Teplov (1966) took the view that perception of melody depends not only on memory and discrimination of the correct intonation of intervals, but also on a harmonic or tonal sense which he saw as an 'emotional experience of the relationships between tones'. By contrast Mursell saw melody as always entirely independent of harmony (1937, p.102) and cited as support of this view the experiments where well-known melodies remain recognizable when translated into non-tonal microsystems of intervals (Révész, 1935; Werner, 1926). A recent experiment by Dowling and Fujitani (1971) showed that preserving direction but not size of melodic steps also yields recognition of well-known melodies. On the whole this manifestation indicates only the importance of the directional factor in melody recognition while not invalidating Teplov's notion of an affective dimension to the use of the tonal language. Studies are needed where recall rather than recognition is the perceptual measure used.

Many studies show the relative indifference to harmonic factors exhibited by young children (Rupp, 1915; Valentine, 1962). Furthermore, there is evidence that harmonic perception consistently emerges at a later age than melodic perception. Franklin (1956) interpreted this as indicating that an ear for tonality is preceded by the ability to perceive pitch, or consonance and dissonance; true perception of tonality is not achieved until the child can listen both horizontally and vertically, which is a later stage of development. In experiments using a rather imprecise interpretation of the concept of conservation, Pflederer (1964, 1966) also showed the perception of harmony to be a relatively late acquisition.

This sequence of attaining these perceptual skills in childhood reflects, in the history of music, the advance from monophonic to, eventually, harmonic music. The problem still remains: how far are children learning a tonal language with or without help from the psychoacoustic factors underlying the relations between the musical intervals of that language? The major source for embarking on a synthesis of the historic, ethnomusicological and psychoacoustic consideration of this problem remains Helmholtz (1863, pt.3).

III. Memory. This is the nervous system's retention of a dynamic physical record of previous experience, experience that may be perceptual, cognitive, emotional or kinaesthetic. Musical memory includes all these varieties of experience, since music functions both as a perceptual–motor skill and as a language that expresses subjective states and employs a symbol system. Memory includes learning that has occurred either intentionally or unintentionally, self-directed or by instruction, and either by repetition or once-for-all (one-trial learning).

Musical memorizing is an intentional registration in memory which, except for a very few individuals who have total recall, usually involves repetition, since it is essential to reliability, in performance or recall, that there should be some degree of overlearning (that is, repetition beyond the criterion of a single correct reproduction).

1. Encoding, storage, retrieval. 2. Codes. 3. 'Rehearsal'. 4. Retention of the single auditory image. 5. Tonal memory. 6. Melody. 7. Melody and temporal order. 8. Attention. 9. Long-term memory organization. 10. Perceptual–motor memory. 11. Sight-reading. 12. Memorizing: (i) The nature of memorizing (ii) Intentionality (iii) Distribution of sessions. 13. Conclusion.

1. ENCODING, STORAGE, RETRIEVAL. Memory may be regarded as having three aspects, its registration (or encoding), its storage, and lastly its retrieval, which may be manifest at different levels. For instance, one may be unable to recall a phrase, either vocally or by any other representation, yet be able to relearn it in a much shorter time than the original learning had taken. Penfield (1951), from his extensive research correlating memory with topographical stimulation of the cortex in open brain surgery, derived a strong indication that all that has been attended to sufficiently to have been originally encoded survives in storage through a lifetime, so that unavailability of a specific memory (forgetting) may be seen as a failure of the retrieval process rather than as a loss of the original trace. His view of memory storage would apply more to music seen as a non-representational language than to verbal or visual experience where representation or meaning renders it, in the long term, more susceptible to 'schematization' (Bartlett, 1932), a process whereby the original registration is progressively modified over time through subsequent recollections and a process of paraphrase, so that a specific memory more closely resembles its latest recollection than the original event. That 'schemata' thus undergo transformations, as memories are reactivated over the years, presents an objection to the theory of memory as stored by discrete 'traces' each theoretically identifiable by its vintage numbering. Nevertheless, the dominance of recall by the most recent version of a memory may be due to its availability in retrieval rather than to its metamorphosis during storage; previous versions need not be lost even though superseded in conscious memory. After a very long interval of time, for instance, it is frequently an original fingering that is recalled rather than any subsequently learned and improved version, though this spontaneous recovery of an earlier trace possibly exemplifies persistence of perceptual–motor skill memory, as being stronger than that for the syntactic aspects of music. However, since the absence of dictionary meaning in music renders the notion of paraphrase meaningless as applied to it, to regard a purely musical memory trace as enduring without schematization is less problematic than to do so for language memory traces, since any transmutations of a musical phrase can be seen only as inaccuracies similar to misquotations of a text. Impediments to retrieval may include the interference of material subsequently learned (retroactive inhibition) or previously learned (proactive inhibition), or, as psychoanalysis has shown, repression – the blocking from consciousness of material that has some emotionally disturbing association. How far there can be attribution of forgetting to the decay of stored memory traces, say with age, is still a matter of dispute.

Memory refers to retention for seconds, hours or a lifetime. Memory is used even in making sense of a musical work heard for the first time, since unless a theme or configuration can be carried until its next appearance (whether it recurs transposed, embellished, inverted, augmented, reversed or simply repeated), every such recurrence will sound like a totally new event.

The human capacity for retaining immediate sensory information is limited, and the initial coding into memory is a complex process now thought to have at least two phases. First there is a sensory or 'echoic' image outlasting the stimulus by only milliseconds, which is not unlike a rapidly fading after-image and can occur whether or not attention is being paid to that particular stimulus; according to Neisser (1967), sensory stores are 'preattentive'. Second there is a short-term or 'primary' memory in which the rapidly fading trace is coded into more durable form, but which also fades (though not so rapidly) unless it can be rehearsed. Any simple subsequent task which prevents mental rehearsing causes loss of the encoded trace (Peterson, 1963); and the instability of this second stage is also shown by the fact that in cases of concussion or electric-convulsive therapy for mental illness, learning is lost which took place immediately before the accident or treatment, whereas long-term memories are recovered (Williams, 1970). Without this short-term memory one could no more make sense of music as one is hearing it than one could carry on a conversation, which involves retaining and responding to what has just been said.

Long-term memory stores not only our repertory of music, whether retained from intentional learning or from a casual hearing, but also our grammatical comprehension of music, those implicitly acquired rules of musical syntax which govern our expectancies while hearing an unfamiliar work. It is therefore the basis upon which sensory memory is coded into 'primary' short-term memory, since experience of musical grammar progressively improves the skill by which coding by larger groupings or chunks can be accomplished. Miller (1956) has shown that the capacity of short-term memory is limited to a small number of items (7 ± 2), whatever the sense modality receiving them, but that this capacity is extended by the chunking of adjacent items into larger units. Clearly, in diatonic music, scale sequences or triadic steps, for example, are easily chunked, so that experience progressively extends the span of immediate memory. There is evidence that rhythm and even subjective rhythm imposed upon arhythmic material plays a considerable part in chunking both verbal and musical material. Indeed, rhythmic grouping is one basis of mnemonics. Bower and Winzenz (1969) demonstrated that chunked digits (e.g. 384, 25, 18) would not be recognized if presented in different segments (e.g. 38, 42, 518). Dowling (1973), using 20-note melodies originally presented in four groups each of five notes, found similarly poor recognition when the test item was a new grouping (using the second half of one original group and the first half of its successor). Dowling's subjects were music students with a mean of 2·85 years of training; further experiments using subjects of different levels of musical training might show how coding strategies are built up and how versatility in perceiving configurations and their transformations is acquired.

Both long- and short-term memory function in absolute pitch, as they do also in improvisation, where long-term familiarity with grammatical constraints combines with short-term retention of thematic material to produce that hierarchically ordered immediate planning which is used in improvised music much as it is in impromptu speaking upon a theme.

A view widely held in physiological psychology is that short-term memory is the transient reverberation of neuronal circuits (which may be kept reverberating by mental rehearsal) and that long-term consolidated memory consists in structural changes at synapses. However, although the characteristic differences between short-term and long-term memory are well documented, one may object to models of memory which are overdetermined by the computer analogy in regarding sensory memory, primary memory and long-term memory as sharply distinguishable separate storage systems, necessitating an operation of transfer of discrete items from one such store to another. The modes of transition from sensory to primary, or from primary to long-term, are as yet far from clear, and the limitation to retention may either occur in 'processing' or be set by 'storage capacity'. Particularly for music it is difficult to distinguish between sensory (or 'echoic') memory and its coded form, even more difficult to conceive of the former yielding place to the latter. It is probably more useful to regard the persistence of memory traces as dependent upon the depth of immediate analysis made possible by the actual nature of each individual's long-term pattern book, as it were, of musical configurations and forms (against which incoming sensory experience is matched) and the versatility of his coding processes. There are great differences in the estimated duration of auditory and visual sensory memory; moreover, visual and kinaesthetic factors coexist in long-term memory with those auditory cognitive structures responsible for the immediate understanding and retention of music. Instrumentalists particularly will recognize the force of an argument, when applied to music, that it is essentially the depth of perceptual analysis made possible by the nature and organization of the long-term memory store that determines the durability of memory (Craik and Lockhart, 1972). It is this immediate perceptual analysis combined with further 'working' (i.e. analysis), not 'practising' (i.e. mere repetition) (Schnabel; see Wolff, 1972) that constitutes overlearning in the daily experience of all executant musicians.

2. CODES. In remembering a musical phrase, the mental representation may pass through several stages, and to a musician the psychologist's formulation of sensory 'echoic' memory becoming coded raises the all-important question: What is the nature of the musician's code? The distinction between short-term and long-term memories, particularly the initial transition from sensory to primary memory, can be seen in an experiment where visual letter forms were coded into a spoken 'names of letters' code (Sperling, 1960), and since acoustic confusions rather than visual ones account for mistakes (Conrad, 1959) it had been assumed that the visual code yields place in memory storage to the acoustic one. But Posner and Warren (1972) presented evidence that successive codings are laid down and maintained in memory in parallel. When a visual representation (a printed word) leads to a 'name' code and thence to the semantic significance of that name, the earlier representation of sensory attributes is not lost. Although the echoic memory of a tune is preserved when one recalls it (perhaps days after a single hearing), the distinction between this 'remembering' and a musician's

'memorizing' is that the musician does not rely only on echoic memory or even on only an auditory-coded one; he has a highly integrated and multiply-determined set of codes in parallel. This type of memorizing has to some extent become involuntary by virtue of his long established skill, though over and above that capacity the musician commits the different codings consciously to memory in the process of overlearning necessary to flexible concert performance. Equally, being literate, he may possibly translate his auditory-coded memory trace of what he hears into a visual mental image of the symbolized code.

'A code consists of a population or alphabet of symbols and a system of rules or constraints among them' (Fitts and Posner, 1967, p.91). This definition accounts for codes of conventional symbols, but there are also codes of physical action as yet without notation. Although the accomplished musician has acquired a technical control of his instrument that is largely unconscious, his original acquisition went through stages of cognitive effort and integration of subroutines into larger action-sequences before autonomy was reached. Motor sequences, like languages, have a grammar; components of movements fall into groupings with specific constraints as to their orders; kinaesthetic aspects may therefore be considered as codes in which mistakes or reversals of order lead to technical difficulties or muscular fatigue. The highly integrated code of the musician (the pianist, for instance) may at once be (a) echoic-auditory; (b) 'grammatical-auditory' (in the sense that he formally understands tonal and rhythmic relations by several possible coexistent symbol systems – name of note, interval, figured bass, sol-fa, counting rhythmic patterns etc); (c) kinaesthetic without awareness (i.e. that his skilled fingers may go on when he has intellectually forgotten what comes next); (d) kinaesthetic with awareness (i.e. that he has memorized a consistent fingering); (e) visual (in remembering the printed page); (f) visual (in remembering the pattern on the keyboard); and (g) rote learning using other symbol systems (in that he may, for instance, have memorized that there are seven bars of a certain figuration before the pattern changes). Individual musicians vary in the degree to which any aspect assumes dominance in consciousness, and this dominance may fluctuate with the characteristics of particular pieces, as well as with the habits acquired through training. How these several codes in parallel have become integrated throughout a musical eduction is a basic psychological question.

But what is the code of the person who has no musical education? An untutored person may remember a tune, perhaps one heard long ago, having neither a name by which to identify it, nor a name-of-interval code nor a name-of-note code. This preservation of the auditory image from sensory trace into primary and thence long-term memory must have happened in the first instance through mental (or even vocal) rehearsal (intentional or unintentional) and have remained in this specific form in long-term memory. Yet it is doubtful whether tunes are retained at the pitch level at which they were heard, even (on occasion) by those possessing absolute pitch. Given therefore that it is a transposable version which has been retained, it is arguable that rehearsal has transformed the original sensory stimulus (the 'rapidly fading after-image') into a coded form based on interval recognition, even though that person may not know the names of the intervals. Such a capability is often called 'having a good ear'. (Cuddy and Cohen, 1976, showed that more highly trained musicians have a greater amount of interval information available than less trained ones; but non-musicians use intervals as long as they have a high familiarity value: Attneave and Olson, 1971.)

Is there a particular order in which the codes should be integrated? In some primitive societies learning to play a musical instrument is accomplished without formal teaching: indeed, notation does not exist; but furthermore there is little or no verbal instruction (Merriam, 1964). The child learns to be a drummer by sitting next to the adult drummer, listening and watching; only very much later is he allowed to take over. Thus the receptor–effector feedback is the main vehicle of learning, even though in this instance it is an image of action which precedes action itself. Bruner (1967) described how in child development 'enactive' representation, or learning to perceive by doing, is dominant in the first year of life, and soon 'iconic' representation emerges, when a child 'can represent the world to himself by an image or spatial schema that is relatively independent of action'; 'temporal schema' should be added to this description to account for auditory representation. It is evident that there is a tight link between perception and action from the first and that mimicry depends on the internalization of an auditory or kinaesthetic image. The acquisition of the symbolic codes of reading and writing belongs to a later stage of development. In the learning of primitive music we see enactive and iconic internal representation as sufficient to learning a relatively complex musical skill which is at once a new language skill and a perceptual–motor one acquired concurrently. Suzuki, in teaching violin to young children, recognizes the problem of skill-integration, for his method follows the sequence: listen, remember, play. Only later does it become: listen, remember, play, read; his pupils who play by ear and later watch the music while doing so are said to learn to read naturally and easily. This is to follow the sequence of the child's learning of natural language, first acquiring spoken words to which he later learns to match printed symbols in reading and writing. There is quite a strong argument for phasing the process of learning the many operations in instrumental music in this way.

3. 'REHEARSAL'. The psychological use of the term 'rehearsal' does not invariably carry the connotation of overt or subvocal repetitions, though this is frequently the form rehearsal takes. Experiments have shown that after one hearing of a short sequence of words (or digits or letters) considerable loss of retention is caused by any intervening activity that effectively prevents immediate 'rehearsal' (Peterson, 1963). Merely prefacing immediate recall by saying the word 'zero' significantly impairs performance (Conrad, 1960). If one has either been told or looked up a telephone number it is difficult both to retain it and to carry on a conversation, for the interpolated activity seems to erase the telephone number. Broadbent (1958) calls the rehearsal necessary to holding the number in immediate memory 'recirculation in the buffer storage'. There is a limit to the amount which can be kept in this rehearsal loop of repetition: if too many items are attempted, then the last items will have decayed before the rehearsal process has gone through all the first ones. Although subvocal repetition is likely to be the form of rehearsal with

verbal or musical temporal patterning (and there is evidence that memory coding from a visual source is frequently auditory) one could, for instance, rehearse the telephone number, or a phrase in musical notation, by reactivating a visual image of the printed page. Experiments on mental imagery show that instruction to keep a visual memory in activation (e.g. 'visualize an orange') considerably impairs the capacity to take in other visual information from an external source (Segal and Fusella, 1970). This illustrates 'limited channel capacity'. It is conceivable that a musician whose visual notational coding is strong might use this feature as at least a component of immediate rehearsal. Toscanini, who in later life was compelled to learn scores almost bar by bar, using a magnifying glass, is known to have had this visual memory. He was said to be able to read off it as if reading off a preserved after-image, though of course it was inextricably amalgamated with auditory memory.

Advocates of initial silent study away from the instrument should bear in mind that channel capacity is limited where simultaneous auditory mental imagery with visual sensory intake is concerned, though it may be precisely because of the extra effort needed in silent study that this form of learning is found by some to be effective. Silently reading a score is a fairly ubiquitous skill, possibly more difficult than but analogous to silently reading a book, and it presents fewer problems than an instrumentalist's rehearsing silently to memorize a score. Here the plurality of images places a heavier load on channel capacity and may vary with habitual patterns of dominance in using auditory, visual and kinaesthetic codes, and with the technical exigencies of the music. Experimentally nothing has yet been done specifically to tease out the components of this skill.

Rehearsal of an item presented for immediate recall is, therefore, a process of keeping the categorized sensory trace in present activation. The sensory trace has physical properties which may very well co-exist with a name code (Coltheart and Allard, 1971). The category used depends upon the categories already stored in the individual's long-term memory. To remember a musical phrase immediately after it is heard, one is to some extent reactivating it element by element from one's long-term memory vocabulary. The nature of one's rehearsal of it (how much the conscious activation of it is auditory, subvocal, kinaesthetic or visual) depends upon the various categories in one's long-term memory store and the way in which this is organized.

4. RETENTION OF THE SINGLE AUDITORY IMAGE. Memorizing a melody is a process of encoding it into a series of musical intervals from a succession of sensory images which are at an absolute level of pitch. What is known of the survival of each sensory trace? Evidence from masking experiments (see §2) and from those on recognition memory for pitch is relevant. But as yet there are no systematic studies using absolute pitch subjects who are equipped to code instantaneously by name of sensation (as in colour-naming, rather than by pattern-recognition, as in letter-naming). A listener possessing absolute pitch can immediately 'pigeon-hole' (Broadbent, 1971) by sensory category and for him rehearsal of a melody is possibly a tagged auditory reverberation as well as an interval-coded one. Such studies might help to distinguish, by the temporal factors involved, masking (i.e. immediate erasure of the

sensory trace) from loss by interference with already continuing memory-coding processes. How does one retain a single note?

Given no interference either from masking or from subsequent tonal stimuli, the sensory trace decays slowly (Harris, 1952). But holding the single note in memory when it is followed by a number of others is more difficult even when small intervals of time are involved (Wickelgren, 1969); and the difficulty increases with the number of interpolated notes, not with the time interval before the recognition test. However, the sensory trace may be given, as it were, a boost by the subsequent occurrence of a note of the same pitch, even though it is ignored as irrelevant (thus involving no attempt by the subject to distinguish that it, rather than a different pitch, has occurred). Musicians (not necessarily with absolute pitch) performed much better than non-musicians at retaining the image of one tone in order to detect its occurrence as a weak signal through a mask of white noise in a series of trials. Specifically they detected it after a longer series of blank (i.e. noise without signal) trials; it would seem that they retained an image which was then boosted by the next signal occurrence, whereas non-musicians had lost the trace. Deutsch (1972) found a similar 'boosting' effect on a fading trace when her subjects judged a comparison pitch, the standard having been followed by six other tones, the second of which was, in different trials, systematically varied between identity with the standard to a pitch separation of two-thirds of a tone. Identity with the standard of the critical interfering tone acted as a boost, and errors increased with the degree of its pitch separation from the standard. Furthermore, the boost was more effective when in the second place than in the fifth of the six interfering tones (Deutsch, 1975).

There are two possibilities to consider here concerning musical memory. Musicians may almost certainly have better category-systems in long-term memory but this, for musicians without absolute pitch, would be effective only with intervals, not with the single note. Or (one is forced to express it vaguely at present) they are better at hanging on to a sensory trace. But then, in which way are their sensory traces better attended to than those of non-musicians? Deutsch (1970) found that an interpolated task of listening to spoken digits – which had to be memorized – had almost no interfering effect upon pitch retention, whereas interpolated tones not required to be memorized had a much greater disruptive effect. This suggests a mechanism for attenuating verbal input while musical analysis is in progress, for it indicates that interference upon memory for pitch is not simply due to unspecific distraction of attention.

The possible mechanism for musical attention relates to the separate storage sites in the cortex for music (non-dominant hemisphere) and language (dominant hemisphere), though this is not a totally simple and clearcut distinction. But from clinical evidence this hemispheric distinction seems to apply to perception of melodies yet not to pitch alone, timbre alone or rhythm alone (Spellacy, 1970; see AMUSIA) and indeed pitch perception (as also timbre and rhythm) are necessary to the perception of language. Acoustic properties are processed in both hemispheres but further linguistic features are extracted by the dominant hemisphere (Studdert Kennedy and Shankweiler, 1970), further musical features, probably, by the non-dominant hemisphere. The nature of cortical memory storage

influences ear dominance by descending neural pathways according to whether a sound pattern is being analysed according to the linguistic code or the musical one. Where the evidence is not from clinical cases of brain pathology but from healthy musical subjects in attention experiments, musical perceptual analysis is clearly applied to the single note. Either a disposition to enjoy sounds or musical training, or both, may develop in the musician a superior capacity to retain the sensory trace whether or not a coding label is available for it.

Nevertheless, individual differences in coding processes for melodic pitch are clearly involved where more than the single note is being retained in memory, for intervals are relied upon to a different extent according to the degree to which they or the single note can be labelled. The effect of interference by subsequent tonal events on intervals and melody is not only upon the sensory trace itself but also upon the continuing coding processes. These processes are different for untutored musical people, musicians, and musicians with absolute pitch.

Pitch is basic to both the verbal and the musical memory systems and in both it is the relationality of pitch levels which is important. Just as we perceive speech, whether that of a child's voice or a man's, by the pitch relations within one voice range, so we recognize and retain transposed melodies by contour and interval within a certain range. Speech becomes incomprehensible if presented by splicing segments of tape recordings of different voices. Also, in music, given that the range of distortion is not made too large, it appears that contour alone (i.e. preserving the direction of melodic steps but not precisely their intervals) is a strong factor in recognition memory for familiar tunes (Dowling and Fujitani, 1971). Very few people in the world are musically literate, i.e. possess labels for the notes or intervals of the music of their culture, yet large numbers remember the melodies quite accurately. This fact, together with that of the existence of tonal languages, suggests that relational pitch perception is a natural process. That a great many people cannot sing the intervals of Western tonal harmony 'in tune' is not too surprising, for what can be called acceptably 'in tune' is itself a relational question as well as one of auditory acuity. But through familiarity with the music of our culture it is likely that most untutored musical people have an interval code without verbal labels. Musical training provides those labels, and some people have in addition the absolute pitch categorizing system. Thus the question of how each of the intervals of a melody is coded into memory has at the least three possible answers depending on the individual's degree of musicality. How many intervals can be memorized in one span depends partly on those coding differences and partly on the limit to human memory.

5. TONAL MEMORY. Tests which measure the immediate memory span are an essential part of measuring musical aptitudes. Carl Seashore (1919) insisted that tonally unrelated sequences should be used as test material, since familiar interval patterns would not be a pure measure of memory; whereas the Kwalwasser–Dykema test uses simple melodies on the gound that the disposition to memorize music as such is the object of the test. However, the two elements – memory and the disposition to think in the diatonic language – should be con-

sidered separately, since the problem of what can be considered a single item is confounding the measure of memory. The nature of the singly coded items changes with musical education. Seashore's estimate was five to six separate notes, but Kwalwasser–Dykema's estimate is 12 related ones. The psychological question is that of how notes become related in musical learning. Seashore's planned musical IQ test led him to write: 'Intelligence is musical when its background is a storehouse of musical knowledge', which, translated into the language of this article, would be the assertion that capacity to relate adjacent notes in a melody in order to extend the span of immediate memory depends on the content and organization of the long-term memory store. To a highly sophisticated musician any three consecutive notes might be musically related. However, even he might have difficulty encoding them if they were widely spaced in frequency and presented at a rapid rate. Attention to musical intervals does seem to be affected by their pitch range; this is perhaps related to the critical band, perhaps to a limit on receptivity to the range of one human speaking voice. Subjects required to count the number of notes which alternated between a' (440 Hz) and b'' (988 Hz) performed poorly compared with their score when counting repetitions of a single note (Massaro, 1976). Pederson (1975) found performance in a recognition test for 12-note rows to be at chance level when they were spread between many levels, except for one subject who had absolute pitch.

6. MELODY. We have seen with the retention of the single note how subsequent input interferes with holding an item in memory so that a melody, as a series of intervals, has the property that each successive interval can act as interference upon its predecessor. In verbal learning experiments, as well as the pitch recognition ones mentioned above, difficulty increases with number of items, though where a serial list is being learnt speed of presentation is also a factor. Slower rates give more processing time for each item, faster rates leave less time for the decay of the earlier part of the sequence (Aaronson, 1967). That a fugue subject in music is presented initially without the perceptual interference factor (or at least complexity) of the counter-subject shows intuitive psychological wisdom concerning the problem of coding into immediate memory. For instance, the most chromatic subject in Bach's '48' (the B minor, Book 1), which further is tonally ambiguous in that it modulates to F♯ minor, is conceived at a moderate tempo; this gives time for the processing of each interval.

Miller's limit to immediate memory, 7 ± 2, is reflected in Seashore's six items in tonal memory. In verbal learning experiments this estimated limit is borne out, for separate letters act as items unless they can be chunked into larger groupings (words or word-like sequences); and similarly, related words can be chunked into sentences, thus lengthening the span of immediate memory. The same process can be seen in musical learning, depending on the musical vocabulary of the listener. But it is extremely difficult for the methodology of musical psychology to find a basis for defining intervals as 'related'. This limit on the number of items raises the question, for instance, of whether the 11 intervals of the 12-note row of serial music are beyond the limit of the immediate memory span of most people, and what is the nature of the individual's chunking or coding

strategies used to make it wholly and immediately memorable. Opinions differ among 12-note composers as to the degree to which the listener may be expected to retain the note row; nevertheless upon its retention depends the fullest appreciation of its various transformations. Themes may be cumulatively coded into memory by their recurrence throughout a work, but how much transformation can a theme undergo and yet remain perceptually salient? Dowling (1972) found, as any musician would expect, that with transformations of musical themes the order of perceptual difficulty increases from inversion, to retrograde, to retrograde inversion. Do some people consciously or unconsciously use tonal strategies to code atonal music into memory? If so, how is an expectancy for tonality eradicated in order that transformations of the row may be perceived in an atonal context? In our culture musical education has started in tonality, so that, however emancipated or sophisticated a musical ear becomes, the tonal system is basic, since childhood, to the individual's cognitive structures. Learning to perceive atonally is not a parallel to learning a second language, since there is no systematic correspondence between atonality and diatonic music in a syntactic or dictionary sense. At all events, almost nothing is known experimentally about tonal coding strategies (the rhythmic influence on coding has been mentioned earlier).

7. MELODY AND TEMPORAL ORDER. The learning of a series of musical intervals (assuming with Seashore that they are 'tonally unrelated', though this is difficult to achieve) can be seen as analogous to verbal serial learning. In a typical serial learning experiment 20 unrelated words are flashed on a screen at a fixed rate and recall may be required in that order or in any order ('free recall'). In the presentation order items seem to be remembered in chunks a few at a time and in free recall most people retrieve the last items first, as if these were still echoing and could therefore be removed to unburden the rehearsal 'circulation in buffer storage'. If an error score for each item is plotted against its serial position, the graph is a U-shaped curve. The first few items are well learned and free of proactive interference since there had been no items in memory process preceding the list. The left arm of the curve is generally attributable to more long-term coded memory (Glanzer and Cunitz, 1966). This U-shaped curve might possibly represent performance after one hearing in a musical dictation test.

A further serial learning experimental technique specifically investigates recognition memory by presenting a list, and after some delay a single item which is to be judged as having occurred or not occurred in the list. This is known as the probe technique: the subject is assumed to be searching the serial list in his immediate memory, matching the probe to each item. Berg (1975) applied it to eight-note melodies generated by a computer, using a randomizing method to avoid 'tonal relatedness', and presenting them at a fast rate. His subjects were musically literate but were not professional musicians. Where the probe was a single note the typical U-shaped curve emerged, but where the probe was a musical interval of two tones the curve was a zigzag U shape. This indicates that probes starting on the odd position numbers were better recognized than those starting on even ones and suggests a spontaneous coding strategy of chunking in pairs (couplet phrasing), thus reducing the eight-note melodies to four items. A probe which crossed the boundaries was poorly recognized, as in the Dowling (1972) experiment mentioned above. This phenomenon was not found to be a conscious strategy; indeed, a professional musician might find this subjective organization not only simplified but imprudent. Nevertheless the experiment suggests one paradigm for investigating musical coding in recognition memory.

Not only the grouping but, much more, the serial order in which a sequence is learnt has considerable influence on the way it is stored. Recall of a serial list either of words or tones is significantly poorer if the entire second half is required to be recalled first (Morton, Crowder and Prussin, 1971; Berg, 1975). Although a musician may ideally think of a retrograde melody as resembling an after-image Gestalt which he should be able to read off backwards, this is far from being the case. To recognize a palindrome its first half must remain entire in the memory, so its length as well as its subjective grouping is of importance to its recognition in reverse. The determining force of forward temporal order on organization in long-term memory is easy to demonstrate if one attempts to say backwards the most overlearned thing one knows, the alphabet. The difference is not only in speed but also in the fact that a stumble generally evokes a forward search through neighbouring items. These are considerations which apply to the recognition memory used in listening to music.

8. ATTENTION. In listening to music we hear both vertically and horizontally (and perhaps, as Boulez says, 'diagonally'). With contrapuntal music the listener follows a number of melodies which conform harmonically in different ways according to the idiom, and his expectancies are based upon familiarity with the constraints that govern that particular idiom. This familiarity, a product of long-term memory, enables him to make sense of more than one line at a time. It is also a faculty which may help the performing musician to overcome the vicissitudes of untoward concert-room acoustics when he listens for a melodic line he must accompany and experiences only its intermittent audibility. The process somewhat resembles the famous 'cocktail party' problem, when one wishes to listen to a conversation which is not that in which one is engaged but nevertheless succeeds in making sense of both lines of discourse, possibly by intermittent sampling. However, to a musician it is probably an easier task to make continuous sense of music than of two or more concurrent speech messages, at least where the music includes not only timbre and melodic continuity but also harmonic relations. To discover which of the principles of continuity may give priority access to the short-term memory channel (by which we make sense), how many concurrent sequences can be monitored, and to what extent attending or ignoring is under the individual's control are experimental tasks that have not as yet been undertaken in the psychology of music. But the research in verbal memory and attention suggests possible approaches and relevant findings.

When different verbal messages are presented simultaneously one to each ear in a dichotic listening experiment, different priorities of timbre and syntax are shown to operate. Broadbent (1971) distinguished two processes by which incoming information is sorted so

that the subject excludes that which he has been instructed to ignore. If he must follow one of two or more voices and repeat only what the chosen voice says, the pitch and timbre characteristics of the source are used; this Broadbent calls 'filtering' from echoic to primary memory. But if a response is required only to 'digits', regardless of which voice utters them, then categorizing on the basis of the vocabulary content of long-term memory storage takes place; this he calls 'pigeon-holing'. 'Filtering' using acoustic clues occurs at an earlier stage in the system, yet it is less reliable than the more cognitive 'pigeon-holing', for mistakes do not occur in 'pigeon-holing' experiments but do occur when the subject is 'filtering' a certain voice, if the actual sense of the sentence is suddenly switched to another voice or if a category item of importance to the individual (like his own name) occurs in the unattended channel. Thus sense seems to have an analysing priority over physical characteristics, 'sense' consisting in categorizing on the basis of a long-term, constantly used memory store. There is as yet no experimental evidence for music to distinguish any priority the contextual constraints and familiarity of sense might have over timbre; indeed, from the everyday experience of music it seems counter-intuitive that it should, for the same timbre with changing pitch is melody whereas the same pitch with changing timbre gives the impression, as Boulez says, of 'a kind of analysis of one component by another'. Yet understanding the mechanisms of musical attention depends upon understanding the precise relations between cognitive and acoustical analysis in perception.

The fact that in these experiments attention can be deflected by a word in the unattended channel, because it is important to the person or because it has been recently activated, has led to a model of attention (Treisman, 1960) in which the long-term memory store is conceived as a 'neural dictionary' where words have different strengths according to importance or recency. Since one hears one's own name when it is whispered or when one is asleep, its strong memory trace has a lower threshold (i.e. needs less physical stimulus to reactivate it). Clearly, the 'neural dictionary' is a semantic or experiential organizing system thought to govern accessibility to long-term memory. One way in which it might operate in listening to and remembering music is on the basis of the expressive melodic element. Depending on the flexibility or intentional control of the listener's attention, his ear might to some extent be drawn to certain melodic passages for associative reasons. Treisman's recency effect on attention is not unlike the effect of boosting a fading sensory trace, mentioned earlier: reactivation by recency thus links the category process with the sensory one. However, this observation raises questions which can only be answered by direct experiment on music sequences with musical subjects: What is the nature of a musical 'item' in the long-term memory? Is it a note, an interval, a chord, a configuration? What are the principles governing the organization of the long-term memory for music?

9. LONG-TERM MEMORY ORGANIZATION. The account of memory given by a psychologist 'item by item, chunk by chunk' will perhaps appear to a musician as the imposition of an alien methodology upon the natural process of music. He will object that what he recalls is not chunks but melodic, harmonic and rhythmic progressions, that these form the elements of mental

representation or improvisation, and that the information-processing model is still too atomistic an approach. But there is reason to suppose that chunks come in phrase-like shapes, that 'items' in the musical 'neural dictionary' are susceptible to retrieval by segments that owe their identity to natural phrasing. The atomism is more apparent than real, for one appropriate approach to studying the structure of the musical vocabulary in long-term memory is to look at its original acquisition. Just as a young child's first language consists of two-word sentences, 'topic and comment', and this planned sequence is progressively expanded as he becomes able to generate more elaborate sentences (Brown, 1973; McNeill, 1966), so it is likely that the phrases of music emerge by the expansion of simpler structures.

In the absence of direct research on the content and organization of musical long-term memory, one line of psychological inquiry is worth considering, that of the phonological and phrase structure in verbal memory.

Experimental phonetics research shows that the individual speech sounds are in planned sequences and that the speaker makes generative decisions only at certain points. Although phonemes are heard as discrete, there is no such clear indication of boundaries between them in the production of speech; they appear to be pre-programmed in small groups. The flow of speech as it is heard gives little clue to the placing of these generative loci at the phoneme level, but such groupings are certainly heard at the higher organizational level of accented speech. The distribution of accents in speech falls at roughly equal intervals of time. Hitherto in this article memory has been considered primarily in its aspect of pitch relations. But it is clear that rhythmic grouping in real music (rather than in computer tunes in the laboratory which may be subjectively chunked) may prove to be a powerful determinant of chunking strategies. In musical interpretation one can see the part that subjective rhythm plays in making a particular artist's performance distinctive, so that one can recognize a recorded performance as his. It is as individual as his gait, his gesture and the placing of accents in his speech rhythms. Stravinsky, in his most formalist period, wrote: 'The sight of the gestures and movements of the various parts of the body producing the music is fundamentally necessary, if it is to be grasped in all its fullness'. What the artist perceives as a rhythmic grouping is likely to have at least some resemblance to his speech rhythms, and to have been the basis upon which the extension of his memory capacity was developed. Nevertheless composer and interpreter share a musical language in which the patterns of pulse, stress and accent have some commonality of origin and of response. The basic pattern of rhythmic phrasing in music is likely to produce, therefore, similarities in the segmentation pattern of their memory coding.

The second relevant area of research to be considered in (what must be at this stage) speculating on the organization of long-term musical storage is that of the role of imagery in the cross-indexing, as it were, which attaches both visual and kinaesthetic imagery to the auditory-coded memory trace. The auditory memory is to some extent organized by vocal phrasing, the visual one is likely to be predominantly concerned with symbolic codes used in reading the music, and the kinaesthetic one with the movements necessary to its production. In the case of a non-executant music-lover the kinaesthetic

response is based more on expressivity (mediated partly by rhythmic response, partly visually), but for the instrumentalist the memory is one of more elaborate and precise action feedback sequences. Little is known of the limits to the role of imagery in recall from long-term memory. But it can to some extent be measured by experiments designed to disrupt the perception of input by simultaneous conflicting imagery. Performance on detecting signals from the environment is up to a point affected by imagery in the same sense modality, but detection of an auditory stimulus is in fact poorest when the conflicting imagery is visual (Segal and Fusella, 1970). If, instead of being conflicting, imagery is synchronized, as it is in recalling learnt music, then the problem is rather: how does the central control apportion attention between the visual, the auditory and the kinaesthetic memory?

10. PERCEPTUAL–MOTOR MEMORY. It is surprising that there has been so little work on musical skill since that of Seashore's laboratory, particularly since the cybernetic model is appropriate and the skill of the pianist is often cited as an example by psychologists reviewing the problem of serial order in behaviour (Craik, 1948; Lashley, 1951). Seashore's work (1938, chap.27) is well worth consulting as a point of departure; he made a notable contribution in providing equipment as well as techniques for recording sound patterns of instruments in a musical rather than a psychoacoustic approach. Moreover, he was fully aware of the importance of feedback in skill learning and was careful to provide extrinsic feedback as a teaching aid. By watching a visual display the singer or violinist could monitor his own intonation and correct it, in the course of which activity his pitch discrimination was refined; this tonoscope is thus an example of 'augmented' feedback. The cybernetic approach (see §I, 5, ii) applies to the self-directed aspects of learning. External or 'augmented' feedback, sometimes also called 'knowledge of results', is essential to motivation, though the actual refinement of skill is mediated by intrinsic feedback circuits in the nervous system. A great deal has been discovered about intrinsic feedback from experiments in which it is distorted, causing severe disruptions in performance. Even with reduced feedback the subject has effectively to learn a new skill to reach the stage of autonomy he had before the systematic distortion (Fitts and Posner, 1967). Delayed auditory feedback at intervals of less than a second makes music or speech impossible; thus the vital role of feedback is evident. Mainwaring (1933) showed that feedback from singing while listening to a tune was an aid to memorizing, and Teplov (1966) gave numerous examples of the need for motor feedback as such an aid where a voluntary effort is needed to retrieve a musical memory.

The taxonomy of gradual shifts in skill learning which is generally accepted is of three phases, which merge into each other. The 'cognitive' phase of verbal instruction is one of setting up a plan or series of feedback units (as described by Miller, Galanter and Pribram, 1960), the second phase that of practice of the particular codings or associations, which gradually leads to the final phase where the skilled sequences are executed autonomously. The relation between verbal instruction and the development of a skill is under-researched in psychology generally (Annett, 1969), and in the psychology of music such information is to be found only in the educational literature.

Research on skill learning of many varieties seems unanimous in emphasizing the need for overlearning in counteracting the possible disintegration of habits in situations of stress. This view of skill acquisition as passing through three stages (Fitts, 1964) – the cognitive phase, the period of fixation of habits and finally autonomous action – applies equally to music, but with a difference. As technical mastery becomes autonomous, attention is freed and, in times of the high arousal associated with performance, it may have less to hold it anchored to the sequence unless musical concentration is absolute. Contrasted for instance with the acquisition of the autonomous phase of overlearning in driving a car, where attention capacity is liberated for the greater environmental monitoring necessary to the task, in music, with autonomy, attention passes from details of how to play to the direct intentions engaged in what is being played. The ubiquitous precepts in the pedagogic literature (for instance, 'Never play a note without meaning it') are indeed paramount and become more so as the optimal autonomy of technical mastery is achieved. Thus overlearning is indispensable to freedom in performance but yields greater attention capacity, which needs to be fully occupied by a rich substrate of previous musical analysis and understanding of the work; this is the protection against possible intrusion or distraction capturing an attention channel which by virtue of high arousal is of greater capacity.

11. SIGHT-READING. For good sight-readers the visual coding of a printed page is likely to be as closely integrated with memory for sound as it is with memory for speech. Both music and language employ arbitrary visual symbols to represent sound patterns, and learning to read takes a considerable time. With language it progresses from the categorization of items to the ability to take in words and sentences, and with music configurations or perhaps phrases. If the subject is an experienced reader, naming letters is automatic in perceptual tasks where they function as items (Keele, 1972) whereas symbols without names are more difficult to retain (Grindley and Townsend, 1973). It would seem that immediate visual coding takes 20 milliseconds per letter up to a maximum of four items, whereas naming requires 100 per item (Coltheart, 1972). Sloboda (*Music Reading*, 1974; 1976) asked whether musicians develop a superior visual coding for printed music or whether they are better able to translate into a name code. He found the 20-millisecond visual coding to differ very little between musicians and non-musicians, whereas with a two-second exposure musicians can retain six items almost perfectly, non-musicians at best one or two. Possession of a name code, however, is not the facilitating factor, for neither an interpolated task of memorizing pitches nor one of naming letters was effective interference upon the musicians' memory coding. He thought it unlikely to be motor memory coding, since the response required was writing; however, written and motor codes have reached such a high degree of integrated automaticity for musicians that it cannot be ruled out: implicit playing may be almost as likely as implicit singing. Since concurrent shadowing of prose does not interfere with sight-reading performance by good musicians (Allport, Antonis and Reynolds, 1972), one may question whether, for some, the playing motor code might dominate the auditory one. Long-term tests of

memory for the shadowed prose or the music might, for instance, illuminate the degree to which motor skill is occupying channel capacity; how does it compare for instance with the degree to which typists or Morse code operators take in the meaning of the message they are transmitting? Though the musician knows by introspection that several memory codes may be concurrently operative, exactly how they are integrated is the subject of different pedagogic precepts, and research is needed to distinguish the components of this highly overlearned and automated skill.

A study of eye–hand span (i.e. how many notes are played by a sight-reader when the light is suddenly switched off) indicates the tendency of good sight-readers to take in the music phrase by phrase (Sloboda, 'The Eye-Hand Span', 1974). In so far as sight-reading is a skill akin to simultaneous translation, the lag between visual intake and playing represents time taken to perform mental operations upon the intake. Psychologists might approach the problem of whether auditory or visual code is dominant by a brief visual display followed by an auditory recognition task: a 'spot the mistake' test where the measure used is response time might distinguish auditory-code dominance; the subject translating first into kinaesthetic code might take longer. Differences between coding from familiar and unfamiliar instruments are also relevant variables.

12. MEMORIZING. Memorizing will be discussed here in terms of overt recall or performance: a scholar may never have occasion for overt reproduction and such inaccessibility of learning enables only a subjective assessment to be made of his memorizing.

(*i*) *The nature of memorizing.* The characteristics that distinguish memorizing from memory are intentionality, analysis and synthesis, long-term consolidation, and the integration of imagery or internal representations, which may be symbolic, auditory, visual and kinaesthetic. This integration is of particular concern to vocal or instrumental memorizing. Memorizing is a relatively long-term project in contrast to those aspects of memory already discussed. A memory available at will, as opposed to recognition or involuntary recall, necessitates a higher degree of overlearning; and the most productive, economical and natural way of attaining dependable retrieval processes is related to the manner of encoding and to the timing of practice sessions which repeatedly reactivate the memory traces. Thus questions concerning the value of rest periods, the type of repetition and the type of internal representation assume importance.

The psychologist's view of memory as encoding, storage and retrieval indicates that the type of forgetting associated with a well-learnt piece of music is a failure of retrieval from a consolidated store, as contrasted with the loss of items from the short-term process, or failures of encoding. A pace and manner of acquisition are needed that avoid imposing an overload of information at any one time; on the other hand, it is possible to do insufficient overlearning. Easy retrieval from memory depends upon methods of encoding: certain methods are mnemonically better than others.

(*ii*) *Intentionality.* Motivation in learning music may be intrinsic to the pleasure of committing enjoyable music to memory or to the dynamic forces described in psychoanalytic terms. But frequently there are extrinsic factors which may have a helpful or a detrimental effect on memorizing, including the expectations and instructions of teachers, or the projected ambitions of others. To be effective, memorizing requires continuity of attention as opposed to its distraction, and a realistic pacing of the work, rather than the pressures of deadlines or of too exigent aspirations. Fluctuations of attention according to the intricacies of the music are also a factor brought under intentional control where memorizing rather than remembering is concerned; this is closely related to the analysis and synthesis process, for remembering may or may not include an understanding of the relation of the part to the whole, whereas such comprehension is implicit in memorizing. The performance of a work which has been entirely memorized and is under intentional control is characterized by steady attentional processes unaffected by changes in complexity (or information load).

Some years ago Gestalt psychology inspired an enthusiasm among some musicians for whole learning (versus part learning), which seems a pseudo-dichotomy since it depends entirely upon the length of the whole. A series of experimental studies by Rubin-Rabson (1940) seemed to show no advantage to either method but only eight bars were learned by the musician subjects, whereas O'Brien (1943) found a time saving of between 25 and 65% for the part-learning method where 32 bars were to be learned. Two learning factors are involved. One is the transfer of training factor by which the amount of music learnt hitherto and its similarity to the work now being studied affect the speed with which component parts can be learnt. The other is familiarity with musical forms, which affects the comprehension of the place of each part within the whole piece. The size of each 'part' (which in memorizing usually means each phrase) combines with the span of immediate memory to determine the number of repetitions necessary to its retention; a phrase longer than the immediate memory span of that particular person will need more repetitions.

However, the fact that good memorizing depends upon the analysis of the shape of each phrase, the progression from interval to interval and the precise rhythmic values in the onward-moving time pattern is a truism, and this aspect of memorizing may be much better expressed by the various pedagogic treatises on learning music. At this stage an experimental psychologist can assert only that memorizing depends upon depth of analysis of the acoustic pattern, a grasp of the various hierarchically ordered larger structures, and the imposition upon the material of the individual's habitual pattern of structuring and restructuring. As interpretation is a creative pursuit this restructuring involves a process of hearing a phrase in a variety of possible patterns of form and emphasis, by which subtle shifts of harmonic balance or of timing make significant differences in eloquence. Thus the conscious encoding phase of memorizing involves the remaking of each phrase rather than mere repetition. An analogy may be drawn with experiments requiring master chess players to recall a complex chess position, having seen it for five seconds. The less experienced players recalled what little they could at once; the master invariably paused for some seconds before recall (De Groot, 1965). It has been suggested that this pause is occupied by the process of recoding into higher order more meaningful chunks by reactivating long-term memory structures of past experience (Posner and Warren, 1972). A similar process may distinguish the memorizing habits of good musicians, whose search to find the most expressive diction for a phrase constitutes a perceptual reshaping at each repetition.

Another process that must form part of the analysis period of memorizing is the integration of auditory with kinaesthetic imagery. This is particularly apparent where the desired sounds are not expressive of the gesture or body movements necessary to produce them. This is a feature, for example, of some piano music where a very sudden move of the hand, arm and body to a new position must nevertheless be used to produce a calm and mellifluous sound. Although such technical factors become unconscious, they have to be incorporated into the memorizing. Mainwaring (1933) emphasized (possibly unduly) the kinaesthetic factors in musical recall; nevertheless they are a considerable feature of the memorizing process.

Early work was done by Rubin-Rabson (1937) on the value of pre-study away from the instrument as an aid to memorizing. The notion was that the learning processes are thereby taken one at a time and kinaesthetic problems are not encountered until the music can be written down from memory. Rubin-Rabson found it was effective, whereas hearing the work did not make any difference. A further point of view is that mental rehearsal, particularly at a point roughly halfway through the learning process, gives an opportunity for restructuring at points which are not yet properly integrated into the sequence and for 're-seeing' the smaller configurations. Unfortunately these studies rather assume that the principal form of overt repetition is without such analysis and that attention is withdrawn from the smaller groupings as they became pre-programmed.

Without going into the details of musicianship, it is worth mentioning other intentional processes of synthesis which are necessary in memorizing (as opposed to remembering). First, though a piece of music may already be fully appreciated as an organic whole, the synthesis phase of learning requires the intentional memorizing of joins between phrases. Syntactic boundaries, whether of speech or of music, are markers of the groupings at the various architectonic levels and, as in cybernetic processes, they are decision points. The phrases that lie on either side of such syntactic markers are kinaesthetically relatively autonomous through learning (though musically they should never be allowed to become so). Both the joining of phrases and the correcting of mistakes may be seen as processes similar to the integrating of subroutines into an overall plan. A correction of a mistake is a return to analysis at the lowest architectonic level, which then has to be re-integrated at each higher level in turn. That misreadings are sometimes so resistant to correction is partly because spontaneous recovery of an earlier associative response is an ubiquitous psychological phenomenon, and partly because it is not realized how wide-ranging in the grammatical structure the effect of one mistaken element can be.

(iii) *Distribution of sessions.* Rubin-Rabson (1943) studied the relative efficiency of massed versus distributed practice for learning short passages of music, and found that after a delay of time relearning was quicker for those who had initially learned in short sessions punctuated by rest periods. She found that the degree of advantage in having rest periods varied inversely with the proficiency of the pianist. This is only to say that proficiency at music varies directly with experienced capacity to master complexities. However, at whatever level of proficiency, distributed practice is more efficient than massed practice according to the findings in music, in verbal learning (Underwood, 1954) and above all in perceptual–motor skills (Fitts and Posner, 1967; Welford, 1968).

In learning an unfamiliar piece of music, the materials out of which it is fashioned (pitch levels, rhythms etc) are largely familiar from one's entire previous experience; they are simply arranged in a unique order in that particular piece. One is learning a new ordering of responses (Hovland and Kurz, 1952; Underwood and Schultz, 1960). The 'interference theory of forgetting' goes some way to explaining why distributed practice is the more efficient, and why also one should not embark upon learning too much new material at one time. If the whole piece is large, the method of learning the whole rather than successive parts is unlikely to be the most efficient.

In verbal learning experiments that vary the method of learning a first list of paired words between the massed and distributed practice method, in order to assess its effect on subsequently learning a second list, it emerges that the difficulty of learning the second list varies directly with the number of repetitions of the first one learned by massed practice. But this effect of 'proactive interference' increases only up to 80 trials of learning the first list, after which the second is learnt more easily; at this point the first one is sufficiently overlearnt or consolidated as to cause no response competition. However, if the first list has been learnt with distributed practice (over four days), it has no interfering effect on the learning of a new one (Underwood and Eckstrand, 1966). Thus material already well stored in one's musical memory, and learnt over some time, may not impede progress with the new material, but music learnt quickly (though intensively) may do so unless it has been brought to a high degree of overlearning. This may apply at every stage of musical development, but no general prescription can be given as to length of practice sessions or of rests since they depend on the experience (ease of coding) of the individual. The length of each section of music to be brought to an overlearnt level before embarking on the next is equally a matter of previous training.

There are varying estimates of the degree of overlearning necessary to reliable recall in both the psychological and the pedagogic literature, but the psychologists discuss it in rather simplified terms. The degree of overlearning necessary depends upon what is being learnt and what is required to be available for easy recall. One suspects that there is an implicit assumption that 'knowing the right notes' according to the notation in the score is the criterion used in estimates that only 50% overlearning is effective, and more is a waste of time (Rubin-Rabson, 1943). But this criterion gives quite an unrefined representation of the piece of music and can be achieved relatively quickly, as an actor can 'learn his lines'. The artist is also learning every shape, inflection and tone quality, and the significance of the timing of every note, by selecting each attribute out of many alternatives at the analysis stage of working.

It is worth pointing out that there are conflicting theories in the general psychological literature regarding massed versus distributed practice and that two reserva-

tions must be made. First, the variable to note in reading the psychological literature is whether minutes, hours or days are the time-intervals which are being differentially considered in the experiment. Secondly, verbal learning produces interference of a different kind from music, because of the associative networks in long-term memory of the denotative meaning of words. Underwood (1957) attributed the 80–90% of forgetting which occurs over 24 hours in verbal learning experiments, not to the interpolated activity of the 24-hour interval, but to the number of experimental lists the subject had previously learnt; and Underwood and Postman (1960) attributed to the rest interval a spontaneous recovery of the non-experimental verbal learning of a lifetime, and they concluded that new materials which clash with former verbal habits are forgotten more easily, the resulting errors often closely resembling prior habits or associations.

In the learning of music the possible prior habits cannot be described in terms of associative networks of representational character. But at least this finding illuminates the difficulties inherent in learning a work in an idiom which is unfamiliar. It involves the unlearning of strong prior habits concerning the sequential character of the familiar idiom.

13. CONCLUSION. Attention was drawn in §1 to the need for studying the integration of affective and cognitive aspects when considering musical memory, but there has been no discussion of how this might be done by experimental psychology. Hitherto psychologists have dealt with the affective aspects of musical experience separately, for the fact that emotional experience is idiosyncratic has led principally to a search for common factors in individual verbal descriptions of moods evoked when listening to music. Clearly both affective and aesthetic forms of long-term memory, and their influence upon cognition, play a very great part in the retention of music. But each person's life history and musical life history are unique, as are the consequent associations by which particular emotional response and therefore intensity of attention is evoked.

Studies of emotional response to music have included those which use a physiological measure (increase in heart rate, respiration etc) and which do indicate a greater 'arousal' particularly to strongly rhythmic music (Hyde, 1927; Washco, 1933; Ellis and Brighouse, 1952). But while it indicates greater alertness, this evidence of arousal or higher activation level is unspecific as to mood or cognitive impact. Verbal reports where appropriate adjectives are chosen for the subjective experience of different passages of music (Schoen, 1927; Farnsworth, 1928; Hevner, 1937) show a more or less conventional response to such factors as major versus minor mode, and although more sophisticated research methods now exist this has not proved a fruitful line of inquiry. Yet it is clear that emotional factors play a large part in the memorability of music. Similarly studies of aesthetic responses (Schoen, 1927; Farnsworth, 1950; Valentine, 1962) are subject to these difficulties of the complex and individual determinants to such responses.

It is likely that the study of individuals, whether of precocious or highly creative talents, or the clinical studies associated with music therapy, will yield more specific information as to the integration of emotional and cognitive factors in musical memory. In both these areas the role of attention is stressed, and particularly so in those cases of the phenomenal musical memory of the idiot–savant (Anastasi and Levée, 1959). But the view that strength of attention owes its origin to some emotionally charged circumstance in early life, which in extreme cases leads to an overriding bias upon intellectual development, must apply in some measure to less extreme cases. Attention is dependent upon motivation in developing a capacity for musical memory, and the roots of this motivation may be complex and even mysterious for each individual.

IV. Assessment. Among the pioneers of testing in music were Stumpf and Révész; both experimented with tests which closely resembled those traditionally given by music teachers (see Révész, 1944). The development of standardized tests of general intelligence and other intellectual abilities led to attempts to see whether similar methods might apply in music. In a well-standardized test procedures for administering and scoring the test are laid down and tables of norms based on testing representative samples are presented so that an individual's score can be compared with those made by a more general population. The test manual or other supporting publications should also provide evidence of reliability (consistency of results over time) and of validity (extent to which the test measures what it purports to test and not, for example, general intelligence rather than musical ability; see Whybrew, 1962). It has been claimed (Vernon, 1968) that 'we can probably make better predictions from childhood to adult accomplishment in music than in any other specialist field'.

Extensive reviews of tests of musical abilities and attainments can be found in Lehman (1968) and Shuter (1968). The present account summarizes the more important developments.

1. Aptitude and appreciation. 2. Attainment and performance.

1. APTITUDE AND APPRECIATION. Musical aptitude can be said to be concerned with those qualities that are developed over a long period of time; achievement consists of those that are measurable within short periods. Identification of sufficient tasks that are characteristic of musical people whether inherited or learnt slowly is at the heart of determining the validity and usefulness of tests of musical aptitude (Colwell, 1970). Certainly a main aim of prognostic tests has been to help identify gifted children who would be most likely to benefit from opportunities for special music tuition and to save the unmusical from the discouragement of failure. Thus Seashore (1938) declared that one of the purposes of his *Measures of Musical Talent* was 'to measure native and basic capacities in musical talent before training has been begun, and, therefore, to make them independent of musical training'.

The *Seashore Measures of Musical Talent* (1919) were the first standardized tests to be published. They were intended to measure the subject's capacity to perceive differences in pitch, time, intensity and consonance, and to judge which tone in a sequence had been altered on a second playing. A rhythm test was later added. The revised version of 1939 replaced the consonance test (the least satisfactory of the earlier battery) by one on timbre. A typical example from the current form (1960) is the pitch test. Two tones free of harmonics are sounded, one after the other, the differences being graded down to 2 Hz; the subject is asked to state if the second is higher or lower than the first. Seashore insisted that the *Measures* should be used to provide a profile showing the separate score on each capacity. In practice many users have found a general classification based on a composite score satisfactory. The tests have enjoyed widespread use. For example, in Rochester, NY, they formed part of a programme for selecting talented pupils for instrumental instruction and for helping to grade students into homogeneous groups. However, the relevance of capacities for fine sensory discrimination of musical elements to functional musical ability has been continually questioned.

For this reason later test authors have sought to devise tests based on musical materials which would still satisfy the criteria of objective testing. Thus in the *Kwalwasser–Dykema Music Tests* (1930) the stimuli were more musical, but the discriminating power and the reliability of the battery are suspect. Much more successful are the *Wing Standardised Tests of Musical Intelligence* (1948). These are played on the piano; the latest tape-recorded version to appear was in 1960. The seven tests are intended to be used to provide an overall assessment of level of musical ability, but the first three (chord analysis, pitch change and musical memory) can be used alone. The last four seek to measure appreciation of rhythmic accent, of harmony, of intensity and of phrasing. In each case the subject is asked which of two playings of the same musical extract he prefers, one being the original, the other a version distorted (e.g. by weakening the harmonic structure). Evidence of the reliability and validity of the tests is summarized in Wing (1948) and in Shuter (1968). Where only about an hour is available for testing, the Wing tests are perhaps the most satisfactory ones to choose. Other tests based on musical material that have won esteem are the *Drake Tests of Musical Aptitude*, of memory and rhythm (1957), and the *Gaston Test of Musicality* (1958), which includes questions on interest in music as well as tonal items.

Rather similar to the Wing appreciation tests are the *Oregon Music Discrimination Tests* (1935). Two versions of a musical extract are played, one as composed, the other mutilated either in rhythm, harmony or melody. The subject has to judge, first, which is the original, and second, which element has been changed. With the help of Hevner, the original author, an updated version was prepared by Long (1971).

The most ambitious attempt to provide tests that will not only identify the musically gifted but also diagnose individual students' specific strengths and weaknesses is the *Gordon Musical Aptitude Profile* (1965). The tests are classified into three main divisions: 'Tonal Imagery' (melody and harmony); 'Rhythm Imagery' (tempo and metre); and 'Musical Sensitivity' (phrasing, balance and style). Thus seven sub-test scores can be obtained, as well as three totals and a composite score. Gordon himself composed the music, which includes modern as well as traditional styles; it is played by a professional violinist and cellist. In the melody test, for example, the subject has to listen to a tune and answer and then judge whether the answer is a melodic variation of the tune or whether it is different. The test manual provides extensive evidence of the test's reliability and validity. Further data come, for example, from a three-year longitudinal study (Gordon, 1967). Some 250 ten- and eleven-year-old pupils from eight classes in five different schools were tested before the beginning of instrumental music lessons. At the end of three years their achievements in music were compared with their initial test scores. The criteria used to evaluate progress were, first, adjudicators' ratings of melodic, rhythmic and expressive aspects of tape-recorded performances of short studies, some prepared, some sight-read; second, teachers' ratings of each student's progress as compared with that of other students in the group; and third, scores on a musical achievement test designed to assess ability to compare tape-recorded passages with notation, and knowledge of musical terms and signs. The conclusion reached was that the test was indeed a valuable predictor of achievement. Even better results might have been obtained had the test scores been revealed to the teachers for their guidance. The test tapes take nearly two hours to play and should, if possible, be administered over three sessions. If this amount of time is available, the test certainly seems to give excellent results.

All the above tests are intended for subjects at least eight years old, if not ten. To meet the need for tests designed especially to suit younger children, the *Bentley Measures of Musical Abilities* were published (1966). The four tests (pitch discrimination, tonal memory, chord analysis and rhythmic memory) require only 21 minutes' playing time. The recorded instructions are very clear. The *Bentley Measures* enjoy considerable use and seem to be successful in providing satisfactory indications of musical level.

The *Gordon Musical Aptitude Profile* and the *Bentley Measures* were the major developments during the 1960s. Among more recent ones, the battery described by Davies (1971) is of interest in using non-musical materials, sine-wave for tests of melody, pitch and intervals, tapping for rhythm. The melody test, for example, requires the subjects to judge whether or not a sequence of three or four notes is contained within a tonal sequence of four to eight notes. Karma (1975) reported promising results from a test based on ability to structure acoustic material. The subjects have to divide the first section of each item into three similar parts in their minds and then decide whether the second section is similar. Pitch, intensity or length of note may be changed in the 'answer'. Both Davies's and Karma's tests can be used with younger children.

All the above tests aim at providing total scores or a profile of various aspects of musical abilities. Thackray (1969, 1972) focussed on several kinds of rhythmic ability. As well as perceptual tests he produced performance ones, such as asking his subjects to reproduce the rhythm of a short melodic phrase. His performance tests are among the few such tests to appear as part of a standardized battery, no doubt because they have to be administered individually.

How far the authors of prognostic tests have succeeded in producing tests unaffected by previous experience with music raises the nature–nurture question. Studies of family trees suggest that musical talent tends to run in families; on the other hand, it can be argued that musical parents tend to provide musically stimulating environments. Many studies of the influence on test results of home music, of music lessons and of specific coaching with material similar to the test have been carried out (see Shuter, 1968). In general, it seems to be true that previous experience with music tends to improve scores. On the other hand, many students with no formal training make higher scores than do some

after considerable tuition. Individual differences of test scores do not appear to be consistently related to the amount or quality of previous experience. Gordon believed that by the time a child has reached the age of ten whatever capacity he has tends to remain relatively stable. In a report of a five-year study (1974), he stated that children from culturally disadvantaged schools could, given opportunities for instrumental instruction, ultimately achieve significantly better results than pupils from heterogeneous schools with similar musical aptitude profiles. The music lessons appeared to provide the former with an activity by which they could compensate for their culturally deprived backgrounds.

Research seems to confirm the importance of laying foundations for future musical attainment at an early age. Michel (1973, 1975) suggested five or six years as the most favourable age for the development of musical abilities under optimum conditions. He concluded that if all children experience music at an early age, the selection of children for intensive training can be assessed over a period under normal educational conditions. 'Artifical' testing methods are not then required. While this may be the ideal situation, tests can often improve selection, if only by providing additional relevant information.

2. ATTAINMENT AND PERFORMANCE. Since measures of achievement have to be closely linked to what students have been learning, teachers have often preferred to construct their own tests. But some standardized measures have been devised; some authors have recommended schools and colleges to establish their own norms rather than rely on those provided.

Many tests of achievement require not only some previous training in music, but also considerable aural ability. Thus the *Colwell Music Achievement Tests* (1967–70) are designed to measure certain basic skills of aural perception generally regarded as important in the school music curriculum. They are graded from short pitch tests to recognition of cadences. The *Iowa Tests of Musical Literacy* (1971) have six levels each with two parts: tonal and rhythmic concepts. Each part consists of three sub-tests: aural perception, reading recognition and notational understanding.

At the college entrance level, Aliferis (1954) published a respected and successful test. He aimed at assessing the student's power of auditory visual discrimination, that is, his ability to visualize the musical notation of what he hears and to hear inwardly what he sees. The tests are divided into three sections: melody, rhythm and harmony. A similar test for college midpoint level was published in 1962. A promising new development at the tertiary entrance level is the *Australian Test for Advanced Music Studies* designed by Bridges (1975). In its 'provisional final form' it consists of three 45-minute sections: first, tonal and rhythm memory, musical perception; second, aural and visual discrimination, understanding of notation; and third, comprehension and application of learnt musical material. Interest is sustained by the use of music from a variety of cultures.

Performance tests, as noted above, require individual application. The *Watkins–Farnum Performance Scale* (1954) is an important attempt to provide an objective grading of performance on woodwind and brass instruments. The test consists of 14 sight-reading exercises graded by difficulty. The easiest is intended for pupils who have been studying the instrument for three months, while the most difficult would be an exacting test after several years of study.

PUBLISHED TESTS

Seashore Measures of Musical Talent (New York, 1919, rev. 2/1939 by C. Seashore, D. Lewis and J. G. Saetveit as *Measures of Musical Talents*, rev. 3/1960)

The Kwalwasser–Dykema Music Tests (New York, 1930)

The Oregon Music Discrimination Test (Chicago, 1935, rev. 2/1971 as *Indiana–Oregon Music Discrimination Test*)

The Wing Standardised Tests of Musical Intelligence (London, 1948, rev. and recorded, 1960)

The Aliferis Music Achievement Test (Minnesota, 1954)

The Watkins–Farnum Performance Scale (Minnesota, 1954)

The Drake Tests of Musical Aptitude (Chicago, 1957)

The Gaston Test of Musicality (Lawrence, Kansas, 1958)

The Aliferis–Stecklein Music Achievement Test (Minnesota, 1962)

The Gordon Musical Aptitude Profile (Boston, 1965)

The Bentley Measures of Musical Abilities (London, 1966)

The Colwell Music Achievement Tests (Chicago, 1967–70)

E. Gordon: *The Iowa Tests of Musical Literacy* (Iowa, 1971)

Australian Test for Advanced Music Studies (Melbourne, 1975)

BIBLIOGRAPHY

INTRODUCTION, GENERAL

J. Dollard and N. E. Miller: *Personality and Psychotherapy: an Analysis in Terms of Learning, Thinking, and Culture* (New York, 1950)

R. Frances: *La perception de la musique* (Paris, 1958)

G. Miller and S. Isard: 'Free Recall of Self-embedded English Sentences', *Information and Control*, vii (1964), 292

I. Whitfield: *The Auditory Pathway* (London, 1967)

A. Lomax: *Folk Song Style and Culture* (Washington, DC, 1968)

K. H. Pribram: 'The Foundation of Psychoanalytic Theory: Freud's Neuropsychological Model', *Brain and Behaviour*, iv: *Adaptation* (London, 1968), 395–432

R. Plomp and G. Smoorenburg, eds.: *Frequency Analysis and Periodicity Detection in Hearing* (Leiden, 1970)

J. Tobias, ed.: *Foundations of Modern Auditory Theory* (New York, 1970–72)

P. Lindsay and D. Norman: *Human Information Processing* (New York, 1972)

S. E. Gerber: *Introductory Hearing Science* (Philadephia, 1974)

Z. Lissa: 'Zur Theorie der musikalischen Rezeption', *AMw*, xxxi (1974), 157

K. H. Pribram and M. Hill: *Freud's 'Project' Reassessed* (London, 1976)

HISTORICAL BACKGROUND UP TO WORLD WAR I, MENTALISM, BEHAVIOURISM AND GESTALT THEORY

M. Mersenne: *Harmonie universelle* (Paris, 1636–7/R1963; Eng. trans., 1957)

[J. Sauveur]: 'Sur la détermination d'un son fixe', *Histoire de l'Académie royale des sciences* [1700] (Paris, 1703), 131

J. Sauveur: 'Systême general des intervalles des sons, et son application à tous les systêmes et à tous les instruments de musique', *Histoire de l'Académie royale des sciences* [1701] (Paris, 1704), *Mémoires*, 297–364

——: 'Table generale des sistemes temperez de musique', *Histoire de l'Académie royale des sciences* [1711] (Paris, 1714), *Mémoires*, 309

J. P. Rameau: *Démonstration du principe de l'harmonie* (Paris, 1750)

G. Tartini: *Trattato di musica* (Padua, 1754/R1966; Ger. trans., 1966)

——: *Dei principi dell'armonia musicale* (Padua, 1767/R1970)

C. Delezenne: 'Mémoires sur les valeurs numériques des notes de la gamme', *Recueil des travaux de la Société des sciences, de l'agriculture et des arts, de Lille*, i (1826–7), 1–56

A. Seebeck: 'Beiträge zur Physiologie des Gehör- und Gesichtssinnes', *Annalen der Physik und Chemie*, lxviii (1846), 449

H. Spencer: 'The Origin and Function of Music', *Fraser's Magazine* (1857), Oct; repr. in *Essays*, ii (London, 1901), 400–51

G. Fechner: *Elemente der Psychophysik* (Leipzig, 1860)

H. von Helmholtz: *Die Lehre von den Tonempfindungen* (Brunswick, 1863; Eng. trans., 1875, 2/1885/R1954 as *On the Sensations of Tone*)

F. Galton: *Hereditary Genius* (London, 1869)

C. Darwin: *The Descent of Man* (London, 1871)

G. Fechner: *Vorschule der Aesthetik* (Leipzig, 1876)

C. Stumpf: *Tonpsychologie* (Leipzig, 1883–90/R1965)

E. Mach: *Beiträge zur Analyse der Empfindungen* (Jena, 1886, 2/1900 as *Die Analyse der Empfindungen*, 9/1922; Eng. trans., 1914)

C. von Ehrenfels: 'Ueber Gestaltqualitäten', *Vierteljahrsschrift wissenschaftlicher Philosophie*, xiv (1890), 249–92

C. A. T. Billroth: *Wer ist musikalisch?*, ed. E. Hanslick (Berlin, 1895, 4/1912)

K. Blücher: *Arbeit und Rhythmus* (Leipzig, 1896)

W. Wundt: *Grundriss der Psychologie* (Leipzig, 1896)

E. Tichener: *A Textbook of Psychology* (New York, 1909)

G. Révész: *Ervin Nyiregyházy: psychologische Analyse eines*

musikalisch hervorragenden Kindes (Leipzig, 1916; Eng. trans., 1925/R1970, as *The Psychology of a Musical Prodigy*)

C. Seashore: 'The Sense of Rhythm as a Musical Talent', *MQ*, iv (1918), 507

K. Koffka: *Principles of Gestalt Psychology* (New York, 1935)

J. L. Mursell: *The Psychology of Music* (New York, 1937)

C. Seashore: *Psychology of Music* (New York, 1938/R1967)

C. Huyghens: *Musique et mathématique*, Oeuvres complètes, xx (Haarlem, 1940)

M. Schoen: *The Psychology of Music* (New York, 1940)

S. Langer: *Philosophy in a New Key* (Cambridge, Mass., 1942)

D. Hebb: *Organization of Behavior* (New York, 1949)

A. Ehrenzweig: *The Psycho-analysis of Artistic Vision and Hearing* (London, 1953)

S. Langer: *Feeling and Form* (London, 1953)

R. Lundin: *An Objective Psychology of Music* (New York, 1953)

C. Sachs: *Rhythm and Tempo: a Study in Music History* (New York, 1953)

P. Fraisse: *Les structures rythmiques* (Paris, 1956)

H. Lenneberg: 'Johann Mattheson on Affect and Rhetoric in Music', *JMT*, ii (1958), 47–84, 193–236

N. Chomsky: Review of B. F. Skinner: *Verbal Behavior*, *Language*, xxxv (1959), 26

C. Valentine: *The Experimental Psychology of Beauty* (London, 1962)

P. Kivy: 'What Mattheson Said', *MR*, xxxiv (1973), 132

PSYCHOANALYTIC THEORY

W. James: *The Principles of Psychology* (London, 1890)

A. Adler: *Study of Organ Inferiority and its Psychical Compensation* (New York, 1917)

W. Bardas: 'Zur Problematik der Musik', *Imago*, v (1919), 364

S. Pfeifer: 'Musikpsychologische Probleme', *Imago*, ix (1923), 453

S. Freud: *The Ego and the Id* (London, 1927)

S. Yates: 'Some Aspects of Time Difficulties and their Relation to Music', *International Journal of Psycho-analysis*, xvi (1935), 341

R. Sterba: 'Die Problematik des musikalischen Geschehens', *Internationale Zeitschrift für Psychoanalyse und Imago*, xxiv (1939), 428

I. H. Coriat: 'Some Aspects of a Psychoanalytic Interpretation of Music', *Psychoanalytic Review*, xxxii (1945), 408

P. Bregman and S. K. Escalona: 'Unusual Sensitivities in Very Young Children', *Psycho-analytic Study of the Child*, iii–iv (1949), 333

H. Kohut and S. Levarie: 'On the Enjoyment of Listening to Music', *Psychoanalytical Quarterly*, xix (1950), 64

A. Michel: *Psychoanalyse de la musique* (Paris, 1951)

H. Racker: 'Contribution to Psychoanalysis of Music', *American Imago*, viii (1951), 129–63

E. Kris: *Psychoanalytic Explorations in Art* (New York, 1952)

A. Ehrenzweig: *The Psycho-analysis of Artistic Vision and Hearing* (London, 1953)

E. Gutheil: 'Music as an Adjunct to Psychotherapy', *American Journal of Psychotherapy*, viii (1954), 94

H. Kohut: 'Some Psychological Effects of Music and their Relation to Music Therapy', *Music Therapy 1955*, ed. E. T. Gaston (Lawrence, Kansas, 1956), 17

W. G. Niederland: 'Early Auditory Experiences, Beating Fantasies and Primal Scene', *Psycho-analytic Study of the Child*, xiii (1958), 471–504

R. Hinde: 'Energy Models of Motivation', *Symposia of the Society for Experimental Biology*, xiv (Cambridge, Mass., 1960), 199

A. Freud: *Normality and Pathology in Childhood* (New York, 1965)

R. Spitz: *The First Year of Life* (New York, 1965)

P. Noy: 'The Psychodynamic Meaning of Music', *Journal of Music Therapy*, iii (1966–7), 126; iv (1967–8), 7, 45, 81, 117

——: 'A Revision of the Psychoanalytic Theory of the Primary Process', *International Journal of Psycho-analysis*, l (1969), 155

E. Peterfreund: *Information Systems and Psychoanalysis* (New York, 1971)

INFORMATION THEORY

F. Densmore: *Teton Sioux Music* (Washington, DC, 1918/R1972)

C. Morris: *Signs, Language and Behavior* (New York, 1946)

C. Shannon and W. Weaver: *The Mathematical Theory of Communication* (Chicago, 1949)

F. Attneave: *Applications of Information Theory to Psychology* (New York, 1956)

G. Miller: 'The Magical Number 7 ± 2: some Limits on our Capacity for Processing Information', *Psychological Review*, lxiii (1956), 81

H. Quastler, ed.: *Information Theory and Psychology* (Glencoe, Ill., 1956)

D. Broadbent: *Perception and Communication* (Oxford, 1958)

A. Moles: *Théorie de l'information et perception esthétique* (Paris, 1958)

J. Cohen: 'Information Theory and Music', *Behavioural Science*, vii (1962), 137

G. Miller and S. Isard: 'Free Recall of Self-embedded English Sentences', *Information and Control*, vii (1964), 292

L. Meyer: *Music, the Arts and Ideas* (Chicago, 1967), chaps.1 and 10

T. Winograd: 'Linguistics and the Computer Analysis of Tonal Harmony', *JMT*, xii (1968), 2

C. Longuet-Higgins and M. Steedman: 'On Interpreting Bach', *Machine Intelligence*, vi (1971), 221

CYBERNETIC THEORY

N. Wiener: *Cybernetics* (New York, 1948)

W. Ross Ashby: *Design for a Brain* (London, 1952)

G. Miller, E. Galanter and K. Pribram: *Plans and the Structure of Behaviour* (New York, 1960)

P. Fitts: 'Perceptual Motor Skill Learning', *Categories of Human Learning*, ed. A. Melton (New York, 1964), 243–85

J. Young: *A Model of the Brain* (Oxford, 1964)

K. U. Smith: 'Cybernetic Theory and Analysis of Learning', in E. Bilodeau: *Acquisition of Skill* (New York, 1966), 425–82

K. U. Smith and H. Sussmann: 'Cybernetic Motor Learning and Memory', in E. Bilodeau: *Principles of Skill Acquisition* (New York, 1969)

PERCEPTION OF PITCH, LOUDNESS, TIMBRE AND TEXTURE

R. Willis: 'On the Vowel Sounds, and on Reed Organ-pipes', *Transactions of the Cambridge Philosophical Society*, iii (1830), 231–68

H. von Helmholtz: *Die Lehre von den Tonempfindungen* (Brunswick, 1863; Eng. trans., 1875, 2/1885/R1954 as *On the Sensations of Tone*)

E. Mach: *Beiträge zur Analyse der Empfindungen* (Jena, 1886, 2/1900 as *Die Analyse der Empfindungen*, 9/1922; Eng. trans., 1914), 273

W. Rutherford: 'A New Theory of Hearing', *Journal of Anatomy and Physiology*, xxi (1886), 166

C. Stumpf and M. Meyer: 'Massbestimmungen über die Reinheit consonanter Intervalle', *Beiträge zur Akustik und Musikwissenschaft*, ii (1898), 84–167

G. Révész: *Zur Grundlegung der Tonpsychologie* (Leipzig, 1913)

E. Shower and R. Biddulph: 'Differential Pitch Sensitivity of the Ear', *Journal of the Acoustical Society of America*, iii (1931), 275

H. Seashore and J. Tiffen: 'Summary of Established Facts in Experimental Studies of Vibrato up to 1932', *University of Iowa Studies in the Psychology of Music*, i (1932), 344

H. Fletcher and W. Munson: 'Loudness, its Definition, Measurement and Calculation', *Journal of the Acoustical Society of America*, v (1933), 82, 108

M. Wolner and W. Pyle: 'An Experiment in Individual Training in Pitch-deficient Children', *Journal of Educational Psychology*, xxiv (1933), 602

H. Fletcher: 'Loudness, Pitch and the Timbre of Musical Tones and their Relation to the Intensity, the Frequency and the Overtone Structure', *Journal of the Acoustical Society of America*, vi (1934), 59

S. Stevens: 'Equal-pitch-loudness-volume Density Functions', 1934 [fig.1 in Ward, 1970]

R. Seashore: 'Improvability of Pitch Discrimination', *Psychology Bulletin*, xxxii (1935), 546

W. Snow: 'Changes of Pitch with Loudness at Low Frequencies', *Journal of the Acoustical Society of America*, viii (1936), 14

P. Greene: 'Violin Intonation', *Journal of the Acoustical Society of America*, ix (1937), 43

A. M. Small: 'An Objective Analysis of Artistic Violin Performance', *University of Iowa Studies in the Psychology of Music*, iv (1936), 172–231

C. Seashore: *Psychology of Music* (New York, 1938/R1967)

S. Stevens and H. Davis: *Hearing: its Psychology and Physiology* (New York, 1938)

H. Fletcher: 'Auditory Patterns', *Review of Modern Physics*, xii (1940), 47

S. Stevens and J. Volkmann: 'The Relation of Pitch to Frequency: a Revised Scale', *American Journal of Psychology*, liii (1940), 329

H. Blackwell and H. Schlosberg: 'Octave Generalization, Pitch Discrimination and Loudness Threshold in the White Rat', *Journal of Experimental Psychology*, xxxiii (1943), 407

R. F. Wyatt: *Improvability of Pitch Discrimination*, Psychological Monographs, lviii/2 (Evanston, 1945)

W. Garner: 'Auditory Thresholds of Short Tunes as a Function of Repetition Rates', *Journal of the Acoustical Society of America*, xix (1947), 600

G. Miller: 'Sensitivity to Changes in the Intensity of White Noise and its Relation to Masking and Loudness', *Journal of the Acoustical Society of America*, xix (1947), 609

J. Nickerson: *A Comparison of Performances of the same Melody played in Solo and in Ensemble with Reference to Equi-tempered, Just, and Pythagorean Intonations* (diss., U. of Minnesota, 1948)

E. Wever: *Theory of Hearing* (New York, 1949)

J. Egan and D. Meyer: 'Changes in Pitch of Tones of Low Frequency as a Function of the Pattern Excitation Produced by a Band of Noise', *Journal of the Acoustical Society of America*, xxii (1950), 827

G. Miller and G. Heise: 'The Trill Threshold', *Journal of the Acoustical Society of America*, xxii (1950), 637

J. Licklider: 'Basic Correlates of the Auditory Stimulus', *Handbook of Experimental Psychology*, ed. S. S. Stevens (New York, 1951), 811–67

G. Heise and G. Miller 'An Experimental Study of Auditory Patterns', *American Journal of Psychology*, lxiv (1951), 68

J. Corso: 'Unison Tuning of Musical Instruments', *Journal of the Acoustical Society of America*, xxvi (1954), 746

L. Elfner: 'Systematic Shifts in the Judgments of Octaves of High Frequencies', *Journal of the Acoustical Society of America*, xxvi (1954), 270

W. Ward: 'Subjective Musical Pitch', *Journal of the Acoustical Society of America*, xxvi (1954), 369

E. Zwicker: 'Der ungewöhnliche Amplitudengang der nichtlinearen Verzerrungen des Ohres', *Acustica*, v (1955), 67

D. Robinson and R. Dadson: 'A Redetermination of the Equal Loudness Relations for Pure Tones', *British Journal of Applied Physics*, vii (1956), 166

J. Licklider: 'Effects of Changes in the Phase Pattern upon the Sound of a 16 Harmonic Tone', *Journal of the Acoustical Society of America*, xxix (1957), 780

D. Broadbent: *Perception and Communication* (Oxford, 1958)

R. Plomp and M. Bouman: 'Relation between Hearing Threshold and Duration for Tone Pulses', *Journal of the Acoustical Society of America*, xxxi (1959), 749

M. Schroeder: 'New Results concerning Monaural Phase Sensitivity', *Journal of the Acoustical Society of America*, xxxi (1959), 1579

American Standards Association: *Acoustical Terminology* (New York, 1960)

J. Mason: 'Comparison of Solo and Ensemble Performances with Reference to Pythagorean, Just, and Equi-tempered Intonations', *JRME*, viii (1960), 31

G. von Békésy: *Experiments in Hearing* (New York, 1960)

C. Shackford: 'Some Aspects of Perception', *JMT*, v (1961), 162; vi (1962), 66, 295

D. Elliott: 'Backward Masking: Monotic and Dichotic Conditions', *Journal of the Acoustical Society of America*, xxxiv (1962), 1108

R. Plomp and W. Levelt: 'Musical Consonance and Critical Bandwidth', *4th International Congress on Acoustics: Copenhagen 1962*, 55

J. Swets, D. Green and W. Tanner: 'On the Width of Critical Bands', *Journal of the Acoustical Society of America*, xxxiv (1962), 108

R. Christman and W. Williams: 'Influence of the Time Interval on Experimentally Induced Shifts of Pitch', *Journal of the Acoustical Society of America*, xxxv (1963), 1030

J. Swets: 'Central Factors in Auditory Frequency Selectivity', *Psychological Bulletin*, lx (1963), 429

W. Thurlow: 'Perception of Low Auditory Pitch: a Multi-cue Mediation Theory', *Psychology Review*, lxx (1963), 515

C. Watson: 'Masking of Tones by Noise for the Cat', *Journal of the Acoustical Society of America*, xxxv (1963), 167

J. Miller: 'Auditory Sensitivity of the Chinchilla in Quiet and in Noise', *Journal of the Acoustical Society of America*, xxxvi (1964), 2010

E. Saldanha and J. Corso: 'Timbre Cues and the Identification of Musical Instruments', *Journal of the Acoustical Society of America*, xxxvi (1964), 2021

W. Tanner and C. Rivette: 'Experimental Study of "Tone-deafness" ', *Journal of the Acoustical Society of America*, xxxvi (1964), 1465

H. Fletcher, E. Blackham and O. Geertsen: 'Quality of Violin, Viola, Cello and Bass Viol Tones', *Journal of the Acoustical Society of America*, xxxvii (1965), 851

G. Gourevitch: 'Auditory Masking in the Rat', *Journal of the Acoustical Society of America*, xxxvii (1965), 439

T. Littler: *The Physics of the Ear* (Oxford, 1965)

R. Plomp and W. Levelt: 'Tonal Consonance and Critical Bandwidth', *Journal of the Acoustical Society of America*, xxxviii (1965), 548

S. Stevens, M. Guirao and A. Slawson: 'Loudness, a Product of Volume times Density', *Journal of Experimental Psychology*, lxix (1965), 503

G. Henning: 'Frequency Discrimination of Random-amplitude Tones', *Journal of the Acoustical Society of America*, xxxix (1966), 336

R. Plomp: *Experiments on Tone Perception* (Assen, 1966)

B. M. Teplov: *Psychologie des aptitudes musicales* (Fr. trans., Paris, 1966)

J. Goldstein: 'Auditory Spectral Filtering and Monaural Phase Perception', *Journal of the Acoustical Society of America*, xli (1967), 458

D. Norman: 'Temporal Confusions and Limited Capacity Processes', *Acta psychologica*, xxvii (1967), 293

R. Plomp: 'Beats of Mistuned Consonances', *Journal of the Acoustical Society of America*, xlii (1967), 462

W. Dowling: 'Rhythmic Fission and Perceptual Organization', *Journal of the Acoustical Society of America*, xliv (1968), 364

G. Henning and S. Grosberg: 'Effects of Harmonics on Frequency Distribution', *Journal of the Acoustical Society of America*, xliv (1968), 1386

A. Slawson: 'Vowel Quality and Musical Timbre as a Function of Spectrum Envelope and Fundamental Frequency', *Journal of the*

Acoustical Society of America, xliii (1968), 87

R. Plomp and H. Steeneken: 'Effect of Phase on the Timbre of Complex Tones', *Journal of the Acoustical Society of America*, xlvi (1969), 409

L. Jeffress: 'Masking', *Foundations of Modern Auditory Theory*, i, ed. J. Tobias (New York, 1970), 87

R. Plomp: 'Timbre as a Multidimensional Attribute of Complex Tones', *Frequency Analysis and Periodicity Detection in Hearing*, ed. R. Plomp and G. Smoorenburg (Leiden, 1970), 397

R. Ritoma: 'Periodicity Detection', *Frequency Analysis and Periodicity Detection in Hearing*, ed. R. Plomp and G. Smoorenburg (Leiden, 1970)

D. Sergeant: 'The Measurement of Discrimination of Pitch', *10th Conference on Research in Music Education* (Reading, 1970)

J. Tobias, ed.: *Foundations of Modern Auditory Theory* (New York, 1970–72)

W. D. Ward: 'Musical Perception', *Foundations of Modern Auditory Theory*, ed. J. Tobias, i (New York, 1970), 407

F. Attneave and R. Olson: 'Pitch as a Medium: a New Approach to Psycho-physical Scaling', *American Journal of Psychology*, lxxxiv (1971), 147

A. Bregman and J. Campbell: 'Primary Auditory Stream Segregation, Perception of Order in Rapid Sequences of Tones', *Journal of Experimental Psychology*, lxxxix (1971), 244

W. Gulick: *Hearing* (New York, 1971)

A. Houtsma and J. Goldstein: 'The Central Origin of the Pitch of Complex Tones: Evidence from Musical Interval Recognition', *Journal of the Acoustical Society of America*, li (1972), 520

D. Norman: *Human Information Processing* (New York, 1972)

A. Bregman and G. Dannenbring: 'The Effect of Continuity on Auditory Stream Segregation', *Perception and Psychophysics*, xiii (1973), 308

W. Dowling: 'The Perception of Interleaved Melodies', *Cognitive Psychology*, v (1973), 322

S. Gerber: *Introductory Hearing Science* (New York, 1974)

G. Papich and E. Rainbow: 'Research in the Performance Practices of Musicians', *Psychology of Music*, iii/1 (1975), 4

J. Howard and E. Silverman: 'A Multidimensional Scaling Analysis of 16 Complex Sounds', *Perception and Psychophysics*, xix (1976), 193

W. L. Idson and D. W. Massaro: 'Cross-octave Masking of Single Tones and Musical Sequences: the Effects of Structure on Auditory Recognition', *Perception and Psychophysics*, xix (1976), 155

PERCEPTION OF RHYTHM, TEMPORALITY AND TEMPO

W. James: *The Principles of Psychology* (London, 1890), chap.25

H. Munsterburg: 'Vergleichen der Tondistanzen', *Beiträge zur experimentelle Psychologie*, iv (1892), 147

T. Bolton: 'Rhythm', *American Journal of Psychology*, vi (1894), 145

W. Wundt: *Grundriss der Psychologie* (Leipzig, 1896)

C. Squire: 'A Genetic Study of Rhythm', *American Journal of Psychology*, xii (1901), 493

R. MacDougall: 'The Relation of Auditory Rhythm to Nervous Discharge', *Psychological Review*, ix (1902), 460

—————: 'The Structure of Simple Rhythm Forms', *Psychological Review*, (1903), suppl.

E. D. Puffer: *The Psychology of Beauty* (Boston and New York, 1905)

R. H. Stetson: 'A Motor Theory of Rhythm and Discrete Succession', *Psychological Review*, xii (1905), 250, 293–350

K. Dunlap: 'Rhythm and the Specious Present', *Journal of Philosophy, Psychology and Scientific Method*, viii (1911), 348

C. Ruckmick: 'Role Kinesthesis in the Perception of Rhythm', *American Journal of Psychology*, xxiv (1913), 305

G. P. Jackson: 'The Rhythmic Forms of the German Folk-songs', *Modern Philology*, xiii (1915–16), 561; xiv (1916–17), 65; xv (1917–18), 79

K. Bucher: *Arbeit und Rhythmus* (Leipzig, 1919)

E. Jaques-Dalcroze: *Le rythme, la musique et l'éducation* (Paris, 1919, 2/1965; Eng. trans., 1921, 2/1967)

E. Isaacs: 'The Nature of the Rhythm Experience', *Psychological Review*, xxvii (1920), 270–99

M. François: 'Contribution à l'étude du sens du temps: la température interne comme facteur de variation de l'appréciation subjective des durées', *Année psychologique*, xxviii (1927), 186

G. Wedge: *Rhythm in Music* (New York, 1927)

T. Matthay: *The Visible and Invisible in Pianoforte Technique* (London, 1932, rev. 2/1947/R1976)

H. Hoagland: 'The Physiological Control of Judgements of Duration: Evidence for a Chemical Clock', *Journal of General Psychology*, ix (1933), 267

J. Mainwaring: 'Kinaesthetic Factors in the Recall of Musical Experience', *British Journal of Psychology*, xxiii (1933), 284

A. Washco: *The Effects of Music upon Pulse Rate, Blood Pressure and Mental Imagery* (Philadelphia, 1933)

R. Husband: 'The Effects of Musical Rhythms and Pure Rhythms on Bodily Sway', *Journal of General Psychology*, xi (1934), 328

H. Woodrow: 'The Temporal Indifference Interval Determined by the Method of Mean Error', *Journal of Experimental Psychology*, xvii (1934), 167

H. Hoagland: *Pacemakers in Relation to Aspects of Behavior* (New York, 1935)

A. M. Small: 'An Objective Analysis of Artistic Violin Performance', *University of Iowa Studies in the Psychology of Music*, iv (1936), 172–231

L. Vernon: 'Synchronization of Chords in Artistic Piano Playing', *University of Iowa Studies in the Psychology of Music*, iv (1936), 306

C. Seashore: *Psychology of Music* (New York, 1938/R1967)

H. Weaver: 'Syncopation: a Study of Musical Rhythms', *Journal of General Psychology*, xx (1939), 409

H. Hanson: 'Some Objective Studies of Rhythm in Music', *American Journal of Psychiatry*, ci (1944–5), 364

H. Pieron: *Aux sources de la connaissance: la sensation, guide de vie* (Paris, 1945; Eng. trans., 1951, as *The Sensations and their Functions, Processes and Mechanisms*)

W. Garner: 'Auditory Thresholds of Short Tunes as a Function of Repetition Rates', *Journal of the Acoustical Society of America*, xix (1947), 600

J. Black: 'The Effects of Delayed Side-tone upon Vocal Rate and Intensity', *Journal of Speech Hearing Disorders*, xvi (1951), 56

K. Lashley: 'The Problem of Serial Order in Behaviour', *Cerebral Mechanisms in Behaviour*, ed. L. Jeffress (New York, 1951), 112

J. Licklider: 'Basic Correlates of the Auditory Stimulus', *Handbook of Experimental Psychology*, ed. S. S. Stevens (New York, 1951), 985–1039

H. Woodrow: 'Time Perception', *Handbook of Experimental Psychology*, ed. S. S. Stevens (New York, 1951), 1224

E. Haish: 'Über die Psychoanalytische Deutung der Musik', *Psyche*, vii (1953), 81

P. G. Cheatham and C. T. White: 'Temporal Numerosity, iii: Auditory Perception of Number', *Journal of Experimental Psychology*, xlvii (1954), 425

E. Gutheil: 'Music as an Adjunct to Psychotherapy', *American Journal of Psychotherapy*, viii (1954), 94

P. Fraisse: *Les structures rythmiques* (Paris, 1956)

J. Stroud: 'The Fine Structure of Psychological Time', *Information Theory and Psychology*, ed. H. Quastler (Glencoe, Ill., 1956), 174

E. Duffy: 'The Psychological Significance of the Concept of Arousal or Activation', *Psychological Review*, lxiv (1957), 265

I. J. Hirsh: 'Auditory Perception of Temporal Order', *Journal of the Acoustical Society of America*, xxix (1957), 759

D. Broadbent: *Perception and Communication* (London, 1958)

G. Cooper and L. Meyer: *The Rhythmic Structure of Music* (Chicago, 1960)

G. Sperling: *The Information Available in Brief Visual Presentations*, Psychological Monographs, lxxiv/11 (Washington, DC, 1960)

F. Winckel: *Phänomene des musikalischen Hörens* (Berlin and Wunsiedel, 1960; Eng. trans., 1967, as *Music, Sound and Sensation*)

J. Zwislocki: 'Theory of Temporal Auditory Summation', *Journal of the Acoustical Society of America*, xxxii (1960), 1046

C. R. Bell and K. A. Provins: 'Relation between Physiological Responses to Environmental Heat and Time Judgments', *Journal of Experimental Psychology*, lxvi (1963), 572

P. Fraisse: *La psychologie du temps* (Paris, 1963; Eng. trans., 1968)

C. T. White: *Temporal Numerosity and the Psychological Unit of Duration* (Washington, DC, 1963)

A. Liberman and others: 'Some Observations on a Model for Speech Perception', *Models for the Perception of Speech and Visual Form*, ed. W. Wathen-Dunn (Cambridge, Mass., 1964), 68

F. M. Ochberg, I. W. Pollak and E. Meyer: 'Correlation of Pulse and Time Judgment', *Perceptual and Motor Skills*, xix (1964), 861

M. Treisman: *Temporal Discrimination and Indifference Interval* (Washington, DC, 1964)

C. Bell: 'Time Estimations and Increases in Body Temperature', *Journal of Experimental Psychology*, lxx (1965), 232

A. Baddeley: 'Time-estimation at Reduced Body-temperature', *American Journal of Psychology*, lxxix (1966), 475

I. J. Hirsh: 'Audition in Relation to Perception of Speech', *Brain Function*, iii, ed. E. C. Carterette (Berkeley, 1966)

F. Royer and W. Garner: 'Response Uncertainty and the Perceptual Difficulty of Auditory Temporal Patterns', *Perception and Psychophysics*, i (1966), 41

D. Aaronson: 'Temporal Factors in Perception and Short-term Memory', *Psychology Bulletin*, lxvii (1967), 130

E. H. Lenneberg: *The Biological Foundations of Language* (New York, 1967)

U. Neisser: *Cognitive Psychology* (New York, 1967)

W. Garner and R. Gottwald: 'The Perception and Learning of Temporal Patterns', *Quarterly Journal of Experimental Psychology*, xx (1969), 97

R. Ornstein: *On the Experience of Time* (London, 1969)

R. P. and R. M. Warren and others: 'Auditory Sequence: Confusion of Patterns other than Speech or Music', *Science*, clxiv (1969), 586

Biofeedback and Self-control (1970–)

R. L. Birdwhistell: *Kinesics and Context* (Philadelphia, 1970)

J. Patterson and D. Green: 'Discrimination of Transient Signals having Identical Energy Spectra', *Journal of the Acoustical Society of America*, xlviii (1970), 894

H. Schaeffer and M. Parry: 'The Effects of Short-term Familiarization on Infants' Perceptual-motor Coordination in a Simultaneous Discrimination Situation', *British Journal of Psychology*, lxi (1970), 559

D. Berlyne: *Aesthetics and Psychobiology* (New York, 1971)

A. Bregman and J. Campbell: 'Primary Auditory Stream Segregation, Perception of Order in Rapid Sequences of Tones', *Journal of Experimental Psychology*, lxxxix (1971), 244

J. Brener and D. Hothersall: 'Heart Rate Control under Conditions of Augmented Sensory Feedback', *Biofeedback and Self-control*, ed. J. Kamiya and others (Chicago, 1971), 48

W. Colquhoun, ed.: *Biological Rhythms and Human Performance* (New York, 1971)

P. Divenyi: 'The Rhythmic Perception of Micro-melodies', *Experimental Research in the Psychology of Music*, vii, ed. E. Gordon (Iowa City, 1971), 41

E. Gordon, ed.: *Experimental Research in the Psychology of Music*, vii (Iowa City, 1971)

D. Green: 'Temporal Auditory Acuity', *Psychological Review*, lxxviii (1971), 540

J. Kamiya: 'Operant Control of the EEG Alpha Rhythm and some of its Reported Effects on Consciousness', *Biofeedback and Self-control*, ed. J. Kamiya and others (Chicago, 1971), 280

B. Leshowitz: 'Measurement of the Two-click Threshold', *Journal of the Acoustical Society of America*, xlix (1971), 462

C. Longuet-Higgins and M. Steedman: 'On Interpreting Bach', *Machine Intelligence*, vi (1971), 221

D. Perrott and K. Williams: 'Auditory Temporal Resolution', *Psychonomic Science*, xxv (1971), 73

A. Sanford: 'A Periodic Basis for Perception and Action', *Biological Rhythms and Human Performance*, ed. W. Colquhoun (New York, 1971), 179

J. Martin: 'Rhythmic (Hierarchical) versus Serial Structure in Speech and Other Behaviour', *Psychological Review*, lxxix (1972), 487

R. Warren: 'Perception of Temporal Order: Special Rules for the Initial and Terminal Sounds of Sequences', *Journal of the Acoustical Society of America*, lii (1972), 167 [abstract]

R. Warren and C. Obusek: 'Identification of Temporal Order within Auditory Sequences', *Perception and Psychophysics*, xii (1972), 86

A. Gabrielsson: 'Similarity, Ratings and Dimensional Analyses of Auditory Rhythm Patterns', *Scandinavian Journal of Psychology*, xiv (1973), 138, 161

R. Peters and T. Wood: 'Perceived Order of Tone Pulses', *Journal of the Acoustical Society of America*, liv (1973), 315 [abstract]

P. Fraisse: *Psychologie du rythme* (Paris, 1974)

A. Gabrielsson: 'Performance of Rhythm Patterns', *Scandinavian Journal of Psychology*, xv (1974), 63

W. Garner: *The Processing of Information and Structure* (New York, 1974)

A. Gates, J. Bradshaw and N. Nettleton: 'Effect of Different Delayed Auditory Feedback Intervals on a Musical Performance Task', *Perception and Psychophysics*, xv (1974), 21

S. E. Gerber: 'Auditory Temporality', *Introductory Hearing Science* (Philadelphia, 1974), 172

E. Gordon: 'Toward the Development of a Taxonomy of Tonal Patterns and Rhythm Patterns: Evidence of Difficulty Level and Growth Rate', *Experimental Research in the Psychology of Music*, ix (Iowa City, 1974), 39–232

P. Divenyi and I. J. Hirsh: 'The Effect of Blanking on the Identification of Temporal Order in Three-tone Sequences', *Perception and Psychophysics*, xvii (1975), 246

PERCEPTION OF MELODY AND HARMONY

H. von Helmholtz: *Die Lehre von den Tonempfindungen* (Brunswick, 1863; Eng. trans., 1875, 2/1885/R1954 as *On the Sensations of Tone*)

H. Rupp: 'Über die Prüfung musikalischer Fähigkeiten, i', *Zeitschrift für angewandte Psychologie*, ix (1915), 1

F. Brehmer: *Melodieanfassung und melodische Begabung des Kindes* (Leipzig, 1925)

H. Werner: 'Über Mikromelodik und Mikroharmonik', *Zeitschrift für Psychologie* (1926), no.98, p.74

O. Reimers: 'Untersuchungen über die Entwicklung des Tonalitätsgefühl im Laufe der Schulzeit', *Zeitschrift für angewandte Psychologie*, xxviii (1927), 193

P. Farnsworth: 'The Discrimination of Major, Minor and certain Mistuned Intervals', *Journal of General Psychology*, i (1928), 377

G. Révész: ' "Tonsystem" jenseits des musikalischen Gebietes, musikalische "Mikrosysteme" und ihre Beziehung zu der musikalischen Akustik', *Zeitschrift für Psychologie* (1935), no.134, pp.25–61

J. L. Mursell: *The Psychology of Music* (New York, 1937)

G. E. Moorhead and D. Pond: *Music of Young Children, i: Chant* (Santa Barbara, Calif., 1941)

G. Révész: *Inleiding tot de muziekpsychologie* (Amsterdam, 1944, 2/1946; Ger. trans., 1946/R1972; Eng. trans., 1953/R1970)

E. Franklin: *Tonality as a Basis for the Study of Musical Talent* (Göteborg, 1956)

C. Valentine: *The Experimental Psychology of Beauty* (London, 1962)

M. Pflederer: 'The Responses of Children to Musical Tasks Embodying Piaget's Principles of Conversation', *JRME*, xii (1964), 251

——: 'How Children Perceptually Organize Sounds', *Bulletin of the Council of Research in Music Education*, vii (1966), 1

B. M. Teplov: *Psychologie des aptitudes musicales* (Fr. trans., Paris, 1966)

W. Dowling and D. Fujitani: 'Contour, Interval and Pitch Recognition in Memory for Melodies', *Journal of the Acoustical Society of America*, lii (1971), 524

MEMORY AND MEMORIZING

I. Hyde: 'Effects of Music upon Electrocardiograms and Blood Pressure', *The Effects of Music*, ed. M. Schoen (London and New York, 1927), 184

M. Schoen, ed.: *The Effects of Music* (London and New York, 1927)

F. Bartlett: *Remembering: a Study in Experimental and Social Psychology* (Cambridge, 1932)

J. Mainwaring: 'Kinaesthetic Factors in the Recall of Musical Experience', *British Journal of Psychology*, xxiii (1933), 284

K. Hevner: 'The Affective Value of Pitch and Tempo in Music', *American Journal of Psychology*, xlix (1937), 621

G. Rubin-Rabson: 'The Influence of Analytical Pre-study in Memorizing Piano Music', *Archives of Psychology*, xxxi (1937), 220

C. Seashore: *Psychology of Music* (New York, 1938/R1967)

G. Rubin-Rabson: 'A Comparison of the Whole and Part Approach', *Journal of Educational Psychology*, xxxi (1940), 270

C. O'Brien: 'Part and Whole Methods in Memorization of Piano Music', *Journal of Educational Psychology*, xxxiv (1943), 552

G. Rubin-Rabson: 'Studies in the Psychology of Memorizing Piano Music, ii: A Comparison of Massed and Distributed Practice', *Journal of Educational Psychology*, xxxi (1943), 270

K. Craik: 'Theory of the Human Operator in Control Systems', *British Journal of Psychology*, xxxviii (1948), 142

P. Farnsworth: *Musical Taste: its Measurement and Cultural Nature* (Stanford, Calif., 1950)

K. Lashley: 'The Problem of Serial Order in Behaviour', *Cerebral Mechanisms in Behaviour*, ed. L. Jeffress (New York, 1951), 112

W. Penfield: 'Memory Mechanisms', *Transactions of the American Neurological Association*, lxxvi (1951), 15

D. Ellis and G. Brighouse: 'Effects of Music on Respiration and Heart-rate', *American Journal of Psychology*, lxv (1952), 39

J. Harris: 'The Decline of Pitch Discrimination with Time', *Journal of Experimental Psychology*, xliii (1952), 96

C. Hovland and T. Kurz: 'Experimental Studies in Rote Learning', *Journal of Experimental Psychology*, xliv (1952), 31

B. Underwood: 'Studies of Distributed Practice, xii: Retention Following Varying Degrees of Original Learning', *Journal of Experimental Psychology*, xlvii (1954), 294

G. Miller: 'The Magical Number 7 ± 2: some Limits on our Capacity for Processing Information', *Psychological Review*, lxiii (1956), 81

B. Underwood: 'Interference and Forgetting', *Psychological Review*, lxiv (1957), 49

D. Broadbent: *Perception and Communication* (London, 1958)

A. Anastasi and R. Levée: 'Intellectual Defect and Musical Talent: a Case Report', *American Journal of Mental Deficiency*, lxiv (1959), 695

R. Conrad: 'Errors of Immediate Memory', *British Journal of Psychology*, l (1959), 349

L. and M. Peterson: 'Short-term Retention of Individual Verbal Items', *Journal of Experimental Psychology*, lviii (1959), 193

R. Conrad: 'Very Brief Delay of Immediate Recall', *Quarterly Journal of Experimental Psychology*, xii (1960), 45

G. Miller, E. Galanter and K. Pribram: *Plans and the Structure of Behaviour* (New York, 1960)

G. Sperling: *The Information Available in Brief Visual Presentations*, Psychological Monographs, lxxiv/11 (Washington, DC, 1960)

A. Treisman: 'Contextual Cues in Selective Listening', *Quarterly Journal of Experimental Psychology*, xii (1960), 242

B. Underwood and L. Postman: 'Extra Experimental Sources of Interference in Forgetting', *Psychological Review*, lxvii (1960), 73

B. Underwood and R. Schultz: *Meaningfulness and Verbal Learning* (Philadelphia, 1960)

L. Peterson: 'Immediate Memory: Data and Theory', *Verbal Behaviour and Learning*, ed. C. Cofer and B. Musgrave (New York, 1963)

R. Conrad: 'Acoustic Confusions in Immediate Memory', *British Journal of Psychology*, lv (1964), 75

P. Fitts: 'Perceptual Motor Skill Learning', *Categories of Human Learning*, ed. A. Melton (New York, 1964), 243–85

A. Merriam: *The Anthropology of Music* (Evanston, 1964)

A. De Groot: *Thought and Choice in Chess* (The Hague, 1965)

M. Glanzer and A. Cunitz: 'Two Storage Mechanisms in Free Recall',

Journal of Verbal Learning and Verbal Behaviour, lxv (1966), 351

D. McNeill: 'Developmental Psycholinguistics', *The Genesis of Language*, ed. G. A. Miller and F. Smith (Cambridge, Mass., and London, 1966), 15–84

B. M. Teplov: *Psychologie des aptitudes musicales* (Fr. trans., Paris, 1966)

B. Underwood and B. Eckstrand: 'An Analysis of some Shortcomings in the Interference Theory of Forgetting', *Psychological Review*, lxxiii (1966), 540

D. Aaronson: 'Temporal Factors in Perception and Short-term Memory', *Psychology Bulletin*, lxvii (1967), 130

J. Bruner: *Studies in Cognitive Growth* (New York, 1967)

P. M. Fitts and M. I. Posner: *Human Performance* (Belmont, Calif., 1967)

U. Neisser: *Cognitive Psychology* (New York, 1967)

A. Welford: *Fundamentals of Skill* (London, 1968)

J. Annett: *Feedback and Human Behaviour* (London, 1969)

G. Bower and D. Winzenz: 'Group Structure, Coding and Memory for Digit Series', *Journal of Experimental Psychology*, lxxx/2 (1969)

A. Treisman: 'Strategies and Models of Selective Attention', *Psychological Review*, lxxvi (1969), 282

W. Wickelgren: 'Associative Strength Theory of Recognition Memory for Pitch', *Journal of Mathematical Psychology*, vi (1969), 13

G. Bower: 'Organizational Factors in Memory', *Cognitive Psychology*, i (1970), 18

D. Deutsch: 'Tones and Numbers: Specificity of Interference in Short-term Memory', *Science*, clxviii (1970), 1604

D. McNeill: *The Acquisition of Language* (New York, 1970)

S. Segal and V. Fusella: 'Influence of Imaged Pictures and Sounds on Detection of Visual and Auditory Signals', *Journal of Experimental Psychology*, lxxxiii (1970), 458

F. Spellacy: 'Lateral Preferences in the Identification of Patterned Stimuli', *Journal of the Acoustical Society of America*, xlvii (1970), 574

M. Studdert Kennedy and D. Shankweiler: 'Hemispheric Specialization for Speech Perception', *Journal of the Acoustical Society of America*, xlviii (1970), 579

M. Williams: *Brain Damage and the Mind* (London, 1970)

F. Attneave and R. Olson: 'Pitch as a Medium: a New Approach to Psychological Scaling', *American Journal of Psychology*, lxxxiv (1971), 147

D. Broadbent: *Decision and Stress* (London, 1971)

M. Coltheart and F. Allard: *Physical and Code Names of Heard Letters* (paper given at Psychonomic Society meeting, St Louis, Nov 1971)

W. Dowling and D. Fujitani: 'Contour, Interval and Pitch Recognition in Memory for Melodies', *Journal of the Acoustical Society of America*, lii (1971), 524

J. Morton, R. Crowder and H. Prussin: 'Experiments with the Stimulus Suffix Effect', *Journal of Experimental Psychology*, xci (1971), 169

D. Allport, B. Antonis and P. Reynolds: 'On the Division of Attention: a Disproof of the Single Channel Hypothesis', *Quarterly Journal of Experimental Psychology*, xxiv (1972), 225

M. Coltheart: 'Visual Information Processing', *New Horizons in Psychology*, ii, ed. B. Foss (London, 1972)

F. Craik and R. Lockhart: 'Levels of Processing: a Framework for Memory Research', *Journal of Verbal Learning and Verbal Behaviour*, xi (1972), 671

D. Deutsch: 'Mapping of Interactions in the Pitch Memory Store', *Science*, clxxv (1972), 1020

W. Dowling: 'Recognition of Melodic Transformations: Inversion, Retrograde and Retrograde Inversion', *Perception and Psychophysics*, xii (1972), 417

S. Keele: 'Attentional Demands of Memory Retrieval', *Journal of Experimental Psychology*, xciii (1972), 245

M. Posner and R. Warren: 'Traces, Concepts and Conscious Constructions', *Coding Processes in Human Memory*, ed. A. W. Melton and E. Martin (Washington, DC, and New York, 1972), 25

K. Wolff: *The Teaching of Artur Schnabel: a Guide to Interpretation* (London, 1972)

R. Brown: *First Language: the Early Stages* (Cambridge, Mass., 1973)

W. Dowling: 'Rhythmic Groups and Subjective Chunks in Memory for Melodies', *Perception and Psychophysics*, xiv (1973), 37

G. C. Grindley and V. Townsend: 'Visual Imagery and Verbalization with Simple Tachistoscopic Displays', *Quarterly Journal of Experimental Psychology*, xxv (1973), 300

J. Sloboda: *Music Reading and Prose Reading: some Comparisons of Underlying Processes* (diss., U. of London, 1974)

——: 'The Eye-Hand Span – an Approach to the Study of Sight Reading', *Psychology of Music*, ii/2 (1974), 4

P. Berg: *Short-term Memory for Tone Sequences* (diss., U. of London, 1975)

D. Deutsch: 'The Organization of Short-term Memory for a Single Acoustic Attribute', *Short-term Memory*, ed. D. and J. Deutsch (New York, 1975), 108–54

P. Pederson: 'The Perception of Octave Equivalence in Twelve-tone Rows', *Psychology of Music*, iii (1975), 3

M. Critchley and R. A. Henson: *Music and the Brain. Studies in the Neurology of Music* (London, 1976)

L. Cuddy and A. Cohen: 'Recognition of Transposed Melodic Sequences', *Quarterly Journal of Experimental Psychology*, xxviii (1976), 255

D. Massaro: 'Perceiving and Counting Sounds', *Journal of Experimental Psychology of Human Perception and Performance*, ii (1976), 337

J. Sloboda: 'Visual Perception of Musical Notation: Registering Pitch Symbols in Memory', *Quarterly Journal of Experimental Psychology*, xxviii (1976), 1

ASSESSMENT OF MUSICAL ABILITIES AND ATTAINMENTS

C. Seashore: *Psychology of Music* (New York, 1938/*R*1967)

G. Révész: *Inleiding tot de muziekpsychologie* (Amsterdam, 1944, 2/1946; Ger. trans., 1946/*R*1972; Eng. trans., 1953/*R*1970)

H. Wing: 'Tests of Musical Ability and Appreciation', *British Journal of Psychology*, suppl. 27 (1948); pubd separately, rev. (Cambridge, 1968)

W. E. Whybrew: *Measurement and Evaluation in Music* (Dubuque, Iowa, 1962)

E. Gordon: *Musical Aptitude Profile Manual* (Boston, 1965)

——: *A Three-year Longitudinal Predictive Study of the Musical Aptitude Profile* (Iowa, 1967)

P. Lehman: *Tests and Measurement in Music* (Englewood Cliffs, NJ, 1968)

R. Shuter: *The Psychology of Musical Ability* (London, 1968) [foreword with P. E. Vernon]

R. Thackray: *An Investigation into Rhythmic Abilities* (London, 1969)

R. Colwell: *The Evaluation of Music Teaching and Learning* (Englewood Cliffs, NJ, 1970)

J. B. Davies: 'New Tests of Musical Aptitude', *British Journal of Psychology*, lxii (1971), 557

N. Long: 'Establishment of Standards for the Indiana–Oregon Music Discrimination Test Based on a Cross-section of Elementary and Secondary Students', *Bulletin of the Council of Research in Music Education* (1971), no.25, p.26

R. Thackray: *Rhythmic Abilities in Children* (London, 1972)

L. Crickmore: 'A Syndrome Hypothesis of Music Appreciation', *Psychology of Music*, i (1973), 21

P. Michel: 'The Optimum Development of Musical Abilities in the First Years of Life', *Psychology of Music*, i (1973), 14

E. Gordon: 'Fourth-year Results of a Five-year Longitudinal Study of the Musical Achievement of Culturally Disadvantaged Students', *Scientific Aesthetics*, ix (1974), 79

D. Bridges: 'Development of the Australian Test for Advanced Music Studies (ATAMS)', *Music Education for the Very Young Child: IV. International Seminar in Research of Music Education: Wellington 1975*, 32

K. Karma: *The Ability to Structure Acoustic Material as a Measure of Musical Aptitude* (Helsinki, 1975)

P. Michel: 'The Necessity for an Early Development of Musical Talents at Pre-school Age and the Problem of Aptitude Diagnosis', *Music Education for the Very Young Child: IV. International Seminar in Research of Music Education: Wellington 1975*, 26

NATASHA SPENDER (I–III),
ROSAMUND SHUTER-DYSON (IV)

Ptolemaic Kingdom. *See* EGYPT, §I, and HELLENISTIC STATES, §3.

Ptolemy, Claudius [Ptolemaios, Klaudios; Ptolemaeus] (*b* ?Ptolemais, after 83; *d* 161). Greek mathematician, geographer, astronomer and music theorist. He probably had access to an observatory at Alexandria, where he spent his working life. His major work, on mathematics and astronomy, was the *Almagest* (Arabic, *al-majistī*; Ptolemy's original title was *Mathēmatikē syntaxis*). This was a compendium of the work of earlier Greek astronomers; it describes a geocentric universe.

His three-volume *Harmonika* ('Harmonics'), written in the middle of the 2nd century, constitutes the most learned and lucid exposition of music theory in antiquity, its logical, systematic comprehensiveness making it, as Düring said, a 'worthy counterpart' to the *Almagest*. In it Ptolemy discussed the principles and purposes of the theory of harmonics (i, chap.1–2), the principles of acoustics (i, 3–4), interval theory with a critique of the theory of the Pythagorean and Aristoxenian schools (i, 5–11), the theory of the genera with a critique of various divisions of the tetrachord (i, 12–ii, 1), a description of the helicon (a geometrical instrument devised, like the monochord, for measuring interval ratios with stretched strings; ii, 2), the theory of 4th, 5th and octave species (ii, 3), the Perfect System (*systēma teleion*) and the derivation of modes by transposition or modulation, with a critique of the modal theory of Aristoxenus (ii, 4–11), a description of the monochord (ii, 12–13), tables of the genera and the 'mixtures' (*migmata*) of genera usual in practice (ii, 14–16), the use of the 15-stringed 'monochord' (iii, 1–2), comparisons of the relationships between notes and the parts of the human soul (iii, 3–7) and between the heavenly bodies, with tables (iii, 8–16).

Ptolemy adopted as his basic postulate the need for the two criteria of judgment, reason and empirical observation, not to contradict each other. Since, he believed, sense perception is fallible, he sought a precise scientific instrument by which to measure the numerical ratios of consonances, and he found it in the monochord, which illustrates acoustic phenomena in visual, geometric terms. He thus conceived of music theory in terms of precise mathematical calculation.

Citing such authorities as Didymus on the difference between the Pythagorean and Aristoxenian theories of music, he criticized the Pythagoreans for frequently postulating theoretical relationships which do not correspond with reality; on the other hand he criticized the Aristoxenians for designating intervals by *diastēma* ('distance apart', i.e. by summation: *see* GREECE, §I, 7) rather than in terms of precise mathematical ratios.

Ptolemy attacked the Pythagoreans for defining intervals smaller and greater than the octave in different ways. For example, he claimed that they wrongly excluded the 11th (8 : 3) from the consonances while admitting the 4th (4 : 3) because the 11th was a ratio neither multiple (i.e. in the form $nx : x$) nor superparticular (i.e. in the form $(x + 1) : x$ where x is a positive integer): these were the mathematical formulae favoured by the Pythagoreans to define consonances.

Ptolemy arranged intervals between notes of definite but unequal pitch (*anisotonoi*) according to the simplicity of their ratios, as 'homophōnoi', or multiple ratios (e.g. the octave, 2 : 1, or the double octave, 4 : 1); 'symphōnoi', or the first two superparticular ratios which are not multiple (the 4th, 4 : 3, and the 5th, 3 : 2) and their octave extensions (the 11th, $2 : 1 \times 4 : 3 = 8 : 3$, and the 12th, $2 : 1 \times 3 : 2 = 3 : 1$); and finally 'emmeleis' ('in the *melos*, i.e. melodically useful), or the superparticular ratios according to the formula above where x is greater than 3, e.g. the whole tone (9 : 8). He also proved mathematically and acoustically that the Aristoxenians wrongly defined the 4th as two and a half whole tones and the octave as six whole tones.

In examining his predecessors' classifications of the tetrachord, too, he showed that they did not confirm their theoretical results by empirical observation. After citing the classifications of Archytas, Eratosthenes, Didymus and Aristoxenus, he calculated his own tetrachords, using superparticular ratios, as follows:

One enharmonic tetrachord: $(5 : 4) \times (24 : 23) \times (46 : 45)$;

Two chromatic tetrachords: the 'soft' (*chrōma malakon*), $(6 : 5) \times (15 : 14) \times (28 : 27)$, and the 'high' or 'tense' (*chrōma syntonon*), $(7 : 6) \times (12 : 11) \times (22 : 21)$;

Three diatonic tetrachords: the 'tense' (*diatonon syntonon*), $(10 : 9) \times (9 : 8) \times (16 : 15)$, the 'soft' (*diatonon malakon*), $(8 : 7) \times (10 : 9) \times (21 : 20)$, and the 'even' (*diatonon homalon*), $(10 : 9) \times (11 : 10) \times (12 : 11)$.

The enharmonic tetrachord entails the pure 3rd (5 : 4) of Archytas and Didymus; the divisions of the 'soft' and 'tense' chromatic tetrachords are probably very close to the corresponding divisions in Aristoxenus's genera of the same name. Of the diatonic tetrachords, the 'tense' adopts the ratios of Didymus and the 'soft' is a counterpart, though differing in some respects, to Aristoxenus's 'soft' diatonic tetrachord; the 'even' includes a harmonic division by three into intervals of three-quarters of a tone, as in the archaic spondeion scale.

Ptolemy also discussed tuning in instrumental practice, using different genera in the two tetrachords of one octave. Whereas the lyre has two tunings, *sterea* ('hard', ?diatonic) and *malaka* ('soft', ?chromatic), the kithara has six different tunings, called *tropoi* (in the Hypodorian mode), *iasti-aiolia* (Hypophrygian), *hypertropa* (Phrygian), *tritai* (Hypodorian), *parhypatai* (Dorian) and *lydia* (Dorian). Ptolemy's associating them with the ethnic names of the modes suggests that they were commonly used in the imperial era.

For the derivation of the octave species, Ptolemy used a 'monochord' with one string for each of the 15 notes of the double octave making up the Perfect System (*systēma teleion*). The notes can be identified by *thesis*, i.e. their absolute position on the strings, or by *dynamis*, i.e. their function relative to other notes within the mode in question.

In discussing *metabolē* ('alteration', including transposition and modulation) Ptolemy distinguished between a simple transposition of a whole melody to another pitch while retaining the same intervals within it, and a more basic 'modulation' of part of the melody, involving a new sequence of intervals and, thus, a change of genus. Only the second of these two is true modulation, and it alters the ethos.

Instead of the 13 (or 15) transpositional notes, a semitone apart, of the Aristoxenian school, Ptolemy had a system of seven *tonoi*, each spanning a complete octave. They are derived from the three oldest modes (Dorian, Phrygian and Lydian) with the aid of a cycle of 4ths, and result in a sequence of modes pitched either a whole tone (1) or a semitone ($\frac{1}{2}$) apart, in the following order: Mixolydian – ($\frac{1}{2}$) – Lydian – (1) – Phrygian – (1) – Dorian – ($\frac{1}{2}$) – Hypolydian – (1) – Hypophrygian – (1) – Hypodorian. Since the notes *mesē* in each are tuned in the middle octave *e–e'*, Ptolemy's transpositional notes correspond to an octave species.

The *Harmonics* culminates in a metaphysical discussion of the music of the spheres on largely Pythagorean and Platonic lines. Ptolemy drew various analogies between the relationships of the elements of music and those of the human soul (the microcosm) and the movements of the planets (the macrocosm). For instance, he compared the intervals he called *symphōnoi* to the parts of the soul, the genera to the virtues and the Perfect System to the ecliptic. His last chapter, which is fragmentary, contains astrological speculations about the characteristics of planets and musical notes.

A century after the composition of the *Harmonics*, the neo-Platonic philosopher Porphyry wrote an informative commentary on it, referring to Ptolemy's sources, and giving his own evaluation of many earlier authors. He took particular pleasure in discussing such distinctions as the quantities and qualities of notes. The *Harmonics* was translated into Arabic in the 9th century; and two important Byzantine (Greek) editions were made by Nicephorus Gregoras (*c*1335) and his pupil Isaac Argyrus, the former including emendations and original material of his own, interlinear glosses and scholia (annotations).

The various theories put forward by Ptolemy greatly influenced the Byzantine theorists Georgius Pachymeres and Manuel Bryennius, and his influence also extended to western Europe, where he was known in the Middle Ages chiefly through Boethius's *De musica*. His musical and astronomical systems were still current in Kepler's writing. The edition of A. Gogavinus's Latin translation (Venice, 1562) by Wallis was exemplary in its day; the standard modern edition is that of Düring, and is based on 84 manuscripts.

BIBLIOGRAPHY

EDITIONS

Klaudiou Ptolemaiou Harmonikōn biblia gamma, ed. J. Wallis (Oxford, 1682)

'Klaudiou Ptolemaiou Harmonikōn biblia *gamma*', ed. J. Wallis, *Operum mathematicorum*, iii (Oxford, 1699), i ff, 1–152 [with Lat. trans.]

Die Harmonielehre des Klaudios Ptolemaios, ed. I. Düring, Göteborgs högskolas årsskrift, xxxvi/1 (Göteborg, 1930)

Porphyrios Kommentar zur Harmonielehre des Ptolemaios, ed. I. Düring, Göteborgs högskolas årsskrift, xxxviii/2 (Göteborg, 1932)

Ptolemaios und Porphyrios über die Musik, ed. and Ger. trans. I. Düring, Göteborgs högskolas årsskrift, xl/1 (Göteborg, 1934)

CRITICAL STUDIES

F. Boll: *Studien über Claudius Ptolemäus: ein Beitrag zur Geschichte der griechischen Philosophie und Astrologie* (Leipzig, 1894); also pubd in *Jahrbücher für classische Philologie*, suppl.xxi (1894), 66–254

K. von Jan: 'Die Harmonie der Sphären', *Philologus*, lii (1894), 13

R. Issberner: 'Dynamis und Thesis', *Philologus*, lv (1896), 541

C. Stumpf: *Geschichte des Consonanzbegriffes, I: die Definition der Consonanz im Altertum*, Abhandlungen der philosophisch-philologischen Classe der Königlichen Bayerischen Akademie der Wissenschaften, xxi/1 (Munich, 1897), esp. 56ff

T. Reinach: 'La musique des sphères', *Revue des études grecques*, xiii (1900), 432

S. Wantzloeben: *Das Monochord als Instrument und als System, entwicklungsgeschichtlich dargestellt* (Halle, 1911)

L. Schönberger: *Studien zum 1. Buch der Harmonik des Cl. Ptolemäus* (Augsburg, 1914)

J. F. Mountford: 'The Harmony of Ptolemy and the Lacuna in II, 14', *Transactions of the American Philological Association*, lvii (1926), 71

R. P. Winnington-Ingram: 'Aristoxenus and the Intervals of Greek Music', *Classical Quarterly*, xxvi (1932), 195

——: *Mode in Ancient Greek Music* (Cambridge, 1936/*R*1968), esp. 62ff

O. J. Gombosi: *Die Tonarten und Stimmungen der antiken Musik* (Copenhagen, 1939), esp. 98ff

B. L. van der Waerden: 'Die Harmonielehre der Pythagoreer', *Hermes*, lxxviii (1943), 163–99

J. Handschin: *Der Toncharakter* (Zurich, 1948)

J. M. Barbour: *Tuning and Temperament: a Historical Survey* (East Lansing, Mich., 1951/*R*1972), 15ff

K. Ziegler and others: 'Ptolemaios', *Paulys Real-Encyclopädie der classischen Altertumswissenschaft*, xlvi (Stuttgart, 1959), 1840

H. Husmann: *Grundlagen der antiken und orientalischen Musikkultur* (Berlin, 1961), esp. 34ff, 48f, 82ff

L. Richter: *Zur Wissenschaftslehre von der Musik bei Platon und Aristoteles*, Deutsche Akademie der Wissenschaften zu Berlin, Schriften der Sektion für Altertumswissenschaft, xxiii (Berlin, 1961), esp. 181ff

M. Vogel: *Die Enharmonik der Griechen* (Düsseldorf, 1963), esp. i, 33ff, 48ff

B. Alexanderson: *Textual Remarks on Ptolemy's Harmonica and Porphyry's Commentary*, Studia graeca et latina Gothoburgensia, xxvii (Göteborg, 1969)

LUKAS RICHTER

Publishing, music. *See* PRINTING AND PUBLISHING OF MUSIC.

Puccini. Italian family of musicians.

(1) Giacomo Puccini (i) (*b* Celle di val di Roggio, Lucca, baptized 26 Jan 1712; *d* Lucca, 16 May 1781). Composer. The son of Antonio Puccini and the brother of Michele (also a musician), Giacomo was a pupil of Caretti at Bologna and corresponded with Padre Martini. From 1739 to 1772 he was organist at S Martino in Lucca and, from 1739 until his death, director of the republic's Cappella Palatina. His diary, the *Libro delle musiche annue ed avventizie*, now in the Lucca State Archive, illustrates the musical life of the city in his time. From 1743 he was a member of the Bologna Accademia Filarmonica. Pietro Guglielmi was one of his pupils.

Besides being a prolific composer, Giacomo was a good director and organizer of music for the many religious and secular celebrations in and around Lucca that always required new compositions. His sacred music (for chorus and small orchestra) is distinguished by good vocal writing and counterpoint and uses the Baroque technique of contrasting diverse vocal and instrumental groupings, always with marked rhythm. The treatment of the text shows considerable variety, alternating fugal with homophonic sections and brilliant, fast movements with slow, expressive ones. He also composed dramatic music for the *tasche* (elections of the government of Lucca, usually held every two years). The *tasca*, in three parts or *giornate*, each by a different composer, had libretto in praise of liberty drawn from classical history. Musically they consisted of a symphony, a series of recitatives and arias, a chorus and concluding symphony. The orchestra was very small, the recitatives almost always secco, the arias in the standard contemporary forms. Giacomo's arias for these dramas are particularly notable.

WORKS

(in I-Li or Ls unless otherwise stated)

Sacred: 17 masses, 2–8vv, orch, 2 *I-PAc*; Kyrie–Gloria, 4vv, orch; 3 Gloria sections, 1v, some with orch, some with bc; 7 Credo, 4–8vv, orch; 4 Benedictus, 3–4vv, some with orch, some unacc., 1 *PAc*; 1 introits, 4vv, some with orch, some with bc; Gradual, 3vv, orch; Offertory, 4vv, orch; 78 psalms, 2–8vv, some with orch, some with bc, 1 *PAc*; Psalm, 4vv unacc.; 15 hymns, 2–8vv, some with orch, some with bc; 10 Te Deum, 3–8vv, orch, 1 *PAc*; 11 Magnificat, 4–8vv, orch; 22 motets, 2–8vv, some with orch, some with bc, 5 *PAc*, 1 *Bc*; 12 Lamentations: 9, 1v, orch, 3, 1–2vv, bc; 2 Litanies: 4vv, orch, 3vv unacc.; Versi sagri, 4vv unacc.; Improperia, 4vv, bc

Tasche, all perf. Lucca: Dione Siracusano, 1732, rev. 1750; Giunio Bruto, 1735; Marco Genuzio, 1738; Il Solone, 1741; Il Teramene, 1747; Il Curzio Cavalier Romano, 1753; Marco Manlio Capitolino, 1755, rev. 1777; De Tarquinio Collatino, 1758; Roma liberata dalla signoria di rè, 1760; L'Arminio, 1763; La confederazione dei Sabini con Roma, 1765; Il Narsete, 1770; Il Marzio Coriolano, 1773; Roma liberata dalla congiura di Catilina, 1775

Other works: Il martirio di S. Valentino, oratorio, Bientina, Pisa, 1754; Cori da cantarsi in occasione dell'estrazione del primo collegio dopo le tasche, 4vv, orch; Solfeggi in chiave di contralto, 1739, *PAc*

BIBLIOGRAPHY

FétisB

C. Gervasoni: *Nuova teoria di musica* (Parma, 1812), 240

D. A. Cerù: *Cenni storici dell'insegnamento della musica in Lucca e dei più notabili maestri compositori che vi hanno fiorito* (Lucca, 1871), 63f

L. Nerici: *Storia della musica in Lucca* (Lucca, 1880/*R*1969)

A. Bonaccorsi: 'Le musiche sacre dei Puccini', *Bollettino storico lucchese*, vi (1934), 29

K. G. Fellerer: 'Die Musikerfamilie Puccini (1712–1924)', *AMf*, vi (1941), 213

A. Bonaccorsi: *Giacomo Puccini e i suoi antenati musicali* (Milan, 1950)

D. Corsi: 'La dinastia dei Puccini: Antonio Puccini ed alcuni suoi carteggi', *Giacomo Puccini nel centenario della nascita* (Lucca, 1958), 112

E. Lazzareschi: 'La famiglia Puccini e il diario musicale di Giacomo Puccini sen', *Atti dell'Accademia lucchese di scienze, lettere ed arti*, new ser., x (1959), 21–57

H. Handt: 'La confederazione dei Sabini con Roma', *Associazione musicale lucchese*, iii/1 (1965–6), 3

——: 'L'Arminio', *Associazione musicale lucchese*, iv/1 (1966–7), 1

C. M. Gianturco: 'La musica sacra dei Puccini', *La provincia di Lucca*, xiv/2 (1974), 76

(2) Antonio (Benedetto Maria) Puccini (*b* Lucca, 30 July 1747; *d* Lucca, 10 Feb 1832). Composer, son of (1) Giacomo Puccini (i). With financial help from the government of Lucca, he studied under Caretti and Abbate Zanardi in Bologna, where he married Caterina Tesei, an excellent organist. From 1772 he substituted for his father as organist of S Martino and in 1781 became his successor as director of the Cappella Palatina (until its suppression on 31 July 1805). From 1771 he was a member of the Bologna Accademia Filarmonica.

Antonio's sacred compositions consist of a free series of closed movements. His polyphonic technique shows solid training, but does not dominate in his works. The opening symphonies of his *tasche*, which are sometimes in sonata form, employ a harmonious Classical style and an orchestra larger than his father's; the arias are occasionally very beautiful and expressive.

WORKS
(in I-Li and Ls unless otherwise stated)

Sacred: 4 masses, 2–4vv, orch; 4 Kyrie, T, orch, 4vv, orch; 9 Kyrie–Gloria, 4–8vv, orch; 4 Kyrie–Gloria, 2–3vv, bc, 1 *I-PAc*; 3 Gloria, 4vv, orch; 5 Credo, 2–8vv, orch; Benedictus, 4vv, orch; 8 introits, 2–8vv, some with orch, some with bc; Introit, Kyrie for the Mass of the Dead, 4vv, orch; Sequence, 3vv, small orch; Offertory, 2vv, bc; Offertory, Sanctus, Agnus, Communion, Absolution for the Dead, 4vv, orch; 20 psalms, 2–8vv, some with orch, some with bc; 5 hymns, 4vv, some with orch, some with bc; 2 Te Deum, 4vv, orch; Dies irae, 4vv, orch
3 Magnificat, 4vv, orch; Miserere, 4vv, orch; Improperia, 4vv, bc; 10 Lamentations, 1–2vv, some with orch, some with bc; 7 motets, 2–4vv, bc, 1 *PAc*; 2 antiphons, 2–4vv, some with orch, some with org; Responsories, 3vv; Litany, T, B, org, *PAc*
Tasche, all perf. Lucca: Il Narsete, 1770; Il Marzio Coriolano, 1773; Marco Manlio Capitolino, 1777; Cesare in Brettagna, 1779; Il Castruccio, 1781, rev. 1797; Il Leonida re di Sparta, 1783; Emilio, 1785; Lucca liberata, 1787; Bruto, 1789; M. Curzio, 1791; Spartaco, 1793; Enea nel Lazio, 1795
Other works: Il genio, cantata, S, orch; Duetto nella terza giornata delle tasche, 1791

BIBLIOGRAPHY
FétisB

C. Gervasoni: *Nuova teoria di musica* (Parma, 1812), 240f
D. A. Cerù: *Cenni storici dell'insegnamento della musica in Lucca e dei più notabili maestri compositori che vi hanno fiorito* (Lucca, 1871), 71
L. Nerici: *Storia della musica in Lucca* (Lucca, 1880/R1969)
A. Bonaccorsi: 'Le musiche sacre dei Puccini', *Bollettino storico lucchese*, vi (1934), 29
K. G. Fellerer: 'Die Musikerfamilie Puccini (1712–1924)', *AMf*, vi (1941), 213
A. Bonaccorsi: *Giacomo Puccini e i suoi antenati musicali* (Milan, 1950)
D. Corsi: 'La dinastia dei Puccini: Antonio Puccini ed alcuni suoi carteggi', *Giacomo Puccini nel centenario della nascita* (Lucca, 1958), 112
H. Handt: 'Antonio Benedetto Maria Puccini', *Associazione musicale lucchese* (1964–5), 2
C. M. Gianturco: 'La musica sacra dei Puccini', *La provincia di Lucca*, xiv/2 (1974), 76

(3) Domenico (Vincenzo Maria) Puccini (*b* 1772; *d* Lucca, 25 May 1815). Composer, son of (2) Antonio Puccini. He had his first music lessons from his parents and continued his studies in Bologna under Mattei and in Naples under Paisiello, with whom he remained on excellent terms. From 1806 to 1809 he was director of the Cappella di Camera (founded by Napoleon's sister,

Elise Baciocchi, then Regent of Lucca) and of the municipal chapel from 1811 to 1815. His death in that year was sudden and mysterious; some think he was poisoned for political reasons.

In a mid-19th-century illustration published by Breitkopf & Härtel Domenico appears with Grétry and other important contemporary musicians, a sure sign of the esteem that his music enjoyed. His style is completely theatrical, even in sacred and vocal chamber compositions; it differed from that of his father so much that he could not complete his father's unfinished *Te Deum*. The style is very simple and fluid; counterpoint has almost disappeared. In his operas, especially the comic ones, he reveals an outstanding theatrical sense and a fresh and spontaneous inspiration, along with the assimilation of styles present in the comic operas of the time.

WORKS
(all in I-Li and Ls)

Sacred: 5 Kyrie, 3–4vv, orch; Kyrie–Gloria, 8vv, orch; 6 Gloria, 1–4vv, orch; 5 Gloria sections, 1–4vv, orch; Kyrie, Gloria, Credo, 2vv, bc; 2 alleluias, 4–8vv, 1 with orch, 1 with org; Benedictus, 3vv; 8 psalms, 1–8vv, some with orch, some with org; Psalm verse, 1v; 6 Te Deum, 4vv, orch, 1 completed by F. Ravani; 3 Lamentations, S, orch; 2 antiphons, 2–4vv; Motet, 16vv, 2 orchs; 6 motets, 3–4vv, some with orch, some with org
Operas: Le frecce d'amore (opera pastorale, 2), *c*1800; L'Ortolanella, o La moglie capricciosa (farsa buffa), Camaiore, Lucca, 1800; Il Quinto Fabio (opera seria, 2), Livorno, 1810; La scuola dei tutori (farsa), Lucca, 1813, lost; Il ciarlatano, ossia I finti savoiardi (atto buffo), Lucca, 1815
Tasche: Spartaco, 1793, Castruccio, 1797, both perf. Lucca
Secular vocal: La fama, cantata, Inno per la resa di Genova, S, S, orch; Pastorale, 2vv; 6 duettini, S, T, pf/gui; 6 duetti, S, T, pf; 7 comic duets; 6 ariette, S, pf; 6 ariette, S, gui; 2 arias, S, B, pf/orch
Inst: 2 syms.; Conc., hpd/pf; Sonata [wrongly attrib. Domenico Puccini by Bonaccorsi]

BIBLIOGRAPHY

D. A. Cerù: *Cenni storici dell'insegnamento della musica in Lucca e dei più notabili maestri compositori che vi hanno fiorito* (Lucca, 1871), 78f
L. Nerici: *Storia della musica in Lucca* (Lucca, 1880/R1969)
L. Volpicella: 'L'anarchia popolare in Napoli nel gennaio 1799 raccontata da Domenico Puccini', *Archivio storico per le province napoletane*, xxxv (1910), 485
A. Bonaccorsi: 'Le musiche sacre dei Puccini', *Bollettino storico lucchese*, vi (1934), 29
K. G. Fellerer: 'Die Musikerfamilie Puccini (1712–1924)', *AMf*, vi (1941), 213
A. Bonaccorsi: *Giacomo Puccini e i suoi antenati musicali* (Milan, 1950)
D. Corsi: 'La dinastia dei Puccini: Antonio Puccini ed alcuni suoi carteggi', *Giacomo Puccini nel centenario della nascita* (Lucca, 1958), 112
H. Handt: 'Il ciarlatano', *Associazione musicale lucchese*, viii/6 (1971–2), 1
G. Biagi Ravenni: 'Il ciarlatano', *Associazione musicale lucchese*, x/5 (1973–4), 2
C. M. Gianturco: 'La musica sacra dei Puccini', *La provincia di Lucca*, xiv/2 (1974), 76

(4) Michele Puccini (*b* Lucca, 27 Nov 1813; *d* Lucca, 23 Jan 1864). Teacher and composer, son of (3) Domenico Puccini. He began a strict musical education in Lucca under his grandfather Antonio and others. He then continued in Bologna under Pillotti and in Naples under Donizetti and Mercadante. On his return to Lucca he became a teacher at the Istituto Musicale Pacini, where he was director from 1862. For many years he was also organist at S Martino.

Michele Puccini was most important as a teacher, having among his pupils Fortunato Magi and Luigi Nerici. He carried out the first research into the history of music in Lucca, leaving manuscript notes, *Della musica in Lucca: cenni storici* (1863) and *Note ed appunti di musici* (1863), both in the Lucca State Archive;

he transmitted his interest in this subject to Nerici. His treatises on harmony and counterpoint are both lost, but some articles by him were published in *La scena* of Lucca. Although his compositions are well written, they show little imagination; his sacred music (for chorus and large orchestra) mirrors the technique and taste of the contemporary theatre.

Besides the celebrated Giacomo, Michele Puccini had another musician son, Michele (*b* Lucca, 19 April 1864; *d* Rio de Janeiro, 12 March 1891), who studied at the Milan Conservatory and emigrated in October 1889. He lived at Buenos Aires, Juiuy (as a teacher) and Rio de Janeiro, and is known to have composed.

WORKS

Sacred: 7 masses, 2–8vv, some with orch, some with org; 13 Kyrie: 11, 4–8vv, orch, 1, B, T, orch, 1, 4vv, org; Kyrie–Gloria, 4vv, orch; 8 Gloria, 4–8vv, orch, 1 completed by F. Magi; 27 Gloria sections, 1–8vv, orch, some with solo vv; 3 Credo: 1, 4vv, 2, 4vv, orch; 2 Benedictus, 4vv, orch; Agnus Dei, 4vv, orch; 6 graduals: 1, 4vv, orch, 5, 1v, orch, some with 4vv; Gradual, Offertory, Communion, 4vv unacc.; Communion, 4vv, org; 2 sequences, 2–4vv, small orch; 9 psalms, 1–8vv, orch; 25 psalm verses, some for 1–2vv, orch, some for 4–8vv, orch, some for 1–2 solo vv, 4–8vv, orch; 7 hymns, 3–4vv, orch; Magnificat, 4vv, orch; 3 Ave Maria: 2, B, str qt, 1 in canon, 32vv unacc.; 12 motets: some for 4vv unacc., some for 1–8vv with 1 or 2 orchs; Antiphon, S, 4vv, orch; 3 Lamentations, 1–3vv; Litany of the BVM; Mottettone, 2 choruses, orch
Operas: Antonio Foscarini, ?lost; Giambattista Cattani, o La rivoluzione degli Straccioni, Lucca, 1844, 1 romanza extant
Other vocal: 2 cantatas; Scena ed aria con cori; Coro, 5vv, orch; Terzetto, orch acc.; Romanza
Inst: Concertone, fl, cl, hn, tpt, trbn, orch; Sym.

BIBLIOGRAPHY

D. A. Cerù: *Cenni storici dell'insegnamento della musica in Lucca e dei più notabili maestri compositori che vi hanno fiorito* (Lucca, 1871), 89ff
L. Nerici: *Storia della musica in Lucca* (Lucca, 1880/R1969)
A. Bonaccorsi: 'Le musiche sacre dei Puccini', *Bollettino storico lucchese*, vi (1934), 29
K. G. Fellerer: 'Die Musikerfamilie Puccini (1712–1924)', *AMf*, vi (1941), 213
A. Bonaccorsi: *Giacomo Puccini e i suoi antenati musicali* (Milan, 1950)
G. Arrighi: 'Avventure di viaggio di un musicista: Michele Puccini nel Sudamerica', *L'universo*, xliii (1963), 917
G. Biagi Ravenni: 'Michele Puccini, il primo storico della musica lucchese', *Ricordando i Puccini* (Lucca, 1973)
A. Marchetti: *Puccini com'era* (Milan, 1973)
C. M. Gianturco: 'La musica sacra dei Puccini', *La provincia di Lucca*, xiv/2 (1974), 76

(5) Giacomo (Antonio Domenico Michele Secondo Maria) Puccini (ii)

(*b* Lucca, 23 Dec 1858; *d* Brussels, 29 Nov 1924). He was the most eminent member of the Puccini family and the most successful opera composer that modern Italy has produced after Verdi.

1. Education and early compositions. 2. First operas. 3. 'Manon Lescaut'. 4. 'La bohème'. 5. 'Tosca' and 'Madama Butterfly'. 6. Middle years and 'La fanciulla del West'. 7. 'La rondine' and 'Il trittico'. 8. 'Turandot' and Puccini's death. 9. Puccini's concept of opera. 10. Dramaturgy and stage sense. 11. The Puccini heroine. 12. Depiction of atmosphere. 13. Melody and aria types. 14. Harmony and leitmotifs. 15. Use of the orchestra and orchestral mosaic. 16. Use of the chorus. 17. Assessment.

1. EDUCATION AND EARLY COMPOSITIONS. The fifth of the seven children of (4) Michele Puccini, he was a little over five when his father died. As he was expected to follow the family tradition as organist and choirmaster at S Martino, the city fathers in 1864 issued a decree that his uncle Fortunato Magi hold the post until Giacomo should be old enough to take it over. Magi was his first teacher but had little success with the boy, and at the instigation of his energetic mother, Puccini continued his studies with the director of the Istituto Musicale Pacini, Carlo Angeloni, who, like Magi, had been a pupil of Michele Puccini. At the age of ten

Puccini joined the choirs at S Martino and S Michele and four years later started his career as organist at these and other churches in the vicinity of Lucca, including those of Mutigliano, Celle and Pascaglia. When he was 17 he began composing in earnest, writing organ pieces that were largely the result of improvisations into which he worked, much to the surprise of the congregation, snatches from Tuscan folksongs and from operas such as *Rigoletto*, *Il trovatore* and *La traviata*, to which he had been introduced by Angeloni. A performance of *Aida* at Pisa in 1876 made such an impact on him that he decided to break with the family tradition and follow his instinct for operatic composition. He later said that this Pisa performance opened a musical window to him. Lucca, however, was not the place to acquire the operatic craft, and it became Puccini's most ardent wish to go to Milan, which with its Teatro alla Scala and conservatory was the mecca for all aspiring composers. Four years were to pass before his wish could be realized. From those early Lucca days date a *Preludio sinfonico* (1876), a cantata, *I figli d'Italia bella*, written for a competition (1877), and a motet and Credo (1878) which Puccini later used in the Mass in A♭ composed as his final exercise at the Istituto Musicale Pacini (1880). With the help of a scholarship instituted by Queen Margherita for talented sons of poor families and financial support from an uncle, Dr Nicolao Cerù, Puccini entered the Milan Conservatory in the autumn of 1880 and remained there three years. His chief teachers were Antonio Bazzini and Ponchielli. His experiences in those three years had much in common with those of the poor young artists so vividly depicted in *La bohème*. In July 1883 he ended his studies with an instrumental piece, the *Capriccio sinfonico*, which was performed by the student orchestra under Franco Faccio, revealing for the first time his talent for melodic invention and colourful orchestration.

2. FIRST OPERAS. In the preceding April the music publishing firm of Edoardo Sonzogno had announced in its house journal, *Il teatro illustrato*, a competition for a one-act opera (Mascagni's *Cavalleria rusticana* was to be discovered in this way in 1889), and Puccini, then still a pupil at the conservatory, had decided with Ponchielli's encouragement to enter it. Through Ponchielli's intervention he won as librettist Ferdinando Fontana, who suggested to him a subject with fantastic, supernatural features, *Le villi*. Based on a legend first related by Heine, it was used by Adolphe Adam in his ballet *Giselle, ou Les willis* (Paris, 1841) and by Edward Loder in his opera *The Night Dancers* (London, 1846). Such subjects were then in vogue in Italian opera in the wake of the German Romantic operas of Weber, Marschner and early Wagner. (Catalani's *Loreley* of 1880 is another example of this influence.) When the result of the competition was announced early in 1884, *Le villi* was not even mentioned. Soon after, at a party in the house of the wealthy Milan music lover Marco Sala, at which the publisher Giulio Ricordi and the highly influential Arrigo Boito were present, Puccini played and sang his opera at the piano to such general acclaim that it was decided to stage it at the Teatro del Verme. Performed there on 31 May 1884 with resounding success, it was acquired by Ricordi, on whose advice Puccini extended it to two acts (Turin, 1884). Moreover, the publisher commissioned another opera, again with Fontana as librettist. This was the beginning of

Puccini's lifelong association with the house of Ricordi, in whose director he was to find a fatherly mentor and friend. The new opera was the four-act *Edgar*, based on Alfred de Musset's involved and turgid book-drama *La coupe et les lèvres*, apparently chosen by Fontana because of a superficial resemblance of its plot to that of *Carmen*. For Puccini's particular dramatic talent it was a most unsuitable libretto, on which he worked five years. *Edgar* was first given at La Scala on 21 April 1889 and was coolly received, and although the composer subsequently compressed it into three acts (Ferrara, 1892) and further revised it in 1901 and 1905, it has not survived. In Puccini's own words it was 'una cantonata' – 'a blunder'. Into the time of *Edgar* falls the beginning of Puccini's association with Elvira Gemignani, the wife of a wholesale merchant at Lucca, who in 1886 bore him a son, Antonio. It was not until after the death of Elvira's husband in 1904 that her union with Puccini could be legalized.

3. 'MANON LESCAUT'. *Manon Lescaut* was Puccini's first opera for which he chose the subject himself. The international success of Massenet's *Manon* (1884) drew his attention to Abbé Prévost's famous novel, whose narrative, characters and atmosphere he felt to be eminently suited to his particular genius. The libretto was fashioned by five different authors – first Leoncavallo, then Marco Praga and Domenico Oliva, and finally Luigi Illica and Giuseppe Giacosa, with Ricordi lending a helping hand and Puccini controlling the whole operation. Because of the multiple paternity of its libretto, *Manon Lescaut*, so called to distinguish it from Massenet's opera, was published without the names of the librettists. At its first production (Turin, 1 February 1893) it achieved a success such as Puccini was never to repeat, and it made his name known outside Italy. Its London production in 1894 prompted Bernard Shaw, then a music critic, to the prophetic words: 'Puccini looks to me more like the heir of Verdi than any of his rivals'. In 1891, while at work on the opera, the composer acquired a house at Torre del Lago on the lake of Massaciuccoli, where he lived until 1921 and wrote all his later operas except *Turandot*. After Puccini's death his son transformed the house into a mausoleum-cum-museum in which the composer and his wife, who died in 1930, were interred.

4. 'LA BOHÈME'. *La bohème* was the first of the three operas for which Puccini's exclusive collaborators were Illica and Giacosa, an association to which Ricordi jokingly referred as the 'Holy Trinity'. It was perhaps the best team of poets Puccini had in his entire career. There was a clear division of labour: Illica elaborated the scenario and invented picturesque incidents, Giacosa saw to the poetic side and the versification, with Puccini taking a highly active part in the shaping of the libretto. This inevitably led to frequent quarrels among the three, with Giacosa, an eminent writer and poet in his own right, threatening to resign a number of times. In the end, however, it was Puccini who won, because of his extraordinary sense of the theatre. For example, he developed, from a mere hint in Prévost's novel, the unique Embarkation act of *Manon Lescaut*, added a manhunt in the final act of *La fanciulla del West* and invented the character of Liù and her suicide in *Turandot*. The new opera, based on Henry Murger's autobiographical *Scènes de la vie de Bohème*, was first produced at Turin on 1 February 1896 under Toscanini, but did not have an immediate success, since the critics had come expecting to hear an opera in the romantically tragic vein of *Manon Lescaut*. *La bohème*, in its mixture of lighthearted and sentimental scenes and its largely conversational style, was reminiscent of operetta and, in addition, displayed impressionist features in its harmony and orchestration. The progression of parallel 5ths at the opening of Act 3 was particularly castigated. Today the work is considered by some writers to be Puccini's masterpiece.

5. 'TOSCA' AND 'MADAMA BUTTERFLY'. The plan to set Victorien Sardou's *Tosca* to music dates from 1889, shortly after the première of *Edgar*. For some time Puccini seriously doubted whether this blood-and-thunder melodrama suited him at all. It was his first excursion into the sphere of *verismo*. The first night was staged in Rome (Teatro Costanzi, 14 January 1900) in an atmosphere charged with high tension and with wild rumours that a bomb would be thrown. However, nothing happened, and *Tosca* achieved an outstanding success with the Roman public. The critics, on the other hand, attacked it for the sadistic cruelty and brutality of the action, which they thought seriously interfered with the composer's inborn lyricism. Yet they admitted his immense skill in the musical characterization of the atmosphere and the *dramatis personae* and in the ideal adjustment of the music to the swift changes of mood on stage. In the modern view it is the lyricism that Puccini was able to extract from the 'strong' scenes of the libretto that is so admirable.

In the summer of 1900 Puccini saw in London David Belasco's one-act play, *Madam Butterfly*, derived from a magazine story by John Luther Long based on a real incident. Although he knew scarcely any English, he was deeply impressed by the character and fate of the little geisha, and the exotic ambience fascinated him. Following the play, Puccini first thought of a one-act opera with a prologue (the present Act 1), but then decided on two acts, with the second in two parts separated from each other by Butterfly's night vigil. Since he considered this opera the best and technically most advanced that he had written, he looked forward with great expectation to its première at La Scala on 17 February 1904. Yet the evening proved a fiasco rare in the annals of opera, with the public whistling, shouting and making ironic remarks about the heroine. It appears that this pandemonium was engineered by his jealous rivals, who, as in the case of the *Tosca* première, wanted to ruin the performance. Puccini withdrew the opera after a single showing, revised it by judicious cuts in both text and music and recast it into three acts, with an orchestral prelude to Act 3. In this version it was given with great acclaim at Brescia the following May.

6. MIDDLE YEARS AND 'LA FANCIULLA DEL WEST'. Six years were to elapse before his next opera. One of the chief reasons for his slow work was a domestic tragedy which in January 1909 culminated in the suicide of Doria Manfredi, a servant girl of the Puccinis whom the abnormally jealous Elvira had accused of an intimate relationship with her husband. The affair led to a court case which, basing itself on the evidence of the autopsy, established the girl's innocence and found against Elvira. The case provoked an enormous sensation in

Italy, and the publicity associated with it affected the hypersensitive and extremely vulnerable composer to such an extent that for some time afterwards his creative energy and desire to work were impaired. Moreover, he had arrived at a point of his career when he wanted to turn away from the *tragédie larmoyante* of his previous operas and attempt something of a harder, more masculine fibre, such as he had first tried in *Tosca*. He found a subject of this nature in Belasco's *The Girl of the Golden West*, which he happened to see in New York in 1907, where he was attending a Puccini festival at the Metropolitan Opera. What seemed to appeal to him most strongly was the mixture of stark realism and sentimental romanticism of this Wild West melodrama, which takes place among miners at the time of the first California gold rush. Carlo Zangarini and Guelfo Civinini were the librettists, since Illica, after Giacosa's death in 1906, no longer satisfied Puccini as sole collaborator. The fact that *La fanciulla del West* was an 'American' opera prompted Gatti-Casazza, then director of the Metropolitan, to secure the world première for his theatre, where it was given on 10 December 1910 with Toscanini conducting and with Caruso as Johnson and Emmy Destinn as Minnie. With such a cast the opera could not have failed to be a success with the public; the reaction of the critics, however, was guarded. In all technical respects, notably in its Debussian harmony and Straussian orchestration, the opera is a masterpiece and was Puccini's reply to the criticism that he repeated himself in every new opera. What it lacks is the incandescent lyrical phrase, and this is probably the main reason why the opera has never become part of the normal repertory outside Italy.

In the meantime, a new generation of Italian composers was growing up (Pizzetti, Casella, Malipiero) which condemned the native *melodramma* of the 19th century and vocalism in general (it is worth observing, however, that in later years this group of erstwhile firebrands wrote operas themselves). What this anti-operatic movement advocated was a rejuvenating return to the spirit and character of the ancient masters of Italian instrumental music (Frescobaldi, Corelli, Legrenzi, Vivaldi). The chief attack was directed at Puccini, who was accused of bourgeois mentality, lack of ideals and pure commercialism; the intellectual mouthpiece of this movement was the musicologist Fausto Torrefranca, who in 1912 published a book with the significant title *Giacomo Puccini e l'opera internazionale*. As far as is known, Puccini never replied to these attacks in public.

7. 'LA RONDINE' AND 'IL TRITTICO'. Serious differences with Giulio Ricordi's son Tito, who became head of the firm after the death of his father in 1912, were the chief reason that Puccini in 1913 accepted a lucrative offer by the directors of the Vienna Karltheater, Eibenschütz and Berté, to write an operetta for them. He was to compose eight or ten numbers only, the rest to be spoken dialogue. He rejected the first libretto submitted by the Viennese, the next he entrusted to the young writer Giuseppe Adami, who after much rewriting produced an acceptable 'book' with the title *La rondine*. Although it was warmly received at its first production at Monte Carlo on 27 March 1917, it has proved the weakest of Puccini's works, uneasily hovering between opera and operetta and devoid of striking lyrical melody. But it is written with consummate technical skill and possesses a certain allure, notably in the waltz music. *La rondine* is Puccini's only work published by Ricordi's rival Sonzogno. Because of this work Puccini was accused of lack of patriotism by Léon Daudet and his nationalist paper *L'action française* after Italy had entered the war on the side of the Allies.

While still at work on the operetta Puccini began the composition of *Il tabarro*, after the French play *La houppelande* by Didier Gold, which he had seen in Paris in 1913. This was the first of the three one-act operas, known under the collective title *Il trittico*, in which Puccini followed the scheme of the Parisian Grand

1. Giacomo Puccini (centre)
with his wife Elvira and son
Antonio at Torre del Lago

Guignol – a horrific episode, a sentimental tragedy and a comedy or farce. Adami was the librettist of *Il tabarro*, and the texts of *Suor Angelica* and *Gianni Schicchi* are by Giovacchino Forzano, who derived the comedy from a few lines in canto xxx of Dante's *Inferno*. Since the war was still on, with the majority of Italian artists serving in the armed forces, Puccini in early 1918 willingly accepted the offer by the Metropolitan to stage the first production, which took place on 14 December. The first European performance was given in Rome on 11 January 1919. On both these occasions the comedy achieved the widest acclaim, while the reception of the first two episodes was lukewarm. *Gianni Schicchi*, which displays an unexpected *vis comica* in Puccini (a striking parallel to Verdi and his *Falstaff*), was in the following years, much to the composer's dislike, given without the other two, usually in a double bill. But more recently *Il tabarro*, outstanding for its painting of a sombre atmosphere and its dramatic concentration, has come into its own, and occasional productions of the entire triptych have proved the theatrical viability of Puccini's conception.

8. 'TURANDOT' AND PUCCINI'S DEATH. Puccini in his early 60s had arrived at an important turning-point of his style. He was determined to 'tentar vie non battute' ('strike out on new paths') and was looking for a subject with a fantastic, fairy-tale atmosphere, but characters of flesh and blood. His choice eventually fell on Gozzi's *Turandotte*, which was suggested to him by Renato Simoni, an authority on Gozzi and the author of a play on him; Simoni and Adami were to collaborate with the composer. For Puccini this five-act play was the most human of Gozzi's dramatic *fiabe*, and Gozzi himself had felt the same way when writing it. With *Turandot* Puccini felt that he was moving on to a loftier plane, that an 'original and perhaps unique work is in the making', compared with which all his previous music seemed to him 'a farce'. But no other opera cost him so much labour and toil, notably the great love duet in Act 3, and no other opera filled him with such strong doubts about his creative powers. His letters to the two poets expressed a feverish urgency and anguish, and he constantly implored them to get on with the work on the libretto; it was as if he had a premonition that he would not live to complete the opera. In a moment of abject despair he wrote a letter to Adami in which he clearly recognized the limitations of his genius:

I touch the keyboard of my piano and my hands get dirty with dust! My writing desk is a sea of letters – and not a trace of music! Music? It is useless. I have the great weakness of being able to compose only when my puppet executioners [*carnefici burattini*] move on the stage. If I could be a pure symphonic composer, I would then cheat time and my public. But I am not! I was born many years ago – so many, far too many, almost a century . . . and the Almighty touched me with his little finger and said: 'Write for the theatre – mind, only for the the theatre!' And I have obeyed the supreme command. Had he intended me for some other profession . . . well, I should perhaps not now find myself without the essential material. Oh you who say you're working . . . you ought to think of a man who has the earth under his feet, yet feels the ground receding under him with every hour and every day, as if a precipice would swallow him up!

In the midst of his work on *Turandot* Puccini decided to move from his beloved Torre del Lago, where the

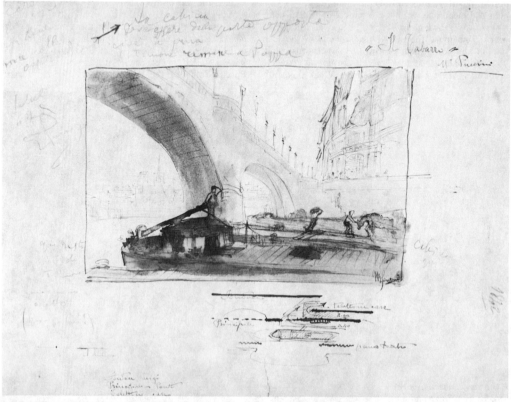

2. *Design by G. B. Santoni for Puccini's opera 'Il tabarro', with annotations by the composer (Museo Teatrale alla Scala, Milan)*

erection of a peat factory had made life impossible for him, and settle in Viareggio (December 1921). Towards the end of 1923 he began to complain of pains in his throat. In the autumn of 1924 three specialists diagnosed cancer. Accompanied by his son, he went to Brussels, where he entered the clinic La Couronne and was treated with X-rays. Though the treatment seemed successful, his heart could not stand the strain and he died on 29 November. The body was brought to Milan and temporarily buried in Toscanini's family tomb. The whole of Italy went into mourning, and Mussolini gave the funeral oration. Two years later his remains were interred at Torre del Lago.

Puccini left three sets of sketches for the final two scenes of *Turandot*, of which one (see fig.4), consisting of 36 pages of continuous music in short score, was used by Franco Alfano for the completion of the opera. The first production was given at La Scala on 25 April 1926, when Toscanini ended the performance with the death of Liù, the last scene Puccini was able to finish. On the following evening the opera was played with Alfano's ending.

9. PUCCINI'S CONCEPT OF OPERA. Puccini had a definite concept of opera, representing a consistent and original point of view in musico-dramatic thinking. To be sure, it was a narrow concept – though in his last period he did try to enlarge it (*Gianni Schicchi* and *Turandot*) – and one tarnished by neurotic features. Compared with the greatest musical dramatists, Puccini worked in an operatic world constricted in subject matter, in variety and range of characters and musical depth. It is significant for the ethos of his operas that of the 12 he wrote, seven are named after their heroines, who, with the exception of Minnie and Turandot, are essentially all of the same type. Puccini does not engage us on as many different levels as do Mozart, Wagner, Verdi and Strauss, but on his own, most characteristic level, the level where erotic passion, sensuality, tenderness, pathos and despair meet and fuse, he was an unrivalled master.

Like every born musical dramatist, he considered work on the libretto a creative act and as important as its musical setting. As he put it: 'The basis of an opera is the subject and its dramatic treatment'. Whatever criticism might be brought against the limitations of the subject matter and his dramatic and psychological handling of it, the fact remains that his librettos are eminently stage-worthy and offered him precisely the opportunities he needed for the full exercise of his imagination. Puccini did not aim at music-drama in the Wagnerian sense, but at musical drama; yet in his own way he thought in terms of a *Gesamtkunstwerk* in which the whole stage apparatus – singing, acting, declamation, facial expression, gesture and movement, costumes, scenery and lighting – should be engaged to create the maximum effect. He thus insisted that the lighting, in following closely the dramatic changes, be regulated 'with an attentive ear', and he was obsessed (as was Berg in *Wozzeck*) with the precise moment at which the curtain should be raised or dropped – 'a curtain dropped too soon or too late often means the failure of an opera'. From *Tosca* onwards his stage directions were far more elaborate than Verdi's, and his operas require singer–actors more flexible in their acting technique than do the majority of the older composer's works.

10. DRAMATURGY AND STAGE SENSE. Puccini's

3. Giacomo Puccini

dramaturgy has much in common with the technique of the short story writer. The plot always develops clearly and logically, showing a definite point of departure, a middle and an end. The story line was for Puccini the chief means of directing and holding the spectator's attention, and he always wanted it to be straightforward and simple so that the action and its motivation remained, as far as possible, self-explanatory. He insisted on what he called 'l'evidenza della situazione', which would enable the spectator to follow the drama even without understanding the actual words. This was one of his supreme criteria when, in his constant searches for a suitable subject, he saw productions of plays in foreign languages, like *Madam Butterfly* and *Tosca*. He wanted dramatic material of the utmost economy and so, except in *La bohème*, sub-plots in the original play or novel were eliminated and historical and local details excised unless they served the evocation of a particular atmosphere. This concern for compression and concentration resulted in a swift unfolding of the drama and a steadily mounting tension. Once the action gets under way in a Puccini opera, there is little lingering or dispersal of interest; suspense and surprise are produced by well-timed incidents and the catastrophe is approached in rapid strokes. Yet in his concern to achieve maximum concentration, he at times overshot the mark. He over-compressed and/or suppressed narrative and psychological details necessary for a fully convincing motivation of the characters. He was not alone in this: over-compression was also the blind spot in the dramaturgy of early and middle Verdi.

Five of Puccini's operas observe the classical unities of action, time and place – an imponderable but important factor contributing subliminally to the concentrated effect on the spectator. In *Tosca* and *Turandot* the action takes place within 24 hours, in *Il trittico* the one-act form of the episodes inevitably compelled the composer to adhere strictly to the classical unities. Each

4. First page of Puccini's autograph sketches for the finale of 'Turandot', completed by Alfano in 1926 (I-Mr)

episode takes less than an hour to perform, yet each is so well constructed that it represents a foreshortened version of a full-length, three-act opera with exposition, development and dénouement.

Puccini's gifts as a man of the theatre include one that many playwrights might envy and that only a few opera composers have possessed. This is what the French call 'l'optique du théâtre', an eye for the purely visual effect of a scene. 'Be sparing with words and try to make the incidents clear and brilliant to the eye rather than the ear', Puccini wrote to Adami about *Turandot*. Every Puccini opera contains at least one scene striking as a stage spectacle, such as the Embarkation act of *Manon Lescaut* or Liù's funeral cortège in Act 3 of *Turandot*. These scenes, in consequence, fired the composer's imagination particularly strongly. From this sense of the purely visual as a dramatic means sprang Puccini's predilection for dumb-shows; in these he relied almost exclusively on the stage action for the intended effect, accompanying it with, as it were, only incidental music.

This is superbly illustrated by the silent scene that follows Tosca's murder of Scarpia and by the arrival and departure of the aunt in *Suor Angelica*. Mention must also be made of the composer's masterly use of the dramatic pause, especially at the point of highest tension, where it achieves an effect far greater than any that words or music could. Puccini called this 'musica sottintesa' – 'implied music'. In this he echoed Verdi's remark that 'there are moments in the theatre where poets and composers must have the talent to write neither poetry nor music'.

For Puccini the theatre had its fixed, immutable laws: it must, he said, interest, surprise, touch or move to laughter. Part of the secret of his success lay in the fact that he fully met these demands in virtually all his operas. Moreover, he was acutely aware that an opera, however dramatic, is not all action, movement and conflict, but must have its moments of stasis and repose, moments to be filled with music of a poetic lyricism. Puccini ranks far above Mascagni, Leoncavallo,

Giordano, Cilea and his other Italian contemporaries because of his superior power of melodic invention, his insight into the imponderables of the musical and dramatic structure and his highly developed sense of the relationship between words and music. Even his *verismo* operas, *Tosca*, *Butterfly*, *La fanciulla* and *Il tabarro*, have a dimension that raises them above the constricted canon of pure realism. Hence his constant demands to his librettists to allow him scope for spreading his colours more lyrically, for an 'affectionate little phrase', for 'episodes delicate, tender, luminous and exquisite' and with a 'touch of gay, fresh laughter'. He possessed most sensitive antennae for 'le cose piccole', the little things in the lives of little, unimportant people and for 'grande dolore in piccole anime'. But this represented only one side of his genius. He was equally strongly drawn to the full-blooded, as is shown by *Tosca*, *La fanciulla* and *Turandot*.

11. THE PUCCINI HEROINE. 'Chi ha vissuto per amore, per amore si morì' sings the street vendor in *Il tabarro*. It might be a description of the fate suffered by his protagonists, notably his heroines, frail creatures who live and die for love. This equation of Eros with Thanatos, or the concept of love as tragic guilt to be atoned for by death, is of course a perennial theme in drama and opera and has nowhere been shown in such grandeur and elaborated to such psychological and metaphysical depths as in Wagner's *Tristan*. With Puccini this concept carried no such implications, but was essentially the expression of an erotic nihilism that stands in marked contrast to the hedonism of his private life. What is striking, however, is the peculiar dramatic pattern in which he presented this theme. In the Puccinian opera the heroine, who is the pivot around which the action revolves, is shown as a woman of true and unbounded love. This, in the composer's view, constitutes a guilt for which she must be punished by physical and mental suffering and gradually ground down until she perishes. It is in this grinding-down process, in which refined cruelty is matched by deep compassion, that Puccini established an individual dramatic pattern. The male characters perform, with one or two exceptions, the role of catalyst (the tenor lovers) or of persecutor (baritone). In *Suor Angelica* and *Turandot* the part of the persecutor is assigned to a female character – the aunt in the former and the Chinese princess in the latter. The fact that Puccini adhered to this dramatic pattern almost from his first to his last opera suggests that it sprang from an image deeply anchored in his unconscious and therefore assumed for him the force of a compulsion.

12. DEPICTION OF ATMOSPHERE. Another fingerprint of Puccini's dramatic style is the projection of atmosphere. Three kinds are apparent in his work: first, documentary atmosphere, like that of the bell music in Act 3 of *Tosca*, for which Puccini made a special journey to Rome to obtain a first-hand impression of the matin bells from the churches around the Castel Sant'Angelo. This is reminiscent of Zola's descending into the coal mines of northern France for his novel *Germinal*. And Flaubert's preparatory archaeological studies for his *Salammbô* are paralleled by Puccini's study of books on the ethnography and music of Japan and China for *Butterfly* and *Turandot*. The musical exoticism of these operas and of *La fanciulla* was, however, not only intended to suggest an authentic atmosphere but also sprang from the composer's desire to evoke a poetic ambience. The Japanese, Chinese and North American tunes employed in these works are not merely quotations, but are organically worked into the fabric of Puccini's own music to saturate it with local colour. Puccini absorbed their melodic, rhythmic and instrumental inflections so completely into his own style that there is no dichotomy between his 'western' and 'exotic' manners. *Butterfly*, *La fanciulla* and *Turandot* are stylistically completely homogeneous. The fertilizing effect of this exotic material on his work can be compared to that of native folksong on the music of Bartók, Falla and Vaughan Williams.

In addition to the documentary and poetic atmospheres there is the psychological atmosphere, which is the nerve centre of each Puccini opera and determines its particular emotional character. Although the dramatic world is small, each opera has its peculiar emotional tone which sets it apart from its sister works. Only a composer possessed of so highly developed a sense of psychological atmosphere could have conceived *Il trittico*, in which three episodes immensely contrasted in their emotional ambience are juxtaposed. Part of the measure of Puccini's stature as a musical dramatist is this ability to bend his inventive power so completely to the psychological character of a libretto. Moreover, virtually every one of his 12 operas opens with a theme, called by him 'motivo di prima intenzione', which catapults the spectator into its ambience. Significant in this context are his words to Adami: 'The difficulty is how to begin an opera, that is, how to find its musical atmosphere. Once the opening is fixed and composed, there is no more to fear'.

13. MELODY AND ARIA TYPES. Puccini once wrote that 'without melody, fresh and poignant, there can be no music'. He thus put his finger on what was perhaps his greatest gift as an opera composer. It is indeed arguable whether his stage works, in spite of his extraordinary theatrical instinct and the attention he paid to the story line, would have achieved such universal and lasting acclaim, had he not possessed remarkable powers as a melodist. In this he showed his deep roots in the tradition of Italian opera and proved himself the true successor of Verdi, although his fund of melody was not as rich and varied as that of the older master. His melodic style can best be studied in his arias, which arise naturally from the action and represent the culmination of a character's lyrical expression. Puccini was too fine a dramatist to subscribe to Giordano's half-joking prescription: 'Find a good song and then write an opera around it!' In later years he even thought that Tosca's 'Vissi d'arte' tended to hold up the drama and wanted to scrap it. Nevertheless, it is the aria that displays his cantilena at its most perfect. Marked by great sensuous warmth and melting radiance, its singability is considerably heightened by the predominantly diatonic movement of the vocal line. His arias most often start in a slow, hesitant manner, with the theme first played by the orchestra, while the voice glides in, chantlike, on softly reiterated notes, as in Massenet and Debussy. Tender, graceful and infinitely supple, Puccini's cantilena in its languor proclaims an affinity with Massenet's typical *phrase décadente* transplanted to Italian soil. Like all born musical dramatists, Puccini concentrated into a single phrase all there was to express at a given point of the drama, thus achieving a close

union of words, sentiment and situation – hence the irresistible impact the Puccinian cantilena has on the listener.

There are various types of aria in Puccini, but the most characteristic is to be found in his 'farewell' and 'death' arias, more particularly in those 'povera faccia' themes reflecting, as it were, the habitual expression of melancholy on his face – so often remarked upon by those who knew him. These themes show certain constant features – a minor key, a slow, dragging pace, a dropping of the melodic line mostly in 4ths and 5ths and an effort to counteract this by a forced screwing-up of the phrase. There is about these limping, spineless themes an air of utter weariness and despair (a characteristic example is already to be found in Le villi). In marked contrast to this are Puccini's ballabile tunes, those dance-like, pirouetting strains in 2/4 and/or 6/8 which are always associated with lighthearted emotions, youthful gaiety (Bohème and Butterfly), playfulness and insouciance (love duet in Tosca, Act 1) and grotesque comedy (the sacristan in Tosca, the three masks in Turandot and innumerable passages in Gianni Schicchi).

14. HARMONY AND LEITMOTIFS. Puccini's harmonic idiom is another element in his superiority over his Italian contemporaries. By turns fragrant, delicate, brilliant, bittersweet and pungent, it displays not only richness and variety but a remarkable flux, reflecting the turns of the drama and, on a more personal level, the rise and fall of the composer's inner tension. It was Puccini's maxim to keep abreast of the innovations of his time, and this is nowhere better seen than in his harmonic vocabulary. He began with chromatic alterations of the triad and chromatic side-slipping of secondary 7ths and 9ths in Le villi and Edgar. He turned to Tristan harmonies in Manon Lescaut, in which he also used parallel 5ths before Debussy. Under the influence of French impressionism he cultivated faburden-like progressions, chords of the added 6th, augmented triads and unresolved dissonances (Bohème). From about 1900 he began to make pointed use of the whole-tone scale (Tosca, Butterfly and La fanciulla) and subsequently experimented with bitonality, chords of the 4th and exposed, naked discords (Il trittico, Turandot). Even the atonality of Schoenberg's Pierrot lunaire, which Puccini heard in Florence in April 1924, seems to have left its mark on the Chorus of Spectres in Act 1 of Turandot. It is significant that the majority of Puccini's most striking harmonic devices occur in situations charged with 'negative' emotions: fear, terror, despair, mental pain and death. Moreover, it is in such situations that the composer resorted, in the orchestra, to ominous, sinister ostinatos, like that accompanying the preparations for the execution of Cavaradossi in Act 3 of Tosca. Puccini obviously derived this device from Verdi, who used it to establish a dramatic mood and impress it on the spectator. The younger composer turned it into a means of creating mounting suspense.

No post-Wagnerian composer could afford to dispense with the leitmotif and Puccini was no exception. His leading motifs are clearcut and sharply defined (the theme of the Bohemians, the 'Scarpia' and 'Turandot' motifs) but his application of this device is not strict, and the same figure may symbolize several things – a character, a situation, an atmosphere, an object (notably in Tosca), or it may be used merely to add interest to the texture without any perceptible relevance to the stage action. Puccini's leitmotifs are employed in the manner of the old 'reminiscence'; they keep their melodic shape and change only in tempo and harmony. Real metamorphosis in the Wagnerian sense is almost entirely confined to the themes of the aunt in Suor Angelica and the Chinese princess in Turandot.

15. USE OF THE ORCHESTRA AND ORCHESTRAL MOSAIC. The orchestra provides a continuous background, but displays only a semblance of symphonic technique. This should not be held against a composer for whom the musical weight of an opera rested on the singers. Orchestral continuity is achieved not so much by the interweaving of different themes as by the juxtaposition of tiny motifs. It is the technique of the mosaic, in which diminutive melodic 'squares' are repeated and treated sequentially, after which the process is repeated with the next square. However, Puccini handled this technique with such consummate skill that it gives the impression of almost organic growth.

In Puccini's orchestral style two basic and strongly contrasted elements can be discerned. There is, on the one hand, the Puccini who, like Strauss, loved rich, saturated colours and, on the other, the Puccini with an ear for the most refined sensory stimuli, who, like Debussy, seemed to relish sound for itself and used his palette with an aristocratic restraint. A characteristic feature of his luxuriant style is the instrumental doubling, trebling and even quadrupling of the vocal melody – a device known as violinata. Puccini was severely criticized for it, yet it had been used by Rossini, Bellini and Donizetti and, indeed, by the 18th-century Neapolitan school (Rousseau, in his Lettre sur la musique française of 1753, mentioned this device specifically). What lay behind these doublings and treblings was the urge to impart to the vocal lines a maximum of sensuousness and vibrancy. However, the impact of a special effect stands in inverse ratio to the frequency of its use, and Puccini's too-frequent use of the violinata tended to become self-defeating.

Puccini always wrote for a large orchestra, one considerably augmented in his 'grand' operas Tosca, La fanciulla and Turandot. As with all the Italian opera composers of the 19th century, the central element of the orchestra is the warm and expressive string section. Often the first half of a Puccini aria or duet is accompanied by strings alone, or supported only slightly by the woodwind. The woodwind dominates in lighthearted scenes, whereas the brass is used mostly to add tension and to underline the dramatic climax. In his three 'exotic' operas Puccini combined brass, woodwind and percussion (including a number of unpitched instruments) to create local colour. Each of his operas has its special orchestral 'tone' or character, and there can hardly be a greater contrast than that between the liquescent and diaphanous timbres of Butterfly and the explosive fauve sound of La fanciulla and Turandot.

16. USE OF THE CHORUS. Like Verdi, Puccini was a master in the handling of big choral scenes. He treated the chorus not as a mere adjunct to the action or as a scenic prop, but as a collective character with an active part in the drama, as for instance in Manon Lescaut (Embarkation Act), La fanciulla (Manhunt, Act 3) and Turandot (Act 1). Even when the chorus represents only a decorative element Puccini enlivened its effect by seemingly effortless musical exchanges between soloists

and crowd, as in the opening acts of *Manon*, *Butterfly* and *La fanciulla* and the splendid Latin Quarter Act in *Bohème*. And what could be more evocative than the humming chorus at the start of *Butterfly*'s night vigil?

17. ASSESSMENT. Puccini was a perfectionist who in all his operas, including the hapless *La rondine*, paid an almost obsessive attention to the minutest technical details. He may well have owed this high level of professionalism to his position as the scion of four generations of most respectable craftsmen, whose history may be said to be the musical history of Lucca. Puccini exemplified Henry James's memorable phrase: 'An artist is fortunate when his theories and limitations exactly correspond'. He was fully aware of his limitations and only once or twice made the mistake of venturing beyond them, since within them he was able to achieve all that he wished to. Yet this does not make him a *petit maître*

any more than it makes a Chopin, a Wolf, a Ravel or, in literature, a Maupassant and a Chekhov minor masters. They were all artists with an acute awareness of the extent of their creative range and were stylists in the true sense of the word, in that they knew how to adapt their imagination and technique completely to the exigencies of their particular medium; this explains Puccini's constant and unremitting search for a subject that would exactly suit his talent. Puccini the man had by no means a fully integrated personality, as had Verdi – there were too many seemingly irreconcilable contradictions in his psychological make-up. But the artist in him succeeded in creating a style that was wholly original, homogeneous and compelling. A lesser genius than Verdi, he represents Verdi's only true successor, and his greatest masterpiece and swansong, *Turandot*, must belong among the last 20th-century stage works that have remained in the regular repertory of the world's opera houses.

WORKS

(published in Milan unless otherwise indicated; detailed bibliographical information in Hopkinson)

OPERAS

Title	Text	First performance	Sources and remarks
Le villi	1, F. Fontana	Milan, Verme, 31 May 1884	autograph, *I-Mr*, unpubd
2nd version	2	Turin, Regio, 26 Dec 1884	vocal score (1885)
Edgar	4, Fontana, after de Musset: La coupe et les lèvres	Milan, La Scala, 21 April 1889	autograph, Acts 1, 3, *Mr*, vocal score (1890)
2nd version	3	Ferrara, 28 Feb 1892	copy of 1st version with autograph changes, *Mr*, vocal score (1892)
final version		Buenos Aires, 8 July 1905	vocal score (1905)
Manon Lescaut	4, Leoncavallo, M. Praga, D. Oliva, L. Illica, G. Giacosa, after Abbé Prévost	Turin, Regio, 1 Feb 1893	autograph, *Mr* (1893), vocal score (1893)
La bohème	3, Illica, Giacosa, after Murger	Turin, Regio, 1 Feb 1896	autograph, *Mr* (1898), vocal score (1896)
Tosca	3, Illica, Giacosa, after Sardou	Rome, Costanzi, 14 Jan 1900	autograph, *Mr* (1899), vocal score (1899)
Madama Butterfly	2, Illica, Giacosa, after D. Belasco's stage version of a magazine story by J. L. Long	Milan, La Scala, 17 Feb 1904	autograph, *Mr*, vocal score (1904)
2nd version	3	Brescia, Grande, 28 May 1904	changes in autograph, *Mr* (1907), vocal score (1904)
La fanciulla del West	3, G. Civinini, C. Zangarini, after Belasco	New York, Metropolitan, 10 Dec 1910	autograph, *Mr* (1911), vocal score (1910)
La rondine	3, G. Adami	Monte Carlo, 27 March 1917	autograph lost (1917), vocal score (1917)
Il trittico		New York, Metropolitan, 14 Dec 1918	autograph, *Mr* (1918), vocal score (1918)
Il tabarro	1, Adami, after D. Gold: La houppelande		
Suor Angelica	1, G. Forzano		
Gianni Schicchi	1, Forzano, developed from a few lines in Dante's Inferno xxx		
Turandot	3, Adami, R. Simoni, after Gozzi	Milan, La Scala, 25 April 1926	autograph, *Mr*, vocal score (1926); inc., finished by F. Alfano

OTHER VOCAL

Sacred: Motet, Credo, in honour of S Paolino, 1878, unpubd; Mass, T, Bar, B, vv, orch, 1880, autograph, *I-TLP*, vocal score (New York, 1951) [incorporating Motet, Credo]; Salve del ciel regina, S, harmonium, before 1880, autograph *Li*, unpubd; Requiem, S, T, B, org/harmonium, before 1905, autograph frag. Ms

Choral: I figli d'Italia bella, cantata, solo vv, orch, 1877; Cantata a Giove (1897)

Songs: Melancolia (A. Ghislanzoni), 1881, unpubd; Allor ch'io sarò morto (Ghislanzoni), 1881, unpubd; Spirto gentil (Ghislanzoni), 1882, unpubd; Noi leggeramo (Ghislanzoni), 1882, unpubd; Storiella d'amore (Ghislanzoni), 1883, in *Musica popolare* (4 Oct 1883); Menti all'avviso (Romani), romanza, 1883; Sole e amore (Puccini), mattinata, 1888, in *Paganini* (1888); Avanti, Urania! (R. Fucini) (Florence and Rome, 1899); E l'uccellino (Fucini) (1899); Inno a Diana (C. Abeniacar [F. Salvatori]) (Florence and Rome, 1899); Terra e mare (E. Panzacchi) in *Novissima* (1902); Morire? (Adami), in *Per la Croce rossa italiana* (c1917–18); Inno di Roma (Salvatori) (Florence and Rome, 1923)

Pedagogical: Solfeggi, 1888, unpubd

INSTRUMENTAL

Orch: Preludio sinfonico, 1876, autograph, private collection of Natale

Gallini, Milan, unpubd; Adagietto, 1883, autograph sketch *Li*, unpubd; Capriccio sinfonico, perf. Milan, 14 July 1883, autograph *Mc*, arr. pf 4 hands (1884); Scossa elettrica, march, 1896, unpubd

Chamber: Scherzo, str qt, c1880–83, autograph *Li*, unpubd; Str Qt, D, c1880–83, autograph parts *Li*, unpubd; Crisantemi, str qt (1890); 3 minuets, str qt (1892), nos.1, 3 rev. (Paris, 1898); La sconsolata, vn, pf, 1883, unpubd

Kbd: several unpubd org pieces, before 1880; Foglio d'album, pf, ?1907 (New York, 1942); Piccolo tango, pf, ?1907 (New York, 1942)

BIBLIOGRAPHY

SOURCE MATERIAL

G. Adami: *Giacomo Puccini: epistolario* (Milan, 1928; Eng. trans., 1931, rev. 2/1974)

G. M. Gatti: *Puccini in un gruppo di lettere inedite a un amico* (Milan, 1944)

E. Gara: *Carteggi pucciniani* (Milan, 1958)

C. A. Hopkinson: *Bibliography of the Works of Giacomo Puccini 1858–1924* (New York, 1968)

G. Pintorno: *Puccini: 276 lettere inedite* (Montecatini, 1974)

BIOGRAPHY AND CRITICISM

F. Fontana: 'Giacomo Puccini', *Gazzetta musicale di Milano*, xxxix (1884), 381; repr. as 'Puccini visto dal suo primo librettista', *Musica d'oggi*, xv (1933), 148

F. Torrefranca: *Giacomo Puccini e l'opera internazionale* (Turin, 1912)

I. Pizzetti: 'Giacomo Puccini', *Musicisti contemporanei: saggi critici* (Milan, 1914)

A. Coppotelli: *Per la musica d'Italia: Puccini nella critica del Torrefranca* (Orvieto, 1919)

A. Weissmann: *Giacomo Puccini* (Munich, 1922)

A. Coeuroy: *La Tosca de Puccini: étude historique et critique* (Paris, 1923)

G. Monaldi: *Giacomo Puccini e la sua opera* (Rome, 1924)

A. Fraccaroli: *La vita di Giacomo Puccini* (Milan, 1925)

A. Neisser: *Giacomo Puccini: sein Leben und sein Werk* (Leipzig, 1928)

R. Specht: *Giacomo Puccini: das Leben – der Mensch – das Werk* (Berlin, 1931; Eng. trans., 1933)

A. Bonaccorsi: 'Le musiche sacre dei Puccini', *Bollettino storico lucchese*, vi (1934), 29

W. Maisch: *Puccinis musikalische Formgebung, untersucht an der Oper 'La Bohème'* (Neustadt an der Aisch, 1934)

G. Adami: *Puccini* (Milan, 1935)

K. G. Fellerer: *Giacomo Puccini* (Potsdam, 1937)

H. Gerigk: *Puccini* (Potsdam, 1937)

V. Seligman: *Puccini among Friends* (London, 1938)

P. Panichelli: *Il 'Pretino' di Giacomo Puccini racconta* (Pisa, 1940, 3/1949)

G. Adami: *Il romanzo della vita di Giacomo Puccini* (Milan, 1944)

M. Carner: *Of Man and Music: Collected Essays and Articles* (London, 1944, 3/1945) [incl. 'In Defence of Puccini', 'The First Version of *Madama Butterfly*', 'The Two *Manons*', 'Puccini's Early Operas', 'Puccini's Chief Symphonic Venture: the *Capriccio sinfonico*', 'A Puccini Operetta: *La Rondine*', 'The Exotic Element in Puccini']

F. Thiess: *Puccini: Versuch einer Psychologie seiner Musik* (Vienna, 1947)

L. Marchetti: *Puccini nelle immagini* (Milan, 1949)

G. Marotti: *Giacomo Puccini* (Florence, 1949)

A. Bonaccorsi: *Giacomo Puccini e i suoi antenati musicali* (Milan, 1950)

W. Dean: 'Giacomo Puccini', *The Heritage of Music*, ed. H. Foss, iii (London, 1951), 153

G. R. Marek: *Puccini: a Biography* (New York, 1951)

D. Del Fiorentino: *Immortal Bohemian: an Intimate Memoir of Giacomo Puccini* (London, 1952)

L. Ricci: *Puccini interprete di se stesso* (Milan, 1954)

M. Carner: *Puccini: a Critical Biography* (London, 1958, rev. 2/1974)

E. Greenfield: *Puccini: Keeper of the Seal* (London, 1958)

C. Sartori: *Puccini* (Milan, 1958)

P. C. Hughes: *Famous Puccini Operas* (London, 1959)

C. Sartori, ed.: *Puccini* (Milan, 1959) [collection of essays by various authors]

N. A. Galli: *Puccini e la sua terra* (Lucca, 1974)

G. Magri: *Puccini e le sue rime* (Milan, 1974)

A. Marchetti: *Puccini: com'era* (Milan, 1974)

L. Pinzauti: *Puccini: una vita* (Florence, 1974)

A. Marchetti: 'Tutta la verità sull'"Inno a Roma" di Puccini', *NRMI*, ix (1975), 396

J. Meyerowitz: 'Puccini: musica a doppio fondo', *NRMI*, x (1976), 3

C. Casini: 'Introduzione a Puccini', *Il melodramma italiano dell'ottocento: studi e ricerche per Massimo Mila* (Turin, 1977)

S. Martinotti: 'I travagliati Avant-Propos di Puccini', ibid

GABRIELLA BIAGI RAVENNI (1–4), MOSCO CARNER (5)

Puccitelli, Virgilio (*b* Sanseverino Marche, 1599; *d* Sanseverino Marche, 26 Dec 1654). Italian writer and priest. As a young man he is said to have lived in Rome and also to have travelled much. About 1630 (or somewhat earlier) he entered the service of Prince Władysław Sigismund of Poland, who reigned from 1633 to 1648 as King Władysław IV. From 1634 he acted as a secretary to the king, for whom he went on private missions (to Italy in 1638–9 and France in 1640) connected with, among other things, the organization of musical life at court. A year after the death of the king, who had granted him an annuity for life, he returned to Italy. He lived first at Naples and then at Sanseverino.

Puccitelli wrote the texts for nine operas performed at the Polish court and for a number of ballet introduc-

tions, three of which are known. The themes of his *drammi* range from the pastoral (*Dafne*, 1635; *Narciso trasformato*, 1638) through the hagiographic (*La Santa Cecilia*, 1637) to the epic (*Il ratto di Elena*, 1636, 2/1638; *Armida abbandonata*, 1641; *L'Enea*, 1641; *Andromeda*, 1644; *Le nozze d'Amore e di Psiche*, 1646; *Circe delusa*, 1648). Their plots are based on a fusion of the neo-Platonic theory of love and Baroque moralism, presented with restraint. They are in three or five acts and are characterized by a combination of elements of different dramatic genres, strong emphasis being laid on tragic hieratic elements; heroic characters are identified panegyrically with the king. The effects possible with the theatrical machinery of the time were widely applied, especially in the mythological *intermedii*. The music of these operas has disappeared. It was composed by members of the royal chapel: Marco Scacchi set *Narciso trasformato*; the composers of the other operas are uncertain but perhaps included Kaspar Förster (ii), Mielczewski, Pękiel and Scacchi.

BIBLIOGRAPHY

G. C. Gentili: *De ecclesia septempedana*, iii (Macerata, 1838)

G. Ranaldi: *Due lettere inedite scritte a Virgilio Puccitelli* (Sanseverino, 1854)

S. Windakiewicz: 'Teatr Władysława IV (1633–48)', *Przegląd Polski*, xxviii (1893), 231–97 [pubd separately (Kraków, 1893); supplement: *Czas*, xlviii (1895), no.285]

K. Targosz-Kretowa: *Teatr dworski Władysława IV* (Kraków, 1965)

A. Panicali: 'Un librettista italiano in Polonia: Virgilio Puccitelli (1599–1654)', *Studi secenteschi*, ix (1968), 287

A. Panicali and A. Szweykowska: 'La maga sdegnata Virgilio Puccitellego', *Pamiętnik teatralny*, xviii (1969), 511

A. Szweykowska: 'Circe delusa: dramma musicale Virgilio Puccitellego', ibid, p.532

——: 'Qualche osservazione sulla struttura letteraria del dramma musicale del primo seicento sull'esempio delle opere di Virgilio Puccitelli', *Quadrivium*, xii (1971), ii, 77

——: 'Twórczość Virgilio Puccitellego dla polskiej sceny (1635–48): problem otwarty', *Studia staropolskie*, xxxi (1971), 84–144

——: 'Il dramma per musica nel teatro di Ladislao IV', *RIM*, vii (1972)

——: *Dramma per musica w teatrze Wazów 1635–1648* (Kraków, 1976)

ANNA SZWEYKOWSKA

Puchner, Hans. *See* BUCHNER, HANS.

Pucitta [Puccitta], Vincenzo (*b* Civitavecchia, nr. Rome, 1778; *d* Milan, 20 Dec 1861). Italian composer. After studying at the Conservatorio della Pietà dei Turchini in Naples, he began as an opera composer in Senigallia in 1799 with a work of unknown title. In the next seven years he wrote, mostly for the theatres of Milan and Venice, at least 17 operas, all but one of them farces or comedies. According to Fétis, he went to Lisbon in 1806, where an *Andromaca* was performed. He was then music director of the Italian opera in Amsterdam and from 1809 to 1814 composer and music director at the King's Theatre, London. In those years this theatre was a showcase for Angelica Catalani, the most famous soprano of the time. For her Pucitta composed a series of operas, both *buffa* and *seria*, tailoring his music to her elaborate vocalism and providing much of the repertory of her highly remunerated solo concerts, at which he often conducted the orchestra. He became her accompanist and went with her on tours of Scotland, Ireland and England and, in 1815, of Holland, Belgium and Germany. In 1814, when she was made directress of the Théâtre-Italien in Paris, he became her house composer. However, the Paris public took such a dislike to him and his music that when Catalani appeared in his new opera *La principessa in campagna* in 1817, she had it advertised without his name. Because of this situation and after disputes with her husband, he returned to Italy in 1817.

In 1819 Pucitta toured Austria and Germany with his pupil, the English soprano Elizabeth Ferron (or Feron), whom he had engaged on a four-year exclusive contract. The tour was successful, Ferron often being compared with Catalani and singing much of the same repertory that Pucitta had formerly composed or arranged for her. In April 1820 she made her début at La Scala in *La principessa in campagna* and was well received, but the opera was not. Shortly thereafter she bought her freedom from the contract for 12,000 francs. The two operas that Pucitta composed for the next carnival season in Rome and Milan were fiascos and he ceased to write for the stage. In his later years he edited collections of popular Marian melodies.

WORKS

Operas: c36 operas, incl. La burla fortunata, ossia I due prigionieri (G. D. Camagna, after B. J. Marsollier: Adolfe et Clara), Venice, 1804, *I-Fc*, perf. as Adolfo e Chiara, London, King's, 1814, *GB-Lbm*, excerpts (London, ?1814); La caccia di Enrico IV (S. Buonaiuti, after Collé), London, 1809, excerpts (London, n.d.); La principessa in campagna, o Il marchese nell'imbarazzo, Paris, 1817, autograph *I-Mr*, excerpts pubd

Other vocal: L'anima penitente ed amante del suo Dio, cantici sacri, solo vv, pf/unacc. (Milan, n.d.); Le mille melodie consacrate a Maria Immacolata (Milan, 1843); Il mese di Maria: cantici popolari su tutti i principali fatti della vita della Santa Vergine (Milan, 1850)

BIBLIOGRAPHY

FétisB
AMZ, xx (1818), 176; xxii (1820), 499
J. W. Klein: 'Pucitta, Vincenzo', *MGG*

ANDREA LANZA

Puebla (de los Angeles). Mexican city, capital of Puebla state and an important musical centre from the 16th century to the 18th. Founded in 1531, it soon became the second largest city in Mexico, surpassed in size, wealth and grandeur only by the capital. By 1640 it had several fine *colegios* for secondary and advanced studies and about 30 sumptuous churches, magnificently decorated by local artists and craftsmen. During the 17th and 18th centuries it welcomed world-famous native painters and writers, including the renowned poetess Sor Juana Inés de la Cruz. About 19 printers published in Puebla during the 17th century, and from 1646 the city had the first public library in the Americas, an extraordinary collection of 5000 volumes donated by Bishop Juan de Palafox y Mendoza (1600–59).

The colonial city also enjoyed the dramatic traditions of Spain; lavish church processionals, costumed *máscaras* (pageants) and sacred and secular *comedias* and *autos* all used music extensively. In the 16th and 17th centuries most were staged in the cathedral plaza, a large area that was also the site of bullfights. Bishop Palafox temporarily interrupted some performances in 1644 by vetoing the city government's plans to stage two *comedias a lo divino* for Corpus Christi in front of the cathedral, 'as had been done since time immemorial'. Local colour was added to the scene by the great dances and pageants performed by Indians, who also participated in some church festivals. The secular *juntas* and *bailes* held by negroes were apparently so frequent and lively as to need periodic official regulation, and their influence is demonstrated by the frequent appearance in the villancico cycles of such song types as the *negrilla* and *guineos*. The churches encouraged the composition of picaresque villancicos and *chanzonetas*, performed at Vespers and Matins on important festivals and saints' days. From the early 17th century secular *comedias* with music were usually staged in a *corral* or *coliseo*; a succession of these theatres operated intermittently in Puebla. The seventh such theatre was the municipal Nuevo Coliseo (1760).

During colonial times musical life centred on the new cathedral with its services renowned throughout the Indies. At the old cathedral (completed 1539) *maestros de capilla* who were also composers included Juan de Victoria (c1567–c1569, a native of Burgos who was Hernando Franco's predecessor as *maestro de capilla* of Mexico City), Pedro Bermudes (1603–c1606), Gaspar Fernandes (1606–29) and the famed Juan Gutierrez de Padilla (1629–64), who ended his service in the new cathedral, dedicated by Bishop Palafox in 1649 and one of the finest examples of Herreriano architecture. There Padilla assembled and composed an extensive library for his choir, which included the brilliant organist–composer Francisco López y Capillas. Padilla was succeeded as *maestro de capilla* by his tenor soloist and assistant, the composer Juan García (1664–c1678). Carlos Valero was given a brief interim appointment in 1678; his successor was the important composer Antonio de Salazar (1679–88). Other *maestros de capilla* who were composers included Miguel Matheo de Dallo y Lana, Francisco Atienza and, at the end of the 18th century, Manuel Arenzana.

As in most Spanish churches the large choir of the cathedral bisects the central nave, and is enclosed on three sides. The musicians, with the *capellanes* and other church officials allowed inside, sat in double rows of seats facing each other. This arrangement encouraged antiphonal effects (with double choirs and alternating plainchant and polyphony) and the extensive use of instruments. During Padilla's time the favoured instruments were the organ, harp ('cross-strung', and capable of chromatic notes) and bass viol, forming a continuo, duplicated for each choir in polychoral music; these were supplemented by recorders, *chirimías* (shawms), cornetts, sackbuts and treble, tenor and bass *bajoncillos* and *bajons* (bassoons), frequently used to double or replace voices. In Spanish and colonial churches the musicians playing shawms, cornetts and flutes were customarily expected to sing during Advent and Lent, when only the organ and bassoon were used with the singers. Padilla's staff in 1651 included ten instrumentalists, six of whom were also singers. Instrumental colour was frequently varied for each verse of such parts of the liturgy as the *Magnificat*, *Salve regina* and psalms. Early in the 18th century violins came into use and by the end of the century the basic cathedral orchestra consisted of violins, flutes, trumpets, horns, double bass and organ, with an occasional viola. Around 1800 Manuel Arenzana frequently added extra violins, clarinets, bassoons and timpani to this group.

Between 1810 and 1821 the wars of independence against Spain caused frequent disruptions, but Puebla remained an important centre. During the rest of the 19th century, however, a constant succession of invasions, battles and political conflicts inevitably caused a decline. Puebla remains a large city but has never regained its earlier cultural leadership. Its cathedral archives, however, contain the largest collection of 16th- to 19th-century polyphony in Mexico, including 20 large choirbooks and quantities of printed and manuscript partbooks, many of them rare. There are extensive holdings of works by Morales, Guerrero, Palestrina and by other composers from the 16th century to the 18th, and one of the largest collections of music by colonial composers working in Mexico. Another extensive collection of 17th- and 18th-century polyphony, the Colección Jesús Sánchez Garza from the Santísima Trinidad convent (founded at Puebla in 1619), was long in private hands; it has since been deposited at the Instituto Nacional de Bellas Artes, Mexico City.

BIBLIOGRAPHY
M. Zerón Zapata: *La Puebla de los Angeles en el siglo XVII* (MS, c1714; enlarged, pubd Mexico City, 1945)
D. A. Bermúdez de Castro: *Theatro Angelopolitano* (MS, 1746; pubd Mexico City, 1908)
M. F. Echeverría y Veytia: *Historia de la fundación de la ciudad de la Puebla de los Angeles* (MS, 1774–80; pubd Puebla, 1931)
A. Carrión: *Historia de la ciudad de los Angeles* (Puebla, 1896–7)
J. T. Medina: *La imprenta en la Puebla de los Angeles: 1640–1821* (Santiago, 1908/R1964)
S. Barwick: *Sacred Vocal Polyphony in Early Colonial Mexico* (diss., Harvard U., 1949)
R. Stevenson: *Music in Mexico: a Historical Survey* (New York, 1952)
A. Ray: *The Double-choir Music of Juan de Padilla, 17th-century Composer in Mexico* (diss., U. of Southern California, 1953)
R. Stevenson: 'Sixteenth and Seventeenth Century Resources in Mexico', *FAM*, i (1954), 69; ii (1955), 10
A. R. Catalyne: 'Music of the Sixteenth through Eighteenth Centuries in the Cathedral of Puebla, Mexico', *Yearbook, Inter-American Institute for Musical Research*, ii (1966), 75
L. B. Spiess and E. T. Stanford: *An Introduction to Certain Mexican Musical Archives* (Detroit, 1969)
R. Stevenson: *Renaissance and Baroque Musical Sources in the Americas* (Washington, DC, 1970)
——: *Christmas Music from Baroque Mexico* (Berkeley, 1974)
ALICE RAY CATALYNE

Puel, Christoph. *See* BUEL, CHRISTOPH.

Puente, Gioseppe de (*fl* Naples, 1606). Italian composer of Spanish extraction. He is known only by *Il primo libro de madrigali* (Naples, 1606), for five voices. The madrigals are shorter and generally more chordal than those of his Neapolitan contemporaries. The identifiable texts are by Marino and Guarini (six each) and G. B. Leoni, A. Parma and Rinuccini (one each). In *Luci seren'e chiare* Puente appears to quote part of Gesualdo's setting of the same text, published in his fourth book of madrigals (1596).

KEITH A. LARSON

Puente, Giuseppe del. *See* DEL PUENTE, GIUSEPPE.

Puerto, Diego del [Didacus a Portu] (*fl* early 16th century). Spanish theorist. He studied in Salamanca where he was *cantor* at the Colegio de San Bartolomé and curate at the church of Laredo. He wrote *Portus musice* (Salamanca, 1504; ed. in Rey Marcos), published in Latin with marginal annotations in Spanish. The last pages, including details on the tuning of the vihuela, are also in Spanish, and it is probably the first Spanish publication to contain polyphonic music. He was more concerned with practical than theoretical aspects of music and his definitions are concise with few digressions. He presented a personal interpretation of the theory of the three *genera*, which he called diatonic, chromatic and compound. He criticized the Guidonian hexachord because of its inadequacies as a training system, but offered nothing better in its place, merely remarking that the use of pitch-names was to be preferred; in this respect he was closer to Ramos than many Spanish theorists. He effectively expounded mensural notation, and his treatise is particularly noteworthy for its explanation, often in markedly aesthetic terms, of the techniques of composing in three and four parts.

BIBLIOGRAPHY
R. Stevenson: *Spanish Music in the Age of Columbus* (The Hague, 1960)
F. J. León Tello: *Estudios de historia de la teoria musical* (Madrid, 1962)
J. J. Rey Marcos, ed.: *Portus musice de Diego del Puerto* (Madrid, 1978)

F. J. LEÓN TELLO

Puerto Rico [Porto Rico, 1898–1932]. Island in the West Indies associated with the USA, with Commonwealth status from 1952. The first contact of Europeans with the Caribbean island was in 1493 during Christopher Columbus's second voyage to America. Colonization by Spain began in 1508, and the seat of government became established at San Juan, now the island's largest city and the centre of commercial and cultural life.

I. Art music. II. Folk music.

I. Art Music. During the first three centuries of Puerto Rican history, musical life centred on the Church and the military garrison. Early records are scarce because many ecclesiastical archives and other sources of information were destroyed in fires, hurricanes, sackings and sieges. Early in the 16th century an organist and a *chantre* were requested for the cathedral, whose construction had begun in 1511. At the end of the 16th century the cathedral, described as being as beautiful as any in England, possessed a fine organ. Capitulary Acts of 1660 indicate that the permanent musical staff of the cathedral consisted of an organist and a *sochantre*, but in 1672 two new posts were created, *maestro de capilla* and cantor. From 1698 until 1756 there is no record of specific nominations to posts in cathedral music. However, from 1756, records show a succession of organists, *maestros de capilla* and other musicians attached to the Church. These musicians, including both clerics and laymen, provided the first regular music instruction in Puerto Rico.

Secular music before the 19th century was connected mainly with public celebrations. Among these were events of religious significance, but mounted at the expense of secular authority: Corpus Christi and the celebration of the patron saints of Spain, of the Spanish West Indies, and of Puerto Rico. In addition, *fiestas reales* were organized on occasions connected with accessions of Spanish monarchs. The accession of Fernando VI in 1746 was marked by processions, balls, *comedias* and other festivities extending over a period of nine days. Similar events occurred in 1789 on Carlos IV's accession to the throne. During the 18th and 19th centuries, military musicians were important figures in the colony's musical life. Attached to Spanish units serving in the Antilles, these musicians also performed for balls and other civil celebrations and provided the nucleus of orchestras formed for opera and concerts. They were among the first teachers of wind instruments in Puerto Rico, and many remained after completion of their military service as teachers, performers and founders of musical families.

Construction of the island's first permanent theatre began in 1824; the building, still in use as the San Juan Municipal Theatre, was officially inaugurated in 1832. A philharmonic society was formed by a group of professionals and amateur musicians. Among the goals of this society (many of which were realized) were the establishment of a music academy, the organization of an orchestra, and the presentation of locally mounted operas and zarzuelas.

One of Puerto Rico's first native composers was Felipe Gutiérrez (1825–1899). He wrote the first opera on a Puerto Rican subject, *Guarionex* (?1856), as well as two other operas, a zarzuela and a large quantity of religious music. Concerts by visiting artists began in 1827 with a series of three recitals by the pianist Eduard Edelman and the cellist Henry Femy. The British tenor William Pearman visited Puerto Rico in 1832, giving performances in the Municipal Theatre. Louis Moreau Gottschalk and Adelina Patti spent a year touring Puerto Rico in 1857–8, during the period when San Juan and Ponce, the island's second-largest city, were becoming regular stops in the itineraries of touring Italian opera companies. Short works of light lyric theatre, including *tonadillas* and *sainetes*, were regularly presented by theatrical companies, and the first complete opera (Rossini's *Il barbiere di Siviglia*) was given by a visiting Italian company in 1835.

19th-century Puerto Rican art music includes symphonic fantasias and overtures, religious music, instrumental chamber music and a considerable amount of piano music. An important species of piano music, cultivated well into the 20th century, is the Puerto Rican *danza*. Originally a social figure dance, the *danza* became a highly stylized form of concert music in the hands of such skilled native composers as Manuel Tavárez (1843–83), Juan Morel Campos (1857–96) and Braulio Dueño Colón (1854–1934). A generation of composers was active during the first half of the 20th century, but economic depression, complicated by the island's change of sovereignty from Spain to the USA in 1898, caused the decline or collapse of traditional agencies of musical patronage. Among these composers, whose production was limited almost entirely to chamber music, piano music and songs, were José Ignacio Quintón (1881–1925), José Enrique Pedreira (1904–59) and Augusto Rodríguez (b 1904).

During the 1940s and 1950s the insular government created a number of new educational and cultural agencies, and as a result music began to regain its traditional importance. A Division of Community Education was created in 1946 and soon began to commission film scores from young native composers. A government-owned radio station began operation in 1949, expanding into television in 1958. In 1955 an Institute of Puerto Rican Culture was created, and a newly organized Puerto Rico SO was established in 1958. These government branches engage performers and commission new works either directly or through grants to such groups as ballet and theatre companies.

Most of the art music composed during the 1950s displays the deliberate use of folk elements in a conscious attempt to create a distinctive Puerto Rican music. Since 1960, however, composers have taken a much more eclectic view, embracing styles and techniques ranging from post-Romantic to serial, aleatory and mixed-media expression. Composers active in Puerto Rico are Jack Delano (b 1914), Héctor Campos Parsi (b 1922), Amaury Veray (b 1922), Luis A. Ramírez (b 1923), Rafael Aponte Ledée (b 1938), Luis M. Alvarez (b 1939), Francis Schwartz (b 1940) and Ernesto Cordero (b 1946).

Music education in Puerto Rico is administered through two governmental programmes and by numerous private academies. One government programme was created in 1947 to provide every elementary school child with an understanding of the basic elements of music. The second programme is a network of junior conservatories, the Free Schools of Music, which offer specialized instruction for children aiming to become professional musicians. Further technical instruction is given at the Puerto Rico Conservatory of Music, established in 1960. University studies in music are conducted, and academic degrees granted in recognition of higher musical studies, at the Inter-American University of Puerto Rico, San Germán, and at the University of Puerto Rico, Río Piedras.

BIBLIOGRAPHY

F. Callejo y Ferrer: *Música y músicos puertorriqueños* (San Juan, 1915, 2/1971)
E. Pasarell: *Orígenes y desarrollo de la afición teatral en Puerto Rico* (San Juan, 1951–67, 2/1969)
M. L. Muñoz: *La música en Puerto Rico: panorama histórico-cultural* (Sharon, Conn., 1966)
R. Fitzmaurice: *Music Education in Puerto Rico: a Historical Survey with Guidelines for an Exemplary Program* (diss., Florida State U., 1970)
F. Caso: *Héctor Campos Parsi in the History of Twentieth-century Music in Puerto Rico* (diss., Indiana U., 1972)
A. Figueroa de Thompson: *An Annotated Bibliography of Writings about Music in Puerto Rico* (Ann Arbor, 1975)
R. Stevenson: 'Music in the San Juan, Puerto Rico, Cathedral to 1900', *Inter-American Music Review*, i (1978), 73

II. Folk music

1. Introduction. 2. African-derived genres. 3. Hispanic genres. 4. Instruments.

1. INTRODUCTION. Until the 20th century interest in Puerto Rican folklore and customs was expressed principally through travellers' descriptions and the introduction of folk themes in 19th-century Puerto Rican *costumbrista* literature; precise knowledge of the island's folk music from the 16th to 19th centuries is therefore slender.

The predominant elements in the folk and traditional music of Puerto Rico have been traced to Spain and west Africa; Spanish settlement and colonization began in 1508, while west African influence is due to the direct importation of African slave labourers until the 19th century and the introduction of American-born blacks at various periods. The indigenous Arawak Indian contribution is minimal; so rapid was the Spanish domination of the island's indigenous population that within a few generations of the Conquest scarcely a trace of Arawak influence could be noted in Puerto Rican life.

Early descriptions of the musical and ceremonial use of Arawak implements are limited to gourd rattles and to the *bastón*, an ornamented stick struck heavily against the ground. The *areito* (a ceremonial dance) was practised throughout the Greater Antilles by pre-Columbian inhabitants and performed on a wide variety of occasions, involving instruments and antiphonal chanting. Attempts to reconstruct Arawak music and chant on the basis of the few extant descriptions or through supposed vestiges in the folk music of later periods have been fruitless.

2. AFRICAN-DERIVED GENRES. African influences have been strong, particularly in the coastal regions. Several Puerto Rican folk music customs clearly display indebtedness to African antecedents, although they have by no means remained unaffected by contact with Spanish music and the Spanish language. Among the most important of these forms are the *bomba*, the *plena* and the *baquiné*.

The *bomba*, which some writers have associated with

the Cuban *conga* and with the more generalized Antillean *bamboula*, is practised in Puerto Rico's coastal lowlands. This dance is characterized by the use of drums as accompanying instruments, by responsorial singing, and by individuals or couples spontaneously dancing within a circle of participants. Song-texts may be improvised by a leader and repeated by the chorus of participants, or they may consist of traditional texts in which leader and chorus sing alternating stanzas:

> Ayá, bombé, quinombó!
> Ohi, ohé, mano Miguel!
> Ayayá, sagú carú!
> Ohé, ohé, quinombó!

Many other names of dances associated with the *bomba* and presumably of African origin have been noted. Among these are the *bamulé, belén, candungo, candungué, cucalambé, cuembé (quembé), cunyá, curiquinqué, gracimá, guateque, holandés, kalindá, leró, mariandá, mariangola, sicá* and *yubá*.

Another form showing marked African influence is the *plena*. The Puerto Rican *plena* is a short narrative song that describes, often with sharply satirical intent, an individual or an event. While somewhat similar in function to the Spanish *romance* (ballad) and the Mexican *corrido*, the characteristic *plena* differs from these in its brevity and its marked use of African-derived rhythms (see ex.1), patterns of vocal usage and dance.

Ex.1 *Los muchachos de Cataño, plena* (Cruz, 1967)

The earliest documented performances of the *plena* date from the first decade of the 20th century. It has been suggested, however, that the style (if not the name) of the *plena* was current in Puerto Rico half a century before. The first known performances are attributed to English-speaking black immigrants from the Virgin Islands and St Christopher, who had settled in Ponce on Puerto Rico's southern coast. The earliest accompanying instruments appear to have been the tambourine and *güiro* with guitar or concertina. The heavy striking of the tambourine, on the beat in binary metre, is believed to have been extremely important in establishing the definitive style of the *plena* developing in the 1920s.

The characteristic form of the *plena* consists of the alternation of stanzas and refrains (either improvised or composed) by soloist and chorus. Many *plenas* have become classics of popular folk music, and have become known throughout Puerto Rico and abroad. Among these is the following text, which refers satirically to the arrival in Ponce of a newly appointed Roman Catholic bishop:

> Mamita llegó el obispo,
> llegó el obispo de Roma.
> Mamita, si tú lo vieras
> que cosa linda que cosa mona!

Baquiné is the communal vigil over the body of a dead child during the night preceding Christian burial. As the child is presumed to have died without sin, the occasion is more one of rejoicing than one of grief. However, songs of consolation are sung to the bereaved parents, and occasionally African deities are invoked in order to repel an evil spirit:

> Huye, huye pronto
> maligno adversario
> en la sombra va el niño
> libre de tu mano.
> Babacó y Ogún
> le tienden los brazos,
> Yeyemá y Changó
> deshojan un ramo.

3. HISPANIC GENRES. In contrast to the African-related folk music of Puerto Rico's coastal lowlands, many of the songs and dances from the interior mountains display relatively pure derivation from Spanish sources. Here, many folksong species are based on the Spanish *décima*, a ten-line stanza of octosyllabic or hexasyllabic structure.

The most important form of folk music practised in the interior is the *seis*. As dance music, the *seis* is in simple binary metre, richly syncopated and frequently overlaid with triplet figurations in melody or accompaniment (see ex.2). Formerly certain types of *seis* were

Ex.2 *Seis del Dorado* (López Cruz, 1967)

performed by couples in two opposite rows. More than 80 types of *seis* have been identified, distinguishable by tempo, rhythmic figuration, melody type or choreography. Many are named after the style of dance-steps associated with them, for example the *seis enojao, seis chorreao* and *seis zapateao*. Others are named after a town or region, such as *seis de Comerío* or *seis de oriente*; still others bear the names of musicians who popularized them, such as *seis de Andino, seis de Villarín* and so on.

As accompaniment to song, the *seis* is closely associated with *décima* texts. The improvisation of *décimas* on family social occasions and during community festivities is basic to Puerto Rican folk custom. In a *seis de controversia* two singers may engage in a contest, improvising *décimas* according to a subject and rhyme established by the contest judge. Subjects for improvisation cover a wide range, from praise of an individual or the celebration of an event to themes of love or popular religion.

The repertory of Puerto Rican *bailes de garabato*, or popular folkdances, also includes the *vals criollo*, the *mazurca* and the *polca*, all modifications of the corresponding 19th-century European social dances.

Folk and popular religious music in Puerto Rico centres on the *aguinaldo* and the villancico, descendants of the 16th-century Spanish villancico. In modern popular usage the two names are almost interchangeable and refer to a specific repertory of well-known songs whose texts deal with the Christmas cycle. The most common themes are the Nativity, the Three Kings and praise of the Virgin or Child. The melodies are usually in simple or compound binary metre; the rhythmic syncopation that many *aguinaldos* or villancicos display may be the result of African influence, although this has not been fully investigated.

The *Cruz de mayo* or Fiesta de Cruz, a popular religious festivity involving a great deal of music, enjoyed a revival during the 1960s and early 1970s after several decades of decline. Dedicated to the Virgin Mary in early May, the *Cruz de mayo* consists of nine consecutive evenings of fiesta. This festival, a form of the traditional Roman Catholic Novena, formerly took place within homes or private patios, but has become a public event sponsored by civic and fraternal groups. The music performed consists of a traditional cycle of songs (19 in one local usage) concerning the Cross, the Virgin, the month of May and the Holy Family. Rhythms, tempos and forms are based on such

traditional species as the waltz and march. The traditional group of accompanying instruments (*conjunto típico*) consists of guitar, *cuatro* and *güiro*, although in some localities this orchestra is expanded to include flutes and violins or instruments associated with popular commercial music. The cycle ends with social dancing and general festivity.

Another religious folk activity, the *rosario cantao* (sung rosary), also involves music of Spanish derivation. It is a family or neighbourhood observance arranged for the purpose of redeeming a vow made to a saint. The event lasts all night, and is divided into periods of singing (*tercios*) and relaxation, the latter consisting of games, stories and banter. After the final *tercio*, at day-break, a dance begins which may last until noon.

4. INSTRUMENTS. Puerto Rican folk instruments include drums of various types, the modern representatives of a continuous tradition of African music in the Caribbean. The isolated use of musical bows has also been observed. The *marímbula*, an Antillean modification of the African LAMELLAPHONE, serves as a bass instrument during many popular festivities involving music. Maracas and *güiros*, descendants of pre-Columbian Arawak instruments, appear in most species of Puerto Rican folk and popular music.

The construction and playing of plucked-string fretted instruments have been skilfully cultivated. Guitar construction, tuning and playing technique follow Spanish usage, but a number of other instruments, unique to Puerto Rico or with counterparts in other regions of Latin America and the Caribbean, have evolved. Among these is the *cuatro* (see illustration), descended from the Spanish vihuela. The modern *cuatro* is made of native woods and exists in a wide variety of shapes while retaining the plectrum technique of the ancestral *vihuela de peñola*. Formerly, the *cuatro* had four double courses of strings tuned in 4ths (*e–a–d′–g′*). At the end of the 19th century a fifth single or double course was added below, giving the pitch *B*.

The *tiple* and *tres* are smaller instruments of the same general type as the *cuatro*. The four or five single-string courses of the *tiple* have had no standardized tuning; there have been as many as 16 generally accepted arrangements. The *tres* has three single strings, tuned *b–g′–d″*. Other plucked instruments that have been used in Puerto Rican folk music are the flat-backed *laúd español* and the *bordonúa*; the latter, which has become rare, has five courses of strings, tuned *A–d–f♯–b–e′*.

Cuatro (guitar) in the Instituto de Cultura Puertor-riqueña, San Juan

BIBLIOGRAPHY

M. Alonso: *El gíbaro* (Barcelona, 1849, 5/1971)

J. A. Mason: 'Porto Rican Folklore: Decimas, Christmas Carols, Nursery Rhymes, and Other Songs', *Journal of American Folklore*, xxxi (1918), 289–450

M. Cadilla de Martínez: *La poesía popular en Puerto Rico* (Madrid, 1933)

——: 'La música popular de Puerto Rico', *Puerto Rico ilustrado* (4 June 1938), no.1473, p.22

G. Durán: 'Romance, corrido y plena', *Boletín de la Unión panamericana* (1942), no.76, p.630

M. Cadilla de Martínez: 'La conga', *Estudios afrocubanos*, v (1945–6), 176

F. López Cruz: *El aguinaldo y el villancico en el folklore puertorriqueño* (San Juan, 1956)

M. Alvarez Nazario: 'Historia de las denominaciones de los bailes de bomba', *Revista de ciencias sociales*, iv (1960), 59

E. Figueroa Berríos: 'Los sones de la bomba en la tradición popular de la costa sur de Puerto Rico', *Revista del Instituto de cultura puertorriqueña*, vi (1963), 46

C. Rosa Nieves: *Voz folklórica de Puerto Rico* (Sharon, Conn., 1967)

F. López Cruz: *La música folklórica de Puerto Rico* (Sharon, Conn., 1967)

C. Marrero de Figueroa: *Tierra y folklore* (San Juan, 1967)
M. Canino Salgado: *La copla y el romance popular en la tradición oral de Puerto Rico* (San Juan, 1968)
J. McCoy: *The Bomba and Aguinaldo of Puerto Rico as they have Evolved from Indigenous, African and European Cultures* (diss., Florida State U., 1968)
L. M. Alvarez: *Bibliography on Puerto Rican Folklore* (MS, Folklore Institute, Indiana U., 1969)
H. Vega Drouet: *Some Musical Forms of African Descendants in Puerto Rico: Bomba, Plena, and Rosario Francés* (diss., Hunter College, NY, 1969)
P. Escabí, ed.: *Estudio etnográfico de la cultura popular de Puerto Rico: morovis: vista parcial del folklore de Puerto Rico* (Río Piedras, 1971)
D. Thompson: 'The Marímbula, an Afro-Caribbean Sanza', *Yearbook for Inter-American Musical Research*, vii (1971), 103
M. E. Davis: 'The Social Organization of a Musical Event: the *Fiesta de Cruz* in San Juan, Puerto Rico', *EM*, xvi (1972), 38

DONALD THOMPSON

Pueyo, Eduardo del (*b* Saragossa, 29 Aug 1905). Spanish pianist. After study in Saragossa and at the Madrid Conservatory, where he won first prize in piano (1918), he continued his musical education in Paris, making his début there in 1921. His piano teachers were Raoul Laparra and Bosch van s'Gravemoer. Retiring in 1927 for a prolonged period of study, he resumed his concert career in 1937. He has earned a distinguished reputation as a concert and recording artist and as soloist with leading orchestras, presenting notable interpretations of Beethoven, Debussy, Albéniz and Granados. Professor (1948) at the Brussels Royal Conservatory, and later at the Chapelle Musicale Reine Elisabeth (Belgium), he has also taught at the Mozarteum, Salzburg. He has been an adjudicator for the Queen Elisabeth as well as the Tchaikovsky and the Busoni international piano competitions.

JOHN G. DOYLE

Pueyo, Salvador (*b* Barcelona, 10 Feb 1935). Spanish composer. He studied at the Barcelona Conservatory with Caminals (piano), Toldrá (conducting) and Zamacois (theory). Among the awards he has received are the Prize of the City of Barcelona (1965 for *Abstracciones*) and the Extraordinary Prize of the Barcelona Conservatory (1968 for *Antitesis*). *Abstracciones* exemplifies the free atonality of his earlier music; later works employ an eclectic synthesis of techniques in music of clear, ascetic structure.

WORKS
(*selective list*)

Opera: Kohelet, 1969
Choral orch: Threnos, 1962; Visperas de S Pedro, 1968
Orch: Abstracciones, 1964; Antitesis, 1965–7
Chamber: Evoluciones, 1963; Trio, 1963; Conceptos, 1966; Wind Qnt, 1968
Pf: Tema con variaciones, 1960; Sonata, 1961

MANUEL VALLS

Puget. French family of organ builders. Théodore Puget (*b* Montréal, Aude, 15 Nov 1799; *d* Toulouse, 31 March 1883) founded in 1834 his organ-building firm at Toulouse. He directed it until 1877 when he passed it to his sons Eugène (*b* Toulouse, 8 Sept 1838; *d* Toulouse, 24 Nov 1892) and Jean-Baptiste (*b* Toulouse, 22 Oct 1849; *d* Toulouse, 22 Sept 1940) who renovated the organ at Albi Cathedral (1904). Jean-Baptiste's son Maurice (*b* Toulouse, 7 Dec 1884; *d* Toulouse, 17 Aug 1960) later took over the firm and carried out the restoration of the organs at Narbonne and Perpignan cathedrals.

GUY OLDHAM

Puget, Loïsa [Louise-Françoise] (*b* Paris, 11 Feb 1810; *d* Pau, 1889). French composer and singer. Instructed in music by her mother, a singer, she became popular as the composer of 300 or more *romances*, most of which have texts by Gustave Lemoine. She sang these works frequently in Parisian salons from about 1832 to 1842. An interest in the theatre led her to study with Adolphe Adam; her one-act *Le mauvais oeil*, to a libretto by Scribe and Lemoine, was performed at the Opéra-Comique on 1 October 1836. Her popularity soon waned, however, and after her marriage to Lemoine in 1842 she composed little apart from an operetta, *La veilleuse, ou Les nuits de milady*, performed at the Paris Théâtre du Gymnase on 27 September 1869. Her *romances* have simple, attractive melodies, appropriate for their humble, sentimental texts.

BIBLIOGRAPHY

FétisB
P. Scudo: 'Esquisse d'une histoire de la romance', *Critique et littérature musicales*, i (Paris, 1850, enlarged 3/1856)
F. Clément and P. Larousse: *Dictionnaire lyrique, ou Histoire des opéras* (Paris, 1867–9, enlarged 3/1905/*R*1969, ed. A. Pougin)

Pugnani, (Giulio) Gaetano (Gerolamo) (*b* Turin, 27 Nov 1731; *d* Turin, 15 July 1798). Italian violinist and composer. His principal teacher was G. B. Somis, a pupil of Corelli. At the age of ten he was admitted to the last chair of the second violins in the Teatro Regio, though his official appointment was delayed until 19 April 1748. A royal stipend enabled him to spend a year in Rome (1749–50) where he studied composition with Ciampi; on his return to Turin he continued to occupy his modest orchestra post, though with doubled salary. He became principal of the second violins in 1763. By that time he had acquired an international reputation through his appearance on 2 February 1754 at the Concert Spirituel in Paris, playing one of his own concertos. The *Mercure de France* wrote: 'the connoisseurs insist that they have never heard a violinist superior to this virtuoso'. In the same year his first published works (the Trio sonatas op.1) appeared in Paris. From 1767 to 1769 he was active in London as conductor of the King's Theatre and he obtained a notable success with his first opera, *Nanetta e Lubino* (1769). He also appeared in concerts with J. C. Bach and other prominent musicians. In 1770 Pugnani achieved his lifelong ambition to become first violinist of the King's Music in Turin, a post once occupied by his teacher Somis and which included the leadership of the Teatro Regio. His duties were expanded in 1776 when he became general director of instrumental music; in addition he was appointed supervisor of military bands in 1786. During these years he also continued his career as composer of operas; works by him were staged in Turin, Naples, Paris, London and Vienna, usually under his direction. From 1780 to 1782 he undertook a lengthy concert tour through northern Europe, accompanied by his favourite pupil, Viotti. After visiting Switzerland, Germany and Russia, Pugnani returned to Turin while Viotti proceeded to Paris. On 22 March 1796 Pugnani conducted a performance in Vienna of his orchestral suite based on Goethe's *Werther*; it was his last foreign journey. His last years were saddened by the decline and ultimate dissolution of Turin's musical establishment due to the war with France.

Pugnani was a vital link in the uninterrupted tradition from Corelli to Viotti. Gratefully, Viotti called himself 'élève du célèbre Pugnani' on his printed music; among

Pugnani's other pupils were Borghi, Bruni and Polledro. His playing was known for its power, eloquence and rich cantilena; his 'arco magno' (grand bowing) became proverbial. He probably played an important part in the development of the modern bow: he himself used a bow (called an 'archetto alla Pugnani') that was straighter, longer and equipped with a screw, and he may have exchanged views with the Parisian bowmaker Tourte *père* in 1754 and with the younger François Tourte in 1772–3, both of whom were engaged in bringing the bow into its present form. Pugnani also preferred to use thicker strings, perhaps because they were better able to withstand the greater pressure of his bowing.

As a composer Pugnani reached far beyond the violin into the field of opera, symphony and chamber music, and must be considered an important representative of Italian pre-Classicism. Burney thought little of his efforts at opera: 'Though an able and celebrated professor on the violin, [Pugnani] seems to have begun writing for the voice too late in life to arrive at great excellence in lyric compositions'. His symphonies show a stylistic resemblance to the schools of Mannheim and Vienna; he preferred a four-movement sequence with a minuet in third place. His chamber music stands midway between that of Sammartini and Boccherini, and often dispensed with a figured bass, though not always successfully. Several of his trios and quintets required an obbligato keyboard part and assorted instruments. His only known violin concerto follows the form established by Tartini but reflects the *galant* style of the 1760s.

WORKS

For thematic index and lost or doubtful works, see Zschinsky-Troxler (1939) with additions in Müry (1941); numbers in square brackets taken from Zschinsky-Troxler; asterisk (*) indicates former MS location.

THEATRICAL

Nanetta e Lubino (opera buffa, C. F. Badini), London, King's Theatre, 8 April 1769; score, *D-Bds*; ov. (London, 1769); Favourite Songs (London, 1769)

Issea (favola pastorale, V. A. Cigna Santi), Turin, Regio, 1771; as Apollo e Issea, London, 30 March 1773; score, *Bds*

Tamas Kouli-Kan nell'India (dramma per musica, Cigna-Santi), Turin, Regio, 1 Feb 1772; lost

Aurora (festa per musica, G. D. Boggio), Turin, 1775, for wedding of Carlo Emanuele IV and Adelaide Clotilde of France; lost

Adone e Venere (opera seria, G. Boltri), Naples, S Carlo, Nov 1784; score, *Bds*, *I-Tf*

Achille in Sciro (dramma per musica, Metastasio), Turin, Regio, 15 Jan 1785; score, *Tf*; arias, *A-Wgm*, *D-Dlb*, *I-Fc*; ov., *CH-Zz*

Demofoonte (dramma per musica, Metastasio), Turin, Regio, 26 Dec 1787; ov., *F-Pc*, *D-Dlb*; arias, *Dlb*, *Bds*, *I-Fc*

Demetrio a Rodi (festa per musica, Boggio), Turin, 1789, for wedding of Vittorio Emanuele and Maria Theresa; score, *Mr*

Correso e Calliroe (balleto eroico), 1792, lost; ballet music to Gluck's Orfeo, lost

OTHER VOCAL WORKS

Betulia liberata (oratorio, Metastasio); score, *D-Bds*

Amore e Psiche, cantata, 2 S, 2 ob, 2 hn, str, *Dlb*; ov., *Bds*, *B-Bc*

La scommessa, cantata, 2 S, chorus, 2 ob, 2 hn, 2 cl, str, *D-B*

6 arias with orch, *A-Wgm*; *B-Bc*; *CH-Bu*; *D-Bds*, *Dlb*

ORCHESTRAL

3 Quintets [25, 11, 27], 2 hn, 2 ob, str, bc (London, 1765 or later); in 6 pièces (Paris, n.d.)

6 Overtures [18, 28, 31, 33, 19, 29] in 8 parts, op.4 (London, ?1768–70); no.5 (London, c1767)

A 2nd Sett of 6 Overtures [13, 20, 34, 21, 32, 22] in 8 parts, op.8 (London, c1769); as op.9 (Paris, c1770)

A 2nd Set of 3 Quintets [26, 12, 17], 2 fl/ob, 2 vn, 2 hn ad lib, bc (London, 1773 or later)

Quintet [40], hpd/pf, fl, vn, va, vc, in 3 Quintetto's . . . by G. Pugnani and . . . J. S. Schroeter (London, 1780); as 3 quintetti, op.1 (Offenbach, n.d.)

Quintette [24], 2 ob, 2 hn, 2 vn, bc (Florence, n.d.)

7 symphonies [14–16, 23, 35–7], *D-Bds*; Werther, orch suite, c1795, *A-Wgm*; vn concerto, before 1766, *B-Bc*; 2 military marches [136–7], Rome, Palazzo Venezia; Marche pour le régiment des gardes [138], *Bc*

VIOLIN SOLO
(all with bc)

6 sonates [100–05], op.3 (Paris, ?1760); no.2, 2nd movt, in Cartier's L'art du violon (Paris, 1798)

6 sonate [106–11], op.7 (London, 1770 or later); as op.5 (Amsterdam, n.d.); as op.6 (Paris, n.d.); no.1 ed. in D. Alard: Die klassischen Meister des Violinspiels (Mainz, 1866); nos.4–6 ed. in K. Witting: Die Kunst des Violinspiels, iii (Wolfenbüttel, n.d.)

6 sonates [112–17], op.8 (Amsterdam, before 1774); as 6 solos (London, n.d.); as op.1 (Paris, n.d.); no.1 ed. in D. Alard: Die klassischen Meister des Violinspiels (Mainz, 1866); no.4 ed. in G. Jensen: Klassische Violinmusik (London, 1889, 2/1911)

2 sonatas, *F-Pc*; 1 sonata, *I-Mc*: see Müry, 95, 107

Praeludium and Allegro, attrib. Pugnani, is by Kreisler

TRIO SONATAS
(all for 2 vn, b, unless otherwise stated)

6 trio [47–52], op.1 (Paris, 1754); as 6 Easy Sonatas (London, ?1763); no.1 in 6 trii da Sebastiano Ferigo ed 1 di Gaetano Pugnani (London, 1760); no.3 ed. E. Schenk, Hausmusik, clxxii (Vienna, 1955); no.4 ed. E. Schenk, Mw, vii (Cologne, c1955); no.6 ed. in A. Moffat: Alte Meister (Leipzig, 1910)

6 Sonatas [53–8], op.2 (London, ?1765); as op.3 (Amsterdam, ?1763; Paris, n.d.)

6 Sonatas [82–7], hpd, vn/fl and vc acc. (London, ?1767); as op.6 (Paris, n.d., Amsterdam, n.d.); no.1 (London, c1775)

A 2nd Set of 6 Trios [65–70], op.9 (London, ?1771); as op.10 (Paris and Lyons, ?1775)

6 trios [80a–f; ? only a, d, by Pugnani], op.11 (Paris, n.d.); as 6 Divertimentos . . . by Pugnani, Vachon, Borghi & Aprile (London, 1772)

6 trios [59–64] (Paris, n.d.), doubtful

9 trio sonata/divertimentos: [71, 78–9], *B-Bc*; [77], *Bc*, *D-ROu*; [72–3], *I-Nc*; [74–6], *Mc*; *GB-Lbm*

OTHER CHAMBER WORKS

3 Quartets [41–3], 2 vn, va, b (London, ?1763); nos.1–3 in 6 pieces (Paris, n.d.)

A 2nd Sett of 3 Quartets [44–6], 2 vn, va, b (London, 1763); as op.13 (Paris, n.d.)

12 Favourite Minuets [88–99], 2 vn/fl, hpd (London, 1768)

6 Sonatas or Duetts [118–23], 2 vn, op.4 (London, ?1770); as op.5 (Paris, n.d.); as op.13 (Paris, ?1776); nos.2, 4–5, ed. A. Bachmann (Paris, 1911)

Minuet [81], 2 vn, 2 hn, b, no.8 in Raccolta di 24 minuetti composti da vari autori (Venice, n.d.)

12 duets, 2 vn: [124–7], *D-Dlb*; [128–34], *I-MOe*; [135], *CH-Bu*

BIBLIOGRAPHY

BurneyH

G. B. Rangoni: *Essai sur le goût de la musique . . . Saggio sul gusto della musica col carattere de' tre celebri sonatori di violino i signori Nardini, Lolli, e Pugnani* (Livorno, 1790, repr. 1932)

F. Fayolle: *Notices sur Corelli, Tartini, Gaviniès, Pugnani et Viotti* (Paris, 1810)

A. Bertolotti: *Gaetano Pugnani e altri musici alla corte di Torino nel secolo XVIII* (Milan, 1892)

D. Carutti: 'Della famiglia di Gaetano Pugnani', *Miscellanea di storia italiana*, iii/2 (Turin, 1896)

M. Pincherle: *Les violinistes compositeurs et virtuoses* (Paris, 1922)

A. Moser: *Geschichte des Violinspiels* (Berlin, 1923, rev. and enlarged, 2/1966–7)

S. Cordero di Pamparato: 'Gaetano Pugnani, violinista torinese', *RMI*, xxxvii (1930), 38, 219, 350, 551 [also pubd separately (Turin, 1930)]

A. Della Corte: *Notizie di Gaetano Pugnani* (Turin, 1931)

——: 'Due inedite opere teatrali di Gaetano Pugnani', *Musica d'oggi*, xiii (1931), 490

E. M. von Zschinsky-Troxler: *Gaetano Pugnani* (Berlin, 1939)

A. Müry: *Die Instrumentalwerke Gaetano Pugnanis* (diss., U. of Basle, 1941)

G. Barblan: 'Ansia preromantica in Gaetano Pugnani', *Chigiana*, xvi (1959), 17–26

W. S. Newman: *The Sonata in the Classic Era* (Chapel Hill, 1963, rev. 2/1972)

S. McVeigh: *The Violinist in London's Concert Life, 1750–1784: Felice Giardini and his Contemporaries* (diss., U. of Oxford, 1980)

BORIS SCHWARZ

Pugni, Cesare (*b* Genoa, 31 May 1802; *d* St Petersburg, 26 Jan 1870). Italian composer. From 1815 to 1822 he studied in Milan, with Rolla (violin) and Asioli (composition) among his teachers. In 1823 he contributed to the ballet *Kenilworth* performed at La Scala, but *Elerz e*

Zulmida in 1826 was the first wholly by him. In the following years he specialized in this genre, but from 1831 to 1834 attempted opera with a series of five works which began successfully with *Il disertore svizzero* and ended with the fiasco of *Un episodio di San Michele*. In this period, and rather unusually for an Italian composer, he also composed orchestral music, publishing two sinfonias, both in one movement and one of them for two orchestras in canon. From 1832 to 1834 he was *maestro al cembalo* and music director at La Scala. Then, however, he left, in disgrace (allegedly because of a passion for gambling), and he spent some years in poverty in Paris, where he was briefly associated with Bellini. In 1843 he began a long collaboration with the celebrated choreographer Jules Perrot, which resulted in more than 30 ballets, principally for Her Majesty's Theatre in London (under Benjamin Lumley). Some of these have remained famous (*Ondine*, 1843; *La Esmeralda*, 1844; *Pas de quatre*, 1845; *Catarina, ou La fille du bandit*, 1846; *Le jugement de Pâris*, 1846), and some are still performed. Other important productions resulted from collaborations with Cerrito, Saint-Léon, Paul Taglioni and Petipa. In 1851 Pugni went to St Petersburg as ballet composer to the imperial theatres. There he produced some 35 works, including revivals of former successes and new ones, such as *Doch Faraona* ('Pharoah's daughter'), 1862, and *Konyok gorbunyok* ('The little hump-backed horse'), 1864.

The reasons for Pugni's success can be found in the *brio*, the imaginative fancy and the expressive quality of his music, rather than in its style, also in its subservience to the functional requirements of the choreography, a subservience which is, at the same time, its greatest artistic limitation. The ballets to which Pugni contributed all or part of the music are said to number more than 300.

WORKS
BALLETS
Only those published in piano excerpts or, where stated, complete piano score

Perf. Milan, La Scala, pubd Milan: Elerz e Zulmida (L. Henry), 6 May 1826 (?1827); Edoardo III, ossia L'assedio di Calais (Henry), 15 Feb 1827, with music by Rossini, Mozart, Meyerbeer (1827); Pellia e Mileto (S. Taglione), 28 May 1827 (1827); Agamennone (G. Galzerani), 1 Sept 1828 (1828, 1832); Adelaide di Francia (Henry), 26 Dec 1829 (1830); Guglielmo Tell (Henry), 19 Feb 1833 (1833); Monsieur de Chalumeaux (Galzerani), 14 Jan 1834 (1834)

Perf. London, Her Majesty's, pubd London: Ondine, ou La naïade (J. Perrot, F. Cerrito), 22 June 1843, complete (1844); La Esmeralda (Perrot), 9 March 1844 (London, Milan, 1845); Eoline, ou La dryade (Perrot), 8 March 1845 (1845); Kaya, ou L'amour voyageur (Perrot, J. Weiss), 17 April 1845 (1845); Catarina, ou La fille du bandit (Perrot), 3 March 1846 (1846), as perf. La Scala, 1847, with addl music by G. Bajetti, complete (Milan, 1847); Lalla Rookh, or The Rose of Lahore (Perrot), 11 June 1846, collab. F. David (1846); Le jugement de Pâris (Perrot), 23 July 1846 (1846); Coralia, ou Le chevalier inconstant (P. Taglioni), 16 Feb 1847 (1847); Fiorita et la reine des elfrides (Taglioni), 19 Feb 1848 (1848); Les métamorphoses (Taglioni), 12 March 1850 (1850)

Stella, ou Les contrebandiers (A. Saint-Léon), Paris, Opéra, 22 Feb 1850, complete (Paris, 1850)

Perf. St Petersburg, Bol'shoy: Voyna zhenshchin [The women's war, or The amazons of the 9th century] (Perrot), 23 Nov 1852, as Wlasta l'amazzone del IX secolo, ossia La guerra delle donne (Milan, ?1855); Faust (Perrot), 14 Feb 1854 (Moscow, n.d.); Doch Faraona [Pharoah's daughter] (M. Petipa), 30 Jan 1862, complete (St Petersburg, n.d.); Théolinda l'orpheline, ou Le lutin de la vallée (A. Saint-Léon), 18 Dec 1862, complete (St Petersburg, n.d.); Konyok gorbunyok, ili Tsar-devitsa [The little hump-backed horse, or the Tsar's daughter] (Saint-Léon), 15 Dec 1864, complete (St Petersburg, ?1864)

OPERAS
Il disertore svizzero, o La nostalgia (melodramma, 2, F. Romani), Milan, Cannobiana, 28 May 1831; vocal score (Milan, 1831)

La vendetta (melodramma tragico, 2, C. Bassi), Milan, La Scala, 11 Feb 1832; autograph *I-Mr*
Ricciarda di Edimburgo (dramma serio, 2, Bassi), Trieste, Grande, 29 Sept 1832
Il contrabbandiere (melodramma, 2, Romani), Milan, Cannobiana, 13 June 1833; autograph *Mr*, excerpts, pf acc. (Milan, ?1833)
Un episodio di San Michele (melodramma giocoso, 2, Romani), Milan, Cannobiana, 14 June 1834

OTHER WORKS
Vocal: c40 masses; other sacred music; Inno alla beneficenza, Milan, La Scala, spr. 1833; songs, some pubd Milan, London
Inst: Sinfonia, D, in canon (Milan, n.d.); Sinfonia, E (Milan, n.d.); pf pieces, pubd London; others

BIBLIOGRAPHY
C. W. Beaumont: *A History of Ballet in Russia (1613–1881)* (London, 1930)
I. Guest: *The Romantic Ballet in England: its Development, Fulfilment and Decline* (London, 1954, 2/1972)
——: *The Ballet of the Second Empire 1847–1858* (London, 1955)
——: *Fanny Cerrito: the Life of a Romantic Ballerina* (London, 1956)
V. Ottolenghi and D. S. Fryer: 'Pugni, Cesare', *ES* [with list of principal ballets]
I. Guest: 'Cesare Pugni', *Dance Gazette* (1979), no.1, p.22

ANDREA LANZA

Pugno, (Stéphane) Raoul (*b* Montrouge, nr. Paris, 23 June 1852; *d* Moscow, 3 Jan 1914). French pianist, teacher and composer. He made his début as a pianist in 1858, and with financial help from Prince Poniatowski he then studied at the Ecole Niedermeyer. From 1866 to 1869 he was a student at the Conservatoire, where he won a *premier prix* for the piano (1866), harmony (1867) and the organ (1869) and a *première médaille* for solfège (1867). However, as an Italian citizen, he could not compete for the Prix de Rome. He took an active part in the Commune of 1871 and in May was made music director of the Opéra. On the fall of the Commune he escaped any retribution and in 1872 became organist and in 1878 choirmaster at the church of St Eugène, a post he held until 1892. In 1874 he also became choirmaster at the Théâtre Ventadour. From 1892 to 1896 he was professor of harmony at the Conservatoire and from 1896 to 1901 professor of the piano there. In 1893 he resumed his concert career and was soon recognized as perhaps the leading French pianist of the time. Excelling in the music of Mozart, Chopin and Franck, which he did much to popularize, he was noted for his lightness of touch and for his extremely flexible and polished technique, demonstrated in the recordings made in 1903 for the Gramophone and Typewriter Co. in Paris. He was also an excellent chamber music player, and his recitals with Ysaÿe, which began in 1896, were celebrated. An early exponent of Wagner in France, he and Debussy provided the two-piano accompaniment for a famous concert performance of parts of *Das Rheingold* on 6 May 1893. He composed, mostly before resuming his concert career, a considerable number of stage works in the lighter genres and salon music, now forgotten, but created a more lasting influence through his many piano pupils.

WORKS

DRAMATIC
Unless otherwise indicated, all first performed Paris and published there shortly afterwards in complete vocal score or excerpts

Comic operas: Ninette (A. Hennequin, A. Bisson), 1883; Le sosie (A. Valabrègue, H. Keroul), 1887; Le valet de coeur (P. Ferrier, C. Clairville), 1888; Le retour d'Ulysse (F. Carré), 1889
Vaudevilles and operettas: A qui la troupe, Asnières, 1877, unpubd; La brigue Dondaine, 1886; La vocation de Marius (Carré, A. Debelly), 1890; La petite Poucette (Hennequin, M. Ordonneau), 1891
Ballets and pantomimes: La fée cocotte (G. Marot, E. Phillipe), 1881; Les papillons, London, 1884; Viviane (E. Gondinet), 1886, collab. C.

Lippacher; La danseuse de corde (A. Scholl, J. Rocques), 1892; Pour le drapeau, 1895; Le chevalier aux fleurs (A. Silvestre), 1897, collab. A. Messager, unpubd; Mélusine, unpubd; Les pauvres gens, unpubd Incidental music: Les rois en exil (P. Delair), 1883; La città morta (La ville morte) (G. d'Annunzio), completed by N. Boulanger, unpubd La résurrection de Lazare (oratorio, E. Favin, C. Grandmougin), 1879

OTHER WORKS

Sonata, d, pf (Paris, 1873); Concertstück, pf, orch (Paris, 1900); numerous pf pieces and songs, pubd Paris
Pedagogical works: L'art de travailler le piano, i: Etude des gammes (Paris, 1908), collab. C. Bresselle; Les leçons écrites de R. Pugno: Chopin (Paris, 1910; Eng. trans., 1911)

BIBLIOGRAPHY

C. Pierre: Le Conservatoire national de musique et de déclamation (Paris, 1900)
H. Imbert: Médaillons contemporains (Paris, 1902) [with list of works]
C. Mauclair: 'Devant la tombe de Pugno', Essais sur l'émotion musicale, ii: Les héros de l'orchestre (Paris, 1919), 110ff
E. Berteaux: En ce temps-là (souvenirs) (Paris, 1946)
G. Samazeuilh: Musiciens de mon temps (Paris, 1947)
H. C. Schonberg: The Great Pianists (New York, 1963)
GUY BOURLIGUEUX

Puhel, Christoph. See BUEL, CHRISTOPH.

Pühler, Johann (b Schwandorf, Oberpfalz, before c1550; d ?c1591). German singer, teacher and publisher. There is evidence that he was a singer in the court chapel of Emperor Ferdinand I at Vienna from 1557 to 1564. From 1564 to 1569 he served in a similar capacity at the court of Archduke Ferdinand of the Tyrol, who transferred his household from Prague to Innsbruck late in 1566. He sang tenor at the court of Duke Wilhelm in Landshut in 1573 and from 1580 he held an appointment as organist and schoolmaster in Regensburg. He was active as a publisher and brought out two sets of compositions by his friend C. Hollander, Newe teutsche, geistliche und weltliche Liedlein (1570) and Triciniorum . . . fasciculus (1573), and a miscellaneous collection of German songs, Schöner ausserlessner geistlicher und weltlicher teutscher Lieder (1585). He also published chansons by Lassus, reputedly his teacher, under the title of Etliche ausserlessne kurtze gute geistliche und weltliche Liedlein (1582); the translation that he provided leaves something to be desired. An MS transcription by Pühler dating from about 1590 was published at Regensburg in 1875 by J. Renner under the title Auswahl deutscher Madrigale von Meistern des 16. Jahrhunderts. It is possible that Pühler was related to the 16th-century composer W. Pühler whose litanies are extant in MSS and in a Munich print dated 1596.

BIBLIOGRAPHY

A. Sandberger, ed.: R. de Lassus: Kompositionen mit französischen Texten, Sämtliche Werke, xii (Leipzig, 1901), p.xxix
B. A. Wallner: Musikalische Denkmäler der Steinätzkunst des 16. und 17. Jahrhunderts (Munich, 1912)
W. Senn: Musik und Theater am Hof zu Innsbruck (Innsbruck, 1954)
W. Boetticher: Orlando di Lasso und seine Zeit, i (Kassel, 1958)
RENATE FEDERHOFER-KÖNIGS

Pui. See PUY.

Puig, Bernardo Calvo (b Vich, 22 Feb 1819; d Barcelona, 1880). Spanish composer. He studied music as a choirboy at Vich Cathedral with José Gallés, whom he succeeded as organist; he later became assistant maestro de capilla there. After further studies in Barcelona he was appointed organist at the church of Nuestra Señora del Pino, and later maestro de capilla of Barcelona Cathedral. In 1853 he was made director of the Escolanía de la Merced. He was a prolific composer: 40 masses and many other sacred works by him are extant in MS at Barcelona Cathedral; his secular compositions include operas and zarzuelas.

ANTONIO IGLESÍAS

Puig, Guillermo de. See PODIO, GUILLERMO DE.

Puilloys, Johannes. See PULLOIS, JOHANNES.

Puishnov, Lev. See POUISHNOV, LEV.

Pujman, Ferdinand (b Nižkov, Bohemia, 23 May 1889; d Prague, 17 Dec 1961). Czech opera producer and writer on music. While studying engineering in Prague he attended Nejedlý's music lectures and later joined Nejedlý's circle, contributing to Smetana and writing reviews for the daily Samostatnost. He was able to put his theories on opera production into practice when he left engineering to become opera producer at the Brno Theatre (1920) and the Prague National Theatre (1921). Here he began a fruitful collaboration with the musical director Otakar Ostrčil; over the next 36 years he produced 88 operas. His spare style, omitting inessentials and making more use of space, motion and lighting resources, had a profound influence on Czech opera production. Pujman also lectured at the conservatory and, after the war, at the academy (AMU), where in his student productions he was able to explore a more adventurous repertory than at the National Theatre. He wrote the libretto for Hába's opera Nová země ('The new country') and translated many Russian vocal texts.

WRITINGS

Lisztovská myšlenka [Lisztian thought] (Prague, 1916)
K zpěvoherní dramaturgii [Operatic dramaturgy] (Prague, 1917)
Poznámky o dramaturgii smetanovských oper [Remarks on the production of Smetana's operas] (Prague, 1919)
Operní sloh Národního divadla [The operatic style of the National Theatre] (Prague, 1933)
Zhudebněná mateřština [The musical setting of one's mother tongue] (Prague, 1939)
Operní režie [Opera production] (Prague, 1940)
Stati o režii a dramaturgii zpívané hry [Essays on the production and dramaturgy of the sung play] (Prague, 1958)

BIBLIOGRAPHY

F. Pala: 'Ferdinand Pujman', HRo, vii (1954), 385
V. Pospíšil: 'Režisér-myslitel' [Producer-thinker], HRo, xiv (1961), 944
——: 'Ferdinand Pujman a moderní režie' [Ferdinand Pujman and modern production], HRo, xvii (1964), 499
List of productions, writings and further bibliography in ČSHS
JOHN TYRRELL

Pujol, David (b Pont de Armentera, Tarragona, 11 April 1894). Spanish musicologist. In 1903 he joined the choir of the monastery of Montserrat as a choirboy, and later became a monk there. He studied sol-fa and piano with Juan Bautista Guzmán, Gregorian chant with Gregorio María Suñol, and composition with Gibert and Barberá. He was director of the boys' choir, and later choirmaster of the monastery. Since 1953 he has lived in Medellin, Columbia. His main work was founding the series Mestres de l'Escolania de Montserrat, of which he published five volumes between 1930 and 1936, and which has recently restarted publication. He has also published Estudios de canto gregoriano (Montserrat, 1955) and numerous articles on sacred music, particularly in the journal Música sacra española, of which he was a director, and in Anuario musical.

EDITIONS
J. Cererols: Obras completas, MEM, i–iii, vi (1930–32, 1975)
Música instrumental, MEM, iv–v (1934–6)

JOSÉ LÓPEZ-CALO

Pujol, Francisco (*b* Barcelona, 15 May 1878; *d* Barcelona, 24 Dec 1945). Spanish choirmaster and composer. He studied solfège and the piano with Font and Buye at the Conservatorio del Liceo, Barcelona, and took composition lessons with Millet. Much of his work centred on the Orfeó Català, which he joined in 1897: in 1900 he was appointed assistant teacher to the conductor and, when the Palau de Musica Catalana was opened as the choir's home, he became administrator and librarian; shortly thereafter he was appointed assistant conductor, succeeding Millet as conductor in 1941. He was also choirmaster of S Felipe Neri from 1902 and of Nuestra Señora de la Merced from 1906. Following the principles of Pius X's *Motu proprio*, he contributed to the dignifying of church music, both in his own works and through promoting the use of Renaissance polyphony. He was president of the Barcelona section of the ISCM, a member of the Spanish Musicology Institute and editor of the folksong collection *Cancioner popular de Catalunya*. Apart from a great number of choral pieces – folksong arrangements as well as sacred and secular works – he produced numerous sardanas, other dances and a few concert instrumental compositions.

A. MENÉNDEZ ALEYXANDRE

Pujol, José (*b* Catalonia; *fl* 1734–98). Catalan composer. In about 1739 he succeeded Francisco Valls as *maestro de capilla* of Barcelona Cathedral. In October 1738 he and other eminent church musicians in Barcelona criticized Bernardo Comes y de Puig's *Fragmentos músicos* (Barcelona, 1739). His most important compositions (main source: *E-Bc*) are 11 oratorios (*La nave del mercader*, 1734, *Hermosa nube del día*, 1745, and *El triunfo de Fael*, 1755, all performed at the Iglesia de Belén in Barcelona; *Ab arce sublimi*, 1750; *De un enigma*, 1762; *Que caiga, que muera*, 1768; *El Juicio particular*, 1770; *El cielo iluminado*, 1771; *La casta Susana*, 1798; *San Felipe Neri*; *Santo Tomás*); three masses and two villancicos also survive (*Bc*).

BIBLIOGRAPHY
LaborD
M. Soriano Fuertes: *Historia de la música española*, iv (Madrid, 1859)
B. Saldoni: *Diccionario biográfico-bibliográfico de efemérides de músicos españoles*, iv (Madrid, 1881)
J. R. Carreras: *El oratorio musical desde su origen hasta nuestros días* (Barcelona, 1906)
R. Mitjana y Gordón: 'La musique en Espagne', *EMDC*, I/iv (1920)
M. Querol: 'Pujol, José', *MGG*

Pujol, Juan (Pablo) (*b* Barcelona, *c*1573; *d* Barcelona, May 1626). Spanish composer. On 19 November 1593 Pujol became *maestro de canto* at Tarragona Cathedral and on 23 January 1596 organist at El Pilar, Saragossa. In March of that year he went to Jaca to receive minor orders, and he became a priest in August 1600. From 1612 until his death he was choirmaster at Barcelona Cathedral: among other duties, he was required to evaluate the music published in liturgical books in the diocese, to attend to the choirboys and to direct the chapel of S Jorge.

Pujol was an exceedingly prolific composer of sacred music. A series of Advent motets written at Tarragona has been lost, and most of his surviving works date from his Barcelona period, when it was his duty to compose a specified number of masses, motets, psalms and villancicos each year. The masses are in the contrapuntal style of the 16th century, particularly in Kyrie, Sanctus and Agnus movements, which are usually related through the use of common opening material; imitation by inversion is particularly frequent. Music for longer texts (psalms, Gloria, Credo) is predominantly more homophonic and features irregular speech rhythms. This is specially true of polychoral works, which are notable for highly resourceful antiphonal and rhythmic effects. Pujol was unusually successful in the treatment of psalm-tone cantus firmi. His secular works reflect the popular style of the early 17th century.

WORKS

Editions: *J. Pujol: Opera omnia*, ed. H. Anglès, PBC, iii, vii (1926–32) [A]
          Cancionero musical y poético del siglo XVII, ed. J. Aroca (Madrid, 1916) [Ar]
          Musica barroca española: polyfonía profana, ed. M. Querol, MME, xxxii (1970) [Q]

SACRED

13 masses, 4, 8vv, *E-Bc*, *Bsm*, *G*; 5 in A
8 Magnificat, 4, 8vv, *Bc*, *CAR*, *MO*; 3 in A
6 Nunc dimittis, 4, 8vv, *Bc*, *Bsm*, *CAR*; 3 in A
12 antiphons, 4, 8vv, *Bc*, *Bsm*, *CAR*, *MO*; 2 in A
12 responsories, 4, 8vv, *Bc*, *Boc*, *Bsm*, *VAcp* (anon.); 2 in A
2 Litaniae BVM, 4, 8vv, *Bca*, *Zs* (anon.)
1 sequence, 8vv, *Bsm*
74 psalms, incl. vesper psalms, 4, 7, 8vv, *Bc*, *Bca*, *Bsm*, *MO*; 27 in A
9 motets, 4, 8vv, *Bc*, *Boc*, *Bsm*, *CAR*, *MO*
11 hymns, 4, 6, 8vv, *Bc*, *Bca*, *Boc*, *Bsm*; 3 in A
3 Lamentations, 4vv, *Boc*, *Bsm*
9 passion settings, 4vv, *Bc*, *Boc*, *G* (inc.)
19 sacred villancicos (1 inc.), 1 responsión, 1 tonada, 4, 6, 8vv: *Bc*, *MO*

SECULAR

12 romances, 3, 4vv, *E-Mn*, *I-Rc*; 4 in Ar
2 letrillas, 3vv, Ar (see Pelinski)
1 liras, 3vv, Q
1 folía, 3vv, *I-Rc*
1 novenas, 3vv, Ar
1 tono, 4vv, Q
16 other works, 3, 4vv, *E-Gp*, *Mn*; 3 in Q

BIBLIOGRAPHY
R. Mitjana y Gordón: 'Comentarios y apostillos al "Cancionero poético y musical del siglo XVII", recogido por Claudio de la Sablonara y publicado por D. Jesús Aroca', *Revista de filología española*, vi (1919), 14–56, 233–67
H. Anglès: Introduction and bibliographical notes to *J.Pujol: Opera omnia*, PBC, iii (1926)
M. Querol: 'El cancionero musical de Olot', *AnM*, xviii (1963), 57
R. A. Pelinski: *Die weltliche Vokalmusik Spaniens am Anfang des 17. Jahrhunderts: der Cancionero de la Sablonara* (Tutzing, 1971)
P. Calahorra Martínez: 'Juan Pujol, maestro de capilla de música de la iglesia de Santa Teresa la Mayor y del Pilar de Zaragoza desde 1595 a 1612', *Tesoro sacro musical*, lxi (1978), 67

BARTON HUDSON

Pujol Vilarrubí, Emilio (*b* Granadella, 7 April 1886). Spanish guitarist, vihuelist, musicologist and composer. At the age of nine he entered the Municipal School of Music in Barcelona, where he studied solfège with Amadeo Badía and the bandurria with Miguel Ramos, making such rapid progress that before he was 12 he gave two bandurria concerts in Paris (1898): in the presence of the president of the French Republic, Felix Fauré, and for the Spanish Queen Isabel II. In 1900 he took up the guitar, studying with the distinguished concert performer Francisco Tárrega (1902–9), and then studied composition with Augustín Campo in Madrid. His performing career began with concerts in Madrid and London (1912); he first toured South America in 1919 and Europe in 1921, and established an international reputation. He gave the first performance of

Falla's *Homenaje a Debussy* in Paris (1922) and of Paganini's guitar quartets (London, 1934). At a memorable concert in the Salle Erard in Paris (1927) he played works by Spanish vihuelists.

From the beginning Pujol Vilarrubí united his performing with research on the technique and history of the guitar, giving numerous lecture recitals. Later he extended his interest to teaching: he was appointed professor of the vihuela at Barcelona Conservatory in 1945 and gave regular courses in the vihuela and Spanish guitar at Lisbon Conservatory (1946–69); he taught the vihuela and early music at the Chigiana Academy, Siena (1953–63), where he also founded the international 'Matilde Cuervas' vihuela competition in memory of his wife; and in 1965 at Cervera-Lérida he began the international courses in the guitar, lute and vihuela, which are extremely popular. He advocated using the flesh of the fingers (rather than the nails) to pluck the strings, and as a result the quality of tone production in classical guitar performance has greatly improved. Pujol Vilarrubí's work as a musicologist remains definitive, both in its usefulness to general readers and in its more scholarly aspects. His outstanding achievements are his editions of early Spanish vihuelists, the account of his technique in his monumental *Escuela razonada de la guitarra* and *El dilema del sonido en la guitarra* and his biography of Tárrega. He has composed several pieces for guitar (mainly studies and dances), many of which appeared in *Bibliothèque de musique ancienne et moderne pour guitarre* (Paris, 1927–), which also contains his arrangements for two guitars of pieces by Albéniz, Granados, Paganini and Pedrell, as well as works for the vihuela from the Spanish classics.

WRITINGS

'La guitare', *EMDC*, II/iii (1927), 1997–2035
El dilema del sonido en la guitarra (Buenos Aires, 1934, 3/1971)
Escuela razonada de la guitarra (Buenos Aires, 1934–) [in Sp. and Fr.]
Estudios para guitarra, grado superior (Barcelona, 1946)
'Significación de Joan Carlos Amat (1572–1642) en la historia de la guitarra', *AnM*, v (1950), 125
'Les ressources instrumentales et leur rôle dans la musique pour vihuela et pour guitarre au XVIe siècle et au XVIIe', *La musique instrumentale de la Renaissance: CNRS Paris 1954*, 205
Tárrega: ensayo biográfico (Lisbon, 1960)
'El Maestro Pedrell: la vihuela y la guitarra', *AnM*, xxvii (1972), 47
Guía para la interpretación de los estudios de Sor (in preparation)
Tablaturas para vihuela, laúd y guitarra del Barroco (in preparation)

EDITIONS

Bibliothèque de musique ancienne et moderne pour guitarre (Paris, 1927–)
L. de Narváez: *Los seis libros del Delfín de Música de cifra para tañer vihuela*, MME, iii (1945)
A. Mudarra: *Tres libros de música en cifra para vihuela*, MME, vii (1949)
Hispaniae citharae ars viva (Mainz, 1955)
E. de Valderrábano: *Libro de música de vihuela, intitulado Silva de Sirenas*, MME, xxii–xxiii (1965)

BIBLIOGRAPHY

J. Riera: *Emilio Pujol* (Lérida, 1974)

JOSÉ LÓPEZ-CALO

Pukhal'sky, Vladimir (Vyacheslavovich) (*b* Minsk, 2 April 1848; *d* Kiev, 23 Feb 1933). Ukrainian pianist and teacher. He graduated from Leschetizky's class at St Petersburg Conservatory in 1874 and taught the piano there (1874–6). In 1876 he moved to Kiev, where the following year he became director of and a teacher at the music school of the Russian Musical Society. Pukhal'sky played an important part in making Kiev a major musical centre; the provincial music school developed into one of the best conservatories in the country. He was director for two years, from its opening in 1913, and then taught the piano there until his death. An excellent pianist whose playing was distinguished for its classical purity, elegance and perfection of finger technique, Pukhal'sky proved an outstanding teacher. Among his pupils were Horowitz, Brailovsky, Leonid Nikolayev, Boleslav Yavorsky, Konstantis Mikhaylov and Grigory Kogan. Pukhal'sky also composed and worked as a music critic in Kiev (1890–1900).

BIBLIOGRAPHY

G. Kurkovsky: 'V. V. Pukhal'sky i G. N. Beklemishev', *Kievskaya konservatoriya: nauchnometodicheskiye zapiski … sbornik 1956* (Kiev, 1957)
G. Kogan: 'Moy uchitel' V. V. Pukhal'sky', *Izbrannïye stat'i* (Moscow, 2/1972)

I. M. YAMPOL'SKY

Pulgar Vidal, Francisco Bernardo (*b* Huánuco, Peru, 12 March 1929). Peruvian composer. He began his musical studies (piano and violin) in Lima, and then studied harmony, counterpoint and orchestration with Andrés Sas. He also studied fugue and composition, with special attention to dodecaphony, with Roberto Pineda Duque in Bogotá. He received the degree of Professor of Music at the Lima National Conservatory, and graduated as a lawyer at the Universidad Mayor de San Marcos, where he also completed studies in art and literature. He twice received the Dunker Lavalle Prize for composition, and in 1971 his cantata *Apu Inqa* won him the only prize at the Choral–Symphonic Composition Contest, organized on the occasion of the 150th anniversary of Peruvian Independence.

Pulgar Vidal belongs to the generation of composers which, during the 1950s, moved away from the exotic trend based on native Indian material. The pre-Hispanic musical culture of Peru is looked upon by these composers quite differently. They are equally concerned with the most advanced contemporary tendencies, using polytonal, polyrhythmic or aleatory elements. Indigenous musical instruments (*antaras*, *putatos*, etc) are used to produce microtones and unusual sonorities. Pulgar Vidal believes that there is no need to draw from folk sources, and above all from the outdated Inca pentatonicism, in order to affirm Peruvian originality.

WORKS

(selective list)

CHAMBER AND INSTRUMENTAL

5 Preludes, pf, 1951; Str Qt no.1, 1953; Str Qt no.2, 1955; 3 Movimientos obstinados, pf, 1955; Taki [Dance] no.1, pf, 1956, arr. str orch, 1960; Pf Sonata, 1958; Paco Yungque, pf, 1960; 3 Piezas, pf, 1964; Detenimientos, 6 pieces, vn, pf, 1967; Takiy Ninchic [Our Song], 60 pieces, pf, 1972

OTHER WORKS

Vocal: 3 Poemas líricos (Quechua, trans. J. M. Arguedas), chorus, 1955; Los jircas (E. L. Albújar), chorus, 1966; 11 piezas corales (Peruvian trad.), chorus, 1968; Vallejiana no.1 (C. Vallejo), 1v, pf, 1969; Apu Inqa (Quechua, trans. T. Meneses), S, reciter, chorus, orch, 1970
Orch: Suite mística (Danzas mestizas), chamber orch, 1956; Chulpas, 7 estructuras sinfónicas, 1968

Principal publishers: Anacrusa, Nueva Música

CÉSAR ARRÓSPIDE DE LA FLOR

Puliaschi, Giovanni [Gian, Giovan] **Domenico** (*b* Rome; *fl* early 17th century). Italian composer, singer and chitarrone player. He entered the papal chapel as a tenor and as a chaplain on 3 May 1612, and he was also a canon of S Maria in Cosmedin, Rome. He was by all accounts one of the most remarkable singers of his time. As he mentioned in a short essay on singing at the end of his *Musiche varie* (1618), he could sing both tenor and bass. He visited the Florentine court in January and February 1620, and an admiring report of his singing there (together with Francesca Caccini and her children) states that he could sing alto as well as tenor and bass and could also play the chitarrone. He is presumably the 'Giovanni Domenico' whom Giustiniani praised as one of the best tenors and basses of his time, and it may have been for him that Caccini composed the two 'arie particolari', covering both tenor and bass ranges, which appear in his *Nuove musiche e nuova maniera di scriverle* (1614).

Apart from a song in *RISM* 1621[14] all of Puliaschi's known music is contained in his *Gemma musicale* for solo voice and continuo (Rome, 1618[13]), which, since it contained so many misprints, he caused to have reprinted about a month later as *Musiche varie* (Rome, 1618[14]); both editions include seven solo motets by G. F. Anerio, who, dedicating the *Gemma* to Puliaschi, commended his 'most beautiful voice' and his songs and stated that he wrote his motets specially for Puliaschi to sing. Puliaschi's own contribution consists of six sectional sonnet settings, four ottava settings over the romanesca, four sets of strophic variations and two madrigals, together with a further madrigal by 'N.' (?G. B. Nanino) to which he provided elaborate embellishments. These contents are typical of Roman songbooks of the period, as are the nobility of the strophic variations and the dullness of some of the other pieces. What is exceptional is the extraordinary virtuosity of some of the songs. Since all are in the tenor or bass clef Puliaschi must have written them to sing himself, and their two most spectacular features – the many leaps, sometimes of two octaves, down to very low notes (on occasion prompted by the words) and the chains of roulades, harking back in their inexpressiveness to the diminutions of the 16th century – are no doubt those that best showed off Puliaschi's phenomenal powers; only a singer of comparable gifts could rescue such music from the contrived and enervating effect it presents on the page, and indeed a reason for publishing it, connected with Puliaschi's concern to have it printed accurately, may have been so that those who had heard his performances could have a record of them. In the concluding essay already referred to (reprinted in Gaspari) he to some extent explained his technique and made other interesting observations about singing that are worth reading in conjunction with Caccini's famous essay in his *Le nuove musiche* (1601/2).

BIBLIOGRAPHY

V. Giustiniani: *Discorso sopra la musica de'suoi tempi* (MS, *I-La*, 1628); in A. Solerti: *Le origini del melodramma* (Turin, 1903/R1969), 110; Eng. trans., MSD, ix (1962), 71
A. Adami: *Osservazioni per ben regolare il coro dei cantori della cappella pontificia* (Rome, 1711), 194
G. Gaspari: *Catalogo della biblioteca del Liceo musicale di Bologna*, iii (Bologna, 1893/R1961), 155f
A. Solerti: *Musica, ballo e drammatica alla corte medicea dal 1600 al 1637* (Florence, 1905/R1968), 152
E. Celani: 'I cantori della cappella pontificia nei secoli XVI–XVIII', *RMI*, xiv (1907), 771
N. Fortune: *Italian Secular Song from 1600 to 1635: the Origins and Development of Accompanied Monody* (diss., U. of Cambridge, 1954)
——: 'Italian 17th-century Singing', *ML*, xxxv (1954), 206
J. Racek: *Stilprobleme der italienischen Monodie* (Prague, 1965), 16, 74, 124, 135, 158, 197f, 211
H. W. Hitchcock: 'Caccini's "Other" *Nuove musiche*', *JAMS*, xxvii (1974), 451, 453

NIGEL FORTUNE

Puliti, Gabriello (*b* Montepulciano, nr. Arezzo, *c*1575; *d* Istria, between 1641 and 1644). Italian composer. He entered the Franciscan order before or at the time of his first appointment as an organist at the monastery at Pontremoli in 1600. In 1602 he was an organist at the monastery in Piacenza and in 1605 he took a similar post in Muggia, near Trieste. In 1609 he was in Koper, in Capodistria, in 1612 in Trieste, and in 1614 back in Capodistria; in 1616 he was in Pirano (now Piran), then in Albona (now Labin) in 1621, in Capodistria again in 1624 and between 1630 and 1638 in Trieste. His death is recorded in the acts of the Franciscan order for the province of Dalmatia, but the exact date and place are unknown. The appellation 'Accademico armonico detto l'Allegro' appears on the title-pages of a number of his works.

Puliti was a prolific composer. However, less than half of his output seems to survive: 15 of his published volumes are extant, and the latest known is marked as op.36. Sacred vocal music outnumbers collections of secular vocal and instrumental music. The quality of the surviving works varies. His early publications are those of an undistinguished beginner. He seems to have been slow in accepting the monodic style, his first known collection consisting entirely of monodies dating from 1618. At least three volumes in the same style followed in quick succession around 1620. These monodies show him at his best: they demonstrate a good sense of balance between syllabic and melismatic passages, although some of them show a bias towards virtuosity. Some of the madrigals in his *Baci ardenti* are in praise of the Archdukes Maximilian Ernst and Ferdinand II of Austria.

WORKS

SACRED

Sacrae modulationes, 4, 5vv (Parma, 1600)
Integra omnium solemnitatum vespertina psalmodia, 5vv (Milan, 1602)
Psalmodia vespertina, 4vv, bc, op.13 (Venice, 1614)
Sacri concentus, 1–3vv (Venice, 1614)
Pungenti dardi spirituali, 1v, bc, op.20 (Venice, 1618)
Lilia convallium B.M.V.: libro terzo delli concerti, 1v, bc, op.22 (Venice, 1620)
Sacri accenti: libro quarto delli concerti, 1v, bc (Venice, 1620)
Il secondo libro delle messe, 4vv, op.30 (Venice, 1620)
Salmi dominicali concertati con il Magnificat, 4vv, bc (org), op.36 (Venice, 1636)
Fragment of a mass, *PL-Kk*

SECULAR

Scherzi, capricci e fantasie per cantar, 2vv (Venice, 1605)
Baci ardenti: secondo libro de' madrigali, 5vv (Venice, 1609)
Ghirlanda odorifera . . . cioè mascherata, 3vv, libro I, (Venice, 1612)
Lunario armonico perpetuo calculato al meridiano et clima delle principali città d'Italia, 3vv, op.16 (Venice, 1615), inc.
Armonici accenti, 1v, bc, op.24 (Venice, 1621); 1 song ed. in Mw, xxxi (1968)
Fantasie, scherzi e capricci, vn, cornett, bc, op.19 (Venice, 2/1624), inc.

BIBLIOGRAPHY

G. Rádole: 'Musicisti a Trieste sul finire del cinquecento e nei primi del seicento', *Archeografo triestino*, 4th ser., xxii (lxxi) (1959), 1–32
——: 'Musica e musicisti in Istria nel cinque e seicento', *Atti e memorie della Società istriana di archeologia e storia patria*, new ser., xii (lxv) (1965), 147–214
D. Plamenac: 'Tragom Ivana Lukačića i nekih njegovih suvremenika', *Rad JAZU*, no.351 (1969), 63

BOJAN BUJIĆ

Puliti, Ornella. *See* SANTOLIQUIDO, ORNELLA.

Pullaer, Louis van (*b* Cambrai, *c*1475; *d* Cambrai, 21 Sept 1528). Flemish choir director and composer. In 1485 he was an *enfant de choeur* at Cambrai Cathedral, where he remained as a singer until 10 October 1494. By the middle of the following year, he had become the director of the children's choir at St Denis, Liège. He returned to Cambrai in 1503 and on 5 April assumed the directorship of the cathedral choir, replacing his former mentor, Denis de Hollain. On 23 April 1507 Pullaer was dismissed for neglect of his duties, but on 17 June 1507 he was appointed choir director at Notre Dame in Paris – a position he assumed on 16 July. In 1509 he received a benefice at St Germain l'Auxerrois, while in 1514 he took part as a singer in the funeral office for Anne of Brittany. He remained at Notre Dame until 1527, when he returned to Cambrai as a canon of the cathedral. His *Missa 'Christe resurgens'* for four voices (with the third Agnus Dei for five) (in *F-CA* 3) is a parody mass based on Richafort's motet *Christus resurgens* in which the pre-existent material is treated rather freely.

BIBLIOGRAPHY

J. Houdoy: *Histoire artistique de la cathédrale de Cambrai* (Lille, 1880/*R*1972)
F. L. Chartier: *L'ancien chapitre de Notre-Dame de Paris et sa maîtrise* (Paris, 1897/*R*1971)
A. Pirro: 'Dokumente über Antoine Brumel, Louis van Pullaer und Crispin van Stappen', *ZMw*, xi (1928–9), 349
J. Delporte: 'La messe "Christus resurgens" de Louis van Pulaer', *IMSCR, i Liège 1930*, 91
——, ed.: *Beilage zur Revue liturgique et musicale* (Paris, 1932) [contains an edn. of the mass]
J. Robijns: 'Pullaer, Louis van', *MGG*

ALLAN W. ATLAS

Pulli, Pietro (*b* Naples, *c*1710; *d* after *c*1759). Italian composer. He made his earliest known musical appearance in autumn 1731 by providing six arias for the revival, with much rewriting, of Vinci's *La mogliere fedele* (text, B. Saddumene; Naples, Teatro Nuovo), the libretto of which calls him 'famosissimo sonatore di arceliuti e contrapuntisto'. In other works he is named simply as Neapolitan *maestro di cappella*. He worked at least until 1734 in Naples, where he set the two dialect operas by Saddumene, *Li zitelle de lo vòmmero* and *La marina de Chiaja*, in 1731 and 1734 respectively, both at the Teatro dei Fiorentini. These works are of some historical interest, since they involve quasi-Arcadian settings, a new, scenographically decorative element.

The remainder of Pulli's operas were produced in north Italy, suggesting that the composer had moved there at least as early as 1739. He probably went first to Modena, where De Brosses found his music for the translation of De la Motte's comedy *Le carnaval et la folie* (*Il carnevale e la pazzia*, Teatro Ducale, carn. 1739–40) not at all to his Gallic taste; he grumbled that only a Pergolesi or a Hasse could have done justice to the play. Pulli's other operas, all serious, were *Le nozze del Piacere e dell'Allegria* (*festa teatrale*, Modena, Teatro Molza, carn. 1739–40); *Caio Marzio Coriolano* (Z. Seriman; Reggio Emilia, Teatro del Pubblico, 1741) – Pulli's most successful work, revived in Naples (1745), Venice (1747) and Modena (1750); *Zenobia* (Metastasio; Milan, Regio Ducal Teatro, 26 December 1748); *Il Demetrio* (Metastasio; the same, carn. 1749); *Vologeso re dei Parti* (Zeno; Modena, for the inauguration of the new Teatro di Corte, carn. 1750); and *Olimpiade* (Metastasio; Modena, Teatro di Corte, January 1751).

A number of arias and sinfonias by Pulli survive (in *B-Bc*, *F-Pn*, *GB-Lbm*, *I-Bc*, *Fc*, *MOe* and *S-Uu*). In addition there are four sonatas for flute and bass, dated 1759 (*I-Nc*). They are transitional in style, combining new and old-fashioned features. All are in three movements, medium–slow–fast; the slow movements are in contrasting keys, and two of them cadence on that key's dominant; the bass of one last movement is written partly in Alberti figuration. Harmonic rhythm is com-

paratively slow, and the composer shows an interesting predilection for the subdominant key area.

BIBLIOGRAPHY

C. de Brosses: *Lettres familières écrites d'Italie en 1739 et 1740* (Paris, 1799), letter to M de Neuilly, Mercredi des Cendres 1740
A. Gandini: *Cronistoria dei teatri di Modena dal 1539 al 1871* (Modena, 1873/*R*1969), i, 22f, 61; ii, 25f
M. Scherillo: *L'opera buffa napoletana durante il settecento: storia letteraria* (Naples, 1883, 2/1916/*R*1969), 171f
O. G. T. Sonneck: *Library of Congress: Catalogue of Opera Librettos printed before 1800* (Washington, DC, 1914/*R*1968), i, 769
V. Viviani: *Storia del teatro napoletano* (Naples, 1969), 294f

JAMES L. JACKMAN

Pullois [Pyllois, Pyloys, Pylloys, Piloys, Puilloys, Pylois, Pillays, Kieken], **Johannes** [Jehan, Jean] (*d* 23 Aug 1478). Netherlands composer. He sang in Antwerp Cathedral, 1442–7, and in 1447 was auditioned by Philip the Good for the Burgundian court chapel but was rejected: the document for this calls him 'maistre des enfans d'Anvers'. He sang in the papal chapel, perhaps as early as 1447, but certainly by 1453, until 1459. Following this he became a member of the Burgundian court chapel, terminating his service in 1463 when he returned to Antwerp. He remained in Antwerp until his death, with the exception of visits to Rome in 1468 and 1469. Besides serving as a member of the Illustrious Confraternity of Our Lady at 's-Hertogenbosch and as head of its chapter from 1476, Pullois served as canon of various churches in the diocese of Utrecht.

His compositions are preserved in a large number of 15th-century sources. The mass is complete in *I-TRmn* 87, but two versions of the Credo exist, of which that in this MS is modally at odds with the rest of the mass. The composer preferred treble-dominated and discant-tenor styles. Among the secular compositions are two with Dutch texts. Two intabulations of Pullois' music appear in the Buxheim Organbook (*D-Mbs*), and several other pieces are instrumental, or at least without text except for incipits. While the sacred compositions are basically in triple mensuration, the secular pieces are often cast in *tempus imperfectum*. The conservative nature of Pullois' compositions is underlined by the use of cadences typical of the earlier 15th century and by his predilection for three-voice structure.

WORKS

Edition: *J. Pullois: Opera omnia*, ed. P. Gülke, CMM, xli (1967)

SACRED

Kyrie, Gloria, Credo, Sanctus, Agnus Dei, 3vv (cyclic mass)
Gloria, 4vv (canonic)
Credo, 3vv (another version of the Cr above)
Flos de spina, 4vv
Globus igneus [= Quelque cose], 3vv
O beata Maria [= De madame], 3vv (anon. in source)
Resone unice genito [= Puisque fortune], 3vv
Victime paschali laudes, 3vv (Easter sequence; inc.)

SECULAR

De ma dame [= O beata Maria], 3vv (rondeau, anon. in source; inst arr. in Buxheim Organbook)
He n'esse pas, 3vv (rondeau)
Je ne puis, 3vv (textless, anon. in source)
La bonté du Saint Esperit, 3vv (sacred ballade)
Le serviteur, 3vv (uses superius of Dufay rondeau)
Les larmes, 3vv (textless)
Op eenen tijd, 3vv (anon. in source)
Pour prison, 3vv (textless; recalls Binchois rondeau)
Pour toutes fleurs, 3vv (rondeau; inst arr. in Buxheim Organbook)
Puisque fortune [= Resone unice genito], 3vv (rondeau)
Quelque cose [= Globus igneus], 3vv (rondeau)
Quelque langage, 3vv (rondeau)
Se ung bien peu, 3vv (rondeau; also in *F-Pn* 15123 and *Pthibault*, Nivelle de la Chaussée, with full text)
So lanc so meer, 3vv (text in German translation as So lang si mir in one source; also attrib. to W. Braxatoris)

BIBLIOGRAPHY

H. Osthoff: *Die Niederländer und das deutsche Lied* (Berlin, 1938/*R*1967)

J. Marix: *Histoire de la musique et des musiciens de la cour de Bourgogne* (Strasbourg, 1939/*R*1972)

J. du Saar: *Het leven en de composities van Jacobus Barbireau* (Utrecht, 1946)

T. Noblitt: 'Die Datierung der Handschrift Mus. ms. 3154 der Staatsbibliothek München', *Mf*, xxvii (1974), 36

G. R. K. Curtis: 'Jean Pullois and the Cyclic Mass – or a Case of Mistaken Identity?', *ML* (in preparation)

KEITH E. MIXTER

Pulsator organorum (Lat.: 'a beater of organs'). The term appears occasionally in 20th-century British literature on the organ together with the explanation that the cumbersome keys of the medieval organ could be depressed only by a blow of the fist. It had appeared earlier meaning simply a player of the organ, as in a number of late medieval references. The Latin verb *pulsare* (which means to beat not only in the sense of to strike but also in the sense of to palpitate) has in fact been associated since classical times with the playing of musical instruments. For example 'pulsare lyram' ('to play the lyre') was in common Roman usage with no connotation of heavy beating. This connotation may have been acquired in the 19th century, when its similarity to the German *Orgelschläger* was observed. The German phrase did indeed mean a beater of organs (it occurs in Johann Seidel's influential *Die Orgel und ihr Bau*, Breslau, 1843; Eng. trans., 1852). It follows a German tradition traceable back to Praetorius, who in his *Syntagma musicum*, ii (1619) claimed that the broad, stiff keys of old organs, such as the one at Halberstadt, could only be depressed by use of the player's fist. It is now believed that even if Praetorius was correct in this particular instance, the majority of medieval organs, whether equipped with the earlier slides or the later keys, were played with the fingers rather than the fist. This is borne out by overwhelming iconographic evidence, by whatever we know of the actual music played, by phrases occasionally encountered which refer to digital dexterity and by the absence of any reference before Praetorius to the striking of organs.

BIBLIOGRAPHY

E. J. Hopkins and E. F. Rimbault: *The Organ: its History and Construction* (London, 1855, enlarged 3/1877/*R*1965)

Ll. S. Lloyd: 'Pulsator organorum', *Grove 1–5*

F. Ll. Harrison: *Music in Medieval Britain* (London, 1958, 2/1963), 43, 160, 166, 177

W. Apel: *Geschichte der Orgel- und Klaviermusik bis 1700* (Kassel, 1967; Eng. trans., rev. 1972)

JAMES W. McKINNON

Pulver, Jeffrey (*b* London, 22 June 1884). English musicologist and violinist. He studied the violin with Ševčik in Prague for a year in 1904, and with Andreas Moser in Berlin in 1908. He made his début in Steinway Hall in 1910, but performing soon gave way to teaching and research. Between 1913 and 1939 he wrote over 170 books and articles on musical subjects, and gave six talks before the Musical Association, on topics ranging from string music and its composers to the music of ancient Egypt and the work of medieval theorists. He collaborated with J. F. Bridge in London while the latter was Gresham Professor of Music, undertaking research for him and illustrating his lectures with his playing. In 1958 blindness forced him to abandon his studies.

In his chief work, *A Biographical Dictionary of Old English Music*, he set out to document musicians and their output up to the death of Purcell. The book is typical of all his work in being notable for its scrupulous annotation of the facts with their sources. In this respect, his publications (though in many cases their content has now been superseded) are exemplary.

WRITINGS

'Music in England during the First Half of the Sixteenth Century', *MT*, lx (1919), 411, 534

A Dictionary of Old English Music and Musical Instruments (London, 1923/*R*1969)

Johannes Brahms (London, 1926)

A Biographical Dictionary of Old English Music (London, 1927/*R*1969) [repr. contains list of Pulver's writings]

'Music in Malory's "Arthur" ', *MMR*, lix (1929), 3

'The Viols in England', *IMSCR*, ii *Cambridge 1933*, 182

Paganini, the Romantic Virtuoso (London, 1936/*R*1970)

Machiavelli: the Man, his Work and his Times (London, 1937)

'Personal Contacts with Paganini and Spohr', *MT*, lxxx (1939), 579

DAVID SCOTT

Punctum. Of the several meanings of the word in classical Latin, 'point' or 'dot' was that which gave rise to the most common medieval usages (§§1 and 2 below). But in oratorical terminology 'punctum' also signified a short clause or brief section (Cicero: *Paradoxa stoicorum*, prooem. §2; *De oratore*, ii, §41, 177; Ausonius: *Idyllia*, 12, prooem.), and this meaning was also taken up by some medieval writers on music (§§3 and 4 below).

(1) In Western chant notations the *punctum* was a neume signifying a single note. It was nearly always written as a dot, and it usually represented a note lower than those on either side (*see* NEUMATIC NOTATIONS, Tables 1 and 2).

(2) A single note of music. 13th-century theorists used 'punctum' to mean not only a note written alone, but also a note joined to others in a ligature.

(3) From the mid-12th century 'punctum' is found in many monastic statutes, always in strictures regarding the phrasing of psalm-singing (*see* INFLECTION, §1). Here it seems to signify a unit less than a half-verse, i.e. a phrase or clause. The words 'punctatim' and 'punctando' mean 'in phrases', 'phrased', etc (see Van Dijk).

(4) In a well-known passage in the treatise by Anonymous IV, 'punctum' is used as the equivalent of CLAUSULA: '[Perotinus] fecit clausulas sive puncta plurima meliora'. This does not agree with classical usage, where 'clausula' had the quite specific and different meaning of 'cadence' (see, besides Cicero, Quintilian: *Institutio oratoria*; Quintilian did not use the term 'punctum'). Nor did theorists up to the middle of the 13th century equate *punctum* and clausula; for instance, the St Martial Anonymous (ed. Seay) used only (2) above, and Johannes de Garlandia likewise, although on one occasion he seems to have meant the tenor note in a piece of organum, implying a phrase of several notes in the duplum part above (Reimer, ii, 36f). The only places where 'punctum' signifies 'phrase' are in those parts of Johannes's treatise designated by Reimer as unauthentic. In the treatise by the Anonymous of St Emmeram (ed. Sowa) 'punctum' still means a single note. Anonymous IV, however, used both meanings side by side, sometimes in the same sentence (Reckow, i, 83, 1.7; 86, 1.20). He specifically identified 'punctum' as a term which instrumentalists used for clausula: 'quidam dicerent: post primam clausulam notarum, quod alii nominant proprie loquendo secundum operatores instrumentorum punctum, et dicerent tunc: post primum punctum' (Reckow, i, 56). 'Clausula' here had its less specific meaning of 'phrase'.

Johannes de Grocheo used 'punctum' to mean a

single note only once, and that in the expression 'finis punctorum', the vertical stroke denoting the end of a section in a composition (Rohloff, 1943, 55). But in his discussion of the textless *stantipes* (*see* ESTAMPIE and DUCTIA) he called the individual sections of these pieces *puncta* (singular *punctus*). He said that each *punctus* consists of two parts, identical except for their endings, called respectively *apertum* ('open') and *clausum* ('closed'). Grocheo seems to have thought six *puncta* were standard for the *stantipes* and three for the *ductia*, but he mentioned some *stantipes* of seven and some *ductiae* of four *puncta* (Rohloff, 1943, 52). Pieces such as these are not rare in medieval music (cf lai, *estampie* and *dansse real*) and the word 'punctus' itself is found by the various sections of two pieces in the Robertsbridge Manuscript (*GB-Lbm* Add.28550) exactly according to Grocheo's usage. The first piece has four *puncta*, the second five.

Both 'clausula' and 'punctum' survived in keyboard music. Several short exercises in a 15th-century Breslau manuscript (*PL-WRu* I F 687) are called 'clausula'; and six short imitative pieces in the 16th-century Mulliner Book (*GB-Lbm* Add.29996) are entitled 'Point'.

See also ANONYMOUS THEORETICAL WRITINGS; CLAUSULA; THEORY, THEORISTS.

BIBLIOGRAPHY

H. Sowa: *Ein anonymer glossierter Mensuraltraktat 1279* (Kassel, 1930)
E. Rohloff: *Der Musiktraktat des Johannes de Grochaeo*, Media latinitatis musica, ii (Leipzig, 1943)
S. J. P. van Dijk: 'Medieval Terminology and Methods of Psalmsinging', *MD*, vi (1952), 7
M. Huglo: 'Les noms des neumes et leur origine', *Etudes grégoriennes*, i (1954), 53
A. Seay: 'An Anonymous Treatise from St. Martial', *AnnM*, v (1957), 7–42
W. Waite: 'The Abbreviation of the Magnus Liber', *JAMS*, xiv (1961), 149
F. Reckow: *Der Musiktraktat des Anonymus 4* (Wiesbaden, 1967)
W. Apel: *Geschichte der Orgel- und Klaviermusik bis 1700* (Kassel, 1967; Eng. trans., rev. 1972)
E. Reimer: *Johannes de Garlandia: De mensurabili musica* (Wiesbaden, 1972)
E. Rohloff: *Die Quellenhandschriften zum Musiktraktat des Johannes de Grocheio* (Leipzig, 1972)
K.-J. Sachs: 'Punctus', *HMT* (1975)

DAVID HILEY

Giovanni Punto: engraving (1782) by S. C. Miger after C. N. Cochin

Punk rock. A type of rock music that developed in the 1970s; *see* POPULAR MUSIC, §III, 7.

Punktmusikschrift (Ger.). BRAILLE NOTATION.

Puntale (It.). ENDPIN.

Puntato (It.). Sometimes *puntato* means that notes are to be played staccato when indicated by 'points' (dots) above or below the notes in question. *Puntato* may also be used for 'dotted' notes in the sense of a dotted quaver (generally followed by a semiquaver). *See also* PIQUER.

Punteado (Sp.; Fr. *pincé*; It. *pizzicato*). The plucking of individual strings of the guitar with the right-hand fingertips, as opposed to RASGUEADO. The *punteado–rasgueado* dichotomy is especially appropriate to the works of the Baroque guitarists, who subdivided their technique into these two basic aspects: the *punteado* element was considered a derivation from lute technique, but *rasgueado* was considered to be indigenous and most natural to the instrument.

ROBERT STRIZICH

Punto, Giovanni [Stich, Johann Wenzel (Jan Václav)] (*b* Žehušice, nr. Čáslav, 28 Sept 1746; *d* Prague, 16 Feb 1803). Bohemian horn player and violinist. His master Count Thun sent him to study the horn, first under Josef Matiegka at Prague, then with Schindelarž at Munich; he completed his studies in Dresden under Hampel, whose recently introduced hand-stopping technique he later improved and extended, and under Haudek, who perfected his high register. After his return home (1763) he served the count for three years and then ran away with four colleagues, crossing the border into the Holy Roman Empire, where he assumed his Italian pseudonym. He began travelling through Europe in 1768, visiting England in 1770 or 1771 and again in 1777. Burney heard him at Koblenz in 1772. For a while he was employed by the prince of Hechingen, and in 1769–74 he was at the Mainz court. In Paris in 1778 he met Mozart, who was much impressed by his playing and composed for him and J. B. Wendling (flute), Friedrich Ramm (oboe) and G. W. Ritter (bassoon) the Sinfonia concertante KAnh.9/297B. In 1781 Punto was a member of the Prince-Archbishop of Würzburg's band, but in 1782 he returned to Paris in the service of the Count of Artois (later Charles X). In 1787 he visited a number of Rhineland towns and in the following year was engaged by Mme Mara to appear in her concerts at the Pantheon, London. From 1789 to 1799 he was again in Paris and under the Reign of Terror held the post of violinist–conductor at the Théâtre des Variétés Amusantes. In 1799 he went to Munich and in 1800 to Vienna, where he met Beethoven, who composed the Horn Sonata op.17 for him; Punto and Beethoven gave its first performance on 18 April. On 18 May 1801 Punto gave a grand concert at the National Theatre in Prague; his performance was highly praised by the *Prager neue Zeitung* (1801, no.39, p.473). In 1802 he toured with J. L. Dussek, with whom he gave a concert at Čáslav (16 September). He made another short visit to Paris, then returned to Prague where he died after an illness of five months. He was given a grandiose funeral, with Mozart's Requiem played at the graveside.

Punto was a *cor basse* player, as were many of the

leading soloists of the day; he used a silver *cor solo* made for him by Lucien-Joseph Raoux of Paris, and was acclaimed by music critics as a virtuoso of the highest order, perhaps the greatest horn player of all time. Mozart's high opinion ('Punto bläst magnifique'), expressed in a letter of 1778, was shared by Beethoven, and all contemporary writers referred to the vocal quality of his playing. Fröhlich's comments are typical:

Punto was remarkable for the purity of his interpretation and the delicacy of his taste no less than for his dynamic control, variety of tone-colour and amazing articulation. He could produce two notes simultaneously, and even full chords, and his tone generally had a quality of silvery brightness that was foreign to any of his predecessors.

In addition to many compositions, mostly for the horn, Punto published Rosetti's solo concerto in E under his name (Paris, 1787), revised Hampel's horn tutor and produced a curious book of daily exercises for the horn. A portrait by C. N. Cochin was engraved by Miger (Paris, 1782).

WORKS
(only those extant)

Hn, insts: 11 concs. (Paris, c1787–?1806), 1 movt ed. in DCHP, ii (1958), no.141; 3 qnts, hn, fl/ob, vn, va, b (Paris, by ?1799); 21 qts, hn, vn, va, b and hn, vn, bn, vc, opp.1–3, 18 (Paris, c1785–96); 20 trios, 3 hn (Paris, ?1800); 56 duos, 2 hn (Paris, 1793–c1803)
Other: 6 trios, fl/vn, vn, b (London, ?1773); 6 [3] duos, 2 vn (Paris, 1782), nos.4–6 by Fodor; 2 Hymne à la liberté (L'Aîné) (Paris, 1793)
Pedagogical: Seule et vraie méthode pour apprendre facilement les élémens des premier et second cors … composée par Hampl et perfectionnée par Punto son élève (Paris, c1795, 3/1798); Etude ou exercice journalière, ouvrage périodique (Paris, 1795, 2/1800)

BIBLIOGRAPHY
FétisB
C. Burney: *The Present State of Music in Germany, the Netherlands and the United Provinces* (London, 1773, 2/1775); ed. P. Scholes as *Dr. Burney's Musical Tours* (London, 1959) [see references to 'Ponta']
G. J. Dlabacž: *Allgemeines historisches Künstler-Lexikon* (Prague, 1815/R1973)
J. Fröhlich: 'Horn', *Allgemeine Encyclopädie*, ed. J. S. Ersch, J. G. Grüber and others (Leipzig, 1818–89)
H. Kling: 'Giovanni Punto, célèbre corniste', *BSIM*, iv (1908), 1066
R. Morley-Pegge: *The French Horn* (London, 1960, 2/1973)
H. Fitzpatrick: *The Horn and Horn-playing* (London, 1970)
REGINALD MORLEY-PEGGE/HORACE FITZPATRICK

Puppet opera, puppet theatre. Usually a mixed genre containing both music and spoken dialogue, performed on a specially designed stage by puppets (string, hand or rod). The works may take the forms of serious or comic operas, plays with incidental music or interpolated songs, or ballets. Because of the caricature nature of puppets, most works written for them have been comic adaptations, mock-heroic dramas or satires of popular dramas. Before the 5th century BC, puppets had a widespread existence in all civilized lands, and they continued to have a place in the performances of mystery plays and liturgical dramas as well as the *commedia dell'arte* throughout the Middle Ages and the Renaissance.

The earliest known Italian operas for puppets (*fantoccini*) were 17th-century burlesques staged in Venice at the Teatro S Moisè by the Florentine nobleman, Filippo Acciaiuoli (1637–1700). *Il Leandro* (1679), *Damira placata* (1680), *L'Ulisse in Feaccia* (1681) and *Il Girello* (1682) were all staged during carnival season by wooden or wax figures while the music was performed by singers behind the stage.

In 18th-century France, the development of the Parisian THÉÂTRES DE LA FOIRE and their continual struggle for survival helped towards the establishment of the puppet (*marionnette*) theatre. The *théâtres de la foire*

were constantly harassed by the licensed Comédie-Francaise and the Académie Royale de Musique, and the puppet theatres, considered beneath official contempt, became a haven for persecuted or aspiring directors, actors, authors and musicians. This state of incessant rivalry stimulated a renewed interest in dramatic parody. When these burlesques and operatic travesties were enlivened by gay VAUDEVILLE, a new genre was born: the *opéra comique*. Without the aid of the *marionnette* theatres at the annual fairs of St Germain and St Laurent, the production of parodies and *opéras comiques* would have been limited only to the short periods of tenure of the human theatres. About 40 puppet *opéras comiques* have survived. Several of them, by such authors as Carolet, Favart, Fuzelier, d'Orneval, Le Sage, Piron and d'Orville, found their way into *Le Théâtre de la Foire ou l'Opéra-Comique* (Paris, 1721–37). The importance of the *marionnette* theatres, however, stood in direct proportion to their necessity. With the establishment of the Opéra-Comique and the Théâtre-Italien and the replacement of the vaudeville by the *ariette*, they were quickly abandoned.

Puppet theatres have played a small but significant role in the history of the English stage. For a short time, during the Puritan control of the interregnum, this form of popular entertainment provided the only home for dramatic activities. Descriptions of the puppet theatres at Bartholomew and Southwark fairs are noted in the diaries of Samuel Pepys and John Evelyn. It was in these humble surroundings that the notable Punch made his début and became synonymous with English puppetry. By the end of the 17th century, puppets had been immortalized in numerous literary works including D'Urfey's *Don Quixote*, Jonson's *Bartholomew Fayre* and Addison's Latin poem *Machinae gesticulantes*.

In the 18th century, operas, satires and artificial heroics filled the puppet theatres, now referred to as 'Punch's theatre'. Martin Powell opened a well-fitted puppet theatre in London in 1710 and both *The Tatler* and *The Spectator* regarded Powell's theatre in Covent Garden and the opera at the Haymarket as the two leading diversions of London. For three seasons, Powell responded to the craze for Italian opera by staging satires of contemporary society, opera burlesques and mock-heroic tragedies. Following Powell's success, Punch theatres opened yearly in unused concert halls or even in converted tennis courts. The Licensing Act of 1737 restricted regular theatrical activities and many actors, musicians and playwrights sought refuge in the less conspicuous puppet theatres. Ballad operas now made up the bulk of the puppet theatres' repertory, and contributions were made by such notable 'proprietors' as Charlotte Charke, Henry Fielding, Samuel Foote and Charles Dibdin.

From 1770 to 1790, London was invaded by Italian *fantoccino* troupes, who mostly staged popular French comedies and light operas. Joseph Haydn visited one of these theatres, the Théâtre des Variétés Amusantes in Savile Row, in November 1791. He wrote in his diary: 'The puppets were manipulated well; the singers were bad, but the orchestra was quite acceptable'. By this time, puppet theatres were as brilliantly fitted as Europe's finest opera houses. It was at this level of existence that puppets found favour with the royal courts throughout Europe.

Puppets were displayed in their own elaborate theatre in plays and operettas at the summer palace of Prince

Nikolaus Esterházy. The theatre flourished between 1773 and 1783 under Haydn's musical guidance. At least two of Haydn's own creations were among the productions: *Philemon und Baucis* and *Die Feuersbrunst*. Other puppet works attributed to Haydn are: *Hexen-Schabbas, Genoveva, Didone abbandonata, Die bestrafte Rachbegierde* and *Demofoonte*. Two more works were included in the puppet repertory: *Alceste* by Carlos d'Ordonez and *Die Fee Urgele* by Ignace Pleyel. In the closing years of the 18th century, the craze for puppets faded. The success enjoyed by the puppet theatre, usually at the expense of the human theatre, had now shifted to its living counterpart.

The late 19th century brought a vivid regeneration of the puppet theatre and in several countries puppetry reached an artistic level of significant potential. Many men of letters turned to the medium as a means of legitimate dramatic expression. Craig, Shaw, Lorca, France and Jarry are among those who found the medium ideal. Composers who added to the puppet repertory include Britten, Casella, Chausson, Copland, Falla, Hindemith, Honegger, Krenek, Liuzzi, Lualdi, Malipiero, Mellers, Satie and Smetana. Of the 20th-century literature for puppets Falla's opera, *El retablo de Maese Pedro*, is perhaps the best known.

See also JAPAN, §III, 3, and SOUTH-EAST ASIA, §II, 4.

BIBLIOGRAPHY
F. Lindsay: *Dramatic Parody by Marionettes in Eighteenth-Century Paris* (New York, 1946)
G. Speaight: *The History of the English Puppet Theatre* (London, 1955)
H. C. R. Landon: 'Haydn's Marionette Operas', *Haydn Yearbook*, i, (1962), 111
J. M. Minniear: *Marionette Opera: its History and Literature* (diss., North Texas State U., 1971)
                                            JOHN MOHR MINNIEAR

Puppo, Giuseppe (*b* Lucca, 12 June 1749; *d* Florence, 19 April 1827). Italian violinist and composer. He received training in Naples at the Conservatorio di S Onofrio di Loreto and in 1768 returned to Lucca as leader of the orchestra. His talent as a soloist soon led to concert tours. An appearance in Paris in 1775 was followed by a tour of Spain and Portugal, where he reportedly made a fortune and quickly squandered it. He was in London in 1777, and in November 1783 he was again in Paris, playing at the Concert Spirituel. Viotti employed him as co-leader of the orchestra at the Théâtre de Monsieur (1789–?92), and he held a similar post at the Théâtre de la République (1793–9). He seems to have remained in Paris until 1811, when he abandoned his wife and children and went to Naples. There he was first violinist at S Carlo until his objection to playing ballets caused his dismissal in 1817. Although he taught for two years at a small school in Pontremoli, he did not succeed in re-establishing his career. He was destitute when the English musician Edward Taylor found him in Florence and generously placed him in a hospice.

Puppo was admired as a soloist, and his career shows his ability as a leader. His playing, said to be at its best in soft, melancholy moods, was occasionally compared to Tartini's; he never studied with that master, however, though he boasted that he had. His only known works, all published without date in Paris, are a set of three violin duos, another of eight studies for solo violin, and six violin fantasies arranged for piano, probably from the preceding studies (Fétis also mentioned two violin concertos). They reflect a fine technique, with originality confined largely to bizarre titles and tempo indications

and to occasional illustrative effects.

BIBLIOGRAPHY
FétisB
A. Choron and F. Fayolle: *Dictionnaire historique des musiciens* (Paris, 1810–11)
A. Moser: *Geschichte des Violinspiels* (Berlin, 1923, rev. 2/1966)
A. Bonaventura: *Storia del violino, dei violinisti e della musica per violino* (Milan, 2/1933)
                                            CHAPPELL WHITE

Purcell. English family of musicians, flourishing in the 17th and 18th centuries. They were possibly of Buckinghamshire origin. Other spellings of the name found in contemporary records are Persill, Purcel, Purcill, Pursal, Pursall, Pursel, Pursell and Pursill.

(1) Henry Purcell (i) (*d* Westminster, London, 11 Aug 1664). Singer. In 1656 he sang the part of Mustapha in Davenant's *The Siege of Rhodes*. On 16 February 1661 he was installed as a 'singing-man' and Master of the Choristers at Westminster Abbey and in the same year was one of the Gentlemen of the Chapel Royal at Charles II's coronation. On 14 November 1662 he was admitted as a musician-in-ordinary for the lutes and voices. He was buried in the east cloister of Westminster Abbey. Since he and (2) Thomas Purcell both had children around 1660 it is probable that they were of the same generation and may well have been brothers. Henry's wife Elizabeth died in August 1699 and was buried at St Margaret's, Westminster. The only offspring for which there is documentary evidence is a daughter, Katherine (*b* March 1662), who married the Rev. William Sale on 18 June 1691. See, however, (3) Henry (ii).

(2) Thomas Purcell (*d* Westminster, London, 31 July 1682). Tenor singer and composer, probably brother of (1) Henry (i). In 1661 he was one of the Gentlemen of the Chapel Royal at Charles II's coronation. On 10 November 1662 he was admitted to the private music for lutes, viols and voices. In 1671 he became a groom of the robes and on 10 January 1672 was appointed composer for the violins jointly with Pelham Humfrey. He also succeeded Henry Cooke as marshal of the Corporation of Music on 24 June 1672 and on 9 March was admitted as a musician-in-ordinary in the King's Private Musick. By his wife Katherine he appears to have had at least four sons – Charles, Edward, Francis and Matthew – and two daughters, Elizabeth and Katherine. For other possible members of his family see (3) Henry (ii).

(3) Henry Purcell (ii) (*b* 1659; *d* Westminster, London, 21 Nov 1695). Composer, organist and bass and countertenor singer. He was one of the greatest composers of the Baroque period and one of the greatest of all English composers.

1. Parentage. 2. Life. 3. Style and development. 4. Dramatic music. 5. Odes and welcome songs. 6. Sacred music. 7. Secular vocal music. 8. Instrumental music. 9. Autographs, publications. 10. Portraits.

1. PARENTAGE. The only contemporary evidence is a letter, dated 8 February 1679, from Thomas Purcell to John Gostling (facsimile in Westrup, *Purcell*, 3/1975), which refers to 'my sonne Henry' and mentions that 'my sonne is composing: wherin you will be chiefly consern'd'. John Hingeston in his will (12 December 1683) left £5 'to my Godson Henry Pursall (son of Elizabeth Pursall)', presumably a son of (1) Henry (i); but he did not identify him as a musician or mention him as his assistant, and there is no certainty that this was the composer (for an alternative view of the parentage of

Henry Purcell (ii) see Zimmerman, 1967, 1f). Henry Purcell (ii) is known to have had three brothers: Edward (*b* 1655 or 1656; *d* 20 June 1717), who, after ten years as a 'gentleman usher daily waiter assistant', joined the army and had a distinguished career as an officer in Ireland, Flanders and Spain; (4) Daniel; and Joseph, who administered Daniel's estate.

2. LIFE. As a boy Purcell was a chorister in the Chapel Royal. He was obviously prodigiously gifted. Playford's *Catch that Catch Can, or The Musical Companion* (1667) includes a three-part song, *Sweet tyranness*, attributed to him. There is no reason to question the attribution, since a version for solo voice was published with his name 11 years later in *New Ayres and Dialogues*. There is nothing inherently improbable in supposing that he was writing music at the age of eight; we also know that boys in the Chapel Royal choir were encouraged to compose.

In 1673 Purcell's voice broke at what was then an unusually early age, and he was appointed an unpaid assistant to John Hingeston, who had charge of the king's keyboard and wind instruments, with the prospect of eventually succeeding him as keeper. Having acquired the necessary experience he was engaged from 1674 to 1678 to tune the organ at Westminster Abbey, where in 1675–6 he was also paid for copying two books of organ parts. In 1677 he was appointed composer-in-ordinary for the violins in succession to Matthew Locke and in 1679 succeeded John Blow as organist of Westminster Abbey – a post which not only entitled him to a salary but also provided the rent of a house. It was probably in 1680 or 1681 that he married. In 1680 he wrote the first of his welcome songs for Charles II and also contributed music to the theatre for the first time. On 14 July 1682 he succeeded Edward Lowe as one of the organists of the Chapel Royal, which meant that he was also a singer in the choir. In February he took the sacrament at St Margaret's, Westminster, before witnesses – perhaps as a result of the recent enforcement of the laws against Dissenters.

In June 1683 he published his *Sonnata's of III Parts*, dedicated to Charles II, and announced that he could supply copies from his house in St Ann's Lane, Westminster. In December that year, on the death of Hingeston, he was appointed organ maker and keeper of the king's instruments. His court appointments were renewed in 1685 by James II, for whose coronation he provided not only music but a second organ. The post of keeper of the instruments was not a sinecure: in 1687 he drew up a detailed statement showing that the cost of cleaning and repairing the Chapel Royal organ and tuning the harpsichords, plus his own salary, would come to £81. On the accession of William III in 1689 he was confirmed in his court appointments and once again had the duty of providing a second organ for the coronation. On this occasion he was involved in a dispute with the dean and chapter of Westminster over the money that he had received for places in the main organ loft: it should have been handed over, after reasonable deductions, more promptly.

Apart from his increased activity as a composer, particularly for the theatre, there is little information about the remaining years of his life. The last royal occasion for which he provided music was Queen Mary's funeral in 1694. He made his will on the day of his death, when he was so feeble that he could hardly hold the pen. His funeral took place in Westminster Abbey on 26 November 1695. The whole chapter attended in their vestments, and the music was sung by the united choirs of the Abbey and the Chapel Royal. Purcell was buried, at no cost to his widow, in the north aisle, adjoining the organ. Lady Elizabeth Howard paid for the erection of a marble tablet, fixed to a pillar above the grave. By his wife Frances, who died in February 1706, Purcell had several children, of whom only two are known to have survived him: a daughter, Frances (*b* May 1688), and a son, (5) Edward.

3. STYLE AND DEVELOPMENT. Apart from a handful of songs and possibly a couple of anthems, the earliest works by Purcell to survive date from 1680. But these – the string fantasias, the music for *Theodosius* and the first welcome song for Charles II – show such a complete mastery of the craft of composition that they must be the result of constant practice over a number of years. They also illustrate two aspects of his work. The music for *Theodosius* and the welcome song were written to order; the fantasias, we may assume, were written either for his own satisfaction or for private performance by friends or colleagues. As the years went on he found himself more and more in demand as a composer. His music for the theatre in particular must have made his name familiar to many people who knew nothing of his church music and had no opportunity of hearing his court odes. He might have been tempted to take some of his duties lightly; but in fact everything he wrote shows the same professional skill and scrupulous attention to detail. His music is sometimes dull, but it is never

1. Henry Purcell's autograph letter of 1686 to the Dean of Exeter (GB-EXc)

slovenly. He clearly learnt much from Locke, Humfrey and Blow and quickly became familiar with the Italian music of his time. But whatever he absorbed from others became transformed in his hands into something that was peculiarly his own. Of all the English composers of his time he was the most individual.

When Henry Playford published the first volume of *Orpheus Britannicus* – an anthology of Purcell's songs – in 1698, he wrote: 'The Author's extraordinary Talent in all sorts of Musick is sufficiently known, but he was especially admir'd for the *Vocal*, having a peculiar Genius to express the Energy of *English* Words, whereby he mov'd the Passions of all his Auditors'. This is a just comment, but it is not the whole truth. In Purcell's early work the vocal music is less remarkable than the instrumental. The songs in *Theodosius* and the writing for voices in the earliest welcome songs have a certain stiffness, which disappeared in his later work as he acquired the art of combining just accentuation with a flexible melodic line. The string fantasias, on the other hand, show a mastery of instrumental writing and an intensity of imagination which he never surpassed. There is a further difference between his songs and his instrumental music. The songs rely for their effect primarily, though not wholly, on melody: the bass, even when figured, provides only a general outline of the harmonic progressions. On the other hand the instrumental writing, including movements in vocal works, is marked by a harmonic subtlety which in vocal music appears only in ensembles. This is very noticeable when Purcell provides an instrumental version of a song, e.g. 'They tell us that you, mighty powers above' in *The Indian Queen*, where the instrumental version introduces dissonances to which there is no clue in the original song. The same thing happens when a song is repeated by a chorus, e.g. 'If love's a sweet passion' in *The Fairy Queen*, where there is a further variant in the instrumental prelude.

Purcell's technical mastery needs no better illustration than his use of canon and ground bass. He employed both with such effortless skill that one can easily listen without being aware that they exist. The examples of canon which he contributed to the 12th edition of John Playford's *Introduction to the Skill of Musick* (1694) do not explain to the reader how to write one: they merely exhibit the finished article. One has the impression that to him such technical devices were instinctive. Perhaps he underestimated the capacity of less gifted practitioners. He described 'Composing upon a Ground' as 'a very easie thing to do, and requires but little judgment', with no hint of the subtlety with which he ensured that the phrases of the melody did not coincide with the repetitions of the bass. He did, however, mention that when, as often, the ground is simply four notes descending, 'to maintain *Fuges* upon it would be difficult', forgetting perhaps how cleverly he had done this in *Dioclesian*.

Purcell's early music, like Monteverdi's, tends to be conservative. The chromaticisms in the string fantasias and in the early anthems, so far from being 'prophetic' or 'curiously modern', are a logical extension of the practice of his immediate predecessors, particularly Locke. He never abandoned chromaticism, but as he became acquainted with the directness and relative simplicity of Italian music he tended to use it much more as a melodic feature within the framework of diatonic tonality. His contribution to Playford's book does not men-

2. Henry Purcell: portrait in black chalk heightened with white, attributed to Godfrey Kneller (1646–1723), in the National Portrait Gallery, London; it is believed to be the only surviving portrait of Purcell drawn from life

tion chromaticism, and there are scarcely any instances of it in his examples. Instead he drew particular attention to the Italians' use of the diminished 7th and the Neapolitan 6th, both of which are basically modifications of diatonic harmony. He was attracted also by the sensuous effect of passages in 3rds, particularly in three-part harmony. He criticized an example from Christopher Simpson's *Compendium of Practical Musick* (1667) on the ground that the alto part moves awkwardly:

Now in my opinion the *Alt* or *Second Part* should move gradually in *Thirds* with the *Treble*; though the other be fuller, this is the smoothest, and carries more Air and Form in it, and I'm sure 'tis the constant Practice of the *Italians* in all their Musick, either Vocal or Instrumental, which I presume ought to be a Guide to us; the way I would have, is thus: [ex.1].

He recommended that a second treble should normally be kept below the first but at the same time pointed out

Ex.1

that in sonatas 'one *Treble* has as much Predominancy as the other; and you are not tied to such a strict Rule, but one may interfere with the other'. Both principles may be illustrated from his own sonatas, e.g. no.9 of the *Ten Sonata's in Four Parts*, where the first and second violins move in 3rds through practically the whole of the second movement. Purcell's vocal writing is also frequently Italianate in character, in both recitative and aria. His recitative, both in church music and in secular works, is often marked by the use of pathetic inflections of the kind found earlier in Locke and Humfrey. Florid writing occurs here, as well as in arias. Its use in arias is not confined to extended pieces like 'Hark the ech'ing air' in *The Fairy Queen* but is found also in such relatively simple songs as 'Dear pretty youth' in *The Tempest* – which may be an argument for accepting as authentic the rest of the music in this work (on which doubts have been cast: see also §7).

In spite of Purcell's emphasis on Italian practice and his publisher's declaration, in the preface to the *Sonnata's of III Parts*, that Englishmen 'should begin to loath the levity, and balladry of our neighbours', he was not unaffected by French music. He may be presumed to have agreed with Dryden's observation, in the dedication to the score of *Dioclesian* (1691), that English music was 'now learning *Italian*, which is its best Master, and studying a little of the *French* Air, to give it more of Gayety and Fashion'. There are plenty of examples of gaiety and fashion in Purcell's dances and entr'actes. But French influence appears also in more solemn passages, notably the introductions to his overtures and the ritual scenes in his dramatic music, as well as in some of the airs of a more popular cast, e.g. 'We come to sing great Zempoalla's story' in *The Indian Queen*. Besides all this there is a strong English element, both in instrumental writing which preserves an older tradition and in songs in the popular idiom of the day. None of these influences accounts for the personal element in Purcell's music, which won him a reputation in his day and has maintained it ever since. This personal element, though often difficult to pin down exactly, has several recognizable features, among them a vein of nostalgia which is not to be explained simply by the use of chromaticism and pathetic inflections, a wide-ranging vocal line and continuity without repetition. Much of his simpler, more direct music does not differ in character from the work of his contemporaries: it merely happens to be better.

The range of Purcell's invention is remarkable. If there were not positive evidence it might be difficult to believe that the same person was the composer of *Ah! few and full of sorrow* and the duet 'Hark! how the songsters' in *Timon of Athens*, or that the man who wrote the chaconne published in *Ten Sonata's in Four Parts* could also produce a series of vulgar catches. If this diversity is not always appreciated, the reason is that although all the surviving music is now in print relatively little of it is performed. The court odes are virtually unknown, the dramatic music, apart from *Dido and Aeneas*, is mainly represented by a handful of songs and a few instrumental suites, and the anthems with strings are heard only at festivals when the necessary resources can be assembled. Only a few of the songs and duets are regularly sung, and then to the accompaniment of 'realizations' which, when not inept or even inaccurate, distract attention from the vocal line by misplaced ingenuity. On the whole the chamber works have fared best, but even here the works with continuo accompaniment have suffered from over-editing. The survival of Purcell's music depends not on factitious additions to his text but on performance by singers and instrumentalists who have the technique and the imagination to do it justice.

4. DRAMATIC MUSIC. Purcell's music for the stage was conditioned by the circumstances of the time. The reopening of the London theatres at the Restoration created a desire to see plays. Songs and instrumental music could be introduced, as they had been in Shakespeare's time, but opera as it was understood on the Continent was not welcomed, nor was it feasible without a substantial subsidy and facilities for training singers. In the 1660s there were various plans for introducing Italian opera to London, but they were not successful. In consequence most of Purcell's dramatic music consisted of overtures, entr'actes, dances and songs. There were, however, a limited number of productions which provided more generous opportunities for music by including masques and scenes of a sacrificial or ceremonial character. Purcell wrote music for five productions of this kind. Four of them – *Dioclesian*, *The Fairy Queen*, *The Tempest* and *The Indian Queen* – were adaptations of existing plays. The fifth, *King Arthur*, was written by JOHN DRYDEN specifically with Purcell's music in mind. It was no doubt Dryden's patronage that stimulated Purcell's work for the theatre in the last five years of his life. Not all his dramatic music can be dated exactly, but it is certain that the greater part of it was written between 1690 and 1695, in contrast to his church music, hardly any of which dates from these years.

The most substantial music is naturally to be found in what Roger North called 'semi-operas' – the five works mentioned above. Some of it is on grandiose lines – for instance, the chaconne at the end of the masque in *Dioclesian*, built on a pompous ground bass with brilliant antiphony between trumpets, oboes and strings, or the setting of 'How happy the lover' in *King Arthur*, where every possibility of the ground bass is exploited by voices and instruments. Particularly impressive are the ceremonial scenes (e.g. the preparations for the sacrifice in Act 5 of *The Indian Queen*), which are not confined to the 'semi-operas'. They occur also in the incidental music written for other plays: examples are the scene for the druids in *Bonduca* and the incantation in *Oedipus*, which includes the song 'Music for a while'. But since many of the plays for which Purcell wrote music were comedies the opportunities for such extended scenes were limited.

Although the settings of some of the plays are exotic, there is no attempt at local colour in the music: any such attempt would have been foreign to the ideas not only of Purcell but of his contemporaries. There is, however, plenty of atmosphere and often lively characterization. The scene in *King Arthur* where the Cold Genius, with chattering teeth, rises slowly from the ground is made more vivid by a throbbing accompaniment for strings and a chorus which follows a little later in the same vein. Equally imaginative is the appearance of Night, with muted strings, in *The Fairy Queen* and the hissing of Envy and his followers in *The Indian Queen*. Purcell was as much at home with comic characters as with allegorical figures: the dialogue for Corydon and Mopsa in *The Fairy Queen* may sound a little too sophisticated for a representation of country life, but it is richly humorous in conception. Some of the instrumental music is clearly designed to illustrate action on the stage, e.g. the Dance of the Furies and the Chair Dance in *Dioclesian*, and the 'Symphony while the Swans come forward' and the Monkeys' Dance in *The Fairy Queen*. But the greater part of the instrumental music has no dramatic significance: for this reason it is included in the general discussion of instrumental music in §8. Similarly many of the songs have no direct relevance to the plays in which they occur. They were not in any case sung by the principal actors, though they might be assigned to priests, spirits, allegorical figures and subordinate characters generally: for a discussion see §7.

Dido and Aeneas is an exception to the general run of Purcell's music in having a libretto which is set to music throughout. It was written for performance 'by Young Gentlewomen' at JOSIAS PRIEST's boarding-school at Chelsea in 1689; though divided into three acts it lasts little more than an hour. Since Aeneas and a sailor are tenors, at least in the copies that have come down to us, and there are parts for tenors and basses in the chorus, the work cannot have been performed entirely by Priest's pupils; and although the music does not make any extravagant demands, some of it calls for a professional standard of technique. Though the opera is a miniature it covers a wide range of emotional expression, from Dido's soliloquies and Aeneas's passionate regret to the sombre utterances of the sorceress and the breezy heartiness of the sailor. Since Priest was a dancing-master there are opportunities for ballet – particularly a Triumphing Dance in chaconne rhythm for the members of Dido's court and a fantastic dance for the witches; there may well have been more in the original production. The work suffers a little from its brevity: the drama moves too rapidly for all the episodes to make their full effect, and Aeneas hardly has time to establish himself as a character. But against this must be set the expressive quality of the recitative, the inspired treatment of ground basses, and the imaginative portrayal of the witches – not least in the use of an echo behind the scenes. Everywhere the music triumphs over a prosaic libretto.

5. ODES AND WELCOME SONGS. The practice of honouring members of the royal family with music was established in the early years of Charles II's reign. The regular occasions were New Year's Day, a royal birthday and the king's return to the capital after a visit elsewhere – generally to Windsor or Newmarket. The only occasion when Purcell set an ode for New Year's Day seems to have been in 1694, when according to the author of the words, Matthew Prior, *Light of the world* was sung; but the music has not survived. During the reigns of Charles II and James II Purcell set nine welcome songs, as well as an ode for the marriage of Prince George of Denmark to Princess Anne. After the accession of William III welcome songs were virtually abandoned, but Purcell wrote six birthday odes for Queen Mary and one for the birthday of Princess Anne's son, the Duke of Gloucester.

The court odes and welcome songs cover almost the entire period of Purcell's known activity as a composer, from 1680 to 1695. Although they do not represent all the facets of his art they give a good general idea of the way in which he was developing. They might properly be described as cantatas for solo voices, chorus and orchestra. Those for Charles II and James II employ mainly strings; however, recorders are used in three of them and in *Swifter, Isis, swifter flow* (1681) an oboe is introduced for the first time. Some of the odes written during the reign of William III are more elaborately orchestrated: five out of the seven have oboes and trumpets. The timpani part found in the only surviving copy (1765) of the last of the Queen Mary odes, *Come, ye sons of art, away*, is probably not authentic. Like the verse anthems the odes include sections for solo voices – in some cases as many as seven – and a limited amount of recitative. By a quaint conceit *Why are all the Muses mute*, the first welcome song for James II, begins with

3. Henry Purcell: portrait (1695) by John Closterman in the National Portrait Gallery, London

recitative and the overture is not heard until after the chorus has sung 'Awake, awake'. The overtures, as in Purcell's works in general, are mostly modelled on the French opera overture, with a pompous introduction, a canzona in fugal style and sometimes an adagio to conclude. Two of the odes introduce popular tunes. In *Ye tuneful Muses* (1686) the melody of *Hey then, up go we* is ingeniously used as the bass of a countertenor solo, then as a counterpoint to a chorus and finally as the bass of an orchestral ritornello. In *Love's goddess sure was blind* (1692) the Scots tune *Cold and raw* is introduced as a bass to the soprano solo 'May her blest example'; according to a tradition reported by Hawkins, it was one of Queen Mary's favourite tunes.

The texts of the odes, most of which are anonymous, are obsequious in the manner of the period. Since Purcell was thoroughly familiar with this conventional attitude to royalty there is no reason to suppose that he was hampered by the words that he had to set. At the same time his imagination was clearly stirred more vigorously by any suggestion of imagery. Examples are the solos 'Welcome, more welcome does he come' in *From those serene and rapturous joys* (1684) and 'See how the glitt'ring ruler of the day' in *Arise, my Muse* (1690), both on a ground bass. The first of these, sombre in tone, refers to Lazarus emerging in a winding-sheet 'from his drowsy tomb'; the second, in minuet rhythm, represents the sun summoning the planets to 'dance in a solemn ball'. For obvious reasons the texts only rarely offer opportunities for a pathetic style. Where they do Purcell clearly welcomed them, e.g. in the countertenor solo 'But ah, I see Eusebia drowned in tears' in *Arise, my Muse*. Here there is genuine emotion, in spite of the fact that 'Eusebia' is the Anglican Church, regretting that William III is compelled to champion her cause in Ireland. Much of the music in these works, however, is in a simple, extrovert style, which nevertheless does not exclude contrapuntal treatment in the choruses. How successful this style could be is best illustrated by *Come, ye sons of art, away*, where there are splendid, swinging tunes which invite the cooperation of trumpets. The same ode also includes one of the most brilliant of Purcell's songs on a ground bass, the duet 'Sound the trumpet' for two countertenors, as well as an elaborate soprano solo, 'Bid the virtues', with an equally elaborate oboe obbligato.

Purcell's odes for other occasions are planned on similar lines. Some of them have rather better texts than the court odes – but not all: Nahum Tate's *Great parent, hail*, for the centenary of Trinity College, Dublin (1694), is a monument of banality, which clearly failed to inspire the composer. Nor did D'Urfey's *Of old, when heroes thought it base*, written for the annual reunion of Yorkshire gentlemen (1690), evoke more than a conventional response. Brady's ode for St Cecilia's Day, *Hail, bright Cecilia* (1692), is superior to these mundane offerings. The text, in praise of music, offers particular opportunities in its references to individual instruments. The passage beginning:

> Hark, each tree its silence breaks,
> The box and fir to talk begin

refers to the recorder and the violin – which led Purcell to accompany his duet setting with an antiphonal treatment of strings and three recorders (one a bass). 'The fife and all the harmony of war' has a martial setting for two trumpets and timpani. The organ, extolled as 'Wondrous machine' over a ground bass, is not specifically illustrated, though it is not impossible that one was present in Stationers' Hall, where the work was first performed. According to the *Gentleman's Journal* the declamatory solo for countertenor, ''Tis Nature's voice', was sung by Purcell himself 'with incredible graces', which are in fact preserved in the score. Though the music for the other soloists is on the whole less arduous it all demands a very proficient technique. The choral writing in this work is more elaborate than in many of Purcell's odes, particularly includes a canon by double augmentation. An earlier St Cecilia ode, *Welcome to all the pleasures* (1683), is much slighter but has a kind of youthful freshness which is very agreeable. It includes a particularly effective song on a ground bass, 'Here the deities approve', which seems to have been popular, since a keyboard transcription was published in *The Second Part of Musick's Hand-maid* (1689) under the title 'A New Ground'.

6. SACRED MUSIC. The repertory of church music at the Restoration was inevitably based on the work of pre-Commonwealth composers, whose anthems and services continued in use, particularly in cathedrals. Purcell himself began at an early age to make copies of anthems by Tallis, Byrd, Orlando Gibbons and other composers of an earlier generation. In the Chapel Royal the need for new music was supplied by composers like Child, Locke and Cooke, who was Master of the Choristers. Cooke was fortunate in having a number of talented boys in the choir, and some of these – notably Humfrey, Blow and Wise – contributed anthems in a style which probably owed something to Cooke's Italian training. A feature of the new style was the extensive use of verse sections for solo voices. Another, found only in music for the Chapel Royal, was the use of a string orchestra in works to be performed when the king was present. Purcell thus became familiar as a boy both with the older tradition of the full anthem and with the newer style, in which solo voices and instruments played an important part. The full anthem could also include sections for a group of solo voices by way of contrast, but they did not call for an independent accompaniment.

Thomas Purcell's letter to Gostling cited in §1 shows that Purcell was writing anthems for the Chapel Royal as early as 1679. In fact it has been shown that the earliest anthem that can be dated, *Lord, who can tell*, was probably written before 1678. Until Purcell was appointed an organist of the Chapel Royal he seems to have divided his attention between full anthems and verse anthems. Some of these must have been sung in Westminster Abbey, since the records for 1681–2 mention a payment 'for writing Mr. Purcell's Service & Anthems'. Once he became a member of the Chapel Royal in 1682 he abandoned the full anthem, either because of the obligations of his new post or because he was inclined to move with the times. His full anthems follow a well-established tradition of vocal polyphony, though not without signs of his individual attitude to harmony, e.g. in the chromatic progressions which illustrate the 'bitter pains of eternal death' in the first version of *In the midst of life*. The early verse anthems with organ are in some respects not unlike the full anthems. Here too there are several instances of an imaginative treatment of the text. These characteristics appear equally in the sacred music designed for private use, which is discussed later in this section. In the Latin psalm *Jehovah, quam multi*, which appears to be an early work, the most remarkable details of the harmony are produced by diatonic clashes between the parts. This work, and *Beati omnes*, may have been written for the queen's chapel at Somerset House, where G. B. Draghi was organist.

Purcell never abandoned his personal response to the texts that he set, but in the larger verse anthems it tended to find its principal expression in recitative. Most of his anthems with strings appear to date from his appointment at the Chapel Royal, and he continued to write works of this kind until the accession of William III. Though James II, as a Roman Catholic, had his own chapel, the Chapel Royal was maintained, but with a declining number of singers, and the string players were ordered to attend when Princess Anne was present. After the accession of William III the use of strings in the Chapel Royal seems to have been abandoned, and only two of Purcell's anthems, both with organ, are known to have been written in his reign.

The main function of the string orchestra was to provide an overture and ritornellos, though it might also on occasion join the voices. Purcell's overtures gen-

4. *Autograph MS of part of Purcell's anthem 'My heart is inditing' composed in 1685 (GB-Lbm R.M.20.h.8, f.60v)*

erally begin in the pompous style of the French opera overture, usually followed not by a fugal canzona but by a brisk, rhythmical movement in triple time – a style which recurs in the ritornellos. The sections for solo voices also have a strongly marked rhythm, but not the symmetrical structure to be found in the odes, no doubt because the words are not in verse. The ground bass, which is a constant feature of the odes, occurs rarely:

one example is in the anthem *In thee, O Lord, do I put my trust*, and there it is used not for the vocal sections but for the introductory symphony. The writing, both for voices and for instruments, is often florid, with a profusion of dotted notes. This style has sometimes been described as 'secular' – a misuse of the term, since music can be sacred or secular only by association. No doubt the Restoration composers, including Purcell,

Ex.2

were endeavouring to satisfy Charles II's desire for a lively, rhythmical style. But this kind of church music had been current on the Continent for a good many years before the Restoration, and in adopting it the English composers were merely showing that they were up to date. Nor was liveliness the only characteristic of the verse anthem. Much of the music is dignified and pathetic in expression, especially in recitative. Like Italian opera composers Purcell obviously wrote for individual singers. He had in JOHN GOSTLING the services of an unusually accomplished bass soloist. Few singers even at the present day would care to tackle a passage like that in ex.2, from *I will give thanks unto thee, O Lord*.

The most complete acceptance of an Italianate style is to be found in *O sing unto the Lord*, with its vigorous antiphony between instruments and chorus. The longest of Purcell's anthems, and certainly the most imposing, is *My heart is inditing*, written for the coronation of James II (see fig.4). Here he had the advantage of two choirs, which made possible extensive subdivision of the voices, and he took the opportunity to produce something both more solid and less episodic than the general run of his anthems. The choral antiphony at 'Hearken, O daughter' is no less impressive than the massive 'Alleluia' with which the work ends. Purcell seems to be completely

Ex.3

involved. This is not always the case in the anthems in general, where the music, however well tailored, often seems to lack conviction and to be marked more by mannerisms than by ideas.

The works written for private performance, several of which date from early in Purcell's career, are rather different in character. For one thing they are more intimate: there is no question of impressing a Sunday congregation in the Chapel Royal. Here one finds more than once a manipulation of harmony which carries even further the ambiguity to be found in many of Purcell's earlier works. The opening of *Plung'd in the confines of despair* is a characteristic example (see ex.3). A number of solo settings establish a similar mood. A penitential attitude to God seems to have been favoured for private devotion. Not all the settings, however, are of this character. Here too, as in the verse anthems, there are jaunty 'Alleluias' and sometimes even a symmetrical tune, as in the four-part *Early, O Lord, my fainting soul*, though it falls a good deal short of the individuality shown in many of Purcell's secular songs. One piece, *In guilty night*, is in effect a dramatic cantata on the subject of Saul's visit to the Witch of Endor. Of the solo songs the *Evening Hymn* ('Now that the sun hath veil'd his light') deserves its high reputation. Founded on a simple descending ground bass, it exhibits Purcell's customary skill in handling this form. The vocal line is adjusted to disguise the repetition of the bass, which modulates in the middle section of the piece. The seemingly endless 'Alleluia' that fills the last 40 bars or so is sufficient to make one forget less happy settings of the word in other contexts.

Since Purcell was an organist for 18 years of his life it is curious that he appears to have written relatively little for the Anglican service. What we have is a complete service in B♭ (including the alternative canticles, Kyrie and the Nicene Creed), an Evening Service in G minor, and a *Te Deum* and *Jubilate* in D. The last is a special case, as it was written for St Cecilia's Day 1694, and is scored for trumpets and strings. Both the services are 'full' settings, but they include many verse sections. They are relatively simple works, even though they include several ingenious canons, and look as if they might have been written for ordinary cathedral choirs rather than for the Chapel Royal: the fact that the B♭ service occurs, either complete or in part, in such a large number of manuscripts suggests that it was welcomed in cathedrals. The verse setting of the *Te Deum* and *Jubilate*, which makes much play with trumpets, was admired at the time and for some years after Purcell's death. But its superficial brilliance does not bear comparison with the best of his anthems: only the more intimate moments are rewarding.

7. SECULAR VOCAL MUSIC. The sheer quantity of Purcell's secular music for one or more voices is almost embarrassing. In the dramatic music alone there are nearly 150 solo songs, and to these must be added more than 100 others, most of which were published in the songbooks of the time. There are also a large number of duets and catches, not to mention a handful of cantatas for two or more voices, some of which have parts for violins or recorders or both. Some of the solo songs are simple ditties, others are themselves cantatas, with a sequence of recitative and aria. Purcell's treatment of recitative was not restricted to a simple enunciation of the words. It was often florid, incorporating in its notation what singers might otherwise have improvised from a simple vocal line. It could more properly be described as arioso, which does not imply that it should be sung in strict time. The opening of *The fatal hour*, published in the second volume of *Orpheus Britannicus*, will serve as an example (see ex.4).

Ex.4

The fa — — tal hour, ____ the fa —

— — tal hour ____ comes on, ____ comes on ____ a —

— pace,   which I had ra-ther die ____

____ than see.

The cantata pattern was particularly suitable for 'mad songs', popular at the time, in which the various stages of frenzy, from dejection to wild fantasy, could be illustrated by contrasted sections of the music. A characteristic example is 'From rosy bowers' in the third part of *Don Quixote*, described when it was published posthumously as the last song that Purcell wrote. D'Urfey, the author of the play, listed the five sections as follows:

1. Sullenly Mad ('From rosy bowers, where sleeps the God of Love')
2. Mirthfully Mad. A Swift Movement ('Or if more influencing, Is to be brisk and airy')
3. Melancholy Madness ('Ah, 'tis in vain, 'tis all, 'tis all in vain')
4. Fantastically Mad ('Or, say ye powers, my peace to crown, Shall I thaw myself or drown')
5. Stark Mad ('No, no, no, no, I'll straight run mad').

Purcell's music faithfully follows these divisions. Sections 1 and 3 are set as a slow arioso, section 2 in brisk duple time, section 4 in triple time, while section 5, marked 'Quick', develops into a miniature aria with an increasingly elaborate bass. Cantata settings other than mad songs did not call for such extravagant gestures. There was, however, no standard pattern. 'Sweeter than roses' in *Pausanias*, for instance, has only two sections: a melting arioso which blazes briefly into fire, and a splendid song of triumph in triple time, 'What magic has victorious love'. Some other examples, particularly dialogues, have more.

The songs which consist of a single movement show a considerable variety of structure. Some are in a simple da capo form, e.g. Belinda's song 'Pursue thy conquest, love' in *Dido and Aeneas*. Some are in the rondeau form familiar from French music, e.g. 'I attempt from love's sickness to fly', in *The Indian Queen*. Others exploit variety over a ground bass, often of the simplest possible form. What is most remarkable is Purcell's power of extending a melody so that one phrase leads effortlessly to the next. He may repeat the first phrase, with or without a different ending; but after that the song frequently goes its own way without looking back, as if propelled by some hidden energy. The popular 'Nymphs and shepherds' in *The Libertine* returns briefly to its opening phrase at the end of the song, but most of it is a continuous and apparently spontaneous flow of new invention. Even a da capo aria like 'Hark how all things in one sound rejoice' in *The Fairy Queen* shows this capacity for uninhibited continuity. Another striking characteristic of many of the songs is the wide range of intervals employed. The traditional precepts of good vocal writing are often flouted with considerable success. An outstanding example is the song 'When I have often heard young maids complaining' in *The Fairy Queen*, which is quoted complete (as ex.5) because it also illustrates the principle of continuity just mentioned. Except possibly at the cadences there are no intervals in the melody that can be predicted, yet they all sound unforced and natural. The modulation in the second half springs no surprises, but the details of its progress and its return to the tonic key are equally unpredictable.

Songs built on ground basses had been used by Italian composers for a good many years before Purcell was born. He was obviously attracted by the challenge which the form presented, since he used it constantly. The difficulty with a short diatonic ground is that the music may be too firmly tied to the tonic key. Purcell did not always avoid this difficulty: the song *O solitude my sweetest choice* hardly ever escapes from the key of C minor. No doubt it was awareness of the problem that prompted him often to modulate and present the bass at one or more different levels, as in Dido's song 'Ah! Belinda', where a temporary switch from C minor to G

minor avoids monotony. At the same time the very flexible vocal line distracts attention from any sameness of key. Where the bass has a less definite tonality there are more opportunities for divergence. The ambiguous ground bass of 'Music for a while' in *Oedipus* allows greater freedom, and Purcell enlarged this by skilful modulation and extension. A particularly striking example of his adroitness in handling the form is the short section of *Gentle shepherds* (an elegy on the death of John Playford) beginning 'Muses, bring your roses hither'. Here the bass is a simple descending scale of C in quavers; but, far from being tied to this key, Purcell managed to make brief allusions to F, E minor and G. In *Cease, anxious world* he not only modulated but used the same formula for the bass of two different sections of the song – one in triple, the other in duple time.

Purcell's increasing preoccupation with Italian music led him to write a good many songs in a florid style, often with quickly moving basses. Examples are the opening sections of *Love arms himself in Celia's eyes* and *Anacreon's Defeat* ('This poet sings the Trojan wars'), both in a heroic vein. These characteristics are strongly marked in the big da capo arias in *The Tempest*, which appear to be too accomplished to be the work, as has been suggested, of some other composer. Though many of his simpler songs can be comfortably performed by amateurs, and no doubt were at the time, it is clear that Purcell was writing primarily for professional singers who, on the evidence of his music, must have had a highly developed technique. He was careful, as the Italians were, to put his runs on an accented syllable and generally chose a long vowel. In passages of this kind music takes precedence over speech; elsewhere he was punctilious in preserving the natural rhythms of English words – over and over again the music fits the text like a glove.

In duets there is the added attraction of two strands of melody woven together, most beautifully in the Latin elegy on Queen Mary, *O dive custos Auriacae domus* and, in a different vein, 'My dearest, my fairest' in *Pausanias*. There are others less serious in intention,

Ex.5

including comic dialogues. The catches, nearly all for three voices, range from the merely convivial to the frankly obscene. The music, though expert, is of minor importance and would hardly be worth mentioning except as an indication of the composer's versatility.

8. INSTRUMENTAL MUSIC. Purcell's instrumental music, whether written in association with choral works or for the theatre or for independent performance, is the most convincing evidence of his genius. In his overtures he favoured the French type, though occasionally inclining to one more nearly related to the Italian. Where there are three movements, the third is normally a solemn adagio, often of a particularly poignant character. In the case of the dramatic music it would be tempting to see some relation between such passages and the play that follows; but in fact there is no obvious distinction between overtures to tragedies and those for comedies. What is common to all of them is a scrupulous attention to details. The same is true of the act tunes (i.e. entr'-actes) and dances. Quite apart from their rhythmical exuberance there are many subtleties of harmony which must have passed unnoticed by many of those who attended the performances. The resources available were limited. In the Chapel Royal Purcell was restricted to strings: the same is true of practically all his incidental music for the theatre. For the odes, recorders, oboes, trumpets and, exceptionally, timpani were available, and he used these resources in all his major works for the stage, with the exception of *Dido and Aeneas*, which is for strings only, and *The Tempest*, which adds to the strings a single oboe. *Dioclesian* is unique in having a part for tenor oboe in the masque, and the symphony in Act 4 of *The Fairy Queen* ('A Sonata plays while the Sun rises') must be one of the earliest instrumental pieces to begin with a timpani solo.

In the dramatic music and the odes Purcell wrote effective obbligatos for wind instruments – for recorders, for example, in the ode *What, what shall be done in behalf of the man*, in the duet 'Hark! how the songsters' in *Timon of Athens*, and in the girl's song 'Why should men quarrel' in *The Indian Queen*; for solo oboe in the ode *Come, ye sons of art, away* and in the air 'Halcyon days' in *The Tempest*; and for trumpet in many pieces of a heroic character. He was also adept at the antiphonal treatment of strings and wind. But since the bulk of his work was for string orchestra it is here that his gift for instrumental writing is most evident – in its dignity, its vivacity and the illumination created by the inner parts.

All this was public music, in which intimacy was incidental. In his chamber music he could give freer expression to his more personal invention. It divides into two obvious categories: works for a viol consort, a medium that was virtually obsolete in his day, and sonatas for the more up-to-date combination of two violins, bass viol and keyboard continuo. The two categories are near to each other in date. Most of the fantasias for viols are exactly dated in the year 1680; and several of the *Ten Sonata's in Four Parts*, published by Purcell's widow in 1697, occur in the same manuscript and in a similar handwriting. The *Sonnata's of III Parts*, published by Purcell himself in 1683, were probably written about the same time, though the autograph does not survive to prove this. Though there are obvious differences between the fantasias and the sonatas, the two categories overlap to some extent, since there are details in the sonatas which are nearer to older

5. *Beginning of 'Celia has a thousand charms': song from 'Orpheus Britannicus'* (London: Pearson, 1706 edition)

English methods than to the current Italian style. It is perhaps not surprising that Corelli was said to have had a 'mean opinion' of Purcell's sonatas: to him the Italian characteristics to which Purcell's publisher drew attention would have seemed less convincing. A similar view is implied by Roger North's reference to Purcell's 'noble set of sonnatas', as 'clog'd with somewhat of an English vein'.

The fantasias, which owe something to the example of Locke, are not only masterpieces of contrapuntal writing but are also passionate revelations of the composer's most secret thoughts. Every possible device of imitation, inversion and augmentation is employed, but the result, far from being an academic exercise, is appealing to the ear and might even be termed romantic in expression. In contrast to the composer's later music the tonality is often ambiguous, not least in some of the homophonic passages which occur by way of contrast. Chromatic movement appears frequently, and virtuosity is not excluded. In the Fantasia upon One Note, where the fourth part repeats middle C throughout, Purcell set himself a severe problem but solved it by exploiting all the possible harmonic progressions and by rhythmic vivacity. The two In Nomines look back firmly to the old English tradition of weaving counterpoint around the plainsong *Gloria tibi Trinitas* as it appears in the Benedictus of Taverner's mass with that title.

The *Sonnata's of III Parts* are described on the title-page as for 'Two Viollins and Basse: to the Organ or

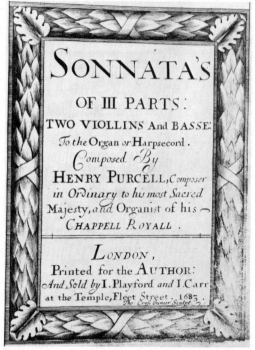

6. *Title-page of Purcell's 'Sonnata's of III Parts'* (*London: Author and John Playford, 1683*)

Harpsecord'. We learn from the preface that Purcell had not originally intended to publish a basso continuo part – a curious observation, since the bass viol part is not always identical with the basso continuo, and in one movement of the fifth sonata the two are completely independent for about 30 bars. If the sonatas were in fact string trios in their original form, a good deal of rewriting must have taken place before they were published. Here, as in the fantasias, there is masterly counterpoint, although the extremes of ingenuity occur less frequently. There are some particularly happy examples of imitation by augmentation. The brisk canzona movements are nearer to the Italian style than the stately introductions, which in general are closer to the older English style. Even though the violin parts are largely confined within a modest range, they show a thorough understanding of the technique of the instrument and, particularly in the *largo* movements, an appreciation of its sensuous qualities.

The *Ten Sonata's in Four Parts* include a single movement in the form of a chaconne which is not a sonata at all. However, no-one is likely to regret its inclusion, as it is one of the very finest, as well as one of the longest, of Purcell's instrumental works. Every possible device of harmonization, figuration and imitation is employed to produce a piece which impresses both by the grandeur of the conception, the wealth of invention and the intimacy of expression. The fact that it was not published until after Purcell's death probably reflects a lack of public support for instrumental music of this kind. This lack of interest would explain why there are no contemporary manuscript copies; and since the autograph has disappeared it is difficult to say when it was written.

Purcell's keyboard music forms only a minor part of

his work. Apart from the eight suites dedicated to Princess Anne, which are agreeable miniatures, there are a number of little pieces presumably designed for amateurs, as well as transcriptions from other works. It is all tasteful but of no great significance when compared with the rest of Purcell's music. Nor do the organ pieces, whether authentic or not, call for more than a passing mention.

9. AUTOGRAPHS, PUBLICATIONS. A detailed list of Purcell's autographs is printed in Holst, pp.106ff. The principal ones are:

(i) *GB-Cfm* 88 (23.H.13), ?1677–82. In addition to anthems by Purcell (some incomplete) it includes his copies of anthems by other composers, including Blow, Locke and Humfrey.

(ii) *GB-Lbm* Add.30930, c1680–83. Sacred music of various kinds and instrumental ensemble music, including 13 fantasias and eight trio sonatas (some incomplete), the latter printed in *Ten Sonata's in Four Parts* (1697).

(iii) *GB-Lbm* RM.20.h.8, c1681–90. Anthems, welcome songs, odes, cantatas and songs (some incomplete). A few items in a copyist's hand.

(iv) *GB-Lgc* VI.6, 1690–95. Songs (some incomplete), mostly from the dramatic music.

Apart from contributions to anthologies and to collective works, and single issues of songs, only a few works by Purcell were published in his lifetime, all of them in London:

Theodosius: or, The Force of Love . . . with the Musick betwixt the Acts (1680) [music anonymous]
Sonnata's of III Parts: Two Viollins and Basse: to the Organ or Harpsecord (1683, 2/1684)
A Musical Entertainment perform'd on November XXII, 1683 it being the Festival of St. Cecilia . . . (1684) [the ode Welcome to all the pleasures]
A Pastoral Elegy on the Death of Mr. John Playford (1687) [Gentle shepherds]
New Songs sung in The Fool's Preferment, or, The Three Dukes of Dunstable (1688)
The Songs of Amphitryon (1690)
The Vocal and Instrumental Musick of the Prophetess, or The History of Dioclesian (1691)
Some Select Songs as they are Sung in the Fairy Queen (1692)
The Songs in the Tragedy of Bonduca (?1695)
The Songs in The Indian Queen: as it is now Compos'd into an Opera (1695)

The following works were published posthumously, also in London:

A Choice Collection of Lessons for the Harpsichord or Spinnet (1696, 3/1699)
A Collection of Ayres, compos'd for the Theatre, and upon other Occasions (1697)
Ten Sonata's in Four Parts (1697)
Te Deum & Jubilate . . . made for St. Caecilia's Day, 1694 (1697)
Orpheus Britannicus: a Collection of all The Choicest Songs for One, Two, and Three Voices (1698–1702/R1967, 2/1706–11, 3/1721)

10. PORTRAITS. The only authentic portraits of Purcell known today are the following:

(i) Portrait in black chalk heightened with white, head, attributed to Godfrey Kneller (1646–1723); it belonged to William Seward (1749–99) and then to Burney, and was acquired by the National Portrait Gallery in 1974. It is believed to be the only surviving portrait of Purcell from life (fig. 2).

(ii) Portrait in oils, head and shoulders, formerly attributed to Kneller. Depicts Purcell as a young man. Inscribed: 'M . Henry Purcell'. National Portrait Gallery, London.

(iii) Engraving, head and shoulders, printed as the

frontispiece to the first violin part of *Sonnata's of III Parts* (1683). Presumably taken from a painting now lost. Description: 'Vera Effigies Henrici Purcell, Aetat: Suae 24'. The engraving in Hawkins's *History* is an inferior copy and like all the portraits in that work is reversed.

(iv) Crayon sketch, head, formerly attributed to Kneller. *GB-Lbm*, Department of Prints and Drawings.

(v) Portrait in oils, head and shoulders, by John Closterman (1656–1713) (fig.3). Traditionally said to have been painted after Purcell's death. National Portrait Gallery. The engraving printed as a frontispiece to *Orpheus Britannicus* (1698) is a copy of this, reversed. Description: 'Henricus Purcell. Aetat: Suae 37.95.'.

WORKS

(*see also §9 above*)

Detailed list, including doubtful and spurious attributions, in F. B. Zimmerman: *Henry Purcell, 1659–1695: an Analytic Catalogue of his Music* (London, 1963) [Z]

Edition: *The Works of Henry Purcell*, The Purcell Society (London, 1878–1965; rev. 2/1961–) [PS]

OPERAS AND SEMI-OPERAS

Z	Title	Text	Type	First performance	Date	PS
626	Dido and Aeneas	N. Tate	opera	London, Josias Priest's School for Young Ladies, Chelsea	1689	iii
627	The Prophetess, or The History of Dioclesian	T. Betterton, after J. Fletcher, P. Massinger	semi-opera	London, Dorset Garden	1690	ix
628	King Arthur, or The British Worthy	J. Dryden	semi-opera	London, Dorset Garden	1691	xxvi
629	The Fairy Queen	?E. Settle, after Shakespeare: A Midsummer Night's Dream	semi-opera	London, Dorset Garden	1692	xii
630	The Indian Queen (final masque by D. Purcell)	Dryden, R. Howard	semi-opera	London, Drury Lane	1695	xix, 1
631	The Tempest, or The Enchanted Island	T. Shadwell, after Shakespeare	semi-opera	—	c1695	xix, 111

PLAYS WITH INCIDENTAL MUSIC AND SONGS

Z	Title	Text	Date	Purcell's contribution	PS
606	Theodosius, or The Force of Love	N. Lee	1680	songs, ensembles, choruses	xxi, 115
589	Sir Barnaby Whigg, or No Wit like a Woman's	T. D'Urfey	1681	1 song with chorus	xxi, 103
581	The History of King Richard II (The Sicilian Usurper)	Tate, after Shakespeare	1681	1 song	xx, 43
593	The Double Marriage	Beaumont, Fletcher	?1682–5	inst music	xvi, 211
590	Sophonisba, or Hannibal's Overthrow	Lee	?1685	1 song	xxi, 109
571	A Fool's Preferment, or The Three Dukes of Dunstable	D'Urfey, after Fletcher: Noble Gentleman	1688	7 songs, 1 duet	xx, 11
572	Amphitryon, or The Two Sosias	Dryden	1690	2 songs, 1 duet, inst music	xvi, 21
577	Distressed Innocence, or The Princess of Persia	E. Settle	1690	inst music	xvi, 122
588	Sir Anthony Love, or The Rambling Lady	T. Southerne	1690	2 songs, 1 duet, inst music	xxi, 87
604	The Massacre of Paris	Lee	1690	1 song (2 settings)	xx, 106
575	Circe	C. D'Avenant	?1690	2 songs, ensembles, choruses	xvi, 95
597	The Gordian Knot Unty'd	—	1691	inst music	xx, 23
598	The Indian Emperor, or The Conquest of Mexico	Dryden, R. Howard	1691	1 song	xx, 41
612	The Wives' Excuse, or Cuckolds make Themselves	Southerne	1691	4 songs	xxi, 162
576	Cleomenes, the Spartan Hero	Dryden	1692	1 song	xvi, 120
580	Henry the Second, King of England	?W. Mountfort, J. Bancroft	1692	1 song	xx, 38
586	Regulus	J. Crowne	1692	1 song	xxi, 51
573	Aureng-Zebe	Dryden	?1692	1 song	xvi, 42
583	Oedipus	Dryden, Lee	?1692	2 songs, 2 trios, choruses	xxi, 1
600	The Libertine	T. Shadwell	?1692	2 songs, ensembles, choruses	xx, 45
602	The Marriage-hater Match'd	D'Urfey	1692	1 duet	xx, 84
579	Epsom Wells	Shadwell	1693	1 duet	xvi, 221
592	The Double Dealer	W. Congreve	1693	1 song, inst music	xvi, 194
587	Rule a Wife and Have a Wife	Fletcher	1693	1 song	xxi, 85
596	The Female Vertuosos	T. Wright, after Molière: Les femmes savantes	1693	1 duet	xx, 7
601	The Maid's Last Prayer, or Any rather than Fail	Southerne	1693	2 songs, 1 duet	xx, 72
607	The Old Bachelor	Congreve	1693	1 song, 1 duet, inst music	xxi, 19
608	The Richmond Heiress, or A Woman once in the Right	D'Urfey	1693	1 duet (dialogue)	xxi, 53
582	Love Triumphant, or Nature will Prevail	Dryden	1694	1 song	xx, 70
591	The Canterbury Guests, or A Bargain Broken	E. Ravenscroft	1694	1 quartet	xvi, 87
595	The Fatal Marriage, or The Innocent Adultery	Southerne	1694	2 songs	xx, 1
603	The Married Beau, or The Curious Impertinent	Crowne	1694	1 song, inst music	xx, 89
632	Timon of Athens	Shadwell, after Shakespeare	1694	songs, duets, inst music, choruses	ii
613	Tyrannic Love, or The Royal Martyr	Dryden	1694	1 song, 1 duet	xxi, 135
611	The Virtuous Wife, or Good Luck at Last	D'Urfey	?1694	inst music	xxi, 148

Z	Title	Text	Date	Purcell's contribution	PS
610	The Spanish Friar, or The Double Discovery	Dryden	1694–5	1 song	xxi, 112
578	The Comical History of Don Quixote, parts i–iii	D'Urfey	1694–5	songs, duets, ensembles, choruses	xvi, 132
570	Abdelazer, or The Moor's Revenge	A. Behn	1695	1 song, inst music	xvi, 1
574	Bonduca, or The British Heroine	after Beaumont, Fletcher	1695	3 songs, 2 duets, ensembles, choruses, inst music	xvi, 45
584	Oroonoko	Southerne	1695	1 duet	xxi, 38
585	Pausanias, the Betrayer of his Country	Norton	1695	1 song, 1 duet	xxi, 44
605	The Mock Marriage	T. Scott	1695	3 songs	xx, 113
609	The Rival Sisters, or The Violence of Love	R. Gould	1695	3 songs, inst music	xxi, 63

ANTHEMS AND SERVICES
(all with bc (org); with chorus 4vv unless otherwise stated)

Z	First line or Title	Type	Date	Forces	PS
1	Awake, put on thy strength	verse	c1682–5	inc., 2 A, B, ?vv, 2 vn, va	xiv, 41
2	Behold, I bring you glad tidings	verse	1687	A, T, B, 2 vn, va	xxviii, 1
3	Behold now, praise the Lord	verse	c1680	A, T, B, 2 vn, va	xiii, 49
4	Be merciful unto me	verse	? before 1683	A, T, B	xxviii, 28
5	Blessed are they that fear the Lord	verse	1688	2 S, A, B, 2 vn, va	xxviii, 42
6	Blessed be the Lord my strength	verse	by Feb 1679	A, T, B	xxviii, 60
7	Blessed is he that considereth the poor	verse	?c1688	A, T, B	xxviii, 71
8	Blessed is he whose unrighteousness is forgiven	verse	c1680–82	2 S, A, 2 T, B	xiii, 71
9	Blessed is the man that feareth the Lord	verse	?c1688	A, T, B	xxviii, 83
10	Blow up the trumpet in Sion	full	by Feb 1679 before 1678	cantoris (S, 2 A, T, B, 5vv), decani (2 S, A, T, B, 5vv)	xxviii, 96
11	Bow down thine ear, O Lord	verse	c1680–82	S, A, T, B	xiii, 103
12	Give sentence with me, O God	verse	by Nov 1681	A/T, T, B	xxxii, 117 (inc.)
13A	Hear me, O Lord, and that soon	verse	c1680–82	S, A, T, B	xiii, 87
13B	Hear me, O Lord, and that soon	verse	c1680–82	S, A, T, B, 5vv	xiii, 90
14	Hear my prayer, O God	verse	before 1683	A, T, B	xxviii, 125
15	Hear my prayer, O Lord	full	c1680–82	inc., 2 S, 2 A, 2 T, 2 B, ?vv	xxviii, 135
16	In thee, O Lord, do I put my trust	verse	c1682	A, T, B, 2 vn, va	xiv, 53
17A	In the midst of life	full	before 1682	S, A, T, B	xiii, 1
17B	In the midst of life	full	before 1682	A, T, B, 2 vn, va	xxviii, 215
18	It is a good thing to give thanks	verse	c1682–5	A, T, B, 2 vn, va	xiv, 1
19	I was glad when they said unto me	verse	1682–3	A, T, B, 2 vn, va	xiv, 97
—	I was glad when they said unto me (incorrectly attrib. Blow in *GB-EL* 6)	full	1685	2 S, A, T, B	ed. B. Wood (London, 1977)
20	I will give thanks unto thee, O Lord	verse	c1682–5	2 S, A, T, B, 9vv, 2 vn, va	xvii, 47
21	I will give thanks unto the Lord	verse	?c1680–82	T, 2 B, 2 vn	xxviii, 139
N67	I will love thee, O Lord	verse		B	xxviii, 157
22	I will sing unto the Lord	full	by Feb 1679	2 S, A, T, B, 5vv	xxviii, 165
23	Let God arise	verse	by Feb 1679	2 T	xxviii, 173
24	Let mine eyes run down with tears	verse	c1682	2 S, A, T, B	xxix, 1
25	Lord, how long wilt thou be angry?	full	c1680–82	A, T, B, 5vv	xxix, 19
26	Lord, who can tell how oft he offendeth?	verse	c1677	2 T, B	xxix, 28
27	Man that is born of a woman	full	c1680–82	S, A, T, B	xxix, 36
28	My beloved spake	verse	before 1678	A, T, 2 B, 2 vn, va	xiii, 24
29	My heart is fixed, O God	verse	c1682–5	A, T, B, 2 vn, va	xiv, 112
30	My heart is inditing	verse	1685	2 S, 2 A, 2 T, 2 B, 8vv, 2 vn, va	xvii, 69
31	My song shall be alway	verse	probably 1690	B/S, 2 vn, va	xxix, 51
32	O consider my adversity	verse		A, T, B	xxix, 68
33	O give thanks unto the Lord	verse	1693	S, A, T, B, 2 vn	xxix, 88
34	O God, the king of glory	full	by Feb 1679	4vv only	xxix, 108
D4	O God, they that love thy name	—		inc.	xxxii, 120
35	O God, thou art my God	full	c1680–82	2 S, A, T, B, 8vv	xxix, 111
36	O God, thou hast cast us out	full	c1680–82	2 S, 2 A, T, B, 6vv	xxix, 120
37	O Lord God of hosts	full	c1680–82	2 S, 2 A, T, B, 8vv	xxix, 130
38	O Lord, grant the king a long life	verse	1685	A, T, B, 2 vn	xxix, 141
39	O Lord our governor	verse	by Feb 1679	3 S, 2 B	xxix, 152
40	O Lord, rebuke me not	verse		2 S	xxix, 168
41	O Lord, thou art my God	verse	c1680–82	A, T, B	xxix, 179
42	O praise God in his holiness	verse	c1682–5	A, T, 2 B, 2 vn, va	xiv, 21
43	O praise the Lord, all ye heathen	verse	by Nov 1681	2 T	xxxii, 1
44	O sing unto the Lord	verse	1688	S, A, T, 2 B, 2 vn, va	xvii, 119
45	Out of the deep have I called	verse	?c1680	S, A, B	xxxii, 8
46	Praise the Lord, O Jerusalem	verse	probably 1689	2 S, A, T, B, 5vv, 2 vn, va	xvii, 146
47	Praise the Lord, O my soul, and all that is within me	verse	c1682–5	2 S, 2 T, 2 B, 2 vn, va	xiv, 131
48	Praise the Lord, O my soul, O Lord my God	verse	1687	A, B, 2 vn	xvii, 166
49	Rejoice in the Lord alway	verse	c1682–5	A, T, B, 2 vn, va	xiv, 155
50	Remember not, Lord, our offences	full	c1680–82	5vv	xxxii, 19
51	Save me, O God	full	by Nov 1681	2 S, A, T, B, 6vv	xiii, 64
52	Sing unto God	verse	1687	B	xxxii, 23
53	The Lord is king, be the people never so impatient	verse		2 S	xxxii, 36
54	The Lord is king, the earth may be glad	verse	1688	B	xxxii, 44
55	The Lord is my light	verse	c1682–5	A, T, B, 2 vn, va	xiv, 78
56	The way of God is an undefiled way	verse	1694	2 A, B, 6vv	xxxii, 58

Z	First line or Title	Type	Date	Forces	PS
57	They that go down to the sea in ships	verse	1685	A, B, 2 vn	xxxii, 71
58A	Thou know'st, Lord, the secrets of our hearts	verse	before 1683	no solo vv	xiii, 6
58B	Thou know'st, Lord, the secrets of out hearts	verse	before 1683	S, A, T, B	xxix, 46
58C	Thou know'st, Lord, the secrets of our hearts	full	1695	flatt tpts (slide tpts)	xxxii, 88
59	Thy righteousness, O God, is very high	full		inc., ?4vv	xxxii, 124
60	Thy way, O God, is holy	verse	1687	A, B, 2 vn	xxxii, 91 (inc.)
61	Thy word is a lantern unto my feet	verse		A, T, B	xxxii, 101
62	Turn thou us, O good Lord	verse		A, T, B	xxxii, 111
63	Unto thee will I cry	verse	c1682–5	A, T, B, 2 vn, va	xvii, 20
64	Who hath believed our report?	verse	c1679–80	A, 2 T, B	xiii, 11
65	Why do the heathen so furiously rage together?	verse	c1682–5	A, T, B, 2 vn, va	xvii, 1
230	Morning and Evening Service, B♭	full	before Oct 1682	cantoris (S, A, T, B), decani (S, A, T, B)	xxiii, 1
231	Magnificat and Nunc dimittis, g	full		cantoris (A, T, B), decani (2 S, A)	xxiii, 80
232	Te Deum and Jubilate, D	verse	1694	2 S, 2 A, T, B, 5vv, 2 tpt, 2 vn, va	xxiii, 90

OTHER SACRED
(all with bc; firm dates are those of publication)

Z	First line or Title	Text	Voices	Date	PS
130	Ah! few and full of sorrow	G. Sandys	T, B, SATB	c1680	xxx, 109
181	Awake and with attention hear	A. Cowley	B	1688	xxx, 1
182	Awake, ye dead	N. Tate	2 B	1693	xxx, 98
131	Beati omnes qui timent Dominum	Ps cxxviii	S, B, SSAB	c1680	xxxii, 137
183	Begin the song, and strike the living lyre	Cowley	B	1693	xxx, 18
184	Close thine eyes and sleep secure	F. Quarles	S, B	1688	xxx, 105
132	Early, O Lord, my fainting soul	J. Patrick	S, B, SSAB	c1680	xxx, 117
185	Full of wrath his threatening breath	J. Taylor	S		xxx, 28
103–6	4 doxologies		canons, 3–4vv	1, in c, c1680	xxxii, 159, 161, 163, 168
107	God is gone up	Ps xlvii. 5	canon, 7vv		xxxii, 170
186	Great God and just	Taylor	S, SSB	1688	xxx, 33
133	Hear me, O Lord, the great support	Patrick	A, T, ATB	1680–82	xxx, 127
187	Hosanna to the highest		B, AB		xxx, 38
188	How have I strayed	W. Fuller	S, SB	1688	xxx, 44
189	How long, great God	J. Norris	S	1688	xxx, 48
134	In guilty night	—	S, A, B, SAB	1693	xxxii, 128
190	In the black dismal dungeon of despair	Fuller	S	1688	xxx, 53
135	Jehovah, quam multi sunt	Ps iii	T, B, SSATB	c1680	xxxii, 147
108	Laudate Dominum	Ps cxvii	canon, 3vv		xxxii, 170
191	Let the night perish (Job's Curse)	Taylor	S, SB	1688	xxx, 57
136	Lord, I can suffer thy rebukes	Patrick	S, S, A, B, SSAB	c1680	xxx, 136
137	Lord, not to us but to thy name	Patrick	ATB	c1680	xxx, 146
192	Lord, what is man?	Fuller	S	1693	xxx, 62
109	Miserere mei	—	canon, 4vv	1687	xxxii, 171
193	Now that the sun hath veiled his light (An Evening Hymn on a Ground)	Fuller	S	1688	xxx, 70
138	O all ye people, clap your hands	Patrick	SSTB	c1680	xxx, 148
139	O happy man that fears the Lord	Patrick	SSAB		xxx, 157
140	O, I'm sick of life	Sandys	A, T, ATB	c1680	xxx, 160
141	O Lord our governor	Patrick	B, SSAB	c1680	xxx, 167
142	Plung'd in the confines of despair	Patrick	T, B, TTB	c1680	xxx, 180
143	Since God so tender a regard	Patrick	T, B, TTB	c1680	xxx, 187
195	Sleep, Adam, sleep and take thy rest	—	S	1683	xxx, 75
196	Tell me, some pitying angel (The Blessed Virgin's Expostulation)	Tate	S	1693	xxx, 77
197	The earth trembled	Quarles	S/B	1688	xxx, 85
198	Thou wakeful shepherd (A Morning Hymn)	Fuller	S	1688	xxx, 88
199	We sing to him whose wisdom form'd the ear	N. Ingelo	S, SB	1688	xxx, 91
144	When on my sick bed I languish	T. Flatman	T, B, TTB	c1680	xxx, 194
200	With sick and famish'd eyes	G. Herbert	S	1688	xxx, 94
120–5	5 chants, Burford psalm-tune, all doubtful	—	SATB		xxxii, 173f

ODES AND WELCOME SONGS
(with 4vv, 2 vn, va, bc, unless otherwise stated)

Z	First line	Occasion	Date	Forces	PS
340	Welcome, vicegerent of the mighty king	welcome, Charles II	1680	2 S, A, T, B	xv, 1
336	Swifter, Isis, swifter flow	welcome, Charles II	1681	2 S, A, T, B, 2 rec, ob, 3 vn	xv, 24
341	What, what shall be done in behalf of the man?	welcome, Duke of York	1682	2 S, A, T, B, 2 rec	xv, 52
337	The summer's absence unconcerned we bear	welcome, Charles II	1682	2 S, 2 A, T, 2 B	xv, 83
325	From hardy climes and dangerous toils of war	wedding of Prince George of Denmark and Princess Anne	1683	B	xxvii, 1
324	Fly, bold rebellion	welcome, Charles II	1683	2 S, 2 A, T, 2 B, 8vv	xv, 116
339	Welcome to all the pleasures (C. Fishburn)	St Cecilia's Day	1683	2 S, A, T, B	x, 1
329	Laudate Ceciliam	St Cecilia's Day	1683	A, T, B, ?no chorus, no va	x, 44
326	From those serene and rapturous joys (T. Flatman)	welcome, Charles II	1684	2 S, A, T, B	xviii, 1
343	Why, why are all the Muses mute?	welcome, James II	1685	2 S, A, T, 2 B, 5vv	xviii, 37
334	Raise, raise the voice	St Cecilia's Day	c1685	S, B, 3vv, no va	x, 26

Z	First line	Occasion	Date	Forces	PS
344	Ye tuneful Muses	welcome, James II	1686	2 S, A, T, 2 B, 2 rec	xviii, 80
335	Sound the trumpet	welcome, James II	1687	2 A, 2 T, 2 B	xviii, 121
332	Now does the glorious day appear (T. Shadwell)	birthday, Mary II	1689	S, A, T, 2 B, 3 vn	xi, 1
322	Celestial music did the gods inspire	perf. at Mr Maidwell's school	1689	S, A, T, B, 2 rec	xxvii, 29
333	Of old when heroes thought it base (T. D'Urfey)	Yorkshire Feast	1690	2 A, T, 2 B, 5vv, 2 rec, 2 ob, 2 tpt	i
320	Arise, my Muse (D'Urfey)	birthday, Mary II	1690	2 A, T, B, 2 rec, 2 ob, 2 tpt, 2 va	xi, 36
338	Welcome, welcome, glorious morn	birthday, Mary II	1691	S, A, T, 2 B, 2 ob, 2 tpt	xi, 72
331	Love's goddess sure was blind (C. Sedley)	birthday, Mary II	1692	S, 2 A, T, B, 2 rec	xxiv, 1
328	Hail, bright Cecilia (N. Brady)	St Cecilia's Day	1692	S, 2 A, T, 2 B, 2 rec, b rec, 2 ob, 2 tpt, timp	viii
321	Celebrate this festival (N. Tate)	birthday, Mary II	1693	2 S, A, T, B, 8vv, 2 ob, 2 tpt	xxiv, 36
327	Great parent, hail (Tate)	centenary of Trinity College, Dublin	1694	S, A, T, B, 2 rec	xxvii, 59
323	Come, ye sons of art, away (?Tate)	birthday, Mary II	1694	S, 2 A, B, 2 ob, 2 tpt, ?timp	xxiv, 87
342	Who can from joy refrain? (?Tate)	birthday, Duke of Gloucester	1695	2 S, 2 A, T, B, 5vv, 2 ob, tpt	iv

SONGS FOR SOLO VOICE AND CONTINUO

Publication dates given only for those published in Purcell's lifetime; all printed works published in London; in PS xxv unless otherwise stated.

Z

352 Ah! cruel nymph, you give despair
353 Ah! how pleasant 'tis to love (1688)
354 Ah! what pains, what racking thoughts (Congreve), inc., bc lost
355 Amidst the shades and cool refreshing streams (1687)
356 Amintas, to my grief I see (1679)
357 Amintor, heedless of his flocks (1681)
358 Ask me to love no more (A. Hammond) (1694)
359 A thousand sev'ral ways I tried (1684)
360 Bacchus is a power divine
461 Beneath a dark and melancholy grove, with SB
361 Beware, poor shepherds (1684)
362 Cease, anxious world (G. Etherege) (1687)
363 Cease, O my sad soul (C. Webbe) (1678)
364 Celia's fond, too long I've loved her (1694)
365 Corinna is divinely fair (1692)
367 Cupid, the slyest rogue alive (1685)
462 Draw near, you lovers (T. Stanley), with SB
368 Farewell, all joys (1685)
463 Farewell, ye rocks (D'Urfey) (1685), with SB
369 Fly swift, ye hours (1692)
370 From silent shades (1683), also known as Bess of Bedlam
464 Gentle shepherds, you that know (Tate), on the death of John Playford (1687), with SB
371 Hears not my Phyllis (C. Sedley) (1695), also known as The Knotting Song
372 He himself courts his own ruin (1684)
465 High on a throne of glitt'ring ore (D'Urfey), ode to the Queen, 1690, with SB
373 How delightful's the life of an innocent swain
374 How I sigh when I think of the charms (1681)
375 I came, I saw, and was undone (A. Cowley)
376 I envy not a monarch's fate (1693)
377 I fain would be free, inc., bc lost
378 If grief has any power to kill (1685)
379 If music be the food of love (H. Heveningham), 3 settings (1692–5)
380 If prayers and tears, on the death of Charles II
381 I lov'd fair Celia (B. Howard) (1694), music same as We now, my Thyrsis
382 I love and I must, also known as Bell Barr
383 Incassum, Lesbia, rogas (Herbert) (1695), also known as The Queen's Epicedium
384 In Cloris all soft charms (J. Howe) (1684)
385 In vain we dissemble (1685)
386 I resolve against cringing (1679)
387 I saw that you were grown so high (1678)
388 I take no pleasure in the sun's bright beams (1681)
389 Leave these useless arts in loving, solo version of duet in Shadwell: Epsom Wells
390 Let each gallant heart (J. Turner) (1683)
391 Let formal lovers still pursue (1687)
466 Let us, kind Lesbia, give away (1684), with SB
392 Love arms himself in Celia's eyes
393 Love is now become a trade (1685)
394 Lovely Albina's come ashore
395 Love's power in my heart shall find no compliance (1688)

396 Love, thou canst hear, tho' thou art blind (R. Howard) (1695)
397 More love or more disdain I crave (Webbe) (1678)
467 Musing on cares of human fate (D'Urfey) (1685), with SB
399 My heart, whenever you appear (1685)
400 Not all my torments can your pity move
468 No, to what purpose should I speak (Cowley), with SB
401 No watch, dear Celia, just is found (1693)
402 O! fair Cedaria, hide those eyes
403 O! how happy's he (W. Mountfort), inc., bc lost, melody from 1st act tune of Dioclesian, 1690
404 Olinda in the shades unseen
405 On the brow of Richmond Hill (D'Urfey) (1692)
406 O solitude, my sweetest choice (K. Philips) (1687)
407 Pastora's beauties, when unblown (1681)
408 Phyllis, I can ne'er forgive it (1688)
409 Phyllis, talk no more of passion (1685)
410 Pious Celinda goes to prayers (Congreve) (1695)
411 Rashly I swore I would disown (1683)
412 Sawney is a bonny lad (P. A. Motteux) (1694)
469 Scarce had the rising sun appear'd (1679)
470 See how the fading glories of the year (1689), with SB
413 She loves and she confesses too (Cowley) (1683)
414 She that would gain a faithful lover (1695)
415 She who my poor heart possesses (1683)
416 Since one poor view has drawn my heart (1681)
471 Since the pox or the plague (1679), with SB
417 Spite of the godhead, pow'rful love (A. Wharton) (1687)
444 Stript of their green our groves appear (Motteux) (1692)
418 Sweet, be no longer sad (Webbe) (1678)
s70 Sweet tyranness, I now resign (1678), solo version of trio
420 Sylvia, now your scorn give over (1688)
421 The fatal hour comes on apace
422 They say you're angry (Cowley) (1685)
423 This poet sings the Trojan wars (1688), also known as Anacreon's Defeat
424 Through mournful shades and solitary groves (R. Duke) (1684)
425 Turn then thine eyes, solo version of duet in The Fairy Queen
426 Urge me no more
427 We now, my Thyrsis, never find (Motteux) (1693), music same as I lov'd fair Celia
428 What a sad fate is mine, 2 settings
429 What can we poor females do? (1694), solo version of duet
472 What hope for us remains now he is gone?, on the death of Matthew Locke (1679)
430 When first Amintas sued for a kiss (D'Urfey) (1687)
431 When first my shepherdess and I (1687)
432 When her languishing eyes said 'love' (1681)
433 When I a lover pale do see (1678)
434 When my Acmelia smiles
D201 When night her purple veil had softly spread, B, 2 vn; PS xxi
435 When Strephon found his passion vain (1683)
436 When Thyrsis did the splendid eye (1675)
437 While Thyrsis, wrapt in downy sleep (1685)
438 Whilst Cynthia sung, all angry winds lay still (1686)
440 Who but a slave can well express
441 Who can behold Florella's charms? (1695)
442 Why so serious, why so grave? (Flatman), inc., bc lost
443 Ye happy swains, whose nymphs are kind (1685)
473 Young Thyrsis' fate, ye hills and groves, deplore, on the death of Thomas Farmer, with SB

SONGS FOR SOLO VOICE AND CONTINUO IN STAGE WORKS
(some with chorus; Z no. of stage work in parentheses)

Aeolus, you must appear [see While these pass o'er]; Ah! Belinda (626); Ah! cruel, bloody fate (606); Ah! how sweet it is to love (613); Ah! me to many deaths (586); All our days and our nights (627); Arise, ye subterranean winds (631); A thousand, thousand ways (629); Begon, curst fiends of hell (630); Beneath the poplar's shadow (590); Blow, Boreas, blow (589); Britons, strike home (574)

Celia has a thousand charms (609); Celia, that I once was blest (572); Charon the peaceful shade invites (627); Come all to me (632); Come, all ye songsters of the sky (629); Come away, do not stay (583); Come away, fellow sailors (626); Come down, come down, my blusterers (631); Come ev'ry demon who o'ersees (575); Come if you dare (628); Come unto these yellow sands (631); Corinna, I excuse thy face (612); Cynthia frowns whene'er I woo her (592)

Dear, pretty youth (631); Dream no more of pleasures past (606); Dry those eyes (631); Fair and serene (631); Fairest isle (628); Fled is my love (571); For Iris I sigh (572); From rosy bowers (578 III); Full fathom five (631); Genius of England (578 II); Great Diocles the boar has killed (627); Great Love, I know thee now (618)

Hail to the myrtle shade (606); Halcyon days (631); Hang this whining way of wooing (612); Hark, behold the heavenly choir (606); Hark how all things (591); Hark, the ech'ing air (629); Hear, ye gods of Britain (574); Hence with your trifling deity (632); Here's the summer, sprightly, gay (629); Hither this way (628); How blest are shepherds (628); How happy is she (609); How happy's the husband (582); Hush, no more (629)

I am come to lock all fast (629); I attempt from love's sickness to fly (630); I call you all to Woden's hall (630); I come to sing great Zempoalla's story (630); If love's a sweet passion (629); If thou wilt give me back my love (571); I'll mount to yon blue coelum (571); I'll sail upon the dog-star (571); I look'd and saw within the book of fate (598); Ingrateful love (612); In vain, Clemene, you bestow (588); In vain 'gainst love I strove (580); I see she flies me (573); I sigh'd and I pin'd (571); I sigh'd and owned my love (595)

Kind fortune smiles (631); Lads and lasses, blithe and gay (578 II); Let monarchs fight (627); Let not a moon-born elf mislead ye (628); Let the dreadful engines (578 I); Let the graces and pleasures repair (627); Let the soldiers rejoice (627); Let us dance, let us sing (627); Love in their little veins (632); Love quickly is pall'd (632); Lucinda is bewitching fair (570)

Man is for the woman made (605); Music for a while (583); Next winter comes slowly (629); No, no, poor suffering heart (576); Now, now the fight's done (606); Now the night is chas'd away (629); Nymphs and shepherds, come away (600); Oft she visits this lone mountain (626); Oh, how you protest (605); O lead me to some peaceful gloom (574); O let me weep (629); One charming night (629)

Pluto, arise (575); Pursue thy conquest, love (626); Pursuing beauty (588); Retir'd from any mortal's sight (581); Return, revolting rebels (632); Sad as death at dead of night (606); Saint George, the patron of our isle (628); Say, cruel Amoret (612); See, even night herself is here (629); See, I obey (629); Seek not to know (630); See my many colour'd fields (629)

See, see the heavens smile (631); See where repenting Celia lies (603); Shake the cloud from off your brow (626); Since from my dear (627); Since the toils and the hazards (627); Sing while we trip it (629); Sound, fame (627); Still I'm wishing (627); Sweeter than roses (585)

Take not a woman's anger ill (609); Tell me no more I am deceived (601); Thanks to these lonesome vales (626); The air with music gently wound (575); The cares of lovers (632); The danger is over (595); The gate to bliss does open stand (606); There's not a swain (587); There's nothing so fatal as woman (571); They tell us that your mighty powers above (630); Thou doting fool (628)

Though you make no return to my passion (601); Thrice happy lovers (629); Thus happy and free (629); Thus the ever grateful spring (629); Thus the gloomy world (629); Thus to a ripe consenting maid (607); Thy genius, lo! (2 settings) (604); 'Tis dark alone can give me ease (571); 'Tis I that have warmed ye (628); To arms, heroic prince (600); Trip it, trip it in a ring (629), also as duet; 'Twas within a furlong (605)

Wake, Quivera (630); What power art thou? (628); What shall I do to show? (627); When a cruel long winter (629); When first I saw the bright Aurelia's eyes (627); When I am laid in earth (626); When I have often heard (629); When the world first knew creation (578 I); While these pass o'er the deep (631); Whilst I with grief (610); Why should men quarrel? (630); Ye blustering brethren (628); Ye gentle spirits of the air (629); Yes Daphne [Xansi], in your looks I find (629); Ye twice ten hundred deities (630); Your hay it is mowed (628)

SONGS FOR TWO OR MORE VOICES AND CONTINUO

Dates given only for those published in Purcell's lifetime; for S, B, and in PS xxii unless otherwise stated.

Z
480 Above the tumults of a busy state
481 A grasshopper and a fly (D'Urfey) (1686); PS xxv

482 Alas, how barbarous are we (K. Philips)
D171 A poor blind woman, 2 S, B
483 Come, dear companions of th'Arcadian fields (1686)
484 Come, lay by all care (1685)
485 Dulcibella, when e'er I sue for a kiss (A. Henley) (1694)
486 Fair Cloe, my breast so alarms (J. Glanvill) (1692)
487 Fill the bowl with rosy wine (A. Cowley) (1687)
489 Go, tell Amynta, gentle swain (Dryden)
541 Hark, Damon hark, 2 S, B, 2 rec, 2 vn; PS xxvii
542 Hark how the wild musicians sing, 2 T, B, 2 vn; PS xxvii
490 Haste, gentle Charon, 2 B
491 Has yet your breast no pity learn'd? (1688)
492 Hence, fond deceiver (1687)
493 Here's to thee, Dick (Cowley) (1688)
494 How great are the blessings (Tate) (1686), also known as A Health to King James
543 How pleasant is this flowery plain, S, T, 2 rec (1688)
495 How sweet is the air and refreshing (1687)
544 If ever I more riches did desire (Cowley), 2 S, T, B, 2 vn; PS xxvii
545 In a deep vision's intellectual scene (Cowley), 2 S, B, also known as The Complaint
496 In all our Cynthia's shining sphere (from E. Settle: The World in the Moon)
497 In some kind dream (G. Etherege) (1687)
498 I saw fair Cloris all alone (W. Strode) (1686)
499 I spy Celia, Celia eyes me
500 Julia, your unjust disdain
501 Let Hector, Achilles and each brave commander (1689)
502 Lost is my quiet for ever (1691)
503 Nestor, who did to thrice man's age attain (1689)
504 O dive custos Auriacae domus (H. Parker), 2 S, on the death of Queen Mary (1695)
505 Oft am I by the women told (Cowley) (1687)
506 Oh! what a scene does entertain my sight, with rec/vn
507 Saccharissa's grown old (1686)
508 See where she sits (Cowley), with 2 vn
509 Sit down, my dear Sylvia (D'Urfey) (1685)
510 Soft notes and gently raised (J. Howe), with 2 rec (1685)
s69 Sweet tyranness, I now resign, 2 S, B (1667)
511 Sylvia, thou brighter eye of night
512 Sylvia, 'tis true you're fair (1686)
513 There ne'er was so wretched a lover as I (Congreve)
514 Though my mistress be fair (1685)
546 'Tis wine was made to rule the day, S, SSB
515 Trip it, trip it in a ring, duet version of solo song in The Fairy Queen
516 Underneath this myrtle shade (Cowley) (1692)
547 We reap all the pleasures, inc., STB, 2 rec; PS xxvii
517 Were I to choose the greatest bliss (1689)
518 What can we poor females do?, also as solo song
519 When gay Philander left the plain (1684)
520 When, lovely Phyllis, thou art kind (1685)
521 When Myra sings (G. Granville) (1695)
522 When Teucer from his father fled (D. Kenrick) (1686)
D172 When the cock begins to crow, 2 S, B
523 While bolts and bars my day control
524 While you for me alone had charms (J. Oldham)
525 Why, my Daphne, why complaining? (1691)

SONGS FOR TWO OR MORE VOICES AND CONTINUO IN STAGE WORKS
(some with chorus; Z no. of stage work in parentheses)

Ah! how happy are we, A, T (630); Art all can do, why then will mortals, 2 S, B (578 I); As Amoret and Thyrsis, S, B (607); As soon as the chaos was made, S, B (602); Behold the man that with gigantic might (A Dialogue between a Mad Man and a Mad Woman), S, B (608); But ere we this perform, 2 S (626); Can'st thou, Marina, leave, A, T, B (606); Celemene, pray tell me, 2 S (584); Come away, no delay, 2 B (627); Come let us agree, S, B (632); Come, let us leave the town, S, B (629)

Fair Iris and her swain, S, B (572); Fear no danger, 2 S (626); For folded flocks, S, B (628); Good neighbour, why do you look awry?, 2 S, A, B (591); Hark! how the songsters, 2 S (632); Hark, my Damilcar, S, B (613); Hear, ye sullen powers below, A, T, B (583); Jenny, 'gin you can love, S, T (571); Laius, hear!, A, B (583); Leave these useless arts in loving, S, B (579), also as solo song; Let all mankind the pleasures share, S, B (627); Let the fifes and the clarions, 2 A (629); Love, thou art best of human joys, S, B (596)

Make room for the great god of wine, 2 B (627); May the god of wit inspire, A, T, B (629); My dearest, my fairest, S, T (585); No more, Sir, no more, S, B (588); No, no, resistance is but vain, 2 S (601); Now the maids and the men (Dialogue between Corydon and Mopsa), A, B (629); O, the sweet delights of love, 2 S (627); Shepherd, leave decoying, 2 S (628); Since times are so bad, S, B (578 II); Sing all ye muses, A, B (578 I); Sing ye Druids all, 2 S (574); Sound a parley, S, B (628)

Tell me why, my charming fair, S, B (627); They shall be as happy, 2 S,

B (629); To arms, your ensigns straight display, A, B (574); To Mars let 'em raise, A, T, B (627); Turn, then thine eyes, 2 S (629), also as solo song; Two daughters of this aged stream, 2 S (628); What flatt'ring noise is this, A, T, B (630); With this sacred charming wand, 2 S, B (578 I); You say 'tis love, S, B (628)

CATCHES

Publication dates given only for those published in Purcell's lifetime; for 3vv and in PS xxii unless otherwise stated.

Z

240	A health to the nut-brown lass (J. Suckling), 4vv (1685)
241	An ape, a lion, a fox and an ass (1686)
242	As Roger last night to Jenny lay close
599	At the close of the evening, 3 B (1691), in Beaumont, Fletcher: The Knight of Malta; PS xx
243	Bring the bowl and cool Nantz, ?1693–4
244	Call for the reckoning
245	Come, let us drink (A. Brome), with bc
246	Come, my hearts, play your parts (1685)
247	Down, down with Bacchus (1693)
248	Drink on till night be spent (P. Ayres) (1686)
249	Full bags, a brisk bottle (J. Allestry) (1686)
250	God save our sovereign Charles (1685)
251	Great Apollo and Bacchus
252	Here's a health, pray let it pass
253	Here's that will challenge all the fair (1680), also known as Bartholomew Fair
254	He that drinks is immortal (1686)
255	If all be true that I do think (1689)
256	I gave her cakes and I gave her ale (1690)
257	Is Charleroy's siege come too? (?1693)
574	Jack, thou'rt a toper (1695), in Fletcher: Bonduca; PS xvi
101	Joy, mirth, triumphs I do defy, 4vv
258	Let the grave folks go preach (1685)
259	Let us drink to the blades (?1691)
260	My lady's coachman, John (1688)
594	My wife has a tongue (1685), in E. Ravenscroft: The English Lawyer; PS xvi
261	Now England's great council's assembled (1685)
262	Now, now we are met and humours agree (1688)
263	Of all the instruments that are (1693)
264	Once in our lives let us drink to our wives (1686)
265	Once, twice, thrice, I Julia tried
266	One industrious insect (?R. Thomlinson), also known as Insecta praecauta, alterius merda
267	Pale faces, stand by (Mr Taverner) (1688)
268	Pox on you for a fop
269	Prithee be n't so sad and serious (Brome)
270	Room for th'express, written on the fall of Limerick, July 1694
271	Since the duke is return'd (1685)
272	Since time so kind to us does prove
273	Sir Walter enjoying his damsel
274	Soldier, soldier, take off thy wine, 4vv
275	Sum up all the delights (1688)
276	The Macedon youth (Suckling), 4vv (1686)
277	The miller's daughter riding (1686)
278	The surrender of Limerick (?1691)
279	'Tis easy to force, 4 B (1685)
280	'Tis too late for a coach (1686)
281	'Tis women makes us love, 4vv (1685)
282	To all lovers of music (Carr) (1687)
283	To thee, to thee and to a maid (1685)
284	True Englishmen drink a good health, 'Song with music on the 7 Bishops' (c1689)
285	Under a green elm lies Luke Shepherd's helm, 4vv (1686)
286	Under this stone lies Gabriel John (1686)
287	When V and I together meet (1686)
288	Who comes there? (1685)
289	Wine in a morning makes us frolic and gay (T. Brown) (1686)
290	Would you know how we meet (T. Otway) (1685)
291	Young Colin cleaving of a beam (D'Urfey) (1691)
292	Young John the gard'ner, 4vv (1683)

STRINGS AND WIND
(in PS xxxi unless otherwise stated)

Z

730	Chacony, g, 4 str
731	Fantasia upon a Ground, D/F, 3 vn/rec, bc, c1680
745	Fantasia upon One Note, F, 5 viols, c1680
732–4	3 fantasias, d, F, g, 3 viols, c1680
735–43	9 fantasias, g, B♭, F, c, d, a, e, G, d, 4 viols, 1680
746	In Nomine, g, 6 viols, c1680
747	In Nomine, g Dorian, 7 viols, c1680

860	March and Canzona, c, 4 flatt (slide) tpt, 1692
770	Overture, G [concert version of introduction to Swifter, Isis, swifter flow], 4 str, 1681
771	Overture, d, 4 str
772	Overture, g, 5 str
752	Pavan, g, 3 vn, bc, c1680
748–51	4 pavans, A, a, B♭, g, 2 vn, bc, c1680
N773	Prelude, g/d, vn/rec
850	Sonata, D, tpt, str, ?1694
780	Sonata, g, vn, bc; reconstructed by T. Dart for vn, b viol, bc
790–801	[12] Sonnata's of III Parts, 2 vn, b viol, bc (org/hpd), c1680 (London, 1683); PS v
802–11	Ten Sonata's in Four Parts, 2 vn, b viol, bc, c1680 (London, 1697); PS vii
770	Suite, G, 4 str, inner parts inc.

HARPSICHORD
(source of transcriptions, with Z no., in square brackets)

Editions: PS vi [unreliable]

H. Purcell: Complete Harpsichord Works, ed. H. Ferguson (London, 1964)

Old English Composers for the Virginal and Harpsichord, ed. E. Pauer (London, 1879)

* – in Ferguson, not in PS
† – in PS, not in Ferguson
†* – in Pauer only

The Second Part of Musick's Hand-maid (London, 1687[7]):

T694		Song Tune, C [Ah! how pleasant 'tis to love, 353]
T695	*	Song Tune, C [Sylvia, now your scorn give over, 420]
647–8		2 marches, C
T689		A New Minuet, d
649–50		2 minuets, a, a
T688		Minuet, d [Raise, raise the voice, 344/6]
655		A New Scotch Tune, G
T682		A New Ground, e [Welcome to all the pleasures, 339/3]
646		A New Irish Tune [Lilliburlero], G
653		Rigadoon, C
656		Sefauchi's Farewell, d
665	*	Suite, C

A Choice Collection of Lessons, hpd/spinet (London, 1696):

660–63, 666–9		8 suites, G, g, G, a, C, D, d [Hornpipe from The Married Beau, 603/3], F [Minuet from The Double Dealer, 592/3]
T687		March, C [The Married Beau, 603/8]
T698		Trumpet Tune, C [The Indian Queen, 630/4a]
T680		Chaconne, g [Timon of Athens, 632/201]
T686		Jig, g [Abdelazer, 570/7]
T678		Trumpet Tune 'Cibell', C
T697		Trumpet Tune, C [Dioclesian, 627/21]
		7 airs:
641		G
T675		d [The Indian Queen, 630/22]
T676		d [The Double Dealer, 592/7]
T693(2)		g [Abdelazer, 570/6]
T696(1)	*	d [2nd version of T675]
T696(2)	*	d
—	*	F [The Indian Queen]
		4 grounds:
645		Ground in Gamut, G
T681		c [Ye tuneful Muses, 344/11]
D221		c, possibly by Croft
D222	*	d [Celebrate this festival, 321/2a]
		3 hornpipes:
T683	*	B♭ [Abdelazer, 570/8]
T684		d 'Round O' [Abdelazer, 570/2]
T685		e [The Old Bachelor, 607/4]
		4 overtures:
T690	†*	c [The Indian Queen, 630/3a]
T691	†*	D [Timon of Athens, 632/1]
T692	†*	D [The Fairy Queen, 629/3ab]
T693(1)	†	g [The Virtuous Wife, 611/1]
		Suite, a:
652	†	Prelude
642	†*	Almand, Corant
654		Saraband
664	†*	Suite, B♭: Almand, Corant, Saraband
644		Corant, G
651		Minuet, G
670	*	The Queen's Dolour, a
T677	*	Canary, B♭ [The Indian Queen, 630/18]

| — | Prelude for the Fingering, C, attrib. Purcell in *The Harpsichord Master*, i (London, 1697), anon. in later vols.; ed. in Petre |
| — | Voluntary, no.9 of *Ten Select Voluntaries* (London, *c*1780), 1 movt of which may be by Purcell; see Cooper |

ORGAN
(all in PS vi)

716	Verse, F
717–20	4 voluntaries, C, d, d (double org), G
721	Voluntary on the 100th Psalm, A

THEORETICAL WORKS

'A Brief Introduction to the Art of Descant: or, Composing Musick in Parts', in J. Playford: *An Introduction to the Skill of Musick* (London, 12/1694/R1972) [partly rev. from earlier work of Campion, Simpson, Playford and others]

(4) Daniel Purcell (*d* London, buried 26 Nov 1717). Composer and organist, brother of (3) Henry (ii). In a list of April 1679 he is mentioned as one of the choristers of the Chapel Royal who attended the king at Windsor in August and September of the previous year. He was organist of Magdalen College, Oxford, from 1688 to 1695 and during this period wrote anthems, and an ode for St Cecilia's Day. He contributed a few songs to collections from 1685, but his principal activity as a composer of secular music began after his brother's death, when he supplied the music for the final masque in *The Indian Queen*, published in 1696. From then until 1707 he wrote incidental music for more than 40 plays. Further activity was probably arrested by the invasion of Italian opera in the early years of the 18th century. Some odes for the court and for St Cecilia's Day date from the same period. In 1700 he was one of the competitors for a setting of Congreve's masque *The Judgment of Paris* and was awarded the third prize (see Lincoln). From 1713 until his death he was organist of St Andrew's, Holborn, London. He was a competent composer, though without his brother's imagination, and wrote some agreeable chamber music.

WORKS
(all printed works published in London)

MASQUES

The Judgment of Paris (W. Congreve), 1700 (1702)

PLAYS WITH INCIDENTAL MUSIC AND SONGS

The Indian Queen (Dryden, R. Howard), 1695; final masque only, rest by (3) H. Purcell (ii); *GB-Lbm*, 1696[5]
Pausanias, the Betrayer of his Country (Norton), 1695
Neglected Virtue, or The Unhappy Conqueror (H. Horden), 1695
Amalasont, Queen of the Goths, or Vice Destroys Itself (J. Hughes), 1696
Brutus of Alba, or Augusta's Triumph (G. Powell), 1696, *Lcm*, *T*; songs (1696)
Cynthia and Endymion, or The Loves of the Deities (T. D'Urfey), 1696
Ibrahim the Thirteenth, Emperor of the Turks (M. Pix), 1696; 1 song in 1696[4]
The Lost Lover, or The Jealous Husband (M. de la Rivière Manley), 1696
Love's Last Shift, or The Fool in Fashion (C. Cibber), 1696; 1 song in 1696[5], 1696[9] and 1699[6]
The Relapse, or Virtue in Danger (J. Vanbrugh), 1696; songs (1707)
The Spanish Wives (Pix), 1696
The Younger Brother, or The Amorous Jilt (A. Behn), 1696; 1 song in Wit and Mirth, iii (2/1707)
The Triumphs of Virtue, 1697
The World in the Moon (E. Settle), 1697; songs (1697)
Amyntas, or The Impossible Dowry (J. Oldmixon), 1698; 1 song in 1699[4] and Wit and Mirth, iv (1706)
Caligula (J. Crowne), 1698
The Campaigners, or The Pleasant Adventures at Brussels (D'Urfey), 1698; 3 songs in The Songs in Phaeton (1698), 2 in 1699[6]
Phaeton, or The Fatal Divorce (C. Gildon), 1698; songs (1698)
Sauny the Scot, or The Taming of the Shrew (J. Lacy), 1698
The Constant Couple, or A Trip to the Jubilee (G. Farquhar), 1699; 1 song in 1699[4] and Wit and Mirth, iv (1706)
Iphigenia (J. Dennis), 1699
The Island Princess, or The Generous Portuguese (P. A. Motteux), 1699; songs (1699)

The Famous History of the Rise and Fall of Massaniello (D'Urfey), 1699; songs (1699)
The Grove, or Love's Paradise (Oldmixon), 1700; songs (1700)
Love Makes a Man, or The Fop's Fortune (Cibber), 1700; songs in A Collection of New Songs (1701), 1 in A Collection of the Choicest Songs (*c*1715)
The Pilgrim [The Secular Masque] (Dryden), 1700; songs (1701)
The Reformed Wife, or the Lady's Cure (W. Burnaby), 1700
The Unhappy Penitent (C. Trotter), 1700; songs (1701)
Psyche, *c*1700
The Emperor of the Moon (Behn), *c*1700
The Rival Queens, or The Death of Alexander the Great (N. Lee), 1701; songs (1701)
The Bath, or The Western Lass (D'Urfey), 1701; 1 song in Wit and Mirth, iv (1706)
The Funeral, or Grief A-la-mode (R. Steele), 1701; 1 song in Wit and Mirth, iv (1706)
The Humour of the Age (T. Baker), 1701; 3 songs in A Collection of New Songs (1701), 1 in A Collection of the Choicest Songs (*c*1715)
The Inconstant, or The Way to Win Him (Farquhar), 1702; songs (1702)
The Modish Husband (Burnaby), 1702; 1 song in Mercurius Musicus (1701)
The Patriot, or The Italian Conspiracy (C. Gildon), 1702; songs (1702)
The Careless Husband (Cibber), 1704
The Faithful Bride of Granada (W. Taverner), 1704; songs (*c*1704)
Macbeth (?W. D'Avenant, after Shakespeare), *c*1704
The Northern Lass (R. Brome), 1705; songs (1705)
The Tender Husband (Steele), 1705
The Basset-table (S. Centlivre), 1706; songs (1706)
The Beaux' Stratagem (Farquhar), 1707
Farewell Folly, or The Younger the Wiser (Motteux), 1707; 1 song in Wit and Mirth, v (1714)

About 75 songs from plays published in single sheets: see *BUCEM*

SACRED VOCAL

O miserable man, 1693[1]
11 solo anthems, *GB-Lbm*: I am well pleased; I will magnify thee, O God; I will sing unto the Lord; In thee, O Lord, have I put my trust; Lord, thou hast searched me (with chorus); Lord, rebuke me not (with chorus); My God, my God, look upon me; O God, thou art my God; O let my mouth be filled; Praise the Lord, O my soul; Put me not to rebuke
Hear my prayer, O Lord, verse anthem, *Lbm*; The Lord gave the word, anthem, *T*
Magnificat and Nunc dimittis, e, ed. J. Stainer (London, 1900)

SECULAR VOCAL

Begin and strike the harmonious lyre (T. Yalden), Oxford, St Cecilia's Day, 1693, *Lbm*
The loud-tongu'd war, welcome song for William III on his return from Flanders, 1697, *Lbm*
Welcome, welcome, glorious day, Princess Anne's birthday, 1698, *Lcm*
Again the welcome morn we sing, Princess Anne's birthday, 1700, *Lbm*
Shepherds, tune your pipes, 1706, *Lbm*, *Och*
Six Cantatas, 1v, bc, 2 with vn acc. (1713)
18 songs and duets in 1685[6], Quadratum musicum (1687), 1687[6], 1688[6], 1687[7], 1688[8], 1688[9], 1689[5], 1690[5], 1696[9], 1699[4], 1700[6]; also in collections and single sheets, see *BUCEM*
2 odes, lost (see Husk); Cecilia, charming saint; Prepare the hallow'd strain

INSTRUMENTAL

6 Sonata's or Solos, 3 for vn, bc (hpd), 3 for fl, bc (hpd) (1698); nos.1–3 in Six Sonatas or Solos, fl, bc (hpd), compos'd by Mr G. Finger and D. Purcell (1709)
Sonata, 2 fl, in A Choice Collection of Airs or Ariett's for two Flutes (1707)
6 Sonatas, 3 for 2 fl, b, 3 for fl, b (*c*1710)
The Psalms Set Full, org/hpd (1718)
Hpd pieces in A Collection of Lessons and Aires (1702)
3 sonatas, tpt, str, *GB-Lbm*

(5) Edward Purcell (*b* Westminster, London, baptized 6 Sept 1689; *d* London, 1 July 1740). Organist and composer, son of (3) Henry (ii). He became an orphan on the death of his mother in February 1706. In her will she left him music and instruments and mentioned that in accordance with her husband's wishes she had given him a good education. On his uncle's death in 1717 he applied for the post of organist at St Andrew's, Holborn, London, but was unsuccessful. A second attempt in the following year, when a vacancy occurred through Maurice Greene's appointment to St Paul's Cathedral, had the same result. From 1726 till his death he was organist of St Margaret's, Westminster. He published a few songs and wrote some chants.

(6) Edward Henry Purcell (*d* London, buried 5 Aug 1765). Organist, son of (5) Edward. Since he is listed as a chorister in the Chapel Royal in 1737 he can hardly be identifiable with Henry, son of Edward and Anne Purcell, who was born in 1716. He worked in London and was organist of St John's, Hackney, from 1753 until his death.

BIBLIOGRAPHY

W. H. Husk: *An Account of the Musical Celebrations on St Cecilia's Day* (London, 1857), 178, 180, 184–6

W. H. Cummings: *Purcell* (London, 1881)

A. Nicoll: *A History of Restoration Drama, 1660–1700* (Cambridge, 1923, 4/1952)

D. Arundell: *Henry Purcell* (London, 1927/*R*1971)

H. Dupré: *Purcell* (Paris, 1927; Eng. trans., 1928/*R*1975)

H. C. Colles: *Voice and Verse: a Study in English Song* (London, 1928)

E. J. Dent: *Foundations of English Opera* (Cambridge, 1928/*R*1965)

A. K. Holland: *Henry Purcell: the English Musical Tradition* (London, 1932, 2/1948)

F. de. Quervain: *Der Chorstil Henry Purcell's* (Berne, 1935)

J. A. Westrup: 'Fact and Fiction about Purcell', *PMA*, lxii (1935–6), 93

——: *Purcell* (London, 1937, rev. 4/1980)

C. L. Day and E. B. Murrie: *English Song-books, 1651–1702* (London, 1940)

S. Favre-Lingorow: *Der Instrumentalstil von Purcell* (Berne, 1950)

W. Meinardus: *Die Technik des Basso Ostinato bei Henry Purcell* (diss., U. of Cologne, 1950)

S. Demarquez: *Purcell: la vie, l'oeuvre* (Paris, 1951)

G. van Ravenzwaaij: *Purcell* (Haarlem and Antwerp, 1954)

H. Wessely-Kropik: 'Henry Purcell als Instrumentalkomponist', *SMw*, xxii (1955), 85–141

R. Sietz: *Henry Purcell: Zeit, Leben, Werk* (Leipzig, 1956)

T. Dart: 'Purcell's Chamber Music', *PRMA*, lxxxv (1958–9), 81

I. Holst, ed.: *Henry Purcell (1659–1695): Essays on his Music* (London, 1959)

M. Tilmouth: 'The Technique and Forms of Purcell's Sonatas', *ML*, xl (1959), 109

J. Wilson, ed.: *Roger North on Music* (London, 1959)

R. E. Moore: *Henry Purcell and the Restoration Theatre* (London, 1961)

M. Laurie: *Purcell's Stage Works* (diss., U. of Cambridge, 1962)

D. Schjelderup-Ebbe: *Purcell's Cadences* (Oslo, 1962)

J. A. Westrup: 'Purcell's Music for "Timon of Athens"', *Festschrift Karl Gustav Fellerer* (Regensburg, 1962), 573

F. B. Zimmerman: 'Purcell and the Dean of Westminster: some New Evidence', *ML*, xliii (1962), 7

——: *Henry Purcell, 1659–1695: an Analytical Catalogue of his Music* (London, 1963)

M. Laurie: 'Did Purcell Set *The Tempest*?', *PRMA*, xc (1963–4), 43

J. A. Westrup: 'Purcell's Parentage', *MR*, xxv (1964), 100

J. Buttrey: *The Evolution of English Opera between 1656 and 1695: a Reinvestigation* (diss., U. of Cambridge, 1967)

F. B. Zimmerman: *Henry Purcell, 1659–1695: his Life and Times* (London, 1967)

——: 'Sound and Sense in Purcell's "Single Songs"', in V. Duckles and F. B. Zimmerman: *Words to Music* (Los Angeles, 1967), 45–90

J. Buttrey: 'Dating Purcell's "Dido and Aeneas"', *PRMA*, xciv (1967–8), 51

R. Covell: 'Seventeenth-century Music for The Tempest', *SMA*, ii (1968), 43

A. H. King: 'Benjamin Goodison and the First "Complete Edition" of Purcell', *Musik und Verlag: Karl Vötterle zum 65. Geburtstag* (Kassel, 1968), 391

G. Rose: 'Purcell, Michelangelo Rossi and J. S. Bach: Problems of Authorship', *AcM*, xl (1968), 203

H. D. Johnstone: 'English Solo Song, c. 1710–1760', *PRMA*, xcv (1968–9), 67

F. B. Zimmerman: 'Anthems of Purcell and Contemporaries in a Newly Rediscovered "Gostling Manuscript"', *AcM*, xli (1969), 55

R. McGuinness: *English Court Odes, 1660–1820* (Oxford, 1971)

F. B. Zimmerman: *The Anthems of Henry Purcell* (New York, 1971)

R. E. Burkart: *The Trumpet in England in the Seventeenth Century with Emphasis on its Treatment in the Works of Henry Purcell* (diss., U. of Wisconsin, 1972)

S. Lincoln: 'A Congreve Masque', *MT*, cxiii (1972), 1078 [on Daniel Purcell]

G. Rose: 'A New Purcell Source', *JAMS*, xxv (1972), 230

R. Savage: 'The Shakespeare-Purcell *Fairy Queen*: a Defence and Recommendation', *Early Music*, i (1973), 200

D. L. Smithers: *The Music and History of the Baroque Trumpet before 1721* (London, 1973) [chap. on Purcell]

I. Spink: *English Song: Dowland to Purcell* (London, 1974)

P. Dennison: 'The Stylistic Origins of the Early Church Music [of Purcell]', *Essays on Opera and English Music in Honour of Sir Jack Westrup* (Oxford, 1975), 44

N. Fortune: 'The Domestic Sacred Music [of Purcell]', *Essays on Opera and English Music in Honour of Sir Jack Westrup* (Oxford, 1975), 62

F. B. Zimmerman: *Henry Purcell 1659–1695: Melodic and Intervallic Indexes to his Complete Works* (Philadelphia, 1975)

R. Savage: 'Producing Dido and Aeneas: an Investigation into Sixteen Problems', *Early Music*, iv (1976), 393

E. van Tassel: 'Two Purcell Discoveries – 1: Purcell's "Give Sentence"', *MT*, cxviii (1977), 381 [with music suppl.]

B. Wood: 'Two Purcell Discoveries – 2: A Coronation Anthem Lost and Found', *MT*, cxviii (1977), 466

The Gostling Manuscript (Austin, Texas, and London, 1977) [facs. edn.]

B. Cooper: 'Did Purcell write a Trumpet Voluntary?', *MT*, cxix (1978), 791, 1073

J. Meffen: 'A Question of Temperament: Purcell and Croft', *MT*, cxix (1978), 504

R. Petre: 'A New Piece by Henry Purcell', *Early Music*, vi (1978), 374

H. Siedentopf: 'Eine Komposition Purcells im Klavierbuch einer württembergischen Prinzessin', *Mf*, xxxi (1978), 446

B. Wood: 'A Newly Identified Purcell Autograph', *ML*, lix (1978), 329

JACK WESTRUP

Purcell Consort of Voices. English vocal ensemble. The group was formed in 1963 with its members drawn from the larger Purcell Singers, which had already become a regular participant at the Aldeburgh Festival under its conductor, Imogen Holst. The consort made its public début there, and in March 1964 appeared in London for the first time at the Wigmore Hall. It tours regularly throughout Europe and has also appeared in Asia. In spite of its name its repertory goes far back beyond the 17th century and extends to the present day: its concerts have included the first performances of commissioned works. As a recording ensemble it has made its greatest mark in English, French and Italian Renaissance music, often in collaboration with the Musica Reservata instrumental group and under the direction of its countertenor, Grayston Burgess. Its early recording, 'Music of the High Renaissance in England', is as fine a representation of the period as can be found on disc.

BERNARD JACOBSON

Purcell Room. London concert hall on the South Bank, opened in 1967; *see* LONDON, §VI, 5(iv).

Purcell Society. English music publishing society. It was founded in February 1876 for the purpose, as the original prospectus states, 'of doing justice to the memory of Henry Purcell; firstly, by the publication of his works . . . and secondly, by meeting for the study and performance of his various compositions'. The idea of performances was abandoned at an early stage, and the society assumed the form simply of a body of subscribers to its publications, all of which from the start have been produced by Novello.

In 1887, by which time only two volumes had appeared, the society was reorganized with W. H. Cummings as editor and W. B. Squire as honorary secretary. Squire continued in office until 1923, by which time 20 more volumes had appeared. He was succeeded by Gerald M. Cooper and in 1923–8 four more were published. On his own account, Cooper began the publication of the Purcell Society Popular Edition in a format for practical performance, which was not part of the main scheme. There was no further activity until 1957 when, the society having been revived by Anthony Lewis, the first of the remaining volumes appeared, leading to the completion of the entire scheme in 31 volumes by 1965. Many of the pre-1928 volumes have stood up well in the light of recent scholarship, though, for example, certain continuo realizations are no longer acceptable. A programme of revision of all volumes is in progress, employing a handier format reduced from the splendid luxury of the original volumes.

WATKINS SHAW

Pürck [Pürk], Wenzel Raimund (Johann). *See* PIRCK, WENZEL RAIMUND.

Purday. English family of music publishers and musicians. The firm of Purday & Button, established at 75 St Paul's Churchyard in about 1805, was the direct successor of the important Thompson firm (founded 1746); it was known as Button & Purday from about 1806 to 1808, when Purday retired from partnership with S. J. Button and it became Button & Whitaker. Purday was probably the father of Zenas Trivett Purday, who succeeded William Hodsoll at Bland's old shop in High Holborn in 1831, and did a large music trade, principally in humorous sheet songs. His business ceased in 1860. Thomas Edward Purday, another member of the family, also traded in sheet songs from about 1834 to 1862 at 50 St Paul's Churchyard, where he took over the music-publishing part of Collard & Collard, having previously been with Clementi & Co. The business was subsequently in Oxford Street as Thomas Edward Purday & Son (*c*1862–4).

Charles Henry Purday (*b* Folkestone, 11 Jan 1799; *d* London, 23 April 1885) was a composer, writer, lecturer on music and singer of some repute. His compositions include songs, rounds, vocal studies and sacred music, although he is now remembered chiefly by his tune 'Sandon' for Newman's hymn *Lead, kindly light*. He was for some time conductor of psalmody at the Scottish Church in Crown Street, Covent Garden. He edited and arranged many sacred and secular vocal works, which were published by his own firm. This was founded in 1854 in Maddox Street, and was continued at various other addresses until 1870 when he apparently retired.

BIBLIOGRAPHY
C. Humphries and W. C. Smith: *Music Publishing in the British Isles* (London, 1954, rev. 2/1970)

PETER WARD JONES

Purdie, John (*d* nr. Stonehaven, 23 Aug 1891). Scottish music publisher, son of ROBERT PURDIE.

Purdie, Robert (*fl* 1809–*c*1837). Scottish music publisher. He was a music teacher at Jollie's Close, Canongate, Edinburgh, in 1804. In 1809 he opened a music shop and publishing house in Princes Street and by about 1820 he had become the leading music publisher in Edinburgh. Besides a great deal of sheet music, he issued the collection *The Scottish Minstrel* in six volumes (1821–4), edited by Robert Archibald Smith (1780–1829); many of the lyrics were contributed by Lady Nairne under the pseudonym 'Mrs Bogan of Bogan'. Purdie also published Smith's *Irish Minstrel* (*c*1825) and *Select Melodies with Appropriate Words* (*c*1827). He acquired and reissued several of the Gow

family's works after the bankruptcy of Nathaniel GOW in 1827.

About 1837 the business passed to Purdie's son John (*d* nr. Stonehaven, 23 Aug 1891), who also published sheet music for the drawing-room market until 1887. Then Methven, Simpson & Co. continued it until 1967.

BIBLIOGRAPHY
F. Kidson: *British Music Publishers* (London, 1900), 191f

FRANK KIDSON/WILLIAM C. SMITH/
DAVID JOHNSON

Pure intonation. *See* JUST INTONATION.

Purfling (Fr. *filet*; Ger. *Einlage*; It. *filetto*). A narrow inlay of wood inset in a trough cut just inside the border edge of the belly and back of certain instruments, notably viols and violins (for illustration *see* VIOLIN, fig.1). This inlay consists of three narrow strips of wood, the middle one being white or yellow and the outer ones being black. The purfling helps to protect the edges of the instrument and serves also as ornamentation. In cheap violins the purfling is sometimes painted on, maintaining the decorative element but reducing the function of the purfling as a strengthening of the edges. Sometimes instrument makers indulged their love for the ornamental by creating a double line of purfling (this is especially characteristic of Maggini violins) or additional inlay in the form of geometric designs. Stradivari (among others) sometimes adorned his violins by inlays of mother-of-pearl as part of the purfling.

DAVID D. BOYDEN

Puschman, Adam (Zacharias) (*b* Görlitz, 1532; *d* Breslau, 4 April 1600). German poet and Meistersinger. He began working as a tailor and later became a teacher. During his journeyman years he devoted himself to Meistergesang, first in Augsburg and later, between 1556 and 1560, in Nuremberg, where his instructor was Hans Sachs. From 1578 he lived in Breslau. Puschman wrote one comedy, *Von dem Patriarchen Jakob, Joseph und seinen Brüdern* (performed in 1583), some 200 Meisterlieder, sacred and secular, and more than 30 *Meistertöne* (*see* TON(i)) for which he also composed the melodies. His importance for the history of Meistergesang rests primarily on his recodification of the artistic rules for Meistersinger (known as the *Tabulatur*) and the laws of the organization (the *Schulordnung*) in his *Gründtlicher Bericht des deutschen Meistergesangs* (Görlitz, 1571, 2/1596; a manuscript copy, dated 1584, is in his *Singebuch*). More important, he made several manuscript collections of the *Meistertöne* melodies which had hitherto almost exclusively been transmitted orally. The most famous of these was his large *Singebuch* (1588), which was in Breslau (Stadtbibliothek, MS 356) and has been missing since 1945. It was set down after the fashion of the great 15th-century collection of Meistersinger melodies, the Colmarer Liederhandschrift, and contained 350 melodies. Further manuscripts containing melodies by Puschman are in Dresden and Strasbourg (*D-Dlb* M 6 and M 207; *F-Sm* V.154/3).

WORKS
Editions: *Adam Puschman: Gründlicher Bericht des deutschen Meistergesanges*, ed. R. Jonas (Halle, 1888)
Der Meistergesang in Geschichte und Kunst, ed. C. Mey (Karlsruhe, 1892, 2/1901) [Me]
Das Singebuch des Adam Puschman, ed. G. Münzer (Leipzig, 1906) [Mu]

1556: 'Verlorene Gimpelweise'
1570: 'Kurze Amselweise'; 'Klingende Buschweise'
1572: 'Stumpfe Lerchenweise'; 'Zeiselweise'; 'Stieglitzweise', Me 191; 'Hänflingweise'; 'Klingende Nachtigallweise' Me 189
1578: 'Geborgte Grasmückenweise', Me 192; 'Lange Kranichweise'
1580: 'Überlange Adlerweise', Mu 55; 'Falkenweise'
1581: 'Jungfrauweise'; 'Meisenweise', Mu 56; 'Rotkelchenweise'
1582: 'Schwalbenweise'; 'Schalmeienweise'
1583: 'Goldammerweise'
1584: 'Stumpfe Starweise', Mu 55; 'Zaunkönigweise'
1585: 'Sperlingweise'; 'Turteltaubenweise'; 'Helle Drosselweise'; 'Meisterweise'; 'Papageiweise'; 'Bachstelzenweise'; 'Finkenweise'
1587: 'Wachtelweise'
1593: 'Aller Vogel Weise'; 'Sittichweise'
1597: 'Birkenhahnweise'; 'Krammetvogelweise'; 'Eisvogelweise'
1598: 'Geborgte Grünspechtweise'

UNDATED MELODIES

'Geborgte Schneekönigweise'; 'Geborgte Wüstlingsweise'; 'Paradiesvögleinweise'

BIBLIOGRAPHY

E. Goetze: 'Monographie über den Meistersänger Adam Puschman aus Görlitz', Neues Lausitzisches Magazin, liii (1877), 59–157
R. Staiger: Benedict von Watt, Publikationen der IMG, Beihefte, 2nd ser., xiii (Leipzig, 1914)
E. Goetze: 'Adam Puschman', Zeitschrift für deutsche Philologie, xlvi (1915), 84
E. Schumann: Stilwandel und Gestaltveränderung im Meistergesang, Göttinger musikwissenschaftliche Arbeiten, iii (Kassel, 1973)
H. Brunner: Die alten Meister: Studien zu Überlieferung und Rezeption der mittelhochdeutschen Sangspruchdichter im Spätmittelalter und in der frühen Neuzeit, Münchener Texte und Untersuchungen, liv (Munich, 1975)
                                                    HORST BRUNNER

Puschmann, Josef (b nr. Bezděz, Mladá Boleslav district, c1740; d Olomouc, ?3 Feb 1794). Czech musician and composer. From early childhood he learnt the violin and other instruments and soon began to compose. About 1762 he entered the service of Baron Skrbenský in Hošt'álkovy, Silesia, as valet and musician. Five years later he transferred to Count Ignác Dominik Chorinský (1729–92) in Velké Hoštice, Silesia, whose castle orchestra he directed until 1777. For the Opava Minorites in 1768 he composed a sacred melodrama entitled Singspiel über das Leben des ... Heiligen Joseph von Copertin. In 1773 Puschmann was sent by Count Chorinský to study in Vienna, and in 1777 he composed a cantata for two voices to celebrate the wedding of the count's daughter Marie with Erasmus Ludwig von Stahrremberg, and in the same year he applied for the post of cathedral musical director in Olomouc to succeed Anton Neumann, taking it up the next year and holding it until his death.

Both as a person and as an artist Puschmann was the most remarkable of the Olomouc Cathedral musical directors. Apart from his duties in the cathedral, he took part in the musical academies which Archbishop Colloredo organized in his palace, and he continued to keep up his musical contacts with his former employer, Count Chorinský. He composed both secular and sacred music, of which his instrumental works are in an early classical style with rococo traits. His dramatic works and cantatas are known only through the printed librettos.

WORKS

(all unpublished; MSS in CS-Bm, KRa, OP)

Instrumental: 7 symphonies, 4 for use as graduals; 5 serenades; 4 partitas for wind insts; 1 vn concerto; 1 va concerto
Vocal: 9 masses; 1 Requiem; 1 Te Deum; 2 litanies; 14 miscellaneous church compositions

BIBLIOGRAPHY

C. d'Elvert: Geschichte der Musik in Mähren und Österreich-Schlesien (Brno, 1873), suppl., 160
B. Indra: 'Šlechtická kapela na zámku ve Vel. Hošticich v 2.polovině 18.století' [The aristocratic orchestra at the castle of Velké Hoštice in the second half of the 18th century], Slezský sborník, liii (1955), 22
——: 'Archivní materiály k starším hudebním dějinám Slezska' [Archival material for the earlier musical history of Silesia], Slezský sborník, lvi (1958), 114
K. Boženek: 'Hudebně dramatická centra ve Slezsku v 18. století' [Musico-dramatic centres in 18th-century Silesia], Časopis Slezského muzea, xx (1971), 138
                                                    JIŘÍ SEHNAL

Pushkin, Alexander Sergeyevich (b Moscow, 26 May 1799; d St Petersburg, 29 Jan 1837). Russian poet. Two factors determine the enormous appeal that his writings have had for Russian composers – the extraordinary breadth and variety of their character and the purely musical appeal of their language. Pushkin combined a knowledge of French and English literature (Shakespeare and Byron in particular) and the sophistication characteristic of the upper class in Moscow and St Petersburg with a deep attachment to the Russian countryside and Russian legends and fairy stories. A free-thinking liberal, he was always suspect to the authorities and spent six years of his short life relegated to the provinces. His writings, prose stories, verse and verse dramas show a protean ability to identify himself with the most widely different characters and temperaments; and the lively, irreverent, sardonic tone of his correspondence, though echoed closely in such works as Graf Nulin and the Gavriliada, The Golden Cockerel and The Queen of Spades, disappears entirely not only in many of the lyrics but in such deeply compassionate and profound dramas as Boris Godunov, The Miserly Knight and Mozart and Salieri, where Shakespeare's influence is unmistakable. In his handling of the Don Juan legend (The Stone Guest) Pushkin combined a Byronic disillusion and worldliness of tone with astonishingly original touches of erotic psychology and an ability to evoke atmosphere by the most economical means.

In his use of words Pushkin emancipated the Russian language from its adolescent conventions and achieved a simplicity and directness of speech and imagery that have few parallels outside the language of ancient Greece. His ear, untrained and uninterested in music proper, had a unique instinct for combining, contrasting and exploiting the multiple vowel sounds and the extraordinary wealth of liquid, sibilant and guttural consonants that give the Russian language its beauty and variety, while he retained a simplicity and a naturalness of expression that often give his poetry and prose an almost conversational character.

Each composer has taken what he needed from Pushkin, beginning with his contemporary Glinka, who set an early fairy story (Ruslan and Lyudmila). Dargomïzhsky also set a fairy story and then took The Stone Guest for his attempt to write an opera purely in recitalter. Musorgsky chose a historical drama (Boris Godunov), Rimsky-Korsakov two fairy stories (Tsar Saltan and The Golden Cockerel) and one of the Dramatic Scenes (Mozart and Salieri); Tchaikovsky a verse novel modelled on Byron's Don Juan (Eugene Onegin), a verse historical romance (Mazeppa) and a sardonic conte (The Queen of Spades); Rakhmaninov another of the Dramatic Scenes and the early, romantic Gypsies (Aleko). Stravinsky made his opera Mavra from the sardonic and mysterious Little House at Kolomna, while Glier and Asaf'yev have written ballets based on Pushkin's works, and Metner's 32 songs to texts by Pushkin show both the fascination exercised by these lyrics and the difficulty of doing them justice. The vein is not yet exhausted but among major latterday composers Prokofiev, apart from incidental and film music for Pushkin dramas, made only three song settings and Shostakovich hardly more.

WORKS SET TO MUSIC

Arap Petra Velikovo [Peter the Great's Moor]: opera by Arapov, ?1949; opera by Lourié, 1958

Bakhchisaraysky fontan [The fountain of Bakchisaray]: Kerim Girci, incidental music by Cavos, 1825; Marie Potocká, opera by Mechura, 1871; opera by Fedorov, Ekaterinoslav, 1895; opera by Zubov, 1898; opera op.46 by Arensky, 1899; opera by A. Il'yinsky, excerpts perf. Moscow, 1899; opera by Krīlov, 1912; opera by Parusinov, 1912; ballet by Asaf'yev, 1934; Girey-Khan, opera by Smetanin, 1934; radio opera by Shaposhnikov, 1937, rev. 1946; incidental music by Atovmyan, 1937; incidental music by Vasilyev, 1938; ov. by Y. K. Arnold

Barīshnya–krestyanka [Lady into peasant girl]: opera by Larionov, St Petersburg, 1875; Ruses d'amour, ballet by Glazunov, 1898; opera by Spassky, 1923; opera by Biryukov, Moscow, 1947; Akulina, operetta by Kovner, 1948; ballet by Bruns, 1955; ballet by Asaf'yev

Boris Godunov: opera by Musorgsky, St Petersburg, 1874; incidental music by Shaporin, 1934; Prokofiev, 1936, Denbsky, 1937, Kenel, 1937, Slonov, 1937, Vasilenko, 1937, Kochurov, 1949; Kozlov

Domik v Kolomne [The little house in Kolomna]: Mavra, opera by Stravinsky, 1922; ballet by Asaf'yev, 1943

Dubrovsky: opera by Nápravnik, 1895; incidental music by Vlasov, 1937; incidental music by Wolfenson, 1937

Graf Nulin [Count Nulin]: comic opera op.44 by Lishen, 1876; opera by Strelnikov, 1938; ballet by Asaf'yev, 1940–41; opera by Koval, 1949

Grobovshchik [The undertaker]: musical comedy by Yanovsky, 1923; comic opera by Admoni-Krasnīy; ballet by Asaf'yev, 1941–3

Kamennīy gost [The stone guest]: opera by Dargomīzhsky, perf. 1872; incidental music by Ferkelman, 1932, Shebalin, 1935, Asaf'yev, 1936, Gnessin, 1936, Denbsky, 1937, Kondratyev, 1937, Radchenko, 1937, Vlasov, 1937; opera by Biryukov, 1941; ballet by Asaf'yev, 1943–6; symphonic poem by Bunin, 1949; incidental music also by Deshevov, Lobachev, Kryukov and Nikolayev

Kapitanskaya dochka [The captain's daughter]: opera by Cui, Moscow, 1914; opera by S. A. Katz, 1936–8, rev. 1946; radio opera by Kryukov, 1944

Kavkazsky plennik [The prisoner of the Caucasus]: opera by Cavos, St Petersburg, 1823; dramatic scenes by Alyab'yev, 1820s; opera by Cui, 1883; ballet by Asaf'yev, 1936–7; sym. poem by Alexeyev

Mednīy vsadnik [The bronze horseman]: Sym. no.10 by Myaskovsky, 1927; sym. poem by Barabshev, 1937; opera by Popov, 1937; opera by Asaf'yev, 1942; Suite, solo v, chorus, orch by Pozdneyev, 1942; vocal frag. by Dudkevich, 1949; ballet by Glier, 1949; 8 pf pieces by Beder

Motsart i Sal'yeri [Mozart and Salieri]: opera by Rimsky-Korsakov, Moscow, 1898; incidental music by Shebalin, 1937

Pikovaya dama [The queen of spades]: incidental music by Cavos, 1836; opera by Halévy, 1850; opera by Tchaikovsky, St Petersburg, 1890; incidental music (for film) by Prokofiev, 1934; film score by Auric, 1948

Pir Petra Velikovo [The feast of Peter the Great]: ?cantata by Verstovsky, 1860; cantata by Afanas'yev

Pir vo vremya chumī [A feast in time of plague]: opera by Cui, 1901; incidental music by Y. F. L'vova, 1932; opera by Lourié, 1933, orch suite arr. 1943; incidental music by Asaf'yev, 1936; suite by Pozdneyev, 1936; incidental music by Kozlov, 1937; opera by Tarnopolsky, 1937; opera by Asaf'yev, 1940; opera by Goldenweiser, 1942, perf. ?Moscow, 1945

Poltava: Maria ili Mazepa, opera by Sokal'sky, 1859; Mazepa, opera by Baron Vietinghof-Scheel, St Petersburg, 1859; oratorio by Vasileyev-Buglay, 1944; music (for radio) by Shebalin, 1945

Rusalka: opera by Dargomīzhsky, 1856; incidental music by Kovner, 1937; incidental music by Lobachev, 1937; music (for radio) by Shebalin, 1937

Ruslan i Lyudmila: ballet by Scholtz, 1821; opera by Glinka, 1842; Volshebnoye zerkalo [The magic mirror], ballet by Koreshchenko, St Petersburg, 1903; Skazka [Story], incidental music by Rimsky-Korsakov, 1879–80

Skazka o mertvoy tsarevne [The story of the dead princess]: sym. poem by Yanovsky, 1902; opera by Krasev, 1924; children's opera by Weisberg, 1937 (radio), Leningrad, 1941; incidental music (for marionette play) by Gelfman, 1940; music (for radio) by Shebalin, 1944; opera by Kotilko, 1946, perf. Saratov, 1947; opera by Chernyak, 1947, perf. Moscow, 1957, rev.; ballet by Deshevov, 1949; children's opera by Tzībin, 1949; film music by Nikolsky, 1951

Skazka o pope i rabotnike yevo Balde [The story of the priest and his workman Balda]: incidental music by Oransky, 1926; incidental music by Kochetov, 1937; radio opera by Bakalov, Moscow, 1938; ballet by Chulaki, 1940

Skazka o zolotoy rībke [The story of the golden fish]: sym. poem by

Krasnoperov, 1943; ballet by V. A. Alexandrov, 1950s; incidental music by Nikolayev, 1951

Skupoy rītsar [The miserly knight]: opera by Rachmaninov, 1921; incidental music by Denbsky, 1937, Deshevov, 1937, Shebalin, 1937, Lobachev, Nikolayev; monologue, B solo, by Tikots, 1936

Stantsīonnīy smotritel [The post stage master]: opera by Kryukov, 1940; Postmeister Wyrin, opera by F. Reuter, Berlin, 1947; ballet by Petrov, 1955

Torzhestvo Vakkha [The triumph of Bacchus]: cantata by Dargomīzhsky, St Petersburg, 1846, rev. as lyric opera-ballet, Moscow, 1867

Tsīganī [The gypsies]: opera by Kashperov, 1850; opera by Lishen, 1876; Aleko, opera by Rakhmaninov, 1893; Aleko, opera by Yuona, 1897; cantata by Khessin, 1899; opera by Ferretto, Modena, 1900; opera by Mironov, c1900; operatic scenes by Shefer, St Petersburg, 1901; opera by Ziks, 1906; opera by Galkauskas, St Petersburg, 1908; opera by Leoncavallo, 1912; suite by Kalafati, 1936; music (for radio) by Shebalin, 1936; ballet by Vasilenko, 1936; incidental music by Denbsky, 1937; sym. poem by Krein, 1937; ballet and orch suite by Sorokin, 1937; opera by Kalafati, 1939–41

Yegipetskiye nochi [Egyptian nights]: Kleopatra, ballet by Glier, 1905, perf. Moscow, 1926; ballet by Arensky, 1908; incidental music by Prokofiev, 1934

Zolotoy petushok [The golden cockerel]: opera by Krasev, 1907; opera by Rimsky-Korsakov, Moscow, 1909; music for children's play, by Zolotaryov, 1923; incidental music by Lobachev, 1937

BIBLIOGRAPHY

M. M. Ivanov: *Pushkin v muzīke* (St Petersburg, 1889)

C. Cui: 'Vliyaniye Pushkina na nashikh kompozitorov i na ikh vokal'nīy stil' ' [The influence of Pushkin on our composers and on their vocal style], *Novosti i birzhevaya gazeta* (26 May 1899); also in *Ts. Kyui: Izbrannīye stat'i*, ed. Yu. A. Kremlyov (Leningrad, 1952), 501

N. Kashkin: 'Znacheniye poezii A. S. Pushkina v russkoy muzīke' [The importance of Pushkin's poetry in Russian music], *Zhizn'* (1899), no.5, p.126

S. Bulich: *Pushkin i russkaya muzīka* (St Petersburg, 1900)

L. Sachetti: 'Otnosheniye Pushkina k muzīke' [Pushkin's attitude to music], *Sbornik statey v chest' D. F. Kobenko* (St Petersburg, 1913), 26

L. Grossman: *Pushkin v teatral'nīkh kreslakh* [Pushkin in the theatre] (Leningrad, 1926)

S. Serapin: *Pushkin i muzīka* (Sofia, 1926)

B. Tomashevsky: 'Pushkin i ital'yanskaya opera', *Pushkin i evo sovremenniki* [Pushkin and his contemporaries], xxxi–xxxii (Leningrad, 1927), 49

A. Glumov: 'Pushkin, Verstovskiy i Viyel'gorskiy' [Pushkin, Verstovsky and Wielhorski], *SovM* (1934), no.1, p.71

V. Kiselyov and S. Popov, eds.: *Pushkin v romansakh i pesnyakh evo sovremennikov (1816–1937)* [Pushkin in the songs and ballads of his contemporaries (1816–1937)] (Moscow, 1936)

I. Eyges: *Muzīka v zhizni i tvorchestve Pushkina* [Music in the life and work of Pushkin] (Moscow, 1937)

M. Pekelis: 'Dramaturgiya Pushkina i russkaya opera', *SovM* (1937), no.5, p.45

B. Yagolim: 'Ukazatel' proizvedeniy sovetskikh avtorov na tekstī i syuzhetī Pushkina' [A catalogue of works by Soviet composers based on texts and subjects by Pushkin], *SovM* (1937), no.2, p.99

V. Yakovlev: 'Pushkin i russkiy opernīy teatr', *SovM* (1937), no.3, p.19; no.6, p.42

G. Abraham: 'Mussorgsky's *Boris* and Pushkin's', *ML*, xxvi (1945), 31

B. V. Asaf'yev: 'Pushkin v russkoy muzīke', *SovM* (1949), no.6, p.7

V. Vasina: 'Lirika Pushkina i puti russkovo romansa' [Pushkin's lyrical poems and the development of the Russian ballad], *SovM* (1949), no.7, p.7

V. Yakovlev: *Pushkin i muzīka* (Moscow and Leningrad, 1949, 2/1957)

E. Berlyand-Chernaya: *Pushkin i Chaykovskiy* (Moscow, 1950)

A. Glumov: *Muzīkal'nīy mir Pushkina* [Pushkin's musical world] (Moscow and Leningrad, 1950)

S. Shlifshteyn: *Glinka i Pushkin* (Moscow and Leningrad, 1950)

B. Shteynpress: 'Kompozitor Pushkinskoy porī: Pushkin v tvorchestve Alyab'yeva' [A composer of Pushkin's time: Pushkin in the works of Alyab'yev], *SovM* (1952), no.11, p.72

I. Bel'za: *Motsart i Sal'yeri* (Moscow, 1953)

N. El'yash: *Pushkin i baletnīy teatr* [Pushkin and the ballet] (Moscow, 1970)

M. Cooper: 'Pushkin and the Opera in Russia', *Opera*, xxii (1971), 96

G. Norris: 'Rakhmaninov's Student Opera', *MQ*, lix (1973), 441 [Rakhmaninov's *Aleko* and Pushkin's *Tsīganī*]

E. Stöckl: *Puškin und die Musik* (Leipzig, 1974)

MARTIN COOPER (text)
APRIL FITZLYON (writings list, bibliography)

Pustet. German firm of publishers. On 30 September 1826 Friedrich Pustet (*b* Hals, nr. Passau, 25 Feb

1798; *d* Munich, 6 March 1882) founded the Pustet publishing firm and retail business in Regensburg (after 1833 the firm also produced paper). The publishing enterprise began with production of popular and academic literature on history and theology, but after 1845 it concentrated on liturgical books and thereby acquired an international reputation. Branches were founded in New York and Cincinnati in 1865 (they became independent concerns in 1912) and in Rome in 1898 (independent since 1916); Pope Pius IX appointed Pustet 'Typographus S. Sedis Apostolicae' in 1862. From 1883 until the publication of the Roman Editio Vaticana in the first decade of the 20th century, Pustet's liturgical books were regarded as the authoritative editions. The firm received a 30-year privilege for the production of all official hymnbooks (1868) and subsequently became 'Typographus Sacrorum Rituum Congregationis' (1870). Despite severe hostility the privilege was extended in 1898 for two years, but expired with the abolition of the so-called Medicaea. The company concurrently developed an equal interest in the publication of church music, serving the Regensburg movement for the restoration of church music; it issued Mettenleiter's *Enchiridion Chorale*, Proske's *Musica Divina* and *Selectus Missarum* and Haberl's continuation of *Musica Divina* and *Repertorium Musicae Sacrae*. The catalogue also contained many works by minor composers. After 1945 Pustet issued the new series *Musica Divina* (edited by Stäblein), *Regensburger Tradition* (Schrems), *Die Chorsammlung* (Haberl and Quak) and the collection of early organ pieces *Cantantibus Organis* (Eberhard Kraus). The firm acquired considerable importance by publishing periodicals and yearbooks of church music including the *Fliegende Blätter für katholische Kirchenmusik* (1866, later *Caecilienvereinsorgan*, 1911–37), *Musica sacra* (1868–1937) and the *Caecilien-Kalender* (1876, later *Kirchenmusikalisches Jahrbuch*, 1886–1932). It also published writings on church music by Haberl, Gottron, Johner, Karl Weinmann, Peter Wagner, Hugo Riemann and Kroyer.

AUGUST SCHARNAGL

Puteanus, Erycius [Ericus] [Putte, Eerryk de; Put, Errijck de; Put, Eryck de; Puy, Henry du; Put, Hendrik van; Putten, Hendrik van der] (*b* Venlo, 4 Nov 1574; *d* Louvain, 17 Sept 1646). Dutch humanist and writer on music. He entered the grammar school at Dordrecht in 1585, whence he moved in 1592 to the Gymnasium Tricoronatum at Cologne. He took the master's degree in the arts faculty of Cologne University in 1595 and obtained his baccalaureate in the law faculty of Louvain University in 1597. After receiving a doctorate in law at Padua University in 1600, he was for six years professor of rhetoric at the Schola Palatina in Milan. He returned to Louvain University in 1607 to succeed his teacher, Justus Lipsius, as professor of history, Roman literature and Roman law. In 1614 Archduke Albert appointed him governor of the nearby Brabantine ducal castle. Besides more than 16,000 letters, Puteanus wrote over 90 works, both long and short, on theological, philosophical, historical and educational subjects. Among them is a treatise on music: *Modulata Pallas, sive Septem discrimina vocum ad harmonicae lectionis novum et compendiarium usum aptata et contexta philologo quodam filo* (Milan, 1599). There are also four adaptations of it, in places drastically abridged:

Modulatae lectionis nova et compendiaria directio ex Modulata Pallade contracta (MS), *Musica Plejas, sive Septem notae canendi Epitome Palladis Modulatae* (Venice, 1600), *Musathena, sive Notarum heptas ad harmonicae lectionis novum et facilem usum* (Hanau, 1602) and *Iter Nonianum, dialogus, qui Epitomen Musathenae comprehendit* (appendix to the 1602 edition; It. trans., Milan, 1603, as *Il Noniano*). The last takes its name from a villa outside Padua and is cast in the form of a dialogue on music conducted between Puteanus and a friend while on their way to it. Puteanus originally conceived the work as a concise musical primer for young people in Milan, but before publication he enlarged it into a comprehensive scholarly study. The salient feature is the extension of the Guidonian system of note names (*ut, re, mi, fa, sol, la*) *by the* addition of *bi* for the seventh note. The titles *Modulata Pallas*, *Musica Plejas* and *Musathena* are explained by Puteanus's diffuse and speculative explanations of the number seven, symbolized in antiquity by the goddess Pallas Athene and the Pleiads.

BIBLIOGRAPHY
P. Sweertius: *Athenae belgicae* (Antwerp, 1628), 230ff
J. F. Foppens: *Bibliotheca belgica* (Brussels, 1729), 265ff
R. Hoche: 'Puteanus, Erycius', *ADB*
A. Roersch: 'Puteanus, Erycius', *BNB*
T. Simar: *Etude sur Erycius Puteanus (1574–1646)* (Louvain, 1909)
J. Kleijntjens: 'Puteanus, Erycius', *NNBW*
M. Vogel: *Die Zahl Sieben in der spekulativen Musiktheorie* (diss., U. of Bonn, 1955), 40, 42
H. Hüschen: 'Der Polyhistor Erycius Puteanus und sein Musiktraktat', *Beiträge zur rheinischen Musikgeschichte*, xxxv (1959), 1
HEINRICH HÜSCHEN

Puteus, Vincentius. See DAL POZZO, VINCENZO.

Puttiputi (It.). FRICTION DRUM.

Putz. German family of organ builders. It comprised Andreas Putz (*fl* 1613–57), his sons Georg Putz (*d* Tulln, Lower Austria, 30 May 1694) and Jakob Putz (*d* Passau, 1706), and the latter's son, Martin Putz (*b* Passau; *d* Passau, 1700). Andreas Putz is known to have built organs in the following places: Bozen (Barfüsserkirche, 1613, two manuals, 16 stops; Franziskanerkirche, with Matthäus Aigner, 1618); Brixen (Klarissenkirche, 1620); Innichen (collegiate church, 1620); Kremsmünster (collegiate church, 1624, two manuals, 20 stops); Schlägel (collegiate church, 1634–8, two manuals, 19 stops, largely extant) and Rohrbach (1635, one manual, eight stops). In 1620 Andreas Putz made alterations to the cathedral organ at Brixen; in 1636 he installed a Hornwerk in the gate-tower of the Benedictine Abbey at Lambach and in 1654 he made a positive organ for the refectory at Kremsmünster. He used the kind of specification which had been known in southern parts of the German-speaking countries in the 16th century, featuring three complete diapason choruses respectively on the Great organ, the 'positive' Choir organ and the Pedal, and adding to these a group of foundation stops (often restricted to 16′, 8′ and 4′ stopped pipes); reed stops and non-diapason mutation stops were rare. Jakob Putz built an organ in Burghausen town church in 1668, one in the collegiate church of Berchtesgaden in 1685 and one in the parish church of Münzkirchen in 1689.

BIBLIOGRAPHY
W. M. Schmid: 'Zur Passauer Musikgeschichte', *ZMw*, xiii (1930–31), 289
J. Mutschlechner: *Die Brixener Domorgel* (Brixen, 1931)

A. Dawidowicz: *Orgelbaumeister und Orgeln in Osttirol* (diss., U. of Vienna, 1949)

R. Quoika: *Die altösterreichische Orgel der späten Gotik, der Renaissance und des Barock* (Kassel, 1953)

O. Eberstaller: *Orgeln und Orgelbauer in Österreich* (Graz and Cologne, 1955)

A. Kellner: *Musikgeschichte des Stiftes Kremsmünster* (Kassel, 1956)

W. Senn: 'Andreas Putz: Beiträge zu seiner Tätigkeit in Tirol', *Acta organologica*, viii (1974), 33

HANS KLOTZ

Puxol, Lucas (*fl* 17th century). Spanish or Portuguese composer. He probably belonged to the Catalonian school, and is known by a single tiento in *P-Pm* 1577, Loc.B, 5 (*Libro de cyfra*), of which there is an edition in M. S. Kastner: *Silva ibérica de música para tecla de los siglos XVI, XVII y XVIII*, i (Mainz, 1954).

BARTON HUDSON

Puy [pui]. The name given to literary and musical societies founded mainly in northern France from the 12th century to the early 17th, and to the contests held by them. The word probably derives from the Latin *podium*, referring to a raised place from which the competitors delivered their chansons, and not from the geographical name of Notre-Dame du Puy in Velay where there was an earlier literary society. The early *puys* were formed in honour of the Virgin Mary and elected a *prince du puy* annually. A contest was held for the best *chanson royale* or serventois and the winner was crowned. 'Puy' could be synonymous with 'confrérie' but the latter was rather more like a religious mutual-benefit society. From the 16th century, *puys* became almost exclusively literary, although a *puy de musique* was founded at Evreux about 1570 in honour of St Cecilia. Mystery plays were performed by some *puys*, for example at Amiens, Paris and possibly Rouen.

There were *puys* in many French cities including Abbeville, Amiens, Arras, Beauvais, Caen, Calais, Dieppe, Paris and Rouen as well as in London. The principal feast of the Amiens *puy* took place at Candlemas (2 February). A new master was elected and a banquet held during which a mystery play was performed and a silver crown offered for the best *chanson royale* based on a previously given refrain. The crown was presented to the winner after a Mass for the Dead the next day. The London *puy* statutes of about 1300 state that the crowned singer must ride through the city after the banquet with the old and new *princes du puy*. The Arras *puy* originated in the early 13th century as a branch of the Confrérie de Notre-Dame des Ardents founded in 1120 by the jongleurs Itier and Norman who miraculously received from the Virgin Mary a candle that cured the citizens of plague. The *puy* was founded by the rich bourgeoisie and two *princes* are known: JEHAN BRETEL and Robert Saumillion. The best *chants royaux* were crowned and jeux-partis (*see* JEU-PARTI) were sung. Bretel composed eight songs and 90 jeux-partis probably for performance at the *puy*. ADAM DE LA HALLE may have been a member; he referred to it and its *princes* in his play *Jeu de la feuillie*.

The CANTUS CORONATUS sung in long notes, as described by Johannes de Grocheo, may refer to trouvère songs crowned at a *puy*. The trouvère manuscript *F-Pn* n.a.fr.1050 has crowns drawn above certain songs with the words 'chanson couronée'.

See also MEDIEVAL DRAMA, §III, 3(ii).

BIBLIOGRAPHY

H. T. Riley, ed.: *Munimenta Gildhallae Londiniensis*, ii/1, Rolls Series (London, 1860)

H. Guy: *Essai sur la vie et les oeuvres littéraires du trouvère Adan de le Hale* (Paris, 1898)

E. Robillard de Beaurepaire: *Les puys de palinod de Rouen et de Caen* (Caen, 1907)

E. Faral: *Les jongleurs en France au moyen âge* (Paris, 1910)

E. Delignières: *Essai sur l'histoire de la confrérie de Notre-Dame d'Abbeville* (Abbeville, 1917)

M. Ungureanu: *Société et littérature bourgeoises d'Arras au XIIe et XIIIe siècles* (Arras, 1955)

JANE M. HARRIS-MATTHEWS

Puy, Henry du. *See* PUTEANUS, ERYCIUS.

Puyana, Rafael (*b* Bogotá, 14 Oct 1931). Colombian harpsichordist. He began to study the piano at the age of six, and in 1949 entered the New England Conservatory (Boston) for advanced training as a pianist. In 1951 he became a harpsichord pupil of Wanda Landowska with whom he continued to study until 1957. Meanwhile he graduated from the Hartt College of Music in Hartford. His New York recital début in 1957 was followed by concert tours in North and South America and Europe. He gave his first London recital in 1966.

Of all Landowska's pupils currently before the public, it is perhaps Puyana who most vividly recalls the rhythmic drive and precision, the sharp musical characterizations and compelling virtuosity for which she was justly famed. His performing style has undergone considerable development since his début. He has tended to forsake the modern harpsichord for traditional instruments which enforce a simpler and more direct style. His wide repertory includes music of all national schools from the 16th century to the 18th, as well as many contemporary works. He has made many recordings, both as a soloist and in ensembles.

HOWARD SCHOTT

Puzzi, Giovanni (*b* Parma, 1792; *d* London, 1 March 1876). Italian horn player. He was probably a pupil of the horn virtuoso Luigi Belloli (1770–1817), who lived in Parma from 1790 to 1812. After a stay in Paris during the 1815–16 season, Puzzi moved to London where he remained permanently. He made his début there in 1817, playing his own Concertante, and soon became the leading soloist of the day, playing principal horn in several London orchestras and appearing (as a soloist on eight occasions and in chamber performances nine times) at the Philharmonic concerts between 1817 and 1837. He also organized a wind quintet which performed a series of concerts known as the Classical Concerts for Wind Instruments. In 1826 he married Giacinta Toso, a prominent Italian soprano. He appeared in public less frequently after about 1840, but drew favourable reviews as late as 1850.

Puzzi is regarded as one of the greatest and most influential horn virtuosos of his time. In 1823 the *Quarterly Magazine and Review* remarked that the horn was 'coming into vogue . . . and owes much of its late celebrity to the beautiful execution of Signor Puzzi'. A Sonata Concertante by Cipriani Potter, written for Puzzi, reveals him as a dazzling exponent of the chromatic late hand-horn technique; the difficulty of the horn part baffles modern valve horn players. Puzzi wrote some works for horn and piano, and Pougin (supplement to *Biographie universelle*) credited him with an unpublished horn method. Only two of Puzzi's horns survive: one, made about 1814 by L. J. Raoux, is in the Carse Collection of the Horniman Museum and the other, made about 1826 by M. A. Raoux, is in the Victoria and Albert Museum.

BIBLIOGRAPHY

FétisB

R. Morley-Pegge: *The French Horn* (London, 1960, 2/1973)
H. Fitzpatrick: *The Horn and Horn-playing and the Austro-Bohemian Tradition 1680–1830* (London, 1970)

REGINALD MORLEY-PEGGE/HORACE FITZPATRICK

Pyamour [Piamor], **John** (*fl* c1418; *d* 1431, before 31 July). English composer. He is known solely for his setting of the Marian antiphon *Quam pulcra es*, for three voices, preserved in *I-MOe* α.x.1, 11 and in the second layer of *TRmn* 92 (no.1526, anon.). He became a clerk of Henry V's Chapel Royal between 1416 and 1419–20, when the king commissioned him to impress boy choristers and take them to him in France: in effect, if not title, he seems to have been the first Master of the Chapel Children. In 1427 he was in the service of John, Duke of Bedford, Henry VI's uncle and Regent of France. The style of his motet suggests that he was a contemporary of Dunstable, who died young. The antiphon chant is not used. The music is astonishingly free from dissonance. The melodic idiom, though intricate in phrasing, is exceptionally smoothly managed with few leaps greater than a 3rd; there are subtle, indeed hidden, imitations. The piece has much in common with Dunstable's more famous setting of the same words.

BIBLIOGRAPHY

J. Harvey: *Gothic England* (London, 1948), 87, 221
M. F. Bukofzer: *Studies in Medieval and Renaissance Music* (London, 1951), 74ff
——: 'Fauxbourdon Revisited', *MQ*, xxxviii (1952), 39 [incl. opening of *Quam pulcra es*]
B. L. Trowell: *Music under the Later Plantagenets* (diss., U. of Cambridge, 1960), i, 33, 65; ii, 191, 290

BRIAN TROWELL

Pyatnitsky, Mitrofan Efimovich (*b* Alexandrovka, Bobrov district, 3 July 1864; *d* Moscow, 21 Jan 1927). Russian folksinger and collector of folksongs. He attended the village school, from 1899 to 1903 was a clerk in a Moscow hospital, and for some years took singing lessons from Camillo Everardi. In 1903 he was invited to join a commission on folk music set up by the Society of Friends of Natural Science, Anthropology and Ethnography, attached to Moscow University. He appeared in folk concerts organized by this commission in Moscow and elsewhere: he had a fine baritone voice and was particularly successful in his interpretations of the songs of the Voronezh government, which he had known since childhood. These concerts captured the interest of Russian audiences, and Pyatnitsky was encouraged to form an ensemble of singers and instrumentalists to give regular performances of folk music. In 1910 he founded a larger choir, whose programmes featured not only folksong arrangements but also choral dances, children's games and dramatized scenes of peasant life. He made more than 400 cylinder recordings of folksongs from the Voronezh government, and also formed an invaluable collection of folk instruments and peasant costumes.

After the 1917 Revolution Pyatnitsky's folk choir was given state support, and similar choirs were set up through the Soviet Union. In 1925 he was created Honoured Artist of the Republic. His choir continued to exist after his death; in 1940 it was renamed in his memory Russkiy Narodnïy Khor imeni Pyatnitskovo.

He published *12 russkikh narodnïkh pesen: Voronezhskoy gubernii, Bobrovskovo uyezda* ('12 Russian folksongs from the Bobrov district in the Voronezh government', Moscow, 1904, 2/1912), and 'Starinnïye pesni Voronezhskoy gubernii v narodnoy garmonizatsii' ('Old songs of the Voronezh government in folk harmonization') in the book *O bïlinakh i pesnyakh velikoy Rusi* (1904). Several of the songs from his phonograph collection were published in the anthology *Russkiye narodnïye pesni* ('Russian folksongs', ed. I. K. Zdanovich, Moscow and Leningrad, 1950).

BIBLIOGRAPHY

'Krest'yanskiye kontsertï v Moskve' [Folk concerts in Moscow], *Moskovskiy listok* (25 Jan/8 Feb 1911)
Kontsertï M. E. Pyatnitskovo s krest'yami [Pyatnitsky's folk concerts] (Moscow, 1914)
I. Martïnov: *Narodnïy khor* [The folk choir] (Moscow, 1944, enlarged 3/1950 as *Gosudarstvennïy russkiy narodnïy khor imeni Pyatnitskovo* [The State Russian Pyatnitsky Folk Choir], 4/1953)
V. Paskhalov: 'M. E. Pyatnitsky i istoriya vozniknoveniya evo khora' [Pyatnitsky and the history of the founding of his choir], *SovM sbornik*, ii (1944)
G. Dorokhov: *M. E. Pyatnitsky: sozdatel' russkovo narodnovo khora* [Founder of the Russian folk choir] (Voronezh, 1950)
P. Kaz'min: 'Mitrofan Efimovich Pyatnitsky', *SovM* (1955), no.1, p.66
N. Rechmensky: 'Vstrechi s M. Pyatnitskim' [Meetings with Pyatnitsky], *SovM* (1961), no.3, p.109; Ger. trans. as '50 Jahre Pjatnitzki-Chor: Begegnungen mit M. Pjatnitzki', *Musik in der Schule*, xiii (1962), 77
M.Sitkovetskaya: 'Iz arkhiva M. E. Pyatnitskovo' [From the Pyatnitsky archive], *SovM* (1964), no.7, p.35
Yu. Zavadsky: 'Priznatel'nost' khudozhniku' [Gratitude to an artist], *SovM* (1964), no.7, p.41

JENNIFER SPENCER

Pybrac, Guy du Faur de. *See* PIBRAC, GUY DU FAUR DE.

Pycard. English composer of the 15th century; *see* PICARD (1).

Pycharde [Pychard], **Thomas.** *See* PICARD, (1) Pycard.

Pye, Charlotte Alington. *See* BARNARD, CHARLOTTE ALINGTON.

Pygmy music. The term 'pygmy' is used by anthropologists for those peoples with an average height of less than 150 cm. It includes certain negrito peoples of India and south-east Asia. This article is concerned only with the music of African pygmies. These, like the Bushmen of southern Africa, are regarded as the autochthonous hunter–foodgathering peoples of Africa. They now live in small groups and hunting bands within the rain-forest areas of Gabon and Cameroon in the west, the Central African Republic, the Congo Republic and Zaïre, and (if one includes the pygmoid Twa) as far east as Uganda, Rwanda and Burundi. They number in all about 168,000, of whom approximately half live in Zaïre, and include the Binga groups near the Atlantic coast, the Central Twa, the Mbuti of the Ituri forest (about whom Turnbull has written extensively), the Ngombe of the Congo Republic and the Aka and Benzele of the Central African Republic.

Many groups now live a partly settled life, having established symbiotic relationships with village-dwelling Bantu and Sudanic neighbours inhabiting cleared areas of the forest zone, among whom they live for limited periods, exchanging forest produce and their labour for agricultural produce, salt and various useful artefacts. Though their musical talents have brought them fame and respect among their neighbours (and earlier among the ancient Egyptians), their inaccessibility has prevented extensive study of their music.

Its most striking features, apparently common to all groups, are an almost unique wordless yodelling, resulting in disjunct melodies, usually with descending contours (see ex.1); and a varied and densely textured multi-part singing, as complex as any other indigenous African style. This choral music is built up from continuously varied repetitions of a short basic pattern, which takes shape as different voices enter, often with apparent informality, and fill out the texture with a variety of techniques that include hocket, ostinato, canonic imitation and parallel part-movement. Penta- or sub-pentatonic forms are used, with harmonies mainly based on 4ths and 5ths. The frequently clear division of the total cyclic pattern between leader and chorus, common in other African styles, is absent in their most typical music, or obscured by the high degree of overlap between parts, by the passing round of what might be regarded as soloistic parts from one to another, and by a considerable freedom to improvise solo within the metrical and harmonic constraints of the pattern. Some scholars see in this a reflection of the essentially democratic, non-hierarchical structure of pygmy social units.

Ex.1 from chorus of Ngombe women; transcr. H. MacDonald

As might be expected among nomadic peoples, their music is primarily vocal, though some groups own and use drums and other instruments, or, as with the Mbuti, readily adopt for a while the instruments of their villager neighbours. Among the Aka and Benzele pygmies of the Central African Republic a distinctive combination of instrument and voice is observed in the use of a single-pitch stopped flute (such as can be fashioned from a piece of pawpaw stem) to make melodies consisting of alternately whistled and sung pitches. Where another performer joins in to make a duet the second flute is tuned to make an interval of approximately a major 2nd with the first (Arom, 1973).

See also ZAÏRE, §3 (in particular for a discussion of Mbuti musical concepts) and CENTRAL AFRICAN REPUBLIC, §4 and ex.2.

BIBLIOGRAPHY

R. Brandel: 'Music of the Giants and Pigmies of the Belgian Congo', *JAMS*, v (1952), 16
P. Schebesta: 'Pygmy Music and Ceremonial', *Man*, lvii/78 (1957), 62
C. M. Turnbull: 'Music of the Ituri Forest', FE 4483 [disc notes]
——: 'The Pygmies of the Ituri Forest', FE 4457 [disc notes]
——: *Wayward Servants: the Two Worlds of the African Pygmies* (New York, 1965)
S. Arom and G. Taurelle: 'The Music of the Ba-Benzele Pygmies', BM 30 L 2303 [disc notes]
M. Djenda: 'Les pygmées de la Haute Sangha', *Geographica*, iv/14 (1968), 27
M. Vuylstèke: 'Musiques du Gabon: Fang, Kota, Masango, Ndjabi,

Obamba, Pounou, Pygmée', OCR 41 [disc notes]
L. G. Strasbaugh: 'Two Lullabies from the Babinga Babenzélé Pygmies', *Mitteilung der Deutschen Gesellschaft für Musik des Orients* (*Berlin*), xi (1972–3), 79
S. Arom: 'Une méthode pour la transcription de polyphonies . . . orale', *RdM*, lix/2 (1973), 165

PETER COOKE

Pygott [Pygot], **Richard** (*fl* 1st half of the 16th century). English composer. By 1516 he was Master of the Children in Thomas Wolsey's household chapel. In a series of letters written by the dean of the Chapel Royal in March and April 1518, the king is reported to have considered Wolsey's chapel choir better than his own, and Pygott is praised for his training of a chorister then in the king's service. Pygott became a Gentleman of the Chapel Royal in 1524, retaining this post for nearly 30 years. He seems to have been deputy Master of the Children in May 1527. He received many marks of royal favour, including a pension from Bridlington Priory (28 February 1526), a canonry and prebend in the collegiate church of Tamworth (12 May 1530), an allowance from the monastery of Coggeshall, Essex (7 October 1532), and, during the 1540s, regular payments from the royal purse. He was present at the funeral of Henry VIII and at the coronation of Edward VI, and was still alive in January 1552, when a payment was made to him by Princess Elizabeth. Morley mentioned him as a 'practicioner' of music in his *Plaine and Easie Introduction to Practicall Musicke* (1597) and printed an extract from one of his compositions.

Pygott's few surviving compositions are of high quality. His technical command was complete, enabling him to create textures of striking complexity without sacrificing logic and beauty of melodic line as, for example, in the final Agnus Dei of his *Missa 'Veni Sancte Spiritus'*; the passage beginning 'ante omnia saecula' in the Credo exemplifies his unusual fondness for imitative writing.

WORKS

Missa 'Veni Sancte Spiritus', 5vv, *GB-Cu* Peterhouse 471–4, *Lbm* Add.34191 (lacks T)
Domine secundum actum (re), 4vv, *WCc* Mun.12845
Gaude pastore, ant, ?5vv, *Lbm* Add.34191 (B only)
Salve regina, ant, 5vv, *Cu* Peterhouse 471–4, *Lbm* Harl.1709 (lacks T)
Quid petis o fili, carol, 4vv, *Lbm* Add.31922, ed. in MB, xviii (1962, rev. 2/1969)
By by lullaby, 4vv, 1530⁶ (B only)
[textless], 2vv, in T. Morley: *A Plaine and Easie Introduction to Practicall Musicke* (London, 1597) (frag.)

BIBLIOGRAPHY
F. Ll. Harrison: *Music in Medieval Britain* (London, 1958, 2/1963)

NICHOLAS SANDON

Pykini (*fl* ?1370). French composer. He is known only for one four-voice virelai, *Plasanche or tost/Or tost aeux*, which appears in two sources in different versions. The higher parts contain imitation. As the ironic text names a 'roussignol' and a 'pape gay' which 'jolyement et doucement escoutes sans desplaysance', this piece may have been written in Avignon for a pope. His identification with Johannes Roqueni, a papal singer in 1372/3, is purely hypothetical, and there are two better possibilities: Gerardus Picquigny, who was in 1335 and 1358 chaplain and *consanguineus* of the Cardinal of Boulogne, and more probably Robert de Piquigny, who from 1374 until at least 1387 was chamberlain to Charles II of Navarre, Machaut's patron.

BIBLIOGRAPHY
R. H. Hoppin and S. Clercx: 'Notes biographiques sur quelques musiciens français du XIVᵉ siècle, *L'Ars Nova: Wégimont II 1955*, 63

U. Günther: 'Zur Biographie einiger Komponisten der Ars subtilior', *AMw*, xxi (1964), 177
N. E. Wilkins, ed.: *A 14th-century Repertory from the Codex Reina*, CMM, xxxvi (1966), no.40
U. Günther: 'Bemerkungen zum älteren französischen Repertoire des Codex Reina', *AMw*, xxiv (1967), 246
W. Apel, ed.: *French Secular Compositions of the Fourteenth Century*, CMM, liii/1 (1970), no.86

URSULA GÜNTHER

Pykke, Thomas. *See* PACKE, THOMAS.

Pylkkänen, Tauno (*b* Helsinki, 22 March 1918). Finnish composer. He studied composition with Madetoja, Palmgren and Ranta at the Helsinki Academy of Music (1937–40) and musicology at Helsinki University (MA 1941). Appointments followed with the music staff of the Finnish Broadcasting Company (1942–61), as music critic for the newspaper *Uusi Suomi* (1941–69) and as artistic director of the Finnish National Opera (1960–70). In 1958 he was appointed chairman of the Association of Musical Artists of Finland, and in 1967 he joined the Helsinki Academy as lecturer in the history of opera. He published *Oopperavaeltaja* ('The opera wanderer', Helsinki, 1953) and opera has been his chief interest as a composer. His style has been categorized as a kind of Finnish *verismo*, a description that applies both to his handling of dramatic situation and to his musical idiom, which is deeply influenced by Puccini. The success of his operas is largely due to his natural theatrical ability; *Varjo* ('The shadow'), his most wholly satisfactory piece, has, for its thrilling dramatic effect, been compared with *The Consul*. In 1950 he won the third Italia Prize for his radio opera *Sudenmorsian* ('The wolf's bride'). The best of his songs are to be found in the cycles *Kuoleman joutsen* ('The swan of death'), *Kuunsilta* ('Moon bridge') and *Yötön yö* ('Nightless night'). His instrumental music clearly reveals the limitations of his style.

WORKS
(selective list)

OPERAS

Batsheba Saarenmaalla [Bathsheba at Saarenmaa], op.10 (1, A. Kallas), 3 solo vv, male chorus, orch, 1940, rev. 1958
Mare ja hänen poikansa [Mare and her son], op.22 (3, Kallas), 1943
Ikaros, op.33 (P. Knudsen), 1956–60
Simo Hurtta, op.43 (E. Leino), 1948
Sudenmorsian [The wolf's bride], op.47 (radio opera, Kallas), 1950
Varjo [The shadow], op.52 (1, H. Bergman), 1952
Opri ja Oleksi, op.61 (3, K. Mäntylä), 1957
Vangit [The prisoners], op.69 (1. A. Kivimaa), 1964
Tuntematon stilas [The unknown soldier], op.73 (V. Linna), 1967

OTHER WORKS

Ballet: Kaarina Maununtytär, 1960
Orch: Lapin kesä [Summer in Lapland], op.15, sym. poem, 1941; Kullervon sotaanlähtö [Kullervo goes to war], op.20, sym. poem, 1942; Sinfonietta, op.25, 1944; Sym. no.1, op.30, 1945; Sym. Fantasy, op.40, 1948; Ultima thule, op.46, tone poem, 1949; Vc Conc., op.48, 1950; Sym. Prelude, op.54, 1952
Choral: Metropolis, op.58 (M. Kuusi), cantata, 3 narrators, chorus, orch, 1955; Maternita, op.65, song cycle, female vv, 1958
Solo song cycles: Kuoleman joutsen [The swan of death], op.21 (Kallas), 1v, pf/orch, 1943; Kuunsilta [Moon bridge], op.55 (Y. Jylhä), 1v, pf, 1953; Visioner, op.63 (S. Kulvik), 1v, pf, 1958; Yötön yö [Nightless night], op.74, 1v, pf, 1969; 1 other cycle; many independent songs, some with orch
Inst: Notturno, op.23, vn, pf, 1943; Str Qt, op.27, 1945; Fantasia appassionata, op.57, vc, pf, 1954

Principal publishers: Fazer, Finnish Broadcasting Co., Westerlund

ILKKA ORAMO

Pyllois [Pylloys, Pylois, Pyloys]**, Johannes.** *See* PUL-LOIS, JOHANNES.

Pyne. English family of musicians descended from two brothers, James Kendrick (i) (?1795–1857), a tenor, and George (?1790–1877), a male alto. James Kendrick's son, James Kendrick (ii) (1810–93), was a composer and organist of Bath Abbey and father of (2) James Kendrick Pyne (iii). George Pyne had two daughters who were both sopranos, Susannah and (1) Louisa Pyne.

(1) **Louisa (Fanny) Pyne** (*b* ?27 Aug 1832; *d* London, 20 March 1904). Soprano. She studied singing with Sir George Smart and made her début when only ten at the Queen's Concert Rooms, Hanover Square, with her sister Susannah. In 1847 she went on a concert tour and in 1849 made her stage début as Amina in *La sonnambula* at Boulogne.

In autumn 1849 she sang Zerlina and Amina at the Princess's Theatre, London, and was the first Fanny in Macfarren's *Charles the Second*. Her success was such that she was dubbed the English Sontag. In 1851 she appeared in an English season at the Haymarket and was then called to the Royal Italian Opera, Covent Garden, to replace Anna Zerr as Queen of Night, where her performance 'in the difficult role quite eclipsed that of her predecessor'. Her voice was said to be beautiful and flexible.

In 1854 she appeared in New York as Amina and as Arline in *The Bohemian Girl*, then made a concert tour of the USA with her sister and the tenor WILLIAM HARRISON. On their return to England in 1857 she and Harrison formed the Pyne–Harrison Opera Company. After appearances at the Lyceum and Drury Lane the company appeared at Covent Garden each winter from 1859 to 1864. During this period she sang the leading soprano roles in the first performances of Balfe's *Rose of Castille*, *Satanella*, *Bianca or The Bravo's Bride*, *The Puritan's Daughter* and *The Armourer of Nantes*, Wallace's *Lurline*, Benedict's *Lily of Killarney* and Glover's *Ruy Blas*.

In 1864 she dissolved her partnership with Harrison and in 1868 married the baritone Frank Bodda, thereafter devoting herself to teaching. She was granted a pension from the civil list in 1896.

(2) **James Kendrick Pyne (iii)** (*b* Bath, 5 Feb 1852; *d* Ilford, 3 Sept 1938). Organist. He studied with S. S. Wesley at Winchester and Gloucester and later became assistant organist at Gloucester. After appointments in Chichester and St Mark's Church, Philadelphia, he settled in Manchester where he succeeded Frederick Bridge as organist at the cathedral, 1876–98. In 1877 he became organist of Manchester Town Hall and was professor of organ at the Royal Manchester College of Music from 1893. He lectured on church music at Manchester University from 1901 and was appointed dean of the Faculty of Music in 1908. He was particularly noted for his Bach playing. His own compositions include a Communion Service in A♭ and a set of Lancashire songs to words by Edwin Waugh.

HAROLD ROSENTHAL

Pyonnier, Joannes. *See* PIONNIER, JOANNES.

Pyrenaeus, Georg. *See* PRENNER, GEORG.

Pyrison Cambio. *See* PERISSONE CAMBIO.

Pyrrhic [pyrrhichē]. Ancient Greek choral dance with accompaniment on the aulos, performed by armed men and boys, and contrasted (as a war dance) with the

EMMELEIA. It was composed as a *hyporchēma* (i.e. a choral dance accompanied by singing) first by Thaletas in Crete, in the 7th century BC: it was common at Sparta, and contests in the pyrrhic were held at the Panathenaea.

BIBLIOGRAPHY
L. B. Lawler: *The Dance in Ancient Greece* (London, 1964), 106ff
GEOFFREY CHEW

Pyrszyński [Pierszyński, Pirszczyński], **Kasper** [Gasparus] (*b* 1718; *d* Leszno, nr. Poznań, 19 Sept 1758). Polish composer. He was the cantor and the organist of the parochial church in Leszno. Only two of his compositions are known: *Sepulto Domino* (copy in *P-Pu*), and *Magnificat*, a large-scale ensemble cantata with virtuoso passages, in the style of the late Italian Baroque. The MSS of both were destroyed in World War II.

BIBLIOGRAPHY
J. J. Dunicz: 'Z badań nad muzyką polską XVIII wieku. 1. Kasper Pyrszyński (1718–1758)', *PRM*, i (1935), 54
ZYGMUNT M. SZWEYKOWSKI

Pysing [Pising(e)], **William** (*b* ?Canterbury, *c*1605–10; buried Canterbury, 6 March 1684). English composer. The family to which he undoubtedly belonged was established in and around Canterbury by the early 17th century. The choirboy Pysing who sang in the cathedral choir during 1617 and 1618 may have been the composer. From 1629 onwards William is mentioned as a teacher of the choirboys, but whether his duties included their general as well as their musical education is not clear. He became one of the six 'substitutes' (men supplementing the lay clerks, but at a lower stipend) in 1631 and was promoted to a full lay clerk's place sometime between 1637 and 1640. In the meantime he had been appointed Master of the Choristers, but not organist, in 1635 or 1636 and held both this post and his lay clerk's place until his death. He was buried in the cathedral on 6 March 1684. His son William (1641–1707) and Richard Pysing (1604–75), probably a relative, were also lay clerks there after the Restoration.

In 1640 Pysing was paid 20 shillings for copying new anthems, but only two of his own survive. They were probably written in the decade or so before the Commonwealth, but are archaic in style and lacking in technical facility. *The Lord hear thee in the day of trouble* (*GB-Och*) has verses and chorus for SSATB and an accompaniment for five viols. In *I will magnify thee* (*Lcm* and *T*) the verses are for two meanes with SAATB chorus and organ. A catch for two trebles and a bass by Pysing – *Come, follow me* – appeared in Playford's 1685 edition of *Catch that Catch Can*.

ANDREW ASHBEE

Pythagoras. Greek philosopher and religious teacher. He emigrated about 531 BC from Samos to Croton (now Crotone) in southern Italy, where he founded a religious, philosophical and political society. The characteristic philosophic doctrine of his school (he appears to have left no written works) was a belief in the importance of numbers as a guide to the interpretation of the world. He may have been led to this view by the discovery, attributed to him, of the numerical ratios corresponding to the principal intervals of the musical scale. He himself may have been content with the definition of the ratios for the octave (2 : 1), the 5th (3 : 2) and the 4th (4 : 3), and for the major tone (9 : 8), which

is the difference between the 5th and 4th. Pythagoreans such as Archytas worked out ratios for the other intervals of the scale (*see* ARISTOXENUS and GREECE, §I, 6).

Another doctrine associated with the Pythagorean school is that of the harmony of the spheres. It was believed that each planet, revolving in its ring or sphere, produced a musical note determined by its velocity and that these notes formed a scale or *harmonia*. Accounts of this doctrine, which may have originated with Pythagoras, differ considerably in detail.

Pythagoras became an almost legendary figure and from the 5th century onwards his followers constituted one of the principal schools of Greek musical theory. It seems unlikely, however, that his work was widely known during his lifetime or that it had any effect on the practice of music in the Greek world: it did not need a Pythagoras to teach string players to use a 'Pythagorean' tuning system.

BIBLIOGRAPHY
B. L. van der Waerden: 'Die Harmonielehre der Pythagoreer', *Hermes*, lxxviii (1943), 163
W. K. C. Guthrie: *A History of Greek Philosophy*, i (Cambridge, 1962), chap.4
W. Burkert: *Lore and Science in Ancient Pythagoreanism* (Cambridge, Mass., 1972), chaps.4–5
J. Mc Kinnon: 'Jubal vel Pythagoras, quis sit inventor musicae?', *MQ*, lxiv (1978), 1
For further bibliography *see* GREECE, §I.
R. P. WINNINGTON-INGRAM

Pythagorean intonation. A tuning of the scale in which all 5ths and 4ths are pure (untempered). Pythagorean tuning provides intonations of several types of scale. A series of five 5ths and 4ths includes the pitch classes of the most familiar kind of pentatonic scale; ascending from F♯ the series would comprise the five chromatic notes of the keyboard. A series of seven 5ths ascending from F yields a diatonic scale comprising the naturals on the keyboard; the 3rds and 6ths in this scale, however, differ from their justly intoned equivalents by a syntonic comma, and therefore do not meet medieval and Renaissance criteria of consonance implied by such terms as 'perfection' and 'unity'. When used as harmonic intervals these Pythagorean 3rds and 6ths are likely to be characterized, on an organ Diapason stop for example, by rather prominent beating, middle C–E or C–A beating more than 16 times per second at modern concert pitch. A series of 12 Pythagorean 5ths provides a fully chromatic scale that is bound to include, however, one sour wolf 5th, smaller than pure by a Pythagorean comma.

Among regular tuning systems Pythagorean intonation has the largest major 2nds and 3rds and smallest minor 2nds and 3rds. Melodically the large major 2nds are handsome and the incisiveness of the small minor 2nds is of potential expressive value. Hence Pythagorean intonation is well suited not only to parallel organum but also to late Gothic polyphonic compositions in which the role of harmonic major 6ths is somewhat analogous to that of dominant 7th chords in later

Ex.1 Adam de la Halle: *Tant con je vivrai*

triadic music, while the use of double leading-note cadences as in ex.1 places a premium on the incisive melodic quality of the small semitones. Nearly all medieval theorists who discussed the arithmetic of musical intervals (*see* MONOCHORD) did so in terms of Pythagorean intonation.

Of particular significance for the development of harmony in Western music was the use of Pythagorean intonation on early Renaissance keyboard instruments. The repertory of the Robertsbridge Codex (*GB-Lbm* Add.28550) shows that a fully chromatic keyboard was in use by about 1340, and passages like ex.2 suggest

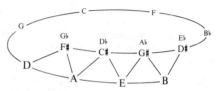

1. *Virtually pure 3rds in Pythagorean intonation on a 12-note keyboard instrument with the wolf 5th between B and G♭*

Ex.2 Robertsbridge Codex

that at that time the tuner would set the chromatic scale by adding pure 5ths at both ends of the chain of 5ths forming the chromatic scale, leaving the wolf 5th perhaps betwen G♯ and E♭. But by the time of the early 15th-century liturgical keyboard repertory of the Faenza Codex (*I-FZc* 117), the five chromatic notes seem to have been tuned to make a chain of pure 5ths among themselves, leaving the wolf 5th between B and F♯. It happens that what might be called a Pythagorean diminished 4th (e.g. the interval between the first and last members of the following chain of pure 5ths or 4ths: B–E–A–D–G–C–F–B♭–E♭) actually forms a much more nearly pure major 3rd than does the diatonic Pythagorean 3rd itself. Hence all the triangles in fig.1 would represent virtually pure triads, or at least particularly sonorous ones, if all the 5ths shown in the spiral were tuned pure (with special care to make none larger than pure). In this disposition of Pythagorean intonation, which may be referred to conveniently as the F♯ × B disposition, each of the five chromatic degrees falls within the lower half of the diatonic whole tone. This disposition was prescribed or referred to by numerous 15th-century theorists, including Prosdocimus de Beldemandis, Ugolino of Orvieto, Johannes Keck, Henri Arnaut de Zwolle, a certain 'librum Baudeceti' cited by Arnaut, Johannes Legrense, John Hothby (referring specifically to the organ), Nicolaus Burtius, Franchinus Gaffurius (in his *Theorica musica* of 1492), and Heinrich Schreiber; its traces are also found in the 1472 portrayal of a clavichord in the ducal palace at Urbino (*see* CLAVICHORD, fig.3). There is corroborating musical evidence, mostly from the first half of the century: exx.3a and b, the conclusions of two organ verses, are typical of the evidence to be found in the liturgical Faenza Codex repertory. Exx.4 and 5 are from two settings in the Buxheim Organbook (*D-Mbs* 3725) of Binchois' *Adieu ma tres belle*; other pieces in the Buxheim repertory that exploit the especially resonant triads of the F♯ × B disposition of Pythagorean intonation include nos.19, 30–31, 126–8, 141, 153–5, 180 and 242. Most of these are keyboard settings of songs initially composed in the first half of the 15th century. (Most of the original keyboard compositions in the Buxheim Organbook, including all the *fundamenta*, seem to require some form of regular mean-tone temperament for their proper effect; *see* TEMPERAMENTS, §2.) The cadence in ex.6, the opening of a Buxheim tran-

cription of Dufay's *Mille bonjours*, would not have, in the F♯ × B disposition, the high leading note cited above as a virtue of Pythagorean intonation in Gothic cadences; nonetheless the pure or nearly pure intonation of the quasi-dominant triad sounds very good in this and other such Dorian contexts. The F♯ × B disposition of Pythagorean intonation, in addition to having perhaps abetted the development of tonality by promoting what might anachronistically be called half-cadences in the Dorian mode, evidently whetted that Renaissance appetite for sonorous triads which only mean-tone temperaments could fully satisfy on keyboard instruments.

Ex.3 Faenza Codex

Ex.4 Buxheim Organbook, no.196

One German source of about 1430 (formerly Breslau, Staatsbibliothek IF 687) contains a set of organ clausulae, two of which are shown in ex.7, suggesting a Pythagorean disposition with the wolf 5th between B♭

Ex.5 Buxheim Organbook, no.144

Ex.7
(a)

(b)

and F and consequently with all those 3rds and 6ths which include a flat being particularly resonant. This tuning appears to have been referred to by Giorgio Anselmi in 1434 (*I-Ma* H 233 Inf.), but no other evidence to corroborate its use is known.

Ex.6 Buxheim Organbook, no.127

Although Gaffurius and other late 15th-century opponents of the theoretical innovations advanced by Ramos de Pareia cited the Pythagorean F♯ × B scheme as the proper alternative to Ramos's new monochord, Gaffurius in 1500 changed to an ostensibly Pythagorean monochord of 14 pitch classes forming a chain of 5ths ascending from A♭ to D♯. In 1496 Gaffurius had acknowledged, however, that organists tempered their 5ths when tuning the instrument. Pietro Aaron and G. M. Lanfranco, the first Italian writers to give tuning instructions for mean-tone temperaments (in 1523 and 1532 respectively), were, like Gaffurius, unabashed upholders of Pythagorean theory in contradiction to their own descriptions of practice. This dichotomy between 'speculative' and practical accounts of musical intervals became so pronounced during the 16th century that when Simon Stevin, the Dutch mathematician and engineer, worked out his precise

calculations for equal temperament around 1600, he was familiar with Pythagorean theory but unaware of the existence of mean-tone temperaments, which were subsequently described to him by a musician friend, Abraham Verheyen. But even though all sophisticated Western composers and performers since the Renaissance have taken for granted the use of tempered tuning on normal keyboard instruments, Pythagorean intonation has persisted in the West as a rustic or provincial practice.

See also CHINA, §IV, 2.

BIBLIOGRAPHY

J. M. Barbour: 'The Persistence of the Pythagorean Tuning System', *Scripta mathematica*, i (1933), 286

——: *Tuning and Temperament: a Historical Survey* (East Lansing, Mich., 1951, 2/1953/R1975)

K.-J. Sachs: *Mensura fistularum: die Mensurierung der Orgelpfeifen im Mittelalter*, i (Stuttgart, 1970)

M. Lindley: 'Fifteenth-century Evidence for Meantone Temperament', *PRMA*, cii (1975–6), 37

——: 'Pythagorean Intonation and the Rise of the Triad', *RMARC* (in preparation)

For further bibliography *see* TEMPERAMENTS.

MARK LINDLEY

Pythian Games. Festival of Apollo at Delphi in ancient times. Musical competitions based on the NOME were held there at eight-yearly intervals until the reorganization of the festival in 586 BC. After that date, it occurred in the third year of each Olympiad (i.e. once every four years), with the additional though temporary feature of aulos contests (both singing to aulos accompaniment and solo aulos playing), and also athletic contests modelled on those of the Olympian Games. The Pythian Games ranked second after the Olympian Games.

BIBLIOGRAPHY

P. J. Meier: 'Agones', *Paulys Real-Encyclopädie der classischen Altertumswissenschaft*, 1st ser., i (Stuttgart, 1894), 836

GEOFFREY CHEW

Q

Qālā. A category of chant in SYRIAN CHURCH MUSIC.

Qālthā. A section of the Assyrian Office of *Lelyā*; *see* SYRIAN CHURCH MUSIC.

Qānūn (Arabic, from Gk. *kanōn*: 'rule'; plural *qawānīn*). The Arabic psaltery. It consists of a right-angled trapezial box about 1 cm deep, 75–100 cm long and 50–60 cm wide (see fig.1), across which are stretched up to 100 gut or nylon strings arranged in triple courses. The belly of the instrument is partly of wood and partly of a piece of parchment to which the vibrations of the bridge are transmitted. The player rests the instrument on his lap with the tuning-pins (usually of wood and mounted vertically) away from him and plucks the strings with plectra fastened to his fingers by rings. Since about the mid-1910s the technique of occasionally stopping courses with the left hand to raise their intonation by a tone or a fraction of a tone has been superseded by the use of small, metal flap bridges, near the tuning-pin end of the strings, to alter their pitch according to the mode. In modern Egypt and further east the *qānūn* rivals the *'ūd* (lute) as a vehicle of classical Arab music. In Egypt, for example, the main melody instruments of the normal classical orchestra are *qānūn*, *'ūd*, *kamānja* (violin) and *nā* (flute); they produce a heterophonic texture in which the *qānūn* plays the melody with great vitality, frequently in octaves.

Although the name of the instrument is of Greek origin, there is no knowledge of its early use in Byzantium. It is mentioned in the tales of the Arabian

1. Qānūn player, Israel

Nights, but the name was certainly not common until a much later period. Even in the Syriac lexica of the 9th and 10th centuries there is no sign of it, in spite of the fact that it was delineated by Bar Bahlul (*fl* 963). According to Ibn Khallikān (*d* 1282) the *qānūn* was invented by al-Fārābī (*d* c950), but al-Fārābī did not write of the instrument by that name in his treatment of instruments with 'open strings', where he mentioned only *ṣunūj* (harps) and *ma'azif* (possibly psalteries). In Moorish Spain, Ibn Ḥazm (*d* 1064) referred to the *qānūn* as the *ra'īs* ('chief') of instruments, and al-Shaqundī (*d* 1231) listed it among the instruments which were exported from Seville. Later in the 13th century Ṣafī al-Dīn (*d* 1294), who was in the service of the last Caliph of Baghdad, invented a rectangular psaltery called the *nuzha*, with 32 strings (for illustration *see* ṢAFĪ AL-DĪN). In the Persian *Kanz al-tuhaf* (14th century) both the *qānūn* and the *nuzha* (*see* ARAB MUSIC, fig.2d) are fully described and delineated, the *qānūn* as having 64 strings, with, apparently, three strings tuned to one note. The *nuzha* was twice the size of the *qānūn* and had 81 strings, tuned trichordally. 'Abd al-Qādir, in his Persian *Jāmi 'al-alḥan* (1418), also wrote of the *qānūn*, the instrument of his day, which 'combined theory with practice', had 105 strings tuned trichordally. Iconographic sources show that it was held with its back against the player's chest, and not horizontally on the knees; this is known to have been the normal playing position from the 13th century to the 15th in the Middle East, and it was also used in Europe (for illustration *see* CANON (ii)). Keyboard instruments superseded the *qānūn* in Europe in the 16th century, although it continued to be played in the East.

The *qānūn* was highly commended in Turkey in the 15th and 16th centuries by the poets Niẓāmī and Rewānī. An engraving by G. Scotin (c1700) of a Turkish girl playing the *qānūn* was copied by Bonanni (*Gabinetto armonico*, 1722; see fig.2), and this type of psaltery was still popular in the 1780s. It then fell into temporary disuse in Turkey until the mid-19th century, when it was reintroduced by an Arab of Damascus. Elsewhere, in Arabic-speaking lands especially, it continued to find favour. In the mid-18th century it was heard in Baghdad; one writer called it a 'tympanon', but his description of the plectra on the fingers as 'ongles d'argent' shows that it was a *qānūn*; and at about the same time it was mentioned as being extant in Syria. In Egypt (c1800) Villoteau gave minute details of its construction and scale: there were 75 gut strings, with three strings to a note, giving a diatonic scale of 25

488

2. Engraving of a rectangular qānūn from Bonanni's 'Gabinetto armonico' (1722)

notes, that is, a range of three octaves and a 4th. Lane delineated the instrument as it was played in the mid-19th century, showing 72 strings; this is the system used on the 19th-century Turkish instrument in the Victoria and Albert Museum, London.

BIBLIOGRAPHY
G. A. Villoteau: *La description de l'Egypte*, i (Paris, 1812), 883
E. W. Lane: *The Modern Egyptians* (London, 1860), 359f
C. Engel: *A Descriptive Catalogue of Musical Instruments in the South Kensington Museum* (London, 1870, 2/1874), 208f
P. Smith: *Thesaurus Syriacus*, ii (Oxford, 1901), 3613
Catalogue of Musical Instruments [in Metropolitan Museum of Art, New York] (New York, 1906), nos.330, 342, 1248
H. G. Farmer: 'Mi'zaf', *The Encyclopaedia of Islam* (Leiden and London, 1913–38, rev. 2/1960–)
G. L. Kinsky, R. Haas and H. Schnoor: *Geschichte der Musik in Bildern* (Leipzig, 1920; Eng. trans., 1930, 2/1951)
J. Rouanet: 'La musique arabe'; 'La musique arabe dans le Maghreb', *EMDC*, I/v (1922), 2788; 2929
R. Yekta Bey: 'La musique turque', *EMDC*, I/v (1922), 3013, 3020
H. G. Farmer: *Studies in Oriental Musical Instruments*, i (London, 1931), 3f; ii (Glasgow, 1939), 88ff
Congrès de musique arabe: Caire 1932, pls.1–4, 17–21
H. G. Farmer: *Turkish Instruments of Music in the Seventeenth Century* (Glasgow, 1937), 33f
C. Sachs: *The History of Musical Instruments* (New York, 1940), 138, 257f
H. G. Farmer: *The Minstrelsy of 'The Arabian Nights'* (Bearsden, nr. Glasgow, 1945), 30ff, pl.12
——: *Oriental Studies: Mainly Musical* (London, 1953), 22f
P. Crossley-Holland: 'Oriental Music on the Gramophone', *ML*, xl (1959), 56
H. G. Farmer: *Islam*, Musikgeschichte in Bildern, iii/2 (Leipzig, 1966, 2/1976)
H. G. FARMER/R

Qanūne yawnāye. A category of chant in SYRIAN CHURCH MUSIC.

Qarna (Aramaic). Ancient Jewish horn; *see* JEWISH MUSIC, §I, 4(iii).

Qaṣaba. A rim-blown flute used in the Maghrib. It is made of cane, is 60 to 70 cm long, and has five or six finger-holes. It is basically the same as the NĀY, found elsewhere in the Islamic world. The *qaṣaba* was known among the Arabs by the 7th century, but it was supplanted in the 9th century by the Persian *nāy*. It continued to be played in the Maghrib and Moorish Spain, and is now widely used in north-west Africa.

See ARAB MUSIC, §II, 4; ISRAEL, §II, 1; NORTH AFRICA, §3.

Qatar. An independent Near-Eastern state on the south-west coast of the ARABIAN GULF.

Qawānīn (Arabic). Plural of QĀNŪN, the Arabic psaltery.

Qawmā. A nocturn in the Office of *Lelyā* of the Syrian Orthodox Church; *see* SYRIAN CHURCH MUSIC.

Qeddasē. A liturgical book of the Ethiopian Church containing the anaphoras of the Eucharist and corresponding to the Latin missal or the Byzantine euchologion; *see* ETHIOPIAN RITE, MUSIC OF THE.

Qenē. Improvised compositions of the Ethiopian *dabtarā*; *see* ETHIOPIAN RITE, MUSIC OF THE.

Qeren (Heb.). Ancient Jewish horn; *see* JEWISH MUSIC, §I, 4(iii).

Qiblī (Arabic: 'southern'). A term describing sections of chant sung by the left-hand half of the choir in the MUSIC OF THE COPTIC RITE.

Qquepa. A Quechua term for a conch trumpet of Peru. It was used from as early as the Chavín era (900–200 BC) through the Inca period to the 20th century. Because of the rarity of the conch in Peruvian waters, instrument makers of Mochica (AD 200–700) and Chimú (AD 1000–1476) used clay to create both imitations of the shell trumpet and vertical and coiled trumpets. The Quechua held the *qquepa* in high regard for its impressive sound and relative rarity; they played it in battle and for warrior initiation ceremonies. Cuzco regional authorities, who call the conch (*Strombus galeatus*) *pututo*, still sound it to gather townspeople in times of crisis or for communal tasks.

JOHN M. SCHECHTER

Quadran pavan. A 16th-century term for the 'passamezzo moderno', one of the forms of the passamezzo ostinato bass (*see* PASSAMEZZO, ex.2). The term derives from the Italian 'passemezzo di B quadro', and refers to the square-shaped natural sign that distinguished the 'passamezzo moderno' from the 'passamezzo antico'.

Quadrat (Ger.). NATURAL.

Quadrille (Fr.). One of the most popular ballroom dances of the 19th century, with an elaborate set of steps and danced by sets of four, six or eight couples. The name, derived from the Italian 'squadriglia' or Spanish 'cuadrilla', was originally applied to a small company of cavalry, subsequently to a group of dancers in a pageant and then to a troupe of dancers in the elaborate French ballets of the 18th century. The popularity of contredanses in ballets led in turn to the description of a set of contredanses in the ballroom as a 'quadrille de contredanses', later shortened to 'quadrille'. The dance was very popular in Paris during the First Empire and was

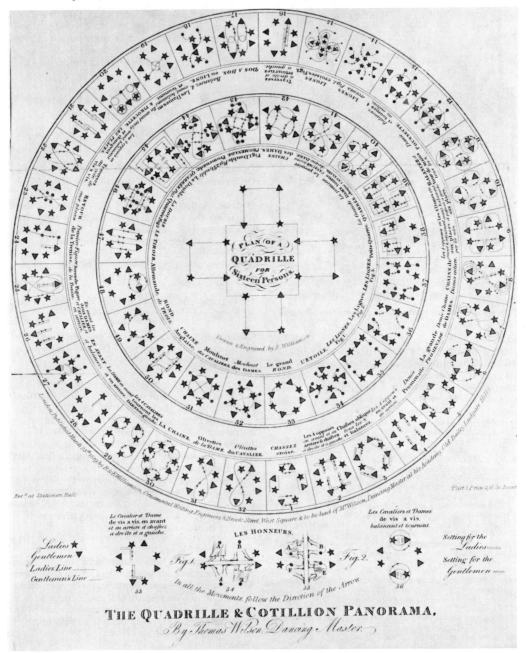

Plan of a quadrille from 'The Quadrille and Cotillion Panorama' (1819) by Thomas Wilson

introduced to London at Almack's in 1815 and to Berlin in 1821. Though known in Vienna around the same time, it did not become the rage there until the carnival of 1840.

The quadrille usually consisted of five distinct parts or figures, which, even when new music was provided, retained the names of the contredanses which originally made up the standard quadrille: *Le pantalon* (adapted from a song which began 'Le pantalon/De Madelon/ N'a pas de fond'), *L'été* (a contredanse popular in 1800), *La*

poule (1802), *La pastourelle* (based on a ballad by the cornet player Collinet) and a lively 'Finale'. *La pastourelle* was often replaced by a further figure, *La Trénis* (named after the dancer Trenitz), but in the Viennese quadrille both were danced, as fourth and fifth figures respectively in a total of six.

The music of the quadrille was made up of lively, rhythmic themes of rigid eight- or sixteen-bar lengths, the sections being much repeated within a figure. Except for *La poule* and sometimes *Le pantalon* (which were in

6/8) the music was in 2/4, and was usually adapted from popular songs or stage works. Among prominent French arrangers were Philippe Musard (1793–1859), Isaac Strauss (1806–88) and Olivier Métra (1830–89). In England the quadrilles of Jullien, such as the *British Army Quadrilles* and the *Grand Quadrille of All Nations* were prominent attractions at his concerts at the Surrey Gardens and Covent Garden. Elsewhere in Europe quadrilles were produced by the Strausses and all other major dance composers of the 19th century.

Hans von Bülow composed a quadrille on themes from Berlioz's *Benvenuto Cellini*, and during his years as conductor at the Powick Asylum (1879–84) Elgar wrote quadrilles which he raided for later works, notably the second *Wand of Youth* suite. The plundering of all sorts of musical sources for themes for new dances and the musical distortions that often had to be made to satisfy the restricted musical form of the quadrille made it a target and vehicle for musical jokes through the arrangement of themes from particularly incongruous sources, as in the *Macbeth Quadrilles* from music attributed to Matthew Locke, the *Bologna Quadrilles* on themes from Rossini's *Stabat mater*, Chabrier's *Souvenirs de Munich* (on themes from *Tristan und Isolde*), and *Souvenirs de Bayreuth* (on themes from *The Ring*) by Fauré and Messager.

See also LANCERS.

BIBLIOGRAPHY
T. Wilson: *A Companion to the Ball Room* (London, 1816)
——: *The Quadrille and Cotillion Panorama* (London, 1819)
M. Schönherr and K. Reinöhl: *Johann Strauss Vater* (Vienna, 1954)
P. J. S. Richardson: *The Social Dances of the Nineteenth Century in England* (London, 1960)
For further bibliography *see* DANCE.

ANDREW LAMB

Quadris, Johannes de. *See* JOHANNES DE QUADRIS.

Quadrupla (Lat.: 'quadruple'). In early music theory, the ratio 4:1. In the system of PROPORTIONS of the late Middle Ages and Renaissance, the *proportio quadrupla* indicated a diminution in the relative value of each note shape in the ratio 4:1. In modern practice, quadruple time has four beats to the bar.

Quadruple croche (Fr.). HEMIDEMISEMIQUAVER (64th-note). *See also* NOTE VALUES.

Quadruplet (Fr. *quartolet*; Ger. *Quartole*; It. *quartina*). A group of four equal notes occurring in place of three equal notes under a time signature where the regular units are divisible by three.

Quadruple time. In modern practice, four beats to the bar; *see* QUADRUPLA.

Quadruplum, quadruplex (Lat.: 'quadruple', 'fourfold'). Terms used in medieval theory to denote principally (1) four-voiced polyphony. In 13th-century theoretical writing both terms were used as nouns in this sense, or as adjectives in phrases such as 'organum quadruplum' and 'quadruplices conductus'. *See* ORGANUM.

(2) The fourth voice of a polyphonic composition – an independent voice composed against a tenor, duplum (or motetus) and triplum. The term 'quadruplum' was thus used in the 13th century with reference to organum and the motet. The English form, 'quadreble' or 'quatreble', was used in the vernacular early 15th-century treatises on English discant.

(3) Diminution or augmentation by a factor of four ('quadrupla', 'proportio quadrupla') in mensural notation of the 14th century to the 16th. *See* PROPORTIONS.

IAN D. BENT

Quaglia, Giovanni Battista (*b* c1625; *d* Brescia, June 1700). Italian composer and organist. He lived at Salò before becoming a musician at S Maria Maggiore, Bergamo, in 1649. He remained until 1690 and from 1677 was *maestro di cappella*. From 1690 he held a similar position at Brescia Cathedral. He was recognized as a diligent teacher and was a more than competent composer. His surviving music consists of 26 solo motets, which are generally in four or five short sections, at least one of which – usually not the first – is set as highly ornate recitative, another is slow, and the finale is an often jig-like 'Alleluia'.

WORKS
[12] Motetti sacri, 1v, bc (org) . . . libro I (Bologna, 1668)
[12] Motetti sacri, 1v, bc (org), . . . libro II (Bergamo, 1675)
Motet, 1v, bc in 1670[1]; motet, S/T, 2 vns, bc (org), in 1695[1]
La vittoria di David contra Golia (oratorio) (Bergamo, 1680)

ROBIN BOWMAN

Quagliati, Paolo (*b* Chioggia, c1555; *d* Rome, 16 Nov 1628). Italian composer and organist. He was born into a noble family of Chioggia and about 1574 settled in Rome, where he remained until his death. During more than 50 years there he worked for wealthy patrician families, as well as for the church, as both musician and bureaucrat. He became a Roman citizen in 1594. In 1606 his *Carro di Fedeltà d'Amore* was performed on a decorated cart in the streets of Rome during the pre-Lenten celebrations. Pietro della Valle, who wrote the text, declared later that it 'was the first dramatic action or representation in music that had ever been heard in that city', an exaggerated claim. Between about 1605 and 1608 Quagliati was in the service of Cardinal Odoardo Farnese, to whom he dedicated his madrigal volume of 1608. The title-page of this publication describes him as organist of S Maria Maggiore, a post he probably held until his death. He is also known to have played the organ at other Roman churches on special occasions. The respect in which he was held by his contemporaries is attested by the dedication to him of *Giardino musicale* (*RISM* 1621[15]), an anthology of songs and duets by eight Roman composers, Frescobaldi among them. During the last years of his life he was in the service of the Ludovisi family. When Cardinal Alessandro Ludovisi became Pope Gregory XV in 1621, he was appointed apostolic prothonotary, and private chamberlain to the pope. For the wedding in 1623 of the pope's nephew Nicolò Ludovisi to Isabella Gesualdo (daughter of the composer) he wrote the collection *La sfera armoniosa*, the print of which includes an engraved portrait of him by Ottario Maria Leoni (reproduced in *MGG*, pl.102/i). When the pope died in that year Quagliati remained in the service of the Ludovisi family. He died a wealthy man and was buried in S Maria Maggiore.

Quagliati's first personal publications were of three-part canzonettas: he published a sacred anthology in 1585 and two secular volumes in 1588, showing himself an enthusiast for the lighter forms that proved to be so important texturally for the emerging Baroque style. He was never a serious madrigalist, so the transition to monody and the concerted madrigal was perhaps easy for him. His one madrigal publication (1608) nevertheless manifests the kind of stylistic uncertainty common in the early 17th century, and its contents are devised so that they can be performed either as concerted madrigals or as monodies; as he stated in the preface:

Seeing that nowadays one group take pleasure in 'full' music with many voices, although it seems that the larger group desire and applaud 'empty' music for solo voices and instruments . . . I have decided to cater to more than one taste.

He was not alone in his attempt to fuse the old and the new, witness, for example, P. M. Marsolo's practice in his second book of four-part madrigals (1614). *Il carro di Fedeltà d'Amore* is a brief festive work, consisting mainly of short solos and duets and ending with a five-part concerted madrigal; it should not be regarded as a miniature or proto-opera. The several other pieces following the *Carro* itself include four solo madrigals that are probably the first in Rome actually composed as such, though the solo versions of the 1608 works preceded them. Quagliati's most substantial secular work is *La sfera armoniosa*, which comprises 25 numbers, mostly solos and duets, with a concerted violin part; five madrigals are variously adapted from the 1608 collection. His *Ricercate e canzoni* (1601, not lost as stated by Kast) display conservative features often associated with the stricter contrapuntal forms. Curiously, the ricercares and canzonas are not differentiated in the body of the publication and cannot easily be distinguished from one another. Quagliati's sacred works, which range from monodies to a 12-part work, have not yet been studied.

In all his works Quagliati used clear, mostly diatonic harmony and adopted a conservative approach to the treatment of dissonance. He favoured modest concertato textures and his melodic style is simple and graceful.

WORKS
(all except anthologies published in Rome)

SACRED VOCAL

Canzonette spirituali de diversi, 3vv (1585[7])
Motecta, 8vv, et psalmus Dixit Dominus, 12vv (1612); 2 ed. J. Killing, *Kirchenmusikalische Schätze der Bibliothek des Abbate F. Santini* (Düsseldorf, 1910)
Affetti amorosi spirituali, 1–3vv (1617)
Motetti e dialogi, 2–4, 8vv (1620)
Motetti, 1, 2vv (1625), lost
Motetti e dialoghi concertati con doi bassi seguiti, libro secondo, 8vv, 2 org (1627)

4 motets; 1 psalm, 8vv, bc; 6 sacred works, 3, 8vv, some with bc: 1592[2], 1599[6], 1616[1], 1617[1], 1618[3], 1621[3], 1627[2], 1639[2]

SECULAR VOCAL

Canzonette per sonare et cantare, libro primo, 3vv (1588)
Canzonette per sonare et cantare, libro secondo, 3vv (1588[26])
Il primo libro de' madrigali, 4vv, bc (1608) [5 rev. in 1623 vol.]
Il carro di Fedeltà d'Amore con aggiunta di alcune arie dell'istesso autore, 1–5vv (1611); ed. in SCMA, xiii (1957); 1 ed. L. Landshoff, *Alte Meister des Bel Canto*, i–ii (Leipzig, 1912)
La sfera armoniosa, 1, 2vv, vn (1623) [incl. 5 from 1608 vol. and 2 by S. Landi]; ed. in SCMA, xiii (1957)

Madrigal, 5vv; 2 canzonettas, 4vv; 3 secular works: 1583[14], 1589[7], 1589[11], 1591[12], 1621[14]; 2 ed. A. Wotquenne-Plattel, *Chansons italiennes* (Leipzig, n.d.)

INSTRUMENTAL

Ricercate e canzoni per sonare et cantare, a 4 (1601); ed. in Swenson
Toccata, kbd, 1593[9]; ed. in AMI, iii (n.d.)

LOST WORKS

Le delizie musicali, aria, Il plettro canoro, Poesie e madrigali, all mentioned in Pitoni

BIBLIOGRAPHY

EitnerQ
G. O. Pitoni: *Notitia de contrapuntisti e de compositori di musica* (MS, *I-Rvat* C.G., I/1–2, c1725)

A. W. Ambros: *Geschichte der Musik*, iv (Leipzig, rev. 3/1909 by H. Leichtentritt), 407, 491f, 707f, 837ff, 856
E. Schmitz: *Geschichte der weltlichen Solokantate* (Leipzig, 1914, rev. 2/1955)
V. Raeli: *Da Vincenzo Ugolini ad Orazio Benevoli nella cappella della Basilica liberiana (1603–1646)* (Rome, 1920)
A. Cametti: 'Paolo Quagliati, organista e compositore', *Rassegna dorica* (1930), Dec, 28
A. Einstein: 'Das Madrigal zum Doppelgebrauch', *AcM*, vi (1934), 110
——: *The Italian Madrigal* (Princeton, 1949/R1971), 690, 724, 855ff, 865
N. Fortune: *Italian Secular Song from 1600 to 1635: the Origins and Development of Accompanied Monody* (diss., U. of Cambridge, 1954)
P. Kast: 'Quagliati, Paolo', *MGG*
A. della Corte: 'Il valore artistico del "Carro di fedeltà d'Amore" ', *Sbornik praci filosofické fakulty brněnské university*, F9 (1965), 55
J. Racek: *Stilprobleme der italienischen Monodie* (Prague, 1965)
F. Testi: *La musica italiana nel Seicento* (Milan, 1970)
M. A. Swenson: *The Four-part Italian Ensemble Ricercar from 1540 to 1619* (diss., Indiana U., 1971)

BRIAN MANN

Quaglio. Italian–German family of stage designers. Giovanni Maria Quaglio (i) (*b* Laino, Como, *c*1700; *d* Vienna, *c*1765) and Domenico Quaglio (i) (1708–73), a portrait and historical painter, were sons of the painter Giulio Quaglio (1668–1751); their descendants constitute two distinct branches of the family.

G. M. Quaglio studied in Rome and Milan, and moved to Vienna, probably in the early 1730s, as an architect and particularly as a stage designer. In 1754 he was appointed royal engineer. He was involved in the reconstruction of the Redoutensaal (1748–52) and designed sets for the Burgtheater and Kärntnertortheater in Vienna (1748–51), becoming the leading designer for both (1752–65). His sets encompassed the Viennese repertory during the transition from courtly to middle-class theatre – *opera seria*, *opera buffa*, *opéra comique* and ballet. He designed nearly all the sets for the reformers Durazzo, Calzabigi, Angiolini and Gluck (*Don Juan*, 1761; *Orfeo ed Euridice*, 1762; *Telemaco*, 1765). His art was rooted in the *opera seria* tradition of formalized illusionistic architecture painting, but he also developed staging as a means of expression, particularly in association with Gluck, through picturesque natural structures aiming at truth and universal appeal.

His son Lorenzo Quaglio (i) (*b* Laino, 23 July 1730; *d* Munich, 2 May 1805) was appointed theatre artist at the Palatinate court of Carl Theodor in 1752. As court theatre architect from 1758 he was responsible for scenery of the Mannheim and Schwetzingen court theatres, and for enlarging the Mannheim court opera (1758) and reconstructing the Nationaltheater (1777). He also worked for theatres at Reggio Emilia (1758), Frankfurt (1764, 1768), Dresden (1768–9) and Zweibrücken (1775). He went to Munich in 1778 when the court moved there, and retired in 1799. As designer for works of the Mannheim school, especially the operas of Holzbauer and the ballets of Cannabich, Quaglio gave a considerable impulse to German musical theatre. He followed his father in continuing to reconcile the courtly formalism of the Galli-Bibiena school with bourgeois intimacy and objectivity, with its genre pieces (Hiller's *Der Dorfbalbier*, 1770) and classical (Schweitzer's *Alceste*, 1775) or national themes (Holzbauer's *Günther von Schwarzburg*, 1777). For late 18th-century *opera seria* (Mozart's *Idomeneo*, 1781; Vogler's *Castore e Polluce*, 1787) extravagances of perspective were renounced in favour of clearly structured neo-classical architectural and landscape views. Carlo Quaglio (*fl* *c*1761–78), son of G. M. Quaglio (i), was assistant and second theatre engineer (1762–5) to his father in Vienna; in 1761 he designed the stage of the palace theatre in Eisenstadt, where Haydn worked, and from 1765 to about 1778 he was stage designer in Warsaw. A third brother, Martin Quaglio (*fl c*1764–73), was assistant to Lorenzo (i) in Mannheim in 1764–8 and then became stage designer in Kassel, where he was still active in 1773. Lorenzo's son Giovanni Maria Quaglio (ii) (1772–1813) was court theatre painter in Munich (1795–9 and 1802–3) and in Mannheim (1800–02).

The family's other line of influential stage designers was founded by Giuseppe (or Joseph) Quaglio (*b* Laino, 2 Dec 1747; *d* Munich, 2 March 1828), son of Domenico Quaglio (i) and nephew of G. M. Quaglio (i), with his brother Giulio Quaglio. Their work was closely connected with Romantic musical theatre and the rise of historical stage design in Germany. Giuseppe went to Mannheim in about 1770 as a theatre painter, probably at the request of his cousin Lorenzo (i), whom he followed to Munich in 1779; until 1823 he was stage designer there, from 1801 court theatre architect. He completed the transition to a pictorially composed scene begun by the older members of the family, especially as regards historical milieu: his sets, using the devices of Romantic landscape painting, exploited mood and local colour and achieved striking expressive variety. This historical eclecticism catered for the contemporary repertory, serving historical opera (Vogler's *Albrecht III von Bayern*, 1781) as well as comic (Winter's *Der Frauenbund*, 1805) and mixed genres (*Don Giovanni*, 1791); it was strongest in the large-scale sets for post-revolutionary grand opera (Paer's *Achille*, 1802; Méhul's *Joseph*, 1809).

His brother Giulio (or Julius) Quaglio (*b* Laino, 1764; *d* Munich, 21 Jan 1801) was a theatre artist in Munich (*c*1781–5), Mannheim (1785–98) and Dessau (1798) before succeeding his cousin Lorenzo (i) as Munich court theatre architect in 1799. His designs, particularly those created after 1785 for the Mannheim Nationaltheater, followed essentially the same principles as those of his brother, but he made less use of historical scenery and his setting of *Die Zauberflöte* (Mannheim, 1794), partly composed of older sets from the theatre's stock, showed a multiplicity of different stylistic elements, notably exotic motifs including a 'Chinese' hall, a 'Gothic' temple and an 'Egyptian' vault.

Giuseppe's son, Angelo Quaglio (i) (*b* Munich, 13 Aug 1784; *d* Munich, 2 April 1815) was an artist at the Munich court theatre from 1801 and also at the Isartortheater after 1812. Like his brothers Domenico (ii) (1787–1837), only very briefly a stage designer, and Lorenzo (ii) (1793–1869), Angelo made a considerable contribution to the popularization of the Gothic style. His work for the stage, which has come down to us mainly through his illustrated inventory of the court theatre (1803–10), inclined (in accord with his father's romantic interest in history) not only towards the Gothic period but also towards other historical epochs – classical antiquity in particular was glorified in the idealized landscapes and architecture of heroic opera (Salieri's *Palmira*, 1814).

A fourth son of Giuseppe Quaglio, Simon (Joseph) (*b* Munich, 23 Oct 1795; *d* Munich, 8 March 1878), was an assistant from 1812 and from 1814 a permanent stage designer at the Munich court theatre, where he supervised the scenery from 1824 up to his retirement in 1877. After his classical early works he devoted himself to Romantic stage painting with mystical char-

1. Stage design for a public square by Lorenzo Quaglio (i) or Giovanni Maria Quaglio (i), c1775, in the Galleria degli Uffizi, Florence

2. Stage design by Angelo
Quaglio (ii) for Act 1 of
'Tristan und Isolde', as first
performed in Munich, 1865

acteristics (*Die Zauberflöte*, Hof- und Nationaltheater,
1818, *see* OPERA, fig.37; *Der Freischütz*, Munich,
1822). Influenced by grand opera, which dominated the
Munich repertory, he later developed a more solemn
historical style (*La juive*, Munich, 1844). His son
Angelo Quaglio (ii) (*b* Munich, 13 Dec 1829; *d* Munich,
5 Jan 1890) was employed from 1850 at the court
theatre, and also managed a commercial scenic studio
which supplied theatres in Dresden, Berlin, Stuttgart, St
Petersburg and elsewhere. His designs remained within
his father's illusionistic historical style. Closely
connected with the aesthetic ideas of Ludwig II of
Bavaria, Quaglio was the principal designer for the
Munich Wagner premières (*Tannhäuser*, 1855; *Lohengrin*, 1858, 1867; *Der fliegende Holländer*, 1864;
Tristan und Isolde, 1865; *Die Meistersinger*, 1868; *Das
Rheingold*, 1869; *Die Walküre*, 1870) and for Ludwig's
private performances (including *Aida*, 1877, and
Oberon, 1881). He worked with his father, Christian
Jank, Heinrich Döll and Franz Seitz. His son Eugen
Quaglio (*b* Munich, 3 April 1857; *d* Berlin, 25 Sept
1942) worked in his father's studio from about 1877,
later (1891) becoming court theatre painter in Berlin, a
post he held until 1923. He carried on the family
tradition of historical stage designs, above all in Wagner
productions (*Tannhäuser*, 1890; *Lohengrin*, 1891;
Rienzi, 1895; *Tristan und Isolde*, 1903). Although
he was influenced by naturalism and *verismo*, his
romanticizing productions were basically historical
idylls (D'Albert's *Der Improvisator*, 1902; Strauss's
Feuersnot, 1902).

See also OPERA, §VIII, 4–5.

BIBLIOGRAPHY

F. Walter: *Geschichte des Theaters und der Musik am kurpfälzischen
    Hofe*, i (Leipzig, 1898/*R*1968), 173ff
L. Malyot: 'Die Künstlerfamilie Quaglio', *Theaterzeitung der
    Staatlichen Bühnen Münchens*, ii (1921), no.56, p.7
J. Kapp: *200 Jahre Staatsoper im Bild* (Berlin, 1942), 68f, 80ff
W. Niehaus: *Die Theatermaler Quaglio* (diss., U. of Munich, 1956)
G. Schöne and H. Vriesen: *Das Bühnenbild im 19. Jahrhundert*
    (Munich, 1959), 9ff, 30ff, 34f, 39ff, 45f [exhibition catalogue]
K. Hommel: *Die Separatvorstellungen vor König Ludwig II von Bayern*
    (Munich, 1963)
F. Cavarocchi: 'Artisti della Valle Intelvi e della Diocesi Comense attivi
    in Baviera alla luce di carte d'archivio del Ducato di Milano', *Arte
    lombarda*, x/2 (1965), 135
G. Schöne: 'Trois mises en scène de la "Flûte enchantée" de Mozart:
    Berlin 1816, Weimar 1817 et Munich 1818', *Anatomy of an Illusion:
    4th International Congress on Theatre Research: Amsterdam 1965*,
    54
D. and M. Petzet: *Die Richard-Wagner-Bühne Ludwigs II* (Munich,
    1970)
B. Król-Kaczarowska: *Teatr dawny polski: budynki, dekoracje,
    kostiumy* (Warsaw, 1971), 123f
G. Zechmeister: *Die Wiener Theater nächst der Burg und nächst dem
    Kärntnerthor von 1747 bis 1776* (Vienna, 1971)
M. Boetzkes: 'Quaglio', *The Age of Neoclassicism* (London, 1972), 938
B. Trost: *Domenico Quaglio 1787–1837: Monographie und
    Werkverzeichnis* (Munich, 1973)

MANFRED BOETZKES

Quallenberg [Qualemberg, Qualenberg], **Johann
Michael** (*b* ?Bohemia, *c*1726; *d* Brühl, nr. Schwetzingen, 16 April 1786). German clarinettist. He learnt the
clarinet in Vienna and from 1759 to 1765 was first
clarinettist in the Mannheim court orchestra. Hiller
noted him as being in the orchestra again in 1767
(*Wöchentliche Nachrichten*, 30 November), and from
1770 his name reappears on the court calendar in this
capacity; he may also have served the court as privy
councillor (*GerberL*). From 1757 he practised forestry
and managed an inn near Schwetzingen; because of
these interests he remained behind in Brühl, at full
salary, when the Mannheim orchestra transferred to
Munich in 1778. He is mentioned in the calendars of the
Bavarian and Palatinate court until 1786, although he
apparently had no further official duties in Mannheim.

Quallenberg was one of the first orchestral performers on the clarinet, which until then had been largely
confined to military bands and outdoor concerts, and as
such played a role in the early development of the
symphony orchestra at Mannheim (Mozart remarked in
particular on the 'glorious effect' of the Mannheim clarinets in a letter of 3 December 1778). The virtuoso
clarinet part in Ignaz Fränzl's Third Symphony (*c*1767)
was probably written for him. Quallenberg himself composed a four-act comedy *Die Schöne am Rhein* (Brühl,
1777, *D-Mbs*) and published a novella 'Die wahre

Geschichte einer Steiner [Jakob Stainer] Geige' in the *Musikalische Korrespondenz der Teutschen filharmonischen Gesellschaft* (1 June 1791, p.169).

BIBLIOGRAPHY

GerberL; *GerberNL* ('Qualemberg')
F. Walter: *Geschichte des Theaters und der Musik am kurpfälzischen Hofe* (Leipzig, 1898/*R*1968)
J. C. von Mannlich: *Ein deutscher Maler und Hofmann: Lebenserinnerungen* (Berlin, 1910, rev. 2/1966)

ROLAND WÜRTZ

Quantz, Johann Joachim (*b* Oberscheden, Hanover, 30 Jan 1697; *d* Potsdam, 12 July 1773). German flautist, composer, writer on music and flute maker.

1. Life. 2. Works. 3. Writings.

1. LIFE. Quantz's life, of which he left an account in F. W. Marpurg's *Historisch-kritische Beyträge* (1754), falls into three distinct periods: 1697–1716, childhood and youth in Oberscheden and Merseburg; 1716–41, growth and maturity, with Dresden as the centre of his activities; 1741–73, peak of fame and old age in the service of Frederick the Great at Berlin and Potsdam.

The son of a village blacksmith, Quantz began his musical training in 1708 after his father's death. He was apprenticed to an uncle, Justus Quantz, a town musician in Merseburg, and then to J. A. Fleischhack. After the completion of his apprenticeship in 1713, he continued to serve Fleischhack as a journeyman until March 1716, with a brief stay in Dresden and Pirna in 1714. He studied most of the principal string and wind instruments, showing considerable proficiency on the violin, oboe and trumpet. He also received harpsichord lessons from J. F. Kiesewetter. He became familiar during this period with works of composers of the preceding generation, such as Biber, J. J. Walther and Corelli, and those of his older contemporaries, such as Vivaldi, Telemann and Heinichen.

In March 1716 Quantz joined the Dresden town band directed by Gottfried Heyne. The following year he paid a brief visit to Vienna, where he studied counterpoint with Fux's pupil J. D. Zelenka. In 1718 he was appointed oboist in the Polish chapel of Augustus II, and for the next six years worked in Dresden and Warsaw. Because he found little opportunity for advancement as an oboist, he turned to the transverse flute, studying briefly with the noted French player P. G. Buffardin. But Quantz credited his friend, the violinist J. G. Pisendel, with the greatest influence on the formation of his musical style. His interest in composition, particularly of works for the flute, continued to grow, and at Dresden he was able to benefit from regular contact with a wide range of Italian and French works then performed at the Saxon court. In 1723, with the lutenist S. L. Weiss and C. H. Graun, Frederick the Great's future Kapellmeister, he played in Fux's opera *Costanza e fortezza* at the coronation of Charles VI in Prague. There he also heard Tartini, whose works he later criticized.

Between 1724 and 1727 Quantz completed his training with a period of study in Italy and shorter stays in France and England. He studied counterpoint with F. Gasparini in Rome and visited the other major Italian music centres, where he heard many important vocal and instrumental performers and works by the principal Italian composers. He impressed A. Scarlatti favourably and met, among many others, the future Dresden Kapellmeister, J. A. Hasse, then studying with Scarlatti.

From August 1726 to March 1727 Quantz visited Paris. Although he found French vocal style disagreeable, he enjoyed the performance of many instrumentalists, such as M. Blavet, A. Fortcroix and J. P. Guignon. While in Paris he had a second key added to his flutes for the first time to improve their intonation. During his ten-week stay in England in 1727 he met Handel, who urged him to stay; he also witnessed the climax of the notable feud between the singers Faustina and Cuzzoni.

Quantz's European tour established his reputation outside Germany, and editions of his works later appeared in France, England and Holland. On his return to Dresden in 1727 he was made a member of the regular court Kapelle, and was recognized as one of its outstanding members for the remainder of his service there.

In May 1728 Quantz, Pisendel, Weiss and Buffardin accompanied Augustus II on a state visit to Berlin. From this time Quantz began to instruct the young Prince Frederick on the flute. Thereafter he made regular visits to Berlin for this purpose, but Dresden remained the centre of his activities for another 13 years. In 1733 he refused an offer to enter Frederick's service, and the following year dedicated his *Sei sonate . . . opera prima* for flute and continuo to Augustus III. In 1737 he married Anna Rosina Carolina Schindler (née Hölzel). The manufacture of flutes was added to his other activities in 1739.

When Frederick became King of Prussia in 1740 he was able to offer his teacher a specially favoured position, and in December 1741 Quantz moved to Berlin. Under his agreement, he took orders only from the king, was exempt from duties in the opera orchestra and received 2000 thalers a year for life as well as special payments for new compositions and flutes. For the

1. Johann Joachim Quantz: portrait by an unidentified artist in Schloss Fasanerie, Fulda

remainder of his career his duties centred on the supervision of the king's private evening concerts, for which he wrote new works and at which he alone had the privilege of criticizing Frederick's playing. After he entered Frederick's service, Quantz seems to have composed almost exclusively for the king. But more than half of the sonatas and concertos in Frederick's collection were probably written before 1741, and a number of them circulated in manuscript copies. During Quantz's Berlin period only a small number of compositions were printed.

Surviving documents show that Quantz was on friendly terms with Lessing and Ramler, and in cordial contact with Telemann and Padre Martini. Quantz's pupils included the composers J. F. Agricola and C. Nichelmann and the flautists A. Neuff and J. F. Lindner. Examples of his instruments are found in Berlin and Washington, DC. Portraits of Quantz include an oil painting by an unidentified artist in Schloss Fasanerie, Fulda (see fig.1), an engraving by D. Schleuen and a sketch by H. Franke.

2. WORKS. Quantz's works consist mainly of sonatas for flute and continuo, trio sonatas and concertos. In style they reflect the transition from a late Baroque to an early Classical idiom. The majority of the trio sonatas and the early solo sonatas are cast in the four-movement slow–fast–slow–fast pattern of the *sonata da chiesa*, but incorporate French dance types characteristic of Quantz's preference for a 'mixed style' containing Italian and French elements. In spite of experiments with three-movement fast–slow–fast arrangements, Quantz continued to use the four-movement scheme in his trio

sonatas. In his solo sonatas he had by 1734 adopted the slow–fast–fast pattern that characterizes his mature works in this form. As to concertos, Quantz acknowledged his debt to Vivaldi, and usually cultivated the three-movement fast–slow–fast form.

In general Quantz's works reflect a modification of late Baroque style through increased use of repeated motifs within themes, simplification of harmony, slower harmonic rhythm and restriction of contrapuntal complexity. Quantz, however, rarely went as far in the direction of simplification as younger contemporaries such as Hasse and Graun. By the time he wrote the *Versuch* (1752), he felt it necessary to defend the importance of counterpoint. In formal organization the sonata movements tend towards the expansion of binary designs to include in the second part an increased return of material from the first. Expansion is also characteristic of his use of ritornello patterns in his concertos. In the quick movements he normally preferred five statements of the ritornello, the last two constituting a kind of recapitulation. Although in form and melodic material some of Quantz's later works suggest an early Classical idiom, the majority of his works retain obvious Baroque features, and his style remains allied with the basic trends of the period from *c*1730 to *c*1755.

3. WRITINGS. Quantz's autobiography and other writings are of considerable interest, but his most enduring contribution to the literature of music is unquestionably his *Versuch einer Anweisung die Flöte traversiere zu spielen*. This work presents a comprehensive programme of musical studies intended for use in conjunction with private lessons; only five of the 18 chapters are exclusively for flautists. The treatise is in three main parts. The first is devoted to performance on an individual instrument, moving from fundamentals to more advanced matters connected with ornamentation and style. The second consists of a review of the 'duties' of the accompanying instruments and their leader. The last part surveys the characteristics of Italian, French and German styles and the principal types of vocal and instrumental music, providing the student with a foundation for the evaluation of works he hears and plays.

In the *Versuch* nearly all phases of performance, from phrasing, ornamentation and dynamics to the seating plan of an orchestra, are discussed. Quantz had models for certain portions of his work, but no similarly comprehensive manual had been attempted before. His detailed approach to matters of performance influenced many later German writers on music, from C. P. E. Bach to D. G. Türk. While later authors explored particulars connected with their own instruments at greater length, none equalled Quantz in his combination of breadth and detail. The *Versuch* clearly mirrors Quantz's wide experience. His views cannot be considered absolute guides for the performance of late Baroque music, but certainly reflect many practices of the period from about 1725 to 1755 as cultivated in Dresden, then one of the finest musical establishments in Europe, and subsequently in Berlin.

2. A page from Quantz's 'Versuch einer Anweisung die Flöte traversiere zu spielen' (Berlin, 1752)

WORKS

INSTRUMENTAL

Solfeggi, unacc. fl; MSS, formerly *D-Bds*, lost in World War II; some survive in Das Flötenbuch Friedrichs des Grossen (Leipzig, 1934); some in *DK-Kk*, ed. W. Michel and H. Teske (Winterthur, 1978)

204 sonatas, fl, bc; most survive, *Bds*; 24 (excluding spurious works) pubd in 18th-century editions, of which only Sei sonate a flauto traversiere solo . . . op.1 (Dresden, 1734) was authorized by Quantz

12 capriccios, 8 fantasias, 20 sonata and suite movts, unacc. fl, *DK-Kk*; ed. T. L. Christiansen (Copenhagen, in preparation)

Variations on Ich schlief da träumte mir, fl, bc, *Bim*
12 duets and 1 minuet, 2 fl/other insts, all pubd in 18th-century editions: the authenticity of Six Sonatas or Duets for Two German Flutes . . . op.5 (London, 1750) is uncertain; the Sei duetti a due flauti traversi . . . op.2 (Berlin, 1759/*R*1967) are genuine
45 trio sonatas, 2 fl, bc, or fl, vn/ob/ob d'amore/rec, bc, and 2 sonatas, 3 fl (the majority in *Dlb*); 9 trio sonatas and 1 sonata for 3 fl pubd in 18th-century editions; 5 trio sonatas arr. fl, hpd, *Bds*; Quantz is known to have composed quartets, but none has been traced
2 concertos, ob, str, bc, ed. (Heidelberg, 1968)
Concerto, ob d'amore, str, bc; lost
2 concertos, hn, str, bc (1 possibly not genuine)
300 concertos, fl, str, bc; the majority, *Bds*
7 concertos, 2 fl, str, bc
Pastorale for Agricola's Die Hirten bei der Krippe zu Bethlehem, orch, *LEm*

VOCAL

Padre perdonna, aria, S, str, bc, *Dlb*
Aria per la Sigra, Astrua: Sembra che il ruscelletto (in Serenata fatta per l'arrivo della Regina Madre a Charlottenburgo), *Bim*
6 songs, v, bc: Ach ich verschmachte – schenket ein; Holde Phyllis, die Göttinnen; Welche Gottheit soll auch mir einen Wunsch gewähren; Wenn ich mir ein Mädchen wähle, all in Oden mit Melodien I. Theil (Berlin, 1753); Kleine schöne, küsse mich!, in Neue Lieder zum Singen beym Clavier (Berlin, 1756); Gewiss der ist beklagenswerth, in Berlinische Oden und Lieder I. Theil (Leipzig, 1756)
22 hymns, with bc, in Neue Kirchen-Melodien zu denen geistlichen Liedern des Herrn Professor Gellerts (Berlin, 1760)
For fuller details on MSS, 18th-century and modern edns., see Reilly (1971)

WRITINGS

Versuch einer Anweisung die Flöte traversiere zu spielen (Berlin, 1752, 3/1789/*R*1952) [various edns. and translations, including *On Playing the Flute* (London, 1966)]
'Herrn Johann Joachim Quantzens Lebenslauf von ihm selbst entworfen', in F. W. Marpurg: *Historisch-kritische Beyträge zur Aufnahme der Musik*, i (1754/*R*1970), 197–250; repr. in W. Kahl: *Selbstbiographien deutscher Musiker des XVIII. Jahrhunderts* (Cologne, 1948), 104–57; Eng. trans. in P. Nettl: *Forgotten Musicians* (New York, 1951), 280–319
Vorbericht, Sei duetti . . . opera seconda (Berlin, 1759/*R*1967; Eng. trans. in Reilly, 1971)
'Hrn. Johann Joachim Quanzens Antwort auf des Herrn von Moldenit gedrucktes so genanntes Schreiben an Hrn. Quanz', in F. W. Marpurg: *Historisch-kritische Beyträge zur Aufnahme der Musik*, iv (1759/*R*1970), 153–91
Quantz may have written a series of articles under the pseudonym 'Neologos' in F. W. Marpurg: *Kritische Briefe über die Tonkunst*, i (1760)

BIBLIOGRAPHY

Anon.: *Catalogue des concerts pour Sans Souci, Catalogue des concerts pour le nouveau Palais, Catalogue des solos pour Sans Souci, Catalogue des solos pour le nouveau Palais* (MSS, *D-Bds*)
J. G. I. Breitkopf: *Catalogo de' soli, duetti, trii e concerti per il flauto traverso* (Leipzig, 1763–87/*R*1966)
C. F. Nicolai, ed.: *Anekdoten von König Friedrich II von Preussen* (Berlin, 1788–92)
A. Quantz: *Leben und Werke des Flötisten Johann Joachim Quantz* (Berlin, 1877/*R*)
R. Eitner: *Katalog der Musikaliensammlung des Joachimsthalschen Gymnasium zu Berlin* (Berlin, 1884)
C. Zoeller: *Thematic Catalogue of the Compositions of Johann Joachim Quantz* (MS, *GB-Lbm*, *c*1886)
R. Eitner: 'Quantz, Johann Joachim', *ADB*
G. Thouret: *Katalog der Musiksammlung auf der Königlichen Hausbibliothek* (Leipzig, 1895)
W. Nagel: 'Miscellanea', *MMg*, xxix (1897), 69
R. Jacobs: *Thematischer Katalog der von Thulemeier'schen Musikalien-Sammlung* (Leipzig, 1899)
A. Raskin: *Johann Joachim Quantz: sein Leben und seine Kompositionen* (diss., U. of Cologne, 1923)
R. Schäfke: 'Quantz als Ästhetiker', *AMw*, vi (1924), 213
G. Müller: 'Die Quantz'schen Königs-Flöten', *ZI*, lii (1932), 238
D. C. Miller: *Catalogue of Books and Literary Material Relating to the Flute* (Cleveland, 1935)
H. Kölbel: *Von der Flöte* (Cologne, 1951, 2/1966)
H.-P. Schmitz: *Querflöte und Querflötenspiel in Deutschland während des Barockzeitalters* (Kassel, 1952)
E. Halfpenny: 'A French Commentary on Quantz', *ML*, xxxvii (1956), 61
K. H. Köhler: *Die Triosonate bei den Dresdener Zeitgenossen Johann Sebastian Bachs* (diss., U. of Jena, 1956)
P. A. Scholes, ed.: *Dr. Burney's Musical Tours in Europe* (London, 1959)
E. E. Helm: *Music at the Court of Frederick the Great* (Norman, Oklahoma, 1960)

E. R. Reilly: 'Further Musical Examples for Quantz's *Versuch*', *JAMS*, xvii (1964), 157
F. Neumann: 'The French Inégales, Quantz, and Bach', *JAMS*, xviii (1965), 313–58
——: 'La note pointée et la soi-disant "manière française" ', *RdM*, li (1965), 66
M. Rasmussen: 'Some Notes on the Articulations in the Melodic Variation Tables of . . . Quantz's *Versuch*', *BWQ*, i (1966–7), 3
E. R. Reilly: *Quantz and his Versuch: Three Studies* (New York, 1971)
——: 'A Realization by J. C. Heck: an Affettuoso di molto by Johann Joachim Quantz (1697–1773)', *Notations and Editions: a Book in Honor of Louise Cuyler* (Dubuque, Iowa, 1974), 154
EDWARD R. REILLY

Quarenghi, Guglielmo (*b* Casalmaggiore, 22 Oct 1826; *d* Milan, 3 Feb 1882). Italian cellist and composer. He studied with Vincenzo Merighi at the Milan Conservatory from 1839 to 1842. He became principal cellist at La Scala in 1850, and a professor at the conservatory in 1851. During 1860–61 Quarenghi was associated with Rossi and Mazzucato in the formation of the Società di S Cecilia, Milan. He succeeded Boucheron as *maestro di cappella* of Milan Cathedral in 1879, but ill-health forced him to resign in 1881.

Quarenghi's only opera, *Il dì di San Michele*, was produced in Milan in 1863, and in the same year he published a mass and other church music. His *Metodo di violoncello* (Milan, 1876) has an interesting preface comparing the earliest bowed instruments, and their evolution, with folk instruments from many countries. He also composed six caprices for solo cello, several original pieces and transcriptions for cello and piano, and some chamber music.

LYNDA LLOYD REES

Quarles, Charles (i) (*d* Cambridge, before 4 July 1717). English organist. He was organist of Trinity College, Cambridge, from December 1688 until his death some time before 4 July 1717, when the College Conclusion Book refers to him as deceased. From August 1709 half the duty of organist was performed by John Bowman, who was to be Quarles's successor. He took the Cambridge degree of MusB in 1698. A pleasing two-movement Lesson in F minor for the harpsichord by him was published by Goodison in about 1790. J. and J. A. Venn (*Alumni cantabrigienses*, Cambridge, 1922–7) suggested that he may have been the son of Charles Quarles, 'builder of the organs at Pembroke and Christ's [Colleges]'. However, the dates when a Charles Quarles was concerned with those instruments do not preclude his being this Quarles, who was allowed £10 'for repairing and fitting the organ' in Trinity College in August 1705.

WATKINS SHAW

Quarles, Charles (ii) (*d* York, *c*1727). English organist; his relationship to Charles Quarles (i) is unknown. He was organist of York Minster from 1722. His successor, Edward Salisbury, was appointed in February 1728, but it is not known for certain whether Quarles was by that time dead. In the *Cathedral Magazine* (1775, iii), an anthem, *Out of the deep*, is ascribed to 'Mr Charles late Organist at York', and it is extremely likely that this really means 'Mr Charles Quarles'. More interesting is a technical study compounded of scales and arpeggios divided between the hands, entitled 'Mr Quarles's way of fingering in Gamut Natural', which occurs in a manuscript (*GB-Ge* R.d.39, f.37*v*) in the hand of Edward Finch, himself of York, and so presumably relates to Quarles of York. In the study free use is made of the thumb and all fingers in the modern way. This evidently struck Finch as sufficiently novel and noteworthy to justify transcription.

WATKINS SHAW

Quarta (It.). FOURTH.

Quartal harmony. A term for a harmonic system based on the interval of a 4th (as in early two-part organum), as opposed to the TERTIARY HARMONY of the major–minor tonal system. *See also* NON-QUARTAL HARMONY.

Quartane. An ORGAN STOP (*Rauschpfeife*).

Quart de soupir (Fr.). A semiquaver REST.

Quart de ton (Fr.). QUARTER-TONE.

Quarte (Fr., Ger.). FOURTH.

Quarte de nasard (Fr.). An ORGAN STOP.

Quarter-note. American term for CROTCHET. *See also* NOTE VALUES.

Quarter-tone (Fr. *quart de ton*; Ger. *Viertelton*; It. *quarto di tono*). An interval or intervallic quantity half the size of a semitone. The term was used by some 17th- and 18th-century theorists to denote the distance between a sharp and enharmonically distinct flat in mean-tone temperaments (e.g. $D\sharp$–$E\flat$). In the context of equal temperament, however, it refers to an interval normally $\frac{1}{24}$ of an octave, or 50 cents. The Czech composer Alois Hába, who used quarter-tones 'to permeate the semitone system with more delicate nuances', taught courses on quarter-tone (and sixth-tone) music at the Prague Conservatory from 1924 to 1951. Bartók used quarter-tones in the last movement of the original, unpublished version of his Sonata for solo violin (1944; see Nordwall, 1965). Other modern composers who have written quarter-tone music include Julián Carrillo (from the 1890s), Ivan Vishnegradsky and Ives, as well as Boulez and many other composers since World War II. (*See also* NOTATION, §III, 6.)

The concept of quarter-tones has been a prominent feature in the analysis of scales by 19th- and 20th-century Islamic music theorists, most notably Mikhā'īl Mushāqa (1800–88), dealing with melodic intervals intermediate in size between a semitone and a whole tone, or in some instances slightly larger than a whole tone. (One early 10th-century theorist, al-Fārābī, described the ostensible use of approximate quarter-tones in the fretting of a long-necked lute, *tunbūr baghdādī*, which he deemed pre-Islamic; *see* ARAB MUSIC, §I, 2.) Many Hindu theorists have considered the octave to be divided into 22 *sruti* which, though seldom regarded as uniform in size, must average about 55 cents (*see* INDIA, SUBCONTINENT OF, §II); some *sruti* may have approximated to this average. The enharmonic genus described by ancient Greek music theory included quarter-tones used melodically (*see* GREECE, §I, and DIESIS (ii)) and their medieval European use is apparent in the 11th-century gradual *F-MO* H159.

BIBLIOGRAPHY

E. Smith: 'A Treatise on Arab Music, chiefly from a Work by Mikhâil Meshâkah, of Damascus', *Journal of the American Oriental Society*, i (1849), 171–218

F. Busoni: *Entwurf einer neuen Ästhetik der Tonkunst* (Trieste, 1907, 2/1910; Eng. trans., 1911/R1962)

J. Gmelch: *Der Viertelstonstufen im Messtonale von Montpellier* (Eichstatt, 1910)

R. Baralli: 'L'episema del ms. H. 159 di Montpellier', *Rassegna gregoriana*, x (1911), 11, 109

H. G. Farmer: 'Musikiya', *The Encyclopaedia of Islam* (Leiden and London, 1913–38)

J. Mager: *Vierteltonmusik* (Aschaffenburg, 1915)

W. von Moellendorf: *Musik mit Vierteltönen* (Leipzig, 1917)

L. Kallenbach-Greller: 'Die historischen Grundlagen der Vierteltöne', *AMw*, viii (1926), 473

L. Sabaneyev: 'The Possibility of Quarter-tone and Other New Scales', *MT*, lxx (1929), 501

A. Wellek: 'Quarter Tones and Progress', *MQ*, xxiv (1938), 528

W. Apel: *Gregorian Chant* (Bloomington, Ind., 1958, 3/1966), 122

C. Ives: *Essays before a Sonata and Other Writings*, ed. H. Boatwright (New York, 1962), 105

O. Nordwall: 'The Original Version of Bartok's Sonata for Solo Violin', *Tempo* (1965), no.74, p.2

Quartet (Fr. *quatuor*, *quartette*; Ger. *Quartett*; It. *quartetto*). A composition or part of a composition for four voices or instruments, or a group that performs such a composition. Many chansons, madrigals and polyphonic lieder of the 16th century and glees of the 17th century are vocal quartets. Partsongs, sometimes (like Pearsall's madrigals) imitating an earlier form, continue the tradition of writing for such combinations through the Classical and Romantic periods. Vocal quartets, like duets and trios, figured prominently in 19th-century domestic music, sometimes in an accompanied form, as in Brahms's two sets of *Liebeslieder* waltzes with piano duet or his *Zigeunerlieder* and Schumann's *Spanisches Liederspiel* with piano solo. Accompanied quartet cycles like Liza Lehmann's once popular *In a Persian Garden* and Stanford's *The Princess* were part of a sizable literature now almost totally neglected.

Vocal quartets accompanied by orchestra are frequent in opera and oratorio from the 18th century onwards. Handel's 'Why dost thou untimely grieve?' in *Semele* is an early example of a form that was subsequently developed as a dramatic confrontation of characters. Independent lines of thought and action on the part of four characters were skilfully portrayed in the music both in ensembles forming an independent number like Mozart's 'Andrò, ramingo e solo' in *Idomeneo* and 'Non ti fidar, o misera' in *Don Giovanni* and Beethoven's 'Mir ist so wunderbar' in *Fidelio*, and in those that are an integral part of a scene such as the quartets in Verdi's *Rigoletto* and *Otello*. Settings of the mass in the Classical period, particularly in Austria, frequently make use of a quartet of solo voices. In his Ninth Symphony Beethoven transferred the device to symphonic music.

The most important chamber music forms are the STRING QUARTET (two violins, viola, cello) and the PIANO QUARTET (piano, violin, viola, cello); these repertories are discussed in separate entries. Closely related to the early string quartet are the many 18th-century works in which one of the violins of the string quartet was replaced by a wind instrument, notably the oboe and flute quartets of J. C. Bach, Vanhal and Mozart or the clarinet quartets of Carl Stamitz and J. N. Hummel. In many of these compositions the wind instrument is treated in a more soloistic manner than would be usual in a string quartet, more in fact in the manner of the *quatuor brillant* (with a virtuoso first violin part). Sometimes both violins were replaced, as in J. C. Bach's quartets for two flutes, viola and cello.

Wind instruments tend to combine with the piano less well than with strings, but there is a handful of quartets for piano and wind, including works by Franz Berwald (with clarinet, horn and bassoon) and Florent Schmitt (with oboe, clarinet and bassoon). For keyboard with mixed ensemble there are various significant modern works such as Hindemith's quartet for piano, clarinet, violin and cello (1938), Messiaen's *Quatuor pour la fin du temps* for the same combination, and Webern's op.22 for tenor saxophone, clarinet, violin and piano.

The repertory of quartets for wind instruments alone is similarly varied in instrumentation. In their divertimentos and cassations Haydn and his contemporaries tended to combine pairs of instruments – two flutes and two horns or two clarinets with two horns, for instance. Rossini's quartets for flute, clarinet, bassoon and horn are mostly arrangements. There are 20th-century works for four different wind instruments by Frank Bridge, Jean Françaix, Egon Wellesz, H. E. Apostel and Henk Badings.

See also CHAMBER MUSIC.   MICHAEL TILMOUTH

Quartetto Beethoven. Italian piano quartet formed in 1968 by FELIX AYO.

Quartetto d'archi [di cordi] (It.). STRING QUARTET.

Quartetto di Roma [Rome Quartet]. Italian piano quartet formed in 1956; *see* SANTOLIQUIDO, ORNELLA.

Quartetto Italiano. *See* ITALIAN QUARTET.

Quartfagott. As mentioned by Praetorius, a large dulcian pitched a 4th below the standard dulcian; similarly, a 'quintfagott' was pitched a 5th below. In the 18th century these terms referred similarly to larger versions of the BASSOON. They are also used to refer to tenoroons pitched at various intervals higher than the standard bassoon, in which case the prefix 'hoch' should be added to avoid confusion (e.g. *Hochquartfagott* in Eb).
                                        WILLIAM WATERHOUSE

Quart flute. A RECORDER pitched in Bb, a 4th above the treble instrument.

Quartieri [Quartiero], **Pietro Paolo** (*b* Rome, *c*1560; *d* ?after 1601). Italian composer. He was probably associated with S Cesareo Cathedral at Terracina, near Rome. Cerreto, in *Della prattica musica vocale et strumentale* (1601), cited him as an outstanding musician. He wrote sacred music for S Cesareo, including psalm settings and motets. Because of his apparent preoccupation with problems of harmony, tonality and form, he often avoided verbal imagery in his madrigals; his interpretation of the texts is reflected in the variation of cadences, textures and metrical changes, and all the pieces demonstrate his mastery of contrapuntal devices.

WORKS
Primo libro de madrigali, 5vv (Rome, 1592); ed. R. Watanabe, *Five Italian Madrigal Books of the Late Sixteenth Century* (diss., U. of Rochester, 1951)
1 madrigal, 5vv, 1606[5]
Many sacred works, formerly *D-KN* Sammlung Heyer, now lost
                                        RUTH T. WATANABE

Quartina (It.). QUADRUPLET.

Quarto di tono (It.). QUARTER-TONE.

Quartole (Ger.; Fr. *quartolet*). QUADRUPLET.

Quartposaune (Ger.). In the strict sense, a trombone pitched a 4th below the ordinary (*gemeine*) trombone. (Similarly the *Quintposaune* is pitched a 5th below.) 'Quartposaune' is mentioned by the maker Georg Neuschel in letters (1541). In the 17th and 18th centuries, from which there survive examples of both *Quart* and *Quint* instruments, 'Quartposaune' might signify whichever of these was available for the occasion. The word 'Quartposaune' came to be used commonly as an equivalent to 'Bassposaune', which was on the whole a rare term before the 19th century. In the early 19th century 'Quartposaune' was still occasionally used (e.g. by Nemetz, *Neueste Posaun-Schule*, Vienna, *c*1830). The pitches of a *Quart-* and *Quintposaune* during the Baroque period were respectively E and D at the old high pitch (*Chorton*); the ordinary trombone was then in A. By the beginning of the 19th century the pitch of the *Quartposaune* had come to be reckoned as F (with the tenor at Bb) at the concert pitch of the time.

Also mentioned, mainly in inventories of instruments from 1580 to 1610, are the *Terz-* and *Secundposaune*, pitched a 3rd and a 2nd below the ordinary trombone. Their purpose was probably to aid transposition of music downwards, though for this an ordinary trombone could be made to serve as *Secund, Terz* or even *Quart* by the addition of crooks, as described in the 1589 inventory of the Stuttgart Hofkapelle (Bossert, *Württembergische Vierteljahrsheft für Landesgeschichte*, new ser., xxi, 1912). 'Terzposaune' in Nemetz refers to a bass trombone in G (the traditional pitch for the bass trombone in England until modern times).
                                        ANTHONY C. BAINES

Quartsextakkord (Ger.). SIX-FOUR CHORD.

Quartzug (Ger.). In Schenkerian analysis a diatonic scalic progression encompassing the interval of a perfect 4th, e.g. $e'-f'-g'-a'$, $eb-d-c-Bb$ (*see* ZUG (i)).

Quasi (It.: 'almost', 'approximately', 'like', 'as though'). A word used both in tempo designations – *andante quasi allegretto, allegretto quasi vivace,* etc – and in piece descriptions – *sonata quasi una fantasia*, 'sonata in the manner of a fantasy'. A curious observation in Koch's *Musikalisches Lexikon* (1802) is that the word 'quasi' scarcely ever appears in music.
For bibliography *see* TEMPO AND EXPRESSION MARKS.

Quassus (Lat.: 'shaken'). An adjective used to describe a neume whose first element is an ORISCUS. For instance, a VIRGA (single note of relatively higher pitch) preceded by an *oriscus* forms two notes in ascending order, a *pes quassus*. As with all neumes which include the *oriscus*, there is doubt as to the exact significance of the *quassus* type. A peculiarity of execution or an ambiguity of pitch may be involved (for illustration *see* NEUMATIC NOTATIONS, Table 1).

Quaternaria (Lat.). A *ligatura quaternaria* or ligature comprising four notes. See LIGATURE (i).

Quatreble (Middle Eng.: 'quadruple'; from Lat. *quadruplus* or *quadruplex*, modified by analogy with 'treble' from Fr. *triple*). A voice or part pitched a 5th higher than the treble. Here the usage is directly related to the Latin *quadruplum* in its sense of a fourth voice, above the *triplum*, in a motet (Franco of Cologne: 'Qui autem quadruplum vel quintuplum facere voluit'). In the 'qua-trebil syghte' of improvised discant, as taught in Leonel Power's *Tretis . . . upon the Gamme*, the child was to sing an octave higher than the notes he imagined on the staff carrying the plainsong; other theorists of the time, however, make this a 12th higher, i.e. a 5th above the treble.

BIBLIOGRAPHY
M. Bukofzer: *Geschichte des englischen Diskants* (Strasbourg, 1936)
JOHN CALDWELL

Quatremère de Quincy [Quatremère], **Antoine-Chrysostome** (*b* Paris, 25 Oct 1755; *d* Paris, 28 Dec 1849). French politician, archaeologist, art historian and writer on music. After preparing for a career in law he studied art and history at the College of Louis-Le-Grand. From 1776 he made several long sojourns in Italy where he was soon drawn towards archaeology and the arts of antiquity. He established himself in 1786 in Paris as an aesthetician and art critic, and his author-ity was soon widespread, both with the public and among artists. His important article 'De la nature des opéras bouffons italiens' (*Mercure de France*, 1789) marked his entrance into the world of musicography, and together with his *Dissertation* that same year led to the recall of the disbanded *Bouffonistes*. He began his political career at the time of the Revolution, persever-ing for freedom of the theatres and for literary, dramatic and artistic copyright. In 1791 he was elected as a deputy to the Legislative Assembly, where he continued his activities on behalf of the arts. He was imprisoned for two years during the Terror, narrowly escaping the guillotine, and again escaped a death sentence in 1795. In 1797 he was appointed to the Council of the Five Hundred. He was made a member of the Académie des Inscriptions et Belles Lettres in 1804, and of the Légion d'honneur in 1808. With the restoration of the Bourbons his honours increased, and in 1816 he was appointed permanent secretary of the Institut de France. In this capacity he delivered funeral orations and bio-graphical notices of deceased members of the academy, including the major French composers of the time. His writings for these occasions were printed separately and later collected in two volumes; based on first-hand documentation and contemporary opinion, they have since become valuable sources for the study of music history.

WRITINGS

(only those relating to music included)
'De la nature des opéras bouffons italiens et de l'union de la comédie et de la musique dans ces poëmes', *Mercure de France* (March 1789), 124
Dissertation sur les opéras bouffons italiens (Paris, 1789) [also in *Archives littéraires de l'Europe*, xvi (1807), 1–39]
Discours . . . sur la liberté des théâtres (Paris, 1790) [also in *Le moniteur* (22 Feb 1790)]
Rapport . . . sur les réclamations des directeurs de théâtres et la propriété des auteurs dramatiques (Paris, 1792)
Dissertation . . . sur le système imitatif des arts et le genre poétique (Paris, *c*1804)
Institut royal de France: . . . funérailles de Paisiello (Paris, 1817); *de M. de Monsigny* (Paris, 1818); *de M. Méhul* (Paris, 1819); *de M. Gossec* (Paris, 1829); *de M. Catel* (Paris, 1830); *de M. Boieldieu* (Paris, 1834)
De l'invention et de l'innovation dans les ouvrages des beaux-arts (Paris, *c*1828)
Recueil des notices historiques lues dans les séances publiques de l'Académie royale des Beaux-arts à l'Institut (Paris, 1834) [notices on Paisiello, Monsigny and Méhul, already pubd separately]; *Suite du Recueil* (Paris, 1837) [notices on Gossec, Catel, Boieldieu, already pubd separately]

BIBLIOGRAPHY
FétisB
A. Maury: 'Quatremère de Quincy, Antoine-Chrysostome', *Nouvelle biographie générale*, xli (Paris, 1862)
A. Boschot: *Le centenaire d'un esthéticien, Quatremère de Quincy* (Paris, 1940)
M. Briquet: 'Quatremère de Quincy, Antoine-Chrysostome', *MGG*
ROGER COTTE

Quatricinium. A term, analogous to BICINIUM and TRICINIUM, applied to a four-part piece, often for wind instruments (e.g. Gottfried Reiche's *24 neue Quatricinia*, Leipzig, 1696). It was also used for didactic compositions, frequently in a contrapuntal style, in treatises of the late 16th, 17th and 18th centuries (e.g. Friedrich Beurhusius's *Musica rudimenta*, Dortmund, 1581).

Quatris, Johannes de. *See* JOHANNES DE QUADRIS.

Quattrini, Jan Ludwik (*b* Brescia, 13 May 1822; *d* Warsaw, 10 April 1893). Italian flautist, singer and teacher, who worked in Poland. He studied with Basili at the Milan Conservatory. From 1839 he was band-master at Mantua, and later at Genoa, Turin, Milan, Venice and Berlin. He moved to Warsaw in 1843 with Rocca's Italian touring opera company and from 1845 to 1891 ran a singing school there, using his own teach-ing methods. From 1845 he was joint conductor of the Warsaw Opera with N. T. Nidecki; after Nidecki's death he became sole conductor and held the title of director of opera, shared simultaneously by a number of other conductors, including Moniuszko. He introduced to Warsaw the operas of Meyerbeer (*Les Huguenots*, *Le prophète*, *Robert le diable*, *L'africaine*), Halévy (*La juive*), Gounod (*Faust*), Verdi (*Aida*, *Don Carlos*), Bizet (*Carmen*) and others. Although Italian by birth, he was a champion of Polish music: he staged Moniuszko's *Loteria* on 12 September 1846 and *Halka* on 1 January 1858, and also Münchheimer's operas. He taught more than 80 distinguished singers, but in 1891 resigned from the opera and became music director of the Piarists' church. He edited collections of Italian airs, composed songs and exercises for singers, and tran-scribed Chopin's Funeral March for chorus, soloists and orchestra (performed in 1856). In 1851 or 1852 he married Kornelia Pion, one of his students, who per-formed at the Warsaw Opera until 1864.

BIBLIOGRAPHY
Echo muzyczne, teatralne i artystyczne, ii (1885), 458
G. Broel-Plater: *Jan Quatrini* (Warsaw, 1887)
T. Błaszczyk: *Dyrygenci polscy i obcy w Polsce działający w XIX i XX wieku* [Polish and foreign conductors working in Poland in the 19th and 20th centuries] (Kraków, 1964)
IRENA PONIATOWSKA

Quatuor (Fr.). QUARTET.

Quatuor à cordes (Fr.). STRING QUARTET.

Quatuor concertant (Fr.). A title used in the late 18th century, especially in France, for a kind of composition for four solo instruments, usually two violins, viola and cello (occasionally a flute, oboe or clarinet replaced the first violin). In this context 'concertant' referred to a piece in which all four instruments were essential to the musical discourse, not primarily, as is sometimes thought, to one which was 'brilliant' and 'showy'. As a title 'Quatuor concertant' was assigned rather loosely – perhaps by the composer, more likely by the publisher – to distinguish this genre from quartets in which the first violin dominated the main melodic action and from quartets in which several instruments might play a single part, perhaps with continuo, in the manner of a chamber sinfonia. The *quatuor concertant* appears to have had one of the first explicitly prescribed scorings in the history of instrumental ensemble music.

Several thousand *quatuors concertants*, by no fewer than 200 composers, appeared on the Parisian musical market (in sets of printed parts) between *c*1770 and 1800; fewer works were so titled in the first decades of the 19th century. Although Paris was the publication capital and also a centre for their composition and performance, many of the same works were published elsewhere, but not always with the designation 'concertant' on their title-pages. Composers of these quartets included E.-B.-J. Barrière, G. M. Cambini, N.-M. Dalayrac, J.-B. Davaux, F. Fiorillo, P. Vachon and G. B. Viotti.

Quatuors concertants, which appealed to amateurs, were normally in two or three movements, the first usually in sonata form. Changes of texture were decisive for formal structure and, particularly in sonata forms, assumed a syntax of their own. The most characteristic texture was that of dialogue in which players exchanged roles, each with his solo moment. Contemporary critics praised such works for being 'bien dialogués'. Conventional treatment of familiar forms accommodated an almost theatrical succession of rapidly contrasting affective gestures – clichés from opera, concerto and other popular sources. A varied palette of sound and a brilliance and elegance of individual moments created structures which at times seem narrative or even episodic.

BIBLIOGRAPHY

L. de La Laurencie: *L'école française de violon de Lully à Viotti* (Paris, 1922–4/*R*1971)

L. Finscher: 'Streichquartett', *MGG*

D. L. Trimpert: *Die Quatuors Concertants von Giuseppe Cambini* (Tutzing, 1967)

D. Klein: *Le quatuor à cordes français au 18ᵉ siècle* (diss., U. of Paris, 1970)

J. M. Levy: *The Quatuor Concertant in Paris in the Latter Half of the Eighteenth Century* (diss., Stanford U., 1971)

JANET M. LEVY

Quaver (Fr. *croche*; Ger. *Achtel-Note*; It. *croma, semicroma*; Lat. *fusa*; Sp. *corchea*). The note that is half the value of a crotchet and twice that of a semiquaver. In American usage it is called an eighth-note. It is the equivalent of the old *fusa*, and is first found in 15th-century music. In sources using black notation it was shown as a minim with two flags, while in 'white' or 'void' notation (post-1450) it is found either as a minim with two flags or as a black or coloured minim with a flag. Some sources use the alternative term *croma*, while in Spanish writings a *fusa* is a demisemiquaver (32nd-note). The quaver is still in regular use, although in common with other notes it now has a round note head. Its various forms and the quaver rest are shown in ex.1*a–e*; the *fusa* rest is shown in ex.1*f*.

Ex.1

(a) (b) (c) (d) (e) (f)

See also NOTATION, §III, 4(ii) and NOTE VALUES.

JOHN MOREHEN

Quebec (Fr. Québec). Canadian city. Founded in 1608, it was Canada's earliest centre of music. Many church and school activities of early times are recorded in the *Relations des Jésuites*. Its first bishop, Monsignor de Laval, brought with him an organ from Paris in 1663. Charles-Amador Martin, a Quebec-born priest, is credited with writing the earliest extant musical composition in Canada, a plainchant *prosa Sacrae familiae* (1670). The Hanoverian Frédéric-Henri Glackemeyer, considered as Canada's first professional musician, probably came to Quebec in 1776 as bandmaster with one of the Brunswick mercenary regiments which came to help the British counter the American Revolution. He was afterwards a teacher and an importer of instruments and printed music. In 1820 he founded the Quebec Harmonic Society. The first Canadian-born conductor is said to have been Charles Sauvageau, who founded an orchestra in 1840 and gave public concerts. Another German-born musician, Theodore Frederic Molt, came to Quebec to teach in about 1823 and returned to Europe for a visit in 1825. In Vienna he met Beethoven and his visit is recorded in the conversation books. Molt published textbooks in French and English and for a time was organist of the basilica. A major development came in 1866 with the founding of the Union Musicale de Québec whose first concert included a performance of Haydn's 'Nelson' Mass. Antoine Dessane, a French-born fellow student of César Franck at the Paris Conservatoire, arrived in 1848 and has been called the 'father of music in Quebec'. In 1869 he founded the Société Sainte-Cécile. The Haydn Septet, consisting of a string quintet with flute and piano, was founded in 1871 and for 30 years played at hundreds of concerts in Quebec and throughout the province. After Glackemeyer, Molt and Dessane, the post of organist of the basilica was held for nearly a century by the Gagnon family, Ernest (1864–76), Gustave (1876–1915) and Henri (1915–61). Claude Lagacé was appointed organist in 1961.

After the death of Sauvageau in 1856, his orchestra was taken over by François Vézina. In 1902 his son Joseph, a pupil of Calixa Lavallée, was in charge of the musical celebrations marking the golden jubilee of Laval University, during which he conducted a performance of Dubois' *Le paradis perdu*. An outgrowth of that performance was the founding of the Société Symphonique de Québec, whose first concert under Vézina was given in Tara Hall on 5 December 1902. Now the Orchestre Symphonique de Québec, it is the oldest existing orchestra in Canada. Vézina was the conductor until his death in 1924, when Jean-Robert Talbot was appointed. Edwin Bélanger became its conductor in 1942, to be succeeded by Wilfrid Pelletier in 1950. Under his tenure the ensemble became fully professional and the season was extended. Françoys Benier took over in 1966 and was succeeded by the Frenchman Pierre Dervaux. During the 1972–3 season, the orchestra gave 55 concerts besides nine performances for the Quebec Opera. Its 70 musicians are under contract for 29 weeks of the year. The orchestra has commissioned major works from Quebec composers, such as Roger Matton's *Te Deum* in 1965.

For opera the Québeçois had to rely on touring companies and sporadic local productions until 1961, when Roger Gosselin founded the Théâtre Lyrique de Nouvelle-France which lasted for ten years. The Quebec Opera, which began with the 1972–3 season, was the first state-subsidized company in North America and operates both in Quebec and Montreal. For many years concerts were given in the Palais-Montcalm or the

Capitol Theatre but the Grand Théâtre (opened in January 1971) now provides a suitable venue. Opera performances and concerts are given in the Salle Louis-Fréchette (1800 seats) or the adjoining Salle Octave-Crémazie (a multi-purpose hall of 500 seats). The complex also houses the conservatory. The CBC has regional radio and television studios in Quebec and also maintains a chamber orchestra. Concert-giving organizations include the Club Musical de Québec and Les Amis de l'Orgue.

The Quebec Academy of Music, an institution aimed at raising the level of music education in the province, was founded in 1868. It awards the annual Prix d'Europe to composers and performers. A private Quebec Conservatory was founded in 1910 and in 1943 was succeeded by a state-subsidized body bearing the same name. Directors have been Henri Gagnon, Raoul Jobin and Paul-Emile Talbot. The School of Music at Laval University was founded in 1922 and its directors have been Gustave Gagnon, J. W. Gilbert, Jean-Robert Talbot, Onésime Pouliot and, from 1962, Lucien Brochu.

BIBLIOGRAPHY
Relations des Jésuites 1632–1673 (Quebec, 1858)
H. Kallmann: A History of Music in Canada, 1534–1914 (Toronto, 1960)
A. Lasalle-Leduc: La vie musicale au Canada français (Quebec, 1964)
A. Walter, ed.: Aspects of Music in Canada (Toronto, 1969; Fr. trans., 1970)

GILLES POTVIN

Quebedo, Bartolomé de. See QUEVEDO, BARTOLOMÉ DE.

Queen Elizabeth Hall. London concert hall on the South Bank, opened in 1967; see LONDON, §VI, 5(iv).

Queen's Hall. London concert hall, opened in 1893; see LONDON, §VI, 5(iii). The Queen's Hall Orchestra was formed in 1895 and renamed the New Queen's Hall Orchestra in 1915; see LONDON, §VI, 2(ii).

Queen's Theatre. (1) The name of the Dorset Garden Theatre, London, from 1689 to its closure in 1706; see LONDON, §IV, 3.

(2) The name of the King's Theatre, London, during Queen Anne's reign; see LONDON, §IV, 3.

Queen's University. The university of BELFAST; it has had a chair of music since 1947.

Queffélec, Anne (b Paris, 17 Jan 1948). French pianist. She studied the piano from the age of five in Paris with Blanche Bascourret de Guéraldi, and in 1964 entered the Paris Conservatoire to study with Lélia Gousseau; a year later she won a premier prix for piano. In 1968 she was awarded first prize at the Munich International Festival, and in 1969 was fifth in the International Competition at Leeds. Her even temperament and light, brilliant style of playing have attracted special praise, notably in performances of French music, and the sonatas of Scarlatti and Mozart.

DOMINIC GILL

Queldryk [Qweldryk] (fl c1400). English composer. He may have been associated with an estate of Fountains Abbey of this name (= Wheldrake, near York). His name is attached to a Gloria and a Credo in the Old Hall MS (nos.30 and 88); there is no other source for his music. The four-part isorhythmic Gloria (troped Spiritus et alme) is in duple time throughout and divides the text between the two upper parts in alternation with

melisma. The three-part isorhythmic Credo has a similar alternation of text and likewise has no identifiable cantus firmus. In both pieces, the color is repeated in halved values and each color has two taleae.

For bibliography and edition see OLD HALL MS.

MARGARET BENT

Quempas (from Lat. Quem pastores laudavere: 'He whom the shepherds praised'). The abbreviated title of a Christmas song popular in Germany in the 16th century, which was used as a generic term for Christmas songs. The custom, performed by the students of Latin schools, of earning alms by singing carols from house to house was known as Quempas singen. A Quempasheft was a collection of Christmas songs that each student copied for his own use.

Quem queritis. The opening words of the celebrated trope to the introit of the Mass of Easter. Around this trope and other similar ones (e.g. its imitation in the third Mass of Christmas) arose a tradition of church drama from at least the 10th century onwards, known rather loosely as 'liturgical drama' (see MEDIEVAL DRAMA, §II, and fig.1). The basic dialogue is as follows (Young, i, p.210):

ANGELS: Quem queritis in sepulcro, o Christicole?
MARYS: Ihesum Nazarenum crucifixum, o celicole.
ANGELS: Non est hic, surrexit sicut ipse dixit; ite, nunciate quia surrexit.

(Whom are you looking for in the tomb, you followers of Christ? Jesus of Nazareth who was crucified, O dwellers in Heaven. He is not here, he has arisen as he himself foretold; go and make it known that he has arisen.)

Various sources have been suggested from time to time for the words of the dialogue (the Gospel narratives, the antiphons and responsories of Easter) and to account for the fact of dialogue itself (the singing of the Passion in Holy Week); but no single source accounts for all its features. The music is similarly a free traditional composition – that is to say, newly composed in the traditional 'neumatic' style of Gregorian chant, using the same tonalities and melodic formulae. In addition to the standard melody found all over Europe, another melody appears in German sources from about 1200 (see Smoldon, 1954, with music example).

Some 14 manuscripts of the 'Quem queritis' can be dated as 10th-century; and of these probably the two oldest are those of St Martial of Limoges (F-Pn lat.1240, dated 923–34) and of St Gall (CH-SGs 484, c950). These and other early sources are written in unheighted neumes but the pitches of the notes can often be deduced from later manuscripts (facsimiles of several versions are reproduced in Smoldon, 1969). Of the two versions just named, the later manuscript presents the simpler. Moreover, they are close in date to a famous description of an Easter ceremony which can with justification be called a Visitatio sepulchri play and which embodies the 'Quem queritis' dialogue: this is to be found in the REGULARIS CONCORDIA, the customary drawn up at Winchester about 970. The co-existence of these three documents in the earliest period of its history argues conclusively against a simple chronological, or elaborate evolutionary, view of the 'development' of the 'Quem queritis' from liturgical trope to representational drama. Indeed, the term 'variants' is safer than 'developments'. Both straightforward and highly complex forms of the dialogue are found throughout the period 900–1300. In some sources prefatory sung sentences (e.g.

'Psallite regi magno, deuicto mortis imperio!') and sentences to ease the transition to the introit 'Resurrexi' (e.g. the antiphon 'Hodie resurrexit leo fortis') are introduced. The sources also vary in the degree to which they rubricate the dialogue, and in the degree to which the rubrics indicate dramatic singing (i.e. by the assignment of singers to roles). In general, so long as the dialogue remains attached to the introit the variants are expressive of 'liturgical rejoicing rather than a sense of drama' (Young, i, p.213).

The elaborate ceremony prescribed in the *Regularis concordia* leads into the singing of the *Te Deum* and the ringing of bells ('una pulsantur omnia signa'). This indicates that the 'play' was part of Matins (it followed the third lesson) and did not in this case precede the introit of the Mass. This and other considerations led Hardison (1965) to suggest that the 'Quem queritis' dialogue began its career as a Resurrection ceremony associated with the Vigil Mass, rather than as a trope – i.e. that it is a separate and independent 'representational ceremony'. This conjecture, put forward on literary and liturgical grounds, was rebutted by Smoldon (1968), who brought forward evidence both palaeographical and musical to confirm the close connection between the dialogue and the Mass introit.

The Easter 'Quem queritis' is paralleled by a Christmas version (Young, ii, p.4, from *F-Pn* lat.887, 11th century):

MIDWIVES: Quem queritis in presepe, pastores, dicite?
SHEPHERDS: Salvatorem Christum Dominum, infantem pannis involutum, secundum sermonem angelicum.

(Shepherds, tell us whom you are looking for in the manger. Our Saviour, Christ the Lord, a babe wrapped in swaddling clothes, as the angels told us.)

There are fewer extant examples of and less variety among the Christmas than among the Easter dialogues. The Christmas dialogue is a trope ending with the direction, *Psalmus* 'Puer natus est' – the first three words of the introit for the third Mass of Christmas Day. The music, which differs decisively from that of the Easter trope, nevertheless displays some of the same motifs: the rising triad *c–e–g* on 'in se-pul[cro]' and on 'Na-za-re[num]' recurs on 'in pre-se[pe]' and 'Chris-tum Do[mi-num]' (The music of *F-Pn* lat.887 is transcribed in *NOHM*, ii, p.196.)

Both the Easter and the Christmas tropes, in their transferred position as part of Matins, underwent expansion and variation. At Easter the result was a group of para-liturgical plays, known collectively as VISITATIO SEPULCHRI; at Christmas the group is entitled the OFFICIUM PASTORUM. Tropes in the 'Quem queritis' genre are found for the feasts of the Ascension and St John the Baptist; and one for the Assumption of the Blessed Virgin was dramatized at Santa Maria del Estany, in Spain, in the 14th century (Donovan).

For bibliography *see* MEDIEVAL DRAMA, esp. Young (1933), Smoldon (1954, 1968, 1969), Donovan (1958) and Hardison (1965).

JOHN STEVENS

Quena. An Andean notched open flute. Dating from the Chavín era (900–200 BC) in Peru, the early *quena* was made from animal, bird or human bone or of gold, silver, clay or gourd. The modern *quena* is longer (25 to 50 cm) and is commonly made of cane, although bone *quenas* are still found; it has five or six equidistant finger-holes located in the lower half of the instrument and one thumb-hole in the centre of the rear. Capable of producing a two-octave chromatic scale, the *quena* is used both for pentatonic melodies of Inca provenance and for mestizo songs. While often played unaccompanied, traditionally by males, it is frequently combined in parallel 3rds with another *quena* and with *bombo* or *caja* (frame drums) to perform *huaynos*, *bailecitos*, *carnavalitos* and other regional dances. The *quena* is found principally in the Peruvian and Bolivian sierra and plateau, although it is also found in northern Chile and Argentina and less frequently in Ecuador, Colombia, Venezuela and the Guianas.

JOHN M. SCHECHTER

Quenes [Quennon] **de Béthune.** *See* CONON DE BÉTHUNE.

Quentin [Cantin]**, Bertin** (*l'aîné*) (*d* ?1767). French violinist and composer, the elder brother of Jean-Baptiste Quentin. He is first heard of in 1706 when he joined the orchestra of the Paris Opéra as a violinist. He is listed as a member of the 'grand choeur' in 1713, and by 1718 he ranked just behind Lalande in the first violin section. On the resignation of Jacques Buret in 1720, Quentin was appointed as cellist to the Vingt-quatre Violons du Roy, from which he retired in 1749. Having received a *privilège général* in 1730, Quentin published in Paris one set of works, ten sonatas for violin or flute and continuo. In 1764 he retired to Ermont, north of Paris. His name disappears from the list of pensioners of the Académie Royale de Musique in April 1767, and it seems probable that he died early that year.

For bibliography *see* QUENTIN, JEAN-BAPTISTE.

LAUREL FAY

Quentin [Cantin]**, Jean-Baptiste** (*le jeune*) (*fl* Paris, 1718–c1750). French violinist and composer, the younger brother of Bertin Quentin. He was a violinist at the Paris Opéra in 1718, and in 1738 he played the viola in the 'grand choeur'. References to him indicate that he was a violinist of high reputation.

As a composer he was prolific. His solo violin sonatas generally consist of four or five movements, usually arranged slow–fast–slow–fast. The trio sonatas are mostly in three or four movements; the later ones have solo indications which suggest the possibility of orchestral performance. Both genres are characterized by a systematic use of *doubles*. There are some particularly distinctive dance movements in lively triple time, labelled 'Allemande' or 'Contredanse', which appear to be the ancestors of the modern waltz. In fast movements Quentin showed a penchant for da capo markings, which produce ternary structures. Technically, his sonatas are moderately difficult, with varied and precisely indicated bowing, and triple and quadruple stops as well as fluid passages in double stops. His use of dynamic markings is careful, and the term 'tendrement' is often appended to arias and gavottes. Despite a certain rhythmic monotony, Quentin's music shows melodic inventiveness and unusually rich harmonies.

WORKS
(*all published in Paris*)

Sonates, vn, bc, 3 bks: 10 each in opp.1–3 (1724–8)
[6] Sonates, vn, rec, bc, op.14 (after 1729)
Sonates en trio, 2 vn, fls, bc, 14 bks: opp.4–7 (1729 and after); opp.8–12, also with sonatas à 4 parties (after 1729); op.13 (after 1729); op.15, with viol, also with sonatas à 4 parties (after 1729); opp.16, 18–19 (c1740)
[3] Sonates et Simphonies en trio et à 4 parties, op.17 (c1740)

BIBLIOGRAPHY
L. de La Laurencie: *L'école française de violon de Lully à Viotti* (Paris, 1922–4/*R*1971)
E. Borrel: 'Quentin', *MGG*

LAUREL FAY

Queralt, Francisco (*b* Borjas Blancas, 1740; *d* Barcelona, 28 Feb 1825). Spanish composer. He was *maestro de capilla* at Barcelona Cathedral for many years until his death. He was a noted teacher, and his students came to occupy posts in various Spanish cathedrals. Queralt's works were all religious in character, often for two or three choirs, and according to Pedrell and Anglès 'reveal the bad taste of their times' in their overuse of appoggiaturas and vocalizations. Four oratorios – one to S Ana, two to S Tomás (1762 and 1779) and another (1785) – survive (*E-C*), as does a *Beatus vir* (*E*); a *Magnificat* setting, motets and psalms, a solo aria *Donzella triunfante*, and 11 librettos for oratorios written for the church of S Felipe Neri, Barcelona, between about 1780 and about 1800, also survive (*Bc*).

BIBLIOGRAPHY
LaborD
F. Pedrell: *Catàlech de la biblioteca musical de la Diputació de Barcelona* (Barcelona, 1908–9), i, 300, 309, 313; ii, 57, 317ff

ELEANOR RUSSELL

Quercu, Simon de [a] [Eijcken, Simon van; Eyken, Simon van] (*b* ?Brabant; *fl* early 16th century). Netherlands music theorist. He was a singer in the chapel of the Duke of Milan, and in 1508 went as tutor to the imperial court in Vienna with Duke Lodovico Sforza's two sons. Quercu wrote a treatise on music, *Opusculum musices* (Vienna, 1509); several copies of each of the four editions survive. It was probably used in the musical education of the duke's sons. The first part, 'Musica plana', deals with the modes, intervals, note names, solmization and solmization syllables, and mutation. The second part, 'Musica mensuralis', deals with note lengths, rests, ligatures, mensuration signs, alteration, imperfection and mensural proportions. The third part, 'Contrapunctus', considers consonances, dissonances and polyphonic writing. His teaching is illustrated with many music examples, though no authorities are named. The use of such unusual terms as 'hexadem' for the 6th and 'heptadem' for the 7th does not contribute to the clarity of the treatise and betrays a singular wilfulness on the part of the author. Quercu also published a book of prayers and monodic liturgical songs of the Paduan rite, *Vigiliae cum vesperis et exequiis mortuorum annexis canticis* (Vienna, 1513).

BIBLIOGRAPHY
R. Eitner: 'Quercu', *ADB*
E. Praetorius: *Die Mensuraltheorie des Franchinus Gafurius* (Leipzig, 1905), 6, 12, 18f, 21f
J. Wolf: *Handbuch der Notationskunde*, i (Leipzig, 1913/*R*1963), 412; ii (Leipzig, 1919/*R*1963), 478
H. Hüschen: 'Simon de Quercu, ein Musiktheoretiker zu Beginn des 16. Jahrhunderts', *Organicae voces: Festschrift Joseph Smits van Waesberghe* (Amsterdam, 1963), 79

HEINRICH HÜSCHEN

Querelle des Bouffons. *See* BOUFFONS, QUERELLE DES.

Querflöte (Ger.). (1) A term for the transverse FLUTE, used to distinguish it from the end-blown RECORDER.
   (2) An ORGAN STOP.

Querflügel (Ger.). SPINET.

Querol (Gavaldá), Miguel (*b* Ulldecona, 22 April 1912). Spanish musicologist and composer. He studied humanities, philosophy, theology and music at Montserrat Benedictine Monastery (1926–36) and counterpoint and composition with Juan Lamote de Grignon in Barcelona (1937–8). After further studies at Saragossa University (1943) he took the BA at Barcelona University (1944–5) and the doctorate at the University of Madrid in 1948 with a dissertation on contemporary Catalan aesthetic theory. He has held appointments as secretary (1946–52), deputy director (1952–69) and director of the Spanish Institute of Musicology (from 1970), assistant (1953), research fellow (1959) and research professor (1971) at the Consejo Superior de Investigaciones Científicas, professor of music history at Barcelona University (1957–70) and adviser to the music department of the Ministry of Education and Science (from 1969). In 1959 he became a member of the Royal Academy of Fine Arts, San Fernando, and in 1973 president of the Catalan Society of Musicology.

Querol's musicological development was guided by Anglès, though he was never formally his student. His main interest is the relationship between words and music, and he has specialized in Renaissance and Baroque Spanish music, especially the songbooks (cancioneros). He has also written a book and several studies on music in the works of Cervantes. Through the Institute of Musicology he has fulfilled an important role in Spanish musicology and participated extensively in international conferences. His compositions, mostly unpublished, include orchestral, choral, chamber and piano music; many are arrangements of folksongs.

WRITINGS
'La música de los romances y canciones mencionados por Cervantes en sus obras', *AnM*, ii (1947), 53
'Cervantes y la música', *Revista de filología española*, xxxii (1948), 367
La escuela estética catalana contemporánea (diss., U. of Madrid, 1948; Madrid, 1953)
La música en las obras de Cervantes (Barcelona, 1948)
'La música religiosa española en el siglo XVII', *1° congresso internazionale di musica sacra: Roma 1950*, 323
'Importance historique et nationale du *romance*', *Musique et poésie au XVIe siècle: CNRS Paris 1953*, 299
'Morales visto por los teóricos españoles', *AnM*, viii (1953), 170
'El romance polifónico en el siglo XVII', *AnM*, x (1955), 111
Introduction to *Canciones y villanescas espirituales de F. Guerrero*, MME, xvi, xix (1955–7)
'Le Carnaval à Barcelona au début du XVIIe siècle', *Les fêtes de la Renaissance I: CNRS Abbaye de Royaumont 1955*, 371
'El villano de la época de Cervantes y Lope de Vega y su supervivencia en el folklore contemporáneo', *AnM*, xi (1956), 25
'La polyphonie religieuse espagnole au XVIIe siècle', *Le Baroque musical: Wégimont IV 1957*, 91
'Nuevos datos para la biografía de Miguel Gómez Camargo', *Miscelánea en homenaje a Monseñor Higinio Anglés* (Barcelona, 1958–61), 707
'Corresponsales de Miguel Gómez Camargo', *AnM*, xiv (1959), 165
'La estética musical de Juan Maragall (1860–1911)', *AnM*, xv (1960), 165
'La música vocal de Juan Cabanilles', *AnM*, xvii (1962), 113
'El cancionero musical de Olot', *AnM*, xviii (1963), 57
'Notas sobre la música en la Iglesia Latina de los siglos III–VI', *AnM*, xix (1964), 155
'La canción popular en los organistas españoles del siglo XVI', *AnM*, xxi (1966), 61
'Lista de los catálogos musicales publicados en España', *FAM*, xiii (1966), 103
'La producción musical de Juan del Encina', *AnM*, xxiv (1969), 121
'La producción musical del compositor Mateo Romero (1575–1647)', *Renaissance-muziek 1400–1600: donum natalicium René Bernard Lenaerts* (Louvain, 1969), 215
'La chacona en la época de Cervantes', *AnM*, xxv (1970), 49
'Dos nuevos cancioneros polifónicos españoles de la primera mitad del siglo XVII', *AnM*, xxvi (1971), 93
'La polifonía española profana del Renacimiento', *Revista musical chilena* (1971), nos.113–14, p.30

'I. Felipe Pedrell, compositor; II. E. Comte Arnau', *AnM*, xxvii (1972), 21
'Los orígenes del Barroco musical español', *Anuario del Conservatorio de música de Valencia* (1972–3), 9
'La producción musical de los hermanos Sebastián y Diego Durón', *AnM*, xxviii–xxix (1973–4)
'Die Musikwissenschaft in Spanien', *ÖMz*, xxx (1975), 208

EDITIONS
Cancionero musical de la casa de Medinaceli, MME, viii–ix (1949–50)
Romances y letras a tres voces, MME, xviii (1956)
Villancicos y romances a 3 y 4 voces de los siglos XV, XVI, y XVII, Música hispánica (Barcelona, 1964)
Música barroca española, i: *Polifonía profana: cancioneros españoles del siglo XVII*, MME, xxxii (1970); ii: *Polifonía policoral litúrgica*, MME (in preparation); iii: *Villancicos y romances de 3 a 16 voces y acompañamiento*, MME (in preparation); iv: *Monodia y dúos con acompañamiento de tecla*, MME (in preparation); v: *Cantatas y canciones para voz solista e instrumentos*, MME, xxxv (1973); vi: *Teatro barroco español*, MME (in preparation)
Cancionero musical de la Colombina, MME, xxxiii (1971)
La música en las obras de Cervantes: romances, canciones y danzas tradicionales a tres y cuatro voces y para canto y piano (Madrid, 1971)
E. de Brito: Motectorum liber primus, Officium defunctorum, Psalmi hymnique per annum, PM, ser. A, xxi (1975)
Cancionero musical de Góngora (Barcelona, 1975)
M. Machado: Romances e canções a 3 e 4 vozes mistas (Lisbon, 1975)
Transcripción e interpretación de la polifonía española de los siglos XV y XVI (Madrid, 1975)
16 tonos humanos del siglo XVII para voz solista y clave (Madrid, 1976)

JOSÉ LÓPEZ-CALO

Querpfeife (Ger.). FIFE.

Quesne, Joseph (*b* St Malo, 15 Nov 1746; *d* Montreal, 3 July 1809). Canadian composer, playwright and poet of French birth. After visiting several exotic countries as a young sailor, Quesnel came to Canada unintentionally in 1779 when the ship *L'espoir*, carrying supplies to the USA, was captured by the British off Nova Scotia. Owing to personal connections, he was allowed to settle in Montreal and later moved to nearby Boucherville. He travelled to the Great Lakes and upper Mississippi and to France, trading in furs and wine. Quesnel was a well-educated amateur anxious to promote music and theatre in a pioneer society. He was a co-founder of Montreal's Théâtre de Société in 1789. On 14 January 1790 this company first performed the 'comédie en prose, mêlée d'ariettes' *Colas et Colinette* with music and words by Quesnel, the first Canadian (and possibly the first North American) opera. After revivals in Quebec in 1805 and 1807 the text was published there in 1808 but the music printing did not continue beyond the first few pages of proof. Only the vocal and second violin parts survive in manuscript; the accompaniment was reconstructed by Godfrey Ridout for a modern revival in 1963, and published at Toronto in 1974. Quesnel also wrote the words and music for the opera *Lucas et Cécile*, of which only the vocal parts survive. His church and instrumental music has been lost. His literary works include the comedy *L'anglomanie* (1802) and the autobiographical poem *Epitre à Mr. Labadie*, a locus classicus for the complaints of the unrecognized Canadian artist. A complete Quesnel edition is in preparation.

WRITINGS
Selected Poems and Songs/Quelques poèmes et chansons (Montreal, 1970)

BIBLIOGRAPHY
H. Kallmann: *A History of Music in Canada 1534–1914* (Toronto, 1960)

HELMUT KALLMANN

Quevedo [Quebedo], **Bartolomé de** (*b* Sahagún, León province, *c*1510; *d* 31 Aug 1569). Spanish theorist and composer. He was *maestro* to the Spanish Infanta Juana at Arévalo from 1549 until 11 January 1552, and was elected *maestro de capilla* of Toledo Cathedral on 5 December 1553, having been spared a competition with Morales by the latter's death. Although the treasurer of the cathedral challenged his appointment claiming a defect in Quevedo's ancestry, the chapter confirmed him in his post, and he remained at Toledo until dismissed for misconduct in 1563.

Quevedo subsequently wrote a commentary in Latin on the portion of Pope John XXII's *De vita et honestate clericorum* devoted to music and musicians. He criticized the modern expansion of the range of polyphonic music to three octaves on the grounds that it obscured the distinction between authentic and plagal modes; he objected to the proliferation of instruments in Spanish cathedrals and to the increased use of chromaticism. Quevedo's only surviving works are an *Asperges* for four and five voices (in *E-Tc* choirbook 9), *Victimae paschali laudes* and an incomplete *Ave verum corpus* for four voices (*Tc* choirbook 12). A lavish volume of his compositions belonged to the estate of Juana.

BIBLIOGRAPHY
C. Pérez Pastor: *Noticias y documentos relativos a la historia y literatura españolas*, ii (Madrid, 1914), 345
R. Stevenson: *Spanish Cathedral Music in the Golden Age* (Berkeley and Los Angeles, 1961)
K.-W. Gümpel: 'Der Toledaner Kapellmeister Bartolomé de Quevedo und sein Kommentar zu der Extravagante "Docta sanctorum" Johannes XXII', *Gesammelte Aufsätze zur Kulturgeschichte Spaniens*, 1st ser., xxi (1963), 294
R. Stevenson: 'The Toledo Manuscript Polyphonic Choirbooks', *FAM*, iii (1973), 103

ROBERT STEVENSON

Quickstep. A fast version of the FOXTROT.

Quijada. A Latin American RATTLE.

Quijongo. A large musical bow of African origin with a wooden arc up to 138 cm long, which is generally made from a flexible wood. A metal string is attached to both ends of the arc and divided a third of the way along by a small attached gourd. Pitches and harmonics are obtained by opening and closing this gourd while striking the taut string with a stick.

LUIS FELIPE RAMÓN Y RIVERA

Quilico, Louis (*b* Montreal, 14 Jan 1929). Canadian baritone. He studied at the Conservatoire de Musique, Montreal, the S Cecilia Academy in Rome and the David Mannes School in New York. His principal teacher was Lina Pizzolongo (who became his wife); he also studied with Martial Singher. He made his débuts with the New York City Opera in 1953, at San Francisco in 1955, Covent Garden in 1961, Paris in 1962 and with the Metropolitan Opera in 1972. By the mid-1970s he had become a leading member of the Metropolitan Opera Company. He is principal baritone of the Canadian Opera Company. Quilico has a clear and ringing dramatic voice, well suited to Verdi. His repertory also includes principal roles in Puccini and Donizetti operas and he sang in the premières of *Pacem in terris* (1963) and *La mère coupable* (1965) by Milhaud and *Les coeurs de la matière* by Jolivet (1965). He has recorded with Birgit Nilsson and Beverly Sills. In 1971 he joined the teaching staff of the University of Toronto.

EZRA SCHABAS

Quilisma (from Gk. *kyliō*: 'to roll', *kylisma*: 'a rolling'). An ornamental neume, usually between two notes a 3rd apart. It is usually written joined to the succeeding (higher) note (usually a VIRGA). Aurelian of Réôme spoke of it as a trembling and rising sound (*GS*, i, 47), and most modern writers have not ventured beyond this. Tack suggested that it concerns a method of voice production no longer practised. Other studies (Wiesli, Cardine) have concentrated on the degrees of the scale on which it is most commonly found, suggesting that it may have been used for tonal orientation (for illustration *see* NEUMATIC NOTATIONS, Table 1; Table 2 shows the *quilisma* in notations of different regions).

BIBLIOGRAPHY

P. Wagner: *Einführung in die gregorianischen Melodien*, ii: *Neumenkunde: Paläographie des liturgischen Gesanges* (Leipzig, 1905, rev., enlarged 2/1913/*R1962*)

H. M. Bannister: *Codices e vaticanis selecti, phototypice expressi*, Monumenti vaticani di paleografia musicale latina, xii (Leipzig, 1913/*R1969*)

G. M. Suñol: *Introducció a la paleografia musical gregoriana* (Montserrat, 1925; Fr. trans., rev., enlarged 2/1935)

M. Huglo: 'Les noms des neumes et leur origine', *Etudes grégoriennes*, i (1954), 53

F. Tack: *Der gregorianische Choral*, Mw, xviii (1960; Eng. trans., 1960)

E. Jammers: *Tafeln zur Neumenkunde* (Tutzing, 1965)

W. Wiesli: *Das Quilisma in Codex 359 der Stiftsbibliothek St Gallen* (Immensee, 1966)

E. Cardine: 'Sémiologie grégorienne', *Etudes grégoriennes*, xi (1970), 1–158

Quill. The PLECTRUM of a harpsichord, made either from leather or from birds' feathers. Harpsichord makers preferred ravens' quills but sometimes had to settle for crows'. For information on quilling a harpsichord, see F. Hubbard: *Three Centuries of Harpsichord Making* (Cambridge, Mass., 1965), pp.226ff.

Quilt canzona. A term adopted by Manfred Bukofzer (*Music in the Baroque Era*, 1947, p.50) as an English equivalent to the German 'Flickkanzone' (literally 'patch canzona') coined by Hugo Riemann (*Handbuch der Musikgeschichte*, ii/2, ed. A. Einstein, 1912) to describe canzonas of several short sections in contrasting styles. Bukofzer, whose choice of word comes from 'patchwork quilt', applied it to the sectional canzonas of Frescobaldi and his contemporaries, and the term's currency seems to follow his usage. Perhaps the clearest and most extreme example of the kind of piece 'Flickkanzone' was meant to denote is the first canzona in Schein's *Venuskräntzlein* (1609; ed. in *Sämtliche Werke*, i, 41): in 125 bars, there are seven changes of metre and at least 14 significant changes in style, figuration or texture. *See also* CANZONA.

Quilter, Roger (*b* Brighton, 1 Nov 1877; *d* London, 21 Sept 1953). English composer. He was educated at Eton, then studied for nearly five years under Knorr at the Hoch Conservatory, Frankfurt, along with Grainger, Scott, Balfour Gardiner and O'Neill, who together constituted the 'Frankfurt group'. Quilter became known to the London public as a song composer late in 1900 when Denham Price sang the *Songs of the Sea* at the Crystal Palace; Gervase Elwes introduced *To Julia* in 1905 and the Seven Elizabethan Lyrics in 1908, and soon several major recitalists had his songs in their repertories. Occasionally Quilter accompanied his songs in public, and he recorded a number with Mark Raphael, his close friend and one of his chief exponents.

Equally successful were the light orchestral pieces which Wood performed at his Promenade Concerts. *A Children's Overture*, a sequence of nursery tunes skilfully treated, remained the most popular. It was inspired by Walter Crane's *Baby's Opera*, an illustrated book of nursery rhymes, as was Quilter's music to the fairy play *Where the Rainbow Ends*, which for many years appeared at Christmas on the London stage, conducted by Leslie Woodgate. The opera *Julia*, however, had no success, and Quilter is remembered primarily for his songs. He loved all that was light and graceful in music from Schubert to Gershwin, particularly the songs of Maude Valérie White, yet his own seemingly effortless style concealed an extreme sensitivity. Composition never came easily to him; *Songs of Sorrow*, for instance, were the painful outcome of a period of illness and depression. Quilter never had to earn a living but was very generous, helping his colleagues both privately and as a founder-member of the Musicians' Benevolent Fund, on whose executive committee he remained until his death, which came after a period of mental decline.

WORKS
(songs complete, remainder selective)
SONGS
(for 1v, pf unless otherwise stated)

op.	
1	4 Songs of the Sea (Quilter): I have a Friend, The Sea-bird, Moonlight, By the Sea (1901)
2	4 Songs of Mirza Schaffy (F. Bodenstedt, trans. W. Creighton): Neig' schön' Knospe dich zu dir, Und was die Sonne glüht, Ich fühle deinen Odem, Die helle Sonne leuchtet (1903); no.2 with new trans. by R. Elkin as The Magic of thy Presence (1911)
—	2 Songs: Come Back, The Secret (1903)
—	The Answer, At Close of Day (L. Binyon) (1904)
3	Love's Philosophy (Shelley) (1905), Now Sleeps the Crimson Petal (Tennyson) (1904), Fill a Glass with Golden Wine (Henley) (1905)
—	June (N. Hopper) (1905)
5	4 Child Songs (Stevenson): A Good Child, The Lamplighter, Where Go the Boats?, Foreign Children (1914)
6	3 Shakespeare Songs: Come Away Death, O Mistress mine, Blow, Blow, thou Winter Wind (1905); no.1 orchd, no.2 also with str, pf ad lib (1944), no.3 also with pf qnt/orch (1945)
8	To Julia (Herrick): Prelude, The Bracelet, The Maiden Blush, To Daisies, The Night Piece, Julia's Hair, Interlude, Cherry Ripe (1906)
10	4 Songs of Sorrow (Dowson): A Coronal, Passing Dreams, A Land of Silence, In Spring (1908)
12	7 Elizabethan Lyrics: Weep you no More, My Life's Delight (Campion), Damask Roses, The Faithful Shepherdess, Brown is my Love, By a Fountainside (Jonson), Fair House of Joy (Fain Would I Change that Note) (T. Hume) (1908); no.7 orchd
14	4 Songs: Autumn Evening (A. Maquarie), April (W. Watson), A Last Year's Rose (Henley), Song of the Blackbird (Henley) (1910)
15	Cuckoo Song (A. Williams) (1913), Amaryllis at the Fountain (16th century) (1914), Blossom Time (N. Hopper) (1914)
18/1–3	3 Songs for Bar or T: To Wine and Beauty (Rochester), Where be you Going (Keats), The Jocund Dance (Blake), pubd singly (1914), as set (1920)
18/4	Spring is at the Door (Hopper) (1914)
18/5–6	2 September Songs (M. Coleridge): Through the Sunny Garden, The Valley and the Hill (1916)
20	3 Songs of William Blake: Dream Valley, The Wild Flower's Song, Daybreak (1917)
22	3 Pastoral Songs (J. Campbell), 1v, pf trio: I will go with my Father A-ploughing, Cherry Valley, I Wish and I Wish (1921)
23	5 Shakespeare Songs: Fear no More the Heat o' the Sun, Under the Greenwood Tree, It was a Lover and his Lass, Take, o Take those Lips Away, Hey, ho, the Wind and the Rain (1921); no.3 as duet (1921), nos.3–4 orchd
—	Fairy Lullaby (Quilter) (1921)
24	There be None of Beauty's Daughters (Byron) (1922), Morning Song (Pack, Clouds, Away) (Heywood) (1922), Go, Lovely Rose (E. Waller) (1923), O, the Month of May (Dekker) (1927), The Time of Roses (T. Hood) (1928)

25	Song of the Stream (A. Williams) (1922), The Fuchsia Tree (Manx ballad) (1923), An Old Carol (I Sing of a Maiden) (15th century) (1924), Arab Love Song (Shelley) (1927), Music, when Soft Voices Die (Shelley) (1927), In the Bud of the Morning-o (J. Stephens) (1927)
26	In the Highlands, Over the Land is April (Stevenson) (1922)
28	5 Jacobean Lyrics: The Jealous Lover (Rochester) (1923), Why so Pale and Wan? (Suckling) (1926), I Dare not Ask a Kiss (Herrick) (1926), To Althea from Prison (Lovelace) (1926), The Constant Lover (Suckling) (1926)
29	I Arise from Dreams of Thee (Shelley), T, orch (1931)
30	4 Shakespeare Songs: Who is Sylvia?, When Daffodils Begin to Peer, How Should I your True Love Know, Sigh no more, Ladies (1933)
—	Music and Moonlight (Shelley), 1935 (1948), Spring Voices (R. Marsh) (1936), Wind from the South (J. Irvine) (1936), Come Lady-day (M. Pemberton) (1938), Wild Cherry (O. M. Denson) (1938)
32	Orpheus with his Lute (Fletcher) (1939), When Icicles Hang by the Wall (Shakespeare) (1939)
—	Trollie, Lollie, Laughter (V. Neuburg) (1939); Freedom (R. Bennett) (1941), also with pf, str; Drooping Wings (E. Sterling-Levis) (1945); Hark, Hark the Lark (Shakespeare) (1946); One Word is too Often Profaned (Shelley) (1947); Tulips (Herrick) [from partsong (1946)] (1947); Music (Shelley) (1948); The Cradle in Bethlehem (Bennett) (1949), also with pf; Come unto these Yellow Sands (Shakespeare) (1951); Tell me, Where is Fancy Bred? (Shakespeare) (1951); Daisies after Rain (J. Bickle) (1951); The Walled-in Garden (A. Heald) (1952); A Song at Parting (When I am Dead) (C. Rossetti) (1952); April Love (Quilter) (1952); My Heart Adorned with thee (M. Schaffy, trans. Quilter) (1953); Full Fathom Five (Shakespeare); Where the Bee Sucks (Shakespeare); If thou Would'st Ease thine Heart (Beddoes); Love is a Bable (anon.); A Secret (Quilter)

CHORAL

—	2 Partsongs (Herrick), SATB: To Daffodils, To the Virgins (Gather ye Rosebuds while ye May) (1904)
7	5 Lyrics of Robert Herrick, SATB: Cupid, A Dirge, Morning Song, To Electra, To Violets (1905)
—	Lead us, Heavenly Father (J. Edmeston), T, chorus, orch, 1908 (1924)
—	Non nobis, Domine (Kipling), SATB, str, pf (1934); arrs. unison vv/male 2vv/SSA
—	The Sailor and his Lass (Bennett), S, Bar, chorus, orch (1948)
—	c11 other partsongs, arrs. of solo songs for 2–3vv

STAGE

—	Where the Rainbow Ends (children's fairy play, C. Mills, R. Owen, [J. Ramsay]), London, Savoy, 21 Dec 1911; orch suite
—	As you Like it (incidental music, Shakespeare), London, 1922; pf suite, op.21 (1920)
—	The Rake, ballet, London, Pavilion, ?1925; pf suite (1925)
—	Julia, light opera, London, Covent Garden, 3 Dec 1936; extracts pubd as Love at the Inn, At the Blue Boar, Rosmé, Love and the Countess
—	Titania, ballet

INSTRUMENTAL

—	Serenade, orch, London, Queen's Hall, 27 Aug 1907
4	3 Studies, set 1, pf (1910)
11	3 English Dances, small orch, Queen's Hall, 30 June 1910 (1910)
16	3 Pieces, pf: Dance in the Twilight, Summer Evening, At a Country Fair (1916)
17	A Children's Overture, Queen's Hall, 1919 (1920)
19	2 Impressions, pf: In a Gondola, Lanterns (1920)
—	3 Studies, set 2, pf (1920)
27	Country Pieces, pf: Shepherd Song, Goblins, Forest Lullaby, Pipe and Tabor (1923)
—	Fairy Frolic, pf trio (1929)
—	Fantasy Quintet 'Gipsy Life', pf, str qt, db (1935)
—	2 Pieces, pf, str: Moonlight on the Lake [Intermezzo from Where the Rainbow Ends], Water Nymph (1937)
—	Tudor March, orch
—	Dickory Dock, suite, str

ARRANGEMENTS

The Arnold Book of Old Songs, 1v, pf (London, 1947)
other arrs. of trad. tunes

BIBLIOGRAPHY

S. Goddard: 'The Art of Roger Quilter', The Chesterian, vi (1925), 213
R. Bennett: 'Song-writers of the Day: II: Roger Quilter', Music Teacher, v (1926), 409
L. Woodgate: Obituary, MT, xciv (1953), 503
M. Raphael: Obituary, Tempo (1953–4), no.30, p.20
Q. Hill: Obituary, ML, xxxv (1954), 15

T. Armstrong: 'The Frankfort Group', PRMA, lxxxv (1958–9), 1
S. Banfield: 'Roger Quilter: a Centenary Note', MT, cxviii (1977), 903
T. Hold: The Walled-in Garden: a Study of the Songs of Roger Quilter (Rickmansworth, 1978)

STEPHEN BANFIELD

Quinart [Quinard], Jean [Jesson] (b 1582 or 1583; d Rheims, 28 April 1670). French composer. He spent his life at Rheims. He was a choirboy at the cathedral, where later he successively held a number of positions: canon (from 1597), deacon and organist (from 1606), vicarial chaplain and master of the boys. In 1624 he became a canon at Ste Balsamie, and according to the title-page of his one extant mass he was still there in 1665. He died at the age of 87 and was buried in a chapel he had had built at Ste Claire. He wrote at least four masses: Columba mea, for four voices, and Surge, propera (Paris, 1665), Dilectus meus and Sonet vox, all for six. They were advertised as published works in Ballard's catalogues of 1707 and 1744, but only Surge, propera is now extant. Its melodic lines have monotonous rhythms and an excessive number of repeated notes, and there are few points of melodic or rhythmic imitation.

BIBLIOGRAPHY

E. de Coussemaker: Notice sur les collections musicales de la bibliothèque de Cambrai et des autres villes du Département du Nord (Paris, 1843/R1970)
C. Cerf: 'La musique dans l'église de Reims', Travaux de l'Académie nationale de Reims, lxxxiv (1887–8), 415

WILLIAM HAYS

Quinault, Jean-Baptiste Maurice (b Verdun, 9 Sept 1687; d Gien, 30 Aug 1745). French composer, singer and actor. He was the son of the actor Jean Quinault (1656–1728) and the brother of Marie-Anne-Catherine Quinault. Quinault (known as 'l'aîné') acted and sang at the Théâtre Français from 1712 to 1728 and at the Comédie Française until 1734. He composed at least 24 divertissements and intermèdes for the French theatre, 1714–32. They include incidental music to plays by Fuzelier, M. A. Legrand and Molière (Le bourgeois gentilhomme, 1716, and La princesse d'Elide, 1722). Quinault had a gift for comic characterization (see for example the laughing recitative 'Enthousiasme de folie' from Legrand's Impromptu de la Folie, 1725). His only work for the Paris Opéra is Les amours des déesses (libretto by Fuzelier), first performed on 9 August 1729 and printed by Ballard the same year; it is a ballet-héroïque consisting of a prologue and four entrées.

BIBLIOGRAPHY

LaMusicaD [includes complete list of works for French theatre]
JAMES R. ANTHONY

Quinault, Marie-Anne-Catherine (b Strasbourg, 26 Aug 1695; d Paris, 1791). French singer. She was the daughter of the actor Jean Quinault (1656–1728) and the sister of Jean-Baptiste Maurice Quinault. Mlle Quinault (known as 'l'aînée') made her début at the Paris Opéra in 1709 in Lully's Bellérophon and remained there until 1713. From 1714 to 1722 she acted and sang at the Comédie Française. According to Fétis (Biographie universelle), she composed several motets for the royal chapel at Versailles, one of which won for her the decoration of the order of St Michel, never before given to a woman.

JAMES R. ANTHONY

Quinault, Philippe (*b* Paris, baptized 5 June 1635; *d* Paris, 26 Nov 1688). French dramatist, librettist and poet. Son of a master baker, he received an excellent literary education from the poet Tristan l'Hermite, whom he served as valet and through whom he was introduced to Parisian *salons précieux*. He was only 18 when his first comedy, *Les rivales*, was performed at the Hôtel de Bourgogne. He became a jurist at about the same time, having, according to Perrault, studied law for only two or three years. After Tristan's death in 1655, Quinault became private secretary to the Duc de Guise, and on 29 April 1660 marriage to a wealthy widow, Louise Goujon (née Bouvet), brought him a degree of economic independence. In 1668 he composed verses for a court divertissement, *La grotte de Versailles*, thereby joining the select group of poets chosen to pay continual homage to Louis XIV. In 1670 he was made a member of the Académie Française and in 1674 of the Académie des Inscriptions et Belles Lettres. In 1671, with Molière and Corneille, he was asked to write the text for Lully to set to music in the spectacular court divertissement, *Psyché*. Thus was inaugurated a 15-year collaboration with Lully; the gap of two years between *Isis* and *Proserpine* is explained by the temporary eclipse of Quinault at court after Juno in *Isis* had been interpreted as an unflattering caricature of Mme de Montespan.

By both temperament and artistic inclination, Quinault was ideally suited to collaborate with Lully. His *livrets*, for each of which he received 4000 livres, were judged first as dramatic poetry. Despite the general agreement that the unities might be overlooked in opera, Quinault was expected to observe unity of action. His subject matter, derived from either mythology or the familiar legends of chivalry, remained fairly constant: a pair of lovers, a powerful rival and the mingling of gods and goddesses in the affairs of men. Although the librettos occasionally treat the Corneillean theme of conflict between 'glory and duty' (*Roland* and *Armide*), the amorous intrigues of gods and men are generally more *galant* than heroic or tragic. This condition precipitated many of the attacks on Quinault's operas by the clergy and the Sorbonne. Ironically, Quinault himself apparently succumbed to the repressive moral climate. After *Armide* he retired from the stage and wrote a long poem on the extinction of heresy which begins:

> Je n'ai que trop chanté les Jeux & les Amours,
> Sur un ton plus sublime, il faut me faire entendu:
> Je vous dis adieu, Muse tendre,
> Je vous dis adieu, pour toujours.

Besides his opera librettos and the 17 tragedies, tragi-comedies and comedies that he wrote between 1653 and 1671, Quinault left several poems and epigrams and over 60 verses set to music by Lully, Le Camus, Bacilly, Lambert, Charles Mouton and others, all found in collections of *airs* issued between 1662 and 1700.

WRITINGS
(*librettos for operas by Lully*)
Later musical settings are indicated; all are *tragédies lyriques* unless otherwise stated.

Les fêtes de l'Amour et de Bacchus, pastoral, 1672
Cadmus et Hermione, 1673
Alceste, 1674; Schurmann, 1719; F.-A. D. Philidor, 1776
Thesée, 1675; Mondonville, 1765; Gossec, 1782; Grenier, 1782
Atys, 1676; Piccinni, 1780
Isis, 1677
Proserpine, 1680; Paisiello, 1803
Le triomphe de l'amour, ballet, 1681; Campra, 1705
Persée, 1682; Philidor, 1780
Phaëton, 1683
Amadis, 1684; De La Borde and Berton, 1771; J. C. Bach, 1779
Roland, 1685; Piccinni, 1778
Le temple de la paix, ballet, 1685
Armide, 1686; Traetta, 1767; Gluck, 1777; Mysliveček, 1779

BIBLIOGRAPHY
F. Lindemann: *Die Operntexte Ph. Quinault's vom literarischen Standpunkte ausbetrachtet* (diss., U. of Leipzig, 1904)
X. de Courville: 'Quinault, poète d'opéra', *ReM*, vi/3 (1925), 74
E. Gros: *Philippe Quinault: sa vie et son oeuvre* (Paris, 1926) [includes most comprehensive lists of 17th- and 18th-century sources]
H. C. Lancaster: *A History of French Dramatic Literature in the 17th Century*, III/ii (Baltimore, 1936)
P. F. Butler: 'Quinault, Philippe', *ES*
R. Schaal: 'Quinault, Philippe', *MGG*
C. M. Girdlestone: *La tragédie en musique considerée comme genre littéraire* (Geneva, 1972)
J. Anthony: *French Baroque Music from Beaujoyeulx to Rameau* (London, 1973, rev. 2/1978)
JAMES R. ANTHONY

Quinby, Benjamin F(ranklin) (*b* Minot, Maine, 3 July 1830; *d* Boston, Mass., 9 July 1890). American brass instrument maker and inventor. Quinby produced large quantities of brass instruments from 1861 to 1884, while associated with several instrument making firms. In 1872 he patented a valve system for brass instruments featuring very simple construction and clear windways. These 'box valves' (as they were called) were not very successful.

Quinby came to Boston as a machinist in 1853 accompanied by his twin brother. In 1861 he was associated for a year with Allen & Hall, and thereafter with D. C. Hall. The firm of Hall & Quinby was very successful from 1866 until 1875 and the business continued as Quinby Brothers after Hall withdrew. Most of the instruments made by these firms were equipped with flat-windway Allen valves. Quinby Brothers ceased making brass instruments in 1884 and began the manufacture of circular machine shoe-brushes.

BIBLIOGRAPHY
H. C. Quinby: *Genealogical History of the Quinby Family* (New York, 1915)
R. E. Eliason: 'Early American Valves for Brass Instruments', *GSJ*, xxiii (1970), 86
ROBERT E. ELIASON

Quinet, Fernand (*b* Charleroi, 29 Jan 1898; *d* Liège, 24 Oct 1971). Belgian composer, conductor and cellist. He showed musical talent at an early age and studied the cello and theory at the Brussels Conservatory (1913–15), completing his studies with d'Indy; in 1921 he won the Belgian Prix de Rome for the cantata *La guerre*. He played in the Pro Arte Quartet from 1916, but gave up his career as a cellist in 1932. He was director of the Charleroi Conservatory (1924–38), professor of harmony at the Brussels Conservatory (1927–38) and director of the Liège Conservatory (1938–63). As a conductor, he had an international reputation in French music; in Belgium he conducted numerous first performances, most of them with the Liège Orchestra, which he founded in 1948 and directed until 1965. He was elected a member of the Belgian Royal Academy in 1954. Throughout his career Quinet gave progressively less attention to composition. One of the first Belgian composers to reject the Franck tradition, he was most indebted to Fauré in achieving his concise art. The harmony of such a piece as the *Trois mouvements symphoniques* suggests an impressionist origin, and Quinet's ironic spirit led to some surprising chord progressions, as well as a lightness of touch and lively, incisive rhythms, as in *L'école buissonnière* for string quartet. These qualities are also found in his vocal music, which avoids extreme lyricism.

WORKS
(selective list)

Orch: Esquisses symphoniques, n.d.; 3 mouvements symphoniques, 1931; 3 pièces, 1952; Fanfare, n.d.
Inst: L'école buissonnière, str qt; Charade, pf trio; Suite, 3 cl; sonatas for vn, pf and va, pf
Vocal: 3 chansons hebraïques, 1v, pf; 5 song cycles, cantata
Incidental and education music

Principal publishers: L'art belge, Salabert, Schott (Brussels)

BIBLIOGRAPHY
R. Wangermée: *La musique belge contemporaine* (Brussels, 1959)
Music in Belgium (Brussels, 1964) [CeBeDeM publication]
R. Bernier: 'La leçon de Fernand Quinet', *Bulletin de la classe des beaux-arts de l'Académie royale de Belgique*, liii (1971), 241
HENRI VANHULST

Quinet, Marcel (*b* Binche, Hainaut, 6 July 1915). Belgian composer and pianist. He began studies at the Mons Conservatory and then transferred to the Brussels Conservatory, where he obtained a *premier prix* for harmony (1936), a *second prix* for counterpoint (1937, under R. Moulaert), a *premier prix* for fugue (1938, under L. Jongen) and a higher piano diploma (1943). Then he studied composition with Absil, and won the Belgian Prix de Rome in 1945 for his cantata *La vague et le sillon*; in 1946 his orchestral Divertissement was awarded the Agniez Prize. He was put in charge of the piano courses at the Brussels Conservatory in 1943, and he also taught harmony (1948) and fugue (1949) there; in 1956 he was appointed professor at the Chapelle Musicale Reine Elisabeth. Awarded second prize in the 1957 Queen Elisabeth Composition Competition, his Piano Concerto no.1 was used as a test piece in the 1964 series of contests.

Quinet's music is distinguished by formal clarity and the absence of lyrical effusion; his objective art has affinities with that of Hindemith. At first influenced by Absil, he began, with the Three Orchestral Pieces (1951), to evolve a more individual style that shows his closeness to French music (particularly Ravel) and his admiration for Bartók's orchestration. He has generally turned to established models, such as the passacaglia or old dance forms: the orchestral Variations are cast as a Baroque suite, and the ballet *La nef des fous* is built as a symphony with a rapid principal theme alternating with slow, expressive passages. Evolving from polytonality to atonality, his music has remained clear in timbre and texture.

WORKS
(selective list)

ORCHESTRAL
Divertissement, 1946; 3 Pieces, 1951; Sinfonietta, 1953; Variations, 1956; Serenade, str, 1956; Divertimento, 1958; Fl Concertino, 1959; Concertino, ob, cl, bn, orch, 1960; Sym., 1960; Ballade, cl, orch, 1961; Va Conc., 1963; Pf Conc. no.2, 1964; Concerto grosso, 4 cl, orch, 1964; Pf Conc. no.3, 1966; Ouverture pour un festival, 1967; Vn Concertino, 1970; Musique, str, timp, 1971; Esquisses symphoniques, 1973; Mouvements, chamber orch, 1973; Gorgone, 1974; Séquence, 1974; Dialogues, 2 pf, orch, 1975; Diptyque, chamber orch, 1975

INSTRUMENTAL
Chamber: Str Trio, 1948; Wind Qnt, 1949; Sonatine, vn, pf, 1952; 4 bluettes, pf trio, 1954; Pf Qt, 1957; Str Qt, 1958; Petite suite, 4 cl, 1959; Sonate à 3, tpt, hn, trbn, 1961; Ballade, vn, pf, 1962; Ww Qt, 1964; Sonata, 2 vn, pf, 1965; Sonatine, vn, va, 1965; Trio, ob, cl, bn, 1967; Pochades, sax qt, 1967; Sonata, fl, pf, 1968; Str Trio no.2, 1969; Polyphonies, pic, 2 fl, ob, eng hn, 3 cl, 1971; Sonatine, cl, pf, 1976; Sonatine, ob, pf, 1976; Sonate à 3, fl, vc, pf, 1977
Pf: Croquis, 1946; 2 impromptus, 1949; Passacaglia, 1954; Improvisations, 1958; Enfantines, 1959; Toccata, 1961; Hommage à Scarlatti, 1962; 5 miniatures, duet, 1964; Partita, 1965; 3 Preludes,

1970; Novelettes, 2 pf, 1973; Badineries, 1974; Petites pièces faciles, 1974; Pour les enfants, 1974; Tableautins, 1974

STAGE AND VOCAL
Les deux bavards, chamber opera, 1966; La nef des fous, ballet, 1969
La vague et le sillon, cantata, 1945; 4 haï kaï, Mez, pf, 1953; Arche de Noé, Mez/Bar, pf, 1955; Comptines, children's chorus 2vv, orch, 1955; Chansons pour rire, children's chorus, orch, 1957; Chanson de quatre saisons, Mez/Bar, pf, 1961; Lectio 'Pro feria sixta', solo vv, chorus, orch, 1973

Principal publishers: CeBeDeM, Universal
MSS in *B-Bcdm*

BIBLIOGRAPHY
R. Wangermée: *La musique belge contemporaine* (Brussels, 1959)
Music in Belgium (Brussels, 1964) [CeBeDeM publication]
HENRI VANHULST

Quinible (Middle Eng.: 'fivefold'; from Lat. *quin*[*que*] and 'ible'). A voice or part pitched an octave above the treble, i.e. a 4th above the QUATREBLE. But the 15th-century English treatises which refer to the quatreble do not mention the quinible; and although *quintuplum* can mean the fifth voice of a motet, or the five-part motet itself (Franco of Cologne: 'Qui autem quadruplum vel quintuplum facere voluit'), the English usage seems to be confined to the general sense of a high-pitched song or voice (Chaucer, *The Miller's Tale*, line 146: 'Ther to he song som tym a loud quynyble'; Skelton, *The Image of Ypocrisy*, iii, line 78: 'They finger ther fidles, And cry in quinibles').

JOHN CALDWELL

Quint. (1) The 4th partial tone of a bell when it is tuned a 5th above the strike note (*see* BELL (i), §2).

(2) When prefixed to the name of an instrument, as in 'Quintfagott' or 'Quintposaune', an indication that the instrument in question plays a 5th lower than the normal type (*see also* QUINTE, §2).

(3) An organ pipe that is sometimes used to produce, when sounded with another pipe tuned at the 5th below, a difference tone imitating – economically though not elegantly – the sound of a pipe an octave below the lower one. *See also* ORGAN STOP.

Quinta (Lat.: 'fifth'). A term occasionally used in medieval writings on music instead of 'diapente' to refer to the interval of a 5th; it has become the standard term in Italian.

Quintadecima (It.). An ORGAN STOP.

Quintadena (Ger.). An ORGAN STOP.

Quintanar, Héctor (*b* Mexico City, 15 April 1936). Mexican composer. He studied at the Escuela Superior Nocturna de Música (1950–56) and played the horn in the Banda de Música del Estado Mayor for eight years. In 1959 he entered the Mexico City Conservatory, where he studied harmony and analysis with Rodolfo Halffter, counterpoint with Blas Galindo and composition with Jiménez Mabarak; he also studied with Chávez (1960–64) and in 1963 served as Chávez's assistant in the composition workshop, which from 1965 to 1972 he directed. A state grant enabled him to study electronic music at Columbia University, New York, with Andrés Lewin Richter (1964), and he studied *musique concrète* with Jean Etienne-Marie in Paris (1967) and Mexico City (1968). He was head of the Secretaría Técnica of the Instituto Nacional de Bellas Artes music department (1965–70), within which he organized major festivals of contemporary music. Founder (1970) and director of the Mexico City Conservatory electronic music studio, he is also sub-director of the Mexico City Opera Orchestra. His conscientious activity as a promoter of new music has included giving concerts in unorthodox locations and, through his group Proa, bringing contemporary music to the church. His works from *Aclamaciones* (1967) have been concerned with non-linear sequences of contrasting materials, such as tape loops of natural sounds (*Ostinato*) and improvisatory or aleatory elements (*Sideral III*). He was the first Mexican to compose an electronic film score, that for *Una vez un hombre*.

WORKS
(selective list)

Mixed-media: Símbolos, cl, a sax, hn, tpt, trbn, pf, vn, tape, slides, lights, 1969; Play Back, vn, pf, perc, tape, slides, photographs, lights, 1970; Sinexas, happening, 1970; Mezcla, orch, tape, 1973; Diálogos, pf, tape, 1973

Orch: Sinfonía modal, 1961; 3 syms., 1961, 1962, 1965; El viejo y el mar, sym. poem, 1963; Galaxias, 1968; Sideral II, 1969

Vocal: Fábula, dramatic cantata, chorus, orch, 1964; Aclamaciones, dramatic cantata, chorus, orch, tape, 1967; Solutio?, S, pf, 1969

Inst: Double Qt, ww qt, str qt, 1965; Str Trio, 1966; Sonata no.1, vn, pf, 1967; Sonata no.2, 3 tpt, 1967; Ilapso, cl, bn, tpt, trbn, perc, vn, db, 1970; Sonidos, pf, 1970; Qnt, pf, vn, db, fl, tpt, 1973

Elec: Sideral I, 1968; Opus 1, 1971; Ostinato, 1971; Sideral III, 1971; Sinfonia, 1971

Principal publishers: Ediciones Mexicanas de Música, Tonos

BIBLIOGRAPHY
Compositores de América/Composers of the Americas, ed. Pan American Union, xv (Washington, DC, 1969), 176

GERALD R. BENJAMIN

Quintatön (Ger.). An ORGAN STOP (*Quintadena*).

Quintavalle, Antonio (*fl* 1688–?1724). Italian composer and organist. In 1703 and perhaps earlier he was chamber organist at the Mantuan court. He wrote music, partly in collaboration with the *maestro di cappella* Caldara, for three operas produced there. According to Lunelli he was *maestro di cappella* of Trent Cathedral from 1712 to 1724. An Antonio Quintavalle, chaplain at Torcello, near Venice, died on 28 January 1721 at the age of 45.

WORKS
(all lost)

OPERAS

L'oracolo in sogno (F. Silvani), Mantua, 6 June 1699; collab. A. Caldara and C. F. Pollarolo, Act 1 only by Quintavalle (pubd lib *I-Bc*)

Il trionfo d'amore, Mantua, 19 Dec 1703 (pubd lib *US-Wc*)

Paride sull'Ida, overo Gli amori di Paride con Enone (F. Mazzari), Mantua, 1704 (pubd lib *I-Bc*)

Partenope (S. Stampiglia), Trent, Teatro Gaudenti, 1713

ORATORIOS

Iefte (P. Giubilei), Rome, Seminario romano, 1688

Sacri amoris triumphus in conversione S Augustini Hipponensis Episcopi, Rome, Oratorio dal Ss Crocifisso, Lent 1694

Il sacrificio di Jefte, Faenza, 1702 [? = Iefte]

BIBLIOGRAPHY
RicordiE; *SchmidlD*

O. G. T. Sonneck: *Library of Congress: Catalogue of Opera Librettos Printed Before 1800* (Washington, DC, 1914)

D. Alaleona: *Storia dell'oratorio musicale in Italia* (Milan, 1945)

A. Liess: 'Die Sammlung der Oratorienlibretti (1679–1725) und der restliche Musikbestand des Fondo San Marcello der Biblioteca Vaticana in Rom', *AcM*, xxxi (1959), 63

U. Kirkendale: *Antonio Caldara: sein Leben und seine venezianisch-römischen Oratorien* (Graz and Cologne, 1966)

R. Lunelli: *La musica nel Trentino dal XV al XVIII secolo* (Trent, 1967)

Quinte (Fr. and Ger.: 'fifth'). (1) The French and German term for the interval of a 5th.

(2) The fifth part of a string ensemble in 17th-century France, generally the first viola part, exceptionally the third viola (*see* CINQUIÈME). J.-B. de La Borde, describing the violin family in his *Essai sur la musique* (1780), referred to the 'Viola (alto) ou Quinte', and numerous references to 'quintes' occurred throughout the 18th century, the term often being applied to the player as well as the instrument. The word was never used in connection with any member of the viol family: it referred solely to violins and was replaced in France by 'alto' in the 19th century.

Quintenzirkel (Ger.). CIRCLE OF FIFTHS.

Quinterne [quintern]. A 16th-century German term for the MANDORE. Praetorius (ii, 1618) mentioned the Quinterne as a kind of guitar. The term is sometimes spelt in English without the final 'e'.

Quinteros, Abelardo (*b* Valparaiso, 10 Dec 1923). Chilean composer. He studied industrial design at the Universidad S Maria, Valparaiso (1936–41) and composition in Santiago with Allende (1942–8) and Focke (1949–51). A scholarship from the Austrian Embassy in Chile enabled him to study serial techniques with Steinbauer and voice with Kern at the Steinbauer Academy in Vienna (1954–6). On returning to Chile he began to take a place among the leading composers of his generation; *Horizon carré*, *Cantos al espejo* and the Piano Studies received awards at successive Chilean Music Festivals. His lyrical and expressive music has its basis in 12-note thinking.

WORKS
(selective list)

Orch: 3 arabescos concertantes, cl, orch; Sinfonema, vn, orch

Vocal: Invocalización (V. Huidobro), A, orch; Las siete palabras, solo vv, org; Horizon carré, 1v, fl, cl, pf, vc; Cantos al espejo, 1v, str qt

Inst: Studies, pf; Balada, vc, pf; 5 epigramas, fl, pf; Str Trio; Ww Trio; Ww Qt

JUAN A. ORREGO-SALAS

Quintet (Fr. *quintette*, *quintuor*; Ger. *Quintett*; It. *quintetto*). A composition or part of a composition for five voices or instruments, or a group that performs such a composition. Vocal quintets include many madrigals, ballettos and other chamber music for voices of the 16th century when there was a certain preference for five-part writing. With the development of dramatic ensemble writing in opera during the 18th century accompanied quintets became frequent and there are several examples in Mozart's mature operas, notably Act 1 of *Così fan tutte*. The most celebrated operatic quintet, however, is 'Selig, wie die Sonne meines Glückes lacht' from Act 3 of Wagner's *Die Meistersinger*.

The most important chamber music forms are the STRING QUINTET (normally for a string quartet of two violins, viola and cello with an additional viola or cello), the PIANO QUINTET (usually for piano and string quartet) and the WIND QUINTET (flute, oboe, clarinet, bassoon and horn); these repertories are discussed in separate entries. Among works for less regular combinations, Mozart's great quintet for piano and wind K452 (oboe, clarinet, bassoon and horn) set a standard, which has not been surpassed, for the euphonious combination of five diverse timbres, though Beethoven imitated it in his op.16 and Danzi, Spohr and Rimsky-Korsakov wrote for similar combinations. A number of works add a wind instrument to the normal string quartet. For example, there are clarinet quintets by Mozart, Reicha, Weber, Reger, Brahms, Hindemith and Bliss, and a horn quintet (with two violas) by Mozart. Quintets formed from various mixed combinations abound especially in the 18th century. It is known that Mozart greatly admired J. C. Bach's six quintets of op.11 for flute, oboe, violin, viola and bass which indulge in charming antiphonal effects between the two wind instruments and bass as against the two strings and bass. The same composer's Quintet in F for oboe, violin, viola, cello and harpsichord, the last sometimes continuo in function, sometimes obbligato, is similarly adept in layout. Mozart's ability to make almost any combination effective is shown in his quintet for flute, oboe, viola, cello and glass armonica. Some of this ability apparently passed to his pupil Süssmayr whose quintet for oboe, english horn, violin, cello and guitar is another engaging contribution to the vast miscellany of such works from the 18th century. Of 20th-century mixed quintets Milhaud's *Les rêves de Jacob*, Nielsen's *Serenata in vano* and Prokofiev's attractive op.39 for oboe, clarinet, violin, viola and double bass may also be mentioned.

See also CHAMBER MUSIC.

MICHAEL TILMOUTH

Quintetto Boccherini. *See* BOCCHERINI QUINTET.

Quintetto Chigiano. *See* CHIGI QUINTET.

Quintiani [Quinziani], **Giulio Cesare** (*b* Piacenza, *c*1550; *d* after 1600). Italian composer. He occupied the post of *maestro di cappella* at Piacenza Cathedral from about 1580 until at least 1600, probably alternating in this position with Luigi Roince who was of French origin. Roince was certainly *maestro di cappella* in the cathedral during the period 1571–97. The title-page of Quintiani's *Sesto Himeneo ingemmato* (Venice, 1600) states clearly that in that year he was *maestro di cappella* in the most important church in Piacenza, and the dedication of the work points to his relationship with the powerful Farnese family, then ruling Piacenza and Parma. His successor was Tiburtio Massaino of Cremona who was appointed *maestro di cappella* at the cathedral in 1605. The ballet *Sesto Himeneo ingemmato* consists of 26 polyphonic compositions for five to eight voices, intended for the wedding celebration of the Duke and Duchess of Piacenza and Parma on 11 August 1600.

BIBLIOGRAPHY
L. Balestrieri: *Feste e spettacoli alla corte dei Farnese* (Parma, 1909)
Piacenza musicale, ed. Liceo Musicale Pareggiato 'Giuseppe Nicolini' (Piacenza, 1940)
F. Bussi: *Panorama musicale piacentino* (Piacenza, 1955)
——: *Alcuni maestri di cappella e organisti della cattedrale di Piacenza* (Piacenza, 1956)
——: 'Piacenza', *MGG*

FRANCESCO BUSSI

Quintiani [Quinziani], **Lucrezio** (*b* Cremona, *c*1555–60; *d* after 1595). Italian composer and friar. He was a member of the Cistercian order; in 1595 he was living in the convent of S Maddalena, near Cremona. In the dedication of his *Primo libro de madrigali*, dated 22 January 1588, he stated that this was his first publication. Considering the time and place at which he was working, his music probably reflects the artistic climate of Venice at that time, with its solemnity, festivity and splendour.

WORKS
Il primo libro de madrigali, 5vv (Venice, 1588)
Le vaghe canzonette, libro primo, 3vv (Venice, 1589)
Cantica deiparae virginis, 8vv (Venice, 1591)
Psalmi decantandi, 8vv (Venice, 1596)
3 missae, liber primus, 8vv, org (Milan, 1598)
Musica in introitus missarum super cantu plano, 4vv, org (Milan, 1599)
Several psalms, madrigals, 1596[1], 1597[24]
1 motet, 8vv, *A-Wn*; 2 madrigals, 5vv, *GB-Och*

BIBLIOGRAPHY
R. Monterosso: *Mostra bibliografica dei musicisti cremonesi* (Cremona, 1951)

For further bibliography *see* QUINTIANI, GIULIO CESARE.

FRANCESCO BUSSI

Quintilian [Marcus Fabius Quintilianus] (*b* Calagurris, Spain, AD 30–35; *d* Rome). Roman orator and writer on rhetoric. He may have begun his studies in Spain; he completed them at Rome, and there went on to gain both fame and wealth. In recognition of his remarkable skill at teaching rhetoric, he received a regular income from the imperial treasury, the first of his profession to be granted this honour. The literary testimonial to his gifts is the *Institutio oratoria*, a treatise in 12 books on the training of the ideal orator from earliest childhood to maturity. In this one surviving work the references to music form an unusual commentary, since they are based on wide reading and sympathetic interest rather than deep knowledge.

The recognition of a relationship between music and rhetoric goes back to earlier Roman writers such as Cicero, and beyond them to Aristotle himself. Quintilian accordingly felt himself to be on firm ground. He did not hesitate to include music, admittedly as a counsel of perfection, among the arts which boys should study before beginning rhetoric (bk 1, §10, i–iv). The extended eulogy of music which follows (1, §10, ix–xxxiii) seeks to demonstrate its antiquity, importance and power through a large number of examples, most of them familiar. The latinized term *musice* used here includes dancing but otherwise conveys much the same meaning as 'music' in modern usage; there is nothing of the broad sense (practically 'culture') that *mousikē* had for Hellenic writers.

Quintilian seldom mentioned details of instrumental technique or construction. These occasional references bespeak close observation of external details, as in the account of a kitharode's movements (1, §12, iii) with its rare evidence for deadening the strings of the lyre. At such times, however, understanding may go no farther than the comprehension of outward appearances or elementary facts of performance. Thus a maladroit lyre player supposedly might find it necessary to 'take the measure' of individual strings (*demensis singulis*, 5, §10, cxxiv) in order to match them with vocal pitches – an apparently meaningless supposition. One finds also the unsupported statement that musicians considered the lyre to have five basic notes (12, §10, lxviii).

Although he reserved the term 'ethos' for a wholly non-musical context (6, §2, xviii–xx), Quintilian clearly assented to a doctrine of musical ethos. He even stated his wish to possess a knowledge of its fundamental principles (*cognitionem rationis*, 1, §10, xxxi). A spirited passage (9, §4, x–xiii) deals with Man's natural affinity for musical sounds and devotes special attention to the *tacita vis*, the secret power of rhythm and melody that gives instrumental music affective power even apart from the voice (so also 1, §10, xxv; cf 11, §3, lxvi, on dancing). Quintilian nevertheless considered it a power which reaches the height of effectiveness in rhetorical eloquence, not in musical performance.

This assessment seems typical. Music has almost no importance in the *Institutio oratoria* save as a propaideutic. Despite express adherence to a belief in musical ethos, Quintilian showed an overriding concern with the spoken word when he dealt with ethical problems. Unquestionably an advocate of *musice*, he views it as the handmaiden of *rhetorice*, and his comments reveal a limited understanding of its secrets.

BIBLIOGRAPHY

H. E. Butler, ed. and trans.: *The Institutio oratoria of Quintilian* (London, 1920, 6/1965)

G. Pietzsch: *Die Musik im Erziehungs- und Bildungsideal des ausgehendes Altertums und frühen Mittelalters* (Tübingen, 1932), 5ff

J. Cousin: *Etudes sur Quintilien* (Paris, 1936)

G. Wille: *Musica romana* (Amsterdam, 1967), esp. 449ff

M. Winterbottom, ed.: *M. Fabi Quintiliani Institutionis oratoriae libri duodecim* (Oxford, 1970)

For further bibliography *see* ROME, §I.

WARREN ANDERSON

Quintilianus, Aristides. See ARISTIDES QUINTILIANUS.

Quintina (It.; Ger. *Quintole*; Fr. *quintolet*). QUINTUPLET.

Quinton. A five-stringed hybrid instrument, in use during the 18th century, that combines characteristics of the viol and the violin. Its body resembles a violin's, save for the sloping shoulders; but its neck is fretted like a viol's. It was tuned *g–d'–a'–d''–g''*. Jacques Aubert (1689–1753) composed sonatas (op.4) for the instrument. For information on the derivation of the word 'quinton' from the fifth ('cinquième') part in French ensemble music of the 17th century, see C. Sachs: *Real-Lexikon der Musikinstrumente* (Berlin, 1913).

Quintposaune (Ger.). A TROMBONE pitched a 5th below the ordinary trombone. *See* QUARTPOSAUNE.

Quintteiler. *See* TEILER.

Quintuor (Fr.). QUINTET.

Quintuplet (Fr. *quintolet*; Ger. *Quintole*; It. *quintina*). A group of five equal notes occurring irregularly, occupying the space of a note or notes of regular metric duration.

Quintuple time. A metre of five beats to the bar. Its irregularity has made it an oddity in Western music. It cannot be divided into equal half-bars, and the common division into alternate groups of two and three beats is as psychologically disturbing as a succession of five unaccented beats. Regular two-bar phrases (as in the Tchaikovsky example mentioned below) tend to mitigate this effect. Quintuple time has been used in a demonstration of technical skill (Tye, Correa, Reicha) or for atmospheric effect (Rakhmaninov, Holst), and it occurs momentarily to suggest unease or unusual excitement (Handel, Wagner). Its common occurrence in folk music (especially east European) was responsible for its more frequent appearance in the works of early 20th-century composers who drew on elements of folk music style. The decline of the use of regular metre has made the occurrence of bars of quintuple time unremarkable in later music.

Passages in five-beat groupings could be written from the 14th century to the 16th by using minor or reversed coloration, and examples of these first occur in

'mannered' notation of the post-Machaut period (see W. Apel: *The Notation of Polyphonic Music 900–1600*, 1942, rev. 5/1961, p.400; for five-beat notes see pp.356, 434; *see also* NOTATION, §III), and, more continuously, in the 'Qui tollis' section of Obrecht's *Missa 'Je ne demande'* and the Sanctus of Isaac's *Missa Paschalis* (see J. Wolf: *Handbuch der Notationskunde*, i, 1913, p.420). The first complete quintuple-time pieces in Western music appear to be seven villancicos in the Cancionero Musical de Palacio (*E-Mp* 2.1.5, *olim* 1335; written 1516–20; ed. in MME, v, 1947, and x, 1951); these are: Pedro de Escobar's *Las mis penas madre* (f.43; time signature 5/2), Juan del Encina's *Amor con fortuna* (f.63; 5/2), the anonymous *Pensad ora'n al* (f.87v; c5/2), Juan de Anchieta's *Dos anades, madre* (f.107; o5/1), Diego Fernández's *De ser mal casada* (f.119; 5/2), Anchieta's *Con amores mi madre* (f.231; o5/1) and Encina's *Tan buen ganadico* (f.280; 3²/5²). The first of these is given as ex.1 (note values reduced). In his *De musica* (Salamanca, 1577/*R*1958), Francisco de Salinas interpreted several ancient Greek metres in quintuple time (p.231); three are found in the above villancicos: bacchic (––./––./etc), palimbacchic (.––/.–––/etc) and cretic metre (–.–/–.–/etc).

Ex.1 Pedro de Escobar: *Las mis penas madre*

1. Las mis pe-nas   ma - dre d'a-mo-res   son.——
5. Que mar-vos á ell   ai - re d'a-mo-res   son.——

2. Sa – lid, mi se – ño - ra,——
3. De so'l na-ran - ja - le,——
4. Que sois tan her – mo - sa,——

Both the first half of a keyboard setting of the offertory *Felix namque* of about 1530 (in *GB-Lbm* Roy.App.56, f.1v; ed. in EECM, x, 1969, p.54) and Christopher Tye's five-part In Nomine *Trust* (?c1540, *Lbm* 31390; facs. in RRMR, iii, 1967) deploy each note of the original plainsong as breve + minim (in ¢ mensuration). Spanish keyboard music provides an early 17th-century example, a section of no.41 of Francisco Correa de Arauxo's *Libro de tientos* (1626; ed. in MME, xii, 1952, p.31).

Quintuple time is used fleetingly in the 'mad scene' in Handel's *Orlando* (1732). In Act 2 scene xi the crazed hero believes himself to have entered Charon's boat on the River Styx and sings the words 'Già solco l'onde' ('Already I am cleaving the waves') to five rising quavers, in unison with the strings, which immediately repeat the figure twice in descending sequence, thus giving three bars of 5/8 time; the figure recurs two bars later. This is within a long accompanied recitative.

Adolfati's opera *Arianna* (Genoa, 1750) contains an aria written in quintuple time, 'Se la sorte mi condanna'. Examples of quintuple time proliferate in the 19th century: it occurs in the ballad *Prinz Eugen* by Loewe, Reicha's 30 Fugues for piano, the air 'Viens, gentille dame' from Boieldieu's *La dame blanche* (1825), Chopin's Sonata in C minor op.4 (1827), and Ferdinand Hiller's Piano Trio op.64 (?1855) and *Rhythmische Studien* for piano. As Tristan awaits Isolde's disembarkation at the beginning of Act 3 scene ii of Wagner's *Tristan und Isolde* (1859) his excitement is expressed through seven bars in 5/4 time. Other notable examples of quintuple time are Anton Rubinstein's *Tower of Babel* (1870), the waltz-like second movement of Tchaikovsky's Symphony no.6 (1893), Rakhmaninov's *The Isle of the Dead* (1907) and the first movement of Holst's suite *The Planets* (1914–16).

DAVID HILEY

Quintus (Lat.: 'fifth'). A fifth part in vocal polyphony, particularly in the era when such music was published in PARTBOOKS. The term was used quite regularly by the 1540s and continued into the second decade of the 17th century. For parts that were additional to the 'standard' four, composers usually preferred designations that indicated ranges or functions: for example 'primus discantus' and 'secundus discantus', or 'contratenor 1' and 'contratenor 2'. In printed partbooks these additional parts, which often differed from piece to piece within a collection, were placed together in a single volume under the general title 'quintus', 'quinto' or 'quinta pars'. Where a sixth voice was involved quintus and sextus were printed on pages facing one another to permit two singers to read from the same book.

OWEN JANDER

Quintzug (Ger.). In Schenkerian analysis a diatonic scalic progression encompassing the interval of a perfect 5th, e.g. $f'-g'-a'-b'-c''$, $e\flat-d\flat-c-B\flat-A\flat$ (*see* ZUG (i)).

Quinziani, Giulio Cesare. *See* QUINTIANI, GIULIO CESARE.

Quinziani, Lucrezio. *See* QUINTIANI, LUCREZIO.

Quire. *See* CHOIR.

Quirsfeld, Johann (*b* Dresden, 22 July 1642; *d* Pirna, 18 June 1686). German composer, writer on music and clergyman. He studied at Wittenberg, where he took a master's degree. He worked at Pirna from 1670 until his death. He was first of all Kantor at the principal church; in 1679 he was made deacon and later became archdeacon. There are three surviving publications by him. *Geistliche Hochzeit des Lammes, bestehend aus 14 Kernsprüchen* (Leipzig, 1677), dedicated to four daughters of a patrician family of Leipzig, contains observations on the love of God and 14 songs for solo voice and continuo (two melodies in Zahn), presumably composed by Quirsfeld, whose texts have as their theme Christ as bridegroom. *Geistlicher Harffen-Klang* (Leipzig, 1679) is a large hymnal whose ten sections are devoted respectively to hymns on the themes of festivals, catechism, psalms, the church seasons, the cross, repentance, thanksgiving, death, Hell and Heaven. It contains 1003 texts with 263 melodies (four in Zahn). About half of the melodies are from the 16th century; most of the others are from collections by Johannes Crüger, to whose example Quirsfeld was indebted for the arrangements for solo voice and bass. Three other tunes are possibly by Quirsfeld himself. Many of the texts are Pietistic hymns of edification. In the preface Quirsfeld praised the origin, purpose and dignity of music. His hymnal was still in use in 1700. *Breviarium musicum* (Pirna, 1675, 6/1717), also much used, is an elementary song textbook for schools. Quirsfeld still dealt with solmization, but he also referred to the method advanced by Ambrosius Profe, an enemy of the old solmization system, in his *Compendium musicum*

(1641) whereby the notes should be sung according to their letter names. The comprehensive examples section includes pieces accompanied by continuo. According to Fétis, Quirsfeld also published *Aurifodina mathematica de sono* (Leipzig, 1675).

BIBLIOGRAPHY

FétisB

C. von Winterfeld: *Der evangelische Kirchengesang*, ii (Leipzig, 1845/R1966), 551f

J. Zahn: *Die Melodien der deutschen evangelischen Kirchenlieder*, vi (Gütersloh, 1893/R1963), 242ff

W. Nagel: 'Die Kantoreigesellschaft zu Pirna', *MMg*, xxviii (1895), 150

A. Schering: *Musikgeschichte Leipzigs*, ii: *Von 1650 bis 1723* (Leipzig, 1926)

reprinted from *MGG* (x, 1820) by permission of Bärenreiter

MARTIN RUHNKE

Quitarra (Lat.). GITTERN.

Quitin, José(-François) (*b* Liège, 28 March 1915). Belgian musicologist. He studied music at the Liège Academy and took a degree in education (1938; 1952, with dissertation) at the University of Liège. He was director of the academy from 1945 to 1952 and in 1946 he became professor of music history at Liège Conservatory. For some time he was also lecturer in music education at the Liège teachers' training college. He has a lively interest in Walloon music and has organized concerts and written disc notes for the music of unknown Liège and other Walloon composers of the 16th-19th centuries. Through his enterprise the Société Liégeoise de Musicologie (originally founded in 1909) was resuscitated in 1972; some notable musicological articles have appeared in the society's quarterly bulletin that he founded. He has written on the teaching of music and on the history of music in Liège, particularly its 17th- and 18th-century church music and its famous school of violinists of the 19th and 20th centuries. His works are the result of long teaching experience and painstaking research in ecclesiastical and other archives, and are well demonstrated in his transcriptions and performances of unpublished music.

WRITINGS

Eugène Ysaÿe (Brussels, 1938, rev. 2/1958)

'Un musicien liégeois, Léonard de Hodemont, *c*.1575–1636: notes biographiques', *La vie wallonne*, xxv (Liège, 1951), 27

'Lambert Pietkin, maître de chant de l'Eglise cathédrale de Saint-Lambert, à Liège, 1613–96', *RBM*, vi (1952), 31

'Les maîtres de chant de la cathédrale Saint-Lambert, à Liège aux XVe et XVIe siècles', *RBM*, viii (1954), 5

Les maîtres de chant et la maîtrise de la collégiale Saint-Denis, à Liège, au temps de Grétry (Brussels, 1964)

'Orgues, organistes et organiers de l'église cathédrale Notre-Dame et Saint-Lambert à Liège aux XVIIe et XVIIIe siècles', *Bulletin de l'Institut archéologique liégeois*, lxxx (1967), 5–58

'Untersuchungen über die Musikpflege Maastrichts im 16. Jahrhundert', *Beiträge zur rheinischen Musikgeschichte*, lxxiii (1968), 39

'A propos de trois musiciens liégeois du 16e siècle: Petit Jean de Latre. Johannes Mangon et Mathieu de Sayve', *Musicae scientiae collectanea: Festschrift Karl Gustav Fellerer* (Cologne, 1973), 451

GODELIEVE SPIESSENS

Quito. Capital of Ecuador. Before the Spanish conquest (1533) Quito was the northernmost outpost of the Inca Empire. As the favourite retreat of Huayna Capac (reigned 1493–1525) it shared the best traditions of Inca court music, panpipes being then as now favourite native ensemble instruments.

The first teachers of European music at Quito, the Flemish Franciscans Josse de Rycke of Mechelen and Pierre Gosseal of Louvain, who arrived in 1534, taught the Indians to read music and play European instruments. At the Colegio de S Andrés (founded 1555) such difficult music as Guerrero's 1570 collection of motets was sung before 1581. In the next century the Quito Franciscan church obtained a 600-pipe organ (completed 1638) and by 1651 boasted a musical culture equal to any in Europe, according to Diego de Córdova Salinas's chronicle published that year at Lima.

The most important 16th-century local musician trained by the Franciscans was the mestizo Diego Lobato (c1538–c1610); the Quito Cathedral authorities paid him 110 pesos a year from 1562 to 1568 for singing 'polyphonic music at the choirbook stand when appropriate' and also asked him to double as organist from 1563. On 3 April 1574 the Quito chapter appointed him *maestro de capilla*, commissioning him to compose new 'motetes y chanzonetas' for all the principal annual feasts. The splendour of cathedral music was further enhanced by a deed of 29 July 1580 stipulating that the *Salve regina* be sung polyphonically with organ every Saturday. Lobato continued as *maestro de capilla* until his death, except for a two-year period (1588–90) when Gutierre Fernández Hidalgo, the greatest South American musician of the epoch, occupied the post.

In colonial Quito, as elsewhere in the Americas, royal commemorations were celebrated with great pomp. Francisco Coronel conducted the polyphony sung at Philip III's commemoration on 30 September 1621. For 70 years from 1653 Quito cathedral music was dominated by the Ortuño de Larrea family, except from 1682 to 1695 when the Jeronymite composer Manuel Blasco was imported from Bogotá to break the family monopoly. Blasco, the most eminent composer in Quito annals after Fernández Hidalgo, left a respectable body of music in the cathedral archive at Bogotá, including some notable versos for two shawms and organ.

The declining interest in *prima prattica* polyphony from 1708 onwards can be traced in the inventories of polyphonic choirbooks; the number declined from 35 to 20 by 1754, and after the disastrous earthquakes of 1755 and 1757 dwindled to none. Bright instrumental ensembles became the rule at cathedral festivals and in local churches. These ensembles, according to the *Compendiosa Relación de la Cristiandad de Quito* by the knowledgeable Bernardo Recio (1714–91), included 'flutes, oboes, trumpets, vihuelas, guitars, harps, harpsichords, violins and other bowed strings' supported by organs. Samuel Fritz (1656–1725), a Bohemian from Trautenau, first popularized violin playing at Quito.

After independence (1822) the same taste for glitter (especially that of opera) that marked the rest of Latin America touched Quito. Although touring troupes visiting Quito en route to other South American capitals never presented entire operas, but only excerpts accompanied by a piano and four or five instruments, the Quito public heard such great stars as Tamberlik and Carlotta Patti. A programme by these and supporting performers, accompanied by a pianist and a chamber group, was announced in *El Nacional* of 25 May 1888 (xii/418, p.1786); it included excerpts from *Die Zauberflöte*, *Rigoletto* and *Les contes d'Hoffmann*. Such programmes generally had 20 numbers, half of them operatic selections, half lighter music such as solo songs in Spanish, comedy skits on the *sainete* pattern, and a few short pieces exhibiting the prowess of local virtuosos.

After various earlier private conservatories had closed, President Gabriel García Moreno (1821–75) decreed the foundation of the Conservatorio Nacional de Música on 28 February 1870. It has been directed by musicians of German, Italian and local origin. Pedro Pablo Traversari Salazar (*b* Quito, 16 July 1874), who administered the conservatory for three periods until 1941, left a superb collection of European and Andean instruments, which forms the nucleus of a unique organological museum given to the Casa de la Cultura Ecuatoriana on 1 May 1951. The leading theory texts published in the early years of the Quito Conservatory by its teachers were Juan Agustin Guerrero's *Nociones de Instrumentación* and *Teoría musical* (both 1873), and Nicolás Abelardo Guerra's *Gramática Musical* (1911, 3/1929). The leading Ecuadorian 20th-century music historian, Luis Segundo Moreno (*b* Cotacachi, Imbabura, 2 Aug 1882; *d* Quito, 18 Nov 1973), was associated with the conservatory in various capacities, first as copyist (1909), then as theory professor (1911–13).

The Sociedad Filarmónica de Quito, organized on 11 June 1952 with the critic Francisco Alexander (*b* 1910) as president, sponsored the founding of the Orquesta Sinfónica Nacional on 2 May 1956. During the first eight years this orchestra gave 120 concerts under its titular conductors Ernesto Xancó (May 1956–August 1958), Georges Gallandres (October 1958–August 1959), Viktor Bürger (July 1960–March 1963) and Paul Capolongo (September 1963–April 1964), all of European extraction. Of the 70 composers represented at these concerts, six were native Ecuadorians – Néstor Cueva, Corsino Durán, Enrique Espín Yépez, Mercedes Silva Echanique, Carlos Bonilla and Claudio Aizaga. In the same eight years Radio Quito encouraged local talent with premières of the early compositions of Mesías Maiguashca and Gerardo Guevara Viteri (*b* 1930). After an absence in Paris (1959–71) financed by a UNESCO grant Guevara became conductor of the Orquesta Sinfónica Nacional in July 1972. While Maiguashca and Guevara have drawn on European styles, one local composer, the Franciscan organist Carlos Alberto Coba (*b* 1937), writes colourful works inspired by South American Indian music.

In the 20th century the chief concerts in Quito have usually been given at the Teatro Sucre (completed 1903, capacity 1500), including those of the pioneer Quinteto Beethoven (reviewed in *El Comercio* 2 and 6 August 1912), the inaugural concert of the Cuarteto Teran (10 August 1925), the début of the Quito-born pianist Leslie Wright (16 July 1953), the concert of the Orquesta Sinfónica of Bogotá (4 December 1953), celebrating the fourth centenary of the founding of Quito, and by international celebrities including Segovia, Rubinstein and Bernstein.

BIBLIOGRAPHY

S. L. Moreno: 'La música en el Ecuador', in J. Gonzalo Orellana, *El Ecuador en cien años de independencia*, ii (Quito, 1930), 187–276; pubd separately as *Historia de la música en el Ecuador* (Quito, 1972)

R. Barbacci: 'Apuntes para un diccionario biográfico musical Peruano', *Fénix*, vi (1949), 479

'El Conservatorio de música, declamación y coreografía de Quito en cincuenta años de existencia (Breve reseña histórica)', *Boletín del Conservatorio de música*, i (1950), 31

A. F. Salgado: 'Músicos nacionales representativos del arte musical Ecuatoriana', *Cuadernos de arte del Conservatorio nacional de música, teatro y danzas*, i (1962), 54

R. Stevenson: 'Music in Quito: Four Centuries', *Hispanic American Historical Review*, xliii (1963), 247

F. Alexander: *Musica y músicos: ensayos en miniatura* (Quito, 1970)
R. Stevenson: *Renaissance and Baroque Musical Sources in the Americas* (Washington, 1970), 7f, 1*ff
Biblioteca musical ecuatoriana, ed. Casa de la cultura ecuatoriana (Quito, 1971)
Museo de Instrumentos Musicales 'Pedro Pablo Traversari', ed. Casa de la cultura ecuatoriana (Quito, 1971)

ROBERT STEVENSON

Quitschreiber, Georg (*b* Kranichfeld, nr. Erfurt, 30 Dec 1569; *d* Magdala, nr. Jena, 1638). German theorist and composer. In 1594 Count Albrecht von Schwarzburg appointed him court and civic Kantor at Rudolstadt. From 1598 to 1614 he was civic Kantor at Jena. Like several such men at this period he then changed to the priesthood, and thenceforward he worked as a pastor, first at Hainichen, near Chemnitz, then, from 1629 until his death, at Magdala.

Quitschreiber is of interest principally for his writings on music. His *Musikbüchlein für die Jugend* goes well beyond the usual school song primer. The range of notes is not limited to the ten-line system but, with a view to the treatment of instrumental music, is expanded to three octaves and a 6th, and the chapters on metre, intervals and word-setting are in advance of the normal level of elementary teaching. The explanations about correct tuning in singing and about transposition, which was specially necessary because of the use of accompanying instruments, are among topics seldom treated by German theorists. The 18 rules for artistic singing set out in *De canendi elegantia* are based primarily on Ornithoparchus and Heinrich Finck, each of whom is named five times as an authority. Quitschreiber still advocated a restrained delivery with fairly even dynamics, and inner parts must not obtrude. He derived from Cyriacus Schneegass the rule that one should in general maintain a regular beat but that occasionally, if the text demands it, one may sing more slowly; he warned against singing too quickly. In ornamental writing the individual notes should not be too strongly accented. *De parodia* is Quitschreiber's most original treatise. Characterizing as inexperienced the opponents of parody, who are not named, he defended the practice by reference on the one hand to Quintilian and parallels in the art of poetry and on the other to compositions by Calvisius and Michael Praetorius. He regarded a thorough knowledge of *musica poetica* as essential if one wished either to add further voices to a pre-existing composition or to reduce the number of voices or if one wanted to base a mass on a motet. Moreover, he emphasized the principle of artistic copyright: nobody may claim another's work as his own, only one's own contribution to a parody may be called one's own work.

Of Quitschreiber's own compositions only five of his 1608 collection of 35 *de tempore* pieces have appeared in a modern edition. Because of the many leaps the bass parts are not very singable, and the inner voices are restricted in range. The pieces are therefore close in style to the simple hymn writing introduced by Lucas Osiander.

WORKS
SACRED VOCAL

Kirchengesänge, Psalmen und geistliche Lieder Luthers, 4vv (Jena, 1608); 5 ed. in *Handbuch der deutschen evangelischen Kirchenmusik*, i/2 (Göttingen, 1942)
8 occasional motets (Jena, 1604–34)
8 other motets, lost

THEORETICAL

De canendi elegantia octodecim praecepta (Jena, 1598)
Musikbüchlein für die Jugend (Leipzig, 1605)

De parodia tractatus musicalis (Jena, 1611)
Quarta exercitatio musicalis: De confusionibus publicis in choro musico (Jena, 1637)

BIBLIOGRAPHY

J. Zahn: *Die Melodien der deutschen evangelischen Kirchenlieder*, vi (Gütersloh, 1893/R1963)
M. Ruhnke: *Joachim Burmeister* (Kassel, 1955)
W. Braun: 'Zur Parodie im 17. Jahrhundert', *GfMKB, Kassel 1962*, 154

MARTIN RUHNKE

Quittard, Henri (*b* Clermont-Ferrand, 13 May 1864; *d* Paris, 21 July 1919). French music historian. After taking his licence ès lettres when he was 24, he went to Paris and, following the advice of Chabrier, studied music with Franck. He soon devoted himself to the history of music, and his first studies appeared in 1898. His special domain was the French musicians of the 16th and 17th centuries. The lutenists of France were of great interest to him; with Michel Brenet he was one of the first to demonstrate their importance. Quittard was lecturer at the Ecole des Hautes Etudes Sociales, archivist at the Opéra from 1912 until his death and music critic to *Le Matin* and from 1909 to *Le Figaro*.

He left unfinished an edition of harpsichord pieces by Louis Couperin. His private collection of lute music, transcriptions, etc, was bequeathed to the Conservatoire library.

WRITINGS

ed.: *Mémoires de musicologie sacrée* (Paris, 1901) [incl. 'Carissimi et le XVIIe siècle italien']
Les années de jeunesse de J.-P. Rameau (Paris, 1902)
Un musicien en France au XVIIe siècle: Henry Dumont (Paris, 1906) [with musical suppl.]
'Un recueil de psaumes français du XVIIe siècle [Signac's 50 psaumes de David, 1630]', *SIMG*, xi (1909–10), 483
Les Couperin (Paris, 1913)
'Notes sur Guillaume de Machaut et son oeuvre', *RdM*, i (1918), 123
'Musique instrumentale jusqu'à Lully', *EMDC*, I/iii (1921), 1176–1260
Numerous articles in *Revue internationale de musique, Revue musicale, Tribune de Saint-Gervais* etc

BIBLIOGRAPHY

L. de La Laurencie: Obituary, *RdM*, i (1919), 242 [with list of writings]

MARIE LOUISE PEREYRA/R

Qūm. A category of chant execution in Ethiopia; *see* ETHIOPIAN RITE, MUSIC OF THE.

Quodlibet (Lat.: 'what you please'). A composition in which well-known melodies and texts appear in successive or simultaneous combinations. Generally the quodlibet serves no higher purpose than that of humour or technical virtuosity, and may thus be distinguished from more serious works in which pre-existing material has a constructive or symbolic function.

Wolfgang Schmeltzl first used the term with specific reference to music (*Guter seltzamer und kunstreicher teutscher Gesang, sonderlich etliche künstliche Quodlibet*, Nuremberg, 1544), taking it from the name of an improvised oral examination in German universities, the *disputatio de quolibet*. Originally the disputation was a serious scholastic exercise at the Sorbonne in Paris during the Middle Ages, but in Germany it became a humorous parody featuring ridiculous lists of items loosely combined under an absurd theme (e.g. objects forgotten by women fleeing from a harem). This general concept was widely accepted in 16th-century German literature, and comical 'catalogue' poems of all kinds (such as *Priamel*) flourished, prompting such definitions of the quodlibet as 'durcheinandermischmäsch'

(S. Roth, 1571). Fischart (*Geschichtsklitterung*, 1575) noted the common element of haphazard combination found in the disputation and the musical quodlibet, probably with reference to Schmeltzl, who followed both academic and literary fashion in stressing nonsensical catalogues in his musical quodlibets.

In France 'quolibet' referred to witty riddles, and 'avoir de quolibet' still means the ability to verbalize quickly a clever, spirited repartee. In this period catalogue poetry was less popular in France than Germany, but lists of 'fools' prefaced theatrical *sotties*, and the lists of dishes and songs in Rabelais' *Pantagruel* were notorious. The citation of chansons and hymn lines (Chesnaye, Molinet, Rabelais) prompted appropriate musical references when such poetry was set to music and both lighthearted inanity and serious or religious symbolism were explored as Renaissance composers sought musical parallels to poetic centonization. Theorists often included quodlibets to illustrate matters such as mensuration, modes and cantus firmus treatment (Tinctoris, *Proportionale musices*, c1472; Glarean, *Dodecachordon*, 1547; Zarlino, *Le istitutioni harmoniche*, 1558; Zacconi, *Prattica di musica*, 1622); but it was Praetorius in his *Syntagma musicum* (1618) who provided the first systematic definition of the musical quodlibet as a mixture of diverse elements quoted from sacred and secular compositions. He presented three categories which he differentiated on the basis of text treatment; a combination of his sometimes abstruse explanation with analysis of his music examples gives the following types: every voice is a completely different *cantus prius factus*; every voice is a different patchwork of quoted fragments; one voice is a patchwork of quotations whose text is shared by the other voices.

Parallel types of quodlibet in the Renaissance were the FRICASSÉE (France), MISTICANZA or *messanza* (Italy), ENSALADA (Spain) and MEDLEY (England). INCATENATURA is a term used by modern scholars to refer to the Italian quodlibet; cento, which survives from classical antiquity, refers specifically to poetry made up entirely of lines quoted from other works, or more generally to any artistic technique that relies on patchwork construction, citations, borrowings, formulae, etc (*see* CENTONIZATION). There are also some isolated terms used from the 17th century to the present that are more or less closely related to the quodlibet, such as *farrago, rôtibouilli, salatade*, fantasia, capriccio, pasticcio, potpourri and miscellany; but this article will discuss only works that fall into one of the three types of quodlibet proper, based on 16th-century German practice: catalogue, successive and simultaneous.

The catalogue quodlibet consists of a freely composed setting of catalogue poetry. Such pieces were rare in the medieval motet, but there is one well-known example, *Moriuntur, oriuntur* (*I-Fl* Plut.29.1), in which a list of nonsense syllables serves as a drinking-song. The onomatopoeic word-play in the 14th-century Italian caccia also prefigured certain aspects of quodlibet hilarity. The closest early parallel, however, is the monophonic setting of *Mon seul plaisir* from the late 15th century (*F-Pn* fr.12744), which is a catalogue of 19 famous chanson refrains (e.g. *Comme femme, J'ay pris amours, Ma bouche rit*). The melody, which does not quote musical material, appeared in a polyphonic arrangement by Ninot le Petit.

Of the 25 quodlibets in Schmeltzl's publication (see above), 15 belong to this category (e.g. *Ein Quodlibet von Eyren* by Matthias Greiter and *Ein Quodlibet von Nasen* by J. Puxstaller; the latter text was also set by Lassus). In 1540 Georg Forster printed two catalogue quodlibets on the theme of Martin's goose, and series of proverbs were also popular, as in Paul Rivander's *Nun höret an* (1615). Both Jacob Reiner's *Venite exultemus* (1581) and Nikolaus Zangius's *Er setzt das Gläslein an den Mund* (1620) set lists of comical drinking-proverbs, and another catalogue of noses was included in J. M. Gletle's *Musica genialis* (1674–85). The simplicity of the musical settings suggests that such pieces were written versions of improvised musical entertainment. In the 17th century many German collections of entertainment music included verbal catalogue quodlibets (e.g. those of J. M. Caesar, J. M. Gletle and Daniel Speer), and the tradition culminated in the 'quodlibeticae' of the *Augsburger Tafelkonfekt* (1733–46).

In the successive quodlibet one voice consists of a patchwork or cento of short musical and textual quotations while the others form a homophonic accompaniment, which is either without a text or else shares that of the patchwork voice. The most striking medieval parallel to this kind of Renaissance quodlibet is provided by the quotation of chanson lines in the refrain motet and *motet enté*. At least one out of every 25 motets contains a patchwork of refrains in one voice (e.g. *Cele m'a mort/Alleluia* and *La bele m'ocit/In seculum*). From the 13th century onwards STREET CRIES were also frequently included among the borrowed materials. In the earliest Renaissance quodlibet, *Wer ich eyn falck*, which appears in the Breslauer Codex (late 15th century), the tenor consists of a cento of fragments from German songs, while the remaining three voices have no text. Another anonymous quodlibet with song quotations in the tenor was published in Forster's second volume of German lieder (1540).

Schmeltzl's collection of 25 quodlibets contains six homophonic centos in which a patchwork in the tenor is surrounded by free voices; but the highpoint of the German type was reached in the works of Melchior Franck. Nine of his ten quodlibets (published in the *Musikalischer Grillenvertreiber*, 1622) are homophonic centos and are more modern in style than earlier examples: the patchwork voice is in the upper part and the quotations are mainly from folksongs. Only two other 17th-century homophonic centos are known, Johann Groh's *Bettlermante* (1606) and Johann Kraut's *Was wöllen wir aber heben an*. In his *Musica genialis* Gletle included a quodlibet citing popular texts, which may also contain musical quotations. Cento technique continued to provide humorous social entertainment, however, as in the quodlibets of Johann Christenius, Georg Engelmann (i) and Johann Theile, and in the street-cry quodlibets of Daniel Friderici, Jakob Banwart, Kindermann and G. J. Werner. Out of the 21 'quodlibeticae' in the *Augsburger Tafelkonfekt* two are musical centos: *Quodlibeticum curiosum* and *Salvete hospices*. Among the best-known examples from the 18th century are the *Hochzeitsquodlibet*, in which J. S. Bach collaborated, and Mozart's *Gallimathias musicum*.

The simultaneous quodlibet consists basically of the polyphonic cento, in which two or more patchwork voices are combined polyphonically, and the cantus firmus quodlibet, in which each voice is a different *cantus prius factus*. A third sub-type, in which a cantus firmus voice is combined with one or more patchwork voices ('cantus firmus cento'), is less common; there are only four cantus firmus centos in German secular music, three of which are in the Glogauer Liederbuch (c1480; the fourth is a bicinium by Paul Rebhuhn published in 1545[7]). These three are among the first examples of the quodlibet proper in Germany; they combine a voice from Dunstable's *O rosa bella* with a patchwork of German songs (see HAM, nos. 80, 82).

The polyphonic cento involves a more complex technique than the homophonic, since several different patchworks of successive quotations must be combined polyphonically – the more centos the more complicated the combination. Schmeltzl included only three such works and they all bear the inscription 'Fürt ein jede stymm jr eygen text'; one of these pieces, *Ein Guckuck*, was reworked by Johannes Eccard (1578). This type of quodlibet corresponds to Praetorius's second category, which he illustrated by referring to a work of Zangius (probably *Ich will zu land ausreiten*, published in Paul Kauffmann's *Musikalischer Zeitvertreiber*, 1609). Zangius also wrote two other polyphonic centos: *Bistu der Hänsel Schütze* (1620) and *Ich ging einmal spazieren* (1613). Franck's *Kessel, multer bilden*, originally published as *Farrago* (1602), brings together many popular songs in masterful six-voice counterpoint.

Juxtaposing several pre-existing melodies, as in the cantus firmus quodlibet, represented in Renaissance thought the ultimate in contrapuntal mastery. This kind of technical virtuosity is evident in Greiter's *Elselein liebstes Elselein*, which appeared in Schmeltzl's collection as an example of a quodlibet composed entirely of quoted melodies; but it may also be seen in contemporary works that quote from two to four simultaneous cantus firmi. Among these are several particularly fine works of Senfl (e.g. *O Elselein/Es taget*), and works by such composers as Jobst vom Brandt, Matthias Eckel, Caspar Othmayr and Matthaeus Le Maistre. Humour is obvious in Othmayr's drinking-songs and technical virtuosity for its own sake in Greiter's, but Senfl's works exude a tender melancholy and represent perhaps a more subtle kind of symbolism than is normally associated with the quodlibet. In such pieces, as in the much larger and older repertory of sacred works using borrowed material for symbolic or purely constructive purposes, the proper boundaries of the quodlibet are difficult to maintain with precision or consistency. In any case, Praetorius limited the category of the cantus firmus quodlibet to works in which every voice is a separate *cantus prius factus*, citing as an example a motet of Göldel that combines five different chorales; Christenius's *Kirchenquodlibet* continued this tradition. The most famous cantus firmus quodlibet of all is the final variation of Bach's Goldberg Variations, in which two popular German songs (*Kraut und Rüben* and *Ich bin so lang nicht bei dir g'west*) are joined with the harmonic framework of the theme. But in a rather different guise the quodlibet took on a new lease of life in the German (and especially the Viennese) theatre of the first half of the 19th century. The term was used in four distinct senses: for the amalgam of (often non-theatrical) items assembled in book form; for a theatrical entertainment in which a popular artist or artists appeared in a series of excerpts from favourite roles; for a pasticcio in which pre-existing musical numbers were grafted on to a libretto for which they were not originally intended (*Rochus Pumpernickel*, 1809, text by M. Stegmayer, music arranged by I. von Seyfried and J. Haibel, is the most famous example); and lastly, for the potpourri or

musical switch. This kind of quodlibet, very popular in Viennese farces and Singspiels between the early 1800s and the 1850s, and probably derived from the same German tradition that enlivened Bach family gatherings and produced J. V. Rathgeber's and G. J. Werner's mid-18th-century examples, consisted of between half a dozen and 50 or more consecutive quotations, usually with altered text; the frequent incongruity of words and music in an unexpected context proved a potent source of parody and entertainment.

Examples of quodlibet-like compositions are not hard to find in 20th-century music. There are a number of works by Ives, for example, in which well-known melodies are combined simultaneously as well as successively (e.g. the last movement of his Symphony no.2); but here, as in 15th- and 16th-century cantus firmus compositions, the dividing line between the serious or symbolic use of borrowed materials and the purely humorous is difficult to draw. There can be little doubt, however, that the essential spirit and form of the genre survives in works such as the *Quodlibet* of Peter Schickele.

BIBLIOGRAPHY

RiemannL 12

M. Praetorius: *Syntagma musicum*, iii (Wolfenbüttel, 1618, 2/1619/*R*1958)

R. Eitner: 'Das deutsche Lied des XV. und XVI. Jahrhunderts', *MMg*, suppls., viii (1876), 1–169; xii (1880), 1–132

A. Raphael: 'Über einige Quodlibete mit dem Cantus firmus "O rosa bella" und über dieses Lied selbst', *MMg*, xxxi (1899), 161

E. Bienenfeld: 'Wolfgang Schmeltzl, sein Liederbuch (1544) und das Quodlibet des XVI. Jahrhunderts', *SIMG*, vi (1904–5), 80–135

F. Feldmann: 'Zwei weltliche Stücke des Breslauer Codex Mf.2016', *ZMw*, xiii (1930–31), 252

H. J. Moser: *Corydon, das ist Geschichte des mehrstimmigen Generalbassliedes und des Quodlibets im deutschen Barock* (Brunswick, 1933)

M. Bukofzer: 'An Unknown Chansonnier of the 15th Century', *MQ*, xxviii (1942), 14–49

D. Plamenac: 'A Reconstruction of the French Chansonnier in the Biblioteca Colombina, Seville', *MQ*, xxxvii (1951), 501–42; xxxviii (1952), 85–117, 245–77

——: 'Deux pièces de la renaissance tirées de fonds florentins', *RBM*, vi (1952), 12

F. Lesure: *Anthologie de la chanson parisienne au XVIᵉ siècle* (Monaco, 1953)

——: 'Eléments populaires dans la chanson française au début du XVIᵉ siècle', *Musique et poésie au XVIᵉ siècle: CNRS Paris 1953*, 169

H. M. Shire and K. Elliott: 'La fricassée en Ecosse et ses rapports avec les fêtes de la renaissance', *Les fêtes de la renaissance I: CNRS Abbaye de Royaumont 1955*, 335

G. Kraft: 'Zur Entstehungsgeschichte des "Hochzeitsquodlibet" (BWV 524)', *BJb*, xliii (1956), 140

J. LaRue: 'A "Hail and Farewell" Quodlibet Symphony', *ML*, xxxvii (1956), 250

H. M. Brown: 'The *chanson rustique*: Popular Elements in the 15th- and 16th-century Chanson', *JAMS*, xii (1959), 16

C. Gallico: *Un canzoniere musicale italiano del cinquecento* (Florence, 1960)

K. Petermann: *Das Quodlibet: eine Volksliedquelle?* (diss., U. of Leipzig, 1960)

H. Albrecht: 'Ein quodlibetartiges Magnificat aus der Zwickauer Ratsschulbibliothek', *Festschrift Heinrich Besseler* (Leipzig, 1961), 215

K. Gudewill: 'Ursprünge und nationale Aspekte des Quodlibets', *IMSCR, viii New York 1961*, i, 30 [see also discussion, ibid, ii, 53]

P. Gülke: 'Das Volkslied in der burgundischen Polyphonie des 15. Jahrhunderts', *Festschrift Heinrich Besseler* (Leipzig, 1961), 179

K. Gudewill: 'Quodlibet', *MGG*

H. M. Brown: *Music in the French Secular Theater, 1400–1550* (Cambridge, Mass., 1963)

——: *Theatrical Chansons of the Fifteenth and Early Sixteenth Centuries* (Cambridge, Mass., 1963)

M. Picker: 'Newly Discovered Sources for *In minen Sin*', *JAMS*, xvii (1964), 133

M. R. Maniates: *Combinative Techniques in Franco-Flemish Polyphony: a Study of Mannerism from 1450–1530* (diss., Columbia U., 1965)

M. Picker: 'The Cantus Firmus in Binchois' *Files a marier*', *JAMS*, xviii (1965), 235

——: *The Chanson Albums of Marguerite of Austria* (Berkeley, 1965)

D. Plamenac: 'The Two-part Quodlibets in the Seville Chansonnier', *The Commonwealth of Music, in Honor of Curt Sachs* (New York, 1965), 163

W. Rogge: *Das Quodlibet in Deutschland bis Melchior Franck* (Wolfenbüttel, 1965)

H. Hewitt: 'A *chanson rustique* of the Early Renaissance: *Bon temps*', *Aspects of Medieval and Renaissance Music: a Birthday Offering to Gustave Reese* (New York, 1966), 376

M. R. Maniates: 'Mannerist Composition in Franco-Flemish Polyphony', *MQ*, lii (1966), 17

——: 'Quodlibet Revisum', *AcM*, xxxviii (1966), 169

W. Elders: *Studien zur Symbolik in der Musik der alten Niederländer* (Bilthoven, 1968)

——: 'Das Symbol in der Musik von Josquin des Prez', *AcM*, xli (1969), 164

H. Deppert and R. Zillhardt: 'Ein weiteres Quodlibet im Glogauer Liederbuch', *Mf*, xxii (1969), 316

M. R. Maniates: 'Combinative Chansons in the Dijon Chansonnier', *JAMS*, xxiii (1970), 228–81

——: 'Combinative Chansons in the Escorial Chansonnier', *MD*, xxix (1975), 61–125

MARIA RIKA MANIATES (with PETER BRANSCOMBE)

Quoshwa. *See* CACHUA.

Ququlion. A category of chant in SYRIAN CHURCH MUSIC.

Quṭb al-Dīn [Maḥmūd ibn Mas'ūd al-Shīrāzī] (*b* Shīrāz, 1236; *d* Tabrīz, 1312). Persian scholar and theorist. The most outstanding pupil of the mathematician Naṣīr al-Dīn Ṭūsī, he is particularly known for his work in medicine, optics and astronomy. His encyclopedia, *Durrat al-tāj* ('Pearl of the crown'), demonstrates his mastery of the whole range of traditional medieval scholarship, and contains within its treatment of the mathematical sciences (Quadrivium) a lengthy section on music. This is mainly a restatement of the musical theory developed by ṢAFĪ AL-DĪN, but is important for its attention to musical practice, particularly in its codification and description of modes and rhythms. In both areas it points to the existence of a wider range of structures than is apparent from the works of Ṣafī al-Dīn; its treatment of the modes in particular is far fuller, and is less restricted by purely theoretical concerns. It ends with the most extended and complex example of notation to be found in the works of the medieval Arab and Persian theorists.

WRITINGS

Durrat al-tāj [Pearl of the crown] (MS, *GB-Lbm* Add.7694); ed. S. M. Mashkūt and N.A. Taqwā (Tehran, 1939–46)

BIBLIOGRAPHY

R. G. Kiesewetter: *Die Musik der Araber* (Leipzig, 1842), viii, 13, 21, 32f, 49f

L. Leclerc: *Histoire de la médecine arabe*, ii (Paris, 1876), 129f

C. Brockelmann: *Geschichte der arabischen Litteratur*, ii (Weimar and Berlin, 1898–1902, 2/1943), 211f

'Ḳuṭb al-Dīn', *The Encyclopaedia of Islam* (Leiden and London, 1913–38, rev. 2/1960–)

H. G. Farmer: *The Sources of Arabian Music* (Bearsden, 1940, rev. 2/1965), 50

O. WRIGHT

Qweldryk. *See* QUELDRYK.

R

R. Abbreviation for *ritardando*, used particularly by Elgar; *see* LARGAMENTE. *See also* RINFORZANDO.

Ra. The flattened supertonic of the prevailing key (or, if this is minor, its relative major), in TONIC SOL-FA.

Raab, Franz de Paula (*b* Pausram [now Puzdřany], 1763; *d* Seitenstetten, 21 May 1804). Austrian composer. The son of a peasant, he was at first an apprentice musician (*Thurnergeselle*) in Purgstall, Lower Austria, and around 1780 obtained a position as a bass singer in the Benedictine abbey of Seitenstetten, where in 1788 he succeeded the organist and composer Christian Widmann. In 1794 he had composition lessons from Albrechtsberger in Vienna. In his sacred music he closely followed the style of Michael Haydn, carefully observing liturgical considerations. His secular compositions consist of patriotic works from the time of the wars with France and functional music for use in the monastery. His music was performed in Seitenstetten until 1875, and his *Graduale pro Dominica III. post Pascha* is still in use in Kremsmünster.

WORKS
(all in MS in A-GÖ, KR, M, SEI, SF, Wgm, D-Bds)

Sacred, 4vv, org, most with other insts: Requiem, e, 1796; 4 Vespers de Dominica, 1800; Vesper de Beata, 1800; Vesper de Dominica, 1800, completed by J. A. Pfeiffer; 16 introits, 1795–6; 12 graduals, 1794–1804; 4 offertories, 1796; Tu fons, origo omnium, 1795

Secular: 16 fugues, pf, org, 1794, lost; 7 variations, hpd/pf; 5 patriotic choruses; 2 occasional cantatas, 1795–7; 3 arias; composition exercises with corrections by Albrechtsberger, 1794; frags.

BIBLIOGRAPHY

Anon.: [Biography of Raab] (MS, 1828, *A-Wgm*)

A. Fuchs: 'Beiträge zur Tonkünstlergeschichte Österreichs', *Allgemeine Wiener Musikzeitung*, iii (1843), nos.14–15

C. von Wurzbach: *Biographisches Lexikon des Kaiserthums Oesterreich*, xxiv (Vienna, 1872), 155

P. Ortmayr and A. Decker: *Das Benediktinerstift Seitenstetten* (Wels, 1955), 293f

J. Haider: *Die Geschichte des Theaterwesens im Benediktinerstift Seitenstetten in Barock und Aufklärung* (Vienna, 1973), 93f, 171f, 180

BENEDIKT WAGNER

Raabe, Christoph. *See* RAB, CHRISTOPH.

Raabe, Peter (*b* Frankfurt an der Oder, 27 Nov 1872; *d* Weimar, 12 April 1945). German scholar and conductor. He studied at the Berlin Hochschule für Musik with Woldemar Bargiel and afterwards worked as a conductor in various towns in Germany and Holland. In 1907 he was appointed court conductor in Weimar, where he became the curator of the Liszt Museum and chief editor of the Breitkopf Collected Edition of Liszt's works, to which he contributed several volumes. In 1916 he received his PhD from Jena University with a dissertation on the genesis of Liszt's orchestral music In 1920 he was appointed general music director of the Aachen Municipal Orchestra, and in 1924 he was made honorary professor of music at Aachen Technische Hochschule. In 1935 he succeeded Richard Strauss as the president of the Reichsmusikkammer, a post which he held until his death. In 1936 he received an honorary doctorate from Königsberg University. Although he conducted a large number of works by contemporary German and foreign composers, most have not survived into the present-day repertory, apart from early pieces by Egk and Fortner. He was a political conservative, and even actively supported the artistic policy of the Nazi regime from the 1930s onwards. He is best remembered for his two-volume study of Franz Liszt. This work, reissued in 1968 in a revised edition by his son Felix, shows considerable scholarship and is a valuable source for research, for as curator of the Liszt Museum Raabe had access to a large number of unpublished MSS. Raabe also wrote songs and piano pieces.

WRITINGS

'Felix Weingartner als schaffender Künstler', *Die Musik*, vii (1907–8), 15

Festschrift zum 50jährigen Jubiläum der Hofkapelle in Weimar (Weimar, 1909)

Die Entstehungsgeschichte der Orchesterwerke Franz Liszts (diss., U. of Jena, 1916)

Grossherzog Carl Alexander und Liszt (Leipzig, 1918)

Franz Liszt (Stuttgart, 1931, rev. 2/1968)

Die Musik im dritten Reich (Regensburg, 1935)

Kulturwille im deutschen Musikleben (Regensburg, 1936)

'Was verdanken wir Franz Liszt?', *AMz*, lxiii (1936), 368

Deutsche Meister (Regensburg, 1937)

'Über die Erziehung von Kapellmeistern und Orchestermusikern', *Musik-Woche* (1937), 1

'Über die Werktreue und ihre Grenzen', *Festschrift für Fritz Stein* (Brunswick, 1939), 153

'Das Problem Unterhaltungsmusik', *ZfM*, Jg.107 (1940), 435

'Etwas über den Solistennachwuchs', *AMz*, cvii (1940), 149

'Der Lindenbaum': Schuberts missverstandenstes Lied', *AMz*, cxiii (1941), 243

Wege zu Liszt (Regensburg, 1943)

Wege zu Bruckner (Regensburg, 1944)

EDITIONS

F. Liszt: Lieder und Gesänge, Musikalische Werke, vii/1–3 (Leipzig, 1917–22/*R*1966)

F. Liszt: Ungarische Rhapsodien, Musikalische Werke, ii/12 (Leipzig, 1926/*R*1966)

BIBLIOGRAPHY

P. Schwers: 'Peter Raabe', *AMz*, lix (1932), 608

A. Morgenroth, ed.: *Von deutscher Tonkunst: Festschrift zu Peter Raabes 70. Geburtstag* (Leipzig, 1942, rev. 2/1944) [with list of writings]

F. Rühlmann: 'Peter Raabe', *ZfM*, Jg.109 (1942), 473

R. Schaal: *Hugo Kaun: Leben und Werk* (Regensburg, 1948), 22ff, 26, 29ff, 111, 168, 171

E. Valentin: 'Musiker, Mensch und Gelehrter: Peter Raabe zum Gedenken', *ZfM*, Jg.113 (1952), 630
F. Raabe: 'Raabe, Peter', *Rheinische Musiker*, iii, ed. K. G. Fellerer (Cologne, 1964)

HUMPHREY SEARLE

Raaben, Lev Nikolayevich (*b* Groznïy, 1 Jan 1913). Soviet musicologist. In 1940 he graduated from Yuly Il'ich Eydlin's violin class at the Leningrad Conservatory, and in 1945 completed his postgraduate studies in the history and theory of string playing. He took his *kandidat* degree in 1948 with a dissertation on violin playing in Russia during the 19th century, and in 1966 was awarded a doctorate for two books on Russian chamber music. In 1946 he joined the teaching staff of the Leningrad Conservatory, in 1949 was appointed senior lecturer and in 1971 professor. In 1949 he became a senior research fellow at the Leningrad Institute of the Theatre, Music and Cinematography, where in 1969 he took charge of the music section. He is also editor of the section's annual research publication, *Voprosï teorii i estetiki muzïki* ('Questions of the theory and aesthetics of music'). In his writings Raaben has made a particularly valuable contribution to research into chamber music and the history of instrumental performance.

WRITINGS

Voprosï kvartetnovo ispolnitel'stva [Questions of quartet playing] (Moscow, 1956, 2/1960)

Instrumental'nïy ansambl' v russkoy muzïke [Instrumental ensemble in Russian music] (diss., Leningrad Conservatory, 1966; Moscow, 1961)

'Esteticheskiye i stilevïye tendentsii v muzïkal'nom ispolnitel'stve nashikh dney' [The aesthetic and stylistic tendencies in the performance of music today], *Voprosï teorii i estetiki muzïki*, i, ed. Institut teatra, muzïki i kinematografii (Leningrad, 1962), 20–51

Leopol'd Auer (Leningrad, 1962)

Sovetskaya kamerno-instrumental'naya muzïka [Soviet instrumental chamber music] (diss., Leningrad Conservatory, 1966; Leningrad, 1963)

'Nauka o muzïkal'nom ispolnitel'stve kak oblast' sovetskovo muzïkoznaniya' [The study of musical performance as a branch of Soviet musicology], *Voprosï teorii i estetiki muzïki*, vi–vii, ed. Institut teatra, muzïki i kinematografii (Leningrad, 1967), 195

Sovetskiy instrumental'nïy kontsert [The Soviet instrumental concerto] (Leningrad, 1967)

Zhizn' zamechatel'nïkh skripachey [The lives of outstanding violinists] (Leningrad, 1967)

Zhizn' zamechatel'nïkh skripachey i violonchelistov [The lives of outstanding violinists and cellists] (Leningrad, 1969)

'Betkhoven i interpretatsii masterov XX veka' [Interpretations of Beethoven by 20th-century performers], *Lyudvig van Betkhoven* (Leningrad, 1970), 82–133

'Instrumental'noye tvorchestvo Sviridova 30-kh–40-kh godov' [Sviridov's instrumental works of the 1930s and 1940s], *Voprosï teorii i estetiki muzïki*, x, ed. Institut teatra, muzïki i kinematografii (Leningrad, 1971), 101ff

Istoriya russkogo i sovetskogo skripichnogo iskusstva [A history of Russian-Soviet violin repertory] (Leningrad, 1978)

Raaff, Anton (*b* Gelsdorf, nr. Bonn, baptized 6 May 1714; *d* Munich, 28 May 1797). German tenor. Originally educated for the priesthood, he sang in several dramas at the Jesuit college in Bonn while still a boy. The Elector of Cologne, Clement Augustus, appointed him to his service in 1736, and took him to Munich, where he studied with Ferrandini and sang in one of his operas. The following year he was sent to study with Bernacchi in Bologna where he met Padre Martini, with whom he initiated a lifelong friendship and correspondence. In 1738 he sang at the betrothal of Maria Theresia in Florence; the following season he was in Venice for three operas. He returned to electoral service in Bonn during 1741–2 and sang for the imperial coronation at Frankfurt am Main and the wedding of

the Elector Palatine, Carl Theodor. In 1749 he left for Vienna, where he sang in several operas composed and directed by Jommelli. Metastasio praised his voice but found him deficient as an actor. He was in Italy at various centres in 1751–2, when he was called to the court of Lisbon; from there he went in 1755 to Madrid, where the opera was directed by Farinelli, with whom he then left for Naples in 1759.

For the next decade Raaff was the principal tenor on the Neapolitan and Florentine stage. The leading masters of *opera seria* vied in pleasing him: de Majo, Hasse and J. C. Bach as well as Sacchini, Piccinni and Mysliveček, the first three of whom were his favourites. He sang Bach's 'Non so d'onde viene' (*Alessandro nell' Indie*, 1762) by preference; another favourite was 'Se al labbro mio non credi' (probably from Hasse's 1760 *Artaserse*). Former ties in Germany were renewed with his appointment in 1770 to Mannheim, Carl Theodor's seat. He was probably instrumental in the commission that brought J. C. Bach to Mannheim to compose *Temistocle* (1772), in which he sang the title role, as he did in Bach's *Lucio Silla* four years later. He was lent to Stuttgart for a revival of Jommelli's *Fetonte* in 1772. Raaff made his début at the Concert Spirituel in Paris singing 'Non so d'onde viene' during June 1778, and was probably responsible for getting its composer a commission for his last opera, *Amadis de Gaule* (1779). Mozart heard him both at Mannheim and Paris, and was severely critical of his singing and acting in the title role of Holzbauer's *Günther von Schwarzburg* (1777), but tried to win his favour by composing a rival setting of 'Se

Anton Raaff: watercolour by an unknown artist in the Theatermuseum, Munich

al labbro mio' (K295). Pleased with the result, Raaff, along with Padre Martini, interceded with the elector to obtain an opera commission for Mozart; the result was *Idomeneo* (1781) for Munich, where the elector had transferred his court. Mozart's letters reveal his struggles to serve his own art while doing the best possible by the venerable tenor, whose attitudes towards singers' prerogatives were those of the mid-18th century. Though Raaff's voice was praised by Schubart as having an uncommon extent from bass to alto, with flexible coloratura throughout, Mozart found it small in range and limited in technique. Yet Raaff sang well enough in 1787 to impress Michael Kelly, who wrote that 'he still retained his fine *voce di petto* and sostenuto notes, and pure style of singing'. He was one of the last and greatest representatives of the legato technique and 'portamento' brought to perfection by Bernacchi and his school.

BIBLIOGRAPHY
C. F. D. Schubart: *Ideen zu einer Ästhetik der Tonkunst* (Vienna, 1806/R1969)
M. Kelly: *Reminiscences* (London, 1826, 2/1826/R1968), i, 282; ed. R. Fiske (London, 1975)
H. Freiberger: *Anton Raaff (1714–1797): sein Leben und Wirken* (Cologne, 1929)
E. Anderson, ed.: *The Letters of Mozart and his Family* (London, 1938, rev. 2/1966)
U. Prota-Giurleo: 'Notizie biografiche intorno ad alcuni musicisti d'oltralpe a Napoli nel settecento', *AnMc*, no.2 (1965), 136
P. Petrobelli: 'The Italian Years of Anton Raaff', *MJb 1973–4*, 233–73
D. Heartz: 'Raaff's Last Aria: a Mozartian Idyll in the Spirit of Hasse', *MQ*, lx (1974), 517
DANIEL HEARTZ

Rääts, Jaan (*b* Tartu, 15 Oct 1932). Estonian composer. After graduating from Sarv's piano class at the Tartu Music Institute, he studied composition at the Tallinn Conservatory under Saar (1952–4) and Eller (1954–7). He worked as a sound director for Estonian radio, and in 1966 he was appointed music director of Estonian television. In 1967 he was made a Merited Artist of the Estonian SSR; five years later his 24 Piano Preludes and Piano Quintet no.3 won him the Soviet Estonia Prize. Rääts's music juxtaposes diverse elements for illustrative effect, often including passages of a neo-classical lyricism, Estonian folk choral writing and improvisatory features taken from jazz. A characteristic work is *Karl Marx*, a through-composed piece uniting popular songs with oratorical numbers.

WORKS
(selective list)

Orch: 7 syms., 1957, 1958, 1959, 1959, 1966, 1967, 1972; 2 concs., pf, chamber orch, 1958, 1971; Oda pervomu kosmonavtu [Ode to the first cosmonaut], 1961; Conc., vn, chamber orch, 1963; Conc., vc, chamber orch, 1966; Pf Conc., 1968
Vocal: Karl Marx, reciter, chorus, orch, 1962–4; Shkol'naya kantata [School cantata], 1968
Inst: 4 str qts, 1956, 1958, 1964, 1970; 3 pf trios, 1957, 1962, 1973; 3 pf qnts, n.d., n.d., 1970; 4 pf sonatas, n.d., n.d.; Nonet, 1967; 24 Pf Preludes, 1968; Pf Sextet, 1972

Principal publishers: Muzïka, Sovetskiy kompozitor

BIBLIOGRAPHY
A. Vakhter: 'Jaan Rääts', *Muzïkal'niye stranitsï* (Tallinn, 1965)
P. Kuusk: 'Jaan Rääts', *Kuus eesti tänase muusika loojat* [Six Estonian creators of modern music], ed. L. Normet (Tallinn, 1970)
H. Olt: 'Jaan Rääts', *Modern Estonian Composers* (Tallinn, 1972)
MARINA NESTYEVA

Rab [Raabe, Rabe], **Christoph** [Corvinus, Christopher] (*b* Zurich, 1552; *d* Herborn, 19 Jan 1620). German printer and publisher. After studying at the universities of Heidelberg, Wittenberg and Vienna (1567–74) he worked in the press of his father Georg Rab (*d* 1580); later he worked with the Frankfurt publisher Sigmund Feyerabend and the printers Johann Wechel and Paul Rab (1581–5). In 1585 he moved to Herborn, where Count Johann VI the elder of Herborn helped him to establish and expand an efficient printing firm. Rab mainly printed works for the new University of Herborn (founded 1584), moving with it to Siegen (1595–9) and then following it back to Herborn. His publications include several editions of hymnbooks and works by Meiland, Melchior Schramm and other composers.

BIBLIOGRAPHY
J. Benzing: *Die Buchdrucker des 16. und 17. Jahrhunderts im deutschen Sprachgebiet* (Wiesbaden, 1963)
H. Hüschen: 'Hessische Gesangbuchdrucker und -verleger des 16. und 17. Jahrhunderts', *Festschrift Hans Engel* (Kassel, 1964), 166
THEODOR WOHNHAAS

Rab [Rabe, Corvus, Corvinus], **Valentin** [Valentinus] (*b* probably Lössnitz, *c*1522; *d* Marienberg, 17 April 1596). German composer. After a time as Kantor in Schneeberg around 1540 he began studies in Wittenberg in June 1542: there he may have attended lectures by Dietrich (1544) and Coclico (1545–6) as well as by Luther, Melanchthon and others. He seems to have remained in Wittenberg until about 1550. From 1554 until his death he was Kantor at the Lyceum Mariaemontanum, Marienberg. With David Köler and Johann Reusch, Rab was one of the important figures in the Upper Saxon circle of composers, which followed Thomas Stoltzer. From 1546 this circle extensively developed the German psalm motet (using Luther's texts), beginning a tradition that still continues. 31 works by Rab are known (mostly in *D-Dlb*, *Z* and *H-BA*), some only as fragments, others only from archival references, while an unknown number of hymn settings have been lost (for full work-list see Dehnhard). His style shows the influence of Josquin's late works. From a technical point of view the German motets do not rise above the average, but the settings of texts with political or Lutheran convictions reach a relatively high level of expressive intensity through heightened word declamation and rhetorical devices. The psalm motets composed between 1547 and 1550 reflect Rab's attitude to the Schmalkalden war (1547), the Augsburg and Leipzig Interims (1548–52) and internal Protestant disputes; they were certainly not conceived as liturgical music and their use as such is limited.

BIBLIOGRAPHY
H. Albrecht: 'Zwei Quellen zur deutschen Musikgeschichte der Reformationszeit', *Mf*, i (1948), 242–85
W. Dehnhard: *Die deutsche Psalmmotette in der Reformationszeit* (Wiesbaden, 1971) [incl. complete list of works]
W. Steude: *Untersuchungen zu Herkunft, Verbreitung und spezifischem Inhalt mitteldeutscher Musikhandschriften des 16. Jahrhunderts* (diss., U. of Rostock, 1973)
WOLFRAM STEUDE

Rabāb. An Arabic term which, with its many variants used throughout the Islamic world, usually denotes a bowed lute (fiddle). The term first appears in the 10th-century treatises of Ibn-Sina and al-Fārābī; al-Fārābī described the *rabāb* as identical with Khurāsānī *ṭunbūr*, having a long neck, with or without frets, a pyriform body and one or two pairs of strings.

There are two main types of *rabāb*: fiddles with wooden, generally pear-shaped bodies; and spike fiddles. In north Africa a *rabāb* of the first type is sometimes carved from a single piece of wood, has a sound-table of skin and is played with a short, heavy, curved bow (*see* NORTH AFRICA, fig.4). In Morocco it is second only to the *'ūd* in popularity. In Turkey similar fiddles were called *rabāb* in the 17th century; they are now usually known as *kemençe* (*see* TURKEY, §2(ii)) and have wooden sound-tables. Synonyms for the Indian *sarod* reveal its Arabic connections; known also as *rabōb* or *rubāb*, it usually has more strings than its African counterparts, including sympathetic strings, and may be bowed or plucked with a plectrum.

Spike fiddles have had the name *rabāb* since early medieval times. Some, like the quadrangular *rabāb* of Egypt, Iraq and Syria, appear to have evolved from frame drums (*see* LEBANON, fig.4). The *rabāb*'s body consists of a wooden frame with a belly and back of skin. It was originally plucked but Ibn Ghaibi (*d* 1435) mentioned it as a bowed instrument. Villoteau distinguished two similar types of *rabāb*, the one-string *rabāb al-shā'ir* ('poet's fiddle') and the two-string *rabāb al-mughannī* ('singer's fiddle'), its strings tuned in 5ths. The *rabāb* of north African nomads may have a quadrangular or circular frame (as is common in Morocco; *see* MOROCCO, fig.5) and a single thick string of horsehair fitted over a thick M-shaped or triangular bridge. A second type of spike fiddle has a hemispherical body of carved wood, gourd or coconut covered with a skin belly. It has a very wide distribution, from north Africa to south-east Asia and the Far East. In many cases the Arabic name has travelled with the instrument, giving for example the *rĕbab*, which has an important melodic role in the gamelan orchestras of Java (*see* INDONESIA, fig.14). Instruments of the *rabāb* type are generally played on the knees with the bow held from underneath. The Arabic two- or four-string *rabāb*, which is used in both folk and classical music, is to some extent being replaced by the European violin: where this has occurred, however, the violin is not necessarily played under the chin in the Western manner, but on the knee like the *rabāb*.

See also 'Rabāb' in Appendix A.

BIBLIOGRAPHY
G. A. Villoteau: 'Description historique, technique et littéraire, des instrumens de musique des Orientaux', *Description de l'Egypte: état moderne* (Paris, 1813)
W. Bachmann: *Die Anfänge des Streichinstrumentenspiels* (Leipzig, 1964, 2/1966; Eng. trans., 1969)
J. Kuckertz: 'Origin and Development of the Rabāb', *Sangeet Natak*, xv (1970), 16
S. Marcuse: *A Survey of Musical Instruments* (Newton Abbot and London, 1975), 477ff
J. Jenkins and P. Rovsing Olsen: *Music and Musical Instruments in the World of Islam* (London, 1976), 33ff
WILLIAM J. CONNER, MILFIE HOWELL

Rabana. Frame drum used in various parts of Indonesia, usually, but not exclusively, in Islamic religious music. The instrument is represented on east Javanese terracotta figurines dating from the Majapahit period (late 13th–early 16th centuries). The frame is deep and may be provided with tinkling metal plates. In west and central Java frame drums are more usually called *tĕrbang* and *genjring*; the *genjring* have tinkling plates. The frame drum is not used in gamelan ensembles but as accompaniment to the *qaṣīda* in religious meetings (*see* ARAB MUSIC, §II, 3(i)) or in Javanese devotional choral songs. Ensembles composed entirely of *rabana* or *tĕrbang* are known from Sumatra and west Java.

ERNST HEINS

Rabassa, Pedro (*b* Barcelona, 1683; *d* Seville, 12 Dec 1767). Catalan composer. He was *maestro de capilla* at Vich before taking the same office at Valencia Cathedral on 24 May 1714. He succeeded Gaspar de Úbeda y Castelay as Seville Cathedral *maestro* on 9 June 1724, remaining there until his death.

According to Soler, Rabassa shared company with Domenico Scarlatti in his ability to modulate effectively. This ability is shown in Rabassa's earliest dated *tono*, *A la festiva noticia*, written to commemorate the victory at Almenar of the Austrian pretender (crowned Carlos III at Barcelona on 24 October 1705), and in his Christmas villancico of 1722, *Que habeis visto pastorcillos*. All of Rabassa's 38 villancicos are multi-movement works, often with recitatives, da capo arias, or duos and ensembles, in an up-to-date cantata style. His Latin works include nine continuo-accompanied masses and numerous smaller works with and without orchestra. In 1869 Hilarión Eslava y Elizondo published his plangent 12-voice continuo-accompanied motet, *Audite universi populi*, as witness to his power in the sublime vein. A manuscript *Tratado de composición*, formerly in the possession of Vicenç Ripollès in Valencia, was lost during the Civil War.

WORKS

A la festiva noticia, tono to commemorate victory of Carlos III at Almenar, perf. Barcelona, Llotja, 1705, ed. in Carreras y Bulbena; O magnum mysterium, 8vv, org; ¡Ay dolor mio!, 1v: all in *E-Bc*
33 Latin works, incl. 9 masses, vv, bc; 15 motets, incl. Audite universi populi, 12vv, bc, ed. in H. Eslava y Elizondo, *Lira sacro-hispana*, ser.1, i (Madrid, *c*1869); 2 psalms [Dixit Dominus, Laudate Dominum]; Magnificat; 2 litanies; Salve regina; hymn; sequence; Miserere: some with orch, all in *Sc* according to Rosa y López
78 Latin pieces, incl. masses, motets, psalms; 38 villancicos, mostly 8/10/12vv, insts, incl. Que habeis visto pastorcillos, 1722, part ed. in Ripollès: all in *VAc*
4 pieces in Guatemala City Cathedral; 3 pieces in Colección Jesús Sánchez Garza, Instituto Nacional de Bellas Artes, Mexico City

BIBLIOGRAPHY
A. Soler: *Carta escrita a un amigo* (Madrid, 1766), 5
J. R. Carreras y Bulbena: *Karl von Oesterreich und Elisabeth von Braunschweig Wolfenbüttel in Barcelona und Girona: Musik, Feste, Geschäfte des Palastes* (Barcelona, 1902), appx 15
S. de la Rosa y López: *Los seises de la Catedral de Sevilla* (Seville, 1904), 328
V. Ripollès: *El villancico i la cantata del segle XVIII a València* (Barcelona, 1935)
R. Stevenson: *Renaissance and Baroque Musical Sources in the Americas* (Washington, 1970), 95f, 176
J. E. Ayarra Jarne: *La música en la Catedral de Sevilla* (Seville, 1976), 63f
ROBERT STEVENSON

Rabaud, Henri (*b* Paris, 10 Nov 1873; *d* Paris, 11 Sept 1949). French composer and conductor. He was born into a distinguished musical family: his grandfather Louis Dorus was a celebrated flautist, his great-aunt was the soprano Dorus-Gras, who created several roles in the operas of Meyerbeer and Halévy, and his father Hippolyte Rabaud was a leading cellist. Rabaud showed prodigious talent and a somewhat academic spirit: 'modernism is the enemy' was his watchword. At the Paris Conservatoire (1893–4) he studied harmony with Taudon and composition with Massenet and Gédalge. Finding Massenet's teaching superficial, he gained more from his studies of the Viennese Classics – the music of Wagner, Franck and Debussy left him indifferent. In 1894 his cantata *Daphne* won him the Prix de Rome, and his sojourn at the Villa Medici opened his mind to newer music; he came to admire Verdi, Mascagni and Puccini. A trip to Bayreuth was enough to complete the demolition of the barriers he had imposed: turning in the direction of Wagner and Franck, he composed a mystical oratorio, *Job* (1900), which enjoyed an immense success. However, he was still capable of writing such drily academic music as the opera *La fille de Roland* (1904). For his second opera, *Mârouf, savetier du Caire* (1914), Rabaud welded together Wagnerian form and oriental picturesqueness; the work was greeted with enthusiasm both in France and abroad. During this period Rabaud was a frequent conductor at the Opéra-Comique and at the Opéra, directing the latter house from 1914 to 1918, in which year he was admitted to the Institut de France. He also interested himself in film music: his first score was for a projection of *Le miracle des loups* at the Opéra in 1924, and this was followed by *Joueur d'échecs* (1925) – both scores were written before the introduction of optical recording. Rabaud succeeded Fauré as director of the Conservatoire in 1922, retiring in 1941.

WORKS
(selective list)

DRAMATIC

La fille de Roland (opera, 4, P. Ferrari after H. de Bornier), 1904
Mârouf, savetier du Caire (opera, 5, L. Népoty), 1914
L'appel de la mer (opera, 1, Rabaud after Synge), 1924
Le miracle des loups, film, 1924
Joueur d'échecs, film, 1925
Rolande et le mauvais garçon (opera, 5, Népoty), 1933
Martine (opera, 5 scenes, J. J. Bernard), 1947
Le jeu de l'amour et du hasard (opera, 3, Marivaux), 1948
Several incidental scores

OTHER WORKS

op.
1 Symphony no.1, d, 1893
— Daphne, cantata, 1894
— L'été (Hugo), S, A, SATB, orch, 1895
2 Divertissement sur des chansons russes, orch, 1899
3 String Quartet, g, 1898
4 Psaume IV, solo vv, chorus, orch, 1901
5 Symphony no.2, e, 1900
9 Job, solo vv, chorus, orch, 1900
11 2ème poème lyrique sur le livre de Job, solo vv, chorus, orch, 1905
— Lamento, orch, 1930
— Prelude and Toccata, pf, orch, 1945
— Trio, ob, cl, bn, 1949

BIBLIOGRAPHY

A. Coeuroy: *La musique française moderne* (Paris, 1922)
J. Tiersot: *Un demi-siècle de musique française* (Paris, 1924)
R. Dumesnil: *La musique française contemporaine* (Paris, 1930)
P. Landormy: *La musique française après Debussy* (Paris, 1943)
G. Samazeuilh: *Musiciens de mon temps* (Paris, 1947)
M. d'Ollone: *Henri Rabaud: sa vie et son oeuvre* (Paris, 1958)

ANNE GIRARDOT

Rabé (Sp.). REBEC.

Rabe, Christoph. *See* RAB, CHRISTOPH.

Rabe, Folke (Alvar Harald Reinhold) (*b* Stockholm, 28 Oct 1935). Swedish composer and trombonist. Active as a jazz trombonist from 1950, he studied at the Stockholm Musikhögskolan under Blomdahl, Wallner and Ligeti (1957–64), and remained there as an assistant teacher (1964–8). He spent some time in San Francisco in 1965, associating with Dewey, Riley, Subotnick and others. In 1963 he co-founded the Kulturkvartetten, a group of four trombonists who have appeared throughout Europe in performances exclusively of their own compositions, some of them theatrical. Rabe has been engaged in work for the Swedish National Concerts since 1968, and for the schools' concerts organization since 1972. One aim of his music, as well as his teaching material *Ljudverkstad* ('Sound workshop'), has been to sharpen awareness of the most subtle variations of sound.

WORKS
(selective list)

Notturno (E. Södergran), Mez, 3 ww, 1959; Pièce, speaking chorus, 1961, collab. L. O'Månsson; Bolos, 4 trbn, 1962, collab. J. Bark; Impromptu, cl, trbn, pf, perc, vc, 1962; Rondes, mixed chorus, male chorus, 1964; Polonaise, 4 trbn, 1965, collab. Bark; Hep-hep, small orch, 1966; Va??, tape, 1967; Joe's Harp, chorus, 1970; Filmmusik I, fl, cl, pf, 1973; Filmmusik II, fl, ob, cl, hn, bn, perc, 1973; Tvaa strofer [2 stanzas] (G. Sonnevi), mixed choir, 1980

Principal publisher: Hansen

WRITINGS

with J. Bark: 'Blåsinstrumentens nya möjligheter', *Nutida musik*, v/2 (1961–2), 20
——: 'Pajasso och Ost funk', *Nutida musik*, vii/4 (1963–4), 18
'Va??', *Nutida musik*, xi/3–4 (1967–8), 33
with A. Mellnäs and L. J. Werle: 'Kann ein Komponist vom Komponieren leben?' *Melos*, xxxvi (1969), 162
'Den svenske tonsättarens situation', *Nutida musik*, xiv/3 (1970–71), 33
with J. Bark: *Ljudverkstad* [Sound workshop] (Stockholm, 1974)

ROLF HAGLUND

Rabe, Valentin. *See* RAB, VALENTIN.

Rabel (Sp.). REBEC.

Rabelais, François (*b* nr. Chinon, 1494; *d* nr. Paris [?St Maur], 1553 or 1554). French satirist, humanist and physician. During the 1520s he was in turn a member of Franciscan and Benedictine orders in Poitou. He studied Greek with the encouragement of Budé and acquired a reputation as a scholarly humanist. Having abandoned monastic life, he graduated in medicine at Montpellier University in 1530, receiving his doctorate there in 1537. He had settled in Lyons by 1532 when he was appointed physician at the municipal hospital and edited medical studies by Hippocrates and Manardi. The humanist Cardinal Jean du Bellay took Rabelais to Rome as his personal physician in 1534 and 1535–6, and between 1540 and 1543 Rabelais attended the cardinal's brother, Guillaume du Bellay, governor of Piedmont.

Rabelais published *Pantagruel*, the first of his novels, in 1532 and the second, *Gargantua*, followed in 1534. The third book of the saga was published in 1546 and part of the fourth two years later; like their predecessors these were censured by the Sorbonne, but the author avoided persecution by fleeing to Metz, rejoining Jean du Bellay in Rome in 1549. Rabelais spent his last years near Paris, probably at the abbey of St Maur-les-Fossés, where he had held a canonry since 1536. The fourth book was completed by 1552, but the fifth book (1562–4) was probably expanded posthumously from a rough draft.

Rabelais' five novels abound in musical description and imagery used for rhetorical effect and witty characterization. Innumerable instruments are mentioned: the bagpipe, shawm, flute, organ and drum are used as physical and often erotic symbols; the strings (lute, harp, spinet, viol) characterize nobility, while trumpets, fifes and drums relate to military and important events. The fifth book includes a list of incipits from 175 dance-songs, 159 of them in the collection of 184 entitled *S'ensuyvent plusieurs basses dances tant communes que incommunes* published in Lyons in the 1530s. Vocal music also figures prominently, with refrains and quotations from noëls and popular chansons used in contemporary theatre, made familiar through polyphonic versions published by Attaingnant and Moderne. As a result of his training, Rabelais was familiar with musical theory, and in the 'Nouveau prologue' to the fourth book he listed 58 of the most distinguished composers of his time. These he divided into two generations, the first including Ockeghem, Obrecht, Josquin, Agricola, Brumel, Mouton, Compère, Févin, Richafort, Conseil, Festa and Berchem, and the second including Willaert, Gombert, Janequin, Arcadelt, Sermisy, Certon, Manchicourt, Villiers, Sandrin, Sohier, Hesdin, Morales, Passereau, Jacotin, Verdelot and Carpentras.

BIBLIOGRAPHY

A. Machabey: 'Rabelais et la musique', *BSIM*, ix (1913), 26
C. van den Borren: 'Rabelais et la musique', *Académie royale de Belgique: bulletin de la classe des beaux-arts*, xxiv (1942), 78–111
N. C. Carpenter: 'Rabelais and the Chanson', *Publications of the Modern Language Association*, lxv (1950), 1212
——: *Rabelais and Music* (Chapel Hill, 1954)
M. A. Screech: *Rabelais* (London, 1979)

FRANK DOBBINS

Rabello, Manuel. *See* REBELLO, MANUEL.

Rabelo, João Soares. *See* REBELO, JOÃO SOARES.

Racchiano, Giovanni Battista (*fl* 1587). Italian priest and composer. He came from Vallata, near Gesualdo's home. On 4 June 1587, Scipione Riccio, a Neapolitan bookseller, contracted to have printed in Venice 200 copies of a book consisting of 17 five-part motets and three masses, including one Requiem, all by Racchiano.

BIBLIOGRAPHY

G. Filangieri: *Documenti per la storia le arti e le industrie delle provincie napoletane* (Naples, 1891), vi, 354f

KEITH A. LARSON

Racek, Fritz (*b* Znaim, Austro-Hungary [now Znojmo, Czechoslovakia], 15 Feb 1911; *d* Vienna, 14 Aug 1975). Austrian musicologist. He studied at the Vienna Academy (1929–35), where he took his conductor's diploma under Oswald Kabasta, and at Vienna University with Orel, Lach and Haas (1931–6), where he took the doctorate in 1939 with a thesis on the modal notation of the Notre Dame School. While studying singing, he worked as a répétiteur and organist. In 1945 he became director of the music department of the Vienna City Library. He ran the music committee of the Wiener Festwoche (1951–4), and organized the 1952 Vienna music congress and the Vienna Mozart celebrations (1956).

Between 1949 and 1964 Racek wrote analyses of 400 works for the symphony concerts of the Gesellschaft der Musikfreunde. As a representative of the Gemeinde Wien he has been responsible for numerous exhibitions and their catalogues, including exhibitions on Johann Strauss (1949), Viennese concert life (1951), Wilhelm Kienzl (1951), Schubert and Wolf (1953), Brahms MSS (1957), Berg (1960), Joseph Marx (1962), *Die Fledermaus* (1967), 100 years of the *Blue Danube* waltz (1967), and Beethoven (centenary exhibition, 1970). In 1967 Racek became general editor of the complete works of Johann Strauss. He was personally responsible for five volumes including those containing the operettas *Eine Nacht in Venedig* and *Die Fledermaus*.

Racek's large output as a composer includes theatre music, songs to his own texts, symphonic and chamber works and choral music. He adapted Hauer's opera *Die schwarze Spinne* and Schubert's *Sakuntala* for performance in Wiener Festwoche (1966 and 1971 respectively). From 1952 to 1956 he was the head of the Österreichischen Gesellschaft für Zeitgenössische Musik.

WRITINGS

Die Clauseln des Wolfenbüttler Codex I (diss., U. of Vienna, 1939)
'Eine wiedergefundene Schubert-Handschrift', *ÖMz*, ii (1947), 18
ed.: *Internationaler Musikkongress: Wien 1952*
'Die Musiksammlung der Wiener Stadtbibliothek', *ÖMz*, x (1955), 171
'Hugo Wolfs erste Chorversuche', *ÖMz*, xv (1960), 55
'Schuberts Singspiel "Der häusliche Krieg" und seine jetzt aufgefundene Ouverture', *Biblos*, xii (1963), 136
'Ein wiederentdeckter Tanz Franz Schuberts', *Die Wiener Stadtbibliothek 1956–1966* (Vienna, 1966), 175
'Die Johann Strauss-Gesamtausgabe', *ÖMz*, xxii (1967), 292
'Das Tagebuch Carl Millöckers', *Veröffentlichungen aus der Wiener Stadtbibliothek*, iii (Vienna, 1969), 137
'Einiges über Lortzings Tätigkeit am Theater an der Wien', *Symbolae historiae musicae: Hellmut Federhofer zum 65. Geburtstag* (Mainz, 1971), 278
'Wo wurde Arnold Schönberg geboren?', *ÖMz*, xxviii (1973), 76
'Zur Entstehung und Aufführungspraxis der "Fledermaus" ', *ÖMz*, xxx (1975), 264
Articles in *MGG*

EDITIONS

Meisterhandschriften aus der Musiksammlung der Wiener Stadtbibliothek (Vienna, 1961) [facs. edn.]
J. Strauss: Instrumentalwerke opp.304–316, Gesamtausgabe, i/19 (Vienna, 1967); *Instrumentalwerke opp.292–303*, Gesamtausgabe, i/18 (Vienna, 1968); *Bühnen- und Vokalwerke: Eine Nacht in Venedig*, Gesamtausgabe, ii/9 (Vienna, 1970); *Instrumentalwerke opp.317–329*, Gesamtausgabe, i/20 (Vienna, 1971); *Die Fledermaus*, Gesamtausgabe, ii/3 (Vienna, 1974)

RUDOLF KLEIN

Racek, Jan (*b* Bučovice, Moravia, 1 June 1905; *d* Brno, 5 Dec 1979). Czech musicologist. He studied under Helfert at Brno University (1924–8) and took his doctorate in 1929 with a dissertation on the concept of the nation in Smetana's music. He then became director of the music archives of the Moravian Regional Museum (1930–48) and was assistant to Helfert at Brno University, where he was appointed lecturer in 1939; in 1948 he became professor and director of the Brno department of ethnography and folk music of the Czech Academy of Sciences; he retired in 1970. Though he obtained his DSc degree in 1957 with a work on Beethoven, his chief interests were stylistic and historical questions of the Baroque era, Czech music of the 17th and 18th centuries and the music of Smetana and Janáček. He was general editor of a number of publications initiated by Helfert, including the journal *Musikologie* and the series of early Czech music, Musica Antiqua Bohemica.

WRITINGS

Idea vlasti, národa a slávy v díle B. Smetany [The idea of the fatherland, nation and glory in Smetana's works] (diss., U. of Brno, 1929; Brno, 1933, enlarged 2/1947)
'Les madrigaux à voix seule de Luzzasco Luzzaschi', *ReM*, xiii (1932), 11
Leoš Janáček (Olomouc, 1938)
Slohové problémy italské monodie [Problems of style in Italian monody] (Prague and Brno, 1938; Ger. trans., d)
ed., with L. Firkušný: *Janáčkovy feuilletony z LN* [Janáček's feuilletons in the *Lidové noviny*] (Brno, 1938, rev. 2/1958 as *Leoš Janáček: Fejetony z Lidových novin*; Ger. trans., 2/1962)
Leoš Janáček a současní moravští skladatelé [Janáček and contemporary Moravian composers] (Brno, 1940)
Česká hudba od nejstarších dob po počátku 19. století [Czech music from the earliest times to the beginning of the 19th century] (Prague, 1949, enlarged 2/1958)
Ruská hudba: od nejstarších dob až po Velkou říjnovou revoluci [Russian music: from the earliest times up to the Great Revolution] (Prague, 1953)
'Zur Frage des "Mozart-Stils" in der tschechischen vorklassischen Musik', *Kongressbericht: Wien Mozartjahr 1956*, 493–524
'Collezione di monodie italiane primarie alla Biblioteca universitaria di Praga', *Sborník prací filosofické fakulty brněnské university*, F2 (1958), 5–58
'Unbekannte Autographen-Fragmente von Mozart', *DJbM*, iii (1958), 41
'Beethoven und Goethe in Bad Teplitz 1812', *SMw*, xxv (1962), 406
Beethoven a české země [Beethoven in Bohemia and Moravia] (Brno, 1964)
'Beethoven auf Schloss Grätz (Hradec) bei Troppau in den Jahren 1806

und 1811: ein Beitrag zur Beethoven und die böhmischen Länder', *Beethoven Symposion: Wien 1970*, 215

'Das tschechische Volkslied und die italienische Barockmusik des 17. und 18. Jahrhunderts', *Symbolae historiae musicae: Hellmut Federhofer zum 60. Geburtstag* (Mainz, 1971), 122

'Skladby Georga Friedricha Händle na zámku v Náměšti nad Oslavou' [Handel's compositions at the castle of Naměšt nad Oslavou], *Časopis Moravského musea, vědy společenské*, lviii (1973), 141

'Z hudební minulosti zámku Hradce u Opavy: příspěvek k hudebním dějinám Slezska' [From the music history of Hradec Castle in Opava: a contribution to the music history of Silesia], *Časopis Slezského muzea*, xxii (1973), 1

'Die Stellung der tschechischen Musik in der Musik Europas und in der Weltmusik', *Convivium musicorum: Festschrift Wolfgang Boetticher* (Berlin, 1974), 254

BIBLIOGRAPHY

T. Straková: 'Soupis prací Jana Racka' [A list of Racek's works], *Sborník prací filosofické fakulty brněnské university*, F9 (1965), 417–519

J. Vysloužil: 'Helfertův nástupce' [Helfert's successor], *HRo*, xviii (1965), 421   JIŘÍ VYSLOUŽIL

Race record. A term used from about 1920 to 1950 (when it gave way to RHYTHM AND BLUES) for a 'single' gramophone record by American black performers, produced specifically for a black audience. Some include non-musical material; most contain GOSPEL MUSIC or BLUES.

Rachelis, Ordo (Lat.: 'Ceremony of Rachel'). The name given in one medieval source (*D-Mbs* lat.6264, 11th–12th century, from Freising) and generally adopted by modern scholars to denote the medieval liturgical play of the slaughter of the Holy Innocents by Herod. The title derives from the central event of the play – a series of laments by Rachel, the archetypal Jewish mother (*Jeremiah* xxxi.15 and *Matthew* ii.16–18).

See also MEDIEVAL DRAMA, §II, 2, and §II, 7(iv), and PLANCTUS.
                                                    JOHN STEVENS

Rachmaninov [Rachmaninoff], Sergey. *See* RAKHMANINOV, SERGEY.

Racholdinger, Elias (*fl* 1623–7). German composer. He probably worked in south Germany, for his only surviving compositions are two motets contained in the second and third parts respectively of Johann Donfrid's *Promptuarii musici* (Strasbourg, 1623–7; *RISM* 1623², 1627²). These compilations contain mostly Italian music, and those German composers who contributed were noteworthy for their complete assimilation of the now popular Italian small-scale concertato idiom. This is clearly seen in Racholdinger's *Ascendens Christus* (1623), scored for the typical trio texture SSB: strongly accented rhythms contrast with a fair amount of melismatic writing in 4/4 time, and there is a jolly central 'Alleluia' section in 3/4.
                                                    JEROME ROCHE

Racine, Jean (*b* La Ferté-Milon, Aisne, 21 Dec 1639; *d* Paris, 21 April 1699). French poet and dramatist. Orphaned at the age of four, he was brought up by his grandmother and an aunt, both of whom had pronounced Jansenist leanings. He was educated at the Collège de Beauvais, at Port-Royal and at the Collège d'Harcourt. Against the wishes of his severe family he wrote poems and plays and became a friend of Molière, La Fontaine and Boileau. Some of his first works celebrated royal occasions, e.g. *La nymphe de la Seine* for Louis XIV's marriage in 1660 and *Sur la convalescence du roi* (1662). He launched his theatrical career with *La Thébaïde* (1664) and scored his first success with

Andromaque (1667). Despite cabals and challenges he maintained his prominent position, composing one dramatic masterpiece after another, until 1677, when, after *Phèdre*, he retired from the theatre and became historiographer royal. He was elected to the Académie Française in 1673. After his introduction to court in 1662 he always found favour there, protected by the king, by Henriette d'Orléans and especially by Mme de Montespan, at whose request he agreed to compose an opera about 1674. A quarrel had separated Quinault and Lully. The latter needed a new libretto, and Racine, aided by Boileau, began work on *La chute de Phaëton*, but because Louis XIV forced Lully to resume working with Quinault it was never finished. During 1677 Racine and Boileau seem to have been working on a theme proposed by Louis XIV. No work by them appears to have been performed in that year, but Racine's *Iphigénie* was played with musical interludes at St Germain on 16 January 1680; and to please the king during the carnival of 1683 Racine and Boileau wrote 'un petit opéra qu'ils ont fait en trois jours'. Two years later Racine wrote the divertissement *L'Idylle de la paix*, which was set to music by Lully and sung at a grandiose reception given by Colbert's eldest son for the king on 16 July 1685.

Although it appears that Racine disapproved of the themes of Quinault's operas, he nevertheless had the opportunity to criticize them in advance from 1683, when he became a member of the Académie Royale des Inscriptions, which 'réglait les actes, distribuait des scènes, plaçait les divertissements' of Quinault's *tragédies lyriques*. His own tragedies contain significant lyrical elements. His considerable knowledge of Greek had given him close acquaintance with the powerful effects of Greek drama, which he tried to recreate in his two tragedies *Esther* (1689) and *Athalie* (1691), both written for Mme de Maintenon and performed before the court by the pupils of the Maison Royale St Louis at St Cyr; Moreau composed the music for both. Racine envisaged *Esther* as 'une espèce de poème où le chant fût mêlé avec le récit' and in *Athalie* he again mingled song and action 'comme chez les grecs'. He also wrote a number of spiritual canticles for St Cyr, and they were frequently performed there in settings by Marchand, Moreau, Lalande and Collasse which were published in 1695.

BIBLIOGRAPHY

J. Orcibal: 'Racine et Boileau librettistes', *Revue d'histoire littéraire de la France*, xlix (1949), 246

J. Vanuxem: 'Sur Racine et Boileau librettistes', *Revue d'histoire littéraire de la France*, li (1951), 78

R. Picard: *La carrière de Racine* (Paris, 1956)

L. Boulay: 'Cantiques spirituels de Racine mis en musique au XVIIe siècle', *Bulletin de la Société d'études du XVIIe siècle*, xxxiv (1957), 79

M. Bert: 'La musique à la Maison Royale Saint Louis de Saint-Cyr', *RMFC*, iii (1963), 55; v (1965), 91–127
                                    MARGARET M. McGOWAN

Račiūnas, Antanas (*b* Užliaušiai, 4 Sept 1906). Lithuanian composer. He graduated from Gruodis's composition class at the Kaunas Conservatory (1933) and continued his studies in Paris with Boulanger, Koechlin and Stravinsky (1936–9). He taught at the Kaunas Conservatory from 1939 and at the Lithuanian Conservatory of Music, Vilnius from 1949 (professor in 1958). In 1953 he was made an Honoured Worker of the Arts and in 1965 People's Artist of the Lithuanian SSR. He has composed four operas (*Trys talismanai*, 1934; *Gintaro krantas*, 1940; *Marytė*, 1953; *Saulės miestas*, compositions, including the large-scale works, he makes use of traditional folk elements such as the *sutartinės*.

Racket [rackett] (Fr. *cervelas*; Ger. *Rackett*, *Rankett*). An ingeniously compact double-reed woodwind instrument of the Renaissance and Baroque periods. The Renaissance type, though never in widespread use, appeared sporadically in central Europe from about the middle of the 16th century to the middle of the 17th. Within its squat cylindrical body (see fig.1), nine parallel bores drilled lengthwise (consisting of eight ranged concentrically around one) connect at alternate ends to form a continuous undulating tube as shown in fig.2; into the central bore is inserted a short staple bearing a bassoon-type reed, surrounded by a large ornamental pirouette of a kind peculiar to the instrument. The double reed causes the cylindrical bore to function as a stopped pipe whose fundamental sounds an octave below that of an open pipe; thus the racket, in spite of its modest size, was rivalled only by the organ in the depth of its compass.

The nomenclature of the instrument is involved. An alternative though less used name is 'rankett', a word also applied to an ORGAN STOP. This register on the organ, first noted as *Rancket* in 1564, bore a confusing resemblance in both tone and construction to the racket. Sachs derived both names from the Middle High German *ranc*, meaning 'to and fro', 'crooked'. However, Seidl argued that although after 1800 the two terms became synonymous, before that they were well differentiated in meaning; he derived *Rackett* from the Italian 'rochetta', a rock, distaff or spinning bobbin. Early forms of the word found in inventories include *ragget*, *rogetten*, *Raketpfeiffen* and *Racquetten* (which suggests 'rocket' to Baines). The French name *cervelat* (later *cervelas*), first used by Mersenne, appears to be derived either from *cervelet*, meaning 'cerebellum' or little brain, or from *cervellato*, an earlier Italian word for a small sausage: whence the German *Wurstfagott*, anglicized as 'sausage bassoon'. Other early names, *cortalli* and *cortaldi*, derive (like *courtaut* and *Kortholt*) from the Latin 'curtus', 'short'. Later German names include *Stockfagott* and *Faustfagott*.

The oldest extant account of the instrument is that given by Praetorius in 1619. He described and illustrated four sizes of *Racketten* and defined a consort as consisting of seven instruments, each with a range of a 12th: two *Diskant*, *c*12 cm (*G–d'*); three *Tenor-Alt*, *c*25 cm (*C–g*); one *Bass*, *c*18 cm (*F'–c*); and one *Gross Bass*, *c*35 cm (*D'–A* or *C'–G*). Three instruments of the type described by Praetorius, which may be termed the Renaissance or pirouette racket to distinguish it from the later type, have survived, two now in Vienna and one in Leipzig. They are all made of ivory rather than the less durable wood and appear to originate from the same workshop (the catalogues of Mahillon and Schlosser give details of their construction). Those in Vienna are a matching pair of descant rackets (fig.3), already listed in 1596 in the Ambras Collection (there are facsimiles in Brussels, New York and Biebrich). The configuration of the bore in each of these instruments is the mirror-image of that in the other. The body of each is 120 mm high and 48 mm in diameter; the nine ducts, each 6 mm wide, are plugged to form a bore totalling a little over a metre long. At intervals along this inner bore 17 holes are drilled at various angles, meeting up to form 11 external orifices which are stopped by the fingers and also three

1. Renaissance racket (with part of a curved cornett): detail of an ivory carving (1618–24) by Christof Angermair in the Bayerisches Nationalmuseum, Munich

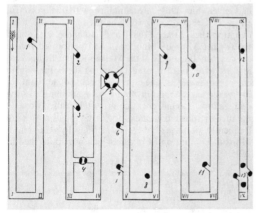

2. Central bore of a racket: diagram from V. C. Mahillon's 'Catalogue descriptif et analytique du Musée instrumental du Conservatoire royal de musique de Bruxelles', iv (1912)

1965), seven symphonies (1933, 1945, 1950, 1960, 1961, 1966, 1969), three symphonic poems (*Vakaras prie Vilijos*, 1937; *Ramunė ir Jurginas*, 1952; *Platelių ežero paslaptis*, 1958), and an orchestral suite (*Gimtinės laukuose*, 1955). His choral works include two cantatas (1945, 1947) and an oratorio (*Tarybų Lietuva*, 1948). He has also written chamber music and piano sonatas. His original solo and chorus songs and folksong arrangements were published in two collections: *Dainuojam* (1935) and *Oi tu, sakale* (1957). Račiūnas's music is rather conservative in harmony and form; in many of his that vent the lowest note. There is also a water hole connecting through the bottom of the first duct. The positioning of the finger-holes enables the player to hold his hands at the same level on either side of the instrument, and to use the middle joints (phalanges) as well as the tips of his fingers where necessary. Each end of these instruments is covered by an ivory plate; through the centre of the upper plate is inserted a tapered metal staple on which the reed is fixed, surrounded by an ornamentally perforated, sleeve-like pirouette with an elliptical slit on top through which the reed-tip protrudes. The third surviving Renaissance racket, in Leipzig (see fig.4), corresponds to Praetorius's *Bass Rackett*. The pirouette of this instrument has a thin, flaring rim 51 mm wide like an eggcup; 20 holes in the bore are arranged to produce 12 finger-holes and four vent holes. Kinsky ascribed this instrument to the same unknown maker of the Viennese pair; its base plate (now missing, but illustrated in de Wit) bore the name and crest of Carl Schurf, a court official of Ferdinand of the Tyrol, active at Ambras in 1596. A replica of the instrument is in Brussels.

The pirouette of the Renaissance racket represents a further stage of development from the wind-cap of the crumhorn (where the reed was entirely outside the player's direct control) and from the pirouette of the

shawm (against which the player pressed his lips, allowing the reed to vibrate freely inside his mouth). With the racket, the player's lips control the reed blades but are supported and helped very effectively by the pirouette to produce and maintain the loose embouchure demanded by the low tessitura; this device also adds, surprisingly, a considerable degree of resonance to the tone. No original reeds survive; Seidl recommended one modelled on a surviving Vienna crumhorn reed: medium arch, rather soft without spine, with a blade about 30 mm long and about 18 mm wide at the tip.

A suggestion of an additional, different technique of blowing can be found in Praetorius. He indicated that although the number of notes would usually correspond to the number of holes, an expert could produce more notes with a good reed, but that 'falsetto' playing was seldom used. This suggests that by using a harder reed and forgoing the support offered by the pirouette in order to control the reed entirely with the lips, an expert player could extend the range upwards by overblowing; it is known that this more modern technique was already coming into use about this time on the shawm. An ivory carving by Christof Angermair in Munich (Bayerisches Nationalmuseum; see fig.1 above), datable 1618–24, shows the instrument apparently being played in this fashion. It is perhaps significant too that Mersenne in

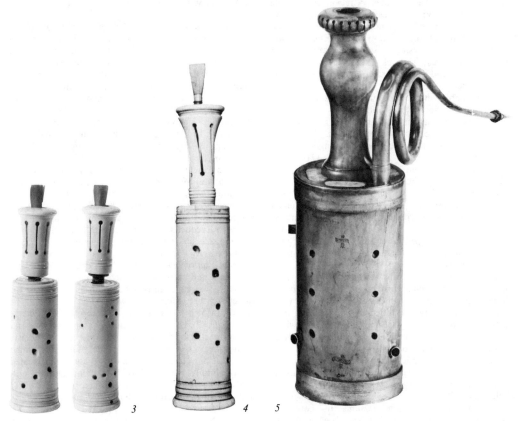

3. *Pair of Renaissance descant rackets (before 1596) from the Ambras Collection (Kunsthistorisches Museum, Vienna)*

4. *Renaissance bass racket, ?c1580 (Musikinstrumenten-Museum, Karl-Marx-Universität, Leipzig)*

5. *Baroque racket by W. Wyne, Nijmegen, c1700 (Staatliches Institut für Musikforschung, Berlin)*

1636–7 showed the racket, which he called the 'cervelat harmonique', without any pirouette at all. Using this technique Seidl claimed to obtain almost an extra octave.

The racket never had a wide distribution; the only other iconographic source of one being played is an illuminated codex (datable 1565–70) by Hans Mielich in Munich (*D-Mbs*; *see* LASSUS, fig.4). References in inventories in Germany, Austria, Bohemia and Italy start to appear in the last quarter of the 16th century, but there is evidence that by about 1630 the instrument had already started to fall out of use, like its other cylindrical relations the kortholt and sordun. Praetorius described the racket's tone as 'quiet, almost like blowing through a comb. The effect of an entire consort lacked grace, but when a gamba was added, or one was used alone with other wind and strings and played by an expert, it was an attractive instrument, especially effective in the bass'. Although its depth of compass exceeded that of the deepest shawms and dulcians, it lacked their tonal strength and expression and became obsolete by the mid-17th century.

A modified version of the instrument, called the Baroque racket or racket-bassoon, has survived in greater numbers. In 1730 Doppelmayr wrote that the elder Denner, Johann Christoph (1655–1707), reproduced in improved form the *Stock-* or *Rackettenfagotte* already known from early times. A racket attributable to Denner, now in Vienna (facsimile in Brussels), shows what the differences of construction were. The wooden body, 190 mm high and 87 mm in diameter, has ten cylindrical bores increasing in size from 10 mm to 23 mm; the narrowest receives a coiled brass crook (missing here) and the widest in the centre a short pepperpot bell made of ivory. The irregularly conical composite bore, with its ten finger-holes taking the range down to *C* and with its ability to overblow at the octave, makes the instrument correspond in range and behaviour to the contemporary dulcian. A Denner racket was among the instruments belonging to the Medici court in Florence (inventory of 1716), and makers in Germany, the Netherlands and France also took up the idea. Specimens survive in the museums of Berlin and Munich (two each; see fig.5), Paris, The Hague and Copenhagen. These substitute a pear-shaped or shortened bassoon-type bell for Denner's perforated capsule; sometimes projecting bushes or 'teats' are added to those holes stopped with the phalanges. Some instruments are covered in leather and have two or three keys. The latest, by Bizey of Paris and Tölcke of Brunswick, are datable to the second half of the 18th century. However, such an instrument, being essentially nothing more than a bassoon in racket form, was never more than a curiosity and failed to survive, even as a mention in contemporary reference works. Hawkins reported that one of the Stanesbys made a *cervelat* according to the dimensions given by Mersenne, 'but it did not answer expectation: by reason of its closeness the interior parts imbibed and retained the moisture of the breath, the ducts dilated, and broke. In short the whole blew up'.

In recent years modern versions of both the Renaissance and Baroque racket have been available, the former usually fitted with a plastic reed. This instrument in particular, with its deep compass and characteristic throaty tone, has been found useful in performing music of the period.

BIBLIOGRAPHY

HawkinsH

M. Praetorius: *Syntagma musicum*, ii (Wolfenbüttel, 1618, 2/1619/*R*1958)

——: *Theatrum instrumentorum* (Wolfenbüttel, 1620/*R*1958) [appx to above]

M. Mersenne: *Harmonie universelle* (Paris, 1636–7/*R*1963; Eng. trans., 1957)

J. G. Doppelmayr: *Historischer Nachricht von den Nürnbergischen Mathematicis und Künstlern* (Nuremberg, 1730)

P. de Wit: *Katalog des musikhistorischen Museums von P. de Wit* (Leipzig, 1903)

V. C. Mahillon: *Catalogue descriptif et analytique du Musée instrumental du Conservatoire royal de musique de Bruxelles*, ii (Ghent, 2/1909); iv (Ghent, 1912)

E. Mandyczewski: *Geschichte der k.k. Gesellschaft der Musikfreunde* (Vienna, 1912) [suppl.]

J. Schlosser: *Die Sammlung alter Musikinstrumente* (Vienna, 1920/*R*1974)

G. Kinsky: 'Randnoten zum Katalog des neuen Wiener Instrumentalmuseums', *ZMw*, iv (1921–2), 162

C. Sachs: *Sammlung alter Musikinstrumente bei der Staatlichen Hochschule für Musik zu Berlin* (Berlin, 1922)

G. Kinsky: 'Doppelrohrblatt-Instrumente mit Windkapsel', *AMw*, vii (1925), 253

A. Buchner: *Zaniklé dřevěné dechové nástroje 16. století* [Obsolete woodwind instruments of the 16th century] (Prague, 1952)

L. G. Langwill: 'Rackett', *Grove 5*

H. Seidl: *Das Rackett* (diss., U. of Leipzig, 1959)

A. Berner: 'Rackett', *MGG*

A. Baines: *European and American Musical Instruments* (London, 1966)

V. Gai: *Saggi di organologia musicale* (Florence, 1970)

WILLIAM WATERHOUSE

Rackstraw, William. *See* ROCKSTRO, WILLIAM.

Racquet, Charles (*b* Paris, 1597; *d* Paris, 1 Jan 1664). French organist and composer. He was the most important member of a family of organists who flourished in Paris during the 17th century. Early in his career he returned from a journey abroad (his will mentions Germany) laden with honours – seven medallions and a silver crown. His early appointment as organist of Notre Dame in 1618, a post he held until shortly before his death, also shows him to have been highly regarded in Paris. Like his father, Balthazar, he enjoyed royal patronage as *Organiste de la musique ordinaire* to Marie de Médicis. He was also much admired by fellow musicians: Denis Gaultier honoured his memory with a *tombeau*; and Mersenne considered him 'one of the best contrapuntists of this age'. In his *Essai sur la musique ancienne et moderne* (Paris, 1780/*R*1972) J.-B. de La Borde called him 'the best organist of his time'.

It is to Racquet's acquaintance with Mersenne that we owe the sole surviving examples of his work: *12 versets de psaume en duo* (music examples in M. Mersenne: *Harmonie universelle*, Paris, 1636–7, chap. 'De la composition') and a piece – called *Fantaisie* in modern editions – written in response to Mersenne's request for something that would 'show what could be done at the organ' (MS in Mersenne's own copy of *Harmonie universelle*: Paris, Bibliothèque du Conservatoire des Arts et Métiers; edns. of all these pieces, L'Organiste Liturgique, xxix–xxx, Paris, 1961). The last-named piece is on a large scale: a single theme is treated contrapuntally over some 100 bars, culminating in brilliant passage-work over dominant and tonic pedals. It well confirms the verdict of the age on its composer.

BIBLIOGRAPHY

A. Tessier: 'Une pièce d'orgue de Ch. Racquet', *RdM*, x (1929), 275

P. Hardouin: 'Notes biographiques sur des organistes parisiens du XVIIe siècle, les Racquet', *RMFC*, iv (1964), 41

EDWARD HIGGINBOTTOM

Radcliffe, Philip (FitzHugh) (*b* Godalming, 27 April

1905). English writer on music and composer. He was a scholar at Charterhouse School (1918–24) and studied under Moule and Dent at King's College, Cambridge, from 1924 to 1929 (BA 1928, MusB 1929). He was a Fellow of King's College from 1931 to 1937 and again from 1948, and was a university lecturer in music from 1947 to 1972. He has contributed music criticism to the *Criterion* (1933–9) and to other periodicals.

As a composer Radcliffe has written mainly vocal music; his works include an anthem for male voices and organ, *I will Lift up mine Eyes* (1931), some partsongs, and many songs for voice and piano. His instrumental compositions include a string quartet (1939) and incidental music for Aristophanes' *The Clouds* (1962), Euripides' *Medea* (1974) and Sophocles' *Oedipus tyrannus* (1965) and *Electra* (1977). Radcliffe's songs (he has written over 100) are perhaps his finest compositions, and of those published *Meg Merrilies* and *Tears, Idle Tears* (both London, 1946) are the best-known. His published work on the music of 18th- and 19th-century composers shows a lucid style and unusual historical breadth. His compact study of Mendelssohn in the Master Musicians series is his best-known work; he has also written sympathetically on John Ireland. In addition he has influenced English musical life through his work as a friend and teacher to several generations of students at Cambridge.

WRITINGS

'The Relationship of Rhythm and Tonality in the Sixteenth Century', *PMA*, lvii (1930–31), 73

'The Scarlattis: Alessandro, 1659–1725, Domenico, 1685–1757', *The Heritage of Music*, ed. H. J. Foss, ii (London, 1934), 20

'Arcangelo Corelli, 1653–1713 and Antonio Vivaldi, 1675/8–1741', ibid, iii (London, 1951), 33

'The Piano Sonatas of Joseph Haydn', *MR*, vii (1946), 139, 280

Mendelssohn (London, 1954, 2/1967)

John Ireland (London, 1954)

'Brahms'; 'Song: 1700–1900', *Grove 5*

Beethoven's String Quartets (London, 1965, 2/1978)

Schubert Piano Sonatas (London, 1967)

'Keyboard Music', *NOHM*, vii (1973), 574–610

E. J. Dent: a Centenary Memoir (Rickmansworth, 1976)

Mozart Piano Concertos (London, 1978)

DAVID SCOTT

Radeck, Johann Martin (*b* ?Mühlhausen, ?1623; *d* ?Copenhagen, 1684). Danish organist and composer of German origin, son of Johann Rudolf Radeck. He became organist of Trinitatis Kirke, Copenhagen, in 1660 and, after his father's death in 1662, of Helligaandskirke there as well. In 1670 he married the sister of Poul Christian Schindler who after his death married his successor Christian Geist. A little manuscript music by him has survived, including a cantata, *Herr, wenn ich nur dich habe* (in *S-Uu*), a set of variations for organ on the chorale *Jesus Christus unser Heiland* (in *D-B*; ed. B. Lundgren, Copenhagen, 1957) and a keyboard suite in German organ tablature (in *S-L*).

BIBLIOGRAPHY

A. Pirro: *Dietrich Buxtehude* (Paris, 1913)

B. Lundgren: 'Helligånds-organisten Christen Geist', *Dansk Kirkesangs Årsskrift 1958–9*, 10

JOHN BERGSAGEL

Radeck, Johann Rudolf (*b* Mühlhausen; *d* Copenhagen, 1662). Danish organist and composer of German origin, father of Johann Martin Radeck. He was Kantor of St Blasien, Mühlhausen, from 1633 to 1635, and of St Marien, Flensburg, from 1635 to 1645. He may have visited Copenhagen in 1638 and 1639, at which time some of his compositions were copied there (see

The Clausholm Fragments, ed. H. Glahn and S. Sørensen, Copenhagen, 1974, pp.40, 42ff). From 1645 until his death he was organist of the Helligaandskirke, Copenhagen. Two keyboard pieces, bearing his initials and added in manuscript to a copy (in *DK-Kk*) of Voigtländer's *Oden unnd Lieden* (Sorø, 1642), are probably by him.

BIBLIOGRAPHY

H. P. Detlefsen: *Musikgeschichte der Stadt Flensburg bis zum Jahre 1850* (Kassel, 1959)

JOHN BERGSAGEL

Radesca di Foggia, Enrico (*b* Foggia, 2nd half of the 16th century; *d* Turin, early 1625). Italian composer and organist. As a young man he served with the Venetian army in Dalmatia. He later turned to a musical career and was appointed organist of Turin Cathedral about 1597. He held this post until about 1615, when he was promoted to the position of choirmaster. By 1605 he was also working as a chamber musician in the service of Don Amadeo, son of the Duke of Savoy. On 20 June 1610 he joined the musicians at the ducal court and by 1615 had become choirmaster of the court chapel. He was naturalized on 14 March 1619, although he had styled himself 'citizen of Turin' as early as 1607.

Radesca seems to have been a popular and admired composer: several of his publications were reprinted, and Banchieri paid him the compliment of including an aria 'in imitation of Radesca' in the second edition of his *La barca di Venetia per Padova* (1623). He was among the earliest composers of sacred music for small vocal ensemble and continuo. His response to Florentine secular monody was, however, more equivocal. He published no real monodies until 1610, preferring instead to issue music for two voices in which the lower voice also served as an unfigured *basso seguente*. This type of duet, which enjoyed some popularity in the early 17th century, appears to have evolved as a reduction to the two outer voices of a three- or four-voice canzonetta texture. The lively and very attractive style that Radesca cultivated in his duet settings of both madrigalian and strophic texts is clearly descended from the 16th-century canzonetta: the music is largely homophonic and diatonic but contains points of imitation 'lightly touched' (to use a phrase of Thomas Morley's) and occasional chromaticism. In an interesting preface to Radesca's 1617 book (not the 1605 book as Schmitz stated) Ludovico Caligari, who had commissioned the work, stated that he had asked the composer to omit complicated passage-work, which could in any case be added by skilled singers. He also mentioned that the three-part pieces could be performed as solos for soprano or tenor or as duets for soprano and bass: the book, which consists entirely of settings of spiritual texts, was thus clearly intended for the widest possible use.

WORKS

SACRED

Messe, libro primo, 4vv, bc (Milan, 1604)

Armoniosa corona: concerti, il primo libro de motetti, salmi, et falsi bordoni, 2vv, bc (Milan, 1607?)

Motets in G. B. Stefanini: Motetti, libro primo, 2, 3vv (Milan, 1606) (see Roncaglia, 295)

Messa con motetti, 8vv, bc; lost, cited in *Indice*

Compieta, 8vv; lost, cited in *Indice*

SECULAR

Thesoro amoroso: primo libro delle canzonette, 3, 4vv (Milan, 1599)

Canzonette, madrigali, & arie alla romana, per cantare & sonare, libro primo, 2vv, chit/spinet (Milan, 1605)

Il secondo libro delle canzonette madrigali, et arie alla romana, per cantare, & sonare . . . con 2 corrente nel fine per ballare, 2vv, chit/spinet (Milan, 1606)

Il terzo libro delle canzonette madrigali, et arie alla romana, per cantare, & sonare, 2vv, spinet, chit, other insts (Venice, 2/1616) [1st edn. lost]

Il quarto libro delle canzonette madrigali, et arie alla romana, per cantare, & sonare, 2–4vv (Venice, 1610)

Madrigali & partito da sonare per chi piacerà, libro primo, 5, 8vv, bc (Venice, 1615)

Il quinto libro delle canzonette, madrigali et arie, per cantare, & sonare . . . op.9, 1–3vv (Venice, 1617)

BIBLIOGRAPHY

Indice di tutte le opere di musica che si trovano nella Stampa della Pigna di Alessandro Vincenti in Venetia (Venice, 1619); repr. in MMg, xiv (1882/R), suppl.

E. Schmitz: Geschichte der weltlichen Solokantate (Leipzig, 1914, rev. 2/1955), 15, 17, 23, 41, 63, 65

S. Cordero di Pamparato: 'I musici alla corte di Carlo Emanuele I di Savoia', Biblioteca della Società storica subalpina, cxxi (Turin, 1930), 80

F. Mompellio: Sigismondo d'India, musicista palermitano (Milan, 1956), 32

G. Roncaglia: La cappella musicale del duomo di Modena (Florence, 1957), 88f, 94, 295

J. Racek: Stilprobleme der italienischen Monodie (Prague, 1965), 15f, 99, 107, 137, 223, 286

O. Mischiati: Adriano Banchieri (1568–1634): profilo biografico e bibliografia delle opere (Bologna, 1971), 98

JOHN WHENHAM

Radić, Dušan (b Sombor, 10 April 1929). Yugoslav composer. He graduated from the Belgrade Academy of Music as a composition pupil of Živković and then spent a short time in Paris, studying with Milhaud and Messiaen. In 1971 he was elected to corresponding membership of the Serbian Academy. After a short period of drawing on Serbian folk music, he has developed an individual style in which the vocal writing and instrumentation are particularly original. He has set poetry by Popa in Spisak ('The list', performed in its revised version at the 1956 ISCM Festival), Uspravna zemlja ('The upright country'), which evokes the ancient beauty of Serbian monasteries, and Ćelekula ('The skull tower'), a cantata concerning the struggle of the Serbs against the Turks in the 19th century. Of his instrumental works, the Divertimento is a neo-classical piece, freshly and wittily orchestrated.

WORKS
(selective list)

Stage: Balada o mesecu lutalici [Ballad of the roaming moon], ballet, 1957; Ljubav, to je glavna stvar [Love, this is the main thing] (musical comedy-ballet, after Molière: M de Pourceaugnac), 1962

Vocal: Spisak [The list] (Popa), n.d., rev. 2 female vv, chamber orch, perf. 1956; Uspravna zemlja [The upright country] (cantata, Popa), 1955; Opsednuta vedrina [The obsessed brightness] (Popa), female chorus, 2 pf, 1956; Ćelekula [The skull tower] (cantata, Popa), solo vv, chorus, orch, 1957; Metamorfoze nastajanja [Metamorphoses of origination], solo vv, chorus, orch, 1971; Vukova Srbija [Vuk's Serbia], cantata, 1971; other choruses, song cycles

Orch: Varijacije na narodnu temu [Variations on a folk theme], 1952; Sinfonietta, 1953; 2 simfonijske slike [2 sym. images], 1953; Cl Concertino, 1956; Divertimento, vib, perc, str, 1961; Sym., 1968; Iz moje domovine [From my country], 6 choreographic poems, 1970

Film scores, pf and vn pieces

Principal publishers: Prosveta, Udruženje Kompozitora Srbije

STANA ĐURIĆ-KLAJN

Radica, Ruben (b Split, 19 May 1931). Yugoslav composer. He studied composition with Kelemen and conducting at the Zagreb Academy of Music, and then continued his training at the Accademia Chigiana, Siena, and in Paris with Leibowitz. In 1959 he was appointed assistant professor at Sarajevo, and in 1963 professor at the Zagreb Academy. After a period of concern with 12-note serialism and isolated-note technique, Radica

came to give more importance to melody. His output is not large, but each work shows an individual approach. Interferencije 19 i 10, for instance, employs the ravings of mental patients, while Extensio is based on modified elements of play.

WORKS
(selective list)

Conc. abbreviato, vc, orch, 1960; Lirske varijacije, str, 1961; Koreografska muzika, orch, 1962; Paean, perc, wind, str qt, 1963; Formacije, orch, 1963; Interferencije 19 i 10, chorus, orch, 1965; Sustanje [Exhaustion], org, orch, 1967; Kompozicija, ondes martenot, chamber orch, 1968; Ranjeni dlan [The wounded palm], opera, 1971; Extensio, pf, orch, 1973

Principal publisher: Društvo Hrvatskih Skladatelja

BIBLIOGRAPHY

E. Krpan: 'Ruben Radica ili borba protiv rasapa' [Radica or struggle against defeat], Novi zvuk (Zagreb, 1972), 254

KREŠIMIR KOVAČEVIĆ

Radical bass. A term used as the equivalent of BASSE FONDAMENTALE, which was used by Rameau (1722) to denote the imaginary bass line produced by linking together the roots of chords in a progression. The term 'fundamental bass' is also used in this sense. See also HARMONY, §2 (ii).

Radical cadence. A CADENCE whose penultimate and final chords are both in root position, as opposed to a 'medial' or 'inverted' cadence, whose penultimate chord is in inversion.

Radicati, Felice Alessandro (b Turin, 1775; d Bologna, 19 March 1820). Italian violinist and composer. The son of an impoverished nobleman, he studied with Pugnani and played the violin in the Turin cappella until it disbanded in 1798. He married Teresa Bertinotti, an operatic soprano, in 1801. The Radicatis travelled for a few years, then spent the years 1805–8 in Germany and Austria, where Felice played and composed chamber music. He was welcomed in Viennese social and artistic circles that included such figures as Haydn, Ferdinand Fränzl, Ludwig Esterházy and Count Moritz von Fries, to each of whom Radicati dedicated one of his works. In 1809 his opera Coriolano was produced in Amsterdam. From 1810 to 1812 the Radicatis were in England, where Felice's next opera, Fedra, was performed at the King's Theatre (5 March 1811). For the next two years they lived in Lisbon, where Teresa sang at the Teatro S Carlo and Felice frequently performed at weekly subscription concerts held in their home. They returned to Italy, and Felice rejoined the Turin cappella on its restitution in 1814; the following year he was appointed leader and director of the Bologna orchestra, maestro di cappella at S Petronio, and violin professor at the conservatory. The Radicatis were in Paris in 1817 and 1818 where Felice learnt a new system of musical instruction, 'mutuel enseignement', from his Turin friend Federico Massimino; he taught by this method in Bologna in 1818–19 and published the Applicazione del mutuo insegnamento alla musica in Bologna in 1819. At the peak of his career as a performer, composer and teacher, he was killed when thrown from a carriage.

Radicati was an accomplished violinist, though not a virtuoso in technique or temperament. As a composer, he was a true disciple of Pugnani in his violin duos; his chamber music is not distinguished, except (according to Moser) for the Grande sonate op.10 for violin and viola and his String Quintet op.17. His enthusiasm for the works of Boccherini, together with his own output of string quartets, earned him the epithet 'Restorer of the Italian quartet'.

WORKS

(all printed works published in Vienna unless otherwise stated)

OPERAS

Il sultano generoso, c1805, unperf.
Coriolano, Amsterdam, 1809
Fedra, London, 5 March 1811
L'intrigo fortunato, 1815
Castore e Polluce (2, L. Romanelli), Bologna, Teatro del Corso, 27 May 1815
Blondello ossia Riccardo Cuor di Leone, Turin, Teatro Carignano, aut. 1816
La lezione singolare ossia Un giorno a Parigi, c1819, unperf.
I due prigionieri, c1820, unperf.
Il medico per forza, c1820, unperf.

OTHER WORKS

Orch: Cl Conc., 1816; Vn Conc., 1819; Sym., n.d.: *I-Bc*
Chamber: 3 qnts, 2 vn, 2 va, vc: op.17 (Mainz), op.21, op.22 (London); 9 str qts, op.8, op.11, 3 as op.14, op.15, 3 as op.16; 5 str trios, 3 as op.7, op.13, op.20; duos and variation sets, 2 vn, opp.1–4, 9, 19; Grande sonate, D, vn, va, op.10

BIBLIOGRAPHY

FétisB; *SchmidlD*
C. Pancaldi: *Cenni intorno Felice Radicati* (Bologna, 1828)
A. Moser: *Geschichte des Violinspiels* (Berlin, 1923, rev., enlarged 2/1966–7)

ALBERT MELL

Radicati, Teresa. *See* BERTINOTTI, TERESA.

Radiciotti, Giuseppe (*b* Iesi, 25 Jan 1858; *d* Tivoli, 6 April 1931). Italian composer and musicologist. He studied music with Faini, his uncle, and then with Baffo and Puccinelli (harmony and counterpoint) at Rome, where he also took an arts degree at the university. In 1881 he taught history at the Ginnasio-Liceo, Tivoli, of which he later became director. He was an active composer (school songs, works for band, church music), but his main work was in musicology, where he implemented a historico-critical approach which was still new in Italy at that time. Much of his research was on the music of the Marche region which he scrupulously documented. He also wrote the first serious monograph on Pergolesi (1910). His most important work was the three-volume *Gioacchino Rossini: vita documentata, opere ed influenza sull'arte* (Tivoli, 1927–9), which, in addition to providing an impressive biography, tried to establish Rossini's originality in musical forms, harmonic language and instrumentation. When difficulties arose in publishing the work Radiciotti offered it to the Istituto Rossiniano, renouncing any commission and promising to cover printing expenses not reimbursed by sales. At his death he was preparing a similarly thorough work on Spontini.

WRITINGS

Il sistema wagneriano (Rome, n.d.)
Teatro, musica e musicisti in Senigallia (Milan, 1893/R1973)
Lettere inedite di celebri musicisti annotate e precedute dalle biografie di Pietro, Giovanni e Rosa Morandi a cui sono dirette (Milan, 1897)
Contributi alla storia del teatro e della musica in Urbino (Pesaro, 1899)
Teatro, musica e musicisti in Recanati (Recanati, 1904)
Il genio musicale dei marchigiani e un giudizio del Prof. Lombroso (Macerata, 1905)
Teatro e musica in Roma nel secondo quarto del secolo XIX (Rome, 1905)
La musica in Pesaro (Pesaro, 1907)
L'arte musicale in Tivoli nei secoli XVI–XVIII (Tivoli, 1907, rev. 2/1921)
I musicisti marchigiani dei secoli XVI–XIX (Rome, 1909)
G. B. Pergolesi (Rome, 1910, 2/1935; Ger. trans.)
'Due musicisti spagnoli del secolo XVI in relazione con la corte di Urbino', *Al maestro Pedrell: escritos heortásticos* (Tortosa, 1911), 225
La cappella musicale del Duomo di Pesaro (Turin, 1914)

Gioacchino Rossini: vita documentata, opere ed influenza sull'arte (Tivoli, 1927 9, 2/1941)

BIBLIOGRAPHY

L. Parigi: 'La musica e il libro: Radiciotti', *Critica musicale*, i (1918), 223
V. Scotti: 'Giuseppe Radiciotti', *Bollettino bibliografico musicale*, vi/5 (1931), 5
A. Belardinelli: *Giuseppe Radiciotti* (Iesi, 1933)

CAROLYN M. GIANTURCO

Radino, Giovanni Maria (*b* mid-16th century; *d* after 1607). Italian composer and organist. From the dedication he wrote for his son Giulio's posthumous *Concerti per sonare et cantare* (1607) we learn that he spent his early life in Carinthia in the service of the family of the Count of Frankenberg. In 1579, according to Tebaldini, he applied unsuccessfully for the post of organist at the Cappella Antoniana, Padua. The title-page of his *Il primo libro d'intavolatura di balli d'arpicordo* (1592) described him as organist of S Giovanni in Verdare, Padua, a post he still held in 1598, when his anthology *Madrigali de diversi* was published.

Radino's most important music is contained in *Il primo libro d'intavolatura d'arpicordo*, the first Italian collection of dances for which the harpsichord is specified. A version for lute, *Intavolatura di balli per sonar al liuto*, appeared in the same year. Each contains a passamezzo paired with a galliard, two paduanas and four separate galliards. The two versions differ, however, not only in details of texture and layout but also occasionally in structure: for example, in the lute version of the passamezzo there is an additional variation, and the order of its sections is changed. Radino's keyboard writing consists mainly of a single-line melodic part in the right hand interspersed with some chords, plus a fuller left-hand accompaniment. But whereas his predecessor Marco Facoli used nothing but plain chords for his accompaniments Radino occasionally introduced imitation between the hands and at times gave the left hand the principal part. He thus made a not unimportant contribution to the development of the keyboard dance in Italy.

WORKS

(all published in Venice)

Il primo libro d'intavolatura di balli d'arpicordo (1592); ed. in CEKM, xxxiii (1968); arr. lute in Intavolatura di balli per sonar al liuto (1592); ed. G. Gullino (Florence, 1949)
ed.: Madrigali de diversi, 4vv (1598⁹), inc. [includes dialogue-madrigal, D'Eugenia almi pastori, 8vv, by him]

BIBLIOGRAPHY

M. L. A[rmitt]: 'Radino', *MT*, xxxv (1894), 663
G. Tebaldini: *L'archivio musicale della Cappella Antoniana in Padova* (Padua, 1895), 14
W. Apel: *Geschichte der Orgel- und Klaviermusik bis 1700* (Kassel, 1967; Eng. trans., rev., 1972), 244, 274
S. Ellingworth: Introduction to CEKM, xxxiii (1968)

HOWARD FERGUSON

Radino, Giulio (*d* before 1607). Italian composer, son of Giovanni Maria Radino. In the dedication of his posthumous *Concerti per sonare et cantare* (Venice, 1607), his father wrote that Giulio had been in the service of a son of the Count of Frankenburg (in Carinthia) until death 'thwarted his just hopes in the flower of his youth'. The volume contains 16 pieces by him – 13 vocal works to sacred texts and two canzonas and a ricercare for instruments; it also includes vocal pieces by four other minor composers. His father included one piece by him in his anthology *Madrigali de diversi* for four voices (Venice, 1598), of which no complete copy survives.

BIBLIOGRAPHY
Å. Davidsson: *Catalogue critique et descriptif des imprimés de musique
. . . à la Bibliothèque de l'Université royale d'Upsala*, iii (Uppsala,
1951), 104
HOWARD FERGUSON

Radio. *See* SOUND RECORDING, TRANSMISSION AND
REPRODUCTION; BROADCASTING; BRITISH BROADCAS-
TING CORPORATION.

Radio Telefis Eireann. *See* DUBLIN, §§3–6, 9.

Radleier (Ger.). HURDY-GURDY.

Radnai, Miklós (*b* Budapest, 1 Jan 1892; *d* Budapest, 4
Nov 1935). Hungarian opera administrator and composer. As a child he learnt the piano and violin; at the
Budapest Academy of Music he studied composition
with Koessler and Herzfeld (1906–11). While teaching
theory at the Fodor Conservatory (1912–21) he won
the Franz Josef Scholarship, which enabled him to study
composition with Mottl in Munich (1916) and in
France, Belgium and the Netherlands; subsequently he
taught at the Budapest Academy of Music (1919–25)
and served as music critic of the journals *Szózat* (1919–
23) and *Nemzeti ujság* (1923–5). In 1925 he was appointed director of the Budapest Opera House (the
youngest to hold that post since Mahler), where he
remained until his death, making an outstanding contribution to Hungarian music. The opera, then the only
permanent company in Hungary, had deteriorated during World War I, and he restored its artistic reputation,
building up a fine team of singers, conductors and
producers; he encouraged new Hungarian operas
(including Kodály's) and mounted many Hungarian first
performances, including works by Debussy, Strauss,
Stravinsky, Milhaud, Malipiero and Hindemith. He was
perhaps the greatest and most important director of the
Hungarian Opera House. In his compositions, including
operas, orchestral works, songs, chamber music and
piano pieces, Radnai showed less response to recent
developments; his best-known work is the ballet *Az
infánsnő születésnapja* ('The birthday of the infanta',
after Oscar Wilde, Budapest Opera House, 26 April
1918).

BIBLIOGRAPHY
J. S. Weissmann: 'Radnai, Miklós', *Grove 5* [incl. full list of works]
JOHN S. WEISSMANN

Radolt, Baron Wenzel Ludwig von (*b* Vienna, baptized
18 Dec 1667; *d* Vienna, 10 March 1716). Austrian
amateur lutenist and composer. He was a nobleman of
independent means, from an old Austrian family of
court and public servants, and was also the heir to
possessions in Italy (his grandmother was an Italian
countess); the Radolt family vault, established by his
forebears, is still in the Dominican church in Vienna.
His only publication is *Die aller treueste, verschwigneste
und nach so wohl fröhlichen als traurigen Humor sich
richtende Freindin* (Vienna, 1701; two works in DTÖ, l,
Jg.xxv/2, 1918/*R*); it consists of five partbooks and is
dedicated to the Emperor Joseph I. It begins with an
explanation of the French lute tablature to which are
appended important instructions about the technique of
embellishment, special fingerings and ensemble playing
in small groups. The volume contains eight concertos –
whose movements are either dance forms commonly
found in the suite, or freer forms – as well as pieces in
the *galant* style showing French influence; simphonie,

capriccio, toccata and tombeau (in place of a sarabande)
are among the forms represented. The music is conceived for two concertante lutes with violin (or flute),
gamba and bass, and it calls for various groupings. In
Austrian and Bohemian court circles around 1700
Radolt was, with Weichenberger, the most important
composer of delicately balanced ensemble writing with
the lute prominently featured. Unlike Weichenberger,
however, he is only rarely represented in MSS.

BIBLIOGRAPHY
A. Koczirz: 'Klosterneuburger Lautenbücher', *Musica divina* (1913),
Aug–Sept, 176
——: 'Österreichische Lautenmusik zwischen 1650 und 1720', *SMw*, v
(1918), 54
J. Wolf: *Handbuch der Notationskunde*, ii (Leipzig, 1919), 153
W. Boetticher: *Studien zur solistischen Lautenpraxis des 16. und 17.
Jahrhunderts* (Berlin, 1943), 178, 234ff
R. Flotzinger: *Die Lautentabulaturen des Stiftes Kremsmünster:
thematischer Katalog*, Tabulae musicae austriacae, ii (Vienna, 1965),
36
WOLFGANG BOETTICHER

Radom [Radomski, Radoluski], **Nicolaus de** [Mikołaj].
See NICOLAUS DE RADOM.

Radomski, Jan (*fl* 2nd half of the 17th century). Polish
composer. He was a canon of the collegiate church at
Łowicz from 1665 to 1676. The manuscripts of two
masses by him for four voices with organ continuo,
Missa de Sanctissima Cruce 'Nos autem' and *Missa
Requiem*, survived (in *PL-Wn*) until 1944, but they have
now disappeared. The first of these was dated 1674. A
fragmentary copy of a *Missa pro feriis Quadragessima*,
which is doubtless identical with it, survives (in *PL-Pu*).
It was performed by Chybiński, in whose opinion
Radomski was a competent contrapuntist.

BIBLIOGRAPHY
A. Poliński: *Dzieje muzyki polskiej w zarysie* [A history of Polish music
in outline] (Lwów, 1907), 144
A. Chybiński: *Słownik muzyków dawnej Polski* [Dictionary of early
Polish musicians] (Kraków, 1948–9), 105
H. Feicht: 'Muzyka w okresie polskiego baroku' [Music in the Baroque
period in Poland], *Z dziejów polskiej kultury muzycznej*, i: *Kultura
staropolska* [From the history of Polish musical culture, i: Early
Polish culture], ed. Z. M. Szweykowski (Kraków, 1958), 193, 211,
213, 278
J. Wieteska: *Katalog prałatów i kanoników prymasowskiej kapituły
łowickiej od 1433 do 1970 r.* [Catalogue of prelates and canons of the
Łowicz primatial chapter from 1433 to 1970] (Warsaw, 1971), 74
MIROSŁAW PERZ

Radoux, Jean-Théodore (*b* Liège, 9 Nov 1835; *d* Liège,
20 March 1911). Belgian teacher and composer. He
began his musical training on the bassoon under Bacha,
whom he succeeded as professor at the Liège
Conservatory in 1856. The same year he took a *premier
prix* for piano and started composition studies under
Daussoigne-Méhul. In 1859 he won the Belgian Prix de
Rome, and he later spent four years in Paris under
Halévy. In 1872 he was appointed director of the Liège
Conservatory, succeeding Soubre. Radoux's compositions include five comic operas, several oratorios and
cantatas, symphonic works and songs.

WRITINGS
Daussoigne-Méhul (Brussels, 1882)
Vieuxtemps, sa vie, ses oeuvres (Brussels, 1891)
La musique et les Ecoles nationales (Brussels, 1896)
BIBLIOGRAPHY
S. Dupuis: *Notice sur J.-Th. Radoux* (Brussels, 1925)
WILLIAM WATERHOUSE

Radoux-Rogier, Charles (*b* Liège, 30 July 1877; *d*
Liège, 30 April 1952). Belgian composer, pianist and

critic. He studied at the Liège Conservatory with his father Jean-Théodore Radoux, and in 1907 he won the Belgian Prix de Rome with his cantata *Geneviève de Brabant*. Appointed professor of harmony at the Liège Conservatory in 1905, he was inspector of music education from 1930 to 1942. He founded a piano quartet, and was for a long time active as a music critic. His interest in Walloon folk music resulted in the publication of several collections of songs with his own accompaniments. Hardly original in musical style, he was at his best in the operas and choral works where his lyrical facility was most pleasing.

WORKS
(*selective list*)

Vocal: 6 operatic works, incl. Les Sangliers des Ardennes, 1905, and Oudelette, 1912; Te Deum, 7 cantatas, 13 other choral works, 65 melodies with pf/str qt/orch, folksong arrs.
Inst: Orch pieces incl. Sym., Triptyche, Burlesque, Impromptu, 2 works for chamber orch, concertante pieces with pf, vn (3), vc (3); Lamentatation on a Bach prelude, eng hn, pf; 2 pf pieces

Principal publisher: Schott (Brussels)

HENRI VANHULST

Radulphus Laudunensis. Theorist. He was from the collegiate church (*de abaco*) at Laon, and is known solely by a conventional music treatise, the last part of which consists of a section on semitones. With another treatise on semitones, it survives in a 13th-century manuscript formerly belonging to the famous abbey of St Victor, Paris (now *F-Pn* lat.15120).

See also THEORY, THEORISTS.

GORDON A. ANDERSON

Radziwiłł, Prince Antoni Henryk (*b* nr. Vilnius, 13 June 1775; *d* Berlin, 7 April 1833). Polish cellist, singer, composer and guitarist. He arranged weekly concerts in his mansion in Berlin, and was friendly with Beethoven, Zelter, Mendelssohn, Goethe and others: Beethoven and Mendelssohn dedicated works to him – the former his Overture op.115, the latter his Piano Quartet op.1. In 1815 Radziwiłł became governor of the Grand Duchy of Poznań, which at that time formed part of Prussia, following the partition of Poland in 1795. His house in Poznań became a centre of cultural life; he himself was an amateur performer of chamber music, including Beethoven's quartets. With his wife Friederike Dorothea Luise (sister of Friedrich Wilhelm, King of Prussia) he gave support to the Polish theatre and encouraged Polish education; but he was nevertheless criticized for adhering to Prussian policy and failing to defend the Polish cause. He was an admirer and close friend of Chopin, whom he first knew in May 1825 and later entertained at his summer residence at Antonin, near Poznań; there Chopin wrote for Radziwiłł his Introduction and Polonaise for piano and cello, and also dedicated to him the Trio in G minor.

As a composer, Radziwiłł is known particularly for his music to Goethe's *Faust* which he began to compose before 1810 and completed in 1831. Extracts were performed in Berlin in 1816, and at Monbijou, near Berlin, in 1820; the whole work was given in Berlin on 25 October 1835, and the score was published there in the same year. Although not uniform in style, *Faust* was admired by some of the Romantics (including Chopin and Loewe). He composed songs, among them *Trois romances* (Leipzig, 1802), the duet *Im hohen Schilfe* (Oranienburg, 1804) and *Do Emmy*, to a Polish translation of a Schiller text; and he also wrote piano pieces,

including the four-hand *Drei National-Polonaisen* (Berlin, n.d.).

BIBLIOGRAPHY
SMP
Z. Jachimecki and W. Poźniak: *Antoni Radziwiłł i jego muzyka do Fausta* (Kraków, 1957)

ALINA NOWAK-ROMANOWICZ

Radziwiłł, Prince Maciej (*b* Szydłowiec, ?1751; buried Nieśwież, 1800). Polish composer and librettist. Around 1780 he lived at Nieśwież, the house of Karol Radziwiłł, governor of Vilnius Province, who maintained a company of actors, musicians and dancers there and at his estates in Alba, Ołyka, Słuck, Biała and elsewhere. At Nieśwież Radziwiłł wrote the libretto (MS in *PL-Wn*) for J. D. Holland's opera *Agatka, czyli Przyjazd pana* ('Agatha, or The master's arrival'), performed on 17 September 1784 during King Stanisław August's visit to Nieśwież. He also wrote the libretto (MS in Zieliński Library, Płock) and presumably the music for the three-act opera *Wójt osady albiańskiej* ('The headman of the settlers at Alba'). Radziwiłł became castellan of Vilnius Province in 1788 and moved to the town of Vilnius where he composed some instrumental and orchestral music.

WORKS

Wójt osady albiańskiej [The headman of the settlers at Alba] (opera, 3, Radziwiłł), Alba, 4 Nov 1786; Sonate, pf, vn, G (Kraków, 1972); Divertimento, D, orch (Kraków, 1970); Serenada, B♭, str qt (Kraków, 1972); 6 polonoises, orch, D-Dlb; 3 polonoises, pf, Dlb

BIBLIOGRAPHY
A. Nowak-Romanowicz and others, eds.: *Z dziejów polskiej kultury muzycznej* [From the history of Polish musical culture], ii (Kraków, 1966)
T. Marek: *Wstęp do sonaty M. Radziwiłła* [An introduction to Radziwiłł's sonatas] (Kraków, 1972)

ALINA NOWAK-ROMANOWICZ

Radziwiłł, Marcelina. *See* CZARTORYSKA, MARCELINA.

Raecke, Hans-Karsten (*b* Rostock, 12 Sept 1941). German composer. He studied composition with Wagner-Régeny, the piano with Walter Olbertz and choral conducting with Fritz Höft at the Berlin Hochschule für Musik (1962–8), and was then appointed lecturer in theory at the musicology institute of Berlin University. His studies were completed in Dessau's master class at the German Academy of Arts (1972–3). In his music since 1969 he has employed serial writing and aleatory elements; some of his pieces were based on geometrical ideas. Works by him have been heard at the Komische Oper, Berlin, and at the 1970 Darmstadt summer courses.

WORKS
(*selective list*)

Theme and Variations, pf, 1965; Die Heinzelmännchen, pf, perc, 1967; Stufenspiele, orch, 1968; Variationssuite, orch, 1968; 5 Variations, pf, 1968; Jazz 1–2, pf, 1969; Klangstücke 1–11, pf, 1969; Klangstücke 12–24, 2 pf, 1969; Extrakte 1–4, pf, orch, 1970; 5 Kanons auf ein Fugenthema von J. S. Bach, str qt, 1971; Formationen, gui, 1971; Formation 6 (Laudse, R. Schwachhofer), speaker, gui, 1971; Vietnam – ein Gesang gegen den Krieg! (Schwachhofer), Bar, speaker, chorus, pf, projections, 1972; Montage, trbn, tape, 1972; Wellen, elec org, tape, 1972; Extrakte 1–2, 2 pf, 1972; Impuls 1–2, 2 prepared pf, 1972; Raster, 1/2 pf (2–6 players), 1973

Raeli, Vito (*b* Tricase, Lecce, 8 July 1880; *d* Tricase, 7 May 1970). Italian musicologist. At the age of five he began piano lessons with his father and theory lessons with C. Minoli; he was then taken to Lecce to study with G. Sarno and C. Preite (piano and theory), and shortly after leaving school he took part, with P. Chillino and L. Cosma, in many educational concerts organized by Sarno in Otranto. He also began to study composition, and in 1904 he took a law degree at the University of Naples. In 1905 he moved permanently to Rome, where he did research in the various archives, writing especially about the Corsiana, Chigiana and Liberiana music collections. He served as secretary of the International Musical Society Congress (1911) and as a member of the council for the Accademia Filarmonica di Roma and of the Association of Italian Musicologists. He founded the *Rivista nazionale di musica* in 1920 and edited it until its end in 1943; he also edited the journal *Musica* and contributed to many music periodicals.

WRITINGS

'La collezione Corsini di antichi codici musicali e G. Chiti', *RMI*, xxv (1918), 345–76; xxvi (1919), 112; xxvii (1920), 60

Collezioni e archivi romani di stampe e MSS musicali (Tricase, 1919)

Da V. Ugolini a O. Benevoli: nella cappella della Basilica Liberiana, 1603–1646 (Rome, 1920)

Nel secolo di Giovanni Pierluigi Palestrina: alla cappella della Basilica Liberiana, 1550–1600 (Rome, 1920)

Da C. Cecchelli a R. Lorenzini (Rome, 1920)

L'Italia musicale prima, durante e dopo la guerra (Rome, 1922)

Maestri compositori pugliesi (Tricase, 1922)

CAROLYN M. GIANTURCO

Raesel, Andreas. *See* RASELIUS, ANDREAS.

Raff, (Joseph) Joachim (*b* Lachen, nr. Zurich, 27 May 1822; *d* Frankfurt am Main, ?24 or 25 June 1882). German composer and teacher. He was the son of a teacher and organist who had fled from Württemberg to Switzerland in the face of French conscription. His family's want of means limited his formal education to a teacher-training course at the Jesuit Gymnasium in Schwyz, and from 1840 to 1844 he taught in Rapperswil. By 1844, when his piano pieces opp.2–6 were printed in Leipzig at Mendelssohn's recommendation, he had already decided on a musical career. He went to Zurich, where he struggled to make a living while educating himself privately. When in 1845 Liszt gave a concert in Basle, Raff made a pilgrimage there on foot. The older composer immediately took him to Germany and secured him a job in a Cologne music shop, although Raff soon had to move to Stuttgart as a consequence of some blunt remarks he had made in the *Wiener allgemeine Musik-Zeitung*. In Stuttgart he met Bülow, with whom he was to enjoy a lifelong friendship, and in 1846 he made Mendelssohn's acquaintance, but plans to study with him in Leipzig were ended by Mendelssohn's death in November 1847. Shortly thereafter Liszt obtained for Raff a new job in Hamburg making arrangements for Schuberth, the music publisher. At the beginning of 1850, he went to live with Liszt, recently made Weimar Kapellmeister, to assist him in such practical occupations as copying parts, putting manuscripts in order and instrumentation. Although understandably Raff felt himself oppressed by Liszt's powerful personality, for a time he exaggerated the importance of his work for the older man.

In 1856 Raff gave up his position in Weimar and went to Wiesbaden to give piano lessons and compose. There he married Doris Genast (1826–1912), descended from an old family of actors and musicians, whose father and paternal grandfather had been closely associated with Goethe's Weimar theatre. Raff now became extremely productive as a composer. In 1877

he was appointed director of the Hoch Conservatory in Frankfurt, a post he held until his death. He also taught composition and was highly esteemed both as teacher and administrator; among his pupils were Edward MacDowell, Johannes Messchaert and Alexander Ritter. In 1903 a monument was erected over his grave in Frankfurt with the help of a generous contribution from Bülow.

As a composer, Raff was at first under the influence of Mendelssohn and, like Schumann, his early works (opp.1–46) were all for the piano. Then, very carefully and critically, he joined ranks with the 'new German school' surrounding Liszt, who offered him strong encouragement. He saw himself as a composer with a historical calling to fuse the great achievements of past and present, and he tried to combine contrapuntal techniques with the structural tendencies of sonata movement composition, while still respecting the 'new German' predilection for programmes. During his lifetime he enjoyed great fame within Germany and abroad and was celebrated along with Wagner and Brahms as one of the leading masters of modern music. Some of his contemporaries, however, observed the weaknesses of his compositions, their critical attitude extending to the discussions in the *Neue Zeitschrift für Musik*, on whose title-page Raff's own name appeared from 1854 until 1861 as a collaborator; but even Max Chop's judgment, severe for the time (1888), praised as significant and ageless certain works which are forgotten today.

Raff's attempt at synthesis led to an unattractive eclecticism and mixture of styles, and his penchant for salon-like music made him susceptible to triviality and sometimes vulgarity. On the other hand, his skilful instrumentation was widely praised, although, in contrast to his fellow 'new Germans' his orchestra did not extend beyond the size of Beethoven's. His work embraces nearly every musical form and genre, and his programme symphonies on rustic subjects had a certain progressive influence on the tone poems of such figures as Strauss and Bruch. In addition to a vast number of compositions, which earned him the rebuke of being too prolific (he withdrew 22 compositions, mostly piano works, from print and destroyed them in a fit of self-criticism), he also produced many arrangements of his own and other composers' works. So great was his confidence in posthumous fame that, according to his daughter Helene, he did not provide for his family after his death. His entire legacy of unpublished material (and that of his daughter, well known as an author) is now in the manuscript department of the Bayerische Staatsbibliothek in Munich.

WORKS

All printed works were published in Leipzig unless otherwise stated; many works also appeared in other arrangements by the composer and full details for these are given in Schäfer (1888); some early opus numbers were duplicated in published and unpublished works; MSS are in *D-Mbs*.

STAGE

(operas unless otherwise stated)

König Alfred (4, G. Logau), 1848–50, Weimar, 1851; rev. 1852, Weimar, 1853

Samson (5, J. Raff), 1853–7, unperf.

Die Parole (3, J. Raff), 1868, unperf.; lib (Wiesbaden, 1873)

Dame Kobold (comic opera, 3, P. Reber, after Calderón), op.154, 1869, Weimar, 1870, vocal score (Berlin, 1871), ov., full score (Berlin, 1870)

Benedetto Marcello (3, J. Raff), 1877–8, unperf.

Die Eifersüchtigen (comic opera, 3, J. Raff), 1881–2, unperf.

CHORAL WITH ORCHESTRA

(all printed works published in full score)

op.
— Psalm cxxi, solo vv, chorus, 1848
— Te Deum, chorus, orch, 1853
— Dornröschen (W. Genast), musical fairy tale, solo vv, chorus, orch, 1855
80 Wachet auf! (E. Geibel), solo vv, male vv, mixed vv, orch, 1858 (Mainz, 1862)
100 Deutschlands Auferstehung (M. von der Werra), male vv, orch, 1862–3 (1864)
141 De profundis (Ps cxxx), mixed vv, orch, 1867 (1868)
171 2 Gesänge, chorus, orch, 1871 (1872): Im Kahn (A. Börner), Der Tanz (P. Flemming)
186a Morgenlied (J. G. Jacobi), chorus, orch/pf, 1873 (1874)
186b Einer Entsachlafenen (Börner), S, chorus, orch/pf, 1873 (1874)
209 Die Tageszeiten (H. Raff), chorus, pf, orch, 1877–8 (1880)
— Die Sterne (H. Raff), chorus, orch, 1880; also arr. pf acc.
212 Weltende, Gericht, Neue Welt (Revelation), oratorio, solo vv, chorus, orch, 1879–81 (1883)

CHORAL UNACCOMPANIED

97 10 Gesänge, male vv, 1853–63 (1865)
122 10 Gesänge, male vv, 1853–63 (1867)
195 10 Gesänge, male vv, 1860–70 (1876)
198 10 Gesänge, mixed vv, 1860–74 (1875)

Kyrie and Gloria, 6vv, Pater noster, 8vv, Ave Maria, 8vv, all 1869

OTHER VOCAL

Vocal ensemble with pf: 12 zweistimmige Gesänge (Hoffmann von Fallersleben and others), op.114, 1860–64 (1865); 6 Gesänge (Geibel), 3 female vv, op.184, 1870–73 (1873)
Songs with orch: Traumkönig und sein Lied (Geibel), op.66, 1854 (Mainz, 1875); 2 scenas (T. Schleiden), op.199, 1875 (1875)
Songs with pf: 3 Lieder (Byron), op.16, lost; 3 Lieder (J. Scheffel), op.18, lost; 3 Lieder (J. G. Fischer), op.47, 1848 (1850); 2 Lieder (G. Logau), op.48, 1848 (1852); 3 Lieder (Fischer), op.49, 1848 (Magdeburg, 1852); 2 italienische Lieder (C. O. Sternau), op.50, 1849 (Magdeburg, 1852); 5 Lieder (Geibel), op.51, 1849–50 (1853); 3 Lieder (Sternau), op.52, 1850 (Berlin, 1853); 2 Lieder vom Rhein (Sternau), op.53, 1849 (Cologne, 1853)
Sangesfrühling (various poets), 30 songs, op.98, 1855–63 (1864); Maria Stuart (M. Stuart), cycle, op.172, 1872 (1873); 8 Gesänge (T. Moore and others), op.173, 1868–70 (1872); Blumensprache (G. Kastropp), 6 songs, op.191, 1874 (1874); Blondel de Nesle (H. Raff), cycle, op.211, 1880 (1880); Ständchen (Sternau), 1859 (Stuttgart, 1861); Frühlingslied (E. Neubürger) (Mainz, 1879)

SYMPHONIES

op.
— Grosse Symphonie, e, 1854, lost
96 Sym. no.1 'An das Vaterland', D, 1859–61 (1864)
140 Sym. no.2, C, 1866 (Mainz, 1869)
153 Sym. no.3 'Im Walde', F, 1869 (1871)
167 Sym. no.4, g, 1871 (1872)
177 Sym. no.5 'Lenore', E, 1872 (1873)
189 Sym. no.6, d, 1873 (Berlin, 1874)
201 Sym. no.7 'In den Alpen', B♭, 1875 (1876)
205 Sym. no.8 'Frühlingsklänge', A, 1876 (1877)
208 Sym. no.9 'Im Sommer', e, 1878 (1879)
213 Sym. no.10 'Zur Herbstzeit', f, 1879 (1882)
214 Sym. no.11 'Der Winter', a, 1876 (1883)

SOLO INSTRUMENT AND ORCHESTRA

Pf: Ode au printemps, G, op.76, 1857 (Mainz, 1862); Conc., c, op.185, 1873 (1874); Suite, E♭, op.200, 1875 (1876)
Vn: La fée d'amour (Die Liebesfee), a, op.67, 1854 (Mainz, 1878); Conc. no.1, b, op.161, 1870–71 (1871); Suite, G, op.180, 1873 (1873); Conc. no.2, a, op.206, 1877 (1878)
Vc: Conc. [no.1], D, op.193, 1874 (1875); Conc. no.2, G, 1876

OTHER ORCHESTRAL

Incidental music to Bernhard von Weimar (W. Genast), 1854, ov., rev. as Ein feste Burg ist unser Gott, op.127, 1865 (1866), 2 marches (Munich, 1885)
Suites: no.1, C, op.101, 1863 (Mainz, 1865); no.2 'in ungarischer Weise', F, op.194, 1874 (Berlin, 1876); Italienische Suite, 1871 (Berlin, 1874); Thüringer Suite, 1877
Other works: Fest-Ouvertüre, 1851–2, lost; Jubel-Ouvertüre, C, op.103, 1864 (1865); Fest-Ouvertüre, A, op.117, 1864 (1865); Konzert-Ouvertüre, F, op.123, 1862 (1866); ovs. to Shakespeare plays, 1879: The Tempest, Macbeth, Romeo and Juliet, Othello; Elegie, 1880 [orig. 3rd movt of Sym. no.10]; Grosse Fuge, 1882, inc.

CHAMBER

Pf, str: Pf Qnt, a, op.107, 1862 (1864); 2 pf qts, G, c, op.202, 1876 (1876, 1877); Pf Trio, g, 1849, lost; 4 pf trios, c, op.102, 1861 (1864), G, op.112, 1863 (1865), a, op.155, 1870 (Berlin, 1872), D,

op.158, 1870 (1871); 5 vn sonatas, e, op.73, 1853–4 (1859), A, op.78, 1858 (1870), D, op.128, 1865 (1867), g, op.129, 1866 (1867), c, op.145, 1868 (1869), all ed. F. David (1876); Aus der Schweiz, vn, pf, op.57, 1848 (Hanover, 1853); 2 Fantasiestücke, vn, pf, op.58, 1850, 1852 (Magdeburg, 1854); 3 duos, on themes from Wagner's operas, vn, pf, op.63, 1853 (Aachen, 1856); 6 morceaux, vn, pf, op.85, 1859 (1862); Volker, cyclic tone poem, vn, pf, op.203, 1876 (1877); Suite, vn, pf, op.210, 1879 (1880); Vc Sonata, D, op.183, 1873 (1873); Duo, vc/vn, pf, A, op.59, 1848 (Hanover, 1855); 2 Fantasiestücke, vc, pf, op.86, 1854 (1862)
Str: Octet, C, op.176, 1872 (1873); Sextet, g, op.178, 1872 (1873); Qt, C, 1849–50, lost; 5 qts, d, op.77, 1855 (1860), A, op.90, 1857 (1862), e, op.136, 1866 (1868), a, op.137, 1867 (1869), G, op.138, 1867 (1869); 3 qts, op.192, 1874 (1876)
Other works: Fest-Ouvertüre, ww, op.124, 1865, arr. pf 4 hands (Bremen, 1865); Sinfonietta, F, 2 fl, 2 ob, 2 cl, 2 bn, 2 hn, op.188, 1873 (1874); 2 Romanzen, hn/vc, pf, op.182, 1873 (1873)

PIANO SOLO

Sérénade, op.1, 1842 (Offenbach, 1843); 3 pièces caractéristiques, op.2, 1842 (1844), rev. as 3 morceaux, 1876 (1877); Scherzo, op.3, 1842 (1844); Fantaisie brillante, on themes from Donizetti's Maria di Rudenz, op.4, 1842 (1844), rev. as Fantaisie, 1881 (1881); 4 galops brillants, op.5, 1843 (1844), rev. as 4 galop-caprices, 1878 (1878); Fantaisie et variations brillantes, op.6, 1843 (1844), rev. as Variations, 1878 (1878); Rondo brillant, on Son sì non ricco e tu sei bella from Donizetti's L'elisir d'amore, op.7, 1843 (1844); 12 romances en forme d'études, op.8, 1843 (1845)
Impromptu brillant, op.9, 1843 (1845), rev. as Introduction et rondeau, 1875 (1876); Grand capriccio, op.10, 1843 (1845); Air suisse, op.11, 1844 (1845); Fantaisie gracieuse, op.12, 1844 (1846), rev. as Fantaisie, 1881 (1881); Sonate avec fugue, op.14, 1844 (1845), rev. as Grande sonate, 1881 (1882); 6 poèmes, op.15, 1845 (Mainz, 1846); Album lyrique, op.17, 1845 (Hamburg, 1846), rev. 1849 (1874–7); 2 Paraphrasen, op.18, 1845 (Cologne, 1846); Fantaisie dramatique, on themes from H. Esser's Les deux princes, op.19, 1845 (Brunswick, 1847)
2 morceaux de salon, op.20, 1845 (Brunswick, 1847); Loreley, op.21, 1846 (Vienna, 1846); 2 rhapsodies élégiaques, op.22, 1846 (Vienna, 1846); 3 pièces caractéristiques, op.23, 1845 (1845); Valse mélancolique, op.24, 1846 (Vienna, 1846); Romance-étude, op.25, 1846 (Vienna, 1846); Den Manen Scarlattis, op.26, 1846 (Vienna, 1846); Angelens letzter Tag im Kloster, op.27, 1845 (1846); Tarantelle, op.31, 1846 (Vienna, 1847); Am Rhein, op.32, 1846 (Vienna, 1846); 6 Lieder, op.34, 1847 (Stuttgart, 1847)
Capriccietto, on themes from Weber's Der Freischütz, op.35, 1847 (Stuttgart, 1848); Fantaisie militaire, on themes from Meyerbeer's Les Huguenots, op.36, 1847 (Stuttgart, 1848); Fantasie, on themes from Bellini's La sonnambula, op.37, 1847 (Stuttgart, 1848); Grande mazurka, op.38, 1847 (1847); Notturno, after Liszt, op.39, 1847 (1847); Capriccietto à la bohémienne, op.40, 1847 (1848); Romance, op.41, 1847 (1853); Le prétendant, after Kücken, op.42, 1847 (1847); Divertimento, on themes from Halévy's La juive, op.43, 1848 (Stuttgart, 1848)
Fantaisie, on themes from Rossini's Il barbiere di Siviglia, op.44, 1848 (Stuttgart, 1848); Reminiscenzen aus Mozarts Don Juan, op.45, 1848 (Stuttgart, 1848); The Last Rose of Summer, op.46, 1849 (Hamburg, 1849); Tanz-Capricen, op.54, 1852 (Berlin, 1853); Frühlingsboten, 12 pieces, op.55, 1850–52 (Magdeburg, 1853); 3 Salonstücke, op.56, 1849 (Hanover, 1854); Schweizerweisen, 9 pieces, op.60, 1851 (1855)
[4 pieces], op.61: 1 Caprice, on themes from Wagner's Lohengrin, 1853 (1855), 2 Reminiscenzen, on themes from Wagner's Der fliegende Holländer, 1853 (1855), 3 Fantasie, on themes from Wagner's Tannhäuser, 1853 (1859), 4 Capriccio in Rondoform, on themes from Schumann's Genoveva, 1855 (1863); 3 Salon-Etüden aus Wagners Opern, op.62, 1853 (Berlin, 1855); Capriccio, op.64, 1855 (1857); [2 pieces], op.65, 1855 (1863): 1 Fantasie, on themes from Berlioz's Benvenuto Cellini, 2 Caprice, on themes from Raff's König Alfred
5 Transkriptionen, op.68, 1857 (1857) [on works by Beethoven, Gluck, Mozart, Schumann and Spohr]; Suite, a, op.69, 1857 (Erfurt, 1857); Trovatore et Traviata, 2 salon paraphrases after Verdi, op.70, 1857 (1857); Suite, C, op.71, 1857 (Weimar, 1858); Suite, e, op.72, 1857 (Weimar, 1858); 3 Klavier-Soli, op.74, 1852 (1859); Suite de morceaux pour petites mains, 12 pieces, op.75, 1858–9 (1859–60); Cachoucha-caprice, op.79, 1858 (1861); [2 pieces from Verdi's Les vêpres siciliennes], op.81, 1858 (1861): 1 Sicilienne, 2 Tarantelle; Mazurka-caprice, op.83, 1858 (Mainz, 1861)
Chant de l'Ondin, op.84, 1858 (1861); Introduction et allegro scherzoso, op.87, 1858 (1862); Am Giessbach, op.88, 1858 (1862); Villanelle, op.89, 1859 (1862); Suite, D, op.91, 1859 (1862); Capriccio, op.92, 1860 (1862); Dans la nacelle, op.93, 1860 (1862); Impromptu-valse, op.94, 1860 (1862); La polka de la Reine, op.95, 1861 (1863); 3 sonatilles, a, G, C, op.99, 1861 (1864–5); Le galop, op.104, 1861 (1864); 5 églogues, op.105, 1861 (1865); Fantaisie-

polonaise, op.106, 1861 (1865); Saltarello, op.108, 1863 (1865); Rêverie-nocturne, op.109, 1863 (1865)
La gitana, op.110, 1863 (1865); 2 Capricen, op.111, 1856 (1857); Ungarische Rhapsodie, op.113, 1863 (1865); 2 morceaux lyriques, op.115, 1864 (1865); Valse-caprice, op.116, 1864 (1865); Valse favorite, op.118, 1864 (1865); Fantasie, op.119, 1864 (1865); Spanische Rhapsodie, op.120, 1864 (1865); Illustrations de L'africaine de Meyerbeer, op.121, 1864 (Berlin, 1866); [3 pieces], op.125, 1865 (1865): 1 Gavotte, 2 Berceuse, 3 L'espiègle; 3 Klavierstücken, op.126, 1865 (Bremen, 1866); 2 études mélodiques, op.130, 1866 (1867)
Styrienne, op.131, 1866 (1866); Marche brillante, op.132, 1866 (1866); Elegie, op.133, 1866 (1867); Vom Rhein, 6 pieces, op.134, 1866 (1867); Blätter und Blüten, 12 pieces, op.135, 1866 (1867); Fantaisie, op.142, 1867 (1869); Barcarolle, op.143, 1867 (1869); Tarantelle, op.144, 1867 (1869); Capriccio, op.146, 1868 (1869); 2 méditations, op.147, 1868 (1869); Scherzo, op.148, 1868 (1869); 2 elégies, op.149, 1868 (1871); Allegro agitato, op.151, 1868 (1871); 2 romances, op.152, 1868 (1871); Valse brillante, op.156, 1870 (1871)
[2 pieces], op.157, 1870 (1871): 1 Cavatine, 2 La fileuse; Suite, g, op.162, 1870 (Berlin, 1871); Suite, G, op.163, 1871 (1871); [3 pieces], op.164, 1871 (Berlin, 1872): 1 Sicilienne, 2 Romance, 3 Tarantelle; La cicerenella, op.165, 1871 (1872); [2 pieces], op.166, 1871 (1872): 1 Idylle, 2 Valse champêtre; Fantasie-Sonate, op.168, 1871 (1872); [2 pieces], op.169, 1871 (1872): 1 Romance, 2 Valse brillante; La polka glissante, op.170, 1871 (1872); Orientales, 8 pieces, op.175, 1872 (1873); Variationen über ein Originalthema, op.179, 1873 (Berlin, 1873)
Totentanz, op.181, 1873 (1873); Erinnerung an Venedig, 6 pieces, op.187, 1873 (1874); Feux follets, op.190, 1874 (1874); [4 pieces], op.196, 1875 (1875): 1 Im Schilf, 2 Berceuse, 3 Novelette, 4 Impromptu; Capriccio, op.197, 1875 (1875); Suite, B♭, op.204, 1876 (Berlin, 1877); Von der schwäbischen Alb, 2 pieces, op.215, 1881 (1882); Aus der Adventzeit, 8 pieces, op.216, 1879 (Berlin, 1885); Valse-rondino, on themes from S. Salomon's Das Diamantkreuz, 1849 (1850); Abendlied von Schumann, 1865 (1866); Valse impromptu à la tyrolienne, 1868 (Mainz, 1869)
30 fortschreitende Etüden, 1868–72 (Hanover, 1883); Improvisation, on L. Damrosch's lied Der Lindenzweig, 1870 (Breslau, 1871); Berceuse d'après une pensée de Gounod, 1872 (1872); Valse de Juliette de Gounod, 1872 (1873); 4 Capriccios über walachische und serbische Weisen, 1875 (1876)

Lost works: 3 fantaisies de soir, 1841; Schicksale, 1841; Fantasie, op.15, 1844; 3 Characterstücke, op.17, 1844; Jarner Fantasie, op.19, 1844; Jaléo and Xeres, Sp. dances, op.22, 1844; Jagd-Fantasie, op.21, 1845; In den Bergen, op.22, 1845; Impromptu, op.16, 1845; 8 Lieder von Mendelssohn, op.19, 1845; 2 airs fameux, from Meyerbeer's Robert le diable, op.28, 1846; Liebesfrühling, op.29, 1846; 2 mazurkas, op.30, 1846; Albumstück, op.33, 1846; Alla tarantella, 1846; Scherzo fantastique, 1846; Sérénade, 1847; Sicilienne, 1847; Fantasie, on themes from Kücken's Der Prätendent, 1847; Grosse Fantasie, on themes from Salomon's Das Diamantkreuz, 1849

OTHER WORKS

Pf 4 hands: Valse-rondino, on themes from Meyerbeer's Les Huguenots, op.13, 1844 (1845); 12 morceaux, op.82, 1858–9 (1861–5); Humoreske in Walzerform, op.159, 1870 (Berlin, 1871); Reisebilder, 10 pieces, op.160, 1870 (1871) Aus dem Tanzsalon, op.174, 1872 (1872)
Other kbd: Chaconne, a, 2 pf, op.150, 1868 (1869); Fantasie, g, 2 pf, op.207, 1877 (1878); Introduktion und Fuge, e, org, 1866 (1867)
Edns./arrs.: J. S. Bach: vn sonata movts, arr. pf, 1865 (1865–9), 6 vc suites, arr. pf, 1868 (1869–71), Chaconne, d, arr. orch, 1873 (1874), orch suites nos.1–3, arr. pf, 1874 (1875), Eng. Suite no.3, arr. orch, 1874; Beethoven: 2 vn romances, arr. pf, 1849 (1849); Handel: 2 marches from oratorios Saul and Jephtha, arr. pf 1859 (1879); B. Marcello: 3 vc sonatas, orig. bc arr. pf, 1875; Wagner: Die Meistersinger, excerpts, arr. pf, 1867, as Reminiscenzen (Mainz, 1868)

WRITINGS

'Die Stellung der Deutschen in der Geschichte der Musik: kunsthistor-ische Skizze', Weimarisches Jb für deutsche Sprache, Literatur und Kunst, i (1854), 171–214
Die Wagnerfrage, i: Wagners letzte künstlerische Kundgebung im Lohengrin (Brunswick, 1854)
Essays in Cäcilia, Jb für deutsche Sprache, Leipziger illustrierte Zeitung, NZM, Signale für die musikalische Welt

BIBLIOGRAPHY

E. Prout, J. S. Shedlock, C. A. Barry: Articles on Raff's symphonies, MMR, v (1875), 32, 46, 61, 77, 93, 121, 147
F. Liszt: Gesammelte Schriften, ed. L. Ramann (Leipzig, 1880–83)
O. Lessmann: Obituary, Allgemeine deutsche Musikzeitung, ix (1882), 215

Obituary, NZM, lxxviii (1882), 319
M. Charles [pseud. of M. Chop]: Zeitgenössische Tondichter, i, (Leipzig, 1888), chap. 'Joachim Raff', 113f
A. Schäfer: Chronologisch-systematisches Verzeichnis der Werke Joachim Raffs (Wiesbaden, 1888/R1974) [comprehensive cata-logue]
F. Liszt: Briefe, ed. M. Lipsius (Leipzig, 1893–1904)
B. Ziehm: 'Raff's "Wagnerfrage" und "Lenore" ', AMz, xxi (1894), 261, 273, 285, 301, 347, 357
H. von Bülow: Briefe und Schriften, ed. M. von Bülow (Leipzig, 1896–1908)
T. Müller-Reuter: Joachim Raff: Im Walde, Symphonie no.3, F-dur, op.153, Der Musikführer, ed. A. Morin, cxxxviii (Frankfurt am Main, 1898)
——: Joachim Raff: Lenore, Symphonie no.5, E-dur, op.177, ibid, cxlix (Frankfurt am Main, 1898)
H. Raff, ed.: 'Franz Liszt und Joachim Raff im Spiegel ihrer Briefe', Die Musik, i (1901–2), 36, 113, 285, 387, 499; ii (1902–3), 688, 861, 977, 1161, 1272, 1423
H. Pohl: 'Joachim Raff: ein Gedenkblatt zur Enthüllung seines Denkmals in Frankfurt am Main', ZIMG, iv (1902–3), 542
H. Raff, ed.: 'Vier Briefe Adolf Jensens an Joachim Raff', Die Musik, iii (1903–4), 94
——: 'Tristan als Briefschreiber: nachgelassene Briefe von Ludwig Schnorr von Carolsfeld an Joachim Raff', Die Musik, iv (1904–5), 97
[Raff–Vischer correspondence], Süddeutsche Monatshefte, ii (1905), 45
P. Raabe: Die Entstehungsgeschichte der ersten Orchesterwerke Franz Liszts (Leipzig, 1916)
M. Bauer: 'Joseph Joachim Raff: zu seinem 100. Geburtstag', Neue Musikzeitung, xliii (1922), 249
P. Marsop: 'Raff, Bülow und die "Frühlingsboten": zum Gedächtnis Joachim Raffs, geboren 27 Mai 1822', AMz, xlix (1922), 439
——: 'Joachim Raff und "Die Wagnerfrage" ', Neue Musikzeitung, xliii (1922), 252
H. Raff: 'Joachim Raff an Kunigunde Heinrich', Neue Musikzeitung, xliii (1922), 256
H. Spangenberg: 'Joachim Raff: Erinnerungen eines ehemaligen Schülers', Neue Musikzeitung, xliii (1922), 254
H. Raff: Joachim Raff: ein Lebensbild (Regensburg, 1925) [with catalogue of works condensed from Schäfer]
K. Huschke: 'Joachim Raff: der Mensch und Künstler im Lichte anderer bedeutender Musiker seiner Zeit', Neue Musikzeitschrift, i (1947), 280
Numerous reviews of Raff's works in NZM, xii–xliii (1845–76)

HORST LEUCHTMANN

Rafi, Claude (b ?Lyons, 1515; d 1553). French flute maker. He worked in Lyons. Most sources give his first name as Claude but at least one instrument ascribed to him bears the initial G. His surviving instruments, all Renaissance in style, include a basset recorder in Bruges (Musée Gruuthuse), a flute in Brussels (Musée Instrumental; see FLUTE, fig.11a), a recorder in Eisenach (Bachhaus), supposedly marked Claude Rafi with a griffin on a shield below the name, and a flute in Verona (Accademia Filarmonica) clearly marked 'G. Rafi', also with a griffin on a shield. A bass flute in Leipzig was destroyed during World War II. He is mentioned in poems by Clément Marot and Jean-Antoine de Baïf.

BIBLIOGRAPHY

G. Tricon: 'Claude Rafi, "fleustier" ', Mémoires de la Société littéraire, historique et archéologique de Lyon, xvii (1896–7), 265
V.-C. Mahillon: Catalogue descriptif et analytique du Musée instrumental du Conservatoire royal de musique de Bruxelles, ii (Ghent, 2/1909)
L. G. Langwill: An Index of Musical Wind-instrument Makers (Edinburgh, 1960, rev. 4/1977)
M. Castellani: 'Two Late-Renaissance Transverse Flutes', GSJ, xxv (1972), 73

FRIEDRICH VON HUENE

Raftor, Catherine. See CLIVE, KITTY.

Rag. See RAGTIME.

Raga (Sanskrit rāga). An Indian term, adopted into English, often translated as 'mode', 'scale' or 'melody type';

see INDIA, SUBCONTINENT OF, §§I, 5(iii); II, 2, 3(ii), and MODE, §V, 1, 2(ii).

Raganella (It.). RATCHET.

Ragazzi, Angelo (*b* ?1680; *d* Vienna, 1750). Italian composer. He studied the violin at the Naples Conservatory of S Maria di Loreto with Giancarlo Chilò (or Cailò), who had moved to Naples from Rome with Alessandro Scarlatti. In 1704 he was employed as a violinist in the royal chapel in Naples (where at some time he was Konzertmeister, according to a Dresden manuscript); when Naples passed under Habsburg rule, he went first to Barcelona and then to Vienna, where he entered the service of Emperor Charles VI. He stayed there from 1713 to 1722, when he returned to Naples, but moved to Vienna again in 1729 (possibly as a result of the transfer of power in Naples from the Habsburgs to the Bourbons); he remained there for the rest of his life, retiring in 1740, ten years before he died.

Ragazzi was one of the leading instrumental composers in 18th-century Naples. His only printed work is a collection of *Sonate a quattro* (Rome, 1736), compositions of considerable interest for a knowledge of the Neapolitan instrumental tradition, and dedicated (as might be expected) to Charles VI. The collection comprises 12 sonatas for first violin, ripieno first violin, second violin, third violin or viola, and violone and continuo. The sonatas are varied in style and broadly representative of Ragazzi's music. Some of them are close to trio sonatas, others to solo concertos; some are in a contrapuntal style, while others are more homophonic. Ragazzi favoured a classical polyphonic manner combined with instrumental virtuosity; some passages show a Venetian influence, but others are in a strict polyphonic idiom. These characteristics of Ragazzi's style need to be seen in the context of contemporary Viennese taste, where the two dominating factors were J. J. Fux's teaching and the popularity of the Vivaldi concertos.

WORKS

Sonate a quattro, vn solo, 2 vn, vn/va, vle, bc, op.1 (Rome, 1736)
Mass, 4vv, 1736, *A-Wn*; Mass, 4vv, 1737, *Wn*; Mass, 8vv, insts, 1739, *Wn*; Inveni hominem, canon, 5vv, *D-Dlb*
Conc. grosso, 3 ob, va, bc, *D-B*; Conc., vn solo, vn, va, bc, *Dlb*; Conc. (C), vn, violetta, bc, 1728, *I-Nc*; Conc. (b), 4 vn, violetta, vc, bc, 1728, *Nc*; Conc. (B♭), vn, violetta, bc, 1728, *Nc*; Conc. a tre (a), 2 vn with ripieni, bc, 1729, *Nc*
Sinfonia, 2 vn, bc, *I-Mc*; Sonate a quattro, *Nc*; 2 sonate a tre, *Nc*; Ricercare, 4 inst, *A-Wn*, *D-B*; Fantasia, vn solo, *Dlb*

BIBLIOGRAPHY

EitnerQ
L. von Köchel: *Die kaiserliche Hof-Musikkapelle in Wien von 1543 bis 1867* (Vienna, 1869), 76
——: *Johann Joseph Fux* (Vienna, 1872), 244, 367
A. Schering: *Die Geschichte des Instrumental-Konzerts* (Leipzig, 1905, 2/1927/R1965), 55f
A. Koczirz: 'Exzerpte aus den Hofmusikakten des Wiener Hofkammerarchivs', *SMw*, i (1913), 289
U. Prota-Giurleo: 'Breve storia del Teatro di Corte e della musica a Napoli nei secoli XVII–XVIII', *Il Teatro di corte del Palazzo reale di Napoli* (Naples, 1952), 72
R. di Benedetto: 'The Sonate a quattro of Angelo Ragazzi (1736)', *IMSCR, xi Copenhagen 1972*, 356

RENATO BOSSA

Ragazzoni [Ragazzono], **Ottavio** (*b* Parma, mid-16th century). Italian composer and publisher. He was a Carmelite monk belonging to the Congregation of Mantua and was probably related to PIETRO PAOLO RAGAZZONI. He supervised the publication of the anthology *Liber primus psalmorum qui in ecclesia*

decantantur ad Vesperas quinque vocibus (*RISM* 1590⁷). This volume contains 20 pieces by 17 composers, including a *Laudate Dominum* by Ragazzoni himself. The dedication is to Padre Maestro Lattanzio Domanino of Mantua.

For bibliography *see* RAGAZZONI, PIETRO PAOLO.

FRANCESCO BUSSI

Ragazzoni [Ragazzono], **Pietro Paolo** (*b* Parma, 28 June 1499; *d* Parma, *c*1580). Italian composer. He lived in Parma, where, with some interruptions, he was a singer in the choir of the Chiesa della Steccata from 1539 to 1564. On 20 March of that year he was appointed *maestro di cappella* of the same church. On 22 November 1566 he was made *maestro di cappella* at the cathedral and was succeeded in that post by Marco Oliva on 3 November 1580. Of his compositions only one volume is extant: *Madrigali di Pietro Paolo Ragazzoni da Parma a quattro voci* (Venice, 1544), dedicated to Girolamo Provosto de la Scala.

BIBLIOGRAPHY

N. Pelicelli: 'Musicisti in Parma nei secoli XV–XVI', *NA*, viii (1931), 201
F. Bussi: *Piacenza, Archivio del Duomo: catalogo del fondo musicale* (Milan, 1967)

FRANCESCO BUSSI

Ragtime. An American popular style, chiefly for the piano, which flourished between about 1890 and World War I.

1. Definition and origins. 2. Characteristics. 3. Piano rolls. 4. Joplin and 'classic' or Missouri ragtime. 5. Eastern ragtime. 6. Roberts, Johnson and Blake. 7. Decline and revival.

1. DEFINITION AND ORIGINS. The term is probably of black origin. In its broadest sense, 'ragtime' is the effect generated by an internally syncopated melodic line pitted against a rhythmically straightforward bass. This phenomenon can, of course, be found in music before the ragtime craze, as its early detractors were quick to point out. But ragtime's importance lies less in what it originated than in what it emphasized: the constant collision between internal melodic and underlying rhythms was its raison d'être, not just a stylistic feature. Ragtime, especially in the 'Missouri style', is primarily a written style, whereas jazz is primarily improvised; even though rag tunes were often used in jazz improvisations it is inaccurate to call ragtime an early form of jazz. Such figures as Jelly Roll Morton bridge the two, and in the 1920s ragtime led directly to popular song (Irving Berlin's 'rag songs' are not true ragtime). While 'ragtime' may be a vague term, 'rag' is not, as that dance form became as definite as (and quite similar to) that of a Sousa march. Composers like Louis Moreau Gottschalk, Dan Emmett and Stephen Foster may have evoked ragtime, but they did not write rags; yet the fact that Gottschalk approached the style as early as 1847 (*La bamboula*) indicates an aural history of ragtime reaching back perhaps to a time when black slaves fused European harmony with African rhythm.

Ragtime's huge popularity was abetted by its wide dissemination in print (Scott Joplin's *Maple Leaf Rag* of 1899 quickly sold a million copies). In 1897 – the year of the first published piano rag (*Mississippi Rag*, by the white bandmaster William H. Krell) – print was still the chief mass medium for music, and the piano was the instrument of musically literate amateurs; thus, although ragtime banjo players (perhaps the style's originators), ad hoc ragtime bands (made up perhaps of

flute, cornet, violin, piano and drums) and ragtime singers like Ben Harney abounded, the style spread mainly
on living-room pianos, where simplified sheet music
guided the amateur pianist through its rhythmic
intricacies. Ragtime's real spawning-ground was
undoubtedly the parlours of bordellos, partly because its
foremost practitioners, the predominantly black 'jig-
pianists', could not find work elsewhere. Most of the
great rag pianists and composers – Scott Joplin, Eubie
Blake, Jelly Roll Morton – started there, and hence the
style was frowned on by the more prudish American
music critics. It is surprising that music springing from
such a 'disreputable' source (and composed mainly by
blacks) should have achieved print at all in those times,
but it did, owing to immense popular demand, and thus
the publication of *Mississippi Rag* marked the beginning
of a rapid worldwide dissemination of the style.

2. CHARACTERISTICS. Krell's rag is rather loosely constructed compared with later examples; however, with
Harney's early rag songs (*You've been a good old wagon
but you've done broke down*, 1895; *Mr Johnson turn me
loose*, 1896) it shares the repeated 16-bar period, or
'strain', that was to endure throughout ragtime's
hegemony. This was usually divided into four clear
phrases with standard cadences, betraying the rag's debt
to 'set dances', quadrilles and marches ('Tempo di
marcia' is a common Joplin heading). With Joplin's
1899 *Maple Leaf Rag* the form was codified into four
strains, sometimes with a four-bar introduction and
similar transitions. Common strain patterns were *AAB
BACCDD* (the *Maple Leaf Rag* form), *AABBCCDD*
and *AABBCCA*. As in a march, the trio or *C* strain is
often in the subdominant; few rags were in the minor
mode, and those that were often finished their strains in
the relative major. This unremarkable format was to
house a fusion of black American folk melody with
fairly complex syncopation, and its simplicity may have
helped make these 'innovations' accessible to a wide
public. Many rag melodies are strongly pentatonic, and
characteristic rhythmic cells, rarely found in white
imitations of the form, abound in black ragtime (see
ex.1). Ragtime waltzes do exist, especially in Joplin, but
until about 1915 most rags were written in 2/4, and
afterwards in common or cut time.

Ex.1 Joplin: *Maple Leaf Rag*

3. PIANO ROLLS. The special magic of the rag form,
then, lies in the richness of imagination that can be
poured into such an inflexible mould, and with its best
composers the rag enjoys a sonnet-like tension between
form and material. With lesser musicians, 'rags' meant
the mere stringing-together of catchy tunes; these commercial 'junk rags' comprised the bulk of the early
mechanical-cut player piano rolls. They were made by
direct transference from printed sheet music without
benefit of a player; later pianists recorded with a device
that left markings on a roll which were then 'translated'
and cut. In both types an 'editor' usually added octave

doublings and counter-melodies to the original, which
resulted in a thick quasi-orchestral texture. 'Penny
arcades' and the like sported mechanical pianos that
churned out ever faster and more hectic ragtime well
into the 1930s, and the impression still remains that
ragtime is a welter of notes at breakneck speed, jingling
over the keyboard.

4. JOPLIN AND 'CLASSIC' OR MISSOURI RAGTIME. To this
level of activity the figure of Scott Joplin stands in
striking contrast. Solidly trained by a German music
teacher (probably sent south by Reconstruction policy),
Joplin distinguished his scores from most popular music
by a more correct orthography, a use of dynamics and
phrasing, and a sophistication of musical content. In
Sedalia, Missouri, and later in St Louis he became the
leader of a style of ragtime notable less for its technical
brilliance than for its folklike, danceable character. At
Tom Turpin's Rosebud Café in St Louis Joplin often
met such rag composers as Arthur Marshall, Scott
Hayden and Louis Chauvin. (Turpin was himself a composer, whose 1897 *Harlem Rag* was the first published
black rag.) Joplin took down strains from Marshall,
Hayden and Chauvin, adding one or two of his own to
complete a rag, and this may account for the stylistic
consistency of the Missouri school; apart from its simplicity on the page, the Missouri style is characterized
by lyrical melodies and relatively slow tempos.

The white New Jersey composer Joseph F. Lamb
(1887–1960) is usually included with the Missouri
group because of Joplin's strong influence; his style
seems almost a fusion of Joplin and Ethelbert Nevin.
James Scott (1886–1938) is considered the third in the
Joplin–Lamb–Scott triumvirate of 'classic' ragtime
composers. Scott, based in Kansas City, Missouri,
shared the same publisher with Joplin and Lamb, John
Stark, who espoused classic ragtime with evangelical
zeal. One of hundreds of music store owners who also
published music, Stark was enabled by the earnings
from *Maple Leaf Rag* to move his small publishing
house from Sedalia to St Louis and finally to New York
(where it eventually foundered). Stark and Joplin, who
had also moved to New York, fell out about 1908, but
Stark continued to publish rags by Lamb, Scott, Artie
Matthews and other 'classic' rag composers until about
1922, several years after the vogue had passed.

5. EASTERN RAGTIME. Apart from a few rag songs and
the 'Red Back Book' ragtime band arrangements of
about 1912, Stark's catalogue was almost exclusively
for solo piano. Considerably less 'good-quality' ragtime
from composers in New York, Baltimore, New Orleans
or Atlantic City was published in that period, so it is
hard to ascertain whether eastern ragtime shared the
orientation towards the piano of its Missouri counterpart; songs, band transcriptions and piano solos are
equally plentiful. 16-bar strains were still the rule in
these rags though it was common to have only three
strains, with the second and trio often extended to twice
their normal length. Otherwise eastern ragtime betrays a
diversity of style that obscures clearcut distinctions between ragtime, 'stride piano' and early jazz. The tendency was towards a fast, brilliant piano style (rarely
reflected in the drastically simplified published scores);
whereas one danced a stately slow drag or cakewalk to a
'classic' rag, only the frenetic 'animal dances' such as
the turkey trot or chicken scratch were suitable for the

more urban tempo of eastern ragtime. Music publishers in the large cities, far more intent on profit than Stark, brought out a stream of 'junk rags', usually imitation black ragtime (with titles like *Bunch o' Blackberries*) by white composers. Courses advertising 'ragtime in ten easy lessons' flourished, with predictable results; for the more professional players, 'cutting contests' (with as many as 30 competing pianists) generated a style remarkable more for surface brilliance than for content. But this is the most familiar form of ragtime, from *Hello ma Baby* (Howard and Emerson, 1899) to *12th Street Rag* (Euday Bowman, 1914), and there is no denying its exuberance.

Title-page of 'The Ragtime Dance' by Scott Joplin

6. ROBERTS, JOHNSON AND BLAKE. If Joplin and his school evince a stylistic unity, three eastern pianists and composers – Luckey Roberts, James P. Johnson and Eubie Blake – show a similar consanguinity. Each adopted a form of ragtime known variously as 'Harlem stride' or 'stride piano', in which an octave is interposed between the on- and off-beats in the left-hand part. Their published rags appeared in the 1910s in simplified form, but all three achieved greater notoriety as composers during the renaissance of the black musical theatre in the 1920s. Roberts is remembered not only for his *Junk Man Rag* and *Pork and Beans* (both 1913) but for his 1941 song *Moonlight Cocktail*. More successful than Roberts's musicals were those of James P. Johnson, but, like Joplin, he later attempted serious opera, to public failure. Blake's earliest rag publications correspond in date with those of his friend Roberts, but his highly successful musical *Shuffle Along* (1921), written with Noble Sissle, instilled the chief characteristic of ragtime, internal melodic syncopation, indelibly into the American musical comedy and popular song.

7. DECLINE AND REVIVAL. The demise of ragtime can perhaps be traced to the moment recordings superseded piano rolls as the principal home entertainment, and to its suppression by jazz about 1915 as the most obviously black-derived musical style. By then it had worked an effect on European composers such as Satie, Stravinsky, Milhaud and Hindemith; but these and other composers seemed primarily attracted by its exoticism rather than its specific manner of syncopation, and in any case took their impressions from printed editions of east-coast junk rags and the misnamed rag pieces of Irving Berlin. (Stravinsky is reported as saying that he had never heard ragtime at the time of his famous rag pieces.) Ragtime's 16-bar strain expanded to the 32-bar chorus of the 1920s and 1930s popular song, which thus retained something of the squareness of the original march form. But more important, ragtime's particular brand of syncopation survived in nearly all forms of American popular music.

The preservation of ragtime as a specific style can largely be credited to Blesh and Janis's book *They All Played Ragtime* (1950), Max Morath's various new editions of rags, and to a few surviving performers. In the late 1960s players and composers such as William Albright, Joshua Rifkin and William Bolcom discovered in classic ragtime an important kind of American serious piano music, a link, as it were, between the native popular and imported classical traditions of American music. Many new rags owing much to the style of Scott Joplin have been written by these and other musicians, less in the spirit of nostalgia than in homage to this recently rediscovered master, and ragtime now appears widely in concert programmes, film scores, and elsewhere in America's musical life. This revival virtually took the form of a craze in the late 1960s and early 1970s and, before subsiding, had established ragtime in the view of music historians as the first clear fusion, and perhaps the most successful, of America's salient musical features.

BIBLIOGRAPHY

I. Schwerke: *Kings David and Jazz* (Paris, 1927), 31ff
I. Goldberg: *Tin Pan Alley* (New York, 1930), 139–77
H. Kaufman: *From Jehovah to Jazz* (New York, 1937), 240ff
J. Moynahan: 'Ragtime to Swing', *Saturday Evening Post*, ccix (13 Feb 1937), 14
W. Sargeant: *Jazz Hot and Hybrid* (New York, 1938, rev. 2/1946), 131ff
W. Cook: 'The Origin of the Cake-walk', *Theatre Arts*, xxxi (1947) Sept, 61
C. Wilford: 'Ragtime: an Excavation', *Jazzbook 1947*, ed. A. McCarthy (London, 1947), 18
S. Campbell: 'Ragtime Begins', *Record Changer*, vii (1948), March, 8
R. Carew: 'Ragtime', *Playback*, ii (1949), July, 6
R. Blesh and H. Janis: *They All Played Ragtime* (New York, 1950, rev. 4/1971)
E. Shapiro: 'Ragtime', *Notes*, viii (1950–51), 457
G. Chase: *America's Music* (New York, 1955, rev. 2/1966)
M. Stearns: *The Story of Jazz* (New York, 1956), 140ff
G. Waterman: 'Ragtime Piano Rolls', *Jazz Review*, i (1958), Dec, 42
C. Wilford: 'Elite Syncopations', *Decca Book of Jazz*, ed. P. Gammond (London, 1958), 29
T. Davin: 'Conversations with James P. Johnson', *Jazz Review*, ii (1959), June, 14; July, 10; Aug, 13; Sept, 26; iii (1960), March–April, 11
G. Waterman: 'A Survey of Ragtime', *The Art of Jazz*, ed. M. Williams (New York, 1959), 11
——: 'Ragtime', *Jazz*, ed. N. Hentoff (New York, 1959), 45
H. Lange: *Jazz in Deutschland 1900–60* (Berlin, 1960), 7ff
S. Charters: 'Negro Folk Elements in Classic Ragtime', *EM*, v (1961), 174
S. Charters and L. Kunstadt: *Jazz: a History of the New York Scene* (Garden City, NY, 1962), 42ff
M. Morath, ed.: *100 Ragtime Classics* (Denver, 1963)
W. Mellers: *Music in a New Found Land* (London, 1964), 276ff
M. Morath, ed.: *Guide to Ragtime: a Collection of Ragtime Songs and Piano Solos* (New York, 1964)
B. Rust: 'Ragtime su dischi', *Musica Jazz*, xx (1964), Aug–Sept, 28

Anon.: 'Sedalia, Mo., Stakes Claim as Birthplace of Ragtime', *Variety* (10 Nov 1965), 1
A. Charters, ed.: *The Ragtime Songbook* (New York, 1965)
S. Grossman: *Ragtime Blues Guitarists* (New York, 1965)
S. Brown: 'Negro Producers of Ragtime', *Negro Music and Art*, ed. L. Patterson (New York, 1967), 49
F. Gillis: 'Hot Rhythm in Ragtime', *Music in the Americas*, ed. G. List (Bloomington, Ind., 1967), 91
H. P. Hofmann and P. Czerny: *Der Schlager: ein Panorama der leichten Musik*, i (Berlin, 1968), 227ff
M. Harrison: 'Early European Ragtime and Jazz Recordings', *Jazz Monthly*, xvi (1970), June, 24
E. Southern: *The Music of Black Americans* (New York, 1971), 310ff
E. Walker: *English Ragtime: a Discography* (Chesterfield, 1971)
R. Blesh, ed.: *Classic Piano Rags* (New York, 1973)
D. Jasen: *Recorded Ragtime 1897–1958* (Hampden, Conn., 1973)
R. Kimball and W. Bolcom: *Reminiscing with Sissle and Blake* (New York, 1973)
M. Morath, ed.: *Giants of Ragtime* (New York, 1973)
W. J. Schafer and J. Riedel: *The Art of Ragtime* (Baton Rouge, 1973)
E. Thacker: 'Ragtime Roots', *Jazz Monthly*, xix (1973), Nov, 6; Dec, 4
T. Waldo: *This is Ragtime* (New York, 1976)
P. Dickinson: 'The Achievement of Ragtime', *PRMA*, cv (1978–9), 63
WILLIAM BOLCOM

Ragué, Louis-Charles (*b* before 1760; *d* Moulins, after 1793). French composer and harp teacher. He appeared on the musical scene in Paris in 1783, when the press described him as an 'amateur distinguished in more than one genre' (*Mercure de France*, October 1784, p.239). He had an active and highly successful career for a decade, after which he disappeared. His first published work, *Trois sonates pour la harpe*, was engraved in Brussels in 1783, and in the same year his op.2, *4 sonates pour la harpe*, was published in Paris, as were all of his subsequent publications. His name appeared frequently in the Parisian press until December 1793, when his ballet *Les muses* was presented at the Opéra. According to Fétis, Ragué retired to the environs of Moulins in 1792 (1794, after the première of his ballet, seems a more likely date).

Although Ragué was not known as a performing harpist, almost all his compositions were for the harp, an instrument much in vogue in Paris at the time, as is shown by the existence of publishers such as Cousineau and Naderman, who specialized in the publication of harp music. Ragué wrote 20 works or groups of works bearing opus numbers, most of them for harp accompanied by another instrument. Other works include two methods for the harp, two rather unsuccessful operas, one ballet and a number of smaller works and arrangements published separately or in periodic collections. His only symphonic work, *Trois symphonies à grand orchestre* op.10, was dedicated to Friedrich Wilhelm II of Prussia. In its preface Ragué called himself 'élève du célèbre Sacchini', who had lived in Paris from 1782 until his death in 1786. These works, which reflect an attempt at more serious composition, were first performed at the Concert Spirituel; the *Mercure de France* (May 1787, p.192), considered them 'very agreeable'. Indeed, all press references indicate that Ragué's compositions were well received both in performance and on publication. The symphonies employ textbook sonata structures with short development sections. The first of the *Trois symphonies*, in D minor, republished in Brook, shows Mannheim influence in the drama of its opening theme, but also exhibits the gentle lyricism of the French *romance* in its second theme, for solo flute. The sonatas and other chamber music for harp rarely have more than two movements, and although somewhat unpretentious and lacking in depth, they are melodic and pleasing, and well suited to the demands of the Parisian salons of the

1780s. The *Mercure de France* (January 1784, p.239) noted Ragué's particular affinity for composing harp music, and found the *Sonates* op.2 'brilliant and agreeable'.

WORKS
(printed works published in Paris unless otherwise stated)

STAGE
Memnon (opéra comique, 3, J. F. Guichard), Paris, Comédie-Italienne, 26 Aug 1784; 3 airs pubd in Le Roy: Airs de Richard Coeur de Lion, Memnon etc (c1785)
L'amour filial (opéra comique, 1, F. de Rozoy), Paris, Comédie-Italienne, 2 March 1786; excerpts pubd in contemporary anthologies
Les muses, ou Le triomphe d'Apollon (ballet, 1), Paris, Opéra, 12 Dec 1793

OTHER WORKS
Vocal: Fin de la captivité de Babylone, oratorio, perf. 1784, lost; airs in contemporary periodicals
Orch: 2 concertos, solo harp, op.6 (1785); 3 symphonies, op.10 (1787)
Chamber: 3 sonates, harp, hpd/vn acc., op.1 (Brussels, 1783); 4 sonates, harp, vn acc., op.2 (1783); 4 sonates, hpd, vn acc., op.3 (1784); 3 sonates et 1 prélude, harp, vn acc., op.4 (1785) [also pubd with op.9 as 4 sonates, op.4]; 2me livre de 3 duos, 2 harp, op.7 (1785); 3me livre de 3 duos, 2 harp, op.8 (1786); Trio, harp, hpd, op.9 (1786) [also pubd as one of the 4 sonates, harp, op.4]; Trio, harp, vn, vc, 1786; 6 duos dialogués, vn, va/vc, op.11 (1787); 2 sets of 3 duos, pf, harp, opp.12–13 (1790); 3 sonates. harp, vn acc., op.18 (1792); Trio, harp, hpd, op.19 (1792)
Harp solo: 4 sonates, op.5 (1785); 2 sets of duos, opp.14, 17 (1792) [arrs. of works by I. Pleyel]; 2 sets of sonates, opp.15–16 (1792) [arrs. of works by Pleyel]; Symphonies et quatuors, op.20 (1792)
Pedagogical: Principes de harpes suivis de 18 airs (1786); Art de préluder, harp (1786)
Arrs. in contemporary periodicals

BIBLIOGRAPHY
EitnerQ; FétisB
Notices in contemporary Parisian periodicals, incl. *Almanach musical* (1783); *Mercure de France* (1783–7); *Annonces, affiches et avis divers* (1783–93); *Journal général de France* (1785–6)
A. Choron and F. Fayolle: *Dictionnaire historique des musiciens* (Paris, 1810–11/R1971)
F. Clément and P. Larousse: *Dictionnaire lyrique, ou Histoire des opéras* (Paris, 1867–9, enlarged 3/1905/R1969, ed. A. Pougin)
B. S. Brook: *La symphonie française dans la seconde moitié du XVIIIe siècle* (Paris, 1962) [vol.iii incl. score of Symphonie, op.10, no.1]
BARRY S. BROOK, SUSAN KAGAN

Raguenet, François (*b* Rouen, *c*1660; *d* 1722). French author and priest. He was tutor to the nephews of Cardinal de Bouillon and remained in the employ of that family for most of his life. His literary production ranges widely: he wrote studies in theology, archaeology and history, as well as a novel. His contribution to music resulted from a journey to Rome with the cardinal in 1698, when he developed a particular fondness for Italian music. His *Paralèle*, published on his return, seeks objectively to compare Italian with French music in favour of the former. With the publication of a reply in support of French music by JEAN LAURENT LE CERF DE LA VIÉVILLE, a literary battle ensued, resulting in Raguenet's rebuttal, *Défense du Parallèle*, additional essays by Le Cerf and a small literature of pamphlets, journal articles, and translations of the arguments propounded. Raguenet's work provides a useful insight into the development of a musical aesthetic in the early 18th century.

WRITINGS
(only those on music)
Paralèle des italiens et des françois, en ce qui regarde la musique et les opéra (Paris, 1702, 3/c1710); Eng. edn. (London, 1709/R1968; repr. in *MQ*, xxxii (1946), 411, and in Strunk); Ger. edns. in J. Mattheson: *Critica musica*, i (Hamburg, 1722/R1964) and F. W. Marpurg: *Kritische Briefe über die Tonkunst*, i (Berlin, 1759/R1967)
Défense du Parallèle des italiens et des françois, en ce qui regarde la musique et les opéra (Paris, 1705)

BIBLIOGRAPHY
Anon.: *La paix de l'opéra, ou Parallèle impartial de la musique françoise et de la musique italienne* (Amsterdam, 1753)

P. M. Masson: 'Musique italienne et musique françoise: la première querelle', *RMI*, xix (1912), 519

M. E. Storer: 'Abbé François Raguenet: Deist, Historian, Music and Art Critic', *Romanic Review*, xxxvi (1945), 283

O. Strunk, ed.: *Source Readings in Music History* (New York, 1950), 473ff

ALBERT COHEN

Raichev, Alexander (*b* Lom, 11 April 1922). Bulgarian composer. In 1947 he graduated from the Sofia State Academy of Music as a composition pupil of Vladigerov. He then participated in the Budapest Conservatory master classes (1947–50) with Kodály, Viski and Ferencsik. In 1952 he was appointed lecturer, in 1962 professor of harmony and in 1972 rector at the Bulgarian State Conservatory. He was a secretary of the Bulgarian Composers Union (1958–65, 1973–5) and vice-president from 1975. His music associates folk elements with novel technical means in a brilliant manner. He has published a two-volume *Kharmoniya* (Sofia, 1963, 1965).

WORKS
(*selective list*)

Orch and cantatas: Toy ne umira [He did not die], sym.-cantata, 1949; Druzhba [Friendship], oratorio, 1954; Sonata-Poem, vn, orch, 1954; Noviyat Prometey [The new Prometheus] (Sym. no.2), 1954–8; Ustremi [Aspirations] (Sym. no.3), 1965; Oktomvri 50, oratorio, 1967; Sym. no.4, str, 1969; Leninski pokoleniya [Lenin's generations], 1969; Siyaina zora [Gleaming dawns], ov., 1970; Sym. no.5, 1971; Leipzig 33, sym. moments, 1972; Septemvriiski rekviem, 1973; Festivalna uvertüra, 1974; Bulgaria – bjola, selena, chervena [Bulgaria – white, green, red], oratorio, 1975

Dramatic: Khaydushka pesen [Khaydush song], ballet, 1952; Slaveyat na orkhideya [The nightingale of the orchid], musical, 1961; Most [The bridge], opera, 1964; Trevoga [Anxiety], opera, 1974; children's operetta, radio opera

Inst: Detski album [Children's album], pf, 1954; Mladezhki album [Youth album], pf, 1955; Burlesque, vn, pf, 1969

*c*500 mass/children's/solo/choral songs, music for plays and films

Principal publisher: Nauka i izkustvo

LADA BRASHOVANOVA

Raichev, Russlan (*b* Milan, 5 May 1919). Bulgarian conductor. Son of the tenor Peter Raichev, he first studied the piano at the Milan Conservatory. In 1943 he graduated from the Vienna Musikhochschule, where he studied under Karl Böhm and Emil von Sauer, while working for two years as répétiteur at the Vienna Staatsoper. He became conductor at the Königsberg (now Kaliningrad) Opera in 1944; he was one of the founders, in 1946, of the Varna SO, which he conducted for some years, and, in 1947, of the state opera company in Varna. He was appointed chief conductor of the Sofia Music Theatre, 1948–50, helped to found the opera company in Plovdiv in 1954 and was conductor of the Russe SO, 1956–8. From 1958 to 1962 he directed the Gusla Male Choir, and was simultaneously conductor at the Sofia National Opera from 1958 and of the Pernik SO, 1960–61. He became chief conductor of the Plovdiv SO in 1968 and, after a competition, he was engaged as general music director at Flensburg for three years from 1974. A natural musician with a wide operatic and symphonic repertory, Raichev has conducted in most European countries and in Cuba.

LADA BRASHOVANOVA

Raick, Dieudonné (baptized Liège, 1 March 1703; *d* Antwerp, 30 Nov 1764). South Netherlands composer and organist. The name Raick appears frequently among canons of the collegiate church of St Paul in Liège during the 18th century. Dieudonné Raick was a choirboy at Antwerp Cathedral, and in 1721 succeeded Jacques La Fosse as organist there. He took minor orders the following year and was ordained priest in 1726. In the same year he left Antwerp to take up the post of organist and trainer of the choristers in the collegiate church of St Pierre in Louvain; he took advantage of his stay in the university town to pursue legal and theological studies, and may have been the master there of Matthias van den Gheyn. At the beginning of 1741 he was appointed organist of St Vincent, Soignies, but did not appear there because he had meanwhile obtained the more rewarding post of organist at the cathedral of St Baaf in Ghent (where he was also required to teach the instrument to the children of the choir). He must have known Pierre-Joseph Le Blan, the bellringer of Ghent, who brought out a harpsichord book there in 1752 with Raick's own publisher. In December 1757, 30 years after leaving Antwerp, he returned there, succeeding his own former successor, Chrétien-Balthazar de Trazegnies; his appointment in Ghent went to Jean-Joseph Boutmy. He remained in Antwerp for the rest of his life.

There is a marked kinship between Raick's music and that of Couperin and Rameau, but it also shows Handel's influence, and this seems to have kept it further from the *galant* style than, for example, that of his fellow countryman and contemporary, Renotte. His op.1 happily exploits a wide range of the expressive and technical possibilities of the harpsichord.

WORKS

6 suites de clavecin, op.1 (Louvain and Brussels, *c*1740), ed. in MMB, vi (1948)

2ème livre de clavecin [6 suites] (Ghent, *c*1745); some ed. in MMB, vi (1948)

3 sonates pour le clavecin (Ghent, n.d.), lost, cited by Eitner and Fétis

6 petites suites, op.3, kbd (Ghent, ?1753), 1 piece ed. in MMB, vi (1948)

6 petites suites, kbd, fl/vn (Ghent, 1753), lost, cited by Vander Straeten

Numerous kbd pieces; motet, vv, orch: mostly in private collections in Brussels, Ghent and Louvain, cited by Eitner and Fétis

BIBLIOGRAPHY

EitnerA; FétisB; RiemannL 12

E. vander Straeten: *La musique aux Pays-Bas avant le XIXe siècle*, iv (Brussels, 1878/*R*1969), 295ff

E. Gregoir: *Documents historiques* (Brussels, 1872)

A. Auda: *La musique et les musiciens de l'ancien pays de Liège* (Brussels, Paris and Liège, 1930)

R. Vannes: *Dictionnaire des musiciens (compositeurs)* (Brussels, 1947)

S. Clercx: Introduction to MMB, vi (1948), pp.xxiiiff

M. de Smet: 'Raick, Dieudonné', *MGG*

PHILIPPE MERCIER

Raidestinos, David (*b* ?Raidestos, nr. Constantinople; *fl* Mt Athos, 1st half of 15th century). Byzantine composer; *see* GREECE, §II.

Raimann, Ferdinand. *See* RAIMUND, FERDINAND.

Raimbaut de Vaqeiras [Vaqeiras] (*b* Vaqeiras, nr. Orange, Provence, ?1150–60; *d* ?Greece, ? 4 Sept 1207). French troubadour poet and composer, companion-at-arms of Boniface, Marquis of Monferrat (1152–1207). According to his *vida* (*I-Rvat* 5232, f.160) he was the son of a 'poor knight' ('paubre cavaillier'), and the fact of his humble origin, at least, is confirmed in his own writings. As a young man, he travelled to the court of Monferrat in northern Italy, where he entered the service of the Marquis of Monferrat and his son Boniface; he remained there probably until the early

1180s. Less is known of his life during the period from about 1183 to 1188, but in 1189 he was again in Provence, possibly in the service of Hugues I des Baux (d 1240). In 1190 he was back in Italy, and in 1192 had returned to Monferrat and the court of Boniface (who succeeded his father as marquis in that year).

It is from the succeeding period that Raimbaut's military exploits are known. His action in saving his patron's life in Sicily in 1194 earned him his knighthood. In 1201 Boniface was elected leader of the fourth crusade, and in 1202 he set off for the Holy Land from Venice. Raimbaut apparently returned to Provence rather than accompany his patron, but when the crusade was diverted into an action against the Byzantine Empire he finally joined the marquis in Constantinople in 1203. In 1205, Raimbaut composed his celebrated 'epic letter' to the marquis (see Linskill, pp.301–44), where there is a description of the events in which he participated during his colourful career. This document (F-Pn fr.856 (anc.7226), f.130) is an invaluable biographical source. Boniface was killed near Messiople on 4 September 1207 during a surprise attack by the Bulgarian allies of the Greeks, and it is generally assumed that Raimbaut died at his patron's side in this battle. There is no direct testimony for this, however, and it may be that he survived and even returned to Provence. A Raimbaut de Vaqueiras who is named as a witness on a document in Provence dated 1243 is thought by some scholars to be the same man.

Of the 35 poems attributed to Raimbaut, seven survive with music. The best known of these is Calenda maya which calls itself an estampida in its last line. A razo states that Raimbaut composed this poem to fit a melody which he had heard played on the vielle (violar) by two French jongleurs. Since many later estampies are instrumental, this story is at least plausible. In any event, Calenda maya is the oldest example of the genre, although it differs in its construction from later specimens. It is uncertain whether Souvent soupire is the original French melody which Raimbaut used as the basis for his poem, or whether it is a later imitation.

WORKS

Editions: Der musikalische Nachlass der Troubadours: I, ed. F. Gennrich, SMM, iii (1958) [G]
  The Poems of the Troubadour Raimbaut de Vaqueiras, ed. J. Linskill (The Hague, 1964) [L]

(all datings are given according to Linskill)

Ara·m requier sa costum' e son us, PC 392.2, G 96, L 10 (composed in Monferrat, 1197–1201)

Ara pot hom conoisser e proar, PC 392.3, G 97, L 19 (crusade-song celebrating the election of Boniface of Monferrat as leader of the fourth crusade, 1201)

Calenda maya, PC 392.9 [contrafactum: 'Souvent soupire', R.1506], G 98, L 15 (composed in Monferrat 1197–1201; for the melody of R.1506, see Gennrich, 1960, p.64)

Eissament ai guerrejat ab amor, PC 392.13, G 99, L 12 (composed in Monferrat, 1197–1201)

Guerras mi plag non son bo, PC 392.18, G 100, L 13 (composed in Monferrat, 1197–1201)

No·m agrad' iverns ni pascors, PC 392.24, G 101, L 22 (composed in Salonika, 1204–5)

Savis e fols, humils et orgoillos, PC 392.28, G 102, L 11 (composed in Monferrat, 1197–1201)

BIBLIOGRAPHY

O. Schultz-Gora: Die Briefe des Trobadors Räimbaut de Vaqueiras an Bonifaz I von Monferrat (Halle, 1893)
A. Jeanroy: 'Sur une pièce de Raimbaut de Vaqueiras', Studii dedicati a Francesco Torraca (Naples, 1912), 483
A. Kolsen: 'Bemerkung zu Raimbaut de Vaqueiras', Archiv für das Studium der neuren Sprachen, cxlv (1923), 274
K. M. Fassbinder: 'Der Trobador Raimbaut de Vaqueiras: Leben und Dichtung', Zeitschrift für romanische Philologie, xlix (1929), 129–90, 437–72
O. Schultz-Gora: ' "En Vaqueiras" in eine Urkunde', Archiv für das Studium der neuren Sprachen, clvi (1929), 100
H. Husmann: 'Kalenda maya', AMw, x (1953), 275
G. Cusimano: 'Poesia di Rambaldo di Vaqueiras', La poesia provenzale in Italia, ed. A. Monteverdi (Rome, 1955–6)
T. G. Bergin: Rambaldo di Vaqueiras: liriche (Florence, 1956)
F. Gennrich: 'Die Bedeutung der Rhythmik der Kalenda-maya-Melodie', Romanica: Festschrift für G. Rohlfs (Halle, 1958), 275
——: Der musikalische Nachlass der Troubadours, SMM, iv (1960)
F. Lecoy: 'Note sur le troubadour Raimbaut de Vaqueyras', Etudes romanes dédiées à Mario Roques (Paris, 1960), 23
F. Gennrich: 'Raimbaut de Vaqueiras', MGG
J. Boutière and A. H. Schutz: Biographies des troubadours (Paris, 1964), 447ff
J. Linskill: The Poems of the Troubadour Raimbaut de Vaqueiras (The Hague, 1964)
G. S. McPeek: 'Medieval Monophonic Song: Kalenda Maia by Raimbault de Vaqueiras (c. 1155–1205)', Notations and Editions: a Book in Honor of Louise Cuyler (Dubuque, Iowa, 1974), 1
For further bibliography see TROUBADOURS, TROUVÈRES.
ROBERT FALCK

Raimo, Padre. See BARTOLI, ERASMO.

Raimon de Miraval (fl 1180–1215). Provençal troubadour. Although his name appears in documents of 1157–1213, these apparently refer to two persons, possibly father and son; it is thus difficult to determine the approximate birthdate of the poet. A member of the lesser nobility, Raimon shared with three brothers a small castle at Miraval, north of Carcassonne. This was taken by the Albigensian crusaders in either 1209 or 1211, and Bel m'es qu'eu chant e coindei refers to its loss. Raimon received the patronage of Count Raimon VI of Toulouse (alluded to in his poetry as 'Audiart') and Viscount Raimon-Rogier of Béziers ('Pastoret'). He was familiar with Uc de Mataplana and, like Aimeric de Peguilhan, visited the courts of Pedro II of Aragon and Alfonso VIII of Castile (perhaps in the company of Raimon VI, following the latter's defeat in 1213). Various noble ladies and men are mentioned in Raimon's poetry under fictitious names. Raimon Vidal and Matfre Ermengaut regarded Raimon de Miraval as the embodiment of the courtly lover, and two of his works are cited by Berenguier de Noia. Francesco da Barberino indicated that a story by Raimon provided the basis for one of his own, but Raimon's work has apparently not survived.

The 48 chansons which can be attributed to Raimon include chansons courtoises, sirventes, coblas échangées, a partimen, and a dompnejaire (salut d'amour). 22 survive with melodies, the largest extant troubadour musical output after that of Guiraut Riquier. All are contained in F-Pn fr.22543, while three occur also in the Ambrosiana Chansonnier (I-Ma R.71 sup.). The poems are normally simple and direct, of excellent craftsmanship, and often elegant. Those with music show a marked preference for heterometric constructions. There is also a clear preference for octosyllabic and heptasyllabic lines, though lines of five, six and ten syllables are also employed. There are usually two different line lengths per strophe, but Ben aja·l cortes esciens has five.

The variety in poetic construction is mirrored by a similar variety in the musical structures. On the one hand there are such tightly organized bar forms as in A penas sai don m'apreing and Chansoneta farai vencutz with symmetrically constituted caudas, and on the other there are non-repetitive settings such as *Cel cui jois taing*, *Entre dos volers*, *Res contr' Amor* and *Si·m fos de mon chantar*. There is a variety of irregular repetition schemes, as well as some interesting examples of phrases which have similar basic contours but display different tonal groupings. There is also considerable variety of modal structure, and two of the three works that survive in both sources vary significantly in their modal organization. In some melodies there is a very strong feeling for a main tonal centre, while in others, such as *Ben aja·l cortes esciens*, *Ben aja·l messatgiers* and *Si tot s'es ma domn' esquiva*, the final is different from the main centre of the opening phrases. Both simple recitations and moderately florid passages are to be found. Only in *Si·m fos de mon chantar* is there a regularity in the disposition of ligatures that suggests symmetry of rhythmic organization.

WORKS

Edition: *Der musikalische Nachlass der Troubadours*, ed. F. Gennrich, SMM, iii, iv, xv (1958–65) [G]

Aissi cum es genser pascors, PC 406.2, G iii, 137; ed. in Anglès (1935), p.401
A penas sai don m'apreing, PC 406.7, G iii, 138; ed. in Anglès (1935), p.402
Ar ab la forsa dels freis, PC 406.8, G iii, 139
Ara m'agr' ops que m'aizis, PC 406.9, G iii, 140
Bel m'es qu'eu chant e coindei, PC 406.12, G iii, 141; ed. in Anglès (1935), p.401
Be m'agrada·l bels temps d'estiu, PC 406.13, G iii, 142; ed. in Gennrich (1959), p.53
Ben aja·l cortes esciens, PC 406.14, G iii, 143
Ben aja·l messatgiers, PC 406.15, G iii, 144
Cel cui jois taing ni chantar sap, PC 406.18, G iii, 145
Cel que no vol auzir chansos, PC 406.20, G iii, 146; ed. in Anglès (1935), p.403
Chansoneta farai vencutz, PC 406.21, G iii, 147; ed. in Anglès (1958), appx 8
Chans, quan non es qui l'entenda, PC 406.22, G iii, 148
Contr' Amor vauc durs et enbroncs, PC 406.23, G iii, 149
D'amor es totz mos consiriers, PC 406.24, G iii, 150; ed. in Anglès (1935), p.402
Entre dos volers sui pensius, PC 406.28, G iii, 151
Lonc temps ai avutz consiriers, PC 406.31, G iii, 152
Res contr' Amor non es guirens, PC 406.36, G iii, 153
Si·m fos de mon chantar parven, PC 406.39, G iii, 154
Si tot s'es ma domn' esquiva, PC 406.40, G iii, 155; ed. in Anglès (1935), p.402
Tals vai mon chant enqueren, PC 406.42, G iii, 156
Tot quan fatz de be ni dic, PC 406.44, G iii, 157
Un sonet m'es bel qu' espanda, PC 406.47, G iii, 158

BIBLIOGRAPHY

P. Andraud: *La vie et l'oeuvre du troubadour Raimon de Miraval* (Paris, 1902)
H. Anglès: *La mùsica a Catalunya fins al segle XIII* (Barcelona, 1935)
——: *La mùsica de las cantigas del Rey Alfonso el Sabio*, iii/2 (Barcelona, 1958)
F. Gennrich: *Lo Gai Saber*, Musikwissenschaftliche Studien-Bibliothek, xviii–xix (Darmstadt, 1959)
For further bibliography see TROUBADOURS, TROUVÈRES.

THEODORE KARP

Raimondi, Gianni (*b* Bologna, 13 April 1923). Italian tenor. A pupil of Gennaro Barra-Caracciolo, he made his début in 1947 at the Teatro Comunale, Bologna, in *Rigoletto*. After appearing at the Comunale, Florence (1952), the Paris Opéra (1953) and at the Stoll Theatre, London (*Rigoletto*, 1953), he has sung almost continuously at La Scala from 1955–6, also appearing at the Vienna Staatsoper (1958 and 1962) and at the Metropolitan Opera (1965–6). Endowed with an ample voice of pure, warm timbre, he has clear enunciation and an exact sense of phrasing. The facility, range and brilliance of his top register have enabled him to take part in many important revivals such as Rossini's

Armida, *Semiramide* and *Guillaume Tell*, Donizetti's *Anna Bolena* and Verdi's *Les vêpres siciliennes*. His other notable roles from the standard repertory include Rodolfo and Pinkerton.

BIBLIOGRAPHY

G. Gualerzi: 'Raimondi, Gianni', *Le grandi voci* (Rome, 1964) [with opera discography]

RODOLFO CELLETTI

Raimondi, Ignazio (*b* Naples, *c*1735; *d* London, 14 Jan 1813). Italian violinist and composer. In Naples, he played in the S Carlo orchestra (1759–62) and studied the violin with Emanuele Barbella, thus coming into contact with the violin school of Tartini. In 1762 he went to Amsterdam, where he appeared as conductor in many subscription concerts and also performed regularly as a soloist. At a concert on 15 January 1777, he conducted, with great success, his symphony *Les aventures de Télémaque dans l'isle de Calypso*. He settled in London in 1780, winning immediate success with his symphony *The Battle* and his concert appearances. In 1789 he went to Paris for the performance of his opera *La muta* and in 1792 gave a series of 12 subscription concerts, as soloist and conductor, at Willis's Rooms. Burney praised Raimondi's playing for its 'sweet tone and polished style'; his chamber compositions are also characterized by sweetness and simplicity. His descriptive orchestration employs a rich variety of effects and techniques.

WORKS

Chamber: 27 trios: 6 for 2 vn, vc, op.1 (Amsterdam, *c*1770, 2/*c*1775 as 6 Sonatas), 6 for (2 vn, b)/(vn, va, vc), op.5, 12 for vn, va, vc, opp.11–13, 3 for fl, vn, vc, op.14; 9 qts, fl, vn, va, vc, opp.7, 10; 21 sonatas: 12 for vn, b, opp.3, 6, 6 for 2 vn, op.4, 3 for pf, acc. vn, vc, op.15; 1 duet, vn, va (London, *c*1790); 6 duetti, 2 vn, *I-Mc*; 6 trios, 2 vn, b, *Mc* (lacking vn 2)
Other works: Sinfonie concertante, 2 vn, orch, op.2; 6 vn concs., opp.8–9; 6 Grand Marches, military band, arr. pf/harp (London, *c*1785); The Favorite Grand Piece called The Battle, orch, arr. pf, opt. vn and vc (London, 1791)

BIBLIOGRAPHY

BurneyH; *GerberL*; *GerberNL*
A. Moser: *Geschichte des Violinspiels* (Berlin, 1923, enlarged 2/1966–7)
E. van der Straeten: *The History of the Violin* (London, 1933)
F. Göthel: 'Raimondi, Ignazio', *MGG*

GUIDO SALVETTI

Raimondi, Pietro (*b* Rome, 20 Dec 1786; *d* Rome, 30 Oct 1853). Italian composer and teacher. Born of poor parents, he was left by his widowed mother in the care of a well-to-do aunt, who sent him to the Naples Conservatory. There he followed Tritto's counterpoint course so assiduously that he is said to have often spent his meagre food allowance on extra lessons. After six years his aunt withdrew her support, and Raimondi returned to his mother in Genoa, where he produced his first operas in 1807–9. In 1811 he was back in Naples, where all but a few of the 40 or so operas that he composed during the next 30 years were to have their first (and usually only) productions. His somewhat plodding reliability in this genre was rewarded in 1824 when he was made music director of the royal theatres of Naples. He also composed sacred operas and oratorios and about 22 ballets for S Carlo.

By 1810 he also had a reputation as a composer of fugues, and a *Christe* from that year for two choruses and orchestra in double canon (in *I-Fc*) shows that he was already interested in contrapuntal complexities. In

1825, after Tritto's death, Raimondi and Francesco Ruggi succeeded him as counterpoint teachers at the Naples Conservatory. In 1833 Raimondi, whom Pacini in 1834 called 'the most celebrated contrapuntist of our time', was chosen counterpoint master and director of the Palermo Conservatory and music director of the Palermo opera house. (According to Fétis, the one resounding operatic success of his career, that of *Il ventaglio* in 1831, had been influential in the choice.) In 1835 he was also named honorary *maestro di camera* to the king's brother, Leopoldo, Count of Syracuse and Viceroy of Sicily. Raimondi seems not to have been happy in Sicily and made several attempts to obtain posts in more important centres (Paris, Milan, Dresden). His operatic style was outmoded, and he was known as a staunch adherent of the old, pre-Rossinian Neapolitan school. Composing no new operas for Naples after 1839 and only a few for Palermo in the years that followed, he turned to didactic works of abstract counterpoint and to religious music (of which he had already composed a fair amount).

From the 1820s Raimondi had progressed from ordinary fugues to four and five independent fugues that could also be performed simultaneously, and finally to the combination (always a consonant one) of up to six independent fugues in different keys and modes. He saw these works as scientific experiments designed to produce 'discoveries' in counterpoint. But he also believed that counterpoint was the essential basis of all music (he thought the new Italian opera styles decadent and arising from young composers' 'heretical' scorn of strict contrapuntal studies); and so to be valid his abstract discoveries had to be suitable for practical application. This he set out to demonstrate in a remarkable series of works, beginning with a mass (in *I-Nc*) performed in 1836 in Palermo; it consisted of two independent masses, each in eight parts with its own orchestra, which could be performed separately and together.

In 1847–8 came three oratorios, *Putifar*, *Giuseppe* and *Giacobbe* (in *I-Rsc*), which could also be performed simultaneously. The musical combinations were made with the utmost boldness, juxtaposing the most disparate tempos, metres, performing bodies and types of musical expression. The work was first performed on 7 August 1852 at the Teatro Argentina in Rome with 430 performers in a concert lasting six hours. When the three groups, each with its own conductor, joined together at the end under Raimondi's overall direction, the resulting grandiosity of sound created a sensation (Raimondi was overcome and fainted). Now a celebrity, he was received by the pope, honoured with a special gold medal and, more substantially, made *maestro di cappella* at St Peter's in December 1852, a post he enjoyed for only a few months before his final illness. He did not finish orchestrating his magnum opus, *Adelasia*, an *opera seria*, and *I quattro rustici*, an *opera buffa*, intended to be performed simultaneously on a divided stage; the orchestration (now in *I-Nc*) was completed by Raimondi's favourite pupil, Pietro Platania, but was never performed.

WORKS

DRAMATIC

Operas: *c*50 operas, principal sources *I-Fc*, *Mr*, *Nc*, incl. Il ventaglio (D. Gilardone, after Goldoni), Naples, 1831, autograph *Mr*, vocal score (Naples, n.d.); Francesca Donata (F. Romani), Palermo, 1842, vocal score (Milan, ?1845)

Other works: *c*13 sacred operas and oratorios, some *Nc*, incl. Il giudizio

universale, Palermo, ?1844, vocal score (Milan, before 1846); at least 4 cantatas, 1 in *Fc*; 22 ballets, incl. Gonsalvo e Zilia, autograph *US-STu*

SACRED

At least 6 masses, vv, orch; 3 requiem; Credo, 16vv; Libera me; numerous vesper psalms; 4 Miserere; 3 Tantum ergo; 3 Stabat mater, 2 pubd (Rome, Naples, n.d.); Le 7 parole, 3vv, str orch; 2 litanies; 2 complines; Veni Creator Spiritus; La salmodia Davidica, 4–8vv, all unacc., inc. [only 1st 60 psalms composed]; hymns; others

DIDACTIC

Fughe diversi (?Naples, n.d., Milan, 2/?1838): pt. i, 20 fughe, 4–8vv, untexted except no.20, Confutatis maledictis, pt. ii, Tu es sacerdos, 4 fughe in una, pt. iii, Et exultavit, 5 fughe in una; Bassi imitati e fugati (Milan, ?1836); Nuovo genere di scientifica composizione: divisa in 12 esempi (?Naples, n.d.); 4 fughe in una dissimili nel modo: opera scientifica, on text Cum sanctis (Milan, ?1846); 6 fughe in una dissimili nel modo, unpubd; 2 fughe in una dissimili nel modo: opera scientifica, 9 pieces (Rome, ?1849); Nuovo genere di scientifica composizione: andamenti di basso numerati con una, due, o tre armonie (Naples, 1852); 2 grandi fughe a 4 voci l'una, e un canone similmente a 4 (12 voci) riunite insieme (Rome, n.d.)

BIBLIOGRAPHY

FétisB

G. Pacini: *Cenni storici sulla musica e trattato di contrappunto* (Lucca, 1834), 23

F. Cicconetti: *Memorie intorno Pietro Raimondi* (Rome, 1867) [incl. list of works]

F. Florimo: *Cenno storico della scuola musicale di Napoli*, i (Naples, 1869), 619ff

O. Chilesotti: *I nostri maestri del passato* (Milan, 1882)

C. Gray: 'Pietro Raimondi', *MR*, i (1940), 25

O. Tiby: *Il Real Teatro Carolino e l'Ottocento musicale napoletano* (Florence, 1957)

DENNIS LIBBY

Raimondi, Ruggero (*b* Bologna, 3 Oct 1941). Italian bass. A pupil of Teresa Pediconi and of Piervenanzi, he made his début at Spoleto on 15 September 1964 as Colline, followed immediately by Procida (*Les vêpres siciliennes*) at the Rome Opera. After having sung at La Fenice, Venice, and other major Italian theatres, he was engaged at La Scala in the 1967–8 season (Timur in *Turandot*), returning there in 1969–70. In 1968 he sang Alfonso at the Royal Festival Hall, London, in a concert performance with Caballé of Donizetti's *Lucrezia Borgia*. He then appeared at Glyndebourne as Don Giovanni in 1969, and at the Metropolitan, New York, making his début as Silva (*Ernani*) on 14 September 1970. He first sang at Covent Garden on 23 February 1972 as Verdi's Fiesco. He has the full, smooth and resonant voice of a *basso cantante* (with a certain baritonal quality and colour in the upper register), a very accurate and stylish technique and an imposing stage presence. He is considered one of the finest contemporary basses in the early 19th-century repertory and has also won great praise as Don Giovanni. In the 1972–3 season in Venice his performance of Boris displayed his singular interpretative talents.

BIBLIOGRAPHY

A. Blyth: 'Ruggero Raimondi Talks', *Gramophone*, 1 (1973), 2030

RODOLFO CELLETTI

Raimund [Raimann], Ferdinand (*b* Vienna, 1 June 1790; *d* Pottenstein, Lower Austria, 5 Sept 1836). Austrian dramatist, actor and theatre director. The son of a carpenter, Raimund as a boy became fascinated by the theatre when he sold refreshments at the Burgtheater. He determined to become an actor, and he spent some years as a member of small touring troupes. In 1814 he was engaged at the Josefstadt Theatre in Vienna, three years later joining the famous ensemble of the Theater in der Leopoldstadt. His rise to pre-eminence was steady rather than meteoric, and was based above all on his remarkable powers of mime and of timing. For some years his rivalry with the older Ignaz Schuster deprived the public of the opportunity to see them both on the same stage in the same performance – Raimund's suspicious, melancholy nature must bear much of the responsibility. He rose to the position of producer and then, in 1828, to that of director of the Leopoldstadt company. In 1830 he left and spent the rest of his life making guest appearances and touring – despite his archetypal Austrian dialect and style he enjoyed remarkable successes in Munich and even in Hamburg and Berlin. During his years at the Josefstadt Theatre he contracted an ill-advised marriage to Luise Gleich which broke up after a year and left him unable to legalize his later union with Antonie Wagner. He died by his own hand, believing that a dog that had bitten him was mad.

Raimund was the most poetic of the dramatists of the Viennese popular theatre, though he only became a playwright out of necessity – the fortunes of Meisl, Bäuerle and Gleich, who had dominated the repertory in the first two decades of the century, were on the wane, and when Gleich failed to provide Raimund with a satisfactory play for a benefit performance, he wrote *Der Barometermacher auf der Zauberinsel* (1823, music by Wenzel Müller, 96 performances in the Leopoldstadt until 1855). Raimund followed this success with a further seven dramas: *Der Diamant des Geisterkönigs* (1824, music by Drechsler, 160 performances until 1854), *Das Mädchen aus der Feenwelt oder Der Bauer als Millionär* (1826, music by Drechsler, 207 performances until 1859), *Moisasurs Zauberfluch* (1827, music by Riotte), *Die gefesselte Phantasie* (1828, music by Müller), *Der Alpenkönig und der Menschenfeind* (1828, music by Müller, 163 performances until 1859), *Die unheilbringende Zauberkrone* (1829, music by Drechsler), and *Der Verschwender* (1834, music by Conradin Kreutzer, 142 performances in the Leopoldstadt until 1859). Raimund himself wrote the melodies for some of his best-known songs (sketches survive in his hand, notated in the treble clef – he was an accomplished if untutored violinist – for the *Aschenlied* and *Brüderlein fein* from *Das Mädchen aus der Feenwelt*, to mention but two of the songs that became *Volkslieder*). Though his voice was neither beautiful nor particularly strong, he was acclaimed for his skill at putting across the songs in his own and other authors' plays. Along with his younger contemporary and antipode, Nestroy, Raimund marks the end and the peak of a long and distinguished tradition; though the most ambitious and tragic of his plays (*Moisasur, Phantasie* and *Zauberkrone*) enjoyed little success in Raimund's lifetime and even now are less popular than the great comedies, his achievement as a dramatist is broad, unified and powerful. The role of music in his plays is considerable, averaging 20 numbers.

BIBLIOGRAPHY

W. A. Bauer and H. Kraus, eds.: *Raimund-Liederbuch* (Vienna, 1924)

A. Orel, ed.: *Die Gesänge der Märchendramen in den ursprünglichen Vertonungen*, [F. Raimund:] Sämtliche Werke (Historisch-kritische Säkularausgabe), vi (Vienna, 1924)

A. Orel: 'Raimund und die Musik', *Raimund-Almanach 1936* (Innsbruck, 1936)

H. Kindermann: *Ferdinand Raimund: Lebenswerk und Wirkungsraum eines deutschen Volksdramatikers* (Vienna, 1940)

K. Goedeke: *Grundriss zur Geschichte der deutschen Dichtung*, xi/2 (Düsseldorf, 2/1953), 314–45

K. Kahl: *Raimund* (Velber, 1967)

D. Prohaska: *Raimund and Vienna: a Critical Study of Raimund's Plays in their Viennese Setting* (Cambridge, 1970)

L. V. Harding: *The Dramatic Art of Ferdinand Raimund and Johann Nestroy: a Critical Study* (The Hague, 1974)

PETER BRANSCOMBE

Rain, Cunz. *See* REIN, CONRAD.

Rainaldi, Carlo (*b* Rome, 4 May 1611; *d* Rome, 8 Feb 1691). Italian architect, composer and instrumentalist. At the wish of his father, the architect Girolamo Rainaldi, he received a humanist education at the Collegio Romano, which he completed by studying geometry at the Sapienza. At the same time he received instruction in music, probably from Virgilio Mazzocchi, *maestro di cappella* of the Collegio Romano. According to Passeri he not only played the organ, harpsichord, double harp and *lira da braccio* 'exquisitely and with great refinement' but also composed 'with exceptional taste and skill'. His known compositions, comprising two Lamentations and 19 cantatas for one or two sopranos and continuo, have only recently come to light. They are similar to the cantatas of Carissimi and Luigi Rossi in their form – alternation of recitative and aria with the inclusion of ritornellos – and in the expressiveness with which the texts are enhanced by the use of rhetorical musical figures and the free use of dissonance. They are, moreover, no less notable than the churches, altars, monuments and triumphal arches that he designed in his principal capacity as an architect.

WORKS

(for 1v, bc, unless otherwise stated)

2 Lamentazioni per la Settimana Santa, *I-Bc*

19 secular cantatas: All'invito d'amata, *A-Wn*; Al vento de' sospiri, *I-Vnm*; Che dici, Amore, 2vv, bc, *Bc*; Chi dice che il foco, 2vv, bc, *Bc*; Ch'io sciolga il nodo, *F-Pthibault*; Dolente pentita, *I-Ra*; E chi m'el crederà, *Rvat*; Entro a stanze reali, *A-Wn*; Fiumicelli che correte, *GB-Ckc*; Ho il cor costante, *I-MOe*; Lorinda al mio ritorno, *Bc*; Luci belle vuò donarvi il core, *GB-Ouf*; Mentre nel mar cadea, *I-Rc*; Non te ne vien pietà, *Vnm*; Occhi belli, s'io v'adoro, 2vv, bc, *Bc*; Pallido muto, *Rvat*; Su le famose sponde, *Vnm*; Uccidetemi, *F-Pn*; Vaghi rai, pupille ardenti, 2vv, bc, *I-Bc*

BIBLIOGRAPHY

G. B. Passeri: *Vite de' pittori, scultori ed architetti, che anno lavorato in Roma morti dal 1641, fino al 1673* (Rome, 1772)

H. J. Marx: 'Carlo Rainaldi als Komponist', *La fabbrica di S. Agnese in Navona*, i, ed. G. Eimer (Stockholm, 1970), 244–78

HANS JOACHIM MARX

Rainbow, Bernarr (Joseph George) (*b* London, 2 Oct 1914). English music educationist and writer on music. While a civil servant, he was a part-time student at Trinity College of Music (1936–40) and after war service became head of music at the Royal Grammar School, High Wycombe (1944). He moved in 1952 to become director of music at the College of St Mark and St John, Chelsea; in 1972 he became postgraduate tutor, and from 1973 to 1978 head of the music department, at Gipsy Hill College of Education (later at Kingston Polytechnic), and then director of the Curwen Institute. He received the PhD from Leicester University in 1967 for his research into the Anglican 19th-century musical revival.

Rainbow's teaching commitments and his research have been closely related. *The Land without Music* was acclaimed as the first work to chronicle convincingly a neglected period of 19th-century musical education, and was responsible for the reassessment of the validity of the title. He brought his wide practical experience of the Anglican liturgy and a sound historical approach to his study of the Anglican choral revival.

WRITINGS

Music in the Classroom (London, 1956, 2/1970)

Handbook for Music Teachers (London, 1964, 2/1968)

The Land without Music: Musical Education in England and its Continental Antecedents, 1800–1860 (London, 1967)

The Choral Revival in the Anglican Church, 1839–72 (diss., U. of Leicester, 1967; London, 1970)

'Education in Music', §VI, 1(i), 'London', §VII, 'Tonic Sol-fa', *Grove 6* ed.: *Classic Texts in Music Education* (1980–)

John Curwen: a Short Critical Biography (London, 1980)

'Music in Education', 'Parochial and Nonconformist Church Music', *The Romantic Age (1800–1914)*, Athlone History of Music in Britain, v, ed. N. Temperley (in preparation)

DAVID SCOTT

Rainer, Jacob. See REINER, JACOB.

Rainey [née Pridgett], **Gertrude (Malissa Nix) 'Ma'** (*b* Columbus, Georgia, 26 April 1886; *d* Rome, Georgia, 22 Dec 1939). Black American blues, jazz and vaudeville singer. Her career began in a talent show when she was 12, and soon afterwards she appeared as a cabaret singer. She married Will 'Pa' Rainey in 1904, and toured with him in F. S. Wolcott's Rabbit Foot Minstrels and other shows until 1916, when they formed their own company. By the time she first recorded (1923) she had become famous throughout the South. In five years she made over 100 recordings, including some with the 'Georgia Jazz Band', which at various times included Tommy Ladnier, Joe Smith, Coleman Hawkins and the young Louis Armstrong (*Jelly Bean Blues*, 1924). These recordings did little justice to her vocal powers, but a majestic phrasing and 'moaning' style close to folk tradition are evident from her first disc (and most celebrated compositions), *Bo-weavil Blues – Moonshine Blues*. She toured throughout the South and in Mexico in the 1920s, establishing a lasting reputation as the most significant early female singer of blues. At an early age Bessie Smith toured with Rainey and became her protégée. Rainey ceased recording in 1928, and in 1935 retired to Columbus, where she was active in the Baptist church. She is best remembered for her classic versions of *See See Rider* (1924) and *Soon this Morning* (1927).

BIBLIOGRAPHY

B. Rust: *Jazz Records: 1897–1942* (London, 1965, rev. 2/1969)

D. Stewart-Baxter: *Ma Rainey and the Classic Blues Singers* (New York and London, 1970)

PAUL OLIVER

Rainforth, Elizabeth (*b* ?23 Nov 1814; *d* Bristol, 22 Sept 1877). English soprano. She studied singing with George Perry and T. Cooke in London. After appearing in concert she made her stage début on 27 October 1836 as Mandane in Arne's *Artaxerxes* at St James's Theatre, London. After a period of further study with Crivelli she continued to sing at Covent Garden until 1843, where her repertory included Zerlina in *Fra Diavolo*, Susanna and the Countess in *Le nozze di Figaro*, and the title roles in Cherubini's *Lodoïska* (in a pastiche version) and Boieldieu's *Barbara, or The Bride of a Day*. In 1843 she joined the company at Drury Lane where she created Arline in Balfe's *The Bohemian Girl* in November 1843. She appeared regularly in oratorio and concerts both in London and the provinces, and sang in Dublin between 1842 and 1849. In 1845 she sang the soprano part in the first performance of Mendelssohn's *Hear my Prayer* at the Crosby Hall, London. She retired in 1856, and two years later went to live in Old Windsor, where she taught music until

1871. Her voice was a high soprano, even and sweet in quality.

HAROLD ROSENTHAL

Rainger, Ralph (*b* New York, 7 Oct 1901; *d* nr. Palm Springs, Calif., 23 Oct 1942). American songwriter and pianist. He studied at the Damrosch Institute, New York, and at Brown University. Among his teachers were Paolo Gallico, Clarence Adler and Schoenberg. He became a lawyer, then performed in Broadway musicals as a piano duettist with Edgar Fairchild (1926–8) and Adam Carroll (1929), and became a pianist in Paul Whiteman's orchestra and an accompanist and arranger for vaudeville singers. As a pianist with Arthur Schwartz's revue *The Little Show* (1929) he wrote *Moanin' Low* (lyrics by H. Dietz). In 1932–42 he wrote songs for about 35 films in Hollywood, mostly with the lyricist Leo Robin; the most successful, some of which were written for Bing Crosby, include *Blue Hawaii* (1937), *Ebb Tide* (1937), *Thanks for the Memory* (1938) and others for the *Big Broadcast* film series (1932–8); he also composed and arranged music for the film biography of Paul Dresser, *My Gal Sal* (1942).

BIBLIOGRAPHY

R. D. Kinkle: *The Complete Encyclopedia of Popular Music and Jazz 1900–1950* (New Rochelle, NY, 1974)

DEANE L. ROOT

Rainier, Priaulx (*b* Howick, Natal, 3 Feb 1903). South African-English composer of English-Huguenot origin. After early childhood in Zululand, she entered the South African College of Music, Cape Town, as a violin student (1913); in 1920 her playing won her the Cape University Scholarship to the Royal Academy of Music. She then settled permanently in London, earning her living as a violinist and teacher until 1935, when an anonymous grant enabled her to concentrate on composition. In 1937 she studied with Boulanger for three months, and she was a professor of composition at the RAM (1943–61).

Rainier has developed a fastidious language drawing little from other 20th-century styles. Rather, the most important influences have been the language and music of the Zulus, and the natural sounds of their country; beyond this, the visual insights of Hepworth and Nicholson, with both of whom she had contact, greatly extended the range of her music. She came to the attention of a wider public after the success of the String Quartet, a work whose originality is particularly clear in the scherzo and in the finale. Crystalline textures and short ostinato rhythms assist in the building of fast movements independent of Bartók and Stravinsky and of more conventional styles. Although Rainier has never consciously used African musical techniques, these movements obviously reflect her origins, and at the same time introduce a characteristic distancing, both literally – as if sounds were being heard across the open air – and metaphorically, the product of classically disciplined musical thinking. Subsequent works of the 1940s emphasize rhythmic novelty, chief among them the Clarinet Suite and the *Barbaric Dance Suite*, where, despite its title, the dominant impression is of delicacy rather than savagery.

At this time Rainier's harmony was triadic and even diatonic; chromaticism was the consequence of melodic inflection and bitonality. Her melodic writing was typified by concise motivic phrases. The promise of functional harmony and extended melodic line was amply realized in *Requiem*, a work of beauty and passion, whose simple yet expressive neo-tonal harmony and incantatory solo part mark the culmination of a period in her output. During the 1960s her music became more compressed, owing in part to a fondness for clusters and an associated emphasis on melodic semitones and minor 9ths, in part to a continuing use of short, pulsating rhythmic figures, but more particularly to the gestures themselves. These retain Rainier's meticulously polished sounds, but are isolated, often abruptly contrasted, and highly concentrated, suggesting an energy activated only briefly. Continuity is achieved more through patterns of timbre and texture than through consistent impulse. A more relaxed expression is evident in the works of the 1970s, although the uncompromisingly objective sounds remain distinctive.

WORKS
(*some early works listed in Grove 5 have been withdrawn*)

Orch: Sinfonia da camera, str, 1947; Ballet Suite, 1950; Phala-phala, dance conc., 1960; Vc Conc., 1964; Aequora lunae, 1966–7; Trios and Triads, 10 trios, perc, 1967–; Ploërmel, wind, perc, 1972–3; Vn Conc., 1974–7; Concertante Duo, ob, cl, small orch, 1977–

Inst: Str Qt, 1939; Suite, cl, pf, 1943; Sonata, va, pf, 1945; Barbaric Dance Suite, pf, 1949; 5 Pieces, kbd, 1955; 6 Pieces, 5 wind, 1957; Trio-Suite, pf trio, 1960; Pastoral Triptych, ob, 1958–9; Quanta, ob, str trio, 1961–2; Suite, vc/va, 1963–5; Str Trio, 1965–6; Quinque, hpd, 1971; Gloriana, org, 1972; Primordial Canticles, org, 1974

Vocal: 3 Greek Epigrams (Anyte of Tegea, trans. R. Aldington), S, pf, 1937; Dance of the Rain (E. Marais, trans, U. Krige), S/T, gui, 1947; Ubunzima (Zulu), S/T, gui, 1948; Cycle for Declamation (Donne), 1v, 1953; Requiem (Gascoigne), T, chorus, 1955–6; The Bee Oracles (E. Sitwell), T/Bar, fl, ob, vn, vc, hpd, 1969; Vision and Prayer (D. Thomas), T, pf, 1973; Prayers from the Ark, T, harp, 1974–5

Principal publisher: Schott

BIBLIOGRAPHY
W. Glock: 'The Music of Priaulx Rainier', *The Listener*, xxxviii (1947), 872
J. Amis: 'Priaulx Rainier', *MT*, xcvi (1955), 354
P. Rainier: 'The New World of Modern Music', *Ideas of Today*, xv (1967), 107
F. Routh: *Contemporary British Music* (London, 1972), 346ff
P. Rainier: [*Requiem*], *The Listener*, lxxxviii (1972), 185
T. Baxter: 'Priaulx Rainier: a Study of her Musical Style', *Composer*, (1977), no.60, p.19
H. van der Spuy: 'Priaulx Rainier', *Musicus*, vii/1 (1979), 7

IAN KEMP

Rains, Robert de. *See* ROBERT DE REINS.

Rais, Jakub de. *See* REYS, JAKUB.

Raisa, Rosa [Burchstein, Rose] (*b* Białystok, 23 May 1893; *d* Los Angeles, 28 Sept 1963). American soprano of Polish birth. When she was 14 she fled from Poland to escape a pogrom and settled in Naples, where she studied with Barbara Marchisio. She made her concert début in Rome in 1912, and was then engaged by Cleofonte Campanini to sing Leonora in *Oberto* during the 1913 Verdi celebrations at Parma. Her success was such that Campanini took her to Chicago for the 1913–14 season, and then to Covent Garden in 1914. She sang regularly in Chicago, 1916–32 and 1933–6, appearing in the first American performances of Mascagni's *Isabeau*, Montemezzi's *La nave* and Respighi's *La fiamma*. In 1936 she sang Leah in the American première of Rocca's *Il dybbuk* at Detroit.

In 1924 Toscanini engaged her for La Scala, Milan, to create Asteria in Boito's posthumous opera, *Nerone*; and she created Turandot in 1926. She returned to Covent Garden in 1933 as Tosca, with her husband, Giacomo Rimini, as Scarpia. In 1937 they opened a singing school in Chicago. She was a thrilling singer and actress; according to the conductor Giorgio Polacco,

she was one of the two greatest dramatic sopranos he had ever heard – the other being Destinn.

BIBLIOGRAPHY
R. Celletti: 'Raisa, Rosa', *Le grandi voci* (Rome, 1964) [with opera discography by J. Swatton]

HAROLD ROSENTHAL

Raison, André (*b* before 1650; *d* Paris, 1719). French organist and composer. His early years were spent at the seminary of the abbey of Ste Geneviève at Nanterre. From about 1666 he was organist at the royal abbey of Ste Geneviève in Paris, and later he also held the post of organist at the convent and college of the Jacobins de St Jacques. He was inscribed in the highest rank of organists in a 1695 tax roll of the keyboard players of Paris. He taught Clérambault, who in 1710 dedicated his *Premier livre d'orgue* to him, paying high tribute to his excellence and influence as a teacher.

The five masses of Raison's first volume follow the usual structure of the French organ mass of the period (versets for alternate phrases of the Kyrie, Gloria, Sanctus and Agnus Dei) but lack plainsong material and are almost entirely secular in character, a feature to which he calls attention when he suggests the relationship of individual pieces to various dance forms of the day. The book's utility is increased by two further features: the 21 versets of each mass can also serve for three *Magnificat* settings of various levels of difficulty; and the five keys of the masses can be adapted to all eight church modes through clef transposition or cadence alteration. The individual versets are in the forms introduced by Nivers and Lebègue – *pleins jeux*, fugues, duos, trios, ornamented solos and dialogues. He also included several ostinato movements, among which the *Trio en passacaille* in the second mass has a theme identical to the first half of that of Bach's C minor Passacaglia. The somewhat weaker *Second livre* begins with a suite of movements invoking David; these include a cantus firmus setting and fugue on *Da pacem* – Raison's only treatment of plainsong – a prelude, an overture, an allemande and additional fugues. There follows a group of noëls, most of which contain introductions and several varied settings of the traditional Christmas melodies.

Raison's organ music is less profound than that of his more famous contemporaries Couperin and Grigny, but it offers charming melody, great rhythmic interest and a sparkling display of the colours of the French classical organ. More than his contemporaries he includes within single pieces rapid changes of tempo and metre and of registration sometimes requiring as many as four manuals. These changes are specially striking in the 'Vive le Roy' acclamations in the *Offerte* of book 1 and the overture of book 2. The preface to the first book (repeated in part in the second and partly translated by F. Douglass) is one of the most valuable guides to the performance of French Baroque organ music; it discusses embellishments, registration and the proper interpretation of each type of movement.

WORKS
Editions: *A. Raison: Livre d'orgue*, ed. A. Guilmant and A. Pirro, Archives des maîtres de l'orgue, ii (Paris, 1899/R1972)
 Premier livre d'orgue, ed. N. Dufourcq, Orgue et liturgie, nos.55–6, 58–9, 61 (Paris, 1962)
 Second livre d'orgue, ed. J. Bonfils, L'organiste liturgique, nos.39–40, 43–4 (Paris, n.d.)
Livre d'orgue contenant cinq messes suffisantes pour tous les tons de l'Eglise ou quinze Magnificats . . . et une Offerte, en action de grâce, pour l'heureuse convalescence du Roy en 1687 (Paris, 1688)

Second livre d'orgue sur les acclamations de la paix tant desirée . . . [auxquelles] l'auteur adjoûte plusieurs Noëls (Paris, 1714)

BIBLIOGRAPHY
A. Pirro: 'L'art des organistes', *EMDC*, II/ii (1926), 1342
G. Frotscher: *Geschichte des Orgel-Spiels und der Orgel-Komposition*, ii (Berlin, 1936, enlarged 3/1966)
N. Dufourcq: *La musique d'orgue française de Jehan Titelouze à Jehan Alain* (Paris, 1941, 2/1949)
W. Apel: *Geschichte der Orgel- und Klaviermusik bis 1700* (Kassel, 1967; Eng. trans., rev. 1972)
F. Douglass: *The Language of the French Classical Organ* (New Haven, 1969)
ALMONTE HOWELL

Raitio, Pentti (*b* Pieksämäki, 4 June 1930). Finnish composer. He studied with Kokkonen and Bergman at the Sibelius Academy, Helsinki. In 1967 he was appointed director of the Hyvinkää music school near Helsinki. His music, most of which is vocal, has a lyrical concentration expressed in a style that makes moderate use of novel techniques.

WORKS
(*selective list*)

Joki [The river], S, ens, 1963; 13 per 13 archi, 1963; Kuun tietä [Along the moon way], S, ens, 1966; Kaksi tanssia unessa [3 dream dances], 1966; Audiendum, orch, 1967; Orfilainen kuoro, Bar, men's vv, 1968; Laulu sadelinnulle [Song to the rainbird], Bar, pf, 1974; 5 kompositioner, str orch, 1975

MSS in *SF-Hmt*

ERKKI SALMENHAARA

Raitio, Väinö (Eerikki) (*b* Sortavala, 15 April 1891; *d* Helsinki, 10 Sept 1945). Finnish composer. He studied at the Helsinki Conservatory (1911–16), in Moscow (1916–17), in Berlin (1921) and in Paris (1925–6). After a period of teaching at the Viipuri Music Institute (1926–32) he lived as a freelance composer in difficult circumstances.

With Pingoud and Merikanto, Raitio was responsible in the 1920s for introducing the first period of modernism in Finnish music. His early output was bound by Romanticism, but in Moscow and Berlin he received new influences that made his style more radical: his harmony was affected by Skryabin and German expressionism, his orchestration by Debussy and other French impressionists. The first work to show these new features was the tone poem *Joutsenet* ('The swans', 1919), still traditional in form and melodic writing. Much more complex and powerful in structure and expression are the *Fantasia estatica* (1921) and the symphonic trilogy *Antigone* (1921–2), which are perhaps his most impressive achievements. They are, without any doubt, influenced by Skryabin's ecstatic visions. 'Chaotic expressionism' is one of the terms that have been used to describe their style, but they also contain sections of sensitive lyricism, often beautifully scored and neither chaotic nor expressionist. Thematic elements, particularly in the *Antigone* trilogy, are short motifs that merge into a complex web whose dissonant character is softened by the mellow use of a very large orchestra. During the 1920s Raitio composed further tone poems, notably *Kuutamo Jupiterissa* ('Moonlight on Jupiter') and *Puistokuja* ('The avenue'), of which the latter, for soprano and orchestra, is perhaps his most impressionist piece and also the one furthest from traditional tonality.

The most important of Raitio's works from the following decade are operas. Some of them suffer from weak texts, but they do not lack a certain musical interest, even if they fall short of the level of the tone poems. Raitio's vocal writing makes extensive use of recitative in order to have every detail of the text faithfully reflected in the music. His ideas on the relationship between drama and music, as well as his use of leitmotifs, were evidently based on Wagner, but in general atmosphere his operas are closer to *Pelléas*. The best of them are the first, *Jephtan tytär* ('The daughter of Jephtha'), and the last, *Lyydian kuningas* ('The king of Lydia'). During the 1930s Raitio also wrote a considerable number of orchestral compositions, but their interest is small: his style became increasingly conventional in these pieces, and his harmony lost the tension which had been the strength of his earlier works.

WORKS
(*selective list*)

Operas: Jephtan tytär [The daughter of Jephtha], op.30 (J. Linnankoski, S. Ranta), 1929; Prinsessa Cecilia (H. Jalkanen, C. Lilius), 1933; Kaksi kuningatarta [Two queens] (L. Haarla), 1937–40; Lyydian kuningas [The king of Lydia] (E. Leino, after Herodotus), 1938
Orch: Joutsenet [The swans], op.15, 1919; Fantasia estatica, op. 21, 1921; Antigone, op.23, 1921–2; Kuutamo Jupiterissa [Moonlight on Jupiter], op.24, 1922; Puistokuja [The avenue], op.29, S, orch, 1926; many other works

Principal publisher: Finnish Broadcasting Co.

BIBLIOGRAPHY
S. Ranta: 'Väinö Raitio', *Suomen säveltäjiä*, ed. E. Marvia, ii (Porvoo, 2/1966), 103
ILKKA ORAMO

Rajeczky, Benjamin (*b* Eger, 11 Nov 1901). Hungarian musicologist and folklorist. After joining the Cistercian order (1917) he studied theology and music history with Ficker at the University of Innsbruck (1920–26), taking a doctorate in theology in 1926; concurrently he was Kapellmeister at the Collegium Canisianum (1924–6). He later studied composition under Kodály in Budapest (1932–5). While teaching in secondary schools in Budapest he also lectured in folk music at the university (1945–50); he then held posts as a research fellow in the music department of the Ethnographical Museum (1950–60) and in the folk music research group of the Hungarian Academy of Sciences (1960–67), of which he was director after Kodály's death until his retirement in 1971. During his years as a teacher (1926–50) he became associated with the reform in music teaching led by Kodály, in which he played a prominent part through his exceptionally successful teaching methods, textbooks and articles, and his organization and training of music teachers.

From 1940 Rajeczky's research, much of it unprecedented in its methods and subjects, was concerned with three main areas: medieval Hungarian music history; plainsong; and the collection, transcription and analysis of Hungarian folk music. His publications have dealt with the plainsong variants in medieval Hungarian manuscripts; the relationship between plainsong and folk music and aspects of plainsong performance; the surviving traces of Hungarian polyphony; dialect forms, laments and other genres of Hungarian folk music; and the international correspondences between certain melody types. He was the editor of the first volume of *Magyar zenetörténet* ('History of Hungarian music'), on the Middle Ages, and has worked on the Melodiarium Hungariae Medii Aevi.

WRITINGS
'A Pray-kódex két Mária-himnusza' [Two Marian hymns of the Pray Codex], *Magyar kórus* (1941), no.11, p.840
'Középkori misszáléink praefatio-dallamai' [The Praefatio melodies of our medieval missals], *Magyar zenei szemle*, i (1941), 233
'Népdaltörténet és gregorián-kutatás' [History of folksong and studies in Gregorian plainsong], *Emlékkönyv Kodály hatvanadik születésnapjára* (Budapest, 1943), 308

'Többszólamu zenénk 15. századi emlékei' [Monuments of Hungarian 15th-century polyphony], *Énekszó* (1950), no.17, p.184

'Adatok a magyar gregoriánumhoz' [Contributions to Hungarian Gregorian chants], *Zenetudományi tanulmányok*, i (1953), 279

ed. with L. Vargyas: *Studia memoriae Belae Bartók sacra* (Budapest, 1956, 3/1959) [incl. 'Parallelen spätgregorianischer Verzierungen im ungarischen Volkslied', 337]

'Descendenzmelodik im Choral und unsere absteigenden Perioden', *Acta ethnographica*, vi (1957), 357

'Typen ungarischer Klagelieder', *Deutsches Jb für Volkskunde*, iii (1957), 31

'Jegyzetek Haydn hat nagy miséjéhez' [On Haydn's six great masses], *Zenetudományi tanulmányok*, viii (1960), 421

with B. Szabolcsi: *Bartók Béla kézirása* [Bartók's handwriting] (Budapest, 1961)

'Spätmittelalterliche Organalkunst in Ungarn', *SM*, i (1961), 15

'Mittelalterliche ungarische Musikdenkmäler und das neue Volkslied', *SM*, iii (1962), 263

'Zu den Monumenta monodica medii aevi', *SM*, vi (1964), 271

'Zur Ambitusfrage der Klagelieder', *SM*, vi (1964), 375

'Mittelalterliche Mehrstimmigkeit in Ungarn', *Musica antiqua Europae orientalis I: Bydgoszcz 1966*, 223

'Le chant grégorien est-il mesuré?', *Etudes grégoriennes*, x (1967), 21

'Ost und West in den ungarischen Klageliedern', *Festschrift für Walter Wiora* (Kassel, 1967), 628

'Sur le "Kyrie ungaricum" du manuscrit no.1267 de la Biblioteka Jagiellońska', *Studia Hieronymo Feicht septuagenario dedicata* (Kraków, 1967), 137

'Über die Melodie Nr.773 der *Monumenta monodica medii aevi*, i', *Festschrift Bruno Stäblein* (Kassel, 1967), 191

'Többszólamúság a középkori Magyarországon' [Polyphony in medieval Hungary], *Magyar zenetörténeti tanulmányok*, i (1968), 125

'Gregorián, népének, népdal' [Plainsong, hymn and folksong], *Magyar zenetörténeti tanulmányok*, ii (1969), 45

'Zur Frage der Verzierung im Choral', *SM*, xi (1969), 350

'Ungarn', §§A, B(i), *MGG*

'Ein neuer Fund zur mehrstimmigen Praxis Ungarns im 15. Jahrhundert', *SM*, xiv (1972), 147

'Choralforschung und Volksmusik des Mittelalters?', *AcM*, xlvi (1974), 181

'Zur Frage der asymmetrischen Rhythmen in der ungarischen Volksmusik', *Neue ethnomusikologische Forschungen: Festschrift Felix Hoerburger* (Laaber, 1977)

'Gregorianik und Volksgesang', *Handbuch des Volksliedes*, i–ii (in preparation)

EDITIONS

Hymni et sequentiae, Melodiarium hungariae medii aevi, i (Budapest, 1956)

with L. Kiss: *Siratók* [Laments], Corpus musicae popularis hungaricae, v (Budapest, 1966)

FOLKSONG EDITIONS

with P. P. Domokos: *Csángó népzene* [Csángó folk music] (Budapest, 1956–61)

BIBLIOGRAPHY

'Benjamin Rajeczky septuagenario sacrum', *SM*, xiii (1971), 176 [with list of writings]

LÁSZLÓ DOBSZAY

Rajičić, Stanojlo (*b* Belgrade, 16 Dec 1910). Yugoslav composer. After piano studies at the Belgrade School of Music he attended the Prague Conservatory as a pupil of Šima (piano) and Karel (composition), also taking part in the master classes of Suk (composition) and Hofmeister (piano). He graduated in 1935 and returned to Belgrade in 1936. At first he taught the piano at the Stanković and secondary music schools; in 1945 he was appointed professor of composition at the academy. He was elected to corresponding (1950) and full (1958) membership of the Serbian Academy. A prolific composer, he has pursued a variety of styles. His Prague training influenced him in the direction of atonality, though he also employed folk elements. Then during the war he wrote a number of symphonic poems based on Serbian traditional epic poetry. This prepared a smoothening of style that gave rise to the tonal, classically formed works of the postwar period, and he continued to employ conventional structures and a language of broadened tonality, sometimes extending to polytonality. His best works are the Third Piano Concerto and the Second Violin Concerto; the orchestral song cycles

Lisje žuti ('The leaves turn yellow') and *Na Liparu* ('On the Lipar') are also often performed. *Simonida*, his first opera, has dramatic, arioso vocal lines and a symphonic accompaniment.

WORKS
(selective list)

Stage: Premija [First prize], ballet, 1940; Poema, ballet, 1944; Simonida (opera, 2, after M. Bojic: Kraljeva jesen), 1956, rev. 3, 1958, rev. 1, 1967; Karadjordje, opera, 1972

Orch: 6 syms., 1935, 1941, 1944, 1946, 1959, 1967; Pod zemljom [Under the ground], sym. poem, 1939; Rhapsody, 1939; 3 pf concs., 1940, 1942, 1950; 3 vn concs., 1941, 1946, 1950; Mali Radojica [Little Radojica], sym. poem, 1942; Zidanje Skadra [Building of Skadar], sym. poem, 1942; Smrt majke Jugovića [The death of Jugovići's mother], 1942; 2 cl concs., 1943, 1962; Vc Conc., 1949; Conc., bn, pf, str, 1972

Vocal: Na Liparu [On the Lipar], 1v, orch, 1951; Lisje žuti [The leaves turn yellow], 1v, orch, 1953; Slepac na saboru [The blind beggar on the Kirmess], cantata, 1961; Magnovenja [Instants], 1v, orch, 1965

Many pf pieces, chamber music, educational works, folksong and dance arrs., music for the theatre and cinema

Principal publishers: Prosveta, Srpska Akademija Nauka i Umjetnosti, Udruženje Kompozitora Srbije

BIBLIOGRAPHY
V. Peričić: *Stvaralački put Stanojla Rajičića* (Belgrade, 1971)

STANA ĐURIĆ-KLAJN

Rajna, Thomas (*b* Budapest, 21 Dec 1928). British pianist and composer. He studied with Kodály, Veress and Weiner at the Liszt Academy of Music (1944–7) and was awarded the Liszt Prize in 1947. That year he moved to London, where he continued his studies under Howells (composition) and Morrison (piano) at the RCM, and then began a career as performer, composer and teacher. He held appointments at the Guildhall School of Music from 1963 and the University of Surrey from 1967; in 1970 he moved to the University of Cape Town and became senior lecturer in music. He has performed widely in Great Britain and South Africa, winning praise for his sympathetic presentation of a repertory that includes all Stravinsky's piano music and works by Messiaen, Skryabin, Liszt and Granados. His compositions exhibit a firm tonal feeling, a keen ear for colour effects and a strong lyrical quality.

WORKS
(selective list)

Orch: Pf Conc., 1962; Movements for Str, 1962; Cantilenas and Interludes, 1968

Chamber and inst: Dialogues, cl, pf, 1947; Music for Vc and Pf, 1950; Music for Vn and Pf, 1957; Capriccio, pf/hpd, 1960

Vocal: Piping Down the Valleys Wild, 1v, cl, pf, 1948; Four African Lyrics, 1v, pf, 1976

Principal publishers: International, Leduc

WRITINGS
'Stravinsky's Piano Work's, *Composer* (1968), no.29, p.5

JAMES MAY

Rajonski, Milton M. See ROGERS, SHORTY.

Rajter, L'udovít (*b* Pezinok, 30 July 1906). Slovak conductor and composer. He began to compose while still a child, studied the piano and cello in Bratislava, and made further study in composition and conducting at the Vienna Academy and Hochschule (1924–9), where his teachers included Clemens Krauss. He also studied with Dohnányi at Budapest, and became conductor of the Budapest Radio Orchestra (1933–45), and professor of conducting at the Music Academy (1938–45). During this time he toured widely in Europe, and he made his New York début in 1936. In 1945 he returned to Bratislava as conductor of the Radio Orchestra there, and became resident conductor of the

Slovak PO on its formation in 1949. He built up the orchestra's standard repertory and added to it the works of Cikker, Suchoň and other contemporary Slovak composers. In 1949 he was appointed to teach conducting at the Bratislava High School of Music. He was named Artist of Merit in 1965. His compositions include symphonic and chamber works, and the ballet *Majales* (Budapest, 1938).

ALENA NĚMCOVÁ

Rakhlin, Natan Grigor'yevich (*b* Snovsk [now Shchors], Chernigov, 10 Jan 1906). Soviet conductor and teacher. He studied the violin at the Kiev Conservatory, conducting under Walerian Bierdiajew and Alexander Orlov at the Lysenko Music School in Kiev (1927–30), and composition with Maximilian Shteynberg in Leningrad (1930–32). After conducting the Khar'kov Radio SO (1932–4) he had two periods as chief conductor of the Ukrainian State SO (1936–41 and 1945–65), spending the intervening years as chief conductor of the USSR State SO in Moscow. He was appointed to teach conducting at the Kiev Conservatory in 1939 and became a professor there in 1947. In 1966 he became chief conductor and artistic director of the Tatar SO at Kazan, and professor of the orchestral class at the Kazan Conservatory. Rakhlin is an intuitive artist whose performances are distinguished by spontaneity and emotional strength and sweep as well as depth. His wide repertory includes new Soviet works. He was made People's Artist of the USSR in 1948.

BIBLIOGRAPHY

N. Matusevich: *Natan Grigor'yevich Rakhlin* (Kiev, 1960)

I. M. YAMPOL'SKY

Rakhmaninov, Sergey (Vasil'yevich) (*b* Semyonovo, 1 April 1873; *d* Beverly Hills, 28 March 1943). Russian composer, pianist and conductor. He was one of the finest pianists of his day and, as a composer, the last great representative of Russian late Romanticism. The influences of Rimsky-Korsakov, Tchaikovsky and other Russian composers in his early works soon gave way to a highly individual, lyrical idiom which, if it has not had any important lasting effect on the development of Russian music, nevertheless is characterized by sincere expression and skilful technique.

1. 1873–92. 2. 1892–1901. 3. 1901–17. 4. 1918–43. 5. Rakhmaninov as a performer. 6. Works.

1. 1873–92. Rakhmaninov's improvident father squandered the family fortune, and they were rapidly reduced to a single estate, Oneg, near Novgorod. It was here that Rakhmaninov had his earliest piano lessons, first from his mother, then from Anna Ornatskaya, a graduate of the St Petersburg Conservatory. In 1882 even Oneg had to be sold to settle debts, and the family moved to St Petersburg, where Rakhmaninov attended the conservatory, receiving a general education and studying the piano with Vladimir Demyansky and harmony with Alexander Rubets. But soon the family was again in turmoil: during an epidemic of diphtheria Rakhmaninov's sister Sofiya died, and, to make matters worse, relations between his parents became so strained that they decided to separate. This emotional upheaval had a decisive effect on Rakhmaninov's future career. With her increased domestic responsibilities, his mother was unable adequately to supervise his homework, and as a result he failed all his general subjects at the end-of-term examinations in 1885. The conservatory hinted that his scholarship might be withdrawn and so, on the recommendation of his cousin Alexander Ziloti, Rakhmaninov was sent to the Moscow Conservatory to study with the strict disciplinarian Nikolay Zverev. Living at Zverev's flat together with two other young pupils, Maximov and Presman, he was subjected to rigorous tuition, beginning practice at 6 a.m., acquiring a basic knowledge of music from four-hand arrangements of symphonies, and attending concerts in the city. It was also at Zverev's, during his Sunday afternoon gatherings, that Rakhmaninov first encountered many of the prominent musicians of the day: Anton Rubinstein, Taneyev, Arensky, Safonov and Tchaikovsky, the most influential figure of his formative years.

In spring 1888 Rakhmaninov transferred to the senior department of the conservatory to study the piano with Ziloti, while still living with Zverev; in the autumn he began to study counterpoint with Taneyev and harmony with Arensky. Zverev, who was concerned solely with the development of Rakhmaninov's piano technique, had never encouraged him to compose, though it was at Zverev's that Rakhmaninov wrote his earliest works, a Mendelssohnian orchestral scherzo (1887), some piano pieces (1887–8) and sketches for an opera *Esmeralda* (1888). But his creative instincts finally led to a breach with Zverev in 1889. In the single workroom at the flat Rakhmaninov found it impossible to concentrate on composition while the others were practising; but Zverev met his request for more privacy with peremptory dismissal from the household, refusing even to speak to him for three years.

Rejecting his mother's idea that he should return to St Petersburg to study with Rimsky-Korsakov, Rakhmaninov remained in Moscow, living for a while with a conservatory colleague, Mikhail Slonov, then with his relatives, the Satins. Here he sketched some ideas for a piano concerto (which came to nothing) and completed two movements of a string quartet (dedicated to Ziloti); and in spring 1890 he composed the six-part motet *Deus meus* and his earliest songs. During the summer he stayed at Ivanovka, the Satins' country estate, where he met the three Skalon sisters, distant cousins by marriage, conceiving a calf-love for the youngest, Vera, and dedicating to her his new cello Romance. It was also for the Skalon sisters that he composed a six-hand piano Waltz (1890) and Romance (1891). Returning to Moscow, he taught for a while in a class for choir trainers, and sketched at least two movements of an orchestral piece, *Manfred*, possibly inspired by the Tchaikovsky symphony, which he had transcribed for piano duet in 1886.

In spring 1891 Ziloti resigned from the conservatory because of constant disagreements with the director, Safonov. Rather than transfer to another teacher for the remaining year of his course, Rakhmaninov was allowed to take his piano finals a year early, and he graduated with honours on 5 June. During the summer, again at Ivanovka, he completed his First Piano Concerto (begun in 1890), and back in Moscow in December he set to work on his first symphonic poem, *Knyaz' Rostislav* ('Prince Rostislav'), which he dedicated to Arensky. Early in 1892 he gave the première of his first *Trio élégiaque* with Anatoly Brandukov and David Kreyn, and also played the first movement of his concerto at a conservatory concert on 29 March. Shortly afterwards he began to prepare for his finals in composition, which, like his piano examinations, he was taking a year early. The main exercise was to be a one-act opera *Aleko*, based on Pushkin's poem *Tsïganï* ('The gypsies'). For his work Rakhmaninov was awarded the highest possible mark, and he graduated from the conservatory with the Great Gold Medal, previously awarded only to Koreshchenko and Taneyev.

2. 1892–1901. After his graduation Rakhmaninov signed a publishing contract with Gutheil, and in the autumn composed what was quickly to become his best-known composition, the piano prelude in C♯ minor, a work to which Rakhmaninov owed much of his early popularity but which became for him a tiresome encore at most of his concerts. In the following spring *Aleko* was given its première at the Bol'shoy. Tchaikovsky, who attended the rehearsals and the performance, was enthusiastic about it, and Kashkin, in his perceptive, not uncritical review in the *Moskovskiye vedomosti* (29 April/11 May 1893), commented that 'of course there are faults, but they are far outweighed by merits, which lead one to expect much from this young composer in the future'.

Spurred by his success, Rakhmaninov composed with ease during the summer and autumn: he completed his op.4 and op.8 songs, the two-piano *Fantaisie-tableaux* op.5, a sacred choral piece *V molitvakh neusïpayushchuyu bogoroditsu* ('O mother of God vigilantly praying'), the two op.6 violin pieces and the orchestral fantasy *Utyos* ('The rock'), which bears a quotation from

Lermontov's poem but was in fact inspired by Chekhov's short story *Na puti* ('On the road'). Tchaikovsky wanted to conduct the piece during the following season; but in November he died, and Rakhmaninov immediately devoted himself to writing a second *Trio élégiaque* to his memory, clearly revealing the sincerity of his grief in the music's overwhelming aura of gloom.

In January 1895 he began work on his first substantial piece, the Symphony no.1 in D minor (which has no connection with a D minor symphonic movement written in 1891). The symphony occupied him until September, and during 1896 Belyayev agreed to include it in one of his Russian Symphony Concerts. The performance, conducted by Glazunov, was on 27 March 1897, and was a disaster: Cui likened the work to 'a programme symphony on the Seven Plagues of Egypt', though other critics acknowledged that its poor reception was due as much to the performance as to the piece itself. Rakhmaninov commented (in a letter of 6/18 May): 'I am amazed how such a highly talented man as Glazunov can conduct so badly. I am not speaking now of his conducting technique (one can't ask that of him) but about his musicianship. He feels nothing when he conducts. It's as if he understands nothing'. Years later Rakhmaninov's wife remarked that Glazunov was drunk at the time. Whatever the cause of the failure, it plunged Rakhmaninov into the depths of depression, and was followed by a three-year period completely devoid of any significant composition: sketches for another sym-

1. Sergey Rakhmaninov (second left) with his teacher Zverev and fellow pupils Presman and Maximov

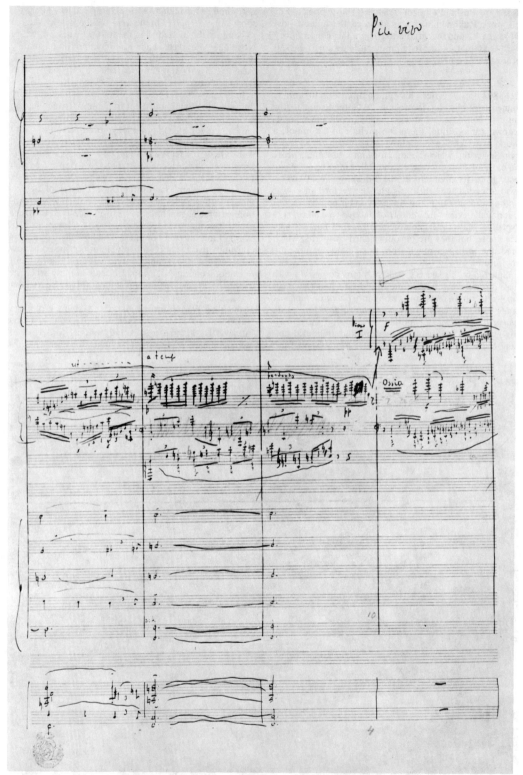

2. *Autograph MS from the second movement of Rakhmaninov's Piano Concerto no.3 in D minor, composed 1909 (private collection); in the printed score the final bar of the piano part is that marked 'Piano I'*

phony were abandoned; ideas for an opera, *Francesca da Rimini*, lay fallow for several years. But just then, thanks to the wealthy industrialist Savva Mamontov, Rakhmaninov was launched on his third career, as conductor, when he was engaged by the Moscow Private Russian Opera for the 1897–8 season. Here he acquired a sound knowledge of Russian and Western opera; he also formed a close friendship with Shalyapin (who sang with the company), and during a summer holiday in 1898 they made intensive studies together of the operas of Rimsky-Korsakov and Musorgsky, particularly *Boris Godunov*.

Rakhmaninov made his London début at the Queen's Hall in April 1899, and, returning to Russia, attended the St Petersburg première of *Aleko*, with Shalyapin in the title role. But even these successes did not inspire him to return to composition. Visits to Tolstoy, intended to stimulate creativity, succeeded only in depressing him further, and finally the Satins decided that he should seek medical help from Dr Nikolay Dahl, who for some years had been specializing in treatment by hypnosis. Dahl, an accomplished amateur musician, had a number of protracted sessions with Rakhmaninov to restore (as Sofiya Satina has recorded in her reminiscences) his 'cheerfulness of spirit, energy, a desire to work, and confidence in his abilities'. The treatment had a rapid effect: in the summer, staying in Italy with Shalyapin, Rakhmaninov composed his anthem *Panteley-tselitel'* ('Panteley the healer') and the love duet for *Francesca da Rimini*. Even more important, he began to compose his most enduringly popular work, the Second Piano Concerto. Ideas were put in order on his return to Russia in August, and he performed the second and third movements on 15 December 1900. Success was such that he was encouraged to add the first movement, and he gave the first performance of the complete concerto on 9 November 1901.

3. 1901–17. Finally reassured of his powers to compose, Rakhmaninov completed his Cello Sonata in December, giving also the first performance (with Ziloti) of a recently composed Second Suite for two pianos. Early the following year he worked at his first important choral piece, *Vesna* ('Spring'), a cantata based on Nekrasov's poem *Zelyonïy shum* ('The verdant noise'), and shortly after completing it announced his engagement to his cousin Natalya Satina. The difficulties of such a marriage were considerable: Rakhmaninov refused to attend church or confession regularly, and in any case the Russian Orthodox Church forbids first cousins to marry. But one of Rakhmaninov's aunts had connections at the Archangel Cathedral in the Kremlin; she made the necessary arrangements, and the wedding took place at an army chapel on the outskirts of Moscow on 12 May.

After a long honeymoon in western Europe, the Rakhmaninovs returned to Moscow, where in May 1903 Natalya gave birth to their first daughter, Irina. During a summer holiday at Ivanovka, Rakhmaninov turned once more to composition, working on his opera *Skupoy rïtsar'* ('The miserly knight'); the piano score was ready by the following spring, when he again took up the threads of his other long-contemplated opera *Francesca da Rimini*. At the same time he agreed to conduct at the Bol'shoy for two seasons (beginning in September 1904), and he spent the summer in frantic efforts to complete *Francesca* in the hope that both it

and *The Miserly Knight* could be staged in December. Largely because of difficulties with the librettist, Modest Tchaikovsky, he managed to complete only the piano score of *Francesca* by August, when he had to devote all his time to learning the operas he was to conduct at the Bol'shoy. His experience with Mamontov's company stood him in good stead for his début in Dargomïzhsky's *Rusalka*; and again Kashkin was complimentary, remarking in *Russkiy listok*: 'the first appearance of the young Kapellmeister this season justified the hopes placed upon him . . . even in the first bars of the overture the audience began to feel a freshness and cheerfulness, clearly revealing the rich and lively temperament of the conductor'.

At Ivanovka in the summer Rakhmaninov worked on the orchestration of *Francesca* and *The Miserly Knight*. Both operas were complete by August, when he again had to prepare for the Bol'shoy; this time his programme included the Moscow première of Rimsky's *Pan Voyevoda*, an interpretation much admired by the composer, who attended the rehearsals and the performance. Rakhmaninov also conducted the premières of *The Miserly Knight* and *Francesca* in January 1906, but in February, because of the increasing political unrest in Russia, he resigned from the Bol'shoy, leaving almost at once for Italy. Staying near Pisa, he contemplated, but abandoned, another opera, *Salammbô*. He then had to return to Russia with his daughter, who from birth had rarely enjoyed good health and had again become ill. She recovered, but the atmosphere in Russia was still not conducive to work, and in the autumn the family decided to leave Russia for a while and take a house in Dresden.

Living there in seclusion for a few months in each of the next few years, Rakhmaninov completed his Second Symphony (1906–7), his First Piano Sonata (1907), his symphonic poem *Ostrov myortvïkh* ('The isle of the dead', 1909) and part of an opera *Monna Vanna*. In May 1907 he took part in Dyagilev's Saison Russe in Paris, then returned to Ivanovka to join Natalya, who in July gave birth to their second daughter, Tatyana.

In 1909 Rakhmaninov made his first American tour, the programmes for which included a new work, the Third Piano Concerto, composed in the previous summer. At the end of the tour, which he loathed, he declined offers of further American contracts, and again he spent the summer at Ivanovka, recently made over to him by his uncle. It was here, during the next two or three summers, that he found the necessary relaxation to compose several important works: the 13 Preludes op.32 (1910), a setting of the *Liturgy of St John Chrysostom* (1910), the *Etudes-tableaux* op.33 (1911), the 14 Songs op.34 (1910–12) and the Second Piano Sonata (1913). The remaining months of the year were generally taken up with a taxing schedule of performing engagements; indeed, during the 1912–13 season he undertook so many concerts and become so tired that he cancelled his final appearance and took the family off to Switzerland. From there they went to Rome, where Rakhmaninov began his choral symphony *Kolokola* ('The bells'). Work on the piece was interrupted when Tatyana and Irina contracted typhoid; but, after they had recovered sufficiently in a Berlin hospital, the family returned to Ivanovka, where Rakhmaninov completed the score, conducting the first performance in December.

During autumn 1914 Rakhmaninov toured southern

3. Sergey Rakhmaninov

Russia with Koussevitzky, giving concerts for the war effort. Although he composed little after the outbreak of World War I, he did manage to write his finest unaccompanied choral work, the *Vsenoshchnoye bdeniye* ('All-night vigil'), in January and February 1915. By the end of 1916 Russia's internal affairs were in chaos: the country was gripped by strikes, and successive governments seemed able only to augment the popular discontent with the tsar. Rakhmaninov wrote to Ziloti in June 1917 asking if he could get him a visa to leave Russia. But Ziloti could do nothing, and after a concert in Yalta on 18 September Rakhmaninov returned to his flat in Moscow, where he revised the First Concerto, something he had been intending for many years. Just then he received an invitation to play in Stockholm and at once travelled to Petrograd to arrange the journey. Natalya, Irina and Tatyana followed a few days later and just before Christmas the whole family left Russia for the last time.

4. 1918–43. Living first in Stockholm, then settling in Copenhagen, Rakhmaninov began to widen his piano repertory, realizing that, without the money and possessions left behind in Russia, his and his family's livelihood depended on a steady income; and he was more likely to achieve that as a concert performer than as a composer. Towards the end of 1918 he received three offers of lucrative American contracts, and, although he declined them all, he decided that the USA might offer a solution to his financial worries. In November the family arrived in New York, where Rakhmaninov quickly chose an agent, Charles Ellis, and accepted the gift of a piano from Steinway, before giving nearly 40 concerts in four months; at the end of the 1919–20 season he also signed a recording contract with the Victor Talking Machine Company. In 1921 the

Rakhmaninovs decided to buy a house in the USA, where they consciously re-created the atmosphere of Ivanovka, entertaining Russian guests, employing Russian servants and observing Russian customs.

For the 1923–4 season Rakhmaninov cut his number of American concerts to allow more time in Europe; and it was while at Dresden in the spring that his elder daughter, Irina, announced her engagement to Prince Pyotr Volkonsky. The wedding was in September, but the marriage ended in tragedy when Volkonsky died less than a year later. It was largely for the benefit of the widowed Irina and for Tatyana that Rakhmaninov founded in Paris a publishing firm, TAIR (derived from his daughters' names), to publish works by Russian composers, particularly himself. Deciding also to limit his American engagements even further and to sell his American property, he found himself with nine months free of all commitments at the end of 1925. His mind turned immediately to composition, for he had long wanted to add another concerto to his repertory; in fact it seems likely that he had been contemplating a fourth concerto as early as 1914. Renting a flat in New York, he worked at the concerto and completed it at Dresden during the summer. Realizing that the piece was too long (he joked to Metner that it would have to be 'performed on successive nights, like the *Ring*'), he made a number of cuts before giving the first performance at Philadelphia on 18 March 1927. The highly critical notices made him take another look at the score, and before its publication by TAIR he made many more alterations and cuts. But it still failed to impress audiences, and he withdrew it from his programmes until he could examine the faults in detail.

In 1931 Rakhmaninov made a rare venture into politics: he had usually avoided comment on the Russian regime, but in January, together with Ivan Ostromislensky and Count Ilya Tolstoy, he sent a letter to *The New York Times* (12 January 1931) criticizing various Soviet policies. This was countered by a bitter attack in the Moscow newspaper *Vechernyaya Moskva* (9 March 1931) and a ban on the performance and study of his works in Russia (the ban lasted for only two years, and his music was restored to favour in 1933). During summer 1931 he revised his Second Sonata and also composed his last solo piano work, the Variations on a Theme of Corelli, performing them at Montreal on 12 October. In the following summers at his Swiss villa (called Senar, from *Se*rgey and *Na*talya *Ra*khmaninov) he composed the Rhapsody on a Theme of Paganini (1934) and the Third Symphony (1935–6, revised 1938); and in 1937 Fokin approached Rakmaninov with the idea of a ballet based on the Paganini legend, using Rakhmaninov's music. The ballet was first given at Covent Garden on 30 June 1939, a performance that the composer could not attend as he had slipped at his home and was lame. In fact he was never again to be in England; he had given his last concert on 11 March 1939, and during the summer the family decided that, in view of the threat of war, it would be safer to leave Europe and return to the USA. There, in the autumn of 1940, he completed his last work, the Symphonic Dances; and in the following year he revised the Fourth Concerto.

Rakhmaninov decided that his 1942–3 season would have to be his last: every year since his arrival in the USA he had undertaken exhausting tours, and recently had been suffering from lumbago, arthritis and extreme fatigue. By January 1943, while on tour, he was clearly unwell. The doctor diagnosed pleurisy, but Rakhmaninov insisted that the tour should continue. On 17 February he gave what was to be his last concert, at Knoxville, becoming so ill afterwards that the family had to return to Los Angeles. There, at his house in Beverly Hills, it became evident that he was suffering from cancer, and he died early on the morning of 28 March.

5. RAKHMANINOV AS A PERFORMER. Rakhmaninov managed to pursue all three of his careers – as pianist, composer and conductor – with almost equal success, admitting, however, that he found it difficult to concentrate on more than one at any given time: certainly the demands of his performing career in his later life precluded much composition. His concert manner was austere, contrasting sharply with the warm and generous personality he revealed in the company of his family and close friends. He possessed a formidable piano technique, and his playing (like his conducting) was marked by precision, rhythmic drive, a refined legato and an ability for complete clarity in complex textures – qualities that he applied with sublime effect in his performances of Chopin, particularly the B♭ minor sonata. The rest of his comparatively small repertory comprised, besides his own works, many of the standard 19th-century virtuoso pieces as well as music by Beethoven, Borodin, Debussy, Grieg, Liszt, Mendelssohn, Mozart, Schubert, Schumann and Tchaikovsky. Whatever music he was playing, his performances were always carefully planned, being based on the theory that each piece has a 'culminating point'. 'This culmination', as he told the poet Marietta Shaginian, 'may be at the end or in the middle, it may be loud or soft; but the performer must know how to approach it with absolute calculation, absolute precision, because, if it slips by, then the whole construction crumbles, and the piece becomes disjointed and scrappy and does not convey to the listener what must be conveyed'.

6. WORKS. Understandably, the piano figures prominently in Rakhmaninov's music, either as a solo instrument or as part of an ensemble. But he used his own skills as a performer not to write music of unreasonable, empty virtuosity, but rather to explore fully the expressive possibilities of the instrument. Even in his earliest works (the three nocturnes of 1887–8, the four pieces probably written in 1888, and the first version of the First Piano Concerto, 1890–91) he revealed a sure grasp of idiomatic piano writing and a striking gift for melody. Some of his early works presage finer achievements: the Prelude in C♯ minor, for example, though less subtle than his mature works, is couched in the melancholy, nostalgic idiom that pervades much of his music. And in some of his early orchestral pieces – Prince Rostislav (1891) and, to a lesser extent, The Rock (1893) – he showed the first signs of that ability for tone-painting which he was to perfect in The Isle of the Dead (1909) and in some of his later piano pieces and songs. In these early years, though, the textures (usually opaque and chordal) lack the variety of later works; his orchestration is often colourless and heavy; and the musical language (notably in his student opera Aleko, 1892) is often redolent of other Russian composers, particularly Tchaikovsky.

With his works of the mid-1890s Rakhmaninov began to strike a more individual tone: the six Moments musicaux (1896) have the characteristic yearning themes, combined with a rise and fall of dynamics and intricate passage-work. Even his First Symphony (1895), however 'weak, childish, strained and bombastic' (as Rakhmaninov himself described it), has many original features. Its brutal gestures and uncompromising power of expression (particularly in the finale) were unprecedented in Russian music; and, although it must be said that the work has a tendency to ramble, nevertheless its flexible rhythms, sweeping lyricism and stringent economy of thematic material ('the meaningless repetition of the same short tricks', Cui called it) were features used with greater subtlety and individuality later on.

After the three vacuous years that followed the poor reception of the symphony in 1897, Rakhmaninov's style began to develop significantly. In the Second Piano Concerto (1900–01) the headstrong youthful impetuosity of the symphony has largely given way to Rakhmaninov's predilection for sumptuous harmonies and broadly lyrical, often intensely passionate melodies. And there are certain technical developments. In place of the often garish orchestration of the symphony, the colours of the concerto are subdued and more subtly varied; the textures are carefully contrasted; and Rakhmaninov's writing is altogether more concise. The idiom of the concerto rubbed off on the other works of the period, notably the Suite no.2 for two pianos (1900–01), the Cello Sonata (1901), the Ten Preludes op.23 (1901–3), the cantata Spring (1902), and the 12 Songs op.21 (1900–02). In these songs he began to achieve a perfect balance between voice and accompaniment, using the piano to echo the sentiments of the text. (Some of the piano parts are, in effect, separate instrumental studies of the poems, and it is significant that Rakhmaninov later transcribed one of the finest, Siren' ('Lilacs', no.5), for piano solo.) This same sensitivity to mood is seen again in his two operas of the period, The Miserly Knight (1903–5) and Francesca da Rimini (1900–05); but here, despite Rakhmaninov's keen dramatic sense – particularly in the central scene of The Miserly Knight and in the love-duet of Francesca – the librettos defy successful stage performance (the former being an almost word-for-word setting of one of Pushkin's 'little tragedies', never intended for the stage; the other an anaemic adaptation by Modest Tchaikovsky of the fifth canto of the Inferno).

The years immediately following the premières of the two operas, spent partly in Russia, partly in Dresden, were Rakhmaninov's most fruitful as a composer, and it was during this period that his style reached full maturity. The Second Symphony (1906–7) and the Third Piano Concerto (1909) display his fully-fledged melodic style (particularly in the slow movement of the symphony), his opulent but infinitely varied and discerning use of the orchestra (notably in the symphony's scherzo), and a greater confidence in the handling of large-scale structures. Like those of the First Symphony, the opening bars of the Second contain pithy ideas that act as unifying elements, but here the material is allowed a far more leisurely expansion and development than in the First Symphony; the long-breathed themes need space to display themselves fully, and the cuts sometimes made in performances of the symphony and the concerto serve only to throw them off balance. The Third Concerto is structurally a more ingenious piece than the Second, not only in the greater continuity achieved through the elimination of the abrupt full stops that occur before important themes in the First and Second Concertos, but also in the subtle recollection and metamorphosis of the first movement material: the fast central section of the slow movement, for example, is a rhythmic mutation of the opening theme.

Certain characteristics of the Third Concerto are brought to mind by the 13 Preludes op.32 (1910), just as the op.23 preludes owe much in style to the Second Concerto. The preludes have the concerto's complexity of texture and flexibility of rhythm, its pungent, chromatic harmony; and, like the concerto, they make extreme demands of agility and power on the pianist. There are extreme emotional demands too, particularly in the more introspective preludes, a mode of expression towards which Rakhmaninov had been developing in the more contemplative of the op.23 preludes and in some of the *Moments musicaux*: the B♭ minor prelude (op.32 no.2), the B minor (no.10) and the D♭ major (no.13) are among the most searching and harrowing music that Rakhmaninov composed. Even the more lyrical preludes have the same hazy quality of his last set of songs (op.38, 1916), while the more ostentatiously dramatic pieces are set in the intense, impassioned idiom of some of the op.39 *Etudes-tableaux* (1916–17). Varied though these pieces are, they all have a common characteristic in that they show Rakhmaninov's ability to crystallize perfectly a particular mood or sentiment: each prelude grows from a tiny melodic or rhythmic fragment into a taut, powerfully evocative miniature. They are, in effect, small tone poems, and it is this vivid portraiture that, in orchestral music, reached a peak in *The Isle of the Dead*. Here the awesome gloom of Böcklin's painting is reflected in the dark colours of the

4. *Sergey Rakhmaninov*

opening section (where the motion of Charon's oars is imitated by the persistent 5/8 metre), enhanced, as in so much of Rakhmaninov's music, by references to the *Dies irae*; indeed, the dénouement of the piece consists of a battle between the chant (symbolizing death) and another, more wistful melody that Rakhmaninov called the 'life' theme. Similarly doom-laden is the long finale of his choral symphony *The Bells* (1913), where he was able to express, with an emotional intensity he never surpassed, the fatalistic sentiments that imbue many other works. In *The Bells* the effectiveness of the subdued finale is heightened by the other three, more vivid, movements; and in all four movements he applied the discriminating orchestration, evident in his other mature works, to convey Poe's sharply contrasting campanological symbols: silver bells for birth, golden bells for marriage, brazen bells for terror, iron bells for death. In the tenor, soprano and baritone solos he also showed the perceptive response to poetry and the sympathetic vocal writing of his two last sets of songs, opp.34 and 38.

For the 14 Songs op.34 (1910–12) he chose poems by some of the principal representatives of Russian Romanticism: Pushkin, Tyutchev, Polonsky, Khomyakov, Maykov and Korinfsky, and also the more modern Bal'mont. Most of the songs are tailored to the individual talents of certain Russian singers: the dramatic, declamatory ones, like *V dushe u kazhdovo iz nas* ('In the soul of each of us', no.2), *Tï znal evo* ('You knew him', no.9), *Obrochnik* ('The peasant', no.11) and *Voskresheniye Lazarya* ('The raising of Lazarus', no.6), are dedicated to Shalyapin; the powerful *Dissonans* ('Discord', no.13) to Felia Litvin; the more lyrical songs, like *Kakoye schast'ye* ('What happiness', no.12), to Sobinov; and the wordless *Vocalise* (no.14) to Nezhdanova. Certain features of the op.34 songs (simple vocal lines; sensitive accompaniments that emphasize certain words and phrases by melodic inflections and harmonic shadings) were developed further in the six last songs (op.38). For these Rakhmaninov chose texts exclusively from the works of contemporary poets – Blok, Belïy, Severianin, Bryusov, Sologub and Bal'mont – all of whom were prominent in the symbolist movement predominant in Russia in the late 19th century and early 20th. Here, as in the op.39 *Etudes-tableaux*, Rakhmaninov was concerned less with pure melody than with colouring; and his almost impressionist style perfectly matches the symbolists' mellifluous, elusive poetry in its translucent piano writing, constantly fluctuating rhythms and ambiguous harmonies.

The op.38 songs and the op.39 studies were the last important pieces that Rakhmaninov wrote before leaving Russia (apart from the substantial revision of the First Piano Concerto, done in 1917). And his friend Vladimir Wilshaw, in a letter written shortly after the Soviet ban on his works had been lifted, perceptively remarked on the difference in style between the extrovert studies (during a performance of which Rakhmaninov had broken a string on the piano) and the Variations on a Theme of Corelli, his last piano work, composed in 1931. In these 20 variations (not, in fact, based on a theme of Corelli, but on the tune *La folìa* which Corelli had used in his Sonata op.5 no.12) the piano textures have an even greater clarity than in the op.38 songs, combined with biting chromatic harmony and a new rhythmic incisiveness. These were to be the characteristics of all the works composed during this

Indian summer of the 1930s and 1940s, and the Corelli Variations were in a sense preparatory exercises for the Rhapsody on a Theme of Paganini (1934), a much more tautly constructed piece than the often diffuse Fourth Piano Concerto (1926). Like the Paganini Rhapsody, the other late works with orchestra – the Three Russian Songs (1926) and the Third Symphony (1935–6) – reveal Rakhmaninov's interest in individual instrumental tone qualities, and this is highlighted by his use of an alto saxophone in his last work, the Symphonic Dances (1940). In the curious, shifting harmonies of the second movement, and in the rhythmic vitality and almost Prokofiev-like grotesquery of the first and last, the Symphonic Dances are entirely representative of his late style; and they also sum up his lifelong fascination with ecclesiastical chants, for he not only quoted (in the first movement) the principal theme from the First Symphony (derived as it is from motifs characteristic of Russian church music), but he also used in the finale the *Dies irae* and the chant *Blagosloven esi, Gospodi* ('Blessed be the Lord') from his *All-night Vigil* (1915), writing at the end of the score the sadly appropriate line 'I thank thee, Lord'.

WORKS

op.

OPERAS

— Esmeralda (after Hugo: Notre Dame de Paris), 1888; Introduction to Act 1 and frag., of Act 3 only, all in pf score
— Aleko (1, V. Nemirovich-Danchenko, after Pushkin: Tsïganï [The gypsies]), 1892; Moscow, Bol'shoy, 9 May 1893
24 Skupoy rïtsar' [The miserly knight] (3 scenes, Pushkin), 1903–5; Moscow, Bol'shoy, 24 Jan 1906
25 Francesca da Rimini (prol, 2 scenes, epilogue, M. Tchaikovsky, after Dante: Inferno), 1900, 1904–5; Moscow, Bol'shoy, 24 Jan 1906
— Salammbô (7 scenes, M. Slonov after Flaubert), 1906, scenario only
— Monna Vanna (Slonov, after Maeterlinck), 1907; pf score of Act 1 and sketches for Act 2 only

CHORAL

— Deus meus, motet, 6vv, 1890
— V molitvakh neusïpayushchuyu bogoroditsu [O mother of God vigilantly praying], 3vv, 1893
— Chorus of spirits for Don Juan (A. K. Tolstoy), unacc., ?1894
15 6 Choruses, female or children's vv, 1895–6: Slav'sya [Be praised] (Nekrasov); Nochka [Night] (V. Lodïzhensky); Sosna [The pine] (Lermontov); Zadremali volnï [The waves slumbered] (K. Romanov); Nevolya [Slavery] (N. Tsïganov); Angel (Lermontov)
— Panteley-tselitel' [Panteley the healer] (A. K. Tolstoy), unacc., 1900
20 Vesna [Spring] (Nekrasov: Zelyonïy shum [The verdant noise]), cantata, Bar, chorus, orch, 1902
31 Liturgiya svyatovo Ioanna Zlatousta [Liturgy of St John Chrysostom], unacc., 1910
35 Kolokola [The bells] (Bal'mont, after Poe), choral sym., S, T, Bar, chorus, orch, 1913
37 Vsenoshchnoye bdeniye [All-night vigil], unacc., 1915
41 3 Russian Songs, chorus, orch, 1926: Cherez rechku [Across the river]; Akh tï, Van'ka [Oh, Ivan]; Belelitsï, rumyanitsï vï moy [Whiten my rouged cheeks]

ORCHESTRAL

— Scherzo, d, 1887
— Piano Concerto, c, 1889, sketches only
— Manfred, sym. poem, 1890, lost
1 Piano Concerto no,1. f♯, 1890–91, rev. 1917
— Suite, 1891, lost
— Symphony, d, 1891, 1st movt only
— Knyaz' Rostislav [Prince Rostislav], sym. poem after A. K. Tolstoy, 1891
7 Utyos [The rock], sym. poem after Chekhov: Na puti, 1893
12 Kaprichchio na tsiganskiye temï [Capriccio on gypsy themes] (Caprice bohémien), 1892, 1894
13 Symphony no.1, d, 1895
— Symphony, 1897, sketches only
18 Piano Concerto no.2, c, 1900–01
27 Symphony no.2, e, 1906–7
29 Ostrov myortvïkh [The isle of the dead], sym. poem after Böcklin, 1909
30 Piano Concerto no.3, d, 1909
40 Piano Concerto no.4, g, 1926, rev. 1941
43 Rhapsody on a Theme of Paganini, pf, orch, 1934

44 Symphony no.3, a, 1935–6, rev. 1938
45 Symphonic Dances, 1940

CHAMBER

— String Quartet, 1889, 2 movts only
— Romance, f, vc, pf, 1890
— Romance, vn, pf
— Piece, vc, pf
— ? String Quintet, lost
— Trio élégiaque, g, pf trio, 1892
2 2 Pieces, vc, pf, 1892: Prélude [rev. of pf piece, 1891], Oriental Dance
6 2 Pieces, vn, pf, 1893: Romance, Hungarian Dance
9 Trio élégiaque, d, pf trio, 1893, rev. 1907, 1917
— String Quartet, ?1896, 2 movts only
19 Sonata, g, vc, pf, 1901

PIANO

— 3 Nocturnes: no.1, f♯, 1887; no.2, F, 1887; no.3, c, 1888
— 4 Pieces, ?1888: Romance, f♯; Prélude, e♭; Mélodie, E; Gavotte, D
— 2 Pieces, 6 hands: Waltz, A, 1890; Romance, A, 1891
— Prélude, F, 1891, rev. 1892 as Prélude, vc, pf
— Russian Rhapsody, e, 2 pf, 1891
3 Morceaux de fantaisie, 1892: Elégie, e♭; Prélude, c♯, arr. 2 pf 1938; Mélodie, E, rev. 1940; Polichinelle, f♯; Sérénade, b♭, rev. 1940
— Romance, G, 4 hands, 1893
5 Fantaisie-tableaux (Suite no.1), 2 pf, 1893
10 Morceaux de salon, 1893–4: Nocturne, a; Valse, A; Barcarolle, g; Mélodie, e; Humoresque, G, rev. 1940; Romance, f; Mazurka, D♭
11 6 Duets, 4 hands, 1894: Barcarolle, g; Scherzo, D; Russian song, b; Valse, A; Romance, c; Slava [Glory], C
16 Moments musicaux, 1896: Andantino, b♭; Allegretto, e♭, rev. 1940; Andante cantabile, b; Presto, e; Adagio sostenuto, D♭; Maestoso, C
— Improvisations, ?1896, for 4 Improvisations, collab. Arensky, Glazunov and Taneyev
— Morceau de fantaisie, g, 1899
— Fughetta, F, 1899
17 Suite no.2, 2 pf, 1900–01
22 Variations on a Theme of Chopin, 1902–3
23 10 Preludes, 1903 (except no.5, 1901)
— Polka italienne, pf 4 hands, ?1906
28 Sonata no.1, d, 1907
32 13 Preludes, 1910
33 Etudes-tableaux, 1911: no.1, f; no.2, C; no.3 (6), e♭; no.4 (7), E♭; no.5 (8), g; no.6 (9), c♯; 3 other pieces intended for op.33 withdrawn before publication; of these, no.4, a, pubd as op.39 no.6; no.3, c, and no.5, d, pubd posthumously
36 Sonata no.2, b♭, 1913, rev. 1931
39 Etudes-tableaux, 1916–17: no.1, c; no.2, a; no.3, f♯; no.4, b; no.5, e♭; no.6, a; no.7, c; no.8, d; no.9, D
— Oriental Sketch, 1917
— Piece, d, 1917
— Fragments, 1917
Cadenza for Liszt: Hungarian Rhapsody no.2, 1919
42 Variations on a Theme of Corelli, 1931

SOLO VOCAL
(for 1v, pf, unless otherwise stated)

— U vrat obiteli svyatoy [At the gate of the holy abode] (Lermontov), 1890
— Ya tebe nichevo ne skazhu [I shall tell you nothing] (A. Fet), 1890
— Opyat' vstrepenulos' tï, serdtse [Again you leapt, my heart] (N. Grekov), 1890
— 2 monologues from Boris Godunov (Pushkin), 1890–91: Tï, otche patriarkh [Thou, father patriarch]; Eshcho odno posledneye skazan'ye [One last story]
— Noch' provedennaya bez sna, Arbenin's monologue from Maskarad (Lermontov), 1890–91
— Mazepa (Pushkin: Poltava), 4vv, fragment
— C'était en avril (E. Pailleron), 1891
— Smerkalos' [Twilight has fallen] (A. K. Tolstoy), 1891
— Pesnya razocharovannovo [Song of the disillusioned] (D. Rathaus), 1893
— Uvyal tsvetok [The flower has faded] (Rathaus), 1893
— Tï pomnish' li vecher [Do you remember the evening] (A. K. Tolstoy), 1893
4 6 Songs, 1890–93: O net, molyu, ne ukhodi [Oh no, I beg you, forsake me not] (D. Merezhkovsky), 1892; Utro [Morning] (M. Yanov), 1891; V molchan'i nochi taynoy [In the silence of the secret night] (Fet), 1890; Ne poy, krasavitsa, pri mne [Sing not to me, beautiful maiden] (Pushkin), 1893; Uzh tï, niva moya [Oh thou, my field] (A. K. Tolstoy), 1893; Davno l', moy drug [How long, my friend] (A. Golenishchev-Kutuzov), 1893
8 6 Songs (trans. A. Pleshcheyev), 1893: Rechnaya lileya [The waterlily] (Heine); Ditya kak tsvetok tï prekrasna [Child, thou art as beautiful as a flower] (Heine); Duma [Brooding]

(Shevchenko); Polyubila ya na pechal' svoyu [I have grown fond of sorrow] (Shevchenko); Son [The dream] (Heine); Molitva [A prayer] (Goethe)

14 12 Songs, 1896 (except no.1, 1894): Ya zhdu tebya [I wait for thee] (M. Davidova); Ostrovok [The isle] (Shelley, trans. Bal'mont); Davno v lyubvi otradï malo [For long there has been little consolation in love] (Fet); Ya bïl u ney [I was with her] (A. Koltsov); Eti letniye nochi [These summer nights] (Rathaus); Tebya tak lyubyat vse [How everyone loves thee] (A. K. Tolstoy); Ne ver' mne, drug [Believe me not, friend] (A. K. Tolstoy); O ne grusti [Oh, do not grieve] (A. Apukhtin); Ona, kak polden', khorosha [She is as lovely as the noon] (N. Minsky); V moyey dushe [In my soul] (Minsky); Vesenniye vodï [Spring waters] (Tyutchev); Pora ['Tis time] (S. Nadson)

— Ikalos' li tebe [Were you hiccoughing] (P. Vyazemsky), 1899
— Noch' [Night] (Rathaus)

21 12 Songs, 1902 (except no.1, 1900): Sud'ba [Fate] (Apukhtin); Nad svezhey mogiloy [By the fresh grave] (Nadson); Sumerki [Twilight] (M. Guyot, trans. M. Tkhorzhevsky); Oni otvechali [They answered] (Hugo, trans. L. Mey); Siren' [Lilacs] (E. Beketova); Otrïvok iz A. Myusse [Fragment from Musset] (trans. Apukhtin); Zdes' khorosho [How fair this spot] (G. Galina); Na smert' chizhika [On the death of a linnet] (V. Zhukovsky); Melodiya [Melody] (Nadson); Pred ikonoy [Before the icon] (Golenishchev-Kutuzov); Ya ne prorok [No prophet I] (A. Kruglov); Kak mne bol'no [How painful for me] (Galina)

26 15 Songs, 1906: Est' mnogo zvukov [There are many sounds] (A. K. Tolstoy); Vsyo otnyal u menya [He took all from me] (Tyutchev); Mï otdokhnyom [Let us rest] (Chekhov); Dva proshchaniya [Two partings] (Koltsov), Bar, S; Pokinem, milaya [Beloved, let us fly] (Golenishchev-Kutuzov); Khristos voskres [Christ is risen] (Merezhkovsky); K detyam [To the children] (A. Khomyakov); Poshchadï ya molyu [I beg for mercy] (Merezhkovsky); Ya opyat' odinok [Again I am alone] (Shevchenko, trans. I. Bunin); U moyevo okna [Before my window] (Galina); Fontan [The fountain] (Tyutchev); Noch' pechal'na [Night is mournful] (Bunin); Vchera mï vstretilis' [When yesterday we met] (Polonsky); Kol'tso [The ring] (Koltsov); Prokhodit vsyo [All things pass by] (Rathaus)

— Letter to K. S. Stanislavsky, 1908

34 14 Songs, 1912 (except no.7, 1910, rev. 1912): Muza [The muse] (Pushkin); V dushe u kazhdovo iz nas [In the soul of each of us] (A. Korinfsky); Burya [The storm] (Pushkin); Veter perelyotnïy [The migrant wind] (Bal'mont); Arion (Pushkin); Voskresheniye Lazarya [The raising of Lazarus] (Khomyakov); Ne mozhet bït' [It cannot be] (A. Maykov); Muzïka [Music] (Ya. Polonsky); Tï znal evo [You knew him] (Tyutchev); Sey den', ya pomnyu [I remember that day] (Tyutchev); Obrochnik [The peasant] (Fet); Kakoye schast'ye [What happiness] (Fet); Dissonans [Discord] (Polonsky); Vocalise, rev. 1915

— Iz evangeliya ot Ioanna [From the Gospel of St John], 1915

38 6 Songs, 1916: Noch'yu v sadu u menya [In my garden at night] (Isaakian, trans. Blok); K ney [To her] (A. Belïy); Margaritki [Daisies] (I. Severianin); Krïsolov [The rat-catcher] (V. Bryusov); Son [A dream] (F. Sologub); A-u! (Bal'mont)

ARRANGEMENTS
(for piano)

Tchaikovsky: Manfred, 4 hands, 1886, lost; *The Sleeping Beauty*, 4 hands, 1890
Glazunov: Symphony no.6, 4 hands, 1897
Behr: Lachtäubchen op.303, pubd as Polka VR, 1911
Smith: The Star-spangled Banner, 1918
Bizet: L'Arlésienne Suite no.1: Minuet, 1922
Musorgsky: Sorochintsy Fair: Hopak, 1924
Schubert: Wohin?, 1925
Kreisler: Liebesfreud, 1925; *Liebesleid*, 1931
Rimsky-Korsakov: Flight of the Bumble Bee, 1931
Bach: Violin Partita, E: Prelude, Gavotte and Gigue, 1933
Mendelssohn: A Midsummer Night's Dream: Scherzo, 1933
Rakhmaninov: Daisies op.38 no.3, 1940; *Lilacs op.21 no.5*, 1941
Tchaikovsky: Lullaby op.16 no.1, 1941
(for piano and violin)
Musorgsky: Sorochintsy Fair: Hopak, 1926

Principal publishers: Editions Russes, Foley, Gutheil, TAIR, Boosey & Hawkes

BIBLIOGRAPHY
V. Belyayev: *Sergey Rakhmaninov* (Moscow, 1924); Eng. trans. in *MQ*, xiii (1927), 359
S. Rakhmaninov: 'Some Critical Moments in my Career', *MT*, lxxi (1930), 557
A. J. and K. Swan: 'Rachmaninoff: Personal Reminiscences', *MQ*, xxx (1944), 1, 174
G. Kogan: 'Rakhmaninov – pianist', *SovM sbornik*, iv (1945), 58
K. A. Kuznetsov: 'Tvorcheskaya zhizn' S. V. Rakhmaninova' [Rakhmaninov's creative life], *SovM sbornik*, iv (1945), 25
D. Zhitomirsky: 'Fortepiannïye tvorchestvo Rakhmaninova'
[Rakhmaninov's piano works], *SovM sbornik*, iv (1945), 80
I. F. Belza, ed.: *S. V. Rakhmaninov i russkaya opera* (Moscow, 1947)
V. M. Bogdanov-Berezovsky, ed.: *Molodïye godï Sergeya Vasil'yevicha Rakhmaninova* [Rakhmaninov's early years] (Leningrad and Moscow, 1949)
J. Culshaw: *Sergei Rachmaninov* (London, 1949)
Z. A. Apetian, ed.: *S. V. Rakhmaninov: pis'ma* [Letters] (Moscow, 1955)
E. Bortnikova, ed.: *Avtografï S. V. Rakhmaninova v fondakh gosudarstvennovo tsentral'novo muzeya muzïkal'noy kulturï imeni M. I. Glinki: katalog-spravochnik* [Rakhmaninov's autographs in the archives of the State Central Glinka Museum of Musical Culture: a reference catalogue] (Moscow, 1955)
S. Bertensson and J. Leyda: *Sergei Rachmaninoff: a Lifetime in Music* (New York, 1956, 2/1965)
Z. A. Apetian, ed.: *Vospominaniya o Rakhmaninove* [Reminiscences of Rakhmaninov] (Moscow, 1957, enlarged 4/1974)
V. N. Bryantseva: 'Gde rodilsya S. V. Rakhmaninov?' [Where was Rakhmaninov born?], *Muzïkal'naya zhizn'* (1969), no.19, p.20
——: *Detstvo i yunost' Sergeya Rakhmaninova* [Rakhmaninov's childhood and youth] (Moscow, 1970, 2/1973)
Z. A. Apetian, ed.: *N. K. Metner: pis'ma* [Letters] (Moscow, 1973) [incl. Rakhmaninov's letters to Metner]
Yu. V. Keldïsh: *Rakhmaninov i evo vremya* [Rakhmaninov and his time] (Moscow, 1973)
——: 'Tvorcheskiy put' velikovo muzïkanta' [The creative path of a great musician], *SovM* (1973), no.4, p.74
G. Norris: 'Rakhmaninov's Second Thoughts', *MT*, cxiv (1973), 364
——: 'Rakhdokhnov's Student Opera', *MQ*, lix (1973), 441
R. Threlfall: 'Rachmaninoff's Revisions and an Unknown Version of his Fourth Concerto', *MO*, xcvi (1972–3), 235
N. D. Uspensky: 'Sergey Vasilievich Rakhmaninov', *Journal of the Moscow Patriarchate* (1973), no.8, p.79; no.9, p.76
P. Piggott: *Rachmaninov Orchestral Music* (London, 1974)
V. Bryantseva: *S. V. Rakhmaninov* (Moscow, 1976)
G. Norris: *Rakhmaninov* (London, 1976)
Z. A. Apetian, ed.: *S. Rakhmaninov: literaturnoye naslediye* [Literary heritage], i (Moscow, 1978)
R. Threlfall and G. Norris: *Catalogue of the Compositions of S. Rachmaninoff* (in preparation)

GEOFFREY NORRIS

Raking. A technique of playing broken chords on the lute, described in Thomas Mace's *Musick's Monument* (1676). *See* ORNAMENTS, §IV, 6.

Rakov, Nikolay Petrovich (*b* Kaluga, 14 March 1908). Soviet composer and teacher. He studied with Glier and Vasilenko at the Moscow Conservatory, where he was eventually appointed professor of instrumentation. His pupils there have included Boris Chaykovsky, Edison Denisov and Andrey Eshpay. As a composer, too, he had given considerable attention to educational work, and his teaching pieces have an important place in the USSR. His music is directly linked with the Russian tradition; his orchestration is masterly in its subtlety and clarity, and he has made many arrangements of Russian, Ukrainian and Estonian folksongs. He is an Honoured Art Worker of the RSFSR and holds the State Prize.

WORKS
(selective list)

Orch: Sym. no.1, 1930; Mkaya syuita [Mari suite], 1931; Tantseval'naya syuita [Dance suite], 1934; Vn Conc. no.1, 1944; Kontsertnaya syuita, 1949; Baletnaya syuita [Ballet suite], 1950; Vn Conc. no.2, 1954; Sym. no.2, 1957; Sinfonietta, 1958; Concertino, vn, str, 1959; Little Sym., 1962
Inst: Sonata v klassicheskom stile, 1950; Sonata, ob, pf, 1951; Sonata, vn, pf, 1951; Sonata no.2, pf, 1954; Sonata, fl, pf, 1970
Vocal music

BIBLIOGRAPHY
I. Popov: 'O tvorchestve N. Rakova' [On Rakov's work], *SovM* (1955), no.10, p.28
A. Solovtsov: *N. Rakov* (Moscow, 1958)
'Nash kalendar': k 60-letiyu kompozitora' [Our calendar: for the composer's 60th birthday], *Muzïkal'naya zhizn'* (1968), no.3, p.23

GALINA GRIGOR'YEVA

Ralf. Swedish family of musicians.
  (1) **Oscar (Georg) Ralf** (*b* Malmö, 3 Oct 1881; *d*

Kalmar, 3 April 1964). Tenor. Son of an organ builder and church musician, he studied in Stockholm with John Forsell (1902–4) and Gillis Bratt (from 1905), and in Berlin and Munich. He made his début in 1905 at the Oscarsteatern, Stockholm's operetta theatre, and sang there until 1915, when he began to study the *Heldentenor* repertory with Bratt. His operatic début was in 1918 as Siegmund with the Swedish Royal Opera, of which he remained a member until 1940, specializing in the Wagner and Verdi repertories and giving notable performances as Florestan and Samson. He was the first Swedish tenor to appear at Bayreuth, as Siegmund in 1927. He translated over 40 operas and 180 operettas into Swedish (many of his translations were still used in Sweden in the 1970s), and published an autobiography *Tenoren han går i Ringen* ('The tenor goes into the Ring', Stockholm, 1953).

(2) **Einar (Christian) Ralf** (*b* Malmö, 24 July 1888; *d* Stockholm, 27 Sept 1971). Choral conductor and teacher, brother of (1) Oscar Ralf. He taught at the Stockholm Conservatory, as its director from 1940. He conducted a student choir, with which he toured abroad several times between 1925 and 1947, and in 1943 was appointed director of the Swedish Choral Association.

(3) **Torsten (Ivar) Ralf** (*b* Malmö, 2 Jan 1901; *d* Stockholm, 27 April 1954). Tenor, brother of (1) Oscar Ralf. He studied in Stockholm and in Berlin with Hertha Dehmlow and made his début at Stettin in 1930 as Cavaradossi. After engagements at Chemnitz (1932–3) and Frankfurt am Main (1933–5) he joined the Dresden Staatsoper, of which he remained a member until 1944; he was appointed a Kammersänger in 1936. At Dresden he created Apollo in Strauss's *Daphne* (1938) and appeared in the première of Sutermeister's *Die Zauberinsel* (1942). He sang regularly at Covent Garden, 1935–9, as Lohengrin, Walther, Parsifal, Erik and Tannhäuser, and in 1936 was heard as Bacchus in a single performance of *Ariadne auf Naxos* given in London by the Dresden company under the composer. He returned to Covent Garden in 1948 as Radamès and was one of the few tenors heard there who ended 'Celeste Aida' with the *pianissimo b♭''* that Verdi wrote. Ralf sang at the Metropolitan Opera, 1945–8, in the Wagnerian repertory and as Radamès and Othello, and appeared at the Teatro Colón, Buenos Aires, in 1946.

HAROLD ROSENTHAL

Rallentando (It.: 'becoming slower'; gerund of *rallentare*, to relax, slacken, slow down). A direction to reduce tempo, often abbreviated to *rall*. In the 18th century the form *lentando* was common. *Rallentando* itself is of relatively recent usage, being scarcely encountered in scores before the 19th century; now it is perhaps the most common of such terms, though *ritardando* and *ritenuto* both occur frequently. Each word has different shades of meaning, but each composer has interpreted these shades in his own way, if at all. From this point of view H. Cahn's excellently documented interpretation of the difference ('Retardando, ritardando', *HMT*) seems a little rigid.

For bibliography see TEMPO AND EXPRESSION MARKS.

DAVID FALLOWS

Ramann, Lina (*b* Mainstockheim, 24 July 1833; *d* Munich, 30 March 1912). German writer and music teacher. The daughter of a wine merchant, she was taught music by the wife of Franz Brendel, the editor of the *Neue Zeitschrift für Musik*. As this publication strongly supported Liszt and his school, she came into contact with Liszt's circle at an early age and was his pupil for a time. She first taught in Gera, then went to the USA for some years. In 1858 she founded a music school in Glückstadt, moving it to Nuremberg six years later. There she continued to work successfully until 1890, when she handed the school over to Liszt's pupil August Göllerich and moved to Munich. Her music school was one of the first in Germany to combine general philosophical education with music teaching.

Ramann wrote a number of books, especially about Liszt, the first of these being a study of the oratorio *Christus*. From 1870 onwards she worked on the 'official' biography of Liszt, *Franz Liszt als Künstler und Mensch*. In this she was very much influenced by Princess Sayn-Wittgenstein, and her account of Liszt's early years with Countess Marie d'Agoult is often inaccurate. Liszt himself annotated the early volumes and pointed out some of their mistakes. Her *Liszt-Pädagogium* reproduces many remarks on piano teaching by Liszt and some of his pupils. Ramann translated Liszt's collected writings into German.

Her cousin Bruno Ramann (*b* Erfurt, 17 April 1832; *d* Dresden, 13 March 1897) was a composer, mainly of songs and piano pieces.

WRITINGS

Aus der Gegenwart (Nuremberg, 1868)
Bach und Händel (Leipzig, 1868)
Die Musik als Gegenstand des Unterrichts (Leipzig, 1868)
Allgemeine musikalische Erziehungs- und Unterrichtslehre (Leipzig, 1870)
Franz Liszts Oratorium Christus (Leipzig, 1874)
ed.: *F. Liszt: Gesammelte Schriften* (Leipzig, 1880–83)
Franz Liszt als Künstler und Mensch (Leipzig, 1880–94)
Grundriss der Technik des Klavier-Spiels (Leipzig, 1885)
Liszt als Psalmensänger (Leipzig, 1886)
Liszt-Pädagogium (Leipzig, 1901)

BIBLIOGRAPHY

A. Seidl: 'Zum Capitel der musikalischen Erziehung: L. Ramann'sche Unterrichtsmethode', *Musikalisches Wochenblatt*, xxi (1890), 169
G. Flachsbart: 'Lina Ramann', *AMz*, xxx (1903), 411
A. Seidl: 'Denkmal der Verehrung und Liebe', *AMz*, xxxix (1912), 415, 439
A. Stradal: 'Lina Ramann: ein Nachruf', *NZM*, Jg.79 (1912), 206
M. Ille-Beeg: *Lina Ramann* (Nuremberg, 1914)
E. von Binzer: 'Lina Ramann', *NZM*, Jg.100 (1933), 758

HUMPHREY SEARLE

Rambert, Dame **Marie** [Ramberg, Miriam] (*b* 1888). English dancer and choreographer of Polish birth; *see* DANCE, §VII, 1(ii).

Rameau, Jean-Philippe (*b* Dijon, baptized 25 Sept 1683; *d* Paris, 12 Sept 1764). French composer and theorist. A close contemporary of J. S. Bach, Handel, Domenico Scarlatti and Telemann, he was the leading French composer (particularly of dramatic music) of his time and an important innovator in harmonic theory.

1. Life. 2. Keyboard music. 3. Sacred music and cantatas. 4. Dramatic style. 5. The tragédies lyriques. 6. Comédie-ballet and opéra-ballet. 7. Theoretical writings.

1. LIFE. His father, organist at St Etienne, Dijon, was the first musician in the family; his mother Claudine Demartinécourt, from the neighbouring village of Gémeaux, belonged to the lesser nobility. Jean-Philippe was the seventh of their 11 children. Their house still stands at 5–7 rue Vaillant. Jean-Philippe was sent to the Jesuit Collège des Godrans, where he spent more time singing and composing than studying, and his parents' hopes of seeing him enter law were dashed when the school asked for him to be taken away. When he was 18

1. Jean-Philippe Rameau: portrait by Jacques Aved (1702–66) in the Musée des Beaux-Arts, Dijon

his father consented to his becoming a musician and sent him to Italy where he spent a few months in Milan. In January 1702 he was temporary organist at Avignon Cathedral; in May he was appointed organist at Clermont Cathedral. By 1706 he was in Paris, where he held posts as organist to the Jesuits of rue St Jacques and the Mercederians of rue du Chaume, and where he published his first book of harpsichord pieces. In March 1709 he was back in Dijon as his father's successor at Notre Dame; in July 1713 he was in Lyons at the organ of the Jacobins, and in April 1715 back at Clermont Cathedral, where he stayed for eight years. To secure his release before the end of his contract he made himself unbearable on a feast day, first by refusing to play and then by pulling out all the most unpleasing stops and adding all possible discords. The chapter allowed him to leave and for the second time he went to Paris, in 1722 or early 1723, and settled there. At Lyons and Clermont he had composed motets and secular cantatas and written his first book, the Traité de l'harmonie, published by Ballard in 1722, in which he was still called organist of Clermont Cathedral.

For his first nine years in Paris he seems to have held no post. He joined forces with his fellow townsman Piron in sketches and farces for the Fair theatres. In 1724 and 1728 he published his second and third harpsichord books. In 1726 he married a girl of 19, Marie-Louise Mangot, a member of a Lyons family of musicians whose brother was later to make Rameau's music known at the court of Parma. In 1727 he competed for the post of organist at the church of St Paul but lost to Daquin. By 1732 he was organist at Ste Croix-de-la-Bretonnerie and in 1736 at the Jesuit novitiate. His Traité and Nouveau système de musique théorique (1726), followed by several articles and discussions in the Mercure, made him famous as a theorist, but his ambition was to compose for the stage. In 1727 he asked La Motte-Houdar for a libretto, without result. About 1726 Piron introduced him to the tax-farmer Le Riche de la Pouplinière who ran a private orchestra and whose wife, Marie-Thérèse Deshayes, was to become a fervent admirer of Rameau. At La Pouplinière's he met the playwright Abbé Simon-Joseph Pellegrin (1663–1745), the author of some 15 tragedies, tragédies lyriques and ballets, and induced him to write a libretto. The outcome was his first opera, Hippolyte et Aricie, played privately at La Pouplinière's in July 1733 and given at the Opéra on 1 October the same year. He was just turned 50 and Pellegrin was 70.

From then on his creative activity was to be divided

between expounding his theories and composing. For 22 years he conducted the financier's orchestra, and from 1744 to 1753 he lived in an apartment in La Pouplinière's mansion (on the site of 59 rue de Richelieu). When he left there he returned to the rue des Bons Enfants where he had lived from 1739 to 1744 and where he was to die in 1764.

Rameau considered his theoretical studies as important as his music and he pursued them unceasingly to his death. Books, articles and operas intermingled in his output from 1732 to the end. Strange though it may seem to those who enjoy his music but do not read his books, it was through his theories that he hoped to win renown and he was more prone to vanity as a thinker than as a composer. In his last years, as he felt his creative powers failing, he told Chabanon that he regretted the time devoted to composition because it had been lost to research into the principles of his art. He courted the commendation of the learned. Two of his books, *Génération harmonique* and *Démonstration du principe de l'harmonie*, were submitted to the Académie des Sciences, which reported favourably on them. D'Alembert thought well enough of them to present them in a more readable form than the originals in *Eléments de musique théorique et pratique selon les principes de M. Rameau* (1752). He sought also the approval of foreign savants, Sir Hans Sloane in London, the younger Jean Bernoulli in Basle, Euler in Berlin, Padre Martini in Bologna, not all of whom reciprocated his own high opinion of them. He engaged in polemics on their account with Father Castel, the inventor of the 'clavecin oculaire', at first one of his supporters, later a severe critic, and with D'Alembert, who passed likewise from approval to condemnation. He made an enemy of Rousseau by slighting his *Muses galantes* when he heard it at La Pouplinière's in 1745, an offence Rousseau never forgave. His attacks on several musical articles in the *Encyclopédie* by D'Alembert and Rousseau between 1755 and 1760 estranged D'Alembert too. On the other hand, he praised the architect and writer Charles-Etienne Briseux, who shared some of his views.

He cannot have been a genial companion, and seems to have enjoyed no close friendships; 'the emptiness he found in society made him avoid it', said Dagoty. Chabanon watched him striding up and down the Tuileries and Palais-Royal gardens without daring at first to speak to him. One day he summoned up courage and, far from being rebuffed, was made welcome and told that the old man would always enjoy being addressed and taken out of his empty, idle existence. But he spoke so little about himself that even his wife knew no details about the first half of his life. Only when discussing musical theory would he open out. The humorous description of him which Piron, who had known him for 40 years, sent to Dr Maret for his obituary and which the doctor dared not use gives the most vivid picture we have of him. Chabanon's *Eloge* is the fullest presentation of the old man's personality. Diderot's portrait of him in *Le neveu de Rameau* is distorted and unreliable (the nephew was for a while a sore trial to his uncle). Rameau's reputed avarice is belied by several acts of generosity to his relations. However unaccommodating he was, no-one ever accused him of acting basely or of time-serving. He faced attacks honestly when they were made openly but was angered by whispering campaigns.

He was a few days short of his 81st birthday when he died. Four months earlier he had been ennobled. Since 1745 he had held the title of *Compositeur du cabinet du roy*. He was buried in his parish church of St Eustache; the bust erected there a century later does not mark the site of his grave, which is unknown.

His physique is familiar. His long thin body resembled Voltaire's; his features, too, were not unlike his contemporary's; they recalled also those of another contemporary, Tartini, like him both composer and theorist. 'He had a sharp chin, no stomach, flutes for legs', said Sébastien Mercier. He was extremely tall and thin, 'more like a ghost than a man', wrote Chabanon. His eagle profile was aesthetically so attractive that hardly any portraits show him full face; an exception is that by Aved in Dijon (fig.1).

2. KEYBOARD MUSIC. Rameau's 65 keyboard pieces, published in four books in 1706, 1724, c1728 and 1741, though all but the last earlier than his first opera, are not unrepresentative and within their narrow scope reflect unmistakably his power and depth. The composer's mark is clear on most of the pages in his first collection and the kinship with Louis Marchand, though recognizable here and there, has been overemphasized. Two-thirds of the 1724 book are genre pieces, the rest dances; they are grouped by keys but do not form suites. The writing looks both forward and backward. Some pieces are almost lute-like, with the harmonies spread out in arpeggios; *Les soupirs* in particular is remarkable for combining *luthé* writing with harmonic boldness. The close linear style of an older generation is found in the Allemande; a more modern linear style in *La joyeuse* recalls Couperin. On the whole the writing is based on arpeggio formation rather than on scalic motion.

It is because of Rameau's attempts to use his keyboard as a sustaining instrument that much of his music sounds well on the piano; indeed the Musette and *Les cyclopes* have a euphonic fullness which presupposes an orchestral imagination. The tone differences between the three parts of *L'entretien des Muses* also suggest differences in timbre. The swirling quavers and smears of semiquaver arpeggios in *Les tourbillons*, the chords prolonged for purposes of colour in *Le rappel des oiseaux* and *Les cyclopes*, all profit from an instrument of greater sustaining power and colour than the harpsichord. *Les niais de Sologne* suggests a hurdy-gurdy tune with a plodding string bass. The Rigaudons and Tambourin are ready for orchestration; indeed the latter, like the Musette, was incorporated in *Les fêtes d'Hébé*.

A wide-spaced left-hand part is prominent in *Les niais*; the hand covers in swift semiquavers as much as two and a half octaves, suggesting its long-legged creator striding in the Tuileries gardens. These great sweeps give Rameau's harpsichord music a spaciousness hitherto lacking in the instrument's literature. Such pieces, with *La Forqueray* in the *Pièces de clavecin en concerts*, are an arsenal of Ramellian virtuosity. He also had a meditative mood, expressed in pieces like *L'entretien des Muses*, while others, like *Les cyclopes* and, in the third (c1728) book, *La triomphante* and *Les sauvages*, call for choreographic rendering.

Of Rameau's four books the second is the freshest and most exuberant. But the third collection contains some of his most ambitious writing. The A minor Allemande and haughty yet emotional Courante are both majestic and contemplative. A dramatic passion not found earlier surges in *La poule*, *Les sauvages* and

L'égiptienne (a gypsy girl dancing). With these the highlights are the Gavotte with six *doubles*, and *L'enharmonique*. All but one are in binary or rondeau form, the binaries being the most adventurous structurally. Each half of the Allemande and Courante is in the through-composed style of suite movements. *Les triolets*, *L'enharmonique* and *L'égiptienne* are more articulated than the others and look forward to the mosaic construction of the Rococo though the general impression is still thematic. They are like sonatas in which the development occurs after the beginning of the recapitulation instead of before. In *L'enharmonique* the second half, which has begun like the first, breaks away from its path and inserts new material; the first of these new passages, a true development, contains the enharmonic change over which Rameau made heavy weather in his preface.

La poule sounds monothematic but is in fact made up of a number of similar themes containing the clucking motif in various forms. It is one of his most powerful compositions. Rameau was in deadly earnest in attempting to transcribe a sound of nature, and nothing in it suggests banter; one should forget the barnyard imagery and hear or play it as pure music, the 'developing' of an unpromising initial cell. It soon becomes clear that the piece is a drama with alternations of hope and despair. After the G minor opening the major intrudes with brutal vigour and reigns for a time before it is displaced by minor keys. The clucking theme, whether in minor or major, is Ramellian in the way it completes its harmony in successive rushes, moments of strain which are followed by easier bars of lighthearted twitterings or by

others with the pursuing-hands motif, after which the repeated notes resume and their inexorable hammering makes a powerful effect. The last *forte* makes clear the seriousness of the piece: the tragic impatience of the climax seems to close the drama in violence.

Except for *La dauphine* all Rameau's harpsichord solo pieces were written before he began composing for the stage. However, eight years after his first opera he published a little volume of 19 pieces grouped in five suites, or 'concerts', for harpsichord, violin or flute, and tenor viol or second violin. They are not trios in the 19th-century sense nor sonatas for two instruments and bass but, as the title says, concerted movements. Their remote forebears were harpsichord suites to which was added an optional violin part; their more immediate ones were the six sonatas op.3 by Mondonville (*c*1734), for harpsichord and violin, in which each instrument has its own part and plays almost continuously; they are not polyphonic and their idiom is 'modern'. After 1734 such harpsichord pieces became fairly common. Though he did not consider the string instruments as mere accessories, Rameau said in his preface that his pieces lost nothing by being played on the harpsichord alone; 'indeed one would never suspect them capable of any other adornment; such at least is the opinion of several persons of taste and skill whom I have consulted'. This is true of most but not quite all.

In some the relation between the two groups results in a situation that may be called symphonic (*La Boucon*). A subtler mode of combination consists in short contrasted wisps and broad 'orchestral' masses (*La Livri*, *La timide*); there is also straightforward accompanying in which one is subordinate to the other (*Le Vézinet*, *La Forqueray*, *La Livri*). In *La timide* and *La Cupis* the harpsichord parts, though of great beauty, do not once touch the melodic material shared by violin (or flute) and viol (or second violin). There are familiar features in the keyboard writing, including wide compass (the second *La timide*, where three and a half octaves are covered within one bar) and triplet runs (*La Laborde*). New are the irregular arpeggios (*La Forqueray*), the scale passages (*Le Vézinet*), and the hand-crossing of various sorts including a hand-over-hand variety not found in the solos (*La timide*, second rondeau; *La Forqueray*). 'Orchestral' writing is of course more common than in the solos.

Most of the pieces are in binary form, but *La pantomime* is a genuine miniature sonata-form movement, with a recognizable 'second subject', a thematic 'development' of 17 bars and a recapitulation in which the first subject returns with full harmony. Several pieces are technically interesting but prosaic, and the collection's general level is not quite as high as that of the earlier ones. Six of the pieces, however, are masterpieces. *La Forqueray*, Rameau's most sustained instrumental work, is like a stiffer, still vigorous version of *Les cyclopes*, full of swinging octaves and downward scales, with alternations between keyboard and strings like solos and tuttis in a concerto. It was perhaps an epithalamium for the viol player and composer Jean-Baptiste Forqueray, who had married in March 1741. The touching *La Boucon* is like the pathetic monologues which open many acts in the *tragédies lyriques*; it is probably a portrait of the distinguished harpsichordist Anne-Jeanne Boucon, who became Mme de Mondonville. *La Livri* is a *tombeau*, a lament for Piron's benefactor the Count of Livry, who had died in July 1741;

2. *Jean-Philippe Rameau: engraving (1762) by Augustin de St Aubin after Jean Jacques Caffieri*

3. Part of 'L'égiptienne' from 'Nouvelles suites de pièces de clavecin' (Paris: Author, Boivin and Le Clerc, c1728)

the cross-rhythms of the keyboard part suggest tolling bells. Each couplet brings a relief dispelled each time by the darkness of the refrain. There are two dreamy menuets, the poignant second one of which is used again in *Les fêtes de Polymnie*. *La Cupis* is another dreamy piece, meant perhaps as a cradle song for Jean-Baptiste Cupis, born in 1741, son of François Cupis, one of La Camargo's brothers. *La timide*, the most haunting of the six, consists of a pair of rondeaux, the first belonging to a large family of French movements in A minor of this period, the second containing a series of remarkable harmonic clashes unique in Rameau's keyboard music.

Most of the titles in the solo collections are either dances or descriptive and characteristic and need no explanation. Dance and character titles also occur in the *Pièces . . . en concerts*. The connection between title and piece is not always obvious, and some titles may have been assigned after the music had been composed. Rameau spoke in his preface of persons 'some of whom have done me the honour of naming some of these pieces', which suggests that he asked his friends for titles after they had been written or that these persons had selected the pieces which they would like to see bear their names. *La La Poplinière* (sic) is certainly a sketch of the flighty financier; Marin Marais (*d* 1728) left many children, one of whom is commemorated in *La Marais*. *La Rameau* is perhaps an unsmiling joke, a parody of the Rameaus practising. These trios have thus an intimate setting and an interest beyond their musical appeal.

3. SACRED MUSIC AND CANTATAS. Rameau's sacred music is the least important part of his output except for his cantatas. It consists of four extant motets, three of which date from between 1713 at the latest and 1723, and a fifth now lost. Three of those that survive are planned on a grand scale, with alternating solos, duets, trios, quartets and choruses, a form evolved by Du Mont and developed by Lully, Lalande and Campra. Though less personal than much of his music they are impressive, especially *Deus noster refugium* (Psalm xlvi).

This, probably the earliest, consists of nine complete numbers and part of a tenth, all in B♭, with two choruses, four solos, a trio, a duet and a quartet. The grandest are the two choruses. The first, 170 bars long, 'Sonuerunt et conturbatae sunt aquae', is built like a concerto grosso with four orchestral ritornellos that alternate with vocal sections, with a key system resembling the later sonata rondo. Its assurance, suggesting that Rameau had already written music like this which must now be lost, deepens the mystery of his formation. This is the kind of chorus which he tried to introduce to the stage with 'Que ce rivage retentisse' in *Hippolyte et Aricie* but never again. The quartet 'Conturbatae sunt gentes' is a dusky ensemble for countertenor, two tenors and bass, unlighted by treble tones. This motet is a noble piece, somewhat unbending and even forbidding except in the countertenor solo 'Vacate et videte'. *In convertendo* (Psalm cxxvi) is the most Ramellian of these motets. Its best numbers are the first, a countertenor solo of dramatic–elegiac character, and a fine chorus, 'Euntes et flebant', complex yet consistent, full of restrained emotion, expressing the contrast between the slow-moving weepers and their joyful return; it is the finest number in all Rameau's church music. The fourth surviving motet, *Laboravi* (from Psalm lxix), polyphonic throughout, was published in the *Traité de l'harmonie*. All four are fine abstract music in which words and sentiments are treated more as occasions for the music than to be interpreted by it.

Of Rameau's six extant chamber cantatas, composed between 1718 and 1728, the best are the sardonic *Les amants trahis* and *Le berger fidèle*. The first is a duet, the others solos; they are accompanied by harpsichord and tenor viol, sometimes with one or two violins. Concerto-like writing for the viol occurs in *Les amants trahis*, *Orphée* and especially *L'impatience*. The only one to show dramatic spirit is *Orphée*, though *Aquilon et Orinthie* has a splendid *air* representing fury, in a rising-scale theme with a brilliant violin part. *Le berger fidèle* is the closest in style to Rameau's operatic music. The interest of most of these products of his first period, however, is much less than that of the contemporary or slightly later harpsichord pieces.

4. DRAMATIC STYLE. Rameau composed in a large number of different dramatic genres: the *tragédie lyrique* (or *tragédie en musique*), the *comédie-lyrique*, the *opéra-ballet*, the *comédie-ballet*, the *pastorale*, the *acte de ballet* and the *divertissement*, and incidental music (to a *comédie-ballet* by Voltaire). The most interesting are the first three *tragédies lyriques*, the first two *opéra-ballets* and the first *comédie-ballet*, though few of his 90 or so acts are without interest.

To experience him at his best one should turn to his first three *tragédies lyriques*, Hippolyte et Aricie, Castor et Pollux and Dardanus. Built on the pattern evolved by Lully and Quinault, they are genuine operas, each act containing an interlude or divertissement of singing and dancing, more or less integrated into the action. The drama is carried on mainly by recitative, generally melodic even when declamatory. From time to time its outline becomes more tuneful for a few bars; such passages were known as *petits airs*. Far from excluding melody, Rameau condemned a slavishly accurate imitation of natural declamation. Its emotional power was often enhanced by its being accompanied. The gradual merging of recitative and melodic passages is typical of his dramatic discourse, and tends towards a quasi-Wagnerian continuity. Thanks to its subtlety it renders, so to speak, the contour of the sentiment, its delicate as well as its massive changes, to a degree unknown to Lully or Gluck. French classical opera does not know the distinction of Italian, so fatal to dramatic illusion, between simple recitative and aria.

The interruption of the action by divertissements was not arbitrary, and they were not always unrelated to the plot; the merit or demerit of a work on this score depends on the librettist. The chief criticism to be made of them on dramatic grounds is not that they are irrelevant but that, by inserting pure music and dancing, they damp down one's dramatic response which has then to be rekindled when the action starts afresh. But a succession of tensions and relaxations, obtained by pathetic scenes alternating with spectacle, whether festive or not, is an essential feature of the genre and not the result of incompetence.

The choruses remain as important as they were for Lully, and they contain some of Rameau's most forceful writing. They too procure tension and release and, by punctuating the scenes, they make up for the lack of contrast between *airs* and recitative. Many of them are bound up with the drama and are themselves action, for example those for the demons guarding Hell in Act 3 of *Castor et Pollux* or the contending good and evil forces in Act 5 of *Zoroastre*. Rameau's most expressive outbursts of passion are attained in some of these action choruses, such as the second one for the Magicians in Act 2 of *Dardanus*, where relentless vigour is linked with a boding sense of danger. Action choruses have their counterpart in action dances, not all of which are violent, and in *ballets figurés*, such as the worship of a divinity, where the music accompanies and underlines dumb show.

Shepherds and shepherdesses enter the temple. The high priestess, preceded by the priestesses and followed by Zais and Zélidie, goes in after them. The god's statue is crowned with garlands and flowers; shepherds and shepherdesses return to the front of the stage [*Zaïs*, Act 1].

The shepherds, bearing baskets full of flowers, strew them before Tiresias's grotto. They embellish the setting by hanging up garlands that compose the monograms of Tiresias and Nais [*Naïs*, Act 2].

Ballets d'action had figured in the Duchess of Maine's festivities at Sceaux early in the century.

The typical Rameau solo resembles the aria in its da capo form, in being preceded by a ritornello and in modulating to the dominant or relative major in its middle section. But its first part is a free repetition rather than a development of the ritornello and the middle section is as long as the first. Though melodic, the vocal line remains near to recitative. The elaborate accompaniment is often concertante, and the instruments compete with the voice on almost equal terms (*Hippolyte*, Act 1 scene i, Act 3 scene i; *Castor*, Act 1 scene iii, Act 2 scene i, Act 4 scene i; *Dardanus*, Act 1 scene i, Act 3 scene i). But this outline is found in only a few of his solos, the diversity of which is too great to be reduced to half a dozen fixed forms. They are often extremely free and unfold like ariosos (*Hippolyte*, Act 2 scene iv, Act 3 scene ix, Act 5 scene i). The freedom, already great in the first operas, increases in Rameau's later works where they blend more and more with their context. Nothing in contemporary Italian opera resembles this untrammelled progress, which only Rameau's organizing power saves from shapelessness. Outside French opera the clearest contemporary analogy is in the ariosos of Bach's Passions. Many orchestral preludes are symphonic units in their own right (*Hippolyte*, Act 5 scene iii; *Dardanus*, Act 3 scene i) and contain some of his most lyrical strains.

Rameau's set duets and trios should be distinguished from his dramatic scenes where two or more protagonists sing together. Though the most interesting of the latter are the divergent ones in which the feelings expressed are contradictory (*Castor*, Act 3 scene iii; *Les Indes galantes*, Act 2 scene vii), the most touching of all is unanimous (*Dardanus*, 1744 version, Act 4 scene iv). There are many further good duet scenes without fixed forms (*Hippolyte*, Act 2 scene i; *Castor*, Act 1 scene i; *Les fêtes d'Hébé*, prologue; *Platée*, Act 3 scene viii). The set pieces occur in dramatic scenes, like the two great Fates' trios (*Hippolyte*, Act 2 scenes iv–v; *Dardanus*, Act 1 scene iii), but are commoner in divertissements; the trio of Dreams in *Dardanus* (Act 4 scene i) is a well-known example.

It is in his *symphonies de danse* that Rameau is least like anyone else and most markedly superior to those who used similar forms. His dances are rich in both choreographic gesture and emotional significance. They impose physical movement rather than express it and dictate the details of the dancers' mimicry. They range from the courtly (gavotte, minuet etc) to the semi-popular (*loure*) and popular (*tambourin*, rigaudon); into his *tambourins*, especially, he often threw a Dionysiac frenzy. Noverre praised the 'witty conversations between the instruments that prevailed in his tunes'.

Formally his most original numbers are his overtures. The earliest keep to the slow–fast pattern inherited from Lully but the 'fast' becomes less and less contrapuntal. The first, *Hippolyte*, is thematically akin to the chorus that follows it. The 'slow' (*fièrement*) of *Castor* returns enlarged in Act 5. Those of *Platée* and *Les fêtes de Polymnie* also presage passages in the operas, and that is true of all his later ones. That of *Les Boréades* is a hunt which runs into the first scene, the formula of Gluck's *Iphigénie en Tauride* ten years later. After *La princesse de Navarre*, with three Italianate movements, he gave up the Lullian pattern. *Zoroastre* has a programme overture depicting Abramane's 'barbarous rule and the groans of the peoples he oppresses', the beneficent power of Zoroaster and the happiness of the liberated. That of *Naïs* portrays the Titans storming Olympus, and *Zaïs*'s evokes chaos. Those of *Pygmalion* (the sculptor's chiselling), *Les surprises de l'Amour* (Vulcan's hammer) and *Acante et Céphise* (gunfire) are also descriptive. Rameau was probably the earliest composer to develop this kind of overture.

As the essential part of Rameau's dramatic achievement is in his operas, as distinct from his one-act ballets, this presentation of it will be based on his *tragédies lyriques* and, more briefly, on his *comédie-ballet Platée* and his two best-known *opéras-ballets*, *Les Indes galantes* and *Les fêtes d'Hébé*.

5. THE TRAGÉDIES LYRIQUES. Though *tragédie lyrique* was regarded as a dramatic genre, Rameau himself was interested in the expressive and descriptive aspects of his texts, not in their architecture. He has usually been pitied for having had such poor librettists; but this pity is not entirely deserved. Neither Pellegrin (*Hippolyte*) nor Bernard (*Castor et Pollux*) nor even Cahusac (*Zaïs*) were negligible playwrights, and both *Hippolyte* and *Castor* have dramatic merits. Of his four performed *tragédies* the only one with a really poor author is *Dardanus* (Le Clerc de la Bruyère). It is of course regrettable that Voltaire's *Samson* should not have survived and that Rameau should have scorned Voltaire's request for him to set *Pandore*. But in the period 1733–56 *tragédie lyrique* had ceased to attract writers of quality, and Rameau had little choice; he had come to the operatic stage 20 years too late.

Pellegrin's *Hippolyte* has the merit of incorporating much of Euripides' *Hippolytus* plays and Racine's *Phèdre*. It is thus in part a Greek tragedy and not just a fairy tale with Greek names. The Abbé took the Hippolytus–Aricia idyll from Racine and made it his chief theme; this led to the obscuring of Phaedra. The lovers come to the fore especially in the non-tragic ending, but the chief gainer is Theseus, whom Pellegrin upgrades enough for Rameau to make him the most monumental figure in all his theatre. Acts 2 and 3 provide Rameau with splendid opportunities and raise the libretto above the mediocre level to which it is usually, and unjustly, assigned. Pellegrin's great stroke of operatic imagination was to stage the judgment of Theseus by Pluto's court. Journeys to Hades had not often figured in French opera. Pellegrin shows the king battling unsuccessfully with Tisiphone until Pluto appears and Theseus begs to be allowed to join Pirithous. Pluto's court meets; guarded by Tisiphone, Theseus is admitted. There follows a brilliant chain of splendid numbers: a warning by the Fates that he must await his hour; an appeal to Neptune; a vengeful chorus of demons; Neptune's request for his release; a second warning by the Fates; and his liberation.

Rameau took full advantage of the opportunities for expressing conflicting and violent emotion. In Theseus he created a character whose music could belong to him alone: his main elements are dignity, assurance and a restrained violence that contrast with the jabbering chorus and Tisiphone's staccato soullessness. His monumental stature is seen in his opening phrases: the recitative strides up and down with vocal leaps which reflect his grandeur. The two *airs* in which he beseeches

Pluto to unite him with Pirithous are masterpieces of rapid declamation, large-limbed and vigorous, in which the utterance of the sentiment is cut to the bone. Then, in a syllabic *air* made up largely of rapid repeated notes, Pluto calls upon the rivers of Hell to avenge Proserpine and himself. The voice part is hammered out, nearer to speech than to song; over it the violins weave a feverish undulating accompaniment, and the words are taken up by a chorus of demons. Theseus is addressed by the Fates in a slow chant whose hollow harmonies convey a sense of doom; his appeal to Neptune is an arioso over an *arpeggiando* accompaniment. The second trio of the Fates is unparalleled in Rameau (the Opéra's mediocre executants could not sing it and he had to substitute something easier); it is the grandest of the ensembles he wrote where the voice parts are rhythmic and syllabic, and expand above a florid orchestral part, and it cries out for plastic interpretation. In the six bars of diatonic enharmony on which the original singers foundered the modulation slides down by semitones from G minor to D minor, a vivid tone-painting of the horror announced by the Fates.

Act 3 consists in Phaedra's confession to Hippolytus and the welcome given to Theseus by his subjects. Phaedra's 'Cruelle mère des amours' is a not unworthy counterpart to Racine's 'O toi qui vois la honte'. The welcome is an expanded divertissement, overshadowed for the spectator by the presence of the sombre king. Its opening chorus, 'Que ce rivage retentisse', is as monumental as the Fates' second trio and also unique in Rameau; here the dramatist gives way to the pure musician, and this is the most highly developed contrapuntal writing in his operas. The tuttis are broken by short homophonic interludes, some for the *petit choeur*, some instrumental. The dancing ends on a bewitching *tambourin*, after which the brooding Theseus comes forward and dismisses his faithful people. A remarkable modulating section of some 30 bars, expressive of his uncertainty, leads to his second appeal to Neptune, another number on a scale that Rameau never dared repeat. 'Puissant maître des flots' is an arioso of 40 bars, grand in its intense emotion, in its breadth, its sustained power and the force of its accompaniment. Much of its strength comes from the opposition between the violin line, with rapid harmonies, and a slow-moving bass. No act in Rameau's operas shows more fully the range of his powers.

The most tragic moment in the opera comes at the end of Act 4: after Hippolytus's death, Phaedra joins the mourning chorus and there is an intense passage of dialogue. Act 5 opens with magnificent scenes for Theseus and Neptune. The rest is peace and love; the most attractive parts are the *symphonie* evocative of Aricia's bower and a haunting musette in seven-beat phrases. The chaconne too is full of charm.

Pierre-Joseph Bernard's *Castor et Pollux* libretto is well constructed and without absurdities, but its plot, based on the theme of brotherly love, is not strictly tragic, and is more narrative than dramatic. The resulting fundamental gentleness is only partly made up for by outbursts of vigour in Acts 2 and 3. In the 1754 version Bernard sought to remedy this by introducing jealousy and bloodshed, with little dramatic gain and some loss for the music. The finest music is in the first three acts. The opening scene by the tomb of the slain Castor is remarkable: such a scene in this position was a novelty in French opera. Its most famous descendant is in *Orfeo*. The music uses the ever-effective symbol of desolation, a descending chromatic scale, which alternates with a lament. The blending of intense grief with ritual movement is one of the secrets of the scene's appeal.

Telaira's 'Tristes apprêts' shows the same union of sorrow and dignity but without rending chromaticisms, dramatic suspensions or minor mode: the line is just a broken fall from tonic to subdominant and thence to tonic (a characteristic example of Rameau's application of his theories about the expressive force of melodic intervals and harmonic progressions). A stark bassoon obbligato adds to its force. The stirring chorus of athletes and warriors is a song of triumph, contrasting with short laments and expressions of vengeance; it is followed by three sinewy dances for the athletes. In Act 2 the best parts are Pollux's elegiac solo in scene i and the divertissement in which Hebe displays the Pleasures with which she regales the Olympians. Entrancing though they be, they seem tantalizingly unreal and one is not surprised that Pollux should repel them: 'Plaisirs, que voulez-vous de moi?'. The lovely vocalises express infinite yearning, not unending bliss. Act 3 unfolds at the gates of Hell and the presence of an unhappy lover, Phoebe, adds human passion, unusual in this opera, to the impersonal violence of Pollux and the devils. Act 4, in the Elysian fields, opens with a beautiful solo for Castor, singing of eternal peace but quivering with Ramellian nostalgia. The recitative, more subtle than in *Hippolyte*, is at its best in the conversation between the brothers. But because of the non-tragic plot the music becomes progressively less stirring and more purely decorative as the opera moves to its close. Throughout, from prologue to chaconne, the abstract dances as well as the *danses d'action* are of the loveliest.

There are more differences than likenesses between Rameau's first two operas. *Hippolyte* is the more vigorous, richer in physical movement (there are five marches), with a strong sense of locality reflected in the music, with well-defined crowds, clashes of feeling and abrupt changes of emotional flavour, as well as some awkwardnesses in the music, relics of barbarity in Phaedra and Theseus. *Castor* has nothing barbaric or awkward: it is homogeneous, exhibits few contrasts, renders fine shades of feeling, is elegiac not tragic; its action is more remote, and unfolds in a world of feeling; its sense of place is weak, its crowds anonymous or ideal. The native sturdiness of the first opera is tamed. Act 2 of *Hippolyte* would be unthinkable in *Castor*, the *Castor* Act 5 apotheosis out of place in *Hippolyte*.

The two versions of *Dardanus*, of 1739 and 1744, amount almost to different works. The contrast between the first, spectacular and rich in pure music, and the second, fuller of action, is striking, and a mark of Rameau's adaptability to his public's requirements. Strength and martial vigour are prominent in both versions. No character is as rock-hewn as Theseus, and no music as brawny as his, but Teucer and Antenor in both versions and the hero in the second have vigorous strains. It makes an impression more consistently forceful than either *Hippolyte* or *Castor*. Moreover, the emotional range is greater. From the dreaminess of the original Act 4, the tragic laments of Iphise and, in the 1744 version, of Dardanus to the warlike or demonic power of the duet in Act 1 (1739), the magicians' choruses (Act 2, both versions), the fury chorus and Antenor's despairing outburst in Act 3 (1744), there is a

tremendous spread of feeling. In the 1744 version the opera is more coherent and dramatic. The best defined character is Iphise. *Dardanus* also excels in its interludes. Rameau's recitative is at its best in the 1744 version, full of variety, expressiveness and intelligent interpretation of the text. Nearly everything is first-rate, but one must single out Iphise's solos and the magicians' choruses in both versions (Act 2), the fury chorus of Act 3 (1744), the well-known dreams sequence in Act 4 (1739) and above all the remarkable 'Lieux funestes' (Act 4, 1744), one of the summits of Rameau's art.

Zoroastre, like *Dardanus*, survives in two versions: not musically the equal of its predecessors, it is nevertheless more dramatic. The contrast between recitative and set pieces is less pronounced than ever: recitative is constantly shading into a few bars of melody, and *airs* and duets break off into recitative. The chorus intervenes more often and more intimately; its most usual appearance is in short outbursts rather than detachable independent ensembles. Cahusac's influence, seeking to integrate drama and spectacle, may be seen in this and in the stress laid on *ballets figurés*.

6. COMÉDIE-BALLET AND OPÉRA-BALLET. *Platée* is a rare example of a comic opera cast in the mould of *tragédie lyrique*. It contains first-rate music and makes a more immediate appeal than *Hippolyte* or *Castor*. Its subject is the discomfiture of an ugly nymph who thinks everyone is in love with her; she is made sport of by Jupiter, and cruelly undeceived. With her ungainliness (depicted in the music), her awkward movements, her mannish gait, her sentimental words set to unsentimental music, her inappropriate emphases and wrong stressing of words and syllables, her ridiculous vocalises, a personality is clearly drawn. Jupiter's courtship is a parody of serious opera. But the constant mockery and caricature, the utter lack of geniality, the sharp edge (frequent even in Rameau's gentle moods and prominent here) and the unremitting cruel fun are somewhat overdone.

Fortunately not all is mockery. There is a lavish display of animal noises, of birds, frogs, cuckoos and a donkey. In sections like the charming, friendly prologue and Folly's entertainment the characters provoke laughter without ridiculing themselves or others. The humour of the Folly episode is nearer to wit though still expressed through movement. Its highlight is Folly's 'Aux langueurs d'Apollon', so absorbingly beautiful that one does not at first realize that it is comic and partly a parody. Folly is the consciously whimsical Fool with the merest touch of the buffoon who infects us with her sturdy gaiety. *Platée* was a triumph in 1749 and, according to D'Alembert, prepared the success of the *bouffons* three years later.

Of Rameau's *opéras-ballets* the first two, *Les Indes galantes* and *Les fêtes d'Hébé*, are the most distinguished; both contain first-rate music though, from the nature of the genre, the level is not as consistently high as in the best *tragédies*. *Les Indes galantes* consists of a prologue and four entrées, each of which is set in one of the 'Indies' (a term which signifies any remote, exotic country). The most stirring is the second, set in Peru. Its central figure, Huascar, is conceived as a theocrat jealous for his power and his love, a vigorous personality worthy to stand beside Theseus. He sings an imperious air, 'Obéissez sans balancer', and joins in a fine divergent trio with his rival and the woman they both

4. Autograph MS from Rameau's pastorale-héroïque 'Daphnis et Eglé', first performed in 1753 (F-Po Rés.208, f.19)

love; he sings in fierce opposition to their smooth 6ths. But it is the spectacle that gives this entrée its chief interest: it consists in an elaborate Feast of the Sun, a *ballet d'action* with solo, choruses and dancing, the most original parts of which are the slow prelude and the *loure*, followed by a sensational meteoric display, the volcanic eruption provoked by Huascar – musically superior to the earthquake and tempest in *Hippolyte* and

the tempest in the first entrée of *Les Indes galantes* itself. The music does not express fear, as in shipwreck choruses, but sheer physical might, untinged by personal emotion. (Here too an enharmonic passage baffled the singers and had to be cut.) Apart from Act 2 of *Hippolyte* there is no passage in Rameau where the tension is kept at such a pitch for so long. The climax of the fourth entrée, *Les sauvages*, is an elaboration for two soloists, chorus and dancing of the harpsichord piece of that name.

Les fêtes d'Hébé presents three forms of art, each in a separate entrée: poetry, music and dancing. No single work of Rameau, not even *Dardanus*, gives so complete a view of his range in lyric, tragic and pastoral. All three entrées are of equal musical interest, but the most surprising episode in such a setting is the miniature tragedy inserted in the second. In the third, the pastoral inspiration floods Rameau's music for the first time: it is much to the fore in his later operas, *Le temple de la gloire*, *Les fêtes de l'Hymen et de l'Amour*, *Zaïs*, *Naïs* and *Daphnis et Eglé*. This less familiar aspect of his art is highly original. His contribution to the pastoral consists in associating with it a tang of longing which implies no promise of happiness; the music seems to yearn after an ideal known to be illusory. In *Les fêtes d'Hébé* that is expressed in the shepherds' dance in honour of Aegle. The prologue marks the first appearance of comedy in Rameau's theatre.

The best of the one-act ballets is *Pygmalion*. In quality it is as good as the *tragédies* and the finest *opéras-ballets*. The drama, usually perfunctory in such works, is treated seriously and at times comes near to tragedy; the hero's 'Fatal amour' is one of Rameau's most searching expressions of grief. The statue's coming to life is followed by a kind of sample book of gavottes, minuets, etc, while she tries each step in turn. The ballet proper shows the throng come to acclaim the prodigy with the usual sparkling chain of contrasted dance numbers. The short *Daphnis et Eglé* is crammed with *ballets figurés* set to enchanting music (see fig.4).

Though graceful, like all his century's art, Rameau's originality does not lie in his grace. Behind the gauze of *fêtes galantes* there stands a sharply defined, austere, almost grim personality, neither sentimental nor frivolous. One must strip him of Watteau-like visions and behold him in all his strength. There is a misfit between his nature and outlook and the frivolous genres to which he had to give himself. His works stand like erratic Baroque blocks in Rococo surroundings. He was denied the opportunities that came to Gluck. His dances and instrumental interludes are what touch us first because of their uniquely immediate, quasi-tactile magic; but they are far from representing the whole of Rameau. He was also intensely human; he was the first French composer to enter with force and sympathy into his characters and situations, and *Hippolyte* is for that reason an important event in operatic history.

Rameau had the impersonality of the true dramatist, and his own unveiled face is seen the most clearly in his *symphonies*. Throughout most of his music, however, including his keyboard pieces, there runs a strain of longing and disillusion, an acerbity present even when the verse speaks of 'volupté' and bliss. It is often distilled in short stretches. A song like Zima's 'Dans nos bois' (*Les Indes galantes*, Act 4) represents the essential Rameau, not just his grace, but also his limitless poignancy, his nostalgia, his power to bring the infinite within the span of an eight-bar phrase.

For illustration of a performance of *La princesse de Navarre*, see PARIS, fig.15.

7. THEORETICAL WRITINGS. Rameau's writings show him as a true product of the Age of Reason. As a theorist he sought to reduce music to a science, and to derive universal harmonic principles from natural causes; as a musician he attempted to adapt these principles to the service of musical practice – notably, keyboard accompaniment and composition. His ideas continued to evolve and mature throughout his career; but they are based on several novel, fundamental concepts already proposed in his earliest and, in many ways, most influential and important work, the *Traité de l'harmonie*.

Rameau maintained that all music is founded on harmony, which arises from natural principles derived from the mathematical and physical bases of a vibrating body (*corps sonore*). Building on Zarlino's earlier work (adopting, in particular, the mathematical proofs of the *senario*), and using Descartes' empirical methodology, he argued the essential unity of harmony, represented in the fundamental sound (*son fondamental*).

Through an understanding of the physical nature of the fundamental sound, he developed the basic concepts that formed the central focus of his harmonic theories: harmonic generation (*génération harmonique*), harmonic inversion (*renversement*) and the fundamental bass (*basse fondamentale*). He noted that each fundamental tone generates a sound that is naturally divisible into component parts, from which are derived the primary consonances in music, in order of relative perfection: octave, 5th and major 3rd. Their combination forms the perfect chord, the major triad. In the *Nouveau système* and later works, using results of the acoustical studies of Mersenne and especially Sauveur, Rameau determined that these intervals are naturally present (as partials) along with the fundamental in the sound produced by a vibrating body. To the primary conson-

TRAITÉ
DE
L'HARMONIE
Reduite à ses Principes naturels;
DIVISÉ EN QUATRE LIVRES.

LIVRE I.   Du rapport des Raisons & Proportions Harmoniques.

LIVRE II. De la nature & de la proprieté des Accords; Et de tout ce qui peut servir à rendre une Musique parfaite.

LIVRE III. Principes de Composition.

LIVRE IV. Principes d'Accompagnement.

Par Monsieur RAMEAU, Organiste de la Cathedrale de Clermont en Auvergne.

DE L'IMPRIMERIE
De JEAN-BAPTISTE-CHRISTOPHE BALLARD, Seul Imprimeur du Roy pour la Musique. A Paris, rue Saint Jean-de-Beauvais, au Mont-Parnasse.

M. DCC. XXII.
AVEC PRIVILEGE DU ROY.

5. *Title-page of Rameau's 'Traité de l'harmonie' (1722);* see also THEORY, THEORISTS, fig.6

ances he added the minor 3rd, which he first obtained from the difference between the natural intervals of the 5th and the major 3rd. Later he offered alternative, though not conclusive, explanations for the derivation of minor. These included: a row of reciprocal tones inversely proportional to the overtone series (in *Génération*), thereby adopting Zarlino's theory of dualism, earlier rejected (in *Traité*); a theory of multiple generation, in which two fundamental sounds a minor 3rd apart are related as generators of a common tone, the third of a major triad being the fifth of its relative minor (in *Démonstration*); and the upper partials of a vibrating body, where the minor triad is formed by the ratios 10:12:15 (in *Code*).

Rameau considered the octave, the most perfect of the primary intervals, to be a replica (*réplique*) of the fundamental, which it represents regardless of position; from this followed the concept of harmonic inversion, applied to both intervals and chords. The primary consonances, through inversion, produce the secondary: 4th, minor 6th and major 6th. Whether or not the fundamental sound is present in the bottom part of an interval or chord, it is understood as its generator tone and harmonic root. In music, a sequence of these roots is called the fundamental bass (distinct from the actual or thorough bass), which provides the foundation for Rameau's theories of harmonic succession.

Basic to harmonic progression in Rameau's system are two chord formations from which all other chords are derived: the perfect triad (*accord parfait*), major or minor, the source for consonance in music; and the 7th chord (*accord de la septième*), the source for dissonance. Normally, chords are not to exceed an octave in fundamental position, nor are they to be without a perfect 5th, an interval that Rameau regarded as the most important harmonic element in music. Chords lacking the 5th were considered incomplete, altered or inverted (including diminished and augmented triads, which he only later admitted to his system). Chords of the 9th or 11th were understood as formed by substitution (*accords par supposition*), where incomplete 7th chords were supplied with fundamental notes added a 3rd or 5th below the chord bass – notes which could not be inverted but determined the harmonic succession of the chord. Only later (in *Code*) did he classify the suspension as a type of *supposition*.

In discussing the construction of the 7th chord, Rameau projected a second theory of chord generation by 3rds: except for two major 3rds in succession, major and minor 3rds may be added to each other or to triads on different scale steps to form various species of 7th. Of these, the major triad with an added minor 3rd is considered the most perfect; it contains the fundamental harmonic dissonances from which all others derive: the major dissonance (diminished 5th) and the minor (minor 7th). The proper resolution of these intervals and, consequently, of this 7th chord to the perfect triad (both in root position) characterizes the perfect cadence (*cadence parfaite*), the most conclusive progression in music. Here the 7th chord, called *dominante tonique*, is found on a root a 5th above the perfect triad, called *tonique*; if the cadence involves inversion, it is considered imperfect (*imparfaite*). Other cadence types described by Rameau include: the irregular cadence (*cadence irrégulière*), where the tonic is followed by the dominant; the broken or deceptive cadence (*cadence rompuë*), where the dominant resolves to a triad on the sixth

degree; and the interrupted cadence (*cadence interrompuë*), where the dominant resolves to another dominant a 3rd below. For Rameau, cadences provided the basis for harmonic progression in music – harmonic motion being regarded as a succession of cadences – as well as for the concepts of key (*ton*) and modulation (*modulation*). Root progression by 5ths is central to harmonic succession; that by 3rds engenders chromaticism and is useful in effecting key change.

The subdominant (*sous-dominante*) has a special place in Rameau's system, though he was never able completely to justify its importance on theoretical grounds. First named in the *Nouveau système*, it is explained through the perfection of the triple geometric progression, 1 : 3 : 9, where the tonic forms the central note of a sequence of 5ths flanked by two dominants, one above and one below. In the *Démonstration* Rameau altered his view of the subdominant and recognized its position as a product of musical experience rather than of nature; he reaffirmed it in later writings. The subdominant was assigned a singular role in harmonic progression. Rameau indicated that in cadences, as a rule, a perfect chord should appear only on the tonic; all other chords require a dissonance, normally the 7th. The dissonance assigned to the subdominant, however, was the added 6th, and there developed in his writings a specific theory of the derivation and use of this chord complex called *double-emploi*, which related to the double meaning of the chord depending on context: as subdominant with an added 6th, and as an inverted 7th chord on the second degree. Thus he justified the direct progression of subdominant to dominant within his harmonic system.

Throughout his writings Rameau continued to resort to 'the judgment of the ear' (*le jugement de l'oreille*) and to 'good taste' (*bon goût*) in seeking resolutions to problems insoluble through scientific or natural means, a recourse which provoked criticism. In his system he considered temperament a practical necessity, as a means of making possible modulation and motion by 5ths of fundamental sounds. Also, while maintaining that melody is derived from harmony, he stressed the need for adding ornamental dissonances (*notes d'ornement ou de goût*) to the harmonic notes of a melodic line in the interest of variety and taste.

Like many of his contemporaries, Rameau asserted that the primary aesthetic purpose of music was to express, to please the ear and to move the passions; he viewed harmony, however, as the fundamental source determining the essential character and coherence of musical expression. Late in his work (particularly in *Observations*, *Code* and *Origine des sciences*), he attempted to relate proportion in music to that in other disciplines, and sought to confirm the derivation of music from a universal, cosmic principle founded on nature and on unity (*le principe de tout est un*).

The influence of Rameau's theories was immediate and widespread. Based on study of both practical and theoretical writings on music and science that appeared in his own time and in the preceding century (principally French, Italian and Latin sources), his ideas underwent continuous re-evaluation and clarification throughout his works, and formed a broad base for the investigation and understanding of the nature of harmony for some 200 years. Rameau corresponded and debated with critics throughout Europe (notably Castel, Montéclair, Estève, Serre, Bollioud-Mermet, Mattheson,

Euler, Martini, D'Alembert and Rousseau) on many issues raised in his works, bringing to a wide, international forum the testing of his concepts on practical and scientific grounds. He also sought approbation, successfully, from the French scientific academy, although he later broke with the Encyclopédistes. Hardly a theorist from the period or from succeeding generations who wrote on harmony escaped the need to relate his work to Rameau's, and the development of several national schools in music theory can be traced directly to his influence (notably in France, England and Germany). His ideas were points of departure for works by such significant theorists as Tartini, Marpurg, Fétis, Day, Hauptmann, Helmholtz, Oettingen, Riemann, d'Indy and Hindemith, and thereby occupy a crucial position in the development of harmonic thinking in Western music.

WORKS

Edition: *J.-P. Rameau: Oeuvres complètes*, ed. C. Saint-Saëns, C. Malherbe [after his death M. Emmanuel and M. Teneo] (Paris, 1895–1924/*R*1968) [OC]

DRAMATIC

All performed at Paris, Opéra, unless otherwise stated; information given only on 1st performances and principal revivals in Rameau's lifetime.
* – autograph

Title, genre	Librettist	Principal sources	Performance	Remarks	Edn.
Samson, tragédie en musique (5 acts)	Voltaire	unpubd, lost	unperf.	composed 1733; pieces used in Les fêtes d'Hébé, Castor et Pollux and Zoroastre; lib pubd (Paris, 1745)	—
Hippolyte et Aricie, tragédie en musique (prol, 5 acts)	S.-J. Pellegrin	print: (Paris, 1733) [copy in *F-Po* with changes, some*]; MSS: *Pn, Po, V, GB-Cfm*	1 Oct 1733 11 Sept 1742 25 Feb 1757	with changes	OC vi
Les Indes galantes, opéra-ballet (prol, 4 entrées): Le turc généreux Les Incas du Pérou Les fleurs Les sauvages	L. Fuzelier	print: (Paris, 1736); MSS: *F-Pn, Po, GB-Cfm*	23 Aug 1735 10 March 1736 28 May 1743 8 June 1751 14 July 1761	prol, 3 entrées 4th entrée added with changes during run, incl. perf. with other works with changes during run, incl. perf. with La guirlande and other works with changes during run, incl. perf. with La guirlande	OC vii
Castor et Pollux, tragédie en musique (prol, 5 acts)	P.-J. Bernard	prints: (Paris, 1737) (Paris, 1754); MSS: *F-Pa, Pn, Po,* Bibliothèque de la Sorbonne, *TLm, GB-Cfm, I-Baf*	24 Oct 1737 8/11 June 1754 24 Jan 1764	no prol, new Act 1, other changes	OC viii [changes in appx]
Les fêtes d'Hébé [Les talents lyriques], opéra-ballet (prol, 3 entrées): La poésie La musique La danse	A. G. de Montdorge	print: (Paris, 1739); MSS: *F-Pn, Po, GB-Cfm*	21 May 1739 27 July 1747 18 May 1756 5 June 1764	2nd entrée rev. during run without prol	OC ix; also ed. in Cyr (1975)
Dardanus, tragédie en musique (prol, 5 acts)	C.-A. Le Clerc de la Bruyère	prints: (Paris, 1739) (Paris, 1744); MSS: *F-Pn, Po, GB-Cfm*	19 Nov 1739 23 April 1744 15 April 1760	2 acts rewritten collab. S.-J. Pellegrin, with addns. and changes without prol	OC x
La princesse de Navarre, comédie-ballet (3 acts)	Voltaire	MSS: *F-Pn*	Versailles, 23 Feb 1745 Versailles, 22 Dec 1745	for wedding of Dauphin with Maria Teresa of Spain rev. as Les fêtes de Ramire; perf. with other works	OC xi
Platée [ou Junon jalouse], comédie-lyrique (prol, 3 acts)	J. Autreau and A.-J. Le Valois d'Orville	print: (Paris, 1749) [copy in *Po*, *annotated]; MSS: *Pn, Po,* Bibliothèque de la Sorbonne	Versailles, 31 March 1745 9 Feb 1749 21 Feb 1754	for wedding of Dauphin with Maria Teresa of Spain lib altered by Ballot de Savot	OC xii
Les fêtes de Polymnie, opéra-ballet (prol, 3 entrées): Le temple de mémoire (prol) La fable L'histoire La féerie	L. de Cahusac	print: (Paris, 1753) [copy in *Po*, *annotated]; MSS: *Pn, Po* [*annotated]	12 Oct 1745 21 Aug 1753		OC xiii
Le temple de la gloire, opéra-ballet (5 acts)	Voltaire	MSS: *Pa, Pmeyer, Pn, Po*, *V, US-BE*	Versailles, 27 Nov 1745 7 Dec 1745 9 April 1746	for victory of Fontenoy without prol in 3 acts with prol	OC xiv
Les fêtes de l'Hymen et de l'Amour, ou Les Dieux d'Egypte, ballet-héroïque (prol, 3 entrées): Osiris Canope Aruéris ou Les Isies	Cahusac	print: (Paris, 1747) [copy in *F-Po* with addns., some*]; MSS: *Pn*	Versailles, 15 March 1747 5 Nov 1748 9 July 1954	for wedding of Dauphin with Maria-Josepha of Saxony without prol	OC xv
Zaïs, ballet-héroïque (prol, 4 acts)	Cahusac	print: (Paris, 1748) [copy in *Po* with annotations, some*]; MSS: *Pn*	29 Feb 1748 19 May 1761	without prol	OC xvi

Title, genre	Librettist	Principal sources	Performance	Remarks	Edn.
Pygmalion, acte de ballet (1 act)	Ballot de Savot, after A. H. de La Motte: *Le triomphe des arts*	print: (Paris, 1748) [copy in *V*, annotated and corrected]; MSS: *AG, Pn, Po*	27 Aug 1748 9 March 1751 31 March 1764	perf. with other works perf. with other works which changed during run; some perfs. at Fontainebleau perf. with other works which changed during run	OC xvii/1
Les surprises de l'Amour, divertissement (prol, 2 acts): Le retour d'Astrée (prol) La lyre enchantée L'enlèvement d'Adonis	Bernard	print: (Paris, 1757); MSS: *Po, Pn*	Versailles, 27 Nov 1748 31 May 1757 10 Oct 1758	 without prol, with Anacréon (ii) as Act 3; from 12 July with Les Sybarites as Act 1 as 31 May 1757 but Anacréon (ii) modified; from 7 Dec with Les Sybarites as Act 3	OC xvii/1
Naïs, pastorale-héroïque (prol, 3 acts)	Cahusac	MSS: *Lm, Pn, Po, US-Wc*	22 April 1749 7 Aug 1764	for Peace of Aix-la-Chapelle with addns. by Berton	OC xviii
Zoroastre, tragédie en musique (prol, 5 acts)	Cahusac	prints: (Paris, 1749) (Paris, 1756) (Paris, 1770) [copies in *F-Pn, V*, annotated]; MSS: *Pa, Pn, Po, TLm, GB-Cfm*	5 Dec 1749 19 Jan 1756	 3 acts rev., without prol	ed. F. Gervaise (Paris, 1964)
Linus, tragédie en musique (3 acts)	Le Clerc de la Bruyère	MSS: *F-Pn* [2 copies of vn I only]	unperf.	rehearsed before 1752; most music lost, MS lib in *Pn*	—
La guirlande, ou Les fleurs enchantées, acte de ballet (1 act)	J.-F. Marmontel	print: (Paris, 1751) [copy in with *Po* *notes]; MSS: *Pn, Po*	21 Sept 1751 11 April 1752 20 July 1762	 with Pygmalion and another work with prol and Les sauvages from Les Indes galantes	—
Acante et Céphise, ou La sympathie, pastorale-héroïque (3 acts)	Marmontel	print: (Paris, 1751) [copy in *Po*, *corrected]; MSS: *Pn*, *Po*	18 Nov 1751	for birth of Duke of Burgundy	—
Daphnis et Eglé, pastorale-héroïque (1 act)	C. Collé	MSS: *Pn, Po**	Fontainebleau, 30 Oct 1753	—	—
Lysis et Délie, pastorale (1 act)	Marmontel	music lost	unperf.	composed Oct 1753; lib pubd (Paris, 1753)	—
Les Sybarites, acte de ballet (1 act)	Marmontel	print: (Paris, 1757); MSS: *Po**	Fontainebleau, 13 Nov 1753 12 July 1757, 7 Dec 1758	 in revival of Les surprises de l'Amour	OC xvii/2
La naissance d'Osiris, ou La fête Pamilie, acte de ballet (1 act)	Cahusac	MSS: *Pn, Po**	Fontainebleau, 12 Oct 1754	for birth of Duke of Berry; with Les Incas du Pérou from Les Indes galantes and Pygmalion	—
Anacréon (i), acte de ballet (1 act)	Cahusac	MSS: *Po*	Fontainebleau, 23 Oct 1754	with other works	—
Anacréon (ii), acte de ballet (1 act)	Bernard	print: (Paris, 1757); MSS: *Pn, Po*	31 May 1757, 10 Oct 1758	in revival of Les surprises de l'Amour	OC xvii/2
Le procureur dupé sans le savoir, opéra-comique en vaudevilles	—	—	privately, 1758/9	music lost; attrib. Rameau in MS lib *Pn*	—
Les Paladins, comédie-ballet (3 acts)	D. de Monticourt	MSS: *Pa, Pn*, Po*, GB-Cfm*	12 Feb 1760	—	ed. in Wolf
Abaris, ou Les Boréades, tragédie lyrique (5 acts)	?Cahusac	*F-Pn**	unperf.	intended for perf. aut. 1764	ed. in Térey-Smith
Nélée et Myrthis [Les beaux jours de l'amour], acte de ballet (1 act)		*Pn*	unperf.	—	OC xi
Zéphyre [Les nymphes de Diane], acte de ballet (1 act)		*Pn**	unperf.	—	OC xi
Io, acte de ballet (1 act)	—	*Pn*	unperf.	—	—

Incidental music to comedies by A. Piron for the Théâtres de la Foire, music by Rameau, collab. others, all lost unless otherwise stated: L'Endriague (3), St Germain, 3 Feb 1723; L'enrôlement d'Arlequin (1), St Germain, Feb 1726; La robe de dissension, ou La faux prodigue (2), St Germain, 7 Sept 1726; Les courses de tempé (1), Comédie Française, 30 Aug 1734, vocal part of airs extant; Les jardins de l'Hymen, ou La rose (1), 1726, Opéra-Comique, 5 March 1744: for details see Sadler (1974)

Aruéris (intermède en musique, 1), Choisy-le-Roi, 15 Dec 1762, lib pubd (Paris, 1762); La cornemuse (ballet-pantomime, P. Sodi), Académie royale; Les jardinières et les ciseaux (ballet-pantomime), Académie royale: lost, for details see Brenner (1947)

OTHER SECULAR VOCAL

Duo paysan (duet), Bar, B, in Recueil d'airs sérieux et à boire de différents auteurs (Paris, 1707)

Avec du vin (canon), in Recueil d'airs sérieux et à boire de différents auteurs (Paris, 1719); pubd in *Traité de l'harmonie* (1722)

Ah! loin de rire (canon), S, S, Bar, B, pubd in *Traité de l'harmonie* (1722)

Thétis (cantata), B, vn, bc, 1718, OC iii

Aquilon et Orinthie (cantata), B, vn, bc, 1719, OC iii

Les amants trahis (cantata), S, B, viol, bc, 1721, OC iii

Orphée (cantata), S, vn, viol, bc, 1721, OC iii

L'impatience (cantata), S, viol, bc, 1715–22, OC iii

Le berger fidèle (cantata), T, 2 vn, bc, 1728, OC iii

Cantate pour la fête de Saint Louis, S, tr, bc, 1740 or later, *F-Pn* Rés.18061 (anon.)

Un Bourbon ouvre sa carrière (ariette), Haute-contre, 2 vn, bc, ?1751, *Pn* Vm⁷3620

Medée (cantata), ?c1720; L'absence (cantata), ?c1720: both lost

Misattrib.: La musette (cantata), B, bc [?by P. de la Garde]; Diane et Actéon (cantata), S, vn, bc [by B. de Boismortier]: both in OC iii

SACRED VOCAL

Hc – Haute-contre

Deus noster refugium (Ps xlvi), S, S, Hc, T, T, B, SSHcTB, 2 vn, va, viol, bc, before 1716, OC v

In convertendo (Ps cxxvi), S, Hc, B, SSHcTBB, 2 fl, 2 ob, bn, 2 vn, va, bc, c1718, OC iv

Quam dilecta (Ps cxxxiii), S, S, Hc, T, B, SSHcTBB, 2 fl, 2 vn, va, bc, c1720, OC iv

Laboravi (part of Ps lxix), SSHcTB, org, pubd in *Traité de l'harmonie* (1722), OC v

Exultet caelum laudibus, c1720, lost

Misattrib.: Diligam te (part of Ps lxix), OC v; Inclina Domine [by François Martin], *F-Pn*

KEYBOARD
(all in OC ii)

Premier livre de pièces de clavecin (Paris, 1706): Prelude, a; Allemande, a; 2e allemande, a; Courante, a; Gigue, a; 1er sarabande, a; 2e sarabande, a; Vénitienne, A; Gavotte, a; Menuet, a

Pièces de clavecin avec une méthode sur la mécanique des doigts (Paris, 1724, rev. 1731 as Pièces de clavecin avec une table pour les agréments): Allemande, e; Courante, e; Gigue en rondeau, e; 2e gigue en rondeau, E; Le rappel des oiseaux, e; 1er rigaudon, E; 2e rigaudon, E; Double du 2e rigaudon, E; Musette en rondeau, E; Tambourin, e; La villageoise, e; Les tendres plaintes, d; Les niais de Sologne, D; 1er double des niais, D; 2e double des niais, D; Les soupirs, D; La joyeuse, D; L'entretien des Muses, d; Les tourbillons, D; Les cyclopes, d; Le lardon, D; La boiteuse, d

Nouvelles suites de pièces de clavecin (Paris, c1728): Allemande, a; Courante, a; Sarabande, A; Les trois mains, a; Fanfarinette, A; La triomphante, a; Gavotte avec 6 doubles, a; Les tricotets, G; L'indifférente, g; Menuet, G; 2e menuet, G; La poule, g; Les triolets, G; Les sauvages, g; L'enharmonique, g; L'égiptienne, g

Cinq pièces pour clavecin seul, extraites des Pièces de clavecin en concerts (Paris, 1741): La Livri, c; L'agaçante, c; La timide, 1er rondeau, a; La timide, 2e rondeau, A; L'indiscrète, B♭

La Dauphine, g, extemporized for the wedding of the Dauphin with Maria-Josepha of Saxony, 1747

OTHER INSTRUMENTAL
(all in OC ii)

Pièces de clavecin en concerts, hpd, vn/fl, viol/vn (Paris, 1741, 2/1752):
Premier concert: La Coulicam, E♭; La Livri, c; Le Vézinet, C
Deuxième concert: La Laborde, G; La Boucon, g; L'agaçante, G; 1er menuet, G; 2e menuet, g
Troisième concert: La La Poplinière, A; La timide, 1er rondeau, a; La timide, 2e rondeau, A; 1er tambourin, A; 2e tambourin en rondeau, a
Quatrième concert: La pantomime, B♭; L'indiscrète, B♭; La Rameau, B♭
Cinquième concert: La Forqueray, d; La Cupis, d; La Marais, D
Not by Rameau: 6 concerts transcrits en sextuor, 3 vn, va, vc, db/vc:
Premier–cinquième concerts = transcrs. of Pièces de clavecin en concerts (Paris, 1741)
Sixième concert = transcrs. of La poule; 1er menuet; 2e menuet; L'enharmonique; L'égiptienne: all from Nouvelles suites de pièces de clavecin, c1728)

WRITINGS

Edition: *Jean-Philippe Rameau: Complete Theoretical Writings*, ed. E. R. Jacobi (Rome, 1967–72)

Traité de l'harmonie reduite à ses principes naturels (Paris, 1722; Eng. trans., 1737); ed. and Eng. trans. P. Gossett (New York, 1971)

Nouveau système de musique théorique (Paris, 1726)

'Examen de la conférence sur la musique', *Mercure de France* (Oct 1729)

'Observations sur la méthode d'accompagnement pour le clavecin qui est en usage, et qu'on appelle échele ou règle de l'octave', *Mercure de France* (Feb 1730)

'Plan abrégé d'une méthode nouvelle d'accompagnement pour le clavecin', *Mercure de France* (March 1730)

'Réponse à la réplique de l'auteur de la conférence; Réplique du premier musicien sur l'harmonie', *Mercure de France* (June 1730)

'Lettre de M . . . à M . . . sur la musique et l'explication de la carte générale de la basse fondamentale', *Mercure de France* (Sept 1731)

Dissertation sur les différentes méthodes d'accompagnement pour le clavecin ou pour l'orgue (Paris, 1732)

'Lettre de M. Rameau au Père Castel', *Journal de Trévoux* (July 1736)

Génération harmonique ou Traité du musique théorique et pratique (Paris, 1737); ed. and trans. in D. Hayes: *Rameau's 'Génération harmonique'* (diss., Stanford U., 1974)

'Remarques de M. Rameau sur l'extrait qu'on a donné de son livre intitulé "Génération harmonique" dans le Journal de Trévoux, décembre 1737', *Le pour et contre*, xiv (1738), 74, 141

'Lettre à M. de Sainte-Albine', *Mercure de France* (July 1749)

Mémoire où l'on expose les fondemens du Système de musique théorique et pratique de M. Rameau (Paris, 1749)

Démonstration du principe de l'harmonie (Paris, 1750)

Nouvelles réflexions de M. Rameau sur sa Démonstration du principe de l'harmonie (Paris, 1752)

'Lettre de M. Rameau à l'auteur du Mercure', *Mercure de France* (May 1752)

'Réflexions sur la manière de former la voix', *Mercure de France* (Oct 1752)

'Extrait d'une réponse de M. Rameau à M. Euler sur l'identité des octaves', *Mercure de France* (Dec 1752)

Observations sur notre instinct pour la musique (Paris, 1754)

Erreurs sur la musique dans l'Encyclopédie (Paris, 1755–6/R1971)

Suite des erreurs sur la musique dans l'Encyclopédie (Paris, 1756/R1971)

Prospectus, où l'on propose au public, par voye de souscription, un code de musique pratique, composé de sept méthodes (Paris, 1757)

Réponse de M. Rameau à MM. les editeurs de l'Encyclopédie (Paris, 1757/R1971)

Nouvelles réflexions sur le principe sonore (Paris, 1758–9)

Code de musique pratique, ou Méthodes pour apprendre la musique . . . avec de nouvelles réflexions sur le principe sonore (Paris, 1760)

Lettre à M. d'Alembert sur ses opinions en musique (Paris, 1760)

'Réponse de M. Rameau à la lettre de M. d'Alembert', *Mercure de France* (April 1761)

'Source où, vraisemblablement, on a dû puiser la première idée des proportions', *Mercure de France* (April 1761)

'Origine des modes et du tempérament', *Mercure de France* (June 1761)

'Suite de la Réponse', *Mercure de France* (July 1761)

Origine des sciences, suivie d'une controverse sur le même sujet (Paris, 1762)

'Lettre aux Philosophes', *Journal de Trévoux* (Aug 1762)

Vérités intéressantes (MS, inc., *F-Pn*)

BIBLIOGRAPHY
GENERAL

F. Raguenet: *Paralèle des italiens et des françois, en ce qui regarde la musique et les opéra* (Paris, 1702; Eng. edn., London, 1709/R1968, repr. in *MQ*, xxxii, 1946, p.411)

J.-L. Le Cerf de la Viéville: *Comparaison de la musique italienne et de la musique française* (Brussels, 1704–6/R1972)

P. L. D'Aquin de Châteaulyon: *Siècle littéraire de Louis XV ou Lettres sur les hommes célèbres* (Amsterdam, 1753)

J.-J. Rousseau: *Lettre sur la musique française* (Paris, 1753)

L. de Cahusac: *La danse ancienne et moderne ou Traité historique de la danse* (Paris, 1754)

J.-A. Bérard: *L'art du chant* (Paris, 1755)

J.-G. Noverre: *Lettres sur la danse* (Paris, 1760/R1952)

J. Le Rond d'Alembert: 'De la liberté de la musique', *Mélanges de littérature, d'histoire et de philosophie*, iv (Paris, 2/1763)

M.-P. G. de Chabanon: *Eloge de M. Rameau* (Paris, 1764)

'Essai d'Eloge historique de feu M. Rameau', *Mercure de France* (Oct 1764)

H. Maret: *Eloge historique de M. Rameau* (Dijon, 1766)

J.-J. Rousseau: *Dictionnaire de musique* (Paris, 1768/R1969)

J.-J. M. Decroix: *L'ami des arts ou Justification de plusieurs grands hommes* (Amsterdam, 1776)

C. Collé: *Journal historique, ou Mémoirs critiques et littéraires* (Paris, 1805)

J. Le Rond d'Alembert: *Oeuvres et correspondances inédites* (Paris, 1887)

E. Bourges: *Quelques notes sur le théâtre de la cour à Fontainebleau (1747–1787)* (Paris, 1892)

M. Brenet: 'La jeunesse de Rameau', *RMI*, ix (1902), 860; x (1903), 185

A. Pougin: *Un ténor de l'opéra au XVIIIe siècle: Pierre Jélyotte et les chanteurs de son temps* (Paris, 1905)

L. de La Laurencie: *Rameau* (Paris, 1908)

L. Laloy: *Rameau* (Paris, 1908)

P.-M. Masson: 'Lullistes et Ramistes', *Année musicale*, i (1911), 187

G. Cucuel: *La Pouplinière et la musique de chambre au XVIIIe siècle* (Paris, 1913)

C. Saint-Saëns: *Au courant de la vie* (Paris, 1914)

A. Pirro: *Les clavecinistes* (Paris, 1924)

J.-G. Prod'homme: 'A French Maecenas of the Time of Louis XV: M. de la Pouplinière', *MQ*, x (1924), 511

J. Tiersot: *Lettres de musiciens écrites en français de XVe au XXe siècles* (Paris, 1924)

——: 'Rameau', *MQ*, xiv (1928), 77

L. Vallos: *Un siècle de musique et de théâtre à Lyon, 1688–1789* (Lyons, 1932/R1971)

P.-M. Masson: 'Rameau and Wagner', *MQ*, xxv (1939), 466

E. Kisch: 'Rameau and Rousseau', *ML*, xxii (1941), 97

J. Gardien: *Jean-Philippe Rameau* (Paris, 1949)

R. Wangermée: 'Lecerf de la Viéville, Bonnet-Bourdelot et l' "Essai sur le bon goust en Musique" de Nicolas Grandval', *RBM*, v (1951), 132

Y. Tiénot: *J.-Ph. Rameau: esquisse biographique, suivie d'un tableau chronologique comprenant une liste complète des oeuvres de Rameau* (Paris, 1954)

P. Berthier: *Réflexions sur l'art et la vie de Jean-Philippe Rameau (1683–1764)* (Paris, 1957)

C. Girdlestone: *Jean-Philippe Rameau: his Life and Work* (London, 1957, 2/1969)

P. Scholes, ed.: *Dr Burney's Musical Tours in Europe*, i: *An Eighteenth-century Musical Tour in France and Italy* (London, 1959)

J. Malignon: *Rameau* (Paris, 1960)

P. Daval: *La musique en France au XVIIIe siècle* (Paris, 1961)

Jean-Philippe Rameau, 1683–1764 (Paris, 1964) [pubd by *F-Pn*]

C. Girdlestone: *La tragédie en musique (1673–1750) considérée comme genre littéraire* (Geneva, 1972)

F. Lesure: 'Iconographie musicale', *L'opéra classique français*, i (Geneva, 1973)

D. Launay, ed.: *La Querelle des Bouffons* (Geneva, 1974) [repr. of pamphlets pubd Paris and The Hague (1752–4)]

WORKS

E. Dacier: 'L'opéra au XVIIIe siècle: les premières représentations de Dardanus', *La revue musicale*, iii (1903), 163

R. Rolland: 'Un vaudeville de Rameau', *Mercure musicale*, i (1905), 19

G. Cucuel: 'La question des clarinettes dans l'instrumentation du XVIIIe siècle', *ZIMG*, xii (1910–11), 280

G. Graf: *Jean-Philippe Rameau in seiner Oper Hippolyte et Aricie: eine musikkritische Würdigung* (Wädenswil, 1927)

P.-M. Masson: 'Le ballet héroïque', *ReM*, ix (1928), no.3, p.132

——: *L'opéra de Rameau* (Paris, 1930/*R*1972)

K. Dale: 'The Keyboard Music of Rameau', *MMR*, lxxvi (1946), 127

C. D. Brenner: *Bibliographical List of Plays in the French Language, 1700–1789* (Berkeley, 1947)

W. Mellers: 'Rameau and the Opera', *The Score*, iv (1951), 26

P.-M. Masson: 'Les deux versions du "Dardanus" de Rameau', *AcM*, xxvi (1954), 36

Z. Klitenic: *The Clavecin Works of Jean-Philippe Rameau* (diss., U. of Pennsylvania, 1955)

E. G. Ahnell: *The Concept of Tonality in the Operas of Jean-Philippe Rameau* (diss., U. of Illinois, 1958)

C. Girdlestone: 'Rameau's Self-borrowings', *ML*, xxix (1958), 52

N. Demuth: *French Opera: its Development to the Revolution* (Horsham, Sussex, 1963)

J. R. Anthony: 'The French Opéra-ballet in the Early Eighteenth Century: Problems of Definition and Classification', *JAMS*, xviii (1965), 197

F. Gervaise: 'La musique pure au service du drame lyrique chez Rameau', *ReM* (1965), no.260, p.21

C. Girdlestone: 'Voltaire, Rameau, et "Samson" ', *RMFC*, vi (1966), 133

J. R. Anthony: 'Some Uses of the Dance in the French Opéra-ballet', *RMFC*, ix (1969), 75

G. Seefrid: *Die Airs de danse in den Buhnenwerke von Jean-Philippe Rameau* (Wiesbaden, 1969)

M. Térey-Smith: *Jean-Philippe Rameau: 'Abaris ou les Boréades': a Critical Edition* (diss., Eastman School of Music, 1971)

J. R. Anthony: *French Baroque Music from Beaujoyeulx to Rameau* (London, 1973, rev. 2/1978)

G. Sadler: 'Rameau, Piron and the Parisian Fair Theatres', *Soundings*, iv (1974), 13

M. Cyr: *Rameau's 'Les fêtes d'Hébé'* (diss., U. of California, Berkeley, 1975)

G. Sadler: 'Rameau's Last Opera: Abaris, ou Les Boréades', *MT*, cxvi (1975), 327

M. Cyr: ' "Inclina Domine": a Martin Motet Wrongly Attributed to Rameau', *ML*, lviii (1977), 318

G. Sadler: 'A Letter from Claude-François Rameau to J. J. M. Decroix', *ML*, lix (1978), 139

M. Cyr: 'A New Rameau Cantata', *MT*, cxx (1979), 907

G. Sadler: 'Naïs, Rameau's "Opéra pour la Paix" ', *MT*, cxxi (1980), 431

R. P. Wolf: *Rameau's 'Les Paladins' (1760)* (diss., Yale U., in preparation)

THEORIES

BurneyH

P. Estève: *Nouvelle découverte du principe de l'harmonie, avec un examen de ce que M. Rameau a publié sous le titre de Démonstration de ce principe* (Paris, 1752)

J. Le Rond d'Alembert: *Eléments de musique théorique et pratique selon les principes de M. Rameau* (Paris, 1752, 2/1762)

J.-A. Serre: *Essais sur les principes de l'harmonie* (Paris, 1753)

Ducharger: *Réflexions sur divers ouvrages de M. Rameau* (Rennes, 1761)

J.-A. Serre: *Observations sur les principes de l'harmonie* (Geneva, 1763)

P.-J. Roussier: *Traité des accords et de leur succession* (Paris, 1764)

J. A. Scheibe: *Über die musikalische Composition*, i (Leipzig, 1773)

F. W. Marpurg: *Versuch über die musikalische Temperatur, nebst einem Anhang über den Rameau- und Kirnbergerschen Grundbass* (Breslau, 1776/*R*)

J.-B. de La Borde: *Essai sur la musique ancienne et moderne* (Paris, 1780/*R*1972)

W. Jones: *A Treatise on the Art of Music* (London, 1784)

M. P. King: *A General Treatise on Music* (London, 1800)

F.-J. Fétis: *Esquisse de l'histoire de l'harmonie* (Paris, 1840)

H. Berlioz: 'De Rameau et de quelques uns de ses ouvrages', *Revue et gazette musicale de Paris*, ix (1842), 321, 329

H. Goldschmidt: *Die Musikästhetik des 18. Jahrhunderts* (Zurich and Leipzig, 1915), 107

J. Tiersot: 'Lettres inédites de Rameau', *ReM*, xvi (1935), 14

A. R. Oliver: *The Encyclopedists as Critics of Music* (New York, 1947)

M. Shirlaw: *The Theory of Harmony* (Illinois, 2/1955)

E. R. Jacobi: *Die Entwicklung der Musiktheorie in England nach der Zeit von J.-Ph. Rameau* (Strasbourg, 1957, 2/1971)

——: 'Harmonic Theory in England after the Time of Rameau', *JMT*, i (1957), 126

J. Ferris: 'The Evolution of Rameau's Harmonic Theories', *JMT*, iii (1959), 231

M. Shirlaw: 'The Science of Harmony: the Harmonic Generation of Chords', *JMT*, iv (1960), 1

M. M. Keane: *The Theoretical Writings of Jean-Philippe Rameau* (diss., Catholic U. of America, Washington, DC, 1961)

E. R. Jacobi: 'Nouvelles lettres inédites de Jean-Philippe Rameau', *RMFC*, iii (1963), 145

H. Pischner: *Die Harmonielehre Jean-Philippe Rameaus, ihre historischen Voraussetzungen und ihre Auswirkungen im französischen, italienischen und deutschen musiktheoretischen Schrifttum des 18. Jahrhunderts: ein Beitrag zur Geschichte des musikalischen Denkens* (Leipzig, 1963)

E. R. Jacobi: 'Rameau and Padre Martini', *MQ*, l (1964), 452

——: ' "Vérités intéressantes": le dernier manuscrit de Jean-Philippe Rameau', *RdM*, l (1964), 77–109

J. W. Krehbiel: *Harmonic Principles of J.-Ph. Rameau and his Contemporaries* (diss., Indiana U., 1964)

C. B. Paul: *Rameau's Musical Theories and the Age of Reason* (diss., U. of California, Berkeley, 1966)

P. Gossett: Preface to *Jean-Philippe Rameau: Traité de l'harmonie* (New York, 1971)

C. B. Paul: 'Music and Ideology: Rameau, Rousseau and 1789', *Journal of the History of Ideas*, xxxii (1971), 395

E. C. Verba: 'The Development of Rameau's Thoughts on Modulation and Chromatics', *JAMS*, xxvi (1973), 69

D. Hayes: 'Rameau's "Nouvelle Méthode" ', *JAMS*, xxvii (1974), 61

——: *Rameau's 'Génération harmonique ou Traité de musique théorique et pratique'* (diss., Stanford U., 1974)

E. C. Verba: 'Rameau's Views on Modulation and their Background in French Theory', *JAMS*, xxxi (1978), 467

CUTHBERT GIRDLESTONE (1–6, bibliography)
ALBERT COHEN (7)
MARY CYR (work-list, bibliography)

Rameau, Pierre (*fl* early 18th century). French dancing-master and author. He was dancing-master to Elizabeth Farnese (1692–1766), who became Queen of Spain on her marriage to Philip V in 1714. Rameau wrote two important works on French court dance, both published in 1725. The first, entitled *Le maître à danser*, is the most authoritative exposition of the early 18th-century French style of dancing, a style which was performed throughout Europe because of its elegance and refinement. The book was read and approved by Louis Pécour, dancing-master for the Paris Opéra, and may thus be taken to represent the central French practice of its day. It gives a clear and detailed account of such matters as the correct way to stand, move and ask a lady to dance, etiquette at court balls and the movements and steps of dances, as well as a complete description of the minuet. It is directed primarily towards the needs of social dancing, and does not discuss virtuoso practices peculiar to ballet. The book, which was several times reprinted, contains many excellent drawings which clarify the verbal descriptions. John Essex translated it into English in 1728; a second edition (1732) contained new drawings by G. Bickham junior, which are used in C. Beaumont's modern English translation (London, 1931/*R*1970).

The second book, *Abrégé de la nouvelle méthode*, concerns dance notation, and it offers improvements upon R. A. Feuillet's system of recording dance. 12 previously published choreographies by Louis Pécour are included, set in these slightly modified symbols.

For pages from *Le maître à danser, see* MINUET, figs.1 and 2.

BIBLIOGRAPHY
FasquelleE
A. Witherell: *Pierre Rameau's French Menuet* (diss., Stanford U., 1973)

MEREDITH ELLIS LITTLE

Ramella, Giovanni Francesco (*fl* Novara, 1601–15). Italian composer. His printed works suggest that he was canon and *maestro di cappella* at Novara. He is known entirely by motets and masses for five to eight voices; one volume of such works, dating from before his 1590 book, is lost. Those that are extant testify to his skill in handling polyphonic textures, especially *cori spezzati* techniques: his eight-part motets, whose harmony is well judged and whose melodies are quite often instrumental in character, display inventive dovetailing of the two choirs, the writing for which is sometimes contrapuntal with complex imitation, and sometimes homophonic. These motets were known as far afield as Pomerania and Silesia.

WORKS

Sacrae cantiones, 5, 6, 8vv, una cum missa & cantico BMV, 8vv, liber primus (Milan, 1590)
Sacrae cantiones cum litaniis sanctorum et duabus missis, lib. 3, 8vv (Venice, 1601)
Missarum, liber primus, 5vv (Venice, 1615)
2 motets, 8vv, 1612³, 1613² (both possibly repr. from earlier vols.)

5 motets, 8vv, *PL-PE*; facs. scores in AMP, vi (1965), incipits in AMP, i (1963)

BIBLIOGRAPHY
EitnerQ
M. Donà: *La stampa musicale a Milano fino all'anno 1700* (Florence, 1961)

MIROSŁAW PERZ

Rami [Ramis] de Pareia, Bartolomeo. *See* RAMOS DE PAREIA, BARTOLOMEO.

Ramin, Günther (*b* Karlsruhe, 15 Oct 1898; *d* Leipzig, 27 Feb 1956). German organist, choral conductor and composer. He sang in the Thomanerchor at Leipzig as a boy, then studied the organ, the piano and composition at the conservatory there. After frequently deputizing at the Thomaskirche for Karl Straube, his organ teacher, Ramin succeeded him as organist in 1918 (when Straube was promoted to Kantor). From the outset Ramin's playing was noted for its vitality, stylish interpretation and brilliant technique. In 1920 he also became organist for the Gewandhaus concerts and taught the organ at the conservatory; and from 1923 his style was significantly influenced by the Schnitger organ at the Jakobikirche in Hamburg, on which he gave many recitals. He undertook tours of other European countries, and of the USA, 1933–4. He also became well known as a harpsichordist and song accompanist, and had a varied career as a conductor, directing the Leipzig Lehrergesangverein (1922–35), the Gewandhaus Choir (1933–4 and 1945–51) and the Berlin Philharmonic Choir (1935–43), as well as conducting numerous orchestral concerts. In 1940 he succeeded Straube as Kantor of the Thomaskirche, the 12th in succession to Bach and one of the most dynamic interpreters of Bach's music. It was thanks to Ramin that the Thomanerchor tradition survived, and he rebuilt the choir in the immediate postwar period, demonstrating its new vitality on many tours, including visits to the USSR in 1953 and South America in 1955. He directed the Leipzig Bach Festivals in 1950, 1953 and 1955, the first of which was a particular artistic triumph for him. In 1950 he received the National Prize of the German Democratic Republic and an honorary doctorate from Leipzig University, and in 1952 he was elected a member of the Academy of Arts. He wrote a few works, mainly organ and choral music. A memorial volume of essays on Bach appeared on the 75th anniversary of his birth (ed. D. Hellmann, Wiesbaden, 1973).

BIBLIOGRAPHY
L. von Koerber: *Der Thomanerchor und sein Kantor* (Hamburg, 1954)
E. Hasse: *Erinnerungen an Günther Ramin* (Berlin, 1958)
H. Heintze: 'Der Organist Günther Ramin', *Musik und Kirche*, xxviii (1958), 193
C. Ramin: *Günther Ramin* (Freiburg, 1958)
M. Mezger: 'Günther Ramin zum 75. Geburtstag', *Musik und Kirche*, xliii (1973), 269

Ramkie. A long-necked unfretted finger-plucked lute with three (subsequently four) strings. It was played by Hottentots in the Cape in the 18th century and later also by other southern African peoples. The name is probably derived from the Portuguese *rabequinha* ('little violin'). Mentzel, who was at the Cape from 1733 to 1741, wrote of it as 'an imitated instrument which the slaves of Malabar brought with them, from whom some Hottentots copied it' (quoted in Kirby). Derivation from the Portuguese *machete* or *machada*, which was also the prototype for the ukelele, has been suggested, though non-European influence seems evident in the body construction. No 18th-century specimens have survived, but the consensus of early reports points to a 'kind of guitar' about 1 metre long, the body made from a half-gourd covered with stretched sheepskin and attached to one end of a straight plank about 10–13 cm broad. The gut or wire strings were raised by a bridge on the body and by a nut near the end of the neck; tuning-pegs were inserted from behind, as on the ukelele.

Bushmen and Bantu-speaking peoples in southern Africa later adopted the instrument from the Hottentots; carved wood or a tin can replaced the gourd body. From all accounts, the *ramkie* was always used for repetitive chord-playing rather than melody, which is not typical of indigenous southern African practice; the player in the illustration seems to be using the chin to produce a

Ramkie: drawing (1834) by Charles Bell in the Africana Museum, Johannesburg

harmonic, following Hottentot musical bow technique. Home-made substitutes for guitars, used by boys throughout southern Africa, often show some constructional resemblance to the *ramkie*. Other names found in the literature include *gabowie, !gutsib, raamakie, rabékin, rabouquin, ramakie, ramakienjo, ramgyib, ramki* and *xguthe*.

BIBLIOGRAPHY
O. F. Mentzel: *Beschreibung des Vorgebirges der guten Hoffnung*, ii (Glogau, 1787), 518
P. R. Kirby: *The Musical Instruments of the Native Races of South Africa* (London, 1934, 2/1965), 249ff

DAVID K. RYCROFT

Ramler, Karl Wilhelm (*b* Kolberg [now Kołobrzeg], 25 Feb 1725; *d* Berlin, 11 April 1798). German poet. After studying at Halle he moved to Berlin in 1745, taught at the cadet school from 1748 and from 1787 until 1796 was director of the Royal Theatre. As friend and correspondent of Gleim, Nicolai and Lessing, and as an exponent of the classical values in lyric verse, he exercised a quiet but important influence. Few of his *Oden* and *Lyrische Gedichte* were set to music, but his collection entitled *Lieder der Deutschen mit Melodien* (1766–8) was highly regarded in its day, and some of his longer texts were frequently set: the cantatas *Der Tod Jesu* by (to name only the best-known composers) Graun, Telemann and J. C. F. Bach, *Die Hirten bei der Krippe zu Bethlehem* by Agricola, Telemann, Türk, Reichardt, Rellstab and Eybler, *Der Mai* by Reichardt, *Die Auferstehung und Himmelfahrt Jesu* by J. C. F. Bach, Agricola, Telemann, Vogler, C. P. E. Bach and Zelter, *Ino* by Telemann, Vogler and J. C. F. Bach, and *Pygmalion* by J. C. F. Bach and F. W. H. Benda; a melodrama *Cephalus und Prokris* was set by Georg Benda. Ramler also wrote many occasional pieces for musical setting, and in 1766 he translated Handel's *Alexander's Feast* into German. One of his earliest published works was an essay 'Vertheidigung der Oper' which was included in F. W. Marpurg's *Historisch-kritische Beyträge zur Aufnahme der Musik* (i, 1754).

BIBLIOGRAPHY
K. W. Ramler: *Poetische Werke*, ed. L. F. von Göckingk (Berlin, 1801–2, 2/1825)
K. Goedeke: *Grundriss zur Geschichte der deutschen Dichtung*, iv/1 (Dresden, 1891), 100
M. Friedlaender: *Das deutsche Lied im 18. Jahrhundert* (Stuttgart and Berlin, 1902/R1970)
A. Schering: *Geschichte des Oratoriums* (Leipzig, 1911/R1966)
E. Schmitz: *Geschichte der weltlichen Solokantate* (Leipzig, 1914, rev. 2/1955)

PETER BRANSCOMBE

Ramondon, Lewis (*fl* 1705–10). English singer and composer. He sang on the London stage from April 1705 to July 1710. He had a small part in the English opera in the Italian style, *Camilla* (1706), and sang in English in the mixed-language productions of *Pyrrhus and Demetrius* (1708) and *Clotilda* (1709). It appears from his published parts that his voice was baritone or low tenor.

Ramondon composed theatre songs, some of which were published as single sheets from about 1705, in *Pills to Purge Melancholy* (mainly in the 1714 edition) and *The Merry Musician* (1716); collected editions of his songs were published by Walsh in about 1720 and 1730. His arrangements of tunes from *Camilla* for harpsichord and for two flutes and bass appeared in 1706 and opera tune arrangements by him were printed in books 1 and 2 of *The Lady's Entertainment*. The

tune of his song *All you that must take a leap in the dark* was used in *The Beggar's Opera*.

OLIVE BALDWIN, THELMA WILSON

Ramoneda, Ignacio (*b* Tarrasa, *c*1735; *d* El Escorial, 19 Oct 1781). Spanish theorist and instrumentalist. On 18 November 1756, he became a monk in the order of St Jerome at the monastery of El Escorial, where he taught plainsong and remained until his death. His brother Pablo Ramoneda, also a monk at El Escorial, was the *maestro de capilla*. Ignacio's treatise *Arte de canto llano* (Madrid, 1778) circulated widely in Spain; a second edition (abridged by Juan Rodó, organist at the monastery) was published in 1827. Ramoneda also compiled the *Indice de la insigne librería del coro de este Real Monasterio de San Lorenzo* (MS, *c*1775, *E-E*), the earliest catalogue of the monastery's music collection. In the same archives are a number of his compositions: a mass, five Lamentations for Holy Week and psalms, some with instruments and continuo. In his lifetime he was renowned for his remarkable skill on the organ and other instruments, but his subsequent reputation is based on his plainsong manual.

BIBLIOGRAPHY
LaborD
F. Pedrell: *Catàlech de la biblioteca musical de la Diputació de Barcelona*, i (Barcelona, 1908), 233ff

JOSÉ LÓPEZ-CALO

Ramon Llull. See LULL, RAYMOND.

Ramón y Rivera, Luis Felipe (*b* San Cristóbal, 23 Aug 1913). Venezuelan ethnomusicologist and composer, husband of Isabel Aretz. He studied at the Caracas Escuela Superior de Música (1928–34) under Vicente Emilio Sojo, Ascanio Negretti, Miguel Angel Espinel and Juan Bautista Plaza, taking a diploma as a viola teacher (1934). For several years he played the viola in various Caracas ensembles such as the Orfeón Lamas and the Symphony Orchestra, before returning to his native state, Táchira, as music teacher at the Escuela de Artes y Oficios de San Cristóbal (1939). There he founded the Táchira Music School in 1940 and directed it until a Venezuelan government fellowship enabled him to study folklore and ethnomusicology with Carlos Vega at the Institute of Musicology, Buenos Aires, and with Isabel Aretz and Augusto Raúl Cortázar at the Colegio Libre de Estudios Superiores (1945–7). On his return to Caracas (1947) he was appointed chief of musicology of the Servicio de Investigaciones Folklóricas Nacionales; with his wife he undertook several field trips in Venezuela before moving to Buenos Aires (1948). There he directed the Americana Orchestra in programmes of Latin American folk music until 1952, when he returned to Caracas and became director of the National Institute of Folklore of Venezuela (1953). During the 1950s and 1960s he travelled extensively throughout the Latin American continent, collecting a considerable amount of material, and taught folklore and ethnomusicology in several Venezuelan and foreign universities. He received a Guggenheim Fellowship (1967), and has been an active member of IFMC, SEM, Chilean and Mexican folklore societies, and president of the Venezuelan Society of Authors and Composers (1972–3).

Ramón y Rivera's main areas of study have been Venezuelan folk and traditional music and Latin American ethnic musics; his extensive field experience has enabled him to make a comparative study of the music of the continent. He has contributed greatly to the knowledge of Venezuelan indigenous, folk and popular music.

WRITINGS

'Consideraciones sobre un instrumento y música de los indios guajiros', *Acta venezolana*, ii/1–4 (1946–7), 104

'¿Es el ritmo una comprobación?', *Revista venezolana de folklore*, i/1 (1947), 57

La polifonía popular de Venezuela (Buenos Aires, 1949)

El joropo, baile nacional de Venezuela (Caracas, 1953)

Cantos de trabajo del pueblo venezolano (Caracas, 1955)

with I. Aretz: 'Viaje de investigación a Pregonero', *Boletín del Instituto de folklore de Venezuela*, ii/1 (1955), 1

——: *Folklore tachirense* (Caracas, 1961–3)

'Cantos negros de la fiesta de San Juan', *Boletín del Instituto de folklore de Venezuela*, iv/3 (1963), 109

Música folklórica y popular de Venezuela (Caracas, 1963)

'El mestizaje de la música afro-venezolana', *2nd Inter-American Conference on Ethnomusicology: Bloomington 1965 [Music in the Americas*, ed. G. List and J. Orrego-Salas (The Hague, 1967)], 176

La música colonial profana (Caracas, 1966)

'Music of the Motilone Indians', *EM*, x (1966), 18

'A Riddle of Cultural Diffusion: the Existence of Inverted Reed Clarinets among the Indians of the Guajira Peninsula', *JIFMC*, xix (1967), 37

'Dos corrientes medievales en la música folklórica de Venezuela', *Revista nacional de cultura*, xix, no.184 (1968), 101

'El culto religiosos en el folklore musical de Venezuela', *Revista venezolana de folklore* (1968), May, 70

'Formaciones escalísticas en la etnomúsica latinoamericana', *YIFMC*, i (1969), 200

La música folklórica de Venezuela (Caracas, 1969)

Música indígena, folklórica y popular de Venezuela (Buenos Aires, 1970)

La música afrovenezolana (Caracas, 1971)

La canción venezolana (Maracaibo, 1972)

La música popular de Venezuela (Caracas, 1976)

Articles for *Grove 6* on Latin American subjects incl. 'Venezuela', §II

GERARD BÉHAGUE

Ramos [Ramis, Rami] **de Pareia, Bartolomeo** (*b* Baeza, *c*1440; *d* in or after 1491). Spanish theorist and composer. The details of his life come from his treatise, *Musica practica* (Bologna, 1482), and some remarks in writings by his pupil GIOVANNI SPATARO and Nicolaus Burtius. His first teacher was Juan de Monte. For a time, Ramos taught at the University of Salamanca, where he came in close contact with Professor Petrus (= Burgo) de Osma, who, according to Ramos, wrote a musical treatise and who probably influenced Ramos in his individual approach to music theory. He seems to have gone to Bologna around 1472. There he was a lecturer in music, so far as is now known, without official connection with the university. Some time after 1484 he went to Rome; he was still there in 1491.

Ramos's sole surviving theoretical work is the *Musica practica*, of which there are two editions, both published in 1482 in Bologna; the first on 11 May perhaps by Enrico di Colonia, the second on 5 June by Baltasar de Hiriberia (facsimile with introduction by G. Vecchi, Bologna, 1969). He is also known to have written an *Introductorium seu isagogicon*. A continuation of the *Musica practica*, a *Musica theorica*, was planned, and in part written, but was never published. Only one complete composition of his, a perpetual canon, is extant (in *I-Fn* B.R.229). From references in his own work and that of Spataro, he is known to have composed a requiem, a mass and a *Magnificat* in Spain, and the motet *Tu lumen* in Bologna.

Ramos is one of the most original music theorists. He was the first to deny the authority of the two great theorists of the past, Boethius and Guido of Arezzo. To Ramos, the tetrachord system of Boethius and the hexachord of Guido were too complicated and difficult for performers. Taking into account the music of his own time, Ramos suggested that the Guidonian solmization method was outdated and useless. In its place he proposed one based on the phrase *Psal-li-tur per vo-ces is-tas*, which supplied the syllables for a complete octave, beginning on C, not on the *Gamma ut* of Guido. (This system is the basis of the fixed *doh* used today in many countries.) With Ramos's system, there would be only one mutation, that of *Psal-* for *-tas* (or the reverse). With this change he wished to avoid the many problems that the Guidonian hexachord system had encountered with the steady increase in the use of semitones at points other than those represented by the traditional *mi* and *fa* (i.e., between E and F, A and B♭, B♮ and C). According to Ramos the solution proposed by JOHN HOTHBY, which allowed hexachords called *coniunctae* to be built on other notes than C, F or G, led to total confusion and to failure to stay on pitch, whereas Ramos's system overcame these difficulties.

His attack on Boethius came primarily on the question of tuning. The basic intervals and ratios were the octave (2 : 1), the perfect 5th (3 : 2), the perfect 4th (4 : 3) and the whole tone (9 : 8). All other intervals were computed by addition or subtraction of these ratios; for example, the major 3rd was 81 : 64 and the minor 3rd 32 : 27. Ramos suggested that these ratios be simplified, the major 3rd as 5 : 4 and the minor 3rd 6 : 5. His assumptions were empirically based on the whole, although he attempted to combine features of Ptolemy's diatonic-syntonic system with the diatonic system of Didymus. (*See* JUST INTONATION and TEMPERAMENTS, §2.)

In addition, Ramos railed against many other traditional procedures of the time: notation, mensuration symbols and classification of the modes. He also suggested the stabilization of intervals of imitation at the 4th below or the 5th above. In all these, Ramos pleaded for practicality and clarity, for he felt that the hallowed procedures of the past were no longer valid for the music and musicians of his own time.

The evidence of the *Musica practica* shows that Ramos was an extremely well-read musician. References are made to all the major writers on music, both of the past and his own day; a partial list includes Aristotle, Plato, Cicero, Macrobius and Boethius from antiquity, Guido of Arezzo, Franco of Cologne and Marchetto da Padova from the Middle Ages, and Ugolino, Anselmi, Johannes Galliculus, Hothby and Tinctoris from his own century. Many of these he mentioned only to sneer at them and their ideas; to Ramos, the supreme insult was to call a man a follower of Guido.

The reaction to Ramos's ideas was vehement; polemics between his followers, principally represented by his student Spataro, and the conventionally minded Hothby, Burtius and Gaffurius, continued on into the 16th century. Nevertheless, many of his ideas were picked up and re-used by later theorists, including Glarean, Aaron and Zarlino.

BIBLIOGRAPHY

N. Burtius: *Musices opusculum* (Bologna, 1487)

G. Spataro: *Honesta defensio in Nicolai Burtii . . . opusculum* (Bologna, 1491) [facs. with introduction by G. Vecchi, Bologna, 1967]

——: *Errori di F. Gaffurio* (Bologna, 1521)

G. Lange: 'Zur Geschichte der Solmisation', *SIMG*, i (1899–1900), 535

J. Wolf, ed.: *Musica practica Bartolomei Rami de Pareia* (Leipzig, 1901/R1968)

O. Strunk: *Source Readings in Music History* (New York, 1950), 202

A. Seay: 'The *Dialogus Johannis Ottobi Anglici in arte musica*', *JAMS*, viii (1955), 86

——: 'Florence: the City of Hothby and Ramos', *JAMS*, ix (1956),

193 [includes transcription of Ramos's canon]
J. M. Barbour: *Tuning and Temperament* (East Lansing, 1959)
F. J. León Tello: *Estudios de historia de la teoría musical* (Madrid, 1962), 343
C. V. Palisca: 'Ramos de Pareja, Bartolomé', *MGG*
A. Seay, ed.: *Johannis Octobi tres tractatuli contra Bartholomeum Ramum*, CSM, x (1964)
U. Sesini: *Monumenti di teoria musicale tra medioevo e rinascimento* (Bologna, 1966)
J. Haar: 'Roger Caperon and Ramos de Pareia', *AcM*, xli (1969), 26
N. Meeùs: 'Bartolomeo Ramos de Pareia et la tessiture des instruments à clavier entre 1450 et 1550', *Revue des archéologues et historiens d'art de Louvain*, v (1972), 26
M. Lindley: 'Fifteenth-century Evidence for Meantone Temperament', *PRMA*, cii (1975–6), 37
D. Fallows: 'Robertus de Anglia and the Oporto Song Collection', *Source Materials and the Interpretation of Music: a Memorial Volume for Thurston Dart* (in preparation)

ALBERT SEAY

Ramovš, Primož (*b* Ljubljana, 20 March 1921). Yugoslav composer. He studied the piano and composition, the latter with Osterc at the Ljubljana Academy of Music (1941), with Frazzi in Siena (1941) and with Casella and Petrassi in Rome (1942–3). In 1945 he joined the staff of the library of the Slovene Academy of Arts and Sciences, becoming its head in 1952. He also taught at the Ljubljana Conservatory (1948–64). An extremely prolific composer, Ramovš began in a neoclassical style, went on to employ 12-note and serial methods, and then established himself as one of the most successful Yugoslav exponents of avant-garde techniques. His earlier lyricism, which became ever more dramatic and expressionist during the 1950s and early 1960s, has given place to 'non-programmatic sound combinations for sound's sake'.

WORKS
(selective list)

Orch: 4 syms., 1940, 1943, 1948, 1968; 3 divertimentos, 1941, 1942, 1943; Sinfonietta, 1951; Musiques funèbres, 1955; Adagio, vc, str, 1958; Concertino, tpt, orch, 1960; 7 Compositions, str, 1960; Vn Conc., 1961; Concertante Music, timp, orch, 1961; Intrada, 1962; Transformations, 2 va, 10 str, 1963; Profiles, 1964; Contrasts, fl, orch, 1966; Antiparallels, pf, orch, 1966; Finale, 1966; Sym., pf, orch, 1970; Syntheses, hn, 3 groups, 1971; Sym. Portrait, 1972

Chamber: Sonatina, cl, pf, tpt, 1953; Sonata, cl, pf, 1953; Trio, 2 vn, va, 1954; Sonata breve, vn, pf, 1956; Wind Qnt, 1959; Sonatina, cl, pf, 1959; Contrasts, pf trio, 1961; Aphorisms, vn, pf, 1961; Sound Portrait, hn, pf, 1962; Enneafonia, 9 insts, 1963; Apel [Call], hn, ens, 1963; Fluctuations, ens, 1964; Prologue–Dialogue–Epilogue, fl, cl, bn, 1966; Oscillations, fl, ens, 1967; Portrait, harp, ens, 1968; Con sordino, tpt, trbn, pf, 1969; Tryptychon, str qt, 1969; Colloquium, harp, str qt, 1970; Signals, pf, ens, 1971; Thème donné, trbn, ens, 1972; Ex uno, 2 pf, 2 perc, 1973

Solo inst: Miniatures, vn, 1943; Prelude and Fugue, org, 1951; Sarcasms, pf, 1951; Tema con variazioni, pf, 1953; Sonatina, pf, 1953; Bagatelles, vn, 1954; Sonatina, harp, 1955; Bagatelles, pf, 1956; Toccata, org, 1960; Pf Variations, 1960; Monologue, vc, 1962; Expansion, fl, 1963; Pentektasis, pf, 1963; Constant and Sequences, pf, 1964; Circulations, harp, 1965; Asymmetry, pf, 1965; Prelude and Return, pf, 1966; Inventions pastorales, org, 1966; Movements, pf, 1967; Extremes, vn, 1970; Acuta, org, 1971; Couple, pf, 1971; 3 nocturnes, db, 1972; Solo, db, 1972; 3 Preludes, pf, 1972; Quadrumanus, pf, 1972; Improvisations, harp, 1973,

Music for the theatre and cinema, songs, choruses

Principal publisher: Edicije DSS

ANDREJ RIJAVEC

Rampal, Jean-Pierre (Louis) (*b* Marseilles, 7 Jan 1922). French flautist. He studied at the Marseilles Conservatory and the Paris Conservatoire. His international career began with his appointment as solo flautist at the Vichy Opéra orchestra (1946–50), the Paris Opéra (1956–62) and with concert tours from 1947 in Europe, Africa, the USA and the Far East. His keen interest in chamber music led to his founding of the Quintette à Vent Française (1945) and the Ensemble Baroque de Paris (1953).

Rampal's great love is music of the 18th century and its performance in authentic style. Even his early performances and recordings were notable for their smooth but unromantic phrasing and stylish ornamentation. His tone on a modern flute is clear but mellow, with a great variety of shading, and delicate, impeccable articulation. His recordings include music by J. S. and C. P. E. Bach, Mozart, Pergolesi, Leclair and Molter; his performance of J. S. Bach's Suite no.2 is particularly fine. He has often edited the music of little-known composers; many of his editions are published.

NIALL O'LOUGHLIN

Rampazetto, Francesco (*d* Venice, ?1577). Italian bookseller and printer. From 1554 until 1568 Rampazetto reprinted the favourite composers, including Rore, Morales, Striggio, Arcadelt, Ruffo and in particular Lassus, as well as popular collections of the time, not without occasional changes. His *Mottetti del fiore a quattro voci* (1564[6]), for instance, is slightly different from that of Gardane (1539). He issued one theoretical work, the third edition of Vicente Lusitano's *Introduttione facilissima et novissima de canto fermo* (1561). Rampazetto's printer's mark, two *putti* bearing laurel wreaths, with the motto 'Et animo et corpore', is absent from many of his books. Much of Rampazetto's printing, musical and otherwise, was done on commission for other publishers, including Marchiò Sessa, Damiano Zenaro, Giovanni Comencino, Plinio Pietrasanta and Filippo Giunta. In 1563, for example, he printed Don Serafino Razzi's voluminous collection of *Laudi spirituali* for the Florentine bookseller Filippo Giunta because Florence lacked a musical press.

In 1572 Rampazetto was elected second Prior of the Guild of Booksellers and Printers. A measure he introduced, severely restricting membership in the guild, caused great dissension among the members, and a lawsuit was instituted against Rampazetto, 'who presumes to be Prior of the Booksellers' (document of 25 February 1575).

Rampazetto's non-musical production was substantial and included books on many subjects, particularly literature, both classical and contemporary, printed in Italian, Latin, Spanish or Greek. He printed or reprinted a number of illustrated books, including Serlio's *Architettura* (1560) and Ruscelli's *Le imprese illustri* (1566), and many writing books. Rampazetto's music books probably do not exceed 50 in number and most are reprints; but apart from the illustrated books they are the most interesting part of his production. Moreover, Rampazetto was the first persistent challenger to the virtual monopoly of Venetian music printing held by Gardane and Scotto.

After his death, he was succeeded by his son, Giovan Antonio Rampazetto, who used the imprint 'heredi di Francesco Rampazetto' from 1578 until 1583, and his own name from then until 1607 or later. In 1579 and 1580 he printed a number of music books, but after that he issued only two theoretical works on music. The firm continued under Rampazetto's name until at least 1662.

BIBLIOGRAPHY
H. Brown: *The Venetian Printing Press* (London, 1891), 87f, 253
C. Sartori: *Dizionario degli editori musicali italiani* (Florence, 1958)
——: 'Rampazetto, Francesco', *MGG*
M. E. Cosenza: *Biographical and Bibliographical Dictionary of the Italian Printers and of Foreign Printers in Italy from the Introduction of the Art of Printing into Italy to 1800* (Boston, Mass., 1968)
C. Marciani: 'Editori, tipografi, librai veneti nel regno di Napoli nel cinquecento', *Studi veneziani*, x (1968), 512, 514, 540

THOMAS W. BRIDGES

Rampini, Domenico (*b* Friuli province, *c*1765; *d* Trieste, 19 Dec 1816). Italian composer. He held posts as harpsichordist at the theatres of S Samuele, Venice (Carnival 1791), and S Pietro, Trieste (1792–1801). When Trieste's Teatro Nuovo was opened in 1801, he became its *maestro di cappella*, a post he held for at least a dozen years, along with that of *maestro* at the cathedral. His many occasional cantatas performed at the Teatro Nuovo suggest considerable public success.

A Vincenzo Rampini (*fl* Venice, 1790) wrote two brief keyboard treatises, *Regole per suonare la spinetta* (including seven sonatinas) and *Regole per accompagnare il basso, e partimenti* (both in Museo Correr Manuscripts, *I-Vc*). He also composed two arias for the pasticcio *Didone abbandonata* performed in Venice in 1790 (copies in *I-Vc*, *D-BFb*, *F-Pc*). Schmidl suggested that he may have been a cousin of Domenico Rampini.

WORKS

Stage, all perf. Trieste: L'impresario di Smirne (dramma giocoso, 2, ? G. Foppa), S Pietro, 3 Feb 1798; Inno popolare (cantata, G. de Coletti), 3vv, S Pietro, 4 Oct 1798; Inno (cantata, Coletti), 3vv, S Pietro, 4 Oct 1799; Pimmalione (dramma giocoso, 2), Nuovo, 6 March 1802; Trieste rasserenata (cantata), Nuovo, 12 Oct 1802; I geni pacificati (cantata), Nuovo, 12 Feb 1808; Minerva consolata (cantata), Nuovo, 28 Jan 1814; Il sogno di corvo (cantata), Nuovo, 12 Feb 1814; La gloria (cantata, D. Rossetti), Nuovo, Feb 1814
Sacred: Easter vespers, 1798; Requiem, 3vv, orch, org, 1808; Mass, Trieste, for Napoleon's visit, 11 Aug 1809; Pastorella for Christmas; Kyrie, 3vv, wind, org, *I-Vsmc*

BIBLIOGRAPHY

FétisB; *SchmidlD*; *SchmidlDS*
C. L. Curiel: *Il Teatro S Pietro di Trieste, 1690–1801* (Milan, 1937), 263, 316, 326, 336, 354, 396f

SVEN HANSELL

Rampini [Rampin], (Giovanni) Giacomo (i) (*b* Padua, 1680; *d* Padua, 27 May 1760). Italian composer, uncle of Giacomo Rampini (ii). Of modest family background, he became a priest when little more than 20 and was elected to succeed P. R. Pignati as *maestro di cappella* of Padua Cathedral on 29 June 1704. He held this position until his death, when Adolfati, who had assumed his duties on 26 April 1760, was named his successor.

Among the relatively few works by Rampini in the cathedral archive is a cycle of graduals and offertories that he compiled in 1710 with music by other composers as well as his own. The archaic choirbook notation of these Propers is unusual, and the contrapuntal style of the music contrasts markedly with the modern homophonic style of Rampini's other works. La Borde described him as an excellent composer of sacred music and a successful one of operas. His reputation as a teacher attracted numerous students, including his nephew.

WORKS

Opere serie: Armida in Damasco (3, G. Braccioli), Venice, S Angelo, 17 Oct 1711; La gloria trionfante d'amore (3, Braccioli), Venice, S Angelo, 16 Nov 1712; Marco Attilio Regolo (3, M. Noris), Verona, Accademia Vecchia, aut. 1713; Ercole sul Termodonte (3, G. F. Bussani), Padua, Obizzi, June 1715
Oratorios: Christo al cenacolo, Padua, Chiesa S Tomaso, 1708; L'angelo di Castiglione (P. Morari), Padua, Chiesa S Leonardo, 21 June 1712; Il trionfo della costanza, ?Padua, 1717; David pentito, Padua, 1728
Sacred: Mass, 4vv; Requiem, 4vv, 1756; Laudate pueri (Ps cxii), 4vv; Salmi di terza (Ps cxviii), SATB, SATB, org; Graduali e offertori per tutto l'anno ... 1710 [incl. works by other composers], all *I-Pc*
Inst: Concerto a cinque, str, bc (Amsterdam, *c*1717)

BIBLIOGRAPHY

EitnerQ; *FétisB*; *SchmidlD*; *LaMusicaD*

J.-B. de La Borde: *Essai sur la musique ancienne et moderne*, iii (Paris, 1780/*R*1972), 226
N. Pietrucci: *Biografia degli artisti padovani* (Padua, 1859), 224f
A. Garbelotto: 'Codici musicali della Biblioteca capitolare di Padova', *RMI*, liv (1952), 311
——: 'Piccola enciclopedia musicale padovanna', *Padova e la sua provincia*, xx (1974), April, 24

SVEN HANSELL

Rampini, Giacomo (ii) (*b* Rovigo; *d* Udine, 15 Nov 1811). Italian composer and organist, nephew of Giacomo Rampini (i). After studying music with his uncle in Padua, he became organist in Latisana and in spring 1775 began substituting for the organist Leonardo Dordolo at Udine Cathedral. When Dordolo died on 18 September 1779, Rampini was named permanent organist. A priest, he also taught at the Udine seminary from 1775 to 1781. On 19 January 1799 he was elected *maestro di cappella* at the cathedral, a post he held along with that of organist until his death.

WORKS

Mass, 3 equal vv, org; Kyrie, 3vv, orch; 3rd Gloria, 3 equal vv, orch; Gloria, 3vv, 2 hn, vle, org; Kyrie–Credo, 3 equal vv, org; De profundis, 3vv, orch; Regina coeli, 2 S, orch; Per silvam ire, motet, B, orch, 1785; Cari affectus, motet, S, orch, 1793, all *I-UD*; 12 sonatas, org/hpd, *VIb*; Sonata, G, org/hpd, *Vnm*

BIBLIOGRAPHY

LaMusicaD
D. Sabbadini: *Dell'origine e delle vicende della musica ecclesiastica e dello stato della medesima in Friuli* (Udine, 1863)
G. Vale: 'La cappella musicale del duomo di Udine', *NA*, vii (1930), 87–201, esp. 143, 168ff

SVEN HANSELL

Rampini, Vincenzo (*fl* Venice, 1790). Italian theorist and composer, possibly a cousin of DOMENICO RAMPINI.

Rampollini, Mattio [Mattia] (*b* Florence, ?2 June 1497; *d* Florence, *c*1553). Italian composer. In 1520 he succeeded Bernardo Pisano as master of the boys at Florence Cathedral; he may have been Francesco Corteccia's composition teacher after Pisano left Florence. Rampollini was also in the service of the Medici family and contributed to the 1539 wedding festival for Duke Cosimo and Eleanora di Toledo, composing two madrigals for their wedding banquet, *Lieta per honorarte* and *Ecco la fida*. Both were published in Gardane's edition of the wedding music (*RISM* 1539[25]). About 1554 Moderne published Rampollini's *Il primo libro de la musica*, dedicated to Duke Cosimo. All the canzoni, with the exception of an anonymous ottava, are by Petrarch and are in the new cyclic canzone form with the stanzas set for a varying number of voices ranging from three to six; the final stanza usually uses all the voices. Several madrigals by Rampollini were published in anthologies.

WORKS

Il primo libro de la musica ... sopra di alcune canzoni del ... M. Francesco Petrarco (Lyons, *c*1554); ed. in CMM, xxxii/7 (1974) [see Pogue for discussion of publication date]
6 madrigals, 1539[25], 1562[8]; 2 ed. A. C. Minor and B. Mitchell, *A Renaissance Entertainment: Festivities for the Marriage of Cosimo I, Duke of Florence, in 1539* (Columbia, Missouri, 1968)

BIBLIOGRAPHY

A. Einstein: *The Italian Madrigal* (Princeton, 1949/*R*1971)
M. Fabbri: 'La vita e l'ignota opera-prima di Francesco Corteccia', *Chigiana*, xxii (1965), 185–217
S. F. Pogue: *Jacques Moderne, Lyons Music Printer of the Sixteenth Century* (Geneva, 1969)
F. A. D'Accone: 'The Musical Chapels at the Florentine Cathedral and Baptistry during the First Half of the 16th Century', *JAMS*, xxiv (1971), 1–50
——: 'Matteo Rampollini and his Petrarchan Canzone Cycles', *MD*, xxvii (1973), 65–106

ANDREW C. MINOR

Ramponi, Virginia. Italian musician, wife of GIOVANNI BATTISTA ANDREINI.

Ramsbotham, Alexander (*b* Leeds, 28 June 1870; *d* London, 3 Sept 1932). English music scholar. He was educated at Charterhouse and at Exeter College, Oxford, where he took his degree (classics and Lit.Hum.) in 1893. In 1894 he took holy orders, and after two Tyneside curacies became vicar of New Seaham (1899–1912), and from 1912 Preacher of the Charterhouse. He was a member of the editorial committee of Tudor Church Music and the index to the collection of photostats relating to that, now in the University of London Library, is his work. He edited the Old Hall Manuscript for the Plainsong and Mediaeval Music Society, the three volumes appearing after his death with help from H. B. Collins and Anselm Hughes (1933–8).

WATKINS SHAW

Ramsey, Robert (*fl* Cambridge, *c*1612–44). English composer. Ramsey graduated at Cambridge in 1616 and was organist of Trinity College, 1628–44. Nothing else is known of his life or ancestry.

His music reflects the influence of contemporary Italian music and the emergence of the early Baroque style in England. The continuo song *What tears, dear Prince* seems to have been intended as an obituary tribute to Henry, Prince of Wales, who died in 1612; if so, it is an early example of English monody. The incomplete *Dialogues of Sorrow upon the Death of the Late Prince Henrie*, dated 1615, are consort songs. The other dialogues are duet monodies on mythological or biblical subjects – embryo operas and oratorios. The setting of *In guilty night*, a paraphrased version of *1 Samuel* xxviii.8–20, anticipates Purcell's similar setting by at least half a century.

Most of his compositions are settings of English or Latin liturgical texts intended presumably for performance in Trinity College. The Latin works embrace the spirit of the *seconda prattica* to a greater extent than the English, but Ramsey did not provide a basso continuo. The two settings of the (Latin) *Te Deum* and *Jubilate* make extensive use of concertante textures and choral recitative which in their rhythmic vitality and harmonic daring recall Monteverdi's new-style church music. The English Service on the other hand is similar in style to Gibbons's Short Service.

Between these extremes of style lie the motets and collects, in all of which imitative points still serve a structural purpose although the textures are not really polyphonic. Expressive dissonance takes precedence over beauty of line or imitative interplay. The anthem *O come, let us sing unto the Lord* is conspicuously modern. Its clearcut phrase lengths, rhythmic patterns, affective melodic lines and concluding Alleluia are characteristic of the Restoration full anthem. The earlier madrigal-anthem is best exemplified in *How are the mighty fallen* and *When David heard that Absalon was slain*. The one complete verse anthem, *My song shall be alway*, is undistinguished.

WORKS

Editions: *R. Ramsey: English Sacred Music*, ed. E. Thompson, EECM, vii (London, 1967) [T]
    English Songs 1625–1660, ed. I. Spink, MB, xxxiii (London, 1971) [S]
    R. Ramsey: Latin Sacred Music, ed. E. Thompson, EECM, xx (London, 1978)

LATIN CHURCH MUSIC

Litany, 4vv, *GB-Cp*
Te Deum and Jubilate, 4vv, *Cp*
Te Deum and Jubilate, 5vv, *Cp*
In Monte Oliveti, 6vv, *Ge*
Inclina, Domine, 8vv, *Ob, Y*
O Sapientia, 5vv, *Cp*
O vos omnes, 6vv, *Ge*

ENGLISH CHURCH MUSIC

Service (TeD, Jub, Ky, Lit, Cr, Mag, Nunc), 4vv, T no.1
Litany, inc., 4vv, T no.12, incipit only
Te Deum, inc., T no.11, incipit only
Almighty and everlasting God, we humbly beseech, 5vv, T no.2
Almighty and everlasting God, which hast given, inc., 5vv, T no.3
Almighty God, which hast given, 5vv, T no.13, incipit only
Almighty God, who through thine only-begotten Son, inc., 5vv, T no.15, incipit only
God, which as upon this day, 5vv, T no.4
Grant, we beseech thee, inc., 5vv, T no.5
Hear my prayer, O Lord, inc., 1/5vv, 4 viols, T no.16, incipit only
How are the mighty fallen, 6vv, T no.6
How doth the city remain desolate, inc., 6vv, T no.17, incipit only
I heard a voice from heaven, inc., 5vv, T no.18, incipit only
My song shall be alway, inc., 1/4vv, org, T no.9
O come, let us sing unto the Lord, 5vv, T no.7
We beseech thee, O Lord, inc., 5vv, T no.19, incipit only
When David heard, 6vv, T no.8
Woe is me, inc., 6vv, T no.20, incipit only

CONSORT SONGS, CONTINUO SONGS AND DIALOGUES

Dialogues of Sorrow upon the Death of the Late Prince Henrie, 1615, inc., v, 5 viols, *GB-Ob*: If plaints, laments or sorrows; O tell me, wretched shape of misery; What dire mishap or unappeased rage; Gone is the world's delight
Songs: Go perjured man (Herrick), v, bc, S no.13; Thou maist be proud (Herrick), v, bc, S no.14; What tears, dear Prince (Raleigh), v, bc, S no.12
Dialogues: Charon, O Charon, 2vv, 3vv, bc; Come, my Oenone, 2vv, bc; Help, O help, kind Abraham, 2vv, bc; Howl not, you ghosts and furies (Herrick), 2vv, bc, S no.15; In guilty night, 3vv, bc, T no.10; Vulcan, O Vulcan, 2vv, bc; Woe's me, alas, 2vv, bc

MADRIGALS

Long ago my heart I gave, 6vv, *GB-Ge*; O how fortunate, 5vv, *Lbm*; Part we must & Yet of us both, inc., 6vv, *Ob*; Since no desert, inc., 6vv, *Lbm, Ob*; Sleep fleshly birth, 6vv, *Ge*; Why dost thou sing aye me, inc., 6vv, *Ob*; Wilt thou unkind now leave me weeping, 6vv, *Lbm*

OTHER WORKS

Canons, *Lbm*

LOST WORKS

Donec gratus eram tibi
O Lord, let me know mine end (only text survives in J. Clifford: The Divine Services and Anthems, London, 1663, 2/1664)

BIBLIOGRAPHY

E. W. Naylor: 'Three Seventeenth-century Poet-parsons and Music', *PMA*, liv (1927–8), 93
E. Thompson: 'Robert Ramsey', *MQ*, xlix (1963), 212
——: Letter in *ML*, xlvi (1965), 289
B. Smallman: 'Endor Revisited: English Biblical Dialogues of the Seventeenth Century', *ML*, xlvi (1965), 137
P. le Huray: *Music and the Reformation in England 1549–1660* (London, 1967), 340ff
K. R. Long: *The Music of the English Church* (London, 1971), 196ff

EDWARD THOMPSON

Ramshā. Office of the Syrian Churches corresponding to Vespers; *see* SYRIAN CHURCH MUSIC.

Ran, Shulamit (*b* Tel-Aviv, 21 Oct 1949). Israeli composer and pianist. She studied composition with A. U. Boskovich and Ben-Haim, and the piano with Miriam Boskovich and Emma Gorochov. In 1962, already an accomplished composer, she was awarded scholarships from the America–Israel Cultural Foundation and the Mannes School of Music, New York, from which she graduated in 1967. During her years in the USA she took lessons with Dello Joio (composition) and with Nadia Reisenberg and Dorothy Taubman (piano). She made concert tours of the USA and Europe that culminated in 1967 with a performance of her Capriccio with the New York PO under Bernstein. In July 1971 she gave the first performance of her Concert Piece with Mehta and the Israel PO. She was artist-in-residence at St Mary's University, Canada (1972–3), and was then appointed assistant professor of composition at the University of Chicago. In her music she has developed from the influence of Ben-Haim to make use of more novel techniques, including electronic music, which she studied with Badings in 1969.

WORKS
(selective list)

Music, fl, hn, str, 1962; 2 pf sonatas, 1962; Capriccio, pf, orch, 1963; Improvisations, fl, pf, 1964; Pf Music, 1965; 10 Children's Scenes, orch, 1966; Qt, fl, cl, vc, pf, 1967; The Laughing Man, television pantomime, 1967; Sym. Poem, pf, orch, 1967; Hatsvi Israel, Mez, chamber orch, 1970; O the Chimneys (after Sachs), Mez, ens, tape, 1970; Structures, pf, c1970; Concert Piece, pf, orch, 1971; 7 Japanese Love Poems, 1971; Fantasy II, vn, pf, perc, 1972; 3 Fantasy Pieces, vc, pf, 1972; Movts, 1v, cl, pf, 1973; Ensembles for 17, S, 16 insts, 1975; Sonata Brevis, hpd, 1975; Double Vision, 2 qnts, pf, 1977; Pf Conc., 1977

Principal publishers: Fischer, Israel Music Institute, Presser

BIBLIOGRAPHY

Y. W. Cohen: Werden und Entwicklung der Musik in Israel (Kassel, 1976) [pt. ii of rev. edn. of M. Brod: Die Musik Israels]
W. Y. Elias: The Music of Israel (in preparation) [bibliography]
WILLIAM Y. ELIAS

Rana, Johannes. See FROSCH, JOHANNES.

Ranalow, Frederick (Baring) (b Dublin, 7 Nov 1873; d London, 8 Dec 1953). Irish baritone. A chorister at St Paul's Cathedral in London from the age of ten, he then trained at the RAM under Randegger. As a leading baritone in the Beecham Opera Company his parts ranged from Hans Sachs to Papageno, and he was one of the best Figaros of his generation in Beecham's Drury Lane production of Mozart's work during World War I. In 1920 he relinquished serious opera for that creation, or re-creation, by which he will be remembered: Frederic Austin's revival of The Beggar's Opera at the Lyric, Hammersmith, began a new epoch in the life of that immortal work, and Ranalow's Captain Macheath was an essential feature of its success. He played the part over 1500 times and set his stamp on it; conversely the part set its stamp on him, to the extent that an enthusiastic public was wont to discover the characteristics of Macheath in the many light operatic parts which Ranalow played later. In his earlier years he was a reliable singer in oratorio at the principal English festivals.

H. C. COLLES/R

Ranāt. A Thai xylophone of which two sizes are played, the high-pitched ranāt ēk and the low-pitched ranāt thum, both with wooden resonators; see BURMA, §2(iii); SOUTH-EAST ASIA, §II, 4(v, vii); THAILAND, §2(i).

Rancalli, Ludovico. See RONCALLI, LUDOVICO.

Randall, Greenwood (b ?Exeter; d after 1645 and before 1660). English cathedral musician. He was a relative (possibly son) of William Randall (i) and brought up in the choir of Exeter Cathedral. On 21 April 1610 he was appointed to assist Edward Gibbons in instructing the choristers in instrumental music, for which he received 25s. quarterly in addition to his salary. He was admitted into a vicar-choral's place on 19 December 1611. On 28 January 1618 he was one of the four vicars-choral who testified to the innocence of John Lugge who was accused of having Catholic leanings. Randall was responsible for music copying at a time when vocal and instrumental music flourished. According to an entry in the Chapter Act Book for 19 December 1618 he received 20s. 'for the newe pricking of services and Anthems for the Quire' and was asked to do 'the rest which are yet undone', and on a later occasion he was paid 17s. 'for 14 bookes covered with parchment and for 7 quire of ruled paper' (Solutions Extraordinary, Christmas 1643). No examples of his work as a copyist are known.

On 10 February 1615 he married Katharine Dunne, a widow; after her death on 17 August 1625 he married Mary, daughter of Edward Gibbons, in a double wedding (4 May 1626) when Gibbons's daughter Jane was also married. Randall's name is mentioned in the last accounts (for 1644–5) kept by the dean and chapter during the Civil War, but does not occur in their new accounts of 1660.

An Evening Service in G has been attributed to William Randall, but a bass part (GB-Lbm Add.17784) bears two clear ascriptions to Greenwood Randall (other parts in WRch). A setting of the Magnificat and Nunc dimittis is in DRc.

BIBLIOGRAPHY
S. Jeans: 'The Musical Life of Exeter Cathedral (1600–1650)', The Organist's Quarterly Record, xliii (1958), 103
SUSI JEANS

Randall, James K(irtland) (b Cleveland, 16 June 1929). American composer. After early training at the Cleveland Institute of Music (1934–47), he studied at Columbia University (BA), Harvard (MA) and Princeton (MFA). He studied the piano with Leonard Shure and composition wwith Herbert Elwell, George Thaddeus Jones, Sessions and Babbitt. In 1958 he was appointed to the staff at Princeton, where he later became professor of music; he has also taught at the US Naval School of Music and the Bennington Composers Conference, and he was one of the founder members of the American Society of University Composers. Since the early 1960s Randall has been principally engaged in the computer synthesis of sound, and has collaborated with Godfrey Winham in developing the Princeton 'Music IV' Facility. He has used the MUSIC 4B (music performing) programme, in which the task of the computer is to simulate numerically the total waveform corresponding to the composer's input. Randall designs his own 'instruments', indeed he specifies every aspect of every sound; then the computer qua performer, supplied with appropriately coded instructions, realizes (or processes) the work. He has said: 'I use the computer solely as an instrument of performance, and not as a composer surrogate'; this is immediately apparent in his Lyric Variations. Composers 'now have the chance to structure developments within any single note exclusively in ways that reflect developments, or principles of development, in a composition as a whole'. Such complexities and originality of thought are finely and cleanly projected in Randall's music, a result of the conjunction of resources afforded by electronic media and Randall's rather special imaginativeness. His computer-synthesized works have been performed throughout the USA, Canada and Europe, and recorded by Cardinal, Composers Recording Inc. and Nonesuch.

WORKS
(selective list)

Slow Movement, pf, 1959; Improvisation on a poem by e.e. cummings, S, cl, sax, tpt, gui, pf/S, pf, 1960; Pitch-derived Rhythm: 7 Demonstrations, fl, cl, pf, 2 vc, 1961–4; Quartets in Pairs, 1964;

Mudgett: Monologues by a Mass Murderer, synth sound, 1965;
Lyric Variations, recorded vn, computer, 1968; Quatersines, 1969;
Eakins, film score, 1972; A Long Story, pf, 1974–6

WRITINGS

'Haydn: String Quartet in D major, op.76, no.5', *MR*, xxi (1960), 94
'Godfrey Winham: Composition for Orchestra', *PNM*, ii/1 (1963), 102
Review of Taneyev: *Convertible Counterpoint in the Strict Style*, *JMT*,
viii (1964), 279
'Two Lectures to Scientists', *Perspectives on Contemporary Music
Theory*, ed. B. Boretz and E. T. Cone (New York, 1972), 116
'Compose Yourself: a Manual for the Young', *PNM*, x/2 (1972), 1; xi/1
(1972), 77; xii/1 (1973)

BIBLIOGRAPHY

R. Swift: 'J. K. Randall's "Demonstrations IV" ', *PNM*, ii/2 (1963), 77
ELAINE BARKIN

Randall, John (*b* 26 Feb 1717; *d* Cambridge, 18 March
1799). English organist and composer. As a chorister
under Bernard Gates in the Chapel Royal, he sang the
title role in Handel's *Esther* given on 23 February 1732
directed by the composer at the Crown and Anchor
Tavern in the Strand. He graduated MusB at Cambridge
in 1744 and later held a variety of posts as organist of
King's College (1745, or 1743 according to Mann), St
John's, Pembroke and Trinity (1777). In 1755 he
succeeded Maurice Greene as professor of music, and
the following year proceeded MusD. On 5 October
1756 he married Grace Pattison. The music that he
composed for Gray's ode for the installation of the
Duke of Grafton as chancellor of the university (July
1769) is now lost. Burney, who originally intended to
set the ode, wrote a spiteful and inaccurate biography of
Randall in *Rees's Cyclopaedia*. Randall edited a collection of psalms and hymn tunes (Cambridge, 1794),
including several of his own; a number of song settings
and hymn tunes (two reprinted in the *English Hymnal* as
nos.93 and 250) survive, as well as the anthems *O be
joyful* (*GB-Cjc*), *O Lord, grant the king* (*Cjc, Ckc*) and
Who hath believed our report? (*D-Hs, GB-Cjc, Ckc*).

BIBLIOGRAPHY

J. D. Brown and S. S. Stratton: *British Musical Biography*
(Birmingham, 1897)
A. H. Mann: Cambridge notebooks (MS, *GB-Ckc*)
P. A. Scholes: *The Great Dr Burney* (Oxford, 1948)
CHRISTOPHER HOGWOOD

Randall, Peter. English music publisher, associated with
JOHN WALSH (i).

Randall [Randoll], William (i) (*b* ?mid-16th century; *d*
Exeter, ?1604). English cathedral musician and composer. He was a lay vicar at Exeter Cathedral as early as
1578, but was deprived of his post (presumably on his
appointment as a Gentleman of the Chapel Royal on 15
February 1584); he was restored to his Exeter post in
1601 after the intervention of the queen. In a Chapel
Royal Cheque Book entry dated 26 July 1592 he is
described as 'organist'. Francis Meres, in his *Palladis
Tamia* (London, 1598) listed Randall among the 16
'excellent Musitians' of his day. He was granted mourning livery for the funeral of Queen Elizabeth on 28 April
1603 and is listed as having attended the coronation of
James I on 25 July 1603; his successor at the Chapel
Royal was appointed on 1 March 1604. Greenwood
Randall, who also worked at Exeter, was probably his
son or otherwise related.

A good five-part In Nomine by Randall survives (in
GB-Ob Mus.Sch.D.212–16), and three keyboard pieces
(two of them arrangements) are in *Cfm* Mus.52.D.25
(Tisdale's Virginal Book). Of his church music only a
six-part full anthem *Give sentence with me* survives
complete (*Lbm, US-NYp*); two verse anthems are

incomplete (*GB-Lbm, Ob, T, US-NYp*) and the words of
a third are known. A full service in G sometimes
attributed to him is clearly ascribed in its source (*GB-
Lbm* Add.17784) to Greenwood Randall.

BIBLIOGRAPHY

E. F. Rimbault: *The Old Cheque-book, or Book of Remembrance of the
Chapel Royal*, Camden Society, new ser., iii (London, 1872/*R*1966)
A. Brown, ed.: *Tisdale's Virginal Book* (London, 1966)
NORMAN JOSEPHS

Randall, William (ii) (*b* London, *c*1728; *d* London, ?Jan
1776). English music seller and publisher. He was a son
or more probably a grandson of Peter Randall, a
London music publisher associated with JOHN WALSH
(i), and was presumably the Randall found among the
Children of the Chapel Royal from 1736 to 1745. At
the death of his cousin JOHN WALSH (ii) in 1766 he and
John Abell inherited the extensive Walsh business,
where they had doubtless been employed. They published for the first time the complete full scores of a
number of Handel oratorios, starting with *Messiah*
(1767). After Abell's death on 29 July 1768 Randall
remained in business alone. Besides reprinting Walsh
publications, sometimes with the original imprint in
addition to his own, he published many interesting
works, including a reissue in 1771 of Morley's *A Plaine
and Easie Introduction to Practicall Musicke*. Collections of country dances and pleasure-garden songs also
came from his press. At his death his widow Elizabeth
carried on the business until 1783, when it was taken
over by WRIGHT & WILKINSON.

BIBLIOGRAPHY

F. Kidson: *British Music Publishers, Printers and Engravers* (London,
1900/*R*1974)
W. C. Smith: *A Bibliography of the Musical Works published by John
Walsh during the Years 1695–1720* (London, 1948)
——: 'John Walsh and his Successors', *The Library*, 5th ser., iii (1948–
9), 291
C. Humphries and W. C. Smith: *Music Publishing in the British Isles*
(London, 1954, 2/1970)
W. C. Smith: *Handel: a Descriptive Catalogue of the Early Editions*
(London, 1960, 2/1970)
W. C. Smith and C. Humphries: *A Bibliography of the Musical Works
published by John Walsh, 1721–1766* (London, 1968)
FRANK KIDSON/WILLIAM C. SMITH/
PETER WARD JONES

Randegger, Alberto (*b* Trieste, 13 April 1832; *d*
London, 18 Dec 1911). English conductor, teacher and
composer of German and Italian descent. He studied the
piano with Lafont and composition with Luigi Ricci.
His first works were masses and other pieces of church
music, together with two operas, one a pasticcio *Il
lazzarone* (Trieste, 1852, in collaboration with three
more of Ricci's pupils), the other a tragedy *Bianca
Capello* (Brescia, 1854). He was also musical director of
theatres in Fiume, Sinigaglia, Brescia and Venice
(1852–4). In 1854 he moved to London, where he
became widely known as a singing teacher, conductor
and composer. His comic opera *The Rival Beauties* was
produced in Leeds in 1864. In 1868 he became professor of singing at the Royal Academy of Music, of which
he was appointed a director and a member of the committee of management; he also became professor of
singing at the Royal College of Music. As an opera
conductor he directed an Italian season at St James's
Theatre (1857) and also worked at the Carl Rosa Theatre
(1879–85) and at Covent Garden and Drury Lane
(1887–98). He also conducted the Queen's Hall Choral
Society and the first two seasons of symphony concerts
at Queen's Hall (1895–7) and was conductor at the

Norwich Festival (1881–1905) and the Wolverhampton Festival (from 1868). He was organist of St Paul's in Regent's Park from 1854 to 1870. His vocal works include a dramatic cantata *Fridolin* (1873), a few scenas and some solo songs.

Randegger did much to encourage a following for Wagner's early operas, and he was admired for his Verdi interpretations: he had known the composer in Italy, particularly in Trieste at the time of *Stiffelio* (1850). At Covent Garden in 1888 he conducted *Die Zauberflöte* with an inserted ballet to Mozart's chamber music; in later Mozart performances he was more scrupulous, discarding for instance the extra orchestration that had been introduced into *Don Giovanni* by Costa and others. He collaborated with T. J. H. Marzials on the libretto for Goring Thomas's *Esmeralda* (1883). But his greatest influence was as a singing teacher: he helped to raise standards at the RAM and RCM, and his textbook *Singing* (London, 1893) remains a useful manual.

BIBLIOGRAPHY
'Alberto Randegger', *MT*, xl (1899), 653
Obituary, *MT*, liii (1912), 17

GEORGE GROVE/JOHN WARRACK

Randel, Andreas (*b* Ramdala, Blekinge, 6 Oct 1806; *d* Stockholm, 27 Oct 1864). Swedish violinist and composer. He was taught the violin by an itinerant player and in 1818 went to Karlskrona, where his talent was noticed. Between 1821 and 1828 he studied at the Paris Conservatoire with Baillot and Cherubini, who thought highly of him. After returning to Sweden in 1828 he joined the royal orchestra in Stockholm as a violinist, becoming deputy leader in 1838 and leader in 1861; he also conducted operas and concerts. Between 1844 and 1864 he taught the violin at the Stockholm Conservatory, becoming professor in 1859. In 1858 he undertook a concert tour in France and Germany.

Randel's compositions include incidental music to about 20 plays, the best known being F. A. Dahlgren's *Värmlänningarne* (Stockholm, 27 March 1846), for which he wrote the overture and arranged many of the songs and dances. This piece was for many years the most popular of its kind in Sweden and is still performed. Among his other works are a *Jubel overture*, three violin concertos, two fantasias on Swedish folk melodies, three string quartets, violin solos, male voice quartets and solo songs. His works show the influence of French Romantic music and Swedish folk music.

BIBLIOGRAPHY
F. A. Dahlgren: *Förteckning öfver svenska skådespel uppförda på Stockholms teatrar 1737–1863* (Stockholm, 1866)
S. Lindström: ' "Vermländingarne" och det svensk-folkliga sångspelet intill 19:de seklets mitt', *STMf*, viii (1926), 94
A. Ringström: 'Källorna till musiken i "Värmlänningarne" ', *Musikkultur*, i (1926), 45

AXEL HELMER

Randel, Don M(ichael) (*b* Edinburg, Texas, 9 Dec 1940). American musicologist. He took the BA from Princeton University in 1962 and the PhD in 1967, studying under Oliver Strunk, Arthur Mendel, Lewis Lockwood, Kenneth Levy and Milton Babbitt. From 1966 to 1968 he taught at Syracuse University. Since 1968 he has been on the staff of Cornell University, where he was chairman of the department of music (1971–6) and then professor. In 1972 he was chief editor of *JAMS*.

Randel's principal fields of research are medieval plainsong, particularly Mozarabic chant, and Renaissance polyphony and theory, especially in Spain. His dissertation, one of the first studies in English on the Mozarabic rite, discusses in detail the relationship of music and liturgy in the responsorial psalm tones. His *Index to the Chant of the Mozarabic Rite* is a basic research tool not only for Mozarabic specialists, but also for students of liturgy and other branches of chant.

WRITINGS
The Responsorial Psalm Tones for the Mozarabic Office (diss., Princeton U., 1966; Princeton, 1969)
'Responsorial Psalmody in the Mozarabic Rite', *Etudes grégoriennes*, x (1969), 87
Review of C. Brockett jr: *Antiphons, Responsories and Other Chants of the Mozarabic Rite* (Brooklyn, NY, 1968), *MQ*, lvi (1970), 125
'Emerging Triadic Tonality in the Fifteenth Century', *MQ*, lvii (1971), 73
An Index to the Chant of the Mozarabic Rite (Princeton, 1973)
'Sixteenth-century Spanish Polyphony and the Poetry of Garcilaso', *MQ*, lx (1974), 61
'Al-Fārābi and the Role of Arabic Music Theory in the Latin Middle Ages', *JAMS*, xxix (1976), 173
ed.: *Harvard Concise Dictionary of Music* (Cambridge, Mass., and London, 1978)
'Mozarabic rite, music of the', *Grove 6*

PAULA MORGAN

Randhartinger, Benedikt (*b* Ruprechtshofen, Lower Austria, 27 July 1802; *d* Vienna, 22 Dec 1893). Austrian tenor and composer. He won a scholarship to the Stadtkonvikt in Vienna in 1813, where he met Schubert. He then studied law at the University of Vienna (1819–25) but continued his music lessons with Salieri. From 1825 to 1832 he was private secretary to Count Széchényi, and during this period composed songs, partsongs and dances that were performed and published in Vienna. After giving up his secretarial duties he entered the Vienna Hofkapelle as a tenor. He became assistant Kapellmeister in 1844 and on the death of Ignaz Assmayer (1862) succeeded him as Kapellmeister, a post which he held until his retirement in 1866.

Although Randhartinger's talents were limited, he was well known in musical Vienna, particularly for his friendship with Schubert. He may have sung *Erlkönig* just after its completion (1815) as Schubert gave him an autograph copy of the song. He kept in touch with Schubert and attended the social gatherings and musical evenings of his circle. His *Ins stille Land* for vocal quartet was composed after Schubert's death and dedicated to his memory. As he grew older, he exaggerated the closeness of his relationship with Schubert, and there is no truth in some of his anecdotes about the composer (such as the story that Schubert composed some songs of *Die schöne Müllerin* overnight after borrowing Randhartinger's copy of the poems). His compositions include symphonies, string quartets, an opera, *König Enzio*, 20 masses, choral works and some 400 songs.

MAURICE J. E. BROWN

Randoll, William. *See* RANDALL, WILLIAM (i).

Rands, Bernard (*b* Sheffield, 2 March 1935). English composer. After studying at the University of Wales, Bangor, to take BMus (1956) and MMus (1958) degrees, Rands travelled to Italy and became a composition pupil of Dallapiccola. In 1960 he took up an appointment as lecturer in music at the University of Wales, continuing his own studies during visits to Germany (conducting and composition with Boulez and Maderna) and Italy (composition with Berio). Awarded a Harkness International Fellowship in 1966, he spent a year each at the universities of Princeton and Illinois. He was made Granada Fellow in Creative Arts at York University in 1969, and from 1970 held an appointment there as lecturer in music; in addition he has been associated with Brasenose College, Oxford, as Fellow in Creative Arts (1972–3). He later joined the staff of the University of California at San Diego. As a composer his career, like his training, has been an international one. He has worked at electronic music studios in Milan, Berlin, Albany (New York) and Urbana; since 1963 his music has been heard at most of the major European and American new music festivals. He has appeared as a conductor of new music and is a co-founder of the London Sonor ensemble.

It was under the aegis of Berio that Rands achieved his first notable success as a composer with *Actions for Six*, and Berio's remains the single influence to have most profoundly marked Rands's work. Extroverted and often virtuoso in character, his music shows great care and skill in the handling of its instrumental combinations. Except in his orchestral pieces for younger players he spurns conventional ensembles, favouring novel and translucent chamber orchestral textures. Like Berio, he has composed works in which the technical potential of a solo instrument is effectively explored, but his closeness to practical realities has also been reflected in an important series of educational works demonstrating the relevance of controlled indeterminacy to music-making in schools.

WORKS
(selective list)

3 espressioni, pf, 1960; Actions for 6, fl, 2 perc, harp, va, vc, 1962–3; Espressione IV, 2 pf, 1964; Formants I – Les gestes, harp, 1965; Wildtrack I, orch, 1969; Espressione V, 1/2 pf, 1969–70; Formants II – Labyrinthe, cl, trbn, 2 perc, cel, pf, va, vc, 1969–70; Tableau, fl + a fl, cl + b cl, perc, pf + cel, va, vc, 1970

Ballad I, Mez, fl + a fl, trbn, perc, pf, db, 1970; Ballad II, 1v, pf, 1970; Metalepsis II, Mez, 6 solo vv, 12 insts, 1971; Memo I, db, 1971; déjà, fl + a fl, cl + b cl, pf/harp, perc, va, vc, 1972; 'As all get out', variable ens, 1972; Mésalliance, pf, small orch, 1972; Serena (music-theatre), singing actress, 2 mimes, fl, elec org, perc, vc, 1972; Ballad III, S, tape, 1973; Memo II, trbn, 1973; Ology, 17 jazz insts, 1973

Response, db, tape, 1973; Wildtrack II, S, orch, 1973; Aum, harp, small orch, 1974; Etendre, db, 11 insts, 1974; Memo III, vc, 1974; Scherzi, cl, pf, vn, vc, 1974; Wildtrack III, speaker, S, Mez, 16vv, orch, 1974–5; Cuaderna, str qt, 1975; Memo IV, org, 1975; Memo V, pf, 1975; Madrigali, inst. ens., 1977; Serenata 75, fl, inst. ens., 1976; Ballad IV, 8vv, 24 players, 1977–8

Educational music incl. Per esempio, orch, 1968; Agenda, orch, 1969–70

Principal publisher: Universal

WRITINGS

'Per esempio', *Music in Education*, xxxiii (1968), 300
'"Agenda" for Orchestra', *Music in Education*, xxxiv (1970), 140
'The Master of New Sounds', *Music and Musicians*, xix/2 (1971), 32 [on Berio]

BIBLIOGRAPHY

C. Small: 'Bernard Rands', *MT*, cviii (1967), 905

G. W. HOPKINS

Ranelagh Gardens. London pleasure gardens; *see* LONDON, §V.

Range. The COMPASS of an instrument or voice, from the lowest to the highest note; the interval between those notes. 'Range' is used particularly of the human voice,

and in this context may be defined in several different ways: according to common practice ('the range of the soprano part in choral writing is usually from *c'* to *a'''*'); in terms of a particular composition or repertory ('the range of the Schubert lied seldom exceeds a 10th'); or according to ability ('her voice had an unusually large range, extending from *a* to *d''''*').

Rangs (Fr.). COURSES.

Rangström, (Anders Johan) Ture (*b* Stockholm, 30 Nov 1884; *d* Stockholm, 11 May 1947). Swedish composer, conductor and critic. He studied composition with Lindegren (1903–4) and with Pfitzner in Berlin (1905–6), where he had singing lessons with Hey (1905–6), continuing these latter studies in Munich (1906–7). As a music critic he worked for the *Svenska dagbladet* (1907–9), the *Stockholms dagblad* (1910–14, 1927–30) and the *Nya dagligt allehanda* (1938–42). In the decade after 1910 he was active as a singing teacher, and he was press adviser at the Swedish Royal Opera from 1930 to 1936. He made his conducting début in 1919 and was chief conductor of the Göteborgs Orkesterförening (1922–5); later he made guest appearances with various orchestras. He was a founder of the Society of Swedish Composers (1918).

Rangström's earliest works reflect the common traits of the time in Scandinavian music; he then absorbed influences from Wagner, Nielsen and others. But it was after his period in Germany that he developed many of the characteristic features of his work: in particular, its primarily homophonic structure and sculpturally clear-cut form. In the symphonic works and operas these tendencies resulted in episodic sequences of large sections, but he achieved concentrated passages of intense expression and pregnant form in the smaller works and in the incidental scores. Only in a few pieces did he attempt a polyphonic technique. Rangström was one of the most important Swedish song composers, showing a thorough knowledge of the expressive resources of the voice. His settings were based on what he termed 'speech melody', a technique of deriving the vocal line from the intonation of an expressive reading. Many of his songs are recitative-like, but there are also numerous exquisitely formed simpler pieces; particularly during the 1930s and 1940s he produced several dramatically intense songs, somewhat in the manner of a free operatic arioso.

WORKS
(selective list)

Stage: Kronbruden [The crown bride], opera, 1915; Stuttgart, 1919; Middelalderlig [In the middle ages], opera, 1918; Gilgamesj, opera, 1943–4, completed and orchd J. Fernström; incidental music

Orch: Sym. no.1 'August Strindberg in memoriam', c♯, 1914; Sym. no.2 'Mitt land', d, 1919; Partita, vn, orch, 1933; Sym. no.3 'Sång under stjärnorna', D♭; Sym. no.4 'Invocatio', E♭, 1936; Ballad, pf, orch, 1937

Inst: Str Qt, 1909; suites for vn/vc, pf; pf preludes and other pieces

Vocal: male/female choruses; c250 songs for 1v, pf (many orchd) incl. sets: 3 Gedichte, 1904; Lyrik, 1904–9; 4 Songs (Strindberg), 1909; 4 melodier (E. Josephson), 1911; Havets sommar (Rangström), 1913–15; Idyll (Runeberg), 1917; 5 dikter (B. Bergman), 1917; Ur kung Eriks visor (Fröding), 1918; Notturno (Rangström), 1918; Romantik (Jacobsen), 1921; Legender, ballader och romanser (O. Levertin), 1922–3; Den mörka blomman (Bergman), 1924; 5 ballader (Bergman), 1924; Trots allt (Bergman), 1933–6; Den utvalda (H. Gullberg), 1938; Sköld och svärd (K. Boye), 1941; Passad (H. Martinson), 1946

Principal publishers: Hansen, Lundquist

BIBLIOGRAPHY

F. H. Törnblom: 'Ture Rangström', *Ord och bild*, lxiii (1934), 551

P. Lindfors: 'Ture Rangström och August Strindberg', *Musikrevy*, x (1955), 75 [Eng. trans. in *Musikrevy International* (1954)]
A. Helmer: 'Ture Rangströms otryckta ungdomssånger', *STMf*, xlii (1960), 76
——: 'The National Romantic School', *Musikrevy*, xv (1963), no.3 extra

AXEL HELMER

Ranieri [Renieri], **Giovanni Simone** ['Mi fiolo'] (*b* Piedmont, 1590–92; *d* Naples, 1649). Italian composer and singer. In 1601 he was a boy soprano at the Annunziata, Naples. His voice broke in 1605, and Macque took charge of his instruction at the royal chapel. In 1609 he entered the chapel officially as a tenor at five (from 1611 seven) ducats a month. Dedicating his 1617 collection to Ascanio Carrafa he thanked him for making him *maestro di cappella* of the church of the Spirito Santo and its convent. In 1621 he was dismissed in the organizational reform of the royal chapel introduced by the viceroy, Cardinal Zapata. In an appeal to Philip IV of Spain for reinstatement he cited his long faithful service, his compositions and the fact that he had been *maestro di cappella* of several Neapolitan churches. He was readmitted to the chapel in 1624 and remained there for the rest of his life, except for an unauthorized visit to Lecce in May 1645. His villanellas all have two sections and generally four stanzas of three, four or six lines and are without refrains. Ranieri advised that they would sound better the faster they were sung.

WORKS

Il primo libro di villanelle e madrigali, 3–5vv, con un dialogo e 3 arie . . . 1–2vv (Naples, 1610)
Il secondo libro delle villanelle, 3–4vv, con una villanella spagnola a 5 . . . et alcune arie, 1v (Naples, 1617)

BIBLIOGRAPHY

F. Strazzullo: 'Inediti per la storia della musica a Napoli', *Il Fuidoro*, ii (1955), 107
U. Prota-Giurleo: 'Aggiunte ai "Documenti per la storia dell'arte a Napoli"', *Il Fuidoro*, ii (1955), 273

KEITH A. LARSON

Ranish, John Frederick (*b* 1692–3; *d* Cambridge, 13 March 1777). English flautist and composer, probably of east European origin (to judge by his name). The subscription list to his first set of sonatas for flute and continuo (London, *c*1735) contains 71 names, including the Musical Society at Cambridge and about 30 names associated with Cambridge colleges, suggesting that by that date he had lived long enough in the city to have achieved considerable standing as a musician. His obituary (*Cambridge Chronicle and Journal*, 15 March 1777, in a column headed 14 March) says: 'Yesterday died aged 84, Mr Ranish, many years an eminent teacher and performer on the German flute in this town. He always supported the character of a gentleman, and was respected by all that knew him'. For illustration *see* HELLENDAAL, PIETER.

His known works comprise two sets of flute sonatas: op.1 (eight works) was dedicated to Jacob Astley; op.2 (12 works) was published *c*1740. Ranish's sonatas are excellently written for the instrument, not difficult but effective, and although they do not possess much individuality they maintain a level of musical substance and do not resort to virtuoso padding. The layout of movements is fairly consistent throughout, generally: 1. slow (Adagio, Andante, etc); 2. Allegro; 3. Giga or Minuet (sometimes both are included). In op.1 several sonatas have a slow movement between 2 and 3. The flute writing in the second set is rather more virtuoso, many pieces including short ad lib cadenzas for the soloist.

RICHARD PLATT

Ranisius [Ranisien], **Sigismund** (*b* early 17th century; *d* after 1653). German amateur composer, organist and lawyer. In his publication of 1652 he stated that he received his first musical instruction from Heinrich Steuccius in the early 1630s (presumably in Naumburg, where Steuccius was living at the time). He was organist at the parish church at Pirna from 1639 to 1645. In his 1652 collection he described himself as a musical dilettante; and indeed from 1648 to 1653 he worked as a lawyer at Cottbus. The 1652 collection contains 16 sacred concertos for one to five voices and continuo, and some include obbligato parts for strings too. The final piece is an arrangement of Rovetta's *Anima Christi*, with a German text, to which he added three instrumental parts to the four vocal parts of the original, and composed an introductory sinfonia. Connections with Italian music or musicians are also suggested by the presence of Ranisius's motet *Veni, Sancte Spiritus* in an MS at *D-Bds* which consists mainly of motets by Monteverdi, Alessandro Grandi (i), Rovetta and other Italians. In this piece Ranisius cleverly exploited the contrasting timbres of the three voices, two violins, two flutes and continuo; it also includes some effective contrapuntal writing and shows a good sense of form. In his 1652 book Ranisius promised seven further publications: they were to include another set of sacred concertos and compositions for lute, organ and harpsichord but apparently none of them materialized.

WORKS

Zu dem allerheiligsten Lobe und Ehren Gottes . . . Sprüche, Lieder und Psalmen, 1–5vv, insts, bc (Dresden, 1652); 1 piece, 4vv, ed. in Ameln and Mahrenholz, 217
Veni, Sancte Spiritus, 3vv, 4 insts, in 1649[6]; also in *D-Bds*
Sacred song, S, bc, in Geistliche Zion (Guben, 1674)

BIBLIOGRAPHY

GerberNL
W. Nagel: 'Die Kantoreigeschichte zu Pirna', *MMg*, xxviii (1896), 148
A. Werner: *Städtliche und fürstliche Musikpflege in Weissenfels* (Leipzig, 1911)
M. Gondolatsch: 'Das Convivium musicum (1570–1602) und das Collegium musicum (um 1649) in Görlitz', *ZMw*, iii (1920–21), 604
K. Ameln and C. Mahrenholz, eds.: *Handbuch der deutschen evangelischen Kirchenmusik*, ii (Göttingen, 1935), 386

A. LINDSEY KIRWAN

Rank. In modern organ terminology, a complete set or row of pipes, usually of the same type, controlled by one stop-knob. Many kinds of stop have more than one rank, notably the compound or MIXTURE STOP; but so have some non-compound stops, such as the several undulating Piffaro stops of the 18th and 19th centuries, or the Principal/Diapason stops frequently doubled in the treble during the 15th–17th centuries. In English sources, 'ranks' was a term usually applied to the rows of pipes in a compound stop such as Sesquialtera or Cornet (Talbot's MS, *c*1695; Hopkins's *The Organ*, 1855); 'stoppes or setts of pipes' (York Minster, 1632) and similar phrases were more usual for 'ranks' in a general sense.

See also ORGAN STOP.

PETER WILLIAMS

Rankett (Ger.). (1) RACKET.
(2) An ORGAN STOP.

Ránki, Dezső (*b* Budapest, 8 Sept 1951). Hungarian pianist. He began piano lessons when he was eight, later studying with Klára Máthé at the Bartók Conservatory (1964–9) and with Pál Kadosa and Ferenc Rados at the Academy of Music (1969–73). In 1969 he won the Schumann International Competition, Zwickau, which led to appearances in Europe, the USA and Japan. His playing is notable for its lyricism, never sentimentalized but always noble, rhythmically vital and stylistically secure; his favoured repertory includes Mozart, Beethoven, the 19th-century Romantics and Bartók (he contributed substantially to the complete Hungarian recording of Bartók's works). He often plays in duet with Zoltán Kocsis, and they are widely considered to be the most gifted Hungarian pianists of their generation. Ránki was awarded the Liszt Prize in 1973.

PÉTER P. VÁRNAI

Ránki, György (*b* Budapest, 30 Nov 1907). Hungarian composer. He studied composition with Kodály at the Budapest Academy of Music (1926–30) and was later concerned with folk music, working with Lajtha at the Museum of Ethnography in Budapest, and with composing for the theatre and cinema. For several years he was in London and Paris (at the Musée de l'Homme), studying oriental folk musics. He directed the music section of Hungarian radio in 1947–8, after which he gave his attention to composition.

Ránki's gift for the grotesque and unusual, the colourful and humorous, may be traced in part perhaps to his studies of eastern music. His greatest successes have been in the theatre, above all with the opera *Pomádé király uj ruhája* ('King Pomádé's new clothes', based on the Andersen story), which draws most of its material from Hungarian folk music. Oriental influences are particularly evident in *Pentaerophonia* for wind quintet, which imitates gamelan effects. In some works he has made use of the Fibonacci series, following (presumably) Bartók; an example is the fantasy *1514* for piano and orchestra, which was based on woodcuts by Derkovits.

WORKS
(*selective list*)

STAGE
Operas, etc: A csendháborító [The rioter] (musical comedy), 1950, rev. 1959; Pomádé király uj ruhája [King Pomádé's new clothes] (opera), 1953, 2 orch suites, 1954; Hölgyválasz [Spoon dance] (operetta), 1961; Egy szerelem három éjszakája [Three nights of love] (tragedy with music), 1961; Az ember tragédiája [The tragedy of man] (opera), 1970
Ballets: Hóemberek [Snowmen], 1939; Cirkusz (sym. dance-drama), 1965

CHORAL ORCHESTRAL
A város peremén [At the outskirts of the city], cantata, 1947; A szabadság éneke [Freedom song], cantata, 1950; Ütközet békében [Battle in peace], cantata, 1951; Dal a népek egyetértéséről [Song on the concord of the peoples], cantata, 1952; A walesi bárdok [The bards of Wales], cantata, 1957; Sóhajtás békesség után [Yearning for peace], cantata, 1959; Békedal [Peace song], cantata, 1960; 1944, oratorio, 1967; Lament in memoriam Zoltán Kodály, 1971; Cantus urbis, oratorio, 1972

INSTRUMENTAL
Orch: Kardtánc [Sword dance], 1949; Hungarian Dances from the 16th Century, 1950; Don Quijote and Dulcinea, ob, small orch, 1960; 1514, pf, orch, 1962; Aurora tempestuosa, 1967; Largo, vn, orch, 1974
Chamber: Aristophanes, vn, pf, 1947; Serenata all'antiqua, vn, pf, 1956; Pentaerophonia, wind qnt, 1958; 1514, arr. 2 pf, perc, 1962
Pf: 2 sonatas, 1931, 1947; Scherzo, 1961; Pas de deux, Circus Gallop, 1966

Principal publisher: Editio Musica

F. ANDRÁS WILHEIM

Rankl, Karl (*b* Gaaden, nr. Vienna, 1 Oct 1898; *d* Salzburg, 6 Sept 1968). British conductor and composer of Austrian birth. He was the 14th child of an Austrian peasant and studied music in Vienna as a private pupil of Schoenberg and later of Webern. He was for all this modern influence a musician in the Kapellmeister tradition, who combined composition with the direction of opera. He was conductor at Liberec (1925), Königsberg (1927) and the Kroll Opera in Berlin (1928–31), where he was associated with Otto Klemperer's advocacy of modern music. After a spell at Graz, he was appointed in 1937 director of the German Theatre in Prague, where in 1938 he conducted the first performance of Krenek's *Karl V*. At the outbreak of war he took refuge in England and became a British citizen.

His experience made him the right man to organize, as musical director, the new establishment of opera at Covent Garden set up in 1946. He recruited a company of British singers and persuaded international singers including Schwarzkopf, Welitsch and Silveri to join it and perform a wide repertory of German, Italian, Russian and English opera, most of it in the vernacular in accordance with the policy first adopted for the reopened London opera house. By 1951 he had made it a going concern in what promised to be a stronger operatic tradition than London had had for decades, but had reached, notably in his 1950 performances of the *Ring*, the limits of his ability as a conductor – he was considered difficult with singers, orchestras and producers. He resigned and in the following year became conductor of the Scottish Orchestra, with which he remained for five years. In 1958 he accepted the post of director of the proposed Sydney Opera, but as the opera house was not built in time he never had the chance to take up the appointment.

His opera *Deirdre of the Sorrows* (based on J. M. Synge's play) won one of the prizes offered by the Arts Council for the Festival of Britain in 1951, but was not produced. He continued to compose symphonies, eight in all, which however, like his string quartet (first performed at Graz in 1936), remain unpublished.

BIBLIOGRAPHY
D. Webster: 'Karl Rankl', *Opera*, xix (1968), 879

FRANK HOWES

Rans [Ranst], van [de] [Vanrans, Vanrrans]. The name of a number of Flemish musicians, active in Mechelen and Brussels in the 16th and 17th centuries. It is assumed that they were related.

Philips [Philippe] van Rans (i) (*b c*1541; *d* 17 Oct 1628) was a town musician at Mechelen from 1559 to 1572; about 1573 he became a bassoon player at the Brussels court. He was described as 'premier maistre joueur de fagot', which suggests that he may have been one of the first bassoon players in the south Netherlands. At the beginning of 1605 he was in receipt of a pension; references to a musician of that name in and after that year must therefore be to Philips van Rans (ii), who was active until at least 1628.

Aert van Rans, an intrumentalist, was a town player at Mechelen from 1570 to 1573.

Nicolas (de) Rans (i) (*b* before 1548) composed music for the lute. Dances by him are in *RISM* 1568²³, 1573²⁴ and *EIRE-Dm* Z.3.2.13 (see Ward); one piece has been edited by Bacher.

Philips [Philippe] van Rans (ii) (*d* after 1628), Nicolas van Rans (ii) and Gaspar [Jaspar] van Rans (*d*

23 Dec 1641) were instrumentalists and regularly listed as 'ministril' in the accounts of the Brussels court chapel, 1605–18. They received payment for extra services in 1605 (including playing at the dance festivities in honour of the English ambassadors) and in 1611, at the official mourning at Brussels for Queen Margaret, wife of Philip III of Spain.

Aureliano van Rans was a singer attached to the Brussels court from 1641 to 1673.

Nicolas van Rans (iii) (b before 1640; d April 1965) was in the service of the Brussels court by 1655, probably as a singer. In 1684 he was assistant *kapelmeester* and in 1686 *kapelmeester*. A *Missa pro defunctis* ascribed to 'Van Ranst' (in *B-Bc*) is probably by him.

BIBLIOGRAPHY

E. vander Straeten: *La musique aux Pays-Bas avant le XIXe siècle* (Brussels, 1867–88/R1969)

——: *Jacques de Saint-Luc, luthiste athois du XVIIe siècle* (Paris, 1887), 15

R. van Aerde: *Ménestrels communaux et instrumentistes divers, établis ou de passage à Malines, de 1311 à 1790* (Mechelen, 1911)

C. van den Borren: 'Le fonds de musique ancienne de la Collégiale SS. Michel et Gudule, à Bruxelles', *Annuaire du Conservatoire royal de musique de Bruxelles 1928–29*, 132

J. Bacher, ed.: *Alte Tänze für Laute* (Kassel, 1939), no.4

S. Clercx: 'Le dix-septième et le dix-huitième siècle', *La musique en Belgique du moyen âge à nos jours*, ed. E. Closson and C. van den Borren (Brussels, 1950), 152, 183

J. M. Ward: 'The Fourth Dublin Lute Book', *LSJ*, xi (1969), 30

G. Spiessens: 'Ranst', *National biographischen woordenboek*, iv (Brussels, 1970)

GODELIEVE SPIESSENS

Rant. A lively, short country dance of the jig variety in binary form and either simple or compound duple rhythm, emanating from the Scottish lowlands and northern England. In contemporary English and Scottish folkdance it is a variety of the polka step in an anacrusic 6/8 or 2/4 rhythm, hopped or skipped. Examples may be seen in *The Scottish Country Dance Book* (vols. vii, x, xii) and in Douglas Kennedy's *English Country Dances of Today* (1948).

Among the earliest printed examples of the rant are four in the 1657 and 1665 editions of John Playford's *The Dancing Master*, which included a supplement of 'Select New Tunes & Jiggs for the Treble Violin'. Two 'new' rants by Thomas Gibbes are printed in Playford's *Courtly Masquing-Ayres* (1662) and others in his subsequent instrumental publications. Matthew Locke included a rant in his *Melothesia* (1673) and dance-tunes entitled 'rant' continued to appear throughout the 18th and 19th centuries. Roger North (*Memoires of Musick*, 1728) said that John Jenkins composed many rants (three in *GB-Lbm* Add.10445), but the assertions made by Rimbault and, hence, by Pulver and others that Jenkins wrote the 'Mitter Rant', 'Peterborough Rant' and 'Fleece Tavern Rant' are unsubstantiated (see J. Wilson: *Roger North on Music*, 1959, p.345, footnote 97). Several rants are extant in 17th- and 18th-century manuscripts of Scottish provenance (e.g. *GB-Lbm* Add.29371). The suggestion that the word 'rant' is derived from 'courant' is erroneous; the Oxford English Dictionary, and Scottish and English dialect dictionaries, all present definitions and usage involving vigorous dancing and singing. The character of the rant is indicated in the oft-quoted passage from Mrs Centlivre's comedy *The Platonick Lady* (1707), when, having mistaken for a request for a rant the dancing-master's request for a courant, Mrs Dowdy says 'Hy, hy, do you call this dancing?

ads heartlikins, in my thoughts 'tis plain walking: I'll shew you one of our country dances; play me a jig'.

MURRAY LEFKOWITZ

Ranta, Sulho (*b* Peräseinäjoki, 15 Aug 1901; *d* Helsinki, 5 May 1960). Finnish composer and teacher. He took the MA at Helsinki University in 1925 and studied composition in Helsinki (with Melartin) in 1921–4, in Berlin, Vienna (with Willner) and Italy in 1926, and in Berlin and Paris in 1930. Back in Finland he was active as a theatre conductor, teacher and music critic, also writing textbooks on the theory and history of music. From 1936 to 1956 he was vice-rector of the Sibelius Academy, Helsinki. As a composer he was one of the first to introduce into Finland such trends as impressionism, expressionism and the use of exotic materials (in his own work he drew on the music of China, Japan and various Finnish regions). But his composing was hindered by his diverse other activities and by the undeveloped state of Finnish culture in the 1930s and 1940s, his most creative period. His best work is in the small-scale songs and chamber pieces.

WORKS
(*selective list*)

Orch: Conc. for Orch, 1928; Sinfonia programmatica, 1930; Sym. no.1 'Piccola', 1932; Kainuun kuvia [Kainuu pictures], 1933; Sym. no.2, a, 1936; Pieni karjalainen sarja [Little Karelian suite], 1940; Sym. no.3 'Dell'arte', 1947; Sym. no.4 (Oratorio volgare), 1951

Music for the theatre and cinema, songs, chamber works

Principal publishers: Fazer, Westerlund

ERKKI SALMENHAARA

Ranz des vaches (Fr.). A Swiss mountain melody sung or played on an alphorn by herdsmen in the Alps to summon their cows. The term is interchangeable with the German *Kuhreigen* or *Kuhreihen*. About 50 melodies survive, characterized by their improvisatory nature and reiterated, short phrases with changes of tempo and accent. Theodor Zwinger quoted an example in his chapter 'De Pothopatridalgia' on the effects of nostalgia (*Fasciculus dissertationum medicarum*, Basle, 1710); another was reproduced in J.-J. Rousseau's *Dictionnaire de musique* (Paris, 1768; Eng. trans., 1771), and he commented that the *ranz des vaches* 'was so generally beloved among the Swiss [mercenaries], that it was forbidden to be play'd in their troops under pain of death, because it made them burst into tears, desert or die, whoever heard it; so great a desire did it excite in them of returning to their country'. Surviving texts for the melodies are rare; Viotti is reported to have heard one performed in Switzerland by a woman singing in unison with an alphorn (see the texted Gruyère *ranz* in King). An early printed example of the famous Appenzell *ranz* melody occurs in Rhau's *Bicinia gallica, latina, germanica . . . tomus primus* (*RISM* 1545[6]), where it begins with the words 'Lobet, o lobet' (from *loba*: 'cow'; hence *Lobetanz*); Meyerbeer used the same melody in his opera *Dinorah* (1859) and it also appears in the overtures to Grétry's and Rossini's operas *Guillaume Tell* (1791 and 1829). The lilting shepherd's piping that opens the last movement of Beethoven's Pastoral Symphony (1807–8) is directly modelled on the Rigi *ranz*; other, more stylized imitations of the *ranz des vaches* occur in the 'Scène aux champs' in Berlioz's *Symphonie fantastique* (1830), Schumann's *Manfred* (1848–9), Liszt's *Album d'un voyageur* (1835–6) and at the beginning of the third act of Wagner's *Tristan und Isolde* (1865).

See also PASTORALE.

BIBLIOGRAPHY

A. H. King: 'Mountains, Music and Musicians', *MQ*, xxxi (1945), 395

Raoul de Beauvais (*fl* ?mid-13th century). French trouvère poet and composer, from the region north and east of Paris. His songs appear only in sources containing the main trouvère repertory, and they are usually grouped with the works of poets active about the mid-13th century. Three of the six poems attributed to him are also attributed to Jehann Erart, but the confusion in this case seems to stem from the sources, and it is likely that all six are the work of Raoul. Although he appears to have composed few songs, and even these were not widely known, they show a refreshing variety of both poetic and musical form. Two of the six are *pastorelles*, and all employ some kind of refrain. *Deles un pre verdoiant* (ex.1) exhibits characteristically imaginative

Ex.1

1. De - les un pres ver - doi-ant. 3. Que fe – rai dist
2. Trou-vai deux da – mes se-ant. 5. Qui pour mon a -

l'une a l'au-tre de mon ort vi-lain pri-ant.
- mi le coin-te me va to - te iour ba-tant.

4. Et vous sa – vez vrai - e – ment jo - lis cuers doit

bien a - mer par a - mis mi - gno - te - ment.

handling of form. While the verse proceeds in paired lines with open cadences (on *b* or *d'*) in every line but the last (line six), the refrain is three lines long and employs closed cadences (on *c'* or *e'*) exclusively. This contrast is thrown into relief by the melodic similarity of lines seven and nine to lines one and two, thus producing both a melodic and tonal symmetry.

WORKS

Au dieu d'amors ai requis un don, R.1862
Quant la sesons renouvelle, R.613 (pastorele)
Remembrance de bone amour, R.1943

WORKS OF UNCERTAIN AUTHORSHIP

Deles un pre verdoiant, R.368
El mois de mai par un matin, R.1375 (pastorele)
Puis que d'Amours m'estuet chanter, R.806

For general bibliography *see* TROUBADOURS, TROUVÈRES.

ROBERT FALCK

Raoul de Ferrières (*fl* 1200–10). French trouvère. A member of the Norman nobility from the département of Eure, he is named in a donation of 1209 to the Abbey of Noé; nothing further is known of his life. Among the 11 chansons ascribed to him, the most important is *Quant li rossignols* – probably the song of that name mentioned by Johannes de Grocheo as a cantus coronatus. (There is a conflicting ascription to the Chastelain de Couci.) It is in bar form, as are all the melodies except two readings of *Si sui du tout a fine Amour*, which may be late modifications. It begins at the upper octave and flows downwards, establishing a firm centre on *d* before concluding. The majority of melodies

attributable to Raoul are in the D modes, while three are in the authentic G mode. There is a similar lack of variety in the poetic construction; with only one exception the first eight lines of all strophes rhyme *ABABBAAB*. Most are octosyllabic throughout, though *Quant ivers* and *Quant li rossignols* are heptasyllabic, and the contested *Quant il ne pert* has alternate eight- and seven-syllable lines. No melodies survive in mensural notation, and hints of regular rhythmic organization are at most sporadic.

WORKS

Encore m'estuet il chanter, R.818
Par force chant conme esbahis, R.1535
Quant ivers a tel poissance, R.243
Quant je voi les vergiers florir, R.1412
Se j'ai chanté, ce poise moi, R.1670
Si sui du tout a fine Amour, R.1956
Une haute amour qui esprent, R.673

DOUBTFUL WORKS

J'ai oublié paine et travaus, R.389
Quant li rossignols jolis, R.1559 [model for: Anon., 'L'autrier m'iere
rendormis', R.1609], ed. in Gennrich (1930), facs. in Gennrich
(*MGG*)
Quant il ne pert fueille ne flours, R.2036
On ne peut pas a deus seigneurs servir, R.1460

BIBLIOGRAPHY

F. Gennrich: 'Lateinische Kontrafakta altfranzösischer Lieder',
Zeitschrift für romanische Philologie, l (1930), 240
——: 'Chastelain de Couci', *MGG*
R. Dragonetti: *La technique poétique des trouvères dans la chanson
courtoise* (Bruges, 1960)

For further bibliography *see* TROUBADOURS, TROUVÈRES.

THEODORE KARP

Raoul de Soissons (*b* ?1210–15; *d* 1270, or shortly thereafter). French trouvère. The second son of Count Raoul le Bon of Soissons, he became Sire de Coeuvres in 1232. He took part in three crusades, the first led by Thibaut IV in 1239. During his ensuing stay in Cyprus, Raoul married Queen Alix, thus becoming a claimant to the Kingdom of Jerusalem. He returned to France after 1243, but took up the crusade led by St Louis (1248–52). In 1270, he embarked on the Second Crusade led by the French king. Since nothing further is known of him, it is assumed that he died on that venture. Raoul exchanged a jeu-parti (R.1393) with Thibaut IV, and dedicated *Rois de Navare* to him. In turn, Raoul's name appears in three envois by Thibaut (R.741, 1811 and 2095). He was the judge of a jeu-parti between Henri III, Duke of Brabant, and Gillebert de Berneville (R.491). In addition to R.1393 (of possible joint authorship), seven chansons are attributed to Raoul in various manuscripts, all but *E, cuens d'Anjou* being contested by other attributions, including four works ascribed also to THIERRI DE SOISSONS, who may be identifiable with Raoul. The ascriptions of R.130 and 1885 to Raoul are undoubtedly erroneous. *Chançon m'estuet* and *Rois de Navare* each served as model for two others; *Quant voi la glaie* was particularly appreciated and provided the model for five other works. Three of Raoul's works comprise isometric, decasyllabic strophes, while the remainder are heterometric, using heptasyllabic lines mingled with shorter ones. All melodies are in bar form: *Quant voi la glaie* is unusual for the repetition (*DEFG DEFG*) constituting the cauda. No melodies survive in mensural notation, and there is no clear evidence of symmetrical rhythmic organization.

WORKS

Editions: *Grundriss einer Formenlehre des mittelalterlichen Liedes*, ed.
F. Gennrich (Halle, 1932) [F]

Troubadours, Trouvères, Minne- und Meistergesang, ed. F. Gennrich, ii (1951; Eng. trans., 1960) [G]

(R) etc   MS (using Schwan sigla – *see* SOURCES, MS) in which a late setting of a poem occurs

Chançon m'estuet et fere et comencier, R.1267 [model for: Anon., 'Par mainte fois m'ont mesdistant grevé', R.462; Anon., 'Chanter m'estuet de cele sans targier', R.1315] (R)

E, cuens d'Anjou, on dit par felonie, R.1154

Quant je voi et fueille et flour, R.1978 (V)

Quant voi la glaie meüre, R.2107 [model for: Anon., 'Deus, je n'os nomer amie', R.1104; Anon., 'Mere, douce creature', R.2091 (without music); ? Phelipe de Remi, 'Ausi com l'eschaufeüre', R.2096; Anon., 'Vierge des cieus, clere et pure', R.2112; Adam de la Bassée, 'O constantie dignitas'], F 212, G 36

Rois de Navare et sire de Vertu, R.2063 [model for: Thibaut IV, 'Bon rois Thibaut, sire, conseilliez moi', R.1666; Oede de la Couroierie, 'Ma derreniere veul fere en chantant', R.321], Van der Werf, 128

WORK OF POSSIBLE JOINT AUTHORSHIP

Sir, loez moi a loisir, R.1423a = 1393 (with Thibaut IV)

BIBLIOGRAPHY

E. Winkler: *Die Lieder Raouls von Soissons* (Halle, 1914)

H. Van der Werf: *The Chansons of the Troubadours and Trouvères* (Utrecht, 1972)

For further bibliography *see* TROUBADOURS, TROUVÈRES.

THEODORE KARP

Raoux. French family of brass instrument makers. They were noted especially for their hand horns (which later developed into the modern French valve horn): they raised them to a standard of design and workmanship never surpassed and rarely equalled in the history of the horn. The family business probably flourished from the late 17th century onwards (a trumpet 'Fait par Raoux seul ordinaire du Roy près de lodiance du ministre à Paris, 1695' is mentioned by Chouquet, no.585), but the family's reputation rests on three members.

Joseph Raoux (*b* c1725; *d* Paris, before 1800) was established as a maker before 1759, for in that and the following year his name appears as a teacher of the horn in *Le tableau de Paris* (together with that of Carlin, another well-known maker of hunting horns). In 1776 Raoux's son Lucien-Joseph Raoux (*b* Paris, 1753; *d* Paris, c1826) left independent premises in rue Mercier to join his father, who moved shop from rue du Petit Lion (now rue Tiquetonne) to rue Froidmanteau (Place du Louvre), the address from which the name of Raoux achieved international renown. It is unlikely that Joseph continued to take an active part in the business later than 1794.

In the spring of 1781, Lucien-Joseph Raoux brought out an improved version of the Hampl-Werner *Inventionshorn* with fixed mouthpipe and centrally inserted crooks in the keys of D, E♭, E, F and G (the most usual keys for solo playing). This instrument was accordingly known as the *cor-solo* and was adopted by its designer Thürrschmidt and many leading virtuosos including LeBrun, Palsa, Punto and Puzzi. A pair of silver *cors-solo* played by Thürrschmidt and Palsa attracted considerable attention at a London Salomon concert in 1786; the next year four in brass were ordered by the court at Trier. In 1794 the firm moved to 8 rue Serpente, where it remained until sold in 1857. In 1798 Lucien-Joseph made the *cor-solo* presented to Dauprat by the Conservatoire. It is now in the museum there and is of brass with silver mounts. Many of Lucien-Joseph's instruments have survived, both *cors-solo* and terminally crooked *cors-d'orchestre*; all show the highest order of workmanship. From 1803 until 1826 they were often dated and signed 'RAOUX A PARIS' bracketed by fleurs-de-lys. Raoux's *poinçon* is a

monogram of the script letters LJR on a small oval shield.

The family business was taken over by Lucien-Joseph's son, Marcel-Auguste Raoux (*b* Paris, 1795; *d* Paris, 3 June 1871), who was both performer and maker. He entered the band of the imperial guard in 1813, and was reputed to have studied with Dauprat. After military service he joined his father in the workshop. In 1822 he was appointed second horn in the Théâtre-Italien and later first horn (a post which he held until his retirement in 1856). Gounod dedicated his *Six mélodies* for horn and piano (1840) to him. In 1839 Raoux won an Exhibition silver medal for a *cor d'orchestre* and in 1844 and 1849 gold medals (in 1849 he became the first brass instrument maker to be awarded the title of Chevalier de la Légion d'honneur). After becoming involved, like many other Parisian instrument makers, in litigation with Adolphe Sax, his disillusionment was so great that he sold out to J. C. Labbaye in 1857.

If Marcel-Auguste Raoux did not surpass his father as a maker, he fully maintained the Raoux tradition of superlative workmanship, and his hand horns, modernized by valves, were in great demand in France and England until supplanted by the coarser but more powerful German instrument. A fine *cor-solo* by him, formerly owned by Puzzi, is now in the Victoria and Albert Museum.

BIBLIOGRAPHY

G. Chouquet: *Le Musée du Conservatoire national de musique: catalogue raisonné des instruments de cette collection* (Paris, 1875)

R. Morley-Pegge: *The French Horn* (London, 1960, 2/1973)

H. Fitzpatrick: *The Horn and Horn Playing* (London, 1970)

HORACE FITZPATRICK

Rapeguero. Stravinsky's term for the GÜIRO in his score of *The Rite of Spring*.

Raphael, Günter (Albert Rudolf) (*b* Berlin, 30 April 1903; *d* Herford, Germany, 19 Oct 1960). German composer. His father was director of music at St Matthäi in Berlin. After initial music studies with Arnold Abel, Raphael attended the Hochschule für Musik in Berlin from 1922 to 1925. There he studied composition with Robert Kahn, organ with Walter Fischer and piano with Max Trapp. From 1926 he taught theory and composition at the State Conservatory and at the Kirchenmusikalisches Institut, Leipzig. He was particularly encouraged in his compositional efforts by Karl Straube, to whom he dedicated his Requiem (1927–8). Raphael's works were banned by the Nazi regime, and in 1934 he resigned his position at Leipzig and moved to Meiningen, and then to Laubach, Oberhessen, in 1945. He continued to compose and teach privately; in 1948 he was awarded the Liszt Prize by the City of Dresden. His return to academic life was in 1949, when he accepted a position in theory and composition at the Conservatory in Duisburg, remaining there until 1953. From 1956 to 1958 he taught at the Mainz Conservatory, and he also held a professorship at the Cologne Hochschule für Musik from 1957 until his death. In his later years Raphael worked on the new editions of Bach, Handel and Reger, and made numerous piano reductions for vocal scores of these composers' works, as well as those of Mozart and Gluck.

Opera was the only major genre to which Raphael did

not turn his attention as a composer. He wrote much choral and organ music for liturgical use, while his more adventurous work is to be found in the chamber and orchestral pieces. Raphael's output may be divided into three periods. Until 1934 he wrote in a late Romantic style reminiscent of Brahms and, particularly as a result of the large amount of chromaticism, Reger. The Requiem op.20 is the masterpiece from this period; its five movements revolve around the keys of G major/minor and B major/minor and their dominants, with some of the movements exhibiting progressive tonality. The second period – that of the exile in Meiningen and Laubach – was a time of transition. Diatonicism, modality, rhythmic ostinatos and sparser textures began to appear in Raphael's music, and he reached further into the past for his models: to Bach (Solo Sonatas op.46) and Schütz (*Geistliche Chormusik*, 1938). Raphael's last 15 years may be considered a third period, in which the new style crystallized and expanded to include some use of 12-note technique. The series is usually found as an ostinato; for example, in *Gesang der Erzengel* op.79, the 12 notes are paired in an ostinato, while in the Viola Sonata op.80 the series serves as a theme in the first and third movements.

WORKS
(*selective list*)

ORCHESTRAL

5 syms.: no.1, a, op.16, 1926; no.2, b, op.34, 1932; no.3, F, op.60, 1942; no.4, C, op.62, 1942–7; no.5, B♭, op.75, 1953
Theme, Variations and Rondo, op.19 (1927); Vn Conc. no.1, c, op.21, 1929; Variations on a Scottish Folktune, E♭, op.23 (1930); Chamber Conc., d, op.24, vc, chamber orch, *c*1930; Divertimento, op.33, 1932; Smetana Suite from dances by Smetana, op.40 (1938); Org Conc., d, op.57, 1936; Sinfonietta, 1938
Symphonische Fantasie, op.59, vn, str, 1940; Jabonah, op.66, ballet suite, 1948, reds. 2 pf and vn, pf; Reger Suite, 1948; Sinfonia breve, op.67, 1949; Concertino, op.71, a sax, chamber orch, 1951; Die vier Jahreszeiten, op.77, str, 1953; Concertino, op.82, fl, chamber orch, 1956; Zoologica, op.83, 1958; Vn Conc. no.2, op.87, 1960

VOCAL

5 Marienlieder, op.15, female chorus 3vv, 1925; Cantata (after Goethe), 2 solo vv, chorus, tpt, hpd, str (*c*1926); Requiem, op.20, 4 solo vv, chorus 8vv, orch, org, 1927–8; Te Deum, D, op.26, S, A, B, chorus 8vv, orch, org, 1930; Wiegenlied der Maria, chorus 4vv, 2 vn, vc, 1930; Psalm cvi, op.29, chorus 12vv, 1931; 2 Motets, op.30, chorus, 1931; 3 Sacred Songs, op.31, A, pf/org (1932); Die Versuchung Jesu, op.35, chorus, 1934; 3 Motets, op.39, chorus, 1935; 3 Sacred Songs, 1v, pf, 1938; Geistliche Chormusik, 12 motets, 1938; Eine deutsche Totenmesse, 1940
Das Kirchenjahr, motets, 1941; 6 Chorale Motets, op.55, chorus, fl, 1945; Psalm cxxvi, op.56, chorus, 1945; Vater unser, op.58, chorus, orch, org, 1945; 4 Motets, op.63, chorus, 1946; Das Glaubensbekenntnis, op.64, chorus 8vv, 1948; Der Minne Lied, chorus, 1949; 20 Advents- und Weihnachtsliedsätze, 1949; Palmström Sonate, op.69, T, cl, vn, pf, perc, 1950; 8 Gedichte, op.72 (Hesse), S/T, orch, *c*1950; Sequenz Dies irae, op.73, chorus 8vv, 1951; 12 Spruchmotette, 1951; Busskantate, chorus, orch, 1952
6 Galgenlieder, op.76 (Morgenstern), 1v, pf, 1953; 10 Männerchöre, op.78, 1954; Gesang der Erzengel, op.79 (Goethe), S, A, Bar, pf/16 wind, 1954; Judica Kantate, chorus, orch, 1955; Von der grossen Weisheit, op.81 (after Laotse), solo vv, chorus, orch, 1955–6; 10 Canons (Goethe), chorus 10vv, 1956; 4 Motets, 1957–8; Herr Gott, dich loben alle wir, op.84, A, Bar, chorus, ob, va, vc, org (1959); Sechsmal Ringelnatz im Drei-Stimmen-Satz, op.85, chorus, n.d.; My dark hands, op.86 (L. Hughes), Bar, pf, drum, db, 1959; 3 kleine geistliche Konzerte, 2 solo vv, 2 rec, org, 1959; Triptychon, chorus 4vv, 1960; Gebet (H. Claudius), chorus, n.d.; 3 Choralpartiten, chorus, org, n.d.

CHAMBER

Str Qnt, f♯, op. 17 (1927); 2 cl qnts, F (Serenade), op.4, 1924, c♯, op.6, *c*1924; 4 str qts, no.1, op.5 (1926), no.2, C, op.9 (1926), no.3, A, op.28, *c*1930, no.4, F, op.54, 1945; Ww Qt, op.61, 1945
Trios: C, op.11, pf, vn, vc, 1925; G, op.44, fl, vc, pf 1938; B♭, op.48, fl, vn, va, 1940; F, op.49, 2 vn, va, 1941; op.70, cl, vc, pf, 1950
Sonatas: op.7, va, *c*1925; e, op.8, fl, pf, 1925; E, G, op.12/1, 2, vn, pf (1926); no.1, E♭, op.13, va, pf (1926); no.1, b, op.14, vc, pf, 1925; b,

op.32, ob, pf (1933); op.36, vn, org (1934); no.3, C, op.43, vn, pf (1968); 9 Solo Sonatas, op.46, vn, va, vc, fl, bn, 1940 46; 6 Duo Sonatas, op.47, 2 vn; vn, va; vn, vc; va, vc; 2 fl; cl, va, 1940–46; G, op.50, cl, vc, 1943; no.2, op.80, va, pf, 1954; sax, pf, 1957
Sonatina, op.52, vn, pf, 1944; 4 Sonatinas, op.65, fl, va, harp; ob, harp/pf/hpd; cl, pf; vn, hn, bn, 1948–9; Dialoge, 2 vols., 2 vn, 1951–7; Divertimento, op.74, a sax, vc, 1952; 3 Pieces, c♯, vc, pf, 1956; Récitatif, sax, pf, 1958; Marche, tpt, pf, 1958; Berceuse, bn, pf, 1958; Sonatina in modo lidico, ob, org, 1959

KEYBOARD

Org: 5 Chorale Preludes, op.1, 1922; 3 Pieces, op.22, 1928–30; 3 Pieces, op.27, 1930–34; 12 Chorale Preludes, op.37, 1934–5; 2 Pieces on Finnish Chorales, op.41, 1939; 7 Preludes on Finnish Chorales, op.42, *c*1939; Toccata, Chorale and Variations, op.53, 1944; Sonata, op. 68, 1949; Kleine Partita Herr Jesu Christ, 1958; Fantasie über den Choral 'Christus, der ist mein Leben' (1968)
Pf: Little Sonata, e, op.2, 1922; Improvisationen, op.3 (1926); Romantische Tanzbilder, op.10, duet (1925); Partita, g, op.18 (1927); Little Sonata no.2, F, op.25 (1930); 2 Sonatas, a, E, op.38, 1939; Toccata, op.45, 2 pf, 1937; 2 Sonatinas, op.51, 1944; 26 Advents- und Weihnachtslieder in leichten Sätzen, 1948

Principal publishers: Breitkopf & Härtel, Müller

WRITINGS

'Deutsche Musik und Weltmusik: zur Geschichte des europäischen Wechselspiels', *Musica*, vi (1952), 10
'Rudolf Mauersberger zum 29. Januar 1959', *Kirchenmusik heute: Gedanken über Aufgaben und Probleme der Musica sacra* (Berlin, 1959), 12ff

BIBLIOGRAPHY
O. Riemer: 'Prophetische Musik: zur geistlichen Chormusik Günter Raphaels', *Musica*, i (1947), 280
M. Mezger: 'Günter Raphaels Kirchenmusik', *Musik und Kirche*, xxiii (1953), 150
H. Klotz: 'Zum Tode von Günter Raphael', *Musik und Kirche*, xxx (1960), 289
F. Högner: 'Günter Raphael', *Gottesdienst und Kirchenmusik* (1960), no.6, 195
W. Stockmeier: 'Raphael, Günter', *MGG*
H. Albrecht: 'Bekenntnis zur Einheit des Glaubens: Günter Raphael', *Credo musicale: Komponistenporträts aus der Arbeit des Dresdener Kreuzchores* (Kassel, *c*1969), 135ff

WILLIAM D. GUDGER

Raphelengius, Christopher (*fl* early 17th century). Flemish printer who managed the Leiden branch of the publishing house founded by CHRISTOPHER PLANTIN.

Rapp, George. Founder of the HARMONY SOCIETY.

Rappoldi. Austrian, later German, family of musicians.

(1) **Eduard Rappoldi** (*b* Vienna, 21 Feb 1831; *d* Dresden, 16 May 1903). Violinist, conductor and composer. He played both the violin and the piano in public at the age of seven but preferred the former, which he studied with Leopold Jansa, Georg Hellmesberger sr (Vienna Conservatory, 1851–4) and Joseph Böhm; he also studied theory and composition with Sechter and Hiller. He played in the Vienna court orchestra (1854–61), and was then leader of the orchestra in Rotterdam (1861–6), in Lübeck (1866), in Stettin (1867) and at the German Theatre in Prague (1869). Joachim took him to Berlin, where he stayed from 1871 until 1877, teaching at the newly founded Hochschule für Musik and playing in Joachim's quartet. He moved to Dresden in October 1877 to become leader of the court orchestra, joint leader of the opera orchestra (with Lauterbach) and professor of violin at the conservatory; of special interest were his historical concerts there (1877–9).

Rappoldi excelled as a teacher and chamber music player. Moser wrote that he had an astonishing left-hand technique 'which would have made him one of the greatest artists of his epoch were it not for the lack of freedom in his bowing … he was one of the most musical persons I have ever met'. His popularity as a teacher was enhanced by his ability to play piano accompaniments. Only a few of his compositions were published, among them two violin sonatas, a piano sonata and some songs, including two settings of poems by Matthisson.

(2) Laura Rappoldi [née Kahrer] (*b* Mistelbach, nr. Vienna, 14 Jan 1853; *d* Dresden, 1 Aug 1925). Pianist, wife of (1) Eduard Rappoldi. At the age of 11, after only one year of musical study, she played one of her compositions for the Empress Elisabeth, who underwrote her studies at the Vienna Conservatory (1866–9), in composition with Otto Dessoff, counterpoint with Bruckner and the piano with Joseph Dachs. In 1868 she won first prize in piano and composition and made her début assisted by Joseph Hellmesberger and David Popper. She studied in Weimar with Liszt in the summers of 1870 and 1873 and, in between, in St Petersburg with Adolf Henselt, who remained a lifelong friend and correspondent. In the summer of 1874 she studied the late sonatas of Beethoven with Bülow, who later wrote a testimonial praising her playing of the Hammerklavier Sonata. In 1874 she married (1) Eduard Rappoldi, with whom she had played in Prague four years before. Extended tours earned her a reputation as one of the finest pianists in Germany. After 1886 she limited her activities to Dresden, giving frequent sonata programmes with her husband and later with her son (3) Adrian Rappoldi. She taught the piano at the Dresden Conservatory for more than 20 years.

Niemann found stylistic characteristics of her three great teachers in her playing: the grand virtuosity of Henselt, the rhythmic energy, brilliance and plasticity of Liszt and the structural clarity and objectivity of Bülow.

(3) Adrian Rappoldi (*b* Berlin, 13 Sept 1876; *d* Bamberg, 1949). Violinist, son of (1) Eduard Rappoldi and (2) Laura Rappoldi. He studied the violin with his father and composition with Felix Draeseke at the Dresden Conservatory, where he won first prize at the age of 14. In 1893 he became leader of the Bilse orchestra in Berlin; there he spent much time in the company of Joachim, who gave him the warmest of testimonials when he left (autumn 1894). After recovering from a serious hand ailment, Rappoldi was leader of the orchestras in Chemnitz, in Teplitz, at the German Theatre in Prague and in Riga. Intermittent tours took him to Germany, Norway and Russia, where he appeared with Brahms, Grieg and Rimsky-Korsakov; he may have studied with Leopold Auer in St Petersburg. In 1912 he succeeded Henri Petri as professor of the violin at the Dresden Conservatory, and from 1915 he was one of its directors. He continued to make solo appearances, but his reputation in Dresden was based primarily on his teaching ability and chamber music playing. He wrote a treatise on violin player's cramp and the origin, treatment and cure of occupational maladies of the violinist; he also co-edited a volume of orchestral studies for the violin.

BIBLIOGRAPHY
W. Niemann: *Meister des Klaviers* (Berlin, 1919)
A. Moser: *Geschichte des Violinspiels* (Berlin, 1923, rev., enlarged 2/1966–7)
L. Rappoldi: *Memorien* (Dresden, 1929)

ALBERT MELL

Rappresentativo. *See* STILE RAPPRESENTATIVO.

Rappresentazione sacra [sacra rappresentazione]. The term was used in the 15th and 16th centuries to designate a kind of religious play with music in the Italian language, cultivated chiefly in Florence. The texts, written mostly in *ottava rima*, were drawn mainly from the Bible or hagiography, but also include secular scenes and even comic elements. Among the best-known authors of the approximately 100 surviving texts were Feo Belcari, Castellano Castellani, Lorenzo de' Medici, Antonia Pulci and Bernardo Pulci. Boys in costume performed the *rappresentazioni sacre* on a stage with sets and in some cases elaborate machinery. Melodic formulae seem to have been used to intone most of the lines (Becherini, 1951), interspersed with *laudi*, frottolas, canzoni and (in the 16th century) madrigals. Most of the musical numbers in 16th-century *rappresentazioni sacre* belonged to the *intermedii*, dramatic interludes with music performed between scenes of the play for the sake of variety and to enlarge upon the events of the drama. The *rappresentazione sacra* is a significant forerunner of both opera and oratorio. Emilio de' Cavalieri apparently intended his opera *Rappresentatione di Anima, et di Corpo* (1600) as a renewal of the *rappresentazione sacra*, by then outmoded.

During the second half of the 17th century in Vienna the term *rappresentazione sacra* was often applied to the *sepolcro*.

See also MEDIEVAL DRAMA, §III, 3(iv), and ORATORIO.

BIBLIOGRAPHY
A. d'Ancona, ed.: *Sacre rappresentazioni dei secoli XIV, XV, e XVI* (Florence, 1872)
A. d'Ancona: *Le origini del teatro italiano* (Turin, 1891)
D. Alaleona: 'Su Emilio de' Cavalieri, la *Rappresentatione di Anima e di Corpo* e alcune sue composizioni inedite', *La nova musica*, iv (1905), 35, 47
V. de Bartholomaeis: *Le origini della poesia drammatica italiana* (Bologna, 1924)
A. Bonfantini: *Le sacre rappresentazioni italiane* (Milan, 1939)
V. de Bartholomaeis, ed.: *Laude drammatiche e rappresentazioni sacre* (Florence, 1943/R1967)
B. Becherini: 'La Rappresentazione di Anima e Corpo di Emilio de' Cavalieri', *RaM*, viii (1943), 1
——: 'Un canta in panca fiorentino: Antonio di Guido', *RMI*, l (1948), 241
——: 'La musica nelle sacre rappresentazioni fiorentine', *RMI*, liii (1951), 193–241

HOWARD E. SMITHER

Rapsodia (It.; Fr. *rapsodie*). RHAPSODY.

Rasa, Lina Bruna (*b* Padua, 24 Sept 1907). Italian soprano. She studied in Padua with Italiano Tabarin and Guido Palombo, and in Milan with Manlio and Gaetano Bavagnoli. Her début at Genoa (1927) as Helen of Troy (*Mefistofele*) was so great a success that Toscanini immediately engaged her for the same role at La Scala later that year. She appeared regularly in Milan from 1927 to 1936, and again in 1940, being especially successful in the *verismo* repertory and as Dolly in Wolf-Ferrari's *Sly*. Mascagni chose her to create Atte in his *Nerone* (1935), and as Santuzza for the *Cavalleria rusticana* 50th anniversary celebrations throughout Italy in 1940, the year in which she also recorded the role under the composer's direction. She sang with success in Holland, Germany and South America. After her mother's death in 1935 she began to suffer fits of depression, and after her performances as Santuzza in 1940 had to leave the opera stage. She attempted a come-back in 1948, with unhappy results.

HAROLD ROSENTHAL

Rasar [Raser, Rasor], William (*b c*?1488). English composer. He was probably the William Rasor who was admitted as chorister to St George's Chapel, Windsor, in 1499. Between 1493 and 1496 there are two references to choristers named Rasar at King's College, Cambridge; of these the first, who left in August 1495, is referred to as 'John Rasar', and no christian name is given for the second (November 1495 to March 1496). William Raser, on the other hand, was admitted clerk of the chapel at King's College, Cambridge, on 1 March 1510 and left between Michaelmas 1514 and Michaelmas 1515. The only extant composition by him is the five-part *Missa 'Christe Jesu'* (ed. in EECM, xvi, 1976) in the Forrest-Heyther Partbooks (*GB-Ob* Mus.Sch.E 376–81) and in the Peterhouse Partbooks (*Cu* Peterhouse 471–4; tenor lacking). The source of the title of this mass is unknown; no plainsong cantus firmus can be identified, and it is perhaps derived from some lost motet. The mass is unusual among English masses of this period in providing a complete setting of the text of the Gloria and Credo and also for being one of the earliest instances in England of a mass composed in duple metre throughout.

BIBLIOGRAPHY
J. Bergsagel: Introduction to *Early Tudor Masses II*, EECM, xvi (1976)
JOHN BERGSAGEL

Rascarini [Lascarini], Francesco Maria (*b* Reggio Emilia; *d* Turin, July 1706). Italian singer and composer. He was a well-known contralto and except for the years 1691–7 was from 1662 until his death a chamber musician in the service of the Duke of Savoy at Turin. He had already sung at Turin in 1660 on the occasion of the marriage of Ranuccio II, Duke of Parma. His popularity as an opera singer took him to Bologna in 1658 (P. A. Ziani: *Le fortune di Rodope e di Damira*), Venice in 1659 (Cavalli: *Antioco*) and 1666 (Cesti: *Tito* and *Orontea*), Milan in 1670 (Busca, P. S. Agostini and P. A. Ziani: *Ippolita reina delle amazzoni*) and Piacenza (Uccellini: *Eventi di Filandro et Edessa*) and Parma (Uccellini: *Giove d'Elide fulminato*) in 1677. The demands of court service interfered with his professional wanderings: in 1667, while engaged by Marco Faustini for performances of Cesti's *La Dori* at the Teatro SS Giovanni e Paolo in Venice, he and a colleague, G. A. Cavagna (Cavagnino), were compelled by the Duke of Savoy to return in haste to Turin for the ballet *Il falso amor bandito* (music by Carisio). His only surviving works are two cantatas for three voices (in *I-MOe*); the second, *Lasciatemi morire*, begins with a clear reference to Monteverdi's *Lamento d'Arianna*. He was a member of the literary Accademia degli Incolti at Turin. Cazzati dedicated a motet to him in *Il quinto libro di motetti a voce sola* (Bologna, 1666).

BIBLIOGRAPHY
V. A. Baronis di Bottigliera: *Applauso delle muse* (Turin, 1665), 29
A. Wotquenne: *Catalogue de la Bibliothèque du Conservatoire . . . annexe*, i: *Libretti d'opéras et d'oratorios italiens du XVIIᵉ siècle* (Brussels, 1901), 74, 80
R. Giazotto: 'La guerra dei palchi', *NRMI*, i (1967), 285
M.-T. Bouquet: *Musique et musiciens à Turin de 1648 à 1775* (Turin, 1968, and Paris, 1969), 44, 215
M. Viale-Ferrero: 'Repliche, a Torino, di alcuni melodrammi veneziani, e loro caratteristiche', *Venezia e il melodramma del seicento: Venezia 1972*, 145
T. Antonicek: 'Die "Damira"-Opern der beiden Ziani', *AnMc*, no.14 (1974), 182
M.-T. Bouquet: *Il teatro di corte dalle origini al 1788* (Turin, 1976), 59, 74, 86
LORENZO BIANCONI

Rasch, Johann (*b* Pöchlarn, Lower Austria, *c*1540; *d* Vienna, ?1612). Austrian writer and composer. He was a boy chorister at the Benedictine monastery at Mondsee in Upper Austria. After two years' study at Wittenberg, he served again at Mondsee from 1561 to 1563 as clergyman. According to his own account, he then studied law. From 1565 he studied astronomy and mathematics at Vienna University and in 1567 he apparently began to study history there. He settled for a while in Neustadt an der Orla, and then in Munich, before becoming organist of the Viennese church Unsere Liebe Frau zu den Schotten in 1570. The Viennese taxation records of 1611 contain the last documented reference to him.

Rasch wrote on the most varied topics, and his writings on wine cultivation bore influence as late as the 19th century. His musical works include several Latin motets and an edition of German Protestant hymns. The motets are not based on cantus firmi; they show much choral writing with very sparing use of polyphony. The German hymns show similar characteristics and thus come close to the genre of the *Kantionallied.*

WORKS
Cantica quaedam ecclesiastica de nativitate Salvatoris nostri Jesu Christi, 4vv (Munich, 1572)
Cantiuncula paschales, 4vv (Munich, 1572)
In monte olivarum, 4vv (Munich, 1572)
Salve regina, 6vv (Munich, 1572)

BIBLIOGRAPHY
J. Seemüller: 'Über den Schottenorganisten Johann Rasch', *Festgabe zum 100jährigen Jubiläum des Schottengymnasiums* (Vienna, 1907)
O. Wessely: 'Johann Rasch', *Das Waldviertel*, xix (1970)
OTHMAR WESSELY

Rascher, Sigurd (Manfred) (*b* Elberfeld [now Wuppertal], 15 May 1907). Scandinavian saxophonist of German birth. After matriculating at the Stuttgart Musikhochschule in 1930, where he studied the clarinet, he decided to become a saxophonist. He taught in elementary schools and played in concert bands before being appointed to teach the saxophone at the Royal Danish Conservatory, Copenhagen (1933), and at the conservatory in Malmö, Sweden (1934); he held both posts until 1938. He made his American début in 1939, and has played with the Boston SO and the New York PO. Ibert, Hindemith and Milhaud composed works for him. Rascher is distinguished for his brilliant agility, sweetness of tone and musical sensibility.

GEORGE GELLES

Raselius [Raesel], Andreas (*b* Hahnbach, nr. Amberg, Upper Palatinate, *c*1563; *d* Heidelberg, 6 Jan 1602). German composer. From 1581 he studied at Heidelberg, and in 1583 became a teacher at the academy there. After taking the master's degree he left Heidelberg in 1584 for religious reasons and found work as an assistant master and Kantor at the Gymnasium Poeticum in Regensburg. In 1600 Friedrich IV, the Prince-Elector of the Palatinate, summoned him back to Heidelberg to serve as court Kapellmeister.

Raselius was among the most outstanding Protestant Kantors of the second half of the 16th century, who, with his extensive humanist cultural background, combined duties both as a pastor and as a teacher with very clear-sighted objectives. The works on music theory are characterized by a systematic approach and contain valuable collections of music examples; compositions range from the age of Senfl to Raselius's contemporary, Lassus. The title of the 1594 work, *Teutscher Sprüche auss den sontäglichen Evangeliis durchs gantze Jar*, reveals a secondary didactic aim even though the music itself was expressly designed for church use.

The two chorale collections of 1591 and 1599 were among the first to take up and continue the efforts initiated by Lucas Osiander in 1586 to present chorale settings suitable for congregational singing. Raselius's compositions in this form, however, are far superior artistically to those of Osiander, not only because they are mainly for five voices, but because of additional, though subsidiary, musical interest in the inner parts. In the 1591 collection the cantus firmus is normally in the tenor; in general it is prominent because of its notation in longer values than the accompanying voices.

Raselius's collections of motets based on texts from the gospels were the first in the German language to comprise, after the example of a corresponding collection in Latin by J. Wanning (1584 and 1590), a cycle for the whole year. Again the settings are often superior to similar works by other composers, even by later masters such as Vulpius, J. Christenius and M. Franck; Demantius only may be considered an exception. In the five-part motets Raselius carefully underlined the emotional impact of the text, and skilfully contrasted repeated words and phrases by an expressive alternation of homophonic and polyphonic textures. Although Flemish and native German influences are most obvious in the 1594 collection, the larger compositions of 1595 show Raselius to have been a master of Italian polychoral techniques.

WORKS

Editions: *A. Raselius: Cantiones sacrae*, ed. L. Roselius, DTB, xxxvi, Jg.xxix–xxx (1931)
        Deutsche sonntägliche Evangelien-Sprüche, ed. H. Nitsche and H. Stern (Stuttgart, 1964)

Teutscher Sprüche auss den sontäglichen Evangeliis durchs gantze Jar, 5vv (Nuremberg, 1594)
Teutscher Sprüche auff die fürnemsten järlichen Fest und Aposteltage . . . 5, 6, 8, 9vv auff die 12 modos dodecachordi (Nuremberg, 1595)
Regenspurgischer Kirchenkontrapunkt, allerley . . . geistlichen Psalmen und Lieder, D. M. Lutheri . . . also gesetzt, dass jedermann . . . ungehindert wol mit singen kann, 5vv (Regensburg, 1599)
Cantionale, 1587/8, *D-Rs* (autograph)
Psalmen und geistliche Lieder, 5vv, 1591, *Rp* (autograph)
Exercitationes musicae . . . et aliae cantiones, 4–6, 8vv, festivitatibus nuptialibus amicorum, 1594, *Rp* (autograph)
Cantica sacra pro nova parochia: geistliche Psalmen und Lieder, 5vv, 1599, *Gs* (autograph)
Lateinische und deutsche Lieder, 1605, *Rp*
6 individual works in *Rp*: Also hat Gott die Welt geliebt, 8vv, 1600; Der Herr ist mein Hirt, 6vv; Der Tag, der ist so freudenreich, 5vv, 1610; Gelobet seist du Jesu Christ, 5vv, 1610; Hosianna dem Sohne Davids, 5vv; Vom Himmel kam der Engel Schar, 5vv, 1610

THEORETICAL WORKS

Hexachordum seu Questiones musicae practicae . . . in welchem viva exempla Dodecachordi Glareani in utraque scala gefunden werden (Nuremberg, 1591)
Dodechachordi vivi, in quo 12 modorum musicorum exempla duodena, 4–6vv (MS, *D-Rp*, 1589)

BIBLIOGRAPHY

J. Auer: *M. Andreas Raselius* (Leipzig, 1892)
B. A. Wallner: *Musikalische Denkmäler der Steinätzkunst* (Munich, 1912)
H. J. Moser: *Die mehrstimmige Vertonung des Evangeliums*, i (Leipzig, 1933/R1968)
G. Pietzsch: *Quellen und Forschungen zur Geschichte der Musik am kurpfälzischen Hof zu Heidelberg bis 1622* (Wiesbaden, 1963)
A. Scharnagl: 'Raselius, Andreas', *MGG*

WALTER BLANKENBURG

Raser, William. See RASAR, WILLIAM.

Rasetti [Razzetti, Razetti], **Amedeo** (*b* Turin, 1754; *d* ?Paris, 1799). French keyboard player and composer, of Italian origin. His father, Piero-Antonio Amedeo Rasetti, moved to France in 1760 to join the 24 Violons du Roi, and later organized performances for the Concert Spirituel (1771–9). Amedeo's mother, who was praised by Casanova for her beauty and sophistication, arranged that he receive training from the composer–harpsichordist C.-F. Clément, and around 1780 Rasetti launched a successful career in Paris as a harpsichordist, pianist and composer. Fétis remarked that his piano trios were in great vogue around the turn of the century.

Most of Rasetti's works feature the piano, and even his ensemble works are primarily accompanied piano pieces. In general his style followed that of Clément. The six keyboard sonatas op.7, each respectively in the style of Eckard, Haydn, Clementi, Cramer, Steibelt and Mozart, show a wide interest in the developing idioms of the piano, and the *Nouveau concert arabe* op.14 for piano and orchestra looks ahead to the keyboard virtuosity of the following era.

WORKS

(all published in Paris, n.d.)

Kbd sonatas: 6 as op.1; 6 with vn ad lib, op.2; 3 with vn ad lib, op.3; 1 with vn, vc, op.6; 6 for pf, op.7; 3 de diférents caractères, pf, no.2 with vn, b, no.3 with 2 vn, vc, b, op.10
Other inst: Pf Qt, op.5; 3e pot-pourri, arr. pf, acc. fl/vn, bn/vc ad lib, op.12; 3 trios, pf, fl/vn, bn/vc, op.13, also arr. str qt; Nouveau concert arabe, pf, orch, op.14; 1 piece in Corrette's *L'art de se perfectionner dans le violon* (Paris, 1782)

BIBLIOGRAPHY

FétisB
M. Brenet: *Les concerts en France sous l'ancien régime* (Paris, 1900/R1969)

DEANNE ARKUS KLEIN

Rasgueado (Sp.; Fr. *batterie*; It. *battute*). The downward strumming of the strings of the guitar with the right-hand thumb or the back (flat side) of the right-hand fingernails, or an upward sweep over the strings with the fingertips or the thumb.

Rasgueado has been an important aspect of guitar technique since the 16th century, when as early as 1555 Bermudo wrote of *música golpeada* ('struck music') for the guitar. The exact nature of this 16th-century *rasgueado* is uncertain. However, by the beginning of the 17th century guitarists began to devise ways of notating *rasgueados*: the direction in which full five-course chords were to be strummed was shown by small vertical lines extending either above or below a single horizontal line – a downward line indicating a strum in a downward direction, and an upward line indicating an upward strum. Notes indicating exact rhythmic values of the strums were often added above the horizontal line. After the middle of the 17th century when guitarists adopted a five-line staff for the notation of their works, *rasgueados* were indicated in two different ways depending on the type of tablature used: in Italian tablature, by small vertical lines extending either above or below the lowest line of the staff; in French tablature, by a note written within the staff, of which the value and direction of the stem indicated respectively the time-value and direction of the strum.

During the 17th and 18th centuries, *rasgueados* could be performed in a variety of ways. Upward *rasgueados* were generally executed by the index finger alone, although the use of several fingers in succession (beginning with the index) was possible on longer chords. Downward strums could be executed either by the thumb alone, by the index finger alone, by several fingers of the right hand playing either simultaneously or successively, or by a combination of thumb and fingers in succession, beginning with the fourth finger. Descriptions of various manners of executing *rasgueados* may be found in the works of Pico (*Nuova scelta di sonate*, 1608), Milioni (1627), Foscarini (1640), Ruiz de Ribayaz (*Luz y norte musical para caminar por las cifras de la guitarra española*, 1677), Visée (1682, 1686) and Corbetta (1671). Statements in the works of Granata (1659) and Derosier (1699) indicate that players often interpreted *rasgueado* chords as PUNTEADO (plucked) arpeggios of varying complexity depending on the length of the relevant chord.

The art of *rasgueado* playing became an important aspect of Baroque guitar technique, and was undoubtedly developed to a high degree of sophistication. During the 19th century it became virtually obsolete in art music for guitar, surviving only in accompaniments of a popular nature. However, *rasgueado* technique has been used in many 20th-century works for classical guitar, owing to its colouristic and evocative qualities, and it has also remained an integral part of flamenco guitar technique.

BIBLIOGRAPHY

S. Murphy: 'Seventeenth-century Guitar Music: Notes on Rasgueado Performance', *GSJ*, xxi (1968), 24

R. Strizich: 'Ornamentation in Spanish Baroque Guitar Music', *Journal of the Lute Society of America*, v (1972), 38

——: Preface, *The Complete Guitar Works of Gaspar Sanz* (in preparation)

ROBERT STRIZICH

Rasheed, Hassan (Ahmed) (*b* Cairo, 1896; *d* Cairo, 1969). Egyptian composer. As a boy in Cairo he played the violin, which he continued to study for many years, both in Egypt and in England, where his wealthy family sent him to be educated: he read agriculture at Durham University, also singing baritone and composing. In 1918 he returned to Cairo and married the pianist and children's-song composer Baheega Sidky. The Rasheeds were among the most active members of the Egyptian Amateur Music Association, which they founded with others in 1942, the aim of the organization being to spread the appreciation of classical Western and new Egyptian music. Besides performing in the association's concerts, Rasheed began to compose vocal music to Arabic texts, an activity which culminated in his single opera *Anthony's Death*, to the first part of Shawky's *Cleopatra's Death*. This was the first opera composed by an Egyptian. Parts of it were produced in 1942 and again in 1973 (by the Egyptian Opera Troupe); the overture is sometimes played as a concert piece, and the aria 'Isis, O fount of tenderness' is also often performed separately. Rasheed was influenced by the Italian opera performed in Cairo, yet his melodic invention is not without originality. However, the Egyptian public found it difficult to accept the conventions of Western operatic style, particularly when associated with familiar poetry in Arabic, and Rasheed's opera has had few successors. He also composed numerous songs, of which the *Songs for Youth* were published; *Time* is one of the best examples of his style, with a piano part that has an essential role in creating atmosphere.

SAMHA EL KHOLY

Rasi, Francesco (*b* Arezzo, probably 4 May 1574; *d* after 1620). Italian composer, tenor, chitarrone player and poet. He was born of noble parents; the probable date of birth derives from a 17th-century manuscript (in

I-Fn). According to Severo Bonini (see Solerti, p.138) he was a pupil of Caccini. During the early 1590s he performed in Rome under the patronage of Grand Duke Ferdinando I of Tuscany. Emilio de' Cavalieri, in a letter from Rome dated 16 December 1593, reported Rasi's great success as a singer and chitarrone player and urged the grand duke to increase his salary, since he was being considered for other positions. In 1594 he entered the service of Gesualdo and subsequently travelled to Ferrara, Venice and Naples. He probably returned to Florence in 1596, when Gesualdo settled permanently in Naples. In a letter of 17 November 1598 Cavalieri reported that Rasi had accepted an offer from the Duke of Mantua. He probably served the Gonzagas for the rest of his life.

Rasi was in Florence in 1600, when he sang in the first performances of Peri's *Euridice* and Caccini's *Il rapimento di Cefalo*. Both composers highly praised his artistry. At Mantua in 1607 he almost certainly created the title role in Monteverdi's *Orfeo* (see T. Carter, *MT*, cxviii (1977), 393) and in 1608 he again sang there, in the first performance of Marco da Gagliano's *Dafne*. He travelled to Austria in 1612, when he dedicated to the Prince-Archbishop of Salzburg a manuscript of sacred and secular songs for one to three voices (now in *D-Rp*, copy by A. Einstein in *US-Nsc*); the solo songs were among the earliest Italian monodies north of the Alps. In 1617 he wrote an opera, *Cibele, ed Ati*, for the wedding of Ferdinando Gonzaga and Catarina de' Medici; however, it was not performed then, and the music is lost, although the text survives in his seven-volume collection of secular and spiritual poetry, *La cetra di sette corde* (Venice, 1619), along with another libretto, *Elvidia rapita*. There is no record of his activities after the publication of his *Dialoghi rappresentativi* in 1620. His death was mourned in an undated poem by Chiabrera.

Rasi's two collections of monodies, *Vaghezze di musica* (1608) and *Madrigali* (1610), contain 42 pieces, all but two for tenor: they comprise 24 madrigals, four sonnets, two ottavas, two settings of terza rima and ten strophic arias. The texts are attributed mainly to Rasi himself; in other cases they are by Petrarch, Chiabrera, Guarini, Marino, Bernardo Tasso, Giulio Strozzi or Alessandro Capponi. The style of the madrigals is generally similar to that of Caccini's. The lyrical vocal lines, with rhythms sensitive to the texts, are occasionally embellished at cadences and important words. Dissonances are restricted mainly to passing notes and suspensions. The short strophic arias, many labelled 'canzonetta', contain numerous sequential patterns and note-against-note movement between the voice and bass line. The most imposing songs are those that are settings of more impressive texts: the sonnets *Che fai, alma, che pensi?* and *Ferma, Tersilla mia* contain more dissonances, vocal leaps and chromatic writing than usual; the two ottava settings, *Ahi fuggitivo, ben come si tosto* and *Vostro fui, vostro son*, are both elaborate variations on the Ruggiero formula, and the terza rima setting for bass, *Quel rosignuol che dolcement'a l'ombra*, is written in a similar virtuoso style with strophic variations.

The manuscript of 1612 contains four Latin motets, six strophic songs and one madrigal, all with continuo. The five pieces for solo voice are primarily syllabic settings and include one strophic recitative. In four of the duets the vocal lines alternate at times in dialogue fashion, at other times combine in parallel motion. The other two ensemble pieces, for two and three voices respectively, are strictly homophonic. The four dialogues in Rasi's *Dialoghi rappresentativi* are for three solo singers, with continuo. In the first three the characters are successively introduced in declamatory recitatives, which are concluded by more lyrical refrains. Later in each dialogue recitative sections are mixed with short independent pieces for various combinations of voices, most of which are simple homophonic settings of strophic texts; but two of the duets (*Fra quanti mai, fra quanti* in the second dialogue and *Chi sprezzi l'empia sorte* in the fourth) include imitative passages and long embellishments. For the final sections of the first and second dialogues respectively Rasi used again the music of the duet *Bel mattin* and the trio *O del sol messaggia aurora* in the 1612 manuscript.

WORKS

SECULAR SONGS

(all for 1v, bc, unless otherwise stated)

Vaghezze di musica per una voce sola (Venice, 1608) [1608]
Madrigali di diversi autori (Florence, 1610) [1610]
Musica di camera et chiesa, 1612, *D-Rp* [*Rp*]

Ahi fuggitivo, ben come si tosto (Rasi), 1608; Arde nel cielo, 2vv, bc, *D-Rp*; Ardo, ma non ardisco il chius'ardore (Marino), 1608; Bel mattin (Rasi), 2vv, bc, *Rp*; Che fai, alma, che pensi? (Petrarch), 1608; Cor mio, mentre vi miro (G. B. Guarini), 1608; Deh chi porge soccorso (Rasi), 1608; Deh com'in un momento (Rasi), 1608; Dolci miei sospiri (Chiabrera), 1608; Dov'è la bella fede (Rasi), 1608; Dove misero mai (Chiabrera), 1610

E si lieto il mio core (Rasi), 1610; Ferma, Tersilla mia (Rasi), 1610; Filli mia, Filli dolce (G. B. Strozzi), 1610; Filli, mira che fuggono (Rasi), 1608; Filli, tu vuoi partire, 1610; Fillide, mira, o come bell'e chiaro (Rasi), 1610; Galatea, mentre t'amai (Rasi), *Rp*; Girate, occhi, girate (Chiabrera), 1608; Hor ch'a noi rimena (Rasi), 1608; Hor ch'è fuggit'è il giorno (Rasi), 1608; Hor sò come da se 'l cor si disgiunge (Petrarch), 1608

Indarno Febo il suo bell'oro eterno (Chiabrera), 1608; Indarno, occhi, girate (Rasi), 1608; Luci liete (Rasi), 1608; Messaggier di speranza (Chiabrera), 1608; Ne l'altrui braccia, ahi lasso (A. Guarini), 1610; Occhi che fia già mai (A. Capponi), 1610; Occhi sempre sereni (Rasi), 1610, *Rp*; Occhi, si dolcemente amor vi move (Rasi), 1610; O che felice giorno (Rasi), 1610; O del sol messaggia aurora, 3vv, bc, *Rp*; O Filli mia, che tanto amai (Rasi), 1608; O dolcezza d'amore (Rasi), 1610; O pura, o chiara stella (Rasi), 1610; O rimembranz'amara (Rasi), 1608

Perchè mia voce (Rasi), *Rp*; Quel rosignuol che dolcement'a l'ombra (Rasi), 1610; Schiera d'aspri martiri (Chiabrera), 1608; Sento l'antica fiamm'incenerirsi (Rasi), 1610; Si da me pur mi desviano (Chiabrera), 1608; S'una fede amorosa un cor non finto (Petrarch), 1610; Un guardo nò troppa pietate (Chiabrera), 1610; Un guardo, ohimè, ch'io moro (Rasi), 1610, *Rp*; Voi che l'anima mia (Rasi), 1608; Voi pur vi dipartite (G. B. Guarini), 1608; Vostro fui, vostro son (B. Tasso), 1608, *B-Bc* 704

OTHER WORKS

Sacred songs, in Musica di camera et chiesa, 1612, *D-Rp*: Egredimini, 2vv; Rorate coeli, 1v; Vox dilecti mei, 2vᵛ; Vulnerasti cor meum, 2vv, also in 1618⁴

Cibele, ed Ati (opera, Rasi), 1617, not perf., lib only extant

Motetti. . . fatti da diversi musici servitori del serenissimo signor duca di Mantova, 1–4vv (Venice, 1618⁴)

Dialoghi rappresentativi (Rasi) (Venice, 1620), MS copy *US-Nsc*: Amoroso; In natività di bella donna; In morte di bella donna; Amante addolorato

BIBLIOGRAPHY

VogelB

P. Canal: *Della musica in Mantova* (Venice, 1881/*R*1977)

A. Ademollo: *La bell'Adriana ed altre virtuose del suo tempo alla corte di Mantova* (Città di Castello, 1888/*R*)

A. Bertolotti: *Musici alla corte dei Gonzaga in Mantova dal secolo XV al XVIII* (Milan, 1890/*R*1969)

A. Solerti: *Le origini del melodramma* (Turin, 1903/*R*1969)

H. Riemann: *Handbuch der Musikgeschichte*, ii/2 (Leipzig, 1912, 2/1922)

A. Einstein: 'Ein Emissär der Monodie in Deutschland: Francesco Rasi', *Musikwissenschaftliche Beiträge: Festschrift für Johannes Wolf* (Berlin, 1929/*R*1973), 31

C. MacClintock: 'The Monodies of Francesco Rasi', *JAMS*, xiv (1961), 31

C. V. Palisca: 'Musical Asides in the Diplomatic Correspondence of Emilio de' Cavalieri', *MQ*, xlix (1963), 339

A. Newcomb: 'Carlo Gesualdo and a Musical Correspondence of 1594', *MQ*, liv (1968), 409

S. Reiner: 'La vag'Angioletta (and others): i', *AnMc*, no.14 (1974), 41, 43

T. Carter: *Jacopo Peri (1561–1633): his Life and Works* (diss., U. of Birmingham, 1980)

WILLIAM V. PORTER

Raskin, Judith (*b* New York, 21 June 1932). American soprano. She studied music at Smith College, Northampton, Mass., and singing with Anna Hamlin, joining NBC Opera in 1957, and making her début as Susanna at Ann Arbor, Michigan. This was followed by television appearances as Sister Constance (*Dialogues des carmélites*), Zerlina and Marzelline. She made her New York City Opera début in 1959 as Despina, and her Metropolitan Opera début in 1962 as Susanna; her Glyndebourne début was in 1963 as Pamina, a role she repeated the next year. In 1963 she created the Wife in Menotti's *The Labyrinth* for television, and sang the soprano role in a dramatized version of the *St Matthew Passion*. A noted exponent of Baroque music, she has appeared in stage and concert performances of Monteverdi's *Orfeo* and *L'incoronazione di Poppea*, Purcell's *The Fairy Queen* and Rameau's *Les Indes galantes*, as well as in much Handel; in the USA she is also an admired recitalist. A performer of charm and refinement, she has been compared with Elisabeth Schumann for vocal flexibility and purity. Her recordings include Anne Trulove (*The Rake's Progress*) under the composer. She wrote 'American Bel Canto' in *Opera News* (xxx/2, 1966, p.6).

HAROLD ROSENTHAL

Rasor, William. *See* RASAR, WILLIAM.

Rasse, François (Adolphe Jean Jules) (*b* Helchin, Hainaut, 17 Jan 1873; *d* Brussels, 4 Jan 1955). Belgian composer and conductor. At the Brussels Conservatory he studied the violin with Ysaÿe and composition with Huberti, winning the Belgian Prix de Rome in 1899 with the cantata *Cloches nuptiales*. After his period in Rome, he took up a career as a chamber music player and conductor, notably at the Théâtre Royal de la Monnaie in Brussels. In 1920 he was appointed professor of harmony at the Brussels Conservatory and he directed the Liège Conservatory from 1925 to 1938; in 1933 he was elected a member of the Belgian Royal Academy. He left a large quantity of music in a late-Romantic style; the many song cycles (the most noteworthy being *La chanson d'Eve*) reveal his sensitivity, while his opera *Soeur Béatrice* and his orchestral music display a considerable dramatic sense.

WORKS

(selective list)

Stage: Déidamia (opera, 3, L. Solvay), 1905; Le maître à danser, ballet, 1908; Soeur Béatrice (opera, 3, Maeterlinck), 1938

Orch: Vn Conc., 1906; Poème concertant, pf, orch, 1918; Une vie, 1925; Improvvisata, tpt, orch, 1928; Pour une tragédie, 1929; Poème concertant, vn, orch, 1935; La dryade, cl, orch, 1943; Lamento, vc, str orch, 1952; 3 syms., 3 sym. poems

Inst: 2 str qts, 1906, 1950; Pf Qnt, 1914; Pf Qt, 1941; 3 pf trios, 1897, 1911, 1951; duo sonatas, kbd pieces

Song cycles: 10 chants de la guerre, 1v, orch, 1914–18; Voix de la terre et du temps, S/T, orch, 1930; Le chant éternel (cantata), S, B, chorus, orch, 1924; La chanson d'Eve, 1v, orch, 1931; Les premières paroles, 1v, orch, 1932

89 separate songs with pf/str/orch, choral works

Principal publishers: CeBeDeM, Lauweryns, Oertel, Schott (Brussels)
MSS in *B-Bcdm*

BIBLIOGRAPHY
Catalogue des oeuvres de compositeurs belges: François Rasse (Brussels, 1954) [CeBeDeM publication]
R. Moulaert: 'Notice sur François Rasse', *Annuaire de l'Académie royale de Belgique*, cxxv (1959), 25
HENRI VANHULST

Rassel (Ger.). RATTLE.

Rastell, John (*b* London, *c*1475; *d* London, 1536). English Member of Parliament, dramatist, writer on law, historian, adventurer, and printer of books and music. Although the quantity of extant music printed by him is small, it is of great historical importance. It consists of a three-part song (see illustration) printed in rough score in his own play, *A New Interlude and a Mery of the Nature of the iiii Elements* (modern edition by R. Coleman, Cambridge, 1971, as *The Four Elements*), and a broadside ballad (unique copies in *GB-Lbm*). Unfortunately the play is also imperfect and lacks a date.

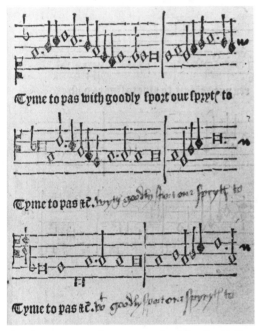

The three-part song 'Tyme to pas' from the play 'A New Interlude' written and printed by John Rastell (GB-Lbm)

The circumstantial and bibliographical evidence is extremely complex, but strongly suggests that neither the play nor the broadside is likely to have been printed much later than 1525 and the play possibly some years earlier. The broadside, a fragment of a much larger sheet (with little more than one line of a voice part) which contained the music of either a two-part or a three-part song, is the earliest known broadside with music printed from type in any country. The music type used by Rastell, though rather rough and produced from twice-struck matrices, enabled him nevertheless to print the staves, notes and directs at the same impression with the text. Since no type of any kind was first cut and cast in England until some time after Rastell's death, he must have obtained the fount from some continental source, possibly in the Low Countries or northern France. But no other trace of its use survives in Rastell's lifetime and

the type is found only once after his death, in a book of psalms printed by John Gough in about 1540.

Rastell's two productions antedate by at least three years the first book of Attaingnant's chansons which appeared in April 1528 and have long been considered the first example of one-impression music printing. Although Attaingnant used type cast from once-struck matrices, and was a better printer, he must on present evidence yield priority to Rastell as the pioneer in the use of this far-reaching innovation in the history of music printing.

BIBLIOGRAPHY
A. H. King: 'Rastell Reunited', *Essays in Honour of Victor Scholderer* (Mainz, 1970), 213
——: 'The Significance of John Rastell in Early Music Printing', *The Library*, 5th ser., xxvi/3 (1971), 197
——: 'An English Broadside of the 1520s', *Essays on Opera and English Music in Honour of Sir Jack Westrup* (Oxford, 1975), 19
ALEC HYATT KING

Rastrelli, Joseph [Gioseffo, Giuseppe] (*b* Dresden, 13 April 1799; *d* Dresden, 15 Nov 1842). Italian composer and conductor. A precocious musician, his first teacher was his father, Vincenzo, who in 1805 displayed him as a violinist in Moscow. He continued his studies in Dresden under Poland (violin) and Fiedler (harmony) and in 1814 went with his father to Italy, where he completed his studies in counterpoint with Padre Mattei in Bologna. In 1816 he made his début as a composer at Ancona with the opera *La distruzione di Gerusalemme*. In 1817 he returned to Dresden, where his opera *La schiava circassa* was successfully performed in 1820, and in the same year he was made a violinist in the royal chapel. He had two more operatic successes in 1821–2. Given a royal grant he went to Italy, where his opera *Amina* had one performance at La Scala. On his return to Dresden Rastrelli devoted himself principally to teaching singing and composing sacred music, and he was made a Knight of the Golden Spur by the pope in 1828 in reward for two motets he had written for the Sistine Chapel. In 1829 he was appointed deputy music director under Morlacchi at the court theatre and in 1830 royal *maestro di cappella*, together with Morlacchi and Reissiger. In 1832 he produced *Salvator Rosa, oder Zwey Nächte in Rom*, a Singspiel whose music reflected both German and Italian influences. This was the first new opera performed in Dresden after the liquidation in that year of the Italian Opera and it was followed by two others, also in German, in 1835 and 1839. Highly esteemed in Dresden, particularly as a conductor, Rastrelli declined in 1836 an advantageous offer from Moscow. With his death and that of Morlacchi, the Dresden dynasty of Italian musicians came to an end. In 1843 they were replaced at the court theatre and at the royal chapel by Richard Wagner.

WORKS

Operas, performed Dresden, Hoftheater, unless otherwise indicated: La distruzione di Gerusalemme, Ancona, 1816; La schiava circassa, 1820, *D-Dlb*; Le donne curiose, 1821; Velleda, 1822; Amina, Milan, 1824; Salvator Rosa, oder Zwey Nächte in Rom, 1832, autograph *Dlb*, vocal score (Dresden and Leipzig, ?1832); Bertha von Bretagne, 1835, *Dlb*; Die Neuvermählten, 1839, *Dlb*; Il trionfo di Nabucco il grande, perf. details unknown, *Dlb*

Other stage works: Intermezzi for Shakespeare: Macbeth, 1836; Der Raub Zetulbeus (ballet), *c*1836–7

Sacred, autograph *Dlb*: Mass, 4vv, orch, 1829; Domine probasti me, 1831; Miserere, 1837; 4 Salve regina; 2 Regina coeli; 2 Ave regina; 2 Alma Redemptoris mater; 2 Litanie Lauretane; Credidi; In exitu Israel; 3 Laudate pueri; 3 Laudate Dominum; 3 Beatus vir; 3 Dixit Dominus; In convertendo; 3 Magnificat; 3 Confitebor

Other works, mostly *Dlb*: arias; songs; choruses; Va Conc.; Va Concertino; 3 military marches; Les charmes de Dresde, rondo, pf (Dresden, n.d.)

BIBLIOGRAPHY

FétisB

G. Schilling: *Encyclopädie der gesammten musikalischen Wissenschaften, oder Universal-Lexikon der Tonkunst* (Stuttgart, 1835–42/R1973)

M. Fürstenau: *Beiträge zur Geschichte der Königlich-sächsischen musikalischen Kapelle* (Dresden, 1849)

M. Börner-Sandrini: *Erinnerungen einer alten Dresdnerin* (Dresden, 1876), 123, 233ff

H. von Brescius: *Die Königl. Sächs. musikalische Kapelle von Reissiger bis Schuch (1826–1898)* (Dresden, 1898)

ANDREA LANZA

Rastrelli, Vincenzo (*b* Fano, nr. Pesaro, 1760; *d* Dresden, 20 March 1839). Italian singing teacher and composer. He completed his earliest musical studies in Fano, where at the age of 18 he became one of the most sought-after singing teachers. From 1780 he studied counterpoint with Padre Mattei in Bologna, becoming a member of the Società Filarmonica in 1786. After holding the posts of *maestro di cappella* at Fano Cathedral and, from 1793, of *maestro al cembalo* at the Teatro del Sole in Pesaro, he moved to Dresden as a teacher of singing and music to Count Marcolini. In 1795 he succeeded Franz Seydelmann in the post of composer to the court church. After four years in Moscow (1802–6) and a short stay in Italy, he returned to Dresden in 1807, reappointed composer to the court church. In 1814, on being refused permission by the provisional Russian government for a journey to Italy, he resigned his post and, on his return, lived as singing teacher to the royal family. Nevertheless, in 1824 his former appointment was restored to him, this time for life. He retired in 1831. Rastrelli wrote an oratorio, *Tobia*, a harpsichord concerto and a large amount of church music, much of it surviving in manuscript in Dresden (*D-Dlb*).

BIBLIOGRAPHY

FétisB

G. Schilling: *Encyclopädie der gesammten musikalischen Wissenschaften, oder Universal-Lexikon der Tonkunst* (Stuttgart, 1835–42/R1973)

M. Fürstenau: *Beiträge zur Geschichte der Königlich-sächsischen musikalischen Kapelle* (Dresden, 1849)

ANDREA LANZA

Rastrum (from Lat.: 'rake'). A pen with a number of nibs or styli, for drawing more than one line at a time. It is particularly useful for drawing staves. Five-line staves were sometimes drawn with rastra in the 15th century, and pens with four nibs also seem to have been used for chant manuscripts. During the 16th century rastra were used with enough nibs to draw more than one staff at a time: two staves were frequently drawn together, and up to six appear in some manuscripts. The use of rastra tended to be the province of the regular music scribe, while the amateur drew most lines separately. The advent of printed manuscript paper later in the century does not appear to have affected this pattern.

The gauge (or spacing of the lines) of one rastrum is seldom identical to that of another; further, such pens leave distinctive patterns at the ends of lines. As a result, the study 'rastrology' has developed, in which the patterns of use of different rastra yield information about, for example, the order of work of the scribe.

See also SOURCES, MS, §I.

BIBLIOGRAPHY

O. Jander: 'Staff-liner Identification: a Technique for the Age of Microfilm', *JAMS*, xx (1967), 112

STANLEY BOORMAN

Rat, Le. *See* LE RAT.

Ratamacue. A technique of side-drumming; *see* DRUM, §3.

Ratchet [cog rattle] (Fr. *crecelle*; Ger. *Ratsche, Knarre*; It. *raganella*). A percussion instrument of indefinite pitch in the form of a scraped idiophone. It consists of a cogwheel which is either revolved by means of a handle against one or more stout tongues of wood or metal (as illustrated), or twirled, when the tongues strike the cogs of the wheel. Instruments of the above type resemble the old type of watchman's rattle. In a larger form it resembles the *matraca*: a cog rattle up to 2 metres high.

Ratchet turned by a handle (see also SCRAPER)

Ratchets serve in the Orthodox Church; in Roman churches they replace the bells during Holy Week. They have served secular purposes over a long period of time: in Europe as the watchman's rattle, as an alarm signal and as a noise-maker at sports gatherings. They are used universally to scare birds and animals, and in a simpler form to amuse children.

With such exceptions as the *Ratsche* in Beethoven's 'Battle' Symphony, where an instrument of the maraca class is used to represent rifle fire, a small cog rattle wound by a handle is used in the orchestra. It occurs for example in the 'Toy' Symphony (now considered to be by Leopold Mozart); Strauss's *Till Eulenspiegel*; Musorgsky's *Pictures at an Exhibition* (orchestrated by Ravel); the finale of Walton's First *Façade* Suite; and in Respighi's *Pini di Roma* – here in a rhythmic pattern (ex.1).

Ex.1 *Raganella*

BIBLIOGRAPHY

F. W. Galpin: *A Textbook of Musical Instruments* (London, 1937, 2/1956)

JAMES BLADES

Ratdolt, Erhard (*b* Augsburg, 1447; *d* Augsburg, late 1527 or early 1528). German printer. According to his own diary covering the years 1462–1523 (*A-Wn* 15473), he first went to Venice in 1462, after the death of his father. Returning there in 1474, he began printing with two German partners, Peter Löslein and Bernardus

Pictor (whether 'Pictor' is a latinized version of the surname, 'Maler', or whether it refers to its bearer's profession of illuminator, remains uncertain). Following the departure of both partners in 1478 or 1479 and after a one-year interim, he resumed business by himself in 1480. In 1485 the diocese of Augsburg commissioned a breviary from Ratdolt, which particularly pleased the bishop; efforts were made to persuade the printer to return to Augsburg, first by Bishop Johann von Werdenberg and, after his death in 1485, by his successor, Friedrich von Hohenzollern. He apparently did so shortly afterwards (his last Venetian publication is dated 18 March 1486) and continued printing until his retirement in 1522, although his son Georg officially took over the business in 1515.

Ratdolt was one of the major craftsmen of his time, known primarily, however, for publications outside the field of music. In Venice his efforts were devoted mainly to writings on astronomy and mathematics (about 50 works), but his Augsburg publications (over 70) are almost exclusively liturgical, principally consisting of missals, breviaries and obsequials for various dioceses in southern Germany, Austria and Switzerland (Augsburg, Brixen, Chur, Konstanz, Freising, Passau, Regensburg and Salzburg). He introduced musical notes into his liturgical books in 1487, using wood blocks at first, in 1491 changing to movable type. Ratdolt was the first printer to employ decorated title-pages and the first to print in three, and even four, different colours, using woodcuts by such prominent artists as Hans Burgkmair and Jörg Breu. A proof sheet of 14 different type models, dated 1 April 1486 (made just before his return to Augsburg and apparently in connection with that offer), is extant (in *D-Mbs*).

BIBLIOGRAPHY
G. R. Redgrave: *Erhard Ratdolt and his Work at Venice*, Bibliographical Society, Illustrated Monographs, i (London, 1894, 2/1899) [incl. list of publications]
R. Proctor: *An Index to the Early Printed Books in the British Museum, Part 2, 1501–1520: Section 1, Germany* (London, 1903/R1954), 74
R. Molitor: *Deutsche Choral-Wiegendrucke* (Regensburg, 1904)
R. Proctor: *Catalogue of Books Printed in the XVth Century now in the British Museum*, ii (London, 1912/R1963), 379
K. Schottenloher: *Die liturgischen Druckwerke Erhard Ratdolts aus Augsburg 1485–1522* (Mainz, 1922) [incl. numerous facsimiles and list of publications]
I. Schwarz: 'Die Memorabilien des Augsburger Buchdruckers Erhard Ratdolt (1462–1523)', *Werden und Wirken: Festgruss K. W. Hiersemann zugesandt* (Leipzig, 1924), 399
R. Diehl: *Erhard Ratdolt: ein Meisterdrucker des XV. und XVI. Jahrhunderts* (Vienna, 1933)
D. C. McMurtrie: *Erhard Ratdolt, the Father of Typographic Decoration* (Chicago, 1936)
K. Meyer-Baer: *Liturgical Music Incunabula* (London, 1962)
J. Benzing: *Die Buchdrucker des 16. und 17. Jahrhunderts im deutschen Sprachgebiet* (Wiesbaden, 1963), 13
T. Wohnhaas: 'Ratdolt, Erhard', *MGG*
A. Layer: 'Augsburger Musikdrucker der frühen Renaissancezeit', *Gutenberg-Jb* (1965), 124

MARIE LOUISE GÖLLNER

Rathaus, Karol (*b* Tarnopol, 16 Sept 1895; *d* New York, 21 Nov 1954). American composer of Polish origin. In 1913 he moved to Vienna to enrol at the University and the Academy of Music, where he studied composition with Schreker. After service in the Austrian army during World War I, he made his début as a composer–pianist in Vienna in 1919, playing his op.1, the Variations on a Theme by Reger. When Schreker moved to Berlin in 1920, Rathaus and other young composers (including Krenek and Hába) joined him to form a select master class at the Hochschule für

Musik. With a brief interruption in 1922 to receive a PhD at Vienna University, Rathaus remained in Berlin until 1932 and established himself as 'one of the strongest hopes of our new music' (Schrenk). Important premières of that decade included those of his Symphony no.2 at the Frankfurt Festival (1924), the Overture op.22 by the Berlin PO under Furtwängler (1928), the Suite op.29 at the Liège ISCM Festival (1930), and two works produced at the Berlin Staatsoper, the ballet *Der letzte Pierrot* (1927) and the opera *Fremde Erde* (1930). In 1931 Rathaus turned to the comparatively new medium of sound film and wrote the score to *The Brothers Karamazov* (directed by Otzep), considered a classic of its kind.

From 1932 to 1934 Rathaus lived in Paris, and from 1934 to 1938 in London, where the Ballets Russes staged *Le lion amoureux* at Covent Garden (1937). In 1938 he settled in the USA (he became a citizen in 1946); after a brief stay in Hollywood (1939) he moved to New York to become professor of composition at Queens College, a position he occupied until his death. There he developed a remarkable curriculum for creative musicianship and shaped the talents of many young composers. He served on the directorate of the ISCM (American section) and on the advisory board of the Fulbright Award. In 1952 the Metropolitan Opera commissioned him to rework the orchestration of *Boris Godunov* wherever the original was impracticable, a task he accomplished with exemplary discretion. After his death a Karol Rathaus Memorial Association was founded, offering a prize for composition students at Queens College, and in 1960 the new music building at Queens College was named Karol Rathaus Hall.

Rathaus's style has many facets not easily classified. Unmistakable is his affinity to the Polish tradition, both in rhythm and melody; the German expressionism of the 1920s coloured some of his earlier works, submerging the Viennese elegance, and in certain scores dealing with Jewish topics (e.g. the incidental music to *Uriel Acosta* for the Habimah Theatre), he drew on Judaic intonations, mixing East European and Near-Eastern influences. But essentially his music is not dominated by national or racial elements: he was in the mainstream of European music. He escaped late Romanticism by stressing rhythmic vitality and angular melodies, without sacrificing emotional appeal. Imagination and colour rather than dogmatic exigencies dominate his music. He skirted atonality but did not abandon the tonal centre, despite a bold use of dissonance. His style is improvisational, rhapsodic and declamatory. Especially noteworthy is his predilection for the piano (he was a masterly pianist) and his sonorous, vivid orchestration. In his chamber music he combined intimacy with intensity.

WORKS
(selective list)

Dramatic: Der letzte Pierrot, op.19 (ballet), 1927; Fremde Erde, op.25 (opera), 1929–30; Le lion amoureux, op.42 (ballet), 1937; 9 incidental scores, incl. Uriel Acosta; 17 film scores

Orch: Sym. no.1, op.5, 1921–2; Sym. no.2, op.7, 1923; Ov., op.22, 1928; Suite, op.27, vn, chamber orch, 1929; Suite, op.29, 1930; Kleine Ouverture, op.30, tpt, str, 1930; Serenade, op.35, 1932; Jacob's Dream, op.44, nocturne, 1938; Pf Conc., op.45, 1939; Music for Str, op.49, 1941; Sym. no.3, op.50, 1942–3; Polonaise symphonique, op.52, 1943; Vision dramatique, op.55, 1945; Salisbury Cove Ov., op.65, 1949; Sinfonia concertante, op.68, 1950–51; Louisville Prelude, op.71, 1953; sym. pieces and suites from dramatic works

Vocal: songs, opp.48, 57; O iuvenes, op.60, academic cantata, T, chorus, orch, 1947; Chorus from 'Iphigenia in Aulis', op.61, vv, hn;

Diapason, op.67 (Dryden, Milton), oratorio, Bar, chorus, orch, 1950; Choral Songs, op.70

Chamber: 5 str qts, nos.1–2 lost, opp.41, 59, 72; 2 sonatas, vn, pf, opp.14, 43; Sonata, op.21, cl, pf; vn pieces, opp.39, 64; Trio, op.53, vn, cl, pf; Rapsodia notturna, op.66, vc, pf, 1950; Trio Serenade, op.69, pf trio; educational pieces

Pf: Variations on a Theme by Reger, op.1; 4 sonatas, opp.2, 8, 20, 58; Ballade, op.40; 4 Studies after Domenico Scarlatti, op.56; Variations on a Theme by Georg Boehm, op.62; shorter pieces, opp.9, 11, 24, 47, 51; educational pieces

Principal publishers: Associated, Belwin-Mills, Boosey & Hawkes, Israeli Music Publications, Oxford University Press, Presser, Universal

BIBLIOGRAPHY

W. Schrenk: *Richard Strauss und die neue Musik* (Berlin, 1924)

K. Rathaus: 'Meine Oper "Fremde Erde" ', *Musikblätter des Anbruch*, xii (1930), 13

C. Reis: *Composers in America* (New York, 2/1947)

B. Schwarz: 'Karol Rathaus', *MQ*, xli (1955), 481 [with complete list of works]

BORIS SCHWARZ

Rathgeber, Johann Valentin (*b* Oberelsbach, nr. Fulda, 3 April 1682; *d* Banz, nr. Coburg, 2 June 1750). German composer. He received his earliest musical education from his father, who held the combined posts of village organist and schoolmaster. In 1701 he entered the University of Würzburg to study theology, and in 1704 became a schoolmaster and organist at the Juliusspital in Würzburg. He went to the Benedictine abbey of Banz early in 1707 as chamber musician and servant to the abbot, and by the end of the year had become a novice. In 1711 he was ordained, and about the same time was appointed choirmaster at Banz, a post which he held, with one interruption, for the rest of his life. In 1721, the Augsburg firm of Lotter issued the first of his many publications, a volume of masses. Eight years later, when he had established a considerable reputation as a composer of church music, he sought permission to leave Banz for a European tour; he was refused and left without it. He visited Würzburg, Augsburg, Bonn, Cologne, Trier and Benedictine houses in Swabia and around Lake Constance. One of his reasons for making this tour seems to have been to gather information about performance conditions and liturgical customs in the Catholic areas of Germany; in the preface to his Vespers op.9, he said that he had added settings of the Compline psalms as, though sung Compline was not customary in his part of Germany, it was more common in the Rhineland and he had been asked to provide music for it. He also turned his attention to secular vocal music. The first two volumes of the *Ohren-vergnügendes und Gemüth-ergötzendes Tafel-Confect*, a collection of popular songs which he edited and arranged, were published by Lotter in 1733 and 1737 respectively.

Although he was reinstated as choirmaster after his return to Banz and readmission to the community, Rathgeber produced no more church music after 1738. He continued to work on the *Tafel-Confect*, whose last volume appeared in 1746, and in 1743 his last original composition was published, a set of short and simple keyboard pieces. He died in 1750 after a long illness.

Rathgeber is remembered mainly in connection with the *Tafel-Confect*, but in his own time he was also an extremely popular and influential composer of church music. Lotter's catalogues show that southern Germany saw a boom in published church music for the average choir in the mid-18th century, and that Rathgeber was the most important and prolific composer in this field in the 1720s and 30s; his first two publications of masses,

opp.1 and 3, had the rare distinction of achieving second editions. Moreover, it is likely that his works started the trend towards simple church music for parish choirs; his op.1 was almost certainly the first publication of its kind, for though some church music was published in Germany before 1720 it was nearly all too elaborate and lavishly scored to be practical for them.

Most of Rathgeber's sacred output is made up of mass settings and Vesper psalms, for which parish churches had the greatest demand; but he also provided for all other liturgical occasions with sets of offertories (general motets, not settings of the Proper), litanies, hymns, antiphons, and settings of the *Miserere* and *Stabat mater*. Each publication contained a great deal of music; most of his mass volumes include eight or more complete settings of the Ordinary, and his Vespers ones at least four complete sets of psalms for various occasions, with *Magnificat* settings and antiphons. Except for the sacred arias op.10, all his church music is scored for SATB solo and chorus, one or two violins and continuo, with optional trumpets and drums in certain pieces. Some publications, such as the Vespers of 1736, however, were intended for country districts, where choirs were often small and incomplete, and in these two voice parts and either one or both violin parts were optional, so that the music could be performed with a minimum of two voices and organ.

Until about 1750, south German published church music had a style distinct from that of the large-scale Catholic church music being written elsewhere, or of that of the Lutheran composers of the north. The first extant publication in this style is Rathgeber's op.1. The style is compact and non-contrapuntal; as the words can be clearly heard and there is little repetition of them, the music is apt for liturgical use. Rathgeber had a considerable talent for writing good melodies, for chorus as well as solo singers, so that although the choral texture is simple, and the solo parts make no excessive demands, the music is not dull. Most of his mass movements and psalm settings are through-composed; he rarely divided them into sections, and, except for the Benedictus in the mass, never wrote self-contained solo arias. In his earlier publications he developed a technique of unifying long movements by means of short recurrent motifs, vocal and instrumental, in melody or bass. But Rathgeber's forms are never stereotyped, and even his settings of the longest and most amorphous psalm texts have a sense of shape. He is further helped by a skilful, if naive, use of word-painting. He showed in his arias op.10 that he could also use the more common contemporary ritornello forms. Each is a da capo movement; but unlike later composers of sacred arias Rathgeber did not imitate the Italian style, and the vocal writing is hardly more difficult than in his larger-scale music.

Despite his cultivation of simple textures and attractive melodies, Rathgeber was not a progressive composer. His melodic and harmonic idioms, and his bass lines, are firmly rooted in the Baroque. This is true also of his instrumental music: the concertos of op.6 are concerti grossi, for various combinations of instruments; and the keyboard pieces op.22, all in binary form, are Baroque in idiom, though as they are not at all contrapuntal, and in only two parts, their effect is rather thin. The *Tafel-Confect* contains a large and varied selection of the popular songs of the period, including solos, duets and choruses, many of which are described as quodlibets. Some have instrumental accompaniments, others merely figured basses. The square, sturdy, often predictable tunes are similar to those of the songs published at about the same time by composers such as Telemann, though the words, often nonsense syllables or in Bavarian dialect, are less distinguished.

WORKS
(all pubd in Augsburg)

op.
SACRED
1 Octava musica, 4vv, 2 vn, bc (1721, 2/1728), 8 masses (in 2nd edn. 2 requiems added)
2 Cornu-copiae vesperarum diversarum, 4vv, 2 vn, 2 tpt ad lib, bc (1723), 6 Vespers, 4 antiphons, litany
3 Novena principalis Constantiniana, 4vv, 2 vn, 2 tpt ad lib, bc (1725), 9 masses
4 Sacra anaphonesis, 4vv, 2 vn, 2 tpt ad lib, bc (1726), 24 offertories
5 Harmonia Mariano-Musica, 4vv, 2 vn, 2 tpt ad lib, bc (1727), 6 litanies, 15 antiphons
7 Decas Mariano-Musica, 4vv, 2 vn, 2 va, 2 tpt, bc (1730), 10 masses
8 Harmonia lugubris, 4vv, 2 vn, 2 tpt ad lib, 3 trbn ad lib, bc (1731), 6 requiems, 2 Libera me
9 Psalmodia vespertina, 4vv, 2 vn, 2 tpt ad lib, timp ad lib, bc (1732), 4 Vespers
10 Vox sonora decantans, 1v, 2 vn, va, bc (1732), 8 Latin arias, 8 German arias
11 Columba sacra, 4vv, 2 vn, 2 tpt ad lib, bc (1732), 36 hymns
12 Missale tum rurale tum civile, 1–4vv, 1–2 vn, 2 tpt ad lib, bc (1733), 12 masses, 2 requiems
13 Cithara Davidis poenitentis, 4vv, 2 vn, 2 tpt ad lib, 3 trbn ad lib, bc (1734), 6 Miserere, 6 Tantum ergo
14 Holocaustoma ecclesiasticum, 4vv, 2 vn, 2 tpt ad lib, timp ad lib, bc (1734–5), 60 offertories, 18 antiphons, 3 Tenebrae
15 Dominicale, 4vv, bc, insts ad lib (1735), 50 offertories
16 Antiphonale Marianum, 4vv, 2 vn, bc (1736), 24 antiphons
17 Psalterium iucundum, 2vv, org, 2vv ad lib, insts ad lib (1736), 4 Vespers, 5 psalms
18 Cultus Marianus, 1–4vv, 2 tpt ad lib, 2 hn ad lib, timp ad lib, bc (1736), antiphons, litany
19 Sacrum quadriformae, 4vv, 2 vn, 2 tpt ad lib, 2 trbn ad lib, timp ad lib, bc (1738), 4 masses
20 Hortus noviter exstructus, 4vv, 2 vn, bc (1739), 30 offertories
— 4 Sanctus, 4vv, 2 vn, 2 tpt, 2 trbn, bc, D-Bds; 3 hymns, 4vv, 2 vn, 2 tpt, bc, PL-WRu; Salve regina, D-Dlb; Requiem rurale, S, A, B ad lib, 2 hn, org, D-WEY

SECULAR
6 Chelys sonora (1728), 24 concertos; 2 vn, bc, 7 with vn solo, 6 with 2 tpt, 2 with tpt solo, 4 with 2 tpt ad lib
— Ohren-vergnügendes und Gemüth-ergötzendes Tafel-Confect (1733, 1737, 1746), 1–4vv, bc/vc, 2 vn ad lib; ed. in EDM, 1st ser., xix (1942)
22 Musikalisches Zeitvertreib (1743), 60 keyboard arias of which the last 10 are pastorals for Christmastide

ELIZABETH ROCHE

Ratisbon. *See* REGENSBURG.

Ratisbonne, George de. *See* CHAMBRAY, LOUIS FRANÇOIS.

Raţiu, Adrian (*b* Bucharest, 28 July 1928). Romanian composer and musicologist. He studied with Chirescu (theory and solfège), Constantinescu (harmony), Negrea and Buicliu (counterpoint), Klepper (composition), Breazul (history), Comişel (folklore) and Rogalski (orchestration) at the Bucharest Conservatory (1950–56), and in 1969 attended the Darmstadt summer courses. He was editor of *Muzica* from 1959 until 1962, when he was appointed to teach harmony at the Bucharest Conservatory. As a musicologist he has produced fine analyses of Romanian and other 20th-century music, and his theoretical ideas are important to his creative work. In early works, such as the Piano Pieces of 1957, he attempted a synthesis of hexatonic modality and serialism. He then passed through a phase of rigorous organization with frequent recourse to folk modes, as in the Oboe and Bassoon Concerto (1963), before reaching a free post-serial style including

aleatory features, original timbres and, again, structures based on folk modality.

WORKS
(*selective list*)
Orch: Sym. no.1, 1956, rev. 1961; Conc., ob, bn, str, 1963; Diptic, 1965; Concertino per la Musica-Nova, 1967; Impresii, chamber orch, 1969; 6 imagini, 1971; Poem, vc, orch, 1972; Pf Conc., 1973
Chamber: Str Qt, 1956; Partita, wind qnt, 1966; Transfigurări, cl, pf, str trio, 1975
Pf: Pieces, 1957; Monosonata I, 1968; Monosonata II, 1969; Constellations, 1970
Vocal: Lieduri (N. Labiş), 1961; Lieduri (T. Arghezi), 1963; Madrigaluri corale (Shakespeare), 1964; Madrigaluri (M. R. Paraschivescu), 1964

Principal publishers: Gerig, Izdatelstvo Muzīka, Muzicală

WRITINGS
'Aspekte der Ausdrücksmittel im Lichte der Entwicklung der zeitgenossischen Musik', *Beiträge zur Musikwissenschaft*, iv (1965), 337
with others: *Georges Enescu* (Bucharest, 1971)
'Le système harmonique de Scriabine', *Muzica*, xxiii (1973), no.1, p.41; no.2, p.43

VIOREL COSMA

Ratner, Leonard G(ilbert) (*b* Minneapolis, Minn., 30 July 1916). American musicologist. He took an MA from the University of California at Berkeley in 1939 and a PhD in 1947; his professors included Bukofzer, Schoenberg, Bloch and Frederick Jacobi. He taught at Berkeley from 1944. In 1947 he joined the faculty of Stanford University, where he was professor of music from 1957.

Ratner specializes in late 18th-century music, particularly its theory, style and performing practice, and is most noted for his studies of harmonic structure in music of the Classical period. His observations on form and analysis are also reflected in his two textbooks, *Music: the Listener's Art* and *Harmony, Structure and Style*.

WRITINGS
Harmonic Aspects of Classic Form (diss., U. of California, Berkeley, 1947)
'Harmonic Aspects of Classic Form', *JAMS*, ii (1949), 159
'Eighteenth-century Theories of Musical Period Structure', *MQ*, xlii (1956), 439
Music: the Listener's Art (New York, 1957)
Harmony, Structure and Style (New York, 1962)
'Approaches to Musical Historiography of the 18th Century', *CMc*, no.9 (1969), 154
'Key Definition – a Structural Issue in Beethoven's Music', *JAMS*, xxiii (1970), 472
'*Ars combinatoria*: Chance and Choice in Eighteenth-century Music', *Studies in Eighteenth-century Music: a Tribute to Karl Geiringer* (New York and London, 1970), 343
Classic Music: Expression, Form, and Style (New York, 1979)

PAULA MORGAN

Ratsche (Ger.). RATCHET.

Ratti, Bartolomeo ['Il Moro'] (*b* Padua, 1565; *d* Padua, 21 April 1634). Italian composer, singer and organist. He attended the school attached to S Antonio, Padua, and studied composition with Costanzo Porta. On 30 October 1591 he became a tenor in the S Antonio choir. On 9 June 1593 he competed unsuccessfully for the post of player of the 'organetto dei concerti' there, but he was appointed to this position on 24 February 1594 and also continued as a singer. On 14 March 1594 he received permission to become *maestro di cappella* at Gemona, Friuli, whence he returned to Padua to become, on 13 December 1600, deputy to Porta at S Antonio. On 1 June 1601, after Porta's death, he succeeded him as *maestro di cappella*, a post he held until 1606. Having apparently been *maestro di cappella* briefly at S Francesco, Piacenza, he returned to his post at Padua in 1608. On 11 December 1613 he was dismissed for neglecting his duties, but he continued to live in the monastery attached to S Antonio until his death. He composed both sacred and secular music in a variety of styles current in his day.

WORKS

Cantiones in laudem deiparae Virginis Mariae (quae vulgo nominari solent motecta) . . . et in fine adjectae sunt litaniae in honorem ejusdem virginis, liber I, 5vv (Venice, 1594)

Amorosi fiori . . . madrigali, 4vv, con uno, 8vv (Venice, 1594)

Ghirlanda de varii fiori amorosi, libro II de madrigali, 4vv, con 1 sonetto, 8vv, et 1 dialogo, 8vv (Venice, 1596)

Ardori amorosi, madrigali e canzonette, 3vv (Venice, 1599)

Li brevi salmi intieri che nelli Vespri di tutte le solenità si cantano secondo il rito del Sacro Concilio di Trento, 5vv, bc (Venice, 1605)

BIBLIOGRAPHY

P. Saviolo and B. Franco: *Arca del Santo di Padova* (Padua, 1765)

G. Tebaldini: *L'archivio musicale della Cappella Antoniana in Padova* (Padua, 1895)

R. Lunelli: 'Nota complementare sul musicista Costanzo Porta', *Miscellanea francescana*, lvi (1956), 282

REGINA F. CHAUVIN

Ratti, Cencetti & Comp. Italian music publishers, active in Rome. Giovanni Battista Cencetti ran a copying business at 8 via Canestrari, established by the second decade of the 19th century and began music publishing with Leopoldo Ratti, probably in 1821. The firm, originally styled Stamperio Litografica di Leopoldo Ratti e Gio: Batta Cencetti, was first at 24 via de' Spagnuoli. From about 1823 to 1830 it was at 23 via della Posta Vecchia (also referred to as 23 via de' Sediari), with additional premises at 17 via della Croce (from c1828); in about 1830 the latter became its main address, with 154 via di Ripetta also in use (c1830–31). Cencetti's name was dropped from the imprint in about 1834, but as Ratti & Comp. the firm continued in business until at least late 1837.

To judge by plate numbers (which appear to be chronological) the firm issued some 600 publications, all probably in lithography, mainly of excerpts from contemporary operas. It is best remembered, however, for the enterprising series of complete full scores of eight Rossini operas: *Mosè in Egitto* (c1825), *L'inganno felice* and *Semiramide* (c1826), *Il barbiere di Siviglia* (c1827), *Ricciardo e Zoraide* (c1828), *L'assedio di Corinto* (c1830), *Matilde di Shabran* (c1832) and *Guillaume Tell* (c1835). Although Rossini probably did not supervise their preparation, they were the first full scores of his operas to appear in Italy (five of them have never been republished in full score). They are landmarks in both Italian and in lithographic music publishing; only a few operatic full scores were published in Italy in the 19th century, and it was at this time exceptional for such large-scale works to be printed by lithography anywhere.

BIBLIOGRAPHY

P. Gossett: *The Operas of Rossini* (diss., Princeton U., 1970), 572ff

RICHARD MACNUTT

Ratti, Lorenzo (*b* Perugia, c1590; *d* Loreto, 10 Aug 1630). Italian composer and organist. He was a pupil of his uncle Vincenzo Ugolino and from 1599 to 1601 a choirboy in the Cappella Giulia at St Peter's, Rome. From 1 May 1614 to June 1616 he was organist of Perugia Cathedral and from 17 June 1619 to between July and November 1620 *maestro di cappella* of the Collegio Germanico, Rome. He then became *maestro* of S Luigi dei Francesi, Rome. He returned to the Collegio Germanico for a further period as *maestro*, which lasted probably from late March 1623 to about 1 December 1629. On 15 December he succeeded Antonio Cifra as *maestro di cappella* of the Santa Casa, Loreto, but he had to resign on 30 July 1630 because of ill-health. He was ordained in the priesthood little more than a month before he died.

The *Sacrae modulationes* contain his most important work: polychoral settings of the Proper of the Mass as well as motets for the Elevation for every Sunday of the year; the four dialogues are the only early 17th-century dialogues to have served a liturgical function.

WORKS
SACRED

Litanie e motetti, 5–8vv (Venice, 1616)

Motecta, 2–5vv, bc (org), libro I (Rome, 1617)

Motecta, 2–5vv, bc (org), libro II (Rome, 1617)

Motetti della cantica, 2–5vv (Rome, 1619)

Motetti, 1–6vv (Venice, 1620)

Litanie della beata virgine, 5, 8vv (Venice, 1626)

Sacrae modulationes . . . pars I, 2–12vv, una cum bc (org) (Venice, 1628)

Sacrae modulationes . . . pars II (Venice, 1628)

Sacrae modulationes . . . pars III (Venice, 1628)

Litanie Beatissimae Virginis Mariae, 5–8, 12vv, una cum bc (org) (Venice, 1630)

Cantica Salomonis, 2–5vv, una cum bc (org), pars I (Venice, 1632)

Missa sine nomine, Missa Do re mi: *I-Rsmt*

Ecce panis angelicus, *Rvat*

SECULAR

Il primo libro de' madrigali, 5vv (Venice, 1615)

Il secondo libro de' madrigali, 5vv (Venice, 1616)

Il Ciclope overo della vendetta d'Apolline, dramma harmonico, Collegio Germanico e Ungarico, Rome, 1628, music lost

BIBLIOGRAPHY

G. Tebaldini: *L'archivio musicale della Cappella lauretana* (Loreto, 1921)

U. Rolandi: 'Il Ciclope, dramma harmonico con musica di D. Lorenzo Ratti (Roma, 1628)', *NA*, x (1933), 253

R. F. Chauvin: 'Six Gospel Dialogues from the Offertory by Lorenzo Ratti', *AnMc*, no.9 (1970), 64

T. D. Culley: *Jesuits and Music, i: A Study of the Musicians Connected with the German College in Rome during the 17th Century and of their Activities in Northern Europe* (Rome, 1970), 13, 128ff, 136f, 168f, 173

REGINA F. CHAUVIN

Rattle (Fr. *hochet*; Ger. *Rassel*, *Schnarre*; It. *nacchere*). A shaken idiophone in a variety of forms and with numerous names (see illustration). In its simplest and earliest form a strung rattle consists of small hard objects such as seeds, shells or teeth bunched together; a GOURD rattle formed from a seed pod in which the dried seeds remain; or a calabash or clay vessel filled with seeds or small pebbles. Certain rattles (such as the beaded calabash) have seeds, shells, or other rattling pieces outside as well as inside the gourd. The shells of gourd rattles, the beaded calabash and similar instruments are provided by the natural fruit. In some cases a handle and bowl are fashioned simply by tying the calabash fruit near its stalk. Modern rattles formed from natural fruit pods, or manufactured from wood or a plastic material, include *maracas*, the *chocalho* (a tube rattle) and the CABACA.

The rattle is the instrument with which we are usually first acquainted as children, and it was among the earliest instruments known to man. Clay objects excavated in Costa Rica point to the use of rattles in prehistoric times. The strung rattle remains an important instrument among the modern primitives of a low cultural standard. It is used to stress dancing, being shaken or hung from the ankle, leg, arm or neck of the dancer. Rattles of this description fashioned from the ears of springbok or dried hide, and containing small pieces of ostrich-egg shell or dried berries as rattling

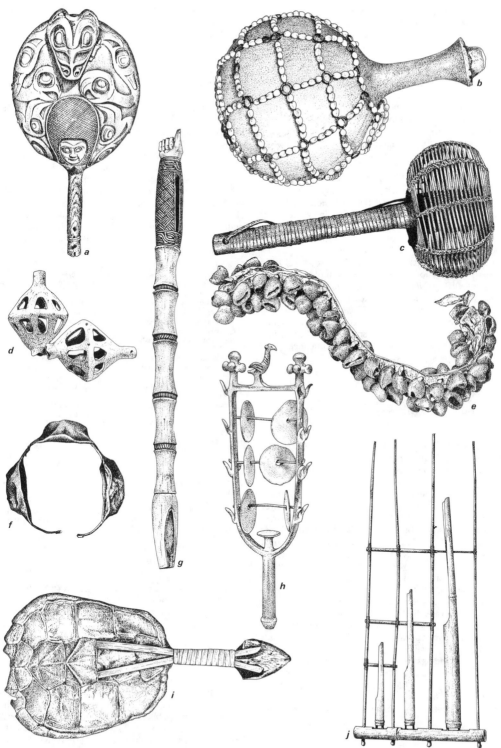

Examples of rattles: (a) *wooden rattle of the Kitksan Indians, British Columbia, Canada;* (b) *gourd rattle (cabaca);* (c)
basket rattle, Zaïre; (d) *bronze rattles, Luristan, Iran;* (e) *nut-shell belt, South America;* (f) *iron rattle, West Africa;*
(g) *ivory stick rattle, Nigeria;* (h) *bronze sistrum (c2100* BC), *Central Anatolia;* (i) *turtle-shell rattle of the Seneca
Indians, New York State;* (j) *bamboo rattle (angklung), Java;* (a),(i) *Museum of the American Indian, New York;*
(c)–(g) *Horniman Museum, London;* (h) *Metropolitan Museum of Art, New York*

pieces, are found among the Bushmen of South Africa. Early travellers to America found the rattle an important instrument in such ancient ceremonial dances as the *tupinamba* (ritual fire dance), and ceremonies connected with burial and sacrifice. In his *Historie of Virginia* (1624) John Smith wrote of rattles made of gourds or pumeone shells which sounded 'Base, Tenor, Countertenor, Meane and Treble'. Rattle worship and the belief in the magical power of this simple instrument is widespread. It is an important item of the equipment used by the African witch doctor and his counterpart, the North American shaman. Rattles are used by Korean priests, and to Brazilians who indulged in rattle worship the rattle was the dwelling-place of the Devil. For a long time man has used numerous elements to make rattles, including such macabre objects as human skulls filled with pebbles, and the jawbone of an ass or zebra in which the loose teeth act as rattling pieces. This instrument survives in the Latin American dance orchestra as the *quijada*, as do gourd rattles (maracas), and instruments such as the cabaca.

Rattles of various descriptions are scored for in modern compositions, outstanding examples being the works of Orff (*Weihnachtsspiel* and *Antigonae*); Varèse (*Ionisation* – maracas, high and low); Henze (*Ode an den Westwind*); and Britten (*The Prodigal Son* – here a conical gourd rattle is used to produce two distinct tones). In certain cases composers are not explicit, and fail to define whether rattle or ratchet is intended.

See also the entry 'Rattle' in Appendix A.

BIBLIOGRAPHY

J. Smith: *Historie of Virginia* (London, 1624)
T. De Bry: *Historia Americae*, iii (Frankfurt am Main, 1932)
G. Chase: *A Guide to the Music of Latin-American Pan American Union and The Library of Congress* (Washington, DC, 1962)

JAMES BLADES

Rattle, Simon (Denis) (*b* Liverpool, 19 Jan 1955). English conductor. Having played percussion from an early age with the National Youth Orchestra and occasionally the Royal Liverpool PO, he studied the piano, percussion and conducting at the Royal Academy of Music, London (1971–4). In 1974 he won the John Player International Conductors' Competition and was then appointed assistant conductor of the Bournemouth SO and Bournemouth Sinfonietta. He made his Festival Hall début with the (then New) Philharmonia Orchestra in 1975, and the next year became associate conductor of the Royal Liverpool PO and assistant conductor of the BBC Scottish SO. In 1979 he was appointed principal conductor of the CBSO. Other orchestras he has conducted include the London Sinfonietta, the ECO and (from 1978) the Rotterdam PO. The youngest conductor to have appeared at the Proms and with Glyndebourne Festival Opera (*The Cunning Little Vixen*, 1977), he has been noted for his fluent style and lucid direction. Haydn, Mahler, Sibelius, Janáček and Stravinsky are among the composers on whom he has concentrated, one of his most acclaimed performances being the première of Maxwell Davies's Symphony (1978).

RUTH THACKERAY

Ratz, Erwin (*b* Graz, 22 Dec 1898; *d* Vienna, 12 Dec 1973). Austrian musicologist. In addition to his musicological studies under Adler at Vienna University (1918–22), he became a private pupil of Schoenberg in 1917 and remained an active supporter of his teacher's work. After organizing the ten public rehearsals in 1918 of Schoenberg's Chamber Symphony op.9, he founded the Verein für Musikalische Privataufführungen (1918–21) with Berg and Paul A. Pisk. The activities of the society prepared for the founding of the ISCM in 1922. When Schoenberg went to Berlin (late 1925) Ratz continued his composition studies with Webern; they were close friends until Webern's death. Ratz's ability in music analysis led to his appointment to teach theory at the Musikakademie, a post he held until his death. His research into the problems of several important works, is demonstrated in his exemplary *Einführung in die musikalische Formenlehre*.

In 1955 Ratz became president of the International Gustav Mahler Society and editor of the complete critical Mahler edition. In connection with this he established a collection of literary and recorded documents. He also prepared critical editions of Beethoven's piano variations and Schubert's piano sonatas. From 1953 to 1968 he was president of the Austrian section of the ISCM.

WRITINGS

Zur Chronologie der Klaviersonaten Franz Schuberts (Vienna, 1949)
Die Originalfassung des Streichquartettes op.130 von Beethoven (Vienna, 1950)
Erkenntnis und Erlebnis des musikalischen Kunstwerks (Vienna, 1950)
Einführung in die musikalische Formenlehre: über Formprinzipien in den Inventionen und Fugen J. S. Bachs und ihre Bedeutung für die Kompositionstechnik Beethovens (Vienna, 1951, 3/1973)
'Zum Formproblem bei Gustav Mahler: eine Analyse des ersten Satzes der IX. Symphonie', *Mf*, viii (1955), 169
'Zum Formproblem bei Gustav Mahler: eine Analyse des Finales der VI. Symphonie', *Mf*, ix (1956), 156
Gustav Mahler (Berlin, 1957)
'Persönlichkeit und Werk: Gustav Mahler zum 100. Geburtstag', *ÖMz*, xv (1960), 282
'Über die Bedeutung der funktionellen Formenlehre für die Erkenntnis des Wohltemperierten Klaviers', *Mf*, xxi (1968), 17
'Analyse und Hermeneutik in ihrer Bedeutung für die Interpretation Beethovens', *ÖMz*, xxv (1970), 756
Gesammelte Aufsätze (Vienna, 1975)

EDITIONS

G. Mahler: *Symphonie Nr. 7*, Sämtliche Werke: kritische Gesamtausgabe, vii (Berlin, 1960); *Symphonie Nr. 4*, ibid, iv (Vienna, 1963); *Symphonie Nr. 6*, ibid, vi (Lindau, 1963); *Adagio aus der Symphonie Nr. 10*, ibid, xia (Vienna, 1964); *Symphonie Nr. 5*, ibid, v (Frankfurt, 1964); *Das Lied von der Erde*, ibid, ix (Vienna, 1964); *Symphonie Nr. 1*, ibid, i (Vienna, 1967); *Symphonie Nr. 10* (Munich, 1967) [facs. of sketches]; *Symphonie Nr. 9*, ibid, x (Vienna, 1969); *Symphonie Nr. 2*, ibid, ii (Vienna, 1970); *Symphonie Nr. 9*, ibid (Vienna, 1971) [facs. of 1st draft in score]; *Symphonie Nr. 3*, ibid, iii (Vienna, 1974); *Symphonie Nr. 8*, ibid (in preparation)

BIBLIOGRAPHY

K. H. Füssl: 'Prof. Erwin Ratz zum 60. Geburtstag', *ÖMz*, xiv (1959), 18 [incl. list of writings]
R. Klein: 'Erwin Ratz zum Gedenken', *ÖMz*, xxix (1974), 44
R. Stephan: 'Erwin Ratz†', *Mf*, xxvii (1974), 151

RUDOLF KLEIN

Rauch. German or Alsatian family of musicians.

(1) Johann Georg Rauch (i) (*b* Sulz, nr. Strasbourg; *d* Strasbourg, 21 July 1710). Organist and composer. He is first heard of in June 1687 when he was appointed organist of Strasbourg Cathedral; about the same time his first extant publication, a volume of motets, was published in Augsburg. Since his subsequent publications appeared at Strasbourg, it may be that his previous appointment had been in the Augsburg region. Though three further publications appeared in the next ten years, Rauch's applications for the post of Kapellmeister were never successful. When Sébastien de Brossard, for whom Rauch had sometimes deputized, left in

1699, he was eventually replaced by Thomas Bourgeois, and when the latter left in 1707 Rauch was again passed over.

Rauch's published church music displays a great variety of textures and a familiarity with all the contemporary styles of church music, from the flowing melodious duet to the massive ceremonial concertato style. It is typical of the Italian-influenced church music favoured by many German composers of the time.

WORKS

Novae sirenes sacrae harmoniae, motets, 2–8vv, insts, op.1 (Augsburg, 1687)
Novae sirenes sacrae harmoniae, motets, 3–7vv, insts (Strasbourg, 1690)
Harmonicus missarum concentus, op.3, masses, 4–8vv, 5 inst parts (Strasbourg, 1692)
Cithara Orphei duodecim sonatorum, 4 parts (Strasbourg, 1697), lost

(2) Joseph Michel Rauch (b Strasbourg, c1685; d Strasbourg, 10 April 1738). Organist and composer, son of (1) Johann Georg Rauch (i). He is first heard of in 1708, when the authorities of Strasbourg Cathedral gave him a bursary to study the organ and composition in Paris. By 1710 he was back in Strasbourg, taking over the post of cathedral organist in September, after his father's death. Unlike his father, he also obtained the post of Kapellmeister; but from a non-musical point of view, he does not seem to have been a very satisfactory employee, as the cathedral frequently had to pay his debts, and he spent six weeks away in Rheims without permission in 1725. His death in 1738 was preceded by 12 years of illness, and though he officially held his posts to the end of his life, much of the work was done by his younger brother, (3) Johann Georg Rauch (ii).

Rauch had a considerable reputation as an organist, but was less well regarded as a composer. None of his compositions, which include a number of masses and a Te Deum for the wedding of Louis XV, is extant.

(3) Johann Georg Rauch (ii) (b Strasbourg, 1702; d Strasbourg 1 July 1779). Organist, son of (1) Johann Georg Rauch (i). He became organist at Strasbourg Cathedral in 1738 on the death of his elder brother, (2) Joseph Michel, for whom he had been deputizing since 1726. He does not seem to have succeeded to his brother's other post of Kapellmeister; in the last years of his life it was held by F. X. Richter, who wrote a funeral motet for him.

(4) Johann Baptist Rauch (fl 1779–96). Organist; his relationship to the earlier members of the family is not known. He succeeded (3) Johann Georg Rauch (ii) as organist at Strasbourg Cathedral in 1779, and still held the post in 1796; no other details of his life are known. He is said to have composed a mass, which is not extant.

BIBLIOGRAPHY

A. Goehlinger: Die Musikpflege an Strassburger Münster (Strasbourg, 1920)

ELIZABETH ROCHE

Rauch, Andreas (b Pottendorf, 1592; d Ödenburg [now Sopron], 1656). Austrian organist and composer. The title-pages of his published works show that he was organist at the Protestant churches at Hernals (1621–5) and Inzersdorf (1627) in the Lutheran region of Lower Austria. Following the expulsion of Protestants from Austria he arrived in 1629 in Ödenburg, where he was the organist of St Michael's Church until his death.

As well as the Venetian polychoral style, which characterizes the hymns of thanksgiving that he wrote to celebrate the Peace of Westphalia in 1648, Rauch em-

ployed both old and new stylistic means as he needed them. Thus the motets of the Thymiaterium (1625) – the title, meaning 'censer', is a play on the composer's name ('smoke' or 'incense') – present pseudo-polyphonic harmonic writing reminiscent of Johannes Eccard, whereas the sacred works of 1641 and 1651 for four or fewer voices only follow Monteverdi and the Kleine geistliche Konzerte of Schütz, and the secular three-part songs (1627) are related stylistically to Italian ballettos. As a minor master of Protestant music in Austria and Hungary, Rauch ranks with such men as Brassicanus, J. F. Fritzius and Lagkhner.

WORKS

Symbolum peccatoris resipiscentis . . . 4vv (Nuremberg, 1621)
Thymiaterium musicale . . . 4–8vv, bc (Nuremberg, 1625)
Musicalisches Stammbüchlein . . . 3vv (Nuremberg, 1627); edns. of 3 secular songs in Das frühdeutsche Lied, ed. W. Vetter, ii (Münster, 1928), and 1 sacred and 2 secular songs in Antiqua-Chorbuch, ed. H. Mönkemeyer, i, ii (Mainz, 1951)
Zwey christlische musicalische Gesänglein (Nuremberg, 1627)
Concentus votivus sub . . . Ferdinandi II (Vienna, 1635)
Missa, vespera et alii sacri concentus concertati, 2vv, hpd (Nuremberg, 1641), includes his portrait 'aet. suae 49'
Currus triumphalis musici . . . 8–12vv, bc (Vienna, 1648)
Newes Thymiaterium . . . 3–4vv, insts (Vienna and Lucerne, 1651)
EitnerQ lists 2 motets: Resonet in laudibus and Incipite Dominum tympanis, copied from prints
A second Musicalisches Stammbüchlein (Ulm, c1649) is cited in contemporary catalogues (see Moser)

BIBLIOGRAPHY

H. J. Moser: Die Musik im frühevangelischen Österreich (Kassel, 1954)

HELLMUT FEDERHOFER

Rauch, Caspar (b Ulm, 1558; d ?Breslau, after 1618). German composer. He is known to have been a citizen of Breslau in about 1618, for he referred to himself thus when he published his only known work, Ein Schatz-Kasten voller Clainodien von allerley schönen Trostsprüchen auss heiliger Schrift dess alten und newen Testaments, in Königgrätz that year. In this publication (a sole copy exists in PL-WRu) there is mention of an extensive collection of songs, although only eight appeared in the appendix in settings for one to five voices; most of the songs deal with the subject of death. The work has also a secondary, didactic purpose, in that Rauch intended the pieces to be used in schools.

BIBLIOGRAPHY

A. Fischer and W. Tümpel: Das deutsche evangelische Kirchenlied des 17. Jahrhunderts, i (Gütersloh, 1904/R1964) [incl. edn. of two songs]; v (Gütersloh, 1916/R1964) [incl. complete list of titles]
H. J. Moser: Die Musik im frühevangelischen Österreich (Kassel, 1954)
R. Quoika: Die Musik der Deutschen in Böhmen und Mähren (Berlin, 1956)

WALTER BLANKENBURG

Rauch, František (b Plzeň, 4 Feb 1910). Czech pianist. He studied the piano with Hoffmeister (1929–31) and composition with Novák (1936–7) in Prague, made his début with the Czech PO in 1932 and then played in most European centres and, after World War II, in India, Japan and Brazil. He has a strong technique, and tends towards balanced and objective, though not unemotional, interpretations. Rauch specializes in Czech music, Beethoven, Chopin and the German Romantics. An excellent chamber player, he has formed duos with the violinist Zika, the cellist Sádlo and the pianist Hubička. He is a member of the Prague Trio, originally with Bělčík (violin) and F. Smetana, then Sádlo (cello); later with Etlík (clarinet) and Tylšar (horn). From 1939 he taught at the Prague Conservatory and from 1946 at the Prague Academy (AMU) where he became head of the department of keyboard instruments; his pupils include Růžičková, Boldocká and Eben. In 1963 he was made Artist of Merit. He occasionally writes reviews and articles for *Hudební rozhledy* and has composed for piano and chamber ensemmbles.

BIBLIOGRAPHY

ČSHS

P. Eben: 'Jubileum umělce-učitele' [Jubilee of the artist-teacher], *HRo*, xiii (1960), 70

J. Kozák: *Československtí koncertní umělci a komorní soubory* [Czechoslovak concert artists and chamber ensembles] (Prague, 1964), 73ff

ALENA NĚMCOVÁ

Rauche, Michael (*fl* London, second half of 18th century). English instrument maker. His extant instruments include two theorbos, one of which, in the Victoria and Albert Museum, London, bears the date 1762 and Rauche's address in Chandos Street, London. It is an elaborate instrument in ivory and ebony. The other, in a private collection, is much plainer, with a finish reminiscent of some of his guitars. One of these, dated 1770, is in the Hill collection at the Ashmolean Museum, Oxford.

Rauch von Schratt, Hans. *See* SCHRATT, HANS RAUCH VON.

Raugel, Félix (*b* St Quentin, 27 Nov 1881; *d* Paris, 30 Dec 1975). French choir director and musicologist. He studied at the Lille Conservatory (1899–1900; *premier prix* for viola in 1900 under Charles Queste), then at the Schola Cantorum in Paris (1900–09), where he was taught the organ by A. M. Decaux, composition by d'Indy and counterpoint by Roussel; he also studied harmony under Libert. Raugel's many posts during his long career were mainly those of organist and choir director: *maître de chapelle* at St Eustache (1911–28) and at St Honoré d'Eylau (1928–40); founder and director of the Handel Society (1909–14), the Chorale Française (1922–4), the Société des Etudes Mozartiennes (1930–39) and the Chorale Félix Raugel (1931); finally choir trainer for French radio (1934–47) and conductor of the Philharmonic Society of Rheims (1926–62).

Raugel wrote some 20 papers on the organ (instruments, organists and makers) and on aspects of choral music. He also made editions of organ works (by Handel, Scarlatti and Buxtehude) and vocal works (by Péchon, Steffani and Brossard). His writings include contributions to several reviews (*Tribune de Saint-Gervais*, *Monde musical*, *Revue de l'orgue*) and important encyclopedias. He was musical director of the Anthologie Sonore (1949–59) and vice-president of the Société Française de Musicologie (1944–59).

WRITINGS

Les orgues de l'Abbaye de Saint-Mihiel (Paris, 1919)
Le cantique français (Tourcoing, 1920)
Les organistes (Paris, 1923, 2/1961)
Recherches sur les maîtres de l'ancienne facture française d'orgues: les Lépine, les Cavaillé, Dom Bédos (Paris, 1925)
Les anciens buffets d'orgues du Département de Seine-et-Oise (Paris, 1926)
Les grandes orgues des églises de Paris et du département de la Seine (Paris, 1926)
Les anciens buffets d'orgues du département de Seine-et-Marne (Paris, 1929, 2/1972)
Palestrina (Paris, 1930)
Les grandes orgues de Notre-Dame (Paris, 1934)
Les anciens buffets d'orgues du département de la Marne (Paris, 1938)
'Les Isnard: problèmes de musique sacrée', *Cahiers de l'art sacré*, vi (1946), 29

'Les maîtrises d'enfants de choeur dans l'ancienne France, des origines au XVIe siècle', *Cahiers de l'art sacré*, vi–vii (1947), 165
Le chant choral (Paris, 1948, 3/1966)
L'oratorio (Paris, 1948)
Les orgues et les organistes de la Cathédrale de Strasbourg (Colmar, 1948)
Les grandes orgues de la basilique de Saint-Nicolas-de-Port (Paris, 1949)
'Une maîtrise célèbre au grand siècle: la maîtrise de la Cathédrale d'Aix-en-Provence' *Revue des études du XVIIe siècle* (1954), nos.21–2, p.422
'L'organiste P. Du Mage', *Mélanges d'histoire et d'esthétique musicales offerts à Paul-Marie Masson* (Paris, 1955), 125
'François Pétouille, maître de musique de Notre-Dame de Paris', *RMFC*, ii (1961–2), 117
'La maîtrise, les orgues et les organistes de la Primatiale Saint-Trophime d'Arles', *RMFC*, ii (1961–2), 99
'Notes pour servir à l'histoire musicale de la Collégiale de Saint-Quentin, depuis les origines jusqu'en 1679', *Festschrift Heinrich Besseler* (Leipzig, 1961), 51
'Les Silbermann facteurs d'orgues et les organistes de leur temps', *Liber amicorum Charles van den Borren* (Antwerp, 1964), 191
'La musique à la Chapelle du Château de Versailles sous Louis XIV', *Revue des études du XVIIe siècle* (1967), no.54, p.19
'Les buffets d'orgues de l'ancien département de Seine-et-Oise', *L'orgue* (1971), no.138 bis, pp.1–43
'Les buffets d'orgues de l'ancien département de Seine-et-Marne', *L'orgue (cahiers et mémoires de l'Orgue)* (1972), no.142, pp.1–40
'Autour de Sauzay, de Boëly et de Reber', *RMFC*, xv (1975), 146

EDITIONS

Les maîtres français de l'orgue aux XVIIe et XVIIIe siècles (Paris, 1933, 2/1949)
P. du Mage: *Livre d'orgue 1676–1751* (Paris, 1952)

BIBLIOGRAPHY

'Pour les quatre-vingts ans de Félix Raugel', *L'orgue* (1962), no.102, p.59 [incl. list of publications]
N. Dufourcq: 'Nécrologie: Félix Raugel', *RMFC*, xvi (1976), 212

CHRISTIANE SPIETH-WEISSENBACHER

Raulin de Vaux (*fl c*1420). French composer. He is known solely through the rondeau *Savés pour quoy suy sy gay* which is found in *GB-Ob* 213 (*Early Fifteenth Century Music*, ed. G. Reaney, CMM, xi/2 (1959), p.104). The work is for three voices with text in the top voice only. The text has a shorter line appearing after the first phrase of the refrain and in the same place in the second section. Both times the music is the same. He is not to be identified with the Raulin of *I-Fn* 176.

TOM R. WARD

Rault, Félix (*b* Bordeaux, 1736; *d* Paris, 1800 or later). French flautist, teacher and composer. A pupil of the flautist Michel Blavet, he acquired great skill in his early youth. He obtained a part-time position in the Paris Opéra orchestra in 1754 and when Blavet retired from this orchestra in 1758, Rault became his full-time successor. He was also employed in the Concert Spirituel orchestra from 1765 to about 1776 and in the royal chapel from 1768 until its dissolution in 1792. In 1781 Rault left the Opéra with a pension and began to devote more time to solo performances. The flute concerto and numerous chamber works that he wrote for these occasions reflect the typical *galant* style of the time, but show little imagination or depth. The cancellation of pensions at the Opéra during the Revolution caused Rault to take a post in the orchestra of the Théâtre de la Cité; when the theatre closed in 1800 he fell into desperate financial straits, and he reportedly died shortly thereafter.

Rault is historically important mainly as a flute teacher; he figured strongly in the evolution of the French school of flute playing from the late Baroque to the Romantic periods. As the most noted pupil of Blavet, he became the principal transmitter of the early 18th-century French tradition. His most outstanding pupil,

Jean-Georges Wunderlich, was one of the first flute professors at the Paris Conservatoire and co-author (with Antoine Hugot) of the official *Méthode* used by the Conservatoire for many years.

WORKS
(*most published in Paris*)

Ier concerto, fl, orch (1793); Fl Conc. no.2, lost

3 trios, 2 fl, bn, op.25 (n.d.); 3 trios, fl, vn, va, op.26 (n.d.); at least 30 duos (of which 6 are lost) in 6 sets, 2 fl; ?6 sonates, fl, b; other works, lost

BIBLIOGRAPHY

GerberL; *GerberNL*

J.-B. de La Borde: *Essai sur la musique ancienne et moderne* (Paris, 1780/*R*1972)

R. S. Rockstro: *A Treatise on ... the Flute* (London, 1890, 2/1928/*R*1967)

A. Girard: *Histoire et richesses de la flûte* (Paris, 1953)

C. Pierre: *Histoire du Concert spirituel 1725–1790* (Paris, 1975)

SHERWOOD DUDLEY

Raupach. German family of musicians and writers.

(1) Christoph Raupach [Veritophilus] (*b* Tondern, 5 July 1686; *d* Stralsund, 1744). Organist, composer and writer on music. He studied the harpsichord, organ and violin with his father Georg Raupach (*b* Kauffung, nr. Liegnitz [now Legnica]; *d* Tondern, 1700), an organist at Zittau and Tondern; in 1701 he went to Hamburg to study composition with Georg Bronner. On 30 April 1703 he was appointed organist at the Nikolaikirche in Stralsund, where he remained until his death. Several compositions, including keyboard suites, oratorios and cantatas (among them *Danket dem Herrn* and *Wünschet Jerusalem Glück*, *B-Bc*), are mentioned in his autobiography (in Mattheson, 1740). He also wrote essays on music, most notably 'Veritophili deutliche Beweis-Gründe, worauf der rechte Gebrauch der Music beydes in den Kirchen und ausser denselben beruhet' (in F. E. Neidt: *Musicalischer Handleitung*, iii, Hamburg, 1717).

(2) Hermann Friedrich Raupach (*b* Stralsund, 21 Dec 1728; *d* St Petersburg, Dec 1778). Harpsichordist and composer, son of (1) Christoph Raupach. On 24 February 1755 he was engaged as deputy harpsichordist in the court orchestra at St Petersburg, and in 1758 succeeded Araia as Kapellmeister and court composer. In the same year he produced his first opera, *Alceste*. On 18 January 1762 Raupach was replaced as Kapellmeister by Vincenzo Manfredini; he then went via Hamburg to Paris, where he met the young Mozart and had some sonatas for violin and keyboard published. Four movements from Raupach's sonatas were arranged by Mozart in his keyboard concertos K37, 39 and 41. In 1768, after Tommaso Traetta had been appointed Kapellmeister, Raupach returned to St Petersburg as deputy harpsichordist and in 1770 was promoted to deputy Kapellmeister. In this post he was required to write ballet music and other stage works; his opera *Dobrïye soldatï* ('The good soldiers') was performed posthumously. Raupach became the director of the music department at the Academy of Fine Arts in St Petersburg in 1777, his students including E. I. Fomin.

WORKS

Stage (all first performed in St Petersburg): Alceste (A. Sumarkov), 1758, *USSR-Ltob*; Siroe (opera), c1760, *B-Bc*; Dobrïye soldatï [The good soldiers] (opera, 3, Khoraskov), ?1778, perf. 29 Feb 1780, *USSR-Ltob*; c15 ballets, some to operas by T. Traetta, lost

Inst: 6 sonates, vn, op.1 (Paris, c1762); 4 sonates, vn, op.2 (Paris, c1765); 4 sonates, 2 vn, b, op.3 (Paris, c1770)

(3) Ernst Benjamin Salomo Raupach [Hirsemenzel, Lebrecht] (*b* Straupitz, 21 May 1784; *d* Berlin, 19 March 1848). Dramatist. He studied at the University

of Halle; in 1804 he moved to Russia as a tutor, and from 1816 taught in the philosophy department of St Petersburg University, where he was appointed professor of history and German literature in 1817. He left Russia in autumn 1822; after travelling to Italy he returned to Germany, settling in Berlin in autumn 1824. He wrote a number of opera librettos, including *Agnes von Hohenstaufen* (set by Spontini, 1829) and *Die drei Wünsche* (Carl Loewe, 1832); his play *Der versiegelte Bürgermeister* (1828) was adapted by Richard Batka and A. S. Pordes-Milo for Leo Blech's opera *Versiegelt* (1908). Other writings by him inspired music by Mendelssohn, K. L. Blumer, H. Proch, F. Hiller, Wagner and Spohr. A four-volume edition of his comedies (Hamburg, 1829–35) and 16 volumes of his serious works (Hamburg, 1835–43) were published.

BIBLIOGRAPHY

J. Mattheson: *Critica musica*, i (Hamburg, 1722/*R*1964), 167ff

——: *Grundlage einer Ehren-Pforte* (Hamburg, 1740); ed. M. Schneider (Berlin, 1910/*R*1969), 282ff

P. Raupach: *Raupach: eine biographische Skizze* (Berlin, 1853)

R. A. Mooser: *Annales de la musique et des musiciens en Russie*, i (Geneva, 1948)

GEOFFREY NORRIS

Rauscher (Ger.: 'rustle'; Fr. *batterie*). An 18th-century term for rapid, broken accompaniment figures.

Rauschpfeife (Ger.). A loud straight capped SHAWM of the 16th and early 17th centuries (*see* WIND-CAP INSTRUMENTS). It was named in at least three 16th-century sources. Burgkmair's woodcuts of the Triumph of Maximilian I (1526) include the only known illustration of the instrument; under the title 'Musica süess Melodey' a group of eight musicians on a wagon play string instruments, pipe and tabor, and two pipes, one larger than the other, of shawm-like appearance save for their reed-caps (see illustration). The caption calls them 'ain klain Rauschpfeiffen' and 'ain grosse Rauschpfeiffen'. Another scene in the same series shows them, again named, in a mounted band with shawms and trombones. A letter dated 1541 from the Duke of Prussia relating to purchases of wind instruments from Georg Neuschel of Nuremberg (see Eitner) mentions the 'grossen lauteschallenden Instrumente oder Rauschpfeiffen' which can be used in six or more parts, and the Baden-Baden 1582 court inventory includes 24 Rauschpfeifen.

See also ORGAN STOP.

Two rauschpfeifen (centre back) with a fiddle, two lutes and a pipe and tabor: detail of a woodcut from the 'Triumph of Maximilian I' (1526) by Hans Burgkmair

BIBLIOGRAPHY
R. Eitner: 'Briefe von Jorg Neuschel in Nürnberg nebst einiger andern',
    MMg, ix (1877), 149
ANTHONY C. BAINES

Rauschquint [Rauschwerk] (Ger.). An ORGAN STOP (*Rauschpfeife*).

Rautavaara, Einojuhani (*b* Helsinki, 9 Oct 1928). Finnish composer. He studied composition with Merikanto at the Sibelius Academy in Helsinki (1948–52) and musicology at Helsinki University (MA 1953). From 1955 to 1956 he studied with Persichetti at the Juilliard School and with Copland and Sessions at Tanglewood, in 1957 with Vogel in Ascona and in 1958 with Petzold at the Staatliche Hochschule für Musik, Cologne. He then took appointments as librarian of the Helsinki City Orchestra (1959–61), director of the Käpylä Music School in Helsinki (1965–6) and lecturer in music theory at the Sibelius Academy (from 1966). In 1971 he was appointed professor in arts, a state office with no fixed duties. Among the awards he has received are the first prize in a competition sponsored by the Brevard Foundation for *A Requiem in our Time* (1954) and the Sibelius Prize of the Wihuri Foundation (1965).

Like many Finnish composers of his generation (and in particular the pupils of Merikanto), Rautavaara was first influenced by the neo-classicism of Hindemith and Stravinsky. But *A Requiem in our Time* also reveals an interest in Russian music, primarily Musorgsky and Borodin. The piano suite *Ikonit* ('The icons', 1956) is permeated by Musorgsky and the atmosphere of the Orthodox faith: the idea of the work is very similar to that of the *Pictures at an Exhibition*. Other sources here are Debussy, Messiaen and perhaps Hindemith; the main stylistic features are resonant parallel chords, bitonality and modal scales. In the late 1950s he became interested in the 12-note method, which he employed in, for example, the Second String Quartet (1958) and the Wind Octet (1964). Rautavaara has compared the sound of his Second Quartet with that of *Verklärte Nacht* or the Bruckner Quintet. An almost Romantic warmth of sound and expression also characterizes the Rilke song cycle *Die Liebenden* (1959), whose style, like that of the television opera *Kaivos* ('The mine', 1963), is very close to Berg, whereas Bruckner's name has often been mentioned in connection with the Third Symphony (1961). Rautavaara could be accused of eclecticism and lack of individual style, and the quality of his output is uneven. But at his best, as, for example, in the Cello Concerto and *The True and False Unicorn*, he can write music that is interesting and distinctive.

WORKS
(selective list)
STAGE AND VOCAL

Operas: Kaivos [The mine], op.15 (television opera, Rautavaara), 1963; Apollon contra Marsyas, op.56 (comic opera, 3, B. V. Wall), 1970; Runo 42 (Kalevala, Rautavaara), 1974; Marjatta matala neiti (Kalevala), 1975; En dramatisk scen (Rautavaara), 1975–6
Ballet: Kiusaukset [The temptations], op.47, 1969
Choral orch: Itsenäisyyskantaatti [Independence cantata], op.29, S, B, speaker, chorus, orch, 1967; Daughter of the Sea, op.49, conc., S, chorus, orch, 1970; The True and False Unicorn, op.58 (J. Broughton), chorus, orch, tape, 1971; The Water Circle, op.65 (Broughton), pf, chorus, orch, 1972
Unacc. choral: Ludus verbalis, op.10, 1957; Nattvarden [Communion], op.22, 1964; 2 Preludes, op.32 (Eliot), 1967; 2 Psalms, op.37, 1968, 1970; Vigilia, op.57 (Orthodox liturgy), 1971; Credo, op.63, 1972; Suite de Lorca, 1973; Hammarskjöld-fragment, 1975
Songs: 5 Sonette and Orpheus, op.9 (Rilke), 1959; Die Liebenden, op.13 (Rilke), 1959; 3 Sonnets (Shakespeare), 1962; October, 1972

INSTRUMENTAL

Orch: A Requiem in our Time, op.3, 1953; Syms. nos.1–4, 1956, 1957, 1961, 1964; Cantos I–II, str, 1960; Arabescata, op.24, 1963; Anadyomene, op.33, 1968; Sotilasmessu [A soldier's mass], op.40, wind, perc, 1968; Vc Conc., op.41, 1968; Pf Conc., op.45, 1969; Dithyrambos, op.55, vn, orch, 1970; Säännöllisiä yksikköjaksoja puolisäännöllisessä tilanteessa [Regular sets of elements in a semi-regular situation], op.60, 1971; Cantus arcticus, op.61, orch, tape, 1972; Taiteilijan muotokuva määrätyllä hetkellä [A portrait of the artist at a certain moment], op.62, 1972; Conc., fl, orch, 1973; Annunciations, org, brass, ww, 1977
Chamber: 4 str qts, op.2, 1952, op.12, 1958, op.18, 1965, 1975; Wind Octet, op.21, 1964; Sonata, op.26, bn, pf, 1965–8; 2 Preludes and Fugues, op.36, vc, pf, 1965; Laudatio trinitatis, op.39, org, 1969; Sonata, op.46, vc, 1969; Sonetto, op.53, cl, pf, 1969; Toccata, op.59, org, 1971; Sonata, fl, gui, 1975
Pf: Pelimannit [The fiddlers], op.1, 1952; Ikonit [The icons], op.6, 1956; 7 Preludes, op.7, 1957; 3 Symmetric Preludes, op.14, 1959; Partita, op.34, 1968; Etudes, op.42, 1969; Sonata no.1 'Christus und die Fischer', op.50, 1969; Sonata no.2 'The Fire Sermon', op.54, 1970

Principal publishers: Breitkopf & Härtel, King, Weinberger
ILKKA ORAMO

Rautenstein, Julius Ernst (*b* Lauenburg, nr. Hamburg, *c*1590–95; *d* ?Stettin [now Szczecin], after 6 March 1654). German composer and organist. An illegitimate descendant of Duke Franz I of Saxe-Lauenburg, he was an organist at Kroppenstedt, near Magdeburg, until 1617, when he moved to Halberstadt to take up a similar post at the church of St Martin. From 24 February 1626 to 1636 he was organist at two churches at Quedlinburg and was also employed during this period in nearby Magdeburg. He then moved north, probably because of hardships caused by the Thirty Years War, and became organist at Bremen Cathedral, where he was acquainted with Jacob Praetorius (ii) and Scheidemann, and which he left in 1642. He finally settled in Stettin and in the occasional compositions that he published there was described as court organist.

Rautenstein enjoyed a considerable reputation as a composer in his day, although little of his apparently large output now remains: he appears mainly to have written occasional works, both with and without continuo. There are three German sacred duets by him in the *Fasciculus secundus geistlicher Concerten* (1637), a war-inspired collection which he may well have been partly instrumental in compiling, for the contents of its two volumes, including music by some of the most famous composers of the time, had been the repertory of a group of amateur musicians at Nordhausen, not far from Quedlinburg. His duets show a real understanding of the medium. The continuo is totally independent of the voices, has its own rhythmic interest and is figured in great detail. The vocal writing is mainly imitative, with short contrasting motifs including dotted melismatic passages, and his treatment of the words is expressive.

WORKS

4 wedding motets, 5, 8vv (Halberstadt, 1617–19), lost
Freuden Gesangk, 3vv, bc (Elbing, 1645)
8 motets for burials, other occasions, 4–12vv (Stettin, 1647–54)
3 motets, 2vv, in 1637[3]
Ich sucht des Nachts, *D-Dlb*

BIBLIOGRAPHY
A. Arnheim: 'Aus dem Bremer Musikleben im 17. Jahrhundert', *SIMG*, xii (1910–11), 389
F. Piersig: 'Die Orgeln der bremischen Stadtkirchen', *Bremisches Jb*, xxxv (1935), 400
G. Kittler: 'Die pommerschen Notendrucke', *Musik in Pommern*, v (1936), 28
A. LINDSEY KIRWAN

Rauthner, Christian Peganius. See KNORR VON ROSENROTH, CHRISTIAN.

Rautio, Matti (Olavi) (*b* Helsinki, 25 Feb 1922). Finnish composer and teacher. He studied at Helsinki University (MA 1945) and at the Sibelius Academy (certificate 1950), where he served as a piano teacher (1947–64), librarian (1947–57), teacher of piano teaching (1951–60), senior theory teacher (from 1956) and director of the school-music department (from 1966). He has also taught at Jyväskylä University as professor of musicology. Although his main contribution has been in the educational field, he has produced some fine, individual compositions, all on a small scale. His music has a lively rhythm, influenced by Prokofiev and Stravinsky. Merikanto is the Finnish composer to whom he owes most, and he has drawn on Finnish folk music (particularly its dance rhythms) and on Chinese music, whose timbres and rhythms are freely imitated in the ballet *Sininen haikara* ('The blue heron').

WORKS
(*selective list*)

Sininen haikara [The blue heron], ballet and suite, 1957; Tanhumusiikkia [Folkdance music], 1960; orch, Divertimento, vc, orch, 1965; Pf Conc., 1971
Radio scores, solo/choral songs, few small pf pieces

Principal publisher: Finnish Broadcasting Corporation

HANNU ILARI LAMPILA

Rauzzini, Matteo (*b* Camerino, nr. Rome, 1754; *d* Dublin, 1791). Italian composer and singing teacher. He followed his more successful brother Venanzio to Munich, where his two comic operas *Il cam cinese* and *Le finte gemelle* were produced in 1772. Hearing the latter, Burney described the music as 'common, but pretty and in good taste'. He was later active in Venice, where he wrote two comic operas in 1775 and 1781 and two oratorios in 1785 for which the librettos name him *maestro* of the Incurabili. He passed his last years as a singing teacher in Dublin where *Il re pastore*, his only *opera seria*, had been performed in the season 1783–4.

WORKS
(*music lost*)

OPERAS

Il cam cinese (comic, G. Fioroni), Munich, Residenztheater, 1772
Le finte gemelle (comic, 2, ? G. Petrosellini), Munich, Residenztheater, 1772; also as I finti gemelli, Le fente gemelli
Li due amanti in inganno (comic, 3), Venice, S Cassiano, carn. 1775; act 2 only, acts 1 and 3 by G. Rust
L'opera nuova (comic, 2, G. Bertali), Venice, S Moisè, carn. 1781
Il re pastore (opera seria, 3, Metastasio), Dublin, Smock Alley, carn. 1784

ORATORIOS

Exitus Israel de Aegypto (azio sacra), Venice, S Salvatore, 20 Feb 1785; lib, *I-Vcg*
Plagae Aegypti (azio sacra), Venice, S Salvatore, 15 May 1785; lib, *I-Vcg*

BIBLIOGRAPHY

C. Burney: *The Present State of Music in Germany* (London, 1773, 2/1775); ed. P. A. Scholes as *Dr. Burney's Musical Tours*, ii (London, 1959)
M. A. Zorzi: 'Saggio di bibliografia sugli oratori sacri eseguiti a Venezia', *Accademie e biblioteche d'Italia*, iv (1930), 534; v (1931), 96

For further bibliography *see* RAUZZINI, VENANZIO.

KATHLEEN KUZMICK HANSELL

Rauzzini, Venanzio (*b* Camerino, nr. Rome, baptized 19 Dec 1746; *d* Bath, 8 April 1810). Italian male soprano, composer and harpsichordist. After early studies in Rome and possibly also in Naples with Porpora, he made his début at the Teatro della Valle in Rome in Piccinni's *Il finto astrologo* (7 February 1765). His first major role was in Guglielmi's *Sesostri* at Venice during Ascension Fair 1766. In the same year he entered the

Venanzio Rauzzini: portrait (1778) by John Hutchinson in the Victoria Art Gallery, Bath; for a watercolour portrait of Rauzzini, see MARA, GERTRUD ELISABETH

service of the Elector Max Joseph III at Munich, where he remained until 1772. He first appeared in Traetta's *Siroe* (Carnival 1767) and later that year was given leave to perform at Venice and at Vienna, where Mozart and his father heard him in Hasse's *Partenope*. It was for Munich that Rauzzini composed his first operas: *Piramo e Tisbe* (1769) and *L'eroe cinese* (1771). Burney, visiting Rauzzini in August 1772, praised his virtuosity and the quality of his voice, but was most impressed by his abilities as a composer and harpsichordist. His last known operatic performance in Munich was in Bernasconi's *Demetrio* (Carnival 1772). According to Michael Kelly he was then forced to leave because of difficulties with noblewomen engendered by his good looks; this is corroborated by no other source. The authenticity of the Munich operas *Astarto* (1772) and *Pompejo* (1773), sometimes attributed to Rauzzini, is likewise doubtful.

Rauzzini performed two more years in Italy before moving permanently to England. Engaged for Carnival 1773 at Milan, he was *primo uomo* in Mozart's *Lucio Silla* (26 December 1772) and in Paisiello's *Sismano nel Mogol* (30 January 1773). In January Mozart wrote for him the brilliant motet *Exsultate, jubilate*, K165/158*a*. Later that year he sang at Venice and Padua, and in 1774 at Turin (Carnival) and Venice (Ascension Fair).

From November 1774 to July 1777 Rauzzini sang regularly at the King's Theatre in London, making his simultaneous début as singer and composer in the pasticcio *Armida*. Bingley reported that his acting in Sacchini's *Montezuma* (7 February 1775) greatly impressed Garrick. Both Burney and Lord Mount-Edgcumbe, however, deemed his voice sweet but too feeble, a defect Burney ascribed to Rauzzini's devoting too much time to composition. Indeed, Rauzzini contributed arias to four other pasticcios in the season 1775–6 and wrote a comic opera, *L'ali d'amore*. *Piramo e Tisbe*, his best-loved opera, was first staged in London on 23 March 1775; it was revived there in three other seasons and performed at many continental theatres. In

1777 Welcker of London published Rauzzini's sonatas op.1. Publications over the next 30 years included string quartets, more keyboard sonatas, keyboard quartets and four-hand duets, in addition to his popular Italian arias and English songs. Rauzzini's singing also gradually won over London audiences. For his last London appearance in 1777 he composed an *Address of Thanks*, presumably the cantata *La partenza* 'sung by him and Miss Storace'.

In autumn 1777 Rauzzini took up residence in Bath, joining with the violinist Lamotte to manage concerts at the New Assembly Rooms. Many renowned performers, among them his famous pupils John Braham, Nancy Storace, Charles Incledon, Mrs Billington and Mme Mara, freely volunteered their services, and Rauzzini himself sang and played his own works. At Dublin in 1778 he met and taught Michael Kelly and promoted his career with advice to study in Naples. In spring 1781, again in London, Rauzzini sang in concerts with Tenducci and others and wrote the second act of the opera *L'omaggio*. With Tenducci and Pacchierotti he performed his cantata *Il tributo* at the Fonthill (Wiltshire) home of William Beckford (29 September 1781), returning with them also at Christmas. Though by this time he had become sole manager of the Bath concerts, Rauzzini was intermittently in London during the following three seasons to stage his operas *L'eroe cinese* (entirely revised from the Munich version), *Creusa in Delfo* and *Alina, o sia La regina di Golconda*, which was heavily criticized by the *Public Advertiser* (10 May 1784). Ballets with music by him were performed at King's Theatre in the season 1783–4, and he also directed the production of Sarti's *Le gelosie villane* (15 April 1784). During this period a scandal arose over his claim that certain arias in Sacchini's operas were his own. He was not in London when his incidental music for Reynold's *Werter* (originally performed at Bath) was used at Covent Garden on 14 March 1786, and after the London première of his unsuccessful opera *La vestale* (1 May 1787) he remained permanently at Bath in his handsome town house and sumptuous country villa in Perrymead. Michael Kelly described his visit there in 1799: 'Everything at Pyramid [sic] ... breathed content and happiness; professional people, of all descriptions, were welcome to his hospitable table'. Among his many guests was Haydn, who wrote the canon *Turk was a faithful dog and not a man* during a visit from 2 to 5 August 1794. Near the end of his life Rauzzini published a set of 12 vocal exercises with an introduction summing up his ideas on the art of singing and reflecting his own tasteful execution.

WORKS

Unless otherwise stated, all theatrical works first produced in London, King's Theatre, and all printed works published in London

OPERAS

Piramo e Tisbe (azione tragico, 2, R. Calzabigi, after M. Coltellini), Munich, Residenztheater, spr. 1769; rev. London, King's Theatre, 16 March 1775; score, *A-Wn, F-Pn, I-Bc*; arias (London, 1775) and in A Select Collection of the Most Admired Songs, Duetts &c (Edinburgh, 1779)

L'eroe cinese (opera seria, 3, Metastasio), Munich, Residenztheater, 1771; rev. London, King's Theatre, 16 March 1782; arias (London, 1782)

L'ali d'amore (opera comica, 3, C. F. Badini), 29 Feb 1776; rev. 13 March 1777; Favourite Songs, op.3 (London, c1777) and in A Select Collection of the Most Admired Songs, Duetts &c (Edinburgh, 1779)

L'omaggio di paesani al signore del contado (opera seria, 3), 5 June 1781; only act 2 by Rauzzini

Creusa in Delfo (opera seria, 2, G. Martinelli), 29 April 1783; aria, Spiegar non posso (London, ?c1783)

Alina, o sia La regina di Golconda (opera seria, 3, A. Andrei, after J. M. Sédaine), 18 March 1784; ov. and arias (London, c1784)

La vestale, o sia L'amore protetto dal cielo (opera seria, 2, Badini), 1 May 1787; 3 arias, *GB-Lbm*

Doubtful: Astarto (opera seria, 3, Zeno, Pariati), Munich, Residenztheater, sum. 1769/72; Pompejo (opera seria, 3), Munich, Residenztheater, 1773

PASTICCIOS

Armida (opera seria, 3), 19 Nov 1774; Favourite Songs (London, c1774)

La sposa fedele (opera comica, 3, P. Chiari), 31 Oct 1775; Favourite Songs (London, c1775)

Didone (opera seria, 3, Metastasio), 11 Nov 1775; Favourite Songs, (London, c1775)

The Duenna or Double Elopement (comic opera, 3, Sheridan), Covent Garden 21 Nov 1775; aria, By him we love offended [= Fuggiam dove sicura], in The Duenna (London, c1775) and A Select Collection of the Most Admired Songs, Duetts &c (Edinburgh, 1779)

Astarto (opera seria, 3, G. Bottarelli), 2 Nov 1776; Favourite Songs, (London, c1776)

Ezio (opera seria, 3, Metastasio), 17 Nov 1781; Favourite Songs (c1781)

The Village Maid (comic opera, 3), lib (London, 1792); aria, Silent I tread, *Cpl*

INCIDENTAL MUSIC

Werter (F. Reynolds, after Goethe), Bath, 3 Dec 1785; revived Covent Garden, 14 March 1786; Epithalamium, lost

Cymbeline (Shakespeare), Bath, before 1797; Dirge (London, n.d.) and in A Periodical Collection of Vocal Music (1797)

CANTATAS

La partenza, 5 July 1777; as op.4 (London, 1777)

La sorpresa, London, 1779; 2 arias, *Lbm*

Il tributo, Fonthill, home of W. Beckford, 29 Sept 1781, music lost

Old Oliver, or The Dying Shepherd (P. Pindar), Bath, c1796 (London, c1796)

OTHER VOCAL WORKS

12 Italian Duettinos, 2vv, bc, op.5 (1778)

4 Favourite Italian duets, 2vv, hpd/pf, also 4 Easy Airs, 1v, hpd/pf/harp, op.13 (1784)

6 Italian Canzonets, 1v, pf (c1785)

A Periodical Collection of Vocal Music (Bath, 1797, 2/1800)

A Set of 12 Solfeggi or Exercises for the Voice (1808)

Miscellaneous Eng. songs and It. arias, pubd singly and in 18th-century anthologies

Miscellaneous It. arias: *A-Wgm*; *B-Bc*; *GB-Lbm, Cpl*; *I-PAc, Rc, Tn*

Requiem, London, Little Haymarket Theatre, 1801; 2 numbers, *Lbm*

INSTRUMENTAL
(thematic catalogue in Reindl, 1961)

15 sonatas, pf/hpd, vn acc.: 6 as op.1 (1777), 6 as op.8 (1781), 3 as op.15 nos.1–3 (1786)

12 str qts: op.2 (c1777), op.7 (c1778)

6 qts, pf/hpd, 2 vn, vc, op.6 (c1778)

4 duets, pf/hpd 4 hands: 3 as op.12 (1783), 1 as op.15 no.4 (1786)

Sinfonia, D, *D-W*

Miscellaneous dances, sonatas and lessons pubd in 4 contemporary anthologies

BIBLIOGRAPHY
BurneyH

Indice de' spettacoli teatrali per il carnovale (Milan, 1772), 35; ibid (1773), 29; ibid (1774), 60

C. Burney: *The Present State of Music in Germany* (London, 1773, 2/1775); ed. P. A. Scholes as *Dr. Burney's Musical Tours*, ii (London, 1959)

W. Bingley: *Musical Biography* (London, 1814), ii, 315ff

M. Kelly: *Reminiscences* (London, 1826, 2/1826/R1968), 10ff, 118ff

Lord Mount-Edgcumbe: *Musical Reminiscences ... respecting the Italian Opera in England ... from 1773 to 1823* (London, 2/1827), 14f, 18

F. D'Arblay: *Memoirs of Doctor Burney ... by his Daughter*, ii (London, 1832), 35f, 39, 47

F. Rudhart: *Geschichte der Oper am Hofe zu München* (Freising, 1865), 149f, 156f

C. F. Pohl: *Mozart und Haydn in London* (Vienna, 1867/R1970)

J. Harris, Earl of Malmesbury: *A Series of Letters of the First Earl of Malmesbury, his Family and Friends from 1745 to 1820* (London, 1870), i, 293, 296

C. S. Terry: *John Christian Bach* (London, 1929, 2/1967), 147ff, 152, 155, 164, 167

M. Sands: 'Venanzio Rauzzini – Singer, Composer, Traveller', *MT*, xciv (1953), 15, 108

J. Reindl: *Venanzio Rauzzini als Instrumental-Komponist* (diss., U. of Vienna, 1961)

The London Stage, 1660–1800 (Carbondale, Ill., 1960–68)

H. Bolongaro-Crevenna: *L'arpa festante: die Münchner Oper 1651–1825* (Munich, 1963), 88, 238f

KATHLEEN KUZMICK HANSELL

Raval [Ravalle], **Sebastián** (*b* Cartagena, *c*1550; *d* Palermo, before 27 Oct 1604). Spanish composer, friar and soldier, who lived in Italy. As a young man he began a military career, serving in the Spanish army in Flanders and Sicily. In July 1579 he was gravely wounded at the capture of Maastricht and entered the Capuchin order, only to find it too onerous for a man in his nearly crippled condition. According to his own statement in a contemporary document (printed in Casimiri), he sought, at first unsuccessfully, to join another mendicant order and at last was accepted in 1592 by the order of St John of Jerusalem (also known as the Knights of Malta), and obtained the appropriate dispensation from the Holy See.

During the period of his petitions, he apparently worked as a musician at the Urbino court of Duke Francesco Maria II della Rovere. In 1592 he went to Rome to receive his knighthood in the order and shortly afterwards brought out his first musical publications: a book of motets, another of canzonets and one of madrigals, all within five months. In the dedication to the madrigals he mentioned that they had been written at Urbino and he referred to the musicians before whom he had performed in Rome, including Cavaliere del Liuto, Scipione Dentice and Marenzio. Other publications from Rome include a book of Lamentations and a set of madrigals, mostly for three voices, which includes compositions intended for the great Florentine virtuoso Vittoria Archilei, for Cavalieri and for Gesualdo. At that time he promised the imminent publication of masses for five and eight voices with canons for eight and 16 voices, but the work seems never to have appeared. So great was Raval's self-esteem that he challenged Nanino and Soriano to a musical competition, but was quickly and resoundingly defeated. Shortly after this humiliation, he left Rome for Palermo in the service of a Sicilian nobleman, G. B. Tagliavia, Duke of S Giovanni and Count of Cammarata. On 28 April 1595 he took the post of *maestro di cappella* at the royal chapel of S Pietro in Palermo, now the Cappella Palatina. He enjoyed great favour among the Spanish viceroys there, partly, it seems, because of his Spanish origins, and he received regular bonuses and salary increases; at his death, the salary reverted for his successor to its original level.

While in Sicily Raval challenged another musician to a competition, a young *maestro di cappella* of Caltagirone, ACHILLE FALCONE of Cosenza. The adjudicator decided in favour of Falcone, whereupon Raval appealed to the viceroy and demanded a new examination. The second time Spanish favouritism apparently decided the victory for Raval, but Falcone prepared to appeal to Nanino and Soriano for still another competition in Rome, which, however, never came to fruition, owing to the death of Falcone. In 1603 Falcone's father, Antonio, published the compositions written by Raval and Falcone in the first competition; these included a madrigal, a motet, various canons and a ricercare. Raval's post at Palermo was filled by Vincenzo Gallo on 27 October 1604, suggesting that Raval had died only a few days previously.

Raval's music aimed at contrapuntal complexity; he favoured canonic devices that seem rather old-fashioned

for his period. His conservative attitude is apparent in the 'corrections' he made to a madrigal by Falcone, of which 'both words and music were improvised at the request of a friend'. Raval's version, according to Antonio Falcone, was 'composed at great expense of time and effort', in order to 'emend the above work of Achille'. The opening of the two pieces (see ex.1) shows

Ex.1

Falcone: A te ve - ne-re il mir-to

Raval: A te ve - ne-re il mir - to

that Raval disliked Falcone's unusual upbeat beginning and preferred a more normal attack on a strong beat; he also rewrote the quaver passage (*) to avoid an accented passing-note dissonance. Nevertheless, his version is heavier and lacks the freshness of Falcone's piece.

WORKS

SACRED

Motectorum liber primus, 5vv (Rome, 1593)
Lamentationes Hieremiae prophetae, 5vv (Rome, 1594)
Motecta selecta organo accomodata, 3–6, 8vv, org (Palermo, 1600)
1 motet, 1609[1]

SECULAR

Il primo libro de madrigali, 5vv (Venice, 1593)
Il primo libro di canzonette, 4vv (Venice, 1593)
Madrigali, 3, 5, 8vv (Rome, 1595)
El primo libro di ricercari . . . 4 o 6 opere con parole spirituali, in canoni ad echo, lutes, hpd, viols (Palermo, 1596)
2 madrigals in Infidi lumi (Palermo, 1603), lost
Several pieces, 1603[11]

BIBLIOGRAPHY

R. Casimiri: 'Sebastian Raval, musicista spagnuolo del secolo XVI', *NA*, viii (1931), 1
H. Anglès: 'Una obra desconocida de Sebastian Raval', *AnM*, iii (1948), 3
O. Tiby: 'Sebastian Raval: a 16th-century Spanish Musician in Italy', *MD*, ii (1948), 217

STEVEN LEDBETTER

Ravel, (Joseph) Maurice (*b* Ciboure, Basses Pyrénées, 7 March 1875; *d* Paris, 28 Dec 1937). French composer. His distinctive style brought lasting popularity, and his scrupulous craftsmanship helped him to a position of eminence among composers of his day. Ravel was an important innovator in pianistic style, an orchestrator of genius, a sophisticated harmonist and, on occasion, a bold and successful experimenter with musical form. But much of his appeal is due to the strong sympathies that inform his work: sympathies with the worlds of children and of animals; and with imagined exotic and antique life. Especially where his music touched on these ideas, Ravel was a decorative artist of the highest order, defining and elaborating musical objects and images which exercise a continuing fascination. He also made appearances as a conductor and as a pianist; and he taught, privately, a few pupils.

1. 1875–1905. 2. 1905–37. 3. Creative personality. 4. Technique and works.

1. 1875–1905. Ravel was the eldest child of Pierre Joseph Ravel, an engineer of unusually cultured outlook, and his wife Marie, née Delouart. Shortly after Maurice's birth at the home of his mother's aunt in Ciboure, his father took up work in Paris, and the family lived permanently in the capital from then on. Whereas his father's background was largely Swiss and his mother's Basque, Ravel's childhood was a thoroughly Parisian one, and when it became clear to the boy's father that Maurice's gifts suggested a possible career in music, the best instructors and, ultimately, the Conservatoire were at hand. It seems that the elder Ravel actively desired such a career for his son: certainly he encouraged it, and in 1882 placed him with a distinguished piano teacher, Henri Ghys. In 1887 Ravel began studies in harmony with the Delibes pupil Charles-René, an association that produced his earliest known essays in composition (Schumann and Grieg Variations, a piano sonatina movement); and two years later, after becoming a piano pupil of Emile Decombes, he gained admission to Eugène Anthiôme's preparatory piano class at the Conservatoire. From here, in a further two years, he graduated to the class of Charles de Bériot, studying harmony with Emile Pessard.

If, during his first years at the Conservatoire (1889–95), Ravel's record as a student of harmony and the piano was patchy and, in terms of the establishment's awards system, ultimately unsuccessful, his record as one who sought experience was very much more impressive. At the Paris World Exhibition of 1889 Ravel, like Debussy, first encountered the music of the Javanese gamelan, which exercised a lasting enchantment on him, if not the deeper influence commentators have found in Debussy's work. At the same event he attended concerts of Russian music given by Rimsky-Korsakov, again an experience that left a distinctive imprint on his own orchestral music. Ravel's early friendship with the remarkable Spanish pianist Ricardo Viñes, a fellow pupil in de Bériot's class, stimulated a mutual exploration of the contemporary arts. In music, Wagner, the Russian school, Chabrier and Satie were objects of enthusiasm; in literature (and aesthetic theory) important links were forged with Baudelaire, Poe and Mallarmé. In 1893 Ravel made personal contact with Chabrier and Satie whose influence on his early compositions (the Sérénade grotesque for piano, the song Ballade de la reine morte d'aimer etc) he himself was the first to point out.

In July 1895 Ravel left the Conservatoire; by the end of the year he had completed three works, the song Un grand sommeil noir, the piano piece Menuet antique and the Habanera for two pianos, in which the distinctive characteristics of his style began to be felt. It has been suggested that this was the time when he made his decision to devote himself primarily to composition. Yet 1896 saw the production of only two songs, Sainte and D'Anne jouant de l'espinette, and it was not until the next year that he decided to return to the Conservatoire as a member of Fauré's composition class, while studying counterpoint and orchestration with André Gédalge. In fact the years 1897–8 seem to have represented a fresh start in his work as a composer; he published none of the works he composed during this period (a violin sonata, Entre cloches for two pianos, the songs Chanson du rouet and Si morne!, the Shéhérazade overture) and it is easy to see in them the admixture of boldness and uncertainty that characterizes most student work of

talent. Of these works the most significant are the sonata, an extended essay in which Orenstein has seen anticipations of the 1914 Piano Trio (a work Ravel dedicated to Gédalge), and the overture, the composer's first orchestral venture, associated with a projected opera.

During the next year a return to Ravel's mock-archaic manner brought a return of his more confident handling of materials; the immediate outcome could be seen in a further Marot setting (D'Anne qui me jecta de la neige) and the instantly popular Pavane pour une infante défunte. It was somewhat as an antiquary, too, that Ravel began his career in the publishers' catalogues. Chabrier's publisher, Enoch, brought out the Menuet antique in 1898; and this was followed by the two Marot songs (as Deux épigrammes) and the Pavane, published by Demets in 1900. More important, the first public performances of Ravel's music date from these years. Habanera and Entre cloches, yoked together as Sites auriculaires, were presented in March 1898; a month later Viñes introduced the Menuet antique; and in May 1899 Ravel himself conducted the Shéhérazade overture. These performances were hardly an outright success with the critics or with the public, but there were gratifying aspects, such as Debussy's interest in the Habanera, and at Shéhérazade there were, by Ravel's own account, 'more applauders than protesters'.

At the Conservatoire Ravel's time was again being well spent in any but the official view. In Fauré he had a truly sympathetic teacher whose undogmatic guidance and encouragement were to be acknowledged in the dedications of Ravel's next important works, the piano piece Jeux d'eau and the String Quartet; but when it came to satisfying the authorities of his abilities in fugue writing he failed abysmally. In 1900 he again found himself excluded from the Conservatoire's rolls through inability to secure a prize. Henceforth, although he continued to attend Fauré's class as an 'auditeur', his main official connection with the Conservatoire consisted in his several attempts to obtain the Prix de Rome for composition. The first of these was in 1900, when he failed to qualify for the principal part of the competition, the composition of a cantata to a set text under specially supervised conditions. He entered again in each of the next three years, producing the cantatas Myrrha (1901), Alcyone (1902) and Alyssa (1903); these were judged inferior to the works of the respective winners, André Caplet, Aymé Kunc and Raoul Laparra. In 1903 Ravel had to leave Fauré's class altogether, having once again failed to pick up a prize for composition.

Contemporary portraits and other documents show that the young Ravel was attracted to dandyism as a way of life (as expounded, for instance, by Baudelaire): he cultivated an impeccably elegant façade, taking fashion as his style. At this period his social life included frequentation of salons. But he was also a member of a côterie known as 'Les Apaches'. Typical of many such bands of artistic allies, it was formed around the turn of the century, and its regular meetings offered its members a stimulating platform for their work as well as a congenial milieu for aesthetic discussion. These members included Falla, Schmitt and Delage (a pupil of Ravel), Inghelbrecht, Calvocoressi and Vuillermoz, the painter Paul Sordes and the poets Fargue and Klingsor. It was Klingsor who supplied the texts for Ravel's orchestral song cycle Shéhérazade. By now Ravel was producing music of mature mastery. The attitude of the Conservatoire authorities towards him was partly dictated by his failure to meet the academic requirements of the time, but largely it was a consequence of irreconcilable artistic ideals. It was not long before the eruption of 'the Ravel affair' heralded the downfall of a regime deaf to the new order of post-Lisztian piano writing so confidently established in *Jeux d'eau*, to the strength and individuality (enough, indeed, to win it a permanent place in the repertory) of the 1903 Quartet, and to the

1. Maurice Ravel, 1907

orchestral brilliance and imaginative range, embracing both breadth and delicacy of effect, which made *Shéhérazade* the most satisfying portent to date of Ravel's potential greatness.

Having neglected to compete for the Prix de Rome in 1904, Ravel again entered the competition the next year. As in 1900 he failed to progress beyond the preliminary round. That in the statutory choral piece and fugue he had flagrantly transgressed academic rules made it virtually impossible for the jury to accept his candidature in the competition proper. Either one must attribute to Ravel an extraordinary degree of naivety or indeed of stupidity, or one must accept that at this point in his career, for one reason or another, he was coolly playing politics; for, to the outside observer, the Conservatoire's refusal to admit to the Prix de Rome a composer already adequately established in the 'outside' world seemed a grotesque blunder. Controversy rapidly ensued, dying down only after Dubois had resigned the directorship to be replaced by Fauré and a more open-minded administration. Ravel, for his part, escaped from Paris to join a yachting cruise in Holland with a party of friends, and plunged into one of the most fruitfully creative periods of his career.

2. 1905–37. Ravel's major battles were now with certain sectors of critical opinion. He had every reason to feel that he was making an original and totally

individual contribution to French music: perhaps such a feeling helped to sustain his current work on a remarkable stream of compositions, the Sonatina and *Miroirs* for piano, the *Introduction et allegro* for harp and ensemble, the cycle *Histoires naturelles* and a number of other fine songs, the orchestral *Rapsodie espagnole* and his first opera, *L'heure espagnole*. Certainly he became irritated by the insistence of certain critics that everything worthwhile in new music must be traced back to Debussy. In 1906 he wrote to the critic Pierre Lalo, pointing out that *Jeux d'eau* could justly claim priority in the matter of a 'special type of writing for the piano' ascribed to Debussy. Whether or not Ravel's work influenced *Jardins sous la pluie* (as Orenstein has suggested), its last ripples certainly left their mark on *Pagodes*. Again in 1907 Lalo persistently found 'the unmistakable echo of Debussy's music' in the *Histoires naturelles*, and this somewhat odd opinion, together with the excessive asperity with which the work was attacked after its first performance, sparked off a further violent controversy in the Paris press. This time, the composer again chose to turn his back on the disputes, though Lalo now published Ravel's letter to him of the previous year.

L'heure espagnole followed a number of abandoned or unfinished opera projects. After his early attraction to the subject of *The Thousand and One Nights*, Ravel's next important project was an adaptation of Hauptmann's *Die versunkene Glocke*; he worked on this sporadically between 1906 and 1914, and eventually used some of the material from it in *L'enfant et les sortilèges*. Another text he seriously considered as a potential libretto was Maeterlinck's *Intérieur*. The literary stimulus behind some of his instrumental works of this period is clear too. *Gaspard de la nuit* was composed 'after Aloysius Bertrand' (his *Histoires vermoulues et poudreuses du Moyen Age*), and *Ma mère l'oye* is based on the fairy tales of Perrault, Mme d'Aulnoy and Leprince de Beaumont. The latter work, dedicated to the children of Ravel's friend Cyprien ('Cipa') Godebski, whom he had first met in 1904, was transcribed for orchestra and ultimately expanded into a ballet score; *Valses nobles et sentimentales* was similarly adapted for the stage. By this time, however, Ravel had composed his most ambitious stage work of all, the ballet *Daphnis et Chloé*, the composition of which occupied about three years (1909–12) and was the result of a commission from Dyagilev. The visit of the Ballets Russes to Paris in 1909 made a considerable impact on the work of several leading composers, some of whom were themselves to write ballets for the company. On Ravel, there was a further impact: his meeting with Stravinsky, the brilliant young composer who had orchestrated music by Grieg and Chopin for Dyagilev, and was soon to produce his own ballet *The Firebird*. (Stravinsky joined Les Apaches in 1909, the year in which Ravel was closely associated with the founding of the Société Musicale Indépendante, a group which, as its title suggests, promoted new music regardless of its aesthetic tendency.)

At this time Ravel undertook a surprising amount of ostensibly unspectacular musical work. He harmonized folksongs and made arrangements and orchestrations of his own and others' music, often for use in ballet productions. One such task, the preparation of a new performing version of Musorgsky's *Khovanshchina*, took him to Clarens (Switzerland) where he collaborated on the task with Stravinsky. This was in 1913, and not only did Ravel there see, and appreciate, the music of *The Rite of Spring*, but he acquainted himself with Stravinsky's *Three Japanese Lyrics*, the third of which is dedicated to him. This work, with its special way of combining voice and chamber ensemble, reflected the influence of Schoenberg's *Pierrot lunaire*, which Stravinsky had recently heard in Berlin; and thus Schoenberg may be said to have been the indirect stimulus behind Ravel's own *Trois poèmes de Stéphane Mallarmé* the first of which was completed in Clarens and dedicated to Stravinsky. The settings contain writing of notable complexity set off against nostalgic reminiscences of the *Shéhérazade* cycle. This work and the subsequent Piano Trio represent the culmination of Ravel's pre-war output, the piano pieces and songs completed within the next year being distinctly lesser productions. When war broke out he was at work on his Piano Trio, a composition more reminiscent (of the String Quartet) than prophetic. But, as seen in a letter to Roland-Manuel, many other schemes were in his head at this time: *Zaspiak bat* (a piano concerto on Basque themes), *Nuit romantique* (a piano work, possibly along the lines of *Gaspard de la nuit*), the two projected operas, *La cloche engloutie* and *Intérieur*, a symphonic poem *Wien* and a 'French suite'. Of these, only the last two were eventually to come to anything, as *La valse* and *Le tombeau de Couperin*.

Meanwhile, however, the war itself was a shattering influence on Ravel's life. Clearly he believed it the duty of the artist to share his nation's experiences to the full. To Jean Marnold he wrote: 'They tell me that Saint-Saëns announces to the avid crowd that during the war he has composed theatre music, songs, an elegy and a piece for trumpets. If instead he had been servicing howitzers, his music might have been the better for it'. Desperately anxious to serve his country, and disqualified from military service (because he was underweight by two kilograms), he made every endeavour to enlist in the air force. But instead he became a driver with the motor transport corps, an occupation he ultimately found less rewarding than 'servicing howitzers': in summer 1916 the urge to compose and the conviction that he was at the height of his powers welled up and filled him with impatience. He fell ill with dysentry, was taken to hospital, and travelled to Paris in order to recuperate. Hardly had he arrived when his mother died; she had been, and would continue to be, the only true focus and sustenance of his sentient being: children, animals, perhaps even treasured objects, but no other adult elicited his deepest affections.

During the war years a number of French artists turned their attention to reviving past national glories. Debussy's sonatas suggest precisely this kind of historical nationalism. In Ravel it is expressed in two works, in the archaism of his *Trois chansons* for mixed chorus (the words of which, like those of the earlier *Noël des jouets*, Ravel wrote himself), and in the Baroque dance forms of *Le tombeau de Couperin*. Each of the six movements of this suite is dedicated to the memory of a victim of the war. The work is the last in which Ravel evoked Baroque forms, and may be seen as a culmination of the tradition that embraced works by Chabrier, Chausson, Fauré, Debussy and of course Ravel himself. A number of causes – the war, sickness, but above all the emotional shock of his mother's death – slowed his creative processes so that the completion of *La valse*

was delayed until 1920, and even then had only been spurred by a commission from Dyagilev.

With Debussy dead, there were many who now saw Ravel as the leading figure in French music. His success with the public had grown steadily since the early *Pavane* and *Jeux d'eau*, both of which had quickly established themselves as favourites with pianists in France and abroad. The String Quartet too was widely performed, and a broader degree of popularity with the concert-going public was won, during the year after the notoriety of the *Histoires naturelles* controversy, with his first important orchestral work, the *Rapsodie espagnole*. The next big landmark came with the production of *L'heure espagnole* at the Opéra-Comique in 1911; a year later, *Daphnis et Chloé* was staged and went into the touring repertory of the Ballets Russes. Ravel's was undoubtedly a position of eminence, and in 1920 the republic proposed to acknowledge the fact by conferring on him the order of the Légion d'honneur. But the proposal was made public before Ravel could either accept or refuse, and his subsequent refusal of the honour, as a matter of principle, created a similarly public stir. Again it seemed that ill feeling bedevilled Ravel's relations with officialdom, but here it is difficult to accuse him of calculated political manoeuvring in his dealings with authority. He must rather have viewed the establishment as a necessary evil, something from which he must find the quickest and shortest line of retreat into artistic privacy. The same need prompted him in 1920 to acquire a home outside Paris and from 1921 he lived in Montfort-l'Amaury.

Such a withdrawal had a peculiar aptness at the time when his work with Colette on *Ballet pour ma fille* (later to become *L'enfant et les sortilèges*) demanded the imaginative creation of a magical world of childhood. Here again the process of composition was slow and a work whose planning dated back to 1918 was not finished until early in 1925; and even then Ravel's work on it had been hastened by a deadline for the Monte Carlo Opera. In the meantime he had responded to three requests for commemorative pieces: a memorial to Debussy, a tribute to Fauré, and a contribution to the celebration of the quatercentenary of Ronsard's birth. The first of these, a duo for violin and cello, was expanded into a four-movement sonata. Other preoccupations of this period were some further orchestrations (including the famous version of Musorgsky's *Pictures from an Exhibition*), ill-fated projects such as that for a concertante work based on Alain-Fournier's novel *Le grand Meaulnes*, and the brilliant violin showpiece *Tzigane*; he had also started work on his Violin Sonata, though again this proved to be a considerably protracted labour. The *Chansons madécasses*, composed to meet a commission from Elizabeth Sprague Coolidge, came more swiftly from his pen; as a cycle for voice and chamber ensemble they are at once a natural continuation of his Mallarmé set and a bold advance on it.

Ravel's American tour of 1928 is important more as a personal and social experience than for any discernible creative stimulus it produced. His music had taken him abroad several times already: to Great Britain in 1909 and again in 1911; to Vienna in 1920; and during the 1920s to Holland, Italy, Spain, Scandinavia, Belgium, Germany, Switzerland and (again) Britain. These professional engagements generally happened after the composition of the work they might have seemed most likely to stimulate; *La valse*, for instance, was written before his visit to Vienna, and the 'Blues' movement of the Violin Sonata predates his tour of North America (one exception is the *Tzigane*, manifestly suggested by the playing of Jelly d'Arányi in London.) The four-month American tour had been arranged by Elie Robert Schmitz, president of the Pro Musica Society, and in addition to a large number of concerts and recitals, it gave Ravel the opportunity to meet many noted personalities in the arts, including the cinema. Undoubtedly the experience was an exhausting one (Ravel referred to it as a 'crazy tour', and his itinerary meant spending many nights on train journeys), but it must have brought home to him the extraordinary acclaim his music had won him overseas. In the same year the conferring on him of an honorary doctorate at Oxford University reinforced the message.

From this time until 1932 Ravel was occupied with a number of projects, some of them commissions of a rather unusual nature. Ida Rubinstein, the dancer, requiring a ballet with a Spanish flavour, first asked Ravel to orchestrate some pieces from Albéniz's *Iberia*, but the upshot was the composition of *Boléro*. The Concerto for the left hand was written for the one-armed pianist Paul Wittgenstein at the same time that Ravel was working on a Concerto in G for his own use. Ravel's collaboration was sought in a film based on Cervantes and featuring Shalyapin, resulting in the songs *Don Quichotte à Dulcinée*; this work and its subsequent orchestration represent the last music Ravel was to complete. Other projects held his interest for varying periods of time. Briefly and impulsively he planned to touch up the orchestration of Chabrier's opera *Le roi malgré lui*. An opera–oratorio on the subject of Joan of Arc was planned in 1929 and remained a serious possibility in his mind at least until 1933; although initially based on a text by Joseph Delteil, the work would undoubtedly have been coloured by Ravel's admiration for Shaw's *Saint Joan*. The last of his projects for the stage, like the first, was drawn from *The Thousand and One Nights*: an opera–ballet *Morgiane*, which seems tantalizingly to have evolved to near-completion in his mind but was not written down.

1932 marks the beginning of Ravel's tragic final period, during which he was totally at the mercy of his last illness, the progressively incapacitating 'Pick's disease'. Some commentators have traced the first warning symptoms back to the insomnia that began to assail him at the end of the war. He complained of 'cerebral anaemia' in 1926, and about a year later his doctor, Pasteur Vallery-Radot, advised him to rest for a year. A road accident in 1932 appeared to precipitate his illness, though this was later denied by the brain surgeon Clovis Vincent; certainly after this date his powers steadily declined, despite numerous efforts of sympathetic friends to stimulate and amuse him, including holidays abroad. Soon he was no longer able to sign his name, and he moved and spoke with increasing difficulty. His life revolved round occasional concert-going, visits from performers seeking advice, and above all the companionship of his brother and a small circle of friends. His death in December 1937 followed an unsuccessful brain operation.

3. CREATIVE PERSONALITY. Ravel always felt an intense

2. Leon Bakst's design (1912) for Act 1 of Ravel's 'Daphnis et Chloé' (Musée des Arts Décoratifs, Paris)

3. Ravel with the group 'Les Apaches', c1908: (from left to right) Robert Mortier, L'Abbé Léonce Petit, Maurice Ravel, Ricardo Viñes and Jane Mortier

need for privacy. His sexual life was shrouded in secrecy; and he made a mystery of the creative process, exposing his music only when the final touch had been applied to its composition. Undoubtedly he felt vulnerable. There is too little evidence for an adequate picture of his sexual relationships to be formed, although one cannot doubt that their nature would be relatable to, and hence liable to shed light on, other instances of self-expression: the music. However, where an over-zealous commentator has been compelled to eke out the slender direct evidence with assumptions deduced from the works, these deductions, in themselves incapable of fresh illumination of the music, fail to be of interest.

Ravel's vulnerability as an artist is more interesting. He felt music was his true vocation: 'It's lucky I've managed to write music, because I know perfectly well I should never have been able to do anything else'. But the peculiar nature of Ravel's creative mind imposed special conditions on the pursuit of that vocation. As Nichols has pointed out, while Debussy gave himself over to 'a search for new styles, new "musics" . . . for Ravel, the search lay not so much beyond him as inside him'. With Debussy music was in evolution; with Ravel it was in crystallization, and a quite exceptional spiritual stillness was needed for the process to be accomplished flawlessly. He worked in solitude and with intense concentration. The music took shape on 'long expeditions in the woods, whatever the weather; nightly walks across Paris'; then, abruptly, he would shut himself off from

the world to transfer his work to paper.

Even to Ravel the process seemed magical, an alchemical distillation; it relied on precarious 'inspiration'. As he grew older composition became more difficult and laboured. On the one hand he matured as an artist, becoming more comprehensively aware of the complexities and contradictions in his own nature; on the other, particularly after the death of his father in 1908, he found it increasingly difficult to escape from the cares and responsibilities of mundane existence. Consequently his capacities as an artist became ever more precarious until at the last total impotence superseded. Ravel's insecurity is reflected in his music in two important ways. Firstly, 'everything had to be done – or seem to be done – by a miracle'. Ravel had extremely scrupulous ideas about professionalism in music. The finished score that came from his workshop had to be just that: finished with the highest degree of craftsmanship, in no need of further attention. It is reported that once the long and secret labour of creation was over Ravel tended to lose interest in the work he had produced. Certainly he saw the quality of that labour as all important. 'If each of you worked as I work', he said, 'you could achieve the same results.' The care expended on the smallest detail of his music, and the thoroughness that induced him, for instance, to ensure that in orchestral works the music for each family of instruments was as satisfactory in isolation as it was when considered as part of the whole, are precautions that most composers would regard as excessive, if not potentially detrimental; for Ravel they were a kind of insurance, perhaps all the more necessary after his academic failures at the Conservatoire.

The second symptom of his insecurity goes deeper, and is inseparable from his approach to composition as manifest in his technique. The idea of composition as crystallization has been suggested above; Ravel expressed it this way:

In my own composition I judge a long period of gestation necessary. During this interval I come progressively, and with a growing precision, to see the form and the evolution that the final work will take in its totality. Thus I can be occupied for several years without writing a single note of the work, after which the composition goes relatively quickly. But one must spend time in eliminating all that could be regarded as superfluous in order to realize as completely as possible the definitive clarity so much desired.

Objective definition was an acute need. And at another level it led him, especially in his more rapidly composed works, to an unusual degree of reliance on objective treatment of his musical components – a feature to be examined more fully in the following consideration of his technique in relation to the works themselves. Here it is necessary only to note that he was aware of the bounds of his objectivity, and of the necessity of such bounds to the vitality of his art: 'If I could explain and demonstrate the value of my own works, that from my point of view at least would prove that they were constructed entirely from elements that were obvious, superficial and tangible, and therefore imperfect works of art'. The mysterious, whether seen as inspiration or as alchemy, was clearly understood to have a leading role in the process of composition.

Reference has already been made to Ravel's adoption of the dress and manners of the fin-de-siècle dandy; it is generally accepted, and certainly probable, that this guise served to compensate for his small stature which he felt to be a social disadvantage, and which did indeed prove a disadvantage when he wanted to join the armed forces. Always meticulous about his personal appearance, he was as unlikely to present himself as he was a composition to the world in an 'unfinished' state. Somewhat spoilt as a child, he retained a longing and an affinity for the pure and uncluttered emotional horizons of childhood. He remained a collector of mechanical toys and other small-scale bric-à-brac. His huge appetite for the exotic and the antique was coloured by a preference that they should be retailed through the distorting glass of a naive intermediary, as in a child's picture book: *Daphnis* was 'less concerned with archaism than with fidelity to the Greece of my dreams which is close to that imagined and painted by the French artists of the 18th century'; and Jankélévitch has expanded on this, pointing out that Verlaine and de Régnier, favourite poets of Ravel, were largely responsible for bringing the 18th century into vogue, that the composer of the *Chansons madécasses* and *Shéhérazade* turned first to the poetry of Evariste Parny and to Galland's translation of *The Thousand and One Nights*, and that *Ma mère l'oye* is reminiscent of Boucher's pictures, the *Menuet antique* of Watteau. Finally, *L'enfant et les sortilèges* shows that Ravel could still understand the child's wilful and dictatorial response to the warm security of his mother's love: and performers associated with him found that not only did he know precisely what he wanted, but also he possessed enough blind determination to settle for nothing less.

4. TECHNIQUE AND WORKS. Ravel's technique relied to an unusual extent on the manipulation of musical objects. The term as used in this context requires some explanation, particularly as Ravel was a pioneer in this respect. A musical object suggests a musical element considered in its own right as self-sufficient (an end in itself, as it were), hence free from the functional roles expected of musical subjects. The nature of the element, like that of the physical object, will be more or less synoptic (in other words, perceivable from a single standpoint), but whereas in physical objects this quality is extensioned by extension in space, in musical objects it is extenuated by extension in time. Since the object cannot actively participate in 'subjective' functions (those normally associated with musical exposition and development), its temporal extension must be constituted either of stasis or of some form of 'objective' (i.e. mechanical, automatic) movement. Examples would be, in the former case, the exceptionally sustained or exceptionally isolated note or chord, and in the latter case rigidly patterned movement as in ostinato figures; an example of the two combined would be a repetitive pedal point. (It is worth distinguishing from an object a 'motif', a term that self-evidently expresses an active function.)

Composition has always made use of musical objects, which in certain epochs have tended to be more synoptic than in others. The tension between the active (subject) and the passive (object) has been a sustaining feature in most styles of Western music. But it would be hard to discover a composer before Ravel who devoted so much of his imaginative passion to the minting of elaborate but virtually tangible musical complexes whose sole role is as passive stabilizer or sheet-anchor, or even as independent mechanism to fascinate the ear (commentators are apt to recall knowingly that Pierre Joseph's work as an engineer held a like fascination for his son). Ravel's consuming artistic concern was a quest for 'l'objet juste', a pursuit of striking musical imagery, which often enough was also required to correspond (in the Baudelairean sense) with some poetic or dramatic conception. The labour expended on this search was imaginatively rather than intellectually intense, and the end result varied from the exhilarating to the platitudinous. (Professionalism is by no means synonymous with artistic self-criticism.) Whether delicate or massive, however, all Ravel's objects give the feeling of beautifully sculptured solidity.

This tendency has been mentioned as being related to Ravel's feelings of insecurity: the artist who lacks confidence in his 'subjective' powers of musical discourse may be expected to take refuge in the presumed strength of impersonal artifice. Confluent tendencies in Ravel's music support this view. He required a near-absolute power of certainty with relation to his work. His frequent recourse to small-scale construction, or adherence to traditional forms, have led some observers to class him as a miniaturist or as a parasitic manipulator; and his penchant for the synoptical and the mechanical, often seen as a corollary to his weakness for figurines and clockwork toys, is also taken into account by Stravinsky's famous description of him as a 'Swiss watchmaker'. A further screen is that of stylization: the use of modes, generally to suggest antique or exotic scales; the application of characteristic gestures from Baroque or national styles (which may be taken to include jazz); and the imitation or development of a

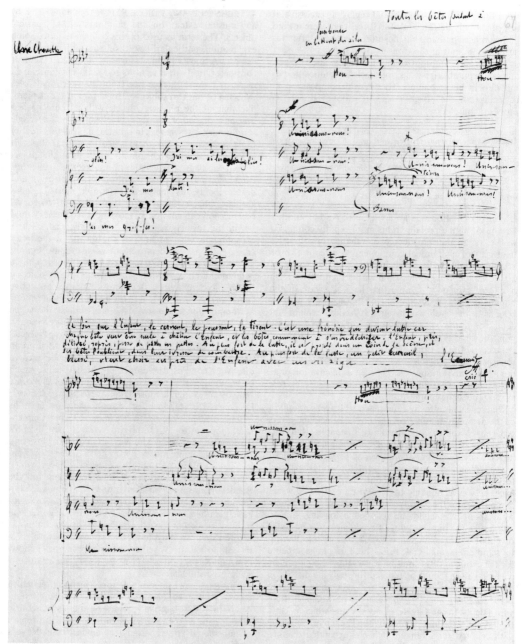

4. *Part of the autograph vocal score of 'L'enfant et les sortilèges' by Ravel, composed 1920–25 (US-NYpm)*

particular stylistic model, generally in homage rather than pastiche. To the extent that this stylization was 'mechanical', candidly imitative, the result would be objective; and referential musical objects, often termed 'symbols', are the materials of irony in music. Hence the link some critics have seen between the composer of the *Histoires naturelles* and Mahler. Yet another mooring, at a period when tonality was being subjected to vigorous and effective questioning, was Ravel's firm adherence to the traditional diatonic system; for all his

harmonic inventiveness, his notions of the permissible and the undesirable were inflexibly dogmatic as compared, for instance, with those of Stravinsky. In all these traits, and in the very professionalism mentioned earlier, one sees Ravel's need to exercise an extraordinary degree of control over his musical output. He spoke of the work of art as a 'ripened conception where no detail has been left to chance'.

This attitude has disturbed many listeners; it is seemingly incompatible with spontaneity of utterance. Jankélévitch has pointed out that even when the style is improvisatory, the means remain strictly under control: in the capricious chromaticism of *Noctuelles* and *Oiseaux tristes*, or the rubato effects in *La valse* and *Tzigane*; to which one might add the jazz-like syncopations in the Concerto for the left hand. However, as Jankélévitch said, there is no justification for confusing calculation and stylization with lack of expressiveness. Indeed, much of the effort Ravel put into the invention of his musical objects was directed towards making them evident and adequate symbols of a wide variety of human feeling and experience. It would be fair to say that he was less anxious to depict external reality than to select those qualities of it that made it peculiarly accessible to a kind of sympathetic perception: he not so much portrayed nature as captured its effect on human sensibilities. There is no lack of expressiveness; it is merely that the sensibilities are frequently borrowed, from children or the naive, Ravel diffidently masking or suppressing his own.

Some of the many possible critical approaches to Ravel's music have been more attractive than others. Perhaps the most obvious is that which maintains that Ravel was a master of musical miniatures, and that his emotional range was correspondingly cramped. Those who find these attributes blameless applaud him most when he was being true to them: in 'gem-like' miniatures (such as the Sonatina, perhaps) or in re-creations of an idealized childhood (as in *Ma mère l'oye*); but those who feel shame at such innocent delights tend to prefer the Ravel of bold, large-scale forms (*La valse*, the Concerto for the left hand) and darker, maturer awarenesses (these same works). Some admire the highly sophisticated preciosity of the *Valses nobles et sentimentales*; others acclaim the broader strokes of *Daphnis et Chloé*. The automatism of *Jeux d'eau* may be weighed against the deliberative invention of the Adagio assai from the G major Concerto. A further approach might concentrate on the sheer quality of his invention, which could veer abruptly between the banal and the original from one piece to the next (*Une barque sur l'océan* to *Alborado del gracioso*, for instance). One doubts whether Ravel would have been unaware of these potential criticisms: but they are likely to be finally irrelevant, as they were seemingly irrelevant to Ravel's own purposes. For these are criticisms proper to the subjective composer. (It is, for instance, a requirement only of subjective truth that a high level of inventive quality should at all times be maintained.)

As a final precaution against insecurity, Ravel adopted a detached attitude to his art: it was for him an 'act', possibly of imitation, possibly of reportage. This left him free to disclaim intimate involvement, free, that is, to place his music beyond the bounds of traditional humanistic criticism. The decisive charge against Ravel would seem to be that of coolness: he was the somewhat disavowing type of artist who stood aside from his creation and 'pared his fingernails'. The weight of this charge will always depend on the general tendency of public and critical opinion at any time. It has been felt that anything less than the earnestness of Debussy and Schoenberg amounted to irresponsibility at a period when music was passing through the intense crisis of dissolving tonality, and it is possible in this light to view the irony, parody, imitation and other 'second-order creation' of Ravel as a facet of that fatally aimless cleverness which is a symptom of cultural decadence.

(One may here aptly quote the epigraph of *Valses nobles et sentimentales*: 'le plaisir délicieux et toujours nouveau d'une occupation inutile'.) However, when cultural values are in doubt it is proper to bear in mind that the vice of one age may be the virtue of another; and that even without such clearcut idealism, the sharp, clear, refining personality of Ravel's music will exert its due attraction.

There are several strikingly recurrent features in Ravel's technique, among the most evident being the musical objects already discussed. One of his earliest surviving manuscripts (the Verlaine setting *Le ciel est, pardessus le toit*, c1892) already shows heavy reliance on the hypnotic reiteration of a single accompaniment figure. In the *Habanera* (1895), however, the object in question is a pedal point on a characteristic Spanish rhythmic ostinato; and in his treatment of it Ravel transcended everything that had gone before. The reiterated note, a dominant C♯, is established as a 'solid' object, so that even a chord featuring its semitonal neighbours B♯ and D cannot quieten it; there arises what a later age would call a 'cluster'. But the clash is far from gratuitous. Although melodically Ravel was here largely working in the Phrygian mode, his harmonies are traditionally, if somewhat elliptically diatonic. The typical quasi-tonic role of the dominant in Spanish folk music provides the explanation of Ravel's cluster as a quasi-Neapolitan 6th over the ostinato pedal. (That this Phrygian melodic inflection was associated with the Spanish idiom in Ravel's mind is confirmed by the shape of the *Boléro* tune; that it may also have Basque connections is suggested by the closing passage of the reportedly Basque-flavoured first movement of the G major Concerto.)

This use of the repeated note was to become a hallmark of Ravel's style, especially in his piano music, and memorably in *Miroirs* and *Gaspard de la nuit*; but as an ostinato device on a dominant (or quasi-tonic) C♯ it was to recur with curious insistence not only in Ravel's own *Alborada del gracioso*, but also in Debussy's *Lindaraja* and *Soirée dans Grenade*. Indeed, it is hardly far-fetched to find echoes of it in Messiaen's *Turangalîla* more than half a century later: such was the impact of the startlingly original *Habanera*, which Ravel incorporated in his orchestral *Rapsodie espagnole* of 1907–8. It should also be noted that such was his feeling for traditional tonality that discords like the clusters of the *Habanera* tend to be both more acute and more tonally unequivocal than comparable clashes in Debussy; only in rare cases does one find the emancipated discord in Ravel: he himself singled out the *Chansons madécasses* as a work he probably could not have composed without the example of Schoenberg. Another work of 1895, the *Menuet antique*, also features (in its opening phrase) the simultaneous use of a tonic pedal with a cadential formula, though the repeated note here, F♯, immediately discloses itself as part of a melody. Again Ravel made play with the contrast between modal melody and diatonic harmony, the latter making an unconvincing attempt to mimic the *style galant* which had already been more smoothly exploited by Fauré (*Clair de lune* op.46 no.2) and Debussy (*Suite bergamasque*), to name but two.

Another early feature of Ravel's harmony which was to persist as a conscious technique was his exploitation of parallel chords; indeed, these, with all the 'forbidden' consecutive intervals they entailed, became such a firm feature of his writing that they are to be found in his otherwise justifiably atypical Prix de Rome essay, *L'aurore* (1905). Satie and, to a lesser extent, Chabrier are the obvious influences in this respect, especially where chords of the 9th and 11th are introduced. *Entre cloches* is an interesting example, summing up Ravel's discoveries of the 1890s. The parallel chords are used as an ostinato pealing figure to support progressions of quite sophisticated chords (for instance the natural 11th of the final plagal cadence) which verge on bitonality. The harmonies are so unrestrained as to suggest the naivety that Ravel later more carefully planned in the parallel triads of *Noël des jouets* (1905), which anticipates a similar device in Stravinsky's *Petrushka*.

Ravel constantly found varied uses both for bare organum-like 4ths and 5ths and for consecutive triads. In addition to *Entre cloches*, the song *Ronsard à son âme* (1924) uses the former for a particular 'programmatic' effect; more subtle is the extract from *L'enfant et les sortilèges* shown in ex.1, where an effect of wistful

Ex.1

aimlessness is achieved by combining bare 4ths with irregular metrical groupings. (An interesting comparison may be made with 'Petit Poucet' from *Ma mère l'oye*, where 'bare' 3rds are used in a similar situation.) Sometimes parallel intervals are designed to yield a purely timbral effect, in imitation of an organ stop ('Fanfare' for *L'éventail de Jeanne*, 1927; *Boléro*).

The use of triads is somewhat more complex. At its simplest there is again the suggestion of mere reinforcement, as in scalic passages in the 'Danse générale' of *Daphnis et Chloé* and at the end of the first movement of the G major Concerto. The same principle applies in more elaborate and thematic patterns, where 'automatic' block harmonization suggests timbre rather than tonality (see ex.2, from the finale of the Piano Trio).

Ex.2

Sometimes, however, a specifically harmonic direction is introduced by admitting irregularities, both in chord position and in mode. Thus a certain harmonic pull (without resolution) is present in the repeated five-chord figure which closes *Frontispice* (1918). An example from the 'Musette' of *Le tombeau de Couperin* (ex.3)

Ex.3

3 Cordes

demonstrates the flexible use of parallel harmonies in a typical confrontation between modal and diatonic elements (the use of a pedal point is not peculiar to this example, and indeed accompanies parallel harmonies quite frequently in Ravel's music).

Before proceeding to more elaborate chords, mention

may be made here of Ravel's early use of parallel octaves (or, more typically, 15ths or 22nds). Where treble and bass are thus coupled (*Habanera, Pavane pour une infante défunte*, the first movement of the Sonatina) it is fair to remark the influence of Chabrier, although, as Cooper has pointed out, it often appears to be Puccini who is invoked (the Quartet's first movement, the *Introduction et allegro, Petit poucet* etc). Of parallel dissonant chords, the most obvious use is again timbral. Perhaps the most typical in Ravel is the diminished octave, which appears in all manner of conjunctions. The consecutives that open *Alborada del gracioso* are particularly striking in that they also illustrate a characteristic harmonic progression, which may be summarized as tonic–dominant–flattened leading note–subdominant. The same progression underlies the chromatically sliding added-note chords of *Le martin-pêcheur* (*Histoires naturelles*), but here Ravel was thinking rather of passing notes and their resolution than of timbres. But a lengthy progression may itself become a mechanical gesture, a mere procession, so that the repeated sequence of dominant chords in the introduction to *L'heure espagnole* once again expresses ironic detachment (and it is again difficult to avoid the thought that the quality of Ravel's musical ideas is often beyond, or beneath, criticism).

Much of Ravel's harmonic language is indeed to be understood in terms of chromatic passing notes and appoggiaturas, often resolving on to further discords or in the 'wrong' octave. There is frequently considerable freedom in the treatment of dissonance and of abrupt juxtaposition of conflicting harmonies. Tritonal contrasts of common chords are evident throughout, from the *Shéhérazade* overture and *Jeux d'eau* to the Concerto for the left hand; there is an instance in ex.2. Ravel was clearly drawn to bitonality, and an effect of distinct and independent tonalities is particularly noticeable in certain postwar works (*Frontispice*, the Sonata for violin and cello, *L'enfant et les sortilèges*). Yet, by a superb paradox, the 'masculine' asperity of key clashes often belies their origins in (unresolved) conventional feminine closes. In a letter to René Lenormand, Ravel showed the monotonal basis of the trio section of the seventh of the *Valses nobles et sentimentales*; and the same principle is applicable to superficially bitonal passages in, for example, the Violin Sonata and the G major Concerto. In Ravel's sensibility there is every justification for analysis in terms of 'yearning' appoggiaturas, whereas one would hardly adopt this approach to a composer like Milhaud.

A similar affective quality, characterized by prominent use of the falling 4th – whether on to, or leading to, resolution (Sonatina, first movement, second-time bar), or unresolved (close of *L'enfant et les sortilèges*) – has been noted as a feature of Ravel's melodic thought. The opening bars of the *Valses nobles et sentimentales* (ex.4) show this feature as a motif related to the harmonic progression remarked on in *Alborada del gracioso*: as a melody it is transposed to different degrees (mediant–leading note–supertonic–submediant); it is subjected to octave displacements (though the altered form in its reappearance in the eighth waltz, tonic–dominant–flattened leading note–dominant, respects the 'true' registers); and chromatic appoggiaturas and passing notes appear in the harmonization (upward-tending in bar 1, downward in bar 2). Such sequences may be classed as 'melodic objects'; so may the pentatonic and

Ex.4

modal motifs used for ironic evocation in 'Asie' (*Shéhérazade*), 'Laideronnette' (*Ma mère l'oye*) and the cup's aria in *L'enfant et les sortilèges* and found also in *Sainte*, *Jeux d'eau* and the Concerto for the left hand. In addition, gapped scales and modes form the basis of many more extended and shapely melodies, a particular favourite being a Dorian lacking second and seventh notes (found by Roland-Manuel in *Menuet antique*, *D'Anne jouant de l'espinette*, *Daphnis et Chloé* and the G major Concerto). Ravel liked to give interest to his melodies by building them on irregular metrical schemes: the Piano Trio contains more than one example; and in his earliest works 5/4 (*D'Anne jouant de l'espinette*), 7/8 (Violin Sonata, 1897), 10/8 (*Entre cloches*) and mixed signatures (*Shéhérazade* overture) are to be found. Sequential writing builds up irregular phrase lengths in the *Pavane pour une infante défunte*. Where Ravel composed melodies of exceptional scope and breadth there is usually a sense of deliberate effort. Notable examples may be found in the 'Rigaudon' from *Le tombeau de Couperin*, the central movement of the G major Concerto (castigated by Constant Lambert as 'artificial melody') and the fine opening passage of the Concerto for the left hand.

Three distinct influences marked Ravel's treatment of the piano. Chabrier's is especially prominent in the 'Spanish' pieces: *Habanera* owes something to Chabrier's piano piece of the same name; but *Alborada del gracioso* is far more redolent of the orchestral *España*. When Ravel came to write his *Valses nobles et sentimentales* it is clear that he was frequently mindful of the *Trois valses romantiques* (there are echoes of the second in particular). There is more than a trace of the piano accompaniments to Chabrier's animal songs in *Histoires naturelles*. And, though it is hard to endorse Jankélévitch's description of *Menuet antique* as 'the twin of the *Menuet pompeux*' (a work orchestrated by Ravel in 1918), it is possible that Chabrier's *Bourrée fantasque* figured in Ravel's mind (alongside Balakirev's *Islamey*) as a precursor of *Scarbo*. Another precursor, and always a significant influence, was Liszt, Ravel's admiration for whom counterbalanced his distaste for Wagner. Apart from their shared taste for virtuoso fireworks, Ravel adopted a Lisztian point of view in many of his paintings from nature (*Jeux d'eau*, *Noctuelles*, *Une barque sur l'océan* and the song *Les grands vents venus d'outremer*, 1907). Finally the Baroque keyboard composers provided models for the more archaic pieces, and it is notable that preparatory to composing *Le tombeau de Couperin* Ravel transcribed a *forlane* by Couperin.

In 1889 Ravel heard Rimsky-Korsakov conduct the *Capriccio espagnol*, and in his own works he combined the Russian's skill in blending and balancing with a personal appreciation of individual timbres. His acute awareness of the expressive potential of each instrument gives high definition to his instrumentation and leads to effects of striking originality. His love of timbral eventfulness could result in moments of trite vulgarity; but

the complex crowding of densities which has offended some in *La valse* and elsewhere is, on the other hand, surely aesthetically justifiable. Ravel took a keen interest in instrumental technique; it must, however, be admitted that it was a composer's interest in what was even barely possible rather than a performer's interest in what was, in terms of instrument design, natural.

On the whole Ravel retained formal models well tested as suitable to diatonic language; the use of ternary and sonata forms generally satisfied his need for formal poise, and where these seemed too obvious he obscured their outlines by rudimentary camouflage or curtailment. On a broader scale, his handling of dramatic forms is ingenious and convincing, though the expansive assurance of *Daphnis et Chloé* is won at the expense of characteristic detail. The design of *La valse* is bold and simple; the *Valses nobles et sentimentales* are enriched by their retrospective finale; and in the Concerto for the left hand he slotted a variety of formal types into a single movement. Better suited to the reception of musical objects is the open-ended type of form typified by *moto perpetuo*. A fairly conventional example is the finale of the Violin Sonata; more suggestive is the brief *Frontispice*, whose closing chords in the manner of Satie are an ill-fitting stopper: Schoenberg more frankly left the third of his 1910 Orchestral Pieces unfinished.

Ravel's few pupils, of whom the most creatively noteworthy were Delage, Vaughan Williams and Roland-Manuel, were disinclined to mimic their teacher: his music was simply too finished to invite emulation, and he himself was a great imitator. His attitude as a composer, however, has been a considerable influence on 20th-century music. As a promoter of musical objectivity he paved the way for Stravinsky and the whole anti-Romantic school which flourished in the 1920s and early 1930s. And at its most extreme (perhaps in the opening of *L'heure espagnole*) his enthusiasm for mechanical precision and perfection anticipated the cogs and springs of later composers – of Ligeti, for example, and Riley. His own music continues to live; its sheer elegance to delight; its pungent 'guilt-edged' sensuousness to speak; and its wistful pursuit of innocence to fascinate.

5. Maurice Ravel

WORKS

Only works published and/or performed are included; for others see Orenstein (1975), 242ff.

OPERAS

L'heure espagnole (comédie musicale, 1, Franc-Nohain), 1907–9; Paris, Opéra-Comique, 19 May 1911

L'enfant et les sortilèges (fantaisie lyrique, 2 parts, Colette), 1920–25; Monte Carlo, 21 March 1925

BALLETS AND ORCHESTRAL

Shéhérazade, ouverture de féerie, 1898

Une barque sur l'océan [after pf work], 1906, 2nd version perf. 1926

Rapsodie espagnole, 1907–8: Prélude à la nuit, Malagueña, Habanera [after pf work], Feria

Pavane pour une infante défunte [after pf work], 1910

Ma mère l'oye (ballet, Ravel) [after pf work, with additional movts and interludes], 1911; Paris, Arts, 28 Jan 1912

Daphnis et Chloé (symphonie chorégraphique, 3 movts, Fokin, after Longus), 1909–12; Paris, Châtelet, 8 June 1912

Suite no.1 from 'Daphnis et Chloé', 1911: Nocturne, Interlude, Danse guerrière

Suite no.2 from 'Daphnis et Chloé', 1913: Lever du jour, Pantomime, Danse générale

Valses nobles et sentimentales [after pf work], 1912; score used for Adelaïde, ou Le langage des fleurs (ballet, Ravel), Paris, Châtelet, 22 April 1912

Alborada del gracioso [after pf work], 1918

Le tombeau de Couperin [after nos.1, 3, 5 and 4 of pf work], 1919; score, excluding no.1, used for ballet, Paris, Champs-Elysées, 8 Nov 1920

La valse, poème chorégraphique, 1919–20; score used for ballet, Paris, Opéra, 20 Nov 1928

Tzigane, rapsodie de concert [after work for vn, pf], vn, orch, 1924

Fanfare (for ballet L'éventail de Jeanne, Y. Franck, A. Bourgat), 1927; Paris, Opéra, 4 March 1929

Boléro (ballet), 1928; Paris, Opéra, 22 Nov 1928

Menuet antique [after pf work], 1929

Piano Concerto for the left hand, 1929–30

Piano Concerto, G, 1929–31

VOCAL

(with orchestra)

Myrrha (F. Beissier), cantata, 3 solo vv, orch, 1901

Alcyone (E. and E. Adénis), cantata, 3 solo vv, orch, 1902

Alyssa (M. Coiffier), cantata, 3 solo vv, orch, 1903

Manteau de fleurs [after song with pf], 1v, orch

Shéhérazade (T. Klingsor), Mez, orch, 1903: Asie, La flûte enchantée, L'indifférent

Noël des jouets [after song with pf], 1v, orch, 1905, 2nd version 1913

Chanson de la mariée, Tout gai [after nos.1 and 5 of song cycle Cinq mélodies populaires grecques], 1v, orch

Deux mélodies hébraïques [after songs with pf], 1v, orch, 1919

Chanson hébraïque [after no.4 of song cycle Chants populaires], 1v, orch, 1923–4

Don Quichotte à Dulcinée (P. Morand), 1v, orch, 1932–3: Chanson romanesque, Chanson épique, Chanson à boire

Ronsard à son âme [after song with pf], 1v, orch, 1935

(with ensemble)

Trois poèmes de Stéphane Mallarmé, 1v, pic, fl, cl, b cl, pf, str qt, 1913: Soupir, Placet futile, Surgi de la croupe et du bond

Chansons madécasses (E.-D. de Parny), 1v, fl, pf, vc, 1925–6: Nahandove, Aoua, Il est doux . . .

(choral)

Trois chansons (Ravel), SATB, 1914–15: Nicolette, Trois beaux oiseaux du paradis, Ronde

(songs with piano)

Ballade de la reine morte d'aimer (R. de Marès), c1893

Un grand sommeil noir (Verlaine), 1895

Sainte (Mallarmé), 1896

Chanson du rouet (Leconte de Lisle), 1898

Si morne! (Verhaeren), 1898

Deux épigrammes de Clément Marot, 1896–9: D'Anne qui me jecta de la neige, D'Anne jouant de l'espinette

Manteau de fleurs (P. Gravollet), 1903

Shéhérazade [after songs with orch], 1903

Noël des jouets (Ravel), 1905

Cinq mélodies populaires grecques (trans. Calvocoressi), 1904–6: Chanson de la mariée, Là-bas, vers l'église, Quel galant m'est comparable, Chanson des cueilleuses de lentisques, Tout gai!; lost nos.: A vous, oiseaux des plaines, Chanson de pâtre épirote, Mon mouchoir, hélas, est perdu

Histoires naturelles (J. Renard), 1906: Le paon, Le grillon, Le cygne, Le martin-pêcheur, La pintade

Les grands vents venus d'outremer (de Régnier), 1907

Sur l'herbe (Verlaine), 1907

Vocalise-étude en forme de habanera, 1907

Tripatos (trans. Calvocoressi), 1909

Chants populaires, 1910: Chanson espagnole, Chanson française, Chanson italienne, Chanson hébraïque, Chanson écossaise; lost nos.: Chanson flamande, Chanson russe

Trois poèmes de Stéphane Mallarmé [after songs with ens], 1913

Deux mélodies hébraïques, 1914: Kaddisch, L'énigme éternelle

Trois chansons [after choral work], 1914–15

Ronsard à son âme, 1923–4

Chansons madécasses [after songs with ens], 1926

Rêves (Fargue), 1927

Don Quichotte à Dulcinée [after songs with orch], 1932–3

CHAMBER AND INSTRUMENTAL

Sonata, vn, pf, 1897

String Quartet, F, 1902–3

Introduction et allegro, harp, fl, cl, str qt, 1905

Piano Trio, 1914

Le tombeau de Claude Debussy, vn, vc (1920)

Sonata, vn, vc, 1920–22

Berceuse sur le nom de Gabriel Fauré, vn, pf, 1922

Tzigane, rapsodie de concert, vn, pf, 1924; also for vn, pf, luthéal

Sonata, vn, pf, 1923–7

PIANO

Sérénade grotesque, c1893

Menuet antique, 1895

Sites auriculaires, 2 pf, 1895–7: Habanera, Entre cloches

Pavane pour une infante défunte, 1899

Jeux d'eau, 1901

Sonatine, 1903–5

Miroirs, 1904–5: Noctuelles, Oiseaux tristes, Une barque sur l'océan, Alborada del gracioso, La vallée des cloches

Gaspard de la nuit, 1908: Ondine, Le gibet, Scarbo

Menuet sur le nom d'Haydn, 1909

Ma mère l'oye, 4 hands, 1908–10: Pavane de la belle au bois dormant, Petit poucet, Laideronnette, impératrice des pagodes, Les entretiens de la belle et de la bête, Le jardin féerique

Valses nobles et sentimentales, 1911

A la manière de . . ., 1913: Borodine, Chabrier

Prélude, 1913

Le tombeau de Couperin, 1914–17: Prélude, Fugue, Forlane, Rigaudon, Menuet, Toccata

Frontispice, 2 pf 5 hands, 1918

La valse [after orch work], 2 pf (1921)

Boléro [after orch work], 2 pf (1930)

ARRANGEMENTS, EDITION

(orchestrations)

N. Rimsky-Korsakov: Antar: excerpts, partly reorchd for use as incidental music, c1910

M. Musorgsky: Khovanshchina, c1913, collab. Stravinsky, lost

E. Satie: Le fils des étoiles: Prélude, 1913

R. Schumann: Carnaval: Préambule, Valse allemande, Paganini, Marche des 'Davidsbündler' contre les philistins, for use as ballet, c1914, other nos. lost

E. Chabrier: Dix pièces pittoresques: Menuet pompeux, for use as ballet, 1918

C. Debussy: Pour le piano: Sarabande, 1922

——: Tarantelle styrienne, as Danse, 1922

M. Musorgsky: Tableaux d'une exposition, 1922

(piano reductions)

F. Delius: Margot la rouge, vocal score, 1902

C. Debussy: Nocturnes, 2 pf, 1909

——: Prélude à 'L'après-midi d'un faune', 4 hands, 1910

(edition)

F. Mendelssohn: Complete works for piano solo and piano concertos, 1915–17

Principal publishers: Durand, Eschig

WRITINGS

'Concert Lamoureux', *BSIM*, viii (1912), Feb, 62

'Concerts Lamoureux', *BSIM*, viii (1912), March, 50

'Les "Tableaux symphoniques" de M. Fanelli', *BSIM*, viii (1912), April, 55

'A propos des "Images" de Claude Debussy', *Cahiers d'aujourd'hui* (1913), Feb, 135

'Au Théâtre des Arts', *Comoedia illustré*, v (5 Feb 1913), 417

'Boris Godounoff', *Comoedia illustré*, v (5 June 1913)

'Fervaal – poème et musique de Vincent d'Indy', *Comoedia illustré*, v (20 Jan 1913), 361

'La sorcière à l'Opéra-Comique', *Comoedia illustré*, v (5 Jan 1913), 320

'A l'Opéra-Comique', *Comoedia illustré*, vi (20 Jan 1914), 390

'Les nouveaux spectacles de la saison russe – Le rossignol', *Comoedia illustré*, vi (June 1914), 811

'Parsifal – version française d'Alfred Ernst', *Comoedia illustré*, vi (20 Jan 1914), 400
'Les mélodies de Gabriel Fauré', *ReM*, iii/11 (1922), 22
'Contemporary Music', *Rice Institute Pamphlet*, xv (1928), April, 131; repr. in *RdM*, 1 (1964), 208
Article on the pf concs., *Daily Telegraph* (16 July 1931)
ed. Roland-Manuel: 'Une esquisse autobiographique de Maurice Ravel', *ReM* (1938), no.187, p.17
ed. R. Chalupt and M. Gerar: *Ravel au miroir de ses lettres* (Paris, 1956)

BIBLIOGRAPHY

CATALOGUES

Catalogue de l'oeuvre de Maurice Ravel (Paris, 1954)
Catalogue de l'exposition Ravel (Paris, 1975)

MONOGRAPHS

Roland-Manuel: *Maurice Ravel et son oeuvre* (Paris, 1914)
——: *Maurice Ravel et son oeuvre dramatique* (Paris, 1928)
W.-L. Landowsky: *Maurice Ravel, sa vie, son oeuvre* (Paris, 1938, 2/1950)
Roland-Manuel: *A la gloire de Ravel* (Paris, 1938, 2/1948; Eng. trans., 1947)
V. Jankélévitch: *Maurice Ravel* (Paris, 1939, 2/1956; Eng. trans., 2/1959)
Colette and others: *Maurice Ravel par quelques-uns de ses familiers* (Paris, 1939)
M. Goss: *Bolero: the Life of Maurice Ravel* (New York, 1940)
K. Akeret: *Studien zum Klavierwerk von Maurice Ravel* (Zurich, 1941)
T. Aubin and others: *Maurice Ravel* (Paris, 1945)
H. Jourdan-Morhange: *Ravel et nous* (Geneva, 1945)
N. Demuth: *Ravel* (London, 1947)
A. Machabey: *Maurice Ravel* (Paris, 1947)
F. Onnen: *Maurice Ravel* (Stockholm, 1947)
R. Malipiero: *Maurice Ravel* (Milan, 1948)
L.-P. Fargue: *Maurice Ravel* (Paris, 1949)
J. Bruyr: *Maurice Ravel ou Le lyrisme et les sortilèges* (Paris, 1950)
L. La Pegna: *Ravel* (Brescia, 1950)
W. Tappolet: *Maurice Ravel: Leben und Werk* (Olten, 1950)
V. Perlemuter and H. Jourdan-Morhange: *Ravel d'après Ravel* (Lausanne, 1953)
V. Seroff: *Maurice Ravel* (New York, 1953)
J. van Ackere: *Maurice Ravel* (Brussels, 1957)
J. Geraedts: *Ravel* (Haarlem, 1957)
R. de Fragny: *Maurice Ravel* (Lyons, 1960)
R. Myers: *Ravel: Life and Works* (London, 1960)
G. Léon: *Maurice Ravel* (Paris, 1964)
H. H. Stuckenschmidt: *Maurice Ravel: Variationen über Person und Werk* (Frankfurt, 1966; Eng. trans., 1969)
P. Petit: *Ravel* (Paris, 1970)
M. Long: *Au piano avec Maurice Ravel* (Paris, 1971; Eng. trans., 1973)
A. Orenstein: *Ravel: Man and Musician* (New York, 1975) [incl. full bibliography]
R. Nichols: *Ravel* (London, 1977)

INTERVIEWS

L. Laloy: 'Wagner et les musiciens d'aujourd'hui – opinions de MM. Florent Schmitt et Maurice Ravel', *Grande revue* (10 May 1909), 160
M. Montabré: 'Entretien avec Maurice Ravel', *L'intransigeant* (28 Jan 1923)
'Entretien avec Ravel', *ReM*, no.113 (1931)
'Tien opinies van M. Ravel', *De telegraaf* (7 April 1932)

OTHER LITERATURE

T. Klingsor: 'Les musiciens et les poètes contemporains', *Mercure de France* (1900), Nov, 430
P. Lalo: 'Encore le Debussysme: une lettre de M. Ravel', *Le temps* (9 April 1907)
Roland-Manuel: 'Maurice Ravel', *ReM*, ii/6 (1921), 1
F. Shera: *Debussy and Ravel* (Oxford, 1925)
ReM, vi/8 (1925) [special Ravel issue]
ReM (1938) [special Ravel issue], no.187
Articles by J.-R. Bloch, Roland-Manuel and H. Sauguet in *ReM* (1939), no.188
M. de Falla: 'Notes sur Ravel', *ReM* (1939), no.189, p.81
M.-D. Calvocoressi: 'Ravel's Letters to Calvocoressi', *MQ*, xxvii (1941), 1
——: 'When Ravel Composed to Order', *ML*, xxii (1941), 54
R. de Fragny: 'Les inédits de Maurice Ravel', *Concorde* (11 April 1946)
Melos, xiv/12 (1947) [special Ravel issue]
P. Boulez: 'Trajectoires: Ravel, Stravinsky, Schoenberg', *Contrepoints* (1949), no.6, p.122; repr. in *Relevés d'apprenti* (Paris, 1966; Eng. trans., 1968)
Roland-Manuel: 'Lettres de Maurice Ravel et documents inédits', *RdM*, xxxviii (1956), 49
Articles by R. Chalupt, R. Dumesnil, V. Jankélévitch, T. Klingsor and

A. Mirambel in *ReM* (1958), no.243
J. van der Veen: 'Problèmes structuraux chez Maurice Ravel', *IMSCR, vii Cologne 1958*, 289
F. Lesure: ' "L'affaire" Debussy–Ravel: lettres inédites', *Festschrift Friedrich Blume* (Kassel, 1963), 231
J. Braun: *Die Thematik in den Kammermusikwerken von Maurice Ravel* (Regensburg, 1966)
A. Orenstein: 'L'enfant et les sortilèges: correspondance inédite de Ravel et Colette', *RdM*, lii (1966), 215
——: 'Maurice Ravel's Creative Process', *MQ*, liii (1967), 467
——: 'Some Unpublished Music and Letters by Maurice Ravel', *Music Forum*, iii (1973), 291–334
H. Macdonald: 'Ravel and the Prix de Rome', *MT*, cxvi (1975), 332
J.-M. Nectoux: 'Ravel/Fauré et les Débuts de la Société Musicale Indépendante', *RdM*, lxi (1975), 295
G. Sannemüller: 'Die Sonate für Violine und Violoncello von Maurice Ravel', *Mf*, xxviii (1975), 408
J.-M. Nectoux: 'Maurice Ravel et sa bibliothèque musicale', *FAM*, xxiv (1977), 199
R. Grouquist: 'Ravel's Trois poèmes de Stéphane Mallarmé', *MQ*, lxiv (1978), 507

G. W. HOPKINS

Ravenna rite, music of the. With Milan and Aquileia, Ravenna was a major ecclesiastical centre of northern Italy during the last centuries of the western Empire and the period immediately following. Ravenna is approximately 160 km south of Venice, a short distance inland from the coast; it came into prominence with its selection as the imperial capital by Honorius in 402. It fell successively to the Goths in 493, the Byzantine Empire in 540, the Lombards in 751 and the Franks in 754; Pepin bestowed it upon Pope Stephen III and thus founded the temporal power of the papacy.

Ravenna reached the heights of its political power and artistic eminence during the 5th and 6th centuries: these are stunningly reflected in combinations of builder's stone and mosaic tile which include the mausoleum of Galla Placidia (*d* 450), the Orthodox and Arian baptisteries, the Archiepiscopal chapel, the tomb of Theodoric and the churches of S Vitale, Sant'Apollinare at the nearby town of Classe, and Sant'Apollinare Nuovo.

Very little remains of Ravenna's liturgical music. Where Milan preserves the full repertory of its medieval liturgical chant (*see* AMBROSIAN RITE, MUSIC OF THE), the early chant dialect of Ravenna has all but disappeared. The city's importance as a liturgical centre up to the mid-8th century, though perhaps exaggerated in Gamber's proposal that the mixed Gelasian sacramentaries originated at Ravenna, suggests that its chant repertory may to some extent have developed independently. Two chants from the Easter Vigil Mass for neophytes can be regarded as possible survivors from this period: an alleluia with verses from Psalm cxxxv, the first of which is *Confitemini Domino quoniam*, and *Qui in Christo baptizati estis* (?offertory), related musically to it. The text and music of the latter are derived from a Byzantine baptismal troparion, *Hosoi eis Christon*, which was adapted musically in other ways in the Beneventan, Old Roman and Gregorian melodic traditions. These two Ravenna chants reveal an elegance of centonate structure (*see* CENTONIZATION) not matched elsewhere in the West among the more sophisticated chants of the Gregorian tradition.

Two other unusual chants found at Ravenna are known also in manuscripts from the Beneventan region of southern Italy (*see* BENEVENTAN RITE, MUSIC OF THE), in the central Italian provinces and in the intervening backwater of the Abruzzi; there is no trace of them in manuscripts reflecting Roman practice. Like parts of southern Italy, Ravenna, during the Byzantine Exarchate (540–751), was a natural point of entry into Italy and the West for chants of Eastern Orthodox origin; one such chant, the Greco-Latin antiphon *Hote tō staurō/O quando in cruce*, is both musically and textually a borrowing of an Eastern hymn for the Good Friday Hours, attributed to Sophronius, Patriarch of Jerusalem (634–8). The other chant is a hymn or *versus* in hexameters (*Lux de luce Deus tenebris illuxit averni*) whose presumably original form, with a single musical pattern repeated for each verse, is found only in the Ravenna sources. It is thought that both of these chants were in use before the mid-8th century, for at that time the Byzantine link between Ravenna and southern Italy was effectively broken by the Lombard conquest of the north. Whether they were introduced in the north before the south, however, is uncertain, but a northern origin is probable at least for *Lux de luce*.

Other survivals of the characteristic Ravenna practice may be distinguished among the Proper chants (in particular, the alleluias, offertories and sequences) for saints venerated locally, particularly Apollinaris, Vitalis, Agricola and Fusca. The alleluia with the verse *Accipe spiritum sanctum* for St Apollinaris is an example of a chant composed later (though before the 11th century) at Ravenna. Although no early antiphoners of the Office from Ravenna survive, there are three fine versions of the *antiphonale missarum* from this region, dating from the 11th and 12th centuries: *US-BAw* W.11 (a *missale plenum*); *I-Pc* A.47; and *MOe* O.I.7. Fragments of Ravenna office-books survive in *I-Rvat* lat.4750 and perhaps *Rvat* lat.85.

Another important possible source of the early Ravenna chant repertory may be the liturgy of Milan. During the late 5th century and the early 6th, the Milanese bishops took refuge from the Lombard occupation of Milan at Genoa, which was at that time strongly influenced by Byzantium by way of Ravenna. There are many chants of eastern origin in the Milanese liturgy which, it has been suggested, were originally introduced under the contemporary influence of Ravenna.

By the early 11th century – and perhaps much earlier – most traces of the older local chants had been extinguished at Ravenna as they had throughout Europe. When St Romuald (c951–1027), a native of the city and sometime abbot of the Benedictine monastery at Classe, founded the Camaldolese order, he seems to have drawn on the monastic rite in use at Classe, which had already been influenced by the Cluniac reform (PalMus, ix, Tournai, 1906, p.13). In the late 11th century, however, there was a local renewal, for which St Peter Damian (1007–72) seems to have been largely responsible; he was himself the author of a number of hymns. A noted Mass Proper for St Apollinaris and a noted Office for St Silvester, appended to an early collection of Peter's works (*I-Rvat* lat.3797, dating from c1100) contain some local material; this may represent a genuine early survival, or perhaps the introduction of new compositions in an archaic style.

BIBLIOGRAPHY

H. M. Bannister: 'Gli inni di S. Pietro Damiano', *Rassegna gregoriana*, viii (1908), 262

C. Blume, ed.: *Analecta hymnica medii aevi*, li (Leipzig, 1908), 238ff

A. Wilmart: 'Le recueil des poèmes et des prières de Saint-Pierre Damien', *Revue bénédictine*, xli (1929), 342

E. Wellesz: *Eastern Elements in Western Chant*, MMB, *Subsidia*, ii (1947), 68ff, 95ff

G. Vecchi: 'Lirica liturgica ravennate', *Studi romagnoli*, iii (1952), 243

B. Stäblein: 'Von der Sequenz zum Strophenlied', *Mf*, vii (1954), 257

M. Huglo: 'Antifone antiche per la *fractio panis*', *Ambrosius*, xxxi (1955), 85

B. Stäblein: 'Italien', §A, *MGG*

P. Borella: *Il rito ambrosiano* (Brescia, 1964), 30ff, 84ff

K. Gamber: 'Das Missale des Bischofs Maximian von Ravenna', *Ephemerides liturgicae*, lxxx (1966), 205

——: *Codices liturgici latini antiquiores*, Spicilegii friburgensis, *Subsidia*, i (Fribourg, 1963, 2/1968), 111f, 119f, 123f, 222

K. Levy: 'The Italian Neophytes' Chants', *JAMS*, xxiii (1970), 181–227

——: '*Lux de luce*: the Origin of an Italian Sequence', *MQ*, lvii (1971), 40

KENNETH LEVY

Ravenscroft, John (i) (*d* not later than 1708). English composer resident in Italy. All that is known about his life is what can be deduced from copies of his works. The first edition of his 12 *da chiesa* sonatas op.1, for two violins, violone or archlute, and organ continuo, in which he is described as 'Giovanni Ravenscroft, alias Rederi Inglese', bears a dedication from Rome dated 1695 to Prince Ferdinando of Tuscany, presumably his patron. In a postscript 'Al Lettore' Ravenscroft describes his work as the product of 'una penna dilettante non professoria', and it seems likely that he was one of the small group of well-to-do British amateur violinists who received some instruction from Corelli, a group which also included Sir John Clerk and, according to Hawkins, Lord Edgcumbe. That Ravenscroft was Corelli's pupil is supported by the evidence of an inscription on a contemporary MS copy of his op.1. Both editions of his six *da camera* sonatas op.2, for two violins and basso continuo, published in London in 1708, make it clear that he was then dead. Whether he had returned to England is not known, but it seems probable.

Einstein expressed a high opinion of Ravenscroft's church sonatas, at the same time acknowledging their derivative nature by describing them as 'more like Corelli than Corelli's own sonatas' (about 1735 Le Cène reissued nine of them as 'Corelli's op.7', and for a long time two were wrongly attributed to Caldara). Their texture is more concentrated and less virtuosic than that of their models, and Ravenscroft allows himself no episodes deviating from the main subject matter. The chamber sonatas exhibit a somewhat unorthodox ordering of movements: in no.4 the Giga is placed second, and no.2 ends with a Sarabanda in 3/8 time marked 'Allegro'. The last is a 'Ceccona', clearly based on Corelli's example in his op.2, but with a short preludial Largo.

BIBLIOGRAPHY

A. Einstein: *A Short History of Music* (London, 1936, 5/1948), 276ff, 376f

W. S. Newman: 'Ravenscroft and Corelli', *ML*, xxxviii (1957), 369

——: *The Sonata in the Baroque Era* (Chapel Hill, 1959, 2/1966/R1972), 311f

M. Tilmouth: *Chamber Music in England 1675–1720* (diss., U. of Cambridge, 1959), i, 301ff; ii, 160ff

MICHAEL TILMOUTH

Ravenscroft, John (ii) (*d* ?1735–45). English violinist. He was a member of the band at Goodman's Fields Theatre, probably from its opening in October 1729, and received benefit performances there in the 1729–30 and 1730–31 seasons. He seems to have been replaced by 1735. According to Hawkins he was also a wait of Tower Hamlets. Hawkins further stated that Ravenscroft was a good player, much in demand for balls and dancing parties. He seems to have composed mainly hornpipes and other dance tunes, though two songs, *Foolish woman* and *Lucinda, say* (both published *c*1725) are probably his. *The Dancing Master*, iii (*c*1727) contains one hornpipe by him, and another, entitled *Ravens Hornpipe*, may also be his. Hawkins printed two more from a collection which seems to be no longer extant; one of these was included in *The Delightful Pocket Companion for the German Flute*, ii (*c*1750).

MARGARET LAURIE

Ravenscroft, Thomas (*b* ? *c*1582; *d c*1635). English editor, composer and theorist. On 2 May 1594, a Thomas 'Raniscroft' became a chorister of Chichester Cathedral. Ravenscroft was a chorister at St Paul's Cathedral under Thomas Giles (both their names appear in a list of the choir included in the report of Bishop Bancroft's visitation, 1598); although his name is, however, absent from a list of members made in 1594, he was still there in 1600 when Edward Pearce became organist and choirmaster.

His appointment coincided with a renewal of activity by the St Paul's company of child actors which, like the children of the Chapel Royal, catered for more sophisticated tastes by including in their plays specially written songs to be performed by trained voices and instrumentalists. Ravenscroft wrote some of the music for these productions and was probably also active as an instrumentalist or actor-singer. We learn from the *Briefe Discourse* that he was a student at Gresham College; the book is dedicated to the 'most worthy and Grave Senators' of that institution. Fellowes and others gave the date of Ravenscroft's Cambridge BMus as 1607, but no-one graduated with the BMus in that year. The University Book of Supplicats, however, shows that a 'Thomas Rangcraft' from Pembroke Hall took the degree in 1605. There are few details of his activities between then and the time when he was music master at Christ's Hospital (1618–22), but it is likely that he continued his association with the theatre. Ravenscroft's date of birth is sometimes given as 1592, but this would be impossible if (as the Cambridge Grace Book E states) he received his degree after ten years of study. Yet the prefatory poem to the *Briefe Discourse* (1614) by 'R.LL.' describes Ravenscroft as a youth of 22, and a marginal note confirming this states that he received the BMus when he was 14; other recipients can be shown to have been at least 21. What may have confused the poet's reckoning was the fact that the necessary period of study was not considered to have begun until after the candidate's 14th birthday.

In 1609 Ravenscroft edited *Pammelia*, which is the earliest English printed collection of rounds and catches, and contains 100 examples, some having sacred texts in English or Latin. There are also vendors' cries, sol-faing pieces, tavern songs and traditional ballads, but a number of them suggest that Ravenscroft's theatrical connections did not cease when he left St Paul's; for example, three of the songs (nos.62, 85 and 100) were sung in Beaumont's *The Knight of the Burning Pestle* (1608). *Deuteromelia* (also 1609) contains 17 catches and 14 freemen's songs for three and four voices. Again there are a few play songs: no.7, for instance, comes from *The Knight of the Burning Pestle*, and no.17 is sung in *Jack Drum's Entertainment* (1601). Also included are *Three Blind Mice* and the

catch *Hold thy peace knave* sung in *Twelfth Night*. *Melismata* (1611) comprises 23 settings of which nine are 'Citie' and 'Countrey' rounds; the others are short madrigalian pieces which attempt to express the 'humour' of the text. Sabol tentatively suggested appropriate dramatic contexts for four of the songs; no.12, however, can definitely be identified with Audrey's song in Act 4 scene v of Middleton's *A Trick to Catch the Old One*.

Whereas the music of these collections is anonymous, 12 of the songs appended to the *Briefe Discourse* (1614) to illustrate Ravenscroft's theoretical ideas are ascribed to him; six others are by John Bennet and two by Edward Pearce. The book itself, despite its impressive array of authorities, is an ambiguous discussion of the contemporary misuse of mensuration signs and an attempt to impose order on the chaos by advocating a return to medieval practice. The music, with the exception of a few madrigalian numbers, is of the consort song variety and includes four play songs (nos.6, 8, 9, 15) and a jig-like cantata in which Hodge Trillindle woos Malkyn in a broad west-country dialect (nos.17–19). Ravenscroft's *The Whole Booke of Psalmes* (1621), with its 105 settings, is one of the most important psalters of the period, though it contains much music from the earlier publications of Day, Parker, East and Barley. The melodies are in the tenor and are named. The new contributors include John and Thomas Tomkins, Peerson, Palmer, the elder John Milton,

Part of 'Hodge Trillindle to his Zweet hort Malkyn' from 'Briefe Discourse' (1614) by Thomas Ravenscroft

Ward, Stubbes, Cranford, Harrison and Ravenscroft himself, who contributed 55 settings. His anthems and instrumental compositions are relatively unimportant and the value of his *Treatise of Musick* (*GB-Lbm* Add.19758) is negligible. The publication *Musalia* (1613), mentioned in a letter to the *Musical World* in 1840 (see King) is fictitious.

Ravenscroft's extant compositions show him to have been a man of great versatility, though of slender talents. His collections of rounds and partsongs are historically important in that they afford an insight into the popular music-making of the day, as well as preserving a number of play songs which would otherwise have been irrecoverably lost. The composer was highly regarded by his contemporaries.

WORKS

8 verse anthems (1 also attrib. M. Peerson), *GB-DRc, Lbm, Ob, Och, T*
3 full anthems, 5vv, *Ob, Och*
3 motets, 5vv, *Lbm, Ob*
4 fantasias, 5 viols, *Lbm* Add.39550–54

THEORETICAL WORKS

A Briefe Discourse of the True (but Neglected) Use of Charact'ring the Degrees ... Examples whereof are exprest in the Harmony of 4 Voyces (London, 1614²¹/*R*); ed. in Mateer
A Treatise of Musick (MS, *Lbm* Add.19758)

EDITIONS

The Whole Booke of Psalmes (London, 1621¹¹); ed. W. H. Havergal (London, 1845)
Pammelia ... [100] Catches, 3–10vv (London, 1609³¹/*R*1961); ed. P. Warlock (London, 1928)
Deuteromelia ... [14] Freemens Songs and ... [17] Catches, 3–4vv (London, 1609³²/*R*1961)
Melismata: Musicall Phansies, fitting the Court, Citie and Countrey Humours, 3–5vv (London, 1611/*R*1961)

BIBLIOGRAPHY

'Dotted Crotchet': 'A Visit to Christ's Hospital', *MT*, xlvi (1905), 573
E. H. Fellowes: *English Madrigal Verse* (Oxford, 1920, 3/1967), 201–55
W. J. Lawrence: 'Thomas Ravenscroft's Theatrical Associations', *Modern Language Review*, xix (1924), 418
J. Mark: 'Thomas Ravenscroft's B.Mus (c. 1583–1633)', *MT*, lxv (1924), 881
H. N. Hillebrand: *The Child Actors*, University of Illinois Studies in Language and Literature, xi/1 (Urbana, 1926)
A. J. Sabol: 'Two Songs with Accompaniment for an Elizabethan Choirboy Play', *Studies in the Renaissance*, v (1958), 145
——: 'Ravenscroft's "Melismata" and the Children of Paul's', *RN*, xii (1959), 3
A. H. King: *Some British Collectors of Music* (Cambridge, 1963), 39ff
D. G. Mateer: *A Critical Study and Transcription of "A Briefe Discourse" by Thomas Ravenscroft* (diss., U. of London, 1970)

DAVID MATEER

Raverii, Alessandro (*fl* early 16th century). Italian music printer. His father Constantin Raverii was a member of a minor printing family and married one of the Bindoni family, famous as Venetian printers though little associated with music. Through them he became related to the Gardane family. Alessandro Raverii printed music only between 1606 and 1609, during which time he printed a large number of volumes of which over 50 are extant. He appears to have had close ties with Angelo Gardane, for many of Raverii's titles are clearly no more than reprints of volumes from Gardane's house after 1588. Raverii also printed three titles (by Bonini, Caccini and Peri) which he seems to have taken from Marescotti in Florence.

BIBLIOGRAPHY

C. Sartori: 'Una dinastia di editori musicali', *La bibliofilia*, lvii (1956), 176–208
——: *Dizionario degli editori musicali italiani* (Florence, 1958)
L. Bartholomew: *Alessandro Raverii's Collection of 'Canzoni per sonare'* (*Venice, 1608*) (Fort Hayes, Kansas, 1965)

STANLEY BOORMAN

Ravn, Hans Mikkelsen [Corvinus, Johannes Michaelii] (*b* nr. Grenaa, Jutland, *c*1610; *d* Ørslev, Zealand, 10 Aug 1663). Danish educationist, scholar and music theorist. He was educated at the grammar school at Slagelse, where the foundations of his interest in music were laid. He read theology at the University of Copenhagen from 1631 to 1634, after which he was appointed to Herlufsholm public school. In 1640 he was called back to his old school at Slagelse as rector. From 1652 until his death he was parish priest at Ørslev. He proved himself an excellent teacher as well as a scholar interested in history, poetry, the Danish language and music. His most important literary work is his *Heptachordum danicum seu Nova solsisatio* (Copenhagen, 1646), which, as he observed in his dedication, was the first attempt at a complete and thorough presentation of the art of music in Denmark. The work consists of a lengthy prolegomena, in which he reviewed the history of music, discussed Danish folksongs and hymns and described ancient instruments; a short section on musical notation ('De notatione'); the main body of the work ('De modulatione'), a presentation of music theory in two parts as it concerns both monophonic and polyphonic music, for which his principal authorities seem to have been Lippius, Crüger, Mersenne, Praetorius and Demantius; and finally the rules governing the behaviour of choirboys which had been drafted by a Copenhagen rector (Olaus Theophilus) in 1573, supplemented by pedagogical advice to choirmasters, suggesting that Ravn intended his book for use in grammar schools. As the title of the work declares, he advocated the seven-note scale, adding the syllable *si* to the hexachord, the introduction of which into Denmark he attributed to Gregorius Trehou. He also subscribed to Zarlino's syntonic scale, as opposed to the diatonic scale of Pythagoras, and presented the triadic system in such a way as to pave the way for an acceptance of the concepts of major and minor tonalities.

BIBLIOGRAPHY

A. Hammerich: *Musikken ved Christian den Fjerdes Hof* (Copenhagen, 1892)
H. Ehrenchrone-Müller: *Forfatter-leksikon*, vi (Copenhagen, 1929), 423
N. Schiørring: 'Ravn, Hans Mikkelsen', *DBL*
B. Johnsson: 'Hans Mikkelsen Ravn's Heptachordum Danicum 1646', *DAM 1962*, 59–92

JOHN BERGSAGEL

Ravvivando (It.: 'bringing back to life'; gerund of *ravvivare*, to revive). As *ravvivando il tempo*, a direction indicating that the pace of a piece of music is to revert at a given point to a faster tempo at which it had moved earlier. *Ravvivando* alone, without *il tempo*, may also indicate a return to a livelier mood, but even so a faster pace is nearly always implied.

See also TEMPO AND EXPRESSION MARKS.

ERIC BLOM/R

Rawlings [Rawlins]. English family of musicians.

(1) Thomas Rawlings (*b c*1703; *d* London, 1767). Instrumentalist and possibly singer. He was a pupil of Pepusch and a member of Handel's orchestra (probably as a violinist) in both opera and oratorio performances. It is likely that he is identical with the Thomas Rawlins who entered the Queen's Chapel as a singer in 1737. On 14 March 1753 he was appointed organist at Chelsea Hospital.

(2) Robert Rawlings (*b* London, 1742; *d* London, 1814). Violinist, son of (1) Thomas Rawlings. He was a pupil of his father and of the Italian theorist Barsanti, who was then living in London. He may have held an early appointment as organist to Chelsea College. At the age of 17 he was appointed musical page to the Duke of York, with whom he travelled on the Continent until the duke's death in 1767. Rawlings then returned to England and was appointed personally by George III as violinist in the king's band; he was also elected to the queen's private band.

(3) Thomas A. Rawlings (*b* London, 1775; *d* London, *c*1850). Violinist, cellist, pianist and composer, son of (2) Robert Rawlings. He was a pupil, first of his father, then (1788–95) of Joseph Diettenhofer, an Austrian theorist who had settled in London in 1780. During these years he had some of his music played at the Professional Concert and met Haydn. He performed as violinist and cellist for all the London concert organizations, including the Opera and the Antient Concerts, and he taught piano, violin and thoroughbass in London. Fétis said that he met Rawlings in London in 1829.

Rawlings's major works seem to belong to the earlier part of his life. After 1800, he poured out a long succession of songs, marches and piano pieces for the salon. According to Brown and Stratton the well-known song *Isle of Beauty* generally attributed to him was by a Major C. S. Whitmore; Rawlings was merely the arranger. It is to the same dictionary that we owe the information that he 'died about the middle of the present century'.

WORKS
(*all published in London*)
3 Sonatas, hpd/pf, vn acc., op.1 (*c*1793)
6 New Waltzes, pf, tambourine and triangle acc., op.2 (*c*1794)
A Cantata on the Death of the Late Unfortunate Marie Antoinette, Queen of France (*c*1794)
A Grand Military March in Score, pf (*c*1795)
Concerto, pf, fl, 2 vn, va, vc, in Concerto da camera, no.4 (*c*1800)
Numerous songs and pieces for pf pubd singly and in 19th-century anthologies; most in *GB-Lbm*

BIBLIOGRAPHY
EitnerQ; *FétisB*
J. Sainsbury, ed.: *Dictionary of Musicians* (London, 2/1825/*R*1966)
J. D. Brown and S. S. Stratton: *British Musical Biography* (Birmingham, 1897)

PETER PLATT

Rawsthorne, Alan (*b* Haslingden, Lancs., 2 May 1905; *d* Cambridge, 24 July 1971). English composer.

1. LIFE. Rawsthorne did not turn to the serious study of music until he was 19, having made false starts in both dentistry and architecture. In 1925 he entered the Royal Manchester College of Music, where he was a pupil of the pianist Frank Merrick and the cellist Carl Fuchs; his piano studies were continued abroad, notably under Egon Petri. On his return to England in 1932 he taught at Dartington Hall School and also composed music for the associated School of Dance Mime. Yet even though he moved to London in order to devote himself primarily to composition, it was not until 1938 (when he was 33) that he achieved wide recognition with the Theme and Variations for two violins, introduced at that year's ISCM Festival in London. At the 1939 festival, in Warsaw, a far more ambitious score, the Symphonic Studies, demonstrated his mastery of orchestral resources, while in the same year the First Piano Concerto (in its original version, with an orchestra of strings and percussion) confirmed the achievement of a

highly individual language and certain structural predilections; both were to remain remarkably constant throughout the rest of his career.

Rawsthorne rescored the concerto in 1942, by which time he was doing military service; despite this he was able to complete the two contrasted overtures of 1944 and 1945. It was only with the end of the war, however, that he was at last able to devote all his energies to composition, and to be confident of receiving performance: within some five years he had produced four concertos, a symphony, several chamber works and a body of film music, and was thus already among the more prolific instrumental composers of an English generation that included Walton and Tippett. The chamber cantata *A Canticle of Man* (1952) was the first substantial evidence of an interest in setting words that was to culminate in the large-scale *Carmen vitale* of 1963; yet vocal writing never displaced instrumental as the basis of Rawsthorne's musical thinking. Two further symphonies (1959 and 1964) and four more concertos head an impressively bulky list of orchestral scores produced in the last two decades of his life, most of them written to commission.

However, it is clear that the emergence of a younger generation of composers with different ideals tended to draw public interest away from a composer so steadfast in his established path and so scornful of 'novelty value'; though Rawsthorne first performances remained notable occasions, they were too little followed up, especially in the recording studio. For whatever reason, beginning with the Concerto for ten instruments, written for Cheltenham in 1961, he showed a heightened interest in chamber orchestral writing and in pure chamber music, the genre that dominated the output of his last years. He also wrote music for youth orchestras (*Overture for Farnham* and Theme, Variations and Finale, both of 1967) and in the same year produced his biggest piano work, the Ballade written for John Ogdon. Rawsthorne was made a CBE in 1961, and was awarded honorary doctorates by the universities of Liverpool, Essex and Belfast.

2. WORKS. From the earliest published scores it can be seen that Rawsthorne was never attracted towards the tasteful 'higher diatonicism' that distinguished most of the composition taught in English conservatories in the 1920s. The finale of the Viola Sonata (completed by 1935, though revised in 1953) openly declares a strong debt to Hindemith, yet in the rest of the work the influence has been assimilated, together with that of Walton's Viola Concerto, and the most prominent traits are Rawsthorne's own. Still more is this true of the Theme and Variations, all that remains of the String Quartet no.1 (1939), and of the piano Bagatelles (1938). As with Hindemith, a music that appears 'chromatic' in its recourse to the 12-note repertory is in fact built from the constant juxtaposition of melodic phrases that individually have clear (but tonally differing) diatonic origins. Their phraseology, though flexible, is essentially traditional, depending much on rhythmic, and sometimes melodic, sequence, and often approaching Baroque ideals of patterned figuration. As in Hindemith's music, too, the harmony appears to be regulated by the convergence of strong linear movements in each strand, yet its avoidance of intense dissonance shows a considered restriction of chord structures. But whereas Hindemith deployed his range

of chord types in a hierarchy so as to create intensifying and relaxing harmonic movements that clarify long-term tonal designs, Rawsthorne used his favoured aggregates with extreme consistency, their nature being to sustain over long spans a sensation of tonal ambivalence. Considering the 'false relation' he seems to have admired in Walton, one finds it not only creating a simultaneous major–minor mode, but built around by the absorption of its 3rds into conflicting triadic structures (e.g. from an A–C–C♯ source can spring superimposed triads of F major and A major–minor; if the A now moves to G♯, the complex has become F minor – C♯ minor–major; and so on). The prevalence, to the point of mannerism, of the augmented triad in Rawsthorne's harmony becomes clear, for its tonally contradictory major 3rds form the basis of this method.

Though in many works two particular tonal emphases may stand out as almost evenly weighted (one of them ultimately proving the more fundamental), Rawsthorne avoided the fatuous tone of so much systematic bitonality by his fluid movement between harmonic units that offer a wide range of subsidiary ambiguities. On the other hand, this constant suspension of tonal commitment does limit the range of mood that Rawsthorne's music can encompass. Meticulous textural craftsmanship ensures that a certain elegance of finish is never lacking, but this reinforces at times a somewhat impassive, even grey, tone. But enigmatic restraint can give way to a resigned pathos, and even an acute anguish; more affirmative or optimistic (as opposed to merely energetic) moods are not so surely caught, except where a less equivocal diatonic stance is adopted.

Such a harmonic method can be used to shape paragraphs, but is not easily magnified so as to shape movements; the classical sonata thesis, for example, is likely to lose much of its original point when argued in these terms. Rawsthorne's early music shows a marked preference for variation structures and for composite movements that largely avoid problems of balancing a single expansively continuous span. Even so, the Symphonic Studies demonstrate impressive powers of organization across and within five linked movements; this is a remarkable first orchestral score by any standards. The colour is highly characteristic, with a steely edge not at all like the sound of Hindemith's *Mathis* symphony – to mention the work most obviously suggested by the agile figuration. Though each section expands developmentally (the finale resorting to fugato), the derivation of so much material from the first allegro theme (and ultimately from the opening epigram) gives the cogency of a set of extended variations. Significantly, it is the central chaconne that remains most memorable in the First Piano Concerto. In the postwar concertos, the sonata principle continues to be sidestepped or modified, by the use of composite movements (Violin Concerto no.1, 1948), or an introductory theme whose recurrence is more crucial than those within the allegro (Oboe Concerto, 1947), or an introductory shape that is so evidently the source of later events as to acquire the primacy of a ritornello (Concerto for string orchestra, 1949). Even in works that acknowledge the sonata's duality of material, Rawsthorne was still able to practise a palpable economy of basic motivic shapes. And when the classical exemplars seem most pertinent, as in the Second Quartet (1954), with its new subject clearly in the dominant, they are likely to be abandoned: the

Alan Rawsthorne

second subject's tonic return is vestigial, merging into a transition that prefigures the following movement. Both this quartet and the Second Violin Concerto (1956) still find an important place for variation structures in their finales.

In both violin concertos the treatment of the orchestra is warmer and more gentle than in the piano concertos, where it strives to match a brittle, percussive pianism. This warmth, and the strain of ardent lyricism it accommodated, can be seen as a general development of Rawsthorne's style in the 1950s. The first extended vocal work, *A Canticle of Man* (1952) is one pointer, the title Four Romantic Pieces (1953) another; most striking of all, however, is the use of a soprano soloist in the finale of the Second Symphony (1959). This work, later called *A Pastoral Symphony*, is far more openly committed emotionally than was its predecessor, and suggested that Rawsthorne could find points of contact with the English tradition of reflective lyricism; but there is no relapse into an amorphous modal rhapsodizing, and an introductory section unifies much that follows with its individual harmonic stamp. From the same period, the Violin Sonata proved to be Rawsthorne's most distinguished chamber work so far, covering his entire expressive range yet firmly organized, with the conflict of tonal fields, now the semitonal relationship D–E♭, made a central issue. Also of note during these years are *Practical Cats* (1954), settings for speaker and orchestra of poems from Eliot's *Old Possum*, and the ballet score *Madame Chrysanthème* (1955); though neither has acquired general currency, both helped to direct towards more specific (and diverse) ends a musical speech that had sometimes been in danger of rendering the 'absolute' as the aloof.

Rawsthorne's two principal works using voices appeared in the early 1960s, the *Medieval Diptych* (1962) for baritone and orchestra and *Carmen vitale* (1963) for soprano, chorus and orchestra. His vocal lines often meet their instrumental counterpoints on little more than equal terms and melisma does not always take wing from the text; nonetheless, there is an effective independence of verbal and metrical stress, while the retention of a dense network of purely musical connections protects this music from the woolly archaism too many English composers would have brought to medieval texts. By this time, all of Rawsthorne's works grow from a very restricted store of motifs, but they are handled with more than the traditional variation and multiplication techniques of his early scores. In the *Medieval Diptych*, for example, a shape of eight different pitches is used melodically in inverted and reversed orders and is conflated into harmonic units; thus the composer is at once appropriating certain devices of pitch serialism and moving into more complex harmonic territory. Yet his characteristic chord structure, resolving itself into two or more traditional units in conflict, is preserved or extended into a wholly symmetrical chord-building (most schematic in the 'Alla ciacona' of the Third Quartet of 1964); the old fastidiousness of spacing ensures that in this late style aggregates of eight and more pitches retain an extreme luminosity.

That certain late pieces (movements more often than works) develop their material from a 12-note set is no more than a rationalization of tendencies which had long been apparent in Rawsthorne's style. The relation to Schoenbergian serial practice is tenuous. Even a movement like the third of the Quintet for piano and wind (1962–3), which is unusually persistent in serial device, contains extensive patterning that shows no concern for 12-note propriety, while the finale abandons the 12-note operations of its introduction for an allegro that is vehemently scalic (casting the faint shadow of Bartók to be detected elsewhere when Rawsthorne uses variable scales); and the first movement's manipulation of a nine-pitch shape is rather more inventive than either. This is Rawsthorne's longest chamber work and among his most powerful; the Quintet with strings (1968), though a beautifully integrated composite structure, does not measure up in the sometimes mechanistic allegro writing to the brooding intensity of its penultimate 'Lento' section. The Oboe Quartet (1970) uses a single set in all three movements, conflating it at the finale opening into a spiky two-part counterpoint that had become a favoured texture (compare it, for example, with the opening of the Quartet no.3). If some of this last harvest has a slightly dry flavour, the biggest orchestral scores, the Symphony no.3 (1964) and the Cello Concerto (1965) have yet to be recognized as achievements at least equal to those that made the composer's name. The concerto revitalizes the lyrical impulse of the previous decade, and shows a new refinement of orchestral colouring; by comparison, the two-piano Concerto (1968), with its importunate 12-note assertions, can appear unsubtle. In the Third Symphony, however, Rawsthorne's recourse to pitch serialism is simply one aspect of a developmental process that is ubiquitous. Though first and last movements are sectional structures in matters of tempo, both are sustained by concentrated musical thinking: comparison with the Symphonic Studies shows how far Rawsthorne had escaped from neat structural frames. The sarabande and scherzo each round out a sharply defined mood across a big span, the sarabande's obsession with its initial E emphasizing a

tonal centre to which the whole symphony is subject with a direct force unusual in Rawsthorne.

The lesser orchestral and chamber works are rarely notably inferior in craftsmanship to the major scores. Indeed, the very consistency of Rawsthorne's sizable output perhaps encouraged its almost uniform neglect during his last years. In a historical perspective of 20th-century English composition it will find a prominent place; that it has failed to accord with fashion does not invalidate the essential qualities of this unostentatious but finely wrought music.

WORKS

DRAMATIC

Madame Chrysanthème (ballet, Ashton), 1955
Scores for 22 films and 4 plays, all unpubd

ORCHESTRAL

Conc., cl, str, 1936; Light Music, str, 1938; Sym. Studies, 1938; Pf Conc. no.1, pf, str, perc, 1939, arr. pf, orch, 1942; Ov. 'Street Corner', 1944; Fantasy Ov. 'Cortèges', 1945; Conc., ob, str, 1947; Vn Conc. no.1, 1948; Conc., str, 1949; Sym. no.1, 1950; Pf Conc. no.2, 1951; Concertante pastorale, fl, hn, str, 1951
Vn Conc. no.2, 1956; Ov. 'Hallé', 1958; Sym. no.2 (A Pastoral Sym.), S, orch, 1959; Improvisations on a Theme of Constant Lambert, 1960; Divertimento, chamber orch, 1962; Elegiac Rhapsody, 1964; Sym. no.3, 1964; Vc Conc., 1965; Theme, Variations and Finale, 1967; Ov. for Farnham, 1967; Conc., 2 pf, 1968; Triptych, 1969

CHORAL

A Canticle of Man (R. Swingler), Bar, SATB, fl, str, 1952; Canzonet (MacNeice), S, SATB, 1953; 4 Seasonal Songs, SATB, 1955; A Rose for Lidice (Swingler), S, SATB, 1956; Lament for a Sparrow (Catullus), SATB, harp, 1962; Carmen vitale, S, SATB, orch, 1963; The Oxen (Hardy), SATTB, 1965; The God in the Cave (Swingler), SATB, orch, 1966

SOLO VOCAL

With orch/inst(s): Practical Cats (Eliot), speaker, orch, 1954; Medieval Diptych, Bar, orch, 1962; Tankas of the Four Seasons, T, ob, cl, bn, vn, vc, 1965; Scena rustica, S, harp, 1967
With pf: 3 French Nursery Songs, 1938; We Three Merry Maidens (Fr. trad.), 1940; 2 Songs (Fletcher), 1940; Carol (W. R. Rodgers), 1948; Two Fish (G. du Bartas), c1970

CHAMBER AND INSTRUMENTAL

For 3–10 insts: Sonatina, fl, ob, pf, 1936; Str Qt no.1 'Theme and Variations', 1939; Cl Qt, 1948; Str Qt no.2, 1954; Conc., 10 insts, 1961; Pf Trio, 1962; Qnt, pf, ob, cl, bn, hn, 1962–3; Str Qt no.3, 1964; Pf Qnt, 1968; Suite, fl, va, harp, 1968; Ob Qt, 1970; Qnt, cl, hn, vn, vc, pf, 1970
For 1–2 insts: Concertante, vn, pf, 1934, rev. 1968; Sonata, va, pf, 1935, rev. 1953; Theme and Variations, 2 vn, 1937; Sonata, vc, pf, 1948; Sonata, vn, pf, 1958; Elegy, gui, 1971
For pf: Bagatelles, 1938; The Creel, 4 hands, 1940; Sonatina, 1949; 4 Romantic Pieces, 1953; Ballade, 1967; Theme and 4 Studies, 1971

Principal publisher: Oxford University Press

BIBLIOGRAPHY

W. Mellers: 'Alan Rawsthorne and the Baroque', *Studies in Contemporary Music* (London, 1947), 171
C. Mason: 'Alan Rawsthorne', *MT*, xci (1950), 137
A. E. F. Dickinson: 'The Progress of Alan Rawsthorne', *MR*, xii (1951), 87
H. Howells: 'A Note on Alan Rawsthorne', *ML*, xxxii (1951), 19
A. Frank: 'Alan Rawsthorne', *Modern British Composers* (London, 1955), 74
L. Berkeley: 'Alan Rawsthorne', *Composer* (1971–2), no.42, p.5
J. McCabe: 'Alan Rawsthorne', *MT*, cxii (1971), 952
G. Green: 'Alan Rawsthorne: a Brief Record of Friendship', *Composer* (1972), no.43, p.1

PETER EVANS

Rawsthorne, Noel (*b* Wirral, Cheshire, 24 Dec 1929). English organist. A boy chorister at Liverpool Cathedral, the centre of his later career, he studied the organ with Harold Dawber at the Royal Manchester College of Music. He became assistant to H. Goss-Custard in 1949 and succeeded him as cathedral organist in 1955. He has won a high reputation as a recitalist with exceptional gifts of improvisation, and has toured the USSR and made frequent visits to the Continent. He specializes in the interpretation of 19th- and 20th-century French organ music, but his BBC recitals on the small Willis organ in the Lady Chapel at Liverpool have shown his skill as a Bach player. His recordings on the main organ, the largest in any English cathedral, include the first in the series Great Cathedral Organs, a programme of 20th-century organ music, ten toccatas for organ, and music for trumpet and organ (with Alan Stringer). He is a senior lecturer in music at St Katharine's College of Education, Liverpool, and a member of the council and examiner for the Royal College of Organists. He has written a booklet, *The Organs of Liverpool Cathedral* (Liverpool, 1962).

STANLEY WEBB

Raxach, Enrique (*b* Barcelona, 15 Jan 1932). Dutch composer of Spanish birth. He served in the army (1949–52) while studying composition and theory with Nuri Aymerich. In 1958 he visited Paris, Munich and Zurich, establishing connections with Boulez, Hartmann, Scherchen and Maderna. He attended the Darmstadt summer courses (1959–64) and from 1961 was involved with the Gaudeamus music weeks. In 1962 he settled in the Netherlands, becoming a citizen in 1969. A state bursary enabled him to study conducting with Hupperts (1962–6).

WORKS
(*selective list*)

Orch: Equinoxial, 1968; Figuren in einer Landschaft, 1972–4; Ad marginem, fl, vn, va, orch, 1974–5; Erdenlicht, 1975

Vocal: The Esoteric Garden, chorus, orch, 1972; Sine nomine, S, chamber orch, 1973; Grand duo concertant, S, db, 1975

Chamber and inst: Fases, str qt, 1961; Imaginary Landscape, fl, perc, 1968; Scattertime, fl + pic, cl + b cl, pf, elec org, perc, vn, vc, 1971; Str Qt no.2, str qt, elec, 1971; Chimaera, b cl, 2-track tape, 1974

Principal publisher: Donemus

ROGIER STARREVELD

Ray. The supertonic of the prevailing key (or, if this is minor, of its relative major) in TONIC SOL-FA.

Raybould, (Robert) Clarence (*b* Birmingham, 28 June 1886; *d* Bideford, 27 March 1972). English conductor and accompanist. He was the first to take the BMus degree at Birmingham University (1912). In that year he joined the staff of the Midland Institute of Music in Birmingham to teach harmony and counterpoint. He assisted Rutland Boughton as pianist, coach and conductor at the early Glastonbury Festivals and after World War I he performed the same service for the Beecham Opera Company and then for the British National Opera Company. His opera *The Sumida River* was produced in Birmingham in 1916. Raybould toured widely as a pianist and accompanist in Britain and abroad, and worked for the Columbia Graphophone Company (1927–31) and in documentary films. He joined the BBC staff in 1936, and from 1939 to 1945 was assistant conductor to the BBC SO. His subsequent work with young musicians included the conductorship of the Royal Academy of Music senior orchestra and of the National Youth Orchestra of Wales, which he founded in 1945 and conducted until 1966.

FRANK HOWES

Raygada, Carlos (*b* Lima, 3 Feb 1898; *d* Lima, 7 Feb 1953). Peruvian music critic and musicologist. He was self-taught in music and began his career as a music critic in 1921, writing regularly for the daily *El comercio* under the pseudonyms 'Mazeppa', 'Semibreve' and others. Subsequently he became art critic of *El Perú* (1931) and was appointed secretary–treasurer of the Academia Nacional de Música 'Alcedo'; he also served as professor of music history at the Bach Institute, Lima (1936). After visiting the USA as a member of the first Latin American Summer School at the University of North Carolina (Chapel Hill) and giving a series of lectures in American universities, he was elected secretary of the Directive Council of Musical Culture (1943) and joined the faculty of the National Conservatory of Music (1946). As secretary of the council and inspector of the Lima Municipal Art Museum (1950), he was influential in furthering music and art education in Peru. As a music critic and lecturer he collected considerable factual information on Peruvian music and musicians, posthumously published as *Guia musical del Perú*. Most of his works, however, remain unpublished.

WRITINGS
'Panorama musical del Perú', *Boletín latino-americano de música*, ii (1936), 169
'Peru: a Decade of Orchestral Growth', *Musical America*, lxix/12 (1949), 12
Historia crítica del himno nacional (Lima, 1954)
'Guia musical del Perú', *Fénix* (1956–7), no.12, p.3; (1963), no.13, p.1; (1964), no.14, p.3
Antología bibliográfica de la música en el Perú (Lima, n.d.)

GERARD BÉHAGUE

Rayleigh, John William Strutt, 3rd Baron (*b* Langford Grove, nr. Maldon, Essex, 12 Nov 1842; *d* Witham, Essex, 30 June 1919). English scientist. He was educated at Cambridge University, where he was Cavendish Professor of Experimental Physics (1879–84); later (1887–1905) he held the professorship of natural philosophy at the Royal Institution, London, and in 1905 he became president of the Royal Society. He received jointly with Sir William Ramsay a Nobel Prize for the discovery of argon.

Rayleigh was perhaps the most versatile of British physical scientists from about 1850 to 1930 and, like Helmholtz, he covered almost all branches of physics and ventured into other disciplines. His monumental *Theory of Sound* (1877–8/R), written over five years, is often termed the 'bible of acoustics' and remains a standard treatise. Among Rayleigh's contributions to acoustics was his extension of Helmholtz's resonator theory. He also made more precise the corrections for open and closed resonating tubes, and gave a theoretical explanation of heat-maintained vibrations in pipes (the 'Rijke sounding-tube' effect). Additionally he carried out investigations on singing and acoustic sensitive flames and gave a more detailed explanation of 'whispering galleries', attributing the effect of the St Paul's gallery to the slight inward slant of the circular containing walls. He also investigated the binaural effect in sound and developed the phonic motor, of considerable value for frequency measurement. Rayleigh's collected papers, which number over 400, were published in 1922.

See also PHYSICS OF MUSIC, §§5 and 6.

BIBLIOGRAPHY
R. J. Strutt, 4th Baron Rayleigh: *Life of John William Strutt, Third Baron Rayleigh* (Madison, 1968)
R. B. Lindsay: *Lord Rayleigh: the Man and his Work* (Oxford, 1970)
——: 'Strutt, John William, Third Baron Rayleigh', *Dictionary of Scientific Biography* (New York, 1970–)

R. W. B. STEPHENS

Raymond, Fred [Vesely, Raimund Friedrich] (*b* Vienna, 20 April 1900; *d* Überlingen, Germany, 10 Jan 1954).

German composer. Self-taught in composition, he worked as a bank official and began composing songs; in 1924 he became a professional cabaret entertainer, accompanying himself at the piano in his songs. The songs *Ich hab' mein Herz in Heidelberg verloren* (1925) and *In einer kleinen Konditorei* achieved outstanding popularity, and he continued to compose for revues and for a series of operettas, having meanwhile settled in Berlin. Of the operettas, *Maske in Blau* (Berlin, Metropoltheater, 27 September 1937) and *Saison in Salzburg* (Kiel, Stadttheater, 31 December 1938) have retained their popularity in Germany, as has a further hit song *Es geht alles vorüber, es geht alles vorbei* (1942), but his postwar compositions were less successful.

BIBLIOGRAPHY
E. Nick: 'Raymond, Fred', *MGG* [incl. list of works]

ANDREW LAMB

Raymundi, Daniel (*b* Liège, *c*1558; *d* Liège, 25 Jan 1634). South Netherlands composer. He came from a long-established Liège family of churchmen and magistrates. He was a *duodenus* at Liège Cathedral and was awarded a bursary to assist his studies at Louvain University; this was withdrawn, however, on 31 April 1578. He was probably a succentor at Liège Cathedral, for on 28 July 1581, despite his youth, he was one of three candidates recommended by the cantor for the post of singing master. The chapter chose, however, in favour of Henri Jamaer. Raymundi nevertheless remained a succentor there for several years longer, and on 27 July 1588 he provided some compositions for the choir for which he was later paid 30 florins. He was particularly interested in ecclesiastical administration and he rapidly advanced his position in the church, obtaining increasingly remunerative benefices: on 30 March 1601 he was appointed canon of St Materne. A year previously the Liège chapter had decided, though with no great enthusiasm, to undertake the revision of the Liège Breviary. They entrusted this work to Raymundi, but no-one, it seems, was particularly anxious to comply with instructions from Rome, and the work progressed slowly. The reforms were discussed several times in 1604 and in 1615, and on 6 March 1615 the completion of the work was entrusted to the two Masters of the Ceremonial at the cathedral, Lambert Scroncx and Raymundi. In 1617 a quarrel between Raymundi and the *Ludimagister*, Charles de Bois, drew attention to the slow progress of the work and the chapter ordered Raymundi to speed up his revision. In 1619 he demonstrated the results of his work to the chapter and the Reformed Breviary was finally adopted in September, 1619. On 23 June 1632 he was declared a Jubilee Canon; his will was made out on 3 April 1633 in favour of his brother Abacuc and his sons.

Raymundi's qualities as a humanist are evident in a quite different field: he made several transcriptions of early chronicles, in which his concern for precision shows a certain critical acumen. To judge from his few extant works, he was an able composer with a certain gift for melody. Three motets of his, for eight voices and continuo, *Ecce panis angelorum, Homo quidam* and *Tantum ergo* are extant in the *Grand livre de choeur de Saint-Lambert* (*B-Lc*) and one five-part motet, *Fiat cor meum*, is edited by J. A. L. de Lafage in *Diphtérographie musicale* (Paris, 1864), 487.

BIBLIOGRAPHY
S. Balau: 'Raymundi', *BNB*
A. Auda: *La musique et les musiciens de l'ancien pays de Liège* (Liège, 1930)
R. Vannes: *Dictionnaire des musiciens (compositeurs)* (Brussels, 1947)
L. Lahaye: 'Les chanoines de Saint-Materne', *Bulletin de la Société d'art et d'histoire du diocèse de Liège*, xxvii (Liège, 1936), 140
J. Quitin: 'Les maîtres de chant de la cathédrale Saint-Lambert a Liège', *RBM*, viii (1954), 1

JOSÉ QUITIN

Raynero de Scarsellis. *See* SCARSELLI, RINIERI.

Razetti, Amedeo. *See* RASETTI, AMEDEO.

Razumovsky, Count **Andrey Kyrillovich** (*b* St Petersburg, 2 Nov 1752; *d* Vienna, 23 Sept 1836). Russian statesman, art collector, amateur violinist and patron of music. He completed his diplomatic career by serving as Russian ambassador to Vienna, starting in 1792. In 1788 he married Countess Elisabeth of Thun-Hohenstein, sister of Princess Lichnowsky. After her death in 1806 he married Countess Constanze of Thürheim. Razumovsky's enthusiasm for music had drawn him to Haydn; he knew Mozart personally and had close associations with Beethoven between 1796 and 1816. His name is associated primarily with the three quartets op.59, in which Beethoven introduced Russian folk themes in honour of his dedicatee. In 1808 Razumovsky established a string quartet, led by Schuppanzigh, which was permanently salaried and which Beethoven was allowed to use. Although Razumovsky had retired as ambassador in 1807, he was Russia's main representative at the Congress of Vienna in 1814. For this he was subsequently made a prince. But on the last day of that year, in preparation for one of his most lavish parties, a fire broke out and ravaged his palace, library and art collection. Despite offers of help, he was forced to discontinue his way of life. The quartet was disbanded and pensioned.

BIBLIOGRAPHY
A. Schindler: *Biographie von Ludwig van Beethoven* (Münster, 1840, enlarged 2/1845, rev. 3/1860; Eng. trans., 1966, as *Beethoven as I knew him*), 59f, 205, 216
T. Frimmel: *Beethoven-Handbuch*, ii (Leipzig, 1926/*R*), 51ff
P. Nettl: *Beethoven Encyclopedia* (New York, 1956), 183ff
E. Forbes, ed.: *Thayer's Life of Beethoven* (Princeton, 1967), 400f, 409, 444, 600ff

ELLIOT FORBES

Razumovsky, Dmitry Vasil'yevich (*b* Tula province, 7 Nov 1818; *d* Moscow, 14 Jan 1889). Russian musicologist. As a young seminarian in Tula (1834–9) and as a student at the Kiev Theological Academy (1839–43), Razumovsky displayed an interest in Russian church music. From 1843 to 1852 he taught physics, mathematics and natural science at the Spaso-Vifanskaya (now Zagorsk) Seminary near Moscow. He took the Master of Philosophy degree (1845) and also taught Hebrew. In 1850 he was ordained priest, and in 1852 transferred to Moscow as a parish priest in the church of St George, where he remained active until his death. In 1858 he was appointed a member of a committee for the inspection and correction of church music publications, and in 1862 he was invited to study photographs of a few select pages of music manuscripts photographed in 1858 by Sevastyanov in the monastic libraries of Mt Athos. In 1863 Razumovsky delivered a public lecture on *Staffless Musical Manuscripts of Church Chants*, which was published in the same year and marked the beginning of his scholarly investigation of the origins of Russian chant. In 1866, when the Moscow Conservatory was founded, Razumovsky was invited to become the first teacher of Russian church music, a position he held to the end of his life. His carefully edited lecture notes were published in three parts (1867–9) and represent the first systematic survey of the history of chanting in Russia. His subsequent publications, though few in number, remain as important documents of his scholarship. In 1916 Razumovsky's collection of some 120 music manuscripts (mostly from the 17th century to the 19th) and his archives and extensive correspondence were deposited in the former Rumyantsev Museum in Moscow (they are now in the Lenin Library, Moscow). An excellent catalogue of this collection was published in 1960, and contains the best survey of his life and activities and a bibliography.

WRITINGS

'O notnïkh bezlineynïkh rukopisyakh tserkovnovo znamennovo peniya' [The staffless musical MSS of the church chant], *Chteniya v obshchestve lyubiteley dukhovnovo prosveshcheniya*, i, ed. L. U. Stepanov (1863), 55 [also pubd separately]

'Materialï dlya arkheologicheskovo slovarya' [Materials for an archaeological dictionary], *Drevnosti: trudï Moskovskovo arkeologicheskovo obshchestva*, i, ed. A. A. Kotlyarevsky (Moscow, 1865–7), 15–78

'Ob osnovnïkh nachalakh bogosluzhebnovo peniya pravoslavnoy Greko-Rossiyskoy tserkvi' [The basic principles of the liturgical chanting of the Greco-Russian Orthodox Church], *Sbornik na 1866*, ed. Obshchestvo drevne-russkovo iskusstva (Moscow, 1866), 107

Tserkovnoye peniye v Rossii: opït istoriko-tekhnicheskovo izlozheniya [Church chant in Russia: an attempt at historical and technical presentation] (Moscow, 1867–9) [collection of lectures]

Patriarshiye pevchiye diaki i poddiaki [Patriarchal singers and singing pupils] (Moscow, 1868, 2/1895)

'Tserkovnorusskoye peniye' [Russian church chant], *I arkheologicheskiy s'yezd: Moskva 1869*, ii, 444

Gosudarevï pevchiye diaki XVII v. [Imperial singers of the 17th century] (Moscow, 1873, 2/1895)

Bogosluzhebnoye peniye pravoslavnoy Greko-Rossiyskoy tserkvi, i: teoriya i praktika tserkovnovo peniya [The liturgical chant of the Greco-Russian Orthodox Church, i: theory and practice of church chanting] (Moscow, 1886)

BIBLIOGRAPHY

I. Kudryavtsev, ed.: *Rukopisnïye sobraniye D. V. Razumovskovo i V. F. Odoyevskovo i arkhiv D. V. Razumovskovo* [The Razumovsky and Odoyevsky MS collections and the Razumovsky archive] (Moscow, 1960) [incl. B. Granovsky: 'D. V. Razumovsky: kratkiy ocherk zhizni i deyatel'nosti' [Life and works], 23]

MILOŠ VELIMIROVIĆ

Razzetti, Amedeo. *See* RASETTI, AMEDEO.

Razzi, Fausto (*b* Rome, 4 May 1932). Italian composer. He studied in Rome under, among others, Petrassi, whose ordinary and graduate courses he followed (1957–63). From 1958 to 1968 he was assistant and then successor to Saraceni as conductor of the Rome University Choir, and in 1966 he began teaching, eventually becoming professor of composition at the Pesaro Conservatory. He won honourable mentions in the composition competition of the Italian section of the ISCM (1963, 1965), and prizes awarded by the Prague Spring Festival (1966) and the Milan Angelicum (1969).

Razzi's music is marked by precise formal design and flexible realization. Sometimes these aspects are exploited separately (*Quattro invenzioni, Tre pezzi sacri*), but usually they interact. The result in the cantata *Die helle Stimme* is an antagonism between choral tautness and instrumental pointillism, and in *Musiche* (nos.1–6) an 'informal' stratification of rigorously ordered materials. Cautious reformulations of his attitude have brought Razzi sometimes to a point of concurrence with certain

new techniques (cf the Ligeti-like choral writing of the *Tre pezzi sacri*), and sometimes to a belated absorption of established procedures (as in the limited aleatory writing of the three *Improvvisazioni*). Later he became interested in computer music, attempting to reassess the structural plan of the *Musiche*. Thanks to its functional and rational qualities, his work in this field is equally distant from abstraction and empiricism (persistent poles in Italian electronic music), marking a development that leaves no more doubt of the worth of a hardwon consistency in approach.

WORKS
(selective list)

Vocal: 3 poesie di H. Michaux, 1 female v, va, b cl, 1959; Die helle Stimme (anon.), chorus, double wind qt, hpd, gui, perc, 1962–3; 3 pezzi sacri, chorus, 1964; Improvvisazione II, chorus, str orch, 1966; Improvvisazione III, S, S, B, fl, hpd, 2 perc, db, 1967; Musica per 18, vv, ens, 1969; other early pieces

Inst: Str Qt, 1958; 4 invenzioni, 7 insts, 1961; Movimento, pf, orch, 1963; Invenzione a 3, E♭-cl, ob, b cl, 1964; Improvvisazione, va, 18 wind, timp, 1965; Musica per pf, 1968; Musica per 10, wind, 1968; Musica per 26, ens, 1968; Musica no.5, str trio, 1970; Musica no.6, orch, 1970; Variante, va, pf, 1973; Musica per pf, 1975; other early pieces, educational music

Elec: Progetto per una composizione elettronica, 1971–3

Principal publisher: Suvini Zerboni

CLAUDIO ANNIBALDI

Razzi, Giovanni [Serafino] (*b* Marradi, nr. Florence, 13 Dec 1531; *d* Florence, 8 Aug 1611). Italian theologian, writer, music editor and composer. He and his brother received a thorough humanistic education; on 28 June 1549 he entered the Dominican monastery of S Marco, Florence, as a novice and adopted the religious name of Serafino. His early career was mostly spent in preaching, and in 1558 he was ordained to the priesthood. Apart from his time at S Marco he spent important periods at S Domenico, Perugia, and later at S Maria Novella, Florence; his numerous appointments and substantial reputation took him to many places both within and outside Italy. His travels in France are described in *Fra Serafino Razzi: la prima parte de suoi viaggi fatti dal 1572–78* (MS, *I-Fc* Palat.37).

Razzi made a considerable contribution to Counter-Reformation literature and was also active in the musical sphere; he assembled, edited and published two collections of *laude*, namely *Libro primo delle laudi spirituali . . . le quali si usano cantare in Firenze nelle chiese doppo il vespro o la compieta* (Venice, 1563[6]/R1969) for one to four voices, and *Santuario di laudi . . . per le feste di ciaschedun santo . . . con eziando delle feste mobili* (Florence, 1609[8]). These, with Animuccia's first book (1563), were the first collections of *laude* published since those of Petrucci. The *Libro primo* contains about 70 anonymous compositions, many of which reappeared in the *Santuario*; this consists mostly of *laude* texts but contains 31 one- and two-voice settings in a music supplement of 24 pages. There are some textual concordances with 15th-century sources, and many of the texts not by Razzi himself are by his contemporaries at S Marco. In addition to the two printed collections, four books of *laude* assembled by Razzi survive in an autograph manuscript (*I-Fc* Palat.173). He originally collected three books of settings of his own texts, to which he then added a fourth book containing *laude* by other authors. The dedication of the first book is dated 15 July 1590 while the second and third are dated 1586 and 1588. The fourth book is dated 17 March 1596 and concludes with an imprimatur of 11 December of the same year, though it is not known to have been published in this form. The first three books contain about 130 compositions, mostly melodies only, some of which also appear in his published collections. Many are accompanied by commentaries and annotations, usually non-musical.

The melodies of some of Razzi's *laude* derive melodically from secular songs of the earlier part of the century. Jeppesen, D'Accone and Slim have pointed out melodic relationships between Razzi's *laude* and madrigals by Francesco de Layolle and Verdelot.

Besides Razzi's extant works, Negri referred to a publication of 1567 containing *laude* (but this is probably an incorrect citation of the *Libro primo*) and to theoretical writings on music.

BIBLIOGRAPHY

G. Negri: *Istoria degli scrittori fiorenti* (Ferrara, 1722/*R*1969), 498
E. Piani: *Brevi cenni biografici d'illustri Marradesi* (Faenza, 1871)
D. Alaleona: 'Le laudi spirituali italiane nei secoli XVI e XVII e il loro rapporta coi canti profani', *RMI*, xvi (1909), 1–54
E. J. Dent: 'The Laudi Spirituali in the Sixteenth and Seventeenth Centuries', *PMA*, xliii (1916–17), 63
K. Jeppesen: 'Laude', *MGG*
G. M. di Agresti: Introduction to *Fra Serafino Razzi O.P.: Vita di S Caterina de' Ricci* (Florence, 1965), pp.xvii ff
J. J. Gallucci: *Festival Music in Florence ca. 1480–ca. 1520: canti carnascialeschi, trionfi and related forms* (diss., Harvard U., 1966)
W. H. Rubsamen: 'The Music for "Quant'è bella giovinezza" and Other Carnival Songs by Lorenzo de' Medici', *Art, Science and History in the Renaissance*, ed. C. S. Singleton (Baltimore, 1968), 163
F. D'Accone: Introduction to *Francesco de Layolle: Collected Secular Works for 2, 3, 4 and 5 Voices*, CMM, xxxii/3 (1969), pp.xiii, xviii
N. Pirrotta and E. Povoledo: *Li due Orfei: da Poliziano a Monteverdi* (Turin, 1969, enlarged 2/1975), 28, 43, 70
W. Osthoff: *Theatergesang und darstellende Musik in der italienischen Renaissance* (Tutzing, 1969), i, 110f, 114, 188, 217f
H. C. Slim: *A Gift of Madrigals and Motets for Henry VIII* (Chicago, 1972), i, 96ff, 184f, 212, 225

IAIN FENLON

Re. The first degree of the Guidonian HEXACHORD; *see also* SOLMIZATION, §I. In TONIC SOL-FA, the sharpened supertonic of the prevailing key (or, if this is minor, of its relative major). In French (as *ré*), Italian and Spanish usage, the note D; *see* PITCH NAMES. (For non-Western usages, see Appendix A.)

Read, Daniel (*b* Attleboro, Mass., 16 Nov 1757; *d* New Haven, Conn., 4 Dec 1836). American composer and tune book compiler. Together with William Billings (1746–1800), Daniel Read was the most significant American composer of psalmody during the 18th and early 19th centuries. A farm-worker and surveyor in his youth, Read served as a private in the Continental Army in 1777–8. Before the war was over he had settled in New Haven, where he stayed for the rest of his life. There he operated a general store and carried on an active career as a musician.

Read began to compose at 19, making his début in print in Jocelyn and Doolittle's *Chorister's Companion* (New Haven, 1782–3). Shortly afterwards he became the first American musician after Billings to bring out a collection devoted entirely to his own music: the *American Singing Book* (New Haven, 1785). The next decade established Read's prominence as a composer. Such works as the *Worcester Collection* (Worcester, Mass., 1786), the *Federal Harmony* (Boston, Mass., 1790) and Nehemiah Shumway's *American Harmony* (Philadelphia, 1793) borrowed freely from his tune books, though not necessarily with his approval, and a small group of his tunes was established by the mid-

1790s as part of the central repertory of American psalmody.

Read is commonly considered to be the most prominent of a group of Connecticut yeoman psalm tune composers who fashioned a unique musical idiom during the late 1770s and early 1780s. Rooted in the *a cappella* tradition of the American singing school, the idiom developed free from the influence of European bass practice and its attendant network of functional harmonic relationships. The American idiom developed by Connecticut composers is distinguished by a straightforward, folklike melodic style, often with a modal tinge; a fondness for incomplete triads – perfect intervals unsoftened by 3rds; a certain tentativeness about chord connections, especially in mid-phrase; and frequent clashes between voices on weak beats. Some of Read's most popular tunes – 'Russia', for example, or 'Greenwich', 'Windham' or 'Sherburne', like the rest of Read's music written for four-voice chorus without accompaniment – are exemplars of the idiom.

Most of the 80-odd pieces Read composed and published date from the 1780s and early 1790s. He seems to have composed little after 1795, and the pieces he did write from that time on reflect his increasing interest in imitating European composers. In fact, though he was a pioneer figure in the formation of an American musical idiom, Read was not moved to defend that idiom when, beginning in the last years of the 18th century, it came under increasingly heavy criticism from musical reformers who considered it inferior to the devotional music then in vogue in Britain. A letter Read wrote in his 71st year explains that although he was no longer publishing music, he had continued to study it, had during the last two decades become familiar with the works of prominent Anglo-American authorities and their standards of 'scientific' music, and had found his own 'ideas on music . . . considerably altered'. A measure of Read's 'altered' ideas appears in the *New Haven Collection of Sacred Music* (Dedham, Mass., 1818), a tune book he did not compile but helped to prepare for the press. The work carries three of Read's better-known tunes ('Judgment', 'Lisbon' and 'Winter'), all marked 'corrected by the author'.

Daniel Read's musical publications span a quarter of a century. The *American Singing Book* was remarkably successful for a collection of original music (2/1786, 3/1787 with suppl., 4/1793, 5/1796). The *Columbian Harmonist*, a larger work, was issued in separate parts, each devoted to a different repertory. Part i (New Haven, 1793) carried 'new psalm tunes of American composition'; part ii (New Haven, 1794) contained the day's most popular psalm tunes, mostly American but with a few British favourites included as well; part iii (New Haven, 1795) was given over mostly to larger works: 'anthems and set-pieces . . . chiefly new'. Bound together and consecutively paged, the three parts made comprehensive whole. They were also available separately. After 1800 Read brought out three more editions of the *Columbian Harmonist*, now a single typeset volume rather than the three engraved pamphlets of the first edition, and now issued from large Massachusetts print shops (2/1804, 3/1807, 4/1810; another issue, 3/1806, was pirated by Joel Read, Daniel's brother, and Herman Mann). He also published *An Introduction to Psalmody* (New Haven, 1790), a pamphlet containing instructional dialogues without music. In collaboration with Amos Doolittle, Read compiled and published the

American Musical Magazine (New Haven, 1786–7) in 12 numbers – the earliest American music periodical.

BIBLIOGRAPHY

Baker 5
F. Metcalf: *American Writers and Compilers of Sacred Music* (New York, 1925/R1967)
J. H. Coursault: 'Read, Daniel', *DAB*
I. Lowens: 'Daniel Read's World: The Letters of an Early American Composer', *Notes*, ix (1951–2), 233; rev. in Lowens: *Music and Musicians in Early America* (New York, 1964)
R. Crawford: 'Connecticut Sacred Music Imprints, 1778–1810', *Notes*, xxvii (1970–71), 445, 671

RICHARD CRAWFORD

Read, Ernest (*b* Guildford, 22 Feb 1879; *d* London, 9 Oct 1965). English educationist. At the RAM he studied the piano with Matthay and conducting with Henry Wood (1896–1906); he also made a close study of eurhythmics, working under Jaques-Dalcroze (1912–13, 1920–21), becoming director of the London School of Dalcroze Eurhythmics and, later, chairman of the Dalcroze Society (1943–65). He was principal of the Watford School of Music (1913–20), lecturer and professor in conducting and aural training at the RAM (1919–50) and a member of its management committee (1924–44), a founder council member of the Northern School of Music (1943–65) and president of the Music Teachers' Association (1943–65).

Read was a pioneer of the youth orchestra movement, founding the London Junior and Senior Orchestras (1926, 1931: *see* LONDON, §VI, 2), a choir (1943), the Ernest Read Children's Concerts (1944; *see* LONDON, §VI, 4) and annual orchestral and chamber music summer courses (1949), all subsequently administered by the Ernest Read Music Association (founded 1960), which his wife Helen Read (*b* London, 28 March 1902) directed after his death (she was made an OBE in 1972). He had a particular talent for communicating the enjoyment of music-making to the young and to amateurs. His publications include *Aural Culture based on Musical Appreciation* (1912, rev. 2/1953) and other textbooks written with Stewart Macpherson, and numerous arrangements for female voices of choral works by Bach, Handel, Haydn etc. He was made a CBE in 1956.

In 1977 the London Junior and Senior Orchestras were renamed the Ernest Read Youth Orchestra and Ernest Read Symphony Orchestra respectively.

BIBLIOGRAPHY

W. Cole: 'Ernest Read', *MT*, cv (1964), 104
Obituary: *MT*, cvi (1965), 971; *The Strad*, lxxvi (1965–6), 293; *The Times* (11 Oct 1965); *Music in Education*, xxx (1966), 29

LYNDA LLOYD REES

Read, Gardner (*b* Evanston, Ill., 2 Jan 1913). American composer. He studied with Copland at the Berkshire Music Center and with Hanson and Rogers at the Eastman School (MusB 1936, MusM 1937). His Symphony no.1, composed at the MacDowell Colony in 1936, won first prize in the American Composers' Contest sponsored by the New York Philharmonic-Symphony Society in 1937 and his Second Symphony the Paderewski Prize in 1943. He taught at the St Louis Institute of Music (1941–3), the Kansas City Conservatory (1943–5), the Cleveland Institute (1945–8), and from 1948 at the Boston University School of Fine and Applied Arts. In 1966 he was visiting professor at the University of California at Los Angeles. A brilliant orchestrator and an excellent musical architect, he early won recognition as one of the most prolific and highly skilled American craftsmen of his epoch.

WORKS
(selective list)

Opera: Villon, op.122 (3, J. Forsyth), 1967
Orch: Sketches of the City, op.26, 1933; Sym. no.1, op.30, 1936; Fantasy, op.38, va, orch, 1935; Prelude and Toccata, op.43, 1937; Suite, str, 1937; Night Flight, op.44, 1936–42; Sym. no.2, op.45, 1942; Ov. no.1, op.58, 1943; Vc Conc., op.55, 1945; The Temptation of St Anthony, op.56, dance sym., 1947; Pennsylvaniana, op.67, 1947; Sym. no.3, op.75, 1948; Arioso elegiaca, op.91, str, 1951; Sym. no.4, op.92, 1958; Toccata giocosa, op.94, 1953; Vernal Equinox, op.96, 1955; Sonoric Fantasia no.2, op.123, vn, chamber orch, 1965; Sonoric Fantasia no.3, wind, perc, 1968
Choral: The Golden Journey to Samarkand, op.41, solo vv, chorus, orch, 1936–9; Jesous Ahatonhia, op.87, chorus, org, 1950; The Reveille, op.89b, chorus, wind, perc, org, 1962; The Golden Harp, op.93, 1952; The Prophet, op.110 (K. Gibran), A, Bar, narrator, chorus, orch, 1960; Chants d'Auvergne, chorus, insts, 1962
Solo vocal: 4 Nocturnes, op.23, 1v, orch, 1934; From a Lute of Jade, op.36, Mez, orch/pf, 1936
Chamber: Pf Qnt, op.47, 1945; Sonata brevis, op.80, vn, pf, 1948; Sound Piece, op.82, brass, perc, 1949; Nine by Six, op.86, 6 wind, 1950; Str Qt no.1, op.100, 1957; Sonoric Fantasia no.1, op.102, cel, harp, hpd, 1958; Los dioses aztecas, op.107, 6 perc, 1959
Pf: 3 Satirical Sarcasms, op.29, 1935; Driftwood Suite, 1942; Sonata da chiesa, op.61, 1945; Touch Piece, op.85, 1949
Org: Passacaglia and Fugue, op.34, 1936; Sinfonia da chiesa, op.61b, org, brass qnt, 1969; Suite, op.81, 1949; 8 Preludes on Old Southern Hymns, op.90, 1950; Variations on a Chromatic Ground, 1964; And there appeared unto them Tongues as of Fire, 1977

Principal publishers: Associated, Colombo, Gray, Presser

WRITINGS
Thesaurus of Orchestral Devices (Westport, Conn., 1953, 2/1969)
Music Notation: a Manual of Modern Practice (Boston, 1964, 3/1971)
'Some Problems in Rhythmic Notation', *JMT*, ix (1965), 162
Contemporary Instrumental Techniques (New York, 1975)
Style and Orchestration (New York, 1975)
Modern Rhythmic Notation (Bloomington, Ind., 1978)

BIBLIOGRAPHY
Compositores de América/Composers of the Americas, ed. Pan American Union, viii (Washington, DC, 1963), 127
G. Read: *Catalogue of Complete Works* (Boston, 1964)

ROBERT STEVENSON

Reade [Read], **Richard** (*fl* 1570–1616). English singer and composer. He is probably the Richard Read who took the BMus from Christ Church, Oxford, on 7 July 1592. Anthony Wood wrote: 'Richard Read, who had studied the musical faculty for 22 years, was admitted the same day. He hath composed certain Church Services, and other matters for instruments, which are scattered in several books' (*Fasti oxoniensis*, 1691). It has been conjectured that this was the same Richard Read who was a 'singing-man' at Christ Church from 1588–1616, and the likelihood of this connection is strengthened by the fact that one of Reade's compositions is named 'Mr Doctor James Deane of Christchurchs paven'.

In his will (proven at Oxford, 5 April 1617) he gave 'unto Martha Gryse one Base Violl wch she hath now in keeping'; this suggests that he may have played this instrument. The Cambridge Consort Books (*GB-Cu*) are the sole source for his instrumental music; the bandora book is now missing from the set and most of the pieces need reconstruction in one or more of the parts, but as far as it is possible to tell, Reade appears to have been a composer well skilled in the contrapuntal style.

WORKS
(for sources see Nordstrom)
(broken consort)

Pavans: Flatt pavan, Mr Doctor James Dean of Christchurchs paven, 9 untitled
Galliards: to the 6th pavan, to the 8th pavan, 1 untitled (2 versions)
Jigs: Eglantine, Sweet bryer, 4 untitled
Allmaine (after Holborne); Battell; La volta; When Phoebus first

(*other insts*)

4 pavens: orpharions (? with viols)

Mag, Nunc 'to Mundy's Short service', *GB-DRc*, *Lbm*; God standeth in the congregation, *DRc*, *Lbm*: doubtful, both by 'Read' or 'Reed'

BIBLIOGRAPHY

I. Harwood: 'The Origins of the Cambridge Lute Manuscripts', *LSJ*, v (1963), 32

L. Nordstrom: 'The Cambridge Consort Books', *Journal of the Lute Society of America*, v (1972), 70–103

DIANA POULTON

Reading, John (i) (*b* Lincoln, *c*1645; *d* Winchester, 1692). English composer and organist. He was admitted junior vicar and poor clerk of Lincoln Cathedral in 1667, and in 1670 was appointed Master of the Choristers. He received regular payments for paper and strings and for repairing viols. He left Lincoln and was on 4 January 1675 appointed organist, 'Shirburn Clerk' and Master of the Choristers at Chichester Cathedral. On 20 March 1675 he applied for a licence to marry Ann Micklethwayte of Lincoln, describing himself as a widower of about 30 years. On 25 November of the same year he became organist and Master of the Choristers at Winchester Cathedral. From December 1681 to the time of his death he was organist of Winchester College. It was at Reading's request that the 20-year-old college organ by Thomas Harris was rebuilt by his son Renatus Harris. Reading set the college's Latin graces as well as the school song *Dulce domum*; both were first printed in Philip Hayes's *Harmonia Wiccamica*. Reading was always described as a gentleman, perhaps to differentiate him from others of the same name.

An organbook compiled by him and finished by Daniel Roseingrave, his successor at Winchester Cathedral, survives (*US-BE*); it contains several sacred works of his composition. He was also the composer of some fine songs, of theatre music and of catches which appeared in many collections and editions. A ground with divisions, called 'Mr. Readings Ground', published in several editions of Playford's *The Division Violin* (1685), can probably be attributed to him.

Several other musicians have been confused with John Reading (i), notably John Reading (ii) and (iii) below; a John Reading (1588–1667), prebendary of Canterbury, wrote a sermon defending church music.

WORKS

3 full anthems, *US-BE* Mus.751A (organbook)

4 verse anthems, *BE* Mus.751B

Choruses to verse anthem by 'Mr Lawe', *BE* Mus.751B

Responses, litany, *BE* Mus.751B; ed. M. Walsh (London, 1972)

Songs, catches etc, 1681[4], 1685[4], 1686[4], 1687[5], *c*1695[10] and 18th-century collections

Ground, 1685[10] (attrib. 'Mr Reading')

BIBLIOGRAPHY

H. Davey: 'Reading, John', *DNB*

J. B. Clark: *Transposition in Seventeenth Century English Organ Accompaniments and the Transposing Organ* (Detroit, 1974)

SUSI JEANS

Reading, John (ii) (*fl* 1684–1717). English bass. He was the first Corydon in Purcell's *The Fairy Queen* (1692) and sang in the first performances of the Purcell duets *Behold the man* and *Since times are so bad*. In 1695 he was involved, with another singer, John Pate (Mopsa in *The Fairy Queen*), in a Jacobite celebration at the Dog Tavern, Drury Lane, which degenerated into a riot; the singers were fined and suspended from the Playhouse as a result. After 1697 he disappears from stage records, but the 'Mr Reading' who appeared intermittently be-tween 1709 and 1717 was probably the same man.

There were occasional appearances by a Mrs Reading between 1709 and 1724, and a Miss or Mrs Reading sang Peace in Clayton's *Rosamond* in 1707. A bass Balthazar Reading was in the Chapel Royal, and a Valentine Reading in the Private Music during the reign of James II.

BIBLIOGRAPHY

N. Luttrell: *A Brief Historical Relation of State Affairs*, iii (Oxford, 1857), 483, 487

OLIVE BALDWIN, THELMA WILSON

Reading, John (iii) (*b* ?*c*1685 or 1686; *d* London, 2 Sept 1764). English composer and organist. He was probably a son of John Reading (i). He was educated at the Chapel Royal under Blow and left the chapel in 1699 when his voice broke (which shows he was unlikely to have been born in 1677, as is usually stated; that date derives from his obituary, where his age was given as 87, probably a printer's error for 78). Reading was organist at Dulwich College from March 1700 to 26 September 1702. Because of difficulties with his predecessor he was never officially appointed, but he showed great loyalty and affection for the school all his life. His next position was at Lincoln Cathedral, where he was appointed junior vicar and poor clerk on 21 November 1702. On 5 October 1703 he was made Master of the Choristers and on 28 September 1704 he was mentioned as singing teacher to the choristers. His name disappears from the cathedral records in 1705; the next reference to him was as chosen organist of St John's, Hackney, in London, on 28 January 1708: he held that position for nearly 20 years in spite of a threat of dismissal on 12 December 1719 and a representation made to him about 'irregularities relating to the execution of his Office as Organist of this Parish, and particularly for playing the Voluntary too long, and using persistently too light, Airy and Jyggy Tunes, no ways proper to raise the Devotion Suitable for a Religeous Assembly'; Reading promised 'to amend'. On 4 April 1727 he was given three months' notice so 'that he may provide himself with another place in that time' and on 29 July the church wardens paid him his salary and 'forbade him either in person or by Deputy playing any more upon the Organ belonging to the Parish'. He was then appointed organist of the combined churches of St Mary Woolnoth and St Mary Woolchurch Haw in the City of London, where he received an annual salary of £20 (dropping to £12 in 1758). In 1728 he took up in addition the organist's post at St Dunstan's-in-the-West with a salary of £21. He held both posts until the end of his life.

Reading was present at the death of his friend, Jeremiah Clark, organist of Westminster Abbey, who shot himself when Reading happened to be passing his house. An anecdote about Reading refers to his illness, supposed to be palsy (but more likely to be epilepsy), caused by the Vox humana stop at St Mary Woolnoth. He lived at various addresses in London: in 1710 at Arundel Street, Strand, in 1715 by 'Swan passage in Orrange Street near Red-Lyon Square in Holborne' and in 1762 in Lombard Street. He was an early member of the Royal Society of Musicians (1738). A portrait of him is in Dulwich College gallery.

Reading collected, transcribed and arranged an enormous amount of music, 12 volumes of which he donated to Dulwich College; three of these form one of the most important sources of English organ music. He was also a skilled and versatile composer, who was as a young man much influenced by Italian music. He remarked in the preface of his earliest published work *A Book of New Songs (after the Italian Manner)* that his sole motive for publishing the work was 'to incite our Great masters to improve ye Design to such perfection yt our English Composers might be inspired with ye utmost delicacy of a *Roman Genius*'. Most of his compositions were intended for use in church. His numerous organ compositions were not frivolous, as suggested by the parishioners of Hackney, but thoughtful and dignified. It is interesting to note that Reading often copied the same piece two or three times and used different ornamentation each time.

WORKS

A Book of New Songs . . . with Symphonies (London, *c*1710)
A Book of New Anthems . . . with Proper Ritornels (London, *c*1715)
2 voluntaries, in Ten Voluntarys . . . by Dr Green, Skinner . . . Reading, org/hpd (London, 1767)
Prelude and fugue, org, ed. J. Pitman, *A Series of Progressive Studies*, viii (London, 1882)

Songs and other works pubd in 18th-century anthologies
Unto thee, O Lord, anthem, *GB- Ldc* (score), *LI* (inc.)
Divine Harmonie, or Choice Collection of Anthems composed by Several Masters, 1717, *Ldc* (incl. works by Reading)
Mr Reading's Great Book of Lessons for the Harpsichord: the Ladys Entertainment, *Ldc*
Readings Book of Lessons for the Harpsichord, 1727, *Ldc*
14 autograph vols. of arrs. of operatic, sacred vocal and kbd music by numerous composers, incl. Reading: 12 in *GB-Ldc*, 1 in *Mp*, 1 in *J-Tn*

BIBLIOGRAPHY

HawkinsH
F. B. Bickley: *Catalogue of the Manuscripts and Muniments of Alleyn's College of God's Gift at Dulwich* (London, 1903)
S. Jeans: 'Reading, John (iii)', *Grove 5*, esp. suppl.

SUSI JEANS

Read School of Pianoforte Playing. See DUBLIN, §10.

Real answer. A term used in fugue, in opposition to TONAL ANSWER.

Realism. *See* VERISMO.

Reaney, Gilbert (*b* Sheffield, 11 Jan 1924). English musicologist. He studied music and French at Sheffield University (1942–3, 1946–52; BA 1948, BMus 1951), taking the MA in 1951 with a dissertation on the ballades, rondeaux and virelais set by Machaut. After studying at the Sorbonne (with a grant from the French government) on the Roman de Fauvel (1950–53) he was a research fellow at the universities of Reading (1953–6) and Birmingham (1956–9) and spent a winter term as visiting professor at the University of Hamburg (1959–60) before being appointed associate professor (1960) and professor (1963) at the University of California at Los Angeles. Having worked for many years in close contact with Carapetyan, he became assistant editor of *Musica disciplina* (1956) and general editor of the series Corpus Scriptorum de Musica of the American Institute of Musicology (1966). While in England he was also active in preparing early music conferences and programmes for the BBC and gave concerts with his London Medieval Group, which visited the Continent.

Reaney's main research interests are medieval and Renaissance music, theory and literature. The range and importance of his outstanding contribution to musicology are demonstrated by his editions of Vitry's and Franco's treatises, the six volumes of *Early Fifteenth-century Music*, and particularly the two

RISM volumes on sources of polyphonic music from the 11th century to the 14th, which comprise the first complete survey of this material. Both his specialized articles and his comprehensive general studies are marked by characteristic objectivity, clarity of argument, a concise style and thorough knowledge of widely varying subjects.

WRITINGS

The Ballades, Rondeaux and Virelais Set to Music by Guillaume de Machaut (diss., U. of Sheffield, 1951); extracts in *AcM*, xxvii (1955), 40
'Concerning the Origins of the Rondeau, Virelai and Ballade Forms', *MD*, vi (1952), 155
'John Dunstable and Late Medieval Music in England', *Score*, no.8 (1953), 22
'The Ms. Chantilly, Musée Condé 1047', *MD*, viii (1954), 59–113; see also *MD*, x (1956), 55
'Musica ficta in the Music of Guillaume de Machaut', *L'ars nova: Wégimont II 1955*, 196
'The Ms. Oxford, Bodleian Library, Canonici Misc. 213', *MD*, ix (1955), 73–104
'The Lais of Guillaume de Machaut and their Background', *PRMA*, lxxxii (1955–6), 15
'Voices and Instruments in the Music of Guillaume de Machaut', *RBM*, x (1956), 3
'The Greek Background of Medieval Musical Thought', *MMR*, lxxxvii (1957), 124
'A Note on Conductus Rhythm', *IMSCR*, vii *Cologne 1958*, 219
'Machaut's Influence on Late Medieval Music', *MMR*, lxxxviii (1958), 50, 96
'The Ms. London, BM, Add.29987 (Lo)', *MD*, xii (1958), 67
'The Poetical Form of Machaut's Musical Works, I', *MD*, xiii (1959), 25 [only pt.I pubd]
'The "Roman de Fauvel" and its Music', *MMR*, lxxxix (1959), 99
'Ars Nova', *The Pelican History of Music*, i, ed. A. Robertson and D. Stevens (Harmondsworth, 1960), 261–319
'Ars Nova in France', *NOHM*, iii (1960), 1–30
'The Ms. Paris, BN, fonds italien 568 (Pit)', *MD*, xiv (1960), 33–63
'Some Little-known Sources of Medieval Polyphony in England', *MD*, xv (1961), 149
'The Medieval Modes in the 14th Century, in particular in the Works of Guillaume de Machaut', *Organicae voces: Festschrift Joseph Smits van Waesberghe* (Amsterdam, 1961), 137
Ch. Jones, the Saint Nicholas Liturgy and its Literary Relationships (Berkeley and Los Angeles, 1963) [incl. essay on the music]
ed. with A. Gilles and J. Maillard: *P. de Vitry: Ars nova*, CSM, viii (1964)
ed.: *The Manuscript London, British Museum, Additional 29987*, MSD, xiii (1965) [facs. edn.]
ed.: *Willelmus: Breviarium regulare musicae; Anon: Tractatus de figuris; J. Torkesey: Declaratio trianguli et scuti* [with A. Gilles], CSM, xii (1966)
'The Performance of Medieval Music', *Aspects of Medieval and Renaissance Music: a Birthday Offering to Gustave Reese* (New York, 1966), 704
'Towards a Chronology of Machaut's Musical Works', *MD*, xxi (1967), 87
'Notes on the Harmonic Technique of Guillaume de Machaut', *Essays in Musicology: a Birthday Offering for Willi Apel* (Bloomington, Ind., 1968), 63
'Accidentals in Early Fifteenth Century Music', *Renaissance-Muziek 1400–1600: donum natalicium René Bernard Lenaerts* (Louvain, 1969), 223
'Text Underlay in Early 15th Century Manuscripts', *Essays in Musicology in Honor of Dragan Plamenac* (Pittsburgh, 1969), 245
'The Italian Contribution to the Manuscript Oxford, Bodleian Library, Canonici Misc. 213', *L'ars nova italiana del trecento II: Certaldo 1969*, 443
ed.: *C. Butler: The Principles of Musik* (New York, 1970) [facs. edn]
'John Wylde and the Notre Dame Conductus', *Speculum musicae artis: Festgabe für Heinrich Husmann* (Munich, 1970), 263
ed. with A. Gilles: *Anon.: Ars musicae mensurabilis secundum Franconem*, CSM, xv (1971)
'Accidentals and Fourteenth Century Counterpoint in England', *Quadrivium*, xii (1971), 195
Guillaume de Machaut (London, 1971)
with A. Gilles: *Franco of Cologne: Ars cantus mensurabilis*, CSM, xviii (1974)
'The Part Played by Instruments in the Music of Guillaume de Machaut', *Studi musicali*, vi (1977), 3

EDITIONS

Early Fifteenth-century Music, CMM, xi/1–6 (1955–76)

URSULA GÜNTHER

Reardon, John (*b* New York, 8 April 1930). American baritone. He was educated at Rollins College, where he received the degree of Bachelor of Music (1952), and then studied further with Martial Singher and Margaret Harshaw. He made his début at the New York City Opera in 1954, at the Metropolitan Opera in 1965, and has sung with numerous opera companies in the USA and in Europe. He has taken part in several opera recordings (he was a strong Nick Shadow under Stravinsky) and appeared extensively on television. The possessor of a well-controlled lyric voice, allied to a notable acting ability, Reardon is best known for his large repertory of over 100 roles (Mozart, Strauss; Scarpia, Pelléas, Britten's Tarquinius) and for the number of first performances he has given, mostly with the Santa Fe Opera Company. He has sung in the premières of *The Wings of the Dove* (Douglas Moore), *Carry Nation* (Douglas Moore), *Summer and Smoke* (Lee Hoiby), *Mourning Becomes Electra* (Marvin David Levy) and *The Sea Gull* (Thomas Pasatieri); and in the American premières of *The Nose* (Shostakovich), *Cardillac* (Hindemith), *Danton's Death* (Einem), *The Devils of Loudon* (Penderecki), *The Bassarids* (Henze) and *Help, Help, the Globolinks!* (Menotti). In the mid-1970s he was artistic director and director of the opera workshop for the Wolf Trap Summer Theater in Virginia.

BIBLIOGRAPHY
'*The Devils* and Reardon', *Time* (22 Aug 1969), 46
J. Reardon: 'The Challenges of Modern Opera', *Music Journal*, xxix/4 (1971), 1

PATRICK J. SMITH

Rebec [rebeck, rebecke, rebekke] (Fr. *rebec, rebecq, rebecquet, rebet*; Ger. *Rebec*; It. *rebeca, ribeca*; Lat. *rebeca, rebecum*; Sp. *rabé, rabel, rebequín*). A bowed string instrument with a vaulted back and no clear demarcation between the body and neck. Derived from the Byzantine *lūrā* and the Arab RABĀB, rebecs have been known in Europe under different names and in various shapes from the 10th century to the present day, but their use in art music was chiefly during the Middle Ages and Renaissance.

1. Terminology. 2. Structure. 3. History. 4. Repertory.

1. TERMINOLOGY. The terminology of early European rebecs reflects their Byzantine and Arab origins. Martin Gerbert, in his *De cantu et musica sacra* (St Blasien, 1774/*R*1968), reproduced a drawing from a 13th-century manuscript (since destroyed) from the monastery of St Blasius. It shows a pear-shaped instrument with one string and a bow, clearly labelled 'lyra'. A related instrument in the slightly earlier *Hortus deliciarum* of Herrad von Landsberg (formerly in *F-Sm*, but now also destroyed) was described as a 'lira'. Jerome of Moravia, in his *Tractatus de musica* (after 1272), gave a tuning for the 'rubeba', which from its description seems to have been similar to the Moorish *rabāb*. Other words of the same derivation, apparently describing instruments of the rebec family, include the French 'rebebe', 'reberbe' and 'rebesbe', and the English 'ribibe', 'ribible', 'rubebe', 'rubible' and 'rybybe'. 'Gigue' appears frequently in literature of the 13th and 14th centuries (leading to 'Geige' in German), and is thought to have applied in general to rebec-type instruments, although it may sometimes have referred also to the medieval fiddle. Its players (*gigatores*) were, however, listed separately from fiddlers (*vidulatores*) in the expense accounts of medieval English kings.

The word 'rebec' was used from about 1300 onwards, one of the earliest instances being in the poem by Aimeric de Peyrac (see §2 below). Tinctoris (*De inventione et usu musicae*, *c*1487) said that some people called the instrument 'marionetta'. As medieval instruments were unstandardized, there was inevitably a great deal of overlap among their names. An example of the rebec's being denoted by the generic use of the word 'fiddle' occurs in Lydgate's *Pilgrimage of the Life of Man* (*GB-Lbm* Cotton Tiberius A.vii, f.79*v*.), where 'ffedle' in the text is illustrated by an unmistakable rebec in the margin. Conversely, John Palsgrave's *Lesclarissement de la langue francoyse* (1530) uses French cognates of 'rebec' to describe not only the rebec, but also the 'fyddell' and 'croude'. Virdung (1511) and Agricola (1528) described rebecs as 'clein [kleine] Geigen', and in 1618 Praetorius used the diminutive 'Rebecchino' for a violin. From the 16th century onwards the rebec was often called by the various names of its offshoot, the KIT.

1. Pear-shaped rebec with lateral drone string: miniature from a 13th-century English MS (GB-Ob Ashmole 1525, f.102r)

2. Rebecs with right-angled pegboxes: miniature from the Cantigas de Santa María, Spanish, 13th century (E-E b.I.2, f.118r)

2. STRUCTURE. The vaulted back of the rebec is generally carved from one piece of hard wood; the instrument tapers in such a way that there is no visible distinction between the body and the neck. The fingerboard, when one exists, is a raised part of the soundboard or is fixed to it from above (sometimes with a wedge as on early violins), but this does not change the frontal outline of the instrument. Early rebecs had no soundpost, but soundposts are found on similar instruments made since the Renaissance, including 20th-century folk instruments such as the Bulgarian *gadulka*. The design of the soundholes, peg-holder, pegs, tailpiece or other string-holder, strings and bow varied during the Middle Ages, presumably according to the function the instrument was to perform, and on the same lines as the medieval FIDDLE.

In the first four centuries of its history there were two main types of rebec (see figs.1 and 2): the completely wooden pear-shaped instrument terminating in a flat peg-holder (similar to the modern Greek *lyra*), and the skin-bellied, narrower instrument with its right-angled pegbox (the latter seems to be the 'rabé morisco', mentioned by the 14th-century poet Juan Ruiz, which has survived in the *rabāb* of North Africa). While continuing their separate existences, both contributed to the traditional type of European rebec that appeared in the late 13th century and became established in the 14th. This type, occasionally fretted, was pear-shaped, with a wooden soundboard, a sickle-shaped pegbox, usually ending in a scroll or carved head, and a tailpiece (see fig.3). It seems to have coincided with the appearance of the word 'rebec', and may have been that type of 'rebecum' which, according to Tinctoris, was invented by the French. Meanwhile experiments continued within the basic type, and the right-angled pegbox, hitherto used mainly in southern Europe, now spread to the north.

Just as the shape varied, so did the size of the instrument and the number of strings. Any number from one to five was quite usual; occasionally there were more. Sometimes they were grouped in pairs, each pair tuned to one note, and a lateral drone was not uncommon. Instruments of the *rabāb* type seem to have kept on the whole to two strings which, according to Jerome of Moravia, were tuned in 5ths, to *c* and *g*. Aimeric de Peyrac, however, indicated a higher pitch by comparing the sound of the rebec to women's voices ('Quidam rebecam arcuabant muliebrem vocem confingentes'). In 1532 Gerle indicated that the rebec was tuned in 5ths, and in 1545 Agricola gave specific tunings for four different sizes: discant *g–d'–a'*, alto and tenor *c–g–d'* and bass *F–G–d–a*. This last example shows that tuning only in 5ths cannot, however, have been universal; indeed those rebecs that had three or more single strings and a flat bridge needed a tuning suitable for regular drones. As the medieval fiddle was often tuned in 5ths and octaves, like the pear-shaped but plucked mandore (according to somewhat later sources of information), it seems reasonable to assume that this tuning may sometimes have applied to the rebec as well. Agricola described a three-string rebec tuned in 5ths because to him it was the most usual, but (owing to lack of space) he did not set out to describe its many variants.

From the time of their appearance, there has been a tendency for instruments of the rebec family in southern Europe and northern Africa to be played down in the lap, with the bow gripped from below. This is clearly seen in the Cantigas de Santa María manuscript (see fig.2) and in the Psalter of Alfonso V of Aragon (see fig.4). However, Giovanni di Nicola's *Virgin and Child Enthroned* is one of several pictures where rebecs of the *rabāb* type are played up at the shoulder. It seems that the latter position was usual in northern Europe, the downward position in the south; also that in the north the strings were pressed down by the fingers and in the south they were touched from the side by the fingernails. However, such generalizations reflect only tendencies and not fixed rules, and everywhere there was considerable variety in the manner of performance. The downward position seems to have been almost unknown in England.

Of the few rebecs which survive from the Middle Ages, one typical of the lira type was excavated in Novgorod on the site of a 14th-century house, and is now, together with fragments of other such instruments, in the Institute of Archaeology of the Academy of Sciences of the USSR, Moscow. An Italian instrument of approximately the same date is so elaborately carved that its tapering outline can be seen only from the back. This is now in the Irwin Untermeyer Collection, New York.

3. HISTORY. Although for some time bowing was not fully accepted in the higher social circles of Asia, it was widely adopted in Europe after the bow's establishment there in the 10th and 11th centuries. Instruments of the rebec family were deemed by Romanesque artists worthy to be played by the Elders of the Apocalypse and by David's minstrels, and at the Porta das Platerias at the Cathedral of Santiago de Compostela David himself is depicted playing one. During the Middle Ages and Renaissance, the rebec was a recognized instrument of professional minstrels who, dressed in special livery, played in royal courts or were attached to a town or noble household. Such was the rebec player carved on the Minstrels' Pillar at St Mary's Church, Beverley, Yorkshire, during its rebuilding after the tower collapsed in 1520. In the *Knight of La Tour Landry* (before 1450) the 'ribible' is referred to as one of the instruments 'as longithe to a mynstralle'. (It was during the Renaissance that the KIT gradually evolved from the rebec.)

In rustic society the rebec was prominent at village revels, and as such can be seen carved, together with a pipe and tabor, round a window in St Mary's Church, Lawford, Essex. While wind instruments were more usual in the fields, the French poem *Bellefoiere* describes the 'hoarse rebec of the cowherds' being played with the bagpipes. Its bucolic associations are many. In Lydgate's *Pilgrimage of the Life of Man* people are taught 'to revelle at taverne on rebube and on symphonie', while in Langland's *Vision of Piers Plowman* Gluttony goes into a tavern and finds there 'a rybibour and a ratoner, a rakere and hus knave'. In 1628 Parisians were forbidden to play any form of violin in taverns, but the rebec was allowed to remain.

Processions, whether sacred or secular, often included rebecs. The 14th-century Tickhill Psalter shows David, holding the head of Goliath, being escorted by musicians singing and playing two rebecs, two gitterns and four trumpets (see fig.5). Gentile Bellini's *Procession of the Reliquary of the Cross in the*

4. Rebec played in the lap: miniature from the Psalter of Alfonso V of Aragon, Italian or Spanish, 15th century (GB-Lbm Add.28962, f.82r)

5. David, with the head of Goliath, escorted by musicians singing and playing two rebecs (left), two gitterns and four trumpets: miniature from the Tickhill Psalter, 14th century (US-NYp MS 26, f.17r)

3. Angel with fully developed European rebec: detail from the painting 'The Virgin and Child with Saints' (early 16th century) by Gerard David, in the Musée des Beaux-Arts, Rouen

Piazza Marco (1496) shows two musicians, one playing trumpets, shawms and sackbuts, and the other, nearer to the Cross, playing a rebec, lute and harp (see CHORUS (i) fig.3). In 1536 the mystery play Les actes des apôtres at Bourges was preceded by a parade round the town: one of the floats represented Heaven, and on it were 'two . . . little angels, singing hymns and canticles, who joined with players of flutes, harps, lutes, rebecs and viols, walking around Paradise'. A painting (1615) by Alsloot of a float in an ommeganck procession at Brussels shows the Muses playing a lute, harp, viola, rebec (? or kit), recorder, bass violin, triangle and tambourine, while Apollo plays a harp (see BRUSSELS, fig.1).

The use of rebecs at feasts, dances and entertainments of the nobility has been widely documented. Johannes de Garlandia listed the 'giga' among other instruments to be seen in the houses of rich Parisians in the 13th century. Edward I had among his regular minstrels three gigatores from Germany, who took part in the celebrations at Westminster on Whitsunday 1306. The French poet Eustache Deschamps wrote that 'at royal courts everyone wants to play the trumpet, gittern and rebec'.

At the court of Henry VIII rebec players (listed in the accounts) included John de Severnacke, Thomas Evans and Great Guilliam, and the types of occasion on which they played were described by court scribes and visiting foreigners; these included a feast where 'in the centre of the hall there was a stage on which were some boys, some of whom sang, and others played on the flute, rebeck and harpsichord'. In the Revels Accounts of 1513 Richard Gibson described a pageant he had produced. Called the 'Ryche Mount', it was an elaborate replica of a mountain, decorated with symbolic plants (such as broom for Plantagenet) and drawn into the hall by two 'mighty woordwossys or wyld men'. Six minstrels stood on it, playing rebecs and 'tambourines' (probably pipes and tabors in this context) while lords and ladies descended from it to dance. At the wedding in Florence in 1539 of Cosimo I, Duke of Florence, to Eleonora of Toledo, the elaborate intermedi ended with the appearance of 20 bacchantes, eight of whom played disguised instruments, one being a stag's head containing a 'ribecchino'. When Mary Queen of Scots returned from France in August 1561 and was trying to sleep, 'five or six hundred scoundrels of the town serenaded her with wretched violins and small rebecs, of which there is no lack in this country; and they began to sing psalms than which nothing more badly sung or out of tune could be imagined'.

4. REPERTORY. The rebec dates from the period when music was seldom written for specified instruments but was played on whatever was available and suitable for the occasion, and although it survived into the Baroque era it did not at that time normally appear in art music. This apart, the earlier ways in which it was used are broadly those described for the medieval fiddle. Its use in Renaissance consort music can be seen from two examples: Hans Gerle left several pieces of four-part music for whole consorts of rebecs (such organized grouping by size was unusual before the 16th century); and its appearance in a broken consort is exemplified by the above-mentioned song from the Florentine wedding. Composed by Corteccia in four parts to the words 'Baccho, Baccho, e u o e', its voices would have been doubled by the instruments (probably playing divisions), and as the rebec was a small one it is likely to have played the top line.

Certainly the music played on the rebec depended to a great extent on the tone of each individual instrument, and as there was no standardization of structure each one's sound must have been very different. Indeed, this is evident not only from modern reconstructions but also by comparison of the 'hoarse rebec' in *Bellefoiere* with the instrument described by Tinctoris:

And I am similarly pleased by the rebec, my predilection for which I will not conceal, provided that it is played by a skilful artist, since its strains are very much like those of the fiddle ['viola']. Accordingly, the fiddle and the rebec are my two instruments; I repeat, my chosen instruments, those that induce piety and stir my heart most ardently to the contemplation of heavenly joys. For these reasons I would rather reserve them solely for sacred music and the secret consolations of the soul, than have them sometimes used for profane occasions and public festivities.

BIBLIOGRAPHY

S. Virdung: *Musica getutscht* (Basle, 1511/*R*1970)

M. Agricola: *Musica instrumentalis deudsch* (Wittenberg, 1528/*R*1969)

H. Gerle: *Musica teusch* (Nuremberg, 1532, rev. 3/1546/*R*1977)

M. Praetorius: *Syntagma musicum*, ii (Wolfenbüttel, 1618, 2/1619/*R*1958)

H. Panum: *Middelalderens strengeinstrumenter* (Copenhagen, 1915–31; Eng. trans., 1939/*R*1971 as *The Stringed Instruments of the Middle Ages*)

J. Rittmeyer-Iselin: 'Das Rebec: ein Beitrag zur Geschichte unserer Streichinstrumente', *Festschrift Karl Nef zum 60. Geburtstag* (Zurich and Leipzig, 1933), 210

E. van der Straeten: *The History of the Violin*, i (London, 1933)

A. Baines: 'Fifteenth-century Instruments in Tinctoris's *De inventione et usu musicae*', *GSJ*, iii (1950), 19

H. Hickmann, B. D. Siedersbeck and H.-H. Dräger: 'Fidel', *MGG*

A. Baines, ed.: *Musical Instruments through the Ages* (Harmondsworth, 1961, rev. 2/1966)

H. H. Carter: *A Dictionary of Middle English Musical Terms* (Bloomington, Ind., 1961)

J. Stevens: *Music and Poetry in the Early Tudor Court* (London, 1961)

H. M. Brown: *Music in the French Secular Theater, 1400–1550* (Cambridge, Mass., 1963)

W. Bachmann: *Die Anfänge des Streichinstrumentenspiels* (Leipzig, 1964; Eng. trans., 1969)

S. Marcuse: *Musical Instruments: a Comprehensive Dictionary* (New York, 1964)

R. Rastall: 'The Minstrels of the English Royal Households, 25 Edward I–1 Henry VIII: an Inventory', *RMARC*, iv (1964), 1–41

D. D. Boyden: *A History of Violin Playing from its Origins to 1761* (London, 1965)

Aspects of Medieval and Renaissance Music: a Birthday Offering to Gustave Reese (New York, 1966)

A. Puccianti: 'La descrizione della *viella* e della *rubeba* in Girolamo di Moravia', *CHM*, iv (1966), 227

L. M. C. Randall: *Images in the Margins of Gothic Manuscripts* (Berkeley and Los Angeles, 1966)

E. Winternitz: *Die schönsten Musikinstrumente des Abendlandes* (Munich, 1966; Eng. trans., 1967 as *Musical Instruments of the Western World*)

A. C. Minor and B. Mitchell: *A Renaissance Entertainment: Festivities for the Marriage of Cosimo I, Duke of Florence, in 1539* (Columbia, Missouri, 1968)

G. R. Rastall: *Secular Musicians in Late Mediaeval England* (diss., U. of Manchester, 1968)

M. Remnant: 'The Use of Frets on Rebecs and Mediaeval Fiddles', *GSJ*, xxi (1968), 146

——: 'Rebec, Fiddle and Crowd in England', *PRMA*, xcv (1968–9), 15; xcvi (1969–70), 149

F. von Glasenapp: *Varia/Rara/Curiosa* (Göttingen, 1971)

H. M. Brown and J. Lascelle: *Musical Iconography* (Cambridge, Mass., 1972)

F. Crane: *Extant Medieval Musical Instruments* (Iowa City, 1972)

K. Kos: *Musikinstrumente im mittelalterlichen Kroatien* (Zagreb, 1972)

M. Remnant: *Bowed Instruments in England up to the Reformation* (diss., U. of Oxford, 1972)

T. Seebass: *Musikdarstellung und Psalterillustration im früheren Mittelalter* (Berne, 1973)

W. Stauder: *Alte Musikinstrumente* (Brunswick, 1973)

S. Marcuse: *A Survey of Musical Instruments* (Newton Abbot and London, 1975)

D. Munrow: *Instruments of the Middle Ages and Renaissance* (London, 1976)

M. Remnant: *Musical Instruments of the West* (London, 1978)

C. Page: 'Jerome of Moravia on the *rubeba* and *viella*', *GSJ*, xxxii (1979), 77

L. Wright: 'Sculptures of Medieval Fiddles at Gargilesse', *GSJ*, xxxii (1979), 66

MARY REMNANT

Rebel. French family of musicians associated with court and stage positions for three generations, from about 1661 to 1775.

(1) Jean Rebel (*b* 1st half of the 17th century; *d* Versailles, before 29 Feb 1692). Singer. His name first appeared in 1661 when he was a tenor in Louis XIV's private chapel, a post which he held for the rest of his life. As an *ordinaire* to the king he had secular singing and, perhaps, dancing duties at court in the ensembles of some of Lully's early ballets. His responsibilities increased sharply from 1670; he began to have larger parts in the ballets (*Le bourgeois gentilhomme*, 1670; *Cadmus*, July 1673; *Alceste*, 1674) and was named a singer to the queen. In December 1670 he also served as conductor of 'La suite de Mars', part of the grand *Ballet des ballets*. In the same period he introduced his musical children (2) Anne-Renée and (3) Jean-Féry to the court. In April 1683 he participated in an elaborate competition to choose four *sous-maîtres* for the royal chapel and was among the 15 finalists required to write a motet while isolated. He did not win any of the positions, and none of his compositions is extant. Jean's brother Robert (*d* c1662) was an *ordinaire de la musique du roi*. Anne-Renée and Jean-Féry, and Jean's grandson (4) François, were prominent musicians. His son by a second marriage, Jean-Thomas (c1676–1718), was a musician and held an appointment with the Prince of Monaco; he is unlikely to be the Thomas Rebel who was a dancing-master in Lyons in 1688 or the Jean who joined the orchestra in that city in 1687. A Robert Rebel was also active in Lyons c1688–1704.

(2) Anne-Renée [Renée Anne] **Rebel** (baptized Paris, 6 Dec 1663; *d* Versailles, 5 May 1722). Singer, eldest child of (1) Jean Rebel. She probably sang at court as early as 1673, and had solo roles before she was 12. Some thought her the best singer in the royal chamber, and Durey de Noinville praised both her voice and her musicality. She was a favourite of the king, who in July 1684 paid the dowry and expenses for her wedding to Michel-Richard de Lalande, his *maître de chapelle* (and later chamber composer). In 1704 their two daughters,

Jeanne and Marie-Anne de Lalande, charmed Louis XIV with their singing; two years later they were awarded pensions for their father's merit and for their own performances in the royal chapel. In 1711, however, the girls died of smallpox at the ages of 24 and 23. Their mother continued to receive a royal pension until at least 1717.

(3) **Jean-Féry** [Jean-Baptiste-Ferry] **Rebel** [*le père*] (baptized Paris, 18 April 1666; *d* Paris, 2 Jan 1747). Violinist, harpsichordist, conductor and composer, son of (1) Jean Rebel. By the age of eight Jean-Féry, who was to be Jean's most famous musical offspring, had astonished the king and Lully with his violin playing; L'Abbé de Fontenay told how Lully played through and approved the youngster's first attempt at opera. By 1699 he was first violinist at the Académie Royale de Musique but he left for Spain in the following year with the troupe formed by the Count of Ayen to attend Philip of Anjou's wedding; on his return in July 1705 he was awarded a place in the king's 24 Violons. This was the first of many court appointments of increasing importance and responsibility awarded to Jean-Féry in his long career. He also played an important role in the orchestra of the Académie Royale. At court his most important position was that of chamber composer; he received the right of succession to the half of this office held by Lalande, his brother-in-law, on 30 March 1718, and the title itself in 1726. His other activities at Versailles often included the administration and direction of the 24 Violons and of large groups brought together for special productions or ceremonies, ranging from funerals to ballets. At the Académie he sometimes played the harpsichord continuo, beginning in 1707, and was chosen to be *maître de musique* in 1716; he also conducted the Concert Spirituel for at least the 1734–5 season. An unusual tribute was paid to the aging man when his son François directed a concert of his works on 22 June 1740.

The changing genres of Jean-Féry's compositions divide his career into three overlapping periods. The

Jean-Féry Rebel: engraving by Moyreau after Valeau

first, up to 1708, was characterized by small, incidental vocal works, and his unsuccessful opera *Ulysse*. Rebel's next published efforts were chamber works, which show his graceful instrumental writing. The manuscript of Rebel's *Sonates à II et III*, dated 1695 but not published until 1712, puts him among the earliest French composers to write string sonatas, although they show no virtuosity. The *Sonates* for solo violin are similar in arrangement to Corelli's op.5 violin sonatas; when the bass viol has important material a true trio texture results.

The final part of Rebel's output consists of choreographed 'symphonies' to use the talents of the dancers in the Académie Royale. *Les caractères de la danse* was composed with Mme Françoise Prévost in mind, and she danced it before Tsar Peter the Great. It was also popular when danced by her two famous pupils, Marie Camargo and Marie Sallé. Jean-Féry's most interesting piece was written when Prince Carignan (Victor-Amédée of Savoy) coaxed him out of retirement in 1737 to write the popular *Les élémens*. In an article accompanying the music the composer explained his intentions in the piece: the first sound heard in the first movement ('Le cahos') was the simultaneous attack of every note in the D minor harmonic scale, representing chaos, which resolved to the single tone representing Earth; each of the other three elements also had its own characteristic motif which it retained throughout the work.

Jean-Féry was greatly esteemed as a composer by his contemporaries, and made important innovations in genres of instrumental music within the conventions of the French style. Le Cerf de la Viéville explained Rebel's appeal to the French: 'Rebel truly has a part of the Italian genius and fire, but he has had the taste and the sense to temper them by the French wisdom and tenderness, and he has abstained from the frightening and monstrous cadenzas which are the delight of the Italians'.

WORKS
(all printed works published in Paris)

INSTRUMENTAL

Pièces . . . divisées par [3] suites de tons (vn, bc)/hpd/viol (1705)
Recueil de 12 sonates à II et III parties (2 vn, b viol, bc)/hpd (1712)
[12] Sonates, vn, bc, . . . mellées de plusieurs récits, b viol (1713)
Choreographed 'symphonies': Caprice, 3 vn, vc, bc (1711); La boutade (2 vn, viol, bc)/hpd (1712); Les caractères de la danse, fantaisie, 2 vn, bc, with opt. fl, ob, bn in some movts (1715); Terpsichore, sonate, vn, fl, bc (1720); Fantaisie, 5 fl, 2 vn, bc, with opt. vc, tpt, timp in some movts (1729); Les plaisirs champêtres, 2 vn, bc, with opt. fl, ob, bn in some movts (1734); Les élémens, simphonie nouvelle (2 vn, 2 fl, bc, with opt. va, ob, bn, hn, vc in some movts)/hpd (1737)
La petite Drôt, 2 vn, b viol, bc, *D-Dlb*, doubtful authenticity; 3 gavottes, 1 rondeau, *F-Pn*

VOCAL

Ulysse (tragédie lyrique, prol, 5, H. Guichard), Paris, Académie Royale, 23 Jan 1703, pubd (1703)
[6] Leçons de Ténèbres, perf. Concert Spirituel, *F-Pa*, collab. M.-R. de Lalande
Numerous serious songs, drinking-songs and chansons pubd in 18th-century anthologies

(4) **François Rebel** [*le fils*] (*b* Paris, 19 June 1701; *d* Paris, 7 Nov 1775). Violinist, theorbist, composer, conductor and theatre administrator, son of (3) Jean-Féry Rebel. Like his father, he gained musical recognition at an early age; he entered the orchestra of the Académie Royale at the age of 13 and three years later received the right of succession to his father's place in the 24 Violons. He also travelled outside France; Quantz observed him with his friend François Francoeur at the festivities surrounding Charles VI's coronation in

Prague in 1723. Francoeur and Rebel were nearly inseparable in their musical careers from that point forward. In 1726 they performed violin duets at the Concert Spirituel, and the same year saw their first stage collaboration, the opera *Pirame et Thisbé*. Dubbed 'l'opéra des enfants' by Beffara because of the youth of its composers, this popular tragedy was followed by five other major operas or ballets and numerous shorter productions. While these were meeting with mixed success, François' career at court continued to flourish. He had much responsibility for royal spectacles, and served as conductor of the Petits-Cabinets theatre orchestra, royal chamber composer (active 1727–55), and *surintendant* and *maître* of the royal chamber music (30 August 1733 until his death). In the latter dual offices he became involved in bitter squabbles with officers of the chapel over the direction of large ceremonial works.

At the Académie Royale de Musique François had both performance and administrative posts. He was a violinist in the orchestra and directed the Concert Spirituel in 1742, but had much more influence on the Académie as *inspecteur général* (with Francoeur as his assistant), 1743–53, and as co-director with Francoeur from 1757. They supported Rameau and the French style in the Querelle des Bouffons, but with limited success. Their venture as directors was further handicapped by deficits, a bad fire and personnel problems, until they finally requested a dissolution of their contract, which was effected on 1 April 1767. In 1760 Rebel had become one of the five musicians ennobled by Louis XV; he was also made a Chevalier of the Order of St Michel. The king's confidence in him was shown when he was called back in 1772 to assist the Académie in the new post of *Administrateur général* with an enormous salary.

By far the most important of François' compositions were those for the stage, of which nearly all were in collaboration with Francoeur. It is impossible to distinguish between their contributions now, but La Borde claimed that Rebel gave their music its 'morceaux de force' while Francoeur added the 'morceaux de sentiment'. Several of their pieces became popular, but none was other than light entertainment. Rebel's greatest achievement lies in his administrative efforts to keep French opera alive in the troubled times of the 1750s and 1760s rather than as a strong and direct influence on theatrical music.

WORKS

STAGE

Music for 18 stage works written in collaboration with François Francoeur
Pastorale héroïque de la fête des ambassadeurs plénipotentaires – d'Espagne à l'occasion de la naissance de Monseigneur le Dauphin (ballet, 1, J.-L.-I. de Laserre), Versailles, 24 Jan 1730 [?music by Rebel only, ?lost]
Intermezzos in Eugénie (comédie), pubd (Paris, 1753), ?collab. Francoeur
Intermezzos in Amour pour amour (comédie), pubd (Paris, 1765), collab. unknown
Addns to Lully's Persée, 1770, collab. B. de Bury and A. Dauvergne

OTHER WORKS

L'amour de Psiché (cantata), 1v, 2 vn, fl, bc; Climène (cantata), S, 2 vn, ?fl, bc: both F-Pc
4 motets, all perf. Concert Spirituel, ?all lost: Domine salvum, 8 Dec 1744; De profundis, March 1752, collab. Francoeur; De profundis, 1 April 1763 (Paris, n.d.); Te Deum, Nov 1763

Recueil des symphonies composées soit pour les opéras de ces auteurs [Rebel and Francoeur], soit pour les opéras d'autres auteurs, F-Pc
Numerous songs and airs pubd in 18th-century anthologies

BIBLIOGRAPHY

EitnerQ
S. de Brossard: Catalogue, *F-Pn* Rés. Vm⁸21
J. L. Le Cerf de la Viéville: *Comparaison de la musique italienne et de la musique françois* (Brussels, 1704–6/*R*1972)
J.-B. de La Borde: *Essai sur la musique française* (Paris, 1780/*R*1972)
P. Aubry: 'Jean-Ferry Rebel', *RHCM*, v (1905), 301
E. Dacier: 'Les caractères de la danse: histoire d'un divertissement pendant la première moitié du xviiie siècle – danseuses d'autrefois: La Camargo, Mlle Prévost, Mlle Sallé, etc', *RHCM*, v (1905), 324, 365
L. de La Laurencie: 'Une dynastie de musiciens aux xviie et xviiie siècles: Les Rebel', *SIMG*, vii (1905–6), 253–307
——: *L'école française de violon de Lully à Viotti* (Paris, 1922–4/*R*1971)
W. C. Gates: 'Jean Féry Rebel's "Sonates à violon seul mellées de plusieurs récits pour la viole" (1713)', *JAMS*, vii (1954), 251
E. Borrel: 'Notes sur l'orchestration de l'opéra Jephte de Montéclair (1733) et de la symphonie des Elémens de J. F. Rebel (1737)', *ReM* (1955), no.226, p.105
W. S. Newman: *The Sonata in the Baroque Era* (Chapel Hill, 1959, rev. 2/1966/*R*1972)
M. Briquet: 'Rebel', *MGG*
M. Le Moël: 'Un foyer d'italianisme à la fin du XVIIe siècle', *RMFC*, iii (1963), 43
F. Robert: 'Scanderberg, le héros national albanais dans un opéra du Rebel et Francoeur', *RMFC*, iii (1963), 171
J. R. Anthony: *French Baroque Music from Beaujoyeulx to Rameau* (London, 1973, rev. 2/1978)
C. Pierre: *Histoire du Concert Spirituel 1725–1790* (Paris, 1975)
J. A. Sadie: *The Bass Viol in French Baroque Chamber Music* (Ann Arbor, 1981)

PEGGY DAUB

Rebello [Rebelo, Rabello, Rabelo], **Manuel** [Manoel] (*b* Aviz, *c*1575; *d* Évora, 1647, before 6 Nov). Portuguese composer. He studied with Manuel Mendes and about 1596 became *mestre de capela* of Évora Cathedral, a post he held until his death in spite of efforts to dismiss him because of old age. In 1644 he was rated by the poet Manuel de Faria e Sousa at Madrid as one of the four best Portuguese composers, the other three being Mendes, Manuel Cardoso and Duarte Lobo. On 16 April 1647 John IV rewarded him with a dowry for his niece. The catalogue of John IV's library (1649) lists by him a 12-part *Missa primi toni*, a *Miserere* on the 4th tone for three choirs, two settings of *Ave regina coelorum*, for four and eight voices respectively, *Ave virgo gratiosa* for six voices, an eight-part psalm, two funerary motets, and seven villancicos (one in Negro dialect) for three to eight voices. His even-verse *Magnificat primi toni* for four voices is extant (in *P-EVc* Choirbook 3 ascribed to 'Manoel Rebelo'); the Sanctus of his five-part mass in the same choirbook is transposed Dorian music of considerable power and expressiveness (ed. in Alegria, 1973).

BIBLIOGRAPHY

M. de Faria e Sousa: *Fuente de Aganipe . . . parte segunda* (Madrid, 1644), f.165
Primeira parte do index da livraria de musica do muyto alto, e poderoso Rey Dom João o IV. nosso senhor (Lisbon, 1649/*R*1967); ed. J. de Vasconcellos (Oporto, 1874–6), 241, 261f, 295, 308ff
D. Barbosa Machado: *Bibliotheca lusitana*, iii (Lisbon, 1752), 348f
F. M. Sousa Viterbo: 'Subsídios para a história da música em Portugal', *O Instituto* (Coimbra), lxxxii (1931), 385
J. A. Alegria: *Arquivo das músicas da Sé de Évora* (Lisbon, 1973), 13
——: *História de Escola da música da Sé de Évora* (Lisbon, 1973), 63ff, 162ff

ROBERT STEVENSON

Rebelo [Rebello, Rabelo, Rabello], **João Soares** [Suárez] or **João Lourenço** (*b* Caminha, 1610; *d* Apelacão [now in Lisbon], 16 Nov 1661). Portuguese composer, brother of MARCOS SOARES PEREIRA; he took his mother's surname. At 14, while still a treble, he joined his brother in the choir maintained at Vila Viçosa by Dom Teodósio II, 7th Duke of Bragança and father of John IV. His earliest known composition, a 12-part *Parce mihi* for the duke's exequies, shows that at the age of 20 he was already addicted to the grandiose polychoralism that dominates his output. In 1646 King John IV made him a nobleman of the royal house, simultaneously bestowing on him several other privileges of rank as well as financial favours; he had his own estate, Santo Amaro, at Apelacão. In 1649, dedicating to him his *Defensa de la música moderna*, John IV praised his vast output of masses, other sacred music and *tonos*. Shortly before his death John provided in his will for the publication of Rebelo's 1657 collection of sacred works. In this volume he frequently called for an independent instrumental part. All the surviving parts abound in dotted and other sharply etched rhythms. When invited to comment on his works Carlos Patiño characterized them as fiery and warlike, an apt description of *Credidi propter quod*, his one polychoral work surviving complete. On the other hand the eight anonymous vesper psalms and *Magnificat* at Vila Viçosa are sober four-part unaccompanied works, as are the *St Matthew Passion*, *Asperges me* and *Panis angelicus*. Like Monteverdi, Rebelo evidently veered at will between the first and second practices.

WORKS

Psalmi tum vesperarum, tum completarum, item Magnificat, Lamentationes, et Miserere, 4–15vv (Rome, 1657) [incl. 2 motets, 6vv, by John IV]

Asperges me, 4vv, *P-VV*

Credidi propter quod, 8vv, harp, *E-LPA*

Panis angelicus, 7vv, *P-VV*

St Matthew Passion, *VV*

8 vesper psalms, Magnificat, 4vv, *VV* (anon.); psalms also at *EVc* (see Joaquim and Alegria)

Many lost masses, incl. Mass, 39vv, 1643 (for John IV's 39th birthday); 6 other masses; Requiem with Dies irae and responsories; motets, hymns; villancicos, tonos

BIBLIOGRAPHY

D. Barbosa Machado: *Bibliotheca lusitana*, ii (Lisbon, 1747), 765ff; iii (Lisbon, 1752), 410f

M. Joaquim: *Vinte livros de música polifónica do Paço Ducal de Vila Viçosa* (Lisbon, 1953)

L. de la Torre de Trujillo: 'El archivo de música de la Catedral de Las Palmas', *El Museo Canario*, xxv/89–92 (1964), 192

J. A. Alegria: *Arquivo das músicas da Sé de Évora* (Lisbon, 1973), 13f

ROBERT STEVENSON

Rebenlein. German family of printers. Georg Rebenlein (1575–1657) was one of Hamburg's four official book printers; his son Jakob Rebenlein (*d* Hamburg, 1662) inherited the printing firm, whose output included music. The business was continued by Jakob's sons, Georg Jürgen Rebenlein (1634–84) and Johann Hans Rebenlein (1637–78). Its chief musicological significance is its connection with the origins and development of the Hamburg school of song.

BIBLIOGRAPHY

J. Benzing: *Die Buchdrucker des 16. und 17. Jahrhunderts im deutschen Sprachgebiet* (Wiesbaden, 1963)

T. Wohnhaas: 'Rebenlein', *MGG*

THEODOR WOHNHAAS

Rebequin (Sp.). REBEC.

Reber, (Napoléon-)Henri (*b* Mulhouse, 21 Oct 1807; *d* Paris, 24 Nov 1880). French composer and teacher. Intended by his family for a career in industry, he already had a thorough scientific grounding when he found his vocation for music and began learning the piano and flute and composing on his own. At the age of 21 he entered the Paris Conservatoire to study harmony under Reicha and composition under Le Sueur, but was

dismissed from their classes with an undistinguished record. His earliest works are chamber pieces dating from about 1835; his music to Act 2 of the ballet *Le diable amoureux* (the rest composed by Benoist) was performed at the Opéra-Comique on 23 September 1840. In 1851 he was appointed professor of harmony at the Conservatoire, and in 1853 the success of *Le père Gaillard* resulted in his election to the Institut as Onslow's successor. Soon after this he gave up writing for the theatre and returned to chamber music. He also began to write on music, and in 1862 he succeeded Halévy as professor of composition at the Conservatoire; from 1871 he was also inspector of the Conservatoire's branches. He was made a Chevalier of the Légion d'honneur in 1855, and an Officier in 1870.

Reber is remembered almost entirely for his *Traité d'harmonie*, which was first published in 1862 and (with additions to the first reissue by Théodore Dubois) went through many editions. His musical output was small, but was distributed throughout his career. It gives a true reflection of its creator, who might be called a belated classicist having small regard for the masters of his own century, except perhaps for Schubert. In spite of the considerable success of his theatrical works and the fact that some of his best music is contained in his vocal melodies (carefully polished and thus a rarity at a time when the *romance* had reached its lowest ebb), his enduring chief interest was in instrumental music. His piano trios were given their first performances by Saint-Saëns, with Dien and Batta; Saint-Saëns, who knew him well, wrote:

With his predilection for the past and his exquisite courtesy of manner, he evoked a bygone age; his white hair looked as though it were powdered; his frock-coat had an air of period dress about it; he seemed like a forgotten man from the 18th century, wandering through the 19th as a contemporary of Mozart might have done, surprised and somewhat shocked by our music and our ways.

WORKS

(selective list; all printed works published in Paris; MSS in F-Pc)

STAGE

Unless otherwise stated, all are comic operas, first performed at the Opéra-Comique, and published (vocal score) shortly after first performance.

Le diable amoureux (ballet), 23 Sept 1840, collab. F. Benoist; 2 extracts (1842)

La nuit de Noël (3, Scribe), 9 Feb 1848

Le père Gaillard (3, T. Sauvage), 7 Sept 1852 (1854)

Les papillottes de Monsieur Benoist (1, J. Barbier), 28 Dec 1853

Les dames-capitaines (3, Mélesville), 3 June 1857

Naïm ou Les maures en Espagne (grand opéra, 5), unperf., unpubd; ov. (n.d.)

Le ménétrier à la cour, unperf., unpubd; ov. (n.d.)

OTHER WORKS

Vocal: Roland (after Quinault), cantata, op.35 (1887); 55 mélodies, 1v, pf, i (1863), ii (1880); 18 vocalises, S/T, pf (1845)

Orch: 4 syms. (1858); Suite de morceaux, op.31 (1878)

Chamber: Str Qnt, op.1, c1835; 3 str qts, op.4 (n.d.), op.5 (n.d.), *F-Pc*; 6 pièces, vn, pf (1849); Pièces de différents caractères en 3 suites, vn/fl/vc, pf, op.15 (c1855); Pf Qt (1866); 9 pièces, vn, pf (1866); 7 pf trios, incl. no.6, op.34 (1876), no.7, a (1881); 2 morceaux caractéristiques, vn, pf (1881); Berceuse célèbre, vn/vc, pf (1901)

Pf: 6 pièces (1845); 9 pièces de différents caractères en forme de valses, op.10; 6 pièces de différents caractères en 3 suites, op.13; Souvenirs d'Alsace, waltzes (1866); Pastorale, 4 hands (1876); Suite de morceaux, 4 hands (1877); Bagatelles, op.36 (1879)

WRITINGS

Traité d'harmonie (Paris, 1862, 2/1889 ed. T. Dubois)

BIBLIOGRAPHY

E. Legouvé: 'Reber', *La France musicale*, vi (1843), 98

C. Saint-Saëns: *Notice sur M. Henri Reber* (Paris, 1881)

F. Noske: *La mélodie française de Berlioz à Duparc* (Paris and Amsterdam, 1954; Eng. trans., rev., 1970)

F. Raugel: 'Autour de Sauzay, de Boëly et de Reber', *RMFC*, xv (1975), 146

FRÉDÉRIC ROBERT

Rebet (Fr.). REBEC.

Rebhuhn [Rephuhn], **Paul** (*b* Waidhofen, *c*1500; *d* Oelsnitz, after 10 May 1546). German teacher, dramatist and composer. Although details of his formal education have not been established with certainty, he is known to have been active in Zwickau from about 1526 to 1529 as a singer and teacher in the Latin school. After serving as Rektor in the school at Kahla, he returned to Zwickau in 1535 and became Konrektor. On the recommendation of Luther in 1542, he was made superintendent of the parishes in the vicinity of Oelsnitz. Rebhuhn was among the vanguard of German writers who used the current Latin school dramas as a prototype and converted them into the vernacular. His German biblical play *Susanna* (1536, published Wittenberg, 1537) contains his own two-voice choruses which were sung to conclude four of the five acts of the play. He also composed eight bicinia with German and Latin texts published by Rhau in his *Secundus tomus biciniorum* (Wittenberg, 1545).

BIBLIOGRAPHY
R. von Liliencron: 'Die Chorgesänge des lateinisch-deutschen Schuldramas im XVI. Jahrhundert', *VMw*, vi (1890), 321, 364 [incl. music from *Susanna*]
W. Thoene: 'Rebhuhn, Paul', *MGG*

CLEMENT A. MILLER

Rebikov, Vladimir Ivanovich (*b* Krasnoyarsk, Siberia, 31 May 1866; *d* Yalta, 4 Aug 1920). Russian composer. He studied with Klenovsky at the Moscow Conservatory and in Berlin. From 1894 to 1898 he lived in Odessa, and thereafter in Kishinev; he founded branches of the Society of Russian Composers in both cities. Then, after a long period in Berlin and Vienna, he took up residence in Moscow (1901–19), appearing as a pianist at home and abroad. His early compositions are in a Tchaikovskian style, but around 1900 he began to be much more experimental. His use of whole-tone harmony earned him a reputation as the finest Russian impressionist, and he also became known as the father of Russian modernism. His most adventurous and cele-brated (though seldom heard) pieces are the 'musico-psycholographic dramas' and the 'mélomimiques' for voice and piano; these are small-scale works in an ex-pressionist style. In the larger stage pieces this manner is combined with the continuing influence of Tchaikovsky, and there is a similar effort at psych-ological probing in some of the piano compositions; *Aspirer et attendre*, for instance, is sub-titled 'tableau musical-psychologique'.

WORKS
(selective list)

STAGE
V grosu [In the storm] (opera, 2, after W. G. Korolenko), 1893; Odessa, 1894
Yolka [The Christmas tree] (fairy play, 1, after Dostoyevsky, Andersen and Hauptmann), 1902; Moscow, 30 Oct 1903
Dramatized Fables (9 pts., I. A. Krilov), 1902
Besdna [The abyss] (musico-psychologographic drama, L. Andreyev), 1907
Thea (A. P. Vorotnikov), 1907
Snow-white (opera); Tbilisi, 1909
Zheneshchina s kinzhalom [The woman with the dagger] (musico-psychologographic drama, after Schnitzler), 1911
Alfa i omega [Alpha and omega] (musico-psychologographic drama, Rebikov), 1911
Narcissus (opera, after Ovid), 1913
Prince Charming and Princess Beautiful (fairy opera)
The Gentry's Nest, op.55 (musico-psychologographic drama, Andreyev)

OTHER WORKS
Pf: Rêveries d'automne, op.8, 1897; Aspirer et attendre, op.25; Chansons blanches, op.48; Les danses, op.51; other pieces

Vocal: Mélomimiques, v, pf, opp.11, 15 and 17; other pieces
Orch suites, liturgical music, etc

BIBLIOGRAPHY
M. Montagu-Nathan: 'Rebikof', *Contemporary Russian Composers* (London, 1917)
A. Rowley: 'Rebikov', *MR*, iv (1943), 112
W. H. Dale: *A Study of the Musicopsychological Dramas of Vladimir Ivanovich Rebikov* (diss., U. of California, Los Angeles, 1955)

Rebillé, Philbert [Philibert]. *See* PHILBERT.

Rebop. *See* BOP.

Recapitulation (Ger. *Reprise*). The third and last main division of a movement in SONATA FORM, in which the thematic material introduced in the first section (the exposition), either in the tonic or in a contrasting key, is restated, normally all in the tonic.

Recercada (Sp.: 'study', 'ricercare'). A term used in Diego Ortiz's *Tratado de glosas* (1553) for 26 didactic pieces. The first four are for solo bass viol, another 14 take the form of counterpoints for viol above dance tenors played on the harpsichord, six are in the form of ornamentation to be played on a string instrument sim-ultaneously with an Arcadelt madrigal or Sandrin chan-son, and two consist of added fifth parts to be played simultaneously with the same four-part madrigal and chanson. None exploits imitation. *See* RICERCARE.

ROBERT STEVENSON

Recercar [recerchar, recerchare]. *See* RICERCARE.

Rech, Géza (*b* Vienna, 25 June 1910). Austrian stage director and musicologist. He studied German and musi-cology at Vienna University with Lach, Orel and Wellesz (1929–35) and took the doctorate in 1935 with a dissertation on the Viennese stage director Friedrich Strampfer. After serving as stage manager and producer at various German and Austrian theatres (1935–44) he was a programme director with Salzburg radio (1946–50). In 1950 he was appointed to the Salzburg Mozarteum to teach opera production and direction, and in 1964 he also began lecturing in drama and elocu-tion at Salzburg University. In 1950 he became editor of the *Mozart-Jahrbuch* and director of the musicology section of the Internationale Stiftung Mozarteum (gen-eral secretary 1968; professor of its Hochschule 1974). He has written numerous articles on exhibitions and Salzburg concerts.

WRITINGS
Friedrich Strampfer (diss., U. of Vienna, 1935)
'Das Mozart-Wohnhaus', *MJb 1951*, 131
Mozart: Lebensweg in Bildern (Munich, 1955)
'Aus dem Briefarchiv der Internationalen Stiftung Mozarteum', *Festschrift Otto Erich Deutsch* (Kassel, 1963), 159
Das Salzburger Mozart-Buch (Salzburg, 1964)
'Mozart auf dem Theater', *Liber amicorum Charles van den Borren* (Antwerp, 1964), 196
'Mozart: Ergebnisse der heutigen Erforschung seines Lebenswerkes', *Universitas*, xix (1964), 925; Eng. trans., *Universitas*, vii (1965), 645
'Bretzner kontra Mozart', *MJb 1968–70*, 186
'Die Bühnen von Mozarts Wiener Opern-Uraufführungen', *Musik und Verlag: Karl Vötterle zum 65. Geburtstag* (Kassel, 1968), 488
'Die Bibliotheca Mozartiana der Internationalen Stiftung Mozarteum', *ÖMz*, xxiv (1969), 641
'Ludwig Alois Friedrich Ritter von Köchel', *Symbolae historiae musicae: Hellmut Federhofer zum 60. Geburtstag* (Mainz, 1971), 260
'Böhm und Schikaneder: zwei Salzburger Theaterimpresarios der Mozartzeit', *Festschrift Walter Senn* (Munich and Salzburg, 1975), 188
'Die Mozart-Opern vor und bei den Festspielen in Salzburg', *Erich Valentin zum 70. Geburtstag* (Munich, 1976)

with R. Thomasberger: *Salzburger Szenenbilder* (Salzburg, 1977)

RUDOLF KLEIN

Recherché (Fr.: 'sought out'). An adjective equivalent to the Italian *ricercato* (from RICERCARE), generally used of a learned fugal style. Beethoven's *Grosse Fuge* op.133 is entitled in the first edition *Grande fugue tantôt libre, tantôt recherchée.*

Récit (Fr.). (1) A generic term used in France during the 17th and 18th centuries which designated either fragments or entire compositions for solo voice or instrument. In the 17th century it was generally restricted to music 'sung by one solo voice and above all by a soprano' (A. Furetière: *Dictionnaire universel,* 1691 edn.). In the 18th century the meaning was extended to embrace solo instrumental sections in larger works: references to a *récit de violon* or to a *récit de flûte* are common. The terms *récit* and 'recitative' are therefore not synonymous. All recitatives are a type of *récit,* but not all *récits* are recitatives. The *récit* may be a solo passage of a few bars' duration or, in the case of some of the *grands motets* of Lalande, a highly developed concert aria (see, for example, 'Amplius lava me' from his *Miserere mei*).

Récit had a more specialized meaning in the 17th-century *ballet de cour*. At first declaimed and after 1605 generally sung by a solo voice, a *récit* was usually placed at the beginning of each act of the ballet and served as commentary.

(2) One of the four manuals normally found on the French classical organ. Like the echo manual it had a compass of two to three octaves and was used for solo stops (Cornet, Flûte, Hautbois, Trompette). It first appeared in the early 17th century on organs in churches in Normandy and the Ile de France.

JAMES R. ANTHONY

Recital. A term used in the 16th century to define a speech or a narrative account; it was transferred to musical terminology in the 19th century and has come to mean a concert given by one performer or a small number of performers. Liszt was the first to popularize the term, in respect of his solo performances, when an advertisement for his appearance in the Hanover Square Rooms, London, on 9 June 1840, read: 'M. Liszt will give Recitals on the Pianoforte of the following pieces'. Although a recital might be thought primarily to imply performance by one executant (e.g. piano recital, organ recital), or by a soloist with accompanist (e.g. song recital, violin recital), the term is used flexibly to indicate almost any kind of small-scale concert.

See also CONCERT (ii).

PERCY M. YOUNG

Recitative (Fr. *récitatif*; Ger. *Rezitativ*; It. *recitativo*). A type of vocal writing, normally for a single voice, which follows closely the natural rhythm and accentuation of speech, without necessarily being governed by a regular tempo or organized in a specific form.

1. Early use to *c*1650. 2. Late 17th- and 18th-century conventions. 3. Germany, England and France. 4. Performance and accompaniment. 5. 19th and 20th centuries. 6. Instrumental recitative.

1. EARLY USE TO *c*1650. *Recitativo* is properly an adjective. As a noun, short for *stile recitativo*, it occurs as early as 1626 (Domenico Mazzocchi, *La catena d'Adone*). It derives from the verb *recitare*, 'to recite',

which was also used in the 16th century for vocal performance, for example in Baldassare Castiglione's *Il libro del cortegiano* (1528), where the phrase 'cantare alla viola per recitare' occurs. The development of music in speech-rhythm was closely associated with the Camerata in Florence at the end of the 16th century, but recitative would certainly have arrived even without the stimulus of opera, for which it was essential. Indeed a kind of recitative, in the form of plainchant, had already existed for centuries in the church, and in liturgical drama and Passion settings this performed a function not unlike that of recitative in secular opera. Recitative differs from plainchant mainly in its precise rhythmic notation, its harmonic support, its wide melodic range and its affective treatment of the words.

The new style of word-setting was not initially known as recitative, though this is implied by Agazzari (*Del sonare sopra'l basso*, 1607) in his reference to 'lo stile moderno di cantar recitativo', and by Gagliano in the preface to *La Dafne* (1608), where he spoke of the 'artifiziosa maniera di recitare cantando'. This style of writing was originally known as *stile rappresentativo*. Monteverdi described two *lettere amorose* in his seventh book of madrigals (1619), which are in the simplest form of recitative, as 'in genere rappresentativo', and added: 'si canta senza battuta' ('to be sung without a beat'). Freedom of interpretation was characteristic of all early 17th-century monody, apart from those pieces that were clearly in a regular rhythm, for example some of the arias in Caccini's *Le nuove musiche* (1601/2). In the preface to that work Caccini claimed to have introduced a style in which one might be said to speak in music ('in armonia favellare'), employing a certain 'sprezzatura di canto' ('a studied negligence in singing'). Peri made a similar claim in the preface to his opera *Euridice* (published in 1600).

Apart from the fact that recitative tended to use a static bass, its harmonic structure in the early 17th century was derived from the madrigal and was marked by similar cadential points. It also borrowed from the madrigal the use of chromaticism, modified, however, by the fact that changes of harmony could take place over a stationary bass. In Monteverdi's music *sprezzatura* often takes the form of anticipation: the voice moves, creating a dissonance, before the accompanying harmony changes to accommodate it (see ex.1, from Act 4 of Monteverdi's *Orfeo*, 1607; the dissonant notes are indicated by asterisks). Although there was as a rule no regular formal organization, repetition of various kinds could be employed to provide coherence. Thus the shepherd's recitative at the opening of Act 1 of Monteverdi's *Orfeo* is in ternary form, while in Penelope's monologue in Act 1 of his *Il ritorno d'Ulisse* (1641) 'Torna, deh torna, Ulisse' serves as a kind of refrain. In Italian monodies of the early 17th century a recitative-like vocal line is frequently organized above a freely repeated sequence of long notes in the bass (*see* STROPHIC VARIATIONS). The result is a piece that combines the rhythmic and harmonic fluidity of recitative with the formal organization of an aria. The technique was frequently employed in opera, too, and such a passage as the prologue to Monteverdi's *Orfeo* (1607), in which the five stanzas are separated by instrumental ritornellos, serves as a reminder that in the early 17th century 'recitative' and 'aria' were by no means exclusive, either as terms or as musical styles. In his opera *La catena d'Adone* (1626) Mazzocchi even used the designation 'aria recitativa di sei parti' ('a six-stanza aria in recitative style').

Ex.1

2. LATE 17TH- AND 18TH-CENTURY CONVENTIONS. In the 17th century the aria became more and more the dominant element in opera, partly through the influence of the solo cantata and partly as the result of the opening of public theatres in Venice from 1637 onwards. By the 18th century, consequently, recitative came to be mainly a vehicle for dialogue and dramatic action and in many cases merely a connecting link between arias. In the earliest operas and cantatas the voice and accompaniment always end together, as in the madrigal. The practice of cutting off the voice before the cadence and leaving the accompaniment to complete the progression seems to have arisen in recitatives of a pathetic character, where the singer was so overcome with emotion that he could not continue; there are examples in Michelangelo Rossi's *Erminia sul Giordano* (1633), Cavalli's *Didone* (1641) and Monteverdi's *L'incoronazione di Poppea* (1642). This soon became a convention applied to all recitative. It also became customary for the singer to add an appoggiatura to his final note or notes, not only at the final cadence but at appropriate intermediate points. In his *Anleitung zur Singekunst* (1757, an enlarged German version of Tosi's *Opinioni de' cantori antichi e moderni*) J. F. Agricola gave examples to show how this was done (ex.2).

Ex.2

(a)

(b)

At a later period it became customary to delay the two final chords in the accompaniment until the singer had finished. In the chapter on recitative in his *Versuch über die wahre Art, das Clavier zu spielen*, ii (1762), C. P. E. Bach printed his example in this form, with a rest under the singer's final notes. Telemann (*Singe-, Spiel- und Generalbassübungen*, 1733–4) said that such delay was usual in his time in cantatas (presumably church cantatas), but he also said that in opera the cadence should coincide with the singer's final syllables. Heinichen (*Der General-Bass in der Composition*, 1728) approved of this, at least in intermediate cadences, on the grounds that delay in playing the chords would hold up the action. A clash with the voice part can be avoided by using 4–3 harmony in the penultimate chord; for instance, the cadence shown at ex.2a can be harmonized as in ex.3. Examples of this treatment of the cadence are

Ex.3

[4   #3]

sometimes actually written out in early 18th-century scores where the accompaniment is for orchestra. Where the orchestra has elaborate figuration, postponement of the final chords is in any case impossible. Bach normally placed the chords after the singer's final notes, which agrees with what Telemann said about cantatas.

One of the functions of 18th-century recitative was to modulate from one key to another in readiness for the next aria; for instance, the first recitative in Act 1 scene ii of Handel's *Serse* (1738) is only nine bars long but it begins in D major and ends in E♭ major. Diminished 7th chords are often used as a means of transition. A change of mood, or a change of speaker, is often marked by the use of the so-called 'interrupted' cadence, ending on a 6-3 chord, as in Act 2 scene vii of the same work (ex.4). Ex.4 also illustrates other conventions of 18th-century recitative. Among these are the cadential for-

Ex.4

mulae in the voice part which almost invariably accompany the completion of a statement in the text – either the falling 4th, as at 'scri-ven-do', or the 4–3–(2)–1 descent (often, though not in this case, preceded by the sixth degree of the scale), as at 'mostro or-ren-do'. This extract also serves to show how the carefully notated rhythmic declamation of early 17th-century recitative (see ex.1) has been replaced by a more rapid and even delivery, notated almost entirely in quavers with occasional crotchets and semiquavers. This trend was developed still further in opera buffa of the late 18th century, until with Mozart a few chords may serve to support a lengthy passage of dialogue, notated (though not necessarily declaimed) in an unbroken string of semiquavers.

While the tendency after about 1650 was towards an ever sharper differentiation between recitative and aria, new ways were frequently sought to link the two more closely. Towards the end of the 17th century the practice arose of beginning a recitative with a 6-3 chord, no doubt to preserve continuity with the preceding aria or, in the case of an initial recitative, to convey the impression of a continuing narrative or dialogue. Recitative could be introduced in the course of an aria for dramatic or poetic effect; a well-known example occurs in 'V'adoro, pupille' in Act 2 of Handel's Giulio Cesare (1724). Conversely, lyricism continued to intrude into recitative in the form of ARIOSO passages.

By its very nature, recitative is designed primarily for solo singing. Examples of recitative in two (rarely more) parts are not uncommon in late 17th- and 18th-century opera, but they are confined to very brief passages in which both characters sing the same words. In a similar way choral recitative is employed for turba interjections in Passion settings, a particularly famous example being the cry 'Barrabam' in Bach's St Matthew Passion.

3. GERMANY, ENGLAND AND FRANCE. Although recitative was a form designed for and ideally suited to the Italian language, it could obviously be adapted to other languages that had a tonic accent, even if, as in English, the vowel-sounds were poor by comparison. Both in Germany and in England the term stile recitativo was known in the early years of the 17th century, but circumstances were for some time against the direct imitation of Italian models. German opera was not established until the later years of the 17th century. Schütz may well have employed a style similar to Monteverdi's in his opera Dafne (1627), but this can only be conjecture since the music is lost. He certainly used recitative in his sacred music, for example in Die sieben Wortte unsers lieben Erlösers (1645), and chorally in the earlier Psalmen Davids (1619), in the preface to which he spoke of 'stylo recitativo' as 'almost unknown in Germany at present'. It was not until the beginning of the 18th century that recitative, under the influence of Erdmann Neumeister, was introduced into the church cantata by Johann Philipp Krieger, whose example was followed by Bach and others. Bach's recitatives, though perfectly geared to the German language, are basically an adaptation of the idioms of Italian opera; and there is no difference in style between his use of it in his sacred and his secular works.

In England monody had its adherents early in the 17th century, particularly in the masque; but though Ben Jonson stated that the music of his Lovers Made Men (1617) was 'sung after the Italian manner, stylo recitativo' by Nicholas Lanier, who wrote it, it is not until Lanier's Hero and Leander (c1630) that the first unequivocal use of recitative is found in English music. The style of the English compositions is, in any case, nearer to arioso than to recitative in the Italian sense, and this is true even of Purcell's music. Italian recitative was a complete novelty to most people when it arrived in England at the beginning of the 18th century. Addison (Spectator, no.29) observed that 'there is nothing that has more startled our English Audience, than the Italian Recitativo at its first Entrance upon the Stage. People were wonderfully surprized to hear Generals singing the Word of Command, and Ladies delivering Messages in Musick.' There is a delicate irony in the prologue to Gay's The Beggar's Opera (1728), when the Beggar says: 'I hope I may be forgiven, that I have not made my Opera throughout unnatural, like those in vogue: for I have no Recitative.' In spite of this Handel had by that time made London audiences thoroughly familiar with Italian recitative and successfully applied the same principles to English.

In France there was resistance, almost from the first, to Italian influence. Saint-Evremond (Sur les opéra) remarked that when Luigi Rossi's Orfeo was performed in Paris in 1647 'the recitative was found to be very boring – so much so that even the Italians were impatient for the attractive parts [les beaux endroits – the arias], which they thought came only too rarely'. Apart from this the character of the French language led inevitably to a type of recitative that was radically different from the Italian form. Its roots lay in the 16th-century musique mesurée (see VERS MESURÉS) and the RÉCIT of the ballet de cour. It tended to avoid the declamatory character of Italian recitative in favour of a more flowing melodic style and achieved both continuity and flexibility by frequent change of time signature. It remained a characteristic form throughout the 17th and 18th centuries.

4. PERFORMANCE AND ACCOMPANIMENT. Though the early 17th-century recitative in Italy was based on speech-rhythm it did not exclude ornamentation, which it had inherited from the madrigal. Examples of such ornamentation are to be found before the end of the 16th century in the solo madrigals Dalle più alte sfere and Io che dal ciel cader from the Florentine intermedi of 1589. The first of these was sung by Vittoria Archilei, who was praised by Peri in the preface to Euridice for her ability to improvise graces that could not be written down. Gagliano, in the preface to La Dafne (1608), approved of ornamentation but urged moderation: it should be used only at the proper time and in the proper place. Monteverdi, in Orfeo, actually provided an ornamented version of Orpheus's scena 'Possente spirto'. In the published text (1638) of Il combattimento di Tancredi e Clorinda (1624) he particularly asked that there should be no ornamentation except at the one place ('Notte che nel profond'oscuro') which he specified. Once recitative had become a series of melodic formulae designed to expedite the drama, improvised ornamentation, apart from appoggiaturas, was out of place, though composers sometimes wrote elaborate passages for dramatic effect. Most later writers on the subject were against it, though there is evidence that some singers used it.

The speed at which recitative was sung depended entirely on the expression. P. F. Tosi, writing about *opera seria*, said that singers should learn 'a certain natural Imitation, which cannot be beautiful, if not expressed with that Decorum with which Princes speak, or those who know how to speak to Princes' (*Opinioni*; Eng. trans., 2/1743). On the other hand Grimm (*Encyclopédie*, xii, 1763, 'Poème lyrique') regarded recitative as the medium for ordinary conversation. These views are not easily reconciled, because neither takes into account the context of a recitative or the type of work in which it occurs.

Jean-Jacques Rousseau, who admired Italian recitative, disapproved of the French form. As an experiment he wrote the play *Pygmalion* (1770), called a *scène lyrique*, in which spoken words alternated with instrumental music by a Lyons amateur, Horace Coignet. Among those who followed his example was Georg Benda in Germany. When Mozart heard Benda's *Medea*, called a *duodrama*, at Mannheim in 1778 he was full of enthusiasm and thought the method preferable to recitative, except where music was essential for the expression of the words. He actually accepted a commission to compose a *duodrama* himself, but there is no trace of the work, though examples of spoken words with instrumental music survive in *Zaide* (1780), where he used the term 'melologo'. Spoken words have been used in this way in 19th- and 20th-century operas, but rarely with any success.

In *Orfeo* Monteverdi prescribed three keyboard instruments for the continuo – harpsichord, organ and regal – in addition to plucked string instruments. With the development of opera as a public spectacle, variety of this kind was impractical. The harpsichord became the standard instrument in secular music, while in church the organ was used; there is no evidence for the general use of the harpsichord in Bach's cantatas and Passions, though he seems to have used it either with or instead of the organ in at least one performance of the *St John Passion*. Recitative accompanied only by the continuo was known as *recitativo semplice* (in France *récitatif simple*); it was not until the 19th century that it was called *secco* (dry). The function of the keyboard instrument was simply to support the voice. The chords might be arpeggiated, and this, as Quantz pointed out (*Versuch einer Anweisung die Flöte traversiere zu spielen*, 1752), would help the singer to find his notes. But C. P. E. Bach emphasized that there is no time for arpeggios in rapid declamation. The accompanist's response to the singer must be prompt: 'if one must make a choice between two evils, it is better to hurry than to drag'. On the organ chords were not arpeggiated, and according to G. H. J. Hahn (*Der . . . General-Bass-Schüler*, 1751) and C. P. E. Bach (*Versuch*, ii, 1762) the player should, after a chord is struck, raise his right hand and rest until the next chord is reached. Other theorists leave the matter to the player's discretion. In the scores of his Passion settings J. S. Bach notated the recitatives in the normal way, with long held notes in the bass, but in the continuo parts of the *St Matthew Passion* he wrote short notes separated by rests.

Until the last two decades of the 17th century there were relatively few examples of recitative accompanied by instruments other than continuo. However, the frequently repeated assertion that *recitativo accompagnato*, as it came to be called, originated with Alessandro Scarlatti's *Olimpia vendicata* (1685) is probably based on a misunderstanding of a passage in E. J. Dent's *Alessandro Scarlatti: his Life and Works* (1905). Even

if the examples in Monteverdi's *Orfeo* ('Possente spirto', Act 3) and *Il combattimento di Tancredi e Clorinda* ('Amico hai vinto') are discounted as being closer to aria than to recitative, there are still enough instances by Cavalli (*L'Ormindo*, 1644; *Il Giasone*, 1649), Cesti (*La Dori*, 1661; *Il pomo d'oro*, 1667), Lully (*Les saisons*, 1661, etc), Steffani (*Servio Tullio*, 1685) and others to show that accompanied recitative was fairly consistently, if not frequently, used throughout the 17th century in stage works. In most contexts it accompanied scenes of grief or death, but Purcell used strings for the witches' scene in Act 1 of *Dido and Aeneas* (1689) to evoke the supernatural, just as in a more expensive production another composer might have used trombones.

Accompanied recitative had a special role to play in settings of the Passion story. Thomas Selle used various combinations of instruments in an attempt at musical characterization in his *St John Passion* (1643), and both Johann Sebastiani and Johann Thiele used string accompaniment for the recitatives in their settings of the *St Matthew Passion* (1672 and 1673 respectively). The convention, however, was to surround the words of Jesus with a 'halo' of string sound, while those of the Evangelist and the minor characters were set to *recitativo semplice*. The convention dates at least from Schütz's *Die sieben Wortte unsers lieben Erlösers* (1645) and is observed in Passion settings by Alessandro Scarlatti (c1680), Johann Meder (c1700), J. S. Bach (1729) and others. Bach's *St John Passion* (1723) is somewhat unusual in accompanying the words of Jesus with continuo only.

The generic term for recitative with orchestral accompaniment was *recitativo accompagnato* or simply *accompagnato* (in France *récitatif accompagné*); the term *stromentato* is also found. The extent to which it could be employed was limited, especially in stage works, by the fact that the presence of instruments inevitably imposed a slower speed of delivery on the singer. The example in Scarlatti's *Olimpia vendicata* is typical of the period in being associated with sleep, where a leisurely delivery is appropriate. In his later operas he employed a more elaborate kind of accompaniment (sometimes known as *recitativo obbligato* or *récitatif obligé*), in which the orchestra has independent passages of a violent or pathetic character. Recitative of this kind was quickly adopted by other composers and became as indispensable a part of *opera seria* as the da capo aria. It is found not only in opera but also in the cantata. A particularly remarkable example is the bass recitative 'Ja! ja! die Stunden sind nunmehro nah' in Bach's secular cantata *Der zufriedengestellte Äolus* ('Zerreisset, zersprenget, zertrümmert die Gruft', BWV205), where the singer is accompanied by the full orchestra, including two horns, three trumpets and timpani, with wild excursions on the woodwind and strings. In recitatives of this kind the singer had only a limited freedom, since there were passages where he was bound to keep in time with the orchestra, though there were others where he was more or less independent. Metastasio was well aware of the dramatic function of *recitativo obbligato*. In a letter to Hasse, dated 1749 and published in his posthumous works, he set out in detail how a scene in *Attilio Regolo* was to be set – where the instruments should accompany, where they should be silent, where they should have ritornellos. In *Orfeo ed Euridice* (1762) Gluck, in accordance with his and

Calzabigi's reform principles, accompanied all the recitatives with orchestra, mostly in a simple and straightforward style. He reverted to continuo accompaniment for some of the recitatives in *Alceste* (1767) but abandoned it in the French version (1776), and in the operas written for Paris (1774–9) the orchestra accompanies throughout.

5. 19TH AND 20TH CENTURIES. The old *recitativo semplice* with keyboard accompaniment survived in Italy until the early years of the 19th century, but its days were numbered; Rossini abandoned it in *Elisabetta, regina d'Inghilterra* (1815), though it reappears in *Il barbiere di Siviglia* (1816), an *opera buffa*. Even when recitative with keyboard accompaniment finally disappeared there was still a distinction between two types, though both were accompanied by the orchestra. One was the *recitativo obbligato* as practised in the previous century; the other might be called *recitativo semplice* with orchestra, where the accompaniment consisted of a few detached and isolated chords. In this latter type, as in 18th-century recitative with harpsichord, the voices were often left without accompaniment for several bars on end; there are many examples in Verdi, for instance the scene between Violetta, Annina and the doctor in the last act of *La traviata* (1853).

Continuo accompaniment was still necessary, however, for the performance of old operas, and this was often supplied by a solo cello, or cello and double bass, without keyboard. The practice was not new; J. A. Scheibe referred to it in connection with the cantata in his *Critischer Musikus* (2/1745), and there is further evidence of its use during the 18th century in Italy, England and France. The *Méthode de violoncelle et de basse d'accompagnement* (1804), written for the Paris Conservatoire by Jean Henri Levasseur, Charles-Simon Catel and Charles-Nicholas Baudiot, and edited by Pierre Baillot, gives instructions for performance: the accompaniment is to be simple and to consist of spread chords. In London Robert Lindley (1776–1855), for many years associated with the double bass player Domenico Dragonetti (1763–1846), was famous for his accompaniments to recitatives, which seem sometimes to have been more elaborate than was strictly justified. It is difficult to say when this practice was abandoned; J. W. von Wasielewski (*Das Violoncell und seine Geschichte*, 1889) mentioned having heard it in Italy as late as 1873. In the 20th century, recitative has sometimes been accompanied by a fully written-out keyboard part, for example for piano in Britten's *The Rape of Lucretia* (1946), and for harpsichord in Stravinsky's *The Rake's Progress* (1951).

A reaction against spoken dialogue in the Singspiel and *opéra comique* led to the addition of recitatives for such works by other composers; examples include Berlioz's recitatives for Weber's *Der Freischütz* and Guiraud's for Bizet's *Carmen*. Gounod himself turned his *Faust* into an opera sung throughout. With the growth of continuous texture in opera in the later 19th century, recitative as an independent form disappeared, except where it was artificially revived. But since there are many passages in a libretto which cannot be set in a lyrical form it remained, though integrated with its context, an essential means of expression. This is true not only of Italian opera but of works by Wagner, Strauss (e.g. the prelude to the second version of *Ariadne auf Naxos*, 1916) and later composers in various countries.

The principles of recitative were also adapted to a continuous setting by Musorgsky and Debussy, each in an idiom dictated by the language. In his *Pierrot lunaire* (1912) Schoenberg introduced a new kind of recitative known as Sprechstimme or SPRECHGESANG which, as its name implies, lies somewhere between speech and song, and is interpreted precisely as regards rhythm but only approximately as regards pitch. Far from being an attempt at a more 'natural' method of declamation than straightforward recitative, Sprechgesang is a highly artificial one, entirely appropriate both to the German language and to the dreamlike or nightmarish situations associated with expressionism. It was soon admitted into opera, notably by Berg (*Wozzeck*, 1917–21; *Lulu*, 1929–34) and by Schoenberg himself (*Moses und Aron*, 1930–51).

6. INSTRUMENTAL RECITATIVE. Recitative-like passages have often been used in instrumental music for special expressive or dramatic effect. Among the earliest examples are those in Kuhnau's *Biblische Historien* (1700). Bonporti wrote a much-ornamented recitative for solo violin in no.5 of his *Concerti a quattro* op.11 (*c*1727), but a more direct imitation is to be found in the works of later composers. Examples include the first of C. P. E. Bach's 'Prussian' Sonatas (1742), Haydn's Symphony no.7 ('Le midi', 1761) and Sinfonia concertante HI:105 (1792), Mozart's Violin Concerto no.3 K216 (1775) and Beethoven's piano sonatas op.31 no.2 (1802) and op.110 (1821). The passage for cellos and basses in the finale of Beethoven's Choral Symphony is marked 'selon le caractère d'un Récitatif, mais in tempo'. Schoenberg's Variations on a Recitative for organ op.40 (1941) explores possibilities that other composers seem to have ignored.

BIBLIOGRAPHY

J. R. Ahle: *Kurze doch deutliche Anleitung zu der lieblich- und loblichen Singekunst* (Mühlhausen, 1690, enlarged 2/1704)

J.-L. le Gallois: *Traité du récitatif* (Paris, 1707, rev. 2/1740)

J. A. Scheibe: 'Abhandlung über das Rezitativ', *Bibliothek der schönen Wissenschaften und der freien Künste*, xi (1764), 209; xii (1765), 217

J.-J. Rousseau: 'Récitatif', *Encyclopédie, ou Dictionnaire raisonné des sciences, des arts, et des métiers*, xiii (Paris, 1765)

——: 'Récitatif accompagné', 'Récitatif mesuré', *Supplément à l'Encyclopédie*, iv (Amsterdam, 1777)

G. J. Vogler: 'Praktische Abhandlung vom Accent im Recitative', *Betrachtungen der Mannheimer Tonschule*, i (Mannheim, 1778/*R*1974)

J. K. F. Rellstab: *Versuch über die Vereinigung der musikalischen und oratorischen Deklamation* (Berlin, 1786)

A. Heuss: 'Bachs Rezitativ-Behandlung', *BJb*, i (1904), 82

B. Zeller: *Das 'Recitativo accompagnato' in den Opern J. A. Hasses* (diss., U. of Halle, 1911)

E. Schmitz: *Geschichte der weltlichen Solokantate* (Leipzig, 1914, rev. 2/1955)

M. Schneider: 'Die Begleitung des Secco-Rezitativs um 1750', *Gluck-Jb*, iii (1917), 88

R. Meyer: 'Die Behandlung des Rezitativs in Glucks italienischen Reformopern', *Gluck-Jb*, iv (1918), 1

C. Spitz: 'Die Entwicklung des *Stile Recitativo*', *AMw*, iii (1921), 237

P. Mies: 'Über die Behandlung der Frage im 17. und 18. Jahrhundert', *ZMw*, iv (1921–2), 286

R. Gerber: *Das Passionsrezitativ bei Heinrich Schütz und seine stilgeschichtlichen Grundlagen* (Gütersloh, 1929)

E. Borrel: 'L'interprétation de l'ancien récitatif français', *RdM*, xii (1931), 13

L. Spinner: *Das Rezitativ in der romantischen Oper bis Wagner* (diss., U. of Vienna, 1931)

S. Wilson: 'The Recitatives of the St Matthew Passion', *ML*, xvi (1935), 208

F. Graupner: *Die Rezitative des Evangelisten in der Matthäuspassion von J. S. Bach* (Greifswald, 1947)

A. Mendel: 'On the Keyboard Accompaniments to Bach's Leipzig Church Music', *MQ*, xxxvi (1950), 339

J. A. Westrup: 'The Continuo in the *St Matthew Passion*', *Bach-*

Gedenkschrift (Zurich, 1950), 103

E. Jammers: 'Zum Rezitativ im Volkslied und Choral', *Jb für Volksliedforschung*, viii (1951), 86

S. T. Worsthorne: *Venetian Opera in the Seventeenth Century* (Oxford, 1954/*R*1968)

A. Melica: 'Del recitativo sinfonico', *Bollettino del centro rossiniano di studi*, ii (1956), 21

J. A. Westrup: 'The Nature of Recitative', *Proceedings of the British Academy*, xlii (1956), 27

H. Melchert: 'Das Rezitativ der Kirchenkantaten J. S. Bachs', *BJb*, xlv (1958), 5–83

E. O. D. Downes: 'Secco Recitative in Early Classical Opera Seria', *JAMS*, xiv (1961), 50

J. Chailley: 'La déclamation théâtrale aux XVIIe et XVIIIe siècles d'après les récitatifs', *Saggi e ricerche in memoria di Ettore Li Gotti*, i (Palermo, 1962), 355

F.-H. Neumann: *Die Ästhetik des Rezitativs* (Strasbourg and Baden-Baden, 1962)

J. A. Westrup: 'The Cadence in Baroque Recitative', *Natalicia musicologica Knud Jeppesen* (Copenhagen, 1962), 243

G. J. Skapski: *The Recitative in Johann Adolph Scheibe's Literary and Musical Work* (diss., U. of Texas, 1963)

J. A. Westrup: 'Rezitativ', *MGG*

H. C. Wolff: 'Die Sprechmelodie im alten Opernrezitativ', *HJb 1963*, 93–134

M. K. Phillips: *Recitative – Arioso: a Survey with Emphasis on Contemporary Opera* (diss., U. of California, Los Angeles, 1965)

F. Giegling: 'Zu den Rezitativen von Mozarts Oper *Titus*', *MJb 1967*, 121

H. VanderWerf: 'Recitative Melodies in Trouvère Chansons', *Festschrift für Walter Wiora* (Kassel, 1967), 231

W. M. Vos: *English Dramatic Recitative before ca. 1685* (diss., Washington U., St Louis, 1967)

S. H. Hansell: 'The Cadence in 18th-century Recitative', *MQ*, liv (1968), 228

P. Mies: *Das instrumentale Rezitativ* (Bonn, 1968)

R. Allorto: 'Il prologo dell'*Orfeo*: note sulla formazione del recitativo monteverdiano', *Congresso internazionale sul tema Claudio Monteverdi e il suo tempo: Venezia, Mantova e Cremona 1968*, 157

J. A. Westrup: 'The Continuo in Monteverdi', *Congresso internazionale sul tema Claudio Monteverdi e il suo tempo: Venezia, Mantova e Cremona 1968*, 497

H. Frederichs: 'Das Rezitativ in den *Hugenotten* Giacomo Meyerbeers', *Beiträge zur Geschichte der Oper*, ed. H. Becker (Regensburg, 1969)

S. Hermelink: 'Bemerkungen zu Bachs Rezitativ', *Musik und Kirche*, xxxix (1969), 98

W. Dean: *Handel and the Opera Seria* (London, 1970)

B. Kinsey: 'Performance Problems in Twentieth-century Recitative', *National Association of Teachers of Singing Bulletin*, xxvi/2 (1970), 26

K.-H. Viertel: 'Singend sprechen – zur Aufführungspraxis von Opern des 18. Jahrhunderts', *Musik und Gesellschaft*, xx (1970), 672

P. Williams: *Figured Bass Accompaniment* (Edinburgh, 1970)

K.-E. Eicke: 'Musik und Sprache: eine didaktische Orientierung am Beispiel des Rezitativs', *Musik und Bildung*, iii/2 (1971), 78

M. F. Robinson: *Naples and Neapolitan Opera* (Oxford, 1972)

H. Seifert: 'Das Instrumentalrezitativ von Barock bis zur Wiener Klassik', *De ratione in musica: Festschrift Erich Schenk* (Kassel, 1975), 103

A. Verchaly: 'A propos du récit françois au début du XVIIᵉ siècle', *RMFC*, xv (1975), 39

M. Ruhnke: 'Das italienische Rezitativ bei den deutschen Komponisten des Spätbarock', *AnMc*, no.17 (1976), 79–118

W. Dean: 'The Performance of Recitative in Late Baroque Opera', *ML*, lviii (1977), 389

M. Murata: 'The Recitative Soliloquy', *JAMS*, xxxii (1979), 45

JACK WESTRUP

Reciting note. The note on which most of a psalm verse is sung; *see* PLAINCHANT; PSALM; *see also* MODE.

Reckow, Fritz (*b* Bamberg, 29 March 1940). German musicologist. After practical musical training he studied musicology from 1959 at the universities of Erlangen, Freiburg and Basle with Eggebrecht, Stäblein, Hammerstein and Schrade. He took the doctorate at Freiburg in 1965 with an edition and interpretative study of the principles of organum purum. From 1965 he represented the Mainz Academy of Sciences and Literature at Freiburg in the preparation of the *Handwörterbuch der musikalischen Terminologie*, for which he has written many articles; in 1970 he was appointed lecturer in musicology at Freiburg. He specializes in music history of the Middle Ages and in musical aesthetics of the 18th–20th centuries, with special reference to the history and principles of musical terminology.

WRITINGS

Der Musiktraktat des Anonymus 4 (diss., U. of Freiburg, 1965; Wiesbaden, 1967)

'Proprietas und perfectio: zur Geschichte des Rhythmus, seiner Aufzeichnung und Terminologie im 13. Jahrhundert', *AcM*, xxxix (1967), 115

'Zu Wagners Begriff der unendlichen Melodie', *Das Drama Richard Wagners als musikalisches Kunstwerk*, ed. C. Dahlhaus (Regensburg, 1970), 81ff

'Aspeckte der Ausbildung einer lateinischen musikalischen Fachsprache im Mittelalter', *IMSCR*, xi *Copenhagen 1972*, ii, 612

Die Copula: über einige Zusammenhänge zwischen Setzweise, Formbildung, Rhythmus und Vortragsstil in der Mehrstimmigkeit von Notre-Dame (Wiesbaden, 1972)

'Das Organum', *Gattungen der Musik in Einzeldarstellungen: Gedenkschrift für Leo Schrade*, i (Berne and Munich, 1973), 434–96

'"Peripherie und Zentrum" aus der Perspective der mittelalterlichen Musiklehre', *GfMKB, Berlin 1974*

'Zwischen Metapher und Terminus: die "Tonsprache": "Sprachähnlichkeit" der Musik als terminologisches Problem', *Zur Terminologie der Musik des 20. Jahrhunderts*, ed. H. H. Eggebrecht (Stuttgart, 1974)

'Organum-Begriff und frühe Mehrstimmigkeit: zugleich ein Beitrag zur Bedeutung des "Instrumentalen" in der spätantiken und mittelalterlichen Musiktheorie', *Forum musicologicum*, i (1975), 31–167

'*Sprachähnlichkeit*' der Musik als terminologisches Problem: zur Geschichte des Topos Tonsprache (in preparation)

HANS HEINRICH EGGEBRECHT

Recorder [common flute, English flute] (Fr. *flûte à bec*, *flûte à neuf trous*, *flûte d'Angleterre*, *flûte douce*; Ger. *Blockflöte*, *Langsflöte*, *Schnabelflöte*; It. *flauto diretto*, *flauto dolce*). A woodwind instrument with seven finger-holes and a thumb-hole. It is the chief member of the class of fipple flutes, that is, flutes with a whistle mouth-piece. Its thumb-hole distinguishes it from most other fipple flutes. It figured significantly in the music of Purcell, Bach, Handel, Telemann and many of their contemporaries, and though it failed to be included in the standard orchestra as it developed in the 18th and 19th centuries it has a place in 20th-century music, even in the works of avant-garde composers.

See also ORGAN STOP.

1. The instrument. 2. History.

1. THE INSTRUMENT. The modern recorder is generally made in three jointed sections: the head, with a beak-shaped mouthpiece and cylindrical inner bore; the middle joint, with the thumb-hole and six of the finger-holes; this tapers from the head to the foot joint, which has the seventh finger-hole (fig.1a). The dimensions of the taper bore and the sizes and positions of the eight holes are critical in the recorder's construction, for they must give the instrument a chromatic compass of over two octaves. No less important are the proportions and voicing of the whistle mouthpiece. The main purpose of the thumb-hole is to assist in the production of the harmonics of the second octave (and higher notes), enabling them to be sounded clearly with only slightly increased breath pressure.

The 20th-century recorder follows the general design of the Baroque type in use towards the end of the 17th century and during the 18th. Before that recorders were generally made of a single piece of wood with near-cylindrical bore (figs.1b and 4b). Without the movable foot-joint a ninth hole was provided for a left-handed player's little finger, the hole not in use being stopped with a wax plug or wooden peg. This gave the instrument the name 'flûte à neuf trous'.

The derivation of the name recorder is uncertain. ('To record', in the sense of 'to sing like a bird' may well derive from the name of the instrument, and not the other way round.) The name is probably derived from the Latin *recordari*: to think over, call to mind, 'remember', or the Italian *ricordo*: a souvenir or memento. Trowell cited a reference in the household accounts of Henry, Earl of Derby (later King Henry IV), dated 1388 to payments 'i fistula nomine Ricordo' ('a pipe called a memento'); this is the earliest known reference to the instrument.

Recorders are made in different sizes, with compasses corresponding to different vocal ranges. Traditionally made of wood, sometimes ivory, the smaller members of the family are now often mass-produced in plastics, particularly for school use.

There are four main instruments in use today: the descant (known in the USA as the 'soprano'; lowest note c''); treble (in the USA 'alto'; lowest note f'), tenor (lowest note c') and bass (f). There are also sopranino (f'') and the great bass (c) instruments. The treble and tenor are written for as non-transposing instruments, but music for the sopranino, descant, bass and great bass is customarily written an octave below their sounding pitch. Besides these instruments in F and C there have been recorders in D: the 'sixth flute' (i.e. lowest note d'', a 6th above the treble) was written for by Woodcock, Baston and Babell, and an octave below was the 'alto' or 'voice flute' (d'). A recorder in B♭, a 4th above the treble, was known as the 'quart flute' or 'flûte du quatre'.

The variety of names in different languages used to denote the recorder at different periods of its history may be classified as follows: (*i*) The French *flûte à bec* and German *Schnabelflöte* derive from the instrument's beak-shaped mouthpiece.

(*ii*) From the 'fipple' or plug which almost closes the upper end of the tube to form the whistle mouthpiece comes the term 'fipple flute' (the generic term covering all whistle flutes, not only recorders); in German *Blockflöte*.

(*iii*) The recorder's characteristically sweet tone quality is alluded to in the Italian: *flauto dolce* and French *flûte douce*.

(*iv*) From the recorder's close association with England, and to distinguished it from the 'German' or transverse flute came the term 'English flute', or *flûte d'Angleterre*.

(*v*) La *flûte à neuf trous* (as explained above) during the 16th century.

(*vi*) The term 'flute' (*flûte, Flöte, flauto*) has sometimes been used as a generic term covering all kinds of transverse and fipple flutes, and in modern times it describes the transverse type rather than the recorder. Until the late 18th century, however, the recorder was known simply as the flute (*flauto*) or 'common flute' to distinguish it from the 'German' flute or *traversa*.

(*vii*) *Flauto diretto* (It.); *Langsflöte* (Ger.); *flety proste* (Pol.) derive from the fact that the recorder is held straight in front of the player.

The normal range of the Renaissance recorder was an octave and a 6th, although Ganassi indicated that a further octave might be possible on some instruments in the hands of expert players. The Baroque recorder could give two octaves and a note, a further 4th being asked

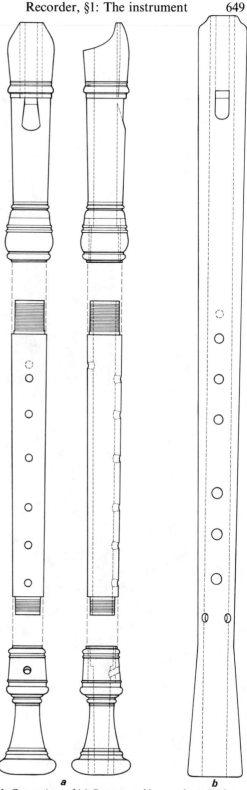

a   *b*

1. Comparison of (a) Baroque treble recorder in F (drawing after von Huene), and (b) Renaissance tenor recorder in C

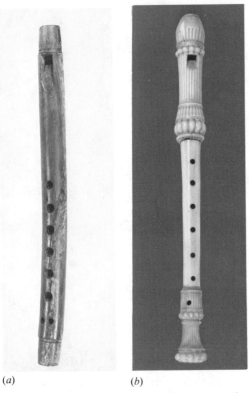

2. Woodcut from the title-page of Ganassi's 'Fontegara' (1535)

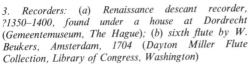

(a)   (b)

3. Recorders: (a) Renaissance descant recorder, ?1350–1400, found under a house at Dordrecht (Gemeentemuseum, The Hague); (b) sixth flute by W. Beukers, Amsterdam, 1704 (Dayton Miller Flute Collection, Library of Congress, Washington)

4. (b) One-piece recorder: detail of the painting 'Vanitas' (1664) by Jan Davidszoon de Heem the Elder, in the Musées Royaux des Beaux Arts, Brussels

4. (a) Renaissance recorder, lute, virginal and bass viol: painting, 'Le concert champêtre', Italian School, 16th century (Hôtel Lallemant, Bourges)

for in some virtuoso works. The modern recorder normally has the same compass, although avant-garde composers extend that range and write for 'chords' and other effects, some of them produced by covering and by closing the lower end of the recorder (see Vetter).

The chromatic range of two octaves and a note makes use of a system of cross-fingerings to give the semitones. This has proved so successful in the case of the recorder, with its relatively small holes and low breath pressure, that attempts to give it a key system (like that of other woodwind instruments) have never met with any success. The only key necessary in the case of the recorder is that for the lowest note of the bass and sometimes the tenor of the family. Double holes (two smaller holes bored side by side in place of one normal hole) are used to give the two lowest semitones where cross-fingering would not work. They are standard on modern recorders, but were first added to the instrument at the end of the 17th century, notably on some recorders by Bressan. Owing to its length the bass is generally fitted with a crook, a metal tube rather like the bocal of a bassoon, to take the player's breath to the head of the instrument (see figs.7 and 8 below).

2. HISTORY. The recorder probably had its origin as an art instrument in northern Italy during the 14th century and was certainly well established there by the beginning of the 16th century. The evidence is circumstantial: the first surviving recorder method, Ganassi's *Fontegara* was published in Venice in 1535 (see fig.2); Praetorius indicated that the great consort of recorders which he described in his *Syntagma musicum* could be bought in Venice for 80 thaler; and the largest number of surviving Renaissance recorders belonged to noble families of northern Italy.

The word 'recorder' appears in English literature in the 15th century in the lists of musical instruments which are a feature of some poems, such as the *Squyr of Lowe Degre* (c1400) and the Scottish *Buke of the Howlate* (c1450), as well as in the *Promptorium parvulorum*, the earliest English–Latin dictionary (1499/R1968), where the recorder is described as a 'lytyl pype' and translated by *canula*.

The evidence of painting and sculpture is sometimes deceptive. For example, the figure from a 12th-century psalter in Glasgow claimed by Galpin and others as a recorder player has more recently been shown to be a bagpiper. In many pictures it is difficult to tell whether the instrument shown is a true recorder or some kind of folk pipe (without thumb-hole). Towards the end of the 15th century and during the 16th century, paintings in which recorders can be seen are more frequent and the instruments themselves more clearly shown (see fig.4a).

Evidence of the recorder in the 16th century is more definite. The earliest surviving recorder is a descant made of elmwood, about 29 cm long, which was found under a 15th-century house at Dordrecht (see fig.3a). It is now in the Gemeentemuseum at The Hague, and is presumed to be at least as old as the house under which it was discovered. The Accademia Filarmonica of Verona owned many fine instruments and a list dated 1569 mentions a chest of 22 recorders and two incomplete chests. One at least of these, a great bass recorder, 2.85 metres long, is in the Biblioteca Capitolare, Verona. At Schloss Ambras near Innsbruck the Archduke of the Tyrol had a collection of musical instruments. An inventory dated 1596 mentions pipes

(*Pfeifen*) made in Germany, others from France and 'ain grosse Flaut per Concert, von Venedig erkauft' ('a large recorder for the consort bought from Venice'). A bass from this collection is now in the Kunsthistorisches Museum, Vienna. Other collections were those of the Correr family of Venice and of the Obizzi family at Catajo near Padua. Most of the recorders from Catajo (39) are now at Vienna.

These instruments, together with the writings of Virdung, Agricola, Ganassi, Jambe de Fer, Praetorius and Mersenne, help to build up a more complete picture

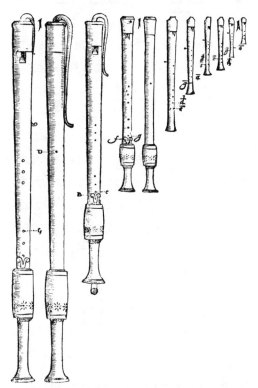

5. *The 'great consort' of recorders from 'Syntagma musicum', ii (2/1619), by Praetorius; (left to right) Grossbass (F), Bass (B♭), Basset (f), Tenor (c'), Alt (f'), Discants (c'', d'), Klein Flötlein (Exilent, g'') and gar klein Flötlein (with one thumb- and three finger-holes)*

of the Renaissance recorder. Virdung and Ganassi both wrote of three sizes: the *diskant* (lowest note g' – the instrument would now be called a treble, and is not the equivalent of the modern 'descant'), tenor (c') and bass (f). Agricola showed a quartet in his illustration but explained that for an alto part one would make use of an extra tenor recorder. Praetorius, describing the family of *Blockflöten* ('latinis Fistula, so von den Italianern Flauto, von den Engelendern Recordor genennet werden'), listed eight sizes (see fig.5): Exilent (g''), Discant (d'', c''), Alt (f'), Tenor (c'), Basset (f), Bass (B♭) and Grossbass (F). It is difficult to imagine all these instruments being played in consort together – the effect of the B♭ Bass playing by the side of the d'' Discant would be almost comparable to that of clarinets in A and B♭ playing together. However Mersenne divided recorders into two sets, *grand jeu* and *petit jeu*, the one beginning

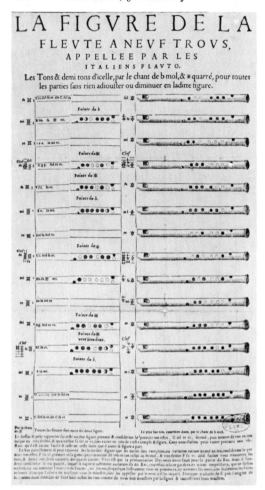

LA FIGVRE DE LA
FLEVTE A NEVF TROVS,
APPELLEE PAR LES
ITALIENS FLAVTO.

Les Tons & demi tons d'icelle, par le chant de b mol, & ♮ quarré, pour toutes les parties sans rien adiouster ou diminuer en ladite figure.

6. Fingering chart for the recorder from Jambe de Fer's 'Epitome musicale' (1556)

where the other leaves off. Praetorius indicated that any three adjacent recorders could be used together (e.g. $F,B\flat$, f; $B\flat,f,c'$;f,c',g'; or c',g',d''), the other two (c'' and g''), and the *gar klein Flötlein* serving as octave instruments.

In England Henry VIII was skilled in music and played the recorders, flute and virginals. His instruments were listed at the time of his death (1547), and among the virginals, regals, horns etc there were 72 flutes and 76 recorders, including 'one great base Recorder of woode in a case of woode' (see Galpin). Most of these recorders were in cases of four, six, seven, eight or nine instruments, undoubtedly made and tuned together for playing in consort. None of the instruments named in the inventory is known to have survived.

The Renaissance recorder was designed for playing in consort rather than as a solo instrument. Its wide, near-cylindrical bore favoured the fundamental sounds, and its range of an octave and a 6th was adequate for the part-music of the time. With a set of recorders tuned together by the maker, each instrument could be made from a single piece of wood. A movable head for tuning was unnecessary, and the ninth hole provided for the left-handed player. Composers generally wrote music without specifying its orchestration. Dance music published by Jacques Moderne (Lyons), Attaingnant (Paris),

Phalèse (Louvain and Antwerp) and Susato (Antwerp), and polyphonic works such as those in the manuscript *Liber Fridolini Sichery* at St Gall or the Regensburg manuscript of *Carmina germanica et gallica* are examples, although Attaingnant did mark some of his chansons with a letter to indicate that particular items were suitable for performance on flutes or on recorders. Susato's *Danserye* (1551) was described as 'zeer lustich ende bequaem om spelen op alle musicale Instrumenten' ('very pleasant and suitable to play on all kinds of musical instruments'). The collection of five-part pavans, galliards and other dances published in 1599 by Anthony Holborne were for 'Viols, Violins or other Musicall Winde Instruments'. Towards the end of this period flutes (i.e. recorders) were sometimes specified, such as the flute (probably a bass recorder: see Dart, 1947–8) part in Morley's *Consort Lessons* (1599), an anonymous 'Sonada a 3 Fiauti' with continuo (from Breslau, c1620), a 'Sonatella a 5 Flauti et Organo' by Antonio Bertali and a 'Sonata a 7 Flauti' by J. H. Schmelzer. There is a short four-part 'Gavote pour les Flustes douces' given by Mersenne as an example of writing for recorders. Morley's *Consort Lessons* and Rosseter's *Lessons for Consort* (1609) were scored for treble lute, bandora, cittern, bass viol, 'flute' and treble viol: three plucked instruments, two bowed and one wind; an example of the use of the recorder in the context of other instruments. Francis Bacon (*Sylva sylvarum*, London, 1627) remarked that 'the *Recorder* and *Stringed Musick* agree well'.

The writings of Virdung, Agricola, Ganassi, Jambe de Fer, Praetorius and Mersenne are consistent in their accounts of the playing technique of the time. Their tables of fingering vary a little in details but reveal the essentials of the system in use today (see fig.6). Ganassi's book gives examples of elaborate Renaissance ornamentation.

Der fluyten lust-hof (Amsterdam, 1654) is a collection of solo pieces and a few duets for *hand-fluyt* (descant in c'') by Jacob van Eyck, the blind carillon player of Utrecht, who also played the recorder in the churchyard to amuse the passers-by. Many of the pieces are variations on Elizabethan tunes, such as Dowland's *Lachrimae* (for solo recorder) and *Comagan* (the song *Come again*). They give evidence of a fluent technique. Where the tunes he gave vary from the originals, it may be assumed that the blind man picked them up by ear, made his own version where his memory failed him and dictated the whole to an amanuensis for publication.

At the French court of Louis XIV (reigned 1661–1715) music was highly organized: the chapel, the chamber music and the *grande écurie*, a large body of musicians administered by the Master of the Great Stables of the King. The *grande écurie* provided the players for ceremonial occasions and for the operas and other entertainments of Lully, and included some who were also skilled as instrument makers, notably members of the Hotteterre family. The Hotteterres were responsible for far-reaching improvements in the design of the oboe, transverse flute and recorder; these were made possible by the use of shorter sections of wood jointed together in place of the earlier one-piece construction. In the case of the recorder, a narrower tapering bore was the first step towards more refined tone and an extended compass. The shorter lengths of wood could be more accurately bored. The joints needed strengthening, which led to the use of ivory mounts. In fact elegance and sophistication were encouraged.

In England the recorder was little used during the Civil War and Commonwealth. But in 1674 Cambert, who had come to England two years before, was engaged to supervise the production of Crowne's masque *Calisto*, and for this brought over from France some oboe players, including Jacques (later James) Paisible. Paisible remained in England and became established as a player of the oboe and (later) the recorder. About 1683 his friend P.-J. Bressan, a French maker of flutes and recorders, also came and settled in England. In the following year John Carr wrote in the preface to his *The Delightful Companion*:

This Delightful Companion the Pipe Recorder hath been for a long time out of use, but now it's beginning to be in a greater repute than ever it was before, and indeed there is no music for so natural a voice. It admits of excellent harmony in consort of two or three parts . . .

About 20 years before this the flageolet had been a popular instrument. In 1661 Greeting's *Pleasant Companion* was published; among Greeting's friends and pupils were Samuel Pepys and his wife, both of whom played the flageolet about this time. In February 1668 Pepys went to see Massinger's *The Virgin Martyr* and was deeply affected by the 'wind-musique'. It is generally assumed that recorders must have played a leading part in this music, since Pepys wrote later that he resolved 'to practice wind musique' and visited the flute maker Drumbleby:

and there did talk a great deal about pipes; and did buy a recorder, which I do intend to learn to play on, the sound of it being of all sounds in the world, most pleasing to me.

In 1679 Hudgebut brought out his *Vade mecum*, in which he compared the recorder with the flageolet to the detriment of the latter; in 1681 John Banister (who had played the flageolet to Pepys in 1668) published his *Most Pleasant Companion* for the recorder; and in 1683 came Humphrey Salter's *The Genteel Companion*. From this it can be seen that the recorder gradually took the place of the flageolet as the amateur musician's favourite instrument.

About this time the recorder shared with the flageolet, as far as these little tune books were concerned, a system of 'dot notation' or TABLATURE, a 'ridiculous and troublesome way' as Pepys described it after he had bought his recorder. The instructions in the published tutors apply to the treble recorder and form the basis from which the technique of present-day recorder playing has developed.

In 1693 Hudgebut published a *Thesaurus musicus* which included a number of duets for treble recorders, but showed on its title-page a quartet of recorders, including the bass (see fig.7). Even though all the music published for the recorder at the end of the 17th century was for the treble, other members of the family were still in use. James Talbot's manuscript (*c*1687) not only gives detailed measurements of tenor and bass recorders made by Bressan, but lists the following 'flutes' (recorders) in relation to the treble (the notes in brackets are given in staff notation in the manuscript):

Fifth higher [*c*″]. Eighth higher [*f*″]. Voice, Third lower [*d*′]. Tenor 5th [sic] lower [*c*′]. Bass [*f*]. Double bass [*c*].

These correspond to the modern descant, sopranino, alto in D, tenor, bass and great bass. A magnificent quartet by Bressan is in the Grosvenor Museum at Chester – treble, alto, tenor and bass (fig.8; see Bridge). Also in that museum is an alto in E♭ by Bressan, and in Edgar Hunt's private collection is a 'fourth flute' in B♭, also by Bressan.

These instruments represent some of the finest work

of instrument makers of the period. They follow the pattern established by the Hotteterres in France by being made in three sections: head, middle and foot. With the adjustable foot-joint the duplicate hole of the *flûte à neuf trous* is no longer needed, although the keys of the tenor and bass retain their double touches. The outward design is more ornamental, with characteristic bulges at the joints and mouthpiece (for added strength as well as ornament), more elaborate turnings and a more pronounced foot. The voicing is exceptionally fine, and gives a full and mellow tone in the lower register, rising to clear, pure upper notes, without shrillness. The treble and alto of the Chester recorders have double holes for the two lowest semitones. The pitch of Bressan's recorders is *a*′ = 408: about three-quarters of a tone below modern pitch.

Bressan's most famous contemporaries in England were the Stanesbys, father and son. The elder Thomas Stanesby, who died in 1734, had been making flutes from about 1690 onwards; his son died in 1754. Hawkins wrote in his *History* of both the Stanesbys and Bressan, but criticized the intonation of the latter's recorders (a criticism not supported by surviving examples):

The flutes of the latter kind [à bec] of the younger Stanesby approach the nearest of any to perfection; but those of Bressan, though excellent in their tone, are all too flat in the upper octave.

Other leading makers of recorders included J. C. Denner of Nuremberg, J. H. Rottenburgh of Brussels, Rippert of Paris, R. Haka and W. Beukers of

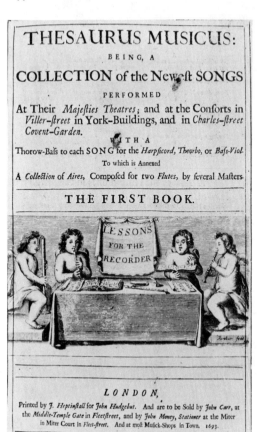

7. *Title-page of John Hudgebut's 'Thesaurus musicus'* (*1693*)

Amsterdam (see fig.3*b* above), and I. Heitz [Heytz] and later J. W. Oberlender of Berlin.

The chief composers for the recorder in England at this period were Daniel Purcell, James Paisible, Robert King, John Banister, Gottfried Finger, Raphael Courteville and William Croft. Their music took the form of duets for treble recorders and sonatas for one and two recorders and continuo.

The 'flute' parts in Purcell's odes and dramatic works

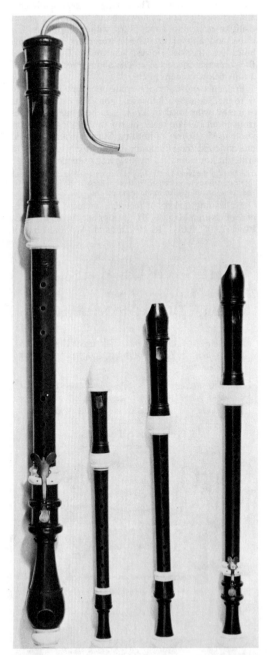

8. Quartet of recorders by Bressan, London, late 17th century (Grosvenor Museum, Chester); (left to right) bass in F, treble in F, alto in D and tenor in C

were for recorders, and the bass recorder is specified in one of the manuscripts of his 1692 Ode for St Cecilia's Day (z328). There is a chaconne in his *Dioclesian* (z627) for two recorders in canon over a ground bass, and a fantasia '3 parts on a ground' for recorders and continuo (z731). Pairs of recorders provide obbligatos to arias and duets in the incidental music for *Dioclesian, King Arthur, The Fairy Queen, The Indian Queen, Theodosius* and *Timon of Athens*, and many of the odes and cantatas. Blow made appropriate use of recorders in his Ode on the Death of Purcell, 1696 (*Mark how the lark and linnet sing*) and in *Venus and Adonis*, where they are associated with Venus and Cupid.

There is a tradition which associates certain instruments with particular dramatic situations: trumpets with battle, horns with hunting, etc. Recorders have been used in love scenes, pastorals (with oboes), funerals, supernatural happenings (concerning goddesses, angels or witches) and to imitate the singing of birds. This tradition underlies the use of recorders by Purcell, Bach, Handel and other composers and its acceptance is shown in the instruments specified in the stage directions of many plays.

In 1707 was published the *Principes de la flûte traversière ... de la flûte à bec ... et du haut-bois* by Jacques Hotteterre 'le Romain', a far more serious and detailed work than any of the series of 'companions' that had appeared during the previous 28 years; the first method for the newly perfected transverse flute and a model for many which were to follow. At about the same time J. B. ['John'] Loeillet, a native of Ghent, settled in London as a performer on the recorder and oboe, and introduced the transverse flute to English audiences. This was the 'German' flute or *traversa* with a conical bore and one key, which had been perfected by the Hotteterres about 1680, and which was eventually to rival the recorder and ultimately to oust it from its position as the favourite instrument of gentlemen of fashion. Loeillet published a number of sonatas for recorder and continuo and trio sonatas with the oboe besides music for the transverse flute. His cousin J. B. Loeillet 'de Gand', who lived in France, also composed a number of sonatas for recorder and continuo. Some of his sonatas were also arranged as duets for two recorders. A third Loeillet, Jacques, was a brother of the London Loeillet and the composer of a quintet for two voice flutes, two transverse flutes and continuo.

The Division Flute, published in 1706 in imitation of Simpson's *Division Violist* (1659), was a collection of variations on popular grounds together with some 'preludes', many of which were extracts from sonatas without the bass part. The great popularity of the recorder at the beginning of the 18th century in England was reflected in the fact that at the foot of most of the song sheets was provided a transposition of the tune to a suitable key 'for the flute' (i.e. recorder). Some years later this became 'for the German flute' and then again 'for the flute' (by now meaning the transverse flute), thus marking the change in taste.

Among 'John' Loeillet's contemporaries as composers for the recorder in England were Robert Valentine and three composers who wrote concertos for the 'sixth flute', a recorder in *d''*: Baston, Woodcock and Babell. Others who came to England from Italy, France and Germany and contributed to the recorder's repertory included Barsanti, Bononcini, Dieupart, Pepusch, Sammartini, Thornowitz and Handel.

In the 18th century the treble recorder was the standard instrument. Apart from the bass, such other recorders as were in use were treated as transposing instruments and named according to their interval of transposition from the *f'* of the treble. About the middle of the century, after giving a table of fingerings for the treble recorder, Tans'ur wrote: 'Of *Flutes* there are many *Sizes*, as a *Concert Flute*; a *Third Flute*; a *Fifth*, and a *Sixth*, and an *Octave Flute*; yet all may be played by the foregoing Rules'. Of these the 'concert' flute is the treble, and the fifth and octave flutes are the modern descant and sopranino instruments. The sixth flute is the same as the smaller of the two *discant* flutes of Praetorius (see fig.3*b* above).

This relating of the recorders to the F of the treble set them apart from other woodwind instruments at the time when the orchestra was being born. Flutes and the oboes played to a system of 'six fingers D'. The corresponding six fingers (and thumb) on the treble recorder gave G. In about 1732, to sustain the recorder's popularity against the rivalry of the German flute, Thomas Stanesby attempted to rationalize the woodwind families by adopting the 'six fingers D' of the flute and oboe as a standard, and to make the descant (fifth flute) and tenor their fundamental instruments. According to Hawkins:

To further this invention of Stanesby, one Lewis Merci, an excellent performer on the flute, a Frenchman by birth, but resident in London, published about the year 1735, six solos for the flute, three whereof are said to be accommodated to Mr Stanesby's new system, but the German flute was now become a favourite instrument, and Stanesby's ingenuity failed of its effect.

This idea has been tried since, but without success.

In France at the beginning of the 18th century music was composed for '2 musettes, vielles, flûtes à bec, flûtes traversières, hautbois ou violons sans basse' in which the individual characteristics of the recorder were submerged in the welter of alternative instruments; the presence of two drone instruments (the musette and the vielle), by limiting modulation, ensured monotony. The principal composers of this school included Bâton, Boismortier, the Chedevilles, Aubert and Naudot, and the tutors by J.-P. Freillon-Poncein and Hotteterre give a valuable insight into the French style of those times.

In Italy Marcello, Alessandro Scarlatti and Vivaldi made significant contributions to the recorder's repertory with solo sonatas with continuo. Scarlatti also wrote a quartet sonata for three recorders and continuo and some concertos with strings; Vivaldi used the recorder in much of his chamber music and concertos.

From Germany there were brilliant solos and six concertos for four recorders and continuo by Schickhardt, a concerto for four recorders and strings by Heinichen, a concerto and other chamber works by Graupner besides the major contributions of Bach and Telemann. Mattheson's op.1 was a set of 12 sonatas for unaccompanied recorders, four of them duets and the remainder trios. They were dedicated to amateur players and are Mattheson's only works for the recorder, although he showed an understanding of its particular virtues in his writings. A trio sonata by Quantz for recorder, flute and continuo is one of a very small number of works in which the two kinds of flute – *à bec* and *traversière* – are heard together.

Bach used both the recorder and flute in his orchestra and clearly distinguished between the two. His chamber music, i.e. the sonatas, trio sonatas and the Suite in B

minor, are all for the flute, but the second and fourth Brandenburg Concertos use recorders. The exact meaning of the 'fiauti d'echo' of the latter is much debated (see Dart, 1960) but the parts can be played on two trebles in F or on a treble in G and one in F. Bach arranged the fourth Brandenburg Concerto as a concerto in F for solo harpsichord, two recorders and strings; comparison between the two versions helps to confirm that recorders in F should be used for both. Bach's recorder parts were marked 'flauto' and were generally written in the French 'violin' clef – the G clef on the bottom line.

There was often a difference in pitch between Bach's organ and the *Kammerton* of his woodwind players. The latter used a flat pitch like that of the recorders of Bressan, Denner and other makers. This difference in pitch was sometimes a whole tone or even a minor 3rd, and to reach agreement in performance Bach often had to write out a transposed organ continuo part for a church cantata. Modern editors, by adopting the key of the organ part and transposing the wind parts, have made it difficult to judge the tessitura of the original parts from a modern score, and it is impossible in some instances to use the original instrumentation in modern performances at the new pitch.

Recorders play a prominent part in 20 of the church cantatas and the birthday cantata *Was mir behagt* (1716). In the *Easter Oratorio* (1736) both recorders and a flute are used, an important obbligato being given to the latter. In the *St Matthew Passion* flutes have most of the work, but recorders are scored for in the tenor recitative and chorus 'O Schmerz'. The *Actus tragicus* (BWV106) is a good example of Bach's use of recorders and of the pitch problem. The orchestra consists of two viole da gamba and continuo. Because of their pitch difference the recorder parts as printed in the score are a tone too low – they should be in C, not B♭ – with the result that much of the work is unplayable on modern-pitched instruments without alteration.

Handel's use of the recorder began with the four sonatas out of the 12 that make up his op.1, and the Italian cantata *Nel dolce dell'oblio*, in which the recorder plays an obbligato. There are three more sonatas known as the 'Fitzwilliam' sonatas from the location of Handel's manuscript in the Fitzwilliam Museum, Cambridge. The second of these was assembled from separate, previously existing movements in the same key. Among Handel's many trio sonatas assigned loosely to two oboes, flutes or violins and bass, there are two for recorder, violin and continuo: op.2 no.1 in C minor and no.4 in F. In the orchestra Handel used the recorder ('*flauto*') as well as the *traversa*; in addition to the treble he occasionally called for the sopranino (*flauto* piccolo as distinct from *traversa* piccolo – in *Rinaldo*, *Acis and Galatea*, etc), descant, and bass (*basso de' flauti*, in *Giustino*). Handel did not write for the recorder in his oratorios.

The Modern Musick-master was published anonymously in 1731 (Hawkins identified the author as Peter Prelleur). It is a compendium of instruction books of which the section on the German flute was a shortened translation of Hotteterre's *Principes* of 1707 while that on the recorder followed the plan of earlier methods. Handel's operas provided many of the tunes which followed the instructions in each section. This book shows the popular instruments of the time, and how the German flute was taking over from the recorder.

9. Recorder player: painting (1778), thought to be a self-portrait of János Kupezky, in the Szépművészeti Múzeum, Budapest

The rivalry between recorder and flute was by no means confined to England. In Italy some of the concertos in Vivaldi's op.10 started as recorder works, though when published later, they were all assigned to the flute. In fact Vivaldi composed a number of recorder concertos – not only for the treble, but also for a *flautino*, a sopranino recorder. Vivaldi's writing demands a high level of virtuosity from his recorder soloists. Sammartini was one of the few composers to write a concerto for descant recorder, treated in the original score as a fifth flute (transposed to be fingered as a treble).

Telemann made extensive and brilliant use of the recorder in sonatas with continuo, in particular the two (D minor and C) from the *Essercizii musici* and four from *Der getreue Musikmeister* (in F, C, F minor and C). Among the trio sonatas there are several for recorder, oboe and continuo, for recorder, treble viol and continuo and for recorder, violin and continuo. In some the recorder is joined by a viola da gamba, in others a horn, with the continuo. There is also one in B♭ for recorder with solo harpsichord and continuo. Of the trio sonatas for two recorders and continuo, one in C, from *Der getreue Musikmeister*, indicates the possibility of performance by a larger group of recorders with doubled parts, as there are solo and tutti indications. There are also quartet sonatas for recorder, oboe, violin and continuo, and one for recorder (or bassoon), two traversi and continuo.

This indication of the bassoon as an alternative to the recorder can be better understood when it is remembered that the recorder parts of Telemann (as well as Bach and others) were written in the French violin clef, and a bass instrument could read it as if prefixed by a bass clef, sounding the music two octaves lower. This use of the French violin clef also aided clef transposi-

tion. For example, a part for flute in G major in the treble clef could be played in B♭ by a treble recorder with the French violin clef and a key signature of two flats in mind. In this way recorder players have been encouraged to 'borrow' from the flute repertory, and have in fact adopted some of the fantasias for solo flute, the canonic sonatas and other duets originally published for flutes.

Like Bach, Telemann used the full range of the recorder in concertos and suites. Of these the Suite in A minor is the best known, since it is played by flautists. In another suite for recorder and strings Telemann scored for a *flûte pastorelle*; this may have been an alto recorder in E♭ or (more effectively) a fourth flute (descant in B♭). He also wrote concertos for two recorders and strings, for two recorders, two oboes and strings and a concerto for recorder, viola da gamba and strings. (In all these 'strings' implies the presence of a harpsichord continuo.)

As early as 1679 John Evelyn wrote that 'The Flute Douce is now much in request for accompanying the voice'. Purcell's and Bach's use of recorders as obbligato instruments in vocal music has been noted, as has Handel's use of the instrument in an Italian cantata and his operas. Telemann's *Der harmonische Gottesdienst* provides a solo cantata for each Sunday of the Christian year and rings the changes between violin, oboe, recorder and flute as obbligato instruments. Other composers who used the recorder with the voice include Arne, Croft and Pepusch. A late use of the instrument is found in C. P. E. Bach's trio for bass recorder, viola and continuo, w163.

The recorder was replaced in popularity by the transverse flute during the course of the 18th century, and the latter found a permanent place in the growing orchestra. In 1780 one of the last known English tutors (*Compleat Instructions for the Common Flute*) was published. By 1800 the recorder was virtually obsolete, except possibly in amateur circles. An attempt at revival among amateurs was made with the flageolets and other novelties of Bainbridge, Simpson, Hastrick and others. Their double and triple flageolets were amusing instruments and beautifully made, but of little musical value.

The recorder went out of fashion with the growth of the orchestra and the concert hall, and because it could not keep pace with the development of other instruments. Its fixed windway and voicing precluded any wide dynamic range, and it could not meet the demand for a stronger tone to fill the growing concert halls. Other woodwind instruments gave the players greater control of pitch and tone. They could compensate for flatness when playing gently or sharpness when blowing strongly with an instant adjustment of embouchure.

The revival of the recorder began towards the end of the 19th century through the researches of Bridge, who discovered the famous Chester recorders; Welch, who studied literary references to the recorder and other flutes; Galpin, who studied the instruments themselves and taught his family to play them; and Arnold Dolmetsch, who realized that the music of early instruments could not be revived without a revival of the craftsmanship which made them. Dolmetsch made his first recorder in about 1919: the treble recorder figured in the first Haslemere Festival (1925) and the quartet was presented in 1926.

These festivals aroused interest abroad; Pater Harlan, a guitarist from Germany, heard the recorders in 1926 and realized their possibilities in the German Youth Movement. Before long imitations of these recorders were being mass-produced in Germany and became very popular. Unfortunately this German revival was not backed by Dolmetsch's scholarship; important details in the design were not understood and changes were made, resulting in the faulty 'German fingering'. In this the fingers are lifted one after another to produce a basic scale and the fourth degree (f'' on a descant recorder) is no longer a forked fingering as it was on all the old recorders. This change entailed modifications to the sizes and positions of other holes with a result that the next semitone ($f\sharp''$) could not easily be produced in tune. The recorder in the 18th century was fully chromatic, responding to a system of cross-fingering, well suited to its light wind pressure and gentle tone. The German fingering, by attempting to simplify the scale of C, prevented modulation on the sharp side and limited the choice of music. Other changes in design affected other notes and alternative fingerings and limited the expressive qualities of the instrument. This mistaken fingering continues to influence recorder playing in Germany and other countries.

Arnold Dolmetsch's younger son, Carl, became a leading virtuoso of the recorder and brought the making of recorders in the 20th century to a high standard. Double holes for the lowest semitones are now normal (they were known in the 18th century but not generally used), and Carl Dolmetsch invented two keys; one to close the lower end of the recorder, primarily to produce $f\sharp''$ on the treble recorder, the other to open a small hole near the mouthpiece and raise the pitch of the recorder, but at the same time make it possible to play more softly without getting flat. Dolmetsch also aimed to produce a recorder with more powerful tone for solo playing, and designed a 'tone projector' which concentrated the tone of the instrument when playing with a modern string orchestra. Meanwhile, Edgar Hunt, working independently, introduced the recorder to schoolchildren and established the teaching of the instrument at Trinity College of Music, London, in 1935. In 1937 the Society of Recorder Players was founded by Dolmetsch and Hunt. This is an association of amateur players and has played an important part in the development of the recorder movement in England, encouraging the publication of music and publishing a journal.

Up to the autumn of 1939 English schools had been supplied mainly with recorders mass-produced in Germany but with a cross-fingering system (very few with German fingering were ever imported). During World War II, when schools were evacuated to the country, the demand for recorders grew at a time when mass-production in wood was impossible, and so a plastic descant recorder was designed. This was originally intended as a stop-gap until such time as inexpensive wood recorders were made available.

The revival of the recorder in England has been based on the music, instruction books and instruments of the 17th and 18th centuries. The new instruments were designed to be fully chromatic, using the well-established system of cross-fingerings which has become known as 'English fingering' (known as 'Baroque' or 'original' fingering on the Continent). At the same time

new music has been written for the recorder. The first was probably written by Robin Milford (in his oratorio *A Prophet in the Land*, 1930). Other English composers who have contributed to a growing repertory have included Stanley Bate, Lennox Berkeley, York Bowen, Britten (Scherzo, Alpine Suite and parts in *Noyes Fludde* and *A Midsummer Night's Dream*), Arnold Cooke (many works, including a concerto), Walter Leigh, Herbert Murrill, Franz Reizenstein, Malcolm Arnold, Edmund Rubbra and Gordon Jacob.

Beside the popular use of the recorder in Germany, Gustav Scheck was playing and teaching the instrument, at first in Berlin and after the war in Freiburg. Among his pupils were Conrad Fehr, the founder of a Swiss firm of recorder makers, Ferdinand Conrad (Hanover), and Hans-Martin Linde (Basle) who became leading performers and teachers. Hindemith included a trio for recorders in his *Plöner Musiktag* (1931) and his example has been followed by many others, including Poser, Bresgen, Badings, von Beckerath, Genzmer and Henze. Rudolf Barthel has developed the recorder orchestra (comparable with the string orchestra and brass band) in which well-balanced groups of sopranino, descant, treble, tenor, bass and great bass recorders perform specially composed and orchestrated music.

In its 20th-century revival the recorder has been cultivated on three levels: as a school instrument, among amateurs, and as an instrument in its own right. At each of these levels there are many subdivisions. In school it can be regarded as a melodic continuation of the rhythmic work of the percussion band, or as a preparation for playing the flute or clarinet. In some schools, under favourable conditions, the recorder is more seriously regarded. Among amateurs there are some good soloists and an even greater number of capable chamber music groups and larger ensembles. As a musical instrument it was first used to give authenticity to performances of early music; then composers began to take note of the instrument. More recently the avant garde has exploited the recorder by the use of tonguing effects ('flutter-tonguing' with the tip or the back of the tongue), alternative fingerings, including those produced by closing the end of the instrument, overblown 'chords', vibrato (with breath, finger and with the hand on the mouthpiece), glissando effects, out-of-tune playing (under- and overblowing), singing while playing etc. These trends probably began with Jürg Baur's *Mutazioni* and *Incontri* about 1962, and have been stimulated by Vetter and Frans Brüggen, whose playing has encouraged Rob du Bois, Andriessen, Berio, Shinohara and others.

The foundations of modern recorder playing in Holland have been laid by Joannes Collette, Kees Otten and Frans Brüggen. Brüggen has done more than any other player to bring the recorder to the virtuoso level of other recital instruments. His repertory has covered Van Eyck, Telemann and the 18th century, including the French school, and the 20th-century avant garde. He has pioneered the use of original 18th-century instruments in his recordings, encouraged the making of copies of these instruments, and through his teaching founded a modern Dutch school and style.

In the USA the recorder movement has been fostered by the American Recorder Society under the leadership of such players as Davenport, Krainis and Wollitz and the quarterly publication *The American Recorder*. Summer schools are an important part of the programme and the influence of Brüggen has been felt.

In England, although recorder teaching has been established for many years at Trinity College of Music and more recently at the RCM, the GSM and the RAM, much valuable teaching has also been done through summer schools, such as those at Downe House (1939–61), The Recorder in Education (from 1946) and the Anglo-French Recorder Courses (from 1962).

In France the movement owes much to the work of Jean Henry and his participation in the Anglo-French courses. Pierre Poulteau and Michel Sanvoisin are notable players, and Alexandre Tansman and Gaston Saux have written for the recorder.

In Vienna, Hans Ulrich Staeps has made a special contribution to the recorder's repertory in such works as his *Sieben Flötentänze* (descant, two trebles and tenor) and Sonata in E♭, besides many other ensemble and didactic works.

Italy has produced a remarkable young player in Amico Dolci, a composer, Eliodoro Sollima, and two societies of recorder players (one in Rome, the other in Turin).

The making of recorders, which started with the aim of producing a modern instrument, as if to make up for those years of neglect in the 19th century, has now turned to a closer study of the best examples from the 18th century, and significant work is being done by individual craftsmen (notably by Friedrich von Huene in Boston and Martin Skowroneck in Bremen) rather than by the larger firms, although there is a constant demand for good mass-produced instruments for school use and among amateurs. There are also wide-bore recorders based on 16th-century models for the performance of music of that period.

BIBLIOGRAPHY

Hawkins H

S. Virdung: *Musica getutscht* (Basle, 1511/*R*1931)

M. Agricola: *Musica instrumentalis deudsch* (Wittenberg, 1528/*R*1896)

S. Ganassi: *Opera intitulata fontegara* (Venice, 1535/*R*1934)

P. Jambe de Fer: *Epitome musical* (Lyons, 1556); repr. in F. Lesure: 'L'epitome musical de Philibert Jambe de Fer', *AnnM*, vi (1958–63), 341–86

T. Morley: *The First Booke of Consort Lessons* (London, 1599, 2/1611)

M. Praetorius: *Syntagma musicum*, ii (Wolfenbüttel, 1618, 2/1619/*R*1958)

J. Evelyn: *Kalendarium: de vita propria* (MSS, private collection, 1620–1706); ed. by E. S. de Beer as *The Diary of John Evelyn* (London, 1955)

M. Mersenne: *Harmonie universelle* (Paris, 1636–7/*R*1963)

S. Pepys: *Diary* (MS, *GB-Cmc*, 1660–69); ed. R. Latham and W. Matthews (London, 1970–)

T. Greeting: *The Pleasant Companion, or New Lessons and Instructions for the Flageolet* (London, 1661)

J. Hudgebut: *A Vade mecum for the Lovers of Musick, Shewing the Excellency of the Rechorder with some Notes and Directions for the same* (London, 1679)

J. Banister: *The Most Pleasant Companion* (London, 1681)

H. Salter: *The Genteel Companion: being Exact Directions for the Recorder* (London, 1683)

R. Carr: *The Delightful Companion, or Choice New Lessons for the Recorder or Flute* (London, 1684, 2/1686)

J. Talbot: *Musica* (MS, *GB-Och* Mus.1187, *c*1687); notes on wind insts repr. in A. C. Baines: 'Fifteenth-century Instruments in Tinctoris's *De inventione et usu musicae*', *GSJ*, iii (1950), 19

J. Hudgebut: *Thesaurus musicus* (London, 1693)

J.-P. Freillon-Poncin: *La véritable manière d'apprendre à jouer en perfection du hautbois, de la flûte et du flageolet* (Paris, 1700/*R*1971)

The Division Flute (London, 1706)

J. M. Hotteterre: *Principes de la flûte traversière, ou flûte d'Allemagne; de la flûte à bec, ou flûte douce, et du haut-bois* (Paris, 1707/*R*1942)

——: *L'art du préluder sur la flûte traversière, sur la flûte à bec, sur le hautbois, et autres instruments de dessus* (Paris, 1719)

P. Prelleur: *The Modern Musick-master* (London, 1730, 2/1731/*R*)

W. Tans'ur: *New Musical Grammar* (London, 1746)

C. Welch: 'Literature relating to the 'Recorder', *PMA*, xxiv (1897–8), 145

J. C. Bridge: 'The Chester Recorders', *PMA*, xxvii (1900–01), 109

C. Welch: '*Hamlet* and the Recorder', *PMA*, xxviii (1901–2), 105

F. W. Galpin: *Old English Instruments of Music* (London, 1910, 4/1965), fig.25

C. Welch: *Six Lectures on the Recorder* (London, 1911)

E. Hunt and R. Donington: *A Practical Method for the Recorder* (London, 1935)

M. Ruetz: 'Die Blockflöte bei Bach', *Zeitschrift für Hausmusik*, iv (1935), 13, 75

The Recorder News (New Malden, 1938–47; London, 1950–63)

D. Degen: *Zur Geschichte der Blockflöte in den germanischen Ländern* (Kassel, 1939)

A. Carse: 'Fingering the Recorder', *MR*, i (1940), 96

C. F. Dolmetsch: 'The Recorder or English Flute', *ML*, xxii (1941), 67

The American Recorder (New York, 1941–)

R. T. Dart: 'Morley's Consort Lessons of 1599', *PRMA*, lxxiv (1947–8), 1

E. Hunt: 'The Recorder and its Music', *PRMA*, lxxv (1948–9), 39

L. H. von Winterfeld: *Die Solo-Blockflöte* (Halle, 1949)

——: *Die Altblockflöte* (Halle, 1950)

W. Hilleman: 'Die Blockflöte bei Händel', *Musik im Unterricht*, xlii (1951), 154

R. T. Dart: 'Four Dutch Recorder Books', *GSJ*, v (1952), 57

H. Peter: *Die Blockflöte und ihre Spielweise in Vergangenheit* (diss., Free U. of Berlin, 1952; Eng. trans., 1958)

L. H. von Winterfeld: 'Die Blockflöte in den Kantaten J. S. Bachs', *Zeitschrift für Hausmusik*, xvii (1953), 106

R. T. Dart: 'A Hand-list of English Instrumental Music printed before 1681', *GSJ*, viii (1955), 13

A. Mendel: 'On the Pitches in Use in Bach's Time', *MQ*, xli (1955), 332, 466

E. Halfpenny: 'The English Baroque Treble Recorder', *GSJ*, ix (1956), 82

C. Dolmetsch: 'Recorder and German Flute during the 17th and 18th centuries', *PRMA*, lxxxiii (1956–7), 49

B. Trowell: 'King Henry IV, Recorder-player', *GSJ*, x (1957), 83

R. T. Dart: 'Recorder "Gracings" in 1700', *GSJ*, xii (1959), 93 [quotes from *GB-Lbm* Add.35043]

——: 'Bach's "Fiauti d'echo" ', *ML*, xli (1960), 331

D. S. Higbee: 'A Plea for the Tenor Recorder by Thomas Stanesby, Jr.', *GSJ*, xv (1962), 55

E. Hunt: *The Recorder and its Music* (London, 1962, rev., enlarged 2/1977)

The Recorder and Music Magazine (London, 1963–)

H. Alker: *Blockflöten-Bibliographie* (Wilhelmshaven, 1967–75)

M. Vetter: *Il flauto dolce ed acerbo* (Celle, 1969)

EDGAR HUNT

Reco-reco. A notched bamboo stem scraper; *see* GÜIRO and BRAZIL, §II, 1(iv).

Recoupe (Fr.). A term used by Attaingnant for the first after-dance of the *basse danse commune*. The recoupe consisted of 12 *mesures* or step patterns, as against the 20 of the basse danse itself. The same section of a basse danse was called a 'moitié' in the Turin basse danse scroll (*c*1517) and in Antonius de Arena's treatise *Ad suos compagnos* (*c*1519), while in the Lyonnais treatise *S'ensuyvent plusieurs basses dances tant communes que incommunes* (*c*1535) it is called 'residue', and in Arbeau's *Orchésographie* (1588) it is called 'la retour de la basse danse'. Arbeau described the dance as being accompanied by repetition of one of the strains of the basse danse itself, but independent music for the recoupe section survives in Attaingnant's *Dixhuit basses danses* (1530), Moderne's *Musicque de joye* (*c*1544) and Susato's *Het derde musycke boexken* (1551).

See BASSE DANSE.

BIBLIOGRAPHY

T. Arbeau: *Orchésographie* (Langres, 1588; Eng. trans., 1948, rev. 2/1967)

D. Heartz: Preface to *Preludes, Chansons, and Dances for Lute Published by Pierre Attaingnant* (Neuilly-sur-Seine, 1964)

Recte et retro (Lat.: 'direct and retrograde'). The use of a theme together with its retrograde version.

Reda, Siegfried (*b* Bochum, 27 July 1916; *d* Mülheim, 13 Dec 1968). German composer and organist. He began his studies in Dortmund and continued them in Berlin under Pepping and Distler at the Spandau Church Music School. In 1946 he took over the directorship of the Institute for Evangelical Church Music at the Essen Folkwangschule, where he also taught the organ and composition. In addition, he was appointed director of church music for Mülheim (Altstadt) in 1953. His compositional work combines an awareness of tradition with contemporary elements such as serial melody, and his major contribution was to introduce recent developments in Protestant church music, previously based on archaic formulae. In the field of organ music, he evolved from the neo-classicism of the concertos, through a novel employment of timbre as a form-building factor (*Triptychon*) to the dense serial writing of aphoristic spareness found in the *Monologe*. His liturgical choral music developed Distler's principles, with a deeply emotional declamatory style, rich in excited gestures, which is relieved at intervals by quasi-instrumental melismas; the choral pieces and the concert works share textures that are constructed in several layers. Reda's greatest achievement was the Requiem, which may be regarded as a summary of his life's work. He exerted a powerful influence on the new currents in Protestant church music from the early 1950s, partly through the Heidenheimer Tage für neue Kirchenmusik which he instituted with Bornefeld in 1946, and partly through the development of an organ style released from archaic limitations.

WORKS
(*selective list*)
ORGAN

Choralkonzert 'O wie selig seid ihr doch, ihr Frommen', 1946; Choralkonzert 'Gottes Sohn ist kommen', 1946; 3 Concertos, 1947–8; Choralkonzert 'Christ unser Herr zum Jordan kam', 1948; Triptychon über das Kirchenlied 'O Welt, ich muss dich lassen', 1950; Marienbilder, 1950; Choralkonzert 'O Traurigkeit', 1952; Monologe, 1953; Prelude, Fugue and Quadruplum, 1957
Gloria Dei 'Ich weiss ein lieblich Engelspiel', 1957; Sonata, 1960; Laudamus te [after Bach: Mass in b], 1961; Servite Domino [after Reger: Psalm c], 1961; Meditationen über das Passionslied 'Ein Lämmlein geht', 1964; Meditationen über das Passionslied 'O Mensch, bewein', 1964; Chorale Fantasia 'Herzlich lieb hab' ich dich', 1965; Toccata novenaria modos vertens, 1966

CHORAL

Choralkantate 'Fröhlich soll mein Herze springen', solo vv, chorus 3–4vv, org, 1946; Chormusiken nach chinesischen Dichtungen, 1947; Chormusik für das Jahr Kirche, 1947–58; Evangelienmusik 'Die heiden Schächer', 1v, 2 chorus, 1948; Evangelienmusik 'Leidensverkündigung und Heilung eines Blinden', 1949; Evangelienmusik 'Die Weihnachtsgeschichte', 1v, chorus 4–6vv, 1949; Ecce homo aus dem 22. Psalm, 1950; Te Deum, 2 chorus, brass, 1950
Die Ostergeschichte, 2S, chorus, 1950; Amor Dei (H. Thoma), S, chorus, org, 1952; Das Göttliche Spiel, 1952; Weihnachtskyrie (J. Klepper), S, female chorus, 2 vn, vc, 1954; Altchristlicher Hymnus, S, chorus 4vv, 2 vn, vc, org, 1955; Meditation und Fuge über das Passionslied 'Wir danken Dir, Herr Jesu Christ', chorus, org, 1959; Requiem, solo vv, chorus, orch, 1963; Psalm viii, solo vv, chorus, org, 1964; Psalmus morte servati (Psalm xxx), Bar, chorus, orch, org, 1966

Principal publisher: Bärenreiter

BIBLIOGRAPHY

S. Reda: 'Selbstbildnis', *Musik und Kirche*, xvi (1947), 81
H. Eckert: 'Gemeinsame Grundlagen des kompositorischen Schaffens von Ludwig Weber, Erich Sehlbach und Siegfried Reda', *Beiträge zur Musikgeschichte der Stadt Essen*, ed. K. G. Fellerer (Cologne and Krefeld, 1955)
S. Scheytt: 'Kommentar zur Musik von Siegfried Reda', *Musik und Kirche*, xxxi (1961), 76
S. Reda: 'Reda, Siegfried', *Rheinische Musiker*, v, ed. K. G. Fellerer (Cologne, 1967) [incl. list of works]
W. Hufschmidt: 'Sehnsucht nach der Harmonie', *Neue Musikzeitung*,

xviii (1969), 7
K. Kirchberg: 'Er stellte sich der Gegenwart', *Musik und Gottesdienst*, xxiii (1969), 89

KLAUS KIRCHBERG

Redcliffe Concerts of British Music. London concert organization founded in 1964 by Francis Routh; *see* LONDON, §VI, 4(iii).

Redding. *See* READING family.

Redel, Kurt (*b* Breslau [now Wrocław], 8 Oct 1918). German conductor. He studied the flute, conducting and composition at the Breslau Hochschule für Musik, and attended a conducting course given by Clemens Krauss. His début as a conductor and as a soloist was at Breslau in 1938. As a flautist he first appeared outside Germany in 1950 at Menton, and three years later as a conductor at the Festival de Royaumont and the Semaines Musicales de Paris. Since then he has conducted at many European festivals, as well as being director of the Munich Pro Arte Orchestra, which he founded, and the Mozart Chamber Orchestra of Salzburg; he has made records with both these orchestras. He specializes in the works of Bach and his contemporaries, and has edited the *Art of Fugue*, the *Musical Offering* and the *Magnificat*, and Passion settings by Telemann, whose *St Mark Passion* of 1759 he reconstructed and recorded.

ALAN BLYTH

Redel, Martin Christoph (*b* Detmold, 30 Jan 1947). German composer. At the Nordwestdeutsche Musikakademie, Detmold (1964–9), he studied percussion with F. Scherz and composition with Kelterborn and Klebe; his composition studies were continued with Yun at the Staatliche Hochschule für Musik, Hanover, in 1970. Never losing links with traditional techniques, his scores are based on free tonal, 12-note and serial procedures. Redel's music is transparent in form and detail and lyrical in feeling, serenity contrasting with tension. He wrote *Grundlagen des Kadenzspiels im Tonsatzunterricht* (Berlin, 1975).

WORKS
(*selective list*)

Musik, pf, perc, 1966; Str Qt, 1967; Symbolismen (R. Huch), S, ens, 1968–9; Dialoge, ob d'amore, hpd, 1970; Strophen, orch, 1970; Epilog (Gryphius), B-Bar, fl, gui, 1971; Dispersion, ens, 1972; Kammersinfonie II, 1973; Konfrontationen, orch, 1974; Interplay, ens, 1975; pieces for pf, org, ens, orch

Principal publisher: Bote & Bock

H. KUNZ

Redestinos, David (*b* ?Raidestos, nr. Constantinople; *fl* Mt Athos, 1st half of 15th century). Byzantine composer; *see* GREECE, §II.

Redford, John (*d* London, will made 7 Oct and proved 29 Nov 1547). English composer and organist.

The earliest known mention of him dates from 20 June 1534 when, as one of the vicars-choral of St Paul's Cathedral, he signed Henry VIII's Act of Supremacy. At his death he was almoner and Master of the Choristers, and had probably succeeded to these posts on Hickman's death earlier that year. There was no specifically named post of organist at St Paul's at this time, but Redford was undoubtedly employed in this capacity in view of the substantial body of works which he composed for the instrument. On his death he was probably immediately succeeded by Sebastian Westcote as almoner, but the duties of organist appear to have been assumed, at least

Ex. 1 *(note values halved)*

(plainsong)

De - us   Cre - a - - - tor   o - - - mni - - - - - um

in part, by Philip ap Rhys. Redford was a poet and dramatist as well as a musician. A morality play with indications for music, *Wyt and Science* (edition in *Tudor Interludes*, ed. P. Happé, Harmondsworth, 1972), with a fragmentary dramatic interlude and other verse, is included in a separate section of a manuscript (*GB-Lbm* Add.15233) which also contains some of his organ music. The morality and the interlude were almost certainly intended for performance by the children of St Paul's, a tradition which was to be continued by Westcote. The latter certainly, and Redford probably, collaborated in dramatic productions with John Heywood, who later became virginalist to Queen Mary. Heywood was a witness to Thomas Mulliner's ownership of the manuscript now known as the Mulliner Book (*GB-Lbm* Add.30513), which is a major source of Redford's music. The principle source (the first section of Add.29996) probably dates from shortly after Redford's death, but before the coming into effect of the Act of Uniformity in 1549.

Redford is one of the earliest English composers whose organ music has survived, and certainly the earliest of any importance. Before his day, organ music was almost completely an art of improvisation, using plainsong as its basis. Its function, as in Redford's own music, was to alternate with, and partially replace, the sung plainsong of the Latin services. In some forms (hymn, *Te Deum*, *Magnificat*), the organ shared the plainsong with the singing on a verse-for-verse basis; but in the offertory only the first few notes were left to be intoned by the cantores. The organ antiphon replaced the singing of such chants at the end of a psalm, a group of psalms, or a canticle. Redford's distinction was to raise this art to the status of written composition. His music is not entirely free from dryness; but it is completely instrumental in idiom and almost completely independent of vocal techniques. Redford often embellished the plainsong in a manner known as 'breaking the plainsong', each note of the plainsong being allotted a specific unit of time, within which the note itself or its octave must appear (special liberties were allowed for

repeated notes and at cadences). Redford is cited as a master of this art by Morley in *A Plaine and Easie Introduction* (1597). His favoured texture consists of two or three parts with the plainsong in the bass or middle part, as may be seen in three successive verses of a hymn, *Deus Creator omnium* (ex.1). The widely-spaced texture of the third verse, in which the middle part or 'mean' is transferred from hand to hand, is characteristic of Redford. Another of his methods was to use the faburden of the plainsong as cantus firmus: this was a melodic line, originally designed to accompany the plainsong, formed mainly by duplicating at a 6th below (or a 3rd above), but falling to the octave (or unison) at cadences and certain other points. In his two settings of the odd-numbered verses of the *Te Deum*, Redford used a highly embellished faburden in varying transpositions according to the tessitura of the original melody, thus creating an immensely sophisticated cantus firmus technique in which the plainsong is thoroughly disguised.

Redford wrote a few four-part works for organ, but did not achieve the fluency of his artistic successor, THOMAS PRESTON, in this respect. Rhythmically he was unadventurous compared with Preston, the main foil to the predominant quadruple metre being the use of sesquialtera proportion (best described as a moderate 6/8 in modern notation). Occasionally, by disposing the plainsong in short notes (crotchets in modern notation) he achieved rhythmic patterns corresponding to the modern 3/4, 5/4 and even 10/4 (see his two settings of the *Te Deum*). The one source which may date from his lifetime (*Lbm* Add.15233) shows greater liberality in the use of accidentals than the other manuscripts, which perhaps indicates a disposition towards a moderate degree of chromaticism in his own performance. His few vocal works show the clear influence of instrumental techniques.

WORKS

Editions: *The Mulliner Book*, ed. D. Stevens, MB, i (1951, rev. 2/1962) [S]

Early Tudor Organ Music I: Music for the Office, ed. J. Caldwell, EECM, vi (1966) [C]

Early Tudor Organ Music II: Music for the Mass, ed. D.
Stevens, EECM, x (1969) [DS]

VOCAL

Ego autem cantabo, 4vv, *GB-Lbm* Roy.App.31–35
Christus resurgens, 4vv, *Lbm* Add.17802–05, *T* 389
Sint lumbi vestri praecincti, 4vv, *Och* 979–83, *T* 389

KEYBOARD

A meane, 1 section, S 67
A solis ortus cardine (hymn), 1 verse, C 25
Aeterne rerum conditor (hymn), 4 verses, C 28
Aeterne rerum conditor (hymn), 1 verse, S 74
Aeterne rex altissime (hymn), 1 verse, S 26
Agnus Dei, 2 sections, DS 4
Angulare fundamentum (hymn), 1 verse, C 29
Aurora lucis rutilat (hymn), 1 verse, S 73
Christe, qui lux es (hymn), 4 verses, C 36, S 31
Christe, qui lux es (hymn), 1 verse, S 40
Christe Redemptor omnium (hymn), 1 verse, C 38
Conditor alme siderum (hymn), 4 verses, C 40
Deus Creator omnium (hymn), 3 verses, C 42
Exsultet caelum laudibus (hymn), 1 verse, S 30
Felix namque (offertory), DS 20
Felix namque (offertory), DS 21
Glorificamus (antiphon), S 54
Iste confessor (hymn), 1 verse, S 48
Iste confessor (hymn), 1 verse, S 63
Iam lucis orto sidero (hymn), 1 verse, S 75
Justus ut palma (offertory), DS 23
Lucem tuam (antiphon), C 8
Lucem tuam (antiphon), S 37
Lucem tuam (antiphon), S 39
Lucis Creator optime ('O Lux with a meane', hymn), 1 verse, S 29
Miserere (antiphon), S 7
Miserere (antiphon), C 19
Miserere (antiphon), C 20
Miserere (antiphon), S 53
O lux beata Trinitas (hymn), 1 verse, S 28
O quam glorifica ('redfordes meane', hymn), 1 verse, C 49
Precatus est Moyses (offertory), DS 25
Primo dierum omnium (hymn), 1 verse, C 52
Salvator mundi Domine (hymn), 1 verse, S 36
Salvator mundi Domine (hymn), 1 verse, S 72
Te Deum, 16 sections, C 2
Te Deum, 16 sections, C 3
[Te lucis ante terminum] (hymn), 1 verse, S 38
Tui sunt caeli (offertory), DS 27
Veni Redemptor gentium (hymn), 3 verses, C 61
Veni Redemptor gentium (hymn), 1 verse, C 60
Verbum supernum prodiens (hymn), 3 verses, C 63

For further information and attributions see Caldwell.

BIBLIOGRAPHY

C. F. Pfatteicher: *John Redford* (Kassel, 1934)
D. Stevens: *The Mulliner Book: a Commentary* (London, 1952)
F. Ll. Harrison: *Music in Medieval Britain* (London, 1958)
J. Caldwell: 'Keyboard Plainsong Settings in England, 1500–1660', *MD*, xix (1965), 129
O. Neighbour: *The Consort and Keyboard Music of William Byrd* (London, 1978)

JOHN CALDWELL

Redhead, Richard (*b* Harrow, 1 March 1820; *d*
Hallingley, Surrey, 27 April 1901). English organist
and composer. He trained as a chorister at Magdalen
College, Oxford, under Walter Vicary. In 1839 he
was appointed organist of Margaret Chapel (now All
Saints'), Margaret Street, London, by the Rev. F. W.
Oakeley, under whose guidance he trained the prototype
surpliced parochial choir which heralded the Tractarian
choral revival. In conjunction with Oakeley, Redhead
produced the first Anglican plainsong psalter *Laudes
diurnae* (1843), and other liturgical music for Anglo-
Catholic use. From 1864 he was organist of St Mary
Magdalene, Paddington, for which he published several
works including the *Book of Common Prayer with
Ritual Music* (1865).

BIBLIOGRAPHY

B. Rainbow: *The Choral Revival in the Anglican Church, 1839–72* (London, 1970)
N. Temperley: *The Music of the English Parish Church*, i (Cambridge, 1979)

BERNARR RAINBOW

Redi, Tommaso (*b* Siena, *c*1675; *d* Montelupone,
Loreto, 20 July 1738). Italian composer. He studied
first with his uncle, G. O. Cini, *maestro di cappella* at
Siena, and then perhaps with G. M. Casini, organist of
Florence Cathedral. A priest, he spent 1706–9 in Spain
with the papal nuncio; then he went to Rome. In 1711
his requiem mass for Francesco Maria de' Medici was
performed in Siena Cathedral. According to Morrocchi,
he was organist in Provenzano; it may have been from
there that he applied to be assistant to Franchi, *maestro
di cappella* at the Cappella Lauretana, in 1731. Caldara
also competed for the position but Redi, supported by
Pitoni, was engaged, on 1 June 1731. On 2 December
1731, on Franchi's death, Redi became *maestro di cappella*, holding the title until shortly before his death.

Redi's music, written in response to the various
demands of his position, ranges from a simple four-part
homophonic *a cappella* sequence to a polyphonic, often
chromatic, mass for two four-part choirs with string
accompaniment. Redi's writing is always competent and
in a clear, rhythmically regular 18th-century style.

But the main interest in Redi comes from his controversy with Padre Martini over the incomplete canon
by Animuccia in an oil painting in the Cappella
Lauretana. The young Martini found a solution (29
September 1732) with which Redi disagreed; his own,
together with Martini's, was then sent to Pitoni (in
Rome), Pacchioni (Modena), Calegari (Venice) and
Vallotti (Padua). While appreciating Redi's proposal,
they nevertheless voted for Martini who then wrote a
long, scholarly defence that closed the question. There
are in all nine letters on the subject, including one from
Tartini. Redi was buried in the church of the Padri
Minori Conventuali, Montelupone.

WORKS

Magnificat, 2 choirs each 4vv, 2 org/vc; Requiem, 2 choirs each 4vv, str, bc, 1713; Mass, 6vv, bc; Mass, 4vv; Dixit Dominus, 2 choirs each 4vv, bc, Rome, 12 March 1731; In passioni Domini, S, vn, bc, Rome, 23 March 1723; Laudate pueri, 2 choirs each 4vv, 2 org, 1713; 2 sequences a 4; various sacred works, incl. antiphons, introits, graduals, offertories etc, all 4vv, bc: all in *D-Bds*
25 introits, 2 choirs each 4vv, str, org, 1731–2; Responsory [Posuit], 8vv; vesper antiphon, 8vv; 3 Introits, 3 Alleluias, all 4vv, org; various hymns [Vexilla regis, Ecce sacerdos magnus, Lauda Sion salvatorem]: all in *I-LT*

BIBLIOGRAPHY

R. Morrocchi: *La musica a Siena: appunti storici* (Siena, 1886/*R*1969)
N. Zanichelli: *Carteggio inedito del G. B. Martini coi più celebri musicisti del suo tempo*, i (Bologna, 1888) [with letters referring to controversy with Martini]
G. Tebaldini: *L'archivio musicale della Cappella lauretana: catalogo storico-critico* (Loreto, 1921)

CAROLYN M. GIANTURCO

Redlich, Hans F(erdinand) (*b* Vienna, 11 Feb 1903; *d*
Manchester, 27 Nov 1968). British musicologist, conductor and composer of Austrian birth. He studied at
the universities of Vienna and Munich in the early
1920s; up to 1921 he also studied the piano privately
with Paul Weingarten and theory with Hugo Kauder
and then studied composition with Carl Orff. In 1931
he obtained a doctorate at Frankfurt University with a
dissertation on the madrigals of Monteverdi. Meanwhile
he had obtained practical experience of conducting as
assistant conductor at the Charlottenburg Opera, Berlin
(1924–5), and at the Stadttheater, Mainz (1925–9); during his years at Mainz a number of modern works,
mainly German and Italian, were produced at his
instigation. His Concerto grosso was first performed at
Krefeld in 1927. He worked in Germany until political

events caused him to return to Austria in 1937, and then to move to England in 1939; he took British nationality in 1947.

From 1941 to 1955 Redlich was a lecturer for the eastern division of the Workers' Educational Association and for the extra-mural departments of Cambridge and Birmingham universities and travelled indefatigably as a lecturer for all three bodies. During this period he lived at Letchworth, Hertfordshire, and became an important figure in the musical life of the area, conducting the local choral and orchestral societies. In 1955 he was appointed lecturer in history of music at Edinburgh University, while at the same time lecturing in eastern Scotland for the university's department of adult education and extra-mural studies. In 1962 he was appointed professor of music at the University of Manchester. He brought new standards to the department and founded the Wissema Ensemble. In 1967 Edinburgh University awarded him the honorary degree of DMus.

Redlich was a man of great energy, humour and charm, who in addition to his practical activities found time to write several books and many articles and to produce a large number of practical editions, most of which stemmed from his position in his later years as general editor of Eulenburg miniature scores. His interests were wide but centred on three main areas. He first made his name as a student of Monteverdi, and some 20 years later his book on the life and works of Monteverdi (1949) and its English translation, supplemented by his editions of the Vespers and L'incoronazione di Poppea, crowned his work on this composer. He was on the advisory committee of the Hallische Händel-Ausgabe, for which he edited two volumes. His enthusiasm for Austrian music of the past 100 years is reflected above all in his books on Bruckner, Mahler and Berg. His personal connections with the composers of the Second Viennese School (a designation that he invented) led to the foundation of the International Alban Berg Society, of which he was vice-president. Much of Redlich's published work has been superseded by that of younger scholars, including those to whom he readily gave encouragement, but his principal achievement was to help popularize in the English-speaking world the music of Monteverdi, Bruckner, Mahler and Berg when it was far less familiar than it has since become, partly as a result of his efforts. His private library now forms the nucleus of the music department library at the University of Lancaster.

WRITINGS

Gustav Mahler: eine Erkenntnis (Nuremberg, 1919)
'Die Welt der V. VI. und VII Symphonie', *Musikblätter des Anbruch*, ii (1920), 265
'Schoenbergs Tonalität: zu Schoenbergs Instrumentierung zweier Bachscher Choralvorspiele', *Pult und Taktstock*, iv (1927)
Das Problem des Stilwandels in Monteverdis Madrigalwerk (diss., U. of Frankfurt, 1931; Berlin, 1931, enlarged 2/1932 as *Claudio Monteverdi: I. Das Madrigalwerk*)
'Neue Monteverdiana', *Musikblätter des Anbruch*, xiii (1931), 127
'Zur Bearbeitung von Monteverdis "Orfeo" ', *SMz*, lxxvi (1936), 37
'Monteverdis "Incoronazione di Poppea" ', *SMz*, lxxvii (1937), 617
'Zu Monteverdis letzte Oper', *Musikblätter des Anbruch*, xix (1937), 108
'Monteverdi's Religious Music', *ML*, xxvii (1946), 208
Richard Wagner: Tristan und Isolde, Lohengrin, Parsifal (London, 1948, 3/1951)
Claudio Monteverdi: Leben und Werk (Olten, 1949; Eng. trans., 1952)
'The Finale of Bruckner's Symphony IX', *MMR*, lxxix (1949), 143
'The Significance of Britten's Operatic Style', *Music Survey*, ii (1950), 240
'Arnold Schoenberg', *MR*, xii (1951), 304

'Notes to a New Edition of Monteverdi's Mass of 1651', *MMR*, lxxxiii (1953), 95
'Der Symphoniker Alban Berg', *ÖMz*, ix (1954), 148
'Monteverdi e l'orchestra', *L'orchestra [in onore Gino Marinuzzi 1882–1945]* (Florence, 1954), 183
'The Editing of Monteverdi', *RN*, vii (1954), 18
'Alle gute Dinge', *Melos*, xxii (1955), 39
'Bruckner and Brahms Quintets in F', *ML*, xxxvi (1955), 253
'Claudio Monteverdi: Some Problems of Textual Interpretation', *MQ*, xli (1955), 66
Bruckner and Mahler (London, 1955; rev. 2/1963)
Alban Berg: the Man and his Music (London, 1957)
Alban Berg: Versuch eine Würdigung (Vienna, 1957)
with F. Walker: ' "Gesu mori": an Unknown Early Verdi Manuscript', *MR*, xx (1959), 233
'The Re-discovery of Monteverdi, on the Occasion of a New Edition of L'Incoronazione di Poppea', *MR*, xxiii (1962), 103
' "Prima la musica . . .?": a Ruminative Comment on Richard Strauss' Final Opera', *MR*, xxiv (1963), 185
'The Meaning and Aims of Musicology', *Manchester Literary and Philosophical Society Memoirs and Proceedings*, cvi (1963–4), 124 [Percival Lecture]
'Alban Berg and Posterity: an Interim Report', *MR*, xxv (1964), 320
'Paul Hindemith: a Reassessment', *MR*, xxv (1964), 241
'Schoenberg's Religious Testament', *Opera*, xvi (1965), 401
'Bergs Briefe an seine Frau', *ÖMz*, xxi (1966), 338
'Bergs Konzertarie "Der Wein" ', *ÖMz*, xxi (1966), 284
'Gustav Mahler: Probleme einer kritischen Gesamtausgabe', *Mf*, xix (1966), 378
' "Messiah": the Struggle for a Definitive Text', *MR*, xxvii (1966), 287
'Wagnerian Elements in pre-Wagnerian Opera', *Essays Presented to Egon Wellesz* (Oxford, 1966), 145
'The Oboes in Handel's Op.6', *MT*, cix (1968), 530
'Alban Berg's "Altenberg" Songs Op.4: Editorial Problems and no End', *MR*, xxxi (1970), 43

EDITIONS

Meister des Orgelbarock, Musica sacra, i (Berlin, 1931) [rev. edn. of F. Commer, ed.: Musica sacra, i (Berlin, 1839)]
with A. Hoffmann: *G. F. Handel: 12 concerti grossi, op.6*, Hallische Händel-Ausgabe, iv/14 (Kassel, 1961); *Wassermusik und Feuerwerksmusik*, ibid, iv/13 (Kassel, 1962)

BIBLIOGRAPHY

W. Szmolyan: 'Hans Ferdinand Redlich', *ÖMz*, xxiii (1968), 162
H. Gál: 'Hans Ferdinand Redlich zum Gedenken', *Mf*, xxii (1969), 3
W. Szmolyan: 'Hans Ferdinand Redlich', *ÖMz*, xxiv (1969), 45 [obituary]
G. Reaney: 'Hans Ferdinand Redlich in Memoriam', *AcM*, xlii (1970), 217

ARTHUR D. WALKER

Redman, Don [Donald Mathew] (*b* Piedmont, West Virginia, 29 July 1900; *d* New York, 30 Nov 1964). Black American jazz arranger, band-leader, saxophonist and composer. He was a child prodigy in a musical family, learnt several instruments and studied music at Storer College. After graduating he joined Billy Paige's Broadway Syncopators and went with them to New York, where he joined Fletcher Henderson as saxophonist and arranger. During his stay with Henderson (1923–7) he developed the basic principles of jazz orchestral arrangement which were to shape not only Henderson's but eventually all big bands. He then became musical director of the Detroit band McKinney's Cotton Pickers, developing for them a style different from Henderson's. From 1931 to 1940 he led his own band, and thereafter worked as a freelance arranger, leading a big band on a European tour in 1946–7 and working as musical director for Pearl Bailey.

Although Redman's playing, singing and compositions were not particularly innovatory or influential, his arranging, band-leading and teaching (musicians who worked with him praised his remarkable lucidity) made a considerable impact. By the late 1920s Redman had confronted and devised solutions for nearly every problem of big band arranging, including that of adapting popular music for the jazz repertory. His use of the reeds and brass in separate 'sections' was not remarkable in itself, but by placing them in opposition he devised a powerful idiom in which the characteristic rhythms of jazz, previously found only in solo improvising, are applied to the full ensemble.

BIBLIOGRAPHY
F. Driggs: 'Don Redman', *Jazz Review*, ii (1959), Nov, 6
C. Fox: 'Don Redman', *Jazz Monthly*, viii (1962), April, 8
J. Grunnet Jepsen: *Jazz Records, 1942–1962*, vi (n.p., 1963)
R. Hadlock: *Jazz Masters of the 20s* (New York, 1965), 194ff
B. Rust: *Jazz Records: 1897–1942* (London, 1965, rev. 2/1969)
R. Atkins: 'Don Redman', *Jazz on Record*, ed. A. McCarthy (London, 1968), 239
G. Schuller: *Early Jazz* (New York, 1968), 256ff
A. McCarthy: *Big Band Jazz* (London, 1974), 25ff

JAMES DAPOGNY

Redonda (Sp.). SEMIBREVE (whole note); *semibreve* is also used. *See also* NOTE VALUES.

Redowa. A Czech dance. It was introduced into Paris about 1840 and quickly attained great popularity for a short time, both there and in London. In Czechoslovakia there are two variants of the dance, performed in succession: the *rejdovák*, in 3/4 or 3/8 time, which is rather like a waltz, and the *rejdovačka*, an after-dance in 2/4 time similar to a polka. The ordinary *redowa* is written in 3/4 time and is similar to the mazurka, but with less strongly marked rhythms.

Reed. An elastic lamina of metal, plastic or natural vegetable tissue (the traditional material from which the name is derived). Under the influence of an airstream from a wind player's lungs or from bellows, this elastic body will vibrate at a frequency determined by its dimensions, mass, etc, and this vibration is used to excite periodic pressure waves in an air column within the tube of an instrument. The frequency of these waves and hence the note sounded is mainly determined by the form and dimensions of the air column which are the more important factors in a coupled acoustic system. Reeds as used today in art music are categorized as 'beating' or 'free', the former being again divided into 'single' and 'double'.

The single beating reed (typified by that of the CLARINET or saxophone) is a narrow slip split from the stem

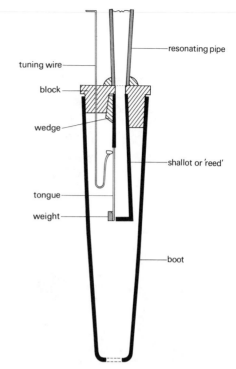

2. *Reed pipe of an organ*

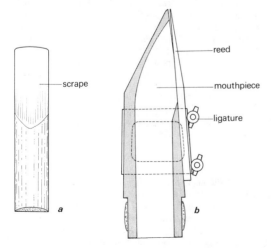

1. (a) *single reed of a clarinet; (b) clarinet mouthpiece with reed in position*

of the large semi-tropical grass *arundo donax* or *arundo sativa*, commonly though inaccurately called 'cane', which is grown for the purpose chiefly in the Var region of France. The stems are harvested when of suitable size and somewhat unripe, and are then matured in the open air, a process which calls for nice judgment on the part of the growers. The rough slips are cut to length, flattened on the inner side, and on the other scraped down to a feather edge at one end (fig.1a). The mouthpiece to which such reeds are allied is roughly conical with a flat 'table' tangential to the base. Towards the tip of the mouthpiece the table or 'lay' is slightly curved in its length and is perforated by a roughly rectangular slot which communicates with the inner bore. The thick end of the reed is bound to the table with cord or a metal ligature (fig.1b). As the thin end vibrates it periodically closes the slot to a greater or lesser extent, thus transmitting bursts of energy to the air column within.

In reed pipes of organs (fig.2) the action is similar but in this case a slight curve is applied to the metal blade or the tongue instead of to the table (*see* REED-WORK). In some cases the tongue is loaded with a supplementary weight to lower its natural frequency. The structure equivalent to the mouthpiece of a woodwind is called the shallot, or by organ builders a reed – a curious reversal of practice elsewhere.

The beating double reed of the oboe or bassoon is made up of two slips of 'cane', hollow on the inside, gouged until quite thin and again scraped to a feather edge on the outside (fig. 3a–b). These are bound together – face to face – with thread, and in the smaller sizes mounted on a short tapered metal tube, or staple. When

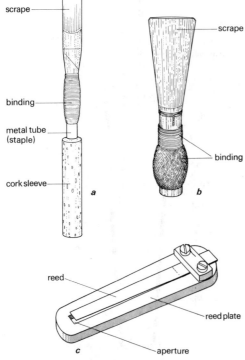

3. (a) double reed of an oboe, and (b) a bassoon; (c) free reed of a concertina

blown the elliptical gap between the ends of the blades opens and closes, again giving bursts of energy to the air column. The form and degree of 'scrape' applied to the tip of the reed has a profound influence on its behaviour and tractability, and varies much from player to player, but there are two principal styles in vogue. In one the chamfer is fairly even from side to side; in the other more of the outer skin is left intact to form a stiffish 'backbone' along the mid-line of the blade.

The body of some folk instruments is itself a length of cane; a reed is formed by cutting and raising a tongue from the tube below a natural knot. This is kept from closing down completely by inserting a hair at the base of the cut. Such instruments are termed 'idioglot', and are exemplified by the Near Eastern *zummarah*. Detached reeds of similar construction are widely used in the drones of Western bagpipes.

In Western musical instruments the free reed (fig.3c) is less common than the beating type and is chiefly found in certain organ pipes and bellows-blown instruments such as the accordion and harmonium. Here the tongue does not close against the slot in the shallot or mounting plate, but can pass freely through it. The common MOUTH ORGAN and the traditional Chinese *sheng* are two of the few examples of mouth-blown free reeds.

For very many years attempts were made to find substitutes for *arundo donax* as the raw material for reeds. Silver, whalebone, lancewood, etc, have all been tried, but until quite lately only the traditional material has proved useful. Other vegetable tissues are commonly employed for folk instruments, but none of them has shown the qualities required by an orchestral player.

The search for a substitute was accelerated after the damage to French reed farms in both world wars, and today, after increasing research into the characteristics of plastic materials, plastic reeds are produced which are found acceptable by some players.

The word 'reed' is also used in two contexts which, though common, are not strictly accurate. Lip-energized brass instruments are not infrequently called 'lip reeds' since the player's lips form with the mouthpieces the vibrating element of the tone generator. Modern research, however, has shown that when in operation the behaviour of the lips and of a reed is not quite comparable. The term 'air reed' for the generating element in organ pipes, recorders, or transverse flutes, while useful, is not strictly accurate either.

For further illustrations *see* REED INSTRUMENTS.

PHILIP BATE

Reed, Richard. *See* READE, RICHARD.

Reed, Thomas German. *See* GERMAN REED, THOMAS.

Reed, William Henry (*b* Frome, 29 July 1876; *d* Dumfries, 2 July 1942). English violinist and teacher. He studied the violin and composition at the RAM in London and became an accomplished solo and chamber music player. In 1904 he joined the LSO on its formation, and served as its leader for 23 years (1912–35), and as chairman of its board from 1935 until his death, enjoying throughout the unswerving support and regard of his fellow musicians. At successive Three Choirs Festivals with the LSO, Reed formed a close friendship with Elgar that brought about his assistance in certain technical aspects of Elgar's Violin Concerto. He took part in the first performances of Elgar's Violin Sonata, String Quartet and Piano Quintet, and wrote two books on Elgar, the earlier of which includes facsimile reproductions of sketches for the composer's unfinished third symphony with Reed's commentary on them, based on first-hand discussions with Elgar. For many years Reed taught the violin at the RCM in London, and was active as a conductor, mainly of amateur orchestras, and as an examiner and adjudicator; he died while adjudicating in Scotland (he was buried in Worcester Cathedral, near the Elgar Memorial Window). His compositions are skilful but not individual, and include orchestral tone poems (some performed at Three Choirs Festivals), a Violin Concerto, a Rhapsody for violin and orchestra, and works for small orchestra and chamber ensembles.

WRITINGS
'Elgar's Violin Concerto', *ML*, xvi (1935), 30
Elgar as I Knew him (London, 1936)
Elgar (London, 1939)

BIBLIOGRAPHY
H. Foss and N. Goodwin: *London Symphony: Portrait of an Orchestra* (London, 1954), esp. 198
J. Creighton: *Discopaedia of the Violin 1889–1971* (Toronto, 1974), 622

H. C. COLLES/NOËL GOODWIN

Reed, William Leonard (*b* London, 16 Oct 1910). English composer. He was educated at Dulwich, Oxford (DMus 1939) and the Royal College of Music (1934–6) where he studied with Herbert Howells (composition) and Constant Lambert (conducting). He won the Cobbett Prize in 1934 and from 1937 spent two years in Scandinavia as a lecturer for the British Council. He later spent some time in the USA. In the 1950s he toured the Far East, Africa and Europe with his musical play *The Vanishing Island* (with G. Fraser, Santa Barbara, 1955). Other successful musicals by him include *The Crowning Experience* (with G. Fraser, Detroit, 1958), *Annie* (London, 1967) and *Love All* (London, 1978). He has also composed orchestral works (*Scherzo*, 1937; *Mountain House Suite*, 1949; *Festive March*, 1978), chamber music (*Concert Piece* for two clarinets and piano, 1936; *Doctor Johnson's Suite*, string quartet, 1944), and pieces for piano (*Concert Waltz*, 1977) and organ. He has also written film music and edited anthologies of sacred vocal music.

Reed-cap shawms. Another term for WIND-CAP INSTRUMENTS, wind instruments in which a reed, usually a double reed, is enclosed by a cap so that the player does not control it directly with his lips.

Reed instruments (Ger. *Rohrblattinstrumente*). A term commonly used for musical instruments in which an airstream is directed against a lamella which is thereby set into periodic vibration and interrupts the stream intermittently (*see* REED). In classifying musical instruments, Hornbostel and Sachs (1914) divided aerophones into two subclasses: free aerophones (*freie Aerophone*) and wind instruments proper (*eigentliche Blasinstrumente*). Reeds appear in both categories, and although the classification may be based on controversial acoustic premises it provides a valuable compendium for surveying various kinds of reed instrument. The relevant excerpts are given here in translation (with minor emendations):

41 *Free aerophones*: the vibrating air is not confined by the instrument

411 *Displacement free aerophones*: the airstream meets a sharp edge, or a sharp edge is moved through the air; it appears that a periodic displacement of air occurs to alternate flanks of the edge (whip, sword-blade)

412 *Interruptive free aerophones*: the airstream is interrupted periodically

412.1 *Idiophonic interruptive aerophones or reeds*: the airstream is directed against a lamella, setting it in periodic vibration to interrupt the stream intermittently. In this group also belong reeds with a 'cover', i.e. a tube in which the air vibrates only in a secondary sense, not producing the sound but simply adding roundness and timbre to the sound made by the reed's vibration; they are generally recognizable by the absence of finger-holes (organ reed stops)

412.11 *Concussion reeds*: two lamellae make a gap which closes periodically during their vibration (split grass-blade)

412.12 *Percussion reeds*: a single lamella strikes against a frame

412.121 *Individual percussion reeds* – found in British Columbia

412.122 *Sets of percussion reeds* (earlier reed stops of organs)

412.13 *Free reeds*: the lamella vibrates through [at] a closely-fitting slot

412.131 (*Individual*) *free reeds* (single-note motor horn)

412.132 *Sets of free reeds*: NB in instruments like the Chinese *cheng* the finger-holes do not serve to modify the pitch and are therefore not equivalent to the finger-holes of other pipes (reed organ, mouth-organ, accordion)

412.14 *Ribbon reeds*: the airstream is directed against the edge of a stretched band or ribbon [the acoustics of this process have not been studied] – found in British Columbia

412.2 *Non-idiophonic interruptive instruments*: the interruptive agent is not a reed

42 *Wind instruments proper*: the vibrating air is confined within the instrument itself

[421 *Edge instruments or flutes*: a narrow stream of air is directed against an edge]

422 *Reedpipes*: the airstream has, through means of one or two lamellae placed at the head of the instrument, intermittent access to the column of air which is to be made to vibrate

422.1 *Oboes*: the pipe has a [double] reed of concussion lamellae, usually a flattened stem

422.11 (*Single*) *oboes*

422.111 *With cylindrical bore*

422.111.1 *Without finger-holes* – found in British Columbia

422.111.2 *With finger-holes* (aulos, crumhorn)

422.112 *With conical bore* (European oboe)

422.12 *Sets of oboes*

422.121 *With cylindrical bore* (double aulos)

422.122 *With conical bore* – found in India

422.2 *Clarinets*: the pipe has a [single] 'reed' consisting of a percussion lamella

422.21 (*Single*) *clarinets*

422.211 *With cylindrical bore*

422.211.1 *Without finger-holes* – found in British Columbia

422.211.2 *With finger-holes* (European clarinet)

422.212 *With conical bore* (saxophone)

422.22 *Sets of clarinets* – found in Egypt (zummāra)

422.3 *Reedpipes with free reeds*: the reed vibrates through [at] a closely-fitted frame; there must be finger-holes, otherwise the instrument belongs to the free reeds, 412.13 – found in south-east Asia

422.31 *Single pipes with free reed*

422.32 *Double pipes with free reeds*

Suffixes for use with any division of this class (aerophones):

–6 *with air reservoir*

–61 *with rigid air reservoir*

–62 *with flexible air reservoir*

–7 *with finger-hole stopping*

–71 *with keys*

–72 *with Bandmechanik* [perforated roll or ribbon]

–8 *with keyboard*

–9 *with mechanical drive*

(For illustrations see p.666.)

In this scheme the word 'clarinets' is used as a generic term for all reedpipes with a single reed 'consisting of a percussion lamella' – regardless of the shape of the bore and regardless of whether there is an air reservoir (as in a bagpipe). Likewise 'oboes' is used as a generic term for all reedpipes with a double reed 'of concussion lamellae'; some writers use the word 'shawm' instead, but others reserve 'shawm' for instruments with a wider bore than an oboe, or with a pirouette, or disc, against which the player's lips may rest, or for Renaissance instruments, etc.

Traditionally, reed instruments often have a rustic or pastoral connotation. Milton evoked 'the sound of pastoral reeds with oaten stops' and Shakespeare referred to those occasions 'when shepherds pipe on oaten strawes'. Children in the country still make their own reed instruments from the stalk of an oat or some other kind of straw by detaching a long, narrow tongue from the wall of the stalk (leaving it rooted to the body).

Reed instruments are often deemed to have common characteristics in timbre. Current sentiment among Western musicians about reed players was summed up by Baines (*Woodwind Instruments and their History*, 1957): they 'are entirely dependent upon a short-lived vegetable matter of merciless capriciousness, with which, however, when it behaves, are wrought perhaps the most tender and expressive sounds in all wind music'. This is certainly true of the modern Western oboe and english horn. Bartók gave a different account, however, when he heard a reed instrument in Algiers: 'its tone is much stronger than that of the lowest notes of the oboe; throughout its registers the tone remains equally piercing and shrill, and indoors it almost bursts one's eardrums'. A Swahili name for double-reed instruments is *parapanda*, an onomatopoeic word that conveys the piercing shrillness described by Bartók. Ethnomusicologists sometimes use the word 'reed' in unfortunate juxtaposition with 'flute', in the term 'reed flute ensemble'. This term refers to the sets of singly-blown, stopped tubes without finger-holes, cut from vegetable stalks. Although made of reed, the instruments are not reed-instruments in the sense defined above, but rather flutes, i.e. edge-blown.

See also ORGAN, §III.

KLAUS WACHSMANN

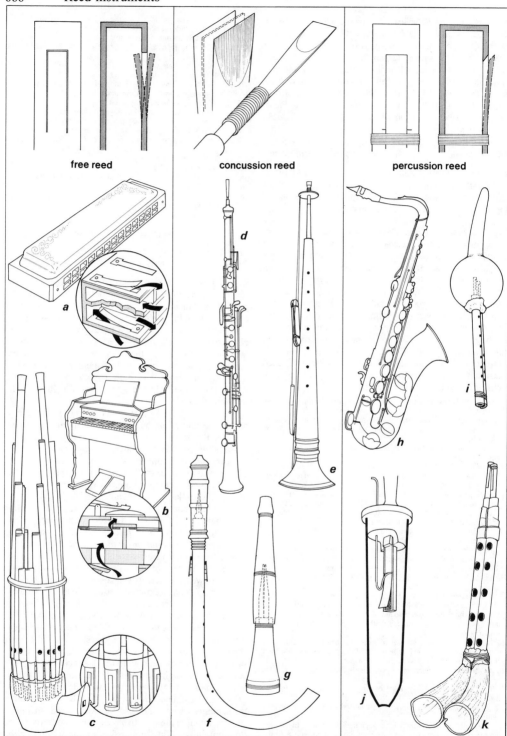

Classification of beating reeds, with examples of instruments in which each are found. Free reeds: (a) mouth organ (harmonica – inset shows airflow: inhale, lower tier; exhale, upper tier); (b) harmonium (cf inset with HARMONIUM, *fig.1); (c) mouth organ (sheng, China – pipes carrying brass reeds shown inserted into common windchamber); concussion reeds: (d) oboe; (e) shahnāī (India); (f) crumhorn (reed enclosed in windcap); (g) sk'a'na (British Columbia – reed enclosed in body of instrument); percussion reeds: (h) saxophone, (i) pungī (India – reed enclosed in windcap); (j) reed pipe of an organ; (k) double reedpipe (Tunisia)*

Reed organ. *See* HARMONIUM.

Reedpipe. In early literature, any simple or rustic musical pipe made from a reed or cane, or from several reeds, for instance the panpipes. More recent studies of ancient, primitive and folk instruments, however, tend to restrict the term to instruments in which the sound is produced through vibration of a reed (single, double or free), the pipe itself being commonly, but not necessarily, made from a reed or cane. By this definition panpipes would be classified with flutes rather than with reedpipes. Organ 'reed pipes' are those provided with a reed (normally of metal) as opposed to the 'flue pipes', which sound on the duct-flute or whistle principle (*see* ORGAN, §III, 2).

See also REED and REED INSTRUMENTS.

ANTHONY C. BAINES

Reedpipe ensemble. *See* STOPPED FLUTE ENSEMBLE.

Reed-work. The reed stops of an organ collectively (as distinct from FLUE-WORK), i.e. those in which sound is produced in each pipe by the wind exciting an elastic metal blade or tongue. The small metal tube cut away longitudinally against which the tongue 'beats' is properly called the reed. Reed-work refers to the Trumpet family of flaring pipes, the Krummhorn family of cylindrical pipes, others of short, fanciful, stopped, half-stopped pipes and all varieties of metal and wooden stops other than those of the flue-work. The term also encompasses the many types of regal and 'free reed' or harmonium stops.

In England the term 'reed' seems to have been systematically used first by James Talbot (MS treatise, *c*1695) sometimes in the phrase 'regals or reed' but referring to all reed stops known by him. Occasionally 'reed pipe' (*ryetpijpen*) was used in the Netherlands (Zwolle, 1505) and hence, probably, in England; certainly 'rede' was used in a sense of 'reed instrument' by Chaucer (*House of Fame*, 1380) and John Gower (*c*1390). It is older than the term 'flue stop' by about two centuries. Burney used the phrase 'reed-work' of the organ in Ulm Cathedral (1773).

PETER WILLIAMS

Reel (Anglo-Saxon *hreol*; Suio-Gothic cognate of *rulla*: 'to whirl'; Gael. *ruidhle, ruidhleadh*). An indigenous and probably very ancient Scottish dance. The reel contains two basic dance elements: a setting step danced on the spot, and a 'travelling' figure, i.e. movement in a particular pattern. One of the earliest specific references to the reel as a dance is in the report of the trial of the witches at North Berwick in 1590 at which Geilles Duncan, a servant girl, was stated to have played the reel *Commer goe ye before*, 'upon a small trumpe called a Jewes trumpe' (jew's harp), for the witches' dance. An early Gaelic reference to the reel occurs in a waulking-song:

> Reels around in endless mazes,
> With the great reed pipe a-straining

It is possible to establish the approximate date of the song because Gillie Calum, Chief of MacLeod of Raasay from 1648 to 1651 is mentioned in it as contemporary.

The reel has existed in Scotland in a number of forms, with qualifying names such as 'threesome', 'foursome', 'sixsome' and 'eightsome'; these indicate the number of

A foursome reel (foreground) danced to the accompaniment of a bagpipe: engraving from 'A Companion to the Ball Room' (1816) by Thomas Wilson

dancers. Many of these forms are now obsolete. The earliest reel, which may go back to medieval times, was probably the Circular Reel for two couples, of the western Highlands and Isles, in which the travelling figure was a circle. This could well have been performed round the fire, which in ancient times was in the centre of the floor. In the eastern Highlands and the Lowlands the threesome reel was danced, using the figure-of-eight as the travelling figure. It has been supposed that the threesome reel is related to the hey or hay, a threesome dance that may have spread from the Continent to both Scotland and England in about 1500. The threesome reel was gradually displaced by the foursome reel, also known as the Scotch Reel, first mentioned in 1776 by Topham; this remained a popular dance until after World War I.

The two reels most often danced today are the Reel of Tulloch and the eightsome reel. The modern version of the latter appears to have come into popular use in about 1868. The Reel of Tulloch (Gael.: *Ruidhleadh Thulachain* or *Hullachan*), as it is now danced, is said to have been devised in about 1880. The original dance, however, must have been older, for the tune *The Reel of Tulloch* appears in the McFarlan MS (*c*1740). A folk-tale attributes the original composition of the dance to Iain Dubh MacGregor of Glen Lyon; this would date the dance from the late 16th century or the early 17th.

Ex.1 *Johnnie made a wedding o't*

The first appearance in print of a reel tune with 'reel' in the title, is in Playford's *A Collection of Original Scotch Tunes* (1700). Other early reel tunes appear in the McFarlan MS, the Young MS (1740), and in Walsh's *Country Dances* (1773). The music of the reel is of a rapid but smooth-flowing quaver movement in *alla breve* time, minim = 120 (see ex.1). Orkney and Shetland have their own species of reels and reel tunes, some of which are obsolete. The 'auld reel' of Shetland, frequently with lines of irregular phrase structure, is thought to have some affinity with the Norwegian *halling* and other Scandinavian dances; this suggests that the reel may have been of Scandinavian origin. It may equally be, however, that the dance is Celtic, and spread from Scotland to Scandinavia and the Netherlands. The reel flourished in Ireland following its introduction from Scotland during the second half of the 18th century, and it is now a favourite dance-tune type among traditional instrumentalists (*see* IRELAND, §II, 5(ii)). In North America the reel is the staple musical fare for square-dances, though in the central and southern USA it is often known by the name BREAKDOWN or HOEDOWN.

BIBLIOGRAPHY

E. Topham: *Letters from Edinburgh Written in the Years 1774 and 1775* (London, 1776)
T. Newte: *A Tour in England and Scotland, 1785* (London, 1788)
J. G. Atkinson: *Scottish National Dances* (Edinburgh, 1900)
D. R. MacKenzie: *The National Dances of Scotland* (Glasgow, 1910)
D. G. MacLennan: *Highland and Traditional Scottish Dances* (Edinburgh, 1950)
H. A. Thurston: *Scotland's Dances* (London, 1954)
J. F. and T. M. Flett: *Traditional Dancing in Scotland* (London, 1964)
J. L. Campbell and F. Collinson: *Hebridean Folksongs*, i (Oxford, 1967)
J. F. and T. M. Flett: 'The Scottish Reel as a Dance-form', *Scottish Studies*, xvi/2 (1972), 91

FRANCIS COLLINSON

Rees, J(ohn) T(homas) (*b* Cwmgiedd, nr. Ystradgynlais, 1857; *d* Bow Street, Cardiganshire, 1949). Welsh conductor and composer. Like his older contemporary Joseph Parry, he came to music after working as a coal miner for many years. He studied music under Parry at Aberystwyth, took a MusBac at Toronto University, taught briefly in the USA and in 1889 settled in Bow Street near Aberystwyth. There he taught music, served as organist and conductor of the choir at 'Y Garn' Chapel, composed, wrote about music in Welsh journals and worked as an editor. For many years he was music editor of *Trysorfa'r Plant*. Of his compositions, which include an opera and most forms of instrumental composition, only his hymn tunes are now known ('Isfryn', 'Bronceiro', 'Llwynbedw', 'Salem', 'Neuadd Las'). Rees was a powerful figure in Welsh musical life, and was reputed to have conducted over many years more *cymanfaoedd canu* than anyone (the *gymanfa ganu* is a distinctive and uniquely Welsh kind of devotional entertainment at which large numbers of people join together in worship to sing hymns in four-part harmony under the direction of a conductor).

BIBLIOGRAPHY

D. H. Lewis: *John Thomas Rees: cofiaut* (Llandysul, 1955)
H. Williams: *Tonau a'u hawduron* (Caernarvon, 1967)

OWAIN EDWARDS

Reese, Gustave (*b* New York, 29 Nov 1899; *d* Berkeley, 7 Sept 1977). American music scholar and teacher. He attended New York University (LlB 1921, MusB 1930) and taught there, with a few interruptions, from 1927. He also served as visiting professor at a number of American universities including Harvard, Duke, California (UCLA), Southern California, Michigan and the City University of New York, and gave courses in musicology at the Juilliard School. He was associate editor (1933–44) and then editor (1944–5) of the *Musical Quarterly*. From 1940 to 1945 he was head of the publication department for the firm of G. Schirmer; from 1945 to 1955 he was director of publication at Carl Fischer, a firm with which he was later connected in an advisory capacity.

Throughout his career Reese was a leading figure in American musicological administration. He was a founder-member of the AMS in 1934; having been its secretary (1934–46), vice-president (1946–50), and president (1950–52), he continued to serve the society as a member of various committees. In 1958 he became a vice-president of the Plainsong and Mediaeval Music Society; from 1967 to 1972 he was a member of the council of the IMS. From 1971 to 1973 Reese served as president of the Renaissance Society of America. He received honorary degrees from the Chicago Musical College (1949) and from Rutgers University (1972). In 1972 he received New York University's 'Great Teacher' award.

With the publication of *Music in the Middle Ages* (1940) Reese established himself as a scholar of the first rank. His *Music in the Renaissance* (1954) did more than simply add to his reputation; the two books taken together gave tremendous impetus to the study of early music and to musicology in general in English-speaking countries. In many respects Reese's work set new standards; the completeness and precision of bibliographic documentation, together with the orderly marshalling and clear exposition of fact in his books, have made them model textbooks for graduate students. His fairness in representing the work of other scholars and his ability to select the best from among conflicting theories are exemplary. Another notable feature of these books is Reese's apt mixture of bibliographic fact with aesthetic judgment based on genuine acquaintance with an enormous body of music (this last no surprise to his students, with whom he always stressed the importance of getting to know the sound of as much early music as possible).

The sense of indebtedness felt by musicologists to Gustave Reese can be seen in the imposing scope and quality of the Festschrift volume presented to him on his 65th birthday.

WRITINGS

'The First Printed Collection of Part-music: the Odhecaton', *MQ*, xx (1934), 39–76
Music in the Middle Ages (New York, 1940)
ed.: *A Birthday Offering to Carl Engel* (New York, 1943) [incl. 'More about the Namesake', p.181]
'Maldeghem and his Buried Treasure', *Notes*, vi (1948–9), 75–117
'The Origin of the English *In Nomine*', *JAMS*, ii (1949), 7
with T. Karp: 'Monophony in a Group of Renaissance Chansonniers', *JAMS*, v (1952), 4
Music in the Renaissance (New York, 1954, rev. 2/1959)
Fourscore Classics of Music Literature (New York, 1957)
Chapters 17–20 in *Music and Western Man*, ed. P Garvie (London, 1958)
'The Polyphonic Magnificat of the Renaissance as a Design in Tonal Centers', *JAMS*, xiii (1960), 68
ed., with R. Brandel: *The Commonwealth of Music: in Honor of Curt Sachs* (New York, 1965) [incl. 'The Repertoire of Book II of Ortiz's *Tratado*', p.201]
'Musical Compositions in Renaissance Intarsia', *Medieval and Renaissance Studies*, ii (Durham, North Carolina, 1968), 74
'Tritonus', *MGG*
ed., with R. J. Snow: *Essays in Musicology in Honor of Dragan Plamenac* (Pittsburgh, 1969/R1977) [incl. 'An Early 17th-century Lute MS at San Francisco', p.253]

'The Polyphonic 'Missa de Beata Virgine' as a Genre: the Background of Josquin's Lady Mass', *Josquin des Prez: New York 1971*, 589

ed., with S. Ledbetter: *Ornithoparchus' Musice active micrologus (1517) and J. Dowland's English Translation (1609)* (New York, 1973)

'An Editorial Problem in a Mass by Heinrich Isaac (c. 1450–1517): *Sanctus* and *Benedictus* from *Missa Misericordias Domini*', *Notations and Editions: a Book in Honor of Louise Cuyler* (Dubuque, Iowa, 1974), 33

'The Opening Chant for a Palestrina Magnificat', *A Musical Offering: Essays in Honor of Martin Bernstein* (New York, 1977)

'Josquin Desprez', §§1–7, *Grove 6*

BIBLIOGRAPHY

J. LaRue and others, eds.: *Aspects of Medieval and Renaissance Music: a Birthday Offering to Gustave Reese* (New York, 1966, 2/1978) [contains biography and bibliography]

A. Mendel: 'Gustave Reese (1899–1977): a Personal Memoir', *JAMS*, xxx (1977), 359

'Tributes to Gustave Reese, 1899–1977', *Early Music*, vi (1978), 99

JAMES HAAR

Reeser, H(endrik) Eduard (*b* Rotterdam, 23 March 1908). Dutch musicologist. He studied at the University of Utrecht with Vogelsang (history of art) and Smijers (musicology); he took the doctorate there in 1939 with a dissertation on the violin and piano sonata in Paris at the time of Mozart. He taught history of music at the Conservatory of Rotterdam (1930–37). He was also editor with Herman Rutters of the monthly *Caecilia en de muziek* and in 1937 he became music editor of the *Nieuwe Rotterdamsche courant*. After World War II Reeser was appointed government music adviser. He held this post until 1947, when the Maatschappij tot Bevordering der Toonkunst offered him a musicology post at the University of Utrecht. Three years later he was made reader, and in 1956 professor; he retired in 1973.

Reeser has continued the work of Smijers in creating a school of musicology at Utrecht, though in a different way from his predecessor since his interests are not limited to his own subject – music since 1600 – but extend broadly through the history of Western culture. A special interest is the Dutch composer Alphons Diepenbrock (1862–1921), whose cause he has promoted through editions of his compositions, writings and letters.

As a member of the board of many organizations Reeser has played a prominent part in furthering Dutch musical life. He has been secretary of the Alphons Diepenbrock Foundation (1940–70, chairman since 1970), president of the Donemus Foundation (1947–57, government adviser since 1957), member of the board of the Holland Festival (1948–68) and president of the Maatschappij tot Bevordering der Toonkunst (1951–69). He has been on the board of the Vereniging voor Nederlandse Muziekgeschiedenis for many years and was its chairman from 1957 to 1971. Since 1958 he has been a member of the IMS council; he was president, 1972–7. He was appointed a member of the Royal Dutch Academy of Sciences in 1961.

WRITINGS

De muzikale handschriften van Alphons Diepenbrock (Amsterdam, 1933)

Alphons Diepenbrock (Amsterdam, 1935)

'Van Bach tot Beethoven', *AMe*

'Guillaume Dufay: "Nuper rosarum flores"', *TVNM*, xv/3 (1938), 137

De klaviersonate met vioolbegeleiding in het Parijsche muziekleven ten tijde van Mozart (diss., U. of Utrecht, 1939; Rotterdam, 1939)

De zonen van Bach (Amsterdam, 1941; Eng. trans., 1946)

'Een "isomelische mis" uit den tijd van Dufay', *TVNM*, xvi/3 (1942), 151

Muziekgeschiedenis in vogelvlucht (Amsterdam, 1942; Eng. trans., 1946)

De Vereeniging voor Nederlandsche muziekgeschiedenis 1868–1943: gedenkboek (Amsterdam, 1943)

De geschiedenis van de wals (Amsterdam, 1947; Eng. trans., 1947)

Muziek in de gemeenschap der kunsten (Rotterdam, 1947)

'Johann Gottfried Eckard', *TVNM*, xvii/2 (1949), 89–125

Een eeuw Nederlandse muziek (Amsterdam, 1950)

ed.: *Verzamelde geschriften van Alphons Diepenbrock* (Utrecht, 1950)

Music in Holland (Amsterdam, 1959)

'Musikwissenschaft in Holland', *AcM*, xxxii (1960), 160

'Alphons Diepenbrock', *Musica*, xv (1961), 259

ed.: *Alphons Diepenbrock: brieven en documenten* (The Hague, 1962–)

'De nalatenschap van Johann Gottfried Eckard', *Anthony van Hoboken: Festschrift zum 75. Geburtstag* (Mainz, 1962), 122

'Nationale kenmerken in de Noord-Nederlandse muziek 1830–1940', *Filologencongres: Antwerp 1963*, 455

'Alexander Voormolen', *Sonorum speculum* (1965), no.22, p.1; no.23, p.18

'Audible Staging: Motion and Gesture in the Music of Richard Wagner', *Essays on Drama and Theatre: Liber Amicorum Benjamin Hunningher* (Amsterdam, 1973), 140

'Idomeneo auf dem Theater', *MJb 1973–4*. 46

'Der junge Mozart und der Alberti-Bass', *Erich Valentin zum 70. Geburtstag* (Regensburg, 1976), 195

'Some Melodic Patterns in the Music of Alphons Diepenbrock', *Key Notes* (1976), no.3, p.16

EDITIONS

Verzamelde liederen van Alphons Diepenbrock (Amsterdam, 1951–9)

J. G. Eckard: *Oeuvres complètes pour le clavecin ou le pianoforte* (Amsterdam, 1956)

W. A. Mozart: *Bearbeitungen von Werken verschiedener Komponisten: Klavierkonzerte . . . und Kadenzen*, Neue Ausgabe sämtlicher Werke, x/28/2 (Kassel, 1964)

Stijlproeven van Nederlandse muziek/Anthology of Music from the Netherlands 1890–1960 (Amsterdam, 1963–)

ELLINOR BIJVOET

Reeve, William (*b* London, 1757; *d* London, 22 June 1815). Prolific English theatre composer of negligible talent. He was organist at Totnes in Devon in the early 1780s, and came to London to help with the music at Astley's Amphitheatre, where the more popular performers were all horses; two songs survive from a burletta called *The Double Jealousy*. In June 1787 John Palmer opened his ill-fated Royalty Theatre. When he found that spoken dialogue would be illegal there, he was forced to present all-sung burlettas in which, being a poor singer, he could take little part. Of Reeve's contributions only *Thomas and Susan* was published in vocal score; most of the song tunes were traditional ballads. Palmer also staged a ballet called *Don Juan* so that he could mime the title role, and Reeve wrote much of the music. Dramatic miming was almost unknown at the playhouses. Covent Garden's first successful attempt at what we would call *ballet d'action* was *Oscar and Malvinia* (1791); the plot, developed from hints in Ossian, was carried on entirely in mine and dance, but a few songs and choruses were added for variety. Shield was to have written the music, but he quarrelled with the management and went abroad, with the result that Reeve, who had been a minor Covent Garden singer for two seasons, was asked to complete the score. The success of *Oscar and Malvinia* and the absence of any rival of the least ability made it possible for him to compose Covent Garden operas and pantomimes for the next 15 years; in their more ambitious productions he was told to collaborate with Mazzinghi. By chance rather than inclination he continued to be involved in ballet experiments. *Hercules and Omphale*, *Raymond and Agnes*, *The Round Tower* and *Joan of Arc* had no spoken dialogue or recitative to carry forward their elaborate plots, though all contained a few songs. As only his songs were published, one cannot tell how Reeve dealt with the more dramatic moments. He was much less interested in ballet than was John C. Cross, the librettist for many of his early operas. Cross devised the action of *The Round Tower* and *Joan of Arc*, and then went off to the Royal Circus Theatre where, with Sanderson, he created much more adventurous story ballets of which all the music survives.

Reeve composed two 'Entertainments' of songs for the Lyceum Theatre, *The Evening Brush* (1792) and *Mirth's Museum* (1794), and continued to provide trivial and undramatic songs for Covent Garden; many of his naive overtures were published in piano arrangement. When an opera of his succeeded, it was not because of the music. *The Caravan* drew crowded houses because, at the climax, a dog jumped into a tank of water and rescued a child. The success of this piece led Charles Dibdin junior, who was running Sadler's Wells from 1803, to instal there a large tank of usually fetid water round which he devised his 'aqua dramas'. From 1808 until his death, Reeve, seldom now wanted at Covent Garden, wrote nearly all the Sadler's Wells music; he had earlier become one of the proprietors by buying five of the 40 shares. Dibdin admired his honesty and benevolence. The George Reeve who also composed for Sadler's Wells was presumably his son; Charlotte Reeve, a passable Ophelia at Covent Garden, was his daughter.

WORKS

Only those theatrical works from which music survives are listed; each entry includes only extant published music, and unless otherwise indicated a published libretto survives. All printed works were published in London shortly after first performance.

(vs–vocal score)

ROYALTY THEATRE ITEMS

Don Juan (ballet, Delpini); 3 dances, 4 songs
Hero and Leander (burlesque, Jackman); ov., 2 songs
Hobson's Choice (burletta, Oulton); 1 song, no lib
Thomas and Susan (short all-sung opera); vs, no lib

PLAYHOUSE ITEMS

(CG–Covent Garden; DL–Drury Lane; LT–Little Theatre)

Tippoo Saib (pantomime ballet, Lonsdale), CG, 6 June 1791; vs (songs), no lib
Oscar and Malvina (pantomime ballet, Byrne), with Shield, CG, 20 Oct 1791; vs (Reeve's contribution), no lib
The Purse (short opera, Cross), LT, 8 Feb 1794; vs
British Fortitude (short opera, Cross), CG, 29 April 1794; vs
The Apparition (short opera, Cross), LT, 3 Sept 1794; vs
Hercules and Omphale (pantomime ballet, Byrne), with Shield, CG, 17 Nov 1794; ov. for double orch, lost; no lib
Merry Sherwood (pantomime, Pearce, O'Keeffe), CG, 21 Dec 1795; vs, no lib
The Charity Boy (short opera, Cross), DL, 5 Nov 1796; ov., 2 songs, no lib
Harlequin and Oberon (pantomime, Wild, Follet), CG, 19 Dec 1796; ov., 1 song
Bantry Bay (short opera, Reynolds), CG, 18 Feb 1797; vs
Raymond and Agnes (pantomime ballet, Farley, after Lewis: The Monk), CG, 16 March 1797; vs (ov., 4 vocal items)
The Round Tower (pantomime ballet, Cross), CG, 24 Nov 1797; vs (vocal items), lib in Cross's Circussiana
Harlequin and Quixote (pantomime, Cross), CG, 26 Dec 1797; ov., 1 song, no lib
Joan of Arc ('historical ballet of action', Cross), CG, 12 Feb 1798; ov., 6 songs in short score, no lib
The Raft (short opera, Cross), CG, 31 March 1798; ov., 2 songs
Harlequin's Return (Cross), CG, 9 April 1798; ov., 4 songs, no lib
Ramah Droog (opera, Cobb), with Mazzinghi, CG, 12 Nov 1798; vs
The Embarkation (short opera, Franklin), DL, 3 Oct 1799; vs, no lib
The Turnpike Gate (short opera, Knight), with Mazzinghi, CG, 14 Nov 1799; vs
Paul and Virginia (short opera, Cobb), with Mazzinghi, CG, 1 May 1800; vs, no lib
The Blind Girl (short opera, Morton), with Mazzinghi, CG, 22 April 1801; vs
The Chains of the Heart (short opera, Hoare), with Mazzinghi, CG, 9 Dec 1801; vs
Harlequin's Almanack (pantomime, T. Dibdin), CG, 28 Dec 1801; ov., songs
Jamie and Anna ('Scots pastoral in 1 act'), c1801; vs, no lib
The Cabinet (opera, T. Dibdin), with Corri, Davy, Moorehead, CG, 9 Feb 1802; vs

Family Quarrels (opera, T. Dibdin), with Braham, Moorehead, CG, 18 Dec 1802; vs
The Caravan (opera, Reynolds), DL, 5 Dec 1803; vs
Out of Place (short opera, Reynolds), with Braham, CG, 1805; vs, no lib
Thirty Thousand (short opera, T. Dibdin), with Davy, Braham, CG, 1805; vs; Reeve also set a pantomime with same title, Sadler's Wells, 18 April 1808
Kais (opera, Brandon), with Braham, DL, 11 Feb 1808; songs
Who's to have her? (short opera, T. Dibdin), with Whitaker, DL, 22 Nov 1813; vs
The Farmer's Wife (short opera, C. Dibdin), with Bishop, CG, 1 Feb 1814; 1 song
Brother and Sister (short opera, Dimond), with Bishop, CG, 1 Feb 1815; songs
Also additional songs for Gluck: Orpheus and Euridice, CG, 28 Feb 1792; Jackson: The Lord of the Manor, CG, 24 Oct 1812

SADLER'S WELLS ITEMS
(all to texts by C. Dibdin jr)

The White Witch, 18 April 1808; ov., songs
The Magic Minstrel ('aqua drama'), Whitsun 1808; ov., songs
Harlequin High Flyer (pantomime), 4 July 1808; ov., 1 song
Castles in the Air (pantomime), 31 July 1809; 2 songs
The Red Reaver (melodrama), 15 April 1811; ov., 1 song
Dulce Domum (pantomime), 15 April 1811; 2 songs
The Council of Ten ('Venetian water romance'), 3 June 1811; vs
Rokeby Castle ('aqua drama', after Scott), 19 April 1813; 2 songs
The Corsair ('aqua drama', after Byron), 1 Aug 1814; 3 songs
30 other items listed in Nicholl, music lost

MISCELLANEOUS

The Juvenile Preceptor (London, c1802) [kbd tutor]
Many songs pubd singly and in contemporary anthologies, probably from theatrical works: see *RISM* and *BUCEM*

BIBLIOGRAPHY

BUCEM
J. S. Sainsbury, ed.: *A Dictionary of Musicians* (London, 2/1825/R1966)
A. Nicholl: *History of the English Drama* (London, 2/1955)
G. Speaight, ed.: *Memoirs of Charles Dibdin the Younger* (London, 1966)

ROGER FISKE

Reeves, Sims (John) (*b* Shooters Hill, now in London, ?26 Sept 1818, baptized 25 Oct 1818; *d* Worthing, 25 Oct 1900). English tenor. He was the son of John and Rosina Reeves; his father, who taught him the piano, cello and bassoon, was principal bassoonist and singer with the Royal Artillery Band at Woolwich. After further musical studies with George Mackenzie, J. B. Cramer and W. H. Callcott, Reeves began to study medicine, but finally decided on a singing career and made his début as a baritone on 14 December 1838 at Newcastle upon Tyne in *Guy Mannering*. After three seasons as a baritone he found that his voice was changing, and trained with J. W. Hobbs and T. Cook. He sang second tenor roles with Macready's company at Drury Lane from 1841 to 1843, and then went to Paris and Milan for further study with Bordogni and Mazzucato. He made his début at La Scala in 1846 as Edgardo in *Lucia di Lammermoor*, returning to London in December that year to sing the same role at Drury Lane, where soon after he created the role of Lyonnel in Balfe's *The Maid of Honour*. In February 1848 he sang Faust in the first performance in England of Berlioz's *La damnation de Faust* under the composer. From 1848 he sang at Her Majesty's Theatre, first under Lumley's and then Mapleson's managements; he sang the title role in *Faust* in the opera's first performance in English in 1864, and Huon in the revival of *Oberon* in 1866. In 1848 he appeared at the Norwich Festival and sang in Handel's *Messiah* at the Sacred Harmonic Society. From 1848 he appeared regularly at the various choral festivals and was particularly admired in Handel oratorios and for his performance of the Evangelist in Bach's *St Matthew Passion*, which he sang under Sterndale Bennett in 1862. He made his formal farewell appearance at the Albert Hall in 1891, but reappeared in a concert in 1893, and made a tour of South Africa in 1896 with his pupil Maud Reve, whom he had married the previous year. His first wife had been the soprano Emma Lucombe (*d* 1895) who performed in operas and concerts. Their son Herbert Reeves, and daughter Constance Sims Reeves, both appeared in concerts.

WRITINGS

Sims Reeves: his Life and Recollections written by himself (London, 1888)

My Jubilee, or Fifty Years of Artistic Life (London, 1889)

On the Art of Singing (London, 1900)

BIBLIOGRAPHY

H. Sutherland Edwards: *The Life and Artistic Career of Sims Reeves* (London, 1881)

C. E. Pearce: *Sims Reeves: Fifty Years of Music in England* (London, 1924)

HAROLD ROSENTHAL

Refardt, Edgar (*b* Basle, 8 Aug 1877; *d* Basle, 3 March 1968). Swiss musicologist. After receiving a doctorate in law in 1901, Refardt devoted himself entirely to musicology, specializing in music bibliography. His *Historisch-biographisches Musikerlexikon der Schweiz* (1928) aimed to assemble as much biographical knowledge on Swiss music as possible. It was the first overall treatment of Swiss musical history and placed him, together with Peter Wagner and Karl Nef, among the first Swiss music historians. Refardt devoted special attention to the work of Theodor Fröhlich (he was really responsible for the rediscovery of this Swiss early Romantic composer) and Hans Huber. From 1921 to 1948 he was director of the Basle Orchestral Society.

WRITINGS

Historisch-biographisches Musikerlexikon der Schweiz (Leipzig and Zurich, 1928) [new edn. in preparation]

Hans Huber: Leben und Werk (Zurich, 1944)

Theodor Fröhlich: ein Schweizer Musiker der Romantik (Basle, 1947)

Brahms, Bruckner, Wolf: drei Wiener Meister des 19. Jahrhunderts (Basle, 1949)

Musik in der Schweiz: ausgewählte Aufsätze (Berne, 1952)

Numerous MS catalogues in *CH-Bu*

BIBLIOGRAPHY

SML

H. Ehinger: 'Edgar Refardt: dem Freund und Gelehrten', *SMz*, lxxxvii (1947), 318

H. P. Schanzlin: 'Edgar Refardt zum 85. Geburtstag am 8. August 1962', *Schweizerische musikforschende Gesellschaft: Mitteilungsblatt*, no.33 (1962), 7–30 [contains complete bibliography]; additions in no.34 (1963), 11; no.38–9 (1966), 15

H. P. Schanzlin: 'Pionierarbeit auf dem Gebiet der baslerischen und der schweizerischen Musikgeschichte: zum Gedenken an Edgar Refardt (1877–1968)', *Basler Stadtbuch 1969*, 233 [includes photograph]

JÜRG STENZL

Refice, Licinio (*b* Patrica, nr. Rome, 12 Feb 1885; *d* Rio de Janeiro, 11 Sept 1954). Italian composer and conductor. He studied composition and the organ at the Liceo di S Cecilia, Rome, gaining his diploma in 1910. In the same year he was ordained. He taught (1910–50) at the Scuola Pontificia di Musica Sacra, Rome, and from 1911 to 1947 was *maestro di cappella* at S Maria Maggiore. In his later years he made several tours as a conductor (sometimes with the Cantori Romani di Musica Sacra), both in Europe and in South and North America. It is improbable that Refice's music would have become widely known had it not been propagated from the Vatican. Influential sectors of Catholic opinion regarded him as Perosi's natural heir, but he had few of the older composer's qualities and most of his defects. Like Perosi, he was a facile keyboard improviser, and

this often shows in his works. Moreover his mingling of archaic and late Romantic styles rarely transcends eclecticism in the bad sense: his two completed religious operas weave lines derived from plainsong into an unashamedly post-Mascagnian musical fabric – which did not, however, prevent *Cecilia* from being staged frequently and in many countries, from Chile to Ireland (Gaiety Theatre, Dublin, 1954).

WORKS
(*selective list*)

Operas: Cecilia (E. Mucci), 1922–3, Rome, 1934; Margherita da Cortona (Mucci), Milan, 1938; Il mago, 1953–4, inc.

Oratorios, cantatas etc: La Cananea, oratorio, 1910; La vedova di Naim (P. Ferretti), cantata, 1912; Maria Magdalena (Ferretti), oratorio, 1914; Martyrium S Agnetis Virginis (Ferretti), oratorio, 1919; Dantis poetae transitus (G. Salvadori), poema sinfonico-vocale, Ravenna, 1921; Trittico Francescano (Mucci), oratorio (1926); La samaritana (Mucci), episodio evangelico (1930); L'oracolo (Mucci), mistero, Milan, 1946; Lilium crucis (Mucci), mistero, Naples, 1952; Pomposia (G. Pascoli), Assisi, 1957; Emmaus (Mucci), episodio evangelico, inc.

Church music: over 40 masses; Stabat mater, 1917; Te Deum, 1918; hymns, motets, psalms, many other pieces

Other works: few secular songs, small inst pieces etc

Principal publishers: Associazione Italiana S Cecilia (Rome), Casimiri (Rome), Mignani (Florence), Pustet (Regensburg), Ricordi

BIBLIOGRAPHY

M. Rinaldi: 'Le opere nuovissime: "Cecilia" di Licinio Refice', *Rassegna dorica*, v (Rome, 1933–4), 143

G. Gavazzeni: 'Lettera da Milano', *RaM*, xi (1938), 28 [on *Margherita da Cortona*]

E. Mucci: *Licinio Refice* (Assisi, 1955)

T. Onofri and E. Mucci: *Le composizioni di Licinio Refice* (Assisi, 1966)

A. Bartocci: 'Licinio Refice, il musicista-sacerdote', *Il mondo della musica*, xiv/1 (Rome, 1976), 31   JOHN C. G. WATERHOUSE

Refrain (Fr. *refrain*; Ger. *Kehrreim*; It. *ripresa*). In poetry, a phrase or verse that recurs at intervals, especially at the end of a stanza. The term has been adopted to describe analogously recurring passages in musical forms, whether or not they involve the repetition of text.

The French term 'refrain', applied to song of the mid-12th century to the mid-14th, has a particular meaning not identical with the usual poetic one cited above. In this usage a *refrain* is a segment of melody, usually two or three phrases, with words. These segments are sometimes found on their own, sometimes as interpolations in other works where they may or may not be repeated as part of a strophic song. The literary nature of the *refrain* is that of a courtly aphorism or amorous proverb, and in courtly romances such as *Guillaume de Dole*, *Roman de la violette* or *Prison d'amours*, the *refrains* are characteristically introduced as part of a dance-song (more often than not called a CAROLE) forming part of a courtly festivity. Variants seem to arise from a tradition half-oral, half-written, and no one version can be regarded as authentic. Some have different melodies to their recurrent text. The purely musical sources for *refrains* include polyphonic motets, which sometimes incorporate *refrains* into the tenor (e.g. Tres joliement/Imperatrix/Cis a cui, no.272 of *F-MO* H 196, f.301*v* with the *refrain* 'Silx a cui je suis ami'), or have *refrains* in their upper parts (the so-called 'refrain motet'); in others the two halves of the *refrain* frame new material (the *motet enté*). *Chansons avec des refrains*, monophonic courtly songs popular with the trouvères, introduced *refrains*, with their proper tunes, into otherwise strictly strophic verses (e.g. Ernoul Caupain's *Ier mains pensis chevauchai* incorporates eight different refrains into its eight stanzas). Other *refrains* of this sort are found in Adam de la Halle's play *Le jeu de Robin et Marion*.

Much scholarship has been devoted to the relation of refrains to the *formes fixes* (RONDEAU (i), VIRELAI and BALLADE (i)), all of which involve refrains in the more usual sense in their poetic and musical structures. The refrains of certain other forms are known by specific terms: that of the BALLATA and FROTTOLA as RIPRESA, that of the VILLANCICO as ESTRIBILLO and that of the CAROL as BURDEN. The later polyphonic French chanson sometimes had a refrain which could be referred to as the 'rechant'.

When the word 'refrain' is applied to more recent vocal music, it usually means that both melody and text are recurrent, as in Schubert's 'refrain lieder'. The refrain is often called a 'chorus', since it is frequently sung chorally after solo verses, but in English music-hall songs the refrains are called 'chorus' whether sung chorally or not. Choral refrains occur in early Christian psalmody in the 'Amen' and other exclamations sung by choir or congregation after each psalm verse or pair of verses; the technique is still common in European music. In instrumental music in rondeau (*see* RONDEAU (ii)) or RONDO form, it consists of a recurrent phrase or melody enclosing couplets or episodes of contrasting material.

BIBLIOGRAPHY

A. Jeanroy: *Les origines de la poésie lyrique en France au moyen âge* (Paris, 1889)
J. Bédier: 'Les plus anciennes danses françaises', *Revue des deux mondes*, lxxvi (1906), 398
F. Gennrich: *Rondeaux, Virelais, und Balladen*, i (Dresden, 1921); ii (Göttingen, 1927); iii (Langen bei Frankfurt, 1963)
P. Verrier: 'La plus vielle citation de carole', *Romania*, lviii (1932), 380–421
H. Spanke, ed.: *G. Raynauds Bibliographie des altfranzösischen Liedes* (Leiden, 1955)
F. Gennrich: *Bibliographisches Verzeichnis der französichen Refrains des 12. und 13. Jahrhunderts*, Summa musicae medii aevi, xiv (Langen, 1964)
N. H. J. van den Boogaad: *Rondeaux et refrains du xiie au début du xive siècle* (Paris, 1969)

JOHN STEVENS, MICHAEL TILMOUTH

Regals [regal] (Fr. *régale*; Ger. *Regal*; It. *regallo*).
(1) A kind of small organ in which the sound is produced by one or more sets of beating reeds provided with little or almost no resonators. It usually has direct-pin action. With this action the key depresses a short rod below the finger-end, which in turn presses down and opens the pallet; the bellows are usually placed on the same level as the keyboard, at the other side of the row of reeds. Thus the whole instrument at its simplest is several centimetres deep, and square or rectangular in horizontal section (of which the shorter side is that of the keyboard); as such it needs to be placed upon a table.
(2) A group of organ stops in a larger flue-pipe organ, built on the same principle as (but without the longer resonators of) reed stops, and often provided in *c*1600 with a prefixed name describing their sound or construction (*Apfelregal, Rackettregal*, etc). *See also* ORGAN STOP.

1. History. 2. Repertory.

1. HISTORY. The terminology, etymology and origin of the regals are equally uncertain, and likely to remain so. Like 'virginals' and *orgues* the plural is the more traditional form of the name. English versions are 'regalles' (1537, etc), 'regalls' (1538, etc), 'reygaals', 'regols' (1554, 1556) and 'regal' (1676); French stop

names include 'ung jeulx de regalles' (Bordeaux, 1531), 'régalle pour servir de voix humaine' (Gisors, 1580) and 'regales ou voix humaine' (Mersenne, 1636); German instrument names were *Regale* (Virdung, 1511), *Regahll* (Praetorius: *De organographia*, 1619), *Rigal, Rygal* (16th century). However, the first post-classical reference to organ reeds, Arnaut de Zwolle's manuscript of *c*1450, uses instead *l'anche*; the word does not appear in England until at least *c*1500; and some later Italian sources call the regals *organi di pivette* (1565). For the more general name 'regal' many explanations have been offered. Praetorius said some people thought it so named because it could serve as a royal gift; more recent authors have related it to *rega* (a 'row' of reeds, cf *Reihe*), to *rigole* (late French term for the reed-pipe shallot), to *rigols/régale* (for Grassineau a kind of xylophone or row of wooden strips, hence *régale à bois*), to *rigabello* (obscure term in one 16th-century source), to *regula* ('regulating' the pitch of the singers, cf *regolo*).

Already by 1511 (Schlick, Virdung) there was a clear distinction in central Europe between reed stops with long resonators, organ stops of the *regall oder super regall* kind (8′ and 4′, Schlick), and the independent keyboard instrument called regals or *Regal*. But it is noticeable that the Flemish and Dutch organ builders who were most inventive in creating reed and regal stops *c*1510 found more picturesque names than simply 'regal' – e.g. the *moesele* ('bagpipes'), *queenkens* ('old woman's voice') and *hommelkens* (? a Zink stop) at Notre Dame in Antwerp (1505). Such names as Vox humana arose as descriptive adjectives for the organ stop regal (or *reael* at Diest in 1530), as seen in the phrase from Gisors above. As far as the organ stop is concerned, both the name 'regal' and its sound are neutral until for the one a prefix and for the other an adequate coupled-system resonator are supplied, as they both were during the 16th century.

As instruments, the regals also underwent certain development. In England from *c*1540 a 'payre of Regalls' was a standard term, while 'Double Regals' almost certainly indicated a compass below *G*; the two phrases are very likely related. Already in the various royal inventories of 1547, etc, it is clear that makers had begun to add other, presumably small-scaled flue stops to the regal rank(s), such as 'one Stoppe of pipes of woode' and 'a Cimball' (high metal Mixture); a set of spinet or virginal strings (8′ or 4′) might also be added,

Regals: woodcut from Praetorius's 'Syntagma musicum' (2/1619)

the whole making an instrument still easy to carry. The regals illustrated by Praetorius may be considered the standard simple type, but clearly the small boxed section holding the reeds would be enlarged if fuller resonators were added. Several German cuts of the 16th century show such resonators as already very fanciful in shape though still rather drastically mitred in scale, i.e. the bass pipes were very short in relation to the treble; also, the resonator, whatever its shape, was basically a half-stopped pipe. The completely open, inverted conical resonator (often of a hard metal such as copper) was a recognized type of regal, the so-called *Trichterregal*; but most ingenuity was to be found in the little cylindrical or square-section stopped or half-stopped regals, right through from 1500 to 1750, and across Europe from Seville to Königsberg. Praetorius noted that Austrian builders were distinguished regals makers, and mentioned others in Augsburg, Nuremberg and Regensburg, as well as an unnamed maker who, to Praetorius's scepticism, claimed to be able to make a regals that would stay in tune.

It was a Nuremberg maker, G. Voll, who was said to have made the first 'Bible regals' towards the end of the 16th century, i.e. a regals whose pair of bellows are shaped like two halves of a book, the whole folding up to resemble a large closed bible. But such inventors were seldom isolated. Praetorius also credited another Nuremberg maker in the late 15th century with inventing a stop that was 'said to sound like a Schalmey' (a regal/reed stop or a flue Rauschpfeife) but which in fact must have been known by many makers before 1500.

2. REPERTORY. In large organs regal ranks served to give varieties of tone-colour, especially in the manual and pedal *Brustwerk* departments. The latter were in many instances before *c*1650 nothing more than a kind of regals instrument incorporated in a church organ. The regals instrument in its own right was used in many ways. By 1713 Mattheson thought it 'extremely disgusting' as a sound ('höchst eckelhafft') and recommended the use of other keyboard instruments for continuo in church; but his remarks make it clear that it was still in use in Hamburg churches. Earlier it had been useful to the writers of *intermedii* in Florence (*c*1589), of music at English guild feasts (Parish Clerks, 1522), pageant plays (Coventry, 1550s) and drama (mourning song in Edwards's *Damon & Pythias*, 1565). It was used in early opera and its later imitations (*Orfeo*, 1607, to accompany Caronte; *Pomo d'oro*, 1667, for the infernal scene) when expense was not spared, in princely chapels with *cori spezzati* groups of instruments for motets (Praetorius, Schütz) or Passions (Selle, 1643), where organ might be used for the chorus, regals for the soloists, or organ for accompanying brass instruments, harpsichord for strings, regals for cornets and oboes, etc.

Although the regals can never have been very common outside Germany, Praetorius (1619, pp.72ff) showed that it was used there for continuo (for which it was better than a harpsichord because more sustained in tone, and could play loud or soft depending on whether the cover above the reeds was open or not), in princely convivial assembly, in large and small churches ('almost better than a positive organ') and portable enough to be taken from one to the other (hence requiring care if taken from a cold church to a warm dining-room).

In England 'tuner of the regalls' was one of the titles in the court appointments until at least 1767, but it is doubtful if it kept its literal meaning beyond the Restoration. To James Talbot (MS, *c*1695) the name was puzzling. He applied it both to full-length reed stops in general and to a little 4′ Vox humana stop, but not to a self-contained keyboard instrument. Many of the organ theorists *c*1700 (North, Muffat, St Lambert) and even *c*1600 (Banchieri, Agazzari) mentioned it as a continuo instrument rarely if at all. Praetorius seems to have preferred the soft sound of the stopped, sweet Dolcian-like regals (*regale dolce* in Munich *intermedii*, 1568); and it is certainly the coarser sound of regals with short, open copper-alloy resonators that helped to make the instrument lose its popularity, even in central and north Germany.

BIBLIOGRAPHY

R. Menger: *Das Regal* (Tutzing, 1973)

PETER WILLIAMS

Regamey, Constantin (*b* Kiev, 28 Jan 1907). Swiss composer and pianist. Born of a Swiss (Vaudois) father and a Russian mother, he studied piano and classical and oriental philology at Warsaw. He received his doctorate in 1936, and directed the Polish review *Muzyka polska* from 1937 to 1939. During World War II he was arrested and deported by the Germans, but he managed to escape to Switzerland in 1944. While holding the chair of Slavonic and oriental languages at the Universities of Lausanne and Fribourg, he pursued his career as a composer, begun in Poland where he had been self-taught. Although his academic work prevented him from producing much music, his works rapidly gained an international audience. His études for female voice and piano were first performed at Donaueschingen in 1955, and he made several tours as a concert pianist. Between 1954 and 1962 he helped edit the *Revue musicale de Suisse Romande*. He was president of the Association of Swiss Musicians (1963–8), and then of the Swiss Council of Music. Numerous voyages to India and the Far East gave him the opportunity to study the music of these countries, and this influenced his sensibility and aesthetics deeply.

His music is a refined synthesis of oriental and Western thinking. Leaving behind the tonal system and traditional forms, Regamey evolved an extremely complex style which makes use of some of the developments of serialism, atonality and modality. In his highly self-critical quest for original expression, he has not stifled the emotive message, but has recoiled from excessive expansiveness and from violent contrasts. Regamey's imagination is deficient neither in a sense of the grotesque nor in a certain spirit of mockery. His orchestration is skilful and his treatment of the voice, which he uses as another instrument, is assured. In order that the verbal content should not intrude, he deliberately chooses poems in languages which his audience will not understand: the études are based on texts in ancient Indian dialects and the *Symphonie des incantations* uses texts from prehistoric, ancient Indian and Mesopotamian sources.

WORKS

(selective list)

2 operas: Don Robott, 1970; Mio, mein Mio, 1973

Vocal works incl. Chansons persanes, Bar, chamber orch, 1942; 5 études, female v, pf/orch, 1955; Poèmes de Jean Tardieu, chorus, 1962; 3 Lieder des Clowns, Bar, orch, 1968; Symphonie des incantations, S, Bar, orch, 1968; Alpha, T, orch, 1970

Inst works incl. Studio da concerto, pf, 1935; Quintet, cl, bn, vn, vc, pf, 1944; String Quartet, 1948; Variationi e tema, orch, 1948; Musique pour cordes, 1953; Autographe, chamber orch, 1962; 4 × 5, ww qnt, brass qnt, str qnt, perc qnt, 1963

Principal publishers: Carisch, Impéro, Mills (New York), Polskie Wydawnictwo Muzyczne

BIBLIOGRAPHY

H. Jaccard: *Initiation à la musique contemporaine: Trois compositeurs vaudois: Raffaele d'Allessandro, Constantin Regamey, Julien-François Zbinden* (Lausanne, 1955)
H. Gagnebin: *40 compositeurs suisses* (Amriswil, 1956), 150
B. Pilarski: *Szkice o muzyce* (Warsaw, 1969)

PIERRE MEYLAN

Regan, Anna (*b* Aich, 18 Sept 1841; *d* Munich, 18 April 1902). Austrian singer, wife of ADOLF SCHIMON.

Regensburg. Bavarian city on the Danube in the Federal German Republic, formerly Ratisbon. The cathedral choir school dates from 975, since when the city has been an important centre of Catholic church music. Outstanding Kapellmeisters of the 17th century were Georg Faber (1674–9) and J. G. Reichwein (1679–91). In the 19th century it was a centre of the CECILIAN MOVEMENT, particularly under Kapellmeister F. X. Haberl (1871–82) and his successors Ignaz Mitterer (1882–5), F. X. Engelhart (1891–1924) and Theobald Schrems (1924–63). Outstanding cathedral organists have included Joseph Hanisch (1829–92), Joseph Renner (1892–1934) and Eberhard Kraus (appointed 1964). J. G. Mettenleiter, choirmaster at the Alte Kapelle from 1839 to 1858, was also a supporter of the Cecilian reforms. Since Haberl's time the cathedral choir, known as the 'Domspatzen', has been one of the leading European ensembles in *a cappella* polyphony. Of the city's many monastic institutions the abbey of St Emmeram was the most important musically.

In 1748 the princes of Thurn und Taxis moved from Frankfurt to Regensburg. Prince Alexander Ferdinand built a court theatre, and French plays (1760–74), Italian opera (1774–8 and 1784–6, directed by Theodor von Schacht) and German plays (1778–84) were performed there. In 1777, when Joseph Riepel was Hofkapellmeister, the Kapelle numbered 35 musicians. The theatre was subsequently used by visiting directors, including Schikaneder (1786–9) and Ignaz Walter (1804–22). In 1806, when the princes lost their sovereignty, the Kapelle was disbanded. In 1851 a new theatre, the Neues Haus, was built; it was run by the city after 1859. Between 1888 and 1935 Prince Albert of Thurn und Taxis was a distinguished patron.

Several music societies have been established in Regensburg since the 19th century. The Regensburger Liederkranz, a male-voice choir founded in 1837, amalgamated with the Damengesangverein in 1880 to form a mixed choir. The Musikverein has been active since 1849, and in 1935 Ernst Schwarzmaier founded a collegium musicum.

In 1537 the city council founded the Gymnasium Poeticum, where music was among the subjects taught. Of its precentors, Raselius (1584–1600), Homberger (1603–43), Stolzenberg (1714–64) and J. K. Schubarth (1781–1810) were outstanding composers. In 1874 Haberl founded the Kirchenmusikschule, which he directed until 1910. He was succeeded by Karl Weinmann (1910–29), Carl Thiel (1929–39) and Ferdinand Haberl (1939–70). Since 1959 the school has been affiliated to the Institut für Kirchenmusik, and since 1968 music has also been taught at the University of Regensburg (founded 1962).

The Proske-Musikbibliothek and the Thurn und Taxis'sche Hofbibliothek offer facilities for musicological research. Regensburg's music publishers include G. Manz, A. Coppenrath, F. Feuchtinger, F. Pustet and G. Bosse.

BIBLIOGRAPHY

D. Mettenleiter: *Musikgeschichte der Stadt Regensburg* (Regensburg, 1866)
K. Weinmann: *Regensburg als Kirchenmusikstadt* (Regensburg, 1928)
J. Hösl: *Einhundert Jahre Regensburger Liederkranz* (Regensburg, 1937)
B. Stäblein: *Regensburg: das Bild einer bayrischen Musikstadt* (Munich, 1948)
R. Doblinger: *Das Evangelium in Regensburg* (Regensburg, 1959)
R. W. Sterl: 'Kirchenmusikstadt Regensburg-Bibliographie', *Musica sacra*, iv (1968), 146
R. W. Sterl: *Musiker und Musikpflege in Regensburg bis um 1600* (Regensburg, 1971)

AUGUST SCHARNAGL

Regent's bugle. A kind of trumpet. In 1815 the *Allgemeine musikalische Zeitung* of Leipzig stated that Johann Georg Schmidt, then solo trumpet in the prince regent's private band, had recently introduced a new brass instrument that he called the 'regent's bugle'. Pontécoulant, Fétis and Billert have all left cursory though somewhat contradictory accounts of the instrument (which was constructed by Percival of London), but no accurate detailed description seems to have survived. Sachs, taking Schmidt's own account as his source (but lacking an authenticated specimen), described the instrument as a slide-bugle, a term that to the strict organologist may seem self-contradictory. Sachs's intention is clear, however, and he may well have coined the word to avoid confusion with Halliday's KEYED BUGLE (1810). Blandford suggested that the 'regent's bugle' was no more than the comparatively well-known 'short model' of the English SLIDE TRUMPET. Morley-Pegge (1956), reviewing all the evidence then available, rejected Blandford's view but offered the interesting suggestion that Schmidt's choice of title might have been motivated by his rivalry with the celebrated keyed-bugle player, John Distin, whose reputation was largely founded on Halliday's instrument, which he had named 'Royal Kent Bugle' after his own patron the Duke of Kent, younger brother to the regent.

There the matter rested until 1966, when Joseph Wheeler investigated an instrument (no.37 of the Spencer Collection in the Brighton Museum; see illustration) that presents all the characteristics mentioned severally by previous writers. The main tubing of this instrument is strictly cylindrical and provided with a graduated telescopic mouthpipe and a U-shaped tuning-slide which, when drawn together and to the same distance put the instrument into C, D♭, D, E♭, E or F. In addition opening one or more of five keys on the bell section furnishes semitones, whole tones and minor 3rds above the natural notes of each slide setting. This instrument – though made not in London but by Curtis of

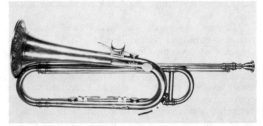

Regent's bugle by Richard Curtis, Glasgow, early 19th century (Spencer Collection, Brighton Museum)

Glasgow – seems to be the true 'regent's bugle', and so far the only recorded example.

BIBLIOGRAPHY

FétisB

L.-G. le D. Pontécoulant: *Organographie* (Paris, 1861)

C. Billert: 'Horn', *Musikalisches Conversations-Lexikon*, v, ed. H. Mendel (Berlin, 1875)

C. Sachs: *Reallexikon der Musikinstrumente* (Berlin, 1913)

W. F. H. Blandford: 'The Regent's Bugle', *MT*, lxvi (1925), 442

R. Morley-Pegge: 'The Regent's Bugle', *GSJ*, ix (1956), 91

J. Wheeler: 'New Light on the "Regent's Bugle" ', *GSJ*, xix (1966), 65

A. Baines: *Brass Instruments: their History and Development* (London, 1976)

PHILIP BATE

Reger, (Johann Baptist Joseph) Max(imilian) (*b* Brand, Upper Palatinate, Bavaria, 19 March 1873; *d* Leipzig, 11 May 1916). German composer.

1. LIFE. He came of Roman Catholic peasant and artisan stock, though by the time of his birth the Regers had attained a certain prosperity: his father, Joseph Reger, was the first member of the extensive family to achieve the status of a schoolmaster. Joseph was a musical amateur, playing the oboe, the clarinet and the double bass, and he made sure that his son learnt to play the piano and string instruments (he was also the author of a valuable harmony text for general schools). Father and son rebuilt a scrapped school organ for use at home, and this was the instrument on which Reger first explored harmonic effects. His mother, Philomena Reichenberger, passed on to him a melancholy sensitivity that often took refuge behind a pronounced sense of humour, and a discriminating literary taste – as well as a tendency to plumpness.

Although his father encouraged his delight in playing musical instruments, Reger's gifts were not systematically developed. Even when, at the age of 11, he played a military march faultlessly from memory, his parents refused to take his talent seriously. Eventually Adalbert Lindner, town organist and teacher of Weiden (where the Reger family had been living since 1874), took an interest in Max and began to give him formal training. In 1922 Lindner published an account of his pupil's early years, and this remains an important help to the understanding of Reger's personal and artistic development, despite its many inaccuracies and well-intentioned exaggerations. In particular, it reproduces letters that clearly show an early maturity and judgment, besides containing humorous but occasionally pessimistic notes on the years of study. Lindner carefully and sympathetically developed Reger's abilities, introducing him to the piano music of Beethoven and the Romantics, and also to Riemann's polyphonic Sonatas op.42 and the inventions of Bach, which stimulated a deep and persistent devotion to that composer's works (in 1903 Reger, collaborating with Straube, added third parts to the two-part inventions to produce a *Schule des Triospiels* for organ, a work which brought much hostile criticism from musicologists). Reger and Lindner worked through the chamber and orchestral repertories in four-hand arrangements, and it was doubtless this experience that caused Reger to favour the duet and two-piano media in later years.

At this time he composed accompanying violin parts to Clementi's Sonatinas op.36, but he failed properly to appreciate Mozart, who was later to mean so much to him. He was, however, greatly influenced by Beethoven and still more so by Brahms, as is evident from the themes and sonorities of his music right down to the last works. Soon he was able to stand in for his teacher as

organist at church services. When he was 15 a visit to the Bayreuth Festival left an abiding impression on him, and confirmed his resolution to devote himself solely to music. After secondary school he entered the teacher training college in Weiden, intending to follow his father as a Volksschule teacher.

Through the agency of Lindner, some of Reger's early compositions were sent to Riemann, who was teaching in Sondershausen, Thuringia; these included an Overture in B minor – composed for the amateur orchestra of Weiden and written directly into a fair copy of 120 pages scored for string quintet, flute, clarinet and piano – and a Scherzo for flute and string quartet. More important than either of these works, however, was a three-movement String Quartet in D minor (1888–9), with a double bass added in the finale, 'Aufschwung'. Since passing an examination in Thuringia would not have qualified Reger to teach in Bavaria, his parents tried to place him with Joseph Rheinberger of Munich. Rheinberger did not refuse him outright, but he did point out the difficulties of making a career as an artist, and so Reger became a pupil of Riemann, soon becoming his teacher's assistant when the latter moved to Wiesbaden. Riemann had a very high opinion of his student and his uncanny speed of comprehension. It was in Wiesbaden that Reger's drinking began; later this gave rise to the popular legend of a perpetually drunk composer, and considerably damaged his international reputation. He made friendships with d'Albert and with Busoni, to whom he promised, but failed to deliver, some piano concertos.

The first of his works which Reger recognized (though he later dismissed all the compositions from op.1 to op.20 as 'hopeless rubbish') was the Violin Sonata op.1 (1890), which aroused animosity and admiration in equal measure. Then came the Trio op.2 for piano, violin and viola, in the finale of which Reger broke new ground in variation technique, the Violin Sonata op.3, clearly modelled on Brahms and dedicated to the composer's friend Theodor Kirchner, and the Cello Sonata op.5, an extraordinarily mature work for its early date. The Lieder op.4 are early examples of a conflict between melody of a traditional kind and the new declamatory style of Wagner and Wolf.

Reger's period of military service in Wiesbaden was not one of the happiest episodes of his life, though he was fortunate in finding in his company commander, Captain Max von Bardeleben, someone who fully appreciated his individual nature. In 1898, sick in body and mind, he returned to spend some time at his parents' home in Weiden, and during the next few years he wrote a long string of works in diverse genres, but with an emphasis on organ music. The Three Pieces op.7 for organ had been composed in 1892, and in 1894–5 Reger produced the Suite op.16, which he sent to Brahms, receiving a benevolent reply. In the organ Reger saw 'a concert instrument of the very first class', and he regarded it as his duty to carry on the tradition of Bach, Mendelssohn and Schumann. A more recent influence was that of the symphonic poem of Liszt, which considerably enriched Reger's organ style and stimulated him to write chorale fantasias, in which, a convinced Catholic, he entered wholeheartedly into the spirit of the Protestant chorale. A good example is the first work in this genre, the Fantasia 'Ein' feste Burg ist unser Gott' op.27. By 1900 most of his major organ works were completed. He found an excellent and devoted interpreter of his organ music in Karl Straube, who was also a lifelong friend. Straube urged Reger to turn his attention to the theatre, but, with the exception of an incidental score for the Rhenish Festival play *Castra vetera* by Johanna Baltz, he composed nothing for the stage.

As a firm supporter of 'absolute' music he came into bitter conflict in Munich (where he settled in 1901) with the Neudeutsche Schule, centred on Thuille, von Schillings and the critic Rudolf Louis. Now a pianist of some note, Reger gave concerts with the violinist Henri Marteau, who became one of his closest friends, the singer Josef Loritz and many other well-known artists, with whose assistance and through much effort on his own part he managed to have his works performed. One of the first critics to form a favourable opinion of Reger was Hugo Leichtentritt, and his work was also admired by Alexander Berrsche, one of his earliest Munich pupils. Reger was a declared enemy of programme music (he later reconsidered his views), but he joined with Strauss, for whom he always had great respect, in writing outspoken articles on modern music and the rights of the composer. In October 1902 he married Elsa von Bercken, née von Bagenski; having no children of their own they adopted two orphans (parts of the *Schlichte Weisen* op.76 and the *Fünf neue Kinderlieder* op.142 express Reger's love for children). Also at this period he struck up a warm friendship with Mottl.

These Munich years were creatively productive: there Reger wrote the Piano Quintet op.64, described by Grieg, whom Reger held in high regard, as a 'plum pudding', the large-scale String Quartet op.74, the often-criticized Violin Sonata op.72 and the Sinfonietta op.90, whose first performance caused a great scandal. Also in Munich he composed his first major work for piano solo and a central contribution to the 20th-century piano literature: the Variations and Fugue on a Theme of J. S. Bach op.81. The work is dedicated to his friend, the pianist August Schmid-Lindner, who was engaged with Reger on a new edition of Bach's keyboard works when the project was terminated by the composer's early death.

Tired of Munich and its bickering, Reger accepted in 1907 an appointment as professor of composition and director of music at Leipzig University. This was the beginning of an intense period of activity as a teacher, which brought him international renown. In his teaching he demanded a close understanding of Riemann's functional theory (although by now Riemann had taken a hostile attitude to his former pupil), but in his compositions he remained true to the tradition of Rameau and Sechter, as the few extant sketches demonstrate. Among his Leipzig pupils were Grabner, Joseph Haas, Hasse, Jora, Kvapil, Lubrich, Rettich, Schoeck, Szell, Unger, Weinberger and Julia Weissberg. Thanks to the efforts of his friend and biographer Fritz Stein, director of music at Jena University, Reger received in 1908 an honorary doctorate from that institution, one of many honours that came his way. In return he composed his greatest sacred work, the setting of Psalm c op.106, the first part of which was performed at the doctorate presentation ceremony (the work was first heard complete in Chemnitz in 1910 under the composer's baton).

Reger's creativity grew apace, as did his reputation in Germany and abroad: concert tours of the Netherlands, Belgium, Austria, Hungary, Russia and England brought him considerable success as a composer, conductor and soloist, and broadened the horizons of a man who was always ready to learn (he won the respect of strangers but earned his companions' despair, spending long hours in the great London art galleries and then giving detailed descriptions of the works, complete with literary and historical considerations). He gave enthusiastic accounts of the receptions accorded to concerts of his music in The Hague, Utrecht, Brussels and London, where there was a Reger concert and dinner at the Royal Academy. Three years previously he had had similar success in Russia: in St Petersburg in December 1906 he conducted the Serenade op.95, played with Siloti the Beethoven Variations op.86, the Introduction, Passacaglia and Fugue op.96 and the Piano Pieces op.94, and performed the Violin Sonata op.84 and the Suite op.93 with Ysaÿe; he also played the keyboard part in a performance of the Brandenburg Concerto no.5. Although Stravinsky took a dislike to him, Reger won the approval of Prokofiev and Myaskovsky; and his prestige in Russia is indicated by the fact that Heinrich Neuhaus could report a memorial concert given in St Petersburg eight days after the composer's death, when Germany and Russia were at war.

Even in his Leipzig period – which saw the composition of important chamber pieces, such as the Clarinet Sonata op.107 and the String Quartet op.109, dedicated to Mendelssohn's son-in-law, Adolf Wach – most of the advances in Reger's language were made in orchestral works: the Variations and Fugue on a Theme of Hiller op.100 constituted the first major example of his new techniques. On the other hand, his organ music was fundamentally retrospective. His last great contributions include the Variations and Fugue on an Original Theme op.73, vaguely reminiscent of Franck, the Introduction, Passacaglia and Fugue op.127 and the Fantasia and Fugue op.135*b*, dedicated to Strauss and, despite its opus number, probably Reger's last completed composition.

In 1911 Duke Georg II of Saxe-Meiningen, who was known as the 'duke of the theatre' because of his enthusiasm for art, appointed Reger conductor of the court orchestra at Meiningen. The orchestra had been established in 1880 by von Bülow, and it performed only concert music; its subsequent conductors had been Strauss, Steinbach and Berger. At first Reger had to contend with the court camarilla, but in the duke he found a kind and understanding friend, who later showed a real concern for his conductor's health. Some of Reger's programmes were very bold; at the duke's wish the music was mainly Austro-German, but the music of Mahler (which Reger could never like) and many of Strauss's works demanded a larger orchestra than was available in Meiningen. Besides the Classics (particularly Beethoven) Reger conducted the symphonies of Brahms and Bruckner, his own compositions, Strauss's *Tod und Verklärung*, Debussy's *Prélude à l'après-midi d'un faune*, pieces by Berlioz, Grieg, Cornelius and Wolf (whose *Italienische Serenade* he rearranged for the Meiningen orchestra), and the waltzes of Strauss, which he is said to have performed with inimitable grace. Willy von Beckerath made some celebrated sketches of Reger rehearsing, and the drawings and paintings of Franz Nölken at Kolberg show the indefatigable composer at his desk. At Meiningen he was able to call on many well-known musicians, among them Flesch and Szigeti. On one occasion he played Bach's Concerto in C major for three keyboards together with his friends Philipp Wolfrum and Fritz Stein – he steadfastly refused to have anything to do with the harpsichord, then just coming back into fashion.

By the end of 1913 Reger was beginning to want to relinquish his strenuous post at Meiningen. In the first place he disliked court life, and also he was ill: 'You have demanded of yourself the superhuman' wrote the duke. Although there was pressure from many quarters for him to stay, he tendered his resignation, but five days before he was due to leave Duke Georg died. World War I had now begun, and the new duke disbanded the orchestra; feeling a keen sympathy with the redundant musicians, Reger gave concerts and collected money to support them. Early in 1915 he took up residence in Jena, where he became a friend of the philosopher Rudolf Eucken. His new home had a beneficial effect, and the 'free Jena style', as he called this phase, gave rise to his most mature works, including the suites for solo cello op.131c and for solo viola op.131d, the Fantasia and Fugue op.135b for organ, the Violin Sonata op.139, the Serenade op.141a, the String Trio op.141b, the *Träume am Kamin* op.143 for piano, the Clarinet Quintet op.146 and the op.144 choral orchestral pieces.

On 10 May 1916, tireless as ever, Reger was returning from a concert tour of the Netherlands and stopped in Leipzig to spend the evening with old friends. At about midnight he suffered a heart attack and shortage of breath; Straube took him back to his hotel, where he died, presumably from heart failure. On the bedside table lay the corrected proofs of the motet op.138 no.1: 'Der Mensch lebt und bestehet nur eine kleine Zeit'. The body was cremated at Jena on 14 May 1916, when Philipp Wolfrum gave the funeral oration. Reger's pupils

Max Reger

Adolf and Fritz Busch played the Aria from the Suite op.103a and the Largo from the Violin Sonata op.139, and the dirge from op.137 was sung by Anna Erler-Schnaudt. In 1930 the ashes were removed to a grave of honour in Munich.

At the Valhalla near Regensburg a bust by Georg Müller was set up. The estate was in the trust of Reger's energetic widow: archives were established in Reger's house in Jena (they were later moved to Meiningen), a Reger Society was founded in 1920 and an Austrian branch soon followed. A notable collection was formed in Weiden, and the Max Reger Archives of the Elsa Reger Foundation found a home in Bonn-Bad Godesberg at the Max-Reger-Institut, whose director, Ottmar Schreiber, has been largely responsible for the collected edition whose publication began in 1954.

2. WORKS. Together with Skryabin and Schoenberg, Reger was one of those composers who grew up under the influence of Wagner's music without following him slavishly. It would be difficult to assign him a specific place in the history of music: in some respects his unruly talent was ahead of its time, but it drew strength from a tradition which he was constantly trying to renew. Though it has been said that Reger had little control over his creative impulse, he was from his youth articulate about his attitude. At the age of 23 he wrote to Busoni: 'I utterly detest all forms of musical prejudice – Brahms versus Wagner' and 'You'll probably be rather surprised at the "turgidity" in my works; one always wants to do too much at first. But I was always in earnest!'. And in 1897 he wrote to Lindner that, as a 'fervent admirer of Bach, Beethoven and Brahms', he was striving 'to develop their style'. Gifted with a true sense of the function of harmony in determining form, combined with an unrestricted melodic gift, he stated when he was only 16 that for him there was no essential difference between harmony and counterpoint. His predilection for counterpoint, derived from an early familiarity with Bach and with Renaissance polyphony, quickly earned him the nickname 'the second Bach', a label which acknowledged his exceptional ability, particularly in the techniques of variation and fugue, but added a suggestion of academicism. This stereotype image was still widely current 60 years after Reger's death.

His prodigious output, produced in a working life of only 26 years, is unparalleled among leading contemporaries, and it covers all genres except opera, in which Reger was little interested, although he was a keen theatre-goer. At once Baroque and Romantic, his music gives an impression of inner disunity, yet it has had an influence which cannot easily be assessed. Reger never escaped the feeling that he was writing under the pressure of time: 'Remember Mendelssohn, Mozart, Schubert, Wolf', he wrote to Edith Mendelssohn-Bartholdy, 'We have little time left, and I must complete my work'. Yet in sum the many letters and reported remarks do little to elucidate his complex creative mind.

Reger's childhood musical experiences were of Classical and Romantic music, particularly Beethoven, whose work played an important part in Reger's composition throughout his life. The influence may be detected in the violin sonatas, a medium to which Reger returned again and again, and string quartets, in the Variations and Fugue on a Theme of Beethoven op.86 for two pianos and in the Variations and Fugue on a

Theme of J. S. Bach op.81, where the human and artistic experience of Beethoven's late piano sonatas is clearly audible. Chopin, Mendelssohn and Liszt also left their mark; their piano techniques and harmonic imaginations constantly engrossed Reger as a highly gifted pianist, and the compositional influences persisted to his very last works. In Schumann Reger saw not only the unsurpassable master of the small form but, in the late works, an increasing tendency to melancholy, also to emerge in Reger's monumental compositions, such as the Piano Concerto op.114 and the *Symphonischer Prolog zu einer Tragödie* op.108. Without feeling any inclination to the stage, Reger learnt much from Wagner, whose chromaticism, particularly in *Tristan*, was of immeasurable importance to Reger's harmonic style. By extending the possibilities of tonality without discarding its framework, Reger moulded an individual idiom which brought him much hostility, as well as widespread recognition and imitation. It was this that brought about the rift with Riemann, who behaved very unpleasantly towards his most gifted pupil, yet Reger never lost his temper; he continued to subscribe to Riemann's teaching, prompted no doubt by his sense of tradition. The strongest influences came from Brahms, in whose music Reger perceived 'new, unsuspected spiritual impressions'. As late as the Violin Sonata op.139 and the Clarinet Quintet op.146, echoes of a genuine reverence for Brahms bear witness to a close stylistic affinity.

The enormous production of organ music at around the turn of the century makes Reger the most important German organ composer after Bach. Although he always emphasized the pre-eminence of the organ as a concert instrument, he composed sacred programme music, for the great fantasias on Protestant chorales (whose musical and moral strength he greatly admired) are essentially symphonic poems in the Lisztian manner. This is also true of the works without chorales, such as the Fantasia and Fugue on B–A–C–H op.46 and the Variations on an Original Theme op.73. His frequently displayed love for the Lutheran chorale led this strict Catholic to join Arnold Mendelssohn as a leader in the renewal of Protestant church music. But he also left valuable Catholic works, such as *Die Nonnen* op.112 and the unfinished Requiem. His other vocal music raises problems: he did not always select texts with due intelligence, though he did make sympathetic settings of Morgenstern, Verlaine and other important poets of his time. In the late choral pieces, *Der Einsiedler* (on Eichendorff) and *Requiem* (on Hebbel), he made deep incursions into spiritual areas close to those of the last works of Beethoven and Brahms.

Reger's chamber and piano music clearly shows his progress as a composer. The works of the early period have a rich sound demanding much of performer and listener; then came the bold ventures of the Munich years, with slow movements of religious profundity and an often broad humour in the scherzos. In the final phase there was a Classical orientation, notable in the string quartets op.109 and op.121, the flute serenades and string trios op.77 and op.141, the String Sextet op.118, the later sonatas for violin or cello with piano, and the many solo string compositions, of which the Suites op.131d for solo viola are decided novelties. Reger produced no grand piano sonata, but the Bach Variations op.81 may be seen as a focal point, proving the composer a worthy successor to the tradition estab-

lished by the large-scale keyboard variation cycles of Bach, Beethoven and Brahms. Other important works for solo piano include the Telemann Variations op.134, the Sonatinas op.89, the four-volume collection *Aus meinem Tagebuch* op.82, the *Episoden* op.115 and the *Träume am Kamin* op.143. There are also major compositions for four hands, among them the Six Pieces op.94, the Beethoven Variations op.86 and the Introduction, Passacaglia and Fugue op.96.

Of Reger's orchestral works, which overshadow the organ music, the exceptionally compact Sinfonietta op.90 and the *Symphonischer Prolog zu einer Tragödie* op.108 might be classed as symphonies. The two concertos also have symphonic traits: the one for violin has always been neglected, but the Piano Concerto op.114 gained international favour in the early 1970s. In the *Romantische Suite* op.125 and the *Tondichtungen nach Böcklin* op.128 there are harmonic and orchestrational influences from Debussy, whose *Prélude à l'après-midi d'un faune* Reger regarded highly, and from Strauss, for whom his admiration was lifelong if not uncritical. After the brilliant Hiller Variations op.100 his quest for a synthesis of styles culminated in the Mozart Variations op.132, which has remained the most frequently performed of his orchestral works.

If it is impossible to define Reger's influence, some indication of the importance which subsequent composers have attached to his work may be drawn from the fact that it has been the subject of study by Berg, Hindemith, Honegger, Schmidt and Schoenberg.

WORKS

Edition: *M. Reger: Sämtliche Werke* (Wiesbaden, 1954–) [R]

ORCHESTRAL

op.	
—	Heroide, d, symphonic movement, 1889, R xxxvii
—	Castra vetera (incidental music, J. Baltz), 1889–90, R xxxvi
—	Symphonic movement, d, 1890, R xxxvii
—	Lyrisches Andante (Liebestraum), str, 1898
—	Scherzino, hn, str, 1899, R viii
26/1	Elegie, e [arr. pf work], R xxxvii
50	2 Romanzen, G, D, vn, orch, 1900, R vii
86	Variations and Fugue on a Theme of Beethoven [arr. 2 pf work], 1915, R vi
90	Sinfonietta, A, 1904–5, R i
93	Suite im alten Stil, F [arr. vn, pf work], 1916, R vi
95	Serenade, G, 1905–6, R ii
100	Variations and Fugue on a Theme of J. A. Hiller, E, 1907, R iii
101	Violin Concerto, A, 1907–8, R vii
103(a)	Aria, A, vn, small orch [arr. vn, pf work], R vii
108	Symphonischer Prolog zu einer Tragödie, a, 1908, R iii
114	Piano Concerto, f, 1910, R viii
120	Eine Lustspielouvertüre, 1911, R iv
123	Konzert im alten Stil, F, 1912, R iv
125	Eine romantische Suite, after Eichendorff, 1912, R iv
128	4 Tondichtungen nach Arnold Böcklin, 1913, R v
130	Eine Ballettsuite, D, 1913, R v
132	Variations and Fugue on a Theme of Mozart, 1914, R v; arr. 2 pf, 1914, R xiv
140	Eine vaterländische Ouvertüre, F, 1914, R vi
147	Andante for Rondo, vn, small orch, inc., R xxxvii

CHORAL

6	3 Choruses, SATB, pf, 1892, R xxx
—	Tantum ergo sacramentum, 5vv, 1895, R xxvii
21	Hymne an den Gesang (L. Steiner), male chorus, orch/pf, 1898, R xxix
—	Gloriabuntur in te omnes, 4vv, ?1898, R xxvii
38	7 Male Choruses, 1899, R xxvii
39	3 Choruses, SAATBB, 1899, R xxvii
—	Maria Himmelsfreud! (J. P. Heuberger), 1899 or 1900, R xxvii
61	Simple liturgical pieces: 61a, 8 settings of Tantum ergo; 61b, 4 settings of Tantum ergo, SA/TB, org; 61c, 4 settings of Tantum ergo, 4vv, org; 61d, 8 Marienlieder; 61e, 4 Marienlieder, SA/TB, org; 61f, 4 Marienlieder, 4vv, org; 61g, 6 Trauergesänge; 1901, R xxx
—	Palmsonntagmorgen (E. Geibel), 5vv, 1902, R xxvii
71	Gesang der Verklärten (K. Busse), SSATB, orch, 1903, R xxix

4 cantatas: Vom Himmel hoch, da komm ich her; O wie selig seid ihr doch, ihr Frommen; O Haupt voll Blut und Wunden; Meinen Jesum lass ich nicht; 1903–5, R xxx

— Auferstanden, auferstanden, cantata, A, chorus, org, 1903–5, arr. J. Haas, R xxx

79 79f, 14 arrangements; 79g, 3 arrangements, female/boys' chorus; 1900, R xxvii

83 10 Gesänge, male vv, 1904, 1909, R xxvii

— Weihegesang (O. Liebmann), A, chorus, wind orch, 1908, R xxviii

106 Psalm c, chorus, orch, org, 1908–9, R xxix

110 Geistliche Gesänge, 5vv: Mein Odem ist schwach; Ach, Herr, strafe mich nicht; O Tod, wie bitter bist du; 1912, R xxvii

— Vater unser, 12vv, 1909, completed K. Hasse, R xxvii

111b 3 Gesänge, female 4vv, 1909, R xxvii; arr. female 3vv as op.111c

112 Die Nonnen (M. Boelitz), chorus, orch, 1909, R xxix

119 Die Weihe der Nacht (Hebbel), A, male vv, orch, 1911, R xxviii

— Lasset uns den Herren preisen (Easter motet, J. Rist), 5vv, ?1911, R xxvii

126 Römischer Triumphgesang (H. Lingg), male vv, orch, 1912, R xxix

138 8 geistliche Gesänge, 4–8vv, 1914, R xxvii

— Abschiedslied (M. von Seydewitz), 4vv, 1914, R xxvii

— Requiem: 1st movt, Totenfeier (trans. H. von Hase), 4 solo vv, 4vv, orch, 1914, R xxviii; 2nd movt, Dies irae, vv, orch, 1914, inc., R xxxvi

144 2 Gesänge: Der Einsiedler (Eichendorff), Bar, 5vv, orch; Requiem (Hebbel), A/Bar, chorus, orch; 1915, R xxviii

— 20 Responsorien (1966)

CHAMBER

— Scherzo, g, fl, str qt, R xxxviii

— String Quartet, d, with db in finale, 1888–9, R xxv

1 Sonata, d, vn, pf, 1890, R xix

2 Trio, b, vn, va, pf, 1891, R xxii

3 Sonata, D, vn, pf, 1891, R xix

5 Sonata, f, vc, pf, 1892, R xxi

— Vn parts for 6 Sonatinas op.36 by Clementi, before 1895

— Piano Quintet, c, 1897–8, R xxiii

28 Sonata, g, vc, pf, 1898, R xxi

41 Sonata, A, vn, pf, 1899, R xix

42 4 Sonatas, d, A, b, g, vn, 1900, R xxiv

49 2 Sonatas, A, f♯, cl, pf, 1900, R xxi

54 2 String Quartets, g, A, 1900, R xxv

— Caprice, a, vc, pf, 1901, R xxi

64 Piano Quintet, c, 1901–2, R xxiii

— Prelude and Fugue, a, vn, 1902, R xxiv

— Romanze, G, Petite caprice, g, vn, pf, 1902, R xx

— Albumblatt, E♭, Tarantella, g, cl/vn, pf, ?1902, R xxi

— Allegretto grazioso, A, fl, pf, ?1902, R xxi

72 Sonata, C, vn, pf, 1903, R xix

74 String Quartet, d, 1903–4, R xxv; 77b, String Trio, a, R xxiv; 1904

78 Sonata, F, vc, pf, 1904, R xxi

79 79d, Wiegenlied, Capriccio, Burla, vn, pf, 1902–4, R xix; 79e, Caprice, Kleine Romanze, vc, pf, 1904, R xxi

84 Sonata, f♯, vn, pf, 1905, R xix

87 Albumblatt, Romanze, vn, pf, ?1905, R xix

91 7 Sonatas, a, D, B♭, b, e, G, a, vn, 1905, R xxiv

93 Suite im alten Stil, F, vn, pf, 1906, R xx; orchd 1916, R vi; Largo arr. vn, org, R xxxviii

102 Trio, e, vn, vc, pf, 1907–8, R xxii

103 103a, Suite (6 Vortragsstücke), a, vn, pf, 1908, R xx, 3rd movt orchd; 103b, 2 Little Sonatas, d, A, vn, pf, 1909, R xx; 103c, 12 kleine Stücke nach eigenen Liedern [op.76], vn, pf, 1916, R xx

107 Sonata, B♭, cl/va, pf, 1908–9, R xxi

109 String Quartet, E♭, 1909, R xxv

113 Piano Quartet, d, 1910, R xxii

116 Sonata, a, vc, pf, 1910, R xxi

117 Preludes and Fugues, b, g, e, g (Chaconne), G, d, a, e, vn, 1909–12, R xxiv

118 Sextet, F, 2 vn, 2 va, 2 vc, 1910, R xxvi

121 String Quartet, f♯, 1911, R xxv

122 Sonata, e, vn, pf, 1911, R xx

131 131a, Preludes and Fugues, a, d, G, g, D, e, vn, 1914, R xxiv; 131b, 3 Duos (Canons und Fugen) im alten Stil, 2 vn, 1914, R xxiv; 131c, 3 Suites, G, d, a, vc, 1915, R xxiv; 131d, 3 Suites, g, D, e, va, 1915, R xxiv

133 Piano Quartet, a, 1914, R xxii

— Allegro, A, 2 vn, ?1914, R xxiv

139 Sonata, c, vn, pf, 1915, R xix

141 141a, Serenade, G, fl/vn, vn, va, 1915, R xxvi; 141b, String Trio, d, 1915, R xxiv

---

146 Clarinet Quintet, A, 1915, R xxvi

— Prelude, e, vn, ?1915, R xxiv

SOLO VOCAL

14 5 Duets, S, A, pf, 1894, R xxx

19 2 geistliche Gesänge, Mez/Bar, org, 1898, R xxxiv

— 3 geistliche Lieder, Mez/Bar, org, 1900, 1903, R xxxiv

— Trauungslied 'Befiehl dem Herrn deine Wege', S, A, org, R xxx

105 2 geistliche Lieder, Mez/Bar, org/harmonium/pf, 1907, R xxxiv

111a 3 Duets, S, A, pf, 1909, R xxx

124 An die Hoffnung (Hölderlin), A/Mez, orch/pf, 1912, R xxxv

136 Hymnus der Liebe (L. Jacobowski), Bar/A, orch, 1914, R xxxv

137 12 geistliche Lieder, 1v, pf/harmonium/org, 1914, R xxxiv

Lieder: 6 Lieder, op.4, Mez/Bar, pf, 1891, R xxxi; 5 Lieder, op.8, S/T, pf, 1892, R xxxi; 5 Lieder 'Der Manen Franz Schuberts', op.12, 1v, pf, 1893, R xxxi; Ich stehe hoch über'm See, op.14b (von Lieven), B, pf, R xxxi; 10 Lieder, op.15, Mez/Bar, pf, 1894, R xxxi; 4 Lieder, op.23, 1v, pf, 1898, R xxxi; 6 Gedichte von Anna Ritter, op.31, Mez/Bar, pf, 1898, R xxxi; 6 Lieder, op.35, Mez/Bar, pf, 1899, R xxxi; 5 Gesänge, op.37, Mez/Bar, pf, 1899, R xxxi; 8 Lieder, op.43, 1v, pf, 1900, R xxxi; 7 Lieder, op.48, Mez/Bar, pf, 1900, R xxxi; 12 Lieder 'An Hugo Wolf' op.51, 1v, pf, 1900, R xxxi; 15 Lieder, op.55, 1v, pf, 1900–01, R xxxi; 16 Gesänge, op.62, 1v, pf, 1901, R xxxi; 12 Lieder, op.66, Mez/Bar, pf, 1902, R xxxii; 6 Gesänge, op.68, Mez/Bar, pf, 1902, R xxxii; 17 Gesänge, op.70, S/T, pf, 1902–3, R xxxii; 18 Gesänge, op.75, 1v, pf, 1903, R xxxii; Schlichte Weisen, op.76, 60 Lieder, 1v, pf, 1903–12, R xxxiii; 8 Kompositionen, op.79c, 1v, pf, 1901–3, R xxxiv; 4 Gesänge, op.88, Mez/Bar, pf, 1905, R xxxiv; 4 Lieder, op.97, 1v, pf, 1906, R xxxiv; 5 Gesänge, op.98, 1v, pf, 1906, R xxxiv; 6 Lieder, op.104, 1v, pf, 1907, R xxxiv; 5 neue Kinderlieder, op.142, S/T, pf, 1915, R xxxiv; other lieder without op. no., 1893–1912, R xxxiv

Orchestrations of lieder opp.31/4, 31/5, 37/3, 43/5, 62/11, 75/11, 76/16, 76/22, 76/35, 76/52, 97/1, 98/1, R xxxv

PIANO

9 12 Walzer-Capricen, duet, 1892, R xiii

10 20 deutsche Tänze, duet, 1893, R xiii

11 7 Walzer, 1893, R ix

13 Lose Blätter, 1894, R ix

17 Aus der Jugendzeit, 1895, R ix

— 111 Canons durch alle Dur- und Molltonarten, 1895, R xii

— Etude brillante, c, 1896

18 Improvisationen, 1896, R ix

20 5 Humoresken, 1896, R ix

22 6 Walzer, duet, 1898, R xiii

— An der schönen blauen Donau, improvisation, 1898

— Grüsse an die Jugend, 1898, R xii

24 6 morceaux, 1898, R ix

25 Aquarellen, 5 kleine Tonbilder, 1897–8, R ix

26 7 Fantasie-Stücke, 1898, R ix

— 3 Albumblätter, 1898–9, R xii

32 7 Charakterstücke, 1899, R ix

34 5 pièces pittoresques, duet, 1899, R xiii

36 Bunte Blätter, 1899, R ix

44 10 kleine Vortragsstücke, 1900, R ix

45 6 Intermezzi, 1900, R x

53 Silhouetten, 7 pieces, 1900, R x

58 6 Burlesken, duet, 1901, R xiii

— 4 Spezialstudien, left hand, ?1901, R xii

— Blätter und Blüten, 12 pieces, 1900–02, R xii

— In der Nacht, 1902, R xii

79a 10 Piano Pieces, 1901–3, R x

81 Variations and Fugue on a Theme of J. S. Bach, 1904, R x

82 Aus meinem Tagebuch, 35 little pieces, 1904–12, R x

86 Variations and Fugue on a Theme of Beethoven, 2 pf, 1904, R xiv; orchd 1915, R vi

— Perpetuum mobile, c♯, 1905, R xii

— 4 Piano Pieces, 1901–6, R xii

— Scherzo, f♯, Caprice, f♯, 1906, R xii

89 4 Sonatinas, e, D, F, a, 1905, 1908, R xi

94 6 Pieces, duet, 1906, R xiii

96 Introduction, Passacaglia and Fugue, b, 2 pf, 1906, R xiv

99 6 Preludes and Fugues, e, D, a, b, G, d, 1906–7, R xi

— Ewig dein!, salon piece, 1907, R xii

115 Episoden, 8 pieces, 1910, R xi

132a Variations and Fugue on a Theme of Mozart, 2 pf [arr. orch work], 1914, R xiv

134 Variations and Fugue on a Theme of G. P. Telemann, 1914, R xi

— Marsch der Stiftsdamen, 1914, R xii

143 Träume am Kamin, 12 little pieces, 1915, R xi

— Fughette über das Deutschlandlied, 1916, R xii

ORGAN

7 3 Organ Pieces, 1892, R xv

16 Suite 'Den Manen J. S. Bachs', e, 1894–5, R xv

27 Chorale Fantasia 'Ein' feste Burg ist unser Gott', 1898, R xv
29 Fantasia and Fugue, c, 1898, R xv
30 Chorale Fantasia 'Freu' dich sehr, o meine Seele', 1898, R xv
33 Sonata no.1, f♯, 1899, R xv
40 Chorale Fantasias 'Wie schön leucht't uns der Morgenstern', 'Straf' mich nicht in deinem Zorn', 1899, R xv
46 Fantasia and Fugue on B–A–C–H, 1900, R xv
47 6 Trios, 1900, R xv
52 Chorale Fantasias 'Alle Menschen müssen sterben', 'Wachet auf, ruft uns die Stimme', 'Halleluja! Gott zu loben, bleibe meine Seelenfreud', 1900, R xv
56 5 Easy Preludes and Fugues, 1904, R xvi
57 Symphonic Fantasia and Fugue, 1901, R xvi
59 12 Pieces, 1901, R xvi
60 Sonata no.2, d, 1901, R xvi
63 Monologe, 12 pieces, 1901–2, R xvi
65 12 Pieces, 1902, R xvi
67 52 Easy Chorale Preludes, 1902, R xvii
69 10 Pieces, 1903, R xvii
73 Variations and Fugue on an Original Theme, f♯, 1903, R xvii
79b 13 Chorale Preludes, 1901–3, R xvii
—   Schule des Triospiels [arr. Bach: 2-part inventions], 1903, collab. K. Straube
80 12 Pieces, 1904, R xvii
85 4 Preludes and Fugues, c, G, F, e, 1904, R xvii
92 Suite, g, 1905, R xviii
127 Introduction, Passacaglia and Fugue, e, 1913, R xviii
129 9 Pieces, 1913, R xviii
135a 30 Little Chorale Preludes, 1914, R xviii
135b Fantasia and Fugue, d, 1916, R xviii
145 7 Organ Pieces, 1915–16, R xviii
Several small pieces, 1893–1906, R xviii

Principal publishers: Augener, Bote & Bock, Breitkopf & Härtel, Junne, Kahnt, Lauterbach & Kuhn, Leuckart, Peters, Schott, Simrock, Tischer & Jagenberg, Universal

EDITIONS AND ARRANGEMENTS
(selective list)

Orch: *H. Wolf: Italienische Serenade*, small orch (Leipzig, 1903); *J. S. Bach: Vn Concs., a, E*, 1911; *G. F. Handel: Concerto grosso in B* (Leipzig, 1912); *A. Corelli: La folia* (Brussels, 1914); *J. S. Bach: O Mensch, bewein' dein' Sünde gross*, str (Leipzig, 1915); *J. S. Bach: Brandenburg Conc. no.5, Kbd Conc., d, 2 Kbd Concs., C, c*, 1915; *J. S. Bach: Suites nos.1–3*, 1915–16; *J. S. Bach: Suite, g* [arr. Kbd Partitas and English Suites] (Leipzig, 1916); *J. S. Bach: Triple Conc., a*, 1916
Chamber: *J. S. Bach: Violin-Sonate, f* (Leipzig, 1915); *J. S. Bach: Violin-Sonate, A* (Berlin and Leipzig, 1922)
Pf: *E. d'Albert: Ouvertüre Esther, op.8*, duet (Berlin, 1895); *J. S. Bach: Orgel-Werke* (London, 1895); *J. S. Bach: Orgel-Werke*, duet (London, 1895–6); *F. Chopin: 5 Spezialstudien* (Munich and Leipzig, 1899); *R. Strauss: Ausgewählte Lieder* (Munich and Leipzig, 1899); *J. S. Bach: 13 Choralvorspiele* (Munich and Leipzig, 1900); *H. Wolf: Penthesilea*, duet (Leipzig, 1903); *H. Wolf: Italienische Serenade*, duet (Leipzig, 1904); *H. Wolf: 12 Mörike-Lieder* (Leipzig, 1905); *J. S. Bach: Brandenburg Concs. nos.1–6*, duet (Leipzig, 1905–6); *J. S. Bach: Orchester-Suiten 1–4*, duet (Leipzig, 1907); *C. P. E. Bach: 4 Symphonien*, duet (Leipzig, 1910); *A. Jensen: 3 Lieder* in *Jensen-Album* (Leipzig, 1910); *R. Wagner: Auserlesene Stücke aus Opern*, 2 pf (Leipzig, 1914); *J. Brahms: 5 langsame Sätze aus den Sinfonien* (Berlin and Leipzig, 1916); *J. S. Bach: 3 Choralvorspiele* (Munich and Leipzig, 1943)
Choral: *9 ausgewählte Volkslieder*, male vv (Munich and Leipzig, 1899); *6 Madrigalen* (Leipzig and Zurich, 1900); *12 Madrigalen*, male vv (Leipzig and Zurich, 1900); *H. Wolf: Christnacht* (Leipzig, 1903); *H. Wolf: 6 geistliche Lieder*, male vv (Leipzig, 1903); numerous unpubd arrs.
Solo vocal with orch: *H. Wolf: 14 geistliche Lieder* (Leipzig, 1908); *7 Lieder* [Brahms, Grieg and Wolf] (Leipzig, 1914); *F. Schubert: 8 Lieder* (Leipzig, 1914); *J. Brahms: 6 Lieder* (Leipzig, 1914–15); *R. Schumann: 5 Lieder*, 1916; *F. Schubert: 7 Lieder* (Vienna, 1926)

WRITINGS

'Analyse des Streichquartetts d-moll op.74', *Die Musik*, iii (1903–4), 244
Beiträge zur Modulationslehre (Leipzig, 1903, 24/1952)
'Hugo Wolfs künstlerischer Nachlass', *Süddeutsche Monatshefte* (1904), no.2
'Ich bitte um's Wort', *NZM*, lxxi (1904), 20
'Mehr Licht', *NZM*, lxxi (1904), 202
'Zum 1. April', *NZM*, lxxi (1904), 274
'Degeneration und Regeneration in der Musik', *Neue Musikzeitung* (1907)
'Musik und Fortschritt', *Leipziger Tageblatt* (16 June 1907)
'Offener Brief', *Die Musik*, vii (1907–8), 12
'Felix Mendelssohn Bartholdys "Lieder ohne Worte"', *Leipziger illustrierte Zeitung* (28 Jan 1909)

ed. E. von Hase-Koehler: *Briefe eines deutschen Meisters* (Leipzig, 1928, 2/1938)
ed. H. and E. H. Mueller von Asow: *Briefwechsel mit Herzog Georg II. von Sachsen-Meiningen* (Weimar, 1949)
ed. O. Schreiber: *Briefe zwischen der Arbeit* (Bonn, 1956, 1973)

BIBLIOGRAPHY
DOCUMENTS AND REMINISCENCES

R. Eucken: *Persönliche Erinnerungen an Max Reger* (Bielefeld, 1916)
J. Haas: *Reger als Lehrer* (Munich, 1920–23)
H. Marteau: *Meine Erinnerungen an Max Reger* (Prague, 1923)
E. Reger: *Mein Leben mit und für Max Reger* (Leipzig, 1930)
C. Brock: *Max Reger als Vater* (Marburg, 1936)
W. Gurlitt: *Aus den Briefen Max Regers an Hugo Riemann* (Leipzig, 1937)
S. Zweig: *Die Welt von gestern* (Stockholm, 1944)
R. Braungart: *Freund Reger: Erinnerungen* (Regensburg, 1949)
F. Busch: *Aus dem Leben eines Musikers* (Zurich, 1949)
G. Busch: *Fritz Busch* (Frankfurt, 1950)
Festschrift für Elsa Reger anlässlich ihres 80. Geburtstags am 25. Oktober 1950 (Bonn, 1950)
W. Strecker: 'Max Reger in London', *Mitteilungen des Max-Reger-Instituts* (1957)
L. Thoma: *Ein Leben in Briefen* (Munich, 1963)
M. M. Stein: *Der heitere Reger* (Wiesbaden, 1969)
K. Laux: 'Max Reger: Erinnerungen – Bekenntnis – Aufgaben', *Musik und Gesellschaft*, xxiii (1973), 129

CATALOGUE, BIBLIOGRAPHY AND MONOGRAPHS

R. Braungart: *Max Reger*, Monographien moderner Musiker, ii (Leipzig, 1907)
M. Hehemann: *Max Reger: ein Leben in Musik* (Munich, 1911, 2/1917)
H. Poppen: *Max Reger* (Leipzig, 1918, 3/1947)
K. Hasse: *Max Reger: mit Regers Schriften und Aufsätzen* (Leipzig, 1921)
H. Unger: *Max Reger: Darstellung seines Lebens, Wesens und Schaffens* (Munich, 1921)
A. Lindner: *Max Reger: ein Bild seines Jugendlebens und künstlerischen Werdens* (Stuttgart, 1922, 3/1938)
G. Bagier: *Max Reger* (Stuttgart and Berlin, 1923)
S. Kallenberg: *Max Reger* (Leipzig, 1929)
F. Stein: *Max Reger* (Potsdam, 1939)
F. Stein: *Thematisches Verzeichnis der im Druck erschienenen Werke von Max Reger einschliesslich seiner Bearbeitungen und Ausgaben* (Leipzig, 1953)
E. Otto: *Max Reger: Sinnbild einer Epoche* (Wiesbaden, 1957)
H. Rösner: *Max-Reger-Bibliographie* (Bonn, 1968)
H. Wirth: *Max Reger* (Hamburg, 1973)

STUDIES

H. Grabner: *Regers Harmonik* (Munich, 1920)
E. Gatscher: *Die Fugentechnik Max Regers in ihrer Entwicklung* (Stuttgart, 1925)
P. Coenen: *Max Regers Variationsschaffen* (diss., U. of Berlin, 1935)
H. E. Rahner: *Max Regers Choralfantasien für die Orgel* (Kassel, 1936)
H. J. Therstappen: 'Über die Grundlagen der Form bei Max Reger', *Festschrift Fritz Stein* (Brunswick, 1939)
H. Distler: *Funktionelle Harmonielehre* (Kassel and Basle, 1941) [incl. analysis of op.82/1, 1st movt]
W. Abendroth: 'Max Reger', *Vier Meister der Musik* (Munich, 1952)
K. Straube: *Briefe eines Thomaskantors* (Stuttgart, 1952)
H. Walcha: 'Max Regers Orgelschaffen kritisch betrachtet', *Musik und Kirche*, xxii (1952), 2
H. J. Moser: 'Max Regers Orchesterwerke', *Beiträge zur Reger-Forschung* (1953), 21
K. Hasse: 'Max Regers unvollendetes "Vater unser" für 12stimmigen Chor a cappella und seine Ergänzung', *Mitteilungen des Max-Reger-Instituts* (1955), no.3, p.2
G. Wehmeyer: *Max Reger als Liederkomponist*, Kölner Beiträge zur Musikforschung, viii (Regensburg, 1955)
O. Schreiber: 'Max Reger in unserer Zeit', *Mitteilungen des Max-Reger-Instituts* (1963)
O. Schreiber and G. Sievers, ed.: *Max Reger zum 50. Todestag am 11. Mai 1966: ein Gedenkschrift* (Bonn, 1966)
G. Sievers: *Die Grundlagen Hugo Riemanns bei Max Reger* (Wiesbaden, 1967)
H. J. Busch: 'Max Reger und die Orgel seiner Zeit', *Musik und Kirche*, xliii (1973), 63
S. Kross, ed.: *Max Reger in seiner Zeit* (Koblenz, 1973) [incl. catalogue for centenary exhibition, Bonn, and six articles]
P. Prince: 'Reger and the Organ', *Diapason*, lxiv/4 (1973), 1
G. Sievers: 'Die Klavierkompositionen von Max Reger', *Mitteilungen des Max-Reger-Instituts* (1973), Sonderheft, p.34
R. Stephan: 'Max Reger und die Anfänge der neuen Musik', *NZM*, Jg.134 (1973), 339

H. Wunderlich: 'Zur Bedeutung und Interpretation von Regers Orgelwerken: ein Beitrag zum Regerjahr 1973', *Musik und Kirche*, xliii (1973), 7

K. Röhring, ed.: *Max Reger 1873–1973: ein Symposion* (Wiesbaden, 1974)

G. Massenkeil and S. Popp, eds.: *Festschrift für Ottmar Schreiber* (Wiesbaden, 1978)

HELMUT WIRTH

Reggae. An urban popular music and dance style, originating in Jamaica in the mid-1960s. In its original context and its general musical style, reggae closely resembles its precursor 'rock steady'.

Reggae is a synthetic style with elements of North American, particularly Afro-American, popular music and traditional Afro-Jamaican music (itself a blend of West African and British elements); it has a Western melodic-harmonic base, West African sound ideals and organizational principles, and American popular and rock music mannerisms including a preference for high volume, particularly in the bass. The characteristic rhythmic texture is an amalgam of short ostinatos performed by an ensemble of organ, piano, drums and three electric guitars (rhythm, lead and bass, the last two usually doubling a bass pattern in octaves). Except for the bass patterns, which are almost as individual as the melodies, the number of instrumental ostinatos used is small. In 4/4 metre, for example, the chordal instruments normally emphasize quaver offbeats, while the drums highlight the second and fourth crotchet downbeats; a characteristic rhythm for compound quadruple metre is more complex (see ex.1). While such accompani-

Ex.1 Compound quadruple metre rhythm

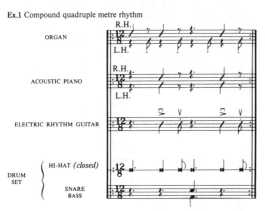

ments are often used to 'Jamaicanize' non-indigenous songs, they are an integral part of the reggae composing style. Other characteristics include a circumscribed harmonic vocabulary (an almost total reliance on primary diatonic triads, and a lack of modulation), and a predilection for short formal and harmonic units, i.e. the repetition of a single three-chord progression occupying two or four quadruple-metre bars (e.g. tonic–subdominant–dominant–subdominant), or oscillation between two chords. Reggae musicians compose and perform in an oral tradition, without recourse to a formalized body of music theory, musical notation or specialized training in music.

Reggae was originally music of the Jamaican lower class. Many of the texts—based on English but laced with creole expressions unintelligible to a non-Jamaican—disclose and affirm that class's values and fundamental concerns (most prominently Rasta-

farianism and extreme social discontent), in such songs as *Revolution, Better must come, Let the Power fall on I* and *Thy Kingdom come*. Several magazines provide coverage of reggae performers and records, among them *Melody Maker* (Britain), *Rolling Stone* (USA), and most importantly *Swing* (Jamaica).

BIBLIOGRAPHY

G. White: 'Rudie, oh Rudie', *Caribbean Quarterly*, xiii/3 (1967), 39

P. O'Gorman: 'An Approach to the Study of Jamaican Popular Music', *Jamaica Journal*, vi/4 (1972), 50

M. Thomas: 'The Wild Side of Paradise: Steaming with the Rude Boys, the Rastas and Reggae', *Rolling Stone*, cxxxix (19 July 1973), 44

ROBERT WITMER

Reggio, Fattorin da. The name under which DOMENICO VALLA published his only known work.

Reggio, Hoste [Spirito da]. *See* HOSTE DA REGGIO.

Reggio, Pietro (Francesco) (*b* Genoa, baptized ?6 July 1632; *d* London, 23 July 1685). Italian composer, singer, lutenist, guitarist and teacher. He sang bass in the troupe of Italian musicians employed by Queen Christina in Stockholm (not Rome, as stated in Eitner, *Grove 5* and *MGG*) from 30 November 1652 to 1 March 1653; he may have stayed in Sweden until the queen's abdication in 1654. He is reported to have travelled to Germany and Spain, and there is documentary evidence dated September 1657 that about that time he sang in the French royal choir. By July 1664 he was in England, where he remained. He settled in London (not Oxford, as stated in Eitner and *Grove 5*) and earned his living by singing, playing and teaching music. The private homes in which he performed included those of Pepys and Evelyn. According to Evelyn he sang tenor as well as bass, and he taught singing to Evelyn's daughter Mary. That he also worked as a music copyist is shown by *GB-Lbm* Harl.1501 and *US-LAuc* fC697 M4. He did not, however, copy *GB-Lbm* Add.31440: although this is called a Reggio autograph in the *Lbm* catalogue and in *MGG*, it dates from an earlier period and contains neither his handwriting nor any of his music. He was among the composers who contributed to Shadwell's adaptation of *The Tempest* in 1674: he wrote the song 'Arise, ye subterranean winds'. This and other songs by him in English and Italian were included in MSS of the period, and 46 of his songs and duets were published in 1680. A treatise on singing by him was advertised for publication in 1678, but no further reference is known, and no copy seems to survive. When he died he was buried in St Giles-in-the Fields, with a handsome inscription on his tombstone.

Reggio had a moderate success as a composer: his output was small, of limited scope and rather ordinary in quality. He was probably more gifted as a singer and player. His main role perhaps was to bring music and musical styles from Italy to countries across Europe: by performing and teaching this music abroad he made it more widely known. In England in particular he contributed usefully to the musical scene.

WORKS

[42] Songs, S, bc [and 4 duets, S, B, bc] (London, 1680) [most to poems by A. Cowley]

1 song, 1v, bc, in 1685⁵; 14 songs, 1v, bc; 2 duets; 1 Lat. motet, 3vv, bc: *GB-Cfm, Lbm, Och, T*

WRITINGS

The Art of Singing, or a Treatise wherein is Shewn How to Sing Well Any Song Whatsoever, and also How to Apply the Best Graces, with a Collection of Cadences Plain, and then Graced (? London, 1678) [possibly never pubd]

BIBLIOGRAPHY
EitnerQ; *HawkinsH*
J. A. Westrup: *Purcell* (London, 1937, rev. 4/1980)
J. Evelyn: *Diary*, ed. E. S. de Beer (London, 1955), iv
E. Sundström: 'Notiser om drottning Kristinas italienska musiker', *STMf*, xliii (1961), 297
M. Tilmouth: 'A Calendar of References to Music in Newspapers Published in London and the Provinces (1660–1719)', *RMARC*, i (1961/*R*1968), 4
P. J. Willetts: 'A Neglected Source of Monody and Madrigal', *ML*, xliii (1962), 329
G. Rose: 'Pietro Reggio—a Wandering Musician', *ML*, xlvi (1965), 207
P. J. Willetts: 'Autographs of Angelo Notari', *ML*, l (1969), 124
GLORIA ROSE

Regina caeli laetare (Lat.: 'Queen of Heaven rejoice'). One of the four Marian antiphons. It is now sung at the conclusion of Compline from Easter Sunday to the Friday after Pentecost; since 1742 it has also been used to conclude the *Angelus* during the same season. Its use as a concluding antiphon during Easter dates from the mid-13th century, although it first appeared in a manuscript dating from about 1200 of the Old Roman chant tradition, where it was used as the *Magnificat* antiphon for the octave of Easter. Of the two versions in the *Liber usualis* the more elaborate (p.275) dates from the mid-13th century; there are polyphonic settings of this version by Dunstable, Busnois, Victoria, Philips and others. The second, simpler version dates from the 17th century and is probably by Henry Du Mont.

See also ANTIPHON and MOTET, §II.

Regino of Prüm (*b* Altrip, nr. Ludwigshafen, *c*842; *d* Trier, 915). German Benedictine monk, historian, canonist and music theorist. The 16th-century annals of Prüm record that he was born of 'very noble parents'; they give no birthdate, but it may be deduced from the date of his abbacy. He probably entered the abbey of Prüm as a youth; there he received instruction under Abbot Markward, one of the most learned men of his time. In 885 he became provost (*custos*) of the monastery; in 892 he was elected abbot, but was forced to resign seven years later. Archbishop Radbod of Trier then appointed him Abbot of St Martin, where he wrote a chronicle of the years from the birth of Christ to 906, a handbook of canon law for bishops to use during diocesan visitations (*De synodalibus causis*) and a musical treatise followed by a tonary (*Epistola de armonica institutione*; *Octo toni de musicae artis*). He died at the abbey of St Maximin at Trier; his tomb was discovered there in 1581.

The musical treatise was written in the form of a letter dedicated to Radbod, hence the title *Epistola*. It must have been compiled about 901, shortly after Regino's arrival at Trier. Only the beginning and the end are original, the main body of the work being a compilation of Boethius, Martianus Capella, Macrobius and (to a lesser extent) Calcidius, Cassiodorus and Fulgentius. Regino's principal intention was to correct the intonations of the antiphons and responsories of the Mass and Office, for the benefit of the clerics of the diocese of Trier; some of these intonations, he claimed, were 'degenerate'. If his claim was correct it may have been because books were lost during the Norman devastations.

Two versions of the treatise survive: the original form as a letter (in a Leipzig manuscript) and a mid-11th-century abridgment (*Breviarium de musica*) which may well be a product of the monastic reforms of GUIL-

LAUME DE DIJON (*d* 1031), modelled on those of Cluny. In the latter version all reference to people's names, even that of the author, was eliminated. Although the treatise is arbitrary and pedantic, it contains two important rules concerning 9th-century plainchant: the tone or mode proper to antiphons, introits and communions is determined by their first note; the tone or mode proper to responsories is determined by their last note.

Regino's is the first comprehensive tonary surviving after the Metz Tonary of about 870 (*F-MZ* 351; ed. Lipphardt, 1965), and together with the Hartker Antiphoner (*c*1000, *CH-SGs* 390–91; ed. in PalMus, 2nd ser., i, 1900) and the Sarum Gradual (ed. Frere, 1894/*R*1966) it is one of the most comprehensive plainchant sources in existence. Modelled on an antiphoner of Trier (now lost), and akin to a later one from the same city (*D-TRs* 1245/597), it contains the incipits of more than 1300 antiphons, 200 introits, 300 communions, 26 responsories and 26 verses; it formed the basis for Gevaert's classification of antiphons into 47 main groups. The tonary appears in full in *B-Br* 2750–65 [2751] (?*c*930), which is notated in Messine neumes, whereas the version of *D-LEu* Rep. I.8.93 [169] (?*c*925), notated in Saxon neumes, contains a classification of approximately the same repertory according to the eight modes within the cycle of the liturgical year, but omits the introits and communions while adding the alleluias, tracts, invitatories and antiphons of special feasts. These two manuscripts contain differing introductions, which cannot safely be ascribed to Regino. The other early sources of the *Epistola*, *Breviarium* and tonary are as follows: *I-Vnm* Z.L.497 [1811] (*Breviarium* without tonary; early 12th century); *F-MO* H.159 (*Breviarium* without tonary; mid-11th century); *MZ* 494 (11th-century copy of the preceding); *I-MC* 318 (short excerpts without tonary; 11th century); *GB-Ob* Lyell 57 and *Ob* 613 (fragments; 13th century). The supposed Ulm manuscript was an invention of Beyschlag (in his *Sylloge variorum opusculorum*, Nuremberg, 1728).

BIBLIOGRAPHY
CS, ii, 1–73 [tonary]; *GS*, i, 230–47 [*Epistola*]; *PL*, cxxxii, 483–502
Wyttenbach: 'Noch ein Wort über Regino', *Archiv der Gesellschaft für ältere deutsche Geschichtkunde*, iii (1821), 291
F. Kurze, ed.: *Reginonis abbatis prumiensis Chronicon cum continuatione treverensi*, Monumenta Germaniae historica, Scriptores rerum germanicarum in usum scholarum, 1 (Hanover, 1890), 885, 892, 899
F. Haberl: *Il tonario di Reginone di Prüm* (diss., Pontificio Istituto di Musica Sacra, Rome, 1937)
E. Oberti: 'L'estetica musicale di Reginone di Prüm', *Rivista di filosofia neo-scolastica*, lii (1960), 336
H. Hüschen: 'Regino von Prüm, Historiker Kirchenrechtler und Musiktheoretiker', *Festschrift Karl Gustav Fellerer* (Regensburg, 1962), 205
H. Reetz: 'Regino von Prüm geboren im pfälzischen Altrip', *Jb des Kreises Prüm*, v (1964), 19
Y. Chartier: *L'Epistola de armonia institutione de Réginon de Prüm* (diss., U. of Ottawa, 1965)
M. P. Le Roux: *The 'De harmonica institutione' and 'Tonarius' of Regino of Prüm* (Ann Arbor, 1970)
C. M. Bower: 'Natural and Artificial Music: the Origins and Development of an Aesthetic Concept', *MD*, xxv (1971), 17
M. Huglo: *Les tonaires: inventaire, analyse, comparaison* (Paris, 1971)
YVES CHARTIER

Regis, Johannes [Leroy, Jehan] (*b* *c*1430; *d* ?Soignies, *c*1485). Netherlands composer. A 'Jehan Leroy' is mentioned in the account books of St Vincent in Soignies in 1458. In 1460 he was appointed *magister puerorum* of Cambrai Cathedral, but it is uncertain whether he actually took up the position, although the cathedral records carry notices of the copying of several of his compositions. In 1463 he was *magister puerorum* at Notre Dame, Antwerp. Regis became Dufay's secretary in Cambrai, living there perhaps for as long as from 1464 to 1474. In 1481–2 he was a canon and *scholasticus* in Soignies.

Johannes Tinctoris referred to Regis in two treatises. In the *Proportionale musices* (before 1475) he censured the composer for using 'notes computed in imperfect tempus' within the sign of *tempus perfectum*. In his *Liber de arte contrapuncti* (1477), however, he ranked Regis with Ockeghem, Busnois, Caron and Faugues, and later praised him for the contrapuntal variety in his motet *Clangat plebs*. Regis was well known, for the text of the *secunda pars* of Compère's *Omnium bonorum plena*, a prayer for composers, includes Regis's name, and Crétin's *Déploration* contains posthumous mention of him.

Regis used cantus firmi and, to some extent, imitative procedures to structure his music. Techniques such as the use of melodic sequence and head-motifs are of secondary importance. *Tempus perfectum* is the basic mensuration, although *tempus imperfectum* is often found. Rhythmic variation and motivic play moderate the general feeling of a homogeneity in texture. Even though the harmony has a degree of independence from the counterpoint, it cannot yet be described as functional. Regis employed dissonance carefully; the dissonant note is never longer than a minim. Parallel perfect consonances are rarely found in part-writing, and 6-4 chords are generally avoided.

In the *Missa 'Dum sacrum mysterium'*, the outer voices have the text of the Ordinary, while the inner ones generally present that of the *Magnificat* antiphon for the dedication of St Michael the Archangel. In addition the melody *L'homme armé* is used, symbolizing St Michael's attributes as a warrior. A three-voice head-motif and the presentation of the secular cantus firmus in the tenor, at times in canon with the contratenor altus, serve as unifying factors. In the *Missa 'Ecce ancilla'* (a more mature work than the *Missa 'Dum sacrum mysterium'*), the tenor and contratenor bassus respectively are based on the Advent antiphons *Ecce ancilla Domini* and *Ne timeas Maria*, although five additional antiphons appear at least in part. The head-motif is less rigorously carried through than in the earlier mass. *Patrem vilayge* is based on Credo I, which is presented in the tenor. It is a compact work, with some textual elision.

The motets are stylistically somewhat more advanced. The cadences are more often of the V–I variety, rhythmic activity is greater, and the scoring, usually for five voices, produces a full sound. In most of the motets the tenor has the cantus firmus and, although it enters late and is rhythmically distinguished by its longer note values, it soon assumes the general character of the other parts. At times the other voices are treated as two pairs. The five-voice *Ave Maria* is rather more contrapuntally orientated than is usual in Regis's style. *O admirabile commercium*, the only motet in three *partes*, shows the influence of Josquin Desprez, to whom it is ascribed in one manuscript. It represents, with its bass-like baryphonus, a departure from the tenor motet procedure. The small *Ave Maria* is found in a collection of examples for Glarean's *Dodecachordon* (*D-Mu* Cim 44a.).

WORKS

Edition: *J. Regis: Opera omnia*, ed. C. Lindenburg, CMM, ix (1956) [L]

MASSES ETC

Missa 'Dum sacrum mysterium'/'L'homme armé', 4vv, L i, 1

Missa 'Ecce ancilla Domini'/'Ne timeas Maria', 4vv, L i, 25

Credo 'Patrem vilayge', 4vv, L i, 62

MOTETS

Ave Maria, 5vv, L ii, 42 (sequence to BVM; 5th v missing)

Ave Maria, 3vv, L ii, 60 (to BVM)

Celsi tonantis/Abrahae fit promissio, 5vv, L ii, 5

Clangat plebs/Sicut lilium, 5vv, L ii, 21 (to BVM)

Lauda Sion Salvatorem/Ego sum panis, 5vv, L ii, 14 (sequence for Corpus Christi)

Lux solempnis adest/Redempti sunt omnes, 5vv, L ii, 30 (for Whitsuntide)

O admirabile commercium/Verbum caro, 5vv, L ii, 49 (for Christmas)

Salve sponsa, 5vv, L ii, 1 (to ?BVM; 5th v missing)

SECULAR

Puisque ma dame/Je m'en voy, 4vv, L ii, 63 (rondeau)

S'il vous plaist, 4vv, L ii, 62 (rondeau; another version for 3vv)

BIBLIOGRAPHY

H. Besseler: *Die Musik des Mittelalters und der Renaissance*, HMw, ii (1931/R1949)

W. Stephan: *Die burgundisch-niederländische Motette zur Zeit Ockeghems* (diss., U. of Heidelberg; Kassel, 1937)

C. W. H. Lindenburg: *Het leven en de werken van Johannes Regis* (diss., U. of Amsterdam; Amsterdam, 1939)

C. van den Borren: *Etudes sur le XVᵉ siècle musical* (Antwerp, 1941)

M. Bukofzer: 'An Unknown Chansonnier of the 15th Century (The Mellon Chansonnier)', *MQ*, xxviii (1942), 14–49

J. du Saar: *Het leven en de composities van Jacobus Barbireau* (diss., U. of Utrecht; Utrecht, 1946)

J. Wouters: *Harmonische verschijningsvormen in de muziek van de XIIIᵉ tot de XVIᵉ eeuw* (diss., U. of Amsterdam; Amsterdam, 1954)

C. W. H. Lindenburg: 'O admirabile commercium', *TVNM*, xvii/4 (1955), 242

A. Seay: 'The *Proportionale musices* of Johannes Tinctoris', *JMT*, i (1957), 22–75

C. Lindenburg: 'Regis, Johannes', *MGG*

M. Caraci: 'Fortuna del tenor "L'homme armé" nel primo Rinascimento', *NRMI*, ix 1975), 171

KEITH E. MIXTER

Register (Ger. *Lage*). A part of the range or compass of an instrument, singing voice or composition. No interval can prescribe the size of a register, though the construction or playing of an instrument and the manner of singing can help to determine whether two notes are in the same or in different register, for example the strings of a violin, the octave key of an oboe, overblowing on a flute, lip tension on a brass instrument, and singing with a 'head' or 'chest' voice, or in falsetto.

In determining the registers of a musical work it is necessary to have some understanding of its style or structure. Medieval plainsong, for instance, distinguishes between higher (authentic) and lower (plagal) modes, thus suggesting that the interval between corresponding pairs of modes – a 4th – defines a difference in register. The 4th is also the difference between successive hexachords (*see* HEXACHORD) in the notational system used in the late Middle Ages and Renaissance. In tonal music the octave became an important register-defining interval; for the first time melodies were repeated in different octaves for contrast. Some were conceived to bring two octave regions together (ex.1).

Ex.1 Mozart: Haffner Symphony K385, opening

One often encounters the expression 'in a higher register' meaning no more than 'in a higher octave', and modern letter notation of pitch (i.e. $C'–B'$, $C–B$, $c–b$, $c'–b'$, $c''–b''$ etc) tends to support the primacy of the octave as a determinant of register. The importance of register to melodic unity was first clearly expressed by Heinrich Schenker, who believed that the fundamental melodic resolution to the key note or tonic is confined to one, 'obligatory' register (*see* OBLIGATE LAGE). In TWELVE-NOTE COMPOSITION the octave is of fundamental importance in giving meaning to 12-note sets, which consist of pitch classes that have no particular registral identity. *See also* REGISTRATION.

WILLIAM DRABKIN

Register key. *See* SPEAKER KEY.

Registration. The selection of different pitches and tone-colours available on an instrument. The two instruments that offer the player a choice of registration are the organ and the harpsichord.

I. Organ. II. Harpsichord.

I. Organ. The musical forces of the organ are available selectively by means of separate stops, or registers, which together provide the entire tonal capacity of the instrument. Each of the registers controls the 'on' or 'off' position for a series of pipes, grouped so that one or more pipes will respond to each key on a manual or pedal keyboard. The term 'organ registration' takes in the large body of advice about what is appropriate when combining organ stops, as well as the aggregate tonal effect of any combination drawn for a particular musical need. There is a rich store of information about registration for the organ that can be classified generally into two categories: practical advice, often supplied by organ builders, which consists of lists of combinations capable of being turned to good use; and instruction from composers or theoreticians about combinations appropriate for performing a particular musical composition.

1. Registration and the organ. 2. Early Spanish organs. 3. Early Italian organs. 4. North-western Europe. 5. Classical French organs. 6. Registration in the 19th century. 7. Authenticity.

1. REGISTRATION AND THE ORGAN. The history of organ registration is inextricably bound up with changing styles in organ building. Its origins lie in the transition between the stopless organ (*Blockwerk*) and instruments equipped with selective registers. In the *Blockwerk* of the early 15th century, the plenum, a mighty mixture of pipes sounding fundamentals and harmonics, was the only registration, and such an organ was indivisible. The introduction of the *fluitwerk-sterkwerk* option, the second manual division (*Positif-de-dos*, or *Rückpositiv*), and Trompes (Bordunen) made some variety in registration possible; but still there was no selectivity in the modern sense within the sections of the instrument. In Italy towards the end of the 15th century there were one-manual organs whose plena had been parcelled out to separate stops, each controlling a rank of pipes. As this new fashion spread northwards through France and Germany, organists were confronted for the first time with the necessity of choosing and blending their registrations, and builders often supplied them with advice about the most attractive combinations available. The earliest known organ music and the earliest instructions for registration date from the 15th century. But until the first decade of the 17th century there was no apparent attempt to identify any registration with a certain musical texture.

Mersenne, in his *Harmonie universelle* (1636–7), opened his section on organ registration by summing up possible combinations of stops for an instrument of 22 registers. Taken in pairs, he said, the individual sounds of the instrument may be varied in 231 ways; taken in threes, 1540 ways; and taken in fives, 26,334 ways. But 'among the many possible combinations there are several which are disagreeable'. This statement suggests that a player of good taste should refer to Mersenne's advice to find the most agreeable registrations, and eventually learn enough about the tonal design of the organ 'to invent several others by experimenting at the keyboard'.

Mersenne's lists of 'agreeable' registrations summed up more than a century of innovatory development for the French organ, a period from which considerable information about habits of registration has survived. A typical organ contract of the 16th century, or a list of registrations made out to assist the player, first described the plenum (called *fourniture* or *plein jeu*). The plenum was the ancient *Blockwerk* split into three or more registers controlling doubled or tripled ranks of 16′, 8′ and 4′, with two mixtures, called Fourniture and Cymbale. These mixtures held diverse ranks of many pitches contributing to the plenum; they were not useful by themselves, but neither was the plenum complete without them. Alongside the plenum, additional registrations developed for newly invented stops – flutes, reeds, bells, birdcalls, drums – bearing the names of their most distinctive components, such as Nasard, Doublette or Cromorne. Names of familiar sounds were applied to certain registrations, as *petit carillon*, 'parrot', 'canaries' or the 'voice of pilgrims of St Jacques'.

Major developments in organ building during the 16th century and the early 17th led to sharp stylistic delineations along national lines. Mersenne's 'agreeable' registrations would not have suited the tastes of Italian or German musicians of his time, whose instruments were designed according to different tonal concepts. Yet organ builders and theorists supplied the broadest range of advice available for playing early organ music. Schlick, in his *Spiegel der Orgelmacher und Organisten* (1511), mentioned that preludes should be played on the plenum, and the cantus firmus could be brought into prominence on the *Hauptwerk*. Numerous characteristic sonorities were discovered and recorded, such as Krumhorn and Zimbel, which appeared in the Netherlands as early as 1505.

2. EARLY SPANISH ORGANS. Two post-Cabezón documents deal fully with possibilities for one- or two-manual organs contemporary with Francisco Correa de Arauxo. They are the *Documents per a la historia*, which relate to the organ in S Juan de las Abadesas, Barcelona (1613), and *Archivo musical* (document 1404 at the cathedral of Lérida) for a 25-stop, two-manual organ built in 1624–5. The latter is most remarkable for its systematic coverage of 117 registrations. One-manual combinations were classified under the following headings: plenum, Flautados, Nasardos and Misturas; two-manual registrations, usually using the *cadira* (*Rückpositiv*) for melodic purposes, were grouped as: *unisonus*; 'other combinations' to be used with or without Tremulant; Flageolets; Gaytilles; Cornetillas; Regalies; and ways of using the 'medio registro partido' (half-registers split between bass and treble). Although Correa's tientos seem to have been written mostly for a one-manual organ with split stops (divided at *c′*), the Lérida manuscript shows richer possibilities for contemporary adaptation to an instrument provided with a *Rückpositiv*.

The introduction of the famous horizontal trumpets of Spanish organs (Clarines, or Trompettes *en chamade*) in the 17th century further heightened the contrasts between those instruments and organs in the other European countries. As early as 1706 directions for using horizontal trumpets were given in the titles of pieces in the *Flores de música ... por Fray Antonio Martín y Coll, organista de San Diego de Alcalá*: 'Cancion de clarín, con eco, a discreción', 'Entrada de clarines' and 'Registro de clarines, mano derecha'.

A late 18th-century Spanish source shows the influence of Bédos de Celles, the third volume of whose *L'art du facteur d'orgues* (1770) gave valuable advice on registration. A series of letters to a friend by Don Fernando Antonio of Madrid, dealing with the construction and maintenance of organs, was published in 1790. Despite his feeling that organists should know how to find suitable registrations for their own playing, Don Fernando was persuaded to add a section on registration. It is, in effect, a Spanish adaptation of Bédos' instructions.

3. EARLY ITALIAN ORGANS. The Italians, the first to use spring- and slider-chests that made registration possible on the organ, called attention to the correlation between certain registrations and suitable musical textures. Diruta, in his *Seconda parte del transilvano* (1609), assigned moods to the 12 modes, and recommended a registration for each. Banchieri, in *L'organo suonarino* (1605), not only noted registrations but even included changes between sections of two compositions, the 'Battaglia' and the 'Dialogo'. But the most significant contribution came from the builder Costanzo Antegnati, in *L'arte organica* (1608), written in the form of a dialogue between father and son. Antegnati explained his 12-stop organ at Brescia Cathedral, and gave instructions on how to play it during the Mass. The stops all spoke from one manual keyboard, typical for Italian organs of the period, with a coupled pedal which controlled the bass section of a Principal stop (see no.2 below):

1. The complete Principale (24′)
2. The split Principale (24′), divided at *d*, the bass played by the pedals
3. Ottava (12′)
4. Quintadecima
5. Decimanona
6. Vigesimaseconda
7. Vigesimasesta
8. Vigesimanona
9. Trigesimaterza
10. Another Vigesimaseconda, to play in concert with the Ottava, and Flauto in ottava and Decimanona, which gives the effect of cornets.
11. Flauto in quintadecima
12. Flauto in ottava

Registrations and important comments were as follows:

1. *Ripieno*, for intonations, introits or preludes: 1.3.4.5.6.7.8.9
2. *Mezzo ripieno*: 1.3.8.9.12
3. 1.3.12
4. 1.12
5. 3.5.6.12 for the concerto style. These four stops resemble a consort of cornets.
6. 3.12. These two are excellent for playing diminutions and for canzonas 'alla francese'.
7. 3.12 + Tremolo; for the same sorts of pieces, but not for diminutions
8. 1 alone. 'I usually play this at the Elevation of the Mass'.
9. 1.2 in unison may be played together.
10. 12 alone
11. 12 + 2. When played in the treble, this makes a kind of accompanied harmony of two stops; then going down to the bass one hears the flute alone ... thus one comes to make a dialogue with the help of the Contrabasse of the Pedal.
12. 11.1 should be played in diminutions; 3 may be added.

Antegnati continued with stop-lists and comments about registration for the nine-stop organ at the Church of S Faustino and the Braces, Brescia, S Grata, Bergamo, the Carmine Church, Brescia, and S Marco, Milan. Additional advice about registration is summarized as follows:

a The *ripieno* should be used at the *Deo gratias*, with toccatas, using pedals.
b For accompanying motets in concertato style: the Principale and Flauto in ottava. For motets with few singers: Principale alone, also with Tremolo, but in that event without diminutions.
c The Tremolo can be used with the Ottava and Flauto in ottava, or Flauto in Ottava alone, but then slowly and without diminutions.
d The Fiffaro should be played only with the Principale, slowly and legato.
e For canzonas 'alla francese', a good effect for flourishes is achieved with the Principale, Flauto in duodecima, Ottava and Flauto in ottava, without Tremolo.
f Finally Antegnati discussed the advantages of split stops for dialogues between the bass and treble ranges.

Italian organ music was seldom annotated with the composer's instructions for registration. Rare examples are found in the organ part for Monteverdi's *Vespro della Beata Vergine* (see the *Magnificat* settings for six and seven voices); in the titles of organ sonatas by Padre Martini; in Zipoli's *Pastorale*; and in the organ sonatas of Gaetano Valeri, the registrations for which were indicated for an organ by Callido. A number of organ builders' registration lists appeared from the mid-17th century until the end of the 19th. These often introduced the innovations of foreign builders, such as Willem Hermans (Como, 1650; Rome, 1666) and Eugen Casparini (Trent, 1687). Although the classic Italian ripieno usually survived intact, there were registers and devices unfamiliar to most Italian organists, such as the Tierce, the mounted Cornetto, the Sesquialtera and the Tromboni, and such toy stops as the Rusignoli and the Cuccù. The second manual division was meant to function as an echo (*organo piccolo*). In the late 18th century the Swell was introduced as an enclosed *organo piccolo*, without powerful reed stops at first. New mechanical devices included the *tiratutti* and the *terza mano* (octave coupler).

4. NORTH-WESTERN EUROPE. The impetus for the development of what are now known as the classical French, the Dutch and the north-west European styles of organ building came from the internationally active group of 16th-century Flemish builders. Virtually all the sources dealing with registration in northern countries before the publication of the second volume of Praetorius's *Syntagma musicum* (1618) apply to the Flemish style before sharp outlines of national development had been manifested. Sweelinck played on an organ of this type built by Heinrich Niehoff, of 's-Hertogenbosch. No comparable advice for registration exists for the magnificent organs built by the Scherer family, of Hamburg, and their successors in north-west Germany, but contractual documents and the surviving instruments may serve to complement the music composed for them. In the Lüneburg tablatures, for instance (*see* SOURCES OF KEYBOARD MUSIC TO 1660, §2, iii), there are references to manual changes, to the *Rückpositiv* for florid melodic passages, or to the *Hauptwerk* as an echo. There were also instructions for registration in the preface to Praetorius's *Musae Sioniae* (1610). Some doubt arises about the authenticity of certain hints found in the organ works of Buxtehude, but Georg Friedrich Kauffmann, in his *Harmonische Seelenlust* (1733–6), left careful recommendations for

specific stops for each piece. There is no evidence of a comprehensive record of the vast possibilities for registration on the greatest instruments built in the 17th century, such as those in the Catharinenkirche, Hamburg, where Heinrich Scheidemann was organist from 1625 to 1663, or the Jacobikirche, where his pupil, Matthias Weckmann, played from 1655 to 1674.

A valuable indication of registration in a related tradition comes from Samuel Scheidt, who played a Compenius organ in Halle, and published the following instructions in his *Tabulatura nova* (1624):

To Organists

Every organist who has an organ with two manuals and pedal can play these *Magnificat* settings and hymns, as well as some of the psalms found in parts i and ii; the chorale melody might be played with a penetrating stop on the *Rückpositiv* (in order to bring it more clearly into relief), particularly when it appears in the soprano or tenor. When it is a bicinium, and the chorale is in the soprano, the chorale is played on the upper manual or *Werck* with the right hand, and the second part with the left hand on the *Rückpositiv*. If the chorale is in the soprano of a four-part verse, it is then played on the *Rückpositiv* with the right hand, the alto and tenor with the left hand on the upper manual or *Werck*, and the bass on the pedal. If the chorale is in the tenor, the chorale is played with the left hand on the *Rückpositiv* and the other parts with the right hand on the upper manual or *Werck*, the bass on the pedal.

In a four-part verse the alto may also be played specifically on the *Rückpositiv*, but the soprano must be played with the right hand on the upper keyboard, with both the tenor and bass voices together on the pedal; it must be specially composed, however, so that the tenor is no higher than C [*c′*], since one seldom finds D [*d′*] in the pedals, and also so that these parts are not spaced too widely apart, only an octave, 5th, or 3rd, since one cannot span a larger distance well with the feet.

But . . . [it is] most beautiful and far more comfortable to play the alto on the pedal. But the advantage of this way depends upon the stops and particular voices in the organ, which must have been disposed knowledgeably in terms of 4′ and 8′ pitch levels. The *Positiv* must always be based on 8′ pitch; and the Pedal on 4′ pitch. Soprano, alto and tenor should be played on the *Rückpositiv* on an 8′ stop. The alto will be played on the pedal with a 4′ stop. Voices of a sharp 4′ tone in the Pedal: 4′ Oktave and Zimmel, 4′ Gedackt and Zimmel, Cornett (bass) 4′, and so on. When such 4′ stops are drawn the alto sounds in the correct pitch relationship. . . .

Certain registers or stop divisions to draw when one will play a chorale on two manuals and hear it clearly:

On the Hauptwerk

Gross Gedackt 8′ ⎤
Klein Gedackt 4′ ⎦ drawn together

or

Prinzipal 8′ alone and other stops according to preference.

Sharp stops on the *Rückpositiv* to hear the chorale clearly: Quintadena or Gedackt 8′ and the Klein Gedackt or Prinzipal 4′, with the Mixtur or Zimmel or Superoktave; these stops together or others according to preference.

To hear the chorale clearly on the Pedal: Untersatz 16′, Posaune 8′ or 16′, Dulzian 8′ or 16′, Shalmei, Trompete, Bauerflöte, Cornett, and others which are found often enough in small and large organs.

The foregoing I would nevertheless prescribe only to those who do not yet know the style and who would like to do it properly. Other distinguished persons and sensible organists, however, will be left to direct such things after their own inclination.

A theoretical work by Mattheus Hertel (1666) refers to and enlarges upon Scheidt's registrations. Hertel wrote that the Tremulant, which was to be used for doleful melodies, also 'can be used for preludes, and also even for fugues'.

In later theoretical works (Werckmeister, 2/1698; Niedt, ed. Mattheson, 1717; Adlung, 1758; Marpurg, 1760) it can be seen that strict rules about the combination of stops of the same pitch were gradually being relaxed. The most important of these limitations to registration had been the exclusion of flute stops from the plenum. Adlung made the point that 'good' wind systems would not cause fluttering when two 8′ stops were drawn together. Registration lists by M. Heinrich Rothe for the Silbermann organ in Fraureuth (1739–

42) and by J. G. Schenke (instructions dated 1780) for Silbermann's organ at Gross Hartmannsdorf (1738–41) reveal the growing taste for combinations of fundamental-sounding stops, such as Principals, Flutes and Gambas.

Towards the end of the century additional information was supplied by Daniel Türk (*Von den wichtigsten Pflichten eines Organisten*, 1787) and J. H. Knecht (*Vollständige Orgelschule*, 1795), in which early attempts at crescendo registration are documented. The 'tutti' concept, employing all the stops and couplers, was firmly entrenched by this time, and eventually replaced the traditional orientation of the organ's tonal design around the plenum.

The classical purity of national styles of organ building was breaking down by the late 17th century, as is shown by the work of several builders who moved from their home countries: Casparini (German) and Hermans (Dutch), who worked in Italy; Riepp (French), working in southern Germany; and the brothers Andreas and Gottfried Silbermann, who moved from Saxony to France (Gottfried Silbermann later returned to Germany with first-hand practical experience of the classical French tradition). Registration lists survive for organs made by these builders: for Casparini's organ at S Maria Maggiore, Trent (1687); Hermans's organ at S Apollinare, Rome (1666); and for Silbermann's instruments at Fraureuth (1739–42) and Gross Hartmannsdorf (1738–41). Riepp himself wrote four lists for organs in Salem, including a 'gourmet' rendition of the classical French tradition, and hints for registrations for particular audiences, such as 'a king', 'an officer', 'a child' or 'an ignoramus' (see Meyer, 167ff). Certain excessive treatments in the construction of organs must have had their effect at least on local habits of registration. For example, Riepp's Trinity organ at Ottobeuren (1757–66) had eight Tremulants, two for each of four manual divisions.

Bach's directions for registration of his organ compositions are comparatively sparse. Names of stops are given in the Concerto in D minor after Vivaldi (BWV596) and the chorale preludes on *Gott, durch deine Güte* (BWV600) and *Ein' feste Burg* (BWV720). Pitch levels are indicated in four of the 'Schübler' chorale preludes (BWV645–7, 650). *Forte* and *piano*, *Rückpositiv* and *Oberwerk*, and *organo pleno* are indicated in several large chorale works and preludes and fugues. It is said that Walther wrote in the names of stops Bach had used for playing his chorale prelude on *Ein' feste Burg* – Fagotto and Sesquialtera. But more interesting speculation arises from the notes in the first movement of the Concerto in D minor. Here the instructions call for separate Oktave 4′ on *Oberwerk* and *Brustpositiv* with Prinzipal 8′ for the Pedal, changing in the course of the movement to Subbass 32′ in the Pedal and Prinzipal 8′ and Oktave 4′ for the *Oberwerk*. The 4′ opening pitches reflect Vivaldi's original score, but did Bach mean to add 16′ and 32′ in the Pedal? The sparse information coming directly from Bach's hand, as indicated above, is best translated into practical use in the light of C. P. E. Bach's statement to Forkel:

No-one understood registration as well as he [J. S. Bach]. Organ builders were terrified when he sat down to play their organs and drew the stops in his own manner, for they thought that the effect would not be as good as he was planning; then they heard an effect that astounded them.

5. CLASSICAL FRENCH ORGANS. The ultimate refinement in registration for composed music is an achievement of

the French, who since the mid-17th century have maintained a precise relationship between the indigenous character of specific registrations and musical textures to which they best respond. While the Germans have left performers more or less free to choose their own registrations, subject basically to the instrument's natural restrictions, the French have wedded timbre and articulation with the musical score to an exemplary degree. Lebègue (*Premier livre d'orgue*, 1676) enjoined his contemporaries to play according to the exact directions for registration: 'There are several pieces in this book that are not useful to organists whose instruments lack the stops necessary for their execution'. Even the more flexible approach of André Raison (*Livre d'orgue*, 1688) provided free choice in registration only within the limitations of the design of organs generally in favour in his own time: 'As I vary the choice of stops and manuals a great deal, it is not necessary to play all my pieces exactly as marked'. The classical French repertory was forgotten during the 19th century because French organs no longer made the sorts of sounds that could articulate that repertory.

Among many excellent sources of information on the classical French tradition of organ registration, Gaspard Corrette's preface to his *Messe du 8e ton* (1703) provides the best available clarification of the important relationships between registration, musical texture, and style of performance. The registrations he specified for particular pieces are as follows:

For the Plein Jeu, couple the manuals. On the *Grand jeu* [sic], the Bourdon 16', Bourdon, Montre, Prestant, Doublette, Fourniture and Cymbale. On the *Positif*, the Bourdon, Montre, Prestant, Doublette, Fourniture and Cymbale.
For the Fugue, couple the manuals. On the *Grand jeu*, the Bourdon, Prestant and Trompette. On the *Positif*, the Bourdon, Prestant or Montre and the Cromhorne.
For the Trio a deux dessus, the manuals are uncoupled; the right hand playing on the *Positif*, and the left on the *Grand jeu*. On the *Grand jeu*, the Bourdon, Prestant, Montre, Tierce, Grosse Tierce, Nazar and Quarte de nazar. On the *Positif*, the Bourdon, Prestant or Montre, Cromhorne and Tremblant doux.
The Duo is played with the manuals uncoupled, the right hand on the *Positif*, and the left on the *Grand jeu*. On the *Grand jeu*, the Bourdon 16', Bourdon, Prestant, Tierce, Grosse Tierce, Nazar and Quarte de nazar. On the *Positif*, the Bourdon, Prestant or Montre, Tierce and Nazar.
The Recit de Nazar is played on the *Positif*, with the accompaniment on the *Grand jeu*. On the *Grand jeu*, the Bourdon and Montre 4'. On the *Positif*, the Bourdon, Prestant or Montre and the Nazar.
The Dessus de Petite Tierce is played on the *Positif*, with the accompaniment on the *Grand jeu*. On the *Grand jeu*, the Bourdon and Prestant. On the *Positif*, the Bourdon, Prestant or Montre, Tierce and Nazar.
For the Basse de Trompette, the manuals are uncoupled. On the *Grand jeu*, the Bourdon, Prestant and Trompette. On the *Positif*, the Bourdon and Prestant or Montre.
For the Basse de Cromhorne, the manuals are uncoupled. On the *Grand jeu*, the Montre and Bourdon. On the *Positif*, the Prestant or Montre, Nazar, Tierce, Doublette, Larigot and the Cromhorne – not the Bourdon.
For the Cromhorne en Taille, on the *Grand jeu*, the Montre, Bourdon, and the Pedalle de flûte. On the *Positif*, the Bourdon, Prestant or Montre and the Cromhorne.
For the Tierce en Taille, on the *Grand jeu*, the Bourdon 16', Montre, Prestant and the Pedalle de flûte. On the *Positif*, the Bourdon, Prestant or Montre, Nazar, Tierce, Doublette and Larigot.
For the Fond d'orgue, the manuals are coupled. On the *Grand jeu*, the Bourdon 16', Bourdon, Prestant and Montre. On the *Positif*, the Bourdon and the Prestant or Montre.
For the Concert de Flûte, the manuals are coupled. On the *Grand jeu*, the Bourdon and Flûte. On the *Positif*, the Bourdon, Flûte and the Tremblant doux.
For the Dialogue de Voix Humaine, the manuals are not coupled. On the *Grand jeu*, the Bourdon and Flûte. On the *Positif*, the Bourdon, Flûte, the Voix humaine and the Tremblant doux.
For the Dialogue a deux Choeurs, the manuals are coupled. On the *Grand jeu*, the Bourdon, Prestant, Trompette, Clairon and Cornet. On the *Positif*, the Bourdon, Prestant or Montre and the Cromhorne.
For the Dialogue a trois Choeurs, the manuals are coupled. On the *Grand jeu*, the Bourdon, Prestant, Trompette, Clairon, Cornet, Nazar, Quarte de nazar and Tierce. On the *Positif*, the Bourdon, Prestant or Montre, Cromhorne, Tierce and Nazar. The third *choeur* is played on the *Clavier d'echo*, and the Tremblant a vent perdu is used.

6. REGISTRATION IN THE 19TH CENTURY. During the 19th century, technological advances and the introduction of machine tools transformed the craft of organ building into an industrial pursuit. To assure their commercial success and artistic recognition organ builders competed for prominence by displaying their latest mechanical innovations in the great industrial exhibitions in London or Paris, and by courting favourable comment from the press. Soon the ancient concepts that had previously limited the musical resources of the organ were abandoned. Vastly expanded tonal capacity resulted from the application of pneumatic, and later electrical, devices to relieve the key-action; stable and practically limitless wind supplies were provided by more and more men at the bellows, by steam engines and eventually by electrical blowers which fed into large reservoirs. Because of these 'advances' and the musical demands of the new Romantic aesthetic, organists were quite content gradually to relinquish the time-worn architectural concepts that had previously governed registration. The *plein jeu* was forsaken in favour of the reed-dominated tutti. Mutations were replaced by wind-hungry ranks at the fundamental pitches: open flutes, harmonic stops and broad strings. Wind pressures rose continually, but no-one dreamt that in the America of the 1920s organs would be built demanding wind more than ten times as strong as the 19th-century maximum.

To respond to the call for a smooth crescendo from the whisper of soft stops speaking behind closed Venetian shutters to the immense roar of the tutti, pneumatic motors were installed to provide the player with pre-set combinations (St Sulpice, Paris, 1863). A single player could move skilfully about, using all the sounds of a mammoth organ with great ease and speed. Registration, by ventil pedals in France, or by *Rollschweller* in Germany, or by electrically operated combinations in England and the USA, was gradually reduced from an art to a formula.

The essential ingredients for the registration of 19th- or early 20th-century organ music were the building blocks of the tutti, beginning with enclosed 8' stops, which were then combined with unenclosed 8' flue stops in the manuals and 16' and 8' stops of the pedal always coupled together. Steps along the way provided for the addition of foundation stops (16', 8' and 4' on all keyboards), followed by reeds and mixtures. The Swell shades were fully opened before the final introduction of the most powerful unenclosed sounds. The *Rollschweller*, or crescendo pedal, did this job efficiently by the gradual 'blind' addition or subtraction of registers in a predetermined order.

The music of Mendelssohn and Rheinberger was written with post-classical registration in mind, while Reger demanded the continuous dynamic alterations inherent in the system described above. Franck, Widor and their successors wrote specifically for Cavaillé-Coll's system of stop-controls, which consisted mainly of mechanical devices for the introduction or blocking-off of wind from sections of the chests (*fonds* and *anches*). Sub-octave coupling was important for the *grand choeur*.

7. AUTHENTICITY. Each new generation has felt a persistent urge to impose new fashions over established tastes. Only since the mid-20th century has there been a perceptible desire to preserve intact or to respect the musical traditions of the past; nor did earlier players scrutinize the evidence relating to those traditions. Whatever was resurrected came dressed in the current fashion. For example, in the 19th century it was not considered inappropriate to adapt the rediscovered works of J. S. Bach to registrations considered suitable for Romantic music. Schweitzer, perhaps the world's best-known Bach lover, wrote: 'What a joy it is … to play Bach on the beautiful Walcker organs built between about 1870 and 1875', and 'how happy Bach would have been could he have had a finer *piano* on his third manual by the Venetian shutter swell!'. Widor, Schweitzer's teacher and collaborator, maintained: 'The organ of Aristide Cavaillé-Coll remains the true organ, the organ of J. S. Bach'. Yet Widor protested at the Americanization of French organs, calling on the Académie des Beaux-Arts to preserve the French (i.e. Romantic) organ heritage, and Schweitzer was influential in helping to preserve the old Dutch and German instruments before the dawn of the classical revival.

The least satisfactory approach to authenticity in registration lies in the notion that it can be achieved by applying information from simple lists of stops to any instrument equipped with stops bearing those names. Equally fallacious is the notion that an all-purpose organ can be devised, suited to the registration needs of the entire literature. Recently, organ building has tended to rely increasingly on inspiration derived from a single historical tradition, rather than a fusion of various stylistic patterns. This approach provides a new hope for authenticity in the registration of early organ music.

See also ORGAN and ORGAN STOP.

BIBLIOGRAPHY

SPAIN

H. Anglès, ed.: *J. Cabanilles: Musici organici . . . opera omnia*, PBC, iv, viii, xiii, xvii (1927–56)
F. Baldello: 'Organos y organeros en Barcelona', *AnM*, i (1946), 225
M. A. Vente and W. Kok: 'Organs in Spain and Portugal', *The Organ*, xxxvi (1956–7), 155, 203
M. A. Vente: 'Mitteilungen über iberische Registrierkunst unter berenderer Berücksichtigung der Orgelkompositionen des Juan Cabanilles', *AnM*, xvii (1962), 41
M. A. Vente and F. Chapelet: 'Connaissance de l'orgue espagnol', *Orgues historiques*, x (1965)
J. Wyly: 'La registrazione della musica organistica di Francisco Correa de Arauxo', *L'organo*, viii (1970), 3
R. Walter: 'A Spanish Registration List of c1170', *Organ Yearbook*, iv (1973), 40

ITALY

A. Banchieri: *L'organo suonarino* (Venice, 1605, rev. 3/1622)
C. Antegnati: *L'arte organica* (Venice, 1608; ed. R. Lunelli (Mainz, 1938, 2/1958)
G. Diruta: *Seconda parte del transilvano* (Venice, 1609/R1978)
C. Gervasoni: *La scuola della musica* (Piacenza, 1800)
P. Gianelli: *Grammatica ragionata della musica* (Venice, 1801)
——: *Dizionario della musica sacra e profana* (Venice, 1801, 3/1830)
G. Serassi: *Descrizione ed osservazioni del nuovo organo nella chiesa posto del SS. Crocifisso dell'Annunziata di Como* (Como, 1808)
C. Gervasoni: *Nuova teoria di musica* (Parma, 1812)
G. P. Calvi: *Istruzioni teorico-prattiche per l'organo e singolamente sul modo di registrarlo* (Milan, 1833/R1970)
R. Lunelli: *Scritti di storia organaria* (Trent, 1925)
Cenni cronistorici intorno agli organi e organisti della Cattedrale di Feltre (Feltre, 1943)
W. Shewring: 'Notes on the Organ in Italy', *The Organ*, xxx (1950–51), 42
R. Lunelli: 'Un trattatello di Antonio Barcotto colma le lacune dell' "Arte organica" ', *CHM*, i (1953), 153
W. Shewring: 'Organs in Italy; Brescia and Verona', *The Organ*, xxxv (1955–6), 161

R. Lunelli: 'Descrizione dell'organo del duomo di Como e l'attività italiana di Guglielmo Hermans', *CHM*, ii (1956), 255
W. Shewring: 'Organs in Italy: Venice, Treviso, Trent', *The Organ*, xxxvi (1956–7), 18
L. F. Tagliavini: 'Il ripieno', *L'organo*, ii (1960), 197
S. dalla Libera: *L'arte degli organi a Venezia* (Venice, 1962)
V. Giacobbi and O. Mischiati: 'Gli antichi organi del Cadore', *L'organo*, iii (1962), 3–59
T. Culley: 'Documenti d'archivio – organari fiamminghi a S. Apollinare a Roma', *L'organo*, v (1967), 213
G. Rádole: 'Note sulla registrazione degli organi nel sei e settecento', *Musica sacra*, xci (1967), 92, 159
L. F. Tagliavini: 'Registrazioni organistiche nei "Vespri" ', *RIM*, ii (1967), 365
G. Rádole: 'L'arte organaria in Istria', *L'organo*, vi (1968), 41–107
——: 'L'arte organaria in Trieste', *L'organo*, viii (1970), 21–63

NORTH-WESTERN EUROPE

A. Schlick: *Spiegel der Orgelmacher und Organisten* (Speyer, 1511/R1959); ed. E. Flade (Mainz, 1931, 2/1951); facs., incl. Eng. trans., ed. E. B. Barber (Buren, 1978)
M. Praetorius: *Syntagma musicum*, ii (Wolfenbüttel, 1618, 2/1619/R1958)
S. Scheidt: *Tabulatura nova* (Hamburg, 1624/R1954)
A. Werckmeister: *Orgel-Probe* (Frankfurt am Main and Leipzig, 1681, 2/1698/R1970 as *Erweiterte und verbesserte Orgel-Probe*, 5/1783; Eng. trans., 1976)
F. Niedt: *Musicalischer Handleitung*, iii, ed. J. Mattheson (Hamburg, 1717)
G. F. Kauffmann: *Harmonische Seelenlust* (Leipzig, 1733–6); ed. P. Pidoux (Kassel, 1951)
J. Mattheson: *Der vollkommene Capellmeister* (Hamburg, 1739/R1954)
F. W. Marpurg: *Historisch-kritische Beyträge zur Aufnahme der Musik* (Berlin, 1754–78/R1970)
J. Adlung: *Musica mechanica organoedi*, ed. J. L. Albrecht (Berlin, 1768/R1961); ed. C. Mahrenholz (Kassel, 1931)
D. G. Türk: *Von den wichtigsten Pflichten eines Organisten* (Halle, 1787/R1966, rev. 2/1838 by F. Naue)
J. H. Knecht: *Vollständige Orgelschule* (Leipzig, 1795)
C. Locher: *Erklärung der Orgelregister* (Berne, 1887; 2/1923/R1971, ed. J. Dobler as *Die Orgel-Register und ihre Klangfarben*)
R. Rudolz: *Die Registrierkunst des Orgelspiels in ihren grundlegenden Formen* (Leipzig, 1913)
G. Schünemann: 'Matthäus Hertel's theoretische Schriften', *AMw*, iv (1921–2), 336
E. Flade: *Der Orgelbauer Gottfried Silbermann* (Leipzig, 1926/R1953)
H. Klotz: *Über die Orgelkunst der Gotik, der Renaissance und des Barock* (Kassel, 1934, 2/1975)
G. Frotscher: *Geschichte des Orgel-Spiels und der Orgel-Komposition* (Berlin, 1935–6, enlarged 3/1966)
H. Meyer: *Karl Joseph Riepp, der Orgelbauer von Ottobeuren* (Kassel, 1938)
J. Wörsching: *Der Orgelbauer Karl Riepp* (Mainz, 1940)
P. Smets: *Die Orgelregister, ihr Klang und Gebrauch* (Mainz, 1943)
U. Dähnert: *Die Orgeln Gottfried Silbermanns in Mitteldeutschland* (Leipzig, 1953/R1971)
M. A. Vente: *Die brabanter Orgel* (Amsterdam, 1958, 2/1963)
M. Blindow: 'Die Trierer Orgelakten, ihre Bedeutung für die deutsche Registrierkunst des 16. Jahrhunderts', *Musik und Kirche*, xxxi (1961), 115

FRANCE

M. Mersenne: *Harmonie universelle* (Paris, 1636–7/R1963; Eng. trans., 1957)
F. Bédos de Celles: *L'art du facteur d'orgues* (Paris, 1766–78/R1965; Eng. trans., 1977; ed. C. Mahrenholz, Kassel, 1934–6, 2/1963–6)
L. Girod: *Connaissance pratique de la facture des grandes orgues* (Namur, 1877)
W. Goodrich: *The Organ in France* (Boston, 1917)
J. Huré: *L'esthétique de l'orgue* (Paris, 1923)
A. Pirro: 'L'art des organistes', *EMDC*, II/ii (1926), 1181–374
A. Cellier: *Traité de la registration d'orgue* (Paris, 1957)
P. Hardouin: 'Essai d'une sémantique des jeux de l'orgue', *AcM*, xxxiv (1962), 29
——: 'Jeux d'orgues au XVIe siècle', *RdM*, lii (1966), 163
F. Douglass: *The Language of the Classical French Organ* (New Haven, 1969)
N. Dufourcq: *Le livre de l'orgue français 1589–1789*, iv (Paris, 1972)
F. Douglass: 'Should Dom Bedos play Lebègue?', *Organ Yearbook*, iv (1973), 101

MISCELLANEOUS

E. Truett: *Organ Registration* (Boston, 1919)
G. A. Audsley: *Organ Stops and their Artistic Registration* (New York, 1921)
N. A. Bonavia-Hunt: *Modern Organ Stops* (London, 1923)

E. H. Geer: *Organ Registration in Theory and Practice* (Glen Rock, NJ, 1957)

C. Clutton and A. Niland: *The British Organ* (London, 1963)

P. Williams: *The European Organ 1450–1850* (London, 1966, 2/1968)

II. Harpsichord

1. Registration and the harpsichord. 2. Resources of the instrument. 3. Written evidence.

1. REGISTRATION AND THE HARPSICHORD. There is an extraordinary disparity between the possibilities for harpsichord registration in early music and the evidence of its use. From the last quarter of the 16th century at the latest to the demise of the instrument about 1800, harpsichords rarely had fewer than three colours (two stops which could be used separately or together). Mersenne (*Harmonie universelle*, 1636–7) wrote of harpsichords with 'seven or eight kinds of stops and two or three keyboards' which were varied and combined like those of the organ. Praetorius claimed to have seen one with four choirs of strings, and Mace (*Musick's Monument*, 1676) described a harpsichord which he called a 'pedall' whose registers were controlled by the feet and gave (with the aid of a hand-operated harp stop) 24 'varieties'. None of these exotic instruments has survived, but any late 17th- or 18th-century harpsichord with two manuals and three choirs (even one lacking such accessories as a BUFF STOP and restricted by a dogleg arrangement; *see* DOGLEG JACK) was capable of at least ten distinct registrations. Documents of every kind, particularly advertisements and inventors' proposals, extol variety of colour and ease in obtaining it as desirable features of harpsichords. And yet, in an age when rules governed so many aspects of music, no conventions of harpsichord registration developed, even in countries where the instrument was relatively standardized. In 18th-century Paris, for example, where a two manual harpsichord nearly always had I: 8′, 4′; II: 8′; coupler, composers who wrote for both instruments and gave detailed instructions for organ registration in their prefaces and in the titles of their pieces were silent on the subject of harpsichord registration. Michel Corrette, in the preface to his *Nouveau livre de noëls* (1753–4) for harpsichord or organ, directed harpsichordists to ignore the registrations provided for the organ and to play always on the same manual, except for two pieces in which the left hand plays on the upper manual and the right on the lower.

Surviving evidence for specific registration practices is of three kinds: negative evidence supplied by known limitations of the instruments themselves, negative evidence implied by the wording of instructions that do exist, and isolated instances of registrations for particular pieces.

2. RESOURCES OF THE INSTRUMENT. Where Italian harpsichords (or instruments modelled after them) predominated, registration must have been of the simplest kind. The norm was a single manual and two registers (8′, 4′ or 8′, 8′) which in earlier instruments may have been fixed, permitting no change at all except for effects produced by accessories such as the buff stop or ARPICHORDUM (metal pins contacting the strings to produce a harsh buzzing). Harpsichords of this kind (mostly without the accessories) prevailed everywhere until the last quarter of the 16th century, in Germany through much of the 17th, and in Italy, Spain and Portugal until replaced by pianos. Thus a very large proportion of the harpsichord repertory, including all Italian and Iberian music, would normally have been played without the benefit of manual changes and with the minimum variety in colour or dynamics.

Flemish harpsichords of about 1575–1625, which evidently influenced English and French designs of the period, resembled Italian instruments in disposition (though they were very different in construction and tone), but their registrational possibilities were considerably increased by the buff (or harp) stop, which muted one of the choirs of strings, giving a pizzicato or harp-like effect; this was particularly true if the buff was divided so that treble and bass could be muted independently. Harpsichords with three choirs (8′, 8′, 4′) are known to have been made in Flanders and England, and the Flemings also built two-manual instruments, but these had their manuals pitched a 4th apart for transposing, making them useless for effects of contrast. In order to engage or disengage one of the registers of a Flemish harpsichord, the player had to reach outside the case with his right hand and move the slide which projected through the cheekpiece.

The so-called 'contrasting' (Ripin) or 'expressive' (Hubbard) double (i.e. a harpsichord with two manuals at the same pitch, or at the octave, playing different registers) probably originated early in the 17th century in France or the Low Countries, whence it spread to England and Germany. The most important determinants of registrational flexibility on such an instrument are the means used to make the upper-manual register(s) playable from the lower, and the damping arrangements. The dogleg, as used by English and Flemish makers throughout the 17th and 18th centuries, plays from both manuals if it is on; it cannot be engaged on one manual and disconnected from the other. In both countries there was often a second register on the upper manual consisting of a row of jacks let into the wrestplank and plucking near the nut to give a thin, intense, almost disembodied sound (the English called it a 'lute' and the Flemings a 'spinett', neither of which instruments it resembles). The use of this register depended upon which choir of strings it plucked and which registers were provided with dampers, since one register cannot play a choir of strings that is damped by another unless they are on the same keyboard or otherwise connected. Large 18th-century Flemish or English harpsichords with two manuals, three choirs of strings, four rows of jacks and a buff stop had far fewer registrational possibilities than arithmetic would predict; most important, on none of these instruments was it possible to play the two normal 8′s independently on two manuals at the same time, as one must in a *pièce croisée* (e.g. Couperin's *Le tic-toc-choc, ordre no.18*, and several of Bach's Goldberg Variations).

The manual coupler, as used by the French and sometimes the Germans, or a dogleg which could be disengaged by drawing the keyboard away from it, as found on German instruments, eliminated all these problems; and although French harpsichords lacked the extreme colour of the lute and did not always even have a buff stop, the remaining stops could be combined much more freely than on English and Flemish instruments. Some 17th-century French doubles, however, seem to have been disposed I: 8′, 8′: II: 4′; coupler, an arrangement which cancelled much of the flexibility conferred by the coupler.

German harpsichords present no very coherent picture, perhaps because not enough have survived, but the registrational possibilities of the majority of doubles (none earlier than 1700) appear to approximate to or exceed those of the French ones. The Germans had a greater fondness for buff stops, they sometimes added the lute, and they were readier to experiment with very elaborate dispositions – up to five choirs (16′, 8′, 8′, 4′, 2′), six registers of jacks, and three manuals. Bach would have known of the 16′, but it was far from standard, and not a single clue to its use is known. It is a curious irony that the German dispositions which limited variety were not those of the Baroque period but 20th-century ones – in particular, the so-called Bach disposition' (I: 16′, 8′; II: 8′, 4′; coupler) found until recently on nearly all large modern German harpsichords. This arrangement, on which neither the Italian Concerto nor the French Overture can be played satisfactorily, was copied from an altered 18th-century instrument which had no connection with Bach and, in its original state, no 16′. Although the Germans have left us the most luxuriously disposed harpsichord made before the 20th century (by H. A. Hass, 1740, having I: 16′, 2′; II: 8′, 4′; II and III: dogleg 8′; III: lute; buff to 16′; two couplers), they were much less inventive than the English and French in matters of stop-control, leaving their stop-levers on the wrestplank where they were neither visible nor easily accessible and required the player to remove both hands from the keyboard to couple or uncouple. The strong implication is that the Germans did not change stops during the course of a movement but accomplished whatever registration was required by passing from one manual to the other.

3. WRITTEN EVIDENCE. In spite of their failure to give general rules or principles of registration, 18th-century French composers occasionally indicated how particular pieces were to be played, and when they did their directions were almost invariably worded so as to imply that the normal way to play was on the lower keyboard with all the registers on and the manuals coupled – in other words, on the full harpsichord. Registers were retired and manuals uncoupled for special effects: *Les bagatelles* from Couperin's second book (1716–17) is to be played with the manuals 'uncoupled' and the octave 'removed'. A passage from the preface to Dandrieu's first book of harpsichord pieces (1724) shows this approach and at the same time seems to suggest that manipulating the registers of a harpsichord was something beyond the ordinary accomplishment of a player and required careful explanation:

It will not perhaps be unprofitable to speak here of a care which one may take in executing the pieces, which I shall point out, if one wishes to play in the style proper to them. It is this: *Le concert des oiseaux* should be played with both hands on the lower manual, but with the two unisons retired, leaving only the octave [by 'two unisons' he means lower 8′ and coupler; a modern player would put the direction in a positive sense: '. . . should be played on the solo 4″']. *Le timpanon* also requires one to leave only the octave, but the right hand plays on the upper manual and the left on the lower. For *Les fifres*, it is necessary on the contrary that the left hand should be on the upper manual and the right on the lower, again leaving only the octave. One may, however, play these pieces in the usual way, if the instrument does not permit what I have just indicated to be observed, because these different ways of disposing the stops and placing the hands are only conceived to render the imitation more perfect.

One of two conclusions imposes itself on the reader: either every other piece in the collection is to be played on full harpsichord or the composer cares only about registration as an aid to 'imitation' of the most obvious sort.

Other than registrations for *pièces croisées* and pieces

imitating effects in nature, only a few scattered general indications can be gleaned from music of the second half of the Baroque period and other sources. Although there is no suggestion that manuals or registration were changed for the repeats in binary forms, there are enough instances of *petites reprises* being marked with a *p* or some other indication of softening to allow a modern player to do the same even where there is no mark. Echo effects can also be achieved by registration, but the characteristic repetition of short phrases so beloved of mid-18th-century Italian composers, especially Domenico Scarlatti, are not echoes and could not in any case be played as such on Italian harpsichords. When accompanying, the harpsichordist was always enjoined to subordinate himself to his soloist; accompaniment treatises sometimes suggest retiring stops or moving to the upper manual in concerts with weak-voiced singers. An isolated comment from England suggests that the 4′ be used only in large ensembles, and that two 8′s are better for 'lessons' (i.e. solo pieces). Finally, the 'pedall' described by Mace must have been known to Purcell, since one figured among the royal instruments in his charge, and it is therefore impossible to deny to his music the possibility of elaborate registration (though probably on a single manual) on grounds of instrumental limitations.

Coarse and insensitive though it may seem, nearly all the evidence derived from the music itself points to the conclusion that the usual way to begin any Baroque piece was on all the registers together, and that changes during the course of the piece were confined to changes of manual, though even these were rare. On the other hand, evidence derived from the instruments refutes this conclusion, but only as it applies to music originating where or when Italian harpsichords were not dominant.

Harpsichords were built in great numbers, however, after the Baroque period, and here the situation changes. In both France and England large harpsichords were fitted with 'machine' stops which when in proper adjustment could not only shift the registration from full to a single 8′ on each manual with one motion of the foot or knee but could respond to the growing demand for graduated dynamic effects – crescendos and diminuendos. Although too cumbersome to provide the kind of shape and nuance to a single line to which the piano was so well adapted, crescendos in busy textures in the style of orchestral allegros were more successful than on the piano because of the complexity of the ensemble sound of a harpsichord. The presence of graduated dynamics in a piece of post-Baroque music does not, therefore, necessarily indicate a preference for the piano; most music was published 'for harpsichord or piano' and was played on both instruments, the tendency towards one or the other depending on the country and date of the performance. One piece, a *Simphonie de clavecins* for two harpsichords by Armand-Louis Couperin from the early 1770s, makes such elaborate demands that it can be played on no instrument other than a French double with the usual disposition plus a fourth register in *peau de buffle* (played from the lower manual and giving a gentle *pianissimo*) and a full complement of knee-levers as developed in the 1760s by Pascal Taskin. This work is altogether exceptional, however, in excluding the possibility of performance on the piano by its demand for two manuals and a particular harpsichord stop (the *peau de buffle*). A few other works (by Tapray and Balbastre) ask for the *peau de buffle*, but not necessarily two manuals.

Another entirely exceptional work is the *Sonata per cembalo a due tastature* WQ69 by C. P. E. Bach (1747), the only example of harpsichord music before the 20th century in which every register to be used is specifically indicated. It is difficult to deduce from the somewhat ambiguous terminology the disposition of the instrument, but the piece is interesting as a unique attempt to register harpsichord music with something of the variety of colour possible on an organ. The first movement is marked 'Das forte unten mit allen Registern, das piano oben', the second 'Das forte mit Octav und Cornet unten, das piano oben'. The third is a set of variations, of which nos.4, 5 and 6 may serve as a sample: 'oben mit der rechten Hand Cornet und Spinet, unten Flöte'; 'oben mit der linken Hand Cornet, unten Flöte'; 'mit der rechten Hand Octav, mit der Linken gedämpftes Cornet'.

See also HARPSICHORD.

BIBLIOGRAPHY

E. Harich-Schneider: *Die Kunst des Cembalo-Spiels* (Kassel, 1939, 2/1958)
E. Bodky: *The Interpretation of Bach's Keyboard Works* (Cambridge, Mass., 1960)
F. Hubbard: *Three Centuries of Harpsichord Making* (Cambridge, Mass., 1965)
K. Gilbert: 'Le clavecin français et la registration', *L'interprétation de la musique française aux XVIIe et XVIIIe siècles: Paris 1969*, 203
E. Ripin, ed.: *Keyboard Instruments* (Edinburgh, 1971)
H. Schott: *Playing the Harpsichord* (New York, 1971)
D. Fuller, ed.: *A. L. Couperin: Selected Works for Keyboard* (Madison, Wisc., 1975)

FENNER DOUGLASS (I), DAVID FULLER (II)

Registre de luth (Fr.). BUFF STOP.

Registre d'hautbois (Fr.). LUTE STOP.

Regnart, Jacob [Jacques] (*b* Douai, ? between 1540 and 1545; *d* Prague, 16 Oct 1599). South Netherlands composer, resident mainly in Austria and Bohemia. His German secular songs, especially those for three voices, were immensely popular, and he was also a notable composer of church music.

1. Life. 2. Works. 3. Family.

1. LIFE. Regnart probably received his first musical education at Douai. He himself stated that he served the Habsburgs from 1557, no doubt at first as a chorister in the Prague Hofkapelle of Archduke Maximilian, which was directed by Jacobus Vaet. He first appears in the household lists in 1560 as a tenor, with a monthly salary of seven guilders, which was raised to the standard 12 guilders in 1564, after Maximilian's election as emperor – if not earlier. It was in that year too that music by him first appeared in print. He now worked at Vienna. He studied in Italy from 1568 to October 1570. The first of his own volumes of music to be published, *Il primo libro delle canzone italiane* (1574), was doubtless stimulated by this visit, and it was quickly followed by a number of other volumes, both sacred and secular. His growing reputation as a composer was matched by success in his professional and personal life at the imperial court during this period. On 1 November 1570 he was appointed music teacher to the chapel choristers; in 1571 he was given a coat-of-arms and in 1573 a salary rise. Following the disbanding of Maximilian's household after his death in 1576, the Emperor Rudolf II

made Regnart a member of his Hofkapelle, which soon moved to Prague; his monthly salary rose to 15 guilders. By October 1579 he had succeeded Alard Gaucquier as vice-Kapellmeister. He continued to publish a good deal of music at this period. In 1580 Lassus recommended him as Scandello's successor as Kapellmeister to the Saxon court at Dresden, but he chose to remain with the Habsburgs.

Soon, however, Archduke Ferdinand persuaded Regnart to succeed Alexander Utendal as vice-Kapellmeister, and he arrived at Innsbruck on 9 April 1582. He was now somewhat less prolific, but among his works at this period was music for a moralizing comedy by the archduke himself (1584). On 1 January 1585 he was appointed Kapellmeister. Under his direction music at the Innsbruck court was reorganized and considerably raised in standard, to general admiration; in particular, new Netherlands singers were engaged, as well as Italian solo singers and instrumentalists. In 1588 he emphasized his commitment to Catholic reform with his motet collection *Mariale*, and another interesting print from this period is a joint collection of motets by Regnart and three of his brothers (1590: see §3 below). Regnart was now becoming a rich man. In 1589 he bought himself a house (now 21 Innstrasse) and a plot of land, and in 1597 and 1598 he was even able to lend large sums of money to the Tyrol revenue office. Archduke Ferdinand decided to elevate him to the nobility for his outstanding services; the archduke's death in 1595 frustrated this intention, which was, however, realized by Archduke Matthias in 1596. After Ferdinand's death the Hofkapelle was disbanded, but Regnart stayed at Innsbruck until at least 27 April 1596. By November of that year he had arrived at Prague, where he again entered imperial service as vice-Kapellmeister, under Monte. From 1 January 1598 until his death he received a monthly salary of 20 guilders.

2. WORKS. Regnart's music continued to be highly regarded after his death and appeared in a number of anthologies up to 1655. It is also listed in several inventories of the 17th century, especially in Germany and Austria. Works by him were admired by Friedrich Weissensee in his *Opus melicum* (1602) and by Michael Praetorius in the third volume of his *Syntagma musicum* (1618, 2/1619), and he is mentioned in Joachim Burmeister's *Hypomnematum musicae poeticae* (1599). Many epigrams were written in his honour by a wide variety of authors. He enjoyed his greatest success as a composer with his *Teutsche Lieder* for three voices. They originally appeared in three volumes over a short period of time (in 1576, 1577 and 1579), the first two being reprinted twice and the third once up to 1580. In 1584 the original publisher, Gerlach of Nuremberg, brought out a complete edition, which was twice reprinted up to 1593. A rival publisher, Berg of Munich, had anticipated him with a complete edition in 1583, and this went into five editions, the last appearing in 1611. These songs were thus continually being published in their original form over a period of 35 years. Moreover, they appeared in several arrangements too, for example in tablatures by E. N. Ammerbach (1583), Gregor Krengel (1584) and Matthäus Waissel (1592). Leonhard Lechner arranged 21 of them for five voices (1579, 2/1586). Johannes Brassicanus quoted three of them in his quodlibet *Was wölln wir aber heben an*, Paul

Title-page and first page of music (discantus partbook) of Regnart's 'Der dritter Theyl schöner kurtzweiliger teutscher Lieder' (Nuremberg: Gerlach and Berg, 1579)

Luetkeman published a pavan on *Ohn dich muss* in 1597, and Francesco Rovigo based a *Magnificat* on *Venus, du und dein Kind* (1583). Two much greater composers also turned to this last song: Lassus drew on it in his four-part lied *Die Gnad kombt oben her*, and Schein published in his *Cantional* of 1627 a contrafactum, *Auf meinen lieben Gott*, which later found its way into Protestant hymnbooks, leading in turn to countless arrangements over many years.

These three-part songs were not only phenomenally popular but also highly important for the development of the lied. Regnart announced on all the title-pages that they were 'in the style of *napolitane* or Italian villanellas'. His achievement in these songs lay in bringing the genre, which with other composers still adhered to the imitative style of classical vocal polyphony, closer to the popular style of the villanella, and thus to do indeed display the essential features of the villanella – simple harmony and melodies, as well as parallel 5ths. In his *Opusculum bipartitum* (1624) Joachim Thuringus classified them as 'sortisatio', which Johannes Nucius (in his *Musices poeticae*, 1613) described as a combination of 'usus' and 'ars', since it was cultivated by both artisans and the best court musicians. This is a useful indication of how to view these songs, which since their first complete modern edition (Eitner's of 1895) have frequently been condemned, both for their partly erotic content and for their compositional errors; they have also been altered and 'improved' as well as compared unfavourably with the apparently more 'artistic' tricinia of men such as Ivo de Vento and Lechner. It is not yet possible to establish how far Regnart relied on Italian models either for the words or the music. Velten, among others, suggested that the departure from normal German octosyllabic verse and the almost exclusive use in the first volume (1576) of Italian poetic forms – for example the decasyllabic or hendecasyllabic triplet with the rhyme pattern *AAA, ABA, ABB*, or else the six-line hexasyllabic or heptasyllabic, divided into three couplets with the rhyme pattern *AA, BB, CC* – betrays Italian influence; this influence is less marked, however, in the second and third books (1577–9). It is difficult to determine how far Regnart was responding to a demand for simple, popular music and how far he actually created a demand, but there can be no doubt that he provided what people wanted to sing and to listen to,

and his success with such music was far greater than that of his contemporaries, Lassus included. In the preface to his 1576 volume he acknowledged that this was an unpretentious kind of music, and Lechner's madrigalian arrangements for five voices can almost certainly be seen as an attempt to enhance their status in the sphere of art music.

It is impossible to say how far Regnart's four-part lieder (1591) resembled his tricinia, since only the treble part survives, but its melodic structure suggests that they were similar in style; they were not reprinted, however, and must thus have been much less popular. The five-part songs (1580), which were reprinted once, are quite different. Osthoff (1938), who rightly called them 'by far the most important monuments of the polyphonic lied', equally rightly saw them as 'the closest approximation until then of the choral lied to the madrigal'. They are full of the refinement and polyphonic artistry that Regnart deliberately shunned in his three-part pieces. The two volumes of *canzone italiane* (1574–81) can also for the most part be classified as madrigals; the first volume was twice reprinted, and both volumes appeared in German translation in 1595.

Regnart's sacred works have generally received far less attention (but see Mossler, and Pass, 1967). Yet they form the greater part of his extant music, and in them he again displayed his outstanding ability. In particular he made masterly use of the possibilities of musical rhetoric, and skilfully employed music to underline the meaning of his chosen texts; his *Mariale* (1588) in particular is one of the most notable products of the Catholic reform movement.

3. FAMILY. Jacob Regnart had four brothers, all of whom were born at Douai at unknown dates, nor is it known where and when they died. One of them, Augustin, a canon at St Pierre, Lille, edited *Novae cantiones sacrae* (Douai, 1590[10]), for four to six voices, which consists entirely of 40 motets by his four brothers; ten are by Jacob. There are three by each of two other brothers, Charles and Pascasius, of whom it is known only that between 1562 and 1565 they were members of the court chapel of Philip II of Spain, the former as a soprano, the latter as a chaplain. The best represented brother in the collection is François, with 24 motets. According to

Augustin he studied at Douai University and Tournai Cathedral, and according to Fétis he served Archduke Matthias of Austria at Tournai, first, about 1573, as acting choirmaster and then as deputy choirmaster. He published a volume of his own music too: *50 chansons*, for four and five voices (Douai, 1575, 2/1579 as *Poésies de Pierre de Ronsard et autres poëtes*; 20 ed. in MMRF, xv, 1902). The publication *Missae tres* (Antwerp, 1582), for four and five voices, of which there is now no trace, was ascribed to him by Fétis, who stated that it was printed by Plantin, but it was rejected by J. A. Stellfeld (*Bibliographie des éditions musicales plantiniennes*, Brussels, 1949, p.231). In a collection of 1568 there is a motet in two *partes* by a Petrus (?Pierre) Regnart, but it is impossible to say whether he belonged to the same family.

WORKS

Edition: *J. Regnart: Opera omnia*, ed. W. Pass, CMM, lxii/4–6 (1972–5) [P]

    J. Regnart: Deutsche dreistimmige Lieder, ed. R. Eitner, PGfM, xix (1895) [E]

(*for full details see Pass, 1969*)

SACRED VOCAL

Sacrae aliquot cantiones, quas moteta vulgus appellat, 5, 6vv (Munich, 1575); P lxii/4

Aliquot cantiones, vulgo motecta appellatae, ex veteri atque novo testamento collectae, 4vv (Nuremberg, 1577); P lxii/5

Mariale, hoc est, Opusculum sacrarum cantionum omnium Beatissimae Virginis Mariae festivitatibus, 4, 6, 8vv (Innsbruck, 1588); P lxii/6

Missae sacrae ad imitationem selectissimarum cantionum suavissima harmonia, 5, 6, 8vv (Frankfurt am Main, 1602) [autograph ded. dated 31 Dec 1599]

Continuatio missarum sacrarum, ad imitationem selectissimarum cantionum suavissima harmonia, 4–6, 8, 10vv (Frankfurt, 1603)

Corollarium missarum sacrarum ad imitationem selectissimarum cantionum suavissima harmonia compositarum (Frankfurt, 1603)

Sacrarum cantionum, 4–8, 12vv (Frankfurt, 1605)

Canticum Mariae, 5vv (Dillingen, 1605); lost, cited in *Walther ML*

Missarum flores illustrium numquam hactenus visi (Frankfurt, 1611); lost, mentioned in Mossler, 16

Magnificat ad octo modos musicos compositum cum duplici antiphona, Salve regina, 8, 10vv (Frankfurt, 1614); lost, cited in *Walther ML*

47 motets, 3–6vv, 5 tricinia, 2 hymns, Ger. work, 5vv: 1564⁴, 1567², 1568², 1568³, 1568⁴, 1568⁵, 1568⁶, 1569⁶, 1580³, 1580⁴, 1590¹⁰, 1596², 1604⁷, 1605¹, 1609¹⁴, 1627¹, 1629⁴, Cantionale sacrum (Gotha, 1646); Ger. work ed. in Cw, xxx (1934); 4 motets ed. in TM, i, iv, x, xxvii (1971–4)

Works in MS, incl. c20 masses, motets, St Matthew Passion, 100 hymns, 2 odes: *A-Wm, Wn*; *D-As, B, Bds, Dlb, LÜh, Mbs, Ngm, Nla, Rp, Z*; *GB-T*; *H-Bn*; *I-Bc*; *PL-GD, PE, WRu* (see also *EitnerQ*)

Motet, lost, cited in F. Weissensee: *Opus melicum* (Magdeburg, 1602)

Works 'de expugnatione Joarini Hexaphonia', lost, formerly Landschaftsschule und Landhauskirche, Linz, see O. Wessely: *Neue Beiträge* (1954)

SECULAR VOCAL

Il primo libro delle canzone italiane, 5vv (Vienna, 1574; Ger. edn. Nuremberg, 1595, as Threni amorum: der erste Teil lustiger weltlicher Lieder, texts by A. Ratz)

Kurtzweilige teutsche Lieder, nach Art der Neapolitanen oder welschen Villanellen, 3vv (Nuremberg, 1576, 2/1578 as Der erste Theyl schöner kurtzweiliger teutscher Lieder); E

Der ander Theyl kurtzweiliger teutscher Lieder, 3vv (Nuremberg, 1577); E

Der dritter Theyl schöner kurtzweiliger teutscher Lieder, 3vv (Nuremberg, 1579); E

Newe kurtzweilige teutsche Lieder, 5vv (Nuremberg, 1580); 1 ed. H. Osthoff (Kassel, 1928)

Il secundo libro delle canzone italiane, 5vv (Nuremberg, 1581; Ger. edn. Nuremberg, 1595, as Threni amorum: der ander Theil lustiger weltlicher Lieder, texts by A. Ratz)

Teutsche Lieder . . . in ein Opus zusamendruckt, 3vv (Munich, 1583) [complete edn. of songs, 3vv]

Tricinia: kurtzweilige teutsche Lieder, 3vv (Nuremberg, 1584) [complete edn. of songs, 3vv]

Kurtzweilige teutsche Lieder, 4vv (Munich, 1591)

46 Ger. songs, 2 madrigals, 2 Lat. odes: 1585¹⁷, 1600⁵, 1600⁶, 1602¹¹, 1609²⁸, 1610¹⁸, Allerley kurtzweilige teutsche Liedlein (Nuremberg, 1614); 1 song ed. in Cw, li (1938/R)

Works, *A-Wm, CH-Bu, D-B, Bds, Dlb, Lr, Mbs, Rp, PL-WRu*

Schoene Comedie: Speculum vitae humanae, aufft teutsch ein Spiegel des menschlichen Lebens genandt (Archduke Ferdinand), 1584, lost; motet, 9vv, ed. in Osthoff (1929)

INSTRUMENTAL

29 intabulations, 1583²², 1583²⁴; 1584¹²; 1584¹⁴; Lautenbuch . . . sampt ausserlesenen deudtschen und polnischen Tentzen, Passamezen, Gaillarden, deudtschen Vilanellen, Neapolitanen und Phantasien, ed. M. Waissel (Frankfurt an der Oder, 1592); Der erste Theil newer lateinischer und deutscher Gesenge . . . nebenst nachfolgenden schönen Fantasien, Paduanen und Galliarden, ed. P. Luetkeman (Stettin, 1597)

BIBLIOGRAPHY

FétisB; WaltherML

O. Kade: *Die ältere Passionskomposition bis zum Jahre 1631* (Gütersloh, 1893)

R. Velten: *Die ältere deutsche Gesellschaftslied unter dem Einfluss der italienischen Musik* (Heidelberg, 1914)

G. Gruber: *Das deutsche Lied in der Innsbrucker Hofkapelle des Erzherzogs Ferdinand 1567–1596* (diss., U. of Vienna, 1928)

H. Osthoff: 'Eine unbekannte Schauspielmusik Jacob Regnarts', *Musikwissenschaftliche Beiträge: Festschrift für Johannes Wolf* (Berlin, 1929/R1973), 153

A. Einstein: 'Italienische Musik und italienische Musiker am Kaiserhof und an den erzherzoglichen Höfen in Innsbruck und Graz', *SMw*, xxi (1934), 34

H. Osthoff: *Die Niederländer und das deutsche Lied* (1400–1640) (Berlin, 1938/R1971)

M. Steinhardt: *Jacobus Vaet and his Motets* (East Lansing, Mich., 1951)

W. Senn: *Musik und Theater am Hof zu Innsbruck* (Innsbruck, 1954)

O. Wessely: Introduction to MAM, ii (1954)

——: *Neue Beiträge zur Pflege der Musik in der evangelischen Landschaftsschule und Landhauskirche zu Linz* (Linz, 1954), 300ff

J. Roth: *Die mehrstimmigen lateinischen Litaneikompositionen des 16. Jahrhunderts* (Regensburg, 1959)

W. Dürr: 'Die italienische Canzonette und das deutsche Lied im Ausgang des XVI. Jahrhunderts', *Studi in onore di Lorenzo Bianchi* (Bologna, 1960), 71–102

H. Federhofer: 'Regnart', *MGG*

G. Gruber: *Beiträge zur Geschichte und Kompositionstechnik des Parodiemagnificat in der zweiten Hälfte des 16. Jahrhunderts* (diss., U. of Graz, 1964)

F. Mossler: *Jakob Regnarts Messen* (diss., U. of Bonn, 1964)

H. Federhofer: *Musikpflege und Musiker am Grazer Habsburgerhof der Erzherzöge Karl und Ferdinand von Innerösterreich* (1564–1619) (Mainz, 1967)

W. Pass: *Jacob Regnart und seine lateinischen Motetten* (diss., U. of Vienna, 1967)

J. Tichota: 'Deutsche Lieder in Prager Lautentabulaturen des beginnenden 17. Jahrhunderts', *MMC*, xx (1967), 63

W. Pass: *Thematischer Katalog sämtlicher Werke Jacob Regnarts*, Tabulae musicae austriacae, v (1969) [incl. full bibliography]

——: 'Jacob Regnarts "Mariale" und die katholische Reform in Tirol', *Festschrift Walter Senn* (Munich and Salzburg, 1975), 158

WALTER PASS

Regnault, Pierre. See SANDRIN.

Regnes, Nicole (*fl* 1530–51). French editor and composer. He worked in Paris as house editor for Nicolas du Chemin between 1549 and 1551, instructing the printer in the rudiments of music in return for his board and a modest salary. Du Chemin also offered Regnes ten golden crowns for several books of his music, including three collections of new chansons and a book of unpublished four-part motets (though there is no evidence that any of this was ever printed). Regnes was succeeded as house editor by Claude Goudimel.

20 of Regnes' compositions survive: all but one are four-part chansons. The three-part *Le berger et la bergere*, to judge from the frequency with which it was reprinted, was his best-known work. A few of Regnes' chansons – *A tout jamais vous faire humble service*, for example – demonstrate competence in handling the chordal texture of the typical Parisian chanson. Most of

the pieces, however, show the composer's woeful lack of contrapuntal skill. Regnes' style suffers from a paucity of harmonic and melodic imagination. The great disparity between Regnes' better work and the many incompetent pieces suggests that there may have been more than one composer involved; the music is attributed variously to Regnes, Rene, Renes, Rennes, Renez, Reveré, Revertz and Revez (generally no forename is given), but there is no consistent correlation between one form of the name and any stylistic traits.

WORKS

1 chanson a 3, Attaingnant: Trente et une chansons (1535)
19 chansons a 4, 2 in 1530[3], 1 in 1531[1], 1536[5], 1538[10], 1543[14], 1546[12], 3 in 1549[24], 1549[25], 1 in 1549[26], 2 in 1550[5], 3 in 1550[7]; 1 ed. in PÄMw, xxiii (1899), 114, 1 ed. in Collegium musicum, ii (1960), 22

BIBLIOGRAPHY

E. Coyecque: *Histoire générale de Paris: Recueil d'actes notaire . . . 1532–1555*, ii (Paris, 1923), item 5795
F. Lesure and G. Thibault: 'Bibliographie des éditions musicales publiées par Nicolas Du Chemin (1549–1576)', *AnnM*, i (1953), 269–373
D. Heartz: '*Au pres de vous* – Claudin's Chanson and the Commerce of Publishers' Arrangements', *JAMS*, xxiv (1971), 193–225
L. Bernstein: '*La courone et fleur des chansons a troys* [*RISM* 1536[1]]: a Mirror of the French Chanson in Italy in the Years between Ottaviano Petrucci and Antonio Gardano', *JAMS*, xxvi (1973), 1–68
LAWRENCE F. BERNSTEIN

Regnier, Nicolas. *See* RENIER, NICOLAS.

Rego, Pedro Vaz (*b* Campo Maior, Transtagana, baptized 19 March 1673; *d* Évora, 8 April 1736). Portuguese composer. He studied with Diogo Melgaz at Évora Cathedral choir school. After a brief period as deputy *mestre de capela* at Elvas Cathedral, he returned in 1697 to assist the ailing Melgaz, succeeding him in 1700. Six years later – now rector of the archbishop's college as well as *mestre de capela* at Évora – he published there a *Relação das festas . . . 2 de Junho 1706*, composing the music for the festivities himself. His other publications include a defence of Valls's use of unprepared dissonance (undated) and two poems (1733), one praising a *Salve regina* by Domenico Scarlatti's patron and pupil Maria Bárbara, the other containing an extremely useful history of music in the Spanish royal chapel. The latter, entitled *Armonico Lazo*, is dedicated to Torres.

Among the many masses, psalms, hymns, motets, Lamentations, Passions and villancicos credited to him by Barbosa Machado, all that survive are four villancicos (*P-EVp*), a four-voice *Missa ad omnem tonum* (*EVc* 8, 1731) and two four-voice psalms, *Beati omnes* and *Credidi* (*EVc* 6). In his mass Rego cited the psalm recitation formula in each of the eight traditional tones, combining all eight in the final virtuoso Agnus (transcribed in Alegria, *História*, 1973; by the ninth tone Rego meant D minor). Although in Portuguese, his *Amante Deus da minh'alma* (*EVp*) follows the custom much more widespread in Spain of being written a 4th higher than it was to be sung.

BIBLIOGRAPHY

DBP
D. Barbosa Machado: *Bibliotheca lusitana*, iii (Lisbon, 1752), 624f
J. Mazza: 'Dicionário biográfico de músicos portugueses', *Ocidente*, suppl. (1945), 99ff
J. A. Alegria: *História da Escola de música da Sé de Évora* (Lisbon, 1973), 87ff, 176ff

——: *Arquivo das músicas da Sé de Évora* (Lisbon, 1973), 8, 14f, 28, 36, 60
R. Stevenson: *Villancicos portugueses* (Lisbon, 1976)
ROBERT STEVENSON

Regola dell'ottava (It.: 'rule of the octave'). A term used by certain 18th-century figured bass theorists to refer to a simplified system of harmony in which each note of a diatonic scale (ascending and descending an octave) considered as a bass part can be assumed to have its own chord above. The 'rule' is thus a rough and ready guide, and a figuring such as that in ex.1 (Rameau, 1722) is only one of several possible. The idea is a

Ex. 1

practical one, and although the phrase itself occurs late (in Campion's *Traité . . . selon la Règle des Octaves*, 1716) and although some writers treated it somewhat theoretically (Mattheson, Heinichen, Schröter, Blankenburg), figured bass players had long been accustomed to thinking that certain bass lines probably indicated certain harmony. Many 17th-century theorists and composers had assumed, for example, that a C♯ rising to a D indicated a particular progression and could be learnt as a formula; such scales as given by Gasparini (*L'armonico pratico*, 1708/*R*1967) merely extended and codified the practice.

PETER WILLIAMS

Regondi, Giulio (*b* Genoa, *c*1822; *d* London, 6 May 1872). Italian guitar, concertina and melophone player. He was brought up in Lyons by a foster-father, who recognized and cultivated his musical ability. He was presented in Milan as a child prodigy of the guitar, then in the major capitals of Europe, achieving fame in Paris in 1830 and London in 1831. His family settled in London, the guitar cult being popular there in the 1830s. This gave him the opportunity of meeting Leonhard Schulz the younger, who was publishing Mauro Giuliani's guitar music in London. Here he also met the Polish guitar virtuoso Marek Sokołowski, whose seven-string instrument may have prompted him to go a step further and take up the eight-string guitar. He played this on a concert tour to Vienna, Prague and Leipzig in 1840–41, in the company of the cellist Joseph Lidel. In his maturity Regondi was a distinguished player of the concertina, an invention of Charles Wheatstone's (1829) which he popularized. Bernhard Molique wrote a concerto for concertina and orchestra, op.46 (London, 1853) for him. Regondi himself wrote two such concertos, and about 12 chamber works for concertina and piano, such as the *Introduction and Variations on an Austrian Air* op.1 (1855), and several concert pieces for solo concertina. He also wrote many solo guitar works, including *Reverie nocturne* op.19 and *Fête villageoise* op.20.

BIBLIOGRAPHY

Harmonicon (London, 1831), 174, 200, 202, 230
J. Zuth: 'Die Leipziger AMZ (1798–1848) als gitarristische Quelle', *Die Gitarre*, i (Berlin, 1920), 123, 140, 156, 168, 183
——: 'Eine Handschrift von Giulio Regondi', *Musik im Haus*, vi (1927), 78 [incl. portrait of Regondi]
THOMAS F. HECK

Regularis concordia. The book of customs and observances, following Benedictine tradition, for the monasteries of England ('anglicae nationis monachorum sanctimonialiumque') drawn up and approved by the Synod of Winchester, about 970; St Dunstan and St Ethelwold contributed to it. The preface acknowledges an indebtedness to the customs of Fleury and Ghent. Of prime importance in the history of liturgical drama are the detailed instructions for the singing of the dialogue QUEM QUERITIS at Easter matins, ending with the *Te Deum*.

See also MEDIEVAL DRAMA, §II, 2.

EDITIONS
W. S. Logeman: 'De consuetudine monachorum', *Anglia*, new ser., i (1891), 365
T. Symons: *Regularis concordia* (London, 1953)

JOHN STEVENS

Rehfuss, Heinz (Julius) (*b* Frankfurt am Main, 25 May 1917). Swiss bass-baritone of German birth, later naturalized American. He was brought up in Neuchâtel, and studied singing with his father, Carl Rehfuss, and operatic production with Otto Erhardt. In 1937–8 he made his début as a singer and producer at the Städtebundtheater in Biel-Solothurn; he sang in 1938–9 in Lucerne and from 1940 to 1952 at the Zurich Opera House, where he undertook more than 80 roles. He was also an outstanding lieder and oratorio singer, particularly admired as a sensitive interpreter of Christ in Bach's Passions. From 1952 he sang at many European opera houses, notably as Don Giovanni, Boris Godunov and Golaud, and went on concert tours to America, Asia and Africa. He also made a point of singing 20th-century music, in such roles as Dr Schön in *Lulu*. Rehfuss taught singing during courses at Dartington Hall and Darmstadt; he became professor of music (head of the singing and opera departments) at the State University of New York at Buffalo, and visiting professor at the Montreal Conservatory and the Eastman School, Rochester. In 1962 the city of Zurich awarded him the Hans Georg Nägeli Medal.

JÜRG STENZL

Rehim, Gamal. *See* ABDEL-RAHIM, GAMAL.

Rehm, Wolfgang (*b* Munich, 3 Sept 1929). German musicologist and editor. From 1948 to 1952 he studied musicology at Freiburg University under Gurlitt and Zenck with medieval history and modern German literature as secondary subjects; at the same time he studied the piano and theory at the Hochschule für Musik in Freiburg. In 1952 he took his doctorate at Freiburg with a dissertation on Binchois' chansons. He then became an unpaid assistant at Breitkopf & Härtel in Wiesbaden; in 1954 he was appointed research assistant and reader with Bärenreiter in Kassel, and he has been head reader and chief editor of this firm. He has been widely active as an administrator: treasurer of the Association Internationale des Bibliothèques Musicales since 1959, a member of the editorial board of the Neue Bach-Gesellschaft since 1962 and deputy chairman since 1974, treasurer of *RISM* since 1964, a member of the international editorial board of the New Berlioz Edition since 1965, secretary of the Internationale Schubert-Gesellschaft in Tübingen, president of the editorial committee for both series of Documenta Musicologica since 1973, and chairman of

the Internationaler Arbeitskreis für Musik since 1974. From 1960 to 1971 he was a member of the editorial commission of the Gluck-Gesamtausgabe, and since 1960, with W. Plath, he has been chief editor of the Neue Mozart-Ausgabe, to which he has contributed several volumes. He was co-editor of the Festschriften for Deutsch (1963), Fédorov (1966) and Vötterle (1968).

WRITINGS
Das Chansonwerk von Gilles Binchois (diss., U. of Freiburg, 1952; extracts in Musikalische Denkmäler, ii, Mainz, 1957)
Afterword to *Codex Escorial: Chansonnier, Biblioteca del Monasterio El Escorial Sign. MsV.III.24*, Documenta musicologica, 2nd ser., ii (Kassel, 1958)
'Über ein Repertorium der Musik', *IMSCR, vii Cologne 1958*, 221
'Der Musikwissenschaftler im Musikverlag', *GfMKB, Kassel 1962*, 325
'Ergebnisse der Neuen Mozart-Ausgabe: Zwischenbilanz 1965', *MJb 1964*, 151
ed. with H. Bennwitz, G. Feder and L. Finscher: *Musikalisches Erbe und Gegenwart: Musiker-Gesamtausgaben in der Bundesrepublik Deutschland* (Kassel, 1975)

EDITIONS
M. Reger: *Werke für Klavier zu vier Händen*, Sämtliche Werke, xiv (Wiesbaden, 1954)
W. A. Mozart: *Werke für Klavier zu vier Händen*, Neue Ausgabe sämtlicher Werke, ix/24, Abt.2 (Kassel, 1955); *Klavierkonzerte*, ibid, v/15/8 (Kassel, 1960); *Streichquartette*, ibid, viii/20, Abt.1/1 (Kassel, 1966) [with K. H. Füssl and W. Plath]; *Klaviertrios*, ibid, viii/22, Abt.2 (Kassel, 1966) [with W. Plath]; *Don Giovanni*, ibid, ii/5/17 (Kassel, 1968) [with W. Plath]
with W. Plath: W. A. Mozart: *Jugendsonaten II: Sechs Sonaten für Klavier (Cembalo), Violine (oder Flöte) und Violoncello, K10–15* (Kassel, 1969)

HANS HEINRICH EGGEBRECHT

Reibtrommel (Ger.). FRICTION DRUM.

Reich, Steve [Stephen] (**Michael**) (*b* New York, 3 Oct 1936). American composer. At Cornell University (1953–7) he studied philosophy, particularly the work of Wittgenstein. He was trained as a composer at the Juilliard School (1958–61) and at Mills College (1962–3), where his teachers were Milhaud and Berio. The summer of 1970 he spent studying African drumming at the Institute of African Studies, University of Ghana. During 1969–71 he was on the staff of the New School for Social Research in New York. He is a performer on keyboard instruments and percussion, and in 1966 founded the group Steve Reich and Musicians. As a composer he is interested in the possibilities of multiples of the same instrument, either live (e.g. in *Four Organs*) or contrived, as in *Violin Phase* for recorded and live violin. He makes large pieces from minimal materials – a single chord in *Four Organs*, a five-word phrase for most of *Come out*. He is particularly concerned with an extension or elaboration of canon, with identical lines proceeding as if recorded on tape loops at different speeds, starting together but gradually becoming separated, and the rhythms are finely and exactly imagined. Reich makes his music available for performance only by ensembles of which he is a member.

WORKS
(*selective list*)
Come out, 2-track tape, 1966; Piano Phase, 2 pf, 1967; Violin Phase, vn, 3-track tape/4 vn, 1967; Pendulum Music, mics, amps, loudspeakers, 1968; Four Organs, 4 elec org, maracas, 1970; Phase Patterns, 4 elec org, 1970; Drumming, 8 small tuned drums, 3 mar, 3 glock, vv, pic, 1971; Clapping Music, 2 musicians, 1972; Six Pianos, 6 pf, 1973; Music for Mallet Instruments, Voices and Organ, 4 mar, 2 glock, metallophone, 3 female vv, elec org, 1973; Music for Pieces of Wood, claves, 1973; Music for 18 Musicians, 1975
Other pieces for tape or ens, film scores
All works unpublished

WRITINGS
Writings about Music, ed. K. Koenig (Halifax, Nova Scotia, 1974) [collected essays]

BIBLIOGRAPHY

M. Nyman: Interview, *MT*, cxii (1971), 229

E. Wasserman: Interview, *Art Forum* (May 1972)

C. Gottwald: 'Signale zwischen Exotik und Industrie: Steve Reich auf der Suche nach einer neuen Identität von Klang und Struktur', *Melos/NZM*, i (1975), 3

MICHAEL STEINBERG

Reich, Willi (*b* Vienna, 27 May 1898; *d* Zurich, 1 May 1980). Swiss music critic and musicologist of Austrian birth. He studied chemistry at Vienna Technische Hochschule and musicology with Lach, Orel and Haas at Vienna University, where he took his doctorate in 1934 with a dissertation on Martini; concurrently he took private lessons in music theory and composition with Berg (1927–35) and Webern (1936–8). From 1920 he worked as a music critic for numerous Viennese and foreign newspapers. From 1932 to 1937, encouraged by Berg, he edited the journal *23 – eine Wiener Musikzeitschrift*, which took vehement issue with the defects of Viennese musical life and supported the new music, particularly that of the Second Viennese School. The journal was in many ways indebted to Karl Kraus and his *Die Fackel*; the opening 'defence' of the first issue outlined its programme: 'We want to rectify everything in the wide circle of the arts and the music business which is at present affected by distortion, half-truths, falsity, malice and hostility to merit'. The journal, which in June 1933 had emphatically criticized national socialism and whose regular authors included Ploderer, Krenek and Adorno as well as Reich, was banned immediately after the Austrian Anschluss. In 1938 Reich moved to Basle where he worked as a freelance writer until the end of 1947 and built up the comprehensive archives which have served as the basis of his numerous documentary books. In 1948 Willi Schuh offered him a post on the *Neue Zürcher Zeitung*, in addition to which he lectured at the federal Technische Hochschule in Zurich (1959–1970; honorary professor 1958, titular professor 1967). In 1961 he became a Swiss citizen.

With Adorno, Erwin Stein and others Reich belonged to a small group of music journalists who had personal contact with the composers of the Second Viennese School and who were quick to champion their work with ceaseless energy and open-mindedness – against an extraordinarily influential press, sworn to 'tradition', within and beyond Vienna. His two monographs on Berg and his book on Schoenberg have been established as fundamental accounts of the life and works of the two composers. His numerous other books attempt to characterize the poets and musicians in their own words; each is presented in a different way to suit the relevant material. Reich also established a reputation as a translator of musical works and in particular of Strindberg's plays into German; the latter are almost always performed by German-speaking theatres.

WRITINGS

'Alban Berg und Anton Webern in ihren neuen Werken', *Der Auftakt*, x (1930), 132; Eng. trans., *MM*, vii/3 (1929–30), 41

Wozzeck: a Guide to the Words and Music of the Opera by Alban Berg (New York, 1931); repr. in *MQ*, xxxviii (1952), 1

Padre Martini als Theoretiker und Lehrer (diss., U. of Vienna, 1934)

'Busoni and England', *MT*, lxxvii (1936), 890

Alban Berg (Vienna, 1937)

ed.: *Mozart: Denkmal im eigenen Wort: Lebensdokumente* (Basle, 1945)

'Dem "Meister des dreifachen Pianissimo" (zum Tode von Anton Webern)', *SMz*, lxxxvi (1946), 27

ed.: H. G. Nägeli: *Von Bach zu Beethoven* (Basle, 1946)

Romantiker der Musik (Basle, 1947)

ed.: *Richard Wagner* (Olten, 1948)

'Ernest Kreneks Arbeit in der Zwölftontechnik', *SMz*, lxxxix (1949), 49

ed.: *Goethe und die Musik* (Zurich, 1949)

ed.: *Johann Strauss-Brevier* (Zurich, 1950)

ed.: *Giuseppe Verdi: aus Briefen und Erinnerungen* (Zurich, 1951)

'Richard Strauss und Romain Rolland', *Melos*, xviii (1951), 70; Eng. trans., *MMR*, lxxxi (1951), 116

ed.: F. Busoni: 'Anmerkungen zum "Wohltemperierten Klavier" ', *SMz*, xcii (1952), 49

'Versuch einer Geschichte der Zwölftonmusik', *Alte und neue Musik* (Zurich, 1952), 120

ed.: *Anton Bruckner: ein Bild seiner Persönlichkeit* (Basle, 1953)

Beschwörungen (Berne, 1955) [trans. of A. Honegger: *Incantations aux fossiles*, Lausanne, 1948]

Musik in unserer Zeit (Munich, 1955) [trans. of A. Goléa: *Esthétique de la musique contemporaine*, Paris, 1954]

ed.: K. F. Zelter: *Selbstdarstellung* (Zurich, 1955)

ed.: *Arthur Honegger: Nachklang – Schriften, Photos, Dokumente* (Zurich, 1957)

ed.: *Béla Bartók: eigene Schriften und Erinnerungen der Freunde* (Zurich, 1958)

ed.: *Gustav Mahler: im eigenen Wort – im Wort der Freunde* (Zurich, 1958)

ed.: *Alban Berg: Bildnis im Wort* (Zurich, 1959)

ed.: *Frédéric Chopin: Briefe und Dokumente* (Zurich, 1959)

'Zur Geschichte der Zwölftonmusik', *Festschrift Alfred Orel* (Vienna and Wiesbaden, 1960), 151

ed.: *Anton Webern: der Weg zur neuen Musik* (Vienna, 1960, 2/1963; Eng. trans., 1963)

Alexander Tscherepnin (Bonn, 1961, 2/1970)

ed.: *Anton Webern: Weg und Gestalt* (Zurich, 1961)

ed.: *Joseph Haydn: Chronik seines Lebens in Selbstzeugnissen* (Zurich, 1962)

Alban Berg: Leben und Werk (Zurich, 1963; Eng. trans., 1965)

'Anton Webern', *NÖB*

ed.: *Beethoven: geistige Persönlichkeit im eigenen Wort* (Zurich, 1963)

'Ein heiteres Dokument aus der Wiener Mahler-Zeit', *Festschrift Otto Erich Deutsch* (Kassel, 1963), 257; repr. in *ÖMz*, xix (1964), 26

ed.: *A. Schönberg: Schöpferische Konfessionen* (Zurich, 1964)

ed.: *Gespräche mit Komponisten* (Zurich, 1964)

'Kleines Mahler-Triptychon', *SMz*, civ (1964), 21

with K. H. Ruppel: 'Paul Hindemith und sein Werk für die moderne Musik', *Universitas*, xix (1964), 137

'Drei Notizblätter zu Alban Bergs Oper "Lulu" ', *SMz*, cvi (1966), 336; cvii (1967), 165

'Gespräche mit Othmar Schoeck', *SMz*, cvi (1966), 23

Richard Strauss: das Opernwerk (Munich, 1967, 2/1969 as *Die Opern von Richard Strauss*) [trans. of W. Mann: *Richard Strauss: a Critical Study of the Operas*, London, 1964]

ed.: *Robert Schumann* (Zurich, 1967)

Arnold Schönberg oder der konservative Revolutionär (Vienna, 1968; Eng. trans., 1971, as *Schoenberg: a Critical Biography*)

ed.: *Felix Mendelssohn im Spiegel eigener Aussagen und zeitgenössischer Dokumente* (Zurich, 1970)

'Von Büchner und Wedekind zu Alban Berg', *Beiträge zur neuen Musik* (Kassel, 1970–71), 71

ed.: *Franz Schubert in eigenen Worten und Betrachtungen seiner Freunde* (Zurich, 1971)

'Musik und Gesellschaft heute', *Melos*, xxxviii (1971), 476

ed.: *Johannes Brahms: in Dokumenten zu Leben und Werk* (Zurich, 1975)

Further Berg, Webern and Schoenberg letters and literary documents in *SMz*, xciii (1953), 49; xcv (1955), 475; xcvii (1957), 259; cvii (1967), 149; *ÖMz*, xiv (1959), 10; xvi (1961), 276; xx (1965), 407; *Melos*, xxxiii (1966), 225; xxxvi (1969), 9

BIBLIOGRAPHY

W. Schuh: 'Willi Reich siebzigjährig', *SMz*, cviii (1968), 201

JÜRG STENZL

Reicha [Rejcha], Antoine(-Joseph) [Antonín, Anton] (*b* Prague, 26 Feb 1770; *d* Paris, 28 May 1836). Czech, later French, composer. Though a prolific composer, he was of particular importance as a theorist and teacher in early 19th-century Paris.

1. 1770–1805. 2. 1805–24. 3. 1824–36.

1. 1770–1805. Reicha was only ten months old when his father Simon, an Old Town piper, died at the age of 30. About 1780 he felt that his education was suffering and ran away to his grandfather Václav Rejcha (1717–98) in Klatovy, Bohemia. Then he went to his aunt and

uncle, Lucie Certelet and Josef Reicha (1752–95), who adopted him. The fragmentary facts of the first 30 years in the life and works of Reicha often have been confused with those of his uncle, a virtuoso cellist, concert director and composer. Reicha learnt the violin and the piano from his uncle and also received instruction in the flute.

After the family moved to Bonn in 1785, Reicha played the violin and the flute (his main instrument) in the Hofkapelle under his uncle's direction, alongside Beethoven and C. G. Neefe, who both may have given him composition lessons, and introduced him to Bach's keyboard works. At first, he had to study composition secretly, against the wishes of his uncle; he may have read at this time Marpurg's *Abhandlung von der Fuge* and Kirnberger's *Die Kunst des reinen Satzes*. In 1787 he conducted his first symphony and several *scènes italiennes* at Bonn, and in 1789 he entered Bonn University. He met Haydn in the early 1790s at Bonn and again in 1795 in Hamburg, where he had moved to at the end of 1794 when the French invaded Bonn. In Hamburg, vowing not to perform any more, he taught the piano, harmony and composition. He also devoted himself to composition, readings in mathematics, philosophy and music, and meditation on the nature of composition and the methods of teaching it. His earliest known opera, *Godefroid de Montfort*, may have received its second private performance in Hamburg in 1796 with the assistance of Pierre Garat and Pierre Rode.

Hoping for operatic success, Reicha went to Paris on 25 September 1799. Despite the well-received performances by his friends (Rode, Garat, Gossec and Devismes) of the symphonies opp.41 and 42 (with thematically connected movements), an overture (probably op.24) and some *scènes italiennes*, Reicha could neither get his Hamburg librettos accepted nor find a suitable new one, even with the influential assistance of Mme St Aubin-Schroeder. On Grétry's recommendation he set Guy's libretto *L'ouragan*, but this met with failure; both the Théâtre Feydeau and the Salle Favart closed in 1801. Distraught, Reicha joined Rode at Montmorency and late that year left for Vienna. His early work had shown the influences of Dalayrac, Grétry and his uncle, Josef Reicha; by op.20, the influences of the Mannheim composers, Gluck, Mozart and Haydn predominated.

In Vienna Reicha first went to visit Haydn, whose current preoccupation with canons and variations provided common ground for a close friendship. He renewed his friendship with Beethoven and took lessons from Albrechtsberger and Salieri. Prince Lobkowitz had *L'ouragan* performed at his palace c1801. Shortly afterwards, Empress Marie Therese commissioned Reicha to write *Argine, regina di Granata*, in which she sang at a private performance at the Imperial Palace. In 1802 Reicha rejected an invitation to become teacher and Kapellmeister to Prince Louis Ferdinand, but during the next two years wrote *L'art de varier* for him. Unified by a large tonal plan, by the common derivation of the 57 variations, and by the occasional recurrence of slightly varied versions of the theme, the work is meant for performance despite its didactic origins.

In Reicha's output individual works defy classification as purely musical, theoretical or didactic; this was a result of his Hamburg meditations. Like *L'art de varier* and Bach's didactic works, the 36 Fugues (1803, dedicated to Haydn) subsume pedagogical examples within artistic conceptions. No.13 offers modal prin-

ciples in which cadences are possible on all but the 7th degree of the scale without further alteration; nos.20, 24 and 28 contribute 'combined metre' (e.g. $6/8 + 2/8$), while no.30 displays polymetre. Beethoven owned a copy of these fugues; though he wrote of them that 'the fugue is no longer a fugue', changes in his style (e.g. Variations op.35) may derive from Reicha's ideas on variation and fugue. The exchange of ideas between them was probably reciprocal.

The 24 compositions in *Practische Beispiele* (1803) include demonstrations of forms and genres, bitonality, and fiendishly difficult sight-reading exercises; the text shows that Reicha foresaw how the art of modulation would pervade the new epoch and it reveals his predilection for mathematics and the philosophy of Kant.

2. 1805–24. In late December 1805 Reicha, acting as interpreter, introduced Baillot and Cherubini (in Napoleon's entourage) to Haydn. Reicha's new cantata *Lenore* could not be performed in occupied Vienna because of Napoleon's censorship of the works of the librettist, Bürger. Reicha therefore went to Leipzig in 1806 to arrange for a performance, stopping en route at Prague to visit his mother for the first time since he had run away. He continued on his way to Leipzig after several days, never to see Prague again. The French army's four-month blockade of Leipzig effectively cancelled his performance. He finally returned to Vienna, but in 1808, when Austria once again prepared for war, he left for Paris, to be welcomed home by Louis Adam and Sébastien Erard.

While in Vienna, Reicha wrote about 50 pieces, mostly chamber works rich in melody and folk elements. Wide-ranging tonal schemes characterize the String Trio in F, while cadentially elided, thematically connected movements shape the String Quartet op.52. The Piano Sonata with violin and cello accompaniment op.47 (1804) approaches the true piano trio (see Newman, 1963); Reicha said of his Six Quartets for flute and strings op.98 (probably before 1815) that they were true quartets, not sonatas or solos for flute with string accompaniment. Haydn's interest in canons and Albrechtsberger's lifelong devotion to writing instrumental fugues apparently reinforced Reicha's predilection, so that many of his chamber works of this period include fugal movements.

Cagliostro (1810) lasted for eight performances, a fate similar to that of Reicha's only other produced operas, *Natalie* (1816) and *Sapho* (1822). The recitatives in *Natalie* and *Sapho* show the influence of Gluck and Spontini. Despite the failure of *Sapho*, Reicha considered it, along with the unproduced *Philoctète*, to be his masterpiece. Berlioz admired a moving duo and several choruses from *Sapho*; Bücken later noted the prominent role of the chorus, the effective orchestration, musical characterization and the use of reminiscence themes, and the well-integrated dances.

Although Reicha's operas failed, his fame increased. By 1817 many of his compositions had been published and were being performed, and the *Traité de mélodie* (1814) was being examined for the Académie by Méhul at the time of his death. Concerned primarily with melodic phraseology, this treatise examines melody apart from its relation to harmony. It distinguishes rhythm from metre, differentiates among cadential goals of unequal strength (using the analogues of 18th-century grammar and rhetoric) and supplies one of the first descriptions of sonata form that emphasizes thematic rather than tonal aspects. Comments on singers' embellishments and the use of national airs to impart local colour round out the treatise.

The Etudes op.97, published several years after the *Traité de mélodie*, are in the 'fugued' genre, and are preceded by remarks aimed at young composers. With the exception of four of the 34 études, all are fugues, each preceded by a kind of prelude that illustrates in most cases a compositional technique or problem, a form, a texture etc. The prelude to no.3, for example, is a theme and variations in which variations 1, 3, 5 and 7 are in invertible counterpoint, their inversions thus producing variations 2, 4, 6 and 8.

Reicha had had few composition pupils before 1809, but by 1817 the Count de Sèze, recommending Reicha for appointment to the Conservatoire, could point out that eight of Reicha's students – probably his friends Baillot, Bouffil, Dauprat, Garaudé, Guillou, Habeneck, Rode and Vogt – already were professors there. These men, most of them accomplished musicians when they began studying with Reicha, spread his reputation for being precise, logical, efficient and strict. Berlioz recalled that Reicha gave reasons for the rules and that, unlike Cherubini, his respect for tradition was not fetishistic, and that he promptly recognized innovation.

Reicha was appointed professor of counterpoint and fugue at the Conservatoire in 1818. His *Cours de composition musicale, ou Traité . . . d'harmonie pratique*, published around 1816–18, replaced Catel's treatise, which had been the official one since 1802. One of the first modern classroom harmony textbooks using examples written expressly for the text, the *Cours de composition* deals with harmony (tempering the proscription against 5ths and octaves), strict and free music, imitation and orchestration. It stresses the point that theory must be justified by practice and that the pupil must learn about contemporary usage, not solely about ancient principles that diametrically opposed what he heard outside the classroom; this resulted in many students believing that serious study of composition was useless because free music permitted anything.

On 15 October 1818 Reicha married Virginie Enaust; they had two daughters, Antoinette Virginie (*b* 26 August 1819) and Mathilde Sophie (*b* 13 April 1824). Reicha's autobiography, *Notes sur Antoine Reicha*, perhaps originally dictated about 1824 to his pupil Henri Blanchard, survives in Antoinette Virginie's hand. In these *Notes* Reicha mentioned having had the idea of writing a 'double quartet' (for wind in E minor and strings in G major) which could be played either as two separate works or as an octet. Though mentioned in several lists of works, this understandably seductive idea (which anticipates Milhaud) may never have materialized.

The autobiography comes from a time when Rossini may have become his friend (1823); when Mendelssohn (who had studied with Moscheles, an owner of the 36 Fugues) sought him out (1825); and when Balzac, in *Les employés* (set in 1824), could have one of his characters, Colleville, first clarinettist at the Opéra-Comique, convince a friend to attend a soirée by promising him the excitement of a performance of a new wind quintet by Reicha. Reicha's wind quintets show his refined sense of instrumental colour and have served as models of their genre.

3. 1824–36. The most important of Reicha's treatises, the *Traité de haute composition musicale* (1824–6), was brought out as a sequel to the earlier published treatises and provoked much controversy. For Reicha, counterpoint was almost synonymous with harmony, but it connoted the elevated work of a savant, a profound harmonist, one who was both creator and scientist; 'haute composition', then, extols invertible counterpoint and practical music while belittling simple counterpoint and 'school music'. The text was the first to use the terms exposition and counter-exposition with regard to fugue; it also extended Reicha's earlier modal principles which in turn expanded the tonal frame of the fugue and promoted a periodically phrased fugue. Reicha's 'fugue phrasée' attempts to reconcile polyphonic continuity with homophonic periodicity. The attempt results from his view of history in which the 'incoherent' phraseology of early music progressively evolved to the clear and regular articulations of forms in their mature, Classical state. Fétis claimed that Reicha had unwittingly rediscovered the 17th-century *ricercare di fantasia* by not giving priority to real and tonal fugues on the tonic and dominant, thereby also weakening the tonality. The text presents a more thematically orientated scheme for sonata form than that found in the *Traité de mélodie*, and gives what may be the first clear description of sonata-rondo form. Reicha demonstrated methods for exposing and developing melodic and harmonic ideas and suggested that the study of mathematics helps regulate the feverish imagination. He proposed speaking choruses, quarter-tone notation for declamation and enrichment of the rhythmic language, he formulated a 200-piece orchestra, and included his setting of Kosegarten's *Die Harmonie der Sphären* for string orchestra, double chorus, and four pairs of timpani tuned to eight different pitches.

Baini severely criticized Reicha's approach to counterpoint. The controversy divided the students and faculty of the Conservatoire into adherents of Cherubini, Reicha or Fétis. Antoine Marmontel recalled the courtyard and corridor battles of looks between 'Italy, Bohemia, and the Netherlands' (see Emmanuel, pp.35, 48, 50). Though their criticisms had historical validity, Baini (sometimes labelled an ultra-conservative), Cherubini and Fétis represented the rearguard while Reicha, in this instance at least, seems to have represented the future. Excerpts of this treatise were published in English in 1830. Czerny, in 1832, edited a French–German version of the first three published treatises, entitling them *Vollständiges Lehrbuch*. Within several years English, Italian and Spanish translations of excerpts or complete treatises had appeared in Europe and America.

In 1826 Berlioz and Liszt began studying with Reicha. Berlioz's frequent fugal passages, his reharmonization of melodies on each recurrence, the asymmetric metre of the 'Dance of the Soothsayers' in *L'enfance du Christ*, his general rhythmic flexibility, his concept of the ideal orchestra, his use of the timpani and his emphasis on the wind instruments, all reflect Reicha's influence, regardless of Berlioz's silence on that subject. Liszt suggested that his own idiosyncratic use of fugue and his attitudes toward formal and rhythmic experiments might derive from Reicha.

Following his naturalization in 1829, Reicha was made a Chevalier of the Légion d'honneur in 1831. In December of that year Chopin, who had wanted to study with Reicha, heard unfavourable comments from some pupils and decided not to work with him. Reicha's health had been failing since about 1828, and a letter to Cherubini from Reicha in July 1832 states that he would welcome his pupils to his home for lessons.

In 1833 *Art du compositeur dramatique*, a manual devoted to the technique of writing opera, appeared. It also describes performing practice at a time when Rossini and Meyerbeer dominated the French musical stage. Typically French, and also typically Czech, is Reicha's attention to declamation. The volume of plates accompanying the manual contains many excerpts in vocal score from *Natalie*, *Sapho* and *Philoctète*. About 1835 Czerny produced a German translation of this treatise.

Stylistic generalizations about Reicha's late works are difficult to make because the dating of many is not certain; some late Parisian publications with high opus numbers contain works whose manuscripts originate in the Viennese period. But it seems clear that Reicha treated fugue more conservatively in works known to be later ones. The influence of Handel is apparent in large choral works such as *Der neue Psalm* and the *Te Deum*.

Reicha succeeded Boieldieu at the Académie in 1835, one year before his death. In June César Franck became a pupil of Reicha for ten months, a period of study that was to affect Franck's formal and tonal conceptions. Both the brevity of personal contact and the late date at which evidence of Reicha's influence surfaces in Franck's work call into question that influence. Franck's notebook (as well as Antoinette Virginie's) attests to Reicha's thoroughness and speed. Further argument for latent influence lies in the fact that Franck's subsequent teachers, Le Borne and Reicha's friend Benoist, continued to use Reicha's treatises in their instruction. Similarly, Ambroise Thomas' notebook indicates familiarity with Reicha's ideas and texts because he studied with Barbereau, a Reicha student.

Hence Reicha's students and the treatises themselves in their many translations broadcast Reicha's theories beyond Paris and beyond his own time. As early as 1815 Meyerbeer wrote to Gottfried Weber about the *Traité de mélodie*; by 1834 Meyerbeer owned at least two other treatises. Schumann noted that Reicha's 'often peculiar ideas about fugue' should not be ignored; Sechter listed Reicha among the most important theorists of his time; and Smetana knew Reicha's ideas through the Czerny edition used by his teacher Joseph Proksch. Until more is known of Reicha's music the judgment of time on his importance as a composer must tacitly be accepted; his role as a seminal figure however seems clear.

For illustrations from *Traité de mélodie*, see ANALYSIS, figs. 3–5.

WORKS

Unlocated works mentioned in:
A. Reicha: *Traité de haute composition musicale* (Paris, 1824–6) [H]
——: *Art du compositeur dramatique* (Paris, 1833) [A]
J. Vysloužil, ed.: *Zápisky o Antonínu Rejchovi/Notes sur Antoine Reicha* (Brno, 1970) [R]

THEATRICAL
Armide (scene, R. di Calzabigi), c1787, lost, mentioned in R, ?scène italienne
Godefroid de Montfort [Godfried von Montfort] (opera), ?c1794, Hamburg, ?1796, mentioned in *FétisB*
L'ermite dans l'île Formose (Singspiel, A. von Kotzebue), ?1794–8, lost, mentioned in R
Obaldi, ou Les français en Egypte (opera, 2), before 1798, *F-Pc* 12011, 12044
Amor, der Joujou-Spieler (Singspiel), before c1800; Ach! Amor

Herzenzieler, aria, *D-Lr*, ed. in Auswahl der besten Compositionen für das Clavier, i/3 (Hanover, c1800), no.20; ?by J. Reicha
Rosalia (Singspiel), ?before 1800, *Rtt*
L'ouragan (opera, 3, J. H. Guy), c1800, Vienna, Prince Lobkowitz's palace, c1801 [in Ger. trans.], *F-Pc* 12016
Télémaque (grand opera, ?Devismes), ?1800–01, inc., lost, mentioned in R
Argine, regina di Granata (heroic opera, 2, ?Calzabigi), Vienna, Imperial Palace, c1802, *Pc* 12034 (autograph), *A-Wn* 9993 (copy)
Cagliostro, ou La séduction [Les illuminés] (opéra comique, 3, J. A. Reveroni de Saint-Cyr and E. Mercier-Dupaty), 1808–10, Paris, Théâtre Feydau, 27 Nov 1810, *F-Pc* 2509, 12018; Act 1 by V. C. P. Dourlen
Gusman d'Alfarache (opéra comique, 1, E. Scribe, J. H. Dupin), after c1809, *Pc* 12017
Bégri ou Le chanteur à Constantinople (opéra comique, 1), after c1809, *Pc* 12014
Natalie ou La famille russe (grand opera, 3, Guy), c1810–12, Paris, Opéra, 30 July 1816, *Pc* 2585 (frag.), *Po* 415 (2 versions), A 447.II–III; excerpts in A ii, 28, 75; ov. and selected scenes (Paris, n.d.)
Olinde et Sophronie (opera), c1819, inc., mentioned in Emmanuel
Philoctète (grand opera, 2, ? after Sophocles), before 1822, lost except for 3 choruses in A ii, 59, 62, 68
Sapho (opera seria [tragédie lyrique], 3, H. Cournol, A. J. S. Empis), Paris, Opéra, 16 Dec 1822, *Pc* 12024 (almost complete), *Po* 435, A 468.I–IV; excerpts in A ii, 24, 40, 65, 72; ov. and selected scenes (Paris, c1822)
Gioas, re di Giuda (opera, Metastasio), before 1826, aria and chorus in H ii, 188, 198; ? never composed as complete opera
Venne ed il nostro addio, frag., ? scène italienne, ? from Argine, *A-Wn* 10687–8
Unidentified frag., *F-Pn* fr.12760, 419–20

CHORAL
with orch
Requiem, ?1802–8, ?lost, mentioned in R; ? same as Missa pro defunctis
Lenore (G. A. Bürger), cantata, with solo vv, c1805, *F-Pc* 10096 (1–2)
Der neue Psalm (A. Mahlmann), cantata, with 2 S, A, T, B, 1807, *Pc* 2504
Missa pro defunctis (Requiem), with S, A, T, B, ? after 1809, *Pc* 12023
Hommage à Grétry, cantata, with S, 2 T, B, 1814, *Pc* 12010
Choeur dialogué par les instruments à vent, E♭, chorus, fl, ob, cl, bn, hn, vc, db, before 1824, ed. in H i, 74
Te Deum, with S, A, T, B, org, 1825, *Pc* 6185
Die Harmonie der Sphären ('Horch, wie orgelt') (L. G. Kosegarten), double chorus, str, 8 timp, before 1826, *D-B* 18176, ed. in H ii, 331
Le peuple saint (C. Ménard), with org, before 1826, *B* 18175, ed. in H ii, 168
2 fugues, D, F; double fugue; e; Cum sanctis tuis in aeternum; Dona nobis pacem, chorus, str: all before 1826, ed. in H ii, 133, 138, 143, 151, 182
Passion oratorio, with S, A, T, B, pf score in *Rtt*

with kbd
Urians Reise um die Welt (M. Claudius), unison vv, pf, op.56 (Vienna, ?1804)
Do–do, l'enfant do, S, chorus, pf/harp, ? after 1810 (Paris, n.d.)
Regina coeli, double chorus, org, bc, before 1818, in *Cours de composition musicale*, 217
Fugue, g, 8vv, org, bc, 1822, *A-Wn* 16458, ed. in H ii, 116
Fugue, e, double chorus, org, bc, before 1824, *D-Dl* 4234/G/1, ed. in H i, 80
Prière, chorus, org, ded. Cherubini, before 1826, ed. in A ii, 98
Sonetto: Hymnus an den Karfunkel, 2 S, T, B, chorus, pf, *SW* 4405A

unacc.
Das lacedämonische Lied ('Einst fühlen wir') (Plutarch), fugue, 4 male vv, 3 Jan 1805, *Bds*
Je prends mon bien partout, canon, 4vv, ed. in *Euterpe vosgienne*, iv (Paris, c1823), 41
Duo dans le style rigoureux, E♭, S, A, T, B, before 1824, ed. in H i, 10
2 fugues, 4vv: F, E♭, before 1826, ed. in H ii, 49, 68
Fugue, double chorus, *Dl* B.262.11
Cantique, 4 solo vv, double chorus, mentioned in Emmanuel; ? same as Hommage à Grétry

SOLO VOICES
with orch
Donne, donne, chi vi crede (cavatina), S, orch, ?1786–94, *F-Pc* 12021, ? scène italienne
Basta ti credo. . .Quanto e fiero (recit and aria, ? P. L. Moline), 1v, orch, ?1800, *Pc* D.14855, arr. 1v, pf (Leipzig, 1807), ? scène italienne
Abschied der Johanna d'Arc (melodrama, Schiller), S, musical glasses, orch, 12 March 1806, *Pc* 12045
Aure amiche ah non spirate (scena and aria), S, orch, c1810, ? autograph in *D-Rtt*, copy in *Hs*, ? scène italienne
Prelude, T, orch, before 1826, ed. in H ii, 322
Voici le moment favorable (? opera frag.), S, T, 3 B, orch, *F-Pc* 13107

without orch

Romance nouvelle 'Quel est, hélas! la tourmente que j'endure!, 1v, pf (Paris, ?1800)

Das Andenken (Matthison), S, pf, ?1801–9 (n.p., n.d.), mentioned in Bücken (1912)

Der Brüder Graürock und die Pilgerinn (cantata, G. A. Bürger), S, pf, ?1801–9, *Pc* 2503

Die Sehnsucht (C. L. Reissig), 1v, pf, after 1809 (Vienna, ?1817)

Hamlets Monolog ('Sein oder nicht sein'), 1v, pf (Leipzig, *c*1810)

Air, S/ob, pf, before 1818, ed. in *Cours de composition musicale*, 158

Je vais cherchant pour rencontrer un coeur, 1v, pf/harp, ed. in *Euterpe vosgienne*, iii/1 (Paris, *c*1822), 30

Voi sole o luci belle, canon à 2, S, T, bc, before 1824, ed. in H i, 210

Das Grab (Salis), 1v, pf, ed. in *Euterpe vosgienne*, v/2 (Paris, *c*1824), 60

Fra mille vari moti, 2 S, T, B, db ad lib, bc, ed. in *Euterpe vosgienne*, viii/1 (Paris, *c*1827), 90

Circé, cantata, S, pf, mentioned in Emmanuel

12 Gesänge, 1v, pf (Brunswick, n.d.)

Liebe und Freundschaft [Láska a přátelství], ed. O. Pulkert, *Písně* (Prague, 1962), 56

Raccolta di [6] arie, di [5] duetti e di [13] terzetti, 2 S, T, pf, *Pc* 10942, ? scènes italiennes [2 terzettos unacc.]

Quatuor vocal, mentioned in Emmanuel [Ger., Fr., It. texts]

ORCHESTRAL

symphonies

Sym., perf. Bonn, 1787, lost, mentioned in R

Sym. à grand orchestre ('First Symphony'), E♭, ?1799–1800, *F-Pc* 13107; op.41 (Leipzig, 1803)

Sym. à grand orchestre, E♭, ?1799–1800, op.42 (Leipzig, 1803)

Sym. no.1, G, completed 13 July 1808, *Pc* 14498 (inc.)

Sym. no.2, ?before 1808, mentioned in Emmanuel

Sym. no.3, F, completed 4 Sept 1808, *Pc* 14499

Grande symphonie no.2, ?1808, mentioned in Borrel

Sinfonie à grand orchestre, D, ?1809, *Pc* 13107 (1st movt)

2/?4 syms. à grand orchestre, no.1, 1809, no.2, 1811, mentioned in Emmanuel and Borrel

Sym., C, before 1824, frag. in H i, 141

Sym., C, before 1824, frag. in H i, 166

Sym./Ov., C, before 1824, frag. in H i, 175

Sym. à petit orchestre, no.1, c, *Pc* 14500

Sym., E♭, *Pn* 9153

Sym., f, *Pc* 14501

Sym., *US-Bp* ** M.403.107

Undated sym. movts and frags., *CH-E* 19.08, *F-Pn* 9152–3, *Pc* 13107

overtures

Ov., C, op.24 (Brunswick, ?*c*1795)

Grand Ov., D, d'un concert ou d'une académie de la musique, *c*1803–23, versions in *Pc* 2511, *Pn* 9154, *Pc* 13107, 12037, *B-Bc* X 8128 [in estimated order of completion]

Ov. en l'honneur de l'Impératrice Marie Thérèse, ?*c*1805, mentioned in Emmanuel, ? an ov. for Argine; see 'Doubtful and spurious works'

Ov., C, before 1810, orig. for Cagliostro, *Pc* 12036

Ov., C, before 1822, orig. for Sapho, *Pc* 12039

Ov., E–e, ? op.34, ? after 1813, *GB-Lbm* RPS loan collection 854

Ov., D, ?1823, *F-Pc* 12038

Ov./Sym., C, before 1824, frag. in H i, 175

Ov., D, ?1824, *Pc* 13107

Ov., E♭, ?1824, *Pc* 12041

Ov., E♭, ?1824, *Pn* 9151

Ov., C, ?1825, mentioned in Emmanuel

Undated ovs. and frags., *Pn* 9152, *Pc* 12040, 12042–3, 13107

concertos etc

Pf: Conc. ('no.1'), E♭, 1804, *Pc* D.11708(1–2), inc.; Conc., ?1815, mentioned in *MGG*

Vn Conc., E, ? *H-Bn*, mentioned in Bücken (1912), ? by J. Reicha

Va Conc., mentioned in *RiemannL 12*

Vc: Conc., ded. de Lamare, ?1803 (?1823), mentioned in Emmanuel; Conc., D, perf. before 1789 or between 1812 and 1814 (Paris, n.d.), ? by J. Reicha; Conc., D♯, *D-Rp*, ? by J. Reicha; Variations on a theme of Dittersdorf, *F-Pc* 12013

Fl: Andante varié, mentioned in Emmanuel, ? for pf

Eng hn: Scène, 22 Jan 1811, *Pc* 2515

Cl Conc., ?1815, mentioned in Emmanuel

Hn; Rondo, ?1820; 2 Solos (no.1, alto horn in G, ?1823): all mentioned in Emmanuel

Musical glasses: Grand solo, 25 June 1806, *Pc* 12019

Pf, vn: Grand duo concertant, *Pc* D.11709

Fl, vn: Concertante, G, *Pc* 13107, inc.

2 vn: Concertante, op.1 (Bonn, n.d.), ? by J. Reicha

2 vc: Concertante, ?1807, mentioned in Emmanuel

Wind qnt: Concertante, mentioned in Emmanuel, but see 'Chamber music without piano: wind instruments'

other orchestral

Musique pour célébrer la mémoire des grands hommes, military band, ?1809–15, *Pc* 2495, 8425

Befiehl du deine Wege, str, in *Cäcilia*, ii (1824), 272

Rondo del Sigre A. Reicha, small orch, *CH-E* 19.08

Mesdemoiselles, voulez-vous danser?, air, mentioned in Emmanuel

CHAMBER MUSIC WITHOUT PIANO

wind instruments

op.

12   Qt, D, 4 fl (Brunswick, ?1796–8)

18   Harmonique imitée ou 3 adagios, 4 fl (Brunswick, ?1796–8)

19   Sonata, 4 fl (Brunswick, ?1796–8)

20   Variations, 2 fl (Brunswick, ?1796–8)

21   Three Romances, e, G, D, 2 fl (Brunswick, ?1796–8)

22   [12] Little Duos, 2 fl (Brunswick, ?1796–8)

25   Eight Duos, 2 fl (Brunswick, ?1796–8)

26   Trios, 3 fl (Brunswick, ?1796–8)

27   Qt, 4 fl (Brunswick, ?1796–8)

—   Sonata, 4 fl, ?*c*1797, mentioned in Bücken (1912), ? *A-Wgm*, ? op.19

82   Twenty-four Trios, 3 hn/(2 hn, bn) (Paris, before 1815)

—   Concertante, fl, ob, cl, bn, hn, ?1817, perf. Paris Conservatoire, 13 Jan 1819

—   Two Andantes, Adagio, eng hn, fl, cl, bn, hn, 1817–19, *F-Pc* 12022

88   Six Qnts, e, E♭, G, d, B♭, F, fl, ob/fl, cl, bn, hn, 1811–17 (Paris, 1817)

91   Six Qnts, C, a, D, g, A, c, fl, ob/fl, cl, bn, hn (Paris, ?1817–19)

99   Six Qnts, C, f, F, D, b, G, fl, ob/fl, cl, bn, hn, 1811–19 (Paris, 1819)

100   Six Qnts, F, d, E♭, e, a, B♭, fl, ob/fl, cl, bn, hn, ?1820 (Paris, 1820)

—   Four movts, G, f, G, D, wind qnt, before 1826, ed. in H ii, 263, 274, 293, 312

strings

1   Six Duos, vn, vc (Bonn, *c*1796), ? by J. Reicha

3   Three Duos, vn, vc (Bonn, ?1796–8), ? by J. Reicha

4   Three Duos, G, D, D, vn, vc (Bonn, ?1798), ? by J. Reicha

90   Six Qts, E♭, G, C, e, F, D, ?1801–8 (Paris, 1819)

94   Three Qts, ?1801–8 (Paris, 1824)

95   Three Qts, ?1801–8 (Paris, 1824)

45   Three Duos, A, D, B♭, 2 vn (Leipzig, 1804)

48   Three Qts, C, G, E♭ (Leipzig, 1804)

49   Three Qts, c, D, B (Leipzig, ?1804–5)

52   Qt, C, *I-Bc* RR 539.1 (Leipzig, ?1804–5)

53   Grand Duo, C, 2 vn (Leipzig, ?1804–5)

58   Qt, A (Leipzig, ?1804–5)

—   Variations on a Russian theme, vc, str qt, 26 Aug 1805, *F-Pc* 12015

—   Six Qnts, *Pc* 12027–31, 12033; nos.1–2 for vc, str qt (no.1, 1805), nos.3–6 for va, str qt (1807)

92   Three Qnts, va, str qt, F, D, E♭, ?1805–7 (Vienna, 1820)

—   La pantomime, fantasia, str qt, 24 April 1806, *Pc* 12020

—   Quatuor scientifique, str qt, ?1806, *Pc* 12020 [incl. nos.3, 4, 7 of 36 Fugues for pf]

—   Qnt, E, vc, str qt, 1807, *Pc* 12026

—   Trio, 3 vc, 15 June 1807, *Pc* 12009

—   Fugue on a theme from Les deux journées, str qt, *c*1808, lost, perf. Paris Conservatoire, ?1808–9

—   Trio, F, vn, va, vc (Vienna, before 1809)

84   Twelve Duos, vn, vc (Paris, *c*1814)

—   Ouverture générale pour les séances des quatuors, str qt, 1816, *Pc* 12035

—   Harmonie retrograde à 4 and Marche funèbre, both ? for str qt, before 1824, ed. in H i, 220, 181

—   Four fugues and a variation set, str qt, before 1826, ed. in H ii, 73, 92, 127, 223, 305

—   Fugue, a/C, à 2 sujets en contrepoint à la 12ième, str qt, before 1826, *Pc* 2518 (4); ed. in H ii, 78

—   Canon, vn, va, vc, 22 June 1833, *Pc* w.23, 22 (37–8)

—   Armonia al revescio, ? str qt, 11 June 1834, *US-Wcm* ML 96.D44, 29

—   Six Duos, 2 vn (? op.1), mentioned in Bücken (1912)

—   Five or six str trios, mentioned in Bücken (1912)

—   Qt, frag., *F-Pc* 12014

string and wind instruments

51   Eighteen Variations and a Fantasia on a theme of Mozart, G, fl, vn, vc (Leipzig, 1804)

89   Qnt, B♭, cl, str qt, ?before 1809 (Paris, *c*1820)

93   Twelve Trios, 2 hn, vc, after 1810 (Paris, *c*1820)

—   Double Qt, fl, ob, cl, bn, str qt, ?1811, mentioned in R and Emmanuel, ? never written

98   Six Qts, fl, vn, va, vc, *c*1813 (Paris, before 1815)

—   Grand Trio, fl, vn, vc (Vienna, before 1815)

96   Octet, E♭, ob/fl, cl, bn, hn, str qt, ?1817 (Paris, 1820)

107   Qnt, F, ob/cl, str qt, ?1821–6 (Paris, 1829) [as cl qnt, in G]

105   Qnt, A, fl, str qt, ?1824–6 (Paris, 1829)

106   Qnt, E, hn, str qt (db ad lib), ?1824–6 (Paris, 1829)

—   Grande symphonie de salon, ob, cl, bn, hn, str qt, ?1825, mentioned in Emmanuel

— Qnt, bn, str qt, 1826, *Pc* 12032
— Grande symphonie de salon [no.1], fl, ob, cl, bn, hn, str qt, db, ?1827, mentioned in Emmanuel
— Grande symphonie de salon no.2, fl, ob, cl, bn, hn, str qt, db, ?1827, mentioned in Emmanuel
— Diecetto, A, fl, ob, cl, bn, hn, str qt, db, ?1827–8, mentioned in Emmanuel; ? same as Grande symphonie de salon no.1 or 2
— Qnt [no.4], E♭, fl, cl, bn, hn, va, *A-Wn*
— Two qts, fl, vn, va, vc, ? from op.98, *F-Pc* 9154
— Variations, bn, str qt, *Pc* 12012
— Grand duo concertant, B♭-cl, A-cl, str qt (?db ad lib), mentioned in R and Bücken (1912) [? never written]
— Octet, ob, cl, bn, hn, str qt, db ad lib, mentioned in Emmanuel
— Concertante, *Pc* 13107

CHAMBER MUSIC WITH PIANO

— Rondeau, vn, pf, ?1800, *F-Pc* 2514
47 Sonata, C, vn, vc, pf, ?1800 (Leipzig, 1804)
44 Vn Sonata, C, ?1802–3 (Leipzig, 1804)
54 Fl Sonata, G, ?1802–3 (Leipzig, ?1804–5)
55 Two Vn Sonatas, B♭, E♭, ?1802–3 (Leipzig, ?1804–5)
62 Vn Sonata, A, ?1802–3 (Leipzig, 1808)
— Qnt, 2 vn, va, ?va/vc, musical glasses, ?1806, mentioned in Emmanuel and Bücken (1912)
— Duo, bn, pf, B♭, ?1810–15, *Pc* 2513
— Solo, e, hn, pf, ?1810–15, *Pc* 2500
103 Grand duo concertant, D, fl, pf, ?1818–20 (Paris, 1824)
104 Grand quatuor concertant, E♭, fl/vn, vc, bn/vc, pf (Paris, 1824)
101 Six trios concertants, vn, vc, pf, E♭, d, C, F, D, A, 1824 (Paris, 1824)
— Grand Trio no.6, vn, vc, pf, 1824, *Pc* 12008
— Grand duo concertant, A, vn, pf, 1826, *Pc* 2499
— Pf Qnt, 1826, *Pc* 12025
— Twelve Vn Sonatas, mentioned in *RiemannL 12*
— Adagio from a vc conc., arr. for vc, pf (Berlin, n.d.), mentioned in R
— Trio, vn, vc, pf, *C* 1075

PIANO SOLO

(dated)

23 Différentes pièces (Brunswick, ?1796–8)
— Rondos, Fantasia (Brunswick, ?1796–8)
— Twelve Fugues, ?1799 (Paris, 1800–01)
30 Etudes ou Exercices (Paris, c1800–01) [incl. nos.2, 9, 23–4 of Practische Beispiele: see 'Theoretical works']
31 Etude de transitions et 2 fantaisies (Paris, 1802)
32 Fugue on a theme of D. Scarlatti (Paris, 1802)
— Thirty-six fugues (Vienna, 1803) [incl. op.32, fantasia from op.31, no.9 from op.30, nos.10 and 22 of Practische Beispiele (see 'Theoretical works') and 12 Fugues, 1799]
40 Sonata, E (Leipzig, 1803)
57 L'art de varier (Leipzig, ?1803–4) [57 variations on an original theme]
43 Sonata, E♭ (Leipzig, 1804)
46 Three Sonatas, G, B♭, E (Leipzig, 1804)
— Sonata, E♭, ?1804–5, *F-Pc* 2497
59 [2] Fantasias, C, F (Leipzig, 1805)
61 Fantasia, e (Leipzig, 1807) [no.13 of Practische Beispiele: see 'Theoretical works']
81 Six Fugues (Paris, 1810)
83 Variations on an original theme (Paris, before 1815)
85 Variations on the air 'Charmante Gabrielle' (Paris, before 1815)
86 La victoire (Allegro brillant) (Paris, before 1815)
87 Variations on a theme of Gluck (Paris, before 1815)
— L'enharmonique, 1815, *Pc* 12069, no.16 of op.97
97 [34] Etudes dans le genre fugué [La fugue et le contrepoint; 34 études de fugues et contrepoint], ?1815–17 (Paris, n.d.)
— Fugue analysée sous le rapport de l'harmonie, before 1818, in *Cours de composition musicale*, 263
102 Etudes de piano ou 57 variations sur un thème [by Grétry], suivies d'un rondeau (Paris, c1820)
— Allegretto, A, 1822, *US-NH*
— Harmonie retrograde, 18 Nov 1825, *F-Pc* w.7(9)
— Fugue à 3 dans le style moderne, before 1826, ed. in H ii, 41

(undated)

— Air de ballet, *Pc* 12067
— Allegretto, *Pc* 12065
— Andante varié, *Pc* L.13.810
— Andantino, A, *Pn* 3830(2)
— Capriccio, *Pc* 12077
— Fantaisie sur l'harmonie précédente, 5 fantasias, *Pc* 12068
— Fantaisie sur un seul accord, *Pc* 12063
— Fantasia on a theme of Frescobaldi, *Pc* 12062
— La chercheuse d'esprit, arr. of 13 Fr. 16th-century ariettas, *Pc* 12066
— L'espiègle, *Pc* 12070

— Marche funèbre, G, *Pc* 2501
— Marche funèbre, *Pc* 2516; ? from Musique pour célébrer, see 'Other orchestral'
— Prelude, E♭, *Pn* 3830(3), inc.
— Three rondos, *Pc* 12064, 2 in *Pc* 12078(1–2)
— Sonate facile (La pastorale), *Pc* 12061
— Sonata, F (Variations on a theme of Mozart), *Pc* 2501
— Six sonatas, C, *Pc* 2498, D, 1st movt and finale ('La folie'), *Pc* 2502, 3 in *Pc* 8458, *Pc* 12072
— Variations, E♭, *Pc* L.13.809
— Untitled pieces, sonata movts, *Pc* 12065, 12069, 12071, 12073–6, 12079(1–7)
— Fugue à 2 sujets en contrepoint à la 12ième, mentioned in Bücken (1912), = Fugue α/C, str qt; see 'Chamber music without piano: strings'

ORGAN

— Fugue, A, ed. H. G. Nägeli, *Die Contrapunktisten des 19. Jahrhunderts* (Zurich, n.d.)

OTHER WORKS

Scènes italiennes, 1787, mentioned in R
Canons, 5 Dec 1804, *F-Pc* 2517
Canon à 3 on the air 'Charmante Gabrielle', before 1824, H i, 194
Canon à 6, in *Cäcilia*, ii (1824), after p.272
Fugue à 3 octaves, before 1826, H ii, 177
Ressources harmoniques, 6 Nov 1835, *Pc* w.24.44, p.72
Ariette, mentioned in Emmanuel
Ariettes italiennes, mentioned in R
Canon à 4 voix, ed. M. Pincherle, *Musiciens peints par eux-mêmes* (Paris, 1939), 89
Many sketches and frags. in *Pn* 3828–32

DOUBTFUL AND SPURIOUS WORKS

(probably by Josef Reicha)

Concertante, 2 vn/?vn, vc, orch, op.1 (Bonn, n.d.)
6 Duos concertants, vn, vc, op.1 (Bonn, ?1796–8)
3 Concertos, vc, op.2 (Offenbach, ?1799)
Sinfonie concertante, 2 vn/vn, vc, orch, op.3 (Bonn, ?1795)
4 Duetti concertanti, vn, vc, op.3, *CS-Pnm* xxvi D 306 [nos.1–3]; copy in Tepelského monastery archives
2 vc concs., *D-Mbs* 1268–9
Adagio à la mort de la grande Marie-Thérèse, impératrice d'Autriche, vc, mentioned in R, almost certainly by J. Reicha
See also 'Chamber music without piano: strings', opp.1, 3, 4; 'Orchestral: concertos'

THEORETICAL WORKS, WRITINGS

(dated)

Practische Beispiele: ein Beitrag zur Geistescultur des Tonsetzers ... begleitet mit philosophisch-practischen Anmerkungen, Vienna, 1803, *F-Pc* 2496, 2510
An Joseph Haydn, poem in preface to 36 Fugues, pf (Vienna, 1803)
Über das neue Fugensystem, foreword for 1805 edn. of 36 Fugues, pf
Sur la musique comme art purement sentimental, ?before 1814, *Pc* Rés.F.1645–6
Traité de mélodie (Paris, 1814); ed. C. Czerny as *Vollständiges Lehrbuch der musikalischen Composition*, ii (Vienna, 1832) [Fr. and Ger. text]
Petit traité d'harmonie pratique à 2 parties, op.84 (Paris, c1814)
Cours de composition musicale, ou Traité complet et raisonné d'harmonie pratique (Paris, ?1816–18; Eng. trans., 1854/R1977); ed. C. Czerny as *Vollständiges Lehrbuch*, i (Vienna, 1832)
Traité de haute composition musicale (Paris, 1824–6); ed. C. Czerny as *Vollständiges Lehrbuch*, iii–iv (Vienna, 1832)
A messieurs les membres de l'Académie des beaux-arts à l'Institut de France (Paris, 1831)
Art du compositeur dramatique, ou Cours complet de composition vocale (Paris, 1833); ed. C. Czerny as *Die Kunst der dramatischen Composition* (Vienna, 1835)
'Contrepoint', *Encyclopédie des gens du monde*, vi/1 (Paris, 1836), 716

(undated)

Cours de mélodie, *F-Pc* Rés.1935
Die Grundsätze der practischen Harmonie, *Pc* 2512
Haute composition musicale, *Pc* 8°: C2.244
Kunst der practischen Harmonie, *Pc* 13376
La musique chez les grecs dans l'antiquité, lost, mentioned in Emmanuel
Notes et exemples musicaux sur la permutation, *Pc* Rés.F.1647

BIBLIOGRAPHY

AUTOBIOGRAPHY, LETTERS

A. Reicha: *Notes sur Antoine Reicha* (MS, c1824, *F-Po* Carton 2073)
J. B. T. Weckerlin: *Musiciana* (Paris, 1877), 307
La Mara [pseud. of M. Lipsius]: *Musikerbriefe aus fünf Jahrhunderten* (Leipzig, 1886), i, 350
H. Jouin: *Les maîtres peints par eux-mêmes* (Paris, 1902), 214
J. G. Prod'homme: 'The Baron de Trémont: Souvenirs of Beethoven and Other Contemporaries', *MQ*, vi (1920), 374

——: 'From the Unpublished Autobiography of Anton Reicha', *MQ*, xxii (1936), 339

M. Pincherle: *Musiciens peints par eux-mêmes* (Paris, 1939), 85ff

J. Vysloužil, ed.: *Zápisky o Antonínu Rejchovi/Notes sur Antoine Reicha* (Brno, 1970) [with annotated edn. of A. Reicha: *Notes sur Antoine Reicha*]

LIFE AND WORKS

ČSHS; *RiemannL 12*

E. Bücken: *Anton Reicha: sein Leben und seine Kompositionen* (Munich, 1912)

M. Emmanuel: *Antonin Reicha* (Paris, 1937)

OTHER STUDIES

J. Sainsbury: *A Dictionary of Musicians* (London, 1824/*R*1966, 2/1827)

G. Baini: *Memorie storico-critiche della vita e delle opere di Giovanni Pierluigi da Palestrina* (Rome, 1828/*R*1966), ii, 363ff

[?H. Blanchard]: 'M. Reicha et l'Institut', *Revue musicale*, ix/23 (1835), 180

H***** [H. Berlioz]: 'Antoine Reicha', *Journal des débats* (3 July 1836)

H. Blanchard: 'Des successeurs de Reicha', *Revue et gazette musicale de Paris*, iii/24 (1836), 200

J. A. Delaire: 'Notice sur Reicha', *Annales de la Société des beaux-arts*, vii (Paris, 1836); pubd separately (Paris, 1837)

H. Berlioz: 'Biographie d'Antoine Reicha', *Revue et gazette musicale de Paris*, v/28 (1838), 287

J. G. Kastner: 'Reicha: biographische Skizze', *Zeitschrift für Deutschlands Musikvereine und Dilettanten*, iv/8–9 (1844), 116

H. Berlioz: *Mémoires* (Paris, 1870; Eng. trans., 1969)

H. Ludwig: *Johann Georg Kastner* (Leipzig, 1886)

E. Bücken: 'Beethoven und Anton Reicha', *Die Musik*, xii (1912–13), 341

——: 'Anton Reicha als Theoretiker', *ZMw*, ii (1919–20), 156

L. de Flagny: 'Notes sur Antoine Reicha', *ReM*, vii/1 (1925), 37

L. Schiedermair: *Der junge Beethoven* (Leipzig, 1925, 3/1951)

C. Engel: Review of J. W. Christern: *Franz Liszts Leben und Werke* (Hamburg, 1841), *MQ*, xxii (1936), 354

N. Demuth: 'Antonín Reicha', *ML*, xxix (1948), 165

N. Dufourcq: *César Franck* (Paris, 1949)

M. M. Laing: *A. Reicha's Quintets for Flute, Oboe, Clarinet, Horn, and Bassoon* (diss., U. of Michigan, 1952) [with trans. by G. Hallman of A. Reicha: *Notes sur Antoine Reicha*]

K. Blum: 'Bemerkungen Anton Reichas zur Aufführungspraxis der Oper', *Mf*, vii (1954), 429

E. Borrel: *La symphonie* (Paris, 1954)

D. W. Packard: *Seven French Theorists of the 19th Century* (Rochester, NY, 1954)

Č. Gardavský: 'Liszt und seine tschechischen Lehrer', *Liszt–Bartók: 2nd International Musicological Conference: Budapest 1961* [*SM*, v (1963)], 69

W. S. Newman: *The Sonata in the Classic Era* (Chapel Hill, 1963, rev. 2/1966)

E. Werner: *Felix Mendelssohn* (New York, 1963)

I. Horsley: *Fugue: History and Practice* (New York, 1966)

W. Kirkendale: *Fuge und Fugato in der Kammermusik des Rokoko und der Klassik* (Tutzing, 1966)

V. J. Sýkora: 'Tschechische Musik der Beethovenzeit', *IMSCR, x Ljubljana 1967*, 209

S. Kunze: 'Anton Reichas "Entwurf einer phrasirten Fuge" zum Kompositionsbegriff im frühen 19. Jh.', *AMw*, xxv (1968), 289

U. Sirker: *Die Entwicklung des Bläserquintetts in der ersten Hälfte des 19. Jh.* (Regensburg, 1968)

F. Ritzel: *Die Entwicklung der 'Sonatenform' im musiktheoretischen Schrifttum des 18. und 19. Jh.* (Wiesbaden, 1968)

M. S. Cole: 'Sonata-rondo, the Formulation of a Theoretical Concept in the 18th and 19th Centuries', *MQ*, lv (1969), 180

S. Grossmann-Vendrey: *Felix Mendelssohn-Bartholdy und die Musik der Vergangenheit* (Regensburg, 1969)

W. S. Newman: *The Sonata since Beethoven* (Chapel Hill, 1969, rev. 2/1972)

H. Becker, ed.: *Giacomo Meyerbeer: Briefwechsel und Tagebücher* (Berlin, 1970)

HV, vii (1970) [Reicha issue]

J. Vysloužil: 'Antonín Josef Rejcha', *Opus musicum CS*, iii (1971), 1

S. Kunze: ' "Die wirklich gantz neue Manier" in Beethovens Eroica Variationen, op.35', *AMw*, xxix (1972), 124

J. Vysloužil: 'Antonín Josef Rejcha und die tschechische Musik', *Sborník prací filosofické fakulty brněnske university*, H7 (1972), 53

J. R. Stevens: 'Theme, Harmony, and Texture in Classic–Romantic Descriptions of Concerto First-movement Form', *JAMS*, xxvii (1974), 26–60

O. Šotolová: *Antonín Rejcha* (Prague, 1977) [incl. thematic catalogue]

PETER ELIOT STONE

Reicha [Rejcha], **Josef** (*b* Chudĕnice, nr. Klatovy, 13 March 1752; *d* Bonn, 5 March 1795). Czech cellist,

composer and conductor, uncle of Antoine Reicha. He lived in Prague with his elder brother, and, as a boy soprano at the church of the Knights of the Cross, received cello lessons from J. Werner and piano lessons. In 1774 he became the leading cellist of the orchestra of Count Kraft Ernst von Oettingen-Wallerstein at Harburg, Swabia, which was directed by F. A. Rössler and included the violinist Antonín Janič and the oboist Josef Fiala. Reicha made several tours with both these musicians; Leopold Mozart praised his playing in Mozart's Divertimento for piano trio in B♭ K254, which he performed with Janič and Nannerl Mozart in Salzburg in 1778. Reicha was married in 1779.

In April 1785 Maximilian Franz appointed Reicha cellist and leader of the electoral court orchestra in Bonn under Gaetano Mattioli. Reicha replaced Mattioli in June, and in 1789 became the director of the new theatre orchestra; in the following year he was named director of instrumental music and opera. Under his direction, Bonn's church, concert and theatre organizations performed sacred works by Caldara and Pergolesi, Italian and French instrumental music and operas (particularly Gluck, Salieri and Mozart) and German music. When the French occupied the Rhineland in 1794, the court was dissolved; Reicha died several months later.

Influenced by the Mannheim school and by Austrian music, Reicha exploited the sonorous capacity of string instruments, and his use of chromatic melodies points up his expressive style. In the instrumentation of his partitas he influenced his nephew Antoine, and in his Second Cello Concerto (op.2 no.2), as well as in other works, he may have influenced the young Beethoven. Some of the works attributed to him, in particular the duos opp.1 and 4 for violin and cello, may be by his nephew.

WORKS

Orch: 3 syms., large orch, op.5; 3 syms., 10 insts, op.7; 2 concertants, 1 for 2 vn, 1 for vn, vc; 3 symphonies concertantes, 1 for 2 vn, 1 for vn, vc, 1 for 2 hn; 4 concs., 1 for va, 1 for vc, 1 for 2 hn, 1 for vc, 10 insts

Chamber: 12 Partitas, most for 2 fl, 2 ob, 2 cl, 2 hn, 2 bn; duos concertants, vn, vc; 9 duos, vn, vc (6 as op.1, 3 as op.4)

Adagio ('Overture') [written on the death of Empress Maria Theresia]

See also REICHA, ANTOINE, 'Doubtful and spurious works'.

BIBLIOGRAPHY

ČSHS [with bibliography]

L. Schiedermair: 'Die Blütezeit der Öttingen-Wallersteinschen Hofkapelle', *SIMG*, ix (1907–8), 83

E. Bücken: *Anton Reicha: sein Leben und seine Kompositionen* (Münich, 1912)

L. Schiedermair: *Der junge Beethoven* (Leipzig, 1925, 3/1951)

J. G. Prod'homme: 'From the Unpublished Autobiography of Anton Reicha', *MQ*, xxii (1936), 339

E. Forbes, ed.: *Thayer's Life of Beethoven* (Princeton, 1964, 2/1967)

J. Vysloužil, ed.: *Zápisky o Antonínu Rejchovi/Notes sur Antoine Reicha* (Brno, 1970) [with bibliography]

PETER ELIOT STONE

Reichard, Heinrich Gottfried (*b* Schleiz, 22 June 1742; *d* Grimma, 22 May 1801). German classical philologist, Kantor and composer, son of Johann Georg Reichard. He began his studies in Leipzig in 1761 and graduated in 1768; he was appointed Kantor and *Quartus* in 1769, *Tertius* in 1782 and, in 1799, co-rector of the electoral school of St Augustin at Grimma. In addition to writing numerous literary works, Reichard composed church cantatas (37 survive, two in fragmentary form; some are of considerable proportions), nine Sanctus settings, a secular cantata, an aria and an instrumental symphony (all now in *D-Dlb*). The cantatas, of which he wrote the text himself (in free, rhyming verse) show a wide variety of treatment; those composed for the Grimma school festival were celebrated in their time. His music was influenced by that of Johann Friedrich Doles, Kantor of the Thomaskirche in Leipzig. Skilful orchestration and elements of the *empfindsamer Stil* on the one hand, and operatic virtuoso and ornamental vocal writing on the other, are the chief characteristics of his somewhat stiff but soundly constructed compositions.

BIBLIOGRAPHY

Akten des Pfarrarchivs Schleiz
C. G. Lorenz: *Series praeceptorum illustris* (Grimma, 1849)
R. Hoche: 'Reichard, Heinrich Gottfried', *ADB*
B. Schmidt: *Geschichte der Stadt Schleiz*, iii (Schleiz, 1916)
W. Steude: preface to J. G. Reichard: *Weihnachts-Weissagung* (Leipzig, 1974)

WOLFRAM STEUDE

Reichard, Johann Georg (*b* Oels, Silesia, 1710; *d* Schleiz, 2 June 1782). German jurist, composer and Kapellmeister. He studied law at Leipzig where he matriculated 5 May 1732, then moved to Schleiz where he held various juridical positions and in 1736 was appointed director of the court chapel of the counts of Reuss (in succession to Gottfried Siegmund Liebich). Seven church cantatas and occasional compositions, in part autographs, are in the music collection of the former electoral school at Grimma (now in *D-Dlb*). These are almost the sole surviving testimonies of the early musical life of Schleiz to have survived World War II.

For bibliography *see* REICHARD, HEINRICH GOTTFRIED.

WOLFRAM STEUDE

Reichardt, Bernhard (*b* Wolfersdorf, nr. Berga an der Elster, 11 March 1840; *d* Waldenburg, Saxony, 22 Feb 1907). German conductor, teacher and organist. He studied music first with his father, the Kantor Ernst Theodor Reichardt, then in Weimar with Chélard, Montag, Sulze and J. G. Töpfer before becoming teacher, Kantor and organist in Werdau, Elsterberg, Adorf and Hohenstein. From 1872 he was senior lecturer at the Waldenburg seminary, where he was appointed royal music director in 1887. He was also a music historian (an expert on organs and bells), liturgist and hymnologist. He founded the Glauchau Diocesan Society for Church Music.

Reichardt's son Ossian (*b* Waldenburg, 31 Dec 1874; *d* Löbau, 18 Dec 1942) studied at the Waldenburg seminary, where he won early recognition as an organist. He taught in Glauchau and wrote and conducted his own orchestral pieces before studying at the Leipzig Conservatory with Bose, Homeyer, Jadassohn, Kretzschmar and Reinecke. His career as a music lecturer took him to Waldenburg, Grimma, Bischofswerda and finally to Löbau. He was also a proficient practical musician and critic.

BIBLIOGRAPHY

G. A. Naumann, ed.: *Neue sächsiche Kirchengalerie, die Ephorie Glauchau* (Leipzig, 1910)
Festschrift zur Feier des 75jährigen Bestehens und der Weihe des Um- und Erweiterungsbaues des Königlichen Lehrerseminars (Grimma, 1913)
F. Nagler: *Das klingende Land* (Leipzig, 1936)

WALTER HÜTTEL

Reichardt, Johann Friedrich (*b* Königsberg [now Kaliningrad], 25 Nov 1752; *d* Giebichenstein, nr. Halle, 27 June 1814). German composer and writer on music.

1. Life. 2. Music. 3. Writings.

1. LIFE. His father Johann (*c*1720–80) belonged to the last generation of outstanding lutenists. Under his tutelage, Johann Friedrich rapidly became a violin prodigy and, at the same time, a good lutenist and singer to his own lute accompaniment; from about the age of ten he began to develop some reputation in nearby cities as a travelling violinist and keyboard player. His early teachers also included J. F. Hartknoch (a young musician from Riga then learning the publishing trade in Königsberg), a local musician named Krüger, the organist C. G. Richter, who introduced Reichardt to the music of C. P. E. and J. S. Bach, and the violinist F. A. Veichtner, a pupil of Franz Benda. But all these teachers somehow failed to give Reichardt a systematic grounding in composition, and he remained handicapped in some aspects of composition technique all his life.

Reichardt's formal education was similarly fragmented, though he made good use of his considerable intellectual gifts and was accepted into the nearby home of the Count and Countess von Keyserling almost as another son. At 15 he enrolled, with difficulty, at Königsberg University, where he led an undistinguished student life for three years. He later wrote that it was Kant's influence there which enabled him to avoid 'the customary degrading path followed by most artists of our time'.

Like other young artists of the 'Sturm und Drang' era, Reichardt began his career with years of travel. The first of his journeys began in spring 1771 with a performing tour of north German and Bohemian musical capitals; he met J. A. P. Schulz, Ramler, Friedrich Nicolai, Franz Benda, J. A. Hiller, J. G. Naumann, C. P. E. Bach, Lessing, Klopstock and Claudius. During this journey he spent two long periods in Berlin, where he attended performances of Graun and Hasse operas at the declining royal opera and French theatre, studied briefly with Kirnberger and was deeply impressed by his first substantial hearing of Handel's music. In Leipzig he began, and quickly terminated, a programme of study at the university, attended Hiller's concerts and immersed himself in the composition of vocal music and Singspiels; in Dresden he studied briefly with Homilius, a former pupil of J. S. Bach. At a concert in Prague he had to play a borrowed violin, having pawned his own. He returned to Königsberg in September 1774 with a sheaf of youthful compositions, a monograph on German comic opera and a large collection of travel notes. The monograph was published in that year as *Über die deutsche comische Oper*; a selection from his travel notes, along with letters written at the same time, was published in two volumes in 1774 and 1776 under the title *Briefe eines aufmerksamen Reisenden die Musik betreffend*.

For about a year Reichardt held a post as a government official. In September 1775, having learnt that Frederick the Great was seeking a Kapellmeister for the royal Berlin opera to succeed J. F. Agricola, he wrote to Frederick, boldly recommending himself as a worthy perpetuator of Graun's style and enclosing the score of his opera *Le feste galanti*, composed in imitation of Graun and Hasse during his stays in Berlin. By the end of the year, his 23rd, the important post was his.

Never having intended to continue his youthful imitation of the old styles beyond *Le feste galanti*, Reichardt nonetheless found himself directing operas by Hasse and

1. Johann Friedrich Reichardt: engraving (1814) by Riedel after a painting (1794) by Anton Graff

Graun, occasionally adding to them under the king's close supervision to suit aging, uncooperative singers; his own more progressive operatic creations were ignored. By way of compensation he devoted more of his energies to writing, and to the composition of dramatic works as much unlike the old Italian operas as possible. In 1777 he wrote a melodrama *Cephalus und Prokris* for the flourishing new German opera house. He was able to leave Berlin for long periods, and spent time in Hamburg, Dessau, Weimar and Königsberg. He married Juliane Benda, Franz Benda's daughter, in 1776, and remarried soon after she died in 1783. During these years he avidly pursued friendships with such illustrious contemporaries as Goethe, Herder, J. G. Jacobi, Lavater and Moses Mendelssohn. His home was a meeting-place for artists and intellectuals; as a boy Ludwig Tieck was a playmate of his stepson and was strongly influenced by the cultural atmosphere of the Reichardt home, where Goethe was already spoken of with reverence.

A leave of absence in 1782–3 allowed Reichardt to visit Klopstock and Lavater in Baden, Goethe in Weimar, Galuppi in Venice, and Gluck and the Emperor Joseph II in Vienna. In Italy he was strongly affected by the newly rediscovered works of Palestrina; in Vienna he listened devotedly to Haydn symphonies, Mozart operas and the aging Gluck's personal demonstrations of poetic vocal declamation. In 1783 he founded the Berlin Concert Spirituel in imitation of the Paris institution of that name, featuring his own music and that of such composers as Haydn and Handel. Another leave of absence in 1785 took him to England and France. In Paris he had begun to compose on commission two operas, *Tamerlan* and *Panthée*, when he had to return to Berlin in October 1785. Further leave was granted, and he returned to Paris in early 1786, finishing *Tamerlan* on the way; but contract difficulties delayed the production, and he soon realized that the fickle Parisians had lost interest in him during his

absence. He gave vent to his disappointment and indignation in an indictment addressed 'to the musical public' which went far to earn him a reputation for arrogance.

With the death of Frederick the Great in 1786 the new king, Friedrich Wilhelm II, gave Reichardt full authority as Kapellmeister, raised his salary, hired new musicians, renovated the opera house and allowed Reichardt's music to be heard at last. Reichardt became more closely associated with Goethe, Schiller and Herder. He collaborated with Goethe on the Singspiel *Claudine von Villa Bella* (1789); it was the first German opera successfully presented to the Prussian court by its own Kapellmeister, and for Reichardt it represented his metamorphosis from conductor of Italian court opera to composer of German Singspiel and lied.

But this era, the highpoint of his career, ended prematurely. During another trip to Italy at the end of the 1788–9 season a substitute Kapellmeister was appointed, and resentment and jealousy broke out among the musicians. To avert open conflict Reichardt was granted a three-year leave of absence, with full pay, in October 1790. He travelled to Paris and London again, and to Stockholm and Copenhagen. In 1792, the year of the Terror, he made himself known in Paris as a political liberal; and on his return to Berlin he even published, under the pseudonym 'J. Frei', a book sympathetic to the Revolution (*Vertraute Briefe über Frankreich*). His numerous enemies at court denounced him to the king as a Republican, and Reichardt was finally dismissed in 1794 without salary. By 1795 he had also alienated both Schiller and Goethe through what Goethe called 'his forward and impertinent nature'.

Reichardt left Berlin in 1794 to settle on a country estate in Giebichenstein, near Halle. In 1796 he was pardoned by Friedrich Wilhelm and appointed director of the Halle salt mines, a position which gave him leisure to pursue his own interests. Giebichenstein became a 'hostel of Romanticism' for such artists and intellectuals as Goethe (now reconciled), von Arnim, Brentano, E. T. A. Hoffmann, Tieck, the brothers Grimm, Fichte, Jean Paul, Schleiermacher, Novalis, Schlegel and J. H. Voss. It was a centre of lieder and romantic poetry, folksong and folk art, Singspiel and German opera.

In 1806 Napoleon's troops occupied parts of Prussia, and also Halle and Giebichenstein. Reichardt and his family fled to north Germany, and returned in October 1807 to find Giebichenstein in ruins. Within a few months the now destitute Reichardt was brought to Kassel by Jérôme Buonaparte as *Directeur général des théâtres et de son orchestre*. He faced his work there with little enthusiasm, and by autumn 1808 he had once again set out on travels, supposedly to hire new singers for the opera; but he was held in disfavour by his new patron – who offered the post, in vain, to Beethoven at about this time – and never returned to Kassel. He spent several months in Vienna, where he visited the great names of his acquaintance and was entertained as a famous musician. At this time he wrote one of his most substantial travel diaries, the *Vertraute Briefe geschrieben auf einer Reise nach Wien*, an account of Vienna's music at the height of its most celebrated era. Returning to Giebichenstein in July 1809 with barely enough money to support his family, he had to depend on income from writing and composing until 1811, when he was given a small pension. He made several more journeys, to Berlin, Leipzig and Breslau, but his brilliant reputation had gone. He died largely forgotten.

2. MUSIC. In at least two categories Reichardt's abandonment of the typically limited outlook of the German Kapellmeister proved beneficial: his songs departed from the rigid plainness of the 'Berlin School' odes towards the folk styles and dramatic gestures of early Romanticism; and his stage works, instead of centring on older styles of *opera seria*, favoured forward-looking Italian opera, Singspiel and other German theatrical forms.

The songs – he composed about 1500 of them, on texts by some 125 poets – cover a range of styles probably unsurpassed until Schubert, whom he influenced importantly. One extreme of this range is represented by the *Lieder für Kinder aus Campes Kinderbibliothek*, settings of edifying or pious verses by such poets as Gleim, Claudius, Hölty and Kleist. Uniformly strophic, seldom harmonized in more than two or three parts (with the voice doubling the upper part), and with melodies so folklike that some are still sung in German schools, this set shows Reichardt as one of the sincerest and most effective composer–propagandists in the early history of modern music education. At the other extreme are songs which present dramatic scenes: in the Goethe settings, for instance, *Prometheus* contains declamations against static harmonies, quick-changing dynamic indications and sudden alterations of tempo; the *Monolog des Tasso* is through-composed like an operatic scena; the rondo-like form of *Johanna Sebus* is determined by alternate representations of a flood and a child's attempt to rescue its mother. (Goethe was to write of Reichardt as 'the first to make my lyrical work known to the world through music'.) Reichardt's songs of all sorts show their composer's preference for strophic form, a vocal part that doubles or varies the upper line of the accompaniment (though this is less common after 1795), a style of text-setting whose clarity is probably still unexcelled, a

deference to the spirit and structure of the poem, and an idealistic adherence to the dignified simplicity that he admired in folk art.

Reichardt broke away from *opera seria* in 1785–6 with *Tamerlan* and *Panthée*, both composed in imitation of Gluck. *Andromeda* (1787) was a fortunate attempt to combine the best of the French (Gluckian) and Italian styles. Of *Brenno*, performed before the new king with great success in 1789, the composer wrote: 'more than any other [of my operas], it was conceived and worked out according to my own taste, with confidence in my own powers and with faith in a great new epoch of noble musical theatre'. Richly scored and staged, celebrating military heroism with bravura arias and an impressive triumphal procession, and demanding vocal virtuosity in the old bel canto style while prefiguring the pomposity of Spontini, *Brenno* was obviously designed to please the public in general, and the Prussian court in particular. With *Claudine von Villa Bella* (1789, libretto by Goethe) the court gave its approval in principle to opera in German, and a signal to Reichardt that the future lay in German works. Ironically, the syllabic, folklike settings and deliberately thin instrumentation were criticized by Goethe as not close enough to the 'noble example of the Italians'. A more successful Reichardt–Goethe collaboration was the Singspiel *Jery und Bätely*, first performed in 1801. Goethe's text was shortened against his will by the composer, who allegedly 'set the naive Goethe verses to several unaltered Swiss and French folk melodies'. Reichardt's aptitude for Singspiel lay in his peculiar ability to evoke folk melody in simple yet not banal songs, though he was equally capable of larger effects (as in the orchestral 'storm scene' of *Die Geisterinsel*, his most successful Singspiel). His invention of the LIEDERSPIEL, a kind of mirror reflection of the vaudeville in which already existing poems are set to new music, proved to be a dead end, as did his

2. Part of Reichardt's setting of 'Erlkönig' from 'Göthe's lyrische Gedichte' (Berlin, 1794)

experimentation with melodrama. The incidental music for plays fared better; the 'Hexenscenen' for *Macbeth*, very popular until well into the 19th century, sets the outburst of the witches against a large orchestra with rushing string figures and chromatic harmonies, foreshadowing the mood of *Der Freischütz*.

Although Reichardt was deeply impressed by the newly discovered music of Palestrina and believed with the Cecilians of the 19th century that church music should return to the *a cappella* ideal, his own sacred works were composed mainly for large chorus and orchestra and presented in non-denominational public performances; at times they even adopt operatic style. He remained a relative stranger to fugue and other contrapuntal devices even in the most conservative of these works.

The virtuoso violinist and much admired keyboard player in Reichardt was overshadowed by the *littérateur*. He clearly believed that his epoch would produce ever more valid combinations of music and literature, and that pure instrumental music would take second place. His instrumental works suffer in general from flippancy and haste, and in particular from his curiously doctrinaire adherence to the old notion – an inheritance from *Affektenlehre* – that contrasting moods do not belong in a single movement. The Classical principles of contrast, balance, development and restatement remained virtually foreign to him. His symphonies, chamber music and keyboard pieces are mainly retrospective; his concertos are not as progressive as those of C. P. E. Bach.

3. WRITINGS. Reichardt's importance as a writer and a cosmopolitan was probably equal to his importance as a composer. While much of his writing exhibits the worst along with the best characteristics of reportage – ephemeral value and immediacy, disorganization and freedom, vagueness and ardour – he must nevertheless be listed with Burney and Forkel as a pioneer of modern music journalism. His programme notes for the Berlin Concert Spirituel are among the first essays in audience instruction. The *Briefe eines aufmerksamen Reisenden* (intended, at Nicolai's suggestion, to counteract Burney's uncomplimentary remarks on German music in *The Present State of Music in Germany*) show his characteristic want of scholarly pretension: 'Do not look for organization in these letters, but instead take pleasure in the stream from my overflowing heart'. The 'intimate letter' was an ideal vehicle for such communication, one he never abandoned, though some found it offensive: in the *Vertraute Briefe* of 1808–9 the mere pleasure-seeker and flatterer was so much in evidence that the work was called a 'scrawl' by Beethoven and held in contempt by von Arnim, Brentano and Goethe.

In his work as an editor Reichardt rose to a higher level. The *Musikalisches Kunstmagazin*, a mixture of musicography and newly printed music, is still regarded as an epoch-making work; it was unusual in being addressed to the connoisseur rather than the amateur, and was still being read with interest by Schumann and his generation. It shows Reichardt as one of the journalist creators of the Romantic folk ideal in the lied, and as a music critic devoted to a new objective of the Enlightenment and of the Revolution: the improvement of the public's taste.

WORKS

DRAMATIC

Hänschen und Gretschen (Singspiel, 1, J. G. Bock, after M. J. Sedaine:

Rose et Colas), ? perf. Leipzig, Stadt, 1772; score lost, vocal score (Riga, 1773); ov., *A-Wgm* (entitled Simphonia II, 1801), ed. in DM, xcvii (1964)

Amors Guckkasten (La lanterne magique de l'amour) (Singspiel, 1, J. B. Michaelis), ? perf. Berlin, 1773; score lost, vocal score (Riga, 1773) [pubd with Hänschen]

Le feste galanti (La gioja duopo il duolo ò Le feste superbe) (3, Villati), Potsdam, Hof, 1775, *D-B*, *F-Pc*

Der Holzhauer oder Die drei Wünsche (Singspiel, after J. F. Guichard: Le bucheron), 1775

Cephalus und Prokris (melodrama, 1, K. W. Ramler), Hamburg, 7 July 1777, *D-B*; vocal score (Berlin, 1777)

Ino (melodrama, 1, J. C. Brandes), Leipzig, 4 Sept 1779, *B*, *DK-Kk*; vocal score (Leipzig, 1779)

Der Hufschmied (Singspiel, 2), Hamburg, 1779

Liebe nur beglückt (Singspiel, 3, Reichardt), Dessau, Hof, aut. 1781 (Dessau, 1780), autograph, *D-Bds*

Tamerlan (tragedy, 4, M. de Mandenville, trans. J. O. H. Schaum), 1785–6, Berlin, Königliches, 16 Oct 1800, *B*, *US-Wc*

Panthée (lyric tragedy, 4, Berquin), Paris, 1786, *F-Pc*

Andromeda (3, A. Filistri), Berlin, Königliches, 11 Jan 1788, *D-B*, *Bds*, *Mbs*, *US-Wc*

Orfeo (tragedy, 3, R. de Calzabigi), Berlin, Königliches, 31 Jan 1788, *D-B*, collab. F. G. Bertoni

Protesilao (2, G. Sertor), Berlin, Königliches, 26 Jan 1789, *B*, *Bds* [Act 1, Reichardt, Act 2, J. G. Naumann]

Claudine von Villa Bella (Singspiel, 3, Goethe), Berlin, Charlottenburg, 29 July 1789, *B*, *Bds*

Brenno (3, Filistri), Berlin, Königliches, 16 Oct 1789; vocal score (Berlin, 1789), full score (Berlin, c1797)

Jery und Bätely (Singspiel, 1, Goethe), 1789, Berlin, National, 30 March 1801, *A-Wn*, *D-B*, *WRdn*, *US-Wc*; vocal score (Berlin, ?1789)

L'Olympiade (3, Metastasio), Berlin, Königliches, 2 Oct 1791, *D-B*, *Bds*

Lila (Singspiel, Goethe), 1791, ?unperf., music lost

Erwin und Elmire (Singspiel, 2, Goethe), Berlin, ?March 1793, *B*, *WRdn*, *US-Wc*; vocal score (Berlin, 1791)

Macbeth (tragedy, 3, G. A. Bürger), Munich, Hof, spr. 1795

Die Geisterinsel (Singspiel, 3, F. W. Götter, after Shakespeare: The Tempest), Berlin, National, 6 July 1798, *D-B*, *Bds*, *WRdn*; vocal score (Berlin, 1798)

Lieb' und Treue (Lieb' und Frieden) (Liederspiel, 1, Reichardt), Berlin, National, 31 March 1800, *B*, *Dlb*; vocal score (Berlin, 1800)

Der Jubel oder Juchhei (Liederspiel, 1, Reichardt), Berlin, National, 21 June 1800, *B*, *DT*; vocal score (Strasbourg, 1805)

Rosmonda (tragedy, 3, Filistri), Berlin, National, 6 Feb 1801, *B*, *Bds*

Das Zauberschloss (3, A. von Kotzebue), Berlin, National, 2 Jan 1802, *F-Pc*

Hercules Tod (melodrama, 1, after Sophocles), Berlin, National, 10 April 1802, *D-B*, *Bds*, *US-Wc*

Kunst und Liebe (Liederspiel, 1, Reichardt), c1803, Berlin, National, 30 Nov 1807; vocal score (Strasbourg, 1805)

L'heureux naufrage (comedy, 1), ? Kassel, Hof, aut. 1808, *D-Bds*

Bradamante (4, H. J. von Collin), Vienna, 3 Feb 1809, *Tu*

Der Taucher (2, Bürde, after Schiller), Berlin, National, 18 March 1811, *B*, *Bds*

Sakontala (L. Tieck), 1812; ov. only, lost

Artemisia (3, G. A. Migliavacca), Berlin, 1785 [Hasse's opera altered by Reichardt]

Musik zu J. F. Reichardts Liederspielen (Strasbourg, 1804)

Incidental music: Einige Hexenscenen aus Schackespears Macbeth, Berlin, National, 28 Dec 1787 (Berlin, 1787), vocal score in Olla Potrida für Clavierspieler, ed. J. C. F. Rellstab (Berlin, 1789); Götz von Berlichingen (Goethe), c1790, lost; Faust I (Goethe), 1790, *DT*, *S-Skma*; Torquato Tasso (Goethe), 1791 [pubd in Göthe's Lieder, Oden, iv]; Egmont (Goethe), 1791, Weimar, Hof, 25 April 1796, *D-DÜk*, *WRgs*; Clavigo (Goethe), 1791, Berlin, National, 15 July 1803, lost; Angelica liberata oder Der Sturz des Ungeheuers, Leipzig, Stadt, 16 Oct 1797, lost; Iphigenia (Goethe), c1798, *B*; Die Kreuzfahrer (Les croisés) (Kotzebue), Berlin, National, 1 Jan 1802, lost; Die Räuber, Die Jungfrau von Orleans, Wallenstein (Schiller) [pubd in Schillers lyrische Gedichte]

Other: 2 ballets: Orpheus, Trippstrill, 1763–4, lost; Il genio della Russia e il genio della Prussia (Landi), prol to C. H. Graun: Angelica e Medoro, Berlin, 24 July 1776; Ein französischer Prolog von Madame Aurore Bursay: Venez plaisirs charmants, Kassel, Hof, 20 Feb 1808, *LEm* (inc.)

For individual dramatic arias of uncertain origin, see Pröpper, ii, 329ff

LIEDER AND SONGS

Vermischte Musicalien (Riga, 1773) [incl. 7 solo songs, 1 aria]; Gesänge fürs schöne Geschlecht (Berlin, 1775); Oden und Lieder, i–iii (Berlin, 1779–81); Gedichte von K. C. L. Rudolphi . . . mit einigen Melodien (Berlin, 1781); Frohe Lieder für deutsche Männer (Berlin, 1781); Lieder für Kinder aus Campes Kinderbibliothek, i–ii (Hamburg, 1781); iii (Wolfenbüttel, 1787); iv (Brunswick, 1790); Oden und

Lieder von Uz, Kleist und Hagedorn (Grotkau, 1782); Lieder von Gleim und Jacobi (Gotha, 1784); Kleine Klavier- und Singestücke (Königsberg, 1783) [incl. 9 songs]; Deutsche Gesänge (Leipzig, 1788)

Geistliche Gesänge von Lavater (Winterthur, 1790); Cäcilia, i–iv (Berlin, 1790–95); Göthe's lyrische Gedichte (Berlin, 1794); Deutsche Gesänge beim Clavier von Matthisson (Berlin, 1794); Gesänge der Klage und des Trostes (Berlin, 1797); Lieder der Liebe und der Einsamkeit, acc. harp, kbd, i–ii (Leipzig, 1798, 1804), ed. W. Serauky (Halle, 1951); Wiegenlieder für gute deutsche Mütter (Leipzig, 1798); Lieder für die Jugend, i–ii (Leipzig, 1799); Sonetti e canzoni di Petrarca (Berlin, n.d.); 12 deutsche Lieder (Zerbst, 1800), collab. L. Reichardt

6 Romances, acc. pf/harp (Paris and Berlin, 1805); Romantische Gesänge (Leipzig, 1805); Le troubadour italien, français et allemand, i–xxxvi (Berin, 1805–6); Göthe's Lieder, Oden, Balladen und Romanzen, i–iv (Leipzig, 1809–11), ed. in EDM, 1st ser., lviii–lix (1964); Schillers lyrische Gedichte (Leipzig, 1810); 3 Lieder von C. L. Reissig (Leipzig, 1812); Lieder von T. Körner, autograph, D-DÜk

Songs in anthologies ed. Reichardt: Musikalischer Blumenstrauss, i–iv (Berlin, 1792–5), iv as Musikalische Blumenlese für 1795; Lieder geselliger Freude, i–ii (Leipzig, 1796–7), ed. G. Ochs (Halle, 1948); Neue Lieder geselliger Freude, i–ii (Leipzig, 1799, 1804)

Other songs and arias in anthologies and MSS, see EitnerQ

CHORAL

Oratorios: La Passione di Gesù Cristo (Metastasio), 1783, D-Bds, USSR-KA; Auferstehungs-Oratorium, 4vv, double choir, orch, 1785

Cantatas: Gott ist unser Gesang (Burmann), 4vv, orch, 1778, D-Bds [for birthday of Frederick the Great]; Ariadne auf Naxos (Gerstenberg) (Leipzig, 1780); Der May: ein Wettgesang (K. W. Ramler), 2vv, 2 fl, 2 ob, 2 hn, 3 bn, 1780; Die Hirten bei der Krippe (Ramler) (Gotha, 1782); Der Sieg des Messias (Tode), 1784, SWl; Cantata in the Praise of Handel (J. Lockman), S, chorus, orch, 1785; Weihnachts-Cantilene (M. Claudius) (Berlin, 1786)

Cantus lugubris in obitum Friderici Magni borussorum regis, 4vv, chorus, orch, Sept 1786 (Berlin, 1787) [on death of Frederick the Great]; Cantata per giorno natalizio della Principessa Frederica de Prussia, 4vv, orch, 1787; Eine Geisterstimme (A. Iffland), 1787; Miltons Morgensang, 4vv, chorus, orch (Kassel, 1808) [arr. by Reichardt of C. Fasch: Hymne]; Cantate auf die Einweihung der Berliner Universität (C. Brentano), 15 Oct 1810; Cantate auf den Tod der Königin Luise von Preussen (Brentano), 1810

Sacred: Requiem, 6vv, lost; Der Säemann säet den Saamen, c1784; Der Mensch lebt und bestehet (Claudius), c1784; Der 8. Psalm, 4vv, insts, org, ?lost; Der 165. Psalm (trans. M. Mendelssohn), 1784; Der 64. Psalm, 1784; Der 65. Psalm, chorus, orch (trans. Mendelssohn), 1784, A-Wn, B-Bc, D-Bds, SWl; Te Deum laudamus, double choir, orch, 1786, A-Wn, D-Bds (autograph), KA [for coronation of Friedrich Wilhelm II of Prussia]; Te Deum zur Feier des Sieges bei Leipzig 1813, 2vv, double choir, orch, ?lost

Other vocal: An die Musik (Ebeling), 1778, lost; La danza, 2vv (St Petersburg, c1788); Il consiglio, 1788; Amor timido, 1788; Musikalische Feier zum Andenken Friedrich's den Grossen (Berlin, 1788); Trauerode auf den Tod der Grossfürstin Helena (Penig and Leipzig, 1805); Das neue Jahrhundert: eine prophetische Ode von Klopstock, 2vv, double choir, orch, autograph 1814, Bds

INSTRUMENTAL

MSS of unpublished works in D-Bds unless otherwise stated; thematic index in Dennerlein

Concs.: 9 for kbd: 6 concerts . . . à l'usage de beau sexe, hpd/pf, op.1 (Amsterdam, 1774), Bb (Riga, 1773), g, 1774, for Juliane Benda (Leipzig, 1777), G, autograph 1772; Concerto VIII, 2 kbd, 1773; 1 for hpd, vn, autograph c1773; 1 for vn (Riga, 1773), ed. in NM, clxxxi (1955)

Other orch: 6 syms.: nos.1 and 2, autograph 1773, e, c1774, ?lost, no.6, autograph 1776, D, autograph 1782, Schlachtsymphonie, 1814; Overtura di Vittoria, 1814; 2 ovs., 1776; Trauermarsch, c1797

Chamber: 3 qnts, 2 vn/fl/ob, c1774, D-SWl; 6 trios, 2 vn, b, 1774 (2 lost, 2 pubd Offenbach), 1 ed. in Collegium musicum, lii (Leipzig, 1926); 6 sonatas, 2 vn, vc, op.1 (Cffenbach, 1778); 3 sonatas, vn, va, vc, op.4 (Berlin, 1782); 6 sonatas, vn, b (Berlin, 1778), 2 ed. in NM, lxiv (1930); 6 hpd sonatas, vn acc., op.2 (Amsterdam, 1777); 4 sonatas, hpd/pf, vn acc. (Paris, 1785); 2 sonatas, fl, kbd, D (Berlin, 1787), C, c1787, ed. in Collegium musicum, cviii (Wiesbaden, 1957); 100 leichte Übungsstücke, 2 hn (Leipzig, ?1810); Vermischte Musicalien (Riga, 1773), [incl. str qt, str trio, vn sonata with vc, 2 vn sonatas with kbd; works for glass harmonica]

Kbd: Sonate der Herzogin . . . Annen-Amalien (Berlin, 1772); 2 hpd sonatas in Vermischte Musicalien (Riga, 1773); 6 hpd sonatas (Berlin, 1776); 6 hpd sonatas (Berlin, 1778); 6 sonatas, hpd/pf, op.3 (Berlin, 1782); 6 rondeaux, pf/hpd (Paris, 1785); 4 pf sonatas (Berlin, 1793); 12 variations sur l'air . . . de l'opéra Die Geisterinsel, pf (Berlin, c1800); Grande sonate, pf (Leipzig, ?1813); 4 kbd sonatas, USSR-KA, D-Bds, incl. 2me sonate . . . pour Madame la Baronne de Ertmann, autograph 1814; Kleine Klavier und Singestücke (16

works) (Königsberg, 1783); miscellaneous smaller works in anthologies

WRITINGS

Über die deutsche comische Oper (Hamburg, 1774/R1974)

Briefe eines aufmerksamen Reisenden die Musik betreffend, i (Frankfurt and Leipzig, 1774/R); ii (Frankfurt and Breslau, 1776/R)

Schreiben über die Berlinische Musik (Hamburg, 1775)

Ueber die Pflichten des Ripien-Violinisten (Berlin and Leipzig, 1776)

Leben des berühmten Tonkünstlers Heinrich Wilhelm Gulden (Berlin, 1779) [?autobiographical]

Der Weltbürger (Berlin, 1780) [lib of Lustspiel, after Goldoni]

Musikalisches Handbuch auf das Jahr 1782 (Alethinopel [?Hamburg], 1781)

ed.: Musikalisches Kunstmagazin, i–ii (Berlin, 1782–91/R)

Georg Friedrich Händel's Jugend (Berlin, 1785); ed. in HJb, v (1959)

Schreiben an den Grafen Mirabeau . . . Lavater betreffend (Hamburg, 1786)

An das musikalische Publikum seine französischen Opern Tamerlan und Panthée betreffend (Hamburg, 1787)

Vertraute Briefe über Frankreich, i–ii (Berlin, 1792–3) [under pseud. 'J. Frei']

ed., with F. L. A. Kunzen: Studien für Tonkünstler und Musikfreunde (Berlin, 1793/R) [incl. Musikalisches Wochenblatt 1791 (Berlin, 1791), Musikalische Monatsschrift 1792 (Berlin, 1792)]

Über die Schändlichkeit der Angeberei (Berlin, 1795) [pubd anon. in protest against his dismissal]

ed., with P. Poel and others: Frankreich (Lübeck and Hamburg, 1795–1805)

ed.: Musikalischer Almanach (Berlin, 1796)

ed., with F. Schlegel: Deutschland (Berlin, 1796)

——: Lyceum der schönen Künste (Berlin, 1797)

Vertraute Briefe aus Paris, geschrieben . . . 1802–3, i–iii (Hamburg, 1804)

Liederspiele (Tübingen, 1804) [libs of Lieb' und Treue, Der Jubel, Kunst und Liebe]

ed.: G. von Schlabrendorff: Napoleon Bonaparte und das französische Volk unter seinem Consulate (Hamburg, 1804)

ed.: Berlinische musikalische Zeitung, i–ii (Berlin, 1805–6)

ed.: G. von Schlabrendorff: Napoleon Bonaparte wie er leibt und lebt und das französische Volk unter ihm (St Petersburg, 1806)

'Der Rheingraf oder Das kleine deutsche Hofleben' [5-act play], 'Offene Briefe des Freiherrn Arminius von der Eiche und seines Leibjägers Hans Heidekraut', Haupt- und Staatssittenspiegel für Gross' und Kleine (Hamburg, 1806)

Vertraute Briefe geschrieben auf einer Reise nach Wien und den österreichischen Staaten zu Ende 1808 und zu Anfang 1809, i–ii (Amsterdam, 1810); ed. G. Gugitz (Munich, 1915)

'Autobiographie', AMZ, xv–xvi (1813–14) [also in Berlinische musikalische Zeitung]

For articles, reviews, editorial works in journals, monographs and collections, see Pröpper, ii, 19ff

For details of correspondence, see Pröpper, ii, 29ff

EitnerQ   BIBLIOGRAPHY

H. M. Schletterer: Johann Friedrich Reichardt (Augsburg, 1865/R)

C. Lange: Johann Friedrich Reichardt (Halle, 1902)

W. Pauli: J. F. Reichardt: sein Leben und seine Stellung in der Geschichte des deutschen Liedes (Berlin, 1903)

W. Merian: 'Johann Friedrich Reichardt und Isaac Iselin', ZMw, i (1918), 698

M. Faller: Johann Friedrich Reichardt und die Anfänge der musikalischen Journalistik (Kassel, 1929)

F. Flössner: Reichardt, der Hallische Komponist der Goethezeit (Halle, 1929)

W. Dennerlein: Johann Friedrich Reichardt und seine Klavierwerke (Münster, 1930)

P. Sieber: Johann Friedrich Reichardt als Musikästhetiker: seine Anschauungen über Wesen und Wirkung der Musik (Strasbourg, 1930/R1971)

W. Salmen: Johann Friedrich Reichardt (Freiburg, 1963)

R. Pröpper: Die Bühnenwerke Johann Friedrich Reichardts (Bonn, 1965)

N. B. Reich: A Translation and Commentary of Selected Writings of Johann Friedrich Reichardt (diss., New York U., 1973)

EUGENE HELM

Reichardt, Louise (b Berlin, 11 April 1779; d Hamburg, 17 Nov 1826). German composer and singing teacher. She was the daughter of Johann Friedrich Reichardt and his first wife, née Juliane Benda. By 1813 she had settled in Hamburg, where she became a well-known singing teacher and taught and directed a women's chorus which became the nucleus of the Hamburg Singverein (1819). She was known particularly for her untiring efforts in the production of Handel oratorios, whose texts she translated and whose choruses she prepared for performances conducted by her male colleagues. She also composed over 90 songs and choruses, both sacred and secular, to texts mainly by Romantic poets such as Novalis, Tieck and Arnim. The songs, tender and often melancholy, were popular throughout the 19th century, and have unusually graceful and lyrical vocal lines with inappositely simple piano accompaniments. Several, notably *Hoffnung* ('*Wenn die Rosen blühen*') and *Nach Sevilla*, still appear in many anthologies.

WORKS
(*printed works published in Hamburg, unless otherwise stated*)

Editions: *L. Reichardt: Ausgewählte Lieder*, ed. G. Rheinhardt (Munich, 1922)
            L. Reichardt: Selected Songs, ed. N. B. Reich (New York, 1978)
Songs: 12 deutsche Lieder (Zerbst, 1800), collab. J. F. Reichardt; 12 deutsche und italiänische romantische Gesänge (Berlin, 1806); 12 Gesänge (c1806); 6 Lieder (Novalis) (c1819); 12 Gesaenge (c1819); 6 canzoni (P. Metastasio) (n.d.); 7 romantische Gesänge (L. Tieck) (n.d.); 6 deutsche Gesänge (n.d.); Des Schäfers Klage, song (n.d.); Christliche liebliche Lieder (n.d.); 12 Gesänge, gui acc. (Breslau, n.d.); 6 geistliche Lieder unsrer besten Dichter, arr. 4 female vv (1823); 6 deutsche Lieder (c1827); Choralbuch (Basle, c1827); Choral Buch, 1822, *D-Hs*
Arr. of J. F. Reichardt: Weihnachtscantilene (Hamburg, 1827)

BIBLIOGRAPHY
M. G. W. Brandt: *Leben der Luise Reichardt* (Karlsruhe, 1858, 2/1865)
H. Weber: 'Luise Reichardt', *Neujahrgeschenk von der Allgemeinen Musik-Gesellschaft in Zürich*, lxviii (1880), 3
A. Krille: *Beiträge zur Geschichte der Musikerziehung und Musikausübung der deutschen Frau (von 1750 bis 1820)* (Berlin, 1938), 175ff
F. Lorenz: *Die Musikerfamilie Benda: Franz Benda und seine Nachkommen* (Berlin, 1967), 123ff

NANCY B. REICH

Reiche, Gottfried (*b* Weissenfels, 5 Feb 1667; *d* Leipzig, 6 Oct 1734). German trumpeter. Nothing is known about his early training, but it should be noted that Weissenfels produced many good trumpeters, among them the Altenburgs, father and son. Reiche arrived in Leipzig in 1688, apparently as journeyman to the local *Stadtpfeifer*. In 1700 he was named *Kunstgeiger*, in 1706 city piper, and in 1719 senior city piper. Between 1723, the date of J. S. Bach's arrival in Leipzig, and his own death in 1734, Reiche played all Bach's first trumpet parts. He was the composer of *Vier und zwantzig neue Quatricinia* (1696; modern edition 1927, rev. 3/1958), as well as many five-part sonatas and other pieces now lost.

His importance for the city of Leipzig was such that as early as 1694 the city council paid him a sum of money to prevent him from seeking employment elsewhere during a period of mourning. It was probably on his 60th birthday that the council engaged E. G. Haussmann, an artist who later painted a portrait of Bach, to do an oil portrait of Reiche; in that year an engraving was made from it by C. F. Rosbach (see illustration).

Although we have no reason to doubt that Reiche was a great trumpeter, modern scholars have tended to overrate his historical importance, especially as regards the coiled trumpet he displays in the portrait. Even if it should be shown (which is by no means certain) that Reiche favoured the coiled trumpet in performance, other trumpeters using the natural trumpet in its common long form, notably Heinisch in Vienna, greatly surpassed Reiche in the use of the high register, as written for by composers such as Fux, Caldara, Michael Haydn and the younger Georg von Reutter.

Gottfried Reiche: engraving (1727) by C. F. Rosbach after E. G. Haussmann

BIBLIOGRAPHY
A. Schering: 'Zu Gottfried Reiches Leben und Kunst', *BJb*, xv (1918), 133
M. Rasmussen: 'Gottfried Reiche and his *Vier und zwantzig neue Quatricinia* (Leipzig, 1696)', *Brass Quarterly*, iv (1960), 3 [with extensive bibliography]
G. Karstädt: 'Das Instrument Gottfried Reiches: Horn oder Trompete?', *GfMKB, Kassel 1962*, 311
E. H. Tarr: *Die Trompete* (Berne, 1976)

EDWARD H. TARR

Reichel, Bernard (*b* Neuchâtel, 3 August 1901). Swiss composer and organist. He studied with Charles Faller in Le Locle, Hermann Suter in Basle, Emile Jaques-Dalcroze and William Montillet in Geneva and Ernst Lévy in Paris. Having returned to Geneva in 1925, he has remained there as a Protestant church organist and a teacher at the conservatory and at the Jaques-Dalcroze Institute. His music has been influenced by the rhythmic ideas of Jaques-Dalcroze, and it bears witness to a deep religious conviction. Sensible to the work of Honegger, Hindemith and Stravinsky, Reichel has retained an individual style, producing in his later years works of youthful spontaneity and expressive clarity.

WORKS
(*selective list*)

Choral music incl. La vision d'Ezéchiel, oratorio, unpubd; Emmaüs, oratorio, unpubd; Magnificat, chorus, 1955; Récit de Noël, oratorio, 1970; cantatas, psalms, motets
Orch works incl. Concerto, org, str, 1946; Sym. Piece, 1947; Concertino, pf, orch, 1949; Sym. Suite, 1954; Pièce concertante, 1955; Concerto, va, orch, 1956; Concerto, hpd, small orch, 1961; Suite, chamber orch, 1969
Org pieces incl. Aria and 2 Variations; Theme and Variations, 1941, unpubd; Chorale Variations 'Der Herr ist mein getreuer Hirte', unpubd; 11 Chorales
Sonatas and chamber pieces; 20 Préludes, pf

Principal publishers: Bärenreiter (Basle), Henn (Geneva)

BIBLIOGRAPHY
H. Gagnebin: *40 compositeurs suisses contemporains* (Amriswil, 1956), 155ff
A. Châtelain: 'Bernard Reichel', *Revue musicale de Suisse romande*, xx (1967), 9
E. Muller-Moor: 'Pour le 70ème anniversaire de Bernard Reichel', *Revue musicale suisse*, cxi (1971), 222

PIERRE MEYLAN

Reichenau. Benedictine monastery founded in 724 on the island of the same name in Lake Constance; a prominent centre of intellectual life until the 10th century.

According to tradition, Charles Martel made the island over to the missionary Pirmin after defeating the Alemanni in 722. Charlemagne was another early patron: he made the monastery independent of the diocese of Constance. In 815 Reichenau received the privilege of immunity and the freedom to elect its own abbot. From 786 to 849 the connections of the monastery reached as far as St Denis, Corvey and Fulda in the north and Rome in the south; but by the middle of the 9th century Reichenau was already becoming second in importance to the monastery of St Gall.

The monastery school, modelled on that of Tours, was set up under Abbot Waldo (786–806) in accordance with the aims of Carolingian educational reform. Liturgical, mathematical and musical writings were produced by men associated with the Reichenau monastery school; they are of interest to historians of medieval musical theory and they contain important information about the introduction and propagation of Roman plainsong, as well as methods of instruction and performance. Such treatises, and also liturgical compositions (hymns, antiphons, responsories and sequences) were written by Abbot BERNO OF REICHENAU (1008–48) and his pupil HERMANNUS CONTRACTUS (1013–54).

The school ensured the reputation and influence of the monastery, as did the library, which was one of the largest of the Carolingian era. Its organization began under Abbot Petrus (782–6); in 821, 415 volumes were listed, including 58 sacramentaries, 12 lectionaries, 10 antiphoners, 50 psalters and 7 books with special Offices. This stock was considerably increased under Abbot Friedrich von Wartenburg (1427–53); but only about a quarter was still to hand after the secularization of the monastery in 1802–3. A few MSS dating from the 10th–15th centuries, some of which certainly belonged to Reichenau, survive in the State Library at Bamberg, the archiepiscopal archives at Freiburg, the Heidelberg University Library, and, above all, in the Badische Landesbibliothek at Karlsruhe. Most are fragments of a few pages; an exception is the MS *D-BAs* Lit.5, written in 1001, which contains tropes, sequences, offertory verses and a tonary. The identification of Reichenau MS fragments rests on the presence of festivals of saints whose relics were acquired by Reichenau in the 9th century (Pirmin, Genesius, Valens (Marcus), Januarius, Fortunata, Pelagius and Meinrad) and of the feasts of the Virgin, the feast of the Precious Blood and the feasts of the patron saints of the churches (Peter, Paul, Mark and George).

BIBLIOGRAPHY
P. von Winterfeld: 'Die Dichterschule St. Gallens und der Reichenau unter den Karolingern und Ottonen', *Neue Jahrbücher für das klassische Altertum, Geschichte und deutsche Literatur*, iii (1900), 341
A. Holder: *Die Handschriften der Grossherzoglichen Badischen Landesbibliothek* (Leipzig, 1906–18)
K. Beyerle, ed.: *Die Kultur der Abtei Reichenau: Festschrift zur 1200sten Wiederkehr des Gründungsjahres* (Munich, 1925)
R. Stephan: 'Aus der alten Abtei Reichenau', *AMw*, xiii (1956), 61
H. Oesch: *Berno und Hermann von Reichenau als Musiktheoretiker* (Berne, 1961)
H. Husmann: *Tropen- und Sequenzenhandschriften* (Munich and Duisburg, 1964)
KARLHEINZ SCHLAGER

Reicher-Kindermann, Hedwig (*b* Munich, 15 July 1853; *d* Trieste, 2 June 1883). German dramatic soprano. A daughter of the baritone August Kindermann (*b* Potsdam, 6 Feb 1817; *d* Munich, 6 March 1891), she studied with her father, and in 1870 sang in the chorus of the Munich Court Opera. The following year she was engaged at Karlsruhe and in 1874 sang in Berlin as Pamina in *Die Zauberflöte* and Agathe in *Der Freischütz*. Returning to Munich, she appeared at the Gärtner Theatre as Mlle Lange in Lecocq's *La fille de Mme Angot*, in Offenbach's *Die Schwätzerin von Saragossa* (*Les bavards*) and as Orlofsky in the first Munich performance of *Die Fledermaus* (10 July 1875). She sang Grimgerde, one of the Valkyries, in the first complete *Ring* cycle at Bayreuth in 1876 and took over the part of Erda in *Das Rheingold* and *Siegfried* for the second cycle. In 1877 she sang at Hamburg, making her début there as Orpheus in Gluck's *Orfeo ed Eurydice*, and the following year appeared in Vienna.

Engaged by Angelo Neumann for his company at Leipzig from 1880, she sang Fricka in Neumann's production of the complete *Ring* at the Victoria Theatre, Berlin (1881), Isolde in the first Leipzig performance of *Tristan und Isolde* (1882), Ortrud in *Lohengrin* and Eglantine in Weber's *Euryanthe*. When Neumann's company gave the first complete performances of the *Ring* in London, at Her Majesty's Theatre in May 1882, she sang Fricka and Waltraute in the first cycle, and Brünnhilde in the second and third. She accompanied Neumann's Wagner tour through Europe, singing Brünnhilde at the opening performances in Breslau during September. Forced to leave the company for a time because of illness, she rejoined it for the Italian part of the tour, which began in Venice on 14 April 1883 with *Das Rheingold*, in which she sang Erda. After performances of the *Ring* in Bologna, Rome and Turin, she sang Leonore in *Fidelio* at Milan (15 May) and Erda in *Das Rheingold* at Trieste (18 May) and, though too ill to appear in *Die Walküre* or *Siegfried*, she appeared as Brünnhilde in *Götterdämmerung* on 21 May. 12 days later she died, aged only 29.

Her passionate intensity, dramatic abandon and glorious voice, so Neumann wrote in a letter to Wagner after a performance she had given of Isolde, combined to make her the outstanding operatic artist of her generation. Her untimely death, only a few months after the composer's own, occasioned the remark that 'Wagner has summoned his Valkyrie to Valhalla'.

BIBLIOGRAPHY
H. Klein: *Thirty Years of Musical Life in London* (London, 1903)
A. Neumann: *Erinnerungen an Richard Wagner* (Leipzig, 1907; Eng. trans., 1908)
H. von Wolzogen: *Lebensbilder* (Regensburg, 1923)
E. Newman: *The Life of Richard Wagner* (London, 1933–47)
H. Wagner: *200 Jahre Münchner Theaterchronik 1750–1950* (Munich, 1958)
G. Skelton: *Wagner at Bayreuth* (London, 1965)
ELIZABETH FORBES

Reichert, Georg (Nikolaus) (*b* Šupljaja, 1 Dec 1910; *d* Würzburg, 15 March 1966). German musicologist of Yugoslav birth. After attending German, Hungarian and Yugoslav schools he studied at the Vienna Academy of Music and Performing Arts and with Haas, Lach, Ficker, Orel and Wellesz at Vienna University, where he took his doctorate in 1935 with a dissertation on Viennese settings of the mass in the first half of the 18th century. In 1936 he became musicological assistant to Ernst Fritz Schmid and then Carl Leonhardt (1937) at

Tübingen University, where he helped to establish the Swabian music archive and completed his *Habilitation* in 1940 with a study of the Swabian composer Erasmus Widmann. After war service he was a lecturer and assistant professor there (1946–60), and was then appointed to the newly established chair of musicology at the University of Würzburg (1960–66); he also served as acting professor at Tübingen (1951–2, 1958–9) and visiting professor at Munich (1954–6). His research was mainly concerned with sacred music (an interest which led him to consider the relationship between words and music in medieval music), tonality, dance and the music of Swabia.

WRITINGS

Zur Geschichte der Wiener Messenkomposition in der ersten Hälfte des 18. Jahrhunderts (diss., U. of Vienna, 1935)

Erasmus Widmann: Leben, Wirken und Werke eines württembergisch-fränkischen Musikers (Habilitationsschrift, U. of Tübingen, 1940; Stuttgart, 1951)

'Strukturprobleme der älteren Sequenz', *Deutsche Vierteljahrsschrift für Literaturwissenschaft und Geistesgeschichte*, xxiii (1949), 227

'Der Passamezzo: Probleme der Instrumentalmusik im 16. Jahrhundert', *GfMKB, Lüneburg 1950*, 94

'Beziehungen württembergischer Musiker zum Hamburger Organistenkreis', *Der Barock, seine Orgeln und seine Musik in Oberschwaben: Ochsenhausen 1951*, 70

'Kirchentonart als Formfaktor in der mehrstimmigen Musik des 15. und 16. Jahrhunderts', *Mf*, iv (1951), 35

'Martin Crusius und die Musik in Tübingen um 1590', *AMw*, x (1953), 185–212

Minnesang des 13. Jahrhunderts: aus Carl von Kraus' 'Deutschen Liederdichtern' ausgewählt von H. Kuhn (Tübingen, 1953)

'Die Preces-Primarie-Register Maximilians I. und seine Hofkapelle um 1500', *AMw*, xi (1954), 103

'Mozarts "Credomessen" und ihre Vorläufer', *MJb 1955*, 117

'Das Verhältnis zwischen musikalischer und textlicher Struktur in den Motetten Machauts', *AMw*, xiii (1956), 197

'Vom Anteil der Geschichte am Wesen der Musik', *Deutsche Vierteljahrsschrift für Literaturwissenschaft und Geistesgeschichte*, xxxv (1961), 483

'Wechselbeziehungen zwischen musikalischer und textlicher Struktur in der Motette des 13. Jahrhunderts', *In memoriam Jacques Handschin* (Strasbourg, 1961), 151

ed. with M. Just: *GfMKB, Kassel 1962*

'Giacomo Gorzanis' "Intabolatura di Liuto" (1567) als Dur- und Molltonarten-Zyklus', *Festschrift Karl Gustav Fellerer* (Regensburg, 1962), 428

'Tonart und Tonalität in der älteren Musik', *Musikalische Zeitfragen*, x (1962), 97

'Harmoniemodelle in Johann Sebastian Bachs Musik', *Festschrift Friedrich Blume* (Kassel, 1963), 28

'Literatur und Musik', *Reallexikon der deutschen Literaturgeschichte*, ii, ed. P. Merker and W. Stammler (Berlin, 2/1965 ed. W. Kohlschmidt and W. Mohr), 144

ed. M. Just: *Ausgewählte Aufsätze* (Tutzing, 1977)

EDITIONS

E. Widmann: *Ausgewählte Werke*, EDM, Sonderreihe, iii (1959)

Der Tanz, Mw, xxvii (1965; Eng. trans., 1974)

BIBLIOGRAPHY

H. Beck: 'In memoriam Georg Reichert', *Mf*, xix (1966), 243

Reichmann, Theodor (*b* Rostock, 15 March 1849; *d* Marbach, 22 May 1903). German baritone. He studied in Berlin, Prague and with Lamperti in Milan, making his début in 1869 at Magdeburg. After singing at Rotterdam, Strasbourg and Hamburg, he appeared for the first time in Munich on 17 May 1874 in *Guillaume Tell*, and the following year began a permanent engagement there with Marschner's *Hans Heiling* (10 June 1875). He sang Amonasro in *Aida* (13 May 1877) the Wanderer in *Siegfried* (10 June 1878) and the title role of Nessler's *Der Rattenfänger von Hameln* (15 March 1881), all first Munich performances. He sang Amfortas at all 16 performances of *Parsifal* at Bayreuth in 1882, returning to the festival in that role regularly until 1902, as Hans Sachs in *Die Meistersinger* in 1888–9 and as Wolfram in *Tannhäuser* in 1891. He

made his London début in 1882, when he substituted for Scaria as Wotan in the second and third complete *Ring* cycles presented by Angelo Neumann at Her Majesty's Theatre. He first sang at Covent Garden in 1884, appearing as Telramund in *Lohengrin* (11 June), as the Dutchman and as Hans Sachs and returned in 1892 to sing Wotan (*Die Walküre* and *Siegfried*) in the *Ring* cycles conducted by Mahler. From June 1883 to April 1889, and again from September 1893 until his death, he was engaged at the Vienna Court Opera, where he sang Iago in the first Vienna performance of Verdi's *Otello* (14 March 1888). He made his New York début at the Metropolitan on 27 November 1889 in *Der fliegende Holländer*, and during his two seasons there he sang 16 parts, which included Don Giovanni, Di Luna in *Il trovatore*, Renato in *Un ballo in maschera*, Solomon in *Die Königin von Saba*, Amonasro, Werner in *Der Trompeter von Säckingen*, Nelusko in *L'africaine* and Escamillo in *Carmen*, as well as his Wagner roles. His final appearance in Munich was at the Prinzregententheater as Hans Sachs on 11 August 1902, when the resonance of his magnificently warm and even voice was said to have been as powerful as at the beginning of his career, 30 years earlier.

BIBLIOGRAPHY

H. Klein: *Thirty Years of Musical Life in London* (London, 1903)

T. W. Elbertshagen: *Der Roman eines Sangesfürsten* (Brunswick, 1932)

E. Newman: *The Life of Richard Wagner* (London, 1933–47)

W. Beetz: *Das Wiener Opernhaus 1869 bis 1945* (Vienna, 1949)

W. H. Seltsam: *Metropolitan Opera Annals* (New York, 1949)

E. Pirchan, A. Witeschnik and O. Fritz: *300 Jahre Wiener Operntheater* (Vienna, 1953)

H. Rosenthal: *Two Centuries of Opera at Covent Garden* (London, 1958)

H. Wagner: *200 Jahre Münchner Theaterchronik 1750–1950* (Munich, 1958)

G. Skelton: *Wagner at Bayreuth* (London, 1965)

ELIZABETH FORBES

Reid, John (*b* Straloch, Perthshire, 13 Feb 1721; *d* London, 6 Feb 1807). Scottish amateur flautist, composer and musical benefactor. He combined a long and successful army career with extensive amateur music-making. He read law *c*1740 at Edinburgh University, where, on his own testimony, he spent the happiest days of his life. In June 1745 he joined the army as a lieutenant and was active in the Jacobite Rebellion (1745–6), in Flanders (1747–8) and on the American continent (1756–67). He retired from the army in 1770 intending to settle in New York State, but this plan was upset by the War of Independence; he returned to the army in 1780 and subsequently reached the rank of general.

Reid was renowned as a flautist, and his compositions were all written for that instrument. Probably he had help, at least with the harmonization of his sonatas, from James Oswald, who (like Reid) was a member of the composers' secret society 'The Temple of Apollo' in London. The second set of sonatas, originally published in 1762 as 'by I. R. Esqr', are attributed to Oswald in a later edition (*c*1775); since Oswald had died in 1769 it would seem that the reattribution was made by Reid himself as a recognition of Oswald's part in the composition of the pieces.

Reid's marches are, unusually for the period, tinged with the Scottish folk style: the opening phrases of many of them recall contemporary folktunes. The most famous is the *March for the 42nd or Old Highland Regiment*, later fitted with words beginning 'In the garb of Old Gaul' by Sir Henry Erskine of Alva (*d* 1765).

Reilly, Edward R.   711

Reid's most lasting contribution to music was, however, the endowment in his will of a chair of music at Edinburgh University. In 1839 the university acquired £68,000 from his estate and the Reid Professor was appointed; but it was not until 1861, after the fourth holder of the chair, John Donaldson, had conducted a lengthy court case against the university, that a full teaching department was set up which formed the basis of Edinburgh University's present Faculty of Music. Donald Tovey was the seventh Reid Professor, holding the post from 1914 to 1940.

WORKS
(all published in London)

6 sonatas, fl/vn, bc (2 sets, 1756, 1762)
16 marches, 2 fl/ob/cl, bn, 2 hn (1778)
19 minuets, 2 vn, 2 hn, bc; 3 marches, 2 ob, 2 hn, bc (1781)

BIBLIOGRAPHY
K. N. Murray, Marchioness of Tullibardine: *A Military History of Perthshire 1660–1902* (Perth, 1908), 387ff
H. G. Farmer: *A History of Music in Scotland* (London, 1947), 337f, 389ff

DAVID JOHNSON

Reigenlied (Ger.). Medieval round-dance song. It played an important role in the texts of Neidhart von Reuental's summer songs and was also one of the structural constituents of songs by, among others, Gottfried von Neifen and Ulrich von Lichtenstein (known as *tanzwîsen*: 'dance-tunes') in the 13th century.

The Reigenlied is not a form, in the conventional sense of that word, but rather a conceptual mould for performance – a model for oral realization. For this reason it survives only very rarely in direct musical sources. However, the choice of this manner of realization by such authors as Frauenlob, der Harder and Michel Beheim for their Meisterlieder makes it possible to establish its characteristics. Musically it is characterized by ternary rhythm, the use of repeated notes and an unusual amount of melodic phrase-repetition. Poetically, its stanzas are marked by the cumulative effect of a single monosyllabic rhyming sound, and by a preference for lines containing four stresses. The result is a uniformity which corresponds appropriately with the regular movement of the round-dance.

How this conceptual mould for performance related to existing practice in the singing of songs remains an open question in view of the scarcity of primary source-material. The cries of 'He' or 'Hei' which occur in *Ich spring an disem ringe* (Lochamer Liederbuch, no.42), for example, and also stamping and clapping, belonged to the actual presentation of a Reigenlied. They reflect its basic function as a means of expressing *joie de vivre* in springtime.

The use of *reien* (*Reigen*) as a model in performance was a test of versatility for authors of Meisterlieder. In a number of songs it clearly relates to the content of the poem. These include songs whose texts celebrate joy at the Redemption, at the Virgin, or even at mortal woman. Particularly instructive is an anonymous Meisterlied *Die dryzehen reyen* in the Colmar Liederhandschrift (Runge, no.57), in which God's plan for salvation is cast as an initial *reien* which is then followed by a series of *reien* from the fall of Lucifer through the Redemption to the Last Judgment. The characteristics listed above are particularly clear in this example.

BIBLIOGRAPHY
P. Runge, ed.: *Die Sangesweisen der Colmarer Handschrift* (Leipzig, 1896/R1965)

C. Petzsch: 'Rufe im Tanzlied', *Zeitschrift für deutsches Altertum*, xcv (1966), 204
——: 'Frühlingsreien als Vortragsform und seine Bedeutung im Bîspel', *Deutsche Vierteljahrsschrift für Literaturwissenschaft und Geistesgeschichte*, xlv (1971), 35–79 [cites earlier bibliography, which should be taken in conjunction with a monograph on the Reigenlied in the *Handbuch des deutschen Volksliedes*]
——: 'Eine Möglichkeit des Wiedergewinnens mittelalterlicher Reigenmelodien', *SM*, xiii (1971), 225

CHRISTOPH PETZSCH

Reihe (Ger.). SERIES.

Reihungsform (Ger.). Form which relies on proportion and symmetry; *see* ANALYSIS, §III, 4.

Reilich, Gabriel (*b* St Georgen [now Sîngeorzu-Nou], Bistriţa Năsăud, between 1630 and 1639; *d* Hermannstadt [now Sibiu], 12 Nov 1677). Transylvanian composer and organist of Saxon descent. He studied the organ with various Transylvanian teachers at St Georgen and Bistriţa and was organist of Protestant churches at St Georgen (1664–5), Bistriţa (1665) and Hermannstadt (1665–7). He continued to live at Hermannstadt, where he was active as a composer. His fame was assured by the *Geistlich-musicalischer Blum-und Rosenwald*, which appeared in numerous editions. It is in effect a practical demonstration of the art of composition; in the preface Reilich set out his views about the role of the composer in musical life and insisted on the necessity for rigorous technical training. He was primarily a composer of sacred vocal concertos, which are coloured by melodic elements from Transylvanian folk music. Yet they are firmly grounded in more universal Baroque practices and illustrate the distinct stylistic unity of 17th-century Transylvanian church music.

WORKS

Geistlich-musicalischer Blum- und Rosenwald partea I: bestehend in etlichen herrlichen Liedern über welche neue Melodeyen sind gemachet worden (A. Silesius), 1v, bc (Hermannstadt, 1673)
Geistlich-musicalischer Blum- und Rosenwald, anderer Theil: bestehend in etlichen herrlichen Liedern, 1v, bc (Hermannstadt, 1677)

Vesperae brevissimae, 4vv, 2 vn, bc, 1664, *R-Sb*
Ein neu-musicalisches Wercklein, von der Geburt unseres lieben Heylands, Erlösers und Seligmachers Jesu Christi, 2vv, 5 vn, welche auch auf allerhand Instrumenten, als auf Zincken, Posaunen, Fagoten und dergleichen, können gespielt werden, bc (org, lutes, hpd), 1665 (printed Hermannstadt, 1775)
Neu-musicalische Concerten, 1–5vv, vns, bc, Hermannstadt, 1668, in private collection, Freiburg
74 Concerte bisericeşti pentru întregul an, 4vv, org, 1665–73, *R-Sb*

BIBLIOGRAPHY
J. Trausch and F. Schuller: *Schriftsteller-Lexikon der Siebenbürger Deutschen*, iv (Sibiu, 1902), 348f
E. Hajek: *Die Musik, ihre Gestalter und Verkünder in Siebenbürgen* (Braşov, 1927), 124
G. Brandsch: 'Die Musik unter der Sachsen', *Bilder aus der Kulturgeschichte der Siebenbürger Sachsen* (Sibiu, 1928), ii
V. Cosma: *Muzicieni români: lexicon* (Bucharest, 1970), 380f
O. L. Cosma: 'Creaţia muzicală din Transilvania în secolul XVII', *Muzica*, iii (1972), 11

VIOREL COSMA

Reilly, Edward R(andolph) (*b* Newport News, Virginia, 10 Sept 1929). American musicologist. He was educated at the University of Michigan, where he studied with Louise Cuyler and Hans David; he received the BM in 1949, the MM in 1952 and the PhD in musicology in 1958. He taught at Converse College from 1957 to 1962. During summer 1962 he was visiting professor at San Francisco State College, and in autumn that year he joined the faculty of the University of Georgia, where he remained until 1972. For the academic year 1970–71 he was a visiting professor at

Vassar College; he was appointed professor there in 1972.

Reilly's scholarly interests range from 18th-century theory and performing practice to such 19th- and 20th-century figures as Musorgsky, Mahler and Guido Adler. His principal contributions have been the first complete English translation of Quantz's *Versuch* and a companion volume in which he investigates Quantz as a composer, traces the later history of the treatise and considers several of its more neglected or misinterpreted areas.

WRITINGS

Johann Joachim Quantz's 'Versuch einer Anweisung die Flöte traversiere zu spielen': a Translation and Study (diss., U. of Michigan, 1958)

'Composers and Congregations', *Georgia Review*, xviii (1964), 26

'Further Musical Examples for Quantz's *Versuch*', *JAMS*, xvii (1964), 157

ed. and trans.: *J. J. Quantz: On Playing the Flute* (New York, 1966)

Quantz and his Versuch (New York, 1971)

'Mahler and Guido Adler', *MQ*, lviii (1972), 436–70

PAULA MORGAN

Reilly, Tommy [Thomas] (**Rundle**) (*b* Guelph, Ont., 21 Aug 1919). British harmonica player of Canadian birth. He first studied the violin but soon became interested in the harmonica. In 1935 he settled in England and the next year toured both there and abroad. Among the finest harmonica players in the world, he has played with many of the leading European orchestras and has encouraged composers to write for the instrument: Michael Spivakovsky's Harmonica Concerto (1951) was the first such concerto to be broadcast in England; Reilly also gave the première of Robert Farnon's Prelude and Dance for harmonica and orchestra in Oslo (1966). In 1967 the world's first silver concert harmonica was made in London to a specification by Reilly. An eminent teacher, he has written books on harmonica playing and has composed incidental music for radio and television as well as film scores.

IVOR BEYNON

Reimann, Aribert (*b* Berlin, 4 March 1936). German composer and pianist. The son of the Berlin church musician Wolfgang Reimann, he studied at the Hochschule für Musik in West Berlin (1955–9) with Blacher for composition, Pepping for counterpoint and Rausch for the piano. In 1958 he also undertook musicological studies in Vienna. After completing his education he established himself as a freelance composer and pianist, being most active in the latter role as an accompanist to Fischer-Dieskau and other singers. In composition he began as a follower of Webern, but in 1967 he renounced serialism. His encounter with Indian music has left a mark on the rhythmic aspect of his music. He shows a preference for vocal music, and his important works include three notable operas, *Ein Traumspiel*, *Melusine* and *Lear*, much praised when given at Munich in 1978. Among the awards he has received are the Rome Prize (1963) and the Schumann Prize of Düsseldorf (1964).

WORKS

(*selective list*)

Operas: Ein Traumspiel (C. Henius, after Strindberg, trans. Weiss), 1965, Kiel, 1965; Melusine (4, C. H. Henneberg, after Goll), 1970, Schwetzingen, 1971; Lear (Henneberg, after Shakespeare), Munich, 1978

Ballet: Stoffreste, 1957, rev. as Die Vogelscheuchen (3, Grass), 1970

Orch: Vn Conc., 1959; Pf Conc., 1961; Rondes, str, 1967; Loqui, 1969; Conc., pf, 19 insts, 1972; Variations, 1975

Choral: Verrà la morte, cantata, solo vv, 2 choruses, orch, 1966; John III 16, unacc., 1975

Solo vocal: Ein Totentanz, Bar, chamber orch, 1960; Hölderlin-Fragmente, S, orch, 1963; Nenia, Sprechstimme, orch, 1966; Inane, monologue, S, orch, 1968; Zyklus, Bar, orch, 1971; Lines, S, str orch, 1973; Wolkenloses Christfest, requiem, Bar, vc, orch, 1974; Fragmente aus Lear, Bar, orch, 1979; Nachtstück 2 (J. von Eichendorff), Bar, pf, 1980; Unrevealed (Byron), Bar, str qt, 1980; many lieder and smaller pieces

Chamber and inst music, incl. Piano Sonata, 1958; Reflexionen, 7 insts, 1966; Spektren, pf, 1967; Invenzioni, 12 players, 1979

Principal publisher: Schott

BIBLIOGRAPHY

W.-E. von Lewinski: 'Aribert Reimann: "ein Weg in die Freiheit"', *Melos*, xxxviii (1971), 129 [on *Melusine*]

RUDOLF LÜCK

Reimann, Heinrich (*b* Rengersdorf, nr. Glatz [now Kłodzko, Poland], Silesia, 14 March 1850; *d* Berlin, 24 May 1906). German organist, teacher, writer on music and composer. He was the son and pupil of Ignaz Reimann (1820–85), a teacher and church musician, and began conducting orchestras and choirs as a schoolboy. At his father's wish he studied classical philology in Breslau from 1870 to 1874, during which period he also studied the organ with Moritz Brosig and directed the choral society Leopoldina. He graduated with the dissertation *Quaestiones metricae* in 1875 and spent the next nine years as a teacher in Strehlen, Wohlau, Ratibor and Berlin, becoming headmaster of the Gleiwitz grammar school in 1885. Following an argument with the authorities he changed both his profession and his religion, and after living privately in Leipzig for a year he went again to Berlin in 1887.

During his first stay in Berlin, Reimann had become well known as a writer (under the pseudonym Erich Reinhardt) in the *Schlesische Zeitung* and other publications, and in Ratibor he had founded a choral society. He now began to expand his musical activities, working as an organist (of the Berlin PO and in solo recitals), composer, music critic of the *Allgemeine Musikzeitung* (until 1895), at the Berlin Royal Library, where he was curator from 1893 until his death, and in 1893–4 as organ and theory teacher at the Klindworth–Scharwenka Conservatory. In 1895 he was appointed organist of the newly built Kaiser-Wilhelm-Gedächtniskirche and from 1898 to 1902 he directed the church's choir. From 1896 he gave weekly organ concerts, and in 1898 he founded the Bach-Verein, whose performances he also conducted. For his many services to the musical life of Berlin, he was awarded the title of professor by the emperor in 1897.

Reimann's musical aesthetics, expanded in his critical and analytical writings (he also wrote programme notes for the Berlin PO's concerts), were strongly influenced by his studies of Bach, but he also supported the music of Wagner, Brahms and Reger. Although most of his writings were intended for the general public, his scholarly ability equipped him to edit a volume in the third edition of Ambros's music history and to produce some valuable work on Byzantine music. He edited a series of monographs on composers (*Berühmte Musiker*), for which he wrote the volumes on Bach and Brahms. With his best-known edition, a collection of international folksongs, he became the first compiler of such a volume to present the texts in their original language. In his organ teaching he passed on Brosig's approach to the playing of Bach, with its subjective emphasis on musical expression; his most famous pupil was Karl Straube. As a composer he shared with Reger a concentration on formal principles grounded in a thorough study of Bach's music.

WORKS
(selective list)

Choral: 4 Lieder, mixed vv, op.5 (Breslau, ?1881); 2 male choruses, op.6 (Leipzig, c1885); 4 Lieder, male vv, op.7 (Leipzig, c1885); Drei altdeutsche Minnelieder, male vv, op.13 (Berlin, ?1888); [8] Liebesszenen in Walzerform (Heyse), mixed vv, pf, op.14 (Berlin, 1889); Lieder, mixed vv, op.15 (Berlin, 1889); male choruses, op.19 (Berlin, ?1889); 3 motets, mixed vv, op.22 (Berlin, 1889)

Other vocal: 4 Lieder, op.1 (Breslau, 1880); 3 duets, female vv, op.2 (Breslau, 1880); 5 Lieder, S, pf, op.3 (Breslau, 1881); 2 ballads, Bar, pf, op.16 (Berlin, 1889); Goldene Zeiten, 8 children's songs, op.21 (Berlin, 1889); Ps cxxvi, A solo, org/pf, op.26 (Berlin, 1897)

Org: Studies, op.8 (Leipzig, 1887); Sonata, d, op.10 (Leipzig, 1887); Suite, E, op.12 (Leipzig, ?1888); Toccata, e, op.23 (Berlin, c1890); Wie schön leuchtet der Morgenstern, chorale fantasia, op.25 (Berlin, 1895); Prelude and Triple Fugue, d, op.31 (Leipzig, 1905); Chaconne, f, op.32 (Leipzig, 1905)

WRITINGS

Studien zur griechischen Musikgeschichte (Ratibor, 1882)
Robert Schumanns Leben und Werke (Leipzig, 1887)
'Zur Geschichte und Theorie der byzantinischen Musik', *VMw*, v (1889), 322, 373
ed.: A. W. Ambros: *Geschichte der Musik*, ii (Leipzig, 3/1891/R1968)
Johannes Brahms (Berlin, 1898, 4/1911, ed. B. Schrader, 6/1922)
Musikalische Rückblicke (Berlin, 1900) [collected essays]
ed. H. Meisner: *Aus Hans von Bülows Lehrzeit* (Berlin, 1909)
ed. B. Schrader: *Johann Sebastian Bach* (Berlin, 1912)

Reviews and essays, *AMz* (c1887–1903); programme notes, *Philharmonische Concerte* (Berlin, 1891–)

EDITIONS

Das deutsche Lied: eine Auswahl aus den Programmen der historischen Lieder-Abende der Frau Amalie Joachim (Berlin, 1892)
Internationales Volksliederbuch: eine Sammlung ausländischer Volkslieder (Berlin, 1893)
Das deutsche geistliche Lied von der ältesten bis auf unsere Zeit (Berlin, 1895)
J. S. Bach: St John Passion (Leipzig, 1903)

BIBLIOGRAPHY

A. Lindner: *Max Reger* (Stuttgart, 1922, rev., enlarged 3/1938)
H. E. Rahner: *Max Regers Choralfantasien für die Orgel* (Kassel, 1936), 22ff
K. Straube: *Briefe eines Thomaskantors*, ed. W. Gurlitt and H.-O. Hudemann (Stuttgart, 1952), 7ff, 132f, 234f
G. Frotscher: *Geschichte des Orgel-Spiels und der Orgel-Komposition*, ii (Berlin, 1936, enlarged 3/1966), 1216
W. M. Freitag: 'An Annotated Biography of Hans von Bülow in the Harvard College Library', *Harvard Library Bulletin*, xv (1967), 246ff

HORST LEUCHTMANN

Reimann, Margarete (*b* Schiltigheim, nr. Strasbourg, 17 Oct 1907). German musicologist. After qualifying as a private music teacher at the Gumpert Conservatory in Düsseldorf (1930 piano, 1931 violin), she continued her practical training under J. Neyses and B. Eldering. From 1933 she studied musicology with Kroyer, German philology with E. Bertram and philosophy with H. Heimsoeth at the University of Cologne; she spent the summer semester of 1938 studying under Pirro in Paris. She took a doctorate at Cologne in 1939 with a dissertation on the development of form in the French keyboard suite. She then worked as a research assistant at the State Institute of Musicology (1940–45), and in 1945 took up an appointment teaching piano at the Berlin Hochschule für Musik. Later she joined its department of church and school music as a lecturer in musicology, becoming professor in 1955; she retired in 1973. She has written valuable articles on source materials and various topics connected with analysis and the history of ideas, and notably on 17th-century keyboard music.

WRITINGS

Untersuchungen zur Formgeschichte der französischen Claviersuite (diss., U. of Cologne, 1939; Regensburg, 1940)
'Zur Entwicklungsgeschichte des Double', *Mf*, v (1952), 317–332; vi (1953), 97–111
'Zur Deutung des Begriffs Fantasia', *AMw*, x (1953), 253
'Zur Spielpraxis der Klaviervariation', *Mf*, vii (1954), 457

'Pasticcios und Parodien in norddeutschen Klaviertabulaturen', *Mf*, viii (1955), 265
'Materialien zu einer Definition des Terminus und des Begriffs der Intrada', *Mf*, x (1957), 337
'Zur Editionstechnik von Musik des 17. Jahrhunderts', *Norddeutsche und nordeuropäische Musik: Kiel 1963*, 83
'Ein italienisches Pasticcio von 1609', *Mf*, xix (1966), 289
'Musik und Spiel', *AMw*, xxiv (1967), 253
'Couperin, Familie', 'Fantasie', §V, 'Frescobaldi, Girolamo', 'Invention', *MGG*

EDITIONS

Die Lüneburger Orgeltabulatur KN 208¹, EDM, 1st ser., xxxvi (1957)
Die Lüneburger Orgeltabulatur KN 208², EDM, 1st ser., xl (1968)

HANS HEINRICH EGGEBRECHT

Reimann, Matthias. *See* REYMANN, MATTHIAS.

Reimar von Hagenouwe. *See* REINMAR VON HAGENAU.

Reims (Fr.). RHEIMS.

Rein [Rain], Conrad [Cunz] (*b* ?Arnstadt, c1475; *d* before 3 Dec 1522). German composer. On 21 September 1502 he became rector of the Lateinschule at the Heiliggeist-Spital, Nuremberg, where two of his pupils were Hans Sachs and Hektor Poemer, a patrician and trained musician who later became prior of St Lorenz. Rein was in charge of choral and polyphonic music at Heiliggeist and occasionally helped with the music at the parish churches of St Sebald and St Lorenz. In 1515 he relinquished his posts and probably went to Erfurt, although he still received the income from his livings until 1522. His compositions are found exclusively in mid- and south-German sources, none of them dated before 1538. Ornithoparchus in his *Musicae activae micrologus* (1517/R1973) numbered Rein with Ockeghem, Obrecht, Josquin, La Rue, Isaac, Heinrich Finck and others as a composer whose works realized an 'ideal balance between "sensus" and "ratio" '. His few extant works are all sacred with Latin texts. Their style, though following Isaac's tradition, clearly reflects the tensions felt in German lands between the scholastic tradition and newer humanist tendencies; they are seldom unified and show occasional archaic figures, but are normally concordant and use sequential melodies.

WORKS

Missa 'Accessit ad pedes Jesu peccatrix', 4vv, *D-ERu* 473, 1
4 mass sections, 4vv, Kreisbibliothek (formerly Karl Alexander-Bibliothek), Eisenach; 2 mass sections, 2vv, 1549¹⁶; 1 ed. in HM, lxxiv (1951)
2 Magnificat, 4vv, Kreisbibliothek, Eisenach
10 motets, 4vv, 1538⁶, 1538⁷, 1539⁹, 1539¹⁴, Kreisbibliothek, Eisenach, *ERu*, *Mbs*, *Rp* A.R.886, A.R.940–41, *Rtt* F.K. Musik.76, II Abtlg., *PL-WRu*

BIBLIOGRAPHY

R. Wagner: 'Wilhelm Breitengraser und die Nürnberger Kirchen- und Schulmusik seiner Zeit', *Mf*, ii (1949), 141–77, esp. 150

FRANZ KRAUTWURST

Rein, Walter (*b* Stotternheim, nr. Erfurt, 10 Dec 1893; *d* Berlin, 18 June 1955). German composer and teacher. He turned from teaching to composition studies in 1920 with Erwin Lendvai. He was subsequently the pupil of Wetz at Weimar (1922–3) and of von Baussnern at the Berlin Akademie für Kirchen- und Schulmusik (1923–4). While at Berlin Rein became associated with Jöde, and during the 1920s was increasingly involved with the youth movement in music, ultimately emerging as a leading composer of the group. Returning to Weimar in 1925 he assumed responsibilities as Dozent, director and organizer of the Thüringen Musikantegilde. In 1930 he was made professor at the Pädagogische Akademie, Kassel, Frankfurt and Weilburg, and after 1935 taught at the Hochschule für Musik-Erziehung in Berlin. He left teaching in 1945 to devote himself exclusively to composition. Tribute was paid to his pedagogical influence after his death by the founding of Walter Rein choirs in Stotternheim and in Erlangen, where a Walter-Rein-Archiv was also established. A large part of Rein's compositional activity was devoted to folksong arrangements for chorus, many of which were published in Jöde's *Musikant* and in the *Lobeda-Chorbuch*. Even in works not openly dependent upon folksong, Rein worked with elements of peasant music.

WORKS
(for fuller list see Stilz)

Venuskränzlein, Bar, female chorus (1921); Die heilige Flamme, male chorus (1928); Erntefeier, Bar, chorus, small orch (1938); Bojen-Ballade, male chorus (1950); Minnelied, male chorus (1953); Mörike-Zyklus, male chorus, 3 horns (1953); Heimat, children's/female/male chorus, wind orch (1954); Wir spielen Zirkus (children's Singspiel, M. Barthel) (1957); Guten Morgen, 12 choral canons, n.d.; Totentanz, small chorus, fl, str orch, triangle, n.d.

Principal publishers: Eres, Greifenverlag, Schott, Schwann, Tonger

WRITINGS
'Brief', *Hausmusik*, xv (1951), 27
'Meine Erinnerungen an A. Knab', *Deutsche Sängerbundeszeitung*, xl (1951), 179
'Jugenderinnerungen eines Komponistens', *Die Kulturgemeinde*, iv (1954), no.10
'Musikalische Laienbildung', *Handbuch der Musikerziehung*, ed. H. Fischer (Berlin, 1954), 125ff

BIBLIOGRAPHY
E. Stilz: 'Walter Rein', *Musica*, vi (1952), 44
H. Gappenach: 'Walter Rein: zur 5. Wiederkehr seines Todestages am 18. Juni', *Musica*, xiv (1960), 302
——: 'Rein, Walter', *MGG*

JOHN MORGAN

Reina, Sisto (*b* Saronno, nr. Milan; *d* ?Modena, after 1664). Italian composer and organist. He was a minorite monk. From 1648 until at least 1653 he was organist of S Maria dei Miracoli, Saronno. In 1656 he was at S Francesco, Milan, and in 1660 was *maestro di cappella* of S Francesco, Piacenza. From 1662 he worked at Modena, at first both as organist of S Bartolomeo and as *maestro di cappella* of S Francesco, but from 1664 he retained only the first of these positions. It can be seen that he spent a good deal of time at Franciscan churches in northern Italy, and his fairly extensive output of sacred music was no doubt intended for performance at these and the other churches at which he worked: five of his collections – of which op.2 is lost – appeared while he was employed at Saronno. This music is typical of that produced at the time for churches where only small forces were available, and shows that he was isolated from the influence of Assisi and Padua. Several of his volumes have fanciful titles, among them op.9. The sonatas show that, unlike his contemporaries, who were writing solo and trio sonatas in a lighter style, he preferred more solid contrapuntal textures and the weightier forces of four violins and continuo, perhaps feeling that they were more suited to church performance.

WORKS
Novelli fiori: ecclesiastici concertati nell'organo all'uso moderno . . . messa, salmi, motetti, Magnificat et letanie, 8vv, op.1 (Milan, 1648)
Armonicae cantiones, 1–5vv, cum missa, Magnificat, litaniis BVM, 5vv, bc (org), op.3 (Milan, 1651) [also called Il secondo libro de concerti at the foot of p.3]
Marsyae et Apollinis de musices principatu certantibus triumphus quartus, 2–5vv, bc (org) [op.4] (Milan, 1653)
Armonia ecclesiastica, 2–5vv, bc, op.5 (Milan, 1653)
Rose de' concertati odori: germoglio VI [i.e. op.6] (Milan, 1656), inc.

Fiorita corona di melodia celeste, 1–4vv, insts, op.7 (Milan, 1660)
La pace de numeri, pubblicata con l'armonia di 5vv, bc, nel Vespro del Signore, nel Tantum ergo e nell'hinno delle grazie, vns, op.8 (Venice, 1662)
La danza delle voci regolata ne salmi de Terza e di Compieta in un Te Deum nelle tanie, 8vv, altri salmi, 1, 3vv, vns, le 4 antifone, 4vv, e in 2 sonate, 4 vns, 2 sonate, 2 vns, bc, op.9 (Venice, 1664)

BIBLIOGRAPHY
W. S. Newman: *The Sonata in the Baroque Era* (Chapel Hill, 1959, rev. 2/1966/*R*1972)

NONA PYRON

Reinach, (Salomon) Théodore (*b* St-Germain-en-Laye, nr. Paris, 3 July 1860; *d* Paris, 30 Oct 1928). French historian, archaeologist and musicologist. He was educated in Paris and worked as editor-in-chief of the *Revue des études grecques* (1888–1907), director of the *Gazette des beaux-arts* and a professor of numismatics at the Collège de France. In 1928 he was elected president of the Société Française de Musicologie, and he was also a member of the Institut. His writings contain virtually all contemporary knowledge of Greek music, and his account of classical music theory and transcriptions in modern notation in *La musique grecque* (1926) have retained their value. In his surveys of Greek notation, modes and the rhythmic relations of Greek poetry and music he emphasized his belief in the moral value of music and its influence on the development of human character, and his view of Athens as a leading centre of art in ancient Greece. His publications include the librettos for Roussel's *La naissance de la lyre* (1922–5, after Sophocles), and Maurice Emmanuel's *Salamine* (1929, after Aeschylus's *Persae*).

WRITINGS
with E. d'Eichthal: 'Notes sur des problèmes musicaux d'Aristote', *Revue des études grecques*, v (1892), 22; see also xiii (1900), 18
'La musique des hymnes de Delphes', *Bulletin de correspondance hellénique*, xvii (1893), 584; see also xviii (1894), 363
'La guitare dans l'art grec', *Revue des études grecques*, viii (1895), 371
'Deux fragments de musique grecque', *Revue des études grecques*, ix (1896), 186–215
'L'hymne à la Muse', *Revue des études grecques*, ix (1896), 1
'Fragments musicologiques inédits', *Revue des études grecques*, x (1897), 313
ed. with L. Boëllmann: *Le second hymne delphique à Apollon* (Paris, 1897)
with H. Weil: *De la musique* (Paris, 1900) [Plutarch's *Peri mousikēs*: Gk. text with Fr. trans.]
'La musique des sphères', *Revue des études grecques*, xiii (1900), 432; see also *Congrès international d'histoire de la musique: Paris 1900*, 60
'Nouveaux fragments de musique grecque', *Revue archéologique*, 5th ser., x (1919), 11
'Un ancêtre de la musique d'église', *ReM*, iii/9 (1922), 8
'Les doléances d'un professeur de musique il y a 2000 ans', *RdM*, vi (1925), 145
La musique grecque (Paris, 1926)
'Un cercle de musique militaire dans l'Afrique romaine', *RdM*, ix (1928), 12

Further articles in *Dictionnaire des antiquités grecques et romaines*, ed. C. V. Daremberg and E. Saglio (Paris, 1873–1919), *Ami des monuments* (1892), *Annales des Fouilles des Delphes* (1912), *Bulletin de correspondance hellénique* (1893–1910), *Revue bleue*, *Revue critique* (1887), *Revue de Paris*, *Revue des études grecques* (1888–1928)

Reina Codex (*F-Pn* n.a.fr.6771). See SOURCES, MS, §VIII, 2.

Reinagle. English family of musicians, of Austrian descent.

(1) Joseph Reinagle (i) (*b* nr. Vienna; *d* after *c*1775). Trumpeter. He is said to have served in the Hungarian army. By the mid-18th century he had settled at

Portsmouth, where most of his children were born. Through the influence of the Earl of Kelly he was appointed trumpeter to the king in 1762, and he appears to have moved to Edinburgh about 1763. In 1774 his daughter was married there to the cellist Johann Schetky.

(2) Alexander Reinagle (*b* Portsmouth, baptized 23 April 1756; *d* Baltimore, 21 Sept 1809). Composer, pianist and teacher, son of (1) Joseph Reinagle (i). He was a pupil of his father and of Raynor Taylor, musical director of the Theatre Royal in Edinburgh where Reinagle made his first known public appearance on 9 April 1770, playing a harpsichord sonata. By 1778 he was teaching the harpsichord in Glasgow, and his interest in keyboard teaching is reflected in his first publications, two sets of 24 'short and easy' pieces. About 1782 he brought out *A Collection of . . . Scots Tunes with Variations*, issued probably from Glasgow (not London, as the title-page indicates). He was in London in 1783, when he published six sonatas with violin accompaniment resembling the Italianate manner of Clementi and J. C. Bach while exhibiting surprising originality. Reinagle visited C. P. E. Bach in Hamburg (*c*1784), and a brief correspondence between the two ensued. He accompanied his brother (4) Hugh Reinagle to Portugal, arriving in Lisbon on 23 October 1784 (his memorandum of the journey is in *US-Wc*); on 8 January 1785 he appeared in a public concert and a week later performed for the royal family. After Hugh's death Alexander returned to England and became a member of the Royal Society of Musicians in London.

In late spring 1786 Reinagle arrived in New York, advertising himself as a teacher of the piano, harpsichord and violin; he gave a concert there on 20 July 1786. Two months later he was in Philadelphia, where on 21 September 1786 he took part in a concert given by the cellist Henri Capron. Reinagle settled there and revived the defunct City Concerts with a series of 12 evenings during the 1786–7 season. The programmes listed orchestral works by leading European composers of the time and smaller works by Reinagle himself. He was in demand as a music teacher to Philadelphia's upper class (George Washington is said to have engaged him to teach his adopted daughter, Nellie Custis) and brought out in rapid succession four publications probably intended for use in teaching: a smaller edition of his *Scots Tunes* variations; two collections, each in two books, of song arrangements; and a collection of pieces arranged for keyboard. He gave many concerts, appearing not only in Philadelphia but also in New York (1788–9), Baltimore (1791) and Boston (1792).

From 1790 or 1791 until his death Reinagle was a partner with the English actor Thomas Wignell (*d* 1803) and Wignell's successors in a theatrical company operating in Philadelphia and Baltimore. The New Company, as it was called, erected spacious and elegant theatres in Philadelphia (the New Theatre in Chestnut Street, February 1793) and Baltimore (Holliday Street, September 1794). The company's repertory was divided equally between spoken and musical works, the latter usually English light opera or ballet. In his 15 years with the company Reinagle directed the theatre orchestra from the piano, and composed or arranged music for hundreds of productions, the extent of his responsibility ranging from a single incidental song to a completely new score, or the orchestration of an existing

score. All this music, except for a few published excerpts, perished in the fire that destroyed the Philadelphia New Theatre on 2 April 1820. Three major non-theatrical works from the theatre years are also lost: the *Concerto on the Improved Pianoforte, with the Additional Keys* (1794), a *Monody* commemorating Washington's death, and an unfinished oratorio on excerpts from Milton's *Paradise Lost*.

In 1803 Reinagle moved to Baltimore, where on 20 September he married Anna Duport. His second wife, she was the daughter of Pierre Landrin Duport, a colourful French dancing-master who went to the USA after the French Revolution. Reinagle was a master mason and a member of the St Andrew's Society of Pennsylvania. His grave is in St Paul's Burying Ground, Baltimore.

Reinagle's most significant extant works are the four piano sonatas written in Philadelphia about 1790, bearing traits of C. P. E. Bach's *empfindsamer Stil*. They have been called 'the finest surviving American instrumental productions of the eighteenth century' (Krohn, *DAB*), and are the first piano pieces composed in America, perhaps the first sonatas written in the USA. Reinagle's *Scots Tunes* variations were the first solely secular musical publication in the USA, and he was first in America to replace the harpsichord with the piano in the orchestra pit. His high standard of performance and refined taste, greatly admired by his contemporaries, widely influenced the musical life of the young republic.

WORKS
(*printed works published in Philadelphia unless otherwise stated*)

STAGE
(*first performed at Philadelphia, New Theatre; music mostly lost*)
* – partly adapted

*Robin Hood, or Sherwood Forest (comic opera, 2, L. Macnally), after W. Shield, 10 March 1794

St Patrick's Day, or The Scheming Lieutenant (farce, 2, R. Sheridan), 17 March 1794, ov.

La forêt noire (pantomime), 26 April 1794

Slaves in Algiers, or A Struggle for Freedom (incidental music, 3, S. H. Rowson), 30 June 1794

*The Spanish Barber, or The Fruitless Precaution (comic opera, 3, G. Colman after Beaumarchais), collab. B. Carr after S. Arnold, 7 July 1794

*Harlequin Shipwreck'd, or The Grateful Lion (pantomime), 2 Jan 1795

*The Purse, or Benevolent Tar (melodrama, 1, J. C. Cross), after W. Reeve, 7 Jan 1795

The Volunteers (comic opera, 2, Rowson), 21 Jan 1795, vocal score (1795)

*Auld Robin Gray, or Jamie's Return from America (comic opera, 2), after Arnold, 4 May 1795, ov.

The Sicilian Romance, or The Apparition of the Cliffs (musical play, 2, H. Siddons), 6 May 1795

Harlequin's Invasion (speaking pantomime, 3, D. Garrick), 12 June 1795, ov.

The Warrior's Welcome Home (pantomime), 10 Feb 1796

The Witches of the Rocks, or Harlequin Everywhere (pantomime), 26 Feb 1796

*The Lucky Escape, or The Ploughman Turned Sailor (pantomime), after C. Dibdin, 14 March 1796, ov.

Pierre de Province and La belle Magulone (ballet, 2), 2 May 1796

Columbus, or The Discovery of America (melodrama, 5, T. Morton), 30 Jan 1797, selection (1797)

The Savoyard, or The Repentent Seducer (musical farce, 2), 12 July 1797

The Italian Monk (melodrama, 3, J. Boaden), ? after Arnold, 11 April 1798

The Arabs of the Desert, or Harlequin's Flight from Egypt (pantomime), 13 April 1799

The Constellation, or A Wreath for American Tars (dramatic sketch), 30 Dec 1799, selection arr. pf, in Mr Francis's Ballroom Assistant (c1802)

A Wreath for American Tars, or Huzza Again for the Constitution (dramatic sketch), 8 April 1800, selection arr. pf, in Mr Francis's Ballroom Assistant (c1802)

The Double Disguise (musical farce, 2, H. H. Hook), 18 April 1800
*Harlequin Freemason (pantomime, ?2, J. Messink), after Dibdin, 21 April 1800
Pizarro, or The Spaniards in Peru (incidental music, 5, R. Sheridan after Kotzebue), collab. R. Taylor, Dec 1800
Edwy and Elgiva (incidental music, tragedy, C. J. Ingersoll jr), 4 April 1801
The Sailor's Daughter (comedy, 5, R. Cumberland), 10 Dec 1804, selection (1807)
The Wife of Two Husbands (melodrama, 5, J. Cobb after Pixérécourt), collab. Carr and Taylor, 1 March 1805, ov.
Mary, Queen of Scots (tragedy, 5, J. St John), 15 Jan 1806
*The Travellers, or Music's Fascination (comic opera, 5, A. Cherry), ? after D. Corri, 20 April 1807

OTHER VOCAL

Choral: Chorus Sung before Gen. Washington, 3vv, pf/hpd (1789); Monody on the Death of Washington, 4 solo vv, chorus, ?orch, Philadelphia, 23 Dec 1799, collab. R. Taylor, lost; Masonic Ode, 1803, lost; oratorio (J. Milton) (unfinished), lost

Songs (1v, pf): A Collection of [22] Favorite Songs, 2 vols. (?1789), partly arr.; A Collection of [32] Favorite Songs, 2 vols (?1789), partly arr.; patriotic, theatrical etc songs (some pubd, some lost), incl. America, Commerce and Freedom, The Bleeding Nun, Claudine, Dear Anna, First Baltimore Hussars, Hunting Song, I Have a Silent Sorrow Here, Notes of the Linnet, Rosa, The Tars of Columbia (Columbia Triumphant; Perry's Victory), Winter; arr. songs by S. Arnold, M. Kelly, C. Dibdin, W. Shield, N. Piccinni, W. Reeve, others, some pubd, some lost

INSTRUMENTAL

Orch (all lost): Pf Conc., 1794; Occasional Ov., 1794; others

Chamber (pf/hpd unless otherwise stated): 24 Short and Easy Pieces, op.1 (London, c1780, 2/c1815, repr. c1823); A Second Set of 24 Short and Easy Lessons, op.2 (London, c1781); A Collection of . . . Scots Tunes with Variations (London, c1782; abridged 2/1787 as A Selection of the Most Favorite Scots Tunes with Variations); 6 sonatas, pf/hpd, vn (London, 1783); 12 Favorite Pieces (?1789), partly arr.; 4 sonatas, c1790, US-Wc, ed. in Recent Researches in American Music, v (Madison, Wisc., 1977); La Chasse (1794); Preludes, in Three Classes (1794); Mrs Madison's Minuet (c1796); Mr Francis's Ballroom Assistant (c1802), partly arr.; marches (mostly pubd), incl. Faederal March, Jefferson's March, Madison's March; others, mostly pubd, some lost

(3) Joseph Reinagle (ii) (b Portsmouth, 1762; d Oxford, ?12 Nov 1825). String player and composer, son of (1) Joseph Reinagle (i). He was at first intended for the navy; after the family moved to Edinburgh he was apprenticed to a jeweller there, but decided to concentrate on music. He learnt the horn and trumpet from his father and the cello from his brother-in-law, Johann Schetky, becoming a noted player at the Edinburgh concerts. He abandoned the cello because he considered his brother (4) Hugh Reinagle to be a more skilful player, though he resumed after Hugh's death. He became a violin and viola player and the leader of the orchestra at St Cecilia's Hall, Edinburgh. Some time before 1784 he went to London, where he played at the Handel Commemoration that year; he then went to Dublin, playing at the concerts there under the patronage of the Earl of Westmorland. He stated in a letter (GB-Ge) that he stayed in Ireland for two years; he was back in London in 1796 and played at Salomon's Haydn concerts. He noted that he 'had the honour of Haydn's friendship and received many serviceable hints on composition from the great master'. In the 1790s he moved to Oxford where, according to Crotch, 'J[ohn] Mahon was clarinet of the 1st band & Reinagle one of the horns. . . . Thus we kept away Bonaparte'. On the advice of Lord Abingdon (d 1799) and some other amateurs he decided to remain in Oxford.

WORKS

(printed works published in London unless otherwise stated)

6 Duettos, vc/vn, vc, op.1 (c1795) [attrib. A. Reinagle in GB-LEc, H. Reinagle in EitnerQ]; 6 Easy Duetts, 2 vc (c1797), ed. O. Huttenbach: Moeck's Kammermusik, xlviii–xlix (Celle, c1955); 3 Duetts, vn, vc, op.3 (1799); New Grand Medley Overture, pf score (1799); March [for the Oxford University Volunteers] (c1800); A Concise

Introduction to the Art of Playing the Violoncello, [incl.] 30 Progressive Lessons (c1800); Dumfries Races, other tunes, in Gow's Fifth Collection of Strathspey Reels (Dunkeld, 1809); others pubd, lost, incl. 6 str qts, Duets opp.4–5, Vn Conc., 7 vc concs.

(4) Hugh Reinagle (b Edinburgh, c1764; d Lisbon, 19 March 1785). Cellist, son of (1) Joseph Reinagle (i). He was a pupil of his brother-in-law, Johann Schetky, and became a proficient player. He was sent to Portugal for reasons of health in 1784, accompanied by his brother (2) Alexander Reinagle.

(5) Alexander Robert Reinagle (b Brighton, 21 Aug 1799; d Kidlington, nr. Oxford, 6 April 1877). Organist, son of (3) Joseph Reinagle (ii). He studied music with his father at Oxford, where he became a teacher, organist and well-known figure in musical circles. He was organist of the church of St Peter in the East. He composed a number of sacred pieces including the psalm tune 'St Peter', and at least one piano sonata (London, 1825). He also wrote and compiled many teaching manuals for the violin and cello. In 1846 he married Caroline Orger (b London, 1818; d Tiverton, Devon, 11 March 1892), a pianist and teacher who wrote some technical works for the piano, as well as a concerto, some chamber music and songs.

BIBLIOGRAPHY

W. Crotch: [Annotations to music by J. B. Malchair] (MS, GB-Ob Mus.d.32), f.49
J. R. Parker: 'Musical Reminiscences', Euterpeiad, ii (19 Jan 1822), 170
J. C. Hadden: 'Reinagle, Joseph', DNB
O. G. T. Sonneck: 'Early American Operas', SIMG, vi (1904–5), 465, 486; repr. in Miscellaneous Studies in the History of Music (New York, 1921/R1968), 54, 64ff
——: A Bibliography of Early Secular American Music (Washington, DC, 1905; rev. and enlarged 2/1945/R1964)
'The Tune "St. Peter" ', MT, xlvii (1906), 542 [see also F. Kidson, ibid, 617; O. G. T. Sonneck, ibid, 683]
O. G. T. Sonneck: 'Zwei Briefe C. Ph. Em. Bach's an Alexander Reinagle', SIMG, viii (1906–7), 112
——: Early Concert-life in America (Leipzig, 1907/R1969)
R. R. Drummond: Early German Music in Philadelphia (New York, 1910), 57ff
O. G. T. Sonneck: Early Opera in America (New York, 1915/R1963)
E. C. Krohn: 'Alexander Reinagle as Sonatist', MQ, xviii (1932), 140
——: 'Reinagle, Alexander', DAB
R. J. Wolfe: Secular Music in America, 1801–1825: a Bibliography (New York, 1964)
C. A. Horton: Serious Art and Concert Music for Piano in America in the 100 Years from Alexander Reinagle to Edward MacDowell (diss., U. of North Carolina, 1965)
A. McClenny: 'Alexander Reinagle: an Eighteenth-century Musician with Modern Ideas', American Music Teacher, xix (1969), 38, 49
R. Hopkins: Preface to Recent Researches in American Music, v (Madison, Wisc., 1977)

FRANK KIDSON/R (1, 3–6), ROBERT HOPKINS (2)

Reinberger, Jiří (b Brno, 14 April 1914; d Prague, 28 May 1977). Czech organist and composer. At the Brno Conservatory he studied the organ with Tregler (graduating in 1932) and composition with Petrželka (graduating in 1938). He continued his composition studies with Novák in Prague (1938–40), and had organ lessons with Wiedermann, and in Leipzig with Ramin and Straube who acquainted him with the traditional style of Bach interpretation. He taught at the Brno Conservatory (1945), then at the Prague Conservatory, and from 1951 at the Academy of Musical Arts in Prague. From 1932 he gave concerts and from 1945 toured in most European countries. As well as Bach, whose works he recorded, he promoted early and contemporary Czech music. He was a member of the juries at international organ competitions, and gave master classes in Prague and Zurich. He was also co-designer of organs for Moscow, Leningrad, Cairo,

Beirut and Toronto. Reinberger's playing combined strict German registration and articulation with Czech vigour of expression, intellectual reasoning and an equal measure of feeling and fantasy. He prepared for publication the anthology of organ works *Čestí klasikové* ('Czech Classicists') (MAB, xii, 1953) and the collection *Musica bohemica per organo* (Prague, 1954–7). He also made a series of gramophone records using historical organs in Bohemia, Moravia and Slovakia. In 1964 he was named Artist of Merit. The most important of his compositions are three organ concertos (1940, 1956, 1960), two symphonies (1938, 1958) and a cello concerto (1962).

BIBLIOGRAPHY

ČSHS

J. Kozák: *Českoslovenští koncertni umělci a komorni soubory* [Czechoslovak concert artists and chamber ensembles] (Prague, 1964), 99ff

J. Kříž: 'Bilance zdaleka neuzavřená' [The account is by no means closed yet], *HRo*, xvii (1964), 284

J. Burjanek, P. Zapletal and others: *Svaz českých skladatelů a koncertnich umělců* [Union of Czech composers and concert artists] (Prague, 1975), 188

ALENA NĚMCOVÁ

Reincken [Reinken, Reinike], **Johann Adam** [Jan Adams] (*b* 27 April 1623; *d* Hamburg, 24 Nov 1722). Dutch or German composer and organist, possibly of Netherlands or Alsatian birth. The title-page of his *Hortus musicus* (1687) describes him as a citizen of Deventer in the Netherlands. His father is known to have moved there in 1637 and on becoming a burgess was called 'Adam Reincken van Wilhuisen'. 'Wilhuisen', which may thus have been Reincken's birthplace, has most often been taken to refer to Wilshausen, Alsace, though it may have been a village in the Netherlands or have denoted Wildeshausen, near Bremen, as has also been suggested. Apart from an official grant towards his musical training nothing is known of Reincken's early life. He moved to Hamburg in 1654 to study with Heinrich Scheidemann, organist of St Catharine's and a former pupil of Sweelinck (who had been born at Deventer). Reincken returned to Deventer in 1657 and became organist of the Berghkercke. In 1658 he went back to Hamburg to become Scheidemann's assistant, and in 1663 he became his successor. Only from his 80th year was he assisted in his duties and he was only five months short of his 100th birthday when he died.

There was a change in the balance of musical power in the 17th century with the political decline of Venice and the increasing importance of wealthy northern centres such as Hamburg. Here, as in Venice, the early focal point of musical activity was the church, where fine traditions of organ playing were established by Scheidemann and another Sweelinck pupil, Jacob Praetorius (ii), while such important elements of Baroque organ music as contrast, volume, texture and colour were enhanced by the organ-building families of Schnitger and Scherer. As a Scheidemann pupil, as a commentator on Sweelinck's composition primer (his copy of which was destroyed in World War II) and, predominantly, as a concert organist, Reincken was a second-generation inheritor of the Sweelinck tradition. His quite small amount of surviving organ music invariably displays a virtuoso element overriding artistic or religious considerations. This resulted from his own superb technique and his exploitation of the harmonically rich four-manual instrument, praised by Bach, over which he presided; there may well, moreover, have been a dramatic streak in his character, for he was co-

founder, with Johann Theile, of the Hamburg Opera in 1678.

Scheidemann, in treating a melody, was content, in the interests of clarity, to retain its original tonal and rhythmic contours; Reincken, with the obsessive mid-Baroque search for novelty and display, altered the rhythmic placing of the notes, subjecting them also to octave transposition and even omitting some and distributing others among the inner parts. These methods can be seen in the *partite* on *Schweiget mir* and in the lengthy fantasia *An den Wasserflüssen Babylon*, which is a compendium of the compositional and performing techniques of the north German organ school, a fine work in its own right and a memorial to Reincken's powers of execution. Techniques that became associated with this school appear in the Fugue in G minor and the Toccata in C. The subject of the former is compounded of figuration patterns of a type employed by Sweelinck, simulating the then novel string tremolo. In the five-section toccata, toccata-like passages alternate with fugal writing; after the bandying about of uninspired ornamental passages between the parts, it gets under way with a fugue, the subject of which is varied to form the basis of another, 12/8 fugal section at the end. Both works exemplify the unsurpassed finger technique of the north German organists.

Since Reincken owned a copy of a composition manual attributed to Poglietti and wrote *partite* on the Mayerin theme (*Schweiget mir*) similarly used by Froberger, he may have had as yet unidentified links with Vienna. The last three variations in his brilliant *partite*, like the corresponding ones in Froberger's more compact work, assume the character of a courante, saraband and gigue without being so named. He also wrote three keyboard suites which consist of a thematically linked allemande and courante, a saraband and a gigue, instead of adhering to the earlier, Froberger type of suite, in which the gigue follows the allemande. The forceful subjects of the gigues in the suites in G and C are inverted in the second sections.

Weckmann's amateur collegium musicum together with professional civic musicians afforded abundant encouragement to chamber music in Hamburg, but only one such publication by Reincken survives, *Hortus musicus*, comprising six suites. These exhibit certain Baroque tendencies: the customary grouping of such works in multiples of three to form an opus, the characteristic trio-sonata textures, and improvisation by the players implicit in the music, especially in slow movements. In each work the tempo indications of the *sonata da chiesa* are juxtaposed with the dance sequence of the *sonata da camera*, the former expressed in the pattern of a Grave thematically linked with a fugal Allegro, an Adagio and a toccata-like Allegro. Reincken's dedicatory preface shows that he indeed envisaged this music as suitable for church or home.

Reincken's fame as an organist and organ consultant brought him many pupils, including Andreas Kneller (who became his son-in-law), G. D. Leiding and possibly Georg Böhm. It has been said that as a young man Bach made journeys specially to hear him play and that he later gave tangible expression to his admiration for his art by basing his G minor Fugue (BWV542) on a Dutch folksong. He made masterly keyboard arrangements from *Hortus musicus* – Suite no.1 in full, no.3 in part, and the fugue from no.2 (BWV965, 966 and 954 respectively).

WORKS

KEYBOARD

Edition: *J. A. Reincken: Sämtliche Orgelwerke*, ed. K. Beckmann (Wiesbaden, 1974) [incl. all kbd pieces]

An den Wasserflüssen Babylon
Was kann uns kommen an für Noth
Partite diverse sopra l'Aria 'Schweiget mir von Weiber nehmen', altrimente chiamata 'La Meyerin'
Ballet, e
Toccata, C; Fuga, g
3 Suites, C, e, G
? 6 suites, *S–N* (see J. O. Rudén, *Svenskt Musikhistoriskt Arkiv Buletin*, ix, 1973, p.21)

OTHER INSTRUMENTAL

Hortus musicus (6 suites, a, Bb, C, d, e, A), 2 vn, va da gamba, bc (Hamburg, 1687); ed. J. C. M. van Riemsdijk (Amsterdam, 1888)

VOCAL

Geistlich Konzert 'auf Michael': Und es erhub sich ein Streit, 4vv, 2 vn, va, 2 tpt, timp, bc, *D-B* (transcr. in A. Sittard's collection)
Canon, *Bds* Mus.theor.1190

THEORETICAL WORKS

Musica amica [composition manual], formerly *Hs*, lost

BIBLIOGRAPHY

EitnerQ; WaltherML
J. Mattheson: *Critica musica*, i (Hamburg, 1722/*R*1964)
——: *Grundlage einer Ehren-Pforte* (Hamburg, 1740); ed. M. Schneider (Berlin, 1910/*R*1969)
P. Spitta: *Johann Sebastian Bach* (Leipzig, 1873–80, 5/1962; Eng. trans., 1884–99/*R*1951)
J. C. M. van Riemsdijk: 'Jean Adam Reincken', *TVNM*, ii/1 (1887), 61
M. E. Houck: 'J(e)an Adam(s) Reincken', *TVNM*, vi/2 (1899), 151
M. Seiffert: *Geschichte der Klavier-Musik* (Leipzig, 1899), 255
W. Stahl: 'Zur Biographie J. A. Reinckens', *AMw*, iii (1920–21), 232
A. Pirro: 'Notes pour servir, eventuellement, à la biographie de Reincken', *Gedenkboek aangeboden aan Dr. D. F. Scheurleer* (The Hague, 1925), 257
L. Krüger: *Die Hamburgische Musikorganisation im 17. Jahrhundert* (Strasbourg, 1933)
G. Frotscher: *Geschichte des Orgel-Spiels und der Orgel-Komposition*, i (Berlin, 1935, enlarged 3/1966)
F. W. Riedel: *Quellenkundliche Beiträge zur Geschichte der Musik für Tasteninstrumente in der 2. Hälfte des 17. Jahrhunderts (vornehmlich in Deutschland)* (Kassel, 1960)
W. Apel: 'Neu aufgefundene Clavierwerke von Schiedemann, Tunder, Froberger, Reincken und Buxtehude', *AcM*, xxxiv (1962), 65
——: *Geschichte der Orgel- und Klaviermusik bis 1700* (Kassel, 1967; Eng. trans., rev. 1972)
G. B. Sharp: 'Jan Adam Reincken, 1623–1722', *MT*, cxiv (1973), 1272

G. B. SHARP

Reindl, Constantin (*b* Jettenhofen, Upper Palatinate, 29 June 1738; *d* Lucerne, 25 March 1799). German composer active in Switzerland. The son of an official in the service of the Prince-Bishop of Eichstätt, in 1756 he entered the novitiate of the Jesuit order in Landsberg. He studied philosophy and theology in Ingolstadt, Dillingen and Freiburg and was ordained priest in 1769. In 1770 he became a teacher at the college in Freiburg, and in 1772 was transferred to a teaching post at the Gymnasium in Lucerne; he succeeded Abbé Joseph Bullinger (known for his association with the Mozart family) as the city's director of music (*Musikpräfekt*). Reindl continued in these posts even after the dissolution of the Jesuit order in 1773. From 1775 to 1777 he also worked at the seminary in St Urban. The highpoint of Reindl's creative output consists of stage works – Singspiels and comic operettas in a light *buffo* style (generally without overtures) – which became the characteristic repertory of the Lucerne school theatre in its heyday.

WORKS

Stage (mostly Singspiels, first performed in Lucerne): Die Sempacherschlacht, 1779, *CH-Lz*; Der Dorfschulmeister, 1784, *Lz*; Das Donnerwetter oder Der Bettelstudent, 1787, *Lmg*, *Lz*; Der Dorfhirt, 1789, *Lmg*, *Lz*; Arlequino in verschiedenen Ständen (pantomime), 1790, *Lz*; Der betrogene Dieb, 1791, *Lz*; Der eingebildete Kranke, 1792, *Lz*; Lebet wohl, 1795, *Lz*; Das neugierige Frauenzimmer, 1796, *Lmg*; Abraham und Isaack, frag. *Lmg*;

Pantomimische Oper, *Lz*; 9 others, lost
Vocal: 3 masses, *E*, *EN*, *Lmg*; Laudate Dominum, *E*; 8 other sacred works, *E*, *SAf*
Inst: 1 sym., *Lmg*; 1 sym., *E*; 1 symphonie concertante, 1794, *Lmg*; Divertimento, *Lmg*; 12 Menuette (? n.p., n.d.), lost; 6 str qts (Lyons, n.d.), lost; 26 str qts, Turkish music (orch), Vn Conc., all lost

BIBLIOGRAPHY

A. Geering: 'Von der Reformation bis zur Romantik', *Schweizer Musikbuch*, ed. W. Schuh, i (Zurich, 1939), 54–114, esp. 96
W. Jerger: *Constantin Reindl* (Fribourg, 1955)
——: 'Constantin Reindl, ein unbekannter Zeitgenosse W. A. Mozarts', *MJb 1954*, 143
——: 'Zur Musikgeschichte der deutschsprachigen Schweiz im 18. Jahrhundert', *Mf*, xiv (1961), 303

WILHELM JERGER

Reinecke, Carl (Heinrich Carsten) (*b* Altona, 23 June 1824; *d* Leipzig, 10 March 1910). German composer, teacher, administrator, pianist and conductor. He was given a thorough musical education by his father, J. P. Rudolf Reinecke (*b* Hamburg, 22 Nov 1795; *d* Segeberg, 14 Aug 1883), a respected music theoretician and author of several textbooks. From 1845 Reinecke travelled through Europe, from Danzig to Riga; in Copenhagen he was appointed court pianist in 1846, where his duties included accompanying the violinist H. W. Ernst as well as giving solo recitals. He was given a particularly friendly reception in Leipzig by Mendelssohn and the Schumanns, and Liszt, whose daughter was later taught by Reinecke in Paris, spoke of his 'beautiful, gentle, legato and lyrical touch'. In 1851 he moved to Cologne, where he taught counterpoint and the piano at Hiller's conservatory. He also gave concerts with Hiller, who recommended him to Barmen. There as musical director and the conductor of several musical societies between 1854 and 1859, he significantly raised the standard of the town's musical life. He then spent ten months in Breslau as director of music at the university and conductor of the Singakademie.

By 1860 his growing reputation brought him an appointment to teach at the Leipzig Conservatory, where he became the director in 1897. By selecting capable teachers who shared his conservative views and by improving the facilities and the syllabus, Reinecke transformed the conservatory into one of the most renowned in Europe. Grieg, Kretzschmar, Kwast, Muck, Riemann, Sinding, Svendsen, Sullivan and Weingartner were all pupils there; and to this distinguished list could be added many other names of equal repute, showing how exaggerated was the reproach, made particularly in north Germany, that Leipzig was a hotbed of reaction (although this criticism had some justification after 1880). But it cannot be denied that Reinecke considered it his responsibility as director to perpetuate the example of the Classical composers; he was very conscious of his position as a representative and guardian of tradition, and also made it his business to foster the music of the pre-Classical composers, particularly Bach, even exploring as far back as Palestrina. He was a sympathetic teacher who firmly believed in the necessity of a thorough grounding. In Leipzig, he was also the conductor of the Gewandhaus Orchestra until 1895 (when Nikisch succeeded him); a stern disciplinarian, he achieved a high standard of virtuosity from his players by his insistence on clarity of execution. In 1875 Reinecke became a member of the Berlin Academy, received the honorary doctorate in 1884 and became a professor in 1885. He retired in 1902, though his creative work continued until the end of his life.

As a composer Reinecke was best known for his

Glückskind und Pechvogel (fairy-tale opera, 2), op.117 (1883)
Auf hohen Befehl (comic opera), op.184, Hamburg, 1886, vocal score (*c*1886)
Der Gouverneur von Tours (comic opera, 3, E. Bormann), Schwerin, 1891 (1891)
Incidental music to Schiller's Wilhelm Tell, op.102 (1871)

VOCAL

6 musical fairy-tales, incl. Schneewittchen (Grove), S, A, female vv, pf, reciter, op.133 (1876); Dornröschen (H. Carsten), S, A, Bar, female vv, pf, reciter, op.139 (1876); Aschenbrödel (Carsten), S, Mez, female vv, pf, reciter, op.150 (1878)
Other works, incl. Belsazar, oratorio (Röber), solo vv, chorus, orch, op.73 (?1865); Ein geistliches Abendlied, T, chorus, orch, op.50 (*c*1857); Almansor, aria (Heine), Bar, orch, op.124 (1874); Die Flucht der heiligen Familie (Eichendorff), male vv, orch, op.131 (1874); Hakon Jarl, cantata (Carsten), A, T, B, male vv, orch, op.142 (1877); Das Hindumädchen, aria (Carsten), A/Mez, orch, op.151 (1879); Sommertagsbilder, chorus, orch, op.161 (1881); other works for male, female or mixed chorus, pf acc. or a cappella; songs

ORCHESTRAL

Symphonies: no.1, A, op.79 (?1870); no.2 'Hakon Jarl', c, op.134 (1875); no.3, g, op.227 (*c*1895)
Overtures: Dame Kobold, op.51 (*c*1857); Alladin, op.70 (*c*1865); Friedensfeier, op.105 (1871); Fest-Ouvertüre, op.148 (1878); Zur Jubelfeier, op.166 (1882); Zur Reformationsfeier, op.191 (1887) [variations on Luther's Ein' feste Burg]; Zenobia, op.193 (1887); Ov., op.218 (*c*1892); Prologus solemnis, op.223 (*c*1895)
Concertos: 4 for pf: f♯, op.72 (1879), e, op.120 (1873), C, op.144 (1878), b, op.254 (*c*1900); vn, g, op.141 (1877); vc, d, op.82 (Mainz, 1866); harp, e, op.182 (1885); fl, D, op.283 (*c*1908)
Other works, incl. In memoriam: Introduktion und Fuge mit Choral, op.128 (1874); Trauermarsch auf den Tod des Kaisers Wilhelm I, op.200 (*c*1890)

CHAMBER

Pf, wind: Trio, A, pf, ob, hn, op.188 (1887); Trio, B♭, pf, cl, hn, op.274 (*c*1905); Undine, sonata, fl, pf, op.167 (*c*1885) [also arr. vn/cl, pf]
Ww: Octet, op.216 (*c*1892); Sextet, op.271 (*c*1905)
Pf, str: Qnt, A, op.83 (*c*1866); 2 qts: E♭, op.34 (Brunswick, 1853), D, op.272 (Mainz, *c*1905); 2 trios: D, op.38 (*c*1854), c, op.230 (*c*1895); 2 Serenaden, pf, vn, vc, op.126 (1874); 3 Sonatinen, vn, pf, op.108 (*c*1873); Sonata, e, vn, pf, op.116 (1872); 3 sonatas, vc, pf: A, op.42 (*c*1855), D, op.89 (*c*1869), G, op.238 (*c*1896)
Str: 5 qts: E♭, op.16 (*c*1850), F, op.30 (*c*1852), C, op.132 (1874), D, op.211 (1891), g, op.287 (?1891); Trio, E♭, op.249 (*c*1898)
Trio, pf, cl, va, op.264 (*c*1903)

OTHER WORKS

Pf works, incl. sonatas; sonatinas; variations on themes by Bach, Handel, Gluck and others; studies; pieces for pf 4 hands, org, harmonium; cadenzas to concertos by Mozart and others
Numerous arrs./edns., incl. Klavier-Konzerte alter und neuer Zeit, op.37 (*c*1877–*c*1890); Die Schule der Technik (1870); Bach '48' (1892); Beethoven sonatas for pf (1886), for vn, pf (1891)

WRITINGS

Was sollen wir spielen? (Leipzig, 1886)
Aphorismen über 'Die Kunst, zum Gesang zu begleiten' (Leipzig, 1890)
Rathschläge und Winke für Clavierschüler (Leipzig, 1890)
Zur Wiederbelebung der Mozartschen Clavier-Concerte (Leipzig, 1891)
Die Beethovenschen Clavier-Sonaten: Briefe an eine Freundin (Leipzig, 1895, 9/1924; Eng. trans., 1898)
Und manche liebe Schatten steigen auf: Gedenkblätter an berühmte Musiker (Leipzig, 1900, 2/1910)
Meister der Tonkunst (Berlin, 1903)
Aus dem Reich der Töne (Leipzig, 1907)

BIBLIOGRAPHY

F. Reinecke: *Verzeichniss der Compositionen von Carl Reinecke* (Leipzig, 1889)
W. J. von Wasielewski: *Carl Reinecke* (Leipzig, 1892)
E. Segnitz: *Carl Reinecke* (Leipzig, 1900)
W. Altmann, ed.: *Johannes Brahms: Briefwechsel*, iii (Berlin, 1908, 2/1912) [incl. Brahms–Reinecke correspondence]
H. J. Moser: *Geschichte der deutschen Musik*, ii/2 (Stuttgart and Berlin, 1924)
N. Topusov: *Carl Reinecke: Beiträge zu seinem Leben und seiner Symphonik* (Sofia, 1943)
R. Sietz: 'Reinecke, Carl Heinrich Carsten', *Rheinischer Musiker*, iii, ed. K. G. Fellerer (Cologne, 1964), 68
K. G. Fellerer: 'Carl Reinecke und die Hausmusik', *Studien zur Musikgeschichte des Rheinlandes*, iii: *Heinrich Hüschen zum 50. Geburtstag* (Cologne, 1965), 103
G. Puchelt: 'Der Freund der Jugend: Carl Reinecke', *Verlorene Klänge: Studien zur deutschen Klaviermusik 1830–80* (Berlin, 1969), 50

REINHOLD SIETZ

Carl Reinecke

numerous piano compositions, representing virtually every musical form of the time and stylistically nearer to Schumann than to Mendelssohn. The exercises for young pianists and the piano sonatinas have become classics because of their charming melodies, as have the canons and nursery rhymes which are highly inventive and totally free from bourgeois sentimentality. Reinecke was a master of the so-called 'Hausmusik' and of the simpler forms popular at the time. His chamber music is distinguished, and in the later works in particular, attain a Brahmsian majesty and warmth within a variety of forms. Something of these characteristics is to be found in his overtures and ambitious symphonies. His concertos include works for flute and for harp, and four piano concertos which well display his lucid, Mendelssohnian virtuoso writing, his pleasant melodic sense and his admirable ear for orchestration; his own style of piano playing, with hands still and fingers curved, reflected his belief in classical practice. His operas, despite their Wagnerian trappings, were not successful; his better-known musical fairy-tales, based in part on his own texts (written under the name Heinrich Carsten), were composed in a tasteful folk-style. Gifted in many fields, he was also a talented painter and poet. His lucidly written books and essays contain many observations still of interest.

WORKS
(*printed works published in Leipzig, unless otherwise stated*)

STAGE

Der vierjährige Posten (operetta, 1, after T. Körner), op.45, Barmen, 1855, vocal score (1856)
König Manfred (grand opera, 5, F. Röber), op.93, Wiesbaden, 1867 (?1870)
Ein Abenteuer Händels oder Die Macht des Liedes (Singspiel, 1, W. te Grove), op.104, Schwerin, 1874 (1874); orig. Kathleen und Charlie, Leipzig, 1870

Reinecke, Hans-Peter (*b* Ortelsburg, East Prussia, 27 June 1926). German musicologist and acoustician. From 1946 he attended the University of Göttingen, studying musicology with R. Gerber, philosophy with N. Hartmann, acoustics with E. Meyer, physics with W. Pohl and psychology with J. von Allesch. In 1948 he went to Hamburg University, where he studied musicology with H. Husmann and physics with R. Fleischmann and took the doctorate in 1953 with a dissertation on the concept of loudness. He then became assistant lecturer (1954–5) and lecturer (1955–61) at the musicology institute at Hamburg University and in 1961 he completed his *Habilitation* in musicology with a work on the psychology of musical hearing. In 1965 he was appointed director of the music acoustics department at the Staatliche Institut für Musikforschung Preussischer Kulturbesitz in Berlin, becoming director of that institute in 1967; in the same year he became *ausserplanmässiger Professor* at Hamburg University.

Reinecke's work has been mainly in the area of systematic musicology, particularly the acoustics and the psychology of music, and in organology. His research has been directed towards linking the concept of music as sense impression with the basic tenets of information theory.

WRITINGS
Über den doppelten Sinn des Lautheitsbegriffs beim musikalischen Hören (diss., U. of Hamburg, 1953)
Experimentelle Beiträge zur Psychologie des musikalischens Hörens (Habilitationsschrift, U. of Hamburg, 1961; Hamburg, 1964)
'Über die Eigengesetzlichkeit des musikalischen Hörens und die Grenzen der naturwissenschaftlichen Akustik', *Musikalische Zeitfragen*, x, ed. W. Wiora (Kassel, 1962), 34
Stereo-Akustik (Cologne, 1966)
'Über Allgemein-Vorstellungen von der Musik', *Festschrift für Walter Wiora* (Kassel, 1967), 31
Cents Frequenz Periode: Umrechnungstabellen für musikalische Akustik und Musikethnologie (Berlin, 1970)
'Über Zusammenhänge zwischen naturwissenschaftlicher und musikalischer Theorienbildung', *Über Musiktheorie: Arbeitstagung Berlin 1970*, 59
'Naturwissenschaft und systematische Musikwissenschaft', *Einführung in die systematische Musikwissenschaft*, ed. C. Dahlhaus (Mainz, 1971), 9–51
'Methodische Probleme der akustischen Forschung an Volksmusikinstrumenten', *Studia instrumentarum musicae popularis*, ii, ed. E. Stockmann (Stockholm, 1972), 24
'Einige Überlegungen zum Begriff des musikalischen "Verstehens": Interpretationen einer psychometrischen Untersuchung mit Psychotikern', *Musicae scientiae collectanea: Festschrift Karl Gustav Fellerer* (Cologne, 1973), 472
'Über die Problematik des Testens musikalischer Fähigkeiten', *Festschrift Kurt Blaukopf* (Vienna, 1975), 97
HANS HEINRICH EGGEBRECHT

Reiner, Adam. *See* RENER, ADAM.

Reiner, Ambrosius (*b* Altdorf, nr. Weingarten, Württemberg, baptized 7 Dec 1604; *d* Innsbruck, 4 July 1672). German composer and organist, son of Jacob Reiner. He was given a trial appointment in the archducal Kapelle at Innsbruck on 15 July 1630 and was confirmed as second court organist and teacher of the choirboys there in 1631. In 1635 he was promoted to first court organist. On 1 July 1648 he was appointed court Kapellmeister in succession to Stadlmayr (whose daughter Maria Katharina had become his second wife in 1642). Reiner became imperial director of music at Innsbruck in 1666, following the disbandment of the archducal Kapelle in 1665; he held the post until his death. His works consist exclusively of sacred vocal music. They have not yet been studied in detail, but they probably show the influence of Stadlmayr.

WORKS
(all pubd in Innsbruck)
Sacrae cantiones liber 1, 2–4vv (1643)
Sacrarum cantionum liber 2, 4–6vv, 2 vn, vle (1647)
Sacrarum cantionum liber 3, 8vv (1648)
Psalmi vespertini pro dominica BMV et Magnificat, 8vv, 2 vn, liber 4 (1651)
[5] Missae, 5vv, 3 insts obbl., 3 insts ad lib, liber 5 (1655)
Litaniae BMV, 5–6vv, 2 insts ad lib, 3 insts obbl., cum antiphonis, 1–5vv, insts, liber 6 (1656)
4 sacred odes in 1638[2]

BIBLIOGRAPHY
W. Senn: *Musik und Theater am Hof zu Innsbruck* (Innsbruck, 1954), 434
HELLMUT FEDERHOFER

Reiner, Fritz (*b* Budapest, 19 Dec 1888; *d* New York, 15 Nov 1963). American conductor of Hungarian birth. He studied composition with Kössler and the piano with Thomann at the Liszt Academy of Music, Budapest, and at the same time studied law at the university. In 1909 he was a coach at the Budapest Opera, where he made his conducting début with *Carmen*, and in 1910 he became conductor at the Landestheater in Laibach (now Ljubljana). From 1911 he conducted at the Budapest Volksoper, giving the first Hungarian performance of *Parsifal* in 1914. That year he was appointed principal conductor at the Dresden Staatsoper, where he came into contact with Nikisch (a major influence on his conducting style), Muck, Mahler and Richard Strauss, with whose works he was later closely associated. While at Dresden, he conducted the first German production of *Die Frau ohne Schatten* in 1919, following its Vienna première the same year.

After brief periods in Barcelona, Rome, Buenos Aires and elsewhere, Reiner settled in the USA and took American citizenship. He was principal conductor of the Cincinnati SO (1922–31), then taught until 1938 at the Curtis Institute, Philadelphia, where Leonard Bernstein was among his pupils. A student who completed his course, he claimed, could 'stand before an orchestra he has never seen before and conduct a new piece at first sight without verbal explanation, by means of only manual technique'. He moved to the Pittsburgh SO (1938–48), and to the Metropolitan Opera (1948–53), where he conducted the first American production of *The Rake's Progress* in 1953. That year he took charge of the Chicago SO, which under him became, in Stravinsky's opinion, 'the most precise and flexible orchestra in the world'. Reiner's visits to Europe included his Covent Garden début in 1936–7 at Beecham's invitation, when he conducted *Tristan und Isolde* for Flagstad's London début, and *Der Rosenkavalier* at the rebuilt Vienna Staatsoper in 1955.

Reiner was irascible and impatient with his musicians, but he placed great emphasis on rhythmic precision and clarity of texture, and was uncompromising in his demand for these qualities. His performances were elegant and unsentimental, but capable of great dramatic impact, and his gestures were sparing: his beat ('a short man who used a big baton') was the smallest since Richard Strauss's, and his performances sounded correspondingly alert.

BIBLIOGRAPHY
R. Angles: 'Fritz Reiner', *Audio & Record Review*, iii/7 (1964), 24 [with discography by F. F. Clough and G. J. Cuming]
P. Hart: 'Reiner in Chicago', *High Fidelity*, xiv/4 (1964), 42 [with discography]
H. C. Schonberg: *The Great Conductors* (New York, 1967), 335ff
I. Stravinsky: 'On Conductors and Conducting', *Themes and Conclusions* (London, 1972), 223
F. Bónis: 'Fritz Reiner: an Early Bartók Conductor', *New Hungarian Quarterly*, xvii/63 (1976), 218
ROBERT PHILIP

Reiner [Rainer], **Jacob** (*b* Altdorf, nr. Weingarten, Württemberg, before 1560; *d* Weingarten, 12 Aug 1606). German composer, father of Ambrosius Reiner. According to the dedication of his *Liber cantionum sacrarum* (1579) he was educated as a boy at the abbey of Weingarten. He continued his studies under Lassus in Munich in 1574–5, and on completing them returned to the abbey, where he spent the rest of his life, without, however, taking holy orders. Here he enjoyed high esteem as Kapellmeister, teacher of music and composer.

His numerous workmanlike compositions, nearly all of them sacred, became known beyond the immediate vicinity of Weingarten. They show the influence of Lassus and also of Venetian composers; with the more important Lechner and Eccard, Reiner belongs to the German school of Lassus. Compared with Lassus's penitential psalms, his three-part settings of the same texts have a positively ascetic simplicity. Expressive restraint of this and similar kinds, such as the avoidance of chromaticism, is probably connected with the greater liturgical severity practised at the abbey after a visitation in 1579. But Reiner did use secular models in some of his masses. His secular German songs, compounded of elements of madrigal, villanella and chanson, are weaker examples of the products of the Lassus circle.

WORKS
Liber cantionum sacrarum, 5–6vv (Munich, 1579); ed. O. Dressler (Stuttgart, 1875) and *MMg*, viii (1876), 29
Schöne newe teutsche Lieder, 4–5vv, sambt 2 . . . lateinischen Liedlein (Munich, 1581)
Cantionum piarum septem psalmi poenitentiales, 3vv, 6 mutetae (Munich, 1586)
Christliche Gesänge, teutsche Psalmen, 3vv (Dillingen, 1589)
Selectae piaeque cantiones, 6–10vv (Munich, 1591)
Cantica sive mutetae ex sacris desumptae, 4–5vv, Magnificat (Konstanz, 1595)
Liber mottetarum sive cantionum sacrarum, 6–8vv (Munich, 1600)
Liber motetarum sive cantionum sacrarum, 6vv (Dillingen, 1603, 2/1606)
Sacrarum missarum, 6vv, liber 1 (Dillingen, 1604)
Gloriosissimae viriginis . . . Magnificat, 8vv, antiphona, Salve regina (Frankfurt, 1604)
Missae tres cum litaniis de SS sanguine Christi, 8vv, liber 1 (Dillingen, 1604)
Missae aliquot sacrae cum officio BMV et antiphonis ejusdem, 3–4vv (Dillingen, 1608)
Over 100 hymns, mostly Latin, some from the pubd collections, in *D-As, Bds, Lr, Mbs, Rp, SI; GB-Lbm; PL-GD, WRu*, Legnica (Bibliotheca Rudolfina); *USSR-KA*
Lost works include three Passions, according to Mark, Luke and John, which O. Dressler (1873) demonstrated were in 5 parts

BIBLIOGRAPHY
O. Dressler: 'Jacob Reiner', *MMg*, iii (1871), 97
——: 'Zur 5- oder 4st. Passion von Jacob Reiner', *MMg*, v (1873), 17
A. Kriessmann: *Jacob Reiner: Beiträge zur Geschichte der Musik an den oberschwäbischen Klöstern im 16. Jahrhundert* (Augsburg and Kassel, 1927)
——: *Geschichte der katholischen Kirchenmusik in Württemberg von der ältesten Zeit bis zur Gegenwart* (Stuttgart, 1939)
E. F. Schmid: *Musik an den schwäbischen Zollernhöfen der Renaissance* (Kassel, 1962), 717f

HELLMUT FEDERHOFER

Reiner, Karel (*b* Žatec, 27 June 1910; *d* Prague, 17 Oct 1979). Czech composer, pianist and administrator. He first studied music with his father, cantor of Žatec, then law at the German University, Prague, where he graduated in 1933, and musicology at Prague University. He also attended the conservatory as a student in Suk's master classes (1931) and in Hába's microtone department (1934–5). During the years 1934–8 he was active as a pianist and composer in Burian's theatre D 34 and for

the Esta gramophone company. After imprisonment in concentration camps during the German occupation he returned to Prague to prepare the first Czech performance of Hába's *The Mother* at the Theatre of the 5th of May (1945–7). From 1931 he had been active in promoting new music as a pianist, and after World War II he took part in organizing a new pattern of musical life in Prague. He contributed articles to *Rytmus* (1935–8, 1945–7) and to foreign periodicals. As a composer he closely identified himself at first with Hába, but later he followed a more independent path. In the 1960s he achieved a successful combination of ideas taken from Hába with new post-war techniques.

WORKS
(*selective list*)
Dramatic: Zakletá píseň [Enchanted song] (opera, Beneš), Prague, 5 Feb 1951; film scores, incidental music
Orch: Pf Conc., 1932; Conc., nonet, 1933; Předehra [Overture], Tanec [Dance], 1935; Vn Conc., 1937; Koncertantní suita, wind, perc, 1947; Sym., 1960; Conc., b cl, str, perc, 1965; Concertino, bn, wind, perc, 1969; Promluvy [Utterances], chamber orch, 1975; Music for str, 1976; Diptych, 1977
Inst: 3 pf sonatas, 1931, 1942, 1961; 3 str qts, 1931, 1947, 1951; Sonata, perc, 1967; over 250 other chamber pieces
Political and mass songs

Principal publishers: Český hudební fond, Panton, Státní hudební vydavatelství

BIBLIOGRAPHY
V. Lébl: 'Písňová tvorba Karla Reinera', *HRo*, viii (1955), 917
M. Kuna: 'Z nové sborové tvorby Karla Reinera', *Lidová tvořivost*, viii (1958), 8
——: 'Zrání umělce současnosti: k tvůrčí cestě Karla Reinera', *HRo*, xv (1962), 97
R. Budiš: 'Reinerův koncert pro basklarinet', *HRo*, xxi (1968), 117

JOSEF BEK

Reinhard, Andreas (*b* ?Schneeberg, nr. Zwickau; *d* before 1614). German organist, theorist and notary. He is known to have lived at Schneeberg. He is mentioned by Abraham Bartolus in 1614 as being already dead. In his *Monochordum* he described a clavichord with 36 keys and 12 pairs of strings. To this instrument he applied a tuning system whose semitones are derived from the just intervals by means of arithmetical division. His use of these intervals in terms of string lengths based on 48 units makes him the first post-Renaissance writer to exploit fully these developments derived from the monochord. His tuning was used by Bartolus a decade later.

WORKS
Osculetur me osculo, 8vv (n.p., n.d.)
Uns hat geboren ein Kindlein, 4vv, dated 1596, *D-Z*

WRITINGS
Monochordum (Leipzig, 1604)
Musica sive Guidonis Aretini De usu et constitutione monochordi dialogus (Leipzig, 1604)
De harmoniae limbo, 1610, and *Methodus de arte musica perconcinne suis numeris et notis elaborata*, 1610, both lost (according to Adlung in the Barfüsserkirche Bibliothek, Erfurt, but the library no longer exists)

BIBLIOGRAPHY
WaltherML
J. Adlung: *Anleitung zu der musikalischen Gelahrtheit* (Erfurt, 1758/*R*1953, 2/1783)
C. D. Adkins: *The Theory and Practice of the Monochord* (diss., U. of Iowa, 1963), 269ff

CECIL ADKINS

Reinhard, Kurt (*b* Giessen, 27 Aug 1914; *d* Wetzlar, 18 July 1979). German ethnomusicologist. He studied musicology and composition (under H. Unger) at Cologne (1933–5) and musicology and ethnology at Leipzig and subsequently at Munich under R. von Ficker, K. Huber and H. Ubbelohdé-Doering (1935–6). In 1938 he took his doctorate at Munich with a dissertation on Burmese music. After a period at the Staatliche Musik-instrumentensammlung, Berlin (1939–45), he became director of the Berliner Phonogramm-Archiv (1948–68) and head of the department of private music teaching at the Petersen Conservatory (1947–52). In 1948 he obtained a teaching post at the Free University, Berlin, where he completed his *Habilitation* on musical instruments in 1950; he was subsequently (1957) appointed professor and head of the department of ethnomusicology. His chief research interest in this field was the folk music and art music of Turkey.

WRITINGS

Die Musik Birmas (diss., U. of Munich, 1938; Würzburg, 1939)
Musikinstrumente und Musikkulturkreise (Habilitationsschrift, Free U. of Berlin, 1950)
Die Musik exotischer Völker (Berlin, 1951)
'Die Musik der Lolo', *Baessler-Archiv*, new ser., iii (1955), 195; see also ibid, iv (1956), 105
Chinesische Musik (Kassel and Eisenach, 1956)
'Beitrag zu einer neuen Systematik der Musikinstrumente', *Mf*, xiii (1960), 160
Türkische Musik (Berlin, 1962)
Einführung in die Musikethnologie (Wolfenbüttel, 1968)
with U. Reinhard: *Volkslieder von der osttürkischen Schwarzmeerküste* (Berlin, 1968)
with U. Reinhard: *Turquis* (Paris, 1969)
'Über die Denaturierungstendenz der Musik', *Festschrift zum zehnjährigen Bestand der Hochschule für Musik und darstellende Kunst in Graz* (Vienna, 1974), 204
'Bemerkungen zu den Asik, den Volkssaengern der Tuerkei', *Asian Music*, vi (1975), 189
'Zur Systematik von Tonsystemen und Gebrauchsleitern', *Mf*, xxviii (1975), 173
Articles in Festschriften for Besseler (1961), Wiora (1967), Hoerburger (1977), Marius Schneider (1977), and in *Das orientalische Element am Balkan: 2. Balkanologen-Tagung: Graz 1966, Beiträge zur Kenntnis Südosteuropas und des Nahen Orients*, iv (1973), *Musica antiqua Europae orientalis IV: Bydgoszcz 1975* and *Zeitschrift für Ethnologie*, c (1975)

HANS HEINRICH EGGEBRECHT

Reinhardt [Rheinhardt, Reinhard]. Austrian family of musicians.

(1) Kilian Reinhardt (*b* 1653–4; *d* Vienna, 25 March 1729). Austrian musical administrator. He does not seem to have been a practical musician, and was never employed in that capacity. In 1683 he was given the job of librarian and copyist to the imperial court orchestra in Vienna. Since the musicians tended to treat him as a servant, he petitioned Leopold I for an official title; his request was granted in 1699, and he was thenceforward known as 'Konzertmeister'. In 1712 Charles VI recognized his long service by including him on a commission to consider the reform of the court chapel. He married twice, the second time comparatively late in life.

In 1727 Reinhardt wrote a treatise on the musical customs of the court chapel, *Rubriche generali per le funzioni ecclesiastiche musicali di tutto l'anno, con un appendice in fine dell'essenziale ad uso, e servizio dell'Augustissima Imperiale Capella* (MS, *A-Wn*). It is a valuable source of information on the history of the chapel music in the late 17th and early 18th centuries, dealing particularly with liturgical customs (especially the relative importance of different Sundays and feast days, and the kind of music appropriate for them), and also containing information on performing practice.

(2) Johann Georg Reinhardt (*b* 1676–7; *d* Vienna, 6 Jan 1742). Organist and composer, nephew of (1) Kilian Reinhardt, by whose intercession he obtained a post in the imperial chapel. In October 1701 he was appointed assistant to the organists. From 1710 to 1712 he himself was organist, though after the reorganization of the chapel music in 1712 he took second place to the elder Georg Reutter. He became first organist on the latter's retirement in 1728, and also worked as Kapellmeister at St Stephen's Cathedral from 1727 to 1742. Church music was not his only interest, however, for he was involved with the production of Fux's *Costanza e Fortezza* in 1723, and in 1734 he was appointed court composer with special responsibility for serenades and ballets. He had a number of pupils, though none achieved any great fame, and was a member of the council of the Caecilienbrüderschaft, founded in 1725.

He was an extremely prolific composer, and though the bulk of his output consists of church music – after Fux and Caldara he was the most significant composer of church music in Vienna at the time – he also produced operas and oratorios. His masses, vesper psalms and litanies are almost all for four voices and orchestra, while the antiphons and motets are for various combinations of solo voices and orchestra. His style resembles that of Fux. His church music was extremely popular, being performed not only in Vienna, but also in parish churches and monasteries all over Austria and Bohemia and at the Saxon court at Dresden, and continuing in use until long after his death. He also wrote a number of motets in the polyphonic style taught by Fux, and some German arias whose melodic lines show the influence of German folksong.

WORKS

OPERAS
(all performed in Vienna for imperial name days)
La più bella (P. Pariati), 1715, *A-Wn, D-MEIr*
L'eroe immortale (Pariati), 1717, *A-Wgm, Wn*
Il giudicio di Enone (Pariati), 1721, *Wgm, Wn*

SACRED MUSIC
(all 4vv, insts, unless otherwise stated)
Il divino imeneo di S Catterina, oratorio, 1716, *A-Wn*
Per crucem Jesu sit desperanti vitae restitutio, oratorio, Olomouc, 1726, lost, lib pubd
22 masses, incl. 3 for 4vv a cappella, 1 elsewhere attrib. J. Fux, *A-GÖ, Wn, WIL, CS-Bm, Pnm, D-Dlb*, 4 lost; 4 requiem, 1 in *CS-Bm*, 3 lost
12 Vespers, incl. 1 for 4vv a cappella, *A-GÖ, Wn, WAY, CS-Pnm*; 1 Compline, 4vv a cappella, *A-Wn*
7 Magnificat, *GÖ, Wn, WIL, D-Dlb*; 19 Marian antiphons, incl. 1 for 4vv a cappella, 10 for 1–2 solo vv, insts, *A-GÖ, KN, Wgm, WIL, CS-Bm, Pnm*, 4 lost
7 Miserere, *A-GÖ, KR, Wn, CS-Bm*; 2 Te Deum, *A-GÖ, KN, CS-Bm*; 21 litanies, incl. 1 for 4vv a cappella, 1 elsewhere attrib. Fux, *A-GÖ, SE, Wgm, WIL, CS-Bm, Pnm*, 4 lost
17 psalms, incl. 1 elsewhere attrib. Caldara, *A-GÖ, H, Wn*, 2 lost
4 hymns, incl. 1 for 4vv a cappella, 3 for 1–3 solo vv, 2 vn, bc, *Wgm, Wn*; 32 motets, incl. 10 for 4vv a cappella, 6 for 1–3 solo vv, insts, *GÖ, SE, Wgm, Wn, WIL, CS-Bm, Pnm*, 7 lost
9 German arias, incl. 1 for B, vn, org, *A-GÖ, WIL*, 6 lost
Miscellaneous works: *GÖ, Wgm, Wn*

(3) Joseph Franz Reinhardt (*b* 1684–5; *d* Vienna, 27 Sept 1727). Austrian violinist, son of (1) Kilian Reinhardt by his first marriage. He was a violinist in the court orchestra, which he joined in 1706, and at St Stephen's Cathedral. His reputation as a violinist was very high (Fux described him as a 'distinguished virtuoso') and he seems also to have been a good teacher. It is not likely that he was a composer; though there exists a *Salve regina* ascribed to him, it is more probably by his cousin (2) Johann Georg Reinhardt.

(4) Karl Mathias Reinhardt (*b* Vienna, 1710–11; *d* Vienna, 31 Jan 1767). Austrian organist and composer, son of (1) Kilian Reinhardt by his second marriage. He was a pupil of his cousin and guardian (2) Johann Georg Reinhardt. He became court organist on 6 February 1739, retaining the post until his retirement in 1762. He was active as a composer as well as an organist; though only two compositions can be definitely ascribed to him, a litany and a requiem (both in *A-KR*), it is possible that some of the works signed merely 'Rheinhardt', ascribed to his cousin, may in fact be by him. His litany and requiem are in a smooth melodious style characteristic of much mid-18th-century Viennese church music.

(5) Johann Franz Reinhardt (*b* Vienna, 1713–14; *d* Vienna, 21 April 1761). Austrian violinist, son and pupil of (3) Joseph Franz Reinhardt. He was a sufficiently good violinist to be given a place in the court orchestra in 1730; in 1740 he added to this the position of violinist at St Stephen's Cathedral. Dittersdorf was much impressed by his virtuosity as a soloist.

BIBLIOGRAPHY

L. von Köchel: *Die kaiserliche Hofkapelle in Wien, 1543–1867* (Vienna, 1869)

G. Reichert: *Zur Geschichte der Wiener Messenkomposition in der ersten Hälfte des 18. Jahrhunderts* (diss., U. of Vienna, 1935)

——: 'Mozarts Credo-Messen und ihre Vorläufer', *MJb 1955*, 117

ELIZABETH ROCHE

Reinhardt, Delia (*b* Elberfeld [now Wuppertal], 27 April 1892; *d* Arlesheim, 3 Oct 1974). German soprano. She studied in Frankfurt with Strakosch and Hedwig Schako, and made her début at Breslau in 1913. Three years later she was engaged by Bruno Walter for the Munich Opera, where she remained until 1923, being especially admired in the Mozart repertory. From Munich she went to the Berlin Staatsoper where she appeared regularly until 1938, singing more than 60 roles including Octavian, the Empress (*Die Frau ohne Schatten*), the Composer, Christine (*Intermezzo*), Elsa, Elisabeth (*Tannhäuser*) and Eva, as well as roles in works by Milhaud, Schreker and Weill. She sang at Covent Garden (1924–7, 1929) and was Octavian in the famous London performances of *Der Rosenkavalier* under Bruno Walter, with Lotte Lehmann, Elisabeth Schumann and Richard Mayr. Reinhardt was also heard in London as Cherubino, Freia, Gutrune, Micaela, Mimì and Cio-cio-san. She sang at the Metropolitan Opera, 1922–4. After World War II she lived in California, where she took up painting and anthropology. Her first husband was the baritone Gustav Schützendorf, her second the conductor Georges Sébastian.

HAROLD ROSENTHAL

Reinhardt, Django [Jean Baptiste] (*b* Liberchies, 23 Jan 1910; *d* Fontainebleau, 16 May 1953). Belgian jazz guitarist. He grew up in a gypsy settlement outside Paris and began to work professionally in 1922 with the accordionist Guérino, later appearing with Fredo Gardoni and Jean Vaissade. In 1928 he was badly burnt in a caravan fire; the resulting mutilation of his left hand led him to devise a fingering method to surmount this handicap. After convalescence he was engaged by Stephen Mougin and later worked and recorded with the singer Jean Sablon and the violinist Stephane Grappelli. He and Grappelli were founder-members of the Quintet of the Hot Club de France (1934), which gained considerable renown before World War II. Reinhardt became an international celebrity, appearing throughout Europe and recording with many important American jazz musicians who visited the Continent. Throughout the war he remained in France, enjoying marked success

as leader of his own quintet (in which a clarinettist had replaced Grappelli). In 1946 he visited London, Switzerland and the USA, where he toured as a soloist with Duke Ellington's band and then worked in New York. He eventually settled at Samois near Fontainebleau, retaining his prominent position in European jazz circles, and encouraging younger musicians.

Django Reinhardt

Reinhardt's grasp of harmony, his remarkable technique and his trenchant rhythmic sense made him an excellent accompanist even early in his career. But he also developed into a soloist of unique character, creating a deeply personal style out of his own cultural patrimony. By 1937, when *Chicago* was recorded, he was clearly the first outstanding European jazz musician, a stylist with great melodic resourcefulness, mastery of inflection and a flair for pacing a performance so that the maximum variety could be wrung from it without compromising its homogeneity. He was also a gifted composer of short evocative pieces and could readily combine with visiting American performers without forsaking his essentially romantic style. In the 1940s he changed to the electric guitar, without coarsening his style, as he used its power discreetly. The rhythmic content of his work became more varied, his improvised lines more flexible, and the asymmetrical, occasionally violent playing of some late performances shows the continual widening of his expressive scope.

BIBLIOGRAPHY

C. Delaunay: *Django Reinhardt: Souvenirs* (Paris, 1954; Eng. trans., 1961)

G. McKean: 'Django Reinhardt', *Jam Session*, ed. R. Gleason (New York, 1958), 111

A. Hodeir: *Toward Jazz* (New York, 1962), 186ff

A. Morgan: 'Django Reinhardt', *Jazz on Record*, ed. A. McCarthy (London, 1968), 241

M. Abrams: *The Book of Django* (Los Angeles, 1973)

MICHAEL JAMES

Reinhardt, Heinrich (*b* Pressburg [now Bratislava], 13 April 1865; *d* Vienna, 31 Jan 1922). Austrian composer. The son of a jeweller, he went to Vienna to study at the Conservatory of the Gesellschaft der Musikfreunde where he was one of Bruckner's pupils. He became an accomplished pianist and organist, and his familiarity with several other instruments later served him well as orchestrator of his own works and those of others. Between 1890 and 1900 he published numerous songs, piano and salon pieces, as well as an opera *Die Minnekönigin* (1895). He also wrote music reports for the *Neue freie Presse*, *Neues Wiener Journal* and *Die Zeit*, but abandoned this after the tremendous success of his first operetta *Das süsse Mädel* (Carltheater, 25 October 1901). Somewhat in musical comedy style, it opened a new phase for Viennese operetta, though Reinhardt's dozen later works were eclipsed by those of Eysler, Lehár, Straus and Fall. A comic opera *Der Gast des Königs* (after Dickens) was produced at the Volksoper on 9 January 1916.

ANDREW LAMB

Reinhardt, Jean Baptiste. *See* REINHARDT, DJANGO.

Reinhardt [Goldmann], Max (*b* Baden, Austria, 9 Sept 1873; *d* New York City, 31 Oct 1943). Austrian producer. He began as an actor in Salzburg, but by 1903 he was devoting himself exclusively to production, responding with enthusiasm and taste to the new theatrical ideas and methods then evolving. He is generally associated with stage spectacle, having effectively mounted many scenic extravaganzas with huge casts, such as *Oedipus rex* (1910) in a Vienna circus, *The Miracle* at Olympia, London (1911), and the annual Salzburg Festival presentations of the morality *Jedermann* in the Domplatz. Like Dyagilev he was a remarkable entrepreneur with a talent for choosing the ideal actors, designers, choreographers and musicians for each production. Music played a substantial part in all his productions, and he supervised the choice of music. He carefully stage-managed musicians, concealing them, costuming them to mix with actors, or leaving them in the orchestra pit, as required. He worked closely with the composers he commissioned: Humperdinck for *The Miracle* and *Twelfth Night*; Weill for Werfel's *The Eternal Road*; Leo Blech for *The Taming of the Shrew*; Pfitzner for Kleist's *Kätchen von Heilbronn*; and Einar Nilson, his musical director and staff composer for over 15 years.

One of Reinhardt's most popular productions was *Orphée aux enfers*, which he first staged with singing actors at the Neues Theater, Berlin, in 1906; Klemperer, then a student, was first choirmaster and then conductor. In 1911 he produced Offenbach's *La belle Hélène* in Venice, and in 1930 he produced the first of several revivals of *Die Fledermaus*. He is best remembered on the opera stage, however, for producing the première of Strauss's *Der Rosenkavalier*, with sets and costumes by Alfred Roller (Dresden, 1911); he also staged the première of the original version of *Ariadne auf Naxos* in Stuttgart (1912), with designs by Ernst Stern. His influence on Strauss and Hofmannsthal was considerable; both *Salome* and *Elektra* were directly inspired by his productions of dramatic versions. In 1920 Strauss, Hofmannsthal and Reinhardt united to create the Salzburg Festival. The idea for the festival, its location and its emphases (Mozart and the Austrian dramatic tradition), were his, and he remained active in it until forced into exile in America in 1937. Among his accomplishments there were the annual productions of *Jedermann* and *Faust*, and his last new opera production, Offenbach's *Les contes d'Hoffmann* (1931).

WRITINGS

Ausgewählte Briefe, Reden, Schriften und Szenen aus Regiebüchern, ed. F. Hadamowsky (Vienna, 1963)
Briefe, Reden, Aufsätze, Interviews, Gespräche, Auszüge aus Regiebüchern, ed. H. Fetting (Berlin, 1974)

BIBLIOGRAPHY

H. Herald and E. Stern: *Reinhardt und seine Bühne* (Berlin, 1918)
O. M. Sayler, ed.: *Max Reinhardt and his Theatre* (New York, 1924)
F. Horch, ed.: *Die Spielpläne Max Reinhardts 1905–1930* (Munich, 1930)
E. Stern: *My Life, My Stage* (London, 1951)
H. Jhering and G. C. Castello: 'Reinhardt, Max', *ES*
F. Hadamowsky: *Reinhardt und Salzburg* (Salzburg, 1964)
H. Braulich: *Max Reinhardt* (Berlin, 1969)
G. Reinhardt: *Der Liebhaber* (Munich, 1973)

PAUL SHEREN

Reinhold, Frederick Charles (*b* London, 1737; *d* Somers Town [London], 28 Sept 1815). English bass and organist, son of Henry Theodore Reinhold. On his father's early death he was brought up with assistance from the Royal Society of Musicians. He is said to have been a chorister at St Paul's and the Chapel Royal, but his name does not occur in the Chapel Royal or Westminster Abbey lists. He embarked early on a stage career and appeared regularly at Drury Lane (as 'Master Reinhold') in 1752–5, playing Oberon in J. C. Smith's Shakespeare opera *The Fairies* on 3 February 1755. He received half a guinea for singing in the chorus of *Messiah* at the Foundling Hospital on 27 April 1758, and again on 3 May 1759; he was in several later performances under John Stanley (1775–7). From 1758 Reinhold sang for many years in the summer concerts at Marylebone Gardens, where he enjoyed great success in the elder Storace's version of *La serva padrona* (8 June 1758, benefit on 21 August). He played an organ concerto at his benefit there on 9 August 1759. He returned to Drury Lane the same year (among the operas in which he sang was William Bates's *Pharnaces* in February 1765), appeared at concerts at the Little Haymarket Theatre in summer 1761 and later joined Covent Garden, where he sang in pantomimes and light pieces by Dibdin, Shield and others in the 1770s and 1780s. In 1783 he was appointed organist of St George the Martyr, Bloomsbury. He was a principal bass at the Handel Commemoration of 1784, and was perhaps the Reinhold who appeared frequently at Cambridge Festivals between 1772 and 1788. He retired in 1797. He is described as an admirable singer and a good actor, but a parsimonious man; he left £5 to a surgeon to cut his windpipe lest he be buried alive.

WINTON DEAN

Reinhold, Henry Theodore (*d* London, 14 May 1751). English bass of German birth. His origins are obscure; according to one account he was an illegitimate son of the Archbishop of Dresden. His name is sometimes incorrectly given as Thomas. He may have been related to the Dresden composer Theodor Christian Reinhold. The date of his first London appearance is uncertain; he was possibly the Reynolds (the name appears once as Reynhold) who played in ballad operas, farces and pantomimes, and some straight plays, at the New Haymarket Theatre in 1728–31. He may have sung in Handel's *Deborah* as early as 1734. He played the small part of Mercury in *Atalanta* at Covent Garden on 12 May 1736 and was a member of Handel's company the following season, when he appeared in revivals of *Atalanta*, *Alcina* (Melisso) and *Poro* (Timagene), the new operas *Arminio* (Segeste), *Giustino* (Polidarte) and *Berenice* (Aristobulo), and probably in revivals of *Alexander's Feast*, *Il trionfo del tempo* and *Esther* (Haman). From this time until his death he sang constantly in London theatres in parts of every kind, from burlesques to oratorios, as well as at concerts. He was attached to Covent Garden in 1736–9 and 1740–46, and to Drury Lane in 1739–40 and 1746–51, but often appeared elsewhere. He sang in the first performances of Handel's *Israel in Egypt* (April 1739) and *Jupiter in Argos* (May 1739), both at the King's Theatre, and regularly in Handel's two seasons (1739–41) at Lincoln's Inn Fields, where he appeared in the English two-act version of *Acis and Galatea* in December 1739 (as Polyphemus, one of his most popular parts), the first performances of *L'Allegro* in February 1740, and Handel's last two operas *Imeneo* (Argenio) and *Deidamia* (Lycomede) in winter 1740–41. In spring 1740 he sang in J. C. Smith's *David's Lamentation over Saul and Jonathan* and *Rosalinda* at Hickford's Room.

The principal bass roles in all Handel's oratorios and masques from 1743 to 1750 were composed for Reinhold: Harapha in *Samson* (he sang Manoa as well in revivals), Cadmus, the High Priest and Somnus in *Semele*, Pharaoh and probably Reuben in *Joseph and his Brethren*, Hercules, Gobrias in *Belshazzar* (he sang most of Cyrus's music on the first night, when the casting was upset by illness), the *Occasional Oratorio*, Simon and Eupolemus in *Judas Maccabaeus*, Caleb in *Joshua*, Ptolemy in *Alexander Balus*, Chelsias and the Second Elder in *Susanna*, the Levite in *Solomon*, and Valens in *Theodora*. He sang in many revivals, including all Handel's London performances of *Messiah* during these years, the title role in *Saul*, Haman in *Esther*, and in 1744 Abinoam in *Deborah*. Other works in which he appeared were Pescetti's opera *Angelica e Medoro* (March 1739), De Fesch's oratorio *Joseph* (March 1745) – both at Covent Garden – Boyce's *Secular Masque* (Drury Lane, October 1750), and many theatre pieces by Lampe and Arne, including the latter's *Rosamond* and *Comus*. He played the Dragon in Lampe's *Dragon of Wantley* during the original 1737 run. His last documented appearance was in Burney's version of Arne's *Alfred* at Drury Lane on 23 February 1751, but he probably sang in Handel's Foundling Hospital *Messiah* on 18 April that year. He died at his house in Chapel Street, Soho, leaving a wife and four young children, and was buried in St Anne's churchyard. An obituary in the *General Advertiser* described him as 'a man no less admired for his private character than his publick performance'. A benefit at Drury Lane raised £101 for his bereaved family.

Reinhold's Handel parts suggest that he improved greatly under the composer's tuition. In the first five operas in which he appeared he was confined to a single aria (not always new); in the last three he had two, in the oratorios sometimes as many as five (*Judas Maccabaeus*, *Theodora*, *Susanna*). He was equally at home as a tyrant (Harapha, Ptolemy, Valens), a dignified father or priest (Gobrias, Simon, Caleb, Levite, Chelsias) and a bluff half-comic character (Somnus, Hercules, Second Elder). In *Susanna* he played two parts of strongly contrasted type. He was a genuine bass, not a baritone, with a compass of F to f', though many of his parts do not exceed G to e'.

WINTON DEAN

Reinhold, Otto (*b* Thum, 3 July 1899; *d* Dresden, 27 Aug 1965). German composer and teacher. He attended the Annaberg Teacher Training College (1914–20), taught in Neustädtel, Erzgebirge (1920–25), studied composition with Grabner at the Leipzig Conservatory (1925–9) and taught music in Dresden (from 1929). In 1960 he retired from teaching and in 1962 was awarded the Martin–Andersen–Nexö Arts Prize of Dresden. His

versatile compositional work shows an effective, musicianly approach, with naturally evolving forms and clear, lucid development.

WORKS
(*selective list*)

Ballet: Die Nachtigall, 1958
Orch: Suite, 1930; Vn Conc., 1937; Conc., chamber orch, 1942; Fl Conc., 1947; Sym., 1951; Heiteres Vorspiel, 1952; Festliches Vorspiel, 1952; Tänzerische Suite, pf, orch, 1954; Triptychon, 1954; Ov., 1959; Sinfonietta, 1960; Jugendmusik, str, 1961; Musik für Kammerorchester, 1961; Sinfonische Ballade, 1962; Konzertante Musik, fl, va, orch, 1962
Vocal: Geistliche Musik, 4–8vv, 1932; Altdeutsche geistliche Chorsuite, unacc., 1935; Der Weg, cantata, 1936; 5 Morgenstern-Gesänge, chorus, 1947; Psalm xc, solo vv, chorus, orch, 1949; 2 dramatische Monologe, Mez/Bar, pf, 1952; Kalendarium, cantata, 1956
Chamber: Klaviermusik, 1938; Musik, va, pf, 1939; Trio-Serenade, cl, va, pf, 1939; Sonata, vn, pf, 1940; Pf Trio, 1948; Musik, org, 2 tpt, trbn, 1953; Theme and Variations, 2 tpt, 2 hn, 2 trbn, 1954; Sonatine, rec, pf, 1956; Sonata, vc, pf, 1959; Str Qt, 1960; Wind Qnt, 1960

Principal publishers: Bärenreiter, Breitkopf & Härtel, Peters

BIBLIOGRAPHY
K. Laux: 'Otto Reinhold', *Musica*, iv (1949), 124
H. Böhm: 'Bildnis eines Chorkomponisten: Otto Reinhold', *ZfM*, Jg.115 (1954), 342
K. Laux: 'Dem Leben abgelauscht, Komponistenporträt Otto Reinhold', *Musik und Gesellschaft*, iv (1958), 195

HORST SEEGER

Reinhold, Theodor Christlieb (*b* Eppendorf, Saxony, 13 Sept 1682; *d* Dresden, 24 March 1755). German organist and composer. He came from an old family of clergy, and went to the Dresden Kreuzschule in 1694; possibly he went to university. In 1706 he became organist at the Annenkirche in Dresden; the next year he was appointed Kantor in Alten Dresden, and in 1720 Kantor of the Kreuzkirche, a post he held until his death. In 1725 he took a post at the Lehrerkollegium and also took charge of music at the new Frauenkirche. He wrote cantatas to mark the laying of the foundation stone of the church (1726) and its consecration (1734), as well as the consecration of the new Silbermann organ (1736); like most of his works, they are now lost. In 1741 he took over the direction of a newly founded collegium musicum, mainly for the performance of cantatas and serenades; he had earlier been concerned with a collegium musicum connected with the Kreuzkirche. In 1742 he retired from teaching.

Reinhold was Kantor of the Dresden Kreuzkirche at the time that Bach was Kantor of the Thomaskirche in Leipzig, and was leader of the German forces that resisted the increasing foreign influence in Dresden musical life, especially during the Hasse period. Of his many pupils, J. A. Hiller is particularly important; he dedicated his *Abhandlung über die Nachahmung der Natur in der Musik* (reprinted in Marpurg's *Historisch-kritische Beyträge*, i, 1754) to Reinhold, and printed two four-part motets by him, Reinhold's only surviving works, *Herr, gehe nichts ins Gericht* and *Alle eure Sorgen werfet auf den Herrn* (in Hiller's *Vierstimmige Motetten . . . von verschiedenen Componisten*, i and iv, Leipzig, 1776, 1780). Reinhold was also an outstanding bass singer, and published an essay *Einige zur Musik gehörige poetische Gedanken bei Gelegenheit der schönen neuen in der Frauenkirche verfertigten Orgel* (Dresden, 1736; reviewed in Mizler's *Musikalische Bibliothek*, i, 67). His successor was Bach's pupil A. Homilius.

BIBLIOGRAPHY
J. A. Hiller: *Lebensbeschreibungen berühmter Musikgelehrter und Tonkünstler neuerer Zeit* (Leipzig, 1784), 81

M. Fürstenau: *Zur Geschichte der Musik und des Theaters am Hofe zu Dresden*, ii (Dresden, 1862/R1971)
K. Held: *Das Kreuzkantorat zu Dresden* (Leipzig, 1894), 83ff
E. H. Hofmann: *Capella sanctae crucis – Der Dresdner Kreuzchor in Geschichte und Gegenwart* (Berlin, 2/1957), 76f
H. Böhm: 'Die evangelischen Kreuzkantoren', *Kirchenmusik heute*, ed. H. Böhm (Berlin, 1959), 172f

DIETER HÄRTWIG

Reiniger, (Robert) Meredith. *See* WILLSON, MEREDITH.

Reinike, Johann Adam. *See* REINCKEN, JOHANN ADAM.

Reining, Maria (*b* Vienna, 7 Aug 1903). Austrian soprano. After working in a bank until the age of 25, she began to study singing in Vienna, making her Vienna Staatsoper début in 1931 as a soubrette, and remaining for two seasons. After appearances in Darmstadt, 1933–5, she joined the Bayerische Staatsoper, Munich. She returned to Vienna in 1937, singing there regularly until 1958. She appeared at Salzburg from 1937 to 1941, as Eva, Euryanthe, Elisabeth (*Tannhäuser*), Mozart's Countess and Pamina, and returned as Arabella (1947) and the Marschallin (1949 and 1953). In 1938 she played Elsa at Covent Garden and Eva and Cio-cio-san at Chicago; in 1949, the Marschallin at the Paris Opéra, and the Marschallin and Ariadne at the New York City Opera. She had a beautiful, well-schooled voice and an elegant and aristocratic stage presence.

HAROLD ROSENTHAL

Reinitz, Béla (*b* Budapest, 15 Nov 1878; *d* Budapest, 27 Oct 1943). Hungarian composer, critic and administrator. In accordance with his parents' wishes he studied law in Kolozsvár and Budapest, taking his diploma in 1907. He never attended a music college, though he took piano lessons with Farkas in Kolozsvár and was a composition pupil of Siklos in Budapest. His careers as critic and composer began almost simultaneously: in 1908 he published his first criticism in the Budapest newspaper *Népszava*, and his first compositions were settings of Ady's *Vér és arany* ('Blood and gold'), published in the same year. He worked for *Népszava* until 1914 and then for *Világ* (1917–19) and he was one of the first to recognize the value of the work of Bartók and Kodály. Nonetheless, his most important contribution was his own songs: he worked almost exclusively in that genre, producing more than 500. His songs were first heard at literary gatherings in cafés during the period 1910–20. There he associated with Ady, and Reinitz's songs were partly responsible for bringing Ady's poetry to general acceptance. However, after the first publications (1910–11) a conflict broke out between poet and composer and Reinitz published no more Ady songs until after the poet's death in 1919. His settings of Ady have an improvisatory quality, with the declamatory vocal part taking the leading role, reflecting Ady's manner of delivery. The accompaniments are ill suited to piano or orchestra but, as Kodály suggested, Reinitz's songs were perhaps a necessary step on the way to those of Bartók, who dedicated his own Ady set to Reinitz. During the same period Reinitz wrote cabaret songs for the first Hungarian cabaret theatre, opened in 1907.

Reinitz had always been politically active, and he took a leading part in musical life after the 1919 revolution. On the fall of the new republic he was forced into exile and lived in Vienna and Germany until 1931.

He continued to compose songs to poetry by Ady and others, and from 1925 he was also active in producing left-wing political numbers to texts by Brecht, Mühsam, Herwegh and Tucholsky; his workers' songs had a great impact on their intended audience. In 1931 he returned to Hungary. A Béla Reinitz evening was held on 13 February 1932: the first occasion on which his songs were performed in a concert hall by professional musicians. He gained wider acceptance than he had had before World War I, but he was unable to find again the stimulating atmosphere of those times. Increasingly isolated, he died in an almshouse.

WORKS
(selective list)
(songs unless otherwise stated)

Ady dalok énekhangra, zongorakísérettel [Ady songs for solo voice with piano accompaniment] (Budapest, 1910)
Dalok Ady Endre verseire [Settings of Ady poems] (Budapest, 1911)
Egykor igy volt [It used to be like this] (Z. Somlyó) (Budapest, 1915)
Szomoru tavaszi ének [Sad spring song] (E. Szép) (Budapest and Leipzig, 1915)
Kop-kop (Szép) (Budapest and Leipzig, 1917)
Hét dal Ady Endre verseire [7 Ady songs] (Vienna, 1924)
Lene Levi (A. Lichtenstein), pubd in *Die Bühne* (29 Oct 1925)
Klabund-Lieder (Vienna and New York, 1926)
Es wird gehn . . . (Ça ira . . .), 8 songs (Vienna and New York, 1926)
Die Mädelchen am Fädelchen (Vienna, Berlin and New York, c1926)
Sieben Rappen (F. Wedekind), pubd in *Kunst und Volk* (1926), no.10
Schatten über Harlem (Singspiel, 4, O. Dymow) (Vienna, 1930)
Marsch der ungarischen Bergarbeiter (K. Tucholsky) (Moscow, 1931)
Dalok énekhangra, zongorakísérettel (Budapest, 1956) [incl. introduction by Kodály]
5 other stage pieces, choral work, lost str qt, fugues

BIBLIOGRAPHY
G. Fejes: 'Reinitz Béla zeneműveinek jegyzéke' [Reinitz's works], *Magyar zenetörténeti tanulmányok Szabolcsi Bence 70. születésnapjára*, ed. F. Bónis (Budapest, 1969)
A. Tóth: 'Uj Ady-dalok', *Pesti napló* (14 Feb 1932)
I. Péterffi: 'Reinitz Béla', *Magyar hirlap* (17 Feb 1932)
B. Révész: 'Reinitz Béla élete: az utolsó kottakönyv: "Halottak énekelnek" ' [Life of Reinitz: the last notebook: 'The dead sing'], *Népszava* (1 Jan 1944)

MELINDA BERLÁSZ KÁROLYI

Reinken, Johann Adam. *See* REINCKEN, JOHANN ADAM.

Reinmann, Matthias. *See* REYMANN, MATTHIAS.

Reinmar von Brennenberg [der Brenneberger, der Brannenburger, der Bremberger] (*d* Regensburg, ? before 1276). German Minnesinger. He came from a Bavarian noble family and was in the service of the Bishop of Regensburg. He died in a local feud at Regensburg. In terms of content and form his Minnelieder and *Sprüche* (*see* SPRUCH), rich in imagery and fantasy, belong among the work of those 13th-century Minnesinger connected with the courtly traditions. His work is close to that of Ulrich von Singenberg, REINMAR VON HAGENAU, HEINRICH VON MORUNGEN and WALTHER VON DER VOGELWEIDE. The manuscript tradition for his poems is unconvincing and contains several errors of form as well as a stylistic diversity that casts doubt on some of the ascriptions. There is no evidence to support his authorship for the 'Brennenberger' Ton in Meistergesang sources, but one melody in the Colmar manuscript (*D-Mbs* Cgm 4997, f.672) has the name 'In dem Brannenberger' and may be his even though it survives only with a later text, *In dyser zyt*; the correct text is probably *Wol mich des tages*.

BIBLIOGRAPHY
P. Runge, ed.: *Die Sangesweisen der Colmarer Handschrift und die Liederhandschrift Donaueschingen* (Leipzig, 1896/R1965), 158 [music edn.]

C. von Kraus, ed.: *Deutsche Liederdichter des 13. Jahrhunderts* (Tübingen, 1952–8), i, no.44 [text edn. and commentary]

H. Kuhn: *Minnesang des 13. Jahrhunderts* (Tübingen, 1953, rev. 2/1962), 159

For further bibliography *see* MINNESANG.

BURKHARD KIPPENBERG

Reinmar [Reimar] **(der Alte) von Hagenau** [Hagenouwe] (*fl* 1185–1205; *d* c1205). German Minnesinger. He was presumably a member of the family of imperial ministerial rank from Hagenau in Alsace. He is not attested in documents of the time: the manuscripts refer to him as 'Reinmar' or 'Reinmar der Alte', and Gotfrid von Strassburg described him as 'die nahtegal von Hagenouwe'. He may have participated in Leopold VI's crusade of 1197–8. Reinmar was one of the leading representatives of Hoher Minnesang, the form of which he raised to classic perfection. It was presumably he who brought this art form from his western homeland to Austria, where he was court poet to the Babenbergs. The character of his poetry is original and reveals hardly any influences of Friedrich von Hûsen's Rhenish school of poetry, which was orientated towards the Provençal lyric; all that can be discerned is the adoption of motifs and themes from the Danube school.

Reinmar's virtuosity had a far-reaching effect on contemporary poetry and poets, such as Ulrich von Lichtenstein, Neidhart von Reuental, and above all Walther von der Vogelweide, his pupil and later his rival. The Meistersinger later regarded him as one of 12 old masters. The characteristic features of his style are sensitivity, veiled circumlocutions and affected turns of phrase. His poetry combines themes of glorification of chivalrous virtue and of the lady of courtly society with reflection, self-analysis and autobiographical remarks.

Reinmar's considerable influence on other poets and a problematic manuscript tradition make it difficult to separate the authentic strophes from the inauthentic. C. von Kraus and others believe that of some 60 'Reinmar' poems that have survived, only slightly more than half are to be attributed to the poet; the remaining 'Pseudo-Reinmar' corpus is the work of his many pupils. It is possible to construct some kind of chronological order for his poems from the literary dispute between Reinmar and Walther von der Vogelweide (which is documented in several poems by both men) and from references made in his own poems.

WORKS

Text edition: *Des Minnesangs Frühling*, ed. K. Lachmann (Leipzig, 1857, rev. 30/1950 by C. von Kraus, 35/1970 without annotations) [MF]

POEMS SURVIVING WITH MUSIC

Daz eime wol getzogenen man tzer werl, *D-MÜsa* VII, 51 [melody and text fragmentary but ascribed 'Meister Reymar'; *Ton* not otherwise known among Reinmar's poetry, so text and music are normally considered unauthentic; ed. in Molitor, 500, with facsimile on the facing page

Sage, daz ich dirs iemer lône, MF 177.10, *D-Mbs* clm 4660 (Codex Buranus) [with staffless neumes]

Solde ab ich mit sorgen iemer leben, MF 185.27 (Pseudo-Reinmar), *Mbs* clm 4660 [preceded by Latin poem in same form with staffless neumes]

Ze niuwen fröiden stât mîn muot, MF 203.10 (Pseudo-Reinmar), *Mbs* clm 4660 [with inc. staffless neumes]

POEMS FOR WHICH MUSIC CAN BE RECONSTRUCTED FROM CONTRAFACTA

Der winter waere mir ein zît, MF 35.16 (?Pseudo-)Reinmar: ?contrafactum of Bernart de Ventadorn, 'Can vei la lauzeta mover' PC 70.43 [cf Hân ich iht vriunt]; ed. in A. Aarburg: *Singweisen zur Liebeslyrik der deutschen Frühe* (Düsseldorf, 1956), 39

Hân ich iht vriunt, die wünschen ir, MF 103.3 (pupil of Reinmar, though ascribed in MSS to Heinrich von Rugge): ?contrafactum of Bernart de Ventadorn, 'Can vei la lauzeta mover' PC 70.43 [cf

previous song]; ed. in Aarburg; *Singweisen zur Liebeslyrik der deutschen Frühe* (Düsseldorf, 1956), 32

Mîn ougen wurden lebens alse vol, MF 194.18 (Pseudo-Reinmar): ?contrafactum of Gaucelm Faidit, 'Mon cor e mi e mas bonas chansos' PC 167.37

BIBLIOGRAPHY

R. Molitor: 'Die Lieder des Münsterischen Fragmentes', *SIMG*, xii (1910–11), 475

C. von Kraus: *Des Minnesangs Frühling: Untersuchungen* (Leipzig, 1939), 341ff

H. de Boor: *Geschichte der deutschen Literatur*, ii (Munich, 1953, rev. 5/1962, 9/1974), 282ff [with bibliography, 322, 497]

U. Aarburg: 'Melodien zum frühen deutschen Minnesang', *Der deutsche Minnesang: Aufsätze zu seiner Erforschung*, ed. H. Fromm (Darmstadt, 1961, 5/1972), 378–421

K. H. Bertau: 'Überlieferung und Authentizität bei den Liedern Reinmars des Alten', *Zeitschrift für deutsche Philologie*, lxxxviii (1969), 389

V. L. Ziegler: *Reinmar von Hagenau and his School: a Study in Leitwort Technique* (diss., Yale U., 1970)

For further bibliography *see* MINNESANG.

BURKHARD KIPPENBERG

Reinmar von Zweter [Reymar von Zwetel, Reymar von Zweten, Römer von Zwickau, Ehrenbote] (*b* c1200; *d* c1260). German Minnesinger. The only biographical clues are contained in his poetry. Born of a noble family from Rhenish Franconia, he was an itinerant musician and composed *Sprüche* (*see* SPRUCH) with a variety of themes – religious, instructive, ethical and political. He grew up in Austria and spent time during his later travels at the courts of the Babenbergs in Vienna and of King Wenceslas I in Prague; he also spent periods in Cologne, Mainz and probably in Meissen.

Together with Bruder Wernher, Reinmar von Zweter is the most important *Spruch* poet of the later, less talented generation of poets after Walther von der Vogelweide. The content, style and form of his poetry is based on that of Walther. The later Meistersinger honoured him as one of the 12 old masters, perhaps on the basis of his 'Frauen-Ehren-Ton' for which he himself wrote over 200 *Spruch* stanzas and which formed the basis of many Meistersinger poems until the time of Hans Sachs. His surviving poetry comprises one *Leich*, several love poems and at least 229 authentic *Spruch* stanzas. The surviving musical evidence is small and confusing. The famous 'Frauen-Ehren-Ton' appears with three different melodies: one is in the Colmar and Donaueschingen manuscripts (ed. in Runge, 155; Taylor, i, 71 with facs.), another is in the lost manuscript of Adam Puschman (ed. in Münzer, no.69) and yet another is in *D-B* ms.fol.25. His one *Leich*, entitled *Got unt dîn eben êwikeit*, appears with music only in the Wiener Leichhandschrift (*A-Wn* 2701, ed. in Rietsch, 62; Taylor, i, 72). There is considerable doubt about the authenticity of the 'Sangweise' (*D-DO* 120, ed. in Runge, 184), the 'Schallweise' (*D-Mbs* Cgm 4997, ed. in Runge, 184 and Taylor, i, 148) and the 'Spiegelweise' (*D-Mbs* Cgm 4997, ed. in Runge, 161 and Taylor, i, 72; a different melody is in *D-B* ms.fol.25).

BIBLIOGRAPHY

G. Roethe, ed.: *Die Gedichte Reinmars von Zweter* (Leipzig, 1887) [complete edn. and biographical material]

P. Runge, ed.: *Die Sangesweisen der Colmarer Handschrift und die Liederhandschrift Donaueschingen* (Leipzig, 1896/R1965)

G. Münzer, ed.: *Das Singebuch des Adam Puschman* (Leipzig, 1906/R1970)

H. Rietsch, ed.: *Gesänge von Frauenlob, Reinmar v. Zweter und Alexander*, DTÖ, xli, Jg.xx (1913/R)

R. J. Taylor: *The Art of the Minnesinger* (Cardiff, 1968)

G. Objartel: 'Zwei wenig beachtete Fragmente Reinmars von Zweter und ein lateinisches Gegenstück seines Leichs', *Zeitschrift für deutsche Philologie*, xc (1971), *Sonderheft*, 217

For further bibliography *see* MINNESANG.

BURKHARD KIPPENBERG

Reinspeck, Michael. *See* KEINSPECK, MICHAEL.

Reinthaler, Karl (Martin) (*b* Erfurt, 13 Oct 1822; *d* Bremen, 13 Feb 1896). German conductor and composer. He had early training in music from G. A. Ritter and then studied theology in Berlin, but after passing his state examination devoted himself entirely to music and studied with A. B. Marx. His first attempts at composition attracted the attention of Friedrich Wilhelm IV and procured him a travelling grant. He visited Paris, Milan, Rome and Naples, taking singing lessons from Geraldi and Bordogni. On his return to Germany in 1853 he obtained a post at the Cologne Conservatory and in 1858 became organist in Bremen Cathedral and conductor of the Singakademie. He had already composed an oratorio, *Jephta* (performed in London in 1856 by Hullah), and in 1875 his opera *Edda* was successfully produced at Bremen, Hanover and elsewhere. His *Bismarck Hymne* obtained the prize at Dortmund, and he composed a symphony and a large number of part-songs. His cantata *In der Wüste* was highly successful and his opera *Käthchen von Heilbronn*, based on Kleist's drama, was chosen by competition for the opening in 1881 of the new opera house at Frankfurt am Main. Reinthaler was a member of the Berlin Academy from 1882 and became Royal Professor in 1888. He retired from the Singakademie in 1890.

Reinthaler is today remembered for his friendship with Brahms, of whose *German Requiem* he was the first conductor, in 1868; he had previously failed to persuade Brahms to extend the work with movements of more specifically Christian content.

BIBLIOGRAPHY

H. von Bülow: *Ausgewählte Schriften*, ii (Leipzig, 2/1911), 210ff
Johannes Brahms im Briefwechsel mit Reinthaler (Berlin, 2/1912) [Deutsche Brahms Gesellschaft edn.]

FRANZ GEHRING

Reis, Jakub. *See* REYS, JAKUB.

Reisch, Gregor [Reischius, Georgium] (*b* Balingen, nr. Tübingen, between *c*1465 and *c*1470; *d* Freiburg, 9 May 1525). German scholar and music theorist. He studied at Freiburg University, becoming Magister in 1489, and at Ingolstadt University, and then entered the Carthusian order. He was prior of the monasteries of Klein-Basel (1500–02) and Freiburg (1503–25). He was in close contact with the best humanists of his time, was one of Johannes Eck's teachers, and was considered one of Germany's most learned men; Erasmus referred to him as an 'oracle' among the Germans.

Reisch's *Margarita philosophica* (Freiburg, 1503) was an enormously popular Latin dialogue textbook which was frequently reissued; its last edition appeared in 1600. (It is unlikely that there was an edition produced at Heidelberg in 1496; contrary to *MGG*, the textbook is not the same as St Hawes's *The Passetime of Pleasure*, London, 1509.) The fifth book is divided into two parts, concerning the 'principles' and 'practice' of music, and cites such authorities as Pythagoras, Plato, Augustine, Boethius and al-Fārābī. On the whole it is a typical Renaissance didactic treatise, dealing with definitions and origins of music, divisions into *musica mundana*, *humana* and *instrumentalis*, classification of consonances and dissonances, use of the monochord, medieval church modes and hexachord solmization. Of special interest are the relatively extensive music examples which in the first edition are written in *Hufnagel*. The 1512 edition incorporates a part of Nicholas Wollick's *Opus aureum musicae* (1501) to serve as a section on *musica figurata*.

BIBLIOGRAPHY

Walther ML [incl. complete list of chap. titles]
G. Münzel: 'Der Kartäuserprior Gregor Reisch und die Margarita philosophica', *Zeitschrift des Freiburger Geschichtsverein*, xlviii (1938), 1
K. W. Niemöller: *Nicholas Wollick ... und seine Musiktraktat* (Cologne, 1956)
K. W. Niemöller: *Die Musica figurativa des M. Schanppecher* (Cologne, 1961)

T. HERMAN KEAHEY

Reisenauer, Alfred (*b* Königsberg, 1 Nov 1863; *d* Libau, 3 Oct 1907). German pianist and composer. A child prodigy, he studied music first with his mother and then with L. Köhler. When he was 12 his parents took him to Weimar for an audition with Liszt, whose favourite pupil he soon became and with whom he made his début at Rome in 1881. After a period spent studying law in Leipzig, and after playing in London and throughout much of Germany, he undertook extended tours of Russia, Siberia and China; he settled in 1900 as a teacher at the Leipzig Conservatory. Among his pupils were Sergei Bortkiewicz, Bruno Hinze-Reinhold and Sigfrid Karg-Elert. He continued to give concerts (over 2000 altogether), and died during another Russian tour. His piano playing was highly praised by Niemann, especially his interpretation of Romantic music; as a composer he was noted for many fine songs and the *Reisebilder* op.14 for piano.

BIBLIOGRAPHY

J. von Schwerin: *Erinnerungen an Alfred Reisenauer* (Königsberg, 1909)
W. Niemann: *Meister des Klaviers* (Berlin, 1919)
F. Weingartner: *Lebenserinnerungen* (Zurich, 1928–9)

Reisinger, Barbara. *See* GERL family.

Reiss, Albert (*b* Berlin, 22 Feb 1870; *d* Nice, 19 June 1940). German tenor. He began his career as an actor in Hamburg, where his voice was discovered by the Intendant Pollini and the singer Schumann-Heink. He then studied in Berlin with Wilhelm Vilmar, later with Beno Stolzenburg and Julius Lieban, and made his operatic début at Königsberg in September 1897, as Ivanov in *Zar und Zimmermann*. After engagements at Posen (1898–9) and Wiesbaden (1899–1901) he was engaged by the Metropolitan Opera, where he sang every season until 1920, being especially acclaimed for his David in *Die Meistersinger* and Mime in the *Ring*; he also appeared with success as the Witch in *Hänsel und Gretel*, a role usually sung by a contralto. In New York he created Nick in *La fanciulla del West* (1910), the Broom-maker in Humperdinck's *Königskinder* (1910), Nial in Parker's *Mona* (1912), and Richard in De Koven's *Canterbury Pilgrims* (1917). He sang Alfred in the Metropolitan première of *Die Fledermaus* (1905), Vašek (under Mahler) in the Metropolitan première of *The Bartered Bride* (1909) and Valzacchi in the New York première of *Der Rosenkavalier* (1913). At Covent Garden (1902–5 and 1924–9) he sang David, Mime and Valzacchi. In 1916 Reiss appeared in and produced Mozart's *Bastien und Bastienne* and *Der Schauspieldirektor* in New York with considerable success; this led him to promote a season of opera later that year at the Lyceum Theater, New York, and to organize the Society of American Singers in 1917. After leaving the Metropolitan Opera, Reiss returned to Germany and sang at the Berlin Volksoper, 1923–5, and later at the Städtische Oper. He was one of the most successful *comprimario* tenors of his day.

HAROLD ROSENTHAL

Reiss, Józef (Władysław) [Dembina, Jan] (*b* Dębica, Małopolska, 4 Aug 1879; *d* Kraków, 22 Feb 1956). Polish musicologist. He studied history at Kraków University and musicology with Adler at Vienna University. In addition to his activities as a secondary school teacher from 1901 he lectured on theoretical subjects at the Kraków Conservatory. In 1910 he took the doctorate in Vienna with a dissertation on Gomółka's psalm tunes (1580) and in 1922 he completed his *Habilitation* at Kraków with a work on the Polish polyphonic hymn in the 16th century and worked in the musicology department until 1939. After the war he resumed his post at Kraków; he was appointed professor in 1949, and retired as professor emeritus in 1953.

Reiss united scholarly interests with activities as a popularizer. He published a series of valuable articles on the history of early Polish music as well as discussions of aesthetic and sociological questions, books on acoustics and instruments, monographs on Beethoven and Wieniawski, and numerous popular articles on Polish and foreign composers of the 19th and 20th centuries. He also wrote textbooks on harmony, music history and musical forms for music schools. His publications played a great part in promoting general music education in Poland.

WRITINGS

Nikolaus Gomółka und seine Psalmen-Melodien (diss., U. of Vienna, 1910; extracts in *ZIMG*, xiii (1911–12), 249; Pol. edn. *Melodie psalmowe Mikołaja Gomółki, 1580*, Kraków, 1912)
Problem treści w muzyce [The problem of content in music] (Kraków, 1915, enlarged 2/1922)
Formy muzyczne [Musical forms] (Leipzig, 1917, 2/1929)
Beethoven (Warsaw, 1920)
Historia muzyki w zarysie [A concise history of music] (Warsaw, 1920, rev. 2/1921, enlarged 3/1931)
'Georgius Libanus Lignicensis als musiker', *ZMw*, v (1922–3), 17
Polska wielogłosowa pieśń kościelna w XVI wieku [Polish polyphonic hymn in the 16th century] (Habilitationsschrift, U. of Kraków, 1922)
Harmonia (Warsaw, 1923)
Przyczynki do dziejów muzyki w Polsce [Contributions to the history of music in Poland] (Kraków, 1923)
'Zwei mehrstimmige Lieder aus dem 15. Jahrhundert', *ZMw*, v (1922–3), 481
Encyklopedia muzyki (Warsaw, 1924)
Książki o muzyce w Bibliotece Jagiellońskiej [Books on music in the Jagellonian library] (Kraków, 1924–38)
Skrzypce, ich budowa, technika i literatura [The violin: its construction, technique and literature] (Warsaw, 1924)
'Pauli Paulirini de Praga "Tractatus de musica" (etwa 1460)', *ZMw*, vii (1924–5), 259
ed.: *Listy Imć Pana Grzegorza Kątskiego do Filharmoniey krakowskiey* [Kątski's letters to the Kraków PO] (Kraków, 1930)
Henryk Wieniawski (Warsaw, 1931, 3/1970)
Muzyka w Krakowie w XIV wieku [Music in Kraków in the 14th century] (Kraków, 1931)
Jak Kraków walczył o operę [How Kraków fought over opera] (Kraków, 1934)
Socjologiczne podłoże śląskiej pieśni ludowej [The sociological basis of Silesian folksong] (Katowice, 1935)
Ślązak Józef Elsner, nauczyciel Chopina [The Silesian Józef Elsner, the teacher of Chopin] (Katowice, 1936)
ed.: *Listy Jana Galla do S. A. Krzyżanowskiego w Krakowie* [Gall's letters to Krzyżanowski in Kraków] (Katowice, 1937)
Almanach muzyczny Krakowa 1780–1914 [An almanac of music in Kraków 1780–1914] (Kraków, 1939)
Elementarz muzyczny [Rudiments of music] (Kraków, 1944, rev. 2/1948)
Najpiękniejsza ze wszystkich jest muzyka polska [The most beautiful of

all is Polish music] (Kraków, 1946, 2/1958)
Skrzypce i skrzypkowie [Violins and violinists] (Kraków, 1955)
Mała encyklopedia muzyki [Short encyclopedia of music] (Warsaw, 1960)

EDITIONS

M. Gomółka: Melodie na Psałterz polski (1580) [Tunes for the Polish psalter (1580)] (Kraków, 1923–7)

ZOFIA HELMAN

Reissiger, Karl Gottlieb (*b* Belzig, 31 Jan 1798; *d* Dresden, 7 Nov 1859). German composer, conductor and teacher. He was the eldest son of Christian Gottlieb Reissiger, organist and choirmaster at Belzig. From 1811 to 1818 he was a pupil at the Thomasschule in Leipzig, where he studied the piano and composition with Schicht, the musical director. He began studying theology at the University of Leipzig; in the same year, Schicht advised him to abandon these studies in favour of a musical career and two years later awarded him a bursary to further his musical studies elsewhere. In 1821 Reissiger left Leipzig for Vienna, where he took theory lessons from Salieri, and in 1822 he moved to Munich to study composition and singing with Winter. By this time his songs and piano pieces were gaining public favour, though he failed in his attempts to gain municipal posts at Leipzig in 1822 and Dresden in 1824. However, his first opera, *Didone abbandonata*, was given in Dresden in 1824 under the direction of Weber with moderate success, and Reissiger was given 500 thalers by the King of Prussia to study the methods of musical education in France and Italy and to advise on its reorganization in Berlin. On his return to Berlin in 1825 he taught composition until invited in the following year to succeed Weber as director of the Court Opera in Dresden. As a champion of German opera, he was at first harassed by pro-Italian factions, but his excellent performances of *Oberon* and *Euryanthe* won him approval, and in 1828 he was appointed Hofkapellmeister with responsibility for sacred music, chamber music and the music for the court theatre, a post he held until his death. Under his direction the Dresden Opera became acknowledged as the best in Germany; in 1842 he gave the first performance of Wagner's *Rienzi* and in 1843 welcomed its composer as second Kapellmeister. Relations between the two men deteriorated when Reissiger declined to set Wagner's libretto *Die hohe Braut*, after which Wagner portrayed him, apparently quite falsely, as a philistine opponent of his progressive artistic views. Reissiger was noted as a gifted conductor – in 1854 Berlioz wrote of the high standard of the Dresden orchestra – and was also regularly called upon to direct music festivals, adjudicate at competitions and advise on musical education. Clara Schumann was one of his theory pupils.

As a part-time but prolific composer, Reissiger confined himself mainly to producing works in the fashionable forms of his day or else for use in Dresden. In the former category are his 80 or so published piano solos and his 70 or 80 collections of songs and duets, in the latter his nine masses and numerous smaller sacred choral pieces, 27 piano trios and other chamber music, and eight operas, of which only *Die Felsenmühle* (1831) was successful outside Dresden. His melodrama *Yelva* (1827) enjoyed widespread popularity, as did the fifth of his *Danses brillantes pour le pianoforte* (1822), known as 'Webers letzter Gedanke'. He wrote several male-voice choruses for the Liedertafel.

Reissiger embodied the dying tradition of the

Kapellmeister-composer, and despite sound craftsmanship (Schumann described the construction of his piano trios as 'exemplary') his music has been forgotten, perhaps because of lack of individuality. His chamber music, like that of Spohr and Onslow, remains within the limits of the tradition of Mozart and Beethoven; his solo and choral songs recall those of Weber and Marschner, and his piano music is indebted to the 'brilliant' style of Herz and Hünten. Weak librettos and lack of dramatic sense hampered him in opera, his favourite but least successful form.

Reissiger's younger brother Friedrich August (*b* Belzig, 26 July 1809; *d* Fredrikshald, Norway, 2 March 1883) was also intended for a theological career but turned to music, settled in Christiania (now Oslo) and gained a modest reputation there as a conductor, military bandmaster, composer and teacher; his works include choral and piano pieces and four operas.

WORKS

STAGE
DO – *Court Opera, Dresden*

Das Rockenweibchen (opera), 1821, unperf., ov. pubd
Nero (incidental music), 1822, ov. pubd
Didone abbandonata (opera, 2, Metastasio), DO, 31 Jan 1824
Der Ahnenschatz (opera), 1825, inc.
Yelva (melodrama, T. Hell, after Scribe), DO, 1827
Libella (grand opera, 2, Theophania), DO, 4 Jan 1829
Die Felsenmühle zu Etalières (romantic opera, 2, B. von Miltitz), DO, 10 April 1831
Turandot (grand opera, 2), DO, 22 Jan 1835
Adèle de Foix (grand opera, 4, R. Blum), DO, 26 Nov 1841
Der Schiffbruch der Medusa (opera, 4, after Brothers Cogniard), DO, 16 Aug 1846

VOCAL
David (oratorio), solo v, chorus, orch
Requiem, 9 masses, 4 Ger. masses, motets, hymns, psalms, graduals, offertories, Miserere settings, chorale settings, sacred songs
8 bks of Liedertafel songs, male vv; other partsongs, 1 bk for mixed chorus, 1 bk for male vv; c10 bks of duets, 2vv, pf; c60 bks of songs, 1v, pf; 1 bk of songs, 1v, hn, pf; var. individual partsongs and solo songs

INSTRUMENTAL
Orch: Sym.; many ovs.; Fl Concertino; Cl Concertino; Fantasia, cl, orch
Chamber music: 3 pf qnts; qnt, 2 vn, va, 2 vc; 7 pf qts; 8 str qts; 27 pf trios; 5 sonatas, vn, pf; 2 sonatas, vc, pf; other works: vn solo; vn, pf; vc, pf; cl, pf; hn, pf
Pf solo: numerous rondos; sonatas, variation sets, marches, ovs., other works

BIBLIOGRAPHY
W. Neumann: *K. G. Reissiger* (Kassel, 1854)
R. Prölss: *Geschichte des Hoftheaters zu Dresden* (Dresden, 1878)
A. Kohut: 'R. Wagner and K. G. Reissiger', *AMz*, xxxvii (1910), 53
J. Reichelt: 'R. Wagner und sein Kollege Reissiger', *AMz*, xxxvii (1913), 505
K. Kreiser: *Carl Gottlieb Reissiger: sein Leben nebst einigen Beiträgen zur Geschichte des Konzertwesens in Dresden* (diss., U. of Leipzig, 1918; Dresden, 1918) [with complete list of works]
H. Schnoor: *Dresden: vierhundert Jahre deutscher Musikkultur* (Dresden, 1948)
B. Kortsen, ed.: *Brev fra F. A. Reissiger* (Bergen, 1976)

JOHN RUTTER

Reissmann, August (Friedrich Wilhelm) (*b* Frankenstein, Silesia, 14 Nov 1825; *d* Berlin, 13 July 1903). German writer on music and composer. In Breslau from 1843 he studied principally with Mosewius and E. L. Richter. In 1850 he settled in Weimar, and from 1863 to 1880 lived in Berlin, where he remained (apart from short stays in Wiesbaden and Leipzig) for the rest of his life, teaching at the Stern Conservatory from 1866 to 1874. As a conservatively biassed writer on music he was especially active between 1861 and 1893, but most of his work consists of superficial essays. In his books he showed a preference

for musical analysis rather than research and the presentation of biographical facts, but the *Musikalisches Conversations-Lexikon*, which he edited after the death of its previous editor Hermann Mendel, is still useful as a wide-ranging reference book for 19th-century music. Though he never won a reputation as a composer, Reissmann wrote three operas: *Gudrun* (Leipzig, 1871), based on a German poem, and *Die Bürgermeisterin von Schorndorf* (Leipzig, 1880) and *Das Gralspiel* (Düsseldorf, 1895), both based on historical events. He also composed choral works, a symphony, a violin concerto, music for violin and piano, piano pieces and songs.

WRITINGS
Das Partiturspiel in einem geordneten Lehrgang (Leipzig, n.d.)
Katechismus der Gesangskunst (Leipzig, 1853)
Das deutsche Lied in seiner historischen Entwicklung (Kassel, 1861)
Von Bach bis Wagner: zur Geschichte der Musik (Berlin, 1861)
Allgemeine Geschichte der Musik, i–iii (Munich, 1863–4; Leipzig, 1864)
Allgemeine Musiklehre (Berlin, 1864, 2/1874)
Grundriss der Musikgeschichte (Munich, 1865)
Robert Schumann: sein Leben und seine Werke (Berlin, 1865, 2/1871; Eng. trans., 1886)
Lehrbuch der musikalischen Komposition (Berlin, 1866–71)
Felix Mendelssohn-Bartholdy: sein Leben und seine Werke (Berlin, 1867, 3/1893)
Franz Schubert: sein Leben und seine Werke (Berlin, 1873)
Geschichte des deutschen Liedes (Berlin, 1874)
ed.: *Musikalisches Conversations-Lexikon*, vii–xi and suppl. (Berlin, 1877–80, 3/1890–91/R1969)
Klavier- und Gesangschule für den ersten Unterricht (Leipzig, c1875)
Die königliche Hochschule für Musik in Berlin (Berlin, 1876)
'Form und Inhalt des musikalischen Kunstwerkes', *Sammlung musikalischer Vorträge*, 1st ser., v (Leipzig, 1879), 143
Zur Aesthetik der Tonkunst (Berlin, 1879)
Joseph Haydn: sein Leben und seine Werke (Berlin, 1879)
Johann Sebastian Bach: sein Leben und seine Werke (Berlin and Leipzig, 1881)
Illustrirte Geschichte der deutschen Musik (Leipzig, 1881, 2/1892)
Handlexikon der Tonkunst (Berlin, 1882)
Christoph Willibald von Gluck: sein Leben und seine Werke (Berlin and Leipzig, 1882)
Georg Friedrich Händel: sein Leben und seine Werke (Berlin and Leipzig, 1882)
Carl Maria von Weber: sein Leben und seine Werke (Berlin, 1883)
Die Hausmusik in ihrer Organisation und kulturgeschichtlichen Bedeutung (Berlin, 1884)
Die sociale Lage der Musiker in der Gegenwart (Breslau, 1884)
Die Oper in ihrer kunst- und kulturhistorischen Bedeutung (Stuttgart, 1885)
Die Musik als Hülfsmittel der Erziehung (Wiesbaden, c1888)
Friedrich Lux: sein Leben und seine Werke (Leipzig, 1888)
'Der Naturalismus in der Kunst: eine kritische Studie', *Deutsche Zeit- und Streit-Fragen: Flugschriften zur Kenntniss der Gegenwart*, new ser., vi (Hamburg, 1891), 265–338
'Die Kunst und die Gesellschaft: eine kritische Studie', *Sammlung gemeinverständlicher wissenschaftlicher Vorträge*, new ser., vii (Hamburg, 1892), 33–79
Was wird aus unserer deutschen Musik? (Berlin, 1897)

BIBLIOGRAPHY
J. Göllrich: *August Reissmann als Schriftsteller und Komponist* (Leipzig, 1884)
B. P. V. Moyer: *Concepts of Musical Form in the Nineteenth Century with Special Reference to A. B. Marx and Sonata Form* (diss., Stanford U., 1969), 135ff

MARTIN ELSTE

Reiter, Franz de Paula von. *See* ROSER, FRANZ DE PAULA.

Reiz, Jakub de. *See* REYS, JAKUB.

Reizen, Mark. *See* REYZEN, MARK.

Reizenstein, Franz (Theodor) (*b* Nuremberg, 7 June 1911; *d* London, 15 Oct 1968). English composer and pianist of German birth. He came of an artistic and musical family; in 1930 he went to the Berlin State Academy, where he studied composition with

Hindemith and the piano with Leonid Kreutzer. Unable to remain in Germany when the Nazis came to power, he left for London in 1934. There he studied composition with Vaughan Williams at the Royal College of Music, and took piano lessons privately with Solomon. Interned as an alien at the beginning of the war, he was active in arranging and performing music at his camp. On his release, he worked until the end of the war as a railway clerk, also performing at many wartime concerts. Reizenstein was a professor of piano at the Royal Academy of Music (1958–68) and at the Royal Manchester College of Music (1962–8). He formed his own piano trio, and often appeared as a soloist in concertos and recitals, playing his own works, those of Hindemith and many well-known and unfamiliar 19th-century concertos. He went to Boston University as visiting professor of composition in 1966, and for a time taught composition at Hendon Technical College.

Reizenstein's early output consisted largely of piano and chamber music. In 1951 his first major choral work *Voices of Night* appeared, and this led to commissions for the radio opera *Anna Kraus* and the oratorio *Genesis*. The texts for all three were written or compiled by his close friend Christopher Hassall, to whose memory the slow movement of the Second Piano Sonata was later dedicated. In the 1950s he wrote a number of film scores and two of the most witty and successful pastiche works ever performed at Gerard Hoffnung's musical entertainments. His works for orchestra are relatively few, and the symphony at which he was working in his later years was never completed. He wrote much for specific occasions and performers, as a practical and complete craftsman with a nice sense of the requirements of each occasion. Earlier works show the influence of Hindemith in the use of short motives as units of construction, in almost continuous contrapuntal activity, and more generally in emotional reticence and reliance on workmanlike activity to maintain interest. Even these early works have little of the harmonic acerbity of early Hindemith, while in later years, though there was no sharp break with earlier practices, more genial, romantic and expressive elements and freer types of thematic development and transformation appeared in Reizenstein's music.

In his best works, he found a just balance between professional craftsmanship and creative imagination. Thus the 12 Preludes and Fugues for piano, which takes Hindemith's 'series I' as a basis to order the keys, is technically and emotionally a considerable work, closely integrated by thematic connection between each prelude and fugue, and ending with a sustained and brilliant fugue which provides a true culmination to the series. *The Zodiac* (12 pieces for amateur pianists) reveals Reizenstein as a composer with an economical and precise lightness of touch. *Voices of Night* and the noble Elizabeth Browning Sonnets display his subtle and perceptive word-setting.

WORKS
ORCHESTRAL
op.
8   Cello Concerto, 1936, rev. 1948
—   Capriccio, 1938
15 Ballet Suite, 1940
16 Piano Concerto no.1, 1941
28 Overture: Cyrano de Bergerac, 1951
29 Serenade, F, wind, 1951, arr. as op.29a, orch, 1951
—   A Jolly Overture, 1952
31 Violin Concerto, 1953
—   Concerto popolare, 1958 [for Hoffnung concert]
37 Piano Concerto no.2, 1959
43 Concerto, str, 1967
Film music

VOCAL
27 Voices of Night (Hassall), S, Bar, chorus, orch, 1951
30 Anna Kraus (radio opera, Hassall), 1952
—   Let's Fake an Opera, 1958 [for Hoffnung concerts]
35 Genesis (Hassall), S, Bar, chorus, orch, 1958
36 Five Sonnets of E. B. Browning, T, pf, 1959

CHAMBER
1   Sonata, vc, 1931, rev. as op.44, 1967
2   Theme, Variations and Fugue, cl qnt, 1931, rev. 1960
5   Wind Quintet, 1934
7/1 Three Pieces [arr. from Piano Suite, op.6], vn, pf, 1936
7/2 Elegy, vc, pf, 1936
9   Divertimento, str qt, 1936, arr. as op.9a, 2 tpt, hn, tuba, 1937
10   Three Concert Pieces, ob, pf, 1937
11   Sonatina, ob, pf, 1937
12   Prologue, Variations and Finale, vn, pf, 1938
13   Partita, fl/rec, pf, 1938, arr. as op.13a, fl, str trio, 1938
18   Cantilena, vc, pf, 1941
20   Sonata, vn, pf, 1945
22   Sonata, vc, pf, 1947
23   Piano Quintet, 1948
25   Trio, fl, ob, pf, 1949
33   Fantasia concertante, vn, pf, 1956
34   Piano Trio [1 movt], 1957
38   Duo, ob, cl, 1963
39   Trio, fl, cl, bn, 1963
42   Concert Fantasy, va, pf, 1966
45   Sonata, va, 1967
46   Sonata, vn, 1968
47   Arabesques, cl, pf, 1968
48   Sonatina [2 movts], cl, pf, 1968

PIANO
Fantasy, op.3, 1933; 4 Silhouettes, op.4, 1934; Suite, op.6, 1936; Impromptu, op.14, 1938; 5 Imaginative Pieces, 1938; Intermezzo, op.17, 1941; Sonata no.1, op.19, 1944; Scherzo, op.21, 1947; Legend, op.24, 1949; Scherzo fantastique, op.26, 1950; Musical Box, 1952 [educational pieces]; 12 Preludes and Fugues, op.32, 1955; Sonata no.2, op.40, 1964; The Zodiac, op.41, 1964

Principal publisher: Boosey & Hawkes

WRITINGS
'Composer and String Player', *The Listener*, lxxvii (1967), 304

BIBLIOGRAPHY
J. Weissmann: 'The Music of Franz Reizenstein', *The Listener*, xlvii (1952), 977
A. Jacobs: 'Reizenstein's "Voices of Night" ', *MT*, xciv (1953), 505, 561
J. Weissmann: 'Reizenstein's Recent Music', *The Listener*, lvii (1957), 133
——: 'Reizenstein's "Genesis" and its Antecedents', *The Listener*, lx (1958), 357
R. Henderson: 'English by Adoption', *The Listener*, lxv (1961), 201
F. Routh: *Contemporary British Music* (London, 1972), 137ff
HUGO COLE

Rejcha, Anton [Antonín]. *See* REICHA, ANTOINE.

Rejcha, Josef. *See* REICHA, JOSEF.

Réjouissance (Fr.: 'rejoicing' or 'merrymaking'). A movement of a lively and joyous character, generally in binary form, sometimes included in the *Galanterien* of the 18th-century suite. Most réjouissances occur in suites in the French style for orchestra where the mood of rejoicing can be enhanced by brass and woodwind instruments (J. S. Bach: Ouverture no.4 in D, BWV 1069; Telemann: Ouverture in D, complete edn., x, p.62). Timpani contribute further to this effect in 'La réjouissance', appropriately included by Handel in his Royal Fireworks music written to celebrate the Peace of Aix-la-Chapelle in 1749.

MICHAEL TILMOUTH

Relative key (Ger. *Paralleltonart*). A key with the same key signature as another given key: C major is the relative major of A minor; E minor is the relative minor of G major. *See also* KEY (i) and TONALITY.

Rellstab, Johann Carl Friedrich (*b* Berlin, 27 Feb 1759; *d* Berlin, 19 Aug 1813). German music publisher and composer. From 1768 to 1775 he performed in student concerts at the Joachimsthal Gymnasium, playing keyboard concertos by J. S. and C. P. E. Bach. He studied with J. F. Agricola from 1773 (mainly the keyboard) and with C. F. C. Fasch in 1776–8 (mainly composition). In 1779 his father, who had acquired Berlin's oldest printing firm, had a stroke, and Rellstab was forced to step into the business and to abandon plans for study with C. P. E. Bach. Soon he enlarged the business, adding a new printing press, a publishing firm and a music shop where keyboard (both English and German), string and wind instruments, musical clocks and tuning forks were sold, and where from 1792, harpsichords, pianos, harps and violin bows were manufactured. In 1783 he established a music lending library, and his firm issued music prints at least as early as 1785. In 1787 he acquired G. L. Winter's publishing firm and in the same year instituted a series of weekly public subscription 'Concerts for Connoisseurs and Amateurs' at the English House, a series he was forced by financial necessity in 1788 to continue as private fortnightly concerts at members' homes. The concerts were often attended by Fasch, Reichardt, Zelter and others, and included both sacred and secular works such as Bach's *Magnificat* and Gluck's *Alceste*. Unfortunate political conditions forced the temporary cancellation of the concerts in 1806 and the sales of many instruments in 1808; in 1812 the lending library almost ceased to function and the press was permanently shut down. Rellstab continued selling some music and wind instruments, giving lessons in singing, declamation, composition and continuo realization. In his views on theory, he backed Marpurg over Kirnberger and hence maintained a close adherence to the tenets of Rameau regarding chord generation. From 1808 to 1813 he was critic for the *Vossische Zeitung*, for which he wrote 155 reviews and 155 other articles.

Rellstab's eldest daughter, Caroline Rellstab (*b* Berlin, 18 April 1793; *d* Breslau, 17 Feb 1813), was a singer noted for her extraordinary range extending to *f'''*. She was at the Breslau Opera from 1811, and was particularly well known for her role as the Queen of Night in Mozart's *Die Zauberflöte*. His son LUDWIG RELLSTAB was a poet and an important music critic.

WORKS

All printed works published by Rellstab in Berlin; complete list in Guttmann (1910); op. nos. are those of the publisher unless otherwise stated.

VOCAL

Stage: Die Apotheke (Singspiel, 2, J. J. Engel), unperf., 1 selection as op.16 in Clavier-Magazin für Kenner und Liebhaber (1787), 2 selections as op.28 in Melodie und Harmonie (1788), 5 selections as op.111 (Rellstab op.8) in Lieder und Gesänge verschiedener Art (1791)

Cantatas, Odes: Zum Geburtstag eines Greises, Zu einer Hochzeitsfeyer, Am Geburtstag einer Mutter, in Lieder und Gesänge verschiedener Art (1791); An die Freude (Schiller), in 14 Compositionen zu Schillers Ode an die Freude (Hamburg, 1799–1800); 4 others, lost

Songs (some 4vv or more): 9, in Clavier-Magazin für Kenner und Liebhaber (1787); 11, in Melodie und Harmonie (1788); 18, in Lieder und Gesänge verschiedener Art (1791); 6, in Winterblumen am Clavier (1793–5); 3 as opp.290, 311, in Blumenkranz dem neuen Jahrhundert geflochten (1800–01); 4 as opp.320, 329, 330, in Frohe und gesellige Lieder (1802–3)

Other: Te Deum, mass, other frags., lost

INSTRUMENTAL

Orch.: Sym., 2 orchs, 1806, lost; 5 syms., 2 ovs., before 1790, lost; 12 marches, pf, arr. orch without strs, lost

Other: 6 character pieces, pf, op.16, in Clavier-Magazin für Kenner und Liebhaber (1787); Sonata, org/hpd, op.39 (Rellstab op.5), in Melodie und Harmonie (1788); 12 marches, pf, op.79 (Rellstab op.12), in Neue Olla Potrida (1790); 6 solfeggi, kbd, in Neue Olla Potrida (1790); Sonatine, pf, fl, in Neue Olla Potrida (1790); Fantasia, glass harmonica (n.d.); 24 short pieces, 2 vn, b, lost

WRITINGS

Versuch über die Vereinigung der musikalischen und oratorischen Declamation, hauptsächlich für Musiker und Componisten mit erläuternden Beyspielen, op.7 (Rellstab op.1) (Berlin, 1786)

Ueber die Bermerkungen eines Reisenden, die Berlinischen Kirchenmusiken, Concerte, Oper und königliche Kammermusik betreffend (Berlin, 1789)

Anleitung für Clavierspieler, den Gebrauch der Bachschen Fingersetzung, die Manieren und den Vortrag betreffend, op.62 (Rellstab op.4) (Berlin, 1790)

BIBLIOGRAPHY

GerberNL

C. von Ledebur: *Tonkünstler-Lexicon Berlin's* (Berlin, 1861/R1965)

H. F. L. Rellstab: *Aus meinem Leben* (Berlin, 1861)

O. Guttmann: *Johann Karl Friedrich Rellstab: ein Beitrag zur Musikgeschichte Berlins* (Berlin, 1910)

W. Hitzig: 'Ein Berliner Aktenstück zur Geschichte des Notendruckverfahrens', *Festschrift Peter Wagner* (Leipzig, 1926/R1969), 81

R. Elvers: 'Die bei J. K. F. Rellstab in Berlin bis 1800 erschienenen Mozart-Drucke', *MJb 1957*, 152

H. Heussner: 'Rellstab', *MGG*

C. H. Porter: *The Rhenish Episode in the Romantic Lied: An Expression of German Identity in the Wake of Napoleon* (diss., U. of Maryland, 1975)

SHELLEY DAVIS

Rellstab, (Heinrich Friedrich) Ludwig (*b* Berlin, 13 April 1799; *d* Berlin, 27 Nov 1860). German music critic and poet, son of J. C. F. Rellstab. As a child he excelled in keyboard performances of Bach and Mozart. In 1816 he studied the keyboard with Ludwig Berger and theory with Bernhard Klein, and with both of them helped found the Jüngere Liedertafel in 1819. In 1823 his first published set of poems appeared, and he completed the libretto for Bernhard Klein's *Dido*. In March 1825 he met Beethoven, and although Beethoven expressed interest in having an opera libretto by Rellstab no further progress was made. In 1826 he became the music critic for the *Vossische Zeitung*. As an outspoken proponent of Germanic opera, in 1826 he satirized the singer Henriette Sontag who had created a vogue for Rossini, and in 1827 severely criticized Spontini who, as general music director in Berlin, presented an obstacle to the German school; these attacks twice led to Rellstab's incarceration. In 1828 Schubert set ten of Rellstab's poems, including seven in the *Schwanengesang* cycle. Besides many independently published works, Rellstab wrote articles and reviews for numerous periodicals, edited the periodical *Berlin und Athen* (1836), and in 1830 founded *Iris im Gebiete der Tonkunst*, a weekly periodical issued until 1841, aimed at sophisticated readers.

In his musical opinions Rellstab was generally conservative; among composers he most admired Berger, Klein, Cherubini, Spohr, Weber and Mendelssohn. He sometimes expressed views against the new Romanticism of Schumann, and considered that Chopin emphasized difficulty for its own sake in the Piano Concerto op.11, comparing it unfavourably with Mendelssohn's Piano Concerto in G minor. He had some praise for Liszt (who set several of his texts), and though at first his attitude towards Meyerbeer was unfavourable he later wrote opera librettos and translated Scribe librettos (*Der Prophet* and *Der Nordstern*) for him. According to Wilhelm von Lenz, Rellstab was the first to refer to Beethoven's Piano Sonata op.27 no.2 in terms of moonlight: 'a boat visiting, by moonlight, the primitive landscapes of Vierwaldstättersee in Switzerland'.

WORKS SET TO MUSIC

Libs: Dido (opera, 3), music B. Klein (Berlin, 1823); Festmusik zum Fest der Naturforscher (cantata), music Mendelssohn, 1827; Irene (opera, 3, ballets E. Hoguet), music C. Arnold and Klein, 1832; Festspiel zur hundertjährigen Feier der Einweihung des Opernhauses (Berlin, 1842); Ein Feldlager in Schlesien (Singspiel, 3, after E. Scribe), music Meyerbeer, 1844; Die Sündfluth (oratorio, 3), music H. Dam, 1849

Song texts: 10 set by Schubert, 1828: Auf dem Strom, Herbst, Lebensmut (frag.), nos.1–7 of Schwanengesang (Liebesbotschaft, Kriegers Ahnung, Frühlingsbotschaft, Ständchen, Aufenthalt, In der Ferne, Abschied); 3 set by Liszt: Es rauschen die Winde, c1845, Wo weilt er?, c1845, Nimm einen Strahl der Sonne (Ihr Auge), 1856

WRITINGS

Henriette, oder die schöne Sängerin (Leipzig, 1826) [under pseud. F. Zuschauer]
Über mein Verhältniss als Kritiker zu Herrn Spontini (Leipzig, 1827)
Berlins Dramatische Künstler, wie sie sind, pt.1 (Berlin, 1829)
Gesänge der jüngeren Liedertafel zu Berlin (Berlin, 1835)
Beurtheilung der Kompositionen des Fürsten Anton Radziwill zu Goethes Faust (Berlin, 1836)
Franz Liszt: Beurtheilungen–Berichte–Lebensskizze (Berlin, 1842)
Gesammelte Schriften, 12 vols. (Leipzig, 1843–4); Neue Ausgabe, 24 vols. (Leipzig, 1860–61) [vols.6, 9–10: reviews, etc; vols.20, 24: biographies of musicians]
Ludwig Berger: ein Denkmal (Berlin, 1846)
Die Gestaltung der Oper seit Mozart (Sondershausen, 1859)
Aus meinem Leben (Berlin, 1861)

Numerous articles in journals

BIBLIOGRAPHY

C. F. Müller: *Spontini und Rellstab: einige Worte zur Beherzigung der Partheien* (Berlin, 1833)
L. E. Kossatz: *Aphorismen über Rellstabs Kunstkritik* (Berlin, 1846)
W. von Lenz: *Beethoven et ses trois styles* (Paris, 1855)
M. Bendiner: 'Rellstab, Heinrich Friedrich Ludwig', *ADB*
E. König: *Ludwig Rellstab: ein Beitrag zur Geschichte der Unterhaltungsliteratur in Deutschland* (Würzburg, 1938)
K. Goedeke: *Grundriss zur Geschichte der deutschen Dichtung aus den Quellen*, xi/1 (Düsseldorf, 2/1951), xiv (Berlin, 2/1959)
H. Heussner: 'Rellstab', *MGG*
W. Franke: *Der Theaterkritiker Ludwig Rellstab* (Berlin, 1964)
C. H. Porter: *The Rhenish Episode in the Romantic Lied: An Expression of German Identity in the Wake of Napoleon* (diss., U. of Maryland, 1975)
——: 'The *Rheinlieder* Critics: a Case of Musical Nationalism', *MQ*, lxiii (1977), 74

SHELLEY DAVIS

Remacha, Fernando (*b* Tudela, 15 Dec 1898). Spanish composer. He studied the violin and composition in his home town and later with Aramendía in Pamplona. His studies were continued at the Madrid Conservatory under del Hierro (violin) and del Campo (composition). In 1923 the Prix de Rome took him to Italy to study with Malipiero. On his return to Spain in 1928 he joined the Madrid SO as a violist and began to compose film scores. He won the National Music Prize in 1932. A member of the 'Eight', he established himself as one of the outstanding musical personalities of his generation, but the Civil War caused him to take refuge, in 1939, in Tudela where he lived in obscurity until he was invited to direct the Pamplona Conservatory in 1957. He made it into a model institution and his efforts were acknowledged by the award of an honorary doctorate from the University of Navarre (1973). Although his creative work was hampered by circumstances, his small output is of high quality. At first influenced by the later works of Stravinsky and Falla, he arrived at an expressionist atonality of great strength, well displayed in his masterpiece, *Jesucristo en la cruz*.

WORKS
(selective list)

Str Qt, 1925; Pf Qt, 1932; Visperas de S Fermin, chorus, orch, 1954; Gui Conc., 1955; Rapsodia de Estella, pf, orch, 1958; Jesucristo en la cruz, S, T, chorus, orch, 1964

BIBLIOGRAPHY

A. Salazar: *La música contemporánea en España* (Madrid, 1930)
T. Marco: *La música de la España contemporánea* (Madrid, 1970)
——: *Música española de vanguardia* (Madrid, 1970)

TOMÁS MARCO

Rembt [Remd, Rempt], **Johann Ernst** (*b* Suhl, 26 Aug 1749; *d* Suhl, 26 Feb 1810). German organist and composer. He studied under J. P. Kellner and in 1768 presented himself in Holland and France as an organ virtuoso in the tradition of Bach. From 1772 until his death he was the organist in Suhl. As a performer he specialized in Bach's music, but he also collected and performed earlier organ music, which (according to his obituary in *AMZ*) he succeeded in popularizing in a style freely altered to fit late 18th-century taste.

Rembt based his compositions on Bach's chorale settings and devoted himself to preserving the 'Bach style'. Most of his output consists of simple chorale harmonizations, fughettas and organ trios, in rather free forms characterized by pronounced melody and simple partwriting. Rembt knew C. P. E. Bach and J. A. Hiller and was influenced by their stylistic advances; his smaller organ works show something of the increasingly prominent keyboard character-piece. The fughettas combine contrapuntal and harmonic elements in the spirit of the organ *versetti*; their brevity conforms to the requirements of church services and they seek above all to simplify pedal technique. The piano and organ pieces (1774), trios (1787), fughettas (1791) and choralepreludes (1797) are character-pieces in contrapuntal style, with clearly articulated small forms and a lyrical melodic style symptomatic of the increased vocality of late 18th-century music. This particular genre of short organ pieces for use in church has continued to the present day, both in new works and in reprintings of Rembt's own pieces, some of which retain a permanent place in the organ teacher's repertory.

WORKS
(for org unless otherwise stated)

Edition: *Rembt-Album*, ed. K. Becker (Wolfenbüttel, n.d.)

Sammlung kleiner Clavier- und Singstücke, i–ii (Leipzig, 1774); VI [12] Trios (Dresden and Leipzig, 1787); 50 vierstimmige Fughetten (Leipzig, 1791); 18 vierstimmige Fughetten (Leipzig, n.d.); XII leichte triomässige Choralvorspiele, i–ii (Leipzig, 1797); XII leichte triomässige Choralvorspiele (Leipzig, n.d.); VI fugierte vierstimmige Choralvorspiele (Leipzig, n.d.); Vorspiel (n.p., n.d.); others

BIBLIOGRAPHY

GerberNL
Obituary, *AMZ*, xii (1809–10), col.736
K. G. Fellerer: *Studien zur Orgelmusik des ausgehenden 18. und frühen 19. Jahrhunderts* (Kassel, 1932)
H. Kelletat: *Zur Geschichte der deutschen Orgelmusik der Frühklassik* (Kassel, 1933)
G. Frotscher: *Geschichte des Orgel-Spiels und der Orgel-Komposition*, ii (Berlin, 1936, enlarged 3/1966)

KARL GUSTAV FELLERER

Remedios, Alberto (*b* Liverpool, 27 Feb 1935). English tenor. He studied at the RCM, London, and made his début as Tinca in *Il tabarro* with Sadler's Wells Opera in 1957, having won encouragement from Norman Tucker, then the company's managing director. Alfredo followed in 1960, Bacchus in 1961; the latter role was more indicative of the way he was to develop, and he soon added Erik and Max to his repertory. With the Sutherland–Williamson company in Australia in 1965 he sang Faust and Lensky. Then in December that year came his Covent Garden début, as Dimitri (*Boris Godunov*), followed in successive seasons by Erik and by Mark (*The Midsummer Marriage*). But the richness of his voice and talent was first fully established by his Walther in *Die Meistersinger* at Sadler's Wells (1968), which led to two years at the Frankfurt Opera. While there he returned to Sadler's Wells (at the Coliseum) to sing Walther again, and Faust in Berlioz's dramatic oratorio. When in 1970 the Sadler's Wells Company planned a new *Ring* under Goodall, Remedios was naturally cast as Siegmund and Siegfried, and his portrayal and singing of the latter role was considered among the most successful in recent years. Also in new productions he has sung Lohengrin (1971) and Massenet's Des Grieux (1973) at the Coliseum, and in 1975 Othello with the Welsh National Opera. He made his début at the Metropolitan, New York, in 1976, as Bacchus. Remedios's approach to the singing of Wagner emphasizes the music's lyricism, and he is able to sustain an unfaltering line even in the most powerful passages. If not intense, his acting is expressive in a forthright way. His brother Ramon (*b* Liverpool, 9 May 1940), also a tenor, joined the English National Opera (as the Sadler's Wells Company was renamed in 1974) in 1975.

BIBLIOGRAPHY
E. Forbes: 'Alberto Remedios', *Opera*, xxiv (1973), 15
ALAN BLYTH

Reményi [Hoffmann], Ede [Eduard] (*b* Miskolc, 17 Jan 1828; *d* San Francisco, 15 May 1898). Hungarian violinist. After studying in Eger he attended the Vienna Conservatory, where he was taught by Joseph Böhm (1842–5). He made his début in Pest in 1846 and played in Paris in 1847 and London in 1848. In that year he was involved in the Hungarian uprising against Austria, as a result of which he was exiled and left for the USA, where he resumed his career as a virtuoso. In 1852 he toured Germany with Brahms, and in the following year went to Weimar to visit Liszt. The latter at once recognized his genius and became his artistic guide and friend; he composed an *Epithalam* for Reményi's wedding and began writing a concerto for him. In 1854 Reményi again visited London, where he was appointed solo violinist to Queen Victoria, a post he held until 1859. In 1855 he was in the USA, and in 1860 obtained an amnesty and returned to Hungary, where he was subsequently appointed to a court position by the Austrian emperor. After his return he seems to have retired for a time to his estate; however, in 1865 he made a sensational appearance in Paris and made further tours through Germany and the Netherlands. In 1875 he settled temporarily in Paris. Two years later he went again to London, where he appeared only once in public, though he was greatly acclaimed in private circles. The next year he returned to play at the Promenade Concerts on his way to the USA, where he took up residence. In 1887 he undertook a world tour, returning to Hungary for the last time in 1891. He died while playing at a concert in San Francisco.

Reményi's playing combined technical mastery with a strongly pronounced individuality and was soulful and fiery, not least as a result of his strong nationalistic feelings. However, like Liszt, he confused true Magyar music with gypsy music (consequently Brahms's Hungarian Dances, strongly influenced by Reményi's playing, are indebted to the gypsy tradition). Reményi's few compositions are of little value; they include three books of Hungarian melodies and *csárdás* for piano (sometimes mistaken for genuine Hungarian popular melodies), a violin concerto and numerous solos and transcriptions for violin.

BIBLIOGRAPHY
La Mara [pseud. of M. Lipsius], ed.: *Franz Liszts Briefe* (Leipzig, 1893–1904)
G. D. Kelley and G. P. Upton: *Edouard Reményi: Musician, Littérateur, and Man* (Chicago, 1906)
K. Stephenson: 'Der junge Brahms und Reményis "Ungarische Lieder" ', *SMw*, xxv (1962), 520
O. Goldhammer: 'Liszt, Brahms und Reményi', *SM*, v (1963), 89
J. Bouws: 'Eduard Reményi in Suid-Afrika (1887–1890)', *Lantern*, xvii/1 (1967), 26
——: 'Ein ungarischer Violinmeister in Süd-Afrika', *SM*, x (1968), 353
E. HERON-ALLEN/R

Remer. *See* RÖMER family.

Remigio de' Girolami [Remigius Florentinus] (*b* Florence, *c*1245; *d* Florence, 1319). Italian philosopher and theorist. He was a Dominican friar, and studied at Paris, perhaps under St Thomas Aquinas. He taught at Florence, at S Maria Novella, and perhaps had Dante as a pupil. Music is discussed in two chapters of two of his works, the *Divisio scientie* and the *Contra falsos ecclesie professores*. In the former, music is considered as one of the sciences of the Quadrivium; the chapter in question is a compilation of passages from Isidore, Boethius, Papias and Aristotle. In the latter, the author attempted to demonstrate that all the human sciences were represented in the Church; the musical element, or *modulatio*, corresponded to the chants of the liturgy, preaching, and a well-regulated church order.

BIBLIOGRAPHY
C. T. Davis: 'An Early Florentine Political Theorist: Fra Remigio de' Girolami', *Proceedings of the American Philosophical Society*, liv (1960), 662
F. A. Gallo: 'La musica nell'opera di frate Remigio fiorentino', *L'ars nova italiana del trecento: convegni di studio 1961–1967*, ed. F. A. Gallo (Certaldo, 1968), 85
F. ALBERTO GALLO

Remigius Autissiodorensis. *See* REMY OF AUXERRE.

Remigius Florentinus. *See* REMIGIO DE' GIROLAMI.

Remington, Emory (*b* Rochester, NY, 22 Dec 1891; *d* Rochester, 11 Dec 1971). American trombonist. He was taught by Gardell Simons (first trombone, Philadelphia Orchestra), Edward Llewellyn (first trumpet, Chicago SO) and Ernest Williams (first trumpet, Philadelphia Orchestra). In 1922 he joined the faculty of the Eastman School of Music, where he taught until his death; he also played first trombone in the Rochester PO, 1923–49. Remington was perhaps the most influential teacher of his time, taking a prominent role in the worldwide revolution in playing technique caused by the abandonment of the so-called 'peashooter' small-bore trombone and the adoption of a larger-bore instrument with F-valve attachment. He emphasized a vocal approach to the instrument and complete relaxation while playing.

EDWARD H. TARR

Remmer. *See* RÖMER family.

Remoortel, Edouard van (*b* Brussels, 30 May 1926; *d* Paris, 16 May 1977). Belgian conductor. He studied harmony, the cello and chamber music at the Brussels Conservatory (1945–9), where he was a pupil of Cassadó and Galliera; he also studied conducting at the Geneva Conservatory and privately with Krips. His début was at the Concerts Populaires of the Palais des Beaux-Arts in Brussels. In 1951 he was appointed principal conductor of the Belgian National Orchestra and his concert tours with many different orchestras established his reputation as a versatile interpreter. From 1958 to 1963 he was principal conductor of the St Louis SO, and in 1965 he was appointed musical adviser to the Orchestre National de l'Opéra in Monte Carlo.

Remouchamps, Henri de (*b* *c*1600; *d* early 1639). South Netherlands organist and composer. He is recorded as a *duodenus* at the cathedral of St Lambert, Liège, from 1617 to 1620. From 1625 to 1630 he was paid a salary as second organist there. An undated document states that he was *maître de chant* at the collegiate church of St Paul, Liège. Only one piece by him is extant, the motet *Salve matrona nobilissima Anna* for eight voices and continuo (in the *Grand livre de choeur de St Lambert*, 1645, in *B-Lc*). It is doubtless an early work, but it shows him to be a skilful contrapuntist, writing in a style popular at the cathedral about 1620–30. Such works were performed with some doubling by instruments. He is also known to have written a requiem for eight voices and continuo.

BIBLIOGRAPHY

J. Quitin: 'Orgues, organiers et organistes de la cathédrale Notre-Dame et Saint-Lambert à Liège aux 17ᵉ et 18ᵉ siècles', *Bulletin de l'Institut archéologique liégeois*, xxx (1967), 5–58

JOSÉ QUITIN

Rempt, Johann Ernst. *See* REMBT, JOHANN ERNST.

Remunde [Ruremunde; Endoviensis], **Christophe van** (*b* Eindhoven, ?1475–1500; *d* London, 1531). Dutch printer. He worked in Antwerp from 1523 to 1531, where he published an important series of liturgical books 'ad usum ecclesie Sarum' – a series which helped to establish Antwerp as a rival to Paris in liturgical music printing. It includes: *Manuale* (1523), *Processionale* (1523), *Hymnorum cum notis opusculum* (1524), *Psalterium cum hymnis* (1524), *Breviarium* (1525), *Missale* (1527) and *Horae Beatae Mariae Virginis* (1530). Remunde had two sizes of type with Roman neumes and one with Gothic neumes (used for the Utrecht Missal of 1527). All were printed by double impression, with black notes on red staves. The smaller of the two Roman faces (found in his publications from 1528 onwards) was also used by SYMON COCK for his first music publication of 1539.

Besides liturgical books, Remunde published an English translation of the New Testament, an English almanac and Lyndewood's *Provinciale seu constitutiones Anglie*. Many of his books were printed for Peter Kaetz and Francis Birckmann, booksellers in London. In 1531 Remunde himself visited London where he was arrested for selling English New Testaments. He was sent to prison where he died. His widow Catharine continued to manage the business in Antwerp from 1532 to 1546. Her publications were similar to those of her husband and included some reprints of his books.

BIBLIOGRAPHY

F. van Ortroy: 'Remunde, Christophe van', *BNB*

P. Bergmans: *La typographie musicale en Belgique au XVIᵉ siècle* (Brussels, 1929)

H. D. L. Vervliet: *Sixteenth Century Printing Types of the Low Countries* (Amsterdam, 1968)

S. Bain: *Music Printing in the Low Countries in the Sixteenth Century* (diss., U. of Cambridge, 1974)

SUSAN BAIN

Rémy, W. A. [Mayer, (Benjamin) Wilhelm] (*b* Prague, 10 June 1831; *d* Graz, 23 Jan 1898). Austrian composer. The son of a Prague lawyer, he studied with C. F. Pitsch and belonged to the group of Davidsbündler which included Hanslick and Ambros. He first appeared in public as the composer of an overture *Die Fanatiken in der Cevennen* for Eugène Sue's drama *Jean Cavalier*. At his parents' wish he studied law, taking his degree in 1856, and did not turn to music professionally until he became conductor of the Steiermärkischer Musikverein in Graz (1862–70). There he wrote many orchestral works, including the overture *Sardanapal*, the symphonic poem *Helena* and a Symphony in F: all three, which showed the influence of Schumann, were performed with success in Leipzig. He also wrote more symphonies, a *Phantasiestück*, *Slawisches Liederspiel* and *Östliche Rosen* for solo voices and chorus with two pianos, a concert opera *Das Waldfräulein* (Graz, 1876) and many songs. He published his music under the pseudonym W. A. Rémy. After retiring he taught privately, his pupils including Busoni, Kienzl, Heuberger, Rezniček and Weingartner. He was a learned and strict but inspiring teacher: his theories of counterpoint were based on Cherubini, his orchestration principles on Berlioz, though he was anti-Wagnerian. Busoni's obituary speaks gratefully of his teaching, and observes, 'His universal erudition enabled him to elucidate, embellish and bring to life points in music and the history of music by drawing upon the entire history of civilization, giving character sketches of the masters where it was relevant, and adding his own highly personal observations, some factual, some joking, some poetic'.

BIBLIOGRAPHY

W. Kienzl: 'W. A. Rémy', *Neue Musikzeitung*, xi (1890), 262

R. Heuberger: 'Nachruf', *Biographisches Jb und deutscher Nekrolog*, iii (Berlin, 1900), 261

F. Busoni: 'Nachruf für Dr. Mayer', *Von der Einheit der Musik* (Berlin, 1922), 41

F. Weingartner: *Lebenserinnerungen* (Vienna and Leipzig, 1923), 63–106

W. Suppan: 'Wilhelm Mayer (W. A. Rémy)', *Neue Chronik zur Geschichte und Volkskunde der innerösterreichischen Alpenländer*, x (Graz, 1961) [with further bibliography]

E. Hilmar: *Eine stilkritische Untersuchung der Werke Ferruccio Busonis aus den Jahren 1880–1890* (diss., U. of Graz, 1962)

J. A. FULLER MAITLAND/JOHN WARRACK

Remy of Auxerre [Remigius Autissiodorensis] (*fl* 862–*c*900). Latin writer, author of a commentary on the *De nuptiis Philologiae et Mercurii* of Martianus Capella, the ninth book of which deals with music. In 861–2 Remy was at the monastery of St Germain in Auxerre as a pupil of Heiric of Auxerre. In 876 he succeeded Heiric as master of the school, and in 883 (893, according to some) was given the task of reorganizing the school at Rheims. In the period just before his death he taught in Paris where, for example, he instructed Odo of Cluny in dialectic and music.

The commentary on Martianus Capella was but one among many commentaries on Latin grammarians and poets (e.g. Donatus, Priscian, Juvenal, Cato) by Remy. He also wrote biblical commentaries and several works on religious subjects, including an essay on the ceremonies of the Mass sometimes ascribed to Alcuin. This last work is of some interest for the early history of plainsong (Migne, *Patrologia latina*, ci.1246ff).

Remy's treatment of Martianus's book 9 is disappointing, for only infrequently did he do more than set down synonyms for individual words or brief phrases of the earlier writer's often overripe vocabulary, and only rarely did he refer to the musical world of his own time. One finds an interesting and early use of *vidula* to designate a musical instrument, and a brief observation on differences between the singing of Goths and Germans. One point of particular interest long went unrecognized, due to the inadequacy of Gerbert's old edition. Remy employed neumatic notation in about a dozen cases, to demonstrate intervals and to explain obscure terms such as *anesis* and *paracterica*.

The extent to which the glosses on music may have become common knowledge in later centuries has not really been studied. The commentary on Martianus as a whole seems to have been a standard and widely distributed work during the Middle Ages.

BIBLIOGRAPHY

M. Manitius: *Geschichte der lateinischen Literatur des Mittelalters*, i (Munich, 1911), 504ff

C. E. Lutz: *Remigii Autissiodorensis Commentum in Martianum Capellam* (Leiden, 1962, 2/1965)

LAWRENCE GUSHEE

Renaissance. In the conventional periodization of Western music history, a term denoting the era from about 1430 to about 1600; this period coincides with the later phases of the broad historical development in Western culture, society, art and technology (c1300–1600) for which the French term 'Renaissance' has been in use since Michelet (1855), who coined it for general history.

1. Introduction. 2. Music historiography and the Renaissance. 3. Music and the concept of rebirth. 4. Conditions and trends. 5. Current views of the Renaissance as a period.

1. INTRODUCTION. The perspective adopted by Michelet was given world-wide currency by Burckhardt (1860), whose influential essay portrayed Italy as the source of a vast cultural transformation that began in the 14th century, gradually spread new forms of thought to northern Europe after 1500 and marked the emergence of a period of civilization that extended in some spheres until the later 17th century.

That the term literally means 'rebirth' is not an anachronistic exaggeration but is justified by the tendency of influential thinkers and writers in the period 1400–1600 openly to repudiate the 'Middle Ages' (a term not then invented) and to venerate antiquity as a model. In view of divergent approaches to the problem it is useful to distinguish two meanings that historians often attach to the term 'Renaissance': a narrow view that holds that it was primarily a movement, which aimed to restore the philosophical and artistic values of classical antiquity; and a broader view – that it can effectively denote an era of fresh beliefs and attitudes in individuals and ultimately in society, an age of discovery and accelerated change, in which innovations were justified by an appeal to their affinity to a 'golden age' of the past.

Although there are controversies over the degree to which the developments stressed by Burckhardt and other Renaissance historians were literally epoch-making, none have denied their importance. Among them are the rise of secular humanism as an educational programme emphasizing rhetoric, grammar and moral philosophy, in opposition to the metaphysical scholasticism of the Middle Ages; the growth of historical thought and the recovery and criticism of ancient texts as a basis for the 'new learning'; the spread of literacy and alteration of patterns of thought signalled by the invention of printing; the break with traditional spatial concepts in cosmology and geography through the discovery of the New World and the Copernican revolution; the upheaval of the formerly stable though complex world of medieval Christianity through the definitive break embodied in the Protestant Reformation; and in the visual arts a new interest in classical principles of form and in the expression of immediately perceptible human situations and feelings, as opposed to the more spiritual, abstract and attenuated expressive modes of medieval art.

2. MUSIC HISTORIOGRAPHY AND THE RENAISSANCE. The spell cast by Burckhardt on mid-19th-century intellectuals soon captured music historians as well as others and led to pursuit of the problem of the 'Renaissance' in music. That users of the term then and now have often failed to distinguish the broad and narrow meanings mentioned above is not peculiar to music history but is an inevitable consequence of the rapid popularization, and eventual decline in force, of Burckhardt's original concept, which soon came to be applied to virtually any phenomenon that fell within the accepted chronological limits. As early as 1868 Ambros conceived the 15th and 16th centuries as a substantially unified period, a view adopted by many later writers, including Pirro, whether or not they employed the term 'Renaissance' (for a survey see Blume). The divergent thoughts on periodization in the generations after Ambros are illustrated by Riemann's proposal to set the 'Early Renaissance' as far back as 1300–1500, and by Edward J. Dent, who (in *Alessandro Scarlatti*, 1905) identified the 'Renaissance' with the rise of monody about 1600. However, with the subsequent borrowing of the term 'Baroque' from the history of art (especially by Curt Sachs in 1919) the rise of opera and its concomitant developments came to be seen as the opening of a new era, while the end of the Renaissance was set in the first decades of the 17th century. Attempts have been made (e.g. by Wellesz) to date the beginnings of the Baroque period as far back as about 1540. Other scholars have tried to interpose a distinctive period of 'Mannerism' (yet another term borrowed from art history) between the Renaissance and Baroque periods, but this proposal has met with wide opposition and is far from being generally accepted. It now seems to be agreed that in music a period marked by substantial unity of outlook and language came into being in the second half of the 15th century and that its principles were not definitively displaced until about 1625. It is also agreed that this period can be called the 'Renaissance', yet often for no better reason than that it falls within the later phases of the Renaissance in the broad sense; this neutral approach, which is no more than an assertion of chronological coincidence, is tacitly adopted by Reese in his *Music in the Renaissance*. A more controversial though more challenging view is that the 'Renaissance' in the narrow sense – the revival of antiquity – did have a perceptible influence on musical thought and, to some extent, practice, and that certain aspects of the cult of classicism affected music, though

'La Musica': fresco (c1494) by Bernardino di Betto Pintoricchio in the Sale Borgia, Palazzo Vaticano, Rome. A typical high Renaissance painting, it portrays by traditional means several aspects of music: the personification of 'Musica', playing a viol; a group of instruments opposite a group of singers (perhaps representing the Three Ages of Man); and Pythagoras, representing the natural laws of harmony

inevitably less directly than in art and architecture.

3. MUSIC AND THE CONCEPT OF REBIRTH. In literature and the visual arts the idea of 'rebirth' gained ground much earlier than in music. From the mid-14th century, Italian and especially Florentine writers often claimed that a single extraordinary artist or writer had recalled to life an art that had been neglected during the 'dark ages' that had intervened since ancient times. Thus about 1350 Boccaccio (*Decameron*, vi, 5) said of Giotto that he 'brought back to light that art which for many centuries had lain buried under errors', and in 1400 the Florentine historian Filippo Villani wrote of Dante that he 'recalled poetry as from an abyss of shadows into the light'. In the 16th century this idea was widely repeated, receiving its most authoritative formulation from Vasari in the preface to his *Lives of the Painters* (1550). For him the earlier history of painting had been marked by utter decline in the period of the 'barbarian' invasions of Italy and by rebirth in the 13th century, beginning with Cimabue and Giotto, followed by later stages of improvement leading to its summit of perfection, exemplified by Raphael and Michelangelo, in his own time. (For a full account of the growth of this idea see Ferguson.)

Among writers on music the first to reflect something of this view was Tinctoris, though his linked treatises (written c1474–84) still seem largely medieval in approach and form a kind of summa of the musical knowledge of his time. Yet they also reveal his considerable

inclination towards humanist learning, probably reflecting the environment of late 15th-century Naples, in which they were written. In the preface to his *Proportionale* (c1476) he cited Plato as an authority for the Greek view that the science of music was 'the mightiest of all' and that no one ignorant of music could be considered truly educated. He mused on the fabled power of music to move 'gods, ancestral spirits, unclean demons, animals without reason, and even things insensate' and observed that in recent times, specifically around 1440, thanks to Dunstable and his generation, there had been a marvellous increase in the possibilities of music. In the preface to his counterpoint treatise (1477) Tinctoris stated flatly that in the opinion of the learned no music composed before about 40 years earlier was worth hearing. The music of Dunstable, as followed by Dufay, Binchois and later masters, began a 'new art'.

In the 16th century the notion of rebirth borrowed more heavily from literary and artistic sources, presumably as musicians came to know and appreciate them better. The Florentine academician Cosimo Bartoli, in a heavily eclectic passage (published in 1567, though the fictitious date of the dialogue is 1543), said of Ockeghem that he 'rediscovered' music, which had virtually died out, and compared him with Donatello as the rediscoverer of sculpture; Bartoli then compared Josquin and Michelangelo as 'prodigies of nature' who followed in the paths of the pioneers and excelled all others in their respective arts. In 1558 Zarlino, evidently following Vasari not only in general line of argument but perhaps more specifically as well, fully embraced the anti-medieval position. He described the music of the ancients as representing a 'height of perfection' and medieval music as reaching the 'lowest depths' and portrayed Willaert, his own teacher at Venice, as a 'new Pythagoras' who had sought out new possibilities and brought music to its flourishing state.

More significant than these claims and comparisons is the actual contribution of the humanist movement to the gradual recovery of the ancient texts on which modern writers could base their knowledge of Greek music. Thin and inaccurate as such knowledge inevitably was, in the absence of practical monuments of ancient music itself, the writers of the period nevertheless did acquire or make available the greater part of the entire literature of ancient theory or commentary, so much so that by the end of the 16th century they knew about as much of this literature as is now known. Until about 1470 the central authority for knowledge of ancient music was Boethius. In the last third of the 15th century, however, the new printing of pedagogical and encyclopedic works brought into circulation the writings of Isidore of Seville and Quintilian, published in 1470; the latter was specially important for Renaissance theories of education. By 1500 Plato's complete works were available for the first time in Latin in the translation by Marsilio Ficino, along with the *Poetics* of Aristotle. While the influence on scholasticism of Aristotle's methods had long been felt in medieval music theory, his *Poetics* had not been known; in the 16th century his views of music were rivalled in importance by those of Plato, which, however, were less visible in tradition-bound music theory than in writings by literary men and were only later adopted directly by musicians. By 1518 Gaffurius had arranged for the translation of the surviving treatises on music by Baccheus, Ptolemy and Aristides Quintilianus. By 1588 Zarlino could claim (in his *Sopplimenti musicali*) to have read these men, as well as Euclid, Nicomachus and a number of others; in 1562 the first translation of Aristoxenus's *Harmonics* had been brought out at his instigation. Salinas in 1577 was able to produce an elaborate discussion of Greek theory, and in 1581 Vincenzo Galilei's *Dialogo della musica antica e della moderna* was the first to publish three Greek compositions – the hymns of Mesomedes, known through the Byzantine tradition.

The 'classicizing' trend is also visible in numerous other treatises of the period, though less as antiquarianism than as justification for innovation. One is Glarean's *Dodecachordon* (1547), the broadest attempt of the period to modify the traditional modal system by extending the Boethian eight-mode system to 12 modes, identifying the names of these with the so-called ancient modes insofar as these could be understood. Nicola Vicentino's treatise *L'antica musica ridotta alla moderna prattica* (1555) is a more radical work, an attempt to demonstrate the validity not only of the diatonic tone system but of the chromatic and enharmonic genera of the ancients and to show how these could be used in contemporary polyphony. The spirit of classical revival is still strong in the series of writings on the nature and ethos of ancient music produced by Girolamo Mei, Vincenzo Galilei, Giovanni de' Bardi and others connected with the Florentine Camerata, which gave intellectual substance and authority to the experiments in expressive settings of dramatic poetry that led to the emergence of opera in the 1590s.

4. CONDITIONS AND TRENDS. As prevailing concepts of music were gradually transformed in the late 15th century and early 16th, they were also affected by a vital change in the technological basis of the production and transmission of music from composer to public. The beginnings of music printing as a commercial activity (1501), with Venice as the initial and leading centre but with rapidly growing competition elsewhere in Europe, not only brought more music into circulation but ensured its distribution more widely, more rapidly and in more uniform texts than before. Printers often produced editions of substantial size (press runs of 500 to 2000 copies are documented throughout the 16th century), and the scope of consumption must have increased enormously. A new and vast bourgeois public was rising, made up largely of performing amateurs for whom music was essentially a higher form of recreation, and it was served by a tide of polyphonic collections, principally of secular music. This trend is visible in successive stages in Italy, France and Germany, and, late in the century, in England, during the latter part of Elizabeth I's reign and much of James I's (roughly 1588–1620), when the aesthetic and technical traditions of the Italian madrigal were imported wholesale into England to meet the demands of a newly curious and cultivated public. Side by side with this secular development went the increasing publication of sacred music in all its forms and varieties, both Catholic and Protestant, devotional and liturgical, Latin and vernacular. Though the social conditions for the performance of sacred polyphony are less well understood than those governing secular music, it must be assumed that many amateurs who sang madrigals and chansons also sang motets and that the flow of publications was in part designed for the use of religious institutions of all kinds, in part for laymen aware of the heightened role of music in the intensified religious atmosphere engendered by the wars of religion that racked the century. By the mid-16th century, then, music had shed its former identity as a pure science of relationships, in the medieval sense, and had settled into the European consciousness as a form of expression closely allied to poetry and religion and suitable for ritual and festive occasions, and as a form of pleasurable leisure activity normally carried on in the home or academy. There naturally followed an increasing market for handbooks that would teach amateurs the rudiments of music; in the Elizabethan period, in some ways a microcosm of the age as a whole, the chief example is Morley's aptly named *Plaine and Easie Introduction to Practicall Musicke* (1597).

This social role was matched by a new view of the function of music, beginning in the late 15th century and taking firm hold in the 16th – that the main aim of music was to heighten the meaning of a text. For this the central classical authority was Plato, chiefly *The Republic*, book 3, in which the thesis is laid down that 'the *harmonia* and the rhythm must follow the sense of the words'. At least some 16th-century writers were aware that this was inherent in the Greek view of music as including not only melody and the characteristic *harmoniae* of various regional idioms, such as 'Dorian' or 'Phrygian', but also the text and even the physical gestures of mime or dance that accompanied the recitation of lyric or dramatic poetry. As Isobel Henderson put it, 'Greek music was mimetic or representative – a direct photography (as it were) of mental objects formed by the ethos and pathos of the soul' (*NOHM*, i, p.385). The union of poetry and music was seized upon as an ideal by Renaissance musicians and by many poets (e.g. Ronsard), and Plato's words were cited by many musicians, including Zarlino (see Strunk, p.256), Bardi (ibid, p.295) and G. C. Monteverdi (ibid, p.407). That this view emerged from the humanist revival of Plato is evident from its appearance as early as 1506 in a passage by Vincenzo Calmeta (cited by Pirrotta, p.38), and it was soon given much wider currency by Sir Thomas More (*Utopia*, 1516) in a passage stressing the capacity of music to express the inner meaning of words. That not only bookish musicians but seasoned practitioners with few literary pretensions subscribed to it is shown by much evidence, including a letter written by Palestrina to the Duke of Mantua (on 3 March 1570) praising a motet composed by the duke both for its 'beautiful workmanship' and for the 'vital impulse that it gives to its words, according to their meaning'.

Related to this was the notion that it is through text expression that music has power to move the soul and to reproduce the marvellous effects attributed to it by the ancients, in the arousal and subduing of the passions. An oft-told tale was one in which Alexander the Great was said to have been unwittingly aroused by music from his banquet table to arm himself for war and was then restored to the banquet when the musician changed his 'tune' and manner of performance; still more pervasive were the legends of Orpheus, the favoured mythical musician. While Zarlino and other moderate critics believed that music of their time, if properly allied to words, could move the souls of its hearers, others denied that polyphony could accomplish anything of the sort, citing principally the relative unintelligibility of the text resulting from overlapping declamation caused by contrapuntal imitation.

This complaint came from many sides, including (in 1549) the Italian Bishop Cirillo Franco, who argued that in the Mass 'when one voice says "Sanctus" another says "Sabaoth" so that they more nearly resemble cats in January than flowers in May', and Galilei expressed similar views in 1581. In sacred music solutions of various types are found, the most drastic of which was the writing of extended or entire sections or movements in a strict or slightly modified chordal style; this approach was explicitly attempted by certain north Italian composers (e.g. Vincenzo Ruffo) working in the aftermath of the Council of Trent. The famous *Missa Papae Marcelli* by Palestrina was evidently intended as an attempt to reconcile the claims of text intelligibility with those of inherent musical interest, and the perhaps apocryphal tales of its success in persuading churchmen at Trent not to abolish polyphony can be taken as a special instance of the general belief in the power of music when properly adjusted to words. A more drastic solution was the complete break with polyphony implied by the Florentine Camerata, whose spokesmen also rejected the efforts of even the most expressive-minded madrigalists to achieve rhetorical effects through word-painting, as in the later madrigal in Italy and in England. The monodists, on the other hand, sought to convey the expressive meaning of a text as a whole. What is actually involved is two opposed aesthetic positions: the word-painting of the madrigalists, whether Marenzio or Weelkes, may seem excessively preoccupied with the

single word only if it is not seen as a means of obtaining maximum variety of tempo, harmonic content and texture within a normal framework of five or six voices; while the expressive purposes in monody, lacking all possibility of textural variety, are achieved through means that make the most of the nuances of the solo voice.

It is increasingly clear that solo singing with instrumental accompaniment, far from being a 'discovery' at the end of the 16th century, had long been practised and indeed had never been completely displaced by polyphony. The varied methods of performing polyphony regularly included the singing of a principal vocal part (at times the tenor but more often the soprano) of a chanson or madrigal to the accompaniment of a lute or other instruments. The tradition in Italian secular music for this type of performance not only went back to the frottola but predated the coalescence of that mixed genre into a semi-polyphonic literature, and it was above all in Italy that it continued to flourish. What Einstein called 'pseudo-monody' was 'pseudo-' only in the sense that it was not regularly written out and was rarely published in this form, though there are important exceptions, such as Willaert's arrangement of madrigals by Verdelot for solo voice and lute (1536). How important solo singing was may also be judged from the writings of such observers as Paolo Cortese (1510) and the famous words of Castiglione (*Il cortegiano*, 1528): polyphony is good but 'to sing to the lute is much better, because all the sweetness consisteth in one alone and a man ... understands the better the feat manner and the air or vein of it when the ears are not busied in hearing more than one voice ...' (Hoby translation: *The Book of the Courtier*, 1561). The new monody around 1600 can thus be seen partly as a change in the norms of representing music – for now the melodic line and the harmonic progressions of its accompaniment were fixed in notation for the first time – and partly as the raising of a long-established tradition to a higher level of dramatic intensity, adapted to dramatic poetry. Thus the roots of 'Baroque' music can be discovered to be buried deep in the 16th century. However, even if the overlapping of polyphonic and monodic tendencies can be seen to have endured much longer than is commonly thought, the full decline of polyphony as a form of expression did not set in before the early 17th century, and the 'Renaissance' can thus be justified as a period extending to about that time. A factor that is still poorly understood is the presumed change in social conditions for music that may have accompanied the decline of vocal polyphony; but this would doubtless have to be studied on a regional basis, as it differed sharply from one country to another.

While the 16th century witnessed a vast growth of solo and ensemble instrumental music for keyboard, string and wind instruments, this kind of music had little place in the aesthetic notions associated with the 'Renaissance', even though justification could have been found in ancient texts for admitting some degree of ethical power to instrumental music. On the whole, instrumental music remained subordinated to vocal music, and much of its repertory was in varying ways derived from, or dependent on, vocal models. Nevertheless the continued cultivation of accompanied solo singing tended from early in the period to glorify the virtuoso instrumentalist as well as singer, whether or not these were embodied in the same person, as in the case of such virtuosos as the lutenist–singer Pietrobono of Ferrara. His followers in the 16th century were similarly admired, though most of them specialized as singers, lutenists or keyboard players. By 1536 it was conventional rhetoric, yet characteristic of the time, when the renowned vihuelist Luis de Milán was compared in the preface to his *Libro de vihuela* with 'el grande Orpheo'.

5. CURRENT VIEWS OF THE RENAISSANCE AS A PERIOD. Even among scholars whose views coincide on the basic musical developments of the period, there is frequent disagreement on the relative importance of the various technical and aesthetic features that are cast into relief and thus in the resulting historical profile of the entire era. Reese saw in Renaissance music essentially a series of significant further advances upon the conquests of the Middle Ages, among them, in the later period, 'a rhythmic fluidity and complexity that part-music has never surpassed', the fuller realization of the potentialities of the triad, the regulation of dissonance and thus the rationalization of intervallic content, the expansion of tonal range and the growing homogeneity of voices through contrapuntal imitation. He saw the Renaissance as a period of matchless cultural unification in music, a period in which composers throughout Europe in the 16th century 'spoke one musical language'.

To this gradualist and evolutionary thesis can be contrasted a theory of the Renaissance that stresses its departure from the Middle Ages and its revolutionary importance as an era, a view that has been advanced chiefly by Edward Lowinsky in a number of articles (most comprehensively in 1954). He saw the age as not merely embodying a decisive array of transformations that set it off definitively from the period of medieval scholasticism but also as a period in which musicians desired 'to arrive at a musical expression free from all shackles'. He submitted the following 'theses' in justification of the use of the term and concept 'Renaissance' for the later 15th century and the 16th: (1) that in the 15th century there was a steady growth and reorganization of musical institutions related to the migration of northern composers to Italy and the interaction of northern and southern traditions; (2) that music of the period was characterized by a broad 'emancipation' from medieval constraints, including the *formes fixes* of poetry, rhythmic modes, isorhythm, the cantus firmus principle and Pythagorean tuning; (3) the criticism of medieval aesthetics; (4) 'emancipation' from the older modal system, and the development of harmony – *musica ficta* and the introduction of chromaticism and modulation; (5) a transition from a 'successive' to a 'simultaneous' conception of part-music; (6) the enlargement of tonal space; (7) the rise of expressivity and a new relationship between words and music; (8) the development of vocal and instrumental virtuosity; (9) the increasing autonomy of instrumental music; and (10) a repudiation of authority on the part of musicians.

While some of these 'theses' refer to broadly identifiable properties of music of the period, others are exaggerated and inflated, for the question of whether they were absolutely new or were only newly developed phases of formerly existing tendencies requires substantially greater evidence than is presented for them, and in some cases evidence for continuity is simply omitted. For example, while the cantus firmus principle undoubtedly receded in importance as a compositional device in the 16th century compared with the 15th, it not only maintained a role of some substance in both sacred and secular polyphony but if anything grew in importance as a didactic device and in instrumental music. Further, the sharp distinction that Lowinsky drew between the 'successive' and 'simultaneous' conception of parts is a conceptual distortion, since it is not really clear what 'simultaneous' could literally mean in the actual work of composition. Moreover, the insistent use of words such as 'shackles' and 'emancipation' is tendentious and one-sided; it fails to allow for the possibility that the Renaissance can be distinguished from the Middle Ages by other means than as a period of alleged 'freedom' in contradistinction to – the contrast is inevitable – 'tyranny'. A more fruitful way of treating the evidence may be to suggest that a new era came into being through the exposure of music and musicians to a new set of prevailing aesthetic and philosophical impulses, combined with a new set of social and technological conditions and with steady developments in the autonomous aspects of musical technique. There is no reason to claim that this was a 'better' age than its predecessor, yet it does appear to have been new in sufficient measure to warrant a separate historical identity, in part carrying forward certain tendencies of the Middle Ages, in part breaking with them. The refinement of these perceptions, together with the creation of new knowledge on which they may be based, is a major task of further research.

BIBLIOGRAPHY

J. Michelet: *Histoire de France* (Paris, 1833–67)

J. Burckhardt: *The Civilization of the Renaissance in Italy* (Ger. orig., 1860; Eng. trans. in numerous edns., incl. London, 1944; Oxford, 1945; New York, 1958)

A. W. Ambros: *Geschichte der Musik* (Breslau and Leipzig, 1862–78, 1882, rev. 3/[except vol.iii] 1887–1911; iii, rev. 2/1893)

T. Kroyer: *Die Anfänge der Chromatik im italienischen Madrigal des XVI. Jahrhunderts* (Leipzig, 1902)

H. Zenck: 'Zarlino's "Istitutioni harmoniche" als Quelle zur Musikanschauung der italienischen Renaissance', *ZMw*, xii (1929–30), 540

H. Besseler: *Die Musik des Mittelalters und der Renaissance*, HMw, ii (1931)

L. Schrade: 'Von der Maniera der Komposition in der Musik des 16. Jahrhunderts', *ZMw*, xvi (1933–4), 3, 98, 152

A. Pirro: *Histoire de la musique de la fin du XIVe siècle à la fin du XVIe* (Paris, 1940)

E. E. Lowinsky: 'The Concept of Physical and Musical Space in the Renaissance', *PAMS 1941*, 57

D. P. Walker: 'Musical Humanism in the 16th and Early 17th Centuries', *MR*, ii (1941), 1, 111, 220; iii (1942), 55; Ger. trans. (1949, as *Der musikalische Humanismus*)

E. E. Lowinsky: 'The Goddess Fortuna in Music', *MQ*, xxix (1943), 45

——: *Secret Chromatic Art in the Netherlands Motet* (New York, 1946)

P. O. Kristeller: 'Music and Learning in the Early Italian Renaissance', *JRBM*, i (1946–7), 255

W. K. Ferguson: *The Renaissance in Historical Thought* (Boston, Mass., 1948)

A. Einstein: *The Italian Madrigal* (Princeton, 1949/R1971)

M. F. Bukofzer: *Studies in Medieval and Renaissance Music* (New York, 1950)

O. Strunk: *Source Readings in Music History* (New York, 1950)

L. Schrade: 'Renaissance: the Historical Conception of an Epoch', *IMSCR, v Utrecht 1952*, 19

E. E. Lowinsky: 'Music in the Culture of the Renaissance', *Journal of the History of Ideas*, xv (1954), 509; repr. in *Renaissance Essays*, ed. P. O. Kristeller and P. Wiener (New York, 1968)

G. Reese: *Music in the Renaissance* (New York, 1954, rev. 2/1959)

C. V. Palisca: *Girolamo Mei (1519–1594): Letters on Ancient and Modern Music to Vincenzo Galilei and Giovanni Bardi*, MSD, iii (1960)

E. Panofsky: *Renaissance and Renascences in Western Art* (New York, 1960, 2/1965)

J. Haar, ed.: *Chanson and Madrigal, 1480–1530: Isham Memorial Library 1961*

H. Hucke: 'Das Problem des Manierismus in der Musik', *Literaturwissenschaftliches Jb*, ii (1961), 214

E. E. Lowinsky: *Tonality and Atonality in Sixteenth-century Music* (Berkeley, 1961)

J. Kerman: *The Elizabethan Madrigal* (New York, 1962)

F. Blume: 'Renaissance', *MGG*; Eng. trans. in F. Blume: *Renaissance and Baroque Music: a Comprehensive Survey* (New York, 1967)

N. Bridgman: *La vie musicale au Quattrocento* (Paris, 1964)

F. Masai: 'La notion de Renaissance: equivoques et malentendus', *Revue belge d'archéologie et d'histoire d'art*, xxxiv (1965), 137–66

H. Besseler: 'Das Renaissanceproblem in der Musik', *AMw*, xxiii (1966), 1

L. Lockwood: 'On "Parody" as Term and Concept in 16th-century Music', *Aspects of Medieval and Renaissance Music: a Birthday Offering to Gustave Reese* (New York, 1966), 560

E. E. Lowinsky: 'Music of the Renaissance as Viewed by the Musicians', *The Renaissance Image of Man and the World*, ed. B. O'Kelley (Columbus, 1966)

J. Shearman: *Mannerism* (Harmondsworth, 1967)

H. Federhofer: 'Zum Manierismus-Problem in der Musik', *Renaissance-muziek 1400–1600: donum natalicium René Bernard Lenaerts* (Louvain, 1969), 105; repr. in *Deutsche Vierteljahrsschrift für Literaturwissenschaft und Geistesgeschichte*, xlix (1970), 393

N. Pirrotta and E. Povoledo: *Li due Orfei: da Poliziano a Monteverdi* (Turin, 1969, rev. 2/1975)

W. Salmen: 'Komponist und Musicus im Renaissance-Zeitalter', *ÖMz*, xxx (1975), 569

M. R. Maniates: *Mannerism in Italian Music and Culture* (Durham, NC, 1979)

LEWIS LOCKWOOD

Renaldi, Giulio [Renaldis, Giulio de] (*d* July or Aug 1576). Italian composer and organist. In 1570 he was chosen to succeed Sperindio Bertoldo as organist at Padua Cathedral. His contract was renewed in 1575. He was active as a madrigalist of considerable repute; a few of his compositions were popular enough to be printed after his death. Among his madrigals is a curious piece (1569) described as composed 'twice for four voices; and one can add any voice whatsoever from one piece to the other, or else sing all eight voices at once'.

Maurice Renaud in the title role of Massenet's 'Hérodiade'

WORKS

Il primo libro de madrigali, 4–6vv, con 2 dialoghi, 7vv (Venice, 1567)

Il primo libro de madrigali, 4vv (Venice, 1569)

Madregali et canzoni alla napolitana, 5vv (Venice, 1576), 1 intabulated for lute in 1599[19]

2 greghesche in 1564[16]; 1 madrigal, 5vv, in 1568[16]; Magnificat, 5vv, in 1576[7]; 1 madrigal, 12vv, in 1584[4]; 2 madrigals, 3vv, in 1587[3]; motet intabulated for lute in 1593[11]

BIBLIOGRAPHY

R. Casimiri: 'Musica e musicisti nella cattedrale di Padova nei sec. XIV, XV, XVI', *NA*, xviii (1941), 53; pubd separately (Rome, 1942)

KLAUS SPEER, JAMES HAAR

Renaud, Maurice (Arnold) (*b* Bordeaux, 24 July ?1861; *d* Paris, 16 Oct 1933). French baritone. He studied at the Paris and Brussels conservatories and made his début in autumn 1883 at La Monnaie, where he took part in the first performances of Reyer's *Sigurd* (1884) and *Salammbô* (1890) in addition to singing a wide variety of roles in French and Italian operas and in Wagner. From 1890 (début 19 September as Karnac in *Le roi d'Ys*) to 1891 he sang with the Opéra-Comique and from 1891 (début 17 July as Nelusko in *L'africaine*) to 1902 he was a member of the Opéra, to which he returned frequently until 1914. He sang at Monte Carlo from 1891 to 1907 and at New Orleans in 1893. His début at Covent Garden was in 1897 and he returned for the next two seasons and again from 1902 to 1904, as, among other roles, Don Giovanni, Wolfram, Nevers (*Les Huguenots*), Escamillo, Rigoletto and Lescaut (*Manon*). He sang with the Manhattan Opera (1906–7 and 1909–10), at the Metropolitan Opera (1910–12), in Boston and also in Chicago, where he sang Rigoletto, Athanaël in *Thaïs*, Rance in *La fanciulla del West* and the roles of Coppelius, Dapertutto and Miracle in *Les contes d'Hoffmann*. Towards the end of his life he taught singing. The leading French baritone after Faure, Lassalle and Maurel, Renaud had a warm and expressive voice and was considered one of the most versatile singing actors of his day. Over 40 published recordings were made between 1901 and 1908 and a few have been transferred to LP.

BIBLIOGRAPHY

A. de Cock and P. G. Hurst: 'Maurice Renaud', *Record Collector*, xi (1957), 75–118 [with discography by L. Hevingham-Root]

R. Celletti: 'Renaud, Maurice', *Le grandi voci* (Rome, 1964) [with opera discography by R. Vegeto]

HAROLD BARNES

Rencontres Internationales d'Art Contemporain. Summer music festival held at La Rochelle from 1973; *see* ROYAN FESTIVAL.

Rendall, (Francis) Geoffrey (*b* Dulwich, 20 Sept 1890; *d* London, 3 Dec 1952). English organologist. He grew up in a musical home and was taught the clarinet by the woodwind instructor at Charterhouse School, where his father was music master and organist. In 1914, having taken the MA in classics at Cambridge, Rendall joined the staff of British Museum; after war service he rose progressively to the position of Keeper of Printed Books. In spite of increasing professional duties Rendall always maintained a wide range of other interests, chief among them being the study of wind instruments. In this he was much encouraged by Galpin and he eventually became the leading clarinet authority of his time; his book *The Clarinet* (London, 1954, 3/1971) is a standard work on the instrument. He was a founder of the Galpin Society and wrote extensively on music (including an important article 'The Saxophone before Sax', *MT*, lxxiii, 1932, p.1077), incunabula, church decoration and liturgiology.

BIBLIOGRAPHY

P. Bate: 'F.G.R. 1890–1953 [sic]', *GSJ*, vi (1953), 7

PHILIP BATE

Rendano, Alfonso (*b* Carolei, nr. Cosenza, 5 April 1853; *d* Rome, 10 Sept 1931). Italian pianist and composer. He had his first musical education in Caserta, and in 1863 entered the Naples Conservatory (for only six months). He made his début as a pianist at the age of 11, but in 1866 resumed studying with Thalberg, who had become very much attached to him and who at that time lived in Naples. In 1867 he went to Paris to establish himself as a virtuoso, and there he took lessons with Georges Mathias, to whom he was introduced by Rossini; in the same year he performed in London. He took other advanced courses in 1868 at the Leipzig Conservatory under Reinecke and Richter. From then on he won success as a concert artist on tours to all the major cities of Italy. He also performed at the Leipzig Gewandhaus (8 February 1872), the Musical Union (30 April 1872), the New Philharmonic Society (9 March 1873), the Crystal Palace and elsewhere in London, including at court and in private circles. Further appearances followed in Paris and Budapest.

In 1874 he returned to Italy, but continued his brilliant activity abroad at regular intervals. During this period he became friendly with Bülow and Liszt in Vienna, benefiting greatly from a stay with the latter for about two months. He returned to play there in 1882. In 1883 he was called upon to teach the piano at the Naples Conservatory, but, eager to reform the method of teaching, he soon tendered his resignation over disagreements with the committee at the conservatory. Immediately afterwards, he founded and directed (for three years) his own school of piano in Naples, and established his personal method of teaching. Finally he settled in Rome, where he continued to teach privately.

Rendano introduced the *pedale indipendente*, also called the *pedale Rendano*, which is a third pedal that makes it possible to prolong the vibrations of a given sound or a particular chord. A celebrated interpreter of Scarlatti, Bach, Beethoven, Weber, Schumann, Chopin, Mendelssohn, Liszt, Rubinstein (who also had a liking for Rendano) and others, Rendano was among the best Italian pianists of the period because of his technical skill, and above all because of his exquisite and delicate touch. He was, moreover, a diligent propagator of culture and musical education in the 19th-century revival of instrumental music in Italy.

WORKS
(selective list)

Consuelo (opera, F. Cimmino, after G. Sand), Turin, Teatro Vittorio Emanuele, 25 May 1902

Inst: pf conc.; pf qnt; numerous piano works

Vocal: chamber ensembles, incl. Serenata in gondola, solo v, small chorus, vn, pf

BIBLIOGRAPHY
L. Torchi: ' "Consuelo" di Alfonso Rendano', *RMI*, x (1903), 564
A. Longo: 'Alfonso Rendano', *L'arte pianistica* (Naples, 1917)
G. Puccio: *Alfonso Rendano* (Rome, 1937)
F. Perrino: 'Alfonso Rendano', *Rassegna musicale Curci*, xv (Milan, 1961)
S. Martinotti: *Ottocento strumentale italiano* (Bologna, 1973)
FRANCESCO BUSSI

Rener [Reiner], Adam (*b* Liège, *c*1485; *d* Altenburg, *c*1520). South Netherlands composer and singer. In 1498 he was a boy chorister at the court of Emperor Maximilian. In 1500, probably after his voice broke, he went to Burgundy to study, but was at the Habsburg court again by 1503 as a composer. He was a singer and composer at the court of the Saxon Elector in Torgau from 1507, apparently succeeding Adam von Fulda, who died in 1505. Records of Rener's tenure in Torgau stop in 1517 and the last documented evidence of his life is the appearance of his name in the Altenburg court records of 1520.

Rener is historically important because like his contemporary Isaac he took the spirit of Netherlands music into Germany soon after 1500. Under his direction the Saxon chapel became an important musical centre, its up-to-date repertory clearly shown by the music in the so-called Jena choirbooks, some of which Rener may have helped to edit. His compositions sometimes show a tendency to depart from strict cantus firmus in favour of freer construction, following the tendencies of the time. This is especially apparent in his settings of the Ordinary of the Mass and the *Magnificat*, but less so in his settings of the Proper, which were probably closer to specifically German traditions of Proper settings. His extant works include nine Mass Ordinaries, a *Magnificat* cycle, three German secular songs and over 30 motets, some of which are cycles for the Proper. They all represent a considerable contribution to the 16th-century Netherlands and German repertory and can stand alongside the larger body of work by Isaac, with which, in many technical aspects, they are comparable.

WORKS
Edition: *A. Rener: Gesamtausgabe/Collected Works*, ed. R. L. Parker, Gesamtausgaben, ii (Brooklyn, 1964–) [vol.i incl. all the motets, vol.ii incl. Magnificat settings]

9 masses, 4vv, 1 inc. Credo, 4vv, 1539[14], 1541[1], *D-Ju* 33, 36; 1 ed. in Cw, ci (1965)

8 Magnificat (1st–8th tones), 4vv, 1544[4]; ed. in *Rhau: Musikdrucke*, v (1970), 2 ed. in Werner

4 Proper motet cycles (each incl. 4 motets), 4vv, 1545[5], *Ju*

18 other motets, 3–6vv, 1539[14], 1540[5], 1542[8], 1542[12], 1544[4], 1545[5], *Ju*, *Rp*; 4 ed. in *Rhau: Musikdrucke*, iv (1960)

3 lieder, 4vv, *A-Wn* 18810; 2 ed. in PÄMw, ix (1880)

BIBLIOGRAPHY
G. Eisenring: *Zur Geschichte des mehrstimmigen Proprium Missae bis um 1560* (Düsseldorf, 1912), 118–73
T. W. Werner: 'Die Magnificat-Kompositionen Adam Reners', *AMw*, ii (1919–20), 195–265
W. Gurlitt: 'Ein Lütticher Beitrag zur Adam-von-Fulda-Frage', *IMSCR, i Liège 1930*, 125
——: 'Johann Walter und die Musik der Reformationszeit', *Luther-Jb*, xv (1933), 1–112, esp. 19f
K. E. Roediger: *Die geistlichen Musikhandschriften der Universitäts-Bibliothek Jena* (Jena, 1935)
W. Schulze: *Die mehrstimmige Messe im frühprotestantischen Gottesdienst* (Kiel, 1940)
J. Kindermann: *Die Messen Adam Reners* (diss., U. of Kiel, 1962) [incl. complete list of works]
——: 'Rener(us) Leodiensis, Adam', *MGG*
R. L. Parker: *The Motets of Adam Rener, c.1485–c.1520* (diss., U. of Austin, Texas, 1963)
MARTIN STAEHELIN

Renesse, George van (*b* Zaamslag, Zeeuws-Vlaanderen, 21 Feb 1909). Dutch pianist. He was a pupil of Ulfert Schults at the Amsterdam Conservatory, where he won the *prix d'excellence* in 1928 and taught from 1930. He completed his studies with Ricardo Viñes and Leonid Kreutzer. In 1928 he made his début, and subsequently toured Europe and the USA several times. His interpretations of Romantic music, especially Schubert's, won him acclaim. As an accompanist, too, he was unusually gifted; he has performed with such soloists as Schwarzkopf, Seefried, Bernac, Feuermann and Piatigorsky, and in 1947 and 1948 he made concert tours with Menuhin. He has also performed with the Amadeus Quartet in Amsterdam, Paris and Munich. His improvisations have been especially popular.

TRUUS DE LEUR

Renier [Regnier], **Nicolas** (*d* ? Paris, *c*1731). French composer. He was active in Paris during the first half of the 18th century. Renier's reputation as a composer rested upon his large output of *airs* and his eight cantatas, two of which (*Le jugement de Paris* and *L'Amour aveuglé par la folie*) were performed at Philidor's concerts at the Tuileries in 1729, the year after their publication. On these occasions (January 5 and 22) the two soloists were well-known singers, Mlles Le Maure and Bourbonnais. In the previous year the same series of concerts included a divertissement by Renier (performed 7 February, repeated 9 February) but its title was not given by the *Mercure de France* when it reported these concerts. No divertissement by Renier survives. Of his cantatas, *Ulisse et Pénélope* (for soprano and bass with continuo) is perhaps the most attractive; its seven movements are fused into one, after the manner of an operatic scena. Renier's *airs* are contained in 11 books of *airs sérieux et à boire* and in anthologies issued by Ballard and others. The inclusion of *airs* by Renier in various collections published posthumously confirms their popularity. A retrospective catalogue issued by the publisher J.-P. Le Clerc in 1742 lists two 'concerts' of sonatas for two flutes by Renier but they are lost. An opera *Thésée* was attributed to him by Eitner but doubts have been cast on its authorship.

WORKS
(all printed works published in Paris)

Collected cantatas (1728): Le jugement de Paris; L'indifférence punie; L'Amour aveuglé par la folie; Ulisse et Pénélope
Separate cantatas: Sémélé (1719), La communauté bachique (lost), Les hommes (lost), Mars et Vénus (parody, lost)
11 recueils d'airs sérieux et à boire (1714–23); airs in Ballard's Recueils (1708–18) and other collections
Divertissement (*c*1728, lost); Laudate Domine (lost); 2 concerts, 2 fl (lost)

BIBLIOGRAPHY
RiemannL 12
Mercure de France (1728–9)
D. E. Tunley: *The 18th Century French Cantata* (London, 1974)
DAVID TUNLEY

Renieri, Giovanni Simone. *See* RANIERI, GIOVANNI SIMONE.

Renn, Samuel (*b* Kedleston, Derbyshire, 10 June 1786; *d* Manchester, 11 Jan 1845). English organ builder. About 1800 Renn was apprenticed to his uncle, James Davis, a successful London organ builder who had migrated from Preston, Lancashire, about 1790. In 1808 Renn became Davis's foreman and supervised organ installations and maintenance in London and Lancashire; he was working on Davis's largest organ, in Stockport parish church, when Davis retired on inheriting his brother David's wealth made in partnership with Clementi. Renn, with John Boston, took over Davis's Lancashire contracts and traded as Renn & Boston, first in Stockport (1822–5) and then in Manchester; Boston left the partnership about 1835. Renn's nephew James Kirtland had joined the firm as apprentice in 1826; after Renn's death Kirtland continued trading and was joined in 1846 by Frederick Wincott Jardine. The name Kirtland & Jardine was used until 1867, when the title Jardine & Co. was adopted; this firm flourished in Manchester until 1976.

Renn adapted the Lancashire factory system to organ building, using standardized dimensions for pipes, soundboards, consoles and cases; in this way he reduced the cost of organs to £30 a stop, 12% less than London prices, while evolving artistic designs from a range of modules. At least 100 organs were built by Renn (1822–45) and critics have always praised their musical qualities. F. W. Jardine refused to modify Renn's Chester Cathedral organ of 1829 and organ builders have persistently re-used Renn material in spite of changing taste in organ design. The closure of urban churches has resulted in the loss of many Renn organs; the best surviving example is in St Philip's, Salford.

BIBLIOGRAPHY
M. Sayer: *Samuel Renn, English Organ Builder* (Chichester, 1974)
MICHAEL SAYER

Rennagel, Johann Wilhelm. *See* RÖNNAGEL, JOHANN WILHELM.

Rennert, Günther (*b* Essen, 1 April 1911; *d* Salzburg, 31 July 1978). German producer and administrator. He was educated in Essen, Buenos Aires and Cologne, and from 1930 to 1933 in Munich, Berlin and Halle where he studied law, music, drama and theatre. In 1933 he began directing short comedy films, but came under the influence of Walter Felsenstein who persuaded him to turn to opera. After appointments in Wuppertal, Frankfurt am Main and Mainz between 1935 and 1939, he was appointed chief producer at Königsberg (1939–42). He was chief producer at the Berlin Städtische Oper from 1942 to 1944, and held the same position at the Bayerische Staatsoper in its first postwar season, staging its opening *Fidelio* in 1945. From 1946 to 1956 he was general administrator and chief producer at the Hamburg Staatsoper, where he staged many modern works, including *Peter Grimes*, *The Rake's Progress*, *Mathis der Maler*, *Wozzeck* and *Lulu*. In 1959 Rennert produced *Fidelio* at Glyndebourne, where in 1960 he was appointed head of production and joint artistic counsellor with Vittorio Gui; he remained at Glyndebourne until 1967, and with Raymond Leppard he staged the successful productions of *L'incoronazione di Poppea* and *L'Ormindo*. In 1967 he became Staatsintendant of the Bayerische Staatsoper. He also produced opera in New York, San Francisco, at the Salzburg Festival, Vienna and Milan. In Munich as at Hamburg, Rennert laid special emphasis on 20th-century opera, and also on Rossini, though his new versions of the latter's works did not please musical purists. His handling of crowd scenes in such works as *Fidelio*, and *Peter Grimes*, his unfailing instinct for character, a strong pictorial sense and a light touch in comedy marked his productions.

WRITINGS
Opernarbeit: Inszenierungen 1963–1973 (Munich, 1974)
HAROLD ROSENTHAL

Rennes. Composer, possibly identifiable with NICOLE REGNES.

Rennes, Catharina van (*b* Utrecht, 2 Aug 1858; *d* Amsterdam, 23 Nov 1940). Dutch composer, educationist and singer. After studying the piano, singing and composition at the Utrecht music school, she briefly pursued a singing career (from 1878) and later became a pupil of Johannes Messchaert in Amsterdam. In 1887 she founded her own singing school, Belcanto, in Utrecht. She became celebrated as a teacher of children, first in Hilversum (until 1902), and later in

Amsterdam and The Hague; for five years the future Queen Juliana was one of her pupils. At the coronation of Queen Wilhelmina in 1898 she conducted her *Oranje-Nassau-Cantate* op.33 with a choir of 1800 children and orchestra. Together with Hendrika van Tussenbroek (1854–1934) she did pioneer work in composing more than 100 children's songs with simple melodies and conservative, though suggestive, piano accompaniments; these and her 'matinées' were responsible for inspiring a love of music in generations of young people. Her songs, choruses and children's cantatas were published in Utrecht and Strasbourg; especially popular in its time was her *Zonnelied* from *Drie liederen* op.8 (1890; Utrecht, 1898).

BIBLIOGRAPHY
A. Annegarn: 'Rennès, Catharina van', *MGG*

JAN TEN BOKUM

Renosto, Paolo (*b* Florence, 10 Oct 1935). Italian composer. He studied at the Florence Conservatory (1949–62) with Nardi for the piano and with Fragapane, Dallapiccola and Lupi for composition, at the Accademia Chigiana in Siena (summers of 1956 and 1957) with Lavagnino for film music, and at the Salzburg Mozarteum (summer 1969) with Maderna for conducting. He has taught in Pescara (1974–7), Pesaro (from 1977) and at the Conservatorio de L'Aquila. His music draws rather eclectically on the avant-garde developments of the 1950s and later, without being particularly radical; indeed, the influence of his friend Maderna may be discerned in his recourse to stylistic and formal methods not entirely foreign to tradition. His vocal works are concerned with contemporary themes (the opera *La camera degli sposi*, for example, treats the crisis of a couple in an alienated society) or else with the total liberation of man, following the poetry of Blake, Whitman and Ginsberg.

WORKS
(selective list)

Stage: Andante amoroso (theatre event, A. Rosselli), 1970; La camera degli sposi (opera, P. Rostagno), 1971–2, Milan, Piccola Scala, 1972; Ah, l'amarvi, cari oggetti (chamber play), 1972–3; L'ombra di Banquo, ossia La lezione di potere (scena lirica, B. Cagli), Spoleto, 1976

Orch: Differenze, 1963; Scops, va, orch, 1965–6; Forma, op.7, 1968; Nacht, 2 orch/female v, str orch, 1969; Nachtblau, cl, orch, 1973; Soli, 1974; Pf Conc., 1975–6

Vocal: Love's Body, Mez, 2 reciters, orch, tape, 1972; setting of text from Leaves of Grass (Whitman), S, insts, 1974

Ens: Dissolvenza, 9 insts, 1964; Mixage, fl, a fl, pf, 1965; Du côté sensible, 11 str, 1966–7; The Al(do)us Qt, str qt/trio, 1967; Players, any insts, 1967; Fast, 2 vn, va, 1973; Addii, qnt, 1973–4; Gesta, 11 str, 1973–4; Str Trio, 1975

Inst: Dinamica I, fl/a fl, 1961; Ar-loth, ob + eng hn + musette/ob d'amore, 1967; Per Marisa T, pianista, pf, 1970

Principal publisher: Ricordi

PAOLO PETAZZI

Renotte, Hubert (*b* Liège, baptized 24 Feb 1704; *d* Liège, before 23 June 1745). South Netherlands composer and organist. According to Terry, he was *maître de chant* of the singing at Tongres. In February 1730 he was *phonascus* at the church of St Martin, Liège. Five years later he became organist at St Lambert Cathedral, succeeding Henri Godet; he was also a minor canon and holder of a benefice there. On 23 June 1745 his appointment was announced as vacant. Stylistically, Renotte's music falls between the French art of Couperin and Rameau and the Franco-Italian *galant* style; his most interesting work is the manuscript collection of *Pièces de clavecin* in which – without exhausting the expressive or technical resources of the harpsichord, and in spite of weak passages – he achieved a happy blend of the French and Italian tastes.

WORKS

VOCAL

Vespers, 1–6vv, 1733, Notre Dame, Maastricht; Magnificat, 4vv, vns, org, 1738, *B-Lc*; Magnificat, Litanies, both Namur Cathedral
Mass, 4vv; Mass, double chorus, 1733: both lost

INSTRUMENTAL

6 sonates, hpd/(vn/fl, bc), op.1 (Liège, *c*1739)
6 sonate a 3, op.2 (Liège, n.d.)
Sonates, 2 vn, bc (Liège, n.d.), lost
Pièces de clavecin, *B-Lc*

BIBLIOGRAPHY
FétisB
J.-L. Terry: *Simples notes pour servir à l'histoire des beaux-arts au pays de Liège* (MS, *B-Lc*)
A. Auda: *La musique et les musiciens de l'ancien pays de Liège* (Brussels, Paris and Liège, 1930), 965
R. Vannes: *Dictionnaire des musiciens (compositeurs)* (Brussels, 1947)
J. Quitin: 'Orgues, organiers et organistes de l'église cathédrale Notre-Dame et Saint-Lambert à Liège aux XVIIe et XVIIIe siècles', *Bulletin de l'Institut archéologique liégeois* (Liège, 1968), 56
P. Mercier: 'Hubert Renotte: pièces de clavecin', *Musique en Wallonie*, MW 15 [disc notes]

PHILIPPE MERCIER

Rentia, Anna. *See* RENZI, ANNA.

Rentius de Ponte Curvo. Composer, probably from Pontecorvo (between Rome and Naples). He is known only as the composer of two out of the three or four voices of a Gloria built, with great skill, on a liturgical tenor. The piece appears on the flyleaf of a late 14th- or early 15th-century MS, *I-CF* 63, which comes from the Cathedral of Cividale del Friuli.

KURT VON FISCHER

Renvoisy [Renvoysy], Richard de (*b* Nancy, *c*1520; *d* Dijon, 6 March 1586). French composer and lutenist. From February 1545 he served as a musician at Besançon Cathedral; in 1554 he was appointed 'maître des enfans de choeur' at the Sainte-Chapelle, Dijon, where he remained until his death. He must have taken holy orders for he was a canon from 1559 and a chaplain from 1573. On 13 February 1586 he was arrested on the charge of committing sodomy with his young choirboys and was burnt at the stake three weeks later. The circumstances of his death were related in a manuscript journal by Pépin, a fellow 'chanoine musical' at the Sainte-Chapelle from January 1571; Pépin described his colleague as a clever music master and one of the finest lutenists of his day – a view supported in some Latin verses by Philibert Colin.

Renvoisy's only surviving music, *Quelques odes d'Anacréon poète ancien, nouvellement mise en françoys après le grec … et depuis mises en musique* (Paris, 1559), is a collection of settings of 13 odes ascribed to Anacreon (but probably by later Greek lyric poets) and a canon. The preface, though defensively moralistic, betrays the hedonism of both the composer and the Greek poet who sought 'not to instruct but to entertain'. The French translation of the odes may be by Renvoisy himself, though it was attributed in the 18th century to Jean Bégat, president of the Dijon Parlement until 1572; it lacks the style of Belleau's version of 1556 but its unpretentious language, subtle metre and varied rhyme schemes recapture the spirit and charm of the Greek lyric poet. Renvoisy made no attempt to imitate anacreontic or other classical metres in his settings, but he exploited with great ingenuity the rhythmic innovations of the polyphonic chanson and homophonic *voix de ville*; not only does a dance-like triple metre alternate with the more conventional duple, but compound metres are introduced (e.g. *Mignarde colombelle*) sometimes alternating with simple metres (e.g. *Attendu que suis*). The odes vary greatly in length and Renvoisy adopted the formal scheme of dividing the longer odes into two, three or four sections or *membres*, all set in the same mode including some for three or five voices in contrast to the normal four-part settings; this technique was common in the mass but had only recently affected the more extended types of Italian and French secular vocal music. The shorter pieces and the sections of longer ones are generally through-composed with the conventional repeat of the last line; in several pieces the initial strain is repeated for the second couplet, and the three pieces in *voix de ville* style have extra strophes not set to music. Apart from a few consistently homophonic pieces (e.g. *Mignarde colombelle* and *Vulcan fondz*) and one four-voice canon at the end of the contratenor part-book, most of the odes are in the style of the four-voice chansons of Sermisy and Sandrin; they are suave and generally homophonic with rare imitative entries and pre-cadential melismas. In some of them variety is achieved by setting lines in rapid syllabic counterpoint in the manner of Janequin's and Passereau's narrative chansons; in others the more dance-like metrical, treble-dominated style of Arcadelt, Clereau and the new *voix de ville* is evident, and elsewhere all three styles alternate. Also characteristic of the mid-century chanson is the frequent choice of the Ionian mode (often transposed), but Renvoisy showed a predilection for chords on the flattened 7th degree; only five odes are in the minor mode.

The collection was issued in a revised edition entitled *Les odes mises en musique à quatre parties* (Paris, 1573). The order of the pieces was altered, perhaps to follow a sequence according to mode, the rhythm and orthography were occasionally modified and the preface was omitted. Fétis referred to *Psalmi Davidici* for four voices by Renvoisy published in 1573, but no trace of it has been found.

BIBLIOGRAPHY
FétisB
M. Cauchie: 'Note sur Richard de Renvoisy', *ReM*, x (1929), nos.10–11, p.56
G. Thibault: 'Un recueil de musique imprimé en caractères de civilité par Richard Breton (1559)', *Bibliothèque d'humanisme et Renaissance*, ii (1935), 302

FRANK DOBBINS

Renzi [Rentia, Renzini], **Anna** (*b* Rome, *c*1620; *d* in or after 1660). Italian soprano. She is said to have been still a girl when she began her career as an opera singer in performances at the house of the French ambassador to Rome, probably in one or both of Ottaviano Castelli's dramas *La sincerità trionfante, overo L'Erculeo ardire* (music by Angelo Cecchini, 1639) and *Il favorito del principe* (music by Filiberto Laurenzi, 1640). She sang the role of Lucinda in the latter at the French embassy that year. Late in 1640 she went to Venice with Laurenzi, her teacher. She may have been under the protection of members of the Accademia degli Incogniti, the circle of libertines and sceptics who dominated the early years of Venetian public opera, and was in any case promoted by their propaganda machine (Loredan, for example, published a

fable of her exclusion from Parnassus by Apollo so as not to make the Muses jealous). Among her leading roles was Deidamia in *La finta pazza* (Teatro Novissimo, 1641, music by Sacrati, who is given credit in the libretto, by Giulio Strozzi, a member of the Incogniti, for bringing her from Rome), Archimene in *Bellerofonte* (Teatro Novissimo, 1642, libretto by Vincenzo Nolfi, music by Sacrati), Aretusa in *La finta savia* (Teatro SS Giovanni e Paolo, 1643, libretto by Strozzi, music largely by Laurenzi), Octavia in *L'incoronazione di Poppea* (Teatro SS Giovanni e Paolo, 1643, libretto by Busenello, music probably largely by Monteverdi) and the title part in *Deidamia* (Teatro

Anna Renzi: engraving from G. Strozzi's 'Le glorie della signora Anna Renzi romana' (1644)

Novissimo, 1644, libretto by Scipione Errico, music by an unknown composer). Strozzi's encomiastic compilation of 1644, designed to show that Venetian opera boasted singers on a par with those of the wealthiest courts, eulogizes these performances in verse and includes an engraved portrait (see illustration), Orazio Tarditi's *Canzonette amorose* (1642) is dedicated to her. In 1645 John Evelyn heard her sing in *Ercole in Lidia* (Teatro Novissimo, libretto by Maiolino Bisaccioni, music by Rovetta) and subsequently invited her to a fish dinner. Again at the Teatro SS Giovanni e Paolo, after the probable closure of Venetian theatres during the first years of the war over Crete, she took part in *Torilda* (1648, libretto by P. P. Bissari) and *Argiope* (dedicated to her in 1645 but not performed until 1649), the libretto of which was partly by the Incognito G. B. Fusconi, whom she named as one of her executors in a will of 1652. The assertion that she married the composer of *Argiope*, Alessandro Leardini (see *Notes and Queries*), has not been substantiated and seems unlikely.

In 1653 she probably sang at Genoa (in *Torilda* and *Cesare amante*), and from October 1653 to August 1654 and again from August to December 1655 she was at the Innsbruck court. On the first occasion she would have sung the title role in *Cleopatra* (music by Cesti, a new production of Varotari's *Cesare amante*), and on the latter she was Dorisbe in *Argia* (libretto by Apolloni, music by Cesti), performed for the visit of Queen Christina of Sweden, who gave her her medal and chain. She returned to Venice to take part in *Le fortune di Rodope e di Damira* (Teatro S Apollinare, 1657, libretto by Aureli, music by P. A. Ziani) and may have been the 'Madonna Anna' whose death a letter to the impresario Marco Faustini lamented in November of the following year; but a statement by the Venetian agent of the Austrian Archduke suggests that she was still at the Innsbruck court in January 1660.

According to Strozzi her performances were distinguished by understanding of the text, a sweet but unaffected pronunciation, easy ornamentation and the ability to repeat a role many times with no loss of enthusiasm or finesse.

BIBLIOGRAPHY

G. Strozzi: *Le glorie della signora Anna Renzi romana* (Venice, 1644)
Will, 4 Oct 1652 (MS, *I-Vas*, Notarile, Testamenti chiusi, Atti Francesco Beacini, no.69)
Letter to Marco Faustini (MS, *I-Vas*, Scuola Grande di S Marco, busta 188, f.1)
Statement of Biasio Montanuzzi (MS, *I-Vas*, Notarile, Alessandro Pariglia, busta 10865, f.81*v*)
G. F. Loredan: *Bizzarrie academiche*, ii (Bologna, 14/1676), 180
Notes and Queries, 12th ser., xi (1922), 415
W. Senn: *Musik und Theater am Hof zu Innsbruck* (Innsbruck, 1954)
E. S. de Beer, ed.: *The Diary of John Evelyn* (Oxford, 1955)
W. Osthoff: 'Neue Beobachtungen zu Quellen und Geschichte von Monteverdis "Incoronazione di Poppea"', *Mf*, xi (1958), 129
C. Sartori: 'La prima diva della lirica italiana: Anna Renzi', *NRMI*, ii (1968), 430
L. Bianconi and T. Walker: 'Dalla *Finta pazza* alla *Veremonda*: storie di Febiarmonici', *RIM*, x (1975), 379–454

THOMAS WALKER

Réôme, Aurelian of. *See* AURELIAN OF RÉÔME.

Repeat (Fr. *reprise*; Ger. *Wiederholung*; It. *replica*; Lat. *repetitio*). The restatement of a portion of a musical composition of any length from a single bar to a whole section or occasionally the whole piece. Since the Classical period, repeated passages have not usually been written out; instead they are enclosed within the signs ||: and :||, although the first is generally omitted if the repeat is to be made from the beginning of a movement. Repeats commonly indicated include those made of both sections of a binary movement, that made of the first section of an *ABA* movement such as the minuet and trio (usually indicated by the words 'da capo'), the refrain of a rondeau on its initial appearance, and one or both halves of a movement in sonata form. The evolution of the notation, its exact interpretation and the practice of making repeats nevertheless raise certain problems, not all of which have obvious solutions.

In medieval and Renaissance music, repeats are often required even though no specific instructions to this effect are given. In a medieval chanson the performers must generally deduce the pattern of repeats needed from the poetic form of the text. Repeats are rare in Renaissance vocal music, but when they occur in bicinia or in pieces with, for example, two soprano parts, an interchange of the equal parts is sometimes called for in the repetition; as a result an element of variation is introduced into it. This may well have been accompanied by the addition of further embellishments during the repeat, a practice which became universal during the

Baroque period, when the da capo of an aria would be lavishly ornamented and repeats in dance music were often elaborately varied, as François Couperin's numerous versions of pieces 'plus orné' and the *doubles* to some of J. S. Bach's sarabandes and courantes show. For C. P. E. Bach the variation of repeats was mandatory, and he showed how this should be done in his *Sonaten ... mit veränderten Reprisen* (1760). Composers resisted such decoration during the 19th century, at any rate in more serious compositions such as sonatas, and they showed any modifications that they required by a special direction (e.g. Beethoven's direction that the minuet in his Quartet in C minor op.18 no.4 be played faster when it returns after the trio) or by completely rewriting the passage in question.

The notation of repeats was very imprecise up to the 17th century and in certain respects remained so even into the 18th century. In virginal music repeats are often implied even when no indication is given. The double bar, with or without dots, may imply repeats but may on the other hand merely be a calligraphical ornament (see Ferguson).

Georg Muffat stated in 1701 that a Grave should never be repeated but that lively movements could be repeated in their entirety two or three times if necessary. Handel actually specified this in some of the quick dances in the Water Music, and the last movement of Corelli's op.1 no.4, which is in one continuous section, has a terminal repeat sign that suggests a similar treatment.

Although both halves of 18th-century sonata-form movements are marked to be repeated, following the pattern of the binary structure from which they derived, there is evidence that such repeats were soon regarded as vestigial survivals not necessarily to be strictly observed. Grétry took exception to the automatic observation of these signs, and Hüllmandel and Guénin suppressed them altogether in certain works. By 1800, with few exceptions, the repeat of the second half was no longer indicated, and even that to the first half was sometimes not observed, though up to this date composers often continued to make provision for it. Beethoven's requirements are not always clear, for example as to whether or not the opening Grave is to be included in the repeated section at the beginning of the *Sonate pathétique*, op.13. But the extraordinary repeat of the second half only of the finale of the 'Appassionata' Sonata, op.57, cannot simply be dismissed as an absurdity; and his deliberate modification of the first movement of the 'Eroica' Symphony to include the usual repeat of the exposition suggests intention, not convention.

Clearly the observation of repeats and the possibility of ornamentation within them are problems of importance in interpretation. The requirements of structure – tonal balance and the lengths of sections – must always be observed. In variations where 'conventional' repeats may blossom into written-out double variations in the course of the work, failure to observe them in the theme results in a certain distortion. The practice of making only the first repeats in each movement of Bach's Goldberg Variations set is patently absurd. Before suppressing a composer's written indications in a sonata-form movement the performer must consider whether the proportions of the movement will suffer as a result, whether significant material from first-time bars will be discarded or interesting changes in the course of harmonic events will be lost or whether a meaningful juxtaposition of material between the close and the opening of the exposition may be sacrificed.

In 18th-century terminology a repeat (presumably a modification of the earlier REPORTS) also denotes an entry of the subject in a fugue or other imitative piece.

BIBLIOGRAPHY

F. Praeger: 'On the Fallacy of the Repetition of Parts in the Classical Form', *PMA*, ix (1882–3), 1

R. T. Dart: *The Interpretation of Music* (London, 1954, 4/1967)

H. Ferguson: 'Repeats and Final Bars in the Fitzwilliam Virginal Book', *ML*, xliii (1962), 345

W. S. Newman: *The Sonata in the Classic Era* (Chapel Hill, 1963)

N. Temperley: 'Tempo and Repeats in the Early Nineteenth Century', *ML*, xlvii (1966), 323

MICHAEL TILMOUTH

Répertoire International de Littérature Musicale [RILM; International Repertory of Music Literature; Internationales Repertorium der Musikliteratur]. An international bibliography of scholarly writings on music. It covers both current and older literature, provides abstracts (sometimes annotations or keywords) for each entry, and is published and indexed with computer assistance. *RILM* is an attempt by scholars and librarians to meet and master the explosion in musicological documentation, using modern technology and with international cooperation. It is the second of three such international bibliographical ventures in music, the first being *Répertoire International des Sources Musicales* (*RISM*), founded in 1952, and the third *Répertoire International d'Iconographie Musicale* (*RIdIM*), founded in 1971.

RILM was established in 1966 under the joint sponsorship of the International Musicological Society and the International Association of Music Libraries; it is governed by a ten-member Commission Internationale Mixte (president, Barry S. Brook; vice-presidents, Harald Heckmann, François Lesure). It enjoys the official sponsorship of numerous national musicological and library societies throughout the world, and financial support has come from most of these professional societies, though primarily from the American Council of Learned Societies (ACLS), the National Endowment for the Humanities (NEH) in Washington, DC, and the City University of New York Graduate School, where the International RILM Center is. *RILM* was designated by the ACLS as the pilot project for the development of a computerized, bibliographical system in the humanities to serve as a model for the more than 30 constituent scholarly societies of the ACLS; similar methods are used in other disciplines, notably *Répertoire International de la Littérature de l'Art* (*RILA*). *RILM* has two sections: one for current literature, entitled *RILM Abstracts* (founded in 1967), the other a series of specialized volumes for pre-1967 material, *RILM Retrospectives* (which began to appear in 1972).

RILM Abstracts of Music Literature is a quarterly consisting of three issues of abstracts each covering four months and an annual cumulative author–subject index, with a cumulative index every five years. *RILM Abstracts* aims to inventory and index all significant writings on music published after 1 January 1967, in all languages, embracing writings on all aspects of music and related topics, and drawn from periodicals, collective volumes or individual works, as well as miscellaneous significant scholarly publications of other kinds.

The *RILM* system involves data collection; transla-tion into English, editing and indexing; computer operations; photocomposition and printing; and specialized information retrieval. Collection of material is undertaken by national *RILM* committees in 43 countries, which are responsible for gathering abstracts of works published in their countries, and also by some 30 area editors, who report on specialized monographs or articles in non-musical publications.

Entries in the index are prepared using the *RILM* International Thesaurus, a body of terms developed to serve the needs not only of *RILM* but also of other internationally orientated books and periodicals with the reference number of each abstract. This provides much specific information about the content of the book or item indexed.

RILM Retrospectives, the project's other section, has two main subdivisions. One is the publication of specialized bibliographies with accompanying abstracts of annotations, of which the first to appear was *Thematic Catalogues in Music: an Annotated Bibliography*, by B. S. Brook, published in 1972. The other is the compilation and eventual publication of union periodical indexes for pre-1967 material not adequately covered elsewhere.

BIBLIOGRAPHY

B. S. Brook, A. Lönn and N. Schiødt: RILM reports 1–9, *Notes*, xxiii (1966–7), 462; *FAM*, xv (1968), 2; xvi (1969), 24; xvii (1970), 41; xviii (1971), 73; xix (1972), 192; xx (1973), 15; xxi (1974), 19; xxii (1975), 56

T. J. Condon: 'Abstracting Scholarly Literature: a View from the Sixties', *ACLS Newsletter*, xviii/8 (1967), 1

H. Spivacke: 'A New Journal of Abstracts for Musicologists', *Computers and the Humanities*, ii/3 (1968), 120

B. S. Brook: 'Music Literature and Modern Communication: some Revolutionary Potentials of the RILM Project', *AcM*, xlii (1970), 205; Ger. trans., *BMw*, xiii (1971), 18

N. Schiødt: 'RILM: Répertoire International de Littérature Musicale', *Dansk musiktidsskrift*, iv (1970), 168

L. Schneiderová: 'Projekt RILM', *Hudební nástroje*, iii/7 (1970), 94

R. T. Bottle and W. Chase: 'Some Characteristics of the Literature on Music and Musicology', *Special Libraries* (1972), 469

BARRY S. BROOK

Répertoire International des Sources Musicales [RISM; International Inventory of Musical Sources; Internationales Quellenlexikon der Musik]. The inventory, generally known as *RISM* from its French title, is a publication project jointly sponsored by the International Musicological Society (IMS) and the International Association of Music Libraries (IAML). The sources catalogued include manuscript and printed music and writings about music, divided into two categories, Series A and B. Series C includes a directory of the libraries whose material is listed in Series A and B.

The project had its beginnings in Robert Eitner's fundamental publications for the location of musical source material: *Bibliographie der Musik-Sammelwerke des XVI. und XVII. Jahrhunderts* (Berlin, 1877/R1963) and *Biographisch-bibliographisches Quellen-Lexikon der Musiker und Musikgelehrten der christlichen Zeitrechnung bis zur Mitte des 19. Jahrhunderts* (Leipzig, 1898–1904/R1947, 2/1959–60). These had become less useful because of their incompleteness and their errors (multiplied by the devastation of two world wars). A revision had been discussed in the interwar years, but a committee to consider the possibility was formed only after Hans Albrecht presented a paper on the subject at the first post-World War II Congress of the IMS (Basle, 1949). Independently, the subject was discussed at a first international meeting of music librarians in Florence in October 1949, and in 1951 the IMS and the newly formed IAML agreed to undertake the project jointly. The first joint committee consisted of Higini Anglès, Friedrich Blume, Vladimir Fédorov, Richard S. Hill, A. Hyatt King, Leopold Nowak, Nino Pirrotta and Albert Smijers; their initial planning session was held in 1952 under the auspices of the International Music Council, and the following year a secretariat directed by François Lesure was established in Paris. In 1960 a second secretariat was founded in Kassel for collecting, organizing and editing the material for Series A; Friedrich W. Riedel was director of this office until 1968, when Karlheinz Schlager was appointed. The Paris secretariat has since been disbanded.

The first joint committee soon decided to abandon Eitner and plan an entirely new inventory (which would however retain Eitner's general scheme of two sets of publications as the basis for the *RISM* Series A and B). For practical reasons, the committee accepted various limits and compromises: biographical information, even composers' dates, is excluded; many areas of non-Western music have been abandoned because of the difficulty of finding the required experts and locating sources.

The research, bibliographical, organizational and financial aspects of planning and executing the project on the international level are administered by a joint committee which receives support from 26 autonomous national groups who gather and submit material from their respective countries. Financial support has been provided chiefly by the Ford Foundation, the Volkswagen Foundation, the Kassel Municipal Council, the Council for Philosophy and the Humane Sciences and the International Music Council (both UNESCO), the Paris Bibliothèque Nationale, the Council of Library Resources, the Martha Baird Rockefeller Foundation and the American Musicological Society. Some governments and private foundations have supported the appointment of music catalToguers to visit selected libraries in order to make their uncatalogued backlogs available for inclusion in *RISM*.

Series A (published by Bärenreiter in Kassel) is devoted to works that appeared under the name of a single composer; it is subdivided into printed (A/I) and manuscript (A/II) sources, with the volumes of each arranged in alphabetical sequence by composers' names. The printed works are restricted to those published between 1500 and 1800, although composers whose most productive period fell before 1800 have their post-1800 publications included; this extends coverage to Haydn, but excludes Beethoven (extension to a cut-off date of 1830 would have increased the length of Series A/I by another 50–100%). About 200,000 works by about 8000 composers, in over 1100 libraries in 29 countries, will be listed in eight volumes (and supplementary volumes) when the series is complete. Series A/II lists manuscripts from before 1800. Although about 30,000 entries for manuscripts were on file in Kassel by 1975, publication will probably not occur before 1985, as cataloguing of manuscripts is still incomplete in many countries.

Series B (published by Henle in Munich and Duisburg) consists of catalogues of various self-contained groups of source material, each published independently. Apart from four volumes of Series B, edited by François Lesure at the first *RISM* secretariat in Paris, the volumes of Series B are being prepared by outside specialists. Further planned volumes include *Dépouillement der Drucke des 16. und 17. Jahrhunderts* (H. M. Brown), *The Theory of Music in Arabic Manuscripts up to 1850* (A. Shiloah), *Processionaux* (M. Huglo), *Polyphonic Works of the 15th and 16th Centuries* (N. Bridgman and M. Bent), *Kirchengesangbücher in polnischer Sprache* (K. Hlawiczka and L. Witowski), *Hebrew Sources: Notated Sources in MSS and Prints* (I. Adler), *Kirchengesangbücher in tschechischer Sprache* (J. Kouba) and *Handschriften zu einstimmiger weltlicher und geistlich-nichtliturgischer Musik des Mittelalters* (K. Schlager).

Series C, the libraries directory, was initiated by the Commission of Research Libraries of IAML and edited by Rita Benton. The first three volumes were issued in a preliminary version (R. Benton, ed.: *Directory of Music Research Libraries*, Iowa City, 1967–72). This was taken over by Bärenreiter in 1976 and at the same time officially made a part of *RISM* Series C; the series has continued under Benton's editorship, and the fourth volume appeared in 1978.

While *RISM* offers great advantages over Eitner in terms of accuracy and the number of libraries surveyed and works catalogued, it is by reason of its present boundaries an incomplete work. Supplementary projects to follow the first fiscal and administrative plan (which ended in 1975) have been considered. But even with the present limitations, *RISM* could be described (by King in 1959) as 'one of the boldest pieces of long-term planning ever undertaken for the source material of any subject in the humanistic field'.

PUBLICATIONS: SERIES A AND B
(published in Munich and Duisburg unless otherwise stated)

A/I	*Einzeldrucke vor 1800* (Kassel, 1971–)
A/II	*Handschriften vor 1800* (in preparation)
B/I/1	F. Lesure: *Recueils imprimés, XVIᵉ–XVIIᵉ siècles: liste chronologique* (1960) [index in C. Briguglio: *Indice del R.I.S.M.* (*Répertoire international des sources musicales*), *Recueils imprimés XVIᵉ–XVIIᵉ siècles di François Lesure, 1960: G. Henle Verlag, München-Duisburg, stampato in Germania* (diss., U. of Messina, 1970)]
B/II	F. Lesure: *Recueils imprimés, XVIIIᵉ siècle* (1964) [suppl. of 140 items in F. Lesure: 'Recueils imprimés – XVIIIe siècle (RISM, B II) Supplement', *Notes*, xxviii (1971–2), 397]
B/III/1	J. Smits van Waesberghe: *The Theory of Music from the Carolingian Era up to 1400*, i: *Descriptive Catalogue of MSS* (1961)
B/III/2	P. Fischer: *The Theory of Music from the Carolingian Era up to 1400*, ii: *Italy* (1968)
B/IV/1	G. Reaney: *Manuscripts of Polyphonic Music: 11th–Early 14th Century* (1966)
B/IV/2	G. Reaney: *Manuscripts of Polyphonic Music (c1320–1400)* (1969) [incl. suppl. for B/IV/1]
B/IV/3–4	K. von Fischer and M. Lütolf: *Handschriften mit mehrstimmiger Musik des 14., 15. und 16. Jahrhunderts* (1972)
B/V/1	H. Husmann: *Tropen- und Sequenzenhandschriften* (1964)
B/VI/1–2	F. Lesure: *Ecrits imprimés concernant la musique* (1971)
B/VII	W. Boetticher: *Handschriftlich überlieferte Lauten- und Gitarrentabulaturen des 15. bis 18. Jahrhunderts* (1978)
B/VIII/1	K. Ameln, M. Jenny and W. Lipphardt: *Das deutsche Kirchenlied: kritische Gesamtausgabe der Melodien*, i: *Verzeichnis der Drucke von den Anfängen bis 1800* (1975)
B/IX/2	I. Adler: *Hebrew Writings Concerning Music in Manuscripts and Printed Books from Geonic Times up to 1800* (1975)

BIBLIOGRAPHY

H. Albrecht: 'Zur Frage eines neuen Quellenlexikon', *IMSCR, iv Basle 1949*, 37

M. F. Bukofzer: 'Towards a New Inventory of Musical Sources', *Notes*, viii (1950–51), 265

A. H. King: 'The Music Librarian, his Tasks, National and International', *FAM*, vi (1959), 54

D. Heartz: 'The Répertoire International des Sources Musicales', *JAMS*, xiv (1961), 267

'*RISM*: the Washington Meeting', *FAM*, xi (1964), 3

F. Blume: 'Report on the Current Organizations and Plans of *RISM*', *JAMS*, xvii (1964), 415

F. W. Riedel: 'Zur Geschichte der musikalischen Quellenüberlieferung und Quellenkunde', *AcM*, xxxviii (1966), 3

W. D. Shirley: '*RISM*: a Report on U.S. Activities', *Notes*, xxiii (1966–7), 477

F. Blume: 'Zwanzig Jahre RISM', *AcM*, xliv (1972), 171

'Neue Pläne für RISM', *FAM*, xxii (1975), 83

H. Rösing: 'Zur Planung und zum gegenwärtigen Stand des RISM Handschriftenprojekts', *FAM*, xxiii (1976), 2

K. Schlager, J. Kindermann and H. Rösing: 'RISM: zur Katalogisierung von Musikdrucken und Musikhandschriften der Serie A', *AcM*, li (1979), 173

RITA BENTON

Répertoire International d'Iconographie Musicale [RIdIM; International Repertory of Musical Iconography; Internationales Repertorium der Musikikonographie]. An international project, founded at a meeting of the International Association of Music Librarians, 1971, to develop methods, means and research centres for the classification, cataloguing, reproduction and study of iconographical material relating to music. It is designed to assist performers, historians, librarians, students, instrument makers, record manufacturers and book publishers to make the fullest use of visual materials for scholarly and practical purposes.

The cataloguing of musico-iconographic documents has until recently been largely a private, uncoordinated affair, and has been poorly equipped with methodology and research tools. Several systems of cataloguing visual materials have been proposed, but *RIdIM* appears to have become firmly established for two reasons: because it uses new technologies that facilitate the cataloguing and reproduction of vast numbers of sources; and because *RIdIM* could follow *RISM* (1952) and *RILM* (1966) as the third important international cooperative bibliographical venture in music. Like them, *RIdIM* is sponsored by the International Musicological Society and the IAML, as well as the International Council of Museums, and it is supported by an international advisory commission of art historians, museum directors, musicologists, iconologists and private collectors. It is governed by a Commission Internationale Mixte, appointed by the executive boards of its three sponsoring societies.

RIdIM seeks to establish musical iconography as a discipline in its own right; this requires an internationally agreed approach to cataloguing and classification, an organized body of source material, a tested and proven methodology, bibliographical controls, training schools and inexpensive methods for the reproduction and exchange of documents.

RIdIM functions through national committees and active individuals or working groups and works on two research project series: an inventory of Western art with musical subjects from 1300 to the present (with subseries on paintings, drawings, prints etc); and specific topics (Greek vases, medieval wall paintings, the viol family, musical inscriptions, drums and drummers, Caravaggists, portraits, the meeting of Eastern and Western instrumentaria, 18th-century ensembles, and iconographical sources in the periodical *L'illustration*). Other specialized publications are sponsored by *RIdIM*.

The oldest and by far the largest national centre is the Centre d'Iconographie Musicale in Paris, founded by the Countess of Chambure (Geneviève Thibault). The Research Center for Musical Iconography established in 1972 at the City University of New York serves as both the American National Centre and *RIdIM* international headquarters; it has a photographic archive, *RIdIM* Master Catalogue, and a computer-operated information retrieval system.

BIBLIOGRAPHY

RIdIM reports repr. in *FAM*, xix (1972), 196; xx (1973), 18; xxi (1974), 22; xxii (1974), 58

B. S. Brook: 'RIdIM: a New International Venture in Music Iconography', *Notes*, xxviii (1971–2), 652

V. Ravizza: 'Zu einem internationalen Repertorium der Musikikonographie', *AcM*, xliv (1972), 101

B. S. Brook and R. Leppert: 'RCMI/CUNY: the Research Center for Musical Iconography of the City University of New York', *College Music Symposium*, xiii (1973), 105

Reports on *RIdIM* conferences, *ARLIS/NA* [Art Libraries Society of North America] *Newsletter*, i/3 (1973), 7; ii/3–4 (1974), 46; iii/4–5 (1975)

B. S. Brook and J. Golos: 'Research in Musical Iconography', *AMS Newsletter*, iv/2 (1974)

H. M. Brown: 'An Archive for Iconographers', *Times Literary Supplement*, no.3772 (1974), 660

——: 'What is RIdIM?', *Early Music*, ii (1974), 51

RIdIM/RCMI Newsletter (1975–)

BARRY S. BROOK

Repetendum (Lat.: 'to be repeated'). In Western chant, a section to be repeated, such as the refrain in hymns or the last part of the respond of a responsory, which is repeated after the psalm verse. In the *Ordo romanus I* (second half of the 8th century) and later, the term *versus ad repetendum* designated extra psalm verses added as needed to the mass introit and communion. According to Husmann, the words *ad repetendum* were used in the Middle Ages also for additional tropes added to the introit antiphon.

BIBLIOGRAPHY

W. Apel: *Gregorian Chant* (Bloomington, 1958, 3/1966), 190ff

H. Husmann: 'Sinn und Wesen der Tropen', *AMf*, xvi (1959), 135

RICHARD SHERR

Repetitive music. *See* SYSTEM (ii).

Rephuhn, Paul. *See* REBHUHN, PAUL.

Repiano (It.). Variant spelling of 'ripieno', used in band music to denote players (particularly clarinettists and cornet players in military bands) not at the leading desk; *see* RIPIENO (ii).

Reports. A term formerly used in England and Scotland to mean points of imitation or imitative entries (it seems not to have been used in the singular). There are, however, eight examples of reports in the Scottish Psalter of 1635 where the word appears to have been used in a more general sense for settings in which the parts move in free polyphony rather than in strictly imitative style. In Purcell's revision of the treatise that appears in the third part of Playford's *Introduction to the Skill of Musick* (12/1694) the term is mentioned as being synonymous with imitation, without further explanation.

See also PSALMS, METRICAL, §IV, 2.

Reprise (Fr.; Eng. and Ger. by adoption). (1) A repetition. Originally the word was applied quite generally. In C. P. E. Bach's *Sonaten für Clavier mit veränderten Reprisen* (1760) it refers to all the repeats in first and last movements that are written out in full in varied form. Subsequently it was applied to the return of the main thematic material after the development section of movements in sonata form, but for this sense RECAPITULATION has for long been the accepted term.

The word reprise is also used of the re-entry of a subject in a fugue; in the phrases *point de reprise* (double bar) and *chanson à reprises* (catch); and of the revival of a play or opera.

(2) In the music of Chambonnières, Rameau and other French composers of harpsichord music the word often appears at the beginning of the *couplets* in a rondeau or of the second section of a binary movement. Here it simply indicates the point to which the player returns – a useful additional guide to performing practice, especially in rondeaux, in which refrains were printed only once, at the beginning; it does not, as has sometimes been stated, refer to the *couplets* themselves.

The *petite reprise*, found mainly in French or French-influenced music of the 17th and 18th centuries, is the repeat of a short phrase, usually of four bars at the end of a binary movement, rondeau or similar form, to add to the effect of finality, much as echo phrases were used in Italian music of this period. It is occasionally written out in full (especially if the repetition is varied), but usually it is denoted by a sign or the words *petite reprise*.

See also IMPROVISATION.

MICHAEL TILMOUTH

Reproaches [Improperia]. A series of chants sung on Good Friday during the Veneration of the Cross, the texts of which tell of God's generosity to his chosen people and man's faithlessness. The low Latin word 'improperia' originally meant vulgar insults, but in this context signifies reproaches. It is possible to distinguish three different series of Reproaches in the MSS; these may be designated the greater, the lesser and the Aquitanian.

The greater Reproaches begin with the verse 'Popule meus, quid feci tibi? aut in quo contristavi te? responde mihi' set to a 1st-mode melody in neumatic style in which there are four balanced phrases, with a melodic climax reached in the third of them. There are three more sections, beginning 'Quia eduxi te de terra Aegypti', 'Quia eduxi te per desertum' and 'Quid ultra debui facere tibi'. The first of these immediately follows 'Popule meus'; in it, the two halves of the 'Popule meus' melody are slightly modified, and stated in the form *ABB'*. The next begins again with *A* and *B*, then new material is introduced (to accommodate the longer text); but the ending is the same as before, in both words and music: 'Parasti crucem Salvatori tuo'. In the last section, the character of the earlier melody is preserved but there is less literal borrowing from it. It is customary for the greater Reproaches to be sung in alternation with the trisagion. In modern liturgical books (for example, the *Liber usualis*, pp.704ff) and some medieval MSS, the trisagion is sung in full, in both Greek and Latin, after the second, third and last sections of the Reproaches. In other MSS, the trisagion is also sung before 'Popule meus'.

There are nine lesser Reproaches. Each begins with the word 'ego' and tells of one instance of God's generosity and, in parallel terms, of man's ungrateful response: for example, 'I give you a royal sceptre, and you place on my head a crown of thorns'. The melody, an irregular psalm tone (described in PalMus, xiv,

p.318), is constant throughout. The lesser Reproaches appear almost exclusively in Italian MSS. The 'Popule meus' verse is usually sung as a refrain after each of them.

The Aquitanian Reproaches resemble the greater Reproaches in style, form and character. There are three sections, beginning 'Popule meus' (with a somewhat different melody), 'Dic mihi' and 'Vinea mea', all ending with the same words and music, 'Parasti crucem Salvatori tuo'. In place of the trisagion between sections, a refrain beginning 'Vae nobis' is sung. The Aquitanian Reproaches are found in *F-Pn* lat.903, f.70 (PalMus, xiii, 139), where they are apparently an optional substitute for the greater Reproaches. In *Pn* lat.1240 (see PalMus, i, fig.XXVII) the Aquitanian Reproaches are given immediately after the trisagion, but only in a series of incipits, while the greater Reproaches, which follow them, are written in full.

There is a striking parallel in text and in liturgical use between the Reproaches and a certain Byzantine troparion, which appears in some Beneventan sources faulty both in transliteration – 'Otin to stauron' (instead of 'Otan tō staurō') – and translation ('O quando in cruce'). Interesting evidence concerning this troparion is found in the missal *I-Lc* 606 (beginning of the 11th century), where the liturgy for Good Friday is described in some detail (see PalMus, xiv, pp.300, 304, 308 and pls. XLI–XLIII). The lessons (including the Passion according to St John) and the chants of the Mass of the Presanctified are preceded by one ceremony of the Veneration of the Cross, and followed by another. In the first ceremony, the action is stylized and the rubrics read almost like stage directions: the chants are the antiphon *Ecce lignum* and the psalm *Deus misereatur*, the trisagion, and the greater and lesser Reproaches. In the second ceremony, in which everyone participates (the rubric reads 'et omnes adorent ipsam crucem'), there are three antiphons with psalms. 'O quando in cruce' follows them, sung before the Cross, and a fourth antiphon. The service continues with the Lord's Prayer and Communion.

In some MS graduals, the Reproaches appear between the Mass chants for Good Friday and Holy Saturday. This is true, for example, in the 11th-century Toulouse Gradual (*GB-Lbm* Harl.4951). In it (ff.207*v*–208*v*) the Reproaches are presented in an unusual order: first, the trisagion, in Greek and Latin; two of the greater Reproaches, with the Greek trisagion as refrain; one of the lesser Reproaches, with 'Popule meus' as refrain; another of the lesser Reproaches, with 'Quia eduxi' as refrain; the third of the greater Reproaches and the Greek trisagion; six more of the lesser Reproaches, each followed by one of three refrains, 'Parasti', 'Popule meus' and 'Quia eduxi'. There follow the refrain of the Aquitanian Reproaches, 'Vae nobis', and the second and third of the Aquitanian Reproaches, 'Dic nobis' and 'Vinea mea'. In the Aquitanian Reproaches refrains are borrowed from the greater Reproaches, in addition to 'Vae nobis'. The mixture of different traditions in this source is quite remarkable.

The Reproaches are sometimes also found in tropers, among the processional chants; an example is the St Martial troper *F-Pn* lat.909, ff.145*v*–146*v*. It is rare to find two MSS of the 10th or 11th century in agreement on the number and order of Reproaches or their precise liturgical use; for example, *GB-Lbm* Harl.4951 prescribes the Veneration of the Cross to take place only after the Reproaches have been sung.

BIBLIOGRAPHY

R.-J. Hesbert: 'La tradition bénéventaine', *PalMus*, xiv (1931), 266, 306, 318

L. Brou: 'Les impropères du Vendredi-Saint', *Revue grégorienne*, xx (1935), 161; xxi (1936), 8; xxii (1937), 1, 44

R.-J. Hesbert: 'L'"Antiphonale missarum" de l'ancien rit bénéventain', *Ephemerides liturgicae*, lx (1946), 103–41

E. Wellesz: *Eastern Elements in Western Chant: Studies in the Early History of Ecclesiastical Music*, MMB, *Subsidia*, ii (1947)

Y. Rokseth: 'La liturgie de la passion vers la fin du Xᵉ siècle', *RdM*, xxxi (1949), 48; xxxii (1950), 35

The Liber usualis with Introduction and Rubrics in English (Tournai, 1950)

H. Schmidt: *Hebdomada sancta*, ii (Rome, 1957), 794ff, 940ff

E. Werner: 'Zur Textgeschichte der Improperia', *Festschrift Bruno Stäblein* (Kassel, 1967), 274

W. Schütz: ' "Was habe ich dir getan, mein Volk?": die Wurzeln der Karfreitagsimproperien in der alten Kirche', *Jb für Liturgik und Hymnologie*, xiii (1968), 1–38

RUTH STEINER

Requeno (y Vivès), Vicente [Vincenzo] (*b* Calatorao, nr. Saragossa, 4 July 1743; *d* Tivoli, 17 Feb 1811). Spanish theorist. He joined the Society of Jesus on 2 September 1757, and with the expulsion of the Jesuits from Spain in April 1769 he settled in Rome. In the late 1790s he returned to Saragossa as numismatic curator of the Royal Aragonese Society, but on learning that the Jesuits were re-established on 30 July 1804 in the Two Sicilies he embarked again for Italy.

The first volume of his *Saggi sul ristabilimento dell'arte armonica de' greci e romani cantori* (Parma, 1798) professed to be a history of Greek music; the second is a critique of his contemporaries' 'mistaken' ideas on that subject. He argued that the whole step was not the Pythagorean ratio 9 : 8, but rather the difference between a 5th and a 4th. This equally divisible difference permitted the Greeks' knowing equal temperament. He further maintained that they knew the rudiments of counterpoint, Lysander having been its inventor (i, 100). Among the many authorities cited by Requeno, only one Spaniard is mentioned, Salinas, and he rarely (ii, 275, 311). He took Burney and Rousseau to task for their errors (ii, 120, 174) but praised among his contemporaries Vincenzo Capdagna, *maestro di cappella* at Bologna (ii, 133). In a smaller treatise, *Il tamburo stromento di prima necessità* (Rome, 1807), which drew liberally on F. A. Lampe's *De cymbalis veterum libri tres* (1703), he extolled tuned drums as a means of recapturing the splendours of Greek music. He also wrote a *Scoperta della chironomia ossia dell'arte di gestire con le mani* (Parma, 1797), discussing possible applications of this lost art to theatre and dance.

BIBLIOGRAPHY

J. Masdeu: *Requèno, il vero inventore delle più utile scoperte della nostra età* (Rome, 1806)

C. Sommervogel, ed.: *Bibliothèque de la Compagnie de Jésus* (Brussels and Paris, 1895), vi, 1670ff

F. Pedrell: *Catàlech de la Biblioteca musical de la Diputació de Barcelona* (Barcelona, 1908), i, 43f

M. Menéndez Pelayo: *Historia de la ideas estéticas en España*, iii (Madrid, 1940)

F. J. Léon Tello: *La teoría española de la música en los siglos XVII y XVIII* (Madrid, 1974)

ROBERT STEVENSON

Requiem Mass. The Mass for the Dead (*Missa pro defunctis*) of the Roman Catholic Church, taking its name from the first word of its introit, *Requiem aeternam dona eis, Domine* ('Give them eternal rest, O

Lord'). Settings of its texts (as well as the Mass itself) are frequently referred to by the name 'Requiem' alone, as, for example, are those of Mozart and Berlioz.

1. Liturgical function and structure. 2. Polyphonic settings to 1600. 3. After 1600.

1. LITURGICAL FUNCTION AND STRUCTURE. The Requiem Mass is celebrated in memory of the faithful departed on All Souls' Day, 2 November, and is classed with the votive masses; that is, it is not related to the Office of the day. It may be sung also on the day of burial and on succeeding anniversaries, as well as on the third, seventh and 30th days following the death. Gradually church law rather rigidly proscribed celebration of the Requiem, owing to excesses during the 13th and 14th centuries when all types of votive masses proliferated: in an extreme case, a priest might have celebrated several masses each day, including several requiems.

The sections of the Mass are: introit (*Requiem aeternam*); Kyrie; gradual (*Requiem aeternam*) and tract (*Absolve, Domine*); sequence (*Dies irae, dies illa*); offertory (*Domine Jesu Christe*); Sanctus and Benedictus; Agnus Dei; and communion (*Lux aeterna luceat eis, Domine*); the responsory *Libera me, Domine*, follows the communion on solemn occasions. Except for variant local, musical and liturgical dialects, the Requiem reached its essential structure by the 14th century, the sequence being the last section that was added.

Before the reforms of the Council of Trent (1543–63), an alternative gradual (*Si ambulem in medio umbrae mortis*) and tract (*Sicut cervus desiderat ad fontes aquarum*) could be used, reflecting Sarum tradition. Since the Council, only *Requiem aeternam* and *Absolve* have been approved. The Council also permitted retention of the sequence DIES IRAE, one of the four sequences that remained of the many in use before the Council's actions. The Office for the Dead, a separate liturgical rite separate from the Requiem Mass, aroused comparatively little interest in composers (although polyphonic settings were composed, for example, by Victoria and Gregor Aichinger).

2. POLYPHONIC SETTINGS TO 1600. Antedating the first complete polyphonic setting are single requiem mass movements from the late 15th century (such as those in *I-Fn* Panchiatichi 27). The earliest reference to a complete polyphonic requiem is in the will of Dufay (*d* 1474), which directs 'that twelve or more capable men . . . on the day following my funeral sing my requiem mass in the Chapel of St Stephen (Cambrai) and for this I bequeath four pounds Parisian'. The composition does not survive.

The oldest extant requiem is Ockeghem's, written before 1500, possibly around 1470. Although it is a work of small scope, it nonetheless provided a model for later 16th-century composers, particularly in its use of chant in relatively conservative cantus firmus and paraphrase techniques. Ockeghem set only the introit, Kyrie, gradual (*Si ambulem*) and tract (*Sicut cervus*), and varied the texture frequently, ranging from two to four voices in the sub-sections of the main movements.

The requiems of Brumel, La Rue and Johannes Prioris immediately followed Ockeghem's. Brumel set the sequence polyphonically, the only composer to do so before the Council of Trent, and indeed, one of very few during the entire 16th century. In a manner analogous to traditional settings of the polyphonic hymn, Brumel adopted an alternation scheme for the sequence whereby the odd-numbered strophes are polyphonic, the even-numbered chanted (most hymn cycles reverse this alternation pattern). Exceeding Ockeghem's formal boundaries, Brumel and Prioris both included the Sanctus, Agnus Dei and communion; Prioris set the gradual (*Si ambulem*) and offertory as well. La Rue's setting (for two to five voices) added the tract (*Sicut cervus*) while omitting the gradual. This particular setting is extraordinary in its dramatic juxtaposition of various voice combinations, its use of imitative procedures and in the tessitura for the bass voice (or perhaps doubling instruments) which extends downwards to B♭'. The general avoidance of high pitches in the upper voices coupled with the unusual bass range give the work a sombre, sonorous quality that is unusual for the period.

Several anonymous settings survive from the 16th century (e.g. *I-MOe* α N.1.2 *olim* Lat.452 and *A-Wn* Mus.16196.31, 16205.29–30, 15587, 16698.27). Among known contributors to the repertory in the early and middle decades of the 16th century are Antoine de Févin, Morales (two settings), Richafort, Sermisy, Certon, Clereau, Clemens (non Papa), Jean Maillard (i) and S. de Bonnefond. Richafort was first to expand the number of voices and, of more importance, contributed the sole setting from the Renaissance that employs canon to a significant degree. The Sarum chant *Circumdederunt me gemitus mortis* recurs as cantus firmus throughout the setting. Equally unusual is Richafort's musical and textual quotation from Josquin's chanson *Faulte d'argent*: 'C'est douleur non pareille' is sung in canon by the tenors while the other voices have the liturgical text.

In the later decades of the 16th century there were settings by G. F. Anerio, Giammateo Asola (three settings), Giulio Belli (three settings), Guerrero, Kerle, Lassus (two settings), Mauduit, Manuel Mendès, Monte, Palestrina, Porta (two settings), Ruffo, Jacobus Vaet and Victoria (two settings). The three settings each by Belli and Asola exceed the individual output of any other contemporary composer. By contrast, Palestrina's four-movement requiem, in his most refined style, stands alone among his 104 settings of the Ordinary. A setting by Moro of 1599 is unique for the time in its use of the entire text of the sequence. Victoria's second requiem, written on the death of Empress Maria and published in 1605, is partly a reworking of his earlier setting, but may be considered the masterwork that closes the 16th-century requiem mass history, as well as Victoria's own masterwork.

Some 41 requiem masses survive from Ockeghem to the end of the 16th century. Stylistically, they generally show conservative attitudes: total avoidance of parody procedures, retention of increasingly archaic cantus firmus practice and comparatively little imitative writing (until after about 1550).

3. AFTER 1600. Whereas the number of requiem masses composed before the end of the 16th century is under 50, the number composed during the 17th century is in the hundreds; and whereas composers in the Renaissance were relatively slow to incorporate new musical styles within requiems, their 17th-century counterparts were eager to expand the range of musical expression. They rapidly assimilated concertato principles and the use of continuo and equally rapidly incorporated instrumental forces, producing dozens of settings

within the first half of the 17th century. The requiems from 1619 by Jean de Bournonville and Antonio Brunelli (three settings from 1619), all use continuo. Belli's requiem from 1595 had its fourth printing in 1622, at which time an unfigured continuo was added.

Many requiems were printed and as many or more remain in manuscript, notably in monastic collections such as those at Klosterneuburg, Kremsmünster and the Schottenkloster, Vienna. These collections, with both 17th- and 18th-century settings, document the rising interest shown by composers in setting the requiem mass, often in very dramatic fashion. But the legacy of 16th-century style, the old *prima prattica*, was strongly felt well into the 1640s, a legacy whereby settings retained the austerity of 16th-century polyphony, adding few instruments beyond the continuo. As late as 1680 Joan Cererols composed two requiems (for four and for seven voices) that are cast in a pseudo-Renaissance style, embellished with modest Baroque polychoral writing.

Apparently the first instance of independent instrumental sections in a requiem occurred at the funeral of Cosimo II de' Medici on 21 May 1621. The setting was a composite of sections written by Monteverdi (who conducted at least the *Dies irae*), Giovanni Grillo and Francesco Usper. According to Leo Schrade (*Monteverdi*, New York, 1950/*R*1964), Giulio Strozzi, who was at the service, reported that:

the ceremonies began with a plaintive instrumental sinfonia which moved the listeners to tears; it imitated the ancient Mixolydian mode which Sappho discovered. After the sinfonia, Don Francesco Monteverdi, son of Claudio, sang most delicately these words of sorrow: 'O vos omnes attendite dolorem nostrum . . . Requiem aeternam'. The introit, frequently interrupted by the sinfonia, was most attentively listened to . . . The delicate 'De profundis' [was], as it were, a dialogue between souls in purgatory and visiting angels; [it was] profoundly admired for [its] novelty and exquisiteness.

Requiems written for special occasions proliferated after 1600. Examples in the earlier style are Richafort's setting, probably composed on the death of Josquin, Victoria's second requiem, and the requiem of Du Caurroy, which was used for the funerals of French kings until the end of the 18th century. Other notables specifically commemorated by composers in later centuries include Empress Maria Theresia (by C. A. Campioni and by Salvador Pazzaglia); Mozart (by Antonio Rosetti, among others); Louis XVI (by Cherubini, 1816); Marie Louise of Belgium (by F.-J. Fétis, 1850); and Alessandro Manzoni (by Verdi, 1874). Dozens of less illustrious people were commemorated too, such as the Duchess of Württemberg (by Jommelli, 1756); and Vincenzo Bellini and Niccolò Zingarelli (each by a separate setting by Donizetti, 1835 and 1837 respectively).

Noteworthy among the many composers of requiems in the 17th century are Aichinger, G. B. Bassani, Antonio Bertali (eight settings), Giovanni Cavaccio, P. A. Cavalli, Cazzati, G. A. Ferrari, P. A. Fiocco (three settings), Santino Girelli, Joachim Heller, J. K. Kerll (two settings), Duarte Lobo, Marcin Mielczewski, Etienne Moulinié, José Pujol, Johann Stadlmayr and Viadana.

Georg von Reutter (ii) left a Requiem in G minor (*A-Wn* 16.623) that is in the vocal and instrumental concertato tradition. Instrumental virtuosity, especially in the instrumental solo sections, marks clearly how independently some composers were considering the role of the orchestra in their requiems. The instrumental filigree over choral homophony or vocal duets emphasizes the independence of the instruments. A setting by Francesco Durante also incorporates a concertato use of vocal choirs, sometimes with each other and sometimes with the orchestra. J. K. Kerll's requiem for voices and instruments (published 1689, ed. in DTÖ, lix, Jg.xxx/1) is well within the conservative Venetian concertato style. His other requiem, for voices alone, survives in manuscript (*A-Wn* 16.988) and is a much smaller and considerably less successful work; it has the archaic trait of alternating chant with polyphony. The published work was dedicated to Emperor Leopold I, who himself composed a modest requiem (*A-Wn* 15.054) that, in spite of its limitations and probably because of the distinction of its author, was performed several times in the years 1737–40.

Besides the hundreds of more or less complete requiems from the 17th century onwards, there are dozens of separate settings of the sequence and of the responsory *Libera me*. Both these highly emotive texts seem to have drawn the attention of composers, and the resulting settings were used to great effect when inserted into the usual chanted Requiem service. Comparably, 'Motetti pro defunctis' were composed for use between movements of the requiem mass, in the general manner of motets designed for optional use. Typical of the genre is *Heu! Ah! Eheu!* by the 18th-century composer C. Pachschmidt (*A-Ws*).

Continuing a convention begun in the Renaissance, composers from the 17th century onwards established what became a tradition for some 200 years: the use of fugal technique – or at the very least, clear imitation – in the offertory at the words 'Quam olim Abrahae promisisti' (the most familiar examples are the settings by Mozart and Berlioz). Composers of requiems in the 18th century incorporated into their settings the widespread changes of musical style seen in other church music, instrumental music and opera, albeit more gradually.

The principal musical change was simple expansion of the settings through more frequent text repetition and, in particular, through more lengthy treatment of the sequence. The requiem by G. A. Bernabei treats each verse of the sequence as an individual movement. Jommelli, in his requiem of 1756, set the full sequence in a large quadripartite form within a generally dramatic, florid and sometimes lyric style. The alto solo at 'Mors stupebit' in the sequence is virtuoso in the use of runs, trills and ornaments. The expressive adagios of the 'Libera me' contrast with the florid writing in the other parts of the work. As a whole, Jommelli's setting shows him to have been a very skilled contrapuntist. Giuseppe Bonno's Requiem in C minor (*A-Wn* 15.885 A.C.38.B.18) includes trombones which contribute to the extraordinarily dynamic opening of the sequence; elsewhere the orchestra is usually relegated to the role of accompaniment for the voices; the setting suffers from an overuse of tremolo effects. Bonno's more successful work is the Requiem in E♭ (*A-Wn* 15.923 A.N.33.A.43) which contains one of the longest settings of the sequence in the 18th century. The verses are treated as separate movements, and especially striking is the manner in which the 'Tuba mirum' is set off by a complete break followed by a 13-bar instrumental introduction. Carlo Campioni's memorial requiem for Empress Maria Theresia is similarly dominated by an extended treatment of the sequence. Gossec's Requiem is large and Romantic in concept, and its dramatic intensity anticipates Mozart's, more so than do A. C. Adlgasser's settings that survive in Salzburg. Paisiello's Requiem for soloists, double chorus and orchestra (1789) is a moderately large work with an extended sequence that is weakened by being too sectionalized, by too frequent use of uninteresting strophic variation and by static harmony with little richness of colour; there is evidence that Paisiello's funeral symphony is intended to be performed before the Requiem. Giuseppe Moneta's Requiem (*A-Wn* 16.647) is dramatic and operatically conceived, and is specially notable for making extensive use of instrumental introductions to various movements, almost in the nature of curtain-raisers; it is one of the earliest settings to do so to such a degree. The vocal writing is florid, but not to the extent of, for instance, Hasse's. The treatment of the sequence is in keeping with Moneta's dramatic conception: this section comprises more than two-thirds of the score, and includes a 26-bar horn introduction to the 'Tuba mirum'.

Among the many predecessors and contemporaries of Mozart who contributed to the repertory of the requiem in the 18th century are Albrechtsberger, J. C. Bach, Campra, Cimarosa, Nicola Fago, J. F. Fasch, Feo, Fux (several settings), Gassmann, Galuppi (five settings), Pietro Gnocchi (six settings), J. A. Hasse, Michael Haydn, Heinichen, J. A. Kobrich (six settings), Marianus Königsperger (four settings), Kozeluch (five settings), G. B. Martini, Leopold Mozart, Pergolesi, Perti, Josef Preindl, Reicha and Vogler.

Mozart's Requiem (1791) was unfinished at his death and was completed by F. X. Süssmayr; uncertainty persists over precisely what each contributed. Complicating the matter further are various additions made by Joseph Eybler, a contemporary Kapellmeister in Vienna and a composer of requiems. The composition is among the most important of Mozart's works as well as the most widely performed of all 18th-century requiems. The expressiveness and intensity of the work match the poignancy of the circumstances surrounding its composition during the final months of Mozart's life. Eybler's own Requiem in C minor (*A-Wn* 16.591, and in the Schottenkloster) dates from 1803 and is an ambitiously large setting for eight voices, strings and organ. It is a sophisticated and skilfully composed work, as might be expected from one who contemplated dealing with Mozart's unfinished Requiem. The instrumental writing is often independent of the voices, and all sections are full of sharp, dramatic contrasts gained through dynamic markings. The Requiem was performed several times at the Schottenkloster up to 1870. Johann Gänsbacher was also at the Schottenkloster; but his Requiem in E♭ reveals little beyond a basic musical craftsmanship. Musical skill is shown in the Requiem in C minor by Franz Bühler (*D-Mbs* 3204).

Two requiems were composed by Cherubini, in C minor and in D minor. The Requiem in C minor (first performed on 21 January 1817, at the commemoration of Louis XVI's execution) anticipates the later large-scale requiems by Berlioz and Verdi. Beethoven thought Cherubini's C minor Requiem a masterpiece, greater than Mozart's, and Berlioz held it to be Cherubini's greatest work. The setting departs from earlier and contemporary practice in that soloists are not used, and the sequence is a single continuous movement. The use of a Chinese gong to begin the sequence lends theatricality to the work and also foreshadows Berlioz's spectacular effects. The Requiem in D minor, for men's voices, was composed in 1836 and is much simpler in style; it set a precedent for many such settings, of which Liszt's Requiem for men's voices is one example.

The Portuguese composer João Domingos Bomtempo (d 1842) published a Requiem (1819, op.23), of which Fétis aptly remarked in his *Biographie universelle*, 'C'est un ouvrage bien fait'. The composer's rich harmonic palette is used very successfully in this sizeable and dramatic work. Friedrich Kiel's first Requiem op.20 (written 1859–60) is more lyric than dramatic, but his second Requiem op.80 (1881), returned to the mainstream of theatrically conceived sacred music. Joseph Kaintz and Joseph Krottendorfer, two somewhat later colleagues of Eybler at the Schottenkloster in Vienna, composed several requiems that, though generally undistinguished, were given many performances in the mid-19th century in Vienna.

The requiems of Berlioz (1837) and Verdi (1874) are both large-scale, opera-dominated pieces that call for vocal and instrumental resources equal to or exceeding their operas. Berlioz's setting (entitled *Grande messe des morts*) stretches liturgical propriety in its gargantuan orchestra and chorus; Verdi's does so in its rearrangement of the requiem text. Both works have survived the initial intense musical, aesthetic and liturgical criticism to become staples of the repertory.

The requiems by Liszt, Saint-Saëns, Bruckner and Dvořák are more conservative than those of Berlioz and Verdi, and are in the expressive tradition of Cherubini. Liszt's Requiem in D minor (1867–71), for men's voices with organ, is a contemplative and restrained composition when compared to his more dramatic works. Louis Théodore Gouvy's Requiem op.70, is an extraordinarily chromatic and tense work that, for effective contrast, includes sections of great lyricism. The piece is symphonically conceived and, musically, calls for large forces in performance; in sheer size and breadth of conception it approaches Verdi's Requiem and perhaps exceeds Dvořák's. Fauré contributed the most widely-performed requiem of the late 19th century (op.48, 1887–8), a work that has secured a permanent niche in the repertory, at least partly because of its songlike character and simplicity and the composer's restraint in vocal and instrumental requirements. George Henschel (d 1934), the first conductor of the Boston Symphony Orchestra, produced a curious requiem (op.59) that juxtaposes chant and chant-like vocal sections against bombastic passages. Written in 1902, it seems to have been performed rather often within a short period.

Other important requiem composers in the 19th century include J. K. Aiblinger, Francisco Andrevi y Castellar, N. C. Bochsa, J. B. van Bree, Canetti, Catelani, Carlo Coccia, Fétis, John Goss, Gounod, J. E. Habert, Teodulo Mabellini, Meyerbeer, Sigismund Neukomm, Giovanni Pacini, Carl Reinecke, F. A. Reissiger and Joseph Rheinberger.

The influence of the 19th-century Cecilian movement continued well into the 20th century, and may be seen in the almost countless issues of religious music from regional and denominational publishing houses in Europe and America. The Cecilian influence, resulting in the simplification of church music, was, in the largest framework, yet another attempt to reform church music in order to make it immediately understandable, easy to perform and safely within the (so-called) bounds of liturgical propriety. Cecilianism thus stands in sharp contrast to the drama and force of the requiems by Cherubini, Berlioz and their successors, whose works to say the least stretch the boundaries of liturgical fitness. The movement stands in still sharper contrast to the requiem-derived compositions of the 19th and 20th centuries, such as the compositions by John Foulds, Britten and León Schidlowsky.

Notable contributors to the 20th-century repertory are Cesar Bresgen (for Webern), Duruflé, Guido Guerrini, Sigfrid Karg-Elert, Ligeti, Lutosławski (*Requiem* and *Lacrymosa* only), Witold Maliszewski, Heinrich Sutermeister, Randall Thompson, Virgil Thomson, Riccardo Zandonai and Amilcare Zanella. Of these only Duruflé has achieved wide success with his setting (1947), a success that is comparable to Fauré's; their settings are often compared because of their restraint, lyricism and general musical style.

Some 1600 requiems may be identified for the period from Ockeghem to the mid-1970s: to about 1620, 70 works; 1620–1750, 325; 1750–1825, 250; 1825–1910, 620; and 1910 to the mid-1970s, 335. In addition to the general influence of Romanticism that may have provoked interest in setting such a dramatic text, the 19th-century Cecilian movement doubtless accounted for dozens, if not hundreds, of works. The publishing houses of Pustet and Coppenrath in Regensburg, and Böhn in Augsburg, issued the widest possible variety of requiem compositions, ranging from settings for mixed voices, men's voices, children's voices and solo voice to settings with optional instruments, with and without organ, *a cappella*, accompanied and so forth. Most of these requiems were used for only a short time and then discarded, with very few remaining in the active repertory.

Non-liturgical but related are the numerous so-called 'German requiems' and other compositions bearing in some form the title 'Requiem'. Composers such as Schütz, Praetorius, Thomas Selle, Michael Haydn, Schubert, J. I. Müller, C. Bütner, J. F. Fasch and Brahms contributed to this category. These 'German Requiems' may derive their texts from the Lutheran Bible, as Brahms's did, or from a variety of Protestant liturgical sources and ceremonies. John Foulds's *A World Requiem* and Britten's *War Requiem* are not appropriate for liturgical presentation. The latter work and Brahms's *German Requiem* are probably the most widely-performed of all non-liturgical settings bearing the name 'Requiem'. A popular poem by the German poet and dramatist Friedrich Hebbel (1813–63), *Requiem: Seele vergiss sie nicht*, has been confused with German requiems in its many settings, by composers such as Reger, Geilsdorf, Cornelius and Gebhard. A *Deutsches Helden-Requiem* (1937) by Hermann Erdlen (d 1972) sets a Nazi theme in a text by A. Thieme. Hanns Eisler's *Lenin: Requiem* (1970) is a tribute to the Russian leader. John Tavener's *Celtic Requiem* (1972) is a composite of liturgical text, Irish poetry and children's singing-games, and is a work for the stage.

BIBLIOGRAPHY

F. Cabrol and H. Leclerq, eds.: *Dictionnaire d'archéologie chrétienne et de liturgie* (Paris, 1907)

A. Schnerich: *Messe und Requiem seit Haydn und Mozart* (Vienna and Leipzig, 1909)

P. Wagner: *Geschichte der Messe*, i (Leipzig, 1913/R1963)

G. Reese: *Music in the Middle Ages* (New York, 1940)

C. W. Fox: 'The Polyphonic Requiem before about 1615', *BAMS*, vii (1943), 6

M. Bukofzer: *Studies in Medieval and Renaissance Music* (New York, 1950)

K. G. Fellerer: *Die Messe: ihre musikalische Gestalt vom Mittelalter bis zur Gegenwart* (Dortmund, 1951)

R. J. Schaffer: *A Comparative Study of Seven Polyphonic Requiem Masses* (diss., New York U., 1952) [incl. transcr. of requiem by Du Caurroy]

G. Reese: *Music in the Renaissance* (New York, 1954; rev. 2/1959)

S. Barwick: 'Puebla's Requiem Choirbook', *Essays on Music in Honor of Archibald Thompson Davison* (Cambridge, Mass., 1957), 121

H. Luce: *The Requiem Mass from its Plainsong Beginnings to 1600* (diss., Florida State U., 1958) [incl. transcrs. of requiems by Brumel, Prioris, Sermisy, Clereau, Certon, Vaet, Guerrero, Asola, Lassus and Belli]

J. Bruyr: 'Les grands requiems et leur message', *Journal musical français musica disques*, no.116 (Nov 1963), 4

A. Seay: 'Requiem', *MGG*

S. Günther: 'Das säkularisierte Requiem', *Musica*, xviii (1964), 185

F. Sopeña Ibañez: *El réquiem en la música romántica* (Madrid, 1965)

E. A. Wienandt: *Choral Music of the Church* (New York, 1965)

M. Schnoebelen: *The Concerted Mass at San Petronio in Bologna: ca. 1660–1730: a Documentary and Analytical Study* (diss., U. of Illinois, 1966)

A. Cornides: 'Requiem Mass, Liturgy of', *New Catholic Encyclopedia* (New York, 1967)

A. Robertson: *Requiem: Music of Mourning and Consolation* (London, 1967)

R. Snow: 'Requiem Mass, Music of', *New Catholic Encyclopedia* (New York, 1967)

S. Girard: 'Algunas fuentes de musica de requiem en el nuevo mundo', *Heterofonia*, iii (1971), 10, 42 [Eng. abstract]

R. Münster: *Musikhandschriften der ehemaligen Klosterkirchen Weyarn, Tegernsee, Benediktbeuern* (Munich, 1971) [lists 35 requiems]

S. Girard: *The Requiem Mass and Music for the Dead in Venezuela* (diss., U. of California, Los Angeles, 1975)

JAMES W. PRUETT

Rescue opera. The name given to a type of opera (more strictly *opéra comique*), very popular in France during the years after the 1789 Revolution, in which the hero or heroine is delivered at the last moment either from the cruelty of a tyrant or from some great natural catastrophe (or both), not by a *deus ex machina* but by heroic human endeavour. It reflected the secular idealism of the age and often carried a social message. The genre was anticipated before the Revolution in Grétry's *Richard Coeur-de-Lion* (1784), but its earliest true representative is Berton's *Les rigueurs du cloître* (1790), in which the inhabitants of a nunnery are rescued from the 'tyranny' of the church and sent into the world to rear families. Some rescue operas were based on contemporary real-life incidents, among them Gaveaux's *Léonore, ou l'amour conjugal* (1798) and Cherubini's *Les deux journées* (1800), both with librettos by J. N. Bouilly. The former became the source of Beethoven's *Fidelio* (1805), the most famous example of the class. The rescue opera was imitated in Italy by Mayr, Paer and others, who often used librettos translated or adapted from the French, and became a major influence on the *opera semiseria*.

WINTON DEAN

Res facta (Lat.: 'created matter'). A term used in medieval and early Renaissance music to designate that which is written down as opposed to that which is improvised or passed on by some less rigid means. It seems to have been first used by Tinctoris who distinguished it from improvised discant on a tenor (*CS*, iv, 129) and equated it with *cantus compositus* (*CS*, iv, 179, 187). Similar usages and definitions are found in the works of several early 16th-century theorists (see Ferand). In looser parlance *res facta* can designate a written part (e.g. a basse danse tenor or SQUARE) that served as a basis for improvisation; but the implication in Tinctoris is that *res facta* is one kind of music – for practical purposes that which survives in written form –

and is to be distinguished from the vast quantity of unwritten music from the Middle Ages for which only iconographic or documentary evidence survives. There is also some justification for suggesting that much medieval secular monophony is not *res facta* inasmuch as the sources suggest that the music was composed – or rather devised – in the mind and not written down until it was already established in the repertory.

BIBLIOGRAPHY

E. T. Ferand: 'What is *Res Facta*?', *JAMS*, x (1957), 141

C. Petzsch: 'Das mittelalterliche Lied: res non confecta', *Zeitschrift für deutsche Philologie*, xci (1972), *Sonderheft*, 1

DAVID FALLOWS

Residue tone. The lower-pitched tone that may be heard when a group of harmonically related tones is sounded quietly together. It can be distinguished from the difference tones because if all the components are raised in frequency by the same amount, the residue tone also rises, though not by the same amount. If a difference tone were present it would remain constant in frequency. *See also* SOUND, §9.

Resimbala (Port.). AN ORGAN STOP (*Zimbel*).

Resin. *See* ROSIN.

Resinarius [Hartzer, Harzer], **Balthasar** (*b* Tetschen, Bohemia, *c*1485; *d* Leipa, 12 April 1544). German composer for the early Protestant Church. As a boy he sang and received his musical training under Heinrich Isaac in the chapel of Maximilian I. In 1515 he entered Leipzig University and returned to Tetschen in 1523 to become a Catholic priest. Despite earlier conflict with the local Lutheran preacher, Resinarius converted to the new faith, became a member of its clergy, and was made Bishop of Leipa.

His compositions, all of which appeared in the last two years of his life, are known from the publications of Georg Rhau who was apparently directly responsible for their commission. As responsories, hymns, chorale settings, motets and a Passion, all fill the immediate liturgical needs of the early Lutheran Church, and as such are highly representative of the concepts of the Wittenberg theologians, emphasizing the significance of the Word in musical composition. They are mainly cantus firmus works, stylistically conservative and characterized by frequent archaisms; the cantus firmus, most often found in the tenor, is only sparingly ornamented. In his concern for careful presentation of the text, Resinarius set each phrase in concise, clear units; after initial imitation of the cantus firmus, most of the voices come to a melodic cadence when the cantus firmus ends its phrase. Only seldom does the writing approach the pervading imitation characteristic of a Josquin motet. Accented declamation of the text in humanistic manner, however, is frequently in evidence. Rhau particularly praised the suavity of Resinarius's style and the artfulness of his cadences. Holtheuser in his *Encomion musicae* (1551) cited Resinarius as being one of the outstanding masters of his day. The popularity of his works is suggested by the number of responsories and chorale settings which appeared in manuscript copies after their publication by Rhau.

WORKS

Editions: *G. Rhau: Newe deudsche geistliche Gesenge*, ed. J. Wolf, DDT, 1st ser., xxxiv (1908/*R*) [W]
    B. Harzer (*Resinarius*): *Johannes-Passion*, ed. F. Blume and W. Schulze, Cw, xlvii (1938) [B]

G. Rhau: *Sacrorum hymnorum liber primus*, ed. R. Gerber, EDM, 1st ser., xxv (1943/*R*1961) [G]

B. *Resinarius: Responsorium ... libri duo*, ed. I.-M. Schröder, G. Rhau: *Musikdrucke aus den Jahren 1538 bis 1545 in praktischer Neuausgabe*, i–ii (Kassel, 1955–7) [S]

Responsorium numero octoginta de tempore et festis iuxta seriem totius anni [80 responsories and St John Passion], 4vv, libri duo (Wittenberg, 1544), S, B [St John Passion]

Introit, Deus misericordiam, 4vv, 1545[5]

Motets, 4vv, 1545[5]: Factum est autem; In principis erat verbum; Liber generationis

30 chorale settings, 3, 4vv, 1544[21], W

Hymns: Ceduntur gladiis, 4vv, G 55; De nativitate domini hymnus: Beatus author saeculi, 4vv, *D-Dlb*; Deus tuorum militum, 4vv, G 57; Jesu corona virginum, 4vv, G 62; Urbs beata Jerusalem, 4vv, G 66; 4 hymns, 4vv, *H-BA*

Versus, 2vv, 1549[16]: Eya inquit Paulus; Tradiderunt; Vigila te ergo

BIBLIOGRAPHY

W. Gosslau: *Die religiöse Haltung in der Reformationsmusik* (Kassel, 1933)

G. Pietzsch: 'Zur Pflege der Musik an den deutschen Universitäten', *AMf*, iii (1938), 302

I.-M. Schröder: *Die Responsorienvertonungen des Balthasar Resinarius* (Kassel, 1954)

V. H. Mattfeld: *Georg Rhaw's Publications for Vespers* (Brooklyn, 1966)

VICTOR H. MATTFELD

Resnik, Regina (*b* New York, 30 Aug 1922). American mezzo-soprano (formerly soprano) and producer. She studied at Hunter College, New York, and later with Rosalie Miller, who introduced her to Fritz Busch; he engaged her to sing Lady Macbeth with the New Opera Company, New York, in 1942. After appearances in Mexico City under Kleiber, she joined the Metropolitan in 1944, making her début as Leonora in *Il trovatore*. During the next ten years her roles there included Ellen Orford in the first New York performance of *Peter Grimes*, Alice Ford in *Falstaff* under Beecham, Leonore in *Fidelio* under Walter, Anna and Elvira, and Sieglinde; she sang Sieglinde at Bayreuth in 1953. In 1955, finding her voice changing, she concentrated on the mezzo-soprano repertory, and as well as singing such roles as Eboli, Laura in *La gioconda* and Herodias in *Salome*, she created the part of the Countess in Barber's *Vanessa* (1958), and was also heard as Lucretia in Britten's *The Rape of Lucretia* at Stratford, Ontario (she had sung the Female Chorus in the opera's American première in Chicago in 1947). In 1972 at San Francisco she sang the role of Claire in the American première of von Einem's *The Visit of the Old Lady*.

In 1957 she made a very successful Covent Garden début as Carmen; from then she was a regular visitor to London, where her roles included Marina in *Boris Godunov*, a brilliant Mistress Quickly and a decadent Clytemnestra. She also appeared regularly in Vienna, Salzburg and in the leading American and German opera houses. In her prime, Resnik had a warm, vibrant voice with a firm, strong upper register. Her acting was full of subtle detail and her fine musicianship and keen intelligence were apparent in all her work. These last two attributes led her into the field of production and in 1971 she produced *Carmen* at the Hamburg Staatsoper and *Elektra* in Venice.

BIBLIOGRAPHY

I. Cook: 'Regina Resnik', *Opera*, i (1963), 13

H. Rosenthal: 'Regina Resnik', *Great Singers of Today* (London, 1966)

HAROLD ROSENTHAL

Resolution. The conclusive ending of a musical idea, be it a melodic line on the keynote or a chord progression on the tonic. In counterpoint a resolution converts a dissonant configuration (e.g. a suspension) into a consonance (ex.1).

Ex.1

See also CADENCE.

Reson [Rezon], **Johannes** (*fl c*1425–35). Composer, probably of French origin. It is unlikely, though possible, that he is to be identified with the Johannes Reson [Reesone] who was a member of the London Gild of Parish Clerks at the compilation of its first membership list in 1448/9 and whose death was reported between Ascension 'Day 1459 and Ascension Day 1460.

His two compositions with French texts are in the third fascicle of *GB-Ob* 213, one of the latest portions of the manuscript. If the text of his rondeau is autobiographical, we may assume that Reson was not a court musician ('en court n'ay pas mon temps perdus'), although at some stage he travelled away from his native country ('Il est temp que je me retraye/au pais dont je suis venus'), and obviously met with little material success ('Je n'ai or, argent ne monnoye/de biens, d'avoir je suis tous nus'). The setting of this poem is typical of the polyphonic song type which gained prominence in northern France during the early decades of the 15th century. As in the rondeaux of Malbecque, each line of text is begun with a characteristic rhythmic motto, and untexted interludes alternate regularly with texted segments. In the rondeau refrain *Ce rondelet*/*Le dieu d'amours*, a miniature duo in celebration of spring, two matched voices engage in voice-exchange.

Reson's most significant composition is an early cyclic mass all the movements of which are found uniquely in *I-Bu* 2216. Whereas the Kyrie alone is ascribed to the composer in the source, and although some of the movements are separated from each other by several folios, Charles Hamm has shown convincingly that they were conceived as a unit. The substantial melodic and tonal recurrences from one movement to the next, as well as the use of common clefs and mensurations, leave no doubt as to the authorship of the unattributed movements. The Sanctus includes the trope 'Deus Pater cuius praesentia' (Analecta hymnica medii aevi, xlvii, no.326); the Agnus Dei has a more obscure interpolation beginning 'Alme Patrem rex iustificans'. Hamm's attribution to Reson of the *Ave verum corpus* adjacent to this Agnus Dei in *I-Bu* 2216 is made on the basis of melodic structures that recur prominently in the mass. The *Salve regina* shows Reson's characteristic use of melodic lines with overt sequences, and simplicity of formal design. He is seen at his best in the three-voice *Ave verum corpus* in which chains of suspensions create a relatively high level of dissonance, and where formulaic structures are less pronounced.

WORKS

Edition: *Early Fifteenth-century Music*, ed. G. Reaney, CMM, xi/2 (1959) [R]

SACRED

Kyrie, 3vv, R
Gloria, 3vv, *I-Bu* 2216 (anon.; attrib. by Hamm)
Credo, 3vv, *Bu* 2216 (anon.; attrib. by Hamm)
Sanctus 'Deus pater', 3vv, *Bu* 2216 (anon.; attrib. by Hamm)
Agnus Dei 'Alme Patrem', 3vv, *Bu* 2216 (anon.; attrib. by Hamm)
Gloria, 3vv, R
Ave verum corpus, 2vv, *Bu* 2216 (anon.; attrib. by Hamm)
Ave verum corpus, 2vv, R

Ave verum corpus, 3vv, R
Salve regina, 3vv, R

RONDEAUX

Ce rondelet/Le dieu d'amours, 2vv, R
Il est temps, 3vv, R

BIBLIOGRAPHY

G. Reaney: 'Reson', *MGG*
C. Hamm: 'The Reson Mass', *JAMS*, xviii (1965), 5
F. A. Gallo: *Il codice musicale 2216 della Biblioteca universitaria di Bologna*, MLMI, iii/3 (1968)

RICHARD LOYAN

Resonance. A large amplitude of oscillation built up when a vibrating system is driven by an outside periodic force of frequency close to the natural frequency of the system. It plays an important part both constructively and destructively in all acoustic systems and musical instruments. It can be used to enhance tone but in the wrong place it can produce disastrous effects. *See also* FORMANT and SOUND, §5.

Resonanzboden (Ger.). SOUNDBOARD.

Resonanzsaiten (Ger.). SYMPATHETIC STRINGS.

Resonator. A body showing the properties of RESONANCE. Common usage refers to the air column in a wind instrument as a resonator, though strictly speaking this requires a reservation. In most wind instruments, which are all 'coupled acoustic systems', the frequency of impulses created by the 'generator' element (be it a reed, the player's lips, or an air jet impinging on a sharp edge, as in clarinet, trumpet and flute respectively) does not correspond to a natural period of the air column in the body tube. Nevertheless, the cumulative effect of these impulses is to put that air column into a state of forced vibration at a compromise frequency near to one of those proper to it, the note sounded being governed mainly by its form and dimensions.

Air columns of reed organ pipes are resonators in the strict sense, since these are designed to respond accurately to a frequency (fundamental or harmonic) of the reed tongue, and they have little or none of the coercive effect exercised by, for example, a woodwind air column on its reed.

The bodies of string instruments and the soundboards of pianos and harpsichords etc, whose main function is the efficient radiation of sound energy, are also frequently referred to as resonators. This is perhaps less justifiable since under playing conditions these structures are subject to forced vibration at frequencies foreign to them, except perhaps over limited areas and which are determined by the length, mass and tensions of the strings; they are of course intended to radiate as evenly as possible over a wide frequency range (*see* WOLF).

The word resonator is also used of partly closed air vessels designed to respond to specific vibration frequencies and thus reinforce selected elements of a complex tone. These form an essential part of such instruments as the xylophone and vibraphone, and they have also been used in qualitative sound analysis (*see* HELMHOLTZ, HERMANN VON).

PHILIP BATE

Reso-reso. A notched bamboo stem scraper; *see* GÜIRO.

Respighi, Ottorino (*b* Bologna, 9 July 1879; *d* Rome, 18 April 1936). Italian composer. He studied at the Liceo Musicale, Bologna (1891–1901), where his teachers included Torchi and Martucci. In 1900–01 and again in 1902–3 he visited Russia, where he had lessons from Rimsky-Korsakov that crucially influenced his orchestration. He was widely active as a string player and pianist in the first decade of the century, and he began to take an interest in neglected Italian music of the remoter past. In 1908–9 he was in Berlin, where he absorbed much from the rich musical environment but little from the few of Bruch's lectures that he attended. After a further period in Bologna, he settled permanently in Rome in 1913, having been appointed professor of composition at the Liceo (later Conservatorio) di S Cecilia. In 1924 he became director of the same institution, but resigned two years later to devote himself mainly to composing. During the last decade of his life he nevertheless continued to teach, to conduct his works in many countries on both sides of the Atlantic, and to accompany singers, notably his wife Elsa Olivieri-Sangiacomo (*b* 1894), herself a composer and later her husband's biographer. In 1932 he was honoured with membership of the Reale Accademia d'Italia.

Though not the most important Italian composer of his generation, Respighi was much the most successful internationally, thanks above all to the advocacy of certain conductors (from Toscanini downwards). The undeniable limitations of Respighi's art are closely bound up with the limitations of his personality. Though a man of considerable culture, he remained at heart (as his widow's biography reveals) very simple, even childish. He was not so much a thinker as an avid observer of things, being especially receptive to visual impressions. It was therefore natural that the best aspects of his work tend to be 'sensory' in character: his preoccupation with vivid orchestral colours, and his eager, magpie-like appropriation of the more decorative elements in the styles of predecessors and contemporaries, were symptomatic. And when deeper emotions break through the music's glittering surface, they often recall the fresh, radiant emotions of a child. Even his faults can seem childlike: the notorious *Feste romane*, despite certain fascist overtones (probably unconscious), basically reflect nothing worse than the uninhibited self-indulgence of an infant with a box of gaudy toys.

Most of Respighi's earliest works show little sign of his real nature. Before 1910 he was absorbing the influences of various composers, from Martucci and Sgambati to Strauss; but only a few songs of those years, notably the very early *Nebbie* and the slightly later *Nevicata* and *Stornellatrice*, already have the freshness and inevitability of personal statements. It was, indeed, in a rather larger song that Respighi's mature individuality began to emerge: *Aretusa*, his earliest important composition, is still eclectic, yet the composer's personality comes through strongly, as in the twittering trills and tinsely diatonic dissonances of the opening bars. Some years were to elapse before he attained comparable individuality in instrumental music: the huge *Sinfonia drammatica*, which pays longwinded tribute to the more ponderous side of Strauss, has understandably made little headway. Then, in 1916, he completed the justly celebrated *Fontane di Roma*, in which influences from, among others, Ravel and Strauss (notably the Silver Rose music in *Der Rosenkavalier*) are completely assimilated; here Respighi showed both a perfect knowledge of his limitations and a superb command of his gifts.

Later works did not always maintain the standard of the *Fontane*. Not that they revealed nothing new: the later symphonic poems may resemble their prototype in their hedonistic pictorialism, but such things as the vivacious Children's Playground section in *Pini di Roma*, the vernal radiance of the *Trittico botticelliano*, and the eerie squeaks and slithering sounds of the Snake Garden movement in the *Impressioni brasiliane* show that Respighi was constantly exploring new possibilities within the same general aesthetic. The years immediately following the appearance of the *Fontane* were indeed a turning-point in one basic respect, for it was then that he began to let more and more deliberately archaic elements enter his music. This trend is probably best known through his use of Gregorian motifs in the later symphonic poems (notably *Vetrate di chiesa*) and his arrangements of early music (which tend, typically enough, to be decorative rather than scholarly). One should not, however, ignore the series of large and unexpectedly sober abstract works of these years, which also in their way reflect archaic tendencies (the *Concerto gregoriano*, the *Quartetto dorico*, the *Concerto in modo misolidio*), while the most perfect embodiment of Respighi's 'archaizing' principles is the radiantly charming *Lauda per la Natività del Signore*, in effect a large Christmas carol, pervaded throughout by suggestions of 16th-century madrigals, Monteverdian arioso, and other pre-Classical music.

In later years Respighi also turned his attention increasingly to opera. The results usually reflected his basic nature in being better in picturesque or idyllic than in dramatic or passionate scenes. Yet they contain many points of interest, ranging from the unwontedly 'modernist' angularities of the devil music in *Belfagor* to the unusual, highly stylized conception of *Maria Egiziaca*, reminiscent of an early *sacra rappresentazione*. Respighi's operas for adults all, however, pale in comparison with the unassuming yet wholly captivating *La bella dormente nel bosco*, originally conceived for puppets and later adapted for child mimes, accompanied by offstage voices. This, alone among Respighi's dramatic works, can rank alongside the *Fontane di Roma*, the *Lauda per la Natività* and a few other things, as one of his best compositions.

WORKS

STAGE

Re Enzo (comic opera, A. Donini); Bologna, 1905; unpubd
Semirama (opera, A. Cerè); Bologna, 1910
Marie-Victoire (opera, E. Guiraud), 1913–14, unperf., unpubd
Scherzo veneziano (Il ponticello dei sospiri) (ballet, I. Leonidoff); Rome, 1920
La bella dormente nel bosco (La bella addormentata nel bosco) (opera, G. Bistolfi), 1916–21; marionette version, Rome, 1922; child mime version, Turin, 1934; adult singer version, rev. G. Tocchi, 1966
Belfagor (opera, E. L. Morselli and C. Guastalla), 1921–2; Milan, 1923
La campana sommersa (opera, Guastalla, after Hauptmann), 1923–7; Hamburg, 1927
Belkis, regina di Saba (ballet, Guastalla), 1930–31; Milan, 1932; orch suite, 1934
Maria Egiziaca (mistero, Guastalla), 1929–32; concert, New York, 1932; staged, Venice, 1932
La fiamma (opera, Guastalla), c1930–33; Rome, 1934
Lucrezia (opera, Guastalla), 1935, completed E. Respighi, 1936; Milan, 1937

ORCHESTRAL

Pf Conc., a, 1902; Suite, D, org, str, 1902–5; other juvenilia, 1900–13, unpubd; Sinfonia drammatica, 1913–14; Fontane di Roma, 1914–16; Ballata delle Gnomidi, 1918–20; Adagio con variazioni, vc, orch [arr. early vc, pf work], 1920; Conc. gregoriano, vn, orch, 1921; Pini di Roma, 1923–4; Conc. in modo misolidio, pf, orch, 1925; Belfagor Ov. [concert work after opera] (1925); Poema autunnale, vn, orch, 1920–25
Vetrate di chiesa [first 3 movts after 3 preludi sopra melodie gregoriane, pf], 1925; Trittico botticelliano, 1927; Impressioni brasiliane, 1928; Toccata, pf, orch, 1928; Feste romane, 1928; Metamorphoseon modi XII, 1929–30; Conc. a 5, ob, tpt, pf, vn, db, str, 1933

VOCAL

With ens/orch: Aretusa (Shelley), Mez, orch, 1910; La sensitiva (Shelley), Mez, orch, 1914; Il tramonto (Shelley), 1v, str qt/str orch, 1914; La primavera (C. Zarian), solo vv, chorus, orch, c1918–19; Lauda per la Natività del Signore (?Jacopone da Todi), S, Mez, T, chorus, pic, fl, ob, eng hn, 2 bn, pf duet, 1928–30; orch versions of some songs with pf
For 1v, pf: Nebbie, Nevicata, Stornellatrice, 5 canti all'antica (1906); 6 melodie (1909); 6 liriche (1909); 6 liriche (1912); 4 rispetti toscani (A. Birga) (1914); Deità silvane (A. Rubino) (1917), arr. 1v, 11 insts (1925); 5 liriche (1917); E se un giorno tornasse (V. Aganoor Pompily) (1919); 4 liriche (D'Annunzio) (1920); 4 liriche su parole di poeti armeni, 1920; 3 vocalizzi, 1933

CHAMBER AND INSTRUMENTAL

Many early works, incl. Str Qt, D, 1907, and Adagio con variazioni, vc, pf; 3 preludi, org (1912); Sonata, vn, pf, 1916–17; 3 preludi sopra melodie gregoriane, pf, 1919; 3 preludi, org (1921); Quartetto dorico, str qt, 1924; smaller pieces

ARRANGEMENTS AND REALIZATIONS

Operas: realizations of Paisiello, 1920, unpubd, Cimarosa, 1920, pubd posth.; *Monteverdi: Orfeo*, free transcr. (lib modified Guastalla), Milan, 1935
Ballets: La boutique fantasque [after Rossini], London, 1919; La pentola magica [on Russ. melodies], Rome, 1920; Sèvres de la vieille France [after Fr. 17th–18th century], Rome, 1920
Orch: Antiche arie e danze per liuto, set 1, pf duet/orch, 1917, set 2, small orch, 1923, set 3, str, 1931; Rossiniana, 1925; Gli uccelli [after Rameau, Pasquini, etc], small orch, 1927; Passacaglia, c [arr. Bach], 1930–31; 5 études tableaux [arr. Rakhmaninov], 1931
Other arrs. of works by Bach, Frescobaldi, Locatelli, Monteverdi, Tartini, Vitali, Vivaldi, etc

Principal publishers: Bongiovanni, Bote & Bock, Ricordi, Sonzogno, Universal
MSS in *I-Bc*, *Vgc*
For fuller list see de Rensis, 99ff; also references to other minor works in E. Respighi (1954)

WRITINGS

with S. A. Luciani: *Orpheus* (Florence, 1925) [elementary textbook]

BIBLIOGRAPHY

I. Pizzetti: 'Semirama di Ottorino Respighi al Comunale di Bologna', *Il secolo* (Milan, 21 Nov 1910), 2
G. Bastianelli: 'Le nuove tendenze dell'opera italiana: Semirama di Ottorino Respighi', *Musicisti d'oggi e di ieri* (Milan, 1914), 48
E. Desderi: 'Musicisti contemporanei: Ottorino Respighi', *Il pianoforte*, iii (Turin, 1922), 143 [followed by 'Nota bio-bibliografica', 148]
S. Luciani: *'Belfagor' di Ottorino Respighi* (Milan, 1923)
——: 'Ottorino Respighi: note biografiche e bibliografia', *Bollettino bibliografico musicale*, i/3 (Milan, 1926), 3
A. Lualdi: ' "Belfagor" di Ottorino Respighi alla Scala', *Serate musicali* (Milan, 1928), 34
G. Sallustio: 'Respighi', *Revista de musica*, iii/1 (Buenos Aires, 1929), 1
M. Barbieri: ' "La campana sommersa" di Ottorino Respighi', *L'Italia musicale*, iii/7 (Genoa, 1930), 2
M. Saint-Cyr: 'Ottorino Respighi', *Rassegna dorica*, iii (1931–2), 22
M. Mila: 'Un musicien italien au tournant des époques: Ottorino Respighi', *ReM* (1933), no.135, p.250
——: 'Problemi di gusto e d'arte in Ottorino Respighi', *RaM*, vi (1933), 95
M. Rinaldi: ' "La fiamma" di Ottorino Respighi', *Rassegna dorica*, v (1933–4), 100
R. de Rensis: *Ottorino Respighi* (Turin, 1935; Fr. trans., 1957) [incl. work-list and short bibliography]
R. Bernard: 'Ottorino Respighi (1879–1936)', *ReM* (1936), no.167, p.32
A. Capri: 'L'arte di Ottorino Respighi', *Bollettino mensile di vita e cultura musicale*, x (Milan, 1936), 65
C. Clausetti: 'Ottorino Respighi', *Musica d'oggi*, 1st ser., xviii (1936), 153
M. Labroca: 'Ottorino Respighi', *RaM*, ix (1936), 159
G. M. Gatti: 'Ottorino Respighi', *International Cyclopedia of Music and Musicians* (New York, 1938, 10/1975)
E. Respighi: 'D'Annunzio, Respighi, e "La vergine della città" ', *Scenario*, iv (Milan and Rome, 1938), 214
A. Gasco: *Da Cimarosa a Strawinsky* (Rome, 1939), 243ff
H. Amano: *Gendai itaria ongaku* [Contemporary Italian music] (Tokyo, 1939)

D. de' Paoli: *La crisi musicale italiana* (Milan, 1939)

M. Rinaldi: 'Ottorino Respighi, pittore del suono', *All'ombra dell' Augusteo* (Rome, 1944), 39

A. Capri: 'L'arte di Ottorino Respighi', *Musica*, i (Rome, 1946), 61

J. Marx: 'Ottorino Respighi', *Betrachtungen eines romantischen Realisten* (Vienna, 1947), 315

D. Maxwell White: 'Ottorino Respighi', *The Music Masters*, ed. A. L. Bacharach, iv (London, 1954), 291; (2/1957), 283

E. Respighi: *Ottorino Respighi: dati biografici ordinati* (Milan, 1954; Eng. trans., abridged, 1962)

C. Guastalla: 'L'opera di Ottorino Respighi nei ricordi di Claudio Guastalla', *Ricordiana*, new ser., i (1955), 44

F. Abbiati: 'Il teatro di Ottorino Respighi', *Ricordiana*, new ser., ii (1956), 279

E. Respighi: 'L'influence du chant grégorien dans la musique de Respighi', *SMz*, xcvi (1956), 161

V. Terenzio: 'Appunti su Respighi', *RaM*, xxvii (1956), 27

A. Capri: 'Lineamenti della personalità di Respighi', *Immagini esotiche nella musica italiana*, Chigiana, xiv (1957), 77

M. Labroca: 'Respighi cordiale e solitario', *L'usignolo di Boboli* (Venice, 1959), 67

H. Amano: *Gendai itaria ongaku* [Contemporary Italian music] (Tokyo, 1960), 356–86 [different book from Amano, 1939]

M. la Morgia: 'Ottorino Respighi 25 anni dopo', *La Scala* (1961), no.145, p.29

M. Rinaldi, R. Rossellini and C. Rostand: *Musica d'oggi*, new ser., iv (1961), 146 [special number]

Ottorino Respighi: catalogo delle opere (Milan, 1965)

G. Manzoni: *Guida all'ascolto della musica sinfonica* (Milan, 1967), 357ff

S. Martinotti: *La musica moderna*, i (Milan, 1967), 193 [special number]

J. C. G. Waterhouse: *The Emergence of Modern Italian Music* (*up to 1940*) (diss., U. of Oxford, 1968), esp. 552ff

A. Gentilucci: *Guida all'ascolto della musica contemporanea* (Milan, 1969), 352ff

JOHN C. G. WATERHOUSE

Respond (Lat. *responsa*). In literature on the music of Western Christian rites the term is sometimes used synonymously with RESPONSORY. A clearer practice (e.g. as found in W. Apel: *Gregorian Chant*, 1958, 5/1973) uses 'respond' for the first part of a chant in responsorial form (e.g. the gradual at Mass and the responsory of Matins) as distinct from the verse that follows. 'Respond' and 'verse' are often abbreviated to 'R' and 'V', each crossed with a diagonal slash (see illustration; the same abbreviations are commonly used for versicles and responses). For the brief 'responsae' associated with early responsorial psalmody, *see* ANTIPHON, §1.

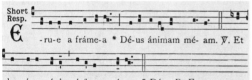

Short responsory, Terce on Passion Sunday and Palm Sunday, from 'Liber usualis'

See also VERSICLE.

Responsa (Lat.). A response sung, originally by the congregation, in the preces of the Gallican rite; *see* GALLICAN RITE, MUSIC OF THE, §13.

Response. In Christian liturgies the short text spoken or sung by the congregation or choir in reply to the VERSICLE.

Responsorial psalmody. The chanting of a psalm by alternation between a soloist (cantor), who sings a verse

or verses, and a chorus (congregation, choir), who sing a refrain ('respond'). As with antiphonal psalmody the term implies both a style of performance and a formal structure. It has recently been established that the psalms were written for cultic purposes; thus responsorial performance may be as old as the texts themselves, for the response of a group to a leader in prayer is a fundamental and universal manner of worship. Many of the psalms have refrains within their texts (e.g. Psalms cxxxvi, lxxx and cvii), and the psalmody described in the earliest Jewish sources (Talmudic) was responsorial. The first clear descriptions by Christian writers (Tertullian, Egeria) reflect a similar practice, and so suggest a natural continuity of responsorial psalmody from synagogue to church.

The oldest responsorial forms in Christian liturgy (corresponding to the gradual and great responsory in the Roman use) immediately followed the lections of Mass and Office, other chants on the same model (alleluia and short responsory) being introduced at a later date. The respond might be taken from the psalm itself, as in the gradual, or it might be an added text, as in the alleluia. Many of these chants are only loosely styled psalmody, their texts being taken from non-psalmodic sources. The gradual, though melodically complex, has the simplest structure: R–V–R, where R is the respond and V the verse. The alleluia, in which the word 'alleluia' is itself the respond, has the form R–R'–V–R'; the respond is sung first by the cantor without its melisma. More complex and variable formal structures involving the use of partial responses (R½) and the lesser doxology (D) are found in the great and short responsories, though the latter are melodically quite simple and formulaic. The great responsory commonly has the form R–V–R½–R or R–V–R½–D–R, the short responsory the form R–R–V–R½–D–R. The doxology is treated as a verse and sung by the cantor, who also intones the incipit in each chant. For the relationship between early antiphonal psalmody and responsorial psalmody, *see* ANTIPHON, §1.

See also PSALM, §II.

THOMAS H. CONNOLLY

Responsorium graduale. *See* GRADUAL (i).

Responsory [great responsory of Matins; responsorium prolixum]. A category of Western chant serving at Matins and monastic Vespers as musical postludes to the reading of lessons, as the gradual and alleluia do at the Mass. Responsories make up, indeed, the greater part of Matins, and in the total repertory of Roman chant are surpassed in quantity only by Office antiphons. From about 600 in their earliest musical source, the Hartker manuscript of *c*1000 (PalMus, 2nd ser., i), the number of responsories increased to nearly 1000 in the 13th-century Worcester Antiphoner (PalMus, 1st ser., xii).

1. History of the form. 2. Sources of the texts. 3. Modality of the melodies. 4. Structural principles of the melodies. 5. Polyphonic settings.

1. HISTORY OF THE FORM. The responsories of the Office, like the graduals and alleluias of the Mass, are termed responsorial chants because in them choir responds to cantor. Isidore of Seville (*c*559–636) gave this early definition: 'Responsories are so called because a chorus responds in consonance to a soloist'. In the medieval chant tradition the responsory usually com-

prised a choral respond, a single solo psalm verse and the *repetendum* (the last part of the respond repeated), yielding a ternary structure. It is likely that the responsory originally included the entire psalm with the verses, sung by a soloist, separated by a brief congregational refrain. Its abbreviation from the complete psalm to a single verse must have come about owing to a change in its melodic nature. When the congregation relinquished its singing role to the trained choir, the respond section probably became more elaborate in style (and therefore longer) and required fewer verses in order to avoid excessive overall length. Isidore of Seville indicated that only one verse was sung in his time, and Peter Wagner suggested that analogous changes occurred in the graduals of the Mass as early as the 5th century.

An approximation to the original practice was maintained at Rome in the 9th century, nevertheless. Amalar of Metz gave the following account of responsory performance in Rome at that time:

First a soloist sings the respond, which the choir repeats; the soloist next sings the verse, following by choral repetition of the respond; then the soloist sings the doxology, with the choir now repeating only the second part of the respond; and finally soloist and choir, in turn, each sing the complete respond.

Amalar also reported that the doxology, which had long been part of the responsory in France, had only recently been added to responsories in Rome.

In France, evidently, the repeat had become only partial after the verses as well as the doxology. Moreover, the original twofold initial statement of the respond had been reduced to a single statement, intoned by the soloist and continued by the choir. Thus the Frankish responsory in the early 9th century must have been performed as follows: respond (solo–chorus), verse (solo), latter half of respond (chorus); or with doxology: respond (solo–chorus), verse (solo), latter half of respond (chorus), doxology (solo), latter half of respond (chorus).

Rome maintained the earlier form of fuller performance well into the 12th century, at least for major feasts; rubrics in the Roman antiphoner (*I-Rvat* S Pietro B79, *c*1175) call for the complete respond after the doxology in the first three responsories for the first Sunday of Advent, and after the verse in all the responsories of Epiphany, Easter, Ascension, and SS Peter and Paul. This manuscript reveals, however, that considerable abbreviation had occurred even in Rome. The soloist now only intoned the respond, though a full choral statement still followed; moreover, for the bulk of the responsories the *repetendum* was indicated after the verse(s). Evidently, by the 12th century, Roman practice had come to conform almost entirely to Frankish. How far it conformed is well illustrated by the responsory *Aspiciens a longe* which, doubtless by virtue of its position as first responsory of the liturgical year, had three verses and doxology. The text of the respond reads: 'Aspiciens a longe, ecce video Dei potentiam venientem, et nebulam totam terram tegentem. Ite obviam ei, et dicite: Nuntia nobis si tu es ipse qui regnaturus es in populo Israel'. Both the Roman and Frankish versions have successively shorter *repetenda*. The *repetendum* after verse 1 begins with 'Ite obviam'; that after verse 2 with 'Nuntia'; that after verse 3 with 'qui regnaturus'. But there is a divergence in practice at the fourth *repetendum*; in the Frankish version, the *repetendum* after the doxology comprises only 'in populo Israel', whereas in the Roman version – as a vestige of an earlier practice –

the respond is repeated in full.

2. SOURCES OF THE TEXTS. Unlike the chants of the Mass, which take their texts principally from the book of *Psalms*, Office chants draw upon other sources, particularly the historical books of the Old and New Testaments (for the feasts of the Proper of the Time), and non-biblical sources such as martyrologies and the lives of the saints (for the Proper and Common of the Saints). The following list shows sources for the texts of responsories for the Proper of the Time:

Advent: the prophets: *Isaiah, Jeremiah, Baruch, Daniel, Micah, Zechariah, Habakkuk*

Christmas to Epiphany: the Gospels and Christian ecclesiastical literature

The Sundays after Epiphany: the book of *Psalms*

Septuagesima to the fourth Sunday in Lent: the Pentateuch, *Joshua*

Passion Sunday, Palm Sunday: *Psalms, Jeremiah, Job, Wisdom*

Maundy Thursday to Low Sunday: the Gospels

The Sundays after Easter: first ('de auctoritate') mainly from *Revelations*; also from *Sirach*, the *Song of Solomon*, *Wisdom*, *Tobit*, *Lamentations*; second onwards ('de psalmis') from *Psalms*

Ascension to Whitsunday: the Gospels, *Psalms, Acts*

The Sundays after Pentecost: *Kings, Wisdom, Job, Tobit, Judith, Esther, Ezra, Maccabees*, and finally, as Advent approaches, the prophets again round out the cycle.

3. MODALITY OF THE MELODIES. The Roman chant exists in two versions: Gregorian, found particularly in music manuscripts copied in Carolingian domains from the 10th century, and Old Roman, found in a small group of manuscripts (including the S Pietro Antiphoner mentioned above) produced in Rome from the mid-11th century to the mid-13th. Old Roman and Gregorian are liturgically nearly identical but reveal two distinct yet cognate melodic traditions. The similarities, often approaching identity, bespeak a common origin; the differences, on occasion quite striking, show the stylistic independence of the two repertories (*see* GREGORIAN AND OLD ROMAN CHANT). The following analysis takes into account both versions of Roman chant.

Responsories possess two distinct parts, respond and verse. For the latter, each repertory has a set of eight recitation formulae or 'tones', one for each mode. All Old Roman and all but a few freely composed, late examples of Gregorian verses, and the doxologies, were sung to these tones (see ex.1, pp.762–3: Gregorian, after

TABLE 1

Tone	Responsories	Percentage
1	64	10
2	84	14
3	32	5
4	82	14
5	29	5
6	27	4
7	118	19
8	175	28
Conflicts among sources	5	
No music given	1	
	617	

Frere: *Antiphonale sarisburiense*, 4; Old Roman, from *I-Rvat* S Pietro B79). Neither melodic tradition is entirely stable; moreover, the Old Roman tones are based on a transcription of only part of the repertory and are thus no more than tentative as yet.

The Old Roman chant manuscripts contain 617 Old Roman responsories together with 15 borrowings from the Gregorian repertory. The distribution of the verses among the eight tones is shown in Table 1. The corresponding figures from the Hartker manuscript, the earliest known Gregorian antiphoner with modal indications, are shown in Table 2.

TABLE 2

Mode	Responsories	Percentage
1	91	14
2	79	12
3	62	10
4	78	12
5	38	6
6	22	4
7	125	20
8	139	22
	634	

Essentially, both repertories have the same modal distribution, and the picture is not affected significantly by the great increase in the number of responsories in later Gregorian sources. The Roman responsories show a predilection for the *tetrardus* modes with a corresponding neglect of the *tritus* modes.

4. STRUCTURAL PRINCIPLES OF THE MELODIES. Melodically, the responds can be grouped in three categories: their melodies may be standard adaptations to many different texts, centos composed of stock phrases or patterns arranged in varying order from piece to piece (*see* CENTONIZATION) or freely composed. Since examples of the latter are rare, 'the art of responsorial composition is, to a very large extent, the art of adapting the different clauses of a liturgical text to different well-defined but plastic and adaptable musical phrases' (Frere, p.5). The following general remarks can be made about these basic formal units. In both the Gregorian and the Old Roman the pattern is essentially a recitation whose foundation is the reciting-note. The text dominates and straightforward declamation is the rule. The recitation is framed by an introduction and a conclusion which permit greater musical development. Although the introduction normally carries only the first two or three syllables of the text phrase, the cadence commonly takes the last five or six syllables, and both range in style from neumatic to melismatic.

The single standard melody of the 2nd mode, used for more than 50 responsories in each of the two repertories, appears in ex.2. The melody ranges from a neumatic to a melismatic style. (Late compositions frequently had more extended melismas, sometimes borrowed from other chants, but generally Office responsories were not so melismatic as responsorial Mass chants.) The structure consists of units themselves made up of an intonation, a recitation and a cadence. There are fundamental principles of textual adaptation identical in both repertories. A very close relation between text and music is achieved by placing the first and the last accented syllable of the text always in the same position (marked 'x' in ex.2) in the intonation and cadence of each pattern. The other syllables at the beginning and end of the phrase are adapted to the rest of the musical elements, some of which may be added, divided or omitted if necessary. In patterns 2 and 6 of ex.2, an element (marked '+') is added in the cadence when the antepenultimate syllable is accented; in patterns 1 and 3, a cadential melisma is divided when there is such an accented syllable. Patterns 4 and 5 of ex.2, however, have musically autonomous cadences: the text is set to them without regard for the accent. The responsories using the standard melody of the 2nd mode, then, were essentially the same in both repertories. They agree in structure, text adaptation and melodic contour; moreover, their patterns are similarly ordered.

Ex.2

Some points of difference also emerge from ex.2. First, pattern 4 of ex.2 and the second part of the 2nd tone (see ex.1) are identical in their Gregorian versions. Since the *repetendum* usually begins at pattern 5, this identity must represent a conscious attempt to make a smooth return from verse to respond. No such relationship is found in the Old Roman version. This fact supports the theory of the Frankish invention of the

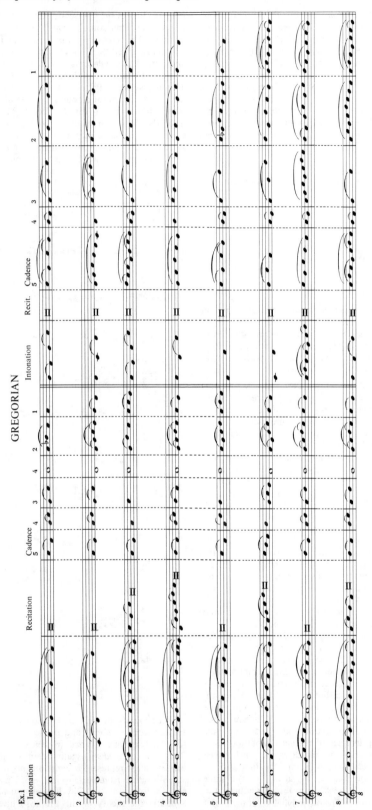

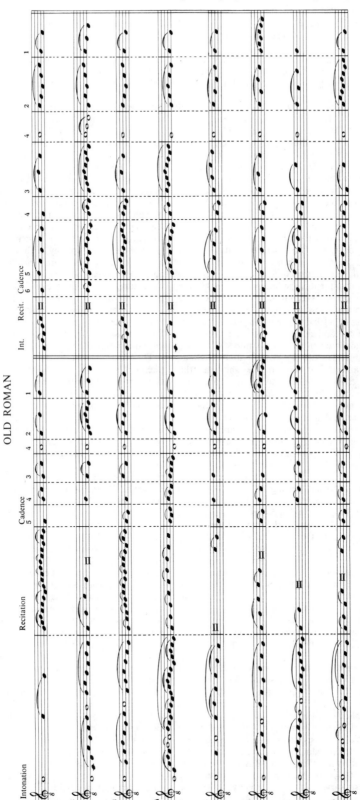

repetendum. In the Old Roman versions, however, the end of verse and the end of respond are similar and probably point to an ancient relationship between the two. Second, the Old Roman version tends to be diffuse at the cadence; most patterns end with a melisma as a transition to the subsequent phrase. The Gregorian version is more direct at the termination, the final element usually being a *clivis*. Third, in recitation practice, the Gregorian version prefers the third or final modal degree, and the Old Roman the fourth or second. The Old Roman recitation, nevertheless, normally resolves to the third or final at the start of the cadence. As ex.2 shows, the first or preparatory element in Old Roman cadences (absent from Gregorian) releases the tension built up on the reciting-note and at the same time introduces the cadence. Thus both chants emphasize the third and the final: the Gregorian directly, and the Old Roman, with more dramatic effect, by a recitation one tone higher.

Ex.1 shows that this latter difference applies also to the responsory tones. The Old Roman recitation occurs on the 5th and 6th in the authentic modes, and on the 4th and 2nd in the plagal; the Gregorian chooses the 4th and the 5th in the authentic, the 3rd and the final in the plagal. In both repertories recitation on *b* is avoided; the Old Roman 3rd tone, however, may be exceptional.

A comparison of all the Old Roman and Gregorian responsories of the 2nd mode, moreover, reveals that the former are built up from fewer patterns which are much more stable than the Gregorian patterns, admitting far fewer variants. Furthermore, they show that the Old Roman gives more attention to melodic continuity by adjusting the beginnings and endings of patterns for smooth transition between phrases. Hence, for the responsories of the 2nd mode Gregorian yields to Old Roman in matters of economy, stability and melodic development. Further investigation will reveal how far this is true also of responsories of the other seven modes.

5. POLYPHONIC SETTINGS. Settings of responsory texts survive from the earliest periods of polyphonic music. The Winchester Troper contains 59 responsories which cannot be transcribed accurately. Léonin and Pérotin set many responsories in the *Magnus liber*, providing polyphony for the intonation of the respond and for the verse; the remaining music of the respond was to be sung in plainchant when it occurred both after the intonation and in shortened form (the *repetendum*) after the verse. This practice of setting soloist music to polyphony and leaving the choral music in plainchant obtained until the 16th century. The anonymous *Descendit. . .Tamquam sponsus* (possibly by Pérotin or a contemporary) is an example of a responsory set as *organum triplum*.

From the time these early examples appeared until the 16th century very few responsories were set polyphonically. In England during the late 15th century, however, there developed in the Sarum Office a distinct place for polyphonic responsories, and they became a major feature of English music in the first half of the 16th century. Various responsories survive in *GB-Lbm* Eg.3307 (*c*1450), including two settings of *Audivi vocem*, a text set by most important English composers over the next 100 years. Numerous late 15th-century responsories also survive in *GB-Cmc* Pepys 1236. The Sarum responsories most frequently set are *Audivi*

vocem (All Saints); the verse *Gloria in excelsis* (from *Hodie nobis*, a Christmas responsory); *Dum transisset Sabbatum* (Easter); and the two compline responsories for Lent, *In pace* and *In manus tuas*. Apart from the latter two compline responsories, the great majority are settings of matins texts.

Responsories by Taverner are the first to show a reversal of the traditional roles of soloist and chorus, in that the intonation of the respond and the verse are monophonic while the remainder of the respond and the *repetendum* were set polyphonically, as in his *Dum transisset Sabbatum*. This practice became the norm for later 16th-century English settings. Not only did it in effect reintroduce a formal parallel to the plainchant responsory (the progression from solo plainchant to polyphony paralleling that from solo to choral plainchant), but it also represented a change in the nature of polyphonic singing. During the 15th century most English polyphony had been soloists' polyphony, designed to be sung by one singer to a line. The development of choral polyphony, with more than one singer to a line, occurred later in England than on the Continent, and its effects can be seen in this change of responsorial procedure, and in the style of choral polyphony which is noticeably different from that of soloists' polyphony. Nevertheless, smaller responsories, notably the two compline texts, continued to be set in the old manner: of Sheppard's three settings of *In manus tuas*, one uses only the intonation and verse.

The most magnificent responsory from this period is Sheppard's *Gaude gaude gaude Maria virgo cunctas*, (Vespers of the Purification); it includes the long *prosa Inviolata et integra* set in *alternatim* style, and is the only surviving example of such a *prosa* set in its responsorial context. The manner in which Sheppard devised alternative cadences for the repeated sections of the responsory itself, and the clear tonal structure of the whole, help make this an unsurpassed example of tonal and thematic architecture in music of this period. Its text suggests that it was composed during the Sarum revival of Queen Mary's reign (1553–8). Many of the responsories of Tallis and Sheppard (which seem to fit together into a more or less complete liturgical cycle) probably date from this revival (but Doe argued against this, 1968–9, 1970).

Although it was normal for the plainchant to be laid out in equal note values in the tenor, one exception is Byrd's *Libera me*, the last of his contributions to his and Tallis's *Cantiones sacrae* of 1575. By this date the Sarum rite had been finally abolished (when Byrd was 15) and it is not surprising to find that his few responsories show little liturgical propriety. Although *Libera me* maintains the internal cadences typical of earlier settings (necessary before the point where the *repetendum* begins), the intonation is nevertheless incorporated into the main body of the polyphony. The independent responsory motet was thereby created in a different manner from its already current continental counterpart. This responsory motet form was commonly adopted by English composers in the remainder of Elizabeth's reign, the most notable example being Tallis's great 40-voice *Spem in alium*, probably dating from the 1570s.

On the Continent the history of polyphonic responsories was quite distinct, more complex and less liturgically orientated. Interestingly, one of the earliest full settings was by an Englishman, Walter Frye, though he belonged clearly to continental traditions more than English ones, and his responsory motet form bears no relation to that of the Sarum rite. Frye's *Ave regina* (one of the most famous pieces of the late 15th century) sets the complete text of the familiar antiphon, but includes a repetition of lines 3 and 4 at the end. The result is in fact not an antiphon, but the responsory for Compline (from Candlemas to Maundy Thursday). His music sets the whole text in polyphony (intonation, respond, verse and *repetendum*), a practice that became standard on the Continent from that time onwards. The resulting *aBcB* motet form also became a prototype for longer motets in general, especially in the later 16th century, regardless of whether the texts were in fact responsories.

Ockeghem's *Gaude Maria* is an *aBcB* responsory with cantus firmus in the tenor. Obrecht's *Ave Maria* preserves the plan of Frye's, but this is not surprising since its tenor was taken from Frye's (though Obrecht laid out the tenor in long notes). During the Reformation and the Council of Trent, numerous examples of *aBcB* motets are found among the works of most major composers, notably Clemens non Papa. Not all of these pieces can be identified as having normal liturgical responsory texts. The structural repetition inherent in the form seems to have been attractive for purely musical reasons, and many of the 'manufactured' motet texts of these years are shaped into responsory form, without any liturgical necessity.

Perhaps the most important set of responsories in the 16th century was Kerle's famous *Preces speciales*, sung at the Council of Trent in 1562 (the year when the future of complex polyphonic Catholic church music was under strong debate). These extraordinary pieces are all based on newly written non-liturgical texts, in the form of large responsories. This shows that Kerle, at least, was well aware of the structural value of responsory form in longer movements; he treated the basic repetition formulae with great freedom and imagination. Many of Palestrina's and Victoria's larger motets in two *partes* are based on liturgical responsory texts, such as Palestrina's famous six-part *Tu es Petrus*, *Tribulationes civitatum*, *Sancta et immaculata* and *Dum complerentur*. The *aBcB* form is found also in many shorter motets, in one *pars*, notably in the works of Palestrina and Monte.

The period 1550–1650 saw the publication of many complete sets of responsories in Italy, either for Christmas or, much more frequently, for the 27 responsories of Holy Week's Tenebrae services (Matins of the Thursday, Friday and Saturday, which were at that time sung in the increasing darkness and 'shadows' of the previous evenings; thus many sets are described as being for Wednesday, Thursday and Friday, although liturgically they are indeed for the *triduum sacrum*). The earliest published set of Tenebrae responsories is that of Paolo Animuccia, probably published around 1555. Over the next 100 years, nearly 100 sets of Holy Week responsories were published, almost entirely by very minor Italian figures: Giovanni Alcarotto, Ruggerio Argilliano, Michele Falusi, Manuel Cardoso, Girolamo Bartei and many others. The three most famous sets are those of Ingegneri (1588), which were assumed for centuries to be by Palestrina (who seems not to have set the texts), Gesualdo (1611), set in a considerably more restrained and refined style than his madrigals, and Victoria's justly admired set (1585), which has never been equalled for concision, liturgical propriety and

sombre intensity. Victoria was one of the few composers to set only 18 of the complete 27 Tenebrae responsories, those for the second and third Nocturns of each day. Other composers occasionally set only the first Nocturn, but most set all three. Most settings are in the unaccompanied manner associated with the Sistine Chapel, though several were published with organ part. Some even state on their title-page that they are 'alla Palestrina'.

Among 18th-century sets are those by Alessandro Scarlatti (1708), Pompeo Cannicciari (1709), Giovanni Bononcini (c1730), Nicolò Jommelli (c1740), Leonardo Leo (c1740) and Michael Haydn (c1774–1796). Some survive only in manuscript and were virtually the exclusive property of the Sistine Chapel choir.

Other responsories frequently set include those from the Mass for the Dead. These have a polyphonic history as old as polyphony itself, and such responsories (e.g. the *Libera me*) continued to be set during the 18th and 19th centuries in complete settings of the Requiem Mass. Neither responsories nor complete requiems, nor indeed liturgical Office music, have exerted much attraction over leading composers of the last 100 years. Furthermore, the gradual abolition of Tenebrae during the 1950s, and the final restructuring of the whole Catholic liturgy from 1970 onwards, have left little place for such music and little incentive for its composition.

BIBLIOGRAPHY

C. Proske, ed.: *Liber vespertinus*, Musica divina, i/4 (Regensburg, 1862)
P. Wagner: *Einführung in die gregorianischen Melodien*, i: *Ursprung und Entwicklung der liturgischen Gesangsformen* (Fribourg, 1895, 3/1911/R1962); ii: *Neumenkunde* (Leipzig, 1905, 2/1912/R1962); iii: *Gregorianische Formenlehre* (Leipzig, 1921/R1962)
W. H. Frere, ed.: *Antiphonale sarisburiense* (London, 1901–25/R1966)
P. Ferretti: *Estetica gregoriana ossia Trattato delle forme musicali del canto gregoriano*, i (Rome, 1934/R1977; Fr. trans., 1938)
O. Strunk: 'Some Motet-types of the 16th Century', *PAMS 1939*, 155
J. M. Hanssens: *Amalarii episcopi opera omnia liturgica*, Studi e testi, cxxxviii–cxl (Rome, 1948–50)
W. Apel: *Gregorian Chant* (Bloomington, Ind., 1958, 3/1966)
F. Ll. Harrison: *Music in Medieval Britain* (London, 1958, 2/1963)
H. J. Holman: *The Responsoria Prolixa of the Codex Worcester F.160* (diss., Indiana U., 1961)
R.-J. Hesbert: *Corpus antiphonalium officii*, i: *Manuscripti 'Cursus romanus'*, Rerum ecclesiasticarum documenta, main ser., *Fontes*, vii (Rome, 1963)
H. Hucke: 'Responsorium', *MGG*
P. Doe: 'Latin Polyphony under Henry VIII', *PRMA*, xcv (1968–9), 81
P. F. Cutter: *The Old-Roman Responsories of Mode 2* (diss., Princeton U., 1969)
P. Doe: 'Tallis's "Spem in alium" and the Elizabethan Respond Motet', *ML*, li (1970), 1
J. Stenzl: 'Antiphonen und Responsorien', *Geschichte der katholischen Kirchenmusik*, ed. K. G. Fellerer, i (Kassel, 1972)
H. Hucke: 'Das Responsorium', *Gattungen der Musik in Einzeldarstellungen: Gedenkschrift für Leo Schrade*, i (Berne and Munich, 1973), 144–91
R. Steiner: 'Some Melismas for Office Responsories', *JAMS*, xxvi (1973), 108
T. F. Kelly: 'Melodic Elaboration in Responsory Melismas', *JAMS*, xxvii (1974), 461
G. A. Anderson: 'Responsory Chants in the Tenors of some Fourteenth-century Continental Motets', *JAMS*, xxix (1976), 119
P. F. Cutter: 'Oral Transmission of the Old-Roman Responsories?', *MQ*, lxii (1976), 182

PAUL FREDERICK CUTTER (1–4), DAVITT MORONEY (5)

Rest (Lat. *pausa*, *suspirium*; Fr. *pause*; Ger. *Pause*; It. *pausa*). A notational sign that indicates the absence of a sounding note or notes; in traditional notation every note value has an equivalent form of rest. A rest may, but need not, imply a silence; nor need silence in music be indicated by rests. In some cases rests may convey technical or physical information about sound production to the performer (e.g. the movement of hands over the keyboard or articulation) but need not result in any audible break in the music. On the other hand certain techniques of sound production (e.g. staccato or breathing for singers and wind players) will result in silence that is not indicated by rests.

Plainchant notation in the Middle Ages contained no sign for the rest, though in 12th-century square notation a vertical line drawn through the staff indicated a phrase ending and thus articulatory silence. This vertical line was taken over into the notation of RHYTHMIC MODES in the same century. As a small stroke intersecting only one or two lines of the staff, it signified the cessation of a reiterated modal pattern and thus usually a rest of some unspecified length. Rests specifying duration became necessary only when durations could not be deduced from the modal context; they first occur in the mensural notation of the 13th century. Franco of Cologne referred to the rest as *vox amissa* (i.e. 'lost' note, as distinct from *vox prolata*, 'sung' note), and he presented the six signs shown in ex.1 as the *pausa perfecta* (equal in

Ex.1

duration to the perfect *longa*), the *pausa imperfecta* (equal to the imperfect *longa* and to the altered *brevis*), the *pausa brevis* (equal to the *recta brevis*), the *pausa maior semibrevis* (equal to the major *semibrevis*, i.e. two thirds of the *brevis*), the *pausa minor semibrevis* (equal to the minor *semibrevis*, i.e. one third of the *brevis*), and the *finis punctorum* (which was unmeasured and indicated the end of a section or composition). The rest signs of mensural notation, therefore, expressed absolute durations; by contrast, the durations of pitches were decided not only by the written note values but by the metrical context which might dictate the application of the processes of imperfection and alteration.

When in the next century the *minima* became a note value in its own right, the *semibrevis* rest became a vertical line of half a space depth hanging down from a staff line, while the *minima* rest became a line of the same depth placed on a staff line (exx.2*a* and 2*b*). Thereafter the rests for the *semiminima* or *fusa* and for the *semifusa* took the form of *minima* rests with, respectively, a single and a double flag to the right (exx.2*c* and 2*d*). By the 15th century the name 'fusa' was given to a note of half the value of a *semiminima*; the new *fusa* and *semifusa* rests took the form of *minima* rests with, respectively, a single and a double flag to the left (exx. 2*e* and 2*f*).

Ex.2

(a) (b) (c) (d) (e) (f)

Although the duration of a rest was not conditional on context, its temporal position within a metrical unit was. Two devices were used to clarify this: the location of a rest on a particular staff line and the dot of division. Thus in ex.3*a* the two *minima* rests are placed on the staff line of the following note and have no effect of imperfection on the preceding note. In ex.3*b* one of the two rests is placed on the staff line closest to the preceding note and has the effect of shortening that note; at the same time there is now only one *minima* rest in the

following perfection, and so the note *c'* has to be altered (doubled in length) to fill out the perfection. In ex.3*c* the dot of division indicates where the end of one perfection and the beginning of the other falls, and thus achieves the same effect as ex.3*b* but by different means.

Ex.3

(a)   (b)

(c)

Thus there existed by the 15th century a set of signs in which, for the smaller values, the number of flags to the left of a rest corresponded with the number of flags to the right of the same note form. The only subsequent changes to the set of rest signs was the addition of still shorter values by addition of further flags, and the horizontal elongation of the vertical lines for semibreve and minim rests for clarity. The resulting forms that arose in the 17th century are shown in ex.4 together with their note forms.

Ex.4

semibreve		
minim		
crotchet	ʳ or ⸾	
quaver		
semiquaver		
demisemiquaver		
hemidemisemiquaver		

The only significant changes since that time have been the conventional use of the semibreve rest to represent a full bar's rest in whatever time signature; the use of the breve rest to represent two such bars and the long rest to represent four, usually with the number of bars indicated above the staff as well; and the notating of still longer rests as a horizontal bar on the middle staff line with the number of bars given above (ex.5). When an instrumental

Ex.5

part is silent for a whole movement of a work, this is usually indicated by the word *tacet* and no staff is provided. A rest of long duration (conventionally of one bar or more) in all parts of a work for large forces, especially orchestra, is often called a 'general pause' and marked 'G.P.' above the staff.

For further information and bibliography see NOTATION, §III.

Resta, Agostino (*b* San Severo, *c*1550; *d* after 1586). Italian composer. He was an Augustinian friar who served in the 1580s as *maestro di cappella* of S Marco, Milan (not at St Mark's, Venice, as erroneously stated in *LaMusicaD*). He published *Madrigali a cinque e sei voci* (Venice, 1580). His only other known music is included in Vincenzo Ruffo's *Soavissimi responsorii della Settimana Santa* (Milan, 1586⁵). He wrote the preface to this publication, which makes clear that Ruffo composed responds for S Marco, Milan. A book of motets for five and six voices is cited in Kast.

BIBLIOGRAPHY
P. Kast: 'Die Musickdrucke des Kataloges Giunta von 1604', *AnMc*, no.2 (1965), 41
L. Lockwood: *The Counter-Reformation and the Masses of Vincenzo Ruffo* (Venice, 1970)
LEWIS LOCKWOOD

Resta, Natale (*fl* ?Milan, 1748). Italian composer. The only known evidence of his existence is one comic opera, *Li tre cicisbei ridicoli* (text, C. A. Vasini; Bologna, carn. 1747–8), the libretto of which names him as 'Maestro di Cappella Milanese'. The work is noteworthy because it enjoyed some popularity (with further performances in Venice, Bologna and London) and earned contemporary praise (Burney said it 'had great comic merit' among the works introduced in London's first season of Italian comic opera in 1748–9; La Borde called it 'charming'), and because a score has survived – one of the few north Italian comic operas to do so before Galuppi pre-empted the field.

Though the score (*I-MOe*; catalogued under Galuppi's name) represents a later version of the opera, it retains approximately half the original musical numbers, including all the finales. These show Resta to have been an able composer. The arias are written in short-breathed, often irregular phrases, with a sharp ear for expressive rhythms; some are in da capo form and some, which repeat the entire text, are in a shape resembling binary sonata form. In the finales Resta departs from the 'chain' arrangement of musically independent segments usual for this time, and makes some attempt at internal formal organization.

BIBLIOGRAPHY
BurneyH
J.-B. de La Borde: *Essai sur la musique ancienne et moderne* (Paris, 1780/*R*1972), iii, 226
JAMES L. JACKMAN

Restoration of instruments. *See* INSTRUMENTS, RESTORATION OF.

Restz, Jakub de. *See* REYS, JAKUB.

Resupinus (Lat.: 'bent backwards'). An adjective describing a neume of more than two notes where notes in descending order are followed by a final turn upwards. Thus a TORCULUS *resupinus* has four notes forming the following steps: up, down, up (for illustration *see* NEUMATIC NOTATIONS, Table 1).

Retardation. An obsolete term used by some theorists for a SUSPENSION whose dissonance is resolved by one of the parts moving upwards by step. In the 17th and 18th centuries it was called *retardatio* (Lat.). *See also* NON-HARMONIC NOTE.

Retford, William Charles (*b* Milton, Hants., 20 June 1875; *d* London, 17 Sept 1970). English bowmaker. He

joined W. E. Hill, London, in 1892. Working in the bow department, he gave almost a lifetime of faithful service, learning, improving, influencing and teaching. In origin Hill bows reflected the knowledge and taste of the Hill brothers themselves; Retford was one of the perfectionist craftsmen who carried out their suggestions, applying practical knowledge of the specialized skills of bowmaking, and the day-to-day experience of, as he put it, 'one whose homeland is the workshop, his appliances the plane, the knife and the lathe; [his] material Brazil wood and ebony, gold and silver'. He retired in 1956, but continued the craft he loved at his home in Hanwell, at the same time preparing his book *Bows and Bow Makers*, published in 1964. This is a valuable account of bowmaking, with interesting notes on the work of many excellent makers.

BIBLIOGRAPHY
M. R. Sadler: *The Retford Centenary Exhibition* (London, 1975)
CHARLES BEARE

Rethberg, Elisabeth [Sättler, Lisbeth] (*b* Schwarzenberg, Saxony, 22 Sept 1894; *d* Yorktown Heights, NY, 6 June 1976). German soprano. She studied the piano and singing at the Dresden Conservatory, and then pursued her vocal studies with Otto Watrin, a pupil of August Iffert. In 1915 she made her début with the Dresden Opera as Arsena in *Der Zigeunerbaron*, and remained with the company for seven years, during which time she is said to have mastered over 100 roles, ranging from Octavian and Sophie in *Der Rosenkavalier* (she was later to be a distinguished Marschallin) to Mozart's Constanze, Weber's Agathe and the popular Puccini heroines.

On 22 November 1922 Rethberg made her Metropolitan début as Aida, and soon became one of the most warmly appreciated members of the company, with whom she remained as leading soprano for 20 consecutive seasons, making her last appearance there, again as Aida, on 6 March 1942. During this long period she was heard in 35 roles, German, French and Italian, and was acclaimed by many musicians, including Toscanini, as the greatest soprano of her time. Her Verdi roles, besides Aida, were Desdemona, Amelia in *Un ballo in maschera*, Maria Boccanegra and the Leonoras of *Il trovatore* and *La forza del destino*; in Wagner she was a famous exponent of the 'youthful-dramatic' parts, Elisabeth, Elsa, Eva and Sieglinde, and in her last season she even tackled the *Siegfried* Brünnhilde. She was also an accomplished Mozartian (Constanze, Countess, Donna Anna, Donna Elvira, Pamina) and a notable Rachel (*La juive*), Maddalena (*Andrea Chénier*), Marguerite, and Selika (*L'africaine*). In Respighi's *La campana sommersa* her florid singing was so remarkable that Gatti-Casazza tried unsuccessfully to make her study such coloratura roles as Gilda, Amina and Lucia.

During these years she frequently sang elsewhere in the USA, and also returned regularly to Dresden, where, on 6 June 1928, she assumed the title role in the première of *Die aegyptische Helena*. She sang at Covent Garden in five inter-war seasons, and also appeared in the major Italian theatres, and in Mozartian and other roles at the Salzburg Festival. After her retirement from the Metropolitan, she continued to sing in concert for two more years; in 1957 she married George Cehanovsky, a *comprimario* baritone who enjoyed an even longer Metropolitan career than her own.

Rethberg's beautiful *lirico spinto* soprano was perfectly equalized between the registers, and a combination of natural musicianship and thorough training enabled her to maintain an unusually even legato in the most difficult passages. The most valuable of her many fine records are the acoustic recordings of 1924–5, a pair of couplings of the two *Aida* arias and of arias from *Tannhäuser* and *Lohengrin* made in Berlin in 1927, and several of her earlier American records, notably the arias from *Otello* and *Un ballo in maschera* and an almost complete Nile Scene from *Aida* with Lauri-Volpi and De Luca. It can fairly be claimed that many of these recordings have not been surpassed in beauty of tone and purity of style.

BIBLIOGRAPHY

H. Henschel and E. Friedrich: *Elisabeth Rethberg: ihr Leben und Künstlertum* (Schwarzenberg, 1928/R1977)

J. B. Richards: 'Elisabeth Rethberg: the Discography', *Record Collector*, iii (1948), 51

——: 'Elisabeth Rethberg's Recordings', *Record Collector*, viii (1953), 5

——: 'Rethberg, Elisabeth', *Le grandi voci* (Rome, 1964) [with opera discography by W. Smolian]

DESMOND SHAWE-TAYLOR

Réti, Rudolph [Rudolf] (*b* Uzice, 27 Nov 1885; *d* Montclair, NJ, 7 Feb 1957). American writer on music, pianist and composer, of Serbian birth. In Vienna he studied the piano and music theory at the Academy of Music and musicology at the university. As a concert pianist he gave the first performance of Schoenberg's op.11 piano pieces (1911). He was an initiator of the Salzburg Music Festival (1922), which led to the founding of the International Society for Contemporary Music. Later he became chief music critic of the Vienna newspaper *Das Echo* (1930–38), and after emigrating to the USA he was a contributing editor to the *Musical Digest*. Réti's theory of composition was based on his analyses of Beethoven's sonatas, some of which were published posthumously as *Thematic Patterns in Sonatas of Beethoven* (1967). In *The Thematic Process in Music* (1951) he suggested that composers since the 18th century have based works not on a structural design but on the conscious evolution of motivic cells of melody into a thematic pattern. This recurs with transformation throughout the work, determining modulations, chords, bridges, 'emotional strength' and form; composition is viewed as a linear process and the motifs are identified without regard for rhythm. In *Tonality–Atonality–Pantonality* (1958), a partly prescriptive and partly analytic work, Réti considered early atonal music and its potential unity of form.

See also ANALYSIS, §§II, 7, III, 3, and figs.23–6.

WRITINGS

'Die tonalen Wege der Modernen: von Impressionismus in der Musik und am Klavier', *Der Merker*, ii (1911), 383

The Thematic Process in Music (New York, 1951)

'Egon Wellesz: Musician and Scholar', *MQ*, xlii (1956), 1

'The Role of a Duothematicism in the Evolution of Sonata Form', *MR*, xvii (1956), 110; Ger. trans., *ÖMz*, xi (1956), 306

Tonality–Atonality–Pantonality (London, 1958)

'Zwölfton-Dämmerung', *ÖMz*, xiv (1959), 457

Tonality in Modern Music (New York, 1962)

ed. D. Cooke: *Thematic Patterns in Sonatas of Beethoven* (London, 1965)

'Die thematische Einheit in Verdi's "Don Carlos"', *ÖMz*, xxx (1975), 342

BIBLIOGRAPHY

D. M. Schwejda: *An Investigation of the Analytical Techniques Used by Rudolph Réti in 'The Thematic Process in Music'* (diss., Indiana U., 1967)

Retirada (It.: 'withdrawal'). A title sometimes used in the 17th and 18th centuries, particularly in eastern Europe, for the closing dance of a suite. Examples may be found in Baron Wenzel Ludwig von Radolt's lute-book *Die aller treueste verschwigneste und nach so wohl fröhlichen als traurigen Humor* (1701) and in the 18th-century lute manuscript *PL-Wu* Rps.55.

Retransition (Ger. *Rückführung*). In any work or movement said to be in SONATA FORM, the last part of the development section, which prepares for the return of the opening idea (recapitulation). In tonal works the retransition normally consists of a passage leading to the dominant of the key of the movement and then a passage that emphasizes the dominant just before the recapitulation begins.

Retro. *See* RECTE ET RETRO.

Retrograde (Ger. *Krebsgang*, from Lat. *cancrizans*: 'crab-like'). A succession of notes played backwards, either retaining or abandoning the rhythm of the original. It has always been regarded as among the more esoteric ways of extending musical structures, one that does not necessarily invite the listener's appreciation. In the Middle Ages and Renaissance it was applied to cantus firmi, sometimes with elaborate indications of rhythmic organization given in cryptic Latin inscriptions in the musical manuscripts; rarely was it intended to be detected from performance. Even the most famous secular example of retrograde, Machaut's *Ma fin est mon commencement*, whose text gives away its design, has been admired more for the finesse with which the technique is used than for the chanson's other artistic merits. There is only one well-known example of retrograde in tonal music, apart from its use in puzzle canons: this is in the last movement of Beethoven's Hammerklavier Sonata, where an entire fugal exposition is based on the retrograde form of the original subject, retaining its 'backward' rhythm but being converted to the minor mode. This retrograde can be recognized by the listener, owing to the striking leap of a 10th to a minim trill at the beginning of the original form of the subject. In the 20th century, retrograde has played an important part in the theory of TWELVE-NOTE COMPOSITION, being one of three basic operations that can be performed on a 12-note set and often used in conjunction with the other two, inversion and transposition.

WILLIAM DRABKIN

Retroncha. *See* ROTROUENGE.

Rettich, Wilhelm (*b* Leipzig, 3 July 1892). German composer. He studied with Reger at the Leipzig Conservatory and also with Didom, Hoyer, Grabner, Davido and La Capria. He was a répétiteur at the Leipzig Opera (1912–13), then served in World War I and was taken prisoner by the Russians in Siberia. He returned to Leipzig in 1921 by way of Shanghai and Tientsin, taking with him Russian and Chinese soldiers' songs which he used in the opera *König Tod*. After a further period at the Leipzig Opera he worked in Plauen, Königsberg, Bremerhaven and Stettin, and then went back to Leipzig to join Central German Radio. In 1931 he was appointed accompanist, composer and conductor to Berlin Radio, and conductor to the Schillertheater. His first major choral work, *Fluch des Krieges* (after Chinese verse), made a deep impression, but its rejection of the soldier as hero found little favour with the Nazis, and he was forced to flee to Amsterdam, where he taught music, conducted for Hilversum Radio and accompanied Else Barther, the finest performer of his lieder and later his wife. He moved to Haarlem in 1945 and returned to Germany in 1964. His works include symphonies and concertante pieces, many choral compositions, orchestral songs and lieder, some of them published by Schott.

WRITINGS

'Mein Chorschaffen', *Deutsche Sängerbundeszeitung*, xliii/9 (1951)
'Max Reger als Lehrer', *Lied und Chor*, lviii/7 (1966)

BIBLIOGRAPHY

K. Funk: 'Dem Komponisten W. Rettich zur Vollendung seines 75. Lebensjahres', *Lied und Chor*, lix/7 (1967)
F. Baser: *Grosse Musiker in Baden-Baden* (Tutzing, 1973)

FRIEDRICH BASER

Retz, Jakub de [du]. *See* REYS, JAKUB.

Reubke. German family of musicians.

(1) Adolf Reubke (*b* Halberstadt, 6 Dec 1805; *d* Hausneindorf, nr. Quedlinburg, 3 March 1875). Organ builder. Together with E. F. Walcker, F. Ladegast and W. Sauer, he was one of the most important 19th-century German organ builders. His business was based in Hausneindorf, and his son Emil (1836–85) was in partnership with him from 1860. The firm built organs at Jakobikirche, Magdeburg (1855–8; three manuals, 53 stops), Magdeburg Cathedral (1856–61; four manuals, 81 stops), the Gewandhaus, Leipzig (1860), Quedlinburg (1870), Kyritz (1873) and elsewhere. Ernst Röver took over the firm in 1885; his instruments include the organ of the Nikolaikirche, Hamburg (1892; three manuals, 101 stops). In their early years the Reubkes built sliderchests, but soon began to use the Sanders type of tubular-pneumatic action, and eventually developed their own kind of sliderless chest ('Hahnenlade'; the 'Hahnen' (cocks) are anglepieces for opening the pipe-valves). A. G. Ritter and W. Sauer had a high opinion of Reubke organs.

BIBLIOGRAPHY

E. F. Richter: *Katechismus der Orgel* (Leipzig, 1864, 4/1896)
C. Elis: *Orgelwörterbuch* (Kassel, 1933, 3/1949)
T.-M. Langner: 'Reubke', *MGG*

(2) (Friedrich) Julius Reubke (*b* Hausneindorf, nr. Quedlinburg, 23 March 1834; *d* Pillnitz, nr. Dresden, 3 June 1858). Composer, pianist and organist, son of (1) Adolf Reubke. He received his early musical training from Hermann Bönicke in Quedlinburg, and his Trio in Eb for two manuals and pedal dates from this period. In 1851, already proficient as an organist, he entered the newly founded Berlin Conservatory, where he studied the piano with Theodor Kullak and composition with Adolf Bernhard Marx. He was awarded high honours and Hans von Bülow considered him the school's most gifted student. Two compositions of this period, a mazurka and a scherzo, are fluently written for the keyboard in the style of Chopin. After teaching the piano at the conservatory he went in 1856 to Weimar, where he became one of Liszt's favourite pupils. Close acquaintance with works of the new German school transformed his own style. In the spring of 1857 he completed his two most important works, the piano sonata in Bb minor and the organ sonata in C minor; the latter was first performed by him on the Ladegast organ in Merseburg Cathedral in June of that year. Both works were highly esteemed by members of the Weimar circle; Liszt was particularly fond of the

piano sonata and regarded Reubke as a composer of unusual promise. Reubke moved to Dresden at the end of the year; he joined the Dresdner Tonkünstlerverein and participated as pianist in its concerts. His failing health forced him to retire in the spring to Pillnitz, where he died in June. Peter Cornelius, a close friend, dedicated a poem to his memory.

The two sonatas are masterpieces of the German Romantic style. While they are directly influenced by Liszt in both thematic and formal structure, they are distinguished by formal development of a very personal kind. Each work shows an individual approach to one-movement sonata form, the organ sonata with strict monothematicism, the piano sonata with the technique of thematic metamorphosis. Although the latter is somewhat more adventurous, both works share a harmonic language comparable to the most advanced contemporary works of Liszt and make virtuoso demands on the performer. The organ sonata is based on nine verses from Psalm xciv, though no indication is given as to the precise connection between text and music. As an organ composition with extra-musical content, it belongs to the tradition of instrumental settings of psalm texts and, in a general sense, is heir to the Baroque *Affektenlehre*; for its period it is perhaps the finest example of a programmatic work for organ. Its single movement is divided into three sections – fantasia, adagio and an impressive, broadly planned fugue – all based on the same theme. While Liszt's influence is apparent not only in the thematic development but also in the keyboard figuration, the work is nevertheless genuinely original and effective, revealing a maturity and imaginative power remarkable for so young a composer. It has been described as one of the truest manifestations of Romantic aesthetic thought, following the principles of Wackenroder and Ludwig Tieck, and it certainly represents a high point in 19th-century organ literature.

Reubke's two sonatas display a musical conviction and promise which was regrettably unfulfilled through the composer's early death. Both works were published posthumously by Schuberth in Leipzig and both have been reissued, the piano sonata edited by August Stradal (Berlin and Stuttgart, 1925), and the organ sonata by Herbert Ellinford (London, 1932), Casper Koch (New York, 1934), Hermann Keller (Frankfurt, 1958) and Daniel Chorzempa (London, 1976).

(3) Otto Reubke (*b* Hausneindorf, 2 Nov 1842; *d* Halle, 18 May 1913). Organist, pianist, conductor and composer, son of (1) Adolf Reubke. He studied the organ with A. G. Ritter in Magdeburg and then attended the Berlin Conservatory, where he studied the piano with Bülow and composition with Marx and Weitzmann. From 1864 to 1867 he studied composition with Moritz Hauptmann in Leipzig. He then settled in Halle as a performer and teacher, and in 1877 was made assistant to Robert Franz, music director of the university, where Reubke lectured in musicology, harmony and composition. In 1876 he founded his own choral society and from 1881 to 1911 was conductor of the Robert Franz Singakademie. He was officially appointed university music director in 1892 and professor in 1895. He was renowned for his organ improvisations and admired as a conductor; his compositions, all published in Leipzig, consist mainly of piano music and songs and show the influence of Schumann.

BIBLIOGRAPHY

H. von Bülow: 'Julius Reubke: Scherzo', *NZM*, xlviii (1858), 40

R. Pohl: 'Nachruf: Julius Reubke', *NZM*, xlviii (1858), suppl. after 272

H. Grace: 'Reubke's Organ Sonata', *MO*, xxxviii (1914–15)

H. Böhm: 'Julius Reubke: zum Todestag des vergessenen Kleinmeisters am 3. Juni', *Musica*, xii (1958), 360

H. Keller: 'Der Orgelkomponist Julius Reubke', *Musik und Kirche*, xxix (1959), 36

W. Rackwitz: 'Die Singakademie in den Jahren 1860–1911', *Festschrift zum 150jährigen Bestehen der Robert-Franz-Singakademie* (Halle, 1964)

D. Chorzempa: *Julius Reubke: Life and Works* (diss., U. of Minnesota, 1971)

HANS KLOTZ (1), DANIEL CHORZEMPA (2, 3)

Reuental, Neidhart [Nîthart] **von.** *See* NEIDHART VON REUENTAL.

Reulx [Reux, Rieu], **Anselmo** [Anselme] **de** (*b* ?Reulx, Hainaut; *fl c*1524–57). South Netherlands composer, active in Italy. He served in about 1524 at the Spanish court chapel of Charles V. His output consists solely of madrigals. His second book for four voices concludes with a 'bataglia moresca' which Einstein considered 'one of the intermediary links between the *canzone villanesca* and the freer and more fully developed *moresca*'. On the evidence of this piece Einstein assumed that he spent a period in Naples in the mid-1540s.

WORKS

Madrigali, 4vv (Venice, 1543)

Secondo libro di madrigali, 4vv (Venice, 1546) [b only extant]

Works in 1543[17], 1549[31], 1556[22], 1557[16]

BIBLIOGRAPHY

A. Einstein: *The Italian Madrigal* (Princeton, 1949/*R*1971)

DON HARRÁN

Reusch, Johannes [Johann] (*b* Rodach, nr. Coburg, *c*1525; *d* Wurzen, nr. Leipzig, 27 Feb 1582). German composer. The preface to his *Elementa musicae* states that as a boy about 1538 he was a pupil of Heinrich Faber at Naumburg. He matriculated at the University of Wittenberg in April 1543. He then worked at the Stadtschule, Meissen, as Kantor from that year until 1547 and as headmaster from 1548 to 1555; in 1547–8 he was Kantor at the Fürstenschule there. From 1555 until his death he was chancellor to the Bishop of Meissen, whose residence was at Wurzen. His principal work is *Zehen deudsche Psalm Davids* (1551), which has a preface by Philipp Melanchthon. Apart from some similar pieces by Thomas Stoltzer and one by Johannes Heugel, its contents are the earliest examples of German-language psalm settings, a genre that was to become particularly popular in the Lutheran heartlands. They broke new ground in being published in an individual print, which was followed in 1554 by David Köler's *Zehen Psalmen Davids*, whose title was certainly modelled on it. It is known that Reusch's collection dates back to 1546 and that to some extent it is closely linked with the political situation of the Protestants immediately after the death of Luther in that year. Reusch sent an informative letter (reproduced in Dehnhardt) to Prince Georg of Anhalt with a copy of his volume in 1551. His motets exhibit considerable compositional skill; in accordance with the Netherlands style of the time of Josquin, their characteristic linear flow is interrupted by expressive homophonic interludes closely related to the sense of the words. All of Reusch's output, which also comprises odes, occasional pieces and an elementary manual of *musica practica*, dates from his years at Meissen; he seems to have abruptly given up composing after he settled at Wurzen.

WORKS

Epitaphia Rhauorum (Wittenberg, 1550)

Zehen deudscher Psalm Davids, 4vv (Wittenberg, 1551)

Carminum nuptialium liber I (Leipzig, 1553)

Melodiae odarum Georgii Fabricii (Leipzig, 1554)

Grates nunc omnes, motet, 1545[5]

Christus ist um unserer Sünde willen gestorben, *D-Dlb*; ed. in *Handbuch der deutschen evangelischen Kirchenmusik*, ii/1 (Göttingen, 1935)

THEORETICAL WORKS

Elementa musicae practicae pro incipientibus (Leipzig, 1553)

BIBLIOGRAPHY

W. Dehnhardt: *Die deutsche Psalmmotette in der Reformationszeit* (Wiesbaden, 1971)

WALTER BLANKENBURG

Reuschel, Johann Georg (*fl* 2nd half of the 17th century). German composer. He is first heard of working in Annaberg, Upper Silesia, probably as Kantor and schoolmaster; about 1667 he held similar posts at nearby Markersbach. Only the titles are known of his collections *Erfüllendes Chor-Gethön* for six to 18 voices and the five- and nine-part *Teutsche Kirchen-Lieder ... Complementen sampt ihren Fundament*, which apparently were never printed. They nevertheless indicate that he cultivated the large-scale concerted style in Protestant church music, as is confirmed by his only surviving collection, *Decas missarum sacra ... in usum ecclesiae ... evangelicae prelo subiecta* (Freiberg, 1666–7), which consists of masses typical of the Protestant *missa brevis* (i.e. Kyrie and Gloria only); his brother Gabriel appended to it a poem in praise of Schütz.

BIBLIOGRAPHY

E. Schild: *Geschichte der protestantischen Messkomposition im 17. und 18. Jahrhundert* (Wuppertal-Elberfeld, 1934)

H. J. Moser: *Die evangelische Kirchenmusik in Deutschland* (Berlin, 1954), 114

O. Wessely: 'Ein unbekanntes Huldigungsgedicht auf Heinrich Schütz', *Anzeiger der phil.-hist. Klasse der Österreichischen Akademie der Wissenschaften*, xcviii (1961), 132

OTHMAR WESSELY

Reusner [Reussner], **Esaias (i)** (*d* ?Silesia, between 1660 and 1680). German composer and lutenist, father of Esaias Reusner (ii). His only known work is *Musicalischer Lust-Garten, das ist Herren D. Martini Lutheri, wie auch anderer gottseliger (der Reinen Augspurgischen Confession zugethaner) Männer geistliche Kirchen- und Hauss-Lieder* (Breslau, 1645), a collection of 98 Protestant chorales transcribed for lute in a simple chordal style. This publication contains the only known biographical information about him, a reference to his employment as lutenist at the court of the Duke of 'Buestat in Silesia'. He was presumably living at Löwenberg, Silesia, when his son was born there on 29 April 1636.

BIBLIOGRAPHY

K. Koletschka: 'Esaias Reussner Vater und Sohn und ihre Choralbearbeitungen für die Laute: eine Parallele', *Festschrift Adolf Koczirz* (Vienna, 1930), 14

GEORGE J. BUELOW

Reusner [Reussner], **Esaias (ii)** (*b* Löwenberg, Silesia [now Lwówek Śląski, Poland], 29 April 1636; *d* Cölln, Berlin, 1 May 1679). German composer and lutenist, son of Esaias Reusner (i). He was taught the lute by his father and became a child prodigy. About 1645, after the death of his mother, the family moved to Breslau, where at about the age of 12 he entered the service of the Swedish general Count Wittenberg as a page. He spent the next year in the household of the royal war commissioner, Müller. In 1651 he was employed in Poland as a valet at the court of Princess Radziwiłł, where he became a pupil of an unidentified French lutenist. He returned to Breslau in 1654 and in the following year became lutenist to Georg III, Duke of Silesia, an appointment he retained until 1672. He then moved to Leipzig, where he taught the lute for a year at the university. From 5 February 1674 until his death he was a chamber musician at the court of the Elector Friedrich Wilhelm of Brandenburg in Berlin. His two collections of suites for the lute, *Delitiae testudinis* and *Neue Lauten-früchte*, are important as showing the first application of French lute style by a German composer and also as early documents in the development of the instrumental suite. They contain a total of 28 suites, varying in number of movements from four to nine. Each suite is unified by a major or minor tonality. They all include the basic structure of later dance suites, allemande–courante–sarabande–gigue. Most of the longer suites begin with another dance, such as a paduana or ballo, or the characteristically French improvisatory prelude, and many conclude with a dance other than the gigue. Reusner's influence was widely felt in Germany in the 17th century, and the style of his music established a precedent evident in the works of subsequent lutenists such as Silvius Weiss.

WORKS

Delitiae testudinis, praeludiis, paduanis, allemandis, courantis, sarabandis, giguis, et gavottis (n.p., 1667; Breslau, 2/1668 as Delitiae testudinis, oder Erfreuliche Lauten-Lust; Leipzig, 3/1697 as Erfreuliche Lauten-Lust); suite ed. in Der Lauten-Kreis, ii/2 (Berlin, 1933); 4 suites, 1 couranta ed. in EDM, 1st ser., xii (1939)
Musicalische Taffel-Erlustigung, bestehend in allerhand Paduanen, Allemanden, Couranten, Sarabanden, Gavotten, Balletten, und Giguen ... in 4 Stimmen gebracht, also das dieselben nach frantzösischer Art auf Violen füglich können gebraucht werden, durch Johann Georg Stanley, vn, 2 viols, bc (Brieg, 1668) [arr. of 10 lute suites]; ed. F. J. Giesbert (Mainz, 1938)
Musicalische Gesellschafts-Ergetzung bestehend in Sonaten, Allemanden, Couranten, Sarabanden, Gavotten, und Giguen, 3 str, bc (Brieg, 1670) [10 suites]; 1 suite ed. F. J. Giesbert (Neuwied, c1950)
Musicalischer Blumenstrauss (Bremen, 1673) [100 suite movts for various insts], lost
Neue Lauten-Früchte (Berlin, 1676) [copy in *D-Bds* incl. new lute works written in by Reusner, perhaps for a 2nd edn.]; 1 suite ed. in Alte Meister der Laute, iii (Berlin, 1927); suites 1–5 ed. W. Gerwig (Wolfenbüttel and Berlin, 1928); 4 suites, incl. 1 from holograph, ed. in EDM, 1st ser., xii (1939)
100 geistliche Melodien evangelischer Lieder, welche auf die Fest- und andere Tage, so wol in der christlichen Gemeine, als auch daheim gesungen werden (Berlin, 1676 or 1678); 9 chorales, lv, lute, ed. in EDM, 1st ser., xii (1939)

BIBLIOGRAPHY

G. Sparmann: *Esaias Reusner und die Lauten-Suite* (diss., Free U. of Berlin, 1926)
F. Blume: Introduction to *E. Reusner: Sämtliche Suiten für die Laute, i: Suite 1 bis 5 aus den 'Neuen Lautenfrüchten (1676)'*, ed. W. Gerwig (Wolfenbüttel and Berlin, 1928)
K. Koletschka: 'Esaias Reusner der Jüngerer und seine Bedeutung für die deutsche Lautenmusik des XVII. Jahrhunderts', *SMw*, xv (1928), 7–45
——: 'Esaias Reussner Vater und Sohn und ihre Choralbearbeitungen für die Laute: eine Parallele', *Festschrift Adolf Koczirz* (Vienna, 1930), 14

GEORGE J. BUELOW

Reuss, August (*b* Liliendorf bei Znaim, Moravia, 6 Mar 1871; *d* Munich, 18 June 1935). German composer. He first entered his father's construction business but later decided on a musical career. In 1899, until then self-taught, he went to Munich where he became a pupil of Thuille. He resigned from positions as Kapellmeister in the theatres of Magdeburg and Augsburg because of poor health. After a brief stay in Berlin he settled in Munich in 1909 as a freelance composer. In 1927 he was appointed teacher of composition at the newly

established Trapp Conservatory. Two years later he began teaching at the Akademie der Tonkunst where he stayed until his death. His late Romantic music is thoroughly tonal and above all lyrical. The tone poems are Straussian in their formal design and particularly in their display of lush orchestral sonority, but most of his output was of chamber music and lieder. He also wrote journalistic essays on musical subjects.

WORKS
(selective list)

Orch: Der Tor und der Tod, op.10, sym. prologue, Hofmannsthal, 1901; Johannisnacht, op.19, tone poem, 1903; Judith, op.20, tone poem, after Hebbel, 1903; Sommeridylle, op. 39, 1920; Serenade, A♭, op.41, vn, chamber orch, 1921; Glasbläser und Dogaressa, op.46, ballet-pantomime, perf. 1925; Romantische Ballett-Suite, op.46a, n.d.; Pf Conc., g, op.48, 1924
Chamber and inst: Cl Qnt, f, op.12, 1901; Landsommertage [variations on theme from Herzog Philipps Brautfahrt], op.22, pf, 1904; Str Qt, d, op.25, 1906; Sonata, D, op.26, vn, pf, 1909; Pf Sonata, c, op.27, 1911; Pf Trio, G, op.30, 1912; Str Qt, E, op.31, 1914; Fantasie, op.42, 2 pf, 1914; Romantische Sonate, D, op.35, vn, pf, 1918; Octet, B, op.37, 2 ob, 2 cl, 2 bn, 2 hn, 1918; Str Trio, G, op.40, 1921; Pf Sonata, C, op.55, n.d.; Trio, g, op.61, fl, vn, va, n.d.
Vocal: Herzog Philipps Brautfahrt, opera, 3, perf. 1909; 3 Melodramas, op.21, speaker, pf, n.d.; 4 Duets, op.24, S, A, pf, n.d.; 4 Trios, op.32, female chorus, n.d.; Trost der Nacht, op.38/1, S/T, pf, 1921; Lied des Einsiedels, op.38/2, S/T, org/pf, vn, 1921; Kinderlieder, op.49, chorus, n.d.; 9 Pieces, op.53, male chorus, n.d.; c50 lieder, opp.28–9, 33, 36, 44

Principal publishers: Brockhaus, Eulenberg, Hieber, Kahnt, Kistner & Siegel, Ries & Erler, Schott, Tischer & Jagenberg, Verlag Musikalische Kunst und Wissenschaft

BIBLIOGRAPHY

H. von Waltershausen: 'August Reuss', *Gesammelte Aufsätze* (Munich, 1926)
A. Würz: 'August Reuss', *ZfM*, Jg.98 (1931), 215
——: 'Gedenkblatt für August Reuss', *ZfM*, Jg.112 (1951), 183
——: 'Reuss, August', *MGG*

CHARLOTTE ERWIN

Reussner, Esaias. *See* REUSNER, ESAIAS (i) or (ii).

Reuter, Fritz (*b* Dresden, 9 Sept 1896; *d* Dresden, 4 July 1963). German musicologist, teacher and composer. He studied with Teichmüller and Krehl at the Leipzig Conservatory and at the same time with Riemann and Schering at Leipzig University, where he took the doctorate under Abert in 1922 with a dissertation on early German opera in Leipzig. After conducting a theatre orchestra in Allenstein (1917–18), he taught music theory, composition, music education and music history at Leipzig Conservatory and Leipzig University (1921–33). In 1933 he lost these positions and became a schoolmaster, at first in Leipzig, and from 1937 in Dresden. After serving as conductor and Dramaturg at the Dresden Volksoper (1945–8) he became professor and director of the music education institute at Halle University (1949–55) and then director of the music education institute at the Humboldt University, Berlin (1955–62). In 1955 he was awarded the arts prize of the town of Halle and in 1962 the East German National Order of Merit.

Reuter achieved an early reputation in German music education and did much to establish its scientific basis. As a theorist he relied chiefly on Karg-Elert's system of functional harmony. Although some of his early compositions show expressionist influence, Reuter belonged as a composer to the polyphonic school based in Leipzig and was essentially a Romantic. His many works include oratorios, stage works, cantatas, choruses and songs, as well as orchestral and chamber music.

WRITINGS

Stephan Krehl (Leipzig, 1921)

Geschichte der deutschen Oper in Leipzig (1693–1720) (diss., U. of Leipzig, 1922; *ZMw*, v (1922–3), 1 as 'Die Entwicklung der Leipziger, insbesondere italienischen Oper bis zum siebenjahrigen Kriege')

Die musikalische Hören auf psychologischer Grundlage (Leipzig, 1926, 2/1942)

Musikpädagogik in Grundzügen (Leipzig, 1926)

Beethoven im Lichte des Zeitgeistes (Leipzig, 1927)

Zur Methodik der Gehörübungen und des Musikdiktats (Leipzig, 1927)

Harmonieaufgaben nach dem System Sigfrid Karg-Elerts (Leipzig, 1928)

Praktische Gehörbildung auf Grundlage der Tonika-Do-Lehre (Leipzig, 1928)

Die Beantwortung des Fugenthemas (Leipzig, 1929)

Methodik des musiktheoretischen Unterrichts auf neuzeitlichen Grundlagen (Stuttgart, 1929, 2/1950)

Praktisches Partiturspielen (Halle, 1951, 2/1954)

Praktische Harmonik des 20. Jahrhunderts (Leipzig, 1952)

Praktisches Generalbass-spielen (Halle, 1952, 2/1954)

'Über die Lage des musiktheoretischen Unterrichts an den Ausbildungsstätten für Musik', *Festschrift Richard Münnich* (Leipzig, 1957), 58; also in *Musica*, xii (1958), 80

Grundlagen der Musikerziehung (Leipzig, 1962)

Articles in *Kongressbericht: Leipzig 1925* and Festschrift for Max Schneider (1955)

BIBLIOGRAPHY

P. Mies: 'Fritz Reuter, der Komponist und Pädagoge', *Musica sacra*, lxxx (1960), 75

W. Busch: 'Nachruf zum Tode Dr. Fritz Reuters', *Musik in der Schule*, xiv (1963), 424

H. Grabner: 'Briefwechsel mit Fritz Reuter', *Wissenschaftliche Zeitschrift der Humboldt-Universität zu Berlin: Gesellschafts- und Sprachwissenschaftliche Reihe*, xv (1966), 343

P. Mies: 'Das Konzert für Violine und Orchester von Fritz Reuter', ibid, 419

H. Seidel: *Das Fritz-Reuter- und Richard-Wagner-Museum in Eisenach* (Eisenach, 1968)

DIETER HÄRTWIG

Reutter, Georg (von) (i) (baptized Vienna, 3 Nov 1656; *d* Vienna, 29 Aug 1738). Austrian organist and composer, father of Georg Reutter (ii). He may have been a pupil of Kerll, whom he succeeded as organist at St Stephen's Cathedral, Vienna, in 1686. In 1695 he spent some time in Italy. According to the patent of nobility for his son, he was ennobled in Rome on 8 January 1695 by Prince Sforza; unlike his son, he did not use his title. Between 1696 and 1703 Reutter was employed in the Viennese court chapel as continuo player on the theorbo. The principal Kapellmeister, Antonio Draghi, recommended him to the emperor as 'a virtuoso player able to play many instruments'. Draghi's successor as court Kapellmeister, Fux, also noted Reutter's virtuoso abilities and mentioned that he was an experienced opera accompanist. He was married three times and was the father of 15 children, of whom two became musicians (Karl and the younger Georg). In 1700 Reutter was formally appointed court organist at a yearly salary of 900 florins, supplemented by about 300 florins as theorbo player. In 1712 he succeeded Fux as vice-Kapellmeister and in 1715 as first Kapellmeister of the cathedral; he retained that position until 1728. For housing and instruction of six choirboys at St Stephen's he received 1200 florins and his salary as Kapellmeister was 550 florins. When he relinquished one of the two Kapellmeister positions of the cathedral in 1728 his income remained relatively high as he kept the six choirboys. He passed on the position of cathedral organist to his son Georg in 1720. A kind and affable man, according to Mattheson (*Grundlage einer Ehren-Pforte*, 1740), he remained active up to his last years, though his son Georg substituted for him increasingly often.

As a composer Reutter is best known for his collection of toccatas (*D-Bds* P 407; one ed. in DTÖ, xxvii, Jg.xiii/2). They show that he was a capable organ composer who combined technical brilliance with skill in the use of counterpoint and florid melodic invention. He also composed a large number of so-called *Versetteln* or short organ preludes. Some of the larger sacred works ascribed to him by Eitner may have been composed by his son Georg, and of the compositions published by Botstiber (in DTÖ, xxvii, Jg.xiii/2) two capriccios, one ricercare and probably the canzona on *Christ ist erstanden* are by N. A. Strungk. Hofer may have gone too far in attributing most of the compositions extant under the name Reutter to his son, particularly as regards those sacred works in a traditional polyphonic style. Some of Reutter's secular works must be lost; Draghi mentioned in his recommendation that Reutter had composed ballet music, and no traces of such pieces are known.

BIBLIOGRAPHY

EitnerQ

L. von Köchel: *Die kaiserliche Hof-Musikkapelle in Wien von 1543 bis 1867* (Vienna, 1869)

C. F. Weitzmann and M. Seiffert: *Geschichte der Klaviermusik* (Leipzig, 1899)

F. Berend: *N. A. Strungk* (diss., U. of Munich, 1915)

N. Hofer: *Die beiden Reutter als Kirchenkomponisten* (diss., U. of Vienna, 1915)

G. Frotscher: *Geschichte des Orgel-Spiels und der Orgel-Komposition*, i (Berlin, 1935–6, enlarged 3/1966)

F. W. Riedel: *Quellenkundliche Beiträge zur Geschichte der Musik für Tasteninstrumente in der 2.Hälfte des 17. Jahrhunderts* (Kassel, 1960)

For further bibliography *see* GEORG REUTTER (ii).

EVA BADURA-SKODA

Reutter, (Johann Adam Joseph Karl) Georg (von) (ii) (*b* Vienna, baptized 6 April 1708; *d* Vienna, 11 March 1772). Austrian composer and organist, son of Georg Reutter (i). Of his five baptismal names he generally used only the last; attempts have been made to distinguish between father and son by ascribing two Christian names to the latter, e.g. Karl Georg (Pohl, Köchel) or Johann Georg (Eitner).

Reutter's musical training began in his father's house, where he grew up with other cathedral choristers. His instruction in composition, he later said, came solely from Caldara. By the time he was 14 he was deputizing for his father as court organist; in 1726 he was referred to in the *Wiener Diarium* as organist of the Himmelspforte convent. His attempts to be accepted as a court scholar or to find employment as court organist were frustrated by the disapproval of Fux, the first court Kapellmeister, whose only application to Charles VI on Reutter's behalf concerned support for the continuation of his studies in Italy. This may not have been granted, but Reutter went in 1729 or 1730 to Italy, where he evidently stayed at Venice and Rome. He was back in Vienna by the beginning of 1731, when he obtained his desired position as court composer (with an annual salary of 600 florins) and married the gifted court singer, Theresia Holzhauser. From his oratorio *La morte d'Abele* in 1727, Reutter was prominent as a composer of operas and oratorios, with 38 of his operas performed up to the death of Charles VI in 1740; during that time he was the most prolific of the Viennese court composers after Caldara. His frequent requests for a salary increase found little or no support from Fux and were mostly rejected.

In about 1736, Reutter took over the duties of first Kapellmeister at St Stephen's Cathedral, and the post was made over to him officially on his father's death in

1738. Soon after, in 1739–40, when looking for choristers, he heard and engaged the young Haydn in Hainburg. In 1740 he was ennobled. On Fux's death in 1741, L. A. Predieri was promoted to first Kapellmeister and from then on Reutter occasionally undertook the Kapellmeister's duties in the hope of being appointed second Kapellmeister, a hope that was realized in 1747. Predieri was pensioned off in 1751 and Reutter assumed full control of the court Kapelle, although he bore the title of first Kapellmeister only after Predieri's death in 1769. When Reutter took over the court Kapelle, Maria Theresia introduced a new system of administration and remuneration of musicians. Reutter's contract stipulated that he should appoint musicians at his own discretion and should fix their salaries and duties, but that all expenses must be covered by an annual sum of only 20,000 florins. This represented not only an administrative simplification but also a severe reduction in the budget for court music, though under these regulations the remuneration of orchestral musicians for opera performances was covered from extra funds (ticket sales or by way of leasing the Kärntnertortheater to impresarios; see Zechmeister, 1971). Reutter tried several times to obtain subsidies, and opposed (successfully) a budget reduction planned in 1754. However, he renewed his contract in 1757, apparently without making adequate reference to the decline of the court music. He left unfilled posts that fell vacant through death or resignation; the number of court musicians steadily declined and the level of performance sank lower and lower. When he died in 1772, the Kapelle consisted of a mere 20 members (under Fux there had been over 100), and the neglect was further evident in the fact that there were no cellists or bassists, nor even an organist, among them, although Reutter had been responsible for chamber and church performances.

Under regulations introduced in 1751, the administration of the court theatre ceased to be one of his duties and was handed over temporarily to the city authorities. In any case the number of Italian opera performances had dwindled to a minimum since the beginning of Maria Theresia's reign. When Durazzo was appointed director of court and chamber music in 1760, and took over the supervision of both theatres, the city council retained control of the Kärntnertortheater. Durazzo's efforts to appoint Gluck in Reutter's place, or to transfer to him as second Kapellmeister the direction of court secular music, failed, and the consequent dispute was resolved in Reutter's favour (see Haas, *Gluck und Durazzo*, 39ff).

Reutter seems to have been little concerned with his obligations at the cathedral; perhaps his activities as Kapellmeister left him little time for this. During the decade that Haydn spent in Reutter's house, the boy received two composition lessons at the most (which Reutter was not obliged to teach), and his talent remained unnoticed. The city council often complained that Reutter was seldom to be seen in the cathedral. He was nevertheless able to appropriate to himself, in 1756, the remunerative position of second cathedral Kapellmeister; from then he held not only both Kapellmeister positions at court but also both those at the cathedral, a situation which had not existed before in Vienna and was never to again. When Reutter died, he was accorded an elaborate funeral in accordance with his status. There is a pastel portrait of him at the

Heiligenkreuz monastery; an oil painting and an engraving also survive (*A-Wgm*).

Reutter was one of the most prolific composers of his time, but his work is uneven in quality. His operas were modelled on those of Caldara, but lack the cantabile mellifluousness that distinguishes Caldara's arias. His harmonic progressions are rather simple and he overused sequence. Though talented, he apparently lacked self-criticism. His church music, all of it written to meet immediate needs, enjoyed wide circulation in manuscript; it did not make severe technical demands on the performers and the use of trumpets, trombones and drums assured a festive quality. His busy violin parts ('rauschenden Violinen à la Reutter': Pohl) became proverbial. His contribution towards the development of sonata form was insignificant; although his *Sinfonie* of 1757 (described as 'Servizio di tavola', DTÖ, xxxi, Jg.xv/2) corresponds in the number and arrangement of its movements to the Classical form evolved by Haydn, in content it has little in common either with Haydn's works of the time or with those of the Mannheim symphonists. Numerous Baroque features persist, alongside a certain naive simplicity characteristic of this transitional period. Frequent use of sequence, the absence of independent middle voices (except in fugato sections, which however are usually very short), the habitual progression of the melodic line in 3rds and 6ths, and the straightforward harmony, seldom seasoned with chromaticism, show Reutter to be an experienced and gifted musician but with limited creative abilities. Burney's harsh judgment of 'much noise and little meaning', though often justified, stands in sharp contrast to the reputation Reutter seems to have enjoyed at the court and perhaps in Vienna generally (the *Diarium* once described him as 'incontestably the greatest composer to sing the praise of God'). His historical significance is negative rather than positive, in that the imperial Kapelle declined during his Kapellmeistership; further, because of him, Gluck, Haydn and other talented men were unable to obtain positions at the Viennese court. None of Reutter's compositions was printed during his lifetime.

WORKS

DRAMATIC

(all first performed in Vienna)

Archidamia (festa teatrale, 1, C. Pasquini), 22 Nov 1727, *A-Wgm, Wn*
La forza dell'amicizia (3, Pasquini), 17 Aug 1728, collab. Caldara, *Wgm, Wn*
Dialogo tra Minerva ed Apollo (Pasquini), 25 Oct 1728, *Wn*
Alcide trasformato in dio, 1729, *Wn*
La magnanimità di Alessandro (Pasquini), 1 Oct 1729, *Wn*
Plotina (festa teatrale, 1, Pasquini), 19 Nov 1730, *Wn*
La pazienza di Socrate con due moglie (3, N. Minato), 17 Jan 1731, collab. Caldara, *Wn*
Dialogo tra l'Inclinazione ed il Bene (Pasquini), 26 June 1731, *Wn*
La generosità di Artaserse con Temistocle (Pasquini), Oct 1731, *Wn* (only Act 1 by Reutter)
Dialogo tra Aurora ed il Sole, festa di camera, 1731
Il Tempo e la Verità (Pasquini), 15 Oct 1731, *Wn*
Pastorale a 2 voci (Pasquini), 30 Aug 1732
Alessandro il Grande (Pasquini), 1 Oct 1732, *Wgm, Wn*
Zenobia (festa teatrale, 1, Pasquini), 19 Nov 1732, *Wgm, Wn*
Ciro in Armenia (festa teatrale, 1, Pasquini), 1 Oct 1733, *Wgm, Wn*
La gratitudine di Mitridate (1, Pasquini), 1 Oct 1734, *Wn*
Dafne (festa teatrale, 1, Pasquini), 19 Nov 1734, *Wgm, Wn*
Il Palladio conservato (azione teatrale, 1, Metastasio), 1 Oct 1735, *Wn*
Il sacrifizio in Aulide (festa teatrale, 1, P. Pariati), 19 Nov 1735, *Wn*
La Speranza assicurata (serenata, Pasquini), 13 May 1736, *Wgm, Wn*
Diana vendicata (festa teatrale, 1, Pasquini), 19 Nov 1736, *Wgm, Wn*
Statira (3, ? A. Zeno), 1736
Il Parnaso accusato e difeso (festa teatrale, 1, Metastasio), 28 Aug 1738, *Wn*
L'Alloro illustrato (festa teatrale, 1, Pasquini), 19 Nov 1738, *Wgm, Wn*
L'eroina d'Argo (Pasquini), 15 Oct 1739, *Wgm, Wn*

Amor prigioniero (dialogo, 1, Metastasio), aut. 1741, *Wn*
La gara (1, Metastasio), 13 May 1755, *Wn*
Other stage works, libs by Metastasio: Complimento, 1748; L'augurio
  di felicità, 1749; La rispettosa tenerezza, 1750; La virtuosa
  emulazione, 1751; Primo omaggio di canto, 1753; Complimento,
  1754; Il tributo di Rispetto e d'Amore, 1754; La corona, 1754, *Wn*;
  Il sogno, 1757, *Wgm*, *Wn*; Le Grazie vendicate, 1758; Complimento,
  1759; Complimento, 1760
Works to German texts (inc.): Wasser, Feuer, Luft und Erde, 1730;
  David, 1735; Verlöbnis, Segen, Freude, Ehre, 1738; Die drei
  Grazien; Judith; Die wahre Huldigung
Oratorios (principal source *HE*): Die Grablegung Christi [Oratorium
  Germanicum], 1726, *KR*; La morte d'Abele (G. Salio Padovano),
  13 March 1727, *Wn*; Elia (Villati), 24 Feb 1728, *Wgm*; Bersabea
  ovvero Il pentimento di David (Catena), 12 March 1729; Il martirio
  di S Giovanni Nepomuceno (Pasquini), 17 June 1731; La divina
  provvidenza in Ismael (Lucchini), 6 March 1732 (Ger. version of lib
  with different music, *HE* (inc., autograph)); La Betulia liberata
  (Metastasio), 8 April 1734, *Wgm*, *Wn*, *D-Rp*; Gioas, re di Giuda
  (Metastasio), 1735; La Maria lebbrosa, 1739; Ger. oratorio, *A-HE*
  (frag.)

OTHER WORKS
(*for further details and sources, see DTÖ, lxxxviii, 1952*)

Sacred: 81 masses, incl. Missa S Caroli, 1734, *HE* (autograph), *Gd*,
  GÖ, *KN*, *KR*, *Wn*, *D-Bds*, ed. in DTÖ, lxxxviii (1952); 6 Requiem,
  A-GÖ, *HE*, *KN*, *Wn*, 1 ed. in DTÖ, lxxxviii (1952); 7 It. cantatas, *HE*; 17 graduals, *KN*; 31 offertories, *Gd*, *KN*; 126 motets, *GÖ*,
  KN, *Wn*, 1 ed. in DTÖ, lxxxviii (1952); 151 psalms, canticles, *GÖ*,
  KN; 63 hymns, sequences; 48 antiphons, *HE*, *KN*, 1 ed. in DTÖ,
  lxxxviii (1952); 7 responsories; 20 litanies, *GÖ*, *KN*; other sacred
  works, *Gd*, *KN*, *D-Bds*, *Dlb*
Chamber: 6 syms., partitas, str, wind insts, *A-Wgm*, incl. Servizio di
  tavola, 1757, ed. in DTÖ, xxxi, Jg.xv/2 (1908/*R*); 5 syms., single
  works, str, *Wgm*; 2 hpd concs. (1 inc.); 2 clarino concs.; wind qnt; 14
  hpd suites, *D-Bds*; 15 single hpd works; other single orch. works

BIBLIOGRAPHY

EitnerQ
L. von Köchel: *Die kaiserliche Hof-Musikkapelle in Wien von 1543 bis
  1867* (Vienna, 1869)
——: *Johann Joseph Fux* (Vienna, 1872)
C. F. Pohl: *Joseph Haydn* (Berlin, 1875)
La Mara [M. Lipsius]: *Musikerbriefe aus fünf Jahrhunderten* (Leipzig,
  1886)
L. Stollbrock: 'Leben und Wirken des k.k. Hofkapellmeisters und
  Hofkompositors Johann Georg Reutter jun.', *VMw*, viii (1892), 161–
  203
A. Schering: *Geschichte des Oratoriums* (Leipzig, 1911/*R*1966)
N. Hofer: *Die beiden Reutter als Kirchenkomponisten* (diss., U. of
  Vienna, 1915)
R. Haas: *Gluck und Durazzo im Burgtheater* (Vienna, 1925)
K. Geiringer: *Haydn: a Creative Life in Music* (New York, 1946)
L. Nowak: *Joseph Haydn* (Vienna, 1951)
F. Raugel: 'Les véritables auteurs d'oeuvres religieuses attribuées à
  Mozart', *RdM*, xxxviii (1956), 146
F. W. Riedel: *Quellenkundliche Beiträge zur Geschichte der Musik für
  Tasteninstrumente in der 2.Hälfte des 17. Jahrhunderts* (Kassel, 1960)
E. Schenk: 'Ist die Göttweiger Rorate-Messe ein Werk Joseph Haydns?',
  SMw, xxiv (1960), 87
G. Zechmeister: *Die Wiener Theater nächste der Burg und nächst dem
  Kärntnerthor von 1747 bis 1776* (Vienna, 1971)

EVA BADURA-SKODA

Reutter, Hermann (*b* Stuttgart, 17 June 1900). German
composer and pianist. From a musical family, he had
piano and cello lessons from his uncle. From 1920 he
lived in Munich, where he studied at the academy with
Franz Dorfmüller for the piano, Walter Courvoisier for
composition, Ludwig Mayer for the organ and Karl
Erler for singing. In 1923 he came into contact with the
Donaueschingen circle, in particular with Hindemith,
and there his first compositions (mostly songs and
chamber music) received notice. He soon made a name
for himself as both a composer and a pianist, especially
as an accompanist in lieder; between 1930 and 1935 he
made seven tours of the USA with the singer Sigrid
Onegin. Meanwhile he had taken an appointment to
teach composition at the Stuttgart Musikhochschule
(1932); in 1936 he moved to Berlin to take direction of
the Hoch Conservatory (Staatliche Hochschule für
Musik from 1938).

Teaching, accompanying and composing were now
established as Reutter's principal activities. He played
the piano for Alma Moodie, Marta Fuchs, Lore
Fischer, Henry Wolf, Karl Erb and Rudolf Nel, and
after 1945 for Elisabeth Schwarzkopf, Hans Hotter,
Dietrich Fischer-Dieskau and others; he had retired to
the neighbourhood of Heilbronn after the war. In 1952
he took over classes in lieder and composition at the
Staatliche Hochschule für Musik in Stuttgart, where in
1956 he was appointed director. From 1960, he also
occupied guest appointments at various American universities and Japanese conservatories.

Reutter is among the most productive German composers of his generation, and the most traditionalist. At
first influenced by the Hindemith school, he returned
around 1930 to a simplified late Romantic style eschew-
ing any experiment. The clarity of his music comes from
Orff, the harmonic manner from Pfitzner and the tonal
structure from Hindemith. His music is distinctly
formed, and adapts itself equally to lyrical and dramatic
modes. His versatility, which is based on the sure knowledge of the craftsman, has led him to compose in all
genres, but he is particularly admired for his stage
works and songs; he may, indeed, be considered one of
the foremost proponents of the lied tradition in the
second half of the 20th century.

The essential value of a combination between
progress and historical consciousness in art has been
summed up by Reutter himself: 'any artist, no matter
how progressive, is bound and obliged as the spiritual
heir of his ancestors'. He acknowledges the human content of artistic creation, which lies beyond any question
of style, theoretical consideration or criterion of the day.

WORKS
(*selective list*)
STAGE

Saul (opera, A. Lernet-Holenia), Baden-Baden, 1928; rev., Hamburg,
  1947
Der verlorene Sohn (opera, Gide, trans. Rilke), Stuttgart, 1929; rev. as
  Die Rückkehr des verlorenen Sohnes, Dortmund, 1952
Doktor Johannes Faustus (opera, L. Andersen), 1934–6, Frankfurt,
  1936; rev., Stuttgart, 1955
Die Kirmes von Delft, op.48 (ballet), 1937; orch suite
Die Prinzessin und der Schweinehirt (fairy play), Mainz, 1938
Odysseus (opera), 1940–42, Frankfurt, 1942
Der Lübecker Totentanz, Göttingen, 1948
Der Weg nach Freudenstadt, Göttingen, 1948
Don Juan und Faust (Grabbe), Stuttgart, 1950
Topsy (piece for actors and dancers), 1950
Notturno Montmartre (ballet), 1951, Frankfurt, 1952; orch suite
Die Witwe von Ephesus (opera, after Petronius), 1953; Cologne, 1954;
  rev., Schwetzingen, 1966
Die Brücke von San Luis Rey (opera, after Wilder), 1954, Essen, 1954
Der Tod des Empedokles (conc. scenico, after Hölderlin), 1965,
  Schwetzingen, 1966

ORCHESTRAL

Pf Conc., op.19, 1925; Pf Conc., op.36, 1929; Vn Conc., op.39, *c*1930;
  Sinfonische Fantasie, op.50, pf, orch, 1938; Pf Conc., g, 1944;
  Concertino, op.69, pf, str, 1947; Concerto, E♭, 2 pf, orch, 1950;
  Konzertvariationen, pf, orch, 1952; Tanz-Variationen, op.76, 1952;
  Prozession, vc, orch, 1956; Sym., str, 1960; Capriccio, aria e finale,
  pf, orch, 1963; Figurinen zu Hofmannsthals 'Jedermann', 1972

CHORAL

Der neue Hiob, op.37, Lehrstück, 1930; 4 Bettellieder, op.38b, unacc.,
  1930; Der grosse Kalender, unacc., 1930–32, rev. 1970; Der glück-
  liche Bauer, op.44 (M. Claudius), cantata, *c*1935; Gesang des
  Deutschen, op.49 (Hölderlin), cantata, 1938; Chorfantasie, op.52
  (Goethe), S, Bar, chorus, orch, 1939; Hochzeitslieder, op.53, 1941
3 Madrigäle, unacc., *c*1949; Pandora, op.72 (Goethe), cantata, 1949; 3
  laudes, unacc., 1964; Jesu Nachtgespräch mit Nicodemus, unacc.,
  1968; Phyllis und Philander (P. Squentz), chorus, 6 wind, pf, 1970

SOLO VOCAL

with orch: Lyrisches Konzert, op.70, S, fl, pf, str, timp, 1949; Monolog
  der Iphigenie, op.74, *c*1950; Spanischer Totentanz (Lorca), 2vv,

orch, 1953; Aus dem Hohelied Salomonis, conc. grosso, A, va, pf, orch, 1956; Kleine Ballade von den drei Flüssen (Lorca), S, orch, 1960; Andalusiana (Lorca), S, orch, 1962; Szene und Monolog der Marfa aus Schillers 'Demetrius', S, orch, 1968

with insts: 3 Gesänge, op.3; Missa brevis, op.22, c1926; 5 antike Oden, op.57, c1940; Der himmlische Vagant (Klabund), A, Bar, insts; Weltlicht, B, insts, 1959; Ein kleines Requiem (Lorca), B, vc, pf, 1961; Gesänge aus Prediger Salomo XII:1–9, A/B, fl, pf, 1973

with pf: opp.21, 23, 31, 54, 56, 58–61, 64–5, 67–8, 73; 3 Zigeunerromanzen (Lorca), 1956; Die Jahreszeiten (Hölderlin), 1957; Meine dunklen Hände (black verse), 1957; 6 späte Gedichte (Huch), 1957; 3 altägyptische Gedichte, 1962; Ein Füllen ward geboren (Perse), 1962; Epitaph für einen Dichter (Faulkner), 1962; 5 Fragmente (Hölderlin), 1965; Sankt Sebastian, triptych, 1968; 4 Liederzyklen (N. Sachs, Joyce, Huch, M.-L. Kaschnitz), 1973

Also edn. of anthology *Das zeitgenössische Lied* (Mainz, 1969)

CHAMBER AND INSTRUMENTAL

Fantasia apocalyptica, op.7; Variations, op.15, pf; Vn Sonata, op.20, c1925; Die Passion in 9 Inventionen, op.25, pf, c1927; Pfingstmusik, op.41 no.2, 2 vn, c1931; Musik, va, pf; 12 Stücke, wind, pf, 1957–69; Pièce concertante, a sax, pf, 1968; 5 caprichos sobre Cervantes, va, 1968; Sonata monotematica, vc, pf, 1970

Principal publisher: Schott

BIBLIOGRAPHY

H. Lindlar, ed.: *Hermann Reutter: Werk und Wirken: Festschrift der Freunde* (Mainz, 1965)

HANSPETER KRELLMANN

Reux, Anselme de. See REULX, ANSELMO DE.

Revel, Harry (*b* London, 21 Dec 1905; *d* New York, 3 Nov 1958). American songwriter and pianist of English birth. He studied at the Guildhall School of Music, London, and in Paris became a pianist and composer for a 'Hawaiian' dance orchestra which toured Europe. He wrote music for *Was Frauen träumen* in Berlin and for *Charlot's Review* in London before going to New York in 1929. He toured in vaudeville and wrote songs for several revues, notably Ziegfeld's *Follies* (1931). In 1933 he went to Hollywood, where he became one of the most successful composers for films, including *Sitting Pretty* (1934), *Paris in the Spring* (1935), *Stowaway* (1936) and *My Lucky Star* (1938). During World War II Revel organized shows and edited the periodical *At Ease* for the armed forces.

BIBLIOGRAPHY

I. Stambler: *Encyclopedia of Popular Music* (New York, 1965)
R. D. Kinkle: *The Complete Encyclopedia of Popular Music and Jazz 1900–1950* (New Rochelle, NY, 1974)

DEANE L. ROOT

Reverberation time. The time taken for a loud sound to decay to an inaudible level. When a sound is created within a room, the initial waves are reflected back and forth between the walls and so the sound may appear to continue after the source has ceased to produce sound. If the walls are highly absorbent the persistence may be short and the room is then said to have a short reverberation time or a 'dry' acoustic quality. If the walls are highly reflecting (e.g. of glazed tiles and glass as in an indoor swimming pool) the reverberation may be long (up to four or five seconds) and the room is said to be 'lively' or 'reverberant'. Good acoustic design demands (among other things) a balance between these extremes to suit the use for which the room is intended. *See also* ACOUSTICS.

Reveré [Revertz]. Composer, possibly identifiable with NICOLE REGNES.

Révész, Geza (*b* Sofiok, 9 Dec 1878; *d* Amsterdam, 19 Aug 1955). Hungarian psychologist. He studied law in Budapest and then (1901–5) psychology in Göttingen and with Stumpf in Berlin, taking the doctorate in psychology at the University of Göttingen. Subsequently he was assistant lecturer (1906), lecturer (1908), assistant professor (1917) and full professor (1918) of psychology at Budapest University. He left Hungary after the Revolution and in 1921 settled in Amsterdam, where he was in charge of a psychological laboratory. From 1932 he held the post of assistant professor and, later, of full professor of psychology.

Révész was an important exponent of experimental psychology and worked on touch, sight and hearing. His early work concerned pathological disturbances in hearing, the conditions known as amusia (the inability to comprehend or produce musical sounds) and parakusia (disturbances in the perception of individual notes). These investigations stimulated his interest in more general aspects of the psychology of music, and from about 1914 he began studying the problem of musical talent, which he considered extensively in his major work, *Inleiding tot de muziekpsychologie*. He developed a test for gauging musical ability by means of exercises based on the perception of rhythm, the ability to analyse two or more notes played simultaneously, and the capacity to reproduce tunes. He also evolved the important 'dual component theory of pitch', which states that the perception of tonal pitch is characterized by two phenomena: a sound impression which alters with the change in frequency, and a feeling for tonal quality which derives in particular from the recognition of octave similarity. In contrast to Helmholtz, who took common partials as a starting-point, Révész regarded the 'quality' of notes as a basic musico-acoustic characteristic. He became known for his work in general aspects of psychology, but his importance rests primarily on his research into the psychology of music, and some of his writings on that subject are still standard works.

WRITINGS

with P. von Liebermann: 'Über Orthosymphonie: Beitrag zur Kenntnis des Falschhörens', *Zeitschrift für Psychologie*, no.48 (1908), 259; also in *Beiträge zur Akustik und Musikwissenschaft*, iv (1909)
'Über die hervorragenden akustischen Eigenschaften und musikalischen Fähigkeiten des siebenjährigen Komponisten Ervin Nyiregyházy', *4. Kongress für experimentelle Psychologie: Innsbruck 1910*, 224
'Nachweis, dass in der sog. Tonhöhe zwei voneinander unabhängige Eigenschaften zu unterscheiden sind', *Nachrichten von der Königlichen Gesellschaft der Wissenschaften zu Göttingen: Mathematisch-physikalische Klasse* (Göttingen, 1912)
with P. von Liebermann: 'Experimentelle Beiträge zur Orthosymphonie und zum Falschhören', *Zeitschrift für Psychologie*, no.53 (1912), 286–324
——: 'Über binaurale Tonmischung', *Nachrichten von der Königlichen Gesellschaft der Wissenschaften zu Göttingen: Mathematisch-physikalische Klasse* (Göttingen, 1912), 676; also in *Zeitschrift für Psychologie*, no.69 (1914), 234 as 'Die binaurale Tonmischung'
'Über die beiden Arten des absoluten Gehörs', *ZIMG*, xiv (1912–13), 130
Zur Grundlegung der Tonpsychologie (Leipzig, 1913)
'Über musikalische Begabung', *6. Kongress für experimentelle Psychologie: Göttingen 1914*, 88
Ervin Nyiregyházy: psychologische Analyse eines musikalisch hervorragenden Kindes (Leipzig, 1916; Eng. trans., 1925/R1970 as *The Psychology of a Musical Prodigy (Ervin Nyiregyházy)*)
'Das musikalische Wunderkind', *Zeitschrift für pädagogische Psychologie*, xix (1918)
'Prüfung der Musikalität', *Zeitschrift für Psychologie*, no.85 (1920), 163–209
Das frühzeitige Auftreten der Begabung und ihre Erkennung (Leipzig, 1921)
'Über audition colorée', *Zeitschrift für angewandte Psychologie*, xxi (1922), 308
with D. Katz: 'Musikgenuss bei Gehörlosen', *Zeitschrift für Psychologie*, no.99 (1926), 289–324
'Zur Geschichte der Zweikomponentenlehre in der Tonpsychologie', *Zeitschrift für Psychologie*, no.99 (1926), 325–56

' "Tonsystem" jenseits des musikalischen Gebietes, musikalische "Mikrosysteme" und ihre Beziehungen zu der musikalischen Akustik', *Zeitschrift für Psychologie*, no.135 (1935), 25–61

'Gibt es einen Hörraum?', *Acta psychologica*, iii (1937), 137–92

'The Problem of Space with Particular Emphasis on Specific Sensory Spaces', *American Journal of Psychology*, l (1937), 429

'Die psychologische Bedeutung der musikalischen Erziehung bei Mindersinnigen und Sinnesschwachen', *Acta psychologica*, iv (1938–9), 361

'Der Ursprung der Musik', *International Archiv für Ethnographie*, xl (1941), 65

Inleiding tot de muziekpsychologie (Amsterdam, 1944, 2/1946; Ger. trans., 1946/R1972 as *Einführung in die Musikpsychologie*; Eng. trans., 1953/R1970; It. trans., 1954)

'Béla Bartók', *Mensch und Melodie*, i (1946); also in *Revue mensuelle de pédagogie musicale*, iii (1946)

De creatieve begaafdheid (The Hague, 1946)

'Die Beziehung zwischen mathematischer und musikalischer Begabung', *Schweizerische Zeitschrift für Psychologie*, v (1946)

'Colour Mixture and Sound Mixture', *Acta psychologica*, vi (1949), 3–46

Talent und Genie: Grundzüge einer Begabungspsychologie (Berne, 1952; It. trans., 1956)

BIBLIOGRAPHY

H. C. Duijker: 'In memoriam Géza Révész', *Acta psychologica*, xi (1955), 357

P. Lersch: 'G. Révész', *Jb der Bayrischen Akademie der Wissenschaften* (1956)

A. Wellek: 'Nachruf auf G. Révész', *Psychologische Rundschau*, vii (1956), 57

F. Benestad: 'Teorier om musikkens opprinnelse', *Norsk musikktidsskrift*, viii (1971), 1

HELGA DE LA MOTTE HABER

Revista (Sp.). REVUE.

Revival spiritual. A simplified folk hymn used for group singing. It became popular in the early 19th century in American revival and frontier camp meetings; *see* GOSPEL MUSIC, §I; SHAPE-NOTE HYMNODY, §§1–2; SPIRITUAL, §I, 1–2.

Revolutionary hymn. A general term for music sung to embody the idea of revolution. The present article is concerned with the repertory of revolutionary hymns sung at festivals and on other occasions in France around 1790–1800. The title does not refer to any distinct genre, but defines a body of music according to its social function. A remarkably substantial body of such music was created, and much survives. Because the French revolutionary hymn existed only within the social events that called it into being, some understanding of these events is desirable. Singing almost seems to have been the need of a people who suddenly found a common voice. However, the outlawing of Catholicism left gaps in social life which the state in part exploited. The type of music could be the simplest song with figured bass accompaniment, or it could be an elaborately orchestrated semi-dramatic piece designed for use at a state ceremony. Popular revolutionary songs like *La marseillaise* (*see* NATIONAL ANTHEMS) were constantly issued in cheap, rapid printings, while more pretentious music was actually purchased by few people. The great speed of official decision making resulted in a continuous cycle of state requests for music by established composers from 1793 to 1800 (before 10 August 1793 revolutionary music was volunteered, not commissioned). This music was performed at various Parisian and provincial festivals of the Revolution. Thus

Part of the revolutionary hymn 'Aux mânes de la Gironde' (1795) by Gossec

from 1790 the people heard and sometimes participated in a variety of hymns by Gossec, Méhul, Cherubini and many others, for which the music was distributed free at state expense, and for which a more or less elaborate accompaniment was provided, usually by a wind ensemble.

A government directive of January 1796 ordered *La marseillaise* and other songs to be sung before the curtain went up in all theatres of the republic. But spontaneous singing was commonplace at any kind of meeting. The most popular songs were *Ah ça ira* (1790), *La marseillaise* (1792), *La carmagnole* (1792), Dalayrac's *Veillons au salut de l'empire* (1792) and Méhul's *Chant du départ* (1794); no fewer than 1374 songs were composed or, more often, arranged between 1789 and 1803 (see Pierre, 1904). Moreover, such songs were incorporated into stage works, themselves stylized representations of public or military events; and the dividing-line between art and reality was so much further narrowed as to be virtually non-existent. Such works were, for example, Gossec's *L'offrande à la liberté* (Opéra 1792), Rodolphe Kreutzer's *La journée du 10 août 1792* (Opéra 1793) and P. J. Candeille's *La patrie reconnaissante* (Opéra 1793).

The programmes of 86 festivals are listed by Pierre (1904) from 1790 to 1800; as well as annual celebrations of Bastille day (14 July), of the uprising of 10 August 1792 and of the founding of the republic (22 September 1792), occasions such as the reburial of Voltaire in the Panthéon on 11 July 1791, the celebration of various military victories, funerals of notables and of 'martyrs' such as Bara and Viala, Robespierre's festival of the Supreme Being (8 June 1794) and, later, annual festivals under the Directory for 9 Thermidor, for agriculture, youth, marriage and the aged all required music. A limited number of festivals and hymns were also produced by royalists and moderates; in January 1795 Pierre Gaveaux's song *Le réveil du peuple* was taken up by the White reaction, to be banned by the Directory a year later. The number of hymns (not unofficial songs) rose from a handful in 1790–92 to 20 in 1793 and 56 in 1794. In 1795 there were 15 and thereafter the total dwindled gradually.

The first great festival, of Federation (14 July 1790), took in part the form of a Christian Mass celebrated on an 'altar of the fatherland' in the Champ de Mars; much early revolutionary music likewise had links with both church and stage. Gossec's *Te Deum* and his *Chant du 14 juillet* (written for this festival) represent the beginnings of the revolutionary hymn. Each uses a three-part male chorus accompanied by woodwind (including serpents) and brass, with percussion and violas in the *Te Deum* (the violas were eliminated from all subsequent outdoor works). The music is chiefly foursquare in phrase structure and harmony and is largely in common time. Militaristic dotted or dactylic rhythms are already evident. These elements were carried into later hymns; but the plainly chordal vocal writing was later made more flexible and even subject to simple contrapuntal elaboration. Gossec, the 'Tyrtaeus of the Revolution', composed the greatest number of revolutionary hymns, and the majority of those written up to November 1793. At their best they recall a neo-classical ancestry in Gluck's reform operas; this is entirely fitting, since in the festivals directed by the painter David between the Voltaire reburial and Thermidor, costumes and emblems of classical antiquity were the dominant characteristic. But the noble simplicity of Gluck was frequently quickened into a mode of relentless optimism; this style dominates the *Chant du 14 juillet*, ex.1, which thus stands as a prototype for many successors, including *La marseillaise*.

Ex.1 Gossec: *Le chant du 14 juillet*, 1790

Dieu du peuple et des rois, des ci – tés des cam–

–pag – nes de Lu- ther, de _ Cal - vin, des_

en –fants d'Is - ra - el _ etc

Some later musical expansion of the genre is seen in the use of four-part chorus, alternating sections of solo and chorus music and some dramatic word-painting. Departures were sometimes also made from the normal strophic form, with elements of through-composition and varied instrumentation. Parts for two reconstructed antique instruments, the TUBA CURVA and BUCCIN, were often included from 1791; these were confined to notes of the harmonic series. Notable contributions of a more ambitious kind were Cherubini's *L'hymne au Panthéon* (1794; one of only two hymns printed at the time in full score) and *Hymne funèbre sur la mort du général Hoche* (1797), Méhul's *Hymne à la raison* (1793), C.-S. Catel's *Hymne du 10 août* (1795) and Le Sueur's extended *Scène patriotique* (1794). Other composers included H.-M. Berton, François Devienne, François Giroust, the brothers Jadin, J. P. A. Martini and Pleyel.

Copyists' records show that accompanying ensembles could vary between 30 and 70 in number, sometimes with large extra detachments of drummers. No reliable figures exist to show how many voices may have participated. The festival of the Supreme Being, largest of them all, may have included over 1000 singers, but the facts cannot be truly ascertained.

Two large-scale secular cantatas ordered by Napoleon effectively ended the era of the revolutionary hymn: Méhul's *Chant national du 14 juillet 1800* for three choirs and three ensembles, and Le Sueur's *Chant du 1er vendémiaire* (1800) for four choirs and four ensembles. Both were given in the Invalides. Le Sueur's piece survives in fragmentary form while Méhul's was printed in full score at state expense. Their spatially separated orchestras and voices brought under artistic control two essential features of the earlier hymns: grandiose scale and musical assertiveness. Méhul's piece also contains more original material such as an important section for sopranos accompanied by two harps and horn solo.

The revolutionary hymn drew on other forms for most of its stylistic features, though it did raise the problem of extended instrumental writing without the participation of strings. Thus it is impossible to declare that Beethoven came into direct contact with such pieces. Yet the last movement of his Fifth Symphony comes extremely close to the style of some hymns by

Ex.2 Gossec: *Aux mânes de la Gironde*, 1795

virtue of its essential spirit, expressed through straight-forwardly elemental harmony and melody. A piece by Gossec may be quoted for comparison (ex.2). Later revolutions of 1830 and 1848 were too brief to do much except revive the music of the 1790s; but Berlioz noted the spontaneous singing of his own *Chant guerrier* (published in February 1830) during the July Days, and there is no reason to suppose that more contemporary songs were not adapted for use both in 1830 and 1848.

BIBLIOGRAPHY

La révolution française depuis l'ouverture des états généraux jusqu'au 9 brumaire en quinze tableaux gravés par Helman d'après Monnet (Paris, 1838)

H. Berlioz: *Mémoires de Hector Berlioz* (Paris, 1870; ed. and Eng. trans. by D. Cairns, 1969, 2/1970); ed. P. Citron (Paris, 1969), chap.29

H. Welschinger: *Le théâtre de la révolution* (Paris, 1880)

C. Pierre: *Musique exécutée aux fêtes nationales de la révolution française* (Paris, 1893–4)

——: *Le Magasin de musique à l'usage des fêtes nationales* (Paris, 1895)

——: *Musique des fêtes et cérémonies de la révolution française* (Paris, 1899) [inc. 110 hymns in vocal score]

——: *Les hymnes et chansons de la révolution* (Paris, 1904)

J. Tiersot: *Les fêtes et les chants de la révolution française* (Paris, 1908)

H. G. Farmer: *The Rise and Development of Military Music* (London, 1912)

C. Hughes: 'Music of the French Revolution', *Science and Society*, iv (1940), 193

D. L. Dowd: *Pageant-master of the Republic: Jacques-Louis David and the French Revolution* (Lincoln, Nebraska, 1948)

D. Charlton: 'New Sounds for Old: Tam-tam, Tuba Curva, Buccin', *Soundings*, iii (1973), 39

DAVID CHARLTON

Revue (from Fr.; It. *rivista*; Sp. *revista*). A topical, satirical show consisting of a series of scenes and episodes, usually having a central theme but not a dramatic plot, with spoken verse and prose, sketches, songs, dances, ballet and speciality acts. Revue developed in France during the 19th century, was taken up by other countries including Britain and the USA, and enjoyed its greatest acclaim and significance between the world wars. In revue there are elements of other stage forms such as cabaret, variety show, vaudeville, pantomime, burlesque and musical comedy.

1. France, Germany, Spain. 2. Britain. 3. The USA.

1. FRANCE, GERMANY, SPAIN. Revue evolved as a distinct genre in France in the early 19th century, consisting of satirical scenes 'passing in review' of recent events. During the reign of Louis Philippe (1830–48) it gained favour as an annual production, satirizing the theatrical productions of the previous season, and particularly the salient features and chief performers of the larger genres presented at the Opéra and Opéra-Comique. In *Le carnaval des revues* (Bouffes Parisiens, 1860) Offenbach

incurred the wrath of Wagner with his satire of 'the musician of the future'. During the Second Empire (to 1870) theatres increasingly presented revues emphasizing visual spectacle, with expensive costumes, scenery and stage machinery helping to create a more lavish and variegated entertainment. These works stimulated the rapid development of stage technology and set design, one element of the visual splendour being the *tableau vivant*, an allegorical still-life that helped to introduce nudity to the stage.

The typical revue of the 1880s was still a relatively inexpensive and simple entertainment, appealing to audiences mainly by the wit of the dialogue and the vivacity of those who played in it. Apart from the final tableau the scenery was often primitive and the music often a rehash of well-worn tunes. A compère or commère was an essential of the entertainment, interpolating explanatory or cynical remarks throughout – though the commère often had little to do except appear in practically no clothes. In 1886, however, the Folies-Bergère staged the first successful 'outfit revue', which abandoned the satirical bite of earlier shows and replaced it with suave cosmopolitanism, lavish visual effects, extravagant costumes and elaborately staged dances and songs. It prompted many imitations, and during the 20th century the main Parisian revues have followed this model – particularly at the Folies-Bergère and the Casino de Paris. The entertainment revolved round popular entertainers such as Mistinguett (Jeanne Bourgeois) (1873–1956) – famous for her *valse chaloupée* (Apache dance) – Maurice Chevalier (1888–1971), and the black American Josephine Baker (1906–75), who in 1925 first scandalized Paris with her erotic dances in the *Revue nègre*. The revues' texts and scores were compiled from many collaborators, with new material frequently inserted, the wider musical impact deriving from the songs of such composers as Maurice Yvain (*Mon homme* and *J'en ai marre* for Mistinguett), José Padilla (*Ça c'est Paris* and *Valencia* for Mistinguett), Henri Christiné (*Valentine* for Chevalier) and Vincent Scotto (*J'ai deux amours* for Josephine Baker).

By the 1920s revue had also become well established in other countries. During the last decade of the 19th century Berlin had the first of the annual revues at the Metropoltheater. They featured such star performers as Fritzi Massary and Josef Giampietro, who parodied the aristocrats and officials of the empire in songs filled with references to current events; the music was provided by the house conductor–composers including Viktor Holländer (1902–8) and Paul Lincke (1908–10). After World War I the Berlin revue took on more of the lavishness of Parisian spectacle revues, parading semi-nude women, sumptuous and massive sets, and elaborately choreographed production numbers. Similar trends were discernible in other continental countries, notably in Spain, from which emerged the singer Racquel Meller and the composer José Padilla, both of whom consolidated their personal success in Paris during the 1920s.

2. BRITAIN. In Britain burlesque and satire had long been staples of the theatre, and one-man entertainments by Charles Dibdin (from the 1780s to 1804), Charles Mathews (from 1808 to 1835) and others embraced dramatic monologues, songs, topical sketches and a wide variety of themes during an evening's performance.

(1915) (as with many revues the titles reflected their piecemeal nature). Cochran's example was followed by André Charlot, and their productions during the 1920s represented the peak of the genre's success in London, attracting the talents of leading performers, writers, composers, designers and choreographers.

Although the topicality and localized satire of revues made them unsuitable for export, there was considerable interchange of artists and material between London and New York. *Charlot's London Revue of 1924*, using successful material from various London revues, first introduced to New York Gertrude Lawrence (singing Philip Braham's *Limehouse Blues*), Beatrice Lillie and Jack Buchanan. Since the music for revues usually came from various sources the scores were traditionally the responsibility of the theatre's conductor, but specialist songwriters were increasingly used. Among composers of World War I revues were Herman Finck, James W. Tate, Herman Darewski and Nat D. Ayer, whose score for *The Bing Boys are Here* (1916) included 'If you were the only girl in the world'. Later composers included Ivor Novello, whose songs for Charlot's *A to Z* (1921) included 'And her mother came too', and Noël Coward, whose talents as songwriter as well as performer were first highlighted in Charlot's *London Calling* (1924). Coward went on to produce some of his best songs for *On with the Dance* (1925) and *This Year of Grace* (1928) for Cochran, who was also quick to give opportunities to the young Rodgers and Hart (*One Dam Thing after Another*, 1927, with Jessie Matthews singing 'My heart stood still') and Cole Porter (*Wake Up and Dream*, 1929). Cochran's revues also featured ballets; it was *Cochran's 1930 Revue*, for example, that introduced Lord Berners's score *Luna Park*.

Cochran and Charlot continued their series of revues into the 1930s. But the arrival of the talking picture seriously affected the vogue for witty, tuneful, spectacular stage shows, and the name 'revue' survived more securely in the non-stop nudist shows of the Windmill Theatre. The 1930s and 1940s saw some successful productions by George Black and a series of small-scale revues, and the 1950s brought the whimsical shows of Michael Flanders and Donald Swann. The success of the sharply satirical *Beyond the Fringe* (1961), however, showed that the genre was once more surviving on its verbal satire rather than as a source of original music.

3. THE USA. In the USA revue developed mostly from extravagant burlesques and vaudeville in New York during the late 19th century. John Brougham wrote one of the first, *The Dramatic Review for 1868* (1869), an afterpiece burlesquing the previous year's popular theatre, but the show was unsuccessful and prompted no imitations. The first popular revue came in 1894 with *The Passing Show* (music by Ludwig Englander), which, like Brougham's piece, was a satire on theatrical productions but which incorporated some topical songs in the style of Tin Pan Alley. Soon there were many revues on the New York stage. Those starring Joe Weber and Lew Fields (1896–1904) had vaudeville-like farce and pantomime, humorous songs, dances and more travesties on theatrical productions.

But the real establishment of American revue came with the *Follies of 1907*, 'a musical review of the New York sensations of the past season'. Produced by Florenz Ziegfeld junior, it appropriated the name and style of the Folies-Bergère, though the female chorus

1. Richard Dolman and Jessie Matthews singing 'My heart stood still' in 'One Dam Thing after Another' (Cochran's London Pavilion revue, 1927) by Ronald Jeans; lyrics by Lorenz Hart and music by Richard Rodgers

Perhaps the first unified revue in London was *Success, or A Hit If You Like It* (1825), a one-act allegorical afterpiece written by J. R. Planché, who was also responsible for various successors. By the 1890s, however, the form was still scarcely known in Britain, and *Under the Clock* (1893; music by Edward Jones) and *Pot-pourri* (1899; music by Napoleon Lambelet) were both pioneering efforts, modelled on the French form and satirizing recent theatrical productions. During the early 1900s revues began to appear as part of an evening's entertainment at variety theatres such as the Coliseum, but it was the advent of ragtime that finally established the genre in London. In particular, shows like *Hullo, Ragtime* (1912) and *Hullo, Tango* (1913), produced by Albert de Courville as part of the entertainment at the Alhambra Theatre, captured the popular imagination with their fast-moving presentation and as the means whereby new American song and dance styles and performers were introduced to Britain.

A more intimate style of revue had been introduced to London by the Follies, a company led by H. G. Pelissier from 1897 to 1913 and featuring a small cast and sparse sets. More significant shows on a smaller scale were those introduced to London by C. B. Cochran, who based his style on pieces still performed at small Parisian theatres and dependent on more subtle, satirical humour and on the talents of individual, versatile performers. For his one-act prototype *Odds and Ends* (1914) he imported various French performers including Alice Delysia, and the show's success prompted a full-length successor simply called *More* had to attract more by sheer beauty than mere nakedness. It became the first of an annual series of *Ziegfeld Follies* that became progressively more spectacular. Ziegfeld set the standard with very large casts, an emphasis on female glamour, grand costumes and sets (notably by Joseph Urban), fast-paced scenes and star performers like Fanny Brice, W. C. Fields, Eddie Cantor and Marilyn Miller. The shows remained a leading form of American stage entertainment into the 1920s and produced many imitations, notably the Shubert brothers' *The Passing Show* series from 1912, the *Greenwich Village Follies* from 1919, George White's *Scandals* from 1919, Irving Berlin's four *Music Box Revues* (1921–4) and the *Earl Carroll Vanities* from 1922.

The shows' songs and dances were part of the humour and variety element and were rarely satirical: the texts and scores were usually collaborations lacking a cohesive style and having new numbers interpolated as needed during the run of a show. Continental successes were sometimes featured (Fanny Brice first sang Yvain's 'My Man' in the *Ziegfeld Follies of 1921*); but over the years the revues gave opportunities to many up-and-coming American songwriters and introduced songs that have become established favourites. The *Ziegfeld Follies* introduced 'Shine on, Harvest Moon' (1908; Nora Bayes and Jack Norworth), 'Row, Row, Row' (1912; Jimmie V. Monaco), 'A pretty girl is like a melody' (1919; Irving Berlin), 'Second Hand Rose' (1921; James F. Hanley) and 'My Blue Heaven' (1927; Walter Donaldson); *The Passing Show* had 'I'm forever blowing bubbles' (1918; Jean Kenbrovin and John William Kellette) and Donaldson's 'Carolina in the Morning' (1922); and George White's *Scandals* introduced George Gershwin's 'I'll build a stairway to paradise' (1922) and 'Somebody loves me' (1924) and DaSylva, Brown and Henderson's 'The Birth of the Blues' and 'Black Bottom' (both 1926).

It was another series of shows, the *Garrick Gaieties*, that first brought attention to Rodgers and Hart with 'Manhattan' (1925) and 'Mountain Greenery' (1926); but these were shows in which simplicity and economy replaced elaborateness of setting and costume. Smaller-scale but still lavish revues were also given in rooftop theatres and night clubs, notably the Cotton Club in Harlem (music by Jimmy McHugh and later Harold Arlen). From the 1920s more serious, intimate revue came to the fore as lavish productions waned during the economic depression. *The Little Show* (1929) was one of a series that made the name of Arthur Schwartz, another being *The Band Wagon* (1931), which featured the Astaires and the song 'Dancing in the Dark'. *Three's a Crowd* (1930), in which Libby Holman sang Johnny Green's 'Body and Soul', and Irving Berlin's *As Thousands Cheer* (1933) were other noteworthy shows; but the departure of the leading composers for Hollywood hastened the decline of the genre, although giving opportunities to newer songwriters such as Burton Lane, Vernon Duke and Harold Rome (*Pins and Needles*, 1937). After World War II revues were performed less frequently at large Broadway theatres. While the song-and-dance revue found new life on television, satirical intimate revue was fostered by repertory companies throughout the country, notably in San Francisco (The Committee) and Chicago (Second City) in the 1960s. The productions more often favoured improvised sketches and topical commentary on American

society, abandoning complex choreography, elaborate sets and even clothes (in *Oh Calcutta*, 1969): the music increasingly used rock and electronic idioms.

BIBLIOGRAPHY

C. Smith: *Musical Comedy in America* (New York, 1950)
V. Ottolenghi and others: 'Rivista'; 'Rivista da camera', *ES*
R. Baral: *Revue: the Great Broadway Period* (New York, 1962)
R. Mander and J. Mitchenson: *Revue* (London, 1971)
ANDREW LAMB, DEANE L. ROOT

Revueltas, Silvestre (*b* Santiago Papasquiaro, Durango, 31 Dec 1899; *d* Mexico City, 5 Oct 1940). Mexican composer and violinist. At the age of eight he began violin studies in Colima, and at 12 he entered the Juárez Institute, Durango. He studied further under Tello (composition) and Rocabruna (violin) in Mexico City (1913–16), at St Edward College, Austin, Texas (1916–18), and at the Chicago Musical College under Sametini (violin) and Borowski (composition, 1918–20). After a hiatus in Mexico he returned to Chicago in 1922 to complete a four-year violin course under Kochanski and Ševčik. He was again in the USA in 1926 and 1928, playing the violin in a theatre orchestra in San Antonio, Texas, and conducting an orchestra in Mobile, Alabama. Chávez recalled him to Mexico City to take the post of assistant conductor of the Mexico SO (1929–35), and during the years 1931–4 he composed six sophisticated picture-postcard pieces for that orchestra. At the same time he taught the violin and chamber music at the conservatory and conducted a conservatory graduates' orchestra. In 1937 he toured Spain, there allying himself with the Republican cause, and on his return he continued to teach. His early death was due to alcoholism.

Without quoting Mexican folksong, Revueltas's mature works weave melodies of folk type into a gaudy instrumental fabric. In rhythm he not only favoured the hemiola endemic to all Hispanic American popular music (3/4 alternating with 6/8), but also liberally inserted passages in vigorous septuple and quintuple metres. The much played *Sensemayá* – a vocal and orchestral setting of the poem by the Afro-Cuban revolutionary Nicolás Guillén about the killing of a tropical snake, later transcribed for orchestra alone – illustrates his superb rhythmic drive in 7/8 (occasionally 7/16) to an orgiastic climax. Revueltas's principal melodies, no matter how encased in dissonant counterpoint, are always tuneful and repetitive in a manner comparable with that of the *Rite of Spring*. His works are concise, ending *fortissimo* after a hammering crescendo, and there is a play of sardonic humour even in his most wistful moments. Openly confessing his cynicism, he sometimes prescribed 'for the tourist trade' an indigenous instrument such as the huehuetl. But the street music of modern Mexico was his model, not Aztec art. His brother, the muralist Fermin Revueltas (1903–35), closely resembled him in painting bold simplistic designs limned in bright colours.

WORKS

Ballets: El renacuajo Paseador, 1936; La coronela, 1940, 4th and final episode by B. Galindo, orchd C. Huizar
Orch: Cuauhnahuac, 1930; Esquinas, 1930; Ventanas, 1931; Alcancías, 1932; Colorines, 1932; Janitzio, 1933; Toccata, vn, orch (1933); Caminos (Itinerarios), 1934; Planos, small orch, 1934; as Danza geométrica, large orch (1964); Redes, suite [from film score], 1938; Sensemayá, 1938 [after vocal setting of Guillén]
Chamber: 2 str qts, 1930, 1931; Música da feria, 1932; 3 piezas, vn, pf, 1932; 8 x radio (Ocho por radio), 1933; Homenaje a Federico García Lorca, chamber orch, 1935; Toccata, 8 insts (1959); 2 piezas serias, wind qnt (1957); 4 Little Pieces, 2 vn, vc (1969)

Songs: Duo para pato y canario, 1v, small orch, 1931, arr. 1v, pf (1962); Ranas y el tecolete, 1v, pf, 1931; 2 canciones (R. López Velarde, N. Guillén), 1937; Canto a (de) una muchacha negra (L. Hughes), 1938; 7 canciones (Lorca), 1v, insts, 1938

Film scores: Redes, 1935; Vámomos con Pancho Villa, 1936; Ferrocarriles de Baja California, 1938; El indio, 1938; Bajo el signo de la muerte, 1939; La noche de los mayas, 1939; Los de abajo, 1940

Principal publishers: G. Schirmer, Southern

BIBLIOGRAPHY

O. Mayer-Serra: 'Silvestre Revueltas and Musical Nationalism in Mexico', *MQ*, xxvii (1941), 123

H. A. Palencia: *Músicos de Durango* (Durango, 1947)

G. Contreras: *Silvestre Revueltas: genio atormentado* (Mexico City, 1954)

Compositores de América/Composers of the Americas, ed. Pan American Union, i (Washington, DC, 1955), 54ff

ROBERT STEVENSON

Revutsky, Levko Mykolayevich [Lev Nikolayevich] (*b* Irzhavets [now in Chernigov region], 20 Feb 1889; *d* Kiev, 30 March 1977). Ukrainian composer and teacher. He studied the piano with Lysenko at the Kiev Music Institute (1903–5) and also with S. Korotkevich and G. Khodorovsky. In 1916 he graduated from the Kiev Conservatory, in Glier's composition class, and from the law faculty of Kiev University. He took a major part in the administrative and educational activities of the Leontovich Association (1922–8); at this time his creative production was at its height. From 1924 he taught harmony, counterpoint and orchestration, and from 1930 he took a composition class at the Kiev Music-Dramatic Institute. Later he taught at the Kiev Conservatory, from 1935 as professor, and between 1941 and 1944 he headed the composition department at the Tashkent Conservatory. He has also served as president of the board of the Ukrainian Composers' Union (1944–8), as a member of the presidium of that union and as a board member of the Composers' Union of the USSR. Among his honours are a doctorate in musicology (1941), the USSR State Prize (1941), the title National Artist of the USSR (1944), membership of the National Academy of the USSR (1957), the Shevchenko Ukrainian SSR State Prize (1966) and the title Hero of Socialist Labour (1969).

Revutsky's output is small but shows great originality and accomplishment. His music presents a clear poetic vision – the harmonious union of man with nature and art, spiritual dignity or the heroic daring of nation and individual – and it is distinguished by lyricism, a lofty romanticism and finesse in form. His compositions have formed foundation stones for a range of genres in Ukrainian Soviet music. Revutsky is an expert on folklore, considering it the basis of national culture and the source of renewal in contemporary art. His many folksong arrangements, essentially original compositions, display a new synthesis of traditional traits with contemporary instrumental technique and the colourful harmony of the late-Romantics and impressionists. In his Second Symphony he achieved a versatile and vital transformation of folk melodies from ancient ritual and from song, everyday, lyrical and comic. Except for the main theme, which is altered, the tunes are employed in their original forms and developed with a masterly use of thematic elaboration, variation, polyphony, contrast and active interaction. The result is a work which is dynamic and integrated, organic in its progress. Revutsky has also edited many works of Lysenko for the complete edition and other publications; his work on the opera *Taras Bul'ba* (Kiev, 1936) included the composition of an overture.

WORKS

(selective list)

Orch: Sym. no.1, A, op.3, 1916–21, only 1st movt extant; Sym. no.2, E, op.12, 1926–7; Kozachok [Little Cossack], 1929; Pf Conc., F, op.18, 1934

Choral: Khustyna (Shevchenko), cantata, solo vv, chorus, pf, 1923; Shchoroku [Yearly], op.5 (O. Oles'), solo vv, chorus, pf, 1923; Pisnya pro partiyu [Song for the Party] (M. Ryl'sky), chorus, orch, 1949; Oda pisni [Ode to song], vocal-sym. poem, 1957; *c*44 folksong arrs., 32 songs, 5 school choruses

Solo vocal: Sonechko [Little sun], folksong arrs., 1v, pf, 1925; Kozats'ki pisni [Cossack songs], folksong arrs., 1v, pf, 1926; Galits'ki pisni [Galician songs], op.14, folksong arrs., 1v, pf, 1926–7; Monolog Tarasa Bul'bi (Ryl'sky), B, orch, 1936; over 80 folksong arrs., 1v, pf; 2 folksong arrs. for 1v, orch; 2 folksong arrs. for 2vv, pf; 4 folksong arrs. for 4vv

Pf: Sonata Allegro, b, op.1, 1912; 7 preludes, opp.4, 7, 11, 1914–24; 2 Pieces, op.17, 1929; other pieces

Other works: inst pieces, music for the theatre, cinema and radio

For full list to 1938 see *Radyans'ka muzika* (1939), no.1, p.13; for list of main works see Byalik (1963), 130ff

WRITINGS

'Pro moyo robotu nad muzichnim oformlennyam pesi Pogodina *Posle bala*' [On my work on the incidental music for Pogodin's *After the Ball*], *Radyans'ka muzika* (1934), no.8–9, p.35

'Nova redaktsiya opei M. V. Lysenka *Taras Bul'ba*', *Radyans'ka muzika* (1936), no.2, p.6

'Moya robota nad muzikoyo *Taras Bul'ba*', *Visti TsVK URSR*, no.85 (1937), 4

'*Taras Bul'ba*', *Radyans'ka muzika* (1937), no.4, p.16

'Avtobiografichni zapiski' [Autobiographical notes], *Radyans'ka muzika* (1939), no.1, p.8

'Pam'yati V. S. Kosenka' [In memory of Kosenko], *Radyans'ka muzika* (1939), no.5, p.23

'Avtobiograficheskiye zapiski', *SovM* (1940), no.7, p.24

'Pam'yati Grigoriya Mikolayovicha Beklemisheva', *Radyans'ka muzika* (1940), no.1, p.28

'Moy uchitel' [My teacher], *Sovetskaya Ukraina* (20 April 1941) [on Lysenko]

'Moi vikhovantsi' [My pupils], *Molod' Ukrayini* (19 Feb 1946)

'Petro Illich Chaykovs'ky', *Mistetstvo* (1955), no.3, p.30

'Vikhovannya kompozitors'koyi molodi' [The education of young composers], *Mistetstvo* (1956), no.1, p.30

'Struni Lysenka zhiviyi' [The strings of Lysenko are alive], *Mistetstvo* (1967), no.4, p. 28

BIBLIOGRAPHY

E. Stolova: *Druga redaktsiya simfoniy L. Revutskovo* [The second edition of Revutsky's symphony] (diss., U. of Kiev, 1946)

G. Kisel'ov: *L. M. Revutsky* (Kiev, 1949)

A. O. Kolomiets': *Nayvazhlivishi dodatkovi epizodi u noviy redaktsiy operi Taras Bul'ba M. Lysenka* [The most important additional episodes in the new edition of Lysenko's opera *Taras Bul'ba*] (diss., U. of Kiev, 1958)

T. Sheffer: *L. M. Revutsky* (Kiev, 1958)

——: *L. M. Revutsky* (Kiev, 1960, 2/1973)

M. Byalik: *L. N. Revutsky* (Moscow, 1963)

N. Gerasimova-Persids'ka: *Druga simfoniya L. Revutskovo* [Revutsky's Sym. no.2] (Kiev, 1963)

M. Dremlyuga: *Ukrayins'ka fortepianna muzika i fortepianna tvorchist' kompozitora L. M. Revutskovo* (diss., U. of Kiev, 1964)

N. Goryukhina: *Simfonizm L. Revutskovo* (Kiev, 1965)

M. Byalik: *Tvorchestvo L. N. Revutskovo* [Revutsky's works] (diss., U. of Leningrad, 1969)

V. Klin: *L. Revutsky: kompozitor–pianist* (Kiev, 1972)

M. G. Byalik: *L. Revutsky: risi tvorchosti* [Revutsky: the features of creativity] (Kiev, 1973)

LYU PARKHOMENKO

Rexroth-Berg, Natanael. *See* BERG, NATANAEL.

Rey. French family of musicians.

(1) Jean-Baptiste Rey (i) (*b* Lauzerte, 18 Dec 1734; *d* ?Paris, 15 July 1810). Conductor and composer. He was taught at the choir school of St Servin and had become *maître de chapelle* at Auch Cathedral by the age of 17. He resigned after three years and went as a conductor to the opera houses of Toulouse, Montpellier, Marseilles, Bordeaux and Nantes. In 1776 he was engaged as a conductor at the Paris Opéra, where he conducted works by, among others, Gluck and Piccinni.

In 1781 he succeeded Louis-Joseph Francoeur as director of the Opéra orchestra. From 1779 he was master of the *musique de chambre* at the court of Louis XVI, and from 1781 to 1786 occasionally conducted at the Concert Spirituel. In 1792, during the Revolution, he joined the committee in charge of the Opéra. For a brief period in 1793 he conducted at the Théâtre de la République (the Comédie-Française), notably some incidental music by Méhul for André Chénier's *Timoléon*, in which Talma took the leading part. In 1799 he went to the Paris Conservatoire as professor of harmony; he stayed only three years because of a disagreement with the director, Sarrette. He had also antagonized his colleagues through his support of Rameau's theories, which they thought outdated. In 1804 he was appointed *maître de chapelle* to Napoleon, but in 1810, just before his death, he resigned from all his positions.

Rey is best remembered as a conductor. After the revival of one of Gluck's operas in 1786, the *Mercure de France* (4 March 1786) called him 'the foremost conductor in all Europe'. As a composer he mostly limited himself to arrangements of works he was about to conduct. His most important work is the completion of Sacchini's *Arvire et Eveline* (1788); he also made additions to works by J. J. Mouret and his brother (2) Louis-Charles-Joseph Rey, and wrote one opera, *Diane et Endymion* (Opéra, 1791), two motets, masses (now lost) and solfège exercises for the Conservatoire.

(2) Louis-Charles-Joseph Rey (*b* Lauzerte, 26 Oct 1738; *d* Paris, 12 May 1811). Cellist and composer, brother of (1) Jean-Baptiste Rey (i). At the age of 16 he joined the orchestra of the Montpellier opera, probably using his older brother's influence. About 1755 he went to Paris, where he studied the cello with Berteau and had some of his ballets performed in various small theatres. From 1757 to 1766 he was a cellist at the Bordeaux theatre. He then returned to Paris and was a member of the Opéra orchestra from 1767 to 1806 and the orchestra of the royal chapel from 1772. He composed for the stage and for the cello.

WORKS
(all printed works published in Paris)
Stage: Le forgeron (ballet-pantomime), Paris, Comédie-Italienne, 1756; Le suisse dupé (ballet-pantomime), Paris, Opéra-Comique, 1757; Apollon et Coronis (opera, 1, Fuzelier, after J. J. Mouret: Les amours de dieux), Paris, Opéra, 3 May 1781, collab. J.-B. Rey (i)
Vocal: 4 ariettes, 1v, insts (1770)
Chamber: 6 sonates, vc/vn, b (1768); 6 duos, 2 vn/(vn, vc) (1769); Trios, 2 vn, vc (n.d.)

(3) Jean-Baptiste Rey (ii) (*b* Tarascon, *c*1760; *d* Paris, *c*1822). Theorist and instrumentalist, possibly a son of (2) Louis-Charles-Joseph Rey. According to Fétis he was self-taught; he was active as a cellist, violinist, harpsichordist, organist and composer, but is best known as a theorist who followed Rameau's ideas, adapting them to 19th-century musical idioms. He was the organist and *maître de chapelle* at the cathedrals of Viviers and Auch before going in 1795 to Paris, where he was a cellist in the Opéra orchestra from 1796 to 1822. His most important works comprise theoretical studies, a piano method and some piano music.

There were several other musicians in the Rey family. V. F. S. Rey (*b* ?Lyons, *c*1760; *d* ?Paris, after 1816), whose relationship to the family is unknown, was a theorist who popularized Rameau's ideas, and published a *Tablature générale de la musique . . . d'après les prin-*

cipes du célèbre Rameau (Paris, 1795) as well as several other practical books on music. A certain Mlle Rey was a dancer at the Paris Opéra in the early 18th century. Another Mlle Rey, sister of (1) Jean-Baptiste Rey (i) and (2) Louis-Charles-Joseph Rey, married a composer named Pitrot and was a dancer at the Opéra from 1755. A third 'Mlle' Rey, wife of (2) Louis-Charles-Joseph Rey, was a dancer and possibly a singer at the Comédie-Italienne. Louise Rey, probably a daughter of (1) Jean-Baptiste Rey (i), taught solfège at the Paris Conservatoire from 1795 to 1797. Another Louise Rey and Mion Rey, probably daughters of (2) Louis-Charles-Joseph Rey, were well-known dancers at the Comédie-Italienne and later at the Opéra. A certain Rey (first names unknown) was a baritone at the Opéra and a member of the orchestra of the Masonic Lodge 'Le Contrat Social' in 1786.

BIBLIOGRAPHY
Fétis B
C. Pierre: *Le conservatoire national de musique et de déclamation: documents historiques et administratifs* (Paris, 1900)
R. Cotte: *La musique maçonnique et ses musiciens* (Brussels, 1974)
                                         ROGER COTTE

Rey, Cemal Reşit (*b* Jerusalem, 24 Sept 1904). Turkish composer, conductor and pianist. A child prodigy, he went to Paris at the age of nine as a pupil of Marguerite Long. After a period in Switzerland at the Geneva Conservatory, he continued his studies in Paris with Raoul Laparra, Fauré and Henri Derosse (conducting). Returning to Turkey in 1923, he began teaching at the Istanbul Conservatory, where in 1934 he founded the conservatory orchestra. In 1938 he became the music programme director of Radio Ankara, in 1945 conductor of the Istanbul City Orchestra and from 1949 to 1950 music programme director of Radio Istanbul. Between 1949 and 1960 he also undertook concert tours abroad. Since retiring from official positions, he has continued to teach privately and to compose.

Rey's style and expression show the influence both of impressionism and traditional Turkish music. One of the most productive members of the Turkish Five, he has produced works of almost every type, including musicals (mostly to the librettos by his brother, Ekrem Reşit Rey) and music for plays and films.

WORKS
(selective list)
Scènes turques, orch, 1928; Instantanés, sym. poem, 1931; Karagöz, sym. poem, 1931; Chromatic Conc., pf, orch, 1933; Str Qt, 1935; Pf Qnt, 1939; Vn Conc, 1939; 3 syms., 1941–68; Pf Conc., 1948; L'appel, sym. poem, 1950; Fatih Sultan Mehmet, sym. poem, 1953; Colloque instrumental, ens, 1957; Variations on a Theme of an Istanbul Song, pf, orch, 1961; Turkey, sym. poem, 1972
Stage: Vann Marek, 1922; Sultan Cem, 1923; Zeybek, 1926; Tchelebi, 1945; Benli Hürmüz, 1965; Yaygara, 1969

Principal publishers: Ankara State Conservatory, Bosworth, Heugel, Universal (Vienna)
                                         FARUK YENER

Reyer [Rey], (Louis-Etienne-)Ernest (*b* Marseilles, 1 Dec 1823; *d* Le Lavandou, Var, 15 Jan 1909). French composer and critic. His real name was Rey. Having attended a music school in Marseilles from the age of six, he was sent in 1839 to Algiers to work with an uncle, Louis Farrenc, in a government department. There he composed, without the benefit of tuition, a number of minor works, including a mass for the visit of the Duke of Aumale in 1847. In 1848 he defied his parents' and uncle's objections to a musical career and went to Paris, where his kinship with Aristide and

Louise Farrenc was an invaluable introduction to a wide musical circle; Louise Farrenc took charge of his musical studies on an informal basis. Equally important was his early association with a number of literary figures, especially Gautier, Méry and de Cormenin, whose tastes were similar to his own. Reyer had thus had little formal musical training when *Le sélam*, an 'oriental symphony' in four parts to a text by Gautier, was successfully performed in Paris in 1850. Closely modelled on Félicien David's then popular *Le désert*, it won the praise of Berlioz and established Reyer's inclination towards exotic subject matter, repeated in *Sacountalâ*, a ballet by Gautier played at the Opéra in 1858, and in *La statue* (1861), an *opéra comique* based on the *1001 Nights*. *Maître Wolfram* (1854), an *opéra comique*, was a tacit homage to Weber; *Erostrate*, commissioned for the new theatre in Baden-Baden in 1862, tells the legend of how the Venus de Milo lost her arms.

Within 14 years Reyer had established a minor celebrity and composed a substantial body of music, but though he lived another 46 years, only two significant works appeared: the operas *Sigurd* and *Salammbô* together represent his highest achievement as a composer. Both were first produced at the Théâtre de la Monnaie, Brussels, whose management was at that time considerably more adventurous than that of the Paris Opéra. *Sigurd* was begun in the 1860s but had to wait until 1884 to be heard, when the fact that its subject was close to that of Wagner's *Ring* was still not the handicap it might have been a year or two later. Reyer had chosen his material independently of Wagner and from different sources. The success of *Sigurd* was considerable and it put Reyer's name high in public esteem. *Salammbô* (1890), brought his friend Flaubert's highly coloured novel to the stage and enjoyed equal success, both in Brussels and in France – a success also due to the sumptuousness of its settings and the singing of Rose Caron. Both survived in the repertory for 50 years.

Reyer's preferred music was that of Gluck, Weber, Schumann and Berlioz. He had been close to Berlioz in his last years and remained a staunch advocate of his music at a time when it was almost unheard in Paris. He also held Wagner's music in admiration (after early doubts) and made repeated efforts to obtain hearings of the operas in the 1870s. Yet he did not imitate Wagner's style: 'the only composer who can write Wagnerian music is Wagner', he once said, and although he used a clear leitmotif technique it is truly closer to Weber in origin than to Wagner. Nor did he consciously imitate Berlioz, for the same reason. Reyer's music draws on the French tradition of delicately coloured scoring, with its oriental flavour, to be seen also in David, Gounod, Delibes and Bizet; at the same time it has, especially in the last two operas, a breadth and weight that relate more closely to Meyerbeer and Verdi. His fondness for triplets and static bass lines is almost a mannerism. He took particular pains over his orchestration, which is some compensation for his lack of true melodic distinction. Indeed all his work was painstaking and disciplined, despite being accused of amateurishness by his critics. He had a sternly independent spirit and a scorn for what he saw as debased styles. As a composer he was perhaps too conscious of what he did not want to be to establish a positive individuality.

In this respect one can see Reyer's work as a critic in fundamental opposition to his work as a composer, despite the sincerity and constancy of his ideas, for which he earned the widest respect. Undoubtedly, too, his activity as a critic accounts for the small output of his later years. His articles appeared over a span of 40 years, in *Revue française*, *La presse*, *Moniteur universel*, *Courrier de Paris* and especially *Journal des débats*, to which he contributed articles from 1866 to 1898. Some of his articles are in his compilation *Notes de musique* (Paris, 1875), which contains an account of his journeys to Germany in 1863 and to Cairo, for *Aida*, in 1871. (After 1870 he refused to visit Germany again and he never went to Bayreuth.) A posthumous collection, *Quarante ans de musique* (Paris, 1909), contains his essays on Wagner's and Berlioz's operas, and also, interestingly, on his own. Its editor, Emile Henriot, said of Reyer the critic: 'His writing is, like his music, very literary, more literary than musical, more poetic than technical. There lies, perhaps, the source of his genius. He was more a poet than a musician, perhaps even more a painter than a poet'. He distrusted progressive ideas, especially uncritical Wagnerism. He opposed, for example, the introduction of valved brass instruments. He was extremely shy of public appearance and earned a reputation for waspishness, which Adolphe Jullien insisted was false. He was elected to the Institute in 1876 and from 1866 until his death was librarian of the Opéra, a duty to which he seems to have paid scant attention.

WORKS
(all printed works published in Paris)

STAGE

Maître Wolfram (opéra comique, 1, F. J. Méry, T. Gautier), Paris, Lyrique, 20 May 1854, vocal score (1854)
Sacountalâ (ballet-pantomime, 2, Gautier), Paris, Opéra, 14 July 1858
La statue (opéra comique, 3, M. Carré, J. Barbier), Paris, Lyrique, 11 April 1861, vocal score (1861)
Erostrate (opera, 2, Méry, E. Pacini), Baden-Baden, 21 Aug 1862 [in Ger.], Paris, Opéra, 16 Oct 1871 [in Fr.], vocal score (1864)
Sigurd (opera, 4, C. du Locle, A. Blau), Brussels, Monnaie, 7 Jan 1884, vocal score (1884), full score (n.d.)
Salammbô (opera, 5, du Locle, after Flaubert), Brussels, Monnaie, 10 Feb 1890 (1890)

OTHER WORKS

Sacred: Messe pour l'arrivée du Duc d'Aumale à Alger, 1847
Other vocal: Le sélam, symphonie orientale (Gautier), solo vv, chorus, orch, 1850, vocal score (1852); L'hymne du Rhin (Méry), cantata, S, chorus, 1865; La Madeleine au désert (E. Blau), scène, Bar, orch, 1874, unpubd; 40 vieilles chansons du XIIe au XVIIIe siècle (1885) [collected by Reyer]; 30 mélodies in 2 collections; choruses, male vv
Orch: Marche tzigane, 1865 (1882)
Pf works

BIBLIOGRAPHY

H. de Curzon: *La légende de Sigurd dans l'Edda: l'opéra de Reyer* (Paris, 1890)
——: *Salammbô: le poème et l'opéra* (Paris, 1890)
H. Imbert: *Nouveaux profils de musiciens* (Paris, 1892)
A. Jullien: *Musiciens d'aujourd'hui* (Paris, 1892–4)
G. Servières: *La musique française moderne* (Paris, 1897)
A. Bruneau: *Musiques de Russie et musiciens de France* (Paris, 1903)
J. Combarieu: 'Ernest Reyer', *RHCM*, ix (1909), 88
A. Jullien: *Ernest Reyer: sa vie et ses oeuvres* (Paris, 1909)
A. Pougin: *Musiciens du XIXe siècle* (Paris, 1911)
G. Servières: 'Les relations d'Ernest Reyer et de Th. Gautier', *Revue d'histoire littéraire* (1917), Jan–May
J. Tiersot: *Un demi-siècle de musique française* (Paris, 1918, 2/1924)
H. de Curzon: *Ernest Reyer, sa vie et ses oeuvres* (Paris, 1924)
A. Jullien: 'Reyer intime d'après des lettres inédites', *ReM*, v/3 (1924), 12
A. Boschot: *Portraits de musiciens*, i (Paris, 1946)

HUGH MACDONALD

Reyes Católicos (Sp.). CATHOLIC MONARCHS.

Reymann [Reimann, Reinmann], **Matthias** (*b* Thorn, Poland, *c*1565; *d* after 1625). German lutenist and composer. He issued a collection of music in French tablature for eight-course solo lute, *Noctes musicae*

(Heidelberg, 1598) and a second book, now lost, *Cythara sacra* (Cologne, 1612). Three galliards and two *choreae* by him are found in *D-LEm* MS II.6. 15 (the Długoraj Lutebook).

Noctes musicae is dedicated to four Czeykys brothers, from Bohemia, in whose care Reymann spent part of his youth. He was in Leipzig by 1582 and evidently a student of law at the university there. He is mentioned as a lutenist and holder of minor legal positions. He may have gone to Cologne in 1612 for the publication of his second book. He is sometimes confused with Matthias Reymann (1544–97), jurist and counsellor to Rudolf II.

Reymann's surviving collection contains no vocal intabulations, unlike many contemporary lutebooks, but includes among its 74 pieces 23 preludes, 16 fantasias, 12 passamezzo suites, 5 pavans, 10 galliards and 8 *choreae* (the table of contents is faulty). The music is remarkable for the richness and persistence of its figuration, and for the idiomatic treatment of the lute. It is much influenced by Italian forms and instrumental techniques. A tendency towards modern tonality and a harmonic style of rich variety are conspicuous features. A part of the total effect is the frequent use of the lower ranges of the instrument, making use of the two lower strings, a practice discussed in the preface. Nine of the fantasias are more restrained, being motet-like and using (generally without decoration) the successive phrases of well-known Lutheran chorales. (One must assume the composer's Protestant persuasion, especially since his second book was devoted to 152 settings, each with a variation, of psalm melodies taken from Goudimel's Psalter.) The remaining fantasias are monothematic, some with central sections in triple metre. The passamezzo suites are extensive, each with seven sections, including duple and triple metre variations, and a *ripresa*, many of which are wholly unrelated to what has gone before. The eight *choreae* also have noteworthy triple variations. Reymann came close to the use of the terms 'major' and 'minor' in describing his pieces as having 'durum' and 'molle' tonalities. He even went so far as to make use of the key of E♭ minor ('Passemezae 9: ad notam E la mi, melos molle tono ficto').

BIBLIOGRAPHY

R. Wustmann: *Musikgeschichte Leipzigs*, i (Berlin, 1909)
H. B. Lobaugh: *Three German Lute Books* (diss., U. of Rochester, NY, 1968)

H. B. LOBAUGH

Reymar von Zwetel [Zweten]. *See* REINMAR VON ZWETER.

Reynaldus, Fr(?anciscus) [?Frate] (*fl* ?c1400). Italian composer. Only one of his works survives: a two-voice ballata, *L'adorno viso*, in the fragment *D-Bs* 523 (no.4), which shows French influence.

BIBLIOGRAPHY

K. von Fischer: 'Una ballata trecentesca sconosciuta', *L'ars nova italiana del trecento: convegni di studio 1961–1967* (Certaldo, 1968), 39 [with edition]
W. T. Marrocco, ed.: *Italian Secular Music*, PMFC, x (in preparation)

For further bibliography see ITALY: BIBLIOGRAPHY OF MUSIC TO 1600.

KURT VON FISCHER

Reynaldus Tenorista. Composer, possibly identifiable with Ray. de Lantins; *see* LANTINS, DE.

Reyneau, Gacian (*b* Tours, ?c1370; *fl* before 1429). French composer. He entered the royal chapel at Barcelona in the 1390s. His rondeau *Va t'en* fore-

shadows Cordier and Dufay in its conductus-like texture and synchronized dance rhythms (6/8 alternating with 3/4). Likewise, its apparently instrumental interludes and clear sense of tonality presage typical features of the early 15th-century chanson style.

BIBLIOGRAPHY

H. Anglès: 'Gacian Reyneau am Königshof zu Barcelona in der Zeit von 139 … bis 1429', *Studien zur Musikgeschichte: Festschrift für Guido Adler* (Vienna, 1930), 64
U. Günther: 'Eine Ballade auf Mathieu de Foix', *MD*, xix (1965), 80
W. Apel, ed.: *French Secular Compositions of the Fourteenth Century*, i, CMM, liii/1 (1970), XL, 166f

NORS S. JOSEPHSON

Reynolds, Anna [Ann] (*b* Canterbury, 4 Oct ?1931). English mezzo-soprano. A Royal Academy piano student, she later made singing her principal study under Debora Fambri and Re Koster in Rome. Her operatic début was in Parma (Suzuki, 1960); it was in Italy, rather than Britain, that she first achieved an operatic career, with appearances at Vicenza (1961), Rome (1964, 1970), Spoleto (1966), Trieste (1967), Venice (1969) and La Scala (1973). These covered a wide range of roles, including Purcell's Dido, Rossini's Tancredi, Elizabeth I (*Maria Stuarda*) and Charlotte (*Werther*); they indicate the considerable versatility of her style and stage presence. Her first opera appearance in England was at Glyndebourne in 1962 (Geneviève in *Pelléas et Mélisande*, a part later successfully taken at the Aix-en-Provence Festival, with Scottish Opera and in Milan); at Covent Garden she has played Adelaide (*Arabella*, 1967) and Andromache (Tippett's *King Priam*, 1975). As a Wagnerian mezzo-soprano she took part in the Karajan *Ring* cycles, at Salzburg and the Metropolitan; from 1970 to 1976 she regularly appeared at Bayreuth. A concert singer of great distinction, she first sang in London under Barbirolli, as the Angel in *The Dream of Gerontius* (1963). She frequently sings in Mahler's *Das Lied von der Erde* and her many recordings include a collection of his songs, Schumann's Eichendorff *Liederkreis* and Bach cantatas. In this music her true, even vocal production, with its attractively tangy timbre, is at its best; in German, French and Italian, as in English, her enunciation is always clear, idiomatic and expressive.

ALAN BLYTH

Reynolds, Roger (*b* Detroit, 13 July 1934). American composer. After obtaining a degree in engineering at the University of Michigan he studied composition there with Finney and Gerhard (1957–60). He was active in the mixed-media ONCE Festivals in Ann Arbor, and in 1962–3 worked at the Cologne electronic studios under a Fulbright grant. A Guggenheim Fellowship took him to France and Italy in 1964–5; from 1966 to 1969 he was in Japan as a Fellow of the Institute of Current World Affairs. In 1969 he was made associate professor of music and cultural studies at the University of California, San Diego, where in July 1972 he was appointed director of the newly-founded Project for Music Experiment. In 1971 he was visiting professor at the University of Illinois and received an award from the National Institute of Arts and Letters. Reynolds's music can be related generally to that of Ives, Varèse and Cage. He has also drawn on Buckminster Fuller's ideas, notably in *I/O*, based on 'complementary opposites', here relationships between the sexes. *The Emperor of Ice Cream* exemplifies his concern with the structuring and coordination of theatrical and aural elements. He has published *Mind Models: New Forms of Musical Experience* (New York, 1975).

WORKS
(selective list)

Epigram and Evolution, pf, 1959; Wedge, 2 fl + pic, 2 tpt, 2 trbn, perc, db, pf, 1960; Acquaintances, fl, db, pf, 1961; 4 Etudes, pic, 2 fl, a fl, 1961; Str Qt, 1961; The Emperor of Ice Cream (W. Stevens), 8 solo vv, perc, pf, db, 1962; Mosaic, fl, pf, 1962; A Portrait of Vanzetti, narrator, wind, perc, tape, 1963; Fantasy for Pianist, 1964; Graffiti, orch, 1964; Ambages, fl, 1965; Masks, chorus 8vv, orch, 1965; Quick are the Mouths of Earth, 3 pic + fl, ob, tpt, trbn, b trbn, 2 perc, pf, 3 vc, 1964–5; Gathering, wind qnt, 1965

Blind Men, 24 solo vv, 3 tpt, 2 trbn, b trbn, tuba, perc, pf, 1966; Threshold, orch, 1967; . . . Between . . ., chamber orch, elec, 1968; Ping, after Beckett, fl, pf, harmonium, bowed cymbal, tamtam, elec, slides, tape, 1969; Again, 2S, 2 fl, 2 trbn, 2 db, 2 perc, 4-track tape, 1970; I/O: a ritual for 23 performers, 9 female vv, 9 male mimes, 2 fl, cl, 2 technicians, 1971; Compass, T, B-Bar, vc, db, elec, projections, 1972; Small Changes, 4-track tape, 2 16mm films, 1972; Promises of Darkness, 11 insts, 1976; Fiery Winds, orch, 1978

GILBERT CHASE

Reys [Reis, de Rais, de Reiz, de Restz, de Retz, du Retz, Polak], **Jakub** [Jacob] [Jacques le Polonois] (*b* Poland, *c*1540; *d* Paris, *c*1605). Polish lutenist and composer active in France. From archival documents and printed references it is now established that Jakub Reys and Jacques le Polonois were the same person. In 1574 he went to France in the retinue of Henri III, remaining there as lutenist and *valet de chambre ordinaire du roi* until his death. He was married in 1585 to the daughter of a merchant of Blois. In many contemporary references he is praised as one of the foremost lutenists of the period; his invention of a new style of playing is often alluded to, although precisely what this style was is not known.

Reys's skill as a performer is reflected in the many technical difficulties in his extant works. Some long passages and even whole compositions show the emergent major–minor tonal system, for example the fantasias in Besard's *Thesaurus harmonicus*. Even in largely imitative polyphonic compositions, the leading melodic line is clearly shaped by considerations of harmony and colour. He created interesting dissonances through the use of suspensions and retardations of melodic notes, especially at cadences. Many of his fantasias are clearly variational ricercares; interestingly, they appeared in the *Thesaurus harmonicus* at about the same time as Frescobaldi's variational ricercares, showing that the form appeared in both lute and keyboard music simultaneously. Reys's galliards (of which only four are extant) were especially admired by his contemporaries. They show virtually no trace of modality, and three exhibit the two- or three-section structure which was to be the principle of construction for the next two centuries: in the major keys, modulation to the dominant, and in the minor keys, modulation to the relative major. According to Praetorius, two types of courante were designated by the names of their composers, the 'Courante de Perrichon', and the 'duret'; the latter may have taken its name from a variant form of Reys's name, du Ret. His one sarabande, consisting of a theme and seven variations, is particularly interesting; it is the earliest known example of this dance of French provenance.

WORKS

Edition: *J. Polak: Preludia, fantazje i tańce*, ed. M. Szczepańska, WDMP, xxii (1951) [rev. 2nd edn. and fasc.2 in preparation]

Lute: 21 fantasias, 15 preludes, 6 intabulations of vocal pieces, ballet, 2 branles, 8 courantes, 4 galliards, sarabande, 7 volte; in 1603[15], 1610[23], 1612[18], 1615[24], 1617[26], and in *D-BAUk* 1 an 13, 4[0], 85, *D-W* Guelf.18.7–8.Aug.2[0] and *GB-Cfm* 3.1956

Keyboard intabulation by A. Gabrieli of vocal piece, in 1605[19], attrib. 'Jakob', possibly by Reys

BIBLIOGRAPHY
H. Opieński: 'Jacob Polonais et Jacobus Reys', *Riemann-Festschrift* (Leipzig, 1909), 349

F. Lesure: *Recherches sur les luthistes parisiens à l'époque de Louis XII* (Paris, 1958)

K. Wilkowska-Chomińska: *A la recherche de la musique pour luth* (Paris, 1958)

PIOTR POŹNIAK

Reyser, Georg (*fl* late 15th century). German printer. He received a licence to print liturgical writings from the Bishop of Würzburg, Rudolf von Scherenberg, and until about 1503 produced exemplary liturgical prints, some of which included music, for the dioceses of Würzburg, Mainz and Eichstätt. His relative Michael Reyser was the first to print in Gothic Hufnagel notation.

BIBLIOGRAPHY
R. Molitor: *Deutsche Choralwiegendrucke: ein Beitrag zur Geschichte des Chorals und der Notendrucker in Deutschland* (Regensburg, 1904), 49ff

K. Meyer: *Liturgical Music Incunabula: a Descriptive Catalogue* (London, 1962)

THEODOR WOHNHAAS

Reyzen, Mark (Osipovich) (*b* Zaytsevo, nr. Lugansk, 3 July 1895). Soviet bass. He studied with F. Bugamelli at the Kharkov Conservatory from 1917, made his début as Pimen in 1921 at the Kharkov Opera, sang at the State Academic Opera (now the Kirov), Leningrad (1925–30), then with the Bol'shoy Theatre, Moscow (1930–54). Reyzen was a leading Soviet opera singer of his time, winning both popular and critical acclaim. His voice, a *basso cantante* with a range of over two octaves, was warm and powerful, with a rare tonal beauty, and very well schooled. Musically and dramatically his performances were integrated and finely inflected, so that he could convey the confused feelings of Boris Godunov and the militant fanaticism of Dosifey, the satanic irony of Mephistopheles, the stupidity of Farlaf, and the pitiable greed of Don Basilio. His resourceful acting was enhanced by his excellent make-up. Greatest as Boris and Dosifey, he was also outstanding as Susanin, the Miller (*Rusalka*) and Verdi's King Philip. He sang in concerts, toured abroad, was made People's Artist of the USSR in 1937, and taught at the Gnesin Institute, Moscow (1954–8). He published 'Stranitsï vospominaniy' ('Pages of reminiscences'), *SovM* (1965), no.7, p.94.

BIBLIOGRAPHY
M. L'vov: 'Mark Osipovich Reyzen', *SovM* (1951), no.5, p.44

D. Kabalevsky and others: 'K 70-letiyu M. O. Reyzena' [For Reyzen's 70th birthday], *SovM* (1965), no.7, p.89

I. M. YAMPOL'SKY

Řezáč, Ivan (*b* Řevnice, nr. Prague, 5 Nov 1924; *d* Prague, 26 Dec 1977). Czech composer and writer on music. He studied composition with Dobiáš from 1949 to 1953 at the Prague Academy, where he became assistant lecturer in composition and, from 1961, vice-dean. Many of his articles were published in *Hudební rozhledy* and *Literární noviny*. His compositional style was influenced most strongly by Prokofiev, Shostakovich and Honegger. The overture to Mayakovsky's poem *The Right Cause* received a prize at the competition held in 1960 to celebrate the 15th anniversary of the liberation of Czechoslovakia.

WORKS
(selective list)

Orch: 3 pf concs., 1955, 1964, 1972; 2 syms., 1956, 1960; The Right

Cause, ov., 1959; Torzo Schumannova pomníku [Fragments of Schumann's monument], va, chamber orch, 1968; Introduction and Allegro, pf, orch, 1969; Vivace, 1977; Montage, 1977
Chamber: Pf Trio, a, 1958; Wind Qnt, 1971; Duo, vc, pf; Musica da camera, fl, ob, vn, va, vc, 1973; Trio, hn, vn, pf, 1975; Wind Octet, 1976
Pf: 2 sonatas, n.d.; Preludes, n.d.; Suchá jehla (Pointe-sèche), 1961; Sisyfova neděle [Sunday of Sisyphus], n.d.

Principal publishers: Panton, Supraphon

BIBLIOGRAPHY
ČSHS
B. Karásek: 'I. Řezáč: Trio a-moll pro klavír, housle a violoncello', HRo, xviii (1964), 115
J. Dehner: 'S Ivanem Řezáčem o možnostech hudby' [Řezáč on possibilities of music], HRo, xxiv (1971), 272

OLDŘICH PUKL

Rezitativ (Ger.). RECITATIVE.

Rezniček, E(mil) N(ikolaus) von (*b* Vienna, 4 May 1860; *d* Berlin, 2 Aug 1945). Austrian composer and conductor. He read law at the University of Graz from 1878. At the same time he studied music with Wilhelm Mayer (W. A. Rémy) and he completed his studies in 1884 at the Leipzig Conservatory under Reinecke and Jadassohn. He was répétiteur in Graz, then theatre conductor in Zurich, Mainz, Stettin, Berlin, Jena and Bochum. From 1888 he was for seven years military bandmaster in Prague where his comic opera *Donna Diana* was produced in 1894. The work was subsequently produced in several German theatres with great success, and has remained Rezniček's best-known work for its sparkling overture. In 1896 he was for a short time court conductor at Weimar and from 1896 to 1899 at Mannheim where he also conducted the academy concerts. He went to Berlin in 1902 as a conductor and also gave chamber concerts there; for a brief time from 1906 he taught theory at the conservatory. From December 1906 until 1909 he was conductor of the Warsaw Opera and PO, making frequent journeys into Russia. In November 1907 he conducted two concerts in London, introducing his Symphony in B♭. He was conductor of the Komische Oper, Berlin (1909–11), and of the Italian seasons under Hermann Gura until 1912, after which he concentrated on composition. In 1919 he was elected to the Berlin Academy of Arts and from 1920 to 1926 taught at the Hochschule für Musik.

WORKS
(selective list)
STAGE
(most published in vocal score in Leipzig or Berlin)
Operas: Die Jungfrau von Orleans (3, Rezniček, after Schiller), Prague, Deutsches Opernhaus, 19 June 1887; Satanella (2, Rezniček), Prague, Deutsches Opernhaus, 3 May 1888; Emmerich Fortunat (Rezniček), Prague, Deutsches Opernhaus, 8 Nov 1889; Donna Diana (3, Rezniček, after Moreto y Cavana: El desdén con el desdén), Prague, Deutsches Theater, 16 Dec 1894, rev. 1908, 1933; Till Eulenspiegel (2, Rezniček, after J. Fischart: Eulenspiegel Reimensweiss), Karlsruhe, 12 Jan 1902; Eros und Psyche (2, Rezniček), Breslau, Hoftheater, 1917
Ritter Blaubart (3, H. Eulenberg), Darmstadt, 29 Jan 1920; Holofernes (2, Rezniček, after Hebbel: Judith), Berlin, Deutsches Opernhaus, 27 Oct 1923; Tanzsymphonie (2, R. Lauckner), Leipzig, Staatsoper, 13 Jan 1927; Satuala (4, Lauckner), Leipzig, Stadttheater, 1927; Spiel oder Ernst? (1, P. Knudsen), Dresden, 11 Nov 1930; Der Gondoliere des Dogen (1, Knudsen), Stuttgart, Stadttheater, Oct 1931; Das Opfer, 1932; Tenor und Bass, 1, Stockholm, State Opera, 1934
Operetta: Die Angst vor der Ehe, Frankfurt am Oder, 1914
Incidental music: Drömspelet (Strindberg) (Berlin, 1916)
Rev. of Gounod: Le médecin malgré lui as Der Artzt wider Willen, Berlin, Königliche Oper, 3 Sept 1910

OTHER WORKS
Vocal: Requiem, d, n.d.; Der Sieger, A, chorus, orch (1913); In memoriam, A, Bar, chorus, org, str (1915); Vater unser, chorus, orch (1919); songs

Orch: Sym. no.1 'Tragic', 1904; Nachtstück, vn/vc, orch (1905); Sym. no.2 'Ironic', B♭ (1905); Sym. no.3, D (1918); Sym. no.4, f (1919); Serenade, G, str (1924); 4 Sym. Dances (1925); Vn Conc., e (1925); Raskolnikoff, ov. (1932); Lustspiel, ov., n.d.; 2 sym. suites, e, D, n.d.
Inst: 3 str qts, c (1921), d (1923), B (1932); Präludium und chromatische Fuge, C, org (1921); Org Fantasy (1930)

BIBLIOGRAPHY
O. Taubmann: Emil Nikolaus von Rezniček (Leipzig, 1907)
M. Chop: Emil Nikolaus von Rezniček: sein Leben und seine Werk (Vienna, 1920)
R. Specht: Emil Nikolaus von Rezniček: eine vorläufige Studie (Vienna, 1923)
H. Killer: 'Gedanken über einen Meister: E. N. von Rezniček', Die Musik, xxxii (1939–40), 224
W. Altmann: 'Emil Nikolaus von Rezniček zum Gedächtnis', Neue Musik-Zeitschrift (1950)
F. von Rezniček: Gegen den Strom (Vienna, 1960) [with survey of works by L. Nowak]

ANDREW LAMB

Rezon, Johannes. See RESON, JOHANNES.

rf [rfz]. *See* RINFORZANDO.

R. H. Right hand (also Ger., *rechte Hand*).

Rhapsode. A professional declaimer of the epic poetry of Homer in ancient Greece; *see* AOIDOS.

Rhapsody (Fr. *rapsodie*; Ger. *Rhapsodie*; It. *rapsodia*). Originally the song of the ancient Greek rhapsodist, or professional reciter and chanter of epic poetry. An epic poem such as Homer's *Iliad* consists of a number of rhapsodies recited or written down in sequel. The term was applied to instrumental music early in the 19th century and is among the innovatory titles employed by Tomašek; it was first used by him in a set of six rhapsodies for piano (*c*1803). His pupil Alexander Dreyschock added other works to this repertory.

The rhapsody had no regular form and was not confined to any particular medium. Early examples are restrained in character, but free fantasias of an epic, heroic or national character were later often given the title, and during the 19th century its utterance became more ebullient and high-flown and its emotion more uncontrolled.

A piece whose nature shows the beginnings of the extravagance found later in the century, and which certainly influenced Liszt, is Schubert's *Divertissement à l'hongroise* for piano duet (D818), composed in 1824. The identification of the rhapsodic quality in music with Hungarian or gypsy violin playing reached its zenith in the 19 Hungarian Rhapsodies of Liszt (1846–85); he wrote them for orchestra and arranged most of them for the piano. They are characterized by remarkable changes of mood, supposed to be typical of the Slav temperament, moods which range from deep gloom to joyful excitement. This is perhaps why rhapsodies by composers such as Dvořák, Dohnányi, Bartók and Enescu display the same temperamental variety of mood, whereas those by the German Brahms are more disciplined. Dvořák composed his rhapsodies for orchestra; there is a Rhapsody in A minor (1874), but the important ones are the three Slavonic Rhapsodies of op.45 (1878), based on folktunes. Dohnányi composed four rhapsodies for piano in 1910, which were published as his op.11. The rhapsodies of Bartók, similar in style to concertos, are op.1 for piano and orchestra (1904) and two for violin and orchestra (1928). Enescu published his two Romanian Rhapsodies (1901–2) as his op.11. Brahms's *Rhapsodie* op.53, for contralto, men's chorus and orchestra, justifies its title, in the Greek sense, inasmuch as it is a setting – a recitation, or rhapsody – of a portion of Goethe's poem *Harzreise in Winter*. He composed three rhapsodies for the piano, the two of op.79 (1879) earning him the description of 'the young heaven-storming Johannes'. Many of his Hungarian Dances are rhapsodies in all but name.

Folktunes and popular music or material influenced by their idioms have also been the basis of a number of pieces in this form, usually for orchestra, by English nationalist composers of the 20th century (Vaughan Williams: *Norfolk Rhapsody*, George Butterworth: *A Shropshire Lad*), and comparable works have also been written by composers in other countries apart from those already mentioned. Chabrier's *España* (1883) is one of the most celebrated and successful of them. Other examples of the form display little or no folk influence and are more akin to symphonic poems; an example is John Ireland's symphonic rhapsody *Mai-Dun* (1920–21).

BIBLIOGRAPHY

V. Jankélévitch: *La rhapsodie, verve et improvisation musicale* (Paris, 1955)

MAURICE J. E. BROWN

Rhau [Rhaw], **Georg** (*b* Eisfeld an der Werre, Suhl, 1488; *d* Wittenberg, 6 Aug 1548). German publisher, primarily of music and books on musical theory and theology. Working in Wittenberg, rather removed from the main centres of European music publication, Rhau became one of the most important publishers of music, particularly for the Reformation church. Working with church leaders, he provided them with an extensive repertory of music that would meet the liturgical requirements of the service, and the artistic and educational needs of their schools.

On 15 April 1512 he enrolled at the University of Wittenberg, and in 1514 completed requirements for the BA degree. He then began a long association with the publishing business, working for four years in the publishing house of Johann Rhau-Grunenberg (presumably his uncle). In the summer of 1518 he left Wittenberg to become Kantor of the Thomasschule and Thomaskirche in Leipzig, a position he held until at least 1 May 1520. On 18 September 1518 he also joined the faculty of the University of Leipzig, lecturing in music theory.

Whether Rhau was associated with the circle of theologians surrounding Luther in Wittenberg is not clear. Nevertheless, as a former student at the University of Wittenberg and a resident of that city at the time of the nailing of the 95 theses, Rhau was certainly aware of Luther's position. In Leipzig, he seems to have become more directly involved. In June 1519 he wrote the *Missa de Sancto Spirito* for the service at the Thomaskirche which marked the opening of the disputations between Luther and Eck. This in itself implied no particular sympathy towards Luther's position, since such activity would have been normal to his duties as Kantor of the cathedral church. However, the growing enmity towards the Wittenbergers and Rhau's apparent sympathies put his position at the Thomaskirche in jeopardy, and it was necessary for him to leave Leipzig in 1520. He moved to Eisleben, where he accepted the post of *Ludimagister* of one of the Winkelschulen of the city. In 1521 or 1522 he became a teacher at Hildburghausen, and in 1523 he returned to

publishing in Wittenberg, where he remained until his death.

Rhau's publishing activities reflected his relationship to the new church. Publications with respect to both the literary and musical needs of the church appeared in large quantities, including many books on theology, exegeses of the books of the Bible written by Luther, Melanchthon and Bugenhagen, editions of Luther's Catechism, his sermons, the Augsburg Confession and doctrinal treatises, both apologetic and polemic. Rhau's close association with the Wittenberg theological circle is further demonstrated by the prefaces by Luther, Melanchthon and Bugenhagen for his various musical publications; also a number of the young theologians, while studying at the university, worked in varying capacities in Rhau's shop.

Georg Rhau. woodcut from 'Postremum vespertini officii opus' (1544)

The degree and extent to which Rhau's publications served the needs of early Protestantism is also reflected in the esteem accorded Rhau by his contemporaries. At his death, university classes were dismissed so that student body and faculty could participate in funeral observances. Caspar Creutziger, who as a student had also been employed by Rhau, acclaimed Rhau for his piety, for the extensive contributions to theology, mathematics and music provided by his publications, and for his services as a citizen. Rhau had served as town councillor from 1541 till his death in 1548. Nine years later, at the death of Rhau's daughter Margareta, the rector of the university also required that the students attend the funeral as an indication of respect for her father.

Rhau's enthusiasm for music had begun at an early age; he remarked in the preface of his *Postremum vespertini officii opus* that he had been occupied with music 'a pueritia'. It is also likely that, since the music curriculum at the University of Wittenberg was well developed, Rhau attended lectures in music. No known compositions of Rhau are extant, but his accomplishments as composer as well as performer are suggested by his having been appointed to the position of Kantor at the Thomaskirche. Even as late as 1548 (the year of his death), he assumed direction of the electoral choir in Torgau succeeding Johann Walter – a fact which suggests his continuing ability and interest in musical performance.

In publication of musical materials, Rhau's first efforts were directed towards theory. In 1517, while still employed in the offices of Grunenberg, he published the first part of his own treatise on musical theory, *Enchiridion utriusque musicae practicae*, devoted to the subject of plainchant (*musica choralis*). The second part, *Enchiridion musicae mensuralis*, appeared in 1520, while Rhau was in Leipzig. Although neither portion of the treatise was innovatory, the work enjoyed considerable success, appearing in successive editions – even after his death, as continued in publication by his heirs – until 1553. Beginning in 1517, he also brought out publications or new editions of theoretical works by Martin Agricola, Nicolaus Listenius, Wenceslaus Philomathes, Johann Galliculus and Johann Spangenberg.

In 1538 Rhau's interest turned chiefly to the publication of collections of polyphonic music. In his preface to *Vesperarum precum officia* he stated that it had always been his desire particularly to assist schoolboys by providing them with materials through which they might praise God and learn the truths of the Scriptures, and through which they might also love and study the honourable discipline of music. He further stated that from their early years the pupils should be exposed to the precepts of the musical art and through the singing of worthy examples learn to apply the rules to practical experience.

To fulfil these intentions Rhau published 15 major collections between 1538 and 1545, ranging from very simple works to those representative of the most highly developed Franco-Flemish polyphony, and which in keeping with his aims provided an extensive repertory of artistically significant music for both Mass and Vespers, arranged for the most part according to the seasons of the church year. The *Opus decem missarum* furnished settings of the Ordinary of the Mass in general, while the *Officia paschalia, de resurrectione et ascensione Domini* and the *Officiorum . . . de nativitate, circumcisione, epiphania Domini, et purificationis, etc.* supplied settings of both Ordinary and Proper, as complete services, for the Mass on the high feasts from Christmas to the Purification and from Easter to the Ascension respectively. The *Selectae harmoniae quatuor vocum de passione Domini* provided similar works, as well as appropriate motets, for Lent.

Three of the collections were for Vespers. The *Vesperarum precum officia* included complete settings of the choral portions (opening responses, antiphons and psalms, responsory, hymn, versicle, *Magnificat* with antiphon and *Benedicamus Domino*) for each day of the week; the *Sacrorum hymnorum* contained 134 settings of vesper hymns; and the *Postremum vespertini officii opus 25 Magnificat* settings. Three other collections provided settings by single composers of specific portions of Vespers: the *Novum ac insigne opus musicum* with settings by Sixt Dietrich of antiphons for each day of the week; the *Responsorum numero octoginta* with two volumes of responsories by Balthasar Resinarius; and the *Novum opus musicum* with three volumes of hymns by Sixt Dietrich.

Of the remaining volumes, four comprised materials for more general use within the school. The *Symphoniae iucundae* contained 52 motets, many of which were appropriate for use in the service. The *Tricinia* and *Bicinia*, each of two volumes, however, contained secular materials only, selected for their artistic merit, to serve in the development of the pupils' musical ability and taste. The final volume, the *Wittembergisch deudsch geistlich Gesangbüchlein*, constituted a new and enlarged edition of Johann Walter's *Gesangbüchlein* which had appeared in earlier editions (1524, 1525 and 1535) from other presses, but which now, because of its continuing usefulness, was issued by the press which had come to represent the very centre of publishing activities for the new church.

Rhau's musical publications as a whole present compositions which reflect procedures that had been traditionally associated with settings of liturgical texts at the beginning of and just before the Reformation, as seen in the works of the generation of Obrecht and Josquin. This generation is rather well represented in the publications. However, there is also a fairly extensive literature representative of a younger generation of German composers associated directly with the new church, and whose compositions are known through Rhau's publications. The publications are important, not only for the general quality and accuracy of the musical printing, but also for the preservation of a repertory useful for the study of the early Reformation worship service, its music, and the conservative attitudes towards musical style held by its composers.

WRITINGS

Enchiridion utriusque musicae practicae (Wittenberg, 1517; 2/1518 as
  Enchiridion musices ex variis musicorum libris depromptu, 9/1558,
  facs. edn., ed. H. Albrecht, Kassel, 1951; 13/n.d., but after 1553)
Enchiridion musicae mensuralis (Leipzig, 1520, 10/1553)

PUBLICATIONS
(all published in Wittenberg unless otherwise stated)

THEORETICAL

V. Philomathes: *Liber musicorum quartuor* (Leipzig, 1518)
J. Galliculus: *Isagoge de compositione cantus* (Leipzig, 1520; 2/1538 as
  Libellus de compositione cantus, 6/1553)
M. Agricola: *Ein kurtz Deudsche Musica* (1528; 3/1533 as *Musica
  Choralis Deudsch*)
——: *Musica instrumentalis deudsch* (1529); ed. R. Eitner (Leipzig,
  1896); 5/1545, ed. R. Eitner, 1896)
——: *Musica figuralis Deudsch* (1532)
——: *Von den Proporcionibus* (1532)
N. Listenius: *Rudimenta musicae* (1533; 3/1537 as *Musica Nic[olai]
  List[enii] denuo recognita*, 11/1557)
V. Philomathes: *De nova domo musicorum libri quatuor* (1534)
J. Spangenberg: *Quaestiones musicae in usum scholae Northusianae*
  (1536, 2/1542)
——: *Prosodia in usum iuventutis Northus* (1538)
J. Walter (i): *Lob und Preis der löblichen Kunst Musica* (1538, repr. 1938
  with commentary by W. Gurlitt)
M. Agricola: *Rudimenta musices* (1539/R1966)

MAJOR COLLECTIONS OF POLYPHONIC MUSIC

Edition: *G. Rhau: Musikdrucke aus den Jahren 1538 bis 1545 in
  praktischer Neuausgabe* (Kassel, 1955–) [individual vols. cited
  below]

Selectae harmoniae quatuor vocum de passione Domini (1538[2])
Symphoniae iucundae atque adeo breves quatuor vocum (1538[8]); ed. H.
  Albrecht (Kassel, 1959)
Officia paschalia, de resurrectione et ascensione Domini (1539[14])
Vesperarum precum officia: Psalmi feriarum et dominicalium dierum
  tocius anni, cum antiphonis, hymnis et responsoriis (1540[5]); ed. H. J.
  Moser (Kassel, 1960)
S. Dietrich: Novum ac insigne opus musicum triginta sex antiphon-
  arum (1541); ed. W. Buszin (Kassel, 1964)
Opus decem missarum quatuor vocum (1541[1])
Tricinia . . . latina, germanica, brabantia et gallica (1542[8])
Sacrorum hymnorum liber primus (1542[12]); ed. R. Gerber, EDM, 1st
  ser., Reichsdenkmale, xxi, xxxv (1942–3/R1974)
B. Resinarius: Responsorum numero octoginta de tempore et festis
  iuxta seriem totius anni, libri duo (1542); ed. I.-M. Schröder (Kassel,
  1955)
Newe deudsche geistliche Gesenge CXXIII. Mit vier und fünff Stimmen
  für die gemeinen Schulen (1544[21]/R1969 with commentary by L.
  Finscher); ed. H. J. Moser (Wiesbaden, 1958)

Postremum vespertini officii opus. . .Magnificat octo modorum seu
tonorum numero XXV (Wittenberg, 1544[4]); ed. P. Bunjes (Kassel,
1970)
J. Walther: Wittembergisch deudsch geistlich Gesangbüchlein. Mit vier
und fünff stimmen (1544); *J. Walter: Sämtliche Werke*, ed. O.
Schröder, i–iii, v (Kassel, 1953–61)
Bicinia gallica, latina, germanica. . .tomus primus (1545[6]); ed. H.
Mönkemeyer (Wilhelmshaven, 1963)
Secundus tomus biciniorum/quae et ipsa sunt gallica, latina, germanica
(1545[7]); ed. H. Mönkemeyer (Wilhelmshaven, 1963)
S. Dietrich: Novum opus musicum. Tres tomos sacrorum hymnorum
continens (1545); ed. H. Zenck (St Louis, 1960)
Officiorum (ut vocant) de nativitate, circumcisione, epiphania Domini,
et purificationis, etc (1545[5])

MINOR COLLECTIONS, WORKS CONTAINING MUSIC, ETC
J. Murmellius: Protrepticus studiosorum poetices (1517, 2/1533)
J. Greff: Ein geistliches schönes neues Spil (1537)
——: Mundus: ein schönes neues kurtzes Spiel von der Welt Art
(1537)
Christlike Kerken-Ordeninge, im Lande Brunschwig Wulffenbüttels
(1543)
Etliche Psalmen sampt den Symbols . . . inn Gesang bracht (1544)
J. Walther: Cantio septem vocum (1544); *J. Walter: Sämtliche Werke*,
ed. O. Schröder, v (Kassel, 1961)
J. Spangenberg: Zwölff Christliche Lobgesenge und Leissen (1545)
J. F. Petsch: Ein schön Lied von Dr M. Luther (1546)

BIBLIOGRAPHY
J. Reusch: *Epitaphia Rhauorum* (Wittenberg, 1550)
F. W. Rost: *Was hat die Leipziger Thomasschule für die Reformation
getan?* (Leipzig, 1817)
R. Eitner: 'Georg Rhaw: Biographie', *MMg*, x (1878), 120
O. Kade: 'Georg Rhaw', *MMg*, xi (1879), 27
G. Buchwald: 'Stadtschreiber M. Stephan Roth in Zwickau', *Archiv für
Geschichte des deutschen Buchhandels*, xvi (1893), 6–246
F. Spitta: 'Die Chorsammlung des Georg Rhaw 1544', *Monatschrift für
Gottesdienst und kirchliche Kunst*, xv (1910), 2
T. W. Werner: 'Die Magnificat-Kompositionen Adam Reners', *AMw*, ii
(1919–20), 235
W. Wölbing: *Der Drucker und Musikverleger Georg Rhaw: ein Beitrag
zur Drucker- und Verlagstätigkeit im Zeitalter der Reformation*
(diss., U. of Berlin, 1922) [includes complete list of Rhau's theological
publications]
H. Zenck: *Sixt Dietrich, ein Betrag zur Musik und Musikanschauung
der Reformation* (Leipzig, 1928)
W. Gosslau: *Die religiöse Haltung in der Reformationsmusik, nachge-
wiesen an den 'Newen Deudschen Geistlichen Gesengen' des Georg
Rhaw* (Kassel, 1933)
H. Albrecht: 'Sacrorum hymnorum liber primus, Besprechung der
Neuausgabe', *Mf*, i (1948), 201
L. Schrade: 'The Editorial Practice of Georg Rhaw', *The Musical
Heritage of the Church*, iv (1954), 31
I.-M. Schröder: *Die Responsorienvertonungen des Balthasar Resinarius*
(Kassel, 1954)
H. Albrecht: 'Zur Rolle der Kontrafaktur in Rhaus "Bicinia" ',
Festschrift Max Schneider (Leipzig, 1955), 67
A. Boes: 'Die reformatorischen Gottesdienste in der Wittenberger
Pfarrkirche von 1523 an', *Jb für Hymnologie und Liturgik*, iv (1958–
9), 1–40; vi (1961), 49–61
M. Geck: 'Rhau, Georg', *MGG*
V. H. Mattfeld: *Georg Rhaw's Publications for Vespers* (Brooklyn,
1966)
C. Parrish: 'A Renaissance Music Manual for Choirboys', *Aspects of
Medieval and Renaissance Music: a Birthday Offering for Gustave
Reese* (New York, 1966), 649
C. T. Gaines: *Georg Rhau: Tricinia, 1542* (diss., Union Theological
Seminary, 1970)
B. A. Bellingham: *The Bicinium in the Lutheran Latin Schools during
the Reformation Period* (diss., U. of Toronto, 1971)
W. Steude: *Untersuchungen zur Herkunft, Verbreitung und spezifi-
schem Inhalt mitteldeutscher Musikhandschriften des 16. Jahrhun-
derts* (diss., U. of Rostock, 1973)

VICTOR H. MATTFELD

Rhazes. *See* AL-RĀZĪ, ABŪ BAKR.

Rheims (Fr. Reims). City in northern France. It was
long France's ecclesiastical capital, and a city of prime
political importance while royal power depended
heavily on church support. It was less significant
musically, probably because it was never a royal
residence. Rheims achieved episcopal status towards the

end of the 3rd century under St Sixtus. It was an event
of crucial importance in European history when St
Remi (Remigius) baptized the Frankish King Clovis in
Rheims Cathedral on Christmas Day, 496. The political
importance of the city increased steadily in the
Carolingian era, and Pope Sylvester II (999–1002, formerly Gerbert of Aurillac, archbishop of Rheims 991–
5) published a bull recognizing the right of the arch-
bishops of Rheims to crown the kings of France. The
sacred ampulla of balm used in this ceremony was kept
at the monastery of St Remi and brought to the cathedral for the occasion. The Bibliothèque Municipale in
Rheims contains many manuscripts concerned with the
ceremony. The details of the ceremonial for the coronation of Charles V in 1365 (*F-RSc*, 1489) may be compared with those of a formulary in a British Museum
manuscript (Cotton Tiberius B VIII), which bears
Charles's own signature (see Dewick). Although it was
natural enough that Machaut's rise to fame should culminate in a canonicate at Rheims, there is no evidence
for the assertion that his setting of the Mass Ordinary
was composed for this occasion. Another splendid coronation was that of Louis XIV in 1654 (see illustration).

The Carolingian cathedral built through the zeal and
munificence of Hincmar and dedicated in about 860 was
destroyed in 1210. Notre Dame Cathedral was built
between 1211 and 1311; the chapter took over the choir
in 1241. At the time of Gerbert, Rheims was the first of
the great cosmopolitan medieval schools. Gerbert gave
the cathedral an organ in 992, and there was an organ
on the screen in the 13th century. In 1469 a larger two-
manual instrument was built in the north transept by
Etienne Enoque and restored after the fire of 1481 by
Oudin Hêtre. Further rebuildings took place in 1570
(Denys Collet of Rheims), 1619 (Nicolas Hocquet of
Nancy), 1647 and 1765 (Péronard). Between 1845 and
1849 John Abbey built an instrument of 53 stops, with
three manuals and pedals. Plans for further rebuilding
by Mutin, a pupil of Cavaillé-Coll, were stopped by
World War I, and it was not until 1937 that Gonzalez of
Châtillon-sous-Bagneux, advised by the cathedral organist L. Lartilleux, Marcel Dupré and Norbert Dufourcq,
constructed an 87-stop instrument, with the biggest
pedal organ in France (20 stops).

Although the office may have been established earlier,
the first recorded *maître de chapelle* was Jean Petit, who
was sent to Cambrai for training in 1465 and made
master of the choristers on his return. The Clicquot
family of organ builders and Pascal Collasse, Lully's
assistant, came from Rheims, and Nicolas de Grigny
was organist of the cathedral from 1697 to his death in
1703. In 1749 Henri Hardouin, *maître* from that year,
formed a music society which performed ballets, symphonies, motets and other works in the Grande Salle
Basse of the Hôtel de Ville; in 1752 the society became
the Académie de Musique de Reims, and Hardouin
directed its activities for nearly 20 years. For the coronation of Charles X in 1824 Cherubini composed a
setting of the mass for three-part choir and orchestra, a
motet, *Confirma hoc Deus*, and a *Marche religieuse*
played during the communion. Louis Fanart, *maître de
chapelle* of the cathedral, founded the Société
Philharmonique in 1833. In 1902 the new church of Ste
Clotilde was made a basilica by Pope Leo XIII, who
granted to France a national jubilee and composed for it
a Latin 'Ode to France', which inspired Théodore

A L'Autel où le Roy est sacré.
B Le Roy ayant receu l'Onction se
   releue pour prendre la Cou-
   ronne.
C Monsieur l'Euesque de Soissons
   tient la Couronne du Roy,
   tandis que tous les Ducs &
   Pairs s'approchent, pour y
   mettre tous la main, afin de la
   poser sur la teste du Roy.
D Monsieur le Chancelier.
E Monsieur le Connestable.
F Messieurs les Pairs Ecclesiastiques.
G Messieurs les Ducs & Pairs laics.
H Monseigneur le Cardinal Gri-
   maldi.

I Monseigneur le Cardinal Maza-
   rin.
K Plusieurs Euesques en rochet, qui
   n'officioient pas.
L Les trois Mareschaux de France
   portans les honneurs.
M Les quatre Secretaires d'Estat.
N Messieurs les Barons qui furent
   querir la sainte Ampoulle,
   ayans chacun vn Guidon à la
   main armorié de leurs armes,
   estoient M. de Richelieu, M.
   de Biron, M. de Coaslin, & M.
   de Manchiny.
O Les Maistres des Ceremonies.

P Loge proche l'Autel, où estoient
   les Reines de France & d'An-
   gleterre.
Q Les Gardes Escossoises de la Man-
   che.
R Les Herauts.
S Les Trompettes, Tambours,
   Hautbois & Fifres.
T Exempts & Gardes du Corps du
   Roy, estans vers la porte du
   Chœur, pour empescher le des-
   ordre.
V Pavillon où le Roy fut se confes-
   fer.
X Messieurs les Ambassadeurs, de
   Rome, Portugal, Venise,
   Genes, &c.

Y Toute la Musique de la Chapelle
   du Roy.
Z Lieu où estoient les Filles de la
   Reine.
1 Les Chanoines dans leurs hautes
   & basses chaires.
2 Echaffaut autour du Chœur, où
   estoient toutes sortes de per-
   sonnes de qualité.
A droit & à gauche du Chœur
   estoient les cent Gentilshommes dits
   Becs de Corbin, & Monsieur le Marquis d'Humieres à la teste; & dans ce
   grand nombre d'Officiers qui sont
   necessaires auprés du Roy, vous y
   remarquerez tous ceux dont i'ay par-
lé dans la Seance: sçauoir, le Grand
   Chambellan, le Grand Maistre de
   la Maison du Roy, le Premier Gentilhomme de la Chambre, & les deux
   Capitaines des Gardes du Corps,
   les deux Huissiers de la Chambre, &
   les premiers Valets de Chambre du
   quartier, qui ne se peuuent pas mon-
   trer par lettres de renuoy n'estans
   plus dans la seance, & estant meslez
   les vns parmy les autres, comme aussi
   les Euesques assistans, celuy de Rennes, de Coutances, de Rhodes, de S.
   Pol, d'Agde, & celuy de Leon.

The coronation (1654) of Louis XIV in Rheims Cathedral: engraving by Antoine Le Pautre

Dubois' oratorio *Le baptême de Clovis*. In 1913 an Ecole Municipale de Musique was founded, which became the Ecole Nationale de Musique de Reims in 1951.

BIBLIOGRAPHY

G. Marlot: *Histoire de la ville, cité et université de Reims* (Rheims, 1843–6)
C. Cerf: *Histoire et description de Notre-Dame de Reims* (Rheims, 1861)
——: 'Anciens usages dans quelques églises de Reims', *Travaux de l'Académie nationale de Reims*, xciii (1894), 315
E. S. Dewick: *The Coronation Book of Charles V of France* (London, 1899)
B.-E. Kalas: *La musique à Reims* (Rheims, 1910)
——: *La Société philharmonique de Reims* (Rheims, 1924)
J. Leflon: *Henri Hardouin et la musique du chapitre de Reims au XVIIIe siècle* (Rheims, 1933)
——: *Gerbert, humanisme et chrétienté au Xe siècle* (St Wandrille, 1946)
J. Wörsching: *Die Orgelwerke der Kathedrale zu Reims* (Mainz, 1946)
N. Dufourcq: *Le livre de l'orgue français, 1589–1789*, i (Paris, 1971), 65f, 261ff

DAVID HILEY

Rheinberger, Joseph (Gabriel) (*b* Vaduz, 17 March 1839; *d* Munich, 25 Nov 1901). German composer, organist, conductor and teacher. He was the son of the Prince of Liechtenstein's treasurer Johann Peter Rheinberger and Elisabeth Carigiet, who came from the Rhaeto-Romanic canton of Grisons. The first to discover his talent was the organist and teacher Sebastian Pöhli, from whom he had his first lessons at the age of five. He made such startling progress that when he was seven he was able to take on the post of organist in Vaduz; he also began to write music, including a three-part mass with organ accompaniment. But it was not until 1848 that he received further training from the choir director of Feldkirch, Philipp Schmutzer, who taught him harmony, the piano and organ, also introducing him to the works of Bach and the Viennese Classical composers. Although by this time he was making frequent public appearances as a pianist, it was only through pressure and persuasion from the composer Nagiller that, after much delay, the boy's father decided to send him for further study to Munich, where he moved in 1851, making it his permanent home.

At the Munich Conservatory, where Franz Hauser was director, Rheinberger studied theory with J. H. Maier, the organ with J. G. Herzog and the piano with J. E. Leonhard; later he also had occasional private instruction from Franz Lachner. Even in his student days (up to 1854) his rapidly developing talent, as an organist and in such techniques as counterpoint, fugue and score-reading, won much admiration. Among those who played an active part in his development K. F. E. von Schafhäutl in particular had an important and beneficial influence on the intellectual and spiritual growth of the young artist. As early as 1853 Rheinberger was employed as an organist at a number of churches and also earned his living as a private music teacher. Above all, he devoted himself with great zeal to composition, and in the next few years he wrote well over 100 works of the widest variety; but he was critical of all these early works and did not release them; his op.1, four piano pieces, appeared only in 1859. That year he was taken on the staff of the conservatory, first as a piano teacher and then in theory subjects as well; in addition he became organist at St Michael's Church and soon achieved some notable early successes as a composer with a *Stabat mater* and incidental music to Calderón's *El mágico prodigioso*. In 1864 he succeeded

Perfall as conductor of the Munich Choral Society, a post he held until 1877; during this period he proved himself an able choral conductor, especially of works by Handel. He also worked for a time as a coach at the court opera and thus witnessed at close quarters the events and feuds surrounding Richard Wagner's stay in Munich, which culminated in the première of *Tristan und Isolde*. In 1867 he became a professor at the conservatory, where he remained until his death a highly revered, much sought-after and increasingly renowned teacher. Bülow, who was a friend of his and also did much to promote his compositions, said 'Rheinberger is a truly ideal teacher of composition, unrivalled in the whole of Germany and beyond in skill, refinement and devotion to his subject; in short, one of the worthiest musicians and human beings in the world'.

In 1867 Rheinberger married his former pupil Franziska von Hoffnaass (1832–92), a socially influential and widely cultured woman who was also a gifted poetess (Rheinberger set much of her poetry). Her diary is of biographical as well as contemporary historical interest. Rheinberger was now frequently plagued by ill-health; he nevertheless continued to compose indefatigably, enjoying the company of a few valued friends, as befitted his retiring, somewhat melancholy nature. His career was accompanied by many, if not all spectacular, successes which brought him numerous honours and marks of recognition. In 1877 he was appointed Hofkapellmeister, and thereby acquired considerable influence on the cultivation of sacred music. In 1894 he was ennobled and awarded the title of privy councillor; in 1899 the University of Munich awarded him an honorary doctorate. He was also a member of the Berlin Royal Academy (1887) and a corresponding member of the Paris and Florence academies. He died a few weeks after his retirement. His grave in Munich was destroyed during World War II and since 1950 he has lain buried in his birthplace. His entire artistic legacy went to the Bayerische Staatsbibliothek.

Rheinberger's lasting fame resulted primarily from his teaching. Many important musicians and musical scholars were the product of his rigorous schooling, including Humperdinck, Wolf-Ferrari, Thuille, Sandberger, Kroyer, Trunk, the Pembaurs, Schmid-Lindner, Buonamici, Horatio Parker, G. S. Chadwick and Furtwängler. At a time when young people were pressing towards new goals with a thirst for freedom and a belief in progress, he imparted to his students a sound and extensive knowledge based on classical tradition. It was typical of his generous nature that, although he himself disliked the work of Wagner and Liszt and was no partisan of the New German School, he never tried to influence the young artists in his care through his personal views. Bonds with tradition are also characteristic of Rheinberger's work as a composer, which derives from Bach, Mozart and the middle-period Beethoven as well as other early Romantics; he consciously remained aloof from the new currents that developed in the mid-19th century. The strength of his works, in every sphere, lies in the indisputable mastery and the planned coherence of his compositional style, which is imbued with the spirit of polyphonic thinking rather than compelling inventiveness or vivid conception. The survival of his work is thus prejudiced not so much by an absence of links with the musical development of his time as by a certain academic approach and want of lively intensity of expression. Nevertheless, even his best works are only rarely heard: his work remains valued chiefly by organists and Catholic choirmasters. Certainly he produced his most outstanding and highly individual work in the 20 organ sonatas, which are rich in artistry and ideas, but he also made a significant contribution to sacred music, especially in the works written after 1877, in which he went his own way in contrast to the stylistic inflexibility of followers of the Cecilian movement. The wide range of his compositions offers many worthwhile opportunities for the rediscovery of his work.

WORKS

Principal MS collection is in *D-Mbs*. All printed works were first published in Leipzig. For a complete list of works, see H.-J. Irmen: *Joseph Rheinberger: thematisches Verzeichnis seiner Kompositionen* (Regensburg, 1975).

INSTRUMENTAL

Orchestral: Wallenstein, sym. poem, op.10; Der Widerspenstigen Zähmung, ov., after Shakespeare, op.18; Sym. no.2, F, op.87; Pf Conc., A♭, op.94; Demetrius, ov., after Schiller, op.110; 2 org concs., F, op.137, g, op.177; Akademische Festouvertüre in Form einer Fuge mit sechs Themen, op.195

Chamber without pf: Nonet, fl, ob, cl, bn, hn, vn, va, vc, db, op.139; Str Qnt, a, op.82; 3 str qts, c, op.89, g, op.93, F, op.147

Chamber with pf: Qnt, C, op.114; Qt, E♭, op.38; 4 trios, d, op.34, A, op.112, B♭, op.121, F, op.191a; 2 vn sonatas, E♭, op.77, e, op.105; Cello Sonata, C, op.92

For pf: 4 sonatas, 'Symphonic', C, op.47, D♭, op.99, E♭, op.135, 'Romantic', f♯, op.184; numerous other pf pieces, incl. Studien über ein Thema von Händel, op.45

For pf 4 hands: Tarantella, op.13; Aus den Ferientagen, op.72; Fantasia, op.79; Sonata, c, op.122

For 2 pf: Duo, op.15; arr., Bach: Goldberg Variations, ed. M. Reger (1915)

For org: 20 sonatas, c, op.27, 'Fantasie-Sonate', A♭, op.65, 'Pastoral-Sonate', G, op.88, a, op.98, f♯, op.111, e♭, op.119, f, op.127, e, op.132, b♭, op.142, b, op.146, d, op.148, D♭, op.154, E♭, op.161, C, op.165, D, op.168, g♯, op.175, 'Fantasie-Sonate', B, op.181, A, op.188, g, op.193, 'Zur Friedensfeier', F, op.196; other works, org solo; Suite, org, vn, vc, op.149; 2 suites, vn, org, opp.150 and 166

VOCAL

Stage: Die sieben Raben (opera, 3, F. Bonn and F. von Hoffnaass), Munich, 1869, op.20; Der wundertätige Magus (incidental music, Calderón), op.30; Die unheilbringende Krone (incidental music, F. Raimund), op.36; Der arme Heinrich (children's Singspiel, Bonn), op.37; Türmers Töchterlein (opera, 4, M. Stahl), Munich, 1873, op.70; Das Zauberwort (children's Singspiel, 2, Hoffnaass), op.153

Masses: 1v, org, op.62; d, 4vv, op.83; E♭, 3vv, op.109; 'Ss Trinitatis', F, 4vv, op.117; 'In nativitate Domini', A, 3 female vv, org, op.126; 'Ss Crucis', G, 4vv, op.151; 'Ss Reginae Rosarii', E♭, 3 female vv, org, op.155; f, 4vv, org, op.159; C, solo vv, chorus, orch, op.169; B♭, male vv, org/wind insts, op.172; 'Sincere in memoriam', g, 3 female vv, org, op.187; F, 4 male vv, org, op.190; 'Misericordias Domini', E, chorus, orch, op.192; a, chorus, orch, frag., completed by L. A. Coerne as op.197

Other sacred: 3 Requiem, b♭, op.60, E♭, op.84, d, op.194; 2 Stabat mater, solo vv, chorus, orch, op.16, chorus, str orch, org, op.138; Das Töchterlein das Jairus, children's cantata, op.32; Christophorus (Hoffnaass), legend, solo vv, chorus, orch, op.120; Der Stern von Bethlehem (Hoffnaass), Christmas cantata, solo vv, chorus, orch, org, op.164; hymns, motets, sacred songs

Secular vocal: Das Tal des Espingo (P. Heyse), ballad, 4 solo vv, male chorus, orch, op.50; Toggenburg (Hoffnaass), cycle of romances, solo vv, chorus, orch, op.76; Klärchen auf Eberstein (Hoffnaass), ballad, solo vv, chorus, pf, op.97; Wittekind (F. Halm), ballad, male vv, orch, op.102; Die Rosen von Hildesheim (Hoffnaass), ballad, male vv, brass insts, op.143; Montfort, 'Eine Rheinsaga' (Hoffnaass), solo vv, chorus, orch, op.145; Vom goldenen Horn, Turkish Liederspiel, solo vv, chorus, pf, op.182; other choral songs, ballads; c70 songs, 1v, pf, various op. nos.; 30 Children's Songs, op.152

BIBLIOGRAPHY

A. Hinger: 'J. Rheinberger', *Jb des Historischen Vereins für das Fürstentum Liechtenstein*, ii (1903)

R. Molitor: *Joseph Rheinberger und seine Kompositionen für die Orgel* (Leipzig, 1904)

T. Kroyer: *Joseph Rheinberger* (Regensburg and Rome, 1916)

A. Sandberger: 'Joseph Rheinberger', *Ausgewählte Aufsätze zur Musikgeschichte* (Munich, 1921)

H. Grace: *The Organ Works of Rheinberger* (London, 1925)

W. Altmann: *Handbuch für Streichquartettspieler* (Berlin, 1928)

——: *Handbuch für Klaviertriospieler* (Wolfenbüttel, 1934)

H. W. Kaufmann, ed.: 'Joseph Rheinberger: Gedenkschrift zu seinem 100.Geburtstag', *Jb des historischen Vereins für das Fürstentum Liechtenstein*, xl (1940)

H. Wanger, ed.: *J. Rheinberger: Briefe an seine Eltern (1851–1872)* (Vaduz, 1961)

H.-J. Irmen: *Gabriel Josef Rheinberger als Antipode des Cäcilianismus* (Regensburg, 1970)

H.-J. Irmen, ed.: *J. Rheinberger: Briefe an Henriette Hecker* (Vaduz, 1970)

A. Schmid-Lindner: 'Aus meinen Erinnerungen an Joseph Rheinberger', 'Joseph Rheinbergers polyphonie Klaviermusik', *Ausgewählte Schriften* (Tutzing, 1973)

H.-J. Irmen, ed.: *Engelbert Humperdinck als Kompositionsschüler Josef Rheinbergers* (Cologne, 1974–)

H.-J. Irmen: *Joseph Rheinberger: thematisches Verzeichnis seiner Kompositionen* (Regensburg, 1975)

ANTON WÜRZ

Rheineck, Christoph (*b* Memmingen, 1 Nov 1748; *d* Memmingen, 29 July 1797). German composer. He received musical training during his youth, but his father decided that he should become a merchant. After practising this trade in St Gall (1768), in 1769 he settled in Lyons, where he composed and successfully presented two *opéras comiques*, Le nouveau Pygmalion and Le fils reconnoissant (1774–5); the latter attracted the attention of Turgot, the French minister of finance, who promised to obtain for him a position in Paris. After a preliminary visit in 1775, however, Rheineck arrived in Paris to find Turgot in disgrace and unable to fulfil his promise. He returned to Memmingen, where he became proprietor of the inn Zum weissen Ochsen. There he frequently presented concerts in which he himself participated as singer, pianist and clarinettist, and which featured such eminent virtuosos as Clementi and Vanhal. In 1776, for his own marriage, he composed a wedding cantata to a text by his friend and admirer C. F. D. Schubart, who conducted the performance. Until 1790 he also served as music director of St Martin's Church.

Rheineck was a successful lied composer, and was particularly adept at setting humorous and folklike poetry. The keyboard accompaniment of these predominantly strophic works is frequently independent of the voice and the harmonic writing often imaginative, but there are occasional awkward progressions. Rheineck also wrote sacred music, now mostly lost, and a number of unpretentious instrumental pieces for amateurs.

WORKS

Operas, lost: Le nouveau Pygmalion (opéra comique, B. Desgagniers), Lyons, 9 Aug 1774, lib publd; Le fils reconnoissant (opéra comique), Lyons, 1775; Rinaldo (Singspiel, C. Städele), Wolfegg, 12 Sept 1779

Choral: Wedding cantata (C. F. D. Schubart), Memmingen, 15 July 1776, lost; Der Todesgang Jesu (Städele), Augsburg, 8 April 1778, only lib extant; Missa solemnis, *D-B*, *HR*

Lieder: Lieder mit Clavier Melodien, i (Nuremberg, 1779), ii–vi (Memmingen, 1780–92); 56 neue Melodien zu den zwoten vermehrten Ausgabe Schelhorns geistliche Liedersammlung (Memmingen, 1780) [incl. lieder by C. P. E. Bach, J. A. Hiller, J. H. Rolle, Heinsius, Wernhammer]; 19 in Blumenlese für Klavierliebhaber, ed. H. P. Bossler (Speyer, 1782–4); others in *B*

Inst: 3 kbd concs., 3 sonatas, kbd 4 hands, *B*; kbd pieces in Blumenlese für Klavierliebhaber (Speyer, 1782–4), Sammlung vermischter Clavierstücke, ii (Nuremberg, 1784)

BIBLIOGRAPHY

GerberL

C. F. D. Schubart: *Ideen zu einer Ästhetik der Tonkunst* (Vienna, 1806/*R*1969)

B. Schelhorn: *Lebensbeschreibungen einiger des Andenken würdigen Männer von Memmingen* (Memmingen, 1811)

M. Friedlaender: *Das deutsche Lied im 18. Jahrhundert* (Stuttgart and Berlin, 1902/*R*1970)

H. Kretzschmar: *Geschichte des neuen deutschen Liedes*, i (Leipzig, 1911/*R*1966)

F. Oberborbeck: *Christoph Rheineck: ein Beitrag zur Musikgeschichte suddeutscher Reichsstädte im 18. Jahrhundert* (diss., U. of Bonn, 1923; extracts in *ZMw*, v, 1922–3, p.598, and *Memminger Geschichtsblätter*, ix/3, 1923)

E. F. Schmid: 'Christoph Rheineck', *Lebensbilder aus dem bayerischen Schwaben*, vii (1959), 324

DAVID OSSENKOP

Rheinhardt. *See* REINHARDT family.

Rheinische Philharmonie. Orchestra founded in 1945 in KOBLENZ.

Rhete, Jerzy. *See* RHETUS, GEORG.

Rhetoric and music. The connections between rhetoric and music have often been extremely close, notably in the Baroque period. The influence of the principles of rhetoric profoundly affected the basic elements of music. (*See also* ANALYSIS, §II, 1.)

1. Introduction. 2. Musical-rhetorical concepts. 3. Musical figures. 4. The Affections. 5. Conclusion.

1. INTRODUCTION. Interrelationships between music and the spoken arts – *artes dicendi* (grammar, rhetoric, dialectic) – are at once obvious and unclear. Until fairly late in the history of Western civilization, music was predominantly vocal and thus bound to words. Composers have therefore generally been influenced to some degree by rhetorical doctrines governing the setting of texts to music, and even after the growth of independent instrumental music, rhetorical principles continued for some time to be used not only for vocal music but for instrumental works too. What still remains to be fully explained is how these critical interrelationships often controlled the craft of composition, at least until well into the 18th century. These developments are unclear partly because modern musicians and scholars are untrained in the rhetorical disciplines, which since the beginning of the 19th century have largely disappeared from most educational and philosophical systems.

All rhetorically related musical concepts originated in the extensive literature on oratory and rhetoric by ancient Greek and Roman writers, especially Aristotle, Cicero and Quintilian. The rediscovery in 1416 of Quintilian's *Institutio oratoria* provided one of the primary sources on which the growing union between rhetoric and music was based in the 16th century. Quintilian, like Aristotle before him, stressed the similarities between music and oratory. The goal of his work and all other studies of oratory since antiquity was the same: to instruct the orator in the means of controlling and directing the emotional responses of his audience or, in the language of classical rhetoric and also later music treatises, to enable the orator (i.e. the composer or even the performer) to move the 'Affections' (i.e. the emotions) of his listeners (see §4 below).

While early Christian sacred music has not been adequately studied to consider the potential influence on it of rhetorical concepts, it appears certain that Gregorian chant itself displays frequent and varied reflections of rhetorical expression. There is some evidence (see Flotzinger) for believing that a similar influence was exerted on early polyphony. The direct impact of classical rhetorical thought on music first became unmistakable, however, with the advent of Renaissance humanism in the late 15th century. It was then that classical as well as contemporary books on rhetoric became the basis of an important part of European educational curricula. This development occurred both in Catholic countries as well as in those regions that became Protestant after the Reformation. Elementary Latin schools and universities placed similar emphasis on the study of oratory and rhetoric, and every educated man was a skilled rhetorician. This universal development had a profound impact on composers' attitudes to text-bound music, sacred as well as secular, and led to new musical styles and forms of which the madrigal and opera are only the most obvious products.

These dramatic changes in music, which can in general be traced to humanist influences, confronted music theorists with problems foreign to all traditional music theory. Music, which since antiquity had belonged, with arithmetic, geometry and astronomy, to the Quadrivium – the mathematical disciplines – of the Seven Liberal Arts, was forced to adopt new theoretical values if it were to embrace these new rhetorically orientated musical styles. While music remained closely allied to mathematics up to the 18th century, it was German theorists in particular who raised musical composition to a science based on the relationship of words to music. As early as 1537 Listenius introduced a broad new division of music theory, which he called *musica poetica*, into the former Boethian duality of *musica theoretica* and *musica practica*. Another German, Joachim Burmeister, first proposed a systematic musical-rhetorical basis for such a *musica poetica* in his *Hypomnematum musicae* (1599) and its later versions, *Musica autoschediastikē* (1601) and *Musica poetica* (1606). His theory included the significant new idea of musical figures, which were analogous to the rhetorical figures found since antiquity in treatises on rhetoric (see §3 below). Johannes Lippius suggested in his *Synopsis musices* (1612) that rhetorical doctrine was not only the basis for an effective musical setting of words but also for the basis of the *forma* or structure of a composition. It is particularly revealing that many German theorists of this period observed that rhetorical expression occurred in the music of many Renaissance composers. Johannes Nucius, in his *Musices practicae* (1613), for example, considered Dunstable first among the composers belonging to a new tradition of rhetorically expressive music, a tradition in which he also included Binchois, Busnois, Clemens non Papa, Crecquillon, Isaac, Josquin, Ockeghem and Verdelot. Lassus, however, was the composer whom theorists most often singled out as a master of musical rhetoric.

Not until the Baroque period did rhetoric and oratory furnish so many of the essential rational concepts that lie at the heart of most compositional theory and practice. Beginning in the 17th century, analogies between rhetoric and music permeated every level of musical thought, whether involving definitions of styles, forms, expression and compositional methods, or various questions of performing practice. Baroque music in general aimed for a musical expression of words comparable to impassioned rhetoric or a *musica pathetica*. The union of music with rhetorical principles is one of the most distinctive characteristics of Baroque musical rationalism and gave shape to the progressive elements in the music theory and aesthetics of the period. Since the preponderantly rhetorical orientation of Baroque music evolved out of the Renaissance preoccupation with the impact of musical styles on the meaning and intelligibility of words (as for example in the theoretical discussions of the Florentine Camerata), nearly all the elements of music that can be considered typically

Baroque, whether the music be Italian, German, French or English, are tied, either directly or indirectly, to rhetorical concepts.

2. MUSICAL-RHETORICAL CONCEPTS. As early as 1563, in a manuscript entitled *Praecepta musicae poeticae*, Gallus Dressler referred to a formal organization of music that would adopt the divisions of an oration into *exordium* (opening), *medium* and *finis*. A similar structural plan appears in Burmeister's treatise of 1606. In both instances rhetorical terminology was raised to the level of defining compositional structure, and such a viewpoint remained valid until well into the 18th century. In 1739, in *Der vollkommene Capellmeister*, Mattheson laid out a fully organized, rational plan of musical composition borrowed from those sections of rhetorical theory concerned with finding and presenting arguments: *inventio* (invention of an idea), *dispositio* (arrangement of the idea into the parts of an oration), *decoratio* (the elaboration or decoration of the idea) – called *elaboratio* or *elocutio* by other writers – and *pronuntiatio* (the performance or delivery of the oration). Dressler's structure of *exordium*, *medium* and *finis* was only a simplified version of the more usual sixfold division of the *dispositio*, which in classical rhetoric as well as in Mattheson consisted of *exordium*, *narratio* (statement of facts), *divisio* or *propositio* (forecast of main points in a speaker's favour), *confirmatio* (affirmative proof), *confutatio* (refutation or rebuttal) and *peroratio* or *conclusio* (conclusion).

While neither Mattheson nor any other Baroque theorist would have applied these rhetorical prescriptions rigidly to every musical composition, it is clear that such concepts not only aided composers to a varying degree but were self-evident to them as routine techniques in the compositional process. Nor was rhetorical structure limited to German music theory. Mersenne, for example, in his *Harmonie universelle* (1636–7) emphasized that musicians were orators who must compose melodies as if they were orations, including all of the sections, divisions and periods appropriate to an oration. Kircher, writing in Rome, gave the title 'Musurgia rhetorica' to one section of his highly influential encyclopedia of the theory and practice of music, *Musurgia universalis* (1650); in it he also emphasized the analogy between rhetoric and music in the common divisions of the creative process into *inventio*, *dispositio* and *elocutio*.

The vitality of such concepts is evident throughout the Baroque period and even later. Just as an orator had first to invent an idea (*inventio*) before he could develop his oration, so the Baroque composer had to invent a musical idea that was a suitable basis for construction and development. Since each musical idea must express an inherent or sometimes an imposed affective element of the text to which it was joined, composers often required aids to stimulate their musical imagination. Not every poetic text possessed an affective idea suitable for musical invention, but again rhetoric provided the means to assist the *ars inveniendi*. In *Der General-Bass in der Composition* (1728), Heinichen extended the analogy with rhetoric to include the *loci topici*, the standard rhetorical devices available to help the orator uncover topics – i.e. ideas – for a formal discourse. The *loci topici* are rationalized categories of topics from which suitable ideas for invention could be drawn. Quintilian described them as 'sedes argumentorum' –

sources of argument. On the most elementary level they were symbolized by the well-known questions that he posed for any legal dispute: whether a thing is (*an sit*), what it is (*quid sit*) and of what kind it is (*quale sit*). Heinichen (see Buelow, 1966) employed the *locus circumstantiarum*, namely the use of a textual antecedent, concomitant or consequent – i.e. a preceding recitative, the first (*A*) section of an aria, and the second (*B*) section or a subsequent recitative – as sources of musical ideas for aria texts. In *Der vollkommene Capellmeister* Mattheson criticized him for limiting himself to only the *loci* of circumstance and urged the full employment of several other *loci* commonly used by rhetoricians, such as the *locus descriptionis*, *locus notationis* and *locus causae materialis*. It is not unimportant that both Heinichen and Mattheson were practical theorists with long and distinguished careers as composers, during which they wrote vocal music for the opera house as well as for the church.

3. MUSICAL FIGURES. The most complex and systematic transformation of rhetorical concepts into musical equivalents originates in the *decoratio* of rhetorical theory. In oratory every speaker relied on his command of the rules and techniques of the *decoratio* in order to embellish his ideas with rhetorical imagery and to infuse his speech with passionate language. The means to this end was the broad concept of figures of speech. As early as Renaissance music, both sacred and secular, there is ample evidence that composers employed various musical-rhetorical means to illustrate or emphasize words and ideas in the text. Indeed the whole musical literature of the madrigal unequivocally depends on this use of musical rhetoric. In recent discussions, some authors (e.g. Palisca) have connected the late 16th-century practice of musical rhetoric to the definition of a musical 'mannerism', suggesting that this particular approach to composing may well be the explanation of the obscure term 'musica reservata'. Of all the late Renaissance composers, Lassus was undoubtedly the greatest musical orator, as was frequently recognized by his contemporaries, and in the first treatise attempting to codify musical-rhetorical practices, by Burmeister, one of his motets, *In me transierunt*, was analysed according to its rhetorical structure and its employment of musical figures. For more than a century a number of German writers, following Burmeister, also borrowed rhetorical terminology for musical figures, with both Greek and Latin names, but they also invented new musical figures by analogy with rhetoric but unknown to it. In this basically German theory of musical figures there are thus numerous conflicts in terminology and definition among the various writers, and there is clearly no one systematic DOCTRINE OF MUSICAL FIGURES for Baroque and later music, notwithstanding frequent references to such a system by Schweitzer, Kretzschmar, Schering, Bukofzer and others. The most detailed catalogue of musical figures (in Unger) lists approximately 160 different forms, taken from definitions and descriptions of varying degrees of exactness in many 17th- and 18th-century treatises, among the most important of which are J. Burmeister: *Musica autoschediastikē* (Rostock, 1601), expanded as *Musica poetica* (Rostock, 1606); J. Lippius: *Synopsis musicae nova* (Strasbourg, 1612); J. Nucius: *Musices practicae* (Neisse, 1613); J. Thuringus: *Opusculum bipartitum* (Berlin, 1624); J. A. Herbst: *Musica moderna prattica* (Frankfurt am Main,

2/1653) and *Musica poetica* (Nuremberg, 1643); A. Kircher: *Musurgia universalis* (Rome, 1650); C. Bernhard: *Tractatus compositionis augmentatus* (MS); J. G. Ahle: *Musikalisches Frühlings-, Sommer-, Herbst-, und Winter-Gespräche* (Mühlhausen, 1695–1701); T. B. Janovka: *Clavis ad thesaurum magnae artis musicae* (Prague, 1701); J. G. Walther: *Praecepta der musicalischen Composition* (MS, 1708) and *Musicalisches Lexicon* (Leipzig, 1732); M. J. Vogt: *Conclave thesauri magnae artis musicae* (Prague, 1719); J. A. Scheibe: *Der critische Musikus* (Leipzig, 2/1745); M. Spiess: *Tractatus musicus compositorio-practicus* (Augsburg, 1745); and J. N. Forkel: *Allgemeine Geschichte der Musik* (Leipzig, 1788–1801).

Attempts by writers such as Brandes, Unger and Schmitz to organize the multitude of musical figures into a few categories have not proved successful. The following list aims only to give the most frequently cited musical figures in an equally arbitrary but somewhat broader group of seven categories: (A) Figures of melodic repetition, (B) Figures based on fugal imitation, (C) Figures formed by dissonance structures, (D) Interval figures, (E) Hypotyposis figures, (F) Sound figures, (G) Figures formed by silence. No effort has been made to enumerate all of the many variant names under which some of these figures appear in the literature, and the indication of a theorist's name following the figure gives only one of often several sources in which the term is defined and discussed (see Unger for a more complete list of figures and sources).

A. FIGURES OF MELODIC REPETITION

1. Anadiplosis (Vogt). The repetition of a closing melody at the beginning of a new section, but see also no.55.

2. Anaphora (Kircher) = *Repetitio* (Nucius). The repetition of a melodic statement on different notes in different parts (see ex.1). Thuringus, however, limited it in his definition to the repetition of a bass part only (see ex.5).

3. Auxesis. See no.4.

4. Climax (Nucius) = *Auxesis* (Burmeister). The repetition of a melody in the same part a 2nd higher (see ex.2), which is a special case of *Synonymia* (no.17). As *Gradatio* (no.9) (Burmeister), a continuing *Climax* in sequence (see ex.3).

5. Complexio (Nucius) = *Symploce* (Kircher) = *Epanalepsis* (Gottsched) = *Epanadiplosis* (Vogt). The repetition at the end of a melody or a whole musical section from the beginning.

6. Epanadiplosis. See no.5.

7. Epanalepsis. See no.5.

8. Epistrophe. See no.10.

9. Gradatio. See no.4.

10. Homoioptoton (Kircher) = *Epistrophe* (Scheibe). The repetition of a closing section at the end of other sections.

11. Hyperbaton (Scheibe). The removal of a note or musical idea from the expected order for underlining of the text.

Ex.2 Carissimi: *Jonas*, 'Miserunt ergo sortem'

Ex.1 Schütz: *Freuet euch des Herren, ihr Gerechten; Symphoniarum sacrarum 2a pars* (1647)

Ex.3 Bach: Cantata no.78, *Jesu der du meine Seele*, 'Wir eilen mit schwachen, doch emsigen Schritten'

12. Paronomasia (Scheibe). The repetition of a musical idea on the same notes but with new additions or alterations for emphasis (see exx.4–5).

13. Palillogia (Burmeister). The repetition of a melodic idea on the same notes and in the same part (see ex.5).

14. Polyptoton (Vogt). The repetition of a melodic idea in a different register or different part (see exx.5–6).

15. Repetitio. See no.2.

16. Symploce. See no.5.

17. Synonymia (Walther). The repetition of a melodic idea on different notes in the same part (see ex.7).

Ex.4 Viadana: *Exaudi me, Domine*; *Cento concerti ecclesiastici* (Venice, 1602)

Ex.7 Schütz: *Ich liege und schlafe*; *Kleine geistliche Concerte*, i (1636)

Ex.6 Bach: Cantata no.65, *Sie werden aus Saba alle kommen*, 'Gold aus Ophir ist zu schlecht'

Ex.5 Schütz: *Nun komm, der Heiden Heiland*; *Kleine geistliche Concerte*, i (1636)

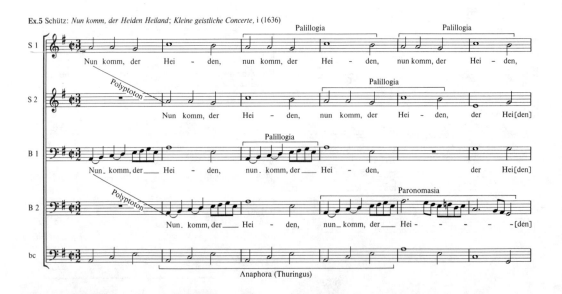

B. FIGURES BASED ON FUGAL IMITATION
(all from Burmeister)

18. *Anaphora.* A form of fugue in which a subject is repeated in some but not all of the parts. See also no.2.
19. *Apocope.* Fugal imitation in which the repetition of the subject is incomplete in one part.

20. *Fuga imaginaria.* Canon.
21. *Fuga realis.* Regular fugal imitation.
22. *Hypallage.* Fugal imitation in contrary motion.
23. *Metalepsis.* Fugue with two subjects.

C. FIGURES FORMED BY DISSONANCE STRUCTURES

24. *Cadentiae duriusculae* (Bernhard). Unusual dissonances occurring before the final notes of a cadence (see ex.8).
25. *Ellipsis* (Bernhard). The omission of an otherwise essential consonance which alters the normal formation of a suspension or passing-note passage (see ex.9). More generally (Scheibe), an unexpected new direction taken by a passage that has led up to an expected conclusion.
26. *Heterolepsis* (Bernhard). A leap or stepwise movement into a dissonance from a consonance; in effect the adoption of the note of a second voice part that would have arrived on the same note as a passing note (see ex.10).
27. *Pleonasmus* (Burmeister). An abundance or piling up of harmonies

that in the formation of a cadence, between preparation and resolution, is made up of *Symblemas* (see no.34) and *Syncopes* (see no.29), over two, three or more half-bars (see ex.11).
28. *Prolongatio* (Bernhard). The extension of the normal value of a dissonance, whether a suspension or a passing note (see ex.12).
29. *Syncope* (Burmeister). An ordinary suspension.
30. *Syncopatio catachrestica* (Bernhard). This occurs when a suspension fails to resolve according to the rules (i.e. down a 2nd) but instead (*a*) resolves down a second but to another dissonance, (*b*) is prepared on a dissonance or (*c*) resolves by some other form of melodic movement (see ex.13).

Ex.8 Schütz: *Saul, was verfolgst du mich?*; *Symphoniarum sacrarum 3a pars* (Dresden, 1650)

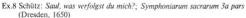

Ex.9 Peri: *Euridice*, 'Funeste piaggi'

Ex.10 M.-A. Charpentier: *Dialogue entre Madeleine et Jésus*

Ex.12 from Bernhard: *Tractatus compositionis augmentatus* (MS, see Hilse)
(a)

(b)

Ex.11 Lassus: *In me transierunt,* from Burmeister: *Musica poetica* (Rostock, 1606)

Ex.13 from Bernhard: *Tractatus compositionis augmentatus* (MS, see Hilse)
(a)

(b)

(c)

D. INTERVAL FIGURES

31. *Exclamatio* (Walther). A melodic leap up by a minor 6th. In general practice, however, any leap up or down by intervals larger than 3rds and either consonant or dissonant, depending on the character of the exclamation. As a dissonant leap sometimes called *Saltus duriusculus* (see exx.14–15).

32. *Inchoatio imperfecta* (Bernhard). An initial harmonic interval that is other than perfect.

33. *Interrogatio* (Scheibe). A musical question, a melodic ending or entire harmonic passage ending a 2nd or some other interval higher than the previous note or notes (see ex.16); also a Phrygian cadence.

34. *Parrhesia* (Kircher). A false relation, a stark dissonance, especially a tritone between parts (see ex.15). More specifically, according to

Burmeister, a mixture among other consonances of a single dissonance half the value of a tactus. In this sense *Parrhesia* is a special case of *Maius symblema*, a dissonance on the second half of a half-bar to the value of a minim.

35. *Passus duriusculus* (Bernhard). This occurs (a) when a part ascends or descends by a minor 2nd and (b), more generally, when a part moves by an interval too large or too small for the scale (see ex.17).

36. *Pathopoeia* (Burmeister). Movement through semitone steps outside a harmony or scale to express affections such as sadness, fear and terror.

37. *Saltus duriusculus*. See no.31.

Ex.14 Bach: Cantata no.155, *Mein Gott, wie lang, ach lange*

Ex.16 Schütz: *St Matthew Passion*

Ex.15 Bach: Cantata no.1, *Wie schön leuchtet der Morgenstern*

Ex.17 Bach: Cantata no.23, *Du wahrer Gott und Davids Sohn*

E. HYPOTYPOSIS FIGURES

38. *Hypotyposis* (Burmeister). A large class of musical-rhetorical figures, many without specific names, all serving to illustrate words or poetic ideas and frequently stressing the pictorial nature of the words. The rhetorical term is more accurate than the commoner expressions 'madrigalism' and 'word-painting'. All of the following figures in this section are in the *Hypotyposis* class.

39. *Anabasis* (Kircher). This occurs when a voice part or musical passage reflects the textual connotation of 'ascending' (see ex.18).

40. *Catabasis* (Kircher). The opposite of *Anabasis* (see ex.19).

41. *Circulatio* (Kircher). The musical description of circular or crossing-over motion (see ex.20).

42. *Fuga* (Kircher). In the sense of 'flight', not as fugal imitation, a

melodic figure illustrating flight, escape etc. (see ex.21).

43. *Hyperbole, Hypobole* (Burmeister). A melodic passage that exceeds the normal ambitus of a mode either above or below.

44. *Metabasis* (Spiess) = *Transgressus* (Bernhard). The crossing of one part by another.

45. *Passaggio*. See no.47.

46. *Transgressus*. See no.44.

47. *Variatio* (Bernhard) = *Passaggio* (Walther). A passage of vocal embellishment emphasizing the text, it can include forms of melodic ornamentation such as *accento, cercar della nota, tremolo, trillo, bombo, groppo, circolo mezzo* and *tirata mezza*. Walther (*Praecepta*) referred to musical 'amplification' of a text.

Ex.18 Bach: Cantata no.31, *Der Himmel lacht, die Erde jubilieret*

So ste-he denn, du gott-er-geb-ne See-le, mit

Chri-sto geist-lich auf!

Ex.20 Bach: Cantata no.131, *Aus der Tiefe rufe ich, Herr, zu dir*

- bung, dass man dich fürch -   - te,

Circulatio = Anaphora (Thuringus)

Ex.19 Carissimi: *Jonas*, 'Miserunt ergo sortem'

Et prae-pa-ra - vit Do - mi-nus ce-tum gran-dem,   ut

Catabasis

de - glu - ti - ret Jo - nam,

Ex.21 Cavalieri: *Rappresentatione di Anima, et di Corpo*

ANIMA

A - ma il mon-dan pia-cer   l'huom sag - gio ò

Fuga

fug - ge? fug - ge?

F. SOUND FIGURES

48. *Antitheton* (Kircher). A musical contrast, to express things contrary and opposite, occurring successively or simultaneously. It can be characterized by contrasting registers in a voice part, contrasting thematic ideas in a contrapuntal texture, contrasting musical textures etc.

49. *Congeries* (Burmeister). This occurs when a 5-3 chord moves to a 6-3 chord, which then moves back to a 5-3 chord, up and down. Burmeister defined the figure as 'an accumulation of perfect and imperfect consonances, the movement of which is permitted [by the rules of counterpoint]'.

50. *Fauxbourdon* (Burmeister). Parallel motion between parts in 3rds and 6ths.

51. *Mutatio toni* (Bernhard). The sudden shifting of mode for expressive reasons (see ex.22).

52. *Noema* (Burmeister). A purely homophonic section, usually consonant, within polyphony, for textual emphasis. Four special types can be distinguished:

53. *Analepsis*. Two immediately adjacent *Noemas* (see no.52).

54. Two successive *Noemas* (see no.52), the second of which is at a different pitch.

55. *Anadiplosis*. A double *Mimesis* (no.54), but see also no.1.

56. *Anaploce*. A repetition of a *Noema* (no.52) heard in chorus A by chorus B while chorus A is silent.

Ex.22 Schütz: *Saul, was verfolgst du mich?*; *Symphoniarum sacrarum 3a pars* (1650)

G. FIGURES FORMED BY SILENCE (RESTS)

57. Abruptio (Bernhard) = *Aposiopesis* (Burmeister) = *Homoioteleuton* (Nucius) = *Tmesis* (Janovka). A general pause or silence within a musical texture where silence is not expected (see ex.8).
58. Aposiopesis. See no.57.
59. Homoioteleuton. See no.57.

60. Suspiratio (Kircher). Usually the breaking up of a melody by rests to illustrate the text (see ex.23); it is closely related to all the other musical-rhetorical figures in this class.
61. Tmesis. See no.57.

Ex.23 Monteverdi: *L'incoronazione di Poppea*, Act 3 scene vi

Many of the musical figures, especially those from the earlier sources such as Burmeister and Bernhard, originated in attempts to explain or justify irregular, if not incorrect, contrapuntal writing. Although proceeding contrary to the rules of counterpoint, such passages were found to be suitable for dramatizing affective expression of the texts. Another large group of figures, the *Hypotyposis* class, have often been called madrigalisms (see under no.38 above) because they occur so frequently in Italian madrigals of the 16th century and later; word-painting occurs in music as early as medieval plainchant and continues unabated in the music of today. Finally, it should be stressed that while German theorists were almost solely responsible for the terminology of musical figures, this is not to say that similar figurative guidelines were not followed by composers in other countries in the 17th and 18th centuries (see, for example, the detailed analysis in Massenkeil, 1952, of musical figures in the oratorios of Carissimi). What German theorists rationalized was a natural and common element in the craft of every composer. Whether or not composers of other countries made such precise terminological associations between rhetorical figures and musical equivalents cannot be established, but that such musical-rhetorical emphases exist in their music cannot be questioned.

4. THE AFFECTIONS. As a result of its intricate interrelationships with rhetorical doctrines, Baroque music assumed as its primary aesthetic goal the achieving of stylistic unity based on emotional abstractions called the Affections. An affection ('Affekt' in German, from the Greek 'pathos' and the Latin 'affectus', consists of a rationalized emotional state or passion. Beginning in antiquity the purpose of rhetoric and subsequently, therefore, all rhetorically inspired music, was to imitate human passions. The extent to which Renaissance composers were influenced by rhetorical principles related to the Affections remains unclear, but theorists as early as Cochlaeus (1511) and throughout the 16th century (see Ruhnke) had connected rhetoric with musical expression. Zarlino (*Le istitutioni harmoniche*, 1558) urged composers to 'muover l'animo & disporlo a varij affetti'. After 1600, however, the representation of the

Affections became the aesthetic necessity of most Baroque composers, whatever their nationality, and the fundamental basis of numerous treatises. During the Baroque period the composer was obliged, like the orator, to arouse in the listener idealized emotional states – sadness, hate, love, joy, anger, doubt and so on – and every aspect of musical composition reflected this affective purpose. While it was easier to appreciate it in music associated with a text, the aim in instrumental music was the same. It needs to be stressed, however, that to compose music with a stylistic and expressive unity based on an affection was a rational, objective concept, not a compositional practice equatable with 19th-century concerns for spontaneous emotional creativity and equally spontaneous emotional responses on the part of an audience. The Baroque composer planned the affective content of each work, or section or movement of a work, with all the devices of his craft, and he expected the response of his audience to be based on an equally rational insight into the meaning of his music. All the elements of music – scales, rhythm, harmonic structure, tonality, melodic range, forms, instrumental colour etc – were interpreted affectively. The styles, forms and compositional techniques of Baroque music were therefore always the result of this concept of the Affections.

Since the 19th century, writings on Baroque music have often referred to a so-called DOCTRINE OF THE AFFECTIONS (or 'Affektenlehre' in its commoner German equivalent), though in fact no one comprehensive, organized doctrine of how the Affections were to be achieved in music was ever established in Baroque theory. It has been assumed incorrectly, especially by writers such as Pirro and Schweitzer and those influenced by them, that composers worked with stereotyped musical-rhetorical figures – analogous to the Wagnerian leitmotif – in order to create a predetermined form of tone-painting. Other writers including Bukofzer continued to believe that such a stereotyped set of musical figures was an essential aspect of a Baroque Affektenlehre. More recent research has clearly shown that a concept of stereotyped musical figures with specific affective connotations never existed in the Baroque composer's mind or in theoretical ex-

losè agebant. In Congratulamini 6. vocum 2. parte ad textum : Mulier quid ploras ? In convertendo 8 vocum secunda parte sub textu Et flebant &c. & infinita alia apud eundem.

XIV. DE HYPOTYPOSI.

Hypotypofis est illud ornamentum, quò textus significatio'im deumbratur ut ea, quæ textui subfunt & animam vitamq; non habent, vita esse prædita, videantur. Hoc ornamentum usitatissimum est apud authenticos Artifices. Vtinam eádem dexteritate ab omnibus adhiberetur Componistis. Exemplum est in Orlandi Benedicam Domino altera parte ad textum, Et lætentur. Alia videantur apud eundem in Confitemini 2. parte ad textum : Et letetur cor. Item in Deus qui sedes : ad textum : Laborem & dolorem. In Sicut mater, &c. 5. voc. ad textum : Et gaudebit cor vestrum.

XV. DE APOSIOPESI.

Apofiopefis ἀποσιώπησις est quæ silentium totale omnibus vocibus signò certò positò confert. Vt apud Orland. in Angelus ad pastores 5. vocum. Simile vide apud eundem in Surgens Iesus 5. vocum. In Christe patris verbum, &c. 6. vocum. In principio erat verbum. tertia parte.

XVI. DE ANAPLOCE.

Anáploce ἀνάπλοκη est in Harmonijs ex Octo præsertim vocibus, & duobus choris constantibus propè clausulam vel in ipsâ etjam Clausulâ Harmoniæ unius Chori in altero replicatio, repetitione ad binas ternasve vices inculcata. Exemplum est in Orlandi Deus misereatur nostri Harmoniâ 8. voc. quò textus ; Et metuant eum, expolitur. Item in Handl. Quam dilecta tabernacula, sub textu : Qui sperat in te.

De Ornamentis sive figuris Melodiarum.

I. De Parembole.

Parembole παρεμβολη est quando duabus vocibus vel etjam pluribus, fugæ affectionem ab mitio cantus persequentibus, admiscetur alia voc, quæ cum illis alteris pariter procedit, nihil ▬ ad Fugæ naturam vel rationem conferens, sed tantum vacua concordantiarum loca inter illas voces Fugæ ▬ exsequentes, replens. Exem-

Exemplum est apud ORL. in Surrexit pastor. 2. Disc. Simile est apud eundem in Cantione Sicut mater.

II. De Palillogia.

Palillogia παλιλλογια est ejusdem τοῦ μέλος affectionis sive tractuli in ijsdem fonis, nonnunquam omnibus, interdum vero initialibus, in una eadem; voce intercalatis quibusdam pausis, vel etjam nullis, iteratio, quæ in unica saltem fit voce :

Exemplum.

Et fanctum nomen ejus.   ij

Et fanctum nomen ejus.

Simile est apud Orlandum in Mirabile mysterium 5. voc. quod hic ascribemus.

Deus homo factus est.

III. De Climace.

Climax κλίμαξ est, quæ per gradus intervallorum similes fonos repe-

Pages 62–3 from J. Burmeister's 'Musica poetica' (Rostock, 1606; the expanded edition of 'Musica autoschediastikē', 1601)

planations. Musical-rhetorical figures were devices meant only to decorate and elaborate on a basic affective representation and to add dramatic musical stress to words and poetic concepts. They functioned in music just as figures of speech function in oratory – as part of the *decoratio*.

The concept of the Affections was at least partly shaped by the writings of 17th-century philosophers of such diverse national backgrounds as Descartes, Francis Bacon and Leibniz. In an ever-growing stream of natural-philosophical studies in the 17th century, Descartes' *Les passions de l'âme* (1649) became perhaps the most decisive in its influence on the art of music. This resulted from the belief that he had discovered a rational, scientific explanation for the physiological nature of the passions and the objective nature of emotion. Nor was music unique, for a similar concern for the Affections dominated all the arts in the 17th century. The attempt to understand the passions lies deeply buried in the history of Western art long before Descartes, however. The connection with the ancient concept of the four temperaments or humours should not be overlooked, and the ancient Greeks wrote at great length about the control of human emotions. They believed that music possessed an ethical force, or ethos, that was bound together with the modes. The Renaissance witnessed a convergence of the Attic philosophy of Ethos, the theory of the temperaments and a developing theory of the Affections, for example in the numerous definitions of the modes according to their affective nature. In later treatises these ideas

ultimately became doctrines of affections associated with keys, the best known of which was Mattheson's in his *Neu-eröffnete Orchestre* (1713).

The association of rhetoric with the concept of the Affections can be found almost continuously in the history of music from at least the end of the 15th century. It is explored in most of the major treatises on Baroque music (see Buelow, 1973–4, for a selective bibliography). By the turn of the 17th century, for example in Caccini's preface to his *Le nuove musiche* (1601/2), the musical goal of the singer became the moving of the affections of the soul ('di muovere l'affetto dell'animo'). The German theorist Michael Praetorius, in *Syntagma musicum*, iii (1618), warned that a singer must not simply sing but must perform in an artful and graceful manner so as to move the heart of the listener and to move the affections. An Italian theorist, Cesare Crivellati, in *Discorsi musicali* (1624), devoted a chapter to 'Come con la musica si possa movere diversi affetti' (chap.11), and the English writer Charles Butler, in *The Principles of Musik* (1636), gave the purpose of music as 'the art of modulating notes in voice or instrument. De wie, having a great power over de affections of de minde, by its various Modes produces in de hearers various effects'. Among the many works contributing definitions of the Affections in the 17th century is Kircher's *Musurgia universalis*, an extraordinarily big work, full of valuable information, where a theory of intervals as related to the affections was proposed for the first time (see Scharlau). Of equal value are the several treatises of Werckmeister, who attempted to combine the rationality of mathematics with the rhetorical concepts of the Affections, providing a definition of particular value to an understanding of German late Baroque music.

In 1706 the German writer Johann Neidhardt, in his work on the tuning of a monochord, *Beste und leichteste Temperatur des Monochordi*, asserted that 'the goal of music is to make felt all the affections through the simple tones and the rhythms of the notes, like the best orator', and this remained the aesthetic credo of writers on music for much of the 18th century. Perhaps the most succinct and effective statement regarding the role of the affections in music was made by Mattheson (in *Der vollkommene Capellmeister*): 'everything that occurs without praiseworthy affections [in music] can be considered nothing, does nothing and means nothing'.

5. CONCLUSION. Musical-rhetorical concepts continued to figure prominently in music theory and terminology after 1730–40, when Baroque style was fading away. Even though the vitality of rhetorical doctrines weakened progressively during the course of the 18th century, a rhetorical viewpoint continued to influence the music aesthetics of the *galant* style and of early, as well as advanced, stages of Classicism. As late as 1770 J. F. Daube, a German theorist living in Vienna, continued to urge composers 'to consider carefully the rules of oratory' (*Der musikalische Dilettant*). For many writers on music, among whom C. P. E. Bach, Quantz and Leopold Mozart were the most prominent, it was that part of rhetorical theory concerning execution or delivery – the *pronuntiatio* – that received new emphasis. Performers were reminded that music was an oration in sound and that the singer or instrumentalist must, like the orator, employ the techniques of good delivery: distinctiveness, pleasing variety of tone, contrasts of emphasis and a comprehension and expression of the affections in an appropriate style (see, for example, Quantz's *Versuch einer Anweisung die Flöte traversiere zu spielen*, 1752, chap.11). Forkel, however, in his *Allgemeine Geschichte der Musik* (1788–1801), thought that much of the important knowledge formerly associated with musical rhetoric had already been forgotten. To restore it he published an outline of musical rhetoric which in many of its details returned to concepts that had been set out in the works of Mattheson, Scheibe and other Baroque theorists.

Although the writers of the later 18th century constantly reaffirmed the continuing validity of the affections as the primary aesthetic force governing musical styles and expression, their definitions of them showed subtle changes (see Dammann, chap.6). The affections lost their objective quality as rationalized emotional states that acted as unifying forces in every work. After 1750 they frequently became identified instead with subjective, personal emotions originating within the composer. There were conservative theorists who still proposed a basic affection for each work or section of a work, but there were other authors who advocated contrasting affections within the bounds of a single work, and it is clear that the old unity of the affections gradually lost its relevance to composers of the late 18th century.

While some of the terminology as well as the basic ideas about rhetoric remained part of compositional technique until well into the 19th century, the understanding of rhetorical expression was almost entirely forgotten. It was only early in the present century that music historians, beginning with Kretzschmar, Goldschmidt and Schering, rediscovered the importance of rhetoric as the basis of aesthetic and theoretical concepts in earlier music. An entire discipline that had once been the common property of every educated man has had to be rediscovered and reconstructed during the intervening decades, and only now is it beginning to be understood how much Western art music depended on rhetorical concepts at least until the beginning of the 19th century.

BIBLIOGRAPHY

B. F. Richter: 'Eine Abhandlung Johann Kuhnaus', *MMg*, xxiv (1902), 147

A. Schering: 'Die Lehre von den musikalischen Figuren im 17. und 18. Jahrhundert', *KJb*, xxi (1908), 106

H. Kretzschmar: 'Allgemeines und Besonderes zur Affektenlehre', *JbMP 1911*, 63; *JbMP 1912*, 65

H. Goldschmidt: *Die Musikästhetik des 18. Jahrhunderts* (Zurich, 1915/R1968)

J. M. Müller-Blattau: 'Zum Verhältnis von Wort und Ton im 17. Jahrhundert', *Kongressbericht: Basel 1924*, 270

G. Frotscher: 'Bachs Themenbildung unter dem Einfluss der Affektenlehre', *Kongressbericht: Leipzig 1925*, 436

A. Schering: 'Geschichtliches zur "Ars inveniendi" in der Musik', *JbMP 1925*, 25

——: 'Bach und das Symbol, insbesondere die Symbolik seines Kanons', *BJb*, xxii (1925), 40; xxv (1928), 119

G. Frotscher: 'Die Affektenlehre als geistige Grundlage der Themenbildung J. S. Bachs', *BJb*, xxiii (1926), 90

J. M. Müller-Blattau: *Die Kompositionslehre Heinrich Schützens in der Fassung seines Schülers Christoph Bernhard* (Leipzig, 1926, 2/1963)

F. Stege: 'Die deutsche Musikkritik des 18. Jahrhunderts unter dem Einfluss der Affektenlehre', *ZMw*, x (1927–8), 23

W. Serauky: *Die musikalische Nachahmungsästhetik im Zeitraum von 1700–1850* (Münster, 1929)

K. Ziebler: 'Zur Aesthetik der Lehre von den musikalischen Figuren im 18. Jahrhundert', *ZMw*, xv (1932–3), 289

H. Brandes: *Studien zur musikalischen Figurenlehre im 16. Jahrhundert* (Berlin, 1935)

H.-H. Unger: *Die Beziehungen zwischen Musik und Rhetorik im 16.–18. Jahrhundert* (Würzburg, 1941/R1969)

W. Gurlitt: 'Musik und Rhetorik', *Helicon*, v (1944), 67

A. Schmitz: *Die Bildlichkeit in der wortgebundenen Musik J. S. Bachs* (Mainz, 1950)

——: 'Die oratorische Kunst J. S. Bachs – Grundfragen und Grundlagen', *GfMKB, Lüneburg 1950*, 33

G. Toussaint: *Die Anwendung der musikalisch-rhetorischen Figuren in den Werken von Heinrich Schütz* (diss., U. of Mainz, 1950)

G. Massenkeil: *Die oratorische Kunst in den lateinischen Historien und Oratorien Giacomo Carissimis* (diss., U. of Mainz, 1952)

H. Federhofer: 'Die Figurenlehre nach Christoph Bernhard und die Dissonanzbehandlung in Werken von Heinrich Schütz', *GfMKB, Bamberg 1953*, 132

F. Feldmann: 'Untersuchungen zum Wort–Ton Verhältnis in den Gloria–Credo Sätzen von Dufay bis Josquin', *MD*, ix (1954), 141

M. Ruhnke: *Joachim Burmeister: ein Beitrag zur Musiklehre um 1600* (Kassel, 1955)

H. H. Eggebrecht: 'Zum Wort–Ton-Verhältnis in der 'Musica poetica' von J. A. Herbst', *GfMKB, Hamburg 1956*, 77

F. Feldmann: 'Divergierende Überlieferungen in Isaacs "Petrucci-Messen", als Beitrag zum Wort–Ton Verhältnis um 1500', *CHM*, ii (1956), 203

——: 'Mattheson und die Rhetorik', *GfMKB, Hamburg 1956*, 99

G. Massenkeil: 'Zur Frage der Dissonanzbehandlung in der Musik des 17. Jahrhunderts', *Le Baroque musical: Wégimont IV 1957*, 151

F. Feldmann: 'Das "Opusculum bipartitum" des Joachim Thuringus (1625) besonders in seinen Beziehungen zu Joh. Nucius (1613)', *AMw*, xv (1958), 123

H. Lenneberg: 'Johann Mattheson on Affect and Rhetoric in Music', *JMT*, ii (1958), 47, 193

H. H. Eggebrecht: 'Zum Figur-Begriff der Musica poetica', *AMw*, xvi (1959), 57

H. Leuchtmann: *Die musikalischen Wortausdeutungen in den Motetten des 'Magnus Opus Musicum' von Orlando di Lasso* (Strasbourg and Baden-Baden, 1959)

K. Darenberg: *Studien zur englischen Musikaesthetik des 18. Jahrhunderts* (Hamburg, 1960)

F. A. Gallo: 'Pronunciatio: ricerche sulla storia di un termine retorico-musicale', *AcM*, xxxv (1963), 38

G. J. Buelow: 'The "Loci topici" and Affect in Late Baroque Music: Heinichen's Practical Demonstration', *MR*, xxvii (1966), 161

R. Dammann: *Der Musikbegriff im deutschen Barock* (Cologne, 1967)

U. Scharlau: *Athanasius Kircher (1601–1680) als Musikschriftsteller* (Marburg, 1969)

C. V. Palisca: '*Ut oratoria musica*: the Rhetorical Basis of Musical Mannerism', *The Meaning of Mannerism*, ed. F. W. Robinson and S. G. Nichols (Hanover, New Hampshire, 1972), 37

W. Hilse, trans.: 'The Treatises of Christoph Bernhard', *Music Forum*, iii (1973), 1

G. J. Buelow: 'Music, Rhetoric and the Concept of the Affections: a Selective Bibliography', *Notes*, xxx (1973–4), 250

R. Flotzinger: 'Vorstufen den musikalisch-rhetorischen Tradition im Notre-Dame Repertoire?', *De ratione in musica: Festschrift Erich Schenk* (Kassel, 1975), 1

W. Pass: 'Jacob Vaets und Georg Prenners Vertonungen des "Salve regina" in Joanellus' Sammelwerk von 1568', *De ratione in musica: Festschrift Erich Schenk* (Kassel, 1975), 29

K. Schnürl: 'Musikalische Figuren in den vierstimmigen "Harmoniae morales" des Jacobus Gallus', *De ratione in musica: Festschrift Erich Schenk* (Kassel, 1975), 50

G. G. Butler: 'Music and Rhetoric in Early Seventeenth-century English Sources', *MQ*, lxvi (1980), 53

For fuller bibliography see Buelow, 1973–4

GEORGE J. BUELOW

Rhetus [Rhete], **Georg** [Jerzy] (*b* Stettin [now Szczecin], 16 Jan 1600; *d* Stettin, 5 June ?1645). German printer. He came from a family of printers living in Stettin; in 1619 he purchased Georg Rhode's printing house, the most eminent in Danzig (now Gdańsk), and in 1629 he was appointed 'Reipublicae et gymnasii typographus'. After his death the firm was run by his widow and then by his sons until the end of the 17th century. His music publications included volumes by Eccard and Stobaeus (*RISM* 1634³), Opitz (1639), Stobaeus (1640), Siefert (1640) and Spielenberger (1641). He used a high quality of type and his publications present an attractive appearance.

BIBLIOGRAPHY

M. Przywecka-Samecka: *Drukarstwo muzyczne w Polsce do końca XVIII wieku* [Music printing in Poland up to the end of the 18th century] (Kraków, 1969)

I. Treichel, ed.: *Słownik pracowników książki polskiej* [Dictionary of Polish printers] (Warsaw and Łódź, 1972)

TERESA CHYLIŃSKA

Rhiemann, Jacob. *See* RICHMANN, JACOB.

Rhodes, Helen. *See* HARDELOT, GUY D'.

Rhodes, Jane (Marie Andrée) (*b* Paris, 13 March 1929). French mezzo-soprano. She made her stage début in *La damnation de Faust* at Nancy in 1953, and took part in the première of Landowski's *Le fou* (1956). Her Opéra début was in 1958 as Berlioz's Marguerite; incursions into the dramatic soprano repertory, notably as Strauss's Salome (Opéra, 1958), though – perhaps invited by her lissom figure and attractively piquant stage presence – were not invariably successful; as an internationally admired Carmen, at the Metropolitan (where she made her début on 15 November 1960) and on American television, and in Tokyo and Buenos Aires as well as widely in France, she has developed an impressively 'French' portrayal, aided by a voice not large or intrinsically beautiful, but capable of exquisitely seductive inflections. In addition to an operatic repertory that includes *Bluebeard's Castle*, *L'incoronazione di Poppea*, Ravel's *L'heure espagnole* and Poulenc's *La voix humaine* (the last two played in a 1968 Opéra-Comique double bill), she has appeared in much Offenbach. An important recorded role has been Renata in Prokofiev's *The Fiery Angel* (in French). She married the conductor Roberto Benzi in 1966.

MAX LOPPERT

Rhodes, Willard (*b* Dashler, Ohio, 12 May 1901). American ethnomusicologist and educationist. He studied at Heidelberg College, Tiffin, Ohio (AB, BMus, 1922), the Mannes School of Music, New York (1923–5), and Columbia University (MA 1925). He then went to Paris (1925–7) where he was a pupil of Cortot and Boulanger. On his return he worked with opera companies, including the Rhodes Chamber Opera in Chicago in the early 1930s. He was director of music in the public schools of Bronxville, New York, 1935–7; then he joined the music department at Columbia University, where he remained until his retirement in 1969. Concurrently, from 1938, he was adviser to the Bureau of Indian Affairs in its project for recording American Indian music; this resulted in the issue of a notable series of recordings by the Library of Congress and Folkways. He has also done fieldwork in Africa (notably Nigeria) and India. Rhodes was a co-founder of the Society for Ethnomusicology (1953) and its president, 1956–8; he was also president of the Society for Asian Music (1961) and the International Folk Music Council (1968), and has served on the committees of other organizations such as the American Musicological Society, the American Folklore Society, the African Music Society and the International Institute for Comparative Musical Studies and Documentation.

WRITINGS

'Acculturation in North American Indian Music', *Acculturation in the Americas: New York 1949*, 127

'North American Indian Music: a Bibliographical Survey of Anthropological Theory', *Notes*, x (1952–3), 33

'On the Subject of Ethno-musicology', *Ethno-musicology Newsletter* (1956), no.7, p.1

'The Christian Hymnology of the North American Indians', *Men and Cultures: 5th International Congress of Anthropological and Ethnological Sciences: Philadelphia 1956*, 324

'Towards a Definition of Ethnomusicology', *American Anthropologist*, lviii (1956), 457

'A Study of Musical Diffusion based on the Wandering of the Opening Peyote Song', *JIFMC*, x (1958), 42

'The State of African Music in the Federation of Rhodesia and Nyasaland', *Transactions of the New York Academy of Sciences*, 2nd ser., xxiii (1961), 464

'Music as an Agent of Political Expression', *African Studies Bulletin*, v/2 (1962), 15

'North American Indian Music in Transition: a Study of Songs with English Words as an Index of Acculturation', *JIFMC*, xv (1963), 9

'The Use of the Computer in the Classification of Folk Tunes', *SM*, vii (1965), 339

'The "New" Folk Music', *Artistic Values in Traditional Music: Berlin 1965*, 100

'Folk Music, Old and New', *Folklore and Society: Essays in Honor of Benjamin A. Botkin* (Hatboro, 1966), 11

with P. Collaer and others, eds.: *Amerika: Eskimo und Indianische Bevölkerung*, Musikgeschichte in Bildern, i/2 (Leipzig, 1967)

'La musique noire dans le nouveau monde', *La musique dans la vie*, ii (Paris, 1969), 24

'Music of the North American Indian Shaker Religion', *Festschrift to Ernst Emsheimer* (Stockholm, 1974), 180

with others: *María Sabena and Mazatec Mushroom Velada* (New York, 1974)

'The Compositional Techniques of a Mazatec Curandera', *Studien zur Phänomenologie der musikalischen Gestaltung: Festschrift für Marius Schneider* (Regensburg, 1977)

'Musical Creativity of Hausa Children', *YIFMC*, ix (1977), 38

'North America', §I, Grove 6

BIBLIOGRAPHY

EM, xiii (1969) [issue dedicated to Rhodes, incl. R. Korson and J. C. Hickerson, 'The Willard Rhodes Collection of American Indian Music in the Archive of Folk Song', 296, and list of writings, 305]

Rhodesia. *See* ZIMBABWE.

Rhombe (Fr.). BULLROARER.

Rhumba. *See* RUMBA.

Rhymed office. A comprehensive view of the rhymed office, or *historia*, is not possible yet: a substantial number of sources upon which such a view might be based is recorded in the *Analecta hymnica* editions, but in a half-century including two world wars, many MSS must have been lost or scattered into new locations. Moreover, many rhymed offices were purely local productions, perhaps adapted from unique musical sources according to ad hoc principles, and thus a general history may be almost impossible to write. Little work has been done, apart from the edition of about 1000 texts in *Analecta hymnica*.

Amalar of Metz was the first to use the term *historia*, referring to a liturgical text drawn from the historical books of the Bible. Historical narrative, usually drawn from the *vita* of a saint, often of only local importance, characterizes most later offices, whose musical items, mostly antiphons and responsories, are provided with rhymed and metrical texts; otherwise the services are quite normal.

Antiphons, and the 'refrain' sections of responsories, appear to have been centonized or adapted from standard formulae, and Frere regarded this procedure as a debasement, modally, stylistically and formally. The conventional tones for the verses of responsories were discarded in favour of newly composed tunes. In later offices the melodies for many of the items were borrowed, complete or in part, from earlier widely distributed offices. Thus rhymed offices, like tropes, provided composers with opportunities to practise adaptation and new composition, from the 9th century.

The antiphons and responsories were sometimes arranged in a strictly modal order, usually with a return to the 1st mode after the eighth item (*see* ANTIPHON). This practice appeared even in the 9th century and soon became normal; it was perhaps started by the earliest compilers of rhymed offices, such as Stephen of Liège or Hucbald. The office for Trinity Sunday, one of the earliest, not being votive to a local saint, gained general and lasting use.

Rhymed offices, like sequences, continued to be widely used and composed until the 16th century and it seems possible that they exercised some influence on the rhymed and metrical sacred paraphrases of the Renaissance.

BIBLIOGRAPHY

G. M. Dreves and C. Blume, eds.: *Analecta hymnica medii aevi* (Leipzig, 1886–1922/*R*1961), v, xiii, xvii, xviii, xxiv–xxvi, xxviii, xlv
A. Auda: *L'école musicale liégeoise au Xe siècle: Etienne de Liège* (Brussels, 1923)
E. Jammers: 'Die Antiphonen der rheinischen Reimoffizien', *Ephemerides liturgicae*, xliii (1929), 199; xliv (1930), 84, 342
——: *Das Karlsoffizium 'Regali natus'* (Strasbourg, 1934)
W. H. Frere: Review of E. Jammers: *Das Karlsoffizium*, *ML*, xv (1934), 353; [incl. short history of the rhymed office]
S. Corbin: 'L'office portugais de la "Sepultura Christi"', *RdM*, xxvi (1947), 63
——: 'L'office de la Conception de la Vierge', *Bulletin des études portugaises*, xiii (1949), 105–66
R.-J. Hesbert: 'La composition musicale à Jumièges: les offices de S.

Philibert et de S. Aycadre', *Jumièges: congrès scientifique du XIIIe centenaire, Rouen, 1954* (Rouen, 1955), ii, 977
R. Weakland: 'The compositions of Hucbald', *Etudes grégoriennes*, iii (1959), 155
R. A. Ottósson: *Sancti Thorlaci episcopi officia rhythmica* (Copenhagen, 1959)
A. Önnerfors: 'Zur Offiziendichtung im schwedischen Mittelalter', *Mittellateinisches Jb*, iii (1966), 55–93
R. H. Hoppin: *Cypriot Plainsong* (Rome, 1968)
R. Jonsson: *Historia: études sur la genèse des offices versifiés* (Stockholm, 1968)
M. Huglo: Review of R. Jonsson: *Historia*, *RBM*, lv (1969), 226
K.-H. Schlager: 'Reimoffizien', *Geschichte der katholischen Kirchenmusik*, ed. K. G. Fellerer, i (Kassel, 1972), 293

ANDREW HUGHES

Rhys, Philip ap [Aprys, Apprys, Apryce] (*fl* 1545–60). English composer. He was organist of St Mary-at-Hill in the city of London (as 'Philipp Ryse'), a post from which he resigned in 1547; 'Ryse William', presumably a relative, took over in 1548. In *GB-Lbm* Add.29996, f.28*v*, he is described as being 'Off Saynt poulls in london'. John Redford, almoner of St Paul's Cathedral, died in 1547, and it is reasonable to suppose that Philip ap Rhys took over his duties as organist there. He is last heard of on 17 July 1559, when 'Mr. Phillip of Poles' was paid 1s. 4d. for playing at Evensong at St Mary-at-Hill.

Rhys's surviving compositions consist entirely of liturgical organ music in the section of *GB-Lbm* Add.29996 which, because of its wholly archaic repertory, appears to have been compiled before the Act of Uniformity of 1549. He was not an imaginative composer but he wrote an 'organ mass' which because of the effect of the Reformation has turned out to be unique in the English repertory. It consists of a troped Kyrie, Gloria, offertory, Sanctus and Agnus Dei. Staves for the Credo were ruled in the MS, but the piece (if composed) was not entered. The offertory is, by continental standards, an unusual item in an organ mass, being from the Proper rather than the Ordinary. It consists of a setting of the plainsong *Benedictus sit*, the Offertory for Trinity Sunday. The setting omits the opening phrase, which was intoned by a cantor. The other movements consist of organ verses played in alternation with plainsong sections of the chant. Most of Rhys's organ music is in a simple three-part texture with the plainsong in the middle or lowest voice.

WORKS

Editions: *Early Tudor Organ Music I: Music for the Office*, ed. J. Caldwell, EECM, vi (1966) [C]
      Early Tudor Organ Music II: Music for the Mass, ed. D. Stevens, EECM, x (1969) [S]

ORGAN WORKS

Missa 'In die Sanctae Trinitas' (Ky 'Deus Creator omnium', Gl, off: Benedictus sit, San, Ag), S no.1
Antiphon: Miserere, C no.21
Offertory: Felix namque, S no.22

BIBLIOGRAPHY

D. Stevens: 'A Unique Tudor Organ Mass', *MD*, vi (1952), 167
H. Baillie: 'A London Church in Early Tudor Times', *ML*, xxxvi (1955), 55

JOHN CALDWELL

Rhythm (from Gk. *rhythmos*). The subdivision of a span of time into sections perceivable by the senses; the grouping of musical sounds, principally by means of duration and stress. Together with melody and harmony, rhythm is one of the three basic elements of music; but since melody and harmony both contribute to the rhythmic organization of a work, and since neither melody nor harmony can be activated without rhythm, the three must be regarded as inseparably linked processes.

Etymologically the word probably implies 'not flow, but the arresting and the firm limitation of movement' (Jaeger, 1959). The widely accepted view of *rhythmos* as deriving from *rheō* ('flow') has now lost ground in favour of an older derivation from the root *ry* (*ery*) or *w'ry* ('to pull'). The history of the word *rhythmos* shows that it was close in meaning to *schēma* ('shape', 'form', 'figure' – Leemans, 1948). Petersen (1917) has characterized *rhythmos* as 'immobile form which arises through motion', thus suggesting an artistic origin of the word as well.

This article is concerned almost exclusively with rhythm in Western music. For rhythmic systems in other cultures see relevant articles; *see* especially ARAB MUSIC, §I and INDIA, SUBCONTINENT OF, §II.

See also ANALYSIS; DANCE; NOTATION; PSYCHOLOGY OF MUSIC, §II, 4.

I. The nature of rhythm. II. History of rhythm in Western music.

I. The nature of rhythm

1. Manifestations of rhythm. 2. Autonomy of the concept of rhythm in music. 3. Rhythm and tempo. 4. Rhythm and metre: recent views. 5. Additive and divisive rhythm. 6. Upbeat and downbeat. 7. Conflict between rhythm and metre. 8. Rhythm and counterpoint. 9. Interaction with melody and harmony.

1. MANIFESTATIONS OF RHYTHM. The human mind seeks to interpret continuous time generally as a succession of durations; it assumes that a rhythmic principle operates in the whole of man's environment. This operation seems particularly evident in constructions built on the repetition of an event at more or less regular intervals, sometimes called 'periods'. Modern psychologists have suggested 12 seconds as the longest span of time which can be distinctly perceived as a single unit. Periods of time whose individual units are far too long to be perceived directly – for instance, the change of the seasons – require rational abstraction. Similar conceptual processes further permit rhythmic categories to be translated into space, surface and line (the symbols of musical notation are a good example of this) and, conversely, spatial categories to be translated into time. One thus speaks of rhythm in drawing and painting, and of rhythmically ordered columns in architecture.

The relationship between rhythm and the human organism (see §2 below) is essential to an understanding of rhythm. Heartbeat, breathing and walking order the passage of time in regular units, and have been used time and again to illustrate this relationship despite their variability and complexity. External and internal events alike affect pulse and breathing rate; conversely, regular rhythm has its physiological manifestations. Other processes in the human body that have been examined as possible internal time-keepers, as 'biological clocks', include neurological ones such as the phase-length of the alpha rhythm in the brain, and chemical ones such as the rate of metabolism of body cells, particularly of brain cells. None of these has yet been shown to provide the basic time unit, the 'ticking' of the biological clock, by which all spans of time might be measured and rhythms understood.

If rhythm pertains to, indeed originates in, Man's organic being, then – according to Bücher (1897) – the rhythm of work results from the interaction of object and breathing. In this way a parallel rhythmic–musical structure arises, in work and in dance, directly from rhythmic formations imposed by physiological necessity: the work song, the dance-song.

The alteration of tension and relaxation that is characteristic of physiological rhythms is experienced and registered in the mind. Psychological rhythmic constructs tend to form in groups; related to this is the tendency to impose rhythm subjectively upon a series of equally spaced beats of equal strength by hearing them as divided into pairs (but those who have been used as subjects in experiments to this effect have always belonged to Western culture with its predominantly binary musical metres). This subjective process is probably traceable back to a preconsciousness in the subconscious. Whether or not it favours weak–strong rhythms over strong–weak remains open to debate.

In modern terminology, poetry, music, dance, mime and drama are temporal arts and therefore directly rhythmic. The interrelationships of the first three of these art forms are very close. This has occasionally led to the idea that the origin of poetry lies in music, or of music in poetry, or that both derive from dance. There are doubtless some speech constructions that arose directly from music, just as music may have had as its basis the impulse of dance, work processes or elevated speech delivery. Dance translates acoustic (i.e. musical) rhythms into an optical–spatial medium, whereas poetry demonstrates its independent, individual nature much more clearly. The constructions of musical rhythm in the West are orientated to an inherent unit value, whether divisible (e.g. Riemann's *Taktmotiv*) or indivisible (e.g. the *chronos prōtos* of ancient Greek music: see §II, 2 below). Every complex rhythmic pattern in music is divisible – in the mathematical sense – by the unit value. By contrast, the rhythmic organization of speech is based chiefly on approximate values, the unit of measure defying exact definition. In some individual cases the actual duration of a spoken long syllable may hardly exceed that of a short one; in others the ratio may be as much as 3:1. The identifying of accent-by-stress (dynamic accent) with accent-by-duration (agogic accent), and the frequently vague discussion of the two made by earlier theorists, have added considerably to the difficulties of understanding the rhythm of ancient and medieval music, which was based on procedures of speech. Interpretations and systems of rhythm in speech and music have become much interwoven; this gives the history of vocal music a special character, and reflects the autonomy and heteronomy of the two spheres of art (see §7 below).

2. AUTONOMY OF THE CONCEPT OF RHYTHM IN MUSIC. In physiology and psychology there has in the past been a strong concern to subsume musical rhythm under a system involving rhythm in all its aspects. Such a system would start from basic facts and experiences of the human organism that have already been cited: not only the involuntary actions of breathing and heartbeat, but also voluntary activities such as walking and jumping, that is, processes that involve visual and spatial concepts. The psychological effects of rhythm are predominantly temporal. Human beings do not perceive objective time-spans as vacant; despite the lack of actual

'content' they tend to invest them with subjective experience, which occurs as an alternation between tension and relaxation. All tangible rhythmic phenomena experienced through the sensory organs are based on this fundamental principle of rhythm which has served as a basis for theories of the origin and classification of all the temporal rhythmic arts.

Musical rhythm, however, cannot successfully be explained by abstraction from a general system. It is rather something specifically musical in origin, and must be conceived as such. Rhythm cannot be separated from music as if it were just one of a number of factors or elements that exist side by side in the totality of music. Melody, harmony and rhythm, traditionally regarded as such elements, are special effects or facets of music which are inseparably linked and made to work together. These manifestations of music as a whole must always be kept in view if the function of rhythm is to be understood. To the listener music is not an object, but something that is realized in time. Those of its processes which involve movement – melodic, harmonic and rhythmic – create a specifically musical type of temporal experience; and they do so by the simultaneous enactment of all of these processes. They give rise to meaning but a type of meaning that is peculiarly intangible. The impulse of motion manifests its meaning in musical sounds, just as rhythm manifests itself in the relationships between units of time and between points of emphasis. Thus duration and stress – in other words constructions in time and gradations in strength – are the central determinants of rhythm, its constituent factors.

3. RHYTHM AND TEMPO. Tempo regulates the absolute duration of notes, hence of successions of notes, and thus the relative pace latent in, or characteristic of, any given rhythmic structure. The system of musical tempos clearly has its origins in functions of the human body and mind. It is related in particular to the speed of a normal heartbeat, between 60 and 80 beats per minute; on either side of this lie the sensations of 'fast' and 'slow' which are the starting-point of all musical movement. Using a basic pulse (set by a conductor or by a numerical marking), tempo proceeds to interpret rhythm by means of small fluctuations in this pulse without necessarily itself taking on a particular rhythmic quality. More drastic variations in tempo, created by accelerandos, rallentandos and so on, do indeed affect rhythmic organization – by displacing implied accents. The regulating of tempo has been effected in different ways at different times in history. In the successful realization of tempo marking, objective and subjective events intersect. Tempo affects a musical work as well as its performance, and is associated with a complex of issues involved in basic decisions on music-making (*see* TEMPO AND EXPRESSION MARKS).

4. RHYTHM AND METRE: RECENT VIEWS. The meaning of the terms 'rhythm' and 'metre' – and the relationship of the one to the other – are extremely controversial issues. This is true of their use in general, and of their more specialized use in music and in musical theory. The bewildering variety of definitions of rhythm in the literature of numerous disciplines reflects basic attitudes which are widely separated in time as well as in approach. The many attempts to distinguish between the two concepts may be classified under three definitions: rhythm is similar to metre – some would say identical; rhythm is 'animated' metre, and thus is a sub-category of

metre; metre is organized rhythm, thus a necessary organizing principle through which rhythm can express itself and assume form.

At the root of the first definition is the notion that similar procedures return at periodic intervals, despite the variety of content they may engender. Rhythm, then, is a natural process, experienced and manipulated by Man as metre. This enables music theory to bring the two concepts roughly into proximity. This view often occurs when a predominantly mathematical view of music is expressed.

The thesis that rhythm is subordinate to metre, which underlies the second definition, was posited by Hegel in the third part of *Ästhetik*:

Regarding the purely temporal aspect of musical sound, we must agree that time reigns supreme in music, that the beat is simply intelligently regulated tempo, and that rhythm is that which begins to give spirit to these abstract rules in that it renders certain parts of the beat more prominent and causes others, by contrast, to recede.

For Hauptmann (1873), who adopted this view in his teachings, metre was the actual measure, rhythm the type of movement within the measure. He transmitted these ideas to Lussy (1874) and later to Riemann.

Riemann set out from the idea of a normal unit of time – a bar – which can be filled in a variety of ways; from the 'rhythmic motif' (*Taktmotiv*) as the smallest 'constructional unit of significant content and definite expressive value'. The perception of rhythmic motifs, their size and the points at which they begin and end is thus basic to his comprehensive system of thematic structure, and provides the link between rhythm and 'phrasing' – the division of music into units of sense. Definite rhythmic and metric qualities (besides melodic and harmonic ones) characterize each rhythmic motif, namely qualities of duration and stress. The motif comprises two distinct but indivisible events: up and down, light and heavy, question and answer, *arsis* and *thesis*. Riemann built his system of rhythmic and metrical theory dialectically on this basis: rhythmic theory explored the inner workings of the motif, the various combinations of longs and shorts; metrical theory investigated the combining of individual motifs to fill larger spans of time and create larger forms. The contrast of upbeat and downbeat was 'the basic principle at work in the creation of all musical form'.

Following Riemann, Schering (1925) made a distinction between the principles of rhythmic emphasis and metrical weight. Höweler (1952, 1953) also related rhythm and metre closely to one another: in his view the metrically ordered passage of time became rhythmic 'by means of more intricate gradation of degrees of stress'. Similar notions were put forward frequently in late 19th- and early 20th-century music theory, clearly mirroring the fundamental musical ideals of the time. At a time when a broadly comprehensive concept of rhythm that would account for free verse and rhythmic prose was being formed by such literary theorists as Heusler (1925–9), musical analysis long concerned itself with the dialectic of rhythm and metre.

The third definition maintains that metre is external, rhythm internal. Thus metre is merely one possible manifestation of rhythm, whose role is to arrange time in units perceptible to the senses. In modern theories of music, this notion of rhythm – as able to exist independently of metre – is based chiefly on the work of Steglich (1927), who defined rhythm as a 'meaningfully formed musical line of force' which is free of fixed models. Klages (1934) adopted a special position by comparing rhythm to such natural phenomena as wave motion, where only similar, never identical events are bound to occur regularly; the beat participated in the rhythmic process by alternating strong with weak, and by providing a time continuum which bridged the gap between 'crest' and 'trough'.

Cooper and Meyer (1960) maintained that rhythm is independent of metre in the sense that it can exist without the regularly recurring accents that measure metrical units of equal duration, and also in the sense that any particular rhythmic grouping can occur in any type of metrical organization. For them, rhythm concerned grouping; it was 'the way in which one or more unaccented beats are grouped in relation to an accented one' (p.6). On the other hand, metre can also exist independently of rhythm, and the two can thus exist temporarily side by side in conflict. An interactive process occurs: metre is projected by the elements that make up rhythm; at the same time, metre is the 'matrix out of which rhythm arises' (p.96).

The growing favour the third thesis has found in recent decades reflects the elemental use of rhythm in much contemporary music. But it is also documentary evidence of an increased knowledge of rhythmic formulae and models and independent metric patterns in many non-Western cultures. It has brought deeper insight into the historical aspects and manifestations of rhythm.

Whereas the mensural system had previously been seen as a development preliminary to the rhythmic and metrical system of the 18th and 19th centuries, it is now generally viewed as having arisen in its own right from prevailing factors and conditions. Much earlier music is basically vocal in character, with texts that are often in prose form or proceed in a free rhythm. For these reasons the study of rhythm in this music has been closely allied to the doctrines of poetic rhythm.

In order to do justice to the many-sided nature of the phenomenon, rhythm is now generally understood as the subdivision of time into sections perceivable by the senses, wherein objective time (i.e. time as measured by a clock) is translated into subjectively tangible duration (Bergson, 1920). Thus every duration and every passage of time is rhythmic; and if these durations are rationalized, they are also incidentally metrical. Accordingly, rhythm is chiefly experienced passively, whereas metre demands the action of a form-giving principle or formal interpretation. In this sense every formal scheme is metrical, whether or not one unit stands in opposition to another, or whether rhythm is articulated by the deployment of strict beats and accents or determined merely by relative lengths. In Classical music, for instance, PERIOD structure is as much a metrical phenomenon as is the succession of beats; the same is true of the ISORHYTHM of the 14th and 15th centuries.

Yeston (1976) evolved an approach to rhythm that involves pitch very fully as a criterion of interpretation. For Yeston, metre is not an independent force, but something that comes into being in the 'middleground' of the rhythmic structure of a piece. Yeston's analytical method first divides texture into 'rhythmic strata', each stratum being determined by consideration of pitch recurrence, and secondly deduces a middleground from each of these foreground strata by the Schenkerian process of reduction to essentials. Metre arises from the interaction of the middleground strata. Such strata

may be rhythmically 'consonant' (so that their values relate to each other by direct multiplication or division) or 'dissonant' (in which case they fail to do so at some level of value). If consonant, metre will be unambiguous; if dissonant, determining its identity may involve a valuation of one stratum over another or be impossible.

5. ADDITIVE AND DIVISIVE RHYTHM. Even if musical rhythm is considered all of a piece, as an entirety, as something elemental, there still remains the crucial question of whether the individual note values that constitute it are to be regarded as divisible into smaller units or as absolute and indivisible. To assume that rhythmic elements are divisible is to postulate a rational, measurable structure, usually based on division by two or three, and, implicitly, a beat that organizes the music metrically by establishing an even, regular pulse. The notion of an indivisible small-scale note value as a rhythmic starting-point, on the other hand, admits of irregular constructions of any type. Music whose rhythmic elements are divisible into smaller units and multipliable into larger ones is 'qualitative', since the unit of measure always fills the duration between two points of stress. Additive music, on the other hand, uses one (and only one) unit of time to measure durations and to define phrase lengths – even the lengths of asymmetrical phrases.

In a coherent succession of notes, certain notes stand out from the others and serve to divide the succession into sections: these notes carry accents, whose chief property is the ability to stress the notes. At the opposite pole stand rests: the rest functions as a sort of negative accent, whose special dynamic has played a significant role in recent rhythmic theory. Dynamic accents are considerably more important in metrically organized music, since they are a part of the regulating mechanism of metre. The other qualities by which accents may be ranked – duration (agogic accent) and pitch (tonic accent) – may either be closely linked to one another in a musical work, or they may be intentionally isolated. The diverse systems of accentuation in European music probably arose from the different relationships between strong and weak perceivable in different languages.

Ex.1

stress   duration   pitch

The organizing power of the accent has far-reaching consequences. The two-note iambic figure, for instance, can appear in three different ways, as shown in ex.1. Additive music recognizes such note successions without necessarily combining them to form a higher unity. In divisive music, however, the rhythmic motifs are combined to form phrases whose individual components stand in a dialectical relationship to one another (ex.2): here the motifs are related to each other as single accents, while at the same time they contribute to, and are experienced as, a higher unity. As a result, a dialectical relationship is established: motif repetitions and

Ex.2 Beethoven: Sonata for violin and piano, op.96, 2nd movt

sequences are by the above reasoning additive, serial formations, but they share with multiplicative phrases a coalescence into groups, in direct analogy with the component parts of motifs.

Additive and divisive principles join together when several successions of notes (i.e. phrases) are juxtaposed, as in ex.3. The rhythmic character of such a higher formation is preserved so long as each individual component can be perceived on its own rhythmic level.

Ex.3 Bach: Sonata for violin and harpsichord BWV1015

6. UPBEAT AND DOWNBEAT. It was Riemann who classified rhythmic motifs as 'on-stressed' (*anbetont*), 'off-stressed' (*abbetont*) or 'interior-stressed' (*inbetont*), depending on whether their accent fell at the beginning or end or in the middle. Such a classification takes for granted the presence of an underlying metre by which the location of an accent can be determined. On the other hand, in rhythmically free music, where section simply follows section, the question as to whether a particular rhythmic component is off-stressed or on-stressed can be decided only from its musical content.

The relationship of 'upbeat' (that is, of off-stressed and interior-stressed) rhythms to 'downbeat' (on-stressed) rhythms has been the subject of much investigation since Riemann's formulation. The theory that an increase in the frequency of upbeat rhythms brings an increase in energy and a decrease brings a decrease in energy suggests that the upbeat rhythm is the 'norm', the fundamental, for all music. But this theory has been shown in practice to be of only limited validity even for metrically organized music. The third movement of Beethoven's Pastoral Symphony offers an example of continuous alternation between upbeat and downbeat constructions by means of changes in the quality of accent. In ex.4 the transition from the upbeat opening to the downbeat continuation is effected by two devices: by the fourfold repetition of the rhythmic motif, and by reinforcement of the main accent – which is itself a tonic accent as well as a metrical accent – by the sforzati.

Ex.4 Beethoven: Symphony no.6, op.68, 3rd movt

Even where there is no repetition of pitch content, and where the form of a passage is asymmetrical, such a transition can be effected provided that there is a prevailing metre. The change from upbeat to downbeat in ex.5 brings about a definite rhythmic accent. In this Italian folksong the change, signalled by a rest, has the effect of a strengthening of the cadence, so that the change of metre underlines a poetic 'conceit'.

Ex.5 *Dove te vett, o Mariettina*

7. CONFLICT BETWEEN RHYTHM AND METRE. The relationship of rhythm to any metrical system which involves ordering is of great interest. Temporal formations may indeed follow exactly regular procedures without necessarily belonging to a metrical system, or the system may cut across mathematically definable divisions. Thus Riemann's normative 'period' consisting of eight bars belongs to metre, even though it concerns itself with rhythmic motifs and phrases, and not with actual bars. As such, it often conflicts with the regular ordering of bars; in ex.6, for instance, the fourth motif of the phrase has to be doubled to ensure a return to the regular succession of four bars which is threatened by the use of binary units within a ternary bar.

Ex.6 Beethoven: Piano Sonata, op.14 no.2, 3rd movt

Another type of rhythm that interacts with a metrical ordering is that of speech-rhythm in the context of vocal music. It is not of general relevance whether the sung text is itself in metre. If the music is allied to the rhythmic structure of the text, then it can choose either to reproduce syllables which would be lengthened in speech as strong accents, or to introduce a quantitative system of metre into the system of bars made up of equal beats of different quality. Ex.7 shows a quantitatively expressed poetic metre fitted into 16 bars of 4/4, each pair of lines occupying eight bars. The significance of verse and strophe arrangement for music is testified to by the repeated attempts to derive rhythmic systems for music directly from the constructive forms of speech itself (see especially Westphal, 1861). Poetry organized by syllable count has a special place in the rhythmic relationship of music to speech. Whether and to what extent music observes the innate accentual relationships of the text depends mainly on the nature and intensity of the accents in the language in question. Italian music theory of the high Renaissance condemned the violation of word accent by music as 'barbarism'. If the metre of the spoken word is linked rigidly to the musical beat, conflicts of this sort arise frequently. In ex.8 the accent on 'einsam' is highlighted both melodically and harmonically, and so asserts itself against the normal accent of the beat.

The phenomenon of SYNCOPATION also arises from a struggle between the course of rhythm and the ordering of bars. Whereas a strong accent usually falls at the beginning of a long note value, syncopation displaces its weight so that an additional harmonic accent is admissible.

8. RHYTHM AND COUNTERPOINT. The coincidence of the individual voices in a polyphonic texture can be described according to one of three basic rhythmic situations: identical, complementary or conflicting. The identical rhythms of homophonic music are distinct from the rhythm of monophony only in that the harmony contributes to the way the rhythm is felt. Complementary rhythms produce a dense continuum of motion corresponding to the metrical system that governs the texture (for instance, the continuously flowing 6/8 pattern of ex.9). They are exploited particularly fully in the 'colotomic' structures of gamelan music in south-east

Ex.7 Britten: *Holy Sonnets of John Donne*, no.9 'Death'

Death be not proud,   though some   have cal - led thee Migh - ty and dread - full, for,⸻ thou art not   soe,

For, those, whom thou think'st, thou dost o - ver throw, Die not, poore death,   nor yet canst thou kill mee.

Ex.8 Schubert: *Harfenspieler I* D478

Ach   werd,   ich erst ein - mal   ein -

- sam   im Gra - be sein,

Ex.9 Bach: '48', ii, 19

Ex.10 Obrecht: *Missa Graecorum*, Opera omnia, i/2 (1954), 110

[mun-]di pec - ca - ta mun - di
[mun-]di   qui tol-lis pec-ca-ta mun - di,⸻ do-[na]
mun - - - di⸻

Ex.11 from A. M. Jones: *Studies in African Music* (1959), ii, 12

VOICE
ATSIMEVU
SOGO

Ex.12 from B. Szabolcsi: *Bausteine zu einer Geschichte der Melodie* (1959), 228

Ex.13 Beethoven: Piano Sonata, op.10 no.1
(a) 2nd movt
      Adagio molto

(b) 3rd movt
      Prestissimo

Ex.14 Bach: *Schmücke dich, O liebe Seele* BWV654

Man. II

Pedal

Asia. Conflicting rhythms are those polyrhythmic formations among different voices, such as the juxtaposition of triplet quavers and ordinary semiquavers, which bring into contrast rhythms involving different divisions of the same numerical order, as in ex.10, and formations of voices involving the superimposition of different orders, as in ex.11.

9. INTERACTION WITH MELODY AND HARMONY. Both melody and harmony are in their own way temporal elements of a musical work, and therefore dependent on its rhythmic organization. Every change of pitch or of harmony brings with it, broadly speaking, a rhythmic accent. Although both harmony and melody, seen in this light, are functions of rhythm, music conceived primarily in melodic or harmonic terms results in significantly different ways of effecting a change of direction in a composition. Basically, music that is primarily melodic is more complicated in rhythm than harmonically based music; if, on the other hand, the rhythmic forces are dominant, both melodic and harmonic elements are subdued.

A subtle melodic style which distinguishes clearly between crucial and decorative notes will, in general, be more complex rhythmically (ex.12). In florid music, whether rhythmically free or organized in a qualitative metre, dynamic accents recede in favour of agogic accents. In spite of the clear orientation to a beat, the peaceful flow of the Adagio molto from Beethoven's op.10 no.1 (ex.13a) and the consequently slow succession of dynamic accents permits the melodic style to be luxuriant. The quick movement of the ensuing Prestissimo (ex.13b) on the other hand, relates rhythm and melody directly to a focal point on the downbeat; musical interest shifts from the detail to the forward motion of the music.

Harmony in music that is governed by tonal function conveys a sense of progression. The impulse that underlies this sense originates in a desire for resolution. Examples of non-Western polyphony and also contemporary Western music, however, show that the course of harmony can rest entirely on 'chance events'. If it is functionally designed, harmony has a retarding effect. The author of De organo (CS, ii, 74), from the time of Hucbald, remarked that the introduction of organal performance of plainchant destroyed rhythmic distinctions in its execution – evidence suggesting that plainchant was beginning to be performed in equal note values. The effect of certain harmonic progressions causing an apparent cessation of motion is an innate tendency of the harmonic accent. In a system where beats are linked to a metrical order, harmonic accents usually coincide with the regular accent of the beat. In ex.14 a new harmonic function coincides with the beginning of virtually every beat, that is, a change of harmony accompanies each move into a new time unit.

In general, rhythmic elements as objectified through the medium of notation leave considerable room for interpretative freedom. They may even demand it. Thus, for instance, improvised melodic roulades shift the listener's interest from dynamic accent to agogic accent. Inflections of tempo allow the harmonic structure to exercise a greater effect than usual. Finally, an exaggeration of dynamics limits the effect of an accentuation based on gradations of loudness and can seriously threaten the metrical arrangement, to the extent of giving the impression of a change in metre.

II. History of rhythm in Western music

1. General historical remarks. 2. Theory of classical antiquity. 3. Sacred and secular monophony in the Middle Ages. 4. 13th-century polyphony: modal rhythm. 5. 14th century. 6. The tactus. 7. 15th- and 16th-century theory. 8. 16th-century practice. 9. The Baroque period. 10. 17th-century theory. 11. Baroque practice. 12. 18th-century theory: the galant era. 13. Principles of Classical and Romantic music. 14. 20th century.

1. GENERAL HISTORICAL REMARKS. By the very nature of the subject, an attempt to write a history of musical rhythm would be doomed to failure. More emphatically than any other element of music, rhythm resists classification along lines of development, thereby testifying to its autonomous nature. Historical demonstrations in music that are based on the notion of progress of ideas largely ignore factors that are inherent to rhythm. The self-contained, immutable character of each historical epoch is expressed with particular clarity in the sphere of rhythm; and so rhythm should be studied more from the point of view of its historical development within epochs than from that of its development from one epoch to the next. Historical studies have been concerned with the elementary premises of rhythm: corporeality and feeling of density, and motion in space and time. Musical form takes shape from the type of motion it engenders – hence, in time. In other words, any musical form is necessarily linked to its inherent rhythm. It must also be remembered that the establishment of any systematic set of concepts in itself requires a historical outlook.

Theoretical study alone cannot deepen one's understanding of rhythm: actual participation in music-making is necessary. Becking (1928), inspired by the resonance analysis (Schallanalyse) of the Germanist Eduard Sievers, placed so-called accompanying movements (Begleitbewegungen) at the centre of his work and, following the example of Ottmar Rutz and Herman Nohl, used rhythm to define personal and national constants, as well as fixed features of certain historical periods. Accordingly, then, the main historical epochs will be investigated from the point of view of their rhythmic structures and hierarchical types, without attempting to discover universally valid laws by interpreting theoretical writings or making detailed musical analyses. Whatever descriptive concepts are used are intended to be significant only for the actual historical period under discussion. Finally, only the most characteristic rhythmic manifestations of each period are discussed.

2. THEORY OF CLASSICAL ANTIQUITY. The ancient Greeks discussed the fundamental issues in the arts coherently and comprehensively. They distinguished between two 'logical' systems which embraced all the arts: harmony and rhythm. These systems were closely related to each other, as well as to the Pythagorean grouping of numbers. The concept of harmony, as outlined by the Pythagoreans, was older than that of rhythm and at one time embraced all elements of form, including the later 'rhythmic' form. 'Rhythm' is found as an art–historical term at least as early as the academician Xenocrates (4th century BC). The aisthēsis rhythmos kai harmonias ('feeling for rhythm and harmony') was, according to Plato (in the Nomoi) that which distinguished man from beast; he defined rhythm as 'order within movement'.

Until the time of Aristotle, Greek antiquity knew no independent system of musical rhythm, but instead derived it from speech. The most comprehensive and definitive formulation goes back to Aristoxenus of Tarentum, who gathered and systematized the artistic traditions of the 'classical' period and arranged them in his own way. Rhythm linked harmony, metre and orchestics, rendering them the 'imitative' arts. As opposed to rhythm as a general, ideal principle, there was the medium of motion, the *rhythmizomenon*, upon which rhythm acted. This was a characteristically Aristotelian division of form and matter, law and perceivable manifestation. Rhythm was therefore superior to the medium through which it was manifested; but it could appear only through the *rhythmizomenon* to which it had given form. The ways in which rhythm was manifested aesthetically were to be found in the natural organization of the world of the senses. Rhythm was felt as motion, through the senses of touch, sight and hearing. One might also speak of rhythm in a translated sense as it concerned motionless objects. Thus rhythm, as the order-giving principle of 'matter' with respect to time, could be perceived in three ways: in speech, declamatory delivery and song, known as *poiēsis*, or rhythmically formed speech; in singing and playing, known as *mousikē* (music); and in body movement, known as *orchēsis* (dance) or, more specifically, *rhythmopoiia* (orchestics). These three types of manifestation might appear in combination. When combined, however, they belonged to the same rhythm they would normally have manifested in the three *rhythmizomena*. The most important of these was the rhythm of speech, whose semblance was adopted by those of singing and dance. This was the basis of the superiority accorded to speech-rhythm in Greek theory.

The smallest rational time value was designated by Aristoxenus as the *chronos prōtos*. This was not further divisible, being a minimum unit analagous to the quarter-tone in the system of pitches; it also did not have an absolute value, being dependent (in performance) on tempo. Rhythm consisted in the particular joining together of minimum values into a unified group; this was done along the lines of the additive principle. The union had, however, to be perceptible to the senses; only a certain number of events could be comprehended as a unity. Thus clarity was a significant element of rhythm. The combination of several events relied on differing intensity (stress), by which one event was emphasized more than the others. The names *thesis* (or *basis*) and *arsis* were derived from orchestics, where they represented the rhythmic elements of dance steps. In *thesis* the foot touched the ground, in *arsis* it was lifted off the ground. Through *arsis* and *thesis* one experienced a certain grouping in 'feet' (1 plus 1, 2 plus 1, 2 plus 2, 2 plus 3, etc) by the faculty of perception called *taxeis chronōn*. The feet, as proportions, formed the basis of rhythmic formations. The starting-point of rhythmic theory was therefore the irreducible elements based on the minimum units; these were added together to form certain types and species.

Aristoxenus permitted rests only at the beginning and end of a verse. In late antiquity, however (e.g. in St Augustine's time), they could occur at any point in a verse, as long as they did not threaten to destroy its metric shape. It was through this process that the verse feet came to resemble one another, a development in which the changeover from quantitative to qualitative rhythm may also be discerned for longer time-spans.

The particular ethos of rhythms, which distinguished

them from colours, odours and flavours, testified to the characteristics of motion that they possessed. St Augustine (*Musica*, chap.6) interpreted the manifold character of rhythm, the ethical power of which was felt at work in nature, in the soul of man and in the origins of the universe, as the image of the Creation and the Creator, and thus explained the power of music to purify the soul.

Before the time of Aristoxenus, the general rules of speech-rhythm were differentiated as follows: the doctrine peculiar to speech was called metrics and was thus a sub-species of rhythm. Rhythm in general concerned categories of *chronoi prōtoi* (of *arsis* and *thesis*, and the genera) in the abstract; metrics, on the other hand, had concrete application in the area of speech. In the post-classical period the close connection between metrics and rhythmics was loosened; metrics was isolated by the grammarians. Their interest was concentrated on older literature known by written transmission rather than from direct contact. Thus they considered measurement only by longs and shorts. The differentiation between rhythm and metre, which was characteristic of late antiquity and the Middle Ages, became evident. The term 'metre' was ultimately restricted to describing quantitative poetry; 'rhythm' was used for syllable counting, for accented poetry and often for rhyming.

3. SACRED AND SECULAR MONOPHONY IN THE MIDDLE AGES. The formation and stabilization of new languages, and the concomitant growing tendency towards dynamic accent and away from agogic accent, caused a change both in the concept of rhythm and in what it comprised. Thus, although the Venerable Bede (*d* 672) knew St Augustine's definition 'a certain rhythm may lack metre, but a metre cannot lack rhythm', he nevertheless essayed an interpretation of Ambrosian hymns by syllable count rather than by quantity. In the 9th century Aurelian made the following distinction between metre and rhythm in *Musica disciplina*: 'Metre is measure with modulation [*ratio cum modulatione*]; rhythm, on the other hand, is modulation without measure [*modulatio sine ratione*] and is discerned by the number [*numerum*] of the syllables' (*GS*, i, 33). The idea of rhythm as a simple delimitation of durations was far from what St Augustine had believed: to him it had rather meant a limitless continuum. In the high Middle Ages the thesis was again posited that rhythm was 'a consonance of speech with similar endings [i.e. rhyme], ordered within a certain number [*numero*] without metrical feet' (Johannes de Garlandia: *Poetria*).

The division of music into harmony, rhythm and metre was retained; rhythm concerned the succession of words, metre the verse feet. Compared with classical antiquity, however, the concepts of metre and rhythm had become exactly reversed: metre was peculiar to music ('A song is executed with beats [*plaudatur*] according to metrical feet': *Musica enchiriadis*, *GS*, i, 182), whereas rhythm was peculiar to verse. Metre was theoretically limitless; rhythm, on the other hand, signified a definite syllable count, usually ending in a rhyme.

A second branch of the tradition kept the two concepts closer to their original meaning: 'There are some rhythms in which the number of syllables is taken into consideration without any regard for their length or shortness ... Other rhythms are metrical as well' (*D-Mbs* lat.14784, f.92*v*). In the *Micrologus*, chapter 15,

Guido of Arezzo developed a detailed system of musical rhythm. The syllable was, as usual, fundamental to rhythms that were allied to speech. Taken together or on their own, syllables constituted neumes, which in turn made up the melody. From several neumes a *distinctio* was formed; this was a 'fitting place for a breath'.

The duration of individual neumes varied: 'some notes [*voces*] have a duration twice as long or twice as short as others, or have a tremolo [*tremulam*], that is, a varying tenor'. 'Tenor' here probably refers to the duration of the last note of a *distinctio*. *Musica enchiriadis* enlarged on this: 'It is necessary to know where a longer and where a shorter duration should be used; and to what extent short and long syllables are used; and which notes should be lengthened [*producti*] and which shortened [*correpti*]' (*GS*, i, 182). In this context it is worth noting that the terms 'productus' and 'correptus' in poetic theory referred to dynamic accents. Thus Johannes de Garlandia said of the cadence in verse: 'One rhythm falls like the iambic metre, another like the spondaic metre. Iamb here is to be understood as a verse [*dictio*] whose penultimate syllable is shortened [*corripiatur*] . . . for an iamb consists of a short and a long' (ed. Mari, 408).

That metres based on quantitative measure were systematically applied to accented verse at this time is proved by the use of the term 'percussio', for instance 'rithmus trispondaicus . . . habet tres percussiones' ('a trispondaic rhythm . . . has three beats'). The combination of dynamic and agogic accents converted stressed spoken accents into long musical note values. In the *Metrologus* (see *Musicologica medii aevi*, i, 1957, p.86) the verse feet were built into a musical–metrical system with examples such as the following: 'A dactyl has one long succeeded by two shorts' (see ex.15). In the *Micrologus* durational relationships were ordered according to the rhythmic species of antiquity, with the substitution of the term 'neume' for 'foot', whereby the musician clearly had some freedom of choice as to which rhythmic species to use. This was so for prose texts; metrical texts were often sung so 'that the verses seemed to be scanned in feet'.

Ex.15

The practical application of the above theory to monophonic Latin and vernacular music is still controversial. The freedom of interpretation available to the performer was clearly considerable, and depended on circumstances only partly reconstructable. This accounts for the scholarly dispute regarding the nature of both plainsong rhythm and secular monophonic song. It is possible that the equalized rhythm of 'plain' chant became prevalent at a relatively late date, as a by-product of the more widespread cultivation of organal polyphony. As for secular song, the vernacular courtly love lyric, cultivated mainly by lay people, could hardly have depended directly on the learned theory propagated in the monastic schools. The influence of musical folklore may be assumed for at least the early development of the courtly love lyric.

The rhythmic character of medieval monophony was, furthermore, closely bound up with tempo, which could be deduced from the text: 'The execution of the song should imitate the thing it concerns, so that for sad things the neumes shall be grave, for tranquil things jocund, for happy things exultant, etc' (*Micrologus*, chap.15). The double meaning of *gravis* ('deep' and 'long') goes back to antiquity, which associated both deep and long notes with slow movement.

See also NOTATION, §III, 1; PLAINCHANT; SOURCES, MS, §§II, III.

4. 13TH-CENTURY POLYPHONY: MODAL RHYTHM. With the advent of a variety of sophisticated polyphonic styles, no longer based on any techniques of improvisation, it was necessary to define precisely the rhythmic relationships between the individual voices. It is not clear to what degree the rhythm of St Martial polyphony was based on quantitative measure, though the beginnings of a quantitatively measured system seem to go back to the early 12th century. For the last quarter of the century, the polyphonic repertory of the Parisian masters at Notre Dame is documentary evidence of a new rhythmic significance for the note symbols; theoretical witness, however, is known only from the 13th century. Just as the nature of Gregorian chant is reflected in the neumatic style of script that was used to notate it, so modal rhythm found expression in a characteristic written form.

Generally, historical rhythmic types can be recognized primarily by the palaeographic stage of development of each epoch; a change in the appearance of the notation is usually evidence of a rhythmic crisis. The origins of modal rhythm are obscure, but its discovery was one of the most significant achievements in the history of Western music – a discovery comparable only with the rise of polyphony, with which it was definitely connected. Metrical hymns may be cited as an early application of rational measurement of duration and weight; more important, however, is the extensive repertory of monophonic dance music, resistant though this is to historical investigation. But measured rhythm in polyphonic music had revolutionary implications for the future.

At least two phases of modal development may be distinguished. The first, which reached back well into the 12th century, was contemporaneous with the Latin rhythmic proses and sequences; here the rhythm cannot be read from the note shapes themselves but is dependent on the metre of the text. Performing instructions were conveyed orally for each piece, just as for plainchant from neumatic sources: 'They worked solely by intellect, saying: "I understand this to be long, I understand this to be short"' (see *CS*, i, 344). The second, later practice, in which certain procedures or types of motion (*modi*) were represented by the shapes of the ligatures, was described by the theorists as rhythmic schemata and related back to the metres of classical poetry: 'whence is mode the understanding of sounds in terms of levity [*acuitate*] and gravity [*gravitate*], according to the length and shortness of time . . . a proper mode is one that is related with one of the six ancient modes' (Johannes de Garlandia: *De musica mensurabili positio*, *CS*, i, 97). The modal system comprised the six rhythmic patterns given in ex.16.

These references should in no way be overrated. They were commentaries by theorists writing in a period later than that in which modal rhythm flourished. Moreover, modal rhythm found its ideal expression in the melismas of organum, which are untexted. To derive the modes directly from classical metre makes for some difficul-

Ex.16 The six rhythmic modes

ties: the modal long did not always equal two breves but sometimes three, and in certain circumstances the breve could be measured as two time units instead of one. Furthermore, the binary genera of classical antiquity were transposed to a musical system that was exclusively ternary in metre. The dactylic rhythm of ex.17

Ex.17 *Alleluia, Pascha nostrum*, Publikationen älterer Musik, xi (1940), 61

would correspond to the classical choriamb in the form long–short–short–long with the first two syllables conflated to a ternary long, and would thus belong to the iambic genus. The relationship of this 3rd mode (and also of the 4th mode: quaver–crotchet–dotted crotchet) to the 2nd mode (quaver–crotchet) would then be confirmed in theoretical terms: 'The second mode interlocks [*convenientiam habet*] with the third, for after one long in the third mode or after two breves there may immediately follow a breve and an altered long; and thus one mode may be made from the third mode and the second mode by equivalence [*equipollentiam*]' (Anonymous VII: *CS*, i, 379). Surviving polyphony supports this correspondence (ex.18). The predominantly iambic accentual declamation of Latin poetry yielded matching music in triple time throughout, with the 1st, 2nd and 6th modes enlarged to trochaic, iambic and tribrachic dipodes respectively.

Ex.18 *Et illuminare*, Publikationen älterer Musik, xi (1940), 135

Whether the fluctuation of stress and long accents known in poetry passed into musical rhythm may be disputed. The music of the 13th century certainly shows a developed dynamic accent, but this does not necessarily correspond to the long. This is shown by the sharp distinction between 1st and 2nd mode, and the interchangeability of the 2nd and 3rd modes. But without doubt it is the dynamic accent that is the regulating principle. The symmetry of a regular succession of longs and breves gives the dynamic accent its very prominence, as a point of reference.

In the course of the 13th century new motivic im-

pulses came to the fore. Short notes became increasingly subdivided. Composers avoided isolating the modes strictly from one another, and mixed them instead to form 'irregular' modes (Anonymous IV, ed. Reckow, i, 85ff). The ternary principle was, however, retained. In speculative thought this had its origins in the *perfectio* of the number 3, which goes back theologically to the Holy Trinity. A growing freedom of movement and flexibility in mensural polyphony of the 13th century can be perceived particularly in the greater possibilities of subdivision and the consequent increase in rhythmic independence in the individual voices. The binary superior order resulting from the dipode beat resolved itself into single beats, thereby strengthening the underlying ternary order (ex.19a). The relationship between two voices was often one of complementary rhythms, as in ex.19b, where the 1st mode has been superimposed on the 3rd.

Ex.19 P. Aubry, ed: *Cents motets du XIIIe siècle* (1908), ii

(a) no.105

(b) no.107

5. 14TH CENTURY. In 14th-century France and Italy music theory and practice severed all links with the metres of classical antiquity. A new idea of rhythm, illustrated by an unusually complicated notation, was announced by Philippe de Vitry (*Ars novae musicae*, *CS*, iii, 41), ranking duple time equally with triple time, which had previously dominated art music. A mode was called perfect if a long was worth three time units (*tempora*), imperfect if it was worth two.

Ex.20 Philippe de Vitry: *Cum statua/Hugo/Magister*, PMFC, i (1956), 82

Neither in syllabic text declamation nor in melismatic sections was the rhythm of the Ars Nova orientated to any formal scheme; on the contrary, it was free. One of the most basic changes in musical procedure was the subdivision of the unit value. Ex.20, from a motet by Vitry, shows one particular level on which this might occur. Each beat of a basic duple metre is divided along the lines of a 1st-mode pattern, which predominated in the 14th century to an even greater extent than before. As the perceived speed is faster, the superior duple time registers conclusively on the mind even though the principal structure of the piece remains trochaic. Dynamic accent is notably diminished in strength. A richer variety of note values, the self-sufficiency of duple time and

– most of all – the independent rhythmic life of the individual voices all contribute to weakening the dynamic accent and to allowing melody to play a more decisive role in rhythm.

Ex.21 Machaut: *Qui es promessus/Ha, Fortune/Et non est*, PMFC, ii (1956), 134

Et non est qui adjuvet

In some works, such as ex.21 by Machaut, in which rhythmic subdivision is binary on all levels, there is a free-flowing quality to the melodic lines and an independence of phrase structure in the individual voices which makes for a considerably reduced dynamic accent. These and other features such as the frequent overlapping of sections of music and text in ex.22 (from the same piece) are prerequisites for unified rhythmic flow throughout a whole piece.

Ex.22 (ibid)

de-hors luist et   de-dens est or - du - re. Une   y - dole _ est de _

As modal rhythm began to disappear as a governor of movement, the principle of ISORHYTHM, realized in numerous forms, effected a unique focal organization on whole pieces. Even if its spiritually abstract factors were largely inaudible, its relevance for the relationship between melody and harmony, and at the same time for the sense of a general metric periodicity, can hardly be overestimated.

See also NOTATION, §III, 3, and SOURCES, MS, §§VII, VIII.

6. THE TACTUS. In the music of Dufay and his contemporaries the rhythmic interweaving of the voices became an inherent part of the construction. Melodic and rhythmic imitation contributed to a musical continuity based on 'motifs', which were developed chiefly according to the principles of variety and alternation. Ex.23 illustrates the juxtaposition of two different rhythmic figures which are nevertheless linked by a continuity of movement; this is an unmistakable characteristic of divisive rhythm.

Ex.23 Dufay: *Missa Sancti Iacobi*, Alleluia, CMM, ii/4 (1949), 15

sis   stel-la.

sis   stel-la.

From the mid-15th century eight note values were distinguished in so-called 'white' notation, of which in fact only five had independent value (ex.24). Only the four larger values were susceptible to both duple and triple division, while the minim was a theoretically indivisible minimum value. This particular method of notation expressed a particular view of rhythm.

Ex.24

maxima   longa   brevis

semibrevis   minima

Two branches of tradition are discernible in Dufay's work: a primarily melismatic flowing line predominant in the Latin motets and masses, and a more syllabic, declamatory style, nearer to speech, in the secular pieces. These two trends persisted into the work of his successors. By the end of the 15th century, rhythmic–melodic imitation was the essential structural principle of polyphonic composition. Surviving traces of the old functional differentiation of the individual voices, with corresponding rhythmic individuality, were ignored; the voices came to resemble each other more and more closely.

The development towards equality in part-writing ushered in the period of classical mensural polyphony, whose uniqueness lies in the fact that the notes were disposed according to an unalterable, regular beat according to certain prescriptions (*mensurae*), which indicated in what relationship the notes stood to the theoretically unvarying beat. In other words, the value of the notes was relative, in each case regulated by the *mensura*. The actual tempo of the music was indicated by signs which defined the relationship of the notes (from the beginning of the century, the semibreve in particular) to an unchanging, regular beat. The relative value of the note symbols and their corresponding rests was therefore clearly visible in the notation, but not the speed at which they progressed. The somewhat abstract interrelationships among the various kinds of notes retained their actual significance throughout any one piece of music by reference to an understood 'tactus', which was the basic measure of time.

Different theorists understood the measure of the tactus differently, though most agreed that constancy and moderation of motion in the beating hand were equally important. The succession of gentle single beats had only a time-measuring function. Each tactus consisted of a downbeat and an upbeat, which were inextricably joined. The speed of the beat was described in numerous treatises and derived in various ways (see Chybiński, 1912). The tactus, as a single time-beat, constituted a temporal regulator comparable to the human pulse or the pendulum of a clock. In all this, it contrasts with the modern beat, which unites many time units of differing weights at a higher level. Surrounded by bar-lines, the modern beat forms recurring groups whose rhythm is accentual. Mensural rhythm, on the other hand, is characterized by an inherently accentless floating which contains its own kind of energy.

Measuring time by the tactus was a necessary aid to performance and the correct discernment of the rhythm. Within the regular strokes the linear movement of the individual voices unfolded outwards, each voice independently. The forward flow of choral polyphony, as usually executed by men's voices, is destroyed by expressive conducting gestures.

7. 15TH- AND 16TH-CENTURY THEORY. For a long time theory had approached the subject of rhythm primarily by explaining problems of notation. Some time elapsed before insight was gained into a metrical system to which musical rhythmics might be related. In the

speculations and ideals of the humanists about a theory of speech, the forgotten doctrine on rhythm of antiquity was taken up (Gaffurius: *Theorica musicae*, 1492, i/4):

There is also music in the metres employed by the poets, called metric music; St Augustine wrote of this at sufficient length. For by it they knew the logic of the various feet such as the iambic, the tribrachic and the dactylic, as well as appropriate measure of these.

This change of view led at this time to intensive debate about the rhythmic structure of music. John Hothby (*d* 1487) suggested that rhythm should be measured not only quantitatively but also qualitatively. Ramos de Pareia (*d* after 1491) disagreed: 'The diversity of music is not in quality but in quantity' (*Musica practica*, vi). Giovanni del Lago related musical form expressly to grammar, not only in questions of syntax, the *distinctiones* ('for why the cadence is like the point in grammar'), but also in the handling of individual words ('and be careful not to make a barbarism . . . that is, do not place a long accent on a short syllable, nor a short accent on a long syllable, which would be contrary to the art of grammar'; letter to Fra Serafino, 26 August 1541). The ideal of setting correctly the longs and shorts of the words of a Latin text brought into being numerous compositions based on the metrical system of the ancients: 'In this way the poets of sapphic lyrics performed song, pronouncing long syllables each to a complete measure of beaten time, which we set with breves. And those syllables which were demonstrably short we set to semibreves, which correctly contain half as much as proper breves' (Gaffurius: *De harmonia musicorum instrumentorum*).

Francisco de Salinas (*De musica*, 1577) brought the various views together in a comprehensive theory of music. As in antiquity, rhythm began from a *chronos prōtos*: 'now there is a time element in rhythm, that is an origin of rhythm'. Salinas touched on one musical issue of his time, the problem of translating word-linked rhythms into instrumental music: 'for two notes of equal duration, even if the sounds themselves be not articulated, may be written not in letters but by certain notes: they make a pyrrhichius, according to musicians. Three make a tribrach, four a proceleusmaticus' (p.283).

Quantitative reading of Latin verse is possible only up to a certain point. Musical practice, apart from the special category of ode settings, held to the word accent. Zarlino also supported this theoretically. He distinguished three types of accent, rhetorical (*árma vírumque cáno*), grammatical (*ármă vīrúmquĕ cănó*) and musical. The last of these corresponded to the enunciation of a spoken sentence, emphasizing the weightiest syllables of a verse (*Sopplimenti musicali*, collected edn., iii, 322ff). The musician should in the first place observe the rhetorical accent: 'In his compositions he should follow the rhetorical accent in his organization of time, and not the grammatical'.

8. 16TH-CENTURY PRACTICE.

The classification of music into two broad areas, sacred (mass and motet) and vernacular ('cantus parvus') is appropriate for a historical survey of rhythm in the high Renaissance. While sacred music developed from ideals established by Josquin and his contemporaries, vernacular music – especially the frottola and madrigal – tended towards patterns induced by declamatory rhythm. Along with this, the frottola and later certain forms of the canzonetta took over features from the rhythmic style of associated instrumental music, features that, towards the

end of the century, brought about the establishment of instrumental music in its own right. Declamation formed one of the pillars of the doctrine of imitation which was characteristic of Renaissance aesthetics. According to Sebastiani Minturno music should respect the syllabic count, the spacing of the voices and the accentuation of the text (*L'arte poetica*, 1563, p.176). In order to preserve the nuances of spoken declamation, madrigalists organized verses in groups. These groups corresponded to the syntax of the versified text, and might even exceed the length of the verse, since for the musician only the rhetorical word accent and the accent in the music carried weight. Typical groupings derived from Italian speech forms arose; the commonest rhythms are shown in ex.25a–b. Tactus and mensuration affected the distribution of note groups, primarily because of the natural emphasis of the thesis: all important cadences ended on the tactus, which also regulated rests and endings. This was also true for the motet and smaller song forms. The motet was richer in melismas even on unaccented syllables (so long as these did not then become longer than accented ones). The canzonetta and the lied concentrated on syllabic declamation and often used rhythmic formulae.

Ex.25

(a) and

(b) Marenzio: *Deh vezzose*, Publikationen älterer Musik, iv/1 (1929), 124

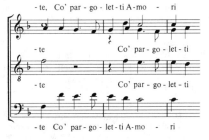

The concern for correct declamation culminated, both speculatively and practically, in MONODY. Its programmatic aim was to convey both the sense and feeling of the text, and to free declamation from all polyphonic hindrance. Thus Vincenzo Galilei summoned Plato to witness: 'He expressly commanded in his rules that one should sing and play *proschorda* and not *simphone*: that is, in unison and not in harmony [*consonanza*]'; he further explained that this did not mean that one should sing unaccompanied, but that 'one should never pronounce the same syllables of the same word one after the other, nor mutilate them, nor split up the order and measure of the verses as is the custom nowadays' (*Dialogo della musica*, 1581, p.83). In monody, as in homophonic polyphony, it was possible to keep a verse

Ex.26 Caccini: *L'Euridice* (1600)

Nin-fe ch'i bei crin d'o-ro scio-glie-te lie - te   al- lo scherzar de'

intact despite its division into clauses (ex.26). The rhythmic pathos of this 'new' art was manifest as much in flowing declamatory motion as in the extreme emphasis laid on some individual words and their meaning.

9. THE BAROQUE PERIOD. The revolutionary new relationship between speech and music which now arose touched the very foundations of both arts. It bore ripe fruit in the genres of monody, the concertante style and the recitative. Monteverdi formulated a distinction that contrasted a freely declamatory 'tempo dell' affetto de l'animo' with measured music making 'della mano' (eighth book of madrigals, 1638). This deep-rooted musical change, symbolized in the key words 'monody' and 'basso continuo', manifested itself as far as notation was concerned in the introduction of new, smaller note values (especially for instrumental music) and in the abandonment of ligatures. Diverging procedures in vocal and instrumental music were apparent. In the former, particularly in music in the *stilus gravis*, the old mensural system survived longer; in the latter progress was more rapid. While the respective paths of rhythmic development call for special attention, the actual intensive exchange between the two is itself also characteristic of the Baroque era.

The mensuration signs of the 16th century were for the most part retained; the special temporal–rhythmic significance of proportion theory fell into oblivion, since a fixed content of beats was implied by bar-lines which now came more and more into use. Around 1680 the last vestiges of mensural notation disappeared. In the early Baroque period, time signatures no longer indicated the relative values of notes but instead represented the 'content' of the bar. At first this was done rather loosely, that is the bars contained varying sums of note values. And in place of the strict time relationships of mensural music, regulated by arithmetical proportions, choice of tempo became a matter of freedom of expression.

The contrast with the impersonal rhythm of mensural music, which seemed to lack the element of human responsiveness, made a deep impression. Thus Daniel Friderici said (*Musica figuralis*, 1618, 4/1649, vii, Regula 19):

In singing one should not feel a single beat throughout: the beat should rather be ordered according to the words of the text. Thus Kantors err if they measure off bars as strictly as a clock the minutes, and observe no decorum whatever nor concessions to the text or the harmony. For sometimes a rapid beat is needed, and sometimes a slow one.

10. 17TH-CENTURY THEORY. Early Baroque theory of musical rhythm again harked back to antiquity. But while Michael Praetorius cited Aristides Quintilianus in the first volume of *Syntagma musicum* (1614–15, p.166), he then proceeded to introduce his own system of classification, deviating from the 'rhythmicians' by dividing music into *harmonica* and *metrica* (p.168). Understanding and sensitivity were to be the arbiters of rhythm: 'Rhythm: that of which a part orders time, motion and fractions of durations according to mathematical rules; and of which a part elicits perception and pleasure for the senses' (G. B. Doni: *De praestantia musicae veteris*, 1647, p.77). Mersenne, for Book 10 of

his *Traité de l'harmonie* (1627), had planned a comprehensive treatise on the effect of rhythm, starting from the interrelationship of its mathematical and its emotional components, which would have culminated in a system of musico-rhythmic psychotherapy. Descartes (*Compendium musicae*, 1618) understood musical form as an aggregation of periods whose scope was formally determined. W. C. Printz (*Compendium musicae*, 1668) developed a doctrine of quantities; rhythm had its place as 'quantitas temporalis'.

There was a stronger leaning towards a mathematical interpretation of rhythm, since it respected and covered the specific declamation of concerted vocal music that was not imitative. The regular course of an ostinato bass figure (a development from dance music) restricted the freedom of movement of the declamatory upper voice, obliged though the latter was to observe the emotional state of the words, and brought it into line with a rhythmic model. Such ostinatos obviously originated in dance. The ritornello, the identical or transposed return of large, self-contained musical sections, is at the opposite pole to the exact, usually uninterrupted repeat of a melodic–rhythmic figure as ostinato. The writings of, in particular, Caroso (1581) and Arbeau (1588) give information about dances and dance rhythms of the late 16th century. Arbeau noted a number of rhythms char-

Ex.27
(a)
Basse dance 3
Pavane

(b)
Allemande
Corrente

acteristic of the various dances: they may be reduced to two basic types (ex.27a). These rhythms, to be beaten out on a 'tambourin', branch out into two further types (ex.27b).

The impulse of dance gave rhythm its life in the Baroque era. The suite and the *sonata da camera* were directly dance-inspired from the point of view of rhythm; virtually every genre and form of Baroque music was affected at least indirectly by dance. The rational character of the era of dance, inclining towards standardization, recalls the procedures of the late Middle Ages when fixed 'modes' made out of stock rhythmic figures were presented additively in series (see §4 above). Ex.28 supports the postulate that in the German Baroque it was the total rhythmic flow, in which the beat was embedded, that set the pattern, rather than the separate beats themselves. Musicians looked on the power of rhythm as something bestowed 'from above', and used it as a superhuman force about whose effects the artist could not concern himself.

In theory the semibreve remained the basic value until well into the 17th century. But after about 1540 the minim tended to replace it in practice. Three main

Ex.28 Schütz: *O bone Jesu, fili Mariae* swv471

categories of beat were distinguished: *tactus maior* (ex.29a), *tactus minor* (ex.29b) and *tactus proportionatus* (ex.29c). Listenius (*Musica*, 1549, ii/10), deviating from this usage, cited the so-called breve beat as '*tactus totalis . . .* which others call *maior*'; he called the normal semibreve beat *tactus minor*, and put all other beat relationships into a category '*specialis . . .* which they call proportional, for why I know not'. The once carefully ordered hierarchy of proportions broke down, and at the end of the 16th century fused with the concepts *tempus perfectum* and *imperfectum, diminutum* and *non diminutum*. The change between even and uneven beats was effected in a 2:3 ratio (*proportio sesquialtera*); these were supplemented by the quick *tripla* (1:3), which came from the dance.

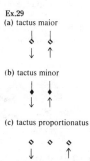

Ex.29
(a) tactus maior

(b) tactus minor

(c) tactus proportionatus

The bar-line, originally confined to instrumental tablatures, was used in scores (Cipriano de Rore, 1577) from the last quarter of the 16th century, and for orientation in partbooks ('ad discernendum tactum', Praetorius), frequently at regular intervals. If at first the line served the purpose of clarity, from the middle of the 17th century it was used increasingly to display internal periodicity. Gradually time signatures lost their significance for tempo and proportion. Giovanni Gabrieli systematically notated *tripla* in *tactus maior* and *sesquialtera* in *tactus minor*; since both time indications related to the semibreve, they amounted to the same relationship. For Frescobaldi, time signatures indicated merely the subdivision of the semibreve.

TABLE 1

de deux temps	2	¢	$\frac{2}{4}$		
de trois temps	$\frac{3}{1}$	$\frac{3}{2}$	$\frac{3}{4}$	$\frac{3}{8}$	$\frac{3}{16}$
	3		(triple simple = $\frac{3}{4}$)		
de quatre temps	C	¢	$\frac{4}{8}$		
de six temps	$\frac{6}{4}$	$\frac{6}{8}$	$\frac{6}{16}$		
de neuf temps	$\frac{9}{4}$	$\frac{9}{8}$	$\frac{9}{16}$		
de douze temps	$\frac{12}{4}$	$\frac{12}{8}$	$\frac{12}{16}$		

Alongside this development a deliberately archaizing system was established, which claimed support from the old rhythmic genera. Thus W. C. Printz postulated spondaic and trochaic, duple and quadruple time signatures that were related to tempo: 3/1 was slow, 3/4 fast. Loulié (*Eléments ou principes de musique*, 2/1698) offered a developed time-system in which he distinguished signatures as shown in Table 1.

11. BAROQUE PRACTICE. Between beat and declamation there now existed a relationship of rare instability. A feeling for heavy and light underscored the rules of prepared dissonance (syncopation) and harmonic resolution, and of passing notes. Use of rests, and cadence formations (usually on the *thesis*), also showed the regulating power of the beat, especially when a whole composition might have the feeling of being driven towards cadences. Correct declamation ran in parallel with the beat.

Serial rhythm and heavy accent were amalgamated. In ex.30a the beginning and the middle of the bar are marked both by long accents and by harmonic emphasis; the inner dynamic of each bar unfolds in a straightforward way and without interruption. The figuration is variable; each rhythmic element remains isolated, like a building-block. Until the late Baroque period, figuration was orientated to the unit of one beat. There was a characteristic preference for dotted rhythm (e.g. ex.30b), which was often exaggerated in performance, and for its inversion, the Lombard rhythm or 'Scotch snap' (e.g. ex.30c).

Ex.30
(a) Purcell: *Dioclesian*, Works, ix

(b) and

(c)

Ex.31 Bach: *Jesu, meine Freude* BWV227

fleischlich, ihr a – ber seid nicht fleischlich, nicht fleisch - lich,

(fleisch) –   –   –   –   – lich, son -

sondern geistlich, ihr

- dern geist-lich,

In contrast to music influenced by dance, which was regulated by beat accents, polyphonic compositions retained a distinctly egalitarian rhythmic style. In ex.31, for instance, the continuous complementary movement sets up an even pulse – rhythm by complementation – in which the quaver (which governs the declamation of the text) seems almost to be the basic unit. The displacement of a single rhythmic series throughout the different registers, which is characteristic of Baroque polyphony, establishes a pulse in which all the beats are equally heavy, except those on which a new harmony falls. Bach's music lacks differentiated nuances of emphasis; its rhythm moves evenly, 'objectively', without personal additive – in short, like a heartbeat. The performer allows it to express itself and take effect without actually obstructing it; he does not rebel against its authority by placing an accent contrary to it. Bach's music adheres typologically to the character of such a pulse: a continuous, unbroken inner dynamism.

In Italian music, the long drawn-out type of movement of a piece in slow tempo gains point from the strong accent, and the way is prepared for decorative melodic ornamentation by the simultaneous use of differentiated rhythmic quantities in the texture below (ex.32).

Ex.32 Vivaldi: Concerto no.41 RV106

12. 18TH-CENTURY THEORY: THE GALANT ERA. Mattheson developed an encyclopedic theory of rhythm in *Der vollkommene Capellmeister* (1739; ii/6–8). His attempt to create a musical *rhythmopöie*, again based on classical verse theory, led him to the concept of the *Klangfuss*, or 'foot expressed in sound'. He wrote: 'That which feet signify in poetry is what is represented in music by rhythms, for which reason we should like to call them "sound-feet" [*Klang-Füsse*]'. Following the example of the metre of speech, he arranged these feet in twos, threes or fours according to the number of syllables they contained, relating them to music of a particular character (e.g. spondee for 'most sacred songs', iambic mixed with trochee for the 'minuet'). A separate discipline in rhythm was concerned with beat and tempo. Mattheson attached a special significance to the complex of issues related to agogic accent and dynamic accent. Dynamic accent determined declamation, since 'where a speech accent occurs in the text, a singing accent must also be entered without fail', even around a series of short notes.

Marpurg's observation on 'good' and 'bad' parts of the bar (*Anleitung zur Musik*, 1763, pp.76f) is particularly informative: 'In every duple bar only one good part of the bar is available, namely the first. In every quadruple bar there are two, namely the first and third parts'. One of the main stumbling-blocks in a differential system of beats was thus overcome in theory, and was not to be a problem again for a long time. Kirnberger's theory of rhythm, as explained in the second volume of *Die Kunst des reinen Satzes* (1776, pp.105ff), assumed a temporary division: motion was the rate of speed, beat the order of accents which organized the sounds of words and rhythm the periods, that is, the pieces formed from words. In music, which Kirnberger likened to

language, the beats and their periodic recurrence were the analogues of the laws of composed speech. He also distinguished periods, which ended in the key of the tonic, from rhythms, which ended in a related key. Kirnberger's theory marks the end of an era based on the regularity imposed by the principles of dance (in particular, the aesthetic of a binary division). The renewed ascendency of dance-tunes characterized the era of the *galant* style, whose theory of the arts saw beauty as the image of reason, hence of order, and thus explains the general desire for clarity and simplicity of technique in musical form. Ex.33 shows a passage from a composition with all the marks of eight-bar period structure. The clarity with which the extent of each rhythmic motif can be recognized and the strong accentuation point to the world of dance music; the apparent extension of the penultimate bar interrupts the rationalized succession of bars in the sequence and throws into the foreground the accent which is being built up.

Ex.33 Rameau: 'Les niais de Sologne', *Pièces de clavecin* (1724)

13. PRINCIPLES OF CLASSICAL AND ROMANTIC MUSIC. While the beat was a constituent framework for rhythm in the *galant* style, the groundplan it provided was often deliberately overlaid, for variety, by agogic and tonic accents. Period structure and the beat entered into a fruitful, intensive relationship with each other which, covertly or openly, served to intensify rhythm. When J. G. Sulzer, in his *Allgemeine Theorie der schönen Künste* (pp.1771ff) applied to rhythm the old idea of unity within diversity, rhythmic theory acquired a widely applicable tool of knowledge, which became characteristic of the epoch. Metre and beat, that is, regularity, were the representatives of simple uniformity; rhythm, on the other hand, represented diversity within uniformity. The manner of filling out the beat defined the character, indeed the very ethos of the music, and formed rhythms from shorter and longer components. The rate of succession of those components had to be dependent on the feeling (*Empfindung*) of the music; in this way the concept of beat avoided the danger of falling into mere schematicism: the period structure was open to free rhythmic events.

Early theoretical witness for this freedom is given in the writings of H. C. Koch and J.-J. de Momigny. Momigny took the dialectical organization of music back to the *cadence*, the smallest musical unity, seeing in it a contrast of beginning (*antécédent*) and end (*conséquent*): 'Music moves from a lift [*levé*] to a beat [*frappé*], not the other way round'. The law of the upbeat thus postulated freed the notion of rhythm from being tied to the bar, and gave the motifs freedom to negate and override the boundary of the bar-line. But Momigny understood the bar-line as signifying a joining, not a separation; he taught that the visual bar should be distinguished from the aural, and that the bar-line was a notational device, like the comma or full stop in language. From the *cadence* Momigny derived the period, whose chief feature was its symmetry. It arose from the inner dynamic of a regular alternation of contrasting

Ex.34 Mozart: String Quartet in F κ590, 1st movt
Allegro moderato

Ex.37 Wagner: *Parsifal*, prelude

formal units. In ex.34, for instance, the alternation of rising and falling motion serves as a model example: a rising chordal motif built of long note values is answered by a falling scale motif in short, lively note values. Upbeat and downbeat give depth to the picture. In slower, more drawn-out motion (ex.35) the rhythmic–

Ex.35 Beethoven: Piano Sonata, op.101, 3rd movt

metrical layering is more complex: here an echo of the Baroque era can be found, the bar-scheme formally containing the motif, and the attenuation of the crucial beats lessening the dynamic accents in favour of a more embellished melody. The Beethoven example is an arioso – it verges on recitative, which Momigny specifically excluded from his theory of periodicity on the grounds that recitative was more closely related to prosody.

In musical performance, motifs were functionally ambivalent. Romantic music offered a great internal realm to the motif, by its flexible treatment of upbeat and downbeat and by the freedom with which it discovered and employed melodic–rhythmic forces (ex.36). It is in

Ex.36 Schumann: *Kreisleriana*, op.16, 2nd movt

the manifold internal musical relationships that an individual flowing dynamism may be expressed. It was an attribute of the Romantic era that the regularity of the beat was often only a fragile setting for music whose rhythmic life followed – and expressed – a will of its own. A step beyond this, Wagner's 'unending melody' could overflow with utmost expressiveness into a rhythmically seamless, limitless vision (ex.37). At about the same time irregular beat groupings (such as 5/4) began

to appear, particularly in music inspired by folk or nationalist elements. Their wavering, aperiodic accentuation heralded the supercession and decline of Classical–Romantic metre. Such irregular beat groupings were prepared by irregular phrases which were often declamatory and ran contrary to balanced periodic structure.

In 19th-century rhythmic theory, Joseph and Anton Gersbach tried to relate rhythm to general number theory in their *Reihenlehre oder Begründung des musikalischen Rhythmus aus der allgemeinen Zahlenlehre* (1834). Westphal's preoccupation with Greco-Roman metrics was rich in consequences, leading him to show its validity for contemporary rhythm by showing the analogy of the modern beat to the classical poetic foot. Hauptmann's theory, on the other hand, neglected the organization of *Klangfüsse*, which had previously occupied a central position in the theory of rhythm. Lussy went another way in his *Traité de l'expression musicale* (1874), basing his ideas chiefly on Momigny's theory of phrase construction.

Riemann was avowedly indebted to both Hauptmann and Lussy. His *System der musikalischen Rhythmik und Metrik* (1903), the most significant document on Classical–Romantic rhythmic theory, views the motif as embodying the cell of living musical matter. For Riemann the motif was related to, yet not defined by, the beat. In contrast with the ancient verse foot, it was based either on a definite succession of *arsis* and *thesis*, or on a fixed order of rhythmic qualities: a motif might be embellished by figuration without changing its shape. The phrase developed from an interplay between question and answer. Metrics developed by analogy with musical rhythmics: the beat, like the phrase, came from the succession of light and heavy and culminated in the eight-bar period which Riemann called the 'normative basic schema' (see §I, 4 above). It might be extended by extrapolation or interpolation, or shortened by conflation or elision. Thus Riemann held it to be a 'welcome unit measure' for the analysis of more complex structures. In his interpretation, music of the Classical period held an unassailably high rank: most of his examples were drawn from Beethoven, and from Mozart and Haydn. Therein lay the greatness and individuality – as well as the limitations – of Riemann's theory of rhythm.

14. 20TH CENTURY. New types of rhythmic procedure began to emerge at the beginning of the 20th century. The rhythmic interest of a work was becoming increasingly focussed on its surface; instead of being concerned with a combination of different rhythms (especially faster rhythms within slower ones) operating on many levels of a work – that is, carrying out a quiet, profound, structural function – rhythm functioned noisily as a part of the musical foreground. The *locus classicus* of this development is the 'Danse sacrale' from Stravinsky's *The Rite of Spring* (1913), and others of his early scores showed this tendency towards surface rhythm, as did Bartók's *The Wooden Prince* (1916) and *The Miraculous Mandarin* (1919), though these works were written in direct reaction to *Petrushka* and *The Rite of Spring*. As early as 1905, however, in his first Suite for

orchestra (fifth movement), Bartók used asymmetrical alternations of 2/4 and 3/4 bars in a fast, giddy tempo. Additive rhythms, based usually on a small unit such as the quaver and forming constantly varying sizes of large-scale unit, led naturally to styles incorporating folk idioms, jazz and ostinato. These were used by a wide spectrum of composers up to World War II; in this tradition the unchanging element (the small duration) generally moves fast, involving the listener at an exhilarating, sometimes hectic level.

In another tradition the constant element was a longer duration that was subdivided. Frequently in Debussy, for instance, a basically slow tempo is subjected to a great degree of rubato, and evokes a lyrical rather than mechanistic mood. As Bartók and Stravinsky were composing increasingly sharp, hard rhythmic shapes, Debussy was composing softer, vaguer ones. In another branch of this tradition, exemplified by much of Webern's early music (especially the short pieces of opp.6–11), rhythm is held together by a reasonably constant, often slow beat. But the movement across and within the beat is of an extraordinary intricacy and subtlety that has hardly been equalled since: the timing of each event bears so much structural meaning that the listener used to a simpler, one-dimensional clarity is often baffled by it.

The crisis caused by the recession of tonal (i.e. harmonic) rhythm, which had precipitated the expansion of surface rhythm, was followed by a general move back in rhythmic style in the period between the two world wars. Neo-Classicism was born. In his rigorous 12-note compositions Schoenberg seriously attempted to match the all-embracing function of rhythm in tonal music, though in completely new terms. His much-criticized rhythmic 'conservatism' was the result of a deliberate spurning of what he would have considered superficial rhythmic stopgaps plastered on to an ailing music to give it a semblance of life; in his own music he sought a genuinely 'deep' rhythmic structure to articulate the complex symmetries of his serial pitch technique, for instance by applying the same rhythm to different orderings of pitch classes to show that one ordering is the result of a direct operation (inversion, retrograde, transposition, repeated registral or timbral selection) on another.

If the first crisis was brought about by largely musical issues, a second was caused by largely political and cultural events. World War II produced a reaction towards technology, science and the objective paradigm: total serialism was born, and with it electronic music. One of the most important leaders of the new movement was Messiaen. Before the war he had used his own additive techniques, and a personal version of the folk idiom practice – rhythms drawn from the remote world of Hindu music as found in the pitchless abstracts tabulated by Shargadeva in Lavignac's *Encyclopédie de la musique*. With the piano piece *Mode de valeurs et d'intensités* (1949), however, Messiaen systematically fixed durations to pitches, and in the *Livre d'orgue* (1951) he formalized the additive technique to an extreme degree, by the systematic permutation of 64 durations (from one hemidemisemiquaver to 64 hemidemisemiquavers, totalling one semibreve: 61, 62, 63, 64, 4, 3, 2, 1, 57, 58, 59, 60, 8, 7, 6, 5 and so on); and other permutation systems abound in other pieces. The marriage of such systems with 12-item serialism quickly took place in the 1950s, in the music of Stockhausen, Boulez, Nono,

Berio, Maderna and others. Rhythm seemed finally to be freed of its servitude to the pressures of pitch and other musical dimensions; it was no longer the rhythm 'of' something so much as a layer in its own right, determined on an equal basis with other layers. Of course this was an intellectual illusion, and the holistic Stockhausen quickly saw it as such. His reaction was characteristic: rather than withdrawing, he took the idea further, envisaging the realm of duration as a unity encompassing everything from the slowest perceptible duration (which he fixed at eight seconds) through the realm of pitch frequency (up to 14,000 cycles per second). In *Gruppen*, for three orchestras, he used the same serial principles to govern both tempo and pitch. Also, the division of a slower fundamental duration into its component subdivisions was equated with the acoustic nature of timbre (fundamental frequency plus harmonic partials) – especially in his electronic music – and degrees of non-harmonicity (or noise) were equated with random incidence across out-of-time layers of music. These techniques were not confined to Stockhausen's music of the 1950s; they have continued to enrich it – *Inori* (1974), for instance, offers a clearer realization of many of the tempo techniques first tested in *Gruppen*. Stockhausen has persistently tried to enlarge the domain of time-consciousness, particularly the consciousness of slower rhythms. Fibonacci series govern the durations in several of his works. *Telemusik*, for tape, uses 13 sections lasting 13 seconds, eight lasting 21 seconds, five lasting 34 seconds, three lasting 55 seconds, two lasting 89 seconds and one lasting 144 seconds; these are interlaced in a slow symmetrical rhythm, each length of which is introduced by its appropriate high or low Japanese percussion instrument (apparently as a re-creation of 'noh' time).

By far the most consistent use of serial rhythm has been by Milton Babbitt who, since his Three Compositions for piano (1948) has developed independently of European composers. His 'time-point' system offers an exact analogy to his serial-pitch procedures, allowing, with its placement of an attack on a serially-determined unit (which is one of a 12-unit module), for equivalents to octave transposition of pitch – that is, the difference and similarity between the intervals shown in ex.38*a* and their analogous expression as rhythmic intervals in ex.38*b*. This works particularly well when sets are superimposed combinatorially.

Ex.38

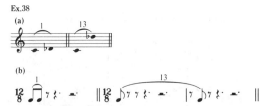

Of the numerous other ramifications of rhythmic practice in recent years it is possible to touch on only a few. Xenakis has enlarged the concept of statistical tendencies in rhythm with large numbers of 'voices' controlled by laws of probability. This has been widely influential on the Continent. Cage, with chance operations, has tried to 'let sounds be uniquely themselves' and to liberate them altogether from the continuity of rhythm. Feldman's use of slowness and silence is an attempt to get sounds to 'exist in space unimpeded by one another'. Again, paradoxically, new rhythmic structures are born. La Monte Young has extended the single sound, a continuous drone for instance, to become the duration of the entire piece. Interesting rhythm arises by a new route – as an acoustic by-product: beating rhythms, illusory changes produced by the listener as he moves his head or changes his mental mode of perception. Terry Riley (influenced by jazz), Steve Reich (influenced by oriental and African music) and Philip Glass have reinstated periodicity in such a simple and clear way that the perceptual ground is similarly cleared for subtle changes to be heard. Changes from rhythms that are in phase to rhythms that are out of phase, a favourite device of Reich, were originally discovered by playing the same tape loop on two tape recorders and subtly desynchronizing one of them. Glass's lengthy additive and cyclic processes set up clear large-scale rhythms lasting several hours. The creation of new rhythmic patterns is no problem, particularly in an age of computer-synthesized music; the ability to perceive them and find them significant has developed more slowly. The USA continues to offer the most uninhibited psycho-acoustic experiments in this direction. Alvin Lucier cast a new light on involvement with rhythm in Music for a Solo Performer (1965), in which the rhythms heard were the performer's alpha brain waves monitored by EEG electrodes. David Rosenboom and others have extended this concept to give the musician an even stronger feeling that his psychic life is in fact the music, that his brain waves activate all sorts of other sounds and sights – to perform a rhythm is to be a rhythm.

BIBLIOGRAPHY

BIBLIOGRAPHIES

A. Ruckmich: 'A Bibliography of Rhythm', *American Journal of Psychology*, xxiv (1913), 508; xxvi (1915), 457

D. Seckel: *Hölderlins Sprachrhythmus* (Leipzig, 1937) [with bibliography of rhythm research]

M. Schoen: 'Bibliography of Experimental Studies on the Psychology of Music', *MTNA Proceedings*, xxxv (1940); xxxvi (1941); xxxvii (1943)

H. C. Wolff: 'Das Problem des Rhythmus in der neuesten Literatur (ca. 1930 bis 1940)', *Archiv für Sprach- und Stimmphysiologie*, v (1941), 163–95

S. Winnick: *Rhythm: an Annotated Bibliography* (Metuchen, 1974)

ETYMOLOGY

E. Petersen: 'Rhythmus', *Abhandlungen der Königlichen Gesellschaft der Wissenschaften zu Göttingen: philologisch-historische Klasse*, new ser., xvi/5 (Berlin, 1917), 1–104

E. Wolf: *Die Bedeutung von 'rhythmos' in der griechischen Literatur* (diss., U. of Innsbruck, 1947)

E. A. Leemans: 'Rythme en rhythmos', *Antiquité classique*, xvii (1948), 403

W. Jaeger: *Paideia*, i (Berlin, 4/1959), 174f

NATURE OF RHYTHM

A. F. L'vov: *O svobodnom ili nesimmetritschnom ritme* [On free or asymmetrical rhythm] (St Petersburg, 1858; Ger. trans., 1859)

R. Westphal: *Die Fragmente und die Lehrsätze der griechischen Rhythmiker* (Leipzig, 1861)

——: *Elemente des musikalischen Rhythmus mit besonderer Rücksicht auf unsere Opern-Musik*, i (Jena, 1872)

M. Hauptmann: *Die Natur der Harmonik und Metrik*, ed. O. Paul (Leipzig, 1873; Eng. trans., 1888)

M. Lussy: *Traité de l'expression musicale* (Paris, 1874, 8/1904; Eng. trans., 1885)

R. Westphal: *Allgemeine Theorie der musikalischen Rhythmik seit J. S. Bach* (Leipzig, 1880)

M. Lussy: *Le rythme musicale, son origine, sa fonction et son accentuation* (Paris, 1883, 4/1911)

R. Westphal: *Aristoxenos von Tarent: Melik und Rhythmik des klassischen Hellenentums* (Leipzig, 1883–93) [vol.ii, ed. F. Saran]

H. Riemann: *Musikalischen Dynamik und Agogik: Lehrbuch der musikalischen Phrasierung* (Leipzig, 1884)

M. Lussy: 'Die Correlation zwischen Takt und Rhythmus', *VMw*, i (1885), 141

H. Riemann: 'Wurzelt der musikalische Rhythmus im Sprachrhythmus?', *VMw*, ii (1886), 488; repr. in *Präludien und Studien*, i (Frankfurt am Main, 1895/R1967), 104

H. L. Bergson: *Essai sur les données immédiates de la conscience* (Paris, 1889, 19/1920)

P. Souriau: *L'esthétique de mouvement* (Paris, 1889)

E. Meumann: 'Beiträge zur Psychologie des Zeitsinns', *Philosophische Studien*, viii (1893), 431–509; ix (1894), 264–306

——: 'Untersuchungen zur Psychologie und Ästhetik des Rhythmus', *Philosophische Studien*, x (1894), 249–322, 393–430

——: 'Beiträge zur Psychologie des Zeitbewusstseins', *Philosophische Studien*, xii (1896), 127–254

K. Bücher: *Arbeit und Rhythmus* (Leipzig, 1897)

J. Combarieu: *Etudes de philologie musicale*, i: *Théorie du rythme dans la composition moderne d'après la doctrine antique* (Paris, 1897)

T. Lipps: *Grundlegung der Ästhetik*, i (Hamburg and Leipzig, 1903)

H. Riemann: *System der musikalischen Rhythmik und Metrik* (Leipzig, 1903)

——: 'Ein Kapitel vom Rhythmus', *Die Musik*, iii (1903–4), 155

C. S. Myers: 'A Study of Rhythm in Primitive Music', *British Journal of Psychology*, i (1905), 397

R. H. Stetson: 'A Motor Theory of Rhythm and Discrete Succession', *Psychological Review*, xii (1905), 250, 293–350

J. Combarieu: *La musique, ses lois, son évolution* (Paris, 1907; Eng. trans., 1910)

K. Koffka: 'Experimental-Untersuchungen zur Lehre vom Rhythmus', *Zeitschrift für Psychologie*, lii (1909), 1–109

H. Wetzel: 'Zur psychologischen Begründung des Rhythmus und die aus ihr fliessende Bestimmung der Begriffe Takt und Motiv', *Riemann-Festschrift* (Leipzig, 1909), 100

H. Woodrow: 'A Quantitative Study of Rhythm', *Archives of Psychology*, xiv (1909), 1–66

E. Landry: *La théorie du rythme et le rythme de français déclamé* (Paris, 1911)

O. Rutz: *Musik, Wort und Körper als Gemütsausdruck* (Leipzig, 1911)

——: *Sprache, Gesang und Körperhaltung* (Munich, 1911)

E. M. von Hornbostel: 'Arbeit und Musik', *ZIMG*, xiii (1911–12), 341

V. Benussi: *Psychologie der Zeitauffassung* (Heidelberg, 1912)

E. Sievers: *Rhythmisch-melodische Studien* (Heidelberg, 1912)

A. Halm: 'Rhythmik und Vortragsdynamik', *Von Grenzen und Ländern der Musik: Gesammelte Aufsätze* (Munich, 1916)

T. Wiehmayer: *Musikalische Rhythmik und Metrik* (Magdeburg, 1917)

G. Becking: ' "Hören" und "Analysieren": zu Hugo Riemanns Analyse von Beethovens Klavier-Sonaten', *ZMw*, i (1918–19), 587

H. Bergson: *Réflexions sur le temps, l'espace et la vie* (Paris, 1920)

O. L. Forel: *Le rythme: étude psychologique* (Leipzig, 1920)

G. Becking: *Studien zu Beethovens Personalstil: das Scherzothema* (Leipzig, 1921)

R. Dumesnil: *Le rythme musical* (Paris, 1921, 2/1949)

H. Bergson: *Durée et simultanéité* (Paris, 1922)

R. H. Stetson: 'Teaching of Rhythm', *MQ*, ix (1923), 181

G. Becking: 'Über ein dänisches Schul-Liederbuch, über Mitbewegungen und Gehaltsanalyse', *ZMw*, vi (1923–4), 100

A. Orel: 'Zur Frage der rhythmischen Qualität in Tonsätzen des 15. Jahrhunderts', *ZMw*, vi (1923–4), 559–607

A. Schering: 'Betonungs- und Gewichtsprinzip', *Kongressbericht: Leipzig 1925*, 460

F. Rosenthal: 'Probleme der musikalischen Metrik', *ZMw*, viii (1925–6), 262

A. Heusler: *Deutsche Versgeschichte* (Berlin, 1925–9)

R. Hönigswald: *Vom Problem des Rhythmus* (Leipzig and Berlin, 1926)

E. Tetzel: *Rhythmus und Vortrag* (Berlin, 1926)

W. Bund: *Einige strittige Probleme der musikalischen Rhythmik und Metrik* (diss., U. of Vienna, 1927)

3. Kongress für Ästhetik und allgemeine Kunstwissenschaft: Halle 1927 [*Zeitschrift für Ästhetik und allgemeine Kunstwissenschaft*, xxi (1927)] [incl. articles and discussions on the problems of rhythm]

R. Steglich: 'Über Dualismus der Taktqualität im Sonatensatz', *Beethoven-Zentenarfeier: Wien 1927*, 104

G. von Keussler and A. Orel: 'Rhythmus in der Musik', *3. Kongress für Ästhetik und allgemeine Kunstwissenschaft: Halle 1927* [*Zeitschrift für Ästhetik und allgemeine Kunstwissenschaft*, xxi (1927)], 260

G. H. Wedge: *Rhythm in Music: a Textbook* (New York, 1927)

T. Lamm: 'Zur experimentellen Untersuchung der rhythmischen Veranlagung', *Zeitschrift für Psychologie* no.118 (1930), 209–82

H. Mersmann: 'Zeit und Musik', *4. Kongress für Ästhetik und allgemeine Kunstwissenschaft: Hamburg 1930* [*Zeitschrift für Ästhetik und allgemeine Kunstwissenschaft*, xxv (1931)], 216

R. Steglich: *Die elementare Dynamik des musikalischen Rhythmus* (Leipzig, 1930)

W. Heinitz: *Strukturprobleme in primitiver Musik* (Hamburg, 1931)

G. Becking: 'Der musikalische Bau des Montenegrinischen Volksepos', *1st International Congress of Phonetic Sciences: Amsterdam 1932* [*Archives néerlandaises de phonétique expérimentale*, viii–xi (1933)], 144

A. W. de Groot: 'Der Rhythmus', *Neophilologus*, xvii (1932), 81, 177, 241

L. Klages: *Vom Wesen des Rhythmus* (Kampen auf Sylt, 1934)

A. Verwey: *Rhythmus und Metrum* (Halle, 1934)

W. Heinitz: 'Berichte der Gesellschaft zur wissenschaftlichen Erforschung musikalischer Bewegungsprobleme, i–v', *Vox*, xx/1 (1934), 54; xx/2 (1934), 120; xxi (1935), 70; xxii (1936), 22; appx, *Archiv für Sprach- und Stimmphysiologie*, i (1937), 249

H. Schenker: *Neue musikalische Theorien und Phantasien*, iii: *Der freie Satz* (Vienna, 1935, rev. 2/1956 by O. Jonas)

G. Flik: *Die Morphologie des Rhythmus* (diss., U. of Berlin, 1936)

J. L. Mursell: *The Psychology of Music* (New York, 1937)

A. Arnholtz: *Studier i poetisk og musikalisk rytmik*, i (Copenhagen, 1938)

H. Mersmann: *Musikhören* (Potsdam and Berlin, 1938, 2/1952)

E. Schmidt: *Über den Aufbau rhythmischer Gestalten* (Munich, 1939)

H. E. Weaver: 'Syncopation: a Study in Musical Rhythms', *Journal of General Psychology*, xx (1939), 409

G. Brelet: *Le temps musical* (Paris, 1949)

W. Heinitz: 'Vom Takt zum Rhythmus', *Studium generale*, ii (1949), 96

R. Steglich: 'Über Wesen und Geschichte des Rhythmus', *Studium generale*, ii (1949), 141

Studium generale, ii/2–3 (1949) [on rhythm and periodicity]

H. Conradin: 'Das Problem der Bewegung in der Musik', *GfMKB, Lüneburg 1950*, 189

J. Kunst: *Metre, Rhythm and Multipart Music* (Leiden, 1950)

A. Schoenberg: *Style and Idea* (New York, 1950; enlarged 1975)

R. Steglich: 'Über den Rhythmus Beethovens', *Studium generale*, iii (1950), 135

C. Alette: *Theories of Rhythm* (diss., U. of Rochester, 1951)

B. C. Benward: *A Proposal for the Analysis of Motion Factors in Music* (diss., U. of Rochester, 1951)

K. Lashley: 'The Problem of Serial Order in Behaviour', *Cerebral Mechanisms in Behaviour*, ed. L. Jeffress (New York, 1951), 112

L. Schrade: 'Das Rätsel des Rhythmus in der Musik', *Melos*, xviii (1951), 304

C. Höweler: *Het rhythme in vers en Muziek* (The Hague, 1952)

——: 'Zur internationalen Uniformität der Begriffe Metrum und Rhythmus', *GfMKB, Bamberg 1953*, 47

H. von Lüttwitz: *Untersuchungen zum Körperausdruck und Tonsatz* (diss., U. of Cologne, 1953)

E. Willems: *Le rythme musical* (Paris, 1954)

A. Briner: *Der Wandel der Musik als Zeit-Kunst* (Vienna, 1955)

P. Fraisse: *Les structures rythmiques* (Paris, 1956)

L. B. Meyer: *Emotion and Meaning in Music* (Chicago, 1956)

W. Wiora: 'Musik als Zeitkunst', *Mf*, x (1957), 15

N. Cazden: 'The Principles of Direction in the Motion of Similar Tonal Harmonies', *JMT*, ii (1958), 162

W. Gerstenberg: 'Grundfragen der Rhythmus-Forschung', *IMSCR*, vii *Cologne 1958*, 113

K. Hlawiczka: 'Die rhythmische Verwechslung', *Mf*, xi (1958), 33

IMSCR, vii *Cologne 1958* [incl. articles on categories of musical rhythm]

J. LaRue: 'Harmonic Rhythm as an Indicator of Rhythmic Function', *IMSCR*, vii *Cologne 1958*, 176

M. Schneider: 'Prolegomena zu einer Theorie des Rhythmus', *IMSCR*, vii *Cologne 1958*, 264

R. Steglich: *Über die 'kantable Art' der Musik J. S. Bachs* (Zurich, 1958)

M. Schneider: 'Studien zur Rhythmik im *Cancionero de Palacio*', *Miscelánea en homenaje a Monseñor Higinio Anglès* (Barcelona, 1958–61), 833

F. Neumann: *Die Zeitgestalt* (Vienna, 1959)

R. Steglich: '"Rhythmische Verwechslung?" ', *Mf*, xii (1959), 92

G. W. Cooper and L. B. Meyer: *The Rhythmic Structure of Music* (Chicago, 1960)

P. Benary: 'Musikalische Werkbetrachtung in metrischer Sicht', *Mf*, xiv (1961), 2

I. Bengtsson: 'On Relationships between Tonal and Rhythmic Structures in Western Multipart Music', *STMf*, xliii (1961), 49

P. Creston: *Principles of Rhythm* (New York, 1961)

F. Klugmann: *Die Kategorie der Zeit in der Musik* (diss., U. of Bonn, 1961)

Werner Dürr: *Untersuchung zur poetischen und musikalischen Metrik* (diss., U. of Tübingen, 1962)

B. Kippenberg: *Der Rhythmus im Minnesang: eine Kritik der literar- und musikhistorischen Forschung* (Munich, 1962)

P. Westergaard: 'Some Problems in Rhythmic Theory and Analysis', *PNM*, i/1 (1962), 180; repr. in *Perspectives on Contemporary Music Theory*, ed. B. Boretz and E. Cone (New York, 1972)

E. Jammers: 'Takt und Motiv: zur neuzeitlichen musikalischen Rhythmik', *AMw*, xix–xx (1962–3), 194

P. Fraisse: *La psychologie du temps* (Paris, 1963; Eng. trans., 1968)

M. Rothärmel: *Der musikalische Zeitbegriff seit Moritz Hauptmann* (Regensburg, 1963)

Walther Dürr: 'Rhythm in Music: a Formal Scaffolding of Time', *The Voices of Time*, ed. J. T. Fraser (New York, 1966), 180

A. A. Pierce: *The Analysis of Rhythm in Tonal Music* (diss., Brandeis U., 1968)

J. L. Hanson: *An Operational Approach to Theory of Rhythm* (diss., Yale U., 1969)

R. E. Ornstein: *On the Experience of Time* (Harmondsworth, 1969)

E. Apfel and C. Dahlhaus: *Studien zur Theorie und Geschichte der musikalischen Rhythmik und Metrik* (Munich, 1974)

G. Hennenberg: *Theorien zur Rhythmik und Metrik: Möglichkeiten und Grenzen rhythmischer und metrischer Analyse, dargestellt am Beispiel der Wiener Klassik* (Tutzing, 1974)

W. Seidel: *Über Rhythmustheorien der Neuzeit* (Bonn, 1975)

——: *Rhythmus: eine Begriffsbestimmung* (Darmstadt, 1976)

M. Yeston: *The Stratification of Musical Rhythm* (New Haven, 1976)

HISTORY: GENERAL

E. Vogel: 'Zur Geschichte des Taktschlagens', *JbMP 1898*, 67

O. Rutz: *Sprache, Gesang und Körperhaltung: Handbuch zur Typenlehre Rutz* (Munich, 1911)

A. Chybiński: *Beiträge zur Geschichte des Taktschlagens* (Kraków, 1912)

G. Schünemann: *Geschichte des Dirigierens* (Leipzig, 1913/R1965)

O. and K. Rutz: *Typenstimmbildung* (Leipzig, 1920)

O. Rutz: *Menschheitstypen und Kunst* (Jena, 1921)

G. Becking: *Der musikalische Rhythmus als Erkenntnisquelle* (Augsburg, 1928)

W. Gurlitt: 'Die Epochengliederung in der Musikgeschichte', *Universitas*, iii (1948), 533

J. Müller-Blattau: *Das Verhältnis von Wort und Ton in der Geschichte der Musik: Grundzüge und Probleme* (Stuttgart, 1952)

C. Sachs: *Rhythm and Tempo: a Study in Music History* (New York, 1953)

W. Gurlitt: 'Form in der Musik als Zeitgestaltung', *Akademie der Wissenschaften und der Literatur, Mainz: Abhandlungen der Geistes- und sozialwissenschaftlichen Klasse*, no.13 (1954), 651

F. Neumann: 'Die Zeitgestalt als Grundbegriff der musikalischen Rhythmik', *GfMKB, Kassel 1962*, 268

CLASSICAL ANTIQUITY; EARLY MIDDLE AGES

Aristides Quintilianus: *Peri mousikēs*, trans. R. Schäfke as *Von der Musik* (Berlin, 1937)

Augustinus: 'De musica', *PL*, xxxii (1841), 1081–194

Grammatici latini, vi: *Scriptores artis metricae*, ed. H. Keil (Leipzig, 1874)

F. A. Gevaert: *Histoire et théorie de la musique de l'antiquité*, ii (Ghent, 1881)

G. Mari: 'I trattati medievali di ritmica latina', *Memorie del Reale Istituto Lombardo di Scienze e Lettere: Classe di lettere, scienze storiche e morali*, xx (Milan, 1899), 373–496

H. W. Smyth: *The Greek Melic Poets* (London, 1900)

W. Meyer: *Gesammelte Abhandlungen zur mittellateinischen Rhythmik*, i–iii (Berlin, 1905–36/R1970)

C. F. A. Williams: *The Aristoxenian Theory of Musical Rhythm* (Cambridge, 1911)

H. J. Moser: 'Zur Rhythmik der altdeutschen Volksweisen', *ZMw*, i (1918–19), 225

J. G. Schmidt, ed.: *Haupttexte der gregorianischen Autoren betreffs Rhythmus* (Düsseldorf, 1921) [orig. texts and Ger. trans.]

H. Edelstein: *Die Musikanschauung Augustinus nach seiner Schrift 'De musica'* (diss., U. of Freiburg, 1929)

C. M. Bowra: *Greek Lyric Poetry* (Oxford, 1936, rev. 2/1961)

E. Jammers: *Der gregorianische Rhythmus: antiphonale Studien* (Leipzig, 1937)

——: 'Rhythmische und tonale Studien zur Musik des Antike und des Mittelalters', *AMf*, vi (1941), 84, 151; viii (1943), 27, 87

T. Georgiades: *Der griechische Rhythmus, Musik, Reigen, Vers und Sprache* (Hamburg, 1949)

L. Kunz: 'Dürfen die Melodietöne des gregorianischen Chorals gezählt werden?', *Mf*, v (1952), 332

H. Husmann: 'Die musikalische Behandlung der Versarten im Troubadourgesang der Notre Dame-Zeit', *AcM*, xxv (1953), 1

T. Georgiades: *Musik und Sprache* (Berlin, Göttingen and Heidelberg, 1954)

H. Husmann: 'Das System der modalen Rhythmik', *AMw*, xi (1954), 1–38

L. Kunz: 'Beda über reinrhythmische und gemischtrhythmische Liedtexte', *KJb*, xxxix (1955), 3

F. de Meeûs: 'Le problème de la rythmique grégorienne, à propos de travaux récents', *AcM*, xxviii (1956), 104–75

R. Monterosso: *Musica e ritmica dei trovatori* (Milan, 1956)

R. L. Crocker: 'Musica rhythmica and Musica metrica in Antique and Medieval Theory', *JMT*, ii (1958), 2

T. Georgiades: *Musik und Rhythmus der Griechen* (Hamburg, 1958)

H. Husmann: *Einführung in die Musikwissenschaft* (Heidelberg, 1958) [with bibliography]

J. W. A. Vollaerts: *Rhythmic Proportions in Early Medieval Ecclesiastical Chant* (Leiden, 1958)

T. Georgiades: 'Sprache als Rhythmus', *Die Sprache*, ed. Bayerische Akademie der Schönen Künste (Munich, 1959), 109

H. Anglès: 'Der Rhythmus in der Melodik mittelalterlicher Lyrik', *IMSCR, viii New York 1961*, i, 3

J. Rayburn: *Gregorian Chant Rhythm: a History of the Controversy Concerning its Interpretation* (New York, 1961)

W. Vetter: 'Antike', *Mythos-Melos-Musica*, ii (Leipzig, 1961), 349–500

L. Gamberini: *La parola e la musica nell'antichità* (Florence, 1962)

B. Kippenberg: *Der Rhythmus im Minnesang: eine Kritik der literar- und musikhistorischen Forschung* (Munich, 1962)

E. Jammers: 'Der Choral als Rezitativ', *AMw*, xxii (1965), 143

H. Vanderwerf: 'Deklamatorischer Rhythmus in den Chansons der Trouvères', *Mf*, xx (1967), 122

W. Anderson: 'Word Accent and Melody in Ancient Greek Musical Texts', *JMT*, xvii (1973), 186

E. Jammers: 'Gregorianischer Rhythmus, was ist das?', *AMw*, xxxi (1974), 290

LATE MIDDLE AGES TO PRESENT DAY

G. Baini: *Saggio sopra l'identità de'ritmi musicale e poetico* (Florence, 1820)

J. Gersbach: *Reihenlehre oder Begründung des musikalischen Rhythmus aus der allgemeinen Zahlenlehre*, ed. A. Gersbach (Karlsruhe, 1834)

A. Czerwinski: *Die Tänze des XVI. Jahrhunderts* (Danzig, 1878)

R. von Liliencron: 'Die Horazischen Metren in deutschen Kompositionen des 16. Jahrhunderts', *VMw*, iii (1887), 26–91

H. Bergson: *Introduction à la métaphysique* (Paris, 1903; Eng. trans., 1912)

F. Busoni: *Entwurf einer neuen Aesthetik der Tonkunst* (Trieste, 1907; Eng. trans., 1911)

E. Borrel: *Contribution à l'interpretation de la musique française du XVIIIe siècle* (Paris, 1914)

A. Schering: 'Takt und Sinngliederung in der Musik des 16. Jahrhunderts', *AMw*, ii (1919–20), 465

H. Besseler: *Beiträge zur Stilgeschichte der deutschen Suite im 17. Jahrhundert* (diss., U. of Freiburg, 1923)

A. M. Michalitschke: *Theorie des Modus* (Regensburg, 1923)

A. Orel: 'Zur Frage der rhythmischen Qualität in Tonsätzen des 15. Jahrhunderts', *ZMw*, vi (1923–4), 559–607

J. Handschin: 'Zur Notre Dame-Rhythmik', *ZMw*, vii (1924), 386

A. Schering: *Die metrisch-rhythmische Grundgestalt unserer Choralmelodien* (Halle, 1924)

H. Besseler: 'Studien zur Musik des Mittelalters', *AMw*, vii (1925), 167–252; viii (1926), 137–258

F. Blume: *Studien zur Vorgeschichte der Orchestersuite im 15. und 16. Jahrhundert* (Leipzig, 1925)

A. Schering: 'Betonungs-und Gewichtsprinzip', *Kongressbericht: Leipzig 1925*, 460

——: 'Zur Metrik der "Psalmen Davids" von Heinrich Schütz', *Festschrift Peter Wagner* (Leipzig, 1926/R1969), 176

K. G. Fellerer: *Die Deklamationsrhythmik in der vokalen Polyphonie des 16. Jahrhunderts* (Düsseldorf, 1928)

R. Gerber: 'Wort und Ton in den *Cantiones sacrae* von Heinrich Schütz', *Gedenkschrift für Hermann Abert* (Halle, 1928), 57

A. Schering: 'Musikalischer Organismus oder Deklamationsrhythmik?', *ZMw*, xi (1928–9), 212

O. Gombosi: 'Zur Deutung gewisser rhythmischer Figuren des 16. Jahrhunderts', *ZMw*, xii (1929–30), 380

H. Cowell: *New Musical Resources* (New York and London, 1930, 2/1969)

P. F. Radcliffe: 'The Relation of Rhythm and Tonality in the 16th Century', *PRMA*, lvii (1930–31), 73

E. Lowinsky: 'Zur Frage der Deklamationsrhythmik in der a-cappella-Musik des 16. Jahrhunderts', *AcM*, vii (1935), 62

E. Jammers: 'Die Barockmusik und ihre Stellung in der Entwicklungsgeschichte des Rhythmus', *Festschrift für Martin Bollert* (Dresden, 1936), 225

E. Schwarzmaier: *Die Takt- und Tonordnung J. Riepels* (Wolfenbüttel, 1936)

G. Langer: *Die Rhythmik der J. S. Bachschen Präludien und Fugen für die Orgel* (Dresden, 1937)

H. C. Wolff: 'Der Rhythmus bei J. S. Bach', *BJb*, xxxvii (1940–48), 83

——: 'Die Sprachmelodie im alten Opernrezitativ', *Archiv für Sprach- und Stimmheilkunde*, iv (1940); also in *HJb 1963*, 93

D. P. Walker: 'Musical Humanism in the 16th and Early 17th Centuries', *MR*, ii (1941), 1, 111, 220, 288; iii (1942), 55; Ger. trans. as *Der musikalische Humanismus im 16. und frühen 17. Jahrhundert* (Kassel, 1949)

A. Einstein: 'Narrative Rhythm in the Madrigal', *MQ*, xxix (1943), 475

O. Messiaen: *Technique de mon langage musical* (Paris, 1944; Eng. trans., 1950)

R. von Ficker: 'Probleme der modalen Notation', *AcM*, xviii–xix (1946–7), 2

H. Rosenberg: 'Frottola und Deutsches Lied um 1500: ein Stilvergleich', *AcM*, xviii–xix (1946–7), 30–78

F. Gennrich: *Musikwissenschaftliche Studien-Bibliothek* (Nieder-Modau, 1946–8, Darmstadt, 1953–65)

M. Bukofzer: 'Rhythm and Metre in the Notre Dame Conductus', *BAMS*, xi–xiii (1946–8), 63

H. Engel: 'Ein Beitrag zur Prosodie im 16. Jahrhundert', *IMSCR, iv Basle 1949*, 83

A. Auda: 'Le tactus, principe générateur de l'interprétation de la musique polyphonique classique', *Scriptorium*, iv (1950), 44

H. Besseler: *Bourdon und Fauxbourdon* (Leipzig, 1950)

W. H. Austin: *Harmonic Rhythm in Twentieth-century Music* (diss., Harvard U., 1951)

B. Blacher: 'Über variable Metren', *ÖMz*, vi (1951), 219

R. F. Goldman: Review of *E. Carter: Cello Sonata*, *MQ*, xxxvii (1951), 83

S. Babitz: 'A Problem of Rhythm in Baroque Music', *MQ*, xxxviii (1952), 333

W. Gerstenberg: *Die Zeitmasse und ihre Ordnungen in Bachs Musik* (Einbeck, 1952)

J. Handschin: 'Zur Frage der Conductus-Rhythmik', *AcM*, xxiv (1952), 113

H. Heckmann: *W. C. Printz und seine Rhythmuslehre* (diss., U. of Freiburg, 1952)

F.-J. Machatius: *Die Tempi in der Musik um 1600* (diss., Free U. of Berlin, 1952)

W. Eberhardt: *Das Prinzip der Metrik Beethovens* (diss., German U. of Berlin, 1953)

R. Elvers: *Untersuchungen zu den Tempi in Mozarts Instrumentalmusik* (diss., Free U. of Berlin, 1953)

H. Heckmann: 'Der Takt in der Musiklehre des 17. Jahrhunderts', *AMw*, x (1953), 116

H. Beck: *Studien über das Tempoproblem bei Beethoven* (diss., U. of Erlangen, 1954; *BeJb 1955–6*, 24–54, as 'Bemerkungen zu Beethovens Tempi')

H. Heckmann: 'Influence de la musique instrumentale du XVIe siècle sur la rythmique moderne du XVIIe', *La musique instrumentale de la Renaissance: CNRS Paris 1954*, 339

P. Horn: *Studien zum Zeitmass in der Musik J. S. Bachs: Versuche über seine Kirchenliedbearbeitungen* (diss., U. of Tübingen, 1954)

L. Schrade: 'Sulla natura del ritmo barocco', *RMI*, lvi (1954), 3

T. B. Steunenberg: *Rhythmic Continuity in Slow Movements from Beethoven's Symphonies* (diss., U. of Rochester, 1954)

W. C. Waite: *The Rhythm of Twelfth-century Polyphony* (New Haven, 1954)

H. Zingerle: *Zur Entwicklung der Rhythmik und Textbehandlung in der Chanson von ca. 1470–1530* (Innsbruck, 1954)

E. Carter: 'The Rhythmic Basis of American Music', *Score*, no.12 (1955), 27

A. Feil: *Satztechnische Fragen in den Kompositionslehren von F. E. Niedt, J. Riepel, und H.Chr. Koch* (Heidelberg, 1955)

S. Goldthwaite: *Rhythmic Patterns and Formal Symmetry in the Fifteenth-century Chanson* (diss., Harvard U., 1955)

F.-J. Machatius: 'Über mensurale und spielmännische Reduktion', *Mf*, viii (1955), 139

W. Serauky: 'Die Affekten-Metrik des Isaac Vossius in ihrem Einfluss auf J. Kuhnau und J. S. Bach', *Festschrift Max Schneider* (Leipzig, 1955), 105

I. M. Bruce: 'A Note on Mozart's Bar-rhythms', *MR*, xvii (1956), 35

M. C. Burton: *Changing Concepts of Rhythm in English Musical Writings, 1500–1700* (diss., U. of Rochester, 1956)

Werner Dürr: *Studien zu Rhythmus und Metrum im italienischen Madrigal, insbesondere bei Luca Marenzio* (diss., U. of Tübingen, 1956)

A. Elston: 'Some Rhythmic Practices in Contemporary Music', *MQ*, xlii (1956), 318

F. Feldmann: 'Mattheson und die Rhetorik', *GfMKB, Hamburg 1956*, 99

E. Lowinsky: 'On Mozart's Rhythm', *MQ*, li (1956), 162

H. Keller: 'Rhythm: Gershwin and Stravinsky', *Score*, no.20 (1957), 19

J. LaRue: 'Harmonic Rhythm in the Beethoven Symphonies', *MR*, xviii (1957), 8

A. Palm: *J.-J. de Momigny* (diss., U. of Tübingen, 1957)

K. Stockhausen: '. . . wie die Zeit vergeht . . .', *Die Reihe*, iii (1957), 13; Eng. trans., iii (1959), 10–40

Walther Dürr: 'Zum Verhältnis von Wort und Ton im Rhythmus des Cinquecento-Madrigals', *AMw*, xv (1958), 89

——: 'Zwei neue Belege für die sogenannte "spielmännische Reduktion" ', *Quadrivium*, ii (1958), 76

G. Ligeti: 'Pierre Boulez: Entscheidung und Automatik in der Structure 1a', *Die Reihe*, iv (1958), 38; Eng. trans., iv (1960), 36

C. Petzsch: 'Die rhythmische Struktur der Liedtenores des Adam von Fulda', *AMw*, xv (1958), 143

N. W. Powell: *Rhythmic Freedom in the Performance of French Music from 1650 to 1735* (diss., Stanford U., 1958)

C. Dahlhaus: 'Zur Rhythmik der Mensuralmusik', *Musik und Kirche*, xxix (1959)

L. A. Dittmer: 'Änderung der Grundrhythmen in den Notre-Dame-Handschriften', *Mf*, xii (1959), 392

S. Hermelink: 'Rhythmische Struktur in der Musik von Heinrich Schütz', *AMw*, xvi (1959), 378
I. Herrmann-Bengen: *Tempobezeichnungen: Ursprung, Wandel im 17. und 18. Jahrhundert* (Tutzing, 1959)
A. Copland: *Copland on Music* (New York, 1960)
H. E. Smither: *Theories of Rhythm in the Nineteenth and Twentieth Centuries, with a Contribution to the Theory of Rhythm for the Study of Twentieth-century Music* (diss., Cornell U., 1960)
G. Vecchi: *Dalle Melopoiae sive harmoniae tetracentiae orazione di Tritonio (1507) alle Geminae undiviginti odarum Horatii melodiae (1552)* (Bologna, 1960)
J. Cage: *Silence* (Middletown, Conn., 1961)
P. Creston: *Principles of Rhythm* (New York, 1961)
C. Dahlhaus: 'Zur Entstehung des modernen Taktsystems im 17. Jahrhundert', *AMw*, xviii (1961), 223
M. L. Perkins: *Changing Concepts of Rhythm in the Romantic Era: a Study of Rhythmic Structure, Theory and Performance Practices Related to Piano Literature* (diss., U. of Southern California, 1961)
A. Verchaly: 'La métrique et le rythme musical au temps de l'humanisme', *IMSCR, viii New York 1961*, i, 66
M. Babbitt: 'Twelve-tone Rhythmic Structure and the Electronic Medium', *PNM*, i/1 (1962), 49–79
E. Karkoschka: 'Zur rhythmischen Struktur in der Musik von heute', *GfMKB, Kassel 1962*, 379
D. Lewin: 'A Metrical Problem in Webern's Op.27', *JMT*, vi (1962), 125
M. B. Collins: *The Performance of Coloration, Sesquialtera, and Hemiolia* (diss., Stanford U., 1963)
R. Erickson: 'Time Relations', *JMT*, vii (1963), 174
A. Pike: 'The Time Set as a Rhythmic Agent for the Series', *MR*, xxiv (1963), 168
M. Rothärmel: *Der musikalische Zeitbegriff seit Moritz Hauptmann* (Regensburg, 1963)
K. Stockhausen: 'Die Einheit der musikalischen Zeit', *Texte zur elektronischen und instrumentalen Musik*, i (Cologne, 1963), 211
I. Stravinsky and R. Craft: *Dialogues and a Diary* (Garden City, NJ, 1963)
K. von Fischer: 'Das Zeitproblem in der Musik', *Das Zeitproblem im 20. Jahrhundert*, ed. R. W. Meyer (Berne, 1964), 296
C. Jacobs: *Tempo Notation in Renaissance Spain* (Brooklyn, 1964)
H. E. Smither: 'The Rhythmic Analysis of 20th-century Music', *JMT*, viii (1964), 54–88
C. Dahlhaus: 'Probleme des Rhythmus in der Neuen Musik', *Zur Terminologie der Neuen Musik* (Berlin, 1965)
A. Hughes: 'Mensuration and Proportion in Early Fifteenth Century English Music', *AcM*, xxxvii (1965), 48
J. M. Perkins: 'Note Values', *PNM*, iii/2 (1965), 47
P. Westergaard: 'Some Problems Raised by the Rhythmic Procedures in Milton Babbitt's *Composition for Twelve Instruments*', *PNM*, iv/1 (1965), 109
P. Aldrich: *Rhythm in Seventeenth-century Italian Monody* (New York, 1966)
S. G. Davis: 'Harmonic Rhythm in Mozart's Sonata Form', *MR*, xxvii (1966), 25
A. Feil: *Studien zu Schuberts Rhythmik* (Munich, 1966)
P. Friedheim: 'Rhythmic Structure in Schoenberg's Atonal Compositions', *JAMS*, xix (1966), 59
C. F. Haenselman: *Harmonic Rhythm in Selected Works of the Latter Half of the Nineteenth Century* (diss., U. of Indiana, 1966)
F. Reckow: 'Proprietas und perfectio: zur Geschichte des Rhythmus, seiner Aufzeichnung und Terminologie im 13. Jahrhundert', *AcM*, xxxix (1967), 115
R. J. Rittenhouse: *Rhythmic Elements in the Symphonies of Johannes Brahms* (diss., U. of Iowa, 1967)
E. Varèse: 'Rhythm, Form and Content', *Contemporary Composers on Contemporary Music*, ed. E. S. Schwartz and B. Childs (New York, 1967), 201
D. B. Anthony: *Microrhythm in the Published Works of Anton Webern* (diss., Stanford U., 1968)
J. B. Marks: *Harmonic Rhythm as a Factor in Form Delineation in Selected Instrumental Works from 1775 to 1850* (diss., Indiana U., 1969)
R. P. Morgan: *The Delayed Structural Downbeat and its Effect on Tonal and Rhythmic Structure of Sonata Form Recapitulation* (diss., Princeton U., 1969)
N. Rubenstein: *A Fortran Computer Program for Transcribing Franconian Rhythm* (diss., Washington U., 1969)
R. F. Erikson: *Melodic Structure in Organum Purum: a Computer Assisted Study* (diss., Yale U., 1970)
D. Finke-Hecklinger: *Tanzcharaktere in Johann Sebastian Bachs Vokalmusik* (Trossingen, 1970)
B. Boretz: 'In Quest of the Rhythmic Genius', *PNM*, ix/2 (1971), 149
P. Boulez: *Boulez on Music Today* (London, 1971)
F. Rzewski: 'Nonmetrical Rhythm since 1950', *Dictionary of Twentieth Century Music*, ed. J. Vinton (New York, 1971), 622
H. E. Smither: 'Rhythm', *Dictionary of Twentieth Century Music*, ed. J.

Vinton (New York, 1971), 618
A. Sommer: *Die Komplikationen des musikalischen Rhythmus in den Bühnenwerken Richard Wagners* (Giebing am Chiemsee, 1971)
J. A. Bank: *Tactus, Tempo and Notation in Mensural Music from the 13th to the 17th Century* (Amsterdam, 1972)
G. Henneberg: *Theorien zur Rhythmik und Metrik: möglichkeiten und Grenzen rhythmischer und metrischer Analyse, dargestellt am Beispiel der Wiener Klassik* (Tutzing, 1974)
C. Schachter: 'Rhythm and Linear Analysis: a Preliminary Study', *Music Forum*, iv (1976), 281–334
W. Seidel: *Rhythmus: eine Begriffsbestimmung* (Darmstadt, 1976)

§§I and II, 1–13 based on *MGG* (xi, 383–419) by permission of Bärenreiter

WALTHER DÜRR, WALTER GERSTENBERG (I; II, 1–13),
JONATHAN HARVEY (II, 14)

Rhythm and blues. A term coined for the music most popular among American blacks in the 1950s and 1960s, but now carrying wider applications. The term (or 'R & B') came into use in 1949 when the music-trade paper *Billboard* proposed it as a replacement for 'race music'; it was in turn supplanted in 1969 by 'soul'. The phrase stresses the prominence of BLUES and blues-related styles, particularly those of the Mississippi River delta as they were developed in Chicago and other Midwestern industrial centres.

Unlike traditional blues, rhythm and blues is entirely ensemble music, usually with, first, a 'melodic carrier' (a vocalist or small vocal group, a lead instrumentalist, or both); second, a 'rhythm section' (a string or electric bass; a drum set; a piano, organ or electric guitar, or a combination of them), delineating and elaborating the basic pulse and metre, and providing harmonic support; and third, a 'filler unit' (any combination of a small vocal group, one or more wind instruments, an electric guitar or a keyboard instrument) providing responsorial phrases, riffs and other ostinato-like figures, and additional harmonic and rhythmic support. Most rhythm and blues music is basically in the major mode (with such variants as 'blue notes'); it uses non-modulatory forms modelled on the blues, or Tin Pan Alley popular songs, and is in quadruple metre. Even-numbered beats are emphasized. Much rhythm and blues is vocal; the lyrics range from typical American mainstream popular music with 'escapist' themes to the blues vision of the human condition.

The large number of professional performers who practised the style represent a considerable diversity of musical sub-styles. Recorded anthologies include the *History of Rhythm and Blues* series, *This is how it all Began* and the *Oldies but Goodies* series. Rhythm and blues played an important part in the rise of ROCK AND ROLL in the 1950s; the distinctions between the two styles during that decade are often obscure.

See also SOUL MUSIC; RACE RECORD; MOTOWN.

BIBLIOGRAPHY
C. Keil: *Urban Blues* (Chicago and London, 1966)
C. Gillett: *The Sound of the City* (New York, 1970)
A. Shaw: *The World of Soul* (New York, 1970)
L. McCutcheon: *Rhythm and Blues* (Arlington, Virginia, 1971)
B. Millar: *The Drifters* (London, 1971)
P. Grois: *They all sang on the Corner: New York City's Rhythm and Blues Vocal Groups of the 1950s* (New York, 1973)
S. Propes: *Those Oldies but Goodies* (London and New York, 1973)
J. Whitburn: *Top Rhythm and Blues Records 1949–71* (Menomonee Falls, Wisc., 1973)
C. Gillett: *Making Tracks: Atlantic Records and the Growth of a Multibillion-dollar Industry* (New York, 1974)
L. N. Redd: *Rock is Rhythm and Blues: the Impact of Mass Media* (East Lansing, Mich., 1974)

ROBERT WITMER

Rhythmic modes [modal rhythm]. The modern name

for a medieval concept of rhythm in which the durations of individual notes were determined by their place within a succession of long and short values. The concept is associated particularly with polyphony of the late 12th century and early 13th, but has been applied by scholars also to medieval secular monophony.

The principal exposition of the rhythmic modes is by Johannes de Garlandia in *De mensurabili musica* of about 1240 (ed. E. Reimer, 1971–2). Garlandia equated the three Latin terms 'modus', 'species' and 'maneries': '*maneries* is the term given to that which, by the measurement of time, that is by longs or by shorts, runs together' (p.36). This 'measurement of time' involved the regular reiteration of a given rhythmic pattern. It thus provided continuity – a regularly recurring succession of long and short values. Moreover, the six rhythmic patterns that were available were subsumed within a single system by a common unit of time, the 'perfection', equal to three short notes (breves). By this common unit, the different patterns could literally be 'run together'.

A single statement of any one of these six patterns was termed an *ordo*. The last duration of an *ordo* (shown below in italic), or in the case of the fourth the last two, when fully stated was a repetition of the first duration. These six patterns constituted the six rhythmic modes. They were, each stated as a single *ordo* (L = long, B = breve): 1st mode: L–B–*L*; 2nd mode: B–L–*B*; 3rd mode: L–B–B–*L*; 4th mode: B–B–L–*B–B*; 5th mode: L–L–*L*; 6th mode: B–B–B–*B*. When one of these patterns was reiterated, the last duration was omitted until the final *ordo*. Thus a succession of three *ordines* of the 1st mode was: L–B–L–B–L–*B–L*; two *ordines* of the 3rd mode: L–B–B–L–B–B–*L*.

The regular long was equal in duration to two breves. Thus in the 1st and 2nd modes the reiteration of a long and a breve produced a metrical unit worth three breves (the 'perfection'). The same was true of the 6th mode, in which a succession of three breves was reiterated. These three modes were called by Garlandia the 'right' or 'measurable' modes (*modi recti* or *mensurabiles*: see ex.1). In the other three modes, reiteration occurred

Ex.1

1. L B L B L B L

2. B L B L B L B

6. B B B B B B B B B B

after two perfections: each pattern lasted for six breves' duration. These were the *modi non recti* or *non mensurabiles* or *ultra mensuram* ('beyond measure'), so-called because each used a long that was worth three breves (thus more than the regular long of two breves), and because two of them used a breve (always the second of a pair) that was double its regular value (ex.2).

Modal rhythm, which is rightly described as one of the foremost achievements of Western music, has often been accredited to Léonin. But as a conceptual system it must have existed for some time before his day; it is even doubtful whether Léonin could have invented the notational system that came into existence in the 12th century to represent the six modes. This system took

Ex.2

3. L B B L B B L B B L

4. B B L B B L B B L B B

5. L L L L L L L

over the existing ligature shapes of square notation, using prescribed successions of two-, three- and four-note ligatures or single notes to designate each of the modal patterns, as follows: 1st mode: 3–2–2 ... 2; 2nd mode: 2–2–2 ... 3; 3rd mode: 1–3–3 ... 3; 4th mode: 3–3–3 ... 2; 5th mode: 3–3–3 ... 3, or 1–1–1 ... 1; 6th mode: 4–3–3 ... 3. For examples of two *ordines* of each see ex.3.

Ex.3

1.   4.

2.   5.

3.   6.

Modifications could be made to the strict basic patterns, in particular by subdividing notes of two or three breves' value into separate, short notes. This distortion of the archetypal proportions of values was codified by Anonymous IV as 'irregular modes' (*modi irregulares*), and there were notational devices for representing them. In addition, Anonymous IV spoke of a 7th mode 'which is the "mixed" or "common" mode, and is made up of two or three or four etc of the above' (ed. F. Reckow, *Der Musiktraktat des Anonymus 4*, i, 1967, p.85).

The patterns of the rhythmic modes go back to classical antiquity and to the 'feet' of Greek poetics. The system of poetic feet was transmitted to the Middle Ages through the writings of St Augustine. Other theorists of the 13th century who contributed to the literature of modal rhythm are Anonymous VII (c1260–80; CS, i), Alfredus (c1275), Magister Lambertus (before 1279) and the St Emmeram Anonymous (1279).

See also Notation, §III, 2; Rhythm, §II, 4.

BIBLIOGRAPHY

W. G. Waite: *The Rhythm of Twelfth-century Polyphony: its Theory and Practice* (New Haven, 1954)
F. Reckow: *Der Musiktraktat des Anonymus 4*, ii: *Interpretation der Organum Purum-Lehre* (Wiesbaden, 1967)
W. Frobenius: 'Modus (Rhythmuslehre)', *HMT*
G. A. Anderson: 'Johannes de Garlandia and the Simultaneous Use of Mixed Rhythmic Modes', *MMA*, viii (1975), ii

For further bibliography *see* Notation.

IAN D. BENT

Rhythmik (Ger.). The study of or approach to Rhythm; the rhythmic resources of a composer, a school, a piece or set of pieces, a genre etc.

Rhythm Kings. *See* New Orleans Rhythm Kings.

Riadis [Eleftheriadis; Khu], **Emilios** (*b* Salonica, 1 May ?1886; *d* Salonica, 17 July 1935). Greek composer. His father, Erricos Khu, was of Austro-Hungarian origin. Riadis took his first lessons in harmony and the piano in Salonica with Dimitrios Lalas (1848–1911), a friend and disciple of Wagner. He then studied at the Munich Academy (1908–10) with Walbrunn (form, instrumentation, fugue), Mayer-Gschrey (piano), Becht and Stich (choral singing). Afterwards he was a pupil of Charpentier and Ravel in Paris (1910–15) where he established a reputation among French and exiled Greek composers: Schmitt is said to have described him as 'the Musorgsky of Greece'. Temporarily arrested as a Turkish subject at the outbreak of World War I, he returned to Salonica (1915) where for the rest of his life he was professor of the piano at the State Conservatory. He is reported to have been also sub-director of this institution, but no documentary confirmation of this appointment is available. In 1923 he received the National Award for Arts and Letters. Although he gave occasional lectures – on Chinese music (1921 or 1922), on Mozart (1924) and on ancient Egyptian music (1926) for example – his enthusiasm for work is said to have slackened. Yet it seems that some of the chamber works were composed after his return to Greece, and on his deathbed he spoke of a complete string quartet existing in his head. He died at Salonica City Hospital from a variety of Malta fever.

Riadis, whose sensitivity had much in common with that of Cavafy, sought to express a personal vision bound up with experience of the orient and of Greece: 'One is only perfect in opposing nature. The other natural bears no good fruit', as he wrote on one of his MSS. His renown rests largely on his songs, particularly those with a national or oriental flavour, which were envied by Kalomiris. They are masterpieces of the Greek national school, with a lyricism combining 'oriental sensuality with western "restraint"' (Anoyanakis). Their vocal lines, influenced by folk music and full of poignant nostalgia, are enhanced by subtle harmonies and arabesques in the piano accompaniments. Impressionist and avoiding harsh dissonance, these accompaniments often adroitly imitate folk instruments and attain an extreme simplicity and transparency, as in *La chanson du vieux Bey*. The chamber music, inasmuch as the state of Riadis's MSS allows any stylistic description, incorporates modal polyphony, occasional ostinatos and clear textures without sophisticated effects. Most of the major works are in an unfinished condition. Many are in several versions, often written in light pencil and much corrected; Riadis also made corrections to published works and these are incorporated in Anoyanakis's edition of 16 songs (1973). The MSS include poems and other texts, among them a 200-page history of music.

WORKS

STAGE

Galateia (music drama, 3, P. Ch. Jablonski), 1912–13; act 1 in vocal score, act 2 in orch score, act 3 in vocal score sketches
La route verte (opera, 1, J. Valcler), ?1914; vocal score sketches
Un chant sur la rivière (opera, 1, Riadis), n.d.; 55 bars of prelude for 2 pf
Incidental music: Salome (Wilde), 1922, ?lost; Hecuba (Euripides), 1927; Riquet à la houppe (Banville, trans. Riadis), 1929

INSTRUMENTAL AND CHORAL

Orch: Invocation à la paix, inc., n.d.; Symphonie agreste, pf score sketches, n.d.
Fugue, c, 1909; 3 danses grecques, pf, no.2, 1925; Sonate pour 4, B, pf qt, *c*1928–35; Hommage à Ravel, pf, n.d.; 2 sonatas, vc, pf, inc., n.d.; Sonate pour 4, C, pf qt, 1 movt extant, n.d.; Str Qt, G, 3 movts extant,

n.d.; Str Qt, D, inc., n.d.; fragments of other str qts
Choral: Liturgie de St Jean Chrysostome, men's and boys' chorus, 5vv, perf. 1931; Little Doxology, men's and boys' chorus, n.d.; Good Friday Service, SATTBarB, n.d.; Christos anesti [Christ is risen], TTBarB, n.d.; all pubd Athens, 1952

PUBLISHED SONGS
(for 1v, pf unless otherwise stated)

Chansonette orientale (M. Malakassis, Fr. trans.), pubd in *Les feuilles de mai* (1912–13), no.1, p.28
Jasmins et minarets (Riadis): Raïka, L'odalisque, Salonique (Paris, 1913); no.3 orchd C. Brailoi, n.d., unpubd
Berceuse (Riadis) (Paris, 1913); orchd, n.d., unpubd
La fiancée de l'ombre (Riadis) (Paris, 1913)
5 chansons macédoniennes (Riadis): Au métier, Les plaintes de la jeune fille, L'esprit du lac et le roi, La fiancée de l'ombre, Berceuse (Paris, 1914)
3 chansons macédoniennes (Riadis): L'aveugle au métier, L'orpheline, L'esprit du lac et le roi [= no.3 of previous set] (Paris, 1914)
13 petites mélodies grecques (Riadis, except where otherwise stated), 2 vols.: Ni 'kalimera', ni 'ora kali' (Nerval), Luth, Demande, Automnal (Malakassis), Chansonette (Malakassis), Musique (Malakassis), Rencontre (Belle s'en va puiser de l'eau), La chanson du vieux Bey, Sérénade, La chanson de l'odalisque, La chanson de l'adolescent, La fille et le chasseur, La danseuse (Paris, 1921, 1924)
12 Greek and 3 Albanian folksongs in *Das Lied der Völker*, ed. H. Möller (Mainz, after 1928), 265ff
Greek songs (?trad.): Ehe ya [Farewell], Pali synnefias' o ouranos [Again the sky clouded over], Garoufalia, S, A, T, B, pf (Salonica, n.d.)
Dance songs: Pothos [Desire] (D. Christopoulos), Tryghos [Grape harvest] (?trad.), S, Mez, A-cl, pf qt (Salonica, n.d.)
9 mikra romeika tragoudia (A. Pallis, except where otherwise stated): Hira [Widow] (Riadis), Erofili (Cambyssis), Tourkala [Turkish woman], Missiriotissa [Egyptian woman], Arvanitissa [Albanian woman], Patrinoula [Patras girl], Haide, hourdhe [Onward, Kurd], Tsigana, Kori sti vryssi [The maid at the fountain] (Riadis) (n.d.)
Miroloya [Laments] (Palamas): Afkiasto ki astolisto [Uncared and unadorned], Ta mallia sou olohyta [With hair flowing], Sto taxeidhi pou se pasi o mavros kavallaris [On the journey with the black rider] (1921)
Last two collections, with nos.3, 10, 11, 12 from 13 petites mélodies grecques, pubd as *E. Riadis: Songs*, ed. F. Anoyanakis (Salonica, 1973)

UNPUBLISHED SONGS

Ode à Cassandre (Ronsard), 1911
Remainder n.d.: Les Odalisques (?Riadis); [3] Nocturnes (Nocturnes chinoises, Chansons chinoises), sketches; San paramythi [Like a fairy tale] (Gryparis); Danse biblique (Riadis) 1v, 2 pf; [3] Pèlerinages fantasques (Riadis); [5] Intermedia (Gryparis); [4] Ta tragoudia tis tourkissas [Songs of the Turkish women] (?Riadis); 3 tsiganika tragoudia (no.1 R. Ghil, trans. Riadis); [3] Mélodies antiques (J. M. de Heredia); [4] Chansons exotiques (J. Valcler); [3] Mélodies simples (Valcler); 3 songs (Ronsard, trans. Riadis); 3 songs (Moréas, trans. Riadis); 2 songs (Fort, trans. Riadis); Epitaphe de pernette de juillet (M. Scève), others
Principal publishers: Chapelier, Institut français d'Athènes, Romaeos, Senart, Techni

WRITINGS

'I moussiki apo tou tetartou mehri tou dekatou ogdoou aeonos ke malista en Italia' [Music from the 4th century to the 18th, particularly in Italy], *Makedonikon imerologion 1926* (Salonica, 1925), 183ff

BIBLIOGRAPHY

O. Merlier: Foreword to score of *Liturgie de St Jean Chrysostome* (Athens, 1952), 8ff
F. Anoyanakis: 'I moussiki stin neoteri Hellada', in K. Nef: *Einführung in die Musikgeschichte* (Gk. trans., Athens, 1958), 588
M. Dounias: 'Riadis, Emilios', *MGG*
'Costí Palama: grammata ston Emilio Riadi (1926–1927)' [Kostis Palamas: letters to Emilios Riadis (1926–1927)], *Epitheorissi technis*, xix/111–12 (1964), 279

GEORGE S. LEOTSAKOS

Ribafrecha, Martín de. *See* RIVAFRECHA, MARTÍN DE.

Rïbakov, Sergey Gavrilovich (*b* Samara, 9 Oct 1867; *d* Moscow, 28 Dec 1921). Russian musicologist. He graduated from St Petersburg University, where he had studied history and philosophy; he also attended Rimsky-Korsakov's composition classes at the conservatory. In 1893 he was invited to join a folksong commission set up jointly by the Russian Geographical Society and the Academy of Sciences, and during the next few years he travelled extensively in the Urals, Siberia and other parts of south-east Russia. On his first journey (1895–7) he noted down over 200 folk melodies of the Bashkirs and Tatars, and in 1899, using a phonograph, he collected folk music of the Tajiks, Turkmens and Uzbeks. He wrote many articles on folk music in Russian journals, and also an essay on Russian church bells.

WRITINGS
'O narodnïkh pesnyakh tatar, bashkir i teptyarey' [The folksongs of the Bashkirs, Tatars and Teptyars], *Zhivaya starina*, iv (1894), 325–64

O poeticheskom tvorchestve ural'skikh musul'man: tatar, bashkir, teptyarey [The poetry of the Ural Muslims: the Tartars, Bashkirs and Teptyars] (St Petersburg, 1895)

Kuray: bashkirskiy muzïkal'nïy instrument [The kuray: a Bashkir musical instrument] (St Petersburg, 1896)

Tserkovnïy zvon v Rossii [The church bell in Russia] (St Petersburg, 1896)

Muzïka i pesni ural'skikh musul'man s ocherkom ikh bïta [The music and songs of the Ural Muslims with an essay on their way of life] (St Petersburg, 1897)

'Russkaya pesnya' [Russian song], *Entsiklopedicheskiy slovar' Brokgauza i Efona*, liii (1899), 310–21

JENNIFER SPENCER

Ribári, Antal (*b* Budapest, 8 Jan 1924). Hungarian composer. He studied composition at the Budapest Academy of Music (1943–7, under Rezső Kókai) and later with Ferenc Szabó. From 1953–5 he taught at the Academy of Dramatic Arts. His First Violin Sonata won the composition prize at the World Youth Festival in Warsaw in 1955.

WORKS
(selective list)

Stage: Lajos király válik [The divorce of King Louis] (opera, 1), Budapest, 1959; Liliom (F. Molnár), opera, 1960; Az aranypróbás legény [Fortunio] (ballet, 1), 1969

Orch: Szimfonietta, 1956; Vc Conc., 1958; Sym. no.1, 1960; Musica per archi, 1961; Pantomime, 1962; Sym. no.2, 1964; Vn Concertino, 1965; Metamorphosis, S, orch, 1966; Dialogues, va, orch, 1967; Sym. no.3, 1970; Sinfonia festiva, 1972; Conc. grosso, fl, cl, harp, orch, 1975; Variations, 1976; 6 Improvisations, 1977

Vocal: A megsebzett galamb és a szökőkút [The wounded pigeon and the fountain] (G. Apollinaire), cantata, T, chorus, orch, 1962; 5 Shakespeare-szonett, 1v, pf, 1972; Requiem for the Lover (after Blake, Shelley, Swinburne), cantata, A, T, chorus, orch, 1973; Hat sor a Satyriconból, 2 A, chorus, insts, 1975; 5 songs (Villon), S, pf, 1977

Inst: Vn Sonata no.1, 1953; Vn Sonata no.2, 1954; Str Qt no.1, 1955; Str Qnt, 1956; Va Sonata, 1958; Vc Sonata, 1959; Str Qt no.2, 1964; 9 Miniatures, str qt, 1966; All 'antica, pf, 1968; 5 miniatures, wind trio, 1969; Fantasia, vn, va, vc, 1971; Sonata, pf, 1971; Vn Sonata no.3, 1972; Vc Sonata no.2, 1973; Doppelquartett, str, 1977

Ribaupierre, André de (*b* Clarens, 29 May 1893; *d* Rochester, NY, 17 Jan 1955). Swiss violinist. He studied the violin with his brother Emile (*b* 1887), with Władislav Górski and with Ysaÿe. After his début at the age of 17 in Lausanne and London his first tours were of New Zealand and Australia. He held master classes at the Lausanne Conservatory (1914–19), then he continued his studies in Cincinnati under Ysaÿe, whose master class he took over from 1921 to 1924. In 1923 he joined the staff of the Cleveland Institute of Music, where he also led the orchestra. In 1929 he returned to Switzerland where he became director of the Institut de Ribaupierre, a private music school founded by his family in Lausanne, with branches in Montreux, Vevey, Aigle and Château d'Oex, and gave many concerts. During a further tour of the USA he was made director

of the violin department of the Eastman School of Music, Rochester, where he remained until his death.

BIBLIOGRAPHY
SML

W. Schuh, ed.: *Schweizer Musikbuch*, ii (Zurich, 1939), 171

F. Walter and L. Montandon: 'André de Ribaupierre', *SMz*, xcv (1955), 122

'André de Ribaupierre†', *Feuilles musicales*, viii (1955), 27

JÜRG STENZL

Ribayaz, Lucas Ruiz de. See RUIZ DE RIBAYAZ, LUCAS.

Ribeca (It.). REBEC.

Ribeiro, Mario Luis de Sampayo. See SAMPAYO RIBEIRO, MARIO LUIS DE.

Ribera, Antonio de (*fl* early 16th century). Spanish composer and singer. Between 1520 and 1527 he was a papal singer during the pontificates of Leo X and Clement VII. (2 August 1514, suggested by F. X. Haberl as the date he started, must now be considered erroneous.) The lists of singers between that of 1 March 1509 (when he is not mentioned) and that of 3 September 1522, in which he is cited in the penultimate place just before Josquinus Dor, are missing. However, a record of payment, undated but placed after one of 1520, indicates that he had recently joined the chapel. He is mentioned for the last time in December 1526 in a list that is particularly important, since all singers signed it to certify receipt of payment. The next record of chapel members (July 1529) no longer cites Ribera, Bernardo Salinas and many others, probably a result of the serious disturbances that took place during the sack of Rome on 6 May 1527.

Ribera's works, particularly his secular compositions, effectively communicate the text by simple means. His style is archaic but nonetheless highly expressive. The pieces for the Elche Mystery, with their harmonizations of popular tunes, are typically Spanish in character.

WORKS
Misa, 4vv, *P-Cug* 12; Misa, 4vv, *E-TZ* 3

Ave Maria, 4vv, *P-Cug* 48; Ave Maria, 4vv, *E-TZ* 2; O bone Jhesu, 4vv, *TZ* 2; Patris sapientia, 4vv, *TZ* 2

Music for feast of the Assumption, Elche Mystery (see Pomares): Cantem senyors, 4vv; Flor de virginal bellEça, 4vv; Jueus, aquesta gran novetat, 3vv; Nosaltres tots creiem, 4vv; O Déu adonai, 4vv; Promens Jueus, 3vv

Nunca yo, señora, os viera (villancico), 3vv; ed. in MME, v (1947), no.192

Por unos puertos arriba (romance), 4vv; MME, v, no.107

BIBLIOGRAPHY
Archival records, *I-Ras* Mandati camerali, 857, 859, Protocolli delli uditori di camera 409; *Rvat* C.S. 652, 681

F. X. Haberl: 'Die Kammermusiker Leo's X., das Personal der Capella Sistina und Giulia bis Paul III (1513–1534)', *VMw*, iii (1887), 251

H. W. Frey: 'Regesten zur päpstlichen Kapelle unter Leo X. und zu seiner Privatkapelle', *Mf*, viii (1955), 62

J. Pomares: *La festa o misterio de Elche* (Barcelona, 1957), 215ff

R. Stevenson: *Spanish Music in the Age of Columbus* (The Hague, 1960)

JOSÉ M. LLORENS

Ribera, Bernardino de (*b* Játiva, province of Valencia; *d* ?Toledo, ?late 1570 or before 9 Feb 1571). Spanish composer. He became choirmaster of Avila Cathedral on 2 June 1559. He thus taught the young Victoria, who was then a pupil at the cathedral choir school, and he appears to have influenced him considerably. In November 1562 he left Avila Cathedral and in April 1563 was appointed choirmaster of Toledo Cathedral; his successor at Avila was Juan Navarro (i). On 9

February 1571 Andrés de Torrentes succeeded him at Toledo, so he may well have died shortly before this. A number of sacred works by him survive in manuscript, including two masses and some *Magnificat* settings (in *E-Tc*), while most of the other works are motets (in *E-P*, *Tc*, *V*, *VAcp* and *Zs*); two motets and a *Magnificat* setting are ed. H. Eslava y Elizondo, Lira sacro-hispana, siglo XVI, 1st ser., i (Madrid, 1869).

BIBLIOGRAPHY

F. Rubio Piqueras: *Música y músicos toledanos: contribución a su estudio* (Toledo, 1923), 58, 60

———: *Códices polifónicos toledanos* (Toledo, 1925), 21f

R. Stevenson: *Spanish Cathedral Music in the Golden Age* (Berkeley and Los Angeles, 1961), 239, 324, 332, 351f, 450, 467

GUY BOURLIGUEUX

Ribera (y Tarragó), Julián (*b* Carcagente, nr. Valencia, 19 Feb 1858; *d* Carcagente, 2 May 1934). Spanish Arabist and writer on history, literature and music. He studied at Valencia University and took a doctorate at Madrid. He then taught Arabic at Saragossa University (from 1887) and Arabian-Spanish literature at Madrid (from 1905). He was appointed a member of the Real Academia Española in 1912 and of the Real Academia de la Historia in 1915.

Ribera's studies of Islamic influence on medieval Spanish literature and history are still held in esteem; he was one of the first to precipitate the present debate about the origins of European lyric poetry and song by drawing attention to the *mūwashshaḥ* and the *kharjas*, Spanish-Muslim lyrics written in a mixture of cultured and popular styles. He did not begin to write about music until he was over 60 and becoming deaf. His musicological theses are now generally held to be wayward. His theory of the influence of Hispano-Arabic music on European song from the 11th century has been repudiated by Schneider, Spanke and in particular Anglès, who censured Ribera's methods of transcription; his theories of the Arabic origins of Iberian folksong, even extending into modern popular songs, are likewise suspect. However, parts of his survey of Arabian music in *La música de las cantigas*, and of the *jota* and the *muñeira*, at least, are still valuable to modern scholars.

WRITINGS

La música de las cantigas [de Santa María de Alfonso el Sabio], iii, (Madrid, 1922, 2/1927 without music transcr. as *Historia de la música árabe medieval y su influencia en la española*; Eng. trans., abridged, as *Music in Ancient Arabia and Spain*, 1929)

Disertaciones y opúsculos: edición colectiva que en su jubilación del profesorado le ofrecen sus descípulos y amigos (Madrid, 1928) [incl. 'La música andaluza medieval en Europa', 'De música y métrica gallegas', 'Para la historia de la música popular', 'El cancionero de Abencuzman', 'Epica andaluza romanceada', 'La enseñanza entre los musulmanes españoles']

La música de la jota aragonesa (Madrid, 1928)

EDITIONS

La música andaluza medieval en las canciones de trovadores, troveros y minnesinger (Madrid, 1923–5/*R*1974) [text repr. in *Disertaciones*]

BIBLIOGRAPHY

M. Asín Palacios: Introduction to *Disertaciones y opúsculos* (Madrid, 1928)

H. Spanke: 'Die Theorie Riberos über Zusammenhänge zwischen früh-romanischen Strophenformen und andalusisch-arabischer Lyrik des Mittelalters', *Volkstum und Kultur der Romanen*, iii (Hamburg, 1930), 258

V. Castañeda: 'Don Julián Ribera y Tarragó', *Boletín de la Real academia de la historia*, civ (1934), 401 [incl. list of works]

H. Anglès: *La música de las cantigas de Santa María del rey Alfonso el Sabio: facsímil, transcripción y estudio crítico*, iii (Barcelona, 1943), 35–8, 454ff [incl. H. Spanke: 'Die Metrik der *Cantigas*', refuting some of Ribera's theories]

M. Schneider: 'A propósito del influjo árabe: ensayo de etnografía

musical en la España medieval', *AnM*, i (1946), 31–141

JACK SAGE

Ribible. *See* REBEC.

Ribniczki, Jacobo Christophoro. *See* RYBNICKÝ, JAKUB KRYŠTOF.

Ribó, Jesús A. Occasional pseudonym for JOSÉ SUBIRÁ.

Ribock, Justus Johannes Heinrich (*b* Egestorf, nr. Lüneburg, 1743; *d*? Hanover, *c*1785). German physician and flute designer. After study at Helmstedt, Rinteln and Halle, he graduated as a doctor of medicine in Göttingen in 1763. About 1780 he practised at Lüchow, the home town of his family, and betwen 1777 and 1783 he had an animated correspondence with J. G. Tromlitz in Leipzig. His book on the flute compares contemporary flutes by Tromlitz, Quantz, Kirst and Grenser and makes many proposals for better design and treatment of the instrument; it also contains the first German fingering chart for the five-key flute.

WRITINGS

Bemerkungen über die Flöte, und Versuch einer kurzen Anleitung zur bessern Einrichtung und Behandlung derselben (Stendal, 1782/*R*)

'Über Musik, an Flötenliebhaber insonderheit', *Magazin der Musik*, i (Hamburg, 1783), 686–736

BIBLIOGRAPHY

K. Ventzke: 'Dr. J. J. H. Ribock (1743–1785)', *Tibia*, ii (1976), 65

KARL VENTZKE

Ribs (Fr. *éclisses*; Ger. *Zargen*; It. *fascie*). The term may be used in two senses when describing musical instruments. (1) In instruments like the violin, the ribs are the sides which connect the back and the belly.

(2) In instruments like the lute, the ribs are the curved strips of wood (often thinner than 1·5 mm, and from nine to nearly 40 in number) that form the internal frame of the lute's swelling body.

Applied to lute-like instruments, 'ribs' has almost an anatomical meaning. The first meaning could not be applied to a lute whose convex back is jointed directly to the belly without ribs; and to make this distinction clear the strips of wood that support the lute's belly are generally called bars. The first meaning is more prevalent, being proper to all members of the violin and viol families and to those plucked instruments, such as guitars, whose back and belly are clearly separated by 'sides', a term somewhat more common in this connection than ribs.

In instruments of the violin family proper (violin, viola, cello and sometimes the double bass) both the top and back overhang the ribs, while in most other string instruments, including the viols, the belly and back are flush with the ribs. In viols and violins the ribs are generally made of hardwood, particularly maple, and should be of the same texture as the back, preferably from the same piece of wood. In the violin, the ribs consist, as a rule, of six curved strips: two for the upper curves (bouts), two for the inner C-bouts of the waist and two for the lower bouts.

The height of the ribs varies greatly, having been determined in the past, largely on empirical grounds, by generations of craftsmen and players who were influenced by such factors as the sound desired, the ease of tone production, and the anatomy of the intended player. For example, the sound of a violin built with a relatively flat-arched belly and back (as in a typical

Stradivari violin) generally 'carries' better than one of high-modelled arch (e.g. an Amati or a Stainer). In practice, this means that the ribs are higher in a Stradivari than in an Amati violin because, in general, the lower the arching, the higher the ribs should be (the ribs of an 'average' Stradivari violin made after 1700 are from 3 to 3·17 cm).

The height of the ribs generally increases with the size of the instrument, provided it is of the same family and is played in the same manner. For instance, the height of the ribs of the viola, which is played under the chin, cannot exceed a certain limit (in practice, rarely more than 3·13 cm) without causing the player some discomfort. On the other hand, the height of the ribs is not important as a playing factor to the player whose instrument is played at the knee, such as the cello, the height of whose ribs is about 11·5 cm or even more. Similarly, the viols, all of which are played at the knee, are constructed with ribs whose height exceeds that of the corresponding member of the violin family, especially the violin and viola. A typical treble viol has ribs whose height is 7 cm as compared to less than half that for the ribs of a violin.

For illustration see VIOLIN.

DAVID D. BOYDEN

Ricartsvorde, Jean. See RICHAFORT, JEAN.

Riccati, Count **Giordano** (b Castelfranco Veneto, nr. Treviso, 25 Feb 1709; d Castelfranco Veneto, 20 July 1790). Italian mathematician, music theorist, physicist and architect. Born into a family of mathematicians, he attended the Collegio dei Nobili in Bologna from 1720 to 1726 and, in 1729, Padua University, at the same time studying music theory and various instruments. He corresponded widely with scholars, in particular F. A. Vallotti, with whom in 1735 he discussed a theory of the generation of the major and minor scales and the tonal function of chords similar to that propounded by Rameau two years later in his *Génération harmonique*. From 1747 he taught mathematics, physics, architecture and music in Treviso; G. B. Bortolani and Ignazio Spergher studied the piano and counterpoint with him. The first of his writings on music, the *Saggio sopra le leggi del contrappunto*, appeared at Castelfranco in 1762 and was followed by other theoretical works, a biography of Steffani and critiques of the theories of Rameau, Tartini and Vallotti. Riccati held that, in the construction of theoretical musical systems, abstract reasoning needed to be tempered with empirical data, and he adversely criticized the systems of Rameau (in the *Génération harmonique*) and Tartini for being at variance at some points with music as it was actually practised. Riccati was a member of the Treviso Accademia dell'Arcadia under the name of Erbistide Callistamio.

BIBLIOGRAPHY
D. M. Federici: *Commentario sopra la vita e gli studi del Conte Giordano Riccati nobile trivigiano* (Venice, 1790)
P. Petrobelli: 'Riccati, Graf Giordano', *MGG* [incl. complete list of writings on music]

FERRUCCIO TAMMARO

Ricchezza, Donato (b 1648; d 1716). Italian composer. He was active in Naples. His surviving works consist of sacred vocal music and oratorios, apparently written for the Oratorio dei Filippini (now Girolamini). His oratorios from the 1680s show his familiarity with progressive idioms of his time: characteristic features include the use of obbligato accompaniments in the orchestra, the independent melodic character of the bass line in continuo arias, and the inclusion of sicilianos, an aria type becoming popular just at this time. Later oratorios show regressive tendencies, with static bass lines and a relative abundance of arias in 3/2 time similar to those popular during the composer's youth. The sacred music features a variety of combinations, from solo voice with continuo to large concerted works for soloists, chorus and orchestra.

WORKS
(all in I-Nf)

31 sacred compositions, incl. 2 masses
11 oratorios: La fede trionfante, 1683; S Giusto, 1683; S Eustachio, before 1689; Vita di S Eustachio, 1689; Il martirio di S Eustachio, after 1689; La ruina degli Angeoli; La madre di Maccabei; La gara degli elementi; In honore del glorioso S Francesco Saverio; Nabucco; S Martino vescovo

THARALD BORGIR

Ricci, Cesarina (b Tingoli; fl 1597). Italian composer. Her only known work, *Il primo libro de madrigali a cinque voci con un dialogo a otto* (Venice, 1597), is dedicated from Monte Colombano to Cardinal S Giorgio and includes the only two known compositions of Alberto Ghirlinzoni.

Ricci, Federico (b Naples, 22 Oct 1809; d Conegliano, nr. Treviso, 10 Dec 1877). Italian composer, brother of Luigi Ricci. Like Luigi he was educated at the Naples Conservatory, which he entered in 1818. His teachers included Zingarelli, the great contrapuntist Pietro Raimondi and, in their capacity as *maestrini*, his own brother and Bellini. His talent first showed itself in two masses and a symphony composed while he was still a student. In 1829 he cut short his studies to follow Luigi to Rome, where he became intimate with the painter Horace Vernet and his circle and sat more than once for Vernet himself. About this time he was recommended to Bellini, then in Milan, who, it was hoped, might secure him an opera contract at La Scala. But Bellini was either unable or unwilling to do this, and the start of Federico's theatrical career was delayed until the production in 1835 at the Teatro Fondo, Naples, of *Il colonello*, the first of four comedies composed jointly with Luigi. This was followed by Federico's first venture on his own, *Monsieur de Chalumeaux* (Venice, 1835), and a second collaboration, *Il disertore per amore*, written for Naples in 1836. Then came one of his most sensational successes, *La prigione di Edimburgo* (Trieste, 1838), an *opera semiseria* drawn from Scott's *The Heart of Midlothian*. Besides the popular barcarolle 'Nella poppa del mio brick', it contains a remarkable mad role for the second prima donna (Madge Wildfire in the novel), in which the singer Rita Gabussi created a furore.

Federico's La Scala début with *Un duello sotto Richelieu* (1839) was not specially glorious, but in 1841 he scored a double success with *Luigi Rolla* (Florence), written for and dedicated to the tenor Napoleone Moriani, and *Corrado d'Altamura* (Milan), based on the same plot as Verdi's *Oberto, conte di San Bonifacio* and widely considered to be his masterpiece in the tragic genre (it was the only one of his serious operas to be printed outside Italy). Its success resulted in a commission from Carlo Alberto, King of Savoy, to provide for his court two occasional cantatas, the first of which was performed in 1842 to celebrate the wedding of the crown prince, Vittorio Emmanuele. Ricci was now famous; he travelled widely and was known in the salons of Paris. But his serious operas written subsequently aroused less and less interest. Like his brother he succeeded mainly in comedy, to which he devoted himself exclusively after 1847. Two years after *Crispino e la comare* (Venice, 1850), his final collaboration with Luigi, Federico triumphed in Vienna with *Il marito e l'amante*, not surprisingly, perhaps, for what is an obvious forerunner of Strauss's *Die Fledermaus*. But the utter failure of *Il paniere d'amore* (Vienna, 1853) decided him to accept the offer of an appointment as *maître de chapelle* of the imperial theatres at St Petersburg, a high-sounding title whose duties involved no more than the supervision of vocal studies at the conservatory. His compositions of the next 16 years include vocal chamber works and exercises for his students, but nothing for the stage. In Italy he was by now regarded as one of the most skilful composers of the older generation. In 1869 Verdi invited him to contribute a piece to the *Album Piave*, a set of romances to be published in aid of the librettist, then paralysed by a stroke, and a Milan committee, with Verdi's approval, asked him to supply a Recordare to the requiem commemorating the anniversary of Rossini's death. After Federico left Russia for Paris in 1869 he enjoyed an Indian summer of popularity as a composer of French *opéra bouffe*. The most famous of these, *Une folie à Rome* (Paris, 1869), was originally composed in Italian as *Carina* (though first performed in Italian as *Una follia a Roma*) and was also performed with great success at Genoa under Angelo Mariani. In 1876 he retired to Conegliano in the Veneto, where he died the following year leaving his last opera, *Don Quichotte*, uncompleted.

Less obviously original than his brother, Federico was the more accomplished and versatile composer. In comedy he had a lighter, more graceful touch, which would make his contributions to *Crispino e la comare* relatively easy to pick out, even if they were not indicated in the first printed score. His serious works are worthy to stand beside Mercadante's, though they do not aspire to the same grandeur. Late offshoots of the Bellini tradition, they were inevitably among the casualties of the post-*Nabucco* era. But *La prigione di Edimburgo*, which holds a delicate balance between pathos and comedy, might well bear revival. The late *opéras comiques* show an unexpected ability to keep up to date in matters of harmony and scoring, but they remain tied to the expansive traditions of Italian *opera buffa*.

WORKS

OPERAS

Il colonello [La donna colonello] (opera giocosa, 2, J. Ferretti), Naples, Fondo, 14 March 1835, collab. L. Ricci; *I-Mr, Nc*, excerpts (Milan, 1835), vocal score (Paris, c1840)

Monsieur de Chalumeaux (melodramma comico, 2, Ferretti), Venice, S Benedetto, 14 June 1835; autograph *Mr*, excerpts (Milan, 1835)

Il disertore per amore (opera giocosa, 2, Ferretti), Naples, Fondo, 13 Feb 1836, collab. L. Ricci; *Mr, Nc*, excerpts (Milan, 1836)

La prigione di Edimburgo (melodramma semiserio, 3, G. Rossi), Trieste, Grande, 13 March 1838; autograph *Mr*, vocal score (Milan, 1840); rev., Milan, *Mr*

Un duello sotto Richelieu (melodramma serio, 2, F. dall'Ongaro), Milan, La Scala, 17 Aug 1839; autograph *Mr*, excerpts (Milan, 1839)

Luigi Rolla [Michelangelo e Rolla] (melodramma tragico, 3, S. Cammarano), Florence, Pergola, 30 March 1841; vocal score (Milan, 1841)

Corrado d'Altamura (dramma lirico, prol, 2, G. Sacchéro), Milan, La Scala, 16 Nov 1841; autograph *Mr*, vocal score (Milan, 1842); rev., Paris, 1844, *Mr*, added nos. (Milan, 1844), vocal score (Paris, n.d.)

Vallombra (dramma lirico, 2, Sacchéro), Milan, La Scala, 26 Dec 1842; autograph *Mr*, excerpts (Milan, 1843)

Isabella de' Medici (opera seria, 3, A. Gazzoletti), Trieste, Grande, 9 March 1845

Estella di Murcía (melodramma serio, 3, F. M. Piave), Milan, La Scala, 21 Feb 1846; autograph *Mr*, vocal score (Milan, 1846); rev., Venice, *Mr*

L'amante di richiamo (opera giocosa, 2, dall'Ongaro), Turin, d'Angennes, 13 June 1846, collab. L. Ricci

Griselda (melodramma serio, 4, Piave), Venice, La Fenice, 13 March 1847; autograph *Mr*, vocal score (Milan, n.d.)

Crispino e la comare (melodramma fantastico-giocoso, 4, Piave), Venice, S Benedetto, 28 Feb 1850, collab. L. Ricci; autograph *Mr*, vocal score (Milan, 1850); in Fr. as Le docteur Crispin, Paris, 1869, with added nos. by F. Ricci, vocal score (Paris, n.d.)

I due ritratti (opera buffa, 2, ?Ricci), Venice, S Benedetto, 21 Nov 1850

Il marito e l'amante (melodramma comico, 3, Rossi), Vienna, Kärntnertor, 9 June 1852; autograph *Mr*, vocal score (Milan, 1852); in Fr. as Une fête à Venise, Paris, 1872, with added nos. by Ricci, vocal score (Paris, n.d.)

Il paniere d'amore (opera buffa, 2, ?Ricci), Vienna, Kärntnertor, 25 May 1853

Une folie à Rome (opéra bouffe, 3, V. Wilder), Paris, Fantaisies-Parisiennes, 30 Jan 1869; in It. orig. as Una follia a Roma, perf. Paris, 1870; autograph *Nc*, vocal score (Paris, n.d.; Milan, n.d.)

Le docteur Rose, ou La dogaresse (opéra comique, 3, E. de Najac), Paris, Bouffes-Parisiens, 10 Feb 1872; vocal score (Paris, n.d.)

Don Quichotte, 1876, inc.

SONGS

Le rendez-vous au salon (Milan, 1840), 6 ariettes: 1 Ballata antica, 2 Una postilla al vocabolario d'amore, 3 Il carrettiere del Vomero, 4 La preghiera d'un bandito, 5 Je ne rêve qu'à toi, 6 Il ritorno a Napoli; 6 nocturnes, 2vv: 7 La solita conversazione, 8 La mia felicità, 9 Consiglio all'amica, 10 Gli spazzacamini, 11 Perchè, 12 La traversata del lago

Etrennes à l'objet de ma pensée (Milan, 1841): 1 Il suonatore di campane, 2 Il n'est jamais content, 3 Vicino e lontano, duettino, 4 I cacciatori, duettino/chorus, 5 Propositi d'amanti, notturno, 3 B, 6 Serenata, 2 S, A, B, 7 Le tue carezze!, 8 Con quanto si contenta un lazzarone!, duettino

Grida dei venditori di Napoli (Naples, ?1846): 1 Venditori d'ostriche e d'uova, 2 di gelse gelate, 3 di castagne, 4 di broccoli, sarde e cetone, 5 di ciliegie e di ricotte, 6 di fichi secchi, 7 di mele e di carne di maiale, 8 di fave, 9 di frutti secchi, carciofi e franfellichi

Album, in Venetian dialect (Milan, 1850): 1 La colomba di Venezia, 2 La morosa, 3 La vezilia del Redentor, 4 Amor, 5 La bigolante, 6 El dì di S Marco

Album (Milan, 1850): 1 Una fontana a Roma, 2 L'indifferenza, 3 Desiderio di pace, 4 Sentite che idea!, 5 Non è tutt'oro quello che luce, 6 Voi siete la più bella ragazzina, serenata, 2B

Canti (Milan, 1864): 1 Giuramenti, 2 Una preghiera, 3 Un arancino, 4 Un cuore, 5 Solito scioglimento, 6 Alla fenestra affacciate

C'est pour vous (Milan, n.d.): 1 Sta bene all'erta, 2 Il pescator veneziano, 3 La fioraia, 4 Il immagine di Lei, 5 Dolente istoria, 6 Il disinganno, 7 La mia bella è morta, 8 Un ricordo a mezzanotte, duettino

Several individual It. and Fr. songs and duets, most pubd (Milan, St Petersburg, Paris)

OTHER WORKS

Cantatas: La felicità (F. Romani), Genoa, for wedding of Vittorio Emanuele, 1842; Cantata (di Negro), Genoa, commissioned by King Carlo Alberto; Cantata (G. Pepoli), St Petersburg, in praise of Italy, 1854

Sacred: 2 masses, 4vv, orch, 1819, 1829; Dies irae, 4vv, orch; Recordare, S, A, Bar, B, orch, for Rossini requiem, 1869; hymn

Others: Solfèges (St Petersburg, n.d.); Canto patriotico triestino, collab. L. Ricci; pf pieces

BIBLIOGRAPHY

L. Escudier: *Mes souvenirs* (Paris, 2/1863), 20f

F. de Villars: *Notices sur Luigi et Federico Ricci, suivies d'une analyse critique de 'Crispino e la comare'* (Paris, 1866)

A. Heulard: *Etude sur 'Une folie à Rome'* (Paris, 1870) [with work-list]

F. Florimo: *Cenno storico sulla scuola musicale di Napoli* (Naples, 1869–71, repr. 1880–81 as *La scuola musicale di Napoli e i suoi conservatorii*, i, iv)

P. Cambiasi: 'Prospetto delle composizioni musicali del maestro cav. Federico Ricci', *Gazzetta musicale di Milano*, xxxii (1877), suppl. to no.51

L. de Rada: *I fratelli Ricci* (Florence, 1878)

G. Cottrau: *Lettres d'un mélomane pour servir de document à l'histoire musicale de Naples de 1829 à 1847* (Naples, 1885)

A. Cametti: *Un poeta melodrammatico romano: appunti e notizie in gran parte inedite sopra Jacopo Ferretti e i musicisti del suo tempo* (Milan, 1898)

JULIAN BUDDEN

Ricci, Francesco Pasquale (*b* Como, 17 May 1732; *d* Loveno di Menaggio, Como, 7 Nov 1817). Italian composer. Born of a middle-class family, he received a liberal education, then concentrated on music under Vignate at Milan. He joined the Franciscan Order of the Friars Minor and used the title Abbate. Appointed *maestro di cappella* at Como Cathedral in 1759, he was nevertheless able to travel extensively and was absent from his duties during much or all of the time between early 1768 and December 1777. He visited Paris, London, and, most importantly, The Hague, where he appeared in concert (1766–80) and dedicated works to the prince and others attached to the court. In the 1760s and 1770s a number of works, including symphonies, string trios and quartets and accompanied keyboard sonatas, were published there or in Amsterdam. Many of these appeared also in Paris and London, generally in the same edition with altered title-page. According to Brook, a work by Ricci was probably the first to be published as a 'symphonie concertante'. However, despite this title, the piece was probably an ordinary symphony, perhaps a reprint of a piece from the sets published in The Hague (*c*1765) and Amsterdam (op.2, *c*1767). His fame was spread by the impact of the first performance of his *Dies irae*, which was published and widely distributed. According to Fayolle, the audience was struck with a 'saint effroi' by the introduction at the 'Tuba mirum' of a trumpet sounding from the cupola (the printed score calls for horns). Ricci was not the first to attempt this effect, however.

Ricci's name appears with that of J. C. Bach in the *Méthode . . . pour le forte-piano* (Paris, *c*1788), devised for one of the conservatories at Naples. The nature of the collaboration is uncertain, but it is likely that the two musicians had become acquainted at Milan through Count Litta, a patron of both, and had continued their friendship in London. Ricci may merely have arranged and edited the work in memory of his deceased friend; the ascription to Bach may in any case be false.

WORKS

INSTRUMENTAL

Orch: 9 syms., str, 2 ob, 2 hn, 3 as op.[1] (The Hague, *c*1765; also pubd separately as Periodical Symphonies, no.1, 1763, no.2, 1780), 6 as op.2 (Amsterdam, *c*1767); [3] Symphonies concertantes, op.9 (The Hague, London and Paris, *c*1775); Fl. Conc., *D-KA*; Vc Conc., *D-B*
Chamber: 12 trios, 6 for 2 vn, vc, op.3 (Amsterdam, *c*1765), 6 for vn, va, vc, op.10 (The Hague, *c*1775); 12 sonatas, 6 for hpd, vn, vc, op.4 (London, *c*1768), 6 for hpd, vn, op.6 (The Hague, *c*1770); 6 Qnts, various insts, op.5 (London, *c*1768); 6 str qts, op.8 (The Hague, *c*1773); [2] Divertimento, hpd, vn (The Hague, *c*1770); Minuetti ballabili e Notturni, 2 vn, bc (The Hague, *c*1775); others, *D-B, KA, I-Mc*

OTHER WORKS

Vocal: Dies irae, 4vv, orch, op.7 (The Hague, *c*1773), Recordare, ed. C. LaTrobe in *Selection of Sacred Music*, ii (London, 1806); Mass, g, ed. S. Webbe, *A Collection of Masses* (London, 1792), also in *Sacred Music* (London, 1811); 6 ariette, 2 vv, bc (The Hague, *c*1777); Canzone buffa (n.p., n.d.), mentioned by Gerber; ?Mass, *A-Wn*; other sacred works
Pedagogical: [Méthode ou] Recueil de connoissances elementaires pour le forte-piano ou clavecin (Paris, *c*1788/*R*1973); Aux plus heureux jeux harmoniques pour composer des menuets ou des contredanses, mentioned by Gerber

BIBLIOGRAPHY

EitnerQ; *FétisB*; *GerberL*; *La MusicaD*
G. B. Giovio: *Gli uomini della Comasca diocesiantichi, e moderni, nelle arti, e nelle lettere illustri* (Modena, 1784)
A. Choron and F. Fayolle: *Dictionnaire historique des musiciens* (Paris, 1810–11/*R*1970)
C. Gervasoni: *Nuova teoria di musica* (Parma, 1812)
E. Ostinelli: *Sulla fondazione di una scuola popolare-musicale in Como* (Como, 1875)
B. Studeny: *Beiträge zur Geschichte der Violin-Sonate im 18. Jahrhundert* (Munich, 1911)
C. S. Terry: *John Christian Bach* (London, 1929, rev. 2/1967)
R. Münster: *Die Sinfonie Toeschis* (diss., U. of Munich, 1956), 148
B. S. Brook: *La symphonie française dans la seconde moitié du XVIIIe siècle* (Paris, 1962)
C. Cudworth and F. Göthel: 'Ricci, Francesco Pasquale', *MGG*
W. S. Newman: *The Sonata in the Classic Era* (Chapel Hill, 1963, rev. 2/1972)
R. Kidd: *The Sonata for Keyboard with Violin Accompaniment in England: 1750–1790* (diss., Yale U., 1967), 157
——: 'The Emergence of Chamber Music with Obbligato Keyboard in England', *AcM*, xliv (1972), 141
M. de Smet: *La musique à la cour de Guillaume V, Prince d'Orange (1748–1806)* (Utrecht, 1973)

RONALD R. KIDD

Ricci, Luigi (*b* ?Naples, 8 June or 8 July 1805; *d* Prague, 31 Dec 1859). Italian composer, brother of Federico Ricci. At the age of nine he entered the Naples Conservatory, where he studied the violin before turning to the keyboard and to composition. His masters included Furno, Zingarelli and, privately, Generali, at whose instance he composed his first comic opera, *L'impresario in angustie*, to the same libretto set by Cimarosa. Performed in 1823 by the students of the conservatory, it is said to have incensed the austere Zingarelli, who had to be placated with a cantata written in his honour. In 1824 Ricci made his début at the Teatro Nuovo, Naples, with *La cena frastornata*, in which Generali had a hand; it was followed by four more works there in 1825–7. His attempt to capture the S Carlo with *Ulisse in Itaca* in 1828 failed, as did most of his essays in the serious genre. The moderately successful *Colombo* (Parma) and *L'orfanella di Ginevra* (Rome) in 1829 were followed by four disasters in a row: *Il sonnambulo* and *L'eroina del Messico* (Rome), *Annibale in Torino* (Turin) and *La neve* (Milan). But with *Chiara di Rosembergh* (Milan, 1831), an *opera semiseria* composed for the mezzo-soprano Giuditta Grisi, Ricci not only redeemed his reputation but also created one of the favourite pieces of the decade. From then on he continued mainly in comedy, scoring a notable success with *Un avventura di Scaramuccia* (Milan, 1834), written to a witty libretto, part romance, part theatrical satire, by Felice Romani. A performance at Pavia the following year earned him a benefit night, for which he added the one-act *farsa La serva e l'ussero*, an amusing piece that has enjoyed amateur revival. In the same year *Il colonello*, the first of four works written jointly with his brother Federico, was produced in Naples. The series culminated in the fantastic comedy *Crispino e la comare* (Venice, 1850), which held the stage until the end of the century.

In 1836 Ricci accepted the post of *maestro di cappella* at Trieste. After the predictable disaster of his *Le nozze di Figaro* (Milan, 1838), written to a new and undistinguished libretto by Gaetano Rossi, he gave up composing operas for seven years and devoted himself to religious music, also serving as *maestro concertatore* at the Teatro Grande (in this capacity he directed the première in 1848 of Verdi's *Il corsaro*).

In 1843 the twins Franziska (Fanny) and Ludmilla (Lidia) Stolz (*b* 1827), after leaving the Prague Conservatory, were also engaged at the Teatro Grande. They then accompanied Ricci to Odessa, where he directed the 1844–5 opera season. There he lived more or less openly with both, so causing confusion as well as scandal. After returning to Trieste, the three were in 1847–8 at Copenhagen, where the sisters' engagement at the Opera was cut short by the king's death. Back in Trieste, Ricci married Lidia in 1849 without discontinuing the *ménage à trois*. Lidia's daughter Adelaide (1850–71) had a brief career as a singer, appearing at the Théâtre-Italien, Paris, in 1868–9. Fanny's illegitimate son Luigi (1852–1906) earned a modest reputation as a theatre conductor and composer of operas and operettas. He called himself Ricci-Stolz after becoming the heir of his aunt, the soprano Teresa Stolz (who was a pupil of Luigi Ricci in the 1850s).

By the middle of the century Ricci was once more doing well with *opere buffe* such as *Il birraio di Preston* (Florence, 1847) and, more notably, *La festa di Piedigrotta* (Naples, 1852), whose tarantella remains a popular classic of light music. After the appearance of his last opera *Il diavolo a quattro* (Trieste, 1859), which had been commissioned at Copenhagen in 1847–8, but not performed then, symptoms of mental illness became evident. He was transferred to an asylum at Prague, his wife's birthplace, where he died, like his idol Donizetti, of general paralysis of the insane.

Luigi Ricci's is one of the more individual voices in Italian opera of the period. His chief gift was for comedy, to which he brought not only a complete mastery of the traditional devices but also a new, robust *buffo* manner characterized by a wealth of bouncing *allegretto* melodies, mostly in duple time, and a not infrequent use of folktune. Not even at his most sophisticated, as in *Scaramuccia*, did he match Donizetti's elegance and sentimental charm. He was clearly the leading spirit in the collaborations with his brother Federico, and most of *Crispino* is by him. The comic numbers of *Chiara di Rosembergh* were the most celebrated, but elsewhere there are bold strokes of harmony and rhythm that show an ability to rise to the serious dramatic occasion.

WORKS
OPERAS

NN – *Naples, Teatro Nuovo*   MSc – *Milan, Teatro alla Scala*

L'impresario in angustie (farsa, 1, G. M. Diodati), Naples, Conservatory, 1823; *I-Nc*
La cena frastornata (opera semiseria, 2), NN, aut. 1824; *Nc*
L'abbate Taccarella [La gabbia de' matti; Aladino] (opera buffa, 2, A. L. Tottola), NN, carn. 1825; *Mr, Nc*, excerpts (Milan, 1832)
Il sogno avverato (azione teatrale, Tottola), NN, for king's return, sum. 1825, collab. D. Pogliani-Gagliardi
Il diavolo condannato a prender moglie [Il diavolo mal sposato] (opera semiseria, 2, Tottola), NN, 30 Jan 1826; *Mc, Nc*
La lucerna di Epitteto (opera semiseria, 2, G. Checcherini), NN, carn. 1827; *Nc*
Ulisse in Itaca (opera seria, 2, D. Gilardoni), Naples, S Carlo, 12 Jan 1828; *Nc*
Colombo (melodramma serio, 2, F. Romani), Parma, Ducale, 27 June 1829; *Mr*, excerpts (Milan, 1830)
L'orfanella di Ginevra [Amina] (melodramma semiserio, 2, J. Ferretti), Rome, Valle, 9 Sept 1829; *Mc, Mr, Nc*, excerpts (Milan, 1830), rev. version, *Mr*
Il sonnambulo (opera semiseria, 2, Romani), Rome, Valle, 26 Dec 1829; excerpts (Milan, 1830)
L'eroina del Messico [Fernando Cortez] (melodramma serio, 2, Ferretti), Rome, Tordinona, 9 Feb 1830; autograph *Mr*, excerpts (Milan, 1830)
Annibale in Torino (melodramma serio, 2, Romani), Turin, Regio, 26 Dec 1830
La neve (commedia lirica, 2, Romani), Milan, Canobbiana, 21 June 1831; ?autograph *Mr*
Chiara di Rosembergh (opera semiseria, 2, G. Rossi), MSc, 11 Oct 1831; autograph *Mr*, vocal score (Milan, 1832)
Il nuovo Figaro (melodramma giocoso, 2, Ferretti), Parma, Ducale, 15 Feb 1832; autograph *Mr*, excerpts (Milan, 1832)
I due sergenti (opera semiseria, 2, Romani), MSc, 1 Sept 1833; autograph *Mr*, excerpts (Milan, 1833)
Un avventura di Scaramuccia (melodramma comico, 2, Romani), MSc, 8 March 1834; autograph *Mr*, copy *Mc*, vocal score (Milan, 1834)

Gli esposti [Eran due, or son tre] (melodramma buffo, 2, Ferretti), Turin, d'Angennes, 3 June 1834; autograph *Mr*, excerpts (Milan, 1839)
Chi dura vince [La luna di miel] (melodramma eroicomico, 2, Ferretti), Rome, Valle, 26 Dec 1834; autograph *Mr*, vocal score (Milan, 1841); as La petite comtesse, Paris, 1876, vocal score (Paris, n.d.)
Il colonello [La donna colonello] (opera giocosa, 2, Ferretti), Naples, Fondo, 14 March 1835, collab. F. Ricci; *Mr, Nc*, excerpts (Milan, 1835), vocal score (Milan, c1840)
La serva e l'ussero (farsa, 1), Pavia, Compadroni, spr. 1835; autograph *Mr*, vocal score (Milan, 1841)
Chiara di Montalbano (melodramma semiserio, 2, Rossi), MSc, 15 Aug 1835; autograph *Mr*
Il disertore per amore (opera giocosa, 2, Ferretti), Naples, Fondo, 13 Feb 1836, collab. F. Ricci; *Mr, Nc*, excerpts (Milan, 1836)
Le nozze di Figaro (melodramma comico, 2, Rossi), MSc, 13 Feb 1838; autograph *Mr*, excerpts (Milan, 1838); rev., MSc, 1841, autograph *Mr*, excerpts (Milan, 1841)
La solitaria delle Asturie (opera seria, 2, Romani), Odessa, Italiano, 20 Feb 1845
L'amante di richiamo (opera giocosa, 2, F. dall'Ongaro), Turin, d'Angennes, 13 June 1846, collab. F. Ricci
Il birraio di Preston (melodramma giocoso, 3, F. Guidi), Florence, Pergola, 4 Feb 1847; *Mo*, vocal score (Milan, ?1847)
Crispino e la comare (melodramma fantastico-giocoso, 4, F. M. Piave), Venice, S Benedetto, 28 Feb 1850, collab. F. Ricci; autograph *Mr*, vocal score (Milan, 1850); in Fr. as Le docteur Crispin, Paris, 1869, with added nos. by F. Ricci, vocal score (Paris, n.d.)
La festa di Piedigrotta (opera buffa napolitana, 4, M. d'Arienzo), NN, 23 June 1852; *Nc*, vocal score (Naples, n.d.)
Il diavolo a quattro (melodramma comico, 3, Rossi), Trieste, Armonia, 15 May 1859; autograph *Mr*, vocal score (Milan, 1859)

OTHER WORKS

Sacred: Mass, 4vv, orch, before 1823; Messa pastorale; Requiem; Messa di S Luigi, ATBarB, org, *Mr*; more than 20 masses for Trieste Cathedral, after 1836; Credo, 3vv, orch, *Nc*; Litany, S, S, B, org, *Nc*; others

Vocal: Mes loisirs, 6 songs, 5 duets, 1 quartet (Milan, 1840); Les inspirations du thé, 5 songs, 1 trio (Milan, 1845); other songs; I contrabbandieri, 1/3vv (Milan, n.d.); Serenata (Milan, 1845): 1 Un eco divino, 3vv, 2 Non risplende, duettino, 3 Anche un zeffiro, romanza, 4 Poichè siam vicino al mare, canzone; Parthenope, hymn, *Nc*

Inst: Gran concertone, for opening of Teatro Italiano, Odessa, 1844, *Bc*

BIBLIOGRAPHY
V. dal Torso: *Luigi Ricci* (Trieste, 1860)
L. Escudier: *Mes souvenirs* (Paris, 2/1863), 20f
F. de Villars: *Notices sur Luigi et Federico Ricci, suivies d'une analyse critique de 'Crispino e la comare'* (Paris, 1866)
F. Florimo: *Cenno storico sulla scuola musicale di Napoli* (Naples, 1869–71, repr. 1880–81 as *La scuola musicale di Napoli e i suoi conservatorii*, i, iv)
L. de Rada: *I fratelli Ricci* (Florence, 1878)
G. Cottrau: *Lettres d'un mélomane pour servir de document à l'histoire musicale de Naples de 1829 à 1847* (Naples, 1885)
A. Cametti: *Un poeta melodrammatico romano: appunti e notizie in gran parte inedite sopra Jacopo Ferretti e i musicisti del suo tempo* (Milan, 1898)
F. Walker: *The Man Verdi* (London, 1962)

JULIAN BUDDEN

Ricci, Ruggiero (*b* San Francisco, 24 July 1918). American violinist. After studies with Persinger from the age of eight, he made his débuts at San Francisco (1928) and Carnegie Hall, New York (1929), playing the Mendelssohn concerto. Further studies with Michel Piastro and Georg Kulenkampff were followed by a tour of Europe in 1932, when he visited London, Paris, Berlin, Vienna, Rome and Scandinavia with distinct success. He studied next with Paul Stassevitch (1933–7), as well as with Persinger again, and made the transition from prodigy to mature virtuoso without apparent difficulty, eventually specializing in the 19th-century bravura repertory. He has been widely acclaimed for the uncanny accuracy, ease and elegance of his playing, especially in demanding, extrovert challenges. He toured the USSR three times, made his first world tour in 1957, and appears regularly in the USA and Europe. His première performances include Ginastera's concerto

(1963) with Bernstein and the New York PO at Lincoln Center, and von Einem's concerto (1970) with Ozawa and the Vienna PO at the Vienna Festival. With a special affinity for Paganini, he introduced the rediscovered Fourth Concerto to American audiences in 1971, and he was the first to record the 24 Caprices in their original version. He has taught at Indiana University (1970–73) and, from 1975, at the Juilliard School, New York. He plays a violin dated 1734 by Guarneri del Gesù which formerly belonged to Huberman.

BIBLIOGRAPHY
J. Creighton: *Discopaedia of the Violin, 1889–1971* (Toronto, 1974)
MARTIN BERNHEIMER

Ricciarelli, Katia (*b* Rovigo, 16 Jan 1946). Italian soprano. She studied at the Benedetto Marcello Conservatory, Venice. Her stage début was at Mantua in 1969, as Mimì. After winning the Giuseppe Verdi Award for Young Singers (1970) at Parma, she sang Leonora in *Il trovatore* there. Her fame spread throughout Italy as a result of the 1971 television New Verdi Voices Contest, which she won. She made her American début at Chicago in 1972, as Lucrezia in *I due Foscari*. She has taken part in two new Covent Garden productions: *La bohème* (1974, her début), and the 1975 *Un ballo in maschera*, as Amelia. As Elisabeth de Valois she has appeared in Paris and Munich, as Desdemona in Brussels. Her warmly attractive *spinto* voice can be heard on record in the roles of Suor Angelica, Amelia in *Simon Boccanegra*, Luisa Miller and Mimì, but her technical control is not always faultless. She is an appealing and thoughtful actress.

ALAN BLYTH

Riccieri, Giovanni Antonio. See RICIERI, GIOVANNI ANTONIO.

Riccio [Ricci], Benedetto (*b* ?Naples, ?1678; *d* after 1710). Italian composer. He was listed by Prota-Giurleo among the 'dilettanti' (together with Faggioli, Orefice and de Mauro) who originated the Neapolitan dialect *opera buffa*. His *L'alloggiamentare* (text, N. Gianni; Teatro dei Fiorentini, ?autumn 1710) belongs, formally speaking, among the earliest members of the genre, with its many (57) short musical numbers, frequent ensemble pieces, use of short and probably sometimes strophic arias, lack of exit arias, and in general rapid, fluid movement between recitative and song. As far as can be judged from the libretto, however, it is progressive in intent: the arias' verse forms are often longer and more complex than those in the opera's predecessors; the possibilities of onstage music begin to be exploited, for example in Act 3 a serenata (which Viviani considered possibly a popular song of the day) and a dance, and there is some evidence of shaping the dramatic material in terms of the musical, as in Act 2 scene iii, with its increasingly complex series of numbers. Riccio had earlier composed a serious opera, *L'Ateone* (I. Romani; Fiorentini, 1708) and two *melodrammi sacri*: *L'Iride in cielo* (1704) and *L'umanità consolata* (O. Pinto; Congregazioni di S Maria del Porto dei Dottori, cloister of SS Apostoli dei PP Teatini, Christmas season, 1704; both in *I-Nf*). Two cantatas survive (in *I-Gi(l)* and *I-Nc*); that in Naples, *Clori, vorrei narrarti quel che sò*, consists of a recitative and aria for soprano and continuo and is a conventional but skilful exercise in pastoral

pathos with a neatly contrapuntal bass part. Some works by a 'Riccio' (*I-RI*) may also be his.

BIBLIOGRAPHY
SchmidlDS
M. Scherillo: *L'opera buffa napoletana durante il settecento: storia letteraria* (Naples, 1883, 2/1916/*R*1969), 90ff
B. Croce: *I teatri di Napoli: secolo XV–XVIII* (Naples, 1891/*R*1968), i, 201
U. Prota-Giurleo: *Nicola Logroscino: 'il dio dell'opera buffa'* (Naples, 1927), 16
A. Sacchetti-Sassetti: 'La cappella musicale del duomo di Rieti', *NA*, xvii (1940), 170
V. Viviani: *Storia del teatro napoletano* (Naples, 1969), 266
JAMES L. JACKMAN

Riccio, David. See RIZZIO, DAVID.

Riccio [Rizzo], Giovanni Battista (*fl* 1609–21). Italian composer and instrumentalist. He was appointed organist at the Venetian confraternity of S Giovanni Evangelista in 1609. His contract describes him as a violinist. No further details of his life are known.

Psalms and antiphons are the main textual sources for his motets; Marian antiphons are especially emphasized in the third book. A two-part mass and a *Magnificat* appear in the second. All three volumes contain instrumental pieces. He employed a style developed for relatively large numbers of performers in works for few, usually two, performers: there is, for example, frequent use of echo and dialogue techniques, instruments and voices are employed in the concertato manner, and there are occasional ritornellos. In these respects his style seems to be an adaptation of that of Giovanni Gabrieli to the small ensemble. His later works show an increasingly stronger response to the *seconda prattica* vocabulary associated with Monteverdi, but his writing is never as florid as that of some of his contemporaries.

Riccio's instrumental works are chiefly canzonas, a few of which are based on themes by Gabrieli. Most are for two violins, or violin and trombone, but he also scored for sopranino recorder (*flautino*), cornett and bassoon. Although his writing is again not florid, he employed such relatively modern devices as trills and tremolo figures and frequently wrote cadenza-like flourishes at final cadences.

WORKS
Il primo libro delle divine lodi . . . con l'aggiunta . . . d'alcuni concenti armonici spirituali, 1–3vv, bc (org) (Venice, 2/1612)
Il secondo libro delle divine lodi . . . con alcune canzoni da sonare, 1–4vv, bc (org), 2, 4 insts (Venice, 1614)
Il terzo libro delle divine lodi musicali . . . et alcune canzoni da sonare, 1–4vv, bc (org), 14 insts (Venice, 1620/21); ed. R. Ewerhart (Celle, 1976); Jubilent omnes ed. in NM, lxxv (1931)
1 echo canzona in Otto ordini di letanie della Madonna, ed. V. Bona (Venice, 1619⁶)

BIBLIOGRAPHY
E. Selfridge-Field: *Venetian Instrumental Music from Gabrieli to Vivaldi* (Oxford, 1975)
ELEANOR SELFRIDGE-FIELD

Riccio, Teodore [Teodoro] (*b* Brescia, *c*1540; *d* Ansbach, *c*1600). Italian composer, active mainly in Germany. He referred to himself as 'Brixianus Italus'. He may have worked at Ferrara, and according to the preface of his first book of madrigals he was *maestro di cappella* of S Nazaro, Brescia, in 1567. In 1575 he arrived at the Ansbach court of Margrave Georg Friedrich of Ansbach-Brandenburg, probably after spending some time in Vienna and Dresden. It is possible that he was recommended to Ansbach by Antonio Scandello, at that time Kapellmeister to the Dresden court. In 1578, when the margrave became administrator of the duchy of Prussia, the musicians were sent to Königsberg in Prussia where Riccio became a Protestant. From 1580 he was acquainted with the composer Johannes Eccard who is cited in the household register as vice-Kapellmeister. In 1585 Riccio married and became a householder near the town; in that year he was appointed Kapellmeister of the court for life. In 1586, at the end of his term as administrator, Margrave Georg Friedrich returned to Ansbach with most of his musicians. Riccio was mentioned as being in Ansbach in 1599, but had died by the time the margrave died in 1603.

Riccio was one of the many Italian composers who took important posts in Germany in and after about 1550; he was evidently a reliable and esteemed Kapellmeister. Apart from his madrigals, his works are in the traditional Lutheran style; polychoral writing was one of his chief preoccupations.

WORKS

SACRED

Sacrae cantiones, 5–8vv (Nuremberg, 1576)
Missarum liber primus, 4–6vv (Königsberg, 1579)
Magnificat octo tonorum, 4–8vv (Königsberg, 1579)
Secundus liber sacrarum cantionum, 5–12vv (Königsberg, 1580)
Paraphrases psalmorum graduum cxxxiii ... et cxxxiv, 5vv (Königsberg, 1582) [Ps.cxxxiv is by Eccard]
Hymnaeus in honorem, Phil. Davveli, 5vv (Königsberg, 1584)
17 psalmi ... motectae et 4 Magnificat ... cum Litaniis, 8vv (Venice, 1590)
Several motets, 1578[1], 1583[2], 1589[17], 1591[1]
Several works in MSS: B-Bc, D-B, NLa

SECULAR

Il primo libro di madrigali, 5vv (Venice, 1567)
Il primo libro di madrigali, 6vv (Venice, 1567)
Il primo libro delle canzone alla napolitana ... con alcune mascherate, 5, 6vv (Venice, 1577)
Several further madrigals, 1583[23], 1586[22], 1590[11], 1590[27], 1594[19], 1600[5a], 1600[6]

BIBLIOGRAPHY

R. Eitner: 'Teodore Riccio', MMg, xii (1880), 135, 175, 191
E. Krause: 'Zur Biographie T. Riccios', MMg, xiv (1882), 56
G. Schmidt: Die Musik am Hofe der Markgrafen von Brandenburg-Ansbach (Kassel, 1956)

WALTER BLANKENBURG

Ricciotti, Carlo [Bacciccia] (b c1681; d The Hague, 13 July 1756). Italian violinist and impresario active in the Netherlands. He is first heard of with a French opera company at The Hague in 1702, where he worked, ultimately as director, until 1725. On 26 February 1740 the states of Holland and West Friesland awarded him a patent for the printing of six concertos. According to the register he was 75 at the time of his death. There are no records of the composer Ricciotti, while of the practising musician we know only that he was violin teacher to Count Willem Bentinck. His name was unfamiliar until recently, when Concerti armonici or 'Concertini', also ascribed to Pergolesi, were attributed to him.

Furnished with Ricciotti's patent, the VI concerti armonici a quattro violini obligati, alto viola, violoncello obligato e basso continuo were published in The Hague. The title-page mentions only that the concertos are dedicated to Count Bentinck by Ricciotti, at whose expense they were printed: no composer is named. In the dedicatory letter to Bentinck, Ricciotti begged the count 'to take even greater pleasure in accepting these works since they stem from an illustrious hand [Illustre mano] which your Excellency esteems and honours, and to which I am bound out of respect'. In 18th-century Italy the word 'Illustre' indicated high social standing (particularly when written with an initial capital) rather than artistic renown. This interpretation is supported by a newspaper advertisement in The Hague on 18 August 1749 in which a performance is announced at The Hague (Ricciotti's own domain) of some Concerti armonici, composed by 'een voornam Heer' ('a distinguished gentleman') and printed by Ricciotti. One must assume that the Concerti armonici were written by a composer of high social class and that Ricciotti paid for their printing only in order to dedicate them to his former pupil, the rich and influential Count Bentinck.

When the concertos were reprinted by the London publisher Walsh, Ricciotti was named as the composer; but, particularly in view of the feeble provisions for international copyright, the attribution can have no significance whatever. An early 19th-century MS (now in US-Wc) lists these concertos as 'Septetti' by 'F. G. Handel'; a second title-page is stuck over, on which the works are ascribed to Pergolesi as 'Concertini'. An MS of the concertos in Paris (F-Pc), owned previously, like the Washington MS, by Franz Commer, also bears an ascription to Pergolesi. This MS is probably based on the Washington one, and dates from c1850. A further copy, of c1900, in the private possession of Hans Hoesch of Hagen, Westphalia, also contains Pergolesi's name.

The ascription to Pergolesi may have been conjectured by the first owner of the Washington MS, François Lessel. The name of Handel, which appeared in the first version of the title-page, is likewise probably no more than a speculation, later retracted by the copyist or the first owner. Through the Washington MS the Concerti armonici worked their way into the Pergolesi collected edition (Kassel, 1942), as 'Concertini', and have since enjoyed great popularity (they are also published in HM, Kassel, 1951–9). From the external circumstances we can be certain only that Count Bentinck valued and esteemed the composer, and that the composer was 'Illustre', or 'of high social standing'; the present state of stylistic criticism does not provide a secure foundation for solving the problem of authorship on internal evidence alone (see Larsen). Taking external factors into account, H. J. Moser suggested Count von Erbach or Prince von Bückeburg as possible composers, and also mentioned the possibility of the authorship of J. A. Birckenstock, 12 concertos by whom were announced in Walther's Musicalisches Lexicon (1732) as soon to appear in Amsterdam, with the same scoring as the Concerti armonici. Birckenstock's concertos were never published.

An auction catalogue produced by a book dealer at The Hague in 1749 lists the Concerti armonici under the name of Willem de Fesch. No other MS or printed sources of the Concerti armonici give his name, and the style is foreign to the rest of his work. Hinnenthal's conjecture that Ricciotti himself was the composer would seem to be refuted by the dedicatory letter already quoted. Dunning has suggested that Fortunato Chelleri might have been the composer. Bentinck met him in 1726 and valued him highly. With the honorary title of Hofrat bestowed on him by the Swedish king in 1734, Chelleri would fulfil the condition of 'Illustre'. The style provides no evidence against Chelleri's authorship, and the appearance in the A major concerto of the canonic melody Non nobis Domine (popular in England, and attributed to William Byrd) is consistent with Chelleri's visit to London in 1726–7. Cudworth was probably closest to the truth when he said these concertos can only be ascribed to 'that most prolific of all composers, Signor Anonimo'.

BIBLIOGRAPHY

J. P. Larsen: *Die Haydn-Überlieferung* (Copenhagen, 1939)

C. L. Cudworth: 'Notes on the Instrumental Works attributed to Pergolesi', *ML*, xxx (1949), 321

F. Walker: 'Pergolesiana', *ML*, xxxii (1951), 296

C. L. Cudworth: 'Pergolesi, Ricciotti and the Count of Bentinck', *IMSCR*, v Utrecht 1952, 127

H. O'Douwes: 'Carlo Ricciotti: Italiaans musykmeester en burger van s'Gravenhage', *Mens en melodie*, xiii (1958), 244

H. J. Moser: 'Die Zukunft der deutschen Musikforschung', *Mf*, xii (1959), 179

A. Dunning: 'Zur Frage der Autorschaft der Ricciotti und Pergolesi zugeschriebenen "Concerti Armonici"', *Anzeiger der phil.-hist. Klasse der Österreichischen Akademie der Wissenschaften*, c (1963), 113

F. Degrada: 'Le messe di Giovanni Battista Pergolesi: problemi di cronologia e d'attribuzione', *AnMc*, no.3 (1966), 65

J. P. Hinnenthal: 'Ricciotti und die Concerti Armonici', *Mf*, xxi (1968), 322

A. Dunning:' "Ricciotti und die Concerti Armonici": eine Erwiderung', *Mf*, xxii (1969), 343

J. P. Larsen: 'Über Echtheitsprobleme in der Musik der Klassik', *Mf*, xxv (1972), 4

ALBERT DUNNING

Rice, 'Daddy' [Thomas Dartmouth] (*b* New York, 20 May 1808; *d* New York, 1860). American minstrel performer. As a travelling actor and comedian he introduced in 1828 the song-and-dance skit *Jim Crow*, probably in Louisville, Kentucky, and became one of the first blackface negro impersonators to win fame, even outside the USA, performing several times to great acclaim in Britain (*see* MINSTRELSY, AMERICAN; POPULAR MUSIC, §II, 5, and fig.9). The character Jim Crow became a symbol for a degraded black in the USA. Rice has been called the 'father of American minstrelsy'; he was the first to develop an entire show round black-face impersonation and dancing to the accompaniment of an orchestra or solo fiddle. In addition to performing burlesques of well-known works and of such performers as Sarah Bernhardt ('Sarah Heartburn'), he compiled minstrel tunes into extended sketches called 'Ethiopian operas', precursors of the full-scale minstrel show. Rice was briefly a member of Charley White's Serenaders and Wood's Minstrels; he played the title role in a New York production of *Uncle Tom's Cabin* before he retired in 1858.

Rice, Edward Everett (*b* Brighton, Mass., 21 Dec 1848; *d* New York, 16 Nov 1924). American composer and producer. By 1879 he had produced several operettas in New York and on tours in the USA. Among his first compositions were songs for John Brougham's burlesques *Pocahontas* (1870s) and *Lotos* (1878). Rice's best-known burlesque is *Evangeline* (1874, libretto by J. C. Goodwin), one of the first works to be called a 'musical comedy' and perhaps the first of the genre in America to have a fully original score without adapted or interpolated songs. *Adonis* (1884, W. Gill and H. E. Dixey) was popular in New York and London. In the 1870s Rice formed a troupe that revived his works for many years, continually adding new dialogue and topical songs. Although his burlesques succeeded largely for their comic routines, his music adeptly portrays the humorous and sentimental natures of the characters. Irving Berlin first appeared on stage in Rice's *Show Girl* (1902).

BIBLIOGRAPHY

C. Smith: *Musical Comedy in America* (New York, 1950)

D. L. Root: *American Popular Stage Music 1860–1880* (diss., U. of Illinois, 1977)

DEANE L. ROOT

Ricercare [ricercar, recercar(e), recerchar(e), ricercata] (It.: 'to search for'; Sp. *recercada*; Fr. *recherché*). In its widest sense, a piece of an esoteric nature; a technical exercise either of a practical nature or illustrative of some device of composition.

1. Introduction. 2. The preludial or rhapsodic ricercare. 3. The imitative ricercare.

1. INTRODUCTION. The general notion of musical composition as a process of seeking or finding is ancient: it is referred to in the Vulgate by the very word from which 'ricercare' is derived ('requirentes modos musicos', *Ecclesiasticus* xliv.5; Revised Standard Version: 'those who composed musical tunes'; Authorized Version: 'such as found out musical tunes') and is presumably the concept expressed in the terms 'troubadour' and 'trouvère', although these were primarily used of poets or poet–musicians rather than simply of composers. The idea reappears in the term INVENTION, and there is much to be said for the view that links the tradition of the didactic duet, often called 'ricercare' (see §3), with Bach's two-part inventions.

Originally the term 'ricercare' was used for a piece of preludial character for lute or keyboard instrument (as in the expression 'ricercare le corde', 'to try out the strings'), giving it a meaning comparable to that of 'tastar', 'tañer', 'tiento' etc (*see* TOCCATA). The commonest type subsequently was the imitative ricercare, similar in scope to the fantasia and fugue. Some uses appear to combine two different meanings of the word, as, for example, imitative ricercares designed as exercises in vocalization, or elaborate and technically difficult compositions for viola da gamba illustrating the technique of setting a cantus firmus.

Few early authors attempted a comprehensive definition of the ricercare. For Vincenzo Galilei (*Dialogo*, 1581, p.87) it was a fugal form, comparable in its excessive complexity to the verse form known as the sestina. For Michael Praetorius also (*Syntagma musicum*, iii, 1618, pp.21f) it was imitative, the equivalent of the *fuga*, which by that date had come to acquire something like its present-day meaning. Many 18th- and early 19th-century compilers of dictionaries mentioned its preludial function, often without referring to its fugal connotation; they include Brossard (1703), Walther (1732; his is a fuller definition than most, citing among others Galilei, Praetorius and Brossard), Rousseau (1768) and Lichtenthal (1826). All referred to the literal meaning of the Italian verb, which is usually glossed by the Latin 'exquirere' and similar words; and Rousseau, who gave only the French form 'recherché', added that it was also used as the equivalent of 'cadence', a cadenza or improvisatory flourish over a cadential pedal-point (see the full title of Giovanni Bassano's *Ricercate* referred to in §2 below).

2. THE PRELUDIAL OR RHAPSODIC RICERCARE. The term first occurs in Spinacino's *Intabulatura de lauto, libro primo* (Venice, 1507). The 17 ricercares are placed at the end, and while in most of them the title is unqualified, in two cases it suggests a preludial function by referring to a chanson intabulated earlier in the volume (e.g. *Recercare de tous biens*). There are another ten in Spinacino's second book of the same year. In J. A.

Dalza's *Intabolatura de lauto* (1508), four of the pieces called 'tastar de corde' are followed by ricercares, usually called 'ricercare dietro' ('following'). Thus there may already have been a distinction between the most primitive kind of 'trying-out' and the more artistic, purely rhapsodic piece. Most of these early ricercares, like those in the Capirola Lutebook (*see* CAPIROLA, VINCENZO), include both chordal and scale passages and are as much ancestors of the toccata as of any other type.

The preludial style of ricercare was transferred to the keyboard in M. A. Cavazzoni's *Recerchari, motetti, canzoni . . . libro primo* (1523). Here the two ricercares serve as preludes to two motet transcriptions, *Salve virgo* and *O stella maris* respectively. They are extended compositions of considerable interest, with passages of imitation but not primarily based on an imitative principle. One of their chief attractions is the idiomatic keyboard writing, chords and runs being blended together with great skill into a full yet clear texture. Several similar pieces, including another by M. A. Cavazzoni and one by 'Jaches' (perhaps Jacques Brunel, organist at Ferrara, 1533–64) are found in a source from Castell'Arquato (*see* SOURCES OF KEYBOARD MUSIC TO 1660). That source also includes some of the earliest surviving examples of the imitative ricercare, including one by 'Jaches' and four by Giacomo Fogliano.

The non-imitative ricercare did not entirely die out after the early 16th century; examples for solo viol are found in the works of Sylvestro di Ganassi dal Fontego and Diego Ortiz. The former included eight solo ricercares in his two instruction books of 1542–3. Ortiz, in his *Trattado de glosas* (1553), used the term 'recercada' not only in the sense of a rhapsodic piece for solo viol but also for viol and keyboard works based on various grounds (in which case the keyboard player added chords above the bass line), and transcriptions of vocal polyphonic pieces for the same medium. The six pieces based on the basse danse melody known as 'La Spagna' belong to a whole tradition of didactic works using this widespread cantus firmus. Those of Ortiz are perhaps the first to be designated ricercares; most of their successors, however, belong to the imitative type rather than to the improvisatory type cultivated by Ortiz. The close association between the ricercare and the Renaissance practice of diminution is exemplified in Giovanni Bassano's *Ricercate, passaggi et cadentie* (1585).

3. THE IMITATIVE RICERCARE. The precise origin of the imitative ricercare is disputed. Many scholars have assumed that it was the instrumental counterpart to the motet and derived directly from it. The study of the earliest instrumental ricercares has cast doubt on this premise and suggests that the purely imitative type arose from the use of occasional imitation in the rhapsodic type, but such a hypothesis ignores the place of the ensemble ricercare in the development of the form. *Musica nova* (*RISM* 1540²²) contains 18 compositions (out of 21) labelled 'R' for 'ricercare', all of which (together with two of the untitled works) are in motet style with pervading imitation. When it is remembered that the term 'motet' does not exclude cantus firmus and chordal techniques, its relevance to the history of the ricercare is seen to be considerable. The ricercares of M. A. Cavazzoni are strikingly similar to what one might expect of a keyboard arrangement of an inconsistently imitative motet; they are indeed closely related in style to the motet arrangements which follow them in the printed source. Thus the motet has a direct bearing on the early history of both the imitative and (at least in the case of keyboard music) the non-imitative or partly imitative forms. A similar transition from the non-imitative to the imitative type of ricercare is found in lute sources, probably through the influence of the keyboard form, as for example, in the publications of Simon Gintzler (1547), Bakfark (1552) and Galilei (*Intavolature de lauto. . .madrigali e ricercate*, 1563).

The ricercares of *Musica nova*, by Julio Segni, Willaert, Girolamo Cavazzoni and others, have the form of a consistently imitative motet. Several short themes are given fugal treatment in turn. Although some works use more themes than would a motet of the same length, the general similarity to the sacred vocal style of the generation of Clemens and Gombert is unmistakable. The parts (all but one of which have to be reconstructed from a French reprint, *Musicque de joye, RISM* c1550²⁴) show severe melodic lines, but these may have been ornamented in performance.

The early type of imitative organ ricercare is represented by the four examples in Girolamo Cavazzoni's *Intavolatura cioe recercari canzoni himni magnificati* (1543). They differ from the ensemble form only in the provision of ornamented melodic lines, notably at cadences. Sometimes the ornamentation blossoms out into lengthy scales and runs, resulting in a climactic effect peculiar to the early keyboard form, as, for example, towards the end of no.2. Although a few organ works of this period are virtually unornamented in the sources, there can be little doubt that they would have been lightly embellished in performance.

The title-page of *Musica nova* indicates that its contents could be sung, or played on organs or other instruments, and the implied flexibility is found in the title-pages of many of its successors. These include Jacques Buus, *Recercari . . . da cantare et sonare d'organo et altri stromenti* (1547 and 1549); Giuliano Tiburtino, *Fantasie et recerchari . . . da cantare et sonare per ogni instrumento* (1549); Willaert, *Fantasie recercari contrapunti a tre voci di M. Adriano et de altri autori appropriati per cantare et sonare d'ogni sorte di stromenti* (1551); and Annibale Padovano, *Il primo libro de ricercari a quattro voci* (1556). One of the pieces from the second volume of Buus's work is actually included in his *Intabolatura d'organo di recercari* published in the same year (1549); thus it is possible to compare an embellished intabulation of the period with its plain original. The technique of ornamentation, in this as in his other organ ricercares, is more elaborate than in those of Cavazzoni. A written-out and embellished keyboard score of an ensemble ricercare is a rarity, and organists normally had to make their own copies from the printed partbooks, until in the late 16th century publishers took to providing an open score ('partitura'), either in addition to or instead of the separate parts.

Singers could perform these works to the appropriate solmization syllables. The term 'ricercare da cantare' occurs as late as Claudio Merulo's third book (1608), while the four-part ensemble ricercare itself was cultivated at least until the publication of Antonio Cifra's *Ricercari e canzoni franzese. . .libro primo* (1619), published in four partbooks, with a separate organ score.

(The second book, also 1619, is in score only and was probably originally for keyboard, though considered an ensemble work by Frotscher and Apel, 1967.) Of particular interest in the history of the ensemble ricercare are the works on 'La Spagna' by Mayone (1609) and Trabaci (1615). The element of vocal exercise is also provided by numerous collections of duets in imitative style, such as Francesco Guami's *Ricercari a due voci* (1588), Lassus's *Motetti et ricercari* (1585) and the famous *Ricercari a canto e tenore* by Grammatio Metallo (possibly first published in 1591; a 1595 edition, also lost, is mentioned by Fétis; for extant 17th-century editions see below). Such didactic duets do not always bear the heading 'ricercare': there are no specific titles to the pieces in Eustachio Romano's *Musica duorum* (1521) nor to those in Morley's *Plaine and Easie Introduction* (1597) (*see also* BICINIUM).

The use of the term 'fantasia' to denote a piece in fugal style probably arose from the development of the monothematic ricercare, in which the main structural feature of the motet, the contrapuntal treatment of several themes in turn, was abandoned in place of a much stricter design. Later still, when the term 'ricercare' had acquired an archaic connotation, 'fantasia' was used even for monothematic works (such as those by Sweelinck and Frescobaldi) if they were in a modern style or contained elements of rhythmic liveliness. Nevertheless, at least one of Sweelinck's fantasias is called 'ricercare' in its two sources, and one should not set too much store by the vagaries of 16th- and 17th-century nomenclature.

One of the earliest examples of a monothematic ricercare comes from Buus's first book. It is an arid piece, as one might expect of a lengthy experimental composition devoted to the exploration of a new technique. The form was further developed by Andrea Gabrieli, whose organ music first appeared in six volumes (all now lost) during the 1560s and early 1570s. The three volumes containing ricercares were reprinted posthumously in 1595, 1596 and 1605. The *Libro secondo* (1595) contains 11 ricercares (together with two by his nephew Giovanni); the *Libro terzo* (1596) has a further six; the *Libro quinto* (1605; a fourth book of which the contents are unknown has disappeared altogether) gives seven more, while the *Libro sesto* of the same year includes one. Gabrieli's ricercares illustrate a gradual reduction in the number of subjects, five actually being monothematic. Gabrieli made frequent use of inversion, augmentation, diminution and other fugal techniques. Moreover, he was perhaps the initiator of the device which can only be called the counter-subject, invertible and appearing with most occurrences of the subject. Although the technique is not used with the regularity found in the later fugue, it clearly foreshadows that treatment. Gabrieli did not introduce the counter-subject until the second entry of the subject (in other words, it is a continuation of the first voice), but later composers introduced two, three or even four subjects simultaneously from the outset. This technique is the ancestor of the double, triple and quadruple fugue and is not to be confused with the earlier method of working several themes in succession. In a sense, works such as these are monothematic fugues on a single two-, three- or four-part subject.

Andrea Gabrieli's fifth book contains seven works described collectively on the title-page as 'ricercari ariosi'. In the body of the book four of them are designated simply 'ricercar arioso', while the remaining three

are based on French chansons: 'Ricercar sopra Martin menoit', '. . . Orsus au coup' and '. . . Pour ung plaisir'. Each follows a canzona based on the same material; but whereas the canzonas are fairly strict intabulations of their vocal models, the ricercares are rather freer fugal paraphrases and use longer note values. The 'ricercari ariosi' may also be based on vocal models. Although most organ music of the 1560s and later tended to use shorter note values, semiquavers now being as frequent as quavers had been in the works of Girolamo Cavazzoni, the development in the organ ricercare stopped short at the point reached by Buus, and in some cases reverted to a still plainer manner, perhaps as a conscious archaism.

The ricercares of Annibale Padovano, Sperindio Bertoldo and Claudio Merulo, like those of Andrea Gabrieli, survive only in posthumous prints or reprints. Merulo's ricercares (originally published in 1567) are not representative of his best work and include no monothematic examples. The ricercares of the Neapolitans Rocco Rodio (1575) and Antonio Valente (1576) are more significant. Rodio, particularly, included passages requiring virtuoso technique and extremes of chromaticism which recall the pedagogic significance of the term 'ricercare'. The collections of Mayone and Trabaci follow in the same tradition.

Volumes six and seven of the Giordano collection in Turin (*see* SOURCES OF KEYBOARD MUSIC TO 1660, §2, (iii)) are devoted to ricercares. Although the word is there also applied to non-Italian works, given other designations by their composers, there are genuine examples of the form, including six that may be attributed to Giovanni Gabrieli with some confidence. These ricercares, like two by Giovanni Gabrieli printed in Andrea's *Libro secondo* (1595), use shorter note values than do those of his uncle and include antiphonal passages between high and low groups of parts in a manner reminiscent of Giovanni Gabrieli's ensemble music.

The high point of the organ ricercare was reached in the works of Frescobaldi. His *Recercari et canzoni* was first published in 1615 and was reprinted with the capriccios in 1626. Some of the ten ricercares have several sections devoted to different subjects; others treat one or more subjects simultaneously from the beginning or nearly the beginning of the piece. In the first, three subjects are combined in this way. The ninth is based on four subjects; the fourth, sixth, seventh and tenth are based on solmization syllables; in the last case the subject is repeated throughout in the top voice only, against a multisectional ricercare which unfolds in the lowest three voices. The second consists in effect of three double fugues in which both subject and counter-subject are treated alternately in their original form and in inversion. The eighth is subtitled 'obbligo di non uscir in grado': that is, no part may at any time proceed by step. These ricercares, in spite of their severity, their archaic flavour and their comparative immaturity, are interesting for their single-minded pursuit of the contrapuntal ideal. The ricercares of Frescobaldi's *Fiori musicali* (1635), which were to replace the liturgical offertory, give a rather different impression. Four are multisectional in form. The sections are marked off by pauses, probably to indicate possible terminations in the context of liturgical performance. The ricercare of the first mass is an example of what may be called the variation ricercare: in each of its two sections the main theme is combined with different counterpoints. This technique is seen to perfection in the magisterial 'recercar cromaticho' from the second mass, which is in three sections and is preceded by a short toccata. The first ricercare of the third mass is similar in scope. In the alternative piece from the second mass, on the other hand, the main subjects, presented separately in the first three sections, are combined in the last. The last of these works has an optional fifth part, an ostinato which the performer must not only fit correctly into the polyphonic texture but also sing himself.

The tradition of the keyboard ricercare continued in Italy with such composers as Giovanni Salvatore (1641), G. B. Fasolo (1645), Bernardo Storace (1664), Luigi Battiferri (1669), Fabrizio Fontana (1677) and Gregorio Strozzi (1687). It seems fairly clear that one of its main functions in this period was to replace the liturgical offertory, and perhaps also other items of the Proper, when these were not explicitly provided for in the numerous organists' handbooks of the day; indeed, it is explained in Fasolo's *Annuale* that they may be used instead of the short substitutes provided for both the Gradual and the Offertory. Though the regular four-part ensemble ricercare virtually disappeared after Giovanni Cavaccio's *Sudori musicali* (1626), the two-voice type continued with G. B. Calì (1605), Giorgio Gentile (1642), Cristofano Piochi (1671 and 1673) and Stefano Corti (1685), as well as with Metallo's ricercares, which passed through at least 12 editions between 1605 and 1685. Piochi's 1671 volume also includes three-part works, to which his publication of 1675 is devoted. The character of a technical exercise is preserved in the 12 short unaccompanied fanfare-like ricercares from Girolamo Fantini's *Modo per imparare a sonare di tromba* (1638), and in such later publications as G. B. Degli Antoni's *Ricercate sopra il violoncello o cembalo* (1687) and *Ricercate a violino e violoncello o cembalo* (1690), as well as in the manuscript *Ricercari per violoncello solo* by Domenico Gabrielli (1690).

In Austria and Germany the severe manner of Frescobaldi was continued by Froberger, whose 14 ricercares are monothematic and employ the variation principle. The works in C♯ minor and F♯ minor exhibit the growing tendency towards tonal experimentation (both the severity and the tonal adventurousness are reflected in the fugues of J. C. F. Fischer's *Ariadne musica*). Other German composers of ricercares include Johann Krieger and Pachelbel; but the form did not undergo any rejuvenation until the time of Bach, who was probably thinking of its monothematic aspect when he revived the term in the *Musical Offering*. The king's subject, unsuited to stretto, is surrounded by a wealth of different counterpoints in the three-part work which begins the collection and in the massive six-part work which is its culmination. Though the latter exists in a two-stave version in Bach's own hand and was certainly intended primarily for the keyboard, he published it in open score and in so doing (as in the *Art of Fugue*, where the term 'contrapunctus' is chosen) revived an old Italian notation with all its implications of an idealized counterpoint irrespective of medium. The few modern composers who have used the term have generally implied by it a severe fugue with archaic mannerisms.

BIBLIOGRAPHY

BrownI; *FétisB*; *SartoriB*

A. G. Ritter: 'Die "Ricercari sopra li toni" von G. P. Palestrina(?)', *MMg*, vi (1874), 134

H. Opieński: 'Quelques considérations sur l'origine des *Ricercari* pour luth', *Mélanges de musicologie offerts à M. Lionel de la Laurencie* (Paris, 1933), 39

E. Meyer: *Die mehrstimmige Spielmusik des 17. Jahrhunderts in Nord- und Mitteleuropa* (Kassel, 1934)

A. Einstein: 'Vincenzo Galilei and the Instructive Duo', *ML*, xviii (1937), 360

K. Jeppesen: *Die italienische Orgelmusik am Anfang des Cinquecento* (Copenhagen, 1943, rev. 2/1960)

G. Sutherland: 'The Ricercari of Jacques Buus', *MQ*, xxxi (1945), 448

W. Apel: 'The Early Development of the Organ Ricercar', *MD*, iii (1949), 139

H. H. Eggebrecht: 'Terminus "Ricercar"', *AMw*, ix (1952), 137

——: *Studien zur musikalischen Terminologie* (Mainz, 1955, 2/1968)

O. Gombosi: Preface to *The Capirola Lute-Book*, Société de musique d'autrefois, i (Neuilly-sur-Seine, 1955)

R. M. Murphy: 'Fantaisie et ricercare dans les premières tablatures de luth du XVIe siècle', *Le luth et sa musique: CNRS Neuilly-sur-Seine 1957*, 127

I. Horsley: 'The Solo Ricercar in Diminution Manuals: New Light on Early Wind and String Techniques', *AcM*, xxxiii (1961), 29

H. C. Slim: *The Keyboard Ricercar and Fantasia in Italy, ca. 1500–1550* (diss., Harvard U., 1961)

——: 'Keyboard Music at Castell'Arquato by an Early Madrigalist', *JAMS*, xv (1962), 35

R. S. Douglass: *The Keyboard Ricercare in the Baroque Era* (diss., North Texas State U., 1963)

E. E. Lowinsky: Foreword to *Musica nova*, ed. H. C. Slim, MRM, i (1964)

W. Apel: *Geschichte der Orgel- und Klaviermusik bis 1700* (Kassel, 1967, Eng. trans., rev. 1972)

S. Bonta: 'The Uses of the *Sonata da Chiesa*', *JAMS*, xxii (1969), 54–84

H. R. Chase: *German, Italian and Dutch Fugal Precursors of the Fugues in the 'Well-tempered Clavier I', 1600–1722* (diss., Indiana U., 1970)

D. Kämper: 'Studien zur instrumentalen Ensemblemusik des 16. Jahrhunderts in Italien', *AnMc*, no.10 (1970) [whole vol.]

H. M. Brown and E. E. Lowinsky: Introduction to *Eustachio Romano, 'Musica duorum', Rome 1521*, MRM, vi (1975)

E. Selfridge-Field: *Venetian Instrumental Music from Gabrieli to Vivaldi* (Oxford, 1975)

W. Kirkendale: 'Ciceronians versus Aristotelians on the Ricercar as Exordium, from Bembo to Bach', *JAMS*, xxxii (1979), 1–44

JOHN CALDWELL

Rich, Buddy [Bernard] (*b* Brooklyn, 30 June 1917). American jazz drummer and singer. A child prodigy, he appeared on stage in his parents' vaudeville act before his second birthday, played the drums and tap-danced on Broadway at four, and from the age of six toured the USA and Australia, leading his own stage band at 11. He joined Joe Marsala's band in 1937 and then played briefly with Bunny Berigan, Harry James, Artie Shaw and Benny Carter, and somewhat longer with Tommy Dorsey (1939–42). After serving with the US Marines he rejoined Dorsey in 1944–5 and then led his own band intermittently until 1951, also playing with Norman Granz's 'Jazz at the Philharmonic', Les Brown and Charlie Ventura. From 1953 to 1966 he was with Harry James's group except for spells with Dorsey (1954–5) and with his own small group (1957–61), when he also appeared as a singer in a style resembling Sinatra's. In 1966 he formed a second big band, and achieved remarkable international success with it until its dissolution in 1974. Thereafter he played mainly with a small group ensemble in his own New York club, 'Buddy's Place'.

Rich's playing is characterized by phenomenal speed and dexterity which made him one of the outstanding drummers of the 'swing' period. Favouring an extrovert style, he performs complex patterns with metronomic clarity and simpler lines with an exquisite precision.

JOSÉ HOSIASSON

Rich, John (*b* ?London, 1691 or 1692; *d* London, 26 Nov 1761). English theatre manager and dancer. He was the son of Christopher Rich (*d* 1714), the manager of the company which staged Purcell's later dramatic operas and the early English-Italian operas. In 1714 John opened the new theatre at Lincoln's Inn Fields, which his father had built. He kept a full repertory of plays, but his real preferences were music, dance and spectacle. These elements were combined in his famous pantomime afterpieces, most of which had music by Galliard. Under the name of Lun, Rich danced Harlequin in them for many years, and he was highly praised for his artistry in mime and movement. Pepusch wrote music for him at Lincoln's Inn Fields, and it was here that *The Beggar's Opera* (1728) made 'Gay rich, and Rich gay'. Rich built the first Covent Garden Theatre and continued to produce ballad operas, panto-mimes and burlesques there from 1732. Handel hired his theatres for some opera seasons between 1734 and 1741 and his Lent oratorio seasons were at Covent Garden in 1743, 1744 and yearly from 1747. In his will Handel left Rich his 'Great Organ' which was installed at Covent Garden. After Rich's death the theatre was managed by his son-in-law, the tenor John Beard.

OLIVE BALDWIN, THELMA WILSON

Richafort [Richauffort, Rycefort, Ricartsvorde], **Jean** (*b* ?Hainaut, *c*1480; *d* ?Bruges, *c*1547). Franco-Flemish composer. The inference that he was born in Hainaut is derived from the conflation of two documents. A Flemish translation published in 1698 of Guicciardini's *Storia d'Italia* lists Richafort among distinguished Netherlanders (and states that he was dead by 1556) whereas the 16th-century Swiss humanist Aegidius Tschudi described the composer as 'Gallus' in a manu-script in St Gall (*CH-SGs* 463). If both sources are accurate, Richafort was a French-speaking Netherlander and hence might have been a native of Hainaut. In 1507 he was appointed *maître de chapelle* at St Rombaud in Mechelen, the city where Margaret of Austria had taken up residence as regent of the Netherlands during the same year. His choir there included his two brothers, Guillaume and François. Richafort, who is called 'Magister' in the documents, did not stay there long – Noel Bauldeweyn replaced him in 1509 – but his whereabouts for the years immediately following are unknown.

Richafort was connected with the French royal chapel, although when and in what capacity is unknown, for no documentary evidence from the court mentions him. He composed the motet *Consolator captivorum*, which praises 'Ludovice piissime' and offers a prayer for him. The subject was clearly Louis XII of France and the motet may have been written for his funeral in 1515. Richafort was mentioned as a singer in the French chapel by Pope Leo X. When Leo met with François I in 1516 to devise the Concordat of Bologna, the pope demonstrated his graciousness by rewarding many members of François' entourage. He made two of the leading French composers, Longueval and Mouton, apostolic notaries, and he gave lesser gifts to various other singers, among them Claudin de Sermisy and Richafort. Later in the century Vincenzo Galilei reported that many musicians including Richafort came to Rome from France and Flanders at the time Leo was elected (*I-Fn* Anteriori Galilei, vol.I, f.138*v*). His statement has been challenged on the grounds that some

of the men that he mentioned cannot possibly have been in Rome in 1513, but insofar as it applies to Richafort it contains at least a grain of truth: Richafort was in Bologna in 1516, shortly after the pope's election, albeit as a member of the French royal chapel, and Leo was evidently impressed with his ability.

It is not known when Richafort entered or left the service of the French kings and his activities during the 1520s remain a complete mystery. He may have been in Brussels in 1531, at the court of Queen Mary of Hungary, regent of the Netherlands after the death of her husband, Louis II of Hungary. In that year her account books list a 'Jean de Rycefort prêtre et chantre de la Reine', but they may contain a scribal error, for a Joachim de Rycefort held a position at her court for a number of years and Jean is not known to have been a priest. The composer's last known position was as *maître de chapelle* from 1542 to 1547 at St Gilles in Bruges. Since Jean Bart was appointed to take his place in 1548 and nothing more about Richafort is found in archives, he is presumed to have died about that time, probably in Bruges.

The only volume of music dedicated exclusively to Richafort is one containing 19 motets, *Joannis Richafort modulorum quatuor quinque & sex vocum, liber primus*, published posthumously in 1556 by the Parisian firm Le Roy & Ballard. The remainder of his music is dispersed through some 70 anthologies printed between 1519 and 1583, and a number of manuscripts.

In the dedication to *Livre des meslanges* (Paris, 1560), Pierre de Ronsard mentioned that Richafort had been a student of Josquin Desprez. Although there is no reason to take Ronsard's rhetorical remark as literal truth, the style of Richafort's music clearly identifies him as one of those gifted younger disciples of Josquin, eager to explore the ground broken by the master. More-over two pieces of evidence suggest that Richafort may indeed have had personal contact with the older com-poser. Richafort's motet *Misereatur mei* is based on the same ostinato as that in Josquin's *Miserere mei*, trans-formed rhythmically in the same way and transposed systematically in the same pattern, an obvious act of homage to the master. And Richafort's Requiem Mass uses as its structural scaffolding a canon on the Sarum chant *Circumdederunt me*, one adopted by Josquin on several occasions for similar sorts of pieces. The mass also quotes the text, 'c'est douleur non pareille', and the melody associated with it in Josquin's chanson *Faulte d'argent*. Because of these borrowings, Kast suggested that Richafort actually composed the mass as a requiem for Josquin.

Richafort's pre-eminence, affirmed by Glarean and others, is revealed most clearly in his motets, which exhibit all those features one might expect from a fer-vent admirer of Josquin. They include works based on sequences, responsories (some, free of borrowed mater-ial, in the new *aBcB* form), antiphons and psalms, as well as some that set apparently non-liturgical devotional texts. As structural devices, Richafort em-ployed cantus firmi, ostinatos, canons, paraphrase tech-nique or simply points of imitation without any pre-existent material. A master contrapuntist following Josquin's lead, Richafort was among those who at-tempted to deepen and enhance the relationship between words and music. His best-known motet is probably *Quem dicunt homines*, a model of formal clarity, which survives in numerous sources and served as model for parody masses by Divitis, Mouton, Lupus or Pierkin de Raedt, Pseudo-Josquin, Charles d'Argentille, Morales, Vincenzo Ruffo and Palestrina. The two earliest of these masses, by Divitis and Mouton, may have been composed in competition and possibly for performance before François I and Leo X at Bologna in 1516. In any case they are among the earliest masses using the full-fledged parody technique of the 16th century, a fact that suggests the French royal chapel as the cradle of the technique. Richafort's own masses (except for the Requiem) are also parodies built on his own motets. Some of Richafort's predominantly motet-like chansons for three to five voices are based on pre-existent melodies, whereas others are composed with entirely new melodic material. One of his two secular Latin pieces, *Vinum bonum et suave*, sets an 11th-century goliard poem, a parody of the famous sequence *Verbum bonum et suave*.

WORKS

Edition: *Treize livres de motets parus chez Pierre Attaingnant en 1534 et 1535*, ed. A. Smijers and A. T. Merritt (Paris and Monaco, 1934–64) [SM]

MASSES

Missa 'O Dei genetrix', 4vv, 1532[4] (on his own motet; entitled Missa 'O gloriosa' *F-CA* 3)
Missa 'Veni sponsa Christi', 4vv, 1532[8]
Requiem mass, 6vv, 1532[6]

MAGNIFICAT SETTINGS

10 Magnificat, 4vv, *D-MÜs* 2784
Magnificat, 4vv, SM vi
Magnificat, 4vv, *NL-Lu* E
2 Magnificat verses in 1534[19]

MOTETS

Modulorum quatuor quinque & sex vocum, liber primus (Paris, 1556) [1556]
Ave Maria, 5vv, SM viii; Ave virgo gloriosa, 4vv, 1556; Beata dei genitrix, 5vv, 1540[6]; Christe totius dominator, 4vv, SM ii; Christus resurgens, 4vv, H. Glarean: *Dodecachordon*, ed. and Eng. trans. C. A Miller, MSD, vi (1965); Cognoscimus, 4vv, SM iv; Congratulamini, 4vv, *I-Bc* Q19, ed. R. van Maldeghem: *Trésor musical*, xvii (Brussels, 1881) (attrib. Josquin in 1537[1]); Consolatur captivorum, 4vv, 1556
Ego sum qui sum, 5vv, *E-Tc* (anon. in *NL-Lw* B); Emendemus in melius, 4vv, MRM, iii–v (1968); Exaudiat te Domine, 4vv, 1538[6]; Gloria, laus et honor, 4vv, SM i; Homo quidam, 4vv, *E-Tc*; Iam non dicam, 5vv, 1532[9]; Laetamini in Domino, 5vv, 1540[6]; Misereatur mei, 5vv, 1532[9]; Non turbetur, 5vv, 1545[3]
O beata infantia, 6vv, 1556 (attrib. Willaert in *I-Rv* E.II,55–60); O genitrix, 4vv, *DK-Kk* 1848–2°; O praesul egregie, 4vv, SM ii; O quam dulcis, 4vv, SM ii; Pater noster, 5vv, SM iii; Peccata mea Domine, 4vv, 1532[10]; Philomena praevia, 4vv, 1528[2]; Quem dicunt homines, 4vv, Cw, xciv (1963); Salve regina, 5vv, SM xii; Sancta Maria, succurre nobis, 4vv, *GB-Lbm* 19583, inc.; Sufficiebat, 4vv, SM iv; Veni electa mea, 6vv, SM viii; Veni sponsa Christi, 5vv, MRM iii–v (1968)

CHANSONS

Cuidés vous, 5vv, 1540[7]; D'amours je suis desheritée, 1572[2]; De mon triste et desplaisir, 4vv, ed. H. M. Brown: *Theatrical Chansons of the Fifteenth and Early Sixteenth Centuries* (Cambridge, Mass., 1963); En revenant du bois, 3vv, 1578[15]; Gentilz gallantz, 3vv, 1578[15]; Hors de plaisir, 4vv, 1538[16]; Il n'est sy doulce vie, 4vv, ed. H. M. Brown: *Theatrical Chansons* (Cambridge, Mass., 1963); J'ay vue que souloye, 3vv, 1569[11]; Je fus, je fus, 3vv, 1536[1]; Je veulx laysser melancholie, 4vv, MME, iii (1945) (intabulated for vihuela)
L'amour de moy, 3vv, 1578[15]; La rousée du moys de may, 3vv, 1578[15]; Le temps qui court, 4vv, 1545[16]; N'avez point beu mal, 3vv, 1536[1]; Ne vous chaille mon cueur, 5vv, 1544[13]; Or vray Dieu, 3vv, 1569[11]; Qui est celuy, 3vv, 1536[1]; Sour tous regretz, 4vv, PÄMw, ii (1873–5); Sy je m'y plain, 5vv, 1572[2]; Tru tru trut avant, 3vv, 1536[1]

SECULAR MOTETS

Laus tua, non tua fraus, 2vv, 1549[16]; Vinum bonum, 5vv, 1540[6]

DOUBTFUL WORKS

Gaudent in caelis, 8vv, attrib. Richafort in 1564[1], attrib. Phinot in *D-Mbs* 2875
Hierusalem luge, 5vv, attrib. Richafort in 1532[9], attrib. Lupus in SM viii, attrib. Caen in *Rp* A.R.891
Miseremini mei, 4vv, attrib. Richafort in 1519[1], attrib. Mouton in H. Glarean: *Dodecachordon*, MSD, vi (1965), anon. in SM i

BIBLIOGRAPHY

Y. Rokseth: 'Un fragment de Richafort', *RdM*, vii (1926), 28
G. van Doorslaer: 'Jean Richafort, maître de chapelle-compositeur',
Bulletin de l'Académie royale d'archéologie de Belgique, 1929 (1930), 103
M. E. Kabis: *The Works of Jean Richafort, Renaissance Composer (1480?–1548)* (diss., New York U., 1957)
P. Kast: 'Richafort, Jean', *MGG*
L. Lockwood: 'A View of the Early Sixteenth-Century Parody Mass', *Twenty-fifth Anniversary Festschrift (1937–1962)* (Queens College of the City University of New York, Department of Music, 1964), 53

HOWARD MAYER BROWN

Richard I, Coeur-de-lion (*b* Oxford, Sept 1157; *d* Limoges, 11 April 1199). King of England from 1189 to 1199, Duke of Aquitaine from 1171 and Count of Poitou from 1169, poet and composer. Though born in England, he never learnt English and spent most of his time in Aquitaine. He was the son of Henry II of England and Eleanor of Aquitaine, whose grandfather was Guillaume IX, Count of Poitou and the earliest troubadour poet. Richard's reputation as a poet and singer has been much enhanced and exaggerated by the wholly fictitious story of his rescue from prison in Austria by Blondel de Nesle in 1194; the story is nevertheless accurate in claiming that he was in fact a poet and composer.

Two poems by Richard are extant of which only *Ja nus hons pris* survives with music. Both poems are topical, or 'political' – Richard was concerned to pursue his political goals even as a poet. In *Dalfin, je'us voill deresnier* (R.1274a, PC 420.1) he chided Robert, the Dauphin of Auvergne, for not coming to his aid against King Philippe Auguste of France. *Ja nus hons pris ne dira sa raison* (R.1891, PC 420.2; ed. in Gennrich) – a rotrouenge – is a complaint about his fate as a prisoner in Austria, and was apparently written during his period of captivity (1192–4). Both poems survive in trouvère as well as in troubadour sources, and *Dalfin* appears in the latter in Provençal. Though a minor artistic figure, he nevertheless belonged to the earliest generation of trouvères and has left one of the earliest examples of the rotrouenge.

BIBLIOGRAPHY

F. Gennrich: *Die altfranzösische Rotrouenge*, Literarhistorisch-musikwissenschaftliche Studie, ii (Halle, 1925), 20f
B. Broughton: *The Legends of King Richard I Coeur de Lion* (The Hague, 1966)
For further bibliography see TROUBADOURS, TROUVÈRES.

ROBERT FALCK

Richard, Balthazar (*b* Mons, *c*1600; *d* after 1660). South Netherlands composer and cornettist. He served the royal chapel at Brussels as cornettist and composer apparently from 1620 onwards: in a document of 1660 he referred to his 40 years of service as a musician there. In a list of chapel musicians dated 1641 he is recorded as receiving a salary as high as those of the assistant director of music and the organist. He was involved in a legal action in 1657–60. In 1657 a protégé of his, Jean Corbisier, was named *maître de chant* at Notre-Dame du Sablon on his recommendation and with his guarantee that he would be fully capable of holding the position within a year. Corbisier's incompetence rapidly became evident, however; the matter was taken to court (see vander Straeten, ii, 71ff), and Richard's reputation suffered in the process. Except for an instrumental piece attributed to him in the Rost Codex (*F-Pn* Rés. Vm[7] 65z), none of the considerable quantity of music that he appears to have written seems to survive. It included *Litaniae beatissimae Mariae Virginis Lauretanae V. VI. VII. VIII. IX. et XII. tam vocibus, quam instrumentis modulatae, quibus missa octonis vocibus adjuncta est* (Antwerp, 1631). There were works by him in the library of King John IV of Portugal that was destroyed in the Lisbon earthquake of 1755, and there seem at one time to have been two or three by him in *I-Rvat*. An inventory of works belonging in 1666 to Jean Tichon, *maître de musique* of the Brussels royal chapel (in *B-Ba*), includes a mass for 17 voices and 20 other pieces by 'Baltazar Ritchart', and an eight-part canzona for violins and cornetts in the same list may have been by him too. An inventory compiled in 1677 at St Jacob, Antwerp (now in *B-Aa*), includes the reference 'Richard, Balthasar, 18 boecken'.

BIBLIOGRAPHY

Primeira parte do index da livraria de música do muyto alto, ed poderoso Rey Dom João o IV. nosso senhor (Lisbon, 1649/R1967); ed. J. de Vasconcellos (Oporto, 1874–6)

E. vander Straeten: *La musique aux Pays-Bas avant le XIXe siècle* (Brussels, 1867–88/R1969)

A. vander Linden: 'Un fragment d'inventaire musical du XVIIe siècle', *RBM*, iii (1949), 43

MARY ARMSTRONG FERRARD

Richard, Cliff [Webb, Harry Roger] (*b* Lucknow, India, 14 Oct 1940). British popular singer. He first sang and learnt the guitar with a skiffle band, and when rock music became popular he and his group became professional, taking the name Cliff Richard and the Shadows (1958). In the 1960s he recorded 50 hit songs, beginning with *Livin' Doll* (by Lionel Bart), and was the most successful British popular singer of the postwar generation. Cultivating a moderate, 'clean-cut' image in contrast to such rock groups as the Rolling Stones and The Who, he also performed as an actor and singer in several films and musicals in London, and participated in evangelical religious programmes.

BIBLIOGRAPHY

B. Ferrier: *The Wonderful World of Cliff Richard* (London, 1964)

D. Winter: *New Singer, New Song: the Cliff Richard Story* (London, 1967)

ALASDAIR HAMILTON

Richard, Etienne (*b* Paris, *c*1621; *d* Paris, ?May 1669). French composer and organist. He came of a family of organists, who appear not to have been related to the family of musicians of the same name (to which François Richard belonged) who worked in Paris at the same period. From 1645 he was organist to Chancellor Séguier in Paris, a post that he shared with his brother Charles, whom, on his death in 1652, he succeeded as organist of St Jacques-de-la-Boucherie, Paris. He also succeeded his father, Pierre Richard (*d* 1652), as organist of two other Paris churches, St Nicolas-des-Champs (from 1651) and St Martin-des-Champs (from 1655). From 14 February 1657 until his death he was also *maître-joueur d'épinette* to the king, and he was a viola player to the king's brother: he enjoyed considerable prestige at court. Several keyboard pieces – allemandes, courantes, etc – by him are extant, primarily in the Bauyn MS (*F-Pn* Rés.Vm⁷ 674–5) and in the Parville MS (*US-BE*; 13 in *L'organiste liturgique*, xviii, 1957).

BIBLIOGRAPHY

N. Dufourcq: 'Notes sur les Richard, musiciens français du XVIIe siècle', *RdM*, xxxvi (1954), 116

A. Curtis: 'Musique classique française à Berkeley', *RdM*, lvi (1970), 123

EDWARD HIGGINBOTTOM

Richard, François (*d* Paris, buried 22 Oct 1650). ?Composer and lutenist. He was apparently not related to the family of musicians to which Etienne Richard belonged. He had a son, also called François (*b* Paris,

*c*1604; *d* Paris, buried 9 Nov 1646), who was also a lutenist (like another son, Louis) but probably not a composer. They both worked at the French court, where their activities are sometimes difficult to disentangle. As early as 1614 the elder François is cited as *ordinaire de la musique de la chambre et de la chapelle*. In 1628 he is styled *ordinaire de la musique du roi*, while his son is named *compositeur de la musique du roi*. The latter was later appointed successor to his father, but in fact he died first. Two volumes of *airs de cour* by François Richard, most likely the elder, were published in Paris in 1637, one for solo voice and lute, the other containing arrangements of the same pieces for from two to four voices (six solo versions ed. in A. Verchaly, *Airs de cour pour voix et luth (1603–1643)*, Paris, 1961, nos.82–7). Several other *airs* by him appear in collections printed by Pierre Ballard in 1626 and 1628 and in an MS at the Bibliothèque Nationale. Some of his *airs* were republished with new words in sacred anthologies in 1629 and 1631–2.

BIBLIOGRAPHY

N. Dufourcq: 'Notes sur les Richard, musiciens français du XVIIe siècle', *RdM*, xxxvi (1954), 116

I. Spink: 'The Musicians of Queen Henrietta-Maria', *AcM*, xxxvi (1964), 177

EDWARD HIGGINBOTTOM

Richard de Bellengues. See CARDOT.

Richardinus, Robertus (*fl c*1530). Scottish Augustinian priest. He was a canon of Cambuskenneth near Stirling, and after 1522 was sent to Paris by his abbot, Alexander Mylne, to study with the Augustinians. He has been tentatively identified, but not on firm evidence, with a Robert Richardson who was sent to Scotland in 1543 to preach against the pope.

He wrote a commentary on the Rule of St Augustine, *Exegesis in canonem diui Augustini recens aedita* (Paris, 1530), which includes evidence of contemporary practice in church music. In it he advocated a reformed monastic life in which church music had a place as part of the etiquette owed to God. He felt, however, that the time-consuming church music usual in England and Scotland (apparently, florid polyphony) and organ music on feast days should be replaced by Gregorian chant, or by settings where 'litera una intelligitur cum nota' (a phrase perhaps implying comprehensibility of the text to the listener). He wrote, moreover, that praise of God is void unless accompanied by praise in spirit ('laus interior hominis', his quite unhistorical interpretation of St Augustine's 'jubilus').

The interest of his commentary lies largely in the specific examples he gave. He described a Vespers of the Assumption at Notre-Dame, a service he evidently attended in the 1520s. It was celebrated in the presence of John, Duke of Albany, regent of Scotland, and French notables, and the *Magnificat* was sung to simple Gregorian chant; this, he implied, was unusual; he reported moreover that no music but Gregorian chant was used at Sens at that time. He cited the (now lost) masses of Alexander Paterson of the Chapel Royal at Stirling as examples of acceptable musical settings.

BIBLIOGRAPHY

W. Fraser, ed.: *Registrum monasterii S. Marie de Cambuskenneth* (Edinburgh, 1872), pp.lxxxviii–xcii

G. G. Coulton, ed.: *Commentary on the Rule of St. Augustine by Robertus Richardinus*, Publications of the Scottish History Society, 3rd ser., xxvi (Edinburgh, 1935)

H. G. Farmer: *A History of Music in Scotland* (London, 1947/R1970), 100f

GEOFFREY CHEW

Richards, (Henry) Brinley (*b* Carmarthen, 13 Nov 1819; *d* London, 2 May 1885). Welsh pianist. The son of Henry Richards, organist of St Peter's Church, Carmarthen, who also kept a music shop, he was encouraged to abandon plans for a medical career when he won a composition prize at the Gwent and Morgannwg Eisteddfod in 1834. Gaining the patronage of the Duke of Newcastle he entered the RAM, where he was twice awarded the King's Scholarship (1835 and 1837). He went briefly to Paris for further study, becoming acquainted with Chopin, and on his return was appointed a teacher of the piano at the RAM, and later a director. He instigated the RAM's regional examination system and became superintendent of examinations for Wales and Scotland. He was said to be the finest pianist in Britain in the mid-19th century and also enjoyed a good reputation as a teacher. He was a prolific composer of undistinguished vocal and symphonic music, now forgotten. He kept his connections with Wales and was prominent as an adjudicator at the competitive eisteddfods, took an interest in Welsh triple harp playing and was a leading member of the Cymmrodorion. His *Songs of Wales* (London, 1873), published in response to the success of Caradoc's Choir at Crystal Palace in 1872, was widely sold, but his only lasting composition is *God Bless the Prince of Wales* (1862).

BIBLIOGRAPHY
J. C. Haddon: 'Richards, Henry Brinley', *DNB*
R. D. Griffith: 'Richards, Henry Brinley', *Dictionary of Welsh Biography* (London, 1959)

OWAIN EDWARDS

Richardson, Alan (*b* Edinburgh, 29 Feb 1904; *d* London, 29 Nov 1978). Scottish composer and pianist. After practical experience with the BBC in Edinburgh he moved to London where he became a pupil of Harold Craxton and studied at the RAM (1929–30). In 1931 he toured Australia and New Zealand, and he was accompanist to Flesch from 1936 to 1939. He wrote a large amount of piano music, including two sonatinas (the earlier of which was given its première by the composer at the 1949 Edinburgh Festival), a *Sonata elegiaca* and numerous shorter pieces. The picturesque titles of many of these (*The Dreaming Spires, Adventures in Space, Silver Night, Over the Moors*) give a good idea of their character, though some of the names were apparently added as afterthoughts. Richardson was married to the oboist Janet Craxton, who (like Leon Goossens) inspired him to compose several works for that instrument. In later years, indeed, the oboe had an increasingly important role in his music, though his interest in it dates back as far as 1946, when he wrote his French Suite, a euphonious, melodious work in five movements, paying graceful tribute to the early French masters. Here, as in many other works, he wrote with brevity, civility and polish. In addition to his compositions he produced viola transcriptions of pieces by Purcell, Bach, Handel and other composers, in collaboration with Watson Forbes. In 1960 he was appointed professor of piano at the RAM.

WORKS
(*selective list*)
Orch: Junior Conc., pf, orch, 1960
Chamber: French Suite, ob, pf, 1946; Sonata, vn, pf, 1948; Sonata, ob, pf, 1950; Sonata, va, pf, 1954; Sonatina, ob, pf, 1965; Suite 'In the Lowlands', tuba, pf, 1968; Sonata, bn, pf, 1968; Sonatina, fl, pf, 1968; Suite, fl, ob, pf, 1969; 3 Inventions, fl, ob, 1970; 2 books of ob solos, 1971, 1972, collab. J. Craxton; Trio, ob d'amore, a fl, b cl, 1972; Trio, va, b cl, pf, 1973; Duo, ob, vc, 1973; Ov., Coronach and Capricietto, b cl, pf, 1973

Pf: Suite, D, op.38, 1955; Sonata, op.26, 1956; 3 Pieces, op.35, 1957; Rhapsody, op.37, 1958; Sonatina, F, op.27, 1960; Sonata elegiaca, 1960; Kaleidoscope, 10 tone sketches, 1967

Principal publishers: Associated Board, Augener, Chester, Oxford University Press, Weinberger

CONRAD WILSON

Richardson, Arnold (*b* Ely, 6 Jan 1914; *d* London, 26 June 1973). English organist and composer who specialized in the interpretation of modern French music. He studied with G. D. Cunningham and Benjamin Dale at the Royal Academy of Music, of which he was a Fellow and where he joined the teaching staff and became an examiner in 1961. His first post (1934) was at St Alban's, Holborn, to which church he invited Messiaen to give the first complete English performance of *La nativité du Seigneur* in 1938. Richardson became borough organist of Wolverhampton in 1938 and succeeded Percy Rideout as organist of the West London Synagogue in 1955. He played frequently at the Promenade Concerts, at one of which (1949) he gave the first performance of a Carillon by Herbert Murrill, dedicated to him. He was one of four British organists chosen to give the opening recital at the Festival Hall in March 1954 and appeared there regularly afterwards. As conductor of the Wolverhampton Civic Choir from 1949 to 1972 he directed major choral works with the City of Birmingham Orchestra. He was made an honorary Fellow of the Royal College of Organists in 1971. His own compositions include a mass in A (1935), a pastorale for organ (1936) and a three-part mass for men's voices (1939).

STANLEY WEBB

Richardson, Ferdinand [Heybourne (Heaburn), Sir Ferdinando] (*b c*1558; *d* Tottenham, Middlesex, 4 June 1618). English composer. He was a pupil of Tallis (to judge from his prefatory poem to the Tallis–Byrd *Cantiones sacrae*), became a groom of the Privy Chamber in 1587, and was pensioned in 1611. He wrote two pavan–galliard pairs, each with a 'Variatio', which survive in the Fitzwilliam Virginal Book. One of these pairs, without its 'Variatio', is in *GB-Lbm* Add.30485 (which also includes another pavan–galliard pair and an 'Alman'). He arranged a pavan and galliard by Thomas Morley (*GB-Cfm* Mus.782, 52.d.25, 'set by Mr. Heybourne'), printed in EKM, xiv (1958).

Richardson appears as the dedicatee of Farnaby's *Canzonets*, published in 1598 by Peter Short. His brother, Christopher Heybourn(e), was in some way associated with Morley's patent (for the printing and importation of music).

BIBLIOGRAPHY
R. Marlow: 'Sir Ferdinando Heybourne alias Richardson', *MT*, cxv (1974), 736

JOHN CALDWELL

Richardson, Marilyn (*b* Sydney, 10 June 1936). Australian soprano. She studied singing at the New South Wales State Conservatorium of Music. In 1971, on winning a Churchill Fellowship, she studied with Bernac in Paris and Conchita Badía in Barcelona, and took opera repertory instruction in Austria. An outstandingly versatile singer with a rich voice of nearly three-octave range, she performs medieval, Renaissance and Baroque music, lieder and oratorio. She is, in addition, the leading Australian exponent of 20th-century music, with a repertory that includes works by

Pousseur, Dallapiccola, Messiaen, Berio, Cage and Maxwell Davies (she gave many of their first Australian performances). She performs much Australian music and has inspired many compositions. Her opera performances include the title roles of *Lulu* (1972) and *Salome* (1974) at Basle, Malinka in Janáček's *The Excursions of Mr Brouček* (Adelaide Festival, 1974) and, for the Australian Opera Company, Aida (1975), Salome and the Marschallin (both 1976).

ANN CARR-BOYD

Richardson, Vaughan (*b* ?London, *c*1670; *d* Winchester, June 1729). English organist and composer. From 1678 he was a chorister in the Chapel Royal, where he was a pupil of John Blow; his voice broke in 1688. It has been suggested that he may have been related to a Thomas Richardson, Gentleman of the Chapel Royal from 1664 to 1712, or a William Richardson who was his fellow chorister (and who later published harpsichord music and psalm tunes). He was temporary organist at Worcester Cathedral from 1686, and from June 1688 until his death organist at Winchester Cathedral. Among his students at Winchester was James Kent, who later became organist there.

Richardson wrote *An Entertainment of New Musick, composed on The Peace* (of Ryswick) performed at York Buildings, London, in 1697 and published *A Collection of Songs* for one to three voices (London, 1701). Foster listed 21 of his anthems, including *O how amiable*, which was traditionally sung as a processional at Winchester and edited in John Page's *Harmonia Sacra* (London, 1800); one anthem, *O Lord God of my Salvation*, and a service in C 'composed upon ye Peace [of Utrecht], 1713' are included in Thomas Tudway's collection (*GB-Lbm*), and another anthem, *To God on High*, is at St Paul's. J. S. Bumpus possessed an autograph volume, now apparently lost, containing 14 anthems, the Service in C, *A Song for the King* (dated 1697), *A Song for St Cecilia's Day* (performed at Winchester about 1700) and six sonatas for strings. Another Cecilian ode survives (in *GB-Lcm*). Supposed autographs of four anthems were given to the British Museum by Ralph Griffin in 1930; other works are to be found in various cathedral libraries.

Richardson's few extant compositions are of little importance. He was a typical English composer and organist of the transition period between the Restoration and Georgian eras.

BIBLIOGRAPHY
EitnerQ
J. W. West: *Cathedral Organists* (London, 1899)
M. B. Foster: *Anthems and Anthem Composers* (London, 1901/*R*1970)
J. S. Bumpus: *English Cathedral Music*, ii (London, 1908)
W. H. Husk: 'Richardson, Vaughan', *Grove 5*
CHARLES CUDWORTH

Richard-Wagner-Verband. *See* WAGNER SOCIETIES.

Richart de Fournival (*d* 1260). French trouvère poet, composer and author. He is often given the title *maistre* in sources and was the son of Rogiers de Fournival, personal physician to King Philippe Auguste of France. In 1240 he was recorded as 'Magister Richardus de Fournival, Canonicus' of the chapter of Notre Dame in Amiens, and in 1246 became chancellor. Like his father, he was a surgeon, and continued in that profession throughout his life. In addition to the 22 lyric poems ascribed to him in a substantial number of sources, he

wrote a Latin *Biblionomia* and a *Bestiaire d'amour*.

Even without the large number of monophonic songs attributed to him, Richart would be of interest to the music historian because of his association with the early motet. Although none of his motets may be traced directly to a clausula as its source, one, *Chascuns qui de bien amer*, is based on a tenor from the Notre Dame repertory. Two of the motets are found in a collection (*D-W* 1206) which contains the earliest layer of French motet composition; thus, Richart may be regarded as one of the earliest poet-composers associated with the genre. (Neither the tenor nor the music for *Renvoisiement i vois a mon ami* is extant, and indeed it is uncertain whether this is a motet at all.)

Richart's 18 monophonic songs are remarkable for the variety of their structure matched by equally varied and subtle musical treatment. One song, *Mere au roi omnipotent*, is a Marian contrafactum of a song by Richart's contemporary, Moniot d'Arras, while another, *Oiés, seigneur, pereceus, par oiseuses* is based on a celebrated crusader's song which was composed in the year 1188. Richart's contrafactum employs one of four melodies surviving with the model.

WORKS
CHANSONS

Adés m'estoie a ce tenus, R.2130
Ains ne vi grant hardement, R.685
Amis Richart, j'eusse bien mestier, R.1290 (no melody)
Gente m'est la saisons d'esté, R.443
Joie d'amours ne puet nus esprisier, R.1278
L'amour de ma douce enfance, R.218
L'autrier avint en cel autre pais, R.1574 (two melodies survive)
Lonc tens me sui escondis, R.1541
Mere au roi omnipotent, R.713 [modelled on: Moniot d'Arras, 'Ne me dones pas talent', R.739]
Oiés, seigneur, pereceus, par oiseuses, R.1020a [modelled on: Conon de Bethune or Chastelain de Couci, 'Ahi, Amours, con dure departie', R.1125]
Par mainte fois pensé ai, R.53
Puis qu'il m'estuet de ma doulour chanter, R.805
Quant chante oisiaus tant seri, R.1080
Quant chiet la fueille en l'arbroie, R.1689
Quant ie voi, R.1677a
Quant la justice est saisie, R.1206
Se je pooie aussi mon cuer doner, R.847
Talent avoie d'amer, R.760
Tels s'entrement de garder, R.858

MOTETS

Chascuns qui de bien amer, 2vv, R.759
Onques n'amai tant con je fui amee, 2vv, R.498
Renvoisiement i vois a mon ami, 2vv, R.1143a (no music; ?motet)

BIBLIOGRAPHY
P. Aubry: *Trouvères and Troubadours* (New York, 1914), 118f
F. Gennrich: 'Trouvèrelieder und Motettenrepertoire', *ZMw*, ix (1926), 14, 17
ROBERT FALCK

Richart de Semilli (*fl* late 12th or early 13th century). French trouvère. Mention of Paris in three chansons seems to indicate that Richart was a native of that city. Ten works are ascribed to him in *F-Pa* 5198 and a few related sources, and *L'une est la chastelaine*, which is anonymous, may also be his. The re-use of the same poetic structure and melody in *Chancon ferai* and *Je chevauchai*, and in *De chanter* and *Quant la sesons*, is unusual within the work of one poet but not without parallel in the repertory. Richart's musical structures stand apart from the mainstream of trouvère music in their heavy reliance on repetition. *J'ain la plus sade* is constructed of one phrase and a variant, while *L'autrier chevauchoie* uses three phrases and their variants for 11 lines of text. *L'autrier chevauchoie*, *Molt ai chanté* and *Nous venions* each present the last melodic material three times in varied form. *Chancon ferai* and *L'autrier* *tous seus* are examples of rotrouenge form. Most melodies are quite simple, *Molt ai chanté* being somewhat more ornate. The patterns of *De chanter* suggest that the 2nd mode may be suitable, although no melodies survive in mensural notation. The authentic D mode and plagal F mode are favoured, although *L'autrier chevauchoie* concludes the main body of a strophe based on *d* with a refrain ending on *c*, while *Molt ai chanté* concludes the main body of a strophe emphasizing *g*, with a refrain preparation and refrain ending on *f*. *Je chevauchai, L'autrier chevauchoie, L'autrier tous seus* and *Nous venions* provided the models for other chansons. *Par amors* employs the same structure and melody as two other chansons, the question of priority being uncertain.

WORKS

Editions: *Die altfranzösische Rotrouenge*, ed. F. Gennrich (Halle, 1925) [A]

       Troubadours, Trouvères, Minne- und Meistergesang, ed. F. Gennrich, Mw, ii (1951; Eng. trans., 1960) [G]

(V) – MS (using Schwan sigla – *see* SOURCES, MS) in which a late setting of a poem occurs

Chancon ferai plein d'ire et de pensee, R.538 [contrafactum: no.4; model for: Anon., 'Chanter vous vueil de la vierge Marie', R.1182], A 58 (V)

De chanter m'est pris courage, R.22 [contrafactum: no.10], Aubry, 102 (V)

J'ain la plus sade riens qui soit de mere nee, R.533

Je chevauchai l'autrier la matinee, R.527 [contrafactum: no.1; model for: Anon., 'Chanter vous vueil de la vierge Marie', R.1182], A 54 (V)

L'autrier chevauchoie delés Paris, R.1583 [model for: Anon., 'L'autrier m'en aloie', R.1680], A 35 (V)

L'autrier tout seus chevauchoie mon chemin, R.1362 [model for: Anon., 'De la tres douce Marie vueil chanter', R.835], A 56, G 32 (V)

Molt ai chanté, riens ne m'i puet valoir, R.1820 (V)

Nous venions l'autrier de joer, R.868 [model for: Anon., 'On doit la mere Dieu honorer', R.822], Gennrich (1937)

Par amors ferai chanson, R.1860 [contrafacta: Moniot de Paris, 'Qui veut amours maintenir', R.1424; Moine de St Denis, 'D'Amour me doit souvenir', R.1468] (V)

Quant la sesons renouvele, R.614 [contrafactum: no.2] (V)

DOUBTFUL WORK

L'une est la chastelaine, devers Mont le Heri, R.1044a (most of first strophe and music missing)

BIBLIOGRAPHY

G. Steffens: 'Der kritische Text der Gedichte von Richart de Semilli', *Festschrift für Wendelin Toerster* (Halle, 1902), 331

P. Aubry: *Trouvères et troubadours* (Paris, 1909)

F. Gennrich: 'Grundsätzliches zu den Troubadour- und Trouvère-Weisen', *Zeitschrift für romanische Philologie*, lvii (1937), 45

For further bibliography *see* TROUBADOURS, TROUVÈRES.

THEODORE KARP

Richauffort, Jean. *See* RICHAFORT, JEAN.

Richault. French music publishing firm. It was founded in Paris by Charles-Simon Richault (*b* Chartres, 10 May 1780; *d* Paris, 20 Feb 1866). After an apprenticeship with the publisher J. J. de Momigny, Richault set up on his own in 1805 at 7 rue Grange-Batelière, occasionally also publishing jointly with Momigny for up to 20 years afterwards. His firm, normally styled 'Simon Richault', moved to 16 boulevard Poissonnière some time between August 1823 and July 1825; between 14 and 28 November 1841 it moved (or the house was renumbered) to no.26; and on 19 October 1862 it had just moved to 4 boulevard des Italiens. Meanwhile, in November 1839, Richault purchased the business of J.-J. Frey, many of whose publications he subsequently reissued. On his death, Charles-Simon was succeeded by his son Guillaume-Simon (*b* Chartres, 3 Nov 1805; *d* Paris, 7 Feb 1877) and the firm became known as Richault & Cie. Guillaume-Simon was in turn succeeded by his son Léon (*b* Paris, 6 Aug 1839; *d* Paris, 7 or 10 April 1895), who traded as Richault & Cie or Richault Fils & Cie. After Léon's death the firm was managed by his widow or mother until in June 1898 it was acquired by Costallat & Cie (still in existence in the mid-1970s).

Particularly under the management of Charles-Simon, Richault was one of the most important music publishers in Paris during the 19th century, putting out a total of some 20,000 publications. It was specially concerned with orchestral, chamber and vocal music, concentrating chiefly on important non-Italian contemporary composers, such as Beethoven, Czerny, Fesca, Liszt, Mendelssohn, Schumann, Spohr, Weber and notably Schubert. Among the French composers it encouraged were Alkan, Massé, Reber, Thomas and Berlioz; Richault was the first to publish Berlioz's *La damnation de Faust*, *L'enfance du Christ*, *Lélio*, four of the overtures and several vocal works, as well as a collection of his *mélodies* with piano accompaniment. Rather less attention was paid to opera, but full scores or orchestral parts or both were published of works by Adam, Monpou, Onslow and Thomas, as well as the handsome critical edition of Gluck operas edited by F. Pelletan and others (issued in association with Breitkopf & Härtel, 1873–96). Piano–vocal scores of at least 30 operas were published. According to Pougin (*FétisBS*) the firm acquired and reissued many editions previously published by Naderman, Sieber, Pleyel, Erard and others and, after Pacini's death in 1866, at least part of his stock, including his operatic publications. Richault's plate numbers were applied chronologically and are generally reliable for dating purposes.

BIBLIOGRAPHY

FétisBS

C. Hopkinson: *A Bibliography of the Musical and Literary Works of Hector Berlioz* (Edinburgh, 1951), 197ff

——: *A Dictionary of Parisian Music Publishers 1700–1950* (London, 1954), 104

——: *A Bibliographical Thematic Catalogue of the Works of John Field* (London, 1961), 168f

RICHARD MACNUTT

Riche, Anthoine le. *See* DIVITIS, ANTONIUS.

Richée, Philipp Franz le Sage de. *See* LE SAGE DE RICHÉE, PHILIPP FRANZ.

Richmann [Rhiemann, Riemann], **Jacob** (*d* after 1720). Flemish or German viola da gamba player and composer. He was employed as a chamber musician, first in the service of the Princess of Orange and later to the Elector of Hessen-Kassel. Out of five collections of works, mostly published in Amsterdam, referred to in contemporary sources only his *Six sonates à une viole de gambe et basse continue* op.1 (1710) are known to have survived. The lost works are *Sonate à violino e basso continuo* op.2 (*c*1710–12), *Sonate à violino, viola di gamba e basso continuo* op.3 (*c*1712–15), *Suites de preludes pour la basse de viole* (1727) and psalms of David (*c*1718). Richmann's instrumental music was frequently advertised in Roger's catalogues; all four collections were still available in Le Cène's catalogue of 1737.

Op.1 consists of six sonatas, each of five movements (Preludio, Allemanda, Corrente, Sarabanda and Giga); the figured bass part is marked 'Organo'. These works, technically less difficult than those by Schenck, were written for a six-string viol in an idiomatic style using many chords. They nevertheless show a strong Italian influence in the use of semiquaver passage-work, successions of chords marked 'Arpeggio', and changing tempo indications within a movement.

BIBLIOGRAPHY
K. Pauls: 'Richmann, Jacob', MGG
F. Lesure: Bibliographie des éditions musicales publiées par Estienne Roger et Michel-Charles Le Cène (Paris, 1969)
LUCY ROBINSON

Richter, Anton Karl. Austrian composer and organist, son of FERDINAND TOBIAS RICHTER.

Richter, Ernst Friedrich (Eduard) (*b* Gross-Schönau, Lausitz, 24 Oct 1808; *d* Leipzig, 9 April 1879). German theorist, teacher and composer. From about 1818 he attended the Gymnasium at Zittau, where he directed the choir. In 1831 he went to Leipzig University to read theology, but received musical instruction from Weinlig, who was then Kantor. He conducted the Leipzig Singakademie (1843–7) and became a professor of harmony and counterpoint at the newly founded conservatory. Fétis stated that he directed the university music. He was organist of different churches and in 1868 became Kantor of the Thomasschule. The oratorio *Christus der Erlöser* (8 March 1849) and the cantata *Dithyrambe* op.48 (for the Schiller Festival, 1859) were the best known of his many compositions. He also wrote songs, keyboard and sacred choral works, and Fétis mentioned an overture (1836), string quartets and a Cello Sonata op.37. Richter's manuals, especially the *Lehrbuch der Harmonie*, translated into at least six languages, became textbooks for several generations of students in Europe and the USA.

Richter's son Bernhard Friedrich Richter (*b* Leipzig, 1 Aug 1850; *d* Leipzig, 16 April 1931) worked as an organist and as a teacher at the Thomasschule. He published studies on music in Leipzig and the performing practice of Bach's music, contributing articles to the *Bach-Jahrbuch* (1905–11) and the *Monatshefte*.

WRITINGS
Die Grundzüge der musikalischen Formen und ihre Analyse (Leipzig, 1852)
Lehrbuch der Harmonie (Leipzig, 1853, 36/1953; Eng. trans., 1864); *Aufgabenbuch zu E. F. Richters Harmonielehre*, ed. A. Richter (Leipzig, 1879, 64/1952)
Lehrbuch der Fuge (Leipzig, 1859, 9/1921)
Katechismus der Orgel (Leipzig, 1868, 4/1896/R1977)
Lehrbuch des einfachen und doppelten Kontrapunkts (Leipzig, 1872; Eng. trans., 1874)

BIBLIOGRAPHY
FétisB; *FétisBS*
H. Riemann: *Geschichte der Musik seit Beethoven* (Berlin and Stuttgart, 1901)
F. Lampadius: *Die Kantoren der Thomasschule zu Leipzig* (Leipzig, 1902)
[B. F. Richter]: Obituary, *BJb*, xxviii (1931)
FRANZ GEHRING/DAVID CHARLTON

Richter, Ferdinand Tobias (*b* Würzburg, 22 July 1651; *d* Vienna, 3 Nov 1711). Austrian composer and organist of German birth. It seems reasonable to assume that he received his musical training from his father, Tobias (*d* 1682) – vice-Kapellmeister at the court of the Elector of Mainz from before 1651 and later Kapellmeister there – as well as from his godfather, P. F. Buchner. On 25 August 1675 he was appointed organist of the Cistercian monastery of Heiligenkreuz, Lower Austria, and from June 1676 he was also prefect of the choirboys; he remained there until 31 August 1679. It is not

known why he left or where he spent the next four years, but on 1 July 1683 he was appointed court and chamber organist at the court of the Emperor Leopold I in Vienna (the retrospective decree is dated 1 January 1684). In 1690 he was promoted to first organist at the court chapel, a position he held until his death. During his tenure he was entrusted with the musical education of, among others, several of Leopold I's children, including the future emperors Joseph I and Karl VI. A number of south German organists visited Vienna to study with him, and Pachelbel too recognized his significance when he dedicated his *Hexachordum Apollinis* (Nuremberg, 1699) jointly to him, as a representative of the south German school of organists, and to Buxtehude, representing the north.

Richter's fame during his lifetime and immediately after his death rested on his accomplishments and reputation as an organist and as a composer of keyboard music. Most of this music consists of suites, which begin with a prelude and fugue and continue with a succession of dance movements. Although clearly influenced by Froberger and Poglietti, these works also adumbrate the stylistic changes that were soon to come to fruition in the music of composers such as Fux. They show a feeling for the dramatic that is not unexpected in a composer who wrote a fair amount of stage music. For, together with J. B. Staudt, Richter was one of the leading composers of music for the Latin school plays produced by the Society of Jesus. These works were among the most important and effective agencies of the Counter-Reformation in Austria, and they enjoyed immense popularity and prestige in the 17th century. The music is usually restricted to overtures, prologues and epilogues and occasional arias, ensembles, choruses, instrumental interludes and dances. In style it follows late 17th-century operatic practice, but Richter shows a remarkable sense of musical drama that elevates his work above much of the frequently mass-produced dramatic music of his Viennese contemporaries.

Richter's eldest son, Anton Karl (*b* Vienna, 1690; *d* Vienna, 11 Nov 1763), was accepted into the Vienna court chapel as a pupil of his father in 1699. He did not, however, enjoy the success expected of him, and when he was appointed sixth and last organist at court in 1718 it was mainly because of his father's long and meritorious service. With the reorganization of the court music in 1741 he was promoted to the position of second organist, from which he retired in 1751. As a composer he is known by a suite and two character-pieces (in *A-Wn*), all for keyboard and all of poor quality.

WORKS

MUSIC FOR JESUIT SCHOOL PLAYS
(*in A-Wn unless otherwise stated*)

Passio Christi, armatura fortium, Linz, 1 April 1684; lost, lib *A-Wn*
Altera Bethlehem, sive domus panis, Linz, 9 June 1684
Invicta christiani herois fortitudo, Vienna, 3 Dec 1688
Humilitas arcanum gloriae in Clodoveo, Vienna, 25 Feb 1691
Themistocles, Atheniensium dux (J. B. Adolph), Vienna, 1 Jan 1696
Otto magnus Romanorum imperator, Vienna, 1696; lost, lib *Wn*
Hymenaei de marte triumphus (J. Sellenitsch), Vienna, 26 Feb 1699
Amor in Aenea pro Livinia, Vienna, 3 Dec 1706
Laureatus fidei et amoris, Vienna, 3 Dec 1708; lost, lib *Wn*
Sacer hymenaeus de profano amore victor, Vienna, 31 July 1710
Mala livoris perfidiosi, Krems, 1710; lost, lib *GÖ*

OPERAS
L'istro ossequioso, Vienna, 21 May 1694, *A-Wn*
Le promesse degli dei (N. Minato), Vienna, 9 June 1697, *Wn*

ORATORIOS
Santo Ermenegildo (D. Cupeda), Vienna, 1694, *Wn*

La caduta di Gerico, Vienna, 1695; lost, lib *Wn*
L'incoronazione di Salomone (S. Amerighi), Vienna, 1696; lost, lib *Wn*
S Teresa (P. A. Bernardoni), Vienna, 1706, *Wn* [only final chorus by Richter]

OTHER SACRED
(*in A-GÖ unless otherwise stated*)

Requiem, 4vv, insts
Vesperae de BVM, 5vv, insts
Tenebrae, 5vv, insts
Magnificat, 5vv, insts, formerly *D-DS*, now lost
Miserere, 4vv, insts

INSTRUMENTAL

Sonata, a 7; Balletti, a 4, 5: dated 1685, *A-Wn*
Sonate, a 4, 6–8, dated 1685, *Wgm*
Balletti, *CS-KRa*
5 Suites, kbd, *A-Wm*; 3 ed. in DTÖ, xxvii, Jg.xiii/2 (1906/*R*1959)
Toccata, d, with 10 versetti, kbd, *Wm*; ed. in DTÖ, xxvii, Jg.xiii/2 (1906/*R*1959)
Capriccio, Toccata, d, kbd, *D-Bds*
Ricercare, kbd, *A-Wn* (copy)
Versetti, kbd, *Wm*

BIBLIOGRAPHY

L. von Köchel: *Die kaiserliche Hof-Musikkapelle in Wien von 1543 bis 1867* (Vienna, 1869)
A. von Weilen: *Zur Wiener Theatergeschichte: die vom Jahre 1629 bis zum Jahre 1740 am Wiener Hofe zur Aufführung gelangten Werke theatralischen Charakters und Oratorien* (Vienna, 1901)
H. Botstiber: Introduction to DTÖ, xxvii, Jg.xiii/2 (1906/*R*1959)
A. Koczirz: 'Exzerpte aus den Hofmusikakten des Wiener Kammerarchivs', *SMw*, i (1913), 278
E. Wellesz: 'Die Opern und Oratorien in Wien 1660–1708', *SMw*, vi (1919), 5–138
P. Nettl: 'Die Wiener Tanzkomposition in der zweiten Hälfte des siebzehnten Jahrhunderts', *SMw*, viii (1921), 45–175
——: 'Zur Geschichte der kaiserlichen Hofmusikkapelle von 1636–1680', *SMw*, xvi (1929), 70; xvii (1930), 95; xviii (1931), 25; xix (1932), 33
E. H. Meyer: *Die mehrstimmige Spielmusik des 17. Jahrhunderts in Nord- und Mitteleuropa* (Kassel, 1934)
F. Hadamowsky: 'Barocktheater am Wiener Kaiserhof, mit einem Spielplan (1625–1740)', *Jb der Gesellschaft für Wiener Theaterforschung, 1951–2* (1955)
A. Kellner: *Musikgeschichte des Stiftes Kremsmünster* (Kassel, 1956)
G. Frotscher: *Geschichte des Orgel-Spiels und der Orgel-Komposition*, i (Berlin, 1935, enlarged 3/1966)
F. W. Riedel: *Quellenkundliche Beiträge zur Geschichte der Musik für Tasteninstrumente in der 2. Hälfte des 17. Jahrhunderts* (Kassel, 1960)
——: *Das Musikarchiv im Minoritenkonvent zu Wien* (Kassel, 1963)
W. Kramer: *Die Musik im Wiener Jesuitendrama von 1677–1711* (diss., U. of Vienna, 1965)
H. Knaus: 'Franz Mathias Techelmann (1649–1714): kaiserlicher Hoforganist in Wien', *SMw*, xxvii (1966), 186
F. W. Riedel: 'Die Libretto-Sammlung im Benediktinerstift Göttweig', *FAM*, xiii (1966), 105
W. Apel: *Geschichte der Orgel- und Klaviermusik bis 1700* (Kassel, 1967; Eng. trans., rev. 1972)
H. Knaus: *Die Musiker im Archivbestand des kaiserlichen Obersthofmeisteramtes (1637–1705)* (Vienna, 1967–9)
C. D. Harris: 'Problems in Editing Harpsichord Music: *Suite in D* by Ferdinand Tobias Richter (1649–1711)', *Notations and Editions: a Book in Honor of Louise Cuyler* (Dubuque, Iowa, 1974), 142
S. Wollenberg: *Viennese Keyboard Music in the Reign of Karl VI* (diss., U. of Oxford, 1975)

RUDOLF SCHNITZLER

Richter, Franz Xaver (*b* ?Holleschau [now Holešov], 1 Dec 1709; *d* Strasbourg, 12 Sept 1789). German composer and singer of Moravian–Bohemian descent. His birth is not recorded in the church archives in Holešov and the death certificate cited by Vogeleis refers to him as 'ex Kratz', so that his origin is uncertain. He had received a musical education based on Fux's *Gradus ad Parnassum* (and perhaps under the personal supervision of Fux in Vienna) by 1740, and on 2 April that year became vice-Kapellmeister for the Prince-Abbot Anselm von Reichlin-Meldegg in Kempten, Allgäu; he was married there in February 1743 to Maria Anna Josepha Moz. By 1747, however, his name appears

Franz Xaver Richter: engraving (1785) by Christophe Guéru

among the court musicians of the Elector Palatine Carl Theodor in Mannheim. He is listed as a bass in some published librettos of the Mannheim court opera, including that of Galuppi's *L'Olimpiade* (January 1749), which refers to him as *virtuoso di camera*. F. W. Marpurg included him as a second violinist in the Mannheim orchestra list of 1756 (*Beyträge*, ii), but perhaps this was a mistake, as he is not mentioned elsewhere as an instrumentalist. Six of his symphonies had been published in Paris by 1744, but he also obtained recognition at the Palatine court for his sacred compositions. In 1748, his second year there, he was given the honour of composing an oratorio for Good Friday at the elector's request, *La deposizione dalla croce*. Between 1761 and 1767 he wrote a composition method which he dedicated to the elector, who appointed him chamber composer (probably in 1768, when his name is dropped from the list of court singers). Although he was able to make concert tours to the Oettingen-Wallerstein court (1754) and later to France, the Netherlands and England, he was displeased with the prevailing attitudes of virtuosity, stereotyped musical effects and modishness at Mannheim. On 24 April 1769 he succeeded Joseph Garnier as Kapellmeister at Strasbourg Cathedral, where both his performing and composing activities turned still further to sacred music, but he also continued to influence secular musical life. During his last years Ignace Pleyel served as his assistant at the cathedral.

Richter has been called one of the foremost Mannheim composers (Burney), although he consciously avoided that court's fashionable style. His early works were conservative, and in an outmoded Viennese Baroque style that found a warmer reception in England and northern Germany than in the southern regions. His instrumental counterpoint, which he used either in fugal outer movements or introduced into otherwise homophonic movements, was particularly admired; Burney found his melodic lines in the Baroque style inventive but spoilt by too many sequences. The string quartets (published in 1768, although Kirkendale suggested that they may have been composed by 1757) are remarkably advanced for their time, with a balance of the four parts presaging the Classical period. Among the Mannheim composers, only Richter and Ignaz Fränzl frequently used the minor mode for either the principal or secondary key of symphonies. In his sacred compositions he contrasted polyphonic *a cappella* movements with harmonically rich arias and duets, and placed choral or orchestral fugues beside choral movements with concerted instruments in the Neapolitan style.

Richter was also a highly respected teacher whose pupils included J. M. Kraus, H. J. Riegel, Carl Stamitz (1770) and Ferdinand Fränzl (1785–6). His *Harmonische Belehrungen* is the only 18th-century theoretical work produced in Mannheim (excluding Vogler's), although it does not represent the Mannheim style. This extensive work, based on Fux's textbook, contains many practical examples and is similar to the writings of Meinrad Spiess in its defence of the church modes and its accessible manner.

WORKS

ORCHESTRAL

Syms. [thematic catalogue in DTB, iv, Jg.iii/1 (1902)]: 6 grandes simphonies . . . en 4 parties (Paris, 1744); 6 Symphonys in 8 Parts, op.2 (London, 1760), lost (Amsterdam, c1765); 6 sinfonie, op.3 (Paris, 1760); 6 simphonies, op.4 (London, c1765), 2 ed. in DTB, iv, Jg.iii/1 (1902), 1 ed. in DTB, xiii, Jg.vii/2 (1906); 6 sinfonie, op.7 (Paris, 17677) [incl. 1 from op.4]; 20 in contemporary anthologies (c1758–c1775); c32 syms., *A-LA, ST; B-Bc; CS-Bm, Pnm; D-Bds, Dlb, DS, HR, Mbs*, [1 ed. in DTB, iv, Jg.iii/1 (1902)], *Rtt; F-Pc*

Concs.: 6 Concertos . . . in 5 Parts, hpd (London, c1765); 8 hpd concs., now lost, 1 ed. H. Höckner (Berlin, 1933); 8 for fl, *D-KA, Rtt* [1 ed. D. Sonntag (Heidelberg, c1965)], *F-Pc*; 1 for ob, *D-Rtt*; 1 for clarino, *US-Wc*; 6 for hn, 1754, lost; 1 for vc, before 1766, lost

Other orch: A Third Set of 6 Favourite Overtures (London, c1775); 12 minuets, 1779, offered by Breitkopf

CHAMBER

(thematic catalogue in DTB, xxviii, Jg.xvi, 1915)

6 Sonatas, hpd, vn/fl, vc (London, 1759); A Second Set of 6 Sonatas, hpd, vn/fl, vc (London, c1763), 1 ed. H. Riemann, Collegium musicum, xviii (Leipzig, 1904), 1 ed. in DTB, xxviii, Jg.xvi (1915); 6 sonates, 2 fl/vn (Paris, 1763); 6 solos, fl/vn, bc (London, 1764); 6 Sonatas, 2 vn, vc, hpd (London, c1764), as op.3 (Amsterdam, c1675)

A Second Set of 6 Sonatas, 2 vn, vc, hpd, op.4 (London, c1765); 6 Quartetto's, 2 vn, va, vc (London, 1768), ed. in DTB, xxvii, Jg.xv (1914), as op.5 (Paris, c1772); 3 sinfonie a 4, *D-Bds, Mbs*; Divertimento, hpd, fl, vc, *B-Bc*; works for kbd, *D-HR, DO*; 8 trios cited in catalogues

VOCAL

Oratorios: La deposizione dalla croce (C. Pasquini), Mannheim, 12 April 1748, only lib extant; Oratorium in 2 partes divisum, Stams, 1762, lost

Other vocal: 39 masses, most in *F-Sg(sc)*, others *D-Bds, Mbs, OB, F-Pc, I-Fc*; 3 requiem, *F-Sg(sc)*; Magnificat a 4 (Paris, c1790), lost; Dixit Dominus, 4vv, chorus, orch/org (Paris, n.d.); over 50 cantatas and motets, c30 smaller sacred works, most in *F-Sg(sc)*, others *B-Bc, CH-E, F-Pn, I-Mc*, for details see Mathias (1909), *EitnerQ*; 1 aria in The Summer's Tale (London, 1765); arrs. of sacred works by Fux, Jommelli, Hoffmann, Caldara, 'Bordier', all *F-Sg(sc)*

THEORETICAL WORKS

Harmonische Belehrungen oder gründliche Anweisung zu der musikalischen Ton-Kunst oder regulären Composition (MS, *B-Bc*); ed. and trans. C. Kalkbrenner as *Traité d'harmonie et de composition* (Paris, 1804)

BIBLIOGRAPHY

GerberL; GerberNL

C. Burney: *The Present State of Music in Germany, the Netherlands and the United Provinces* (London, 1773, 2/1775); ed. P. Scholes as *Dr. Burney's Musical Tours* (London, 1959)

J. N. Forkel: *Musikalischer Almanach 1784* (Leipzig, 1783/R)

F. X. Mathias: 'Franz Xaver Richter', *Caecilia*, xv (1907)

——: 'Thematischer Katalog der im Strassburger Münsterarchiv aufbewahrten kirchenmusikalischen Werke Fr. X. Richters (1769–1789)', *Riemann-Festschrift* (Leipzig, 1909), 394

M. Vogeleis: *Quellen und Bausteine zu einer Geschichte der Musik und des Theaters im Elsass 500–1800* (Strasbourg, 1911)

K. G. Fellerer: *Der Palestrinastil und seine Bedeutung in der vokalen*

Kirchenmusik des 18. Jahrhunderts (Augsburg, 1929/R1972)

W. Barth: *Die Messenkompositionen Franz Xaver Richters (1709–89)* (diss., U. of Munich, 1941)

W. Gässler: *Die Sinfonien von Franz Xaver Richter* (diss., U. of Munich, 1942)

E. Schmitt: *Die Kurpfälzische Kirchenmusik im 18. Jahrhundert* (diss., U. of Heidelberg, 1958)

R. Münster: 'Vier Musiker der Mannheimer Schule', *Musica*, xiv (1960), 488

R. Fuhrmann: *Mannheimer Klavier-Kammermusik* (Marburg, 1963)

E. Schmitt: 'Franz Xaver Richter', *Caecilia*, lxxii (1964), 14, 139

W. Kirkendale: *Fuge und Fugato in der Kammermusik des Rokoko und der Klassik* (Tutzing, 1966; Eng. trans., 1979)

ROLAND WÜRTZ

Richter, Hans (*b* Raab [now Györ], 4 April 1843; *d* Bayreuth, 5 Dec 1916). Austro-Hungarian conductor. He was born of musical parents: his father was Kapellmeister at the cathedral in Raab, and his mother, Josephine Csazinsky (*d* 1892), sang Venus in the first Vienna *Tannhäuser* (1857). In 1853, the year of his father's death, Richter began his schooling at the Löwenburg Konvikt in Vienna; for four years he was also a chorister in the Vienna Hofkapelle. From 1860 to 1865 he studied the violin, the horn and theory (the last under Simon Sechter) at the Vienna Conservatory, also playing the horn in the Kärntnertor Theater (1862–6). Then in 1866 the theatre's conductor, Heinrich Esser, recommended him to Wagner; Richter spent over a year (1866–7) in Tribschen, preparing a fair copy of the score of *Die Meistersinger*. In the following year he worked as conductor at the Munich Opera under the aegis of Bülow, and after a short stay in Paris and a memorable *Lohengrin* performance in Brussels (March, 1870), he returned to Wagner and Tribschen to assist in the completion of the *Ring* score. While at Tribschen, he played the trumpet in the first performance of the *Siegfried Idyll*. From 1871 to 1875 he was chief conductor at the National Theatre, Pest, and in 1875 he made a triumphant début in Vienna, which led to his being appointed to the Hofoper in succession to Dessoff. In 1876 he conducted the first performance of the entire *Ring* cycle in Bayreuth; he remained one of the regular conductors at the Bayreuth festivals throughout his life. In appreciation of his achievements on behalf of Wagner's music, Ludwig II of Bavaria awarded him the Order of Maximilian and the Grand Duke of Weimar that of the Falcon.

Concurrently with his appointment to the Vienna Hofoper in 1875, Richter took over the Philharmonic concerts (until 1898), and from 1880 to 1890 he also held the post of conductor of the Gesellschaft der Musikfreunde. From 1877 onwards he was a regular visitor to England, first appearing (with Wagner) in the Albert Hall in a Wagner festival. Between 1879 and 1897 he conducted an annual series of concerts first known as Orchestral Festival Concerts, later as the Richter Concerts, and from 1885 to 1909 he was music director of the triennial Birmingham Music Festival. In 1897 he settled in Manchester as conductor of the Hallé Orchestra, a post which he retained until 1911, and from 1904 to 1911 he also conducted the LSO. At Covent Garden he conducted German opera in 1882 and 1884, introducing English audiences to *Die Meistersinger* and *Tristan*, and appearing there regularly from 1904 until his retirement. One of his outstanding achievements during that time was a performance of the complete *Ring* cycle in 1909, sung in English for the first time. He withdrew from the English

Hans Richter (right), with Felix Mottl (centre) and Hermann Levi (left)

scene in 1911 and ended his artistic activities with a magnificent *Die Meistersinger* performance in 1912 at Bayreuth, where he lived in retirement until his death.

Together with Hans von Bülow (1830–94), Hermann Levi (1839–1900), Felix Mottl (1856–1911) and Karl Muck (1859–1940), Richter belongs to that first group of great international conductors to shed the relative anonymity which, until then, had been the conductor's lot, a group that reached its culmination in Arthur Nikisch (1855–1922). Richter's strong personal association with Bayreuth gave him a deep insight into Wagner's music, which he performed with the utmost enthusiasm and precision throughout his life. On the concert platform he impressed mainly by the clear profile he gave to the music he conducted, and his knowledge and performances of Beethoven's symphonies were by all accounts remarkable. Richter also spared no effort in propagating the music of Brahms, and he was one of the few musicians of his day who also appreciated Bruckner: he conducted the first performances of Bruckner's Symphonies no.1 (Vienna version), no.3 (1889 version), no.4 and no.8. His repertory consisted almost entirely of German music and he is reputed to have said that there was 'no French music'; he also conducted works by Dvořák, whose music he introduced to English audiences with overwhelming success, and Elgar. Richter admired Elgar greatly, frequently playing his major works, and Elgar showed his appreciation by dedicating his First Symphony 'to Hans Richter, true artist and true friend'.

BIBLIOGRAPHY

E. Hanslick: *Concerte, Componisten und Virtuosen der letzten 15 Jahre: 1870–1885* (Berlin, 1886, 4/1896)
L. Karpath, ed.: *R. Wagner: Briefe an Hans Richter* (Vienna, 1924)
R. Newmarch: 'The Letters of Dvořák to Hans Richter', *MT*, lxxiii (1932), 605, 698, 795
O. Šourek: *Antonín Dvořák a Hans Richter* (Prague, 1942)
R. Nettel: *The Orchestra in England* (London, 1946, 3/1956)
                                    HANS-HUBERT SCHÖNZELER

Richter, Johann Christoph (*b* Dresden, 15 July 1700; *d* Dresden, 19 Feb 1785). German organist and composer. He lived in his native city throughout his career, becoming court organist in 1727 and remaining in that position for over 50 years. In 1750 his duties were expanded to include the direction of the Protestant court services, and in 1760 he was named Kapellmeister. Nothing is known about Richter's education beyond the fact that the Dresden aristocracy sent him to Italy in 1716 in order to enrich his musical education. In 1726 Augustus I (the Strong), Elector of Saxony and King of Poland, ordered him to learn to play Pantaleon Hebenstreit's invention, the Pantaleon, a musical instrument resembling a large, tonally impressive dulcimer, which was a great favourite at the Dresden court. After 1734 Richter replaced Hebenstreit as Court Pantaleonist. He also became the principal performer on another instrumental novelty created by Hebenstreit, a porcelain glockenspiel.

Richter became widely known as an organist and he also wrote instrumental music and operas for court performances. Two opera MSS are in *D-Dlb*: *Il re pastore* (Metastasio), and *Opera drammatica per festeggiare il gloriosissimo giorno natalizio della real altezza principesse, imp. di Sassonia* [Maria Antonia], given in Dresden in 1764. A *Concerto con echo* in 15 parts is in *Dlb*; a trio for two harpsichords and bass, and a group of dances, survive in *D-B*. This composer is sometimes confused with the Dresden oboist Johann Christian Richter (1689–1744).

                                    GEORGE J. BUELOW

Richter, Johann Paul Friedrich. See JEAN PAUL.

Richter, Karl (*b* Plauen, 15 Oct 1926). German organist, harpsichordist and conductor. After studying in Leipzig with Rudolf Mauersberger, Karl Straube and Günther Ramin, he became choirmaster of the Christuskirche, Leipzig, in 1946 and a year later was appointed organist of the Thomaskirche. In 1951 he began to teach at the Hochschule für Musik in Munich (where he was organist of the Markuskirche), and he was appointed professor there in 1956. As an organist and harpsichordist, as choirmaster of the Munich Bach Choir and as conductor of the Munich Bach Orchestra, of which he was the founder, his musical activity has extended far beyond the city of Munich. Highpoints of his numerous concert tours include the performances in Moscow and Leningrad, in 1968, of Bach's *St John Passion* and Mass in B minor. Although he has also conducted Classical and Romantic orchestral works, his primary interest is the music of J. S. Bach. His harpsichord playing is characterized by an avoidance of a would-be 'historical' style, and by the use of flexible registration and dynamic contrasts on a large scale. Some critics have found his style romantic, and others have considered it rhythmically rigid; but his recordings of Bach's major choral works and harpsichord concertos, and of Handel's *Messiah*, have met with some praise.

                                    HANS CHRISTOPH WORBS

Richter, (Hermann) Lukas (*b* Bärenstein, Saxony, 22 Feb 1923). German musicologist. He studied musicology under Meyer, Vetter and Dräger at the

Humboldt University of Berlin (1949–52), taking his doctorate there in 1957 with a dissertation on Plato's and Aristotle's teachings on music. He completed his *Habilitation* at Berlin in 1966 with a study of Berlin street songs (*Gassenhauer*). In 1963 he became research fellow at the Institut für Altertumskunde of the Akademie der Wissenschaften der DDR; he was appointed director of research in 1966. His chief interests are ancient music (both its sources and its sociological aspects), German folksong (including urban song) and Schoenberg's *Harmonielehre*.

WRITINGS

Zur Wissenschaftslehre von der Musik bei Platon und Aristoteles (diss., Humboldt U. of Berlin, 1957; Berlin, 1961)
'Antike Überlieferungen in der byzantinischen Musiktheorie', *DJbM*, vi (1961), 75
'Berliner Tanzstücke des Biedermeier', *DJbM*, x (1965), 31–65
Der Berliner Gassenhauer (Habilitationsschrift, Humboldt U. of Berlin, 1965; Leipzig, 1969)
'Griechische Traditionen im Musikschrifttum der Römer', *AMw*, xxii (1965), 69
'Zwischen Volkslied und Schlager', *BMw*, viii (1966), 193
' "Des Psellus vollständiger Kurzer Inbegriff der Musik" in Mizlers "Bibliothek" ', *BMw*, ix (1967), 45; Eng. trans. in *Studies in Eastern Chant*, ii, ed. M. Velimirović (London, 1971), 112
'Die neue Musik der griechischen Antike', *AMw*, xxv (1968), 1, 134
'Musik der Griechen und Römer', *Knaurs Weltgeschichte der Musik*, ed. K. Honolka (Munich and Zurich, 1968), 57
'Schönbergs Harmonielehre und die "freie Atonalität" ', *DJbM*, xiii 43; abridged in *Leoš Janáček et musica europaea: Brno III 1968*, 339
'Beethoven und die Gassenhauer seiner Zeit', *II. Internationales musikologisches Symposiums: Piešt'any 1970*, 217
'Beethovens britische Volksliedbearbeitungen für Gesang und Klaviertrio', *Musica cameralis: Brno VI 1971*, 373
'Das Musikfragment aus dem Euripideischen Orestes', *DJbM*, xvi (1971), 111–49; abridged in *Muzyka*, xiv (1969), 3
Minnesang und Spruchdichtung (Berlin, 1971) [disc notes]
'Musikalische Aspekte der attischen Tragödie', *BMw*, xiv (1972), 247–98
'Literatur zur Geschichte des Volksliedes', *BMw*, xv (1973), 281 [review]
'Zur Musikanschauung von Stanislaw Przybyszewski', *DJbM*, xviii (1973–7), 59
'Karl Straubes Bearbeitungen Bachscher und vorbachscher Orgelwerke', *Karl Straube: Wirken und Wirkung*, ed. C. and J. Held (Berlin, 1976), 157–91
'Die mehrstimmige Vokalmusik im 15. und 16. Jahrhundert' (in preparation)
Geschichte des altdeutschen Volksliedes (in preparation)

HORST SEEGER

Richter, Nico (Max) (*b* Amsterdam, 2 Dec 1915; *d* Amsterdam, 16 Aug 1945). Dutch composer. From an early age he showed a great talent for composition. He won the Henri Leboeuf Prize at the International Composition Competition in Brussels (1935) with the Concertino for clarinet, horn, trumpet, piano and two violins. Subsequently he studied conducting with Scherchen, and in 1941 he took the arts diploma. He was arrested by the Germans in 1942; in 1945 he returned to Amsterdam from a concentration camp, gravely ill, and he died a month later. His small body of works includes a Trio for flute, viola and guitar (1935), the Sinfonia-Divertimento (1936) and the chamber opera *Amorijs* (1937); these were published by Donemus.

BIBLIOGRAPHY

E. Helm: 'Memorial Concert', *Sonorum speculum* (1970), no.43, p.18

ROGIER STARREVELD

Richter, Sviatoslav (Teofilovich) (*b* Zhitomir, Ukraine, 20 March 1915). Soviet pianist. Although grounded in the rudiments of music by his father, an organist and composer, Richter taught himself the piano. At the age of 15 he became a répétiteur at the Odessa Opera and at

18 chief assistant conductor; he gave his first piano recital the following year. His formal instrumental training began in 1937, when he entered the Moscow Conservatory as a pupil of Heinrich Neuhaus. In 1942 he gave the first performance of Prokofiev's Sixth Sonata; his championship of Prokofiev continued with the premières of the Seventh and Ninth Sonatas (the latter is dedicated to him) and with the first performance of the Symphony-Concerto for cello and orchestra (1952), in which Rostropovich was the soloist and Richter made a single public appearance as conductor. He published a book of recollections, *S. S. Prokofiev* (Moscow, 1961). Richter won the USSR Music Competition in 1945 and the Stalin Prize in 1949. In the 1950s he played throughout the USSR and eastern Europe, gaining increasing eminence and a reputation that was not tested in the West until he performed in Finland in May 1960 and in Chicago (with the Chicago SO) and New York that October. Concerts in Italy, Germany, France and Britain soon followed. The keen expectancy aroused by announcements of Richter's appearances in the West has often been disappointed by cancellations, ill-health being the reason most frequently given; a liking for intimate performing conditions has led him several times to the Aldeburgh and Spoleto Festivals and to become, from 1964, the guiding inspiration of the Fêtes Musicales held annually at the Grange de Meslay, near Tours.

Richter, among the outstanding pianists of the 20th century, is one of the rare performers whose ascendancy over his instrument is expressed in every aspect of his playing. His technique, consummate in its virtuosity, allows him an extraordinary freedom, plasticity and

Sviatoslav Richter

poetry of phrase shaping; he draws from the piano a range of tone-colours varied, distinctive and recognizable from first utterance to last. A deeply introspective musician, he is at his most creative in 19th-century Romantic music, in particular Schubert and Schumann, whose *Phantasie* he invests with the wealth of significance and quiet intensity of the greatest interpretations. Also admired for the subtlety and finesse of his Debussy and Ravel performances, and a Bach player of definite and forceful personality, he brings to the more extrovert vehicles of keyboard virtuosity, such as the concertos of Rakhmaninov and Prokofiev, a coruscating flair and wit – his recordings of Liszt's concertos, among the first he made in the West, stand unchallenged for their blend of magnetism and aristocratic style. On occasion, the searching, self-communing qualities that make his Schumann playing so rewarding can seem to deprive his Beethoven of natural energy and spontaneous force; even here, however, the mastery of his playing is always in evidence. Richter is also a chamber pianist, and has appeared in concerts and on record as accompanist to such singers as Schwarzkopf and Fischer-Dieskau, and in piano duets with Britten.

MAX LOPPERT

Richter-Haaser, Hans (*b* Dresden, 6 Jan 1912). German pianist. He inherited manual skill from his mother's musical and his father's carpentering forebears. After family tuition, he entered the Dresden Academy at 13 to study the piano with Hans Schneider (winning the coveted Bechstein Prize at 18), also the violin, percussion and conducting. He made his début in Dresden at a Schubert centenary concert in 1928 playing the Wanderer Fantasy, but his career was interrupted by World War II: his first appearance before an American audience was in a French prison camp (with 'POW' written on the back of his uniform). In 1946 he became conductor of the Detmold SO, and in 1947 professor of piano, accompaniment and ensemble at the newly founded North-west German Music Academy.

International acclaim came after a highly successful concert in Holland in 1953 conducted by Paul van Kempen. Since then Richter-Haaser has toured widely, particularly in the USA and South America. Though he believes in a varied repertory, his laurels have mainly been won in late Classical and early Romantic music. His complete cycles of Beethoven's sonatas and concertos were in great demand well before the bicentenary (1970) of the composer's birth. Though he is equally committed, his style is lighter, crisper and cleaner than that of such an ardently demonstrative Beethovenian as Schnabel.

JOAN CHISSELL

Ricieri [Riccieri], Giovanni Antonio (*b* Venice, 12 May 1679; *d* Bologna, 15 May 1746). Italian composer and singer. His name also appears (incorrectly) as Rizzieri and Rizieri. Son of Francesco Ricieri and Chiara Stella Bettanini, he was baptized on 23 May 1679 in the church of S Silvestro near the Rialto bridge. Two months later the family moved to Bologna; seven years later to Imola, and then to Faenza, where Giovanni began his musical studies with Count Fabio Naldi. In about 1688, frightened by an earthquake, the family moved back to Venice; after a brief sojourn there they settled in Vicenza. There Ricieri continued studying music, first with Giovanni Castelfranco, then with

Pietro 'tedesco di Baviera', as well as Matteo Zanoli. He later studied counterpoint with Domenico Freschi, *maestro di cappella* at Vicenza and Francesco Alghisi. In 1700, after his father's death, Ricieri went to Ferrara where he sang soprano during the carnival opera season at the Bonacossi theatre, as well as some concerts at the Accademia di S Spirito. In July of the same year, he moved to Bologna, recommended by G. B. Bassani to his Bolognese colleague G. A. Perti, *maestro di cappella* at S Petronio. Ricieri was admitted to this *cappella musicale* on 1 March 1701 as a soprano.

In the same year he became a member of the Accademia Filarmonica as a singer; he was promoted to the rank of composer on 17 May 1704. However, because of his inclination to excessively frank criticism of his contemporaries and to violent outbursts of temper (it is recounted that, in fury over a singer's error in a church service he was directing, he snatched his wig off and threw it into the congregation), he was banished from the Accademia Filarmonica on 2 July 1716. In 1722 he went to Poland in the service of the field-marshal Count Stanisław Rzewuski. According to his own eccentric account (*Istorica narratione della casa Ricieri*) he organized a small theatre in Luboml, the winter residence of Rzewuski, and composed two operas entitled *L'inganno punito* and *L'imeneo preteso*. After four years he returned to Bologna, and in 1728 he was asked by his former patron to compose an opera. This he evidently did (the libretto of *L'Armidoro* exists in MS in *I-Bc*), but by the time it arrived in Poland Count Rzewuski had died, and it was probably never produced.

Four years later, Ricieri decided to enter the Franciscan Order. However, after only three months of novitiate, he returned to his more mundane life as a musician. In 1733 he left Bologna for Venice and Padua, and, becoming acquainted with Francesco Antonio Vallotti there, discussed Vallotti's harmonic theories with him. By 1738 he had returned to Bologna, where he disputed with his pupil, Giovanni Battista Martini, in 1740: he accused Martini of not being able to answer a fugue theme given to him; Martini, in self-defence, sent him 12 answers to the same theme. Martini's judgment of Ricieri was that 'although he was a mediocre soprano singer, he became a skilful composer'.

His works demonstrate a mastery of counterpoint as well as concertato style. Martini praised his ability to combine the older church modes with the newer tonal ideas of his time. Among his pupils, besides Martini, were Angelo Caroli, Antonio Bernacchi and Giuseppe Maria Nelvi.

WORKS

OPERAS

L'inganno punito, ?1722, lost
L'imeneo preteso, ?1722, lost
L'Armidoro, 1728, *I-Bc* [lib only]

ORATORIOS
(all lost)

Il difensor della fede (U. M. Nini), Bologna, Congregazione di S Gabriele, 19 March 1713
La nascità di Gesù Bambino, Bologna, Congregazione di S Gabriele, Christmas, 1713
La tentazione d'incredulità, Bologna, Congregazione di S Gabriele, 11 March, 1714
Il core umano (G. B. Neri), Bologna, Congregazione di S Gabriele, Lent 1716
Il sacrificio d'Isacco, Castel S Pietro, Arciconfraternità di S Catterina, Pentecost, 1738

OTHER WORKS
1 canzona in La ricreazione spirituale (Bologna, 1730)

1 psalm, Domine, inc., in G. B. Martini, 1774
Concerted masses, motets, psalms, antiphons, litanies, madrigals, canons, *A-Wn, D-Dlb, Mbs, I-Ac, Baf, Bc, Bsp, Pca, PL-SA*
Letters, *I-Bc*

BIBLIOGRAPHY

Istorico narratione della casa Ricieri (MS, *I-Bc* H/66)
Invettiva contro il carattere impertinente e maledico di G. A. Ricieri (MS, Bc I/29)
Controversia occorsa fra il P. Martini ed il Sig. G. A. Riccieri per un soggetto di fuga (MS, Bc HH/6)
G. B. Martini: *12 risposte diverse a un soggetto di fuga dato dal Ricieri* (MS, Bc HH/72)
——: *Esemplare o sia Saggio fondamentale pratico di contrappunto sopra il canto fermo* (Bologna, 1774, 1776), i, 71f; ii, 156ff
C. Ricci: *I teatri di Bologna* (Bologna, 1888/R1965)
F. Parisini: *Carteggio inedito del P. G. B. Martini* (Bologna, 1888), 30, 34, 52, 81
G. Gaspari: *Catalogo della Biblioteca del Liceo musicale di Bologna,* i–iv (Bologna, 1890–1905/R1961); v, ed. U. Sesini (Bologna, 1943/R1961)
L. Busi: *Il Padre G. B. Martini* (Bologna, 1891/R1961)
G. Mantese: *Storia musicale vicentina* (Vicenza, 1956), 75f
M. Perz: 'Materiały do dziejów muzyki i opery na dworze Stanisława Mateusza Rzewuskiego' [Material for the history of music and opera at the court of Rzewuski], *Opera w dawnej Polsce na dworze Władysława IV,* ed. J. Lewański (Wrocław, 1973), 61ff
——: 'Arie "polskie" Giovanni Antonio Ricierego', *Pagine,* iii (in preparation) [in Pol. and It.]

ANNE SCHNOEBELEN

Ricketts, Frederick Joseph. *See* ALFORD, KENNETH J.

Ricochet (Fr.). In string playing, a bowstoke that bounces off the string; *see* BOW, §II, 3(x).

Ricordi. Italian firm of music publishers.

1. History. 2. Publications.

1. HISTORY. The firm of Ricordi was founded in Milan in 1808 by Giovanni Ricordi (*b* Milan, 1785; *d* Milan, 15 March 1853); it was directed from 1853 to 1888 by his son Tito (i) (*b* Milan, 29 Oct 1811; *d* Milan, 7 Sept 1888), from 1888 to 1912 by Tito's son Giulio (*b* Milan, 19 Dec 1840; *d* Milan, 6 June 1912) and from 1912 to 1919 by Giulio's son Tito (ii) (*b* Milan, 17 May 1865; *d* Milan, 13 March 1933). The firm was managed from 1919 to 1940 jointly by Renzo Valcarenghi and Carlo Clausetti, from 1940 to 1944 by Valcarenghi and Alfredo Colombo and from 1944 to 1952 by Colombo, Eugenio Clausetti and Camillo Ricordi. In 1952 it became a limited company, under the presidency first of Colombo, then from 1961 of Guido Valcarenghi and from 1976 of Carlo Origoni.

Giovanni Ricordi, a violinist, was leader of the orchestra of a small Milanese theatre, the Fiando. Probably in 1803 he had started a *copisteria* (copying establishment) beneath the portico of the Palazzo della Ragione. From 1804 to 1807 he was under contract as official copyist and prompter to the Teatro Carcano and in 1807 to the Teatro del Lentasio. In 1807 he spent several months in Leipzig studying the techniques of Breitkopf & Härtel and, after returning to Milan, on 16 January 1808 he formed a publishing partnership with Felice Festa, an engraver and music seller. Their first, and probably only, joint publication was a duet from Farinelli's *Calliroe,* which they issued as the first in a series entitled Giornale di Musica Vocale Italiana; the imprint gave Ricordi's address as Contrada di S Margherita (not mentioning the house number, 1108) and Festa's as Pantano no.4705. The partnership was terminated on 26 June 1808, and at about the same time Ricordi took a shop at 4068 Contrada di Pescaria Vecchia, from which address his plate number 1

(Antonio Nava's *Le quattro stagioni*) was issued. In 1811 he was appointed publisher to the Milan Conservatory. In the following year, probably in August, he moved to 1065 Contrada di S Margherita, and in the winter of 1815–16 to no. 1118 of the same street. About 1824 the shop, which he used as his publishing address, transferred to Ferdinando Artaria's former premises, favourably located opposite La Scala (Dirimpetto all'I.R. Teatro alla Scala no.1148), and in 1828 he moved his printing works from 1118 Contrada di S Margherita to 1635 via Ciovasso. From 1838 Ricordi's imprints read '1720 Contrada degli Omenoni', but after about 1860 the firm's address was normally omitted from its publications. In 1844 a new shop was opened at the side of La Scala, 'di fianco alla Scala', and soon became known as the Casino Ricordi. By 1867 the main offices, and probably the works too, were at 1 via Omenoni; from 1875 at the latest there was a shop at the Galleria Vittorio Emmanuele; in 1884 new printing works were erected at 21 viale Porta Vittoria; and in January 1889 a shop was opened at 9 via S Margherita. In 1910 the works were moved to 42 viale Campania and the offices to 2 via Berchet. Both these premises were bombed in 1943, with the loss of machinery and the stock of unsold copies, hire material and almost all the non-autograph manuscripts. The reconstructed via Berchet premises were reopened in February 1950. The most valuable of Ricordi's rich archives survived the war and are still in the possession of the firm; they include some 4000 music manuscripts (chiefly autograph), a large quantity of correspondence, and approximately 25,000 printed editions; details of much of the collection are listed at the Ufficio Ricerca Fondi Musicali (the Italian *RISM* centre) in Milan.

During his first decade in business Giovanni Ricordi issued an average of 30 publications a year; in his second the yearly average was about 300. This expansion was largely the result of a succession of contracts, starting from December 1814, in which he won as prompter and exclusive copyist to La Scala, giving him the right to publish the music performed there; in 1825 he purchased their entire musical archives. In 1816 he had a similar contract as copyist to the Teatro Re, and in the 1830s and 1840s concluded highly favourable agreements with the opera houses of Venice and Naples. By the end of 1837 he had not only purchased the stock and plates of Ferdinando Artaria but was able to advertise more than 10,000 publications, the exclusive rights to operas written for Milan and Naples, an archive of 1800 autograph manuscripts and a branch in Florence. The latter, Ricordi Grua & Co., was opened towards the end of 1824; its name was changed to Ricordi Pozzi & Co. (1827), to G. Ricordi & Co. (1828) and to G. Ricordi & S. Jouhaud (*c*1840). In 1860 the association with Jouhaud was terminated, and in 1865 Tito (i) opened an independent branch in Florence. A London branch, Grua Ricordi & Co., had been opened (1824), but it was closed four years later. In December 1840 Ricordi purchased the small business of Gaetano Longo (of Este), and expansion within the firm continued at such a rate that by his death in 1853 Giovanni had issued 25,000 publications.

Tito (i), a good pianist, had worked in the firm since 1825. Under his management, new printing methods were introduced, branches in Naples (1860), Rome (1871), London (1875), Palermo and Paris (both 1888) were opened, and the substantial businesses of Clausetti

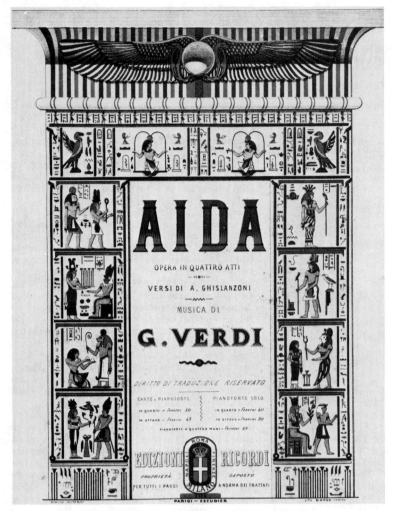

Title-page of the first edition of the vocal score of Verdi's 'Aida', published by Ricordi in 1871

(1864), Del Monaco and Guidi (both 1887) and finally Lucca (30 May 1888) were taken over. The acquisition of Lucca, which had been Ricordi's chief rival from the 1840s and had itself between 1847 and 1886 absorbed five firms (including Canti), brought to the Ricordi catalogue some 40,000 editions as well as the Italian rights to Wagner's operas.

Shortly before his death, Tito (i) gave over the management of the firm to his son Giulio, a highly cultured man and the best musician in the family. Usually under the pseudonym J. Burgmein (or sometimes Grubmeni), he composed many piano pieces and songs as well as some orchestral music and stage works, culminating in a comic opera *La secchia rapita*, performed at Turin in 1910. He worked for his father for a short time from 1856 and permanently from 1863. It was he who regularly dealt with Verdi on the firm's behalf (from c1875) and who played a central role in Puccini's artistic development. Under his management, branches at Leipzig (1901) and New York (1911) were opened, part of the stock of Escudier, Ricordi's former Paris agent, was acquired (1889), and the firms of Pigna and Schmidl (both 1902) and Carelli (1905) were taken over. His son Tito (ii), who succeeded him, appears to have lacked both charm and judgment. He and Puccini disliked each other, and Puccini had *Le rondine* published by Ricordi's rival Sonzogno. When Tito (ii) retired in 1919, the management of the firm passed out of the hands of the Ricordi family. Business expansion continued, however, and in South America the publishers Breyer-Hermanos (1924), Canulli (1925), Harrods (1928), Oerthmann (1935), Balerio y Bonini (1940) and Romero y Fernandez (1947) were all taken over; the Walter Mocchi musical archives were acquired in 1929, and the Naples firm of Pasquariello absorbed in 1946. Further branches were set up in Buenos Aires (1924), São Paolo (1927), Basle (1949), Genoa (1953), Toronto (1954), Sydney (1956) and Mexico City (1958). Since then branches or agencies have been opened in Bari, Florence, Turin and Munich, while those in New York and Leipzig have closed. By 1975 the firm had published more than 132,000 editions and included gramophone records and light music in its catalogue.

2. PUBLICATIONS. The firm's earliest editions were

printed from engraved plates, but in 1821 or 1822 several publications were printed by lithography. About 1824 Ricordi took over Ferdinando Artaria's lithographic department, and a year or so later Tito (i) was sent to Germany to study the process. Nevertheless the firm only rarely used lithography and printing direct from engraved plates remained the normal practice until the 1870s, when chromolithographic and offset processes were introduced. In their publications of vocal music Ricordi invariably used, until about 1844, the soprano and tenor clefs in addition to the treble and bass, and it was a further 20 years before the former were finally dropped. In 1877 the firm devised a new modification of the treble clef to indicate a line sung an octave lower, by a tenor. Ricordi's plate numbers are in general reliably chronological (but certain caveats are sounded by Gossett and Hopkinson). The sudden, curious leap in 1890 from about 55,000 to about 94,000 is explained by the application in that year of Ricordi numbers to their recently acquired Lucca stock. Another useful Ricordi practice was the blind-stamping of dates on most of their publications issued between about 1860 and 1932; in all probability these stamps related not to the date of printing but rather to that of the binding or wrappering of a particular batch of copies. In the Ricordi archives there is a further valuable (and largely unexplored) source of precise chronological information – a series of manuscript notebooks giving the dates on which many works to be published by the firm were sent, apparently, for engraving or printing.

Ricordi's first catalogue (1814) lists his first 176 publications. These were mainly piano arrangements of and variations on operatic tunes, pieces for one and two guitars (including several by Antonio Nava), and the operatic numbers that formed part of his Giornale di Musica Vocale Italiana (which did not run beyond its fourth volume). The most notable single items from these early years were Asioli's *Trattato d'armonia* and Pollini's *Metodo per forte-piano o clavicembalo*, both published for the Milan Conservatory, and Ricordi's first complete vocal score, Mayr's *Adelasia ed Aleramo*, issued in association with the firm of G. C. Martorelli. Several supplementary catalogues were printed during the next few years, and then, in 1825, appeared a major catalogue of Ricordi's total production (more than 2300 items) to the end of 1824. By this time the firm was offering a range of instrumental music by international composers, methods and theoretical works for students, a large selection of Italian operatic numbers for piano solo and piano and voice (including many pieces by Rossini), and dance and ballet music for piano solo. Especially noteworthy are the first appearances of Paganini's works in print (opp.1–5), many pieces for violin by Rolla and for guitar by Nava and Giuliani, and vocal scores of five complete operas. The catalogue lists in full score about 60 operatic excerpts but only two complete works: Weigl's cantata *Il ritorno d'Astrea* and Beethoven's *Christus am Ölberge*. Much of the music in the catalogue first appeared in the series Biblioteca di Musica Moderna, a periodical collection offered by subscription in four (1820) and six (1821–30) categories, three consisting of piano music and one each of vocal, violin and flute music.

The next general catalogue appeared in 1838 and advertised the firm's 10,000 publications to the end of 1837. During this period Ricordi had, through his connections with opera houses, established both extremely powerful position for himself in the operatic world and a highly profitable business. Rossini had effectively retired and Bellini was dead; but Ricordi had published vocal scores and was in a position to hire out performing material of 19 operas by Rossini and eight by Bellini. Donizetti was still flourishing, and Ricordi either already had published, or was about to publish, all but a handful of his works composed after 1830. Also on Ricordi's books were the best of the other Italian opera composers – Mercadante, Vaccai, Pacini and Luigi and Federico Ricci – as well as Meyerbeer, whose *Crociato in Egitto* had been published by the firm in 1824 and whose French operas were now achieving widespread success. In 1839, by publishing Verdi's first opera, *Oberto, Conte di S Bonifacio*, Ricordi took the most significant single step in the entire history of the firm. Except for *Attila*, *I masnadieri* and *Il corsaro*, published by Lucca between 1846 and 1848, Ricordi published all Verdi's remaining operas, the Requiem and, after 1848, almost all his smaller works.

Shortly afterwards Italy's first regular musicological and critical journal, the *Gazzetta musicale di Milano* was founded by Ricordi. From 2 January 1842 it was weekly, with monthly published musical supplements that were reissued annually, until 1848, in a series entitled Antologia Classica. For a short time in 1848 it appeared as the *Gazzetta musicale di Milano ed Eco delle notizie politiche*, the greater part being given over to political comment, but, after a break in publication, it reverted in 1850 to exclusively musical content. Apart from occasional breaks, it survived until 25 December 1902, after which it merged with Ricordi's *Musica e musicisti*, which had been started in June 1902. This was renamed *Ars et labor – Musica e musicisti* from 1906 until December 1912, when it merged with *Il secolo XX*. From 1865 to 1883 the firm had published a second periodical, the *Rivista minima*, a fortnightly review of politics, literature, art and theatre; it was edited until 1874 by Verdi's librettist Antonio Ghislanzoni, then by Ghislanzoni and Salvatore Farina, and from 1878 by Farina alone. In 1919 *Musica d'oggi* was launched, quarterly for its first year and thereafter monthly, until 1942, when it lapsed temporarily. From 1951 to 1957 it reappeared as *Ricordiana* and in 1958 reverted to *Musica d'oggi*; it ceased publication in December 1965.

The Italian passion for operatic and vocal music coupled with the paucity of original instrumental works composed in Italy during the 19th century was not unnaturally reflected in Ricordi's catalogues, and during the second and third quarters of the century a large proportion of the immense quantity of instrumental music, especially for piano, put out by the firm consisted of operatic arrangements. Specially large contributions were made by Czerny, Liszt, Döhler, Henri Herz, the Strauss family, Golinelli, Prudent, Truzzi, Adolfo Fumigalli, Ascher, Bonamici and Martucci; the firm also published numerous methods and exercises for all instruments. The Ricordi catalogue of 1875 advertised the Biblioteca di Musica Populare, which came to be known as the Edizioni Economiche. Designed to be produced inexpensively, this at first consisted only of vocal and piano solo scores of opera, printed in a new, smaller format (subsequently used for all Ricordi's vocal scores); later, publications in all genres were added to the series. This catalogue shows that in the second half of the century the firm was maintaining its operatic tradition. Pedrotti and Boito had already been taken on, and from the 1870s Ponchielli and Catalani operas were published. In 1884 Ricordi published Puccini's first opera, *Le villi*, after it had been turned down by Sonzogno; and, apart from *Le rondine*, the firm went on to publish all Puccini's operas. After Verdi, Puccini has been Ricordi's most valuable asset by far. Sonzogno, however, proved to be their strongest rival since Lucca; he was the main publisher of Puccini's most successful contemporaries, Mascagni and Leoncavallo, leaving Ricordi the less profitable Alfano, Franchetti, Montemezzi and Zandonai.

After World War I the character of Ricordi's catalogue altered: much more emphasis was now given to new editions of earlier composers, both Italian and foreign. These undertakings included editions of Domenico Scarlatti, Beethoven and Chopin, and an anthology of early music; in 1947 an important collected edition of Vivaldi's instrumental works was launched. At the same time Ricordi continued to publish, though with far more competition and perhaps rather less energy and inspiration than in the 19th century, the works of contemporary Italian composers, including operas and other music by Pizzetti, Malipiero, Respighi, Wolf-Ferrari, Rocca, Tosatti, Rossellini, Bettinelli, Rota and Testi, and non-operatic works by Arrigo, Bussotti, Casella, Castelnuovo-Tedesco, Gentilucci, Ghedini, Maderna, Mannino, Nono, Petrassi, Turchi, Veretti and Zafred. The firm's output of literature has been small; the more substantial items include Franco Abbiati's useful biography *Giuseppe Verdi* (1959) and the *Enciclopedia della musica*, edited by Claudio Sartori (1963–4).

Between 1700 and 1770 Italian music publishing was in eclipse. Marescalchi and Zatta brought about a temporary revival, but both had retired before Giovanni Ricordi opened his business in 1808. At this time Italian music normally circulated in manuscript copies; it needed a man of Ricordi's training, taste, energy and ambition to realize, after himself spending four years as a copyist, that through publication music could be circulated much more accurately, widely, swiftly and cheaply, as well as far more profitably, to everybody's advantage. His rise to power in his first 20 years seems to have been achieved with a simplicity and orderliness that are hard to believe; it is interesting to speculate what sort of opposition, if any, he encountered in clinching that useful appointment to the conservatory and those vital contracts with La Scala and other theatres. The fact is, however, that he brushed aside, and continued to brush aside, almost all competition, just as his son and grandson were to do after him. All three had the happy knack of recognizing quality when they saw it; they also had the tact, the persistence and the influence to patronize and market it. In the entire history of music publishing there has been no other firm that through its own efforts, astuteness, initiative and flair has achieved a position of dominance such as Ricordi enjoyed in Italy in the 19th century, nor of power such as it has been able to maintain (on account of its rights on Verdi's and Puccini's operas) in the 20th.

Yet with power should go responsibility, and it must be noted that Ricordi have been criticized for allowing considerations of art to take second place to those of commerce. Verdi himself complained bitterly about the

elder Tito's sanctioning, for financial gain, mutilated performances of his works. There is a clear moral obligation for the publisher owning the rights and autograph manuscripts of almost every one of Verdi's and Puccini's operas to make those works available, and in correct texts. All but three of Ricordi's Puccini operas were by 1975 available in orchestral score; the final three were in preparation in 1976. But the Ricordi catalogue of 1975 advertised the full scores of only seven Verdi operas; the others had never been put on sale and were available only for hire. Further, there is a widely held view that the existing scores of these composers' operas, whether on sale or for hire, contain inaccurate texts. From 1958 to 1963 there raged a battle at least as fierce as the Querelle des Bouffons between, on the one hand, Denis Vaughan and his supporters, who maintained that the scores were riddled with actual errors (Vaughan claimed to have counted 27,000 in *Falstaff*) and, on the other, Ricordi and their defenders, who held that the alleged divergences between autograph and printed texts were authorized modifications that had gradually evolved over successive contemporary performances and productions. The dispute could be resolved only by Ricordi's allowing unfettered access to their Verdi and Puccini archives and publishing a critical edition of the works of both composers. The critical edition of Rossini's operas in preparation for Ricordi under the general editorship of Philip Gossett and Alberto Zedda, and the plan for a Verdi critical edition, to be published from 1980 in association with the University of Chicago Press, represent promising developments.

CATALOGUES
(selective list; all published in Milan)

'Catalogo della musica stampata nella nuova calcografia di Giovanni Ricordi', in A. Rolla: *Tre divertimenti a violino e viola* (1814)
Catalogo della musica di fondo e degli spartiti di Giovanni Ricordi (1825)
Catalogo della musica pubblicata . . . di Giovanni Ricordi (1838)
Catalogo delle opere pubblicate . . . di Giovanni Ricordi (1844)
Catalogo generale degli spartiti manoscritti d'opere teatrali (1844, suppl. c1847)
Secondo catalogo delle opere pubblicate (1848; suppls.1–32, 1848–55)
Catalogo delle opere pubblicate (1855–64)
Catalogo (in ordine numerico) delle opere pubblicate (1857–c1896)
Catalogo delle pubblicazioni (1875)
Catalogo generale delle edizione G. Ricordi e C. (c1893–7, suppls. 1904–23)
Catalogo generale delle edizioni economiche e popolare (1919)
Catalogo di musica sinfonica, sinfonico-vocale e da camera (1965, suppl. 1969)
Edizioni Ricordi: catalogo (1975)

BIBLIOGRAPHY
RicordiE
E. Rosmini: *Legislazione e giurisprudenza sui diritti d'autore* (Milan, 1890)
Internationale Musik- und Theater-Ausstellung 1892 Wien . . . G. Ricordi & C. (Milan, 1892)
N. Tabanelli: 'Giurisprudenza: la causa Ricordi–Leoncavallo', *RIM*, vi (1899), 833
——: 'Giurisprudenza teatrale: la ditta Ricordi contro il tenore Bonci', *RIM*, viii (1901), 703
'Fascicolo dedicato al centenario della ditta Ricordi & C. di Milano', *Il risorgimento grafico*, v (1907), 169
G. Cesari and A. Luzio: *I copialettere di Giuseppe Verdi* (Milan, 1913/R1968)
G. Adami, ed.: *Epistolario di Puccini* (Milan, 1928; Eng. trans., 1931, rev. 2/1974)
G. Adami: *Giulio Ricordi e i suoi musicisti* (Milan, 1933)
A. Luzio, ed.: *Carteggi verdiani* (Rome, 1935–47)
G. Adami: *Giulio Ricordi: l'amico dei musicisti italiani* (Milan, 1945)
O. Vergiani: *Piccolo viaggio in un archivio* (Milan, 1953)
M. Carner: *Puccini* (London, 1958)
E. Gara, ed.: *Carteggi pucciani* (Milan, 1958)
C. Sartori: *Casa Ricordi* (Milan, 1958)

——: *Dizionario degli editori musicali italiani* (Florence, 1958)

D. Vaughan: 'Discordanze tra gli autografi verdiani e la loro stampa', *La scala* (1958), no.104, pp.11, 72

G. Gavazzeni: *Problemi di tradizione dinamico-fraseologica e critica testuale, in Verdi e Puccini* (Milan, 1961). [in It., Eng. and Ger.]

C. Sartori: 'Ricordi', *ES*

F. Walker: *The Man Verdi* (London, 1962)

C. Sartori: 'Ricordi', *MGG*

G. Martin: *Verdi* (New York, 1963, rev. 2/1964)

H. Weinstock: *Donizetti and the World of Opera* (New York, 1963)

C. Gatti: *Il teatro alla Scala*, i (Milan, 1964), 49ff

C. Hopkinson: 'Bibliographical Problems concerned with Verdi and his Publishers', *I° congresso internazionale di studi verdiani: Venezia 1966*, 431

J. J. Fuld: *The Book of World-famous Music* (New York, 1966, 2/1971), 67ff

C. Hopkinson: *A Bibliography of the Works of Giacomo Puccini* (New York, 1968)

H. Weinstock: *Rossini* (New York and London, 1968)

C. Sartori: 'The Bibliographer's Occupation', *Notes*, xxvi (1969–70), 711

P. Gossett: *The Operas of Rossini* (diss., Princeton U., 1970), 594ff

T. F. Heck: 'Ricordi Plate Numbers in the Earlier 19th Century', *CMc*, (1970), no.10, p.117

——: 'The Role of Italy in the Early History of the Classic Guitar: a Sidelight on the House of Ricordi', *Guitar Review* (1971), no.34, p.1

H. Weinstock: *Vincenzo Bellini: his Life and his Operas* (New York, 1971)

J. Budden: *The Operas of Verdi* (London, 1973–)

C. Hopkinson: *A Bibliography of the Works of Giuseppe Verdi* (New York, 1973–8)

M. Chusid: *A Catalog of Verdi's Operas* (Hackensack, 1974), 192

RICHARD MACNUTT

Ridderbusch, Karl (*b* Recklinghausen, 29 May 1932). German bass. His original intention to become an engineer was changed when he took part in a competition for amateur singers. Rudolf Schock, who recognized his talents, partly financed his studies at the Folkwang-Schule, Essen. He made his début at the Städtisches Theater, Münster, in 1961. He was a member of the Essen Opera from 1963 until 1965, when he moved to Düsseldorf–Duisburg and made the Deutsche Oper am Rhein his artistic base. His international reputation grew rapidly; he made his first appearances at Bayreuth (1967) as King Henry, Titurel and Fasolt, at the Metropolitan Opera (1967) as Hunding, and at Covent Garden (1971) as Fasolt, Hunding and Hagen. He has sung regularly at the Vienna Staatsoper since his first appearance there in 1968, and was a notable Hans Sachs in Karajan's production of *Die Meistersinger* at the 1974 and 1975 Salzburg Easter festivals. Ridderbusch's voice is firm, clear, sonorous and rich in timbre; his style is direct, his stage presence imposing. He has taken all the standard roles of the German repertory and many in Verdi; he has appeared successfully in *buffo* roles, including Ochs and Mozart's Bartolo, but is at his best in the serious, dramatically demanding repertory, for example Pizarro, Hunding, Hagen, Sachs and Caspar (*Der Freischütz*). He has made several recordings, and his concert repertory includes works by Mozart, Beethoven, Bruckner and others; he is a notable Christ in the *St Matthew Passion*.

GERHARD BRUNNER

Riddle, Frederick (Craig) (*b* Liverpool, 20 April 1912). English viola player. After studying at the RCM, he joined the LSO in 1932. He became principal viola of the LPO in 1938, and was appointed to the same position in the RPO in 1953. In the 1940s and 1950s he played in a trio with Jean Pougnet and Anthony Pini, with whom he made several recordings. He has also had a distinguished career as a soloist, playing not only the well-known repertory by Mozart, Berlioz, Walton, Bartók and Hindemith, but also works by modern British composers such as Fricker and Rubbra. In 1937 he made the first recording of Walton's concerto with the composer conducting. Concertos have been written for him by Martin Dalby (first performed 1974) and Justin Connolly. Riddle is a strong player, combining a virile tone with a real sense of poetry. In 1948 he began teaching at the RCM and the Royal Manchester College of Music. Many leading younger viola players have been his pupils. He plays on violas by the Grancini brothers and P. A. Testori.

WATSON FORBES

RIdIM. *See* RÉPERTOIRE INTERNATIONAL D'ICONO-GRAPHIE MUSICALE.

Řídký, Jaroslav (*b* Liberec, 25 Aug 1897; *d* Poděbrady, 14 July 1956). Czech composer and teacher. At the Prague Conservatory he studied with Jirák, Foerster and Křička (1919–23), continuing his training in Foerster's master classes in 1926. He worked as harpist of the Czech PO (1924–38) and conductor of the Czech Philharmonic Choir (1925–30), but his most important activity was in teaching composition at the Prague Academy of Music (1929–56), where he was appointed professor in 1955; in the previous year he had received the K. Gottwald State Prize. Řídký's music was in the tradition of Dvořák: lyrical, folklike in its melody and finely crafted.

WORKS
(selective list)

Orch: 7 syms., op.3, 1924, op.4, 1925, op.8, 1927, op.10, 1928, op.17, 1931, op.35, 1938, op.47, 1956; Vn Conc., op.7, 1926; 2 vc concs., op.14, 1930, op.36, 1940; Pf Conc., op.46, 1952

2 nonets, 5 str qts, wind qnt, pf trio, other inst pieces

Light music incl. polkas, marches, folksong arrs.

Principal publishers: Panton, Supraphon

BIBLIOGRAPHY
ČSHS

'Jaroslav Řídký', *Rytmus*, vii (1941–2), 54 [incl. worklist]

J. Řídký: 'Několik slov k mé činnosti učitelské a skladatelské' [Some words about my activities as a teacher and composer], *Rytmus*, x/4 (1945–6), 11

B. Karásek: 'Jaroslav Řídký: čtyři kapitoly o slohu jeho symfonické a komorní hudby' [Řídký: four chapters on the style of his symphonic and chamber music], *Rytmus*, xi (1947–8), 98

K. P. Sádlo: 'Dočká se Jaroslav Řídký?' [Will Řídký's day come?], *HRo*, xx (1967), 456

MILAN KUNA

Ridler, Philipp Jakob. *See* RITTLER, PHILIPP JAKOB.

Ridout, Alan (John) (*b* West Wickham, Kent, 9 Dec 1934). English composer and teacher. He went to the RCM in 1951, where he studied composition with Jacob and Howells; he also studied privately with Fricker and Tippett. In 1957 he was awarded a Netherlands government scholarship and worked for a year with Badings. Since 1960 he has taught composition at the RCM; he also taught it at Cambridge University, 1963–75. He became well known for his broadcast talks 'Background to Music'. Ridout's career as a composer has been closely linked with residence at Canterbury, where he has composed seven settings of the canticles, concise versions of the Matthew and John Passions, organ music and three choirboys' operas. His choice of style and idiom is always related to the needs of the occasion and reflects his interest in music of many types, from medieval polyphony to 12-note serialism.

WORKS
(selective list)

Operas: The Rescue (D. Holbrook), 1963; The Pardoner's Tale (N. Platt, after Chaucer), 1971; Creation (P. Dickinson), 1973; Phaeton (radio opera, P. Dickinson), 1975; Wenceslas (P. Dickinson), 1977; 6 children's operas

Choral and vocal: 6 cantatas, incl. The Quarrel (P. Dickinson) and C.3.3. (Wilde, Goethe); Christmas Oratorio; 12 melodramas with narrator; 8 song cycles

Orch: 6 syms.; Fl Conc., 1973; Db Conc., 1974; concertinos, pic, dbn, fl, ob, eng hn, cl, b cl, sax, bn, hn, tpt, trbn, tuba, all with str, 1975–9; Tr Rec Conc., 1979; Fl and Harp Conc., 1979

Org: The Seven Last Words, 1965; Dance Suite, 1969; Resurrection Dances, after a picture by S. Spencer, 1969; Sinfonia, 1970; 6 Studies, 1976; 14 Stations of the Cross, 1978

Other works: 5 works in 31-note temperament; 3 works, perc ens; pf and chamber music

Principal publishers: Stainer & Bell, Oxford University Press, Schott, Cramer, Chappell, Scotus

HUGO COLE

Ridout, Godfrey (*b* Toronto, 6 May 1918). Canadian composer. He studied with Ettore Mazzoleni, Charles Peaker and Healey Willan at the Toronto Conservatory, where in 1940 he began teaching theory and history. His first major work, the Ballade for viola and string orchestra (1938), was widely performed in Canada and the USA by William Primrose, and in Britain under Boult. During the 1940s he gained valuable experience writing and conducting film scores for the newly created National Film Board, arranging popular music for symphony orchestra for 'big band' shows and providing over 200 background scores for CBC radio dramas. In 1948 he was appointed to the Faculty of Music of Toronto University, where he became senior professor.

Ridout is proud of his status as the eccentric traditionalist among Canadian composers. He has acknowledged the particular influence, conveyed to him by his English-trained teachers, of such Victorian and Edwardian composers as Sullivan, Elgar and Holst. But his music is much more widely informed, even to the extent of occasional forays into serial techniques – without, however, following their stylistic implications. His preferred medium is the full orchestra, augmented where possible by solo voice or choir with texts that are likely to be scriptural in fact or in feeling, or of romantic impulse. Of the works without text, some of the most engaging are programmatic or ceremonial. His tunes are often unashamedly tonal, but his bold harmony, syncopated rhythms and brilliant orchestration are contemporary and North American. However, rhythmic ostinatos can be sustained over a whole movement with almost Baroque consistency. Ridout's forms tend to be sectional, closed and symmetrical. His work is characterized by a striving not for newness but for mastery of style, which perhaps partly explains the historical rightness of his reconstruction of the orchestral score of Quesnel's Canadian opera *Colas et Colinette* (1790) from an extant second violin part.

WORKS
(selective list)

Orch: Ballade, va, str, 1938; Festal Ov., 1939; Dirge, 1943; 2 Etudes, str, 1946, rev. 1951; Music for a Young Prince, 1959; Fall Fair, 1961; Colas et Colinette, ov. for opera by Quesnel, 1964; La prima ballerina (ballet), 1966, 2 suites, 1967; Partita accademica, band, 1969; Frivolités canadiennes [after melodies by Vézina], 1973; Jubilee, 1973; Conc. grosso, pf, str, 1974; George III his Lament, 1975; Tafelmusik, wind ens, 1976

Choral: Esther (H. Voaden), dramatic sym., S, Bar, vv, orch, 1952; Coronation Ode (Voaden), vv, orch, 1953; The Dance (Carmina burana cxxxvii, trans. J. A. Symonds), vv, orch, 1960; Pange lingua, vv, orch, 1960; 4 Sonnets (J. E. Ward), vv, orch, 1964; When age and youth unite (C. Bissell), vv, orch, 1966; Cantiones mysticae no.3 'Dream of the Rood', Bar/T, vv, orch, 1972; many smaller pieces

Solo vocal: Cantiones mysticae (Donne), S, orch, 1953; The Ascension (Cantiones mysticae no.2), S, tpt, str, 1962; In memoriam Anne Frank, S, orch, 1965; 4 songs of Eastern Canada, S, orch, 1967; many songs and folksong arrs.

Other works: chamber pieces, inst music, arrs.

Principal publishers: Chappell, Harris, Novello, Thompson, Waterloo

HARVEY OLNICK

Rieck, Karl [Carl] **Friedrich** (*d* Berlin, 14 July 1704). German composer, violinist and harpsichordist. Besser reported that Rieck soon mastered to the highest degree both the keyboard and the violin. According to Mattheson, he became director of music to Counts Fug and Räder in Silesia. From 20 January 1683 he worked for the electoral Brandenburg court at Berlin, in the first place as chamber musician. On 14 September 1698 he became director of the elector's chamber music and in 1701 Oberkapellmeister of what had become the royal Kapelle. About 1700 several servants of the Berlin court bore the name Rieck, but the relationship between them is as yet unknown; Karl Friedrich was sometimes known as 'the younger Rieck'. He is known to have composed for court festivities a vocal ballet and three cantatas; all but the ballet are now lost. The ballet was *La festa del Hymeneo* (*D-Bds*, to a text by Ortensio Mauro), composed jointly with Attilio Ariosti for the wedding of Princess Louise Dorothea Sophie; for the same occasion at Oranienburg, Rieck wrote a dramatic cantata, *Peleus und Thetis, oder Das Glück der Liebe* (to a text by Besser). He wrote his cantata *Der Streit des alten und neuen Saeculi* (with words by Benjamin Neukirch) for the birthday of King Friedrich I on 12 July 1701. His other cantata was called *Triumph der Liebe*.

BIBLIOGRAPHY

J. von Besser: *Des Herrn von Besser Schriften Beydes in gebundener und ungebundener Rede* (Leipzig, 1732)

J. Mattheson: *Grundlage einer Ehren-Pforte* (Hamburg, 1740); ed. M. Schneider (Berlin, 1910/R1969)

C. Pluemicke: *Entwurf einer Theatergeschichte von Berlin* (Berlin, 1781)

L. Schneider: *Geschichte der Oper und des königlichen Opernhauses in Berlin*, with appx: *Geschichte der kurfürstlich Brandenburgischen und Königlich Preussischen Kapelle* (Berlin, 1852)

C. von Ledebur: *König Friedrich I. von Preussen* (Leipzig, 1878)

A. Ebert: *Attilio Ariosti in Berlin* (Bonn, 1905)

THOMAS-M. LANGNER

Riedel, Carl (*b* Kronenberg, nr. Wuppertal, 6 Oct 1827; *d* Leipzig, 3 June 1888). German chorus master and composer. He received his main musical education at the Leipzig Conservatory (with Hauptmann, C. F. Becker and others) from 1849 to 1852. In 1854 he founded a choral society (the Riedel-Whistling Verein) which in the following year became known as the Riedel'scher Verein and gave its first public concert. The choir performed sacred music of all periods, but Riedel gave special emphasis to Protestant works by J. S. Bach, Johannes Eccard, J. W. Franck and Schütz, as well as Liszt, Raff, Draeseke and other composers of the 'new German school', whom he supported as president (from 1868 until his death) of the Allgemeiner Deutscher Musikverein. He arranged and published the *Sieben Worte* and a compilation of selected pieces from the four Passions by Schütz (including the St Mark Passion later discovered as spurious) in the early 1870s. These rather free adaptations and his successful performances of them became very famous and stimulated further interest in Schütz among musicians and musicologists, including Chrysander, and Philipp and Friedrich Spitta.

BIBLIOGRAPHY

E. Kneschke: *Zur Geschichte des Theaters und der Musik in Leipzig* (Leipzig, 1864), 302ff

F. Spitta: *Die Passionen nach den vier Evangelisten von Heinrich Schütz: ein Beitrag zur Feier des 300jährigen Schütz-Jubiläums* (Leipzig, 1886), 54ff

H. Ehrlich: *Aus allen Tonarten: Studien über Musik* (Berlin, 1888), 137ff

P. Simon: 'Zur Erinnerung an Prof. Dr. Carl Riedel, ehemaligen Vorsitzenden des Allgemeinen deutschen Musikvereins', *NZM*, lxxxv (1889), 297

S. Kümmerle: *Encyklopädie der evangelischen Kirchenmusik* (Gütersloh, 1888–95/R1974)

A. Göhler: *Der Riedel-Verein zu Leipzig: eine Denkschrift zur Feier seines fünfzigjährigen Bestehens* (Leipzig, 1904)

F. Spitta: 'Die Passionen von Schütz und ihre Wiederbelebung', *JbMP 1906*, 15

La Mara [pseud. of M. Lipsius]: *Durch Musik und Leben im Dienste des Ideals* (Leipzig, 1917, 2/1926)

MARTIN ELSTE

Riedel, Friedrich W(ilhelm) (*b* Cuxhaven, 24 Oct 1929). German musicologist. He studied church music with J. Brenneke and E. Zillinger at the Schleswig-Holstein State Music School in Lübeck (1949–50), and musicology under Blume and Albrecht at Kiel University (from 1951) with history and theology as auxiliary subjects. He took a doctorate at Kiel in 1957 with a dissertation on source writings on keyboard music in the second half of the 17th century. He directed the central secretariat of RISM in Kassel (1960–67) and was an assistant lecturer at the musicology institute of Mainz University (1968–71), where he completed his *Habilitation* in 1970 with a dissertation on church music at the court of Charles VI. Since then he has worked at Mainz University, first as official *Privatdozent*; in 1972 he became an *ausserplanmässiger Professor*, and in 1973 a research fellow. He is a member of the international RISM committee for the 19th century. In addition to his extensive studies of source materials and regional music, he specializes in the history of church and keyboard music and has edited early organ music (K. Krieger, Muffat etc) for Die Orgel.

WRITINGS

Quellenkundliche Beiträge zur Geschichte der Musik für Tasteninstrumente in der zweiten Hälfte des 17. Jahrhunderts (diss., U. of Kiel, 1957; Kassel and Basle, 1960)

'Aloys Fuchs als Sammler Bachscher Werke', *BJb*, xlvi (1960), 83; see also *Mf*, xv (1962), 274; xvi (1963), 270

'J. G. Fux und die römische Palestrina-Tradition', *Mf*, xiv (1961), 14

'Der "Reichsstil" in der deutschen Musikgeschichte des 18. Jahrhunderts', *GfMKB, Kassel 1962*, 34

'Die Bibliothek des Aloys Fuchs', *Hans Albrecht in memoriam* (Kassel, 1962), 207; see also *Mf*, xv (1962), 274; xvi (1963), 270

'Musikpflege im Benediktinerstift Göttweig (Niederösterreich) um 1600', *KJb*, xlvi (1962), 83

'Neue Mitteilungen zur Lebensgeschichte von A. Poglietti und J. K. Kerll', *AMw*, xix–xx (1962–3), 124

Das Musikarchiv im Minoritenkonvent zu Wien (*Katalog des älteren Bestandes vor 1784*) (Kassel, 1963)

'Musikgeschichtliche Beziehungen zwischen Johann Joseph Fux und Johann Sebastien Bach', *Festschrift Friedrich Blume* (Kassel, 1963), 286

'Alessandro Pogliettis Oper "Endimione"', *Festschrift Hans Engel* (Kassel, 1964), 298

'Beiträge zur Geschichte der Musikpflege an der Stadtpfarrkirche St. Veit zu Krems', *950 Jahre Pfarre Krems* (Krems an der Donau, 1964), 300–341

with H. Federhofer: 'Quellenkundliche Beiträge zur Johann Joseph Fux-Forschung', *AMw*, xii (1964), 111

'P. Virgil Fleischmann OSB (1783–1863), ein unbekannter Schüler Michael Haydns', *KJb*, l (1966), 165

'Zur Geschichte der musikalischen Quellenüberlieferung und Quellenkunde', *AcM*, xxxviii (1966), 3

'Der Einfluss der italienischen Klaviermusik im 17. Jahrhunderts auf die Entwicklung der Musik für Tasteninstrumente in Deutschland während der ersten Hälfte des 18. Jahrhunderts', *AnMc*, no.5 (1968), 18

'Ein Skizzenbuch von Alessandro Poglietti', *Essays in Musicology: a Birthday Offering for Willi Apel* (Bloomington, Ind., 1968), 145

Kirchenmusik am Hofe Karls VI (1711–40) (Habilitationsschrift, U. of Mainz, 1970)

'Zur "Missa SSmae Trinitas" von Johann Joseph Fux', *Symbolae histor-icae musicae: Hellmut Federhofer zum 65. Geburtstag* (Mainz, 1971), 117

'Musikpflege im Stift Göttweig unter Abt Gottfried Bessel', *Gottfried Bessel (1672–1749)* (Mainz, 1972), 141–72

'Siegfried Wilhelm Dehns Besuche in Wien 1841 bis 1846', *Beiträge zur Musikdokumentation: Franz Grasberger zum 60. Geburtstag* (Tutzing, 1975), 391

'Hasse, Peter', 'Klavier', §§I–V, 'Kuhnau, Johann', 'Muffat, Gottlieb', 'Notation', §C, I, IV, 'Orgelmusik', §A, §B, IV, V, 'Poglietti, Alessandro', 'Reincken, Johann Adam', *MGG*

EDITIONS

J. J. Fux: *Werke für Tasteninstrumente*, Sämtliche Werke, vi/1 (Graz, 1964)

J. M. Kraus: *Etwas von und über Musik fürs Jahr 1777* (Munich, 1977)

HANS HEINRICH EGGEBRECHT

Riedel, Georg (*b* Sensburg, East Prussia, 6 June 1676; *d* Königsberg, 5 Feb 1738). German composer. In 1694 he entered the University of Königsberg, where he studied theology and philosophy. He received his musical training from Georg Raddäus, director of the Königsberg court musical establishment, with which Riedel subsequently held a position as precentor for a time. One of his first occasional works was a serenade written for the Königsberg student community for the celebrations of the coronation of King Frederick I in January 1701; later there followed arias, canons, cantatas and other works for weddings, birthdays and funerals (as well as for his own obsequies). On 24 May 1709 Riedel became Kantor at the Altstädter church, thereby obtaining one of Königsberg's leading musical posts, of whose reversion he had already been assured since 1706. He occupied this office for nearly 30 years, until his death. He was apparently a wilful and eccentric musician. His settings of the entire Gospel according to St Matthew, of the complete Psalter and of the whole of *Revelation*, partly written in his own artistic hand (he was also a calligrapher), are unique in the history of music.

Erroneous biographical particulars in Döring are partly based on a confusion with another Georg Riedel (*b* Neidenburg, East Prussia, 12 Sept 1715; *d* Königsberg, 21 July 1791), who, having previously been a Kantor in Wehlau, East Prussia, was Kantor in the Löbenicht church in Königsberg from 1749 to 1753 and at the cathedral there from 1753 to 1791.

WORKS

Evangelium Sancti Matthäi, solo vv, chorus, insts, completed 1721
Psalmen Davids . . . auff alle Sonn- und Fest Tage, solo vv, chorus, insts, completed 1724
Die geistreiche geheimte Offenbarung des heiligen und hocherleuchteten Evangelisten Johannis, solo vv, chorus, insts, completed 1734
Numerous occasional works, some of above average quality (prints are known from the years 1702–19), incl.: Der für die Erlösung des menschlichen Geschlechtes gemarterte Jesus (Passion cantata, J. V. Pietsch), 1719; Reformationskantate (J. C. Gottsched), 1723

BIBLIOGRAPHY

G. Döring: 'Die Musik in Preussen im XVIII. Jahrhundert', *MMg*, i (1869), 150

A. Mayer-Reinach: 'Zur Geschichte der Königsberger Hofkapelle in den Jahren 1578–1720', *SIMG*, vi (1904–5), 77

G. Küsel: *Beiträge zur Musikgeschichte der Stadt Königsberg in Preussen* (Königsberg, 1923)

H. Güttler: *Königsbergs Musikkultur im 18. Jahrhundert* (Königsberg, 1925)

——: 'Die Monumentaloratorien des Königsberger Kantors Georg Riedel (1676–1738)', *Kongressbericht: Leipzig 1925*, 373

——: 'Die Gelegenheitskompositionen Georg Riedels', *Königsberger Beiträge: Festgabe zur vierhundertjährigen Jubelfeier der Staats- und Universitätsbibliothek zu Königsberg Pr.* (Königsberg, 1929), 181

J. Müller-Blattau: 'Die Musik im 18. Jahrhundert', *Deutsche Staatenbildung und deutsche Kultur im Preussenlande* (Königsberg, 1931), 341

W. Reich: *Die deutschen gedruckten Leichenpredigten des 17. Jahrhunderts als musikalische Quelle* (diss., U. of Leipzig, 1963), 40, 94ff, music suppl., ex.23

GÜNTER THOMAS

Riederer, Johann Bartholomäus (*b* Nuremberg, baptized 3 March 1720; *d* Altdorf, *c*5 Feb 1771). German theologian, clergyman and writer. After studies at Altdorf and Halle he held posts at the Dominican church at Nuremberg and parish church at Rasch before becoming professor of theology and deacon (later arch-deacon) at Altdorf in 1752. His principal work on music was his *Abhandlung von Einführung des teu-tschen Gesangs in die evangelischlutherische Kirche überhaupts und in die Nürnbergische besonders* (Nuremberg, 1759). Supplementary material appeared in the first, third and fourth volumes of his *Nachrichten zur Kirchen-gelehrten- und Bücher-Geschichte* (Altdorf, 1764–8). Though based on earlier studies and per-petuating many of their errors and omissions, Riederer's work remains useful for the study of the chorale and related texts.

HOWARD SERWER

Riedl, Josef Anton (*b* Munich, 11 June 1927). German composer. He composed a number of piano, organ and vocal works as a boy, and studied with Orff. However, a more determining influence was that of Schaeffer, whose work he first heard at the 1951 Aix-en-Provence Festival. He was soon composing studies in *musique concrète*, and in 1953 he joined Schaeffer's research group in Paris. Subsequently he worked in the West German radio electronic music studio in Cologne (from 1955), in Scherchen's experimental studio in Gravesano (1959) and at the Siemens studio in Munich (1960–66), of which he was a founder-member. During these years he continued to compose electronic works, but his es-says in 'optical music' (using lighting as an additional means) were leading to the mixed-media compositions and environmental pieces that occupied much of his time in the late 1960s and early 1970s. In 1966 he joined the Institut für Klangforschung und Elektroni-sche Musik in Munich, and in 1974 he was appointed to direct the new youth centre at the Bonn Centre.

WORKS
(selective list)

Environments: Spielstrasse, Munich, 1972; other events in various German cities
Elec: Studie, 1951–2; Studie, 1958–9; Zyklus von 4 Studien, 1962; Polygonum, 1v, tape, 1968; Paper Music, 1970; Silphium, tape, live elec, 1972
Optical music: Lautgedichte, 1960; Vielleicht-Duo 1963–70; Stroboskopie, light environment, slides, 1971; Rhilapsis, metal-lophone, 1972
Film scores: Impuls unserer Zeit, 1959; Stunde X, 1959; Kummunikation, 1961; Geschwindigkeit, 1963; Unendliche Fahrt, 1965; Thunder over Mexico, 1966; Sekundenfilme, 1968; Adam II, 1968
Incidental music: Leonce und Lena (Büchner), Munich, 1963; Der Sturm (Shakespeare), Berlin, 1968
Radio scores: Kains Bruder ist umsonst gestorben (M. Y. Ben-Gavriël), 1960

Riedt, Friedrich Wilhelm (*b* Berlin, 5 Jan 1710; *d* Berlin, 5 Jan 1783). German flautist, writer on music and composer. Like his father, he was a keeper of the silver (*Silberdiener*) in the service of Frederick the

Great. He studied composition with Johann Gottlieb Graun and Christoph Schaffrath and was admitted into Frederick's Kapelle in 1741 as a flautist. He was also a founder of the Musikübende Gesellschaft becoming its director in 1749. Though he composed much chamber music for his own use and for the society, relatively little was published in his lifetime. Colleagues, like F. W. Marpurg, spoke favourably of his compositions, but later commentators like Charles Burney found them dry and mechanical.

Riedt's main theoretical work, the *Versuch über die musikalische Intervallen* (1753), was an attempt to cal-culate, systematize and evaluate all possible intervals used in composition. Like Rameau and others, Riedt engaged in considerable arithmetical manipulation to generate 21 pitches, 52 intervals, and various scales and chords. Of greater historical significance is his essay on ornamentation and variation in performance, *Betrachtungen über die willkührlichen Veränderungen der musikalischen Gedanken* (1756), which is notable for asserting that in a given melody only insignificant ideas may be varied by the performer. Riedt was ex-plicitly critical of the contemporary practice of exten-sive improvisation and variation, and held that no changes should contradict the underlying harmony of the original idea, which must always remain recogniz-able. Riedt's position may be taken both as a reflection of the court's opposition to excessive improvisation and as a manifestation of the developing belief that the com-poser's written score must be rendered unchanged in performance. Riedt's suggestions for the application of his ideas tend however to be both pedantic and mechani-cal. He also published a few chamber works for flute, both singly and in Marpurg's *Musikalisches Allerley* (Berlin, 1761–3).

WRITINGS

Versuch über die musikalische Intervallen, in Ansehung ihrer wahren Anzahl, ihres eigentlichen Sitzes, und natürlichen Vorzugs in der Composition (Berlin, 1753) [tables repr. in F. W. Marpurg: *Historisch-kritische Beyträge*, ii (1756/R1970), 387]
'Beantwortung der in des Herrn Capellmeisters Scheibe historischen-critischen Vorrede zu seiner . . . Abhandlung von dem Ursprung und Alter der Musik sec. 9 befindlichen Anmerkung', in F. W. Marpurg: *Historisch-kritische Beyträge*, i (1755/R1970), 414
'Betrachtungen über die willkührlichen Veränderungen der musikali-schen Gedanken bey Ausführung einer Melodie', in F. W. Marpurg: *Historisch-kritische Beyträge*, ii (1756/R1970), 95
'Zwo musikalische Fragen . . . beantwortet', in F. W. Marpurg: *Historisch-kritische Beyträge*, iii (1757/R1970), 371
'Beytrag[-Fortsetzung] zum musikalischen Wörterbuche', in F. W. Marpurg: *Kritische Briefe über die Tonkunst*, iii (1763/R1973), 105
'Antwort, auf Herrn Sorgens Verantwortung gegen Ihn, so in des letz-tern Anleitung zur Fantasie S. 76 befindlich ist', in J. A. Hiller: *Wochentliche Nachrichten und Anmerkungen die Musik betreffend*, iii (1769/R1970), 331

BIBLIOGRAPHY

F. W. Marpurg: 'Lebensnachrichten', *Historisch-kritische Beyträge*, i (1755/R1970), 549
C. Burney: *The Present State of Music in Germany, the Netherlands and the United Provinces* (London, 1773, 2/1775); ed. P. Scholes as *Dr. Burney's Musical Tours* (London, 1959)
S. Lowenthal: *Die musikübenden Gesellschaft zu Berlin und die Mitglieder . . . Friedrich Wilhelm Riedt* (diss., U. of Basle, 1928)
T.-M. Langner: 'Riedt, Friedrich Wilhelm', *MGG*

HOWARD SERWER

Illustration Acknowledgments

We are grateful to those listed below for permission to reproduce copyright illustrative material, and those contributors who supplied or helped us obtain it. Every effort has been made to contact copyright holders; we apologize to anyone who may have been omitted. Brian and Constance Dear prepared the maps and technical diagrams, and Oxford Illustrators the typographic diagrams (except where otherwise stated). Photographs acknowledged to the following sources are Crown copyright: Her Majesty the Queen, the Victoria and Albert Museum (including the Theatre Museum), the Science Museum and the National Monuments Record. The following forms of acknowledgment are used where the copyright of an illustration is held by a contributor:

photo John Smith – John Smith is contributor and photographer
John Smith – John Smith is contributor and copyright holder
photo John Smith, London – John Smith is a contributor (not of the article concerned) and photographer
John Smith, London – John Smith is a contributor (not of the article concerned) and copyright holder.

Where illustrations are taken from books out of copyright, the full title and place and date of publication are given, unless in the caption.

Playford *1*, *2* British Library, London; *3* English Folk Dance and Song Society, London

Pleyel (i) *1* Royal College of Music, London; *2* British Library, London; *3* Richard Macnutt, Tunbridge Wells

Poland *2*, *3* Polskie Wydawnictwo Muzyczne, Kraków: (*2*) after W. Kamiński, 'Instrumentarium muzyczne w Polsce średniowiecznej', *Musica medii aevi*, ii (1968); (*3*) from J. Banach, *Tematy muzyczne w plastyce polskiej*, ii: *Grafika i rysunek* (1962); *4*, *6* Alexandr Buchner, Prague; *5* Wydawnictwo Poznański, Poznań: from J. Burszta, ed., *Kultura ludowa Wielkopolski*, iii (1967); *7*, *8* Państwowe Muzeum Etnograficzne, Warsaw / photo Zbigniew Kamykowski (*7*, *8a*), Lech Trojanowski (*8b*)

Poliphant British Library, London

Polynesia *1* photo Mervyn McLean; *3* Nouvelles Editions Latines, Paris: from P. O'Reilly, *Dancing Tahiti* (1978); *4* photo Axel Poignant, London; *5–9* photo Bernice P. Bishop Museum, Honolulu; *10* photo Richard M. Moyle, Canberra; *11* photo Gerd Koch, Berlin

Ponchielli, Amilcare Archivio Storico Ricordi, Milan

Ponselle, Rosa Stuart-Liff Collection, Tunbridge Wells

Popular music *1*, *10* Mansell Collection, London; *2* Richard Macnutt, Tunbridge Wells; *3* Bildarchiv Preussischer Kulturbesitz, Berlin; *4*, *6*, *8* Mander and Mitchenson, London; *5* Andrew Lamb; *7* Mary Evans Picture Library, London; *9*, *11*, *12* Bodleian Library, Oxford; *13* Theatre and Music Collection, Museum of the City of New York; *14* photo *Old Time Music*, London; *15* Duncan Schiedt, Pittsboro, Ind.; *17* Popperfoto, London; *18* London Features International Ltd, London; *19* photo Valerie Wilmer, London; *20* Rex Features Ltd, London

Porpora, Nicola Conservatorio di Musica S Pietro a Majella, Naples / photo Wanda Parise

Porta, Costanzo *1* Museo Civico, Padua; *2* Bayerische Staatsbibliothek, Munich

Portative Memlingmuseum, Bruges / photo ACL, Brussels

Portugal *1* Smithsonian Institution, Washington, DC / photo Joanne B. Purcell; *2*, *5*, *6* Fundação Calouste Gulbenkian, Lisbon; *3* photo Joanne B. Purcell; *4* English Folk Dance and Song Society, London

Post horn *1* Conservatoire National Supérieur de Musique, Paris; *2*, *3* Museum of Fine Arts (Leslie Lindsey Mason Collection), Boston; *4a* The Post Office, London; *4b* Royal Pavilion, Art Gallery and Museums, Brighton

Punto, Giovanni photo Horace Fitzpatrick

Poulenc, Francis Popperfoto, London

Pousseur, Henri Universal Edition (London) Ltd

Praetorius, Michael *1* Bayerische Staatsbibliothek, Munich

Prague *1* Národní Muzeum, Prague / photo Olga Hilmerová; *2* Archiv

für Kunst und Geschichte, Berlin; *3* Theatre Museum, Victoria & Albert Museum, London

Prepared piano Henmar Press Inc., New York (1960)

Price, Leontyne San Francisco Opera / photo Pete Peters

Printing and publishing of music *1*, *2*, *5*, *7* (below), *10*, *16*, *19*, *23*, *24*, *27* British Library, London; *3a–f* Museum Plantin-Moretus, Antwerp; *4* Newberry Library, Chicago; *6*, *8* Bibliothèque Nationale, Paris; *7* (above) Giraudon, Paris; *9*, *11*, *14* Edmund Poole; *12* Österreichische Nationalbibliothek, Vienna; *13* Guildhall Library, London; *15* G. Henle Verlag, Munich, and H. Stürtz AG, Würzburg; *17*, *26* Bayerische Staatsbibliothek, Munich; *18* photo St Bride's Printing Library, London (*18a* from C. Wagner, *Alois Senefelder, sein Leben und Wirken*, Leipzig, 1914); *20a* Breitkopf & Härtel (London) Ltd; *20b* Boosey & Hawkes Ltd, London; *21* Armando dal Molin, Music Reprographics Ltd, Oyster Bay, NY; *22* Music Print Corporation, Boulder, Colorado; *25* Richard Macnutt, Tunbridge Wells

Prokofiev, Sergey *1* H. Roger-Viollet, Paris; *2* M. I. Glinka State Central Museum for Musical Culture, Moscow, and Boosey & Hawkes Ltd, London; *3* Novosti Press Agency, London

Psalmodikon Musikhistorisk Museum, Copenhagen

Psalmody (ii) *1* British Library, London; *2* Victoria and Albert Museum, London

Psalms, metrical *1* Württembergische Landesbibliothek, Stuttgart; *2* Dean and Chapter, Westminster Abbey, London; *4* British Library, London; *6* Tracy W. McGregor Library, University of Virginia, Charlottesville

Psaltery *1* Bibliothèque Municipale Classée, Angers; *2* Trustees of the National Gallery, London; *3* Städelsches Kunstinstitut, Frankfurt-am-Main; *4a* Koninklijk Museum voor Schone Kunsten, Antwerp / photo ACL, Brussels; *4b* Alexandr Buchner, Prague

Psychology of music *2* Academic Press Inc., New York (from P. Lindsay and D. Norman, *Human Information Processing*, 1972), and Institute of Physics, London

Puccini *1*, *4* Archivio Storico Ricordi, Milan; *2* Museo Teatrale alla Scala, Milan

Puerto Rico Instituto de Cultura Puertorriqueña, San Juan

Purcell *1* Exeter Cathedral Library; *2*, *3* National Portrait Gallery, London; *4*, *6* British Library, London

Qānūn *1* International Institute for Comparative Music Studies and Documentation, Berlin / photo H. H. Touma; *2* British Library, London

Quadrille British Library, London

Quaglio *1* Soprintendenza alla Gallerie, Florence

Quantz, Johann Joachim *1* Kurhessische Hausstiftung, Kronberg; *2* British Library, London

Raaf, Anton Theatermuseum, Munich
Racket *1* Bayerisches Nationalmuseum, Munich; *2* British Library, London; *3* Kunsthistorisches Museum, Vienna; *4* Musikinstrumenten-Museum, Karl-Marx-Universität, Leipzig; *5* Staatliches Institut für Musikforschung Preussischer Kulturbesitz, Musikinstrumenten-Museum, Berlin
Rakhmaninov, Sergey *1* Novosti Press Agency, London; *3* Royal College of Music, London; *4* RCA Ltd, London
Rameau, Jean-Philippe *1* Musée des Beaux-Arts, Dijon; *3, 5* Richard Macnutt, Tunbridge Wells; *4* Bibliothèque Nationale, Paris
Ramkie Africana Museum, Johannesburg
Rastell, John British Library, London
Rauzzini, Venanzio Victoria Art Gallery, Bath Museums Service
Ravenscroft, Thomas Bodleian Library, Oxford
Ravel, Maurice *1* Madame Alexandre Taverne, Rougemont, Switzerland; *2* Musée des Arts Décoratifs, Paris; *3* photo Editions du Seuil, Paris; *4* Pierpont Morgan Library (Robert O. Lehman Collection), New York, and Editions Durand & Cie, Paris; *5* Luciana Frassati, Turin: from L. Frassati, *Il Maestro: Arturo Toscanini e il suo mondo* (Turin, 1967)
Rawsthorne, Alan photo John F. P. Blake, Saffron Walden
Rebec *1* Bodleian Library, Oxford; *2* Patrimonio Nacional, Madrid; *3* Giraudon, Paris; *4* British Library, London; *5* New York Public Library at Lincoln Center, Astor, Lenox and Tilden Foundations (Spencer Collection)
Rebel photo Musées Nationaux, Paris
Recorder *1a* Friedrich von Huene, Brookline; *1b* after E. Hunt; *3a* Gemeentemuseum, The Hague; *3b* Music Division, Library of Congress, Washington, DC; *4a* Giraudon, Paris; *4b* Musées Royaux des Beaux-Arts de Belgique, Brussels / photo ACL; *5* British Library, London; *6* Bibliothèque Nationale, Paris; *7* Mansell Collection, London; *8* Grosvenor Museum, Chester; *9* Szépművészeti Múzeum, Budapest
Reel British Library, London
Regals British Library , London
Regent's bugle Royal Pavilion, Art Gallery and Museums, Brighton
Reger, Max Archiv für Kunst und Geschichte, Berlin
Regnart, Jacob Staatsbibliothek Preussischer Kulturbesitz, Musikabteilung, Berlin
Reichardt, Johann Friedrich *1* Deutsches Musikgeschichtliches Archiv, Kassel; *2* Bayerische Staatsbibliothek, Munich
Reiche, Gottfried Metropolitan Museum of Art (Gift of Mrs John Crosby Brown, 1901), New York
Reinecke, Carl Royal College of Music, London
Renaissance Mansell Collection, London, and Alinari, Florence
Renaud, Maurice Stuart-Liff Collection, Tunbridge Wells
Renzi, Anna Edizioni RAI, Rome: from C. Sartori, 'La prima diva della lirica italiana: Anna Renzi', *NRMI*, ii (1968), 430
Respond Desclée Editeurs, Tournai
Revolutionary hymn British Library, London
Revue Mander and Mitchenson, London
Rheims Bibliothèque Nationale, Paris
Richter, Franz Xaver Cabinet des Estampes, Strasbourg
Richter, Hans Harold Rosenthal, London
Richter, Sviatoslav photo Erich Auerbach, London
Ricordi Richard Macnutt, Tunbridge Wells